D1614261

THE NEW INTERPRETER'S BIBLE COMMENTARY

In Ten Volumes

EDITORIAL BOARD

* The credentials listed here reflect the positions held at the time of the original publication.

THE NEW INTERPRETER'S™ BIBLE
COMMENTARY

VOLUME ONE

Introduction to the Pentateuch
Genesis
Exodus
Leviticus
Numbers
Deuteronomy

ABINGDON PRESS
Nashville

CONTRIBUTORS

JOSEPH BLENKINSOPP
John A. O'Brien Professor of Biblical Studies
Department of Theology
University of Notre Dame
Notre Dame, Indiana
(The Roman Catholic Church)
Introduction to the Pentateuch

TERENCE E. FRETHEIM
Professor of Old Testament
Luther Seminary
Saint Paul, Minnesota
(Evangelical Lutheran Church in America)
Genesis

WALTER BRUEGGEMANN
William Marcellus McPheeters Professor of
Old Testament
Columbia Theological Seminary
Decatur, Georgia
(United Church of Christ)
Exodus

WALTER C. KAISER, JR.
President and Colman M. Mockler
Distinguished Professor of Old Testament
Gordon-Conwell Theological Seminary
South Hamilton, Massachusetts
(The Evangelical Free Church of America)
Leviticus

THOMAS B. DOZEMAN
Professor of Old Testament
United Theological Seminary
Dayton, Ohio
(Presbyterian Church [U.S.A.])
Numbers

RONALD E. CLEMENTS
Samuel Davidson Professor of Old Testament
King's College
University of London
London, England
(Baptist Union of Great Britain and Ireland)
Deuteronomy

* The credentials listed here reflect the positions held at the time of the original publication.

CONTENTS

VOLUME I

INTRODUCTION TO THE PENTATEUCH

JOSEPH BLENKINSOPP

THE PENTATEUCH IN THE BIBLICAL CANON

The designation Pentateuch, deriving from the Greek ἡ πεντάτευχος βίβλος (*hē penta-teuchos biblos*, "the fivefold book"), is not attested before the second century CE, though the fivefold division was in place much earlier. Josephus gives pride of place to the five books of Moses among authoritative Jewish records, which he compares favorably with those of the Greeks, but does not name the individual books.[1] The titles were, however, known to his older contemporary Philo, who refers to Deuteronomy as "The Protreptics," a not inappropriate title.[2] Occasional allusions in the New Testament (NT) to "the law and the prophets" (e.g., Matt 5:17; Luke 16:16; Rom 3:21) reflect contemporary Jewish usage, but the NT nowhere refers to the fivefold division or names any of the individual books. This division was, nevertheless, in place no later than the time of Ben Sira, who wrote his treatise in the early decades of the second century BCE; the fact that this author is familiar with the division of Latter Prophets into three and twelve (Sir 48:20–49:10) creates a strong

presumption that he also knew the fivefold division of Torah. Frequent allusions to "the law," "the law of Moses," and "the book of the law" in earlier Second Temple composi-tions (e.g., 2 Chr 30:16; Ezra 10:3; Neh 8:3) refer to the legal content of the corpus, most frequently the Deuteronomic law, rather than to the entire Pentateuch.

Designations current in Judaism—חמישה חומשי התורה (*ḥămîšâ ḥûmšê hattôrâ*, "the five fifths of the Law") or, more briefly, חומש (*ḥûmāš*, "the fivefold book"), and, of course, תורה (*tôrâ*, "instruction, law")—imply the preeminence of the legal material that takes up more than one fifth of the Pentateuch. And since all the laws were believed to have been delivered to Israel through Moses, it was practically inevitable that the entire corpus came to be attributed to him as sole author.

In due course, the Pentateuch, or Torah, became the first and most important seg-ment of the tripartite canon for Jews, and it alone enjoyed canonical status in the Samari-tan community. We should add, however, that the term *canon,* meaning an authorita-tive corpus of sacred writings, originated in a Christian milieu no earlier than the fourth century (in Athanasius's *Decrees of the Coun-cil of Nicaea,* c. 350), though lists of bibli-cal books were in circulation from the early

---

1. *Against Apion* 1:37-41.
2. *De Fuga et Inventione* 170.

second century. In Judaism there is nothing comparable prior to the well-known passage in *b. B. Bat.* 14b-15a listing the biblical books and their reputed authors. The process by which the canon in its different forms (Jewish, Protestant, Catholic, Eastern Orthodox) reached its final formulation is now acknowledged to have been much more complex and less clearly defined than was once thought, and the role of "the men of the Great Assembly" at the time of Ezra and "the Council of Jamnia [Yavneh]" after the fall of Jerusalem to the Romans in 70 CE is now known to be anachronistic and unhistorical. In any case, the Pentateuch had in all essentials reached its final form much earlier in the Second Temple period.

THE PENTATEUCHAL NARRATIVE

In spite of the designation Torah current in Judaism, the Pentateuch is basically a narrative. The sequence of events begins with creation and the early history of humanity in which the structurally decisive event is the deluge, after which the descendants of Noah are dispersed around the earth. In the tenth generation after the deluge, Abram (later Abraham) is called by God to leave Mesopotamia for a new land, with the promise of divine blessing and numerous progeny contingent on his answering this call. The history of Israel's ancestors is traced through four generations, particular attention being devoted to the twenty-year exile of Jacob (later called Israel) in Mesopotamia, his eventual return to the promised land, and the emigration of his family, now seventy in number, to Egypt. The story of the ancestors, therefore, begins and ends outside the land, hence the promise made initially to Abraham and often repeated awaits fulfillment in the future. In Egypt the original settlers grow into a numerous and powerful people until a new pharaoh ascends the throne and, for reasons that are not entirely clear, launches a genocidal campaign against them.

One of Jacob's descendants called Moses, son of Levitical parents, survived the massacre of Hebrew male infants decreed by Pharaoh and, after killing an Egyptian overseer, was forced to take refuge in Midian. There he had the extraordinary experience of a deity's self-revelation to him as Yahweh, God of the ancestors, who sent him on a mission to persuade Pharaoh to let the oppressed Hebrews leave Egypt. A first attempt proved unsuccessful, but with the assistance from his brother, Aaron, and after a series of ecological disasters visited on the Egyptians culminated in the death of their firstborn, a second mission succeeded. The Israelites headed out into the wilderness and the pursuing Egyptians were destroyed as they attempted to cross a body of water. After further vicissitudes, the Israelites, now 600,000 strong, not counting women and children, reached the wilderness of Sinai. There Moses received laws from Yahweh: First, ten commandments promulgated to the people at once; then a collection of laws communicated to Moses alone. There followed a covenant ritual and the revelation of the plan for the construction of the sanctuary and detailed instructions for the cult to be carried on in it. During Moses' absence on the mountain, an act of apostasy by the people, aided and abetted by Aaron, led to the breaking and remaking of the Law tablets and the giving of further statutes, mostly of a ritual sort. The cult was then set up as prescribed, the priesthood under Aaron was inaugurated, and after a lapse of about a year the Israelites continued on their way.

After an abortive attempt to invade Canaan, the Israelite throng under Moses arrived in Moab, east of the Jordan. The attempt of the Moabite king to block their passage by hiring a seer to curse them was thwarted, and those Israelites who succumbed to the temptation to engage in sexual rites were executed. Preparations were made for occupying land both east and west of the Jordan, and on the last day of his life Moses addressed the people, reminding them of past favors bestowed on them by their God and the obligations they had thereby incurred. This last address included a new set of laws and was followed by a new covenant. Moses commissioned Joshua as his successor before his death and burial in an unmarked grave at the age of 120.

NARRATIVE ANOMALIES

The uneven narrative tempo of the Pentateuch story will be obvious even on a cursory reading. According to the chronology provided by the narrative itself, the events unfold over a period of 2,706 years, yet the sojourn at Sinai, the account of which occupies about one fifth of the total length, lasts less than one year (Exod 19:1; Num 10:11), while another fifth is dedicated to the last day in the life of Moses (Deut 1:3; 32:48). The most obvious explanation of this anomalous feature is that all laws, whenever promulgated, came in the course of time to be backdated to the lifetime of Moses. But the narrative also contains numerous repetitions and digressions and is punctuated at frequent intervals by genealogies and lists. These features suggest that the Pentateuchal story has been formed as the result of an incremental process over a considerable period of time.

Another structural problem is that the ending, with Moses and his people camped in Moab, east of the Jordan, appears to leave the promise of land, prominent in the history of the ancestors, up in the air. According to the Deuteronomic author-editor of Joshua, the conquest of Canaan was viewed as the fulfillment of that promise (see esp. Josh 21:43-45), so that it might seem more appropriate to speak of a Hexateuch (Pentateuch plus Joshua) as the basic literary unit and explain the omission of the conquest from the Pentateuch as a later move dictated by the needs of the post-exilic community. But in the context of the dominant documentary hypothesis (see below), we then have the problem that the principal continuous early sources—namely, J and E—are not clearly attested in Joshua, which reflects, rather, the language and ideology of Deuteronomy. This has led several scholars, conspicuously Martin Noth, to read Deuteronomy as the preface to the Deuteronomic History (Joshua–2 Kings) and the first four books as a more or less self-contained Tetrateuch. But a glance at the conclusion of Numbers will suffice to show that the Tetrateuch is no more a well-rounded and self-contained narrative than the Pentateuch; indeed, less so, since it not only leaves Israel outside the land but also omits the death of Moses. Noth's Tetrateuchal hypothesis would

be further weakened if, as several scholars have since argued, the Deuteronomic hand is much more in evidence in Genesis–Numbers than he and others at that time were prepared to allow.

It is at least clear that the present divisions in the narrative continuum from creation to the Babylonian exile resulted from successive editorial adjustments. The most important of these was the inclusion of the Deuteronomic law and its homiletic framework in the narrative of Israelite origins, a move that necessitated the displacement of the commissioning of Joshua and the death of Moses from their original position in the Priestly narrative (Num 27:12-23) to the end of Deuteronomy (32:48-52 and 34:1, 7-9, also of P origin). Once this was done, Moses' death marked the closing of the normative epoch in which everything necessary for the sustenance of the Israelite commonwealth had been revealed and promulgated. In its final form, therefore, the Pentateuch is centered on the law and the unique mediatorial role of Moses.

STRUCTURE, DIVISIONS, THEME

The chapter divisions of the Pentateuch begin to appear in Hebrew MSS in the later Middle Ages, but had already been introduced into the Vulgate by Stephen Langton, Archbishop of Canterbury (1150–1228). By the Talmudic period, individual sentences or brief pericopes were being identified by words or phrases (סימנים *sîmānîm*, "signs"), but verse numbering is first attested in Christian Bibles at the time of the Reformation. The division of the Hebrew Bible (HB) into longer pericopes for liturgical reading is also attested from an early date. These sections (סדרים *sĕdārîm*) were subdivided into short paragraphs (פסקות *pisqôt*) separated by a space of at least three letters, a practice already attested in the Qumran biblical texts. According to an early tradition, this had the purpose of giving Moses time to reflect on the meaning of the text between each subsection.[3]

While the division of the Pentateuch into five books clearly owed something to the need for convenient scroll handling, it

---

3. *Sipra* 1:1.

is equally clear that the material could have been divided in a different way. Genesis and Deuteronomy have their own distinctive character as self-contained narratives, though the former could as well have concluded with the recapitulating genealogy of the Israelite family in Egypt in Gen 46:8-27. This is not the case with Exodus and Numbers, which are almost exactly equal in length. The break between Exodus and Leviticus is quite artificial, for the latter falls within the Sinai pericope that ends only in Numbers 10. Moreover, the ordination ceremony in Leviticus 8 is the sequel to the prescriptions for carrying out that ceremony in Exodus 29. It is possible that the fivefold arrangement had the purpose of highlighting Leviticus, by far the shortest of the five books, as the central panel defining Israel as a holy community distinct from other nations. The structure itself could then be read as encoding an important aspect of the self-understanding of the emergent Jewish commonwealth after the return from exile.

Another significant structural feature is the division of Genesis into sections entitled תולדות אלה (ʾēlleh tôlĕdôt, "these are the generations . . ."). They are arranged in two pentads (groups of five) covering, respectively, the early history of humanity (Gen 2:4a; 5:1; 6:9; 10:1; 11:10) and the ancestral history (Gen 11:27; 25:12, 19; 36:1; 37:2). As with the fivefold division of the Pentateuch itself, this arrangement draws attention to the central panel of each pentad—namely, the deluge in the first and the vicissitudes of Jacob/ Israel in the second. While the title tôlēdôt is particularly apt for genealogical material, most of these sections contain far more narrative than genealogy.

A structuring and periodizing feature of a different kind is the series of precise chronological markers punctuating the narrative, especially in Genesis (e.g., Gen 7:6, 11; Exod 12:40-41; Num 10:11). Attempts to decode this chronological schema are complicated by the different numbers in the MT, LXX, and Samaritan Pentateuch, and no one solution has won universal acceptance. What can be said is that the schema is undoubtedly fictive and that it extends beyond the Pentateuch, taking in the building of Solomon's Temple (1 Kgs 6:1) and the 430 years between the

construction and the destruction of the Temple, identical with the length of the sojourn in Egypt, according to Exod 12:40. It has also been observed that the interval of 2,666 years between creation and the exodus is two-thirds of a total of 4,000 years, which may have been thought of as a world epoch or "Great Year." Whatever the solution, this chronological grid expresses the conviction that the course of events has a direction and a goal predetermined and willed by God.

Since the Pentateuch contains materials from successive periods in the history of Israel and early Judaism that have been combined and reshaped in response to different situations, it is difficult to identify a single theme or organizing principle. The fact that it concludes with the death of Moses prior to the occupation of and residence in the land suggests that what is centrally important is the complex of institutions and laws that serve as a kind of blueprint for the commonwealth and polity to be established. But the story of the ancestors begins with the command to Abraham to go to a land in which his descendants would become a great nation replete with blessing and a source of blessing for other peoples (Gen 12:1-3). For those who postulate a Hexateuch from which the Pentateuch was formed by detaching Joshua, the fulfillment of these promises would be seen in the conquest and settlement of Canaan (see Josh 21:43-45, which reads like a finale to the story); and for those who postulate a Yahwist (J) source from the early monarchy, the terminus would be the "Greater Israel" of David and Solomon. If, however, the Pentateuch *in its final form* is read in the context of the emergent Judaism that produced it, the ancestral promises would reflect the aspirations of those who elected to return to the homeland under Persian rule. The addition of the early history of humanity in Genesis 1–11, in keeping with well-established historiographical tradition in the Near East and the Levant (the countries bordering the eastern edge of the Mediterranean Sea), placed the history of the nation in the context of world history and allowed for a realistic and profound diagnosis of the human condition.

THE FORMATION OF THE PENTATEUCH

From Ibn Ezra to Wellhausen. The view long traditional in both Judaism and Christianity, and still maintained in the more conservative denominations of both religions, is that Moses authored the entire Pentateuch with the possible exception of the last verses recounting his death and burial. The beginnings of this belief can be traced to the close association between Moses and the law. From a fairly early time, it became standard procedure to attribute all laws to Moses in the same way that sapiential compositions came to be attributed to Solomon and Psalms to David. And since the laws are embedded in narrative, it was a short step to assigning the entire corpus to Moses in spite of the fact that this is nowhere affirmed in the Pentateuch itself.

One of the earliest to raise questions about the attribution was the twelfth-century Jewish scholar Abraham Ibn Ezra, who alluded cryptically, in his commentary on Deuteronomy, to certain passages that presuppose situations and events long after the time of Moses; e.g., the remark that at that time the Canaanites were in the land (Gen 12:6) and the allusion to the iron bed of King Og of Bashan, which was a tourist attraction at the time of his writing (Deut 3:11). Further difficulties were raised by other commentators in the following centuries, with the result that by the seventeenth century writers as diverse as Spinoza and Hobbes simply rejected Mosaic authorship altogether. Even scholars within the ecclesiastical mainstream, while not denying the traditional view outright, were beginning to acknowledge the composite nature of the Pentateuch. One of the earliest of these was the French Oratorian priest Richard Simon. In his *Histoire Critique du Vieux Testament* (1678), he acknowledged the role of Moses in the production of the Pentateuch but went on to suggest that it owed its final form to scribes at the time of Ezra. The outcome was that his work was placed on the Roman Catholic Index of Prohibited Books and most of the copies printed were destroyed. One of the surviving copies was, however, translated into German by Johann Salomo Semler about a century later

and, in that form, contributed significantly to research on the Pentateuch, then well underway in German universities.

By the early eighteenth century, evidence for the use of sources was becoming more and more apparent. Repetitions, parallel versions of the same event, and notable differences in language and point of view seemed to render this conclusion inevitable. The first to exploit the occurrence of divine names—Elohim and Yahweh—as a means of distinguishing between sources was Henning Bernhard Witter, Lutheran pastor of Hildesheim, who wrote a monograph on the subject in 1711 that remained practically unnoticed until rediscovered by the French biblical scholar Adolphe Lods in 1925. Somewhat along the same lines, the French physician and amateur Old Testament (OT) scholar Jean Astruc published a book forty-two years later in which he distinguished three sources in the Pentateuch, the first two of which were characterized by use of the names Elohim and Yahweh respectively. By assuming that these sources were used by Moses in compiling the Pentateuch, Astruc sought to preserve the traditional dogma. By the end of that century, nevertheless, the existence of parallel sources was widely acknowledged, at least for Genesis and the first part of Exodus up to the point where the divine name YHWH (Yahweh) was revealed to Moses (Exod 3:13-15).

A minority opinion, first proposed by the Scottish Roman Catholic priest Alexander Geddes in the late eighteenth century and developed by J. S. Vater, professor at Halle in the early years of the following century, rejected the hypothesis of two continuous parallel sources in favor of a much greater number of quite disparate blocks of material that were combined long after the time of Moses to form the Pentateuch (the Fragmentary Hypothesis). Another alternative assumed that a single base narrative, or *Grundschrift,* was subsequently filled out with additional material (the Supplementary Hypothesis). But in whatever form it was proposed, the view that the Pentateuch is the result of a long process of literary formation was firmly established by the early nineteenth century, in academic if not in ecclesiastical circles.

During that period of political and cultural upheaval, the most important contribution to understanding the formation of the Penta-teuch was that of Wilhelm Martin Leberecht de Wette (1780–1849), colleague of Schlei-ermacher at the newly founded University of Berlin. De Wette's study of Chronicles persuaded him that the legal and cultic sys-tem that the author of Chronicles presumes to have been in place since Mosaic times or, with respect to the Jerusalem cult, from the time of David, is unattested in the early records and must, therefore, be a projection into the past of the situation obtaining at the time of writing in the post-exilic period. The greater part of the legal and cultic material in the Pentateuch, therefore, belongs to the early history of Judaism rather than to that of Israel. In keeping with this conclusion, de Wette divided his *Biblical Dogmatics* (1813) into two sections entitled "Hebraism" and "Judaism." True to the dominant Romanti-cism of the time, de Wette contrasted the spontaneity and vigor of early Israelite reli-gion with the formalism and empty ritualism that he believed characterized early Judaism and Judaism as a whole, a contrast that would be set out in much starker terms by Wellhau-sen toward the end of the same century. In another important monograph, de Wette identified the lawbook that the priest Hilkiah claimed to have found in the Temple during the reign of Josiah (640–609 BCE) with an early draft of Deuteronomy (see 2 Kgs 22:8-10). According to de Wette, this composi-tion claimed for itself Mosaic authorship but was actually a recent pseudepigraphal work "planted" by the priests to serve as a basis for the religious reforms that followed its "dis-covery." By thus placing the Deuteronomic Law (Deuteronomy 12–26) in the seventh century BCE, de Wette believed it possible to distinguish between earlier legislation unfa-miliar with this compilation and later laws that presupposed it.

Throughout the nineteenth century OT scholars concentrated on the identification and dating of sources, rather less so on the editorial processes by which they were assem-bled into a coherent whole. Briefly, the most important advances following de Wette were, first, the discovery that the Elohist source (E), by most considered the earliest, contained an earlier and a later strand. First suggested by Karl David Ilgen in 1798, the distinction was

worked out in detail about a half century later by Hermann Hupfeld, resulting in the emer-gence of a priestly and theocratic source (later to be known under the siglum P). The second and decisive proposal, already implicit in the results obtained by de Wette at the beginning of the century, was that this newly discovered Priestly source was to be located at the end, not the beginning, of the process of forma-tion. First advanced by Edouard Reuss in lectures delivered at the University of Stras-bourg, the hypothesis of the late P source appeared in print in a book published by Karl Heinrich Graf, student of Reuss, in 1866. The way was thus cleared for the definitive for-mulation of what came to be known as "the newer documentary hypothesis," with the sources in the chronological order JEDP, in the *Prolegomena to the History of Israel* of Julius Wellhausen (1883).

With benefit of hindsight, it is not too dif-ficult to detect the philosophical and cultural determinants of this lengthy and persistent attempt to identify and date sources. It is important to bear in mind that the goal of this massive effort to identify and date sources was not so much a theological or aesthetic appreciation of the texts in themselves but rather the reconstruction of the history, and especially the religious history, of Israel. Throughout the nineteenth century, schol-ars emphasized development, specifically of ideas. Although sometimes exaggerated, the impact of Hegel's dialectical philosophy of his-tory was felt in both OT and NT studies. It can be detected, for example, in the tendency for a tripartite periodization of the history—typically, Mosaism, propheticism, early Juda-ism. As noted above, influences were also felt from the Romantic movement, especially in the positive evaluation of the early and naive stage of religious development, the high esti-mation of the prophet as the religious indi-vidualist *par excellence,* and the marked lack of enthusiasm for post-exilic Judaism, gener-ally characterized as a decline into religious formalism and ritualism. While, perhaps, few OT scholars professed to be anti-Jewish, aca-demic study of the Pentateuch, and the OT in general, was carried on in an atmosphere decidedly unfavorable to Judaism. It is, there-fore, not surprising that Jewish scholars, with few exceptions, turned their attention elsewhere.

From Wellhausen to the Mid-Twentieth Century. The four-source or newer documentary hypothesis as set out by Wellhausen soon became the critical orthodoxy, though opposed by scholars of more conservative ecclesiastical affiliation. It was not clearly perceived at the time, but the Graf-Wellhausenian construct was threatened less from conservative reaction than it was from the ongoing analysis of the sources themselves. The requirement of a fairly high level of consistency in terminology, style, and theme had already led to the division of an originally unitary E source into P and E, and it was not long before the E source itself suffered the same fate,[4] resulting in E[1] and E[2]. However, J proved to be especially friable, resulting either in J[1] and J[2] as constituent sources[5] or in the postulation of a more primitive strand within J, variously described as of lay origin,[6] or of Kenite,[7] Edomite,[8] or nomadic provenance.[9] Wellhausen himself had argued for two strands in Deuteronomy, and the existence of a Josian and exilic redaction, from the seventh and sixth centuries BCE respectively, is now widely accepted. At the beginning of the century, Bruno Baentsch identified as many as seven strands in P, each with its own redactional history, and while few were prepared to press source division to that extreme, many agreed that additions were made at different times to the P narrative and laws,[10] though there is still no agreement as to whether P is a distinct source or an editorial reworking of earlier material.

The problem inherent in this kind of detailed analysis of sources is not difficult to detect. To the degree that the requirement of inner consistency is pressed, the sources tend to disintegrate into a bewildering variety of smaller units or strands, and the entire hypothesis is undermined. A challenge of a different nature emerged from the work of Hermann Gunkel (1852–1932), the first edition of whose commentary on Genesis appeared in 1901. Gunkel accepted the Graf-Wellhausen construct, but the innovative study of literary forms, in his work and that of his students Gressmann and Baumgartner, was to create serious problems for the documentary hypothesis. The influence of the History of Religions school on Gunkel can be seen in his first significant publication, entitled *Creation and Chaos* (*Schöpfung und Chaos,* 1895); following the lead of this school, Gunkel brought a comparative study of genres to bear on the narrative material in Genesis, concentrating on the smallest literary units, their oral prehistory, and the social situations that generated them. His description of these narratives as saga has occasioned difficulties, since in English the term applies to medieval Icelandic prose narratives, not necessarily composed and transmitted orally. In German, however, the corresponding term *Sage* can have a more general meaning, including legend and folktale, and it is in this sense that Gunkel used it, depending on the work of the Danish folklorist Axel Olrik. Gunkel's application of this kind of literary analysis, which he called *Literaturgeschichte* (literary history) or *Gattungsforschung* (the investigation of genres), but which has since been known as *Formgeschichte* (the history of forms, form criticism), shifted the emphasis away from extensive written documents to individual pericopes and the oral tradition underlying them. Although it was not clearly perceived at the time, Gunkel's investigations were to lead in a quite different direction from that of Graf and Wellhausen.

The concept of oral tradition also played an important role in the work of von Rad, whose study entitled "The Form-Critical Problem of the Hexateuch," published in 1938, proved very influential, and whose ideas were further developed in his commentaries on Genesis and Deuteronomy as well as in the first volume of his *Old*

---

4. See Abraham Kuenen, *Historisch-Kritische Einleitung in die Bücher des Alten Testaments ihrer Entstehung und Sammlung* (Leipzig: J. C. Hinrichs, 1887); Otto Procksch, *Das nordhebräische Sagenbuch. Die Elohimquelle* (Leipzig: J. C. Hinrichs, 1906).

5. See Karl Budde, *Die Biblische Urgeschichte (Gen. 1–12, 5)* (Giessen: A. Töpelmann, 1883); Rudolph Smend, *Die Erzählung des Hexateuch. Aufe ihre Quellen untersucht* (Berlin: Walter de Gruyter, 1912); Cuthbert Simpson, *The Early Traditions of Israel: A Critical Analysis of the Pre-Deuteronomistic Narrative of the Hexateuch* (Oxford: Blackwell, 1948).

6. *Laienquelle* is a source of the Pentateuch, according to Otto Eissfeldt. See his *The Old Testament: An Introduction* (Oxford: Blackwell, 1965).

7. Julius Morgenstern, "The Oldest Document of the Hexateuch," *Hebrew Union College Annual* 4 (1927) 1-138.

8. Robert Pfeiffer, "A Non-Israelite Source of the Book of Genesis," *Zeitschrift für die alttestamentliche Wissenschaft* 48 (1930) 66-73.

9. Georg Fohrer, *Introduction to the Old Testament* (Nashville: Abingdon, 1968).

10. See Gerhard von Rad, *Die Priesterschrift im Hexateuch literarisch untersucht und theologisch gewertet* (Stuttgart: W. Kohlhammer, 1934).

Testament Theology.[11] According to von Rad, the Hexateuchal narrative was elaborated on the basis of the kind of liturgical and confessional statement found in Deut 26:5-9, the form of words pronounced by the Israelite farmer at the offering of the first-fruits. He observed that this "Hexateuch in a nutshell," as he called it, memorialized the descent into Egypt, the exodus, and settlement in the land but omitted any mention of the giving of the Law. To explain this omission, he postulated two separate streams of tradition that came together only in the work of the Yahwist author (J): the exodus-occupation tradition rooted in the Festival of Weeks at Gilgal; and the Sinai tradition, originating in the Festival of Tabernacles at the ancient tribal sanctuary of Shechem. The Yahwist prefaced the literary elaboration of these conflated traditions with the early history of humanity in Genesis 1–11 and the ancestral history in Genesis 12–50, thus laying the groundwork for the Hexateuch as we have it. Cultic recital rooted in the tribal federation of the prestate period was thus transformed into religious literature, the catalyst for the transformation being what von Rad called "the Solomonic enlightenment."

Von Rad's high evaluation of the Yahwist as a literary and religious genius was very influential, especially during the heyday of the "biblical theology movement" in the two decades following World War II and residually down to the present. Books and articles began to appear on the kerygma, or the theology, of the Yahwist.[12] There were even attempts to penetrate the veil of anonymity by identifying him as a member of Solomon's entourage, the favored candidates being Nathan, Abiathar, and Ahimaaz. In recent years serious questions have been raised about the date, extent, and even existence of J as a continuous and integral narrative source.

Other proponents of a cultic origin for the narrative and legal traditions of ancient Israel were the Norwegian scholar Sigmund

Mowinckel, who located the Decalogue in a pre-monarchic New Year festival; Johannes Pedersen, who read Exodus 1–15 as the deposit of cultic recital for Passover; and Albrecht Alt, whose influential essay "The Origins of Israelite Law"[13] grounded the apodictic laws in the cult of the Israelite amphictyony. Following the same form-critical and traditio-historical procedures, Martin Noth[14] identified five major themes (guidance out of Egypt, progress through the wilderness, entry into the arable land, promise to the ancestors, and the revelation at Sinai) whose origin and early development were in the tribal amphictyony and its cult. These traditions were combined and molded into a consecutive narrative to form the Tetrateuch. Noth's acceptance of the documentary hypothesis was fairly laconic, since he maintained that the essential lines of the narrative tradition had been present from the beginning, whether in oral or written form is unclear (his reference to a base narrative or *Grundschrift* remained undeveloped).

Noth's studies provided the basis for his account of the origins and early development of Israel in his *A History of Israel.*[15] His main point was that the combination of the five themes, originating in different segments of what later became Israel, went hand in hand with the consolidation of these diverse groups into the Israelite tribal federation, or amphictyony, of the pre-monarchic period. Here, too, more recent studies have called into question Noth's amphictyonic thesis, first advanced in 1930, and his understanding of Israelite origins in general. His hypothesis of a Deuteronomistic historical work (Dtr) covering Joshua through 2 Kings, first advanced in 1943, has on the other hand stood the test of time and is still almost universally accepted.

We can see now how von Rad and Noth, neither of whom questioned the regnant documentary hypothesis, followed Gunkel in shifting the emphasis back into the preliterary origin of the Pentateuchal traditions. While this displacement has had important

11. Published in English in *The Problem of the Hexateuch and Other Essays* (New York: McGraw-Hill, 1966) 1-78. See *Genesis: A Commentary,* rev. ed. (Philadelphia: Westminster, 1973), first published in 1953; *Deuteronomy: A Commentary* (Philadelphia: Westminster, 1966), first published in 1964; *Old Testament Theology,* vol. 1: *The Theology of Israel's Historical Traditions,* trans. D. M. G. Stalker (New York: Harper and Row, 1962), first published in 1957.
12. See Hans-Walter Wolff, "Das Kerygma des Yahwisten," *Evangelische Theologie* 24 (1964) 73-98; Peter Ellis, *The Yahwist: The Bible's First Theologian* (Collegeville: Liturgical Press, 1968).

13. Albrecht Alt, "Die Ursprünge des israelitischen Rechts," *Bericht über die Verhandlungen der Sächsischen Akademie der Wissenschaften zu Leipzig. Philologisch-historische Klasse,* vol. 86, 1 (Leipzig: S. Hirzel, 1934).
14. Martin Noth, *A History of Pentateuchal Traditions* (Englewood Cliffs, N.J.: Prentice-Hall, 1972). First published in 1948.
15. Martin Noth, *A History of Israel,* 2nd ed. (New York: Harper and Row, 1960), first published in 1950.

consequences, many of the specific conclusions of both scholars have since been called into question. The creedal statements von Rad took as the starting point of the literary development eventuating in the Hexateuch, especially Deut 26:1-15, are now seen to be Deuteronomic and, therefore, no earlier than the seventh century BCE. The separate origin of the exodus-occupation and Sinai traditions has been generally abandoned, and the high antiquity of the covenant formulation can no longer be taken for granted. More recent comparative studies of oral tradition have given us a better understanding of the relation between oral and written transmission and have made it more difficult to determine the oral origin of written narrative.[16] Moreover, one might ask how the cult, which can certainly serve to transmit a narrative tradition, can also originate it.

During the same period, more radical theories of oral tradition were popular with Scandinavian scholars, especially with respect to the Pentateuch and the prophetic books. Drawing on the work of the Uppsala scholars H. S. Nyberg and Harris Birkeland, Ivan Engnell argued strongly for a traditio-historical approach rather than the Wellhausenian emphasis on literary sources. Engnell maintained that the narrative material in the Tetrateuch was transmitted orally throughout the pre-exilic period and was committed to writing only after the Babylonian exile in what he called "the P circle." This final redaction was quite distinct from the roughly contemporary "D work" comprising Deuteronomy and Dtr. At some point Deuteronomy was detached from the history and built into the Priestly Tetrateuch, resulting in the Pentateuch more or less as we have it. Some aspects of Engnell's critique of the documentary hypothesis are reproduced in recent revisionist writings, but his extreme advocacy of oral tradition has since been abandoned.

Recent Developments. While there have always been those who rejected the documentary hypothesis outright[17] and others who were critical of some aspect of it,[18]

it is only in the last two decades or so that the Graf-Wellhausen construct can be said to be in serious and possibly terminal crisis. The main line of attack has focused on the existence of *continuous* sources from the early period of the monarchy. It has become apparent that Otto Eissfeldt's description of J as expressing "enthusiastic acceptance of agricultural life and national-political power and cultus"[19] may apply to some parts of the narrative but not at all to the substantial J component of Genesis 1–11, which speaks of the curse on the soil and emphasizes the vanity of human pretensions in general and in the political sphere in particular. Considerations such as this have led several scholars— Norman Wagner, Rolf Rendtorff, Erhard Blum, among others[20]—to argue that the several narrative blocks in the Pentateuch had their own distinctive processes of formation until they were redacted together at a late date. Doubts about the early dating of J (in the tenth or ninth century BCE) have coalesced to the point where such an early date can no longer be taken for granted. The Canadian scholar F. V. Winnett[21] argued for a post-exilic J in Genesis, while John Van Seters, one of his students, postulated an exilic J whose work reflects the exigencies and aspirations of the Jewish community at that time. In later studies, Van Seters went on to argue that the Yahwist, an individual author and not a school or circle, produced a historiographical work that can be profitably compared with, and was influenced by, early Greek mythography and historiography, including Herodotus and the Hesiodic *Catalogue of Women*.[22] It is still too early to evaluate adequately this new direction, but at least one scholar of note has taken a similar line.[23]

Another development threatening to undermine the existing paradigm involves

---

16. Robert Culley, *Studies in the Structure of Hebrew Narrative* (Philadelphia: Fortress, 1976).
17. E.g., the Jewish scholar Umberto Cassuto, *Torat hatte 'udot vesiddurim shel sifre hattorah* (Jerusalem: Magnes, 1941).
18. E.g., Wilhem Rudolph and Paul Volz, *der Elohist also Erzähler. Ein Irrweg der Penteteuchkritik? An der Genesis erlautert* (Berlin: Walter de Gruyter, 1933).

19. Eissfeldt, *The Old Testament*, 200.
20. Norman E. Wagner, "Pentateuchal Criticism: No Clear Future," *Canadian Journal of Theology* 13 (1967) 225-32; Rolf Rendtorff, "Pentateuchal Studies on the Move," *JSOT* 3 (1977) 2-10, 43-45; Erhard Blum, *Die Komposition der Vätergeschichte* (Neukirchen-Vluyn: Neukirchener Verlag, 1984), and *Studien zur Komposition des Pentateuch* (Berlin: Walter de Gruyter, 1990).
21. F. V. Winnett, "Re-examining the Foundations," *JBL* 84 (1965) 1-19.
22. John Van Seters, "Recent Studies on the Pentateuch: A Crisis in Method," *JAOS* 99 (1979) 663-67; and *In Search of History: Historiography in the Ancient World and the Origins of Biblical History* (New Haven: Yale University Press, 1983).
23. R. N. Whybray, *The Making of the Pentateuch: A Methodological Study* (Sheffield: JSOT Press, 1987).

the contribution of Deuteronomic authors to the narrative in the first four books of the Bible. We have seen that Martin Noth made a sharp distinction between the Tetrateuch and Dtr prefaced by Deuteronomy; until recently, this position was widely accepted. In recent years, however, several scholars have argued for a substantial D contribution to the narrative continuum in Genesis–Numbers, especially in key passages such as "the covenant of the pieces" in Genesis 15 and the Sinai/Horeb pericope in Exodus 19–34.[24] Others have noted prophetic and Deuteronomic features in passages routinely attributed to J—e.g., the call of Moses in Exodus 3–4, reminiscent of prophetic commissionings—and have concluded that the first consecutive account of the founding events was put together by members of the Deuteronomic school who linked existing units of tradition by means of the promise of land, nationhood, and divine blessing.[25] These conclusions—the displacement of J to a much later period, a significant D component in Genesis–Numbers, the absorption of J into the D school—are still open to debate, but if they are sustained it is difficult to see how the documentary hypothesis can survive in anything like its classical form. And it goes without saying that they would lead to a very different way of reconstructing the history and religion of Israel.

A more radical attack on the documentary hypothesis, and the historical-critical methods employed by its advocates, has come in recent years from a quite different direction, that of literary-critical theory. The emergence of the New Criticism in the twenties and thirties of this century marked a decisive turning away from the historical, philological, and referential approach to literature with an emphasis on the circumstances of the production and first reception of texts, the psychology and intention of the author, and the like. The proponents of this theory, including such major figures as I. A. Richards and William Empson, favored a text-immanent approach that concentrated on the internal organization and aesthetics of the literary composition without regard to its social and psychological coordinates. A similar concentration on "the text in itself," the text as a closed system, characterizes more recent trends in formalist, structuralist, and post-structuralist interpretation, and it was inevitable that sooner or later such approaches would be applied to biblical texts. This is not the place to evaluate the many essays in interpretation of Pentateuchal narratives of these kinds that have appeared over the last two decades or so. Several (e.g., Roland Barthes's analysis of the Jabbok ford narrative in Genesis 32) have been stimulating, but the results have been uneven, and the best readings have come from professional literary critics familiar with and sensitive to the original language.[26] Synchronic analysis, which takes the text as it is, can open up valuable new perspectives, but without disposing of the need for diachronic—i.e., historical-critical—reconstructions, the principal aim of which has never been aesthetic appreciation of the text.

Similar in some respects is the approach that, since the 1970s, has come to be known as "canonical criticism."[27] Both the new critical and the canonical approaches concentrate on the final form of the text, but with the difference that the latter has an explicitly theological agenda. The contribution of Brevard S. Childs in particular seems to aim at reaffirming the nature of the Bible as a confessional document originating in a faith community. Attention is, therefore, focused on the final form, rather than on the hypothetical origins or sources, of the biblical texts as the proper object of theological inquiry. With respect to the Pentateuch, therefore, Childs seeks to show how the five books are related thematically and how the final editorial stage was based on a reading of the Pentateuch as a whole.[28]

The Final Stage of Formation. It is generally agreed that the Pentateuch achieved its final form during the two centuries (538–334 BCE) when Jews in the province of Judah, and most Jews elsewhere, were subject to Iranian rule. Some, including Wellhausen himself,

24. See Lothar Perlitt, *Bundestheologie im Alten Testament* (Neukirchen-Vluyn: Neukirchener Verlag, 1969); and Ernst Kutsch, *Verheissung und Gesetz* (Berlin: Walter de Gruyter, 1973).

25. See esp. Hans Heinrich Schmid, *Der sogenannte Jahwist: Beobachtungen und Fragen zur Pentateuchforschung* (Zurich: Theologischer Verlag, 1976).

26. E.g., Robert Alter, *The Art of Biblical Narrative* (New York: Basic Books, 1981).

27. Brevard S. Childs, *Introduction to the Old Testament as Scripture* (Philadelphia: Fortress, 1979); and *Old Testament Theology in a Canonical Context* (London: S.C.M., 1985).

28. Childs, *Introduction to the Old Testament as Scripture*, 112-35.

have been prepared to go further and identify the Pentateuch, or at least its legal content, with the law, which Ezra was commissioned to teach and enforce in the Transeuphrates satrapy of the Achaemenid Empire (Ezra 7:1-26). This hypothesis has ancient precedent in the Ezra Apocalypse (late first century CE), which depicts Ezra's reproducing under divine inspiration the sacred books after they had perished in the fall of Jerusalem (2 Esdras 14). The law administered by Ezra was certainly no innovation, since it was presumed to be familiar to Jews in the area under Ezra's jurisdiction (Ezra 7:25). It would be reasonable to assume that, at least in the mind of the author of the Ezra narrative, it was identical with the law referred to on numerous occasions elsewhere in Chronicles–Ezra–Nehemiah, and therefore included legal material from both Deuteronomy and the Priestly writers. But there is no evidence that Ezra "canonized" the law in such a way that no further additions or modifications could be introduced into it. Thus the Temple tax, which is a third of a shekel in Neh 10:33-34, has increased to half a shekel in Exod 30:11-16 (see also 38:25), and the solemn day of fasting and repentance occurs on the twenty-fourth of Tishri, according to Neh 9:1, and on the tenth of the same month in the Priestly law (Lev 16:29; 23:27-32; Num 29:7-11). Admittedly, these divergences could be explained otherwise, but they are consistent with the conclusion that the Pentateuchal law had not attained its final form by the mid-fifth century BCE but was well on its way to doing so.

Our knowledge of Achaemenid imperial administration also suggests that the Pentateuchal law came to serve as the civic constitution of the Jewish ethnos at that time. It was the Persian custom to insist on the codification of local and traditional laws and entrust their implementation to the provincial authorities, including priesthoods, with the backing of the central government. A document example comes from Egypt, since we know from the Demotic chronicle[29] that Darius I appointed a commission composed of representatives of the different orders charged with the task of codifying the traditional laws. After a labor of several years, these laws were

redacted in Aramaic and demotic Egyptian. While there is no direct evidence of such activity in Judah, the proximity of Judah to Egypt and its location in the same satrapy, as well as the consistency of Persian policy in this respect, suggest that something similar may have happened in Judah.

The circumstances under which the narrative achieved its final form are even more obscure. The great importance of the laws as the civic constitution of the nascent Jewish commonwealth would help to explain why the story ends with the death of the lawgiver, and the exclusion of the conquest narrative would be understandable in view of the delicate situation of a small subject province in the vast Achaemenid Empire. The need for a comprehensive corpus of laws resulted in the incorporation of the Deuteronomic law with its historical and homiletic framework into the structure of the Priestly work, which also features law and narrative. This was accomplished by the simple expedient of adding a date of the P type at the beginning of Deuteronomy (1:3), which aligned the book with the overall P chronology. It appears that in the original form of the P narrative Moses' death, preceded by the commissioning of Joshua as his successor, occurred at an earlier point in the wilderness itinerary (Num 27:12-23), following on the deaths of Miriam and Aaron (Num 20:1, 22-29). God commands Moses to ascend Mount Abarim, view the land, and die; the natural implication is that this is to happen at once, delayed only by the need to appoint a successor. But Moses' death is not recorded at this point, because he must first promulgate the second law and covenant in Moab. Only toward the end of Deuteronomy, therefore, do we find a revised version of the appointment of Joshua as successor (32:48-52) and an account of Moses' death (34:1, 7-9), both passages from the hand of a later P writer. The work is then rounded off with a statement denying parity between the Mosaic revelation and prophetic revelations subsequent to Moses' death; a statement that, in effect, establishes the Mosaic age as normative and confers authoritative status on the record of Moses' life and work (Deut 34:10). By this means the post-exilic commonwealth laid a firm foundation in the past for its own

---

29. Papyrus 215 of the Bibliothèque Nationale in Paris.

self-understanding as a community based on covenant and law.

If, then, we view the process of formation beginning with this final stage and working backward, we must assign a decisive role to the Priestly and Deuteronomic writers. The former, whose contribution is relatively easy to detect, were responsible for the basic structuring of the work. The narrative framework within which the massive corpus of Priestly law is presented begins with creation and ends with the establishment of the sanctuary in the promised land (Joshua 18–19). The Deuteronomic contribution is not confined to the book of Deuteronomy but is in evidence elsewhere in the Pentateuch (e.g., Genesis 15; Exodus 32–34), though to what extent still remains to be clarified. If, for the sake of continuity, we continue to speak of J and E, we must now acknowledge that there is no longer any certainty about the origin, date, and extent of these sources. Some of the material assigned to them is either Deuteronomic or of unknown provenance. The J material in Genesis 1–11 may even be later than P, serving as a reflective supplement and commentary in the manner of the later stages. Both D and P have certainly incorporated early traditions and written sources in prose and verse, but the entire issue of pre-exilic source material in the Pentateuch—its extent, its origins written and oral, and its editorial history—remains to be clarified.

READING THE PENTATEUCH THEOLOGICALLY

A theological reading of the Pentateuch must take account not only of the final form but also of the successive restructurings, re-editings, and expansions that, according to a historical-critical reading, eventuated in the final form. This process implies that any theologically significant theme will have undergone a process of development. In addition, different traditions, notably those of the Priestly and Deuteronomic writers, have been allowed to coexist even where they differ in significant respects. Reducing these perspectives to a common theological denominator

would risk missing the richness and variety of religious thinking in the Pentateuch.

Theological understanding is also conditioned by the point of view, the perspective, of the reader and the convictions of the community within which the text is read. Neither Judaism nor Christianity has assigned absolute and exclusive authority to the Pentateuch. In Judaism functional canonicity includes Mishnah, Gemarah, and Toseftah, understood as the deposit of the oral law. Early Christianity continued to regard the Law and the Prophets as authoritative but read them in the light of the new reality in Christ. Persons and events in the Pentateuch were interpreted as prefiguring this new reality and the prophets as predicting it. The laws in the Pentateuch were evaluated in widely different ways from the apostolic period on. From an early date, the Decalogue served as a compendium of moral teaching (e.g., in the *Didache*), a circumstance that, when taken with the neglect of the ritual laws, explains why it played a very minor role in Jewish teaching. (It is mentioned only twice in the Mishnah.) This issue came to the fore with particular clarity at the Reformation. The Lutheran distinction between law and gospel, reinforced by Luther's own often-expressed aversion to Judaism, resulted in a distinct undervaluation of the legal content of the Pentateuch. Calvinism, on the other hand, tended rather to overestimate the place of law in Christian theology and church polity. The result is that only in recent years have Christian biblical scholars begun to give serious and unprejudiced attention to the legal material, including the ritual law.

While this is clearly not the place to attempt a comprehensive survey or synthesis of religious ideas in the Pentateuch, which would be tantamount to writing a history of Israelite religion, some account should be given of the leading theological symbols and ideas in the major literary strands.

The Priestly Writers (P). While several Jewish scholars have followed Yehezkel Kaufmann[30] in dating P to the pre-exilic period, the majority opinion has placed this school in the sixth or fifth century BCE while allowing that much of the legal and cultic

---

30. Y. Kaufmann, *The Religion of Israel from Its Beginnings to the Babylonian Exile* (New York: Schocken, 1972).

material may have originated earlier. There is no consensus on the issue of P's relation to earlier narrative material, some viewing it as basically commentary and editorial expansion and others as an independent narrative source. In favor of the latter alternative, at least with regard to the narrative core of the P material, are the thematic and linguistic correspondences between the creation account in Gen 1:1–2:3, the construction of the wilderness sanctuary in Exodus 35–40 (see especially 39:32; 40:33), and its establishment at Shiloh in the land of Canaan (Josh 18:1; 19:51).[31] One implication of this structural feature is that the created order exists for the worship and praise of God. The seven days of creation represent the liturgical week. Sabbath is rooted in the created order, and the fact that its celebration concludes the construction of the wilderness sanctuary signals a close association between world building and sanctuary building (Exod 31:12-17). The heavenly bodies are created on the fourth day as a means of establishing the religious calendar. If we confine ourselves to the P strand, the Sinai event consists exclusively in the reception by Moses in a vision of the specifications for the sanctuary and its cult (Exod 19:1; 24:15-18; 25–31), which can be inaugurated only after the ordination of priests, a ceremony that also lasts seven days (Leviticus 8–9).

Even if it is argued that the P version was intended to be read together with other, and presumably earlier, accounts of the Sinai/Horeb event, it is still remarkable that this source omits any reference to a covenant. The P source in fact represents a rather radical rethinking of the covenant idea, no doubt in response to the situation of exile. The first covenant is made with the new humanity after the flood, long before Israel appears on the historical scene (Gen 9:8-17). All of humanity had received a religious qualification at creation (Gen 1:26-28), and now is offered a new dispensation, including the so-called Noachide laws, and an unconditional commitment on the part of God to preserve the new creation. The only covenant with Israel recorded in P is with Abraham, to whom is promised nationhood, land, and the divine presence (Gen 17:1-21). Both of these covenants, with humanity and with Israel, are unilateral and unconditional, since circumcision is the sign of Israel's covenant and not a stipulation on the observance of which God's promise is contingent. Both are also "everlasting covenants" (Gen 9:16; 17:7-8, 13) that, therefore, do not require periodic renewal as do most covenants. All that is called for is that God *remember* the covenant commitment, which God does when the people are languishing in exile (Exod 2:24; 6:5; Lev 26:42, 45).

According to P the covenant promise of divine presence is fulfilled through the erection of the sanctuary and the inauguration of the cult, a conclusion implicit in the structure of the core narrative. Throughout the wilderness journey, presence is signified by the mysterious glory or effulgence (כבוד *kābôd*) that comes to rest in the sanctuary (Exod 40:34-35), appears when important decisions have to be taken (e.g., Num 14:10; 16:19), and guides Israel in its progress to the land. In P, all aspects of the liturgical life of the people are revealed in orderly fashion. Only rituals not requiring presence in the sanctuary and the participation of the priesthood are revealed before the cult is inaugurated; namely, sabbath (Exod 31:12-17; cf. 16:22-30), circumcision (Gen 17:9-14), and Passover (Exod 12:1-28). The P version of the flood story, therefore, omits mention of the distinction between clean and unclean animals and Noah's sacrifice on leaving the ark. The basic rationale for the sacrificial cult, as of the laws governing clean and unclean and sexual relations, is to preserve and, where necessary, restore the cosmic order established at creation. That order is disturbed by sin, even involuntary sin (e.g., bodily discharges), and can be restored only by the mandatory purgation and reparation sacrifices (Lev 4:1–6:7). The tenfold occurrence in the creation recital of the phrase "according to its/their kind" suggests that the distinction between clean and unclean fauna (Leviticus 11–15) was intended to preserve the norms established in creation and to inculcate a reverent regard for the created order. Although often dismissed as archaic and irrational, these and similar regulations reflect an ecological concern in the broadest sense, a discriminating ethical attitude to the taking of life for human

31. J. Blenkinsopp, "The Structure of P," *CBQ* 38 (1976) 275-92.

nourishment, and a concern for the body as that part of the world for which each one is more directly responsible.

The Deuteronomists (D). A significantly different perspective is apparent in the Deuteronomic corpus, consisting in Deuteronomy, the Deuteronomistic History (Joshua–2 Kings), additions to the narrative in the Tetrateuch, and editorial accretions in several prophetic books, especially Jeremiah. Deuteronomy presents not so much a law as a program or polity for the future Israelite commonwealth. Endowed with the authority of Moses as lawgiver and founder of the nation, it grounds the social existence of the people on the new covenant made on the eve of entry into the land. Unlike the P covenant, that of the Deuteronomists is genuinely bilateral and conditional in that its maintenance is contingent on a faithful and trustful commitment on the part of Israel to the observance of the Law. In this respect, it is comparable to, and was probably influenced in its formulation by, more or less contemporary Assyrian vassal treaties. The emphasis, therefore, is on Israel as a moral community. The connection between the fulfillment of the promises and faith that finds expression in fidelity to the law is already clearly articulated in the Deuteronomic profile of Abraham (Gen 18:17-19; 22:16-18; 26:4-5), the starting point for the presentation of Abraham in both Judaism and Christianity as the model and paradigm of faith (e.g., Heb 11:8-12). On numerous occasions, the Mosaic homilies in Deuteronomy emphasize that the gift of land is contingent on fidelity to the Law, and it is made abundantly clear that without faith Israel cannot fulfill its destiny (see Deut 1:32; 9:23).

The covenant is also the basis for Israel's election and its consequent special status vis-à-vis the nations of the world. While the dangerous ambiguities inherent in this idea of election are abundantly clear, the Deuteronomists emphasize repeatedly both its origin in a divine initiative (see Deut 4:32-40; 7:7-11) and the obligations it entails (7:7-11). The uniqueness of Israel, thus defined and circumscribed, is emphasized at every turn. Thus the law is seen as the counterpart of the intellectual tradition or wisdom of other peoples (Deut 4:5-8), and prophecy is contrasted with divination and similar forms of mediation

practiced elsewhere (13:1-5; 18:9-22). Most important, Deuteronomy insists on an exclusive relationship with one God: Yahweh, God of Israel. This conviction, of immense significance for the future, is enshrined in the שמע *šěma'* (Deut 6:4-9), a confessional formula that has sustained the faith of the Jewish people down to the present.

The incorporation of Deuteronomy into the framework of the P narrative resulted in the juxtaposition within the same corpus of different theological perspectives, those of the two major schools and those of their sources. Thus the covenant of obligation of D is balanced against the promissory and indefectible covenant of the P writers, and the more limited and nationalistic perspective of Deuteronomy is offset by the more universalistic range of the P work. The extension of the narrative back to creation and the early history of humanity also permitted the grounding of institutions—sabbath and covenant—in antecedents of unimpeachable antiquity. This combination also provides an illustration of the tension between tradition and situation. Like Israel, both synagogue and church draw their self-understanding, their ability to survive and flourish, from the myth of their origins, constantly repeated and reactualized in recital and ritual. Appeal to a shared memory, so prominent in Deuteronomy, is a central feature of the Pentateuch. It appears with particular clarity in the festivals that memorialize the founding events of the community. It is also a prominent feature of the legal tradition. It is noteworthy, for example, how care for the rights of the resident alien is enjoined on the grounds of collective memory: "You shall not oppress a resident alien; you know the heart of an alien, for you were aliens in the land of Egypt" (Exod 23:9 NRSV). But allegiance to the past must also allow for openness to the demands imposed by life in a changing world, requiring an ongoing testing and reinterpreting of what has been received. A careful and critical reading of the Pentateuch shows that this process of incorporating and reinterpreting the past continued throughout the history of Israel.

Other Sources. While the existence of *continuous* early, pre-exilic sources can no longer be taken for granted, the Pentateuch in its final, post-exilic form has clearly incorporated much pre-exilic narrative and legal source material. With the possible exception of Abraham, of whom we first begin to hear in exilic texts (Ezek 33:24), traditions about the ancestors were in circulation from an early time (e.g., Hos 12:4-5, 13), as also about the exodus (e.g., Amos 3:1; 9:7; Hos 2:15; 11:1) and wilderness period (e.g., Hos 2:14-15; 9:10). In whatever form these traditions circulated, they served to sustain a sense of corporate identity strong enough to survive the destruction of the state and the experience of exile, and they have continued down to the present to exercise this function for the different "interpretive communities" that have accepted them.

The J version of the early history of humanity in Genesis 1–11 has generally been assigned a date in the early monarchy period, perhaps as early as Solomon's reign, though we have seen reason to suspect that a much later date would be more appropriate. Using ancient Mesopotamian mythic traditions as a model, the author projects on to human origins a psychologically profound and disturbing diagnosis of human existence. In a manner reminiscent of some of the later prophets (e.g., Jer 17:9-10) and sages (e.g., Job 14:1-6), the author emphasizes both the ineradicable human tendency to evil (see especially Gen 6:5 and 8:21) and the reality of divine mercy and forgiveness. In their own quite different way, the stories about the ancestors (however they originated and in whatever form they were known to the post-exilic redactors) also succeed in rendering the richness and complexity of human existence in the presence of God. These stories are unified by the promise of land, progeny, and divine blessing, announced at the outset (Gen 12:1-3) and repeated at regular intervals throughout (e.g., 13:14-17; 15:7-21; 26:2-4; 46:2-3). Yet at the crucial points of the narrative—at the beginning, in the middle, and at the end—the protagonists are outside the land, and the story ends with exile in Egypt. In this situation of deferred fulfillment, Abraham is presented as the model of trust and fidelity, especially in the climactic scene of the near-sacrifice of Isaac (Genesis 22). The Jacob narrative, less schematic and psychologically more realistic than that of Abraham, is organized around the twenty-year exile of the protagonist and

the transformation he must undergo in order to bear the name Israel (Gen 32:22-32; cf. 35:9-15 P).

The "Song at the Sea" (Exod 15:1-18), one of the oldest poems in the HB, celebrates deliverance from slavery in Egypt by miraculous, divine intervention. The accompanying prose account narrating the sequence of events leading up to this point is also based on ancient tradition, though we are no longer able to identify its earliest formulation or trace its development in detail. These events were decisive for Israel's self-identity and its relationship with its God ("I am Yahweh your God from the land of Egypt" [Hos 12:9; 13:4]). Commemorated in the Passover ceremony, they achieved paradigmatic status for both community and individual: "In every generation one must look upon oneself as if one had in one's own person come out of Egypt." Something similar can be said of the wilderness narratives (Exod 15:22–18:27; Num 10:29–36:13), also based on ancient tradition, as exemplifying divine guidance and providence and legitimating the institutional life of the community. This context, then, confers on the law given at Sinai/Horeb its character as gift and grace.

BIBLIOGRAPHY

Alter, Robert. *The Art of Biblical Narrative.* New York: Basic Books, 1981.

Blenkinsopp, Joseph. *The Pentateuch: An Introduction to the First Five Books of the Bible.* Anchor Bible Reference Library. New York: Doubleday, 1992.

_____. *Prophecy and Canon.* Notre Dame: University of Notre Dame Press, 1977.

Knight, Douglas A. "The Pentateuch." In Douglas A. Knight and Gene M. Tucker, eds. *The Hebrew Bible and Its Modern Interpreters.* Chico, Calif.: Scholars Press, 1985.

Noth, Martin. *A History of Pentateuchal Traditions.* Englewood Cliffs, N.J.: Prentice-Hall, 1972.

Rendtorff, Rolf. "Pentateuchal Studies on the Move," *JSOT*3 (1977) 2-10, 43-45.

Van Seters, John. *In Search of History: Historiography in the Ancient World and the*

Origins of Biblical History. New Haven: Yale University Press, 1983.

————. "Recent Studies on the Pentateuch: A Crisis in Method," *JAOS* 99 (1979) 663-67.

von Rad, Gerhard. "The Form-Critical Problem of the Hexateuch." In *The Problem of the Hexateuch and Other Essays.* New York: McGraw-Hill, 1966, 1-78.

————. *Old Testament Theology.* Vol. 1: *The Theology of Israel's Historical Traditions.* Translated by D. M. G. Stalker. New York: Harper & Row, 1962.

Whybray, R. Norman. *The Making of the Pentateuch: A Methodological Study.* Sheffield: JSOT, 1987.

Winnett, F. V. "Re-examining the Foundations," *JBL* 84 (1965) 1-19.

THE BOOK OF GENESIS

INTRODUCTION, COMMENTARY, AND REFLECTIONS
BY
TERENCE E. FRETHEIM

THE BOOK OF
GENESIS

INTRODUCTION

T he book of Genesis stands at the head of the canon. Its range is breathtaking, moving from cosmos to family, from ordered world to reconciled brothers, from the seven days of the creation of the universe to the seventy descendants of Jacob entering the land of their sojourn. Hence, it stands as a monumental challenge to the interpreter.

The canonical placement of Genesis is important for various reasons. Genesis is a book about beginnings, from the beginnings of the universe and various orderings of humankind to the beginnings of the people of Israel. It also witnesses to the beginnings of God's activity in the life of the world. But creation is more than chronology. Genesis stands at the beginning because creation is such a fundamental theological category for the rest of the canon. God's continuing blessing and ordering work at every level is creational. Moreover, only in relationship to the creation can God's subsequent actions in and through Israel be properly understood. The placement of creation demonstrates that God's purposes with Israel are universal in scope. God's work in redemption serves creation, the *entire* creation, since it reclaims a creation that labors under the deep and pervasive effects of sin. Even more, the canonical placement makes clear that God's redemptive work does not occur in a vacuum; it occurs in a context that has been shaped in decisive ways by the life-giving, creative work of God. Redemption can never be understood as *ex nihilo* without denigrating God's gifts given in creation.

THE CRITICAL STUDY OF GENESIS

For more than two hundred years, *source criticism* has provided the predominant literary approach to the study of Genesis and the Pentateuch. In fact, Genesis has often been studied only as part of this larger literary whole. Hence, Genesis is usually seen as a composite work, consisting primarily of three interwoven sources (Yahwist [J], Elohist [E], Priestly [P]), with some texts attributed to other traditions (e.g., chaps. 14 and 49). Genesis thus grew over time, with

19

these sources gradually brought together by redactors over five hundred years or more, from the United Monarchy to the post-exilic era.

This long-prevailing scholarly consensus has come under sharp challenge from a number of perspectives in the last generation. From within the source-critical perspective, the nature, scope, and dating of the sources have been regular subjects of debate. Few doubt that Genesis consists of traditions from various historical periods, but there is little consensus regarding the way in which they have been brought together into their present form.[1]

I view Genesis as a patchwork quilt of traditions from various periods in Israel's life. The earliest stories date from before the monarchy; over time certain traditions began to coalesce around key figures, such as Abraham and Jacob, and more extensive blocks were gradually built up. The fact that the major sections of Genesis (generally, chaps. 1–11; 12–25; 26–36; 37–50) remain identifiable clusters within a relatively thin, overarching framework sustains this theory. A redactor (probably J) wove these clusters of tradition together into a coherent whole, provided a basic framework (perhaps focused on the ancestral promises), and integrated them with the larger story of the Pentateuch. While J probably worked early in the monarchical period, arguments for a later date for the Yahwist are attractive (not least because of the sophisticated form of its anthropomorphisms). Over the centuries reworkings of this collection took place, drawing on other, as yet unintegrated, traditions (the Elohist may be one such supplementary reworking). One major redaction is to be identified with P (probably during the exile); this redactor drew on materials from a wide variety of sources, older and more recent, and placed a decisive stamp on the entire corpus. It is possible that deuteronomistic redactors worked over this material at a later time, integrating it into a still larger collection with only minor touch-ups.

The purpose of these retellings of the material is not entirely clear and may vary, involving sociopolitical and religious issues. Each reworking made it ever more difficult to discern where the inherited traditions and the retellings begin and end. It is likely, however, that theological and kerygmatic interests come more and more into play, so that finally one must speak of the essential testimonial character of the material, a witness to the complex interrelationships of divine action and human response.[2]

Newer literary approaches have also called into question many of the assumptions and conclusions of the source-critical consensus. These strategies focus on issues of literary criticism rather than literary history, on the texts as they are rather than any history prior to their present shape. Such readers attempt to hear the texts as we now have them and to discern their various rhetorical features as they work together to form a coherent whole. At times, this analysis has been undertaken with an eye to literary parallels in other ancient Near Eastern literature (e.g., the *Gilgamesh Epic*).[3]

The book of Genesis has been one of the most popular workshops for these approaches. Over the last two decades hundreds of articles and sections of books have mined the literary riches of these chapters and unearthed many insights into the ways in which they can be read with greater profit. Yet, it is not so clear how these gains are to be integrated with the more historical approaches. While historical issues continue to be important, this commentary will emphasize literary approaches in order to perceive what makes these texts work.

Literary studies and analyses of the theological movement within these texts have not kept pace with one another. For example, many literary (and other) studies simply work with the assumptions and conclusions of classical theism in the analysis of the theological material the texts present. On the other hand, some studies take pains to treat the theological elements at the same level as any other (e.g., God becomes a character like every other). I will attend to the theological dynamic of the text and recognize its special stature in view of the community of faith that produced it and the canonical place eventually given to it.[4]

1. For a recent survey, see R. N. Whybray, *The Making of the Pentateuch* (Sheffield: *JSOT*, 1987); and J. Blenkinsopp, *The Pentateuch: An Introduction to the First Five Books of the Bible* (New York: Doubleday, 1992) 1-30.

2. See W. Brueggemann and H. W. Wolff, *The Vitality of Old Testament Traditions* (Atlanta: John Knox, 1982).

3. On new literary approaches, see R. Alter, *The Art of Biblical Narrative* (New York: Basic Books, 1981). On extra-biblical parallels, see D. Damrosch, *The Narrative Covenant* (San Francisco: Harper & Row, 1987).

4. On theology and narrative, see Terence E. Fretheim, *Exodus,* Interpretation (Louisville: Westminster/John Knox, 1990) 10-12.

Another lively concern in Genesis studies has to do with ancient Near Eastern parallels (and beyond, possibly even Greece). Since the unearthing of the Mesopotamian accounts of creation and the flood over a century ago, augmented since by numerous discoveries, scholars have devoted considerable attention to discerning possible links with Genesis. While this is true of Genesis as a whole, parallels to chaps. 1–11 have constituted a special focus. Although direct points of dependence do not seem common, it is clear that Israel participated in a comprehensive ancient Near Eastern culture that had considerable impact on its ways of thinking and writing, both in details and with larger themes. Apart from more formal links, such as language, some have tended to view these parallels largely in negative terms. At the same time, Israel's deep dependence upon its cultural context extends even to theological matters (e.g., the understanding of moral order or creation by word) and to the very creation-disruption-flood structure of chaps. 1–11. Interpreters must maintain a fine balance between recognizing such dependence (finally, a witness to the work of the Creator) and Israel's genuinely new and imaginative ideas and formulations.

Feminist scholarship has produced important studies that have influenced this commentary at numerous points. This work has attended particularly to the place of the woman in chaps. 1–3 and the prominent role of women in the ancestral narratives. Phyllis Trible's work, in particular, has had an immense and salutary influence. In addition, anthropological and sociological studies have expanded our knowledge of the issues of kinship and culture.[5] Generally, a proliferation of approaches is elucidating ever new dimensions of these important biblical materials.

LITERARY FORM

There are basically two types of literature in Genesis, narrative and numerative, to use Westermann's language.[6] Poetic pieces are integrated into the narratives as well (e.g., 2:23; 3:14-19; 16:11-12; 25:23; 27:27-29, 39-40; 49:1-27).

1. Narratives. Little consensus has emerged regarding the proper label for these narratives, though *saga* has been used often. The issues in chaps. 1–11 are particularly complex (see below). "Family narrative (story)" emphasizes the family unit as central to these texts, and in a way that has no real parallel elsewhere in the OT. While not historiographical in character and with much imagination used in the telling, the narratives do possess certain features associated with history writing, e.g., a chronological framework and some cumulative and developmental character.[7]

The language of story may be most helpful in determining how these materials functioned for Israel.[8] They are told in such a way that they could become the story of each ensuing generation. The readers could participate in a great, yet often quite hidden, drama of divine action and human response. At this juncture of past story and present reality Israel came to know what it meant to be the people of God. The faith was not fundamentally an idea, but an embodiment, a way of life. The language and experience of faith thus remained concrete and personal. Thus it has the capacity to keep the reader anchored in this world. It does not dissolve into myth, into some mystical world of the gods that suppresses the human or the natural, or some religious world far removed from the secular sphere. By and large, the world reflected in these stories is ordinary, everyday, and familiar, filled with the surprises and joys, the sufferings and the troubles, the complexities and ambiguities known to every community.

At the same time, the story form allows (in a way that history proper does not) an admixture of Israel's story and God's story. But even the latter is seen to be this-worldly, as God works toward the divine purposes in and through less than perfect individuals and world. And God's

5. Phyllis Trible, *God and the Rhetoric of Sexuality* (Philadelphia: Fortress, 1978) 72-143; see also the work of R. Hendel and C. Meyers, listed in the bibliography.

6. C. Westermann, *Genesis 1–11: A Commentary* (Minneapolis: Augsburg, 1984) 6.

7. On the Pentateuch as a historiographical work in comparison with early Greek histories, see the assessment of John van Seters in Blenkinsopp, *The Pentateuch*, 37-42.

8. See T. Fretheim, *Deuteronomic History* (Nashville: Abingdon, 1983) 39-40; R. W. L. Moberly, *The Old Testament of the Old Testament: Patriarchal Narratives and Mosaic Yahwism* (Minneapolis: Fortress, 1992) 130-46; D. Steinmetz, *From Father to Son: Kinship, Conflict and Continuity in Genesis* (Louisville: Westminster/John Knox, 1991) 134-55.

story has the ultimate purpose, not of bringing people into some heavenly sphere, but of enabling a transformation of this life.

The capacity of the story to draw one into it in such a way as to encompass the full life of the reader has the effect of overcoming the distance between past story and present reader; the horizons merge. At the same time, readers will encounter that which is often different from their own stories; there are surprises and discontinuities as past and present life stories come into contact with one another. Some hearers may reject the story, but for those who respond positively the story may provide a means of shaping identity (a constitutive function), a mirror for self-identity (a descriptive function), or a model for the life of faith (a paradigmatic function). One may thereby not only become a member of the people of God, but also come to know who one is, and what shape the life of faith ought to take in the world.

The narratives offer an exercise in self-understanding. They become a vehicle through which a new generation can learn its identity once again as the people of Abraham, a people who have trod in his footsteps, who have taken his journey. It is one more retelling of the past, not to find patterns for moral behavior, but to understand who we are as the people of God who have inherited these commands and promises, who have ventured down similar paths. We can thereby see where we have been, who we now are, and the shape of our paths into the future.

2. Genealogies. "Genesis is a book whose plot is genealogy."[9] Israel formulated family trees, often with social and political overtones. As with us, they were concerned about kinship interrelationships and tracking family origins and "pedigrees," especially for important figures. Also similar is the way in which genealogies are woven into family stories. Major portions of seven chapters in Genesis consist of genealogies, an interest evident in other OT texts (e.g., Chronicles) as well as in the NT (see Matthew 1; Luke 1).

The ten תולדות (*tôlēdôt* translated either "genealogy"/"generations" or "account"/ "story")—2:4 (heaven and earth); 5:1 (Adam); 6:9 (Noah); 10:1 (Noah's sons); 11:10 (Shem); 11:27 (Terah); 25:12 (Ishmael); 25:19 (Isaac); 36:1, 9 (Esau); 37:2 (Jacob)—constitute a prominent structuring device in Genesis. These Priestly genealogies are supplemented by a few others (e.g., that of Cain, 4:17-26). Genealogies have an enumerative style, but at times they are "broken" by narrative pieces (e.g., 10:8-12). They usually introduce a section, but at times they look both backward and forward (2:4; 37:2). One type of genealogy is linear (one person in each generation, 5:1-32); the other is segmented (multiple lines of descent), characteristic of branches of the family outside the chosen line (table of nations; Ishmael; Esau). Because genealogies cut across the break between chaps. 11 and 12, they witness to the fundamental creational unity of Genesis.

The historical value of the genealogies is much debated, but their function of providing continuity over these chapters probably means that they were understood as some kind of historical anchor for the larger story. Their original setting was the family or tribe, those most interested in such matters, and within which they were often transmitted orally over many generations. They show that every character is kin to every other, a key to Israelite self-identity, especially in times of conflict or dispersion. Hence, Genesis is fundamentally about one big extended family. The genealogies also demonstrate that Israel is truly kin to all the surrounding peoples, a fact that helps to develop the meaning of the people's special role. The genealogies thus are integrally related to the essential concerns of the narratives.

Because genealogies order people into families, and witness to the continued existence of families in spite of much difficulty and dysfunctionality, they fit most fundamentally within a theology of creation (so explicitly in 5:1-2). They present "the steady, ongoing rhythm of events which stamp the course of human existence—birth, length of life, begetting, death" in which both God and human beings participate.[10] Moreover, because the first of the *tôlēdôt* includes the nonhuman, genealogies link human and nonhuman into a larger *creational family*, in which every creature is, in effect, kin to every other. Even more, because genealogies also encompass

---

9. N. Steinberg, "The Genealogical Framework of the Family Stories in Genesis," *Semeia* 46 (1989) 41. Generally, see R. Wilson, *Genealogy and History in the Biblical World* (New Haven: Yale University Press, 1977).

10. Westermann, *Genesis 1–11*, 7.

larger human groupings (10:1-32; 25:12-18), they witness to the range of the divine creative activity in the ordering of the world.

The narratives, on the other hand, "are inherently messy . . . take account of much that is problematic and contingent, all the vagaries of human life . . . pursuing a far less predictable course of surprise and unanticipated events."[11] Naomi Steinberg speaks of genealogies reintroducing equilibrium into such messy family lives, restabilizing them for the next journey into a volatile future. Yet, she shows that this perspective is too simple. Some genealogies also contain elements of disequilibrium, contingency, and open-endedness (see 11:30; 25:19-26; 37:2); hence, the genealogies do not witness so univocally to order and stability as one might initially think.[12] Indeed, most genealogies contain such an unusual element (e.g., 5:24 on Enoch; 5:29; 6:9 on Noah; 10:8-12 on Nimrod). Such features integrate narrative messiness into the very heart of the genealogical order. They show thereby that the genealogies do not witness to a *determined* order of reality. Cain's genealogy (4:17-26) testifies further to this integration; it *intensifies* the contingencies of the prior narratives. Genealogies are finally *insufficient* for ordering purposes; another type of divine activity will be needed in order to reclaim the creation— namely, redemption.

FAITH AND HISTORY IN GENESIS

The book of Genesis does not present the reader with historical narrative, at least in any modern sense. Its primary concerns are theological and kerygmatic. Those responsible for the material as we now have it (and no doubt at other stages in its transmission) were persons of faith concerned to speak or reflect on a word of God to other persons of faith. The voice of a living community of faith resounds through these texts. Rooted in history in this way, Genesis is not socially or historically disinterested; it was written—at each stage of transmission—with the problems and possibilities of a particular audience in view.

Although scholars have a difficult time discerning those audiences, the text is linked to specific times and places. While the latest redactors may well have made the witness of the text more generally available to ongoing communities of faith, the material has not been flattened out into generalities. The most basic shaping of Genesis probably occurred in exile. Traditions in Genesis are consistent with other examples of creation language during this era, as evidenced by Isaiah 40–55, which relates Israel's future to the universal purposes of God. Affirmations of divine faithfulness to ancient promises—a veritable litany in these texts—speak volumes in a time when the future appears to stand in jeopardy. In attending to Israel's ancestral heritage, both in narrative and in genealogy, the authors address sharp issues of communal identity. The various stories of the ancestors often seem to mirror the history of Israel, assisting the exiles in coming to terms with their own past (this will often be noted in the commentary; e.g., the parallels between 12:10-20 and the exodus). These texts spoke a clear word of God to exiled people.

The literary vehicle in and through which this word of God is addressed narrates a story of the past. Although the ancient writers were not concerned with reconstructing a history of this early era, modern scholars have had a great interest in determining the extent to which these texts reflect "what actually happened" (on chaps. 1–11, see below). This task has been made difficult by the nature of the texts themselves as well as by the difficulties of assessing extrabiblical parallels.

Scholarly efforts at historical reconstruction of the ancestral period have had mixed results.[13] A period of some confidence in the basic historicity of these texts within the second millennium BCE has faded in recent years in view of the character of the texts and challenges to the interpretation of putative archaeological evidence. Since the biblical texts underwent a long period of transmission, they reflect aspects of Israel's history all along the way. For example, relationships

---

11. R. Robinson, "Literary Functions of the Genealogies of Genesis," *CBQ* 48 (1986) 597.

12. Steinberg, "The Genealogical Framework of the Family Stories in Genesis."

13. See a survey in G. Ramsey, *The Quest for the Historical Israel* (Atlanta: John Knox, 1981) 28-43. See also K. McCarter, "The Historical Abraham," *Int* 42 (1988) 341-52.

between these texts and other tribal and genealogical OT materials suggest that various historical realities from both before and after the United Monarchy are reflected in them. Various ancient Near Eastern parallels to patriarchal names, customs, and modes of life have at times been overdrawn; yet they are not finally without historical value, even for a second-millennium dating at some points. While it is not possible to determine whether the women and men of Genesis were actual historical persons, it seems reasonable to claim that the narratives carry some authentic memories of Israel's pre-exodus heritage. At the same time, Israel's valuing of these materials for its own faith and life appears not to have centered on issues of historicity; however, it is likely that Israel thought these traditions derived from pre-exodus times.

The religion of the ancestors reflected in the texts also figures in this discussion about historical background. The religious (and other) practices of these chapters are often distinctive when compared to later Israelite convention.[14] Hence, later Israelites did not simply read their own religious lives back into these texts (though nothing seems to be incompatible with later Yahwism). They preserved some memories of earlier practices, including worship of God under various forms of the name El (see 16:13; 21:33; 33:20; El is the high god in the Canaanite pantheon), referred to as the God of my/our/your father(s), the God of Abraham, the God of Isaac, and the God of Jacob. The ancestral God was understood to be a personal deity who accompanied this family on its journeys, providing care and protection. Some traditions understand that Yahweh was a name revealed only at the time of Moses (Exod 3:14-16; Exod 6:2-3) and that El was an earlier name for God (although the OT generally understands El to be an alternate name for Yahweh). The frequent use of Yahweh in Genesis is anachronistic in some ways, but it conveys an important theological conviction—namely, that the God whom the ancestors worshiped under the name El had characteristics common to Yahweh and, in fact, is to be identified with Yahweh.

UNITY, STRUCTURE, AND THEME

It has long been the practice in Genesis study to drive a sharp wedge between chaps. 1–11, the so-called Primeval History (Story), and chaps. 12–50, the Patriarchal (Ancestral) History. More recently, under the impact of literary-critical readings, there has been renewed interest in the integrity of Genesis as a whole.[15]

In some ways this division is appropriate, with chap. 12 marking a new stage in God's relationship with the world. Even those who sharpen this division often note that 12:1-3 is a fulcrum text, linking Abraham with "all the families of the earth." Hence, it has been common to claim that God's choice of Abraham had a universal purpose: to extend God's salvific goals through this family to the entire world. Even more, this theme has been tracked through chaps. 12–50, with particular attention not only to its verbal repetition (e.g., 18:18; 22:18; 26:4; 28:14), but also to the numerous contacts made between Israel's ancestors and the "non-chosen" peoples. Remarkably little polemic is directed against outsiders in the Genesis text. The promises of God to Abraham are intended for the world. The way in which Israel's ancestors did or did not respond to this intention served as a negative or positive model for every generation.

The focus of such discussion has been so sharply placed on "salvation history" that creation themes have been neglected. Even more, it is striking the extent to which the more emphatic themes of chaps. 12–50 are grounded in chaps. 1–11, wherein God promises and blesses, elects and saves. God first establishes a covenant and makes promises, not to Abraham, but to Noah (6:18 and 9:8-17); God's promissory activity in Israel participates in God's promissory relation to the larger world (see the manifold promises to Ishmael and Esau). God's work of blessing in the world does not begin with Abraham; it is integral to chaps. 1–11 (see 9:1, 26) and so God's blessing work through Abraham must involve intensification and pervasiveness, not a

---

14. For a review, see Moberly, *The Old of the Old Testament.*

15. See D. Clines, *The Theme of the Pentateuch* (Sheffield: *JSOT*, 1978); B. Childs, *Introduction to the Old Testament as Scripture* (Philadelphia: Fortress, 1979) 136-60; B. Dahlberg, "On Recognizing the Unity of Genesis," *TD* 24 (1977) 360-67; T. Mann, "All the Families of the Earth: The Theological Unity of Genesis," *Int* 45 (1991) 341-53; and Overview sections in this commentary.

new reality. Since God saves Noah, his family, and the animals (Ps 36:6), God does not become a savior with Abraham or Israel. Issues of creation and redemption are integrated throughout Genesis. God's promises and salvific acts must finally be seen as serving all of creation. God acts to free people, indeed the entire world, to be what they were created to be.[16]

Scholars have noted various forms of evidence for structured unity in Genesis, especially in the genealogies (extending from 2:4 to 37:2) and the divine promises (from 8:21 to 50:24). More refined efforts to discern structures throughout the book have been less successful, with the focus of attention on the four major, distinct sections.[17] Links within Genesis have been discerned in chaps. 1–11 and 37–50, from family discord/harmony, to fertility (1:28 and 47:27), to the extension of life to a flood/famine-filled world (41:57), to the "good" that God is about in the creation and through this family (50:20); in some sense Joseph functions as a new Adam (41:38).

At the same time, the Joseph story does not occasion a return to Eden. Sin and its ill effects remain very much in place. Human life, more generally, becomes ever more complex as one moves from Adam to Joseph. These developments are matched by shifts in the imaging of God, whose words and deeds become less direct and obtrusive. God's actions are never all-controlling in Genesis, but a more prominent role is given to the human in the Joseph story, from the transmission of promises to the exercise of leadership. These developments correlate with narratives that become less and less episodic.[18]

The following themes in Genesis as a whole may be gathered; creation themes remain prominent throughout. (1) The presence and activity of God in every sphere of life, among nonchosen and chosen, for purposes of judgment and salvation. These two themes tie chaps. 1–11 closely to chaps. 12–50: God responds to ongoing human sinfulness through sentence and judgment (often involving creational realities, from flood to plague to fire and brimstone); God also responds in a gracious way to humankind, even though their lives have been deeply affected by sin and its consequences. (2) Blessing is a creational category in which both God and humankind, nonchosen and chosen, are engaged. This theme includes the continuity of the family through the struggles of barrenness and birth, and the fertility of fields and animals, often juxtaposed with famine. Blessing also relates to land, raising ecological considerations that are not far from the surface (from the flood to Sodom and Gomorrah). (3) The pervasive concern for kinship and family, an order of creation. One contemporary way of looking at chaps. 12–50 is through the lens of family systems theory and the manifestations of a dysfunctional family one sees throughout. The various dimensions of family life belong within the sphere of God's concern. God is at work in and through family problems and possibilities for purposes of reconciliation (50:20). (4) Concern for the life of the nation also entails one of the most basic orders of creation. In the Joseph story especially, the writers devote attention to issues of economics, agriculture, and the dynamics of political and governmental life more generally, in and through which God is at work for blessing (41:53-57; 47:13-26). (5) The role of the human in the divine economy. It is not uncommon to denigrate the importance of human activity in these chapters. For example, von Rad states: "The story of Hagar shows us a fainthearted faith that cannot leave things to God and believes it necessary to help things along. . . . [A child] conceived . . . in little faith cannot be the heir of promise."[19] But divine promise, appropriated by faith, does not entail human passivity in working toward God's goals for the creation. The high place given to the human role, from creation to Joseph, testifies to the depth of God's engagement with human beings as the instruments of God's purpose.

16. See T. Fretheim, "The Reclamation of Creation," *Int* 45 (1991) 354-65.
17. See Overview sections; G. Rendsburg, *The Redaction of Genesis* (Winona Lake: Eisenbrauns, 1986).
18. See R. Cohn, "Narrative Structure and Canonical Perspective in Genesis," *JSOT* 25 (1983) 3-16.
19. Von Rad, *Genesis* (Philadelphia: Westminster, 1972) 196.

BIBLIOGRAPHY

1. The following are standard commentaries that deal with the full range of issues faced by the interpreter. Those by Westermann contain the most extensive discussions of issues the text presents, from textual matters to the history of interpretation.

Hamilton, Victor. *The Book of Genesis, Chapters 1–17.* NICOT. Grand Rapids: Eerdmans, 1990.

Sarna, Nahum. *Genesis.* JPS Torah Commentary. Philadelphia: Jewish Publication Society, 1989.

Von Rad, Gerhard. *Genesis.* OTL. Philadelphia: Westminster, 1972.

Wenham, Gordon. *Genesis 1–15.* Word Biblical Commentary. Waco: Word, 1987.

Westermann, Claus. *Genesis 1–11: A Commentary; Genesis 12–36: A Commentary;* and *Genesis 37–50: A Commentary.* Minneapolis: Augsburg, 1984–86.

2. The following are commentaries or studies on Genesis geared for use in preaching, teaching, and personal study. The commentary of Brueggemann should be cited for its thoughtful discussions of the text in view of the issues presented by contemporary American culture.

Brueggemann, Walter. *Genesis.* Interpretation. Atlanta: John Knox, 1982.

Fretheim, Terence. *Creation, Fall and Flood: Studies in Genesis 1–11.* Minneapolis: Augsburg, 1969.

Gowan, Donald E. *From Eden to Babel: A Commentary on the Book of Genesis 1–11.* Grand Rapids: Eerdmans, 1988.

Jeansonne, Sharon. *The Women of Genesis.* Minneapolis: Fortress, 1990.

Mann, Thomas. *The Book of the Torah: The Narrative Integrity of the Pentateuch.* Atlanta: John Knox, 1988.

Rogerson, John. *Genesis 1–11.* Old Testament Guides. Sheffield, England: *JSOT,* 1991.

Roop, Eugene F. *Genesis.* Scottdale, Pa.: Herald, 1987.

3. The following are studies of special issues in Genesis from a particular angle of vision. Various articles of interest are cited in appropriate sections of the commentary.

Alter, Robert. *The Art of Biblical Narrative.* New York: Basic Books, 1981.

Anderson, B. W., ed. *Creation in the Old Testament.* IRT 6. Philadelphia: Fortress, 1984.

Blenkinsopp, Joseph. *The Pentateuch: An Introduction to the First Five Books of the Bible.* ABRL. New York: Doubleday, 1992.

Bonhoeffer, Dietrich. *Creation and Fall: Temptation.* New York: Macmillan, 1966.

Brueggemann, Walter, and H. W. Wolff. *The Vitality of Old Testament Traditions.* Atlanta: John Knox, 1982.

Clines, David. *The Theme of the Pentateuch.* JSOTSup 10. Sheffield, England: *JSOT,* 1978.

Coats, George W. *From Canaan to Egypt: Structural and Theological Context for the Joseph Story.* CBQMS 4. Washington: Catholic Biblical Association of America, 1976.

_____. *Genesis: With an Introduction to Narrative Literature.* The Forms of the Old Testament Literature 1. Grand Rapids: Eerdmans, 1983.

Damrosch, David. *The Narrative Covenant.* San Francisco: Harper & Row, 1987.

Fishbane, Michael. *Text and Texture: Close Readings of Selected Biblical Texts.* New York: Schocken, 1979.

Fokkelman, J. P. *Narrative Art in Genesis.* Assen: Van Gorcum, 1975.

Fretheim, Terence. *Deuteronomic History.* Nashville: Abingdon, 1983.

Gunkel, Hermann. *The Legends of Genesis: The Biblical Saga and History.* New York: Schocken, 1964. This is a translation of the introduction to his 1901 commentary.

Hendel, Ronald. *The Epic of the Patriarch: The Jacob Cycle and the Narrative Traditions of Canaan and Israel.* HSM 42. Atlanta: Scholars Press, 1987.

Humphreys, W. L. *Joseph and His Family: A Literary Study.* Studies in Personalities of the Old Testament. Columbia: University of South Carolina Press, 1988.

Levenson, Jon. *Creation and the Persistence of Evil.* San Francisco: Harper & Row, 1988.

Meyers, Carol. *Discovering Eve: Ancient Israelite Women in Context.* New York: Oxford University Press, 1988.

Miller, Patrick D., Jr. *Genesis 1–11: Studies in Structure and Theme.* JSOTSup 8. Sheffield, England: *JSOT,* 1978.

Moberly, R. W. L. *The Old Testament of the Old Testament: Patriarchal Narratives and Mosaic Yahwism.* Minneapolis: Fortress, 1992.

Niditch, Susan. *Chaos to Cosmos: Studies in Biblical Patterns of Creation.* Chico: Scholars Press, 1985.

_____. *Underdogs and Tricksters: A Prelude to Biblical Folklore.* San Francisco: Harper & Row, 1987.

Rendsburg, Gary. *The Redaction of Genesis.* Winona Lake, Ind.: Eisenbrauns, 1986.

Rendtorff, Rolf. *The Problem of the Process of Transmission in the Pentateuch.* JSOTSup 89. Sheffield, England: *JSOT,* 1990.

Steinmetz, Devorah. *From Father to Son: Kinship, Conflict and Continuity in Genesis.* Louisville: Westminster/John Knox, 1991.

Sternberg, Meir. *The Poetics of Biblical Narrative.* Bloomington: Indiana University Press, 1985.

Thompson, Thomas. *The Historicity of the Patriarchal Narratives.* BZAW 133. Berlin: de Gruyter, 1974.

Trible, Phyllis. *God and the Rhetoric of Sexuality.* Overtures to Biblical Theology. Philadelphia: Fortress, 1978.

Turner, Lawrence. *Announcements of Plot in Genesis.* JSOTSup 96. Sheffield, England: *JSOT,* 1990.

Van Seters, John. *Abraham in History and Tradition.* New Haven: Yale University Press, 1975.

Wallace, Howard. *The Eden Narrative.* HSM 32. Atlanta: Scholars Press, 1985.

White, Hugh C. *Narration and Discourse in the Book of Genesis.* Cambridge: Cambridge University Press, 1991.

Whybray, R. N. *The Making of the Pentateuch.* JSOTSup 53. Sheffield, England: *JSOT,* 1987.

Wilson, R. R. *Genealogy and History in the Biblical World.* New Haven: Yale University Press, 1977.

OUTLINE OF GENESIS

I. Genesis 1:1–11:26, The Primeval Story

    A. 1:1–6:4, The Creation and Disruption of the Universe
        1:1–2:3, The Creation
        2:4-25, Another Look at Creation

A. 37:1-36, Joseph and His Brothers
B. 38:1-30, Tamar and Judah
C. 39:1-23, Joseph, God, and Success
D. 40:1-23, Joseph, Interpreter of Dreams
E. 41:1-57, Joseph's Elevation to Power
F. 42:1-38, Joseph Meets His Brothers
G. 43:1-34, The Second Journey to Egypt
H. 44:1-34, Joseph's Final Test
I. 45:1-28, Joseph Makes Himself Known
J. 46:1–47:26, The Descent into Egypt
K. 47:27–50:26, The Emergence of Unified Israel
     47:27–48:22, Joseph and His Sons
     49:1-33, The Last Words of Jacob
     50:1-14, The Burial of Jacob
     50:15-21, The Full Reconciliation of Israel's Sons
     50:22-26, The Promise Transmitted

GENESIS 1:1–11:26

THE PRIMEVAL STORY

OVERVIEW

The last century has seen a proliferation of new directions in the study of these chapters, including comparative studies based on the discovery of ancient Near Eastern creation and flood accounts, new literary approaches and historiographical methods, innovative theological developments, and issues generated by scientific research, environmentalism, feminism, and other liberation movements. These realities have sharply complicated the interpretation of these chapters: Did Israel inherit theological perspectives from the larger ancient Near Eastern culture? How old is the earth? What about evolution? Does the dominion passage commend the exploitation of the earth? Are these texts inimical to the proper role of women in church and society?

It will not do to suggest that such questions violate the integrity of the text, which knew of no such modern problems. Every question asked of the text is contemporary; every reader will study the text through modern eyes. Indeed, personal questions can often make a text come alive. Nonetheless, the public canons of accountability, which historical-critical approaches provide, can introduce some objectivity into the interpretive process.

Even though the rest of the OT makes few specific references to these chapters (see Isa 54:9), rather too much can be made of this fact. The same may be said for other narratives in the Pentateuch. There is, for example, no mention of the Akedah (Genesis 22) and only passing reference to Jacob's wrestling with God (see Hos 12:3-4). This situation stands in some contrast to the prominent use made of these texts in intertestamental literature, which may explain NT interest in them, at least in part (e.g., Mark 10:6-8; Rom 5:12-21).[20] The NT use of these passages will,

no doubt, shape one's angle of vision in some way. Yet, the fact that these NT citations cannot be allowed to have a privileged position in interpreting the OT seems clear from the use of Genesis 2–3 in 1 Tim 2:8-15. Each NT interpretation must be integrated with other evidence and methods as one attends to the meaning of these chapters.

TYPE OF LITERATURE

Determining the type(s) of literature present in these chapters has proven difficult. One confronts terms as diverse as a report of actual events or myth. Scholars generally agree that there is an admixture of narrative and numerative materials, but a more precise understanding of the former has been difficult to achieve, whether it be in terms of saga, legend, myth, fairy tale, etiology, story, or theological narrative. This discussion has not been very fruitful in helping readers understand the texts themselves, not least because there is no agreed-upon definition of words like *myth.* The word *story,* though imprecise, will probably serve us best.

One may identify these materials in two distinct, but not unrelated, ways:

1. They are *typical* or archetypical stories; that is, they explain aspects of human life in every age, including interhuman, human-nonhuman, and creature-Creator relationships. The various uses of the word אדם (*'ādām*) point the reader in this direction (generic—1:26-27; 2:5; 3:22-24; 5:1-2; 6:1-7; the first man—2:7–4:1; Adam—4:25–5:5). This movement back and forth between humankind and first man suggests an effort to portray the human in both typical and atypical ways. The admixture of symbolic (e.g., the tree of knowledge) and literal language

---

20. For a survey of texts, see D. Gowan, *From Eden to Babel: A Commentary on the Book of Genesis 1–11* (Grand Rapids: Eerdmans, 1988) 3-6.

also pushes in this direction, as do the parallels with ancient Near Eastern myth.[21]

Clines emphasizes this typicality. "Genesis 1-11 is not for [Israel], as it is for us, universal history; it is their own history."[22] For example, the flood symbolizes the destruction of Jerusalem for its sinful ways, and the dispersion in chap. 11 alludes to Israel's own Diaspora. Yet, while these texts may indeed mirror Israel's own reality, the claims of the text are more extensive. The past and the present are not simply collapsed into each other.

2. These texts tell *a story of the past,* more particularly a story of beginnings. They speak, not simply of the general human condition, but also of the beginnings of life.[23] This is not to say that the material is historical in any modern sense, nor does it necessarily make any historical judgments. Rather, these narratives offer Israel's own understandings.

(a) There are *atypical* aspects to some texts, showing that Israel did not simply collapse their own (or any later) time into the time of the text. The long-lived patriarchs would be one clear example; Israel knew that it would never live through such a time again. Such a reality belonged to the irretrievable past; indeed, to live such a long life was *totally* beyond Israel's experience. Other texts showing that the time of the text was understood to be different from Israel's own include 2:25 (nakedness and shame); 3:23-24 (driven from Eden, never to return); 6:1; and 11:1 (explicitly unique world situations). On the other hand, 6:4 speaks of continuity between the primeval era and a later time.

(b) There is an etiological concern, wherein the origins of later practices or phenomena are rooted in the distant past. We could cite 4:20-22 and the origins of certain cultural activities, or marriage practices (2:24), or national origins (10:2-31), even certain divine decisions that God will "remember" (8:21; 9:14-16). More generally, we could cite the creation itself; e.g., the actions of God in 2:7 and 2:22 will never be repeated. Creation is not an annual event, but a once-for-all moment that stands at the beginning of time. Somewhat different are the sentences in 3:14-19, which are etiological. They too are typical,

but such typicality will not happen *whenever* people sin; rather, these distorted relationships reflect a *common* human reality.

(c) The concern for chronology is evident in the various genealogies, which allow us to track the years from Adam (5:5) through every generation to Israel. We can discern this same motif in the flood story (7:11; 8:13-14). The presence of such chronology in chaps. 1–11 and chaps. 12–50 means that these two sections of Genesis share a fundamental understanding regarding typicality and atypicality.

In sum, these texts present an interweaving of the typical and what belongs to the past. The interpreter must regularly walk a fine line between these two possibilities.

STRUCTURE AND THEME

Numerous efforts have been made to discern the structure in Genesis 1–11.[24] Most basic is the interweaving of genealogies and narratives.

Narrative pattern provides one type of structure. What transpires in 3:1-24 recurs in subsequent stories (4:1-16; 6:1-4; 6:5–8:22; 9:20-27; 11:1-9): Sinful Act (3:6); Speech (Decision) of Judgment (3:14-19); Act of Mercy/Blessing (3:21); Act of Punishment (3:22-24). While this pattern highlights a certain rhythm in the texts, it is not exact and leaves chaps. 1–2 dangling.

Another type of structure consists of parallel panels: A/A′—Creation from watery chaos (1:1–3:24) stands parallel to the flood (6:9–9:17); B/B′—discordant sons of Adam (4:1-16) to the sons of Noah, a second Adam (9:18-29); C/C′—technological development of humankind (4:17-26) to ethnic development (10:1-32); D/D′—ten generations, Adam to Noah/three sons (5:1-32) to ten generations, Noah to Terah/three sons (11:10-26); E/E′—downfall, Nephilim (6:1-8) to the Tower of Babel (11:1-9). The Shem genealogy and Babel story are reversed in order to connect Abram in 11:26 with 12:1-3. However, this theory presents difficulties,

---

21. See J. Rogerson, *Genesis 1–11* (Sheffield: *JSOT,* 1991) 41-55.
22. Clines, *The Theme of the Pentateuch,* 98.
23. Von Rad, *Genesis,* 65.

24. See Clines, *The Theme of the Pentateuch,* 61-79; T. Fretheim, *Creation, Fall and Flood: Studies in Genesis 1–11* (Minneapolis: Augsburg, 1969) 18-22; Rendsburg, *The Redaction of Genesis.*

as may be seen in the prominent role given to 6:1-8 as over against 3:1-24, which is collapsed into the creation accounts.

These structures may be linked to a more general one wherein chaps. 1–11 depict an ever-increasing growth of sin and severity of punishment. Yet, the Babel story seems anticlimactic after the flood; this episode suggests a modification, with a distinct break after the flood, and then a recapitulation. The first movement is the primeval era, moving from sinful individuals (3:1-24) through family (4:1-26) out into the larger world (6:1–8:22), ending in catastrophe. Then there is another beginning (9:1-17, parallel to 1:1–2:25), moving also through sinful family and individuals (9:18-27) out into the world (10:1–11:9), only this time into a world that Israel clearly knows. The genealogy of Shem (11:10-26), once again, provides an individual point of reference that reaches out into the world (12:3*b*).

The larger structure is particularly helpful because it accounts for both stories and genealogies. It also attends to a variety of themes within these chapters: the growth and spread of sin, to which God's acts of judgment are explicitly related (and hence not arbitrary), accompanied by continuing acts of divine grace, as well as the themes of creation-uncreation-new creation (see 6:5–8:22).

Fundamental to Genesis is the divine creative activity, which involves not only the beginnings of the cosmos and all of its creatures but also God's continuing ordering and blessing activity within and without Israel. This anchor gives a horizon, scope, and purpose to God's particular act of election and words of promise to Israel's ancestors (see Reflections on 1:1). Indeed, even God's promises to Israel are grounded in God's promissory relationship to the world more generally (8:21–9:17), as is the activity of God as Savior (6:5–8:20).

Throughout these chapters issues of relationship are addressed from every conceivable perspective. Most basic are the relationships between God and the creatures, especially humans. The recurrent litany that all is created "good" stands as a beacon regarding the nature of God's creative work and the divine intentions for the creation. The *subsequent* entrance of human sin, while not

finally effacing the God-human relationship or the important role human beings play in the divine economy, has occasioned deep and pervasive ill effects upon all relationships (human-God; human-human at individual, familial, and national levels; human-nonhuman) and dramatically portrays the need for a reclamation of creation. Through the experience of the flood story, God rejects annihilation as the means to accomplish this reformation and graciously opts instead for a more vulnerable, long-term engagement, working from within the very life of the world itself. The world continues to live and breathe because God makes a gracious, unconditional commitment to stay with the world, come what may in the wake of human sinfulness.

GENESIS 1–11 AND MODERN SCIENCE

To claim that God created the world and all that exists is a matter of faith, grounded fundamentally in God's self-revelation (see Heb 11:3). At this level the opening chapters of Genesis are a confession of faith. At the same time, in witnessing to God's creative activity the biblical writers made use of the available knowledge of the natural world. Israel had no little interest in what we today would call "scientific" issues (see 1 Kgs 4:33). These chapters are prescientific in the sense that they predate modern science, but not in the sense of having no interest in those types of questions. "Pre-scientific" knowledge is evident in God's use of the earth and the waters in mediating creation (1:11, 20, 24), the classification of plants into certain kinds and a comparable interest in animals, as well as the ordering of each day's creation. Despite claims to the contrary (often in the interest of combating fundamentalism), such texts indicate that Israel's thinkers were very interested in questions of the "how" of creation, and not just questions of "who" and "why."

Israel's theologians used this kind of "scientific" knowledge to speak of creation. They recognized that the truth about creation is not generated simply by theological reflection; we must finally draw from various fields of inquiry in order to speak the full truth about the world. The key task, finally, becomes that of integrating materials from various fields into one coherent statement about the created order. In effect, Genesis invites every generation to engage in this same process.

Difficulties arise when it becomes evident that not everything in these chapters can be made congruent with modern knowledge about the world (recognizing that no field of endeavor has arrived at the point of full understanding). If our view of the Bible insists that all information in it, of whatever sort, must correspond to scientific reality, then we will have to engage in all sorts of exegetical antics to make it work. But if we recognize that those authors did not know everything about the world (e.g., a source for light independent of the luminaries; the age of the world), then

we just recognize that and move on. We have to take all the additional knowledge we have gained or will gain about the world (e.g., some form of evolution) and integrate it with our confession about God the Creator.

We are not called to separate the theological material from the "scientific" material and rewrite the chapter from our own scientific perspectives (however much that task must be accomplished for other purposes). The Genesis text remains both an indispensable theological resource and an important paradigm on the way in which to integrate theological and scientific realities in a common search for the truth about the world.

GENESIS 1:1–6:4, THE CREATION AND DISRUPTION OF THE UNIVERSE

Genesis 1:1–2:3, The Creation

COMMENTARY

Many scholars consider the opening two chapters of Genesis as two creation stories, assigning 1:1–2:4*a* to the Priestly writer and 2:4*b*-25 to the Yahwist. Moreover, considerable effort has been expended in comparing and contrasting them (see commentary on 2:4-25). Newer approaches to biblical texts, however, have raised anew the question of the shape of the present form of the text. While the two accounts certainly have different origins and transmission histories, they have also been brought together in a coherent way by a redactor. As such, they function together to provide the canonical picture of creation. We cannot be certain that either account ever appeared in their present form, so theological perspectives based on these accounts in isolation are speculative and problematic.

Israel was not the only people in the ancient Near East to compose stories of creation. Sumerian, Mesopotamian, and Egyptian accounts have been unearthed in the nineteenth and twentieth centuries. As a result of comparing these extra-biblical texts with the biblical accounts, it is apparent that Israel participated in a culture with a lively

interest in these questions. While in the past some claimed that Israel depended directly on one or more of these accounts, it is now more common to speak of a widespread fund of images and ideas upon which Israel drew and shaped into its own creation account(s). Early scholarly efforts focused on the Babylonian *Enuma Elish* in the century following its appearance in 1876; more recent efforts have concentrated on the Babylonian *Epic of Atrahasis* (about 1600 BCE), primarily because its sequence of creation-disruption-flood corresponds to the biblical account. Special attention has also been given to Egyptian parallels (e.g., creation by means of the word).

It is important to examine all such accounts and seek to determine their relationship, if any, to the biblical texts. The delineation of similarities and dissimilarities has long belonged to such work. Such dissimilarities as the basic purpose (e.g., the absence of explicit Israelite political interests), the lack of a theogony and a conflict among the gods, the absence of interest in primeval chaos, the prevailing monotheism, and the high value given human beings have often been noted.

At the same time, to conceive of the biblical account's relationship to these other stories fundamentally in disjunctive or polemical terms can miss their genuine contribution to a perception of Israel's own reflection about creation.

Israel itself conceptualized the beginnings of things and told creation stories in several ways. Creation by word (followed by deed) is majestically presented in chap. 1; God as potter and builder working with already existing materials occurs as a prominent image in chap. 2. We may also discern traces of a creation account in which God fought with and achieved victory over chaotic forces (see Ps 74:12-15). It is notable, however, that these references are allusive in character, may refer to the exodus, and are present only in poetic literature. To assume that Israel understood such imagery in a literal way is as profound a mistake as to think of these Genesis chapters as journalistic prose.

Despite this important comparative and historical-critical work, we must not forget that these texts are most fundamentally the product of a community of faith engaged in theological reflection on creation. God is the primary subject of this chapter, which relates God in various ways to every creature. Even more, the chapter, with its rhythmic cadences, has a certain doxological character. Hence, the material may have grown out of liturgical use and the regular round of the community's praise of God the Creator (see Job 38:7). Worship interests also clearly appear in the links among creation, tabernacle, and temple as well as in sabbath and religious festivals.[25] Although these roots seem clear, we should not identify this chapter as an actual liturgy. While it may be identified as a didactic account, it has been shaped by liturgical use and worship interests.

At the same time, we should not collapse every concern in chapters 1 and 2 into a theological mold. This material provides considerable evidence of what we today would call scientific reflection on the natural world. Israel takes the available knowledge of that world and integrates it with theological perspectives, recognizing thereby that both

25. See J. Levenson, *Creation and the Persistence of Evil* (San Francisco: Harper & Row, 1988) 66-99.

spheres of knowledge must be used to speak the truth about the world (see Overview).

Structure. The first account possesses an obvious seven-day structure, signifying unity and comprehensiveness (the number 7 also serves this purpose). But other structures have been observed. Eight creative acts on six days (two acts occur on days three and six) may reflect originally diverse accounts, though such a scheme is more likely a deliberate structure in view of certain natural correspondences:

Day 1: Light   Day 4: Luminaries
Day 2: Waters/   Day 5: Fish/Birds
        Firmament   Day 6: Land animals/
Day 3: Dry land/   People
        Vegetation   Vegetation for food

In addition, the repetition of phrases provides a discernible rhythm: "God said . . . let there be . . . and it was so . . . and God made . . . and God saw that it was good . . . and it was evening and morning." It is important to note that this rhythm is not absolutely regular (additions in the LXX sought to make it so). In sum, various structures overlap and, together, betray a less than perfect symmetry.

1:1-2, The Beginning. The difficulties in translating vv. 1-3 are evident in the NIV and the NRSV, each of which is grammatically defensible. We may note three possible translations. (1) Verse 1 is a temporal clause, subordinate to the main clause in v. 3, with v. 2 a parenthesis regarding prior conditions (see JPS). When God began to create heaven and earth, God said, "Let there be light" (v. 2). Although this translation may be compared to 2:4-7 (cf. 5:1*b*-2) and ancient Near Eastern texts, each of these parallels is inexact (e.g., using the phrase "in the day"). Moreover, such a long opening sentence is uncharacteristic of the style of this chapter and other genealogies. (2) Verse 1 is a temporal clause, subordinate to the main clause in v. 2 (NRSV; also NAB; NEB; GNB). This rendering is less problematic, especially with the emphasis provided by the phrase "in the beginning." (3) Verse 1 is an independent sentence (NIV; also KJV; RSV; JB; NJB; REB). We could interpret v. 1 as depicting the first act of creation followed by further phases, though such a view breaks up the seven-day pattern.[26] Or, preferably, v. 1 may be seen as a summary of the chapter (v. 2 describes the prior conditions and v. 3 narrates the first act of creation). The most convincing evidence for this position derives from the genealogies in 5:1; 6:9; 10:1; and 11:10, all of which begin with an independent clause that provides a summary of what follows.

The word *beginning* probably does not refer to the absolute beginning of all things, but to the beginning of the ordered creation, including the temporal order. Time began with God's ordering, and the seven-day time of God's creating establishes a temporal pattern throughout all generations (see 2:1-3). The author does not deny that God created all things, but God's creative work in this chapter begins with something already there, the origins of which are of no apparent interest. Also, the writer presupposes the existence and basic character of God.

The first of two primary words for God's creative activity is introduced in Gen 1:1 (ברא *bārā*). Only God serves as the subject of this verb in the OT, and the verb has no object of material or means (though some uses refer to re-creation or a transformation of existing realities; see Pss 51:10; 102:18; Isa 41:20; 65:18). The word *bārā'* may be a technical term used to speak about the fundamental newness and uniqueness of what God brings into being. This view has sometimes led to the formulation of a *creatio ex nihilo* view of creation. While the word *bārā'* may speak of what only God can do, it remains metaphorical language. That God's creating is analogous to the human sphere is shown by the common use of the everyday word *make* (עשה *'āśâ*; integrated in 1:26-27; 2:1-3; Isaiah 41–45) and the images of creating present in chap. 2 (e.g., God as potter or builder). Yet, no analogy from the human sphere can exhaust the meaning of God's creative activity.

"Heaven and earth" specifies the ordered universe (see Ps 89:11), the totality of the world in which everything has its proper place and function. This phrase also testifies to a bipartite structure, wherein "the heavens are the LORD's heavens,/ but the earth he has given to human beings" (Ps 115:16). The heavens are an integral aspect of the world

as created. Other texts show that heaven as God's abode is built into the very structure of the created order (Ps 104:1-3; Isa 40:22; Amos 9:6), a shorthand reference to the abode of God *within* the world.

Verse 2 describes the conditions before God began to order the cosmos. The language used to describe this pre-creation state of affairs is difficult to comprehend. There are three parallel descriptions: (1) The "formless void" (תהו ובהו *tōhû wābōhû*) is neither "nothing" nor an undifferentiated mass; the earth, the waters (deep), the darkness, and the wind are discrete realities (see Jer 4:23-26). As a parallel to 2:4-7, but with a watery image, it refers to the earth as "void/ empty" in the sense of something desolate and unproductive. The earth, present here, only "appears" in v. 9. (2) The "deep" (תהום *tĕhôm*) has often been compared with Tiamat of the Babylonian creation story, but a specific link seems unlikely in view of both language and content. Yet, the motif of water as the primal element in other ancient accounts no doubt influenced this writer. In Genesis 1, the "deep" may be equated with the waters that cover the earth (see v. 9; cf. 49:25; Deut 33:13; Prov 8:24). Darkness may not be an absolute absence of light, given the act of separation in v. 4. As with the other realities in this verse (except wind), darkness becomes an integral part of God's ordered world; darkness is not called "good" in v. 4, but neither are the creations of the second day; "everything" is included in the "very good" evaluation of 1:31.[27]

(3) A "wind/spirit from/of God" are common translations of the רוח אלהים *rûaḥ 'ĕlōhîm* (NIV's capitalized "Spirit" implies a Trinitarian view; the superlative "mighty wind" would be unique for this phrase in the OT). The verb (used in Deut 32:11 and Jer 23:9 for a hovering eagle and a drunken walk) may be translated in various ways— "move," "sweep," "hover over"—suggesting the ever-changing velocity and direction of the wind. But to what end? Since the wind is related to God, it involves purposeful movement. God was present, hence the activity was in some sense creative (which tips the translation toward "spirit"). A comparable

26. See G. Wenham, *Genesis 1–15* (Waco: Word, 1987) 11-13.

27. See D. Tsumara, *The Earth and the Waters in Genesis 1 and 2: A Linguistic Investigation* (Sheffield: *JSOT,* 1989).

use of this language occurs in the flood story (8:1) and at the Red Sea (Exod 14:21; see the creative use of spirit in Job 33:4; Ps 104:30).

The writer placed the three clauses in v. 2 in grammatical parallelism; yet the third clause works differently because the wind is the sole entity not picked up in the rest of the chapter. The reference to God moves toward the rest of the chapter; it brings God and raw material together, in motion rather than static, preparing for the ordering process to follow.

1:3-13, Days One–Three. God as speaker is another key metaphor for God's creative activity (see Pss 33:6, 9; 148:5; 2 Esdr 6:38; 2 Cor 4:6). The centrality of the Word means that the creation is not an accident, but a deliberate act of the divine will; it expresses what God intends. The Word personalizes the activity; God enters into the creative deed. The Word bespeaks transcendence, expressing the separateness of God from the created order, which is not a divine emanation or birth. At the same time, God's speech reveals divine vulnerability, for God's speaking does not occur in isolation or function as command. The use of the jussive "let there be" leaves room for creaturely response (vv. 11, 24); the cohortative "let us make" leaves room for consultation (v. 26); the "let them have dominion" (v. 26) entails a sharing of power. God's way of speaking creation communicates with others, makes room for others, with the attendant risks. God no longer chooses to be alone.

God's speaking does not stand isolated from God's making (e.g., 1:6-7, 14-16; see also Ps 33:6; Isa 48:3). This speaking-doing rhythm may reflect earlier forms of the text that have now been decisively integrated. Hence, the word itself does not explain sufficiently what comes to be; the word is accompanied by the deed. God does not create by "word events" but by "word-deed events." Hence, existing in the image of God means having a vocation that consists of both word and deed.

The divine speaking often involves a speaking *with* whatever is *already* created (vv. 11, 20, 22, 24, 28) in such a way that the receptor of the word helps to shape the result. The earth itself assists importantly in creative activity (vv. 11, 24). While God's

work creates the potential for this creaturely response, it is creation from within the creation, not from without. Both human and nonhuman creatures are called to participate in the creative activity made possible by God.

Light. On "day" and "evening and morning," see the commentary on 2:1-3. Inasmuch as the sun had not yet been created, this verse probably refers to a divine manipulation of light as a creative act. Light was thought to have another source (Job 38:19; Isa 30:26; e.g., light on cloudy days and before and after sunset). The sun, when created, augmented the already existing light. Israelites believed light, often a symbol of life and salvation (Pss 27:1; 56:13) and characteristic of the presence of God (Ps 104:2), was fundamental to the creation, pushing back the darkness and making life possible. Every morning was a kind of new creation.

"And God saw that it was good." God acts as an evaluator. In this remarkable and recurring phrase, God responds to the work, making evaluations of it (2:18 implies that the evaluation is part of an ongoing process, within which improvement is possible). The "subdue" language (1:28) implies that "good" does not mean perfect or static or in no need of development. This statement carries the sense of achieving the divine intention, which includes elements of beauty, purpose, and praise. This evaluative move (as with naming or blessing) means that God remains involved with the creation once it has been brought into being. God sees the creature, experiences what has been created, and is affected by what is seen. God's response leads to the further development of the creation and of intra-creaturely relationships. God's creative activity may thus in part be determined by that which is not God.

"And God separated . . . " (vv. 4, 7). In this activity, too, God works with what has already been created to develop the creation still further, suggesting a continued unfolding of the creation. This divine cosmic activity may be intended to ground certain ritual distinctions (e.g., clean and unclean).

God acts as name-giver in vv. 5-10; God names the day, the night, the sky, the earth, and the seas. God's naming stands parallel to, but does not overlap, the human naming in 2:19-20. The naming (either divine or human) does not thereby create these realities. In naming, the deity *responds* to the creation. In effect, God looks at what has come into being, evaluates it, and discerns its place in the creation. The Creator thus not only speaks and acts, but also reacts to what has been brought into being and continues further. The act of creation constitutes, thus, no simple punctiliar act, but also involves a process of action and interaction with what has been created. In this process, naming entails knowledge of and relationship with the thing named.

Dome, Expanse, Firmament. Having no idea of infinite space, the writer thought the sky was something solid (Job 37:18), either metal or ice, held up by pillars (Job 26:11). This "dome" provided living space between the waters above (the source of rain and snow, flowing through windows, 7:11) and the waters on and below the earth.

The irregular placement of the recurrent phrase "and it was so" makes it likely that the divine speech announces the divine *intention* to create. Yet, the creative act is not complete until this phrase has so informed the reader.[28] Sometimes this phrase occurs as a summary; sometimes it occurs between God's speaking and acting (vv. 11, 14, 24). Even the creation of light is not complete until it is separated from the darkness (v. 4).

The creative word functions as an ordering word, especially in v. 9, where the dry land *appears* after the waters have been gathered into seas (the earth is already present in v. 2).

Verses 11-13 witness to a shift in God's way of creating; the earth itself participates in the creative process (see above). The description of the plants and trees with their capacity to reproduce by themselves gives evidence for a probing interest in what we would call "natural science" (see 1 Kgs 4:33). Israel had not yet related plant growth to the sun, ascribing it entirely to the powers of the earth.

1:14-23, Days Four–Five. In vv. 14-19—arranged in a chiasm—the heavenly lights are created to divide day and night, to give (additional) light, and to serve as signs (i.e., time markers) for days, years, and fixed seasons (the word for "season" is also the word for religious festival). The tasks of separating and

ruling (משל *māšal*) are, notably, also divine roles, here delegated to certain creatures. Once again, the involvement of the nonhuman in the continuing ordering of the world achieves prominence. The fact that the sun and moon are not specifically named, and the stars are just mentioned, may reflect a polemic against religious practice in Mesopotamia, where heavenly bodies were considered divine and astrology played an important role in daily life. All are here acclaimed as the creations of the one God.

In vv. 20-23 two new elements are introduced: life and blessing. Animals and human beings alike (not plants, whose reproductive powers are inherent) share a blessing—the power of sexual reproduction. The NRSV and the NIV offer different understandings of the verbal form used in v. 20. In the NRSV, the waters would be parallel to the earth in vv. 11 and 24 in mediating the creative work of God. The NIV's "teem" specifies a more direct creative act. In either case, ultimate responsibility lies with God. The fact that the sea monsters (תנינם *tannînîm*) are specifically mentioned may polemicize theories of a divine chaos monster in other creation stories, ascribing their creation to God; imagery associated with this myth occurs in some poetic texts (e.g., Isa 27:1; Isa 51:9; Ps 74:13). In language similar to 1:28, God's blessing extends to birds and fish, focusing on the life-giving powers. That no land animals receive a specific blessing is something of a puzzle.

1:24-31, The Sixth Day. God's creations on the sixth day all share the habitat of dry land. It may be something of a disappointment to human beings that they have to share this day! As with the vegetation in v. 11, the earth mediates the creation of the land animals (2:19 will speak of God's forming the animals). The NIV interprets "creeping things" accurately with its "creatures that move along the ground."

On the last half of the sixth day, God creates human beings. God's way of speaking and acting signals the importance of this development—namely, inner divine reflection, the cohortative "let us make" (followed by "our"), and the speaking/doing rhythm continues. The plural may refer to the divine council or heavenly court (see Job 38:7; 1 Kgs

---

28. Rogerson, *Genesis 1–11*, 58-60.

22:19; Jer 23:18-23).[29] Other interpretations of the plural are not convincing (the plural of *majesty* is without parallel, and the plural of *deliberation* does not account for 3:22; see 11:7; Isa 6:8).

The "let us" language refers to an image of God as a consultant of other divine beings; the creation of humankind results from a dialogical act—an inner-divine communication—rather than a monological one. Those who are not God are called to participate in this central act of creation. Far from either slighting divine transcendence or concealing God within the divine assembly, it reveals and enhances the richness and complexity of the divine realm. God is not in heaven alone, but is engaged in a relationship of mutuality within the divine realm, and chooses to share the creative process with others. Human beings are the product of such a consultation (אדם *'ādām* is used generically here). The "let us make" thus implicitly extends to human beings, for they are created in the image of one who chooses to create in a way that shares power with others.

The phrase "image of God" has been the subject of much discussion over the centuries.[30] This language occurs only in Genesis 1–11 (though implied elsewhere, e.g., Psalm 8). In describing the relationship between Adam and Seth (5:3; cf. 5:1; 9:6), the words *image* and *likeness* are reversed, suggesting that the second word dominates. In 1:26, *likeness* may specify the meaning more closely, so that *image* should not be construed in the sense of identity. Fundamentally, it means that "the pattern on which [human beings are] fashioned is to be sought outside the sphere of the created."[31] The inner-divine communication, which makes interhuman and God-human communication possible, constitutes one basic element of the pattern. Generally, human beings are given such gifts that they can take up the God-given responsibilities specified in these verses. The "image" refers to the entire human being, not to some part, such as the reason or the will. As for likeness in body, one may suggest that this

notion appears in the later physical appearances of the "messenger of God" (see 16:7).

The image functions to mirror God to the world, to be God as God would be to the nonhuman, to be an extension of God's own dominion. In the ancient Near East the king as image of God was a designated representative of the gods, ruling on their behalf. Genesis 1 democratizes this royal image so that all humanity belongs to this sphere and inter-human hierarchical understandings of the image are set aside. That both male and female are so created (see also 5:2) means that the female images the divine as much as the male; both are addressed in the command of v. 28. The reference to both implies that their roles in life are not identical, and that likeness to God pertains not only to what they have in common but also to what remains distinctive about them (the emergence of both male and female images for God could be grounded in this text). The fact that the words *male* and *female* are not used for animals indicates that both sexuality and procreation are involved.

The involvement in the creative process of those created in the divine image takes the form of a command (1:28). These first divine words to human beings are about their relationship, not to God, but to the earth. They constitute a sharing of the exercise of power (dominion). From the beginning God chooses not to be the only one who has or exercises creative power. The initiative has been solely God's, but once the invitation has been issued, God establishes a power-sharing relationship with humans. This initiative remains in the post-sin world as demonstrated in the use of God language in 5:1-3 and 9:6 as well as the use of these themes in Psalm 8. Hence, God appears less meticulously present in the life of the world; God serves as the supreme delegator of responsibility (for becoming like God in chap. 3, which bears negative connotations, see commentary on 3:22).

The command to be fruitful, to multiply, and to fill the earth immediately follows the word of blessing and involves a sharing of the divine creative capacities. God has brought the first human beings into existence, and the powers of propagating their own kind are now given over to the creatures (see 1:22; continued after the flood, 9:1, 7). The writer was obviously concerned about populating

29. P. Miller, *Genesis 1–11: Studies in Structure and Theme* (Sheffield: *JSOT*, 1978).

30. For a survey, see G. Jonsson, *The Image of God: Genesis 1:26-28 in a Century of Old Testament Research* (Lund: Gleerup, 1988).

31. G. von Rad, *Old Testament Theology* (New York: Harper, 1962) I:145.

the earth. There was plenty of room for the human race to expand and grow. But should the point arrive at which the earth appears to be filled (the definition of which would need discussion), then the human responsibility in this area would need adjustment. New situations will teach new duties regarding the created order.

A study of the verb *have dominion* (רדה *rādâ*) reveals that it must be understood in terms of care-giving, even nurturing, not exploitation. As the image of God, human beings should relate to the nonhuman as God relates to them. This idea belongs to the world of the ideal conceptions of royal responsibility (Ezek 34:1-4; Ps 72:8-14) and centers on the animals. The command to "subdue the earth" (כבשׁ *kābaš*) focuses on the earth, particularly cultivation (see 2:5, 15), a difficult task in those days. While the verb may involve coercive aspects in interhuman relationships (see Num 32:22, 29), no enemies are in view here. More generally, "subduing" involves development in the created order. This process offers to the human being the task of intra-creational development, of bringing the world along to its fullest possible creational potential. Here paradise is not a state of perfection, not a static state of affairs. Humans live in a highly dynamic situation. The future remains open to a number of possibilities in which creaturely activity will prove crucial for the development of the world.

When God conveys blessing (see 1:22; 2:3) God gives power, strength, and potentiality to the creatures. Such action, therefore, constitutes an integral part of the power-sharing image, a giving over of what is God's to others to use as they will. God will not pull back from this act of commitment, which God renews after the flood (9:1).

God as a giver (נתן *nātan*, 1:29-30) provides vegetation to human beings and animals to sustain their lives. When combined with 9:2-3, we discover that human beings were intended to be vegetarians (Isa 11:7; Isa 65:25 imply that animals would be herbivorous in the new creation).

2:1-3, Creation and Sabbath. The repetitive character of this segment stresses the importance of the seventh day. The divine *act* of finishing the creation occurs on the *seventh* day (the NIV's pluperfect, "God

had finished," is possible but not likely). The divine resting concludes creation—namely, sabbath belongs to the created order; it cannot be legislated or abrogated by human beings. "Finishing" does not mean that God will not engage in further creative acts (the absence of the typical concluding formula cannot be appealed to, for the structure of the creation account is not exact). These days did not exhaust the divine creativity! The seventh day refers to a specific day and not to an open future. Continuing creative work will be needed, but there is a "rounding off" of the created order at this point.

The meaning of the word *day* (יום *yôm*) has occasioned much debate. The days, with evening and morning rhythm, are "to be understood as actual days and as a unique, unrepeatable lapse of time in this world."[32] Other possibilities (symbolic; sequential but not consecutive; liturgical) are less likely. While seven-day patterns of various sorts are present in ancient Near Eastern texts, no sabbath day or seven-day week or seven-day creation account has been discovered. Yet, the writer highlights not individual days, but the seven-day pattern. This very temporal framework, a work/rest rhythm, inheres as a part of the created order of things. Creation thus has to do, not simply with spatial order, but with temporal order as well.

Exodus 20:11 and 31:17 (which make sense only if the days are actual days) appeal to Genesis in order to claim that sabbath observance belongs to the creation as God intended it to be; hence its importance for all peoples, not just Israel. As with God, so with human beings; their six days of work are brought to fulfillment when integrated with keeping sabbath. On the far side of sin, resting on the sabbath becomes a *sign* that God's creative order continues to exist in the present. When all the world rests on the sabbath (a sign that all are in right relationship with the Creator—Exod 31:12-17), God's created order will once again be complete, will be realized as at the beginning. Yet, the noun for "sabbath" does not occur; this does not constitute its *earthly* institution (God does not command human beings about the sabbath here).

32. Von Rad, *Genesis*, 65.

The divine act of blessing the sabbath is an unspoken report of God's act of giving power and potentiality to a particular temporal order, in the sense that human honoring of the work/rest rhythm has the capacity of deeply affecting life itself (as does its neglect). The setting aside of one day when human beings attend, not to their own responsibilities and freedoms, but to God's ordering of life honors the larger creative purposes of God and integrating oneself into them. It acknowledges that God is indeed the Creator and provider of all things.

In the act of sanctifying, God sets aside one day as different from other days, the full significance of which becomes apparent only later in the Pentateuch (e.g., Exod 20:11; 31:17). This work stands parallel to other divine acts of separation in the account.

Genesis 2:4-25, Another Look at Creation

COMMENTARY

In the present form of the text, this section is probably intended to describe in detail several days of chap. 1, particularly the sixth one. Genesis 2 was likely not understood as a parallel creation account; it probably was once part of a larger story, evident particularly in vv. 5-6, which could describe a state of affairs after 1:9-10 (with dry land in place, but the separated waters not yet providing fertility).

Differences from chap. 1 have often been observed (e.g., literary type; structure, style, and vocabulary; center of concern). But there are also key similarities: God as sole Creator of a good and purposeful world, the key place of the human among the creatures, the co-creative role of the human and the non-human, the social character of the human as male-female. The chapter focuses on humankind and the particularities of their life, signaled by the shift from "heaven and earth" to "earth and heaven" (v. 4). Elohim, the generic term for the deity, occurs throughout 1:1–2:3. In linking the names Yahweh and Elohim in 2:4-25, the writer may have intended to identify Israel's special name for God with the creator of the world (allowing Elohim to stand alone in 1:1–2:3 makes clear that we are dealing with pre-Israel realities).

While no parallel to this story exists elsewhere in the ancient Near East, certain paradise motifs, e.g. the tree of life, may be found elsewhere. Other OT passages suggest that this was once part of a more comprehensive story (see 13:10; Isa 51:3; Ezek 28:13-19; 31:8-9).

2:4-9, The Role of the Human. Verse 4 has long been considered the point of division between the two creation stories, with v. 4a usually associated with what precedes—with "genealogy" and "create"—and v. 4b with what follows. Some scholars view v. 4 as an introduction to the following story. I construe it as a hinge verse that looks both backward and forward (2:25 may play a similar role), signaled by the reversal of heaven/earth, the creation of which is *assumed* in chap. 2. The phrase "in the day that" (NIV, "when") in v. 4b reaches back into the account of the creation of earth and heavens at a point before everything had been sorted out. Verse 5 functions similarly to v. 18, providing a perspective on the creation process before "not good" became "good."

The word used for "generations"/ "account" (תולדות *tôlēdôt*) is the first of ten such occurrences in Genesis (see Introduction), each of which introduces what is to follow. The phrase, though, remains linked with someone/something that has already been introduced in the narrative. The usage in Gen 2:4 functions most like 25:19 and 37:2, which also introduce new developments in story form.

Verse 5 startles the reader due to the parallel it draws between the rain and human labor (עבד *ʾābad*), both of which are considered indispensable to produce edible plants/ herbs ("stream[s]" is of uncertain meaning, but insufficient for vegetation). The earth remains in a pre-creation state, not only because God has not yet done something, but also because no human beings are active.

The divine purpose for the man in 2:15 is expressed with the same word (שמר *šāmar*, "keep," "protect"). This change gives responsibility to the human being, not simply for maintenance and preservation, but for intra-creational development, bringing the world along toward its fullest possible potential. God intends from the beginning that things not stay just as they were initially created. God creates a paradise, not a static state of affairs, but a highly dynamic situation in which the future lies open to various possibilities.

Various images of God as Creator are presented in this section. (a) God as a potter (יצר *yāṣar*; see Isa 41:25; Isa 45:9; Isa 64:8; Jer 18:1-6) shapes the man according to the divine design (2:7) and forms *every* animal and *every* bird (2:19) from the dust or clay (see Job 10:9) of the ground. The writer uses the same verb to narrate both human and nonhuman creation. The image of the deity as a potter creating humankind from clay occurs elsewhere in the ancient Near East. This image reveals a God who focuses closely on the object to be created and takes painstaking care to shape each one into something useful and beautiful. At the same time, the product of the potter's work remains very much bound to the earth and bears essential marks of the environment from which it derives (see 3:19). This combination of being made from clay and the image of God, being made of the same substance as the earth but made for dominion over it, constitutes a profound statement about human identity (links to royal themes have been noted). (b) God as a bellows breathes life into what has been formed. This "breath of life" is not the air in general, but God's own living breath. God shares this divine "breath of life" with the human and with the animals (see 7:22, which adds רוח *rûaḥ*). The result for both human beings and animals is "a living being" (נפש חיה *nepeš ḥayyâ*; 2:7, 19; 1:20-30; 9:12-16). The divine act of breathing into the human (though it may be implied in 7:22) provides the only distinction between humans and animals. (c) God as farmer/gardener (נטע *nāṭaʿ*, 2:8-9) plants a garden and makes the trees grow out of the ground (אדמה *ʾǎdāmâ*, the source of trees, animals, and human beings). Here the garden lies *in* Eden (probably meaning "luxuriant"), a wider geographical area (in 3:22-24 the garden and Eden seem to be equated).

These verses refer to the trees of the garden and not to vegetation generally (see 1:11-12, 29, where the earth itself acts). Verse 5 refers to edible plants/herbs of the field, which God planted, but they do not grow apart from rain and human toil. The writer devotes special attention to the beauty of the trees and to their provision of food (two characteristics of the tree of knowledge noted by Eve in 3:6), and hence placed there for the good of the human inhabitants. God provides for bodily nourishment and also for other pleasures of life—more than food and clothing! People will find that they depend on that which is outside themselves in order to live fully. The theme of a primeval paradise occurs only rarely elsewhere in the ancient Near East.

The tree of life (2:9; 3:22, 24). The awkward syntax of these texts, which occur at the beginning and end of the story, suggests that stories with different trees have been combined. Some think that only one tree is intended ("the tree of life, namely, the tree of knowledge"), but most interpreters discern two trees in the middle of the garden. The first tree mentioned symbolizes the fullest possible life, the eating of which would grant continuing life (such a tree or plant occurs in the *Gilgamesh Epic* and elsewhere). The reference in 3:22 indicates that one would need to eat from that tree only once, as was also the case with the tree of knowledge.

The narrator gives no indication that the man and woman know of this tree's existence until 3:22. Readers encounter the tree of life in 2:9 and then again only in 3:22-24. Genesis 3:22 implies that the man and woman, having eaten of the other tree and knowing that death has become a near possibility, would with their new knowledge become aware of the tree of life and its import and, by eating of it, live forever.

The relationship between the tree of life and the breath of life (2:7-9; חיים *ḥayyîm*) remains uncertain. When humans are excluded from the tree of life (3:22), they obviously retain God's breath of life. Hence, the tree must represent possibilities for life not entailed in the breath of life. The fact that more is at stake than issues of quality of life seems clear since the deity expresses concern in 3:22 regarding the possibility of humans living forever. Having the breath of life does not entail immortality. Human beings are created mortal, but eating of the tree of life was a means by which human beings might receive a special blessing—namely, ongoing life; no ontological change seems in view, hence *immortality* would not be the right word to describe the result of their eating the fruit. Some this-worldly form of "eternal life" (not an afterlife) may be in mind.

The tree of the knowledge of good and evil (2:9, 17). (The woman refers to it in 3:3 as implied by 3:6; the changes she makes in the command mean that her description of the trees may be less than exact.) The name of this tree gives it a symbolic value, but that value has proved to be difficult to discern. In view of 3:22 (which the serpent affirms, 3:5), God knows good and evil, and human beings attain that godlike knowledge upon eating of the tree, though it is a knowledge with which they cannot live very well. Any meaning assigned to the tree must recognize that it has to do with a "knowledge" that God has. This makes it unlikely that it has to do either with sexual knowledge/experience, which 2:24-25 and 1:27-28 already imply, or knowledge of/experience with sin or wickedness.

The phrase "good and evil" functions as an idiomatic expression in which the individual words do not have their normal meanings (hence the phrase does not speak to the question of the existence of evil; a knowledge of the "good" is assumed from 2:9; 3:5). For example, the NIV translates the phrase in 24:50 with "one way or the other," referring to a divine decision, not the servant's (see 31:24, 29). The phrase with the verb *know* (ידע *yāda'*) occurs twice elsewhere (Deut 1:39; 2 Sam 19:35; cf. Isa 7:15-16), specifying those too young or too old to decide for themselves what serves their own best interests. Comparable phrases in 1 Kgs 3:9 and 2 Sam 14:17 speak of kings discerning the best interests of those who come within their jurisdiction.

For the writer, the key issue involves the discernment of what is in one's own best interests, not the fruit of the tree as fruit or any specific content of the knowledge or knowledge generally.[33] The text defines who

finally decides what is in the best interests of the human. The tree and the command *together* define the limits of creatureliness; to transgress these limits entails deciding about one's own best interests, to become autonomous, independent of the will of God for one's life. To refrain from eating recognizes creaturely limitations and the decisiveness of the will of God for true human life. This creational command presents a positive use of law, wherein certain limits are recognized as being in the best interests of human life and well-being.

2:10-14, The Rivers. This material both retards the action of the narrative and prepares for the end of chap. 3. The narrator creates a specific link between the beginning of things and the later world (see 2:24); vv. 10-14 belong to an identifiable place on the map (though its location is disputed). The Garden of Eden does not equate with the world. We have a glimpse of the world outside the garden. The river that waters the garden flows out of Eden and through the major sections of the then known world, making the latter dependent on the former. Even more, things in the garden are "good" *in their own right* (v. 12), hence in continuity with the good and diverse creation of chap. 1. Moreover, the worlds out beyond Eden already have names, suggesting that they were believed to be inhabited (which would coincide with the fuller population in chap. 4). Rivers and places no longer known to us (Pishon, Gihon, Havilah, and Cush[34]) combine with the known—Assyria and the Tigris-Euphrates valley. Even life outside the garden (eventually to be home to Adam and Eve) has significant continuities with life inside the garden. The two humans will not move from a world of blessing to one devoid of blessing.

2:15-17, Permission and Prohibition. God places the man in the garden—resuming v. 8—to work/serve (*'ābad*) the ground and care for it (*šāmar*) in fulfillment of the command to subdue the earth (ארץ *'ereṣ* and *'ădāmâ* are often interchangeable). Given the use of *'ābad* in v. 5, this role involves not only simple maintenance or preservation, but a part of the creative process itself. The role

---

33. See W. M. Clark, "A Legal Background to the Yahwist's Use of 'Good and Evil' in Genesis 2–3," *JBL* 88 (1969) 266-78; Fretheim, *Creation, Fall and Flood*, 73-77.

34. See Sarna, *Genesis* (Philadelphia: JPS, 1989) 19-20.

given the human in v. 15 may be compared to the dominion/servant role in 1:28.

God addresses the man in vv. 16-17 (given the anthropomorphisms, God is probably embodied), giving permission to eat from every tree (which would include the tree of life) except the tree of knowledge, and a prohibition; in effect, this constitutes a version of the first commandment (see commentary on 2:9), a concern not evident in chap. 1. God's first speech to humans does not center on God's place in the world, but focuses instead on the creatures, on their place and role, and the gifts they are given. The deity expresses no concern that the creature might exalt itself at God's expense.

The permission establishes an incredible range of freedom for the creatures; hence, the command that follows certainly does not seem repressive. The command may appear surprising, but it indicates the important role law has to play as a creational, pre-sin reality; command inheres as an integral part of the created order. To be truly a creature entails limits; to honor limits becomes necessary if the creation will develop as God intends. Yet, while the language takes the form of command, the issue involves trust in the word of God. Decisions faced by the humans will concern not only themselves, but also choices that have implications for their relationship with *God.* The command involves the visible and tangible (see the testing of Abraham, 22:1). Trust in God will often manifest itself in concrete matters.

Over against the tree of life, the tree of knowledge raises the possibility of human death. The two trees represent two possible futures: life and death. To be separated from the tree of life (3:22-24) represents the broken nature of the relationship, with death being inevitable. "The fruit of the righteous is a tree of life,/ but lawlessness takes away lives" (Prov 11:30 RSV; see Prov 3:18; 13:12; 15:4; Dan 4:10-12). The metaphor of eating, so prominent in this text, signifies the taking of something into one's very self with effects on one's total being ("you are what you eat").

"You shall surely die" stipulates a negative consequence, a specific penalty for eating, but the meaning remains difficult to discern. It does not mean "you shall become mortal"; they already are mortal beings. Death as such

belongs to God's created order. It seems to imply capital punishment without delay (though "in the day" could mean "when" more generally, so the NIV); yet, they do not die and God nowhere takes back the threat. It may be that death (and life) has a comprehensive meaning in this story (as in the OT generally; see Hos 13:1), associated with a breakdown in relationships to God, to each other, and to the created order.[35] This larger view of death comes to a climax when humans are excluded from the tree of life and lose the opportunity to overcome their natural mortality. So death does become pervasive within their lives even in the garden. At the same time, physical death would not have occurred had they managed to eat from the tree of life. If God had not acted, the serpent would have been right regarding physical death.

If humans obey the command, they recognize that they do have limitations in the exercise of their God-given responsibilities and that a right relationship to God provides an indispensable matrix for the proper exercise of that power.

2:18-25, The Creation of Woman. God evaluates the situation and declares that something is not (yet?) good; the man remains alone (God's presence does not suffice).[36] God, probably, speaks within the divine council; so the reader, again, overhears the inner divine reflective process (see 1:26). The man's not being alone correlates with God's not being alone. God identifies a problem with the state of creation at this point and moves to make changes that would improve it.

For the woman to be called "helper" (*'ēzer*)—a word used by both God and the narrator—carries no implications regarding the *status* of the one who helps; indeed, God is often called the helper of human beings (Ps 121:1-2). The NRSV's "partner" may capture the note of correspondence more than "suitable" or "fitting." The notion of Eve as "helper" cannot be collapsed into procreation, not least because the immediate outcome specified in vv. 24-25 does not focus on this concern; the term does not offer evidence of a hierarchy.[37]

35. See R. Moberly, "Did the Serpent Get It Right?" *JTS* 39 (1988) 1-27.
36. See W. Brueggemann, *Genesis* (Atlanta: John Knox) 47.
37. For an opposing view, see D. Clines, *What Does Eve Do to Help?* (Sheffield: *JSOT,* 1990).

Initially, God "forms" *every* animal and bird. Indeed, God does not simply create them, but "brings" them to the human in a kind of parade (the same verb is used in 6:19). This is a remarkable image of God. Twice, God "brings" a creature—first the animals, then the woman—before the man. God thereby is placed at the service of the "good" of the human being, presenting creative possibilities before him. Twice, God lets the human being determine whether the animals or the woman are adequate to move the evaluation from "not good" to "good." And *whatever*— without qualification—the man called every living creature, that was its name (v. 19). Phyllis Trible observes that God, who dominates the narrative up to this point, now recedes into the background, "not as the authoritarian controller of events but as the generous delegator of power who even forfeits the right to reverse human decisions."[38] In the first case, the man does not accept what God presents; God accepts the human decision and goes back to the drawing board.

The man recognizes that the woman will address the stated need. God recognizes the creational import of this human decision, for no additional divine word or act follows. God lets the man's exultation over the woman fill the scene; the *human* word (the first one uttered) serves as an evaluation that this situation may be termed "good." The narrator (vv. 24-25) then draws the reader into the closeness of the male-female bond, citing the implication of the human decision for the future. These verses show that the bond involves more than issues of procreation; the relationship includes companionship, intimate and otherwise.

The naming by the human parallels God's naming (1:5-10); it belongs as a part of the creative process, discerning the nature of intra-creaturely relationships. For the woman to be named by the man does not subordinate the named to the namer, any more than does Hagar's naming of God subordinate the deity to her (16:13).[39] Naming involves *discernment* regarding the nature of relationships (the male "rule" over the female derives from sin, 3:16).

God designs and builds (בנה *bānâ*) woman out of already existing material. This image may be compared to that of the potter who both designs and fashions an object. The "rib" is only one step removed from the dust, and hence stresses common ultimate origins, but the different image may reflect differences in design (no known ancient parallel exists for the separate creation of woman). The relationship of the woman to the "rib" entails no subordination, any more than man's being created from the ground implies his subordination to it. (Some suggest "side," Exod 25:12-14, but "rib" best links with the bone/flesh reference. See "boards" in 1 Kgs 6:15-16; the word usually occurs in architectural descriptions.) Unlike the dust, the rib is living material. The theological force of this creation is implied in 1:26-27—namely, the explicit equality of man and woman in the image of God (being created first or last remains immaterial). This description of the human creation emphasizes the personal attention implicit in the image of God as builder.

Contrary to some recent opinions,[40] the אדם (*'ādām*) ought not to be considered an "earth creature" without sexual identity until after the creation of woman. Without an explicit linguistic marker that the meaning of *'ādām* changes from "earth creature" to "the man," this word should be read with the same meaning throughout. Indeed, the word *'ādām* would have to be read with two different meanings *within* v. 22 if this distinction were licit. Moreover, v. 22, which speaks explicitly of God's creation of the woman, would lack a comparable creation account for the man. Verse 23 also refers to the man by the word איש (*'îš*, unambiguously male) as the one from whom the woman was taken.

The point at which *'ādām* becomes the proper name Adam remains uncertain. Genesis 4:25 provides the first unequivocal instance of *'ādām* without the definite article (so NRSV), though the NRSV provides footnotes for 2:20 (NIV begins Adam here); 3:17 (so RSV); and 3:21 (so NEB). These three texts are ambiguous (the NIV also uses the proper name in 3:20 and 4:1, but footnotes "the man"). The movement of the meaning of *'ādām* back and forth between generic

38. Trible, *God and the Rhetoric of Sexuality*, 93.
39. See G. Ramsey, "Is Name-Giving an Act of Domination in Genesis 2:23 and Elsewhere?" *CBQ* 50 (1988) 24-35.

40. Trible, *God and the Rhetoric of Sexuality*, 79-81.

humankind (1:26-27; 5:1-2), the first man, and Adam probably reflects an effort both to tell a story of a past and to provide a mirroring story for every age.

The language of "one flesh" (v. 24) functions as a literal reference at one level. The man is less than what he was before this surgery, and yet humankind has become more than it was—i.e., now male and female. The writer has not depicted a "birth" of the woman from the man, as if the man's creative powers were now in focus. The man was in a deep sleep; not to guard the mystery, but to stress that *God* was working creatively! The deity's initiative remains as central in the creation of woman as it was with the man.

In the wake of this divine act, the man's first words are recorded (note the assumption of a full-blown vocabulary), unlike the "silent" naming of the animals. The naming entails a difference from but no authority over the woman. The use of אִישׁ (*'îš*, "man") and אשה (*'iššâ*, "woman") in the naming discerns and formally *recognizes* the sameness and difference within humanity; the similarity in sound may emphasize equality. The narrator had already so named the woman in v. 22, contrasting the *'iššâ* with the *'ādām* from whom she was made *and* to whom she was brought.

The man's words recognize that the "not good" situation of v. 18 has now become good. "Bone of my bones and flesh of my flesh," a phrase that specifies kinship (29:14; 2 Sam 19:12-13; a broader reference than in English idiom), literally highlights mutuality and equality. The immediately recognizable bodily differences between them occasions the difference in the name. The man thereby has a new level of knowledge of his identity as a sexual being in relationship to the woman.

One Flesh. Verse 24 stands out from its context by the way in which it makes explicit reference to a later time—namely, when children are born and one can speak of fathers and mothers (the NRSV is more explicit than the NIV). The narrator thereby links God's original intention for creation and later practice in providing an etiology of marriage. The previous verses provide the reason for this practice—namely, a man leaves his parents and clings to his wife. Inasmuch as it was usually the woman who left the parental home, such departure probably does not have a spatial reference, but alludes to leaving one family identity and establishing another with his wife. These verses make no mention of children; rather, the writer focuses on the man-woman relationship, not on the woman as the bearer of children. God's creation values sexual intimacy as being good. Although the text does not speak explicitly about single human existence, it does not imply that, in order to be truly human, one must be married.

"One flesh" does not refer to sexual intimacy in a narrow way, but recognizes that man and woman constitute an indissoluble unit of humankind from *every* perspective. Hence the author refers to but does not focus on the sexual relationship. Leaving one's parents certainly implies marriage in that culture, and marriage certainly entails sexual intimacy. Being naked in the presence of the other was natural, with no embarrassment attached to total bodily exposure. Inasmuch as this is still generally true for married persons, nakedness must be understood in both literal and metaphorical senses (3:7, 10, 21); spouses also have no fear of exposure in the broader sense, no need to cover up.

REFLECTIONS

1. Is Genesis 1–2 an adequate statement about creation for the modern or postmodern context in which we live? In many ways this question must be answered in the negative. We have learned truths about the origins, development, and nature of the world from modern science of which the biblical authors never dreamed. We are confronted with issues never faced by these authors, from the environment to the role of women. In some ways the text, at least as it has been commonly interpreted, creates problems for any adequate consideration of these issues. While the commentary suggests that these problems have been created more by interpreters than by the text itself, the reader must not discount the history of the *negative effects* of such interpretations, from the exploitation of the environment to a second-class place for women. It will take generations for newer readings to overcome these effects.

In seeking finally to address these issues in a responsible manner, we must go beyond the text and draw on insights from other parts of the Scriptures and from our own experience in and through which God continues to speak. At the same time, these chapters will continue to provide the modern reader with an indispensable foundation for these reflections, including the images of God and the human, the relationship between God and the world, and human and nonhuman interrelationships. Perhaps, above all, these chapters provide a paradigm that we can use to integrate truths about the world gathered from all spheres of life.

2. The fact that the creation account rather than the birth of Israel stands at the head of the canon remains of considerable importance. The theological factors reflected in this ordering include the following: (a) The Bible begins with a testimony to the universal activity of God. God's creative activity not only brought the world into being but also was effectively engaged in the lives of individuals and peoples long before Israel came into being. The canonical ordering reflects the actual sequence of God's activity in the world. God was at work on behalf of the divine creational purposes before Israel understood what this activity was all about. (b) *God's* actions in the world achieve priority of place over human knowledge of what God has done. When Israel does begin to articulate the place of creation in the divine economy, this amounts to Israel's "catching up" with what God has long been about. The development of a creation theology in Israel occurs secondary to God's actual engagement with the world. At the same time, such a creation theology probably emerged much earlier in Israel than has commonly been supposed. Creation theology seems to be a given for those who first formulated a theology of Israel's redemption (see Exodus 15). (c) This canonical ordering corresponds to human experience of God's activity. Human beings in all times and places have experienced (even if they have not known) God's creative acts prior to and alongside of God's redemptive acts. Human beings receive their life and all their native gifts from the Creator quite apart from their knowledge of its source. The redemptive work of God takes place within a world and individual lives that have been brought into being and sustained by God's care. God's redemptive activity does not occur in a vacuum, but within a context decisively shaped by the life-giving work of God within and without Israel. (d) The position of Genesis 1–2 demonstrates that God's purpose in redemption does not, finally, center on Israel. God as Creator has a purpose that spans the world, and since divine deeds are rooted in the divine will, God's redemptive activity must be understood to serve this universal intention. Israel's place in the purposes of God are clear only from within this creation-wide perspective. Israel's election furthers God's mission on behalf of the entire universe.[41]

3. Traditional interpretations of Genesis have tended to favor the lofty formulations and familiar cadences of chap. 1 at the expense of the more "naive" story in chap. 2. Critical decisions, which tend to see the latter as older and more primitive (J) while considering the former (P) to be the product of more sophisticated theological reflection on creation, tend to fortify this tendency. Such views reinforce the traditional image of God as a radically transcendent Creator, operating in total independence, speaking the world into being.

Whatever the history of the transmission of these accounts, they now stand together as a single witness to the creation of the world. In this canonical perspective on creation each chapter stands in interaction with the other. Praiseworthy language about a

---

41. Fretheim, "The Reclamation of Creation," 355-57.

transcendent Creator has been placed in a theological context in which other images for God and the God-creature relationship come more clearly into view, providing for a more relational model of creation than has been traditionally presented.

Both God and the creatures have an important role in the creative enterprise, and their spheres of activity are interrelated. God has shaped the created order in such a way that the Creator and the creatures share overlapping spheres of interdependence and creative responsibility.[42] Moreover, the creatures are interdependent among themselves. Both human beings and animals depend on vegetation for their food (1:29-30); humans are to preserve the independent role of the animals (1:22). In addition, the nonhumans depend on varying forms of dominion exercised by the humans.

God is God and freely brings into being that which is not God. The creatures depend on the Creator for their existence and continuing life. Chapter 1 stresses divine initiative, imagination, transcendence, and power in a way that chap. 2 does not. The position of chap. 1 implies that these divine characteristics should stand at the beginning and in the foreground in any discussion. Yet, no simple or static hierarchy emerges, since some features of chap. 1 already lean toward chap. 2.

On the other hand, the realm of the divine and the realm of the creature are not two radically unrelated spheres; there are overlapping powers, roles, and responsibilities, to which image language testifies. God is not powerful and creatures powerless, as if the Godness of God could be bought at the expense of creaturely diminishment. In the very act of creating, God gives to others a certain independence and freedom. God moves over, as it were, and makes room for others. Creation involves an ordered freedom, a degree of openness and unpredictability wherein God leaves room for genuine decisions on the part of human beings as they exercise their God-given power. Even more, God gives them powers and responsibilities in a way that *commits* God to a certain kind of relationship with them. Divine constraint and restraint operate in the exercise of power within the creation (e.g., God will not singlehandedly be involved in procreation), still further restrained by the promise at the end of the flood story.

Human beings have been given freedom enough to destroy themselves, though God does not will such destruction. God does not have a final and solitary will in place from the beginning regarding every aspect of the created order. Things may develop, divine and human creativity may continue (see Ps 104:30), in view of which God will make adjustments in the divine will for the world. Yet, these divine acts will always be in tune with God's absolute will regarding the life and salvation of all.

These chapters imply that the divine sovereignty in creation is understood, not in terms of absolute divine control, but as a sovereignty that gives power over to the created for the sake of a relationship of integrity. Such a view involves risk, since it entails the possibility that the creatures will misuse the power they have been given, which does occur. A reclamation of creation will be needed.

4. Some observations on "chaos": The "deep" is probably not related to Tiamat in the Babylonian story in terms of either language or content (see commentary). Yet, some claim that "chaos" is a reality that persists beyond God's ordering activity, providing a negative backdrop and/or a potential threat to God's creation. Such language of "chaos" seems problematic, since *God* decides when to destroy (and promises not to). No reality independent of God is a threat to the creation. Such allusions do, later, provide deeply negative *images* for the world (e.g., Jer 4:23-26), but these are subsumed under the wrath of God in response to creaturely wickedness. Moreover, once Noah finds favor with God (6:8), the deity no longer threatens to destroy all creation, and specific temporal limits are placed on the flood (7:4, 12, 17). In 7:11 the fountains and windows function in an intensive way; they do not break down. When the flood waters abate, the created order of chap. 1 emerges into the light of day.

42. See M. Welker, "What Is Creation? Rereading Genesis 1 and 2," *TToday* 45 (1991) 56-71.

A different perspective on v. 2 seems appropriate. God's creative activity in the rest of Genesis 1 makes use of the "raw material" in v. 2 for new purposes. The author may not have had the philosophical perspective to call it "matter," but this verse testifies to a pre-temporal reality. As such, it describes a state of affairs prior to God's ordering that is *not yet* consonant with the divine purposes in creation (see the "not good" of 2:18).

God relates to this pre-ordering situation in and through the wind/spirit. The writer thus confesses that God constitutes a reality prior to the "beginning," and in the form of an active reality (wind or spirit). Even at this point, God acts creatively. Genesis 1:2 thus leans toward the rest of the chapter when God makes use of raw materials. Hence, the situation does not run out of control or in opposition to God. God does not reject it or say no to it; God simply uses it as part of a more comprehensive creative activity. Once God has ordered creation, the realities of v. 2 become part of a new world order. No independent threat to the cosmos (or to God) occurs at any stage.

Although the doctrine of "creation out of nothing" has often been grounded in this verse (see 2 Macc 7:28; Rom 4:17; Heb 11:3), it speaks almost exclusively of the ordering of already existing reality. We may justify a very limited use of this notion, only if we think of certain creative acts (sky and its luminaries). God brings everything else into being out of the not-yet-ordered reality, in the ultimate origins of which the author has no apparent interest. Any comprehensive doctrine of *creatio ex nihilo* must be found in other texts or theological perspectives.

(On relationships between these chapters and contemporary science, see the Overview.)

5. In 2:18-23, God takes the human decision into account when shaping new directions for the creation. Divine decisions interact with human decisions in the creation of the world. Creation involves process as well as moment; it is creaturely as well as divine.

The future stands genuinely open here. All depends on what the humans does with what God presents. The question of not only *how,* but indeed whether humanity *will* continue beyond this first generation remains open-ended, suspended in this creative moment. What the humans decide will determine whether there will be a next human generation. Human judgment will shape the nature of the next divine decision, indeed the future of the world.

This situation is similar to our own, where ecological sensitivity or the use of nuclear weapons may have a comparable import for the world's future. Such decisions could put an end to the human race as decisively as the man's choice of the animals would have. Human beings do not have the capacity to stymie God in some absolute way. But God has established a relationship with human beings such that their decisions about the creation truly count.

Genesis 3:1-24, The Intrusion of Sin

COMMENTARY

This chapter does not stand isolated. It has long been recognized as an integral part of the story, stretching from 2:4 to 4:16 (24). Some scholars have suggested that the story had an earlier form, particularly in view of the role of the trees, but no consensus has emerged. Given the high value this text has had through the centuries, the reader may be surprised to learn that the OT itself never refers to it (Eden is mentioned in 13:10; Isa 51:3; Ezek 31:9, 16, 18; 36:35; Joel 2:3). The closest parallel to the story is Ezek 28:11-19, a lamentation over the king of Tyre: "You were in Eden, the garden of God . . . were blameless in your ways from the day that you were created, until iniquity was found in you . . .

and the guardian cherub drove you out" (vv. 12, 15-16). Ezekiel 28, however, includes no mention of prohibited trees, the serpent, eating, or cursing of the ground. Genesis 3 offers no mention of riches, precious stones, or holy mountains. Some version of Ezekiel 28 was probably a source for the writer of Genesis 3. Unlike the Mesopotamian parallels, this story develops a sharp sense of human responsibility for the disruption of God's good creation.

One may discern a similar structure in Genesis 3 and 4:7-16. There is an unusual ordering in the appearance of the principals: vv. 1-7: Transgression—serpent, woman, man; vv. 8-13: Inquest—man, woman, (serpent); vv. 14-19: Sentence—serpent, woman, man.[43] That the woman plays the lead role in the transgression and the man in the inquest may suggest an interest in balance.

No word for "sin" occurs in the chapter (though in some ways that would defeat the art of storytelling; to have to name the game means one has not told the story very well). This situation parallels, in some ways, the absence of language about feeling; the chapter focuses instead on what the humans see and know and hear and do.

3:1-7, The Temptation. Verse 1 reaches back into the previous chapter in several ways. The writer identifies the serpent ("snake" would probably present fewer connotations) as a "beast"/"animal of the field" that God had formed and the man had named (the NRSV and the NIV introduce the word *wild* in 3:1 but not in 2:19-20, probably reflecting the history of the interpretation of the serpent). The serpent is characterized as "more crafty" (ערום *'ārûm*) than any of the others God formed; this is a play on the word for "naked" (ערומים *'ărûmmîm*) in 2:25. The link suggests that human beings may be *exposed* at times to shrewd or crafty elements in the world, language often associated with temptation.

Much debate has centered on the identity of the serpent. While the OT has no interest in this question, the situation changes in the intertestamental period. The association of the serpent with the "devil" in Wisd 2:24 (see Rev 12:9; 20:2) has enjoyed a long history. While this interpretation may be a legitimate extension of the relationship between

43. Fretheim, *Creation*, 82.

the serpent and temptation (see below), the text does not assume such metaphysical considerations.

The text does not focus on the serpent per se, but on the human response to the possibilities the serpent presents. As such, the serpent presents a metaphor, representing anything in God's good creation that could present options to human beings, the choice of which can seduce them away from God. The tree itself becomes the temptation, while the serpent facilitates the options the tree presents.

The author introduces the serpent abruptly, in a rather matter-of-fact way. The woman shows no fear or surprise or concern; conversations with snakes about God are presented as nothing unusual. Indeed, the reader receives an initial impression that the serpent is not a villain, but a neutral observer of the God-human relationship and a conversation partner, positively disposed toward the woman. The serpent only *becomes* a facilitator of temptation as the conversation progresses.

The reader appears to be overhearing the middle of a theological dialogue, leaving questions about the source of the serpent's knowledge unsettled, but suggesting that these words have grown out of a broader conversation. The reader first hears a question from the serpent to the woman (why the woman was chosen to play this role remains unknown, perhaps because she did not receive the prohibition firsthand; see 1 Tim 2:13-15; Sir 25:21-24). The question focuses on the prohibition, explicitly referring to God. The serpent raises a question about the amount of freedom God has given humans (always a sensitive topic). This tactic sets the agenda, which centers on God, and provokes a response by suggesting that the woman knows more about the prohibition than the serpent does: "Have I got this straight? Did God really say that you were not to eat of *any* tree?" The question is clever, to which a simple yes or no response is impossible, *if* one decides to continue the conversation (a key move in such situations). The "you" is plural in Hebrew, so that both the man and the woman are implied (the man stands "with her," v. 6, and so acts as a silent partner to the entire conversation).

Eve's response (vv. 2-3) seems motivated by an effort to explain the situation to the serpent. We may deem her response noteworthy in a number of ways. She evidences familiarity with the prohibition (not established to this point in the narrative); she both paraphrases the permission/ prohibition in her own words and quotes God directly. In quoting God, she uses the plural "you," understanding that the prohibition applies to her (as in the "we"), though God's original prohibition was in the singular (2:16-17). One puzzles over the reference to touching (the serpent interprets her indefinite reference to the tree in the middle of the garden—see commentary on 2:9—as the tree of knowledge). She may have heard it this way from the man; yet, because the text does not settle the issue, we do not know that *either* the man or the woman misstated it. The text does not offer a judgment or a defense of God, as the word order shows ("God" is delayed until after the second "garden"; the NRSV and the NIV advance the reference; see TNK, NAB). That she (or the man) makes the prohibition more severe than God made it has been explained in various ways (from anxiety to confusion to innocent defensiveness to hyperbole to a contribution in the search for truth). Most likely, the woman's reasons are revealed in the serpent's reply, which immediately focuses on death. The reference to touching thus reveals a key vulnerability—namely, anxiety about death. She exaggerates because she wants to avoid death at all costs (anxiety does not necessarily involve sin). The exaggeration offers evidence of reflection that the woman (and/ or the man) has had about the prohibition.

The serpent responds (vv. 4-5) precisely at the point of exaggeration and vulnerability, and with a promise at that: The humans will not die. This response could be a contradiction of what God has said (but not all that the woman has said). But it may be more subtle than that. In 3:22, God recognizes that they could eat and not die, *if* they eat of the tree of life. Expulsion from the garden becomes necessary for death to occur. So the serpent speaks a word that has the potential of being true (at least at the physical level). The reason: They will be like God/divine beings (1:26 and 3:22 include both), knowing good and evil (the phrase could refer either to God

or to minor deities, and may be purposely ambiguous). Inasmuch as God said nothing about being like God(s) a new element has been drawn into the picture (3:22 confirms that the serpent was right); yet, because this issue plays no role in the woman's reflection (v. 6) we have difficulty assessing its importance. Hence, we should temper efforts to see the primal sin as a desire to become like God. The serpent was subtle in holding out the possibility of avoiding death, while not conveying all the possible futures, not least a broader definition of death and another option that God had available (expulsion).

The serpent, then, is correct in saying the humans would become like God(s), knowing good and evil, and that eating in itself would not necessarily mean death in at least some sense. The serpent speaks a key phrase: "God knows." It claims that God has not told them the full truth about the matter, that God keeps something back. In this, the serpent acts not as a deceiver but as *a truth-teller.* But what was God's motivation for not telling them the whole story? The serpent makes it sound as if God's motivation is self-serving; the humans will become like God. Has God, in keeping the full truth from them, divine interests more at heart than interest in humans? The issue of knowledge thus becomes at its deepest level an issue of *trust.* Is the giver of the prohibition one who can be trusted with their best interests? Can the man and the woman trust God even if God has not told them everything, indeed not given them every possible "benefit"?

The writer leaves the woman to draw her own conclusions. The serpent has only presented some possibilities. The serpent engages in no coercion here, no arm-twisting, no enticement through presentation of fruit from the tree; everything happens through words. The word of the serpent ends up putting the word of God in question. At the same time, the issue focuses on the visible and tangible, which belong to God's creation.[44]

The woman does not speak (the lack of communication reinforces the element of mistrust); she only looks, contemplates, and eats. She considers explicitly neither God nor the prohibition, in terms of either complaint

44. See H. White, *Narration and Discourse* (Cambridge: Cambridge University Press, 1991) 133-37.

or rejection; she focuses only on the potential the tree offers. The observation that the tree was good for food and pleasant to the sight means, in view of 2:9 (see 1:29), that this tree becomes like other trees to her; it also happens to be "desirable for gaining wisdom." While one may "desire" (נחמד 'neḥmād, 2:9) the trees for their beauty, the humans shall not "desire" wisdom (i.e., knowledge of good and evil). The command seems to forbid an immediate acquisition of knowledge, though without suggesting that humans should not have wisdom. The issue involves *the way in which wisdom is gained.* The fear of the Lord is the beginning of wisdom (see Rom 1:20-21). By using their freedom to acquire wisdom in this way, they have determined that the creational command no longer applies to them. That command refers primarily, not to the intellect, but to success in making decisions in life—true wisdom involves knowing good and evil, the discernment of what is one's own best interests (see at 2:9). What it means can be seen from the result. Only God has a perspective that can view the created order as a whole; human beings (even with their new knowledge) will never gain that kind of breadth, for they make their decisions from within the creation.

The woman takes some of the fruit and gives it to her husband. As a silent partner "with her" throughout this exchange, the man puts up no resistance, raises no questions, and considers no theological issues; he simply and silently takes his turn. The woman does not act as a temptress in this scene; they both have succumbed to the same source of temptation. They stand together as "one flesh" at this point as well.

The result is fourfold: Their eyes are opened (as the serpent had promised, v. 5); they know that they are naked; they make loincloths for themselves (an interhuman act); and they hide from God's presence. With eyes opened, they see the world differently, *from a theological perspective.* They realize that, now having to decide for themselves what is in their own best interests, everything looks somewhat different. Having decided to be on their own, they see the world entirely through their own eyes. They now operate totally out of their own resources.

The humans first see each other's nakedness. It becomes clear (v. 10) that nakedness has more than a bodily reference. It reverses the lack of shame between them in 2:25 (see 9:21-23; Isa 20:4; Lam 1:8; Ezek 16:37). They respond initially by providing garments for themselves, which involves more than a physical act; they attempt to cover up their shame. This response addresses only the symptoms of the problem. Their human resources prove inadequate, as they recognize in seeking to hide their nakedness from God (3:10)—their clothing reveals more than it conceals—as God's action in clothing the already clothed indicates (3:21).

3:8-13, The Inquest. In this section God conducts a judicial inquiry. Whereas the woman functioned as the dialogue partner in vv. 1-5, the man serves that function in vv. 9-12. Hence, the author creates a certain balance between them in the story as a whole.

The Creator of the universe and all creatures chooses not to relate to the world at a distance, but takes on human form, goes for a walk among the creatures, and personally engages them regarding recent events. The writer presents no naive theology, but a deeply profound understanding of how God chooses to enter into the life of the world and relate to the creatures. Even more, this God comes to the man and the woman subsequent to their sin; God does not leave them or walk elsewhere.

Hearing God walking about in the garden, the man and woman try to hide from the divine presence. Not encountering the couple (as usual?), God calls for the man (the "you" is singular). The man interprets the question correctly as a probing inquiry and attempts to deflect the conversation away from what has happened. But his response reveals that something disastrous has occurred. He is afraid—the fear is explicit—because he was naked and, feeling shame at what has happened, hides himself, even though he is now clothed (v. 7). While the nakedness in v. 7 focuses on their relationship to each other, in v. 10 it shifts to their relationship with God. Although the feelings about nakedness are new, their clothing prompts the response; "clothedness" must be hidden from God. (It is ironic that the words for "hearing" and "fearing" can also be used for "obedience" and "awe.")

God's response centers on their nakedness, not on their fear. How would the man have known that he was naked? Something must have happened so that nakedness had become a problem *to the someone who told him* so (namely, the woman). God immediately puts the right question (again, to elicit a confession), asking whether he has eaten of the prohibited tree.

The responses could be viewed as a consequence of achieving autonomy; the man could not handle the new "knowledge." He appears fearful, insecure, and ashamed, seeking to justify himself and deflecting blame, both to God for giving him the woman and to the woman for giving him the fruit to eat, which had been guaranteed to alienate them from each other. Yet he does admit having eaten (though without mentioning motives). This situation attests to a breakdown in interhuman relationships as well as in the relationship with God, whom he does not engage in a straightforward manner.

God then turns to the woman, again asking a leading question. The woman deflects the responsibility as well (though she does not blame God as the man does), this time laying the blame on the trickery of the serpent (blaming it on the source of temptation), yet admitting that she too has eaten. That there is no inquiry of the serpent may show that the purpose in the interrogation of the humans was to elicit confession.

3:14-19, The Sentence. God proceeds with the sentencing, accepting full human responsibility and bringing all parties within the scope of the announcement. God acts as judge, calling each of the participants before the bench (in the order of vv. 1-6) and pronouncing sentence on each in typical courtroom speech (which immediately takes effect). Yet, even in the sentencing, God remains in relationship with the creatures involved, connected and concerned enough to identify further what has just happened.

What are the effects of the sentencing? Most basically, the sentences pertain to their primary roles in life (in that culture), roles of stature among the animals, roles of wife and mother, roles of tiller of soil and provider of food. Every conceivable relationship has been disrupted: among the animals; between an animal and humans; between the ground and humans; between human beings and God; between an animal and God; within the individual self (e.g., shame). More abstractly, one could speak of humiliation, domination and subordination, conflict, suffering, and struggle. The sentences touch every aspect of human life: marriage and sexuality; birth and death; work and food; human and nonhuman. In all of these areas, one could speak of death encroaching on life. Disharmony reigns supreme.

We may deem the judgment announced to the serpent unusual in a number of ways. First, God does not interrogate the serpent, although the judgment recognizes some responsibility on the part of the serpent for what happened. Second, the serpent receives a curse, becoming isolated from the community of animals (a word play with the initial description: "more crafty" [ערום *ʿārûm*] becomes "more cursed" [ארור *ʾārûr*]), a moral order correspondence—what goes around comes around. Third, in the future the serpent will move on its belly and "eat" dust (given the role that eating plays in the temptation, this is moral order talk). While this sentence may present an explanation of why the snake crawls on its belly, it signifies humiliation; eating dust symbolizes degradation (see Mic 7:17; cf. Ps 72:9; Isa 49:23). In some sense, vv. 14-15 create a symbol out of the serpent, which will remind all who encounter it of the subtleties of temptation as well as of the humiliating and conflicting consequences.

God places enmity between the serpent and the woman, and between the offspring of both. On the surface, the writer may be offering an origin of the legendary revulsion human beings have for snakes, which may relate back to 1:28 and show how the human task of dominion has been much complicated (see 9:2-3). Interpreters through the centuries (who have often linked the serpent and the devil) have seen in this text an ongoing struggle at a deeper level, even considering the text messianic, foretelling the struggle between the seed of the woman (i.e., the Messiah) and Satan. Yet, the word for "seed" functions as a collective noun (9:9; 12:7) or refers to the immediate offspring (4:25), not a distant one. It probably refers more generally to ongoing centuries of conflict between people and various sources of temptation. The "head" and "heel" are the natural targets against each other and point to no resolution of the conflict (the NRSV correctly reflects the fact that the same verb is used in both). Yet, striking the head of the serpent would more likely prove decisive and would give at least potential superiority to the human over the animal (perhaps reflecting 4:7).

The sentence on the woman—with whom no curse language is associated—has also been much discussed. Carol Meyers has placed this material in a sociohistorical setting just before the monarchy, a time when the place of women was related to the harsh realities of agricultural life in the central highlands.[45] She translates (with help from different versions) the first line of v. 16 to reflect the arduous field work in which women had to participate ("I will greatly increase your toil and your pregnancies"), and thinks it has an etiological force originally not present in Gen 3:16. While this view has not been fully tested, most scholars continue to translate along the lines of the NRSV and the NIV, so that the first clause in the poetry refers only to the pain of childbirth (hence paralleling the second clause). In any case, whatever the sociohistorical background of the text, the final literary context presents these verses as a consequence of the man's and the woman's sin. The fulfillment of the command to multiply in 1:28 has become more difficult.

The "desire" of the woman for the man remains unclear. It could involve a desire for mastery (as with this verb in 4:7), which will be thwarted by the husband. More likely, it means that, despite the pains of childbirth, she will still long for sexual intimacy. The "rule" of the husband could be a more general reference to patriarchy, which would be a departure from what God intended in creation (see 2:18-23). Trible states that the rule of the male "is neither a divine right nor a male prerogative. Her subordination is neither a divine decree nor the female destiny. Both their positions result from shared disobedience."[46] The "rule" of the man over

the woman is part and parcel of the judgment on the *man* as much as the woman. This writer understood that patriarchy and related ills came as a consequence of sin rather than being the divine intention. How easy it would have been to build patriarchy into the created order!

God allocates the most extensive sentence to the man, whose attempt to pass off the blame to his wife the deity has rejected out of hand. One may discern moral order talk, since eating plays a role in both sin and sentence. Although the man does not receive the curse, the ground from which he was formed does. The ground brings forth thorns and thistles as well as the plants of the field, which human beings will continue to need for food, but the thistles will make it more difficult to obtain. This also means that God's command to subdue the earth will be more difficult to fulfill. A concern for relief from the curse on the ground appears in 5:29 and 8:21. The same word that was used for "toil" in v. 16 for woman's pain in childbirth occurs in this sentence as well (both striking at a primary role in life). The man's work does not receive a curse (he still does in 3:23 what he was called to do in 2:15), but it has become more difficult and more energy has to be expended to gain a living from the soil.

"All the days of your life . . . You are dust and to dust you shall return" expands upon "until you return to the ground." This part of the sentence stipulates that the toil shall not let up until death. Death seems to be assumed rather than introduced as a part of the sentence. While the word *death* does not occur here, certain features of death within life are evident, beginning even before the sentencing. It remains to be seen whether the still remaining possibility of eating from the tree of life and gaining immortality will be realized.

3:20-24, The Expulsion. The note about Eve in v. 20 seems intrusive, but it probably functions as a positive development in the midst of the judgment, anticipating that life will still go on (a negative assessment of this verse incorrectly associates naming with subordination). The NIV future tense seems correct (since the perfect verb expresses certainty). Adam gives his wife the more personal name Eve ("Eve" resembles the word

45. C. Meyers, *Discovering Eve: Ancient Israelite Women in Context* (New York: Oxford University Press, 1988) 117-19.
46. Trible, *God and the Rhetoric of Sexuality*, 128.

for "living"), as a way of expressing confidence that children will be born; indeed, the unity of the human race ("all") appears implied, which would fulfill the command in 1:28.

Verse 21 has both positive and negative dimensions. The use of clothing is a common thread throughout Genesis as a sign of many things (see Tamar in 38:14, 19; Joseph in 37:3). Here God is imaged as a tailor, using animal skins (not necessarily killing to procure them). This same image for God is used in Ezek 16:8-14, where it is a profoundly gracious act, assuring continuing divine presence in the midst of the judgment; that is likely one theme here. If nakedness has to do with shame, exposure, and vulnerability, and they already had made clothes for themselves, God's act of clothing them may relate to issues of salvation (Job 29:14; Ps 132:16). God acts to cover their shame and defenselessness. At the same time, this act recognizes continuity in their estranged relationship; this is something with which they must now live (the more substantial skins may also stress this).

Verse 22 introduces inner-divine communication once again (see 1:26 for the "us"; see also 11:6-7). The sentence could break off abruptly (see NRSV), matching the effect of the action—namely, expulsion from the garden. Or it could be concluded with an exclamation point (see TNK). We should note that 'ādām functions generically here. The expulsion becomes necessary because God envisions radical possibilities regarding the tree of life and human immortality. Expulsion does not mean that an innate immortality has been lost; rather, the possibility of ever attaining it has been eliminated. Preventing humans from living forever might seem to be a defensive move by the deity, yet if death (in the comprehensive sense) has already become a significant part of life, then never-ending life offers no blessing. God continues to protect human beings. In apocalyptic literature, this motif recurs in an eternal frame, and when eternal life becomes a reality, it is not accompanied by sin and its consequences.

The author provides no specific description of the apparently coercive means used to drive the humans out of the garden. Yet, the divine vocation for the human remains the same: tilling the ground (see 2:15) from which he was taken (2:7-8). Hence, the humans leave the garden with a certain integrity, remaining an integral part of the divine purpose for the world (2:5). While being "like God" carries tremendous burdens and ambiguities, it also bears some potential for good and advancement. The cherubim—a human and animal/bird composite (a common phenomenon in the ancient Near East)—are usually associated with sanctuaries in Israel, associated with the divine presence in the ark, the tabernacle, and the temple. They assumed various functions, including guarding the sanctuary from unauthorized intrusion. The turning sword (unique in the OT) may or may not be in the hands of the cherubim, but its purpose is clear: to prevent human beings from returning to Eden; paradise on earth no longer remains a possibility.

The ending of this chapter bears some remarkable similarities both to Israel's being sent/driven out of Egypt (Exod 6:1) and to Israel's exile to Babylon, a banishment from the land (see Leviticus 26). The latter, in particular, may have been viewed as a parallel experience to this primeval moment in Israel's eyes.

REFLECTIONS

1. Inasmuch as God made the serpent, the text raises the issue of God's responsibility for what happens. God holds ultimate responsibility in the sense that God did not create puppets, but made human beings in such a way that they could resist the will of God (human beings would not be commanded not to eat if they were unable to do so). The temptation to reach beyond the limits of creatureliness belongs to created existence for the sake of human integrity and freedom (and God does not have absolute knowledge of future human behaviors, 22:12). At the same time, the text does not bring God's responsibility closer to hand and speak of God as the tempter or the instigator of the serpent's wiles or the source of sin and evil. The author does not use the language of evil to describe the serpent; indeed, the word about the serpent as God's creature recalls the litany of the goodness of all that God has created. Sin and evil have emerged only subsequent to the creation of the world. The first human beings are presented as individuals who are not sinful, but with clear choices available to them, with no response coerced or inevitable; they live in a world where choices count and God has not programmed the divine-human relationship.

We may see the serpent from a number of angles. The word *crafty* seems purposely ambiguous, as words like *clever, cunning,* and *shrewd* commonly are; it depends on the use to which these characteristics are put. Although used to describe human beings in both a good and a bad sense (e.g. Job 5:12; esp. Prov 12:16), no other biblical writer used this word for an animal; yet people often associate animals with characteristics usually reserved for humans (a sly fox; a wise owl). The serpent stands as an ambivalent symbol, associated with both life and death (see Num 21:4-9), often used figuratively for evil people (Pss 58:4; 140:3). Serpents were considered dangerous and probably always poisonous, a threat to life (Ps 91:13); they were "naked" in appearance, silent and "innocent" in their approach, suddenly there with little or no warning. As occasional symbols of deity, they could have been associated with that which was religiously seductive and hence dangerous to Israel's religious health.

The writer views the serpent as an animal of the field, and when God sentences the serpent (v. 14) it is included again among these fauna. Yet, this animal's knowledge and abilities seem not to outmatch those of any other animal. It may have been thought, however, that animals had unusual capabilities in paradise, or even beyond (see Balaam's ass [Num 22:22-30] and animals that have a knowledge of God, Job 12:7-9). When it comes to actions, however, the serpent seems to stand in a class by itself. Yet, a question remains: Is the serpent out to seduce human beings and challenge God or is it more of a neutral figure, serving to mediate possibilities within God's good creation? We should note that the woman occasions no surprise or fear or wonderment about the serpent. From every sign in the text, the woman understands it to be a natural part of her world.

The serpent, neither divine nor human, stands over against both as a "third party." In some sense, Genesis 3 reverses or makes less certain the dominion of humans over animals (1:28). God's sentence makes enmity a part of life. The serpent elicits certain characteristics in the human. "The serpent's 'subtlety' is the ability to provoke reflection on the true meaning of freedom, to reveal by means of conversation that the woman had the ability to think for herself, to suggest to her that she had the power to decide for herself. So it is the course of the conversation that is truly important, and not the existence of a talking serpent. . . . The serpent is a tempter in a sense, but only as a catalyst, assisting the woman's own mental processes to discover the freedom she had the power to grasp."[47]

The identification of the serpent as a "beast of the field" means that the reality embodied in the serpent should not be viewed as either primordial or transhistorical. It is not an evil being or supernatural/metaphysical force opposed to the divine purposes. The serpent exists within this world and is encountered by humans there. Nevertheless, the reality embodied in the serpent is transpersonal, not simply a product of the individual will. Language about the seed of the serpent, as well as God's judgment upon it, prevents us from seeing here *simply* an externalization of an inward struggle. In one sense, the serpent becomes transgenerational. The serpent may be a metaphor, yet no "mere metaphor"; it bears some correspondence with reality beyond the individuals involved.

47. Gowan, *From Eden to Babel,* 52.

2. Descriptions of paradise have, at times, been drawn in overly romantic terms. The text, however, shows remarkable restraint. It emphasizes basics: life, freedom, food, a place to call home, a family, harmonious relationships, and a stable natural environment. The contrast with the situation portrayed in 3:7-19 stands sharp and clear; yet, care must be used not to overdraw the differences. For example, suffering is often considered to be only part of the broken world. But it would be truer to the text to speak of the effects of sin as an intensification of suffering, so that it becomes a burden, tragic, no longer serving life. Eden, though, does include suffering. D. J. Hall speaks of four Edenic dimensions of "the suffering of becoming" (and draws parallels with the life of Jesus): loneliness (2:18); limits (not only the command in 2:17, but the very nature of creaturely existence); temptation; and anxiety (of ignorance, dependency, uncertainty). "Life without suffering would be no life at all; it would be a form of death. Life depends in some mysterious way on the struggle to be."[48] Genesis 1 may recognize this reality in the language of "subdue" (1:28).

3 What is the sin? Although the word *sin* or other such words do not appear in the chapter (4:7 is the first occurrence), we should not overvalue its absence. Stories are similar to games in that certain things do not need to be named. Nonetheless, interpreters have had difficulty identifying the nature of the primal sin. The story remains complex and devoid of abstract reflection. Even God's responses focus on the act of eating itself and its effects (vv. 11, 13, 17). God deems what they have done to be clearly wrong. But no single word appears to be satisfactory to describe it.

Disobedience may be the most common suggestion. Yet, though humans transgress God's prohibition (2:17), that action symptomizes a more fundamental problem. The vocabulary of pride (or hubris) also appears frequently, centered particularly in the "becoming like God(s)" theme. The serpent does mention this issue (3:5), but as part of a larger point being made regarding the divine motivation for the prohibition (for "God knows"). Moreover, the woman does not mention it in her own reflection; she uses language that normally would not be associated with pride (3:6). Even God mentions their having become like God(s) in a matter-of-fact way (3:22). Finally, language of rebellion also presents problems. No storming of the heavens language occurs here, no expressed effort to take over the divine realm. We might speak of their desire for autonomy, but not to run the universe. Even then, the reader finds no declaration of independence and no celebration of a newfound freedom.

The primal sin may be best defined as mistrust of God and the word of God, which then manifests itself in disobedience and other behaviors (e.g., blaming others). The serpent, in telling the truth about God (v. 4, "God knows"), informs the humans of something that God had not conveyed to them. This information centers on certain benefits that would accrue to them upon eating from the tree, benefits that appear to be in their best interest. This raises the question of God's motivation; even more, it suggests that God's motivation might be more focused on God than on their welfare. Can the humans trust that God has their best interests at heart even if they do not know everything? Even more, can the humans trust that God will be able to discern that not all such "benefits" are in their best interests, that true creaturely freedom entails acknowledging limits?

4. Commentators often use the language of "fall" with reference to this chapter. Such language begins to emerge only in post-OT interpretation, both in Judaism (Sir 25:24; Wis 2:24; see 2 Esdr 3:7-22; 7:118) and in Christianity (Rom 5:12-21; 1 Cor 15:21-22, 45-49), and has been a staple of Christian theological reflection through the centuries.[49]

48. D. J. Hall, *God and Human Suffering* (Minneapolis: Augsburg, 1986) 53-62.
49. See S. Towner, "Interpretations and Reinterpretations of the Fall," *Modern Biblical Scholarship,* ed. F. Eigo (Villanova: Villanova University Press, 1984) 53-85; G. Tucker, "The Creation and the Fall: A Reconsideration," *LTQ* 13 (1978) 113-24.

Readers, thereby, have given this text a level of significance found nowhere else within the OT (some themes are picked up here and there). But care must be used not to overdraw this statistical observation (this would be particularly the case if the Yahwist wrote in the exilic period!). Canonical placement has given to this text a certain theological stature (as with chaps. 1–2). Moreover, frequency of reference does not provide an absolute criterion for determining theological importance (one thinks of the suffering servant songs in Isaiah). We can only decry the elevation of this story into a dogma, though that often develops on the basis of many other considerations. Further questions need to be raised: To what extent does the "Fall" constitute a metaphor grounded in this text? This question relates to issues raised by the postbiblical language of "original sin." We take up the latter first.

This chapter in itself cannot support a notion of original sin. "Original" refers to the universality or inescapability of human sinfulness, not to its point of origin or to a particular mode of transmission—say, genetic (though the claim has often been made). At most one could speak of an "originating" sin (see below). Chapters 3–6 together, however, support a view approximating this, especially as seen in the snowballing effects of sin, climaxing in the statement of 6:5, "Every inclination of the thoughts of their hearts was only evil continually" (reaffirmed in 8:21). This suggests a process by which sin became "original."

The text includes the image inside/outside the garden to probe this issue, with progressively greater distances from the near presence of God (3:22-24; 4:16; see also the decreasing ages of human beings).[50] Humans live outside the garden (3:14-19 describes such conditions). Cain makes his decision to kill outside the garden, in a state of alienation from the relationship with God that presence together in the garden implies; 4:7 even gives "sin" an enticing, possessive character. At the same time, 4:7 implies that being "outside the garden" does not exhaust the analysis of a sinful act. Hence, something approximating a distinction between "sin" and "sins" is made; at the least, sin cannot be reduced to individual acts in these chapters.

What, then, of the "Fall" as a metaphor for what happens in this text? At least two issues present themselves: (1) the congruence of this metaphor with the metaphors in the text, and (2) the idea of the sin of Adam and Eve as a decisive rupture in the history of the relationship between God and humans. I believe that we may speak of a fundamental disruption, though this specific metaphor finds no textual basis. The most basic theological issue at stake involves whether sin is collapsed back into God's creational work and intention.

"Fall" theorists commonly assume that the text presents straightforward chronological terms: creation, paradise, fall. I have sought to show that these chapters, for all their typological character, tell a story of the past. They are placed within a *temporal framework,* particularly in the distinctions drawn between past and present and in the common chronological references.

Other readers assume that human beings were not created as sinful or evil creatures. If they were "perfect," how could they have failed? Rather, they were "good," which entails considerable room for growth and the development of potentialities. By the way human responsibility for what happens is lifted up, the writer does not assign the problem of human sinfulness to God or consider it integral to God's creational purposes. Certainly God creates the potential for such developments for the sake of human freedom. Especially important are the effects of this human decision, which range in an amazingly wide arch; it disrupts not only their own lives, but (given the symbiotic character of creaturely relationships) that of the entire cosmos as well, issuing in disharmonious relationships at every level. The narrative signals some kind of fundamental break by the journey of the nakedness theme from 2:25 through chap.

50. Fretheim, *Creation,* 97-99.

3, to which 9:3-5 also testifies. At the same time, the attention given to "process" noted above means that such human developments are not simply collapsed into a single moment.

The metaphor of "fall" does not do justice to these texts. Traditionally, this metaphor has been used to refer to a fall "down." Others typically emphasize the "becoming like God" theme, where human beings strive for and, indeed, assume godlike powers for themselves. This kind of a fall "up" (see above) violates the basic thrust of the metaphor (perhaps one could speak of a reaching up only to fall down, for the humans are not able to handle what they have become).

Such an upward move in the texts has been interpreted positively (at least since Irenaeus) in the sense that human beings move out from under the parental hand of God; they are pioneers on the road to moral autonomy and maturity, a necessary move if they are to become truly human. "The position reflects the mounting consciousness of the last few decades that rebellion against the yoke of authority is both an inevitable and a necessary element in human maturation."[51] However, one has difficulty in sustaining a totally positive view of God's response to the human violation of the prohibition. We would have to assign the problem to God, who acts arbitrarily in the setting of limits, and who opposes maturity and overreacts to what has happened. There are, in fact, few signs that the human lot improves, from either the divine or the human perspective. All the signs are that death (in the comprehensive sense) has become a pervasive reality with which humanity must deal, and that far from being marked by a new maturity or freedom, human life now entails broken relationships with God and every other creature (see 9:3-5 as well).

Perhaps these themes allow a variation on the "Fall" metaphor—namely, a fall "out." The primary images in the text are those of separation, estrangement, alienation, and displacement.[52] In these respects, the story is written not only to reflect a story of the past, but also to claim that in fundamental ways it reflects the character of human life in every age, which is filled with disharmonious relationships at all levels of life. Human beings always "reject their God-given vocation, scorn their permission modestly to enjoy the good gifts of the Garden, and break across into the area of prohibition outside the sphere of human competence."[53]

In view of these suggestions, does the text wish to claim that these events have *universal* effects on *all* subsequent generations? This combination of considerations, particularly the cosmic motifs present in chaps. 3 and 6, suggests that it does (reaffirmed in 8:21). The possible negative consequences for one's view of God need to be considered in the light of the moral order rather than a forensic divine decision. To this end, a consideration of 3:14-19 is helpful.

5. Finding the right language to describe vv. 14-19 has been difficult. Some would say that the language functions descriptively, but not prescriptively. The language does describe what has been commonly true about the human situation; it serves more as a statement about *condition* than a typical effect of specific human sins. Hence, this dimension of the story has a more than typological force; it works as a story of the past, presenting consequences of human sin that have taken hold in human life.

Some interpreters have hesitated to use the language of judgment (or punishment), often narrowly conceived. Yet, God's judgment facilitates the moral order, the working out of the effects of sinful acts. The man and woman reap the consequences of their own deeds. They wanted control over their own lives; they now have control in grievously distorted and unevenly distributed forms. They wanted to transcend creaturely

51. Towner, "Interpretations and Reinterpretations of the Fall," 80.
52. See A. Hauser, "Genesis 2–3: The Theme of Intimacy and Alienation," *Art and Meaning*, ed. D. Clines et al. (Sheffield: *JSOT*, 1982) 20-36.
53. Towner, "Interpretations and Reinterpretations of the Fall," 78.

limits, but they have found newly intensified forms of limitation. They now have the autonomy they so desired, but neither the perspective nor the wherewithal to handle it very well.

The language of prescription does not help if it means that God puts this particular state of affairs into place for all time to come. These judgments are not a divine effort to put a new order of creation into place. And these effects are not cast in stone, determining human fate forever. The judgment of Jerusalem in 587 BCE did not mean that it should remain forever in ruins, for it was soon rebuilt. Correspondingly, the toil of the man and the pain of the woman are not such that no effort should be made to relieve them. In fact, the intense efforts, particularly in recent years, to overcome these effects of sin harmonize with the creational intentions of God. At the same time, continuing human sinfulness impedes these efforts, and other forms of the distorting effects of sin break out among us with extraordinary regularity. We have a smoldering forest fire on our hands.

6. What about death in particular? In some sense this story includes an etiology of death (at least for human beings). Human beings were created mortal; nothing inherent in human beings would have enabled them to live forever. Death per se belongs as a natural part of God's created world. At the same time, the tree of life presents the possibility of continuing life as a special blessing. Since humans violate the prohibition, God cuts off that possibility by excluding them from access to the tree of life (3:22). In effect, sin leads to a death that would have been possible to avoid. It would be a mistake to think of death in these chapters as defined solely in terms of the cessation of heartbeat; death becomes a pervasive reality within life before the exclusion. Yet, these intrusions of death into life would not have led to physical death if the human beings had discovered the tree of life. Only God's act of exclusion in 3:22-24 forecloses that option.

The interpretation of Rom 5:12-21 ought not to be set up in such a way that it presents Paul as either all wrong or all right in his interpretation of the Genesis story. He certainly develops these themes beyond the scope of the story. Paul is, after all, basically interested in soteriological issues and develops an Adam-Christ typology as a way of interpreting the significance of what God has done in Jesus.[54] But, in some sense, he was right to read the story in terms of an etiology of *the reality of* death, if not death as such.

7. In vv. 17-18 the moral order bears a close relationship to the cosmic order, since human sin has ill effects upon the ground. While human behaviors today may affect the nonhuman order in ways different from then, or the cause-and-effect relationship may have been conceived differently, the link remains important.

The concern for the relationship between the human and nonhuman, often neglected, pervades these texts. This connection ranges from the deep concern evident in the detail regarding God's creating of the various creatures, to the assignment of the human to the further development of and care for the nonhuman world. The naming of the animals, while not finally solving human loneliness, establishes a "by name" relationship between the human and the nonhuman. God's continuing concern for the animals in the story of Noah's ark shows that God's delegation of responsibility does not issue in a deistic perspective regarding the divine care for the world. The symbiotic relationship among the creatures, in which humans participate, remains a prominent theme throughout the OT (see Lev 18:24-28; 26:14, 20; Hos 4:1-3; Rom 8:19-23).

---

54. See Ernst Käsemann, *Commentary on Romans,* trans. and ed. Geoffrey W. Bromiley (Grand Rapids: Eerdmans, 1980) 139-58 for a balanced view.

Genesis 4:1-26, Cain and Abel

COMMENTARY

This story of conflict between brothers (assigned to J) has long captivated interpreters. Many factors no doubt contribute to this popularity, from the way in which it mirrors the reality of family life in every age to the many puzzles the text itself presents.

The story has long been recognized as having origins independent of its present context. The verses presuppose a much more densely populated world than the immediate context would allow (e.g., the potential killer of Cain, vv. 14-15; Cain's wife and building of a city, v. 17). Moreover, Adam and Eve are active in the opening and closing verses, but do not appear in vv. 2b-24. Many have suggested that the conflict between a shepherd (Abel) and a farmer (Cain) betrays its origin, but God's regard for Abel's offering has nothing to do with Cain's occupation; after all, tilling the soil (עבד 'ābad) was Adam's vocation (2:15) and what the creation needed (2:5).

The story clearly sets themes such as primogeniture and sibling rivalry in place, providing continuity across the whole of Genesis. Yet the narrator seems especially concerned not in the brief notice of the murder itself, but in God's interaction with the words and deeds of Cain.

The chapter combines various types of literature: a tale of two brothers (vv. 2b-16), enclosed by genealogical materials and expanded by etiological elements regarding various cultural realities (vv. 17-22), concluded by a song (vv. 23-24) and the introduction of the line of Seth (vv. 25-26), which links this genealogy to that in chap. 5. It seems likely that a more compact genealogy has been expanded along the way to include the story of Cain and Abel and the song of Lamech.

Structurally, vv. 7-15 are similar to chap. 3, moving from temptation to sinful deed to divine interrogation and response to divine sentence and its mitigation to expulsion to the east.[55] This and other thematic links (e.g., 3:16 and 4:7; the pervasive concern for the

55. See Fretheim, *Creation,* 93-94.

ground, אדמה 'ădāmâ) imply that the two chapters, though having different origins, are to be interpreted in the light of each other.

Chapter 3 establishes a pattern that will befollowed down through the generations. What happens in the garden in chap. 3 and begins to manifest itself in disharmonious relationships of all sorts accompanies the history of humankind outside the garden in chap. 4. The reality of sin continues and intensifies Cain's problematic relationship to God, to other people (especially to family), to his own feelings and actions, and to the ground. On the structural similarities with other stories in chaps. 1–11, see the Introduction.

4:1-16. The rather abrupt transition to life outside the garden appears initially positive, with the intimacy between wife and husband and the birth of a child; these themes recur in the chapter (vv. 1, 17, 25). Eve lives up to her name (3:20), and the divine blessing of creation (1:28) develops appropriately. In addition, Cain and Abel, in their professions, take up the creational commands to have dominion over the animals and to subdue the earth (1:28).

Readers may find the relation between God and Eve in v. 1 ambiguous. The verb קנה (qānâ, "produced, acquired") plays on Cain's name, but its meaning as well as the preposition *with* remain uncertain. The context suggests a creational theme, "I have created a man with the LORD" (see Exod 18:22; Num 11:17). The verb can refer to God's creative activity (14:19, 22); the preposition can have the sense of "together with" (see BDB, 86; Exod 18:22; Num 11:17). Eve's word implies human-divine cooperation in fulfillment of 1:28 (see 16:2; 17:16). Her words also refer to Adam's cry that woman was taken out of man (איש 'îš; 2:23); now the woman cries out that she has produced an 'îš (the link explains the unusual use of this word for a child). Her cry expresses no more a prideful boast than does that of the man. Eve's response appears similar to that of Leah and Rachel (29:32–30:24), expressing gratitude to Yahweh (a woman first speaks this name) for the child and acknowledging divine participation, which probably refers generally to God's blessing of fertility and child-bearing capability.

The writer handles the birth of Abel more perfunctorily as the narrator quickly moves toward the heart of the story. Abel's status as the younger brother sets the stage for the issue of primogeniture in the rest of Genesis. The brothers grow up to become shepherd and farmer (see 1:28). Although these occupations were often at odds with each other, the text presents no specific signs of such conflict.

The text initially focuses on their worship, thereby placing the reality of worship within a *creational* context, distinct from God's revelation to Israel. They bring offerings without any command to do so; the writer assumes that human beings worship and conduct sacrifices. No altars or cult personnel are evident, and it seems unlikely that later Israelite regulations would apply. The narrator stipulates no motive, but gratitude seems likely. Since the offerings derive from the yield of their labors, they are an extension of the two brothers. All seems to be in order. Cain even brings his offering "to Yahweh" (which entails invoking the name, see v. 26). God clearly could accept both kinds of offerings (as in Israel's worship); neither appears inherently right or wrong.

It thus comes as something of a surprise that God accepts Abel's offering but not Cain's. Two puzzles emerge: (1) We are not told how Cain discovered that neither he nor his offering was accepted. Given God's way of responding in the story, Cain may have been told directly. (2) No rationale is given, hence God's action appears arbitrary (to readers and probably to Cain).[56] Most commonly, scholars have appealed to differences in their offerings. Abel offers the firstlings (Exod 22:19) and choice fat portions (Lev 3:3-17); Cain's offering is not described in such detail. Yet it seems unlikely that later Israelite practice would apply. Their motivation or attitudes may have differed; God looks at both the offerer and the offering (so Heb 11:4; cf. 1 Sam 16:7). God's response suggests that Cain did not "do well." In any case, God makes a decision for the younger brother. Cain's response to that decision sets the rest of the story in motion.

56. For a survey of opinion, see Wenham, *Genesis 1–15*, 104.

Cain's response (NAB, "resentful"; TNK, "distressed")—the downcast face (the external manifestation of the inner feeling [see 3:7])—reveals more the idea of dejection, feelings associated with rejection, than anger. Cain must care about what God thinks of him and his sacrifice. But the basic issue becomes *not* that Cain acts in a dejected fashion, but how he responds to God's interaction with him about his dejection. That God responds at all reveals a divine concern for Cain, and God's questions (v. 6)—repeating the description of v. 5b—disclose an insightful empathy for his situation. They imply that God's decision should not be the occasion for dejection, that a further response from Cain can put the situation right.

Although clearly a key to the entire story, v. 7 presents difficulties. In view of Cain's rejection and dejection, God graciously lays out Cain's options and their consequences. If he acts properly in response to his brother's acceptance and his own rejection (see Jer 7:5), then he will be accepted (namely, God will have regard for him and he can lift up his head again). On the other hand, if he does not do what is right, sin—occurring here for the first time in Genesis—lurks/crouches at the door (of his life), desiring to gain entrance. The image of sin lurking (the "enmity" of the serpent in 3:15 may be in mind; see Deut 19:11) symbolizes temptation. The reality of temptation is portrayed as something active, close at hand, predatory, eager to make inroads into Cain's life; it can consume his life, take over his thinking, feeling, and acting. Cain must not let it rule his life; he (the "you" is emphatic) can or must master it (see Ps 19:13). The text reflects the implications of 3:16 in the use of the words *desire* and *rule/master,* specifying continuity in such post-sin realities. Cain responds to a particular situation—namely, the working out of his feelings toward his brother.

Cain does not attend well to God's warning. When the brothers are in open country, Cain overpowers Abel and kills him (note the lack of emotion or drama). Cain may have invited Abel, but the explicit invitation was not preserved in the Hebrew text. Although God warns that the violation of the command will lead to death (2:17), the fact that a human being and not God sounds death into the world introduces an ironic note.

Once again, God immediately interrogates the offender in order to elicit Cain's response (cf. 3:9-13). Cain takes the road of denial rather than hiding from God; even more, he turns the question back to God ("Am I my brother's keeper?"), implying impropriety in God's question. "Keeping" is not something human beings do to one another in the OT; only God keeps human beings (see Num 6:24; Ps 121:3-8); hence *God* should know the answer to the question. In effect, if God does not know Abel's whereabouts, God has not been "keeping" him and should be blamed for his present situation. Cain seeks to relieve himself of any responsibility for Abel by focusing on God's task of "keeping."

God ignores the counterquestion and offers a sharp reply that keeps the conversation on course. Human actions are evaluated by the deity. Once again, God asks Cain a question (actually more an accusation), prompted by Abel's blood crying out *to God* from the ground (see Job 16:18; the verb often describes those experiencing injustice, see commentary on 18:20-21; 19:13; see also blood as polluting the land in 6:11-13; Num 35:33). This idea assumes that blood as the conveyor of life belongs to God and spilled blood cannot be covered up, leaving the issue of exacting justice in divine hands. God knows Abel has been killed by Cain and seeks to elicit from him a confession to that end. God does not wait for a response, but proceeds to sentence Cain for his crime (vv. 11-12)—though technically he has violated no law against murder (9:6). Nonetheless, Cain's acts certainly violated God's creational intentions. The penalty in 9:6 does not apply to Cain.

God does not curse Cain directly ("from the ground"; unlike 3:17), but the ground, which has opened its mouth and received Abel's blood, mediates the curse to him by rejecting his labors and no longer yielding its fruit (vv. 11-12 belong together). In effect, the earlier curse of the ground (3:17) applies to Cain in an intensified way so that it does not yield produce at all (the banishment, the hiddenness from God, and the journey east are also intensifications of earlier judgments on humanity). God condemns Cain to be a

"restless wanderer" (the NIV captures the hendiadys), rootless, living from hand to mouth, away from the supportive relationships of family. As Cain recognizes, he has received the equivalent of a death penalty. The breakdown of the human relationship to the ground, begun in 3:17, continues here and reaches a climax in the flood story (6:11-13).

Cain does not passively accept the divine sentence. He complains that his punishment—i.e., the consequences of his sin (the word עָוֹן *ʿāwôn*, a common word for "sin," refers to a continuum from sinful act to its effects; see 1 Sam 28:10) is greater than he can bear. (When faced with his own murder, the murderer laments!) In his use of sin language, he accepts the relationship between his sin and God's sentence; he admits guilt. He picks up on language God has just used: If the ground will not yield its produce and he must wander, he will be the target of Abel's avengers (perhaps God or siblings, 5:4). Even more, being driven away from the soil will break his basic relationship to the land itself. Speaking theologically, he will be hidden from the face (i.e., presence) of God (note the implied relationship with God, v. 16), i.e., driven from the near presence of the garden. God will no longer be available to him for care and protection, or even prayers relating thereto.

God disagrees emphatically, though without taking back the basic sentence. Cain's plea occasions a divine amelioration of the sentence, reflecting a divine responsiveness to a human cry, an openness to taking a different way into the future in view of what human beings have to say (see 18:22-33; Exod 32:9-14). God promises ("Not so" could be translated, "I promise," so TNK) that should anyone kill Cain, he will be avenged sevenfold (an idiom expressing intensity or severity). The story depicts not vengeance in the sense of revenge, but an effort to stop the violence from spiraling out of control by intensifying the workings of the moral order. The legal formulation gives it the force of law, hence applicability to all people. God will be Abel's brother's keeper. God's mercy embraces the murderer.

God then puts a mark on Cain as a *protective* device (the "mark of Cain" mistakenly carries a sense of public stigma). Only he would know why he received it; probably this mark (tattoo?; see Exod 12:13; Ezek 9:4-6) would be understood by any who encountered him. The mark does not protect him absolutely, as the word about vengeance shows.

The narrator leaves him as one who has been placed under the very special care of God. Hence, the story ought not to be interpreted in basically negative terms, but rather as the activity of one who lives under divine protection and care.

Cain leaves the presence of the Lord—i.e., the region of the garden, where God's presence was especially evident (see v. 14). This move does not refer to an absolute separation from God; indeed, God remains present in the conception and birth described in v. 17 (see Jonah [1:3], who does not leave God's presence absolutely either). The divine blessing follows Cain through all his wandering. He settles still further to the east of Eden (see 3:24), in a place called Nod (location unknown; it means "wandering" and plays on the word נד [nād, "wander"] in vv. 12, 14). To "settle" in "Wandering," an ironic comment (see also the city he builds), may refer to a division within the self, wherein spatial settledness accompanies a troubled spirit (see Isa 7:2). That Cain founded a city (nothing is said about the nature of this city) suggests that rootlessness means more than simple physical wandering. Those who live in cities can also be restless wanderers.

4:17-26. This section begins as did 4:1 (see v. 25). The genealogy of Cain, seven generations in all, occurs in linear form, with only the firstborn mentioned until Lamech, whose wives and three sons are named (5:32; 11:26). We hear nothing of Cain or any of his descendants beyond this chapter (an association with the Kenite peoples is problematic and of no evident concern here; on the relationship to similar names in chap. 5, see commentary on 5:1-32).

What are we to make of the origins of certain cultural advances—namely, urban life, animal husbandry (a more general reference than Abel's work), music (both stringed and wind instruments) and metallurgy? Inasmuch as such developments were ascribed to divine beings in the Mesopotamian world, this genealogy may provide a demythologized form of that tradition.

Many scholars have suggested that, inasmuch as these developments belong to the genealogy of Cain, these cultural achievements should be interpreted negatively. However, a positive assessment seems more likely. The seven generations of Cain may mirror the seven days of creation, thus placing human creativity parallel to the divine. Just as one may marvel at the great diversity of God's creation, so also human creativity mirrors God's in producing numerous gifts and interests (and to which the Creator God seems related). This relation may be evident even in the names of Lamech's four children; the similar names of the three sons are related to a semantic root having to do with capability and productivity, while the name of the daughter, Naamah, means "pleasant" or "beautiful."

The writer does not condemn Lamech for having two wives (cf. Abraham; Jacob). Lamech's song, probably of ancient origin, occurs in poetic form; in its parallelism, the second line uses different words to repeat the essential point of the first (e.g., listen to me/hear my words; wounding me/injuring me). He probably makes reference to only one incident (though "man" and "young man" are not strictly identical). The piece may be identified as a taunt song by one about to do battle (hence translated future, NIV footnote) or a boasting song upon completion of a mission (revenge), a macho song performed before women. Commentators usually interpret it negatively.[57] Whereas God avenged the death of Abel, Lamech takes vengeance into his own hands; he exacts death only for an injury; he appropriates God's own measures and intensifies the level of retribution, so much so that only a blood feud could ensue (see Matt 18:21-22 for Jesus' reversal of Lamech's boast). The song shows how Cain's violence had been intensified through the generations. Progress in sin and its effects matches the progress in civilization.

The birth of Seth constitutes an important moment; through him the human line will move into the future. Yet, his line involves no less evil than Cain's, as the introduction to

---

57. See J. Sailhamer, *The Pentateuch as Narrative* (Grand Rapids: Zondervan, 1992) 115.

the flood story soon reminds the reader. Eve's response at his birth, recalling the names of all her children, plays on Seth's name (שׁית *sît*, "put," "set") as God's replacement for Abel. The word translated "child" (זרע *zeraʿ*) may also be translated "seed" or "offspring" (see 3:15). Genesis 4:25 offers the first certain instance of אדם (*ʾādām*) as a proper name (without article or preposition; so NRSV, with footnotes to possible prior instances in 2:20; 3:17, 21). The name of Seth's son, Enosh, has the same meaning as *ʾādām*; there is no good reason for giving it a sense of weakness or frailty.

"To invoke" the name of Yahweh (v. 26*b*) refers in general to worship. Such activity should not be linked to Seth in any special way.

The phrase refers to this primeval period and parallels other notes about the beginnings of culture. Cain's offerings to Yahweh (4:3; see also 4:1) already imply the invocation of the deity's name. Yahweh's name was probably first associated with Israel at the time of Moses (see Exod 3:14-16; 6:2-3); using the name here attests that Israel's God should be identified with the God active from the morning of the world. Even more, pre-Israelite worship should not be written off as illegitimate. It was genuine and stands in continuity with Israel's later worship (see also the phrase in 12:8; 13:4; 26:25). This language testifies to a relationship with God that people had before there ever was an Israel and must, in some ways, have continued alongside Israel at a later time (see Mal 1:11).

REFLECTIONS

1. The first story of human life outside the garden includes elements regarding human potential for the best and the worst: from creating life to destroying life, from intimacy to jealousy and resentment, from invoking the name of the Lord to lying to God, from the development of the arts and culture to the use of human ingenuity for violent purposes, from living in the presence of God to alienation from God, from being at home to being displaced.

2. Gowan proposes that the story provides an illustration of the often savage inequalities that life inexplicably visits upon equally gifted or qualified people and the issue of how people should appropriately respond.[58] Yet, the narrator understands that *God* created the problem, and one ought not risk the inference that divine action lies behind each inequality of life. Hence, the text may address more narrowly ways of approaching seemingly unjust and arbitrary *divine* preferences (e.g., God's choice of the younger son in the stories that follow).

3. Verse 7 presents difficulties, but to claim that it is secondary or that God's response is "feeble" is not helpful. God's word evidences a deep concern about Cain's future and the two courses he can take with his life. God gives a gift to Cain by naming his feelings (v. 6) and pointing out the character of his inner struggle. Cain now knows that God understands him. Cain knows how God relates to people in the midst of such struggles; God will not intervene and force Cain to decide one way or another. Cain must decide how to respond, with the help of the knowledge God has given him. More generally, Cain ought not to view even such a divinely generated moment in life as devastating; God wills people to move on from such moments and be on with life.

The text implies that human beings are able to make decisions about *specific* matters of temptation (the issue is not whether to be sinless or not); we do *not* have to do with compulsion here, as if God holds out illusory possibilities to Cain. God clearly speaks an "if" and an "if not"; what human beings decide to do makes a difference regarding the shape of the future.[59]

---

58. See Gowan, *From Eden to Babel*, 67.
59. For a discussion of Steinbeck's use of the statement "you can master it" in *East of Eden*, see Brueggemann, *Genesis*, 58.

4. Cain's feelings or actions are not directed toward God, the one who made the decision, but misdirected toward Abel. In effect, Abel becomes a scapegoat, the one who takes the blame for something God did. In some sense, *God's* action leads to Abel's death. Does this fact explain why God mitigates the penalty for Cain? We should note the importance of the lament psalms and remonstrating responses on the part of persons like Abraham and Moses when confronted with difficult circumstances. In these expressions, God takes the "guff"; the deity helps prevent the blame from being misdirected toward other human beings. The suffering and death of Jesus, who takes on himself the violence and blame for something human beings have done, can be helpfully related to this text (see Heb 12:24 for the Abel-Jesus link).

5. The fact that the first murder arises over a conflict regarding religious practices, between two worshipers of God, presents another ironic twist in the story. Sin lurks within the community of faith, too, and no little conflict has developed over the centuries within that community over disagreements regarding worship and who is being true to God's will in such matters. In the wake of such experiences, the "losers" should be especially watchful, for the temptation to retaliate may be especially powerful.

6. Cain, guilty of murder and standing outside the line of promise, becomes the recipient of a promise from God (see also Ishmael, Esau). Even more, rather than exacting an eye-for-an-eye retribution on Cain, God protects him from an avenger. This incident raises questions about the appropriateness of later eye-for-eye legislation (see Exod 21:23-24) and capital punishment (see 9:6).

7. The sevenfold use of "brother" in the story intensifies concern for that relationship. These two persons are not strangers; they grew up in the same household, had the same family environment, were exposed to the same family values over many years. Yet, even such deep commonalities do not prevent hatred and violence. If sin can have this kind of effect on those who are so close and who share so many values, it presents a deep and pervasive problem for all human beings (see 1 John 3:11-15; Matt 5:21-25 links worship and conflict between brothers and sisters). Cain's act violates the family, an integral part of God's created order. Even more, by taking a life, Cain arrogates to himself a godlike power over Abel's life.

This story sets a key theme for the rest of the book of Genesis, with intrafamilial conflict moving from an exception to the norm. The stories of Abraham, Isaac, Jacob, and Joseph are filled with the legacy of the relationship between Cain and Abel, often involving primogeniture.

8. Once again, the story reflects the close relationship between humans and the land, an intimate link between moral order and cosmic order. Humans and the non-human world live in a symbiotic relationship. Although Cain's behaviors are not specifically directed against the land, the shedding of human blood adversely affects the productivity of the soil (see Hos 4:1-3). Even human behaviors that do not come to the attention of other persons have such an effect; they will in any case come to the attention of God.

9. Advances in civilization are not made ambiguous by being incorporated into a narrative so centered on violence. These references, as well as continuing testimony to intimacy and new life (vv. 1, 17, 25), suggest a powerful rhythm within life that works for good. Although material progress "frequently outruns moral progress and that human ingenuity, so potentially beneficial, is often directed toward evil ends,"[60] such a point moves beyond these verses. We must keep the positive accomplishments of Cain and his descendants *alongside* the negative word about Lamech. While the latter can have a negative impact on the former, it does not so contaminate the other

60. Sarna, *Genesis*, 36.

that the products of human creativity become innately evil. The positive point needs to be made clearly: "The story of civilization . . . is ennobled by the fact that it is a human being, God's creature, who leads the way along the path of progress, invention and discovery."[61] The redactor probably did not think that the pre-flood origin of the arts of civilization was a problem; knowledge was passed down through the family of Noah, finally to be inherited by Israel. In this, Israel acknowledges its debt to earlier creative efforts (Deut 6:10-11).

10. Those long-asked questions about who endangered Cain, where Cain got his wife, and who would have purchased all the houses he built are difficult. We may explain these disjunctions by appealing to the original setting of the story; it originated at a time when the world was populated, and the disjunctions were not smoothed over when it was incorporated into its present context. Yet, it seems unlikely that the redactor would have overlooked these elements. The redactor may have thought of Cain's siblings (see 5:4), but more likely these texts belong with those (e.g., 2:24) that collapse the distance between the "then" of the story and the "now" of the redactor. They are evidence that the story functioned, not as a straightforward account of ancient events, but as a mirror for human reality in every age. Cain may not have been threatened by anyone, but he reflects a concern that would have been voiced by later generations. Cain may not actually have built a city, but urban existence was a reality with which all subsequent generations lived.

61. Westermann, *Genesis 1–11*, 326.

Genesis 5:1-32, Adam's Family Tree

COMMENTARY

This, the second of ten genealogies in Genesis, presents ten generations from Adam to Noah, the hero of the flood (see 11:10-26). The genealogy is linear/vertical in form (see Introduction). The author created a generally consistent pattern, except for the first and last, with Enoch, the seventh entry, a special case. This list, commonly identified with the Priestly (v. 29 is a J fragment) source, bridges creation and the flood. In the present narrative it provides a link between major stories and accounts for every generation from the creation. The immediately preceding verses (4:25-26, J) clarify that the Seth of chap. 5 is actually Adam's third child.

Mesopotamian traditions also feature ten (or so) generations before the flood. In a similar list, eight to ten kings live a total of 432,000 years in one version, 241,200 in another (the kings in post-flood lists have much shorter reigns). Major differences from the biblical lists include the names; semi-divine kings vs. human beings (a motif of democratization comparable to the image of God); shorter lifespans (777-969 years; approx. a ratio of five years to one week). The biblical list participates in a common folklore about the ages of early humans. The ages were probably understood literally (see below). The ancient texts do not agree about the years involved; the years in the Hebrew text total 1,656; the Samaritan text, 1,307; the Septuagint, 2,242.

Some of the names in the Cain genealogy in 4:17-24 are similar to those in Genesis 5. Certain parallels are based in sound, others in form: Cain-Kenan; Irad-Jered; Mehujael-Mahalalel; Methushael-Methuselah; Lamech-Lamech; Enoch-Enoch-Enosh. Moreover, the last person in each list (Lamech, Noah) has three sons. Many scholars consider these lists as doublets (J and P), having a common origin but with different developments, or one being a reworking of the other or having differing forms because of differing functions (variations in the length of genealogies are common). Whatever the history, the present redaction regards them as two separate family lines.

After the murder perpetrated by Cain and the vengeful response of Lamech, Genesis 5 may represent a fresh start, building upon the reference to the worship of Yahweh at the end of chap. 4. The two narrative elements in the chapter are positive (vv. 22-24, 29), though the language regarding Enoch suggests he is something of an exception (so also Noah).

5:1-3. The opening sentence may refer to a larger book that included the other genealogies in Genesis. The "written account" of NIV may more accurately reflect the Hebrew ספר (*sēper*).

Verses 1-2 essentially repeat 1:26-28. The variations may only be stylistic, but the divine naming of male and female parallels the naming in 1:3-9, and gives male and female a decisive place within the created order (*'ādām* functions both generically and as a proper name). This delayed report may affirm humanity in the wake of the preceding stories. The absence of a specific blessing (see 1:28; cf. 9:1, 7) may also show that the creational command remains intact, as does image and likeness of God language. The words *image* and *likeness* in v. 3 are reversed from their order in 1:26. If the second word helps us to understand the phrase, the relationship between son and father embodies the notion of image (only "likeness" appears in v. 1 with reference to God).

5:4-32. Two elements stand out in an otherwise rhythmic genealogy, the notes about Enoch and Noah.

Enoch. Twice he is said to have walked with God (the phrase is used elsewhere only of Noah [6:9; see 17:1; 48:15]), which testifies to a close relationship with God in the midst of a "fallen" world. That God "took" this one who "walked with God" anticipates God's saving of Noah (see "take" in 7:2), a special act of divine deliverance. "He was not" may refer to death (Job 7:8; Pss 39:13; 104:35; Ezek 28:19) or an uncertain disappearance (42:13, 32, 36). It could mean that he died prematurely or disappeared unexpectedly. "God took him" (no place is

noted) could be a way of speaking of death (Jonah 4:3), but it has been linked with God's "taking" of Elijah in 2 Kgs 2:1 (see Pss 49:15; 73:24), which may be how the postbiblical traditions of Enoch's escaping death and receiving divine secrets arose (see Sir 44:16; 1-2 Enoch; Jubilees; Heb 11:5; Jude 14-15). His living 365 years (see the year-long flood, 8:13-14) depends on the solar year, but explanations are only speculative. It may refer to a complete or fulfilled life as well.

Noah. The name is a word play on נחם (*niḥam*, "relief, comfort"), though it probably means "rest." His father, Lamech, who anticipates Noah's role in the following chapters, expresses confidence—or a wish—rather than prophecy (it may stand in contrast to the word of the other Lamech in 4:23-24). The nature of the relief remains ambiguous, but may include a dual reference to 8:21 and 9:20. The former refers to a promise that provides for a constant natural order within which life can develop; the latter offers a specific instance—namely, Noah's development of viticulture and less onerous methods of farming (not the pleasure that wine-drinking brings). The "relief" would ameliorate the curse on the ground (3:17), but not remove it. From another angle, the author uses the Hebrew root for "toil"/"pain" that refers to Yahweh's grief in 6:6; both human beings and God suffer the painful effects of human sin. Moreover, the root for "comfort"/"relief" repeats the vocabulary of God's sorrow/repentance in 6:6-7. God's grieving/repenting actions concerning the human situation are more decisive than anything Noah might do. At the same time, Noah, the one who "walks with" this God, becomes the vehicle in and through which God enables a new beginning for humankind.[62]

Noah, who is unusually old at the time he begins a family, is the first person to be born after the death of Adam. Noah's genealogy brackets the flood story with its resumption in 9:18. Due to the location of his story, Noah is also the ancestor of all human beings.

---

62. See H. Wallace, "The Toledot of Adam," *Studies in the Pentateuch,* ed. J. Emerton (Leiden: Brill, 1990) 28.

REFLECTIONS

1. We may compare the structure of this genealogy with that of Shem in 11:10-26, which also climaxes in a key juncture within the larger story. These two genealogies balance each other, each bringing an era to a close, and with a key figure (Noah, Terah) having three sons. They serve both a literary and a chronological purpose in uniting key elements in the story (see Introduction). Scholars dispute the theological significance of this structure. Three developments may be noted: (1) The fulfillment of the divine blessing (1:28), which entails both human and divine elements. Divine in origin and empowering the creature to fulfill the command, it cannot be effected without human participation (the importance of which is clear in a negative way in 38:8-10). (2) The continuing creation. The order and stability that God the Creator initially brought to the world continues in the shaping of the human community. Even more than in chaps. 1–2, this creational activity involves human participation. Although not absent in this move from one generation to the next, the lack of God language gives the human a special place. (3) Some concern to express the unity of humankind may be present. Yet, because all but Noah's family are lost in the flood, it would not be a point well made. The table of nations (10:1-32) seems more clearly to be concerned about this matter.

2. Readers often puzzle over the long lives of these patriarchs. While they might be idealizations of the world's early history, the overall concern for chronology suggests that they are meant to be taken literally. The decrease in lifespan as time goes along constitutes a notable feature of the ages of these and other ancestral figures: Adam to Noah (969-777); Noah to Abraham (600-200); Israel (100-200); Ps 10:10 (70 years). The author may use these statistics to chart the effects of sin upon human life (see the above discussion on "Fall"), though diminishing life spans are also characteristic of Mesopotamian lists. Most basically, these ages are consonant with other features of chaps. 1–11 that indicate that this age differs from later ages; indeed, it belongs to an irretrievable past. In fact, the ages of these individuals lies *completely* beyond our experience (if not our desires).

The repetitive references to the image/likeness of God are important in several ways (see 1:26). First, it indicates that the identification of the human in the image of God has not been effaced by the events of chaps. 3–4. Not only Adam and Eve, but all subsequent generations (also affirmed at 9:6) are to be so described. Second, the use of likeness/image language to speak of the relationship between Adam and Seth establishes a link between the creativity of God and that of humans. The dialogical character of the divine creation of the human in 1:26 here explicitly draws the human up into that creative enterprise.

Genesis 6:1-4, Sin Becomes Cosmic

COMMENTARY

This brief segment is one of the most difficult in Genesis both to translate and interpret. Certain words are rare or unknown ("abide"/"contend with" and "for" in v. 3; Nephilim in v. 4); issues of coherence arise at many points. These verses may be a fragment of what was once a longer story, or scribes may have added to or subtracted from the text. The fact that the text presents ambiguity may be precisely the point, however: The mode of telling matches the nature of the message.

This fragment may reflect mythical roots, yet parallels in West Semitic cultures (unlike

Greek) have been hard to come by, and very little help has been gained from such comparative work. The text has been traditionally assigned to J, yet links with Priestly material can be discerned.

Consistent with other sections in chaps. 1–11, this material reflects an era no longer accessible to Israel. The text does not mirror a typical human situation (though parallels to specific items may be noted; see "also afterwards" for the Nephilim), but speaks of a time long past when God decreed a specific length to human life.

6:1. The narrative follows naturally what has preceded it. The divine blessing of 1:28 on humanity (האדם *hā ʾādām*) to be fruitful and multiply moves ahead. The language of birth and the reference to daughters pervaded chap. 5. The link of human beings to "the face of the ground אדמה [*ʾădāmâ*]" continues the creational theme of chaps. 2–4. Yet, these themes become distorted in what follows. The blessing to be fruitful and multiply catches up those who are not part of the human realm. Moreover, the earthly character of creaturely existence is compromised with an apparent breakdown of the earth-heaven distinction.

6:2. The author introduces the "sons of God" (or "sons of the gods") as a matter of course, as if the reader needs no explanation. But the modern reader does; indeed, much depends on their proper identification. There are three basic options: (1) The sons of Seth in chap. 5—the daughters are descendants of Cain; the godly sons are Sethites who sin by mixing with unbelievers. Or the daughters are referred to in chap. 5, while the "godly sons" are descendants of Cain (Eve's son "with the help of the LORD," 4:1). Or the "sons of God" are those who have "become like God" (3:22), assuming divine prerogatives. (2) They may be royal or semi-divine figures who accumulated women in their harems. Texts such as Psalms 2 and 82 have been related to this discussion; the links between semi-divine kings in the lists comparable to chap. 5 are also noted. (3) They are divine beings of the heavenly court (see 1:26). This widely held view, which seems most likely, may be grounded in the use of the phrase elsewhere in the OT (Job 1:6; Job 2:1; Job 38:7; Ps 29:1; as old as the LXX) and at Ugarit. These

divine beings take the initiative and breach the boundary between heaven and earth by taking human wives. The strangeness of such events in and of themselves (e.g., actual marriages are in view) should not count against this interpretation.

The reader may observe other links with the preceding narrative. The sons of God "see" the daughters who are "fair, beautiful" (טוב *ṭôb*, "good") and "take" them. These three words occur together in 3:6, describing Eve's eating of the fruit from the tree of knowledge. This parallel must mean that the actions described are inappropriate. The "seeing" narrows the appreciation of women to their beauty or, simply, physical desire. Their "taking" of multiple wives seems arbitrary ("take" is ambiguous; it can mean proper or forced behavior; the parallel with 3:6 suggests the latter); it implies the misuse of women (the "seeing" and "taking" of Sarai by Pharaoh in 12:15 and of Bathsheba by David in 2 Sam 11:2-4 have been cited). At the same time, more is at issue here than the acts of the sons of God. Why should human beings, who did not initiate this matter, bear a divine judgment?

6:3. The placement and interpretation of this verse provide a major crux. Regarding placement, some have thought that God's judgment should be a conclusion to the entire segment and that vv. 3 and 4 should be interchanged. The present placement, however, signals that the judgment relates most fundamentally to the problem, not the product.

The expression "my spirit shall not abide in mortals forever" presents another problem. The NRSV translation "abide," following the LXX and Vulgate, fits the context best. The mortals are humans generally (including any offspring of these unions). Spirit (רוח *rûaḥ*) signifies the breath of life as in 6:17; 7:15, 22 (a variant of 2:7), that divine life that enables life for both humans and animals.

"Forever" refers to 3:22 and the concern that God expresses regarding access to the tree of life. The divine-human link in this text has become another way in which immortality (or very long lives?) might be realized by human beings. Whether they have taken initiative in this matter may be finally irrelevant, for immortality would become a reality in any case (hence, the question of the assignation of fault does not pertain to the basic issue). God issues a decree that such a union will not result in human beings who live forever; indeed a specific limit is set. Without the animation of the divine spirit, the flesh will perish.

If we translate *"for* they are flesh" (as in the LXX), we understand why God thought it necessary to set this more limited lifespan. Immortality raises the issue of humans being able to live such a length of time with their fleshly nature (bodies wear out; see Isa 31:3 for flesh as weakness, not sinful nature). The divine decree becomes necessary, and has in mind what it would mean for a body of flesh to be animated by a spirit that lives forever. God, again, acts graciously.

6:4. Scholars dispute the identification and place of the Nephilim (literally it could be "fallen ones"; Num 13:33 suggests persons of gigantic stature). The first line may be an aside to the reader, giving a contemporary reference ("also afterward") concerning the offspring of these unions. This interpretation seems more likely than that they were actually the offspring of this union; the latter are identified as warriors of renown. Hence this verse does not present an etiology of any persons known to Israel. But if the ancient reader wanted to know what these warriors were like, the Nephilim would be a good analogy.

REFLECTIONS

1. Readers have usually thought these verses illustrate the increasingly ungodly state of affairs before the flood. Although words for "sin," "evil," or "judgment" are not present, they are implied, as was the case in chap. 3.

This downward development occurs at three levels: (1) Human sin has drawn the entire cosmic order into its orbit. Chapter 3 showed that human sin has an effect on the natural order; here those effects move even into heavenly places and entrap divine beings. In effect, the separation between divine and human worlds has broken down; the orders of creation have become confused. Evil has become cosmic in its scope. The flood must have a comparable scope. (2) The text illustrates the "becoming like God" theme only indirectly, for the initiative in the text comes from the divine realm. Likeness to God entails the possibilities for immortality (though still limited, for they are flesh). In this regard, the text relates to 3:22. Whereas that divine action had cut off humankind from the tree of life as a means to immortality, this divine decree cuts off another way in which that end might have been accomplished. The number 120 may also relate to the long life spans of chap. 5. (3) The resulting violence constitutes another level. The reference to heroes and warriors in v. 4 may relate to vv. 11-13. The mix of divine and human resulted in new forms of human life with intensified capacities for violence. The actions of these Nephilim-like figures thus signify another distorting effect of sin on the life of the world.

2. This text became the source of much speculation in postbiblical reflection (and it may have informed such texts as Job 4:18-19 and Isa 14:12-20). Indeed, it became the focus of interpreters more than did Genesis 3 (see 1–2 Enoch; Jubilees 5; 2 Pet 2:4; Jude 6). This text pushed speculation in the direction of dualism, wherein sin and evil are realities for both divine and human realms. Stories associated with a revolt in heaven followed by the casting out of these beings from the heavenly realm led to conclusions regarding the demonic sphere (which did not solve the problem of the origin of evil; it was only pushed back one step). Regarding the fate of the divine beings involved in this episode, however, the text remains remarkably silent. We may assume that they, too, were destroyed in the cosmic flood; indeed they may have precipitated its cosmic character. However, Gen 11:7 suggests that the heavenly council was again in proper working order after the flood.

GENESIS 6:5–8:22, THE FLOOD: THE GREAT DIVIDE

COMMENTARY

Literary analysts consider this narrative an admixture of differing versions of a single story (J and P). Other literary readings have discerned unity in the story, including elaborate chiastic structures.[63] While such schemas are often forced, unified readings of this composite text remain an important task.

That Israel would have preserved several versions of the flood story is not surprising since numerous versions circulated in the ancient Near East. The most widely known today occurs as part of the *Gilgamesh Epic*. An older, but less complete, version may be found in the *Atrahasis Epic*. The 3rd-century BCE history of Babylon by Berossus contains a retelling of the story. A Sumerian version of the flood also exists. Similarities in the basic creation-flood structure between *Atrahasis* and the biblical story are particularly striking (creation; early proliferation and disruption of humankind, including long-lived antediluvians; the gods sending a flood to stop human disruption; the saving of a hero). This structure, as well as commonalities in theme and vocabulary, indicate that these stories are in some way interdependent, though questions of direct dependence remain unresolved.[64]

The existence of numerous flood stories has stimulated efforts to discern the basis of the story. The above-noted stories are set in the Tigris-Euphrates River valley; alluvial deposits show that it was periodically flooded in ancient times. No such deposits have been found in the land of Canaan, and archaeological and geological remains provide no evidence of a worldwide flood. These factors suggest that the Genesis account should be related to a major flood in the Mesopotamian valley, which in time was interpreted as a flood that covered the then known world (one severe flood has been dated around 3000 BCE). Stories from other cultures should be tracked back to their own local flood

traditions. No credence should be given to the occasional rumors regarding the discovery of Noah's ark.[65]

Some interpreters think the flood story is enclosed by the genealogical references in 6:9 and 10:1. Other interpreters, however, argue that the story begins at 6:5. Certainly the repetitions of 6:5 in 8:21 are linked formally and thematically, centering in God's relationship to a sin-filled world. Many readers view God's remembrance of Noah and the animals in 8:1 as the pivotal center of the story. The rising of the waters leads up to 8:1, and their subsidence leads to a newly ordered world.

The story's characteristics include a repetition of key scenes, words, and phrases that focus attention on important aspects of the story; little direct speech (no speaking between 7:4 and 8:15) and no dialogue; no words from Noah, and he assumes little initiative, simply doing what he is told—so his portrayal is rather flat; no description of Noah's family members; a minimum of description of the disaster itself, with little attention given to the plight of the victims or the scene of death or Noah's family's reaction to what must have been a fearful and heart-rending time (how different from the way in which the media would have handled it today!); no communication with or reaction from those most affected negatively by these events—only the one to be saved is told what is coming; the images of God focus less on judgment (no anger language) than on sorrow, pain, disappointment, regret, and mercy.

On the other hand, the author devotes repeated (four times in 6:18–7:15!) attention to the boarding of the ark, to lists of people and animals and birds that are saved, and to the chronology of the event (though not for the construction of the ark). Attention centers on salvation rather than on judgment, on what God does to preserve the creation.

63. See Wenham, *Genesis 1–15*, 155-58.
64. For a summary, see Westermann, *Genesis 1–11*, 399-406.
65. For more details, see L. Bailey, *Noah: The Person and the Story in History and Tradition* (Columbia: University of South Carolina Press, 1989).

6:5-8, Prologue to the Flood. These verses (assigned to J) are central to an interpretation of the flood story.[66] Together with 6:11-13, they provide the deity's rationale for the flood. God's seeing (v. 5; see 6:12) reflects an inquiry into the human situation (see 11:5; 18:21), which issues in a general indictment of humankind (not a specific sinful act). In contrast to "all" the "good" that God "saw" in 1:31, here God sees that "every inclination of the thoughts of their hearts was only evil continually" (v. 5; see 8:21 for a comparable assessment at the end of the flood). "Wickedness" refers to both sinful acts and their consequences. The indictment encompasses not simply actions, but the inner recesses of the human heart. "Inclination" (יצר *yēṣer*) denotes the conceiving of possibilities for thought, word, and deed. The words *only, every,* and *continually* specify the breadth and depth of the sinful human condition (see Jer 17:9-10 for a similar appraisal). These assessments signify that God does not act from sudden and arbitrary impulses.

Having made this evaluation, the narrator describes the inner-divine reaction stunningly. The basic character of the human heart is set alongside the response of the divine heart. God appears, not as an angry and vengeful judge, but as a grieving and pained parent, distressed at what has happened. God "regrets" having proceeded with the creation in the first place, given these tragic developments (repeated in vv. 6-7; the NIV's "grieved" seems too weak a translation of נחם [*niḥam*]; the force of the verb has to do with genuine change; see 1 Sam 15:11, 35). We may discern divine consternation and disappointment, since God's vision for what the world might have been has been dashed by a narrow and self-centered human vision.[67]

Even more, and the NIV says it best, God's "heart was filled with pain" (used of human grief and pain, 45:5, as well as divine, Ps 78:40; Isa 63:10; Eph 4:30). God experiences the pain characteristic of man and woman in 3:16-17. These developments strike deeply into the divine heart and create tensions regarding the shape the future should take. How can God's deep suffering

be reconciled to the forthcoming judgment (see Hos 11:8-9)? God does not stand in an indifferent or remote relationship to what has happened, but personally enters into its brokenness and works on it from within. The future of the creation that becomes a possibility in and through Noah and the ark is rooted in this divine pain and sorrow, leading first to the divine choice of Noah (6:8) and finally to the promises in 8:21–9:17.

God, whose heart has been broken, announces a judgment (v. 7), which is nonetheless thorough going and uncompromising. The verb ("blot out, wipe away") may carry the sense of erasing away, as written letters (Num 5:23); it is used positively for washing away sins (Ps 51:2, 9). Hence the image of the flood would involve cleansing. This action seems to leave no room for qualification or exception (as in 7:4, 23, also followed by a note on Noah). God's showing favor to Noah (v. 8), however, moderates the judgmental decision (see Moses' argument on the relationship between finding favor in God's sight and judgment in Exod 33:12-17; חן [*ḥēn*] is a play on Noah). God's action does not depend on Noah's character (though Noah's potential in God's eyes cannot be discounted). God's gracious choice of Noah results from the divine agony over what to do about the creation. Yet, having been chosen, Noah's *subsequent* faithfulness (v. 9) is not just a blip on the cosmic screen, somehow irrelevant to God (see 7:1). Verse 9 is not presented as Noah's response to the divine choice, but as a consequence of God's prior action.

The relationship between vv. 5-8 and vv. 11-13 is comparable to that between 8:21-22 and 9:8-17, with a divine soliloquy followed by direct divine speech (cf. Exod 2:23-25 with 3:7-10).

6:9-10, Genealogy of Noah. These verses begin in a way typical of the P genealogies in the book of Genesis; they pick up on 5:32, but with the new information (anticipated in 5:29) that Noah's faithful relationship with God provides a channel through which God can start afresh. The negative evaluations of creation (vv. 5, 11-12) enclose the positive reference to Noah. Even in the midst of such a tragedy, one individual faithfully walks with God. But, most fundamentally, God's choice of Noah enables a glimmer

66. See von Rad, *Genesis,* 116-17.

67. See T. Fretheim, "The Repentance of God," *HBT* 10 (1988) 47-70; *The Suffering of God* (Philadelphia: Fortress, 1984) 107-26.

of hope in the midst of all that makes for decay and deterioration.

The descriptions of Noah say essentially the same thing from different points of view. He is a righteous man (צדיק ṣaddîq). God matches this judgment by the narrator (7:1). The point is not that Noah measures up to certain moral standards. Rather, he stands in a right relationship with God and has done it justice in various dimensions of his life (see 38:26). He acts blamelessly (תמים tāmîm) as compared to his contemporaries (see 1 Kgs 9:4; Ezek 14:14-20). This term, typical in ritual contexts for an unblemished animal, does not mean that Noah is sinless; rather, he is a person of high integrity (see Ps 15:2-5). He walks with God, suggesting an unusually close relationship (Enoch, 5:24; see 17:1; 48:15; Mic 6:8). These characteristics are exemplified by Noah's response to God's commands in the narrative that follows (6:22; 7:5, 9, 16; 8:18).

6:11-22, Preparations. Scholars often view vv. 11-13 to be a P version of the divine rationale for sending the flood, a vision of the world from God's viewpoint (see 6:5 for God's seeing). These verses belong with 6:5-7; the latter more clearly specify the depths of human sin, the former the cosmic implications. The indictment followed by the announcement of judgment appears prophetic in form, but only Noah hears the word.

The author focuses on what has happened to the *earth,* a word repeated six times. God deems the earth to be corrupt (vv. 11*a*, 12*a*) because it is filled with violence. Corruption (שחת šāḥat) involves ruin, decadence, or decay, the effect of violence; it stands over against the "good" God saw in chap. 1. The earth (not just the creatures) has not continued as it was created to be (on defiling or polluting of the earth, see 4:10-12; Num 35:33-34; Isa 24:5-7; Jer 3:1-3). Violence (חמס ḥāmās) includes lawlessness or injustice, a willful flaunting of the moral order, manifested in deeds that violate the lives of others, perhaps especially murder (in view of 9:5-6; see 49:5; Ezek 12:19-20).

Some interpreters understand the phrase "all flesh" to refer to both humans and animals, as in 6:17, 19; 9:11, 15-17 (9:2, 5 is at times appealed to). The NIV, however, translates "flesh" as "people" in vv. 12-13 ("life"

or "[living] creatures" elsewhere). Here, the place of animals is not explicit; yet it means that v. 13 (unlike v. 17) would not refer directly to animals. Hence, the inclusion of the animals in the promise (9:8-17) does not appear symmetrical with the pre-flood scene. In either case, at least some animals suffer innocently in the corruption of the earth and in the destruction. Because the moral order does not have a tight causal weave, and given the interconnectedness of life, the innocent often suffer with the guilty (see 18:25).

According to the NIV and the NRSV, the earth along with the creatures will be destroyed (v. 13*b*). However, this seems problematic (cf. NAB, "destroy them and all life on earth"), because v. 13*a* refers only to "all flesh"; people and animals are destroyed "*from* the earth" (7:23), the waters swell and recede from the earth (7:24; 8:3), and the earth is not re-created. The violence does corrupt the earth, and so judgment must be comparably comprehensive, but the effect on the earth functions more as a cleansing than a destruction.

God informs Noah of the "end of all flesh" (i.e., doom, see Amos 8:2; Lam 4:18). The verb *destroy* derives from the same root as "corrupt" (*šḥt*, "ruin/ruined," would capture the point well), which signals the functioning of the moral order (what goes around comes around). God does not need to introduce judgment into the situation (God does not act to trigger the destructive elements). The seeds of destruction are contained within the very nature of the situation. Unlike some biblical figures (e.g., Moses), Noah does not interact with God's announcement. But he must decide whether to obey God's command, trusting God enough to build the ark when nary a cloud is in the sky. God the architect tersely lays before Noah the plans for the ark. The dimensions (450 x 75 x 45 feet, a cubit is about 18 inches; the boat in the *Gilgamesh Epic* was a perfect cube) and other features suggest the image of a floating house rather than a boat, with no rudder, sail, or crew. The word for "ark" (תבה tēbâ) occurs elsewhere only for Moses' basket of rushes (Exod 2:3-5), where Moses becomes a new Noah.[68] Noah faced a daunting task in

68. On this and parallels between the ark and the tabernacle, see Fretheim, *Exodus,* 38, 268-69.

constructing this enormous boat (five times longer than the *Mayflower!*) and getting all the animals and necessary food on board in a short time—and the narrator tells the story in a matter-of-fact way, unlike many extra-biblical versions of the story. The significant issue for the narrator is that Noah obeyed the divine directive (v. 22).

In v. 17 God specifies the means for the destruction of all living creatures (those with the "breath of life" are human beings and animals) by means of a "flood of waters" (מבול *mabbûl*, probably the waters above the firmament [1:7], used elsewhere only in Ps 29:10). Death will overwhelm everyone everywhere, except the occupants of the ark. The covenant (v. 18) assumes a right relationship, as do all of God's covenants in the OT. The covenant probably refers to God's commitment to Noah and his family at this moment of danger and anticipates 9:8-17 in a general way. Noah can move into this horrendous experience surrounded by a promise from God that ensures a future relationship with him and, by implication, the entire creation.

God commands Noah to bring onto the ark his family of eight persons, a pair (or pairs) of "every living thing, of all flesh," and food for all (see 1:29-30). Noah does all that God has commanded him; in view of 7:5, this compliance refers to vv. 14-16 and the completion of the ark, regarding which the author provides no details; vv. 17-21 provide some information about what God intends to do and what will be expected of Noah when the ark is completed.

7:1-10, The Embarkation. These verses stem mostly from J (except vv. 6, 9). God's recognition of Noah's unique righteousness (v. 1) derives from Noah's trust in God and obedience in building the ark (see Heb 11:7). The righteous Noah of 6:9 has done justice to the relationship with God in which he stands. If he had not responded positively to the command, presumably he would have perished like the rest (see the assessment of Abraham in 22:12; cf. 38:26). God's confidence in Noah is seen to be well placed.

Verses 2-4, wherein God actually gives the command to board the ark, introduce problems of coherence with 6:17-20. While 6:19-20 spoke of pairs of animals and birds, here God directs Noah to take seven pairs of clean animals and birds (on clean birds, see 8:20) and a pair of unclean animals (in view of 9:3, clean and unclean refer to sacrifice rather than diet). Also, whereas 6:17 spoke of a "flood of waters" (see 7:11, 24) as the cause of the flood, 7:4 (see v. 12) speaks of forty days and nights of rain. Noah, once again, does all that God commands him (7:5).

Source criticism has explained this variety in terms of a shift from P to J materials; a redactor retained both versions. Yet, the redactor may not have thought this to be a problem; 6:19-20 speaks of pairs of animals generally, while 7:2-3 specifies the number and kind of pairs (needed for the sacrifice, 8:20). Verse 5 may be paired with v. 9*b*, which encloses the act of obedience to God's command. Verse 10 indicates that God does what God promised (v. 4).

The author provides a precise chronology, but contemporary readers have had difficulty in sorting it out, probably due to our lack of information about ancient calendars. Some details suggest a symbolic level of meaning. According to v. 4 the rain would come in seven days and last forty days; God *applies a temporal limit* to the flood from the beginning. Hence, the "flood" (vv. 6-7) does in fact come in seven days (v. 10) and lasts forty days (vv. 12, 17). The forty-day mark of v. 17 concludes the entry of water, the mountain-covering results of which are described in vv. 17-20. The 150-day mark of v. 24 marks the end of the time the flood had such an effect; in 8:3, these 150 days also mark the time the waters had subsided enough for the ark to rest on the mountains. These periods equal the five thirty-day months from the second month of 7:11 to the seventh month of 8:4. This sequence suggests that the forty days are included within the 150 days. The earth was dried up in the 601st year, the twenty-seventh day of the second month (8:14), totaling some 365-370 days (perhaps a solar year). The New Year's day of 8:13 marks the key point in the abatement of the flood (see Exod 40:2). Several scholars have noted the chiasm of seven waiting days (twice, 7:4, 10), forty days of rain (7:12, 17), 150 days of flood prevailing (7:24; 8:3), forty days of waiting (8:6) to seven days (twice, 8:10, 12).[69]

69. Wenham, *Genesis 1–15*, 157, 179-81.

7:11-24, The Flood. The editor created in this section an admixture of J (vv. 12, 16*b*) and P, with the renewed reference to the entry into the ark and Noah's obedience somewhat intrusive (vv. 13-15). Verses 6-9 are recapitulated in vv. 10-16 in more precise detail. The writer makes clear that all those specified had indeed gotten on board and were delivered from the flood. Yahweh shut the door of the ark (unparalleled in the Mesopotamian versions), signifying divine care (v. 16).

Right on God's announced schedule the flood begins, with water pouring in from below and above. The bursting forth (or splitting open) of the deep (תהום *tĕhôm*, v. 11; cf. Ps 78:15; Isa 51:10) suggests a breakdown of the division between waters above and below (1:6-7). The windows of the heavens, however, seem simply to be the source of rain (Mal 3:10; but see Isa 24:18). The presence of this event within a time frame remains important, for it keeps the destruction within created temporal limits.

The swelling of the waters (vv. 17, 24) encloses reference to death for all living creatures; the earth itself receives no mention, but there is repeated mention of the animals in the destruction (drowning language does not appear). The water rose above the highest mountains, and all living creatures died (language from 2:7 and 6:17 is used in v. 22). The writer describes the flood in quite natural terms; only with the subsiding of the waters does God's explicit activity now become apparent.

8:1-12, God Remembers Noah and the Animals. In 8:1-5 (essentially P), v. 1 constitutes the turning point in the story: God remembers (see 9:15; Exod 2:24; Lev 26:42-45) Noah and the animals, both wild and domestic. (God's remembering may be compared to that in Ps 25:7). While this divine act is of no little import, the promise of God's covenant with Noah (6:18) and the placing of a temporal limit on the waters (7:4, 12, 17) means that God's remembering would occur.

Verses 1-2 describe divine activity prior to the end of the 150 days (reference to which brackets these verses; the NIV partially recognizes this action of the deity by putting v. 2 in the pluperfect). God made a wind (רוח *rûah*) to blow over the earth, and it began to dry things up; indeed v. 2 reverses the deeds

of 7:11. This divine activity recalls 1:2; it suggests that the creation had begun to fail, and that God now begins the task of restoration. The *rûah* has a re-creative effect, bringing the cosmic "plumbing" back into proper repair. Unlike the frightened gods of the Mesopotamian stories, Israel's God remains in charge of the situation.

Five months after the flood began, the ark came to rest on a mountain in an area called Ararat (2 Kgs 19:37; Jer 51:37), most likely in extreme northeastern Turkey, near the sources of the Tigris and Euphrates rivers. The waters continue to abate for some months thereafter (v. 5 speaks of seventy-three more days until the tops of the mountains were seen; this chronology implies that the ark was grounded seventy-three days before the mountain on which it was grounded actually could be seen, though the two sources do not seem coherent here).

In vv. 6-12 (J), after forty more days, Noah sends out a succession of four birds (one raven, and a dove three times) to discern the condition of the earth (a comparable scene appears in an extra-biblical account and corresponds to a practice of ancient mariners). Note the use of practical wisdom rather than divine direction to discern the nature of the situation, as well as the salvific use of animals. The raven's going to and fro suggests it made various trips out from the ark, finally stopping when the waters dried up. Noah could probably determine whether the dove had found land by examining its feet when it returned. The olive branch brought back by the dove has long been deemed a symbol of peace (see Pss 52:8; 128:3 for its symbolic value of strength, beauty, and new life).

8:13-22, Disembarkation and Promise. In vv. 13-19 (essentially P), the author provides notice about varying stages of drying, from the appearance of the dry land (on New Year's Day, v. 13, an important moment for the beginning of the new creation) to a completely dry earth (v. 14); the verb stems from the same root as "dry land" in 1:9, hence it parallels the first creation.

God personally gives the directive for everyone to leave the ark (see 7:1, 16). The birds and animals are released for the purpose of multiplying on the earth (see 1:22, where birds but not land animals are blessed). Upon their release they find an earth accommodating to the purposes God intended for them.

In vv. 20-22 (J) Noah responds by building an altar and offering burnt offerings of every clean animal and bird (given the number of animals, this is an offering of consequence!). In the Babylonian epic the gods "gather like flies around the sacrifice," having been without food for many days. Here, God's smelling the odor of the sacrifice provides a lively metaphor for God's positive reception of the sacrifice (cf. Lev 26:31 with Amos 5:21-22) Noah remained unaware of this response. The offering in gratitude serves as a means for God to act on behalf of the worshiper, and hence has atoning value for Noah and his family. To claim, however, that it has perduring, universal significance, shifting God's future relation to *all* humankind and the world, isolates the sacrifice from other features of God's relationship to Noah.[70]

God initially responds with an internal commitment to the future of the creation (vv. 21-22), conveyed as an unconditional promise to Noah in 9:8-17 (formally comparable to 6:7 and 6:13). God's response expresses faithfulness not only to Noah but also to the larger creation. According to 6:18, God's commitment to Noah remains firm and involves more than his personal future. God's recognition of Noah's righteousness (7:1) and God's remembering of Noah *and* the animals (8:1) also reveal a committed relationship. Noah's sacrifice is thus not simply an occasion for or the cause of God's response; it symbolizes a vital relationship. The totality of Noah's relationship with God (not just the sacrifice) mediates God's new relationship with the creation.

Verse 21 has occasioned much discussion. The phrase "never again curse the ground [or hold it in contempt]" (קלל *qālal*) could refer to no more floods, to no additional curses on the ground (ארר *'ārar*, 3:17), to the abandonment of the existing curse, or, more generally, to the end of the reign of the curse. The last seems likely; curse will no longer be the decisive divine relationship to the earth. God enters into the unfolding effects of the curse (of which the flood was a climactic instance), not allowing it to control the future

of humankind or the creation. In effect, God places an eternal limit on the functioning of the moral order. Positively, the divine blessing and promise enter anew upon the scene and begin to break down the effects of the curse.

God's internal reason for giving the promise of no more floods appears highly unusual: "For the inclination of the human heart is evil from youth" (v. 21). A comparable statement occurs in 6:5, which serves as the reason for the flood; it now becomes the reason for *not* sending a flood. The differences between 6:5 and 8:21 are minimal (omission of "every"; replacement of "continually" with "from his youth"). The flood has not changed the basic human character. No new people are in view in 8:21, just fewer of them!

God chooses to take another course of action. The deity does not resign to the presence of sin (God sets only a certain type of judgment off limits), but offers a new way of relating to a wicked world. In view of this, God changes the ways and means of working toward divine goals for the creation.

God promises that the rhythm of the natural order—disrupted by the flood—will continue "as long as the earth endures" (v. 22)—literally, "as long as all the days of the earth." At first glance, one wonders what kind of promise this is, if another flood could simply be one way in which the earth no longer endures! But this phrase does not qualify the promise. It does not have an "end of the world" in view (though 2 Pet 3:6-7 suggests one could think of "the fire next time"); it speaks only of the life of the earth in an indefinite future. The phrase alludes to the "permanence" of the earth.[71] The promises focus on matters ecological, involving agricultural life, climate, seasons, and the daily rhythm. The first implies the continuing existence of human work in seeding and harvesting. All elements are necessary for continued life in the world, providing a basic rhythm as life reaches forward to the future. Come what may, the cosmic order will remain steady and regular.

70. Wenham, *Genesis 1–15*, 190.

71. See Westermann, *Genesis 1–11*, 457.

REFLECTIONS

1. The situation that led to the flood is described clearly enough. The wickedness of God's creatures had become so deep and broad (by the tenth generation) that the creation was reeling in negative response. God had to do something. Scholars have suggested overlapping interpretations for the purpose of the flood.

(a) God intended to *purge* the world of its corruption. Water may thus be understood in both a literal and a metaphorical way, as flood and as a cleansing agent, i.e., the language of blotting out or wiping away, wiping the slate of the world clean of its wickedness and beginning anew. This interpretation has some merit, but 8:21 reminds the reader that the flood did not cleanse human beings of sin. If God's purpose was to cleanse, it was in some sense a failure.

(b) God wanted to *undo* creation ("uncreation") and to begin again ("recreation"). Water functions literally and metaphorically, as flood and as instrument of destruction. Wenham's language conveys this interpretation: The flood was "the day when the old creation died"; it "destroyed the old world, God's original creation, and out of it was born a new world."[72] This could be seen in the return of a watery chaos (תהום *těhôm*) and the collapse of the division of the waters (7:11). Then, in a recreative act, God reverses the movement toward chaos, evident in the use of the רוח (*rûaḥ*) and the return of the waters (8:1-2), the emergence of dry land (8:13-14), and the blessings of 8:17 and 9:1, 7.)

This interpretation also presents some problems. The journey back from chaos works differently from the journey depicted in chap. 1. The old world was not destroyed; major continuities with the original creation remain (vegetation [the olive leaf]; light; firmament; luminaries; the ark occupants). *God sets limits to the flood from the start,* from the saving of a remnant of human beings and animals, to the covenant with Noah (6:18), to placing a temporal limit to the onrush of the waters (7:4). Hence, from a point early in the account, God did not intend to undo the creation, or for that matter to re-create an undone world according to some design. There is a beginning again, but the pre-flood creation remains.

(c) Another approach appeals to mythological or typological elements. Water often occurs as an archetypal symbol of chaos: "The potency of water as a symbol for the threat to all ordered life . . . lurks at the edges of controlled, meaningful existence."[73] Water appears in various texts (e.g., lament psalms) as an image for difficulty and suffering. The story reflects this-worldly reality of every age. For Westermann the story is the product of "a series of identical or similar events which have been fashioned into a type. The flood is the archetype of human catastrophe."[74] The flood story illustrates how God relates to the world in judgment and grace, from the prophetic indictments and announcements of judgment and salvation to the apocalyptic images of the end of the world.

While flood language can indeed be appropriated to depict such moments (see Isaiah 24–27; Matt 24:37-44), this approach to the story is deeply inadequate. The promises that chart God's new relationship to the world indicate that the flood was a not-to-be-repeated event. As such, the flood should *never* be used as a type or illustration of divine judgment. The flood has a unique character, frozen in place by the divine promise never to do this again. Hence, the flood functions for Israel as an illustration of the certainty of God's promises (Isa 54:9-10). The flood typifies the inviolability of God's promises.

The biblical authors did not consider the flood as simply one event among others. It was an epoch-making event that deeply affected the future relationship between God

---

72. Wenham, *Genesis 1–15,* 177, 206; see also Clines, *The Theme of the Pentateuch,* 73-76, who notes this theme in chaps. 3–6 as well.
73. Gowan, *From Eden to Babel,* 92.
74. Westermann, *Genesis 1–11,* 398-99.

and the world (see below). Such a perspective may explain why the flood story is so long, when compared with other narratives in Genesis 1–11.

(d) Another approach to the story involves its relationship to other flood stories in that world. However, we must do more than probe similarities and dissimilarities, and speculate regarding issues of dependence and interdependence. One often finds a tendency to show the "obvious" superiority of the biblical account to the other stories, or to reduce everything to Israelite polemic against other religions. While the task of comparison remains important, the hegemonic agenda does not prove helpful.

A more useful approach recognizes that the Israelites drew on understandings generated by other peoples and cultures. This angle of vision acknowledges that God the Creator was at work among other peoples before Israel appeared, and appreciates that significant insights, even theological insights, have been borrowed and developed by Israel. Israel inherits a way of thinking about beginnings—including the very structure of the account—that enables the community of faith to think about the creation in innovative ways.

From another perspective, we must recognize that God's saving act occurs in the world outside Israel. God *as Creator* acts in *saving* ways on behalf of creational goals. Such actions are not confined to Israel and need not be mediated by the community of faith.

(e) The flood story focuses on God as well as God's decisions and commitments regarding the creation. "The beginning and goal of the event lie with God."[75] The images of God developed in the story are striking: a God who expresses sorrow and regret; a God who judges, but doesn't want to, and then not in arbitrary or annihilative ways; a God who goes beyond justice and determines to save some creatures, including *every* animal and bird; a God who commits to the future of a less than perfect world; a God open to change and doing things in new ways; a God who promises never to do this again. The story reveals and resolves a fundamental tension within God, emphasizing finally, not a God who decides to destroy, but a God who wills to save, who is committed to change based on experience with the world, and who promises to stand by the creation.

The ascription of human feelings to God (see 6:5-7 in particular) reveals something about God. The grieving divine response at *Israel's* sin (Ps 78:40; Isa 63:10) harks back to the morning of the world and relates to all creatures. God, from creation on, continues to be open to and affected by the world. "God's judgment is not a detached decision . . . like flicking a switch or sending an impersonal command through a subordinate. God is caught up in the matter . . . the judgment is a very personal decision, with all the mixed sorrow and anger that go into the making of decisions that affect the people whom one loves. Grief is always what the Godward side of judgment looks like."[76] God experiences such sorrow *as God,* but real continuities with human sorrow exist.

Even more fundamental to the story is "the change wrought in God which makes possible a new beginning for creation. . . . The flood has effected no change in humankind. But it has effected an irreversible change in God. . . . It is now clear that such a commitment [to the creation] on God's part is costly. The God-world relation is not simply that of strong God and needy world. Now it is a tortured relation between a grieved God and a resistant world. And of the two, the real changes are in God."[77] What God does "recharacterizes" the divine relationship to the world. "God decides to put up with this state of evil."[78] This divine commitment signals the end of any simple sin-consequence schemas; this story does not exactly fit that way of construing other narratives in chaps. 1–11.

75. Westermann, *Genesis 1–11,* 394.
76. Fretheim, *The Suffering of God,* 112.
77. Brueggemann, *Genesis,* 73, 81.
78. Westermann, *Genesis 1–11,* 456; see von Rad, *Genesis,* 133-34, who speaks of "forbearance" and cites Rom 3:25.

But the issue involves something other than a patient tolerance of human sin. For God to promise never to do something again, and to be faithful to that promise, entails self-limitation regarding the exercise of divine freedom and power. God thereby accepts limited options, in this case, the way in which God relates to evil in the world—no more flood-like responses. But God does not simply resign to evil (see below). Therefore, God *must* find a new way of engaging evil. Genesis 6:5-7 suggests that God takes the route of suffering. Deciding to endure a wicked world, while continuing to open up the divine heart to that world, means that God will continue to grieve. God thus decides to take suffering into God's own self and bear it there for the sake of the future of the world.[79]

God's regretful response assumes that humans have successfully resisted God's will for the creation. To continue to interact with this creation involves God's decision to continue to live with such resisting creatures (not your typical CEO!). In addition, God's regret assumes that God did not know for sure that all this would happen. As is evident throughout Genesis and the OT, God does not know the future in some absolute way (see commentary on 22:12). The text provides no support for a position that claims that God knew, let alone planned, that the creation would take this course.

God decides to go with the world, come what may in the way of human wickedness. God makes this promise, not simply in spite of human failure, but *because* human beings are sinful (8:21). The way into the future cannot depend on human loyalty; sinfulness so defines humanity that, if human beings are to live, they must be undergirded by the divine promise. Hence, *because* of human sinfulness, God promises to stay with the creation (see 34:9 for an identical understanding of God's future with Israel in the wake of the golden calf debacle).[80]

We find an admixture of realism and promise here. On the one hand, human beings remain sinful creatures through and through. The flood cuts them off from any Edenic paradise; access to that world cannot be bridged or developed by gradual improvement. For the sake of creation, God must formulate laws to restrain negative human tendencies and behavior. On the other hand, human beings remain in the image of God (9:6); they are so highly valued that commands must be put in place to conserve their life, and they retain fundamental responsibility for the larger created order. But humans do not possess sufficient resources for the task; only God can assure creation's future. To this end, God ameliorates the workings of divine judgment and promises an orderly cosmos for the continuation of human and nonhuman life. Humans may, by virtue of their own behaviors, put themselves out of business, but not because God has so determined it or because the created order has failed.

2. There are significant ecological dimensions in the text. Human behavior has had a deeply adverse impact on the created order. The growth of thorns and thistles in the wake of human sin (3:18) has here grown to cosmic proportions. A close relationship exists between moral order and cosmic order, a point needing little argument in the modern world. Positively, it is striking that God puts such stock in the saving of the animals; indeed, God's remembrance of the animals belongs to the same initiative as God's remembering Noah. The lives of animals and humans are so interconnected that our future on this planet is linked to one another's well-being. Although human sin has had significant negative consequences for the earth, if humans assume appropriate responsibility we may anticipate significant potential for good.

3. The theme of God delivering through dangerous water is in a number of biblical texts: e.g., Exodus 14–15 (and the other texts dependent on this tradition, e.g., Isa

79. Fretheim, *The Suffering of God*, 72, 112.
80. Fretheim, *Exodus*, 303-5.

43:2); Jonah; various lament psalms; Jesus stilling the storm and walking on the water (Mark 4:35-41); baptism (1 Pet 3:18-22). Flood water imagery also appears in later divine judgments (Isa 8:7-8). Nonetheless, God's promise remains sure: never again will there be the like of Noah's flood.

GENESIS 9:1–11:26, A NEW WORLD ORDER

Genesis 9:1-17, God's Covenant with Noah

COMMENTARY

These speeches of God to Noah are conventionally assigned to the Priestly writer, but must now be read in view of 8:21-22 and other non-Priestly texts. Recalling key elements from chap. 1 in the light of the experience with a devastated creation, God lays out the dynamics of a renewed relationship to the post-flood world. Although Noah is in some sense a new Adam, God must take into account that the inclination of his heart is evil (8:21). The world is no new Eden. Generally, these texts seek to assure Noah and his family (and readers) that God has not withdrawn from the creation; God still rules and the basic shape of the divine relationship to the world still holds, with its blessings, commands, and promises.

God chooses to safeguard the creation, making provisions from the human (vv. 1-7) and the divine sides (vv. 8-17). Verses 1-7, with their recognition of murder and human-nonhuman conflict, assume that the pre-flood, but post-Eden, state of affairs will continue in post-flood times. God's continuing valuing of and care for the creation, regarding both animals and humans (vv. 1-7) and then more universally with respect to the future of the entire created order (vv. 8-17), provides the primary link between these two sections. The God who blesses (v. 1) and the God who promises (v. 11) come together in this text, and lay the foundations for the future of the post-flood world.

9:1-7. This segment is enclosed by formulations from chap. 1: to be fruitful, to multiply, and to fill the earth; v. 7 even speaks of "swarming" (used for sea creatures, 1:20; cf. 8:17 with 1:22). As in 1:28, God blesses Noah and his sons before offering commands.

This blessing language stresses that, in the midst of death and destruction, God wills life; that will remains firmly in place even with the "inclination of the human heart" (8:21) and the negative effects of continuing violence, injustice, and disorder.

Verse 2 assumes the charge to have dominion, though now complicated by the "fear and dread" of the violence of which human beings are capable (military language, Deut 11:25), and developed in the wake of sin's effect on human domination (v. 5 also knows about violence against humans by animals). Human dominion over that world has often been more a matter of tyranny than benevolence. That all animals are "given/delivered" into human hands (also military language, Deut 20:13) entails power over their life, though not a license for exploitation nor a diminution in the task of dominion. This verse recognizes that the realities of fear make relationships to the animal world much more difficult and complex, with new levels of responsibility. The prophets envision a return to the deity's earlier plan, according to which humans would relate to the animals (see Hos 2:17-18; Isa 11:6-9).

Human diet constitutes another issue carried over from chap. 1. Earlier, God grants green plants to humans for food (v. 29); here God expands that to include *"every* moving thing that lives." A vegetarian diet is supplemented with meat, probably a concession to the need for food in a famine-ridden world. Yet restrictions remain (the formulation of vv. 3-4 is similar to 2:16-17). No distinction between clean and unclean occurs (see 8:20), but the flesh of a living animal or the meat of a slaughtered animal may not be eaten if the blood remains in it, since blood equals life (see Lev 17:11; external evidence for the ancients would be the pulse). Humans must drain animal blood before eating meat. This directive, without parallel in the ancient Near East, recurs in the OT (see Lev 17:10-14; Deut 12:15-27) and has authority in the NT (Acts 15:20; 21:25). It was not uncommon for ancients to drink blood for the renewal of vitality it was thought to bring. Israel, however, believes that life belongs to God and should be returned to its source. This proscription regarding blood—and the attention needed to fulfill it—stands as a sharp reminder that killing animals ought not to be taken lightly, for God is the source of their life. As such, it guards against brutality, carelessness, and needless killing. Concern for the life of animals immediately leads into the concern for human life.

The lifeblood of human beings should not be shed, much less eaten (v. 5). Using personal language, God declares that murderers will be directly accountable to God; indeed, the writer states three times that *God* will require a reckoning. This includes even the animals (for a case, see Exod 21:28-29). Although the text does not specify an executor in v. 5, yet "by a human" in v. 6 assumes, in a matter-of-fact way, that human beings will administer the sanctions. The chiastic formulation of v. 6 provides a shorthand expression, probably proverbial, of the repercussions that fall upon a murderer (v. 6): If a human life is taken, the life of the one taking it shall be required (see Matt 26:52). The chiasm formally expresses the point; in such cases, justice will involve the principle of measure for measure. No persons shall be allowed to pay their way out of such a situation (see Num 35:31). Capital punishment, though referred to here, remains limited compared to many other cultures (e.g., never in property cases). This text does not advocate or authorize or justify capital punishment; rather, it recognizes the way in which human beings would participate in the moral order as executors of the divine judgment (later laws institute a legal system; see Rom 13:4). This saying expresses God's point of view regarding the high value of human life.

The writer links the rationale given for this command to the fact that human beings have been made in the image of God (see 1:26), an understanding that still pertains in a postflood world. In the killing of a human, the created order is threatened; the status and role of humans within God's creation is violated. At the same time, humans are not absolutely inviolable; they can forfeit their right to life if they take a life. The divine image rationale may relate to both halves of v. 6*a* —"for" may refer both to the victim and to the human executor on God's behalf, providing a deeper link with 1:26.

9:8-17. God moves to promises, a personal witness to humans regarding what they can expect from God. The covenant God establishes fulfills the promise God made in 6:18. Originally a doublet of 8:21-22, the latter verses now serve as divine reflection that leads to this public statement of promise (cf. 6:7 with 6:13).

Similar to vv. 1-7, these verses are enclosed by reference to the covenant being established (v. 8) and, in a final peroration, to having been established (v. 17) with all flesh. The many repetitions of key words and phrases emphasize the promissory character of the covenant and the inclusiveness of the recipients throughout all generations, assuring the listeners (and readers) of a hopeful future. The promises may be compared to those given Israel after the fall of Jerusalem (see esp. Isa 54:9-10, which describes this covenant in terms of a divine oath). God stands as the subject of the verbs throughout; God establishes/makes the covenant, sets the bow in the clouds, and remembers the covenant.

We may observe a basic structure: vv. 8-10, the recipients of the covenant; v. 11, the content of the covenant; vv. 12-17, the sign of the covenant, in chiastic form; vv. 12-13, 17, the sign; vv. 14-15, God's remembering when the bow is in the clouds; v. 15*b* is the essence of the promise.

God establishes this covenant, not only with Noah, his sons, and all their descendants, but with "every living creature"—that is, "all flesh"—and with the earth as well (v. 13). The involvement of the nonhuman in the promise parallels their presence in the expectations of vv. 1-7 (see also 6:11-13). We hear a word of comfort and reassurance in the wake of the horrendous experience of the flood (and readers can plug in their own disasters).

Covenant functions as an equivalent to promise; God is obligated, unilaterally and unconditionally. God initiates and establishes the covenant, and remembering it becomes exclusively a divine responsibility. The covenant will be as good as God is. God establishes it in goodness and love and upholds it in eternal faithfulness. It will never need to be renewed; it stands forever, regardless of what people do. Humans can just rest in the arms of this promise. And the promise offers this (comparable to 8:21-22): Never again will God send a flood to destroy the earth. There may well be judgments yet to come, but not one that will annihilate everything (see Isa 54:6-10).

God did not create the rainbow for this moment; it had existed but was now filled with new significance for the future. Although elements of the natural order could function as virtual signs (see Jer 31:35-36; 33:19-26), the bow is different since it reminds God (see Exod 12:13), not human beings (see 17:9-14). When God sees the rainbow, God remembers the covenant. This does not mean that God forgets in between rainbows. Yet, at times Israel believed that God had in fact forgotten them (see Ps 13:1; Lam 5:20). To attest God's remembering assures those who think that God appears to have forgotten. God's remembering entails more than mental activity; it involves action with specific reference to a prior commitment (see 8:1; Exod 2:24; 6:5; Lev 26:42). As a sign for God it

becomes a secondary sign for people, one in which they can take comfort and hope.

In the ancient Near East and Israel (in poetic texts; see Pss 7:12-13; 18:14; 144:6; Lam 2:4; 3:12; Hab 3:9-11) the (rain)bow was a divine weapon, and lightning bolts were arrows that exacted judgment. Hence, possible interpretations of the bow in this text arise: (a) Associating the rainbow with *promise* rather than judgment changes the meaning of the symbol, becoming a sign of peace rather than war; God will not use the bow for this judgmental purpose again. This view seems difficult since the *broken* bow becomes a symbol of peace (Ps 46:9); (b) Associating the rainbow with *both* promise and judgment keeps the normal meaning of the symbol intact, but focuses it on the means by which God keeps the promise—namely, God uses the bow to *protect* creation from such disasters.[81] This interpretation also presents problems because the buildup of clouds in vv. 14 and 16 implies that the divine judgment gathers momentum (see Jer 4:13; Ezek 38:16; Joel 2:2) and the appearance of the bow occasions a shift in God's direction. No bow appears unless there are clouds; the bow thus suggests restraint in the midst of deserved judgment. It thus seems best to retain it as a symbol of peace and divine good will toward the creation. In either case, the bow serves as an important sign of God's ongoing, deep commitment to the life of the creation, and in such a way that God is limited regarding its possible futures (see below).

81. E. Zenger, *Gottes Bogen in den Wolken* (Stuttgart: Katholisches Bibelwerk, 1983).

REFLECTIONS

1. Since the commands in vv. 1-7 are formulated for a pre-Israel world, they present a universal dimension. In fact, God must only be formalizing an already existing "natural law," for such allowed the author to speak of responsibility and accountability in the earlier chapters. For example, Cain was held accountable for his murder of Abel, as were the pre-flood generations for their violence. Numerous other instances occur in Genesis (e.g., 20:1-10; 26:5, 10) and in the rest of the OT (e.g., the oracles against the nations, Amos 1–2). The NT seems cognizant of the status of these laws in such texts as Acts 15:20; 21:25.[82]

82. For a discussion of the so-called Noachic commandments (often idolatry, blasphemy, bloodshed, incest/adultery, robbery, injustice, eating flesh with blood), see Sarna, *Genesis*, 377.

2. In the wake of the troubles caused by human beings, God continues to place confidence in them by giving them hope (vv. 1-7). They are neither reduced to automatons nor considered untrustworthy in any respect, but are directly addressed in light of responsibilities they have within the created order. Whatever else one might say about the effect of the fall on human beings, it does not mean that God has ceased to trust them or refuses to work in and through them.

3. Since God calls the murderer to account, the deity serves as the final arbiter concerning the taking of human life. Although humans have been made the executors of this divine reckoning, they should examine the situation in these terms: Do we understand that such a penalty in this case is the will of God? Are we willing to carry it out in the name of God?

4. Although God promises never again to punish the earth with a flood, that affirmation does not invalidate what human beings might do with nuclear power at their disposal, or by despoiling the environment. This promise also does not speak to issues regarding the "wearing out" of the physical universe over billions of years, or the "Big Crunch." It has been suggested that the text speaks only to a destruction of the earth by water. A recent song has the line, "God gave Noah the rainbow sign—no more water—the fire next time" (see 2 Pet 3:17). But such a perspective would violate the text, which speaks clearly not simply of the means of destruction, but of the end: Earth's destruction (v. 11) or the destruction of all flesh (v. 15).

5. The covenant with Noah involves all people. God, active in this way with all creation quite apart from Israel's life and mission, upholds this covenant *independent* of the community of faith. All people experience its effects, even though they may not have heard Genesis 9. Israel occupies a privileged position because it knows the promise, but is not to keep that knowledge to itself.

This universal covenant provides the context within which other covenants become possible. Since God has covered the earth with promises, other and more particular promises can be made. The creational promise to Noah makes possible, provides grounding for, the promise to Abraham. God's promissory relationship with the world *generates* more particular promises in order to enable these universal promises. Nonetheless, all covenants are directed to the same end—namely, the good creation intended by God. There are correspondences between this covenant and the one with Abraham (chap. 17). There, too, God "establishes" an "everlasting" covenant. However, the sign of Abraham's covenant—circumcision—becomes a sign for Abraham to keep, whereas the sign of the rainbow serves to remind God.

6. The covenant has significant ecological implications because God has established it with "all flesh," with birds and animals and the earth itself, even though they are now alienated from human beings. What does it mean for our ecological considerations that God has made promises to nonhumans? God cares for their life and seeks to enhance it in various ways.[83] Human beings should follow the divine lead. For another, humans, with our knowledge of the promise, have a responsibility to the nonhuman recipients of the promise to tend to the earth and all of its inhabitants. Hosea 2:18 envisions a future in which all the recipients of this covenant will no longer be estranged and can experience God's salvation together.

7. Von Rad speaks correctly here of divine forbearance, calling attention to Rom 3:25.[84] God's power in response to evil in the world restrains itself in a permanent fashion (see 8:21-22). God's use of power in dealing with evil is eternally self-limited. No simple retributive system applies. God will not respond with total destruction, no

---

83. See T. Fretheim, "Nature's Praise of God," *Ex Auditu* 3 (1987) 16-30.
84. Von Rad, *Genesis*, 133-34.

matter the human response. God's internal musings (8:21) make clear that God makes this move with eyes wide open, regarding human possibilities for evil; God remains a realist. But God cares so much for creation and its potential that God determines to take a new direction. As noted above, God changes over the course of the flood, not human beings, and this for the sake of the creation.

Genesis 9:18-29, Curse and Blessing in Noah's Family

COMMENTARY

On the far side of the flood story, the texts begin to reflect known historical realities. Even more, stories of individuals within a family begin to extend into relationships among larger communities. Although especially evident in chap. 10, such a move occurs *within* this text (assigned to J): intrafamilial conflicts within Noah's family (vv. 20-24) lead to communal difficulties among his descendants (vv. 25-27). Noah's sons may be understood in both individual and eponymous terms, thus preparing the way for the table of nations. Both Noah and Adam remain "typical" characters. Moreover, both their families produce sharp repercussions for their descendants. Even more, the relationships anticipated among the descendants of Noah's sons apply to various historical situations. The narrative thus serves complex purposes, including typological, ethnological, and etiological issues.

This brief text consists of an unusual admixture of literary types, from genealogy to story to curse and blessing. This multiform text reflects a complex tradition history, which no redactor has smoothed over. Whether a fuller form of this story ever existed remains uncertain. The text presents numerous difficulties, often so intractable that little scholarly consensus has been achieved. What is the nature of Ham's indecent act? Why is his son Canaan cursed? Why is Canaan to become a slave to his brothers? Why does Noah refer to what his "youngest son" has done, when Ham seems to be the second son (see 7:13; 9:18)? Why are Shem and Japheth aligned?

The redactor may have worked with two different traditions regarding the identity of Noah's sons: (1) Shem, Japheth, and Canaan; (2) Shem, Ham, and Japheth. Two ways of conceiving the resulting amalgamation are thus: The first has been overlaid by the

insertion of "Ham, the father of" (vv. 18, 22); or the second has been overlaid with material about Canaan, based on Israel's later experience in the land. The latter seems more likely, but uncertainty abounds. No known parallels to this story exist in other ancient Near Eastern literature.

The story is enclosed by brief genealogical notices. Verses 18-19 resume earlier references to the sons of Noah and announce the spreading out of their families (detailed in chaps. 10–11). Verses 28-29 give chronological notes about Noah's life and death, completing the genealogy of chap. 5. The references to grape-bearing vines and Canaan as a mature grandson make clear that the story takes place many years after the flood. Also, these verses present the first Genesis story in which God does not appear directly.

The story involves the themes of blessing and curse.

1. Blessing pertains to both nonhumans and humans in this text. God's post-flood blessing begins to take effect amid the world of the curse in all its aspects, hence ameliorating the effects of the curse.

Noah is the first to plant a vineyard and practice winemaking, discoveries ascribed to the *gods* elsewhere in the ancient Near East. Noah's skill at farming and crop development provides some relief from being totally at the mercy of what the ground brings forth on its own, so intimated in the words of his father, Lamech (5:29). As such, he stands in the tradition of the family of Cain (4:21-22), founders of other cultural blessings. He also functions as a new Adam, whose original calling was to till the ground and keep it (2:15).

This focus on vineyards and wine may seem a small matter for modern people, but these were important economic realities for Israel, celebrated in the feast of Booths

(Deut 16:13-16). Vines, the grape harvest, and wine symbolize God's blessings of life and fertility (see Pss 80:8-16; 104:15; Isa 5:1-7; 27:2-6; Hos 2:15; 9:10). Blessings can be abused, however; that which makes the heart glad can also promote drunkenness (see the warnings in Prov 20:1; 23:31-35; 31:6-7; Isa 5:11). What is good within God's creation can be made perverse by inappropriate human behavior.

At another level, the blessing on Shem (v. 26) first hints at God's blessing of Israel. Shem begins the line that will lead to Abraham, in and through whom this blessing will reach out to all the earth (see 12:1-3).

2. Sin and the Curse. The flood did not rid the world of sin (so 8:21). In this text, sin manifests itself in the effects of drunkenness, disrespect of parents, and familial conflict.

The narrator offers no explicit judgment about Noah's drunkenness; yet, it opens Noah to victimization and provides the occasion for all the suffering and conflict that follow. He has drunk himself into an unconscious state and lies naked in his tent (see Lam 4:21; Hab 2:15). The theme of nakedness (chaps. 2–3) involves issues of shame and exposure, an issue of no little consequence in Israel, in both religious (Exod 20:26) and social (2 Sam 6:20; 10:4-5) life. The prophets use this same theme to portray Israel's apostasy (Ezek 16:36) and the resulting divine judgment, in which Israel's shameful behavior will be exposed for all to see (Isa 47:3; Ezek 16:37-39).

What Noah's youngest son "had done" has prompted numerous conjectures. Some readers hypothesize about an inappropriate sexual act, from sodomy to incest. Some even appeal to Lev 18:7-8, which condemns "uncovering the nakedness of one's father," a reference to sexual activity with one's *mother.* Yet, the OT does not normally shrink from "telling it like it is" (see chaps. 18–19). Here the text makes clear that Noah uncovers himself. Moreover, Ham's *seeing* his father naked constitutes the problem, as confirmed by the detailed report of how his two brothers make sure they do not (v. 23; a chiasm of v. 22). Yet, the problem involves more than seeing (which may have been inadvertent); Ham errs in what he does with what he has seen. Rather than keep quiet or seek to remedy the situation,

Ham tells tales to a wider public. The matter entails not simply a breach of filial piety, but the *public* disgrace of his father. Parent-child relationships were considered to be of the highest importance in Israel (see Deut 21:18-21, which prescribes capital punishment for sons who rebel).

When Noah awakens from his stupor, he learns what has been done, probably because it is now public knowledge, and speaks his first and only words. The reference to his "youngest son" may mean that earlier references to Shem, Ham, and Japheth (5:32; 6:10; 7:13) do not occur in chronological order. Noah's blessing and cursing words stand in the tradition of Isaac (27:27-29, 39-40) and Jacob (49:1-27), though one cannot help wondering whether he is overreacting. The curse on Canaan appears most prominent; indeed, his enslavement also becomes part of the blessing of Shem and Japheth. Yet, for Canaan to become a slave of his brothers in an individual sense seems difficult. It almost certainly bears an eponymous force at this point, condemning the wickedness of the Canaanites in advance (see 15:16; Deut 9:4-5). In the blessings of Shem and Japheth (the NIV more literally translates that *God* is being blessed/praised, as in 24:27, but for unstated reasons), Noah calls for God to act (unlike the curse). The blessings *request* a future divine action and are not understood to be inevitably effective (see 25:23; chap. 27).

Noah's cursing of Canaan is most puzzling: He does not curse Ham, but Ham's son, Noah's grandson. Perhaps both father and son were responsible in an originally longer text; this telescoping would be a way of involving both. Perhaps the author alludes to the effects of the sins of the parents on the children (see Exod 20:5). More probably, those reading the text in terms of ethnic units as much as individuals would not have made a clear distinction between Canaanites and Hamites (see 10:6). An original reference to Ham was narrowed to one Hamite group, the Canaanites, when they came into conflict with Israel. Not changing the details keeps the Hamite link intact.

Although chap. 10 identifies many peoples in the lineage of Noah's sons, the author focuses on a narrower range, which is most prominent here: Shem represents the Israelites (but this is unique in the OT); Canaan the Canaanites; Japheth the seafaring peoples, such as the Philistines; Ham the Egyptians, probably. The first three are the most prominent groups occupying Palestine in the early years of Israel's life in the land; their relationships may be foreshadowed in these verses. The Israelites and the Philistines entered Canaan from east and west, respectively, in this period, resulting in the subjugation (i.e., enslavement?) of the Canaanites. The blessing regarding Japheth may represent a qualification of the fulfillment of the promise. Japheth's dwelling in the tents of Shem may mean that Israel does not have the land to itself, but shares it with others, a situation prevailing at various times (as with the Philistines). Ham was the progenitor of nations in the Egyptian orbit (10:6; see Pss 78:51; 105:23-27); Canaan was controlled by (was the son of) Egypt from 1550 to 1200 BCE. The various nations in chap. 14 may represent another level of the fulfillment of vv. 25-27, since all three branches of Noah's genealogy are represented in that conflict.

REFLECTIONS

1. The often-cited parallels between this narrative and the Eden story, especially as interpreted through 5:29, make it typical. Noah, a new Adam, takes up the creational task once again in "planting" and tilling the "ground"; his skill leads to a taming of what the ground produces and hence ameliorates the curse (3:17; 5:29). Yet, Noah as the new Adam (and one child) also fails as miserably as the old Adam. Similar themes appear in both stories: nakedness after eating fruit, and intrafamilial conflict, including human subservience and its affect. The curse on the serpent and the ground parallels the curse on Canaan, both of which affect life negatively. Yet, the act of Shem and Japheth in covering the naked one mirrors earlier action of the deity (3:21).

These parallels strongly suggest that, in the post-flood movement to the world of nations, "good and evil" patterns in life persist. God's work of blessing influences the worlds of human and nonhuman, family and nation; but there are also deep human failures due to the "evil inclination of the human heart" (8:21). This mix of goodness and evil will accompany every human endeavor, whether familial or sociopolitical, and every relationship, whether personal or communal, down through the ages to our own time.

2. It seems incredible that this story could have been used to justify the enslavement of Africans. Suffice it to say that, inasmuch as Canaan among all the sons of Ham, is not the father of a Negroid people (see 10:15-19, where all the peoples listed are Semitic or Indo-European), any attempt to justify the slavery of African peoples is a gross misuse of this text. Regarding slavery in general, however, neither the OT nor the NT condemns this inhumane institution. Various OT laws seek to regulate (never commend) this practice (Exod 21:1-11). And an increasing concern for issues of humaneness may be discerned in later laws (see Deut 15:12-18; Lev 25:39-46). The "enslavement" of Canaanites envisaged in this text probably reflects their later subjugation rather than any practice of slavery.

This text mentions enslavement in the wake of sinful behavior; such a human practice is thus clearly set at odds with God's creational intentions. As with the sentence in 3:14-19, humans should, appropriately, work to overcome this effect of sin.

3. Noah's word (no word from God occurs here) about the future of his sons should not be interpreted in fatalistic terms. What happens over the course of history affects what in fact will happen in the aftermath of such a word (see 25:23).

4. The chief point of this text may involve relationships between children and their parents,[85] a negative illustration of the commandment, "Honor your father and your

85. Westermann, *Genesis 1-11*, 494.

mother." Israelites considered the family of extreme importance in the created order; any deterioration in the quality of family life could only disrupt the creational intentions of God. Such a perspective would be in line with chaps. 3–4, which speak of other familial relationships that have been distorted in the wake of human sin. At the same time, the author has in view broader relationships among peoples and nations, which are profoundly affected by what happens within families. Dysfunctional families affect our communal life together.

Genesis 10:1-32, The Table of Nations

COMMENTARY

This, the fourth *tôlēdôt*, introduces the reader to the world of nations, the history of the world "after the flood." Noah's three sons provide the outline, each point of which closes with statements about land, language, family, and nation (vv. 5, 20, 21). Opening and closing summary verses bracket the chapter (vv. 1, 32). The author provides Shem with a double introduction because of his importance for the Hebrews (Eber), significance also attested by the extension of his genealogy to six generations, while those of his brothers continue for only three. Other elements are embedded in the genealogy (cf., v. 19), usually associated with later Israelite history (i.e., Babylonians/Assyrians; Philistines; Canaanites). Scholars think the chapter consists of interwoven strands of P and J. The beginning verse establishes a connection with the end of the Adam genealogy in 5:32.

Many names in this list function eponymously, whereby the origin of a city/people/nation is explained by derivation from an individual progenitor. The names stand for peoples or nations, represented as "sons" of the group ancestor; smaller groups are represented as "grandsons" (cf. fatherland, mother country). The reader may discern this strategy most clearly in the use of the plural ending (*-îm;* vv. 13-14) and the use of a definite article and a suffix that specifies ethnic identification (vv. 16-18). This same feature also occurs in the genealogies of Abraham (25:1-4), Ishmael (25:12-16), and Esau (chap. 36).

The horizon of the list extends from Crete and Libya in the west to Iran in the east, from Arabia and Ethiopia in the south to Asia Minor and Armenia in the north. However, there are many problems in identifying peoples and places. The peoples seem to be listed on the basis of various factors: geographical, sociocultural, political, and commercial relationships (literary factors may also be at work; i.e., the similar names of v. 7). Issues of language, color, and race do not appear significant; e.g., the Canaanites are not listed with Shem, but the Elamites (whose language was non-Semitic) are. We do not know whether the narrator thought these peoples were actually genealogically related. Scholars dispute the historical situation that this list reflects. The most likely candidates are the end of the second millennium or a time after 600 BCE.[86] On the significance of this chapter's location, see commentary on 11:1-9.

10:2-5. Japheth represents the peoples in Asia Minor (and even farther north) and Greece, to the north and west of Palestine; it includes seven "sons" and "grandsons." Many are maritime peoples. The movement of the "coastland peoples" may reflect population shifts in the Aegean and Mediterranean islands around 1200 BCE.

10:6-20. Ham serves as progenitor of the peoples (thirty in all) within the Egyptian political and commercial orbit, including sections of Africa, Arabia, and Mesopotamia. The inclusion of the latter (who are Semitic) may be attributed to similar-sounding names, Cush in Africa and the Kassites, who ruled in the Mesopotamian region during 1600 to 1200 BCE. Canaan may be included here because it came under Egyptian control in 1500–1200 BCE.

Verses 8-12, associated with Mesopotamia, include prose fragments about a warrior named Nimrod, who established a kingdom

---

86. Some names occur in Ezekiel 27; for details about the various names, see Sarna, *Genesis*, 70-80.

in Shinar (Babylonia) and Assyria (see Mic 5:5). The results of scholarly efforts to identify him with a god or a king are uncertain; legends of the heroic exploits of various figures may have resulted in a composite figure. The specific and repeated reference to Yahweh (v. 9) is unusual, but probably indicates that Nimrod's activity should be interpreted in a positive light, as are references to the deity in chap. 5 (a negative construal would see v. 9 as anticipating 11:1-9, with links to Cain as builder and to the warriors of 6:4).

The peoples mentioned in vv. 15-19 include a number who occupied Canaan, whose boundaries may be specified because of later history (though they correspond to no other boundary list); some are mentioned in the promises to the ancestors (see 15:19-21; Heth = Hittites; Jebusites; Amorites; Girgashites; Hivites).

10:21-31. The double introduction to Shem's genealogy, with the premature introduction of Eber (v. 21), signals its importance

for what follows. Shem stands as the ancestor of peoples in Syria/Assyria/Iran and environs as well as part of the Arabian peninsula (twenty-six are listed in two groups of thirteen). His genealogy encloses the story of the city of Babel. This is a branched or segmentary genealogy, with all the descendants of Shem listed; 11:10-26 presents his genealogy in linear form only through his third son, Arpachshad.

The author places Eber, who is the progenitor of the Hebrews (see 11:16) as well as other tribal groups, among the descendants of Shem. The genealogy of Eber's son Peleg continues in 11:18-26 (the division of the earth in v. 25 remains unexplained, though it has been linked to the scattering in 11:1-9). Eber's other son, Joktan, had thirteen sons, also related to the Hebrews; they may be linked with various Arabian groups near Yemen and had important commercial links to Israel (e.g., Seba, v. 10).

REFLECTIONS

1. These figures are understood in political, rather than mythological, terms; they come into being by virtue of human activity, not divine initiative. Such political structures are part of the ordering work of God the Creator, which promotes good and checks evil in the life of the world. Yet, they are not structured into the created order itself, but participate in all the foibles and flaws of human leadership, hence "they can be changed and are subject to criticism."[87]

2. For the first time in these chapters Israel comes into view, though with no special virtues assigned to its ancestors; indeed, the author provides no reference to God's relationship with them. The repeated reference to "families" (vv. 5, 20, 31-32) links up with 12:3*b:* through the family of Abraham all the families of the earth shall be blessed. At the same time, the chapter testifies to God's work of blessing already active in the lives of these peoples (v. 9); hence, the blessing brought through Abraham continues an earlier reality.

The isolation of the family of Shem places no negative judgment on the families of Ham and Japheth (on Canaan, see commentary on 9:20-27). The writer focuses on the commonalities of the family of Shem (hence of Israel) with all other persons, not on their differences. Shem shares his humanity "before the LORD" with all others, who are given a place in the life of God's creation independent of any relationship to Israel.

3. The fact that seventy peoples are mentioned (excluding Nimrod) is probably important, but its explanation remains uncertain (see 46:27; Exod 1:5; 24:9). The number may signify that the entirety of the known world has been included (even if some were omitted, v. 5) and that all peoples share ultimate unity in spite of the differences of language, race, and color. That the geographical areas appear to overlap and

87. Brueggemann, *Genesis*, 93.

interlock to some degree may testify to a genuinely international community, an integration of peoples across traditional boundaries. In spite of significant differences, we belong to one world. The table thus becomes a natural extension of the creation account. This chapter constitutes a theological witness to a common humanity shared by all.

4. The repeated phrase "before the LORD" (v. 9) probably connotates the help of Yahweh (see TNK, "by the grace of the LORD"). The narrator believed that God the Creator was involved in the lives and activities of such kings and peoples. This would not mean that Nimrod had explicit knowledge of Yahweh, but that the deity associated with his life would later be identified with Israel's God (Isa 10:5; 45:1; Acts 17:26-27 may be dependent on this chap.).

5. The multiplication of peoples across the face of the earth constitutes a fulfillment of the divine blessing and the divine command to "fill the earth" (1:28; renewed in 9:1, 7).

Genesis 11:1-9, The City of Babel

COMMENTARY

The reader may find difficulty in fathoming the import of this final narrative of chaps 1–11. The first problem involves its relationship with chap. 10. The linguistic division of peoples has already appeared in 10:5, 20, 31, as has the spreading abroad (פרד *pārad*, 10:5, 32) or scattering (פוץ *pûṣ*; נפץ *nāpaṣ*, 9:19; 10:18; cf. 11:4, 8-9) of the nations; moreover, Babel has already been named (10:10). Source critics provide a "solution" by assigning the sections to P and J. In the text's present form, however, interpreters often view 11:1-9 as a supplement to 10:1-32 (and 9:18-19), perhaps especially the segment concerning Nimrod and Babel (10:8-12).

The two sections do not stand in chronological order; rather, the second reaches back and complements the first from another perspective. In 10:1-32 the author has associated the realities of pluralism with the natural growth of the human community after the flood. This positive word may have seemed important to state first (structural considerations may also have dictated placement). Genesis 11:1-9, however, gives these developments a negative cast in terms of human failure and divine judgment. The writer depicts the same reality from different points of view (11:1-9 does not cover all that happens in 10:1-32) by juxtaposing texts rather than interweaving them.

This same literary tactic also occurs elsewhere in chaps. 1–11 (see Overview). Genesis 2:4–4:16 relates to chap. 1 in this way (cf. also 6:1-8 with 4:17–5:32; 9:20-29 with 9:18-19; 12:1-9 with 11:10-32 breaks the pattern). In the admixture of story and genealogy, the editor places continued creational blessing in the ongoing generations alongside continuing evidence of breakdown in various relationships. These images do not occur simply as pictures in white and black; genealogies contain elements of disequilibrium (see 10:8-12) and stories exhibit acts of human goodness and divine graciousness. As we will see, Gen 11:1-9 returns to the concerns of creation in chaps. 1–2, providing an inclusio for chaps. 1–11.

No other story like this has been found in the ancient Near East, but some parallels in detail exist, such as the origin of languages, matters of building construction, and the function of towers in Mesopotamian culture. Traditional links between creation and temple building in Mesopotamia may be reflected in the structure of chaps. 1–11, though Gen 11:1-9 does not refer explicitly to a temple. In the flood story preserved by Berossus, the survivors migrate to Babylon, as in the biblical account. The journey of Abraham's family from Ur (11:31) could be understood as a part of the migration from Babel (11:9).

The author clearly intends the text to be a typical story of humankind ("whole earth"), not a reflection on a specific event. Hence, we may read the text from a variety of contexts. From an exilic perspective, the city could represent Jerusalem and the exile, a theme prominent in prophetic materials from that era (Ezek 11:16-17; 12:15; 20:34, 41; 34:5-6, 12). Less probably, the text might be viewed as a critique of royal building programs in Israel or as a negative comment on the history of the Babylonians, a judgment on the prideful stance of such nations in the world. Yet, the text offers no sign of this building project as an imperial enterprise; in fact, the discourse and motivation are remarkably democratic, reinforcing the view that the problem here is generally human, not that of any particular institution or nation.

The writer has structured this narrative symmetrically, wherein the situation of vv. 1-4 is reversed in vv. 6-9.[88] The direct speech of the people's plans in vv. 3-4 parallels that of God's plans in vv. 6-7 (note esp. the consultative "come, let us"). The divine decision to conduct a judicial inquiry (v. 5) sits between these speeches; its central position constitutes the turning point. The bracketing verses (vv. 1-2, 8-9; note the reversal "language" and "whole [all the] earth") describe the human situation before and after the discourses of vv. 3-7, from the human (vv. 1-2) and the divine perspective (vv. 8-9). The fact that the divine and the humans do not stand in dialogue with one another constitutes one of the most ominous elements in this text (in contrast to the divine-human conversation that begins once again with Abraham). The careful structure suggests that this story should not be read as an amalgam of originally distinct narratives.

11:1-4. The story describes the "whole earth" from a communal perspective (no individuals are mentioned), which is consistent with the emphasis on families, soon to be noted (12:3). All members of this community, relatively few in number, speak the same language and have a common vocabulary. They migrate to (13:11; or in, 2:8; or from, 4:16) the east and settle in the land of Shinar (Babylonia; see 10:10). Verses 8-9 specify that this "whole earth" community moves from

this one place (now called Babel), and various peoples who speak different languages (see 10:5, 20, 31) emerge across the "whole earth." Hence, the narrative describes how peoples of common origin had come to speak various languages (despite the historical unlikelihood).

The building of a city with a tower (vv. 3-5, in v. 8 only the city is mentioned, an instance of synecdoche, though the import of the tower is thereby diminished) reflects knowledge of Mesopotamian construction methods. In the absence of natural stone, people made bricks of kiln-baked clay; burning gave them greater durability. The text offers no reason to suppose that the building efforts as such are pernicious; we might in fact think of human creativity and imagination in developing such materials and projects. The author focuses on their motivations, not that they build or what they build. The precise nature of their failure remains elusive, however, resulting in various scholarly formulations.

The effort to secure a place to call home seems natural enough, not even new (see 4:17), and the builders raise no explicit theological issues. Even the tower may not be an issue, as either a fortified city tower (see Deut 1:28; 9:1; Judg 9:46-47) or a temple tower (ziggurat), a stepped, mountain-shaped structure. In Babylonian culture, the latter provided for communication between earthly and heavenly realms through priestly intermediaries. The base of the tower was on earth and "its top in the heavens"— a popular description of ziggurats.[89] The ziggurat represents an *indirect* relationship between heaven and earth; in 28:10-22, a writer implicitly faults the ziggurat for the *distance* it creates between God and the world. As such, it seems insufficient to carry theories about a storming of heaven or transgressing the limits of creatureliness or usurping the place of God. There may be some gibes at Babylonian religious practice, but this seems too specific to constitute a "whole earth" problem. Besides, Babylon appears at the *end* of the story; thus it does not stand at the center of attention.

The objective of "making a name (שׁם *šēm*) for ourselves" is more problematic. This phrase may recall the renown that accrued to

---

88. On literary features, see Wenham, *Genesis 1–15*, 234-35.

89. See Sarna, *Genesis*, 82-83.

kings associated with major building projects in Mesopotamia and Israel or other heroic efforts (see 6:4). It may signal an autonomous attempt to secure the future by their own efforts, particularly in view of the use of *šēm* in 12:2, where God is the subject of any accrued renown (note also that the genealogy of Shem encloses the account). The name they actually receive—though not a divine judgment—becomes Babel ("confusion"), ironically testifying to the futility of their efforts. The project may also intimate a search for the kind of immortality implicit in a famous name (but not in the sense of 3:22, which implies a literal immortality). Yet, David does not come under judgment for such efforts in 2 Sam 8:13 (see 18:18); the desire for fame, even self-generated, does not seem reprehensible enough *in and of itself* to occasion the magnitude of God's response.

The key is in the motivation, "otherwise we shall be scattered abroad upon the face of the whole earth." This central human failure inheres in the straightforward moral-order talk (the punishment fits the crime); it corresponds precisely to God's judgment (vv. 8-9). Most basically, humans fear what the future might bring, evincing deep anxiety and insecurity about what lies ahead. We do not discover fear of other human beings, but fear of not being able to keep their community intact in the face of a perceived peril of dispersion into a threatening world. Only because of this motivation do their objectives of building a city/tower and making a name for themselves become problematic. The building projects constitute a bid to secure their own future as a unified community, isolated from the rest of the world.

Hence, their action constitutes a challenge to the divine command to fill the earth (1:28, renewed in 9:1; already seen by Josephus. *Antiquities* I.iv.1), but *not* simply in a spatial sense. Their resistance to being scattered (this word occurs positively in 10:18; cf. 9:19; 10:5, 32) occasions a divine concern for the very created order of things, for only by spreading abroad can human beings fulfill their charge to be caretakers of the earth. According to 1:28 and 2:5 (cf. 2:15), the proper development of the creation depends on human activity. For the builders to concentrate their efforts narrowly on the future

of the (only) human community places the future of the rest of creation in jeopardy. An isolationist view of their place in the world, centered on self-preservation, puts the rest of the creation at risk. The building project thus understeps rather than oversteps human limits, for it prevents scattering and taking up the creational command that put the creation at risk.

11:5-9. In v. 5 God "comes down" to conduct a judicial inquiry (see 18:21; their project was *not* so meager that God, ironically, had to descend to see it). God's descent (see Exod 3:8) demonstrates God's deep engagement on behalf of the creation. Heaven is that place *within* the created world where God's presence remains uncontested.[90] The relation between this descent and that of v. 7 represents the difference between inquiry and action. As in 18:21, the inquiry appears genuine, preliminary to a final decision (the NIV's "were building" recognizes that the project was incomplete, v. 8).

Verse 6 constitutes a summary of the results of the inquiry; v. 7 calls on the council to assist in taking the necessary actions. Verse 7 indicates that in v. 6 God speaks to the divine council (see 1:26; 2:18; 3:22), with whom God consults about the matter (Abraham assumes the role of the divine dialogically between God and the council. While Yahweh carries out the sentence (vv. 8-9; the text does not report the actual act of confusing, suggesting that the scattering is central), v. 7 indicates that this punishment stems from the divine council.

God's response focuses, not on their present project, but on other possibilities of united human endeavor (v. 6). The *unity* of peoples with isolationist concerns for self-preservation could promote any number of projects that would place the creation in jeopardy. Their sin concentrates their energies on a creation-threatening task; even the finest creative efforts can subvert God's creational intentions. Although the text does not impugn cities, it does recognize that sin and its potential for disaster accompanies human progress of whatever sort.

In response, God judges, but in the interests of the future of the creation, "the face

90. See Fretheim, *The Suffering of God*, 37-39.

of all the earth" (vv. 8-9). God's judgment, though creating difficulties, has a fundamentally gracious purpose. The garbling of languages and consequent scattering prevents any comparable projects that could be carried out by a self-serving, self-preserving united front; humans might engage in feats that could be even more destructive of themselves and God's creation (Job 42:2 uses similar language of God). God's gracious action places limits on human possibilities for the sake of creation (see 3:22; 6:3).

God thus counters their efforts to remain an isolated community by acting in such a way that they have no choice but to obey the command. God does this by making their languages so diffuse that they can no longer communicate, having to leave off what they are doing, move apart from one another, and establish separate linguistic communities. The confusing that leads to their scattering (confusion is the only means cited by which God does this) thus becomes a means to another end: the filling of and caring for the earth in fulfillment of the creational command. God thereby promotes diversity at the expense of any form of unity that seeks to preserve itself in isolation from the rest of the creation.

The divine action of scattering corresponds exactly to what the people sought to prevent (v. 4). The verb *bālal* ("confuse"; vv. 7, 9, see footnotes) plays on the word *Babel* (in English it would approximate "babble"). The very name they sought to make for themselves becomes a name for confusion, making them famous for their failure. (The literal meaning of *Babel,* "gate of god" [see 28:17] is given an ironic, if imaginative, etymological link.) Verse 9 functions similarly to 2:24 ("therefore") by the way the narrator steps outside of the story and summarizes what has happened.

REFLECTIONS

1. The story has a universal ("whole earth") perspective, speaking of what is true of humankind generally; yet the function of that universalism in a context where historically identifiable peoples are very much in view, and itself speaks of Babel, makes it somewhat different from the other primeval narratives. This universalistic/specific combination probably shows that 11:1-9 serves as an *illustration* of the typical developments in 10:1-32; this darker side of developments among the peoples of the world could be multiplied indefinitely. In other words, what is described here characterizes the peoples mentioned in the previous chapter.

2. One tension in the text involves an ambivalent view of unity and diversity. On the one hand, the spreading abroad correlates with God's creational intentions of filling the earth. On the other hand, such scattering constitutes God's judgment. One should distinguish between divine judgment and punishment in any conventional sense. God evaluates the situation negatively and moves to correct it.

Brueggemann notes that human unity is a complex reality in this text.[91] Ordinarily, we regard unity in the human community as desirable and in tune with God's purposes for the creation. But here, because the unity desired and promoted stands over against the divine will to spread abroad throughout the world, a unity that seeks self-preservation at all costs, God must resist it and act to advance the divine will for scattering. Those who seek to save their life will lose it. The right kind of unity occurs only when the community encompasses the concerns of the entire world and encourages difference and diversity to that end. Proper unity manifests itself in an ability to live together without conflict, oppression, and having common objectives in tune with God's purposes for the world. At the same time, scattering should not result in fragmentation or divided loyalty to God. The story of the chosen one, Jacob, also conceives of a false unity that focuses on self-preservation; he also receives the call to "spread abroad" (*pāras,* 28:14) throughout the world so that all the families of the earth can be blessed.

91. Brueggemann, *Genesis,* 99.

Diversity inheres in God's intention for the world, as is evident from the marvelously pluriform character of God's creation in the first place or the blessing evident in the table of nations. In tune with those creational intentions, God makes a decisive move here on behalf of diversity and difference.[92]

3. We find a contemporary parallel in the often-isolated way in which the church relates to the world. In the interests of unity and preserving its own future, the members often stay close to home and don't risk venturing forth (see Jonah). The command of Matt 28:18-20 calls for the church to scatter across the face of the earth. If the church refuses this call, God may well enter into judgment against the church and find some way of getting us beyond our own church cliques out into the world on behalf of the creation. The unity of the church is not to be found by focusing on unity, building churches and programs that present a unified front before the temptations of the world. We receive true unity finally as a gift, found in those things that are not tangible or centered on one's own self-interests. Unity will be forged most successfully in getting beyond one's own kind on behalf of the word in the world.

4. At Pentecost (Acts 2), each of the peoples present heard the gospel in their native tongue. The gift of the Spirit results in a linguistic cacophony, but all receive the gospel. This gift of a new hearing transcends language barriers, but at the same time maintains the differences that languages reflect. The testimony of Acts 2 does not then overturn the multiplicity of languages, but enables people who speak various languages to hear and understand the one gospel for all the earth. The people are then scattered over the face of the earth (Acts 8:1-4) to proclaim the gospel rather than their own concerns (Acts 2:11).

Speaking different languages probably presents more blessing than bane, more gift than problem. Linguistic diversity enriches people's understanding of the world around them and is expressed in the world's literature. Speaking and hearing, broadly conceived, become a more complex reality in everyday life, and include not simply hearing other languages, but truly hearing others in their various life situations. Difficulties in communication can often lead to difficulties in relationships, but this usually involves the failings of people who seek to communicate than the reality of differences in language as such.

92. See B. Anderson, "Unity and Diversity in God's Creation: A Study of the Babel Story," *CTM* (1978) 69-81.

Genesis 11:10-26, From Shem to Abraham

COMMENTARY

This is the fifth of the ten genealogies in Genesis. We find a line of nine (or ten) generations, matching the line before the flood (5:1-32), except in one basic respect: The ages of the figures have been scaled down considerably, with a consequent younger child-begetting age (after Seth's 600 years, the next three live 433-464 years, the last six 148-239 years; as with chap. 5 the versions differ regarding ages).

In linear form, the genealogy moves from Shem, one of three sons of Noah, to Terah, who also has three sons, one of whom is Abraham. A branched genealogy of Shem precedes the story of the city of Babel (10:21-31), the basic elements of which are now included in vv. 10-17 (note that Arpachshad is not Shem's oldest son, a pattern in Genesis). Some names in the genealogy are associated with names in the upper reaches of the Euphrates River valley, from which Abraham migrates and with which Isaac and Jacob continue to associate (e.g., Haran, Serug, Nahor).

REFLECTIONS

1. In a fashion similar to other genealogies, this one brings an orderly, stabilizing rhythm into the scattering images of 11:8-9. The fact that the name *Shem* has a form identical to the word for "name" (in 11:4 and 12:2) may suggest even more—namely, that this family line will be a vehicle in and through which God will magnify the human name.

2. The author does not present Abraham's family line in isolation but sets it in the midst of all the family units of the known world and, in so doing, keeps the chosen line embedded in the life of the world. These are deep roots, which Israel ought not to forget or set aside. God as Creator has been active all the way with this line leading to Abraham (note that Abraham's family is already on the way to Canaan when God's call comes in 12:1-3). God chooses Abraham, not to escape the world out of which he was hewn, but to return to it. All the contacts that Israel's ancestors have with this world in chaps. 12–50 are certainly intended to say something about the nature and scope of this task.

GENESIS 11:27–25:18

THE STORY OF ABRAHAM

OVERVIEW

P ostulating a sharp division between chaps. 1–11 and 12–50, between "primeval 'history' " and "patriarchal history," has long been a staple of Genesis study. While the exact dividing point has been disputed (from 11:10 to 11:27 to 12:1), there certainly are good reasons for such a division as the narrator's eye now focuses on the progenitors of Israel. The text, which has had the world as a stage, narrows down to a small town in Mesopotamia, to a single family, to the mind and heart of a single individual—Abraham. At the same time, the world stage remains very much in view. Abraham is both deeply rooted in that earlier history and continues to be in contact with the peoples of that larger world. The narrator ties these two parts of Genesis together in ways that are rich and deep. Too sharp a distinction between these two "histories" will not serve the interpreter well (see Introduction).

We might claim that God chooses to begin with chap. 1 all over again, except that this time around Abraham steps onto a world stage out of tune with God's creational intentions. The downward spiral that began in Eden plunged the world into a cosmic catastrophe, and the post-flood world seems once again on the way into a negative future. Not much of a future seems to be in store for the family of Terah, with early death, infertility, and interrupted journeys (11:27-32).

Yet, the continuities are positive as well. God did not abandon the creation to the consequences of its own sins within that "primeval" time. The genealogies testify that life, however troubled, continues. Even more, God's covenant with Noah has given the post-flood world a sign, in the shape of a rainbow, wherein God's promise ensures its future. This shift to Abraham does not mean a new world or a new divine objective for the world. God's goal of reclaiming the world so that it

reflects its original divine intention remains in place. However, we now have a clearer view about the *divine strategy* for moving toward this objective. God devises a means by which the creation will be reclaimed through Abraham's family.

We do not know why God chose Abraham rather than another person or family. But we do know that God chose him so that the human and nonhuman creation might be reclaimed and live harmoniously with the original divine intention. God's choice of Abraham constitutes an initially exclusive move for the sake of a maximally inclusive end. Election serves mission.

The Abraham cycle appears episodic in character, often with little discernible coherence. While it is less episodic than chaps. 1–11, the reader does not encounter as sustained a narrative as that of Jacob and especially Joseph. This development coincides with the characterization of the chief personalities, with Abraham least well developed (but more than Noah); Jacob and especially Joseph are more fully portrayed. Moreover, the God who directly engages the life of Abraham is depicted in more unobtrusive ways in the remainder of Genesis, especially in the story of Joseph.

Classical source criticism has identified J, E, and P materials scattered throughout the Abraham cycle (with some texts undesignated, chap. 14). With the recent demise of the Elohist, scholars have discerned J (or JE) and P as the primary sources. Whatever the identity and perspective of these sources at one level or another,[93] they have now been decisively reshaped by theological viewpoints that encompass the entire cycle. We may identify three basic perspectives:

93. See Brueggemann and Wolff, *The Vitality of Old Testament Traditions.*

1. A Theology of Creation. We have already identified some of the links between chaps. 1–11 and 12–50 (see Introduction). The call of Abraham does not narrow God's channel of activity down to a history of salvation. These texts speak to creational issues such as life and death, birth and marriage and burial, family and community, economic and political realities, human conflicts and ambiguities and joys, and divine blessings that reach into every sphere of life. These are matters characteristic of the human community as a whole, matters in and through which God works to carry forth the larger divine designs for the world, and often in ways independent of the chosen community.

More specific modes of God's activity in the world are handled well theologically only in the context of this all-pervading presence and activity of God in the created order. Without this perspective as a given, the idea of a God who works in more focused ways can be perceived only as an interruption of the created order of things, or as radically discontinuous from life in creation generally. These broader creational understandings provide the necessary context for understanding more specific and concrete ways of divine presence in the community of faith.

2. Promise. While God's promises to Abraham are decisive for the future of this community (and through it, the world), they continue the promising and saving activity in which God has been active earlier, i.e., especially in the unconditional word of *promise* to Noah and all flesh and the *salvation* of a family from the ravages of the flood. These divine actions signal a new divine commitment concerning the future of the world. This divine *promissory* relationship with the entire world grounds and generates the more particular promises to Abraham. In order for God to oversee the promise to the world, God must make particular promises. These promises now specify *how* God will relate to the larger world, which now rests secure from destruction, enfolded within the divine promise. Indeed, the God who acts with Abraham is so familiar to the narrator (and implicitly, to Abraham) that God does not even have to be (re)introduced (12:1).

Promises stand at the beginning of the narrative (12:1-3), at the climax (22:16-18),

and are repeated at key junctures throughout (12:7; 13:14-17; 15:1-7, 18-21; 17:1-21; 18:10-14, 18; 24:7). They even give decisive shape to the Hagar-Ishmael texts (16:10-12; 21:13, 18). In their present form and arrangement—the rationale for which is not always discernible—these theologically charged texts reflect the perspective of the final redactor, who thereby gives one internal hermeneutic for the interpretation of the whole (the other is faithfulness).

Interpreters regularly consider the promise of a son to be the oldest; the promises of nation, name, many descendants, and land are extensions that depend on new times and places. In other words, the traditio-historical process *enhances* the promissory element. This process of development extends the promises beyond Abraham's own lifetime (within which only the promise of a son was fulfilled) to an open future. For every new generation the promises continue to function *as promises* independently of specific fulfillments, though with sufficient experience of fulfillment to ground the community's hopes (e.g., land).

David Clines speaks about the *partial* fulfillment of the promises to Israel's ancestors.[94] This insight helps, but such an analysis places too much emphasis on fulfillment and gives insufficient attention to the way in which the promise *functions as promise.* A passage such as 12:1-3, for example, does not really announce a plot for the story of Abraham. These verses attest to the generative event, a profoundly creative moment in his life in which God speaks command and promise, and it propels a faithful Abraham and his family into a future, which takes shape most fundamentally by living with promises. What shape the future takes will depend on many things, but Abraham can be assured that, amid all that makes for trouble in his life and the world, it holds promise for goodness and well-being. And that makes a profound difference for all life.

Son. This promise, though presupposed in the promise of descendants, comes specifically only in chap. 15 and provides the focus for chaps. 16–21. Even then we do not immediately know which son it will be (Ishmael, then Isaac), and the resolution does

94. Clines, *Theme.*

not appear until near the end of Abraham's journey (chap. 22). Initially it appears that Ishmael will be *the* son, then Isaac comes into focus; but even Isaac does not appear as a fulfillment until God tests Abraham's fidelity.

Land. We may discern this theme in the opening chapters (12:7; 13:14-17; 15:7, 18-21; 17:8). God does not make this promise to a landless individual, at least initially. Abraham starts from a homeland (see chaps. 24, 29–31), becomes a sojourner and resident alien, and looks toward a new land for the future. Yet, though he knows the identity and size of the land and procures a down payment (chap. 23), he lives and dies only with the promise. But, again, living with the promise *as promise* profoundly shapes his life and thought; the promise constantly generates new possibilities for living short of fulfillment. Moreover, although God promised to give the land "forever," faithfulness is not an option for participation in the fulfillment. The promise of land functions much like this in Hebrews; those who, like Abraham, journey in faith do not finally need an enduring city (11:8-16; 13:14).

Nation, Name, Kings, Descendants. The promises of nation, name, and kings probably find an initial fulfillment in the Davidic empire. At the same time, Christians claim this language, recognizing that "Jesus the Messiah" may be linked through David to Abraham (Matt 1:1). Moreover, the language of descendants is much broader than the descendants of the "son"; it includes the descendants of Ishmael and Abraham's children by Keturah.

Even more, "descendants" has taken on a much broader spiritual meaning than the text probably knows. The legacy of Abraham includes not only both testaments, but also the Koran. Abraham became the father of the religious heritages embodied in Judaism, Islam, and Christianity. The various religious appropriations of the story of Abraham must be cognizant of not only their similarities and differences in interpreting this story, but also the possibilities that this commonality may hold for continuing conversation with one another. Christians also should recognize among themselves that the NT does not draw on the story of Abraham in a univocal way,

as comparisons of Paul, James, and Hebrews show.

Blessing. The specific language of blessing appears nearly one hundred times in chaps. 12–50 and undergirds a key theme in the fulcrum text of 12:1-3 (see Reflections there). *Blessing* becomes a catchall word, encompassing all the promises noted heretofore, as well as a host of creational blessings (e.g., life and fertility). At the same time, simply to collapse the promises into blessing would fail to recognize the prior role of promise. The specific divine promises enable blessing to be brought into the sphere of redemption. Blessing is basically a creational category; all of God's creatures, to one degree or another, experience blessing apart from their knowledge of God (it rains on the just and the unjust alike). The promises bring a particular focus to God's activity in and through a chosen people, ultimately for the purpose of redemption.

The mediation of the blessing to those outside of the chosen family becomes a centerpiece in the chapters that follow.[95] To that end, these texts relate Abraham with virtually every people in Israel's sociohistorical context, from Egypt (12:10-20) to numerous Near Eastern nations, including the king of Jerusalem (chap. 14); Hagar and Ishmael (16; 21); Sodom and Gomorrah (18–19); Lot, and sons Moab and Ammon (19:30-38); Abimelech and the Philistines (20:1-18; 21:22-34). The biblical authors are interested in the way Abraham relates to these peoples and how he does or does not function as a mediator of God's special blessing to them. The relationship between Abraham and Lot may have the special purpose of relating Abraham to land issues and to the larger world scene.

3. Faithfulness. Abraham's faithfulness also functions centrally in these stories, a centrality made especially evident in the story of Isaac (26:3-5, 24). Key texts provide the center for this concern: 15:1-6; 12:1-9; 22:1-19; they appear at the beginning and end of the cycle, and in the key covenant section. The shape of the future is determined, not simply by the one who speaks the promise, but by the way the recipient responds to it. Abraham does not act as the passive recipient of

95. See Brueggemann and Wolff, *The Vitality of Old Testament Traditions*, 41-66.

a drama shaped solely by the divine will and word. What Abraham does and says has an effect on what happens in the future beyond the promise. Nonetheless, Abraham can neither preserve nor annul the promise, since God will be faithful to promises made.

None of the ancestral figures (Abraham, Sarah, Rebekah) is perfect, but familial strife proves more inimical to God's intentions than isolated actions of individuals. The text presents the story of a family, with all the flaws and foibles characteristic of such institutions. The fact that this conflicted family still mediates God's promise and blessing to the world constitutes one of the marvels in God's way of relating to the world.

The general way God states promises (e.g., nation, blessing, descendants) highlights the human role. God leaves room for human freedom in response, so that the track from promise to fulfillment cannot be precisely determined in advance. Hence, when God promises descendants, but is not specific regarding Sarah, especially in view of her barrenness, the reader must struggle with the other possibilities. To suggest, for example, that if Abraham and Sarah had simply settled back in their married life, God would have seen that a son was born in due time remains (a) pure speculation; (b) insufficient regard for the narrative where Ishmael appears as a fulfillment; (c) a denial of a *genuine* and active role God has given to the human (e.g., God takes Abraham's counsel into account regarding Sodom and Gomorrah). What human beings do makes a difference to God, and hindsight may not reveal the value their actions actually had. In considering matters of this sort, the God portrayed in these texts does not have absolute foreknowledge of the future (see 22:12). Once again (1:26-28), God uses human beings as instruments in and through whom to carry out the divine creational intentions. God gives them responsibilities within this intention, choosing to trust humans with a significant role, while continuing to see to the promises in an attentively personal way.

The NT picks up on the Abrahamic narrative at the points of promise and faithfulness, from Romans 4 to Galatians 3–4 to Hebrews 11 (see 11:27–12:9; 15:6 esp.). Paul grounds some of his basic understandings of faith on narratives that are pre-Mosaic and pre-Sinaitic, giving Abraham a profound relationship with the faith of which he speaks.

Structure. Scholars have made numerous efforts to discover the structure of the Abrahamic narratives.[96] While a certain chiastic ordering may be discerned, we must use care not to overdraw the parallels or neglect overlapping structures. Most efforts have had difficulty incorporating 22:20–25:18 into any finely tuned chiasm. Generally, we may observe a doubling of key stories over the course of the narrative:

1. As with other major sections, genealogies enclose the story of Abraham, those of his ancestors (11:10-32) and of his descendants (25:1-18), although 22:20-24 is a complicating factor.

2. The story of the endangering of Sarah (12:10-20; 20:1-18).

3. Stories pertaining to Lot (13–14; 18:16–19:38).

4. Chapters focusing on covenant (15; 17). Most analyses find the center of the text in these covenants.

5. Stories focusing on Hagar and Ishmael (16; 21:8-21).

6. Segments focusing on the birth of Isaac (18:1-15; 21:1-7).

7. Stories relating to Abimelech (20; 21:22-34).

8. Stories providing a "test" and a journey for Abraham (11:27–12:9; 22:1-19).

9. Stories pertaining to land (13; 23).

These doublings give to the narrative an ongoing mirroring effect, inviting another look at Abraham and the development of God's purposes in and through him from different perspectives along the course of his journey.

More generally, the Abrahamic story may be structured by the parallels regularly drawn with the history of Israel. That is to say, the overall structure of Israel's history provides a grid into which the various Abrahamic stories are fit (see Introduction and each episode).

96. See Rendsburg, *The Redaction of Genesis*, 27-52.

GENESIS 11:27–12:9, THE CALL OF ABRAM

COMMENTARY

Genesis 11:27, beginning with the genealogy of Abraham's father and enclosing the story with genealogies (cf. 25:1-18), provides the likely starting point for the story of Abraham. The story of Jacob (25:19) and the story of Joseph and his brothers (37:2) also begin this way. This segment is an admixture of P and J materials.

11:27-32. These genealogical, geographical, and travel notes introduce 12:1-9 and anchor Abram in the story of the nations (Genesis 1–11). Starting the story at 12:1 would give the impression that the call of Abram marks a highly disjunctive event in his life, a bolt out of the blue. But 11:27-32 makes it clear that his family had already begun a journey to Canaan from their home in "Ur of the Chaldeans" (probably the ancient center about 70 miles south of modern Baghdad; Chaldea was a less ancient name of Babylonia from neo-Babylonian times [see Jer 50:1, 8]). Such movement links the call of Abram to the Tower of Babel story and may also relate to the exiles in Babylon. Terah and his family had gotten stalled along the way, settling in Haran (in southeastern Turkey, on a tributary of the Euphrates). God's call thus spurs Abram to complete the journey once begun (in which God had been involved, 15:7), only now leaving all but his immediate family (which included Lot, who was under Abram's care because his father had died) behind in Haran. These details indicate that efforts to portray Abram's move as especially agonizing may be overdrawn; moving on was a way of life with this family (though verbal links with 22:1 suggest it was not altogether easy).

Other important elements that specifically link up with chaps. 12–50 include the infertility of Sarai (see commentary on 29:31–30:24), which becomes a central theme for the story, and Lot, whose enigmatic place in this family the author explores at key points (chaps. 13–14; 18–19). More generally, links with the family in Haran continue through the story of Abraham (22:20-24; 24) and Jacob (27:43–28:7; 29–31), as both Isaac and Jacob return to marry members of their family (Rebekah; Rachel).

Interpreters dispute whether Abram's call at age seventy-five (12:4) occurred before or after Terah's death (11:32). The NIV pluperfect in 12:1 ("had said") apparently derives from the interpretation of Acts 7:2-4 that Abram received his call in Ur rather than Haran (perhaps based on the general observations of divine leading in 15:7; Neh 9:7). But Terah takes the initiative in 11:31, and Abram leaves from Haran in 12:4-5 (*if* Abram is Terah's firstborn, 11:26, then Terah lived for sixty more years, which may not be the case).[97]

At the end of this short passage, the author reports Terah's death, his uncompleted journey to Canaan, the death of one of his sons, the barrenness of the wife of another, and an orphaned grandson (Lot). The word of God (vv. 1-3) enters into a point of great uncertainty for the future of this family.

12:1-4a. Interpreters universally consider vv. 1-3 to provide the key for the rest of Genesis, indeed the Pentateuch. They constitute a fulcrum text, thoroughly theological in focus, especially written to link chaps. 1–11 ("all the families of the earth") with the ancestral narratives, and to project forward to the later history of Israel ("a great nation"). Although Abram will never see this future, his response will shape it (see 26:4-5, 24). The promises focus on nationhood, renown, and blessing for Abram's family and others through them. The promises are somewhat general, yet the emphasis on greatness entails a level of particularity that can be discerned by others. The promises are brought into play in the following narrative again and again in various formulations, with the implied themes of descendants and land made more specific; further imperatives also play a role (17:1; see 22:1).

The command/promise structure of these verses seems most like 26:2-6*a;* it is similar to others (e.g., 46:1-5*a*) but surprisingly

---

97. See Victor Hamilton, *The Book of Genesis 1–17*, NICOT (Grand Rapids: Eerdmans, 1990) 366-68.

lacks a divine self-identification. The narrator assumes that Abram knows the one who speaks these words. Verses 1-3 serve as the narrator's summary of the "call" (cf. Isa 51:2), laying out a theological agenda in general terms, rather than an actual report thereof. The passage may be outlined as follows:

(1) An imperative. God appears suddenly and without introduction, calling Abram to leave (in order of increasing level of intimacy) his country, his clan, and his home (as in 24:4), and journey to a land God will reveal to him (22:1-2), which must happen quickly given their travel plans (v. 5, as in 22:3-4). Verse 4a reports Abram's positive response to the divine directive.

(2) A series of four cohortative verbs that express emphatically the intention of the speaker, each of which provides gracious divine promises to Abraham, but whose full realization lies beyond his own lifetime (see Overview). *God* will (note the recurrent "I") make Abraham a great nation; bless him; make his name great; and bless those who bless him (and curse anyone who abuses him). God, in essence, promises a new community with a new name (unlike 11:4, given by God). The author, here, recognizes that Abram embodies later Israel (in the subsequent narratives, Abraham's life will mirror that of later Israel). How these promises are related to Sarai's infertility (11:30) sets up a key issue, though the promises at this point do not necessarily involve Sarai in the fulfillment. Lot possibly came to mind for Abram (this is pure speculation), but so much is open-ended in what God says that the point seems to be the *absence* of calculation on Abram's part and a simple trust that God will find a way (Abram's first concern is expressed in 15:2).

The reader might conceive all the promises to encompass the promise of blessing, so that the promises of nation and name are more precise forms of that blessing. Yet, placing the "I will bless you" in second position implies that the promise of "a great nation" (גוי *gôy;* as a political entity it has later Israel in view) creates a key to what follows ; fulfillment of the other promises will follow on the heels of that fulfillment. It is *as a nation* that Israel will be blessed and given a great name or renown. One may discern royal connotations in these

materials (2 Sam 7:9; Ps 72:17). This promise of future blessing, however, does not involve moving from night to day at some future date; the divine promise will already begin its work within Abram's own life and continue on in the lives of his descendants (see Overview).

The promise of "blessing those who bless you" brings Abraham into relationship with those outside the chosen community. Those who treat Israel in life-sustaining ways will receive a response of blessing from God.

The intervening imperative could express either result or intention "so that [and] you will be a blessing," or retain its imperative sense ([you are to] be a blessing). In either case, it (a) indicates that God's fulfillment of the three previous promises will enable Israel's life to take the shape of blessing in the world; and (b) stands as preliminary to v. 3, which specifies that other peoples will experience blessing through their relationship with this family, who are to play an active role on behalf of this divine intention.

(3) The statement "the one who curses you I will curse" makes two shifts, to the singular (the one who, NRSV) and to an imperfect verb. This phrase does not offer another free-standing promise, but a note on the previous promise—namely, should any persons treat Israel with contempt they will reap the consequences of their deed (see Deut 5:9-10; 7:9-10); to put it positively, part of Israel's blessing means that they will be protected from those who mistreat them. The first word for "curse" (קלל *qālal*) has reference to any form of mistreatment; the second (ארר *'ārar*) is the opposite of blessing, reaping the consequences of such behaviors.

(4) Verse 3b, which presents translation difficulties, shifts to the perfect tense, and "families" serves as the subject of the verb. The NRSV has changed to the passive voice (so the NIV throughout) from the reflexive RSV (see footnote), as in the other texts where the Niphal form of the verb occurs (18:18; 28:14). With the Hithpael form, the NRSV shifts to the middle voice (the response of the other is more in play), "gain blessing for themselves" through Abram's offspring (22:18; 26:4). The RSV (NRSV footnote) translation makes Israel's role more passive; Abraham's blessing will become so commonplace that people will bless themselves by

invoking his name (see 48:20). Yet, even here the blessing received by Abram extends to all the families of the earth.

This final phrase presents the objective of all the previous clauses—God's choice of Abraham will lead to blessings for *all* the families of the earth (see 10:32; note the corporate focus). God's choice of Abram serves as an initially exclusive move for the sake of a maximally inclusive end. Election serves mission (in the broadest sense of the term).

12:4b-9. These verses report Abram's silent, but actively positive, response to God's call and review his travels to and through the land he has been shown, during which he is accompanied by God, builds altars, and worships God. Thereby God's promise does not float above the life experience of the recipient; the author emphasizes Abram's faithful and worshipful response at the onset of the story. Indeed, Abraham's fidelity shapes God's promised future (see 22:16-18; 26:4-5, 24).

Sarai and Lot accompany Abram, along with slaves and possessions (all his wealth does not come from Egypt; v. 16). When Abram reaches Canaan, God appears to him to inform him that this is the land promised to his descendants. Abraham then moves through the land, from north to south, anticipating God's request in 13:17 and perhaps the eventual Israelite settlement—from Shechem to near Bethel, toward the Negeb in the south (eventually Hebron, 13:18). The reference to Canaanites (i.e., all pre-Israelite inhabitants; see 15:19-21) reflects the perspective of a later period, long after Moses. The basically positive view of Canaanites in Genesis probably reflects v. 3*b* more than later problems. At this point the future seems open-ended.

Abram's journey functions paradigmatically for the one made by Jacob/Israel in chap. 35, including attention to trees and altars. Worship is obviously an integral part of his life and gives a shape to what will come. This journey seems not to be associated with the founding of sanctuaries, but with building altars at known sacred sites (without personnel or buildings), marked by trees (commonly associated with oracles; Moreh is probably a well-known site, 35:4; Josh 24:26) or stones. The later association of these natural markers with idolatry (Deut 12:2; 16:21) does not characterize this early period. Abraham's altar building belongs to a personal and familial act of worship, probably with sacrificial acts (see 8:20; 22:13), here a vehicle for expressing gratitude to God for the promise (each is built "to the LORD," 13:18). "Invoking the name of Yahweh" (4:26; 13:4; 26:25) refers to worship generally. These forms of early worship allow for movement, and are not tied down to priests or sanctuaries. The altar also functions as a continuing marker, perhaps a kind of public sign of God's promise of land.

Verse 7 speaks of a divine appearance to Abraham (in human form, see 16:7; cf. 17:1; 18:1; 26:2, 24; 35:9) in which the deity promises *this* land to Abraham's descendants (the corporate view of later Israel, evident in vv. 1-3, remains). God continues to give promises; as life moves along, new times and places elicit new promises. Although land is implied in the promise of nationhood (and descendants!) and in God's directive, this promise now refers to the land of Canaan. What God would *show* Abram is now *given.*

REFLECTIONS

1. Verses 1-3 link chaps. 1–11 with Israel's ancestral story. This is most evident in the relationship Abram is to have to "all the families of the earth" (cf. 10:32). This family does not come onto the world scene out of the blue; it has deep familial connections to *all* the nations of the world. This family thereby enables God's cosmic purposes and activity. The author does not even introduce the God who speaks to Abram in 12:1; we assume that this is the God who created the world and who has been engaged in the life of all peoples in the previous chapters. The call of Abram may be understood as

God's response to the dilemma created by the sin and evil that had become so pervasive among all the families of the earth.

2. Blessing becomes a key theme in the narratives that follow, used eighty-eight times in Genesis, with many indirect references (see Overview). It shapes the life of this family in varying ways as well as the lives of the many outsiders they encounter. Blessing stands as a gift of God (mediated through a human or nonhuman agent) that issues in goodness and well-being in life. It involves every sphere of existence, from spiritual to more tangible expressions. Blessing manifests itself most evidently in fertility and the multiplication of life, from herds and flocks, to field and forest, to new human life; it embraces material well-being, peace, and general success in life's ventures (see the list in Deut 28:3-15).

Blessing belongs fundamentally to the sphere of creation. The creation narratives make clear that blessing inheres as an integral part of God's purposes for the world, human and nonhuman, both before (1:22, 28; 2:3) and after (5:2; 9:1) the entrance of sin. The emphasis on blessing in the ancestral narratives (signaled by the fivefold reference in these verses) shows that God's original intentions for the world are being mediated in and through this family. Yet, the "families of the earth" are *not* totally dependent on their relationship to the chosen for blessing; the blessings of God the creator (e.g., sun and rain) continue to flow to all independently of their relationship to Abraham's family. The genealogies of chaps. 1–11 testify amply to the presence and power of blessing within even a fallen creation. The difference remains this: Blessings will be intensified or made more abundant (30:27-30) by this contact, made even more correspondent to God's intentions for the creation.

3. While blessing appears central in Genesis, it is inadequate and incomplete without *promise.* Promise is the most basic category with which this and the following narratives work.[98] The blessing that God promises to Abram has deep levels of continuity with the blessing he has experienced in his life to this point. But his new promise is something more, something beyond what the creation in and of itself can provide. Within creation, blessing is powerful, life-enabling, and life-sustaining, but finally insufficient for the fullest possible life. *The promises bring blessing into the sphere of redemption.*

God speaks to Abram, but very little has been said about him; he has spoken no words and has barely acted. By calling him, God brings Abram into the new day provided by promise. The divine word of command and promise newly constitutes Abram (though, as we have seen, not a *creatio ex nihilo*). God's new commitment to the relationship with Abram that promising entails makes for a new identity for the one who now responds in trust and obedience. Abram now takes into his life the character of the promises made; *he is now one whose future looks like this.* The future is not yet, but because God has been faithful to earlier promises, Abram's very being takes on the character of that future, though not apart from his own faithful response to the word of God, which created his faith in the first place. More generally, the promise stands at the beginning of Israel's ancestral story. We may understand not only the stories that follow, but also the entire history of Israel, as constituted and shaped by God's promises.

Even more, promise as promise serves as a key here. What counts about God's promises finally is their *continuing status as promise,* which can then be appropriated by the community of faith in later generations as still applicable to them and their future (see Overview).

4. Abram's trust in the promise and his move from Haran to Canaan will certainly mean a new level of meaning and life for him. But the God who commands and

---

98. See White, *Narration and Discourse,* 107-12, 169-73.

promises will also change forever as well. Having made promises, and being faithful to those promises, means that God is now committed to a future with the one who has faithfully responded. The text describes not only human faithfulness, but also divine faithfulness to promises made to a specific family. God will never be the same again. By his word, God has created a new family, indeed a new world for both Abraham and God, which gives to *each* a revised job description, though the goal of a reclaimed creation remains the same.

5. This text has many children in both the OT and the NT. It works itself out in the kingship of David and the associated promises (2 Sam 7:9; Pss 47:9; 72:17). The prophets address the theme of blessing on the nations (see Isa 19:24-25; Jer 4:2), which in turn arises in the NT and grounds the inclusion of Gentiles in the community of faith (see Acts 3:25; Gal 3:8).

On another point, Heb 11:8-16 celebrates Abraham and Sarah's journey of faith, but also recognizes its unfinished character. Their pilgrimage becomes one of faith and hope in the promises, but they do not live to see their fulfillment (a theme also present in Acts 7:2-5). As such, the pilgrimage of Abram and Sarai becomes a metaphor for the Christian life, a journey that reaches out toward a promised future, but comes up short of final fulfillment within one's own lifetime. Not that there are no signs of that future along the way; indeed, God provides blessings for the journey in an amazing range of sizes and colors. But persons of faith will realize that hope never becomes obsolete, for "here we have no lasting city" (Heb 13:14); the "better country" (Heb 11:16) will remain stretched out before us until our dying day.

GENESIS 12:10-20, ABRAM AND SARAI IN EGYPT

COMMENTARY

This is a thrice-told tale. In 20:1-18 Abraham will again seek to pass Sarah off as his sister; Isaac does the same with respect to Rebekah (26:1-11). Many interpreters view this as a single story retold in somewhat disparate ways and set into the narrative at different points by later redactors (chaps. 12 and 26 are J; chap. 20 is E). Genesis 12 may be the more original, with chaps. 20 and 26 being reworkings in view of issues in different locales. Stories of this sort were common in the ancient world, however, and these may reflect such a convention.[99] These stories now serve three distinctive, but not unrelated, functions within the narrative.

In addition, the Exodus story provides a structure for the narrative. The text is bracketed by Abram's descent to and return from Egypt (12:10; 13:1) and by the only speaking in the narrative, between Abram and Sarai (vv. 11-13) and between

Abram and Pharaoh (vv. 18-19). Historically, journeys from Canaan to Egypt at a time of famine (usually occasioned by drought) are known from Egyptian sources.

The next two chapters follow naturally this narrative by showing an interest in problems with the land that Abram has been promised.

12:10-16. The promise of the land has just been made to Abram (12:7), and he has been moving about its various territories (cf. the journeys of Jacob in chap. 35). His worship has expressed his gratitude to God (12:8). But now this land of promise cannot support him; the repetition (chiastic) of famine language in 12:10 stresses its severity. He must move out of the land in order to survive.

The narrator has yet to put a word in Abram's mouth. His first words, spoken to Sarai, are difficult to understand (vv. 11-13). The issue is not that Abram lies; in 20:12, we are informed—probably correctly—that Sarai was his half-sister (forms of sister marriage

99. On type scenes, see Alter, *The Art of Biblical Narrative*, 47-62.

in the Near East are not applicable). Abram does, however, ask (not demand) that Sarai speak less than the full truth, to conceal the nature of their relationship, because the Egyptians might kill him to procure such a beautiful woman (the redaction puts her age at sixty-five!). This presupposes a situation where adultery is forbidden, but a murder might be arranged (cf. David and Bathsheba).

Abram's premonitions about Egypt are on target in some respects. Both the populace and the officials of the unnamed pharaoh do make the anticipated judgment about Sarai's beauty. They praise Sarai so much that she is taken into Pharaoh's house to become his "wife" (v. 19; cf. 16:3; 2 Sam 11:27, with possible parallels with David); the lack of any marker to distinguish the uses of "wife" in v. 19 means they have the same force. These references, as well as the time that passes (v. 16), make it likely that the marriage is consummated (to deny this seems a case of special pleading). Because of Sarai ("for her sake"), Pharaoh treats Abram well (anticipated in v. 13, but with a different scenario). Prosperity comes to Abram at the expense of Sarai; indeed, Pharaoh makes Abram a wealthy man (cf. 24:35; 16:1 implies that one slave was Hagar). His life is preserved from famine and Pharaoh, but it has cost him the loss of Sarai, and it has cost Sarai her honor and dignity.

Abram fails to anticipate the Egyptian situation in other respects: (a) Pharaoh himself enters the picture. There is no hint in this scenario that any other than Egyptians generally are in view (confirmed by the broad reference in v. 14). The problem appears cultural, certainly out in the open, and not a peculiarly royal issue. To suggest that Abram intends to entrap Pharaoh goes beyond the text. (b) An Egyptian takes her for a wife. Abram does not even suggest this as a possibility. If it had been any Egyptian but Pharaoh, he may have thought he could negotiate as Sarai's "brother" (cf. 24:55) and been able to forestall her marriage. (c) Abram expects the worst from the outsider. From the way Pharaoh responds when the ruse becomes known, it seems unlikely he would have mistreated or killed Abram, if he had told the truth from the beginning. Pharaoh's response (vv. 18-20) seems genuine, even if offered under some

duress. (d) Abram underestimates the consequences of his actions. Note the disastrous effects of Sarai's presence on Pharaoh and his household. If Sarai should be taken, one must doubt that Abram thought the moral order would function in some mechanical way and would deliver Sarai back quickly (v. 16 assumes no little time) or would gain him considerable wealth.

12:17-20. Pharaoh's action is relationally inappropriate, even though he participates unknowingly, so that it brings divine judgment in its wake (objective guilt). While we do not know the identity of the "serious" plague, diseases are probably in mind (see 2 Chr 26:20; Ps 73:5, 14). The phrase "because of Sarai" (v. 17) points in two directions, God's working within the moral order and the saving of Sarai. God's action constitutes the turning point in the story, in spite of Abram's duplicity. A comparison with the plague stories (Exod 11:1) brings out a notable contrast. While plagues are visited upon the Egyptians in both cases, the reasons differ. In Exodus, the conduct of the Egyptians elicits them. Here the behavior of God's own chosen one leads to Pharaoh's action, which engenders the plagues. Abram brings a curse rather than a blessing upon the nations (12:3). In his very first contact with outsiders, Abram fails in his response to the call of God. Even more, Pharaoh cuts the Egyptians off from this source of blessing.

Nonetheless, Abram does not reap the full negative effects of his behavior; this happens because of Sarai (v. 16) and Pharaoh (v. 20). No mechanically conceived moral order at work here! Human activity can cut into the act-consequence spiral and ameliorate its effects. We do not know how Pharaoh establishes the link between his actions toward Sarai and the plagues; yet, the immediate juxtaposition of the plagues and his interrogation shows that it involves *his own insight* (note the stress on "wife").

Pharaoh asks Abram exactly the same question that God asked Eve in the garden (3:13; similarly of Cain, 4:10). His "sending away" (שׁלח *šālaḥ*) Abram and his family is similar to God's banishing Adam and Eve from the garden (3:23). Not unlike them, Abram (in this only recorded meeting with Pharaoh) may have experienced shame and dread at being peppered by the (nonjudicial) questions of an angry emperor, but the narrator makes a different point. Just as Sarai had no response in vv. 11-13, so also Abram offers no response in this, the only other dialogue. Abram is reduced to silence too! They are sent away abruptly and ignominiously, escorted to the border; yet, Pharaoh exhibits a remarkably generous spirit. While the plagues no doubt prompt this treatment of Abram, Pharaoh also acts in a way more liberally than he has to. Pharaoh not only lets Abram off the hook, but also lets him keep all the possessions he had accumulated because of the ruse (v. 20). Ironically, Pharaoh proves to be more of a behavioral model in this instance than Abram, alleviating the negative consequences that might well have befallen Abram. God's purposes are also served by Pharaoh.

REFLECTIONS

1. Many readers sympathize with Abram's equivocation; after all, he not only comes to Egypt with hat in hand, but he understands his life to be in danger as well. Faced with such a dilemma and preparing for the worst, he puts life ahead of honor, life for himself at the potential expense of Sarai's honor. That this entails the potential loss of the promised future seems unlikely, given her barrenness and her not yet being associated with the promise. At this point the promise need not be fulfilled through Sarai; his death, on the other hand, would be decisive.

Other readers have pronounced his actions cowardly and lacking in integrity (see chap. 20). At what price does he seek to assure his personal safety? A repeated focus on self fills his speech. He puts Sarai at the disposal of his personal concerns. In fact, as his sister, she seems even more likely to be taken; he may lose her altogether (see below).

The truth probably rides the cusp between these two views. Abram had few options, none of them perfect. He chooses to enter into a situation fraught with danger and ambiguity and devises a careful strategy, albeit imperfect, self-serving, and dishonoring of Sarai.

2. The parallels with Exodus are striking: (a) Abram goes down to Egypt because of famine (see 42:1-5; 43:1, 15; 47:4, 13). To "sojourn" (גור *gûr*) is also used in 20:10 and 47:4. In 26:1-3 God tells Isaac *not* to go down to Egypt and sojourn there. Is it not yet the appropriate time? (b) Egypt is both life-threatening and life-enhancing. (c) Use of a ruse (Exod 5:1-3). (d) Sarai like Moses is taken into Pharaoh's house. (e) Conflict with Pharaoh. (f) Plagues on Egypt (כגע *nāgaʿ*; cf. Exod 11:1). (g) Enrichment/despoiling in Egypt. (h) "Take and go" (לקח *lāqaḥ*; הלך *hālak*; 12:19 and Exod 12:32). (i) Let Abram/Israel go (*sālaḥ*).

Abram's story prefigures the experience of Israel. Abram functions as the father of Israel in more than a genealogical way; Israel's story plays out Abram's story. Yet, the author portrays the Egyptians more positively here; indeed, throughout Genesis, the Egyptians appear in a positive light (see chaps. 39–50), which seems remarkable, given what is to come in Exodus. The Egyptians are not the embodiment of evil; they are not destined to a certain way of being. Other futures are available to them. Given the number of links with the Exodus story, the chosen family itself may in some respects be responsible for what the Egyptians become. In some sense Abram (and others) is to blame for the Egyptian oppression.

The chosen ones are not inevitably the bringers of blessing to others. They can so comport themselves in daily life that others will suffer, rather than be blessed. How the people of God respond to others has great potential for both good and ill. In addition, just because a given people are not believers ought not occasion suspicion or a lack of basic human trust. Benevolent behavior by those who are unchosen testifies to the continuing work of God the Creator in the lives of all people. Those who are instruments of God's redemptive activity ought to recognize these wide-ranging positive effects of God's creative work, and seek to join hands with such persons in working toward God's goals of a reclaimed creation. The most basic root of these problematic ways of relating to others, according to this text, lies in a deeply rooted centering on self.

3. We do not know why the narrator gives Sarai no voice. It could reflect the patriarchy of the time. Yet, the powerful voice given women in Genesis (e.g., Rebekah) intimates that Sarai's silence may be intentional (see 20:5). Either it is a characteristic of her relationship to Abram or she chooses to suffer silently, tacitly agreeing to risk her honor and her life for Abram's sake. In view of later initiatives she takes (16:2), the latter is more likely. It is striking that Abram has no response when Sarai is "taken" (cf. his reaction to Lot in 14:14).

Even though she remains silenced, the story unfolds around Sarai; as such, the author gives her a position of no little power and influence. It is because of her that Abram feels threatened, that things may go well with him and that his life may be spared (v. 13), that Pharaoh is "good" to him (v. 16), and that God afflicts Pharaoh (v. 17). The story refers to her thirteen times, moving from being Abram's wife to his sister to "the woman" to Pharaoh's wife and back to Abram's wife. This focus on the silent, but nonetheless powerful, role of Sarai should be allowed to have its full interpretive import. She is no minor figure and should be given a prominent role in any retelling of the story.

4. While Abram can depend on the *promise* of land (12:7), he cannot depend on the land itself. God offers a creational gift that almost immediately fails the recipient— no land of milk and honey for Abram. Does God promise Abram a fractured gift? The very gift has a certain precarious character. In this case, the land does not sustain—at least consistently—the human population so dependent on its riches. The fruitfulness of the land seems precarious; the gifts of God can become something other than what they were created to be.

5. The author intends such talk of famine to recall aspects of the creation story (1:11-12, 29-30; 3:17-18). The land (ארץ *'ereṣ*) was created to bring forth every green thing; it did so, and God saw that it was good. The land was to supply all living creatures with food. Genesis 1 claims that God does not intend famine for the creation. Genesis 3, however, claims that the creation has become at odds with that intention. More specifically, Gen 3:17-18 speaks of an inescapable link between sin and the fruitfulness of the land; human sin has negative creational effects. Ever since, the land has not produced as God originally intended; human beings may indeed suffer famine. Such was the creational situation within which God's promise to Abram occurs. God promises a land, but it falls short of paradise.

Abram committed no sin that led to this famine; this is the way things are in the land when God makes the promise. While the land is full of creational potential, presently it falls short of its promise and contributes to human suffering. So God's gift to Abram can fail, having been spoiled through what human beings have done (see Lev 26:18-20; Deut 11:13-17). The land needs healing, as it often does during Israel's history. In eschatological vision, when God's promises are fulfilled on a cosmic scale, famine will be no more (Isa 65:21; Amos 9:13-14).

6. Abram no sooner receives the promise than he has to leave it behind. Promises often work this way. The promises are real and reliable, because God has made them. But one cannot settle into what has been promised, forever secure in its reality. Promises do not result in certainty; certainty exists only in myth. Promises can only be trusted, believed in; the journey toward the fulfillment of the promise involves faith, not sight (Hebrews 11). This text describes the first of a number of such journeys into alien and dangerous territory for Israel, away from the land of promise. Israel's way of being in the land often appears this way; it will not be otherwise for many another sojourning community of faith.

7. Some have suggested that the absence of reference to God by Abram should be important in evaluating his actions; he should have appealed to or shown confidence in divine help as he faced this dilemma. This direction of thought does not prove helpful. Characters in Genesis often make decisions and pursue actions without specific reference to God, and without being judged for it. In fact, Abram's actions here meet with no little success and wealth (v. 16). Humanly devised strategies are not in and of themselves out of order; in fact, "the narrator presents his character in a world where natural crises arise with no relation to the divine, and where the person of faith makes independent decisions in response to them."[100] It ought not to be thought that Abram's actions entail taking the divine promises into his own hands; that would be a docetic way of viewing God's way of working in the world. Moreover, the alternative could be viewed as tempting God to provide miracles (Exod 17:1-7) or an unreal divine protection plan of some sort. The narrative speaks not one word of Abram's faith in God or lack thereof; it centers on the way he handles a problem in daily life, with all of its complexities and ambiguities.

8. Given the correspondence between act and consequence, one might expect the plagues as an appropriate response (see Exod 11:1; 1 Kgs 15:5; Isa 53:4). Both act and consequence occur within the sphere of creation; an unnatural relationship leads to disease. The consequence inherently follows the deed. Yet the text does not present a deistic process; God midwifes the consequences. A contemporary restatement of such divine action should call on the fuller language of the nature of the divine involvement evident in other biblical texts: "[You] have delivered us into the hand of our iniquity" (Isa 64:7; cf. Rom 1:24-32); "I am going to bring disaster on this people,/ the fruit of their schemes" (Jer 6:19; cf. 21:14). God delivers Pharaoh into the hands of his own iniquity, the fruit of which is disease.

One might well wonder about the fairness of this effect, given both Abram's success and Pharaoh's unwitting activity. Abram has occasioned this problem, as Pharaoh discerns (v. 18). He blames Abram, not Abram's God! He puts the blame right where it belongs (and only Pharaoh does so). But the workings of the moral order do not discriminate between those who commit sins knowingly or unknowingly. This has been true generally throughout human history. People do experience great disasters in life "through no fault of their own." They also experience great benefits.

---

100. White, *Narration and Discourse*, 179.

GENESIS 13:1-18, ABRAM AND LOT

COMMENTARY

Bracketed by an itinerary (vv. 1-4, 18), this text (mostly J) includes a quarrel narrative (vv. 5-13) and an oracle of promise (vv. 14-17). Verse 1 serves as a hinge verse. This report of Abram and his family leaving Egypt and settling in the land again mirrors later events. What Abram does, his descendants will do; he anticipates Israel's history in his own life. This takes its most concrete form

in the promises of land and posterity in vv. 14-17. Jacob's journey from Bethel to Hebron in chap. 35 replicates Abram's and links both patriarchs to these important centers in later Israel and Judah.

The author has included some ethnological features in the story inasmuch as Lot is the progenitor of the Moabites and the Ammonites (19:37-38), peoples often at odds with

Israel (Deut 2:9-19; 23:3-4). Lot's "separation" anticipates that of Ishmael and other sons of Abraham (25:1-18) and Esau (36:6-8), and continues that evident more generally in the table of nations (10:32). This story works as an integral part of the larger story of Lot continued in chaps. 14 and 18–19, though it probably never existed apart from an Abramic context.

13:1-4. Verses 1-4 are ordered in terms of Israel's early history.[101] Abram's going up (עלה *ʿālâ*) from Egypt presents language used of Israel (Exod 13:18); note also the belongings, in detail (12:35-38). In both cases, *Egypt* has willingly enabled this prosperity (12:36). Abram's journeying in "stages" toward the promised land (and the tents) mirrors the exodus and wanderings (17:1; Num 10:12). Lot's being "with him" with "flocks and herds" recalls Exod 12:38. When Lot compares the Jordan valley to "the land of Egypt," the wilderness murmurings come to mind (Exod 16:3; see below), as does the strife (מריבה *mĕrîbâ*, used only for the murmurings; Exod 17:7). Israel encounters the descendants of Lot along the way (Deut 2:9-19). The references to Bethel and Ai (v. 3) and to Canaanites (v. 7; cf. 12:6), as well as the theme of strife, call to mind the early narratives in Joshua, albeit initially without violence (cf. chap. 14; cf. also vv. 14-15 and the language for the land in Deut 3:27). The repeated language concerning Abram's "beginnings" (vv. 3-4) in the land links this family to this land from the start. Neither Lot nor Sarai should be evaluated negatively in view of their absence in v. 4 (or in 12:7-8).

13:5-13. Strife arises between the families of Abram and Lot (vv. 7-8 speak of strife between groups, only potentially between the individuals) because "their possessions were so great that they could not live together" (v. 6; note the repetition). Other groups no doubt intensified such tension (v. 7; cf. 26:12-22), reference to which helps explain why the land is already too small for Abram's family.

Abram takes the initiative to settle the intrafamilial squabble. The explicit motivations are twofold: (1) They are brothers (kinsmen) and hence should not be quarreling (see Ps 133:1); (2) an interest in peace: "Let there be no strife between you and me" (v. 8). The

101. See Wenham, *Genesis 1–15*, 300.

herdsmen extend the family unit. Abram's enlightened self-interest maybe a third reason. This separation would probably lead to greater prosperity, as all would have recognized. Abram makes the first move, given his seniority; it entails no evaluation of Lot (in view of 12:7, the story does not imply that Lot was Abram's heir).

Abram's resolution creates family separation (the verb occurs in vv. 9, 11, 14), with each group occupying different territories. Historically, quarreling among nomads over pastures and wells for their cattle was commonplace in that era (see chaps. 21; 26), and it was common for families to separate (see 10:5, 32). Hence, one ought not think of either Lot or Abram as especially quarrelsome, as if different temperaments would have enabled them to live together. The text does not blame either person, or even regard separation as unfortunate; it works as a responsible way of responding to crowded conditions. The criterion for evaluation should be whether the act helps to achieve peace and well-being.

Abram allows Lot to choose between two lands (given Abram's settlement in Hebron and v. 11, the axis seems to be east-west, though some think it to be north-south). This ploy appears magnanimous, but is it? Too many unresolved questions remain. Did Abram have a sense for the choice Lot might make? He may not have wanted the land that Lot was apt to choose. Or was he tired of strife and willing to take anything for the sake of peace? Did Abram know what the implications of Lot's choice might be? Does he know about Sodom, and if so, does he set up Lot to fail (v. 13)? That Lot thinks through his reasons rather than talking them through relieves Abram of some responsibility for the choice, but his motivations remain ambiguous.

Some think that Abram puts the promise in jeopardy: If Lot had chosen the other portion of land, the promise would have failed. This seems problematic for at least three reasons: (1) Given what became of Lot, his decision could hardly be "right." (2) On the basis of 12:7, Abram does not know what "this land" includes. (3) The promised land does not become co-extensive with either of these options. Verse 9 ("the whole land") and

vv. 14-15 (what Abram sees includes what Lot saw, more than the "Canaan" of v. 12) show that the choices of *both* Lot and Abram were included within the land promised at this point, though Lot journeys to the eastern edge.

Lot's silence appears striking. Yet, v. 10 reports his thoughts regarding the choice Abram has put before him. What are the crucial factors in his decision? Some say that Lot was drawn by the beauty of the land and his own greed. But this explanation works too simplistically. What Lot sees occasions his choice, but so also does other knowledge he has regarding the garden of the Lord (see 2:8; Isa 51:3) and the land of Egypt.

If it were like the Garden of Eden, why would that be a bad choice? There can be no going back to Eden; but even more, v. 13 makes clear that Sodom is no Eden. Lot does not perceive accurately the reality of things. His "seeing" provides too limited a perspective (see 3:5). Regarding Egypt, the links to Exodus point the way. The issue focuses on Egypt as a garden, from which Lot has recently returned (13:1; cf. Deut 11:10). In view of Israel's wandering in the wilderness begging to return to Egyptian flesh pots, Egypt represents a desire for a pre-redemption state of affairs. Likeness to Egypt connects with the later language of "outcry" about Sodom (18:21; 19:13; cf. Exod 3:7-9); note also Abram's identification of a problem in Egypt (12:11-13), of which Lot would have been aware. The narrator's comments about Sodom (vv. 10, 13) say something about Lot's choice, rather than simply anticipating a later aspect of the story. Lot's ethical-theological perspective creates the problem. While this perspective does not determine how Lot will respond within his new locale, his behavior in chap. 19 suggests he begins to take on the character of his new environment. The reference to "eastward" may link up with Abraham's sons by Keturah (25:6) rather than with Adam, Eve, and Cain (3:24; 4:16).

13:14-18. Verses 14-15, 17 consist of a repeated promise of land, enclosing a promise of posterity (v. 16). The dust image relates to the land in which Abraham lives; it provides a traditional image for an unimaginably large number (a new emphasis from 12:1-3; see 15:5; 28:14). The promise to Abram comes

as a direct, unconditional proclamation. It extends the promise that appears in 12:7, with a new word about perpetuity. Three factors contribute to its reiteration: (1) It signals another key transition in Abram's journey. The promise stands just as clearly after Abram's Egyptian sojourn as before. This anticipates what the situation will be after the next Egyptian sojourn. Generally, the promises are repeated so often and in such variety over the course of chaps. 12–50 in order to assure readers from later generations, perhaps especially exiles, that God's promises still stand, no matter the experience.

(2) Lot's decision makes necessary greater precision regarding the extent of the promised land. The promise includes Lot's land (hence his departure?)! The decision by Lot may be a division *within* the promised land; in some sense the family of Abram remains intact within this land. The promise does not express a divine approval of Abram's treatment of Lot; his conduct toward Lot remains much too ambiguous.

(3) The author uses legal language for the transfer of property.[102] Abram lifts up his eyes, looks around, and walks through the land. These actions are probably a legal way of concretely laying claim to something (cf. Lot in vv. 10-12; Josh 1:3; 24:3). They also highlight the fact that heavenly visions are related to earthly realities—i.e., an actual piece of real estate. God thereby transfers the land to Abram; it is *actually given* to him. The text does not describe simply a promise of what will belong to Abram's descendants, but a gift now in place (the NRSV has future tense in v. 17; the NIV is closer to the mark with its "I am giving"). This may explain Abram's inclusion in the promise at this point; only his descendants were in view in 12:7.

Abram follows through on God's instructions in a somewhat oblique way as the narrator reports his journey to Hebron (cf. Jacob in chap. 35; Deut 11:24). Abram "moves his tent" (as did Lot, vv. 12, 18) and settles near a stand of trees, where he (unlike Lot) builds an altar—his third!—in the open air, not at a sanctuary. Mamre, near Hebron, is not mentioned outside of Genesis. The text attests to the importance of this area with Abraham's later

102. For Near Eastern parallels, see Sarna, *Genesis*, 99-100.

purchase of land for a burial place (chap. 23). Lot begins life in the land from essentially the same point as Abram, recipient of the blessings of God in great bounty. What will the two individuals now make of the blessings they have received?

REFLECTIONS

1. This text harks back to Genesis 1–11. The language of "beginning" and the declaration "Abram called on the name of the LORD" (v. 4; cf. 12:8; 4:26) recall creational texts. Note also the strife between "brothers" (cf. vv. 8, 11 with 4:8-11) and the explicit reference to the "well watered . . . garden of the LORD" (v. 10; cf. 2:6). Abram's well-being and wealth and his settlement in the promised land constitute a claim that basic *creational* intentions are being realized (see Exod 3:8).

The author uses the word *evil* (רע *ra'*, cf. 2:9) for the first time since the flood (v. 13; cf. 6:5; 8:21), and the root חטא (*ḥaṭṭāʾ*, "sin[ner]") for the first time since 4:7. The Sodomites are the first historical people described in this negative way and to experience the destruction (שחת *šḥt*) of the divine judgment as a result (v. 10; cf. 6:12-17; 9:11, 15). The author points to continuity with the primeval period. The language of sin/evil/destruction occurs only in these texts in the Abraham cycle. Whatever lack of trust in God that Abram or his family exhibit in these chapters, the writer never uses the language of sin and evil to describe it (see 20:9).

This positive/negative reference back to chaps. 1–11 indicates that the ancestral stories have been placed within a creational matrix and are to be interpreted through the lens provided by the opening chapters of Genesis. This means not only that God's creational activity manifests itself in the life of this family, but also that the forces that make for evil and sin hover near and threaten its future (see 4:7). Israel lives in a world in which the forces of evil are very much a reality; Lot's being drawn into that orbit of life serves as a reminder of negative possibilities for the people of God and the importance of the choices they make. At the same time, these texts look forward to a reclamation of what God has created through Abram's family.

2. The reference to Sodom and Gomorrah (v. 10) also emphasizes the drastic change in the ecology of the area within Abram's lifetime (see chap. 19). Zoar also anticipates this change (see 19:22-23, 30). In some sense the Sodom story, begun here, continues the history of the interweaving of human choices and cosmic effects sketched in Genesis 3–8. Lot's beautiful land will become an ecological disaster, which the author relates implicitly to the wickedness of Sodom (v. 13). Verse 10 (which assumes readers know the Sodom story) does not imply that Lot moves into a situation already doomed before his arrival, but suggests a link between his decision and the future of the area. What characterized humankind as a whole has intruded into the very heart of the family chosen by God to reclaim that creation. It should remind the community of faith that the choices its members make with respect to the land and economic issues have a potential ecological impact on God's blessings of the land.

3. The blessings God showers on people create problems as well as possibilities. The families of Lot and Abram have been blessed with many possessions, but the blessing provides the occasion for strife and separation. A situation of material well-being does not necessarily mean that life will go well; it raises its own set of problems. What people do with their blessings will determine whether they remain blessings or become curses. The text gives a strong premonition of what will happen to Lot's choice. At the same time, the promise to Abram includes Lot's land (vv. 14-15); thus he does not stand outside the reach of God's special blessing (see 14:14). Even more, Abram's land is also potentially within reach of a Sodom and Gomorrah experience. Israel will later be visited with judgments that are described in such terms (see chap. 19).

4. Westermann suggests that this text stands over against later Israelite ways of using war as a way of settling disputes; Abram shows a different way, achieving peace without violence. "The narrative of Abraham, who brought a dispute to peaceful solution by personal renunciation, still spoke across the era of Israel's wars; it was a pointer to another way of solving a conflict. The promise of a king of peace had a predecessor."[103] If this theological background can be assumed, then one might extend it to include an implicit critique of the Joshua parallels noted above. In any case, chap. 14 makes clear that Abraham was not a pacifist.

5. "Forever" language occurs for the first time with the land (see 17:8; 48:4), linked to a countless posterity. This language does not carry the sense of eternity, however, but indefiniteness into the future. This motif should be tied to such issues as who are the heirs of the Abrahamic promises, especially in view of Romans 4. While the gift of land remains always in place, disloyal recipients can remove themselves from the sphere of fulfillment (see 22:15-19; 26:5).

103. Westermann, *Genesis 12–36: A Commentary* (Minneapolis: Augsburg, 1985) 181.

GENESIS 14:1-24, ABRAM AND MELCHIZEDEK

COMMENTARY

This chapter stands among the most difficult in the book of Genesis, evident not least in the unusual number of its unique or rare words and phrases. Scholars have not been able to identify all of these persons and places. To the extent that they are known, and may be set in the second millennium BCE, they are not simply to be taken at face value, but have some typological significance. Moreover, the portrayal of Abram as a military leader stands in some tension with the rest of the cycle (see 23:6). The historical basis of the story remains difficult to discern.[104] The chapter derives from several traditions, but the component parts are usually not associated with the pentateuchal sources (occasionally J, as part of a Lot-Abram tradition). The silence regarding Abram in vv. 1-11 has often led to their separation from vv. 12-24, set entirely within the land of Canaan. Within the latter, vv. 18-20 interrupt reference to the king of Sodom and are associated commonly with

Davidic/Zion traditions. While probably originally unrelated, the three segments in the chapter have been verbally and thematically integrated into a broader story by an editor.[105]

Regarding form, vv. 12-24 may stem from an old hero story about Abram, similar to liberation stories from the period of the judges. Verses 18-20 may have been added as a midrash to link David and Jerusalem with Abram. Verses 1-11 are a report of a military campaign, though with few details; it may have been non-Israelite in origin, perhaps Babylonian. The dating (vv. 4-5) and other stylistic features accord with royal inscriptions from the ancient Near East. Dialogue comes into play only in the aftermath of the entire affair (vv. 21-24).

An editor has integrated this chapter into Abram's story for several reasons: (1) It belongs to a larger pattern wherein Abram mirrors the early history of Israel in his own life, especially the conquest of the land (see below). (2) It serves as an integral part of the larger story of Lot and Abram. (3) The

104. For detail, see Sarna, *Genesis*, 101-11; Wenham, *Genesis 1–15*, 318-20.

105. See Wenham, *Genesis 1–15*, 305-7.

kings' responses prepare us for the response of God in chap. 15. (4) It gives Israel a role in the world of nations, which attests to God as creator. While the chapter may well exalt Abram "as a great and powerful prince who encounters victoriously the united kings of the great kingdoms of the east,"[106] it also says something about Israel. God's call to Abram (12:1-3) has a purpose that spans the globe. This chapter and the table of nations (10:1-32) have many links; together they enclose chaps. 11–13, placing Israel's beginnings through Abraham within a universal context.

This redaction involves Israel's self-understanding, not least within a probable exilic provenance, when the Abrahamic tradition receives renewed attention (Isa 41:8; 51:2). While one concern may be to "awaken a glorious past which opened broader horizons to those currently humiliated,"[107] the focus should be placed on mission rather than on national self-aggrandizement.

14:1-16. Verse 1 presents names and places that are otherwise unattested (Shinar is Babylon, see 10:10; 11:2). Also, we know of no such international coalition, apparently from the Mesopotamian region. Whatever the historical basis, this coalition could be viewed as a gathering of forces that endangers Israel's future in the land.

The names of the five kings of the Pentapolis in the region of the Dead Sea (v. 2) remain unidentified. The five cities occur together only here (four appear in 10:19 and Deut 29:23); in the report of events (vv. 10-11) only Sodom and Gomorrah appear (as in chap. 19). Scholars have been unable to locate the valley of Siddim, but it must be near the Dead Sea. The author depicts Abram as a Hebrew (v. 13), probably to distinguish his people from the others mentioned.

The eastern kings (v. 1) go to war against the Pentapolis (vv. 2-3), which had rebelled after twelve years of subjugation (v. 4). On their way to putting down that rebellion (described in vv. 8-12), they conquer six peoples in the area (vv. 5-7), who may also be participating in a general rebellion against the eastern kings. The first three are original inhabitants of the land, described

in legendary terms as giants (Deut 2:10-12, 20); the next three are well-known. The land of two of these six peoples had been promised to Abram (15:18-20). The reference to Kadesh recalls a stopping place of the Israelites in the Negeb (Num 20:1), in which area the Amalekites were also subdued by the Israelites (Exod 17:8-16; Num 13:29). The reference to the Amorites seems unusual in that it refers to a city near the Dead Sea (see 2 Chr 20:2) rather than a region (Num 21:13; Deut 1:27, 44). Abram is allied with some Amorites (14:13)!

The reference to the "four kings against five" (v. 9) suggests something of the power of the four; this reference highlights Abram's later victory against those four kings (vv. 14-16). The plight of the kings of Sodom and Gomorrah, mentioned in vv. 10-11, may anticipate chaps. 18–19, as does the reference to the geology of the valley of Siddim. Also, the fleeing to the hills anticipates what happens to Lot (19:17-20, 30).

In conquering the Pentapolis, the eastern kings capture people and possessions, including Lot, and leave the area. When Abram hears this report, he takes his trained men, joins forces with other "allies," pursues the kings to the vicinity of Damascus, and brings back all that had been captured, including Lot. In effect, Abram thereby assumes control over the promised land.

Verse 14 provides the reason for Abram's entrance into this perilous situation: He acts on behalf of Lot, who remains very much a part of the family in spite of chap. 13. The story here moves from the world of nations to a single individual. Lot's fate moves Abram to act against the armies of four major nations!

The reference to the wickedness of Sodom (13:13) hangs over this story. Just as Abram would later intercede for these cities for the sake of the righteous in them (18:22-33), so also here he risks his life in ways that will benefit them. Abram centers his efforts on Lot's freedom, but in the process he liberates "great sinners." The move from Sodom and Gomorrah to just Sodom in 14:10-17 (as in 13:10, 13) shows that Lot's domicile is clearly in view.

In this military exploit Abram forms a coalition with non-Hebrews (vv. 13, 24). Living in community means cooperating

---

106. Westermann, *Genesis 12–36*, 192.
107. Westermann, *Genesis 12–36*, 207.

with other families. These allies join Abram's trained group of 318, "born in his house" (14:14). The latter are dedicated and trained persons who serve the family of Abram. In view of this text (see also 15:2; 17:12-13, 23, 27; 24:2), Abram's household appears large, perhaps several thousand with women and children, although historically Abram's retinue was probably somewhat smaller.

14:17-24. When Abram returns from battle, the king of Sodom meets him (vv. 17, 21-24), soon joined by the king of Salem (vv. 18-20) in the King's Valley, of uncertain location but probably near Jerusalem. They respond in different ways to the liberation. Their appearance together, although probably not original, invites comparison. Yet, the king of Sodom has reaped too much negative comment from commentators; inasmuch as he appears with Melchizedek, the reader ought not adjudge his response in an isolated way.

The king of Salem, Melchizedek (vv. 18-20), also serves as a priest of God Most High (*El Elyon*). He brings Abram food and drink, blesses him in the name of God Most High, the Creator, and blesses Abram's God for delivering Abram. These verses give a theological interpretation of the previous events.

Melchizedek is a mysterious figure, mentioned elsewhere only in Ps 110:4 (a royal psalm) and Hebrews 5–7, where the author interprets him in messianic terms. His name, similar to the Canaanite king Adonizedek (Josh 10:1), probably means "my king is salvation [righteousness]." His priest/king status may mean that the Canaanite kingship was understood as a sacral/political office, an understanding not foreign among Israel's kings (see Ps 110:4).

These verses may be traced to Davidic-Solomonic apologists, when relationships with the pre-Israelite leaders of Jerusalem (i.e., Salem; see Ps 76:2) were important. They sought to anchor new forms of royal/temple practice in Abrahamic times in order to legitimize them, perhaps in view of questions raised about "new" practices associated with the Davidic regime.

The priestly name Zadok (2 Sam 8:17; 15:24-35) also derives from this root; he was a pre-Israelite Jerusalem priest associated with David. His descendants, the Zadokite priestly line, were linked with the Davidic dynasty through the centuries. Abram's encounter with Melchizedek may have been understood as legitimizing the Zadokite priesthood.

In view of these links, ancient readers may have viewed Melchizedek as a precursor of both the royal and the priestly lines in the Davidic empire. Melchizedek is a priest of El Elyon, God Most High. Elyon is probably an epithet rather than a name (it is usually translated "Most High," see the NRSV footnote). *El* occurs as the general word for "deity" throughout the ancient Near East (*Elyon* was also used outside of Israel). The two words occur together elsewhere only in Ps 78:35, but *Elyon* appears in parallel with *El* (Num 24:16; Ps 73:11), with other divine names (Pss 18:13; 46:4), and independently (Deut 32:8; Ps 82:6).

Melchizedek's bringing of bread and wine, intended to refresh Abram after his battles, also had a religious import because Melchizedek was a priest. The meal cannot be separated from the blessing by Melchizedek that follows. It is (a) a blessing on Abram by God the Creator. Melchizedek thus exercises a truly mediatorial function. An outsider blesses Abram (cf. Balaam, Num 24:1); he does not do the blessing. (b) It blesses God in direct address; this is an act of praise and thanksgiving for their deliverance from a common enemy. In both cases, the blessing increases power and renown; it bestows strength on Abram from God and fosters an increase of God's renown in the world. Praise is always a word to God and a word about God; it witnesses to God and thereby increases the divine renown in the world (see Exod 18:10, also spoken by a nonchosen one in the wake of an experience of salvation). The text sets both dimensions of blessing in Israel's later worship during the time of Abram.

The tithe Abram gives to Melchizedek refers to the spoils; Abram leaves the other 90 percent with the king of Sodom, except for what the young men take (v. 24). Abram thereby gratefully acknowledges what Melchizedek has proclaimed to him on behalf of God and implicitly recognizes the legitimacy of Melchizedek's priesthood of the same God whom Abram worships. The OT mentions the tithe elsewhere only in connection with regular worship practices; hence we may infer that it functions here as part of the larger ritual of meal and blessings.[108] In this typical exchange, the priest gives the blessing and the worshiper responds. Tithing serves as an act of worship, not a military-political settlement. This account may legitimize later worship practices by rooting them in the story of Abram (cf. Jacob's vow of a tithe in 28:22).

Verse 17 introduces the king of Sodom, but then he drops into the background after Melchizedek's arrival. The two kings have different agendas. The king of Sodom represents the cities liberated by Abram. With worship completed, he generously indicates that Abram should keep the recaptured goods, but the persons (such as Lot) are to be returned. The king focuses on the disposition of the booty (v. 21), a major portion of which was Lot's (vv. 11-12, 16). The problem of who should keep the spoils of war troubled Israel at various times (see Joshua 7), though here it is a matter of getting their own goods back.

The issue here is not simply whether Abram will take the spoils, but whether he

108. Westermann, *Genesis 12-36*, 203.

will take Lot's goods and use them (and that of others) for gaining hegemony in Lot's land, a matter that had just been settled (13:6-12). In some sense, this discussion recapitulates chap. 13: Abram refuses an explicit opportunity to invest himself in Lot's land. Abram would thereby have become rich at Lot's expense and complicated his relation to Lot's land (e.g., he would have been obligated to the king of Sodom; cf. Gideon, who refuses to accept the offer of kingship for himself, Judg 8:22-23). Abram's refusal also gives his later intercession on behalf of Sodom a higher level of credibility. Abram refuses to go back on his agreement with Lot. His refusal depends on an oath, sworn to God Most High, the Creator, that he would not take anything, not even a thread or a shoestring (the smallest items). Abram did let his allies take their share, however.

This text, then, does not simply focus on Abram's choosing not to enrich himself, but centers on an issue of justice—his own agreement with Lot. The author presented Abram's behavior as a model for later Israelite leaders (see 1 Kings 21).

REFLECTIONS

1. As with chaps. 12–13, this chapter also mirrors a subsequent period of Israel's history: the land settlement, the judges, and the Davidic empire.

The six peoples listed in 14:5-7 (from the region around the Pentapolis of 14:2, 8) are among those encountered by Israel on its journey to Canaan. For the four kings (14:1, 9)—representing the world powers known from that era—to have conquered these peoples means gaining control of routes and lands that are integral to Israel's later movement into the promised land. Abram, in conquering the kings, not only frees the peoples there, but clears that region of powerful outside forces. More basically, Abram, as military leader, embodies later Israel. In effect, Abram takes over the promised land by conquest!

We have noted the formal similarity of this story with those of the judges. In this way Abram becomes *a savior figure* for Israel. Continuities with the Gideon story are especially strong. The 300 men of Gideon (Judg 7:7) face a situation not unlike that encountered by Abram's 318 men, and they effect comparable liberation. Moreover, the link between Abram and Melchizedek anticipates later relationships between David and the Jebusites of Jerusalem (Psalm 110; 2 Sam 5:6-10); compare also David's campaign against the Amalekites (1 Samuel 30). The covenant in chap. 15 occurs now with good reason. Abram's own history also parallels that of David.

2. In Abram's military action against the four kings, a solitary individual comes into view: Lot. For Abram, the individual does not get lost amid all the movements of kings and armies. His actions could be ascribed to human foolishness, but Abram's concern for his nephew reaches beyond simple common sense or a careful calculation of possible gains and losses. Moreover, when it comes to the disposition of the booty, Abram remains true to his agreement with Lot and returns his goods.

Moreover, Abram does not pursue a strategy of rescuing only Lot from among those captured. He acts in such a way as to liberate all captives from Sodom and Gomorrah, apart from an assessment of whether they deserved it, or whether their behaviors up to this point would justify the risk. This action links up with Abram's intercession on behalf of these cities in chap. 18.

3. The author describes Abram's group almost entirely in the language of the family. The story pits family against nation. When combined with the focus on Lot, family interests take priority over those of nations and kings. For the sake of the family, it may be necessary to challenge efforts made by national forces. Peace and war are matters that affect nations because they deeply affect families. It is for the sake of the family that Abram finally makes his decisions regarding war and peace.

This text presents issues of war and peace not as matters for chosen people only; all who oppose the subjugation of others (e.g., v. 24) become involved, whether they are people of God or not. God the Creator has an impact on the lives of "outsiders" so that they work toward the peace and well-being of communities not their own. The "goodness" of the creation as stated by God in Genesis 1 manifests itself in the lives of communities outside those who have been specifically called and chosen.

4. Although v. 20 attests that God is effectively engaged in this conflict, the text offers no reference to divine intervention (or speaking). The report of the battle recalls only Abram's abilities as a military strategist and leader. Hence, the battle involves multiple (divine and human) agencies. Nonetheless, Melchizedek ascribes the victory to God. In fact, the battle is not simply a victory, but a rout. The reader receives the image of kings and armies tumbling all over themselves to get away (the same language describes the victories of these kings in vv. 5, 7!)—no doubt designed to impress the reader with the boldness and cleverness of Abram in defeating a much larger force and rescuing the kidnapped persons and their possessions. Abram, as a Gideon-like figure, comes through in larger-than-life proportions. Although Abram's talents and skills are not to be played down, God makes the victory possible.

5. El Elyon probably carries the sense of "God of gods." While Melchizedek's God language is not new to Abram—indeed he claims it as his own in the oath he swore prior to his encounter with Melchizedek (v. 22)—he also claims that *Yahweh* is the name of El Elyon. Each worships the same God; even more, Melchizedek confesses their God as both creator (v. 19) and redeemer (v. 20). But Abram *knows* that the name of this God of gods is Yahweh.

This narrative confesses God the Creator, maker of heaven and earth (קנה *qānâ*; see Exod 15:16; Deut 32:6; Ps 139:13), as the *liberator.* Earlier confessional language for the Creator, evident in both Abram's earlier oath (v. 22) and Melchizedek's blessing (v. 19), appears in doxological service for this moment of salvation. The God confessed as creator of heaven and earth (not simply of human beings) becomes central to the faith of principals from this early period, including both Abram and Melchizedek; the narrator does not introduce a later theological development. The fact that both men worship God with this language also indicates that ancient Israelites presumed some commonality in faith to exist between the progenitors of the later Israelites and Canaanites. This shared belief, too, witnesses to the work of God the Creator in both communities; even more, it is witness to the *knowledge* of God the Creator, indeed a Creator who liberates, outside of the chosen family.

6. The theme of blessing relates to its use elsewhere in Genesis. In 12:1-3, God promises blessing to Abram; Melchizedek helps to fulfill that promise, mediating the divine blessing to him. Although Abram earlier experienced God's blessing in his life,

Melchizedek explicitly does what God has promised to do. Moreover, he thus recognizes Abram as the blessed one of God, even though Melchizedek stands outside that family. Consistent with 12:1-3, Abram has been a blessing to Melchizedek (and others) in and through what he has done in ridding the country of its predators. The text presents a triangular repetition of blessing, from God to Abram to Melchizedek (representing the nonchosen), and then back again from Melchizedek to Abram to God. Significant religious links are thus made between Israel and at least some elements of the Canaanite populace.

7. Why would Abram make the disposition of the booty a matter of oath to God (v. 22)? We have suggested that Lot's presence explains much here, though in the context of other factors. Some look to Abram's generosity of spirit, or a recognition that Sodom's goods were not his to do with as he would, for Sodom was not the defeated one; it would be improper for the liberator to enrich himself at the expense of the liberated. Is there a concern here for the enrichment of the "church" at the expense of its liberated members? The Sodomites had just experienced deliverance; to take away from that experience by keeping all their goods would be to intrude on the salvific experience itself. It might even appear to make the liberation conditional upon receiving the gift! How religious leaders handle the issue of "giving" may obscure the graciousness of the saving experience.

8. Hebrews 5–7 depends more heavily on Ps 110:4 than on Genesis 14. Basically the argument runs like this: Abram (hence his descendant Aaron, father of the Levitical priesthood) acknowledged the primacy of Melchizedek and his priesthood through the giving of a tithe. Hence, Jesus Christ, who belongs to the priestly order of Melchizedek, reaches back beyond Aaron's priesthood in typological (not historical) fashion. This establishes ancient, pre-Abrahamic, pre-Israelite priesthood roots for the Christly priesthood, thereby declaring its preeminence, and so Hebrews uses Melchizedek not unlike David and Solomon did.

GENESIS 15:1-21, THE COVENANT WITH ABRAM

COMMENTARY

From a source-critical perspective, vv. 1-6 have at times been considered the beginning of the E source, with much of vv. 7-21 assigned to J. In recent years, scholars have advanced many differing proposals regarding the history of this material, but no consensus has emerged. An ancient author may have woven a narrative around three originally independent God speeches. Links with the Davidic tradition seem particularly prominent, and suggest one stage for the material. The final redaction presents perceptible unity, centering on promise, possibly with an exilic provenance (cf. Lev 26:44-45).

This chapter differs from the usual ancestral story, being more like 18:16-33 or chaps. 1–3;

therefore, it could be called a theological narrative. The reader may discern movement within the chapter in the dialogue between God and Abram (the first recorded in the Abraham story), centering on key questions Abram raises regarding offspring and land. The two narrative segments (vv. 1-6, 7-21) have similar structures: divine promise (vv. 1, 7), Abram's questioning (vv. 2-3, 8), and God's response with reassuring words and deeds (vv. 4-5, 9-21). At another level, the chapter moves from Abram's vision (vv. 1-11) to his sleep (vv. 12-21).

Some scholars identify this structure as the lament-salvation oracle pattern;[109]

109. Westermann, *Genesis 12–36*, 216-17.

however, each section *begins* with a divine promise. They are more like narratives in which a question or objection follows the promise (e.g., Judg 6:12-13). Hence, this text should be viewed more in terms of theological disputation (see 18:23-33). The text's mood may reflect exilic discussions regarding divine promises.

15:1-5. The expression "the word of the LORD came" (vv. 1, 4), so common in the prophets, occurs only here in the Pentateuch (cf. Abraham as prophet in 20:7 and the link to Davidic promises in 2 Sam 7:4). This link to prophetic texts gives to the promises a special status; this is not "just another" divine word. That the word comes in a "vision" (see 46:2) reinforces this prophetic quality. Theophanies share similar formal features: the divine self-identification, the reassuring word not to fear, and the promise (see 26:24; 46:3). The vision may continue through v. 11.

The phrase "after these things" attests a close relation to the preceding narrative (see 22:1). This word provides God's response to Abram's actions in chap. 14, confirming the judgment of Melchizedek.[110] The link between the identification of Yahweh as "shield" (מגן *māgēn*) in 15:1 and 14:20, where God Most High has "delivered" (*miggēn*) Abraham, is especially important (for God as shield in Davidic contexts, see 2 Sam 22:3, 31, 36; Ps 144:2). Abram had refused any spoils, but God now sees to Abram's "reward." God promises that Abram will receive his "spoils" from God (cf. v. 14; Psalm 132 for David; Isa 40:10). (The NIV has God as the reward, but no such image for God occurs elsewhere.)

The "reward" in v. 1 thus involves neither deliverance nor a promise of land or posterity (those have already been promised). In the context provided by chap. 14, God's "reward" introduces a promise of spoils—the content of which is not made clear—in recognition of Abram's faithful action on behalf of others, including the king and people of Jerusalem. The promises of offspring and land come later, not in view of what Abram has done, but in response to his questions.

God's promise prompts Abram's question in vv. 2-3 ("Lord GOD" is rarely used, and

110. For ties between the chapters, see Sarna, *Genesis*, 112.

its import uncertain). In royal terms, Abram raises the question of dynasty: What good will spoils be, if I cannot pass them on to my children? (Cf. Davidic texts: 2 Sam 7:11-16; Ps 132:11-12, 17-18.) The question turns the issue from "reward" generally to an unfulfilled promise, God's promise of offspring (12:7; 13:15-16). This impatience is repeated in v. 3, but now centered on "seed," suggesting the depth of his concern; the focus of the verb—now in a statement rather than a question—has moved to what God has *not* given rather than to what God will give. The repetition about his servant may be designed to motivate God, as if to make sure God understands the implication of nonfulfillment: Eliezer will be Abram's heir. Is the promise of offspring still in place? The text focuses not on whether there will be an heir (Eliezer of Damascus—a difficult Hebrew phrase—could be adopted), but whether the heir will be from Abram's own line, a matter of great importance in that culture. What God had promised was "seed," not simply an "heir."

God speaks to Abram's concerns, with "heir" repeated and word order designed to emphasize the point: No, Eliezer will not be your heir. Yes, one whom you will father will be your heir (see 2 Sam 7:12). Indeed, his "seed" will be as numerous as the stars in the sky. The stars are not a sign to Abram, but a rhetorical move to make a point about the promise in the face of his questions: God keeps promises (cf. Deut 1:10; 10:22 for fulfillment). The image does not center on power, but on stability and sheer numbers (note the repetition). This rhetorical shift from dust (13:16) to stars suggests stability and security in a way that dust does not (see Jer 33:20-26 for its reference to Davidic offspring; 31:35-37).

15:6. This verse is commonly cited, not least because of its prominent use in the NT (Rom 4:3, 20-24; Gal 3:6; James 2:23).

Unlike his response to the promise of v. 1, Abram *believes* God; i.e., he trusts in the one to whom his faith clings. Abram fixes his heart on God, rests back in the arms of the promise-giver. The narrator, and not Abram, states this, perhaps to move more naturally (from within the vision) into theological reflection. Here the narrator interprets Abram's faith. This does not speak to the (need for such) faith in the narrator's own time; Abram's faith is not restricted to this later generation.

Abram's faith was "reckoned to him as righteousness." The verb for "reckon" likely has a cultic background wherein the priest formally declares that a gift has been properly offered (Lev 7:18; 17:4).[111] In response to Abram's faith, God in effect functions as a priest, although outside of a worship setting, and *formally* declares that Abram is righteous (cf. Ps 106:31). Righteousness (צדקה *ṣĕdāqâ*) often involves doing justice to a relationship in which one stands (cf. 38:26; 18:23-26; 7:1); here it refers to what Abram *becomes* by virtue of God's declaration *in view of his faith*. (Credit language [see NIV] is less than adequate because it suggests a divine keeping of account books.)

15:7-21. The author structures this section in a way similar to vv. 1-6. It begins with a divine self-identification: "I am the LORD who brought you [יצא *yāṣā*] from Ur of the Chaldeans" (v. 7; see 11:28). This language may also refer to the exodus, so that Abram's journey anticipates Israel's (see v. 14; Exod 3:7-10; 6:6-7; 20:2). God's promise here focuses on the gift of a land, a creational goal—life in a land he can call his own.

Abram requests a sign, some concrete indication that this will be so (v. 8), to which God responds positively. While the question in v. 2 focuses on *God's giving,* this question focuses on *Abram's knowing.* God clearly responds to this new issue (v. 13): *Know* for certain (with infinite absolute verb, cf. 24:14). A key point: Abram's knowing will come not only from what God says, but also from what God *does.*

God's response to Abram's question involves a rite, for which Abram must prepare. *God,* rather than the human being, goes through the rite and submits to its terms. While there are extra-biblical parallels to some of the details,[112] Jer 34:18-20 provides the only biblical analogy, where participants walked between divided animals and thereby invoked death upon themselves should they be unfaithful to the terms of the covenant. Not a regular sacrificial act (animals used for sacrifice are specified, but too many elements of the sacrificial ritual are missing), it is a special rite for the formalization of a

solemn oath or promise, which is what "making a covenant" entails in this context (v. 18). The promise works itself out as a ritual event, involving both word and deed.

God asks Abram to become involved in the preparation of the rite. The narrative focuses not simply on what God will *say;* the *entire rite* will constitute an answer to Abram. He goes beyond the divine directive (v. 10), suggesting that he is familiar with the rite. Note that Abram brings the animals directly *to God* (v. 10), so that we should think of the messenger of God in human form. We do not know why the birds were the only animals not divided, why the animals had to be three years old, or the meaning of v. 11. It does evoke some basic themes of the rite, involving a life-and-death matter. At the least, it stresses Abram's vigilance and care in the preparation. An allegorical interpretation, where, for example, the birds of prey are foreign nations, perhaps Egypt, whom Abram drives away, seems strained in view of Jer 34:18-20.[113]

The rite (vv. 12-19) begins at sunset (v. 12) and concludes in total darkness (v. 17). The darkness in v. 5 seems at odds with v. 12, but vv. 1-11 are visionary (so v. 1).

Abram falls into a deep sleep, with all dark and foreboding (see Job 4:12-16). Darkness appears integral to the rite, perhaps to shroud what God does. Such darkness symbolizes dreamlike seeing and knowing (cf. 28:10-22), which penetrates to the deepest recesses in Abram's being.

God, symbolized by the smoke and fire, actually passes through the divided animals (v. 17). God here acts alone; this specifies the unilateral character of the promise. The deity takes on the only obligation in this covenant (royal grants in the ancient Near East are a possible parallel). God's personal involvement constitutes the unusual character of the rite. In an act of self-imprecation, God in effect puts the divine life on the line, "writing" the promise in blood! "God's swearing by his own self" refers to this promise (and 22:16; 24:7; 26:3; 50:24). The author uses this phrase because God cannot invoke a higher power regarding the penalty. In some sense Abram functions as a witness, because he is involved in the preparations. God's "swearing" also

111. Von Rad, *Genesis,* 184-85.
112. See Sarna, *Genesis,* 114-15.
113. See Wenham, *Genesis 1–15,* 332.

alludes to promises to David (2 Sam 3:9; Pss 89; 100:4; 132:11) and to Noah (Isa 54:9).

Verses 13-16 are a divinely spoken word about the future, for Abram personally (v. 15) and his descendants (vv. 13-14, 16). Then, in conjunction with God's passing through the divided animals (v. 17), the deity proclaims an unconditional promise of the land (vv. 18-21).

We may discern that vv. 13-16 (and not just vv. 18-21) are integral to Abram's request expressed in the language of knowing (v. 13). The upshot of this prophetic word resides in v. 16b (the only proper name occurs here), because it explains the long delay before the fulfillment of the promise of v. 7. The sins of the Amorites (i.e., Canaanites) will not have "yet reached [their] full measure"; it takes time for sins to have their full effects (see Exod 20:5, note the reference to the fourth generation; Lev 18:24-25). Verses 13-16 involve the nations, as does chap. 14; God judges them, whether they oppress Israel (v. 14) or are iniquitous more generally (v. 16), and thereby delivers Abram's descendants (this time with spoils) and enables them to have a home of their own.

The relationship between the 400 years of v. 13 (Acts 7:6; 430 years in Exod 12:40; cf. Gal 3:17) and the fourth generation of v. 16 remains uncertain and may reflect different traditions. The "generation" probably refers to a lifetime (more or less than 100 years, see 6:3; Ps 90:10; Isa 65:20). It could, however, refer literally to the fourth generation—namely, Jacob's sons; they come back from a kind of exile (in Haran) and begin to settle in the land (cf. the "Amorites" in 48:22), a process not completed for centuries. Since "Egypt" does not appear in v. 13, the author does not appear concerned to speak about the future with precision. Hence, readers might apply the word to more than one life situation (fourth-generation language would work well for the exiles).

Abram himself will not see the land, and his descendants will do so only after considerable delay. Abram's relationship to the land remains tied to a much larger divine purpose than his own personal life. Because Abram knows that God will continue to be at work on behalf of the promise, he can die in peace after a full life and will "go to" his ancestors

(see 25:8, "gathered to his people"; on Sheol, see 37:35). This personal note about a good life and death also responds to Abram's question about knowing, for in some sense it prefigures that of his descendants (and that may be why v. 15 comes before v. 16). His descent into death will be the experience of his descendants as well. Unlike him they will return to the land, but Abram will receive a kind of immortality.

The ancestral promise, yet delayed in its fulfillment, will come to pass. Verses 18-21, which recollect an earlier moment in the rite ("on that day"), return to the basic promise in greater detail and in specific association with God's commitment (v. 17). The narrative here returns to the beginning (v. 7) in its reiteration of the promise. This involves more than an inclusio; the situation at the end of this text has changed from the beginning. The promise depends decisively on the very nature of God; God has staked God's very own life on the promise.

These boundaries are important to the people of God at various times in their history (cf. Deut 11:24; Josh 1:4; Isa 27:12). They extend from the Euphrates to the "Brook of Egypt" (not the Nile, but of uncertain location). That God has promised such a land, however, does not necessarily mean that they *must* possess every territory noted or at all times. Only with Solomon does the land even approach this size, and then not totally (1 Kgs 5:1, 4; 8:65). This list of ten peoples stands unique and in contrast with most OT lists, which have five to seven names enumerated; they all lived within a territory smaller than that envisaged in v. 18.

We do not hear Abram's response to God's unilateral promise. This may be because of the way God enables Abram's knowing. The event functions at levels of consciousness deeper than in vv. 1-6. Yet, the point of this rite lies elsewhere. God's response to Abram more than matches Abram's faith in God (v. 6). God, in swearing by the divine self, does justice to the relationship with Abram and thereby shows forth the divine righteousness. Abram trusts, and God can be trusted. Abram's faith is matched by God's faithfulness.

REFLECTIONS

1. If our analysis of Genesis 12–14 is correct, wherein the later history of Israel from the descent into Egypt to the kingship of David is prefigured in Abram's own life, then Genesis 15 caps that story off in its talk about covenant. The covenant with Abram prefigures the covenant with David. The latter exists in fundamental continuity with God's commitments to Abraham; in the Davidic kingship, God's promises to Abram find a renewed realization.

The covenant in these chapters parallels that of David. God chooses Abram (12:1-3); God chooses David (1 Samuel 16). God saves Abram from Egypt (12:10-20); God saves David from his enemies (2 Sam 5:24-25; 7:1). Abram worships God (12:7-8; 13:18); David worships as well (2 Sam 6:15-17). God establishes the covenant with both (15:18; 2 Samuel 7). We may discern a consistent order: election, deliverance, faith/worship, covenant. God's choosing and saving actions constitute the foundation of the covenant; God establishes the covenant with those who have faith, evidenced not least in worship. The covenant does not establish the relationship; it becomes a moment where God's promises spoken to faithful ones carries an obligation for God.

Moreover, God's "bringing out" Abram from one land to another (v. 7) prefigures more than exodus and land settlement. The prophets use similar language to speak of a new bringing out of Israel by God (Jer 16:14-15; 23:7-8; Ezek 34:13). Abram prefigures the return of the exiles from that same far country to the land promised them. The specification of boundaries in vv. 18-21 proclaims that God's promises concerning this expanse of land are still in place (cf. Lev 26:44-45).

2. Regarding Abram's "reward," God expresses concern about the faithfulness of human beings, since they affect the future of God's intentions for the world. What people do counts for God as well as for the world. Hence, reward ought not to be thought of in simplistic terms, a "stars in my crown" mentality. The matter remains interrelational, not unlike the role that recognitions play among human beings. God, too, recognizes the contributions people make toward realizing God's plans for the world.

3. Abram believes in God without having any concrete evidence that God's promise will come to pass (Heb 11:1, 8-12). Abram's faith (v. 6) has been enabled by what God has done in the previous verses. God's word makes Abram's faith possible, indeed creates faith; faith arises not from within him or by his own resources. Rather, God particularizes the promise for Abram by *addressing the specific situation* opened up by Abram's question. Abram has expressed some very particular needs concerning the future of his family, and God responds directly to those questions. Not just any word from God will do; the promise of v. 1 did not issue in v. 6. God put the promise in relation to the need, and in a particular rhetorical fashion.

This way of speaking of Abram's faith may be related to the context in which the passage was written. It could be the exile or any time of great difficulty for the Israelites' faith. How can anyone believe the promises of God in such a time? Nothing in the present situation provides a reason to believe. The task for the proclaimer of promises is to link the promise to actual life situations using the most penetrating rhetorical images possible. One may so speak the promises that the hearer will come to believe that nothing is so difficult in the present circumstance as to prevent God from seeing them through to completion.

4. Upon reading v. 8, one may well ask, What has happened to Abram's faith, so amply evident in 15:6? Should such faith be seeking signs? Evidently, believing and seeking signs do not necessarily stand over against each other (see Exod 3:11-12). It is not unnatural to faith, or unbecoming to the believer, that questions persist in the midst of belief. Indeed, if the just-declared statement of righteousness indicates that the God-Abram relationship exists in good order, then his question is appropriate.

5. In this context, covenant means a promise under oath, solemnly sworn, not an agreement or contract, and the making ("cutting") has reference to the rite with cut animals. God unilaterally declares and swears to it at his own initiative. The promise grants the land with specific boundaries to Abram's descendants. Not a future gift, it is now theirs (they are in a land that is "not theirs," v. 13). God makes the covenant with one who has faith.

God will never nullify this promise. It is *by* Yahweh, as God assumes obligation (and hence not strictly "legal"). Yet, the covenant has been made *with* Abram, a person whose faith has just been acclaimed, though not in a contractual sense. The relational element cannot be divorced from the content of covenant. Making and keeping promises to Abram entails a relationship of consequence, an ongoing attending to the promise as it relates to the lives of Abram and his descendants. Yet, while the promise is everlasting, God does not guarantee that every person or generation will participate in its fulfillment. The promise always remains available for believers to cling to, knowing that God remains available to fulfill it, but a rebellious generation may not live to see it. Faith does not function as a condition for the giving of the promise, but one can, by unbelief, leave the sphere of the promise. "Unconditional" promises do not make faithfulness irrelevant (see chaps. 17; 22; Exodus 26:5).

6. When compared to 12:7 and 13:14-17, the divine oath constitutes the new reality in this reiteration of the promise. God enters into that promise at a depth not heretofore evident, at least from Abram's perspective. This kind of divine involvement responds to Abram's question! Abram thereby moves God to take steps to assure Abram of the irrevocable nature of the promises. Abram should now "know" how deeply God has entered into this commitment.

7. Some commentators have had difficulty conceiving of God as a participant in an oath of self-imprecation; one's view of God does affect one's reading. However, that God would swear that the animal's fate would apply to God should the promises be broken is the most natural, and the more difficult, reading of the rite. This should give the reader pause before backing away from it. God commits to the promise at such a depth that God considers an experience of suffering and even death. This reveals the depth of the divine faithfulness to Abram and the divine willingness to become vulnerable for the sake of the promise. This text should be associated with other passages about divine suffering (e.g., Hos 11:8).[114] These levels of divine vulnerability resonate in the minds of Christians because of a comparable move that God makes in the incarnation and at the cross. In that event, God actually does enter into suffering and death on behalf of the promises. In Jesus Christ, those possibilities are not only a potential divine move, but they become actual as well, and all for the sake of the promises.

8. In v. 16, the descendants of Abram will receive the land, not because of their own qualities of being or life, but because the sins of its present inhabitants will reach such proportions that they will be engulfed in their effects (see Deut 9:4-5; Lev 18:24-28; 1 Kgs 21:26). The relationship between sin and judgment means that sins do not necessarily have immediate deleterious effects. The judgment of God may work in an accumulative way, as a buildup of forces, and not as the result of a forensic divine act. Particularly in thinking about communities, it may take time for the effects to build up and overwhelm its perpetrators. The story of Sodom and Gomorrah may be considered the beginning of the fulfillment of this word, and the prophets did not hesitate to apply the very same principle to Israel itself. It invites reflection by the reader on the various

114. See Fretheim, *The Suffering of God.*

communal contexts to which one belongs; how close might we be to experiencing the "completion" of our iniquities?

The text remains open regarding some details of these matters, given the virtual absence of proper names and the ambiguity regarding timing. If so, the "plan of God" language for this text can be used only in a general way as well.[115] There is no effort to lay out the future with precision. As such, it opens up the text to generations of the people of God other than those of Abram. The text allows us to speak of comparable ways in which the people of God will experience life in the world, often as exiles and sojourners, oppressed and under just judgment. It also speaks to the way in which God will be involved in their lives, judging oppression and iniquity, delivering the people of God, and giving them a home in which to dwell.

9. God makes clear to Abram that there will be a delay in the fulfillment of the promise; 400 years is a long time. The story of God's people during those centuries attests that God's promises will move through dark and complex times. The people of God often want immediate fixes, instant gratification; this text might help teach the faithful to live with delay.

10. This chapter, particularly v. 6, is central to the apostle Paul (Romans 4; Galatians 3). For Paul, faith does not earn or merit righteousness. God's gracious action preceded anything that Abram is or does, and the word announcing that gracious action creates Abram's faith; at the same time, God's word can be resisted. Abraham becomes the father of all who have faith (see Eph 2:8-9). God observes Abraham's faith and declares Abraham to be righteous.

The Epistle of James uses this material for somewhat different reasons (2:18-24); he focuses not on faith but on response in life on the part of one who has faith. Faith should issue in a shape for life that corresponds to what God wills for the world. James draws on a common understanding of righteousness: to do justice to the relationship in which one stands. Abraham's works do justice to the relationship and thereby witness to his righteousness.

115. See Westermann, *Genesis 12–36*, 227.

GENESIS 16:1-16, HAGAR AND SARAI

COMMENTARY

Interest in this story has at times focused on the history of the Ishmaelites, bedouin tribes to the south and east of Canaan (see 25:12-18). More recent interest in Islam, which traces its religious heritage to Abraham through Ishmael, has renewed study in Ishmael's heritage in this and related texts (17:15-25; 21:8-21). Whatever its history, the present narrative has been decisively shaped by theological interests and integrated within the story of Abraham. The story has often been identified with the J source (with Priestly framing elements).

In terms of form, scholars have described the story as a "conflict narrative," centering on a conflict between two women, Sarai and Hagar.[116] The nature of this conflict has been much debated in recent years, not least by feminist scholars, who have provided much insight into the text.[117] At the same time, the conflict should be more broadly conceived in terms of the family of Abraham. This text must

116. See Westermann, *Genesis 12–36*, 235.
117. For a survey see K. P. Darr, *Far More Precious Than Jewels: Perspectives on Biblical Women* (Louisville: Westminster/John Knox, 1991).

be placed within the whole of Genesis, which reveals, in contemporary terms, a highly dysfunctional family system in which individuals—both male and female—are caught up in swirls of dissension beyond their own making or ability to control. This text narrates, fundamentally, a family problem. Yet, because the story occurs in a patriarchal system, the males involved deserve special blame, and this does not go entirely unrecognized by the narrator.

In terms of structure and plot, the story begins with a statement of the problem, and in a highly compact way moves through various difficulties toward an ambiguous resolution. While a division might be made between vv. 1-6 and vv. 7-14 from the perspective of the history of traditions, the inclusio provided by the repeated word *bear* (ילד *yālad*) in vv. 1-2 and 15-16 ties the chapter together into a unified whole. The chapter relates to what precedes by references to Egypt (12:10-20; 13:1, 10; 15:18) and the promise of a son—linking son with the blessing on nations. The text now shifts from a focus on land in chaps. 13–15 to a focus on a son in chaps. 16–21.

16:1-6. Sarai remains barren (see 11:30), and Abram has no children. The story moves quickly to Sarai's strategy, as she (not Abram) takes the initiative to resolve the matter. The author does not mention previous discussions or the shame associated with childlessness in that culture; nor does Sarai raise a moral issue, as if she were being judged for something she did. She raises only a theological issue; she *interprets* her situation to mean that God has kept her from having children, whether such were actually the case (see 20:18; 25:21; 29:31; 30:2, 22). At the same time, she recognizes that God does not act alone, that human agency is important ("by her"; cf. 4:1; 17:16; 19:32; 30:3-4). Humans can thwart the will of God concerning progeny by their sexual practices (38:9-10).

Sarai certainly knows that God has promised *Abram* offspring (15:4), but not necessarily by her. At the same time, she wants to have children she can call her own. To accomplish this, she makes a self-sacrificing move. She not only shares her husband sexually, but allows Hagar to be a *wife* to Abram; 16:3 portrays a formal act on Sarai's part. Ancient Near Eastern parallels show that

this was common practice.[118] Rachel and Leah take a similar initiative in 30:3-13, with God's apparent approval (30:6, 18). Since Sarai's strategy appears customary, she should not be condemned. Her decision stems not only from an interpretation of God's action, so that "she must do as she does,"[119] but from a recognition that God works through human agents.

Abram accedes to the plan, though without speaking. A problem arises when, after becoming pregnant with Abram's child, Hagar's attitude toward Sarai changes. The verb קלל (*qālal*) describes her action (also used in 12:3 for contempt shown to Abram's family), which would bring Hagar under the divine curse. Hagar somehow diminishes Sarai's status in view of her new place as mother-to-be of Abram's child (cf. Prov 30:23).

Hagar's *qālal* action certainly justifies Sarai's sharp raising of the issue with Abram (v. 5). Rather than voice her objections to Hagar, she speaks to Abram, the husband of both of them, presumably with the authority in such matters (and 12:3 was spoken to him). In language from the legal sphere, she accuses Abram and gives a rationale; he bears responsibility for this distressful situation (see the NIV). It was within his power to stop this kind of treatment of Sarai and his to settle now, and God will be the judge of how he handles the issue. By so appealing to God, Sarai gives evidence of her own relationship with God.

Abram's only speech in the chapter comes at this point (v. 6). Admitting no responsibility, he puts Hagar into Sarai's hand (i.e., power), giving Sarai authority to do as she wills. Abram thus tips the balance in favor of Sarai, giving no apparent regard for the effect it might have on Hagar. Abram has not handled this conflict very well, to say the least. Sarai seeks no reconciliation with Hagar, but treats her harshly. Sarai acts strongly (ענה *ʿānâ*, vv. 6, 9, 11) against the Egyptian and invites comparison with Exodus texts, for the author uses this verb to describe Israel's oppression *by Egypt* (15:13; Exod 1:11-12; Deut 26:6-7). Hagar, taking her future and

118. See Sarna, *Genesis*, 119.
119. See Westermann, *Genesis 12–36*, 238.

that of Sarai and Abram's child into her own hands, flees (see Exod 14:5) toward her home in Egypt (Shur is near the border). She prefers the dangers of the wilderness to continuing life in Abram's household. Ironically, she thinks she can find more freedom in Egypt than among God's chosen people! With this problem seemingly resolved, the issue of v. 1 seems to be front and center again, but not in this narrative. God remains focused on Hagar. Sarai and Abram have sent Hagar away, not God. God appears on the scene on behalf of this oppressed one, as one day God would for oppressed Israel.

16:7-16. Out in the same wilderness where Israel would later wander, Hagar encounters the "angel of the LORD" (repeatedly introduced, vv. 7, 9-11; cf. Moses in Exod 3:2). This figure, better called a messenger, should not be confused with later angelic beings. The narrator's report in v. 13 shows that Yahweh speaks to Hagar, and Hagar recognizes that she has seen God. This messenger is God in human form (cf. 21:17-19; 22:11-12, 15-16; 31:11, 13).[120]

Hagar's partial reply to God's inquiries (v. 8)—God does not predict her reply—suggests that she envisions no future; she can speak only of the past. God responds by focusing on the future. First, God directs Hagar to return to Sarai and to submit to her (Hagar's return is not noted). Given her treatment of Sarai in view of 12:3, she needs to get this matter resolved. She will not find salvation in being freed from Sarai and Abram as yet (though in her faith she stands on her own).

Instead of following through on the curse, as a mechanical view of the moral order might suggest, God responds to her affliction and makes promises to her (vv. 10-12). In fact, God names Hagar's affliction in exoduslike terms ('ānâ, v. 11). Unlike Abram and Sarai, God addresses her by name, and for the first time she speaks. God is present to her and draws her into conversation rather than reducing her to silence (vv. 8, 13).

The salvation Hagar receives focuses on the promise of a son. We can recognize the Abrahamic promises regarding offspring in v. 10 (13:16; 15:5), while in v. 11 we hear the familiar cadences of the annunciation in

Isa 7:14. Although the oracle in v. 12 is more difficult, Hagar's response remains positive (the narrator has a comparable view).[121] Ishmael will be free, roving the wilderness (the "wild ass" is celebrated by God in Job 39:5-8), and he will not be submissive to oppressive people like Sarai and Abram. He will be frequently at odds with others, but such tension often occurs between sedentary and nomadic groups in that world (OT texts project similar difficulties for the other side of Abram's family, too; cf. 25:23; 27:28-29, 39-40). He will live at odds with his kin (some translations [TNK] have him living "alongside"), but no OT text speaks of a fulfillment in these terms; such oracles are not interpreted as a precise shaping of the future (see 25:23).

Hagar will follow through on bearing the child for Abram; the possibilities for a future of nonoppression will thereby be opened up for her own family (see 21:13-21). While the reader might wish for a freer future for Hagar at this point, she moves with what has become possible in that situation, trusting in the word of God that the future will contain a new form of freedom. Salvation for Hagar must take the form of waiting, but she knows that God sees and hears the afflicted, and so she can rest in the knowledge that God keeps promises.[122]

Hagar's response in v. 13 shows her not only as a trusting spirit but a person of faith. She recognizes the messenger as the voice of God, though he offers no word of self-identification (cf. 31:11-13). Moreover, she publicly confesses that God has come to her rescue ("You are El-roi"—that is, a God of seeing or a God who sees me). The last phrase in v. 13 presents difficulties, but at the least it speaks of a mutual seeing on the part of God and Hagar (so the NIV), and may include the idea of still living after having seen God (so the NRSV; cf. Exod 33:20).

Hagar's new name for God presents a metaphor born of her experience of having been given a future and a hope, rather than an already existing name/epithet. This is not a "new" God who needs a name; the word to her from the messenger uses the name Yahweh (v. 11), as does the narrator (v. 13).

121. See von Rad, *Genesis*, 195.
122. See J. G. Janzen, "Hagar in Paul's Eyes and the Eyes of Yahweh (Genesis 16)," *HBT* 13 (1991) 1-22.

120. For detail, see Fretheim, *The Suffering of God*, 79-107.

Her confession focuses on a God who sees rather than a God who speaks. Her experience mirrors that of Leah and Jacob (29:32; 31:42) and Israel in Egypt, whom God also "sees" and delivers (Exod 2:25; 3:7; 4:31). The name she gives to the well also centers on the God who sees "me" (see the NRSV footnote to v. 14). By these namings the event is pressed into the memory of succeeding generations in terms of a seeing God. A parallel theme is sounded about a God who hears (v. 11). The name Ishmael, meaning "God hears," witnesses to God's hearing one in distress (see 17:20; 21:17; 29:33; 30:6, 17, 22). In this naming of God, Hagar (like Sarai) shows that she has an independent relationship with God.

The text presents God's promises of a son and descendants as *a genuine fulfillment* of God's promise to Abram (cf. v. 10 with 13:16; 15:5; cf. also 17:20; 21:13). Abram has a son in Ishmael and numerous descendants through him (25:12-18). In addition, v. 10 picks up on the promise in 1:28; God's designs for the creation are being fulfilled in and through him. One may assume that the promise of nationhood includes land (17:20),

although language about covenant does not occur. Hence, we ought not to minimize or set aside the vigorous promises given to Hagar and Ishmael.

Verses 15-16 confirm this understanding; they form an inclusio with vv. 1-2, with the verb *bear* (ילד *yālad*) occurring five times. Hagar bears "Abram a son," and Abram gives "his *son*" the name that *God* had given him (v. 11). This assumes that Abram was told of the encounter between Hagar and God and that Abram knows the significance of the name. Sarai does not appear; her intention (v. 2) seems not to be realized.

Genesis 17:15-27 allows such questions at this stage of the narrative (and to some extent in 21:10-13), where the decision as to Ishmael's status remains up in the air; only a new word from God resolves the issue. The reader of chap. 16 must not underinterpret these developments, as if Ishmael were a dead-end issue. Chapter 17 must be interpreted with the understanding that God's promise to Abraham has apparently been fulfilled. The passing of thirteen years between 16:16 and 17:1 reinforces this judgment.

REFLECTIONS

1. Hagar is Sarai's trusted servant; she no doubt came out of Egypt with Abram and his family (see 12:16). With this status, she possesses no choice and has no voice in becoming a surrogate mother; she is simply taken and given to Abram (v. 3). However much she may have accepted the customs of the time, her vulnerability ought not to be played down. She has no powers or rights should she be mistreated by those in authority over her. Since neither Abram nor Sarai ever names her (only God does, v. 8), and even though the narrator never calls her a slave, we are to be mindful of her precarious situation. Even more, the text stresses that Hagar is an *Egyptian* (vv. 1, 3; 21:9)! She is thus an outsider and an African.[123]

Hagar is the first person in Genesis to be encountered by the angel of God, and the first woman to be given promises (see 25:23). In response, Hagar becomes the *only* person in the OT to name God. She engages in theological formulation, using her own experience with God and the knowledge of God gained thereby to shape new language for God. She thereby shapes contemporary language for God in view of ever-changing human experience and new experiences of God in the midst of that change. Being open to naming God in new ways based on personal experience was not a luxury, but a necessity if God would accompany people in their changing lives.

2. At the same time, Sarai comes onto the scene for the first time as a character in her own right. She takes the initiative with her husband, taking charge on the issue of

---

123. For a portrayal of Hagar, see P. Trible, *Texts of Terror: Literary-Feminist Readings of Biblical Narratives* (Philadelphia: Fortress, 1984) 9-35.

offspring and not backing away from issues that need to be addressed. Although she treats Hagar harshly, Abram tacitly participates as well. Many commentators are hard on Sarai, claiming that she seeks to fulfill the promise by her own efforts. Von Rad is typical: Sarai's is "a fainthearted faith that cannot leave things with God and believes it necessary to help things along . . . a child so conceived in defiance or in little faith cannot be the heir of promise."[124] Such a judgment reflects a docetic view of God's ways of working in the world. God often works in and through humans to carry out the divine purposes in Genesis (and the rest of the OT). Theologically, it should be stated as strongly as possible: Sarai should not in any way be faulted for taking the initiative, and the means she uses are typical for that culture.

3. Language about Sarai's (and tacitly Abram's) mistreatment of Hagar (ענה *'ānâ*, v. 6) also describes Israel's oppression by the Egyptians (15:13; Exod 1:11-12) and commandments that forbid oppression binding on Israel (Exod 22:21-22). The story of the outcast contains themes and experiences parallel to that of the insider. Given the prefiguring concerns played out in chaps. 12–15, this chapter may also reflect how Israel, or any who have been delivered, can quickly deny their own history. It is a sad dimension of Israel's story and that of the people of God in every age that the liberated so often become the oppressor.[125] While this kind of behavior can occur at the level of community or society, this text would have us examine the family sphere more closely, not least the relationship between husband and wife or parents and children.

4. The author gives this tale, so attentive to persons outside the chosen family, considerable space in the story of Abraham; it will not be the last time. In terms of the usual recounting of the salvation history, this story doesn't belong; it's a dead end. At best, the story seems to have only a negative purpose. The fact that women play a key role in this story has probably meant for a certain neglect as well.

Such narrow perspectives will not do. Israel's God plays an important role in the lives of these "unchosen" ones. Indeed, God appears to Hagar, converses with her, and makes promises to her that approximate those given to Abram (vv. 10-11). This divine concern will continue in chap. 21. The author portrays God as a *Creator* who makes *promises* to those who do not belong to the "people of God" (which should include their descendants, both physical and spiritual, in Islam). God acts in *both word and deed* outside the boundaries of what we normally call the community of faith. God's attentiveness to Hagar and Ishmael comes more in spite of what Abram's family has done than because of their concern for outsiders and their welfare. Indeed, God enters the picture most decisively at precisely that point when *exclusion* from the chosen family has taken place (the move from v. 6 to v. 7). The chosen people cannot confine God's works and ways—even words of gospel and promise (vv. 10-11)—within their often oppressive and narrowly conceived structures. One ought to recognize that "God has not exclusively committed himself to Abram-Sarai."[126]

What does it mean that Hagar and Ishmael receive the *continuing* promises of God? What might the fulfillment of such promises mean for the people of God, not least for their continuing relationships to the descendants of Ishmael in Islam? What might it mean to continue to confess in and through the retelling of this story that the Ishmaelites are who they are because God has kept promises? A key question for the modern interpreter thus becomes, Has God been faithful to these promises made to Hagar and Ishmael? In search of the answer, we should remember that Ishmael does not receive negative treatment in the rest of the OT, and the Ishmaelites never seem to be in conflict with Israel. When Isaac and Ishmael bury their father, no sign of conflict

124. Von Rad, Genesis, 196.
125. See Westermann, *Genesis 12–36,* 241.
126. Brueggemann, *Genesis,* 153.

appears (25:9). One of David's sisters married an Ishmaelite (1 Chr 2:17), and an Ishmaelite and a Hagrite were administrators for David (1 Chr 27:30-31).

5. At times the community of faith can so center on the speaking God that the theme of the seeing God is left aside. Not so with Hagar, and not so with Israel either. Israel's confession includes the claim that its God sees the human situation and responds to it (see 29:31-32; 31:12, 42; Exod 2:25; 3:7; 4:31). God's seeing (and hearing) remains crucial, because it means that God's speaking will address the human need in a precise way. God's word can bring a future and a hope because God has seen the situation and, hence, has been able to address actual needs in a specific way. God's saving acts respond directly to creaturely need.

On Paul's use of this story in Galatians 4 and other aspects of its significance, see commentary on chap. 21.

GENESIS 17:1-27, COVENANT AND CIRCUMCISION

COMMENTARY

Interpreters usually understand this chapter (assigned to P) as an alternate version of the covenant in chap. 15. Although the two texts do have distinct origins, the redactor of the present text probably does not so view the matter. Most likely we should view this covenant as a *revision* (not simply a renewal) of the earlier covenant in view of events that seem to take the future of the promise in directions not fully satisfactory (cf. the relationship between the covenants in Exodus 24 and 34, with the intervening sin in Exodus 32). The promise of a son (15:4) has been fulfilled, and thirteen years pass between 16:16 and 17:1 (vv. 24-25), during which time Abram lives with what 16:15-16 and 17:18 suggest to be a settled matter. It may be that, during these years, everyone—including God—lives with Ishmael to see what opens up regarding the future. Experience shows (for reasons unknown) that Ishmael will not do. The story begins again, this time with Sarai as mother (v. 19), not simply Abram as father. In a new moment for God, he reveals a new name and shapes a somewhat different future. This new divine identity, correlating with newly shaped promises, associates with *both* Abraham and Sarah, who are also given new names.

God particularizes the promises in other new ways. For example, the promise focuses less on land and more on Abraham as a progenitor of a *multitude* of nations and kings

(vv. 4-6), which also involves a promise to Sarah (v. 16). The covenant as *everlasting* is new, though the land was so viewed in 13:15. The links with creation (cf. 1:28) are also new; in some sense the command within creation is focused in this family (cf. Exod 1:7). God being God to Abraham and his descendants (mentioned thirteen times) provides a new element, or at least a new formulation (v. 7). Finally, the text highlights Abraham's response within this covenant.

17:1-22. The author structures this segment as a typical theophanic narrative. (a) God's appearance: Given the appearances in human form elsewhere in the cycle (e.g., 16:7; 18:1) the reader should think of the divine messenger (note that God "went up" in v. 22). (b) Self-identification (El Shaddai): the meaning of this name remains uncertain, perhaps "God of the Mountains" (Breasts?; recalled in Exod 6:3), commonly translated "God Almighty" (based on Greek and Latin renderings). (c) A word to the recipient, including commands as well as promises: The three introductions focus on God (v. 4, "as for me"), Abraham (v. 9, "as for you"), and Sarah (v. 15, "as for Sarah"). (d) Abraham responds to the word (vv. 17-18), occasioning a more emphatic and particular divine word (vv. 19-21), after which God departs. The narrative concludes with a report of Abraham's obedience to God's command (vv. 23-27).

The word of God dominates the narrative. (1) God begins with imperatives (v. 1; cf. 12:1-2). As Noah did (6:9; cf. Pss 15:2; 101:2; Prov 20:7), Abraham is to walk before God (i.e., be loyal; 24:40 and 48:15; cf. 5:22-24) and be blameless (i.e., unreserved faithfulness in every aspect of the relationship, but not sinless; so also Jacob, 25:27, and David, 2 Sam 22:24; cf. 1 Kgs 3:6). The second imperative presents the consequence of obeying the first (and you *will be* blameless). Walking before God does not constitute a condition for giving the covenant, but Abraham intends to do so; walking before God becomes obligatory for relationship *within* the covenant. As in chap. 15, God establishes the covenant with one who has faith (15:6; the same pattern occurs in covenants with Noah, Israel, and David). For Abraham to fall on his face (v. 3; cf. v. 17) involves a response of faith, agreeing to what God expects for one in a covenant relationship. Hence, v. 2 provides an announcement of what God will do if Abram acknowledges in faith that he intends to walk before God.

(2) God, having taken the initiative, makes (literally, gives) a covenant (i.e., speaks promises) with Abraham and with his descendants (note the ABBA structure in vv. 4*b*-5). The content of the covenant consists of vv. 4*b*-8 (note the colon at the end of v. 4*a*). One should understand covenant here as a royal grant, attested elsewhere in the ancient Near East. It bears close similarities to the covenants with Noah (9:10-17; see 6:9) and David (2 Sam 23:5; 7:8-17) involving stability, eternity, and unconditionality (though not apart from faithfulness). These are the components of this word of God:

(a) Abraham will be exceedingly fruitful (vv. 2, 6). These words recall the creation account (1:28; 9:1, 7). But that creational command here becomes a promise (and in 22:17). Looking forward, it will be conveyed to Isaac in 26:4, 24, from Isaac to Jacob in 28:3, but restated as a command by God in 35:11, and again as promise in 48:4. It also involves a promise made to Ishmael in 16:10 and 17:20. This command/promise is fulfilled in Exod 1:7 (anticipated in Gen 47:27). In other words, in Abraham's family the commands of creation are being fulfilled because of God's promise. The command reaches fulfillment because promise accompanies

it. "Abraham is the first fruit of the new creation."[127]

(b) Abraham and Sarah will be ancestors of a multitude of nations and kings, those whose physical ancestry can be traced to Abraham (see 28:3; 35:11; 48:4), for example, Edomites and Ishmaelites. Yet, as Sarna notes, the phrase "has a more universal application in that a larger segment of humanity looks upon Abraham as its spiritual father," including Christians and Muslims (see John 1:13).[128] "Kings" has Davidic links (see 49:8-12) and later takes on messianic overtones (see Matt 1:1).

(c) God will be God to Abraham and his descendants (vv. 7-8), a statement of divine commitment (see Exod 6:7). The repeated emphasis on descendants (vv. 7-10, 20) understands this promise to stand for all generations.

(d) Abraham will receive the land in which he now resides as an alien for an everlasting possession (v. 8; NRSV "perpetual holding"; cf. 13:15; 48:4). And so he lived in the land, but could not yet consider it his. The promise was for the future; it would not be fully realized in his lifetime (see chap. 23). This would have been an especially important word for landless exiles.

(3) God changes Abram's name to Abraham, a dialectal variation of the name Abram ("exalted father"), but here understood to carry a different meaning: "father of a multitude." A name change does not refer to a change in personality or character, but marks a new stage in his identification with the divine purpose. He must now live up to his new name, which focuses not on his personal relationship with God but on his relationship to the nations. The name looks outward, centered on the lives of others. Abraham's election involves mission.

(4) Abraham and his descendants (including Ishmael) are commanded to keep (שמר *šāmar*) the covenant. Genesis 18:19 and 26:5 articulate more precisely Abraham's "keeping," which involves more than circumcision (cf. Exod 19:5, referring to this covenant).[129] Generally, "keeping" means doing justice to, being faithful to, the relationship

127. Brueggemann, *Genesis*, 153.
128. Sarna, *Genesis*, 124.
129. See Fretheim, *Exodus*, 209-11.

with the promising God. Verse 10 does not identify covenant with circumcision (cf. v. 4); v. 13 b signifies that the covenant is marked in the flesh, an instance of synecdoche, a physical sign referring to the whole (covenant).

Circumcision serves as a *sign* of faithfulness to the covenant from the *human* side (different from the rainbow in 9:12-17, which is a sign for God); it resembles the sabbath of Exod 31:16-17. Although we read about Isaac's (21:4) and Jacob's sons' circumcisions (34:15), the OT seldom mentions the practice elsewhere.

The last clause in v. 14 does not derive causally from the first clause. Neglecting circumcision does not constitute the essence of breaking the covenant; such neglect signifies unfaithfulness, a mark of an already broken relationship. An act of omission symbolizes an act of commission. Those who are unfaithful can remove themselves from the sphere of the covenant; the promises of God, however, will always remain in place for the faithful to cling to.

God will never be unfaithful, yet human unfaithfulness can lead to severe consequences (v. 14). What being "cut off" from the people entails is not certain (note the play on "cut"). The text does not refer explicitly to any action by court or cult—execution or excommunication; the matter is left up to God (see Lev 20:1-6). One has difficulty imagining that noncircumcised children would have "broken" the covenant. Rather, the text refers to the community in which circumcision functions as a sign (see the admixture of singular and plural "you"). The author may have in mind a situation where Israel had become lax, perhaps the exile. The repeated reference to slaves (vv. 12-13, 23, 27; is their status in question?) indicates that presence in the community is what matters, not racial stock or social standing.

(5) Sarai receives a new name and promises of blessing (twice!), nations, and kings (v. 16). The name Sarah (princess?) presents a less archaic form of Sarai; it may be related to the name Israel, and hence recognizes Sarah as the forebear of Israel and other nations. These promises are repeated for Sarah (even if spoken to Abraham); the text does not subsume her under Abraham, finding her importance for the future only through him. She participates genuinely in the covenant.

Abraham first responds by *internal* musing and laughter based on their ages as potential parents (v. 17; cf. 18:12; יצחק [*yiṣḥāq*], a play on the name for Isaac ["he laughs"], becomes a narrative theme, 18:12-15; 19:14; 21:6, 9). Then, he asks God (or claims?) that Ishmael be the one who bears the promise (v. 18). While Abraham responds by falling on his face in obeisance in v. 3, here he falls on his face in laughter. His questions suggest that this laughter expresses incredulity (contrast 15:6), or possibly bewilderment. Abraham's laughter appears similar to Sarah's (18:12), demonstrating that Sarah was not told what he here learns. He accepts the goal but not the means of gaining descendants.

Remarkably God does not chide Abraham; he simply says no, and speaks of a new son, to be named Isaac (God also names Ishmael, 16:11), with whom God will establish the covenant. God responds to Abraham's concerns, however. He speaks promises regarding Ishmael similar to those given Isaac; these amount to a covenant (though that word does not appear), which includes nationhood and royalty (see 21:13, 18; 25:12-16 lists the twelve princes). The heart of the difference would seem to be 12:3 b, the role of mediating blessing to the nations.

God answers Abraham's questions of v. 17 by asserting again that Sarah will be the mother of his son (21:1-7), and Isaac the one with whom the covenant will be continued (26:3-5). God's own decision results in the selection of Isaac. The reference to a male son (cf. 18:14) does not testify to absolute foreknowledge, but to God's knowing what God will do.

After the conversation, God leaves the scene, and the narrator repetitively reports that Abraham follows through on the divine command, himself wielding the knife for all male members of his household. The author refers to the circumcision of Ishmael, "his son," *three* times, and to that of the others twice (vv. 23-26). Abraham responds to the covenant on behalf of his own generation.

RELECTIONS

1. The common translation "God Almighty" (from Greek and Latin renderings) presents an unfortunate abstraction; it unpacks (and hence limits) the concrete image of mountains in a single direction; the image should be retained in translation or (typical for names) transliterated. The image of mountains for God occasions a variety of reflections (cf. Ps 36:7). As Hagar gave a new name to God in 16:13, so here God reveals a new name. God's new name matches the new names for Abraham and Sarah, signaling a new beginning in their relationship. The community of faith must be open to new names for God, names that may be more congruent with the life experiences of people in new times and places.

2. Circumcision was common among Israel's neighbors (and beyond), often as a rite of passage (see Jer 9:25-26; God assumes that Abraham knows the rite). God does not institute a new rite that would set Israel apart from its neighbors. God takes an existing practice—a sign from the world of creation—and "baptizes" it for use within the community of faith.

Circumcision provides a mark on the body, which symbolizes the command to walk before God, involving all aspects of the person's life. Relationship with God does not express itself simply as a spiritual journey; it draws in the bodily dimensions of life to which God lays claim. Women are included only by virtue of being members of a household where the males are circumcised (clitoridectomy, female circumcision, was and is practiced in other cultures). Yet, the later metaphoric use of circumcision (see below) becomes a way of including women.

The physical act of circumcision does not provide the primary sign of faithfulness to the covenant (v. 11). Although external and ineradicable, it was not a visible sign of belonging. Hence, it was, essentially, a sign of belonging for the individual, though also a sign for the community, who are thereby true to God's command. The eighth day may refer to the completion of creation in seven days, here applied to the individual, so that covenant becomes the realization of creation.

Having fulfilled this obligation, the way one's life is shaped remains consequential. Circumcision never guarantees; other traditions will speak of judgment on circumcised ones with an "uncircumcised heart" (Jer 4:4; 9:25; Ezek 44:7-9; cf. Deut 10:16; 30:6). One senses the danger in isolating religious forms from faith, as if the sign in and of itself will suffice. Circumcision will not be a sign if it points to nothing; it becomes an empty sign. The NT picks up on this spiritual circumcision (Phil 3:3; Col 2:11-13 links it to baptism). The NT neither condemns nor makes the sign decisive for membership in the Christian community (1 Cor 7:18-19; Gal 5:6; 6:12-15), a principle framed against those who thought it essential. Paul argues (Rom 4:9-12) that Abraham's faith was decisive for inclusion in the community before he was circumcised.

3. The use of the word *everlasting* with respect to the covenant (vv. 7, 13, 19) and the land (v. 8; cf. 13:15) may occasion questions about continuing applicability. These "terms" involve the promises *from God's side.* If those to whom such promises are made do not walk before God (namely, remain faithful) they can remove themselves from the sphere of promise and *everlasting* no longer applies to them in terms of either covenant or land. This possibility does not take away from the unconditionality of the covenant. Nonetheless, humans must remain faithful (22:16-19; 26:5, 24).

4. Ishmael, the one who stands outside the chosen line, remains integrally related to it due to his circumcision. Generally, the rite provides democratization: slaves as well as sons, foreigners as well as family, chosen as well as unchosen—are all included within its scope. Circumcision allows for a genuine openness to the outsider.

GENESIS 18:1-15, GOD VISITS ABRAHAM AND SARAH

COMMENTARY

Since Abraham's name does not occur until v. 6 (on v. 1, see the textual notes), we may judge that the editor has fully integrated this narrative into the larger story. While the story may not have originally centered on an appearance of God, it now does (18:1). While it differs in some ways from typical theophanic narratives (e.g., no self-identification of the deity), we may view the story as a variant of the form (cf. 16:7-14; 26:24). The divine appearance reaches completion when the deity leaves (18:33). We are not certain at what point Abraham recognizes that God has appeared to him.

Scholars often think this narrative (usually J) centers in the announcement of the birth of a son. Yet, inasmuch as the promise of a son through Sarah has just been emphasized (17:16), a somewhat broader function for the story seems likely. Both biblical and nonbiblical parallels combine the themes of hospitality and birth announcement; 2 Kgs 4:8-17, a story of a "man of God" and a Shunammite woman, provides a good example. Parallels in Greek literature—perhaps late developments of Near Eastern prototypes—include a story in which three gods in human form are received hospitably and give the childless host a son.[130] Stories about visits from strangers are found in many cultures.

The relationship between vv. 1-8 and vv. 9-15 remains difficult to discern. Chapter 17 makes it unlikely that the promised son constitutes a "reward" for Abraham's hospitality or a "gift" from the guests. Verses 1-8 set the issue as one of hospitality extended to strangers; Abraham may pass a "test" of some sort in this. Verses 9-15 retain some interest in hospitality, with their focus on Sarah's *reception* of the announcement: How hospitable will Sarah be to this word? Will her response be similar to Abraham's (17:17)? Issues of hospitality relate to both receiving others and the words they may speak.

This theme (with men/angels) plays a key role in 19:1-3 (Lot) and 24:18-20 (Rebekah). Moreover, in 18:16-33, issues of *divine* hospitality are raised, especially regarding God's reception of the human. God receives the "outcry" from those affected by the conduct of the people of Sodom and Gomorrah and moves to deal with it. God tends to Abraham's words and takes them into account when moving into the future. Another link with vv. 16-33 involves the prominence of questions, from Abraham and God. In all cases, the questions are serious, posed for the purpose of continuing the conversation. God's conveyance to Abraham of matters concerning the future also tie vv. 10-13 with vv. 17-19.

18:1-8. From the narrator's point of view, Yahweh appears to Abraham at his home (v. 1). From Abraham's point of view, however, three men stand near him (v. 2). Yahweh has assumed human form (see 16:7), appearing among the three men;[131] the other two are angelic attendants (so 19:1; perhaps presented in abstract form in Pss 23:6; 43:3). The separation between Yahweh and two of the messengers in 18:22 and 19:1, 13 supports this, as does the singular "you, your" in v. 3 and the shift from plural (v. 9) to a single spokesman (vv. 10-15; a comparable move occurs in 19:17-19, cf. NIV footnotes). All are involved in destroying the city, as the angels mediate God's action (cf. 19:13 with 19:14, 24). But Abraham does not yet know these identities, so the reader understands more at this point than he does. Abraham does not act hospitably due to a desire to please a divine visitor. Sarah's response (vv. 9-15) also must be interpreted with this same intentionality in mind.

Abraham's hospitality has several characteristics: It extends to strangers, toward those who appear unexpectedly; it follows a certain protocol: seeing, running to meet, honoring,

---

130. See Westermann, *Genesis 12–36,* 275-76.

131. For the idea that "Yahweh appeared in all three," see von Rad, *Genesis,* 204.

inviting, refreshing, preparing, serving. Bowing, an everyday gesture, was appropriate for all visitors, not only for important people. "Haste" language appears five times (vv. 2, 6-7; cf. 24:18-20). Abraham gives of the best he has (a calf!), makes and serves food, remains available to them and concerned about their welfare, and accompanies them on their way (v. 16). The phrase "find favor in your eyes" (v. 3; see 19:19; 32:5; 33:8-15) includes courtesy; it gives the visitors a higher status and so the freedom to respond without embarrassment. Abraham depicts what the visitors may expect (vv. 4-5), in view of which they accept the invitation, and he goes beyond what he promised in providing meat—these heavenly beings eat! As the visitors stand near Abraham (v. 2), so he stands near them (v. 8); he reciprocates in being attentive. He understands himself to be their servant (vv. 3, 5).

18:9-15. The home setting integrates Sarah into the conversation. Yet (unlike 17:16), neither Sarah nor Abraham seems to be clear that God speaks. Initially, all three persons are involved (v. 9), then one takes the lead (the NIV's "LORD" in v. 10 is an inference drawn from the words that follow). In v. 13 only the narrator identifies the speaker as Yahweh; v. 14 speaks about Yahweh, but the identity of the "I" remains unclear. The fear shown by Sarah (v. 15) comes from knowing what this person has said about her (including her laughing to herself where she could not be seen). This introduces an element of mystery, amazement that this one could speak for God.

The reader will remember that God had spoken such a promise to Abraham and that he had also laughed to himself, asking essentially the same questions (17:16-17). Abraham's falling on his face implies a more explicit negative response, however. The narrator inserts a word about their age (cf. 17:17) and that Sarah no longer menstruates (v. 11), as if to provide an objective view on Sarah's own comments (v. 12). These comments soften Sarah's response, making it more understandable, as does her observation about the end of sexual pleasure (note that Abraham fathers other children, 25:1-4). For Sarah, the issue has become more than barrenness (cf. 11:30).

All of the questions directed to Abraham in this section seem genuine. The question in v. 9 ensures Sarah is within earshot of what will be said; the narrator states (v. 10) that she listens "off camera." God inquires about Sarah's laughter in v. 13. If an accusatory question, then it could claim that Sarah should know better than to laugh, for nothing is too wonderful for God. Yet, it seems unlikely that God would be critical of Sarah if not of Abraham in 17:19. More likely, the "why" introduces a genuine question designed to continue the conversation, especially if one or both of them do not know God speaks in v. 10. God's question in v. 14, also a genuine question, moves Abraham and Sarah beyond their limited view of the future to a consideration of God's possibilities. Then the author repeats v. 10, as if to start over again in the light of the intervening conversation.

That the deity directs the questions of vv. 13-14 to Abraham means that God seeks a response from *him* regarding Sarah's laughter. God holds him accountable for her response. This may be due to Abraham's not informing her of the events of chap. 17, which means that he shares blame for Sarah's response. Abraham remains silent, as questionable a response as Sarah's. At the same time, if the author intended Sarah to hear the promise expressed in v. 10, the same must be true for vv. 13-14 as well, as her response suggests (v. 15). She does not step forward to speak, so hers may be a voice from "off stage." Her denial of laughter (v. 15) could be a lie, or an attempt to withdraw her laughter,[132] now being more aware of the nature of the moment and the probable identity of the one who has spoken. But the messenger says it remains a fact. This affirmation keeps both Sarah and Abraham on the same level regarding the reception of the promise and also links her response to the naming of Isaac ("he laughs").

Sarah's incredulous response belongs to a literary convention for such announcements, (e.g., the Shunammite woman to a "man of God" [2 Kgs 4:16] and Mary to an angel [Luke 1:34!]); so also the "due time" reference (2 Kgs 4:16), which is the one innovation beyond chap. 17. The relation between

---

132. See Westermann, *Genesis 12–36,* 282.

the twice-stated temporal—but general—reference "due time" (vv. 10, 14) and Sarah having a son finds its explanation in 21:1, which speaks of God visiting Sarah "as he had said." Although God enables Sarah to become pregnant, the normal time for the child to develop in the womb is not set aside.

The precise meaning of the verb פלא (*pālē*), translated "to be wonderful" or "to be hard/difficult" (v. 14), remains obscure. Does the word push in the direction of competence (Deut 17:8) or ability to accomplish something (Jer 32:17, 27) or something

extraordinary or marvelous (Pss 118:23; 139:14)? The related plural noun commonly refers to God's wonderful deeds of redemption and judgment (Exod 3:20; 34:10), not a claim that only God possesses power, or that the divine power is irresistible. The term claims God's promises will not fail, that God will always find a way into the future.

The end of this segment seems incomplete, but the intent may well be to leave the reader (and Sarah and Abraham) in a state of some uncertainty concerning what the future will bring.

REFLECTIONS

1. The motif of hospitality extends into the NT. Jesus specifies that the lack of hospitality serves as grounds for judgment (Matt 25:43). Hebrews 13:2 stresses its importance, for "some have entertained angels without knowing it" (see Acts 14:11; 28:1-6; those visited by Paul say, "The gods have come down to us in human form!"). Hospitality is commended to all Christians (see 1 Pet 4:9; 3 John 5-8), especially leaders (1 Tim 3:2; Titus 1:8). See Luke 24:29 on welcoming the risen Christ.

This text involves not only human hospitality, but also hospitality toward God. One could speak in terms of Matthew 25; acting on behalf of one of "the least of these" constitutes an act on behalf of God. Hospitality toward God is not simply a spiritual matter, but a response of the whole self in the midst of the quite mundane affairs of everyday life. Although we are not always able to identify the presence of God in the midst of life, God assumes flesh and blood in the neighbor (1 John 4:20).

Modern culture presents numerous challenges to the practice of hospitality toward others. Hospitality may be defined as acts of benevolence toward those outside of one's usual circle of family and friends. In North American culture, people live increasingly isolated lives, seldom reaching out beyond a very close circle. We live in a self-protective age where parents must warn their children about strangers; who knows what might be lurking beneath a kind and gentle facade? Hence, we seldom move out toward strangers. Hospitality in the modern world entails some risk of moving toward the stranger with less than full certainty as to how one might be received. Such hospitality should be especially important in the life of worship; worship ought to be a setting in which the stranger is welcomed in premier ways.

2. A text such as this calls for sentences in which God appears as the subject. God makes the promised future possible. God serves as the source of hope in situations where the way into the future seems entirely blocked off. God gives shape to possibilities when all around us seems impossible. The active engagement of God in the midst of the problems of daily life opens up the future rather than closing it down.

3. The question "Is anything too wonderful [hard] for the LORD?" (v. 14), is difficult to understand. The text probably presents a genuine question designed to continue the conversation, not a rhetorical question, which would declare that nothing is too hard. Brueggemann recognizes that the question has no simple yes or no answer.[133] If the answer is yes, then we could delimit in a specific way what is possible for God. No human construct can finally define God's possibilities in a given situation. If the answer

---

133. Brueggemann, *Genesis*, 159.

is no, "that is an answer which so accepts God's freedom that the self and the world are fully entrusted to God and to no other." It would fail to recognize that God has given *genuine* power into the hands of the creation (so 1:28) and that what is possible for God must be consistent with who God is.[134] One must deal with the issues of divine self-limitation raised by many OT texts. But, in this text, God finds a way into the future of a promised son. And this, in spite of the seemingly insurmountable hurdles of human bodily limits (postmenopausal births have been documented in modern times) and the uncertain responses of both Abraham and Sarah. No situation can *finally* stymie the divine purposes.

New Testament texts use such language, e.g., Mark 10:27 and Luke 1:37. We also need to consider texts such as Matt 17:20 (nothing is impossible for faithful *human beings*); Matt 26:39 (where Jesus' "if it is possible" raises questions of divine self-limitation), and Mark 6:5 (where Jesus' healing powers are limited by the dynamics of a situation).

4. Male commentators discussing this passage have often been unfair to Sarah, excusing Abraham's laughter (17:17) but judging Sarah severely.[135] Neither Abraham nor Sarah responds in exemplary ways to the word of God; at the same time, we should not call it unbelief, especially given the conventional form present here (see Mary in Luke 1:34). Many OT texts depict humans questioning God as a natural part of a genuine God-human conversation, and Abraham will shortly do just that (vv. 23-25; cf. Moses; Gideon in Judg 6:13). In this case, God's response continues the conversation, and God makes no judgment, even when Sarah denies that she laughed.

---

134. For the larger OT context, see Fretheim, *The Suffering of God*, 72.
135. See examples in S. Jeansonne, *Women in Genesis* (Minneapolis: Fortress, 1990) 121n 28.

GENESIS 18:16–19:38, ABRAHAM, LOT, AND SODOM

Genesis 18:16-33, Abraham's Intercession

COMMENTARY

This passage picks up a narrative thread from chaps. 13–14. The author introduces an intercessory dialogue between God and Abraham concerning the fate of Sodom and Gomorrah (vv. 23-33) by means of divine reflections on the role of Abraham as God's chosen one (vv. 17-21). The entire text constitutes a *judicial inquiry.* Abraham's intercession functions as a judicial rather than a worshipful act (prayer formulae are absent). More broadly, in this theological narrative, the author does not report an event in Abraham's life, but reflects on theological issues by juxtaposing an ancient tradition about a natural disaster and a religious crisis in the community of the redactor. This tactic grounds theological reflection deeply within Israel's ancestral heritage.

The crisis prompts the question, Will the righteous fare as the wicked? (v. 25; cf. Job 9:22-24). Such issues were prominent at those points in Israel's history when its future seemed to be at stake, from the fall of Samaria (Amos 7:1-9, also an intercessory dialogue regarding a "shower of fire") to the fall of Jerusalem (Jer 5:1; Ezek 14:12-20; 18:1-32). Why would God sweep away the faithful with the wicked, not save all of Israel for the sake of the righteous few? So, while commonly assigned to J, the narrative in its present form is also a relatively late composition.

The shift from Sarah's laughing to the long episode on Sodom and Gomorrah seems abrupt. The fulfillment of God's promise remains up in the air. Perhaps Sarah's laughing and the jesting of Lot's son-in-law (19:14) are linked to highlight the potentially devastating effects of taking God's words lightly (note the prophetic parallels). The road to fulfillment is precarious, through many a dark valley, and faith and hospitality will not be irrelevant. Perhaps, too, the reader catches a glimpse of the kind of world within which this new son of Abraham is to be a blessing.

18:16-19. The men of v. 16 are the three who had appeared to Abraham (v. 2). Three transitional phrases mark developments regarding the fate of Sodom: The three men/angels (then two) "looked toward Sodom" (18:16; cf. 19:28); "went toward Sodom" (18:22); and "came to Sodom" (19:1). This progression correlates with developments in the judicial inquiry. While both Sodom and Gomorrah are in view in the larger narrative, the author focuses on Sodom, the home of Lot.

Verses 17-21 are spoken by Yahweh to the other two men and are overheard by Abraham (v. 23 presupposes their content). In effect, these verses work as inner divine reflection about the situation in Sodom and Abraham's relationship to it (cf. 1:26; 2:18; 11:6-7). We receive insight into God's thoughts as background for the dialogue.

Abraham should not be kept in the dark regarding what God is "about to do," for God has chosen him (ידע [yādaʿ, "known"]; cf. Amos 3:2) and made promises to him. God does not intend human ignorance of God's work (cf. Amos 3:7). Even more, God consults with Abraham because he *and his descendants* are chosen to have a role among the "nations" ("families" in 12:3; cf. 22:18; 26:4). Abraham responds by interceding on behalf of the righteous, none of whom would be among the chosen, not even Lot (as in 20:17).

God calls Abraham to charge his family "to keep the way of the LORD by doing righteousness [צדקה *ṣĕdāqâ*] and justice [משפט *mišpāṭ*]" (v. 19; cf. Ps 33:5; Prov 21:3). These key words—uncommon in Genesis—are picked up in the dialogue, *mišpaṭ* in v. 25 and the root *ṣdq* seven times in vv. 23-28

(cf. 6:9; 7:1; 15:6; 20:4; 30:33; 38:26). The two words are closely related, characterizing individuals and communities that exemplify and promote life and well-being for all in every relational sphere, human and non-human. As such, their lives would correspond to God's creational intentions for the world order, including blessing on all nations. After so charging Abraham, God brings to his attention a case where these divine purposes are being subverted. To be a blessing to all nations, Abraham must become involved in situations of injustice. Just as God enters into the life of the chosen regarding these issues, so also God identifies the divine way with the world more generally.

The author deems the transmission of the faith to subsequent generations an appropriate topic in view of the imminent birth of Isaac. This brings *Israel's* life into view and its practice of "justice and righteousness" and the implications thereof (including judgment). Hence, the question of Sodom's fate could become a question of the fate of Israel (Isa 1:10; Jer 23:14; Ezek 16:49) or any people.

The fact that God raises the issue of justice (in vv. 17-19) before Abraham does is important. If God chooses Abraham to address issues of justice within his household, then God's ways of relating to these issues must be clear (raised by a non-Israelite in 20:4). God's people are to walk in all of God's ways (v. 19; cf. Deut 8:6; 10:12; Jer 5:4-5) and so they should know what justice means for God.

Verse 19 may seem to make God's promises conditional. Yet, the text focuses on Abraham's *transmitting the faith to the next generation,* without which there would be no community to whom the promises apply. The promises are not genetically transmitted. The community of faith can continue only if children receive instruction. If the generations to come are not faithful, they remove themselves from the sphere of the promise. Nonetheless, the faith of Abraham and his descendants will survive (see commentary on 22:16-18 and 26:5, 24).

18:20-22. God reports the cries of unidentified persons about the gravity of the sins of Sodom and Gomorrah (against their own?). Outcry language (also 19:13) describes the oppressed (4:10; 27:34), including Israel in

Egypt (Exod 2:23; 3:7, 9). The sins of Sodom involve social injustice (to which Jer 23:14 and Ezek 16:49 also testify).

Verse 20, with a new introduction, reports the decision of God as Judge (v. 25) formally to investigate the situation; Abraham will be involved in this judicial inquiry (11:5; Num 12:5; on "seeing" as judicial activity, see 6:5, 12; Exod 3:7-9; 32:9). God will consult with him to discover whether the situation is in fact so grave that it warrants the judgment that God has *preliminarily* drawn.[136] The dialogue thus follows naturally from this divine intent. Abraham understands that he has been invited into such a conversation.

This inquiry is not just rhetorical, so God's words, "and if not, I will know [acknowledge, recognize]" (v. 21). This divine knowing for judicial purposes depends on the inquiry. God admits the possibility of an "if not." For God to use "if" language means the future remains open (Exod 4:8-9; Jer 7:5; 22:4-5; Ezek 12:3). God holds out the prospect that the inquiry will issue in a verdict other than that preliminarily drawn. Abraham presumes the integrity of this consultation; what he has to say will be taken seriously (cf. Exod 32:9-14; Num 14:11-20).

The departure of two of the men marks the transition to dialogue (cf. 19:1, v. 16). Abraham now stands before God, though originally the text read that God stood before Abraham (NRSV footnote). The subjects were reversed by scribes who thought it indecorous for God to stand before a human being. "Remained" refers more appropriately to God, who remains behind while the two men depart. God seeks to communicate with Abraham, not the other way around.

18:23-33. Abraham proceeds to raise very specific questions regarding God's preliminary decision. He is blunt, persistent, and nontraditional. His questions (vv. 23-25) pull no punches; he gets right to the point without preliminary niceties. The author stresses this confrontative approach by the "indeed?" (vv. 23-24; cf. 18:13; Job 34:17), as well as the repeated "far be it from you" (cf. 44:7, 17). Abraham understands his relationship with God to be such that direct questions are not only in order but welcome (cf.

Exod 32:11-14). Indeed, God exhibits no disapproval. Abraham does become more deferential as the dialogue proceeds. His motives for this shift are not stated, but God's positive response to his candor may have humbled him. We may not know enough about ancient methods of argumentation to assess this shift properly.

One could suggest that God plays with Abraham, for God knows the number of righteous persons in Sodom. But this would deny the integrity of the inquiry. Something may emerge out of this consultative interaction that calls for a different divine direction. Given the divine "if," God does not appear certain just how far and in what direction Abraham might push the discussion.

Abraham's argument moves in stages to its climactic question at the end of v. 25. Abraham first expresses concern that God not "sweep away" (19:15, 17) the righteous (not sinless—righteousness is measured in terms of creational relationships, cf. 38:26) with the wicked; they must not be treated in the same way. He raises a more specific question: How many righteous must there be in order for God to save the city (see below)?

While Lot may have prompted Abraham's action (as in 14:14, see 19:29), he places the matter on a much broader canvas of concern, i.e., the number of righteous he mentions (fifty!) and the absence of Lot. The "righteous" are any who had not participated in the behaviors that led to the "outcry." While Abraham focuses on them, he knows their deliverance would mean the saving of many wicked. In not suggesting that the few righteous simply be removed (which is what happens) he shows his concern for the many. God's fourfold "for the sake of" carries a double meaning: God will not destroy for the sake of saving the few; for the sake of the few, the many will not be destroyed (in 12:13, 16, Pharaoh dealt well with Abraham *for the sake of* Sarah; see 26:24; 1 Sam 12:22; 2 Sam 5:12; 9:1, 7). The verb נשא (*nāśā',* "spare") means to annul the decision to destroy. The righteous do not exercise an *atoning* function for the others, yet the effect is comparable. Certainly God's mercy toward those who deserve another future grounds this divine response.

Abraham's most direct question is, Will not the Judge of all the earth do right (*mišpāṭ*)? (cf. 1 Sam 2:10; 1 Kgs 8:32; Ps 9:7-8). If God expects Abraham and his family to do *mišpāṭ* (v. 19), justice must be God's own way. Only then would "doing justice" be keeping "the way of the LORD." Abraham's question does not accuse; it provides a debating point, warranted by what God has said (v. 19).

This question suggests an implicit theology. Abraham considers God to be subject to an existing moral order. God has freely created that order but is bound to attend to it faithfully. That is, God cannot ignore doing justice to established relationships (i.e., righteousness) and still be faithful, not least because God expects this of Abraham and his family. God thus is held to certain standards in dealing with issues of justice. Hence in Abraham's eyes, God cannot ignore differences between the righteous and the wicked in acts of judgment. God accepts Abraham's argument.

As Abraham continues to raise the numbers question, God responds in a consistently positive way. Abraham's concerns are matched by God's. The author reveals here the ends to which God will go to save the righteous and the divine patience in matters of judgment. God's will to save over the will to judge so predominates that no reward-punishment schema can explain what happens. The text is making one basic point: No retributionary schema will explain why disastrous events do *not* occur. The wicked may not suffer the consequences of their own sins because of the presence of the righteous.

We should not move too quickly past this point, not least because it answers most clearly why Abraham cut the questioning off at ten, a number not to be taken literally. It may be that "the number ten represents the smallest group"[137] and that a smaller number

137. Westermann, *Genesis 12–36*, 292.

would be dealt with as individuals, who could be (and were) led out of the city. It may be that it represents the point at which Abraham saw that God's justice had been established beyond the shadow of a doubt; he could now leave the fate of the few righteous up to God. It may be that Abraham realizes that this "numbers game" cannot be pressed exactly, for that would mean a precise number "out there," which would trigger a divine decision, as if all that counts is "counting noses." God has no quota system in these matters.

Most basically, however, the numbers speak to the issue of a critical mass in relation to the moral order. The wickedness of a few can have a contaminating effect on the larger group of which they are a part (cf. Deut 21:1-9). Here the issue is reversed; the righteousness of a few can so permeate a wicked society that they can save it from the destructive effects of its own evil ways. However, a buildup of wickedness can become so deep and broad that nothing can turn the potential for judgment around. The "critical mass" effect of the presence of the righteous can be so diminished as not to be able to affect positively the shape of the future. There may come a point where even God cannot turn the situation around and still be just; judgment must fall. Abraham recognizes this by not taking the numbers lower than ten. He tacitly admits that a few righteous may indeed "fare as the wicked" (v. 25). Eschatological thinking will speak finally of a distinction in the world to come rather than in this world.

God does not reappear as an agent until 19:24. Abraham, too, reappears only in 19:27, looking down on the destroyed cities. Chapter 19 now brings readers into the city of Sodom. They will be given an example of behaviors that occasioned the "outcry" and be asked to judge for themselves whether God's judgment appears just. (See Reflections at the end of the next section.)

Genesis 19:1-38, Sodom and Gomorrah

COMMENTARY

This chapter brings the story of Lot to an end, concluding with the faintest of hopes for the future. Lot was part of Abraham's journey of faith (12:5). A conflict over land rights concludes when Lot picks the region around Sodom. The author makes three telling comments (13:10-13): a fertile area like the garden of the LORD; like "the land of Egypt," where *Israel's* "outcry" will be heard by God; its people are "wicked, great sinners against the LORD" (see 18:20). From this chapter, it appears that Lot has taken on some qualities of his environment.

This text (assigned to J) is the most frequently cited Genesis passage in the rest of the Bible. Sodom and Gomorrah become a conventional image for heinous sins and severe disaster. Apparently these cities symbolize the worst that can be imagined. The nature of Sodom's sins may vary, but the mistreatment of other human beings tops the list; inhospitality lends itself to diverse development (Jer 23:14). Later texts recall Sodom's judgment, even its specific form (see Ps 11:6; Ezek 38:22; Rev 21:8).

We do not know where these cities were located, but some now place them southeast of the Dead Sea (rather than under the southern part of the sea). The area lies in a geological rift, extending from Turkey to East Africa, the Dead Sea being its lowest point (1,305 feet below sea level). The area has extensive sulphur and bitumen deposits and petrochemical springs, which the text points out (14:10; 19:24; cf. Deut 29:23; Zeph 2:9). An earthquake with associated fires (19:28; brimstone is sulfurous fire) may have ignited these deposits, producing an explosion that "overthrew" these cities.

The tradition has taken up tales of some such ecological disaster and woven them into the story of Abraham and his family. The area around the Dead Sea had not always been desolate, and its present state was due to *human* wickedness. Such an interrelationship of human and cosmic orders stands in continuity with 3:16 and the flood story (see 13:10). Scholars have noted parallels with

the latter, from the lack of sexual restraint (6:1-4), to natural disaster (note v. 24, "rained" on Sodom), to the saving of a remnant (and God's remembering, 8:1; 19:29), to the drunken aftermath (cf. 9:20-27 with vv. 30-38). The NT also appropriates these texts (see Luke 17:26-32; 2 Pet 2:5-8, which identifies Lot as righteous). We may also discern continuities with the exodus events, such as the outcry of the oppressed, the ecological disasters (plagues), the fate of the Egyptians, and Lot's being brought out of the city (יצא *yāṣā*), vv. 12, 16, 17).

We may also view this chapter from the vantage of its close parallel in Judg 19:22-30, a text that depends heavily on this passage.[138] Sexual abuse comes from Israelites, however, not from foreigners. While the inhospitable mistreatment of others in the two stories contains similar components, the focus in Genesis on divine judgment through a natural disaster and the preservation of a remnant push the story in somewhat different directions.

19:1-11. Readers are not explicitly informed about the upshot of the conversation in 18:23-33. For all they know, God has found ten righteous people in Sodom and the city will be saved. The narrator now gives readers an inside view, enabling them to judge for themselves what ought to be done to Sodom. So 19:1-11 develops an *illustration* of Sodom's character; in view of this, readers should have little difficulty agreeing with the verdict—even Lot comes off as one whose righteous behavior we might question.

The author develops this illustration in relationship to 18:1-15. Both chapters share the basic thematic link of *hospitality,* which should not be narrowly conceived, as if it were a matter of putting out a welcome mat. Hospitality involves a wide-ranging image, revealing fundamental relationships of well-being for individuals and society. Abraham shows hospitality in exemplary fashion. Lot follows suit to some extent, but he fails at a

138. See S. Lasine, "Guest and Host in Judges 19," *JSOT* 29 (1984) 37-59.

key juncture. The people of Sodom show no sign of what hospitality entails at all.

It seems wise not to overdraw the differences between Abraham's hospitality in 18:1-8 and Lot's in 19:1-3. Initially, Lot's hospitality parallels Abraham's; thus, when the differences appear, they have a greater shock value. Lot does engage the crowd on behalf of his guests, and he names directly the sin of the Sodomites (v. 7; רע *ra*ʿ). At the same time, his language to them as "brothers" raises problems, and his treatment of his daughters reveals deep levels of inhospitality.

Abraham had welcomed his visitors wholeheartedly and treated them in an exemplary way. Lot behaves in a basically similar way: He rises (but does not run), bows before them, speaks of them as "lords," provides for their rest and refreshment (the preparations are less thorough and the provisions less sumptuous). He also invites them to stay the night to protect them from the street, which also makes for problems. The visitors accept only upon his strong urging. The word brought to Abraham was one of hope (18:9-10); the word to Lot is one of destruction (19:13-14). Both words are introduced with a question regarding the whereabouts of others (18:9; 19:12). Both households respond to the word in similar fashion; they consider it laughable (צחק *ṣāḥaq*), both Sarah (and Abraham) and Lot's sons-in-law (v. 14). While the response to Sarah was left up in the air (18:15), the narrative pursues the issue of Sodom to its disastrous conclusion. Is the reader invited to draw parallels?

The author makes the depth of Sodom's inhospitality immediately evident. Verse 4 (cf. v. 11) shows that *every* man (!) in the city was caught up in this threat of violence through homosexual activity (they even threaten Lot himself, v. 9). If the assault had succeeded, the result could only be described as gang rape, not a private act. The text presents the sins of Sodom more as social than individual, something that characterizes the entire city. This deed would be but one example of Sodom's sins, as other texts show (see below). Inasmuch as Sodom serves as the evil counterpart to Abraham's hospitality, we trivialize the narrative if we focus on this one sin.

Lot's reply (v. 8) borders on the incredible. Interestingly, he thinks that the men of Sodom would be satisfied with *heterosexual* abuse (as in Judges 19–20, where it is condemned). The offer of his daughters to be abused "as you please" provides but another example of the depravity of Sodom (ironically, Lot will become the abuser of his own daughters, see below). His daughters were betrothed (v. 14); Israel condemned to death those who rape betrothed women (Deut 22:23-24). Threatened sexual abuse and violence, both homosexual and heterosexual, constitutes sufficient evidence to move forward with judgment.

The men of Sodom now raise the issue of justice, which God and Abraham had broached earlier (v. 9); the men of Sodom alone can judge the rightness of their own action—no external standard obtains here. The strangers save Lot—who sought to save them—from their violence and strike them with temporary blindness, perhaps a sudden flash of light (see 2 Kgs 6:18; Acts 9:3-9). We hear no more from the men of Sodom; they are left still blindly groping for the door to complete their objective! But God (and the reader) who came to "see" them has seen enough for the judgment to fall.

19:12-23. The angels mediate *God's* destruction (v. 13; so also Lot and narrator, vv. 14, 24); they save Lot and his family. In spite of Lot's warning, the sons-in-law treat it as a laughable matter (cf. 18:12-15). The word for "punishment" in v. 15 is עון ('*āwōn*,) a common word for "sin" (cf. 4:7). The effects of sin flow out of the sin itself; they are not introduced by God from outside the situation.

These are tension-filled moments, emphasized by the use of imperatives alongside Lot's lingering. Lot's dallying ends only when he is forced to leave the city, an effort due to the undeserved mercy, graciousness, and kindness (חסד *ḥesed*) of God (vv. 16, 19). Commanded not to look back lest his family be delayed and engulfed by the fallout, Lot still hesitates out of fear of the open hills (to which he later retreats, v. 30); the angels agree to exclude the city of Zoar. They are "not able" to do anything until Lot is safe (v. 22). In view of v. 29, God's delay for Lot's sake testifies to the efficacy of Abraham's intercession.

Verses 18-23 explain the meaning of the name Zoar ("little"), but more remains at stake. Because of Lot, one of the smaller cities to be destroyed is saved from destruction, *as are the wicked living there.* Hence, God honors one of the principles for which Abraham argued in 18:22-33. The emphasis on its smallness suggests that the presence of Lot and his family were sufficient to provide the "critical mass" of righteous among the wicked.

19:24-26. The author describes the destruction only briefly. The repetition in v. 24 suggests that the brimstone and fire—a traditional expression—come from the very presence of God. Verse 25 describes its calamitous effects, from the cities and environs to the people and the vegetation. The verb *overthrow* may not fit the nature of the event precisely (but cf. *catastrophe,* which has the same meaning; see Jon 3:4).

The fate of Lot's wife echoes a common motif in folklore. Lot's wife mirrors his irresoluteness, only she lingers to the point of death. The nature of the cataclysm could explain the salt pillar; she was engulfed in the fallout of fire and chemicals. Human-shaped pillars of salt still found in the area may have prompted this element in the story (see Wis 10:4).

19:27-29. Abraham retraces his steps (18:33) and "freezes in the awe-inspiring horror of the sight."[139] He says nothing. He simply witnesses the judgment of God, and his silence speaks volumes. The nations of the earth are to find blessing through him, but not inevitably so. In spite of his efforts, intercession could not turn the situation around (cf. Jer 11:14; 14:11).

God rescues Lot *both* because God is merciful toward him (19:16, 19) and because God remembers Abraham (19:29). God does attend to his prayers; without him Lot would have been lost. The repetition in v. 29 stresses the destruction from which he escaped. Both judgment and rescue witness to the universal work of God the Creator, here powerfully at work outside of the chosen community.

19:30-38. The author/editor has integrally related this text to the preceding story (cf. Zoar). Interpreters have tended in two directions. Most commonly, they understand this passage as the conclusion to the story of Lot, the final stage of a downward spiral,

showing the depths to which this man of faith had fallen. It presents one possible journey for any person of faith, and in view of 18:19, even for Abraham. Lot meets an end as destructive as the cities from which he is taken, having taken on their character in his own life. Yet, his fear of dwelling in Zoar may mean he was not accepted among these people either. He is a person without a home. The man who had chosen paradise (13:10) ends up in a barren cave, far removed from others, utterly destitute.

Lot, who earlier had offered his daughters for sexual abuse, ironically becomes the one who engages in such acts, but passively so. He becomes the passive sexual object he had determined his daughters should become. The narrator thereby passes sharp judgment on Lot for offering his daughters; his fate corresponds precisely to his earlier deed. What goes around comes around. The only "positive" note involves his lack of knowledge; his daughters get him drunk to engage in incest.

Other interpreters see the story as a new beginning; Lot's daughters take the initiative to continue the family line, a larger narrative theme (vv. 32, 34). Parallels with 9:18-27 have been noted, including drunkenness, sexual impropriety, ethnological concerns, and the issue of continuing progeny (the emphasis on Zoar in v. 30 shows that the daughters are concerned about their family line, not a repeopling of the earth). Such a "desperate deed" resonates, especially, with that of Tamar (chap. 38; cf. also the midwives in Exodus 1). Westermann speaks of "acts of revolt against prevailing standards of morality and customs" for the laudable goals of life and family well-being.[140] Given the precarious situation into which their father had led them, their options had narrowed to a single one. Hence, no negative judgment on them seems to be in order, except the judgment of Judah regarding Tamar, "She is more righteous than I" (38:26 NIV).

The reader should also note the genealogical interest in the text. The reference to the Moabites and Ammonites (vv. 37-38) may attest that these peoples were rarely on friendly terms with later Israel (see Deut 23:3). Yet, Ruth was a Moabite, making this

---

139. Westermann, *Genesis 12–36,* 307.

140. Westermann, *Genesis 12–36,* 315.

son of Lot's daughter an ancestor of both David and Jesus (Ruth 4:18-22; Matt 1:5). The messianic line has one of its roots in this initiative by Lot's daughter. Even out of the worst of family situations, God can bring goodness, life, and blessing to the world.

REFLECTIONS

1. Abraham concerns himself with the future of the nonchosen, both righteous and unrighteous, those who are outside the community of faith, almost all of them strangers. He does so by focusing, not on narrowly religious matters (e.g., idolatry), but on issues of justice. This testifies to an interpretation of 12:1-3 that involves the chosen in their relationship to the nations. The fact that God also enters into the lives of others *on the issue of justice* sets a pattern for those who are "to keep the way of the LORD" (18:19).

Sodom is condemned, not because they have no faith in God, but because of the way in which they treat their brothers and sisters. God holds the nonchosen accountable for such behaviors. This assumes an understanding of natural law, wherein God's intentions for all people are clear in the creational order (cf. the oracles of the prophets against the nations, e.g., Amos 1–2).

2. One wonders whether those who think God's decision about Sodom is final from the beginning do so because of a view of God that does not allow for consultation. But God takes Abraham's thinking into account in deciding what the divine action will finally be. God takes seriously what human beings think and say, which can contribute in a genuine way to the shaping of the future. While God would have thought of all the options, to have them articulated by Abraham gives them a new level of significance that God will take into account. Abraham brings new ingredients into the situation— energies, words, insights—that give God new possibilities with which to work. This interaction has the potential of changing the divine decision (see Exod 32:9-14).

Abraham participates with God in matters of divine judgment. Hence, Abraham's role may be compared to that of the pre-exilic prophets (cf. 18:17 with Amos 3:7). We are accustomed to thinking about God working through human beings on behalf of what is positive and good. The nature of the continuing role of the people of God in matters of judgment needs closer scrutiny (see Rom 13:4).

3. This text centers on the future of a corporate entity, not individuals in isolation. It does not deny that individuals are to be held accountable, but it focuses on communal responsibility, on what happens when sin and its effects become so pervasive that the entire community is caught up in it.

The text links corporate responsibility and ecology, a strikingly contemporary concern. Human behavior affects, not simply the human community, but the entire cosmos (though the link may be difficult to discern). Although we often consider individual sins in an analysis of environmental problems, the ecological issue may involve a social dimension in which the innocent (from children to the ozone layer) are caught up in the disastrous consequences. Historical evil can cause creational havoc, as moderns know all too well.

But does not *God* cause all the damage? The text links God to this catastrophe (19:24) as an ecological disaster of divine judgment. God sees to a *creational* form for this disaster; it corresponds to the *anticreational* form of human wickedness, focused especially in the language of outcry and the deprivation of life and well-being (18:20-21; 19:13). God midwifes or sees to the moral order, through already existing human or nonhuman agents.[141] Many such events are just part of the normal workings of the

141. See discussion of plagues in Fretheim, *Exodus*, 105-12.

natural order (the rain falls, or does not fall, on the just and the unjust, Matt 5:45). Yet, both Israelites and moderns know that human behaviors have led and will lead to cosmic disaster (flood story; plagues). The devastation of Sodom and Gomorrah and their environs offers a major instance; the depletion of the ozone layer may be another.

The destruction of Sodom and Gomorrah serves as a warning of what could (and did) become of Israel's own land; the text may allude to the fall of Jerusalem (Deut 29:22-23; Jer 4:23-26). The link between the practice of justice and righteousness and the future of the land remains very close, as the prophets often point out (see Hos 4:1-3). They focus their message of judgment in a sharply corporate manner, rooted in God's concern for the oppressed, deeply embedded in the law (Exod 22:21-23). The prophets do voice a hope regarding the regardening of the land (Isa 51:3; Ezek 36:35), but only on the far side of ecological and historical disaster.

While judgment language may be difficult to accept, for God not to be concerned about the oppression of people would mean that God does not finally care about evil and its effects. What are misdemeanors to us may be disasters to God, not least because God sees the evil effects they have on the creation in a way that we do not. At the same time, this story shows that God is not eager that judgment fall. God consults with Abraham about the possibility of another future short of judgment; God appears open to alternatives. The speech of God in Ezek 18:32 (NRSV), "I have no pleasure in the death of anyone," also characterizes the God of this text. This cuts against the grain of any notion that Israel's God acts as a punitive God focused on the punishment of the wicked. Israel's God is "slow to anger," even with the nonchosen.

4. This text *illustrates* the situation in Sodom as homosexual activity (condemned for males in Israel [Lev 18:22; 20:13]), but refers specifically to the abusive violence and savage inhospitality. The text does not talk about homosexual activity or orientation generally, or nonviolent sexual behavior. Other biblical references to Sodom lift up a wide range of behavior, from neglect of the poor and needy to lies, greed, luxury, heterosexual abuse, and inhospitality to strangers (Isa 1:9-10; Jer 23:14; Lam 4:6; Ezek 16:48-55; Zeph 2:9). Jesus remains true to the text in condemning a town to a fate like Sodom's because of its refusal to receive strangers who bear the word of God (Matt 10:14-15; 11:23-24; Luke 10:12; 17:29; 2 Pet 2:8; only in Jude 7 does the reference to homosexual behavior possibly become explicit).

5. Abraham forthrightly raises the issue of theodicy. He brings questions about the justice of God directly to God, who fields them in a way that does not close off conversation. These issues are raised so sharply because of crisis contexts in which this material functioned. The fate of the righteous, not least the children (Lam 2:20; 4:10), in the judgment of Samaria (Amos 7:1-6) or Jerusalem (Ezek 14:12-20) was a lively issue, as was the saving role of the few for the many (see Isa 53:1-12; Jer 5:1). In such events the innocent (many more than ten!) often have perished with the guilty. Would it be Abraham's view that the Judge of all the earth has *often* not acted correctly?

We usually conceive of the relationship between act and consequence in individual terms, letting the judicial system "take care of" the penalty. We think less often about corporate sin and judgment, but actions against a corporate aggressor (e.g., war) are rooted in such understandings. In God's concern for the moral order at this level, the righteous are caught up in the judgment of the wicked and suffer with them, e.g., children in the fall of Jerusalem (or the World Wars). In such cases, we are seldom able precisely to sort the innocent and the righteous from the wicked. More generally, the interconnectedness of life means that evil actions will have dire consequences for those who are not guilty. The innocent often suffer the consequences of acts committed by the wicked.

Abraham's question focuses on the fairness of the moral order. Should the innocent perish when the wicked are judged? But Abraham argues for the saving of not only the righteous, but also the entire city because of the presence of the righteous, more precisely in order to save the righteous. The priority ought to be given to the righteous. In effect, the presence of the righteous would lead to the extension of the divine mercy upon all. This, of course, would mean that the wicked would not receive their just deserts. So Abraham seeks to abandon any exact retribution system, but discovers in the process that no such system exists.

Abraham, however, introduces a qualification. He raises the precise *number* of righteous people that ought to be present. The numbers ought not to be taken literally; that would establish a kind of quota to which divine judgment would be bound. Yet, the numbers are important (the dialogue focuses there) and indicate the kind of issue Abraham raises. Two questions will help to address this issue:

Why does Abraham not *begin* with one righteous person or take it all the way down to one? If he wanted to reverse this approach completely, the presence of one would be sufficient to make his case. He must want to make another point. Moreover, he stops at ten. God takes leave at that juncture, with Abraham and God in apparent agreement. Why are fifty or ten righteous persons enough to spare the city, but one or so not? Sarna pushes in the right direction.[142] Ten represents the limit of the number of righteous who could outweigh the cumulative evil of the community. Ten constitutes the "minimum effective social entity," a critical mass, *for this situation* (for other situations, the number would vary considerably). The buildup of wickedness and its effects in Sodom are such that ten righteous would not be able to turn around the potential for judgment. So few righteous could not affect the shape of the future in a positive way.

Through this conversation, Abraham recognizes that God will indeed act justly concerning Sodom, and indeed any corporate entity. But, with respect to corporate justice, there comes a point when justice must be done, even radical surgery undertaken, even if some righteous people get caught up in the judgment. Other options are not finally tolerable, especially an option where the Sodomites would not be brought to account in any way for the terrible injustice they are visiting upon people. To avoid judgment would allow evil to go unchecked in the world.

God agrees that the righteous few can often save a city. But Abraham recognizes that there comes a point when even the righteous are too few to turn a situation around (fewer than ten). Even then, what the righteous do in such situations will make a difference, but not a predictable one. Perhaps even ten (or whatever) will not finally be enough. Abraham persuades God to think of a lower number of righteous that might make a difference in Sodom's situation, but finally he chooses not to seek to overturn the moral order, recognizing the justice in it.

Genesis 19:29 presents one other point of persuasion when God remembers Abraham and saves Lot. Abraham is concerned about *all* righteous persons who may have been in the city (he begins with fifty!). Although Abraham does not specifically mention Lot, neither does the author identify Lot as righteous; one has difficulty in linking God's remembering in 19:29 with anything other than Abraham's expressed advocacy. Does God then make an extraordinary exception to the judgment that will catch up the righteous in Sodom? Does God save Lot (and the people of Zoar!) arbitrarily?

For one thing, the fact that the righteous will suffer judgment with the wicked does not belong, necessarily, to the order of things. The moral order does not involve a tight causal weave, with no room for chance or randomness, for the serendipitous or the extraordinary event.

For another, intercession counts for something; Abraham's intercessory advocacy makes a difference. The community of faith tends to intercede for those of whom it approves or causes it endorses. We do not often intercede for the Lots and Sodoms of this world, persons who have disappointed us by the direction they have taken with

142. Sarna, *Genesis*, 134.

their lives. Jesus identifies our obligation: "Love your enemies and pray for those who persecute you" (Matt 5:44-47 NRSV; see Jer 29:7).

At the same time, such activity cannot be separated from the kind of response to the warnings one sees in Lot and his family in chap. 19. If such alarms are deemed to be in jest, the potential effect of intercession will be cut off. Lot illustrates how the journey of faith may end on a very tragic note. Choices people make can adversely affect the power of intercession and the divine engagement in their lives.

This text witnesses to the significance of the presence of the righteous in any situation; they can subvert the effects of sin and evil *from within the city* so that the consequences are less severe, perhaps even sparing the wicked and reclaiming the city. This author argues against fatalism among the righteous, the belief that nothing can be done about society's problems, that plays down the potential impact of human activity and resigns itself to sin's consequences. The righteous can indeed make a difference, to the world and to God.

The positive note in vv. 30-38 entails an understanding of a God who works for good in the midst of great evil (50:20). The decision of Lot's daughters correlates to their father's earlier abuse of them. A father who would offer them to the entire male population of the town for the purpose of sexual services could hardly have had an appropriate relationship with them, no matter how patriarchal the family structures may have been. Their father showed them the way, as have abusive fathers over the centuries; it takes little imagination to recall abusive situations just as devastating in our own society. In such moments, hope in a God who keeps promises through the worst of times can sustain one through to another day. Even then, the journey of a family may continue to be filled with troubles, as the Genesis narrative unfolds. Yet, that one grandson of Lot (Moab), an ancestor of David and Jesus, witnesses to what God can bring out of the worst of situations. Someday God will raise up a single innocent one who does have the power to save the many unrighteous, not by resigning himself to that wickedness or ignoring it, but taking it into himself and exploding the powers of death from within (Isa 53:5, 10: Hos 11:8-9).

GENESIS 20:1-18, ABRAHAM, SARAH, AND ABIMELECH

COMMENTARY

This text (often assigned to E) closely parallels 12:10-20 and 26:1-11 but includes more dialogue and theological reflection. These ties invite a comparison, but such analyses ought to center on the text's role within its present literary context. The narrative provides a return look at Abraham after all that has happened in chaps. 12–19. Given these events, especially Abraham's developing relationship with God, how might he fare in a situation like the one he faced in 12:10-20?

Links with chaps. 18–19 are especially strong: issues of justice, human and divine

(Abraham proves to be closer to the Sodomites than Abimelech!), sin and consequence, Abraham as intercessor. Chapter 21 will return to contact between Abraham and Abimelech (vv. 22-34), but sandwiched in between is a narrative of birth and separation. Focus on the closing of wombs in 20:18 leads into the story of the conception and birth of Isaac (21:1-7), where God's action and Abraham's paternity reinforce 20:4-6.

The author builds this story around three dialogues: Abimelech with God (vv. 3-7),

Abimelech with Abraham (vv. 9-13), and Abraham and Sarah (vv. 15-16).

20:1-7. Abraham journeys (נסע *nāsaʿ*) and sojourns (גור *gûr*) for the first time since 12:9-10, which introduced the previous story of threat to Sarah. Now Abraham sojourns in the city-state of Gerar (in the southwestern corner of Canaan in what became Philistine territory, see 21:34).

In 12:10-20, the narrator presented early the reasoning behind Abraham's calling Sarah his sister; here the rationale is delayed until vv. 11-13. Abraham, already in Gerar, initially claims that Sarah is his sister. Only in v. 5 are we told that Abraham spoke these words to Abimelech, the king of Gerar, and that Sarah had concurred. Placing Abraham's claim at the onset of the story suggests that he has not learned from the previous experience. Once again, he deliberately betrays Sarah. Her acquiescence notwithstanding, Abraham knowingly places her life and well-being in jeopardy. Even more, he apparently still does not believe that God's promise of a son includes Sarah (see 17:16-17). In spite of all the divine words and deeds in his life, Abraham does not address the issue in theological terms. Even more, he fails to consider the effects of his actions on outsiders. These actions may well provide some of the backdrop for the testing in chap. 22.

In view of what Abraham does, and Abimelech's taking Sarah, God abruptly enters the situation to protect Sarah. God speaks to Abimelech in a dream (see 28:10-22; 37; 40-41; dreams were considered a medium of divine revelation and no less real or personal than a direct divine encounter). Abimelech and God carry out a conversation within the dream; Abimelech claims innocence since he did not know that Sarah was married to Abraham. This interchange (vv. 3-7) appears unusual in a number of respects.

(a) God speaks to one who stands outside the community of faith (cf. 31:24; Num 22:20), indeed engages in dialogue with him. Abimelech's response (vv. 4-5) occasions a positive response in God (vv. 6-7), which opens up the possibilities for life rather than death.

(b) Similar to Abraham in 18:22-33, Abimelech acts in a situation of perceived injustice. He not only pleads with God, but sharply

questions God and flatly states his innocence ("pure heart and clean hands" may be a legal formula; cf. 17:1; Pss 24:4; 78:72); he places his action in the context of his general loyalty to interhuman relationships. He refuses to acquiesce in the face of a divine decision or resign himself to the announced fate of death. He expects his innocence to be acknowledged if justice is to be served. His question in v. 4 appears like Abraham's in 18:25: "Lord, will you destroy an innocent people [גוי *gôy*]?" Verses 7, 9, 17-18 indicate the events have affected more than Abimelech as an individual. God acknowledges Abimelech's innocence.

(c) Verse 6 states that God has been so active in his life that Abimelech was prevented from touching Sarah (we learn from v. 17). Because God states this reason, the claim is incontestable.

(d) God announces that Abimelech is a dead man because of what he has done (v. 3), even though v. 6 makes clear that God knew he was innocent. Hence, the announcement of v. 3 serves not as a forensic judgment, but as a matter-of-fact divine statement regarding the moral order and its effects on Abimelech. We learn from vv. 17-18 that Abimelech's death would have been caused by a malady that was capable of being healed and that the women of his household were unable to conceive. The moral order means that certain deeds have an effect just by virtue of their having happened, and people reap the consequences quite apart from their intentions or their knowledge of what they have done (a reality just as true today as then).

(e) God devotes attention to the *effects* of the deeds apart from questions of guilt or innocence. In preventing Abimelech from touching Sarah through an illness, God has prevented a worse deed from occurring and even more serious effects. So the situation is not as bad as it might have been! Possibilities for the future are more hopeful as a result.

God specifies that two things must happen for Abimelech's life to be preserved (v. 7): He should restore Sarah to Abraham, and then Abraham, a prophet, should pray for him. Indeed, if he does not so proceed, his entire family will be claimed by death. Abimelech must do more than restore the situation to the point where it started. He also must consider all the effects that his action has let loose. God deems prayer necessary in order to deal with such realities (see v. 17).

God's word about Abraham's being a prophet serves a double purpose. It protects Abraham from any precipitous judgment that Abimelech may wish to pass, for it makes his life dependent on Abraham's intercession. It also shows God's concern for Abimelech, providing a means by which he can be brought through this difficulty alive. To use the word *prophet* for Abraham is anachronistic, and may be used because prophets were commonly associated with intercessory activity (cf. 1 Sam 12:23; Jer 11:14).

20:8-18. Abimelech reacts in two basic ways. (1) He calls *all* his servants together and reports the event to them (cf. 41:8). Their response is fear; the fallout from this act will adversely affect their lives (see v. 17). (2) Having been assured by God that he has acted innocently, Abimelech confronts Abraham and in effect conducts a judicial inquiry. He does this with knowledge regarding Abraham's complicity that Abraham does not know he has. He does not reveal where he got the information, however, and seeks to get Abraham to tell the story from his own point of view. His charges, expressed as assertions and as rhetorical questions, are on target. Given what Abimelech knows and has suffered, he shows notable restraint and magnanimity toward the guilty one.

Two striking things occur in this: (1) the outsider pronounces Abraham guilty: "You have done things to me that ought not to be done" (v. 9). Abimelech's sin language reveals the essence of the problem. He has not sinned (חטא *ḥāṭāʾ*) against Abraham, but Abraham has brought a "great guilt" (חטאה *ḥăṭāʾâ*) on him. *Abraham's* sin lies at the root of the problem, and its effects have reached out through Abimelech's innocent deed and engulfed his entire kingdom. Gerar faces a situation not unlike Sodom and Gomorrah, but this time due to *Abraham's* unrighteousness. (2) God uses the outsider as a confessor, eliciting a confession from Abraham himself.

In responding (vv. 10-13), Abraham does not deny his guilt, but becomes very defensive and seeks to justify his actions. He gives three reasons: (a) He had determined with certainty (רק *raq*) that there was no fear of God in this place and so had to protect himself (as in 12:10-20, killing an alien was considered less an offense than adultery). In view of what *Abraham* has done, and what the reader has learned about Abimelech, this reason appears highly ironic (and may explain its delay). The "fear of God" may indeed be found in this place. Not all cities are like Sodom! It is *Abraham* who has not exhibited the fear of God; this lays the groundwork for the testing of Abraham's fear of God (22:12; to distinguish between Abimelech's and Abraham's fear of God misses this point).

(b) Sarah, his half-sister, became his wife (a permissible practice, later forbidden, Deut 27:22). This rationale does not speak to the point being made. Abraham had not given Abimelech sufficient knowledge to make a proper decision regarding Sarah.

(c) Genesis 20 does not offer a special case; Abraham has done this at every place where they have sojourned! His focus on kindness (חסד *ḥesed*) to himself, and laying the blame back on God for making him wander (not the full truth of the matter), have a self-serving ring. This suggests a less than trusting relation to God, let alone an inability to develop strategies for life that are in the best interests of all those who might be affected.

Given the defensiveness of Abraham's reply, Abimelech's response seems magnanimous indeed. He not only restores Sarah (the use of "brother" means he either accepts Abraham's explanation or keeps his deed front and center in the midst of the generosity), he gives Abraham a significant sum of money for the purpose of vindicating her within her family (literally, a "covering of eyes")—a public demonstration that she has not been wronged and hence can be held in honor within her community. He also gives them animals and servants and offers them a place to live in his land (unlike 12:19-20).

Abraham responds by interceding on Abimelech's behalf (see 18:22-33; Num 12:13; 21:7). God responds to his prayer and heals Abimelech (of an uncertain malady) and his wife and female slaves so that they can once again bear children (illness? Was Sarah included?). Instead of being an agent of blessing, Abraham had been an agent of curse; but by praying he can begin to turn around what he has done. Note that the narrator uses the name Yahweh for the first time in this narrative (v. 18), perhaps to make clear that this activity functions consistently with the work of God, whom Abimelech's community confesses. This community of outsiders receives, thereby, order (salvation).

REFLECTIONS

1. God attends to what Abimelech has to say in vv. 4-5; it affects the shape of the future. God takes seriously religious questioning by the "unchosen" ones. Moreover, God engages them directly, albeit through less than "orthodox" channels (such as dreams). The fact that Abimelech is a Canaanite ruler makes this point even more notable.

The reader finds goodness and a keen sense of justice among the outsiders. "The Canaanite king hears the voice that speaks as God's voice because it says what he recognizes to be just and valid."[143] The narrator, of course, understands this voice as that of the God of Abraham. Throughout the ages, nonchosen people often have had a profound sense of justice and truth, and they have often been teachers of the community of faith regarding such matters. The text functions with a sense of natural law as a part of the created order of things that can be discerned and observed apart from faith. (See Jesus' evaluation of the centurion in Matt 8:10: "In no one in Israel have I found such faith" [NRSV].)

Once again, God uses an outsider to convict the chosen ones of their sinful deeds (see 12:18-19). Persons of faith have not listened to outsiders as often as they should, perhaps thinking that they cannot be called to account by such persons on moral issues. Many people who are not a part of the community of faith have consciences more sensitive than the people of God, who do not have a corner on discerning right and wrong. One might claim that Abimelech is motivated by self-interest, for he needs Abraham's intercession to be healed. Yet, the overall portrayal of Abimelech suggests a person of character. Although not the root cause of this problem, he seeks to bring healing to the situation far beyond the level of his own involvement.

2. For God to hold an individual back from sinning (v. 6) raises a theological issue. If God can enter into people's lives and, at will, prevent them from sinning (in this case, through Abimelech's illness), then human sin reflects a divine choice, occurring only when God chooses *not* to hold individuals back from doing so. A more likely interpretation would be that Abimelech does not sin because he responds to the work of God in his life.

Texts such as this should prompt reflection concerning God's relationship with those outside the chosen community. It should prevent easy assumptions about God's presence and activity in their lives. Whether such persons recognize the transcendent reality at work is another matter, of course. They often may be unable to name the experience for what it is. The community of faith faces a challenge to speak about the faith with these persons in such a way that connections can be made with the God experiences they have already had, enabling them to move toward naming that experience for what it in fact has been. God speaks with Abimelech fundamentally to preserve Sarah, but also because of a concern for Abimelech.

3. References to the effect of Abimelech's deed upon his people highlight the communal impact of an individual's sin, insufficiently recognized in modern individualistic understandings of sin and guilt. Words for "sin" can refer to any point on a continuum from the sinful act (the first reference in v. 9) to its far-reaching effects (the second). An innocent person, indeed an entire nation, has been caught up in the effects of another's

143. Westermann, *Genesis 12–36,* 322.

sin. Because of the seamless web of life, the interconnectedness of all things, those who are innocent are often caught up in the consequences of the sinful deeds of others (from personal abuse to wars).

In a related matter, this narrative clarifies the importance of distinguishing between forgiveness and salvation. One may be forgiven for a sin committed and thereby be restored within the broken relationship; but forgiveness, however many positive results it may have, does not wipe out with one stroke the *effects* of the sin. Those effects have to be dealt with in other ways, the result of which may be called salvation. Isaiah 40:1-11 is an illustration: God announces forgiveness in vv. 1-2, but salvation still lies in the future. A contemporary illustration: A parent may be forgiven for the abuse of a child, but the effects of that abuse in the child's life will need considerable attention over the months and years to come before the child is healed.

4. Abraham, once again, has brought trouble rather than blessing to outsiders (v. 9). He has not attended very well to the call to be a blessing to all families. This no doubt mirrors the people of God in later generations, who have often mistreated strangers and aliens in their midst (a concern deeply rooted in Israel's law, cf. Exod 22:21-27). Deeds of the chosen have all too often led to the suffering of others.

5. God does not heal directly, but works through Abraham's prayers. The prayer of a righteous person may avail much (James 5:16), but here the prayer of an *unrighteous* Abraham proves effective. The righteous one needs the prayers of the unrighteous chosen one. God has chosen to work through even such persons to carry out the divine purposes. Other texts will speak of additional means (e.g., 2 Kgs 20:7), but prayer appears here as a powerful vehicle through which God works to heal.

6. God works for life and goodness, both within and without the community of faith, and often in spite of the words and deeds of the chosen ones. Although they may complicate and frustrate the divine activity, they cannot finally stymie it; God will find a way to work toward the divine purposes. The next narrative speaks about other ways in which God continues this task.

GENESIS 21:1-34, ISAAC, ISHMAEL, AND ABIMELECH

OVERVIEW

The three episodes in this chapter are sewn together by word plays and other verbal and thematic links. The stories of the birth of Isaac and the expulsion of Hagar and Ishmael are internally linked, and together they are enclosed by stories about Abimelech. The first (20:1-17) is tied to 21:1-7 by the references to God's involvement in the lives of women having difficulty bearing children; the second (21:22-34) follows a story in which water and wells, and relationships between insiders and outsiders, also play a role. The birth of Isaac is surrounded by many texts associated with nonchosen people, suggesting that issues of Israel's relationship to such people (see 12:3) are central. The story of Hagar and Ishmael also has many links with chap. 22 (see below).

Genesis 21:1-7, The Birth of Isaac

COMMENTARY

Isaac's birth brings a key aspect of the story of Abraham to a climax. The writer depicts it in quite straightforward fashion, considering all the problems and possibilities that have led up to this moment (some twenty-five years have passed since 12:4).

The work of the redactor (the narratives are a mix of JEP) includes cross-references, with four citations back to earlier narratives (vv. 1, 2, 4). They stress that God has made good on the promises (17:15-21) and that Abraham has been obedient in naming and circumcising Isaac (17:12, 19; cf. 17:23). Readers will recall the ages of Sarah and Abraham; that constitutes the wonder of the occasion (see 24:36; barrenness is no longer in view). The theme of laughter associated with Isaac's name continues. Only Sarah speaks in response to Isaac's birth (vv. 6-7). Abraham remains silent here and throughout much of the chapter, for reasons that are not entirely clear.

The distinct divine acts in v. 1 (cf. Luke 1:68) stress that God has made Isaac's birth possible. The first verb (פקד *pāqad*, various translations are possible) links this act of God with Exodus events (50:24-25; Exod 3:16; 4:31), showing the import of Isaac for the larger divine purpose. The promise language in 17:16 focuses on blessing, so one should think of a divine *creative* activity that makes Sarah's pregnancy possible (see 11:30).

God's naming of Isaac leads to his naming by both Abraham (v. 3) and Sarah (implicitly in v. 6). Whether vv. 6-7 contain one or two explanations of the name *Isaac* is debated, but the element of shame is unlikely. Verse 6 refers to Sarah's joy at the *birth* of Isaac; others who hear about the birth will rejoice *with* her. Verse 7 gives the reason: No one would have dreamed of announcing to Abraham that two such old people would become parents. They themselves did not believe it could be so!

Isaac's name thus expresses the joy at his birth, with only an indirect reference to the earlier laughter at God's promise of a son. Indeed, the author construes the former disbelief as something anyone would do. We best understand the final line in v. 7 (an inclusio with v. 2) as a cry of joy: "I have borne him a son in his old age" (see Reflections).

REFLECTIONS

1. Isaac, though the son of promise, will also cause problems, tearing this family apart. But at this moment he is the source of deep joy. The cynical laughter of these parents has not been held against them; it has been turned into genuine joy at this new life made possible by God. God has brought an end to cynicism and despair of the future; joyful hope fills the scene.

2. God does not act independently when dealing with Sarah (v. 1). The author uses the verb *bear/beget* (ילד *yālad*, used five times, twice in v. 3, but obscured in NRSV/NIV; cf. 17:17) to describe the roles of both Abraham and Sarah. At the same time, this event occurs only because God has become involved in some way, when all the roads into the future seem blocked (the text stresses their age). God works in and through human beings to carry out his purposes in the world, with all the complications and potential difficulties related thereto. The unusual cross-references stress not only the fulfillment of God's word, but also that this was not the only future possible for God. The faith of Abraham and Sarah remains relevant to all of this (as Rom 4:16-21 and Heb 11:11-12 make clear).

A modern question arises, however: In what sense can we (do we!) still speak of God's involvement in bringing a new life into being? The question is especially poignant for those parents who have had difficulty having children. The OT speaks graphically of this in some texts (e.g., Job 10:8-12; Ps 139:13). One might speak of multiple agency; both God and parents are involved in the shaping of new life. We do not normally understand God's power as all-determinative; the parental situation can profoundly affect matters, e.g., cocaine babies. Genetics or unknown factors appear more complicated. One should think of God's creative involvement in and through the medical community seeking to overcome these realities, resulting in breakthroughs for many parents.

This text might suggest that God can set aside natural processes (in this case, age) for his own special purposes. At the same time, the NT texts noted above indicate that this divine action relates to human response (in this case, faith in a specific promise). A likely reason for the long delay in the fulfillment of the promise relates to the developing response of Abraham and Sarah (including their lack of trust in 17:17; 18:12). Generally, God's perseverance within a human situation may find openings into the future that seem impossible to us, but God's will may also be frustrated in view of human response.

Genesis 21:8-21, Hagar and Ishmael

COMMENTARY

This story has often been considered a doublet with chap. 16 (J and E versions; see the distinctive use of Yahweh and Elohim). Through this "doubling," Hagar and Ishmael become more prominent figures in the story of Abraham, receiving almost as much attention as Isaac. They cannot be set aside as minor diversions in the larger story.

The fulfillment of the divine promise in Isaac's birth occasions problems as well as possibilities. The immediate problem has to do with the relationship between Abraham's two sons. Ishmael and Isaac are both children of promise (see their parallel genealogies in 25:12, 19). In 17:19-20, however, God has made clear to Abraham the difference between the sons. God would make a covenant with Sarah's son, the yet-to-be-born Isaac. But God would not overlook Ishmael; indeed, God makes promises to him as well (16:10; 17:20; 21:13, 18). God's redemptive purposes on behalf of the world (including Ishmael!) will manifest themselves through Isaac. Some of the dynamics associated with this divinely determined distinction are worked out in these verses.

21:8-14. The author begins by noting that Isaac is growing up; hence, the relationship with Ishmael will need attention. At the same time, the relationship between Sarah and Hagar (16:3-9) was either not resolved

amicably or has deteriorated in the three years since Isaac's birth. The references to Hagar as an Egyptian and bearer of Abraham's child are linked to the conflict in chap. 16, as is Sarah's repeated reference to Hagar as the "slave woman" (cf. 16:2, 5) and her concern about inheritance rights (legally, both sons would inherit). Sarah expresses concern about her maturing son's future.

These factors are sufficient explanation for Sarah's action. Yet, the difficulty in translating v. 9 (see Gal 4:29, where Ishmael "persecutes" Isaac) prompts a closer look. The verb צחק (*ṣāḥaq*, "mocking" [NIV]; "playing" [NRSV, adding "with her son Isaac," see footnote]) can have positive or negative senses (cf. 19:14). The verb has appeared in earlier narratives—the name *Isaac* and Sarah's and Abraham's laughter (17:17-19; 18:12-13). The word play associated with Ishmael's activity may have reminded her of the divine decision (17:19-20). Not unlike Rebekah (cf. 25:23), she decides it is time to act; Abraham must choose between his sons. Inasmuch as God will support her objective, at least in this regard the author views Sarah's action in positive terms.

Sarah's *strategy* is also difficult to understand, however. She demands that Abraham send Hagar and Ishmael away, using language that recalls Pharaoh's action in Exod 12:39

(and led to Israel's freedom!). She also chooses the festival associated with the weaning of Isaac, a time of rejoicing because he has survived the difficult first years. Her timing and means seem unnecessarily harsh, and (unlike chap. 16) she does not speak to Hagar. Yet God, agreeing with Sarah's objective, chooses not to interfere with her strategy.

Abraham appears distressed at Sarah's request (v. 11). His concern centers on Ishmael rather than Hagar (cf. 17:18), because Sarah insists that he choose between his two sons; God's reply (v. 12) expresses concern about Hagar as well. The narrator's use of "his son" (i.e., Ishmael) intensifies his anguish. Abraham is genuinely torn. This characteristic of Abraham has recurred in the narrative (cf. 16:6; 17:18). He has difficulty taking decisive action or following through on what God has said; yet, he shows deep levels of concern for the plight of the persons involved, and he does not finally stand in the way of God's directive.

In responding to Abraham (perhaps in a dream, v. 14), God sides with Sarah, adopts some of her language, and tells him to do as she says! God supports her objective and lets her set the strategy; Abraham must set his own feelings aside. God's rationale basically repeats what had been told to Abraham earlier (17:19-21), making it doubly clear that Abraham must make a choice. Both sons are recognized as Abraham's offspring (vv. 12-13; literally, "seed"), but God's particular future will be worked out through Isaac, however difficult or unpleasant that may be. God announces that it is through Isaac that descendants will be "named" for Abraham (NRSV), which probably refers to the covenantal line. At the same time, Abraham can be assured that God will care for the future of Ishmael. God will make of him a great nation also (vv. 13, 18).

This divine concern appears immediately (vv. 15-21). Abraham does as God tells him (שלח [šālaḥ, "send away"] again—see chap. 16—is language for Israel's *freedom* in Exodus, e.g., 5:1-2). The author creates a poignant picture in v. 14—not a single word is spoken (the text remains ambiguous as to whether Ishmael—now about sixteen years old—is placed on Hagar's shoulder). This verse stands parallel to 22:3, as do other elements in this text (see below).

21:15-21. The parallels with Exodus continue in Hagar and Ishmael's "wandering in the wilderness," again mirroring Israel's later experience (as does the provision of water). With water supplies depleted, Hagar puts Ishmael under a bush and moves away in deep sorrow; she cannot bear to watch him die. God hears "the voice of the boy" (her lament and Ishmael's are telescoped) and responds to "her" (by name; no "slave-girl") with a salvation oracle: God quells her fear and assures her of Ishmael's future in words used with Abraham (v. 13). God opens Hagar's eyes and she sees (cf. the seeing in 16:13) the source of water needed to save Ishmael's life. The now-familiar God/messenger of God rhythm appears (see 16:7).

The story closes with three themes that bode well for the future of both mother and child: "God was with the lad" (as with Abraham in v. 22); Hagar exhibits no little strength in continuing to care for his needs (finding a wife for him among her own people, the only time a mother does this in the OT); and he becomes an expert hunter. All these are important for shaping Ishmael's life well, but God's presence with him and God's promise to be creatively at work in his life stand out. His twelve sons parallel Jacob's progeny (25:12-18). Ishmael and Isaac, both as "sons," will return for the burial of their father (25:9).

REFLECTIONS

1. The modern reader may tend to side with Abraham rather than Sarah on the issue of sending Hagar and Ishmael away. Yet, some such move must occur if the sons are to shape their separate futures consistent with God's choice (17:19-20), a historical and theological reality for the narrator. Her objective seems to be on target, even if the means are unnecessarily harsh. It may be more troubling that God lets Sarah set the strategy for the separation. Here, again, God chooses to work through complex situations and imperfect human beings on behalf of the divine purposes. God works with individuals on the scene; God does not perfect people before deciding to work through them. God may see Sarah's strategy, however inadequate, as the best possible way into the future for this particular moment in the life of this family.

2. Although Genesis 22 has received most of the attention, this story of Ishmael is certainly just as difficult and heart-rending. The father-son relationship between Abraham and Ishmael is close and strong. Note some of the parallels between the episodes: In 21:14 and 22:3 Abraham rises "early in the morning" and wordlessly proceeds to put his son's future in jeopardy; both seem to move relentlessly toward death. In both cases, Abraham obeys God's command and trusts in the divine promise, leaving the future of his sons in the hands of God. Hagar voices her lament, while Abraham voices his confidence that God will provide; the sons voice laments, though only Isaac speaks. The angel of the Lord calls from heaven and speaks of a role for their hands, assuring each parent that the son will live. The eyes of both see a source of life that saves their sons.

These are parallel events in Abraham's life. What he endures as a parent of what is now an "only son" (22:2, 12, 16) appears all the more extraordinary. The character of God's "test" of Abraham in chap. 22 is intensified; God's promises are placed in jeopardy in both cases. This should occasion reflection about why the threat to the life of the "outsider" (see chap. 16) is so widely neglected compared to the threatened life of the chosen one of God. The narrator thinks otherwise. The narrative holds us to "the tension between the one *elected* and the not-elected one who is *treasured*" by God.[144]

3. Hagar's lament ensues in the assurance of salvation. This typical rhythm characterizes *Israel's* communal and individual life, so evident in the Psalms. In this story the people of God should recognize and rejoice that God's saving acts are not confined to their own community. God's acts of deliverance occur out and about in the seemingly godforsaken corners of the world, even among those who may be explicitly excluded from the "people of God." Here we see God at work among the outcasts, the refugees of the world—who fill our world as much as they did then. Persons of faith are to participate in their lives, to lift them up and hold them fast until the wells become available. They are also to discern where God's delivering activity may have occurred, to name these events for what they are, and publicly to confess them as such to the participants and to all the world. Once again, we see how Genesis witnesses to the workings of the *Creator* God. Telling and retelling stories like this one keeps that testimony alive and serves to remind the chosen that their God is the God of all the world, including the outcasts.

Phyllis Trible speaks eloquently about Hagar's becoming many things to many people (see chap. 16): "Most especially, all sorts of rejected women find their stories in her. She is the faithful maid exploited, the black woman used by the male and abused by the female of the ruling class, the surrogate mother, the resident alien without legal recourse, the other woman, the runaway youth, the religious fleeing from affliction, the pregnant young woman alone, the expelled wife, the divorced mother with child, the shopping bag lady carrying bread and water, the homeless woman, the indigent relying upon handouts from the power structures, the welfare mother, and the self-effacing female whose own identity shrinks in service to others."[145] How does the community of faith respond to these Hagars of our world?

The text does affirm that God chooses the line of Isaac, not that of Ishmael. This is a strong claim, and it occasions a sharper question for Isaac's descendants than if the treatment had been more "even-handed." What one does with the Ishmaels of this world in the face of the claims for Isaac comes front and center. Abraham was chosen

144. Brueggemann, *Genesis*, 183.
145. Trible, *Texts of Terror*, 28.

so that all families might be blessed through him. This means that the children of Abraham who are also the children of *Isaac* are so to comport themselves that blessing rather than curse comes upon the nations.

4. This text reminds us that the world is filled with both physical *and spiritual* (as Christians relate to Abraham) descendants of Ishmael. Nearly one billion Muslims, 85 percent of whom live outside the Middle East, call Abraham father, too. Even more, they are the descendants of God's promise to Ishmael, which remains a contemporary theological reality. How is the other half of Abraham's family going to relate to these brothers and sisters in ways that acknowledge this ongoing work of God? Our words and actions may run so counter to God's activity that the divine will for this people, embodied in the promises, is thereby frustrated and hence less effective than it might otherwise be.

Paul's use of this text in Gal 4:21-31 picks up on the story in a somewhat narrow way, but does not finally stand over against this point. Using an allegorical approach, Hagar and Sarah symbolize two different ways of conceiving of life in God's world: Hagar, the way of slavery and law (Sinai); and Sarah, the way of promise and the freedom of the Spirit. Ishmael was produced in natural, humanly planned ways; Isaac came only as a gift of God's promise. Paul uses this contrast to address differences between Christianity and Judaism, with Christians belonging to the line of promise. From another angle, Hagar could be the embodiment of Paul's argument, with her combination of necessity (her return to Sarah) and freedom.[146] Paul's word in Gal 3:28-29, that there are neither slave nor free, but that all are one in Christ Jesus, could provide another perspective on Hagar, who bears public witness to the God of Abraham and Sarah.

146. See Janzen, "Hagar in Paul's Eyes."

Genesis 21:22-34, Abraham and Abimelech

COMMENTARY

This episode explores the relationship between Abraham and Abimelech, which began in chap. 20 (cf. Isaac in 26:1-33). It may be an interweaving of two covenant stories (from J and E?) that explain the name Beersheba (cf. 26:33) as the "well of the oath" and the "well of seven [ewe lambs]."

Abimelech appears as a character in two separate episodes, a common feature in the Abraham cycle (witness the wife-sister theme, covenant, Lot, Hagar, and Ishmael). This "doubling" brings greater coherence to the larger story. Here it suggests that the relationship between Abraham and other peoples (especially those in Canaan) matters. Isaac's birth occurs in the midst of a world filled with various problems. The story also highlights Abraham's initial acquisition of land in Canaan (cf. chap. 23). Beersheba, at the southernmost boundary of Judah, did not become a city until later times.

The transition between vv. 21 and 22 is abrupt but presupposes the problems created for Abimelech by Abraham in chap. 20. There are few links to the story of Hagar and Ishmael, but both relate Abraham to non-Israelite peoples, and in ways that exhibit the importance of positive relationships about which God expresses concern.

We may compare the content of vv. 22-24 to the report about Isaac and Abimelech/Phicol in 26:26-33. Abimelech's testimony regards God's presence with Abraham and Abimelech's concern that the basic human loyalty (חסד *ḥesed*) he has shown Abraham be returned to his family (and to the land!). Abraham swears that he will do so. The reference to posterity brings the problematic relationships between Israelites and Canaanites over the years into view. Abraham serves as a mirror in which those generations can reflect about such relationships.

Within the relationship just established, Abraham complains to Abimelech about his servants' actions in seizing a well (v. 25), an important resource in that world (see 26:27). Abimelech pleads ignorance, but also notes that he had not been informed until this moment (in view of chap. 20, this response is not evasive). This exchange concludes with a nonaggression pact, according to which the two agree to maintain a relationship of integrity. Abraham contributes sheep and oxen for his part, but from among them sets seven ewe lambs apart and gives them a special significance.

Abraham's reply to Abimelech's natural query about the lambs indicates that, by accepting them as an addendum to the oath, Abimelech makes a public witness that the well is not his but Abraham's. This shrewd move settles the conflict over the well. Beersheba receives its name based on this sworn oath and the gift/acceptance of the seven lambs. In this way, the story provides grounding for *both* meanings—well of seven or well of the oath (NRSV)—of the name Beersheba.

Abimelech and Phicol return to their own territories. The "land of the Philistines" could be an anachronism (the Philistines settled in that land around 1200 BCE), yet it probably represents the knowledge of the Abrahamic era available to the narrator. Philistines may represent all pre-Israelite inhabitants of the land. Abraham plants a tree at Beersheba as a permanent sign of the treaty and worships God. The epithet used for God (only here)—El Olam, the Everlasting God—may testify to the appropriation of an epithet/name of the god El for Yahweh (cf. Ps 102:24-29). When related to the nature of this specific event, it expresses a confidence in God's tending to this relationship long after the death of the present participants. The final note that Abraham sojourned for an extensive period of time in Abimelech's land testifies not only to the effectiveness of the treaty, but also to Abraham's continuing alien status in a land included in the promise (15:18-21).

REFLECTIONS

Abimelech again discerns the character of Abraham's situation theologically. He *interprets* Abraham's relationship with God: "God is with you in all that you do" (v. 22), in language identical to the narrator's interpretation of Ishmael in v. 20. In other words, God has blessed Abraham in all observable circumstances of life. In spite of the way Abimelech was treated in chap. 20, he discerns that God's presence functions decisively in Abraham's life. Given God's promise (12:3), Abimelech participates in God's blessings to Abraham and Abraham gains some rights in the land. That an outsider like Abimelech makes such a confession and treats Abraham well in spite of what happened earlier testifies notably to God's work as Creator in his life.

Abraham enters into a mutually agreed-upon covenant with outsiders. God's purposes in the world are for the good order of the creation, which includes relationships with all, regardless of their faith commitments. The story implies that Abraham is not somehow inevitably trustworthy; specific agreements will be needed by the outsider, because loyalty on the part of chosen ones all too often fails.

In response to the *secular* event of reconciliation, Abraham worships Yahweh. This connection made by Abraham between peacemaking events of everyday life and the worship of God is significant. Linking such events of peace and justice explicitly to God recognizes that God has been involved behind the scenes, enabling such salutary effects. The OT regularly refuses to separate sacred and secular, though God-talk is often reserved for explicitly religious matters in the modern world. The confession of the community of faith should be clear: "All things work together for good for those who love God" (Rom 8:28 NRSV). This should issue in worshipful gratitude to God whenever *any* good thing happens.

GENESIS 22:1-19, THE TESTING OF ABRAHAM

COMMENTARY

Recent readers of this famous story have been particularly interested in delineating its literary artistry.[147] Significant gains have resulted, but one wonders whether this approach has overplayed its hand by over-dramatizing the story and reading too much between the lines. Likewise, religious interpretations, especially in the wake of Kierkegaard's *Fear and Trembling,* seem often to intensify the contradictoriness of the story, perhaps in the interests of heightening the mystery of the divine ways. While the frightening, even bizarre, character of the divine command ought not to be discounted, it should not be exaggerated either.

This story (commonly assigned to E, with supplements) remains firmly within the circle of the family, which suggests an original pre-Israelite setting. At the same time, the theological force of the story takes on new contours as it is passed through many generations (especially vv. 15-19).[148] Exilic Israel may have seen itself in both Abraham and Isaac: God has put Israel to a test in which many children died, has called forth its continuing faith, has delivered it through the fires of judgment and renewed the promises.

Israelite ritual regarding the firstborn informs this text. Israel knew that God could require the firstborn (Exod 22:29), but that God had provided for their redemption (Exod 13:13; 34:20). Here, God does just this: God asks that Isaac be sacrificed and provides an animal "instead of" Isaac. This issue belongs indisputably to the story, but with a metaphorical understanding of *Israel* as God's first-born (see below). The text bears no mark of an etiology of sacrifice (see 4:3-4; 8:20) or a polemic against child sacrifice, clearly abhorrent to Israel, though it was sometimes a problem (cf. Lev 20:2-5; 2 Kgs 3:27; Jer 7:31; 32:35).

This text fits into the larger sweep of Abraham's life. The relationship between God and Abraham is in progress; it has had its ups and downs, in which each has affected the other. Abraham has exhibited a deep faith and engaged God in significant theological conversation, while God has consulted with Abraham regarding the fate of Sodom and Gomorrah. At the same time, Abraham's response has been less than exemplary, even distrusting the promise (17:17) and not showing the "fear of God" in relationship to outsiders (see 20:11). His response has raised an issue for God, indeed what God truly knows (v. 12).

Generally, though, this text presupposes "familiar mutual trust" built over no little experience together.[149] From Abraham's perspective, the God who commands has filled his life with promises; he understands that God has Abraham's best interests at heart. He has already learned to trust this God. He has no reason to distrust the God from whom this word comes, however harsh and frightening it may be.

The test appears especially poignant in view of the parallels with the story of Ishmael (see 21:8-21). Abraham has just lost his son Ishmael, hence the repeated reference to Isaac as "only son." Now he is asked to sacrifice his remaining son. We may view these stories as mirrors of each other, focusing on the potential loss of both sons, as well as on God's providing for both children.

Parallels between Gen 12:1-4 and Genesis 22 provide an overarching structure. Although this divine command does not appear as abrupt as in 12:1, they are similar in other ways, in vocabulary ("take, go" to a "place that I shall show you"), along with Abraham's silent, but faithful, response. Both are ventures in faith and enclose the story of Abraham; Abraham begins and ends his journey with God by venturing out into the deep at the command of God. The former cuts

---

147. Most influential is E. Auerbach, "Odysseus' Scar," in *Mimesis* (Princeton: Princeton University Press, 1965) 1-22.

148. See R. Moberly, "The Earliest Commentary on the Akedah," *VT* 38 (1988) 302-23.

149. Westermann, *Genesis 12–36,* 356.

Abraham off from his past; the latter threatens to cut him off from his future.

We may observe the structure of the entire text in the threefold reference to "your son, your only son" (vv. 2, 12, 16). Also, the repetition of Abraham's "Here I am," spoken to God (v. 1), then Isaac (v. 7), and finally God (v. 11) highlights basic moments in the story.

22:1-14. God commands Abraham not to kill or murder his son, but to present him "on the altar" as a burnt offering to God (עלה *'ōlâ*; cf. Exod 29:38-46; Lev 1:3-17). The offering language places this entire episode within the context of the sacrificial system. The deed will be a specifically religious act, an act of faith, a giving to God of what Abraham loves (only then would it be a true sacrifice). Inasmuch as sacrifice involves a vehicle in and through which God gives back the life that has been given, the hope against hope for Abraham would be that God would somehow find a way of giving Isaac—or another life—back (hence the link made to the resurrection by Heb 11:17-19). We should note that Abraham does, finally, offer a sacrifice.

Abraham's silent response to God's command (on test, see below) may be designed to raise questions in the mind of the reader. Why is Abraham being "blindly" obedient, not raising any questions or objections (especially in view of 18:23-25)? Abraham's trust in God seems evident in his open stance ("Here I am") and unhesitating response. At the same time, the text gives us no clue as to his emotional state (e.g., whether he was deeply troubled).

God's command is accompanied by נא (*na'*), a particle of entreaty or urgency. Rarely used by God (cf. Judg 13:4; Isa 1:18; Isa 7:3), God thereby may signal the unusual character of the moment and the relationship of mutual trust. It may help Abraham to see that God has as much stake in this matter as he does; God needs to know about Abraham's faith. This may account for Abraham's silence. However, God does not engage in a ploy, but offers a genuine command. Yet, the command pertains to a particular moment; it is not universally valid. Moreover, God does not intend that the commandment be fully obeyed. Hence, God revokes the command when the results of the test become clear and

speaks a second command that *overrides* the first (v. 12).

We should note the emphasis on "seeing." Twice, Abraham lifts up his eyes (vv. 4, 13), and five times the verb "to see" (ראה *rā'â*) is used of Abraham (vv. 4, 13) and God (vv. 8, twice in 14). From a distance, Abraham sees the place where God told him to sacrifice Isaac and then, close up, he sees the ram provided at that very place. This process testifies to a *progressively clearer seeing*. Abraham places his trust in *God's seeing* (v. 8) and that trust finally enables him to see the lamb that God has seen to. Seeing saves the son (cf. Hagar's seeing in 16:13; 21:19, which saves Ishmael).

The writer offers another important feature: "the mountains that I shall show you" (v. 2; cf. 12:1). The narrative stresses it early on (vv. 3-5, 9) and returns to it in v. 14, when a name appears: God will provide. *God* shows Abraham that place (by v. 3 NRSV). It is as if God has prepared the scene ahead of time, ram and all, and hence Abraham must be precisely directed to it. Moriah, three days' journey away (a general reference), a place unknown to us, but not to him, may refer to Jerusalem (2 Chr 3:1; cf. "the mount of Yahweh" [v. 14] in Ps 24:3; Isa 2:3). The place name *Moriah* gives the command a special quality: Abraham will not sacrifice at any altar, but in a specific God-chosen place a great distance away. Might this arrangement have given Abraham a clue to what God intended?

Verses 7-8 are central. The statement "the two of them walked on together" encloses this interchange between Abraham and Isaac. Abraham's statement of faith that God will provide (v. 8) is the only time Abraham responds more fully than "Here I am." This is also the only time that Isaac speaks. Note also the movement from the more distancing language of "boy" in v. 5 to the repeated "my son" in vv. 7-8, perhaps testifying to a shift in perspective.

By this point Abraham stays on course because he trusts that God will act to save Isaac. He conveys to Isaac what he believes to be the truth about his future: God will provide. He testifies to this form of divine action in v. 14, as does Israel's witness to the event "to this day" (v. 14). God tests precisely the nature of Abraham's response as unhesitating trust in the deity. As God puts it (v. 12), it involves Abraham's fear of God, a faithfulness that accords with God's purposes and works itself out in daily life as truth and justice (see 20:11). Abraham obeys because he trusts God; trust out of which obedience flows remains basic. Disobedience would reveal a lack of trust. At least by v. 8 Abraham's obedience is informed and undergirded by a trust that God will find a way through this dark moment.

Anticipations of this trust occur earlier. In v. 5 Abraham tells his servants that both of them will worship and both will return; the servants *witness* to this conviction. The author relates the trustful reference to worship with the worship in v. 8. To suggest that Abraham is equivocating or being ironic or deceptive or whistling in the dark finds no basis in the text; such ideas betray too much interest in dramatization. It would be strange for a narrative designed to demonstrate Abraham's trusting obedience to be punctuated with acts of deception.

Verses 7-8 also focus on Isaac. The author initially devotes attention to Isaac as a child (without recalling the promise). Abraham loves this child (in *God's* judgment, v. 2); we should not assume an abusive relationship. Although ignorant of the journey's purpose, Isaac does not remain entirely passive. He breaks the silence with a question of his father (v. 7)—the only recorded exchange between them. He senses that something is not right (his lack of reference to the knife no more suggests this than does the absence of fire in vv. 9-10). Yet, Isaac does not focus on himself. (Isaac's emotions are often overplayed.) Isaac addresses Abraham as a loving father, mirroring Abraham's trusting relationship to God. Abraham responds in like manner.

Abraham centers on what his son has to say, attending to him as he has attended to God ("Here I am"). He does not dismiss Isaac's question, as if inappropriate. It even elicits Abraham's trust in God in a *public* form. Isaac enables his father's trusting action to be joined with trusting words. While not telling him everything, Abraham does answer Isaac's question directly and conveys to him what he believes will happen. What had been implicit (v. 5) here becomes explicit.

Their walking on together conveys indirectly Isaac's response. He exhibits no resistance, even later when his father prepares him for the sacrificial moment (some descriptions of the knife go beyond the text). Isaac believes his father's trust to be well placed. Abraham's trust in God has become Isaac's trust: God will provide a lamb, which is God's intention from the beginning, of course, and Abraham and Isaac are now both attuned to that intention and trust it.

The text also focuses on Abraham's *continuing* trust in God. The trusting departure does not settle the issue, or God could have cut off the journey much earlier. The question becomes: Will Abraham stay with the journey? The author stresses the journey as such, which provides opportunity for second thoughts (vv. 6, 8) following each expression of trust (vv. 5, 8). Abraham exhibits his trust in God by staying the course. Only at the end of the journey can God say, "Now I know."

Tensions in the text also center on God. *What is at stake in this for God?*

1. God's testing. God and the reader know this is a test; Abraham does not. God intends not to kill Isaac but to test Abraham's faithfulness, which is essential if God is to move into the future with him. In responding, Abraham no doubt observes (as do all commentators) the apparent contradictory character of the command: God, having fulfilled the promise of a son, asks Abraham to sacrifice that son and the future that goes with him. The fact that Abraham obeys shows that he trusts God will find a way into the future. God had found a way to fulfill the promise of a son when nothing seemed possible (see 18:14); given that experience, Abraham trusts that this comparably impossible situation will not be beyond God's ability. Abraham trusts that God's promise and command are not finally contradictory; whatever conflict there may be, it is up to God to resolve it, and God is up to it.

If Abraham had known in advance that it was a test, it would have been no real test; for he (or anyone) would respond differently to a test from a more indirect method of discernment. Moreover, the test would not work simply at the verbal level; words might not lead to action. Abraham may recognize this fact by his silence, responding in deed rather than word. In the OT, God tests Israel to discern whether they will do justice to a relationship in which they stand (Deut 8:2-3). God can test by discerning the human response to a command: Is Abraham's loyalty undivided? God initiates the test to gain certainty.

2. God's knowledge. Brueggemann notes correctly that this test "is not a game with God; God genuinely does not know. . . . The flow of the narrative accomplishes something in the awareness of God. He did not know. Now he knows."[150] The test is as real for God as it is for Abraham.

The test is *not* designed to teach *Abraham* something—that he is too attached to Isaac, or that Isaac is "pure gift," or that he must learn to cling to God rather than to the content of the promise. Experience always teaches, of course, and Abraham certainly learns. But nowhere does the text say that he now trusts more in God or has learned a lesson of some sort. Rather, the test *confirms a fact:* Abraham trusts deeply that God has his best interests at heart so that he will follow where God's command leads (a point repeated in vv. 12 and 16). The only one said to learn anything from the test is *God:* "Now I know" (v. 12; on the angel, see commentary on 16:7). God does not teach; rather, God learns. For the sake of the future, God needs to know about Abraham's trust.

While God knew what was likely to happen, God does not have absolute certainty as to how Abraham would respond. God has in view the larger divine purpose, not just divine curiosity or an internal divine need. The story addresses a future that encompasses all the families of the earth: Is Abraham the faithful one who can carry that purpose along? Or does God need to take some other course of action, perhaps even look for another?

Is the promise of God thereby made conditional? In some sense, yes (see vv. 16-18). Fidelity was not optional. God could not have used a disloyal Abraham for the purposes God intends.

3. God's vulnerability. Some people read this story as if God were a detached observer, a heavenly homeroom teacher watching from afar to see if Abraham passes the test. But God puts much at risk in this ordeal. *God* had

chosen Isaac as the one to continue the line of promise (at one point Abraham would have chosen Ishmael, 17:18; 21:11). Although God does not intend that Isaac be killed, the test places *God's own* promise at risk, at least in the form of the person of Isaac. The command has the potential of taking back what God has taken so many pains to put in place.

This story presents a test not only of Abraham's faith in God, but of God's faith in Abraham as well, in the sense that Abraham's response will affect the moves God makes next. God places the shape of God's own future in Abraham's hands. Given his somewhat mixed responses to God up to this point, God took something of a risk to put so much on the line with this man. As E. Roop puts it: "God took the risk that Abraham would respond. Abraham took the risk that God would provide."[151] One cannot project what God would have done had Abraham failed, or if Abraham had actually killed Isaac, but God would have had to find another way into the future, perhaps another way with Abraham.

Why would God place the promise at risk in order to see whether *Abraham* fears God? Why not just get on with it, or wait to put Isaac to the test? But, according to vv. 16-18 (and 26:3-5, 24), it is not enough for the sake of the history of the promise that Isaac be born. There are also other promises to be fulfilled. Abraham's continuing faithful response to God remains a central issue. God waits upon him before getting on with the promised future.

The interpreter may find difficulty in relating Genesis 22 to the divine promises of chap. 15, where God participates in an act of self-imprecation; God's potential sacrifice there (reinforced here by God's own oath) correlates with Abraham's potential sacrifice of Isaac. While the promises are not given a new shape in Genesis 22, they receive a new emphasis in view of Abraham's response.

4. God's trustworthiness. The test raises the question of whether God can be trusted. This God promises, proceeds to fulfill that promise, and then seems to take it back. Can readers trust this God only because they know this is a test, and that God does not intend to kill Isaac? For Abraham, trust

150. Brueggemann, *Genesis*, 187; on the less than absolute character of divine foreknowledge, see Fretheim, *The Suffering of God*, 45-59.

151. Eugene F. Roop, *Genesis* (Scottdale, Pa.: Herald, 1987) 151.

158

was there without this knowledge. What will God's response be?

Abraham departs for the place of sacrifice because he believes that God can require Isaac of him (and of God!); yet he trusts that God will somehow find a way to fulfill the promises. By v. 8 in his long journey, his trust has taken the form that God will provide a lamb. His public confession constitutes *a new situation* with which God must work. This ups the ante for *God.* The test no longer involves simply Abraham's trust but becomes a matter of God's providing as well. Will Abraham's trust in God be in vain? Is God free to ignore Abraham's trust? If God did not provide, then that would constitute *another kind of test,* at a much deeper level than the one initiating this journey.

If God tests within relationship to determine loyalty, then God cannot disdain the expression of such loyalty. Given God's previous commitments (especially in chap. 15), God is bound to stay with a trusting Abraham. So God does speak, forbidding the sacrifice of Isaac and providing an animal; even more, God provides it as a substitute for Isaac, "instead of his son."

5. God's providing. Why should God be praised as a provider for following through on God's own test? God appears praiseworthy for being faithful to the commitment to Abraham. But why was the ram even necessary? After discerning that Abraham did fear God, God stopped him *before* he saw the ram (vv. 12-13). Yet, God provided the ram, and Abraham offered it "instead of his son." A sacrifice

seems necessary, even if not expressly commanded. If not Isaac, then it must be another.

The redemption of the firstborn remains as a concern in this text (Exod 13:13; 22:29; 34:20). But the interest is not etiological or historical. This motif underscores *Israel* as the firstborn of God (Exod 4:22), an issue faced by the exiles (Jer 31:9, 20; cf. 2:3). This story presents a *metaphor* for Israel's life with God, in which Israel becomes both Abraham and Isaac (see below).

22:15-19. These verses report God's response in straightforward language (reinforced by 26:3-5, 24, but often obscured by efforts to wiggle out of the implications), twice spoken as if to ensure the point: *Because* Abraham has done this, previously spoken divine promises can be reiterated. The promises were originally made (12:1-3) independently of Abraham's response. God's promises create his faith (15:6), though Abraham could still be unfaithful. That is not reversed here so that his faith creates the promises. The covenant in chap. 15 was made with Abraham as a person of faith (as all covenants in the OT are). Here the promises are reiterated (in an emphatic way) to a trusting Abraham. If he had been unfaithful to God, we do not know what would have happened (God may have given Abraham another opportunity), but we do know that the promises would always be there for Abraham to cling to. Having seen Abraham's faithfulness, God swears *an oath* for the first time in the narrative, in effect laying the divine life on the line, putting the very divine self behind the promise.

REFLECTIONS

1. This is a classic text. It has captivated the imaginations of numerous interpreters, drawn by both its literary artistry and its religious depths. It has played a special role in both Jewish and Christian traditions. Before its depth and breadth one stands on holy ground. But this text also presents problems. It has occasioned deep concern, especially in a time when the abuse of children has screamed its way into the modern consciousness.

Psychoanalyst Alice Miller claims this text may have contributed to an atmosphere that makes it possible to justify the abuse of children. She grounds her reflections on some thirty artistic representations of this story over the centuries. In two of Rembrandt's paintings, Abraham faces the heavens rather than Isaac, as if in blind obedience to God and oblivious to what he is about to do. Abraham's hands cover Isaac's face, preventing him from seeing or raising a cry. Not only is Isaac silenced, but only his torso shows—his personal features are obscured. Isaac "has been turned into an *object*. He has been dehumanized by being made a sacrifice; he no longer has a right to ask questions and will scarcely even be able to articulate them to himself, for there is no room in him for anything besides fear."[152]

We may not simply dismiss the possible negative impact of this text; it would not be the first time the Bible has been used knowingly or unknowingly for such purposes. The text contributes to such an understanding, as God asks and then twice commends Abraham for not withholding his son, his only son (vv. 2, 12, 16). Abraham asks no questions, and God offers no qualifications. The child seems to be a pawn in the hands of two "adults" who need to work out an issue between them.

Yet, while moderns might wonder about the psychological abuse Isaac endures in all of this, the narrator gives him a questioning voice, and his father attentively responds to his query. This dialogue leads Isaac to place himself trustingly in the arms of his father and his God. The text offers no evidence that trust in God ever wavers for either father or son. We must be careful to stress these elements for the sake of a proper hearing of the text. Children must be allowed to ask their questions about this text, to which adults should be highly alert.

2. Once again, an Abrahamic text mirrors a later period in Israel's life. Israel, God's firstborn, had been sentenced to death *by God* in the fires of judgment. But exilic Israel remains God's firstborn (so Jeremiah affirms, 31:9), the carrier of God's purposes into the future. As Isaac was saved from death, so was Israel delivered from the brink of annihilation. But what of the future? Out of this matrix the Israelites developed an understanding that a sacrifice was necessary to assure Israel's future, shaped most profoundly in Isaiah 53 (see the use of שׂה (*śeh*), lamb, in 53:7 and vv. 7-8; cf. Jer 11:19). Israel's redemption would not occur without cost. At the same time, Israel's faithfulness was not an optional matter as it moved into a future shaped by God's promises. The emphasis on descendants in v. 17 also connects well with these exilic concerns (see Isa 51:2, and the renewed interest in Abraham in exile). The NT use of this story to understand the sacrifice of God's only Son constitutes an appropriate extension of the text (see John 1:14).

3. To trust God does not mean always to respond in an unquestioning way; this text does not commend passivity before God. Chapters 18 and 22 must be kept together, showing that Abraham's faithfulness to God works itself out in various ways. Perhaps Abraham responds as he does in chap. 22 because he learned from the encounter in chap. 18 that God is indeed just, and that he need only trust on this occasion. The confession that God will provide pertains as much to times of questioning and challenging as to moments of "blind" trust. It may well be the *reader* who, having learned from Abraham in chap. 18, responds with questions to God's command to sacrifice Isaac.

Abraham does not simply obey; he obeys because he trusts. He could have obeyed because he was ordered to do so; if God commands, he had better respond. But v. 8 makes clear that he obeys because he trusts God, that God will be faithful and will act in his best interests. Hebrews 11:17-19 posits the Resurrection at this point; if necessary, the promises will remain in and through death. Moreover, Abraham does not claim ownership of the promise, as if it were his possession, as if his faithful response counts for little or nothing (see Jas 2:18-26).

4. This story presents the last dialogue between Abraham and God and between Abraham and Isaac. It follows closely on the heels of the birth of Isaac and precedes Sarah's death (23:2). The narrative's literary setting intimates a concern for the (unprecedented) turning of the generations; Isaac now moves out into the world on his own. The absence of an explicit reference to Isaac at the end (v. 19) may witness to a future

---

152. Alice Miller, *The Untouched Key: Tracing Childhood Trauma in Creativity and Destructiveness* (New York: Doubleday, 1990) 139.

open to the next generation, with uncertainty as to what will happen to the promises as Abraham moves off the scene.[153]

One promise has been fulfilled. Yet, promises of land, numerous descendants, and being a blessing to the nations remain. What status do these other divine promises have now? Are they a matter of course, to be fulfilled irrespective of Abraham's (or anyone else's) faith in God? Are God's promises now to be carried by genetics, by a natural biological succession? What happens if Abraham ceases to trust God? At times scholars speak of the unconditionality of God's promise to Abraham in such a way that faith becomes irrelevant. Verses 16-18 together with 26:3-5, 24 make clear, however, that God reiterates the promise to Isaac because of the way in which Abraham responded in faithfulness. Hence, the promise does not automatically or naturally carry on into the family's next generation.

Although God will never invalidate the promise, people do not participate in the sphere of the promise independently of a faithful response. Abraham could have said no to God, and complicated God's moves into the future, though not finally stymied them. While the divine word of promise inspires Abraham's trust (15:6), he could resist the word of God; if that were not the case, then the command would have been no test at all, for the outcome would have been settled in advance. God, however, does not coerce or program Abraham's fidelity.

The apostle Paul incorporates this point when making the claim that the promises of God cannot be reduced to genetics (Rom 4:16-25; Gal 3:6-9). Those who have faith in the God of Abraham have received the promises irrespective of biological succession.

At the same time, the text does not imply a spiritual succession across the centuries, for the promise takes shape in the actual lives of people, whose *own words and deeds* are centrally involved in its transmission. This means that the word of God, in some general way, does not provide for the continuity across the generations. God places the promise in the hands of those who are faithful, and their witness ought not to be discounted.

Another way of putting the issue: What happens to faith when the promise reaches fulfillment? Granted, other promises reach out to the future. But receiving the promised son could have tempted Abraham to push other promises to the side: I now have what I want. How do promises already fulfilled affect the relationship with God? Will Abraham's trust in God still be the core of his life? Will Abraham still ground his life in the divine promises rather than bask in the sunshine of fulfillment? In order to explore these questions, the test focused precisely on the point of fulfillment: Isaac.

5. Testing must be considered relationally, not legalistically. Life in relationship will inevitably bring tests; individuals will often find themselves in situations where their loyalty is tested. What constitutes testing will be determined by the nature of the relationship and the expectations the parties have for it. As a relationship matures and trust levels are built up, faithful responses to the testing of the relational bond will tend to become second nature. Yet, even in a mature relationship, sharp moments of testing may present themselves. Abraham may have faced this kind of moment.

Is the relationship with the deity one in which the people of God can expect to be put to the test again and again? Are there absurd, senseless experiences in life that can become the occasion to turn away from God? There may well be a deep, dark, and seemingly hopeless valley through which we travel. Maybe we think God protects us from such moments, especially those who have been given promises; if God does not protect us, then we will turn away from God. We should learn from this story that receiving promises does not entail being protected from moments where those promises seem to be called into question.

153. See White, *Narration and Discourse*, 187-203.

To move to the NT, God does not expect of Abraham something that God would be unwilling to do. God puts Jesus through a time of testing to see if he will be faithful, and hence could be a vehicle for God's redemptive purposes in the world. God risked that Jesus would not be found faithful. Even more, God put Jesus through a time of testing in the Garden of Gethsemane. How was it possible for Jesus to believe that God would be faithful to promises in such a time? Jesus trusts himself to the will of God, trusting that God will find a way to be faithful to the promises even in the face of death. And God does prove faithful in raising Jesus from the dead.

Some NT words on testing may be helpful: "Because he himself was tested by what he suffered, he is able to help those who are being tested" (Heb 2:18 NRSV; cf. 4:15). We are promised by 1 Cor 10:13, "God is faithful, and he will not let you be tested beyond your strength, but with the testing he will also provide the way out so that you may be able to endure it" (NRSV). These affirmations do not make trust an option, but we can count on the faithfulness of God, who in the midst of the worst possible testings will provide a way through the fire.

GENESIS 22:20-24, REBEKAH'S FAMILY

COMMENTARY

The author encloses this section (22:20–25:18), having to do with concluding events in Abraham's journey, with genealogies (22:20-24; 25:1-18; cf. 33:18–36:43 and 47:27–50:26 for other closing accounts). The stories share a common focus: the preparation for the future of the family, as that involves both land and posterity.

This brief genealogy chronicles the family of Abraham's brother Nahor, including children of his wife Milcah and his concubine Reumah (see 11:27-29; 31:53). As with Jacob, Nahor has twelve sons; their names later become associated with tribes and places (see Job 1:1; Job 32:2).

The insertion of the genealogy at this point anticipates the role of Rebekah (granddaughter of Nahor), shortly to be introduced (see 24:15, 24). The writer thus makes clear that Isaac's wife comes from the same family (cf. Ishmael, 21:21). The genealogy lists the children of both the wife and the concubine; the list identifies Rebekah as a granddaughter of the wife.

GENESIS 23:1-20, ABRAHAM BUYS LAND IN CANAAN

COMMENTARY

Within the inclusio provided by the death and burial of Sarah, the chapter (usually assigned to P) provides a report about negotiations between Abraham and the Hittites for purchase of a family burial place. Since Sarah is the first member of the core family of promise to die, the textual moment is appropriate. The prominent use of burial language (thirteen times), especially the expression "bury your [my] dead," demonstrates the centrality of this concern. The matter concludes (23:20) with this particular space within the promised land transferred legally to Abraham. No explicit theological language occurs in the chapter; any such understandings must be developed out of the larger context.

Ancient Near Eastern documents provide parallels to aspects of this transaction.[154] Abraham negotiates with the Hittites, a people infrequently encountered in the OT.

154. See Sarna, *Genesis*, 156-60.

Their eponymous ancestor Heth, the second son of Canaan, appears in 10:15, while 28:1 seems to equate Hittites and Canaanites (see Judg 1:10). Esau marries two Hittite women (26:34), and Rebekah expresses concern that Jacob might do the same (27:46). Although the Hittite kingdom was centered in Anatolia, and their empire did not extend into Canaan, there may have been enclaves of such non-Semitic peoples in Canaan. To the ancient reader of Genesis, the Hittites would have been one of the pre-Israelite peoples living in the promised land; here the author calls them "the people of the land" (vv. 7, 12-13; see 15:20).

Abraham's chosen burying place, Machpelah, was located in the southern part of Canaan near Mamre. This became the burial place not only of Sarah and Abraham (25:9), but also of Isaac, Rebekah, Jacob, and Leah. It was an important site during the biblical period and has remained so during subsequent centuries. Jacob's request to be buried there underscores the importance of a person's burial site (49:29-33; 50:13). And although Joseph is buried at Shechem (Josh 24:32), the importance of burial in the promised land is similarly evident (50:24).

The Story. Sarah has died, and the report of the purchase of land for her burial place begins with Abraham acting much as he did in chap. 14. While he identifies himself as a lowly outsider without property rights, the Hittites immediately recognize and acknowledge his reputation ("mighty prince," v. 6; cf. 24:35). Perhaps in view of his status, the Hittites openly receive his initially quite general request for a burial place (v. 4; "give" probably means "sell"). Abraham negotiates with them as an apparent equal, but with proper deference, at the place for such legal transactions, the city gate (v. 10).

The Hittites grant Abraham's request in a general way; in fact, they offer him the pick of available tombs (v. 6). But Abraham has his sight on a particular cave. One of the elders, Ephron, owns the burial cave he wants to buy, and Abraham requests that he be allowed to proceed with negotiations for it. Ephron twice publicly offers to "give" him not only the cave for burying, but the surrounding field as well (v. 11). This may be an opening gambit for a sale, not generosity. In any case, Abraham, who will not be obligated to strangers (cf. 14:22-24) and wants use of the land, insists on paying for it. Ephron, seemingly not concerned about payment, claims that it is worth 400 shekels; we do not know whether this was a fair price (cf. Jer 32:7). Abraham agrees and, without speaking a word, gives him the money on the spot, carefully measuring it according to local standards.

Verses 17-18 summarize the transaction, with the narrator specifying that the entire plot of land—field, cave, trees—is deeded to Abraham "in the presence of the Hittites," who have been witnesses to all that has transpired. After Sarah's burial, which confirms the agreed-upon use of the land and makes the transaction firm, v. 20 seems concerned to attest Abraham's legal claim to this land one more time.

REFLECTIONS

1. This account has generated a number of interpretations. The text provides no evidence that Machpelah was a hallowed spot or sanctuary. A more theological explanation relates the text to the land promise.[155] In death, these Israelite ancestors are no longer strangers and aliens in the land (Abraham's self-identification in v. 4), but heirs; they come to rest in the land promised them by their God. The repeated language of "possession" (אחזה *ăḥuzzâ*, vv. 4, 9, 20; cf. 49:29-30; 50:13) relates to its immediately prior use in 17:8, where God promised the land to Abraham as an "everlasting possession" (repeated in 48:4; cf. 36:43; Lev 14:34; 27:24; Num 32:32; Josh 22:4, 19). Hence, one can make an explicitly theological interpretation on intertextual grounds (cf. also Jacob's purchase in 33:19 and Jeremiah's in Jer 32:1-15, a text of similar antiquity that bears an explicitly theological meaning).

155. Von Rad, *Genesis*, 250.

2. When one places the repetitive burial language within an exilic context, other meanings may emerge.[156] The text may address the issue of exiles' having to bury their dead outside of the land and their interest in having a special burial place in both exile and Canaan (cf. the interest in transporting bodies from Egypt back to Canaan in 50:12-14, 24-25). These exiles were, like Abraham, sojourners and aliens; Israelites may have understood burial places in Canaan in terms of the land as an everlasting possession. This text shows that Abraham comes by the land on terms that were both legal and fair, and hence should be honored by future generations.

The chapter may also involve issues of family life, as do 17:9-14 (circumcision) and 27:46–28:9 (marriage). Burial practices were an important matter in ancient societies, and texts such as these grounded customs in ancient times.

While these factors may seem to be nontheological, they relate in direct ways to creation, particularly the proper ordering of individual, family, and communal life. A comprehensive theology of creation includes concerns for social order, which in the ancient (and modern!) world is intimately connected with cosmic order. If the social fabric is in disrepair, deleterious effects on the cosmic order may ensue. So the good order of the entire cosmos may be at stake. Hence, this chapter relates to chap. 1 and creational concerns. There are also connections between creation and the promise of the land as an everlasting possession. For the promise to be fulfilled, land must be available. The promise of a specific land for one's own possession presupposes the creational activity of God.

3. Abraham's purchase of a plot in the land does not stand over against God's promise to give the land to his descendants. Again and again, God works through humans on behalf of divine purposes. The purchase of land provides a symbol of hope, a concrete anticipation of what God has in store for those who trust in the promises.

156. See Westermann, *Genesis 12–36,* 376.

GENESIS 24:1-67, THE WOOING OF REBEKAH

COMMENTARY

In this lengthy family story, Joseph-like in character (assigned to J), the author focuses on the search for a wife for Isaac among family members back in the old country (the Nahor of v. 10 is near Haran). In the course of this last story in which Abraham plays a role, interest passes to "master" Isaac (v. 65). Abraham's good and faithful servant (possibly Eliezer, 15:2) serves as the mediator of this transition. The story follows a pattern ("type-scene") similar to that of Jacob/Rachel in 29:1-14 and Moses/Zipporah in Exod 2:15-22—a meeting between a man and a woman at a well that results in a marriage (cf. John 4; Ugaritic parallels have also been noted). We may also discern a literary form used to depict the commission of a messenger, a pattern similar to the calls of the prophets (cf. Exodus 3; Isaiah 6), evident not least in the objection that the servant raises (vv. 5, 39).

Within the larger story of Abraham, this chapter (esp. vv. 1-7, 35-41) provides an inclusio with 12:1-7, with specific references to the call and initial journey, as well as the promises of land and blessing. Genesis 24 provides a similar introduction to the beginning of the second generation. In some sense, however, *Rebekah* rather than Isaac parallels Abraham; she continues the faithful response of leaving home and family that furthers God's purposes. The story also includes recapitulations of scenes that have already occurred (cf.

vv. 17-19 with 13-14; vv. 34-49 with 1-27), a technique that retards the action and helps to interpret the event, especially God's important role.

Abraham initiates the journey by commissioning his servant to find a wife for Isaac (vv. 1-9). The servant carries out the commission (vv. 10-27), and Rebekah and her family respond (vv. 28-61), resulting in the marriage of Rebekah and Isaac (vv. 62-67).

24:1-9. Abraham's final days provide an occasion to note how God has filled his life with blessings. God has indeed kept the promise to him, a promise worked out largely through God's work as Creator.

Abraham now focuses on finding a proper wife for Isaac. Functioning without divine directive, he commissions the most senior of his servants for the task. (In what follows, God's leading actually responds to Abraham's initiative!) He binds the servant with an oath (placing his hand under the genitals, a vehicle of life, vv. 2, 9; cf. 47:29) to find a woman only among family members, not from among the resident Canaanites (see 28:1, but not applicable to Jacob's sons; cf. Deut 7:3-4 for Israel's later history). After an objection by the servant and Abraham's response (note his emphasis on the woman's own decision, v. 8; cf. v. 58), the servant takes the oath. The author explains in v. 7 the twice-expressed concern that Isaac not be brought back to Haran (vv. 6, 8; not recalled in vv. 34-41): for Isaac to settle in the place from which Abraham migrated would be untrue to God's call and the promise for the land. Abraham follows through faithfully on the implications of his own call and subjects Isaac to the same call. At the same time, *Rebekah* will follow exactly in Abraham's footsteps (cf. v. 38 with 12:1) and will receive the same blessing (cf. v. 60 with 22:17). In all things, the servant will prove to be loyal to his commission, while unafraid to take appropriate initiatives.

Abraham, in his last words, does not know what will come of this venture. He makes his servant swear (not) to do certain things (vv. 3-4, 6, 8), but his conduct and that of others are not predetermined. In fact, Abraham considers it possible that this venture might fail because "the woman" might refuse to cooperate (v. 8; in v. 41, the woman's family can decide). Failure might result, even though

God would "send his angel before you" (see 32:1; Exod 23:20; 32:34). The servant takes human behaviors into account when carrying out the task—what people customarily do counts (v. 11), and the numerous gifts (v. 10) are certainly an effort to persuade. These factors suggest that one should not say that "the success or failure of the commission depends on whether God grants success or not."[157] Although success may well depend on God, the activity of human beings may occasion failure even though God intends success.

24:10-27. The author encloses this episode with prayer and doxology. Having arrived at his destination, the servant prays that he will be successful in this venture, which would mean that God show kindness or steadfast love (חסד *ḥesed*) to Abraham—namely, manifest love in this particular way. Without God's steadfast love there would be no success (cf. v. 21). The author presents no claim that lack of success would mean that God had withheld kindness; it could simply result from human decision making (vv. 8, 41). Divine providence does not mean that the future is somehow predetermined or that human decision making can never frustrate the divine designs. The servant refers to Yahweh as "God of my master Abraham," an explicit reference to the language used in vv. 3, 7; only a God of heaven and earth, active throughout those spheres, could grant success in Aram-naharaim (v. 10).

Verse 13 does not constitute a naive effort to inform God; it states the servant's present situation, in which he hopes success will be forthcoming. He then prays in a way that is less precise than it sounds (and may still be too precise for a good prayer) that the woman to whom he will speak *in a certain way* and who will respond *in a certain way* (the words of vv. 17-19 are not identical; cf. vv. 42-46) will be the one whom God has chosen to be Isaac's wife. Note that this interchange will not necessarily signal the presence of the right woman (v. 21). He also hopes and prays that *God will let her be* the chosen one, which implies additional divine action. "By this" (v. 14) refers to the entire complex of events. The servant's prayer to God correlates well with his own sense of what might take place at the well.

---

157. See Westermann, *Genesis 12–36*, 382.

The narrator's description of Rebekah (vv. 15-16) enables the reader to know she will be Isaac's wife before the servant does; the focus thus falls on the servant's faithful handling of the situation. When the anticipated conversation does occur (vv. 17-19; it is not represented as an answer to prayer), the servant does *not* immediately know that this is the woman. Rather, he gazes "at her in silence to learn whether or not the LORD had made his journey successful" (v. 21; not reported in vv. 46-47). In other words, he deems a period of reflection and observation necessary. We do not know how he gained this knowledge, but an inner certainty through God-given insight regarding the divine decision seems likely (and leads to the giving of gifts before he is absolutely certain, vv. 22-24).

When it becomes clear to the servant that Rebekah is the woman (and he had all the time it would take to water *all* those camels with a pitcher!), he immediately gives public thanks to the Lord, praising (i.e., blessing; see v. 48; Exod 18:10) God for his kindness (*ḥesed*), faithfulness (אמת *'ĕmet*), and guiding presence. Rebekah's hospitality mirrors that of Abraham in 18:2-8 (vv. 18-20; cf. also vv. 23, 25).

Relationships in Rebekah's family are not easy to discern, but the following seems likely: Rebekah is the granddaughter of Nahor, Abraham's brother; her father, Bethuel, and Isaac are cousins; her "mother's household" (v. 28) refers naturally to a girl's family (Cant 3:4). The leading role of her brother Laban and minor role of Bethuel (only v. 50) may reflect that culture (in 29:5 Laban is called the son [NIV "grandson"] of Nahor; in 24:48, the NIV has granddaughter-brother; the NRSV has daughter-kinsman).

24:28-61. Rebekah, having informed her family, leaves the official welcoming to her brother, Laban. His theological language, coming after he has observed the expensive gifts, may be more calculated than sincere (v. 31). Yet, his welcome testifies that such symbols of prosperity result from God's work of blessing in the servant's life, a perspective again voiced in v. 50.

The servant insists on telling his story to Rebekah's family, the better to persuade them that Rebekah should marry Isaac (enclosing it with words of blessing, vv. 35, 48). In giving

God such a prominent role, he testifies publicly to all the blessings God has wrought on Abraham's behalf (cf. psalms of thanksgiving, e.g., Ps 66:16). He also lifts up Abraham, his "master" (ten times; twenty-four times in the chapter; "servant" fifteen times) rather than himself. He repeats in somewhat different language the conversation he had with Abraham prior to leaving (cf. vv. 37-41 with vv. 3-8); one difference occurs in v. 41, which places the onus of responsibility on the family, whereas v. 8 had spoken of Rebekah (the decisions of both prove to be important, vv. 51, 58). He also does not repeat Abraham's charge (vv. 6, 8) to avoid taking Isaac back to the home country. Both of these shifts are politic deployments of Abraham's directives.

The servant then recalls his prayer upon arriving at the well in basically the same words (vv. 42-44) and rehearses the events that followed (vv. 45-48), including his acts of worship. This fifteen-verse rehearsal of the story comes to a climax in v. 49: The servant asks Laban and Bethuel to give their daughter to become Isaac's wife. The servant's request includes language he had used of God—to show kindness and faithfulness to Abraham (cf. vv. 12, 27; the NIV retains this verbal link). In other words, Laban and Bethuel will be acting toward Abraham as God does if they allow Rebekah to go. Turning either "to the right hand or to the left" expresses an idiom captured well in the NIV's paraphrase, "so I may know which way to turn." What he does next depends on their response.

Laban and Bethuel respond directly; they believe the witness of the servant constitutes a word from Yahweh (vv. 50-51). As a consequence, "nothing one way or the other" (NIV; the NRSV's "bad or good" is more literal, which the NIV retains in 31:24, 29) can contribute to the discussion, except to formalize the matter (v. 51). These statements testify to a rich and deep faith in Yahweh present in this family, about which we have not heard since Abraham left the home country (cf. 31:53).

Having heard their response, Abraham's servant again worships God (v. 52). He does not respond verbally, but distributes gifts (a dowry?; cf. 34:12) and takes part in a meal. Note the reference to her mother in vv. 53, 55, whereas v. 50 speaks of Bethuel, her father. In vv. 59-60 they refer to Rebekah only as a sister.

In v. 55, Rebekah's family seeks to delay her departure for a few days, as was the custom (cf. Tob 7:15). When the servant insists on leaving so the good news can be brought to Abraham, they call on Rebekah to make her own decision. When she agrees, they send her and her attendants (her nurse Deborah [35:8] anticipates later children) away with their blessing. This blessing takes a traditional form, focusing on victory over enemies and fertility (as in God's word to Abraham in 22:17-18). It lacks explicitly religious language, as befits a narrative addressing everyday family concerns.

24:62-67. The author concludes the story in a brief and direct way. The servant identifies Isaac as the "master," an indication of the transition from Abraham to Isaac. The servant's retelling the story one more time (v. 66) becomes an occasion for the next stage of the story. Isaac and Rebekah are married, and what might have been just an arranged marriage grows into a loving relationship. The veil may be a signal from Rebekah that she accepts Isaac as her husband; her presence in Sarah's tent signifies her new role as matriarch of this family.

REFLECTIONS

1. This novella highlights in an unusually expansive way the motif of divine guidance, especially in the servant's prayers and in his rehearsal of earlier events (vv. 1-27) in vv. 34-48. This retelling constitutes a public testimony to the presence and activity of God, to which Laban and Bethuel respond with their own witness (v. 50). The repetition of vv. 12-14 in vv. 17-19 links prayer for divine guidance with daily life and highlights the place given to worship and prayer, both petition and thanksgiving, throughout the narrative (vv. 12-14, 26-27, 42-44, 48, 52). While these witnessing and worshiping actions of the servant in the story provide a model for the life of God's servants in every age, the servant remains anonymous, subservient to the divine action in the life of this family. The servant illustrates what life is like for many servants of God. They enter into the service of their master and proceed faithfully in quite ordinary situations, remaining anonymous in the overall scheme of things, but they are crucial vehicles for the leading and blessing work of God in daily affairs.

2. The narrator initially portrays God as one who has a history of blessing Abraham. Because blessing involves creation, this history testifies to God's work as creator, which is consonant with the characterization of Yahweh as "the God of heaven and [the God of] earth" (v. 3) and more briefly as "the God of heaven" (v. 7 NRSV). Such universal claims for the God of Abraham match those of 14:19, 22. While these divine epithets are often considered late because of their use in post-exilic literature (e.g., Ezra 1:2; 5:12), the narrator thought that such universal understandings of God were necessary in order to speak adequately about God's activity in this ancestral period.

The material content of these verses may further explain this usage. Abraham's servant is to swear regarding matters that reach out into the wider world of Mesopotamia (vv. 4, 7). Such a universal understanding of God becomes necessary if matters relating to the larger world of this family are to make theological sense. In other words, the theological affirmations of Genesis 24 correlate with the opening chapter of Genesis and its claim about God as creator of heaven and earth.

In addition, we may discuss God's work as creator in and through the ordinary, everyday workings of this family rather than in miraculous or extraordinary events. We do not have here a divine "management of events";[158] to the contrary, our exposition has shown that human activity can shape the future, though not finally stymie God's

158. Von Rad, *Genesis*, 260.

purposes. We can speak of God's highly effective work behind the scenes without resorting to such deterministic descriptions.

3. The story understands Abraham's wealth to result from the blessing of God (vv. 1, 31, 35-36, 60). Moreover, the author emphasizes that God gives success (vv. 12, 21, 40, 56). Blessing and success involve tangible realities, from wealth and property to posterity. "The blessings of heaven come packaged for earth."[159] The author does not claim that wealth and success are always due to the blessing work of God. People can come by possessions and prosperity through evil means. Humans *interpret* whether or not one can ascribe such material well-being to the blessing work of God. The servant attempts to convince the family in Haran that the wealth they see is indeed due to God's work in Abraham's life, but finally they themselves must make an interpretive judgment in faith.

4. The variations in the servant's retelling (vv. 34-49) say something important about the continuing use of this story in our own time. We use biblical texts properly not simply by quoting a biblical passage or providing an exact rendering of this or that biblical story. The biblical materials themselves provide the reteller sanction to play with the details of the story in view of the context in which the teller stands.

5. The God language of Laban and Bethuel (vv. 31, 50-51) invites speculation; certainly the narrator understands that the Yahwistic faith was established within Abraham's family before Abraham left for Canaan (see 31:53). Such faith apparently continues outside of Abraham's family and the specific promises that undergirded his relationship with God. Once again, this situation testifies to the work of God the Creator.

6. Many commentators have observed the importance of prayer in the life of the servant; it is spontaneous, personal, and focused on the individual's relationship to God. Westermann puts its well: These prayers indicate that "spontaneous address to God in petition and thanks arising there from is the natural expression of life with God. . . . Just as the personal relationship of trust in God and his guidance remains the same throughout the Bible, so too does prayer as a response to this guidance when experienced in one's personal life."[160]

7. Regarding v. 67, we must say more than that a new generation is appearing, or even that God's promises of posterity through Isaac can now be realized. Isaac loves Rebekah! Life in God's good creation involves more than divine promises and religious practice; it includes such creational gifts as the love between husband and wife. We should relate this theme to that of faithfulness and steadfast love. While these words depict God's relation to this family (vv. 12, 14, 27), they also characterize human relationships (v. 49) and are integral to God's purposes for all creation.

159. Brueggemann, *Genesis*, 198.
160. Westermann, *Genesis 12–36*, 392.

GENESIS 25:1-18, THE DEATH OF ABRAHAM AND THE FAMILY OF ISHMAEL

COMMENTARY

The story of Abraham ends as it began, with genealogies (a mix of J and P). They link up with 22:20-24 and enclose the final segment of the Abraham story. Although commentators often view v. 18 as the break point, a better ending may come at 25:11, with its reference to the divine blessing of Isaac (cf. 24:1). Verses 12-18 would then be an interlude (vv. 12 and 19 are parallel). This pattern occurs also with Isaac; after his death and burial by his sons (35:29) comes an interlude with the genealogy of Esau (36:1-42), a secondary line parallel to Ishmael (25:19 could be considered parallel to 37:2 as well; cf. also 25:11 and 37:1). One may view Ishmael's genealogy as a new beginning, much briefer than that of Isaac, naturally, but exactly parallel (the same might be said of Esau and Jacob). Generally, the narrator has so closely linked these genealogies and stories that no separation seems finally satisfactory.

An editor has placed the death and burial of Abraham (vv. 7-10) between genealogies, as if to suggest that Abraham's life continues on in many children (cf. 17:5). These names may refer primarily to peoples with whom Israel as a nation was engaged over the years.[161] Most involve various Arabian groups, but the historical setting remains unclear; they do not seem to be sharply distinguished geographically, as might be expected of groups that are partly sedentary, partly nomadic. The various peoples by whom Israel was surrounded were, ultimately, a part of their family.

25:1-6. In vv. 1-6, the narrator introduces us to a side of Abraham's life hitherto completely unknown. Given all the divine and human activity necessary for Abraham to have a son, the reader may be surprised to read about Keturah, who bore him six more children. These names (developed in part to the third generation) are generally associated with the Syro-Arabian desert; we know most about the Midianites (see 37:28, 36). *Keturah* is closely related to the Hebrew word for "spice"; this and other biblical and extra-biblical evidence links these peoples to the lively commerce in these commodities.

We do not know when this marriage of Abraham's occurred, though its place after the death of Sarah suggests that the narrator understood it to postdate that event; Abraham did live seventy-five years after the birth of Isaac and thirty-eight after Sarah died (17:17; 23:1). But, if so, the previous

comments about having a son in his old age (cf. also 24:1) seem trivial. Perhaps the segment (vv. 1-6) provides nothing more than an addendum, a tradition that the narrator chose not to integrate into the major story itself. The apparent reference in v. 6 to the sons of both Hagar and Keturah ("concubines"; perhaps correlated with "wife" [v. 1; 16:3] to set them off from Sarah) draws Ishmael and the sons of Keturah together as those whom Abraham "sent away" (cf. 21:14). They are sent away to "the east" (as are Cain and Lot). This action settles the place of Isaac and issues of inheritance (cf. 21:10 with 25:5). Yet, they receive largess from Abraham, which attests to a relationship of concern and generosity.

25:7-11. Abraham died at the ripe old age of 175, a nice round 100 years after he had responded to the divine call (12:4). The writer describes his death in quite matter-of-fact ways. Death appears not as the enemy, but simply as the end of a good and full life (see 15:15; cf. 47:9). Being "gathered to his people" (vv. 8, 17; 35:29; 49:33; a phrase unique to the Pentateuch) does not refer to death or burial, but probably alludes to Sheol or some other form of afterlife. Isaac and Ishmael, with no sign of disharmony between them, see to his burial beside Sarah in the cave he had purchased (chap. 23). The return of Ishmael but not the sons by Keturah is striking, testifying to the special place of Ishmael as a child of promise (see 17:18; 21:11).

25:12-18. The author depicts Ishmael (v. 12) in terms identical to Isaac (v. 19); both are "sons of Abraham." The reference to his life span is unique outside of the chosen line (v. 17). Moreover, the twelve princes (v. 16) mirror the twelve tribes of Israel. The many descendants of Ishmael testify to the fulfillment of God's promises (17:20; 21:18). Ishmael has a future, too. Some of the names are unknown, but other identifications have been made with Arabian tribal groups to the east and south of Canaan. The translation of v. 18 remains uncertain (see the footnotes), but may be linked to an earlier pronouncement about Ishmael's future, anticipating intrafamilial difficulties (16:12).

161. For details, see Sarna, *Genesis*, 170-77.

REFLECTIONS

The story of Abraham ends by specifying his role as the father of a multitude of nations; his descendants are numerous, indeed. While the author does not recall the language of promise, it goes without saying that these descendants are a fulfillment of key divine promises to Abraham. At the same time, vv. 12-18 witness to the fulfillment of God's promises to Ishmael (17:20; 21:13, 18). God has been faithful to those both within and without the chosen family.

The story of Abraham does not culminate with reference only to Isaac, an important theological affirmation. Given the variety of negative and positive relationships Israel will have with these peoples over the years, it is striking that, at the beginning of Israel's history, stands this word about their place in the family of Abraham. The relationships among people in that part of the world ought to be conceived most fundamentally in familial rather than national or political or religious terms. Differences have emerged over the years that cannot be lightly set aside. But there are significant commonalities as well, to which very deep roots in Abraham's family testify. These links should provide some continuing basis for working with differences among these peoples in a creative and peaceful way.

GENESIS 25:19–36:43

THE STORY OF JACOB

OVERVIEW

J acob is Israel; that overriding consideration informs and propels these chapters. The biblical authors present a story about an individual, one whose character and personality emerge in ways both subtle and direct over the course of the story. Jacob remains very much a person in his own right, but in time he *becomes* Israel. Finally, Jacob is more than an individual.

In another sense, Jacob also becomes Israel during the development of these traditions. The experiences of later, corporate Israel have shaped the telling of this story. The narrative portrays the story of Jacob-Israel as *both* a story of the past—whatever the degree of historicity modern historians say the story may have—and a story of every contemporary Israelite. Israel understands itself as possessing characteristics that are often mirrored in the story of Jacob-Israel (one could make similar, but less fully developed, statements about Esau-Edom and Laban-Aram).

This portrayal presents self-critical realism. The traditions do not whitewash Jacob-Israel, as if to suggest an Eden-like origin for itself. The story possesses remarkably little pretense. Here Jacob stands with qualities negative and positive, clear and ambiguous, simple and complex. Take him or leave him. The most astounding claim of the story is that God takes him.

A writer introduces this section of Genesis with a summary reference to the story of Isaac (see the NIV), yet the reader quickly discovers that his sons, especially Jacob, overshadow him. The story of Isaac himself exists only in an abbreviated form (chap. 26), almost as an interlude in the larger family chronicle. It may be that few Isaac traditions actually existed or that one or more storytellers, for unknown reasons, chose to leave them aside; the obscure references to Isaac in 31:42 and

Amos 7:9, 16 suggest that more was available at one time.

The stories of Jacob in chaps. 25–36 are presented in a somewhat episodic fashion, tied together by itineraries (primarily) or genealogical references, yet less so than with the Abraham stories. Chapters 29–31 provide a sustained narrative that bears similarities to the Joseph story. Moreover, a plot pervades most of the chapters and provides internal cohesion. Any attempt to depict the complex history of the story must come to terms with evidence for both compositeness and unity.

Scholars commonly agree that the story betrays diverse origins, pieced together from a variety of sources, though each part retains its character as a family narrative. These scholars think of J, E, P, and redactors, who used various Jacob traditions that had already been brought together from oral and written materials composed over an extensive period of time. More specific theories of origin remain quite uncertain, though special associations with the northern kingdom seem likely (e.g., the special interest in the northern cities Bethel and Shechem).

During the past two decades there has been increasing interest in reading the Jacob story as a unity. As a literary entity, the text has a life of its own, and we have to come to terms with its final form. This approach does not deny the need to consider issues of source and redaction, but the basic concern involves hearing the text as we now have it. That will be the perspective of this commentary.

We have already noted that the overriding theme is Jacob as Israel. Interpreters often suggest that family conflict provides the basic focus of the story. This may be so, but we must resist the temptation of reducing the text to a sociological phenomenon, to claim that the story fundamentally addresses dysfunctional family systems. Or we may reduce the discussion to moral issues, regarding the ethical behavior of the characters. As important as these matters are, the story makes certain theological claims regarding this family's relationship to God and to God's purposes in the world through them. Most basically, *God's choosing and speaking* generates and propels the story of this family, yet without discounting the important role humans play.

1. The Divine Promise. As with the Abraham stories, promises function at two levels. (a) The basic ancestral promises continue—promises of land, descendants, and blessing on them and through them to the families of the earth (28:3-4, 13-14; 35:11-12). (b) Promises directed to Jacob's particular situation also occur—promises of divine presence and care in his journeyings (28:15; 31:3). Without these promises, and God's tending to them, there would be no story of Jacob. The promises for this family exist for the sake of God's mission in the world. Election and promise involve, finally, the other "families" (12:3; 28:14) of the world, so that they too might receive the life that God intends for creation.

2. The Divine Blessing. The narratives treat blessing basically in creational terms, whether of fertility in the field (26:12; 27:27-28), among the animals (30:30), in the birth of children (29:31–30:24; 33:5), or more generally (26:13, 29; 30:27, 43; 33:11). The blessing extends through Isaac to Jacob (27:28-29; 28:1-4) and Esau (27:39-40), from God to Jacob (32:29; 35:9), and even from Laban to his family (31:55). It constitutes the central issue between Jacob and Esau (27:1-45). God's promises as continuing blessings remain basic for this family and to others through them (26:3-4, 24; 28:4, 14). Blessings are conveyed through both the spoken word and God's working in creational processes, both human and nonhuman. The divine purpose behind the blessings functions identically to that of the promises: to enable the fullest possible life for all the families in God's good creation.

3. God. God speaks promises, brings blessing, and accompanies this family along its various journeys. Even more, God engages this conflicted family directly in the service of these promises. God not only puts these promises in verbal form, but also enters into

the fray on their behalf, even if it means engaging Jacob himself in "hand-to-hand combat."

As with Abraham, God appears in order to speak; this speaking defines the story. God speaks two times to Isaac, to command and to promise (26:3-4, 24), and six times to Jacob to promise (28:13-15; 31:3; 35:11-12), to command (31:3, 13; 35:1), to bless (32:29), to name (32:28; 35:10) and to advise (31:12). God also speaks to Rebekah (25:23) and to Laban (31:24). The response of the various principals to this divine speaking helps give shape to the development of the story.

Attention to God language helps us to understand the story. It appears most pervasively with the birth of the children (29:31–30:24), where Leah and Rachel witness powerfully to the gracious activity of God in responding to their laments. These women also interpret the Jacob-Laban conflict theologically (31:16). Other individuals offer theological interpretations of events: Isaac (26:22), Abimelech (26:28-29), Laban (30:27), and Jacob (30:30; 31:5-9, 42; 32:2, 30; 33:5, 11). These persons testify to a pervading divine presence working in and through people and events within and without the community of faith on behalf of the divine purposes. God language also appears in connection with prayers and rituals by Isaac (27:28; 28:3-4), Jacob (32:9-12), and Laban (31:49-50, 53); though twice Jacob uses God language in less than appropriate ways (27:20; 30:2). We find God language when God speaks to Jacob (28:16-22; 31:11; 35:3) and Laban (31:29). Nonetheless, the narrator uses God talk relatively infrequently, aside from divine appearances (the birth of the children [29:31; 30:17, 22; 31:53; 33:20] and events in chap. 35 [vv. 5, 7, 15]). The narrator obviously prefers that the characters themselves give voice to the place of God in their lives.

4. Conflict. The conflict theme arises from within these theological matters. In the Abraham/Sarah stories, barrenness and childbearing, and their implications for the promise, constitute the prevailing motif; parents rather than sons stand at the center of the conflict. In the Isaac and Jacob stories, while issues of barrenness and birth continue, the narratives focus more on conflict between sons. At the same time, the intrafamilial conflict often extends beyond the brothers, and catches up parents, wives, children, more extended family members (e.g., Laban), the neighbors (from Abimelech to Shechem), and even God. The vital and positive role that women—especially Rebekah, Leah, Rachel, and Dinah—play in these conflicts has only recently received significant attention.

The Jacob story begins with conflict (25:19-34), which sets the stage for much of what follows, issuing finally in a less than full reconciliation. Conflict begins with issues of kinship and inheritance, especially primogeniture, which in turn catches up the characters in acts of deception and all of their spiraling consequences. We might, today, call this a dysfunctional family, with all of its relational difficulties, complexities, and ambiguities. One of the difficulties in interpreting this conflict has to do with character depiction.

Commentators have tended to portray virtually every individual in extreme and unfortunate directions: Jacob is a cheat and rascal, Esau an idiot, Isaac a dottering old man, Rebekah a manipulator. To be sure, there are no gods or demons among these people, but the interpreter will be truer to the text by striving for as much balance as possible in sketching out the ways these characters work in and through the conflict.

At the same time, these texts witness to a God who engages this family in the very midst of its conflicted life from the start. In fact, God's oracle to Rebekah (25:23) stands at the beginning. While the oracle presents a divine interpretation of already existing conditions, and the characters do inherit a way of being a family from their Abrahamic forebears, in some sense it becomes God's own word that generates and intensifies the conflict. The entire story involves a divine decision to elect one person rather than another to carry on the Abrahamic line of promise. At its most profound level, the problems and possibilities created by the divine election constitute the essence of the conflict in the story of Jacob and Esau. We should understand the conflicted relationships in the story as a result of God's decision to choose one family.

The way in which the principals involved respond to this divine election can, of course, intensify the conflict even further. They can complicate and frustrate the divine purpose, even place it in jeopardy. The story should not be seen as "the actualization of a predetermined fate."[162] God is, indeed, bound to this family, but they are to respond faithfully (see 26:5), and the way they work through the divine choices and promises shapes the future, including God's future, in significant ways. Not least, the chosen ones themselves must come to see that election should not be understood in isolated terms. Such a perception could only lead to exclusivistic understandings, to an isolation from the world while basking in the glory of having been divinely chosen (an understanding not foreign to later Israel, cf. Amos 3:2; 9:7). Election always serves mission, the choice of one family for the sake of all other families (12:3; 28:14). This orientation outward helps to explain why these chapters "reveal an astounding degree of empathy with Israel's antagonists."[163]

Structure. One may outline the Jacob story broadly as a journey: flight from Canaan to Haran and back to Canaan. To this we should add the journey through the land of promise in 33:18–35:27, after the return. This itinerary gives to the story a strong sense of movement, presenting a person and a family on the go, never staying in one spot for too long. The journeys both within and without the promised land mirror the life of later Israel, especially the experiences of exodus and exile. The most basic movement in the Jacob story is linear, climaxing in the settlement of Jacob and his family in the land of promise.

Others have observed a chiastic structure within the story (especially as refined by Fishbane and others). However, though certain patterns can indeed be observed, we must be highly cautious about forcing the material into complex and detailed chiasms. A number of structures overlap and help to prevent any easy reading of the story according to a single model.

In discerning structure (and content) one should note the prominent parallels between

---

162. Michael Fishbane, "Exodus 1–4: The Prologue to the Exodus Cycle," *Text and Texture: Close Readings of Selected Biblical Texts* (New York: Schocken, 1979) 62.

163. John Gammie, "Theological Interpretation by Way of Literary and Tradition Analysis: Genesis 25–36," *Encounter with the Text*, ed. M. Buss (Philadelphia: Fortress, 1979) 130.

this story and that of Moses in Exod 2:1–4:31.[164] The following brief observations may be helpful.

Genealogies, those of Ishmael (25:12-18) and Esau (36:1-43), bracket the Jacob story. The former provides a link with the Abraham story, as does the latter for the Joseph story. This bracketing of the chosen by the non-chosen may be a way in which these groups of people are held together, not least in the service of God's mission of blessing *all* "families" (28:14).

One may discern a similar interest in the two chapters that occur at comparable points early and late in the story. They relate the Canaanite peoples to Isaac and Jacob (26; 34), drawing out ways in which Israel's relationship to outsiders takes both positive and negative (mostly) directions.

The centerpiece of the story may well be the birth of Jacob's children (29:31–30:24). This judgment is supported by the sudden and pervasive use of God language, by the lament-deliverance-thanksgiving rhythm revealed in the responses of Leah and Rachel,

164. Ronald Hendel, *The Epic of the Patriarch: The Jacob Cycle and the Narrative Traditions of Canaan and Israel* (Atlanta: Scholars Press, 1987) 140.

and by the overriding concern for the birth of Israel. Different elements of the Jacob-Laban conflict enclose this birth narrative (29:1-30; 30:25–31:54).

Some scholars have suggested that two texts focusing on Jacob and Esau are also parallel (27:1-45; 33:1-17), moving from conflict to some sort of resolution. This judgment, however, tends to reduce the important conflict story in 25:23-34 to the status of an introduction.

The appearances of God constitute the "pillars" of the story. Here the structure becomes more complex than typical chiasms allow. Some interpreters view the dream at Bethel (28:10-22) and the struggle at the Jabbok (32:22-32; or encounters with angels of God, 32:1-2, 22-32) as parallel, enclosing the Jacob-Laban story. However, one may discern more significant levels of correspondence between the texts related to Bethel (28:10-22; 35:1-15). Moreover, the divine oracle to Rebekah (25:23) regarding "struggling" is linked to the struggle at the Jabbok, especially the text's mirroring of the Jacob-Esau and the Jacob-God struggle (see 33:10). One should view these four instances of divine speaking as informing each other in complex ways and propelling the story along.

GENESIS 25:19-34, JACOB AND ESAU

COMMENTARY

These verses introduce in almost snapshot fashion the leading figures of the chapters to follow: Isaac, Rebekah, Jacob, and Esau. Events associated with the birth of Jacob and Esau (vv. 21-26) and their early life (vv. 27-34), while presented in brief and episodic fashion, set the stage well for the conflicted family relationships that ensue. The oracle in v. 23 specifies that national issues are at stake (Edomite and Israelite relationships), but the text grounds those realities in the experiences of individuals. The two principals shape history both before and after birth, with not a little help from their parents.

25:19-26. The story begins with genealogical notes, wherein Abraham's relationship to Isaac is stated twice (the NIV is probably correct

in seeing v. 1*a* as a summary statement of the chapters that follow, cf. 37:2*a*). Verses 19*b*-20 recapitulate earlier material (cf. 24:67), though Isaac's age is new information and Rebekah's family roots are described in greater detail.

The story of Rebekah/Isaac parallels that of Sarah/Abraham. Isaac and Rebekah are identified with some precision (cf. 11:27-32). Like Sarah, Rebekah is barren (cf. also 30:1-2), though that does not become a major motif in this story. Isaac, like Abraham, is old when he becomes a father (sixty years). Unlike Abraham, Isaac prays concerning the barrenness of Rebekah, and God, the narrator testifies, responds to (more precisely, is moved to answer) his prayer so that she conceives.

Rebekah's prayer soon follows Isaac's prayer. God responds differently to the two prayers, however. In the first, God enables conception; hence, one might speak of an "answer." The second involves a more complicated issue. The pregnancy is difficult for Rebekah; the story dictates that the (fraternal) twins' subsequent relationship has its *roots* in genetic rather than environmental factors. To suggest, however, that genetics equals destiny goes beyond the text, especially given the parental favoritism. She brings her lament to God in prayer (the language suggests a trip to a sanctuary), wondering whether life is worth all this suffering (the NRSV and the NIV differ on whether this has become a life-and-death matter for her; cf. 27:46).

God responds directly (an inner voice?) to her with an oracle. The oracle responds to an already existing situation; it does not start from "scratch." God explains to her the reason for the painful pregnancy (twins) and *interprets* this as a sign of the future relationship between them and their descendants (v. 23); the struggle itself does not result from divine action. More specifically, the narrative moves beyond laws of primogeniture; either the older (Esau) will be the weaker of the two and will serve the younger (Jacob), or, more likely, the older will be the stronger but will serve the weaker and younger. If the latter, there would be a play on the word for "strength." Either Esau is stronger physically—he wins the battle in the womb—and Jacob is stronger in other ways, or the one shall be stronger initially (Esau) but not finally (2 Sam 8:13-14). God is not described as an agent in these developments, which underscores the importance of human activity.

This oracle (consonant with Isaac's later blessings on the sons, 27:29, 40; cf. also 49:8), as well as the plays on words, reflects later conflict between the two "nations" (i.e., peoples) of Israel and Edom and the hegemony of the former over the latter (see 2 Sam 8:13-14). They help to ground (perhaps even justify) that later reality in these ancient family events. At the same time, the move from present oracle to future reality was not necessary or inevitable. This oracle will inform Rebekah's subsequent relationships to her sons in significant ways (see 25:28; 27:5-15, 42-46; 28:7).

When the twin boys are born, the narrator portrays them with features of their subsequent relationship: Esau, physical features; Jacob, action (this is reversed to some degree in v. 29). The Hebrew word for "red" (אדמוני *'admônî*, [or "ruddy"]; see 1 Sam 16:12) is a play on *Edom*, linked to the "red stuff" at v. 30 (see 36:1). The word for "hairy" (שׂער *śēʿār*) is a play on *Seir*, the region where the Edomites lived, and is linked to the deception in 27:23. Why he is named Esau is uncertain. The meaning of *Jacob* (יעקב *yaʿăqōb*), also uncertain, plays on the word for "heel," עקב (*ʿāqēb*), "grasp the heel," or, less likely, the verb *ʿāqab* ("he supplants, deceives"; see Esau's interpretation in 27:36; Hos. 12:4). The name *Jacob* is associated with a feature of his birth and implies a uterine struggle to be born first, a struggle that Esau wins.

25:27-34. The following two vignettes not only illustrate this birth relationship between the two brothers, but establish specific grounds for later conflict. The first (vv. 27-28) speaks to issues of life-style and intra-familial relationships, the second (vv. 29-34) to economics and personal values.

The author describes the young men by referring to ways of life that often stood in tension: Esau with those who are at home in the wild, on the move with animals, and Jacob with those who live a more settled, pastoral way of life. The writer characterizes Jacob with the word תם (*tām*), which both the NRSV and the NIV translate as "quiet" or mild-mannered; it normally means "innocent, upright" (see Job 1–2), which seems appropriate, at least at this point in his life. The writer juxtaposes the twins' different interests and temperaments with the love of the parents (cf. 37:4), a realistic note, common among parents. Isaac's love of Esau involves his ability to provide food (see Rebekah's use of this knowledge in 27:7, 14), but also remains independent of the oracle, of which Isaac was unaware. The author offers no specific reason to explain Rebekah's love for Jacob, but we may suppose it relates to what she knows about Jacob from the oracle.

How the second vignette is related to the oracle presents somewhat of a problem: Neither man was aware of the oracle or of the promise. Jacob does not act directly on the basis of the oracle, but Rebekah's favoritism may have helped to shape the way he acts toward his brother. His "cooking" (an ambiguous word) scene may even be contrived on the basis of his knowledge of Esau's habits.

The birthright—namely, the conferral of rights and privileges on the eldest son (normally)—entails a leadership position in the family and establishes claims regarding inheritance, indeed a double share of it—no small matter in view of 25:5 (see Deut 21:15-17). This story (and ancient Near Eastern parallels) indicates that such rights could be forfeited by the one born into such a privileged position. Esau and Jacob relate to the birthright in different ways. Esau comes across as callous and uncaring, easily outwitted regarding what might "naturally" be his, desiring more a satisfied present than a secure future (though his reference to death may not be as hyperbolic as is usually thought). He sells or barters his birthright for Jacob's lentil stew (i.e., "red stuff," another play on his identity); that Esau initially identifies the "red stuff" as

blood stew seems possible, but too uncertain to guide interpretation. Five verbs depict the moment: *ate, drank, rose, departed,* and *despised.* The last verb specifies the narrator's judgment that more is at stake than a lapse in judgment. Although not justifying Jacob's actions, that final verb demonstrates that Esau bears responsibility for what happens here. At the same time, Esau continues to live, in the light of the oracle that he, like Jacob, will become a people or nation (v. 23).

The author, on the other hand, presents Jacob as a clever and opportunistic individual, who knows what he wants. He takes advantage of a brother in need (of which Esau is later rightfully critical, 27:36) and his hospitality to his brother contrasts with both Abraham and Lot (chaps. 18–19). He carefully covers the legal bases when the opening for advancement presents itself, having Esau swear an inviolable oath in the urgency of the moment regarding the transfer of the birthright.

REFLECTIONS

1. The story of Jacob and Esau begins with a struggle, which sets the stage for a complex and difficult journey for everyone within this conflicted family. At the same time, the texts witness to a God at work in and through this situation. The problems and possibilities created by the interaction between God and this family constitute the essence of the story of Jacob and Esau.

We should not cast struggle and conflict in totally negative terms. Hence, for God to subvert the law of primogeniture for the sake of the divine purposes opens the situation up to conflict; those who hold on for dear life to the way things are will not give up easily, not least because they have law and custom on their side. At the same time, we may have difficulty in discerning when and how change (and hence often conflict) stands in service of God's purposes. The furtherance of God's mission in the world would be one basic criterion.

2. We are not told what sort of divine action Rebekah's conception was thought to entail. "Barrenness" means childlessness, but not necessarily infertility. We do not know the degree to which physiological or psychological factors, or some combination, faced these parents. They had been childless for twenty years. Rebekah's conception witnesses to God's work as Creator, enabling new life to emerge.

3. The role of prayer on the part of *both* Isaac and Rebekah continues an emphasis of chap. 24, and demonstrates its importance in the lives of these figures; they obviously believe God would be concerned about such matters and had resources to do something about them (see 18:22-33). Prayer occurs prominently in Genesis as an unself-conscious practice of nearly every major figure, attesting to the personal nature of their relationship with God.[165]

165. On prayer, see S. Balentine, *Prayer in the Hebrew Bible: The Drama of Divine-Human Dialogue* (Minneapolis: Fortress, 1993).

4. God's oracle to Rebekah achieves a profound effect; it sets into motion a certain *direction* for the future. This oracle recognizes that what happens in one generation (especially a word from God) may have a profound influence on those that follow, particularly with respect to certain formative periods in Israel's (or any people's) life. Later Israel understood the ancestral period to be such a time.

One might claim that the future of the two boys has been predetermined by this divine word. Yet, it shortly becomes clear that Rebekah does not understand that the oracle absolutely determines her sons' futures. What she does or says assumes that she thinks she can shape that future. She enters into their lives in decisive, at times manipulative, fashion, acting in ways that she thinks will contribute toward the future of which God has spoken (the narrator passes no judgment on her activity). The oft-suggested idea that just by pursuing such activities one seeks to take the divine promises into one's own hands constitutes a docetic view of the way in which God works in the world. God chooses to work in and through human activity in pursuing the divine purposes.

The future about which God speaks is not set in concrete. This is true of divine announcements about the future generally, particularly in prophetic material (see 2 Kgs 20:1-7; Jonah 3).[166] These utterances express the future as God sees it (or would like to see it). God's knowledge of future human behaviors is not absolute (evident in other texts; see 22:12). Moreover, the divine will can be frustrated by human behaviors (e.g., sin); though God's way into the future cannot, finally, be stymied.

Why would God speak directly to Rebekah about such matters? God takes sharp risks in being misunderstood. Giving Rebekah (or any human being) such information will tend to predispose her to act in certain ways toward her sons. Although she could have ignored God's word or actively worked against it, she chooses to tilt toward Jacob. God knows such behavior is likely, of course. The narrator has already reported Rebekah's preference (25:28), where she is said to love Jacob, and she doubtless knows that this runs counter to Isaac's "love." So God apparently gives Rebekah this information because God wants her to speak and act in such a way that this oracle will have a greater likelihood of coming to pass! The oracle expresses the future that God desires, and he hereby enlists Rebekah to work with God toward that end. That God chooses Rebekah rather than Isaac seems remarkable, given this patriarchal society; it suggests that God has more confidence in Rebekah than in Isaac. The reader might ask: Is this fair? Not according to any known human standard. At this point we are smack up against the mysteries of the divine election of Jacob (or Abraham or Israel . . .).

5. The narrator depicts the situation in such a way as to demonstrate that the inversion of priorities in the oracle does not derive from the boys' behaviors. The decision occurred pre-birth. Both act in ignorance of the oracle. The writer portrays both Jacob and Esau in such a way that disinterested readers would probably disagree on who acted the most reprehensibly. Both are guilty of violating basic family relationships, and any effort to excuse either one cuts against the grain of the text. Jacob takes egregious advantage of another person in need and sets the stage for major family conflict. Esau comes off as the dullard, careless with family interests and despising of the birthright. We do not know why God would choose either one to carry out his purposes. From another angle, inasmuch as God typically chooses weak instruments, then both Esau and Jacob would qualify! It would be precarious to talk about God's choosing the weak to shame the strong on the basis of this passage (unless *strength* is defined in a very narrow way).

The narrator probably "sets up" the reader with this text. The temptation for later Israel (and all who consider themselves to be God's elect) would certainly be to side with Jacob against Esau, to somehow justify his behaviors or even to suggest that

---

166. Contrary to H. White, *Narration and Discourse*, 207, it can be a question of what as well as how.

whatever he did to obtain the birthright was appropriate to or congruent with God's choice. At one level, such thinking is ethically dangerous, for it suggests that the elect are free to act as they please, without regard for the consequences. At another level, such thinking is theologically wrong-headed, for personal behaviors did not ground God's choice to have the elder serve the younger.

Moreover, to note with Brueggemann, the pottage and the birthright ought not to be interpreted "as a contrast of spiritual and material . . . the birthright is fully as historical and material as is the pottage. It concerns security, prosperity, fertility and land."[167]

6. The reader must also use care in discussing primogeniture and the reversal of the rights of the firstborn. To be sure, the oracle overturns traditional customs and understandings and opens the future to possibilities not inherent in existing structures and institutions. But it is just as true that one can idolize the reversal of the traditional for its own sake. Even more, one can be tempted to understand election in terms comparable to primogeniture! Election, too, can be used as a vehicle to exclude others and exalt one's rights and privileges. Against such an understanding the prophets will speak very sharply (Amos 3:2; 9:7).

7. Family conflicts have far-reaching consequences, extending into personal, political, economic, and religious spheres. The conflict within this family will become more and more sharply evident as the narrative moves on. What will this mean for the future of God's people? Are seeds being sown in these dim recesses of history that will one day reap bitter fruit for the descendants of this family? What the people of God do with the conflicts with which they are inevitably presented will make a difference. And, amid all of this intrafamilial difficulty, what will become of the promises of God? Will they transpire as God intends? Neither the oracles nor the promises of God give a precise shape to the future. God will be faithful, that will never be in doubt; but what the recipients of the promise do and say along the way will make a difference regarding the shape of fulfillment.

167. Brueggemann, *Genesis*, 219.

GENESIS 26:1-33, STORIES ABOUT ISAAC

COMMENTARY

Isaac is the least well known of the ancestral figures. We are most familiar with Isaac as the boy portrayed in the stories of Abraham. Chapter 26 presents the only block of material devoted solely to Isaac. Even then, it occurs after the introduction of Jacob and Esau and their emerging conflict, so it has the feel of an interlude within that more comprehensive story. The fact that the two boys are not yet born seems evident from 26:7, so an editor has positioned this chapter in a nonlinear fashion.

Whatever the origins and history of these materials (scholars typically point to J), many interpreters now consider the chapter a unity. Isaac's contacts with Abimelech provide episodes that highlight the promises to Isaac and the formation of peaceful relationships with "nonchosen" people of the land. There are numerous links between this chapter and the story of Abraham. In some basic sense, Isaac is a mirror of Abraham.

26:1-5. The chapter begins with the first of several links to the story of Abraham and the initial famine (12:10). Isaac also leaves his home in time of famine and heads for Egypt, but he gets only as far as Gerar, in Philistine country, when God appears to him. We have previously encountered Gerar, Abimelech, and the Philistines. (See chaps. 20–21. Some have questioned whether this can be the same king, given the expanse of some seventy-five years; yet, the ages of people in Genesis [Abraham died at 175] and the absence of any report to the contrary means the author thinks this Abimelech is probably the same person.)

God appears to Isaac twice (vv. 2, 24), probably in the form of a messenger (see 16:7). In both cases, the deity extends to Isaac the promises previously given to Abraham.

The first instance (vv. 2-5) contains both a command regarding a journey (which Isaac obeys) and a promise, mirroring Abraham's word from God in 12:1-4a; both are also followed by famines and journeys during which the patriarchs place their wives in danger. God intends to *stop* Isaac from doing what Abraham did, going down to Egypt for relief from the famine (see 12:10). He should "sojourn" (be a resident alien) among the Philistines. Enduring the famine here would seem to entail more hardship for the family, but such does not happen. While the command may be intended to deter Isaac from repeating Abraham's experience (that would be ironic in view of what happens), it also highlights God's blessings even in the midst of famine. In another such time God approves Jacob's journey to Egypt (46:3). Looking to Egypt for relief may be a difficult political question for later Israelites.

This divine word fulfills the promise to Abraham regarding the covenant with Isaac (17:19). God's promises are confirmed to Isaac: (a) I will be with you. God offers this word for the first time to Isaac, and then, later, to Jacob (28:15; 31:3); (b) I will bless you (see 12:2); this promise pertains to the goodness that comes to Isaac as well as to his descendants; (c) I will give "all these lands," a collocation peculiar to this context and stated twice; it includes the lands of the various peoples noted earlier (15:18-19), but focuses on the land in which Isaac lives now as an alien; (d) the multiplication of descendants as the stars (see 15:5), i.e., too numerous to count; (e) the blessing upon the nations in and through Isaac and his descendants (see 12:3). This promise takes concrete form in this context in Isaac's relationship to the Philistines.

On the difficult v. 5, see Reflections.

26:6-11. We have already encountered two similar episodes involving the endangering of a wife of a patriarch (12:10-20; 20:1-18). This story begins with language that links it to Abraham's sojourn in the same city, Gerar (20:1-18). The juxtaposition of command/promise and the endangerment episode also occur in chap. 12 (vv. 1-9, 10-20). Moreover, all three versions are followed by texts concerned with land (13:1-18; 21:22-34; 26:12-33). This version of the story presents minimal complexity: little tension, no divine involvement, no actual contact with Rebekah by the king, and less disparagement of the patriarch, who responds only when confronted with interest in Rebekah (and apparently for good reason, v. 10).

Once again, an ancestor of Israel tries to pass off his beautiful wife as his sister in the presence of foreigners. Once again, fear for his own life (twice stated) leads him to do this. This guise had been successful for "a long time" when Abimelech (unlike chap. 20, he was not personally involved) quite by chance observes intimate behaviors between them that suggest a husband/wife relationship. He immediately challenges Isaac, insists on an explanation but ignores it, and berates him for endangering that community. If someone had thought Rebekah was unmarried and had had sexual relations with her, that would have brought "guilt" on his people. In the face of this threat, Abimelech warns all citizens to keep their hands off both Rebekah and Isaac. This edict assures a safe setting in which God's blessings now flow to Isaac. Here, as in chaps. 12 and (especially) 20, the author portrays a foreign king in congenial terms, both personally and religiously.

26:12-22. As with Abraham in Egypt (12:16) and in Gerar (20:14-16), Isaac emerges from this potentially disastrous situation not only unscathed, but also immeasurably enriched. His material prosperity occurs quickly in the very midst of the famine and enfolds every aspect of his life. Unlike chaps. 12 and 20, Isaac's wealth derives only indirectly from the king (the edict protected him, v. 11), whereas the author highlights God's blessing activity. This prosperity attests to the promise in v. 3; the blessing comes in spite of the patriarch's actions. This result qualifies Abimelech's concern about guilt, at least if he thought the moral order functioned mechanically. If people *always* reaped the effects of their deeds, then Isaac (and Abraham) would have reaped disaster rather than blessing.

This picture of great wealth (mentioned three times in v. 13) has become important to these stories. God's promise of blessing works itself out in every sphere of their life. The sojourning life experienced by Israel's ancestors on that land gives a foretaste of what it will be like when Israel lives in the land of milk and honey.

However, not everyone receives well God's work of blessing. Isaac's wealth becomes the object of envy by the Philistines, who stop up some wells Abraham's servants had dug (see 21:22-34; the NIV translation of v. 15 is clearer than the NRSV). Given this tension, Abimelech thinks that Isaac's power endangers (again, cf. v. 10) the Philistine hegemony, and asks him to leave the area. This he does without hesitation, but he remains close by, in territory adjacent to Gerar (v. 17), where Abraham had spent some time (21:34) and had also dug wells.

Conflict over wells and water rights continues in this new territory (vv. 17-22). Isaac and his servants reopen other wells (opposed to those in v. 15) that Abraham had dug and that the Philistines had stopped up; he gave them their old names as a sign of renewed ownership (v. 18). Verses 19-22 speak of Isaac's digging three new wells (finding fresh water in one); the Philistines in the area quarrel over the first two, but not the third (reasons are not given, but v. 16 suggests Isaac's power). Isaac gives names to the wells that correspond to this life experience (see NRSV and NIV footnotes). The author explains the third name (Rehoboth) as a divine gift of land, in which they will be able to spread out and be fruitful. These incidents may reflect Israel's later experience with the people of the land, but we should observe that Isaac does not use his stronger position to claim every well. Verse 22, with its reference to room and fruitfulness in the land of promise, leads into a fuller statement of the promise in v. 24.

26:23-33. The second divine appearance to Isaac (vv. 24-25) occurs after his return to Beersheba (22:19). The author presents a typical theophanic narrative, with self-identification, quelling of fear, and word of God. For the first time, God is identified as "the God of your father." Abraham is the first such

"father," and the epithet now becomes common in referring to the continuity of God's promise. The epithet (used as well for other gods in the ancient Near East) specifies the singularity of this deity from one generation to the next and the faithful response of each "father" to God. The link with persons rather than places emphasizes the personal character of the faith between God and these persons.

The God of Isaac's own father reiterates the basic promises spoken in vv. 2-4 (except the land promise, just treated in v. 22). The promises may recur at this point because the conflicts seem to jeopardize Isaac's relationship to the promises and because land that Abraham held has been reclaimed. The phrase "for the sake of [on account of] Abraham" refers to v. 5. Because of Abraham's faithfulness, the promises are transmitted to Isaac. The designation of Abraham as a servant, an image with a focus on loyalty, stresses exactly this point. This does not involve a "fund of spiritual credit" upon which subsequent generations may draw.[168] For the first time, Isaac responds with worship (v. 25), calling on God as Yahweh (see 4:25). This appearance also establishes Beersheba as a cultic center (Jacob stops here in 46:1). The digging of a well by Isaac's servants (v. 25*b*) may have prompted the visit from Abimelech. The well brackets his visit (vv. 25*b*, 32-33).

Verses 26-33 closely parallel 21:22-34. Abimelech and his top advisers leave their own area to initiate better relationships with the more powerful Isaac; Isaac exhibits caution in view of their history with each other. For all Abimelech's concern about future relations with Isaac, however, he emphasizes another motivation. He observes that *Yahweh* has been with Isaac and has blessed him (vv. 28-29); these affirmations enclose his words and signal their import—they are more than flattery. Because of what God has done—and the reiteration of the promises in v. 24 reinforces this—Isaac draws Abimelech into a peaceful relationship.

The two men express some difference of opinion regarding their common past. Isaac speaks of hostility and expulsion (cf. v. 16); Abimelech claims that no harm, indeed nothing but good, has been done—Isaac was sent

168. Sarna, *Genesis*, 187.

away in peace (cf. v. 11). Isaac ignores the differences (no further words between them are reported) and takes a peaceful initiative by preparing a meal for all concerned (common in treaty making; cf. 31:46). The next day they formally enter into a covenant, a bilateral, nonaggression pact. It results in peace (שלום *šālôm*) between Isaac and Abimelech (cf. 31:44-54), less than idyllic but still peace.

The references to well digging and finding water (vv. 32-33), begun in v. 25, symbolize the newly won peace. Isaac's servants dig a well and discover water, thereby supporting life, and no conflict ensues. Isaac gives essentially the same name to the place—Beersheba—reported in 21:31 (as was his practice, 26:18), testifying to the sworn oath that enables peace rather than conflict to prevail.

REFLECTIONS

1. This chapter as a whole testifies to the way Isaac, exhibiting both weakness and strength, yet repeatedly surrounded by the promises and blessings of God, works through relationships with outsiders and enables peace to prevail amid numerous possibilities for conflict.

2. Verse 5 provides two sorts of difficulties. (1) It seems to indicate that the continuance of the promise depended on Abraham's obedience. (2) The various words for the law seem to presuppose the giving of the law at Sinai.

The initial "because" has been used before in 22:18 (cf. Deut 7:12; 8:20), though there associated only with obeying the "voice" of God. Westermann states that Abraham is "the exemplar of obedience to the law in return for which God bestowed the promises on him." Similarly, Coats states that obedience "offers the basis for the promise."[169] This should be stated differently. God gave the promise to Abraham independently of his obedience (12:1-3). Similarly, God repeats the promise twice to *Isaac* because of the obedience of *Abraham* (vv. 5, 24). Isaac's obedience does not enable him to be the *recipient* of the promise. God announces the promise to him because of someone else's faithfulness. The community of faith throughout the centuries has also received the promise because of someone else's faithfulness.

The issue involves the transmission of the promise to the next generation. Genes, independent of the faithfulness of the one to whom the promise has been given, do not transmit the promise (see commentary on chap. 22). Isaac's faithfulness will be as important for generational transmission as was Abraham's. The reference to the "God of Isaac" in 28:13-15 covers the same point, as does 48:15, where Jacob confesses that Isaac walked before God. This chapter, in its various parallels to Abraham's story, illustrates Isaac's faithful response. Isaac responds to the initial command/promise of God as does Abraham (12:1-4a); he moves through comparable times of failure, but nevertheless remains blessed by God and receives anew the divine promises; and he responds in worship and peacemaking.

The language about the law certainly means that the author knows about the law given at Sinai. But this is no simple anachronism; it carries significance for understanding the place of law in the pre-Sinai period. God introduces law initially at creation (1:26-28; 2:16-17) and other divine commands emerge along the way (e.g., 9:1-7). The law given at Sinai does not emerge as a new reality; it stands in basic continuity with earlier articulations of God's will for the creation.[170] Abraham's conforming to the will of God shows that his life is in tune with God's creational purposes and models for later Israel the right response to law, which cannot be collapsed into that given at Sinai. The fivefold "my" shows that obedience to law is seen in terms of interpersonal response.

---

169. Westermann, *Genesis 12–36*, 424; George W. Coats, *Genesis: With an Introduction to Narrative Literature* (Grand Rapids: Eerdmans, 1983) 189.
170. See Fretheim, "The Reclamation of Creation," 362-65.

---

3. The author presents Abimelech as the only named outsider who extends across more than one generation. He must have grown weary encountering this family, who had a habit of passing off wives as sisters and with whom he had to negotiate about water and wells one more time. One more pre-Israelite, nonchosen inhabitant of the promised land receives remarkably good press, and acts with integrity that often matches the patriarch.

4. The story in vv. 6-11, as others in Genesis, assumes the idea of objective guilt. Even if a sinful act is unknowingly committed (in this case, sexual relations with a married woman), one incurs guilt. Whether the text also presumes corporate guilt ("us") remains unclear. The word translated "guilt" (אשׁם *'āšām*) may only refer more generally to negative communal consequences. Isaac, in protecting himself from danger, places an entire city under threat from the fallout of sins committed because he has not considered fully the possible effects of his action. Yet, this was only a risk, for the moral order does not function in a mechanical fashion.

5. Verse 22 foreshadows settlement in the land, but it also describes a preliminary *fulfillment* of the promise of a "broad" land (cf. Exod 3:8) and their growth as a people (see 17:6; 47:27), which in turn fulfills God's word in creation (1:28; 9:1, 7). Isaac's utterance also provides a good word for people in exile, whose lives often parallel the ancestors. To have a home, a place one can call one's own, means to "make room" (give space). The OT construes the experience of salvation in similar ways (see Pss. 4:1; 18:19, 36; 31:8 ["You have set my feet in a broad place," NRSV]); the blessing that comes in the midst of famine attests to an experience of salvation.

6. Abimelech confirms that the divine promises (v. 3) have been fulfilled (vv. 28-29)! Even more, we see Isaac/Israel as one with whom the kings and nations of the world must come to terms. But this claim does not function simply at the political level; whatever greatness comes to Israel (see v. 13; 12:2) comes because of God's blessing and not its own powers. Even more, if and when power or greatness comes, it does not necessarily involve establishing hegemony over others or undermining their reconciling efforts, perhaps in retaliation for past actions. Israel should be an instrument of peace among the nations (vv. 29, 31).

GENESIS 26:34–28:9, JACOB, ESAU, AND THE BLESSING

COMMENTARY

The author has enclosed this major story of Isaac's deception (27:1-45, assigned to J or JE) by reports associated with the wives of the two sons (26:34-35; 27:46-28:9; assigned to P). These reports intensify the conflicted character of the family. At the same time, Isaac's freely given blessing of Jacob (28:3-4) softens the impact of Jacob's deception in gaining the blessing. The origin of these texts remains obscure, but they may reflect later Israel/Edom alignments. Two old poetic pieces provide the focus for the chapter (vv. 27-29, 39-40).

26:34-35. Chapter 26 concludes on a negative note. Family relationships remain conflicted in spite of peace in the larger community. Esau's act of marrying, without parental consent, two Hittite (Canaanite) women (cf. 24:3; 28:1, 6) first provides evidence of difficulties. Esau's wives' making life bitter for both parents involves more than their family lineage. Yet, placement of these verses before chap. 27 reinforces a negative sense about Esau and disposes the reader to be less critical of the moves made by Jacob and Rebekah. Moreover, Esau's actions create sympathy for the dilemma Isaac faces as a parent. However, one must be careful not to fall into the trap of placing Esau and Jacob on some kind of "fitness" scale, as if God's choices were determined by measuring morality. Jacob is no plaster saint either.

27:1-40. Jacob and Esau never appear together in the four major scenes of this story, nor do Rebekah and Esau, which symbolizes a lack of communication within the family. The author uses vocabulary to create a sensuous story: seeing, hearing, tasting, touching and smelling make it a story one can almost feel. Also, repeated language of blessing (twenty-eight times) demonstrates its centrality in the story.

The relationship between the story of the birthright (בכרה *běkōrâ*; 25:29-34) and this story of the blessing (ברכה *běrākâ*) appears problematic. They may be two different ways of thinking about the same reality, but that may be too simple. Esau distinguishes them but thinks they bear comparable importance (27:36); to lose both produces a double loss. The former relates basically to issues of inheritance; the latter to deathbed blessing (cf. 48:22 with 49:22-26). Both deal with issues raised by the oracle in 25:23, the overturning of primogeniture; both involve Jacob in an active role; his actions are duplicitous in both cases. The former reflects, initially, a private arrangement (of which Isaac is not aware until 27:36), the latter a more public matter.

27:1-4. Isaac, advanced in years, takes steps to prepare his family for the future (cf. 24:1; he does not die until 35:29). Isaac directs Esau to hunt for game and prepare his favorite food (cf. 25:28); then Isaac would give him a personal (נפשי *napšî*) blessing. The provision of a meal constitutes an essential part of the blessing ritual (see below).

27:5-17. Overhearing Isaac's request, Rebekah reports its essentials to Jacob, including Esau's absence, but she adds "before Yahweh" (v. 7). This interpretation sets Isaac over against God's speech (25:23) and establishes Rebekah's theological motivation; she responds to the word of God, which Esau's behaviors have reinforced (26:34-35). Blessing is not a justice issue for her. Taking the initiative, she devises a ruse by which Jacob can receive the blessing, and "commands" him to help out (v. 8; "obey" in v. 13). He should act

in just the way Isaac commanded Esau, but before Esau returns.

Jacob does not immediately agree, not because he thinks it wrong, but because he doubts its feasibility. His participation becomes explicit when he raises a complicating issue; Esau is hairy and Jacob is not, and their nearly blind father can still feel (an ironic touch since "smooth" can also mean deceptive, Ps 55:21). Jacob worries that Isaac may pronounce a curse on him. Their mother's willingness to bear the brunt of any response (note that the curse could be transferred!) reassures him, and he quickly (conveyed by three verbs in rapid sequence, v. 14) "obeys" her directives. Only then does Rebekah address her son's concern by "clothing" him so that he feels and smells like Esau (cf. Jacob's being deceived by clothing in 37:31-33; 38:14). Jacob proceeds without hesitation. We cannot help wondering whether such crude disguises will do the trick.

27:18-29. Carrying out the ruse is now up to Jacob, and he executes it without hesitation. His verbal deception takes two forms: He lies about his identity (vv. 19, 24), and he sanctimoniously draws God into the deceit by claiming, with supreme irony, that *Isaac's* God, Yahweh, has granted him success (v. 20). But from v. 20 on, Jacob utters only one word (v. 24); otherwise he only acts in response to Isaac's queries and commands.

These verses are informed by a blessing ritual (though without magical allusions):[171] the command of the father, here recalled by the son (vv. 18-19); identification of the son (vv. 19, 24); a shared meal—for communion, not strength (v. 25); approach and kiss—to seal the blessing, not to transfer life (vv. 26-27*a*); pronouncement of blessing (vv. 27*b*-29). The various elements of the ritual are essential for the transmission of blessing. At the same time, Isaac utilizes this ritual in remarkable ways to pursue his questions. Isaac may be an unknowing vehicle for Rebekah's wishes, but he has not thereby turned into an automaton!

Interpreters often adjudge Isaac's behavior to be naive, even bumbling, yet the repeated questions and ritual delays reveal that he pursues his deep suspicions carefully. He uses all the senses available to him (in this order:

---

171. Westermann, *Genesis 12–36,* 439.

sound, touch, taste, smell) to discern the truth. He trusts hearing less than touching (vv. 22-23); his blindness and age create varying sensitivities. We should note especially his manipulation of the ritual. Rather than wait for full clarity before proceeding, he uses its various elements to test his suspicions. Twice he questions Jacob's identity; in the meal and kiss rituals he probes with taste and smell. The smell (mentioned four times in v. 27!) *seems* finally to be sufficient, if not conclusive evidence. The smell recalls a fertile field and then moves to the blessing of fertility!

In view of what follows, v. 23 proves startling. If it means what it says, then Isaac utters the blessing, but quickly has further doubts, the import of which would be that a blessing once spoken may not be final. But these words could also refer to Isaac's decision to proceed with the blessing ritual even in the face of uncertainty. In either case, Isaac begins the ritual once again, still concerned with the issue of identity (v. 24).

Isaac never calls Jacob by the name *Esau* (contrast chap. 49) or concludes that he now knows this is Esau. The (sevenfold) "my son" remains constant from beginning (v. 18) to end (v. 27); in fact, its use in v. 25 seems unusual, since "your game" would have been more natural. The narrator claims nonrecognition only at the story's mid-point (v. 23). Isaac probably gives the blessing with less than full certainty, and probably suspects he is dealing with Jacob (note his musings in v. 22).

Although Isaac reacts strongly when he finds he has been tricked (v. 33); and calls it deceit (v. 35), he never chides Jacob. In fact, the next time he speaks to him (28:1-4), Isaac proceeds as if all is well. He then reinforces the blessing, explicitly linking it with Abraham. Isaac's acceptance seems to lie, not in a magical notion of blessing, but in a conviction that he acted properly (vv. 33, 37). After all, he has just learned about the birthright incident for the first time (v. 36); another factor may have been the parental pain Esau's marriages caused (26:35).

The blessing centers on fertility (v. 28) and dominion (v. 29; cf. 24:60). The parallels between this blessing and those Jacob extends to both Judah and Joseph in 49:8-12, 22-26 are noteworthy. Verse 28 (cf. 49:25;

Deut 33:13-16, 28) speaks of divine blessing as rain and mist (i.e., the dew of heaven), rich produce (i.e., fatness of the earth), and a plentiful harvest of grain and grapes. Progeny and land are assumed, but are not mentioned as part of the ancestral promises. Isaac calls upon God the Creator, who blesses in the agricultural sphere, to be active in the life of Jacob. Verse 29 (cf. 49:8)—with only an implicit reference to God—speaks of blessing as dominion over other nations/peoples, including his "brothers/mother's sons" (cf. v. 37; the plural may refer to family members, so NIV). At this point, Isaac unknowingly echoes God's word to Rebekah (25:23) and anticipates the blessing of Judah (49:8). Then, in the only explicit reference to 12:3*a* in Genesis (see Num 24:9), Isaac links his blessing with God's promise: Whether people are cursed or blessed depends on their treatment of Jacob/Israel.

27:30-40. These verses begin as did vv. 18-19. Having obeyed his father's directive, Esau approaches him with the prepared food and requests a blessing, to which Isaac responds with questions about his identity. His inquiry about the perpetrator is only rhetorical (v. 33), for he identifies him as "your brother" immediately (v. 35). Yet, Jacob remains blessed; Isaac refers not simply to the word of blessing but to the accompanying ritual meal as reasons why Jacob remains blessed (v. 33).

Crying out in exasperation and deep disappointment, Esau pleads that his father bless him also. Isaac replies that, even though his brother was deceitful, he has taken his blessing. Esau bitterly retorts that Jacob is rightly named (see 25:26), for he deceived him of both blessing and birthright—news for Isaac. Esau begs for his own blessing, believing it possible that Isaac might have "reserved" a blessing for him (see 49:1-28 on open and multiple blessings). Since Isaac's blessing does, in principle, extend to him, Esau correctly pursues the matter.

Isaac summarizes the blessing given Jacob (v. 37); Isaac acts as the agent, not mentioning God. He has said "I do" to Jacob; in view of the prevailing convention regarding blessings, what can he do for Esau now that Jacob is his lord? Yet, when Esau insistently cries out, Isaac responds to his lament with a secondary blessing (vv. 39-40). Esau will dwell in an area without (or with, NRSV footnote; the Hebrew may be purposely ambiguous) rich land and adequate rainfall, and his life will be filled with violence. Although he will be subject to his brother, at times he will break free from that yoke (see 33:3-7; 2 Kgs 8:20-22). This statement *qualifies* Jacob's blessing (v. 29) in response to Esau's plea; it becomes somewhat less comprehensive than it was. Esau's deep lament proves to be potent, and Isaac responds. "Here is a clear theology of liberation—for Esau/Edom!"[172] For all the negative correspondence to Jacob's blessing, Esau will have a (fruitful?) land in which to dwell, life, progeny, and periods of freedom from his brother. Esau receives blessing—attenuated, compared to Jacob's—but not a curse or even nonblessing.

27:41-45. We can understand why Esau hates Jacob, but Esau's vow to kill him once Isaac has died (cf. 50:15) threatens the future of the promise. Once again Rebekah hears Esau's plans (speaking "to himself" expresses his resolve), and her actions shape the next scene. She informs Jacob and directs him to flee to her home in Haran until Esau's fury has passed (repeated for emphasis). When time has healed the wounds, she will send for him again. She remains hopeful; Esau will drop his threat, but Rebekah will not see Isaac again. Her lament shows a concern for Esau too (though she never speaks to him); if Esau were to kill Jacob, he would be executed. Once again she believes she must act, for the divine oracle of 25:23 will not inevitably protect Jacob. Nor will Isaac's blessing.

27:46–28:9. This section relates to 26:34-35 with its concern about wives, and to the immediately preceding 27:41-45. Her differing motivations are true to the story; she remains anxious about both Jacob's life

172. Gammie, "Theological Interpretation by Way of Literary and Tradition Analysis: Genesis 25–36," 130.

and wife. Rebekah does not speak to Isaac about the threat to Jacob, perhaps to conceal her own involvement. She raises the issue of Esau's marriages, which had "made life bitter" for *both* Isaac and Rebekah (26:35). If Jacob follows suit, her life will not be worth living; she may be thinking about the way she became Isaac's wife (24:2-4). Her concern about wives gives Jacob's departure a sense of legitimacy.

Isaac responds positively. Speaking with Jacob for the first time *as Jacob* in Genesis, Isaac enjoins him from marrying a Canaanite and directs him to go to Haran and marry a cousin, a daughter of Rebekah's brother, Laban. Using language that derives from God's covenant with Abraham in chap. 17, he blesses Jacob for the journey based on the promises he had received from God (26:3-4, 24). This blessing elaborates the blessing in 27:27-29, only Isaac knowingly and freely blesses Jacob this time and without reproach for his deceit; this softens Jacob's deception in obtaining Esau's blessing. Although similar in form ("May God . . . "), the language this time appears more specifically Abrahamic (the link is with v. 29c). Isaac conveys promise in the form of a blessing. Isaac does not transmit the promises formally, but anticipates God's own speaking "the blessing of Abraham" to him, which occurs in 28:13-15. Jacob obeys without a word.

Meanwhile, Esau catches wind of what has happened to Jacob. Suppressing the hatred expressed in 27:41, Esau focuses on his father's concern about wives for his sons and Jacob's obedient response to *both* parents. In an effort to please his *father* (v. 8), he takes a (third) wife from within the family, the family of Ishmael, his father's brother (25:12-18). This favorable portrayal of Esau appears similar to that given to Ishmael (21:8-21). Yet, like Ishmael, he remains on the fringes of the family.

REFLECTIONS

1. This story has long been a favorite of Bible readers. It is well told and filled with intrigue. Some readers think it tells of a cheat and a rascal who, nonetheless, remains the chosen of God. That has occasioned both wonderment and hope on the part of the elect in every age: Why would God choose such a character? If God includes Jacob, who can be excluded? This may be an appropriate direction to take with this text, yet one cannot help wondering if such a negative picture of Jacob is justified.

2. How should one assess Jacob's and Rebekah's actions? They are motivated by an oracle from God (25:23), by Esau's treatment of his parents (26:35; 28:8), and by the birthright (25:33). Jacob's experience and self-understanding link up with Rebekah's theological convictions and familial sensitivities; this is a formidable duo. But, while the end they achieve may be fitting in view of the oracle, do not the means lack integrity, even basic decency (cf. Deut 27:18)? While their actions can be explained, can they be justified? White claims that they may be justified in opening a closed system: "Deception and desire may now have positive roles to play so long as they are subservient to the contingency of the promissory Word and faith, rather than serving the interest of symbiotic personal behavior and structures of power."[173] One thinks of Tamar and the midwives, whose deception was not only tolerated but commended (38:26; Exod 1:20).

One often hears this attractive approach, but it is sometimes bought at the expense of "demonizing" Esau and even Isaac or "whitewashing" Jacob and Rebekah. Neither demons nor plaster saints are here, and the way the story pursues blessing for Jacob retains no little ambiguity. The way in which "what goes around comes around" for Jacob in 29:25-26 and 37:31-33 suggests that Jacob reaps the consequences of his deceptions of Esau and Isaac. At the same time, pursuance of the "right" often carries negative consequences, and with respect to Rebekah one must reckon with issues of patriarchy (see below). One must be careful not to become too defensive regarding Jacob's actions, lest God's choices be grounded in "righteousness" or "uprightness of heart" (cf. Deut 9:4-5). God chooses to work in and through what human beings make available. This reveals a deep divine vulnerability, for it links God with people whose reputations are not stellar and opens God's ways in the world to sharp criticism.

3. Readers should note some additional features of Rebekah's actions.[174] Rebekah could have conceivably pursued other, less deceptive options, such as informing Isaac about God's oracle. But, while we are not privy to her reflections, she doubtless thought this matter through carefully. She had to consider, above all, Isaac's special relationship to Esau (25:28), even though 28:8 (cf. 26:35) indicates Isaac's displeasure with him. Another likely factor involves the prevailing patriarchy, which rendered her opinions on such matters of little import. She must rely on secondary means to discover what goes on in the family (vv. 5, 42), and must be careful in approaching Isaac about Jacob's predicament (27:46; cf. also Isaac's reaction in 27:33—because his authority has been undercut?). In the face of the powerlessness patriarchy engenders, manipulation often remains the only route open to the future. On another matter, her response to Jacob's hesitance in 27:13 indicates a resolve to take upon herself any curse that Isaac might pronounce. She expresses an openness to suffering, even death, on behalf of both her son and the divine purposes she serves.

4. Blessing. This motif probably has its origins in the leave-taking of everyday life (24:60) or in the departure from life itself (see chap. 49). It is important to stress, however, that the word of blessing does not have a magical sense—either in terms of (a) the transmission of vitality from blesser to blessed, so that Isaac has no life left to give Esau; or (b) the speaking of a word that becomes an autonomous force, independent of Isaac or God.

Yet, the latter view especially has been popular. The blessing of the father "inexorably determined destiny: the father's horror [v. 33] stands powerless before the

173. White, *Narration and Discourse*, 225.
174. See Jeansonne, *Women in Genesis*, 53-69.

unalterable."[175] So also the Oxford Annotated NRSV notes: "The blessing, like the curse, released a power that effectively determined the character and destiny of the recipient . . . the spoken blessing, like an arrow shot toward its goal, was believed to release a power which could not be retracted."[176]

However, this understanding of the word is incorrect, both generally and in this text. Acts of blessing in the OT rest on accepted *conventions*. Such words produce effects because of certain social understandings about the function of these speech-acts. These words must be spoken in a particular situation by the appropriate person in the proper form to be effective.[177] If the blessing *could* not be revoked by Isaac, it was because no convention was available for its revocation. If there were such a convention, Isaac chooses not to make use of it. Esau, in asking for *another* blessing, appears to believe that no such convention exists. Even then, Isaac's response to Esau (vv. 39-40) demonstrates that actions can be taken to qualify the impact of a blessing already spoken.

One basic reason cited by Isaac for not retracting the blessing involves the consumption of a meal (v. 33; cf. vv. 4, 7, 10, 19, 25, 31). The meal was an integral part of a conventional blessing ritual (see above), without which it would not have been valid. In this understanding of ritual, we are not far from certain realistic views of, say, the Christian sacraments, or liturgy more generally.

5. It would be too simple to suggest that the known histories of Israel and Edom are here retrojected into early times and thought to have been determined by these early oracles (see 25:23). Certainly the text recognizes that words and deeds do shape history, but not in some detailed, inevitable way. For example, Israel over the course of its history did not always have "plenty of grain and wine" (v. 28; see Deut 11:13-17), nor were the nations of the world, including Edom, always subservient. Esau has Jacob over the barrel not infrequently (see Psalm 137)! Moreover, Esau is not alone in living by the sword (see 34:25; 48:22).

6. It may be that the issue of marrying within one's own community, so evident in this segment, arose at a time when this issue was a lively concern for readers during the exile and later. However, Genesis does not present a consistent picture regarding the matter. Judah and Joseph marry outside the family, with no censure or criticism. The same openness could be claimed for the relationship between Dinah and Shechem in chap. 34, where two of her brothers are rebuked for their actions against Shechem and his family. The issue involves, not a general principle regarding such marriages, but certain moments in the life of a community when a distinctive identity is deemed to be crucial to ensure the future. Such may be the case for the first two generations of Abraham's family, but before the end of Genesis, the issue no longer seems so important.

7. The blessing extended to Esau by his father testifies to blessing as a reality outside the community of chosen ones. Esau's blessing, though attenuated, should be linked with other Genesis narratives, where the "outsider" becomes the recipient of divine blessing (e.g., Ishmael; see chaps. 16; 21). God the Creator works among these peoples with blessings that take various forms, the most basic of which is life itself, often apart from contact with the community of faith (though such contact may produce special blessings, v. 29). The interests of the people of promise are not served well by finding ways of speaking negatively about those outside that community, or seeking to limit the blessing activity of God among them.

175. So Westermann, *Genesis 12–36*, 442.

176. *The New Oxford Annotated Bible*, eds. B. Metzger and R. Murphy (New York: Oxford University Press, 1991) 34-35.

177. See T. Fretheim, "Word of God," in *The Anchor Bible Dictionary*, vol. 6, ed. D. Freedman (New York: Doubleday, 1992) 961-68, and literature cited therein.

8. Jacob's receiving the birthright and the blessing does not issue in a trouble-free life. In fact, they expose his life to more conflict than would probably otherwise have been the case, not least because of what he does with it. God's choices are not always well received, by both the chosen and the not chosen. Certainly, God designs blessing for all the peoples of the world. But, because of the recalcitrance and deception of the chosen themselves, blessing sometimes has the effect of dividing as often as uniting. One should reflect deeply on this story from the perspective of those who believe themselves to be chosen and how they relate to those who are the "unchosen." The degree to which religious convictions have provoked strife in the modern world should occasion deep shame on the part of members of the community of faith and a renewed sense of what it means to be a responsible recipient of divine blessing.

GENESIS 28:10–22, JACOB'S DREAM AT BETHEL

COMMENTARY

This text stands as one of the pillars of the Jacob story. God transmits to him the ancestral promises, fulfilling the expressed wish of his father (28:3-4). This is the first time Jacob appears by himself; hence it represents a new beginning for the larger story. Jacob flees from the hatred and threats of his brother, seeming to reap the consequences of his own duplicity, and the future does not seem bright. At precisely this deeply vulnerable moment in his life, God appears, not in judgment, but to confirm him as the one chosen to carry on the promise.

Some readers think this story has its roots in a concern to ground the later Bethel sanctuary and worship life in the ancestral period (see 1 Kgs 12:26-33). Although possible, the episode has now been drawn into the larger orbit of stories about Jacob (often assigned to JE) and serves a more comprehensive purpose. It shares a basic structure with the fragment in 32:1-2 (cf. 32:22-33), an encounter with angels on his way back home. Together with another appearance of God to Jacob at Bethel on his return journey (35:1-15), this episode brackets the narrative. A note about setting (vv. 10-11) is followed by the dream (vv. 12-15) and Joseph's response to it (vv. 16-22).

The author introduces Jacob en route. He is traveling from Beersheba to Haran, from which the Abrahamic family migrated and where he will find a temporary home and two wives. While still within Canaan, he spends the night out in the open, using an ordinary, if large, stone to support and protect his head. The text does not depict it as a holy site, but "place" anticipates vv. 11, 16, 17, and 19 and "stone" anticipates vv. 18 and 22; God transforms an ordinary stone and an ordinary place. It probably was a religious center for people in earlier times (cf. the name change in v. 19), but the text stakes a claim for Bethel's religious importance on the basis of this event (and perhaps Abraham's visit in 12:8; 13:3-4).

A remarkable dream fills Jacob's night. He dreams that a ladder (better, a stairway or ramp) extends from earth to heaven. We may compare this stairway to those attached to temple towers (ziggurats) elsewhere in the ancient Near East; these were microcosms of the world, with the top of the tower representing heaven, the dwelling place of the gods. Such structures provided an avenue of approach from the human sphere to the divine realm. Priests or divine beings traversed up and down the stairway, providing communication between the two realms. This text polemicizes such an understanding.

Ascending and descending divine beings are a part of Jacob's dream, but they have no specific function. In fact, their presence makes a negative point. While such beings may serve as messengers, here they do *not* serve as intermediaries for divine revelation. Rather, Yahweh stands beside Jacob and speaks directly to him (so NRSV; the NIV's "above it" is possible but unlikely in view of the immediacy in the deity's communication to Jacob). The angels do not speak; God does. Jacob hears the divine promises directly from God, who in turn promises God's very own presence rather than that of a surrogate. "Earth is not left to its own resources and heaven is not a remote self-contained realm for the gods. Heaven has to do with earth. And earth finally may count on the resources of heaven."[178]

God is identified in terms of Jacob's family, referring to Abraham as father rather than Isaac. Jacob thus has the same relationship to Abraham and Abraham's God as his father, Isaac, has had (see 26:3-4, 24). The use of the name *Yahweh* provides clearer continuity with Abraham (cf. 15:7) than the generic word for God.

God's word to Jacob moves directly from self-identification to promise, which fulfills Isaac's benedictory wish of 28:3-4 and constitutes *God's* confirmation of Jacob's gaining of birthright and blessing. God's promises are unusually extensive (eight different elements), to which Jacob adds another (v. 20, food and clothing). The promises are: land; many descendants; dispersion of posterity throughout the land (not the world, cf. 13:14-17); the extension of blessing to others through him; presence; keeping; homecoming, and not leaving. All the promises spoken in the narrative to this point are gathered up and focused on Jacob. The last four (v. 15) relate directly to Jacob's status as a traveler, extending the promise given to his father in comparable circumstances (26:3, 24).

Upon awakening, Jacob realizes the import of his dream, and he proceeds to *interpret* its significance. He recognizes that he has some new knowledge; he has moved from not knowing to knowing that God has been present with him. (Except for the ruse in 27:20, this is the first time he mentions God.) He also expresses awe that in this ordinary place he has been confronted by the God of whom his father spoke (28:3-4), indeed granted direct access to God's promise-speaking (see Reflections). His "naming" of the place occurs in two stages. The first (v. 17) attests to his encounter with the divine presence: the "house of God" (i.e., *Beth-el*)

and the "gate of heaven." These building metaphors represent concretely his experience of direct divine access. The stairway and the angels have been reduced to props, metaphors now inadequate for depicting the dynamics of immediate divine-human communication. The second (v. 19), more formal, naming emphasizes the continuity between the immediate experience and the ongoing significance of this particular place.

Jacob's response the next day takes more concrete forms. He sets up as a pillar the stone that had supported him as a "pillow." What was quite ordinary now becomes a sacred symbol for his experience. (Such standing stones are often set up at Israelite sanctuaries and at other places of historical import; cf. 35:14, 20.) The stone has now become recognizable for use by others who may pass by this way. The anointing with oil consecrates or sets the stone apart from others (cf. 31:13; Exod 40:9-11). The oil also stains the stone so that it can be properly identified by those who follow. Although not itself a sanctuary, the stone can become an integral part of a worship center; Jacob vows he will establish such a site (v. 22; Exodus 35:1-15). At the same time, the stone becomes a public witness to his own experience (on stones as witness, see Josh 24:27).

Finally, Jacob makes a vow (recalled by God in 31:13). Although vows are common in the OT (cf. Num 21:2; Judg 11:30-31; 1 Sam 1:11; 2 Sam 15:8, all spoken at sanctuaries), this vow seems unique since God has already unconditionally promised what Jacob states as a condition. By repeating God's promises in the vow, Jacob *claims* them as his own. Hence, to see this as bargain language does not do justice to the vow; rather, Jacob wants to hold God to his promises (those associated with his journey, v. 15). If God does *not* do these things, of course, then *God* will not have been faithful, and Jacob's relationship to such a God would be problematic, to say the least. If God keeps the promises, then Jacob will do certain things: Yahweh will be his God (namely, Jacob will remain loyal); he will construct a sanctuary (fulfilled in 35:7, 14-15) and offer a tithe (see 14:20; Deut 26:12-15), apparently a one-time gift, perhaps for the care of the sanctuary. In essence, if God acts faithfully, Jacob will be faithful.

178. Brueggemann, *Genesis*, 243.

From this point on, Jacob's journeys are filled with a new sense of vocation, for he now bears the promise. At the same time, he remains Jacob and does not know immediately what this experience entails for his life.

REFLECTIONS

1. God's relation to Jacob, through both his father and his grandfather, stresses not only a familial link, but *divine* continuity across the generations as well. The story involves *God* as well as Jacob's ancestors. God's own self is identified in the context of a divine journey, which God now promises to continue with Jacob. And this journey exists outside of the land of promise, "wherever you go" (see Josh 1:9; Psalm 23; Isa 43:1-2; Isa 46:3-4).

2. The dream (see 31:11-3; chaps. 37; 40-41). Dreams do not witness to the dreamer's psychological state, working out stress or anxiety or subconscious fears; they are external forms of divine communication, in which actual encounters with God take place. They are one means by which God's own self is revealed. When Jacob refers to this event, he speaks of divine appearance but never of dream (35:1-9; 48:3; cf. also 1 Kgs 11:9), apparently understanding God's appearance in the dream to be comparable to other such appearances (cf. 35:9). When Jacob awakens, he does not speak of God's presence in his dream; he speaks of God's presence in this *place!* The dream reflects not simply a mental world, but an actual world that can be slept on, touched, and built on.

Jacob's dream contains both symbolism and divine verbal communication. Jacob interprets the significance of *both* dimensions in his response in vv. 16-22. In turn, he mirrors the dream in responding both verbally and in more concrete terms. The visual and auditory aspects of the dream belong together, not least because human beings are not simply minds or "big ears," and God chooses to address the whole person (e.g. Incarnation; sacraments). The visual "speaks" in its own way, and the word gives "concreteness" to the visual.

The dream comes entirely at the divine initiative; Jacob was asleep, not in control of what happened *within* him (in contrast to the nocturnal wrestling of chap. 32). At the same time, Jacob's responses to God's word of promise shape the future. It may be tempting to explain away such dream experiences, though dreams are much less difficult for the modern consciousness to accept than are direct divine appearances. The text helps us to recognize that "the world is a place of such meetings," and God can use such moments as a vehicle for getting through to us, even today.[179]

3. The word of promise involves more than simply a word about a communal future; God also particularizes the promise for Jacob as an individual, for the specific situation in which he finds himself. God's promises of being with and keeping/protecting Jacob (v. 15) are distinct, for God can also be present to judge, which Jacob may have expected. Yet they are not separate, for God's presence never means passivity. God's "not leaving" gathers up the three previous promises to Jacob, yet it constitutes a further promise centering on the temporal unbrokenness of the divine presence.

4. In Jacob's response to the dream, awesomeness and the themes of presence and access come together. The transcendence of God is not compromised by closeness to humans. The awe that Jacob expresses depends on the fact that *God has come near.* The confession of God as transcendent and awesome correlates this text to God's

179. Brueggemann, *Genesis*, 242.

coming to be present rather than God's remaining afar off. Far from being a place forbidden to human beings, this site becomes a place where humans can be assured of the divine presence.

5. The importance of places of worship. Setting aside a place for a sanctuary does not stand at odds with the God who is with Jacob wherever he goes. Both are significant dimensions of God's being present in the world. Specific places for worship are needed because human beings are shaped by place as well as time. A sanctuary provides (a) order, discipline, and focus to the worship of God; (b) a tangible aspect to worship; (c) assurance that God is indeed present in this place because God has so promised. At the same time, such understandings must guard against a "house of God" syndrome, as if the divine presence could be fixed or localized, as if this were the only place where God could be found. God's being present at the sanctuary is not coextensive with God's presence in the world. Jacob can count on God's being present at this place (hence he returns in 35:1-15) *and* with him during his journey. The rhythms of the ancestors include the rhythm of journeying and worship; their journeys are punctuated by moments of worship at specific places. Yet the place never becomes a final objective, where one settles in; it provides sustenance for the ongoing journey.

6. This text also says something about God. God can bind God's own self with unconditional promises to tricksters and deceivers. Although Jacob leaves this moment with divine promises ringing in his ears, God leaves this moment with the divine options for the future more limited than before, because God will be faithful to these promises Jacob has just spoken. God's promises may have come to Jacob as a surprise, but Jacob will not know them again as such. God can be counted on to be faithful. Jacob need no longer wonder about God; God is a promise-keeper, as Jacob must be also. There is a "must" for God in this text, and a "must" for Jacob as well.

7. To understand this vow, we would remember it as a word spoken by a person in dire straits, concerned about his safety and his future. Such vows are common in the lament psalms (e.g., 7:17; 13:6) and have been used by people in distress in every age!). Because of the context in which they are uttered, we should not press them for theological niceties. But we, as Jacob, should expect God to keep the promises unconditionally.

GENESIS 29:1–31:55, THE BIRTH OF JACOB'S CHILDREN

COMMENTARY

These three chapters constitute a unified "novella" or short story (assigned to J or JE). They follow Jacob's flight from Esau and lead the reader quickly through Jacob's twenty years in Haran to the point of his return to Canaan. Family ties to "the old country" continue (chap. 24), but with Jacob there will now be a permanent break from this part of the family. The text maintains strong ties with Mesopotamian customs and culture; it may reflect Israelite/Aramaean relationships of a later era.

The narrator's primary interest lies in the birth of eleven sons (all but Benjamin), progenitors of the tribes of Israel. The sudden and pervasive God talk (29:31-30:24), as well as structural considerations, underline the importance of these chapters. The story may be outlined as follows: Jacob's arrival in Haran (29:1-14); Jacob's struggles with Laban over Leah and Rachel (29:15-30); the birth of the sons (29:31-30:24); Jacob's struggle with Laban over the departure (30:25-43); preparations for the return to Canaan (31:1-54). The birth of the children stands as the central text, surrounded by parallel narratives arranged chiastically. The text begins and ends with Jacob's arrival in and departure from Haran.

29:1-14. In a type-scene reminiscent of other well stories issuing in marriage (24:15-33; Exod 2:15-22), Jacob meets Rachel, who keeps sheep for her father, Laban. An emerging problem involves watering rights for shepherds. A stone covering the well is so large that only when all shepherds using the well are present can they remove it; this protects fair community access to the water (note the repetition in vv. 2-3, 8, 10; cf. the interest in stones in 28:10-22; 31:45-50). Jacob becomes impatient with waiting for all the shepherds and rolls the stone away so Rachel can water her flock. This becomes a feat of some consequence; it also violates community customs (v. 8). This act establishes Jacob as a person of both strength and authority within this unfamiliar community. Jacob, the father of Israel, is a man to be reckoned with.

Jacob's inquiry about welfare (שלום šālôm, v. 6; cf. 28:21), the wordless and emotional recognition scene of kissing and weeping with Rachel (v. 11-12), and the warm welcome and acknowledgment of kinship by Laban (vv. 13-14) depict familial harmony. It contrasts sharply with the story of deception and conflict that follows. This sense of a developing relationship seems preferable to the idea that Laban was duplicitous and self-serving already in his welcome.

29:15-30. This scene begins on a harmonious note, with Laban expressing concern about Jacob's welfare in view of what would certainly be a lengthy stay (v. 15). His use of "serve" language (and the aside introducing Leah and Rachel) signals the conflict to come; that Jacob "serves" anyone in view of prior oracles seems ironic (25:23; 27:29, 37, 40). Yet, Laban invites Jacob to name his own "salary," and Jacob himself suggests that he "serve" Laban as a free man under contract for seven years for Rachel's hand. This length of time, unreal to readers in a less family-oriented world, reveals both the depth of Jacob's love for Rachel (v. 18) and what he deems to be the equivalent of a dowry for her (see 31:15; 24:53). Jacob considers it no burden at all (v. 20).

Laban's warm welcome and open offer may have created an ironic, unsuspecting trust in Jacob; on the other hand, if Jacob told Laban *everything* ("all") that had happened in Canaan (v. 13; cf. v. 26), Laban would have had good reason to be wary of Jacob. This combination of factors may bring out the worst in Laban. He thinks he can take advantage of Jacob, perhaps even that Jacob should "pay" for his deception of Isaac. The relationship quickly deteriorates as Laban, through deceit (concealing a local custom, v. 26), gets Rachel and Leah married off. The deceiver has been deceived (v. 25; 27:35).

At the end of seven years, Jacob not only must request payment of "my wife" (v. 21; betrothed women have the status of wives, Deut 20:7), but receives Leah rather than Rachel (the NRSV and the NIV in v. 17 reflect the uncertainty as to whether Leah's eyes were "weak" or "lovely"). The brief report of the surprise on the "morning after" is stunning (v. 25a); it seems ironic that Leah knows what Jacob does not know. One can sympathize with Jacob's accusatory questioning, while realizing that what goes around comes around.

Laban's appeal to tradition after the fact (v. 26) appears duplicitous, but by directly raising firstborn issues he establishes an explicit link with Jacob's own deception on the same matter. His reference to "our country" functions similarly. In matching deception for deception, the narrator must have understood Jacob's activity in chap. 27 as reprehensible. Jacob must now know something of how Esau felt. At the same time, he has met in Laban someone not unlike himself.

Jacob's desire for Rachel and his reflection about deception result in his agreement—without a word!—to Laban's terms: He can wed Rachel at the end of seven days, if he completes the bridal week with Leah and serves Laban for seven more years. Jacob thus gains two wives in a week (cf. Lev 18:18 on marrying sisters). Yet, the narrator makes clear that Jacob loves Rachel more than Leah (v. 30; the "unloved" of v. 31 may also refer to preference), which Leah interprets as no love at all (vv. 32-33). Laban's devious orchestration could not force Jacob to love both women; love cannot be so manipulated. Once again, an appeal to custom (v. 26) fails to satisfy. The narrator gives love between a man and a woman a high role here, but it remains complicated by other issues that make for conflict and rivalry: between Laban and Jacob, Leah and Rachel, and Jacob with each wife.

Laban's ruse, made possible through the use of veils (see 24:65) and heavy festival drinking, violates Rachel and Jacob and their love for each other. It violates Leah as well, whose feelings about the matter are not considered, but whose suffering in all of this will shortly be voiced (29:32-35). God responds to her laments first of all (29:31), while Rachel remains childless initially (29:31; 30:1). Neither woman speaks directly in vv. 1-30 (cf. v. 12); their lives are arranged for them. The same also obtains for Zilpah and Bilhah (vv. 24, 29), maids customarily given to a bride by her father. The fact that God responds in so many ways to Leah's suffering in the next episode reveals the divine perspective on her mistreatment and an implicit judgment on her oppressors. She bears seven children, more than all the others. But in so doing, the Leah-Rachel conflict intensifies.

29:31–30:24. This section reads rather like a genealogy, but the conflict between Leah and Rachel and the divine *response* to the oppression of the women provide a basic story line. While these elements may have had separate origins, the interweaving of a gracious divine action in and through a complex fabric of human love and conflict mirrors the story of Israel's life.

The author has made this segment the centerpiece for chaps. 29-31. It narrates the birth of eleven sons and one daughter to Jacob and his wives, Leah and Rachel, and their maids, Bilhah and Zilpah (on Benjamin, see 35:16-18). Leah and Rachel name the children, including the children of their maids, usual Israelite practice. The word plays on the children's names (see the NIV and NRSV footnotes) are not really etymologies, but reflections on the familial conflicts and God's actions related thereto. While their tribal descendants may be in view, the text remains remarkably familial in its orientation, with the mothers playing the major role throughout. Jacob, in fact, appears remarkably passive (speaking only in 30:2).

The conflicting elements both recapitulate and anticipate other intrafamilial struggles. The friction between Leah and Rachel bears resemblances to both the Sarah/Hagar (16:1-6) and the Jacob/Esau conflicts (27:1-45); it anticipates the conflict between Joseph (a child of Rachel) and his brothers. Issues of succession bubble beneath the surface: Will just one of Jacob's sons be the inheritor of

the blessing (as has been the case up to this point)? If so, which one? At the same time, the conflict remains personal in its focus, as Leah struggles with her esteem in the eyes of Jacob (29:32, 33, 34; 30:15, 20; the issue for her moves from love to honor), and Rachel with the reproach of childlessness in the eyes of Jacob (30:1-2, 6, 23). While Laban's deception set up the conflict in the first place, Jacob perpetuates it.

God is now mentioned for the first time in this story, and the interweaving of divine and human roles will shape the rest of our discussion of this section. God is invoked thirteen times by Leah (29:32, 33, 35; 30:18, 20), Rachel (30:6, 23, 24), Jacob (30:2), and the narrator (29:31; 30:17, 22)—the maids never speak—in connection with the birth of seven of the twelve children. These references to God underline the importance of this section for the larger story.

God serves as the subject of the following activities: God sees the affliction of the women, hears their cry, remembers them, takes away their disgrace, and vindicates/rewards them. God both opens the womb and withholds (cf. 16:2) and gives/adds a son. The God language occurs as a gracious response to the women's laments (a common OT rhythm, cf. Exod 2:24-25; 3:7). The eight references to God by the women are always in the spirit of praise and gratitude for the gift of a child; the only reference by Jacob—surely an important statistic—is negative and in the form of an angry question.

The narrator does not mention God at the births of Levi, Naphtali, Gad, Asher, or Dinah. Combined with other factors, this suggests that the author did not think God to be the sole, or even the initiating, agent in conception. For the narrator (29:31; 30:17, 22), God *responds* to concrete human situations, but does not initiate a process. For example, God acts with a specific view to the women's cries. Even when God is not mentioned, the mother's response normally assumes the human need (the author offers no explanation of Dinah in 30:21). From another angle, when *both* the narrator and the women do mention God, it occurs only in connection with the births of Reuben, Joseph, and Issachar (the firstborn of Leah and Rachel and the first child born to Leah after she had "ceased bearing"). The narrator apparently thinks God's agency to be decisive, even if not initiatory, in connection with the firstborn or in problematic cases (see 16:2).

We should note other important factors regarding divine and human involvement:

In 30:1-2, Rachel blames Jacob for her childlessness (see 11:30). Her reference to death may reflect concerns about security and inheritance. Jacob's response could be a theological corrective (but can he speak for God?), yet the deep anger suggests otherwise. It probably constitutes a blatant attempt to lay the blame elsewhere (the narrator makes no such claim for God).

First-person references (e.g., "I have borne"; 29:34; 30:20) highlight the importance of human activity. God and the women are brought together in the blessing of Ruth 4:11: "May the LORD make . . . like Rachel and Leah, who together built up the house of Israel" (NRSV). The author specifically mentions Jacob in connection with only six sons (the four sons by the maids and Leah's last two).

Leah and Rachel—in the tradition of Sarah (16:2)—give their maids to Jacob to bear children for them; even God approves (30:18). Why Leah did this after bearing four children stems from issues of equality in her conflict with Rachel (v. 8). She may have "ceased bearing" (29:35; 30:9) because Jacob avoided her (see 30:15). The reference to bearing on "my knees" (v. 3) legitimates the maids' children (cf. 48:12; 50:23). The reference to good fortune (30:11; text uncertain) may suggest an element of chance in issues of birthing.

Conflict between the two women emerges explicitly in 30:1. It consists of envy (30:1) and "wrestling" (30:8; cf. 32:28), climaxing in the discussion over the use of mandrakes (a wild fruit used as an aphrodisiac, v. 14) provided by Reuben, Leah's oldest. This exchange indicates that the women—for all their theological conversation—thought that nondivine factors might be effective in enhancing potency. The narrator makes clear (vv. 17-19, 22) that God enables Leah and Rachel to conceive, and probably, though not necessarily, independently of the mandrakes (but certainly not Jacob!). Rachel—who had access to Jacob in a way that Leah

did not—makes a deal with Leah—who still desired Jacob's love—so as to improve her chances of having children: Leah's mandrakes for one night with Jacob ("lie" has negative associations, v. 15)! This hiring/bartering results in a fifth child for Leah. Verses 19-21 show that it turned into more than one night, but we see no sign of Jacob's love for Leah—ever. The conflict between Leah and Rachel may be resolved, given their concerted action in 31:14. It finally works itself out at the familial level, however, only when *all* of their children become the children of promise (50:24).

30:25-43. This story of the rivalry between Jacob and Laban no doubt has complex origins, not least because the progression of thought remains unclear. The unit may have been glossed by an editor with agricultural or other interests.

With the birth of Joseph, Jacob decides that the time has come to return home (this now becomes a key theme for the remainder of the story). He asks that, in view of his service, Laban give him his wives and children and "let him go" (echoing Moses' word to Pharaoh). This constitutes a request for a separation of families. Laban is reluctant to do so, for God has prospered him because of Jacob's labor, and Laban would like that to continue (v. 27; the NIV captures the sense with its "please stay"; cf. 39:2-5, 21-23). Laban even offers to renegotiate Jacob's wages if he will stay (v. 28; cf. 29:15). Laban's reference to divination (v. 27), however, is theological hocus-pocus. Jacob tells it straight: Laban knows that God has blessed him through Jacob from his own experience (without divine revelation); he can see for himself what has happened. As for wages, Jacob needs to make provisions for his family, and he wonders when he can be about that responsibility (v. 30). Once again, Laban asks Jacob to set his own "salary" (v. 31*a*).

Jacob realizes that Laban will not let him go easily, and so he devises a cunning plan that will get him out of the country and provide for his family's future (vv. 31*b*-33). In all of this, the deceiver who has been deceived turns the tables one more time. Jacob refuses any wages, but agrees to work for Laban if, at the end of the work period, he can take his "wages" in multicolored animals and black sheep from the flock he tends. He suggests an onsite inspection plan to demonstrate his honesty (צדקה *ṣĕdāqâ*)—that is, his loyalty to the relationship.

Since animals with such markings are uncommon, Laban thinks he has a deal, but to be on the safe side he deceitfully puts all such colored animals he presently has under his sons' care (three days journey away!) so they would not breed stock for Jacob (vv. 34-36). Jacob responds by devising a plan that produces such animals (vv. 37-43). While difficult to understand, it may assume an ancient belief that what animals look toward when breeding (either striped rods for multicolored animals, vv. 37-39, or the flock tended by Laban's sons for the black or partly black animals, v. 40) determines the coloration of their offspring. In this process, Jacob separates the weaker animals from the others and breeds only the strong animals for his purposes (vv. 41-42; cf. modern efforts at genetic manipulation). Hence, over time, Laban ends up with feebler animals and Jacob has the strong ones (ironically mirroring Laban's manipulation of "weak" Leah).

At the same time, it becomes clear (31:7*b*-12) that God has been involved in and through this process (see below). Jacob's means—through which God works—are effective; he manipulates the flocks to outwit Laban, free himself from dependence on him, and become a wealthy man (over a six-year period, 31:41).

31:1-55. An editor or author has united various traditions here in order to maintain the narrative tension of 30:25-43. The text centers on the continuing dispute both Jacob and God have with the oppressive behaviors of Laban and the difficulties associated with Jacob's flight. The narrative reaches its climax in Jacob's speech (vv. 36-42), especially his witness to a God who sides with him in his affliction. It concludes with a covenant of peace between Jacob and Laban (vv. 43-54).

Jacob's successful breeding practices raise suspicions in the minds of Laban's sons, and conflict with Laban intensifies. In the face of these developments, God tells Jacob to return home (in effect, reinforcing Jacob's own decision, v. 25); God will make good on his promise of presence (v. 3). Jacob consults with Leah and Rachel—a high tribute to them and to the importance of their opinion—about

leaving (vv. 4-13) and fills in the details of the story, to which they respond positively (vv. 14-16). The differing agendas of Laban's sons and daughters brackets the central episode. The daughters prove to be stronger and more independent than their brothers.

Jacob testifies that their father has cheated him and changed his wages many times (given Laban's invitations to Jacob, this seems hyperbolic). God, on the other hand, has been working behind the scenes against Laban's arbitrary decisions regarding wages so that whatever changes Laban made actually worked to Jacob's advantage (v. 8); God's activity in vv. 7*b* and 9 encloses Laban's deceit. God has transferred the animals from their father to him. Jacob then recalls a dream in which God revealed how it was that the multicolored animals were the active ones in the breeding process. (Verses 11-12 report the actual dream introduced in v. 10—"once had"; the author telescopes the command to leave the land with the directions about breeding the animals.) God has been so involved because Jacob has been oppressed (v. 12).

Verses 7*b*-12 provide a theological interpretation of the events reported in 30:35-43. God as Creator has been involved in the natural order, in the actual breeding behaviors of animals, resulting in the increase of Jacob's multicolored flock. But God did not give full instructions; Jacob took this divine word and used it to develop effective procedures with the animals. Although Jacob's techniques were important, Jacob gives all the credit to God in this report to his wives.

God's involvement in Jacob's life correlates to promises made at Bethel (28:10-22): "I am the God of Bethel" (v. 13; the angel in v. 11 is identified as God). God has been faithful to the promises made to Jacob (28:13-15), witnessed to in 31:3*b*, 5*b*, 7*b*, 9, 12*b*, and 13. The divine command to return can be trusted in view of Jacob's own experience. These verses also reveal a faithful Jacob, whose witness to God's faithfulness in the presence of his wives remains pervasive and without equivocation.

Jacob's wives—acting in concert!—respond with comparable trust: "Do whatever God has told you" (see vv. 14-16). But they base their case on their father's abuse of them rather than on Jacob's experience. In a rhetorical question they use legal language to renounce their father (v. 14; see 1 Kgs. 12:16). He has engaged in false dealings, misappropriating their dowry (money Laban did not have available to give to Jacob; 29:15) and regarding them as aliens; Laban has treated them as property. Such a strong, public stand on the part of these women against the abuse of their father seems remarkable. When Jacob gained wealth, God acted on their behalf as well! In the face of such oppression, God and Jacob have acted justly and properly. The implication: They will accompany Jacob back to Canaan. Their comments put the lie to Laban's later claims (vv. 26, 43).

Upon hearing Rachel and Leah, but without telling Laban, Jacob gathers his family and possessions and begins to flee (vv. 17-21). Unbeknownst to Jacob (v. 32), and after Laban had left the area, Rachel steals Laban's household gods—human-shaped images of gods that were symbols of Laban's authority over his household, perhaps tokens of inheritance. This mirrors Jacob's action of "stealing" Laban's heart (vv. 20, 26)—namely, deceiving him. Because Laban never discovers what Rachel did, her act functions symbolically (see v. 35).

When Laban hears of the flight, he and his men pursue the family for seven days, to the hills of Gilead where Jacob was encamped (east of the Jordan). At this point, God speaks to Laban in a dream in order to protect the fleeing family (cf. 20:3), commanding him not to speak good or bad to Jacob (vv. 22-24)—namely, to do Jacob no harm (v. 29). The question now is whether Laban will obey the word of God. When Laban overtakes Jacob, he adheres to God's word, but his emotional language appears designed to turn Rachel and Leah against Jacob.

Laban has a list of complaints against Jacob (vv. 25-30). He begins by accusing Jacob of deception and handling his daughters like prisoners. He also berates Jacob by appealing—once again—to custom: Jacob fled in secret; hence, Laban could not give his own flesh and blood a proper send-off. His charge of foolishness (v. 28) seeks to shame Jacob in the presence of his daughters. Self-righteously he appeals to the word from God as a reason for his kindness, but he still could ignore it.

He continues in this vein; by suggesting that they have fled out of a desire to see Jacob's family (v. 30), he dissociates himself as a factor in the flight. Then, he concludes with a question designed to turn the entire situation to his own advantage: Why did you steal my gods? Why would he even need them if he was returning to Canaan?

Again, Jacob does not equivocate (vv. 31-32); he fled out of fear of what Laban might do. But he heightens the tension when he unwittingly condemns to death anyone caught stealing Laban's gods (cf. 44:9). Laban pokes around for the gods in the tents (vv. 33-35). But the gods are nowhere to be found, primarily because of Rachel's cleverness; Rachel had put the gods in the camel's saddle, sat on them, and then used menstruation (see NIV) as an excuse for remaining seated. This interchange symbolizes Rachel's defeat of her abusive father and, should the occasion ever arise, provides evidence that he has no claim to their possessions (see vv. 14-16).

Jacob now takes the initiative and angrily makes countercharges. He presents a legal defense of his rights (vv. 36-42), calls on witnesses, and challenges Laban to find cause to prevent him from proceeding to Canaan with his possessions and wives. There is no evidence that anything has been stolen, and he has worked very hard and long (twenty years is stressed, vv. 38, 41) for what he has, going beyond what he was obligated to do. He brings his defense to its high point by claiming that the God of his father has been with him in all of this. (The Fear [or Refuge] of Isaac is an epithet for the God of Israel's ancestors, appropriated for Yahweh.) This God has sided with him, the oppressed one, rather than with Laban; God has sent him away rich rather than empty-handed (see Deut 24:14-15; 1 Sam 2:1-10; Psalm 124). In fact, God spoke to Laban in order to rebuke him, not simply to protect Jacob.

Laban, refusing to admit defeat publicly, claims that everyone and everything really belongs to him (he views all in terms of property), but that he will be magnanimous and conclude a nonaggression pact with Jacob (vv. 43-44). Laban no doubt realizes that he has been had and seeks to protect his own future from further maneuvers by Jacob.

Although Jacob appears as an equal partner in what follows, the author gives Laban alone direct speech, specifying the terms of what appear to be two forms of the treaty: (1) interfamilial relationships (vv. 49-50); in effect, they ask God to keep watch over them when they are unable personally to keep track of one another (this "Mizpah Benediction" is not all that positive!); (2) land boundaries (vv. 51-52), which both are to recognize as inviolate.

In connection with each are (a) two sets of stones (vv. 45-46, 51), only the first of which is named (vv. 47-49, cf. NRSV and NIV for different attempts to resolve a textual difficulty), which function as continuing witnesses to the treaty; (b) two communal meals (vv. 46,

54), in which only Jacob's kin appear to participate; (c) two invocations of God (vv. 50, 53; Nahor is Abraham's brother). Isaac adds the Fear of Isaac to replace Laban's second name, not to designate a different God, but to replace Laban's epithet in view of his own experience. This act effectively cuts off Jacob and his family from this particular strand of religious tradition. Jacob's relationship to the family in Haran now ends.

The fact that these two individuals, after deception upon deception, could part in peace, however strained the relationship (note that Laban does not speak to Jacob in v. 55), testifies to the work of God. They go their separate ways; Laban is not heard from again.

REFLECTIONS

1. The story reports a watershed period in the life of this family. We find a thoroughgoing break between the family in Haran and the family in Canaan. Although 27:46–28:9 lifted up the importance of Jacob's marrying within the family, resulting in his journey to Haran, that concern now ends. Marital relationships outside the family now become a part of their reality (34:1-24; 38:1-11; 41:45; 46:10). Indeed, a number of texts suggest that Jacob's family are aliens in Haran (31:15; 32:4); the families are distinct from one another (30:30; 31:37, although Laban claims otherwise, 31:43), and even their deities are distinct (31:53). God stresses the importance of Jacob's returning to his own homeland (30:25; 31:3, 13, 18).

This text witnesses to profound changes, even with respect to family structures and human relationships, to which God often calls the community of faith. As those changes develop, however, they may well entail considerable anxiety and conflict. Discerning God's call into a different future may prove difficult and take considerable time and effort.

2. These chapters continue the theme of sharp and deep levels of intrafamilial conflict and deception, with focus now on the family in the "old country." The family in Haran more than matches the family in Canaan. They are chips off the same block; such familial tendencies run deep. At the same time, this picture derives in many ways from Jacob's own duplicity in chap. 27; Jacob is the only link between chaps. 25–28 and chaps. 29–31. Jacob reaps the fruits of his own deception of Esau and in the process intensifies the problems in another community.

The author creates this central text, highlighting the birth of the tribes of Israel, permeated with negative realities. How easy it would have been to paint a rosy, idyllic picture of Israel's origins, a Garden of Eden sort of beginning. But the narrator, with a realistic understanding of the human condition, knew that this would not be realistic. The more deeply the probe into Israel's own past, the more the present looks like more of the same. Yet, precisely because of this continuity, at the level of both human and divine action, readers can see themselves as if in a mirror, gaining new levels of self-understanding and being assured of God's continuing involvement in their troubled lives.

3. At the same time, human love (stressed in 29:18, 20; cf. 24:67) and human service (forms of עבד *'ābad* occur thirteen times) can counter human deception. And we ought not to overlook the humor sprinkled throughout (e.g., 31:33-35). Moreover, as we shall see, God makes use of human wisdom and ingenuity in effecting the divine purposes in and through this family. Both human beings and God act with favorable consequences, from the women (29:31–30:24) to Jacob (30:27, 30). Even people like Laban listen to God's voice and participate in the divine purposes (31:24, 29). Jacob may not be entirely free of arrogance (30:30; 31:42), but God extends abundant blessings through Jacob's service. God's blessings are always mediated, whether through created orders (e.g., the fertility of animals) or human activity or a combination thereof.

4. The author emphasizes the role of the women as mediators of the divine blessing in and through their bearing of children. Jacob, though indispensable, remains deeply in the background, as the voices and actions of the women fill these verses (remembered in Ruth 4:11). In the midst of a patriarchal culture, the tradition gives these women a central place in the story of the birth of the people of Israel. " 'Israel' has emerged out of the intense struggle between Rachel and Leah, just as 'Israel' will emerge from the struggle between Jacob and God."[180] These mothers order the Jacob genealogy (46:8-26).

At the same time, the important role that Leah and Rachel play in the story is not limited to their role as mothers. The text recognizes their abuse at their father's hand and that they give this abuse public voice (31:14-16); such action is of no little importance for a community of faith that has all too often engaged in a cover-up regarding such abusive familial situations. Their sharp critique of their father and renunciation of his authority in their lives witnesses to a possible avenue of approach to abusive situations. Their renunciation takes not only verbal form but also courageous, concrete action in Rachel's theft of the gods and her defiance of him when he comes looking for them. When Leah also voices her abuse at the hands of her husband, Jacob (29:31-34; 30:20), she adds an additional positive dimension to the way in which these women confront tragic situations in their lives.

In addition, the use of God language by the women, both in connection with the birth of their children and with Jacob (31:16), testifies not only to their personal faith, but also to their ability to engage in theological formulation and discussion. The women make confessions, not on the basis of some special revelation, but by the deep-down links they see between their experience and what they know their God to be about in the world.

5. The community of faith is fortunate in having a God who does not insist on perfection before choosing to work in and through it. Israel has a God who blesses this family in the very midst of its conflicts (29:31–30:24; 30:27, 30; 31:3, 5, 7, 9, 42), making life possible even within a dysfunctional system. God does not work in isolation, but within a complex context to bring about the birth of Israel's children and enable goodness to emerge.

In the births of these children we may see God at work on behalf of new life and families. This *creative* work of God remains indispensable for the history of the promise, for it enables the coming into being of persons to whom promises can be given and for whom they can be realized. God's promises are given on behalf of "families" (12:3*b*; 28:14). God's most fundamental objective in giving the promises to Abraham, Isaac, and Jacob—and Leah and Rachel—is the blessing of families. In all of this, of course, God is at work in quite unobtrusive ways, hidden from public view (in this respect, these chapters are similar to the Joseph story).

180. Thomas W. Mann, *The Book of the Torah: The Narrative Integrity of the Pentateuch* (Atlanta: John Knox, 1988) 57.

The author places the birth of Israel as a community of faith within an admixture of familial conflict, human love and service, and ongoing divine blessing in the midst of failure. As such, the story is not simply about origins; it reveals the fundamental character of Israel's continuing life with God through the generations. And it shapes the very heart of Israel's understanding of God as one who works on behalf of families like this one. Indeed, it speaks about and to the community of faith in every age.

6. This mirroring function of the text occurs at another level. Jacob's journey to a foreign land and his return reflect Israel's later journey to Egypt and back. For example, Israel's founding family, though virtually in place in 30:25-43, resides in a foreign land. The situation appears similar to that faced by the adult "children of Israel" in Egypt (Exod 1:1-8). They are not free to leave. Jacob's request of Laban to let his family go echoes Moses' request of Pharaoh (30:25-26; the verbs שלח [šālaḥ, "send"] and הלך [hālak, "go"] are used by Moses with Pharaoh, e.g., Exod 5:1-3; cf. also ['ābad, "serve"] used twice here and often in Exodus). We may compare Moses and Jacob in the ways they gain freedom from Pharaoh and Laban. They begin with relationships in good order, but end with angry exchanges, threats, involvement of women and children, pursuit and interrupted flight, and carrying the wealth of the land with them as they go (cf., 31:18 with Exod 12:35-38). We have seen this mirroring before in Genesis, e.g., Abraham's journey to Egypt (12:10-20). These parallels suggest that the great rhythms of life are usually not unique to any historical period. Human life has a way of returning ever again to face problems and possibilities that are comparable to those of their predecessors in the faith. When we study carefully these texts, we receive a potential source for a word from God to address our own problems and possibilities.

7. The identity of the oppressor and oppressed varies. Jacob, for example, can be both. Initially Laban and Jacob oppress Leah. Her own father uses her for his deceptive purposes (29:23; 31:15), forcing her into a marital situation that he knows will bring trouble. Jacob, in turn, accepts the marriage and relates to her sexually (four children in quick succession), but treats her as nothing compared to Rachel. Leah's cries of affliction (עני 'ānî) are heard (שמע šāma') by God (29:32-33; 30:17). Rachel's cries concerning the distress of her childlessness are also heard (30:6, 22) and remembered (זכר zākar, v. 22) by God. This pattern is later matched by Jacob's affliction (31:42), which is seen (ראה rā'â) by God (31:12). Such language reflects the Exodus events (Exod 2:24-25; 3:7, 17; 4:31), as well as psalms of lament and thanksgiving (see 29:35; 30:23).

This divine commitment to the oppressed is already central to the biblical narrative. This is *not* a theme that surfaces for the first time in Egypt; God's remembrance of Abraham, Isaac, and Jacob grounds the divine response in the exodus (Exod 2:24; 3:6, 16; 6:2-8). And the OT includes Leah and Rachel in this remembrance; they "built up the house of Israel" (Ruth 4:11) and Rachel becomes a metaphor for those who lament the death and dying of the children of Israel; indeed, she even becomes a metaphor for the suffering of God (Jer 31:15-20; cf. Matt 2:18).

GENESIS 32:1-21, JACOB PREPARES TO MEET ESAU

COMMENTARY

This text, a unified composition (mostly J), prepares the reader for Jacob's encounters with God (32:22-32) and with Esau (33:1-20). These verses center on the prayer of Jacob (vv. 9-12), the interpretation of which shapes the approach to the narratives that follow. The prayer is framed by encounters with God (vv. 1-2, 22-32) and, within that, by the dispatch of messengers to Esau (vv. 3-8, 13-21). At the same time, the tension in the narrative sharply increases after the prayer, to such an extent that the encounter with God in vv. 22-32 becomes, in turn, the centerpiece of chaps. 32–33. These verses thus combine with 33:1-20 to enclose the encounter with God in 32:22-32. Jacob's "facing" both Esau and God are important to keep together.

Chapters 29–31 have demonstrated that Haran cannot be home for Jacob. Hence, he must return to Canaan, where a hornet's nest may well await him. Nonetheless, he returns under God's command.

32:1-2. The author structures this section similarly to 28:10-22. Jacob experienced angels when he left Canaan (28:12), when he was in Haran (31:11), and now when he returns (32:1). The angels may be God in human form (on the plural, see 18:2). The angels are associated with revelation in the two prior texts, but in this text no word from God is heard. The angels may be linked to the promise of divine presence (28:15) and, less directly, to 31:42, 49. They also point forward to the dangers of the meeting with Esau and his militia-sized group of 400 men, hence the reference to angels in terms of an entire company or encampment, probably with military connotations (see Josh 5:13-15; 1 Chr 12:22), is fitting. The coalescence of some of these themes in Ps 34:7 ("The angel of the LORD encamps/ around those who fear him, and delivers them" [NRSV]) supports their role as protectors.

The name Jacob gives to the place, Mahanaim (its location is uncertain; it must have had some link with Jacob), "two camps [or

companies]," refers to God's company and his own or to the two divisions of his own people (vv. 7-8). The exclamation appears similar to 28:16-17 and conveys Jacob's clear sense of ongoing divine presence and protection. It may embolden Jacob for the dangerous journey ahead; his response suggests that it does.

32:3-8. In conventional language, Jacob sends messengers (the same word as "angels") on ahead to discern from Esau himself the nature of the situation. His actions reflect the memory of Esau's intentions to kill him (v. 11; 27:41-42). Esau is already settled in Seir (i.e., Edom; though see 36:6-8), to the southeast of Canaan. Jacob tells the messengers what to say: where he has been, about his wealth, and his interest in reconciliation. Indeed, Jacob's use of lord/servant language (vv. 4, 6, 18, 20) in the message itself suggests his willingness to reverse the blessing gained by deceiving Esau. The return to this language in chap. 33 shows that Jacob is serious about such reconciliation. The author does not describe the encounter of the messengers with Esau (though note the "brother" language), only that Esau comes to meet Jacob, accompanied by 400 men (v. 6). Jacob appears distressed and uncertain about the meaning of the report, but he prepares for the worst. He divides his company into two parts so that, should Esau attack, at least one group might be saved.

32:9-12. In the midst of this fearful moment, Jacob prays. Scholars are divided about the sincerity of this prayer. A judgment that Jacob is attempting to deceive God depends not on the prayer itself, but on a negative assessment of Jacob in the larger narrative. Such an interpretation seems unlikely.[181]

The structure of the prayer is similar to the individual lament for deliverance from an enemy (cf. Pss 31:15-16; 40:11-13; 69:13-14; 86:13-15): (1) An invocation, with a threefold naming of God, linking him with

---

181. For a negative view, see S. Balentine, *Prayer in the Hebrew Bible: The Drama of Divine-Human Dialogue* (Minneapolis: Fortress, 1993) 64-71.

the God of his fathers; (2) A recollection of God's command to return to Canaan and what God has done for him. The language recalls God's command to Abraham (12:1) and suggests again a break from the family in Haran. Jacob's use of the terms חסד (ḥesed, "steadfast love") and אמת ('ĕmet, "faithfulness") recalls the use of these terms in 24:27 and links Jacob with basic creedal language for God in the OT (cf. the psalms noted above). (3) A confession of his unworthiness for even a modicum ("least") of God's love. The request does not depend on what he brings to this moment. (4) A request for deliverance; Jacob fears not only for his own life, but for his wives and children; (5) A claiming of the divine promises. This grounds Jacob's plea in God's loyalty to promises made. He appropriately claims God's promises (eight in number; cf. 28:13-15) for this moment.

Jacob quotes God two times in his prayer, referring to the command to return to Canaan (31:3) and the promises regarding divine presence and numerous progeny (28:13-15). The word "do you good" (repeated in vv. 9 and 12, stressed in the latter) summarizes the divine promises and frames the prayer. The

reference to posterity derives from this specific situation.

32:13-21. After the prayer, Jacob begins to move his retinue toward confrontation with Esau. In an effort to cover his guilt for past behaviors (כפר kāpar) and to effect acceptance (נשא nāśā') by Esau (v. 20), Jacob sends his servants on ahead in stages with a major gift: over 550 animals! He cleverly designs the threefold staging of the gift in droves to break down any initial resistance that Esau might exhibit. Jacob instructs his servants carefully concerning their response to Esau's questions. He stresses that the animals are a gift to "my lord [Esau]" from "your servant Jacob" (vv. 18, 20, cf. vv. 4, 6), who is coming along behind. The fourfold mention of gift (מנחה minḥâ, vv. 14, 19, 21-22, a play on Mahanaim) may suggest tribute from a vassal to his lord (cf. 2 Sam 8:2, 6; 1 Kgs 4:21 for this combination).

Prior to the encounter between Jacob and Esau, the narrative pauses for a description of an encounter between Jacob and God. How they are to be related will not be easy to resolve (see 33:1-20).

REFLECTIONS

1. The presence of divine messengers (v. 1) does not obviate the need for human messengers (v. 3). This juxtaposition suggests that, in situations of danger and interpersonal difficulty, the coalition of divine presence and human initiative and planning is important. God's presence does not control so much that what human beings think, do, and say in such moments is irrelevant. At the same time, the struggle with the "messenger" (God) in vv. 22-32 makes clear that God may enter anew into human plans.

2. Jacob does not blame God for the problem he now faces (v. 9); he simply states the truth and claims a coherent relationship between the God who commands and the God who promises. The one who promises can be trusted not to subvert the promises in issuing commands; the one who commands will see somehow to the promises (cf. 22:1). Jacob has been faithful to God and in this dangerous moment claims God's promises; hence the appeal to divine steadfastness and faithfulness. The text does not report that Jacob is delivered from Esau until after the struggle with God (32:30). Given that experience, the confrontation with Esau seems anticlimactic. God answers the prayer for deliverance in a way somewhat different from what Jacob imagined.

3. The language the messengers are to speak to Esau implies Jacob's willingness to reverse his earlier deception and return the blessing to Esau (not the blessing in 28:3-4, and nothing is said of the birthright). The reversal in the use of lord/servant language from 25:23 and 29:29, 37, 40, where Esau became Jacob's servant, demonstrates this interest. Also, the word used for Jacob's "gift" in 33:11 is ברכה (bĕrākâ, "blessing";

see 27:36-41). The word פנים (*pānîm*, "face") occurs seven times (vv. 16, 17, 20-21); this anticipates its prominence in the next sections (32:30; 33:3, 10). Seeing the face of God before seeing the face of Esau turns the meeting with Esau into a less dangerous moment, though seeing the face of God presents its own dangers.

GENESIS 32:22-32, JACOB WRESTLING WITH GOD

COMMENTARY

This text has long fascinated commentators. Its meaning is so elusive that a variety of interpretations is credible. The "breaks and joints . . . and the looseness in the inner connection of the statements to one another [make] room for many ideas" and give it an "essential spaciousness."[182]

Although the story has been edited in the course of its transmission (e.g., v. 32), most scholars assign the present passage to J. An early pre-Yahwistic story of a supernatural encounter at a river crossing may have informed the narrative; yet, the relatively sophisticated image of God and the centrality of the name *Israel* make any such links remote. Hosea 12:3-4 may attest to a somewhat different form of the passage. The text also differs from typical stories of attacks to prevent the completion of a mission; in this case, the one who commanded the return (31:3, 13) becomes the assailant.

This text stands between God's two appearances at Bethel (28:10-22; 35:9-13), one of the primary pillars in the story of Jacob. It presents special parallels to the first story. Just as God encountered Jacob when he fled the promised land because of his brother's anger, so also God now encounters him at the point of reentry, with his brother's anger once again focusing his energies. In both cases, Jacob appears deeply vulnerable and alone, in need of divine care. This time, however, God approaches him in a much more ambiguous manner. God's second appearance at Bethel brings Jacob's return home full circle and clarifies the shape of his future. In another sense, this text has its closest relationship to 33:1-17, Jacob's meeting with Esau, which

182. Von Rad, *Genesis*, 324.

constitutes a mirror image of this episode (see chap. 33). This confrontation with God shapes Jacob's final encounter with Esau.

Among its literary features, the story plays on various words, especially the names *Jacob* (יבק [*yabbōq*, Jabbok]; אבק [*'ābaq*, "wrestle"]) and *Israel* (שרה [*śārâ*, "struggle"]), and the word *face* (פנים *pānîm*), especially in 32:21, 30 and 33:10. Also, the author delays identifying the assailant. Initially, he appears only as a "man" (איש *'îš*, v. 24); the reader gradually comes to realize that this is no ordinary assailant; it is God in human form (the מלאך *mal'āk*, cf. 16:7). Ancient and modern readers familiar with the story would hear it with this identification in mind from the beginning, as I will in the exposition.

Having sent his gift to Esau on ahead, later that same night Jacob sends his entire caravan across the Jabbok (an eastern tributary of the Jordan about twenty miles north of the Dead Sea), a frontier point for the promised land (Deut 3:16). Jacob stays behind at the border for reasons unknown. He remains filled with fear and distress (32:7, 11); for all he knows, Esau still plans to kill him (27:41-42). The narrative stresses that Jacob is alone. He will not be able to call for help should trouble come.

And come it does. During the night and in a surprise attack, God wrestles him to the ground. Jacob may well have thought it was Esau. God and Jacob struggle for a considerable period of time. When God sees that daybreak is near and that he has not been able to prevail in straightforward wrestling, God strikes Jacob in the hollow of the thigh (the exact spot is uncertain). The NRSV's "struck" is truer to the context than the

NIV's "touched," though both translations are possible.

This blow has a crippling effect and brings the struggle to its climactic moment, but it does not dictate the terms of the outcome. Jacob retains such a hold that God cannot escape from it; Jacob alone has the power to grant God's request for release. At the same time, God alone has the power to grant a blessing. Jacob's insistence that release be contingent upon blessing results in God's giving the name *Israel* to Jacob (though both names are retained in the narratives that follow) and the gift of blessing. Jacob is forever marked by the struggle, as he limps away toward the promised land. His mark attests to success and not to defeat.

Rather than move through the text verse by verse, we approach it through some questions it raises. God takes Jacob seriously enough to engage him in a struggle, but God seems also concerned not to be revealed fully to Jacob. Why is this the case?

First, it was a commonplace that God's face would not be seen: "no one shall see me and live" (Exod 33:20 NRSV). This reflects a concern not for God, but for the life of the one seeing. In this story, God is not the one endangered by the daylight, it is Jacob! To see God in the full light of day would have meant death for Jacob. If Jacob holds on until daybreak, he is a dead man! At the same time, the continued grasping of God on Jacob's part in the near-dawn light also says something about Jacob. He is willing to risk death for the sake of the divine blessing. Jacob's action suggests that he will risk seeing the face of Esau, too.

Second, Jacob's request to know the name of God is respectful: "Please." Not unlike Moses (Exod 3:13), Jacob knows that he is dealing with God, seen in the request for blessing (v. 26) and from God (v. 28). He wants neither the generic name *God* (אל *'el*) nor the names God has already given him (28:13). As with Moses, Jacob requests a divine name commensurate with this new development in his relationship with God, a new name for God to go with the new name for Jacob (cf. 16:13; 21:33; 31:13).

God replies to the question with a question (as in Judg 13:18): Why do (למה זה *lāmmâ zeh*) you ask my name? The Jacob-Esau

meeting will also end abruptly with such a question (33:15). God does not seek information from Jacob. At the least, God thereby signals the intent to close off the conversation and move on, while leaving Jacob with a question rather than a refusal. The fact that the question is followed by a blessing suggests the latter as an indirect answer; God is a God of blessing, a deity positively disposed toward Jacob.

In what sense does God not prevail (v. 25) and Jacob prevail (v. 28)? Neither emerges as the unqualified winner; God's blow moves the struggle to a new level, yet Jacob is able to prevent God from leaving (v. 26). One could say that Jacob's struggling and holding his own has helped turn a potentially negative situation into a positive, blessing-filled one.

Who is changed because of this struggle? God? Jacob? Both? Certainly their relationship has changed. They hold fast to each other; neither will turn away. Certainly Jacob is not so changed that he loses his identity. We find no evidence of a purging of his sin or his negative character traits. Yet, we can discern important changes.

Jacob has a new name. Although *Israel* may actually mean something like "God rules," the narrator claims otherwise. The NRSV footnotes suggest a purposeful ambiguity in the name: "God strives" (God initiates and engages in the wrestling) *and* "the one who strives with God" (Jacob responds in kind). Jacob cannot struggle with God if God refuses to be so engaged. God's giving this name, then, has implications for God as well as for Jacob. It affirms a divine commitment to stay with Jacob in the struggle. God will be caught up in this relationship. God's promise (28:15) involves not a passive presence, but an active, engaged relationship.

From Jacob's side, the new name attests to and affirms the strength he has exhibited in this encounter with God *and* throughout his lifetime. It is important to note that name changes do not, necessarily, signal a change in character (cf. 17:5); here God gives the name to Jacob in recognition of *who he has been and presently is*, not what he becomes in this moment. The name change immediately follows Jacob's refusal to let God go and his demand for a blessing from God; these responses prompt God's response. God explains the name *only* in positive terms: It represents Jacob's *strength* and *capacity for struggling well.* If Jacob had not struggled and prevailed, there would have been no new name, at least not the name *Israel.*

This change significantly assures Jacob. If he can hold his own even with God, certainly he should be able to live up to his name with Esau. Although the name *Israel* describes part of Jacob, yet he also exhibits Jacob-like characteristics in this encounter by grasping God. Unlike Abram/Abraham, both names continue to be used in the subsequent narrative, suggesting that both aptly describe this individual. (The repetition of the name change in 35:10 reflects a different origin for the name *Israel.*)

Jacob is blessed. Jacob will not let God go until he receives a blessing (v. 26). God responds positively (v. 29), but not until the exchange over names. What is the content of the blessing? Blessings are normally not gained through struggle. However, Jacob here holds God to the freely given promises (see 28:13-15); Jacob claims what God has promised. Intercession occurs here in physical terms, not unlike Exod 32:10-14. Through such blessings (cf. 35:9) God continues the blessing put in place by Isaac, and the strength for life and well-being it implies (27:27-29). In other words, the blessing spoken here by God enables the promises to be realized in Jacob's life.

Just as Jacob enters the promised land, God seals the promise with him (28:15)— at just the point where Jacob's life appears most in danger. At the moment of deepest vulnerability for Jacob, God enters into the very depths of the struggle, *binding God's own self to Jacob at that level.* In fulfillment of the promise, God will go with Jacob into future dangerous moments. God helps to make Jacob ready for the encounter ahead, arming him with continuing blessings for the journey. Jacob can now face any foe, no matter how hostile (cf. Moses). Jacob is about to embark on a life-and-death struggle, and he now knows that God the wrestler will be at his side.

Jacob sees God face to face. Jacob names the place Peniel ("the face of God"; usually spelled *Penuel*, v. 31). Unlike at Bethel, no altar is built nor are issues of holiness raised. He gives it this name not because of any later historical significance (cf. 1 Kgs 12:25), but because he has had a particular experience— namely, seeing God face to face and living to tell the tale (as Moses does in Num 12:8; cf. Judg 13:22). The references to dawn (vv. 24, 26, 31) make clear that God and Jacob parted company before the full light of day. Hence, seeing God's face was for Jacob at best a twilight experience.

Jacob sustains an injury. The author presents a poignant portrayal of Jacob limping down the road toward the promised land as the sun's first rays peek over the horizon. Jacob may now move on toward his goal. At the same time, Jacob has been sharply, and perhaps permanently, marked by this struggle with God (the exact nature of the injury remains unclear). What is the significance of the mark? On the one hand, it signifies Jacob's *success,* not his failure or defeat; he has struggled and prevailed. As such, Jacob does not become a victim of God, reduced to groveling or to nothing before the power of the Almighty. On the other hand, it attests to God's graciousness; Jacob has wrestled with God to the break of day, yet his life is preserved. So the mark symbolizes *both* who Jacob is and who God is.

By means of a dietary regulation (not mentioned elsewhere in the OT) Israel's memory will be continually jogged regarding this struggle between Jacob and God. This regulation institutionalizes the memory. It provides an ongoing mark of self-identification for Jacob's descendants. This memory, associated with bodily ritual, draws attention to Jacob/Israel's self-identity, involving not simply a spiritual reality, but all of Israel's life as well. An animal—part of God's creation—focuses this human memory.

The author does not report that Jacob let go of God or even that God has left him. The story moves immediately into the confrontation with Esau. In some sense this means that God and Jacob remain bound to each other, facing this future.

REFLECTIONS

1. Both God and Jacob identify the "man" as God (אלהים *'ĕlōhîm*; vv. 28, 30). His assailant speaks of Jacob as having striven with *God.* Jacob understands this to mean that he confronted God: "I have seen God face to face" (v. 30). Other texts connect "man" and "God" in a comparable way (see 18:1-8; Judg 13:6, 21-22). The OT links the human figure with the divine messenger (מלאך *mal'āk*), understanding that God is present and active in human form (see 16:7; Hos 12:3-4 identifies the *'ĕlōhîm* figure with the *mal'āk*, messenger).

Some interpreters view this story as involving *only* an inner struggle between God and Jacob. But the stress on the blow to the body and the resultant limp (vv. 25, 31) indicate that Jacob's physical self is affected. The fact that the struggle involves a figure in human form, rather than a disembodied God, also shows that the author describes more than a dark night of the soul, as does the lack of reference to dreaming or sleeping (cf. 28:10-22). This is no nightmare; Jacob remains fully awake. Jacob struggles with more than his own conscience or fears; his entire person is engaged. The dietary etiology also keeps the story grounded in a physical encounter, as does the parallel drawn with Esau's face (33:10).

2. Why does God wrestle with Jacob? Many suggest that God responds to Jacob's history of deception; the story constitutes a disciplinary move on God's part to teach Jacob that he cannot proceed into the future relying on his own devices. Hence, some claim the story presents Jacob's conversion to a life more attuned to the ways of God. Yet, we find no evidence of that in the narrative—no negative judgment of Jacob's behaviors, no repentance on Jacob's part, and no fundamental change in Jacob's subsequent life pattern. Indeed, in giving Jacob a new name, God commends Jacob for struggling and names him in view of who he has been in the past and, given his response to the divine challenge, still is.

God will act in ways that are in the best interests of the life of the chosen one, however undeserving. At the same time, God sharply challenges Jacob in a "let's-see-what-this-guy's-made-of-when-the-going-really-gets-rough" sense. We may compare how Jacob will respond when faced with such a challenge to God's test of Abraham in chap. 22. The way in which Jacob responds to the divine challenge is as relevant as that of Abraham for the future of this family. Just as God's tests of Abraham and Jacob are attuned to their particular way of being and doing (Abraham is no wrestler!), so also is Jacob's response (like Abraham's) true to who he is. And God's commendation responds directly to the strengths they exhibit in this challenge (cf. 22:16 with 32:28).

Others have compared this text with Exod 4:24-26, a divine attack on Moses.[183] The goal there is more explicit ("seek to kill"); here it is, at least, an act of bodily coercion, a challenging of Jacob at the deepest levels of his being. We do not know the motivation of the assailant in either text, but both texts are associated with a dangerous moment of transition in their lives.

Such struggles might be viewed as divinely initiated exercises in human becoming, of shaping and sharpening the faithfulness of the human beings involved for the deep challenges to be faced. God's engagement in such moments in people's lives is always a gracious move, informed most basically by faithfulness to promises made, and in the interests of health, peace, and well-being.

3. How could Jacob even stay in the ring with God? First, this text does not speak of God in all of God's glory; God has taken on human form and stooped to encounter Jacob at his own level. Second, contrary to most commentators, we find no hint that

---

183. See discussion in Fretheim, *Exodus*, 75-81.

God could have overwhelmed Jacob at any moment God chose. God does not play games with Jacob; God actually struggles with him. With human beings such as Jacob (cf. Abraham; Moses), God commits to a genuine encounter, entering deeply into the struggle with Jacob with a kind of power that doesn't simply overpower him. The power God has available appears commensurate with the nondivine power present in the situation. The divine power differs from the human by the way in which it is exercised. We see a divine restlessness and relentlessness in this moment of encounter, and an indomitable divine will at work on behalf of Jacob. God watches for openings, for opportunities to enhance the divine purpose in Jacob's life. Further, God retains certain kinds of power; God is able to do with Jacob's name what Jacob is not able to do with God's. The blessing comes from God; Jacob does not generate blessings for himself. For all of Jacob's powers, he recognizes the need of a blessing that he can finally only receive from God.

4. The confrontation with Esau mirrors the encounter with God. In some sense, God functions as a substitute for Esau, yet the "man" does not equal Esau. Jacob moves from seeing the face of God to seeing the face of Esau, and he testifies that seeing Esau's face is *like* seeing God's face (33:10). The obverse also seems true in retrospect: Seeing God's face is like seeing Esau's face. What Jacob had expected from Esau was hostility; he got graciousness. What Jacob might have expected from God was graciousness (in view of the prayer in vv. 9-12); he did get that, but only on the far side of an attack. The actual encounter between Jacob and Esau proves to be different from the experience Jacob has with God, but there are still a number of similarities (see commentary on chap. 33).

At the same time, the victory appears ambiguous, for Jacob recognizes that, if he had truly seen God, he would have died. Hence Jacob confesses that God has been his deliverer, and he experiences graciousness at God's (and Esau's) hand. God puts him through the encounter in advance.

The prayer for deliverance (נצל *nāṣal*) from Esau (32:11) is realized initially in being preserved (*nāṣal*, 32:30) in the struggle with God. Jacob prays for deliverance from Esau; God delivers Jacob from *God*. This prior deliverance does not resolve the conflict with Esau, however. Jacob still must face that. But the deliverance from God symbolizes Jacob's future deliverance from Esau. Jacob does not say he has prevailed; only God says that. Jacob understands the event, rather, in terms of his own deliverance.

5. God may encounter people in conflictual times by taking the very form of the anticipated difficulty. "In the night, the divine antagonist tends to take on the features of others with whom we struggle in the day."[184] Having been through such a time with God provides a gracious rehearsal for the actual life circumstance. To refuse to engage with God in that struggling moment denies oneself a God-given resource. To go through it with God before we go through it with others provides resources of strength and blessing for whatever lies in the wings of life.

Israel knows that wrestling with God can have both internal and external effects, even though God has not been seen and no blows to the body have been felt. Other texts about a *verbal* wrestling between God and key figures function similarly to this one (one thinks of Abraham in chap. 18 or Moses).

6. While we might conclude that the members of the community of faith ought to learn from Jacob to struggle with God, we should remember that God takes the initiative here. The issue is how Israel will *respond* to God's initiative. At the least, this means that Israel's response to God ought not to be passive or submissive, acquiescent

---

184. Brueggemann, *Genesis*, 267.

in the face of God's engagement with us. Moses appears as a new Jacob in this regard. An individual may hang on to God, claiming the promises, persisting in the relationship.

When it comes to struggles in daily life, we can count on God's mixing it up with us, challenging us, convicting us, evaluating us, judging us. We may have to place our life at risk, knowing that the one who loses life will find it. God honors the relationship both by engaging in the struggle in the first place and by persisting in that struggle through thick and thin. The most meticulous of preparations cannot guarantee a certain shape for the future. God may break into life and force a new direction for thought and action.

7. This text belongs to a larger story about the experience of two communities (Israel and Edom). Jacob's descendants know that this wrestler with God symbolizes their own experience with their neighbors as well as with God and that, somehow, these relationships are interrelated. Conflicts at the interhuman level have an effect on the God-human relationship, and vice versa. Hence we should understand this text not only in terms of the dynamics of the relationship between individuals or between an individual and God, but in communal terms. "This event did not simply occur at a definite biographical point in Jacob's life, but as it is now related it is clearly transparent as a type of that which Israel experienced from time to time with God. Israel has here presented its entire history with God almost prophetically as such a struggle until the breaking of the day."[185]

185. Von Rad, *Genesis*, 325.

GENESIS 33:1-17, JACOB'S MEETING WITH ESAU

COMMENTARY

This chapter (mostly J) concludes the Jacob-Esau segment of the story of Jacob (except for the burial of their father, 35:29). While a reconciliation of integrity does take place between Jacob and Esau, they will not share a future together. They address past offenses (vv. 1-11), but they spar over the shape the future should take, and, finally, part ways (vv. 12-17). Such is the relationship between Jacob and Esau, Israel and Edom.

33:1-11. The opening verse is filled with tension. The gifts of 32:13-21 have arrived (v. 8), but we have not yet heard Esau's response. Jacob sees Esau coming with four hundred men and the reader expects to hear about a fearful Jacob (as in 32:7, 11). But such will not be the case; moreover, the two companies' strategy has disappeared. Rather, Jacob arranges the women and children (only) in such a way that the most esteemed (Rachel and Joseph) come last, and hence will be introduced last (v. 7). Jacob himself goes

ahead of them, bowing seven times like a vassal before his lord (perhaps an acceptance of wrongdoing). The author repeatedly notes that the women and children behave in comparable ways toward Esau (vv. 5-7).

This behavior suggests that Jacob's basic stance toward Esau involves submission and stands as a fulfillment of the oracle in 27:40, a (temporary?) reversal of the oracle of 25:23 and the blessing of 27:29, 37. Key repetitions support this assessment: "lord" for Esau five times (33:8, 13-15; cf. 32:4-5, 18), his self-reference as "servant" of Esau (33:5, 14; cf. 32:4, 18, 20), and his concern to find favor in Esau's eyes (33:8, 10, 15; cf. 32:5). This language continues with that used by Jacob before Jabbok; the struggle at Jabbok introduces no changes in this language.

Yet, there are also points of discontinuity in Jacob from before Jabbok: (1) The encounter with God appears to have stayed his fear of Esau and eliminated fear-based strategies;

Jacob makes himself vulnerable by moving toward Esau alone, unaccompanied by any of his company. (2) The gift remains intact, but the reason for it changes from appeasement (32:20) to gratitude (33:10). Although this development takes place after the encounter (see below), the encounter with God makes it possible. (3) The submissive language appears genuine. (4) Yet, Jacob does not grovel; he seeks to demonstrate through word and deed the change, indeed the reversal in the relationship between the brothers. (5) Jacob now functions more clearly as the progenitor of a people rather than as just an individual.

Jacob's solitary limping toward Esau and bowing to the ground constitutes clearly the vulnerable move that makes possible what happens next. But Esau, too, takes an important initiative: He runs to meet Jacob, embraces him, throws his arms around him, kisses him, and weeps with him. This impressive list of welcoming activities is unparalleled elsewhere in Genesis (the closest is 45:14-15, where Joseph makes himself known to his brothers; see also 29:11-13; 46:29; 48:10; 50:1; Luke 15:20). Hence, one should interpret Esau's moves positively; in fact, in that culture they may well have entailed forgiveness. Then, at Esau's initiative, Jacob's wives and children are introduced (vv. 5-7). Jacob witnesses publicly to God's graciousness (חן *ḥēn*, "undeserved favor") concerning his family's growth (cf. with v. 11 below), language most closely related to his prayer (32:10; cf. 31:5, 7, 42). Previously, Jacob had never done this. Here he attests to the theological role played previously by his wives, Leah and Rachel (29:31–30:24). They have shown him the way.

Esau also asks about the "company" (מחנה *maḥăneh*) he has encountered (v. 8). This query plays on the word מנחה *minḥâ* (32:13, 18, 20-21), meaning the gift or tribute that Jacob sent on before him. Esau wants to know the *meaning* of this gift. Jacob's response repeats the earlier message to Esau (32:5): "to find favor [חן *ḥēn*] in his eyes" (v. 8). Jacob thereby links God's favor (v. 5) with Esau's, but in a wrong-headed manner. God's graciousness had come to him in a quite undeserved way, but now he would seek, in essence, to buy Esau's favor with all this property.

Esau's refusal of the gift on these grounds (v. 9) brings Jacob's response to a new level. Jacob realizes from Esau's reply (e.g., "my brother") that he has *already* found favor with Esau (v. 10): "If I *have found* favor in your eyes . . . now that you *have received* me favorably" (italics added). Verse 10 proceeds from this new ground: Jacob now gives a *new* reason for extending the gift—namely, *gratitude;* because you have received me as God received me, accept my gift. The gift that was originally offered for purposes of appeasement (32:20) is, in fact, not necessary for reconciliation. Esau has forgiven Jacob quite apart from such an "offering." The "sacrifice" can now function as a "gift."

Jacob, once again, experiences the graciousness of God, this time extended through the face of his brother. Verse 11 testifies to this experience: Jacob now offers the gift not simply in gratitude to Esau, but in gratitude to *God*.

Verse 11 extends this discussion along other lines. The "gift" becomes "my blessing" (ברכה *bĕrākâ*), a clear reference to 27:35-37 (note the lord/servant language), but not to 28:3-4. It may be that Esau also accepts the gift because of the language of blessing that Jacob now uses for the first time. God's blessing has been at work in Jacob's life, and he now has all he needs. He now wants to give that blessing to Esau. He does not give the blessing "back" to Esau,[186] but the blessing that he has received has been so bountiful that it can flow through him to Esau as well (he does not give everything he has to Esau, vv. 13-14, 17). Hence, God's word to Jacob (28:14) is specifically fulfilled with Esau: "All the families of the earth shall be blessed through you."

33:12-17. Esau accepts Jacob's offer. Even more, he offers to accompany Jacob on his journey. Surprisingly, Jacob deflects Esau's offer, asking him to pass on ahead to Seir; Jacob will follow with his company, but at a slower pace. Two observations are in order: (1) Jacob uses language that continues to defer to Esau—though not deceptive, it betrays that theirs has not become a truly brotherly relationship; (2) the reason Jacob gives (vv. 13-14) remains somewhat obscure, but it may mean that Jacob's family

---

186. Compare Westermann, *Genesis 12–36,* 526.

needs some independence to develop properly. Now separated from the family in Haran, Jacob's family must establish its own identity (see 30:30). Jacob's response may have been prompted by a perception that Esau's offer (v. 12) suggested a merger of their families. Yet, Jacob does offer to come along to Seir in due time. The fact that he doesn't (v. 17) must have something to do with the next exchange between them.

Esau takes Jacob's hesitation at face value and offers some of his people to help with the journey, thereby insisting on a close, ongoing relationship (v. 15). In response, Jacob puts an end to the conversation rather abruptly, but what he says is puzzling (compare NIV and NRSV). In view of the parallel expression in 32:29 (למה זה *lāmmâ zeh*), the NIV seems best[187]: "But why do that? . . . Just let me

187. Also Compare Westermann, *Genesis 12–36*, 523.

find favor in the eyes of my lord" (v. 15)— i.e., "This is all the further our relationship should go; it ought not to result in the merging of our families. I trust that we are reconciled, but our families and our futures should remain separate." Jacob's decision not to go to Seir comes in the wake of Esau's continuing to press against this matter (unwittingly?). We should also note that going back to Seir would have delayed fulfilling God's command to return to Canaan (31:3, 13).

Jacob and Esau separate, coming together again only at their father's funeral (35:29). But this shared responsibility, as well as the economic factors cited for Esau's return to Seir (see 36:6-8) make it clear that theirs is a separate relationship, but not without conversation and cooperation. Jacob goes to Succoth, on the east side of the Jordan, and settles his company there for an unknown period of time (v. 17).

REFLECTIONS

1. The narrative concludes in *reconciliation with separation and an open-ended future.* In view of what happens over time between their descendants (Edom and Israel; see Obadiah), this text seems remarkably evenhanded in its treatment of the relationship, even drawing an analogy between the graciousness of Esau and the graciousness of God (v. 10)! Overall, the narrator claims that continued conflict between the two is not a *necessary* future, set for all eternity by some word of the distant past. Even more, it claims that no matter how severe the conflict, or how deeply rooted in past history, reconciliation among brothers remains a possibility, even if that does not finally eventuate in a close relationship. The oracles in 25:23 and 27:27-29 stand in continuing tension with 27:40 (see 33:11), and that tension, in fact, describes their history with each other.

2. Seeing Esau's face so graciously turned toward him works not only parallel to, but as *an extension of* God's face, which Jacob finally saw (32:30). In metaphorical terms, Esau's face *is* the face of God for Jacob one more time: (a) their confrontation begins on a note of danger, with the potential of death; (b) they confront each other face to face, not simply at the psychological level, and engage in bodily struggle, involving the whole person; (c) they are both struggles or wrestlings; in fact, for Esau and Jacob it goes back into their mother's womb (25:22, 26). Struggle so characterizes Jacob that it will shape his relationship with everyone; (d) they both end on a gracious note, though only on the far side of the struggle; Jacob does not die—"my life is preserved." (e) Jacob does not deserve the kindness shown by both God and Esau. (f) They both end up on a "crippling" note: Jacob comes up lame in the encounter with God, and Jacob's encounter with Esau ends short of full reconciliation. (g) They both issue in new corporate realities. Jacob becomes Israel, and the families of Jacob and Esau proceed on to their lives in separate lands. "It is hard to identify the players. In the *holy God*, there is something of the *estranged brother*. And in the *forgiving brother*, there is something of the *blessing God.*"[188]

188. Brueggemann, *Genesis*, 272.

The life one lives with God and the life one lives with other human beings are two sides of the same coin. They affect each other in deep and profound ways; what happens in one relationship has effects for good or evil on the other. Life with God cannot somehow be lived in isolation from one's sisters and brothers without harming both relationships (see Matt 5:22-24; 1 John 3:17; 4:20-21). Life with other humans cannot truly be lived out in isolation from God if we are to be what the Creator intended us to be. In either case, God will find a way to engage in such lives on behalf of the gracious divine purposes.

3. In and through Esau, God works to fulfill the promises of life and goodness on behalf of Jacob, not simply through salvation-historical ("churchly") events, but through the way in which individuals—even former enemies, whether within the family or without—respond to one another. This involves God's *creational* activity, at work beyond the borders of churchly properties and promised lands. But such creational activity remains fundamentally related to God's promissory work, not simply with Jacob but with nonchosen ones like Esau. God fulfills the promises through creative activity as well as through redemptive acts. The result for these related types of divine activity is the same: salvation, in this case, reconciliation between former enemies and the extension of blessings that have the potential of shaping families for the good.

GENESIS 33:18–34:31, THE RAPE OF DINAH

COMMENTARY

Many scholars have thought this chapter to be an isolated narrative, inserted haphazardly into the story of Jacob. Newer literary-critical work, on the other hand, tends to view the chapter as an integral part of Jacob's story.[189] Moreover, one may discern continuities with other Genesis narratives—e.g., the interrelationship of this family with outsiders, or the way the narrative helps to fill in the story of the children of Jacob (especially Dinah, Simeon, and Levi). In addition, there are continuities regarding issues of marriage with those outside the family, circumcision, deception, and family conflict and violence. Perhaps most important, the sharp and unambiguous judgment (indeed, a curse!) by Jacob on the violence of Simeon and Levi must stand as the primary clue about how we should interpret this chapter (49:5-7).

Although the narrative may reflect early tribal history, including issues of land settlement in the Shechem area (see Joshua 24), ethnological considerations should play a

minimal role in interpreting the chapter in its present context. Simeon, Levi, and the other sons of Jacob do attack a city (vv. 25-29), but they are not presented as tribes in this text. Moreover, given the basically positive assessment of the Canaanites here and elsewhere in Genesis, later Canaanite issues are probably not mirrored in this chapter, except to suggest that the roots of those later troubles may stem from this ancestral time.

The story consists of six scenes: Jacob's settlement in the Shechem area (33:18-20); Shechem's rape of Dinah and his request to make Dinah his wife (34:1-4); the negotiations between the two families regarding this request (34:5-18); the fulfillment of the agreement by Hamor's family (34:19-24); the rape of the city of Shechem by Simeon and Levi (34:25-29); the exchange between Jacob and his sons (34:30-31). Moreover, since 35:1 appears as God's response to the question broached in 34:31, chaps. 34 and 35 are drawn more closely together.

33:18-20. The transition to vv. 18-20 seems abrupt, introducing a new stage in Jacob's life. No longer associated with the

189. For different readings, see M. Sternberg, *The Poetics of Biblical Narrative* (Bloomington: Indiana University Press, 1985) 445-75; D. Fewell and D. Gunn, "Tipping the Balance: Sternberg's Reader and the Rape of Dinah," *JBL* 110 (1991) 193-211.

land of Laban, he enters the land of promise, safely or "whole" (שלם *šālēm*), fulfilling the divine command (31:3, 13). His purchase of a plot near Shechem parallels the action of Abraham in chap. 23 and signals another claim to the promised land (as a burial ground, see Josh 24:32). Shechem is both the name of the city in which Jacob settles (33:18)—later, a significant Israelite center (Joshua 24)—and the name of the son of Hamor, from whom Jacob buys the land (33:19).

At this auspicious moment of entering the land of promise, Jacob erects an altar and calls it El Elohe Israel ("God, the God of Israel"; cf. 35:7). Inasmuch as *El* was the name of the Creator God worshiped at pre-Israelite Shechem, this act signals yet another claim: The God of this land is the God of Israel. The "Israel" in God's name has a dual reference: to Jacob, whose name is *Israel* (32:29), and to his "household" (34:30), for whom this moment is an important point in their historical journey.

34:1-4. Dinah is the first child of Jacob to whom the narrator devotes attention (30:21). She pays a visit to other (Canaanite) women in the Shechem area; such openness to outsiders is not unusual for Genesis. The author depicts this visit as entirely natural. The reference to Leah alludes to Dinah's full brothers, Simeon and Levi (vv. 25, 31; Judah is also a full brother), and ought not to be viewed negatively. The journey proves to be unsafe. Suddenly, a Hivite (i.e., Canaanite) named Shechem, the "most honored" (v. 19) member of the ruling family of the city-state, rapes her (see below). The narrator may assume that they know each other (see 33:19); he immediately moves to Shechem's next action.

In the *narrator's* words, Shechem proceeds to act in a way atypical of rapists: He clings to Dinah (as in 2:24), loves her (as Isaac and Jacob love Rebekah and Rachel— 24:67; 29:18, 30), and speaks to her heart (as Joseph does to his brothers, 50:21). The latter phrase may cause Dinah's positive response.[190] As revolting as the rape of Dinah is, this turn of events shifts the reader's response to Shechem in more positive directions. Moreover, the presence of love language for Dinah on the part of both Hamor and the narrator (vv. 8,

19, words also used of God's love and delight) reinforces Shechem's sincerity. Sympathy for Shechem continues to develop based on his generous statement in vv. 11-12. At the same time, this language predisposes the reader to be alert to the sons of Jacob.

In asking his father to make arrangements for Dinah to become his wife ("get" is typical language for this; cf. 24:3-7, 37-40), Shechem conforms to Israel's own legal tradition (Exod 22:16-17; Deut 22:28-29). If a man rapes an unbetrothed virgin, he has to pay the father, marry the woman, and is "not permitted to divorce her as long as he lives." This law sought to preserve as much honor in the situation as possible, including the honor of the raped woman, who would live in disgrace if she remained unmarried in her father's house. In that world, Shechem's offer was in Dinah's best interests (cf. 2 Sam 13:16). All indications are that Dinah had been drawn into the house of Shechem and the two had fallen in love. Hence, when the brothers murder Shechem and "take" Dinah (לקח *lāqaḥ*, v. 26, the word also used for the rape, v. 2) without consulting her, they ignore this legal tradition.

34:5-18. When Jacob first hears of the rape of Dinah (by means unknown), he holds his peace (used in 24:21 to buy time for learning); he waits to consult with his sons before taking action. The author understands this reticence positively (cf. v. 30). In the verses enclosing chap. 34 (33:20; 35:1-4), Jacob focuses properly on the God who has made promises to him. One can best assess Jacob's attitude in chap. 34 as one of prudence and care, informed by the worship of God and in view of a future in the land of promise that is in some jeopardy.

Hamor consults with Jacob (vv. 6-8); the sons' entry in v. 7 interrupts the fathers. When they heard what had happened, but without benefit of consultation with Jacob (as he had hoped, v. 5), the sons were upset and angry, expressed in the phrase "an outrage in [or, against] Israel" (v. 7), which clearly has later Israel in view (cf. Deut 22:21; Judg 20:6, 10; 1 Sam 13:12). At this point, they seem to have the interests of the larger community at heart. Yet, the "outrage" focuses, not on Dinah's rape, but on her having been "lain with," something that "ought not to be

190. See Fewell and Gunn, "Tipping the Balance: Sternberg's Reader and the Rape of Dinah," 196.

done." Their response focuses on the past; without apparent concern for the future (vv. 13, 27).

Both Shechem and his father enter into negotiations with Jacob and (now) his sons for Dinah's hand. The rapist and lover of Dinah, as well as the head of his family, seek to make things right; indeed, they go beyond Israel's own law in doing so. Hamor speaks first (vv. 8-10). His proposal is expansive, piling up verbs denoting generosity (cf. Abimelech's offer in 20:15; cf. 13:9). He moves beyond Shechem's marriage to Dinah to include openness to other marriages and an invitation for Jacob's family to live freely among them and to own property. Verses 20-23 make clear that this is sincere, with mutual benefits—theirs will be ours, and ours theirs. Whereupon Shechem enters the negotiations; he is even more generous and open to the future, offering to give any gift (cf. Exod 22:16-17) and to pay any price, perhaps to Dinah, for her hand in marriage. The language of "taking" has turned into the language of "giving." In fact, he opens himself to being cheated by Jacob's sons. Such generosity was certainly not necessary on his part, given the numerical advantage (v. 30).

The sons of Jacob (all of them!), without their father, resume the negotiations (vv. 13-17), even though Jacob had been addressed earlier (vv. 6, 8, and 11). A possible explanation for his absence is the word *deceitfully* in v. 13 (cf. 27:35); that word does not describe Jacob, though apparently he is not opposed to the form of the negotiations. Hamor would not have made the move he does in vv. 20-24 if Jacob had not been included. The fact that the phrase "because he had defiled their sister Dinah" immediately follows the word *deceitfully*—such evaluations are rare for the narrator in Genesis—is instructive. They believe that what Shechem has done justifies a deceitful response. Thus the reader finds no ambiguity regarding their motivation; this is a trick, pure and simple; they intend to exact vengeance. And they use religion as a vehicle for their deception!

What Shechem did to Dinah, "the outrage in Israel," has dropped from view altogether; the uncircumcised status has become the "disgrace"—a disgrace *to the brothers*. Somehow their honor, rather than Dinah's, has

become the issue. In effect, Jacob's sons are promising that Shechem and his family will be incorporated into the family of Abraham: "You will become as we are"; "we will . . . become one people" (repeated in vv. 21-22). If they do not agree, the parties will go their separate ways (the NRSV's "daughter" and the NIV's "sister" are both possible, but see NIV in v. 8). We find no sign of the violence that is to come.

34:19-24. Hamor and Shechem consider the proposal "good," though the reader knows (v. 13) what they consider good will destroy them. But the author presents them as trusting, even naive, persons who deeply want to bring Dinah and Shechem together. Shechem apparently immediately moves to be circumcised (v. 19). The writer places the phrase "most honored of all his family" strategically; it accents the integrity with which he responds. His honor will bring honor to Dinah, precisely what Israel's law called for in such a situation. The fifth (!) reference to his love for Dinah reinforces the sincerity of his desire for this marriage.

In vv. 20-24, Hamor and Shechem take the negotiated terms to their "city council" for ratification (cf. chap. 23). Their speech is marked by hortatory language designed to persuade an understandably reluctant group, hence the emphasis on economic advantage; no deceit appears, for they could simply have confiscated Jacob's goods if they had wanted. They do not mention the rape, but given the extent to which the word had spread (vv. 5, 7), we may presume the council knew about it. Hamor's and Shechem's words about friendship (*šālēm* is translated "safely" in 33:18) stand in ironic contrast with the "deceit" of v. 13. By disclosing what Hamor says in the privacy of his own council, the narrator emphasizes that Hamor negotiates in good faith. This integrity intensifies when the entire council agrees to submit to this painful and *identity-establishing* ritual. In other words, they recognize Israel's peculiar chosenness and make the necessary overtures to join them; hence Israel has made no compromise at this point.

Circumcision as an identity-establishing rite makes it an even greater gesture on the part of the Shechemite community. (Does not their circumcision in fact incorporate them?)

Certainly, for the reader, this would in effect mean—in view of chap. 17 and the repetition of 17:10 in 34:15—the Shechemites have agreed to be integrated into the Abrahamic family. The repetition in v. 24 (the threefold use of כל [*kol,* "all," "every"]) stresses the unanimity of the city council.

34:25-29. Simeon and Levi (two of Dinah's full brothers) take the initiative in following through on the deceit they and their brothers have schemed; they break faith with their new blood brothers, weakened by the circumcision. (Note that the noun for "pain" is also used for Israel in Egypt, Exod 3:7!) Entering the city by stealth (necessary for two people to kill so many), they murder Hamor, Shechem, and all the males of the city in cold blood. The "sons of Jacob" (v. 27; the NRSV inserts "other," but 49:5-7 assumes that Simeon and Levi are also involved) take advantage of the situation and pillage the city, taking all of the women (*lāqaḥ* must include rape, v. 2), children, animals, indeed, everything they could lay their hands on. The text specifically identifies this wholesale action against the city as revenge for what had been done to Dinah (v. 27; the NIV expresses not cause but place, "where"). Yet, the extensive detail (the accusative particle is used nine times!) yields an "overkill," a blood feud mentality. Even more, the fact that the brothers kept their "spoil" for themselves is highly problematic.[191] In addition, they "take" (*lāqaḥ,* cf. v. 2!) Dinah out of Shechem's house without consulting her. The narrative implies that Dinah was not being detained against her will, so this was probably not a happy occasion for her.

34:30-31. In this concluding exchange, Jacob opposes the violent actions of Simeon and Levi because of what it may mean for the future of the family (i.e., Israel); this verse must be read in the canonical context provided by 49:5-7, with its reference to the

sons' violence, murder, anger, and cruelty against people and animals. Israel's reputation has been besmirched and the trust gained has been violated, with developing good relationships between the families, once so promising, now deeply compromised. If the Canaanites should decide to seek revenge, Jacob's family in its minority status would certainly be destroyed. The future may well have been put at risk.

Ignoring Jacob's perspective on the matter, Simeon and Levi voice an opinion: "Should our sister be treated like a whore?" Note that the brothers introduce a new thought—harlotry. What actually happened to Dinah is thereby blurred; what happens to harlots is not usually called rape. The focus thereby shifts from the violent abuse of Dinah and her rights (appropriate legal restitution) to the brothers' own reputation or honor. The brothers may be accusing their father of mistreating Dinah by his comment, "selling" her for "peace at all costs." If so, that would be ironic, for they have just *used* Dinah and her situation and *taken* her without her consent in order to gain for themselves honor and great wealth (cf. God's response to Achan's comparable actions in Josh 7:11, where the language of "trouble" also appears, 6:18; 7:25). By leaving the reader with the sons' question, standing over against the word of the head of the family oriented toward life and promise, the narrator shows how narrow and self-serving their perspective and actions have been. The question also leaves the reader with an agenda to consider: How would they respond?

God responds to the question with a word about settling elsewhere and worshiping God (35:1). Jacob's response exhibits faithfulness, commanding his household (cf. 34:30), including his sons, to put away foreign gods and to purify themselves. The earlier distress Jacob recalls (35:3) may be parallel to this moment; he is in special need of divine protection (forthcoming in 35:5).

191. See Brueggemann, *Genesis,* 278.

REFLECTIONS

1. The literary brackets provided by vv. 1-2 and v. 31 raise the issue of Dinah's abusive treatment. Two types of references to Dinah stand in counterpoint: (1) the many-faceted love that Shechem has for her (vv. 3, 8, 19); it is no small tribute to

Dinah that her rapist goes to the lengths he does (finally giving his life!) to obey the law and arrange for marriage with her; (2) the violence against her: seized and raped (v. 2); defiled (vv. 5, 13, 27); suffered an outrage (v. 7); "taken" by her own brothers (v. 26); treated like a whore (v. 31). The same verb (ענה *'ānâ*) for what Dinah suffered (v. 2) describes Israel's oppression in Egypt (15:13; Exod 3:7); it was also used for Sarah's treatment of Hagar (16:6). Dinah, an oppressed one, prefigures Israel's own violation at the hands of other outsiders (cf. Isa 53:4).

Why is Dinah, the only daughter of Israel, made the victim of rape and then silenced? One could simply decry the patriarchy involved, but this text gives Bible readers permission to talk openly about rape and the sorry history of society's response, including the silencing of victims. Has this text contributed to that silence?

2. The text raises another issue: the role of the family of Hamor and their interaction with Jacob's family. The larger Genesis context helps in assessing the role of this Canaanite family. While outsiders are almost always viewed in a positive light, the relationship of Abraham's family to them has often stood in sharp contrast to the divine intention (12:3*b*). This chapter offers another instance in which the community of faith fails to serve as a channel for the blessing of God to outsiders. Rather than treat the rape of Dinah according to the law, as Hamor's family was openly willing to do, Israel takes the way of anarchy and violence. Rather than honor a genuine change on the part of Dinah's victimizers, the brothers ignore it and take a sharply overdrawn retributive form of behavior that serves to alienate the outsider. Dinah certainly suffered injustice at the hands of outsiders, but her brothers respond in kind. The deep suffering that Dinah had to undergo could have served as a vehicle for a greater good, but the violent response deepens her suffering. Israel loses the opportunity to bring good out of suffering, and Dinah becomes even more of a victim.

The temptation for the oppressed to become oppressors themselves offers an all too prevalent possibility, a turning-the-tables kind of mentality that places them precisely in the position of those who perpetrated the violence in the first place. The frequently used motif that Israelites should treat the stranger as God would treat them reminds them of this temptation (Exod 23:9).

3. The claim that the text expresses concern about intermarriage with Canaanites, or exogamy generally, appears unlikely (Deut 7:2-3 reflects a later concern shaped by particular contextual realities). The generations following Jacob, now cut off from the family in Haran, must necessarily take wives outside the family; witness Judah (and his sons; chap. 38) and Joseph (41:45; cf. Moses). Some may have deemed intermarriage with the Shechemites a positive development, but Dinah's brothers subvert it by their violent behaviors. Issues of the "politics of sex," sexual hospitality for purposes of political advantage, may have informed an earlier version of this story, but not in its present form.

4. Jacob's concern (v. 30) sharply raises the issue of the future of the chosen family. In fact, Jacob envisions the possibility that his family will be "destroyed." Jacob obviously desired a positive relationship with the inhabitants of the land. But how will the promises of God to this family be fulfilled in view of this changed relationship to the people of the land? The relationship between Israel and these peoples, two of whom are mentioned (Canaanites and Perizzites), reaches back to 13:7 and 15:18-21. In the latter text God promises Abraham the land of these peoples. But the fulfillment of the promise does not necessarily entail violence. The divine intention may have included a less violent relationship with the present inhabitants (15:16 lifts up a note of judgment). This chapter may seek to explain one reason for the violent shape of the later conflict between Israel and these peoples. The behaviors of Jacob's family subverted divine intentions and promoted violence in relationship to the Canaanites (again, see 49:5-7). Is it possible that these actions set up the situation in the land in such a way that only violence could bring about the fulfillment of the promise? This would lead to formulations such as those found in Exod 23:23; 33:2; 34:11; and Deut 7:1-5.

5. Jacob's response (v. 30) focuses on the effects of the violence for the larger issues of life and well-being for the *community* ("I and my household"); this implies a judgment on the violence (made explicit in 49:5-7). Communal well-being remains a key issue. How the family relates to its neighbors becomes relevant for the shape that its life takes, both internally (for Israel) and externally (for the fulfillment of 12:3*b*). The brothers have sacrificed long-range objectives for the sake of short-term advantage, using their sister's predicament as an excuse to perpetrate violence. Such settling of accounts sounds suspiciously like modern governments or individuals that use a wrong done at one level to justify a long-contemplated action that seeks to defend "honor."

The author presents issues of violence at multiple levels. The violence against Dinah and the violence against the Canaanites both come in for criticism. The story illustrates how violence begets violence; a response of violence sets in motion even deeper levels of violence and in the end places the future of the chosen family in jeopardy. This makes it necessary for God to enter into a much more compromised situation in order to answer the divine promises. This way of violence on the part of Jacob's sons continues in the story of Joseph. Violence against the outsider leads to violence within the family (cf. Matt 26:52 [NRSV]: "All who take the sword will perish by the sword").

This development would be congruent with Jacob's evaluation in 49:5-7; their violence results in the families of Simeon and Levi being divided and scattered. Simeon does not survive as a tribe, being absorbed into other groups; members of the tribe of Levi do become a priestly class, but with no tribal land.

6. The brothers' use of circumcision in their deception doubtless constituted an effort to make the Shechemites "pay" in the bodily organ that was the instrument of Dinah's rape. Yet, the inclusion of "every male" goes way beyond any measure-for-measure understanding; adding the rape of all the women of Shechem extends the irresponsible character of the brothers' response. Moreover, the use of circumcision for such a purpose appears highly questionable. They use circumcision as a vehicle for death rather than life, for separating people rather than uniting them in a single community. This will not be the first time that the people of God have used religious practice as a vehicle for deception and violence!

7. We find no explicit God language in this chapter. The persons involved are entrusted with decision making that matters, and they will reap the effects of their own behaviors. At the same time, the chapter is bracketed by God language (33:20; 35:1); God is engaged behind the scenes, working in and through even these levels of violence on behalf of the divine purposes. Yet, the actions of Jacob's sons have drawn their God into a highly compromised situation; God now must work in and through the violence in order to move toward the fulfillment of the divine purposes. Explicitly religious concerns are evident in references to defilement and circumcision, implying that theological issues are close to the surface.

GENESIS 35:1-29, THE JOURNEYS OF JACOB

COMMENTARY

Few biblical chapters give such clear evidence of their composite character as this one (all major sources are probably represented). Apparently, bits and pieces of tradition regarding Jacob's journeys and family have been placed at the end of his story, not unlike the way texts have been woven into the seams of the stories of Abraham (chap. 25) and Joseph (chap. 50). Some linkages occur within the chapter. We should note especially the portrayal of Jacob journeying through the promised land from north to south. Jacob's journey basically recapitulates the journey of Abraham. It begins with a similar command of God (12:1). They both journey from Haran to Shechem to Bethel toward the Negeb (12:6-9), include a promise of land (12:7), and travel in stages to Mamre (13:18), with references to oaks and altars all along the way. In addition, the separation of the families of Jacob and Esau because "their possessions were too great for them to live together" (36:7) parallels exactly the land division between Abraham and Lot (13:6). Verses 9-13 parallel significantly the covenant with Abraham in chap. 17 (see below), including a name change, with a focus on circumcision (as in chap. 34). All of these parallels may mean that Jacob has now arrived at that point in his life where he is a true successor in the line of Abraham.

The links with chap. 34 are somewhat indirect, but important. (a) The purification rites may be tied to the defilement of Dinah (34:5, 13, 27) and more generally to what was done to Shechem. (b) The inclusion of people beyond Jacob's own family (v. 2) may refer to the captives of Shechem (34:29), which may in turn explain the presence of "foreign gods." (c) The "terror" (v. 5) may be a divine response to Jacob's fear of revenge at the hands of the Canaanites in 34:30. (d) Reuben's sexual/political act (v. 22) has parallels with the actions of Simeon and Levi in chap. 34. Both are criticized by Jacob in chap. 49 and lose their place in the family. (e) The focus on Jacob's family as a community occurs in both.

Bethel receives some attention in this chapter, which, with 28:10-22, encloses the story of the adult Jacob.

35:1-15. These verses combine segments revolving around events at Bethel (see 28:10-22). God commands Jacob to go from Shechem to Bethel and build an altar; later God appears there, and Jacob again responds with worship. Worship issues frame the section.

The fact that *God* tells Jacob to make an altar is unusual (cf. Exod 27:1); elsewhere in Genesis this occurs as a human response. God

appeared to Jacob (v. 1) and made promises to him there (v. 7). God has fulfilled those promises, answering him in distress and accompanying him (v. 3). These references suggest that God, who has been faithful, now holds Jacob to his own vow at Bethel (28:10-22; 31:13).

In response to God, Jacob commands his household and "all who were with him" (see 34:29) to put away foreign gods, purify themselves (see Exod 19:10; Deut 27:15), and accompany him to Bethel. The presence of persons in his retinue who are not members of Jacob's family explains the reference to "foreign" gods; Rachel's household gods (31:19) may also still be in view. Such a double reference to the "gods" corresponds to the similar command in Josh 24:14-15, 23. This action of Joshua also occurred at Shechem and was associated with entry into the land (cf. Judg 10:16; 1 Sam 7:3-4). This element of the text may also be related to the issues of defilement raised in 34:5, 13, 27 (cf. Lev 11:47; 16:19). These texts support the idea that this ritual involved an internal renunciation, the shaping of thought and life toward what pleases God. The ritual implies an in-depth reading of the divine command relevant to the new family situation in the land. Jacob's action may be understood as a *paradigm* for worship practices in later Israel.

Everybody responds positively to Jacob's request (not all of Jacob's directives are reported in v. 4, and earrings are added). They give Jacob their idols and their golden earrings, a potential resource for making idols (cf. Exod 32:3-4; Judg 8:24-27). Jacob buries them under the oak at Shechem, another link with Abraham (see 12:6). The immediate reference to God's protection implies that God's action responds to these worship activities.

Jacob and his family undertake the journey from Shechem to Bethel (about thirty miles). God's protection on the way may refer to 34:30 and Jacob's fear of the local inhabitants; the "terror" probably refers to a God-inspired fear instilled in those who may have threatened Jacob (see Exod 23:27; Josh 10:10). They arrive at Bethel unharmed and fulfill the command of God, which, in turn, fulfills Jacob's vow (28:22). The name *El-Bethel* is given to the altar site and not to the city. On Deborah, see Reflections.

God appears to Jacob "again" (v. 9; see 28:10-22). The word God speaks alludes to a number of previous promises, especially 17:2-8, which also includes Abraham's name change. It provides a second realization of Isaac's benediction in 28:3-4 (the first, 28:13-15), but this time it has a community-oriented focus (as in Jacob's recollection of this appearance in 48:3-4). The presence of his entire family and others (see vv. 2, 5-6, 16) makes this more of a corporate experience than the others. God gives a promise (vv. 10-12) to a community that has just renounced other gods. This new, corporate setting in the land of promise may have led to the repetition of Jacob's name change.

One senses that all previous appearances of God in Genesis are caught up in this one, especially the promises to Abraham, and are applied directly to one who gives his name to the people as a whole. God gives these promises to Jacob—that is, Israel. (1) The language and form of appearance are similar to those used with Abraham (17:1); God's "going up" (v. 13; see 17:22) no doubt means the appearance of the messenger in human form (see 16:7). (2) The repetition of the promises of the land (17:8; 26:3; 28:13), a nation, indeed a community of nations and kings (cf. 17:4-6), maintains the continuity between Jacob and Abraham/Isaac. (3) It bridges God's earlier appearance to Jacob at Bethel (28:10-22), including parallels to appearance, promise, and Jacob's response. (4) It parallels the Peniel story: being blessed by God (32:29); the change of his name to Israel (32:28). (5) The command to be fruitful and multiply occurs as a command for the first time since chaps. 1–11 (1:28; 9:1, 6); it took the form of a promise to Abraham (17:6) and is recalled *as promise* in 48:4 (cf. 28:3).

Jacob's response (vv. 14-15) also repeats earlier actions; he names Bethel again (28:19), and he erects another pillar and anoints it (28:18-19). Verses 14-15 have as much to do with the fulfillment of the vow as does 35:7 (e.g., the pillar and the name *Bethel*, the house of God, cf. 28:22). These texts establish the authority of the sanctuary at Bethel for a later generation. Jacob pours the drink (wine) offering, unique to Genesis, on the pillar rather than the altar. These cross-references testify to continuities in

Jacob's relationship with God and bracket his life from the point of leaving home until his return. They also establish continuities with Israel's later, more elaborate ritual activities.

35:16-20. These verses portray the birth of Benjamin and the death of Rachel on the way from Bethel near Ephrath/Bethlehem (see 48:5-7); Rachel's grave lies near Ramah in Benjaminite territory in 1 Sam 10:2 and Jer 31:15, however. There were two Ephraths in Israel, Bethlehem and near Ramah, hence the confusion. The immediate family of Jacob is now complete. The comforting words of the midwife about a son inform Rachel that her desires for a second son (30:24) have been fulfilled. Rachel's naming of her son (*Ben-oni*, "son of my sorrow") is partially changed by Jacob (*Benjamin*, "son of the right hand"— i.e., power—or "son of the south" or "son of days," see 44:20), to link the child less closely to the sorrowful past.

35:21-26. Only here, in chaps. 25–36, does the author refer to Jacob by his new name, Israel, but it may well have a corporate reference. Eder is near Jerusalem; it constitutes one more point in Israel's journey through the promised land ("Israel journeyed on"). The shocking note about Reuben's cohabiting with Rachel's maid (and mother of Dan and Naphtali) probably explains why Reuben lost his status as the firstborn son (cf. 48:5; 49:3-4; 1 Chr 5:1). His act appears more a political move than a sexual one. The death of Rachel occasions an effort on Reuben's part to assume the role of the family leader (see Absalom's efforts with his father's concubines in 2 Sam 16:20-22; cf. 2 Sam 3:7; 12:8) and illustrates again the conflict in this family.[192]

Since a list of Jacob's sons follows this note about Reuben, the author may be addressing the transition in leadership from Jacob to his sons; Reuben makes the first move. He also remains on the list in spite of his deed. The point finally would be that, unlike the previous generations, the blessing and the promise will be shared by the sons as a group, rather than be assumed by any one of them (see 49:1-28; 50:24). The fact that Benjamin is included among those born in Paddan-aram may refer to the home of the mother. Dinah's omission from the list indicates that tribal considerations are at stake here. The list is

192. For details, see Sarna, *Genesis*, 244-45.

followed closely by a list of Esau's descendants (chap. 36).

35:27-29. Jacob finally returns to the place from which he left in 28:1-5 (see 31:18), another piece of evidence for the bracketing function of this chapter. The writer reports Isaac's death in terms almost exactly the same as those used for Abraham (25:7-9), being buried by his two sons (from 49:31) in the grave at Machpelah.

REFLECTIONS

1. One best interprets this chapter as a series of snapshots from a Jacob scrapbook that provided an episodic look at his later life. The references to 28:10-22 and the notices of various journeys that take him the length of the promised land in a manner parallel to Abraham (see above) provide linear coherence. The journeys are punctuated by one birth (Benjamin), three deaths (Deborah, Rachel, Isaac), and continuing family trouble (v. 22). God continues to be with Jacob, with appearances to command (v. 1), to panic (v. 5), to name (v. 10), and to promise (vv. 11-12). Jacob always responds in positive ways, by putting away gods (vv. 2-4), building altars (vv. 3, 7), and worshiping God (vv. 14-15). Amid this amazing variety, the author lists the twelve sons of Jacob according to their mothers (vv. 22c-26).

The author seems to say: "Your lives as Israel will be as complex and varied as was that of your father, Israel, but you will be undergirded by the presence of God catching you up in creation-wide purposes." Such a picture is typical of communities of faith; the surface image resembles more a scrapbook than a harmonious, logical presentation. There are the ongoing rhythms of life and death, joy and sorrow, family conflict and unity. Yet, beneath the surface of these apparently incoherent details, the journey moves toward a divinely established goal.

2. The author appends a curious note about the death of Rebekah's nurse, Deborah (see 24:59), to this story; the narrative does not report the death of Rebekah (cf. 49:31). That a name ("oak of tears") is attached to the place where Deborah is buried may be associated with the oak of v. 4. This text provides striking testimony to the memory of a faithful servant that lives on in the community of faith. Amid all the great movements of these major ancestral figures, the author includes a note about "little" people, who are more important in the larger story than one typically appreciates.

3. The renunciation of other gods embeds the first commandment in the heart of the ancestral story. More broadly, it sets the community of faith apart from certain values and commitments of the surrounding cultures. It lifts up the importance of ritual activity for life in the land, as a way of responding to the problems faced by the community of faith, and as a vehicle in and through which God acts on behalf of the community.

The task of "putting away" whatever is harmful to the community moves beyond just "gods" in other texts, incorporating more specific directives for the shape of a faithful life—putting away crooked speech (Prov 4:24), violence and oppression (Ezek 45:9), and sin (2 Sam. 12:13). Israel should move beyond specific ritual activities and speak of daily commitments and responsibilities. The NT picks up this same language, speaking of putting away "your former way of life, your old self" (Eph 4:22-32 NRSV) and, more specifically, putting off anger, wrath, malice, slander, and abusive language (Col 3:8; cf. 1 Pet 2:1). Putting away foreign gods has been translated into the Christian tradition by referring to the renunciation of sinfulness or "devil and all his works and all his ways."

Changing clothes also works as a symbol of moving from the old to the new. Clothing plays an important role in Genesis, symbolizing significant changes in the narrative (from 3:21 to 41:14). The washing of clothes is a symbol of removing defilement (cf.

Lev 15:5-27); all of our own deeds are like a polluted garment (Isa 64:6). Yet, because of what God has done, we are clothed "with the garments of salvation," covered with "the robe of righteousness" (Isa 61:10 NRSV; 52:1). The NT also uses the image of clothing to symbolize this change (cf. Mark 2:21), and persons of faith are called upon to clothe themselves in the characteristics of the new life in Christ (Eph 4:24; 6:13-17; 1 Pet 5:5). "The new community is found by *renunciation, renaming, reclothing*, and finally, *receiving a promise*."[193]

4. Rachel's weeping lives on in Israel's memory, noted not least in the reference to Jacob's pillar, "which is there to this day" (v. 20). This image works powerfully in Jer 31:15-17 to express the deep effects of suffering on Israel and in Matt 2:17-18, in reference to the slaughter of the innocents in and around Bethlehem at Jesus' birth. In Jeremiah, Rachel is used to express feminine and suffering images for God (31:15-20). This devastating moment for both Rachel and Jacob does not slip into the past or remain only a negative memory; it continues to generate fresh theological reflections. It (along with much else in this chapter) witnesses to the generative power of even "scraps" of the tradition for the ongoing life of the people of God.

193. Brueggemann, *Genesis*, 283.

GENESIS 36:1-43, THE FUTURE OF ESAU

COMMENTARY

These highly composite lists (cf. 1 Chr 1:35-54) include Esau's descendants (vv. 1-19); those of Seir the Horite, whose name is given to the region (vv. 20-30); the Edomite king list (vv. 31-39); and an appendix (vv. 40-43). The king list carries the story of Esau and Edom well beyond the narrative in which it is embedded, down to the time of David and Solomon (2 Sam 8:13-14; 1 Kgs 11:14), probably the time of the narrator. This chapter thus constitutes a *projection* of Edomite peoples and leaders into the future.

These lists were probably gathered by the Davidic monarchy after its subjugation of Edom. Over half of these names are not otherwise identifiable, having no connection with an existing narrative; many of the known names have a close relationship with Judah; some are both personal and place names; some have been taken over from other lists; others are used in more than one way in this text; and still others are not in full agreement with the surrounding story (e.g., Esau's wives in 26:34; cf. 28:9 to 36:1-3, 10, 14).

The lists document stages in the history of the people involved, from family (vv. 1-14) to tribal units (vv. 15-30) to more national entities (vv. 31-39). They probably reveal comparable developments in the life of Israel. Generally, the relationships in the list reflect historical developments among tribal groups (e.g., the intermarriage of Canaanites and Edomites, 36:2).

This list parallels that of Ishmael (25:12-18) in both structure and concern for the nonchosen brother. As with Ishmael, Esau's genealogy relates to previous oracles of blessing (25:23; 27:39-40); God attends to their realization in the development of this people. The move from Esau to Edom in this chapter (vv. 8-9, 43) also leads into chaps. 37–50, where the most basic subject is the movement from Jacob to Israel (36:31; see Josh 24:4).

36:1-19. The lists begin with a genealogy of the five sons of Esau and his three wives. Verses 1-5 focus on Esau's family, vv. 9-14 on that of his sons. The parenthetical reference to Amalek (v. 12) reflects antipathetic relationships between the Amalekites and the Israelites (Exod 17:8-16; Deut 25:17-19). In vv. 15-19 the sons are listed in their political role as chiefs (NIV, or as clans, NRSV) over Edomite territories.

Verses 6-8 constitute the major narrative piece within the chapter (cf. vv. 24, 35); they relate back to relationships between Jacob and Esau, established earlier (33:1-17; 35:29); both have been highly successful. The division between the families of Jacob and Esau are here grounded in socioeconomic reality (cf. Abraham and Lot, 13:5-7), with no sign of previous personal conflict evident. Earlier links in the text between Esau and Seir (32:4; 33:14-16; cf. 14:6) are difficult to justify with these verses; some have suggested this text speaks of a permanent settlement of a nomadic people having a sometime relationship to Seir.

The author presents Esau's family positively, highlighting stability, growth, and continuity. The fact that Esau moves, rather than Jacob, says something about their historical relationships as well as the divine promise regarding Canaan; at the same time, the tradition speaks of the land of Seir as a divine gift for Esau (Deut 2:5; Josh 24:4), and the oracle in 27:39-40 assumes a land.

36:20-30. These verses present a genealogy of the seven sons of Seir the Horite (vv. 20-28), also listed as chiefs (NIV) or clans (NRSV), vv. 29-30. The Horites are also known as Hurrians, a non-Semitic people in origin (but here having Semitic names). These people occupied Seir before the sons of Esau subjugated them (described in Deut 2:12, 22; cf. Gen 14:6). We do not know whether individuals or tribes are primarily in view here, but probably the latter.

36:31-39. This list (not a genealogy) of eight nondynastic kings of Edom (vv. 31-39) may be best understood as chiefs similar to Israelite judges; they probably do not always reign successively or over the same territory. They pre-date Israel's entry into Canaan (see Num 20:14; Judg 11:17) and continue down to the time of the United Monarchy, at which time David conquered the Edomites (2 Sam 8:13-14; 1 Kgs 11:14-17). The last of the kings (Hadar [Hadad]) may be a contemporary of Saul, whose son or grandson may be the Hadad mentioned in 1 Kgs 11:14. Reference to the kings of Israel (v. 31) reflects the oracle (25:23) that Esau was the older son who came to serve the younger. One of these groups, the Midianites, descend from Abraham (25:2).[194]

36:40-43. This appendix probably specifies eleven Edomite chiefs (or clans) in terms of their localities at the time of the last-named king. Redactionally, they balance the twelve sons of Jacob in 35:22-26.

194. For details, see Sarna, *Genesis*, 408-10.

REFLECTIONS

To the average reader of Genesis, these lists (with over 200 names!) are to be read quickly while getting on with the story of Joseph. Moreover, it may be thought that because this chapter focuses on those who are "not chosen," whose history seemingly goes nowhere, it need not delay the reader. Yet, the inclusion of the stories of these peoples (known only from Israelite sources) is significant, for it makes the reader pause over the place of nonchosen ones and ponder their relationship to the chosen. Their story is not expunged or reduced to something of no account by the narrators of the story of the chosen people.

The testimony of this chapter, with its references to Esau's land, material blessings, and the succession of generations is that God the Creator is indeed at work outside Israel, giving life and blessing to the nonchosen. The blessings given to Esau (27:39-40) continue to be realized down through the centuries. In fact, the promises to Abraham and Sarah include a promise of kings and nations (17:5, 16), so that the very existence of Edom depends on divine promises. In these respects we may compare Esau's story to the story and genealogy of Ishmael (see chaps. 16–17; 21; 25).

While Esau is not the "chosen," these texts do not forget that the story is about brothers. This is made clear in other texts, where Esau is a "brother" of Israel (Num 20:14), who is not to be "abhorred" by Israel, "because [the Edomites] are your kin" and are even to be welcomed into the "assembly" of Israel (Deut 23:7-8). It is thereby recognized that, though the division between chosen and nonchosen may slice down the middle of a family, that does not nullify the continuing familial relationship and the obligations the chosen ones have for the welfare of the other. Their responsibility to be a blessing to all the "families" of earth (12:3*b;* 28:14) includes those within the family as well as those who stand without. Election is for the purposes of mission.

It is clear from the historical record that severe conflicts between Edom and Israel took place from time to time, from David to the post-exilic period, issuing in some harsh judgments on Edom (2 Sam 8:13-14; Psalm 137; Obadiah; Mal 1:2-5; cf. Rom 9:12-13). Since these basically positive stories of Esau in Genesis continued to be transmitted through difficult times, they demonstrate that family ties cannot finally be subverted by the behaviors of one or more generations of brothers and sisters. This perspective may attest to a countercultural origin and transmission for these texts, not uncommon for Israel's literature. These texts witness to bonds of family that reach across the centuries. They should inform the continuing relationships among all peoples, no matter how difficult they may be at any given moment.

We may observe links between the two excluded sons, Ishmael and Esau, not only in the promises spoken to them, but also in their roles as progenitors of the Arab peoples, many of whom claim adherence to Islam (see chaps. 16–17; 21; 25). These texts may be especially important as the chosen in the modern world seek to relate to these "others" in as positive a way as possible; they demonstrate that we have common roots in the faith of Abraham and Sarah and that heritage may enhance our conversations with each other.

GENESIS 37:1–50:26

JOSEPH, JUDAH AND JACOB'S FAMILY

OVERVIEW

We know this last major section of the book of Genesis as the story of Joseph; and for good reason, since it involves, primarily, the fortunes and misfortunes of Joseph, Jacob's son. At the same time, the text announces that "this is the story of the family of Jacob" (37:2), and concludes with reference to the promises God "swore to Abraham, to Isaac, and to Jacob" (50:24). At the least this means that, despite all the focus on Joseph, the reader must think fundamentally in corporate terms; this story narrates the emergence of Israel's family as Israel, the people of God.

The reader must also seek to come to terms with chaps. 37–50 as a unified whole. Modern scholarship has usually regarded the story as a composite work (J, E, P, and redactors), a view prompted in particular by so-called doublets. There has been a decisive move away from this approach over the past generation, however, with renewed efforts to understand the story as a unity. Hence, for example, we now may read the repetitions as a deliberate literary device, perhaps reflecting an oral culture. This usually does not entail a denial of the composite character of these chapters in some respects (or the need to probe redactional issues).

Yet, for all the talk about unity, many still regard certain sections as intrusive, especially chaps. 38 and 49 (and often portions of chaps. 46–48; 50). Such an approach seems guided especially by a concern to isolate those segments that focus on Joseph or reflect a particular literary style. However, such claims diminish the corporate perspective of the present redaction. For example, chaps. 48–49 have the emergent tribal groups of Israel in view. Chapter 38 highlights Judah, who has a key role in the larger story (43:3-10; 44:18-34) and whose descendants are of central importance in later Israel. These chapters coordinate the pervasive role that the "brothers" play in the story, but because they are so often mentioned as a collective body, they tend to be less visible. Whatever place the story may have had as an independent piece of literature (of whatever length), it now focuses on the move from Israel as an individual to Israel as a family, to Israel as a people.

Chapters 12–36 are basically individual stories, presented in episodic fashion and tied together by genealogies and itineraries. This story, though episodic at some points (38; 46–50), is more a single narrative. As such, we may designate it a short story or novella, with a plot moving from crisis to resolution (similar to books like Ruth and Esther). At the same time, its self-designation as the "story of a family" (37:2) accents continuities with the previous family narratives. Yet, the differences from chaps. 12–36 suggest that the story emanates from different circles than the earlier stories.

What, then, can be said about its origins? Scholars have often pointed to the influence of the wisdom movement on the book.[195] Wisdom influence may be evident at some points, as in the portrayal of Joseph as an ideal young man or a model administrator. Yet, such ideas were widespread in Israel's world and should not be used to support a specific intellectual matrix for its origins. A royal setting is likely, given leading themes; and the Solomonic era (with its positive relationship with Egypt; see 1 Kgs 9:16) affords a probable background. We must remain agnostic

---

195. See von Rad, *Genesis*, 433-40.

about the story's history, except to say that the Priestly writer probably integrated it into its present ancestral context (Priestly influence can be discerned at a few points [e.g., 37:1-2; 47:27-28; 48:3-6]).

Function. The Joseph story functions in several ways within Genesis and the Pentateuch.

1. The story follows the genealogy of Esau, Jacob's brother. The reason for this juxtaposition seems clear: Both present the movement from individual to people. Chapter 36 announces that "Esau is Edom" (vv. 1, 8-9, 43) and assumes a comparable movement for Jacob (36:31; cf. Josh 24:4). Chapters 37–50 trace this movement, depicting the journey from individual Israel to people Israel (from 37:1 to 47:27 to 50:25), which is recapitulated in Exod 1:1-7.

2. The story leads into the book of Exodus. At one level, the story has a narrow geographical purpose, moving the family from Canaan to Egypt, the setting for Exodus events. References to "settling" (יֹשֵׁב *yāšab*) signals this motif. The story begins with Jacob's settling in the land of Canaan (37:1), moves to his settling in Egypt (47:27; cf. vv. 4, 6, 11), and finally shifts to Joseph's "settling" there *with his father's household* (50:22), with a not unimportant aside about the Canaanites as "settlers" in Canaan (50:11). The journeys of this family back and forth between Canaan and Egypt anticipate Exodus journeys.

At another level, the story "sets up" issues for the book of Exodus—for example, the Egyptian context. The story acquaints the reader with a remarkable range of life in Egypt, particularly the court of Pharaoh. Generally, a highly positive portrayal of Pharaoh and the Egyptians emerges, from the pharaonic treatment of Joseph, to the welcome of Jacob's family, to the significant participation in Jacob's funeral (including prolonged and "grievous mourning," 50:3, 11). One should also note the Egyptians' openness to Israel's God (e.g., 39:3; 41:38-39; 43:23). This material provides essential background for events in Exodus 1–15, so 1:8, "A new king arose over Egypt, who did not know Joseph." Genesis prevents us from "demonizing" the Egyptians of Exodus, suggests potentially positive relationships, and may well prepare for such

prophetic words as Isa 19:18-25: "Blessed be Egypt my people" (Isa 19:25 NRSV)!

"Servant/slave" (עֶבֶד *'ebed*) appears as an important theme. The nearly 100 uses of this root in Exodus should make one attentive to its use in Genesis 37–50. Just as Exodus insists that Israel is the servant of God, not Pharaoh, so also Genesis claims that Israel is not the servant of *Joseph* (read any Israelite leader). Life, growth, and blessing are another significant theme. Lifted up in a prominent way in chaps. 37–50 (esp. 45:5-8), it becomes a creational issue around which Exodus revolves (beginning in 1:7), which also relates to the theme of promise. While this theme appears more muted in chaps. 37–50 (except for blessing), it occurs at key junctures (46:3-4; 48:3-4, 21-22), ends on this note (50:24), and grounds God's activity in the Exodus events (2:24; 3:16-17; 6:2-8).

3. The story continues *and develops* the story of Jacob and his forebears in chaps. 12–36. The story of the family of Abraham/Isaac/Jacob moves on, rampant with conflicting relationships, yet chosen by God to be the recipient of promises and responsibilities. Significant developments occur:

Family and promise. Family issues continue to play a primary role, particularly tensions created by intrafamilial conflict. They create a major movement in the story, resulting in brotherly reconciliation, not an end in itself, however; it happens for the sake of the future, particularly as seen in the promises. The families of Abraham and Isaac had been divided over the issue of the promises (Isaac/Ishmael; Jacob/Esau). Will this "tradition" continue in Jacob's family? The story begins that way; Joseph seems to be eliminated (chap. 37), then Judah (chap. 38). But in time, when Jacob first speaks God's promise to Joseph, he refers to *all* of his offspring (48:3-4; cf. 35:12); Joseph follows through on this by speaking the promise to all his brothers (50:24). Family conflicts are resolved for the sake of a *unified family* moving toward those promises.

Individual, family, and nation. The story integrates family history with national and political history.[196] At times the author focuses on the family (chaps. 37; 42–45), at times on the broader political arena (chaps. 39–41; 47). Yet, because there is no interest in

196. Westermann highlights this throughout his *Genesis 37–50*.

foreign affairs (e.g., wars), the focus throughout remains on issues that affect interhuman relationships.

This integration may speak to a conflictual reality in Israel's history. Put generally, the evolution of Israel's history from a family/clan orientation to monarchy occasioned numerous conflicts. This story conveys the importance of a symbiotic relationship between government and family, embodied in the figure of Joseph, who remains both brother and national leader. Government, in its effect on citizens, should function like a good family system. Yet, if the family is conflicted or natural disaster strikes—as with Jacob—it takes wise governmental leaders—as with Joseph—to bring the good order needed for life and well-being. Because his leadership in social and economic spheres and his rise to power are ascribed to the work of God, the story views national structures in a positive light. They, in effect, mirror God in valuing and preserving life in families. Yet, the potential for the misuse of authority appears evident as well (see Exod 1:8). The story could be interpreted as an essay on the use and abuse of power (from Jacob as a father, to the brothers' treatment of Joseph, to the role of the pharaoh and Potiphar's wife, to Joseph in various roles).

In Joseph, especially, the story highlights the importance of the individual; what he says and does has considerable positive impact. Once placed in a leadership position, Joseph is no passive member of the community, but rather becomes deeply engaged on behalf of the public good. He rejects violence and revenge, and hence brings some closure to the snowballing effects of dysfunctionality. Although no angel—himself the product of such a family—Joseph chooses an approach that, however justifiable, causes no little discomfort among the brothers; finally he does not return in kind, though it is within his power to do so. The one who has ample reason to retaliate chooses reconciliation instead of retribution.

God. The action of God and the relationship to God are seen as central, enabling life and well-being for individual, family, and nation. God, not human heroes, provides the unity in the story; the deity works toward the divine purposes in and through these spheres of society and their deep and pervasive levels of sin and evil. Thereby the family is preserved alive and unified, and enabled to move on as the bearer of God's promises to the world. The story highlights God's presence with Joseph (chap. 39), blessing him at every turn; but God has a larger canvas in view. Joseph's relationship with God, accented at key junctures, affects his personal life, but moves beyond him to affect wide ranges of public life. The move from his encounter with Potiphar's wife to his wise leadership in community affairs suggests that personal and public life are to be linked for maximum effectiveness as a leader.

This story depicts God in ways quite different from chaps. 12–36. Although not mentioned less often (some fifty times), God is portrayed differently. Never obvious, God acts unobtrusively, behind the scenes. God does not overpower or offer oracles and miracles; God's presence weaves the threads of goodness, mercy, *and judgment* into the texture of ordinary life, working toward the best possible end.

Moreover, God never appears to Joseph; unlike his forebears in the faith, he receives no word from God. God appears only in 46:1-4 (48:3-4 recalls an appearance), but to Jacob, not to Joseph. The promises seem hidden to ordinary view. Joseph builds no altars and associates with no centers of worship. Yet God is with him, and he is imbued with God's spirit (41:38). Joseph hears the promises for the first time from Jacob in 48:3-4, 21-22. Such differences may help to explain why the text never includes Joseph in the common formula: the God of Abraham, Isaac, and Jacob. Yet, another important dynamic operates in this way of conveying the knowledge of God. Jacob, not God, passes the promise on to Joseph, who in turn passes it on to his brothers (50:24); also, the word of Joseph to the brothers in 45:3-8 is formally similar to a typical theophany. The human community now becomes responsible for the transmission of the word of God. The former mode of revelation will return almost immediately (Exod 3:1-10), but a new method for transmitting the word of God across the generations has developed.

Why does the author present God differently in this story? This story may have been produced in a more secular time, when human thought and action seemed to carry the day, and God was experienced in less direct ways. Or God's actions correlate with the new reality of a people; God relates to the entire people of Israel, not just to individuals. Or it may be an introduction to the opening chapters of Exodus, where God acts in much the same way (cf. 2:23-25). Whatever the case, Genesis does portray the different ways in which God conveys the divine word to the community of faith.

4. The story picks up on key themes from Genesis 1–11 and, together, they enclose the unity of that book. God appears as one who works on behalf of not only the chosen family, but also the Egyptians; indeed the entire world serves as the divine horizon. The primary issues throughout the story are creational, from issues of family order to natural disaster, from socioeconomic crisis to national structures. God's purposes throughout are to preserve life and well-being, which in 45:5-8 includes the world community. The author focuses on divine blessing, blessings of the land, of wise leadership, of family growth, fulfilling the creational words of 1:28 (47:27), which are in turn extended to Pharaoh (47:7-10), the Egyptians (47:13-26), and the world (41:53-57) through this blessed family (cf. 12:3). God's choosing to work through this weak, conflicted family constitutes a divine

irony, using the weak to bless the strong, which leads into important themes in Exodus.

Structure. The story begins with a conflicted family situation; two brothers, Joseph (37:1-36) and Judah (38:1-30), seem to be eliminated from the line of promise. It ends with the inclusion of all of Jacob's offspring within the orbit of the promise (47:29–50:26), grounded in God's word (48:4). Their futures are marked out in chaps. 48–49; chap. 50 depicts the reconciliation that enables their reception of the promise as a corporate entity (50:24).

Chapters 45:1-9 and 46:1-4 stand parallel and establish the divinely ordered creational setting of life and well-being in Egypt that enables the events of chaps. 48–50. The author describes the family's growth in Egypt, summarized in 47:27 and detailed in the genealogy (46:8-27). The setting makes this possible—filled with the blessings associated with Pharaoh (45:16-20; 47:7-10) and the Egyptians (47:13-26), interwoven with reports about their settlement and provision in that land (45:9-15, 21-28; 46:28–47:6, 11-12).

Chapters 39–44 develop *both* the Egyptian context and the family relationships in such a way that the events of chaps. 46–50 become possible; chaps. 39–41 focus on the public, Egyptian setting, with Joseph's rise to power; chaps. 42–44 develop the family issues.

GENESIS 37:1-36, JOSEPH AND HIS BROTHERS

COMMENTARY

The author/editor juxtaposes chaps. 36 and 37–50 because they involve the movement from individual to people. The announcement that "Esau is Edom" (36:1, 8-9, 43) assumes a comparable movement for Jacob (36:31; cf. Josh 24:4). Chapters 37–50 trace this journey from individual Israel to people Israel (cf. 37:1; 47:27; 50:25). Jacob will also migrate from Canaan, as does Esau (36:6-8); unlike Esau, Jacob claims God's promise of an eventual return.

This story begins in a familiar way: Jacob as an inept father; the deception of the father by sons; the conflict among brothers. Will only one brother receive the promise this time, too? Much of chaps. 37–50 addresses this question. Joseph begins the chapter as the leading candidate to succeed Isaac and Jacob, but he seems to be out of the picture at the end.

Scholars have commonly thought that two sources are interwoven in this chapter, suggested by the roles of Reuben/Judah and the Midianites/Ishmaelites, as well as various geographical and familial details. Yet, other explanations are possible. The use of the names *Jacob* and *Israel* also suggests such a theory. However, the emergence of the name *Israel* for a people (e.g., 47:27; 48:20) may mean that later Israel sees itself mirrored in the story. The fact that Rachel remains alive (v. 10; see 35:19) may also create some confusion; yet, Genesis does not always present events in a precisely linear orientation.

Verses 1-4 set the stage for this episode, indeed for the story as a whole. The remainder of the chapter quickly moves through three scenes to a preliminary climax, the exclusion of Joseph; Joseph's dreams intensify intrafamilial conflict (vv. 5-11); the isolation of Joseph and the violence he experiences at the hands of his brothers (vv. 12-28); Jacob's grieving reaction (vv. 29-36).

37:1-4. Jacob settles in the land of promise (v. 1), which is linked with 47:27 and 50:22, where "Israel" and Joseph settle in Egypt. This sets up two themes for the story: the movement from Canaan to Egypt and the development from individual to people.

The reference to *Jacob's* genealogy (37:2) indicates that the story of Joseph unfolds *from within* the story of Jacob's family. Indeed, Jacob himself remains a central character in this story until his death and burial at the end (49:33).

The author introduces Joseph as a teenager and as a shepherd, helping four older brothers (Dan, Naphtali, Gad, and Asher). He first acts as an interpreter, a key role he will play in the story; he brings a criticism of his brothers back to Jacob (which they may or may not have deserved).

Joseph evidently now has a relationship with his father that the others do not have. It suggests that Joseph becomes the chosen son of the promise; the eleven are "Esau." This perception has been fostered by Jacob himself, who "loves" Joseph more than his other children (see 33:2, 7); Joseph was a child of Jacob's old age (see 30:22-24). Although not a problem in itself, it takes public form, specifically the gift of a costly robe, long and sleeved, perhaps with royal connotations (see 2 Sam 13:18; the traditional translation "a coat of many colors" is based on the Greek

and Latin). Once again, an article of clothing plays an important role in a Genesis story.

As it became obvious that Joseph was his father's pet, the brothers grew to hate him (rather than Jacob!) and could not speak to him peaceably (בשלם *běšālôm*; see 45:15; 50:21). Communication breaks down. The stage is set for deep intrafamilial conflict. "In a few short sentences the narrator has sketched out an unusually complex world of fateful familial stratification, relations, and emotions: youth versus old age, intra-familial social hierarchy, concealed realms of discourse, rivalry, betrayal, obsessive love, ill-considered gifts of passion, hatred, shunning. The balance with which this system is presented leaves no heroes and no villains."[197]

37:5-11. Joseph, like his father, is a dreamer, and also an interpreter of dreams. The narrator heightens the importance of interpretation by offering no words (cf. 28:12-15; 31:10-13), only symbols. Dreams play a key role in the story, with three scenes of two dreams each (see chaps. 40–41). Yet, too much can be made of them as well.[198] They do introduce an important external reality into the family situation, but basically they serve a provisional function. They intensify the conflict through Joseph's telling of them and enable Joseph's testing of his brothers (42:9); but Joseph will finally deny the dreams' continuing applicability for shaping the future.

The meaning of Joseph's two dreams may be transparent, but *interpretations,* implied in their questions, are made only by the brothers and the father (cf. 40:8!): Joseph stands in a position of authority over them. That Joseph chooses to share uninterpreted dreams with those most affected makes for deeper misunderstanding; his silence regarding their interpretations intensifies the difficulties. He could have talked about what "rule" might mean (a key issue in the larger narrative); he could have responded to Jacob's comment about "bowing to the ground" before him (which never happens!). Joseph may be seeking to gain an advantage in the intrafamilial conflict, but he acts insensitively, even arrogantly, and only exacerbates the problems.

197. White, *Narration and Discourse,* 242.
198. See Brueggemann, *Genesis,* 298-307.

In the dream about the sheaves—anticipating the food/famine theme—the brothers bow down to Joseph. The brothers understand this as a threat to their place in the family. This provides a variant on the younger/older brother theme so common in Genesis (see 25:23), but finally *no one* —Joseph or brothers—will be excluded (50:24). The brothers respond with repeated, sarcastic, rhetorical questions about Joseph's becoming their ruler.

The second dream expands upon the first: The luminaries (sun and moon are parents; eleven stars are brothers) add Joseph's parents to those doing obeisance (Rachel seems still to be alive). No astrological links are evident, but the use of luminaries suggests that Joseph's role has taken on "astronomical" proportions! Only Jacob responds with rebuking, nonrhetorical questions this time, but finally he ponders what this might mean (v. 11). The dreams are the final step in a buildup of hatred. They are the catalyst for the first voicing of the brothers' attitude toward Joseph. The dreams finally tip the balance toward violence.

37:12-17. The scene changes abruptly; this enables the brothers to act outside their father's purview. The brothers journey some fifty miles from Hebron (35:27) to pasture the flock where there is good grassland, in this case near Shechem (a place with family links, 33:18-20). Joseph stays home, a change from established practice (37:2), about which Jacob wonders. Jacob (certainly not innocent regarding brotherly relationships) sends him to look into the well-being (*šālôm*) of the brothers and of their flocks and to report back (cf. David in 1 Samuel 17). This seems ironic given previous "reports" (v. 2) and the absence of *šālôm* between the brothers (v. 4). Even more, it leads the reader to wonder about Jacob's motivation. Is this the naive, loving father (the giver of the coat) who hopes that the brothers can work things out? Is he completely innocent of possible violence? *Shalom* will be hard to come by before this book, let alone this chapter, is over.

Because the brothers had moved to Dothan (fifteen miles north of Shechem), even farther away from their father, Joseph has difficulty locating them, and only then through the hospitality of a stranger. This delay heightens the drama, leaving Joseph vulnerably "suspended between father and brothers, between love and hatred."[199] It may also show how acts of hospitality are often "neutralized" by the context of trouble in which they occur.

37:18-28. This scene describes the brothers' plotting against Joseph and its convoluted effects. When the brothers see him approaching, they conspire to kill him. Their motivation centers on Joseph's dream (they sarcastically call him a "master of dreams"); by killing him, they will make certain that the dream does not become a reality. Ironically, by selling him to Egypt they enable it to become so! They think that human action can affect the outcome of what has been depicted in a dream.

Interpreters debate the meaning of this section. The brothers agree to sell him to passing Ishmaelites (vv. 27-28); yet, Midianite traders are also mentioned (vv. 28, 36). The text reports that both groups sell him in Egypt (v. 36; 39:1). Also, both Reuben (vv. 21-22) and Judah (vv. 26-27) intervene in comparable ways on his behalf. Some would resolve the issue by identifying the Midianites with the Ishmaelites (see Judg 8:24), or claim that the redactor does. Others posit two interwoven traditions: (1) Reuben and the Midianites, who kidnap Joseph; (2) Judah and the Ishmaelites, to whom Joseph is sold.

Since the antecedent of "they" in v. 28*a* is ambiguous (so NRSV; the NIV interprets "they" as the brothers) we do not know who sold Joseph. The author may have intended ambiguity, the effect being to destabilize the brothers' planning and leave the details of Joseph's transition to Egypt clouded in mystery (as 40:15 and 45:4-5 do). The fact that both groups are descended from half-brothers of Isaac (hence Joseph's kin, see 25:2) suggests an interest in having the descendants of Abraham through each of his three wives involved in the deed.

The brothers prove not to be of one mind in the matter and two voice their misgivings. Reuben, the oldest son (hence responsible to his father), intervenes on behalf of Joseph and begs the brothers not to take his life, but to throw him into a cistern (holes dug out to store rain water). The narrator informs us

---

199. W. Lee Humphreys, *Joseph and His Family: A Literary Study* (Columbia: University of South Carolina Press, 1988) 35.

that his intention is heroic; he will return to the pit at a later time and restore Joseph to their father (if this happened, Joseph's reports to his father would, of course, intensify familial conflict). The brothers agree, and without a word from them or Joseph (though 42:21 refers to his pleas), they strip him of his robe (namely, his status), throw him into a waterless cistern (to a position *below* them), and sit down to eat (cf. 43:31-34 for the next meal).

Judah intervenes, sensing problems. When Ishmaelite traders bound for Egypt (with goods for use in medicine, cosmetics, and embalming; 43:11) enter the scene, he suggests a compromise, designed to appeal to self-interest: a "profit" motive (there is nothing to gain from killing him, though there would be if they sold him); they cannot conceal his blood (cf. 4:10) and will bear guilt; he is a brother, their own flesh and blood. The brothers agree and sell him for twenty shekels (see Lev 27:5) to the Ishmaelites (or the Midianites kidnap him), and he is sold on the Egyptian slave market. (Historically, a lively slave trade existed between Canaan and Egypt.)

37:29-36. This scene describes the effect of the brothers' convoluted conspiracies. Reuben (who was not with his brothers when they sold Joseph; see 42:22) returns to the pit to release Joseph (v. 22). He discovers to his grief (tearing his clothes) that he is gone. What can be done? His brothers are silent, displaying no knowledge or emotion; all of them simply get on with a ruse to convince Jacob of Joseph's death. Together, they dip Joseph's coat—so despised by them—in goat's blood and take it to their father (NRSV—they had it sent on ahead of them) for identification, following a legal process of substantiating

a death. Jacob recognizes it and imagines a story of Joseph's death uncannily similar to the one the brothers had planned (v. 20). He has been tricked just as he had tricked his father (27:9), though 42:36 suggests he may suspect them. Expecting a report from Joseph, Jacob receives a report about him. Hoping for a word of *shalom*, Jacob hears a word that destabilizes his life. The coat, given to confirm love, becomes a confirmation of death.

Jacob cries out for his son with deep intensity. With traditional signs of mourning, Jacob laments for many days; his children (daughters, i.e., Dinah and his daughters-in-law) are unable to comfort him. He will lament until the day of his death, when he will go down to Sheol—where Joseph already is (cf. 42:38). Sheol is the realm of the dead, a shadowy, silent existence (more than the NIV's "grave"). Perhaps Jacob thought his mourning would continue even beyond death. The brothers sought to displace Joseph in their father's affections, but ironically Joseph will retain a preeminent place in his father's love even in death. Will the promise go down to Sheol with him? As if to confirm Jacob's wishes, Jacob disappears from the narrative until 42:1.

The author concludes by noting that the Midianites sell Joseph to Potiphar, one of Pharaoh's officials (anticipating chap. 39). At least Joseph is alive. But his journey to become ruler has taken a detour through slavery; his status at this point mirrors Israel's later life in Egypt. The story will resume again in 39:1, where the Ishmaelites sell him to Potiphar, perhaps another reference to the ambiguity regarding Joseph's fate, noted above.

REFLECTIONS

1. The dual movement from Canaan to Egypt and from individual Israel to people Israel shapes the Joseph story. This episode sets into motion a concatenation of events that will come to a climax in the formation of a people and the exodus from Egypt, and finally conclude in the promised land, with the deposition of Joseph's bones (Josh 24:32). The narrative as a whole witnesses to a God who uses even the evil designs of people to bring about good, indeed leads to events constitutive of the very character of

Jacob's sons. Sinful behaviors do indeed frustrate the divine purposes in the world, but they do not, finally, stymie them.

2. Dreams in that world were usually understood to be externally and divinely generated (cf. Jer 23:25-26), not the result of an interior psychological process. Yet the brothers interpret Joseph's dreams as if they are the product of Joseph's own arrogance rather than a divine word about destiny. This ambiguity provides some of the tension in the narrative. Dreams also create tension by their "prophetic" character, as they move from announcement to realization (see 42:6; 43:26, 28; 44:16-17), yet without the brothers' realizing it! And not inevitably so, for example, since nowhere does *Jacob* "bow down" to Joseph (37:10). Moreover, the brothers *believe* that they can cut off the fulfillment by killing the dreamer, not least because (unlike a prophecy) Joseph himself remains integral to the plot depicted in the dream.

Eventually, Joseph denies the dreams' continuing applicability (see 50:19); the brothers are *not* to be his slaves, for he is not in the place of God. That role will be assumed by Pharaoh in the book of Exodus. Slavery cannot shape the relationship of Joseph to his brothers if they are to move toward reconciliation. Joseph takes the place of honor at the end of the story not least because he gives up on the dream. In so doing, Joseph demonstrates what it means truly to be a ruler.

The dreams do point to a future, but their import depends on the one who hears them and—always a second step—interprets them. One is reminded of the various responses to the visions of the prophets. For the brothers, Joseph's dreams are understood negatively; for Joseph, they are interpreted in a narrowly personal way; for Jacob, they become a matter for reflection. Jacob's response seems particularly admirable. He does not appear gullible, nor does he reject the dreams' potential import. He initially asks questions concerning the nature and implications of the dreams. But he takes these things and ponders them in his heart (see Luke 2:19), revealing an openness to future possibilities.

3. The narratives in Genesis have depicted the exclusion of various family members from the inner circle: Lot, Ishmael, the sons of Keturah, and Esau. On the basis of this chapter, the reader could think Joseph has joined the list. It is not to be so. The fact that the brothers are progenitors of the twelve tribes of Israel does cast their conflicted story in a different light. Eventually no one will be excluded; all twelve carry the promises into the future (50:24). These intrafamilial conflicts mirror exclusivistic efforts among the people of God in every age. This story finally witnesses to reconciliation among the brothers and the end of exclusion.

4. No individual in this story emerges innocent. Even Joseph, though certainly the primary victim, furnishes fuel for his own troubles. Everyone in his own way contributes to the mess in which the family finds itself; at the same time, to level out the sins of the characters and to make everyone equally irresponsible is to fail to consider issues of communal consequence. Or to turn God into an all-determining power undermines human responsibility for sin and encourages human passivity in the face of the power of evil.

5. Once again, the author tells this story without a single reference to God. The reader will learn (45:5) that God has not been absent from these activities. God works in and through even the worst that this family can perpetrate; in everything—even evil—God works for good. This relationship between human action and divine providence characterizes the entire narrative. The reader will be tempted to fall into one ditch or another in interpreting this dialectic: either divine determinism, where God fully controls events, or deism, where God must simply make do with whatever human action turns up and acts with no independent initiative. Neither of these options grasps the theological perspective that governs the story.

The absence of God language in this chapter commonly results in an emphasis on moral lessons, for example, related to parent/child relationships or intrafamilial disputes and deceptions. One must be careful not to draw easy moralisms, say, about parental favoritism—at most it is a lack of commonsense parenting! Favoritism per se does not constitute the problem; rather, the problem involves the way in which favoritism manifested itself publicly, on the part of both chooser and chosen. In some sense, the same problems arise for the electing God and Israel! Does the text mean to speak about problems in the way Israel dealt with its chosenness?

GENESIS 38:1-30, TAMAR AND JUDAH

COMMENTARY

Interpreters have devoted considerable attention in recent years to the human passions and literary tensions presented in this text. A source-critical approach (usually J) no longer seems sufficient. Despite its independent origins, this narrative plays an important role within its present literary context.[200] This is a family story, not tribal history, that has a "wonderful openness to what is human—passions, guilt, paternal anxiety, love, honor, chivalry, all churning up the narrow circle of one family in labyrinthine entanglement."[201]

The preceding narrative centers on the conflict between Joseph and his brothers, concluding with Joseph's being sold to Egypt (37:36). Chapter 38 proceeds as if that were the end of the story for Joseph, taking us into the continuing life of one of the other brothers, in this case Judah (cf. 37:26), who separates himself from the family. It covers some twenty years in his life, and then, in 39:1, the story of Joseph abruptly picks up at the point where it left off in 37:36.

What is accomplished by this break in the story? From a literary perspective, it slows the action of the story and creates suspense concerning Joseph's fate. Moreover, it shows that the story of Jacob's family continues alongside that of Joseph, especially important in view of Judah's later role. It also anticipates and helps to interpret certain features of the story to follow: (a) issues of sexuality (39:9-11); Judah's serving as a foil for Joseph; (b) the theme of recognition, where Joseph "hides" from his brothers for the sake of their future, not unlike what Tamar does with Judah; (c) the

theme of reversal, in view of which Joseph's return from a seemingly impossible situation parallels that of Tamar; and (d) the theme of deception, through the use of tangible evidence (37:32-33; 38:25-26).

At the same time, chap. 38 picks up many themes from the ancestral story: (1) Judah stands over against the tradition of marriage to Canaanites (24:3; 28:1; Joseph also marries outside the family). Although the Canaanites occupy an ambiguous place in Genesis, the line of promise carries on through Tamar, a Canaanite. The repeated reference to Judah's Canaanite "friend" (vv. 12, 20) may also provide a positive rather than a negative note. (2) As with Abraham and Isaac, the firstborn sons of neither Jacob nor Judah continue the line of promise leading to David. (3) Onan's refusal of responsibility toward Er mirrors the conflict between brothers. (4) The symbolic use of Tamar's clothing has parallels throughout Genesis, from Adam and Eve to various incidents in Joseph's life. (6) Other women, like Tamar, confront the problem of childlessness. (7) Other women—e.g., Rebekah, like Tamar—act over against established order, thereby furthering God's purposes. (8) The web of deception, not least those cases where the deceiver is himself deceived, continues.

This story also relates to the development of Jacob's older sons. Judah's older brothers have been sharply criticized up to this point (Reuben in 35:22; Simeon and Levi in 34:30). Judah, the fourth son, played a slave-dealer (37:26), and he here leaves the rest of the family. This raises a question comparable to chap. 37: Is Judah, too, being excluded from the line of promise? But he returns to

200. See Alter, *The Art of Biblical Narrative*, 3-12.
201. Von Rad, *Genesis*, 361.

become a risk-taker for the sake of the family (see 43:3-10; 44:18-34) and receives high praise in Jacob's blessing (49:8-12). The story of Joseph becomes, also, the story of Judah, both of whom receive equal prominence in Jacob's blessing (49:8-12, 22-26).

38:1-5. Judah settles near Bethlehem (the place names in the chapter are all in this vicinity) and marries an unnamed Canaanite woman; they have three children: Er, Onan, and Shelah. Early normality quickly devolves into dysfunctionality.

38:6-11. Tamar (probably a Canaanite) appears on the scene as the wife of Er. Because Er is a wicked man, God puts him to death (through unspecified means; see below). Judah then directs his second son, Onan, to "perform the duty of a brother-in-law to her" (though marriage is not mentioned, consummation probably entails it; cf. v. 14)—namely, to raise up an heir to carry on the name and inheritance of the deceased brother (cf. Deut 25:5-10; Ruth 4).

Onan sabotages the intent of the relationship in order to gain Er's inheritance for himself upon Judah's death—the firstborn would receive a double share. He regularly uses Tamar for sex, but makes sure she does not become pregnant by not letting his semen enter her (*coitus interruptus*, not masturbation). He thereby formally fulfills his duty, lest the role be passed on to his other brother and he lose Er's inheritance in this way. This willful deception would be observable to Tamar, but God's observation leads to Onan's death (again, by unspecified means).

Judah, having lost two sons and perhaps wondering whether Tamar were the problem, seeks to protect his own future by keeping his last son from her. He does so at Tamar's expense, directing her to return to her own father's house, where she would not have inheritance rights or be free to remarry. This act cuts her off from her husband's family and places her future welfare in jeopardy (cf. 30:1). Verse 26 shows v. 11 to be central; Judah deceives Tamar rather than risk his third son.

38:12-23. Tamar does as Judah says, but she does not settle for such an arrangement. When she realizes that Judah has withheld Shelah from her (v. 14*b* delays this notice), she takes the matter into her own hands and

assumes the duty of providing an heir for Er. Having no recourse to the courts, she will move beyond the law to fulfill the law, even at the cost of her honor and her life. As Judah will say (v. 26), Tamar's risk-taking on behalf of her husband exceeds his and proves her to be the righteous one in this situation.

The death of Judah's wife provides the opportunity for Tamar; he will be open to sexual diversion. Hearing of his trip to Timnah, Tamar makes plans to confront him. She dresses in such a way as to attract Judah's attention and situates herself on the way she knows he will take (see Jer 3:2). The narrator does not speak of her intentions. Although her dress and action could imply prostitution (the veil both invites and conceals), the narrator does not mention it. Judah so interprets the veil and propositions her (vv. 15-16). In v. 21, his friend speaks of her as a "temple prostitute," probably only more discreet language for a prostitute (with no official cultic reference). The townspeople deny having seen a prostitute, a matter stressed in the friend's report to Judah (v. 22). When it becomes evident that Tamar is pregnant, "friends and neighbors" of Judah (not the narrator) draw the inference regarding harlotry (v. 24).

Was Tamar playing the harlot? It depends on one's point of view. Judah and his friend understood her to be a prostitute, and Judah's not recognizing her seems startling (did she remain veiled? cf. 29:23-25). But she was not publicly so identified by the people of Enaim. While Judah's friends assume such upon hearing of her pregnancy, the narrator's perspective does not interpret her action as harlotry. Whatever her intentions and actions, she must not be *identified* as a prostitute. Tamar's putting her widow's garments off and on (vv. 14, 19) symbolizes continuity in identification as the widow of Er. Judah's failure to regain the signs of his identity signifies discontinuity. His identity becomes ambiguous; will he gain it back?

Before Tamar allows Judah to have his way with her, she exacts a price; Judah (apparently unprepared for such an eventuality) agrees on a young goat from the flock, but she wisely insists on a pledge. Judah naively agrees to what she suggests: his staff (specially marked) and his signet and cord (a seal, suspended on a neck cord, used to stamp one's "signature" in wet clay), signs of personal identification. Having completed the sexual act, each goes his or her way, with Tamar's identity intact and Judah's identity in the hands of Tamar. The immediate reference to conception establishes her intent in all of this. The narrative draws no moral conclusions about the behavior of either Judah or Tamar (cf. Lev 18:15).

When Judah seeks to fulfill the pledge, he discreetly sends his friend; but he can find no prostitute. Judah contents himself with the fact that he kept his pledge, and he does not risk having his male ego publicly bruised for being taken by a prostitute. He remains a man without identity.

38:24-26. When Tamar's pregnancy becomes evident, she is charged with harlotry. Upon hearing the news, Judah assumes the role of judge (she was under his authority, though with her family) and exacts the death penalty (cf. Lev 20:10; Deut 22:22). The irony is sharp: When Judah saw her as a prostitute (זונה *zônâ*, v. 15), he used her; when he sees her in this capacity as his daughter-in-law (זנה *zānâ*, v. 24), he condemns her. Clearly Judah applies a double standard.

Tamar, however, produces the pledge given her by Judah and sends the items on ahead (less embarrassing?). Judah responds magnanimously; his words and actions go beyond what would have been necessary. His guilt-admitting recognition that Tamar has been more righteous (צדקה *ṣādĕqâ!*) than he means that Tamar has done justice to *this* relationship in a way that he has not in failing to give her to his third son. Tamar and Judah do not speak face to face, and he does not touch her again, though he may have been entitled to (perhaps a reference to the reestablishment of her proper place in Judah's family). We are not informed whether she ever marries again.

38:27-30. The narrative concludes quickly, with the concern for which Tamar fought brought to fruition. Twins are born to Judah and Tamar in an abnormal birth, reminding the reader of the birth of Jacob and Esau (25:22-26). Again we encounter confusion about the firstborn; although Perez is actually born first, Zerah's arm had already come out, and so he is designated firstborn. Once again, the second born carries on the line of promise, for David (Ruth 4:18) and Jesus (Matt 1:3) descend from Perez.

REFLECTIONS

1. The direct statements that God put Er and Onan to death are unusual for the OT. Such divine actions at the individual level seem reserved for moments when the future of the people of God is at stake (see 1 Sam 2:25). The narrator may understand that here, particularly since the line leading to David is at risk. The narrator does not specify the means by which the brothers meet their death (e.g., sickness; cf. God's role in the death of Saul according to 1 Chr 10:14). These texts provide no basis upon which to draw general conclusions about death as God's will. Generally, God wills life, not death (see 45:5-7; Ezek 18:23, 32). Yet, the fact that God may work toward the death of certain persons ought not be ruled out. One thinks of the theological rationale given by some who plotted Hitler's death.

2. This text involves the continuation of the line of promise, which leads to David (see Ruth 4:18). We have noted links with the story of David (e.g., name similarity, such as Tamar in 2 Samuel 13) and with the Abrahamic promises regarding kings (17:6; 35:11). This line continues through the younger son of Tamar and Judah, Perez (Er drops from the genealogy, perhaps because he had never actually received the inheritance). Tamar is specifically mentioned in the genealogy of Jesus (Matt 1:3), along with three other women who engage in sexual activity of a questionable sort: Rahab, Ruth, and Bathsheba. These women contribute in a direct way to the birth of the Messiah. Such an explicit connection with the birth of Jesus affirms that this royal lineage does not somehow float above the maelstrom of life. This fact presents divine irony: God works in and through what appears weak and despised according to worldly standards in order to accomplish God's purposes (see 1 Cor 1:18-31). Tamar distinguishes herself more than does Jacob's own son toward this end.

3. This text lifts up issues of social responsibility and justice in an especially forceful way, with a focus on the plight of women. The text offers two primary perspectives. On the one hand, the ancient author recognized Tamar as one misused by a key authority figure in her life. In spite of her oppression, she possesses resources to find a way into a more hopeful future (see below). She subverts Judah's intentions and accomplishes a stunning reversal of authority. Tamar's resourcefulness occurs within the order of creation; God does not directly act.

On the other hand, the author presents Judah as one who misuses his authority and fails in both his familial and communal responsibilities. He chooses a self-serving route that places in jeopardy the future of both Tamar and the community to which they belong. The text thus speaks sharply about the use and abuse of power within the family and in the community of faith. But the text is not finally pessimistic regarding changes that can take place within individuals to transform such situations into good. Judah does change and acknowledges that the person he had abused is indeed the one who has been righteous. His experience with Tamar, leading to his public confession, may be decisive; when he risks his life for the sake of the family's future (43:9; 44:32), he follows Tamar's example.

4. Tamar's actions constitute a rebellion against established authority and custom and would normally be considered offensive; most religious people would condemn this act out of hand. But the word used for Tamar's act is *ṣādĕqâ* (v. 26). Her action cannot be universalized so as to be declared righteous wherever it is committed; at the same time, such action may be righteous in another time and place if it becomes the way of doing justice to a relationship. It may be necessary to go beyond the law in order to fulfill the law, which should enable life and well-being to a community (see Deut 6:24; Jesus' sabbath-breaking, Mark 2:27). Here the OT narrative gives especially high value to the future of the community, in view of which individual acts, which might be normally condemned, are viewed positively. Relationships are more important than rules; faithfulness may mean going beyond the law. We cannot help wondering whether this story has informed Jesus' saying that "the prostitutes are going into the kingdom of God ahead of you" (Matt 21:31 NRSV) as well as his open response to the woman who was a "sinner" (Luke 7:36-50).

We should not "secularize" this note about righteousness; in v. 10, God is explicitly involved in judgment regarding this matter. Hence, Tamar has been truer to her relationship with *God* than Judah has. Once again in the ancestral narrative, a person who stands outside of the community of promise proves to be faithful to what God intends for human community, indeed for the community of promise. In fact, she is a Canaanite! At least in part because of his evaluation of Tamar, Judah receives a praiseworthy place in the ancestral narrative (49:8), and his staff becomes a scepter that "shall not depart from Judah" (49:10).

GENESIS 39:1-23, JOSEPH, GOD, AND SUCCESS

COMMENTARY

Chapters 39–41 constitute a unified narrative, telling the story of the problems and successes associated with Joseph's rise to a high official in Pharaoh's court. Within this narrative, the author has divided chap. 39 into three scenes, the first two set in Potiphar's home. Verses 1-6 portray Joseph's initial advancement to a position of power, vv. 7-20, his fall associated with encounters with Potiphar's wife, and vv. 21-23, a new rise to prominence in prison.

This story bears some resemblance to the Egyptian *Tale of Two Brothers.* The course of each story is similar; similar phraseology occurs in both, including theological language (e.g., "the strength of a god was in him"; adultery as the "great sin"). Such stories and motifs were probably common in the ancient Near East.

39:1-6. Chapter 37 ended with the reader's being left in some suspense regarding Joseph's fate. Chapter 39 picks up the story at that point. Joseph has been sold by the Ishmaelites to an otherwise unknown Egyptian named Potiphar, an official of Pharaoh, in whose home Joseph takes up residence. Now, through chap. 41, we find no reference to Joseph's home and family. This absence intensifies Joseph's isolation and may explain the emphasis placed on God's presence with him.

When Potiphar observes how he prospers under Joseph's care, he appoints Joseph to a position of authority, entrusting him with the care of his entire household. The narrator interweaves what God has done (vv. 3, 5) with Joseph's rise to power (vv. 4, 6). By this repetition, the narrator stresses that this success has been made possible because of God's involvement. The only concern Potiphar has is eating; this reference hints subtly to a lack of interest in anything else, including his own wife. This could explain her sexual interest in Joseph, who was well built and handsome (v. 6a should not be split off from v. 6b).

39:7-20. This famous episode of Joseph and Potiphar's wife has often been interpreted as a morality tale, designed to specify limits regarding sexuality for persons of faith. A closer look reveals a more complex purpose. The text has also received attention because of the role of Potiphar's wife, the only woman given a role of consequence in the Joseph story. Although she remains unnamed throughout (Potiphar is named only in 37:36; 39:1 and, unlike his wife, never utters a word), she has much independence and freedom and exercises no little power in the confrontation with Joseph and her own husband. Both Potiphar and his wife are almost always defined in terms of their place in life (e.g., master's wife; captain of the guard; master).

The description of Joseph (words used for his mother in 29:17) leads immediately to a scene in which his master's wife—whose appearance the author does not describe—commands Joseph to go to bed with her: "Lie with me." Forgoing all preliminaries, she presents the matter in terms of power rather than love, of command rather than seduction; she is "his master's wife." But she misunderstands the power issues involved. Joseph resists her demands and responds to her in terms of authority (both human and divine; he begins with master and ends with God) rather than sexuality. He emphasizes that her husband has entrusted him with their household. This element of trust appears central, for his relationship with Potiphar—and perhaps his own life—depends on it (as his later reaction shows). But the text also presents an issue of the responsible exercise of his office; he and Potiphar are in effect equals with respect to authority in the household, hence he need not obey her command. At the same time, he has no rights to her. In fact, it appears that Potiphar has explicitly held his wife back from Joseph (v. 9).

Joseph's reply also specifies a "great wickedness" (or evil) against God, almost certainly a phrase designating adultery (cf. 20:9). The author has identified at least an implicit moral standard on this matter (cf. Deut 22:22), though not addressed in the abstract (nor in chap. 38). The focus: If he should commit this act with his master's wife, he would thereby sin against God. He remains true to God by remaining true to his master. He sees adultery as an irresponsible use of power and a violation of the trusting relationship he has both with Potiphar and with God.

The concern for Joseph's relationship with God appears striking, since the author has not mentioned it. Sin (or wrong, blame) elsewhere in the Joseph story refers to sins or offenses against others (40:1; 42:22; 43:9; cf. also 20:6, 9). From the perspective of Potiphar's wife, Joseph was guilty of an outrage or insult (NRSV; NIV, "making sport") not only against her but against "us," presumably the entire household (vv. 14, 17).

Potiphar's wife does not accept Joseph's reply—she continues to request sexual favors from him (v. 12). He persists in refusing her overtures; indeed, he stays away from her. But one day while he is going about his work alone, she encounters him, grabs his cloak, repeats her command, and retains the garment as he flees her grasp. She now finds herself in a position not unlike Tamar (38:25), except Joseph is the innocent one. She holds Joseph's garment as did his brothers (37:23, 31-32), using it in a deceitful way against him. She accuses him falsely, and she gets away with it (note the absence of retribution, a recognition of the loose causal weave in the moral order).

With Joseph's garment in her hand, and Joseph in her power, she immediately calls her servants together and fabricates a story involving an insult to all of them ("us") wherein Joseph is accused of doing what, in fact, she did. The reference to "a Hebrew" may play on their natural suspicion of foreigners (43:32). She also implicitly blames her husband for hiring him in the first place (vv. 14, 17), thereby raising the stakes. She, in turn, repeats the story in more subtle terms to her husband ("his master"), focusing on the insult to her ("me") and calling him *"your servant"* (vv. 17, 19). She cleverly makes it as much Potiphar's problem as Joseph's. If he hadn't hired Joseph, this would not have happened! This assures that Potiphar's response will be driven as much by guilt as by anger.

39:21-23. Potiphar becomes enraged by what he hears (probably for many reasons) and puts Joseph into prison—another pit (37:20)—without either facing him with the evidence or giving him an opportunity to reply to the accusation. Prison (especially the king's prison) was probably a lesser penalty than what was typical in such situations (Israelite law called for death, Lev 20:10; Deut 22:22). Joseph is an innocent victim, reduced to silence. Yet, in time he responds to the prison warden in a way similar to his response to Potiphar (vv. 4-6), with much the same effect (v. 22): The warden entrusts Joseph with responsibility for the warden's prison work (so the NIV; he did not do everything, so the NRSV). The narrator interprets what happens in theological terms; reports of God's enabling activity enclose the chapter (cf. vv. 2-6).

REFLECTIONS

1. These developments in the story are explicitly linked to the activity of God. Many references to God occur at the deepest point of Joseph's journey. Not since 35:1-15 have God's presence and action been so directly reported. Generally, reference to God occurs more often in the story than interpreters commonly recognize (some fifty times). Yet, the type of reference to God pushes in somewhat different directions, as will become evident.

The narrator provides eight of the nine references to God in this chapter, and they enclose the story (vv. 2-5, 21-23). They include the only occurrences of "Yahweh" (eight times) in the Joseph story, none spoken by a character. Unlike the immediately preceding chapters, the narrator thereby gives an explicitly theological interpretation to what occurs and links the story with key "God" texts later in the narrative (45:5-9; 50:20). Moreover, the use of *Yahweh* connects with usage in previous chapters, assuring continuity. More generally, it links up with Israel's subsequent history.

God works at multiple levels in these events—with both Joseph and Potiphar, and in such a way that the relationship between the two of them develops favorably. Moreover, God's work in and through Joseph leads to life and well-being for everything to which Joseph puts his hand, both human and nonhuman.

2. We focus on the nine references to God in this chapter (see vv. 2, 3, 5, 9, 21, 23). Four of these references specify that Yahweh was with Joseph. Even more, God remains present (1) outside the promised land, (2) in the life of one not of the line of promise, and (3) in everyday spheres of life, especially the political. Two passages occur at those points where Joseph's future appears uncertain. Although Joseph was without the support of his family (v. 2) and in prison (v. 21), the narrator assures the reader that Joseph has not been abandoned. Although all human supports have failed, and Joseph is far removed from the community of faith and the land of promise, God stays with him. God's presence, neither localized geographically nor dramatic or spectacular, is an unobtrusive, working-behind-the-scenes kind of presence.

In addition, God's presence with Joseph encompasses human abandonment and prison. Moreover, the text offers no evidence that such sin-generated events are the will of God for Joseph; sin is "against God" (v. 9); hence it is contrary to the divine will. God does not always get God's way in the world. Divine presence does not mean "preventive medicine" or a "quick fix" of whatever may befall a person of faith. There are implications here for how God works in the world: not in overwhelming power, but in and through the ambiguities and complexities of the relationships of integrity God has established.

The narrator thereby speaks not simply of divine presence but of the kind of God who acts in these events. Presence is one thing; the nature and effect of that presence are another. Verse 21 speaks of this God as one who shows steadfast love (חסד *ḥesed*); this word occurs elsewhere in the Joseph story only for human kindness and loyalty (40:14; 47:29). The author emphasizes here divine loyalty to the promise (see 32:10). God also works with Potiphar, so that Joseph finds favor in his eyes. Thus God appears active, not only within the lives of the family of promise, but also within those who do not confess the name of God.

Other references to God's presence are unusual: The Egyptian Potiphar recognizes that Yahweh is with Joseph and that Yahweh has prospered Joseph (vv. 3, 23). How should we explain an Egyptian's making this theological interpretation? It probably presupposes that Joseph's presence "in the house of his Egyptian master" entails theological conversation, or at least sufficient knowledge of Joseph to make the connection between his God and his words and deeds. This may also stand behind v. 21, which witnesses to a divine action within Potiphar—mediated through Joseph's presence at least—that enables him to view Joseph favorably. We should compare this response to those events in Exodus where God acts with Pharaoh and the Egyptians toward a comparable end (7:17; 8:10; 14:4); the Israelites gain favor at least in the eyes of the Egyptians, if not with the pharaoh (11:3; 12:36).

Two further references to Yahweh focus on the divine blessing brought on Potiphar's household and all that he has (v. 5). The author notes that God gives this blessing "because of Joseph" (as with Jacob, 30:27-30). This divine blessing goes beyond the blessings that come to all in and through the created order. Not simply God's presence but Joseph's presence as well makes a difference to the Egyptian situation. We hear this stated explicitly: *From the time that* Potiphar made Joseph an overseer, such blessings were forthcoming. Joseph's activity thus becomes a vehicle in and through which God works to bless in ways *that would not otherwise be effective in the same way.* In other words, Joseph's presence intensifies and enhances the general blessing work of

God. We may relate this understanding to 12:2-3 (and parallels): In and through the members of Abraham's family, blessing extends to those who are not the elect. What God's people say and do makes a difference regarding the welfare of others; God has chosen to depend on them in carrying out the divine work in the world. While God is not explicitly the subject of verbs conveying blessing to the Egyptians, the entire narrative presupposes that God works among them in and through the person and work of Joseph. Indeed, 41:53-57 makes it clear that this blessing extends to include the entire world!

Three references to Yahweh in this chapter involve God's making Joseph's way prosperous, successful (vv. 2-3, 23; cf. 1 Sam 18:14; 2 Kgs 18:7). Once again, this activity of God relates explicitly to what *Joseph does*. Who Joseph is and the way in which Joseph speaks and acts have a positive effect.

The narrative portrays the impact of Joseph's behavior in a number of ways. For example, the narrator does not neglect the effective methods Joseph uses to bring about well-being (e.g., 41:46-49). Joseph works as an efficient, diligent, and competent administrator, which enables God to work more effectively through him. Moreover, the narrator delves into Joseph's character; he is loyal, patient under stress, and filled with wisdom (his loyalty mirrors God's, v. 21). The trust that Potiphar places in him (v. 6), as well as the incident with Potiphar's wife, are probably intended to speak directly to this point. The author provides the reader a clue to this end with the reference to God in v. 9, the only time a human character utters the word *God.* Joseph does justice to relationships, both with human beings and with God—and both are important in their own right. Joseph does not succumb to the very real temptations of power and sex. His actions have considerable effect on how God works in and through him. Who Joseph is and what Joseph does make a difference to God's work in the world. In turn, God's work in Joseph enables him to mature and develop in ways that would not otherwise be possible.

3. Success and prosperity are not a necessary or inevitable result of either God's presence or Joseph's faith or action. Joseph appears genuinely vulnerable and could have failed even with God's presence and the divine intention for success. Joseph's success depends not simply on his own devices, but on God's engagement in the situation.

4. Interpreters have often pointed to thematic parallels with the story of the rise of David (1 Sam 16:18; 18:12, 14, 28). This comparison suggests a particular interest in associating the presence of God with the political sphere. God accompanies this family as it moves out of the domain of the domestic into the broader sphere of national and political life. God works in every aspect of life.

5. Once again a story in Genesis mirrors a later experience of the people of God or an individual Israelite: Israel from Egypt to the kingship of David and Solomon; David from shepherd boy to king. Also parallel are the theological themes of divine presence and blessing. Different, however, is the basically positive assessment of those who stand outside the community of faith, something typical of Genesis. The incident with Potiphar's wife indicates the potential for the misuse of power by those in high positions. Yet, in Genesis, the author views political power, both when Joseph is in power and when he is not, much more positively. Rather than mirroring later Israel, this aspect of the story provides rulers with an ideal toward which to strive. The Joseph figure—particularly as mediated through David—provides images for the development of messianic themes.

GENESIS 40:1-23, JOSEPH, INTERPRETER OF DREAMS

COMMENTARY

This unified episode fits as an integral part of chaps. 39–41. Set in an Egyptian prison, its very inhospitableness provides the context for an important advance in Joseph's return to a position of power in Egypt. Joseph's ability to interpret the dreams of two court officials focuses this development. While Joseph's own dreams have resulted in his slavery, the dreams of others now become the means for his release from slavery.

40:1-8. The occasion commences with an encounter between Joseph and two recently disemployed, unnamed members of Pharaoh's "kitchen" staff: the chief cupbearer and the chief baker. These were important positions in Egypt; the former personally served wine to the pharaoh. Having committed unnamed offenses against Pharaoh (if poisoning, both could be under suspicion), they are detained in the captain of the guard's house where Joseph has been placed in charge of prisoners. Since they are in detention, their futures have not yet been determined (because they still have their status, Joseph serves them as he did Potiphar, 39:4). Joseph is obviously aware of their situation, which shapes his interpretation of their dreams.

After some time, these servants of Pharaoh have dreams on the same night; they are troubled, probably because they relate the dreams to their uncertain fate. Joseph, here the alert caregiver, asks about their dejection. They report having had dreams, but in prison no interpreters are available (v. 8, פתר *pōtēr*, used only in the Joseph story). Joseph replies that interpretations belong to God (interestingly, he does not say the dreams themselves do)—i.e., God gives the gift of dream interpretation (note TNK translation, "Surely God can interpret!"). Without skipping a beat, Joseph urges them to tell him the dreams. In effect he says: I have the gift of divine interpretation (cf. 41:16). Joseph thereby brings a public witness to God to bear on the situation. God works in and through the dreams

of the nonchosen (so also in chap. 41) to develop the future of the chosen.

40:9-19. Joseph proceeds to interpret the dreams (vv. 12, 18). Once again, as in chap. 37, there are two dreams. They are integrally related to the profession of each dreamer. Elements common to both dreams include the number three, food/drink for Pharaoh in a container, and the hand/head body reference. One key difference is that the cupbearer acts in his dream, while the baker does not (though birds do). Another difference is that Pharaoh is served in the first dream, but not in the second. Commonalities in Joseph's interpretations are the use of "three days" to represent a short time and the expression "lift up your head," though in different senses. "Lift up [not off] the head" in v. 13 is a metaphor for freedom from blame; in v. 19 it is literal, to be hanged; in v. 20 it does double duty. This play on words may relate to audiences before Pharaoh, wherein he lifted the bowed head of one seeking royal amnesty.

These dreams provide mixtures of allegorical elements and literal descriptions of what will happen. Allegorical elements in the interpretations include the three branches/baskets (i.e., three days), the instant blossoming and ripening (i.e., soon, the compression of time), and the baked goods (i.e., flesh of the baker). These dreams require an interpreter more so than those of chap. 37; this will be even more the case in chap. 41.

The chief cupbearer tells his dream to Joseph first (vv. 9-15). In it, a vine with three branches, upon budding, immediately puts forth blossoms, and its clusters ripen into grapes. He presses the grapes into Pharaoh's cup and gives it to Pharaoh. Joseph's interpretation is that in three days the cupbearer will be restored to his office and will give Pharaoh his cup as usual.

Joseph uses the interpretive moment to ask the cupbearer to show kindness (חסד *ḥesed*)—hence to act as God does in 39:21—and to intercede for Joseph's release before

Pharaoh. He has been deprived of his rights wrongfully (kidnapping probably refers to the Midianites in 37:28, but may be a general description) and has done nothing to deserve his imprisonment. He thereby anticipates the laments of his people in Egypt.

The chief baker then takes his turn (vv. 16-19), ironically, as it turns out, after the initial favorable interpretation. In his dream, three baskets of baked goods are on his head, and birds are eating from the topmost one. Joseph's interpretation is that in three days Pharaoh will have him hanged (the NRSV's "from you!" captures the point) and will leave him hanging on the tree for the birds to pick clean. Joseph does not ask the baker to remember him to the pharaoh, for obvious reasons!

40:20-23. These verses report what happens after three days. The dreams are realized as Joseph had interpreted them, on a public occasion, Pharaoh's own birthday, when such decisions were regularly announced. Each man has his head lifted, but in quite different ways; for one it means death, for the other life (these are important themes for the story as a whole).

The cupbearer does not remember Joseph, so he remains forgotten in prison; it will take two more years (41:1) for human memory to be jogged. For now, Joseph's future remains uncertain. Joseph's journey from slavery to freedom is filled with frustration and disappointment (it will take thirteen years in all, 41:46).

REFLECTIONS

1. Verse 8 contains the only reference to God in the chapter. Joseph seems to claim that only God can interpret dreams, and then proceeds to have the dreams told to him in order to interpret them. One should read this verse within the context of other references to God in 41:16, 25, 28, and 38-39.

The text suggests that dream specialists are not needed; God does such business: "It is not I [I cannot do it]; God will give Pharaoh a favorable answer" (41:16). Yet, Joseph repeatedly interprets dreams—without explicit reference to any divine inspiration: "This is its interpretation" (40:12, 18). Moreover, others publicly recognize him as an interpreter (41:12-13).

Another perspective draws on Joseph's knowledge of royal protocol. Such statements as Joseph's are polite disclaimers, devices "for detaching the interpretation from the interpreter; the interpreter bears no responsibility but merely announces what is to come. Joseph in each episode shows himself a sure master of the complexities of court protocol."[202] Such political realities would mean that we must be extraordinarily careful so as not to overdraw the theological import of v. 8.

It would seem best to see Pharaoh's statement in 41:38-39 as ironically putting this data together in an appropriate way: "God has shown you all this, there is no one so discerning and wise as you." Both human and divine agents are recognized. The initiative and the "showing" come from God, but human wisdom and discernment remain necessary. Joseph's gifts are not irrelevant (as if any person would do). His abilities come into play and are *used* by God in the interpretive process. Note Joseph's knowledge regarding the royal context, his discernment of the officials' situation, and his skill at word play.

Joseph is thus engaged at two levels: He receives divine inspiration, and his own gifts of discernment come into play in the interpretation. Yet, Joseph does not boast in his own abilities; he diminishes himself and gives the glory to the God who works in and through him, without whom the appropriate interpretation would not be possible. Comparable language in our own time would be the naming of a sermon as the proclamation of the word of God.

202. Humphreys, *Joseph and His Family*, 143.

In addition, we find no evidence of polemic in this chapter, as if dream specialists are being put down, or that only God's people can interpret dreams. Moreover, not all dreams come from God (see Deut 13:1-5; Jer 23:16-17; cf. Eccles 5:7), though in such cases God may choose to enter into the interpretive process. These dreams are so straightforward that special inspiration for their interpretation seems unnecessary for astute persons such as Joseph.

2. The "prophetic" dreams come to pass as Joseph had interpreted them. Unlike modern interpretations, in the OT (and the ancient Near East generally) dreams relate more to the future than the past or present. But would the dreams have been realized apart from Joseph's interpretation? As for the future of the two officials, is what Joseph says finally irrelevant (except in a "pastoral" function, to reduce or intensify anxiety)? Does not the interpretation in some sense activate the dream (cf. the prophetic word)? Might it have some effect on the shape of the realization? Even more, might not subsequent events also shape the nature of the realization? One thinks of the interpretations of the brothers and the father in chap. 37, where Joseph's second dream remains unfulfilled. The narrator finally appears to be interested, however, not in the dreams as such, but in Joseph's interpretive abilities because of the reputation that accrues to him as a consequence (see also 37:5-11).

3. We hear, for the first time, Joseph speaking openly about his own life—for the first time in the narrative (42:21 recalls an earlier moment) he becomes aggressive regarding his situation. Although Joseph has the God-given ability to interpret dreams, he still needs *human* help. The one inspired by God pleads with a fellow prisoner for help. He asks to be remembered by another—as God remembers Noah (8:1), Abraham (19:29), Rachel (30:22), and the people of Israel (also in bondage in Egypt [Exod 2:24; 6:5]). But to be in need of human help also involves being open to human frailties. The one upon whom Joseph depends will forget Joseph (cf. Exod 1:8), but not forever (see 41:9). Human help will finally be a key to Joseph's future, as it will be for virtually everybody.

Joseph's lament anticipates those of his descendants in Egypt, who also are "brought out of the house" of bondage (see Exod 13:14; 20:2). With Joseph, as with the people of Israel, the lament plays an important role in the development of the deliverance (note the integral relationship between lament and divine remembrance in Exod 2:23-25; 6:5). Such language would also recall psalms of lament (and thanksgiving), which often use the word *pit* to refer to the depths of despair (Pss 28:1; 30:3, 9; 35:7; 40:2; 88:4, 6).

GENESIS 41:1-57, JOSEPH'S ELEVATION TO POWER

COMMENTARY

The scene changes from Pharaoh's prison to Pharaoh's palace, mirroring Joseph's rise from weakness to strength. The dreams continue; this time Pharaoh himself has two dreams (vv. 1-7), which enable Joseph's dream to come full circle. After the cupbearer remembers him (vv. 8-13), Joseph is called forth from prison to interpret the dreams and to give advice based on them (vv. 14-36). As a result, Pharaoh elevates Joseph to prime minister (vv. 37-46), in which capacity he proves to be an effective administrator of Egypt's economy (vv. 47-57).

This episode contains a storyline common to many cultures: elevation of a person from low to high status because he or she solves a problem. This chapter has long been considered a composite, but the occasional roughness of expression may be ascribed to its history of transmission. The chapter is a literary unity, thoroughly integrated into the larger segment of chaps. 39–41 (cf. vv. 9-13).

41:1-7. After a note indicating that Joseph has languished in prison for two more years, these verses describe Pharaoh's two dreams. In the first, the setting is the Nile, Egypt's lifeline. Seven sleek and fat cows come out of the Nile and begin to graze; then seven ugly and gaunt cows appear and eat the fat ones. In the second, seven plump and good ears of grain grow on one stalk; then seven ears of grain, thin and scorched by the hot desert wind, sprout on that stalk and devour the healthy ones. Although the second is somewhat shorter, the dreams mirror each other; this becomes an important point in Joseph's interpretation (vv. 25-26, 32). Pharaoh retells the dreams to Joseph in vv. 17-24, with some variations. This same theme, the weak prevailing over the strong, characterized Joseph's own dreams.

41:8-13. Pharaoh is deeply disturbed by his dreams because their bizarre nature may portend a troubled future, an intrusion that he can neither interpret nor control. Such a God-generated intrusion provides the opening that Joseph needs. Pharaoh calls in specialists to sort out their meaning, but none can interpret them to his satisfaction. They are now in over their heads. Although they are decisively bested by Joseph, the story makes little of their failure (unlike Exodus 7–8 or Daniel 1–2).

These events trigger the cupbearer's memory, and he recalls his experience with Joseph (cf. 40:14), both his interpretation and its accuracy. Quite remarkably, he even uses the language of sin (as in 39:9; 40:1) to describe his forgetfulness. This human act changes the future for all concerned.

41:14-36. Pharaoh hurriedly brings Joseph from the "pit" (signaling the end of his journey from the pit in 37:20-29). His shaving and fresh clothing symbolize the change in his circumstance. Pharaoh reports to Joseph what has been said about him; Pharaoh's expectations are high.

Joseph's reply in v. 16 has a number of dimensions: Pharaoh's dreams come from God (cf. vv. 25, 28); he will receive an answer about their meaning, which will

effect שׁלום (*šālôm*) for him (NIV "desired"; NRSV "favorable"). Joseph has not yet heard the dream! *Shalom* thus relates to Pharaoh's troubled spirit, that Pharaoh would be satisfied with Joseph's interpretation because it comes from God. Joseph, not having heard the dream, acts in a straightforward manner here; in effect he puts God on notice that an interpretation will be needed. At stake are the reputations of both Joseph and God.

Pharaoh tells the dream to Joseph (vv. 17-24). The retelling basically matches the first report. Yet, the differences are important; they are in the first person, they anticipate that the meaning is negative, and they reveal Pharaoh's deep concern: exaggeration (the scrawny cows are unprecedented in their ugliness, and the thin ears of grain are even more withered) and additional bizarre information (the eating did not change the ugly cows' appearance). The dreams contain both literal and allegorical elements, though the latter predominate here. The number seven (four times) refers to years, with the healthy cows/grain referring to years of plenty and the sickly ones years of grievous famine. The famine will so consume the land that the years of plenty will be forgotten (vv. 30-31).

The heart of Joseph's interpretation takes the form of announcements about the future (vv. 29-32), though he does not construe them as divine judgment. He gives a fuller theological explanation than that given in chap. 40, followed by a clear recommendation as to what Pharaoh ought to do about the situation the dreams portend (vv. 33-36).

The theological explanations that punctuate this section (vv. 25, 28, 32) accomplish three things: (1) They emphasize that God reveals this meaning; in other words, this is serious business; (2) they indicate that God speaks through Joseph; and (3) they provide a structure for the section.

The enclosing verses (25, 32) stress the dreams' identical meaning and significance. Verses 26-27 focus on the number seven, vv. 29-31 on the sequence of the events; the author introduces each by a statement that God has revealed to Pharaoh what will happen. The interpretation centers on the years of famine, the better to impress upon Pharaoh the need to take action.

Joseph offers more than just an interpretation. Without waiting for Pharaoh's response and using bold speech, yet cognizant of his status (note the repeated "let," stressing Pharaoh's decision), Joseph puts forward a plan whereby these events can effectively be addressed, preventing much damage to the country (vv. 33-36). Pharaoh should not resign himself to the disaster, as if all the famine's effects were a matter of fate. Pharaoh has the freedom to make decisions, though within a context provided by God's decision. Joseph believes that he can persuade Pharaoh to develop a plan of action so that Egypt will be able to endure the famine in a way that brings the greatest possible well-being to all.

Joseph proposes that a wise and discerning person be appointed (used for an obedient Israel in Deut 4:6 and for Solomon in 1 Kgs 3:12). He carefully articulates the plan in the hopes that he himself will be chosen, not some local expert. Other astute overseers should also be appointed to manage the economic policy. He proposes that enough food—20 percent of the crop each year (i.e., the "all" of v. 35)—be stored during the years of plenty to provide a reserve for the years of famine. Everything will be under "the authority of Pharaoh." (A historical note: Egypt was renowned in that part of the world for its granaries.)

41:37-46. Joseph emphasizes throughout that God has revealed the meaning of the dream to *Pharaoh* (vv. 16, 25, 28). Joseph thereby identifies a direct relationship between Pharaoh and God. This emphasis, along with Joseph's candor and bold speech, as well as his concern for *national* well-being (rather than himself), convinces Pharaoh. While he gives all the "credits" to God, Joseph obviously mediates the divine revelation.

Pharaoh astutely puts these matters together; we ought not discount his theological insightfulness. He recognizes that God has revealed these things to *Joseph* (v. 39); hence he must be the one in whom the Spirit of God rests (v. 38). Pharaoh addresses his question to the court (v. 38), thus drawing them into accepting his conclusion.

Hence, Pharaoh chooses Joseph as the "discerning and wise" person Joseph himself had suggested and had modeled through his speech. Pharaoh makes Joseph the prime minister, in charge of both the palace (v. 40) and the country (vv. 41, 43), second in command only to Pharaoh, with wide-ranging authority. Verse 44 specifies the unlimited character of his command, against which no one shall lift up hand or foot—namely, rebel. Once again, the author portrays Pharaoh as a wise and discerning person in his own right due to his elevation and empowerment of Joseph.

Verses 41-44 describe an act of installation. Pharaoh opens and closes with a formal statement of Joseph's authority (v. 41, 44; cf. Jer 1:10) and gives him the symbols of his new office: his signet ring (with Pharaoh's own "signature," cf. 38:18), a royal garment, and a gold chain. His clothing may mirror the cloak given him by his father. He rides in a royal chariot throughout the city, before which Egyptian heralds call to the crowds to acclaim him: "Bend the knee" (or "Attention"). At some point later, he travels through the entire land so that people can recognize him in his new position (v. 46*b;* cf. 13:17). Through all this, Joseph remains silent; only in the naming of his sons will he reveal his reaction.

Pharaoh gives Joseph an Egyptian name to signal his new status, Zaphenath-paneah (i.e., God speaks and lives), and provides him a wife from the nobility, Asenath (i.e., she who belongs to the goddess Neith). She is the daughter of Potiphera (i.e., the one whom Re gave; probably identical in meaning to Potiphar), priest of On (i.e., Heliopolis), a prominent center for worship of the sun god Re.

A historical note: There is some evidence that slaves from the ancient Near East achieved positions of high standing in Egyptian royal circles. The rite of installation also has parallels in that world, and rings, chains, and chariots that were used on such occasions have been found. Finally, famines were not uncommon; a seven-year famine occurs as a literary convention in Israel (2 Sam 24:13), in Egypt, and in Mesopotamia.[203]

41:47-57. Joseph is thirty years old when these events occur, thirteen years after his enslavement (37:2-3). As prime minister, he carries out the economic program needed to prevent the disaster that Pharaoh's dreams portend. During the seven years of

203. See Sarna, *Genesis*, 290.

plenty—more than could actually be measured—he stores up food in all the cities. The image of the sand of the sea continues the blessing of the family of Abraham (22:17).

Verses 50-52 are not intrusive; the fruitfulness of Joseph and Asenath mirrors the fruitfulness of the land. They have two sons, Ephraim and Manasseh. Joseph names them in recognition of God's involvement in this massive change in his life: Manasseh, because God has enabled Joseph's slavery in Canaan and Egypt to be forgotten; Ephraim, because God has prospered Joseph in the very land in which he has experienced so much misfortune. These names reveal Joseph's life experience: God's preserving and prospering activity in the very midst of great personal hardship. External appearances provide no clear barometer of the depth and breadth of God's blessings. This family reference also anticipates the chapters to come.

When the years of famine come, it affects every country, not just Egypt. But only Egypt has grain. The success of Joseph redounds to his reputation. When Egyptians cry out for bread due to the famine's severity, they can get relief from Joseph (note that they buy grain; it is not given away). In fact, Joseph's wisdom enables Egypt to become the bread basket for "all the world" (vv. 54, 56, 57).

REFLECTIONS

1. The Spirit of God rests on Joseph (v. 36). Some have suggested that Joseph was a charismatic personality and should be understood from within the prophetic tradition. One may also appeal to the relationship between God and wise kings like Solomon (see 1 Kings 3–4). Generally, Joseph's empowerment should be understood in terms of Exod 31:3; 35:31 (cf. Dan 5:14), which connect particular *gifts suitable for the task at hand* with the presence of the divine spirit. These texts recognize God-given talents rather than a pouring out of the Spirit for the occasion, a way in which the people of God might well speak of the work of the Spirit of God in every age. Joseph's portrayal has no single antecedent tradition.

2. The realities of dreams and their interpretation issue in a complex configuration of divine, human, and nonhuman agency (see chap. 40). God sets the context, but does not override human discernment, care, and planning. Humans channel the divine blessings to their most effective ends. Dreams and their God-given interpretation do not necessarily shape the future in detail. Creaturely response also shapes the future. Natural disasters (the famine) do not have predetermined effects; wise human planning can ameliorate their negative impact.

3. Policies are to be developed "so that the land may not perish through the famine" (v. 36). The dreams do not determine the future *in every respect*. God has firmly established the future to which the dreams point, and God will act soon (v. 32). At the same time, the full future that the dreams open up depends on more than God's becoming involved. The economic policies adopted during the years of plenty mean that the land will not be consumed, the dreams will not have their fullest possible negative effects.

Inasmuch as famine results from the failure of the Nile's waters to overflow, and the Nile is a pharaonic symbol of fertility, the story calls into question the very future of the pharaoh. The future does not lie within his control; he appears subject to a future that comes from God. Since Pharaoh listens to Joseph, however, and takes appropriate action, he helps to shape his future. Although his choices are limited, he exercises power, and his elevation of Joseph reveals considerable insight.

4. The story reflects the various ways in which God can work in and through people. God works outside the religious sphere, in economics and government. Moreover, Joseph was not the obvious choice, but was raised up from the lowest rungs to lead a people from the highest levels of authority. Joseph becomes part of a hierarchical structure of power (see chap. 47). With the proper leadership, such structures of authority need not be oppressive.

The problems presented by this chapter have been faced by virtually every generation in every country. The issues have to do with agriculture and related industries, with the difficulties of feeding people when crops are not produced in sufficient amounts. It also presents issues of the management of an economy. God's work in the world through wise leaders affects every sphere of life.

5. God's work of blessing in this chapter includes the entire human race, not just the chosen ones. God works in Pharaoh's life in ways Pharaoh does not know, even communicating in and through a dream. This experience testifies to significant levels of divine activity in human lives outside the community of faith. At the same time, the chosen have the God-given mandate and capacity to enhance God's blessings in such a way that enables them to become more than they would be without human participation.

Moreover, Joseph's *work of interpretation,* his wisdom and discernment, provides an entry point into the life of Pharaoh. Deuteronomy 4:6 uses this same language to speak about Israel; other people will see their obedience and say: Surely this great nation is a wise and discerning people. This work of interpretation—not simply of dreams—has the potential to draw outsiders into conversation regarding God and God's ways in the world, and can, as with Pharaoh, actually lead to their public witness regarding God's involvement in their lives. Indeed, Pharaoh becomes a theologian of no little consequence when he interprets these events (vv. 38-39).

6. Joseph does not boast about what he has done or will do: "It is not I, but God." He speaks of God as the one without whom interpretation would be impossible; God has given him the ability to interpret dreams (cf. 40:8). God enables Joseph to play the critical role (v. 16). Joseph links the chosen people with the unchosen people to bring blessing on the latter.

Precisely because of his disclaimers, Joseph appears as an ideal figure: patient through numerous setbacks and deep suffering; loyal to God, honoring of human relationships in the midst of severe trials and temptations. His bold speech, especially in the presence of persons and systems of power, reveals courage and integrity. He acts wisely and in a discerning manner in all of his dealings with people and their problems. Joseph stands as a model for the godly life, but moving far beyond the religious sphere; it is a life lived in the midst of the full range of human problems and the complexities of human existence.

7. In Joseph's naming of his children, the themes of forgetfulness and fruitfulness are highlighted; God has enabled both. What an incredible gift: God enables one to forget, to put the past behind, to move beyond dwelling on misfortunes and get on with the ever-new gifts that God brings. Joseph's confession should guide the reader's interpretation of the way in which he works with his brothers in the following chapters.

As for fruitfulness, *Egypt* becomes the context for this blessing, anticipating Exod 1:7 and the growth of Israel in that same land. Joseph's life anticipates Israel's. Blessing comes in the midst of affliction (ענה *'ānâ,* used for Israel's oppression in Egypt, Gen 15:13; Exod 3:7). These acts of naming could be profitably compared with the naming of Joseph and his brothers in 29:31–30:24, where the mothers do the naming, in view of their life experience and to praise God. Joseph's naming of his sons testifies to the continuing link between tradition and personal life experience and the importance of their interaction.

8. Both Joseph and his brother Judah (see chap. 38) marry women outside the family and its religious heritage. Later legends speak of Asenath's conversion, but Genesis has no interest in this. The text attests to a remarkable capacity for the integration of Yahwistic faith and other religious communities and expressions (similarly 2 Kgs 5:15-19). Many OT texts do not tolerate such practices, but the reasons are contextual rather than normative (e.g., dangers of syncretism). Joseph functions as an ideal for Israel at this point, demonstrating that the later intolerance is *not characteristic of the Yahwistic faith in and of itself.* Joseph illustrates that such integration can be a positive experience and need not carry negative effects.

GENESIS 42:1-38, JOSEPH MEETS HIS BROTHERS

COMMENTARY

Chapters 39–41, focused on Joseph in Egypt, are now balanced by chaps. 42–44, which center on a new relationship for Joseph and his family. The former developments make the latter possible. The two journeys of the brothers to Egypt mirror the doubling of the dreams in the previous chapters.

This chapter may be a composite of J and E, but works now as a unified whole. Linked with chaps. 37 and 39–41, bringing those different scenes and people together, it also reverses the situation of chap. 37; Joseph now has the power, and the brothers are at the mercy of his decisions. The text now addresses Joseph's use of that power. While some scholars have a basically negative view of Joseph's use of authority, we side with those who take a more positive view.

The scene in this chapter shifts back and forth between Egypt and Canaan, between palace and local village. The reader encounters Jacob and Joseph's brothers (except for Judah) for the first time since chap. 37. Famine has affected Canaan, too. Egypt has grain, however, and this means a trip to procure it (vv. 1-5; cf. 12:10-20). The stage is now set for Joseph and his brothers to encounter one another again, described in vv. 6-24. Verses 25-38 portray the brothers' return to Canaan and the associated difficulties occasioned by Joseph's testing of their integrity.

42:1-5. Verse 1 brings the reader into the middle of a conversation—something of a to-do in the family of Jacob. It is the same old story, but unbeknownst to them, a massive change is in the offing. The famine in Canaan has created a problem, and the brothers are reduced to "looking at one another," waiting for a solution. Jacob, a stabilizing influence in this scene, reports that Egypt has grain, telling his sons to journey there and purchase some. Unknowingly and ironically, he tells them to go to Joseph just as he once sent Joseph to them (37:13-14). Only ten of Joseph's brothers go to Egypt; Jacob holds Benjamin back for fear of his life. As the one remaining son of his beloved Rachel, Benjamin is now the favorite; Jacob will not repeat the mistake he made with Joseph. This decision sets up a key development in the story. The end of the chapter will return to his concern about Benjamin.

The life-and-death matter presented here is a theme struck by Jacob himself in v. 2, and it reappears at important points in the subsequent narrative (vv. 18, 20; 43:8; 45:5-7). Jacob articulates thereby a key objective for the entire story, one that will be picked up by Joseph and even by the brothers.

Verse 5 seems to be set already in Egypt. It blends the brothers into a crowd of peoples who have made the journey for the same purpose, picking up on the theme of 41:57. The phrase "sons of Israel" (cf. 46:5, 8) appears purposely ambiguous; it refers to Jacob, but also anticipates the Israel of the exodus. The journeys in and out of Egypt mirror later developments.

42:6-24. These verses describe the first of four dialogues between Joseph and his brothers (cf. 43:27-31; 44:15–45:13; 50:15-21), a scenario not unlike the encounter between Jacob and Esau, only here the recognition is not mutual. In vv. 8-9*a* the narrator provides a key comment to make sure the reader understands who recognizes whom and that Joseph recalls his earlier dream just before the interrogation begins.

Verse 6 immediately brings the brothers into the presence of the highest official in Egypt, upon whom they now depend. The fact that they bow down before Joseph fulfills the dream in 37:7, reinforced by the brothers' repeated use of lord/servant language (vv. 10, 11, 13, 30, 33). Verse 9*a* shows that Joseph recognizes this; his dream has now come full circle. This recognition now propels the story over the next chapters. The brothers' lack of recognition enables Joseph to manipulate the situation toward the objective he chooses.

What will Joseph do in view of his recollection of the dream? *Now that the dream has been realized,* and in view of 41:51, he begins to move toward healing the breach. But this becomes a complex task. He cannot simply speak to them, for he may not discern equivocation (cf. God's test of Abraham). He must set up situations that will enable him to observe them without their realizing it and to bring their common story to the surface so that it can be dealt with properly. Again and again, these situations will mirror their treatment of him, forcing the issue into the front of their consciousness.

Joseph decides to treat them as if they were strangers, thus creating an artificial relationship. He speaks in an abrupt, officious manner, refusing to take them at their word. He questions them sharply, repeatedly accusing them of spying (historically, an Egyptian concern; the "nakedness of the land" refers to exposed borders), ironically exposing *their* defenselessness. The tables have been turned on the brothers; they experience what Joseph did in chap. 37, including the possibility of being assigned to a comparable fate. The accusation achieves its purpose; it draws out information about the family, including Benjamin, and, when combined with Joseph's shifting strategies regarding their future, it leads the brothers into confessional/theological reflection.

The brothers refuse to accept the evaluation and proceed with a defense born of surprise and fear, revealing more than they need to. They repeatedly insist on two things: (1) They are a family ("sons of one man"). This

makes sense as a defense; it would be unusual for an espionage group to place in jeopardy so many from the same family. Ironically, the brothers appeal to family solidarity, so sharply violated in their treatment of Joseph. In this concern they unwittingly join forces with Joseph. (2) They are "honest people," men of integrity. This note recurs (vv. 11, 19, 31, 33, 34)—are the brothers honest or not? This claim recalls that their dealings with Joseph and their father were marked by a lack of integrity. Joseph needs to test this point: "whether there is truth in you" (vv. 16, 20). Joseph sharply continues his accusation and sets up a test. No doubt noting their equivocation regarding his fate ("one is no more"), he picks up on their unnecessary reference to Benjamin. This may have given him a clue that not all was right with his family. If Benjamin had simply displaced him in Jacob's affection, then the problem between father and brothers (see v. 36) had only been papered over. Benjamin thus becomes a passive vehicle for getting this issue out in the open.[204] One brother is to return for him, while the rest remain in prison. Joseph's repeated use of the oath "as Pharaoh lives" mirrors Israel's use of God or kings in their oaths (cf. 1 Sam 17:55; 2 Sam 15:21), and to rhetorical effect. Together with talk about life and death, it emphasizes the seriousness of the conversation. Joseph then has all of them peremptorily taken into custody (v. 17; cf. 40:4). This arbitrary act gives them a taste of the "pit" experience they put Joseph through and helps to prompt their memory (vv. 21-22).

After three days, Joseph approaches them with a less onerous plan, allowing all but one of them to leave. This extends the test: Will the brothers sacrifice one more brother? This plan mirrors still another dimension of his own experience. Yet, in this plan Joseph gives them an experience of graciousness. This combination of judgment and graciousness elicits their confession (vv. 21-22). Joseph's comments this time are positive in tone; he expresses interest in life for them and their family (vv. 18-19), though death still lingers in the air (v. 20). His rationale for these positive directions touches base with their own tradition: "for I fear God" (see 20:11), and

204. See White, *Narration and Discourse,* 260-61.

stands in ironic contrast to their lack of concern for life.

The brothers agree to the plan (are they sincere?) and begin to lament their plight, not realizing that Joseph, having spoken through an interpreter (unique in Genesis), could understand them. They are "paying the penalty" (or are certainly guilty). The word אשם (*'āšēm*; v. 21) means both guilt and its ill effects. Their speech becomes a *public* confession of guilt for what they did to Joseph, whose anguished cries went unheeded. The detailed recollection after so many years is striking; it reveals a stricken conscience. Even more, ironically, their cry now mirrors his. They engage in moral order talk (what goes around comes around). They see that their present experience corresponds to Joseph's (the punishment fits the crime). More specifically, one brother will suffer the same fate as did Joseph. But the brothers do not perceive that Joseph himself executes the moral order.

Reuben enters an "I told you so" speech (cf. 37:21-22) into the conversation, which could only intensify their sense of guilt; he had told them not to harm (i.e., sin against) the boy, for such crimes cannot finally be concealed. He knew there would be a "reckoning" someday (cf. 9:5). His speech is met with silence, suggesting some level of acceptance.

When Joseph hears their guilt-ridden response, he almost gives himself away, turning from them to weep. Having calmed himself, Joseph turns back to the brothers and proceeds with the test. He binds Simeon (the second oldest; because of Reuben's defense?) as the one to stay behind to guarantee their return with Benjamin, which would confirm the brothers as honest men.

42:25-28. Joseph, however, has another gambit. He orders not only that they be given grain and food, but also that the money paid for the grain be placed in their sacks. This ploy explores the theme of integrity rather than being a sign of love or harshness. Even more, it ironically relates to their selling him for silver (כסף *kesep*, 37:28). This elicits further reflections regarding what they have done, including God's activity in their lives (v. 28).

The brothers depart for Canaan without Simeon; en route one brother discovers the money. Their "hearts sink"—they could be accused of being thieves as well as spies. Perhaps catching the irony of the silver, they feel themselves at the mercy of powers beyond their own. But this now takes explicit theological form, not some general disease. Joseph, of course, had done this; yet, his discernment and wisdom are God-given. Hence, the brothers do get it right in one sense: God indeed remains active in these exchanges among the brothers, not least in seeing to the moral order at work in their lives. Their first reference to God represents another advance in their development (cf. 44:16; 50:17, their only other explicit God statements). In 50:20, Joseph will answer this question: God has been at work in their lives for good—a response anticipated by Joseph's steward (43:23!).

42:29-38. The brothers' return to Jacob follows a pattern similar to 37:32-36; they report their encounter with "the man" (vv. 29-34), but with subtle differences, perhaps to protect "their father" (a rare designation). They stress the positive (even exaggerate, v. 34*b*), with no mention of this as a life-and-death matter, and fewer references to Benjamin (two times vs. four times). But the author heightens the issue of honesty (three times vs. two times) in the formula: "By this I shall know" that you are honest men (v. 33). The brothers also do not speak of being jailed or the discovery of the money. The narrator also reports the new discovery of money by the other brothers. These verses (sometimes seen as a doublet) double the effect of Joseph's action; the returned money affects the brothers on their journey and at home, not only themselves but Jacob as well. It also intensifies the memory of the brothers' selling Joseph for silver (Judah's comment in 43:21 that *all* the brothers had discovered money at the lodging place telescopes vv. 27-28 and 35).

Jacob responds by lamenting the tragedies of his family: you are making me childless (does he suspect them?)! Two sons are gone, and now Benjamin is threatened. This sort of thing is always happening to me! He may be concerned about preserving the family, but tones of self-pity are evident. Reuben asks that Benjamin be put in his care and, in a sign of desperation, offers the life of his two sons should Benjamin not return (how could a loss from the *next* generation help?). Jacob refuses the offer, for if harm should come to Benjamin (cf. v. 4), he would die in great sorrow (cf. his comments about Rachel's other son in 37:35). Better that Simeon be lost than risk losing Benjamin, too.

REFLECTIONS

1. Various suggestions have been made regarding Joseph's motive for giving the test: (1) To exact revenge or punish his brothers. This seems unlikely, given the "test" language—and he is up front about this—and given the diminished test, with one brother detained. While his response may be somewhat harsh, the author's emphasis on Joseph's wisdom and discernment (as well as 41:51 and 42:9) suggests that he has everyone's best interests at heart. (2) To learn whether they are spies, but he knows they are not spies. This issue provides a facade, necessary only to serve another purpose. (3) To bring Benjamin to Joseph.[205] He wants to see his brother (vv. 15-16, 20) and weeps when he does (43:30). Yet, in the larger narrative (cf. 50:15-24) Benjamin becomes a means of achieving family unity, presupposed by the events of Exodus. (4) To determine whether the brothers have changed and are acting more like brothers. Although certainly true in part (v. 16), they may act so only to satisfy the needs of the moment—hence the need for more than one test. (5) To achieve a larger objective: the best possible future for this family *as a unit,* whose very future is at stake. The brothers need to pass through an ordeal in order to bring their memories and guilt to the surface, where it can be dealt with adequately, before reconciliation can truly take place, and hence safeguard the future of the family. This process transpires (see vv. 21-22, 28; 44:16; 50:16-17).

2. The recurring theme of Joseph's weeping (43:30; 45:1-2, 14-15; 46:29; 50:1, 17) has two basic purposes: (1) It breaks "the tension with progressing signs of hope for a full reconciliation."[206] The brothers' remorse prompts the first such sign. (2) Even more, it reveals "Joseph's growing feelings of compassion for his brothers behind his harsh facade, so that the reader can be aware that the meaning of Joseph's actions is not to be found in their surface appearance."[207] The author conveys Joseph's thoughts and feelings through this device.

3. The issue of guilt and punishment surfaces in a number of ways. It involves, however, not forensic acts of divine judgment, but the functioning of the moral order. The moral order does not function in some exact temporal way; the brothers' actions against Joseph come home to roost only after some thirteen or more years. Moreover, it does not function mechanically. The brothers certainly reap the consequences of their sins and relive many dimensions of Joseph's own experience of suffering; yet both human and divine actions are capable of breaking into that spiral, and reconciliation among the brothers finally comes. Nor does the moral order function in some deistic way. God works within it to bring about good (see 45:5-9; 50:15-21). Yet, God does not have full control over human behaviors, else one could not speak of sin as in any sense a human responsibility. But human sin cannot finally stymie God, who can draw everything that has happened into the orbit of larger purposes for good.

205. See von Rad, *Genesis,* 382.
206. Coats, *Genesis,* 286.
207. White, *Narration and Discourse,* 259-60.

GENESIS 43:1-34, THE SECOND JOURNEY TO EGYPT

COMMENTARY

This chapter continues the segment begun in chap. 42 and follows a similar outline, though with contrasting content (e.g., the brothers' reception).[208] The chapter begins with a conversation between the brothers and Jacob (43:1-15) and moves to a description of the brothers' journey to Egypt and their encounter with the steward (vv. 16-25), followed by another audience with Joseph (vv. 26-34).

This doubling of the journey to Egypt has raised the question of sources, suggesting to some that there is really only one journey, twice-told. Others insist on two different journeys, which is the shape of the final redaction in any case. Thus, although Simeon is neglected, he is not forgotten (v. 14). Also, the details of the second journey often presuppose the first (e.g., vv. 2-9). One may recognize a delay in returning (v. 10; see Joseph's concern in 45:9), though perhaps no more than a month or so, given the two weeks needed to make a round trip to Egypt.

43:1-15. Because of the severity of the famine (as in 41:57), the need to return to Egypt for food arises once again (as Joseph anticipated). Israel (Jacob's only name in chap. 43) again tells his sons to go to Egypt, but they will not go without Benjamin (whose age is difficult to discern; cf. "boy" in v. 8).

Judah becomes a resolute spokesman for the brothers (cf. Reuben in 42:37) and remains so for the balance of the story. He plays a key role in helping to overcome the impasse centered on Benjamin. This conversation ought not to be considered a doublet of the report to Jacob in 42:29-34, not least because it focuses solely on the condition regarding Benjamin.

Judah forcefully reminds his father of the conversation with "the man" about Benjamin. Joseph had "solemnly" warned them. To reinforce this, Judah repeats Joseph's words: "You shall not see my face [i.e., me] unless your brother is with you" (vv. 3, 5). Israel

wonders why his sons had even mentioned another brother, knowing how he would feel. They (i.e., all the brothers, v. 7) say it was in response to Joseph's questioning. This appears to skirt the truth, for in 42:13 they volunteer the information; yet, Joseph does not object when Judah reports the conversation to him (44:19-20). So we have difficulty discerning whether the brothers are "honest men." This may be exactly the question the narrator intends the reader to raise.

Judah proceeds with what proves to be a highly persuasive speech (vv. 8-10). He pleads with Israel to let Benjamin return with them, claiming this to be a life-and-death matter for the family—even the children (he echoes the words of both Jacob and Joseph, 42:2, 20). Jacob had not heard the matter put in such terms by the brothers before (42:29-34). Then Judah, in a way more laudable and magnanimous than Reuben (42:37), places himself on the line as the personal guarantor of Benjamin's safety (see 44:32). Finally, Judah notes the delay in returning, indirectly pointing to Jacob's own refusal to send Benjamin (42:38). Joseph's concern about the delay (cf. 45:9) could have raised the issue of the *brothers'* integrity (in view of their agreement, 42:20) and prompted further testing.

Israel realizes that he must allow Benjamin to go, but he seeks to assure his return by sending gifts to "the man." They are to bring the best produce available in Canaan (cf. 24:10), ironically acting like Joseph's traders (37:25). They are also to take double the money (including the money found in the sack), a matter not raised by the brothers (unusual in view of their fears in v. 18). Jacob thus rescues his sons' integrity on this matter. They are to do this posthaste. Then Israel pronounces a benediction upon the success of their journey. Having done as much as he can, Jacob resigns himself to whatever may come; if deprived of children, his will be a deep loss indeed. The author does not name Simeon ("your other brother"), leaving room

208. See Humphreys, *Joseph and His Family*, 97.

in the readers' mind for Joseph. The importance of Benjamin to Jacob sharply informs the brothers' subsequent behaviors (see esp. 44:18-34).

43:16-25. The brothers follow Israel's directives and proceed to Egypt, immediately presenting themselves to Joseph. But they do not get an audience with Joseph right away. Joseph, having observed Benjamin's presence without being seen, chooses to have his steward—an alter ego—deal with the brothers first (v. 16). The narrative purpose for the role of the steward allows Joseph to observe his brothers' behavior at some distance. They have fulfilled his demand regarding Benjamin, but the issue of the money and their honesty (so stressed in 42:11-34) remains open.

The brothers are received cordially this time (cf. 42:7). A dinner is to be prepared, and the brothers are to dine with Joseph. Yet, when they are brought in (probably to the courtyard), they become frightened, a fear born of their last experience with Joseph. They suspect a trap, that they will be overpowered and enslaved because of the money, with the means for their return to Canaan (donkeys) taken away. They take the initiative, telling the steward about the money that mysteriously appeared in their sacks; they are returning it and have additional money for grain. They conclude their defense by pleading ignorance of how this happened. They would appear to have passed the honesty test, but Joseph continues to pursue the issue in the next episode. Does Joseph suspect what the reader knows—namely, that Jacob had to see to the return of the money?

The steward responds graciously, even though he keeps them off balance by the way he talks about the money and God. He assures them that everything is in order (literally, "shalom [שלום] be with you"); they need not be afraid. He tells them that God must have put the "treasure" in their sacks. His statement about receiving their money renounces any claim to it; he does not offer a half-truth.[209] He thus does not feign ignorance about the money; rather, he puts the truth in theological terms.

The scene concludes without dialogue. The steward brings Simeon out to fulfill Joseph's pledge to release him if Benjamin

was brought along. The steward sees that the brothers' needs are met, as well as those of their animals, and they ready themselves and their gift for Joseph. They are Joseph's guests. The story invites us to think that everything will now be fine between Joseph and his brothers. But not yet.

43:26-34. When Joseph makes his appearance, the brothers present their gift and again bow before him to pay him honor (two times!). The realization of Joseph's dream continues (37:7). At the same time, the theme of peace (*shalom*), introduced by the steward (v. 23), is repeated by Joseph (v. 27)—recall 37:14—and is picked up by the brothers (v. 28). This marks an important transition in the narrative. At least from Joseph's perspective, the relationship between the brothers has shifted toward the positive. This exchange of peace, which occurs in an everyday context of greeting, outside of the land of promise and apart from a liturgical setting, provides evidence of its importance for interpersonal relationships.

At the same time, the brothers' obeisance (vv. 26, 28), even if now marked by honor rather than simply submission, makes clear that their relationship with Joseph remains difficult. One verb used in v. 28, קדד (*qādad*, "bow down") occurs only with God as the object elsewhere in the Pentateuch (cf. 24:26, 48). Joseph will claim in 50:19 that he does not stand in the place of God, and thereby recognizes that such obeisance is not appropriate to a proper relationship between himself and his brothers.

Joseph begins by asking about their welfare and that of their aged father (see 44:20). Joseph then shifts his attention to Benjamin. Although Joseph recognizes him, he continues the ruse by asking into Benjamin's identity. Without waiting for a reply, he pronounces a blessing on Benjamin in language that echoes Jacob's blessing (v. 14), as well as Joseph's own gracious treatment by Potiphar (39:4, 21).

The encounter with Benjamin, for whom Joseph shows much affection, so moves Joseph that he excuses himself and weeps privately. The second time that Joseph weeps will not be the last (see Reflections on chap. 42). Having composed himself (see 45:1), he returns and directs the meal to begin. The brothers are now guests rather than enemies.

209. Sarna, *Genesis*, 301.

Yet, the one with whom they are eating still appears as a stranger, signaled by the absence of conversation between them (until 45:3). The relationship has progressed, but Joseph still holds back his identity. For reasons not stated, Joseph believes the time is not yet right to reveal himself to his brothers. Given the events of the next chapter, a further test seems necessary. The brothers have not reached the end of their journey.

The author reports no further dialogue, but notes certain unusual incidents. Separate servings are given to Joseph, to the brothers, and to the Egyptians, because of religious scruples (Joseph sits between communities!). This information shows that reconciliation has not yet truly taken place. The brothers are seated at Joseph's direction (i.e., "before him")[210] according to their age, a strange procedure at which the brothers are astonished: How would he know how to seat them without being asked? Benjamin's portion is five times greater than that of his brothers, demonstrating pleasure at Benjamin's presence, though Joseph also wants to see the brothers' reaction to this favoritism. Benjamin may be the guest of honor, but the absence of any speech on his part (in the entire story!) diminishes his role. The comment about this being a happy occasion sets up the not-so-happy turn of events that follows.

210. Sarna, *Genesis*, 302.

REFLECTIONS

1. The tensions created for the reader of this chapter revolve around difficult decisions that deeply affect family life. The author addresses feeding one's family in the midst of famine, but also the danger presented by the strange request that getting more food from Egypt is contingent on the presence of Benjamin. In weighing options, Jacob finally decides that seeing to the future of the community overrides the fate of a beloved individual family member and his own personal well-being (cf. 34:30).

2. In v. 14, Jacob first mentions God (*El Shaddai,* see 17:1) in this story; he uses the language of mercy (רחמים *rahămîm*), undeserved divine favor, a frequent element in Israel's confession about God (cf. Exod 34:6). The success of his sons' journey depends on the mercy of God. The stress on mercy lifts up the reality of this dysfunctional family. Although hopeful, Jacob knows—and wisely so—that things may not work out as well as he anticipates. His hopes have been dashed before, for anti-God forces are powerful, often frustrating divine purposes. Yet, his trust in God enables him to continue to express hope for the future, for he believes that God's work does have good effects in ways beyond his knowing and beyond external observation.

Joseph's use of the verb meaning "be gracious" (חנן *hānan*) in v. 29 recalls an important theological claim made by Israel for the nature of its God (see Ps 86:15-17). As elsewhere in benedictions (see Num 6:25; Ps 67:1), it functions here as a welcoming word. And as in laments (see Pss 4:1; 86:15-17), it suggests here a response to Jacob's lament about Benjamin—God has been gracious. This word relates back to creedal language used by Jacob at the sending of the brothers (v. 14; see above). Israel's creedal statement about its God (Exod 34:6) attests to this kind of experience with God. Jacob also used this language at the reconciliation with Esau and in the wake of God's graciousness at Jabbok (33:5, 11). God, indeed a gracious one, extends blessings to all, freely and undeservingly (see Exod 33:19).

3. The steward's theological observations in v. 23 are noteworthy. The brothers are extended a word of peace (*shalom*) and told that they need not be afraid, for God, the God of their father (namely, their family) has taken care of them by putting the money in their sacks. This announcement of peace and the removal of fear recurs as a motif in other biblical texts, especially in theophanies (see 26:24) and in Second Isaiah (e.g., 43:1-5). One who stands outside the community announces this word of comfort to the people of God (even if he learned it from Joseph). This may be disconcerting to insiders, but they must be open to God's capability of working on their behalf in and through such persons. Outsiders, too, can be the vehicle for a word of God's peace.

We do not know the extent to which the steward's theology reflects that of Joseph or the narrator. It could be a generic reference to God that the brothers can interpret as they please. Most likely (as in 41:38-39), he offers a way of speaking about God, indeed a gracious, rather than a retributive, God (cf. 42:28), that helps us to understand other aspects of the story, particularly 45:8, "It was not you who sent me here, but God." In 43:23, God did not personally insert the money in their sacks (cf. 42:25), but because this human action was in tune with the divine purposes, one could claim God as the subject of the action. Such a claim does not mean that Joseph's decision to fill the sacks was necessary; he could have taken other actions. The author's direct use of God language seems purposely ambiguous, for the divine activity is not obvious, but remains confessional, as no empirical claims can be made. It becomes a statement of faith.

GENESIS 44:1-34, JOSEPH'S FINAL TEST

COMMENTARY

This segment continues the episode of chaps. 42–43. It begins in Egypt (vv. 1-5), moves to a point along the way between Egypt and Canaan (vv. 6-13), and concludes once again in Egypt at Joseph's house (vv. 14-34). Joseph controls the situation from beginning to end. At the same time, Judah, now the leader of the brothers, makes a passionate and persuasive speech before Joseph, in the wake of which Joseph finally reveals himself (chap. 45).

44:1-5. Joseph commands his steward to put food and money (i.e., silver) in the brothers' sacks for their return to Canaan. This repeats the directive of 42:25, except that Joseph's silver cup is also to be placed in Benjamin's sack. An important personal possession allows one more test of his brothers. The return of the money once again has troubled commentators. Yet, while it plays no further role in this chapter, it reinforces the focus on silver and makes clear that Joseph will not keep any money his family has paid for food (see chaps. 42–43).

Shortly after the brothers depart, Joseph sends his steward after them. He takes a hard-line approach, firing questions that assume they stole the silver cup (NRSV/NIV footnotes). The steward's (Joseph's) questions focus on the personal character of the deed; the silver cup is Joseph's own. In some sense

it stands in for him, so that he is more personally violated when they "take" *this* silver; it more sharply mirrors his own violation at their hands when they sold him for silver.

Joseph uses the cup to divine, to seek the meaning of, events through observing patterns in the liquid (cf. the modern use of tea leaves or coffee grounds). God could work through such means, which is linked with Joseph's ability as a dream interpreter (cf. 40:8). It may be that Joseph does not actually practice divination (cf. v. 15), but he certainly wants the brothers to think he does. They must have had an increasing sense of being hemmed in, at the mercy of powers beyond their control (v. 16a).

44:6-13. When the steward repeats Joseph's words to the brothers, they strongly deny their guilt; they are "honest" men (using עבד [ʿebed, "servant"] three times; this word occurs nineteen times in vv. 7-33!). As evidence, they cite their return of the money (cf. 43:12). If they hadn't kept that money, why would they steal again? They naively offer to become Joseph's servants/slaves should the cup be found; indeed, they pronounce a death sentence on the thief (harsher than Israelite law required). By these words they play right into Joseph's hand (see below). Their innocence, which mirrors Joseph's innocence, seems ironic. Moreover, they prescribe *for* *themselves* a double fate that mirrors his—death for one and slavery to the Egyptians for the rest. Their cries of innocence also parallel Joseph's (42:21).

While v. 10 remains ambiguous, the steward does not fully accept their self-sentencing. He speaks graciously before the evidence sees the light of day. He agrees only to the enslavement of the culpable one; the rest are to go free. The steward thereby sets Joseph up for a response (v. 17) that will provide the breakthrough in this prolonged process of testing.

The brothers confidently subject themselves to a search. When the cup is found in Benjamin's sack, the brothers do not respond verbally; they express their distress by tearing their clothes (cf. 37:34). Rather than proceeding to Canaan, all of them return to Egypt for a confrontation with Joseph himself. Their actions are informed by knowing how their father would respond if they returned without Benjamin (see 42:38).

44:14-17. When the brothers prostrate themselves before Joseph (cf. 37:7), he picks up the steward's accusations. Expressing amazement at what they have done, he claims that he could have (has?) discovered their deed through divination (v. 15). Judah interprets this exposure of guilt as a divine act (v. 16).

Judah, the spokesman for the brothers, acknowledges that they are entirely at Joseph's disposal; they can do nothing to clear themselves. Although he never confesses that a crime has been committed, Judah makes a public confession of guilt for *all* the brothers and throws them on the mercy of this "lord." For him to include all the brothers suggests that he has more than this event in mind, including their actions against Joseph (see 42:21), though Joseph does not recognize this dynamic.

Joseph sharply refuses to make them all his slaves, asking only that the possessor of the cup (Benjamin is not named) be made a slave. The other brothers will return to their father in peace (*shalom*), an irony, given what their father has said about Benjamin (see 42:38; 43:14). On the surface, this proposal appears magnanimous, but Joseph knows that they cannot return to their father without Benjamin. Joseph has tightened the screws; how will the brothers respond?

By this action, Joseph has placed Benjamin in a relationship to his brothers not unlike the way his own had once been (see other such parallels in chap. 42). In this test, Joseph will certainly gain knowledge about his brothers. Will they act toward Benjamin as they once had toward him? Will they allow Benjamin to become a slave, while they save their own skins?

44:18-34. Judah responds with a passionate speech, the longest in Genesis and a literary masterpiece, not least in the way it gathers up the story to this point. In a way similar in its rhetorical power to his speech to Jacob in 43:3-10, Judah seeks to persuade Joseph to keep him rather than Benjamin. To this end, Judah makes selective and expansive use of previous conversations, with Joseph himself (cf. vv. 20-23 with 42:12-20) and Jacob (cf. vv. 24-29, 32 with 37:33-35; 42:36-38; 43:2-14). Joseph hears for the first time his father's reaction to his own abduction, and that Jacob still mourns for him (cf. v. 28 with 37:33).

Judah speaks straightforwardly and sincerely, conveying what is at stake for this family in quite direct ways. At the same time, he speaks in a highly deferential manner, in initial approach ("you are like Pharaoh himself"), in general language (lord/servant is used twenty times!), and in omitting any harshness from prior conversations (e.g., Joseph's charge of spying and threat of death). The speech also has strong emotional content, especially regarding the negative effect on their aged father (mentioned fourteen times!), whose life has been so filled with hardship and loss (vv. 19-20, 22, 27-29, 30-31, 34). Judah stresses that this is a matter of life and death for him (vv. 22, 29-31). He also recalls the violence done to Joseph (vv. 20, 27-29) and refers to Jacob's special love for Benjamin, with whom "his life is bound up" (v. 30; cf. vv. 20, 22, 27-29, 31, 34). Judah speaks of this in nonjudgmental ways, recognizing and accepting such preferential treatment by his father. The climax of the speech refers to the suffering their father will endure (v. 34), a contrast to the brothers' concern in 37:31-35.

Judah also underscores the extent to which the brothers have acceded to Joseph's requests, even more, how he has placed his own future on the line (v. 32). This makes clear that he is following through on his promise to his father (cf. 43:9). Judah's speech accents his integrity and gives further evidence of a change in the brothers. Judah's willingness also appears ironic, for he would then become the slave of the very one he had made a slave (cf. 37:26-27).

As with Jacob (43:11-14), Judah's speech persuades Joseph, whose response is detailed in chap. 45. Judah's references to their father seem to have been particularly effective (45:3, 9, 13, 23).

REFLECTIONS

1. Some commentators believe that Joseph turns the test into "an insolent, almost wanton game."[211] This seems unlikely. As noted, testing must involve action and not just words. Whether there has been a change in fact can more readily be discerned by the way people act. Moreover, the testing gives the brothers an experience not unlike Joseph's own (as in chap. 42). This mirroring process enables the brothers to recognize their guilt and makes reconciliation possible.

2. Note the important language in vv 5-6. The brothers have done wrong (רעע *rāʿaʿ*); they have returned evil (רע *raʿ*) for the good (טוב *tôb*) they had received from Joseph. This anticipates the use of good and evil in 50:20. Here the brothers are accused of doing evil (without so intending), and Joseph does good; there they are said to do evil (with intention), and God does good. Regarding the evil, their "innocence" actually mirrors their guilt in selling Joseph for silver, so that this verse and 50:20 are finally parallel. Regarding the good, we see, once again, an elision of divine and human activity; both are engaged in doing good.

3. The author mentions God only once in this chapter (v. 16), but it is significant. Although the brothers had previously acknowledged their guilt to one another (42:21), they now confess before Joseph. Moreover, although the brothers now use God language for the second time (cf. 42:28), previously it took the form of a question. Judah here brings guilt and God together, thereby confessing that God has been engaged in these events, working to expose their guilt in and through what has happened. When we combine this with other changes, we understand that Joseph's testing (though rigorous) has finally served a positive purpose.

It seems somewhat strange to say that *God* has "found out," as if God did not know what had transpired. The author links God and Joseph again (see 43:23). This use of God language also reflects Joseph's speech in 45:8, where human and divine agency are combined. Moreover, in 45:5-9 Joseph will speak of God as one who has been engaged in preserving life; the reference in 44:16 to God as one before whom guilt stands exposed is directed toward the same end. The exposure of guilt serves life and well-being, not to perpetuate self-loathing. God's activity in convicting the brothers, therefore, brings about reconciliation in this family.

4. Judah's speeches (to Jacob, 43:3-10; and to Joseph, 44:18-34) relate directly to the events of chap. 38 and play a critical role in the Joseph story. Genesis 37–50 also involves a story about Judah. In and through what he says, not least his confession of guilt and the changes he exemplifies in his interpretation of what has happened, he enables the story of this family to move to a new level, setting the stage for the reconciliation that follows. Without Judah, Joseph's ensuing speech would not have been possible. Joseph's theological interpretation of events builds upon Judah's confession.

Even more, unlike his earlier attitude (37:26-27), Judah—like Tamar—chooses to risk himself rather than risk the life of another brother. First, he makes this promise

211. Von Rad, *Genesis*, 391.

to his father. Second, he follows through on it, in spite of his innocence. This self-effacing act—certainly not his only option—serves the future of both father and brother. Self-sacrifice in conflicted situations may lead to reconciliation.[212]

At the same time, Joseph refuses to accept this sacrifice in his response in chap. 45. Joseph recognizes that self-sacrifice is not necessarily a good thing, not least because it can be used in abusive ways to promote the elevation of one person over another. And so finally, in 50:19-21, Joseph will reject any hierarchical relationship among the brothers. Nevertheless, this does not discount the integrity of Judah's offer, and it stands in the narrative as a sign of the great change that has come over the brothers.

212. Westermann speaks of "vicarious suffering," *Genesis 37–50*, 137-38.

GENESIS 45:1-28, JOSEPH MAKES HIMSELF KNOWN

COMMENTARY

Chapter 45 provides the climax to the story, but must be seen as closely coordinate with chap. 46 (especially 45:5-8 and 46:1-4). The actual descent belongs together with the preparations for it. After Joseph reveals himself to his brothers (vv. 1-8), Joseph (vv. 9-15, 21-24), Pharaoh (vv. 16-20), the brothers, and Jacob (vv. 25-28) prepare for the descent to Egypt in their own ways.

One of the puzzles regarding this section involves its relationship to 50:15-21. Those verses seem to replicate the events of this chapter, but that is not the case. The key difference lies in Joseph's relationship with his brothers. Three observations make clear that a full reconciliation does not occur here.

First, in this chapter the brothers do not respond specifically to what Joseph says; v. 15 testifies only to general conversation. In 50:15-18, the brothers still fear Joseph; they still stand in a lord/servant relationship with him, in fact, they seek to perpetuate it. This means that Joseph's goal of ameliorating their anxieties was not finally successful.

Second, Joseph, in chap. 45, does not specifically deal with the lord/servant reality. His first question relates to his father, not to his brothers (v. 3). He leaves questions of accountability and penalty aside (cf. 42:21-22). These issues burst forth at the point of their father's death (between 45:26 and 50:15, the brothers speak only at 47:4).

Third, Joseph is the direct object of every verb, with God as subject (vv. 5, 7, 8, 9): God has sent *me;* God has made *me;* indeed, he repeats that God has made him "lord." The author encloses the report that Joseph asks be brought to his father by language that could be described as self-congratulatory (vv. 9, 13). Initially, Joseph calls himself a brother (v. 4), but father/lord/ruler language finally predominates (vv. 8-9, 13; cf. v. 26). Moreover, directives to the brothers abound, and Joseph even appears paternalistic (v. 24; 46:31-33).

The new question addressed in 50:15-21 addresses the nature of the relationship between Joseph and his brothers. There Joseph will reject the ruler/slave image. The dream of 37:7 was earlier realized, without the brothers' knowledge (do they now realize it?), but the images of that dream must not be allowed to shape their ongoing life together.

45:1-3. Judah's speech proves to be highly effective. Joseph can no longer control his emotions, but rather than leave (see 42:24; 43:30), he dismisses all attendants so that family members can deal with these issues privately. Yet, he weeps so loudly that it proves not to be a private affair after all (Joseph's weeping encloses the section, vv. 1-2, 14-15). Standing alone with his brothers, he reveals his identity. All the brothers are alive.

In view of Judah's speech, Joseph asks whether their father is really still alive ("life" could refer simply to good health). His brothers, however, are reduced to an agitated, fearful silence. This silence provides a break in the reunion; how Joseph will move past this awkwardness and deal with his brothers' fear becomes the question. The task of reconciliation is no simple matter.

45:4-15. Joseph asks his brothers to come closer, not to see him more clearly, but thereby to cross the official barrier. He identifies himself further by recalling their common history, going directly to the heart of the issue: You sold me into Egypt (v. 4).

Joseph's next comment (v. 5*a*) proves decisive. He discerns that his brothers are dismayed or terrified (NIV), distressed (cf. 42:21), and angry at each other (42:22), no doubt for many reasons, not least what this means for their own future. Joseph does not scold or blame them; he does not try to make them feel either guilty or shameful. He asks for no confession of sin and issues no absolution.[213] Rather, he wants to allay their fears (see the "for/because"). His formulations are thus designed for pastoral purposes, and they take on a confessional or doxological character; they must be interpreted not unlike other such language (e.g., the hymns of the psalter; oracles of salvation in response to laments). Even so, Joseph does not fully accomplish his objective.

Joseph's speaking takes a form similar to that of a theophany narrative (see 26:24), with self-identification, the quelling of fear, and the announcement of what God has done (not *will* do). The formal parallels between 45:3-8 and 46:2-4 should be especially noted, because they bring creational and promissory themes together.

Joseph says, fundamentally, that in spite of their past history, all will be well because what has happened corresponds to God's purposes. He invites them to view the past from the perspective of the present: Everybody is alive. Hence, their particular past can be interpreted as having a fundamentally (not totally, 50:20) positive dimension. God has "taken over" what they have done and used it to bring about this end. Their actions have *become* God's by being woven into his life-giving purposes. Even more, *Pharaoh's* actions—elevating Joseph as ruler—have *become* God's! The author leaves aside the role of the human for a specific purpose (not unlike referring to a sermon as the word of God)—the role of the human returns in

50:20. Human actions could have resulted in different ends; these ends have come to pass, however, and the result means that the decisive actor has been God.

Some scholars think that the narrator's perspective appears most transparently at this point; yet, it certainly needs 50:15-21 for proper interpretation. The important new developments in 50:15-21 move theologically beyond this text, so that Joseph's perspective becomes more mature (see above). Moreover, we are not fully clear about how God's activity should be interpreted. Certainly, God acts unobtrusively, hidden beneath the ordinary course of events. God is the subject of two verbs, שלח (*šālaḥ*, "send"; vv. 5, 7, 8), and שים (*sîm*, "make"; vv. 8, 9), in every case with Joseph as the object. God acts to preserve life, particularly the life of Jacob's family (vv. 5, 7).

Famine provides the sociohistorical context for the divine activity. Famine, a life-and-death issue, no doubt cost many lives, which explains references to "remnant" and "survivors" (prophetic use of these words links Israel's hardships with the experience of their ancestors; cf. Isa 10:20; 37:32). The author interprets Joseph's being sent to Egypt and his elevation to leadership in Egypt ("father to Pharaoh" is a title for a king's counselor) as God's means of preserving life. What God did provides the *decisive* reality *within* this larger concatenation of events that has led to life and well-being. God's concern for life also embraces Egypt, indeed the entire world, as already evident in Joseph's wise administration (see 41:56-57). The divine objective encompasses every sphere of life within both family and nation.

In vv. 9-13, Joseph now seeks to preserve his family's life in ways that correspond directly to God's activity. Joseph acts as father, lord, and ruler (all used as images for God in the OT) in tune with God's purposes. Joseph tells the brothers to hurry home, report these events to their father, return with family and possessions, and settle in the land of Goshen near him (of uncertain location on the eastern edge of the delta region, near the border facing Canaan). Joseph assures them that he will provide for all their needs—adults, children, animals—during the continuing famine.

213. Westermann, *Genesis 37–50*, 144.

Joseph concludes by repeating his identity, with special notice of Benjamin (v. 12). Joseph's word to hurry to "my father" with the news (so different from the news in 37:32!) encloses his directives to the brothers (vv. 9, 13), revealing deep concern for Jacob. The episode concludes as it began, with a description of the tearful reunion. The author singles out Joseph's reunion with Benjamin, Joseph's only full brother, the only time in the story that we hear about Benjamin's own feelings. The episode also concludes with a reference to the brothers' conversation with one another, harking back to 37:4, where the brothers could not talk peaceably with one another.

45:16-24. Joseph's instructions to the brothers become those of Pharaoh himself. They are to return to Canaan and bring their father and their families back to Egypt, with the assurance that they will have no worries about possessions. The royal household not only rejoices in the good fortune of Israel's family, but also provides the best land and choicest products (i.e., fat) that Egypt has to offer. Both Pharaoh and Joseph will take care of them. Pharaoh's pleased response, filled with generosity and good will, proves startling. In view of events in Exodus, this positive portrayal of the Egyptians commands attention, alluding to possible reconciliation

for nations—even Egypt and Israel—as well as families. Historically, pharaohs were generous to Semitic peoples in time of famine.

Joseph carries out Pharaoh's wishes with respect to his family, perhaps interpreting Pharaoh's directive somewhat generously. He provides for his full brother, Benjamin, in a special way, and seems emphatically lavish in the provisions for his father (which later serve as evidence, v. 27). Reference to the gift of clothing recalls for the reader that Joseph's coat precipitated this family conflict in the first place; clothing now becomes a sign of reconciliation. Finally, Joseph realistically but paternalistically admonishes his brothers not to quarrel among themselves on the journey (cf. 42:21-22).

45:25-28. When the brothers report the news, Jacob is skeptical. But, when they repeat Joseph's words and display the evidence, he believes and resolves to go to Egypt to see his son before he dies. "Enough" is shorthand for Jacob's willing-ness to put the past behind him and get on with the new possibilities presented by this surprising good news. The parental trauma that Jacob experienced in 37:31-35 now comes full circle; life and joy once more fill the family scene. God enables the past to be forgotten (see 41:51) and makes new beginnings possible. Yet, more will come.

REFLECTIONS

1. For the reader following Joseph's development closely over these eight chapters, his theological presentation may come as something of a surprise. Joseph's God talk has been comparatively rare (see 39:9; 40:8; 41:16, 25, 28, 32, 51-52; 42:18; 43:29), but a sufficient basis on which to build. In addition, God talk by other individuals may reveal the narrator's perspective, particularly those texts that mention God as the seemingly exclusive subject (see esp. 41:38-39; 43:23; 44:16). Such a way of speaking is not new to this text.

Joseph's theology involves life, not promise. The latter awaits later developments, for Joseph has not yet been the recipient of the promises given to his ancestors (see 46:1-4; 48:3-4). But life remains necessary for the continuation of the promises.

2. At this climactic point in their relationship, Joseph sits in a position to do with his brothers as he pleases. Yet, he makes no effort to hold their feet to the fire; his language and demeanor (loud weeping) evidence no anger or irritation. He manifests more weakness than strength; he sets aside the trappings of royalty and enters into the pathos of the situation, all for the sake of reconciliation. Whereas Joseph's testings were indispensable in bringing the family to this moment, a display of power and control was insufficient finally to heal them. Joseph must step outside his role as Egyptian ruler (hence the dismissal of others), and join the family at an intimate and vulnerable level. Yet, as we have noted, Joseph's language does not always match these behaviors. The brothers remain uncertain. A full reconciliation must await later events (50:15-21).

Joseph does not require sorrow or regret from the brothers (cf. 50:17-19). Rather, he confesses that God has been at work in all these events to preserve life, and that is the decisive reality in this moment. What God has done stands *independent of the brothers' repentance.* The word, for the brothers, thus serves as a straightforward gospel word, spoken by one who has experienced it deep within his own life: God has acted so that life, rather than death, now abounds. So the activity of the brothers, however reprehensible in itself, has been used by God as a vehicle for sustaining the life of this family.

3. The relationship between divine and human agency in vv. 5-9 is much debated. One view understands v. 8*a* in a literal fashion: God sends Joseph to Egypt, not the brothers. God is the *only* effective agent in this event ("this all-sufficiency of divine sovereignty makes human action almost irrelevant").[214] A number of difficulties attend such a view, however. (1) The text explicitly ascribes effective agency to the brothers: They "sold" (מכר *mākar*) Joseph into Egypt (vv. 4, 5; 37:28; cf. 42:21). The brothers are not considered puppets in the hands of God (see also the agency of Joseph in vv. 9-13). (2) The larger story uses the language of sin (חטא *ḥāṭāʾ*, 42:22; 50:17) and evil (רעה *rāʿâ*, 50:15, 17, 20) to refer to the brothers' action, for which they are guilty (אשם *ʾāšēm*, 42:21; עון *ʿāwōn*, 44:16). To consider God as the actual subject of these words would be problematic and would rule human responsibility for such activity out of order. (3) The notion of testing is integral to understanding the story (cf. 42:15-16). If God serves as absolute subject of events, there would be no real test of the brothers, for God would bend their wills to respond as God saw fit. All of Joseph's activities would be only a facade for a divine game. (4) Later, 50:20 speaks of both human and divine intentions effectively at work in these events, though in the service of different purposes. Joseph's perspective at this point, however, does not seem as mature as it later becomes.

Another view speaks of effective agency on the part of both God and the brothers, but considers God's intentions as inevitably overriding the brothers' intentions. This view could be correct if understood in the sense that no human activity can *finally* stymie God's purposes for life. On the other hand, such a view seems problematic if it means that God's will can never be rejected or frustrated, so that human sin becomes in effect God's will for the moment. The OT as a whole often testifies to the resistibility of God's word and will.[215]

Either of these perspectives would profoundly affect how one portrays the development of the story. Talk about the drama of the story should then be cast so that everything happens consonantly with the divine will, and any analysis of human words and deeds, *even thoughts,* should be peppered with talk about the controlling divine subject. And, of course, no negative judgment should be placed on the activities of any human subjects, for they are only doing the will of God.

A more acceptable view would speak of the effectiveness of both divine and human agency in the drama, in which both can influence and be influenced, resist and be resisted. As with doxological language more generally, however, God acts decisively, and should thus be celebrated.

We should not evaluate the brothers' life-diminishing activity against Joseph as good (see 50:20) or deem irrelevant how they conduct themselves within God's economy. Rather, God's activity *from within the context set in part by the brothers' sinful behaviors* has proved, finally, to be decisive. Hence, what *God* has done *now* counts in

---

214. Von Rad, *Genesis,* 438.
215. See T. Fretheim, "Will of God in the OT" and "Word of God" in *The Anchor Bible Dictionary,* 6:914-20, 961-69.

charting a way into the future. God has preserved life; God has kept this family intact in the threat of death. To use a different image, the brothers' sinful objectives have been thwarted by being drawn into the larger orbit of God's purposes and used by God in such a way as to bring life rather than death. To repeat, God has "taken over" what they have done and used it to bring about this end. Their actions have *become* God's by being woven into God's life-giving purposes. Even more, *Pharaoh's* actions—elevating Joseph as ruler—have *become* God's!

4. The extent to which one can draw inferences from this text concerning God's more general activity in the world (providence) remains difficult to discern. Westermann denies this possibility, claiming that the text focuses on specific salvific actions of God in this situation.[216] Yet, such actions are stretched out over a considerable period of time; they are also "salvific" in creational rather than redemptive terms. The narrator would certainly claim that the way in which God acts in the world more generally bears basic continuities with God's actions at any moment. While the text testifies to God as an actor in human affairs, these acts are understood in ways quite different from, say, the Exodus events (or 46:1-4, for that matter); they are more hidden to ordinary sight, much less disruptive of ordinary life.

Such an understanding of God's involvement in the life of the cosmos seems especially pertinent in our own world, wherein the tracks of God seem so often ambiguous at best. We might confess that God's activity counts as a factor to be reckoned with in all events, but these same events *could* be interpreted without reference to God at all. But those who make this confession would also go on to say that, wherever there are signs of life rather than death, signs of reconciliation rather than estrangement, God has been at work in, with, and under human affairs. Depending on the context, it may be that God should be the only subject of such verbs so that we know whose life-giving purposes and activity have been decisive.

216. Westermann, *Genesis 37–50*, 143.

GENESIS 46:1–47:26, THE DESCENT INTO EGYPT

COMMENTARY

This chapter begins a new episode, but the parallels between 45:5-8 and 46:1-4 (see below) suggest that chap. 45, as preparation for the descent, must be drawn more closely to this section, which describes the actual trip of Jacob's family to Egypt. Joseph's reconciliation with his brothers has been a leading objective of the narrative, but the reunion of father and son has yet to occur. That, too, constitutes an important dimension of the story.

The segment 46:28–47:12 describes issues of settlement in Egypt. After the reunion of Jacob and Joseph (vv. 28-30), Joseph prepares his brothers for conversations with Pharaoh (vv. 31-33); 47:1-12 reports that audience, leading to the settlement in Goshen; 47:13-26 describes Joseph's agrarian reforms to cope with the effects of the famine; 47:27 concludes this episode with a summary of these events and their effect on Jacob's family.

The remaining chapters in Genesis are more episodic than 39–45, with a disparate range of genres, which reveal a composite character. Verses 1-4 link this story with divine appearances and related promises in Genesis 12–35 (cf. 26:23-25), as do the itineraries and the genealogy-like list in 46:5-27. At the same time, these texts point forward to Exodus, toward which these chapters begin to lean more and more. Together, these sections help both to unify Genesis and to integrate it with Exodus.

46:1-7. Jacob initially journeys from Hebron (cf. 37:14) and comes to Beersheba, where God once appeared to his father (26:23-25). Jacob worships at the altar built by Isaac *before* he has his vision (note the sacrifices, rare in Genesis, cf. 31:54). At this juncture in life—once again on leaving the land (cf. chap. 28)—Jacob builds upon the faith of his family heritage, "the God of his father."

God acknowledges this tradition by appearing to Jacob in visions of the night as the "God of your father" (cf. 15:1; 28:11) and affirms the decision to go to Egypt (cf. 26:2). The plural "visions" seems difficult; it may refer to the intensity of the experience, and could be either oral or oral with a visual component. God's double call and Jacob's obedient response are identical to Abraham's experience in 22:11.

These verses appear formally similar to 45:3-8. Both move from self-identification to the quelling of fear to an announcement, only this time regarding the future. While parallel in form, Joseph's word to his brothers and God's word to Jacob are complementary in content. Together they link creation and promise. God's life-enabling work makes possible the continued articulation of the promises. Without life, there would be no promise. The creative work of God stands in service of the promise.

God allays Jacob's fears regarding the move by making promises, drawing on past promises, but adjusting them in view of the changed circumstances that Egypt presents. Hence, "I will make of you a great nation *there*" (v. 3; cf. 12:2; 18:18), indicates that their development into a people will occur in Egypt (see Exod 1:7). Moreover, God will go down with him to Egypt. This statement constitutes a new version of God's promise of presence to Jacob in 28:15; it not only specifies presence, but emphasizes that this will be *a journey for God*. This represents a deep commitment of God to enter into all the dynamics of the Egyptian experience. With the promise that God will bring him back to Canaan, the exodus and related events come into view. Inasmuch as Jacob himself does not return to Canaan alive (cf. 47:30; 50:4-14),

we may interpret the promise of return in corporate terms as well. Finally, Joseph will close his eyes, implying that Joseph will be with him when he dies (cf. 50:1).

Jacob journeys from Beersheba, accompanied by his family and all their belongings (contrary to Pharaoh's expectations? 45:20). While the following roll focuses on the brothers and their children, this introductory list identifies the women accompanying Jacob. The daughters of Jacob include daughters-in-law (clearer in v. 15; cf. 37:35).

46:8-27. The author provides a list of Jacob's descendants—individuals, not clans—who made the migration to Egypt (cf. Exod 1:1). Its relationship to other lists appears to be highly complex (cf. Numbers 26; 1 Chronicles 1–9).[217] It is based on the number seventy (v. 27; cf. Exod 1:5) and ordered according to Jacob's wives (vv. 15, 18, [19], 22, 25; note the double reference to Rachel), who are called the mothers of both children and grandchildren (e.g., v. 22). The list includes Dinah (v. 15), one granddaughter (v. 17), and four great-grandsons (vv. 12, 17). The author names only Joseph's wife (v. 20; cf. v. 26) and mentions that a Canaanite woman bore one of Simeon's children (v. 10). The list assumes knowledge of the previous narratives (e.g., vv. 12, 15, 18, 20, 25), suggesting that an independent list has been adapted to fit this context, breaking the natural continuity between vv. 7 and 28.

Verses 26 and 27 are difficult, perhaps due to several editorial hands; not everything can be sorted out. The numbers in vv. 15, 18, 22, and 25 total seventy (adding Jacob, Joseph's sons, and one other person, possibly Dinah); the number sixty-six (v. 26), however, takes into account that Er and Onan (v. 12) and Joseph's two sons (v. 20) never made a trip to Egypt.

46:28-30. These verses begin an episode that continues through 47:12, describing the settlement of Joseph's family in Egypt.

Jacob recognizes Judah's leadership in having him prepare the way for their entry into Egypt. When Joseph hears of their arrival in the land of Goshen, he takes the initiative to greet his father. Tears—not words—once again flow for this sensitive man as father and son embrace at length, joyfully reunited after

217. For details, see Westermann, *Genesis 37–50*, 158-61.

so many years apart. Joseph appears before his father as a son, not as a public official, with appropriate levels of emotional intensity (no fulfillment of his second dream seems in view).

Verse 30 brings one dimension of the Joseph story full circle. The violence of chap. 37 has been turned into life. Jacob, who had lamented that he would go into death mourning (37:33-35) and whose life has been so pervaded by this loss (42:38; 43:14; 44:28-29), now announces that he can die with the joy of knowing that his son who was lost has been found (cf. 45:28).

46:31–47:12. Joseph takes charge of the situation. Having prepared his father and brothers, he mediates with Pharaoh the settlement in Goshen. Pharaoh might be concerned about a settlement in Goshen, which Joseph wanted because his family would be nearby, but which Pharaoh could find difficult for some reason (a border region?). Because Goshen is somewhat removed from the settled areas of Egypt, Joseph devises a plan that would allow his family to move there (a convenient placement for escape?). He directs his brothers to stress that they are shepherds (i.e., keepers of livestock), because shepherding was an unappealing occupation to Egyptians (v. 34). Thus Pharaoh would be glad to have them at a distance, and Joseph would not compromise his own position among the Egyptians.

Joseph announces to Pharaoh that the family has arrived and are in Goshen (also called Rameses, v. 11, elsewhere referred to as a city, Exod 1:11). The brothers respond to Pharaoh's questions as directed, describing themselves as shepherds (see 46:32, 34) and, going beyond the question, as aliens (גרים *gērîm*, cf. 15:13) in the land, temporary residents seeking pasture for their flocks ("holding" in v. 11 suggests permanence; does Joseph disagree with his brothers here?). The brothers request settlement in Goshen; both Pharaoh and the narrator describe this as "the best part of the land" (vv. 6, 11), which Pharaoh had promised them (45:18).

Pharaoh, speaking officially to Joseph (vv. 5-6), supportively acknowledges his statement of v. 1 and agrees to this arrangement. Moreover, going beyond previous conversations, he offers to allow the capable ones

among them to oversee his own livestock, guaranteeing the security of the family under pharaonic authority. (Historically, pharaohs possessed herds and used such persons.) The Egyptians are the ones who violate the agreement (Exod 1:8-11); hence they have only themselves to blame for the destruction that comes.

Joseph presents his father to Pharaoh, and Jacob proceeds to bless Pharaoh (rather than do obeisance). He also blesses Pharaoh when he departs (v. 10). We should understand this greeting and farewell more broadly in terms of the blessing motif in chaps. 12-50. This prompts Pharaoh's question about his age; Jacob's blessing might speak to issues of longevity. Jacob states that his 130 years have been "few and hard" compared with his ancestors (see 25:7; 35:28), referring to difficulties endured over the years, not least with Joseph. Yet, characteristic of each patriarch has been the sojourning shape of life, its unsettled character, moving toward a goal set by the promises of God. To be a recipient of God's blessing does not in and of itself mean a trouble-free life. Jacob provides a word of realism for Pharaoh.

Joseph settles his family "in the best part of the land" and provides them with food in this time of famine. We do not know whether Joseph's family suffers the effects of the famine that afflicted the rest of Egypt. Inasmuch as the author never mentions the Israelites in vv. 13-26, they probably had enough food.

These conversations attest to the fact that Egypt will not, finally, be the home of these people. They cannot be integrated with the Egyptians. They remain transients, forced by famine to live here and not able to call it home. Yet, Egypt will prove to be hospitable for the growth of many generations (cf. Exod 1:7).

47:13-26. This segment seems unrelated to its present context. It is most closely connected with Joseph's skilled economic leadership in 41:46-57, which it may continue—though links with the seven-year famine are not made (see the inexact reference to years in v. 18; cf. v. 14 with 41:56). These verses illustrate Joseph's administrative wisdom (and show that it continues beyond the climax in chap. 45). At the same time, such harsh measures made necessary by emergency can be abused if successive leaders are not comparably wise (as in Exod 1:8). Joseph could be faulted for having insufficient vision, especially in making his emergency measures permanent "to this day" (v. 26).

An editor may have placed these verses in their present position because of two themes. First is the report about food in v. 11, where Joseph provides food not only for his family but also for all the Egyptians. Second is the blessings on Pharaoh (vv. 7, 10). Through these economic measures, Joseph serves as the channel for blessing on Pharaoh and his people (stated seven times!).

The reader has some difficulties following the text, which may reflect the redactional process and our lack of knowledge regarding ancient Egyptian economics.[218] The interpreter should thus be cautious in drawing conclusions about Joseph's role. His policy results in a concentration of property and power in the crown, but the language of "slavery" appears insufficiently nuanced (note the textual difficulties in v. 21). One should think about "tenant farmers of the state" as well as the draconian measures of nationalization.[219]

218. For details, see Westermann, *Genesis 37–50*, 173.
219. Sarna, *Genesis*, 321-23.

The severity of the famine in Egypt and Canaan (Canaan drops out after v. 15) prompts Joseph to develop new food distribution systems. He responds to the cries of the Egyptian people for bread, and even takes their opinions into account (v. 19). Whatever effects the measures have on the people, the idea has come from them; they affirm it after the actions have been taken (v. 25).

The progressively more severe measures include the money supply's no longer sufficing to buy food; livestock depletion in exchange for food; Joseph's buying their land in exchange for food (actually, for seed to grow food). They make this request even though it will mean that they and their lands will come under Pharaoh's control (v. 19).

Joseph proceeds as they request. All Egyptian lands (the priests had an agreement with Pharaoh) become royal property, and the people become tenant farmers, even though it deprives them of some freedom. Joseph gives them seed for sowing, and they agree that Pharaoh will receive 20 percent of the harvests (making the emergency policy of 41:34 permanent)—not excessive in that world. They are grateful to Joseph for having saved their lives, and ask for his continuing favor, even as they affirm their status as tenant farmers.

REFLECTIONS

1. These chapters begin to move from the story of the person called Israel to the story of the people called Israel. Literarily, the author interweaves Joseph's reunion with Jacob and the list of the seventy members of Jacob's family who migrate to Egypt. Rather than simply juxtaposing these developments, the list occurs before the reunion. Beginning with "the Israelites" (46:8) and concluding with "the house of Jacob" (v. 27; cf. v. 31; 50:8), the list signals the shift to a new era as the family becomes a people, anticipating the book of Exodus (cf. Exod 1:1 with 1:7).

The author provides a preface, grounded in a promise with corporate dimensions. These promises, long absent from the narrative (see 35:9-13), still operate in spite of all that has occurred. The promise of a "great nation" in 46:3 gives divine direction to this development. The elision of the individual and the corporate in v. 4 ("I will bring you up again") anticipates Exodus events. The move from family to people is presented as divinely sanctioned. The reader thereby begins to shift attention to the new reality of Israel as the people of God.

2. The purpose of the story, especially as articulated in 45:5-9, now comes more clearly into view. God's concern in this entire story has been to "preserve life," to make sure that there would be a "remnant," enough "survivors" from this family to move out into God's larger purposes for the world. This divine purpose for life does not relate narrowly to Jacob's family, but to the larger world. All the attention given to Joseph must be related to these overarching purposes. At the same time, the particular promise to Israel now becomes integrated with this purpose.

3. The author integrates Jacob's twofold blessing of Pharaoh (47:7, 10) with the aforementioned dynamic. As announced in 12:2-3, the chosen family will be a blessing to all, not least to those who extend blessing upon them (as Egypt and Pharaoh certainly have). This entails—even if not actually stated—a blessing for life and well-being for Pharaoh and his family and fertility for his lands and animals. One notes no little irony here, as a lowly foreign shepherd pronounces a blessing upon this paragon of wisdom and power who was understood to participate in the very life of the divine. The text does not state explicitly that Pharaoh, potentate though he is, needs blessing (as his question in 47:8 suggests). Moreover, Jacob represents one who is Lord even of Pharaoh, and from whom all blessings flow.

By this action Jacob adheres to the calling of this chosen family, whose words and deeds on behalf of their God should reach out beyond themselves and include within the circle of blessing even *those who seem least in need of it.* The need for God's blessing cuts across socioeconomic strata and political boundaries; Jacob and Pharaoh stand together as recipients of blessing. Even more, the blessing ought to extend to those whose relationship to the chosen may become problematic and difficult. Jacob's blessing of this pharaoh stands in the background of the later conflict with the pharaohs in Exodus; it remains a sign of the desirable relationship with the Egyptians.

4. In 47:13-26, we see comparable, if more concrete, blessing activity on Joseph's part. This Israelite, whose authority extends over a nonchosen people, responds to their cries for bread. The links between this text and 45:7 show that the preservation of life remains important for all people. The issues of life and death for Jacob's family over the course of the narrative have become issues for the Egyptians (note the repeated concern in vv. 19, 25). The place to which Israel has gone to seek relief is now itself caught up in the famine's effects; Joseph, in effect, returns the favor. The people of God are here engaged in seeking to alleviate the devastating effects of the famine on people who stand outside of their own community, by working in and through a variety of governmental structures. Their methods may not be a model of perfection, but taking the opinions of the hurting people themselves into account, they enter into the fray on behalf of life rather than death.

5. The Egyptians view the famine as a life-and-death issue not only for themselves but also for their land (vv. 18-19). Their cry to Joseph involves the future of the land ("that the land may not become desolate") as much as their own. They thereby recognize that such events have important ecological consequences and that the human future is inextricably linked with the future of the land. This testifies to the wisdom of the nonchosen regarding the care of creation—a wisdom often evident through the centuries, including our own, and to which the community of faith should be as responsive as Joseph.

6. We now understand better the statement that a later pharaoh did not "know Joseph" (Exod 1:8). Later generations of pharaohs will not remember that frequently Joseph served as the mediator of blessings for Egyptian royalty. There may be some irony in that, as Joseph makes "slaves" of the Egyptians (though not to himself), so the later pharaohs—who do not have the wisdom and commitments of Joseph—will make "slaves" of his family. While we cannot be certain, this reversal raises the question of whether later pharaohs extend Joseph's economic policy to include the Israelites. Any governmental policy can be twisted in such a way as to become demonic. Yet, that must not be allowed to immobilize people in their efforts to work for life in and through imperfect structures.

GENESIS 47:27–50:26, THE EMERGENCE OF UNIFIED ISRAEL

OVERVIEW

These chapters, evidently a composite, have been pieced together from various sources and given their present unity by the Priestly redactor. We may conclude that they are concerned primarily with the story of Jacob, his final days, his testamentary activities, his death and burial. Certainly they show that Jacob dies in peace (46:30), after numerous indications that it might not be so (cf. 37:35; 42:38; 44:29-31). Yet, Joseph's role remains important as well. One might suggest that 47:27-28 and 50:22-23 lift up both persons by the way they bracket the section (both "settle" in Egypt, are fruitful, and die at a certain age).

But these chapters possess a more fundamental purpose together with chaps. 46–47: They speak of the transition from the individual sons of Jacob to corporate Israel and the tribal dynamics and interrelationships characteristic of a people. This story comes to a climax in 50:24, with the reconciled brothers receiving the promise from Joseph (who had received it from Jacob in 48:3-4, 21-22). As such, chaps. 48–50 provide a bracket with chaps. 37–38 for the entire story, moving from the apparent exclusion of Joseph and Judah to their special role associated with promises in a unified family.

Subsequent *tribal* history has shaped these chapters. Hence, the relationship between Joseph's sons, Ephraim and Manasseh, in chap. 48 plays off the development and history of Israelite tribes with these names, collectively called the house of Joseph (e.g., Amos 5:6). The blessing of Jacob in chap. 49 does so in a comparable way for all of Jacob's sons, though recognizing the ascendancy of the Joseph and Judah tribes in the north and south.

Genesis 47:27–48:22, Joseph and His Sons

COMMENTARY

This segment begins with a summary statement (47:27-28; v. 27 does double duty) then moves to Joseph's oath regarding Jacob's burial (47:29-31), to Jacob's adoption and blessing of Joseph's two sons (48:1-22), to Jacob's "blessing" on all his sons (49:1-28), and his death and burial (49:29–50:14). It closes with the brothers' reconciliation (50:15-21) and the promise to the unified family (50:24) during Joseph's final days (50:22-26).

47:27. This verse serves as a preliminary conclusion to the story (see the parallel with 37:1). The people of Israel—note the corporate reference—not only survive in Goshen, but they thrive, gaining many possessions and, in fulfillment of the divine promise (35:11; 1:28; cf. 48:4), growing considerably (cf. Exod 1:7). The connections with both Genesis 1 and 35 provide a link between God's creative work and God's promissory activity.

47:28-31. This episode begins with a summary statement about Jacob's life and death. He lives his last seventeen years in Egypt (cf. 37:2).

Prior to his death, Jacob requests that Joseph swear an oath regarding his burial in Canaan (cf. 24:2 for the phrase "hand under thigh"). In 49:29-32, Jacob will charge all the brothers with this task, specifying the cave at Machpelah, near Hebron (23:1-20; 50:5, 12-13). Jacob asks Joseph to "show kindness and faithfulness" (חסד ואמת *ḥesed we'ĕmet*), two significant theological terms (v. 29). This oath presents strong commitment language for what seems an insignificant issue to moderns, but burial in Canaan is no minor matter to Jacob (and Joseph, 50:25), not least because of God's own promise (46:4). It may be a not so subtle effort to assure the continuance of his family in Canaan rather than Egypt.

The phrase "lie down with my ancestors [fathers]" is an idiom for death (cf. 15:15; 25:8); the phrase "bow at the head of the bed" (the NIV adopts another text) probably refers to a worshipful gesture in the bed to which Jacob is confined (48:2; cf. Heb. 11:21). It has nothing to do with bowing down to Joseph, as if the dream in 37:9 were partially fulfilled in this gesture; in the immediately following text, Jacob exercises authority over Joseph.

48:1-7. Upon hearing that his father is ill, Joseph takes his two sons to their grandfather for a proper farewell. Because Joseph has not been told of God's promises (or himself received a revelation), at least in the storyline, Jacob recalls God's (*El Shaddai,* 17:1) appearance to him at Luz (Bethel) in Canaan (35:9-13). The major elements of the promise were that his family would experience considerable growth (see 47:27), become a "community/company of peoples" (see 28:3), and receive Canaan as a perpetual holding (see 17:8; perpetuity does not appear in chap. 35).

This report moves immediately to Jacob's adoption of Ephraim and Manasseh as his own sons, "just as Reuben and Simeon are" (Jacob's oldest sons), a legal act with parallels in the ancient Near East (see Ruth 4:16-17).[220] The "therefore" (NRSV) of v. 5 shows that Jacob makes this decision on the basis of the previous promise: As its recipient, he assumes power to designate its inheritors. This act places Joseph's sons on a par with Jacob's own sons. Should Joseph have other offspring, they are to be his own, though for purposes of inheritance they will participate with the families of Ephraim and Manasseh.

Then (v. 7), for reasons not entirely clear, Jacob recalls Rachel's death at the time of his own death (quoting from 35:16, 19, perhaps because it follows the just-cited 35:9-13). The link between Rachel and this adoption of her grandchildren could be rooted in Jacob's special love for the wife who died in childbirth. The fact that the mother of the two sons is

220. Sarna, *Genesis,* 325.

Asenath, the daughter of an Egyptian priest (46:20), may also be a factor.

48:8-20. A ritual of blessing now follows (cf. chap. 27) as a concluding part of the adoption ceremony. It begins with a verification of the boys' identity (cf. 27:18), as Joseph confesses them to be God's gift to him (so 41:51). The nearly blind Jacob (cf. 27:1) asks that they be brought near so that he can bless them. After kissing and embracing the sons and having them placed near (on?) his knees (v. 12, a symbolic act legitimating their status as sons; cf. 30:3; 50:23), he confesses that God has let him live long enough to see both Joseph and his sons. Jacob certainly had had other opportunities to see his grandsons—here understood to be boys. Hence, these chapters should not be conceived in a linear way.

After bowing his face to the earth (a gesture of honor), Joseph stands them next to his father, Ephraim on the left and Manasseh on the right, the place of honor, assuming that the oldest (Manasseh) would be the recipient of Jacob's right hand. Jacob, however, crosses his hands so that his right hand rests on Ephraim (v. 14; cf. Num 27:18, 23). When Joseph sees this (v. 17), he interrupts the ritual, thinking of Jacob's failing sight (ironic, considering his own story; Num 27:1), and begins to switch his father's hands. But Jacob calmly insists, knowing full well what he has done. He explains: Both sons will become a great people, but Ephraim shall be greater, the father of a multitude of nations. Ephraim will truly be preeminent, so prominent that Ephraim becomes a name for the northern kingdom (cf. Jer 31:9; Hosea). "So he put Ephraim ahead of Manasseh" (v. 20). In terms of tribal history, Ephraim and Manasseh replace the nonterritorial tribe of Levi, thus retaining the number twelve.

The two "blessings" of the sons by Jacob are distributed over the course of the action (vv. 15-16, 20). Jacob *verbally* treats Ephraim and Manasseh equally, building on the act of adoption. Only in the ritual and the explanation given to Joseph (v. 19) does a distinction become evident.

In the first, Jacob "blessed *Joseph,*" though it seems that only the sons are blessed (as in v. 20), but, as in vv. 21-22, reference to the father includes the sons (see Deut 33:13-17;

cf. Gen 49:22-26). Jacob begins a threefold invocation, in liturgical language, with a structure similar to the Aaronic benediction in Num 6:24-26. The specific content of the blessing (v. 16) consists of (1) their families' being included within the ongoing traditions that include the names of Abraham, Isaac, and Jacob; and (2) their considerable growth as families, blessed by God with the power of life (already by Num 26:28-37 their numbers exceed those of Reuben and Simeon; cf. also Deut 33:17).

The second blessing (v. 20) is complicated by the use of the singular "you" (see the NRSV footnote); the first instance probably refers to the sons individually (cf. the use of plural and singular in Num 6:23-26), the second to the one being blessed. The sons' names can be invoked when Israel (the people, cf. 47:27) pronounces blessings on others: God bless you as he has blessed Ephraim and Manasseh, with all that means in terms of life, fertility, and well-being (cf. 12:3; 18:18; 22:18; 26:4; 28:14). What God has done to them will be an exemplary instance of divine blessing.

48:21-22. These verses show that the adoption of Joseph's sons does not entail a displacement of Joseph. This elevation of his sons, in effect, represents an elevation of Joseph to the status of firstborn, who *in his sons* receives a double share (cf. 49:26; Deut. 33:13-17; 1 Chr 5:1-2). Double shares go to the firstborn. The placement of this chapter before the blessings of chap. 49, within which the Joseph sayings (vv. 22-26) are really the only ones that directly relate to the

blessings promised his ancestors, attest to this elevation.

Jacob here speaks more directly to Joseph. Jacob has included him in the blessing of his sons up to this point (v. 15), made especially clear in the transmission of the promise of presence and land to Joseph and his family (the "you" is plural). God will be with them; this promise, usually associated with a journey (28:15), anticipates the exodus. God will also bring them back to the land of promise. These are promises heretofore not extended to Joseph; he in turn will transmit them to his brothers in 50:24. In Canaan he will be given one more portion than that received by his brothers (namely, the portions assigned to his two sons; see Josh 17:14-18).

The word translated "portion" (NRSV) or "ridge of land" (NIV) is שׁכם (*šĕkem*), usually meaning "shoulder," but here probably a play on the city of Shechem. Jacob purchased land there (33:18-19), and Joseph will be buried there (Josh 24:32); it became a central city in the northern kingdom (i.e., Ephraim). The defeat of the Amorites (the pre-Israelite population of Canaan; cf. 15:16) may refer to the violent acts of Simeon and Levi in 34:25-29. Yet, it speaks of Jacob's own sword and bow. Jacob judged those actions harshly (34:30; and in the blessing to be pronounced [49:5-7]). It may be a fragment, recognized also in Israel's never having to conquer the Shechem area. If it alludes to Genesis 34, Jacob would now be simply dealing with reality; it is past history and can now be assigned to the family of Joseph (*not* to Simeon and Levi).

REFLECTIONS

1. The close reader of Genesis might have predicted the turn of events in chap. 48. As throughout the ancestral stories, Jacob's included, primogeniture is set aside; the younger has been given priority over the older. The reader will also recall the deathbed blessing of Jacob's father, Isaac (chap. 27). Such a deathbed blessing was believed to have a special efficacy.

Israelites believed that Jacob's act of putting Ephraim ahead of Manasseh accounted, in part, for the later history of these tribes. While both tribes were powerful during the early years, Ephraim became the more powerful by the time of the monarchy. As Westermann says, the account provides a " 'prehistorical' conception of history," wherein "events were explained by the family structures underlying them."[221] Jacob's decision

221. Westermann, *Genesis 37–50*, 191.

shapes the future, yet not in such a way that his decision floats above the realities of history until it comes to pass. Jacob's decision continues to be remembered and has effects on the subsequent history of the family, which involves the relative status of each of these tribes.

2. Jacob's threefold invocation of God (48:15-16) provides a gathering of themes from the Genesis narrative.

God is the one before whom Abraham and Isaac walked (recalling 17:1; 24:40; cf. 5:22; 6:9). The author focuses here *not* on God's action, but on human "walking." Their faithfulness becomes important for what Jacob now has to say. God's action preceded their response; the deity has been engaged in every aspect of the lives of Jacob's grandfather and father. Jacob can now testify twice to God's involvement in his own life (but not his own "walking").

God is the one who has been his shepherd all the days of Jacob's life, thereby placing a concrete image on the promise of 28:15 (cf. 35:3). The image of God as shepherd includes the ideas of guidance, protection, and the provision of sustenance for the journey (cf. 49:24; Pss 23:1; 80:2). Jacob certainly draws this image of God out of his own experience as shepherd. This integration of life experience and divine revelation illustrates how new images for God develop within the community of faith. It prompts reflection on how new images for God might be developed out of the interplay of modern experience and inherited traditions.

God is the one who has redeemed (גאל *gō'ēl*) him from all harm (רע *ra'*). The text actually reads "the angel [מלאך *mal'āk*]," i.e., God who appears in human form (see 31:11-13; cf. 16:7-13; 21:17-19; 22:11-12, 15-16). Jacob's use of "angel" could be informed by his struggle with the "man" at the Jabbok (32:22-33). The language of redemption (*gō'ēl*) rarely refers to God's action on behalf of individuals (cf. Pss 19:14; 103:4). The OT uses it chiefly for God's salvific acts at the Red Sea (Exod 6:6; 15:13), which this anticipates, as well as in the exile (Isaiah 40–55; Jer 31:9-11). Divine activity on behalf of Jacob thus moves beyond the providential, ongoing activity of the second predicate and more specifically speaks of God's activity as one of salvation. The author thus integrates creation and redemption themes in these wide-ranging statements about God.

Genesis 49:1-33, The Last Words of Jacob

COMMENTARY

Many scholars deem this poem—Jacob's final words to his sons—to be one of the oldest pieces of literature in the OT. Its language, aphorisms, metaphors, word plays, and other poetic features make for many difficulties in text, translation, and interpretation. The poem has no doubt had a complex compositional history, evident, for example, in the differing length and character of each saying. One confronts difficulties in assessing the literary and historical relationships with a similar list of tribal sayings in Deuteronomy 33 (cf. Judg 5:14-18).

Only the sayings of Reuben and Judah occur in the second person, directly addressed to them; only in those of Reuben, Simeon/Levi, and Judah does Jacob refer to himself in the first person (also in the interlude, v. 18). The order of the sons corresponds to no other text; Leah's six sons come first and Rachel's last, with Bilhah's sons (Dan, Naphtali) enclosing those of Zilpah. The form of the sayings regarding Reuben, Simeon/Levi, Judah, and Joseph is more oracular, that of the others more aphoristic.

The prose context in which the poem is set occasions further difficulties. Verse 28 names this word of Jacob a blessing; yet curse and censure occur. The "blessings" of Reuben, Simeon, and Levi are sharply negative (cf. vv. 4-7). Jacob's telling his sons "what will happen to you in days to come" presents a similar difficulty. While most of the sayings bear on the future, not all do. Moreover, they also often focus on past events or present circumstance.

The differences among the sayings provide evidence for their independent origins in widely disparate settings. They have been brought together into a larger poem over an extensive period of time, the present composite form emerging sometime late in the period of the judges or in the early monarchy. The sayings were then inserted into a narrative that originally moved directly from 49:1*a* ("Jacob summoned his sons") to 49:28*b*, a reference to blessing but with no specific content. The structural element that most informs the present shape is Jacob's repeated charge regarding his burial that encloses the two blessings of chaps. 48–49, first to Joseph (47:29-31) and then to all the sons (49:29-32). Enclosing each of these in turn are the references to Jacob's death (47:28; 49:33).

These sayings have to do less with the persons in the previous narrative than with tribal entities, reflecting the history of the tribes during the early centuries in Canaan. Only those of Reuben and Simeon/Levi are explicitly related to earlier incidents; otherwise, only Judah and Joseph mention intrafamilial relationships. The negative words about Reuben and Simeon reflect both their ill-begotten behaviors and their later disappearance as tribal entities; they are the only sayings with a crime/punishment schema. The two lengthiest blessings, those of Judah and Joseph (vv. 8-12, 22-26), reflect both their dominance in the ancestral story and their predominance in tribal history. Only the Joseph sayings mention God explicitly (v. 18 is an interlude); they provide the most direct link to the ancestral promises of blessing. Many of the sayings include lively metaphors from the nonhuman world.

49:1-2. Jacob asks his sons to gather around his deathbed to hear a word about their future. Not all the sayings allude to the future, but in all cases they move beyond the

lifetime of the sons. Hence, there is overall movement from individual to tribal entity, which parallels other elements in these final chapters that move from Jacob to Israel (see 46:8; 47:27). This future, already beginning to emerge out of the present, is conceived in historical, not eschatological, terms.

49:3-4. Jacob addresses Reuben directly. Reuben, Jacob's firstborn and the product of his youthful vigor, excels in rank and power. But like sea waters, he seems unreliable, inconsistent in behavior. He will not excel, because he disgracefully lay with Bilhah, his father's wife (35:22). Jacob, in effect, deposes Reuben from his status as firstborn (see chap. 48). That future of instability (see Deut 33:6) works itself out historically: The tribe, whose territory lay east of the Dead Sea, was absorbed by the Moabites.

49:5-7. Simeon and Levi are the only sons considered together, no doubt because of the slaughter at Shechem (34:25-30). The poem includes strong language about them; they were murderous, violent, fiercely angry, arbitrary, cruel, and harsh in their treatment of animals. Consequently, Jacob will not participate in their counsels (cf. 34:30). He curses their anger (i.e., "them," an instance of metonymy) and announces the dispersion of their families throughout the nation. Historically, their "dispersion" appears quite different. Simeon (omitted in Deuteronomy 33) was absorbed into the tribe of Judah. Levi later becomes a nonterritorial priestly group, elect by God (Num 8:14-19; 18:24), a development not in view here (cf. Deut 33:8-11). Jacob's repeated use of the first person reflects a prophetic mode of discourse; strikingly, Jacob himself (namely, his word) serves as the agent of judgment in v. 7.

49:8-12. Jacob praises Judah highly in recognition of his increasingly prominent role in the preceding narrative. The heart of the saying contains a promise: All his brothers will recognize him as preeminent because he will defeat his enemies in battle (i.e., seize them by the neck). The poet employs the image of a lion/lioness/lion's cub for Judah because he is cleverly successful in his ventures (i.e., he always returns to the lair with his prey) and no one dares to provoke him (cf. Num 24:9; "lion of Judah" becomes a messianic image, Rev 5:5).

Verse 10 appears especially difficult, particularly the word שִׁילֹה (*šîlōh*), variously translated as a place (Shiloh) or a person ("ruler," the one to whom rule belongs; so the NIV) or tribute (NRSV). It most likely refers to a person. The basic image is clear: The poet depicts Judah as a royal figure, whose rule (i.e., scepter, staff standing between feet; cf. Ps 45:6) will continue for a lengthy period until a climactic event occurs that assures a glorious future, when he will reign over obedient nations and a fertile earth.

But what will happen to enable this future? Judah experiences some growth over the years, but achieves prominence only during the time of Saul and David. Hence, many scholars suggest that this verse refers to the Davidic monarchy, at which point Judah's preeminence as a tribe will assume a broader sovereignty over the nations. The imagery has also been interpreted in messianic terms—e.g., the Balaam oracles (see Num 24:17). In such contexts, Judah will rule until the Messiah comes, and all the peoples of the world will serve him in a time of great abundance. Historically, an original Davidic reference was probably given a messianic interpretation during the course of Israel's history (cf. Psalm 2; Isa 11:1-9).

Although the images are somewhat obscure, vv. 11-12 speak of the new prosperity brought about by Judah's hegemony. There will be so many vineyards that he can use the tender stalks to tether his donkey (a royal animal, Zech 9:9) and a grape harvest so abundant that he can even wash his clothes in blood-colored wine. He will be a person of surpassing beauty, with dark eyes and white teeth (see Ps 45:2; the images in Num 24:5-7).

49:13. This verse focuses on geographical location (cf. Josh 19:10-16, where Zebulun is not on the coast). Zebulun shall have an advantageous position, with access to the sea, at or near the port of Sidon (=Phoenicia).

49:14-15. The poet describes Issachar as a strong donkey that has been domesticated and rests at ease rather than roaming free (i.e., lives among the sheep, or saddlebags); this may allude to the fertile plain of Esdraelon in northern Canaan. The image suggests one content with his lot, in exchange for which it will (NIV) or has (NRSV) become a servant

to others (e.g., the Canaanites or Solomon's forced levy, 1 Kgs 9:21?). These verses seem to present a negative future (contrast Judg 5:15).

49:16-17. In this positive saying, Dan (a name similar to the word for "judge") will become active in seeking justice for the tribes of Israel (note the tribal reference; cf. Judges 18). The image of a poisonous snake suggests Dan as a small tribe struggling for survival, but which will successfully strike at more powerful groups ("horse and rider") and so advocate the causes it has assumed. The history of this tribe, which had difficulty settling within its original borders and migrated to the north, is very complex.[222]

49:18. This confession of trust in God provides an interlude reflected in the Psalms (25:5; 38:15; 119:166). Jacob waits for God. He interrupts the blessings on his sons with a word of anticipation for the salvation (יְשׁוּעָה *yĕšûʿâ*) that Yahweh (the only occurrence in chap. 49) will bring to him. This is probably not a word about Jacob personally, but a corporate reference, expressing trust in God's eventual salvation on behalf of Jacob's sons.

49:19. Gad settled east of the Jordan and was especially vulnerable to desert marauders. Gad will continue to be victimized by bands of raiders (גְּדוּד יְגוּדֶנּוּ *gĕdûd yĕgûdennû*, a word play on גָּד *Gad*), but will be able to respond effectively by seemingly minor acts of bravery.

49:20. Asher's coastal land was agriculturally fertile, hence he would provide rich food for royalty, including the export of delicacies. The reference appears positive.

49:21. The positive, but puzzling, image of Naphtali as a doe that has been set free and bears beautiful fawns suggests that he will enjoy freedom, vitality, and increase of numbers in the mountain areas of his home (north of the Sea of Galilee).

49:22-26. The relationship between Joseph and his sons in the previous chapter (see 48:15, 21-22) shows that the mention of either could count for both (cf. Deut 27:12; 33:13-17).

The image of a fruitful, well-watered bough whose branches extend ever outward suggests a growing community that moves

---

222. See Westermann, *Genesis 37–50*, 340.

into surrounding territories. Joseph's enemies attacked him (his brothers?), but he held his own with strength, courage, and agility. This response was made possible because of divine aid, specified by an unusually concentrated series of images, drawn from liturgical practice (cf. 48:15-16): (a) Mighty One of Jacob (see Ps 132:2, 5; Isa 49:26; 60:16); God has seen Jacob through thick and thin during his numerous lengthy and troubled journeys. (b) Shepherd (see 48:15). (c) The epithet "Rock of Israel" (cf. Deut 32:15, 31; 1 Sam 7:12) stresses the strength and constancy of God on behalf of the weak and helpless. God's faithfulness remains steadfast even when being buffeted about by people and events. (d) The title "God of your father" (see Exod 3:6) represents continuity from one generation to the next, informed most fundamentally by God's faithfulness to promises made. (e) The Almighty (*Shaddai*, see 17:1).

This God will continue to help and bless Joseph (note the creation and redemption themes). These themes tie Joseph most closely to the promises given to his ancestors (12:2-3) and are expanded (cf. the parallels in Deut 28:3-6; 33:13-16): the blessing of water for crops—so important in an arid land—from both the heavens above (rain) and the earth beneath (springs) as well as the blessing of the fertility of the females (breasts and womb). The word *blessing* occurs six times!

Verse 26 has a benedictory form. The blessings extended by Jacob (received from Isaac, 27:28) are richer than any others (if they exceed the mountains, they exceed all). They are now given to Joseph, who has been set apart from his brothers (a reference to chap. 48). The reference to head and brow may be synecdoche or refer to the laying on of hands (cf. 48:13-18).

49:27. The image of a ravenous wolf for Benjamin, though basically positive, does not correspond to anything in the narrative (cf. Judg 5:13-14; 20:15-25). The poem portrays him as relentless and successful in battle with other peoples, which could be related to his territory's central geographical location between Judah and Ephraim.

49:28. This concluding comment stresses that each of Jacob's blessings was appropriate to the son—i.e., each was suitable to its person, history, and life situation. The narrator here, for the first time, mentions the twelve tribes.

49:29-33. In this final charge to his sons, Jacob reinforces the oath taken by Joseph (47:29-31); he knows that oaths no more control the future than do blessings. Jacob requests that he be buried in the place purchased by Abraham at Machpelah (chap. 23), where three generations are already buried (the only reference to the burial of Rebekah and Leah). The detail in the text makes the charge unmistakably clear; the repeated clause regarding purchase from the Hittites (vv. 29b, 32a) encloses the place reference, emphasizing its legal standing and authenticating the claim that this is the land promised to Jacob's descendants. Having completed this charge, Jacob dies (cf. 27:30).

REFLECTIONS

1. Tribal considerations appear in chap 49. While most scholars think these words were written soon after the history they reflect, the text presents these materials as Jacob's own word. *Prophecy* would not be fully adequate to describe these materials. We understand them better as Jacob's judgment regarding the future of his sons' lives on the basis of his thoroughgoing knowledge and evaluation of them. The past and present life of the son signals the way in which each future will be shaped. While this becomes explicit only with Reuben and Simeon/Levi, these cases function paradigmatically for the others. Hence, the future sketched out does not appear arbitrary, unrelated to experience. The wisdom exhibited by Jacob—an important link with the

Joseph story as a whole—involves discerning how the future for each son grows out of past and present experience.

2. The last words of Jacob in chap 49 unify the book of Genesis in significant ways. Links with the divine promises to each ancestor are drawn up into this poem. The promises regarding a nation/people (cf. 12:2; 46:3), numerous posterity (cf. 26:24; 48:4), and blessings in abundance (22:17) become a reality in the twelve tribes. Within chaps. 37–50, special attention was initially given to both Joseph (chap. 37) and Judah (chap. 38); now in these last words, Joseph and Judah dominate the scene (in terms of quantity of material [some 40 percent]), the extent to which the divine blessing affects their lives, and their role and influence in shaping Israel's future.

Moreover, the efficacy of the word links the beginning and the end of Genesis, from the creative word of God to the effective word of the patriarch. At the same time, just as one finds a certain vulnerability of the divine word as its waits upon creaturely response, so also the patriarch's word waits upon the contingencies of historical process as it moves into the future. This appears particularly evident concerning the role of the tribe of Levi, whose "dispersion" can hardly be considered negative due to its special election by God to priestly status (Num 8:14-19; 18:24; Deut 10:8-9). Thus Jacob's words do not determine fully the future of the tribes.

3. A poet used striking metaphors to depict Jacob's sons, including lion, donkey, snake, deer, fruit, tree, and wolf. We need to ask how such metaphors function. They have been created on the basis of observations made of commonalities between human beings and the animal and plant worlds. In congruence with the use of metaphor, the enemies of the various tribes are never named (the same phenomenon can be observed in Psalms); this gives the poem a more timeless quality, enabling the reader to relate it to a multitude of situations. We must thus be careful not to seek to pin down each saying to a particular historical moment. The movement back and forth between individual personalities and corporate identities also contributes to this fluidity. Hence, the sayings could link the ancestral period with virtually every succeeding period of the tribal history.

4. We should devote special consideration to 49:10-12 and should not consider this text a straightforward parallel to the messianic oracles of the prophets. First, the text is insufficiently clear to establish this claim. Second, it suggests, wrongly, that a full-blown messianism is present wherever these themes occur. It seems better to think that these verses provide early reflections concerning the future, particularly in view of the failure of the monarchy. These traditions of promise are associated with words of indictment and judgment on Reuben and Simon/Levi.

5. While one rightly should attend to the details associated with each of Jacob's sons, one should also consider the overall picture of this family that emerges. The sayings suggest both unity and diversity. One could use the image of a body, moving back and forth between corporate identity and individual expression, with the various members of the body contributing in their own unique way to the functioning of the whole. At the same time, not all the members make equally important contributions; Judah and Joseph are evidently the head and the heart of the people. Moreover, not all play a positive role; among the tribal groups there is excellence and mediocrity, vigor and weakness, goodness and evil. Overall, the author presents a realistic, warts-and-all portrayal of the people of Israel. Yet, the word for the future is positive, most fundamentally because God is at work among them, saving and blessing.

Genesis 50:1-14, The Burial of Jacob

COMMENTARY

The author reports on the events associated with the death and burial of Jacob. Weeping and mourning, on the part of both Joseph and the Egyptians, move in and out of this scene (vv. 1, 3-4, 10-11).

Once again Joseph weeps, marking another major stage in the development of the story (see 42:24). He directs the physicians to embalm Jacob, a forty-day task, included within the seventy days of mourning. The OT reports mummification only for Jacob and Joseph (hence it genuinely reflects the Egyptian setting). Since this practice was customary for Egyptian monarchs, the writer depicts Jacob's receiving a royal funeral. In contrast, it seems ironic that the burial of Joseph, the royal official, is described in the simplest of terms (v. 26). The *Egyptians* mourn for Jacob in a grand way (the brothers are never so singled out).

Joseph attends to the oath he had sworn to his father about burial in Canaan (see 47:29-31). Contrary to usual practice (see 47:1), perhaps because of the mourning, Joseph indirectly asks permission of Pharaoh to go to Canaan to bury his father. Pharaoh grants it, and Joseph proceeds exactly according to his request.

Joseph and a "very great company" (v. 9) make the journey to Canaan with Jacob's body. This return anticipates the exodus and subsequent events, only this time the Egyptians accompany them! The group includes not only all the members of the "household" of both Joseph and Jacob (except children—probably with mothers—and livestock), but also "all" of Pharaoh's servants and "all" the elders of the land of Egypt, with full chariot (i.e., military) accompaniment. Once again, in purposeful hyperbole, the full participation of the Egyptians appears stunning. The Egyptians seem to agree with the claims of Jacob's family to the land of Canaan. The author reinforces this claim (ironically?) by the "objective" observation of the Canaanites that the Egyptians engaged in such "a very great and sorrowful mourning" (vv. 10-11).

Jacob's burial place remains unclear. In v. 5, Joseph quotes his father's request to be buried "in the tomb that I hewed out for myself in the land of Canaan." We do not find this description in either of Jacob's charges (47:29-31; 49:29-32). The language probably reflects Pharaoh's understanding rather than a different burial tradition. For reasons unknown, they hold a wake at the threshing floor at Atad (renamed Abel-mizraim, "mourning of Egypt," by the Canaanites), a place otherwise unknown. While "beyond the Jordan" could mean the Transjordan, if the writer were east of the Jordan it could be Canaan (as the reference to Canaanites suggests). If the latter, the journey would not be a major detour from a direct Egypt-Mamre (Hebron) route. Hence, we would not need to think of another tradition regarding Jacob's place of burial. Only Joseph observes a seven-day time of mourning (the usual Israelite practice, 1 Sam 31:13), and only the sons continue on to the burial place.

The text stipulates that Jacob's sons did exactly what their father had instructed them to do (v. 12). This claim must refer to the following verse, hence v. 12 should conclude with a colon (so NIV). This episode concludes with the return of the entire party to Egypt (as Joseph had promised to Pharaoh, at least regarding himself, v. 5).

REFLECTIONS

It would appear that the positive references to Egyptian participation (indeed, Egyptian burial practices) in Jacob's funeral are intended to stand in sharp contrast to the changed relationship between Israel and the Egyptians in the following Exodus narrative. Genesis speaks of the kind of relationship that can be possible with other, nonchosen peoples. Exodus records an aberration. Genesis, not Exodus, should inform Israel's post-Exodus relations with the Egyptians.

Genesis 50:15-21, The Full Reconciliation of Israel's Sons

COMMENTARY

The author sets this story of reconciliation between two deaths, though it is difficult to relate it to the story in chap. 45. It may be simply a recapitulation, but its purpose seems more complex (see discussion on chap. 45).

In v. 15, the brothers express apprehension about how Joseph will treat them now that their father has died; he may decide to exact retribution (see 27:41). Given the lack of resolution in chap. 45, this is understandable. Moreover, in the face of the death of a common parent, particularly a parent of such influence and renown, typical patterns of behavior may no longer continue. Life among the siblings has to be renegotiated.

In vv. 16-17, the brothers send a messenger (cf. 37:32) to present their concerns to Joseph, suggesting their high anxiety (the NRSV adopts the LXX reading, omitting the messenger). They couch their concerns in terms of their father's deathbed wish, rather than a direct personal request. The upshot of Jacob's request was that the brothers be reconciled, more specifically that Joseph forgive them the crime they committed. No evidence exists that Jacob actually said this, but Joseph remains as much in the dark on this as the reader! This is the only text in which Jacob gives a clear indication that he knows what the brothers did to Joseph (cf. 42:36). Nothing suggests it is a fabrication, spun out of the brothers' anxiety. In fact, the last reference to a report from the brothers about what Jacob said (44:24-29) appears truthful. The progress of the story toward the unified family of chap. 50 reinforces their speech as an honest report.

Building on their father's request, the brothers call themselves "servants" (anticipating a key theme in Exodus) of "the God of your father." The author grounds their appeal in their common faith in the God of Jacob; this binds them to one another in the heritage of their father. The theme of forgiveness occurs twice in v. 17, in Jacob's request and voiced by the brothers. Words for "sin" and "evil" are used four times, in both their father's speech and in their own words. This high consciousness of their crime suggests that the encounter in chap. 45 did not resolve the matter for the brothers. Even with the assurances given them by Joseph, they still live with the guilt of what they have done.

Joseph weeps, though not in the presence of his brothers (cf. NRSV). Once again, this marks a move toward the resolution of the conflict. He had wept with his brothers in 45:1-2, 14-15 at the occasion of a reconciliation. Here he weeps over their message, words revealing an ongoing mistrust. The weeping may also signal to the reader that he will not seek revenge, marking another stage in the development of the story (see 42:24).

The reference to Joseph's weeping leads into the brothers' coming before him (the NRSV's "wept" is based on an emendation of the Hebrew), without waiting for any response from the messenger. The brothers do obeisance before Joseph and declare themselves his servants/slaves (once again, the Exodus theme). They intensify the messenger's words with these personal actions. The brothers' bowing before Joseph does *not* fulfill his dream in 37:7 (as it does in 42:6; 43:26; 44:14). Joseph will now reject such status as an inappropriate relationship between himself and his brothers.

The words to have no fear enclose Joseph's response (vv. 19-21). This signals an oracle of salvation, a word of comfort and assurance. Such language commonly appears as God's first word in theophany (see 21:17; 26:24; 46:3); Second Isaiah uses it to speak to the exiles (41:10-14). We also find this language in an oracle of salvation at the birth of Jesus and at his resurrection (Matt 28:10; Luke 2:10).

Joseph gives three reasons to ease their fears. First, he responds in tones that are both rebuke and reassurance: "Am I in the place of God?" The question portrays a profound human judgment in this matter, not a "humble declaration of noncompetence."[223] It probably has a double reference—to their request for forgiveness and to their offer to become slaves. (a) The latter occurs immediately before his response. Joseph is not God, thus they can be assured that he will not behave as a pharaoh to them. He remains subject to God as the brothers are; they stand together under the authority of a divine other who works purposefully on behalf of them all. This theme anticipates the acts of the pharaoh who did not know Joseph (Exod 1:8) and the fivefold use of servant language in Exod 1:13-14, with the authoritarianism and potential for oppression. The implication here functions as it does in Exodus; the people of Israel will be the servants of God alone. (b) Regarding forgiveness, Joseph seems to reject a guilt/forgiveness approach (as in 45:3-8), leaving that up to God. At the same time, his words and deeds reveal a conciliatory spirit, showing that no revenge on his part is in view.

Second, regardless of their intentions, and Joseph names them evil (רע *raʿ*; see 44:4-5),

they can be assured their actions have been drawn into God's larger purposes for goodness, and these have come to prevail. The God who created the world and called it good has been about life and its preservation in and through all of these events, despite their intentions for death. Joseph, by clearly naming the brothers' actions as "evil"—something not done in 45:3-9—makes this matter public. His positive action has their evil behaviors in clear view, and the brothers now know that the evil they have done no longer counts against them.

Third, they will be cared for. In v. 21, Joseph comforts them and speaks tenderly/kindly to them (both words are used in Isa 40:1-2 in a context of forgiveness), assuring them that he will provide for them, with special attention to the children, and hence their future (as in 45:10-11; 47:12). This involves not just words, but concrete practical realities. The brothers do not respond, and though vv. 24-25 assume a positive response, the brothers' final silence in the narrative may indicate a sense of foreboding, or at least openness, about future relationships.

223. Von Rad, *Genesis*, 432.

REFLECTIONS

1. The theme of goodness in Genesis comes full circle here.[224] In Genesis 1, God created everything "very good." This "good" did not entail perfection or deny the need of development. Throughout Genesis, God has been pursuing these good intentions for the created order. Even more, God recruited human beings to participate in that pursuit of goodness; God's creative work leads to specific vocations. Joseph's work in Egypt, for example, served creation (41:33-37, recognized by Pharaoh as "good"), providing for the daily needs of *all* persons (cf. 45:11; 47:12; 50:21). God's *creational* purposes for goodness, life, and well-being in and through people do not cease even in the face of their weakness or failure.

2. The narrator gathers up a key theme of these chapters (50:20) concerning what both the brothers and God have done (see also 45:5-9). The verb חשׁב (*ḥāšab*) is translated in various ways; either "plan" or "intend" will do, though "plan" lifts up the concrete side of intention more directly. This term also more clearly alludes to the plots of the brothers against Joseph. In their very plans, God, too, has been working on a plan for goodness (see Jer 18:11-12, 18; 29:11).

God does not have a highly detailed plan all worked out that will come to fruition regardless of what humans do. The people involved are not automatons, whose good or evil actions count for nothing. Positively, they can act for good in the face of those who plan for evil. Negatively, they can frustrate God's intentions, so that the future may look different from what would have been the case had only the divine plan been realized. Yet, however much these planners may complicate the divine planning, God's

224. See Brueggemann, *Genesis*, 373-76.

way into the future will never *finally* be stymied. God will persevere, will stay with plans for life, though it may entail changes in the ways and means to that goal in view of human intractability and failure. We should remember this perspective, voiced at the end of Genesis, as we move into the "evil" evident in the book of Exodus.

This divine action has been behind the scenes, unobtrusive. Dissimilar to the rest of Genesis, it has been more subtle, interweaving the threads of goodness and mercy among the various strands of evil in their lives, working toward the best possible end. God can take what such persons do and draw it into God's larger purposes. We do not find a situation in which "even the evil design is included in God's plan." God does not intend human evil. Rather, God's plan "is to bring the evil devised by the brothers to good effect."[225] Paul echoes this text in Rom 8:28: In everything, in even the worst that evildoers may throw God's way, God will draw it into the divine plans for good. For Joseph, finally, one must trust in these persistent divine purposes on behalf of life.

3. God's purposes are not confined to the reconciliation of the brothers. Joseph's word of comfort and assurance does address the context of their fear and guilt. But these words effect salvation in their lives, in the broadest sense of the term, which moves beyond forgiveness to include life and well-being.

This story demonstrates that the moral order does work, but not in any exact or inevitable way. It can be ameliorated by God's reconciling work as well as human comfort and compassion. The brothers do, indeed, reap many consequences for their deeds (cf. 42:14; 44:16); even forgiveness would not bring those to a sudden end. The issue becomes whether the evil consequences (hence the sin that triggered them) will be allowed to claim the day. God's move, in and through Joseph, means that sin and its consequences are not allowed to have the last word. The people of God can trust that, in the midst of sin and evil, God pursues his purposes for good.

Joseph does not deal directly with his brothers' guilt. In spite of their efforts to discern a word of forgiveness, we hear no such word from Joseph's mouth. "The speech transcends their preoccupation with guilt and turns them to a fresh way of understanding what has happened."[226] The narrative seeks to "restore their personal dignity and parity with Joseph"; a confession of sin "would make their status dependent upon his grace and would thus establish them in a position spiritually inferior to him."[227] What the brothers have done, God has been able to transmute into good, so their guilt no longer remains; therefore, no word from Joseph appears necessary. Although a word of forgiveness certainly could be appropriate in a general way, yet such a word may be used (consciously or unconsciously) to initiate or maintain a hierarchical relationship between the forgiver and the forgiven. The author seems concerned to make sure that, in the end, all parties to the dispute maintain their self-respect as moral equals.

4. God finally brings unity to this story. God is the only one who has been active in the story with a constant good purpose from beginning to end—that there might be life for all.

God is the only one who has been active at every level of the story, from the highest tier of governmental authority to the lowest sphere of everyday family life, suffusing them with the divine purposes for good. God holds life together in all of its personal and social complexity and ambiguity.

God has been active among both the chosen and the unchosen, including the Egyptians, with exactly the same purpose in mind: life. Genesis attests to God's universal purpose in this story of Israel.

---

225. Westermann, *Genesis 37–50*, 205.
226. Brueggemann, *Genesis*, 373.
227. White, *Narration and Discourse*, 267.

Genesis 50:22-26, The Promise Transmitted

COMMENTARY

This epilogue portrays Joseph's final years, pulls together a key theme, and serves as a bridge to the next stage of Israel's story. Indeed, the reference to Joseph's bones pushes on to the land settlement (Josh 24:32; cf. Exod 13:19). The first reference to "Abraham, Isaac, and Jacob" presupposes the unity of the previous narrative. Joseph's death at 110 years provides an inclusio for this section (and with 48:28), while Joseph's "staying" (ישׁב *yāšab*) in Egypt in v. 22 ties back to Jacob's "settling" in 37:1, completing the movement from Canaan to Egypt (cf. 47:27).

Joseph remains in Egypt along with the rest of Jacob's family, living long enough to see his great-grandchildren. They were born on his knees—i.e., claimed as his descendants. The future of his family, and hence the promises regarding posterity, relates to the rest of the family. At the same time, the length of time indicates that the family has stayed in Egypt generations beyond the famine, anticipating the hardships of Exodus.

When Joseph is at the point of death, he extends to his brothers (all are assumed to be alive) both a promise and a charge. Jacob had never spoken the promise to his sons, except to Joseph in 48:21, though there are links in chap. 49. He assures them that God will *surely* visit them in Egypt (see Exod 3:16; 4:31; 13:19) and bring them out of the land of Egypt (see Exod 3:8, 17; 13:19) and into the land of Canaan, the land promised to their ancestors in the previous chapters. Egypt was not to be their permanent home. Joseph's words create the bridge to the next stage in Israel's story, just as it has been his actions in this story that have enabled the brothers to go into Exodus as a unified family.

Joseph also charges them that, after these events, they are to take his bones to Canaan (see Exod 13:19). He trusts his brothers to see to his proper burial, as together they had seen to their father's. He does not insist on a replication of his father's burial, but he links his future with that of his father and the rest of the family. According to Josh 24:32, Joseph was buried in Shechem. Joseph's death marks the end of Genesis, but the stage has been set for a series of events that will constitute Israel's family as the people of God.

THE BOOK OF EXODUS

INTRODUCTION, COMMENTARY, AND REFLECTIONS
BY
WALTER BRUEGGEMANN

THE BOOK OF
EXODUS

INTRODUCTION

T he book of Exodus is, according to tradition, the "Second Book of Moses"—i.e., the second book of the Pentateuch. This traditional formula refers not to Mosaic authorship but to the foundational character of the literature in relation to the unrivaled authority of Moses. The book of Exodus stands at the center of Israel's normative faith tradition.

RELATIONSHIPS WITHIN THE PENTATEUCH

We may identify three relationships within the Pentateuch that are pertinent to the book of Exodus.

1. The relation between the books of Genesis and Exodus is important but uneasy.[1] On critical grounds, it is clear that the community of the Exodus has no direct (historical) connection to the "ancestors" of Genesis. Nonetheless, the text itself gives considerable attention to that connection, which is theologically crucial. On the one hand, the God known in Genesis is only in Exodus made fully known by name (see 3:14; 6:2). On the other hand, the text is insistent that the old promises of Genesis are still operative in Exodus—promises made at creation (Gen 1:28; Exod 1:7), and promises of land to the ancestors (Gen 12:1). Indeed, those promises are the driving force that causes God to be engaged on behalf of the slaves (see Exod 2:24; 3:16-17; 6:8). Thus the connection between the two pieces of literature is promissory (i.e., theological rather than historical) but for that no less decisive.

2. The relation of the book of Exodus to the books of Leviticus and Numbers is very different. Insofar as these later books are the extended proclamation of the Torah, they simply continue the work of Moses at Sinai. They belong completely within the orbit of Moses' authorizing work and in fact constitute no new theme.

3. The relation of Exodus to Deuteronomy is again very different. Deuteronomy consists of a restatement of the Ten Commandments (5:6-21), which then receive a full and belated

---

1. R. W. L. Moberly, *The Old Testament of the Old Testament: Patriarchal Narratives and Mosaic Yahwism,* OBT (Minneapolis: Fortress, 1992).

exposition that is placed in the mouth of Moses. There is enormous interpretive freedom in Deuteronomy, so that what we are given is what Moses could have said in a later, very different circumstance.

Thus the book of Exodus reaches in three quite different directions to gather together the main threads and themes of Israel's faith. As the focal point of all this literature, it is the force of the book of Exodus that makes the Torah (Pentateuch) a profoundly Mosaic book, relying primarily upon his authority.

THE DOCUMENTARY HYPOTHESIS

It is not necessary to review here the complex account of recent critical scholarship, which for the past two centuries has been preoccupied with the complex history of the literature that now bears the authority of Moses. Specifically, this complexity is articulated by scholars in "the Documentary Hypothesis," which identifies four major recastings (sources) of the material around four demanding theological crises. This hypothesis is a way of speaking in critical fashion (largely in nineteenth-century modes) about dynamic vitality in the ongoing development of the tradition. Current scholarship finds the hypothesis in its classical form less and less useful. This commentary makes very little use of the Documentary Hypothesis, though it is fully aware of the textual realities that have evoked the hypothesis.

Specifically, it has been necessary to recognize that the "Priestly texts" are of a peculiar kind, easy to recognize, with very specific ideological interests. I have not found any way to avoid the odd juxtaposition of the liberation narrative and the "sacerdotal" accent.[2] Acknowledging the juxtaposition, what has interested me is the way in which the final form of the text has been able to bring these very different accents into serious, sustained interaction.

MAJOR THEOLOGICAL THEMES

We may identify four major theological themes that order the book of Exodus and that provide focal points for interpretation.

1. Liberation. The "narrative of liberation" (chaps. 1–15) is primarily concerned with the transformation of a social situation from oppression to freedom. This liberation is indeed a sociopolitical-economic operation that delegitimates and overthrows the throne of Egypt. The odd claim of this literature is that social transformation of revolutionary proportion is wrought through the holy intentionality of a "new God" (see Judg 5:8), whose name is known only in and through this wondrous happening.

2. Law. The meeting at Sinai (which continues through Num 10:10) is the announcement of God's will for all aspects of Israel's personal and public life. The God who liberates refuses to be limited with reference only to "religion." Three aspects of this proclamation of law may be noted. First, the giving of the Law is situated in a frightening theophany, whereby the holy God intimidates and threatens Israel (19:16-25). The purpose of the theophany, so far as the canonical form of the literature is concerned, is to ground law in holy authority beyond any human agent or construct. This Law is God's law! Second, the Ten Commandments, and only they, come directly from God's own mouth. This is an extraordinary phenomenon, an act of sovereignty that orders the world, and an act of graciousness whereby Israel need not guess about God's intention for it or for the world. Third, the rest of the laws in Exodus (20:22-26; 21:1–23:19; 34:11-26) are given by Moses, who is the designated and accepted mediator (20:18-21). That is, Israel has devised a stable human arrangement whereby God's will and purpose continue to be available.

2. George V. Pixley, *On Exodus: A Liberation Perspective* (Maryknoll, N.Y.: Orbis, 1987) 35 and *passim,* has used the term *sacerdotal* rather than the more conventional *Priestly,* escaping a bit the pejorative usage attached to *Priestly* and suggesting that this layer of tradition is a continuing angle of interpretation, rather than a late, "degenerate" form of faith.

3. Covenant. The proclamation of Law has as its purpose the making of a covenant, a binding relation whereby Yahweh and Israel are intimately, profoundly, and non-negotiably committed to each other. In this act, a social novelty is introduced into the world, a community founded on nothing other than an act of faith and loyalty.

Moreover, the present form of Exodus 32–34 is now positioned as a new or renewed covenant, after the nullification of the covenant of 19–24. The relation between 19–24 and 32–34 suggests that covenant is a once-for-all commitment. It is endlessly impinged upon by the contingencies of history, so that the covenant rooted in fidelity must struggle with the reality of infidelity. This dynamic, on the one hand, permits the savage warning of the pre-exilic prophets that the relation will end because Israel persists in disobedience. On the other hand, this same dynamic of fidelity in the face of infidelity permits the daring assertion in the Exile that the God who "plucks up and tears down" will also "plant and build" a new covenant people (Jer 1:10; 31:27-28). Thus the theme of covenant permits the terrible tension of judgment and hope already anticipated in 34:6-7 and asserted in pre-exilic prophets (e.g., Hosea), but worked out in the great prophets of the Exile—Jeremiah, Isaiah 40–55, and Ezekiel.[3]

4. Presence. The book of Exodus is concerned not only with an *event* of liberation, but with a *structure* that will ensure in some concrete institutional form the continued presence of God in the midst of Israel. This God, however, is not casually or easily available to Israel, and the emerging problem is to find a viable way in which to host the Holy. The second half of the book of Exodus is preoccupied with this problem and this possibility (25:1–40:38). Israel devises, through daring theological imagination, structure (tabernacle) that makes possible "glory" both as abiding presence and as traveling assurance (40:34-38).

These four themes converge to make the poignant claim that Israel is a profound *novum* in human history. It is a community like none that had yet been—the recipient of God's liberating power, practitioner of God's sovereign Law, partner in God's ongoing covenant, and host of God's awesome presence. This astonishingly odd community is, of course, made possible only by this incomparable God who dares to impinge upon the human process in extravagant and unprecedented ways (see 33:16).

LOCUS

The current view of scholarship is that the book of Exodus reached its present, final form during the sixth-century exile or soon thereafter, with the final shaping of the Priestly tradition. This judgment provides a chronological reference point for the literature. More important, however, this critical judgment also suggests a context in which to understand the pastoral intention and interpretive issues at work in the literature as it comes to us.

The exilic (or post-exilic) community had to practice its faith in a context where the primary guarantees of the Jerusalem establishment (both political and religious) had been terminated, and where foreign powers (Babylon, Persia) governed. The book of Exodus thus is to be understood as a literary, pastoral, liturgical, and theological response to an acute crisis. Texts that ostensibly concern thirteenth-century matters in fact are heard in a sixth- to fourth-century crisis.

This judgment that Exodus is an exilic document does two things. On the one hand, it requires a rereading of the main themes of the book. Thus *liberation* now concerns the freedom given in faith in an imperial context of a Babylonian or Persian "pharaoh." *Law* concerns a counter-ethic in an empire that wants to preempt and commandeer all of life. *Covenant* is a membership alternative to accommodation to the empire. And *presence* is a sense of energy, courage, and divine accompaniment in an empire that wants to "empty" life of such resources. In that imperial context, the book of Exodus becomes a counterdocument that voices and legitimates the odd identity of this community in the face of an empire that wants to crush such oddity.

3. See W. Brueggemann, *Hopeful Imagination: Prophetic Voices in Exile* (Philadelphia: Fortress, 1986); Gerhard von Rad, *Old Testament Theology II* (London: Oliver and Boyd, 1965) 188-278.

On the other hand, the identity of the book of Exodus as an exilic document suggests the interpretive vitality that belongs inherently to this text. Our own interpretive work, then, is not to reflect on an ancient history lesson about Egypt or about cult, but to see how this text, in new, demanding, and dangerous circumstances, continues to offer subversive possibilities for our future.

METHOD

The older critical commentaries (of which Noth's is a primary example) largely reflect and build upon nineteenth-century questions and methods.[4] They are especially concerned with the history behind the present text, both concerning what happened as "event," and how the text itself was developed and formed. This commentary is written in a context of great methodological ferment. It is increasingly clear that the older "critical perspective" is a product and example of the prevailing epistemological situation in the service of modernism. Any probe of these commentaries suggests how greatly our epistemological situation is changed by the receding of modernity. We are, however, only beginning to articulate new methods, none of which yet claims any consensus of scholarly support. This commentary seeks to make use of three emerging methods that are more congenial to the intellectual, epistemological context at the turn of the century, and to the context of Jewish and Christian faith communities in a postmodern context.

1. Literary Criticism. The newer "literary criticism" is no longer preoccupied with the history of hypothetical sources and documents, but seeks to focus on the internal, rhetorical workings of the text, assuming that the text itself "enacts a world" in which the reader may participate. Focus is not on external references, but on what is happening in the transactions of the text itself. This approach devotes great attention to the details, dramatic tensions, and rhetorical claims of the text itself. Such an approach requires great discipline to stay inside the world of text, and great patience in noticing the subtle nuances of the text. From a theological perspective, it operates with a "high view" of the text, suggesting that the world inside the text may be more real, more compelling, and more authoritative than other worlds construed behind or beyond the text.

While this method is everywhere important, Exodus 32–34 provides a marvelous example of its fruitfulness. In these chapters the demanding, insistent role of Moses over against God is noteworthy. Such a role requires that God should also be considered a character who can be impinged upon by action in the text, and who is placed at risk by the rhetoric and transactions of the text. Thus the decision of 34:10 that God will grant a new covenant to Israel results from Moses' insistent petition in v. 9, which in turn results from God's statement of available options in vv. 6-7. Moreover, in 32:10, Yahweh seems almost to be seeking Moses' consent or permission to "burn hot" and consume Israel. Such a dramatic treatment of God in the text does not serve well the interests of either conventional historicism or conventional orthodoxy. It does, however, let the text become a field of imagination in which the listening community catches a glimpse of an alternative world that lives in and through the text.

2. Social Criticism. "Social criticism" sees the text itself as a practice of discourse that is loaded with ideological power and interest. Texts are never innocent or disinterested, but are always acts of advocacy. Most especially, textual material about God is never "mere religion," but is discourse in which God is a party to social conflict and social interest.

In Exodus are many such voices of interest and advocacy; we will comment on two. First, in the narrative of liberation (chaps. 1-15), the dominant voice of the text is that of revolutionary criticism, which mounts a vigorous assault on every (Pharaonic) establishment of abusive power. The work of such revolutionary discourse is to expose the power of Pharaoh as null and void, and to assert that other social possibilities are available, if enacted with freedom, courage, and faith.

4. Martin Noth, *Exodus: A Commentary,* OTL (Philadelphia: Westminster, 1962).

Conversely, in chaps. 25–37, 35–40, and more specifically in 28–29 and 39, the centrality of the Aaronide priesthood is established.[5] There can be no doubt that these texts are ideologically interested and that they work hard to establish the preeminence and monopoly of the Aaronide priesthood.[6] Thus even a text about presence is a form of political discourse about power. Theological terms and social forces are always and everywhere intimately connected and cannot be rent asunder. Indeed, to imagine that they can be separated is a maneuver that keeps real power masked in benign God-talk.

In the book of Exodus, the ideological force of the liberation narrative (1–15) and the monopolizing program of the Aaronides (25–40) are in profound tension with each other, one being revolutionary and the other consolidating if not reactionary.[7] It may be that Exodus leaves us with that tension. However, it is also possible that in its final form, the book intends to show the victory of the "liberation narrative" over the "pattern of presence." This may be subtly suggested in the fact that in 25–31 and 35–40, Aaron does nothing, but passively depends on Moses, who takes all the initiatives. Thus the priest of presence is derivative from the authority of the great liberator. More directly, Exodus 32–34 constitutes a massive critique of the Aaronides and establishes Moses' Levites as the faithful priests.

3. Canonical Criticism. "Canonical criticism" is based on the insistence that one gains very little by probing the complexity of the pre-history of the text. One must seek to read the text in its final, canonical form, taking the joints and seams in the text as clues to the intention of the text.

The final form of the book of Exodus follows a definite sequence from liberation to covenantal law to abiding presence. That is, the purpose of liberation is to live in covenantal obedience, in communion with God's glory. As Yahweh "gets glory" over Pharaoh (14:4, 17), the book of Exodus intends to wean Israel away from the glory of Pharaoh to an alternative glory encountered on the mountain of covenantal law. For Christians, that "alternative glory," a "greater glory," is found in Jesus (see 2 Cor 3:10-11). For the book of Exodus, the culmination of glory in 40:34-38 is already in view in Exodus 1. In bondage, as the story begins, Israel has no glory and has no access to glory. By this sequence from liberation through covenantal encounter to assured presence, it is clear that the distinct political and religious themes of liberation, covenant, and presence cannot be kept separated.

In reading from liberation to glory, one may attend to the deep ideological tension present in Exodus. Thus the Mosaic accent on emancipation wrought through the destabilization and overthrow of Pharaoh is uneasy with the stable "presence" linked to Aaron. I suggest that 29:43-46 shows that traditionists are aware of the tension and deliberately establish the juxtaposition of the two. A canonical reading must take seriously a sociocritical reading.[8] The canonical reading does not nullify the sociocritical dimension of the text, but makes a second-level, intentional use of them. Only in this way is the final form genuinely "post-critical."

INTERPRETIVE ISSUES

The fact that the old memory can serve a later (exilic) community in a pastoral, liturgical way suggests that questions of the recurring contemporaneity of the text are not inappropriate, even concerning our own context as "contemporary." From the very beginning, Israel's authorizing text must always be reread and reinterpreted.

1. This text is understood as dynamic and under way, open to a fresh hearing. The mode of such a text is liturgical—i.e., it is used regularly in public worship, where texts are always and inevitably heard with enormously liberated imagination. In worship one does not ask

5. Ellis Rivkin, "The Revolution of the Aaronides," in *The Shapers of Jewish History* (New York: Charles Scribner's Sons, 1971) 21-41.

6. See Frank M. Cross, *Canaanite Myth and Hebrew Epic: Essays in the History of the Religion of Israel* (Cambridge, Mass.: Harvard University Press, 1973) 195-215; Paul D. Hanson, *The Dawn of Apocalyptic* (Philadelphia: Fortress, 1975); O. Plöger, *Theocracy and Eschatology* (Richmond: John Knox, 1968); and Morton Smith, *Palestinian Parties and Politics That Shaped the Old Testament* (New York: Columbia University Press, 1971).

7. See the statement on this ongoing tension between "the constitutive" and the "prophetic" by James A. Sanders, "Hermeneutics," *IDBSup*, ed. Keith Crim (Nashville: Abingdon, 1976) 402-7.

8. Norman K. Gottwald, "Social Matrix and Canonical Shape," *TToday* 42 (1985) 307-21.

historical-critical questions of when and where, nor does one ask scientific questions of rational possibility. For the moment, one agrees to a willing suspension of disbelief, giving oneself over to the voice of the text.

The Exodus text itself shows Israel practicing exactly that kind of imaginative freedom. Thus the "report" of the Exodus eventuates in the festival of remembrance, whereby new generations enter into the memory and possibility of liberations (12–13). In parallel fashion, I imagine many generations of girls and boys, upon hearing the "pattern of the tabernacle," imagine it, construct it, and at least for a moment "see" the glory that is there.

2. There is no doubt that the core claim of the book of Exodus is covenantal liberation. The text, and a long Jewish history of Passover celebration, has been a voice of alternative possibilities in the world. The structures, policies, and agents of oppression that have seemed ordained to perpetuity are here delegitimated and overthrown. The text permits the entertainment of a world that is different, which in turn permits different kinds of behavior. What happens in the text thus serves to make abused, oppressed persons subjects of their own history, able and authorized to take responsibility for their future. In liturgical celebration, one is not given strategies, policies, or procedures for freedom. Rather, what is given are imaginative possibilities in which the God who hears the cries of the abused Hebrews hears the cries of other abused persons as well and enacts promises that authorize and embolden.

There are, to be sure, current objections to the notion that the Exodus text is related to "liberation theology"; Fretheim offers three objections to such a construal of the material.[9] However, his objections are largely based on a caricature, infused by a kind of dualism that splits religious affirmation and social reality. Thus when Fretheim insists that the exodus is God's doing, and not "violent revolutionary activity," he fails to see that Moses is indeed engaged in such activity in the center of the narrative, and that it is precisely Moses' words and actions that delegitimate the Egyptian power structure. No one imagines that it is Moses alone who liberates. But if the text is taken seriously, it also is not "Yahweh alone" who liberates, for Moses, not Yahweh, must "go to Pharaoh." Fretheim's separation of religious idea from social practice ends with a kind of "idealism," an approach that Gottwald has decisively critiqued.[10]

Gottwald has rightly argued that Yahweh is a "function" of the revolution, even as the revolution is a "function" of Yahweh. The text precludes and denies a separation between the powerful intentionality of Yahweh and the determined action of disobedience that brings freedom to the slaves. The same ill-advised split is evident in Fretheim's second objection that separates "anti-God" activity from "political" activity. Such a split fails to see that God-talk is intrinsically and inevitably political talk. I propose, thus, that one can resist the agenda of liberation in the text only by a seriously distorted reading of the text.

3. Conversely, Fretheim is enormously helpful in suggesting that Exodus champions the theme of creation. The book of Exodus is indeed concerned with God's will for creation and with the destructive capacity of Pharaoh to undo creation.[11] In a context where one might think about "sustainable creation," this text is urgent. Just as Pharaoh defeats creation, so also the laws of Yahweh are intended as ways to honor and enhance creation.

4. Because this text refuses to remain "history," but insists on contemporary liturgical engagement, the contemporary interpreter is permitted considerable imaginative maneuverability, disciplined, of course, by the detailed specificity of the text. As hearers of this text, we are like youths entering into the Passover liturgy and hearing with our own ears the wonder of God's power over Pharaoh. Or we are like children in a ritual of covenant renewal, watching again the frightful theophany, frightened to death, hearing the law proclaimed afresh, claimed in innocent obedience. Or we are like children dazzled by the "pattern of presence," free to imagine how the glory comes and where it dwells, in our midst. Then, upon hearing the wonder of liberation

---

9. See Terence E. Fretheim, *Exodus*, Interpretation (Louisville: Westminster/John Knox, 1990) 18-20. See also Lyle Eslinger, "Freedom or Knowledge? Perspective and Purpose in the Exodus Narrative (Exodus 1–15)," *JSOT* 52 (1991) 43-60; Jon D. Levenson, "Exodus and Liberation," *HBT* 13 (1991) 134-74; and in response, Walter Brueggemann, "Pharaoh as Vassal: A Study of a Political Metaphor," forthcoming in *CBQ*.

10. Norman K. Gottwald, *The Tribes of Yahweh: A Sociology of the Religion of Liberated Israel 1250–1050 B.C.E.* (Maryknoll, N.Y.: Orbis, 1979) 592-607.

11. Terence E. Fretheim, "The Plagues as Ecological Signs of Historical Disaster," *JBL* 110 (1991) 385-96. Fretheim has elaborated this suggestive theme in his commentary, *Exodus*.

and the poignancy of the law proclaimed, and being dazzled by the presence, we break out in an innocent *Te Deum,* when it is all "finished" (39:32; 40:33)!

Scholarly niceties are not unimportant, but must, in the end, be mobilized for our own work of contemporary interpretation. The book of Exodus is now, for us in our reading, set down in a context of profane, self-indulgent consumer culture, in which technological capacity is matched and mobilized by self-serving ideology. In such a culture (either in market-driven licentiousness or in state-practiced brutality), human beings, human community, and human possibility are increasingly neglected and muted, if not nullified. In such a culture, the voice of Exodus sounds where it has courageous interpreters, who simply and uncompromisingly voice the alternative intention the Holy One has for creation.

The dramatic rendition of *liberation* takes place in a society where the question of liberation is little honored. Ours is increasingly a shut-down culture in which "freedom" is reduced to a range of "product choices," but in which the soaring of the human spirit, the dignity of the human body, and the health of the body politic are little cared for, honored, or financed. The question posed by the Exodus tradition is whether liberation is possible in such a shut-down world. The answer given by this Jewish voice of God is that God's own will to end the bondage status of the marginated is relentless and cannot finally be resisted.

The revolutionary possibility of *covenant* is resisted when power is closed, settled, and monopolized. Covenant, the text claims, is a revolutionary possibility. Against both authoritarianism and individual autonomy, the Sinai text enacts a covenant rooted in a holy authority that deabsolutizes every other authority. Moreover, in law and command the God of Sinai grounds human dignity and mobilizes the strong for the sake of the weak. Since those awesome days at Sinai, Jews and Christians have believed that a community of mutuality, rooted in the command of God, is indeed a social possibility and a social mandate.

The pattern for *presence* imagines God's awesome magisterial, life-giving glory being present concretely in the world. That "pattern" given us in the text makes its statement now in an utterly profane cultural context in which sacrament is reduced to technique and magisterial "signs" are driven out by mindless slogans and manipulative ideology. The text continues to ask whether sacramental power and presence are possible in an "emptied" culture.[12] This text asserts that God is willing and yearning to be present, but that presence requires a community of generous faith, which gives its best skills, disciplines, and goods for the housing of the holy.

When we depart the text of Exodus, our world is not miraculously transformed by our reading and interpretation. What is effected by our reading and interpretation is only the slow, unnoticed work of transformed imagination. The book of Exodus invites the reader to Passover imagination (i.e., counterimagination), rooted in the sufferings of our ancestors who cried out. It is powered by our ancestors of the Exile who treasured the alternative. Now our reading, amid the suffering of the world, in the presence of exiles and of exile-producing institutions and policies, invites us to leave off the paralyzing fantasy of Pharaoh for the One who will be gracious.

THREE NEW TESTAMENT EXTRAPOLATIONS

Richard Hays has shown with reference to Paul that the Christian use of the Old Testament (OT) is done in rich and varied modes, but always with respect for and a careful reading of the OT.[13] This is clearly true of the New Testament (NT) use of the book of Exodus. The interrelations between the book of Exodus and the NT take many forms, and one cannot reduce that usage to any single interpretive principle of method. Each such usage attends carefully to the claim of Exodus, and each usage focuses on the decisiveness and finality of Jesus. Here I will mention characteristic interactions that refer to each of the three great themes of the book of Exodus.

1. Exodus Deliverance and Liberation. The entire Moses recital of deliverance becomes the center piece and primary material of Stephen's great sermon (Acts 7:17-44). One is especially

---

12. See George Steiner, *Real Presences* (Chicago: University of Chicago Press, 1989). Concerning an "emptied, shut-down" culture, see Herbert Marcuse, *One-Dimensional Man* (Boston: Beacon, 1964).

13. Richard B. Hays, *Echoes of Scripture in the Letters of Paul* (New Haven: Yale University Press, 1989).

impressed with the detailed way in which the Moses narrative is followed all the way from the birth of Moses in the midst of a death-dealing Egyptian regime (v. 19) to the "tent of testimony" (v. 44). The story of Moses is for Stephen the primary model for the work of the Holy Spirit and for the persecution of the prophets. (See a different casting of the same recital in Heb 11:23-29.)

2. The Covenant at Sinai. The Covenant at Sinai is clearly definitional for Christians. Paul, however, in relating "Moses and Sinai" to his own generation of Jews and the continuing community of Judaism, which did not accept Jesus as Messiah, speaks of a "new covenant" (1 Cor 11:25; 2 Cor 3:6; and the subtle argument of Romans 9–11). Yet for all his brave language of "new covenant," Paul can never cleanly and unambiguously declare that the old covenant is null and void.[14]

3. The Presence. The argument of Hebrews 7–10 depends completely on the Levitical-Aaronide theory of priesthood and presence in Exod 25–40. Again, a complete contrast is made between the once-for-all priestly work of Jesus and the priesthood of Aaron, which is said to be unreliable and insufficient.

In these several uses the New Testament writers are passionately focused on the distinctiveness and finality of Jesus. In our ecumenical and reconciling context, this supersessionism is awkward, but nonetheless evident in the text. It is equally clear, however, that for all such bold claims, the New Testament can never freely and fully escape the claims and categories of the Old Testament and the faith of Moses. Even when the claim of Christian displacement is most powerful, the truth of the Mosaic witness persists in the New Testament. Thus, for example, the thematic use of Exodus in the Gospel of Mark argues for a sense of continuity between the narrative of the God of Exodus and the story of Jesus.

---

14. See the carefully nuanced discussion by Paul M. van Buren, *A Theology of the Jewish-Christian Reality. Part 3; Christ in Context* (San Francisco: Harper & Row, 1988); and Norbert Lohfink, *The Covenant Never Revoked: Biblical Reflections on Christian-Jewish Dialogue* (New York: Paulist, 1991).

BIBLIOGRAPHY

The following books will be helpful reading:

Commentaries:

Calvin, John. *Commentaries on the Last Four Books of Moses (Arranged in the Form of a Harmony).* Vols. II, III. Grand Rapids: Baker, 1979. A magisterial evangelical commentary, informed by the best criticism of his time, but undistracted from a theological focus.

Childs, Brevard. *The Book of Exodus.* OTL. Philadelphia: Westminster, 1974. An erudite, comprehensive commentary, the most important of this generation, which summarizes the critical tradition of scholarship and moves boldly to theological (canonical) issues.

Fretheim, Terence. *Exodus.* Interpretation. Louisville: Westminster/John Knox, 1991. An excellent commentary, reflecting newer methods of reading, offering rich suggestion for pastoral interpretation, committed to an accent on creation theology.

Greenberg, Moshe. *Understanding Exodus.* New York: Behrman House, 1969. A discerning statement that makes full use of Jewish interpretive voices, sensitive to the powerful theological voice of the text.

Noth, Martin. *Exodus.* OTL. Philadelphia: Westminster, 1962. The standard critical German commentary, the most influential of the last generation, largely concerned with the prehistory of the text.

Pixley, George V. *On Exodus, a Liberation Perspective.* Maryknoll, N.Y.: Orbis, 1987. A brief, but important, reading with a liberation hermeneutic alive to the sociocritical issues in the text.

Sarna, Nahum. *The JPS Torah Commentary: Exodus.* Philadelphia: JPS, 1991. A discerning, balanced interpretation, critically informed, but paying primary attention to the religious claims of the text.

Other suggested studies:

Bloom, Harold, ed. *Exodus: Modern Critical Interpretations.* New York: Chelsea House, 1987. Offers a rich collection of classic articles, with special emphasis on Jewish contributions, valuable for theological sensitivity and artistic discernment.

Van Iersel, Bas, and Anton Weiler, eds. *Exodus: A Lasting Paradigm.* Concilium. Edinburgh: T. & T. Clark, 1987. A collection of studies, suggesting the varied modes and contexts of a contemporary Exodus hermeneutic.

Walzer, Michael. *Exodus and Revolution.* New York: Basic Books, 1985. A judicious study by a political theorist of the ways in which Exodus has provided impetus for revolution in many parts of the modern world.

OUTLINE OF EXODUS

I. Exodus 1:1–15:21, The Narrative of Liberation

  A. 1:1–4:31, Preparation for Deliverance
    1:1-22, A New King Comes to Power
    2:1-10, The Birth of Moses
    2:11-22, Moses Flees from Pharaoh
    2:23-25, God Hears Their Groaning
    3:1–4:31, Moses Is Sent to Pharaoh
  B. 5:1–11:10, "Let My People Go"
    5:1–6:1, Bricks Without Straw
    6:2-30, "I Am Yahweh"
    7:1-13, Aaron's Staff
    7:14-25, The Plague of Blood
    8:1-15, The Plague of Frogs
    8:16-19, The Plague of Gnats
    8:20-32, The Plague of Flies
    9:1-12, The Plague on Livestock and the Plague of Boils
    9:13-35, The Plague of Hail
    10:1-20, The Plague of Locusts
    10:21-29, The Plague of Darkness
    11:1-10, Warning of the Final Plague
  C. 12:1–15:21, The Lord Will Reign
    12:1-28, The Passover Instituted
    12:29-39, Death of the Firstborn
    12:40-51, Directions for the Passover
    13:1-16, Special Observances
    13:17-22, Pillars of Cloud and Fire
    14:1-31, Crossing the Sea
    15:1-21, Songs of Moses and Miriam

II. Exodus 15:22–18:27, "Is the Lord Among Us or Not?"

  A. 15:22-27, Bitter Water Made Sweet
  B. 16:1-36, Manna and Quail

EXODUS 1:1–15:21

THE NARRATIVE OF LIBERATION

OVERVIEW

This great narrative of liberation voices themes central to the faith of the Bible, the core of Jewish identity, and the categories in which Christians will subsequently articulate their faith. It concerns a process of social transformation wrought by the revolutionary intervention of God.

At the center of this narrative, as its key actor, is Yahweh, a God known provisionally in the book of Genesis, and now known fully by God's proper name (3:14; 6:2). This God initiates a social transformation and effects the power of a new social possibility in the world. The God of the Bible is in fact and in principle deeply embedded in this narrative, and cannot be fully known apart from this narrative.

The beneficiaries of Yahweh's powerful action are "Hebrews," a collection of marginated people who have no communal identity of their own and are powerless to change their social circumstance. In the telling of the narrative, however, these Hebrews are, or become, "Israel," a community for whom God cares and acts in unprecedented ways. Derivatively, it is clear that this story of liberation has a rich variety of social futures, for many other abused peoples, ancient and contemporary, have found this narrative to be their story as well.[15]

While the work of Exodus is clearly God's work, the human Moses is indispensable as an agent in social transformation. As becomes characteristic in the Bible, God's action in the world is undertaken by human agents who are summoned into Yahweh's dangerous service. The book of Exodus is a statement that establishes and celebrates the authority of Moses as the founder and generator of all

things Israelite, including Israel's faith and freedom.

The dramatic power of the narrative is found in its presentation of Yahweh in deep conflict and combat with the gods (the legitimating powers) of Egypt (see 12:12). Thus this is the story of a *theological* triumph, whereby the God of Israel defeats all the powers of death that continue to stalk the earth with threatening authority.

That theological triumph, however, has socioeconomic and political dimensions. The exodus can never be kept safely as a "religious event." Yahweh's conflict is not simply with Egyptian gods, but is with the Egyptian "social system," which is delegitimated and finally nullified through the process of this narrative. This critical dimension of the narrative has fed subsequent prophetic faith. As Michael Walzer has shown, this text has become the *fount* of revolutionary faith and practice right into the contemporary world.[16]

The structure of the narrative of liberation has dramatic force and power. It starts at a certain place (oppression) and ends at a very different place (liberation and celebration). It invites the listener to participate in that dramatic sequence from hurt to joy. The dramatic form of the narrative suggests that it has its function and use in liturgical recital.[17] This means that the text is not primarily interested in the historical facticity of the story, nor can the dramatic claim of the text be reduced to theological proposition. There is no secondary or alternative language by which this tale of God and Israel can be told. It must be kept, transmitted, and received precisely in its dramatic form.

15. See Bas van Iersel and Anton Weiler, *Exodus: A Lasting Paradigm,* Concilium (Edinburgh: T. & T. Clark, 1987). Levenson, "Exodus and Liberation," 169, has agreed that when rightly construed, the exodus is "the paradigmatic instance" of liberation.

16. Michael Walzer, *Exodus and Revelation* (New York: Basic Books, 1985).

17. See J. Pedersen, *Israel, Its Life and Culture III-IV* (London: Oxford University Press, 1940) 728-37.

In the modern world, with its singular preoccupation with the cerebral and the programmatic, we have failed to notice that the concrete, dramatic voicing of social truth and social possibility has enormous transformative power. The liturgical force of the text is now evident in many social revolutions in our time that begin in imagining an alternative. Moreover, as Freud understood, personal transformation happens in the same way, by acts of criticism and possibility that take the form of subverting narrative.

The exodus story is a narrative construal of reality in which the substance of transformative possibility and the form of narrative discourse effectively converge. This means, first, that one cannot communicate or "practice" Yahweh apart from this narrative in which Yahweh speaks and acts in characteristic ways. Second, it means that the text requires listeners (participants in the liturgy) to imagine and construe themselves through the actions of this drama, so that we know ourselves as offspring and children of this narrative. Third, this narrative is in profound conflict with other narratives by which we can imagine and construe ourselves. In our own Western context, one rival story this narrative defeats is that of individual consumerism. It is the intent of this narrative to evoke repentance, whereby one switches stories and so exchanges worlds.

This text is the release into the practicing community of a daring, subversive, alternative imagination. This narrative is a powerful and primary example of what is meant by the "dangerous" stories of the Bible. In its Passover celebration, Israel regularly practices that dangerous imagination that entertains new possibilities, and that delegitimates all that goes against the freedom and justice Yahweh intends.

EXODUS 1:1–4:31, PREPARATION FOR DELIVERANCE

OVERVIEW

These chapters function as an introduction to the liberation narrative of 1–15 and prepare the way for the initial confrontation between Moses (with Aaron) and Pharaoh. This section of text is made up of a collection of quite different materials, expressed in a variety of different genres, but intricately woven together. Michael Fishbane has shown how these chapters introduce the themes that will recur in and dominate chapters 5–19.[18] We may identify four elements of text and assert four primary themes.

1. Chapter 1 characterizes the slave community for the story that follows. On the one hand, the narrator deliberately connects this community of slaves to the Genesis story, indicating that the promise made to the ancestors is still operative and decisive for this community of slaves. On the other hand, in a candid characterization of the present, the community is shown to be in the throes of brutal oppression at the hands of a death-dealing pharaoh. The narrator has deftly juxtaposed the continuing power of an enduring promise and an exposé of current social helplessness. That juxtaposition creates a tension between past promise and present struggle, a tension that the ensuing narrative will adjudicate.

2. In 2:1-22, Moses is introduced. The narrator's interest in Moses is quite limited, treating only two matters. First, is the wondrous birth and survival of the baby who is in severe jeopardy (vv. 1-10). Cheryl Exum and James Ackermann have noticed the way in which the baby Moses survives, due to the courage and imagination of women who preserve his life from the death decreed by the mad king.[19] Moses is kept safe through

18. Michael Fishbane, "Exodus 1–4: The Prologue to the Exodus Cycle," *Text and Texture: Close Readings of Selected Biblical Texts* (New York: Schocken, 1979) 63-76.

19. J. Cheryl Exum, " 'You Shall Let Every Daughter Live': A Study of Exodus 1:8–2:10," *Semeia* 28 (1983) 63-82; James S. Ackerman, "The Literary Context of the Moses Birth Story (Exodus 1–2)," *Literary Interpretations of Biblical Narratives*, eds. Kenneth R. R. Gros Louis et al. (Nashville: Abingdon, 1974) 74-119; and Ana Flora Anderson and Gilberto da Silva Gorgulho, "Miriam and Her Companions," *The Future of Liberation Theology: Essays in Honor of Gustavo Gutiérrez*, eds. Marc H. Ellis and Otto Maduro (Maryknoll, N.Y.: Orbis, 1989) 205-19.

the inscrutable protection of God, which in the narrative is credited only to the women. Second, the adult career of Moses is quickly traced through three social conflicts (vv. 11-22). In these brief episodes, it is evident that Moses has an acute concern for justice and a keen awareness of his own exploited people.

3. Only in 2:23–3:10 does Yahweh, the God of the promise, enter actively and decisively into the narrative. In 2:23, attention is turned from the life of Moses to the crisis of the people. This section is focused on the appearance and speech (theophany) of Yahweh, who now decisively intervenes to connect the life of Moses to the plight of Israel. The element of the narrative that has attracted the most attention is the appearance in the burning bush (3:1-6). But more important are the words spoken from the bush (3:6-10).

That speech includes the following elements: (a) a reiteration of the promise to the ancestors, (b) an acknowledgment of the Israelites' present suffering, and (c) a self-disclosure including the utterance of God's enigmatic name (3:14). These three elements all lead to the fourth climactic accent in 3:10: (d) Moses is abruptly summoned to a decisive and dangerous role in the life of Israel.

4. In 3:11–4:26, the call of Moses into the purpose of God for Israel is further developed. This "call narrative" is reminiscent of the standard genre of call narratives, also utilized in the prophetic materials. The dominant feature of this section is Moses' fivefold resistance to the call. It is in response to Moses' resistance that God's self-disclosure is given (3:13-15), and the question of Moses' authority is posed, a question that will frequently recur in the book. In the end, Moses' resistance is overcome, and he is prepared to address Pharaoh (4:21-23).

This section of text thus lays out the large drama of God versus Pharaoh, which concerns the future of Israel. That large, almost cosmic, drama, however, focuses on the fearful human agent Moses—i.e., the great clash between Yahweh and the gods of Egypt depends on this human agent. Through these chapters we watch and wait while Moses prepares for the confrontation upon which everything depends. The driving energy of the narrative is from Yahweh. When the drama begins, however, it will be Moses (all alone except for Aaron) before the great power of Egypt. We are prepared for an unequal contest, the outcome of which is unclear, especially to Moses.

Exodus 1:1-22, A New King Comes to Power

COMMENTARY

The exodus narrative, as constantly reiterated in the Passover liturgy, portrays an abrupt newness, a liberation wrought by God for this particular body of slaves. That abruptness, however, has important antecedents in Israel's memory. The story of the exodus begins with a brief, dense retrospective on the memory of Genesis.

1:1-7. This people about to be liberated have a memory and a genealogy. More than that, they have a remembered promise from the "God of the ancestors." Thus the abrupt newness about to be narrated in the book of Exodus is framed in vv. 1-7 by the antecedents of genealogy, blessing, and promise. These people, regarded by the empire as nameless slaves, in fact have a powerful shaping pedigree. This treasured past carries

power and potential that the empire does not recognize and cannot in the end contain.

The Exodus narrative begins with remembering. The last of the great fathers, Jacob, had come to Egypt with a great entourage, affluent, dignified, and honored by Pharaoh (Gen 47:7-12). He is indeed somebody of importance! Our narrative quickly lists his sons, born to two wives and two slave-maidens (see Gen 29:31–30:24). This is the family, blessed by God, that carries the promises of God.

In the listing of the sons, Joseph is not mentioned (vv. 2-4). His name is deliberately withheld. There were seventy persons (see Gen 46:8-27). The number bespeaks vulnerability and fragility. At the threshold of liberation, this family is small in number (see Deut

10:22), but then, this family in Genesis was in every generation small in number, vulnerable, and fragile. Such precariousness, however, is matched (or perhaps overridden) by the mention of Joseph (v. 5). His name was absent from the list in vv. 2-4, because it deserves to be mentioned separately.

Unlike his fragile brothers, Joseph's name bespeaks power, authority, and substance to the Israelites. Joseph, as his name indicates, is one who "adds" (יסף yāsap), who expands and accumulates. The name *Joseph* conjures Egyptian royal power, the power of surplus through coercive accumulation, the power of property and military might, the power of severe policy and ruthless enforcement (see Gen 41:37-57; 47:13-26). With Joseph established, Israel (Jacob) need have no fear. Genesis brings Israel to the horizon of Egypt, with all its gifts and, in the end, with its enormous threat.

The threat of the empire is hinted at in v. 6 and voiced in v. 8. Joseph could not last forever; he had died, as even powerful people do. With his death, the favored status of Israel, so deliberately fabricated, collapsed. The move from Genesis to Exodus reflects the flow of the generations, the drastic shift in the fortunes of this special people, and the fickleness of great power.

Verse 7 provides a summary to the book of Genesis. Because of the promise of God, the fidelity of Jacob, and the strategies of Joseph, who took care of his own, the Israelites were filled with vitality. Four verbs describe Israel's powerful position. Two of these verbs, *fruitful* and *multiply* are also used both for God's will for creation (Gen 1:28), and for God's promise to father Jacob concerning Israel (Gen 35:11). Like creation, Israel is to "be fruitful and multiply"; and now, says this narrative, it has happened! The third verb, *prolific,* characterizes teeming life, evidencing the power of blessing in creation (see Gen 1:21; 8:17; 9:7). Israel, like creation, teems with abundant life. The fourth verb, *be strong,* suggests might and staying power. Moreover, the four verbs are reinforced by a double adverb, *exceedingly much*—i.e., "very, very." Israel is the arena in which God's verbs for creation become embodied and enacted.

1:8-14. We are scarcely prepared for v. 8 after the celebrative affirmation of vv. 1-7.

Indeed, the narrative does not intend us to be prepared. Verse 7 left us with a sense of Israel's well-being, its preparedness for a good future. But now, abruptly and decisively, there is a new king with a short memory! He is not committed to any policies of his predecessors. His forgetting Joseph means that state commitments are abandoned; the privileges previously granted to Jacob's family are, in an instant, forfeited.

Now the new king speaks (vv. 9-10). He is the first one to speak in the book of Exodus. The first word is a royal decree addressed to the royal entourage, "his people," concerning the "sons of Israel." The king reiterates the sense of v. 7, "numerous and more powerful." The words that had been signs of blessing in v. 7, however, now come with the force of threat. The fact that Israel is fruitful and powerful makes it a threat to the empire. Thus in the reuse of the terms, the stakes are upped. The new king proposes to counteract the power of blessing under which Israel prospers.

The king worries that, because of its fruitfulness, Israel will be strong and escape. It is odd that the king's worry is escape, for he might have feared being defeated by them, especially since the term *strong* is used to describe them in v. 7. Defeat, however, is not the agenda. It is escape; they might "go up" (v. 10). The king's speech sounds the crucial Exodus word עלה ('ālâ). The new king anticipates the exodus, the departure of cheap labor that the imperial government is no longer able to control.

Out of his anxiety, the new king generates a fresh policy of forced labor toward his feared workers. Two words are used twice to characterize imperial practice. Twice the Israelites are "oppressed" (ענן 'ānôn; vv. 11-12); twice the Egyptians are "ruthless" (עבד 'ābad; vv. 13-14). The forced labor practice whereby some are coerced to serve the ends of others is not mere abusiveness. Rather, it is an essential part of the great state building program. Great governments must build great buildings in order to produce permanent monuments to their power and greatness. Thus the slaves must enhance precisely the power they most fear, resent, and hate.

The program of the new king, however, is more pragmatic than abuse or self-aggrandizement. The forced labor is to build royal storehouses in the royal cities of Pithom and Rameses. Archaeological remains show evidence that the nineteenth dynasty in Egypt did indeed undertake such ambitious building projects, and the name of one city, Rameses, is also the name much used as a royal name of prowess, as in Rameses II or Rameses III. While a great deal of scholarly energy has been given to the specific dating and geography of these cities, such specificity should not mislead us.

The "storehouses" constitute not only grain policies, but are also metaphors for state policy, an elitist control of economic surplus and the means of production. Such storehouses are not an outcome of economic "good luck." They are, rather, evidence of a policy of coercion and accumulation. Already in Gen 12:10, the hungry Israelites know that Egypt controls a monopoly on food, while everyone else suffers from famine.

We are told in v. 12, however, that this aggressive state policy did not work. The more the empire abuses and oppresses, the more this slave community "multiplied and spread." This phrase repeats one of the verbs of vv. 3 and 8, *multiply,* and introduces a new term: *spread*——i.e., to expand over the land. Thus the narrative unobtrusively suggests that the power for blessing is at work in this community, and the empire is helpless either to slow it or to preempt it for its own ends.

The episode functions primarily to establish the fierce adversarial relationship of Israel and Egypt, and to show that disadvantaged Israel has a decisive advantage in the narrative. This rhetorical shaping of the memory, utilized repeatedly in the larger Exodus liturgy, serves to nurture a deep resentment of state power, a deep yearning for an alternative, and a treasured sense of distinctiveness. Moreover, the lack of historical, factual specificity about the king permits the account to become a paradigmatic presentation that, in every new generation of Israelites, can be reapplied and reasserted against whomever is the current agent of abusive power.

1:15-22. Now the narrative becomes more concrete. The king of Egypt (still not named or even called Pharaoh) undertakes a policy of genocide against the slave population, clearly a self-defeating policy. This paragraph thus escalates the harshness of policies, commensurate with an escalation of anxiety.

In this narrative unit, the king speaks three times. The first time, he issues a command to the two midwives who assist in birthing among the slaves (v. 16). His command is that all boy babies should be eliminated. It is of peculiar importance that in this entire unit, "the Israelites" are not at all mentioned (unlike 1:9, 13). Now it is all "Hebrews." This term, with its cognates known all over the ancient Near East, refers to any group of marginal people who have no social standing, own no land, and who endlessly disrupt ordered society. They may function variously as mercenaries, as state slaves, or as terrorists, depending on governmental policies and the state of the economy. They are "low-class folks" who are feared, excluded, and despised. It is the common assumption of scholars that the biblical "Hebrews" are a part of this lower social class of *hapiru* who are known in nonbiblical texts.

The king's second speech is again addressed to the midwives (v. 18). The instruction of v. 16 has been ignored. Now the king, accustomed to obedience, conducts an investigation into this defiance of imperial command. Finally, he speaks a third time and issues a massive and programmatic command (v. 22). In v. 16, the instruction is only to the midwives, but in the third speech it is "to all his people" (as in v. 9). The deep fear of the outcasts has evoked a policy of systematic murder of precisely the babies who might be the most productive workers in the state system. The new policy is indeed irrational, suggesting that fear and rage have produced a deep insanity in imperial policy.

Over against the two royal decrees of vv. 16 and 22, the narrative juxtaposes a seemingly weak counterforce. The midwives, instructed in v. 16 to kill, are said to disobey the king (v. 17). The reason given for such disobedience is that they "feared God" more than they feared the new king, and for that reason they refused to participate in the state-authorized killing. When questioned about their insubordination, they do not explicitly bear witness to their faith in God. Rather, they attest to the surging power for life that is present in the Hebrew mothers, a power for life that is not known among the women of the empire. Hebrew babies, they say, are born with such vigor and at such a rate that the midwives simply cannot be present in time for each birth. In asserting their innocence, however, the midwives do not accuse the Hebrew mothers. The miracle of such births is beyond the fault of any human agent, for the fault is that of the God who will not be deterred by the new king. What counts is that Hebrew mothers are invested with dangerous, liberated power for life, which no one can deter.

The narrative sweep of chapter 1 leads us to the specifics of the exodus in three large concentric circles. In the most comprehensive circle (vv. 1-7), the horizon of the reader is fixed in the large promissory past preceding the book of Exodus. The lines refer to the ancestral memory—i.e., the stories of the fathers and mothers in Genesis 12–50. The verbs, however, look back even to the promises of creation. In this large look backward to treasured roots, the life-force of God's blessing is brought powerfully into the present of this narrative.

In the second, closer concentric circle (vv. 8-14), we are introduced to a concrete, albeit paradigmatic, unnamed character, "a new king." In uttering that phrase, the narrator brings the large memory of Israel immediately into the purview of their ominous oppression by Egypt. What has been a large, unspecified blessing is now transformed into the specificity of Israel versus Egypt. This narrative features the power of a state policy of abusive labor vis-à-vis the power of blessing operative peculiarly in the life of Israel.

In the third, closest circle of textuality (vv. 15-22), the narrative brings us into a quite specific conversation. The exchange is between a desperately fearful king and nervy midwives who are unafraid. The oddest reality in this raw conflict is that the people of Israel are never mentioned. The subject here is not an identifiable political community. It is "Hebrews," that floating mass of unacknowledged, unnamed humanity who are socioeconomic nobodies with not yet enough nerve or wherewithal to claim peoplehood. This is the unformed chaos of social reality that seethes against the ordered empire. Such images suggest that behind the political-ethical conflict is the reality of a class conflict, the center resisting the margin, the "haves" alarmed by the insistent presence of the "have-nots."

The exchange between the king and the midwives is ominous, touching the bottom of social reality. The midwives (whose names we know, Shiphrah and Puah) and the king (who is given no name) voice life and death respectively. Their encounter is a revisit of the drama of chaos versus order (Gen 1:2). Ironically, the champion of imperial order is, in fact, the agent of chaos, for he will terrorize the very possibility of life. The outcome of the confrontation is not certain. The threat of death now stalks this people of promise. Against such a force, there is only an old promise, and the mothering that persists among the outcasts, a mothering force that refuses to halt or capitulate.

REFLECTIONS

This narrative plunges the listening congregation into a world of danger, brutality, and desperation. It is a world into which a settled congregation does not easily go, a world largely screened out for a church that has romanticized the Bible. This text invites the congregation to reenter a world peopled by extreme characters—a frightened king, abused laborers, and defiant midwives. Or the congregation is invited to stand in the company of Jewish boys and girls at Passover as they are permitted to imagine and envisage a world of ominous, high-stakes conflict. Exodus 1 sets the context and shape for a Passover-imagined world.

1. The world in this text is one in which the power of blessing from God is assured and can be trusted. Throughout this narrative, which counts on the newness of Genesis, the verbs of multiplication, fruitfulness, and life are everywhere. Life is understood and affirmed as blessed, hallowed, and authorized by God to be a productive, fruitful place. That power of blessing, which is assured and affirmed, however, is received in deep jeopardy, for there is always some regime that wants to nullify it.

2. This is a world in which irrational destructive power is unloosed in the person and policies of the new king. There is here no romanticism about a world that is "user friendly" or that is "getting better." Moreover, that irrational, destructive power is not the work of a disturbed individual. It is, rather, brutalizing public policy that is legitimated by imperial ideology and exercises the appearance and force of rationality. Pharaoh's program is a corporate, systemic operation that has at its disposal enormous technical capacity and that relies on immense ideological authority, thus generating actions that are mere policy. The practitioners themselves do not perceive it as brutal, for it is all for reasons of state. The narrative is, in fact, an intense critical judgment against such brutalizing policy, exposing it for what it is. Thus the narrative invites the listening congregation to acute social criticism of such "policy."

3. This word of blessing and of destructive power focuses on the little community of promise, which is profoundly vulnerable in this deep dispute. The narrative is not interested in generalized or objective social criticism. Rather, it speaks from and for the powerless, who are victims of state power and who depend on the elusive power of blessing for survival. The narrative makes this little, unnoticed community the focus of our attention, as though the whole world depends on the possible survival of this community in formation.

4. This imagined world of the text shows us the destiny of Israel. It also pushes behind Israel to the inchoate reality of "Hebrews." That is, the text does not let the listeners stay with competing political identities, but goes underneath to the least-formed, vulnerable, and despised. It invites notice that the world is still ordered in terms of threat and violence, and still includes amorphous, ill-formed communities under threat.

5. In this dangerous mix of power and powerlessness, the narrative places Shiphrah and Puah. Amazing! They are nowhere else named or known, and certainly not celebrated. Yet we remember them by name. We remember these two discreet, defiant, cunning, mothering agents. At great risk, they counter genocide; in so doing, they bear witness to the mothering power of God, whose will for life overrides the killing, and whose power for life is undeterred by the death dispensed by the powerful.

6. The purpose of hearing such a text is not to identify the contemporary counterparts of "the new king," though that could be done. It is, rather, to see that the dynamic of this story is a reassuring and pervasive model for social relations. There is no doubt that the text reflects the endlessly jeopardized situation of Jews in a world bent on their destruction. The fact that the state often acts against Jews is a tale that runs all the way from the book of Esther to the modern Holocaust.

The New Testament parallel to this text is "the Slaughter of the Innocents," wherein Herod sets out to eliminate all the young boys who are potential rivals for power (Matt 2:16-18). Thus the story in Exodus has an opening to christological reality, for the baby Jesus is born exactly in such jeopardy, which persists until implemented on Good Friday in a state execution.

The sphere of Passover imagination, however, is not limited to the risk of the Jews or the destiny of Jesus. There are, in our own day, "little peoples" who, as a threat or an inconvenience for established power, are eliminated in wars and invasions, or are simply denied the right to live. In different parts of the world, different peoples play the role of "Hebrew." They are nonethnic, pre-formed, devalued folk who suffer at the hands of violent, legitimated policy.

Genocide can be blatant, as we have often witnessed. We need not neglect, however, the more "respectable" genocide wrought by our admired technology in which the destroyers never contact the victims. So-called "smart bombs" can take out an enormous civilian population without any need for hand-to-hand combat. The listening congregation may wonder about contemporary policies and practices that nullify the innocent.

The power of God is almost hidden in this text and is scarcely made visible. Nevertheless an undeniable "preferential option for the poor" is at work in this narrative. The power for life surges among the hopeless slave community through blessed women. Thus the issue of liberation surfaces inescapably through these "carriers of liberation." The birthing turns the hopeless into powerful, dangerous hopers.

A sermon on this text need not be confrontational. It would, rather, suggest that our common, uncritical reading of social reality ignores powerful class distinctions. That pervasive misreading screens out not only the hidden surprise of God's power for life, but also the faithful women strong enough to withstand genocide. This interpretation invites what may be an unnoticing, unacknowledging community (perhaps unwittingly allied with the policies of Pharaoh) to enter a season of Passover imagination, wherein one baby born overrides the brutalizing fear of Pharaoh.

On that mismatch between brutal power and the defiant miracle of birth that refuses genocide, Zora Neale Hurston comments: "The birthing beds of Hebrews were matters of state. The Hebrew womb had fallen under the heel of Pharaoh. . . . Hebrew women shuddered with terror at the indifference of their wombs to the Egyptian law."[20]

The capacity of the Hebrews to be indifferent to Egyptian law permits the exodus narrative to proceed. If they had submitted, there would have been no narrative of liberation, no Passover imagination, no gospel.

20. Zora Neale Hurston, *Moses, Man of the Mountain* (Chicago: University of Chicago Press, 1984) 11.

Exodus 2:1-10, The Birth of Moses

COMMENTARY

The Exodus story is not fundamentally interested in the person of Moses. It is not a "hero story." The story cannot, however, manage without Moses. In these verses, the quick sketch we are given of Moses' life moves quickly from the startling miracle of childhood survival (vv. 1-10) to the restless, violent urgency of adulthood (vv. 11-22). The story shrewdly conceals God in the life of Moses where that presence is not explicit or visible. Speaking of God's providential care, Calvin concludes, "All things which led to the preservation of Moses, were disposed by his guidance, and under his auspices, and by the secret inspiration of his spirit."[21]

21. John Calvin, *Commentaries on the Four Last Books of Moses Arranged in the Form of a Harmony Volume First* (Grand Rapids: Baker, 1979) 44.

We have just heard the harsh, massive decree of "the new king" (1:22). All male babies, the very ones who could do the slave labor of the empire, are to be drowned in the Nile River. Pharaoh misuses and distorts the Nile, which is characteristically a power for life, just as he misuses and distorts the lives of those around him.

In spite of this royal decree for death, which violates the "natural processes" of life, those processes continue; Pharaoh cannot stop them. There is a marriage (v. 1), and there is a birth (v. 2). These are two quick acts for life that intrinsically defy Pharaoh, even as the midwives had defied him in chapter 1. The marriage does not occupy the narrative for long (v. 1), and the birth receives only slightly more attention than the marriage (v. 2). An incongruity is immediately established. Death is decreed; birth nevertheless happens. The birth, an act of defiance of Pharaoh much like the births of 1:17-19, is also an act of raw danger. Commentaries observe that this narrative recapitulates something of the earlier narratives of Genesis. The nameless mother looked at the baby and saw "that he is a fine [טוב *ṭôb*] baby," the formula closely echoing the familiar verdict of creation, when God found creation "good" (*ṭôb*) (Gen 1:31). This birth is a new act of creation, an act of new creation. The world begins here again, precisely out of the chaos that "the new king" had decreed.

There are limits to hiding this baby, perhaps because the baby has become too big, too active, too noisy. The still unnamed mother, however, is up to this crisis. She makes a waterproof basket of bitumen and pitch. The narrative uses the term *basket* (תבה *tēbâ*), frequently used in the flood narrative. This new "ark" floats on the river, which was intended for his death. This unnamed baby reenacts the flood narrative; thus the basket, in the imagination of Israel, looks back to Genesis. The basket-ark is placed in the reeds (סוף *sûp*) at the edge of the Nile. The term used here for "reeds" is used subsequently in the exodus narrative to name the waters through which Israel came to liberation (13:18). The baby is at the edge of the waters of freedom, there before his people.

The narrative moves to the third crisis of the baby. Abruptly, the daughter of Pharaoh, also unnamed, comes to the river to bathe and finds the baby (v. 5). Was this discovery planned by the mother? Did Pharaoh's daughter bathe in that place regularly? Did she willfully bathe in the very river now burdened by her father with death? What will she do when she sees the baby? Will she replicate her raging father and kill the baby?

No, she sees the baby as the mother before her had seen him. Her reaction to the baby is surprise and immediate recognition: "A Hebrew!" She "had pity" (חמל *ḥāmal*), or as the NIV renders, she "felt sorry." But the word is stronger than these renderings. She spared the baby, entering into an alliance with him, and prepared to be his protector. Moreover, the princess knows exactly what she is doing. She recognizes that the baby is a "Hebrew baby," a child from the slave community, a child under royal ban, a child

under death sentence from her father—and she spares his life!

Princesses, even well-intentioned ones, however, do not tend to babies. They may knowingly save a baby in defiance of a royal decree, but a nursemaid must be found. All this time, watching at a distance, silent but palpably present, the unnamed sister of the unnamed baby takes initiative (vv. 4, 7). She volunteers to get help, and the help she offers is "from the Hebrew women," the same Hebrew women in 1:19 who are so vigorous and productive.

The response of the Egyptian princess is to issue two commands. To the unnamed sister, she says, "Go" (לכי *lēkî*). To the unidentified mother, she says, "Go [הילכי *hêlîkî*] . . . nurse [הינקהו *hêniqihû*]" (v. 9) and she promises to pay. The narrative reports that "the woman" obeyed the princess. The woman is unnamed, but we know her identity; this is the mother. We have come full circle from "the woman" in v. 2 who conceived and bore to "the woman" in v. 9 who took and nursed. She is at the beginning and the end of this rhetorical unit, the key player. The jeopardized baby who had to be taken from the mother because of the royal threat is now safe again with the mother, because of royal sparing.

The narrative permits a considerable time to elapse between vv. 9 and 10. We do not know how much time, but it is the timespan for growth and maturation. The unnamed child is now old enough to leave his unnamed mother. She yields up her child to the care of the princess who had spared him. The future of the baby is now all in the hands of the princess, for the mother has finished her risky work and now disappears from the narrative. In this single climactic verse, Pharaoh's daughter now adopts him as her own son, and by implication makes him an Egyptian prince. Moreover, in the act of adoption, she names him Moses (v. 10), indicating that he is now fully in her orbit.

In this narrative, Moses is the first person named. The name is Egyptian, used as a part of many royal names in Egypt. The etymology given for the name, placed in the mouth of the princess, however, is of another sort. The term *draw* (משה *māšâ*) is not related to *Moses* (משה *mōšeh*), but is in fact a homonym. The term *māšâ* is used only in 2 Sam 22:17 (cf. Ps 18:16) wherein David says of Yahweh, "He drew me out of mighty waters." The strophe of the poem that includes this verse also includes other active verbs with God as subject, e.g., *delivered* (נצל *nāṣal* and חלץ *ḥālaṣ*) and *brought out* (יצא *yāṣā*). Thus the term is used with reference to God's mighty acts of rescue. What may be a royal Egyptian name is transposed by the proposed etymology into Israelite praise for deliverance. Thus the rescue of little Moses from the waters anticipates a larger rescue to be wrought through the power of Moses.

REFLECTIONS

This narrative is framed by two notations that might mislead. At the outset, we are given a priestly genealogy (v. 1). At the conclusion, we are given an Egyptian name (v. 10). Neither of these plays an important part in the narrative, for the crucial action takes place between these notations.

1. God is not mentioned as a character or agent in the plot (before this, God is evident only in 1:20, in a rather understated way). There is no doubt that God is present but quite below the surface of the rhetoric. Although God will be visibly active in the exodus narrative to follow, here the mode of discourse is not unlike the Joseph narrative wherein the outcome of the story is governed by a God who never makes an appearance (see Gen 45:5-8; 50:20).

2. The main action is wrought through a series of three unnamed women, who are to be linked to the two midwives of 1:15-22. The key characters are "the daughter of Pharaoh," who spares; "the woman," who is the mother; and "the sister." Pixley observes that even in the Egyptian "den of death," "allies of life" are found.[22] The narrator has wrought a powerful interface between the hiddenness of God and the daring visibility of the women. One might conclude that the women act out of the hidden providence of God. Or, closer to the voice of the text itself, the women have displaced the providence of God and are the ones who assure the baby's future. They permit Israel's liberated future.

3. The narrative has unobtrusively injected class consciousness into the narrative. The tension in the narrative is not all focused on the baby. Rather, the action takes place between the daughter of Pharaoh—the powerful Egyptian—and the marginal Hebrews, mother and daughter. These latter women have been designated as enemies by the royal decree of the powerful new king. The three women, however, refuse to live out their assigned hostility to one another. In fact, they become unwitting allies, each playing an unexpected role in the life of the baby. It is a story beyond their ken, for the princess hardly wanted liberated slaves, and the Hebrew women scarcely believed liberation to be possible.

4. This is in fact a rescue narrative. While scholars often cite parallels to other birth legends, this story is not much interested in the birth, which receives only half a verse (v. 2*a*). What counts is the jeopardy of the child (because of the decree of 1:22) and the series of small, emergency maneuvers that move the baby from caring hand to caring hand, until he arrives at safety and is named and valued. The listener is left in astonishment at the rescue.

5. The story of Moses' survival is deeply embedded in the larger, communal memory of Israel. We have mentioned the verdict "good," the basket as an ark, and the reference to the watery reeds. Israel is able to hear in this story of a baby the story of its entire life. The last phrase of v. 10 sounds and anticipates the desperate petitions and the glad thanks of Israel for the many rescues made in its life.

22. Pixley, *On Exodus,* 7.

6. This is a people who always live under the threat of chaos, always about to be inundated by the chaotic waters, helpless lest the Lord of chaos act and intervene. Thus the story of Moses is paradigmatic for Israel's life and faith. It not only anticipates the exodus narrative, but it also resonates with the deepest spirituality of Israel, a practice of plea and praise, of need and hope.

Exodus 2:11-22, Moses Flees from Pharaoh

COMMENTARY

The narrative makes an important leap in time from v. 10 to v. 11. In v. 10, Moses is a child who grows up (גדל *gādal*). In v. 11, he is "grown up" (*gādal*), now fully an adult. The narrative is divided into two locations, Egypt (vv. 11-15*a*) and Midian (vv. 15*b*-22).

2:11-15a. In the Egyptian scene, the narrator loses no time coming to the subject, "forced labor" (v. 11; cf. 1:11; 5:4-5; 6:6-7). When Moses went out, forced labor is what he saw, humans forcibly engaged in oppressive labor for the sake of the imperial government. Others might have seen other matters: royal splendor, extravagant living, well ordered society. But Moses saw only forced labor.

Verse 11 twice uses the term *brother* ("people," "kinsman"). In the first use, we cannot tell if "his people" are the slaves or the imperial overlords. Verses 1-10 make it possible for Moses to claim and enact either identity. The second use resolves our uncertainty. It is a "Hebrew" who is "one of his kinsfolk." We now know whose side Moses is on.

Moses' intervention in the beating of the Hebrew produces three sub-scenes in quick succession. First, Moses intervenes to kill the abusive Egyptian (v. 12). Coote and Ord opine that this act of violence in the face of an oppressive, unequal social relation is the core event for Israel's founding memory.[23] The narrative uses the same word, for "kill" (נכה *nākâ*) that was used for the actions of the Egyptian against the Hebrew, "beat." The Egyptian is killing the Hebrew slave, and Moses inverts the power relation and does to the Egyptian what he is doing to the slave.

The second sub-scene is "the next day" (v. 13). Two "Hebrews" (two of Moses' now embraced kinsmen) are fighting. Of course, the marginated dare not strike out at the master, but work out their unresolved violence on each other, an arrangement that reassures and maintains the position of the unthreatened, unassaulted overseers. A second time, Moses intervenes. Unlike the struggle of Egyptian versus Hebrew, slave versus overseer, this dispute is only between Hebrew slaves. In this intervention, Moses already asserts a judicial function in the community (see 18:13-27), for he identifies and addresses the "guilty one" (רשע *rāšā'*).

Note well that Moses does not scold or judge or reprimand; he only stops the violence. He understands very well that any alternative future for the marginated Hebrews depends on solidarity, which is precluded by internal conflict. The "guilty one" predictably is not happy about the intervention, and promptly and daringly rebukes Moses (v. 14). He chides Moses for his presumptuousness, acting as ruler and judge when no one has authorized him to serve such a function.

Then, as an escalation of the rebuke, the one in the wrong lets Moses know that the killing of the Egyptian is no secret in the slave community. While the slaves might be grateful for Moses' intervention, their awareness of his killing the Egyptian is now used against Moses as a threat.

This challenge to Moses has its immediate and desired effect. The speech of the one "in the wrong" questions the authority of Moses, and at the same time threatens him by communicating that his attack on the Egyptian is well known. If his deed is known among the Hebrews, no doubt it is known (or soon will be) in the royal entourage. This threat (which also serves as a warning) abruptly changes the focus of the narrative. The real danger is

23. Robert B. Coote and David Robert Ord, *The Bible's First History* (Philadelphia: Fortress, 1989) 220-30.

not from the knowing Hebrews, but from the Egyptians who will also know.

The narrative thus turns to the third sub-scene (vv. 14b-15a). Moses' own pondering in v. 14 is reinforced by the verdict of the narrator in v. 15: Pharaoh knows. Again, Pharaoh is unnamed, but he is in any case the same new king who had issued the desperate decree of 1:22. Pharaoh now seeks Moses. Pharaoh intends to "kill" (הרג *hārag*). The verbs of this Egyptian episode are relentlessly violent and brutal. At the outset, the Egyptian "strikes" (v. 11), and at the end, Pharaoh seeks to "kill" (v. 15). In between, Moses "strikes" (v. 12), and is accused of murder (v. 14). The Egyptians kill, and the Hebrews are driven into responding brutality.

2:15b-22. In order to escape the killing reach of Pharaoh, Moses flees (v. 15b). His flight changes the venue of the story. We now begin the second scene of Moses' adult life, this time in Midian. We are not told anything about Midian, except that it is not Egypt. It is evidently a pastoral society, and it is free of the dangers, threats, and abusiveness of the Egyptian kingdom.

The narrator immediately situates Moses at a well. In a pastoral economy, a well is a place of well-being and sustenance. The pastoral opening of this narrative account in v. 15b is heightened in v. 16, with a notice that is almost predictable. In a pastoral economy, women invariably come to the well for water. The narrative introduces us to an appropriate "type-scene," and our imagination recalls the servant of Abraham meeting Rebekah (Gen 24:10-21), and Jacob meeting Rachel at the well (Gen 29:9-12). Almost incidentally, we are introduced to "the priest of Midian," but we are told nothing about him. At this point, his only function is to be the father of seven daughters.

The narrative permits the idyllic scene of Moses, daughter, and water to last for only one verse. That type scene, which holds a potential for romance, is immediately and violently interrupted in v. 17 with the arrival of the shepherds. The work of shepherds is to lead their sheep "beside still waters," but the only available water is at the well where Moses is. The shepherds are stronger than the daughters, so they prevail. The NRSV says that Moses "came to their defense," but

that rendering of the Hebrew is weak. The Hebrew term is ישע (*yāša'*); he "saved" them, he rescued them, and so their flocks had water. Moses intervenes powerfully, so that the weak are not deprived of what is needed for their life. Moses is clearly cast as a rescuer.

Now the action moves from the well to the habitat of the priest, the father of the seven daughters. His name is given only here as Reuel (cf. Num 10:29). He notices that his daughters' schedule has varied, and he inquires why. Their response is telling in two regards. First, Moses is identified in their answer as an Egyptian. This is not at all what we expected. In the preceding episode, Moses has clearly identified himself with the Hebrews and has visibly set himself against Egypt. Now, however, he has enough remaining marks of his royal station that this is how he appears to the daughters. This identification is telling, because it suggests that Moses is at a liminal moment in his life, moving to a new identity.

Second, Moses' action is described by the daughters with the verb נצל (*nāṣal*). He "snatches" the daughters from danger at the hands of the shepherds. Again the NRSV's "help" is much too weak. The use of *nāṣal* here echoes *yāša'* in v. 17. Moses is a powerful intervenor who has yet again entered into a dangerous situation on the side of the weak against the strong.

Reuel, the father, immediately recognizes that this "Egyptian" is a remarkable man and that his debt to Moses is very great. Now the story moves quickly. Reuel offers hospitality to Moses, inviting him to "eat bread"—i.e., to enjoy his household and to enter into solidarity with him (v. 20). Moses accepts the proffered hospitality. The narrative promptly escalates hospitality into marriage, and the marriage immediately eventuates in a son.

We can now see, as we arrive at v. 22, that this story has been moving quite intentionally to the name of the son, "alien." The term גרשם (*gēršōm*) appears to be a combination of the word גר (*gēr*, "alien") with the adverb שם (*šām*, "there"). The narrative, which culminates in the term *alien,* is reinforced by the final word of the narrative, *foreigner* (נכרי *nākěrî*). Moses' powerful intervention has transformed him from a well-situated member of Pharaoh's household to a fugitive. His passion for the well-being of the Hebrews has made him a fugitive from Egyptian order and power. He is a hunted, unwelcome man. He has indeed become an alien in his own land.

REFLECTIONS

This narrative concerning Moses' formation as an adult is not much known or read in the church. We tend to skip directly from the idyllic birth story (2:1-10) to the account of the burning bush (3:1-6). Skipping over this material permits the narrative to be a rather romantic tale of religious experience under the hidden protection of God. This material in vv. 11-22, however, forces the narrative of Moses into the arena of deep social conflict, and of violence and brutality that are inescapable in an unjust society.

1. The narrative lets us see that the social reality in which Moses is formed and out of which he emerges is one of conflict in which he is deeply and riskily enmeshed. Moreover, that social conflict is not just because people are mean-spirited. Rather, the conflict concerns real issues of social, economic, and political power. Thus there is conflict between Egyptian and Hebrew over forced labor practices, between two Hebrew men over a "wrong" (רשׁע *rāšā'*), and between daughters and shepherds over water, which is no doubt scarce. In each of these three cases, Moses intervenes on the side of the victim.

2. While this story focuses on the person of Moses, we should not miss the fact that the narrator operates with a larger, acute social analysis. It is, perhaps, too much to say that the narrative does a "class reading" of social power, but it makes unmistakably clear the enormous contrast between the powerful and the powerless, and shows that this contrast assures that social relations are marked by relentless and recurring violence. The narrative does not comment on the violence, but only voices it and lets us see it for what it is. Moreover, Moses' own activities are themselves acts of compensatory violence, effectively countering the violence of the powerful. This overriding ethos of violence does not permit us to romanticize rescue or salvation in the Bible, which regularly consist of an intrusion into cycles of violence taken at great risk, in order to permit a new pattern of social relations.

3. The story is structured as an interplay between Egypt and Midian. Egypt is a place of power, order, and affluence. It is also Moses' "home" in which he is homeless, and from which he must flee because of his passion for justice. By contrast, Midian is a pastoral society. The main point about Midian is that it is non-Egypt, non-imperial, non-stratified. There is no forced labor policy there. It is in this "other place" that Moses finds hospitality and, in the end, his true family and home. Midian is his chance for a new identity, but his vocation drives him always back to Egypt.

4. Like the geography of his narrative, Moses himself is portrayed as a man with something of a fluid and unsettled identity. In this account, no one calls him by name, except the narrator. On the one hand, the rebuke of the Hebrew man seems to identify him as another Hebrew who is reprimanded for acting presumptuously as an Egyptian (v. 14). On the other hand, late in the narrative, the daughters still perceive him to be an Egyptian. Presumably, Moses still had options and choices. Moses did not have to make the choice he did; had he not so chosen, he would not have had to flee to Midian. Thus his choices made from his passion for justice in fact bestow upon him the role of fugitive (*gēr*, "alien").

5. The series of choices through which this liminal character emerges culminates in his final characterization, "an alien am I" (v. 22). Moses never sets out to be an alien, but finds himself so, one choice at a time. While God is nowhere present in the narrative (as also in 2:1-10), it is clear that attention to the freedom and justice intended by God predictably culminates in being excluded as an outsider.

This characterization of Moses' adult life as an outsider has important christological overtones. One becomes an outsider by making choices to continue as savior on the side of the marginated, in order to break the cycles of brutality. It is no wonder that in the story of Jesus, the one who had "nowhere to lay his head" is finally executed "outside the city," almost completely abandoned. Jesus' story is one of choices that make him a feared outsider.

This role of the continuing outsider has important ecclesiastical overtones as well. Whenever the faithful community accepts a role as an intervener for the marginal in order to break cycles of violence, it invariably becomes a community of "resident aliens." The church does not need to give up its "imperial status" in the company of the Egyptians. But whenever it acts in its passion for "the Hebrew," it accepts its own fugitive vocation.

Exodus 2:23-25 God Hears Their Groaning

COMMENTARY

These three verses function as something of a pivotal marker, a transition point between the preliminary narrative of chapters 1–2 and the narrative of liberation that follows. The action of these verses occurs when the oppressive king dies. Such an occurrence is not uncommon. When an oppressive ruler dies, everything comes unglued and there is an opportunity to reconfigure patterns of social power.

This readily observable political pattern, however, is matched by an even more powerful theological reality. The nullification of this pseudo-king makes room for the real king. The historical sequence and theological dynamic of these verses is not unlike the more familiar statement of Isa 6:1, which we may paraphrase: "In the year that King Uzziah died, I saw the real king." In times of social discontinuity, the kingship of Yahweh becomes powerfully active and visible.

After the framing phrase of v. 23, these verses are cast in two parts: the voicing of Israel and the response of God. The first speaker is Israel (v. 23). It is at the moment of the death of the king that Israel finds its voice. Of course, the voice of rage, resentment, and insistence may have been present in Israel, but stifled. A totalitarian regime can keep such voices silent for a long time. When, however, there is a hint of transition

or a show of weakness, that stifled voice can sound with enormous force and energy.

We have not had mention of "Israel" since 1:13. Since that verse, the subject of the narrative has been "the Hebrews." Now, however, the narrative becomes theologically self-conscious and speaks of "Israel." Israel finds its voice and sounds its pain. It dares to engage in a public process of letting its pain have voice. When such pain is voiced, it takes on energy and becomes an active agent in the process of public power. Four terms, two verbs (אנח 'ānaḥ, "groaned"; זעק zāʿaq, "cried out") and two nouns (שׁועה šawʿâ, "cry;" נאקה nĕʾāqâ, "groaning"), are used for Israel's speech, and twice the statement is reinforced by the phrase "from their slavery." The terms themselves are not exceptional. Together they constitute a characteristic vocabulary of those who cry out in rage, protest, insistence, and expectation concerning an intolerable situation. The two terms *groan* and *groaning* serve as an unfocused expression of distress. The other terms serve to summon help. None of the terms, however, is addressed to anyone in particular.

The focus of our reading need not be on the nuance of any particular term. It is much more important that Israel cried out at all. In the moment of crying out, of letting pain become public and audible, the slaves broke with the definitions of reality imposed by the policies and values of the empire. The empire characteristically preferred silent slaves, who present no social embarrassment or administrative inconvenience. Silence among the oppressed means that they have conceded to the oppressors the right to define reality.

The startling moment of this narrative is when the silence is broken. Israel cries out. We are not told why. No theological reason is given; the cry is neither God-induced nor God-directed. The beginning point of the exodus is rooted not in any explicitly theological claim, but in this elemental fact that human bodies can absorb so much, and then will rebel and assert and initiate. The crying, groaning bodies of the slaves found enough voice to say that their circumstance is not right, acceptable, or sustainable. In a quite distinct rhetorical maneuver, the narrator reports that God heard their cry (v. 24). The one who hears was not explicitly addressed. Perhaps there is something about this God that makes hearing possible. Perhaps this God is especially attentive to cries of oppression. In any case, now and only now, God takes a critical role in the narrative. Until now God has been mentioned only briefly in chapter 1 and not at all in chapter 2.

Only now, after the cries, is there a sustained statement about God. God is now the subject of four crucial verbs: God *heard* (שמע *šāma*), God *remembered* (זכר *zākar*), God *saw* (ראה *rā'â*), and God *knew* (ידע *yāda*). God heard their groaning. These were not groans addressed to God, but the hearing caused the remembering. The voicing of pain drives God back into the book of Genesis, to the ones to whom God is already committed. The memory is powered by those unambiguous carriers of the promise who are now named: Abraham, Isaac, Jacob. God connects present slaves and old promises. God has one eye on the old covenant oaths in Genesis. The other eye, however, is on the present circumstance of Israel in bondage. The text does not say, as the NRSV has it, "God took notice *of them*" (emphasis added). It is only, "God knew," without an object. We are left to imagine what God knew. God knew that these slaves were connected to the people of Genesis. God knew that promises were yet to be kept, requiring powerful intervention. God knew, because of old memories, abiding promises, present pain, and audible groans. God knew and so had to act. All of chapters 1–2 have built toward these powerful verbs that witness to God's powerful, sovereign purpose.

REFLECTIONS

The two points I mention are to be taken in reverse order. First, God is moved to care in decisive and powerful ways for this slave community. The good news is that God is motivated to act in a situation of terrible hurt. Priority should be given, however, to the second point: Israel's voice of hurt and rage. That is the catalyst for the entire Exodus story; it is the cry that evokes God's care.

It is difficult to imagine a more radical theological statement than this; it is voiced grief that mobilizes God to act in saving ways. This affirmation, when fully comprehended, challenges us on two fronts. On the one hand, this sequence of events challenges all talk about divine priority and sovereign initiative. The Exodus is not initiated by either the power or the mercy of God. God is the second actor in the drama of liberation. It is Israel's self-assertion that begins the process. That self-assertion is a remarkable matter, for the first task of every marginalized community is to find its voice when it has had its voice, wind, and identity knocked out of it. God is a crucial agent in the story of liberation, but is second and not first.

On the other hand, this sequence of events goes against all of our refined notions of propriety and decorum. There is here no respectful distance from God, no waiting in silence, no trustful awe. The Exodus process begins with a raging cry of self-assertion. The action of Israel in slavery is not unlike blind Bartimaeus (Mark 10:46-52). His well-meaning contemporaries tried to silence him in his need, but he refused. He knew that silence could only mean continued disability. Thus, against a theology that leaves too much to God, and against an etiquette that prefers peaceable waiting, Israel is vigorous and bold, insistent and importunate. Israel shatters the docile silence, asserts its hurt and its hope. In doing so, it not only terrifies the empire, but it mobilizes holiness on its behalf as well. As a result of Israel's cry, God knows now that God must act.

This text is not perceived as overly urgent in most of our bourgeois congregations. If, however, this story is not only a concrete memory of a past time, but also a present paradigm, it might help us to hear differently the disruptive noise of those who cry out of their hurt and voice their insistent hope. The world of Exodus is where the holiness of God lives in staggering response to the hurt of the slaves. For both parties, Israel and God, there must be a voicing!

Exodus 3:1–4:31, Moses Is Sent to Pharaoh

COMMENTARY

3:1-10 After the formal, public notice of 2:23-25, we are taken back into the narrative of Moses. He has made for himself a new life in the service of his father-in-law, Jethro, presumably another name for Reuel in 2:18. Moses herds sheep and comes to new grazing land. The place to which Moses comes is Horeb, here called "the mountain of God." Elsewhere in the tradition, the same mountain is called Sinai, and even here the term for "bush" is סנה (sĕneh), likely an allusion to Sinai.

We are quickly put on notice that this narrative concerns no ordinary happening, and we must not expect to understand it through our usual categories. The narrative features an angel (messenger), a bush that burns but is not burned, and God's own voice. At the outset, we do well to recognize that this narrative is of a peculiar genre, a vehicle for the appearance of God's presence, God's first presence in the exodus narrative. We need not and must not seek explanations for what happens according to the norms of other genre.

The theophany (i.e., "appearance of God") happens in two parts. First, there is the visible element (vv. 2-3). The better-known part of the appearance is the burning bush. But along with the bush a messenger appears. It is odd that the angel appears, but says nothing and carries no message. It is as though the visible presence in the narrative is designed only to get Moses' attention, which it does.

The second part of the encounter is the speech of God (vv. 4-6). This speech is quite extended, but our immediate concern is only vv. 4-6. The narrator is no longer interested in or troubled by the bush. What counts is the speech of God, which contains three elements. First, there is the sovereign summons. God calls Moses in a double summons, not unlike Gen 22:11 and 1 Sam 3:10 (v. 4). Moses' response, following convention, is "Here am I," indicating readiness to submit and obey.[24] This exchange establishes the right relation of sovereign and servant. This is the first hint we have that the life of Moses has a theological dimension, for the categories of his existence until now have been political.

Second, the commanding voice in the bush asserts an awesome limit, caused by the reality of God's holiness (v. 5). The key term is *holy.* The voice in the fire asserts that God's own preemptive presence is here. That presence transforms everything at hand, including the place and the conversation. The crushing, awesome reality of God's holiness requires respectful distance (cf. 19:23). The removal of sandals is an act of willing submission. The place has been transformed by the speech and presence of God. Moses is now taken up into the sphere of that awful holiness.

God now speaks a third time, offering God's own self-identity (v. 6). The formula of v. 6 connects the experience of Moses to the book of Genesis, and to the promises operative there (see 2:24).

Moses' response is abrupt and appropriate; he "hides his face." He would not look at God. Note well, this narrative does not suggest that God is invisible. Quite the contrary. God is

24. Calvin, *Commentaries on the Four Last Books of Moses Arranged in the Form of a Harmony,* 63.

visible, but must not be seen, for to see God is to impinge upon God's holiness and freedom. Thus Moses' act of submissive deference is undertaken so that God's sovereignty is not crowded. Later on, Moses will become daring and emboldened (33:17-23). But this is after a long, troubled history together.

The unit concerning the bush has much occupied commentators.[25] We must not, however, be overly inquisitive about these strange events. In fact, the theophany has no life of its own, but is only the launching pad in the text for what must come next. The voice in the bush, taken by itself, might be evidence of all sorts of religious manifestation, and has been interpreted in many, varied ways. We are told promptly, however, that this is not a generic religious presence. This is the name-able, identifiable voice of the God of Genesis, the one who has made faithful promises, who "goes with," who guards fugitives like Jacob, who keeps outsiders like Joseph, and who births babies to barren mothers.

The God who summons (v. 4) and warns (v. 5) and discloses an enduring commitment (v. 6) now speaks more fully and characteristically concerning the slaves (vv. 7-9). Fretheim observes that this is Yahweh's first direct speech in Exodus, and is indeed prognostic for what follows.[26] In these verses, the tradition has placed in the mouth of God at the bush the standard credo that Israel in its Passover imagination regularly recites. Here it is God's own speech of self-disclosure that makes available to Moses (and Israel) all that needs to be known of God.

God's first self-announcement echoes the great responding verbs of 2:24-25. In v. 7, three of the verbs of 2:24-25 are reiterated, "I have seen . . . I have heard . . . I have known." (The fourth verb of v. 24, "God remembered," is absent here, but is implied in the formula of v. 6.) These are the three actions that God characteristically takes toward Israel, for Israel is the object of God's intense attentiveness. The verbal sentences here differ in important ways from those of 2:24-25. The first verb, "I have seen," acknowledges affliction, and instead of "sons of Israel" claims the slaves as "my people."

The second verb, "I have heard," is roughly the same. The third verb, "I have known," ends cryptically in 2:25, but here has the object, "sufferings." That is, with all three verbs God acknowledges and engages the troubles of Israel: afflictions, cries, sufferings.

The fourth verb here is not paralleled in 2:24-25 and decisively advances the action: "I have come down." God not only knows, but God is now physically(!) mobilized to be present in the midst of the trouble. The verb articulates decisively what is crucial for Israel's understanding of God, which for Christians culminates in the incarnation— God has "come down" into human history in bodily form.

The verb *come down* is followed by two other verbs of enormous power: *deliver, bring up.* The first of these (נצל *nāṣal*) is the same verb used of Moses in 2:19 when he "snatches" the daughters from the destructive power of the shepherds. So God now snatches Israel from the destructive power of Egypt. The second verb, *bring up* (עלה *ʿālâ*) is regularly used for the exodus. This verb is followed by a double use of the term *land*, used both negatively and positively, "from the land" of Egypt "to the land" of promise. In this sequence of verbs, God's speech introduces the major elements in Israel's normative memory, succinctly anticipating the entire story from exodus to the promised land. In v. 8, God's speech fully anticipates the new land, which in every way contrasts the present land of oppression and bondage. The new land that God now promises is "good." It is filled with the power of blessing rather than curse, broad and nonrestrictive rather than confining like the place of the slaves, and filled with plenty, rather than the close rations that must have been the lot of the slaves. This characteristic expression of Israel's faith readily, and without effort or embarrassment, joins what is everywhere else divided: God/ slaves, God's promise/land. The rhetoric of Israel easily holds together the power of religious claim and the needed resources for public life. This linkage redefines both God and human history, a connection that is the driving impetus for the exodus narrative.

The last part of v. 8 moves to the present occupants of the land of promise. The list of peoples is stylized and is not to be taken as

---

25. See the overview of the passage by Samuel Terrien, *The Elusive Presence*, Religious Perspectives (San Francisco: Harper & Row, 1978) 109-12, together with full documentation.
26. Fretheim, *Exodus*, 53.

an actual description of the land. The list is a foil for God's promise, in order to affirm that God's powerful intentionality will override all present power arrangements. (While this warrant for taking the land occupied by others subsequently has dangerous and destructive implications, those implications are not now on the horizon of the land-hungry who desperately believe they are destined by God for land.)

Verse 9 reiterates God's awareness from vv. 7-8, employing the verb *hear* and repeating the verb *see* and introducing yet another word for "oppression" (לחץ *lāḥaṣ*). God knows Israel's present circumstance and is prepared to counter it decisively. Thus 2:24-25 and 3:7-9 portray God as the only and crucial character in creating for Israel an alternative to the situation of oppression in Egypt.

Verse 10 makes a radical and decisive break, which must have stunned Moses when he heard it, and must have stunned Israel each time it was reiterated. What had been all pious promise now becomes rigorous demand: "Come." In one brief utterance, the grand intention of God has become a specific human responsibility, human obligation, and human vocation. It is Moses who will do what Yahweh said, and Moses who will run the risks that Yahweh seemed ready to take. The connection of God and Moses, of heaven and earth, of great power and dangerous strategy is all carried in the statement "I will send you." After the massive intrusion of God, the exodus has suddenly become a human enterprise. It is Moses (not God) who will meet with Pharaoh. It is Moses (not God) who will "bring out" (יצא *yāṣā*) "my people." It is Moses who acts in God's place to save God's people. Again, this is the odd joining of God and human history. The joining is done, however, through the vulnerable, risk-taking body of Moses, on whom everything now depends.

It is no wonder that the narrative that follows shows Moses voicing a series of serious doubts and resistances to the summons, for he has been summoned to do a remarkably dangerous deed. There is, moreover, substantive reason for such resistance, especially in the case of Moses. The call and the imposition of the verb *yāṣā* are a summons for him to return to the dangerous, conflictual arena of Egypt where his own identity is at risk

and where he must frontally challenge the enormous imperial power of the status quo. Clearly, Moses' chances of success in Egypt are modest indeed, and his chances for survival are no better.

3:11–4:17. Moses offers five points of resistance concerning his awesome new vocation. Childs observes that each objection looks to a past reality, and each response of God moves Moses to a new future.[27] The first resistance is that he is a genuine nobody: "Who am I?" Moses' words anticipate the later resistance by Gideon (cf. Judg 6:15). Moses, like Gideon, is nobody important and lacks authority. In his resistant question, Moses juxtaposes his own insignificance to the great task of Exodus, reiterating the awesome verb *yāṣā* and invoking the dreadful name of Egypt. God's response to Moses is equally massive and characteristic: "I will be with you" (3:12). Moses must go, but not Moses alone. This is the same answer later to be given to Gideon (Judg 6:16). Neither text says how God is present. It is enough that Moses' person is fully invested with God's accompanying presence.

Moses' second point of resistance is more substantive and requires a more substantive response (vv. 13-22). Moses must know the name of the one who authorizes such a dangerous mission. The mission is dangerous not only for Moses, but also for the Israelites, who are asked to engage in massive civil disobedience against Pharaoh. Such a risk will require unambiguous warrant. Moses already accepts that he is dealing with "the God of your ancestors"—the promise-making God of Genesis (cf. 2:24; 3:6). But he wants something more explicit. He wants, as Israel will require, a personal name.

God's answer is extensive and complicated (vv. 14-16). The best known and most enigmatic part of the answer to Moses is the formula of v. 14: "I AM WHO I AM." Without pursuing the endless critical opinions about the origin of the formula, it is enough to see that the formula bespeaks power, fidelity, and presence.[28] This God is named as the power to create, the one who causes to be. This God is the one who will be present in faithful ways

---

27. Brevard S. Childs, *The Book of Exodus: A Critical, Theological Commentary*, OTL (Philadelphia: Westminster, 1974) 72.
28. See Dennis J. McCarthy, "Exodus 3:14: History, Philosophy and Theology," *CBQ* 40 (1978) 311-22.

to make possible what is not otherwise possible. This God is the very power of newness that will make available new life for Israel outside the deathliness of Egypt. This reading of the formula is, of course, a theological interpretation, not a philological analysis. Whether by design or by accident, the name in fact tells Moses almost nothing. Moses still depends on more traditional formulations to flesh out what is suggested in this formula.

That fleshing out, as though recognized as needed by the tradition builders, is given in v. 15. The God with the enigmatic name is in fact the one already known in the Genesis narratives concerning the ancestors (see v. 13). Thus we come full circle to what Moses already knows in v. 13. Moses' knowledge of God has advanced little, but the old memory contains everything Israel needs to know. Everything is already present there, and now is freshly enacted in this encounter with Moses. In the formulation of v. 15, the name Yahweh is uttered as a summary of the longer ancestral formulation. The name Yahweh (יהוה) ostensibly derives from some form of the verb to be (היה hāyâ) so that God is the power for life, the power of being, the power of newness. This strange formula leaves the door open toward "being"—toward "ontology."[29]

Childs vigorously holds to a "historical" understanding, seeing that in the *present* crisis, the formulation looks to the *past* in order to envision an utterly new *future*.[30] Israel, however, does not pursue the point, because even its flirtation with ontology is narratively framed. It is a God with a narratively framed name who will be present and decisive for Israel. This reading of the exchange with Moses insists upon the narrative quality of Israel's faith, which refuses to go behind the narrative or to bring the narrative to a question of abstract "being." What Israel receives of God can be appropriated only by the retelling of the stories in which Yahweh is embedded. Thus Yahweh is "told" and "retold" and is about to be retold again in the face of Pharaoh.

The response to Moses' question in v. 13 extends only through v. 15. In vv. 16-22, the narrative departs from the actual exchange

with Moses in order to suggest a three-step strategy for the actual departure from Egypt.

In the first step, Moses is to recruit and mobilize the elders of Israel—i.e., the heads of the families and clans (vv. 16-18a). While Moses is the initiator of action, he does not act alone. Notice that unlike the Hebrews, who appear to be amorphous and without visible social structure, this narrative imagines Israel's already having in place a coherent, visible structure of leadership.

Moses' word to the elders reiterates the fundamental promise of God, already voiced in vv. 7-9. Moses' appeal is to the God of Genesis. (Notice that reliance is placed upon the formula of v. 15, to the neglect of the enigmatic statement of v. 14.) The God of the Genesis ancestors has taken note of the Egyptian situation. The acknowledgment of the situation of oppression is expressed with an infinitive absolute: "I have *really* visited you" (v. 16); NRSV, "given heed"; NIV, "watched over." (See the important reuse of this formula in 13:20, with reference to Gen 50:24-25.) This assurance is followed by a recognition of what has been "done to you" by the Egyptians and by the use of the term *affliction* ("misery"). This verse uses forceful language to sound again the assurance of 2:25 and 3:7: "I know." This is followed by the verb *bring up,* which was assigned to Moses in v. 10. Now it is God who will "bring up." Again, the Exodus verbs are stretched to include deliverance into the new land of well-being and abundance. That is, Moses is to announce that the God of Genesis is about to act to transform the situation of the present slave community. In v. 18, God adds a powerful assurance, "They will listen to your voice." They (the elders) will be persuaded to act in solidarity with Moses and to place themselves at risk even as Moses is at risk.

The second element in the strategy is that Moses with the elders will directly confront the king of Egypt (vv. 18b-19). The elders and Moses are to assert to the king that Yahweh is the "God of the Hebrews." This is the God who is allied with the amorphous, low-class work force. The slave community is to propose a work strategy to worship this counter-God three days' journey into the wilderness. This demand might be read in very different ways. Such a proposed three-day journey may

29. See Childs, *The Book of Exodus,* 83, 88, on the issue of ontology in this formulation.

30. See Childs, *The Book of Exodus,* 87-88.

be a ruse for escape, or it may be that such a proposed act of worship is a dramatic act that delegitimates the religious claims of the empire through the sacramental acknowledgment of a counter-God. This latter reading lacks the intent of a planned escape, but in the end holds a greater threat.

Whatever the intent of the demand, it will, of course, not be granted by the king (v. 19). If it is a ruse for escape, the king will not permit such an escape. If it is an intended assault on royal ideology, the king cannot risk such an assault. Neither the narrator nor God is naive about the stakes of the confrontation or about the possibilities for success. The narrator understands that power is not willingly or easily surrendered. It requires counter-power, "a mighty hand," to force the hand of Pharaoh (v. 19).

The third element in this strategy is that God's own powerful hand will be at work against the empire. This resolve on God's part anticipates the extensive plague narrative that follows. Two elements of God's resolve are worth noting. First, the verb for "strike" (נכה *nākâ*) is the same verb in 2:12 whereby Moses "struck" the Egyptian. Thus Moses' act anticipates the same action of Yahweh against Egypt. Moses' enormous anger against abusive Egypt has penetrated even into the heart of Yahweh, who now also has enormous anger against abusive Egypt. Second, Yahweh resolves to do "all my wonders." The term *wonders* (נפלאת *niplā'ōt*) bespeaks the extraordinary acts of power that violate all present constructions of reality and make possible what the world thinks is impossible. Such acts are staggering ways of shattering the status quo, inexplicable except that they are credited to God's own inscrutable resolve.

As a result of these "wonders," the slave community in Egypt is to be placed in quite a new relation vis-à-vis the resentful Egyptians (v. 21). Likely, this affirmation is laden with heavy irony. The assertion made to Moses is that Israel will have "favor" (חן *ḥēn*) with the Egyptians, believing the threat of the "mighty hand" and "wonders" that intimidate and coerce Egypt.

The provision thus is cast as a grand euphemism. Each slave woman will "ask" for jewelry of silver and gold from her masters, but in fact the asking is taking, and receiving is seizing. The last phrase exposes the euphemism. Thus you shall "plunder" (*nāṣal* in the *pi'el*) the Egyptians." The text anticipates a forcible redistribution of wealth.

This extended digression in the mouth of Yahweh (vv. 16-22) is only loosely related to vv. 14-15, which respond to Moses' question in v. 13. Although vv. 16-22 are a quite distinct piece, they are placed here to function as an exposition of vv. 14-15. It is implicit in the ancestral and enigmatic name of Yahweh that promises are operative now, as in Genesis. The force of the promise will cause the elders to listen, will cause the king of Egypt to resist, and will cause the slave women to take plunder as they depart from slavery. In a less than direct way, all of these rhetorical elements testify to the dynamism and energy of this God, whose name is permeated with promise and with the capacity to work a new thing. Moses asked for a name; in response, he received a scenario of all that comes along with Yahweh's promissory activity.

Moses' third objection is that he fears rejection by his own people (4:1). The NRSV casts the protest conditionally: "Suppose they do not believe me." The Hebrew text, however, does not require such a construction. It may be a straight indicative statement: "They will not trust me." The second negative, "They will not listen to my voice," is a direct refutation of the assurance given by God in 3:18. Thus in raising this objection, Moses refuses the very assurance God has given. Read psychologically, this exchange from 3:18 to 4:1 suggests that because the stakes are very high, Moses' anxiety is equally high. Read as a piece of strategic rhetoric, the protest serves to heighten suspense and to permit (or require) an even more extreme response from God.

Moses is no longer satisfied with verbal assurances from God, so God's response to this third objection is an act that makes its own irrefutable statement. The action is designed to show what Yahweh is capable of. The purpose of the wonders is to evoke belief (v. 5). The first wonder wrought in response to Moses' anxiety is to turn a staff into a snake, and then in the twinkling of an eye, to turn the snake back into a staff. This feat belongs to the genre of "wonder story" to make its own witness. We are offered no hint of the effect or persuasiveness of the wonder. Given Moses' own misgivings about his mission, we may speculate that the miracle is in fact aimed at Moses and not his doubting comrades, but the narrative provides no clue for such a notion.

It is immediately recognized that the first wonder might not be compelling (cf. v. 8). A second miracle is promptly worked, presumably because it will be more compelling. The structure of this miracle report parallels the first. Whereas the first required a stick-made-snake, now the sequence is leprous hand-restored hand. This is the God who can create weal and create woe (cf. Isa 45:7), who can accomplish life and death.

Yahweh, however, is mindful that even two such remarkable wonders may not be convincing. For that eventuality, a third possibility is left open: Moses will turn the water of the Nile into blood. This third wonder, held in abeyance, is remarkable because Moses is said to be the agent, whereas in the first two Moses is the benefactor and recipient of the wonder. The narrative assumes that such wonders will establish Moses' credibility in the eyes of Israel.

Moses' fourth objection concerns his own speech (4:10-12). Moses protests that he cannot speak effectively. This objection sounds more like the making of excuses. The response of Yahweh suggests irritation, if not indignation, as though Yahweh is losing patience with this endless sequence of objections (vv. 4:11-12).

Yahweh's response is in two parts. In the first part, Moses is asked two questions: Who? Who? The subject is not in specifically Israelite categories. Here speaks the creator God, the one who makes, orders, and dispatches all of creation. The topic concerns creation and endowment of all humanity (אדם 'ādām). The answer to the rhetorical question is brief and sweeping: "Is it not I, Yahweh?" Yahweh is the maker of heaven and earth, birds, fish, creeping things, and human persons with speech and sight and hearing (cf. Ps 94:9). Moses' pitiful excuse disregarded his own status as creature, and the fact that all of his life must be referred to the creator God who endows and invests human persons as is expedient for God. Moses is not autonomous

or abandoned in his difficult calling. He need, therefore, have no anxiety about his speech.

On the basis of this sweeping assurance, God issues a command to Moses (4:12). The imperative is the same as the one issued in 3:10, "Go." The God who promised to "be with" him in 3:12 now reiterates that promise and accepts responsibility for Moses' speech. When Moses speaks, it will be God speaking.

Finally, a fifth objection is lodged by Moses (4:13-17). This statement may, perhaps, be a continuation of the same point raised in 4:10. While God has powerfully assured Moses of adequate speech, Moses is unpersuaded. This time in the response, Yahweh is angry (4:14), perhaps impatient and exhausted, but he concedes much of Moses' point. Moses wants another sent, and God agrees to send Aaron along with him. Fretheim terms this God's "Plan B," after Moses has refused "Plan A."[31] That is, Moses' resistance is taken seriously by God, who must adapt.

The actual role of Aaron in the Exodus tradition is more than a little problematic. As a champion and emblem of the priesthood, his entry into the narrative mostly appears to be an intrusion. Indeed, it might be that all of 4:13-16 is an intrusion to accommodate Aaron's entry into the tradition. In v. 11, Yahweh seems to have put to rest any problem with the speech of Moses, but now the concern has resurfaced.

When we take the text as it stands, without reference to any external priestly agenda, we may conclude simply that Yahweh has devised a procedure that honors Moses' anxiety about speech, a problem apparently not finally resolved in v. 11. Moses and Aaron are to share responsibility for speech, but their roles are by no means symmetrical. Aaron is to Moses as a mouth; Moses is to Aaron as a god (see 6:28–7:2). Moses retains unshared and unchallenged authority.

4:18-31. The remainder of chapter 4 is four brief rhetorical elements, all of which serve as a transition, moving Moses back from Midian to Egypt.

In vv. 18-20, Moses seeks permission from his father-in-law, Jethro, to return to Egypt. It is telling that Moses resolves to go back (v. 18) before he is commanded by God to do so (v. 19). We are not told here why he will

31. Fretheim, Exodus, 53, 73.

go back. In the light of the preceding, especially 3:10, the reason given to Jethro in v. 18 is clearly less than candid. He receives an assurance from Yahweh (cf. Matt 2:20) and is authorized by "the staff of God," now an emblem of special power and authority.

Moses is now given instructions by God (vv. 21-23). First, he is told what to do (v. 21). He is to do "wonders" (מפתים *mōpĕtîm*). This is the first use of this term in our narrative, a term different from the one used in 3:12 and 4:9. This term also refers to extraordinary deeds that intrude upon settled, controlled life and generate new possibilities. Nowhere has Moses been instructed about the wonders that are in his power to perform. To be sure, in 4:1-9, we were offered three representative examples, but that is less than "all the wonders."

The mention of "wonders," oddly enough, evokes the first mention of God's resolve to "harden the heart" of Pharaoh. The juxtaposition is striking. The *wonders* are on behalf of Israel against Egypt; the *hardening* is against Egypt, but only indirectly, on behalf of Israel. God works both sides of the street. God does wonders that shatter all present reality, but God also sponsors resistance to the newness on behalf of the status quo. The juxtaposition makes perfectly good sense, even if we judge only by what is visible and conventional. Gestures and acts that violate the present and anticipate newness do indeed evoke resistance in defense of the status quo. Moreover, the response of resistance tends to be proportionate to the threat of the "wonder." As the pitch of wonder intensifies, so the intensity of resistance is sure to increase as well. The text shows that Yahweh intends to escalate both the wonder and the resistance.

The statement of the text, however, is more than a comment upon what is politically visible and conventional in the trouble evoked by revolutionary activity. The additional factor below the surface, and which changes everything, is the fact that the "hardening" does not just happen, is not merely chosen by Pharaoh, but is caused by Yahweh, who is the subject of the active verb *harden.* The narrator is willing to entertain the awareness that Yahweh operates negatively to heighten the drama, to make the clash between oppressor and victim as pointed as is bearable in the narrative. God's speech serves to give the conflict enormous dramatic scope, so that all experienced reality of the characters is gathered into this single momentous abrasion.

Second, Moses is instructed in what to say (vv. 22-23). The words to be uttered by Moses are not his own words, but Yahweh's. The words of Yahweh include three staggering affirmations. First, there is a dramatic embrace of Israel, who is given a stunning identity as firstborn. Previously, Israel has been called by the epithet "my people," but never by this distinctive phrase. In something like a formula of adoption, Israel is marked as the one best loved and most treasured. Pharaoh is put on notice that this oppression is serious business. There are no limits to how far this watchful father will go on behalf of this son. God's second statement is a retrospect. Referring to 3:18, God has asked leave for the "son" to worship the father—i.e., to enact in a liturgic way an alternative loyalty and alternative identity. There God suggests that Pharaoh would, of course, refuse, because he could not bear such a delegitimating gesture. This second statement suggests that Pharaoh would have one last chance, and he would refuse it.

The third statement of God looks back to the first statement, playing again on "firstborn." In the face of Pharaoh's refusal, Yahweh establishes a *quid pro quo:* Your firstborn for my firstborn. It might be contended that Pharaoh's firstborn is to be understood literally, whereas Yahweh's firstborn is a metaphorical reference and, therefore, not as unequivocal. Childs makes this unhelpful contrast between "metaphorical" and "literal," which dissolves the power of the rhetorical point.[32] The narrative, however, will allow no such contrast. The usage of "firstborn" for Israel is no less serious and concrete. This is a son valued like a son, and so Yahweh's statement is severe and uncompromising. That community that appears to be state property is in fact Yahweh's beloved heir. To misidentify them as Pharaoh has done inevitably leads to mistreatment. Pharaoh abuses because he misconstrues who this people is. The cost of such a misconstrual is very high.

---

32. Childs, *The Book of Exodus,* 102.

Exodus 4:24-26 is among the most enigmatic verses in the entire book of Exodus. The episode is not framed in time or space, nor does it seem to be related to its context. Moses is "on the way," but to where we do not know. The narrative concerns a meeting that seems to happen at night. This is no ordinary meeting but sounds not unlike the meetings of Jacob at Bethel (Gen 28:10-22) and Penuel (Gen 32:22-32). The premise of the meeting is indeed odd: Yahweh seeks to kill Moses. The statement is barren and unqualified, and especially odd in the light of the preceding designation of Israel as firstborn. God seems to take action against those most treasured. The best we can do is to let the narrative witness to the deep, untamed holiness of God. In vv. 22-23, that wildness is aimed at the well-being of Israel, but here it is unleashed in all its destructiveness. There is no hint that God is testing or measuring Moses, but only that Yahweh operates in inexplicable, undisciplined freedom. To be present at all in Yahweh's history is a high risk venture, for Moses as well as for Pharaoh.

The response that rescues Moses from the terror of God is as odd as the terror itself. Zipporah, daughter of Jethro and wife of Moses, intervenes to rescue. Perhaps she enacts a very old, primitive rite that requires blood and is connected with sexual organs. She apparently circumcises her son in a crude way. Perhaps this is the son of 2:22, the one signifying displacement (גר *gēr*). It may be that "feet" here is a euphemism for Moses' genitals, which are touched with the blood.

After her act, Zipporah issues a verdict, giving Moses yet another identity, very different from the one suggested in 4:16. She asserts that he is a "bridegroom of blood," variously with the addition "to me" (v. 25) and "by circumcision." Moses' status is thereby changed, and by this curious act, Moses is made safe from the inscrutable threat of Yahweh.

It is conventional to take this narrative as an etiology for circumcision, to explain why (and how) the practice of circumcision came about in Israel. At one level, this may be so, but taken in context this seems an inadequate comment on the text. We should not forget the nature of this text and of the larger narrative. We are dealing with a story built around the resolve of this holy one, who will not be tamed or explained. Yahweh is set loose for the sake of Israel, but Yahweh is also set loose by the narrator in savage ways against Pharaoh and (here at least) in savage ways against Moses. The larger narrative is not solely about liberation. It concerns, rather, the claim that all parties, Israelite as well as Egyptian, must live in the presence of unleashed, unlimited holiness. There are provisional strategies for safety in the face of holiness, but none that will finally tame this dangerous God. One is struck at the end of this brief encounter with the peculiar juxtaposition of threat and safety, a resolve to kill and safety found only in a primitive act of blood and genitalia. But then, holiness is perplexing beyond all explanation.

Now Aaron makes his first active appearance in the narrative (vv. 27-31). He has been previously authorized as Moses' mouthpiece (4:13-17), but now he is directly recruited by God. It is important that he goes to meet Moses and not the other way round. The primary authority of Moses vis-à-vis Aaron is made clear. The meeting between the two is at "the mountain of God," at the place of ultimate encounter (cf. 3:1). The two are about no ordinary business together.

The mandate to Aaron in vv. 14-16 is for him only to speak for Moses. Here, however, Aaron has taken over authority not only to speak the words of Moses, but also to enact the "signs" (wonders) of Moses. The narrative itself, however, pays no attention to such a development or discrepancy. What counts is that the elders and the people believe. The entire discussion of vv. 1-9 had been preoccupied with bringing Israel to faith. Now this people is converted.

Coming to this faith is no small matter for Israel. What is believed is not simply that Moses had been the receiver of an appearance from Yahweh. What is believed is not simply that Yahweh intends to emancipate Israel. What is believed is that Yahweh has attended to (פקד *pāqad*) and has seen (ראה *rā'â,* "taken note of") Israel's oppression. No wonder they "bowed down and worshiped." No wonder they cast their lot with this new God whose name was not even known a chapter ago.

This act of worship is not a frivolous act of religiosity or piety. It is, rather, an extraordinary decision to define authority in a certain way and to embrace a specific view about public reality. The act of worship, already rejected and refused by Pharaoh (cf. 3:19; 4:23), was an act of enormous political courage as well as social credulity. The Yahweh now embraced by Israel is in every way contrasted with Pharaoh. Yahweh is the God who has seen, known, heard, remembered, and come down. This God is so unlike the king of Egypt, who has noticed nothing of the suffering, who has heard nothing of the protest, who has known nothing of their anguish, who has remembered nothing of old promises, and who has never come down to relieve.

This narrative witnesses to possibilities outside imperial totalism. The "signs" are hopes and affirmations that there is life beyond the empire. The narrative invites the people around Moses and Aaron to a high-risk venture, to trust in the God who gives signs, reveals a name, threatens Pharaoh, and even assaults Moses. This trust is no casual undertaking, but it is a formidable act of letting life start from a different point toward a different possibility.

REFLECTIONS

1. This extended narrative invites reflection upon the nature of vocation, and the power of "call" in the life of faith. An uncalled life is an autonomous existence in which there is no intrusion, disruption, or redefinition, no appearance or utterance of the Holy. We may imagine in our autonomous existence, moreover, that no one knows our name until we announce it, and no one requires anything of us except that for which we volunteer. The life of Moses in this narrative, as the lives of all people who live in this narrative of faith, is not autonomous. There is this One who knows and calls by name, even while we imagine we are unknown and unsummoned.

2. The resolve of Yahweh to transform, to let the oppressed go free, is met by Moses' determined resistance. Moses offers reasons, alibis, and excuses against the call of Yahweh, but he never goes behind these excuses to state the reason for his reluctance and refusal. We are left to conclude that Moses understands immediately and intuitively that this summons from the God of promise and liberation is a threat to his very life. So it is with God's call. In our time, the notion of call has often been trivialized, institutionalized, and rendered innocuous as bland calls to "obedience" and to "ministry." Moses, however, knows better than this. A right sense of call (and its danger) derives from a right sense of Yahweh's intention. And when the call of Yahweh is made safe through trivialization (which Moses refuses to do), it is because Yahweh's intention has already been distorted and domesticated.

Moses' excuses are altogether reasonable, the kind anyone might make who understands the risks at hand. In the end, however, the narrative is not much interested in his resistance. Yahweh does not find his excuses compelling, nor does the narrator. The narrative does not answer or refute the reasons of Moses, but simply overrides them with a more vigorous assertion of Yahweh's intentionality, which in fact dismisses Moses' reluctance as unacceptable. Thus Moses' sense of his own inadequacy (3:11) is not met with an assurance of his adequacy, but with an assertion of Yahweh as the God who will be present (3:12). Moses wants to know the name (3:13), but all he receives is a formula already known (3:15; cf. v. 6), and an enigma (3:14) that yields no name at all.

Moses' worry about disbelief on the part of Israel (4:1) is countered by an assertion that Moses will, as he acts in courage, have resources he does not yet know he has (4:2-7). But his possession of these resources will not be evident until he is at risk in his ominous vocation. And even these stunning acts of power are his only by the assurance of God, so that God's sign overpowers the unfaith of Israel.

Moses' protest about poor speech (4:10) is not answered by an assurance of good speech, but by an assurance that Yahweh presides over speech and gives tongues as they are needed (4:11-14). And even the granting of Aaron as spokesperson in response (4:14-17) to the fifth objection (4:13) gives Moses no slack, for he is still the "point man" in the confrontation to come.

This exchange over five objections and five responses produces a powerful drama of vocation and resistance (3:11–4:17). In the end, Moses exercises no freedom of choice, but is compelled by the power and resolve of Yahweh, which is relentless and unaccommodating. The work and character of this human life are settled in God's own intention, and Moses has no vote or voice in the shape of his future.

3. Yahweh's resolve is not just that of a political sovereign (though it is that), but is also the passion of a parent who will see about the honor and well-being of the beloved heir and firstborn. Thus the great political issue of Exodus is given familial intensity. The danger invited by Pharaoh's politics of oppression concerns not simply politics, but Pharaoh's own most intimate treasure, his crown prince. No one and nothing is safe that stands against Yahweh's resolve to act on behalf of this enslaved, oppressed people. It should not surprise us that the God who has been relentless with Moses (3:11–4:17) should be uncompromising in the world of Pharaoh (4:22-23). Yahweh is now playing for keeps, the way only a treasuring, concerned parent can care.

We might reflect on how odd and unlikely this move to familial images is. The anticipated confrontation between lordly Pharaoh and frightened Moses is so unfair and one-sided. Except, of course, that Moses is not on his own, but is simply the voice and agent of this sovereign whom Pharaoh will not acknowledge (5:2), but before whom he must eventually yield (12:31-32). The terrible challenge to Pharaoh and the public outcome of the narrative anticipate the way in which this Easter God will subsequently challenge and defeat the powers of chaos and death in the world. Moses, it turns out, is a tool of Yahweh in that deep, dangerous conflict between fathers over firstborn sons, with its assured outcome in emancipation for Israel and dread death for Egypt (cf. 14:30-31).

4. In the enigmatic account of 4:24-26, we are given a glimpse of Yahweh in raw and devastating power. In these verses, there is nothing of blessing or promise, nothing of liberation, not even an effort to give assurance to Moses. We are at the end of the narrative, and Moses is now on his way in obedience (4:18-20), the very obedience he had so long resisted (3:11–4:17). Yahweh has prevailed, and Moses has yielded.

Nonetheless, in this odd account, Yahweh seeks to kill the very one who has just been recruited for this singular work of emancipation. Whatever may have been the earlier function of this text in terms of the institution of circumcision, now in this locus, we are given to see Yahweh in dread, inexplicable holiness, enemy and threat even to this called one. Yahweh will not finally be thematized even in a narrative of liberation, much less in a single account of creation and redemption. There is indeed something visceral, untamed, and hostile about this God. Those who are called by this God to service find on occasion that more dangerous than the task is the danger of Yahweh's own person, who in inexplicable ways is partly threatened. That threat pertains even to God's closest associate, and Israel must take care not to count unguardedly on God's intimate friendliness.

5. In the concluding notice of this unit (4:27-31), the call process is given a reassuring closure. Sometimes the call process does work! Moses had needed his brother Aaron, and now he has him as an aide (4:27-28). Much more crucially, the people believed (4:31)! Such faith is always a gift and always a mystery. We do not know why the presence of Moses, called by the God of liberation, was credible to these slaves, when he himself feared disbelief (4:1). But the summons is credible, and there arises in the historical process of oppression the conviction that an alternative is offered, rooted in the very holiness of God. Certainly there was nothing on the surface of Moses' words or acts to give credibility. Trust in the prospect of liberation is indeed a theological reality.

6. In this text converge the large themes of divine purpose and human vocation, and the human drama that arises from that purpose and vocation. Thus, this text enunciates some of the largest, most problematic themes of biblical faith.

Israel knows that the one who speaks here is the Lord of creation and the governor of all of Israel's life. The two credo recitals of 3:7-8 and 3:17 announce that this holy one takes as an overriding purpose the transformation of Israel's life from bondage in an alien land to "at-homeness" in its own land. The plot of the text, and therefore the imagination of the listener, is dominated by this resolve for public transformation.

Pursuant to this large purpose of God, the purpose and intent of Moses' life are reshaped and redefined. It may be that Moses in 2:11-22 was already, unbeknownst to him, embracing the holy purpose of his life. Without any divine disclosure, he already acted as the liberator that he subsequently was called to be. God's call to him does not make him something other than he himself truly was. Moses' vocation is not imposed, but is intrinsic to the context of his life.

The two themes of *divine resolve for transformation* and *a human vocation of liberation* converge to assert something decisive about the public, human process. This text announces that the affairs of nations and of human persons (Egypt, Pharaoh, Moses, Israel, Midian) are in fact elements of the large drama where *divine resolve* and *human vocation* conspire for transformation. Both elements matter decisively; when they are both recognized, the public process is inevitably discerned as laden with alternatives yet to be wrought.

7. This narrative is more fully saturated with "signs" than is often noted (see 3:12; 4:1-9, 17, 27-30). The signs assert that there is more at work in the human process than what is defined by conventional power. They are regarded neither as acts of magic nor as violations of "natural law," but as evidences that a surplus of intention is present in human life at the behest of God. They are not acts of overt force or coercion; they do not directly impinge upon human decision making or policy or rationality, but are hints that the historical process is more open than might be imagined. Thus such "gestures of the holy" outdistance any scientific positivism, any hard orthodoxy, or any critical toning down that imagines it already knows the limits of the possible. We may conclude that attentiveness to such gestures of the holy (wrought by God through human persons) is a precondition of liberation and transformation.

The intention of this foundational narrative may be echoed in John 20:30-31. In something of a signature to the Fourth Gospel, the writer describes the move from "sign" to "faith" through text: "Now Jesus did many other *signs* in the presence of his disciples, which are not written in this book. But these are written so that you may come to *believe* . . . and that through believing you may have life in his name" (emphasis added).

Our text in Exodus is closely parallel in its intention and claim. There will be "many signs," which are *written* in order to evoke faith. Note well that they are written, not in this wording, "acted." The telling of signs in Exodus 3–4 (and in 5–12) is to bring listeners into this alternative future. The text grows out of the powerful signs, but the signs themselves continue to have power because they are embedded in and mediated by the text. The text and its interpretation are to bring the people (see 4:31) to believe and to have life.

EXODUS 5:1–11:10, "LET MY PEOPLE GO"

OVERVIEW

The plague narrative is a great dramatic contest between Yahweh, the Lord of liberation, and Pharaoh, the entrenched power of exploitation. The "plagues" are a series of "wonders" (miracles) whereby the stunning power of Yahweh is exhibited in the world, designed to intimidate Pharaoh until the Egyptian empire sees that it cannot withstand God's will for freedom and justice.

As early as 1940, Johannes Pedersen argued that this textual material closely reflects a liturgic drama.[33] That is, the episodes in the plague narrative are highly stylized, repetitive, and cumulative in their dramatic force. This liturgic exercise (which has as its intention the incorporation of the young into the memory) need not have been slavishly disciplined about "what happened" in any specific detail. Liturgical freedom permits the community to engage in grand, sweeping, hyperbolic rhetoric, the subject of which is the inversions that occur in the historical process, inversions of power that are inexplicable by any commonsense reading.

On the one hand, such a regularly re-enacted drama serves to establish these events as paradigmatic for the faith and imagination of Israel. These events become the authoritative reference point and clue by which the community continues to discern its true situation in the world. Israel's shaping of historical reality is characteristically done in the categories of oppressed and oppressor, with Yahweh as the third actor who regularly intervenes to break open and transform a situation in which the oppressor seems endlessly in charge and the oppressed seems endlessly hopeless. (Note well that Israel utilized the categories long before any modern—e.g., Marxist—analysis.) That this paradigmatic event became enduring script thus provides an ongoing counterreading of social reality that generates revolutionary restlessness, unintimidated social criticism, and buoyant hope to be rediscerned in many circumstances and

settings. It is this paradigmatic event that has made Jews characteristically attentive to the "underdog."[34] Because this liturgy is most plausibly situated in Passover (so Pedersen), I have termed the use of this material a practice of "Passover imagination," the continual re-reading of social reality according to this cast of characters and this recital of inexplicable miracles. (Observe Amos 9:7, where Yahweh is said to be a God who causes exoduses for many other peoples and not exclusively for Israel.)

It goes without saying then, that the prospect for asking critical questions about what happened in the plagues is irrelevant. Greta Hort has provided the classic modern attempt to make the plagues scientifically credible.[35] While her analysis is careful, disciplined, and discerning, in the end it does not touch the dramatic issues that are at the center of the narrative. Thus the text does not stress that a number of odd events occurred. Rather, it accents the fact that Yahweh the creator mobilized all of creation to work this liberation. Thus the text insists that the narrative serves a theological point: It witnesses to the power of Yahweh on behalf of the Hebrew slaves, even in the face of Pharaoh and his power to resist.

We may suggest two productive tensions in the long drama that warrant attention. First, while the plagues feature the resolve, activity, and power of Yahweh (and are, therefore, accounts of miracles), the human work of Moses is decisive. The narrative is to be read as a long, studied process of bargaining, negotiation, intimidation, and deception. A careful reading of the text will not sustain the view that the wonder of liberation concerns no human initiative, for Moses has a crucial role to play. Indeed, the juxtaposition of God's initiative and Moses' cruciality is a characteristic

---

33. Pedersen, *Israel*, 728-37.

34. On the Jewish passion for the underdog, see Cynthia Ozick, *Metaphor and Memory: Essays* (New York: Knopf, 1989) 265-83; Herbert N. Schneidau, "Let the Reader Understand," *Semeia* 39 (1987) 140-42.

35. Greta Hort, "The Plagues of Egypt," *ZAW* 69 (1957) 84-103. See critical responses to Hort by Childs, *The Book of Exodus*, 168, and J. Philip Hyatt, *Commentary on Exodus*, New Century Bible (London: Oliphants, 1971) 336-45.

way in which the Bible refuses to cut apart the roles of Yahweh and humanity.

The second tension concerns earnestness and humor. This confrontation is enormously serious, as the stakes are very high. The very future of Israel rests on the outcome of these transactions; as it turns out, Pharaoh's future is also at stake. At the same time, however, the narrator has a good time and wants the listener to have a good time, largely at the expense of Pharaoh, who in the end turns out to be a pitiful character—indecisive, foolish, and self-destructive. The capacity of the oppressed to laugh at their oppressor is a way for the weak to delegitimate the strong.[36]

The plague cycle makes the point that the processes of human power are not as cut, dried, and foreclosed as the powerful imagine. Another power is loose in the world that finally precludes any system of power that overrides the fragility of human persons and human community. This inscrutable power will not finally tolerate such abuse. At the center of public history is "wonder," which no ruthless pharaoh can resist or squelch. It is that wonder wrought by God that in the end creates human possibilities for freedom and justice, for well-being and covenant.

Alongside the stylized series of confrontations and plagues, the text includes three elements that function to introduce the plagues themselves. First, chapter 5 is a series of conversations within the Egyptian labor structure designed to characterize the foolish and brutal Egyptian policy of oppressive labor. That chapter has the effect of heightening the suspense and creating rage toward the empire. Second, 6:2-9 presents a self-disclosing decree of God. This is a formal self-declaration that connects to the Genesis promise, discloses God's name (cf. 3:14), and pronounces a formal covenant formula. As Walther Zimmerli has shown, the passage is dominated by the expression "I am Yahweh," which places God's sovereignty in the center of the narrative.[37] Third, 6:14-25 presents the only genealogy in Exodus, this

one to present the priestly pedigree of the Levitic-Aaronide priests. They will play a larger role later in the book, and are perhaps the community that brought Exodus to its final form.

The drama of the plagues themselves revolves around several recurring formulas. On the one hand, the imperative "Let my people go" states the overriding agenda of emancipation. (While one may eschew "liberation theology," one cannot avoid the fact that liberation stands as the core agenda of this text.) On the other hand, the indicative "You shall know that I am Yahweh" focuses on the power struggle between Yahweh and Pharaoh, without any particular reference to Israel. In this second formula, the liberation of Israel is only instrumental in exhibiting the rule of Yahweh to which Pharaoh inescapably must submit. Moreover, this latter theme of Yahweh's coming sovereignty is served by the odd formula, "Yahweh hardened Pharaoh's heart." This formula indicates that Yahweh's sovereign will is worked, even through Pharaoh's resistance.

The two governing formulas "Let my people go" and "You shall know I am Yahweh" together join the social and theological issues. The imperative of freedom and the indicative of sovereignty cannot be separated in the rhetoric or in the faith of Israel.

While these fixed formulas do recur and provide the rhetorical structure of the passages, one should not imagine that the several episodes are simply reiterations. In fact, each plague episode is distinct and merits careful attention to rhetorical detail. The narrator is able to handle the stable and recurring formulas with great imagination and playfulness. The outcome is not only imaginative rhetoric and bold theological affirmation, but also a cunning articulation of the ways the social crisis develops through deception and negotiation. In the end, it is clear that the forms of power held by and presided over by Pharaoh do not at all match the reality of power, which has now passed to Moses and the Israelites.

The storyline of the plague cycle does indeed subvert all established power by its witness to Yahweh's irresistible will for social transformation. The community that shares in this dramatic recital continues to affirm that public miracles of transformation will still be wrought by God, no matter what the odds.

36. This is a major element in Minjung theology, on which see Kim Yong Bock, ed., *Minjung Theology: People as the Subjects of History* (Singapore: The Commission on Theology Concerns, The Christian Conference of Asia, 1981); and Cyris H. S. Moon, *A Korean Minjung Theology: An Old Testament Perspective* (Maryknoll, N.Y.: Orbis, 1985). See also James C. Scott, *Weapons of the Weak* (New Haven: Yale University Press, 1987).
37. Walther Zimmerli, *I Am Yahweh* (Atlanta: John Knox, 1982) 7-13 and *passim*. See also Zimmerli's study of the formula in his Ezekiel commentary.

Exodus 5:1–6:1, Bricks Without Straw

COMMENTARY

After Moses' extended narrative in Midian, at "the mountain of God" (3:1–4:31), the narrative moves the action back to Egypt and to the court of Pharaoh. This narrative on the surface simply portrays a struggle for political power and influence, and the action in this chapter takes place completely on Pharaoh's terms. This is the last episode in which Pharaoh will be the unchallenged master of his own house and his own policy. The narrative lets us see unambiguously that where Pharaoh works his will, there is sure to be abuse, brutality, and violence. It is striking that Yahweh, the God of the Hebrews, appears nowhere as an actor in this narrative. To be sure, Yahweh is spoken about by the other characters, but in the end, all that is said of the "God of the Hebrews" is that this God is noticeably absent and ineffective. Moses and Aaron, for the extent of this narrative, are left on their own with Pharaoh, and it is not a hopeful picture for those in bondage.

Along with Pharaoh and Moses-Aaron, there are three other "characters" in the narrative: the taskmasters (נגשׂים *nōgĕśîm*), the supervisors (שׂטרים *šōṭĕrîm*), and the slaves. While the taskmasters and supervisors participate in the action and voice important lines in the plot, they occupy no independent place in the narrative. They function to pass along the brutality downward from above, or the indignation upward from below. At the bottom of the vertical arrangement of the narrative are the peasants-slaves-Hebrews. They are a real presence and a "character" in the plot, even though they are not permitted to speak.

The chapter consists of two related, but asymmetrical, conversations. The one conversation is a confrontation between would-be equals, Pharaoh and Moses-Aaron (vv. 1-5). It is a struggle for control and a conflict between competing visions of social reality. The other conversation is a vertical one between Pharaoh and the Hebrews, in which the taskmasters and supervisors are intermediaries who pass information back and forth (vv. 6-19). In this conversation, the Hebrews do not speak, except to sigh and groan under

severe abuse; this in itself, however, is an important voicing, as we have seen in 2:23.

It is important that Moses and Aaron do not participate in this vertical, hierarchial conversation, for they do not share the view that Pharaoh is at the top of power. They stand outside that conversation as the voice of Yahweh, who challenges Pharaoh's claim to priority. Nonetheless, the voice of Moses-Aaron (i.e., the voice of Yahweh) impinges upon the vertical conversation, because it brings to speech the silenced agenda of the muted Hebrews. Yahweh functions to speak with power for the muted slaves, who have no voice of their own. Pharaoh can ignore the slaves' silence, but he cannot ignore the abrasive, demanding, sovereign speech of Yahweh on the lips of Moses and Aaron.

5:1-9. The chapter consists of a series of sharp, brief exchanges, with only occasional narrative elements to connect the speeches. Moses and Aaron speak first (v. 1), voicing Yahweh's decree and the yearning of the Hebrews. They reiterate the most elemental decree of Yahweh: "Send my people." The conventional reading, "Let my people go," sounds like a request or a plea. In fact, it is an imperative on the lips of Yahweh, as though Yahweh addresses a political subordinate (Pharaoh) who is expected to obey. The reason for the "sending" is a festival in the wilderness, with no hint that the festival is a ploy in order to escape, though later an escape is implied (10:10).

What is intended, rather, is a religious observance that will assert loyalty to Yahweh, thereby delegitimating the claims of Pharaoh to loyalty. Thus the proposed worship "in the wilderness"—i.e., outside Pharaoh's controlled arena—constitutes a threat to Egypt, but that threat is not as blatant as an escape. (On subversive energy that comes from the wilderness, outside the governed territory, see Luke 3:1-6).

Pharaoh's defiant response to the imperative is not an inquiry (v. 2). It is, rather, a hostile, high-handed dismissal of Yahweh. The tone is not unlike that of Yahweh's speech in

4:11, wherein Yahweh dismisses a challenge from Moses. Pharaoh insists that Yahweh is a nobody, has no right to issue a decree, and certainly will not be obeyed. Pharaoh imagines that he is autonomous and refuses his role as an underling to Yahweh. Pharaoh makes two interdependent assertions in response. First, "I do not know Yahweh" (i.e., "I do not acknowledge the status of Yahweh as overlord"). *Know* here means not only "to be familiar with," but also "to recognize authority." Second, and consequently, Pharaoh will not release the slaves. The double point of resistance, as is characteristic of the exodus narrative, joins the *theological* ("I do not know") and the *sociopolitical* ("I will not send").

Political transformation derives from theological commitment. Negatively, Pharaoh's brutalizing political policies derive from his sense of autonomy from Yahweh. Pharaoh cannot practice liberation without acceding to the rule of Yahweh, which he cannot do without giving up his claim to power and authority. Thus the first couplet of speeches (vv. 1-2) sets the conflict in its sharpest, most comprehensive and uncompromising form.

In the second couplet of speeches (vv. 3-5), the two positions are stated with greater intensity and both parties receive more elaborate titles. Yahweh is named "God of the Hebrews," and Pharaoh is called "King in Egypt." The speech of Moses-Aaron indirectly answers Pharaoh's haughty question of v. 2, "Who?" Calvin observes that Pharaoh's defiant question is paralleled by Pilate's question, "What is truth?" (John 18:37-38).[38] Yahweh is "God of the Hebrews," the patron, guarantor, and advocate of the silenced slaves. Thus the title both gives information and intensifies the conflict, for Pharaoh cannot countenance such a God in his realm.

Pharaoh's response does not touch the theological issue raised by Moses and Aaron. His answer concerns work, the only thing he has on his horizon. That is, in his answer, Pharaoh refuses to think beyond the technical requirements of the economy of the state. The counter to Yahwistic worship is a greater commitment to the abusive status quo. The ideology of Pharaoh could be affirmed under

either totalitarian socialism or abusive capitalism: "Work makes free." Such work-produced well-being is clearly not the intent of the wilderness festival. Pharaoh's response indicates that the confrontation is now between two systems of reality. It touches everything from religious claim to economic policy. There can be no compromise.

This double exchange in vv. 1-2 and 3-5 leads to a narrative interlude in which Pharaoh intensifies his policy of abusive labor practice (vv. 6-9). Here for the first time the bureaucratic structure of the empire is mentioned, including taskmasters and supervisors. Their presence reminds us that the problem for the slaves is not simply the fierceness of a single leader, but the systemic force and abuse that supports him.

The new policy intensifies the work schedule. Straw is required for the production of bricks. Presumably the production schedule was so organized that straw was supplied for the brickmakers. The necessary supplies were on a regular work schedule, suggesting high efficiency. Now that a continuous supply of straw is curtailed, the brickmakers must add to their own work time in order to gather straw, but nonetheless meet the same schedule of brick production.

This policy is clear enough; the reasons for the policy are more interesting (vv. 8-9). In v. 8, the brick-producing slaves themselves are said to cry, "Let us go and offer sacrifice to our God." Verse 9 takes a different position. It recognizes that it was not the slaves who issued such a cry. The slaves themselves are not the speakers of this yearning, but are only the hearers and receivers of such an option. The verse does not specify, but it is clear that in v. 9 (unlike v. 8) it is Moses-Aaron who have spoken the troublesome words that threaten the empire.

Thus by inference, Moses-Aaron are outsiders in the slave community, troublemakers who come to agitate, and the brick-producing slaves are only exposed to the seduction of their words. Pharaoh concludes his policy statement with the concern that the slaves should be "saved" (ישע *yāša'*) by false words—i.e., should be misled. Moses and Aaron are labeled "false" (שקר *šeqer*) in their appeal to Yahweh (cf. Isa 36:5-7). This conclusion not only dismisses Moses-Aaron,

38. Calvin, *Commentaries on the Four Last Books of Moses Arranged in the Form of a Harmony*, 114.

but in fact dismisses Yahweh as well, as a god who has no power to enact what is decreed. Pharaoh's strategy is not to silence them, but to keep the slaves too busy to heed, to listen, to respond, or to organize. This approach is ideologically self-deceiving, for it assumes that keeping workers on board with intense work keeps the purposes and warrants of the work from scrutiny. It mistakenly assumes that if they are busy, suffering people will not notice what is going on.

5:10-21. After Pharaoh's decree (vv. 6-9), the narrative pauses to expose the working out of the new, aggressive policy. The action is in two parts: the general implementation (vv. 10-14) and the peculiar problem of the supervisors (vv. 15-21). Pharaoh's underlings (taskmasters and supervisors) are loyal to him in implementing the new policy, the purpose of which is to screen out the countervision of Moses and Aaron. The taskmasters, the more senior officers, insist on the punctual and complete fulfillment of the work schedule (v. 13).

In v. 14, it is clear that the supervisors have a different role to play from that of the taskmasters. Indeed, the breaking point between management and labor seems to fall between taskmasters and supervisors and not, as one might expect, between supervisors and slaves.[39] As a result, the supervisors are directly held accountable for production, and are punished for a failure to meet quotas.

Moreover, the supervisors are closer to the exploited work force and sensitive to their lot under the new policy. The supervisors are said to be "supervisors of the Israelites." The language suggests that they are in fact members of the Hebrew community who have been given modest leadership roles. If so, they are most vulnerable. On the one hand, they must answer for the work and are subject to discipline if the work does not go well. On the other hand, they must have been viewed by their own work force with suspicion, as compromisers with and accommodators to the exploitative work schedule and its benefactors.

The double bind of the supervisors is evident in vv. 15-21, where they undertake two quite heroic confrontations. The first confrontation is with Pharaoh. They "cry out" (צעק

ṣāʿaq; cf. v. 8; 2:23). They issue a protest on behalf of the slaves who are beaten for their inability to meet production schedules. Finally, their speech makes a direct accusation against Pharaoh: "You are unjust" (following the Greek text). The Hebrew text asserts, "You have violated ["sinned against," חטא ḥāṭāʾ] your people." Thus royal policy is identified (with either rendering) as inhumane and unacceptable. Such an assertion in such a high place is indeed a high-risk venture. It is clear that Moses and Aaron were not the only daring and courageous voices in the slave community.

Pharaoh is unresponsive and intransigent. He refuses the protest, reiterates the policy, and accuses the protesting supervisors of being lazy and trying to get out of work (vv. 17-18). Pharaoh reiterates the critical proposal of v. 1 (cf. v. 18). The narrator adds that the supervisors were "in trouble" (רע rāʿ, "get evil for themselves"), for they had issued a protest and were left severely exposed when their request was not heeded.

The second confrontation the supervisors undertake is with Moses and Aaron (vv. 20-21). This meeting happens immediately after the first one, perhaps in reaction to it. It is as though Moses and Aaron are waiting to see what comes out of the supervisors' meeting with Pharaoh. Nothing came out of it but trouble and yet one more insidious resolve on the part of Pharaoh. The supervisors are now exposed and in jeopardy. It is for that reason, not surprisingly, that their attack is now turned promptly upon Moses and Aaron.

Speaking out of their own jeopardy, the supervisors issue a charge against Moses and Aaron not unlike the one they made against Pharaoh. Whereas Pharaoh is "unjust," Moses and Aaron need to be "judged"—i.e., shown to be irresponsible. The charge against them is not, as against Pharaoh, abusiveness. Rather, it is that the protesting supervisors (and the slaves they represent) have become a "bad smell" to Pharaoh, loathsome, repellent, and likely needing to be eliminated (cf. 1 Sam 27:12). That is, acting on the word of Moses-Aaron, the supervisors have now called attention to themselves in a terribly dangerous way. The term "bad smell" (באש bĕʾōš) regularly is used for those who become

---

39. See Pixley's shrewd analysis, *Exodus*, 33.

unacceptable to other, stronger people (cf. Gen 34:30; 1 Sam 13:4; 2 Sam 10:6; 16:21).

5:22–6:1. This narrative ends on an odd and unexpected note (vv. 22-23). Moses has just been accused by the supervisors. Indeed, the supervisors leave the impression that Pharaoh was correct in v. 9; their words are "false," without substance. It is odd and telling that Moses makes no response to them, either to defend himself or to refute the charge. Rather, he turns abruptly to a different conversation in which the supervisors have no part. Moses turns to Yahweh, who thus far has been completely absent in this narrative.

Moses issues a severe rebuke to Yahweh, one to which Yahweh makes only a belated response. The accusation turns on the double use of the term *mistreat* (*rāʿ*). We have already seen the term in v. 19, where the protesting supervisors are said to be "in trouble." Now Moses accuses Yahweh: "You are the one who has caused trouble ["evil," *rāʿ*] for this people." In making this accusation against Yahweh, Moses is deftly declaring his own innocence in response to the charge in v. 21.

Moses' accusation is exceedingly harsh. You have not "really snatched" this people. The word used for "snatch" or "deliver" (נצל *nāṣal*) means to drag out of danger at the last minute (cf. 1 Sam 17:37; Amos 4:11). Two items interest us in this statement. First, already in 3:9, Yahweh had used the term *nāṣal* in the initial promise to rescue Israel from the power of Egypt. Thus Moses here accuses Yahweh of not doing what has been promised. Second, the verb here is in the infinitive absolute; it is an intense, strong verb. Moses is very clear about what needs to be done and what Yahweh has not done. This acute address to Yahweh is the first in what will become a series of attacks Moses makes upon Yahweh.

The accusation is that Yahweh has been absent from this dangerous confrontation, in which Yahweh promised to be the decisive player. A quick reading of the chapter indicates that Yahweh has indeed been absent; the risk-taking parties, Moses-Aaron and the supervisors, have been left on their own. As a result, they are dangerously exposed, with no visible gain or assurance. Moses' protest accuses Yahweh of having offered false words, with no follow-through in action; as a result, Pharaoh does indeed seem to prevail.

However, we must read more closely. I suggest that this "interim narrative," between promise and deliverance, is governed by Yahweh's preceding speech in 4:21. In that verse, Yahweh gives Moses his lines to speak to Pharaoh. Yahweh resolves, "I will harden his heart"; "he will not let the people go." That is precisely what has happened in chapter 5. Pharaoh has not, as Yahweh anticipated he would not, let this people go.

But Pharaoh's heart has indeed been made harder and more resistant. This is evident in the dismissal of Yahweh (v. 2), in the policy of "no straw" (vv. 6-9) and in the reiteration of the harsh policy, the maintenance of the production schedule, and the accusation of laziness (vv. 17-18). As in any exploitative regime, Pharaoh has begun a policy of escalation, believing that more repression, applied a little at a time, is a workable policy. Pharaoh apparently does not know that he is facing a revolution, an exodus. All he knows is that there is more protest, shrill outside agitation; and the way to deal with agitation is to tighten control and be repressive. That is all that is visible in the narrative, all that was visible to the slaves, to the supervisors, to the taskmasters, or even to Moses.

The narrator, however, has let us see a bit more than the participants have been able to notice. This seemingly inhumane strategy whereby Pharaoh becomes more demanding is only the visible element of Yahweh's hidden work of hardening. The hardening and escalation of repression are a necessary step in creating a social situation so laden with pressure that it will blow open with rage and liberation. After all, the exodus is not a transcendental occurrence, but a social revolution accomplished by real people through public protests. Yahweh may be invisible in the narrative, but Yahweh is not absent. Liberation is slow, hard work. It entails making the oppressed odious. It requires making the oppressor stupid and abusive and blind to his own real interest. Liberation takes time, but the time is full of the resolve of Yahweh. No party in the narrative can see the painful requirement of time, not even Moses.

The narrator does not, however, leave the narrative with the rebuke of Yahweh by Moses as the last word. Yahweh is permitted to speak one time (6:1), asserting, against this rebuke, that the present situation of the Israelite community is not the last state. There is more to come from Yahweh. On the basis of what Yahweh will do, Pharaoh will act differently. This enigmatic statement seems, in retrospect, to be an allusion to the last plague of chapters 11–12. The other interesting point about Yahweh's response is that Pharaoh will act "by a mighty hand." The first intent of the statement is that the "mighty hand" is that of Pharaoh. Yet the term hand is twice without a pronominal suffix, where we might expect "his hand." Thus the way is open to suggest that the "mighty hand" by which Pharaoh will act is in the end the mighty hand of Yahweh, who is at work through Pharaoh. It is finally Yahweh who mobilizes Pharaoh to become engaged recalcitrantly in the mighty work of liberation. Yahweh acts with high resolve, but in the public process mostly by indirection.

REFLECTIONS

This is an "interim narrative"; it stands between the announcement of God's intention (chaps. 3–4) and the enactment of that intention (chaps. 6–11). In terms of God's own speech, it stands between the resolve to "harden Pharaoh's heart" (4:21) and the time when "You shall see what I will do" (6:1). In this text, Israel must wait in its dangerous, exposed position where Pharaoh is unjust, Moses causes a "bad smell," and Yahweh has "done nothing." Such waiting provides an opportunity for a more reflective perspective on the text, when there is nothing direct to proclaim.

1. This text invites reflection on the integral relation of theological claim and political possibility, or, if one will, the relation between faith and politics. In much of the church that connection is not understood, and is often resisted. The first exchange between Moses-Aaron and Pharaoh makes the linkage in a subtle and knowing way (vv. 1-2). The decree of Yahweh in the mouth of Moses-Aaron understands that "a sacrifice in the wilderness to Yahweh" is not merely a religious act, but in fact is a threatening political act that implicitly delegitimates the deep claims of Pharaoh to command the loyalty of the Hebrews. Pharaoh understands this connection as well, for in his defiant response, he refuses to acknowledge Yahweh and (consequently) he refuses to let the slaves go.

Given the identification of Yahweh with the slaves, it follows that biblical faith is inevitably concerned with political questions, with an inescapable tilt not only toward justice, but also toward liberation. Thus Pharaoh, with his oppressive policies, is accused of being unjust (v. 16) (following the Greek text). This text relates justice to the character of God, and will not let faith stray far from justice questions that focus on oppression and labor policy. This text invites the listening church to rethink the categories through which it practices the future.

2. The strategy of Pharaoh is worth study. His notion is that the pressure of productivity is the way to keep social relations from changing. That is, the lazy and unproductive have time to listen to voices that authorize dangerous change. Productivity numbs attention to the voice of new possibility. This mode of enslavement is worth considering in a society that is aimed at the acquisition of goods in the pursuit of greed and affluence.

Two dimensions of numbing through productivity might be identified. On the one hand, consumerism, the driving ideology of Western society, is based in the capacity to produce and acquire wealth as a sign of personal worth. While production quotas may not be as abusive and demeaning as in this narrative, the pressure to produce and achieve is enormous in our society, so enormous that it robs energy from every chance for justice and freedom. On the other hand (and more subtly), in a moral posture that is focused on "doing," even the doing of "goodness" leads to a passion for busyness that leaves little time for "being." One can imagine that the exodus narrative is an exercise in weaning the imagination of the listening community away from an ideology of productivity, in order to have room and energy to "be."

3. The supervisors in this narrative are of special interest to us. The large drama of Moses versus Pharaoh makes them decidedly subordinate in the plot. Nonetheless, in this narrative, they occupy considerable attention. They are the "persons in the middle," in the uneasy place of having sympathy for those below, but also appearing to be excessively compromised with those above. Many people who look to this text for help are cast in our society precisely as those "in the middle" of such abusive arrangements. Few among us are as powerful or as brutal as Pharaoh, who has the power to change matters by decree. Many more of us are positioned where we notice and care, where we can protest injustice, but only at risk.

The supervisors are bold characters on two counts. On the one hand, they present a strong critique of Pharaoh on behalf of the slaves. On the other hand, they are accountable for productivity and are beaten when schedules are not met. They rely on the word of Moses-Aaron and seem to be left holding the bag when Moses does not triumph. This narrative provides no solution for those cast in this dangerous role. The narrative, however, is illuminating in letting us see precisely where we may be located. The supervisors do not turn their backs on the abused. Nor do they flinch from protest against abusive power. They are the very ones who keep the justice question visible in the narrative, after the extreme "pronouncement" of Moses-Aaron. They live an exceedingly exposed life.

4. Only near the end is this narrative explicitly theological. The story encourages reflection upon some difficult questions: What is God doing in the story? What is God doing in the world? How is God delivering on God's promises? This story holds no brief for an easy kind of supernaturalism that imagines that God will swoop in and cause freedom. Rather, the exodus is wrought slowly, painfully through hurt and risk, through sociopolitical processes that are not unlike our own experience. The notion of "hardening the heart" suggests that God unleashes increasing injustice, stubbornness, and resistance to change, so that the old order must give way to God's new intention. If a benign status quo can be maintained, nothing will ever change. Only when brutality escalates to an unbearable level can genuine public newness surface. The community that trusts this text is invited to think and notice again God's "strange work" in the public process that makes newness possible.

This muted text makes rigorous demands on our theological categories. It is not that the affirmations are so esoteric or subtle. Rather, they are so strange to us in our conventional, status quo perception of the gospel, or in our expectation that healing, liberating change should be visible and developmental. This narrative invites us to enter into that story of the absence of God in a radical and daring way, in order to perceive the very places that seem closed and hopeless as laden with potential newness. The whole of this narrative stands under a relentless promise and a sovereign decree. Along the way to that promise's fulfillment, there is abuse, trouble, and a "bad smell." This is narrative candor on the way to a new possibility. The community watches to see "what I will do" (6:1). The one who will do is the one whom Pharaoh disdainfully refuses to acknowledge.

Exodus 6:2-30, "I Am Yahweh"

Commentary

This chapter, on any reading, constitutes something of a disruptive oddity in the exodus narrative. According to the older source analysis (which in this particular case seems not only cogent but important), this text is by consensus taken as a part of the Priestly source. The evidence for assignment to this source includes the peculiar language for covenant making whereby the covenant is unilaterally imposed by God (v. 4), the name of El Shaddai for God (v. 2), the preoccupation with priestly genealogy (vv. 14-25), and the peculiar prominence of Aaron in that genealogy (vv. 20-25). It is clear that the texture and intent of this chapter is very different from what precedes and what follows.

Priestly texts are commonly dated either to the exile or soon thereafter.[40] They are addressed to a community in exile (or just out of exile) that is rootless and displaced. By appealing to the very old tradition, the P source seeks to construct for the exiles a sense of structured, stable reality, in order to give coherence, order, and legitimacy to communal life. The ordering that is offered is cultic in character, so that it is around liturgic claims that life is said to be properly arranged. Consequently, the antidote offered in the narrative is no longer political emancipation or economic restitution, but a stabilizing sacral order.

This Priestly block of material includes God's speech of self-disclosure (vv. 2-8), an account of resistance to that speech (vv. 9-13), a priestly genealogy (vv. 14-27), and a reprise of assertion and resistance (vv. 28-30).

6:2-8. In this extended speech of God, we have the fullest self-disclosure of God that is offered in the exodus narrative, (a very different speech of God's self-disclosure is given in 34:6-7). W. Zimmerli has shown that this lean utterance, "I am Yahweh," is the complete self-giving God, the full revelation of God's intentionality, and the way in which God makes God's own self available

to Moses and to Israel.[41] The meaning of the name *Yahweh* is endlessly problematic (as we have seen concerning 3:14). Nonetheless, it is clear that as construed in the Exodus tradition, even in the later P casting of the Exodus tradition, the name bespeaks presence, fidelity, and emancipatory power released in the world. Moreover, in his study of the book of Ezekiel, Zimmerli has shown that this theological formula is peculiarly prized by Israel in exile.[42] When all other modes of theological stability and forms of theological identity were in jeopardy, Israel clung to the name of Yahweh as the summary and foundation of its entire structure of faith and identity.

The remainder of this speech (vv. 3-8) is an exposition of the intent and substance of the brief formula of v. 2. Verse 3 makes clear the proposal of this (Priestly) tradition of the self-disclosure of Yahweh, somewhat differently paralleled in 3:14. The tradition wants to affirm the full continuity of God in the exodus narrative with God in the ancestral tales of Genesis. It is God's memory of promises to the ancestors in Genesis that operates in Exodus for liberation. But with equal resolve, the tradition wants to assert a discontinuity between these two sets of narratives. The God now fully known by name was indeed known by the Genesis ancestors, but not *fully* known and not by name.

This hypothesis of continuity/discontinuity in v. 3 is wondrously exposed in vv. 4-5. In v. 4, it is unambiguous that God fully and unilaterally declared and imposed a covenant upon the ancestors of Genesis. They had no choice or option. The covenant results from God's providential, generous sovereignty (cf. Gen 17:7-8). Moreover, the gift of covenant contained, as its key factor, the gift of the land of the Canaanites. That is, the covenant by definition anticipated receiving of land already held by others.

---

40. But see the important alternative proposal by Jacob Milgrom, *Leviticus 1–16: A New Translation with Introduction and Commentary*, AB 3 (New York: Doubleday, 1991) 3-13.

41. Zimmerli, *I Am Yahweh*, esp. 1-28.
42. Walther Zimmerli, *Ezekiel 1: A Commentary on the Book of the Prophet Ezekiel, Chapters 1–24*, Hermeneia (Philadelphia: Fortress, 1979) 406-14. See also Moshe Greenberg, *Ezekiel 1–20: A New Translation with Introduction and Commentary*, AB 22 (Garden City, N.Y.: Doubleday, 1983), 376-88.

The ancestors to whom the promise of the land is made (cf. Gen 17:8) are in fact only aliens ("sojourners," גרים *gērîm*) there. The usage also recalls Exod 2:22; like the ancestors, Moses is required to live where he does not belong, without a home. While v. 3 recalls the laden past, v. 5 focuses on the painful present tense. God has heard the groaning of the people in oppression (cf. 2:7-8, 16, 24); God is fully attentive to the present. The present pain, however, serves primarily to drive God back to the memory of the covenant made in Genesis. Thus there is a dynamic movement back and forth between old covenant commitment and immediate pain, between an authorizing past and a demanding, insistent present.

Out of this meditation on the dynamic of past and present, God issues a powerful promise to Israel through Moses (vv. 6-8). This promise is one more classic formulation of Israel's core faith, not unlike 3:7-8, 17. The promise is dominated by first-person verbs, with Yahweh as subject. God's own action will dominate Israel's future. Before the active verbs, however, there is a second solemn sounding of the basic affirmation: "I am Yahweh." The verbs of hope and liberation arise from this self-disclosure and belong intrinsically to Yahweh's own self:

"I will free you" (יצא *yāṣa*): This is the verb assigned to Moses in 3:10, but characteristically has God as its subject.

"I will deliver you" (נצל *nāṣal*). The verb is the same used by Moses in 5:23 in the infinitive absolute to accuse God of doing nothing.[43]

"I will redeem you" (גאל *gā'al*). The verb has the force of a kinsman who acts for the honor and well-being of a wounded or abused member of the family, thus bespeaking God's intimate solidarity as a member of the slave community.

This recital of active verbs of rescue takes a curious turn in v. 7, which departs from the standard form of the recital. There is another powerful first-person verb: "I will take you" (לקח *lāqaḥ*). This verb, however, is not a "historical deed," but the establishment of a relation, as though elevating liberated Israel to a new status. This verb affirms a covenant relation. The symmetrical formula "You shall

be my people and I shall be your God" is unusual in the Exodus tradition and is known primarily in the exilic formulations of Jeremiah (11:4; 24:7; 30:22; 31:33; 32:38) and Ezekiel (11:20; 14:11; 36:28; 37:23, 27).[44] Israel, who has been a nobody, now is publicly and irreversibly marked and honored as Yahweh's people. Or in the horizon of P, exiles without identity, in this liturgical context, are given a peculiar and treasured identity.

The formulation of relationship and status at the end of v. 7, however, is still derived from a deed. Again, the statement "I am Yahweh" is linked to the exodus. Moreover, it is introduced by a second stylized expression, "You shall know." Zimmerli has shown that this second formulation is a device whereby theological certitude is rooted in and derived from concrete acts of rescue, well-being, and judgment.[45] Thus the exodus is converted into a datum of theological certitude. The exodus event is not only a covenant about Israel's future, but about Yahweh's character as well.

In v. 8, the standard recital is continued from v. 6, which was disrupted by the different sort of speech in v. 7. In v. 8, the promise of the land, already guaranteed in the old promise of Genesis, is now reiterated. The promise of v. 8 is characteristically the counterpart to the deliverance of v. 6. These three verses, then, have an intentional structure:

v. 6 Exodus as	v. 8 land as
emancipation	possession
("bring out,"	("bring in,"
יצא *yāṣā*)	בוא *bô*)
v. 7 covenant formula	

The whole of the disclosure from God concludes with a climactic reassertion, "I am Yahweh" (v. 8), which balances the statement at the beginning of this assertion in v. 6.

Thus the completed affirmation is bracketed by this self-disclosure. Between "I am Yahweh" (v. 6) and "I am Yahweh" (v. 8) is both the usual *recital of Exodus-land* (vv. 6, 8) and the *covenantal formula* of v. 7. The primary intent of the whole is that this hopeless people should have a firm offer of the character and resolve of Yahweh, whose very

43. See commentary above, Exodus 5:22–6:1.

44. See Rudolf Smend, *Die Bundesformel,* Theologische Studien 68 (Zürich: EVZ-Verlag, 1963).

45. Zimmerli, *I Am Yahweh,* 35-36.

self-disclosure completely reshapes and reconstrues Israel's circumstance in bondage (or in exile). The self-disclosure of God to the slaves (vv. 6-8) grows out of the dynamic between past and present, and promise and suffering (vv. 3-5). The entire text pivots on the single root claim "I am Yahweh." This elemental reality of Yahweh makes a whole alternative history available to the hopeless ones.

6:9-13. This powerful, authoritative redefinition of reality might be expected to evoke delight, exuberance, and energy (vv. 9-13). It does not, however. We are in turn given two responses that in sequence fail to resonate with this remarkable self-offer of God.

The first response is that of the people to whom Moses delivered the self-disclosure of God (v. 9). The people "do not listen." Their response, however, is not because of stubbornness or resistance. It is, rather, because of "a broken spirit." The narrative is subtle and sensitive. The slaves, addressed by hope, have become saturated with hopelessness. The adjective *broken* bespeaks "exhausted," "spent," "short-lived." They cannot muster the vitality needed to accept the imagined alternative future just voiced. Why? Because of "their cruel slavery." They have become so deeply enmeshed in their bondage, so burdened by their brick quotas, so overwhelmed by the coercive legitimacy of Pharaoh's system, and so exhausted with survival issues that they are incapable of entertaining the alternative. The response is not one of recalcitrance, but of exhaustion. The text accepts the fact that the depth of despair can (at least in the short term) defeat the hope of God. In this utterance, despair prevails.

Following the negative response of Israel comes a second mandate of God, and a second response of resistance, this time from Moses (vv. 10-12). God, who had sent Moses to the spent Israelites (v. 6), now sends Moses to Pharaoh (v. 11). The verb addressed to Pharaoh is the same used in 4:23, again an imperative addressed to Yahweh's presumed subordinate, Pharaoh.

The message to Pharaoh, however, never gets delivered. This time Pharaoh does not have the opportunity to refuse Yahweh's decree, for the refusal is made by Moses, the messenger (v. 12). Moses has been permeated by Israel's despair. When the ones for whom the word is good news will not heed, surely Pharaoh, for whom the word is bad news, will not heed either. Besides, adds Moses, "I have uncircumcised lips." This self-disqualification is not quite, as the NRSV has it, an appeal concerning poor speech, as in 4:10. Rather, to plead "uncircumcised lips" may mean that his lips are not adequate. Or it may mean that he is an outsider to Pharaoh, who will never take him seriously. In either case, Moses successfully resists the command of God.

The narrative adds a concluding statement (v. 13). This statement is interesting because it introduces Aaron into the chapter, thus preparing the way for the priestly genealogy to follow. Moreover, the move toward Aaron in the narrative means that the refusals of Israel (v. 9) and of Moses (v. 12) are completely ignored. Rather, these lines sound the good news one more time. Yahweh, via Moses and Aaron, has given command to Israel and to Pharaoh to work on Exodus. The construction of this sentence is odd and unclear. What is clear is that both parties to the Exodus, Israel and Egypt, are under the same command. Both are to work the liberation. Neither welcomes the new intrusion into their life, for Yahweh will cause both parties a staggering inconvenience. Freedom is a terribly disruptive gift from God, unwelcome in the midst of bondage, unwelcome for both perpetrators and victims.

6:14-27. Now that Aaron has been introduced into the narrative, we turn abruptly to a list of the "heads of ancestral houses." The genealogy begins with a roll call of the sons of Jacob: Reuben, Simeon, Levi . . . but the list goes no farther than Levi (v. 16), for this is the point of interest and concern for the narrative. In turn, Levi's sons are three (vv. 16-19). The first of these sons, Gershon, is said to have two sons (v. 17), and Merari two sons (v. 19). The remainder of the genealogy is concerned with the lineage of Kohath, who has four sons and who eventually produces Moses and Aaron, the real subject of this piece. (Moses and Aaron are here fully legitimated, deeply rooted in the oldest and most respected priestly lines, which can be traced to the house of Levi.)

We may usefully reflect on why Moses and Aaron are given this emphasis. When we understand that, we shall likely understand the function of the genealogy in its setting. We have seen in v. 9, taken in its canonical context, that despair precludes Israel from hearing Moses' message of Moses. Despair, in fact, dismisses the message. The pedigree of Moses and Aaron argues against such dismissal. The slaves may despair, but this is not adequate ground for disregarding the message of Yahweh's emancipating self-disclosure. Moses and Aaron warrant a hearing, in spite of despair.

Conversely, taken in a critical context—i.e., in the context of exile (according to the P source)—the exiles may be reluctant to hear a message concerning emancipation from the power of Babylon, or from their role of powerless victim. They may prefer to conclude that the old exodus memory is not germane 600 years late in exile, because it seems so remote and liberation is, then as always, a costly inconvenience. If that be so, then the genealogy is a device for bringing the old story inescapably into the present. For Moses and Aaron, as presented in this list, are not simply ancient leaders, but are the focal references for present priestly authority. The genealogy thus provides an interpretive connection between ancient text and present legitimation of the message, making it contemporarily unavoidable.

6:28-30. The concluding verses are stunning, if this suggested battle for authority is cogent. One last time in this unit, the text sounds the root claim "I am Yahweh." Thus the unit ends as it began. There derives from this disclosure the second piece of news: "Tell Pharaoh." The claim of Yahweh is that Yahweh is able to command Pharaoh.

It would be a different matter if this episode ended with the triumphal assertion of v. 29. Verse 30, however, completely reverses field. One more time, Moses voices his resistant doubt, already surfaced in v. 12. Moses and Yahweh seem to have reached a stalemate. In 5:22-23, Moses cannot get Yahweh to save (*nāṣal*). Now in 6:28-30, Yahweh cannot get Moses to speak. We have seen in 3:7-10 that the Exodus is the doing of God, but that doing is through this human agent. At the end of chapter 6, we do not know whether God's resolve can move beyond Moses' resistance.

REFLECTIONS

1. As much as any text in the Exodus tradition, this one invites reflection upon the character of the God of Israel. Childs observes the "tremendous theocentric emphasis" of this text.[46] God's self-disclosure requires Israel to break with every generic understanding of God, with any notion that life with this God is a standard, conventional religious tale. The angular particularity of this God is an abrasion not only in our culture, but in the church as well.

This is God's self-disclosure freely given. God is subject and not object. God is the speaker and the initiator who gives what will be given. Israel's fresh chance derives from Yahweh's initiative.

God discloses a full, complete personal name: Yahweh. This is the surprising risk of particularity in ancient Israel. God has become fully available to Israel. Israel decided subsequently that this name must not be uttered. This refusal is out of awe and fear, not because Israel does not know or because Yahweh has withheld God's own self. The disclosure of the name completely changes the calculus between God and people, for this community now has leverage with God, which God has willingly given.

God's very character is to make relationships, bring emancipation, and establish covenants. The covenantal formulation of v. 7 suggests not only that Israel is now always Yahweh connected, but also that Yahweh is always Israel connected, and will not again be peopleless. Moreover, the fact that this symmetrical formula has most

46. Childs, *The Book of Exodus*, 119.

currency precisely in the exile means that at the time of the deepest rupture of faith, this relatedness persists. The God of Israel is defined by that relatedness.

The utterance of the name of Yahweh contains within it the urge of the exodus. As Käsemann asserted, "Jesus means freedom."[47] So here, "Yahweh means exodus." Liberation is integral and intrinsic in Yahweh's very character. This is what has made the utterance of the name of Israel's God so endlessly disruptive and dangerous. Any talk of narrative theology must come finally to the shape and claim of this narrative. The story that most faithfully characterizes Israel (and Yahweh) is categorically and nonnegotiably a resolve for emancipation.

2. The move in the narrative between vv. 8 and 9 is devastating. It acknowledges that Yahweh's marvelous self-disclosure toward emancipation does not always and everywhere prevail. The reasons for resistance are not to be found in some dark theological category of "original sin" or in a psychological analysis. Rather, resistant despair is understood in terms of a political-economic analysis. It is "cruel slavery," which creates a "broken heart" and makes trust in Yahweh's emancipation impossible.

We may ponder the power of despair in two quite different directions. On the one hand, it seems clear enough that people who live under brutal repression might be reluctant to run the risk of theological talk of freedom, which invites wholesale civil disobedience. On the other hand, the same paralysis of despair may be more common in the Western church, not among the oppressed, but among the seduced who live in the consumptive end of Pharaoh's productive apparatus. Consumer ideology (not experienced quite as "cruel bondage") may also lead to a "broken spirit"—i.e., to the inability to think, believe, hope, or imagine outside the present tense. Despair is no more powerful among the brutalized than it is among those who are psychologically numbed by consumer satiation. Thus the realism of v. 10 concerning "broken spirit" may apply to more than one kind of bondage.

3. In this text, focused on God's self-disclosure, the cruciality of the human agent, Moses, is accented. After God's grand self-disclosure, Moses is dispatched (v. 6). It is again Moses who is sent to Pharaoh (v. 11). It is this "same Moses and Aaron" (vv. 26, 27); it is Moses who is to tell Pharaoh (v. 29). The entire operation intended by Yahweh, that brings the future to political reality, depends on this human agent. And this human agent can doubt and refuse (vv. 12, 30).

The intended emancipation is clearly rooted in God's own character and fully depends on the capability and willingness of Moses. It is, therefore, an intention that is fragile and vulnerable, because Moses is not easily commandeered. This dramatic interplay of divine resolve and human decisiveness, which is left unresolved in this chapter, gives us pause. God's resolve awaits human readiness. The Christian tradition affirms that in Jesus of Nazareth the gospel of God found a ready human agent, but this text leaves the issue where God's emancipatory impetus seems often left, unresolved and still waiting on a willing human agent.

47. Ernst Käsemann, *Jesus Means Freedom: A Polemical Survey of the New Testament* (London: SCM, 1969).

Exodus 7:1-13, Aaron's Staff

COMMENTARY

Now begins the stylized account of the drama between Yahweh and Pharaoh, a struggle for power, control, and sovereignty (Exodus 7–11). The entire corpus of the plague narrative is cast as a response to the exchange between Yahweh and Moses in 6:28-30. Yahweh has uttered a magisterial "I am Yahweh," and Moses has resisted in his paralyzing doubt. The dynamic of resistance (from Moses) and resolve (from Yahweh) is characteristic of calls to obedience, as in the cases of Gideon (Judg 6:11-24) and Jeremiah (Jer 1:4-10).

7:1-7. In vv. 1-2 of our chapter, Yahweh issues to Moses both an assurance (v. 1) and a command (v. 2). The assurance defines Moses' relation to Pharaoh, and it structures Moses' relation to Aaron. Vis-à-vis Pharaoh, Moses is "a god," with enormous magisterial authority and sure to be obeyed. The Hebrew text, unlike the NRSV, does not say "like a god," but only "a god." Moses relates to Aaron as a god to a prophet; there is no doubt to who is superior and who is subordinate in their relationship.

The command, to be transmitted through Aaron to Pharaoh, is dominated by the verb *"let* us go"—i.e., *send* (שׁלח *šālaḥ*). Moses' "office" is instrumental to God's intention for the exodus.

Verse 3 promptly undermines and threatens both the assurance and the command of vv. 1-2. In the very same breath, Yahweh now escalates the power struggle with Pharaoh. On the one hand, Yahweh will "harden" Pharaoh. On the other hand, Yahweh will do "signs and wonders," gestures of dazzling, inscrutable power. The fact that Yahweh both hardens and does signs appears to be simply a literary device for intensification, but there is a quality of political realism in the escalation. That is, action for liberation leads to greater repression, and greater repression produces more intense resolve for liberation. In that process, it is never known who will be first to lose nerve. Moreover, the very sign itself becomes the means whereby the hardening is accomplished, as the very gesture toward liberation is what evokes more repression—i.e., hardening.

Yahweh is undeterred by Pharaoh's refusal to listen (v. 4). Yahweh will (no matter what) bring Israel out from Egypt. Yahweh's "hand" (massive power) will rest on Egypt, and in the end it cannot be resisted. Yahweh's power will be evident in great "acts of judgment." The phrase suggests that the coming plagues are to be understood as acts that enforce Yahweh's sovereign governance, as the punishment of a recalcitrant vassal. (Cf. Ezekiel 28 for a critique of Egypt's imagined autonomy.)

In his abuse of Israel, Pharaoh has sought to secede from Yahweh's magisterium. The sure indication of a "break-away state" is that it refuses to practice justice toward the powerless, a practice to which Yahweh is fully committed in all areas of Yahweh's realm.

The beginning paragraph of 7:1-7 is presented as a general introduction to the extended plague narrative, announcing most of the important theological themes that follow. Verse 6 suggests an important literary device that we shall see repeatedly in the structure of the book of Exodus. The whole of the paragraph is put together as *command and obedience.* Here the command is that Moses and Aaron shall speak to Pharaoh. In v. 6, we are told, they obeyed and confronted Pharaoh. In spite of his doubts and misgivings (cf. 6:12, 30), Moses is fully obedient to Yahweh. The information of v. 7 no doubt reflects the interest of the tradition (P) in such statistical data. More than that, however, the data voices the "scandal of particularity." Speech, to Pharaoh, is not simply generic and paradigmatic; Israel knows exactly when the speech occurred, who did it, and how old they were.

7:8-13. The narrative now becomes specific with the first of the "plagues" (vv. 8-13). Yahweh anticipates Pharaoh's testing of Moses and Aaron and their capacity to perform (v. 9). The anticipated challenge of Pharaoh is almost flippant: "Do a miracle!" Do something extraordinary to show that you are more than an ordinary protesting political figure. Verse 9 constitutes a command of Yahweh ("Take, throw"), and v. 10 is a report of immediate obedience. Moses and Aaron do promptly and exactly as Yahweh intends. Thus the "first wonder" is the amazing feat of transforming a staff, a symbol of authority into a "snake" (תנין *tannîn*).

The translation "snake" is far too innocuous and bland. What Moses and Aaron conjure is not a garden-variety snake. Rather, the term in most of its uses (and surely here) is a great sea "monster," bespeaking God's unleashing of chaos in the midst of Pharaoh's well-ordered realm. The production of the "monster" thus may announce in the empire that God is unleashing powerful disorder and elemental destabilization, which are the outcome of brutal oppression. In Gen 1:21 and

Ps 148:7, the same "monster" is in fact an obedient creature of Yahweh. Thus what is a devastating threat against Egypt is a useful tool of Yahweh in the exercise of rightful sovereignty (cf. 104:26).

It is clear even to Pharaoh that Moses had worked "a wonder." He has demonstrated that he operates with a "surplus" of power given by Yahweh. What Moses has not yet established is whether that "surplus" is great enough to be a serious challenge to entrenched Pharaoh. Repressive regimes always think of the assertion of freedom as an inconvenience to be silenced. Pharaoh counters the wonder of Moses and Aaron by having his own technicians and "intelligence community" (wise men, sorcerers, and magicians who also possess extraordinary "secrets") match the feat of Moses and Aaron (vv. 11-12a).

In fact, the contest that is staged between these functionaries is really between Yahweh and Pharaoh, between the God of emancipation and the awesome power of evil and brutality. That power of brutal oppression also has "tricks" of its own to perform. It is not difficult to imagine that the court of Egypt possessed special skills and techniques, since it no doubt controlled the most advanced "research and development" available. The surprise is that the disadvantaged slaves, dispatched by Yahweh, could do the same as the powers of the empire.

The contest ends in a stalemate; both sides produce "monsters." The narrative, however, will not leave the matter quite at a stalemate. It adds, "The staff of Aaron swallowed the Egyptian one" (v. 12b). That is, the chaos produced by Israel overpowers the chaos sanctioned by Pharaoh. The "swallowing" is an ominous threat to the order of the empire. Yahweh (and Israel) will unleash disorder beyond the control of the empire.

REFLECTIONS

This first episode only introduces an extended drama of the plagues. Nothing yet is resolved here; therefore, too much should not be claimed at this beginning point in the drama.

1. At the most obvious level, we witness here a show of power that concerns authority outside of the ordinary. We may, if we choose, call this show of power "magic," but we may also see that the "holy" enters the political with inscrutable force. The casting of the narrative already suggests that public power is more than arms and brute force. There is another kind of power that will not be denied or explained away; it is this other power that is endlessly troublesome for established tyrannical power. If there were no such "holy power," then might alone would make right, established power with superior weapons would govern to perpetuity, and tyrants would never be overthrown. Indeed, every established power that moves toward tyranny, public or more personally, dreams of such perpetuity. This narrative, however, tells us that there is more to the public process of power than surface control through brute force. There are ominous signs and wonders that are in fact the "hardening" way in which Yahweh does great "acts of judgment." This narrative is a reflection on that other sort of power that is only belatedly acknowledged.

2. The reference to "know" in v. 5 suggests that this episode is about not only the freedom of the slaves, but also the legitimate governance of Yahweh. The power struggle concerns bringing recalcitrant Pharaoh to acknowledge the rule of Yahweh. In recent times, with unlimited weapons capable of untold destruction, we have witnessed powerful political regimes imagine that they can operate autonomously and unchecked, only to be brought to heel by the force and assertion of the brutalized. Moreover, this text gives pause to any supposed super-power that imagines it is free to do what it wants with its seemingly unchecked power and with the lives of those entrusted to its governance.

3. The strategy of the drama depends on the complete obedience and daring of Moses and Aaron, an obedience that requires enormous nerve against ostensibly uneven odds. One need not turn this narrative into a tract for "revolutionary politics," but must observe that the critics of liberation theology are not correct in their insistence that the exodus is done by God and not by human initiative. In this and in the following narratives, all that is visible in the ongoing confrontation is human courage and human claims of authority. Behind that human action are certainly the references, claims, and allusions to the power and purpose of Yahweh, but they function primarily to give authorization and legitimacy to the human actors.

Exodus 7:14-25, The Plague of Blood

COMMENTARY

In this second plague, the ante is upped in the terrible contest of repression and freedom. The episode is arranged as command (vv. 14-19), obedience (vv. 20-21), Egyptian response (vv. 22-23), and verdict (vv. 24-25).

The plague is the out-working of the sovereign command of Yahweh, which will not be retracted (vv. 14-19). Yahweh's speech takes note of the resistance of Pharaoh (v. 14), and Yahweh sends Moses to meet Pharaoh (v. 15). The place of confrontation is "the water." In an arid climate, society depends on the water; therefore, the maintenance of the water is the regime's first order of business. The water is the power for life in Egypt, and so it is the place of most dangerous challenge.

Moses is directed by Yahweh to issue one more time the most elemental demand, so that Pharaoh will not doubt the subject of the confrontation. The conflict concerns the power and will of "the God of the Hebrews," the God who has taken for a people this amorphous band of the marginal whom Pharaoh in his scorn and contempt keeps helpless and powerless. It is the will of this outsider God that this outsider people be permitted to worship Yahweh and so enact their primal and defining loyalty. Yahweh's instruction adds this chiding notice to Pharaoh: "Until now, you have not listened."

This statement suggests two matters. First, Pharaoh is expected to listen. The king of Egypt is assumed to be subordinate to the command of the "king of the slaves." Such listening would signify a complete transfiguration of politics, whereby the strong one becomes an obedient suppliant.[48] Second, the statement is one of ominous teasing: "Until now" implies "Not yet . . . but you will!" The speech of Yahweh is boldly confident, completely without doubt about the ultimate outcome of the power struggle.

In v. 17, Yahweh moves the speech toward the new "wonder." The next wonder will let Pharaoh "know," or acknowledge as sovereign, this outsider. Pharaoh will come to face Yahweh's awesome majesty when he sees that the Nile, the single source of life, is turned to blood and becomes a sign and channel for death. The Egyptians will not be able to drink from the Nile; life will shrivel, death will come, power will evaporate, and Pharaoh will be no more. Yahweh proposes to strike at the jugular of Pharaoh, for no king can survive in Egypt who does not control the Nile. On behalf of the brutalized, Yahweh will sabotage the life-support system of the empire.

Moses and Aaron obey the decree of Yahweh, and the river of life becomes a source of death (vv. 20-21). The description of their act is graphic and realistic. The fish all die and there is a terrible smell—the smell of death. There is, perhaps, some irony in the notion of the "stench," if this text is related to 5:21. In that verse, the supervisors of the labor force dispute with Moses and Aaron, urging that their actions have made the Hebrews a "bad odor" to Pharaoh (i.e., an unwelcome presence in the regime). Now it is clear, however, that the smell of death from the Nile makes

48. See Paul Lehmann, *The Transfiguration of Politics* (New York: Harper & Row, 1975), esp. his exposition of the Johannine Passion narrative, 48-70.

the "inconvenient odor" of the slaves benign and innocent.

Like every entrenched authority under assault, Pharaoh learns very slowly and very little (vv. 22-23). The technical community already knows how to turn the Nile of life into a channel of death. Perhaps that cynical, uncritical technical capacity is anticipated in 1:22. It is astonishing that the agents of Pharaoh have developed the capacity to undo the Nile of life. It is even more astonishing that they do not hesitate to unleash that power and knowledge against their own people in the context of exhibiting and maintaining royal power. But such are the costs of technology when driven by uncritical ideology. It is now clear that Pharaoh will stop at nothing, not even the death of his own people, to refuse and refute this new power threatening his order.

The decisive turn in the narrative that brings the episode to a conclusion is not the responding "wonder" of Egypt. It is, rather, Pharaoh's refusal to listen. He learns nothing, acknowledges nothing, and grants nothing. He just goes home (v. 23).

This confrontation, once again, ends in a stalemate, with both parties having enacted the same wonder. But once again it is an uneven stalemate. The battle has been fought on Pharaoh's home turf. It is *his Nile* that has been polluted. It is *his people* who must scramble for survival. It is *his land* now in the grip of death and its smell. It is *his power* in deep jeopardy. The slaves lose very little in this crisis, for they long ago learned to survive on almost nothing. Chaos threatens most those who have come to prize their own contrived order. As the slaves are not threatened, so Yahweh is not threatened. Yahweh can wait. Yahweh has set in motion a powerful process whereby Yahweh will repossess the Nile and reclaim sovereignty that Pharaoh has usurped.

Yahweh can wait. The narrator adds enigmatically "seven days" (v. 25). The drama is paced. The third episode can wait, to let death sink in, to let the dramatic turn take its full effect on the imagination of Egypt (and those who listen). Imagine, the king shut up for seven anxious days—Egyptians scrambling for water for seven days. Seven days of chaos! It took seven days to enact the old story of creation, seven days to establish a new order of livelihood, seven days to cancel out the terrible deathliness of chaos (Gen 1:1–2:4*a*). Pharaoh loves chaos too much, relies upon it, embodies it. The slaves await a newness from God, who will finally claim the Nile. The slaves will wait for seven days. It is like waiting for sabbath, when even slaves shall not work and shall come to blessed rest.

REFLECTIONS

Our interpretation should focus on what is distinctive in this text—namely, the importance of the Nile. The Nile, taken in its historical specificity, is indeed the source of life for Egypt. Taken metaphorically, the Nile is not only Egypt's source of life, but it is also a symbol of authority. Whoever controls the Nile has power over life.

According to this account, the Nile in fact belongs to Yahweh, and Yahweh can dispose of it according to Yahweh's larger purposes. Conversely, Pharaoh has misunderstood both his own status as a creature who is dependent upon the Nile and his relation to Yahweh as a vassal who must obey Yahweh. The sorry outcome of this narrative makes clear that when the relation of creator and creature is distorted, life is put profoundly at risk (cf. Rom 1:20-25).

The large horizon of this narrative poses the question of arrogant power that tries to dispose of life on its own terms. In a scientific-technological society, it is seductive and easy to mistake the richness of creation entrusted to us, and imagine that it is a possession to be used at will. Conversely, given enormous technical and political power, it is easy to disregard one's status as a creature and to imagine there are no enduring lines of accountability in the use of power.

The result of distorted creaturehood and disturbed creation is the pitiful picture of the empire brought to its knees, humbled by the inescapable smell of death. One wonders whether the smell could penetrate even the sealed-off royal apartments with their up-to-date ventilation systems. There is also the ludicrous picture of formidable members of society digging desperately with their fingernails to find water enough to live. The empire is reduced to a caricature of itself. And, of course, they thought it couldn't happen here!

In the meantime, the creator waits a full seven days, the time of creation. Israel waits the same seven days, to see if God's newness will bring life for them.

Exodus 8:1-15, The Plague of Frogs

COMMENTARY

The structure of the third plague narrative is by now in a general way familiar to us. Verses 1-7 are the full enactment of the plague. The narrative consists of a charge and warning to Pharaoh, an instruction to Moses, an enactment by Aaron, and a matching "wonder" by the Egyptians. The second part of the narrative, however, exhibits a negotiation about the threat that was not present in the first two cases (vv. 8-15). The narrative has become more complex than in the first two plagues, and the center of interest is no longer in the wonder itself, but in the derivative transaction.

8:1-7. At the outset, Yahweh gives a word to Moses that is to be relayed to Pharaoh (vv. 1-4). The primary insistence of Yahweh is unchanged: Pharaoh is to send the people of Yahweh to worship Yahweh (cf. 6:26-27; 7:2, 16). This command is followed, however, as it was not in the preceding scenes, with a quite specific and extensive threat.

The cost of refusing the command of Yahweh is to be a plague of frogs. The commandment concerning the frogs is brief (v. 2), but the portrayal of their coming is designed to produce dismay in the listener. The frogs with their filth, repulsiveness, disease, and smell will permeate everything: palace, bedchamber, bed, houses of the officials and of people, ovens, and kneading bowls. The frogs will be there "when you are at home, and when you are away, when you lie down and when you rise up" (cf. Deut 6:7). The rhetorical power of this catalogue is parallel to that of 7:19; in both cases the intent is to announce, "No escape." It costs a great deal to continue practices of exploitative labor that contradict the intentions of Yahweh. At least Pharaoh now knows the other side of the bargain and can

make an informed decision about the costs he will undertake.

Yahweh's instruction to Moses quickly follows (v. 5). We all know the choice of one whose heart has been hardened, and there is no need to wait. Yahweh's command is to conjure frogs everywhere, all over the land. Aaron's performance follows immediately upon the command of Yahweh (v. 6), and the land is covered. This is saturation bombing with frogs! Almost as an aside, we are told that the Egyptian technicians match the "wonder" (v. 7). Powerful gestures of freedom are matched, so that the regime does not yet perceive itself as being under serious threat, certainly not anything that requires a review or adjustment of oppressive policy.

8:8-15. In the encounter that follows, the tone and mood are profoundly changed. Whereas the frogs had seemed rather routine in v. 7, by v. 8 it is acknowledged that there is indeed a crisis in the realm. It is as though Pharaoh urges, "Remove the frogs, and then we can talk." This first admission of such trouble on the part of the seemingly impervious Pharaoh suggests that Moses has won a first tactical victory. Speakers for the oppressed regularly have a problem receiving even recognition as a presence worthy of conversation. Moses has now made that case.

Pharaoh requests that Moses and Aaron "make supplication to Yahweh" (cf. Isa 19:22). In this appeal, Pharaoh concedes three matters: that the frogs are genuinely a problem beyond his capacity; that Moses and Aaron can do for him what he cannot do for himself; and, most important, that Yahweh can do what he cannot do—namely, revoke the threat and remove the frogs. This is the same Pharaoh who had haughtily dismissed

Yahweh (5:2). But now something is happening in Pharaoh's alleged realm over which he has no competence. Indeed, Pharaoh is urgent about the frogs, so urgent that he will bargain. He offers the most crucial trade-off, the one that Yahweh, Moses, and Aaron all want. Pharaoh will send the people to worship Yahweh, which act will affirm a withdrawal of any alleged loyalty to Pharaoh.

The enactment of Pharaoh's urgent petition is playful and leisurely, and Moses' response to Pharaoh seems mocking (v. 9). The initial term of his response is not *kindly,* as in the NRSV. Rather, it is a term of honor and praise. Either it is a sarcastic comment by Moses to this king who has now come as a suppliant (which seems likely), or it is a no-nonsense address, acknowledging the office of the king, but conceding nothing excessive by the way of honor or authority. Moses' question sounds like he is toying with Pharaoh. "When shall I pray?" invites an indication of how urgent the crisis is in the purview of Pharaoh. Moreover, Moses seems to add a qualification: The frogs will be withdrawn, but they will not be nullified. They will be kept in the Nile, ready at hand to be recalled.

Pharaoh's answer to the question (accepting the condition "only in the Nile" without comment) is "tomorrow"—i.e., "quickly" (מחר *māḥār*), without delay (v. 10). Moses in turn responds quickly and sharply: "As you say!" Moses and Yahweh, the frog removers, will act promptly. The purpose of the removal, however, is not primarily to accommodate the desperate king, or even to liberate the slaves. Rather, the frog removal is so that Pharaoh (and all his ilk) may come to know that "there is none like Yahweh." From the beginning, the plagues have been designed to bring Pharaoh to "knowledge," to acknowledge Yahweh's sovereignty (cf. 7:5). Here, however, the rhetoric is intensified.

The formula of v. 10 voices the incomparability of Yahweh. There is no other like Yahweh, none who proposes what Yahweh does, none who does what Yahweh does. This verse exhibits Israel's characteristic way of doing theology. The doxology moves from a quite specific act, in this case frog removal, to a sweeping theological affirmation. Pharaoh, the outsider and rival claimant to power, is expected to make the same doxological move

as does Israel. Again, Moses adds his uncontested proviso, "left only in the Nile" (v. 11). The addition is to assert that Yahweh has not been duped, nor has Yahweh conceded anything to the power of Pharaoh.

The frog-removal operation is, of course, effective (vv. 12-14). Pharaoh gets what he wants, the lifting of the emergency; Yahweh is shown to be the full and final arbiter of frog deployment. Moses "cried out" to move Yahweh to act, even as the slaves had initially cried out (2:23); Moses' petition depends on this crucial verb. As Yahweh hears the cries of the slaves (3:7, 16), so now Yahweh hears the cries made for Egypt in its vexation. The voicing of effective petition and its positive reception dramatically assert that Egypt and Pharaoh belong to the regime of Yahweh, and that Yahweh is attentive even to their need. This is a God who answers those in trouble, even if it is the voice of the great nemesis, Pharaoh. The frogs are removed, but the land stinks (cf. 7:21)! Yahweh has left a calling card, one to remind Pharaoh, each time he breathes, that he has been bested.

The conclusion of this episode evidences that Moses is not in a fair fight (v. 15). Yahweh had warned Pharaoh in good faith (v. 2). Pharaoh has seemed to bargain in good faith (v. 8). Whether the bargain in v. 8 was a trick, or whether Pharaoh meant what he said at the time and then reneged, we are not told, and we cannot know. In either case, Pharaoh did not do as he said in v. 8. When he saw that the threat of the frogs was withdrawn, he saw no need to keep his part of the bargain.

It may be easy to conclude (because it is most demeaning of Pharaoh) that Pharaoh had indeed tricked Moses and Yahweh. Such a reading, however, is not necessary. The crisis of frogs may have been acute enough to permit a serious promise by Pharaoh concerning the release of the slaves, but when the crisis is relaxed, making an actual concession seems both foolish and unnecessary. Making a promise and then reneging is a perfectly credible sequence for a major power under duress. The episode has, nonetheless, genuinely changed the tilt of the playing field. By his desperate petition and by his willingness to bargain at all, Pharaoh has in fact given recognition of the power, authority, and reality of Yahweh. By the end of this episode, Pharaoh is strategically and psychologically weakened, though not enough so that he knows it, not enough to warrant substantive concessions. Conversely, Yahweh, Moses, and Aaron are in a measurably strengthened position for the continued struggle for authority.

REFLECTIONS

Along with the standard rhetorical elements of the plague episodes, we may identify the following interpretive points:

1. Covering the earth with frogs that swarm is an appeal to Yahweh's sovereign governance as creator. The verb for "swarm" (שרץ *šāraṣ*) is used in 1:7 concerning the fruitfulness of Israel. Here the creator has reversed the process of creation in the face of Pharaoh, the great disturber and distorter of creation. Instead of a creation that teems with life, the teeming now is an invasion of the power of death, sent at the behest of God. God mobilizes the deathly capacity present in creation against this disobedient power.

2. Pharaoh's petition evidences the willingness of Yahweh to be seriously engaged with non-Israelites, even those who have resisted Yahweh's purpose. Pharaoh's petition is heard, honored, and positively answered. Yahweh intends the well-being even of Pharaoh and of Egypt. Note that Yahweh's readiness to hear prayer for Pharaoh is based on the hint in the narrative that Pharaoh has at least in part acknowledged the rule of Yahweh. Prayer is heard from those who accept the rule of Yahweh, to whom prayer is addressed.

3. The willingness of Yahweh to deal with Pharaoh and with Egypt, however, is uncompromising. Graciousness on the part of Yahweh is not to be construed as accommodation to any rival sovereignty. This lesson is so urgent for a "super power," or for any of us who imagine a piece of our lives where we have final say. Pharaoh here imagines he can enlist the goodness of Yahweh and yet retain his imperial turf. The subsequent narrative makes clear that Pharaoh cannot have it both ways.

4. The God who is disclosed here, whom Pharaoh must come to "know," is without rival, partner, competitor, or ally. This God is unlike any other. This affirmation hints at the abrasiveness of biblical faith in a culture that craves "user-friendly," benign religion. The narrative anticipates the poet of the exile in the assertion, "I am the LORD, and there is no other" (Isa 45:6 NRSV). Pharaoh has not yet come to that realization.

5. Perhaps the most interesting dramatic element in this narrative is the wavering of Pharaoh. After making a promise to Moses (v. 8), he promptly reneges on that promise (v. 15). The narrative is on sound psychological ground in this portrayal of Pharaoh. The narrator understands that in a place of acute crisis, we do resolve to make important changes that are responsible, healing, and large-hearted. However, when the pressure lifts, such costly changes are frequently seen to be neither necessary nor practical. (Cf. the same vacillating resolve in Judah [Jeremiah 34].) Pharaoh here exemplifies the way of a powerful agent (person or community) whose life is strewn with unkept promises and unpaid pledges. Without sustained pressure, it is not easy to listen, and less easy to change. The ongoing narrative shows Yahweh's capacity to keep the pressure on.

Exodus 8:16-19, The Plague of Gnats

COMMENTARY

This brief narrative of the fourth plague is introduced abruptly, presumably as a response to the bad faith of Pharaoh in v. 15. Again the narrative is divided as performance of the plague (vv. 16-17) and Egyptian response to it (vv. 18-19).

The affliction of gnats is brief and conventional. Yahweh issues a command to Aaron through Moses; Aaron obeys, and gnats invade the whole land. Of the damage caused by these pesky insects, Calvin comments: "But let us learn from this history, that all creatures are ready at God's lightest command, whenever He chooses to make use of them to chastise His enemies, and again that no animal is so vile and contemptible as not to have the power of doing injury when God employs it."[49]

As Fretheim has noticed, the sweeping rhetoric used to describe the "saturation bombing" of gnats is the language of creation. Fretheim suggests that "dust" refers to death—i.e., the end of the Egyptians (cf. Gen 3:19; Ps 104:29).[50] The gnats cover all the earth, humankind, and beasts. That is, God has sent a crippling vexation upon the whole earth as a response to the distortion of social relations on the part of Pharaoh. The well-being of the earth depends on the well-being of the human community.

The Egyptians' response to this plague is by now predictable. They will match the miracle of Aaron. In what may be a modest irony, the verb rendered "to produce" in the NRSV is יצא (*yāṣā*), the term regularly used for "bringing out"—i.e., the exodus. The Egyptian technicians attempt to cause an exodus of the gnats.

The narrator, however, has set up the listener for a stunning surprise: "They could not!"(18*a*). The Egyptians were unable to match the Israelite miracle. From the outset, the first three plagues have been aimed at this dramatic moment in the sequence when the confrontation between Yahweh and Pharaoh

reaches to the limit of Egyptian scientific-religious capability.

The verb for "could not" (יכל *yākōl*) elsewhere is rendered without the negative as "be able," "prevail," "assert one's way." It is used on occasion for a struggle with God. Thus in Gen 32:22-32, Jacob wrestles with a night-stranger (ostensibly God). In that struggle, the night-stranger does not "prevail" against Jacob (v. 25), but in the end salutes Jacob: "You have striven with God and with humans, and have prevailed [*yākōl*]" (v. 28 NRSV).

Conversely, in Jer 20:7-13, as Fishbane has shown, the same verb is used to very different effect.[51] In this complaint, Jeremiah is "not able" (v. 9). His opponents hope to "prevail" (v. 10), but in the end cannot prevail against God (v. 11). In this poem, unlike the Jacob narrative, God indeed prevails, against both Jeremiah and his opponents. From the outset, Jeremiah has lived with the assurance from God that his enemies would not prevail—i.e., be able to destroy him—because of God's promise (cf. 1:19; 15:20). The poem in 20:7-13 seeks to claim this promise for the prophet one more time.

In these two examples, Gen 32:22-33 and Jer 20:7-13, it is evident that a struggle with the power of God can lead to different outcomes. Thus Jacob prevails, but Jeremiah and his opponents do not. The result of such a struggle is not known ahead of time. In our text, it was not known until v. 18 that Egypt "could not." This moment marks a dramatic turn in the power struggle between Yahweh and Pharaoh. The remainder of v. 18 adds laconically, "There were gnats on both humans and animals." This innocent statement, however, asserts that such a blanketing of the earth accents the power of Yahweh in contrast to the pitiful impotence of Egypt.

As a result of this dramatic and massive defeat, the technicians of the Egyptian empire are required to report their findings to Pharaoh (v. 19). Their report is astonishing,

49. Calvin, *Commentaries on the Four Last Books of Moses Arranged in the Form of a Harmony*, 165.
50. Fretheim, *Exodus*, 118.

51. Fishbane, "Exodus 1–4," 91-102.

doxologically impressive on behalf of Yahweh, and ominous for the Egyptians. To be sure, the Egyptians do not name the name of Yahweh. Their language is more generic, but their statement is an acknowledgment that a power other than their own has been loosed in the empire.

Characteristically and sadly, Pharaoh will not listen, even to his own advisers. Pharaoh now has sufficient evidence, plus the council of his best scientists, to conclude that he cannot win the battle he is engaged in with Yahweh. The reason he cannot prevail is that he labors not simply against "flesh and blood" (i.e., Moses and Aaron), but against the power that drives all of creation. Increasingly, members of the narrative cast know this. Indeed, everyone knows it now except Pharaoh. The isolation of failed, decadent power encourages enormous self-deception.

REFLECTIONS

This brief narrative concerns the sovereignty of God, which overrides the power of the empire. Even the Egyptian scientists discover the limits of their power. It is clear to them that the empire cannot deliver the goods, cannot keep its promises, and cannot guarantee life. The empire, by its religious ideology and its technological posturing, wants to present itself as an ultimate source of life. One of the pastoral tasks invited by this text is the exploration of the limits of every "empire," every concentrated hosting of an illusion of life-power, in order to discern that such empires, public and personal, cannot keep their promises and cannot give life.

Surprisingly, by the very mouth of the Egyptians, the power of Yahweh to give life is confessed. Yahweh, an outsider to the empire, allied only with the marginal in Egypt, is here shown to be the one capable of creative power. The "power of Yahweh" is a strange and difficult theme in our modernist environment. The language of power concerning Yahweh is sure to be misunderstood, given our dominant models of power. In any case, the text suggests that power for life is not reliably situated where there are the usual forms and appearances of power. We are invited to look to the margins of life, among "the Hebrews," for God's power toward life. Publicly this suggests that those excluded from formal power may finally have the capacity to generate newness. More personally, it suggests that we look to the censored, less honorable, and denied parts of self in order to have life.

Exodus 8:20-32, The Plague of Flies

COMMENTARY

The narrative moves on quickly to the fifth plague. Again the narrative may be divided as performance (vv. 20-24) and Egyptian response (vv. 25-32). Note that the response is more extensive than the enactment of the plague itself.

8:20-24. The performance of the plague of flies is peculiar, because here Yahweh speaks (vv. 20-23) and acts (v. 24) without either Moses or Aaron. It is as though the confrontation has now become so urgent that Yahweh must act swiftly and decisively. To be sure, there is an initial command to Moses (v. 20a). Moses is to address Pharaoh at "the water." The king, in his anxiety, is presumably checking the condition of the Nile. Moses, however, is absent from the action and takes no part in the narrative.

In Yahweh's own mouth is a theological statement in three parts. First, Yahweh issues one more time the basic intention of the entire narrative: "Let my people go" (v. 20). All that is required is that Pharaoh act toward Yahweh in obedience as the vassal he is. Second, as in

8:2, Yahweh states the cost of disobedience and warns of flies that will penetrate everywhere (as did the frogs in 8:2-6). The flies will "fill the earth" (and subdue it?). Yahweh is prepared to place all of creation in jeopardy, because of Pharaoh's distortion of the human community. Third, Yahweh now exposits the notion of "my people," named in v. 20 and often in this programmatic command (vv. 22-23a). The creator God who has just exhibited cosmic power now distinguishes and specifies that a particular people (group) in the empire is the object of Yahweh's special attention and concern. The one who speaks is "the God of the Hebrews" (cf. 7:16; 9:1). Thus "my people" who are to be let go are the Hebrews, that amorphous group of marginated outsiders who have not yet become a real community. The distinctions made by Yahweh are exactly the kinds of distinctions refused by the empire.

After the long speech of Yahweh's resolve, the actual implementation of the threat of flies is quick and devastating (v. 24). The flies come everywhere, and the land is "ruined," left like a land invaded and abandoned in the devastation of war. (In Gen 6:11-12, the term for "ruined" describes the land before the flood—"ruined" by corruption.)

8:25-32. The devastation is enough to evoke a desperate concession from Pharaoh (v. 25-28). He cleverly appears to give in and to grant the primal request so frequently stated (cf. v. 20). He will, indeed, let the people offer a sacrifice to their God. That is an enormous admission in itself, one echoing the admission of the scientists in v. 19. As in all such duplicitous bargaining positions, however, a qualification undermines the entire offer. The permit is for sacrifice "within the land," still under the aegis and scrutiny of Pharaoh. This qualification domesticates the act of worship and robs it of its dramatic, ideological power and subverts the entire offer.

Moses, of course, is quick to notice the cunning footnote to the offer, and so he also bargains (vv. 26-27). Moses' words suggest cool-headed negotiations, but in fact Moses abruptly rejects Pharaoh's modest concession. Worship of Yahweh "in the land" would put the slaves at risk, for they would be worshiping Yahweh where the rule of Pharaoh is still evident and assumed. Such an act would be odious and unacceptable (cf. 5:21). If Israel is to worship Yahweh, that worship must be unfettered and unconditional.

Pharaoh counters with a second offer, giving only slightly more ground (v. 28). Now Pharaoh agrees to let the worship of Yahweh take place in the wilderness, outside his domain. Pharaoh's statement indicates that he understands very well what is at stake in the debate about a worship permit. He understands *to whom* the worship is addressed: to Yahweh, his great adversary. He understands *where* the worship is to happen: in the wilderness, outside his domain and beyond his control.

Like every good negotiator, Pharaoh will not grant that much to Moses without getting something in return. Pharaoh seeks to impose two conditions. First, they cannot go far away. He wants to compromise on where, not far removed from his governance. He does not yet understand that a hair's breadth from his rule into the rule of Yahweh is a leap of light years from one governance to another. To this condition, Moses makes no response, and in fact ignores the proposal.

The second condition is "Pray for me." The LXX adds, as in 8:8, "Pray for me *to Yahweh.*" The added condition of the Greek text is astonishing. It is a reluctant, but necessary, admission on the part of Pharaoh that Yahweh holds the power for life and that Pharaoh must finally submit to Yahweh's requirements. Moses is not excessively eager to accept this last proposal, which concedes a great deal.

Moses is very clear about what comes before what (v. 29). First comes the exodus, the departure. Then, only then, comes prayer to Yahweh on behalf of Pharaoh. Prayers to Yahweh are among Moses' few bargaining chips, and he will not use them lightly. Neither Moses nor Pharaoh doubts that Moses' prayer will effect a removal of the flies, but departure of the slaves is a condition of the removal of the flies. The flies come because of social abuses, and the flies can depart only when those abuses are rectified.

With the added warning of v. 29b, Moses proceeds to act out the condition set by Pharaoh: He prays to Yahweh (v. 30), and the prayer is promptly effected. Yahweh answers by removing all the flies from Pharaoh, from the officials, from the people. So far, so good—except that the narrative ends the account with a twist that violates everything negotiated. Moses had been right to be suspicious, but he had not been fearful enough. Moses had shrewdly sequenced matters in this agreement with Pharaoh: first exodus, then prayers (v. 29). But Moses had promptly disregarded his own condition and had made prayers for Pharaoh before there was an exodus. One more time, Pharaoh has triumphed and bested Moses. One more time, Pharaoh refuses to listen. One more time, Pharaoh acts with a hard heart. One more time, Yahweh is refused, and the slaves stay in bondage.

REFLECTIONS

Three new factors appear in this episode:

1. In the mouth of Yahweh is affirmed a distinction between peoples, between Hebrews and Egyptians. This is an exceedingly important and problematic affirmation. It is important because the entire narrative depends on this scandal of particularity. It is problematic because the notion of distinction flies in the face of our pervasive penchant for even-handed treatments.

Two very different readings are possible of this special people. On the one hand, it is conventional to take this people as "the Israelites," which leads directly to the affirmation that the Jews are the treasured people of God. This is the beginning point of the "mystery of Israel," which continues to be important for Christian theology.

A second, less obvious but more expansive, interpretative possibility suggests that this chosen people is not any ethnic community (or about-to-become ethnic community), but is in fact a sociological allusion to the Hebrews, the socially marginated, wherever and whomever they may be.[52] Inside the narrative itself, this later reading of a sociological distinction has peculiar cogency. Such an affirmation leads to a "class reading" of social relations, to the relationships between haves and have-nots, between the center and the margin. Given Yahweh's special care for the marginated, all social relations are now to be transformed, so that the ones conventionally dismissed as unimportant become peculiarly important.

2. The negotiations between Pharaoh and Moses reach new delicacy and subtlety here. Two facets are worth exploring. First, negotiation belongs to the reality of emancipation. Thus Moses' story will eventually culminate in a massive power play by Yahweh that overrides all possible negotiations. But along the way, Moses is prepared to do business with "the evil empire." Second, the negotiations in the end are not conducted in good faith. Pharaoh is endlessly resourceful, imaginative, devious, and deceptive in his zeal to preserve the status quo. At one level, this procedure simply squares with Niebuhrian realism. Power is not readily relinquished. At another level, if Pharaoh can be seen as an embodiment of demonic power, it is evident that historical-political embodiments of evil are massively resistant and do not easily give up privilege. One is left to adjudicate the extent to which Pharaoh is "normal" in the retention of power, and the extent to which he is an embodiment of larger-than-life evil.

We know already from 8:18 that Egypt cannot prevail. From the perspective of the narrator, that crucial point is settled. Pharaoh, however, has not yet conceded the point, and along the way, he still prevails in many immediate skirmishes. Moses and his folk keep their faith in this ultimate verdict of 8:18 to sustain them in the face of

---

52. In a carefully nuanced way, Paul M. van Buren, *A Theology of the Jewish-Christian Reality Part II: A Christian Theology of the People Israel* (San Francisco: Harper & Row, 1983) 179-83, suggests that the suffering of the Jews may indeed be an important learning for marginated African Americans. And even Jon Levenson, "Exodus and Liberation," 169, concludes his polemical study: "The liberation of which the exodus is the paradigmatic instance is a liberation from degrading bondage for the endless service of the God who remembers his covenant, redeems from exile and oppression, and gives commandments through which the chosen community is sanctified." The "paradigmatic" character of the text-event opens its claims beyond its first "Hebrew" participants.

more immediate defeats. Thus the story is a model for enduring resolve in the face of hostile, even demonic, resistance.

3. Given this mismatch between *a special marginated people* and the *resilient bad faith of Egypt,* we may note a third element already evident in 8:28. Moses prays efficaciously, and his prayer matters in the public arena. Indeed, prayer appears to be Moses' major mode of power and point of bargaining. Prayer is a powerful activity in the narrative, deriving from the power of Yahweh, which is inadvertently acknowledged by Pharaoh. This narrative affirms that the public process of power is not reduced to visible imperial might. If it were, the story would have ended before now, and Pharaoh would have been secure and unbothered. There is, however, another sort of power at work in the public arena, according to this narrative. Prayer is where that other power becomes visible and effective.

While the narrative does not permit any easy, pious claim for the "power of prayer," it is nonetheless clear that prayer is a mode of political power that operates as an equalizer between the marginated, seemingly powerless, and the resilient power of Pharaoh's evil. Moses is utterly convinced of Yahweh's will for transformed social relations, and even Pharaoh must from time to time acknowledge the point. The narrative is not yet to the place where Pharaoh will, like Moses, "know that I am Yahweh." But then, the narrator has not yet finished with Pharaoh!

Exodus 9:1-12, The Plague on Livestock and the Plague of Boils

COMMENTARY

This unit consists in two brief plague episodes in which themes familiar to us are reiterated.

9:1-7. The first of these two plagues concerns "a very heavy pestilence," a contagious disease that will be out of control and will kill livestock. Fretheim suggests a play on *pestilence* (דבר *deber*) and *word* (דבר *dābār*), both attesting to the power of Yahweh.[53] This narrative account includes the usual elements of performance (vv. 1-6) and response (v. 7).

Yahweh again announces the primal intention of liberation, as a command of "the God of the Hebrews." The God of the Hebrews wants for them exactly what they have never had: freedom and the end of abusive dependence. Again the cost of disobedience to Yahweh's decree is stated (vv. 2-3). As usual, the promised vexation will penetrate all of Egyptian society—horses, donkeys, camels, herds, flocks—nothing is immune. Pharaoh is given a clear choice.

This plague episode includes a variation. Yahweh sets a deadline—i.e., issues an ultimatum (v. 5). Pharaoh is very much treated like a recalcitrant vassal who needs to come back into obedience to the real authority. Oddly enough, no space or time is allowed between vv. 5 and 6. Pharaoh is given no slack time in the narrative to reflect upon or to ponder Yahweh's ultimatum. The threat of the deadline is followed promptly by execution of the threat. Yahweh does exactly what has been threatened. The contrast is as complete as promised: "all died/not one died."

Only now, and that briefly, is Pharaoh permitted to respond to the disaster. He conducts an investigation concerning the extent of the damage inflicted by Yahweh. One can imagine the imperial statisticians carefully reviewing the numbers, reporting a census of dead cattle. All the numbers are consistent, except for one fluke. One oddity defies normal explanation: In the land of Goshen, among the slave camps, there are no dead cattle. Scientists that they are, they can only give the data, drawing no large conclusions, either political or theological.

53. Fretheim, *Exodus*, 121.

Pharaoh, however, receives the reports and draws conclusions as he must (v. 7). It is true! Yahweh really does make distinctions. The Hebrews really are an exempt people. The evidence makes unmistakably clear that what is happening in his realm no longer has any relation to the policies or interests of Pharaoh. The revolution has happened, and Pharaoh is increasingly ineffective and irrelevant. It is as though power is being wielded from somewhere else.

Pharaoh makes no comment about the odd statistic. But he knows! He nonetheless draws a conclusion, as though he has taken leave of his senses. He will refuse to acknowledge the new, emerging reality. He will persist in what must surely be, clear even to him, a lost cause. A hard heart leads him to maintain his own interest, even if he must refuse overwhelming reality.

9:8-12. The second of these two plague accounts concerns boils caused by soot. This sixth plague report is highly stylized and contains almost no narrative variation from the conventional form. In this account, there is no voicing of a command from Yahweh to Pharaoh, as is usual, nor is any negative condition stated that leaves Pharaoh an option to avoid the threat. In this account, the threat is not undertaken in order to urge an action by Pharaoh. It is simply announced as punishment. The initial speech of Yahweh to Moses moves immediately to "soot," which will cause boils (vv. 8-9).

The language of Yahweh's speech again reflects a comprehensive governance over humans and animals throughout the whole land. The implementation of the threat by Moses and Aaron is as expected (v. 10). The comment about the Egyptian experts utilizes the language of 8:18, though to somewhat different effect (v. 11). As in 8:18, the magicians "are not able" (יכל *yākōl*), but here the sentence does not refer to a counterattempt at a wonder. It suggests only that Pharaoh's experts are routed, cannot compete, and are finally disabled themselves by the boils. Pharaoh's response, even in the light of the failure of his own experts, is as defiant as usual (v. 12).

REFLECTIONS

These two truncated episodes advance no new themes and are among the most stylized and predictable of any of the narrative units concerning the plagues, but this may let us see more clearly the primary theological claims operative here, as elsewhere, in the plague cycle. The principle claim is that Yahweh, little by little, is establishing sovereignty over Egypt as part of Yahweh's rightful realm. Conversely, Pharaoh is being effectively delegitimated and is, little by little, abandoning his claims and his rule. It is for that reason that Pharaoh responds in desperate resistance. The real issue is not even the loss of the slaves but the loss of legitimacy, as Egypt is seen to be a territory over which Yahweh exercises control. The narrative portrays the way in which Yahweh "must increase," growing "stronger and stronger," and Pharaoh "must decrease," growing "weaker and weaker" (cf. 2 Sam 3:1; John 3:30).

Derivative from that main point about conflicting sovereignties are two interrelated subpoints. On the one hand, the Israelites, subjects of Yahweh's exodus intention, are treated distinctively under social protection (v. 4). Nothing bad can happen to Israel (vv. 6-7). On the other hand, Egypt is subject to Yahweh's special assault. Egypt, at the command of Yahweh, is saturated with the power of death (vv. 3-4, 6) and is unable to resist (v. 11).

The interpretive task is to see how the exodus narrative (or the classic Christian proclamation, for there are obvious connections here), touches in pastoral ways the lived reality of contemporary people. In truth, contemporary people, like ancient people, have in endless ways sworn allegiance or found themselves in bondage to false authorities who intend no good, but who only exploit and abuse. The pastoral office has as its work the emancipation of persons from all seductive bondages. This may entail the dramatic disclosure that the old loyalties are discredited. It also invites people to the hard, slow work of boldly withdrawing allegiance and refusing to obey or submit to these loyalties.

In this pastoral work, Pharaoh's role may take many forms. In public life, it may be the demanding, massive ideologies of sexism, racism, ageism, or nationalism or the seductive sloganeering of greed, anxiety, despair, or amnesia. Taken more personally, this false loyalty, which robs one of life may involve a false sense of self that leads to an abusive underliving or a destructive overliving that, in either case, is death-dealing. A popular phrasing of such false loyalties is "addiction" (or "co-dependency"), but the language of these narrative texts has long ago voiced the crisis more poignantly and more powerfully. Our more analytical language is not an advance on the narrative sketching of the conflict between freedom and bondage, life and death.

Exodus 9:13-35, The Plague of Hail

COMMENTARY

This seventh plague narrative is not only more extended than what has gone before, but it is also much more complex. The narrative divides into three parts: (1) decree and announcement (vv. 13-21), (2) implementation (vv. 22-26), and (3) response (vv. 27-35). In large sweep, this account is like all the others. Wholesale destruction of Egypt is wrought by Yahweh, and in the end, Pharaoh refuses to change. What is interesting and important in the narrative is not a changed outcome (which does not occur), but the process of the story itself.

9:13-21. Yahweh's decree (vv. 13-19) receives an initial mixed response from the Egyptians (v. 20-21). In the decree, Yahweh once more dispatches Moses to Pharaoh to issue again the unchanging resolve of the God of the Hebrews to have this people worship Yahweh in freedom (v. 13). What follows functions as a negative threat that is not unlike 8:2 or 9:2, though the actual "if" clause is lacking. That is, Yahweh declares in a straight, unqualified indicative that all the plagues will be sent. But, in fact, a condition is implied. This time, in the event of Pharaoh's resistance, Yahweh will empty the arsenal of plagues and exhaust the entire repertoire of threats. The reason for this wholesale resolve is not God's exhaustion or impatience. It is, rather, that Yahweh now knows that nothing less than this will affect Pharaoh.

The intention of this massive assault on Pharaoh, so far as this decree goes, is not primarily the liberation of the Hebrews, though that is implied as well. Rather, it is that Pharaoh might know (come to knowledge) that there is none like Yahweh in all the earth (v. 14). The plague thus is a means of theological instruction and persuasion. Pharaoh may have mistaken Yahweh to be like other gods, as do the Assyrian theologians later on (cf. Isa 36:18-20). If Yahweh is like the others, then this threat from Yahweh is neither dangerous nor serious, and the power of Yahweh is not much of a threat. The other gods will either fail in their weakness or be bought off in their greed. Yahweh's willingness to engage Pharaoh on behalf of the Hebrews, however, is an incontrovertible message to Pharaoh (if only Pharaoh will pay attention), that Yahweh is not weak, not fickle, not vain, not for sale.

Then the inescapable question arises: If this is Yahweh's intent, why have there been two and one half chapters of only partial action? Why not do the whole job in the beginning? The narrative seems to recognize this wonderment and seeks to respond to it. There is no doubt, according to the narrative, that Yahweh could have obliterated Pharaoh by now. Yahweh's capacity to do this is not in doubt for the narrator. Yahweh, however, has not done so, but has chosen this slower strategy in order to evidence power, to let Yahweh's reputation (name) be noticed by the other nations. It is as though Yahweh always has one eye on public relation gains and knows that the other nations are watching (cf. Num 14:13-16). Moreover, the narrator seems to recognize that the "events" of the plagues are essentially a literary phenomenon and the delay is appropriate in order to generate more texts that provide more material for liturgic reenactment.

After that odd reflection on strategy, the speech of Yahweh returns to criticize Pharaoh and to justify the coming assault (v. 17). The telling indictment against Pharaoh is that he continues to "lift himself up" (סלל *sālal*) at the expense of the slaves, "my people." The verb used here is a quite distinctive one, used nowhere else in the Hebrew text in this way. It refers to the distortion of social relations whereby the high one towers over the low one. The verb suggests actual physical distance, and it is this distance between power and powerlessness that Yahweh will not tolerate in the earth.

The statement in vv. 14-17 is an odd departure from the conventional sequence of these episodes. Very often these narratives move directly from command (v. 13) to attack (vv. 18-19). The intervening verses provide a rich theological reflection, which joins together the incomparability of Yahweh and the indictment of Pharaoh for self-exaltation. That Yahweh is so preoccupied with Pharaoh's self-exaltation provides substance to the claim of incomparability and, in fact, means that Yahweh will tolerate no competitor.

The plague now to be enacted (cf. v. 14 on "all my plagues") is very heavy hail, like no hail that had ever been in Egypt (v. 18). While v. 18 sounds a note of uncompromising severity, v. 19 provides a way out of the threat, suggesting that Yahweh wants not so much to destroy as to send a decisive signal to Pharaoh. The instruction gives the Egyptians a choice. The response to the instruction is mixed (vv. 20-21); some heed it, and some do not. It is interesting that the ones who heed the urging are not said to act simply in prudence or in terror. They are characterized as "fearing the word of Yahweh." It is likely that this fear intends nothing like faith, but means simply that they took wise precautions in the face of a real danger. That they took the threat to be a real danger, however, means they credit the word. They are, the story suggests, in an elemental way converted to the rule of Yahweh.

9:22-26. The implementation of the promised hail happens through word and act (vv. 22-26). The word to Moses is expansive in scope, reflecting the rule of the creator over all the land, over humans, animals, and plants (v. 22). Moses' act yields very heavy hail. True to the warning of v. 19, everything left exposed in the field is completely devastated (v. 25). The negatives of vv. 19 and 25 correlate precisely. The positives of vv. 19 and 26 do not correlate so completely. The positive warning indicates that anyone, any Egyptian could have had protection from the hail. The outcome introduced by "only" (רק *raq*) in v. 26, however, reports respite and protection only in Goshen where the Israelites dwell. Evidently there is some instability in these statements.

Our propensity, however, should be to let the text have its own clear say. Thus the warning in v. 19, now fully implemented in v. 26, suggests that Yahweh has a modest inclination to want to exempt even Egyptians from the assault, if only they "feared the word of the LORD." Calvin suggests that the Egyptians who feared the word of the Lord did so for "immediate and monetary terror," and did not seriously repent. [54] Using a class reading of the text to which I am sympathetic, Pixley suggests that as some of the Egyptians feared the word of the Lord, "we discern a crack in the solidarity of the state bureaucratic class . . . certain sectors of the state bureaucracies were allied with the peasant uprising."[55] Accepting Yahweh as a force for the uprising, Pixley (unlike Calvin) regards their repentance as serious, including its profound political implications. The text itself passes over this odd relation of warning and outcome without comment.

9:27-35. The response of Pharaoh is poignant and urgent (vv. 27-28). The tone of his response is no longer that of a political ploy. Pharaoh moves to first-level theological talk: "I have sinned this time" (חטא *ḥāṭā'*). The statement is direct, unqualified, and unadorned. This initial term is supported by the double statement of Pharaoh: "Yahweh is righteous [צדיק *ṣaddîq*]; I [and my people] are wicked" [רשע *rāša'*]." Taken at face value,

54. Calvin, *Commentaries on the Four Last Books of Moses Arranged in the Form of a Harmony*, 187.
55. Pixley, *On Exodus*, 52.

the words show Pharaoh fully capitulating to Yahweh. The great power of Egypt is in this moment assessed by the covenantal notions of righteousness and wickedness.

Our suspicion about Pharaoh's statement is immediately evoked, however, when we read on into v. 28. The urgency of Pharaoh's full statement is indicated by the fact that no qualifications, conditions, or bargaining points are added. Nonetheless, it is clear that the purpose of Pharaoh's entire theological exercise is to curtail the threat of devastating hail. Pharaoh is being eminently practical. This confession of guilt is not a statement made for its own sake. It functions only to support the imperative petition which comes next: "Pray to Yahweh" (v. 28).

Moses' response and Pharaoh's ultimate resistance enact a sad tale, one we have heard before (vv. 29-35). Again Moses responds, as in 8:29, with the sequence, "First exodus, then intercession." This time Moses adds a phrase, reiterating the claim of v. 29. The purpose of stopping the hail, like the purpose of sending the hail (v. 14), is in order that Pharaoh may acknowledge what he does not want to acknowledge. In v. 14, the purpose is to know the incomparability of Yahweh; here the purpose is to know that all the earth belongs to Yahweh (and none of it to Pharaoh, v. 29). Thus the sending and withholding of hail are here not directly related to the emancipation of the Hebrews. They are, rather, to exhibit the authority of Yahweh in administering the power both to enhance and to diminish creation.

The wondrous doxological statement on the part of Moses (v. 29) is followed by an amazing strategic comment (v. 30). Moses had been conned by Pharaoh in 8:29-29, and he now recalls that occasion. He lets Pharaoh (and the reader) know that he is not unaware that he is being conned. He is under no illusions. He knows that the words of Pharaoh are only a ploy and he does not believe them.

The parenthetical comment of v. 31 is odd; it provides Pharaoh with a rationale for his capitulation to Moses at this time. The hail had already destroyed the flax and barley crops, and this is a land that must worry about famine. It was not too late to save the wheat and spelt. Thus Pharaoh has a most pragmatic reason for his seeming capitulation: He is buying time for the crops. If Moses knows about v. 31, if he is privy to the narrator's parenthetical comment, and if he knows about the crops, he may also know about Pharaoh's pragmatic reason. It happens, however, that Pharaoh's pragmatic effort to save the crops converges with Moses' witness to the power of the creator. How better to save the crop than to honor the God who gives both wheat and spelt!

Moses implements his plan as he said he would (v. 33). He prays, the hail stops, and the wheat and spelt are presumably saved. Moses, however, has not been duped. His theological witness does not depend on the reliability of Pharaoh. Moses wants to exhibit the power of the creator God, and that can happen regardless of what Pharaoh intends. The concluding response of Pharaoh does not surprise us (v. 34-35). Indeed, Moses in v. 30 has led us to expect this response. Pharaoh, who has acknowledged his sin (v. 27), sins more and increases his resistance. He resists Yahweh and he the exodus. He maintains distance between himself and the slaves, exalting himself at their expense (cf. v. 17).

Nothing in the empire has changed by the process of this narrative. Yahweh has delivered his heaviest blow in the hail, to no visible effect. Yahweh has, however, by sending and ending hail, been glorified as creator. Yahweh is about the business of "getting glory." That work of Yahweh, without regard to the exodus, does not depend on Pharaoh's cooperation. Indeed, Pharaoh's stubborn resistance makes the glory of Yahweh all the more spectacular.

REFLECTIONS

The sending of hail is the most extreme and severe plague yet wrought in this larger narrative. The severe hail, however, does not liberate Israel, for at the end of the narrative Pharaoh is as unresponsive as at the beginning (v. 35).

Yet, the episode is not futile. The peculiar accent of this encounter between the God of the Hebrews and the power of Egypt is on the twofold "know" that Moses announces in vv. 14-16 and 29.

1. The first of these affirmations is that Yahweh is incomparable, "There is no one like me in all the earth" (v. 14). The phrase "all the earth" is reiterated in v. 16. The plague is not aimed at the emancipation of the Hebrews, but at the manifestation of Yahweh in Yahweh's complete incomparability, for all of creation to see.

Such an affirmation invites reflection on Yahweh's incomparability. Of what does it consist? On the one hand, Yahweh is *incomparable in power.* The sending of hail of such destructive intensity is a show of force that, according to this narrative, no other hand (and certainly not any god of the Egyptian variety) could match. Yahweh is known not only to be "in all the earth" but, as will be asserted in v. 27, the earth belongs to Yahweh (see 19:5).

On the other hand, Yahweh's incomparability is known in Yahweh's *solidarity with the needy and the marginal.* In this text, this element of Yahweh's character is signaled in the nomenclature "God of the Hebrews." Unlike every other god in Egypt, or anywhere else for that matter, Yahweh's natural habitat is not in the royal palace or royal temple as patron and guarantor of the central establishment. Unlike all such gods, Yahweh's primary habitat is in the slave huts, and Yahweh's primary inclination is to attend to the cries and groans of the abused.

This aspect of Yahweh's incomparability is exceedingly difficult in a theological context of popular religion informed by a "theology of Zeus" and supported by a scholastic notion of God's omnipotence, omniscience, and omnipresence, in which "godness" is flatly equated with power. Clearly there is more to Yahweh's incomparability than raw power, the "more" being the solidarity that subverts and jeopardizes all established power in an advocacy of the powerless.

Israel's witness to the incomparability of Yahweh is delicate and subtle, holding together *power* and *solidarity,* majesty and mercy, so that each impinges upon and modifies the other without either being nullified. In much mistaken and careless trinitarian theology, this awesome dialectic is transposed so that "the Father" is an agent of power and "the Son" enacts solidarity with the weak. That, of course, will not do, for both elements belong everywhere to the wholeness and oneness of God. Both elements together give the Exodus story (and biblical faith more generally) their force and attractiveness. Thus the narrative of devastating hail shows forth not only *the enormous power of Yahweh which impresses Pharaoh,* but *power in the service of emancipation* for the Hebrews, those who have no power to emancipate themselves; and that angers and jeopardizes Pharaoh.

2. The second statement of "know" in this narrative asserts that Yahweh is the creator God who by right owns and administers all of creation: "The earth is the LORD's" (v. 29). This formula, which Pharaoh is supposed to learn and accept from the giving and removing of hail, is an exact parallel to the familiar doxology of Ps 24:1: "The earth is the LORD's and all that is in it,/ the world, and those who live in it."

The phrasing of Psalm 24 is commonly heard as a benign doxological statement to which we all assent in a kind of romantic gesture. The quote of the same claim in our text shows, however, that the formula is not at all benign and should not be heard simply as a vacuous celebration of the doxological loveliness of "nature." Rather, the statement, even in Psalm 24, is essentially confrontational and polemical. To assert that the earth belongs to Yahweh clearly implies as well that it does not belong to Pharaoh; and Pharaoh should not imagine that any part of the land is his to own or control.

In our own context, when oil spills, "smart bombs," and nuclear contamination are on the loose and at our door, the same phrasing is a polemical statement against the abuse of the earth by super powers who have the technical capacity to govern and to ruin the earth. Or closer, the formula draws a line of warning and relief against our compulsive consumerism. The fact that the earth belongs to Yahweh draws a line against our *greed*, for we are not able to possess the earth to satiation. The fact that the earth belongs to Yahweh draws a line against our *anxiety*, for we do not need to worry about our inability to possess (cf. Matt 6:25, 31). Thus the claim about the governance and control of the creator God is not simply a reassurance about the "character of the cosmos." That claim, in this narrative, is a direct warning against idolatrous political-economic aims.

Exodus 10:1-20, The Plague of Locusts

COMMENTARY

This eighth plague narrative contains many rhetorical elements that are by now familiar to us. Indeed, they are so familiar and predictable that we are likely to lose patience in listening and skip over the story too lightly. Liturgy (for which this material was designed) has reiterative, cumulative force. Just when we want to quit with the excessive familiarity of the material, we are addressed yet again. If, as listeners, we place ourselves in the position of the first subjects of the story—the Hebrew slaves—then, of course, the story is not old or boring or repetitious. This community of the marginated is ready to tell and hear the "old, old story" because it has become "the new, new song" of hope and possibility.

The intent of Yahweh, so Moses is to tell Pharaoh, is to keep the confrontation underway (v. 1). It is for that reason that Yahweh continues to harden Pharaoh's heart. The lines seem to suggest that Yahweh could stop this ongoing confrontation at any time. If Yahweh were to quit hardening the heart of Pharaoh (stop propping him up as an agent of resistance), Pharaoh would immediately collapse and the story would end with an uncontested triumph for Yahweh. The reason for continuing to keep this fragile, dependent character afloat is to give Yahweh more opportunities to enact signs and to commit powerful gestures of solidarity with the Hebrews.

Verse 2 moves outside the confrontation, however, to the production of a text. The story of "hardening" and "signs" is kept going so that the confrontation may be "retold" (ספר *sipēr*). It is clear that the purpose of the text that is being generated is not simply to report or to remember, but to instruct coming generations of "Hebrews," "children and

grandchildren," and induct them into the world of wonder, where God's signs override established, oppressive power.

Verse 2 clearly wants subsequent listening generations to participate in this "class reading" of political reality, for this is a story designed for the use and encouragement of the marginated against the establishment. The story tells us that the powerful can be duped, outflanked, overpowered, and made fools of. The playful quality of this statement means that the confrontation is not one of sheer power, but of a strategic mocking and trivialization of Pharaoh's power. Moreover, if Pharaoh stands as a paradigm for all established, oppressive power, then all subsequent generations of text-listeners are inducted into a mocking resentment toward such power. The ongoing story of hardening and sign is to generate a reading of one's own reality that enacts hope and possibility, precisely for those who seem defeated and hopeless.[56]

The process of downgrading Pharaoh, however, is only the penultimate intent of the narrative. Behind that is the hope that the children and grandchildren should come to know (as Pharaoh may come to know in 9:16, 29) that "I am Yahweh." It is, finally, acknowledgment of Yahweh that is the purpose of the narrative cycle. The purpose, astonishingly enough, is not to convert Pharaoh or to liberate the slaves, but to recruit the next generation of Israelites into this daring scenario of courage and confidence,

---

56. Walzer, *Exodus and Revolution*, 149, concludes his stunning exposition with a threefold extrapolation from the text:
"—wherever you live, it is probably Egypt";
"—there is a better place,"
"—the way to the land is through the wilderness."

passion and faith. In this case, the narrative is not aimed at Egypt at all, but is an in-house tale, for faith and against despair, resignation, and capitulation.

After this singularly reflective and candid statement, the narrative resumes with more familiar elements. Again, there are the elements of announcement (vv. 3-6), implementation (vv. 12-15), and Egyptian response (vv. 16-20), with an interlude for bargaining (vv. 7-11).

Yahweh's announcement to Pharaoh, through Moses and Aaron (vv. 3-6), again begins with a demand from the God of the Hebrews that the Hebrews be released (v. 3). Yahweh is uncompromising and unchanging in this resolve. The only new element in this statement is that Pharaoh's acceptance of the ultimatum from Yahweh would be to "humble" himself (ענה 'ānâ)—i.e., give up his haughty, exploitative distance from the Hebrews. The term for "humble" here is the counterpart to that translated "exalt" (סלל sālal) in 9:17. Pharaoh is thus urged to give up his pretensions, which fly in the face of Yahweh's governance.

The cost of Pharaoh's refusal to liberate the Hebrews this time is a locust swarm, which will come with massiveness, to devastate the land and to make the land genuinely uninhabitable. Like the anticipated hail in 9:18, the locust swarm will be unprecedented in severity. The reference to parents and grandparents in v. 6 is especially interesting in the light of "children and grandchildren" in v. 2. It may be that the reference to the generations in Egypt looks back because there is no Egyptian future, whereas the Israelite generations look forward to a people with a liberated future. Whereas the Egyptians have no future, the Hebrews have not been permitted by Egypt to have any past that is "recorded glory." Their whole life lies in front of them.

Moses' departure from Pharaoh is defiant and haughty (v. 6). As the plagues escalate, those closest to Pharaoh begin to catch on: Yahweh (and Moses) will not stop until Egypt is destroyed beyond recovery. Pharaoh's advisers counsel him to cut his losses (v. 7). After all, this pack of Hebrews is not a life-and-death matter to a great empire. The advisers now can see realistically and ask for an end to Pharaoh's obsession. Pixley observes that

Pharaoh's political base is cracking, a base without which he cannot long endure.[57]

Pharaoh gives his advisers no sign of his reaction to their counsel. He does, however, resume his conversation with Moses and Aaron. Such a resumption of talks leads one to expect concessions, as has just been urged. Indeed, Pharaoh's opening statement to Moses and Aaron sounds like acceptance of the advice of his colleagues: "Go, worship the LORD your God!" (v. 8). It is as though Pharaoh just cannot bring himself to follow such a prudent policy, for immediately after his initial permission, he counters it with a question. The question appears to be a negotiating gesture, but it is in fact a nullification of the permit just granted (v. 8). Pharaoh certainly knows, as his advisers know, that Moses will not go unless all go.

There must have been a groan and a sigh and a sinking feeling in the room among both the royal advisers and the Israelite negotiators, when Pharaoh spoke. It is as though Pharaoh is "fated" ("hardened") to resist the simple act that is, among other things, in his own best interest. Pharaoh is portrayed not only as a fool, but as a man destined to self-destruction in his incredible "march of folly." Barbara Tuchman, in her book *The March of Folly,* has used the phrase to describe the pursuit of self-destructive public policy, even when the policy is manifestly self-destructive and when there is visible counsel to the contrary.[58] Our narrator would say that what happens in such cases is the hardening that is inscrutably done by God. So it is with Pharaoh. He is made a fool of (v. 2) in quite a public, pitiful way.

Moses' answer to Pharaoh's bad faith question is hardly unexpected (v. 9). Everybody goes, or nobody goes! It is as though Moses now had assumed initiative in the talks. When a situation of abuse is too far deteriorated, it happens that the party of the victims comes to hold great moral power before which the establishment is largely delegitimated and, therefore, feeble. The narrator, in this case, knows that at a certain point the moral authority of the abused is so unavoidable that the shift of power and influence cannot be

57. Pixley, *On Exodus,* 57.
58. Barbara W. Tuchman, *The March of Folly: From Troy to Vietnam* (New York: Ballantine, 1984).

stopped. At this point, Moses seems to gain a profound edge in the debate with Pharaoh.

Moses' simple, non-negotiable statement evokes in Pharaoh an impossible condition, one he knows will be rejected: "Leave the children," presumably as hostages, to assure the slaves' return. Pharaoh concludes that Moses has "evil" in mind—that he intends to escape (v. 10). Pharaoh asserts that the initial request was for "man" to worship, and he will grant that, but he will not agree to a change in the terms (v. 11). Pharaoh manages a pious rescinding, as though he is the one who has been deceived. He holds to the letter of the request, but flagrantly violates its intention.

The mention of children (טף ṭap) here is especially poignant in the light of v. 2. Pharaoh wants to bargain precisely the children, so as to deny to the slave community its future into the next generation, just as they are at the threshold of receiving such a future. The children and grandchildren in time to come are to be told that Moses insisted that "our sons and daughters" are to go with us, and we will not go without them. Children in coming generations are to know that this beleaguered community, even in the face of this insane overlord, valued its children and refused to negotiate about them.

With negotiations failed, Moses does what Yahweh had promised (vv. 12-16). The invasion of locusts is as Yahweh had indicated. The narrator takes time and energy to give a full description of the invasion. Fretheim calls attention to the deliberate, frequent use of "all" in these verses, voicing a panoramic view of all creation.[59] (For a positive view of creation, see the frequent use of "all" in Ps 145:13-20.) Distorted social relations by the king who would not humble himself evokes the unleashing of chaos.

Pharaoh's response to the devastation of locusts is by now predictable (vv. 16-20). As in 9:27, Pharaoh confesses his sin, this time not only against Yahweh, but also against the Hebrews. The language of his request is intensified from 8:28 and 9:28. Now Pharaoh asks not only that Moses pray "for me to Yahweh," but that Moses should forgive him. This time Moses makes no interpretive comment; he promptly prays, and the locusts vanish.

It is perfectly credible, given what we have seen of recalcitrant tyrants in modern times, that Pharaoh should choose to be destroyed rather than to yield (v. 20). Even such choices, however, do not (according to the narrator) fall outside Yahweh's sovereign intention. The juxtaposition of *fate and choice* in Pharaoh's behavior is not unlike that of Saul in the narratives of 1 Samuel. He is, indeed, fated by Yahweh to fail, but he also chooses his own destruction in a series of choices. Paul Ricoeur has observed about the power of sin in the narrative of Genesis 3 that the human couple are both *victims* and *perpetrators* of their destruction.[60] So it is with Saul, and so it is with Pharaoh. And so it is with all of our hard-heartedness in which we choose what has been given us.

59. Fretheim, *Exodus*, 127.
60. Paul Ricoeur, *The Symbolism of Evil* (Boston: Beacon, 1967) 252-60. On 258, Ricoeur notices that humanity in the primal story of sin is both "author and servant" of ethical demands, but there is more to disobedience than willfulness.

REFLECTIONS

This by now familiar storyline offers three distinct elements, along with the enduring struggle for sovereignty and emancipation.

1. The narrative about the plagues should be understood to have an educational purpose and potential (vv. 1-2). The narrative is enacted and retold as text in order that coming generations of young people can be inducted into this very tendentious reading of historical reality. The purpose of this education is to teach a most controversial angle of vision that plunges the young into radical social awareness that is resentful of cynical power, and militantly hopeful for the marginated. Such education, rooted in the partisan character of God, is a dangerous education in revolutionary evangelicalism. It makes the insistent affirmation that God intrudes against every abusive power for the sake of a reordered world. It is this nurture in a kind of evangelical restlessness that generates missional courage and energy.

2. The notion of using children as potential bargaining chips in power politics, and Moses' refusal of such bargaining, is a telling innovation in this episode.

The affirmation of the value of children is so obvious as not to require comment. Yet, if one probes more deeply into economic and military matters, it is clear that agents of aggressive, ambitious power regularly treat children as bargaining chips in large games of leverage. Such "useful" purposes for children are evident economically, when children become pawns of the market and are devalued in terms of health care, housing, and education because they do not serve the market. Or, more blatantly, children are easy pawns of power militarily, both in sacrificing young boys (and lately young girls) to military escapades, or in the ruthless abuse of "civilians" in wars that serve only the dominant economy. Against such cynical abuse, the community of Moses stands as an enduring witness. No amount of raw, abusive power is worth holding one child as a pawn or a hostage.

Out of the tradition of Moses, Jesus continued to value the "little ones" who had no political significance or market value (see Matt 10:42; 18:6, 10, 14). In his hands, children become an example of how the world will be organized when God's intention is actualized.

3. As Fretheim has so well observed, the plagues concern the undoing of creation. As a case in point, the locusts are indeed the unleashing of chaos. The reduction of biblical faith to pastoral-psychological categories (so widespread among us) leads to the domestication of some of its great themes. The imagination of the church will be well served by a recovery of the large theme of creation and chaos. God's power to undo creation because human power has gone mad in its abuse permits two affirmations. On the one hand, the maintenance of created order is a fragile task. On the other hand, "He's got the whole world in his hand," little-bitty children and massive Egyptian power. Even the terror of chaos, in God's hand, is in the service of a new world of emancipation.

Exodus 10:21-29, The Plague of Darkness

COMMENTARY

In this episode of the ninth plague, no command for emancipation is voiced. The narrative moves immediately to the performance of the plague itself (vv. 21-23), as though God is eager to get on with the escalation. After the plague, there is a twofold confrontation in response (vv. 24-26, 27-29).

10:21-23. In the performance of the plague itself, no message is sent to Pharaoh, no demand, no condition, no threat (vv. 21-23). Moses is commanded by Yahweh to create a darkness; Yahweh's intention is that the darkness should be "felt," palpable, intense, ominous, and impinging (v. 21). In the conjuring of the darkness, what Moses causes is described by a second word, *dense* (אפלה *'apēlâ) darkness,* which is filled with

the dread of God. The same word is used in Amos 5:21, Zeph 1:15, and Joel 2:2 to characterize the coming of God's terrible wrath and judgment.

It is exceedingly difficult in our positivistic, technically controlled, "Enlightenment" environment to grasp the threat of such darkness. In that ancient "peopled" world (a world untamed, not unlike the dark) this darkness is one of unqualified terror. In that world, one is vulnerable, unprotected, and in severe danger in the dark. With the coming of the darkness, the modest, flimsy ordering of reality by Pharaoh is easily dismissed and set aside. Pharaoh and all his company are exposed to the raw, unnoticing, silent power of chaos, from which there is no refuge or escape. The rhetoric wants to bring the listener to a sense of profound threat, where all safeguards of an ordered world are withdrawn and dysfunctional. The empire is completely at risk.

However, "all the Israelites had light where they lived" (v. 23)! The contrast of darkness in Egypt and light in Israel is indeed peculiar. The Egyptians, the ones who bask in blessing and well-being (of the Sun-God?) are destined for the dread of chaos. The Israelites, the ones exposed and unprotected by present power arrangements, are in fact the ones who are given a cosmic safe conduct. This people, who walked in utter darkness, are now given light.

10:24-29. The first exchange between Pharaoh and Moses again gives the impression that Pharaoh is prepared to negotiate (vv. 24-26). Again, as in v. 8, Pharaoh seemingly authorizes the departure of the slaves and then, in the next breath, qualifies his permission in an unacceptable way (v. 24). Pharaoh is determined to have hostages, though this time he proposes keeping only herds and cattle, and not children. Here as in v. 10, the purpose of retaining children or herds and flocks as hostages is never stated. The most likely "evil" that Pharaoh fears (cf. v. 10) is a complete escape with no return. In proposing to keep cattle as hostages, the narrator has Pharaoh acknowledge that this demand is less intense than the previous one concerning children. That is, Pharaoh admits that this time he is not even considering the retention of the children. He lowers his asking price.

Moses' response is quick, unambiguous, and decisive (vv. 25-26). He identifies herds and flocks as material needed for an adequate sacrifice to Yahweh, so that to leave them behind would preclude a proper festival for Yahweh. Moses' language is uncompromising: "Not a hoof [פרסה *parsâ*] shall be left behind," not one small element of Israel can be left in the hands of Pharaoh.

The exodus must be total, comprehensive, uncompromised.

The confrontation between Pharaoh and Moses has moved from the possibility of negotiations (vv. 24-26) to hard hostility and stiff resistance (vv. 27-29). As the negotiations collapse, Pharaoh is once more smitten by Yahweh to refuse any accommodation to Israel at all. Pharaoh promptly retracts even the qualified permission of v. 24. Indeed, Moses' refusal to make a deal has enraged Pharaoh. Instead of sending the slaves away to freedom, Pharaoh sends Moses away from court. Negotiations are over, and Moses is banished from any further negotiations. The narrator has now escalated the issue to its full, most extreme form. Moses will not beg or grovel. In fact, he assents to Pharaoh's hard verdict. Moses agrees that any time for negotiation is past. Both parties now will go for broke, with no accommodation, no bargaining of cattle or children, no concession, and no compromise. In retrospect, perhaps, there never was any chance for a compromise. The narrator, however, has continued to seduce us into thinking a compromise might happen. Now it becomes clear that there was nothing over which Moses could reach an accommodation with Pharaoh. From the outset, given Yahweh's character, the drama concerns a rigorous "either/or," with no middle ground.

This escalation makes perfectly good literary, liturgical, and theological sense. The narrator creates a situation in which Yahweh's victory is spectacular. This escalation also makes perfectly good political sense. Aligned against each other is a liberation movement now confident of victory and a tired, decadent regime unable to see the depth or power of the resistance that still imagines that Moses voices a fringe threat. Resolving this conflict cannot be put off much longer. As Yahweh's patience is exhausted, so the imagination of the narrator must also be near exhaustion, as more ways are needed to sustain the drama.

REFLECTIONS

The struggle for sovereignty takes shape in this episode around the struggle of light and darkness. There is little doubt that the darkness here refers to the portentous threat of chaos, which is what the terrorizing presence of Israel evokes in the empire.

1. Israel is clear that Yahweh governs darkness as well as light, that God can make use of either to effect Yahweh's purpose. This central conviction in Israel works against our "Enlightened," bourgeois theology, which imagines that God is singularly and everywhere light and love. Not so the God of Moses, the God of the Bible. This God works "the darkness" as well as the light (see Isa 45:7).

At the core of this latter affirmation is the assertion "I am Yahweh." The incomparability of Yahweh is as one who presides over heaven and earth, over life and death, over chaos and creation. This same God dispatches both darkness and light, decrees "weal" (שלום *šālôm*) and "evil" (רע *rāʿ*). Or the same affirmation is put by Hannah in more directly sociopolitical category: "The LORD makes poor and makes rich; he brings low, he also exalts" (1 Sam. 2:7 NRSV).

Our narrative is simply one concrete evidence of the two-sided capacity of Yahweh.

This view of God, to be sure, is a scandal to a religious culture that wants to associate only the "good things" with God. But such a cleaned-up version of God is faithful neither to our experience nor to the witness of Scripture itself. In biblical modes, God has a rich interior life and is endlessly processing and adjudicating the available options.

2. While the text itself focuses on the threat to Egypt, the assurance of light to Israel is a positive counterpart in the text. The children and grandchildren who are to be told this narrative are to learn of God's protection from the witness of God's own people. We have no better affirmation of this protective side of God than the statement of trust in Psalm 91.

The psalm, like Israel's faith in general, is content with doxological assurance. No explanation is given. No effort is used on those who are stricken with the darkness. This affirmation grows out of the experience-based confidence of the faithful. Thus the "sign" of darkness and light, in our narrative, is no isolated wonder. This narrative is well situated in the Psalmic tradition of Israel, which knows that God's darkness is ominous, but that light is given to protect the faithful.

This connection between light and trust in God, and darkness and abuse of God's intention is incontrovertible for Israel. Pharaoh, of course, cannot understand this faith. In his arrogant power, Pharaoh seeks to break the connection between obedience and light, but he cannot have his way. Interpreters of this narrative are wise to ponder both the savage release of chaos upon God's abusers and the odd, protective exception made for those who belong to God. Those who have learned to rely on God find the darkness dispelled.

3. Quite incidentally, without anything being made of it, v. 23 asserts that in the darkness, the Egyptians were immobilized "for three days." They could not see enough to move. It is likely that "three days" is a quite incidental time reference and is not intended as a precise measure. It may be worth noting that the same measure of time is used in the story of Jesus' death. Indeed, the whole earth is then like Egypt, for three days in the grip of death that prevented any freedom of action (cf. Matt 27:45-54). In that narrative, Easter is the dawn of God's light, which gives again the possibility of liberated life. The phrase "three days" is not used here with any special intentionality, nor does this text explicitly relate to the Easter narrative. Rather, in this context, it is evident that the Easter drama is not an isolated story. In Israel's narrative imagination, there were other times when chaos was unleashed, when the power of God's light broke in, making new life possible.

Exodus 11:1-10, Warning of the Final Plague

COMMENTARY

This final plague narrative, the most intensive and extreme action by Yahweh against Pharaoh, is brief. The narrative in chapter 11 is not in fact a narrative about the plague itself, but only a statement of Yahweh's intention and resolve. Thus, unlike any of the other plague episodes, here the announcement is separated from the actual implementation, which does not take place until 12:29-36.

This brief narrative is divided into three parts, a conversation between Yahweh and Moses (vv. 1-3), a statement of Moses to Pharaoh, including a comment by the narrator (vv. 4-8), and a second address of Yahweh to Moses (v. 9). The chapter concludes with a brief narrative statement (v. 10).

11:1-3. Yahweh's address to Moses lets Moses see the larger picture of Yahweh's strategy and intent (vv. 1-2). In 10:1-2, Yahweh had told Moses why this dramatic confrontation with Pharaoh continued for so long, scene after scene, crisis after crisis. Now Moses learns that Yahweh intends to conclude the drama. Presumably the encounter has gone on long enough to establish Israel's knowledge of Yahweh (cf. 10:2). Since the drama has continued only because Yahweh has persistently kept Pharaoh in the game by "hardening" him, Yahweh need only stop that action, and Pharaoh will cease to play his defiant role.

The narrative concedes that Pharaoh's position cannot be defended or justified rationally, because it is sustained only irrationally. Thus Yahweh informs Moses that this is the last plague, the most severe, and the one to bring sure results. Indeed, this plague will be so severe that not only will Pharaoh "send" (שׁלח *šālaḥ*) Israel away, but Pharaoh will "forcibly drive" them out. The verb שׁרשׁ (*gāraš*) is stated with an infinitive absolute, indicating that Pharaoh will not only lose his reluctance about the exodus, but will be an adamant advocate of the departure. Pharaoh will finally come around to the view his advisers expressed in 10:7. The departure of Israel from bondage is the price of saving the throne of Egypt.

The exodus turns out to be a high price for Pharaoh. In vv. 2-3*a*, Yahweh instructs Moses that the Israelites are to "ask" from the Egyptians silver and gold. That is, they are not merely to escape, but are to leave with economic support granted by the Egyptians. This anticipation echoes Exod 3:21-22, where the escaping Israelites are authorized by Yahweh to take Egyptian jewelry and clothing when they leave.

David Daube has supplied the most suggestive interpretation of this authorization from Yahweh.[61] Daube observes that the language of 3:31, and the entire idea of 3:21-22 and 11:2-3*a*, is informed by the Mosaic "year of release" in Deut 15:1-11. In that most radical of all Mosaic laws, the Hebrew slave who is being freed from bondage is not only set free, but is "furnished liberally" with economic wherewithal to rejoin the economy in a fully functioning manner. This law is of interest to us because it voices a remarkably humane notion of debt bondage. On the one hand, it affirms that liberated slaves are to be treated with dignity and respect, they are to be measured in the terms that count most: economic terms. On the other hand, the law of Moses assumes that a responsible slaveholder will act fairly, honestly, and generously in respecting those rights. The slave, upon release, is to compensate from the master's goods, sufficient to resume a full and viable life.

Daube has seen that this law lies behind and informs the narratives of 3:20-21 and 11:2-3*a*. Bringing the exodus transaction into the horizon of this law, the tradition has decisively redefined the drama of the exodus. No longer is this a desperate, frantic, forced escape. For an instant, the instant of this interpretive moment, the exodus is pictured as an ordered, proper, regulated "letting go." The two main points of the law are implied: Israel has certain entitlements that will not be denied, and Pharaoh will act like a proper and responsible slave master and will give of his

---

61. David Daube, *The Exodus Pattern in the Bible* (London: Faber and Faber, 1963) 55-61.

wealth for the sake of the renewed, liberated life of the slave community.

This presentation, in its own context, is palpably a fiction. At best, we may imagine that the slaves seized what they wanted on the run and the Egyptians conceded their right to nothing. But such "realism" contradicts the intentional, magisterial construal of these verses. Thus, according to these verses (which contradict the flow of the main narrative), there is no need to seize goods or to hurry, because the slaves are entitled to their well-equipped departure, guaranteed by torah provision. (The same construal is suggested for the exilic indenture in Babylon; cf. Isa 40:2.)

Moreover, the narrative adds that the slave community was granted (by Yahweh) "favor" in Egyptian eyes—i.e., it was well regarded according to legal requirements. Pharaoh's government also participated (for this one instant) in the redefinition of the Exodus crisis as an ordered economic transaction. The comment in v. 3*b* concerning Moses appears to be something of an afterthought to v. 3*a*. As Israel is granted favor, so Moses is respected. Perhaps it is better to reverse the matter: Moses is greatly feared by the Egyptians; *therefore,* the Israelites gain favor. Either way, the narrative makes clear that the authority of Moses (and of Yahweh) is now visible and powerful enough that Pharaoh's government is willing to play the role required by the law of the "year of release"— that of benign, benevolent creditor who respects and rehabilitates the debtor, in spite of Pharaoh's recalcitrance. By the power of Yahweh, Moses has wrought this redefinition of the relationship.

11:4-8. The second part of the narrative, Moses' speech to Pharaoh, fully rejects the benign portrayal of vv. 2-3. In this speech, Israel is not easily granted any rights or "favor." Pharaoh is not credited with any gracious behavior, and Moses does not sound like a greatly respected leader. Thus vv. 4-8, in contradiction to vv. 2-3, rejects any redefinition of the departure according to the law of the year of release and portrays the Exodus as a raw contest of power, with no quarter asked and none given. The fact that vv. 2-3 and 4-8 stand side by side suggests that the Israelite tradition had a variety of narrative-liturgical

options in construing and constructing its past, as does every remembering community. Israel took no great pains to harmonize all of these options, but simply included them. The main tendency is to portray an intensely adversarial relation (as in vv. 4-8), but it is not the only option (as evidenced in vv. 2-3*a*).

Moses' speech to Pharaoh is filled with ominous threat: "At midnight," in the middle of the darkness shaped and governed by Yahweh; "at midnight," when the rule of chaos is most formidable and Pharaoh is most vulnerable; "at midnight," when the covering deception of royal ideology in the daylight ceases to function in a protective way—then will come God's intrusion. God's most ominous, awesome assault against the empire will be hidden; it will be beyond both description and resistance. Pharaoh will be unable to counter the onslaught of Yahweh.

It will also be hidden from Israel and from Israel's storytellers. They will not know what happened or how it happened. They will be given no clues about how to describe the terrible onslaught, for who dares describe how the "rulers of this age" are made weak and finally destroyed! Yahweh's action, nonetheless, is as sure and powerful as it is hidden. Israel is reduced to elusive language.

In Yahweh's speech in the mouth of Moses, Yahweh uses the strong first-person pronoun "I" (אני *ǎnî*). But the "I" of Yahweh with the predicate "go out" is followed only by a stative verb, "shall die." It is not said, "I will kill." Thus the narrative itself is cautious and restrained in telling anything specific. Moreover, for this long and comprehensive threat, the verb is used only once. It is enough for the one verb to govern all of the sentence. The construction of the sentence is enormously elusive, and the relation between the parts of the sentence is enigmatic: "I go out/firstborn die." That is all; we (and Pharaoh) are told nothing more.

Why is such brutal power arrayed against the firstborn? Why is there such a savage departure from the ordered image of vv. 2-3? The answer is suggested already in 4:22. Israel is Yahweh's firstborn. Israel is Yahweh's treasured son and precious heir and the chance for Yahweh's own future in the world. Pharaoh has brought Yahweh's own treasured heir under threat. If vv. 2-3 are informed by the law of Deut 15:1-11, perhaps this image is informed by the law of Deut 21:15-17. The firstborn has certain rights that may not be denied or compromised. The passion of Yahweh in these verses, however, is more than the enforcement of a legal requirement. It is more like the passion of a mother bear in defense of a cub (see Hos 13:8). The mother bear is ferocious and unreasoned in its attack on anything or anyone that threatens the cub. So Yahweh reacts irrationally and beyond measure for Israel. The empire must pay at every level for its refusal to honor this vulnerable heir.

The response to the slaughter of the firstborn in Egypt (slaughter of the innocents? [cf. 1:16-22]) is as might be expected (v. 6). There will be "a cry" (צעקה $s\check{e}^{\,c}\bar{a}q\hat{a}$) like there has never been nor ever will be. The tradition has preferred superlatives as it moves toward this dénouement of the struggle of Yahweh and Pharaoh. Thus both the hail (9:18) and the locusts (10:6) are said to be unparalleled in any part of the empire. The superlative used to describe the cry, however, is more extreme than that for hail or locust, because it reaches into the future: "will ever be again."

This unprecedented cry is a complete and intentional counterpart to the cry of Israel, reported in 2:23-24 and 3:7. Egypt's cry, however, is more intense, more severe, and more pain-filled than even the cry of Israel. Thus the liturgic tradition works an inversion, so that the people who impose the cry upon Israel are now the ones who cry. The one who continues to exalt himself (9:17) and refuses to humble himself (10:3) now has ended in a terrible humiliation. God will not be mocked; therefore, the empire has arrived at its terrible undoing.

The narrative does not go the full extent to complete the syllogism to say that the humiliated are now exalted (cf. Phil 2:9). It is, however, on its way to such an affirmation in v. 7. The terrible invasion by Yahweh at midnight is everywhere, except—! Yahweh does make a distinction! Yahweh does sort out and treat people differently. Even in the pitch dark of midnight, Yahweh can identify Yahweh's own firstborn, perhaps like a mother finding her child in the dark of the night, by smell, by touch, by instinct too deep to identify. Yahweh makes a distinction in the

night, as Yahweh has been doing in the most recent plagues (cf. 8:23; 9:7, 26; 10:24). Israel sleeps through the deathwatch, sleeps so peacefully that not even its dogs are disturbed. Its livestock are valued and protected as well (see 9:7), and now its dogs are as well off as its cows. The contrast with Egypt could not be more complete or dramatic.

Moses goes on to assert that when this stark contrast of death and life is worked against Egypt, Egyptian officials will finally order Israel to leave (v. 8). The Egyptians will bow down to Moses, at long last recognizing his vast authority (cf. v. 3). They will use an imperative form of the Exodus word for "leave" (צא $s\bar{e}$). The officials will finally enact the wisdom they had already reached in 10:7. Perhaps our verse suggests that they will finally overrule or persuade Pharaoh. In any case, they will gladly send Israel away, because the cost of keeping them has become too great. Then, says Moses, "I will go out" (אצא $\,\bar{e}s\bar{e}$)! Moses' tone is not one of defeat. He has not been chased out. Rather, he envisions a triumphal, dignified exit, with the awareness of having prevailed over Egypt.

Moses' speech concludes. And then he goes out (יצא $y\bar{a}s\bar{a}$) "in hot anger"; he enacts his own exodus from Pharaoh. The narrator shrewdly uses the same verb for his exit. It is now clear that initiative in this conversation has passed from Pharaoh to Moses. In this account, Pharaoh and his officials listen in complete silence. They no longer have a voice in the terms of separation. It is no longer the case that Moses is "driven" from their presence, as in 10:12. Now Moses decides when to come and go. Moses "goes out" whenever he will, and Pharaoh is helpless and mute before him.

11:9-10. After this remarkable and defiant announcement by Moses to the court of Egypt, Yahweh is permitted one more reprise. The verses once again juxtapose "signs" and "hardening." Gestures of sovereignty are matched by intensified hardening. Yahweh had announced in v. 1 that this was to be the final plague, the one to resolve everything. But we do not yet know. In v. 9, Yahweh pauses, almost against the promise of v. 1. Yahweh (or the narrator) is not yet ready to have the drama collapse into triumph and liberation. Moses is adamant, but Pharaoh will not yield. There are new threats, but no new yielding. Moses may go out from the presence of the court in defiance, but the larger "going out" of the Hebrews remains still in prospect. Could it be that Yahweh has miscalculated or has second thoughts? Yahweh allows that Pharaoh, even now, will not listen. But if this action against the firstborn will not persuade Pharaoh, it is difficult to imagine anything that will affect the Egyptian king. We are left to wait with oppressed Israel—at least until midnight.

REFLECTIONS

1. The ordered release of slaves (vv. 2-3), informed by the legal provision of Deut 15:1-11, suggests that power relations between slave and master, between power and powerlessness, between center and margin, are here radically revisioned. In the midst of a conventional relation of slave and master, Israel's narrative tradition introduces the very different notion of covenantal mutuality. In this relation, the slave has *rights* in relation to the material substance of the master, and the master has corresponding *obligations* to the slave. The conventional relation of indifference and disconnectedness is undermined and redefined.

This reconstrual of social relations is taken up in the NT in the Pauline formulation of freedom in Gal 3:28 and in the reflections on power relations in the Epistle to Philemon. Further, this undermining of conventional power relations and redefinition in terms of mutuality in rights and obligations is suggestive for power relations in our contemporary world. The notion of creditor and debtor nations, the empowerment of emerging states that move beyond patterns of dependency, and the notion of mutuality in interpersonal relations are all touched by a rearticulation of rights and obligations. If even Pharaoh can, for a moment, be regarded as a responsible slave owner who liberates with dignity, then any contemporary relation based on power is subject to a very different construal.

2. The inversion of Israel and Egypt, in terms of who cries now and those who cried earlier, suggests something like an eschatological proviso on any set pattern of power relations. At the beginning of the Exodus story, one might have thought Egypt would abuse forever, and Israel could cry in agony to perpetuity, but now in this narrative, Egypt becomes the voice of the most extreme cry. The narrative affirms that drastic revision does indeed take place in power relations where no revision seemed possible. They change because in the end, the God of the Hebrews will not stay unengaged where the Hebrews are oppressed.

In an inchoate form, this belated new voice of cry anticipates the ominous words of Jesus: " 'Blessed are you who weep now,/ for you will laugh . . . / Woe to you who are laughing now,/ for you will mourn and weep' " (Luke 6:21, 25 NRSV).

Those who weep now will not weep forever, but will eventually laugh. And those who laugh now in their well-being will not be so joyous forever, for a time for crying will come (cf. Eccl 3:4). There is more to one's social situation than is visible in the daylight. There are nights and midnights, filled with both heavy loses and astonishing gifts.

3. Yahweh's brutal passion for the firstborn may astonish or even offend us. Yahweh is the partisan advocate who is prepared to go to any extreme in defense of this vulnerable child. That commitment is stated in 4:22 and is now to be enacted in a grossly irrational way against Pharaoh, who has sought to damage the firstborn.

This theme does not need to be turned in a christological direction, but it can be. Thus the role of Israel as firstborn in the NT lives in tension with Jesus as "the beloved Son." In christological usage, the irrational passion for the beloved Son who is heir greatly intensifies the risky offer of the Son for the sake of the world. Thus God's passion for the firstborn son in the exodus narrative plays against the offer of the Son in christological images. In Matt 21:33-41, the son who is heir (and therefore presumably the firstborn) is killed by the tenants. That much sounds like a generous risk on the part of the landlord. The hard saying at the end of the parable (vv. 41, 43-44, the part usually skipped in the reading of the church), suggests that the passion for the firstborn in our text persists in the NT metaphor. Contrary to much sweet, romantic Christian faith, this lord and father does not look lightly upon the killing of the son and heir. Just as Yahweh wars against Pharaoh, who has violated the beloved son and heir, so also the landlord in the Gospel story will kill and destroy those who hurt the Son. The metaphor leads to a hard saying for Pharaoh and the Egyptian system, and it becomes no less hard and ruthless in NT use.

EXODUS 12:1–15:21, THE LORD WILL REIGN

OVERVIEW

This material completes the liberation narrative of 1:1–15:21. The section is made up of quite diverse elements. In chapters 12–13, the predominant materials concern specific regulations for cultic remembrance and reenactment of the exodus from bondage, situated in the festivals of Passover and Unleavened Bread. In the midst of the cultic regulations, there are brief notices that form a conclusion to the events left unfinished in chapter 11—the implementation of the final "plague." The position of chapters 12–13 in the larger narrative suggests that the historical event fades off into or has been cast primarily in, through, and for liturgical reenactment. It is, therefore, impossible to sort out what in the narrative is reportage (in a modern fashion) and what is cultic rubric. This means that remembering and celebrating in Israel are acts that have no great interest in the kind of question of historical origin that readily occupies us. Rather, the central concern is that the ancient victory and liberation should be present now and for the coming generations as a way of redefining and reshaping present social reality.

In chapter 14, we have the only specific narrative of the actual crossing of the "sea." The force of reiterated phrases and the different conversations provided in the text suggest that this most dramatic narrative also is designed to serve cultic reiteration and replication. George Coats has argued persuasively that the crossing of the sea is a late entry into the narrative that had no necessary connection to the deliverance from Egypt.[62] Thus

the sea motif tilts the narrative of liberation toward cosmic-mythic themes that are concerned with the struggle for created order against the surging threat of chaos, which is here embodied in Pharaoh.[63] By this interpretive development, the "historical liberation" is shown to be part of the larger enterprise of Yahweh in governing the unruly waters of chaos.[64] Such a theme in this prose narrative prepares the way for the magisterial poetry of 15:1-21.

Exodus 15:1-21 provides a great lyrical conclusion to the recital of liberation. It consists in two poems, connected by the prose remarks of v. 19. These poems are commonly thought to be among the most ancient and most radical in the OT.[65] The earlier poem is most likely the brief lyric of Miriam and the other women (vv. 20-21), providing a poignant counterpart to the role of the women in chaps. 1–2 in initiating the story of liberation through the nurture and protection of the baby Moses. Its doxological intent is to

63. See Frank Moore Cross, *Canaanite Myth and Hebrew Epic: Essays in the History of the Religion of Israel* (Cambridge, Mass.: Harvard University Press, 1973) 112-44; and Patrick D. Miller, Jr., *The Divine Warrior in Early Israel* (Cambridge: Harvard University Press, 1973).

64. For cautious or even negative judgments about the liberation motif in the exodus narrative, see Fretheim, *Exodus*, 18-20; Levenson, "Exodus and Liberation," 134-74; and Lyle Eslinger, "Freedom or Knowledge? Perspective and Purpose in the Exodus Narrative (Exodus 1–15)," *JSOT* 52 (1991) 43-60; and in response, Walter Brueggemann, "Pharaoh as Vassal: A Study of a Political Metaphor," forthcoming in *CBQ.*

65. See David Noel Freedman, "Divine Names and Titles in Early Hebrew Poetry," *Magnalia Dei: The Mighty Acts of God; Essays on the Bible and Archaeology in Memory of G. Ernest Wright*, eds. Frank Moore Cross et al. (Garden City, N.Y.: Doubleday, 1976) 55-107; and Bernhard W. Anderson, "The Song of Miriam Poetically and Theologically Considered," in *Directions in Biblical Hebrew Poetry*, ed. by Elaine R. Follis, JSOTSup 40 (Sheffield: Sheffield Academic, 1987) 285-96.

62. George W. Coats, "The Traditio-Historical Character of the Red Sea Motif," *VT* 17 (1967) 253-65.

celebrate Yahweh's victory over the forces of injustice and chaos.

The second poem (15:1-18) lays down the primary themes that govern the entire Moses tradition. Indeed, the poem may lie behind and generate the longer narrative that now constitutes chaps. 1–15. The poem has as its theme the struggle with Pharaoh, leading to the triumph and glorious enthronement of Yahweh (v. 18). Whereas chaps. 5–11 narrate the *struggle* with Pharaoh, 12–15 narrate the complete *triumph* of Yahweh and the massive defeat of Pharaoh. Whereas the outcome is far from clear in the plague cycle, in these chapters the outcome is sure and unambiguous. It is a triumph and a defeat that this community continued to reenact and reiterate, both as a practice of hope and as an act of powerful, subversive social criticism. Israel is relentless in its conviction of the outcome and restless in the meantime about the pretensions of the chaotic powers.

Exodus 12:1-28, The Passover Instituted

COMMENTARY

These verses interrupt the flow of the plague narrative, continued in vv. 29-39, in order to introduce a regularized liturgical practice that commemorates and reenacts the saving events of the exodus. In these verses we witness the transformation of a specific, concrete, remembered event into a liturgical convention that is available for replication. Indeed, as the text stands, the *liturgical festival* precedes the *saving event*. Thus the saving event itself is, in its very first casting, a liturgical event. The particularity of biblical memory is regularly converted into routine practice. That conversion is never easy or straightforward, as it is by no means obvious how that shift takes place. It is nonetheless a required shift in a community of faith that stakes its identity on once-for-all events that must be kept present-tense in each new generation and in each new circumstance. In the Christian tradition, the obvious parallel is the way in which the "Last Supper" has been converted into the "eucharist," with a host of interpretive problems and possibilities attached to it.

The text is divided into command (vv. 1-27) and obedience (v. 28). It is immediately clear that the relation between the two is disproportionate. It is assumed in the voicing of the command that there will be obedience, so that the second part of the equation does not need much attention.

The first extended command of Yahweh divides into two parts: a description of concrete procedures for the festival (vv. 1-10) and an interpretive comment on the meaning of the procedures (vv. 11-13). Two practices converge: putting of blood on the doorposts and the eating of unleavened bread. Those two practices together are treated now as part of a single event.

12:1-10. It is thought by many scholars that the provision for the protection by the blood of the lamb may reflect a more ancient rite, taken over by the Israelites, that in its origin had nothing to do with the exodus. While that may be so, the text itself exhibits no interest in such pre-Exodus antecedents, nor in offering explanations for what is required in the observance. This text is simply a manual for what must have been a consensus of right practice. The instructions are concerned for a certain kind of *blood* and a certain kind of *food*. For both food and blood, the festival revolves around the importance of the lamb, its supply, its distribution, and its use. For the celebration, each family unit must have a lamb. But since sheep are a treasured commodity in this pastoral economy, the requirement may be financially excessive for a family, so that a lamb might be more generally shared. The important matter is that each family unit, therefore each member of the community, must have access to a lamb.

12:11-13. In the interpretive comment of vv. 11-13, the twofold accent on food and blood is again maintained. Verse 11 suggests the dramatic intention of the eating. Those who share in this festal meal must be ready to go, ready to travel, ready to depart from the empire. Being ready to go requires that traveling clothes be worn, that shoes be on, and that staff be in hand. The entire drama must be done in a hurry in order to reenact the memory that leaving Egypt is a dangerous, anxiety-ridden business.

Verses 12-13 connect the blood, for the first time, with the exodus. The festival of Passover (פסח *pesaḥ*) marks the time when Yahweh "passes over" (עבר *'ābar*) the community of Israel. The two Hebrew terms for "Passover" (*pesaḥ*) and "pass over" (*'ābar*) are not the same, and it is only in our English translation that the terms appear to be equivalent. Nonetheless, the interpretive comment in vv. 11-13 refers to 11:4-7 when Yahweh shall "go out" (יצא *yāṣā'*) through the land as a "destroyer." In all the previous places where Yahweh makes a distinction (8:23; 9:6, 26; 10:23), Yahweh has known where the special people are and has needed no marking signal. Thus in the primal narrative, the sign of blood that is pivotal for the festival is for Yahweh superfluous. Nonetheless, the blood of the lamb has now become a sign, which quite concretely, publicly, and explicitly marks those who are to be exempt from destruction. Moreover, it is a sign that makes visible the promise of God and assures the protection of Israel.

Verse 12 adds a new element to the familiar formula of destruction. The assault of Yahweh against Egypt for the first time now includes "Egyptian gods." Now the narrative is understood as theologically defined. What finally needs to be overcome is not only the rulers and officials, but also the gods of the empire who sanction oppression and legitimate abusive policy. It may be that this inclusion of the gods only refocuses the festival to make it more "religious." Or it may be that the interpreters are now more discerning about the power of ideology and have come to see that political abuse depends on theological warrants.

12:14-20. The second element of command from Yahweh concerns the festival of unleavened bread (as distinct from Passover). The term for "festival" (חג *ḥag*) is now used; the same word was used for "worship" in 5:1 and 10:9. Three items are reiterated for this festival. First, it is important to have unleavened bread. Second, this special diet shall be followed in all generations. Third, anybody who violates this practice and uses leavened bread shall be "cut off" (i.e., excommunicated).

We are not told in the command why this practice is so important and demanding, but in the reflective comment of v. 11 we find out why. The reason for "unleaven" is that the slaves left in a hurry and could not wait around until the yeast worked and the bread rose. Anybody who has leavened bread is not "hurrying"—i.e., is not participating in the urgency and anxiety of the memory. Such a casualness may suggest being at ease in Egypt, where faithful Israel must never be at ease.

12:21-27. The third element of the celebration focuses on the blood and the Passover (vv. 21-27). The blood functions as a sign for the fundamental distinction God makes between Israel and Egypt, thus marking out Israel's special identity. This festival provides for the special status of Israel under the rule of God.

12:28. The narrative ends with the terse, crucial note "Israel obeyed" (v. 28). Israel is prepared to sustain its special identity, and to accept its odd role in the governance of Yahweh.

REFLECTIONS

These verses provide opportunity to reflect on the cruciality of worship for the maintenance of the identity of a historical community and on the importance of doing worship rightly. The text also suggests the wisdom of avoiding excessive explanation for what is done in worship. Much Christian worship is either excessively doctrinal and rational or excessively moralistic and didactic. In either case, it is excessively self-conscious. Worship entails a willing suspension of disbelief, a reentering of a definitional memory, and a readiness to submit to the memory as identity-bestowing for both parents and children. This community, in every time and place, is prepared to reengage this primitive, unreflective act.

1. Such worship requires pre-rational activity that is simply done without explanation or even understanding. Such worship violates our sophisticated rationality whereby we keep control of what we do and screen out less sophisticated gestures. Childs observes that the rites are "uninterpreted."[66] Serious worship requires violating our sophisticated rationality in order to participate alongside our more credulous ancestors.

In these particular provisions, such activity includes eating in a hurry (perhaps standing up), anxious, at risk, ready to leave. Such activity includes blood on a door post to mark specialness, a sense of being wondrously protected, valued, and safe. Both eating in a hurry and being marked for safety are acts in which children can engage. It is no wonder that it is a child who asks, "What do you mean by this observance?" (v. 26).

2. Such pre-rational activity, however, must be accompanied by a storied account that persists through all seasons of fads and criticism. If there is not a storied account that is understood, cherished, and verbalized, then the pre-rational activity may take on magical meanings, as though in and of itself the act has some intrinsic merit. This activity is not generalized religious practice, but belongs to a known time, place, and people.

The storied meaning is twofold. First, the blood marking enacts a large sense of protectedness from the midnight violence that is loosed in the empire. This is an act that lets us confess to each other that we are abidingly cared for in a world that is under profound threat. Second, eating the food asserts that we are able to depart Egypt. If Egypt and Pharaoh are to be understood as references to any and every agent of oppression and abuse (including one's own socioeconomic system), then this festival evokes an important restlessness. Indeed, when the community of faith no longer has this "festival of urgent departure," it runs the risk of being excessively and in unseemly ways at home in the empire. In such a posture, there will never be a departure; therefore, every celebration is an act of bad faith.

Such interpretive commentary is important to prevent these festival acts from degenerating into superstition. Conversely, it will not do simply to have the interpretation without the acts themselves, for then the memory becomes excessively cognitive and cerebral, and we forget that it is in our bellies that we practice the hurried departure and on our door posts that we mark our safety. There must be no cerebral shortcuts away from actual practice, for we hold the precious memories in our bodies, not in our heads. It was our bodies that were oppressed, and it was our bodies that cried out and were liberated.

3. This festival is clearly Jewish. No doubt Christians need Jews to help us concretely engage these practices, but the Christian community needs to move beyond curiosity about Jewish practices in order to claim these festivals as our own. This, of course, does not mean to usurp or preempt them from Jews, but to see that as the OT is Christian Scripture even while it is thoroughly Jewish, so this festival is a part of our Christian memory and identity. Christians, like Jews, are *children of these marked door posts,* marked for safety in the midnight of chaos and crying. Christians, like Jews, are *children of this hurried bread,* postured to depart the empire, destined for freedom outside the norms and requirements of the empire. Such an embrace will not only draw us into closer solidarity with practicing Judaism, but also let us see the peculiar shapes of humanness given us in our narrative theological tradition.

4. The aim of celebrating these marked door posts and hurried bread is that the children may be recruited into this odd angle of vision. Thus the festival is intended to evoke a probing question from the children. The children will not know, unless they wonder and unless they are told, that this community holds an odd identity in the

66. Childs, *The Book of Exodus*, 204.

world—odd over against established power, odd because of the inscrutable protective attentiveness of Yahweh. The practitioners of these festivals and the tellers of these tales are indeed sojourners dreaming of a better land, filled with God's abundance. The engaged memory of pain evokes hope for a transformed world. The children of this community cannot afford to be protected from either the pain or the hope.

Exodus 12:29-39, Death of the Firstborn

COMMENTARY

These verses resume the narrative of 11:8. The passage includes the conventional plague materials of the assault itself (vv. 29) and the Egyptian response (vv. 30-36), plus an initial glimpse into the beginning of the journey from Egypt (vv. 37-39).

12:29. The description of the assault itself is brief (v. 29). It is exactly as Moses had announced in 11:5. At midnight, in the darkness, which Pharaoh cannot control, Yahweh strikes. The term *firstborn* occurs four times and pounds at the listener. The first use is generic and comprehensive. The other three uses are sub-sets of the first: firstborn of Pharaoh (i.e., the heir apparent), firstborn of the cattle, firstborn of all things Egyptian. Nothing in Egypt is protected from the harsh midnight incursion of Yahweh. Of course, the narrative does not tell what happened in the darkness or how it happened. Nobody saw anything!

12:30-36. The response of Egypt is exactly as was anticipated in 11:6, and is what might be expected in such a crisis. There was a great cry from every part of Egypt. The desperate cry of loss and protest began on the lips of Israel (2:23-24; 3:7), and it has now been transferred to the pathos-filled mouths of Egypt. The empire is now saturated with the reality of death; as had been anticipated in 11:5, Pharaoh cannot maintain the life of the empire against the God who gives both life and death. The extreme, brutal loss brings Pharaoh to his first wise decision. He finally gives to Yahweh and Moses all they have been asking. Yahweh had promised in 11:1 that this would be the end of the struggle, and so it is. Pharaoh completely capitulates to the God of Israel.

Pharaoh summons Moses and Aaron "at night," at the time when he is in least control and most subject to the powers of chaos (v. 31). He summons Moses and Aaron with an urgent imperative, so urgent that it cannot wait until morning. The four imperatives he speaks are the ones Pharaoh has most resisted, which he now desperately wants to utter: "arise" (קומו *qûmû*), "go out" (צאו *ṣě'û*), "go" (לכו *lěkû*), "serve" (עבדו *'ibdû*). The words are finally on Pharaoh's lips, but the command has been instigated by Yahweh. They are words of release, departure, permission, and complete capitulation. Here the word *serve* is not "worship" (חג *hag*), but means to accept one as master, to enter a new servitude. Pharaoh is conceding that the Hebrew slaves are no longer in his servitude, but now owe allegiance to a different master. (See the point expressed in Lev 25:42, with a double use of *serve* [עבד *'ābad*].) In v. 32, two more imperatives are sounded by Pharaoh, "take" (קהו *qěhû*) and "go" (*lěkû*).

Finally, Pharaoh utters a seventh imperative, this one most astonishing: "Bless me also!" In this utterance, the role reversal of Israel and Egypt is complete. According to all appearances, it was Pharaoh who carried the power of blessing, the capacity to bestow life and well-being. The blessing, however, is not where it appears to be, but is carried by this band of slaves who seem to possess nothing. This theme of reassigned blessing has been anticipated in the initial encounter between Jacob and another pharaoh (Gen 47:7-12). The old man was ushered into the presence of the great king, who ostensibly possessed everything. Then, however, we are told, "Jacob blessed Pharaoh" (Gen 47:7, 10). Pharaoh needs what Israel has: the gift of life.

The departure scene shows the Egyptians acting desperately and frantically, with the Israelites hurriedly but pointedly taking whatever they are able to carry. The Egyptians' desperation is due to their recognition that the retention of Israel in its midst will only guarantee death (cf. 10:7). The verb for "urged" (חזק *ḥāzaq*) is regularly used against the Egyptians as "harden." Now the Egyptians are subject to the same verb, but to very different effect. Whereas "harden" was to prevent the departure of Israel, here "urge" is to encourage and insist on that same departure. This use of the term bespeaks not power, but a needy supplication to be rid of Israel. The notation in vv. 35-36 has been anticipated in 3:21-22 and 11:2. The statement of v. 36, echoing 11:3, is likely ironic; it is because of favor from Yahweh that they successfully "asked." The language of "favor from Yahweh" and "asking" in fact disguises marauding and plundering, which the erstwhile slaves work against their deeply resented masters. This seizure of goods is driven partly by a desire to have for the first time, and partly by a mocking scorn of triumph that now lets the hated symbols of arrogant indifference pass through their fingers. They "plundered" (נצל *nāṣal*) the Egyptians. The same term *nāṣal* is used to mean "save" or "rescue" elsewhere, connoting "to snatch from." Here, as in 3:22 and 2 Chr 20:25, the term is used negatively, presumably to seize or snatch, to take violently for oneself. The term makes clear that power has now fully shifted to Israel, and Israel may take whatever it wants.

12:37-39. In an almost understated way, the narrative finally has Israel on its way: "Israel journeyed" (v. 37). The actual moment of departure is always a non-moment in the narrative after the enormous conflict to bring it about. This freedom to journey (journey to freedom), however, is what the entire drama has been about. Slaves have no mobility; they are fixed to a place and are kept there. Now the limit has been broken, and the erstwhile slaves can go as they have not been able to do. Verse 37 gives specific detail about place and numbers. Israel departs Rameses, the hated storehouse city on which it had worked; a city that symbolized Egyptian power, accumulation, and monopoly (cf. Gen 47:13-21; Exod 1:11).

A much more interesting and suggestive statement is offered in vv. 38-39. The narrator describes the scene of initial travel, the "long march," noting four aspects of this company of relaxed bond servants. First, it is a "mixed multitude" of great number. The phrase suggests that this is no kinship group, no ethnic community, but a great conglomeration of lower-class folk who have no time or energy for bloodlines or pedigrees. (On the term *mixed* [ערב *'ēreb*], see Neh 13:3; Jer 25:20, 24; 50:37. This term is important for the view that earliest Israel was not an ethnic community, but a sociological grouping of the marginated who had been liberated from their oppressed socioeconomic status.)

Second, they are not only great in number but also have great numbers of herds and cattle. That is, Pharaoh is able to keep back nothing the Hebrews want to take (cf. 10:24; 12:32). They are completely free and without any supervisory restraint. Third, they carry their dough not yet risen. The narrative continues to refer to the unleavened bread as a reference point for their hurried departure. That is, these first actors in the drama of departure are already characters in the liturgy. They do what they do, not only to get out of slavery, but also to authorize and "institute" the ritual meal.

Fourth, they had made no promises, but leave quickly, because they cannot wait. We are not told why, but, clearly, their waiting might have given Pharaoh a chance to change his mind or to regroup or to continue their servitude. They leave with only what they can hurriedly pick up, nothing more than they can carry in their hands and wear on their backs. But it is enough, because they are on their way!

REFLECTIONS

1. The interpreter's core theme in these narratives is this incredible inversion whereby the last and the first change places. The text does not linger over the collapse of Egypt. It is much more preoccupied with the astonishing appearance of Israel as a new reality in the world. The narrative shows that God has relentlessly valued this firstborn son, so devalued by the world of brutalizing power.

2. In this story, the Israelites are the powerless multitude, abruptly transformed into a community of power and significance, "on their way rejoicing." Pharaoh finally recognizes that Moses and Aaron (Israel) now have the power and authority to bestow blessing. We listen and watch power come to this powerless people. This is indeed the people regarded as "having nothing, and yet possessing everything" (2 Cor 6:10 NRSV). The early church was also a feeble community filled with power. Thus in Acts 3:6, Peter is able to say to the lame man, "I have no silver or gold, but what I have I give you" (NRSV). This encounter faithfully reflects how it is that this completely powerless people is filled with power to transform.

3. Conversely, this narrative is a study of how worldly power, the dazzling grandeur of Egypt, turns out to be an empty shell of powerlessness. Who would have thought that this "bread basket" of the ancient world would at midnight suffer an inexplicable, humiliating reversal of fortunes? Who could have known that its silver and gold would be plundered and seized by its oppressed workforce? Indeed, oppressive regimes vanish in the twinkling of an eye and leave only stories told by those newly endowed with power.

Exodus 12:40-51, Directions for the Passover

COMMENTARY

These verses include a ritual provision inside a narrative frame. The narrative frame of vv. 40-42a and 51 envisions the exodus as an ordered departure of all of Yahweh's "companies." The term צבאות (*ṣěbā'ōt,* "companies") is a military usage, referring to regiments and battalions. The most interesting phrase in this narrative is that the night of departure (cf. vv. 29, 31) is for Yahweh "a night of vigil." The phrase suggests that the departure is a time in which Yahweh is especially alert and attentive, supervising to see that all are on the move, acting as a reviewing officer and as a guard to keep all the companies ordered, on the move, and safe from any last-minute Egyptian harassment. Alternatively, the image is one of Yahweh waiting at headquarters, anxiously awaiting the call that slaves have safely crossed the border into freedom. Yahweh is deeply invested in this revolutionary operation.

Inside that narrative is a provision for a ritual practice, designed to remember and to reenact that "night of all nights" (vv. 42b-50). The night was a "vigil for Yahweh"—i.e., done *by Yahweh*— but now it is to become a watch in honor of and reference *to Yahweh.* That is, the same phrase, "vigil for Yahweh," is used in two different senses, the first *by* Yahweh, the second in devotion *to* Yahweh. With the use of the same preposition, the original event has been made into a routine liturgic practice. Fretheim nicely says, "Israel's keeping remembers God's keeping."[67]

The night of vigil—the night of watching, waiting, and glad remembrance—is the night of Passover. These verses, then, institute the festival sacrament of Passover. Emerging in this text are the most elemental remembrances of Israel and the most precise procedural rules to protect that memory. The text suggests that over time, Passover had many interpretations and many practices, many disputes that require careful and authoritative adjudication. The procedures specify who may participate, and the distinctions are drawn quite firmly. Excluded are foreigners (נכרי *nokrî*), bonded or hired servants, and uncircumcised persons. Conversely, those permitted to celebrate include circumcised slaves and circumcised aliens (גר *gēr*). These distinctions are very close, and we do not know why a line is drawn so closely between slave and hired servant, or between foreigner and sojourner. Apparently what matters is a readiness and willingness to be counted an Israelite, and that is signified by a readiness to be circumcised. Thus the regulation is inclusive (though obviously gender specific), but it is not careless or casual. Finally, we are told that Israel obeys and practices Passover as commanded (v. 50).

67. Fretheim, *Exodus*, 145.

REFLECTIONS

1. The primary accent in this text is that the hidden night of liberation, the miracle of transferring public power, must be remembered by a replication of the event. That night was a concrete, specific, unrepeatable event. It becomes, however, a paradigmatic event, continually mediating in the community a passion for freedom and a critical posture toward any practice of oppression.

2. The community must reflect with discipline upon how to maintain the integrity and power of that festival-sacrament. The text clearly struggles with a desire for inclusiveness and a need for some intentional exclusivity. There is no "moral qualification" for participation, and no "doctrinal test," but a readiness to let this festival define one's life in the world. Those who do not want their lives redescribed in this way are not free to participate.

3. The "spill over" of these "words of institution" is evident in rethinking the Christian eucharist. The eucharist does not replace Passover, but may carry many more of the accents of Passover than is commonly recognized. The Passover connection can keep the eucharist focused on this-world reality of emancipation, feeding, and healing, rather than floating off into liturgical escapism.

4. This festival invites a "night of vigil," a watchful, grateful remembering into the darkness, which we cannot control. On the one hand, that it is at night means paying attention to the inscrutable quality of ominous holiness. On the other hand, that it is for watching means an active, glad waiting for an initiative other than our own. The Passover recalls not an act taken by Israel, but a gift received from Yahweh, precisely at midnight when nothing seems possible.

Exodus 13:1-16, Special Observances

COMMENTARY

This passage includes two provisions for ritual, reflecting themes already introduced in the exodus narrative.

13:1-2. The first theme, that of the firstborn, is introduced in v. 1, but is not explicated until vv. 11-16 (see below). The initial decree is flat, comprehensive, and unconditional. The notion that the firstborn, human and animal, belong to Yahweh likely reflects land-ownership practices and rent arrangements. It is instructive that in v. 11 the regulation is linked to the land. In an agricultural economy, the way of rental payment by a tenant farmer is that the owner of land receives the first share of the produce for the use of the land. The payment of the firstborn animal or first fruits of the crop is an acknowledgment of ownership and, by extrapolation, an acknowledgment of sovereignty.

In extending this provision to the human firstborn in the context of the exodus narrative, the provision may signify that members of the human family—i.e., the community of Israel—belong to and owe allegiance to Yahweh and not to Pharaoh. Thus a land practice seems to be extended in the rhetoric of this provision to underscore the radical claim of loyalty, implicit in the event of the exodus. Whether this language of consecration refers at any time to an actual sacrifice of a human life, or rather is metaphorical is open to question. But there is no doubt that in Israel's purview consecration to Yahweh meant loyalty and allegiance, and not the taking of a life. To make the notion more than a metaphor for loyalty and allegiance would be to contradict the core affirmations of Yahwism, and to think in the categories of Pharaoh's abusive practices.

13:3-10. The second theme of ritual is that of the Feast of Unleavened Bread. We have already seen that unleavened bread is a reminder (and reenactment) that the slave community left Egypt in a hurry and did not wait around for the yeast to rise (cf. 12:11). Thus this festival is a reminder and participation in the drama of a hurried departure from bondage. Two sub-points are important in this provision.

First, the festival is especially designed for the time when Israel is settled in the luxurious land already promised in the book of Genesis (cf. Exod 3:8, 17). The dramatic contrast between present-tense settlement in the good land and past-tense memory of hurried departure from oppression is crucial for understanding this text and the intention of the festival. The tradition knows, perhaps from very specific experience, that present-tense well-being causes disregard of past-tense tribulation. Moreover, such forgetting causes a disregard of dependence on Yahweh and a sense of one's independence, autonomy, and self-sufficiency. Thus the festival intends to keep Israel in touch with a more difficult past, so that it will know that its present situation properly evokes wonder and gratitude, and not self-congratulations.

The second element in this provision is that the practice of eating unleavened bread is to evoke in the watching children questions about the festival and its intent. When the child's question is asked, the community of adults has ready and waiting a normative, canonical answer (vv. 8-9). The answer, which the child could never guess ahead of time, is that the festival is practiced because of what Yahweh did in the exodus. Notice that the recital is first-person singular. The answer is, no doubt, communal. But the text envisions that the questions will be asked by a particular child and answered by a particular parent. Moreover, the conversation may be many generations removed from the exodus, but the answer is nonetheless "When I came out of Egypt." The purpose of the festival is to keep the past present, authoritative, and powerfully identity-giving.

In v. 9, it is not clear what the antecedent of "it" is. The "it" no doubt refers to some aspect of the festival that shall be a visible sign and remembrance. The text does not specify. What is important is that the visible reminder on head and hand is to keep *torah* on the lips, which presumably means the recital of the exodus event and its intrinsic obligations.

13:11-16. The text now refers to the theme of the firstborn, introduced in v. 1. This practice, like the feast of unleavened bread, is explicitly related to, and geared for, the land. The primary command of v. 12 reiterates v. 1 with the same flat, non-negotiable tone. In vv. 13-15*b*, the uncompromising quality of the initial command is toned down. These verses introduce the term *redeem* (פדה *pādâ*), which here refers to a transaction whereby a substitute can be made for the firstborn, so that a less valuable object can be offered to Yahweh in place of the more valuable—e.g., a sheep instead of a donkey. In vv. 13*a* and 15*b*, provision is made for the redemption of a male child, but the approved substitute is not named. On this reading, it seems likely that the primary command of v. 1 is taken literally and that these later verses seek an alternative to the costly demand. The relation between vv. 1 and 12 (which give a flat command) and vv. 13 and 15 (which provide alternatives) is of interest, because they place in juxtaposition an unqualified demand and a qualification of the demand made by "trading downward." The qualifying provisions clearly affirm that the substitute is an adequate equivalent and, in fact, reflects no compromise of value, devotion, or commitment.

The practice of committing the firstborn and/or a substitute to Yahweh may be a highly sacramental gesture. Its main use here, however, is its instructional value. Either the offer of the firstborn or the presentation of a substitute serves to evoke in a watching child wonderment about its meaning. Again the adult community has ready its canonical answer to the anticipated question (vv. 14*b*-15*a*). The practice is related in this answer (as it may not have been in origin) to the exodus and to the liberation wrought by Yahweh. The particular work of liberation could be wrought in Egypt only by killing all the Egyptian firstborn. That is, this payment of "rent" is a way to recall the savage act of Yahweh's power in the service of liberation.

Again in v. 16, it is not at all clear what "it" is, except that the text makes a connection between a ritual gesture and an identifying memory.

REFLECTIONS

1. The biblical community of faith is a community of memory, working at its precious identity in a culture devoted to amnesia. The market forces that encourage a consumer consciousness are largely controlled by ideology that wants to abandon the past and forsake the future in order to live in an absolute "now." Those who neither remember nor hope are profoundly vulnerable to consumerism, busy filling the void left by eradication of that extra dimension of historical awareness that belongs to healthy humanness. Thus when the community says, "This do in remembrance," it is not engaged in a mere history lesson or a simple act of piety. It is, rather, engaged in an act of resistance against an ideology that will destroy any Passover-driven humanness. While such a critique of the ideology of amnesia is not explicit in this text, there is no doubt that as the community struggles for its memory, it seeks to resist the forgetful abandonment of peculiar identity to which it is always vulnerable.

2. The festival of unleavened bread is a dramatic affirmation that freedom is given only at the last moment, only at great risk, only by the skin of our teeth, and only by the midnight urgency of Yahweh. An alternative future is never given or received casually. The festival invites reflection upon the urgency of faith, and how late freedom is characteristically given in a world set against liberation.

3. The lesson taught the children in vv. 14-15 requires enormous interpretive agility. The child is told that God must kill all the firstborn in order to bring about their freedom. Such a voicing of violence, especially by the hand of God, may be unsettling to a child. Implicit in the answer, however, is a drastic (albeit subtle) maneuver. The child learns in this telling that the God who killed the firstborn is also the God who has risked everything for the beloved firstborn. This text does not shield the child from the brutal reality of God's work of liberation, which always requires a tough struggle. In the caring process of the telling, however, this text does not fear that children will understand themselves as the ones exposed to such violence. The case is just the opposite. The surrounding action of the community in the festival permits children to experience the inordinate valuing of the firstborn in this community, without deceiving them about the high price and high risk of freedom as the gift of God.

The text is not (as the interpreter also should not be) insensitive to the hazards of this story. Nonetheless, the root story of faith is a story of deep conflict. Unless the community of faith falsely nurtures a kind of romanticism about the real world in which God brings newness, then the children of the community must come to know this story as their own, of being bought at a terrible price. The terrible price bespeaks the inordinant passion of God and the deep expectation of new obedience that belongs to the liberation.

4. The reference to "redeem" obviously introduces important theological vocabulary. The term *redeem* (פדה *pādâ*) refers to a trade-off whereby a substitute is offered to meet God's demand. Peter Stuhlmacher has shown that this metaphorical use of exchange or substitution (ransom) lies behind the christological formulation of Mark 10:45: "For the Son of Man came not to be served, but to serve and to give his life a *ransom* (λύτρον *lytron*) for many" (NRSV, emphasis added).[68]

In this formulation, the Son of Man is accepted as a substitute for others who are in deep need. That same notion of substitution is already evident in our text. Note well, however, that the substitution is not related to any "satisfaction" of God's requirement. It is, rather, an economic transaction, whereby something especially treasured is bought out of hock.

---

68. Peter Stuhlmacher, *Reconciliation, Law, & Righteousness: Essays in Biblical Theology* (Philadelphia: Fortress, 1986) 16-29.

Exodus 13:17-22, Pillars of Cloud and Fire

COMMENTARY

This "journey report" resumes the account of the journey from 12:37-39. That account has been interrupted by a set of procedural regulations for celebration and remembering in 12:40–13:16. Thus the present text intermingles *guidelines for present celebration* with *narrative accounts of the past.* The narrative in its present form is shaped to create a lively interface between past and present, so that even the narratives that remember are given to us with attentiveness to their present "voice."

This unit briefly reports on the route taken in the departure from Egypt. Scholars have spent great energy on the route, and especially on the Sea of Reeds (ים-סוף *yam-sûp*). It is clear, however, that the paragraph that incidentally mentions geography is principally concerned to make a theological statement, pivoting on the word *lead* (נחה *nāḥâ*). Two statements at the beginning and at the end of this unit focus on the leadership of God.

At the beginning, God "leads" by a circuitous route in order to avoid conflict with the Philistines (vv. 17-18a). That decision about an alternative route, however, is not made because of the threat of the Philistines. The reason for this decision is given us by the rhetoric of a divine soliloquy. The expression "God thought" is, in Hebrew, "God said." God said out loud, perhaps only to God's own self. God is mindful that the Israelites, in the face of danger, may have a "change of mind." The verb *"change* their mind" is נחם (*nāḥam*), which in many other places means "repent" (Gen 6:6-7; Exod 32:14; Amos 7:2, 5). Israel may repent of its resolve for freedom, may abandon its liberated destiny, and may accept the bondaged fate of Egypt.

At the end of the unit, *lead* is related to a very different set of images (vv. 21-22). Now God is much more transcendent and impersonal, being present neither personally nor through reflective speech, but only through the cultic devices of "cloud" and "fire." This part of the tradition has devised a sign of God's full presence that is stable and visible. God is not directly available, but only through

mediation. (Clearly this is a very different leadership from that in vv. 17-18a.) Two facets of this leadership are important. First, it is for "day and night," all of the time. Both the day and the night are filled with enormous danger, and this people is completely vulnerable (cf. Ps 91:5-6). The cloud shields from the sun; the fire protects from darkness.

Thus the verb *lead* in vv. 17-18a and vv. 21-22 means that Israel in its journey, like the shape of this text, is surrounded behind and before by reliable, attentive leadership. Within these references to "leading," two items are mentioned. First, the journey is one into conflict (v. 18b). The departure of Pharaoh was only the beginning of battle, for the journey of freedom includes the struggle to stake out a zone of well-being in a busy, crowded world that is already organized without any reference to Israel's existence or freedom. The term rendered "prepared for battle" (חמשים *ḥămušîm*) specifically means organized into military units of fifty, thus conjuring a well-organized, highly disciplined company. Such language is no doubt an overstatement for this "mixed crowd" (12:38), but the term does signal the coming struggle.

The second, rather odd motif is the report that Moses carries the bones of Joseph on the journey. The book of Genesis ends with Joseph's insistence, finalized in a solemn oath, that his bones must be taken up with the departing Israelites and carried to the land of promise (Gen 50:24-26). It is as though at the last moment Joseph, who as an Israelite was an incredible compromiser with Egyptian definitions of reality, finally asserts unequivocally his Israelite identity. He is clearer about this in his death than he was in his successful political career. Most important, Joseph twice uses the same infinitive absolute, "will surely come" (פקד יפקד *pāqōd yipqōd*), to state his firm conviction that God will not leave this people in bondage but will notice them and liberate them. The inclusion of Joseph's bones on the journey once again binds the exodus community to the old promises of Genesis, as in Exod 2:24; 3:16; and 6:3. Moreover, the paragraph appeals to the firm faith of the dying father Joseph, not usually cited as a carrier of faith. The people who make the journey carry with them, in the tangible form of these bones, very old promises and very sure faith.

REFLECTIONS

The departure from Egypt is not the end, but only the beginning of the long struggle for freedom and well-being, a struggle for the identity and destiny of God's beloved community apart from the life-robbing, life-denying definitions of Egypt. The central interpretive point here is that the community that attends to this text is an inheritor and practitioner of this still unfinished struggle for a distinctive identity and destiny.

1. The primary affirmation of this passage is that God's leadership is thoughtful, prudent, and utterly reliable. The form of that leadership in vv. 17-18*a* is not described, but in vv. 21-22 it is given a more concrete, substantive identity. Compare Ps 23:2-3, perhaps the best-known use of the image of God's leadership. The metaphor in the psalm is of a shepherd who leads sheep safely to good pastures and well-supplied water, even though the terrain to be traveled is dangerous and threatening. The notion of God's leadership is a primary datum in Israel's creedal recital, in Deut 8:2-4. Both texts affirm that God supplies every needed thing.

2. Following the dangerous, demanding lead of Yahweh requires continual fresh resolve and reinforcement. Israel is addicted to the order, oppression, and regular food supply of the empire, and Yahweh's leadership is aimed exactly against that death-dealing addiction. Thus the interpretive point of contact concerns those powerful loyalties currently termed "addictions." Every breaking of an addiction is like departing the reassuring structures of Egypt. This text affirms that the departure is difficult, that the temptation to return is great, and that Yahweh takes steps to make the departure as palatable as possible.

3. The "bones of Joseph" invite reflection on the intergenerational character of biblical faith. The exodus is initiated only because "God remembered" (2:24-25; 6:5). The book of Exodus cannot do without the book of Genesis, even if the relation is awkward and disjointed. The generation of emancipation is not the first generation in the story, but depends on the generations of hopeful ones who believe before them and on whose hope we trade as recipients.

There are two dangers to which this motif may be referred. First, there is the danger that the "now generation" in the church (particularly in a mobile, displacing society) may scuttle all the old ancestors (their names and their bones) and seek to live in a vacuum, excessively focused on the present. Second, there is the danger that a preoccupation with ancestors may treat the past like a relic—i.e., an act of nostalgia that resists present-tense requirements. Against both temptations, the bones of Joseph are understood as an urgent, fervent bet on Israel's future with God: "By faith Joseph, when his end was near, spoke about the exodus of the Israelites from Egypt and gave instructions about his bones" (Heb 11:22 NIV).

Joseph trusted in God's coming liberation. He made that bet on God's future by faith. It is in the same way, by faith, that the journey can be undertaken in the present, dangerous as it is.

Exodus 14:1-31, Crossing the Sea

COMMENTARY

The journey to freedom has begun in 12:37-39. Israel, however, is not yet free. Pharaoh will make one last effort to block the departure. This most dramatic narrative of the departure is arranged in a sequence of quite distinct scenes. While the action turns on the two wonders of the waters divided (vv. 21-25) and the waters returned (vv. 26-28), the actual confrontation is concerned with far more than the miracles of the waters.

14:1-4. The narrative begins, characteristically, with Yahweh's command to Moses. Yahweh knows well before the events themselves that one more crisis with Pharaoh is still to be faced. The reason for this last, desperate effort of the king, so far as the narrative asserts, is not in fact Pharaoh's willfulness, but is yet again Yahweh's act of "hardening."

The reason for Yahweh's action is crucial for our interpretation. The last confrontation will be staged so that "I will get glory over Pharaoh!" (v. 4). Yahweh arranges the confrontation as an exhibition of enormous power, not for the sake of Israel. The final, decisive intention is not Israelite freedom, but Yahweh's glory, which is decisive. The outcome of the power struggle (which Yahweh will win!) is that Pharaoh in all his recalcitrance shall come at last to know "I am Yahweh."

14:5-9. With this disclosure to Moses and to the listener, we are given the same scene a second time, this time from Pharaoh's perspective. In this scene, the action gives the surface appearance that Pharaoh has freely chosen this new initiative against Israel. We are told simply that Pharaoh changes his mind (יהפך לבב *yēhāpēk lĕbab*) and acts with new resolve. The Egyptians now focus not on relief that the "troublemakers" are gone, but on the lost slave labor. What a short memory! Pharaoh cannot remember back to 12:31-32, when he was desperate for their departure. So, with a radical change of policy and strategy, Pharaoh seeks to block the departure of Israel with a display of enormous power and resolve.

The narrative, however, insists that Egyptian power, resolve, and strategy are not what they seem. Everything has been preempted by Yahweh, who manages all sides of the drama. This is an enormously heavy dose of sovereignty. But then, the entire meeting concerns competing sovereignties. In this scene, the double use of "heart" (change of heart, hardened heart) nicely calls attention to the conflict of sovereignties. Fretheim observes that Yahweh's impact on Pharaoh strengthens Pharaoh's own proclivity.[69] The hardening by Yahweh does not violate Pharaoh's own intention.

14:10-14. In the third scene, neither Pharaoh nor Yahweh is present. Now the exchange is between Moses and Israel, who appears as a character in the plot for the first time. The speeches are arranged as a petition (vv. 10-12) and a responding salvation oracle (vv. 13-14).

The renewed attack of Pharaoh is an enormous threat to escaping Israel. The erstwhile slave community is completely vulnerable and without resources. Indeed, in this moment the entire departure is once more in profound jeopardy. As a result, the Israelites do the only thing they can do, the thing they always do in fear, and the thing they did in 2:23-24 at the beginning of the emergency: They cry out to Yahweh. Their cry is characteristic of Israel's faith, modeling the way in which the troubled turn to God. The slaves have now found their insistent voice. They cry out to Yahweh in protest, complaint, demand, and hope.

In fact, their speech is not a petition for help; in fact, it is not addressed to Yahweh, as is stated in v. 10. Rather, it is an accusation against Moses (vv. 10-12). The new threat of Egypt is not viewed as a theological emergency, does not even concern Yahweh, who figures more for Moses than for the community. The threat of Pharaoh evokes a crisis of political leadership. The accusation is in three rhetorical questions that are attacks on Moses

---

69. Fretheim, *Exodus*, 155.

for his unwise, dangerous, miscalculated, stupid initiative: Was it because . . . ? What have you done . . . ? Is this not . . . ?

Moses had provided a revolutionary alternative for the slaves, an alternative to the demands of Egypt. In prospect, such emancipation had been attractive. In hand, however, it is only a profound hardship. It is difficult to sustain a revolution, because one loses all the benefits of the old system, well before there are any tangible benefits from what is promised.

In their three angry questions, Moses' opponents utter the name *Egypt* five times. It is the only name they know, the name upon which they rely, the name they love to sound. In the speech of the protesting, distrusting people, the name of Yahweh, however, is completely absent. They do not perceive Yahweh as being in any way a pertinent, active member of the plot. On their own terms, of course, without Yahweh, their reasoning is sound and their complaint is legitimate. Without Yahweh, they have no resources against Egypt and no hope of success. Moses by himself—without Yahweh—is no adequate resource against Egypt.

Moses' response to the challenge, introduced by "fear not," is a characteristic salvation oracle in which the voice of the gospel, rooted in God's own power and fidelity, is offered as a resolution to the voice of protest and trouble (vv. 13-14).

Moses' speech begins with three reassuring imperatives that serve to seize the initiative from the protesters: "Do not fear, stand, see." Moses refuses to accept the despairing picture of reality offered by the protesters. Their picture includes only themselves and the Egyptians, and there is no hope in such a scenario. Moses asserts that such a construal is a severe distortion of reality, for it eliminates Yahweh as an active player. Thus, in his response, Moses twice mentions Yahweh, the very name the protesters were either unable or unwilling to utter. Moreover, Moses' entire self-defense is staked on the claim that Yahweh is indeed a live, active, decisive character in this crisis. Thus the dispute turns on the relevance or irrelevance of Yahweh to the crisis.

Moses' imperatives refuse to respond to the three accusatory sentences just uttered.

The first imperative, "fear not," is an enormously preemptive statement, used to override fear by the giving of assurance that lies outside and beyond fear. His other two imperatives invite Israel to stop and pay attention, to notice a presence in their crisis that they had neither noticed nor acknowledged. Thus Moses reframes the crisis of Israel around the presence, power, and fidelity of Yahweh, whom the Israelites have not permitted on their horizon.

Before the very eyes of fearful Israel, Moses asserts, Yahweh will work a deliverance (ישׁועה *yěšûʿâ*) today. Indeed, in this statement, it is Yahweh alone who acts to deliver. Israel need only "be still and watch." Yahweh's singular action here precludes any other agent in the liberation. The deliverance will be the evaporation of Egypt as a threat, for Egypt will be removed and never seen again. Moses not only introduces into the picture Yahweh, whom the complainers deny, but he in turn denies the Egyptian reality, the one with whom his adversaries are preoccupied. A second time, Moses names Yahweh as the one who will fight for Israel. Israel can desist from its feverish activity and only witness the battle. The Israelites who protest are given no chance to answer Moses, to reject his affirmations, or to quarrel with his leadership. The narrator gives Moses the last word.

14:15-18. Now Yahweh reemerges in the narrative. Yahweh's initial rebuke of Moses is odd (v. 15), because Moses has not cried out and no one, not even complaining Israel, has addressed Yahweh (cf. vv. 11-12). The rebuke is clearly aimed over the head of Moses against the people, whose cry constitutes lack of faith and readiness to credit the reality of Pharaoh over the reality of Yahweh. As an alternative to the cry of fear and the lack of faith, Yahweh issues an imperative that calls for daring action: "Journey!" (נסע *nāsaʿ*; NRSV "go forward"; NIV "move on").

After that word addressed to the community, Yahweh issues a long statement to Moses (vv. 16-18). It includes the imperative "extend your hand" (i.e., power). It is followed by a reiteration of Yahweh's resolve, stated in v. 4, in which the departure of the people from Egypt is seen to be a way of exalting Yahweh. The outcome again will be an acknowledgment, "I am Yahweh." Thus the imperative of v. 15 is an instrument of the glorification of Yahweh, who effectively changes the subject on Moses and on Israel. The real crisis is not the emancipation or survival of Israel, but the triumph of Yahweh over Pharaoh.

14:19-20. The next paragraph is peculiar and without parallel anywhere in the preceding narrative. It concerns two modes of Yahweh's protective presence. On the one hand, "the angel of God" is a rearguard. We have not had an angel in the narrative since the meeting at the burning bush (3:2). The angel here is an escort to assure safe passage (cf. Ps 91:11-13). One might think of a public person walking through a crowd that pushes and shoves to touch, with the angels as those who push the crowd back to make a safe way; no one can lay a hand on Israel with such protection!

On the other hand, the protective cloud is both before and behind Israel as a protective screen. The narrator seems to play on the motif of cloud and fire in 13:21-22, but here there is only a cloud. In addition to being protective covering, the cloud takes over the function of the fire, providing light as well as covering. By appealing to both "angel" and "cloud," these verses are an extravagant way of characterizing the vigilant protection God gives Israel, which Moses promised in vv. 13-14.

14:21-25. Following the command of v. 16, Moses enacts a double "wonder" that both rescues Israel and glorifies Yahweh. First, as commanded, Moses (and Yahweh!) drives back the waters and creates a dry path for escaping Israel (vv. 21-22). Critics have long noted that in v. 21, the "east wind" blew back the waters in something like a natural event, but in v. 22, there is a "wall of water" so that Moses' action is heightened as a miracle. Such an analysis, based on source criticism, is of little help to the interpreter; in fact, it detracts from the narrator's intention. Indeed, making such distinctions is an attempt to read the event through the eyes of explanatory suspicion, whereas the narrative insists on being taken through the eyes of helpless Israel without resources.

Moses' capacity to divide the waters or drive them back suggests that he is replicating the coming of dry land in creation, when

the sea is divided for the sake of inhabitable land. In this moment of liberation, God does a deed as powerful, original, and life-giving as the very newness of creation. Conversely, the Egyptians are caught in the power of the waters and the disorder—the powers of chaos, which are mobilized by Yahweh to foil the enemies of liberation. The narrative shrewdly juxtaposes the waters of the Nile in chaps. 1–2 with the large, ominous waters of chaos and the specificity of liberation with the majesty of new creation. It is no wonder (but a "wonder") that the Egyptians are forced to a confession of Yahweh (v. 25), an Egyptian affirmation of Moses' assurance in v. 14. Indeed, in this utterance over what they have seen, the Egyptians are at long last forced to "know" (as Yahweh intended in vv. 4, 18) that this is Yahweh, that Yahweh is at work on behalf of the Israelites, and that Egypt is helpless in the face of Yahweh's enduring, passionate resolve.

Thus the Egyptians are made to confess what the Israelites themselves had doubted (vv. 11-12), and what Moses himself had affirmed (v. 14). When one hears the Egyptian confession, one may conclude that we have not seen such faith in all of Israel (cf. Matt 8:10). The Egyptians become, against their will, confessors of Yahweh. Thus the miracle of the water is instrumental to the miracle of faith, to which Egypt is resistantly brought. When Egypt comes to this confession, Yahweh is indeed acknowledged, exalted, and glorified as the real sovereign.

14:26-29. The work of faith (for Israel) and glorification (of Yahweh) accomplished, Moses performs his second "wonder": the return of the waters to their proper course, which is, in fact, the unleashing of the power of chaos, the "mighty waters," before which Pharaoh and the Egyptian army are completely helpless. By the conclusion of the narrative, the contrast between these two antagonists, so long locked in an unequal struggle, is complete. Israel is safe on dry land, untouched by the surging waters of chaos. Egypt is completely nullified, so that "not one of them remained" (v. 28).

14:30-31. The narrator adds a reprise that serves as a conclusion to this chapter, and possibly to the entire exodus narrative: "Yahweh saves" (יְשׁ *yāšaʿ*) (v. 30)! Yahweh commits an act of inscrutable power that breaks the power of Egypt. Then the camera does a slow, sweeping survey of the shore, at the edge of the deathly waters. The Israelites are not visible in the deathly scene. They are behind the camera looking in astonishment. All that is visible are dead Egyptians: Egyptian soldiers, Egyptian horses, Egyptian chariots, Egyptian power, and Egyptian arrogance. The term *dead* looms over the picture and over the text. The word is not new, even on Egyptian lips. Already in 12:33, the Egyptians understand that having Israel among them will bring death.

The watching Israelites are driven to two unavoidable conclusions. First, they fear Yahweh. This is the counterpoint to the imperative of Moses in v. 13, "Do not fear." Israel is to fear Yahweh and, therefore, to fear none other. They finally know beyond any doubt that Yahweh, with power and fidelity, will do for them what they cannot do for themselves.

Second, the Israelites "believe in" (אמן 'mn) Yahweh and Moses. While both Yahweh and Moses are named, and Israel comes to rely on both of them, Moses is clearly in a subordinate, derivative position. Nevertheless, the ones who were fearful and doubting in vv. 11-12 have come to faith and confidence in the leadership of Moses. It is most important that fear of Yahweh is linked to the concrete, specific, political leadership of Moses. As early as 4:1-9, Moses had doubted that he would be trusted or believed in. Now that question has been resolved by the massive, decisive action of Yahweh.

REFLECTIONS

The narrative invites silence before this stunning reversal of the processes of power. This outcome is no ordinary turn of affairs, to be explained by any human stratagem or by any natural phenomenon. Any attempt to have the story on such terms is a violation of what we are intended to hear in the narrative. In the purview of this narrative, there is only one possible explanation, and the name of that "explanation" is Yahweh, who brings both life and death.

Interpreting this passage, then, requires that we clear our minds (as much as possible) of any of the haunting misgivings of modernity. One cannot ask merely how this rescue could happen or whether it is possible. One cannot proceed by seeking to explain the miracle of the water, for any convincing explanation would only lead away from the intent of the text itself. This text is not argument, but witness and summons; it is *a witness to the power of Yahweh* and *a consequent summons to faith.*

1. The key actor in this narrative is Yahweh. It is Yahweh who issues the decisive decree to Moses and who is the target of doubt, the goal of defiance, and the focus of faith. It is Yahweh who is the subject of the crucial verbs, even the "hands-on" verbs, like *clogged* (v. 25) and *tossed* (v. 27), as well as the more magisterial *saved* (v. 30).

The explicit purpose of the narrative is to "get glory" over Egypt, so that Egypt will "know" (acknowledge) that Yahweh warrants allegiance. That is, the large purpose of the narrative is not to comfort the Israelites, but to look beyond Israel to the doubting, cynical reality of worldly power. This focus on Yahweh and Yahweh's exaltation is brought to fruition in the Egyptian confession, stated in desperation in v. 25. The confession, a grudging admission of defeat, anticipates the parallel statement in Mark 15:39, whereby the power of Rome at long last concedes the power of Jesus. The story thus culminates in a loud, grand "Gloria!"

2. The story of the stunning triumph of Yahweh over the great power of Egypt is told in order to summon Israel to faith. Gerhard von Rad has shrewdly seen that the assurance of Moses given in vv. 13-14 (and echoed in Isa 7:9) is a formula now removed from the primary context of battle and has become an invitation to faith.[70]

---

70. Gerhard von Rad, *Holy War in Ancient Israel* (Grand Rapids: Eerdmans, 1991) 88-90.

The context and metaphor of battle may at first glance be offensive—faith is to trust the power of God in the face of one's enemies. Yet that same battle metaphor is used by faith in this wondrous and familiar Pauline affirmation of trust in God: "No, in all these things we are more than *conquerors* through him who loved us" (Rom 8:37 NRSV; emphasis added). Paul would likely not have had this triumphant metaphor available to him if not for the exodus narrative.

3. Both the exaltation of Yahweh and the summons to faith are situated in and dependent upon a concrete, public struggle about power. That is, the glorification of Yahweh and the trust of Israel are not religious ideas or affirmations made in a vacuum unscathed by the reality of life. This narrative insists that the celebration of God and the faith of Israel are inescapably mediated through the transformation of public life. Characteristically, the Bible points to specific, concrete places where the triumph of Yahweh is evident. Faith points to transformation, and liturgy recites and replicates these transformations.

The matter is made both more problematic and more compelling because this is a public event in the face of the empire. Even those of us who are inclined to faith are also inclined to reiterate the cynical question of Stalin about the danger of war: "How many divisions does the Pope have?" Pharaoh might have asked the same cynical question: "How many troops does Yahweh have?" The military metaphors and martial rhetoric of the text make the claim that Yahweh has sufficient troops for the battle.

Such a claim sounds like nonsense, except for two matters. First, the text celebrates the outcome. It did happen! Second, over time, it is the marginal, with no other troops, who in all kinds of emergencies have trusted in the strong arm of Yahweh and have not been disappointed. The faith to which Israel is here summoned is not a faith the world easily believes and is arrived at by common sense. It is trust against the evidence, risk in the face of the odds, that life can come even in the public domain, where Yahweh governs.

Exodus 15:1-21, Songs of Moses and Miriam

COMMENTARY

This unit includes a long poem, usually called "The Song of Moses" (vv. 1-18); a short poem, commonly termed "The Song of Miriam" (vv. 20-21); and a brief narrative interlude between the two poems (v. 19).

15:1-18. The Song of Moses is commonly recognized as one of the oldest, most radical, and most important poems in the OT. It not only sounds the crucial themes of Israel's most elemental faith, but it also provides a shape and sequencing of that faith, which we may take as "canonical." The most important recent development in interpretation is to see that the poem holds together a distinctive articulation of *the story of liberation,* with Israel moving from the world of Pharaoh's oppression to the safe land of promise and the undercurrent thematic of *a creation liturgy,* which portrays and enacts God's victory over the powers of chaos and the forming of the earth as a safe, ordered place for life.

The poem begins with an introduction whereby Moses and the Israelites prepare to sing to Yahweh (vv. 1-2). Such an introduction is a standard element in Israel's hymnody. This declaration is itself an exuberant act of self-abandonment, wherein one yields oneself to the subject of praise. That is, the introduction effectively changes the subject of the song from the intention of the singers to the reality of the one praised. There is no doubt that the "I" of the song is the whole community of Israel, now publicly declaring that its life is rooted in and derived from this other one.

The subject of this act of exuberant self-abandonment is Yahweh, named three times in these introductory verses. This Yahweh has been the subject of the entire exodus narrative, in whom Israel has come to believe (14:31), and whom Pharaoh finally comes to know (14:25). This naming of Yahweh is not only an act of praise, but it is also a polemical act, whereby Israel dismisses and nullifies any rival to Yahweh, for no other has undertaken the liberation now being celebrated.

The first verse of the hymn apparently is a quotation from the older independent song of v. 21. The older song is by "Miriam and all the women." Thus Moses, the official leader, has taken over and preempted the singing first done by the women. This act of preemption is not unlike the early witness to the resurrection of Jesus in Luke 24:10-12. The women were the first witnesses, but it took the verification of the male leaders to authenticate their report. The reference to "sea" here no doubt refers to the Egyptian waters of death, but more largely refers to the waters of chaos, which Yahweh has utilized for the purposes of liberation. That single core act of the defeat of "the horse and rider" becomes the elemental claim from which all else in Israel's doxological tradition derives.

From this single event, now celebrated in all its inscrutable wonder, the poem uses a series of first-person pronouns to draw close to Yahweh in adoration and allegiance: Yahweh—my strength, my song, my deliverance, my God, God of my father. The singer knows that all of life is owed to this one who will be lifted up and enthroned in this act of praise. Reference to "my father's God" may be a modest connection to the Genesis tradition, a connection that was decisive in Exod 2:24-25; 3:17; and 6:2-3.

The rhetoric in v. 3 moves into a somewhat more formal statement. Israel's faith depends in important ways on a military metaphor. While such a metaphor may offend our modern sensibilities, the whole claim of rescue, deliverance, and salvation depends on the reality that God can do for us what we cannot do for ourselves. It is as though the utterance of Yahweh's name is a defiant challenge to any power that might try to undo the liberation and force the singer back into bondage. The singer anticipates the Pauline assertion: "I am not ashamed of the gospel" (Rom 1:16 NRSV). This singer is not embarrassed to take a strong stand for the future

in this affirmation. The singer is buoyant and delighted at the new possibilities the reality of this God makes possible. The remainder of the poem explicates this passionate faith and sure confidence.

The body of the song in its first half focuses on the rescue, understood as a victory for Yahweh (vv. 4-10). The victory song, characteristic of Israel, celebrates by retelling the dangerous, hard-fought conflict and its happy resolve. Thus the whole drama of Exodus is summarized briefly in v. 4, looking back to v. 1, reiterating the event whereby the waters governed by Yahweh were used to protect Israel and to defeat the formidable troops of Egypt. In v. 5, we have a dramatic picture of the soldiers and horses of the empire slowly sinking into the waters (cf. v. 10*b*). One can hear in the poem the blub, blub, blub of water as the bodies disappear into the depths, defeated and helpless. That graphic picture is voiced in the boldest terms possible, for "floods" (תהמת *tĕhōmōt*) and "depths" (מצולת *mĕṣôlōt*) are allusions to cosmic waters. By the surging of these waters, the residue of defeated Egypt disappears from creation and succumbs to the resilient, indifferent power of chaos, a power operating here at the behest of Yahweh.

After the description of the pivotal act of defeat, the poem breaks into a fresh doxology, voicing Yahweh's incomparable power (vv. 6-8). These verses, dominated by the pronoun *your*, acknowledge the unrivaled power of Yahweh. The wonder of this rescue is effected by Yahweh's "right hand"—i.e., Yahweh's most potent capacity for action (cf. 14:31 on Yahweh's "great hand"). Accent on Yahweh's power only underscores the pitiful impotence of Pharaoh, who now has no power at all. The rhetoric includes to "your majesty, your adversaries, your fury, your nostrils." All is "yours"! Israel withholds nothing in its glad acknowledgment of Yahweh as the only one capable of working such an inversion. Yahweh's power, moreover, is aimed exactly against "enemy" (אויב *'ōyēb*), a word that occurs without any definite article; against your "adversary" (קמיך *qāmêkā*), the one who "rises up" in opposition (vv. 6-7). Yahweh is at work against rivals for power, or against recalcitrant subjects of Yahweh's rightful governance.

In vv. 7b-8, we are given two contrasting images for Yahweh's power. On the one hand, Yahweh's "fury" (חרון *hārôn*) is like a consuming fire, for which "stubble" (straw) is most flammable. On the other hand, Yahweh is like a great sea monster. The "wind" (רוח *rûaḥ*) out of Yahweh's nostril blows the waters of the sea; the primordial waters stand aside in a wall. The poetry here moves well beyond the specific enactment of the Exodus and appeals to the language of the creator's victory over and administration of chaos. The images of warrior, fire, and monster are attempts to voice the extravagant power of Yahweh.

The struggle with "enemy" (*'ôyēb*) escalates. Yahweh does not prevail easily. The enemy, the surging, recalcitrant power of chaos, issues a resolve against Yahweh in a speech dominated by defiant first-person pronouns, with more than a little arrogance (v. 9):

I will pursue [רדף *rādap*], I will overtake
  [נשׂג *nśg*],
I will divide [חלק *ḥālaq*] the spoil, my desire
  shall have its fill [מלא *mālē*] of them.
I will draw [ריק *rîq*] my sword, my hand
  shall destroy [ירשׁ *yāraš*] them.

The enemy has not yet been defeated or become convinced of Yahweh's power.

The shift from v. 9 to v. 10 is abrupt and complete. There is no conjunction or preposition, but the rhetoric breaks off as it moves from the "I" of the enemy to the "You" of the doxology. "You blew your wind" (*rûaḥ*). That is all, but that is enough. The wind of God moves over the mighty waters, and the enemy is inundated, destroyed, and nullified. The voice of this poem is positioned as a witness who sees and attests to the contest between Yahweh and Egypt, between creation and chaos, and between life and death. It is no contest. In two lines of poetry, the battle is over, and the enemy is not heard from again.

At the center of the poem is a reflective, doxological reprise that looks back on the victory of vv. 4-10 and articulates an exultant affirmation (vv. 11-12). These two verses stand at the center of the poem, poised between the two main elements of vv. 4-10

and 13-17. The conclusion drawn from the struggle just described concerns the incomparability of Yahweh: "Who is like you?" That issue, here voiced as a rhetorical question, has been voiced in an indicative conclusion in 8:10 and 9:14. The hymn is situated in an openly polytheistic context. It does not say there are no other gods, just that there are no parallels to Yahweh. On the other hand, however, Yahweh is named (the only one named) and in truth has no rivals among the other gods. No other people has a doxology about a god who has won a victory for the oppressed against the oppressor in the real world of power politics.[71]

In the drama of the poem, the world is made utterly safe for the adherents of Yahweh. Slavery is banished, and chaos is eliminated. The doxology of v. 11 is sanctioned and legitimated by the specificity of v. 12, which looks back to vv. 4-10. Again there is reference to Yahweh's right hand. Look out for Yahweh's right hand, for it is lethal! The last line of v. 12 reverts to very different language. The verb *swallow* suggests something like a monster that gulps down the enemy. (See the verb poignantly used in 7:12.) In this case, the earth (dry land) swallows up the sea, the surging power of chaos. In the narrative of chapter 14, that is what Israel saw: Dry land swallowed up the water, creation swallowed up chaos, and order swallowed up disorder (14:21-22). Yahweh has won! Earth is ordered! Israel is safe!

In the second half of the main body of the poem (vv. 13-17), the setting and tone have changed. We are not now at the waters as in vv. 4-10, but are moving through occupied territory. In the literary-liturgical antecedents to Israel's song, the genre amounts to *a victory parade, a triumphal procession,* in which the winning God moves in processional splendor to take up his throne. Along the parade route, those who watch the victory parade stand in silent awe, witnesses filled both with respect and dread. These verses portray Yahweh and Israel moving triumphantly on to the land of promise, moving without resistance, because all the potential resisters have seen Yahweh's great victory and are duly intimidated.

The dominant image here is not power, as in vv. 4-10, but the "steadfast love"

---

71. See Herbert Schneidau, "Let the Reader Understand," 140-42.

(חסד hesed) of the God who journeys now in protective leadership (v. 13). This part of the poem characterizes Israel's journey after the exodus on its way to the land of promise, a journey already anticipated in 3:7-9. This brief outline of the journey sketches the itinerary that is later followed in more detail in the book of Numbers. Here, however, the intention is not to recall all of those encounters, but to witness to the power and fidelity of Yahweh. Already in 13:21-22, we have been introduced to the protective leadership of Yahweh for this people that is "between places." The journey is dangerous, because it is through territory already occupied, in the face of peoples who are hostile, threatened, and suspicious. This hostility and suspicion are countered, so says the poem, by the fidelity of Yahweh, which is committed to this people whom Yahweh has "redeemed" (גאל gāʾal, v. 13) and "acquired" (קנה qānâ, v. 16). Both of these verbs connote an economic transaction. Yahweh has purchased the slaves and then has set them free. Yahweh now "possesses" these erstwhile slaves and can dispose of them as Yahweh chooses. What Yahweh chooses is to give them a safe place that is, in fact, God's own "holy abode" (v. 13).

Israel is protected by Yahweh, who embodies cosmic law. The watching peoples hear about this "invasion" and tremble, enormously agitated (v. 14). That is, they are seized by a powerful urge to do something to resist their loss of territory. "The peoples," here treated generically, include Israel's standard list of adversaries whose land they occupy: Philistines, Edomites, Moabites, and Canaanites. The poem assigns to each of these resentful witnesses a verb of anxiety and hostility: *seized, dismayed, trembling, melted.* Then in v. 16, is a summary statement of their common condition: "terror and dread."

The source of their immobilizing fear, however, is not Israel: It is Yahweh! Each of these peoples has its own god who protects its own territory. Each of these peoples, however, now knows that Yahweh is more powerful than their gods. It is the might of Yahweh's arm (which saves, which drowns) that reduces these peoples to sullen submission. They know the sorry tale of the resistant

pharaoh. If the great king of Egypt could not compete with Yahweh, then much smaller peoples and much weaker gods have no chance.

How long must this grim spectacle persist? How long must these watching witnesses remain immobilized by fear? For as long as Yahweh wants; for as long as it takes to get every Israelite—every man, woman, child, cow, and sheep of Israel—safely pastured. The poem uses a double "until" (v. 16). Now, for the first time in the second half, Yahweh is named, and only with reference to Israel: "Until your people, O Yahweh, have passed by." Normal life in all these places is suspended, until this community, which is possessed and treasured by Yahweh, is brought to safety.

It is not completely clear what this poem intends as a destination. While we expect the goal to be the land, the language of the poem suggests, rather, a sanctuary, perhaps the Temple to be established in Jerusalem (cf. the "mountain" in v. 17). Scholars are uncertain whether the reference is to land or sanctuary; perhaps the elusive rhetoric of the poem does not require a decision. The conventional accent on the "credo" (cf. 3:7-9, 17) would tilt our reading toward the land. In the book of Exodus itself, however, the text culminates with the establishment of a right sanctuary (see Exodus 35–40). Taken either way, the goal is a safe place that is marked by the majestic and protective presence of God.

Verse 18 provides a conclusion to the poem that is structurally the counterpart to vv. 1-3. At the outset, the poem celebrates the military prowess of Yahweh. Now in v. 18, Israel sounds a great doxological affirmation of Yahweh's enthronement. That enthronement, however, does not leave Yahweh in splendid isolation. Rather, the enthronement has required both the safe establishment of Israel and the proper deference of the nations. Yahweh's enthronement entails a reordering of human power for the enhancement of those who have been despised by the nations.

The poem is exceedingly difficult and complicated, and many interpretive problems persist. We may, however, see that in one possible reading the poem is organized in a chiastic fashion:

A *The introduction* announces the core theme: that Yahweh is to be praised for throwing the horse and rider into the sea (vv. 1-3).

  B The *first core element* is a *victory song* (vv. 4-10). In a struggle for divine authority, which in the experience of Israel is constituted by exodus; Yahweh has "gotten glory" over all adversaries.

    C At the center is *the doxological reprise* affirming the distinctiveness and incomparability of Yahweh (vv. 11-12).

  B´ The *second core element* is the triumphal entry of the victor in majestic procession on the way to the throne (vv. 13-17). In Israel's experience, this procession is constituted by the journey toward the land of promise; Yahweh's triumphal entry is at the same time the entry of Israel into well-being.

A´ *The conclusion* is an enthronement formula that anticipates Yahweh's very long-term governance (v. 18).

This extraordinary poem dramatizes and reenacts the story of Yahweh. In Israel's imagination, however, the story of Yahweh can never be told without its being at the same time the story of Israel. As the latter, this poem is the account whereby a helpless company of vulnerable slaves traverses the dangerous territory to a safe land of their own. To be sure, Israel's story could not happen unless this was first of all Yahweh's story. But it is equally clear that Yahweh's story can never be told unless it is at the same time the story of Israel. Humanly speaking, one can conclude that Israel is unwilling or unable to tell Yahweh's story unless it is also a story about "us." Theologically, the poem asserts that Yahweh will not undertake this story unless Israel can be its subject. In the end, the two stories—*the story of victory and enthronement* and *the story of liberation and homecoming*—are deeply intertwined and cannot be told apart from each other.

15:19. After Moses' poem, the narrator has added a prose comment that gives closure to the entire unit of the Exodus narrative. This prose comment only reiterates in summary fashion the second wondrous act of Yahweh (there wrought through Moses) in 14:26-29, whereby the waters return. After the rescue, Yahweh puts things back where they belong. Now life goes on with the "normal" arrangement of land and sea, creation and chaos.

15:20-21. Finally, as the great rhetorical climax to this long tale of inversion, we are given a brief poem, commonly called "The Song of Miriam." This poem is regarded by scholars as being very old, perhaps the oldest Israelite poem we have and perhaps composed very close to the time of these remembered events. The poem itself in v. 21 has already been encountered in v. 1, where it is quoted.

This brief hymn follows the convention of Israel's hymns in its two parts. First, there is an imperative summons, in this case, "Sing to Yahweh." The summons to praise is itself an act of praise, an exuberant acknowledgment of Yahweh and a glad ceding over of energy and loyalty to Yahweh. Second, reasons for praise are given, introduced by the particle *for* (כִּי *kî*, "because"). The reason for praise of Yahweh, the incomparable one, is quite specific. Yahweh has overcome the seemingly invincible power of armed might that enforced aggression. The "power" in this poem is not specifically Pharaoh and Egypt. The lack of specificity permits the poem to be readily available as a paradigm for every doxology that celebrates death to tyrants.

The poem (song) is placed on the lips and in the dancing feet of Miriam and the Israelite women. We know elsewhere that there were women especially skilled in the singing required by the community for grief and death (Jer 9:17; 2 Chr 35:25). In the same way, no doubt there were women, perhaps the same ones, skilled in singing and dancing with joy and exultation for liberation, victory, and well-being (cf. 1 Sam 18:7). The OT lets us see a community that is easily and readily evoked into the "surplus" activity of liturgy for the emotional, political extremities of joy and grief, well-being and loss.

It may be that at the exodus itself there was such singing and dancing, such glad release of stifled yearning, such freedom for which bodies in Israel had long ached. How could it be otherwise! There is also no doubt that as the exodus liberation became a stylized liturgical event, this song and its unfettered dancing must have become standard practice. It is the liturgic remembering and hoping of every community of the oppressed that catches a glimpse of freedom and authorizes liturgical (and eschatological) exaggeration to say, "Free at last!" When the song is sung, clearly this is not yet "at last." The community at worship, however, can dare such exaggeration, because its hope is more powerful and more compelling than any present circumstance.

Finally, no doubt, this song, rooted in exodus experience and preserved in exodus liturgy, is taken up for the canonical telling of the biblical story. Now the story of Miriam and the women is placed as the ultimate verdict of Israel's faith. As such, it stands as a massive, lyrical resolution to the grief and cry of 2:23-25. Israel's *initial cry* (which began the liberating work of Yahweh) and *concluding shout* stand in an arc of faith. The larger narrative of Israel—the old, old story that Israel loves to tell (and act out)—is the Passover tale of grief and joy, trouble and resolution, oppression and liberation. Passover imagination, centered in the one who hears the cry and dances in delight, dares to see all of Israel's existence, all of human existence (indeed, the tale of all creation) as a drama from hurt to well-being. Israel claims, moreover, to know the name of the elusive character who makes the story relentlessly and recurrently true, visible, and actualized in the very bodies of the Israelites.

REFLECTIONS

1. God is portrayed here in embarrassingly anthropomorphic categories (i.e., God has qualities of emotion and body that may offend our "metaphysical propensities"). Our Western inclination to portray God as removed from the human drama of our experience, however, is a highly dubious gain. Such anthropomorphic portrayals as we have in this text belong to the core of biblical faith, and are not incidental footnotes. Moreover, such earthiness brings the questions and resources of faith very close to how we experience and live reality. Such speech in this poem opens up the most elemental struggles and hopes that are part of the human enterprise. No other mode of theological speech so well touches the human concreteness of faith.

2. More specifically, the military metaphors for God raise problems. Yahweh is "a man of war," a description that seems to evoke and authorize violence in the world. Our primary way of dealing with this problem is to transpose the political-historical violence into ontological violence—i.e., God's struggle with death. No doubt there is something positive in such an interpretive move (made even in the Bible itself). Such a maneuver, however, may on occasion be a bourgeois device. It is evident that theological rhetoric about God's use of force against the power of oppression is not experienced as violent by those who are, in fact, oppressed. In a situation of victimization, one is not so worried about violence in the power of one's rescuer. Metaphors of violence are problematic, but we must take care not to escape them by ideological dismissal. There is in the gospel a model of conflict and a deep struggle for power and authority. To miss this element is to distort biblical faith into a benign, innocent affair. We are (as the Bible recognizes) caught in a deep battle for humanness, a battle larger than we ourselves can manage. This, finally, is what faith asserts in its claim that "God is for us."

3. The power of God for well-being, in the sub-currents of this text, concerns the power of cosmic ordering in the face of the surging threat of chaos. Thus the imagery of water and the sea are allusions to the elemental disordering that lives all around our safety and well-being. The news of God's management of the waters and the capacity of the dry land to swallow up the threat is good news: The world is not, in the end, chaotic.

4. This affirmation about holy power clearly has a public, political dimension. It is precisely Pharaoh and his tools of domination (horses and chariots) that are destroyed. The good news of the poem is that God's power for life is arrayed against, and victorious over, every enemy of human well-being in every present power arrangement.

5. Derivatively, this poem is good news in our personal dramas as well. The poem asserts paradigmatically that God is for us, that we as listeners are invited into the world of God's fidelity to be a member of this people whom God has now acquired and treasures.

6. The peculiar image for the show of God's rescuing power is God's רוח (*rûaḥ*). The "wind" here refers concretely to the force that blows the waters back. We may see this usage in v. 8 ("blast") and in v. 10 ("wind") as references to God's force, which moves the world toward life. This "spirit" (as the Hebrew may also be rendered) is not to be read as "the third person of the Trinity," but is the active force of God's irresistible intention unleashed into the world. This force is unadministered, unintimidated, undomesticated, insatiable, and able to move the world toward life.

The wind of God is, in the Christian confession, no doubt profoundly focused in the power of Easter, where God's inscrutable capacity to work life in the face of the determined power of death is demonstrated. Indeed, in the categories of Christian faith, this great poem has its counterpart in the Easter narratives of the Gospels and in the great Pauline lyric of 1 Corinthians 15. Paul can scarcely find words with which to utter the inscrutable power of life in the world that refuses the governance of death. Ezekiel 37:1-14 already provides the language whereby the work of the Spirit and the power of the resurrection are deeply linked to each other.

7. This poem, framed around the crisis of exodus liberation (vv. 4-10) and sojourn-conquest (vv. 13-17), shapes the credo tradition of Israel.[72] These verses assert, in what may be Israel's most crucial articulation of its creed, that Israel's life consists in *liberation from* and *entry into.* These are the two points already promised in 3:7-8. That is, life is shaped as departure from bondage and access to liberated well-being. This same modeling of reality is mediated in Christian liturgy and characterizes the Christian pilgrimage of life in Christ. That life consists in dying with Christ and being raised to new life, in taking the form of a servant and being exalted, in denying oneself and having life given abundantly.

72. See Miller, *The Divine Warrior in Early Israel*, 166-75.

EXODUS 15:22–18:27

"IS THE LORD AMONG US OR NOT?"

OVERVIEW

These chapters articulate a subordinate theme in the book of Exodus: the wilderness sojourn. With the book of Numbers, the wilderness sojourn will come to occupy a much larger place in the completed narrative.

Here the wilderness sojourn functions primarily as a geographical device for the larger narrative. It provides a way to move action from one place to another, or to indicate the passage of time. Specifically, these materials and this theme help move the action from the "Sea of Reeds" to Mt. Sinai. Careful attention has been given by scholars to the historical, geographical, and archaeological elements of the narrative.[73] It is, however, completely impossible to assess the "historical" reliability of any of these narratives.

What may have been a transitional literary convenience, however, has become a freighted theme that makes its own contribution to the larger theological claims of the completed tradition. The wilderness through which Israel traverses comes to be a metaphor for a zone of life not properly ordered and without the usual, reliable life-support systems. The several narrative episodes characteristically revolve around the need of Israel, the distrust of Israel (which becomes an attack on Moses' leadership), and the generous, life-sustaining gifts of Yahweh (cf. Ps 78:19-20). Thus the theological issues regularly come to the fore, and the narrative exhibits little interest in geographical, historical details. Moreover, the wilderness metaphor serves as an

effective cipher for exile, thus being crucial for the exilic and post-exilic community that brought the text to its final form.

The paradigmatic narrative in this small grouping of texts is, of course, chapter 16. In that story about manna, the need of Israel is more than met by the powerful generosity of Yahweh. The derivative themes of the sabbath and the fearful hoarding of bread suggest the broad range of issues present in the theme of the wilderness sojourn. The brief episodes concerning Marah, Elim, and Rephaidim witness to the same suppleness of the tradition.

Two narratives do not fit this general pattern of need and gift. First, the encounter with the Amalekites is odd in this context and serves a quite distinct ideological interest (17:8-16). Second, chapter 18, with its reference to Jethro, stands all alone and does not seem to relate to anything in its context. Both 17:8-16, concerning perpetual war, and 18:13-27, concerning judicial procedures, portray Moses as devising new institutional practices (war and justice) in the process of nation building.[74]

Primary interpretive attention, however, will most likely be given to the other narratives concerning need and gift. Yahweh is indeed able to give life, especially in circumstances where resources for life are not evident and where Pharaoh could not give life. Yahweh's capacity to give life where there is none, to give bread from heaven and water from rock, are examples of *creatio ex nihilo,* God's capacity to form a people out of "no people" (cf. 1 Pet 2:9-10).

73. See George W. Coats, *Rebellion in the Wilderness: The Murmuring Motif in the Wilderness Traditions of the Old Testament* (Nashville: Abingdon, 1968); and Graham I. Davies, *The Way of the Wilderness: A Geographical Study of the Wilderness Itineraries in the Old Testament* (Cambridge: Cambridge University Press, 1979).

74. On Moses as a political leader, see Aaron Wildavsky, *The Nursing Father: Moses as a Political Leader* (Tuscaloosa: The University of Alabama Press, 1984).

EXODUS 15:22-27, BITTER WATER MADE SWEET

COMMENTARY

The journey away from bondage to well-being and from Egypt to the new land, begun in 12:37-39, continues. The setting is "the wilderness," the territory not under the control of Pharaoh. It is also, however, the territory where there is no ordered, reliable life-support system. Wilderness habitation is life at risk. This brief unit features Israel at two "watering holes" (oases): Marah (vv. 23-25a) and Elim (v. 27). The two oases reports sandwich a divine oracle voiced by the God who commands and who heals (vv. 25b-26). Another way to see the construction of this passage is that it moves from "no water" (v. 22) to "water" (v. 27), by way of God's speech (v. 26).

The first encounter at Marah concerns a water shortage, which is promptly transposed into a crisis of leadership (vv. 23-25a). The name of the place is Marah ("bitter"). It is commonly thought by scholars that the tale is told to explain how the oasis got its name, "bitter." What may have been such a name-tale (etymological saga) is, however, transposed by the tradition into a serious theological crisis. There is no water, exactly what one might expect in the wilderness where life is at risk. Without water, the people will soon die.

The people "complain" against Moses. They are restless and discontented with his leadership. The trust they have placed in him (v. 14:31) is soon dissipated, perhaps with the general wonderment, "What has Moses done for us lately?" Moses, however, does not respond to the complaint. Rather, he himself turns into a complainer against Yahweh: "He cried out to Yahweh." There is a two-tiered leadership in which the people deal with Moses, and Moses deals with Yahweh. Thus Moses promptly turns the water crisis over to Yahweh.

We have already seen the rhetorical construct of "complaint-assurance" in 14:11-14, wherein Israel's complaint receives from Moses a salvation oracle that overcomes the cause of complaint. This narrative is structured in the same way, except that Yahweh's response is not a speech, but an act: Yahweh provides a means whereby bitter water becomes sweet. The crisis is averted, and Moses' leadership is again accepted. The life-threatening situation of the wilderness is overcome by a "wonder."

The second element of the unit is a decree of Yahweh (v. 25b-26). This decree has no visible connection to the preceding "wonder," except that the God who presides over life-processes is now entitled to assert sovereignty. This verse makes unmistakeably clear that the liberation from Egypt does not lead to autonomy for Israel, but rather to an alternative sovereignty that imposes an alternative regimen on the liberated slaves. This single verse presents Yahweh as the God who commands, and it anticipates the larger tradition of command in the Sinai meeting to come.

The decree of Yahweh issues a comprehensive command and makes an extraordinary promise. The command is introduced with a conditional "if," followed by an infinitive absolute, "if you will *really* hear," exactly the same instruction as in 19:5 and Deut 15:5. This statement of urgency is followed by three additional verbs of command—*do, give heed,* and *keep*—which are all roughly synonymous. These verbs govern the terms *right, commandments,* and *statutes,* which are synonymous references to the intention and purpose of Yahweh, the new possessor of the liberated slaves. In this triad following the conditional infinitive absolute, Israel is bound, securely and finally, to the will and purpose of Yahweh. So far, this mention of Yahweh's commands is given no substance, and the statement remains completely formal. In this utterance, nonetheless, Israel is radically redefined as a community whose single purpose is the doing of Yahweh's command.

The second half of Yahweh's decree is an assurance. It is odd that the second half of the statement is not in any effective way related to the preceding. We expect an "if . . . then" construction, but there is no "then" in the text. Perhaps it is understood; however, it is not certain whether freedom from Egyptian "diseases" depends on the preceding command, though that is likely implied.

As a seal and guarantee of both the command and the promise, Yahweh issues a magisterial statement of self-identity and self-disclosure: "I am Yahweh." This is not Pharaoh, not a god of burdensome obedience, not a power that generates disease, but a genuine alternative power. Moreover, that magisterial formula is now exposited in a new and remarkable way: "who heals you." The participle might also be translated as a noun, "your healer," or "your doctor." Thus there is introduced into Israel's rhetoric God's concern for the therapeutic, which stands in

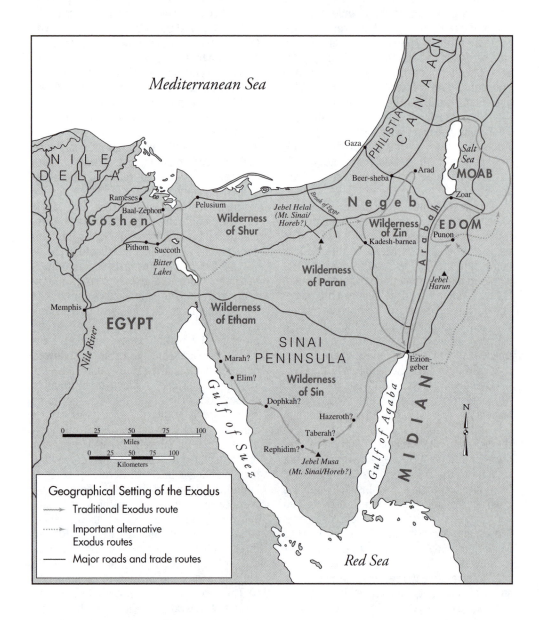

Geographical Setting of the Exodus

→ Traditional Exodus route

⋯▸ Important alternative Exodus routes

— Major roads and trade routes

complete contrast to the Egyptian powers who generate disease.

The final verse of this unit (v. 27), perhaps, has no integral relation to the preceding. It seems to stand alone. In its context, however, Elim, a luxurious oasis, stands in complete contrast to Marah. There is nothing bitter here; therefore, there is no contentiousness among the people. Instead of "no water," there is water. The wilderness contains adequate resources for life! The text itself makes no explicit connection between v. 27 and what precedes. In its present sequence, however, it is fair to think that v. 27 is offered as a case in point of what the new life looks like when the commands and assurances of Yahweh are taken seriously.

REFLECTIONS

1. This is a concrete case of utter dependence. Water is required for life and is urgent in the wilderness. Water cannot be invented, devised, or manufactured. It can only be given and received. These two tales of water assert both Israel's vulnerability and utter dependence, and Yahweh's fidelity in giving what is needed for life. God's people are shown here in their deep precariousness; God is shown in utter, sovereign fidelity. There is no doubt that biblical faith takes "water" as a metaphor for the gift of life in the gospel, most clearly in John 4:7-15.

2. The exodus is construed as a healing, as restoration to healthy existence. The situation of bondage in which Israel finds itself is one of disorder and pathology, not a true state of human existence. This God as "healer" is the one who liberates, redeems, ransoms, restores to the true intention of creation.

So much that is silly and trivial has been said in recent time about therapy.[75] It is indeed a deep misfortune that therapy and healing have in popular parlance become so trivialized. The cost of such a mistaken, truncated notion of "healing" is chronicled in Robert Bellah et al., *Habits of the Heart.*[76] Such caricatures of therapy, however, have nothing to do with the healing intention of God, which is to restore persons, communities, and ultimately the whole of creation to their rightful status of health, as creatures loved by and responsive to the purposes of the creator. This "therapy" is not some act of self-indulgence that touches nothing serious. True therapy, the kind worked by the living God, is a radical reconstrual of reality, a radical recharacterization of self before God, a deep revision of power arrangements in the world, and a demanding embrace of God's good purposes for self and world.[77] This same work of healing, moreover, is entrusted by Jesus to his disciples, who are to do the work of God (Luke 10:9). The claim of the gospel is not only that God is about the work of restoring creation to health, but that God's resolve to effect wholeness is entrusted to human agents.

3. The structure of Yahweh's decree appears to be completely an "if . . . then" statement of conditionality. There is no free offer of healing. One cannot be healed of a pathology if one insists on continuing the practices that initially produced the condition. In this case, the healing of the diseases of Egypt requires coming under the command of Yahweh and renouncing the commands of Egypt.

This statement of conditionality is not a petty supernaturalism that says God will not heal if one does not act right. Rather, it is better understood through serious social criticism. The systemic pathologies of an exploitative system can be escaped only if one stops colluding with the system. The way to stop such collusion, says the decree of Yahweh, is to commit to a different pattern of obedience that is rooted in a different vision.

75. See the critical analysis of Philip Rieff, *The Triumph of the Therapeutic: Uses of Faith After Freud* (New York: Harper and Row, 1966).
76. Robert N. Bellah et al., *Habits of the Heart: Individualism and Commitment in American Life* (Berkeley: University of California Press, 1985).
77. For a classic, public notion of "therapy," see Robert E. Cushman, *Therapeia: Plato's Conception of Philosophy* (Westport, Conn.: Greenwood, 1958).

Specifically, if consumerism is destroying the human spirit among us and crushing the values of family and community, and if consumerism produces a pathology of abused persons in inadequate relations, then there is no remedy within that system. Remedy requires breaking with that system for the sake of a different set of relations that are authorized by the commands of torah. Like the Israelites who lust for Egyptian "fleshpots," so we can be endlessly seduced precisely by the system that generates the disability. The decree of Yahweh invites, authorizes, and requires a deep and intentional break with Egypt in order to be healed. There is no cheap, easy healing, but there is healing. Those who trust the decree of Yahweh and make the break will find themselves at the oasis with an abundance of sweet water.

EXODUS 16:1-36, MANNA AND QUAIL

COMMENTARY

The wilderness continues to be a profoundly troubling place for Israel, where the necessities for survival are not immediately supplied. This long narrative is paradigmatic for the crisis of faith that occurs between bondage and well-being. Israel has no other story that lays out the theme so clearly. We may take this text as representative for the faith issues with which Israel must deal in its times of displacement (e.g., exile). After an introduction, establishing the nature of the crisis (vv. 1-3), there is the giving of the gift of bread (vv. 4-15), the reception of bread (vv. 16-30), and the "sacramentalization" of the bread (vv. 31-36).

16:1-3. The departure from Elim portends the lack of adequate food, water, and life-support. The crisis of the wilderness is a material crisis with great anxiety over what to eat and what to drink. It predictably becomes a crisis over leadership. The beginning point of the narrative is an assault upon the leadership of Moses and Aaron, who have chosen for Israel trouble (liberation) instead of bondage.

The complaint of Israel (which does not mention Yahweh at all) makes a sharp and unfavorable contrast between the wilderness and Egypt. The wilderness is a place of hunger and will inevitably lead to death. By contrast, Egypt is remembered as a place of "pots of flesh" (i.e., meat) and bread, so that even in bondage there may be material satiation. The contrast, so far as it goes, is no doubt correct; there is no hint that the bondaged Hebrews in Egypt lacked bread.

What is striking in this assaulting contrast is how present anxiety distorts the memory of

the recent past. Egypt is known to be a place of deep abuse and heavy-handed oppression. Here, however, none of the oppression or abuse is mentioned, only meat and bread. The seductive distortion of Israel is that, given anxiety about survival, the immediacy of food overrides any long-term hope for freedom and well-being. The desperate, fearful choice that Israel voices in this contrast is reminiscent of Esau, who was willing to forego his birthright for immediate satisfaction in food (Gen 25:29-34).

In its anxiety, Israel is willing to make a very poor trade. Israel is not reprimanded in this narrative for its anxious concern, but receives an immediate, positive response. Israel is not required to repent its yearning for food; rather, they can expect to receive food from another source, one that requires dependence but does not lead to a fresh bondage.

16:4-15. The response to the complaint is the enactment of a "wonder" that redescribes the wilderness as a place of life. It is striking, however, that the response is not made by Moses, to whom the complaint is addressed. Nor does Moses transmit the complaint to Yahweh. Rather, Yahweh takes over the complaint addressed to Moses and answers the complaint directly (vv. 4-5).

Yahweh's promise has two parts. First, there will be bread "from heaven"—i.e., bread given out of God's rich storehouse, so that it need not come from Pharaoh's storehouses (v. 4; cf. 1:11; Gen 47:13-19). Quail is also given in answer to a yearning for meat. (Notice that in Ps 78:26 "the wind of heaven" brings bread and meat. On that wind, see Job 38:24 as well as Exod 14:21.)

Second, there is a special provision for sabbath, so that the bread given on the sixth day is enough for the seventh (v. 5). As we shall see, the theme of sabbath is woven throughout this narrative concerning free bread. Between these two provisions concerning "bread from heaven" and sabbath, God resolves to "test" Israel in order to determine whether Israel is prepared to receive bread and life under wholly new terms and completely changed conditions. The ways of receiving bread in Egypt are completely inappropriate here. Israel will be under scrutiny to see if old ways of receiving bread in Egypt (in anxiety, oppression, hoarding) can be resisted.

On the basis of this promise from Yahweh to Moses, there now follows a speech of Moses-Aaron to the people (vv. 6-8), a statement of Moses to Aaron (v. 9), a statement of Yahweh to Moses (vv. 11-12), and narrative reports on the implementation of God's promise (vv. 10, 13-15). This sequence of exchange reiterates three themes: First, it is affirmed four times that God has *heard* Israel's complaint (vv. 7-9, 12). This is, in fact, the crucial theme in the drama. The narrative insists on this point, because the hearing by Yahweh overrides the complaint. Second, it is twice asserted on the basis of being heard that "you shall know" (vv. 6, 12). You shall *know* that it was Yahweh who rescued. You shall know that the key character in this new, precarious life is precisely Yahweh and none other. Third, the wilderness, which appears bereft of any life-giving presence, will be the host context of God's glory. The glory is promised (v. 7); then the glory is *seen* (v. 10). Israel knows that wilderness is not empty but is inhabited by the powerful presence of God. In these three rhetorical moves of hearing, knowing, and seeing, Israel's complaint is dealt with by a massive disclosure that God is powerfully and decisively present.

Moses (through Aaron) invites Israel, the congregation (עדה *'ēdâ*) to "draw near," or to gather in worship (v. 9). When they do, they see "the glory" (v. 10). This verse is cast in the language of worship, not only with the verb "draw near," but also with an emphasis on "glory" as a real, visible presence in the midst of worship. Although cast in the language of worship, the coming of God's glory is at the same time a remarkable and dramatic turn in the larger narrative. "Glory" bespeaks magisterial and wondrous presence, embodying God's sovereignty. The complaint of v. 3 indicates that Israel still associates "glory" (and the power to give life) with the splendor, wealth, prestige, and extravagance of Egypt. Compared to the glory of Egypt, the wilderness holds little attraction.

In drawing near, however, Israel dramatically turns its face away from Egypt and looks again toward the wilderness. It sees there what it always thought to see in Egypt, and what it never expected to see in the wilderness. It is not an empty, deathly place, but the locus of God's sovereign splendor. The wilderness is more brilliant than Egypt, because Yahweh has "gotten glory over Pharaoh" (14:4, 17). By God's rule, the wilderness is completely redefined.

After these several speeches, there still remains the concrete problem of delivering bread to a hungry, protesting people (vv. 13-15). Everything finally depends not on theological talk or religious manifestation, but on the availability of food for life. And then it happens—enough quail to blanket the camp, meat all over the place! Next morning, there is a kind of bread under the dew that the Israelites have never seen before. Moses must tell them that it is "bread that the LORD has given you to eat" (v. 15). Thus their complaints are answered precisely. In place of Egyptian flesh, they are given quail; in place of Egyptian bread, they have bread from God. The wilderness, which seemed a threat, has become a nurturing place.

The brief exchange of v. 15 about the name of the bread is interesting, though perhaps not very significant. This is bread Israel has never seen; it is not the bread of coercion and affliction. So they say מן הוא (*mān hû'*, "What is it?"), and this question provides the popular name for the bread: *Manna*. That name, however, has no positive content. It is only a question, one that indicates that this is strange, unfamiliar bread without any antecedents or parallels. The positive identification of the bread is in Moses' explanation: It is bread given by Yahweh to eat.

16:16-30. There are, however, two conditions for the right reception of bread. The people shall harvest just enough bread for the day and gather no surplus, so that everyone has enough and nobody has too little. The provision for the bread becomes a model for the right distribution of food and a paradigm for a covenant community that is trustfully organized around God's unfailing generosity. The wondrous reality about the distribution of this bread is that their uncompetitive, non-hoarding practice really does work, and it works for all! The ones who gather a lot do not have too much; the ones who gather a little have no lack (vv. 17-18). The bread has a way of being where it is needed, with everyone having a sufficiency. Thus the bread becomes a means whereby (a) God's reliability is to be trusted, and (b) neighbors are to live together in trustful equity.

Israel, however, refuses to trust the God who promised and supplies the bread. They refuse to live in vulnerable equity with neighbors. Some seek to store up bread in violation of Moses' warning. They want to establish a surplus, to develop a zone of self-sufficiency. The people in the wilderness immediately try to replicate the ways of Egypt by storing up and hoarding out of anxiety and greed. However, this bread (bread of another kind given by God) cannot be stored up. The narrator takes pains to underscore that stored-up, surplus bread is useless. Bread that reflects self-sufficient anxiety and greed will have no food value for Israel, so that the bread of disobedience breeds worms, turns sour, and melts (vv. 20-21).

A special practice is permitted, however, on the sixth day in order to provide food for the sabbath day, which follows (vv. 22-26). What is permitted for the sake of the sabbath directly contradicts what is prohibited for all the other days. What cannot be carried over from one day to the next is now carried over to the day of sabbath. The sabbath authorizes storing up bread, because when designed for sabbath, the extra bread does not reflect either anxiety or greed.

Once again, however, Israel disobeys. In v. 27, some of the people go out to gather on the sabbath, in direct violation of the command just given. Yet, when they go out to gather they find no bread. Not only must the people refrain from working on the sabbath, but also God's own bakeries are closed for the day. Creation is shut down, and the heavens rest. Moses' rebuke of them is sharp: "How long?" The answer is not given, but we may anticipate that the refusal of the commands will last a very long time in Israel.

Verse 30, which concludes this unit, is somewhat surprising. It is as though the community has been converted, as though it has belatedly become convicted to the sabbath command and honors it. This verse is remarkable because it puts a good end to what has been essentially a narrative account of stubborn resistance. (This interpretive maneuver is the antithesis of 17:7, which puts a negative interpretation on a "wonder.")

16:31-36. After the gift of bread and its hard-hearted reception, the chapter ends as the bread is solidified into a sacramental memorial. Now the dispute about the bread has disappeared. A measure of this bread is placed in a jar to be preserved and witnessed to in perpetuity. It is to be kept visible and seen by Israel through the generations as a witness and reminder. Happily, the memory that inhabits the jar is a selective, corrected memory. According to the text, the jar of manna does not allude to the hoarding that violates the provision for dailiness. Nor does the jar refer to the sabbath violation against the provision for rest. Rather, the jar is a positive testimony. It attests only to the generous fidelity of Yahweh in the wilderness after the exodus. It asserts that bread is given, that God is faithful, that life in wilderness is possible, that Israel is safe.

REFLECTIONS

1. The good news of this text is that God gives bread and nourishment for life as the sovereign ruler and governor of all creation. Fretheim wants to insist on the "naturalness" of manna, that it is produced in ways that can be understood according to natural phenomena.[78] By contrast, Calvin takes enormous pains to argue that the bread

78. Fretheim, *Exodus,* 181-82.

of heaven is "contrary to the order of nature."[79] Clearly, Calvin and Fretheim have very different agendas. I suggest that the bread is given according to God's providential ordering of creation. That, however, is an ordering not impinged upon by the mechanisms of technology or bureaucracy. To imagine providence unencumbered by these is well nigh miraculous. God does not depend on the technical apparatus or the bureaucratic arrangements of Egypt for the delivery of bread, but gives bread out of the richness of God's own treasure house.

2. This affirmation of God's good bread pertains precisely to the wilderness, those regions of life wherein Israel is peculiarly dependent and without resources of its own. Verse 35 identifies the zone of free bread as extending "until they came to a habitable land." And Josh 5:12 affirms that on the day they ate the produce of the land, "the manna ceased" for the Israelites. In the wilderness, the primary concern is anxiety about survival; in the land, the temptation is complacency about self-sufficiency. This story of manna is not for all of life. It is for life in those zones of bereftness when the problem is not self-sufficiency but despair, need, and anxiety. From first to last, wilderness is subject to God's ongoing providential generosity.

3. Because the gospel stays so close to concrete, material reality, it is not surprising that this narrative is taken up in powerful ways in the story of Jesus.

On the one hand, the story of manna is replicated in the actions of Jesus. Thus in his feeding of the crowds of 5,000 persons (Mark 6:30-41; John 6:1-4) and of 4,000 persons (Mark 8:1-10), Jesus acts messianically to give bread where there is none. These narratives are cast in eucharistic language, suggesting that the church fully understood the paradigmatic quality of the manna narrative.

On the other hand, in Jesus' discourse about his own person and his mission (John 6:25-59), reference to our text is crucial. The connection to this narrative is direct and explicit: "It is my Father who gives you the true bread from heaven" (John 6:32 NRSV). The narrative is turned in a very different direction with the claim, "I am the bread that came down from heaven" (John 6:41 NRSV). The peculiar mode of discourse in the Fourth Gospel permits the manna story to be taken up and refocused as a christological affirmation. While the listening community in John 6 is bewildered by Jesus' statement, there is no doubt that Jesus is presented as the sign, assurance, and reality of God's generous fidelity, which supplies the need of all those who are faithful (who accept his messianic person).

4. Just as the text provides a model for christology, so also it functions as a model for ecclesiology. In his discussion of the collection for the Jerusalem church, Paul directly quotes this narrative (2 Cor 8:8-15). He suggests that equity in the Christian community results when the ones with abundance and the ones with need live in generosity to each other. The way the bread is distributed in the manna story is a model for the way the church shares and distributes goods with equity and liberality.

5. Woven all through the manna narrative is an argument about the character and cruciality of the sabbath.

I suggest that sabbath is a way of contrasting wilderness with Egypt positively. Egypt is a place where bread is gotten only for labor, where bread is given only as a reward for productivity, and where bread is always received in and with fearful anxiety. The gift of bread, then, is a decisive break with the exploitative conditions of Egyptian bread. "Bread from heaven" is an invitation to break with the destructive politics of bread production and the pressures upon which the empire depends for productivity—namely, fear, abuse, anxiety, and exploitation. Sabbath is yet another opportunity to depart economically and psychologically from Egyptian modes of social reality. The

---

79. Calvin, *Commentaries on the Four Last Books of Moses Arranged in the Form of a Harmony*, 276.

alternative in this narrative is a world of glad dependence and utter fidelity, devoid of all anxiety and threat. The conclusion of the narrative, "So the people rested on the seventh day" (v. 30), is an affirmation that at least for this narrative Egyptian patterns of existence have been nullified.

6. It is striking that in the Sermon on the Mount, Jesus' instructions for prayer (Matt 6:7-15) and against anxiety (Matt 6:25-33) are closely related. In the prayer, the community of disciples is summoned to pray daily for bread. That is, they are to rely on God for each day's supply, without anxious hoarding. The instruction about anxiety thus plays upon the theme from the prayer.

There is a temptation to serve two masters, Yahweh and Pharaoh, and to trust in two bread supplies, the bread of heaven and the bread of the sweat of our brow (cf. Matt 6:24). This teaching of Jesus urges that seeking to have it both ways generates endless anxiety. The only way out of the anxiety is to make a clean, unambiguous decision. The gospel is the affirmation, made earlier in the wilderness, that God knows what is needed and that God faithfully supplies everything required for life.

7. In the life of the church, this narrative that culminates in a jar has been preserved in the form of the "jarring" narrative of the eucharist. The eucharist reenacts and keeps visioning what the world will be like when the bread from heaven is not hoarded, but is trusted in by the human community on a daily basis. Thus the eucharist is not some otherworldly act of spirituality, but a glad affirmation that this counterstory of bread continues to be haunting and, therefore, powerful. This community continues to believe that bread that is broken and shared has power for life that bread does not have when it is unbroken and unshared—when it is guarded and hoarded.

It is not accidental that at the end of the miracle of the bread, Mark reports that they "did not understand about the loaves" (6:52 NRSV). They did not understand because "their hearts were hardened." It is a high irony that in an allusion to the manna story, it is now the disciples, not the people of Pharaoh, who have "hard hearts." Hard hearts make us rely on our own capacity and our own bread. In the end, they render all of these stories of alternative bread too dangerous and too outrageous for consideration. As a result, the bread practices of Pharaoh continue to prevail among us. In the presence of those practices, this community continues to watch the jar, tell the story, and imagine another bread that is taken and given, blessed and broken.

EXODUS 17:1-7, WATER FROM THE ROCK

COMMENTARY

Israel's life in the wilderness, in the aftermath of liberation and in pursuit of Yahweh's promise of the land, is precarious indeed. Israel proceeds "as the Lord commanded" (v. 1), but there is no water to drink. In the wilderness, Israel lacks the most elemental resource for life. This problem leads to two exchanges with Moses (vv. 2-3), which result in a "wonder" (vv. 5-6) and a reflective comment (v. 7).

The first exchange is brief and serves to question the leadership of Moses (v. 2). The people file a complaint (ריב *rîb*) against Moses for his ineffectiveness and his incompetence.

Moses has not and cannot produce drinking water. Moses' response consists in two rhetorical questions that repudiate the charge. The first question asks, in effect, "Why blame me?" We expect Moses to say, as he did in 16:7-8, that he is innocent and that the grievance should be addressed against Yahweh instead of him.

The second question in this case, however, surprises us. Moses reprimands Israel not only for criticizing him, but also for testing Yahweh. What Moses has done is to equate his leadership with that of Yahweh, for the two parts of the question are exactly parallel and equivalent. As it is unthinkable to "test" Yahweh (i.e., to make demands of Yahweh), so it is now unthinkable to challenge Moses.

Because the problem of water is neither acknowledged nor alleviated, it is predictable that there must be a second exchange with Moses (vv. 3-6). Again, the people accuse Moses (as in 16:3) of having caused death by instigating the exodus. Because the escalation of rhetoric is severe, Moses this time turns to Yahweh. His petition, however, is not for the well-being of the people, but for his own safety. Moses petitions Yahweh so that he himself will not be assaulted.

Unlike the first, the second exchange includes Yahweh as a speaker and actor. The second exchange, because of Yahweh's involvement, can have a life-giving outcome as the first exchange, without Yahweh, could not. Yahweh's response to Moses does not address the problem of Moses' leadership or safety, but directly addresses the people's problem of thirst. Moses is to use again his staff, which embodies his authority from Yahweh. Now Moses is to use his staff for a life-giving wonder for Israel.

The center of Yahweh's response, however, is in Yahweh's own commitment to the process: "Behold, I will be standing before you." Yahweh is involved with all the sovereignty that can be mustered to preside over this "wonder." The staff, the rock, the courage of Moses, the witness of the elders, and the guarantee of Yahweh all converge. After Yahweh's careful, detailed instruction, the narrator adds laconically, "He did so." The narrator does not even tell us whether there is water, the people drink, or that the problem is solved. All of that is already certain in the speech of Yahweh, which is much more interesting and crucial than is the implementation. The narrator is clear on the main point: Only Yahweh can give the resources for life, but Yahweh will do so through the work of Moses.

This small, rhetorical unit has the standard structure of *problem* and *resolution,* the movement from the one to the other wrought through a wonder.[80] The presence and power of Yahweh are perfectly capable of transforming rock to water and death to life. It is

likely important that the rock is "in Horeb," located in the peculiar precincts where Yahweh's presence is palpable and immediate. In the sphere of Yahweh's sovereignty, life is wrought in situations of death.

The narrator adds a comment that gives to the narrative an unexpected interpretive direction (v. 7). We might expect the conclusion of the narrative will celebrate in amazement the life-giving wonder wrought by Yahweh. Instead the narrator focuses on the two verbs that concern the plaintiff action of the people: *test* (נסה *nissâ*, thus "Massah") and *quarrel* (ריב *rîb*, thus "Meribah"). The story is slanted as a story of unfaith. It may be that the narrator is preoccupied with a limitation the two verbs impose, which serves to ground a "name tale." In larger context, however, the narrator is not interested in the explanation of place names but with issues of faith and unfaith. It is not that Yahweh must demonstrate a capacity for giving life; that is assumed. What is to be exhibited is not the power of God, but Israel's inappropriate and remarkable lack of faith. In the context of the narrative account of wonders in Egypt, Israel should have known and trusted.

Here, however, Israel is remarkably stubborn and arrogant. Israel dares to ask a demanding question that presumes upon Yahweh (v. 7). The only evidence of Yahweh's presence that Israel will accept is concrete action that saves. Thus Israel collapses God's promise into its own well-being and refuses to allow Yahweh any life apart from Israel's well-being. The question makes the religious issue completely pragmatic, resulting in an affirmation about Yahweh that in fact is a demand that Yahweh must now (right now!) give an account of Yahweh's faithful sovereignty. Thus the focus on *quarrel* and *test* accuses Israel of having inverted the relation with Yahweh, so that Yahweh must now *perform* at Israel's behest. As it turns out, Yahweh does so by producing water. According to the narrator, however, Israel badly misconstrues this act if it imagines that Yahweh's sovereignty can be reduced to meeting Israel's questions and demands.

80. On the narrative structure, see Robert C. Culley, *Studies in the Structure of Hebrew Narrative* (Philadelphia: Fortress, 1976).

REFLECTIONS

1. The story itself provides nearly a model for the structure of evangelical narrative, a structure that is replicated many times in the actions of God and in the saving miracles of Jesus. It is worth considering that the same structure is used as the standard form for television commercials in the United States. The problem is presented, and a need is boldly voiced, in this case thirst. There is a powerful *intervention by God,* here through Moses. There is *a happy resolution* of the problem through a gift of God, in this case water.

At the center of the narrative is the faithful, powerful intervention of God. The story is told as a witness of faith in order to place God's powerful fidelity and attentiveness as the middle term of the whole human drama, as life is moved from hunger to fullness, from thirst to water, from blindness to sight, from leprosy to cleanness, from poverty to well-being, and in the end, from death to life.

The derivative TV use of this structure falsely substitutes for God "the product." The problem may be loneliness, stress, or bad odor. When the "product" is used, life is powerfully transformed to one of companionship, calmness, popularity, peace, joy, and well-being. An evangelical critique of such advertisements is that they are in principle false. Whereas the product may deal with the presenting problem, it cannot in fact generate the joy and well-being that are characteristically promised. Thus the biblical claim in this structure is not only formal, but it is also a substantive claim that only the intervention of Yahweh can work a miracle. There are no other miracle workers.

2. Verse 7 constitutes something of an interpretive problem and offers a fresh interpretive possibility. This "clue" to interpretation suggests that the story is to be understood as a critique of utilitarian religion in which God is judged by the desired outcomes for the asking community. Thus the community in this story would conclude that if the Israelites lack well-being, then God is not present for them. This temptation to reduce religion to utilitarian effect is the problem with which the book of Job struggles. In the end, the whirlwind speeches of Job 38–41 assert (and Job accepts in 42:1-6) that the reality of God is not commensurate with human prosperity. This text provides the ground for criticism of communities of faith that seek to "program" the capacity of God to do the wonders required by the community.

EXODUS 17:8-16, AMALEK IS DEFEATED

COMMENTARY

As we have seen in 15:13-17, Israel's way to the land of promise was not without trouble and conflict. The way is fraught with adversaries, because Israel constitutes a political-military threat to the peoples who already occupy the land. This particular narrative, offensive as it is, identifies the Amalekites as the quintessential enemy of Israel. The narrative consists of two parts: the account of the victory itself (vv. 8-13) and the literary, interpretive process whereby this specific enemy is demonized and turned into a permanent, paradigmatic enemy (vv. 14-16).

17:8-13. The victory account itself makes nothing special or noteworthy out of the defeated Amalekites. It is a report of a confrontation, a battle, and a victory. Even here, however, the narrator presents two very different themes.

First, Joshua is introduced as the warrior who recruits the army, fights with the Amalekites, and defeats them (vv. 9-10*a*, 13). This is the first mention of Joshua in the Bible. He is introduced almost incidentally, as if the reader already knows who he is. His presence at this point in the narrative suggests the overlap of the traditions of Moses and Joshua—i.e., the traditions of exodus and "conquest."

Joshua will subsequently emerge as the pivotal figure in Israel's faith after Moses (and before Samuel). It will be the work of Joshua to lead Israel, to fight its battles as it seizes the land of promise, and to consolidate the victory by dividing the land among the tribes. His name in Hebrew is from יָשַׁע (yāšaʿ, "save"). It is unmistakable in the OT that "save" (i.e., salvation, savior) is first of all military imagery, so that the use of this term bespeaks a struggle with those too strong for Israel. That military metaphor comes in Paul to be a battle against Satan, sin, and death. Even in our contemporary parlance, the same imagery survives, so that we speak not only of the "war" against communism but also of the "war" on cancer and the "war" on poverty. Israel's life does indeed emerge out of struggle and conflict, when Israel wins victories of well-being in situations where one might soberly expect defeat.

Second, in this narrative are the intervening vv. 10b-12, which are sandwiched by Joshua's actions. In these verses, Moses, who does not go into battle, is nonetheless the key figure in assuring Israel's victory. Theologically, these verses not only assert that the power and authority of Moses matter decisively, but also that the battle and the victory are no ordinary military action. What is decisive for the outcome of the conflict is the staff held in the powerful hand of Moses, which bespeaks the power of Yahweh. Childs (with special reference to Barth) sees these two themes, Joshua's leadership and Moses' hands, as "a delicate balance which neither impaired God's will nor destroyed man's genuine activity."[81]

Taken more practically, we may wonder how the raised hands of a leader at a distance from the battle could matter for the outcome of the battle. I have no desire to "explain" the narrative, but to indicate how such a statement might be credible in a self-conscious community in conflict. After all the military strategy, material, and technology is assembled, battles require passion, energy, and sheer adrenalin, which are usually generated not by technicians but by public leaders who

can mobilize imagination and play on the passions of the military community.

17:14-16 The tradition has taken up this particular report of victory and, by a literary, interpretive maneuver, has converted it into an enduring theological passion in Israel. The victory tale itself might have been routine. Moses is instructed by God to reduce the tale of victory to writing, which is to be read to Joshua (to the generation that struggles with the Canaanites), so that it will have enduring authority for all time to come. We are given no reason why this command is issued to Moses. We are told only that from the very mouth of God comes the resolve that God has declared unending hostility toward the Amalekites. God's decree includes an intense infinitive absolute: "I will utterly blot out." The patron and guarantor of Israel has sworn to obliterate an enemy of Israel.

Moreover, as Yahweh has solemnly sworn, so Moses is instructed to create a sign and symbol, rooted in theology, crediting this deep and perpetual hostility, not to any human imagination but to the very God of Israel. Thus the altar and the banner are to make it clear for all time to come that hostility toward Amalek is deep, for perpetuity, and authorized by Yahweh.

When we try to understand this statement, we are reduced to bewildered, awkward silence. We are given no hint of why the report in vv. 8-13, in itself not unusual, leads to the ideological intensification of vv. 14-16. We know of nothing from any other text (except possibly Deut 25:17-19, on which see below) why Amalek is singled out in this way. We have no evidence of more than conventional conflict, and nothing is noticeably barbaric in the relationship between the two peoples. It is as though in an unguarded, undisciplined moment the tradition (or the God of the tradition) has given vent to a deep, irrational hunger to have a permanent enemy.

We may briefly review the sequence of Amalek texts to discern the function of this interpretive maneuver (though we will not find a rationale for this brutal pronouncement).

Verse 14 enjoins Moses to write "in a book" the abiding enmity of God toward Amalek. That written piece is ostensibly found in Deut 25:17-19, which would seem to fulfill the requirement of v. 14. Here we

81. Childs, *The Book of Exodus*, 317.

are given one piece of "information" that we have nowhere else: The Amalekites attack Israel in its weakness and are especially vicious toward stragglers.

But this notice is suspect on at least three grounds. First, such attacks on the vulnerable are not uncommon in war, and it cannot have been the only enemy of Israel who engaged in such a practice. Second, there is no hint of such a criticism of Amalek in the narrative of the battle itself in Exod 17:8-13. Third, and consequently, the reason given comes late in the development of the ideology, thus creating wonderment whether this is rationale after the fact. One gains the impression that this "reason" in itself is not a compelling basis for the enshrinement of hostility in such a remarkable way.

In the curses of Balaam against the enemies of Israel, Amalek is singled out, both as the "first of many nations" and as destined for perpetual destruction (see Num 24:20). The same ideology is clearly at work here.

We can see this powerful ideology most concretely in 1 Sam 15:1-33. As Israel moves toward monarchy (and more ordered, "rational" governance) with Saul, the old tribal ideologies become less compelling. Saul is portrayed as one who, for pragmatic reasons, compromises this piece of old ideology. He "spares" Amalek and takes Amalekite spoils. Saul's explanation of his act to Samuel evidences one who squirms under the power of ideology, because it is difficult to provide rationale for action that contradicts an all-consuming ideology.

By contrast, Samuel is portrayed as the upholder and guarantor of the Amalekite curse. He uses that ideological claim as a ground from which to depose Saul. Moreover, without flinching, Samuel proceeds to execute the curse against Amalek (1 Sam 15:32-33). In v. 33, Samuel suggests that Amalek has in the past murdered pregnant women, perhaps a notion linked to Deut 25:18. There is no way to determine whether this claim is historical. What strikes one about the narrative, rather, is that Samuel is presented as an unconditional adherent to the old ideology, which he fully and gladly implements.

Finally, we may mention David's action in 1 Sam 30:18-31. While it is not the case that David actually "spares" an Amalekite, he does take spoils (herds and flocks) in a quite pragmatic way, to give to "his friends, the elders of Judah." This is a remarkable report, because Saul has been rebuked and finally deposed for daring to keep even Amalekite cattle.

We do not know how to adjudicate David's action. It may be simply that the power of the ideology was weakened and, with the death of Samuel, lost its most passionate, dangerous adherent. Or it may be that David was both pragmatic and strong enough to risk offending old political-theological opinion, and he got away with his pragmatic action. In any case, it is clear that David was able to break the vicious cycle of hate that seems to have persisted long after Amalek constituted any concrete political threat. Eventually, ideological hatred that is no longer connected to political reality may be broken. It can, however, persist for a long time, producing enormous political damage when ideology holds sway without reference to reality.

REFLECTIONS

This is a most problematic text. We may identify four points of interpretive exploration that move from theological affirmation to interpretive suspicion.

1. As we have seen in 15:3 where "Yahweh is a man of war," the military metaphor is crucial in the Bible for making an affirmation that God saves. To the extent that biblical faith is a religion of salvation, the military metaphor is crucial, because it identifies the agonistic context in which God, in power and in fidelity, saves from enemies. Moreover, this way of rhetoric is not an abstract intellectual invention, but arose from quite concrete conflicts. Such concrete conflict is not "nice" but is inevitably brutal and violent. Our capacity to confess the God of the Bible as sovereign depends on the stories of the specific places in which the community has known rescue from those powers that bring death.

2. There is no doubt that the rhetoric of the "victories of Yahweh" has been handled in Jewish faith and certainly in Christian theology by converting such language into metaphor. That is, the concreteness of battle has been transposed into battles against evil and against all the manifestations of evil (personal and public) that take place in human experience. There is no doubt that the process of metaphor is both necessary and legitimate.

Care must be taken, however, when turning these concrete narratives into metaphor, that one does not lose specificity and the connections to socioeconomic reality. When metaphor serves to remove the specific bite of a narrative so that it now becomes "spiritual," remote, or otherworldly, then the metaphor serves to enhance the status quo, and to neutralize the threat inherent in the story. In the end, oppressed communities do not move too quickly away from the conviction that their enemies are God's enemies as well (cf. Ps 139:21-22). That conviction lives close to this sort of text, even as it offends those of us who are less oppressed.

3. The most interesting interpretive point is how the move is made from vv. 8-13 to vv. 14-16. The victory itself is the sort of outcome that happens in the processes of public conflict. The institutionalization of hostility, however, is another matter. This move in the text is the process of *theological demonization,* whereby an enemy in a particular war (perhaps an adversary because of a legitimate conflict of interest) is now absolutized as an embodiment of evil, without regard to any historical circumstance or visible vested interest.

Examples of this in our public life might include the demonizing of Germans ("Remember Munich") or the Japanese ("Remember Pearl Harbor") or the Russians ("Never Trust a Commie"). Perhaps the most blatant example of such demonization has been our fixation on communism, which was uncritically assumed to be monolithic. Such an uncritical act of demonization led us into the morass of the Vietnam war without taking into account the geopolitical realities of China and Southeast Asia. It was far easier to hate "the enemy" than to sort out the nuances of political reality.

In the Persian Gulf War, we watched the ideological demonization of Saddam Hussein of Iraq, an aggressive tribal chieftain, without any acknowledgment of the sorry, shameful imperial history of the West in controlling oil in the Middle East. Saddam was treated as an ontological principle of evil. This demonization justified the defense of other tribal chieftains who practiced an equal brutality. Demonization is easier, quicker, and more immediately satisfying than dealing with political reality.

On a more personal level, our propensity to refuse forgiveness to our enemies causes us to freeze and absolutize relationships, attitudes, and perceptions at one point of hurt and rage. This happens in families, in churches, and in communities of all kinds. Such a freezing and absolutizing precludes any further development in relations and justifies continued irrational negativities that are no longer appropriate. The resolve to remember forever hurt, hate, rage, and fear ensures the shut-down of the political processes of newness.

Forgiveness, by contrast, is the political, creative process of negotiating old wounds in ways that lead to newness. Such negotiations are impossible in a world where hurts are absolutized and institutionalized. David's action toward the Amalekites may be a daring example of de-demonizing, an inclination that may in the end lead even to forgiveness.[82]

---

82. On the larger public issues of forgiveness, see Carter Heyward et al., *Revolutionary Forgiveness: Feminist Reflections on Nicaragua* (Maryknoll, N.Y.: Orbis, 1987).

4. Finally, we are left with the awareness that the interpretive move of v. 14 is on the lips of Yahweh. It is, according to the tradition, none other than Yahweh who has authorized the writing of Deut 25:17-19 and the canonization of this ideology in the imagination of Israel. Of course, it is legitimate to say that some powerful human agent created this text, and no one doubts that the tradition of Deuteronomy was a powerful ideological force in Israel. If, however, we are to think theologically (and beyond critical explanations) about the text, then we must deal with a God who speaks this way and authorizes such a text. I must confess I find responsibility for comment overwhelming. I suggest two lines of thought.

First, the God of the Bible is the source and product of a martial propensity, placing conflict, violence, and brutality in the center of the tradition. The Bible and the God of the Bible are, to a large extent, cast in conflictual categories. This perspective has been most visible in the Christian Crusades (perhaps including twentieth-century examples) and in Islamic rhetoric about "holy war." It may also be that this reality about God is evident in church practice whereby established authority silences those with whom it disagrees, or in the tendency of conservatives and liberals to demonize each other because of passionately held ethical views. As Christians come increasingly into contact with persons of other faiths and become aware that there are other categories through which faith is practiced, we are destined for a dangerous, demanding rethinking of the oppositional mapping of our faith.

Second, it is clear that this propensity of the God of the Bible is not the only way God has been disclosed in the text. Critically, it is easy enough to insist that our understanding of God evolved. But if we are to think theologically (post-critically), we do better to take these texts in tension, as *unresolved issues in God's own heart.* Thus the God who will always remember is also the God who will "remember . . . no more" (Jer 31:34). To be sure, the disparate texts disclosing God differently have arisen in very different contexts and horizons. They are all there, nonetheless, purporting to be disclosures of this God.

EXODUS 18:1-12, JETHRO COMES TO MOSES

COMMENTARY

This entire chapter, which concerns Moses' relation to his father-in-law, Jethro, is most peculiar and seems to disrupt the storyline of the journey from Egypt to "the mountain." The narrative of 17:8-15 has Israel at the oasis of Rephidim, and Israel is still at that oasis in 19:2. Likely chapter 18 is an independent tradition that insisted upon inclusion in the larger narrative.

An older scholarly hypothesis, advocated by Karl Budde, has proposed that it was through Jethro the Midianite that Yahweh was first known and mediated to Israel.[83] We shall not linger over the hypothesis, for two reasons. First, the text as it now stands

is not interested in such a pre-history of Yahweh and will not entertain an alternative to the canonical story of an original revelation to Moses through the burning bush (3:1-6). Second, as the text stands, in v. 11 Jethro makes an exclamation that he now knows about the greatness of Yahweh. Thus, contrary to Budde's hypothesis, the text insists that knowledge of Yahweh has gone from Moses to Jethro.

The text as it stands has as its surface plot the return of Moses to the wilderness after the exodus. However, the weight of the narrative falls on *the witness of Moses* (v. 8) and the *doxological response of Jethro* in word (vv. 10-11) and in liturgic act (v. 12). Whatever pre-history may be reflected here, the function of the present text is to plant in the

83. H. H. Rowley, *From Joseph to Joshua: Biblical Traditions in the Light of Archaeology,* The Schweich Lectures (London: Oxford University Press, 1950) 153-56 and *passim.* Rowley thoroughly reviews the data pertinent to the hypothesis. Note his reference to Budde, 156 n.3.

midst of the larger narrative a pause to permit a model of *testimony and response,* whereby faith in Yahweh is transmitted from Moses to Jethro and the Midianites.

18:1-7 Moses returns to his family. In these verses there is no direct speech but only the narrator's report concerning news of the deliverance shared by Moses and Jethro.

The geographical movements assumed by the text are ambiguous. In 4:18-20 Moses takes his wife and sons with him back to Egypt. In that text, his wife and sons seem to be with him in Egypt, but in our text they are in Midian with Jethro. Several commentaries suggest that in v. 2 Moses sent his wife and sons to Jethro with news and Jethro then returned with them. This would be supported by the name of the second son (v. 4), which reflects Egyptian deliverance and suggests he was born after the deliverance. This, however, runs beyond the explicit statement of the text.

In vv. 3-4, the narrative pauses to elucidate the names of the two sons of Moses. The first, Gershom, is already known in 2:22. The second, Eliezer, is not previously known. The names of the two sons together witness to the shape and destiny of Moses' life. On the one hand, Moses is an "alien there" (גרשם *gēr-šōm*), vulnerable and at risk. On the other hand, God has indeed been Moses' "help" (אליעזר *ʾĕlî-ʿezer*), whereby Moses has survived and wrought the deliverance from Egypt. The name of each son is essential to the characterizations of both Moses and Israel, a people that is both "alien" (גר *gēr*) and "helped" (עזר *ʿāzar*).

Moses' return home is one of joyous hospitality, as well as mutual interest and concern (vv. 5-7). The narrative seems uninterested in such matters, but reports them to create a context for the exchange that happens next. (Cf. the structure in Gen 18:1-15, in which vv. 1-8 function as a narrative preface for the exchange of vv. 9-15.)

18:8-12 The exchange between Moses and Jethro is a model of theological testimony.

Moses' brief speech is an abbreviated form of the narrative credo recital of Israel (v. 8). The phrase "all that Yahweh had done to Pharaoh and to the Egyptians" echoes v. 1, though this is now a direct speech. Moreover, it focuses on Yahweh's action, whereas v. 1 focuses on Moses and "his people Israel." Moses quickly tells of the exodus and the hardship of the wilderness sojourn, and culminates with the verb *deliver* (נצל *nāṣal*), which Moses uses in 5:23 to accuse God of indifference.

Jethro's response to Moses' testimony is more extended (vv. 9-12). He "rejoices in the good"; that is, he is completely taken with the news and delights as in a victory (Ps 21:1-7) or the birth of a child (Jer 20:15). Jethro delivers a conventional doxological blessing that acknowledges and celebrates Yahweh as the giver of new life. Jethro confesses that Yahweh is more powerful, more reliable, and more worthy of allegiance than any other god, even the gods of Egypt. Jethro fully discerns the power struggle that went on between Moses and Pharaoh and between the gods of Egypt and Yahweh. He understands that in the end, Yahweh will not be mocked, dismissed, or belittled. In his exuberant confession, Jethro uses the word *nāṣal* three times (vv. 9, 10, 11), echoing the term Moses used in v. 8. Thus Jethro's speech is a litany of *nāṣal*, whereby he joins in celebration of the God who can override the power of the empire, giving new life and new possibility to the slave community that has no power of its own. Jethro thus becomes a voice for the celebrative faith of Israel.

Verse 12 reports an action that gives liturgical shape to Jethro's doxology. The offerings and sacrifices are not only an act of celebration but of allegiance as well. It is curious that Aaron and the elders, until now absent in the narrative, appear for the official sacrifice. Thus v. 12 serves to give institutional form and stability to the new faith of Jethro. The narrator has recalled the full cast of characters necessary to perform this cultic act of consolidation.

REFLECTIONS

1. The names of Moses' two sons provide an inchoate theological confession that characterizes not only Moses and early Israel, but also the community of faith whenever it is intentional about its dangerous call and destiny. This community is by definition "alien" to every culture, living only by the "help" of God.[84] These names are important reminders against two primary temptations of every established church. On the one hand, "alien" reminds us that the community of faith is not "at home" in any cultural context, any more than Moses dared to be at home in Egypt. On the other hand, "help" reminds us that the community of faith is neither self-sufficient nor abandoned.

2. Moses voices the testimony that comes most readily to Israel's lips: "God delivered," and "God led" on the way. These two verbs are the foundation of Israel's faith, which is astonished by deliverance that is public, concrete, and political. Israel never forgets that its life consists in being saved and that salvation is not any private or otherworldly business. This is a community utterly amazed that it is given life in a context where no real life is on the horizon. Israel's mode of faith is simply to "tell" (ספר *sāpar*) (as Moses did) without justification, proof, or rationalization. There are no larger criteria or categories that make this odd turn of affairs any more credible or palatable.

3. Jethro receives the news and is immediately convicted by it. He is a model for the way in which biblical faith is heard and embraced by those once removed from the events (cf. John 20:29). This second version of the news is the basis of all biblical evangelism. The same verb for "tell" (*sāpar*) is used in 10:2 for communicating to the children and the grandchildren (cf. 9:16). The same dynamic (with the verb בשׂר *biśśar* rather than *sāpar*) is assumed in Isa 52:7 where the "messenger" from exile brings "news" of events to Jerusalem. This is the text by which Paul makes his case for retelling the news of the gospel (Rom 10:14-15).

Moreover, this telling and hearing become the core activity of the early church in Acts, whereby those who have not witnessed the saving events come to share in their reality and their power. Thus in his hearing and in his response in doxology and sacrifice, Jethro becomes a model for evangelism.

---

84. The notion of the community of faith as "alien" to its cultural context, and in some way in an antagonistic relation to it, has been articulated in a contemporary mode by Stanley Hauerwas and William H. Willimon, *Resident Aliens* (Nashville: Abingdon, 1989).

EXODUS 18:13-27, JETHRO'S ADVICE

COMMENTARY

The shift from vv. 1-12 to this rhetorical unit is abrupt. The units have in common the key role of Jethro, but the subject is completely different. This text, in contrast to the preceding, has little explicit reference to the exodus or the God of liberation. Yahweh is nowhere explicitly mentioned. Now the text is concerned with the quite practical matter of judicial procedure. This text shows that Israel has a crucial concern for institution building, for the establishment of stable procedures and due process, which will make justice everywhere available and reliable.

The narrative that Jethro dominates may be divided into three characteristic parts: the statement of a problem (vv. 13-16), Jethro's intervention with a proposed solution to the problem (vv. 17-23), and the resolution by Moses (vv. 24-27).

18:13-16. The problem is that Moses is overworked. The text begins abruptly: "Moses sat as judge." The text affirms and assumes that the practice of justice is a primary concern for his leadership and for Israel from day one. It is worth noting, by contrast, that the matter of justice nowhere comes up as an Egyptian concern.

Moreover, Moses is quite clear that the concern for justice is not simply political pragmatism, but derives from and belongs to the very character of God. Jethro asks Moses why he shoulders such an impossible burden. In his answer, Moses asserts that he is preoccupied with "inquiries of God" (i.e., pronouncing oracles from God) and "instruction [תורה *tôrâ*] of God" (vv. 15-16). Moses is not dispensing mere practical advice or positive law, but the very torah of God. The God of Israel cares about the concrete, day-to-day matters of justice.

18:17-23. Jethro sees immediately that Moses is committed to an unworkable practice. Moses cannot handle the heavy docket. We do not know whether Moses is so concerned with control that he wants to handle all the cases himself, or if he is unreflective and has never thought about a more workable, practical system. Moses seems not to have much common sense about administrative matters. But then, such dominating figures often do not. Jethro fears for Moses that he will "burn out"; Jethro's solution is that Moses must learn to delegate.

Jethro thus proposes a judicial system, distinct from the primitive practice of one-man adjudication. The proposal includes (a) the recruitment of good people (v. 21); (b) their training and preparation (v. 20); (c) a system of courts for different social units (v. 21); (d) a "high court" over which Moses would preside (v. 22); and (e) continued affirmation that the entire system would be referred to the will of God (vv. 19, 23).

Perhaps the most important matter in Jethro's plan concerns the qualifications of the judges (v. 21). They are to be able, God-fearing, haters of dishonest (violent) gain. This list of qualifications is both theologically referenced and aware that corruption is not likely to be about large, theological matters, but about the modest temptations of bribery and economic manipulation.

Such a system will save Moses from burnout, but more important, it will let the community go home in שלום (*šālôm*)—i.e., in harmony and wholeness, free of conflict, enjoying a stable, shared welfare (v. 23).

18:24-27. Moses accepts the proposals of Jethro and implements them. Moses was able to delegate. He does not need to control all details of judicial administration. The text ends with a notice of Jethro's departure, leaving Moses at the mountain of God, ready for the great encounter that comes next.

Two texts are commonly educed to illuminate this encounter with Jethro. First, Deut 17:8-13 shows in more exacting fashion the establishment of a judiciary system with a central high court. In contrast to our passage, which moves from Moses down to "able men," Deuteronomy 17 moves up to levitical priests. The principle espoused is the same, however: a system of courts that permit appeal. It is worth observing that in this text, the occupants of the high court positions are to be levitical priests—i.e., those who claim to survive from the lineage of Moses and Aaron (cf. 6:14-25). Thus we observe that the person of Moses has been converted into an "office" that claims the continuing authority of Moses.

There is here no strict constructionism. The book of Deuteronomy itself is abundant evidence that even the most treasured of all "law" requires continued interpretation and extrapolation in order to be pertinent to new situations. Indeed, if there were no need for continued, authoritative construal, there would be no need for such a high, authorized, trusted court. The text knows very well that the ultimate administration of justice is not the handing out of programmed, fortune-cookie decisions but the articulation of wise, faithful, reasoned, imaginative new judgments. It is ironic that advocates of strict constructionism who want to resist contextual reinterpretation of the law appeal characteristically to the "absolutes" of the Bible. Such a notion itself is not strict constructionism of the text but a bold, self-serving construal of the biblical text. The tradition of Moses knows from the outset that serious justice requires imaginative, unending interpretation.[85]

Norbert Lohfink has suggested that Deut 17:8-13 belongs to the wider text of Deuteronomy 16–19, which serves as something like a constitution in ancient Israel, providing for a constitutional separation of powers.[86] Lohfink sees this as a crucial principle of government in ancient Israel whereby absolutizing authority is resisted and precluded. In Exod 18:13-27, we may see a safeguard against the absolutizing of the Mosaic office, though enormous authority continues to be assigned to it.

85. On the interpretive trajectory of the Mosaic tradition, see Gerhard von Rad, *Studies in Deuteronomy,* SBT 9 (Chicago: Henry Regnery, 1953) 16, and his notion of "preached law." Derivatively, see Walter Brueggemann, *Interpretation and Obedience: From Faithful Reading to Faithful Living* (Minneapolis: Fortress, 1991) 100-18.
86. Norbert Lohfink, *Great Themes from the Old Testament* (Edinburgh: T. & T. Clark, 1982) 55-75.

A second text usefully related to ours is 2 Chr 19:4-11, where King Jehoshaphat in the ninth century institutes an important judicial reform in Jerusalem. Historical-critical judgment may suggest that the Jethro narrative is in fact a retrospect from the narrative of Jehoshaphat. We do not need to accept that judgment in order to let this text illuminate our text. It is enough to cite this text concerning Jehoshaphat to see that this is how Israel at its best characteristically thought and spoke about the matter of social justice.

In this narrative the king establishes a judicial system for his entire realm "from Beer-sheba to the hill country of Ephraim." The most important matter for those newly appointed judges is their moral, personal qualification (vv. 6-7). The new judges are to be clear that justice concerns not human wishes, but Yahweh's agenda. This agenda provides that if Yahweh be "dreaded" (פחד *pāḥad*), taken with ominous seriousness, then it follows that there will be no partiality in judgment or the taking of bribes.

This same provision is fully explicated in Deut 16:19-20, a passage closely connected to Exod 17:8-13: "You must not distort justice; you must not show partiality; and you must not accept bribes, for a bribe blinds the eyes of the wise and subverts the cause of those who are in the right. Justice, and only justice, you shall pursue, so that you may live and occupy the land that the LORD your God is giving you" (Deut 16:19-20 NRSV; cf. Deut. 1:9-18).

Israel (and Jehoshaphat) knows that the judicial system must remain free of the leverage of economic power. Put positively, the courts must be a place where the economically disadvantaged receive an equitable hearing.

These two texts, Deut 17:8-13 and 2 Chr 19:4-11 (see also Deut 16:18-20) provide categories and terms for the ways Israel thinks about justice and its cruciality for maintaining an equitable community. It is astonishing that this issue of fair justice arises so early in the tradition and is dealt with so precisely. Moreover, this concern for justice pays peculiar attention from the very beginning to economic matters. But this is what we might expect in a community that poignantly remembers economic exploitation.

REFLECTIONS

1. We may reflect on the odd juxtaposition of vv. 1-12 and vv. 13-27. As we have seen, the first of these units is a *celebration of the exodus* and the second is about *the institutionalization of justice.* No explicit connection is made between the two texts beyond the fact that both feature the work of Jethro. Their juxtaposition, however, is more than incidental. The exodus celebration of vv. 8-12 clearly looks back to the exodus and the beginning of the sojourn with its "hardships." It exults in God's stunning, sovereign act of liberation. The judicial initiative of vv. 17-23, by contrast, looks forward to the Sinai covenant and its legal provisions for a covenantal ordering of society in the books of Exodus and Deuteronomy.

The juxtaposition affirms that this liberated community must develop institutions that will sustain and stabilize the exodus vision in daily social practice. Moses acts on the assumption that the power and passion that made the exodus possible are the same power and passion that can make possible a society free of exploitation. Biblical faith is not simply a recital of odd, isolated events of rescue. It is also about the hard, sustained work of nurturing and practicing the daily passion of healing and restoring, and the daily rejection of dishonest gain.

2. Israel intends here to institutionalize "exodus-justice." This is a very special kind of justice almost everywhere assumed in the Bible, but not much understood.

Our common understandings of justice are Aristotelian in character, assuming that justice is a system of close retribution in which people receive their "just desserts."

Such a system is especially prized by the well-off and the "deserving," who prefer to see that the "undeserving" get exactly what they "deserve," and nothing else.

Exodus-justice is very different from such retributive justice.[87] The slaves in bondage had no rights and were entitled to no serious consideration. The wonder of the exodus is that Yahweh did not give to the Hebrews what they "deserved," according to settled Egyptian values. Rather, God made a distinction (8:23) and gave the Hebrews what they *needed* in order to have a viable life. Exodus-justice is compensatory, giving to the needy and disadvantaged well beyond what is deserved. For that reason, in Deuteronomy and in the prophets, when justice is urged for widows and orphans, they are not to be given what they "deserve," but what they need for a viable human existence.

87. The best discussion of exodus-justice known to me is José Miranda, *Marx and the Bible: A Critique of the Philosophy of Oppression* (Maryknoll, N.Y.: Orbis, 1974).

EXODUS 19:1–24:18

THE CHARTER OF A HOLY NATION

OVERVIEW

The "Sinai pericope" stands at the very center of the book of Exodus and as the pivotal point for Mosaic faith. The theological claims of this unit are intimately tied to *the liberation of the exodus* (cf. 19:4; 20:1). The God who here commands (20:1-17; 21:1– 23:19) is the God who has liberated (chaps. 1–15). The voice of command that is most decisive here anticipates the *pattern of presence* that is soon to follow (chaps. 25–40). In this text, it is the holy God of command who is known in full, fearful majesty and who speaks a sovereign word. This text, then, is a disclosure of that God, offered in Israel's most characteristic categories. The upshot of Yahweh's command is twofold. First, and most important, a new community is created. In this event, a collection of erstwhile slaves, not identified by common blood, language, or territory, is formed into a community based solely on allegiance to the command of Yahweh. Second, at the center of this unit (20:18-21) stands the authorization of Moses, who is to be the sole legitimator and go-between for Yahweh and Israel. Moses' role, however, is subordinated to the existence of Israel. Through the self-disclosure of Yahweh, the formation of a new community of radical obedience occurs.

There is no doubt that this unit has a complex literary history, comprised of distinct strands of tradition.[88] These difficult matters have been considered by a number of scholars.[89] Given that complexity, however, it is nevertheless possible to trace out something of a coherent, orderly pattern that reflects some theological intentionality.

This was done most boldly by Klaus Baltzer and George Mendenhall, who found in this pericope an orderly form of covenant making.[90] Mendenhall proposed that this form is a reflection of international treaties. It is now commonly agreed that Mendenhall's claim is an overstatement.[91] Nonetheless it is possible to see in these texts a sequence and procedure that aims, in a liturgically stylized way, to form a people newly sworn to obey the radical commands of Yahweh.

The completed form of the text consists in six elements. Chapter 19, after a thematic announcement of covenant obedience rooted in the exodus (vv. 3-6), presents a theophany of the coming of God to the mountain in fearful and devastating sovereignty to meet Israel. This meeting requires ritual preparation and evokes from Israel a preliminary oath of allegiance (v. 8).

The theophany provides the context for God's utterance of the Ten Commandments, the most crucial and authoritative command in the faith of Israel (20:1-17). The text is so familiar to us that we may fail to notice that it is a speech from the very mouth of God. This speech gives to Israel God's full intention for the life of creation. All other law in Israel is reflective commentary upon this decree.[92]

The address of God to Israel in 20:1-17 so frightens Israel that Moses is designated

---

88. Childs, *The Book of Exodus,* 749-51.
89. See, for example, Murray Newman, *The People of the Covenant* (Nashville: Abingdon, 1962); Walter Beyerlin, *Origins and History of the Oldest Sinaitic Traditions* (New York: Oxford University Press, 1965); and Thomas B. Dozeman, *God on the Mountain: A Study of Redaction, Theology and Canon in Exodus 19–24,* SBLMS 37 (Atlanta: Scholars Press, 1989).

90. Klaus Baltzer, *The Covenant Formulary in Old Testament, Jewish, and Early Christian Writings* (Philadelphia: Fortress, 1971); George E. Mendenhall, *Law and Covenant in Israel and the Ancient Near East* (Pittsburgh: The Biblical Colloquium, 1955).
91. See the judicious mediating position of McCarthy and the summary of Nicholson: Dennis J. McCarthy, *Treaty and Covenant: A Study in Form in the Ancient Oriental Documents and in the Old Testament,* Analecta Biblica 21 (Rome: Biblical Institute Press, 1978); Ernest W. Nicholson, *God and His People: Covenant and Theology in the Old Testament* (Oxford: Clarendon, 1986).
92. The most helpful interpretive comment on the Decalogue is Walter Harrelson, *The Ten Commandments and Human Rights,* OBT (Philadelphia: Fortress, 1980). See also Childs, *The Book of Exodus,* 383-439; Johann Jakob Stamm and Maurice Edward Andrew, *TY0he Ten Commandments in Recent Research,* SBT 2 (Naperville: Alec R. Allenson, 1967); and Anthony Phillips, *Ancient Israel's Criminal Law: A New Approach to the Decalogue* (Oxford: Blackwell, 1970).

mediator (20:18-21). From now on, Yahweh will address Israel only indirectly, but Moses will be accepted by Israel as the single, true voice of Yahweh. It is entirely plausible that this text reflects the creation of a Mosaic "office."

The "Covenant Code" of 20:22–23:19 stands in this larger unit as a counterpart to the Decalogue of 20:1-17. However, it is not on a par with the Decalogue in terms of significance or authority; whereas the Decalogue comes out of God's own mouth (before Moses is made mediator), the Covenant Code is Moses' word and comes after the authorization of a mediator. Thus the juxtaposition of the two groups of laws serves to accent both the peculiar authority of the Decalogue and the authority of Moses.

The brief section of 23:20-33 concludes the proclamation of law with a promise and a warning. This speech relates the Sinai pericope to the larger Israelite tradition of promise and land. It indicates how demanding the law of Yahweh is, and how vulnerable Israel is as it seeks to live out its peculiar vocation.

Chapter 24 corresponds to chapter 19 in two aspects. First, it provides contact with God in a theophany. Second, it voices Israel's oath of allegiance to Yahweh (vv. 3, 7). The final verses (vv. 15-18), which situate Moses in the cloud of glory, prepare the way for Exodus 25–31 and anticipate the conclusion of 40:34-38.

In large design this passage is chiastically arranged:

A theophany (19)
  B law (20:1-17)
    C mediator (20:18-21)
    C´ (vv. 22-26)
  B´ law (21:1– 23:19, 20-33)
A´ theophany (24)

The juxtaposition of *theophany* and *law* roots Israel's definitional commands in nothing less than the sovereign voice and will of Yahweh. The law that constitutes Israel's existence originates outside Israel's historical horizon and beyond the reach of Moses or of any king. Israelite life is mandated from the awesome region of heaven, and Moses must enter glory to receive all that is given. The effect of this textual arrangement is to assert that Israel is neither a historical accident nor an ordinary political entity, but a peculiar community willed and destined by God. Its earthly vocation, to be a priestly kingdom mediating God's intention for the world, is grounded in a holy, heavenly purpose. That holy purpose must be practiced in the dailiness of human history.[93]

93. See Martin Buber and his notion of theopolitics, *Kingship of God* (New York: Harper & Row, 1967) 99-107, 121-62, and portions of *Moses: The Revelation and the Covenant* (Atlantic Highlands, N.J.: Humanities Press International, 1988). Echoes of Buber may be sounded in Nicholson, *God and His People*, chap. 10.

EXODUS 19:1-25, AT MOUNT SINAI

COMMENTARY

This extensive, complicated chapter serves as an introduction to the meeting between Yahweh and Israel at "the mountain." Cast in liturgical form, its work is the preparation by Israel to be properly qualified for worship of Yahweh. Rhetorically, the central portion of the text reports a theophany—a disciplined account of the powerful, disruptive, cataclysmic coming of God into the midst of the community. The chapter begins with a geographical note (vv. 1-2), followed by a speech of God to Moses (vv. 3-6). The remainder of the chapter is constituted by a series of

transactions that make the meeting possible (vv. 7-25). We may note three factors operating in this long and not well-ordered narrative of preparation.

First, the meeting is an entry into "the holiness" for the purpose of worship. Such an entry and meeting is a high-risk venture for which careful preparation must be made. This focus on worship makes this chapter pivotal for the entire book of Exodus. On the one hand, this act of worship implements the long-standing, oft-repeated demand of the liberation narrative: "Let my people go that they may worship me" (cf. 5:1; 7:16; 8:1, 20; 9:1, 13; 10:3). On the other hand, and in a very different way, this careful preparation anticipates the detailed enterprise of "sanctification" in Exodus 25–31 and 35–40, whereby a meeting is made possible for Israel.

The fact that this narrative is cast in liturgical categories permits the narrator to hold together two different aspects of Israel's meeting with God. On the one hand, this is a dangerous, once-for-all event, never to be repeated. On the other hand, this is a model meeting that serves as a paradigm for all future covenantal confrontations.

Second, while the meeting is "at the mountain," there is a great deal of movement up and down the mountain. Thus Moses goes up (v. 3) and comes down (v. 14), while the people stand at the foot of the mountain (v. 17). Yahweh descends (vv. 18, 20), and Moses goes up (v. 20) and comes down (v. 25) as commanded in vv. 21, 24. Thomas Dozeman has proposed that movement up and down the mountain in the several literary sources articulates different "geographies of power" among the several parts of this community.[94] Thus the movements up and down are at least scene changes, and likely intend to portray power relations concerning who has access and who stands over whom.

Third, the cast of characters is also complicated. God and Moses are clearly the central protagonists. In addition "the people" are given direct access to God. The elders (v. 7), Aaron (v. 24), and the priests (v. 24) are also specified in their several roles. These various references may indicate, as Dozeman suggests, that in different sources, the distribution of power is differently portrayed; "the people" indicates a broadly based democratic shape of power, "the elders" indicates authorized lay leadership, and the "priests" (Aaron) are a sacerdotal alternative to lay leadership.

19:1-2. These two verses provide a narrative setting of time and place for the meeting to follow. Israel arrives at Rephidim in 17:1 (cf. 17:8), but 18:5 has a narrative episode at the mountain. These verses thus place the meeting at Sinai in the context of the wilderness sojourn. Moreover, the "third full moon" suggests that for this narrative, the events of 15:22–18:27 do not take very long. In any case, the purpose of these verses is to make the mountain the context for what follows. It is futile to try to identify the mountain geographically. More important is the affirmation that the mountain is the place where earth touches heaven, where the human realm makes contact with the abode of God (or the gods). The place thus is laden with holy presence.

19:3-6 God speaks to Moses, abruptly and with sovereign power. This speech is likely the most programmatic for Israelite faith that we have in the entire tradition of Moses. It divides into two parts.

First, v. 4 is an indicative statement recalling the entire narrative of liberation. It affirms that Egypt is now past tense to Israel and that unambiguously the initiative of God has changed Israel's destiny. This verse fully and completely summarizes the memory of the exodus, which is the ground of all that follows. Israel has witnessed God's decisive combat against and triumph over Egypt. Moreover, Yahweh, with enormous power, has taken Israel up, out of Egypt and bondage. Remarkably, the "flight out of Egypt" has not had as its destination the mountain, the land, or any other place, but "to me." That is, the goal of the exodus is presented as a flight from Pharaoh to Yahweh, from one master to a new one.

The metaphor of an eagle for Yahweh's rescue of Israel from bondage is compelling. According to Deut 32:11-14, the eagle (Yahweh) is a nurturing, protective agent who carries, guides, feeds, and protects (cf. Exod 15:4-10, 13-17). The predominant note concerning the eagle here, however, is one of majestic, devastating power (cf. Deut 28:49; Jer 48:40; 49:27). Thus the image holds together majestic power and protective nurturing. The exodus required both power to override the grip of Egypt and nurturing to sustain when there was no other sustenance. Later on, the same image is used in Isa 40:31 very differently, for now Israel itself is like a powerful eagle that does not grow weary or faint (cf. Ps 103:5). That eagle, however, derives its strength from attentiveness to Yahweh, the one who creates and authorizes soaring eagles (cf. Job 39:27).

This extraordinary memory (v. 4) now turns to anticipation of life in devotion to

94. Dozeman, *God on the Mountain.*

Yahweh (vv. 5-6). Two facts of this anticipation interest us. First, the future of Israel is governed by an "if" and by a powerful infinitive absolute; Israel's future is conditional. Everything depends on Israel's readiness to listen (שָׁמַע *šmʿ*; cf. 15:26) and to keep covenant. This strong conditional surprises us after the indicative of v. 4. It is as though the generous God of exodus has abruptly become the demanding God of Sinai; and so it is. While Yahweh's initial rescue is unconditional and without reservation, a sustained relation with Yahweh is one of rigorous demand for covenant. Indeed, the long Sinai text that follows is a statement of condition whereby this rescued people can be a community of ongoing covenant.

The second element of the statement is a promise of Israel's special status. On the one hand, Israel (assuming the conditions are met) is Yahweh's especially prized, peculiar possession. One can see in this verse the faith of Israel, struggling with the tension between universal claim ("all the earth is mine") and the special election of Israel. Indeed, these verses may indicate that Yahweh's own life is a struggle over this tension. Yahweh is indeed the creator who possesses and governs all creation, all peoples. Yahweh also, however, has a special, intimate relation with Israel.

On the other hand, Israel (assuming the conditions are met) is to occupy a position in the world that partakes both of sacral significance and political authority. The two nouns used are specifically political references, *kingdom* and *nation.* Their modifiers, however, move in a sacerdotal direction, *priestly* and *holy.* Israel is to be a community in which worldly power and holy purpose converge.[95] Israel thus has an unparalleled vocation, and Sinai is the meeting whereby that vocation is to be given and accepted.

Verses 5-6 are extraordinary, because they manage in a single utterance to voice both an unthinkable purpose that foresees a people the like of which has never existed, and an unaccommodating condition affirming that Israel's peculiar status is endlessly derivative and never possessed. Israel's holy distinctiveness depends on moment-by-moment listening to the God who commands and authorizes. Whenever Israel ceases to listen and to

keep covenant, and presumes upon its "status," it forfeits its claim in that moment.

These three verses, as James Muilenburg has shown, provide the primary themes and the elemental structure for "Mosaic faith."[96] In the long, sacerdotal section beginning in Exodus 25, this link between promise and demand is not forgotten. Israel is to be holy and priestly; obedience to commands is pivotal even in the sacerdotal tradition, which takes such a high view of Israel (cf. 25:16, 22).

19:7-8. As the go-between, Moses carries Yah-weh's message of vv. 4-6 to the waiting community. While the narrative introduction identifies "the elders" as the addressees of Moses, it is "the people" who answer. Israel's answer is a vow and pledge of loyalty to the commands of Yahweh. Israel has sworn to "really listen" and to "keep covenant" (cf. v. 5). Israel has agreed to its identity and status as subject and vassal of Yahweh, in the full expectation that it will become a new kind of kingdom and a new kind of nation, one marked by priestly, holy marks. This pledge not only binds Israel unequivocally to Yahweh, but also sets Israel apart from all other peoples.

The oracle of Yahweh, voicing saving memory (v. 4), command (v. 5*a*), and promise (vv. 5*b*-6), is matched by the oath of Israel (v. 8). Together the oracle and the oath constitute the foundational acts of Israel's existence. In this moment, a new people is born into the world. Never before has such an offer been tendered to any people; never before has such an oath been taken. It is on the basis of this oracle and oath that preparations for the meeting now begin.

19:9-15. When Yahweh has the oath reported in Yahweh's own ears by Moses, Yahweh announces a stunning resolve: Yahweh will "come to you" (v. 9). The statement is direct and unconditional. We can see that this initial promise of presence, in the final form of the text, looks ahead to Exodus 25–31, which is preoccupied with the presence of God. Even in this direct statement, however, the intervention of Yahweh is immediately hedged about by "a dense cloud." Even God's direct presence will be shrouded in mystery

---

95. Buber, *Moses,* 101-9.

96. James Muilenburg, "The Form and Structure of the Covenantal Formulation," *VT* 9 (1959) 347-65.

and shadow. The most that is intended is that God will speak and Israel will hear. No possibility of Yahweh's being seen is offered.

The intent of Yahweh's direct speech to Israel is not to secure obedience. Yahweh's speech is offered, remarkably enough, only as a way to certify and legitimate Moses, so that Israel may "trust" Moses' words. This text thus has one eye on the authority of Moses and the enduring "office of Moses." The problem of believing Moses has been present in the narrative very early (4:1-9), but seemed resolved in 14:31. The subsequent protests against Moses (16:2-3; 17:2) suggest that because his requirements are so rigorous, issues of authority inevitably recur. This verse makes clear that Moses' radical vision is indeed Yahweh's vision.

Yahweh's resolve to "come to you" is a guarded one, protected by "a dense cloud." As Yahweh takes such precaution that Yahweh's own holiness should not be trivialized, so Israel must make adequate, careful ritual preparation for this spectacular meeting (vv. 10-15). This is not a spontaneous, intrusive, surprising confrontation, but a paced meeting that will be carefully choreographed. On the one hand, such intentionality suggests that the narrator's imagination is under the influence of regular worship, so that every meeting with God, including this one, is imagined in this form. On the other hand, this preparation is so that the initial Sinai meeting can be replicated and reenacted, much as Passover replicates exodus or as eucharist replicates the "last supper."

The work of preparation is to become "holy"—qualified to be in the presence of the holy God (vv. 10, 14). The prescribed preparation consists primarily in ritual cleansing. (On such washing, see 30:17-21. The act of ritual washing has become essential as a dramatic enactment to separate the sphere of worship from all other spheres, to assert that this meeting is different and one must be different to be there.) One can detect here the beginning of the distinctions of "clean and unclean" and "holy and profane," which will come to dominate later sacerdotal thought in Israel (cf. Lev 10:10; Ezek 22:26). One cannot approach this meeting carelessly, as though it were continuous with the rest of one's life.

Around the central preparation of washing, we may observe three other facets on "sanctification." First, the reference to "the third day" likely means as soon as all things are ready and is not to be taken as an exact number. The reference to the third day is perhaps taken up by Hos 6:2, which in turn is influential in the gospel narrative concerning the resurrection of Jesus on the third day. Indeed, "the meeting" of Easter is not unlike a replication of the meeting of Sinai, whereby life begins anew.

Second, the dire warning culminating in "shall surely die" (מות יומת *môt yûmāt*, v. 12) underscores the danger of the meeting and the otherness of God's holiness. Not only is God's "person" dangerous but even the mountain as God's habitat constitutes a great risk for Israel as well. Contact with Yahweh's holiness can be pursued only under intense discipline.

Third, in addition to the general notion of cleanness, the final line of v. 15 gives a powerful masculine tilt to the narrative, for contact with a woman will either profane, weaken, or render them impure. While we can only abhor the sexist reference in this text, which treats women as troublesome and men as "proper worshipers," even this rigorous tradition notices the odd and freighted connection between religion and sexuality; a connection that still operates powerfully among us. That inescapable connection is worth notice here, even though we might propose a very different adjudication of the issue.

19:16-25. Yahweh does what Yahweh says. Yahweh had announced an appearance to Israel (v. 9), and now that meeting happens on the third day as Moses had promised.

What an arrival it is, beyond anything Israel has ever experienced (vv. 16-20). There has been preparation, but the coming seems to override and disregard it. The narrative strains to find language to portray the disruptive, cataclysmic upheaval caused by the entry of God's own holiness. There are hints here of a storm God, causing thunder and lightning. There is evidence of a cultic rendition with the blast of trumpets. The "thick cloud" seems to join these other two accents. All of these images together are enough to cause the camp to tremble (v. 16), to make the entire mountain shake violently

(v. 18). There is now set loose sources of energy, power, and authority so enormous and so fearful that the intended "containers" of God's presence are unable to contain.

The coming of the holy one is unutterable. There are no adequate words, yet all we have left from the meeting is a text. The narrator wants us to see so much. In that hidden holiness, however, as words fail to utter, so vision fails to show, and all that is given is fire, smoke, violent movement, and a trumpet louder and louder. Yahweh is an alien presence, a foreboding, threatening, and destabilizing otherness. The narrator wants to take us up in awe and terror, in the presence of the holy one who is beyond all portrayal.

One more time, echoing vv. 12-13a, Yahweh warns Moses about the danger (vv. 21-25). The warning may be pictured in three concentric circles. First, the whole of the mountain is kept (or made) holy (v. 23). Second, the people are warned not to look (v. 21; vv. 12-13 warn them not to touch). It is not denied that God has a visible form. To see that form, however, is enormously dangerous (cf. 33:22-23)! Third, even the priests, the ones who confidently operate in the zone of God's holiness, are warned to be careful. They must not be complacent or comfortable in the presence of this God. Twice the term "break out" (פרץ *pāraṣ*) is used (v. 22, 24), as though Yahweh is a contained poison, almost substantive, that will break out to contaminate, destroy, and kill. One is struck in by the tumbling out of words and phrases in these verses, without a coherent picture or presentation. As the speech is untamed, so the God who comes in Israel is untamed, and on the loose.

REFLECTIONS

1. The mountain is no ordinary place (vv. 1-2). It is the dangerous environment of holiness, the place where the ordinariness of human, earthly life has contact with the holy that destabilizes and consequently transforms. We have trivialized "mountaintop experiences" as though they are romantic opportunities for religious self-indulgence. This account, against any such domestication, portrays the mountain of holiness as a dangerous meeting place that will leave nothing unchanged. In his study of theophany, Jörg Jeremias has identified two constant factors in theophanic narrative: a cataclysmic coming and a decisive after-effect of transformation.[97] Care must be taken not to reduce, trivialize, or routinize theophany, which here attests to God's terrible confrontation with Israel.

2. Israel's life begins in an oracle of God that is abrupt and without any antecedents (vv. 4-6). Israel is formed by the sovereign speech of Yahweh. This God is as majestic as an eagle, terrible in power, protective of its own treasured people. We are left with the wondrous image of being carried safely (albeit dangling dangerously) out of the reach of bondage.

The gospel premise of v. 4 is matched by a massive gospel demand of v. 5a. The "if" of v. 5 looms large in Mosaic faith. It is easy to treat the promise of v. 4 and the demand of v. 5 as a dialectic of gospel and law. The imposition of these categories, however, can be distorting. It is enough to see that Mosaic faith, i.e., the canonical core of the Bible, is vigorous in its requirement. The powerful verb "really *listen*" ("obey"; שמע *šāmaʿ*), perhaps with an allusion to the tradition of Deuteronomy (cf. Deut 6:4-9), insists that biblical faith focuses on ethical reality. Communion with "the eagle God" takes the form of adherence to the powerful purpose of God, soon to be specified at Sinai but already evidenced in the exodus.

The memory and the demand lead to the promise of vv. 5b-6. As the mountain is not ordinary and this God is not ordinary, so this people is destined not to be ordinary.

---

97. Jörg Jeremias, *Theophanie: Die Geschichte einer alttestamentlichen Gattung*, WMANT 10 (Neukirchen-Vluyn: Neukirchener Verlag, 1965).

The community of faith (synagogue, church) is given a vocation to be a distinct presence in the world on behalf of the world. Specifically, the priestly vocation of this community is to ponder and mediate the presence of the holy God in the midst of the nations, acting to resist any profanation of life that dismisses and banishes the powerful inconvenience of God.

The language of this promise is taken up in 1 Pet 2:9-10, in an attempt to characterize the early church.

3. Israel's response is an appropriate answer to the oracle (vv. 7-8). Israel must decide to accept its odd identity and destiny in the world, and that decision is for complete obedience. The oracle and responsive oath seem to be something like the initial questions asked the bride and groom prior to taking their vows, when each party states the intention and resolve for the relation. In these verses, Yahweh and Israel make an initial commitment to each other that is to be explicated in what follows.

4. The preparation of vv. 9-15 is ordered and severe. Our conventional trivializations of God make God in practice too available, too easy, and too immediate. We drop to our knees or bow our heads, and we imagine that God is eagerly awaiting attention. Or we drop in casually for worship, assuming that God is always there. Most of our worship takes place well short of the mountain, where we can seize and maintain the initiative, imagining God at our beck and call.

This meeting with Yahweh is clearly not one between "buddies." It is more like a meeting with an inscrutable, remote sovereign in which there is a scheduled preparation, a schooling in required steps, and an ordered ushering from chamber to chamber as the awe intensifies.

As the monarch enters the room only after everyone else is appropriately in place and waiting, so Yahweh comes only where disciplined readiness is evident. The text asserts that the holy God of Sinai will not come into the midst of our casual indifference. Some other god might, but it will not be this powerful God of liberation who rescues, demands, and promises.

5. The meeting (vv. 16-25) is cast as a theophany, a cataclysmic confrontation that destabilizes all conventional certitudes. In a society "explained" by the commonalities of the social sciences and received in the assurances of the "therapeutic," theophany is so raw and ragged that we scarcely have access to it. Theophany is by definition disruptive. As an alternative mode of discourse, it employs dramatic images in order to say what cannot be said and to witness what cannot be portrayed.

This raw, pre-rational mode of discourse is crucial for what is uttered in Scripture. First, the pivot points of the Bible are narratives of theophany that witness to the utter holiness of God. Note, for example, the great prophetic encounters with God (Elijah, Isaiah, Ezekiel), the pivot points in the life of Jesus (birth, baptism, transfiguration, crucifixion, and resurrection), and the break points in the life of the church (Pentecost, apocalyptic vision). Our reading of the Bible is often poverty-stricken, either because we exclude these texts as beyond our "realism," or because we trivialize their discourse with our banal exposition. These texts propose that our lives should also be structured by these pre-rational, dangerous comings of God, which lie beyond our capacity for explanation and control.

Second, theophany belongs to a faith-ordered human life. Our lives are not to be lived on a flat plane of bourgeois control. We are visited by the holy in both disruptive and healing ways. What Abraham Maslow too easily calls "peak experiences" are indeed definitional for human life. Persons flattened by modernity require a daring mode of discourse and a more venturesome field of images, whereby intrusions of the holy can be accepted as belonging to our human life. Theophanic texts provide access to experiences in the ongoing life of God to which we have no access without such speech. Israel's sense of humanness does not arise simply from political liberation but from this theophanic incursion that reorders its life.

In the end, however, theophanic discourse primarily serves neither a liturgic agenda nor notions of human personhood. Theophanic discourse is required in order to speak adequately about the character of this holy God who intrudes dangerously and disruptively in order to transform. This God lives neither in easy intimacy with us nor in remote sovereignty over us, but in odd ways comes and goes, seizing initiative and redefining reality.

In this dramatic narrative, Yahweh seizes initiative to establish the relation. This text concerns the freedom of God utterly untamed and undomesticated. In the face of all of Israel's preparations, God is loosed in a sovereignty that evokes trembling. There is something here of Barth's "otherness," an other who is decisively present and who insists that all else must be ordered and reoriented around this coming.

This text seems odd in the bourgeois context of Western Christianity. It witnesses to an extraordinary mountain, an extraordinary God, and an extraordinary people. It invites a reconsideration of our profanation of life whereby we manage and control and leave for religion only innocuous fringes. It models an endangered community that is willing to entertain holiness at its center. The narrative is so dramatic that we may miss its uncommon affirmation. In v. 27, the people "meet God." In vv. 18 and 20, God "comes down." This is an entry of heaven into earth, and earth is never again the same. This is an entry of holiness into Israel, and Israel is never again the same. The unloosing (breaking out) of holiness is so odd for us; the only thing odder is that in chapter 20 this holiness is fully mobilized around succinct and measured demand. The God of Sinai is a revolutionary sovereign who invites this prepared people to come under the discipline of the revolution (cf. Luke 1:17).

EXODUS 20:1-17, THE TEN COMMANDMENTS

OVERVIEW

The terrible, holy God of Sinai is always at the brink of "breaking out" against Israel and spilling over in self-aggrandizing destructiveness (19:22, 24). We are, in the light of that danger, hardly prepared for the proclamation of the Ten Commandments in this next unit. The God who threatens to break out in inexplicable rage instead breaks out in magisterial command. The relation of *theophany* to *law* is an odd one. The juxtaposition of the two genres, however, is definitional for what happens to Israel at Sinai. Command is rooted in theophany. The juxtaposition of theophany and command asserts that, for Israel, there is nothing more elemental or fundamental (even primordial) than the commands that intend to shape and order the world according to the radical and distinctive vision of the God of the exodus.

The Decalogue itself is likely a distinct literary entity that originally was not connected to this theophany. There is, moreover, serious critical question about the date and provenance of the decalogue and, therefore, about its Mosaic authorship. These commands may, like much of the legal material of the OT, have some linkages to already established legal materials of the ancient Near East. None of that, however, takes us very far in interpreting the commands as we have them.

We must, even with all of these critical uncertainties, try to take the corpus of commands as they are given. This means, first, that they are given in the context of the Sinai covenant. They constitute the substantive vision around which the God-Israel relation is ordered. Sinai binds Israel to this vision of social possibility and places Israel under this particular obedience. Second, the commands are given with the authority of Moses. They are in some sense an authentic articulation of what Mosaic faith in its core is all about. Third, even if these two traditions originated separately, the connection of exodus and command in 19:4-6 (and 20:1) binds the Sinai commands to the liberation passion of the exodus narrative. The commands are a decisive way in which Israel (and Yahweh) intend to sustain and institutionalize the revolutionary social possibility that is asserted and enacted in the exodus narrative.

The commands are commonly understood as divided into two "tablets": one concerning relations to God (vv. 1-11), and one concerning the neighbor (vv. 12-17). The relation between the two tablets is of crucial importance to biblical faith. It is self-evident that the second tablet is the more readily available, practical, and pertinent to us. It is risky, however (especially among "theological liberals"), to take the second tablet by itself, as positive law concerning human relations. But such a view misses the primary covenantal point that these "neighbor demands" have their warrant, impetus, and urgency in the character of this particular God. The second tablet is not just a set of good moral ideas. It contains conditions of viable human life, non-negotiable conditions rooted in God's own life and God's ordering of the world. Thus it is important to "get it right" about Yahweh, in order to "get it right" about neighbor. Karl Marx has seen this most clearly and programmatically: "The criticism of heaven is thus transformed into the criticism of earth, the criticism of religion into the criticism of law, and the criticism of theology into the criticism of politics."[98]

Marx means that "God talk" always implicitly asserts neighbor relations and that

every mode of neighbor relations inevitably bootlegs some powerful (even if hidden) notion of God. Thus it is not the case simply that Israel must attend both to God and to neighbor, but that the way of attending to God determines our ways of attending to neighbor and vice versa. It is precisely the worship of the God of the exodus that provides the elemental insistence and passionate imagination to reshape human relations in healing (cf. 15:26), liberating ways.

Norman Gottwald is correct in saying that in its recital of liberation and especially in the actions at Sinai, Israel initiates a revolutionary social experiment in the world, to see whether non-exploitative modes of social relationship can be sustained in the world.[99] In commenting upon the first commandment, Pixley comments:

The problem is not, of course, whether to call the rain God Yahweh or Baal. Behind the conflict of these gods is the social reality of a class struggle. . . . The polemical formulation of the commandment to worship Yahweh, then, has its explanation in the long struggle of the peasantry to rid itself of the domination of a long series of kings . . . who resurrected the old forms of class domination. . . . An Israelite had no choice but to reject any form of loyalty to any god who had not saved the slaves of Egypt.[100]

Thus the Decalogue stands as a critical principle of protest against every kind of exploitative social relation (public and interpersonal, capitalist and socialist) and as a social vision of possibility that every social relation (public and interpersonal, economic and political) can be transformed and made into a liberating relation.

98. David McLellan, *The Thought of Karl Marx: An Introduction* (London: Macmillan, 1971) 22.

99. Norman K. Gottwald, *The Tribes of Yahweh: A Sociology of the Religion of Liberated Israel, 1250–1050 B.C.* (Maryknoll, N.Y.: Orbis, 1979) 200-226 and *passim*.
100. Pixley, *On Exodus*, 129.

Exodus 20:1-7, "No Other Gods Before Me"

COMMENTARY

Israel's destiny under command is rooted in the self-disclosure of God. These commands might be taken not as a series of rules,

but as a proclamation in God's own mouth of who God is and how God shall be "practiced" by this community of liberated slaves.

The speech of God itself is abrupt in its beginning. Except for vv. 5-6, which are quite general, chapter 19 gives no hint that commands are to follow from the theophany. In Israel, however, God's self-giving is in the form of command. Thus the tradition holds closely together "a god so near" and "a torah so righteous" (Deut 4:7-8). God is known in torah; nearness is expressed as righteousness.

20:1-2. The self-disclosure of God begins with a succinct reference to and summary of the recital of liberation (v. 2). The first utterance is, "I am Yahweh." Thus God speaks the same powerful formula that has been reiterated throughout the exodus narrative (cf. 7:5), in which the formula is designed to reassure Israel and to challenge Pharaoh. Here the formula serves to impose a claim upon Israel. The event of the exodus provides the authority for the commands as well as the material claim of those commands.[101]

20:3. This verse (conventionally the first commandment) is programmatic for all Israelite reflection on obedience. Walther Zimmerli and Werner H. Schmidt have taken this command (together with the second command of vv. 4-6) as the essential command, for which all other law is exegesis, and as the *leitmotif* of OT theology.[102] We may identify four related themes.

First, the command requires Israel to mobilize all of its life, in every sphere, around one single loyalty. In the contemporary world, as in the ancient world, we practice a kind of henotheism, which lets different gods have their play in different spheres. This command insists on the integrity, coherence, and unity of all of life. Israel is a community destined to "will one thing."

Second, it is not likely that this command makes any claim about monotheism in any formal sense. That is, it does not insist that there are no other gods.[103] It insists only that other gods must receive none of Israel's loyalty or allegiance. This command thus is in

keeping with Deut 6:4, which also allows for the existence of other gods, but denies them "air time."[104]

Third, the last phrase, "before me," may also be read, "before my face." Because *face* in reference to God often means "sanctuary" or "altar," the command may mean "in my presence"—"in my shrine." On this reading, the command pertains precisely to the practice of worship and asserts that the liturgic life of Israel must be under stringent discipline in order to avoid compromise.

Fourth, H. Graf Reventlow has offered an alternative reading of this command that has considerable merit.[105] Reventlow observes that the formulation of this command is not "Thou shalt not," but rather "there will not be to you." He proposes that the statement is not an imperative command, but an indicative, whereby Yahweh in light of the exodus declares the banishment of all other gods (cf. Psalm 82 for the same motif). On this reading, the statement is a declaration of theological emancipation, whereby Israel can freely and gladly serve Yahweh, without any distracting compromise. One does not need to obey this command but only to hear and trust the good news of triumph and banishment.

20:4-6. The second command (vv. 4-6), often linked to the first, further asserts Yahweh's distinctiveness, which is to be enacted in Israel. The command, in fact, is a series of three prohibitions followed by an extended motivational clause. The three prohibitions are: You shall not make. . . . You shall not bow down. . . . You shall not serve. . . . This threefold prohibition serves as a counterpart to the formula of banishment in v. 3.

Two understandings of the commandment are possible. In the NRSV and NIV renderings, the command precludes "idols," the assignment of theological significance to any element of creation, the investment of ultimacy in what is not ultimate. Clearly, if "no other god" has any real power and, therefore, any real, substantive existence, it is grossly inappropriate that Israel should invest such an object with ultimacy.

101. See Zimmerli, *I Am Yahweh*, 1-28.

102. Walther Zimmerli, *Old Testament Theology in Outline* (Atlanta: John Knox, 1978) 109-40; Werner H. Schmidt, *The Faith of the Old Testament* (Philadelphia: Westminster, 1983) 53-88.

103. On the emergence of monotheism in ancient Israel, see Bernhard Lang, *Monotheism and the Prophetic Minority* (Sheffield: Almond, 1983) 13-59. James A. Sanders, "Adaptable for Life: The Nature and Function of Canon," in *Magnalia Dei: The Mighty Acts of God, Essays on the Bible and Archaeology in Memory of G. Ernest Wright*, eds. Frank Moore Cross et al. (Garden City, N.Y.: Doubleday, 1976) 541-52, nicely speaks of the "monotheizing tendency" in early Israel.

104. On Deut 6:4 in relation to the commandments, see J. G. Janzen, "On the Most Important Word in the Shema," *VT* 37 (1987) 280-300; and S. Dean McBride, "The Yoke of the Kingdom: An Exposition of Deuteronomy 6:4-5," *Int* 27 (1973) 273-306.

105. H. Graf Reventlow, *Gebot und Predigt im Dekalogue* (Gütersloh: G. Mohn, 1962) 25-28.

The word פֶּסֶל (*pesel*), however, need not be rendered "idol." It is more properly rendered "image," a visible representation of Yahweh. The temptation, then, is not the creation of a rival that detracts from Yahweh, but an attempt to locate and thereby domesticate Yahweh in a visible, controlled object. This latter reading, which is the more probable, is also more subtle. It does not fear a rival but a distortion of Yahweh's free character by an attempt to locate Yahweh and so diminish something of Yahweh's terrible freedom.

The motivational clause begins in v. 5*b*, introduced by כִּי (*kî*, "for"). The reason for the prohibition is Yahweh's very own character; Yahweh is a "jealous God" who will operate in uncompromised and uncontested freedom. Yahweh's jealousy is evidenced in two ways in a formula that is more fully stated in Exod 34:6-7. Negatively, this jealous God is one of deep moral seriousness who takes affront at violations of commands, so that the cost of the affront endures over the generations (34:7*b*). Positively, this jealous God is one who practices massive fidelity (חֶסֶד *ḥesed*) to those who are willing to live in covenant (34:6-7*a*). The two motivational phrases are in fact more symmetrical than the NRSV suggests, for "reject me" is in fact "hate" (שֹׂנֵא *śānē'*), as the NIV translates, thus contrasting precisely those who "love" and those who "hate" Yahweh.

Thus the idol (as rival and alternative) or the image (as localization and domestication) is an attempt to tone down Yahweh's jealousy. There are two reasons for toning down God's jealousy: resistance to God's deep moral seriousness or discomfort with God's massive fidelity. Yahweh's character, to which this command witnesses, holds to both moral seriousness and covenantal fidelity. The

measure of both "punishment" and "showing steadfast love" is adherence to the command. The temptation of Israel, here precluded, is to tone down the primacy of command. Israel in covenant must trust itself to the terrible freedom of the God who will be obeyed.

20:7. The third command continues the line of the disclosure of God from the first two commands. This command is often misunderstood and misused, when it is taken to refer to "bad" or vulgar language. While "right speech" is indeed at issue, more is at stake than not cursing or using obscenities. What must be understood is that the "name" of Yahweh bespeaks God's powerful presence and purpose. The utterance of the name is the mobilization of the presence and power of God, an assumption that is still evident in prayers offered "in the name of Jesus." To make "wrongful use of the name," or as Walter Harrelson suggests, the use of the name "for mischief,"[106] means to invoke through utterance the power and purpose of Yahweh in the service of some purpose that is extraneous to Yahweh's own person. That is, the violation is to make Yahweh (who is an ultimate end) into a means for some other end. Such a practice may be done in quite pious ways (without anything like "curse") with an instrumental view of God. This command thus follows well from the first two, because all three concern seductive ways in which the God of the exodus is diminished or trivialized.

The sanction (threat) of this command is ominous indeed: Yahweh will not "acquit" those who seek to use God for their own purposes but will hold such persons guilty to perpetuity. The severity of this threat is congruent with the motivational clause of v. 5.

106. Harrelson, *The Ten Commandments and Human Rights*, 72-76.

REFLECTIONS

These first three commandments are preoccupied with the awesome claims of God's person. God insists, in the light of the exodus, upon being accepted, affirmed, and fully obeyed.

1. It is not always helpful in teaching and preaching the commandments to go through them one rule at a time, as though using a check list. To be sure, there is some need for specificity of interpretation. That, however, is only preliminary to the main interpretive task, which is to voice the large and demanding vision of God that defines biblical faith.

The truth of the matter is that the biblical God is not "user friendly." The theological crisis present in all our modern situations of proclamation and interpretation is that we are all "children of Feuerbach." In the nineteenth century, Ludwig Feuerbach fully articulated the hidden assumption of the Enlightenment, that God is in the end a projection of our best humanness. That Feuerbachian "betrayal" takes more than one form. The "liberal temptation" is to diminish the role of God, either to remove God from public spheres of life and leave God for interpersonal matters, or to make God an object of adoration rather than a subject who can do anything. One signal of such reductionism is the slogan that "God has no hands but ours." The reactive "conservative temptation" is the projection of a settled, sovereign God who in fact is not operative as a political character (as in the drama of the exodus) but is only a set of fixed propositions that give certitude and stability. Either way, in our shared theological failure of nerve, we end with a God very unlike the one who makes a self-disclosure here.

2. Exposition of these commandments has as its topic the voicing of the holy, jealous God of the Bible who saves and commands; a God who is an active, decisive presence in our common public life, but who in holiness is beyond all our most pious efforts at control and manipulation.[107]

There are no analogues, no parallels, no antecedents, no adequate replications or explanations for this God who confronts us in and through the narrative of liberation. It is the majestic act of "getting glory over Pharaoh" (14:4, 17) that bestows upon Yahweh the right to speak and to command. The exodus shows that Yahweh has now displaced every other loyalty, has driven from the field all rivals, and now claims full attention and full devotion from Israel. This people would not have entered history except for Yahweh's demanding solidarity against Pharaoh. The question of this faith in the modern world is whether there is a people, a concrete community, that can embrace and practice this demanding loyalty. Most of the people with whom we preach and teach are (like us) both yearning and reluctant, both ready and hesitant, to embrace these commandments that bespeak a lifetime of ceding over authority.

How, indeed, can a "mystery" be demanding? We expect a mystery to be amorphous and transcendental; we expect a demand to be coercive, visible, and political. In these three utterances, however, Yahweh is indeed holy mystery who, in the very utterance of mystery, enunciates demand.

3. This uncompromising demand is properly voiced in a world of unacknowledged polytheism. We have always lived in a world of options, alternative choices, and gods who make powerful, competing appeals. It does us no good to pretend that there are no other offers of well-being, joy, and security. In pursuit of joy, we may choose Bacchus; in pursuit of security, we may choose Mars; in pursuit of genuine love, we may choose Eros. It is clear that these choices are not Yahweh, that these are not gods who have ever wrought an Exodus or offered a covenant.

In the Christian tradition, baptism is the dramatic form of making a God choice, in which receiving a new name and making promises is choosing this liberating-covenantal faith against any other shape of life. Thus in the Christian tradition, appropriating and living out baptism means living by a single loyalty among a mass of options.

4. The second commandment, in its prohibition, inventories the heavens above, the earth beneath, and the waters under the earth (v. 4; cf. Deut 4:17-18;). The triad, of course, refers to all of creation (cf. Gen 1:28). The command asserts that nothing in creation is usable in making God visible or available. God's sovereign mystery is

107. See Emil Fackenheim, *God's Presence in History: Jewish Affirmations and Philosophical Reflections* (New York: Harper & Row, 1972) 8-19.

discontinuous from everything and anything in creation. The propensity to encapsulate God in creation leads to an attempt to retain for ourselves control over some piece of creation. The clearest, most extensive treatment of this confusion in the Bible is Rom 1:20-25. To imagine that anything in creation could possibly embody the creator God is a result of "futile thinking" and "senseless darkened minds" (Rom 1:21). The outcome is false worship based on a lie instead of the truth (v. 20).

In contemporary church discussions, this powerful, polemical, doxological statement has often been side-tracked and related only to issues of homosexuality. The confusion of creator-creation, however, is much more profound and ominous than an argument about sexuality. Attempts to "image God" by taking creation in our own hands are much more evident in technological abuse of creation and in military exploitation, by which "God as power" comes into play without any restraining awareness that "God as power" is also "God as Holy Mystery." It may in the end be the case that the "shameless acts" men commit with men (cf. Rom 1:27-28) are not sexual as much as they are military and technological. The Mosaic prohibition against idols and images has profound sociopolitical implications, for the practice of worshiping idols is never simply a theological or liturgical matter but always spills over into social, ideological, and political practice, inevitably with the intent of partisan advantage. Carlos M. N. Eire has shown how the prohibition on idols became a driving power for Calvinism as a sociopolitical force.[108] Where the church is soft on idols, it becomes muted on social criticism.

5. The third commandment asserts that God cannot be put to use and is never a means toward an end (v. 7). The notion that the ultimate human purpose is to "glorify and enjoy God" means that God is pure end and never means. Using God's name mischievously however, is an enormous temptation, because the holy God is vulnerable to being made into an ideological tool.

108. Carlos M. N. Eire, *War Against the Idols: The Reformation of Worship from Erasmus to Calvin* (Cambridge: Cambridge University Press, 1986) esp. 276-310.

Exodus 20:8-11, "You Shall Not Do Any Work"

COMMENTARY

The fourth commandment is conventionally included in the first tablet. However, because the sabbath command occupies such a prominent and decisive position in the Decalogue, and because it enjoins rest for humanity as well as honoring God the creator, I take it as a command that stands between and connects to both tablets.[109]

Unlike most of the other commands (see also v. 12), this one is not a prohibition; rather, it enjoins Israel to positive action. Israel is to remember (זכר *zākar*). The act of remembering here, as in the remembering of the eucharist, means to appropriate actively

109. Here I follow Patrick D. Miller, *Deuteronomy*, Interpretation (Louisville: Westminster/John Knox, 1990) 79-84.

as a present reality. The seventh day is to be marked as "holy time"—i.e., as time completely devoted to Yahweh.

The initial command of v. 8 is explicated in three parts. There is first an acknowledgment of six legitimate days of work. Then comes the command for a day of rest for the one addressed, ostensibly a land-owning man, who will provide rest for all creation under his dominion (vv. 9-10). Finally there is a motivational clause (v. 11).

The positive command itself indicates that sabbath remembrance is in fact a complete and comprehensive work stoppage. There is no mention of worship. The way in which this day is to be acknowledged as holy—i.e., different and special—is to separate it from all days of required activity, productivity, coercive performance, self-securing, or service to other human agents. Moreover, this covenantal work stoppage is not a special privilege of the male believer. The entire society that makes up the family, village, or clan is to share publicly in this act.

How is it that a covenantal work stoppage bears witness to this self-disclosing God? The answer is given in the motivational clause: Israel rests because God rests. This God is not a workaholic; Yahweh has no need to be more secure, more sufficient, more in control, or more noticed. It is ordained in the very fabric of creation that the world is not a place of endless productivity, ambition, or anxiety. Fretheim has made the case that exodus liberation is aimed at the full restoration of peaceable creation.[110] There is no more powerful hint of that connection than in this commandment.

While the motivational clause links this teaching explicitly to creation, the preamble of v. 2 links the command to the exodus as well. Such a connection between the command and the preamble hints at a connection made much more explicit in Deut 5:12-15, where the motivation of creation has been subordinated to that of the exodus. In this text the purpose of the covenantal work stoppage is to remember and reenact the exodus. Moreover, Hans Walter Wolff has observed that the phrase "as you" in Deut 5:14 makes the sabbath a great day of equalization in which all social distinctions are overcome, and all rest alike.[111] To be sure, that nice phrase is not present in our version of the command, but it is in any case implicit. The implicit act of equalization in sabbath witnesses to the intention of the creator that creation should be a community of well-being, in which all creatures stand together, equally and in shared rest.

110. This is a main thesis of his commentary; see Fretheim, *Exodus*. See more specifically Terence E. Fretheim, "The Plagues as Ecological Signs of Historical Disaster," *JBL* 110 (1991) 385-96.

111. Hans Walter Wolff, *Anthropology of the Old Testament* (Philadelphia: Fortress, 1974) 139-40. See the helpful exposition of sabbath by Marva J. Dawn, *Keeping the Sabbath Wholly: Ceasing, Resting, Embracing, Feasting* (Grand Rapids: Eerdmans 1989).

REFLECTIONS

1. This sabbath commandment stands at mid-point between two other extended expositions of sabbath in the book of Exodus, both of which are important for explicating the command (16:5, 22-26; 31:12-17). The story of manna (16:5, 22-26) indicates that rest is possible because God gives enough food, and all who gather either little or much have equally enough. The command of 31:12-17 indicates that God needs to be "refreshed," and therefore that those made in God's image also need to have life (נפשׁ *nepeš*) restored (cf. Pss 19:7; 23:3). Sabbath is necessary because of God's own vulnerability. Thus in sabbath, Israel relies on God's generosity and participates in God's vulnerability.

2. The sabbath command is given its foundation in the creation narrative of Gen 1:1–2:4a. That text, commonly taken to be exilic, is part of the development whereby Israel in exile comes to rely on sabbath as one of the two major distinguishing marks of Judaism. (The other is circumcision.) The cruciality of sabbath is further evident in Lev 26:1-2, where it is paired with making images as the preliminary to the great recital of blessings and curses. (Notice that these two verses have a double use of the formula "I am Yahweh.") In Isa 56:4, 6, moreover, sabbath is reckoned as the key mark of keeping covenant in the community after the exile.

Sabbath looms so large in exilic and post-exilic Judaism because the Jews are now politically marginal and vulnerable. They are endlessly at the behest of someone else. Sabbath becomes a way, in the midst of such vulnerability, to assert the distinctiveness of this community by a theological announcement of loyalty to Yahweh. It is also a political assertion of disengagement from the economic system of productivity that never has enough. Thus Judaism in its covenantal work stoppage practices disengagement from the socioeconomic political enterprise that in its endless productivity offers safe, secure rest and well-being.

3. Contemporary practice of sabbath is not concerned to devise a system of restrictions and "blue laws." Rather, sabbath concerns the periodic, disciplined, regular disengagement from the systems of productivity whereby the world uses people up to exhaustion. That disengagement refers also to culture-produced expectations for frantic leisure, frantic consumptions, or frantic exercise.

The pastoral issue for many persons is to develop habits and disciplines that break those patterns of behavior. Sabbath practice is not to be added on to everything else, but requires the intentional breaking of requirements that seem almost ordained in our busy life. Sabbath thus may entail the termination of routines, the disengagement from some social conventions, or even the lowering of one's standard of living. The very concreteness of sabbath is a sacrament witnessing to the reality of exodus and to the governance of the creator who has broken the restless penchant for productive activity. The healing of creation, and of our lives as creatures of God, requires a disengagement from the dominant systems of power and wealth. Sabbath is the daring recognition that with the change of sovereigns wrought in the exodus, such unrewarding expenditure of labor is no longer required. It is only a bad habit we continue in our disbelieving foolishness (cf. Luke 12:16-20).

4. This fourth commandment is commonly placed in the first tablet, honoring the majesty of God. It belongs in the sequence concerning God's sovereignty (first commandment), God's freedom (second commandment), God's holy name (third commandment), and now God's holy time (fourth commandment). It is clear, however, that the neighbor concerns of the second tablet begin here to intrude upon the first tablet. The affirmation about God's rest leads to a command about human rest. In this latter accent, sabbath serves to acknowledge and enact the peculiar worth and dignity of all creatures, and especially of human creatures. Consequently there are limits to the use of human persons, and of all creatures, as instrumental means to other ends. Sabbath is a day of special dignity, when God's creatures can luxuriate in being honored ends and not mobilized means to anything beyond themselves. In the commandments that follow, we shall see that this limit to the "usefulness" of human creatures introduced in the fourth commandment now becomes a *leitmotif* for the second tablet.

Exodus 20:12-17, Neighbor Relations

COMMENTARY

This set of six commands includes one positive command (v. 12), followed by five prohibitions. Calvin offers that charity "contains the sum of the second tablet."[112]

20:12. God enjoins Israel at the mountain to "honor" father and mother. The command consists in an imperative followed by a motivational clause. The command concerns the problematic relationships between one generation and the next. We have seen that the

Exodus narrative is understood as a tale told to ensure that the children and the children's children will know and embrace the memory of liberation (10:1-2). The book of Genesis is preoccupied with the safe transmission of blessing and promise from one generation to the next. Moreover, Michael Fishbane has suggested that the urgent command of Deut 6:4-9 evidences that the children were resistant and recalcitrant to the core teaching of Israel (cf. Ps 78:5-8).[113] And Deut 21:15-17

112. Calvin, *Commentaries on the Four Last Books of Moses Arranged in the Form of a Harmony*, 6-7.

113. Fishbane, "Exodus 1–4," 79-83.

attests to the fact that Israel struggled with the continuity of generations and the valuing of the life-world of the parents by the children. It may be that every society struggles with this issue, but the children's loyalty is peculiarly urgent in a community whose faith works only by remembering unrepeatable events.

The command is to "honor." The Hebrew term כבד (*kābēd*) includes among its meanings "be heavy," suggesting the sense of "give weight to." The negative warning of 21:17 forms a suggestive counterpoint to this command, because the term curse (קלל *qll*) may also be rendered "to treat lightly." Such a nuance is important, because the command does not advocate obeying or being subordinate but treating parents with appropriate seriousness. Childs concludes that it was "a command which protected parents from being driven out of the home or abused after they could no longer work."[114] (Cf. Prov 19:26.) Calvin shrewdly notes that in Eph 6:1, the commandment is quantified, "in the Lord," so that "the power of a father is so limited as that God, on whom all relationships depend, shall have the rule over fathers as well as children . . . Paul . . . indicates, that if a father enjoins anything unrighteous, obedience is freely to be denied him."[115]

The motivational clause concerns keeping the land, which is God's gift. This is the only command of the Decalogue that includes land as a motivation. Several possible connections might be made concerning this command and its motivation. First, the connection may be a quite general one, that distorted relations between the generations lead to a forfeiture of shared well-being. Second, the connection may be a quasi-legal one, suggesting that the capacity to retain the inheritance (נחלה *naḥălâ*) of land depends on embracing the promises of father and mother. Third, if the land is understood as a result of withdrawing from the slave economy for the sake of a covenantal, egalitarian community, then the land will be held only as long as the covenantal vision is held with passion. In any case, socioeconomic security depends on the right ordering of interpersonal relations between the generations, perhaps between the generation of power and that of vulnerability.

20:13. The command against murder is terse and unadorned. While scholars continue to sort out the exact intent of the term *murder* (רצח *rāṣaḥ*), the main point is clear: Human life belongs to God and must be respected. Walter Harrelson (following Barth) takes a maximal view of the prohibition and interprets it broadly as "reverence for life"—i.e., all human life.[116] H. Graf Reventlow suggests that the term *murder* originally referred to blood feuds and epidemics of killings that grew out of an insatiable thirst for vengeance between clans and families.[117] Still other interpretations of this command suggest that murder is precluded within the community of covenant but that the prohibition does not apply outside of one's own community of covenant. It is entirely possible that all such distinctions, in a kind of casuistry, make too fine a point. Appeal to Gen 9:6 suggests that biblical faith has drawn an uncompromising line against the taking of another life, period. Human life is intrinsically of value and may not be ultimately violated.

20:14. The prohibition against adultery concerns distorted sexual relations, or more broadly, distorted human relations. Again, the command is so terse as to invite and require interpretation. Most narrowly construed, "adultery" consists in the violation of the wife of another man. Such a patriarchal reading understands the woman to be the property and trust of a man. For ample reason, of course, the command has been much more broadly understood in Jewish and Christian communities. Most comprehensively, the prohibition points to the recognition that sexuality is enormously wondrous and enormously dangerous. The wonder of sexuality is available in a community only if it is practiced respectfully and under discipline. The danger of sexuality is that it is capable of evoking desires that are destructive of persons and of communal relations. It is inevitable that such a command will be subject to ongoing dispute, because around the subject of freedom and discipline in sexuality we deal with the most intense and elemental mystery of human existence. There is in this command

114. Childs, *The Book of Exodus*, 418.
115. Calvin, *Commentaries on the Four Last Books of Moses Arranged in the Form of a Harmony*, 8.

116. Harrelson, *The Ten Commandments and Human Rights*, 109-10.
117. Reventlow, *Gebot und Predigt im Dekalogue*, 71-77.

neither license for permissiveness nor a puritanical restrictiveness. Everything else is left to the interpretive community.

20:15. The eighth command on stealing is characteristically terse. On the face of it, the commandment concerns respect for the property of another. It does not probe behind the social fact of "property" to notice, as Marx has done so poignantly, the probability that private property arises regularly from violence. It is enough that what is possessed by another must not be seized.

On the basis of Exod 21:16 and Deut 24:7, Albrecht Alt has proposed that the original form of the prohibition was "Thou shalt not steal a person."[118] The gain of such an interpretation is that it focuses on the cruciality of the human and is not drawn away toward lesser "objects." It is, perhaps, neither necessary nor wise to choose between a more conventional focus on property and Alt's focus. The materiality of Israel's faith recognizes that selfhood includes the necessary "goods" to make a life of dignity possible. That, of course, leaves the vexed question of relation between the essential goods of the "have nots" and the extravagant goods of the "haves." This command cannot be used as a defense of "private property" without reference to the kinds of sharing that are required for available human community. Harrelson concludes: "The commandment not to steal means, in effect, that persons are not to whittle down, eat away at, the selfhood of individuals or of families or of communities."[119]

20:16. The ninth commandment (v. 16) is not a general command against "lying" but concerns courtroom practice. The prohibition understands that a free, independent, and healthy judiciary system is indispensable for a viable community. The courtroom must be a place where the truth is told and where social reality is not distorted through devious manipulation or ideological perversion. It is remarkable in this list of prohibitions that concern the sanctity of human life, the mystery of sexuality, and the maintenance of property,

that courts should be so prominent. The prohibition, however, is a recognition that community life is not possible unless there is an arena in which there is public confidence that social reality will be reliably described and reported.

The sphere of this command is narrowly circumscribed. Truth-telling concerns "your neighbor"—i.e., a fellow member of the covenant community. The neighbor is not to be "used" by lying in order to enhance one's own interest. Community requires drawing a line against private interest in order to make social relations workable.

20:17. The tenth commandment, on coveting, is somewhat different from the other elements of the second tablet. It concerns the destructive power of desire. It is not helpful, however, to interpret "desire" as a vague, undifferentiated attitude. Rather, it here concerns desire acted upon publicly, whereby one reaches for that which is not properly one's own. Such reaching inevitably destroys community. The text knows that humans are indeed driven by desire. The commandment regards desire in and of itself as no good or bad thing; its quality depends on its object. The tale of Genesis 3 is the tale of desire misdirected (cf. v. 3).

Notice that desire in ancient Israel is characteristically not directed toward sexual objects (as we might expect) but pertains primarily to economics. Its concern is to curb the drive to acquisitiveness. Thus the object of desire may be silver and gold (Deut 7:25; Josh 7:21) or land (Exod 34:24; Mic 2:2). The supreme and legitimate "desire" of Israel is to do the will and purpose of Yahweh.

In this prohibition, the primary object of desire is the neighbor's house. That "house," however, includes wife (reckoned in a patriarchal society as property), slaves, and working animals. The command expects that within a community of genuine covenanting, the drive of desire will be displaced by the honoring of neighbor, by the sharing of goods, and by the acceptance of one's own possessions as adequate. This commandment, placed in final position in the Decalogue, is perhaps intended as the climactic statement of the whole, referring to Yahweh's claims at the beginning (v. 1). Yahweh's victory over the Egyptian gods in the same action defeated the spiritual power of coveting.

118. See the summary review by Robert Karl Gnuse, *You Shall Not Steal: Community and Property in the Biblical Tradition* (Maryknoll, N.Y.: Orbis, 1985). While Alt has been credited with this reading of the command, in fact the interpretation of "kidnapping" was already proposed in early rabbinic interpretation. See M. H. Gottstein, "Du sollst nicht stehlen," *TZ* 9 (1953) 394-95; and Jacob J. Petuchowski, "A Note on W. Kessler's Problematik des Dekalogs," *VT* 7 (1957) 397-98.

119. Harrelson, *The Ten Commandments and Human Rights*, 42.

REFLECTIONS

This second tablet, anticipated in the fourth commandment, indicates that the holiness of God puts God beyond the reach of Israel, and *mutatis mutandis,* the intrinsic worth of human persons as creatures of God puts humans beyond the reach of abuse and exploitation.

The second tablet is a magisterial assertion that human life is situated in a community of rights and responsibilities that is willed by God. Within that community, human life in all its ambiguity and inscrutability is endlessly precious and must not be violated. This affirmation seems so obvious that we are reluctant to voice it. It is now clear that in the obduracy of totalitarian society and in the rapaciousness of market economy, a humane life of shared rights and responsibilities is exceedingly fragile. The interpretive task is to show that this fragile bonding in covenant that guarantees dignity and well-being is a live possibility among us. The second tablet is indeed an articulation of a more excellent way; it is a way in which human life is intrinsically worthy of respect, in which human persons are honored ends rather than abused means, and in which rapacious desire is properly curbed for the sake of viable community.

1. The fifth commandment concerns the struggle between the generations, a struggle that is inherently filled with tension (v. 12). On the one hand, there can be a kind of traditionalism that submits excessively to "the way we were." On the other hand, there can be a one-generation narcissism that imagines nothing important happened until "us." That intergenerational tension requires a seriousness that does not simply capitulate but that honors in freedom and response. In the angel's announcement to Zechariah, a remarkable transposition of the relation of the generations is anticipated: "With the spirit and power of Elijah he will go before him, to turn the hearts of parents to their children, and the disobedient to the wisdom of the righteous, to make ready a people prepared for the Lord" (Luke 1:17 NRSV).

Here it is not the children who submit to the parents, but the parents who are "turned" to the children. This assertion of the angel does not override Moses' command. Rather, the two statements are in tension, and adjudication requires that both parties, parents and children, must be engaged in the process. The commandment precludes a new generation that disregards the parents and does not give them due weight. The angel's poem precludes a blind, mechanical submissiveness of children to parents.[120] "Honor" is a more delicate, transactive maneuver, whereby both parties grow in dignity through the process.

2. The prohibition on killing asserts that human life is valuable to God, and under God's protective custody (v. 13). No doubt distinctions and differentiations are to be made in enacting this command. The most obvious of these now before us concern capital punishment, war, euthanasia, and abortion. The interpretive community is of no single mind on these great questions, and no consensus is in prospect. The commandment itself states a non-negotiable principle and nothing more. That, however, is a great deal in a society where life is cheap, where technology is impersonal, where economic greed is unbridled, where bombs are "smart," and where ideology is powerful. The murder that makes the newspapers signifies a breakdown of the human infrastructure, which legitimates brutality. The murder behind the headlines—i.e., the killing that happens a little at a time, mostly unnoticed and unacknowledged—is kept ideologically obscure. Such slow, unnoticed destruction diminishes human life among those not powerful enough to defend themselves. The interpretive issue may be this: If human life is precious, what public policies are required in order to enhance and

---

120. Alice Miller, *Thou Shalt Not Be Aware: Society's Betrayal of the Child* (New York: New American Library, 1986), has suggested that the command to honor parents has functioned programatically as a warrant for the abuse of children by parents. Thus the corrective proposed, that the parents turn to the children, counters such a potentially abusive misreading.

protect it? The old-fashioned responses of employment, housing, and health care are not remote from this command. Calvin counts on the positive application of this command, "that we should not only live at peace with men . . . but also should aid, as far as we can, the miserable who are unjustly oppressed, and should endeavor to resist the wicked, lest they should injure men."[121]

Jesus intensified the command to include anger (Matt 5:21-26; cf. 1 John 3:15). One wonders whether in our society Jesus might have focused not on anger but on cynical indifference that is sanctified by a greedy, uncaring individualism that is in its own way killing.

3. The prohibition against adultery concerns the primal mystery of human existence and viable human relationships (v. 14). Our interpretive concern, of course, moves beyond the patriarchal assumption that operates with a double standard. Fidelity should be the guiding theme of interpretation of this command, as distinct from legal arrangements that bespeak old property practices and rights. Formal, legal relations of marriage provide the most durable context and basis for such fidelity. They do not, however, in and of themselves amount to fidelity. Our social context has few models or norms for fidelity of a genuine conventional kind. (It is for that reason that the relation of Yahweh-Israel or Christ-church have become such powerful models and metaphors, though these metaphors are beset with enormous problems in their patriarchal articulation.)

Continuing reflection on this commandment, which concerns genuine fidelity, may go in two directions. On the one hand, there is a struggle with legally constituted relations (marriage), which are not always relations of fidelity because of abusive behavior and a lack of authentic mutuality. On the other hand, there is a struggle concerning the possibility of a genuine relation of fidelity that is outside the conventional sanctions of legal marriage. It is clear on both counts that interpretive issues are not simple and one-dimensional.

In its fullest interpretation, the command against adultery envisions covenantal relations of mutuality that are genuinely life-giving, nurturing, enhancing, and respectful. Such a notion of long-term trust is treated as almost passé in a narcissistic society, preoccupied with individual freedom and satisfaction.

4. There are many ways to "steal a self" (v. 15). Such a focus in the eighth commandment raises important issues regarding what it takes to make a self socially viable. We are, of course, aware of theft and household burglary. We are increasingly aware of white-collar crime whereby large sums of money and property are seized in seemingly "victimless" crimes. Serious covenantal relations preclude such activity.

We must take care, however, that our interpretation of this commandment is not a mere defense of private property and the status quo as a justification for the unjust distribution of goods. Faithful interpretation requires us to probe even the subtle forms of "theft" that rob persons of their future. Here are three facets of theft to which the commandment may point.

First, the terrible inequity of haves and have nots in our society (as in many others) means that babies born into acute poverty are at the outset denied any realistic chance of surviving in a market economy. Because we believe in the goodness of God's creation, we believe such children are intended by God to have what is necessary for an abundant life. Very often, however, they do not—because they have been robbed of their future. They are not robbed by "bad people"; they are robbed by power arrangements and structures that have long since relegated them to the permanent underclass. Over such arrangements and structures, the command speaks out: "Thou shalt not steal!"

---

121. Calvin, *Commentaries on the Four Last Books of Moses Arranged in the Form of a Harmony*, 21.

Second, a like theft continues to occur between developed and developing nations, whereby a long-term pattern of deathly dependence is fostered. For a long time Third World countries have been treated only as colonies, natural resources, or markets, kept in a dependency relation, so that nearly all benefits of the relation go to the developed economy and its colonial agents. Patterns of military control and credit arrangements guarantee not only long-term dependency but a predictable cycle of poverty, hunger, and endless destabilization. There is no doubt that we in the West are the primary beneficiaries of such practice.

Third, in interpersonal relations that lack mutuality, characteristically there is an aggressor and a victim. In that unequal relation, which is carried on by invisible but brutal power, the "self" of the victim is endlessly stolen and diminished. The radical vision of Moses is that covenantal practice does not permit these modes of destructive power in relations, public or interpersonal.

5. The three commands on killing, adultery, and stealing together constitute something of a special group. Not only are they the most tersely expressed commands, but also they all address the ways in which vulnerable persons in community are assaulted, diminished, and destroyed. Such actions, condemned in these commands, are all acts of uncurbed power, which fails to recognize that the perpetrator and the victim share a commonality and a solidarity that preclude destructiveness. Contemporary interpretation need not get bogged down in casuistry about this or that command, but can focus on the shared solidarity that precludes destructiveness, either in the transactions of public (economic) power or in the intimacy of interpersonal relations.

6. Viable human community depends on truth telling (v. 16). This commandment is not concerned with "white lies," but the public portrayal of reality that is not excessively skewed by self-interest or party ideology. The primary point of reference is the court, where witnesses speak and testimony is given. The commandment insists that courts must resist every distortion of reality, every collusion with vested interest (cf. 18:21; Pss 15:2; 24:4), which makes such truth telling prerequisite to worship.

More broadly construed, the commandment enjoins members of the covenant community not to distort reality to each other. The major pertinence of the prohibition in our society is the collapse of truth into propaganda in the service of ideology.[122] That is, public versions of truth are not committed to a portrayal of reality, but to a rendering that serves a partisan interest. Such a practice may take many forms. Among the more blatant practices of "false witness" in recent times has been the use of propaganda through which defeat has been described as military victory or reporting has simply been silenced, so that no truth need be told at all.[123] Such a public tendency is not new. Isaiah 5:20 already addresses those who distorted reality (self-)deception.

Moreover, Jeremiah understood that religious leadership is equally tempted to deception, which both advances institutional interests and seeks to give credence to theological claims (see Jer 6:13-14; 8:10-11). The commandment continues to expect that there is a viable alternative to this deceptiveness in public life.

7. The final commandment on coveting does not address general envy (v. 17), but concerns a kind of acquisitiveness that destabilizes the property and, therefore, the life of another. Marvin Chaney has shown that the oracle of Mic 2:1-5 is, in fact, an exposition of the command.[124] That is, the command concerns primarily land and the development of large estates at the expense of vulnerable neighbors.

---

122. See the critical analysis of propaganda as deception by Jacques Ellul, *Propaganda: The Formation of Men's Attitudes* (New York: Knopf, 1965). See also Neil Postman, *Amusing Ourselves to Death: Public Discourse in the Age of Show Business* (New York: Penguin, 1986).

123. See David Halberstam, *The Best and the Brightest* (New York: Random House, 1972); Neil Sheeham, *A Bright Shining Lie: John Paul Vann and America in Vietnam* (New York: Random House, 1988).

124. Marvin L. Chaney, "You Shall Not Covet Your Neighbor's House," *Pacific Theological Review* 15 (Winter 1982) 3-13. See also D. N. Premnath, "Latifundialization and Isaiah 5:8-10," *JSOT* 40 (1988) 49-60.

The propensity to covet in our society is enacted through an unbridled consumerism that believes that the main activity of human life is to accumulate, use, and enjoy more and more of the available resources of the earth. An undisciplined individualism has taught us that we are entitled to whatever we may want no matter who else may be hurt. Such individualism, however, is driven by a market ideology based on an elemental assumption of scarcity. If there is a scarcity of goods needed for life, then energy and passion are generated to gather and accumulate all that one can (cf. 16:19-21). M. Douglas Meeks has shown that the ideology of scarcity, which drives our economy, is, in the end, an act of theological doubt that does not believe that God's providential generosity is finally reliable.[125] This commandment summons the faithful to break with the practice of acquisitive individualism and to reject the ideology of scarcity upon which it is based. Thus the commandment requires a massive repentance that is theological in substance, but that is manifested economically.

This commandment functions as a crucial conclusion to the entire Decalogue. We may note two important connections to the preceding commands. First, this command is related to the command on sabbath. Whereas coveting is an activity of untrusting restlessness, sabbath resists such anxious activity.

Second, the decision to cease coveting relates to the first commandment. Giving up such a fearful ideological pursuit cannot be accomplished by an act of will. Rather, it may grow out of an affirmation that the powers of coveting and greedy consumption have been defeated. Such powers, then, need have no control over us. In Col 3:5 (NRSV), the first and tenth commandments are nicely joined: "Put to death, therefore, whatever in you is earthly . . . greed (which is idolatry)." Violating the tenth command derives from a violation of the first.

8. In interpreting any of the commandments, it is important to discern clearly the position they occupy in biblical faith. It is possible to conclude simply that these are the most foundational absolutes of God's purpose in the world. That is, the commandments occupy a peculiar and decisive claim, articulated in the categories of revelation. They disclose the non-negotiable will of God.

Alongside that claim, George Mendenhall's political understanding of the Decalogue may be useful. Mendenhall has proposed that these ten commands are "policy" statements.[126] They are not in themselves guidelines for specific action, but provide the ground and framework from which specifics may be drawn. Taking them as policies links the commands quite clearly to the concrete community Moses formed. This means that, rather than contextless absolutes, they are proposals that counter other kinds of policies. Such an understanding invites adherents to this covenant to recognize that they have made, and are making, peculiar and distinctive ethical decisions related to a core decision about covenantal existence.

There are important ecclesiological implications in such a recognition. In fact, in some older Christian liturgies, the commandments are recited at baptism. In baptism, the believer pledges allegiance to a vision of social reality that is rooted in God's wonders and deeply at odds with the dominant assumptions of an acquisitive, individualistic society. The community of faith in our time urgently needs to recover the programmatic intentionality of these commands.

9. In Matt 19:16-22, Mark 10:17-22, and Luke 18:18-30, Jesus alludes to the commandments, though he does not cite them all. Two matters strike us in reading those narratives. First, the reference to specific commandments is kept selective. Harrelson

---

125. M. Douglas Meeks, *God the Economist: The Doctrine of God and Political Economy* (Minneapolis: Fortress, 1989) 170-77 and *passim.*

126. Mendenhall, *Law and Covenant in Israel and the Ancient Near East,* 5-6. See his fuller explication of the decisive difference made by these "policies" in Mendenhall, "The Conflict Between Value Systems and Social Control," in *Unity and Diversity: Essays in the History, Literature, and Religion of the Ancient Near East,* eds. Hans Goedicke and J. J. M. Roberts (Baltimore: Johns Hopkins University Press, 1975) 169-80.

observes that Jesus uses only those commands that pertain to the rich—i.e., the one to whom he speaks.[127] Second, the commandments are, for Jesus, a first-level demand, preparatory to the more rigorous demand, "Go, sell, give, come follow." In these narratives, the commands are not considered unattainable modes of conduct; they are, rather, the threshold to more serious discipleship and a step on the demanding way to "eternal life"!

127. Harrelson, *The Ten Commandments and Human Rights*, 162-64.

EXODUS 20:18-21, MOSES AS MEDIATOR

COMMENTARY

This transitional section consists of a brief narrative about the response of the people to the theophanic coming of Yahweh (19:16-19). While these verses may assume the giving of the commands in 20:1-17, there is no mention of that. For this reason, critical scholarship has often judged this unit to be displaced from the end of chapter 19, before the Decalogue.[128] The fact that it comes *after* the Decalogue serves to enhance the Ten Commandments as words from God's own mouth. In 19:16-19, Israel witnesses thunder, lightning, trumpets, and a smoking mountain, and these items are now reiterated. The people's response is that they see, they tremble, and they keep their distance.

In their fear, the people move to secure protection from Yahweh in the person of Moses (v. 19); they ask Moses to be the go-between. Perhaps, this proposal fulfills God's resolve to Moses in 19:9. Now Israel will "trust" Moses (cf. 14:31). His response to Israel's request is indirect; Moses, in effect, assures Israel that God will not destroy them, but only wants to find out whether their faith is serious (cf. 14:13-14). (According to source analysis, this testing of Israel is parallel to the testing of Abraham in Gen 22:1-14.) While the narrative does not explicitly say that Moses has agreed to be a mediator, v. 21 confirms the fact. Moses is near, and Israel is distant. Israel will not again be exposed to the direct presence of God.

Two matters are important in this narrative unit. First, the office of the mediator is authorized. Hans-Joachim Kraus has made the case that this authorization is not only for the person of Moses, but for a continuing office of mediator, likely occupied subsequently by many persons.[129] The "presence," from now on, will be ordered, formal, and to some extent institutionalized. In the ongoing life of the biblical community, "presence" is characteristically channeled through a recognized instrument. While this led to christology in the Christian tradition, in the Jewish tradition that mediation is through the authority of torah or, in the Priestly tradition, through the priesthood.[130]

Second, an unspoken outcome of the sequence of theophany (19:16-25), commands (20:1-17), and mediation (20:18-21) is the fact that the Decalogue receives a stunningly distinctive place in the tradition. Before this proclamation, there was no formal command. After this, there was command only through mediation (as in 21:1–23:33). Consequently, 20:1-17 stands alone as the only direct, unmediated address of command from Yahweh to Israel. This is the only speech heard directly by Israel. The "ten words" thus are unique as "direct revelation." All the rest is exegesis. Commandments given subsequently by the mediator will be important, but cannot rival in authority this direct address, which constitutes the core of Yahweh's intent and charter for Israel's covenantal existence.

129. Hans-Joachim Kraus, *Die prophetische Verkündigung des Rechts in Israel*, Theologische Studien 51 (Zollikon: Evangelischer Verlag, 1957). See James Muilenburg, "The 'Office' of the Prophet in Ancient Israel," in *The Bible in Modern Scholarship*, ed. J. Philip Hyatt (Nashville: Abingdon, 1965) 74-97.

130. See James A. Sanders, "Torah and Christ," *Int* 29 (1975) 372-90.

128. See Childs, *The Book of Exodus*, 351-60.

REFLECTIONS

1. The narrative of theophany in 19:16-25 suggests that encounter with the Holy One of Israel is ominous and dreadful. The response to the theophany in 20:18-19 affirms the awesome reality of God, which is often trivialized in our "therapeutic" propensity.

2. The characteristic mode of meeting as mediated regularly precludes immediacy with God. This motif may give us pause, given the easy religiosity now evident in our society. Many folk imagine an easily available God who may be readily "experienced." Mediation, by contrast, suggests something like an audience gained with a person of majesty, before whom extra care must be taken.

3. The office of mediator, one who will willingly stand at risk between God and the community, provides a category for the Christian claim concerning Jesus. Jesus is, in a variety of theological modes, understood as the mediator who "opens a way" to the presence of God (see Heb 7:26; 10:20). The argument in Hebrews asserts both the cruciality of the mediator and the direct access Jesus provides to God. A proper theology, of course, handles this tension by the affirmation that this mediator is ultimate and decisive and has dispelled the need for any other mediator. As Moses gives Israel assurance in v. 20, so Jesus offers such assurance with a world-transforming, "Do not be afraid."

EXODUS 20:22–23:19, THE COVENANT CODE

COMMENTARY

This long corpus of laws is regarded as a very old collection, perhaps the oldest legal material in the OT. It probably existed first of all on its own, without reference to the context of the Sinai covenant. It is a miscellaneous collection, no doubt including materials from the general cultural deposit of the Near East, as well as materials that are distinctly Israelite.

It is not possible to identify a coherent structure, pattern, or order for the material. Paul Hanson has proposed that there are competing tendencies, reflecting respectively more exclusive and inclusive tendencies.[131] Hanson's suggestion has merit, as long as those tendencies are seen as simply thematic stresses. If, however, they are viewed as distinct and rival documents, then the argument is quite speculative. Ludger

Schwienhorst-Schönberger believes that a subtle and complicated pattern of organization is at work in the material.[132] While there is no doubt that there are sub-collections in the material that have been joined together with some intentionality, his specific hypothesis is highly speculative and unconvincing. In any case, this miscellaneous collection has now been placed in the center of the Sinai pericope and is made to serve as a series of stipulations specifying the conditions for the covenant between Israel and Yahweh.

In 24:7 the narrative refers to the "Book of the Covenant" as a document for the treaty to which Israel now agrees. On the basis of that reference, chaps. 21–23 have come to be referred to as the Covenant Code, or Book of Covenant.[133] It is not necessary that

131. Paul D. Hanson, "The Theological Significance of Contradiction Within the Book of the Covenant," in *Canon and Authority: Essays in Old Testament Religion and Theology,* eds. George W. Coats and Burke O. Long (Philadelphia: Fortress, 1977) 110-31.

132. Ludger Schwienhorst-Schönberger, *Das Bundesbuch (Ex. 20, 22-23, 33), Studien zu seiner Entstehung und Theologie,* BZAW 188 (Berlin: De Gruyter, 1990).

133. See Dale Patrick, *Old Testament Law* (Atlanta: John Knox, 1985) 63-96.

the reference in 24:7 is to these materials. It is enough that this material be brought into an intentional relation to the covenant. Set in that context, this already extant material now becomes a way whereby Israel thinks and speaks about Yahweh's sovereign intention for its life. The focus on sovereign intention shows that for every part of its life (cultic, ethical, public, personal, economic, and sexual) Yahweh is known to be the governor who intends obedient conduct. This material is, in fact, a series of probes, explorations, and attempts in the community to discern the mind and will of Yahweh. But then, that is often the nature of biblical "law." It is not "relativistic" but manifestly open to revision as Israel more fully discerns the will of Yahweh.

20:22-26. This extended body of laws begins with guidelines for worship. The unit is introduced by a formula that echoes 19:4. In that verse, what is seen is the triumph of the exodus; here what is "seen" is the speech of God at Mt. Sinai.

There are five commands, of which only the third is a positive assertion. The first two commands are arranged chiastically, assuming and reiterating the two commandments of vv. 3-6. In Hebrew the order of the sentences is:

You shall not make alongside me
gods of silver
and gods of gold
you shall not make for yourselves.

The command prohibits other gods as in v. 3, and it prohibits visible forms of a god, as in vv. 4-6.

Then follow three laws concerning a proper altar. While these commands seem less weighty than the preceding two, they are, in fact, of a piece with them. The *character* of God (v. 23) and the *worship* of God (vv. 24-26) are intimately connected. How God is worshiped depends on who God is.

First, an altar of earth (אדמה *ʾădāmâ*) is authorized (v. 24). Apparently this altar is simply a mound of dirt, sufficient to support the activity of animal slaughter and sacrifice. The provision intends that the place of sacrifice should be modest and simple. The last part of the verse has greatly figured in the

classical (Wellhausenian) construction of the history of Israel's religion. The "remembrance of the name" of God is a device (used by the Deuteronomists) to guard against claims of a crass, material presence of God in the shrine. The formula "in every place" has suggested to scholars that altars might be erected and legitimated in many places. This has been taken by scholars to reflect an early form of worship, not yet centralized or carefully administered as in Deut 12:1-7. The picture of worship thus suggested is a widespread, more or less free and spontaneous practice, not yet cramped by hierarchy or complicated procedure.

Second (perhaps as an addendum), it is authorized that the altar may be made of stone, rather than of earth (v. 25). This may reflect subsequent development to a more sophisticated and stylized form of worship. The purpose of the command, however, is not to authorize a stone altar but to preclude the use of hewn stones. Thus a concession to stone is made, but the statement resists excessive craftsmanship or aesthetic concern. We are not told why crafted stone work would profane the altar. The sentence seems to identify simplicity and holiness.

Third, the prohibition warns against having an elevated altar whereby the "nakedness" of the priest would be revealed (v. 26). Concern about nakedness reflects a rigorous concern of the priestly tradition for propriety and discipline. Reference to "profane" in v. 25, along with this reference, suggests an intense priestly agenda and, perhaps, a recognition that worship, especially if undertaken with aesthetic finesse, lives close to the energy and danger of sexuality. We will see this connection brought to full expression in Exodus 32.

21:1-11. The introduction to the main body of material identifies what follows as "ordinances" (משפטים *mišpāṭîm*) (v. 1). The term suggests secular rulings concerned with mundane issues of daily life. Because the text admits of no obvious or compelling coherence, it seems necessary to take up the several ordinances *seriatim*, which in the end leaves us with a lot of fragments, but no systematic interpretive picture.

The corpus begins with two laws concerning debt slaves. It is telling indeed that these laws are placed first. Assuming that this text is old, the community of this text can poignantly remember the exodus and the abuse of debt slaves (cf. Gen 47:13-21). Thus the just treatment of slaves is definitional for the larger practice of justice in ancient Israel. Because of unpaid debts, some eventually become owned by others. The burden of these laws is to affirm that, even in such a sorry situation of debt, these slaves nonetheless have certain rights that must be respected.

The first law concerns a male slave (vv. 2-6) and is structured around a basic principle (v. 2), followed by three contingencies (vv. 3-6). The basic principle, echoed in Deut 15:1, is that a debt slave can be held in servitude for only six years. No matter how great the debt, or how slow the pay-back, or how large the residue of debt at the end of six years, neither servitude nor debt can be sustained more than six years. In this principle, the Mosaic covenant has established the priority of persons over money and has set limits on the ways in which economic reversal can impinge on human well-being.

This principle is clarified (or qualified) in three ways. First, the marital status of the slave is respected (v. 3). Second, a family acquired in bondage is not emancipated with the slave (v. 4). Presumably, the wife given by the slave owner is reckoned still to belong to the owner and not to the slave-husband. Third, the slave may at the end of six years prefer bonded status and forego freedom (v. 6; apparently deriving from v. 4). That is, a slave who acquires a wife in bondage may retain her (and children) in bondage, or he may have freedom without her.

This law reflects the difficult tension between the requirements of the economy and the truth of human dignity. In principle, Israel is willing to curb the demands of the economy (v. 1), but in concrete practice, it does not do so in an unambiguous manner.

The second law concerns a female slave (vv. 7-11), and this time a principle is enunciated (v. 7), followed by four qualifying comments. The principle is that a female slave is to be treated differently and is not subject to the preceding rule on slaves. The case concerns an indebted man who offers his daughter for the debt, presumably in place of himself. It is clear in the qualifying comments

that the female slave is regarded as no person in her own right, as her fate is linked in each case to a man.

In the first instance, she is assigned to the slave owner—to the one who holds the debt (v. 8). But there are limits to his power over her. If the intended marriage is not to his choosing, he may reject her; but he then loses control over her. In the second case, the owner who holds the debt may "assign" her to his son, and the same provision applies (v. 9). In the third case, if the master rejects her and takes a second wife, her rights will be guaranteed (v. 10). In the fourth case, if she is not protected adequately, she shall be freed, without having to buy back her freedom (v. 11).

The careful, if not tortured, reasoning of these laws indicates that Israel cautiously and uncertainly explored a troubled area of public life. Clearly the law wants to set limits to the practice of debt bondage. But it is equally clear that it goes about the problem in a cowardly way, submitting the claims of human dignity to the realities of the economy. The position taken is "reformist," desiring to make debt slavery more palatable and humane, but reluctant to criticize or assault the practice directly and in principle. Patrick is no doubt correct in his conclusion: "The very act of enunciating slave rights laid the foundation for a more radical critique of the institution in later law."[134] The outcome is that a female slave's options are quite narrow. Moreover, in a patriarchal society a daughter-slave is largely at the behest of powerful men. Guarantees are offered her, but they are of a quite circumscribed range.

21:12-17. The next unit consists in four laws that lead to a death penalty, each introduced by an impersonal participle. These laws, unlike the case laws of vv. 1-11, articulate general principles of public policy.

Of the four laws, only the first receives comment and qualification (vv. 12-14). The first law simply provides retaliation for murder: "a life for a life" (v. 12). As in all such provisions concerning capital punishment, however, issues promptly arise that require interpretation and evoke ambiguity. The double "if" of vv. 13-14 inquires about motive: Was the killing intentional, premeditated,

134. See Patrick, *Old Testament Law*, 72.

willful, and treacherous? If the killing is accidental, an "act of God," the perpetrator can flee to a city of refuge (see Deut 4:41-43; 19:1-10). If the killing is intentional, the perpetrator will receive no protection, not even at God's altar, but shall be executed. Thus the text recognizes options in the law. It does not comment on the enormous difficulties in adjudicating the subtle issue of motive.

The second provision appears to be only a special case of the first (v. 15). The third provision uses the verb for "steal" (גנב *gānab*, v. 16). The earlier commentary on 20:15 suggests that the commandment may relate to "stealing a person." The law is concerned with the prospect that it was profitable to kidnap persons and sell them into slavery. Clearly, such an act of depriving one of full life is nearly as serious as killing.

The fourth provision (v. 17) parallels that of v. 15. This time, however, the destructive action is not forceful violence but only destructive speech. In our comment on 20:12, we have contrasted "honor" (כבד *kābēd*) with "trivialize" (קלל *qll*). This is a severe provision for upholding that commandment.

These harsh laws of capital punishment are offered in defense of human life, to preclude actions that would destabilize community. They seek to make killing, kidnapping, or cursing too costly. Whether the emphasis is on punishment or deterrence, Israel takes the maintenance of human life and human dignity seriously.

21:18-27. Four laws concern violent assault by one member of the community upon another.

The first concerns a physical altercation between two men, one of whom injures the other (vv. 18-19). This law is the counterpart of 21:12, where the attacked person dies and a life is required in return. In this law, the attacked person is hurt but recovers. The accent of the law is that the attacker shall be free of liability (נקה *niqqâ*). Restitution is required for only lost time and full recovery (רפא ירפא *rapō' yĕrapē'* is an absolute infinitive). The term for "loss of time" is שבת (*šebet*), i.e., his enforced sabbath rest. The theme of restitution is not, however, the major accent of the law. Rather, it aims to minimize the quarrel. The settlement is to be complete, but not beyond actual damage. No litigious society here!

The second case concerns brutality against one's own slave, male or female (vv. 20-21). While the law indicates there was enough of such brutality to require a ruling, it also indicates that the community pondered the human worth of a slave. This emancipated community is not so far from its liberation that it forgets the emergency created by brutality to slaves. The law makes a distinction between death occurring immediately to a beaten slave, literally "under his hand," and death that occurs sometime later. Noth suggests that the distinction may be between intentional and accidental death, but it may well reflect the severity of a beating.[135] In the case of an immediate death, the slave who dies will "surely be avenged" (infinitive absolute) against the master who killed. The measure of punishment or who inflicts it is not indicated. But the verb for "avenge" is strong, perhaps suggesting a *quid pro quo*—the death of the master for the death of the slave. Although the measure of punishment is unspecified in the Hebrew text, the Samaritan text has "shall surely die" (מות יומת *môt yûmāt*), the same harsh formula we have seen in vv. 12-17. If the Samaritan variant is an interpretation of the MT, then v. 20 suggests that a murdered slave is treated like any other murdered person. This is a remarkable law in a cultural context where slaves characteristically have no such protection, but it is exactly what one might expect from this community of erstwhile slaves.

What v. 20 gives by way of dignity to slaves, v. 21 seems immediately to contradict. In an alternative case where the slave does not immediately die, the brutalizing owner is not punished, and the dead slave is not vindicated. (Again the Samaritan tradition has *yûmāt* for "avenge," נקם *nāqam*.) The rather anemic justification for this ruling is "for he is his property." The term rendered "property" is כסף (*kesep*, "silver"). The slave is the owner's money, and he can do what he wants with it. This latter ruling reflects hardnosed economic thinking without regard to the humanity of the slave. One can either be amazed at the venturesome ruling of v. 20 or dismayed at the conventional relapse of v. 21.

135. Noth, *Exodus*, 181.

The community obviously ponders the value of a "person" who is not fully a person.

The third law in this group concerns bodily harm to a pregnant woman resulting from a quarrel (vv. 22-25). The premise of the case is that a miscarriage is caused. It is important that this constitutes in Mosaic Israel a special case worthy of a ruling.

As in the previous case, distinctions are drawn. On the one hand, a ruling follows if there is "no further harm" (v. 22 NRSV; "no serious injury," NIV). The phrasing seems a bit crass, as though enough harm has not already been done in the miscarriage. The other uses of the term for "harm" (אסון 'āsôn) (see Gen 42:4, 38; 44:29, concerning risk to the beloved Benjamin) indicate that harm is bodily injury resulting in death, here death to the injured mother. Thus the first ruling applies to the mother. If she is not bodily injured, a fine must be paid, as much as the husband requires. The imposition of a fine is an attempt at reparations as an alternative to retaliation. The loss of the pregnancy in and of itself is not judged serious enough to evoke retaliation. The fine constitutes punishment and an attempt at solace, a feeble attempt indeed.

On the other hand, "if harm follows"—if the mother does sustain injury—severe and exact retaliation is required. This is the most complete and extreme statement of retaliation in the Bible, suggesting that punishment for the one who hurts the mother must be exact and point for point. The case permits no misunderstanding as it lists eight illustrative equivalences: life, eye, tooth, hand, foot, burn, wound, and stripe. Childs (following Finkelstein) regards this extensive program of retaliation as a device to ensure equality of treatment for members of the community with unfavorable social standing. The eye, hand, and tooth of any member are protected and valued.[136] In this ruling, one can see the community adjudicating satisfaction to offended parties with the maintenance of a functioning public order. The community moves between honoring wounds and keeping a lid on vengeance.

The fourth law in this group concerns damage done to a slave (vv. 26-27). This law

relates to that of vv. 20-21. It is placed here, perhaps, because it addresses the loss of an eye or a tooth and so picks up the language and theme of v. 24. Again the law reflects a context in which the beating of a slave is not uncommon and is a cause for concern in the community.

This ruling concerns permanent damage, the loss of an eye or a tooth. In the ruling of vv. 23-24 there is exact retribution. In this law the loss of an eye or a tooth leads to the slave's emancipation. If the slave is a debt slave (cf. 21:2), this entails the cancellation of the debt. It may be argued that this is less than exact retribution, for no eye or tooth is required of the brutalizing master. In the context of the exodus, however, the assurance of liberation is greater in value than is retaliation. The cost of an eye or a tooth to the master might deter brutality, but emancipation changes fundamental social relations.

In all of these laws, the community sorts out the tricky and unclear relation between economic value and the elemental, non-negotiable claims of humanness. The economic dimension is evident in payment (vv. 19, 22) and in the power of the slave owner (vv. 21, 26-27). The claims of humaneness are evident in the implied protection of slaves, pregnant women, and injured parties, all of whom are persons at risk. The adjudication of economic and human claims is not clear or unambiguous. It is evident, nonetheless, that the tension between the two is well recognized in Israel and is not easily disposed of.

21:28–22:4. Four laws are voiced concerning either the behavior or the value of livestock. In an agricultural economy, concern for possession, management, control, and disposal of animals is clearly important for the well-being of the community. In the context of covenant, every aspect of daily life pertains to the covenantal rule of Yahweh.

The first law concerns death caused by an ox that gores (vv. 28-32). A farm animal left unattended can do acute damage, and the law reflects upon the resolution of such a problem under several circumstances. Because an agricultural economy is not likely to be litigious, the working principle seems to be to handle damages as simply and directly as possible, so that the disruption of social relations is as minimal as possible.

---

136. Childs, *The Book of Exodus*, 472. See also Pixley, *On Exodus*, 173-74.

The primary ruling concerning an ox that gores is stated in v. 28: An ox that kills must be promptly destroyed. (The verb *stone* is an infinitive absolute.) The important point is that the owner is not held liable. Everyone familiar with animals knows that such damage can happen under the best management.

Four qualifying remarks follow that adjust the primary ruling. First, it is clear that the ruling of v. 28 applies only to first offenders (v. 29). If the animal is a "repeat offender" (which implies that the initial ruling was not implemented), the owner is indeed held accountable. In that event not only is the animal killed, as in v. 28, but the owner is also at fault and may be executed. The community will not endure the continued maintenance of a dangerous animal. Second, in this latter case, the owner may pay a fine instead of execution (v. 30). The terms for "ransom" (כפר *kōper*) and "redemption" (פדין *pidyōn*) here are used in their proper economic sense. Third, the death of a child is as serious, therefore as costly, as the death of an adult (v. 31). Fourth, the death of a slave also requires reparation (v. 32), but here the cost of retribution is limited (30 shekels), while it is left open-ended in the other cases. Further, the reparation is paid to the slave's owner rather than to the slave's family. Economic reality continues to intrude upon human settlements.

While the law does indeed concern the behavior of an ox, and so introduces this series of laws on animals, the subject matter of the law also links it to the preceding section, which concerns assault and death. Thus we are able to detect a certain logic to the present arrangement of the text.

The second law concerns the loss of an animal through human negligence (vv. 33-34). Domestic animals are enormously valuable, and their loss is ominous, particularly to those who own small plots of land. The principle practiced here is restitution, expressed in the verb שלם (*šālam*). Like the noun *shalom*, this verb concerns action that restores balance, harmony, and well-being. Its content is to pay back, correct a wrong, and recover equity. One must pay for one's negligence. The ruling adds that the negligent party, with the payment of restitution, may keep the dead animal. The dead animal, of course, is of small worth compared with a

live animal, but its meat is valuable enough to matter in the process of adjudication. This latter concern suggests that the laws reflect a small agrarian economy.

The third law (vv. 35-36) parallels the first (vv. 28-32). Here, however, the injured party is not a human being but another ox, which is property of another owner. If the offending ox is a first-time offender, then the two owners will share the cost; no fault is assigned. If the offending ox is a repeat offender, then its owner is liable and must restore the damaged ox of the other owner. Again, the one who pays may retain the dead animal.

The fourth law concerns the theft of an ox or a sheep (22:1-4). (The NRSV has rearranged the text of these verses. That rearrangement is helpful, though it rests on no textual basis.) It is impossible to maintain watch over the animals, which are exceedingly valuable. Consequently, the owner's well-being is at risk, and sanctions are severe.

Four principles are enunciated to govern such a case: (1) Extensive restitution is exacted of the thief who has disposed of a stolen animal, by either selling or butchering, so that the animal is not recoverable (v. 1). The price of restitution is fivefold for an ox and fourfold for a sheep, indicating their relative worth to the farmer. (2) If the thief still possesses the stolen animal, then restitution is double. (The extent of penalty indicates a harsh treatment of an adversary, whereas the loss of an ox in 21:33-34, 35-36 is accidental and occurs between friendly neighbors.) (3) If the thief is unable to make restitution, he may be sold into debt slavery. As the text is arranged, this severe penalty applies only to the fivefold or fourfold payment, and not the twofold payment. We may, however, surmise that it applies there as well. (4) Exodus 22:2-3 reflects a social situation in which a farmer is prepared to defend his own property. The farmer is serious, and a potential thief must beware. Again, the ruling makes an important distinction. If the thief comes in the dark of the night, he may be killed, and the farmer is not held accountable. During the daylight, however, the farmer is not free to kill the thief. If the thief is killed in the daylight, it may be assumed that the farmer could have taken less severe measures, and so is guilty of murder. The daytime provision thus provides protection for a thief, even when caught in the act.

This series of laws, two on a dangerous animal (vv. 28-32,v. 35-36) and two on the loss of a valuable animal (vv. 33-34; 22:1-4), reflects a patient struggle with most mundane matters. In precisely such mundane matters, however, the health and well-being of a community is gained or lost.

22:5-17. The dominant theme of the next section, restitution (*šālam*), makes clear that the aim of the laws is to guard against excessive or unfair loss of property, which would disrupt the stability of the community. Such an agenda may suggest a cautious defense of private property, but it also affirms the cruciality of the community and its right ordering, over against personal and private interests. There is here no unbridled individualism in which individual operators may view the community as an arena for ambitious exploitation. Rather, the individual prospers only by maintaining a stable, communal equilibrium.

The first law concerns the violation of someone else's field or vineyard (v. 5). The term rendered "graze" (בער *bi'ēr*) by both the NRSV and the NIV is not used elsewhere for "graze," but regularly means "burn," as in v. 6. In any case, a neighbor's field or vineyard must not be violated. Notice that the law is not concerned with animals that accidentally intrude but with the intentional intrusion of one farmer upon the field of another. There is no severe penalty, but only the return of equilibrium.

The second law concerns the burning of a neighbor's field (v. 6). Here the same verb (*bā'ar*) is used, this time in its normal meaning. A farmer's fire on his own land can get out of hand and spread to the field of another. Again, restitution is required, this time expressed with an infinitive absolute. This suggests a peculiarly serious matter, perhaps because fire can cause much more serious and immediate damage than can grazing.

The third law concerns the loss of goods entrusted to the care of a neighbor (vv. 7-8). In v. 7 the law assumes that the neighbor is not at fault, but that a thief is responsible for the loss. Whereas vv. 5 and 6 require restitution only of equivalence, with a thief the restitution is double (cf. v. 1). Verse 8 adds a proviso: If the thief is not caught, it is possible

there was no thief. In that case, the neighbor who has had the goods in his care is brought to trial to adjudicate his guilt or innocence. The case is brought "before God," i.e., before the tribunal, which enacts and administers covenantal law. In 18:19-22, Moses established a system of courts, presided over by those who "hate dishonest gain." If the neighbor is convicted as the thief, then he must, of course, pay double. If he is acquitted, there is no suggestion that he is liable for the loss.

The fourth case concerns a property dispute (v. 9). In an agrarian community, disputes may arise over such items, particularly in the probation of estates (cf. Luke 12:13). The disputants are not left on their own, but are commended to the court. The court can "condemn" (רשע *rāša'*, i.e., declare guilty) or "acquit" (צדק *ṣādaq*, i.e., declare innocent). (On such language, see Isa 50:7-8 and Rom 8:31-34.) The court's verdict is absolute. The one whose claim is denied must pay reparation to the other party, perhaps to compensate for inconvenience and embarrassment. Again, the cost of a false claim is double payment (cf. vv. 1, 7).

The fifth case, like the third (vv. 7-8), concerns one neighbor having custody of another's goods (vv. 10-13). If there are witnesses to the loss, then the case can be resolved. The difficult cases occur, however, when there are no witnesses. In such a circumstance, the court must decide on the basis of what is not obvious or publicly available.

The case will be decided on the basis of an oath made by the keeper of the goods. This is a specific case of the ninth commandment, concerning false witnesses. In a society that regards taking an oath a high-risk venture, an oath is enough and functions like a lie-detector test. If one asserts innocence in the matter, there is no restitution.

The ruling then adds two other conditional clauses. First, "if it was in fact stolen . . . " (with an infinitive absolute), and if the custodian cannot swear innocence, then he must make restitution. Even in the case of such theft by a neighbor, however, no more than restitution is required. Finally, the ruling notes one other possibility (v. 13): If the goods have been "mangled" (טרף *ṭārap*), i.e., torn by a wild animal, again there is no restitution. The law is willing to allow the caprice of an animal beyond the control of the custodian. Thus the ruling entertains a variety of ways in which goods may be lost—stolen, mangled, killed, injured, or carried off. Only in the case of theft is restitution required.

The sixth case again concerns property damage (vv. 14-15). Presumably the law concerns a work animal that is injured or killed while borrowed. The owner may be "borrowed" along with the animal. If the owner is not present with the animal, then the borrower is responsible for its loss and must repay. If, however, the owner accompanies the animal, then he is responsible and the borrower is without liability. The last line of v. 15 is not very clear, but it seems to make a distinction between borrowing and hiring. An arrangement of paid hire apparently limits liability for the hirer.

The seventh case, concerning a "bride price" (מהר *mōhar*), is very different from the six preceding cases (vv. 16-17). I group it with the others because it does have as its subject the matter of reparations, though the familiar term *šālam* is not used. The case concerns the seduction and violation (rape) of a virgin. The act of violation is not in doubt. Something must be done to the violator, even though in this patriarchal scenario the violation is not against the woman but against her father. In any case, the violator must pay a "bride price" to the father, an unspecified amount of money for the use/abuse of the young woman. For that price, he may receive her as his wife.

But it is the father who has all the options. He may, in response to the payment, make his daughter the man's wife. Or he may refuse the marriage, perhaps finding the man unsuitable, but he still receives the same amount of money. Because the daughter is not engaged, the violation is not a capital crime—i.e., not a serious threat to the community. For that reason, the penalty would seem to protect the family's honor. The law pays no attention to the violated woman herself, and, in that regard, the settlement with the father is not unlike the other cases of retribution for "the owner."

In all seven cases in this group, "property" that belongs to someone is in some way damaged by another: (a) a field is damaged (by grazing?), (b) a field is burned, (c) goods are lost, (d) an animal is wrongly claimed, (e) an animal is lost, (f) an animal is damaged, (g) a young woman is violated.

In each case, restitution must be paid unless exceptional circumstances vindicate the allegedly guilty party. In the last case, the payment is of a "bride price" rather than restitution, but the principle is the same. The practice of restitution, evident in all of these cases, intends to provide guidelines and checks on the abuse of one neighbor by another. The intent is to maintain a community in which all may live in harmony.

22:18-31. Chapter 22 concludes with a series of miscellaneous laws. I am unable to detect any pattern to these commands, for they vary in both form and subject matter. Grouping them together is largely a matter of convenience.

Israel is forbidden to host a female sorcerer (v. 18). It is not specifically clear what a sorcerer does, but it is enough to recognize that sorcery is an attempt to manage and manipulate power that truly belongs only to God. Sorcery is regularly treated as a technique used by foreign peoples who compete with, jeopardize, and seduce Israel away from its proper trust in Yahweh (cf. Deut 18:9-13). Note that in 7:11, sorcerers joined the Egyptian opposition to Moses and Aaron.

Sexual relations with an animal embody a distortion of God's proper ordering of life (v. 19). The commandment concerns a severely distorted and distorting cultural practice (cf. Lev 18:23; 20:15). If the seventh commandment is broadly construed to concern all distorted sexual relations, then this becomes an extreme case in point. Such practices mock the intention of the creator for a rightly ordered, life-giving creation.

The prohibition of sacrifice to the gods is a strong reiteration of the first commandment (v. 20). The punishment of being "devoted to destruction" utilizes the notion of חרם (*ḥērem*), wherein anything that detracts from Yahweh is to be consumed in fire. There is no doubt that the practice of *ḥērem* is a matter of extreme ideological rigor that refuses any compromise at all (cf. Deut 20:16-18; 1 Sam 15:10-33).

Israel's protective affirmation of the socially marginal is rooted in its exodus memory and imagination (vv. 21-24). The paragraph consists in two negative commands (vv. 21-22), followed by interpretive commentary. The first command protects resident aliens—i.e., permanent residents in the community who have no rights of citizenship and, therefore, are vulnerable to all kinds of social pressure. The second command protects widows and orphans, those in the community who have lost their male advocate and protector and so are exposed to endless social threat. The two commands together show that early Israelite law was especially aware of the socially marginated and vulnerable, making it a principle of law that they must be fully guaranteed.

The two commands are supported by two motivational comments. The first, concerning the sojourners, appeals to the exodus tradition. As Israel was protected in its time of marginality, so it is to be the protector of the marginal (cf. Deut 10:19). Cynthia Ozick has observed the way in which the exodus memory has become a powerful metaphor for ethics in ongoing Jewish life.[137]

The second command is supported by a more extended and ominous comment (vv. 23-24). In a less direct way, this command also alludes to the exodus, for it knows that oppressed widows and orphans will cry out as Israel in slavery cried out. Verse 23 is of special interest because it is so emphatic, featuring three absolute infinitives in succession: "If you *truly oppress* . . . if they *truly cry out* . . . I will *truly hear.*" This sequence makes the most decisive appeal Israel can muster for obedience to covenantal ethics. The theological pivot of the exodus narrative is the conviction that God hears and is moved by such cries (cf. 2:23-25; 3:7-8). As the cry of Israel against Egypt mobilized Yahweh against the oppressive Egyptians, so now the cry of widows and orphans will mobilize Yahweh against oppressive Israel. This theological reality posits a God passionately against oppression, no matter where it is found, even in Israel.

The upshot of such a mobilization of God is that when widows and orphans cry out in pain and need, God will destroy husbands and fathers, leaving Israel as helpless as the present vulnerable ones. Thus the punishment fits the crime.[138] The truth is that oppressive

societies have more than their share of violence. And when such violence eventually and inevitably leads to military action, fathers and husbands are killed, producing widows and orphans. This law understands, for all its theological language, exactly the dynamic of social oppression and its outcome. Abuse of the vulnerable has enormous social costs for the abusers that cannot be avoided or denied.

The next group of commands, linked to the preceding by reference to the "poor" (עני ʿānî; cf. vv. 22-23 on the abuse of ענה ʿānâ), consists in three commands set up as a protasis-apodosis (condition-consequence), plus a twofold motivational clause (vv. 25-27): "you shall not deal with them as a creditor; you shall not exact interest from them" (v. 25); "you shall restore it before the sun goes down" (v. 26).

These brief commands are enormously radical. They insist that the workings of the economy must be submitted to the principle of community solidarity. Israelites, in their economic dealings, are not to be conventional bankers and business people. They are to act differently for the sake of the community. Pixley comments: "We are told that basic human rights arise from basic human needs. Misery is not to be trafficked in. The right to life takes precedence over the right to poverty."[139] Specifically, the poor are to have money grants without interest, i.e., without creating economic leverage that will make the poor endlessly indebted and dependent. The law does not argue about the economic viability of such a practice. It simply requires the need for care in concrete ways, and it expects the community to work out the practical details.

The third command cites a quite primitive practice as a case in point. A poor man who has no property may put up his only coat as collateral for the loan. While such collateral may be taken, it may be kept only during the day. It must be returned to the debtor every night. The provision invites a ludicrous scene of the creditor each night going to the house of the poor man to drop off the coat, and returning each morning to pick it up. Since collateral that is held only part-time is no real collateral at all, the practical outcome of such

137. Ozick, *Metaphor and Memory: Essays*, 265-83.
138. On this general principle in biblical ethics, see Patrick D. Miller, Jr., *Sin and Judgment in the Prophets: A Stylistic and Theological Analysis* (Chico, Calif.: Scholars Press, 1982).

139. Pixley, *On Exodus*, 179.

a proposal is to operate without collateral from the poor.

The motivational clause of v. 27 appeals first to a very practical matter. The poor man must not be taken advantage of, for he will be cold in the night. If the retention of his coat is difficult, much more problematic is the charging of interest that deprives the poor of even more than a coat. This pastoral motivation is further supported by a theological affirmation, echoing vv. 23-24. The God who gives these commands does indeed hear on behalf of the weak and against the abusive strong. God is compassionate (חנן ḥānan), willing to act gratuitously (cf. 34:6). God's compassion, however, is only the positive side of God's vengeance.[140] Indeed, Israel has known this about Yahweh since its own origin in the pain of slavery. Now this law daringly applies the lessons of the exodus to ongoing public policy and practice.

Speech is dangerous and power-laden, and must be undertaken prudently (v. 28). In close parallelism, this law prohibits speech that trivializes (קלל qll; cf. 21:17) God or that curses a leader. Both verbs, revile (NIV, "blaspheme") and curse mean to pronounce words capable of diminishing, delegitimating, or damaging their object. No person of power or influence can survive speeches that are derogatory, for they will eventually erode claims of authority. The provision concerning God is related to the first commandment. Clearly one is not permitted to delegitimate the God who has liberated Israel and defeated all the other gods. It is worth noting that the urging of Job's wife (Job 2:9) cannot risk, according to the narrator, the statement "curse God," but must use a euphemism, "bless God." One dare not risk a word of terrible power against the God who commands all power.

The second line of this law shows the clever way in which human, political power is "wrapped in a flag," so that the human leader is placed parallel and in close proximity to God (cf. 1 Kgs 21:10). Thus the two are protected in the same instant by the same prohibition. The term for "leader" (נשיא nāśî) is generic, but likely reflects a pre-monarchical, and thus informal, office.

The command in v. 29a is vague and problematic. The NRSV and the NIV have provided an imaginative, and perhaps correct, extrapolation. The Hebrew text includes only four words: "Your fullness and your flow you shall not delay." The notion that this is an offering to Yahweh may be appropriated from vv. 29b-30, but it is not in the text itself. If the command does concern the firstfruits of crops, then its purpose is to acknowledge that the land belongs to Yahweh.

The law of the firstborn consists in two quite distinct parts (vv. 29b-30). The first line is an apodictic statement (v. 29b). It explains nothing and requires nothing—except the firstborn. It may be that the assertion has a conscious connection to the liberation narrative, where Israel is Yahweh's firstborn son (4:22). In reparation for Israel, Yahweh violently claims the firstborn of Egypt (11:5, 12:29). When the claim of the firstborn is reduced to a cultic regulation, provision is made for the "redemption" of the firstborn son (13:11-16). Thus while the formula of 22:29b makes an important point about God's utter sovereignty and Israel's complete subordination, it is not likely that the statement intends a direct sacrifice of the firstborn. Indeed, v. 29b seems to be a premise for the claim of v. 30. That is, the claim of the firstborn applies concretely to oxen and sheep, not humans. Even so, the requirement is an expensive one, especially in a modest agrarian economy that worries about reparations for one damaged ox.

The final provision in this unit concerns a specific dietary restriction (v. 31). Domestic animals that have been attacked and torn in the field by wild animals are not to be eaten. This quite specific prohibition derives from the very large premise that Israel is a people holy to Yahweh. The text tells us nothing about the relation between the large premise and the specific restriction. (See the same linkage in Deut 14:1-21.) The reason may be hygienic, or it may be that eating such meat is simply beneath the dignity of this people.

23:1-9. Chapter 23 begins with a series of apodictic laws intended to safeguard the well-being of the community through the practice of justice.

A series of five apodictic assertions, four introduced by the negative לא (lō) and one

140. See George Mendenhall, "The 'Vengeance' of Yahweh," *The Tenth Generation: The Origins of the Biblical Tradition* (Baltimore: Johns Hopkins University Press, 1973) 69-104.

by the negative אל (*'al*), provide guidelines for behavior in court that will enhance or diminish equity. While these five assertions are all concerned with false witness, the more general concern is the perversion of justice. These regulations are first aware that false witness can be socially destructive (v. 1) and that following majority opinion can greatly miscarry justice (v. 2).

Two textual questions are of special interest here. In v. 2 the term *justice* is absent in the Hebrew, though is supplied in the Greek. In v. 3, the phrase "partial to the poor" (דל *dāl*) is clear enough in the text, but the reading is odd, because the context does not worry about favoritism to the poor and because such a warning seems superfluous. On the basis of the parallel in Lev 19:15, many scholars read גדל (*gādōl*) for *dāl*, thus, "you shall not be partial to the powerful." If the Hebrew reading is retained, then the text suggests that in its own context even the poor are subject to the demands of justice.

In any case, these laws express Israel's awareness that the life of the entire community is at risk in the practice of injustice. Injustice, which may indeed be the will of the majority, is an enormous seduction, which the covenanted community must intentionally resist.

Two laws are given that reflect an intimate, face-to-face agrarian community (vv. 4-5). In such communities, as in any community, there are "enemies" (v. 4) and those whom one hates (v. 5). One is not inclined to help or enhance the life of one's adversaries. Nonetheless, in an agrarian economy the loss of one's working animals is a most serious matter. Thus even an enemy's stray animal must be returned, and if it has fallen from too heavy a load, then it is to be assisted. These two commands indicate that for the sake of the neighbor, i.e., for the health of the community, one has obligations that override one's emotional propensity. Calvin suggests that believers "should testify their forgiveness of their enemies by being merciful to their animals."[141] The basis of this command is not some romantic "do-gooder" sense, but the practical awareness that the community.

depends on neighborly acts that enhance the life of all

The section concludes with four apodictic requirements and one positive imperative, paralleling the concerns of vv. 1-3 (vv. 6-9). The five rules are: (1) Do not pervert justice due the poor. (2) Keep far from a false charge. (3) Do not kill the innocent or the righteous. (4) Do not take a bribe. (5) Do not oppress a resident alien.

The first, second, and fourth of these pertain directly to courtroom conduct. It is plausible that "murder" in the third law and "oppress" in the fifth are also concerned with court cases. That is, "murder" might include capital execution of the innocent, or less dramatic laws that deny power and access to some.

These five statements intend to maintain the courts as an arena for the true practice of justice, in which manipulation of the law for advantage and private interest is curbed by a genuine commitment to the rights of all the aggrieved. The programmatic phrase "pervert justice" is likely paralleled in v. 2, though the text seems incomplete. (It is also a central concern of the prophet Amos; Leviticus 5:7-15; 8:4-6.) Justice is the commitment of the covenant community to maintaining the viability and integrity of all its members, in this case especially the poor, resident aliens, and those in the right. The text knows that bribery is a powerful tool for distorting the vision of justice (cf. 18:21), tending to serve the powerful, who are most able to provide a bribe.

The last three regulations are supported by powerful motivational clauses. In v. 7, those who damage the innocent are in jeopardy for their guilt; in v. 8 bribery subverts; and in v. 9 the exodus memory is given as impetus for obedience.

The entire section of vv. 1-9 portrays a passionate commitment to the maintenance of a community in which all members are safe and respected, in which due process is guaranteed, and in which selfish interest is curbed for the sake of the weaker, more vulnerable members of society. This section powerfully reflects, in legal form, the ongoing passion of the community of liberation.

---

141. Calvin, *Commentaries on the Four Last Books of Moses Arranged in the Form of a Harmony*, 57.

23:10-19. The Book of Covenant concludes with a series of provisions that are rooted in cultic regulations and practices.

Although not properly cultic, vv. 10-11 are included in this section because of their sabbatical connection to v. 12. While vv. 10-11 do concern regularity of time, they might equally well have been included in the preceding group of laws concerning civil justice. The pattern of seven years may indeed derive from old cultic procedure, but here the law simply concerns crop rotation and the practice of letting the land lie fallow every seventh year. The motivation for such rotation is noteworthy. It is not said that such "rest" is good for the land—which it is. Rather, the fallow land, which will continue to produce some useful volunteer growth, is for the benefit of those who have no property of their own. Thus fields, vineyards, and orchards are, in the "off year," fair territory for the poor and for wild animals. The law resists any practice of "enclosure" that draws too tightly the bounds of private property.[142] Even private property must be managed to keep it sometimes open to the needs and requirements of the community.

The keeping of the seventh day (v. 12) is another form of the sabbath command of 20:8-11. The rhythm of agrarian life requires such a day of rest. The rest is clearly egalitarian, applying to animals and resident aliens. (On the odd term *refreshed,* see 31:17.)

It is curious that v. 13 adds three imperatives of a quite general kind, echoing the first commandment. The present text suggests that other gods will jeopardize sabbath— i.e., lure Israel out of its confident rest—and that sabbath is a way to maintain loyalty to Yahweh.

Finally, this legal corpus concludes with a rather inexact festal calendar (vv. 14-19). Three festivals are specified: (1) Festival of Unleavened Bread (vv. 15, 18), on which see Exodus 12–13; (2) Festival of Harvest, when the firstfruits of the land are brought to Yahweh (vv. 16*a*, 19); and (3) Festival of Ingathering at the end of the harvest season (v. 16*b*).

This festival pattern is likely very old in Israel. While v. 15 connects unleavened bread to the exodus, for the most part the laws reflect the life of an agrarian community. The festivals are not primarily oriented to the memory of liberation but to the patterns of agricultural life. In the festivals, Yahweh is acknowledged as the owner of the land and the giver of crops, i.e., a God of fertility who gives life to all of creation.[143]

Two specific requirements are made for this pattern of festivals. First, no one shall come empty-handed (v. 15*b*). All shall bring an offering, thus acknowledging gratitude and dependence. Second, all males—i.e., all heads of households—shall come to the shrine three times a year, thus regularly enacting their membership in the covenant community as adherents to the covenantal claims of Yahweh (v. 17).

The addendum of v. 19*b* is enigmatic (cf. Deut 14:21*b*). Apparently the prohibited practice is something done in Canaanite ritual. While there is nothing intrinsically evil about the practice, it is known and recognized as an act of devotion to Canaanite gods, so Israel must desist.

The festival ritual is a regular, disciplined demonstration of loyalty to Yahweh, acknowledging that life comes from Yahweh alone and is given back to Yahweh. The memory of the exodus is only marginally important in this pattern for worship. What counts here is land ownership and allegiance, precisely what one expects in an agrarian community. The God of this festal calendar is indeed the creator who "satisfied the desire of everything" (Ps 145:16).

---

142. Karl Polanyi, *The Great Transformation* (Boston: Beacon, 1957), notes the decisive and devastating socioeconomic consequences of practices of enclosure.

143. See Walter Harrelson, *From Fertility Cult to Worship* (Garden City, N.Y.: Doubleday, 1969).

REFLECTIONS

Contemporary interpretation will need to handle these legal provisions with some interpretive distance and freedom. That is, the laws do not "apply" as commandments simply to be acted out by an obedient community, remote from their social context. An ancient law is not precisely and automatically pertinent to new and massively transformed social circumstance.

This does not suggest, however, that there is nothing of value for contemporary interpretation and proclamation in this material. I suggest three avenues of approach to this material. First, one can seek to identify the assumptions and principles that lie behind the concrete laws. For example, the requirement of saving the ox or donkey of one's enemy (23:4-5) recognizes that neighbors who do not like each other are nonetheless bound together in a common good. The principle behind the laws on restitution is that a stable, healthy community requires the maintenance of and respect for property that prevents excessive or catastrophic loss.

Second, law is not a matter of settled conclusion. It is an ongoing process of adjudication to see what will work, what is required, and what is acceptable. In these ancient laws, we are able to observe the processes by which a community does the difficult, ongoing work of adjudicating competing claims and interests. Thus, for example, in the laws of release (21:1-11) the claims and interests of human freedom and dignity are in profound tension with the property rights of slave owners. Quite clearly, these laws do not entertain the notion of abolishing the practice of debt slavery. At best, the laws are reformist, seeking to make a troublesome social practice as humane as possible. One does not need to claim that these legal settlements are right, or that they will not be subject to revision. On the whole, law is not an effort to fix eternal principles but to adjudicate some question at hand. If we understand these laws in relation to the specific case in question, then interpretive practice might allow the church in its moral bewilderment to lower its strident voice and address the human questions before it.

Just as the church has been, in my judgment, excessively busy in recent times stating "absolutes," so also conversation about civil law has fallen into an advocacy of strict constructionism that pretends that law has a once-for-all meaning and intention. These texts are a model for the power of law as a continuing dynamic process. Such a process leaves the community short of absolutes but better able to meet the crises of the day.

Third, because the laws reflect a simple, face-to-face agrarian society, they are not directly applicable to a more complex, urban, technological, and post-industrial society. The temptation is to let the laws pertain to neighbor relations while refusing to interpret them in relation to greater social complexity. These laws require a careful social criticism in order to see how these modes of covenant in a face-to-face community might operate in a complex society. Fretheim suggests that "one is invited by the law to go beyond the law."[144] Thus bond slavery may apply not to a male Hebrew but to a permanent underclass. Thus charging interest may apply not "to the poor among you" but to debtor nations whose economies are rendered hopelessly dependent by creditors. Thus "boiling a kid" may apply not to Canaanite practice but to participation in an extravagantly consumeristic society.

When one exercises interpretive freedom, as well as interpretive responsibility, consideration of these texts can open conversation concerning how the covenantal intention of Yahweh pertains to shared human life. Such consideration might invite the church to ethical reflection in new modes, consisting not in arguments about absolute principles but in provisional decisions to get through the day faithfully, humanely, and covenantally.

Theological conviction eventuates in concrete, ethical reflection. There is no easy, obvious, one-to-one match between them. But the one does necessarily result in the other. On the one hand, theological reflection must come down to concrete decisions concerning worship, economics, and sexuality, for these are the hazardous arenas of loyalty and responsibility. Such a text as the present one undermines the dictum that the church should not mix religion with politics and economics. Politics and economics

144. Fretheim, *Exodus*, 248.

are what these laws are all about. Allegiance to the Lord of the exodus concerns liberation for slaves, humane rates of interest, restitution for crippled oxen, and reparations for a raped woman. Yahweh's exodus sovereignty is daily and concrete, and concerns the ordinariness of life, where covenant becomes visible.

On the other hand, it is equally clear that concrete ethics always lag behind theological conviction. The wondrous claims of liberation that are now available to Israel do not fully function in daily practice. Thus slaves are still "money" (21:21), and women are still property (22:16-17). The ethics of the community is always playing "catch-up" with the theological passions that identify it. The community is always engaged in counting costs, running risks, protecting interests, to see how far it will go with its exodus imagination.

We may now consider in turn the several sections into which the material is divided to see what interpretive possibilities are available:

1. A right understanding of God is closely connected to a right worship of God. I have suggested that the provision for altars is free of hierarchical protocols and concerned for simplicity and modesty as modes of holiness. Altars can be free and spontaneous, yet holy in their simplicity. The God who is worshiped, reflected, and "enacted" in such worship likewise partakes of a holiness free of pretense, extravagance, and grandeur. (We shall see that this mode of worship is in deep tension with the worship proposals of chaps. 25–31.)

2. These two laws on bond servants and their release in 21:1-11 show that the community is aware of the tension between human rights and economic power. In such an economy, slaves represent considerable financial investment. This community, haunted by the exodus, knows that a fettered person can have no full self. It is not willing to forego all economic interest for the sake of full humanness, but it understands the urgency of the question. Such a reformist position is a long way from proclaiming that there is "no longer slave or free" (Gal 3:28), but even Paul was far behind his own lyrical dictum, as demonstrated in Philemon. The interpretive points concern the ways in which persons are held in bondage in economic structures, the costs of liberation, and the high price of keeping persons bonded.

3. The four laws in 21:12-17 are held together by the formula "shall be put to death." They concern any practice of physical or verbal violence in the community. All such violence diminishes persons and thereby destroys community. Thus interpretation might focus on the full human functioning of life in which freedom, dignity, respect, and safety are prized goods.

The means to curb violence is itself an act of violence (capital punishment), albeit an ordered, sanctioned violence. Such a law should not be used to sanction capital punishment in our time and place. Rather, it should help us to consider how a community may be able to maintain human life, human freedom, and human dignity against life-robbing violence.

4. The four laws in 21:18-27 concern violence that does not lead to death. (In two cases, concerning a slave [v. 20] and a miscarried pregnancy [v. 22], a life is terminated. But in neither case is this termination the point of the law.) In all four cases, the community metes out punishment that is equitable without vengeance. The community sets a limit on vengeance and thereby seeks to control violence. We live in an inordinately violent society. In our fearfulness, we seek private oases of security, but we do not want to expend the money or energy on the public infrastructure, which has largely disintegrated. No doubt violence begets violence. These laws take the threat of violence seriously, but they characteristically propose a minimal penalty. Thus the laws seek to de-escalate the violence and have it over and done with.

5. The four laws in 21:28–22:4 concern damage done by an ox or to an ox. These laws suggest that one must control one's "means of production" (oxen) in order to guard the well-being of one's neighbor. The danger to which the law points is a disregard of the neighbor because one is preoccupied with one's own interests.

It requires no great imagination to see that, in a post-industrial society, preoccupation with one's own well-being and profit can lead to neglect of the neighbor's well-being. Thus the "ox that gored" might be understood as water rights, careless chemical pollution, or the introduction of technical "advances" (i.e., smarter oxen) that endanger the environment and destroy another person's context for a good life. "A man and his ox"—that is, a person and his or her possessions—do not exist in a vacuum. We cannot conduct our lives in disregard of our neighbors.

6. Exodus 22:5-17 has to do with restitution. There will be no "communal wholeness" (שלום *šālôm*) until "reparations" are made (שלם *šillēm*). *Shalom* refers to a harmonious equilibrium. But such social equilibrium is not possible in a community that is strongly at odds and in which some are denied what is rightfully and necessarily theirs. Whereas *shalom* characterizes a state of existence, *šillēm* is a very powerful, active intervention to right a wrong.

In these laws, the interventions are domestic and the repayments are modest. They do nonetheless evidence a principle of concrete payment to compensate for an unjust loss. The concreteness of restitution here invites reflection upon the *principle* of reparation and the active work of social redress. In a society that currently resists "affirmative action"—action that compensates for a long, habituated social wrong—the notion of reparations is worth pursuing. The difficulty is in recognizing that those to whom reparations are owed have so long ago lost their ox that we scarcely notice the need to restore it. In a society that dreams of *shalom*, or one that prattles ideologically about *shalom*, those old needs for compensation must be recovered. Thus reparations are due to women from men, to blacks from whites, to the Third World from the first, and to all of those who by the political manipulations of the economy have lost their "ox" without any restitution.

7. In the miscellaneous collection of 22:18-31, attention might most usefully be given to the two provisions in 22:21-24 and 25-27. In both cases, the powerful are warned against exploiting the weak, and the motivation for the instruction is theological. God is wrathful (v. 24), and God is compassionate (v. 27). God's attentive concern extends into the economy. In the second of these laws, it is argued that genuine human concern impinges upon economic transactions. Michael Polanyi has chronicled the way in which the European economy (and by extrapolation the economy of the United States) progressively separated market exchanges from the human fabric.[145] The end result is a market that operates "autonomously," without reference to human costs. The covenantal community will not tolerate such a separation and will insist that economic power be subordinated to the human realities of pain, need, and hope.

These two laws on valuing the needy of the community are framed by laws that insist on singular devotion to Yahweh (vv. 20, 28, 29*a*, 29*b*-30, 31). The two accents are, of course, deeply intertwined. That *Yahweh rules* makes unavoidable that the *poor neighbor counts* (cf. Jer 22:15-16). Israel cannot make the first affirmation without making the derivative ethical commitment.

8. The laws in 23:1-9 rigorously and consistently voice the Mosaic commitment to justice as the norm for the community. In vv. 1-3 and 6-9 that concern focuses primarily on the courts, on honest testimony without distortions to protect vested interest. In vv. 4-5, the practice of justice concerns concrete acts of neighborliness. In neither case, however, is such action mere charity. Rather, it is a discipline that defines the identity of

145. Polanyi, *The Great Transformation.* See Meeks's comments, *God the Economist,* 37-40, 52-55.

this community. The double use of the word *poor* (vv. 3, 6; cf. v. 9) indicates that the law is not unaware of social differentiations; there is no insidious pretense of classlessness. They know very well that money "talks" in court and wherever power is shaped. The laws dare to insist, nonetheless, that voices other than those of money (voices of need, of pain, and of memory) might prevail.

9. Finally, the laws culminate with a festival calendar urging that Israel should "take time to be holy," take time to be whole (23:10-19). This group of laws focuses on the three-festival agricultural cycle, introduced by a seven-year cycle for the land (vv. 10-11) and a seven-day cycle for the economy (vv. 12-13).

The three-festival calendar is explicitly oriented to Yahweh. In it, the crucial times of the agricultural economy become times at which Yahweh's sovereignty is enacted. The two "laws of seven" have a very different orientation, being primarily concerned for God's creation (for the poor and wild animals, for the ox and donkey, for the slave, and for the resident alien). These laws themselves do not say much about Yahweh, aside from the motivational addendum of v. 13. Thus vv. 10-12 (13) concern creaturely well-being, and vv. 14-19 concern the creator who owns the land.

Concerning both creaturely well-being and acknowledgment of the creator, the covenant community practices a rhythm of observations not unlike the church year. The community is enjoined to treat time as holy, both in order to value creation and to honor the creator. (In Gen 2:1-4*a*, *time* is the first element of creation that God makes holy.) All of these times, the festivals of seven and the threefold festival, intend to break the conventional economic practice of working, getting, and spending, or ingathering and harvest. The festivals are an act of faith because they make an ordered acknowledgment that prevents human business from degenerating into an endless effort at management, success, and self-security.

10. It is not clear that this corpus has any intentional shape, though Schwienhorst-Schönberger argues that it does.[146] The corpus begins with the vexed question of human freedom and dignity (21:1-11), and after a powerful accent on justice (23:1-9), it concludes with a pattern for worship and acknowledgment of God's generous sovereignty (23:10-19). If we dare imagine the two units as beginning and end, there is then a move from *human freedom* (21:1-11) to acknowledging *God's governance of creation* (23:10-19). A text that may illuminate this connection is Matt 5:23-24: "So when you are offering your gift at the altar, if you remember that your brother or sister has something against you, leave your gift there before the altar and go; first be reconciled to your brother or sister, and then come and offer your gift" (NRSV).

In this corpus, Israel wants in the end to offer its gift at the altar (23:16, 19). It cannot do so, however, until it has been reconciled to brother and sister, in this case a male slave (21:1-6) and a female slave (21:7-11). The commands of Moses never permit the separation of God and neighbor, or of worship and human justice.

146. Schwienhorst-Schönberger, *Das Bundesbuch,* 22-37 and esp. the summary on 23.

EXODUS 23:20-33, CONQUEST OF CANAAN PROMISED

COMMENTARY

Moses' presentation of God's commandments ends abruptly in 23:19. Now God speaks an enormous promise to Israel, matched by an insistent requirement. Two themes intertwine in this speech: God is going to give land, blessing, and well-being; and Israel must worship Yahweh alone.

God's way of being present in this dangerous journey is in three "sendings": (a) God will send an "angel" (messenger) (v. 20); (b) God will send "my terror" (v. 27); and (c) God will send "the pestilence" (v. 28).

The angel will protect Israel along the way and will guide Israel safely into the land of promise. We have seen the angel in 3:2 as the forerunner of God's holiness and in 14:19 as a protective presence. Clearly the "angel" is a way of speaking about God's own work on behalf of Israel. (Note that in 34:11, a parallel passage, the angel is not mentioned but it is "I" who will do what the angel does in this passage.) The language likely reflects a polytheistic image in terms of a high God with obedient heavenly servants and functionaries. Thus, as in Ps 91:11-12, God is a guardian to keep Israel safe, but the work is done through an angel.

The angel is also the voice of the God who commands, and Israel must listen (i.e., obey). In v. 22, the verb for "hear" is reiterated with an infinitive absolute, as in 19:5. Hearing is made the condition of protection. The God who protects is the God who commands; there will be no protection without obedience.

The purpose of the protected journey, as already anticipated in 3:8 and 17, and as set forth programmatically in 15:13-17, is to situate the former slaves in a productive, secure land. Three affirmations are made about the land in vv. 23-26. First, the land is presently occupied by other, hostile peoples who must be displaced. The list of six peoples in v. 23 is conventional and stylized, although such a list characteristically includes seven nations. Without blinking, God will "blot out" the present occupants of the land. Second, the new land will be a place of rigorous theological decision. Israel must eliminate all the signs, symbols, and seductions of other faith options, must hew to the first commandment, to worship "only Yahweh." Third, the elimination of enemies and the practice of pure loyalty will eventuate in a land that is finally blessed by Yahweh; it will be safe, productive, and fertile. Verses 25-26 cite examples of what a blessed life will be like: good bread

and good water, i.e., adequate sustenance (unlike the jeopardy of the wilderness); no sickness (cf. 15:26); and no miscarriages or barrenness. The land will be saturated with God's good power for life. The rhetoric of vv. 20-26 holds promise and demand in splendid relation.

The speech of God then turns to the strategy whereby the land will be taken. There will be two more "sendings": terror and pestilence, which, unlike the angel, are Yahweh's agents, sent to afflict the enemy. It is not at all clear, however, in what these agents consist. "Terror" (אימה *'êmâ*) is also used in Exod 15:16 and Josh 2:9 concerning the taking of the land; it suggests that Israel's appearance is so formidable that the other peoples will be fearful and retreat. The second term, "pestilence," is equally uncertain. The NRSV also renders it "pestilence" (צרעה *ṣir'â*) in Deut 7:20, but in Josh 24:12 (and here in the NIV), it is rendered "hornet" (both instances are in the context of land seizure). In many other places (including 4:6) the term is rendered "leprosy." It is enough for our purposes that God will cause panic and destabilization, which will cause retreat and withdrawal, making the land available.

Two other motifs appear in this promise of the land. First, vv. 29-30 assert that the displacement of the other peoples will be gradual. The reason given is that in the transition the land will be unoccupied, left to become an unmanageable wilderness; but in the book of Judges three other, very different, reasons for delay are given. The larger attention in Judges is given to the first (and most theological) reason (Judg 2:2-3, 20-23): God is angry at disobedient Israel and will not clear the land. A second, derivative reason is that Israelites inexperienced in war must be given opportunity to learn (Judg 3:1-2). A third, more practical, military reason is that Israel cannot compete against chariots of iron (Judg 1:19; cf. vv. 21, 27-33). It is likely that our verses reflect a situation in which the established population was not easily dislodged, whether the reason is understood theologically, pedagogically, or militarily. The same reasons would pertain, even if the "conquest" is a social revolution of peasants.

Second, the rhetoric concerning the new land is massively escalated (v. 31). Here the narrative envisions a "greater Israel" of the Solomonic Empire. The theological claim is the same (promise and demand), but the dream of Israel has now expanded, and it still drives the ideological claims of many in the contemporary state of Israel.

After discoursing about the wondrous land of promise (vv. 23-31), God's speech returns one more time to a covenantal accent (vv. 32-33). The Mosaic tradition is acutely aware of the theological threat posed by cultural-religious alternatives. It understands that any benign hosting of other peoples, their symbolizations of reality (cf. v. 24; Deut 12:1-7), and their gods will endanger the identity and destiny of Israel.

REFLECTIONS

1. This text, like much of the OT, insists that biblical faith is profoundly materialistic in its intention. This faith is not a "good idea" or a "spiritual relation," but it is about a communal existence of well-being, security, productivity, and prosperity. Israel's faith inherently spills over into politics and economics, thereby raising issues of power. This God intends for this people a good life in a fully bodied existence. A great deal of work on this point is needed in the church in the United States, where there is a large temptation to gnostic-spiritualizing tendencies (e.g., the popular work of Joseph Campbell). This interpretive tendency, not surprisingly, seems to increase commensurate with the affluence of religious practitioners.

2. This sort of text is problematic because it is so savagely hostile and intolerant of other peoples. We are rightly nervous about any such ideology/dream of displacement. Without denying the problem, the best I know to do is to offer a sociocritical comment that issues in a theological claim. The sociocritical discernment of which I am persuaded (as offered by Norman Gottwald) is that Israel's ideology is formed by a revolutionary cadre of Levites to support a peasant uprising against an exploitative city-state system of economics and politics.[147] (On the Levite connection, see 2:1; 6:16-25; and 32:25-29.) That is, the displacement proposed is not of one ethnic community by another but of a hated class of exploiters by those who are too long abused. This peasant community, so the argument runs, intends a "social experiment" to see whether public power can be organized in covenantal ways. The destruction to be wrought for the purpose of the revolution, then, is not to kill Canaanites at random but to destroy the "system," its practices, its symbols, and inevitably its functionaries.

The Israelite system of covenant is totally incompatible with Canaanite modes of exploitative power, and the rhetoric of the text serves the revolutionary cause by making the contrast unbridgeable. It is inevitable, then, that the program of Moses is not only uncompromising, but intolerant. Such a view of Israel's faith may be unpalatable to us. It is, however, more likely to be unpalatable to affluent, established believers who themselves have compromised with dominant power. This is not to excuse the intolerance, but to suggest that our own social location matters enormously in our assessment of this tradition and its rhetoric.

3. The good land now given is conditional. It depends on worship of Yahweh alone (vv. 21, 24-25, 32). Christianity has for so long represented itself as a religion of free grace, that we flinch from the thought that God's gifts are conditional. Mosaic faith, however, is realistically grounded in a comprehensive "if" (v. 22; cf. 19:5). This is not because God is calculating or bargaining but because the gift of a productive, secure land cannot be held carelessly or through patterns of exploitation. Under such practices, the land will soon succumb to self-serving economics that will void any prospect

---

147. It is a primary methodical insistence of Gottwald, *The Tribes of Yahweh*, that Yahwism is deeply enmeshed in and shaped by social relationships in ancient Israel. See esp. 591-621, 700-702.

of peace, security, or justice. The "if" is a realistic understanding that social practice determines social destiny. I will cite three cases in which this conditionality of the good land seems clear enough.

The technological capacity to exploit, distort, and destroy our natural environment is unmistakable. The worship of the gods of military security and unfettered profit does cause a forfeiture of the good land. This is evident in the production of acid rain, and in the environment-threatening residue of modern warfare.

In our day, a variety of obdurate, small tyrants have learned too late that power to govern is not unconditional. When their exploitative system pays no attention to social *conditions*, the land is lost. Super powers, of course, imagine they are immune to such threats. But the turns in the fortunes of the former Soviet Union put even super powers on notice that the conditional quality of the good land in the end has no exceptions, not even for uncommon and unrivaled power.

In the great cities of the United States, the limitless drive of greed and selfishness and the unwillingness to pay taxes in order to sustain the public good have destroyed the infrastructure. As a result, these cities have been overrun with violence. The city cannot be sustained unconditionally. The condition of good life in the good land is adherence to covenantal practices. Israel is always on its way to exile, having learned too slowly. Our own learning is not noticeably swift.

EXODUS 24:1-18, THE COVENANT CEREMONY

COMMENTARY

This chapter concludes the covenant-making process at Sinai (chaps. 19–24), and resumes the themes of theophany, confrontation, and presence, featured in chapter 19. Chapters 19 and 24 thus form a frame that brackets the presentation of law in 20:1-17 and 21:1–23:19.

This chapter holds together two themes, one vertical and one horizontal. The first theme is *communion in the presence of God*, which entails receiving the tablets of commands from God (vv. 1-2, 9-18). The second theme is *covenant making*, whereby Moses dramatically and liturgically binds Israel to Yahweh. These two themes are not, of course, mutually exclusive. But they are expressed in very different forms and rhetoric. According to conventional source analysis, the themes roughly divide into P material (communion) and JE material (covenant making).

24:1-2. God invites Moses to go back up the mountain. According to the analysis of Thomas Dozeman, the movements up and down the mountain not only provide location patterns but also indicate relations of

power and influence.[148] In this brief text we are able to see three levels of approach to the presence of God. At the lowest level are "the people," who do not come up. Second are the priests Aaron, Nadab, and Abihu, and seventy elders. Aaron no doubt signifies a particular priestly interest in the narrative. This priestly company is permitted to "come up" further than the people, but they still must worship "at a distance" (v. 1). Third, Moses is permitted to "come near" (v. 2). Thus the narrative once again enhances the singular authority of Moses and prepares the way for the subsequent polemic against and dismissal of the Aaronides in chap. 32. (This threefold pattern is perhaps distantly echoed in the Gospel narrative of Gethsemane, in which three disciples go part way with Jesus into his ordeal [see Matt 26:36-39; Mark 14:32-35].)

24:3-8. In these verses, however, Moses is not on the mountain but with the people. These verses do not logically follow after vv. 1-2 but seem more appropriate after 20:17

148. See Dozeman, *God on the Mountain*.

or 20:21. In any case, Moses is now preoccupied with binding Israel in fidelity to the rule of God. There is nothing here of "presence," but only of sovereign will. At the outset, the community swears full allegiance (v. 3). Indeed, this oath seems almost a blank check. Israel swears to obey everything God has said, even that which Moses may yet tell them. Anticipated in 19:8, and reiterated in 24:7, the moment of oath taking is the moment of Israel's constitution as a people unlike any other; they are a people not constituted by blood, language, or territory but only by its singular hearing. Its resolve to "hear" is an acknowledgment that Israel is not self-made, self-invented, or autonomous, but is formed by the power, and for the pleasure, of the Holy One.

Three acts of Moses consummate the relation with Yahweh. First, an altar is built (cf. 20:24-26) on which burnt offerings and whole offerings are given, commensurate with the twelve-tribe structure of Israel (vv. 4-5). Second, there is the "book of the covenant," apparently a literary deposit of the commands given by God to Moses (cf. Deut 31:9-13). While it may be constituted by the Decalogue, scholars are inclined to relate this reference to the corpus of 21:1–23:19. Third, in a ritual act, Moses sprinkles blood from the sacrifice upon both the altar (v. 6) and the people (v. 8). The "blood of the covenant" thus creates solidarity between the two parties. This dramatic act is not rationally explicable, but no doubt arises from the recognition that "blood" is the distinctive element that makes life possible. (See the comparable actions of Gen 15:9-11; Jer 34:18-19.) Thus Israel now begins a new life of obedience, signified by sacrifice, the "book of the covenant," and the "blood of the covenant."

24:9-11. As the narrative advances, we return to the scene at the mountain, as in vv. 1-2. The characters are the same as in vv. 1-2: Moses, Aaron, Nadab, Abihu, and the seventy elders. This is the authorized leadership of the community. In the Priestly tradition, we are at an awesome moment of peculiar and dreadful encounter. A. Henton Davies describes these verses as "some of the most astonishing and inexplicable verses in the Old Testament."[149]

The narrative is abrupt: "They saw God!" (v. 10). There God was, fully visible in concrete form. In v. 11, the theme intensifies: "They beheld God," or better, "They gazed upon God." The scene suggests a stunned, astonished silence. They look and are mesmerized. They do not speak; they do not move. Ernest Nicholson quotes Rabbi Hoshoia: "They fixed gloating eyes upon the Divine Presence."[150] This is indeed a foundational moment, not to be repeated in Israel's life.

Then the narrative adds three notes. First, it attempts to say what they see (v. 10) in words that are, as might be expected, stammering and inadequate. The "description" is governed by the double use of "like" (כ *kĕ*), for the scene will not admit of direct reportage. What is seen is unutterable and can only be narrated by indirection. It is not "a pavement of sapphire stone," but it is "like" that. It is not "heavenly clearness," but it is "like" that, even as it is beyond it and unutterable. The most remarkable parallel to this report is Ezekiel's vision, in which "like" is used repeatedly (Ezek 1:13, 16, 22, 24 [three times], 26 [four times], 27 [three times], 28 [two times]). The narrator wants to characterize what is real and visible and tangible. What is given in the meeting, however, is holy and unapproachable.

Second, the narrative reports God's astonishing deference to Israel (v. 11). Ordinarily one may not see God; certainly one may not see God and live (Judg 6:22-23). This is not because God is invisible, but because God is dangerously holy (33:22-23). Thus these priests and elders are at great risk. But God does not lay a land upon them, and they are safe. Presumably it is a moment of God's generous self-giving, not repeatable, but very real.

Third, they eat and drink (v. 11). It is conventional to say that here Israel participates with God in a meal of covenantal solidarity, thus sealing the relation. Harold Bloom, in what may be a slight trivialization, calls this "a picnic."[151] But we are not told the meal was light or celebrative. It may as well have been solemn, ominous, and dreadful.

149. G. Henton Davies, *Exodus: An Introduction and Commentary* (London: SCM, 1967) 193.

150. Ernest Nicholson, "The Interpretation of Exodus XXIV 9–11," *VT* 24 (1974) 89-90.

151. Harold Bloom, "From J to K, or The Uncanniness of the Yahwist," in *The Bible and the Narrative Tradition,* ed. Frank McConnell (New York: Oxford University Press, 1986) 35.

The narrative intends to leave us stunned, bewildered, and awestruck. And it does! We do not know what happened, for here earth entered into face-to-face contact with the Holy One around the most elemental activity of eating (cf. Luke 24:35). It is entirely plausible that in Priestly rhetoric "seeing God" and "eating with God" are understood as cultic actions (cf. Ps 17:15; Isa 6:1). Such recognition, however, explains nothing and diminishes nothing, but only locates the moment of awe. More likely, the narrator invites us to an irreducible moment that allows no useful probing. The outcome is that Israel is even more stunned by the holiness; the leadership is freshly authorized, but, we may imagine, shaken to its respective toes by this Reality so utterly present and so completely, unutterably beyond them.

24:12-14. Then Moses goes farther up the mountain. He is now alone—except for Joshua. The reference to Joshua is odd, for it is "Moses alone" in v. 2. In fact, Joshua plays no role here at all (previously we have him only in 17:14). The narrator is perhaps looking forward to the time when Joshua must be legitimated as Moses' successor. With that peculiar and inconsequential exception, it is "Moses alone." Aaron (and Hur) are left behind. Thus the narrator prepares the way for the crisis of chap. 32. Later, Joshua and Aaron will come to represent conflicting trajectories of Israel's life and faith. There is, moreover, no doubt where the narrator's sympathies lie.

24:15-18. Finally, Moses is alone, now without even Joshua, exposed, at risk, on the mountain, into the cloud. Here, he is to wait in complete obedience to be addressed and to receive.

The counterpoint to Moses in this meeting is not the God who is seen. It is "the glory of the LORD," which is "like" a devouring fire: alive, dangerous, and visible. We have seen the glory of Yahweh arise from combat with Pharaoh (14:4, 17), and we have been surprised to find the glory inhabiting, of all places, the wilderness (16:10). Now, however, the glory is in its natural habitat, high above, inaccessible, in the midst of the cloud.

And "Moses entered the cloud." What a statement! He goes where no one has ever gone. He leaves the zone of humanness and enters the very sphere of God. And there he stays, forty days and forty nights—i.e., a very long time. No one, not Aaron or Israel or the narrator, knows whether he will ever come out again. The rootage of Israel's worship (now to be authorized in chaps. 25–31 and to be actualized in 40:34-38) is not a human device, but a holy gift that comes from God's own awesome intentionality. God wants God's glory to abide, "to tabernacle" (שכן *šākan*) in the realm of the human, in the very life of Israel. But for God to come here, Moses must go there!

REFLECTIONS

This chapter, perhaps by juxtaposing P and JE materials, holds together *awesome presence* and *covenantal demand*. Faithful interpretation must take both seriously, and must perhaps accent the theme that in each context is the more difficult. In a context focused on rigorous obedience, the awesome glory warrants attention; in a context fascinated with glorious presence, the demand of covenant deserves attention.

1. The oath of loyalty (vv. 3-8), together with its dramatic bonding through book and blood, creates a new community in the world. Kutsch has argued strongly that "covenant" (ברית *běrît*) is in fact not a "relationship" (*Bund*) but an "obligation" (*Verpflichtung*).[152] Israel's distinctive life in the world is due to its sworn allegiance to this God alone. Such a hard-nosed claim is exceedingly difficult in a culture that is so fearful of authority, so bent on the therapeutic, and so committed to individual freedom and self-fulfillment. That, of course, has made Israel (and the "New Israel"?) endlessly odd and problematic. The oath of allegiance is access to a radical ecclesiology.

152. E. Kutsch, *Verheissung und Gesetz. Untersuchungen zum Sogenannten "Bund" im Alten Testament*, BZAW 131 (Berlin: De Gruyter, 1973). See the critical summary of his work by Nicholson, *God and His People*, 89-117.

Moreover, that community is finally constituted not forensically but sacramentally. Israel comes into being not primarily by an act of its own will, but by liturgic action taken upon it by God, which bestows upon it a solidarity, a destiny, and an identity that it could not choose for itself. The reference to blood is a witness to profound solidarity, wrought by the initiative of God (cf. Heb 9:18-21). In this self-giving, Yahweh is fully pledged to Israel, as Israel is sworn to Yahweh. See the more formal and symmetrical assertion of this solidarity in 6:7.

2. "Gazing upon God" leads our reflection in a very different direction. At the center of the Sinai tradition is an act of contemplation, an awed, silent, respectful look at God. This tradition is in deep tension with the oath of loyalty and obedience, but it is powerfully present, nonetheless, in the text. Samuel Terrien has poignantly juxtaposed the "ethical ear" and the "contemplative eye" in his study of the presence of God in the OT.[153] The "beholding of God" curtails all the listening and is overwhelmed by the vision. As I write this, a British hostage has just been released from five years of captivity in Lebanon. He reports that after four years of confinement, he and his cohorts were given a bowl of red cherries, the first fruit and the first color they had seen in four years. Despite their eagerness to taste the fruit, he reports, they waited a day, simply to gaze upon the cherries in wonder and gratitude. This mundane report may hint at what the priests and elders did at Sinai: They gazed before they ate.

3. The stammering speech of the narrator is crucial to the telling. The biblical tradition is, of course, eloquent and articulate. It does, however, reach the point of the unutterable. Karl Barth has said of this faith: "As ministers we ought to speak of God. We are human, however, and so cannot speak of God."[154]

This text has perhaps its closest NT counterpart in the narrative of the transfiguration of Jesus, in which the narrator also stammers: "His face shone like the sun, and his clothes became dazzling white" (Matt 17:2 NRSV); "His clothes became dazzling white, such as no one on earth could bleach them" (Mark 9:3 NRSV). Luke then writes, "They saw his glory" and "they were terrified as they entered the cloud" (Luke 9:32, 34 NRSV). Here also there is glory; here also the cloud overwhelms; and here also, finally, a massive, terrifying voice is heard. The narrative of the transfiguration is no ordinary story. It tells of the faithful disciples' being given an intimate glimpse into the reality of God's holiness. This holiness is embodied in Jesus who echoes and replicates the oddity of Sinai.

At the core of Christian faith is an overpowering, unutterable disclosure that gives access to the awesome holiness and moves in the direction of contemplation, wonderment, and grateful awe. Conventional Protestantism, with its moral passion, has been reluctant to probe or consider these matters, being frightened of anything that smacks of mysticism. No doubt such an accent is just now problematic, given the rage of gnostic spirituality. But neglect of this dimension of faith may be equally hazardous. This vision provides the legitimation and energy for Moses and for all who draw life from this vision.

4. The vision of God is inescapably transformative. Martin Smith takes the expression "No one can see God and live" to mean "No one could see God and remain unchanged."[155] The power of God's appearing changes those who see (see 1 John 3:2-3). Those who see become "more like God." But then, seeing God has transformative power, which leads to more dangerous obedience. The presence of God and communion with God are "the real thing" in and of themselves. Nonetheless, they have profound transformative effect on those who "enter the cloud."

---

153. Samuel Terrien, *The Elusive Presence: Towards a New Biblical Theology*, Religious Perspectives (San Francisco: Harper & Row, 1978). On this passage, see 134-36.

154. Karl Barth, *The Word of God and the Word of Man* (New York: Harper and Bros., 1957) 186.

155. Martin Smith, *The Word Is Very Near You: A Guide to Praying with Scripture* (London: Darton, Longman and Todd, 1989) 131.

EXODUS 25:1–31:18

THE PATTERN OF THE TABERNACLE

OVERVIEW

These seven chapters, consisting in seven speeches by Yahweh to Moses, purport to be instructions given on Mt. Sinai (cf. 24:15-18). They are instructions to Moses about how to build a suitable place in which Yahweh will dwell (שׁכן *šākan*) in the midst of Israel (25:8). The consensus of critical scholarship is that these chapters are an exilic or post-exilic piece of the Priestly tradition that describes a notion of a sanctuary suitable to the post-exilic situation of a displaced people.[156]

The noun *tabernacle* (משכן *miškān*) derives from the verb *sākan*, which means "to dwell" or "to sojourn." The verb suggests full presence, but it is not a stable guarantee of a permanent presence. The God who dwells here does so with freedom to leave. The tabernacle is a "portable temple," which is appropriate for a displaced people who are no longer in Jerusalem and are, therefore, in transit. Thus the proposed tabernacle guarantees a combination of presence and mobility.

Recent scholars, however, have not been content to leave this as a descriptive text. With more interpretive imagination, they have asked how this allegedly descriptive account functions in and serves the larger Priestly theology. Joseph Blenkinsopp has proposed that this text is a quite deliberate complement to the creation narrative of Gen 1:1–2:4*a*, both in terms of the rhetoric of "command and performance" and with the affirmation of 39:32 and 40:33 that the work of the tabernacle is "finished" (cf. Gen 2:1).[157] Blenkinsopp proposes that the creation of the tabernacle parallels the creation of the world in P theology. (He also suggests a third parallel in the distribution of the land in Joshua 18–24.) Thus for P, the completion of the tabernacle to house God's glory is as momentous as the creation of the world.

This text can be seen as a theological statement about God's willingness to be present in the midst of the community of Israel, under the custodial auspices of the priests. Frank H. Gorman, Jr., has helpfully shown how liturgic interests are indeed an important public agenda for a community that wants to order its life in intentional ways.[158] Thus the interpreter is invited to think with these texts about how the power and goodness of God are present in the world. The answer to that wonderment given here is that the presence of God is available through a cultic apparatus authorized and designed by God's own self-disclosure, and implemented through skilled, obedient human authority.

Beyond a concern for source analysis and religious history, but also beyond a particular theological strand in the Pentateuch (P), we must at last ask what it means to have a *canonical text* that talks seriously about these matters. As a canonical text, it is no longer an actual description, or even a sixth-century theological strategy, but a revealing, authorizing text for all the generations. As readers of the text, we are not making a tabernacle and have no particular interest in one, per se. So then, what do we do when we read this text?

In the end, the exodus scenario is not only a transformative "event," but also a settled, reliable, sustained "pattern" for God's presence. This text, then, is an act of daring imagination that invites erstwhile slaves to imagine a world in which God is palpably, visibly, wondrously present.

---

156. See the important alternative proposal on the dating of the Priestly material by Jacob Milgrom, *Leviticus 1–16: A New Translation with Introduction and Commentary,* AB 3 (New York: Doubleday, 1991).

157. Joseph Blenkinsopp, "The Structure of P," *CBQ* 38 (1976) 275-92. See also P. J. Kearney, "Creation and Liturgy: The P Redaction of Ex 25–40," *ZAW* 89 (1977) 375-87.

158. Frank H. Gorman, Jr., *The Ideology of Ritual: Space, Time and Status in the Priestly Theology*, JSOTSup 91 (Sheffield: Sheffield Academic, 1990).

Imagining the presence is an invitation to a certain kind of theological sensitivity that is marked by extravagance and aesthetic yearning. This act of imagination is crucial in our own time for two reasons. On the one hand, mainline Christianity in the United States has been preoccupied with either moral or doctrinal matters, giving far less energy to sacramental imagination. In the tradition of the Reformation in particular, an actual cherishing of the presence in and for itself is largely avoided. Such a shunning of the mystery of presence has permitted much faith to become blatant ideology practiced in a tone and posture of coercion. Imagination about the presence may tone down such hard-nosed certitude to permit a less triumphalistic sureness.

On the other hand, a society of technological secularism is increasingly a profaned society, having banished mystery and largely emptied the world of any meaning beyond the small significances we ourselves devise. In such a world, brutality is possible and increasingly palatable, both informally and as official public practice and policy. The mystery of presence does indeed function as a counter to the threat of profanation so powerful among us. This text requires us to think and believe in trajectories largely neglected in most popular religion as well as in most cavalier rejections of religion. This text asserts, against both ideological religious certitude and against confident secularism, that there is a sacramental foundation that makes life possible, that defines life in certain ways, and that precludes the destructiveness and despair that seem so potent among us.

EXODUS 25:1-40, TABERNACLE FURNISHINGS

COMMENTARY

Moses enters the cloud and is in the inscrutable presence for forty days and forty nights (24:18). What happens during that time is hidden from us. We only know that Yahweh speaks and Moses listens. Kearney has observed that the extended address to Moses is divided into seven discreet speeches.[159] By far the longest of these is the first, 25:1–31:11. Since that speech is so long, however, I have chosen to follow conventional chapter divisions, because the discussion will be easier to follow, and because in teaching and/or preaching, the conventional chapter divisions are most likely to be employed. It is important to remember, however, that these chapters do indeed form one long speech.

Two obvious preliminary points merit careful attention. First, these long speeches are dominated by God, the same God who has worked wonders against Egypt (chaps. 1–15) on behalf of Israel (chaps. 16–17). This is also the God who has met with Moses and Israel at Sinai (chaps. 19–24). In that meeting, God has asserted sovereignty over the future of this liberated people, and has bound Israel to a rigorous obedience.

In the process of covenant making at Sinai, however, this God has also been bound to a new loyalty. The bonding of Sinai is a two-way affair, and God has been decisively impinged upon by Israel. Nothing of God's sovereignty has been diminished, but that sovereignty is now differently deployed. The God who has been ferocious and resolute about victory and deliverance is now the God who speaks to an attentive, responsive Moses. The mood of this speech is one of acceptance between friends, albeit friends who live at a respectful distance.

Second, we take special note of what this newly bound, newly impinged upon God does. God *speaks*. God announces God's will and thereby reveals something of God's own self. God discloses a generous provision for how the holiness of God can be hosted in a community that is not easily God's habitat. Thus the speech of God, even cast as an imperative, is an act of inordinant generosity.

25:1-8. God's self-disclosing, generous command is to be initiated through an

159. Kearney, "Creation and Liturgy."

offering (תרומה *těrûmâ*) of the materials out of which the modes of communion will be constructed. The entire program of constructing a fitting place for God's presence begins in an offering from Israel. God does not unilaterally bestow or impose a habitat. Constructing an adequate place for the holiness of God is indeed human work, wrought in generosity. The term *offering* (*těrûmâ*) refers to what is "raised, lifted," here reinforced by the phrase "whose hearts prompt them." The term *prompt* (נדב *nādab*) refers to those who are compelled or motivated gladly to make an offering. The materials to be used are those freely given, without coercion or requirement. These are people who genuinely want communion with God.

The materials of the offering provide an inventory of the kinds of wealth required for what follows and the kinds of wealth available in this economy. We are surprised to learn that this community now possesses all these goods. Perhaps the list here has a counterpart in 3:21-22; 11:3; and 12:35-36, in which Israel is "empty-handed" and able only to take what is needed. Israel is now indeed to "give of its best." Such a requirement means that the development of an adequate place for holiness concerns the center of the economy. While the list of requirements is more than a little obscure, we may note that gold and silver stand at the top of the list (no doubt also first in value) as well as oil for both lamps and anointing. We shall see in what follows that a provision for light will be important, and the "oil for anointing" suggests a concern not only for God's presence, but also for human agents in worship. In this list of things to be produced, the mention of "ephod" and "breast plate" anticipates the dress and, therefore, the centrality of the priestly office. From the outset, this speech focuses on priesthood as the necessary means of communion.

The purpose of the offering (and of this long speech) is indicated in vv. 7-8, with particular attention to three terms. First, this is to be a "sanctuary" (מקדש *miqdāš*). This is a noun formed from the term for "holy" (קדש *qādaš*). Second, and perhaps most important, God uses the phrase "that I may dwell among you"—the governing intention of this long

speech. God intends to be among the people, in the midst of, at the center of Israel's life.

The verb *dwell* (*šākan*) is peculiarly important and delicate. On the one hand, it signifies an abiding presence. That is, God now intends to be "at home" in the midst of Israel. On the other hand, the verb *šākan* implies much less than "to sit permanently" (ישב *yāšab*). It suggests a settling in, but with freedom and capacity to move on at will, i.e., to bivouac.

The use of this term is part of an ongoing, unresolved tension in the OT about the presence of God, a tension that this speech exploits to the full. Thus we may suggest a continuum concerning God's presence:

come/go . . . . . sojourn . . . . . inhabit permanently
בוא (*bô*)   שכן (*šākan*)   ישב (*yāšab*)

There are texts to support each of these views. Our text takes up the middle position, wanting to assure presence, but also carefully avoiding the more crass assumption that God is a permanent occupant. Our text seeks to respect and take seriously the freedom of God, who is committed to Israel but who will not be domesticated by cultic practice.

The third term, *tabernacle* (משכן *miškān*), derives from *šākan*. The term appears to be simply the conversion of a verb into a noun that specifies the place wherein God will bivouac. This term shows the tradition struggling to work out a theory and understanding of God's presence that both honors the freedom of God and takes seriously the need for regularity and reliability of God's presence in the community.

25:9. Finally in v. 9, God says, "I will cause you to see concerning the pattern (תבנית *tabnît*). . . . " This is a remarkable statement in two regards. First, the text that started in speech that Moses can *hear* ends in showing that Moses *sees*. While this statement is presented to us as a speech of God, in fact it is a drawing or picturing by God. In this text, the book of Exodus moves a *recital* of narrative to an *exhibit* of blueprints, and Israel's mode of faith is transformed from conversation to observation. The move negatively suggests a static quality of faith, an attempt to "freeze" the presence. Positively, it introduces, alongside ethical concerns for justice and liberation, aesthetic concerns for symmetry, beauty, and loveliness. Prior to this, Israel had seen what the mighty liberating hand of God did to Egypt. Now what Moses sees is an abiding portrayal that gives durability to the prospect of communion.

This emphasis on "see" is reinforced by the term *pattern* (*tabnît*), a noun from the verb for "build" (בנה *bānâ*). The expression "show the pattern" is important because it suggests that there is an overall plan fully conceived in God's mind as a habitat within the community. The plan is God's own vision of what is required and what is possible. Just as God has seen ahead of time, and as Moses is now permitted to see, so also the community of this text is invited to see what is intended in beauty and symmetry.

Second, the architect charges the engineer: "You do it." The habitat for communion is a human responsibility and a human possibility, but it is a human enterprise undertaken in obedience to a grand, God-given design of proportion.

The remainder of this chapter describes four aspects of the tabernacle, each of which is to serve and enhance presence and communion: the ark (vv. 10-16), the mercy seat (vv. 17-22), a table of acacia wood (vv. 23-30), and a lampstand (vv. 31-40). All four of these pieces of equipment are specified in two ways. First, there is great precision in their construction. Second, nothing is to be spared in extravagant materials. In both precision and extravagance, the making of these objects is an urgent matter that is undertaken gladly by the community in order to enhance the promise of presence.

25:10-16. One can trace through the OT varied and, no doubt, rival understandings of the function and purpose of the ark, though here no interpretation is given. It is plausible that the ark was a dramatic paladin for war. In other uses, it was a throne upon which sat the invisible God, so that a notion of royal presence may have displaced military dynamism. While these two functions can be distinguished, they are not discontinuous. Both attest to the real action and sovereign presence of God.

A third view of the ark, one that seeks to minimize the notion of "presence," is that the ark is a container for the tablets of the commandments (Deut 4:7-8 may suggest holding these two accents together, as it places in parallel "a God so near" and "a torah so righteous.") First Kgs 8:1-13 closely relates to our text. The text seems to have a high view of presence connected to the ark, referring to some of the same features as in our text, and yet also asserts that "the two tablets of stone" were in it (1 Kgs 8:9 NRSV). The fact that such different interpretations of the ark exist side by side indicates that Israel never arrived at a consensus view.

In our text, v. 16 makes a comment not unlike that of 1 Kgs 8:9, suggesting that the ark is essentially a container for "the covenant" (עדת *'ēdūt*). The term *'ēdūt* is elsewhere rendered "testimony," and seems to refer to actual, physical tablets of commands, which endure and testify to and remind Israel of its solemn oath to Yahweh. Thus in this paragraph describing sanctuary furniture, the climactic statement concerns membership in covenant.

25:17-22. The second element in the tabernacle is the "mercy seat" (כפרת *kapōret*). Again we are given the precise shape and measurements, and this second object is again overlaid with gold. The term for "mercy seat" is once more a noun (*kapōret*), from the verb כפר (*kāpar*), which means to "cover." While the term itself may only mean a covering or a place of covering, the verb here means to cover over the power and danger of sin, so that the mercy seat is the place where the power of sin is covered over and neutralized. The cruciality of the term is evidenced by its recurrence in the book of Leviticus at the end of each sacrifice to be enacted by a priest. The noun is a special theological term created by this tradition, and it represents a remarkably imaginative achievement, whereby a verb has been visualized as an identifiable object. The operation of "covering" at the mercy seat is like putting a sealer over a contaminated substance so that it can no longer infect or threaten. Thus "mercy seat" is a place or an object that functions to overcome the danger from sin, wherein sin is treated almost as a material, physical threat. There is a considerable theological development from the primitive, substantive notion of "cover" to the relational notion of conciliation, but they are held together in the term *atone*. The meaning of the cult object depends on interpretive decision, because the text tells us nothing about the function of the tabernacle. In Lev 16:2-16, however, the term is used exactly to describe the liturgic process whereby the power of guilt is overcome in *Yom Kippur*, the day of "covering," i.e., the Day of Atonement.

The mercy seat is encompassed by two "cherubim," perhaps a carving of two winged creatures hovering over the mercy seat. The cherubim are members of the court of the holy God (not innocent, overweight children as in artistic portrayals of cherubs) who function to signify the presence, sovereignty, and protection of God. The visual portrayal of cherubim witnesses to a "peopled" place that mediates a God who is distantly transcendent but palpably available.

The description culminates again in an interpretive-promissory comment (vv. 21-22). Again, there is reference to the "testimony" (*'ēdūt*) in the ark. The mercy seat, however, is the place where God will meet (יעד *yā'ad*) Moses. More than a place of deposit, the purpose of the ark and the mercy seat is "meeting"! Perhaps even more astonishing than the prospect of the meeting is its purpose. While the language of "mercy seat" might suggest a covering of guilt and the gift of forgiveness, the purpose of the meeting is "I will command you to the Israelites" (v. 22)—i.e., the purpose is to issue commandments.

This remarkable interpretation of the "meeting" suggests two things. First, the cult tradition believes that obedience is indeed possible; this tradition is not mired down in a heavy preoccupation with guilt. Second, there is no ground for separating the cultic and the ethical. The purpose of the cult is mediation of torah, to assure that the community of Moses will be a torah-keeping community. The "mercy seat" is concerned with the giving of the torah, itself a profound act of mercy in Israel!

25:23-30. The third piece of furniture in the tabernacle is a table made of acacia wood. Again, we are told not only of its exact measurements, but also about the vessels that are to sit upon it—plates, dishes, flagons, and bowls, all of which are to be gold plated.

Yet a third time (as in vv. 16, 22), the paragraph that contains specifications of measurement and luxurious construction culminates in a statement that gives a theological twist to the provision (v. 30). The purpose of the table is for "the bread of presence," i.e., the bread of faces. The text tells us nothing about this bread. It takes no great imagination to see that the bread is in some sense sacramental, but we are not told more than that. Most plausibly, it is bread that the human community eats (with God) as "table fellowship." Or it may be bread that the people provide for the "care and feeding" of God. Either way, it bespeaks presence and, perhaps, solidarity between God and Israel.

25:31-40. The fourth piece of furniture is a lampstand. It is described in enormous detail, more than the preceding three objects. It is, indeed, an elaborate object, and it as well is to be decorated with pure gold. We are not told much of its precise function, but that perhaps may be taken as obvious. The concluding statement is that it should "give light" (v. 37). It is plausible that the light is understood to have liturgical, sacramental significance, but nothing is said of that. More likely, in a context where there are no other lights and where the darkness is peopled and enormously threatening, the practical function of light and its sacramental significance cannot be easily divided. The light creates a safe place in a world of threat. The light witnesses to and presents a place that God has carved out of the dangerous darkness, where God's good rule is fully established, and where Israel may be fully at ease in well-being.

The final verse of the chapter pertains not only to the last paragraph concerning the lampstand, but to all four items named and described (v. 40). For all four objects, there is a pattern: a visible, precise intention that Moses and the community are permitted to see or imagine. Thus the articulation of these four items is an act of hope and a promise of how the worship and the world of Israel will be when a proper context for community is established.

REFLECTIONS

For many readers, entry into the second half of Exodus is rather like stepping into a dark, dank archive. The texts at first glance appear remote and opaque, without discernible windows of interpretation. This impression may be acutely strong among Christians who imagine that such old texts have been overcome in the Christian gospel, and especially among Protestants who are in any case suspicious of ritual punctiliousness and precision.

The problem of engaging these texts is larger, however, than simply Christian supersessionism or Protestant negativity toward cult. The problem is rooted in modernity's impatience with any notion of holy mystery, or with any offer of holy mystery and holy presence that requires discipline, order, and planning. Or, said another way, modernity is restless with any offer of transcendent meaning and power that must be mediated when, in fact, this text is all about the possibility and the problem of such mediation.

It may be nearly impossible to do so, but the interpreter should attempt to hear these texts as though for the first time (as indeed they will be for many readers)! Imagine that in the context of covenant at Mt. Sinai God should take care to think through, speak about, and propose modes and procedures whereby Israel can count upon with certitude a rendezvous with the Holy One. There is, in our own time and place, a deep hunger and yearning for reliable contact with the holy mystery of God. This text invites the community to imagine that meeting and to receive the offer of presence given in the text.

The text makes two fundamental affirmations. First, such a meeting is possible. Second, such presence is not "immediately" available, but is mediated through the regularized disciplines of the community. Such an articulation does not deny that there may be immediate meetings, but no textual procedure can produce, assure, or generate that possibility. This is presence for "ordinary times" when there is no crisis, but simply the deep, abiding hunger for that which can satisfy and give rest to the restless. This text affirms that there is in God a counterpart to human restlessness—a willingness to meet.

1. As the interpreter moves from liberation to presence, from recital to blueprint, it is worth asking whether there are any counterpoints between the two parts of the text and between cultic offer and contemporary need. I suggest the following possibilities for the four cultic objects listed in this chapter.

The purpose of the **ark** is to provide a place for the "testimonies" ('ēdût) that give Israel its membership in a community with God. The "testimonies" may be commandments or other tokens of identity, but in any case they witness to and voice a peculiar identity as the people of Yahweh.[160] Such a witness needs care and special housing. This special people with this visible membership is what came into being at Sinai, when the slave community was taken as "my treasured possession out of all the peoples," "a priestly kingdom and a holy nation" (19:5-6). That special identity depended on and still depends on hearing and obeying (19:5).

Prior to the hearing, prior to the belonging, there was no special people, no priestly kingdom, no holy nation. Prior to Sinai this was at best a "community of Hebrews." The phrase is almost an oxymoron, for at best to be "Hebrew" meant to have no social identity and no membership except as "surplus" population. Or at worst, this people was a "mixed crowd" (12:38), without identity of any kind. Thus the ark contains the "testimonies" that give membership through which Israel resists being merely a nondescript, powerless, vulnerable "mixed crowd."

---

160. See Frank Moore Cross, *Canaanite Myth and Hebrew Epic: Essays in the History of the Religion of Israel* (Cambridge: Harvard University Press, 1973) 311-14.

The ark of membership (testimony) is *still* an offer in God's fidelity to lost, isolated people who not only want a larger belonging, but who must have a larger belonging in order for their humanness not to shrivel. The ark articulates signs, assurances, and reminders of belonging to a community in a mass of displaced persons.

The **mercy seat** has as its explicit purpose a meeting to receive commandments. It has as its implicit purpose covering—i.e., activity that makes possible reconciliation and forgiveness. In its two functions in relation to *obedience* and *communion*, the mercy seat offers life to this people that is peculiarly congenial to Yahweh, who both commands and treasures.

The Hebrews in Pharaoh's brickyards were exactly a pre-mercy-seat people. Instead of the offer of reconciliation and communion made possible through the mercy seat, the pre-liberated slaves were destined for a life of alienation, not only from their over-lords, but, according to 2:13-15, from each other as well.

The Hebrew slave people had no religious vehicles of their own, no symbolic apparatus with which to break the vicious cycles of abuse and self-hatred. Of course, it is the work of the slave owner to keep the symbolic life of the slaves thin and poverty-stricken, so that there can never be an act of sacramental imagination to let folks begin again. In the mercy seat, Israel now has a vehicle, given in God's graciousness, for periodically beginning again, not only in life with God but in the community of economic reality. (On the economic dimension of כפר [*kāpar*], see Lev 6:1-7.)

The mercy seat is *still* an offer in God's graciousness for life to begin again, out beyond the vicious cycles of dehumanization so visible and powerful among us. "Modern" folk tend to be fated folk, because we believe there is no new thing yet to be enacted. New beginnings cannot be willed; they must arise from great initiatives and gestures of holy otherness. Having eliminated holiness in our modernist narcissism, we cannot imagine how that newness can come. Here, however, provision is made precisely for newness that arises from God's inscrutable, palpable, self-giving presence.

The **table** has on it perpetually the **Bread of Presence.** Whether an offer of bread to God or an invitation to eat in the presence of God, this community has at the center of its symbolic life an enduring sign, offer, and promise of nourishment. In this symbolization, Israel moves from the planned, enforced scarcity of Pharaoh to the guaranteed plenty of Yahweh.

In the completed form of the text, it may be that this table looks back especially to the gift of "bread from heaven" in chapter 16, bread gathered and eaten so that there need never be hunger again. It is a long leap, and the text gives no hint of any intended connection between the two. The reiterated focus on bread nonetheless lets one ponder the two texts simultaneously. Entry into the liturgic presence of Yahweh is a sure offer of nourishment that the world (of Pharaoh) cannot give.

The table of the Bread of the Presence needs to be seen, held up (blessed and broken), in order to remind the community that it is always enough, with seven or twelve baskets left over.

As a community, we are in the grip of an ideology of scarcity. We are either short on bread, or we have plenty of bread but are short on joy and freedom. Our scarcity leads us to do brutal things to each other. The bread of the table, and the Christian extrapolation from the table to eucharist, are about an abundance that breaks our parsimonious fears.

The **lampstand** is in order that there will be "light in the space in front of it." While illuminating the sanctuary, such light is never mere illumination. It is a reference laden with surplus significance, inevitably alluding to God's power to push back darkness and to defeat the death-threatening force of chaos, which is all around in the darkness.

The Israelites who make this lampstand for the tabernacle are no strangers to the crisis of light and darkness. No doubt they remember the "wonder of darkness" (10:21-29) and recall with delight that "all the Israelites had light where they lived" (10:23).

The "darkness," in the exodus narrative, and the wonder of light for the Israelites, concerns the power of God to create a safe place for life in a body of death. The God of this text can "form light and create darkness" (Isa 45:7 NRSV). Around the lampstand, with its glow of well-being, Israel can remember the darkness and the Egyptians who disappeared in it.

The lampstand is *still* an offer of the light-giving God to "people who walk in darkness." The metaphor of darkness bespeaks the endless procession of fears, hurts, hates, enslavements, and despairs that beset us. Already in this text, there is a "light of the world" (cf. John 9:5). There need be no bewildering, terrifying lostness, and no terror before the power of death. The world, in the scope of this light, is redefined as a safe place. The lamp of God gives light that culminates in *shalom*.

2. As the text stands in the book of Exodus, this speech of Yahweh "shows the pattern," anticipating chaps. 35–40, wherein Moses will implement the commands for the tabernacle of presence. The prospective power of this "showing" is not, however, completed or exhausted in these chapters. It continues to operate well beyond the book of Exodus in a way we may call eschatological. Israel and the church continue to wait for the time when the full worship imagined by God will be actualized.

This powerful text thus is generative of intensive anticipation, which comes to its fullest, most lyrical expression in the book of Revelation. This community looks with confidence to the time when the full worship of God will be perfectly established, and all the faithful will share in the joy and in the presence. Thus the whole of this literature is cast in a doxological frame. Revelation 4:1-6 offers a vision of "what must take place after this," which is a vision of the throne of God and "seven burning torches" (lamps, Rev 4:5). In 11:19, the ark is in the temple of God, which is in the heavens. The tent (tabernacle) is in heaven, where the temple is filled with glory (15:5-8). And in the final lyrical vision of "the end," God's own self has become the light (21:24; 22:5), and God's dwelling place (tabernacle) is in the midst of the human community (cf. 21:3-6*a*).

In relation to the book of Exodus, it is instructive that in Rev 11:19 and 15:5 the temple is the source of plagues, which suggests a way in that the two parts of the book of Exodus are held together. Just as chaps. 1–15 are dominated by *plagues*, so also chaps. 25–31 are dominated by *presence*. Both are manifestations of God's sovereign power and God's utter commitment to this people.

The book of Revelation thus relies heavily on the theology of presence in the Priestly tradition of Exodus. It anticipates that the full, perfect, joyous, lyrical goal of humanity is to be in the unending liturgy of praise and celebration, very close to the throne and in intimate contact with the holy Presence. This accent on worship as the quintessence of existence in God's creation is precisely what Exodus 25 intends to evoke and implement.

3. This powerful eschatological anticipation of the "not yet" of worship in the book of Revelation is claimed as "already" in the epistle to the Hebrews, which asserts that in the person of Jesus, the new, full worship of God has already come into existence. Hebrews 9:1-12 makes a powerful claim for the decisiveness and distinctiveness of Jesus in the worship of the holy God. That claim depends for its articulation precisely on the cultic functions of Exodus 25, although it moves in a different order: lampstand, table, bread of presence, tent (tabernacle), cherubim, and mercy seat. These are all attempts at disclosing the way into the holy of holies. This worship arrangement, however, "cannot perfect the conscience of the worshiper" (Heb 9:9 NRSV), but in Christ "a greater and perfect tent" has been offered that is a "new covenant" in "his own blood" (see Heb 9:11-15).

There are, of course, serious problems concerning "supersessionism" pervading the letter to the Hebrews. The point to stress, however, is that liturgy becomes both a way of speaking about the significance of Christ and a metaphor for the fullness and joy of human life. The letter to the Hebrews wants to show forth the inadequacy of the tabernacle arrangement; yet, it cannot speak of the new adequacy of Jesus except in those very same categories.

In both the "not yet" of Revelation and the "already" of Hebrews, it is insisted that worship is what human life is all about and that communion with God is the fulfillment of all human longing. Such a notion of *homo liturgicus* is a polemical alternative to contemporary notions of the human person as maker, as player, as consumer, and as fighter.

EXODUS 26:1-37, TABERNACLE CURTAINS AND FRAME

COMMENTARY

Yahweh's initial speech to Moses continues to "show the pattern" (cf. 25:8, 40). After the more specific furnishings listed in 25:10-39, the speech now returns to the main subject: the tabernacle (cf. 25:8-9). What is called a "pattern" in 25:9 and 40 is here referred to as a "plan" (משפט *mišpāṭ*, 26:30), but the intention is the same.

This chapter contains exceedingly technical and sometimes quite obscure instructions about the proper design and construction of the cultic apparatus.[161] Two dimensions are clear. First, there is care and precision in detail, so that its builders will have no misgivings about what is to be done or how the parts relate to each other. For this concern, the "blueprint" employs vocabulary of curtains, loops, clasps, frames, pegs, bases, bars, and pillars. Not much is to be learned from an analysis of that special vocabulary.

Second, the design intends that the tabernacle should embody the wealth, treasure, and luxury of the community (cf. 25:3-7). For that concern, an unusual vocabulary is also employed with particular reference to colors.[162] These terms for colors (blue, purple, crimson) are rarely used elsewhere in the OT. We may note, however, that their use is characteristically poignant where it is used. Thus see Judg 8:26, wherein Gideon collects the wealth of Israel, but promptly uses it for self-aggrandizement, so that "all Israel

prostituted themselves" (Judg 8:27 NRSV). And in Jer 10:9, the same vocabulary issues as a vigorous polemic against false idols, well-decorated images that are in fact powerless and false.

As color terms are used in religious polemic, so they are also employed in political critique. Thus the king of Tyre is criticized for his arrogant extravagance and pride in making himself and his realm beautiful (Ezek 27:7; cf. also v. 16). In both religious and political criticism, this extravagance is seen to be not only unseemly, but also religiously unacceptable.

In the narrative of Esther, however, we can see a more delicate and complex use of the terminology. In Esth 1:2-8, the king in Susa is critically described as extravagant and cynically self-serving. In this case, however, the narrative goes on to dramatize an inversion of political power, whereby the persecuted Jews come to well-being and prosperity. Mordecai, faithful Jew, is then extravagantly clothed in all the finery previously possessed by the condemned Haman (Esth 8:15-16). Thus the text is able to affirm that what may be seductive and destructive, when properly and faithfully appropriated, is not only acceptable but is a celebrative and legitimate way to express honor.

Thus the pattern given to Moses intends that God's sanctuary be outfitted in the most luxurious way possible, because the sanctuary becomes the promise and embodiment of the new world of abundant blessing and

161. On the technical matters, see Menahem Haran, "The Priestly Image of the Tabernacle," *HUCA* 36 (1965) 191-226.
162. See Athalya Brenner, *Colour Terms in the Old Testament*, JSOTSup 21 (Sheffield: JSOT, 1982).

well-being. There is nothing too good or too costly for the Holy One.

The tradition of Moses is rightly known among us as a tradition of ethical rigor. Here we are able to see that, in its completed form, it is one of great aesthetic concern and sensitivity as well. This part of the tradition does not focus on the "ear of obedience," but on the "eye of loveliness."[163]

In the midst of artistic attentiveness and aesthetic extravagance, we may note especially

163. Samuel Terrien, *The Elusive Presence: Toward a New Biblical Theology,* Religious Perspectives (San Francisco: Harper & Row, 1978), has made the tension between "ear" and "eye" definitional for his understanding of biblical theology. The same contrast is evident in the contrast David Tracy makes between "proclamation" and "manifestation," behind which stands the distinction of Paul Ricoeur concerning a "hermeneutics of suspicion" and a "hermeneutics of retrieval."

the prescribed curtain (פרכת *pārōket*), which is different from the more numerous curtains (יריעת *yĕrî'ot*) earlier listed (vv. 33-34). This curtain (*pārōket*) provides for a separation between "the holy place" and "the most holy place" (i.e., the holy of holiness), wherein are housed the ark and the mercy seat. While we may detect in this design gradations of holiness that inevitably lead to elitism and special priestly privilege, none of that danger is noted here. Rather, what is intended is the creation of the most protected, awesome place to host and entertain properly the very self-giving of God. No doubt the screen was proposed with only the best of liturgical intentions, and it seems first of all to be appreciated for that intention.

REFLECTIONS

1. Worship, the hosting of the holy, requires order, discipline, planning, and forethought. To be sure, there are dangers in excessive preoccupation with liturgical niceties, a danger well and regularly noted in both the prophets and the tradition of the Reformation. While that danger is real, this text invites reflection in the opposite direction. The tradition of the priests, while no doubt aware of prophetic strictures against excessive preoccupation with worship details, nonetheless wants to guard against casual, slovenly, easy access to the holy.

Of course, how one assesses this text depends not only on one's context, but also on one's view of God. If we take God to be a royal sovereign who is to be approached with awe, then care must be taken. The notion of entering into an awesome throne room is, to be sure, not the only imagery of the Bible for worship, but it is an image that carries considerable importance, both for the text and in relation to human yearning.

2. Worship is an exercise in extravagance that depends on the willing generosity of the community and that, as an act of hope, lives in tension with what may have been the leanness of the community in its actual ordering of everyday life. All of us are aware of the abuses of a self-indulgent church that has built great golden edifices out of the bitter sweat of peasant offerings. The text, however, does not focus on the ethics of care for the poor. Rather, it engages in an act of hope that believes the world "in here," in the sanctuary, must be luxurious in contrast to the world "out there," which is mean, thin, and hopeless. Such a liturgic strategy may, of course, be escapist; but it may also function as an antidote to despair, keeping alive a vision of the "other world" of God in which we are welcomed as beloved members.

Such "misdirected extravagance" calls to mind the interaction of Jesus with the woman who anointed him with precious oil (Mark 14:3-9). The woman extravagantly uses the oil to anoint Jesus, presumably for his death. The disciples protest that the money is better used in the service of the poor. Jesus, however, remonstrates his disciples. Something similar operates in this tabernacle provision, which asks for opulence in the celebration of God's holy presence.

3. Attention to the aesthetic dimension of the tabernacle (design, symmetry, color, luxurious materials) invites reflection on worship as a practice of the "beauty of holiness." Our technological, consumeristic society inclines to turn everything (even art objects) into commodities with utilitarian values. As part of that tendency, self-indulgent religion turns God into a commodity and worship into a calculating utilitarianism. The "beauty of holiness" by contrast enacts the truth that God is not a useful commodity. Rather, worship is an end in itself.

Hans-Georg Gadamar underscores three dimensions of the artistic that pertain to our subject.[164] (1) Art is the play and practice of *excess*, the human activity of moving beyond what is managed, to what is inscrutably surplus and transcendent. (2) Art is the act of making oneself "*at home* in the world," where one is largely and deeply homeless. (3) Art is a festival that draws isolated individuals into *unity*.

The tabernacle in the wilderness (exile?) serves such purposes. The design is clearly a *proposal for excess*. Because it is mobile in the wilderness, it is also a *home for displaced persons* who have no other place to belong. And no doubt by offering itself as the core home for exiles, it intends to draw all the scattered, conflicted elements of the exiled community together *into a unity*. In all three ways, the activity and function of the tabernacle propose an alternative existence.

These three points from Gadamar provide contact with the pastoral realities of our own situation of faith. Worship can be an invitation and practice of an "otherness" *beyond fearful utilitarianism*. Worship can be a place of overriding *belonging at home*, even in the face of our powerful and insistent homelessness. Worship can be *a post-rational embrace of oneness* in a world where we are so deeply and angrily divided. Worship that is to enact such transformative possibility must indeed be aesthetically rich.

4. The reference to the "curtain" (פרכת *pārōket*, LXX καταπέτασμα *katapetasma*) that partitions the holy place and the holy of holies (vv. 33-35) directs our attention to Matt 27:51 and Hebrews 10:20.

In Matt 27:51, the cosmic upheaval evoked by the crucifixion of Jesus causes the tearing of "the curtain" (*katapetasma*) of the Temple. There is no doubt that this text directly refers to Exod 26:33-35. The original use of the "curtain" is to make the holy of holies the locus of the core of God's holiness in all the world—the epicenter of cosmic reality. This curtain, never intended to be a barrier, is now destroyed in order to permit access again to God's holiness. In the process of destroying the curtain, the whole of the "system of holiness" is brutally dismantled.

In Heb 10:19-23, the same claim as Matt 27:51 is made for the person of Jesus, who made possible "the new and living way that he opened for us through the curtain" (Heb 10:20). This use serves the larger argument of the letter to the Hebrews that Jesus has displaced the system of worship in the Levitical system.

The way in which Matthew 27 and Hebrews 10 play against Exodus 26 lets us see that Jesus' death is understood in the early church as a largely subversive act, deeply in touch with the institutional context of established religion. Without this reference in Exodus 26, the Gospel portrayal makes little sense. More broadly, the connection of these texts suggests the way in which well-intended religious devices become distorted in their function. The gospel exercises a profound critical function against even our best enhancements of God, which often turn out to be domestications and manipulations.

164. Hans-Georg Gadamar, *The Relevance of the Beautiful and Other Essays* (Cambridge: Cambridge University Press, 1987).

EXODUS 27:1-21, ALTAR, COURT, LAMP

COMMENTARY

God's speech to Moses continues to show Moses the "pattern" for right worship. In this chapter, three further provisions are made for worship: an altar (vv. 1-8), a court for the tabernacle (vv. 9-19), and a lamp, which will be kept burning for all time (vv. 20-21).

27:1-8. The altar of the tabernacle is now mentioned for the first time, as a part of the larger pattern from the mountain (v. 8). This altar is quite in contrast to that authorized by the earlier tradition of 20:24-26, which was to be plain and simple. While its horns were likely ornamental, or serve a symbolic function now lost to us, they come to provide a place of political refuge (cf. 1 Kgs 2:28).

The altar is to be fully equipped with everything necessary for a place of sacrifice, though once again nothing is said about its proper function. (In 30:27-28, a distinction is made between the "altar of incense," described in 30:1-10, and an "altar of burnt offering." While burnt offerings are not mentioned in our passage, presumably this is the altar referred to there.) The design is careful and precise. We may notice that the overlay is of bronze and not of gold, as are most of the other objects in the tabernacle. This suggests that there is a gradation of values whereby the altar is not as important as the other objects covered with gold.

This terse "blueprint" gives us little room or warrant for the theological purpose of the altar. It will become evident in Leviticus 1–7 that the altar is for sacrifices. Moreover, the sacrifices seem to serve two functions: to acknowledge sovereignty ("to glorify God") and to enjoy communion ("enjoy God forever"). But nothing is made here of these characteristic actions.

The inventory of utensils in v. 3 calls attention to two other texts that connect our text to more specific social contexts. In 1 Kgs 7:40-45 (cf. vv. 46-51), a closely paralleled list belongs to the construction and equipment of the Jerusalem Temple. Two things are evident. First, all of this equipment is linked to and evidence for Solomon's enormous opulence. Second, the production of all of these vessels is done by Hiram of Tyre, reflecting Solomon's international connections and likely attesting as well his religious syncretism.

The second telling reference to these utensils is in 2 Kgs 25:13-17 (cf. Jer 52:17-23). It is reported that the Babylonians carry away everything portable from the Temple in Jerusalem. Moreover, Ezra 1:7-11 reports that under Cyrus, the vessels are restored to the reestablished place in Jerusalem. The removal of the vessels signifies not only avarice on the part of Babylon but also ritual humiliation of Yahweh, whose own "treasures" are now confiscated and taken up by a more powerful god. Further, as Peter Ackroyd has seen, the fact that the text reports in detail the return of the vessels to Jerusalem indicates that the Temple utensils function as more than ornaments or equipment.[165] They are, in fact, theological symbols of continuity for a community facing severe discontinuity and tokens of God's resilient fidelity in a time of enormous danger and displacement.

Taken together, 1 Kgs 7:40-45 and 2 Kgs 25:13-17 show that the Temple vessels play a pivotal symbolic role at the beginning of the royal period (the time of Solomon) and at the end of the royal period (exile), articulating, respectively, both the origin and termination of legitimated worship. When read in the light of these texts, moreover, it is evident that our text carries symbolic significance that is enormously vulnerable to historical-political vagaries.

27:9-19. The building of the court of the tabernacle again focuses on structure and design and not at all on its function. Again we note the symmetry and detail of the design, and the fact that it is all of bronze (not gold). In v. 16 we note two special features of the court. First, it is to have a screen (מסך *māsāk*), which again suggests the protectedness of the space and, perhaps, gradation of access and privilege. Second, only the screen is detailed

---

165. Peter R. Ackroyd, "The Temple Vessels: A Continuity Theme," in *Studies in the Religion of Ancient Israel,* ed. by the Board of the Quarterly VTSup 23 (1972) 166-81.

with color through fine needlework. Artistic sensibility is much less evident here than in the preceding chapter on the tabernacle.

27:20-21. The third provision of this chapter is the maintenance of "the light," not to be confused with the lampstand (25:31-39). This particular instruction is a departure from the mode of discourse thus far in chaps. 25–27, for it moves away from design to speak about maintenance. The introduction of questions of maintenance necessarily entails delineation of personnel for the first time. Thus in these two verses there is a significant change of subject. Maintenance involves two functions. On the one hand, the people are to provide pure olive oil for the light; pure olive oil is the offer of one's best, and it likely assured the clearest, most reliable light.

On the other hand, "Aaron and his sons," no doubt a priestly order, are for the first time marked as the ones who will maintain the lamp. This mention of Aaron does not concern a person or a brother of Moses, but a priestly order and office. If this mention grants to "Aaron" special privilege in cultic function, then one may see how this text serves to enhance the authority that "Aaron"

claims as distinct from and perhaps in conflict with other priestly orders (on which see chap. 32).[166]

As with the altar and the court, we are told nothing here of a function or intention for the lamp. It is plausible, however, to suggest three related dimensions to the lamp. First, the light is practical. Second, however, because the light is to be kept burning regularly (תמיד *tāmîd*, "constantly"), it is clear that this light is more than functional. Its symbolism is to provide a safe, reliable place in a world filled with ominous threat. Moreover, if we follow the suggestion of Kearney and Blenkinsopp, the perpetual light signifies the order, safety, and well-being of creation.[167] The tabernacle is the "dry land" in the flood of chaos. Third, the light bespeaks the very presence of God, a bespeaking made possible by the attentiveness of the priests. It is the cooperation of the lay community and the priestly office that does the human work of signifying, actualizing, and assuring the presence of God.

166. On the priestly rivalries, see Cross, *Canaanite Myth and Hebrew Epic*, 195-215, and more broadly Aelred Cody, *A History of Old Testament Priesthood* (Rome: Pontifical Biblical Institute, 1969).
167. See esp. Kearney, "Creation and Liturgy," 375.

REFLECTIONS

1. The altar is essential to the public life of this liberated, covenanted community. Israel must have a place where it regularly submits in gratitude to the sovereignty of God. As in all of these instructions, Israel has long known that *the actual practice* of the presence in and through these objects is essential. It will not do to "think" the presence or intend it; it must be done in bodily engagement.

2. The references to the Temple utensils in 1 Kings 7 and 2 Kings 25, and by extrapolation the entire cultic apparatus, invites reflection upon the ways in which Temple furniture, which arises in concrete circumstance, takes on transcendent power and authority. The theological issue to be explored is the way concrete religious experience acquires or receives transcendental authority, so that a functional arrangement becomes a non-negotiable presence. That theological principle is never confronted in the abstract. It meets us in the concreteness of an altar Bible, a pew hymnal, a picture of Jesus, or a memorial piano.

These texts might permit us to see both the value and the danger in such an unavoidable human process. The value of investing the ordinary with transcendent significance is essential to the development of culture, especially religious culture. The process protects life from becoming finally utilitarian or cheaply relativistic. The danger of such absolutizing, which I infer from 1 Kings 7 and 2 Kings 25, is that a community can take these objects with such seriousness that it assigns ultimate meaning to what is not ultimate. I imagine that the adjudication of symbolizing and criticism, of valuing and seeing the danger, is an endless human process. No doubt in the circumstance of a jeopardized exilic community, exactly a "hermeneutic of retrieval" is urgent. It is precisely the retrieval of symbol that mediates to this community a clear sense of presence.

3. The light is a liturgic gesture of safety and well-being in a world under threat. While the light assures God's presence and God's governance, there is a strand of spirituality in the Bible that insists not only that the light witnesses to God but that, in the end, God is the light. In the Fourth Gospel, the theme of light recurs (see, e.g., John 1:8-9; 8:12). Other NT texts (e.g. 1 John 1:5; Rev 22:5) push even beyond such christological claims, echoing the doxological affirmation of Ps 27:1 that God "is my light and my salvation" (NRSV).

Revelation 21:23-24 plays with the duality of "light" and "lamp" (as we have seen that duality already in Exod 27:20): "And the city has no need of sun or moon to shine on it, for the glory of God is its light, and its lamp is the Lamb. The nations will walk by its light, and the kings of the earth will bring their glory into it" (NRSV).

This text manages to make an affirmation about God as light, yet it uses the same imagery to express a distinct christological claim. This lyrical affirmation anticipates that the power of chaos and evil (in the form of darkness) finally will be banished when God's light prevails everywhere. Thus the light in the Temple is a harbinger of the new creation. That light, so well maintained, anticipates that God's light will move out from the tabernacle, so that the presence will pervade the entire earth.

EXODUS 28:1-43, PRIESTLY VESTMENTS

COMMENTARY

The mention of Aaron and his sons in 27:21 changes the subject of Yahweh's instruction to Moses. The central concern is no longer the objects for worship but the priesthood. This long chapter is primarily preoccupied with the proper appearance of the priests and only incidentally with their function. Taken critically, this text appears to be a self-serving method of enhancing priestly prestige, wealth, and power. Taken theologically, the priest is the one who shall enter into the holy presence of God, an awesome and dreadful undertaking.

The chapter begins with a summary about equipping Aaron for his office (vv. 1-5) and concludes with a like statement concerning the sons of Aaron (vv. 40-43). The material between these two sections deals in close detail with priestly garb: ephod (vv. 6-14), breastplate (vv. 15-30), robe (vv. 31-35), rosette (vv. 36-38), tunic, and turban (v. 39). The way in which these paragraphs grow progressively shorter may be evidence that the priestly inventory received *ad hoc* additions as time went on, as the expectations of

priestly garb continued to develop in more ambitious and punctilious ways.

28:1-5. Aaron, with his sons, is to serve Yahweh as priest. It is decisive that in this speech of Yahweh, they are called to "serve me." That is, the priestly office is not concerned first of all with Israel; the priests exist for the sake of Yahweh.

Unlike the early period, Israel in the later period of the OT, with its profound sense of dislocation, works overtime to be sure that legitimating genealogies are clear and in order. This concern is likely related to the crisis of legitimacy alluded to in chapter 27. No genealogy is provided for Aaron in this text, because in 6:14-25, Aaron is already fully connected to Levi, and his authority here can be assumed. The four sons of Aaron, who are named in 6:23, reappear here.

In other narratives related to the sons of Aaron, we may distinguish two pairs of sons. On the one hand, Nadab and Abihu are quickly disposed of in Lev 10:1-5, for what appears to be an unauthorized priestly act (cf. Num 3:4). We may imagine this narrative of execution is reflective of struggles between priestly orders concerning authority and power.

On the other hand, Ithamar and, especially, Eleazar continue to be important for the function and history of the priesthood. In 1 Chr 24:1-6 these two sons are assigned considerable priestly power and are said to be the progenitors of the later (so far as this text stands) priesthood of Zadok and Abiathar. In particular, Eleazar is the successor to Aaron (cf. Num 20:25-28), who functions along with Moses (Num 26:1, 3, 63) and Joshua (Num 27:18-23).

The other element in this introduction is a concern that Aaron as priest should be properly clothed. The elliptical language of v. 3 (not fully reflected in English translations) suggests that the proper vestments contributed to the holiness that is acknowledged in consecration. The comprehensive catalogue of vv. 3-5 suggests that the dress of the great priest is carefully arranged in every detail, and that only the very best, most extravagant materials may be used. It is a matter of serious concern to the community that Aaron be made into the most impressive, attractive official possible, one who is "glorious in adornment" (v. 2).

The body of the chapter now consists for the most part in characterizing in detail elements of the inventory of v. 4. Very little is said about the function of these pieces of dress; the appearance itself counts. Five elements are named, with most of the attention given to the first two.

28:6-14 The Ephod. Nobody knows what an ephod is. Apparently it is a priestly garment, but the specificity of the apparel is known only from biblical texts that are notoriously unclear and often contradictory. It is enough for us that the ephod was worn to announce and enhance the authority of Aaron and the Aaronides. We may observe two important matters in its description. First, it is exotically decorated in gold, precious stones, and rich coloring. Second, inscribed upon it are the names of the "twelve sons of Israel"—i.e., the twelve tribes (cf. 1:1-5). Moreover, the inscribed stones are said to be "stones of remembrance." In its intention, the ephod serves to bring Israel, with all its generations gathered in a moment, into the holy presence of God, where Israel can be reconciled, basking in light that it can find nowhere else.

28:15-30 The Breastplate. This priestly garment again is exceedingly odd in its design, and is known only here and in Lev 8:6-9, where Moses finally gives Aaron all these authorized insignia of office and authority. Again we meet with the two features we have come to expect in description: precision of design and extravagance of ornamentation.

Having become accustomed by now to extravagant decoration, this particular object is nonetheless relatively excessive. The text proposes that here the community must mobilize all its wealth and the best of its imagination. All the best materials and all the most dramatic colors are to be used. What is most striking, however, is the symmetrical list of twelve precious stones, all contained in gold.

The vocabulary of these stones is exceedingly obscure, with many of the terms unknown in the OT beyond this cluster of texts. We may refer to three other places in the Bible where mention is made of some of these stones. A like list occurs in Ezek 27:16 to characterize the rich commerce of Tyre. The list is used to state the huge economic success of Tyre and to condemn it as arrogance. In Job 28:16-19 is a list of precious stones used as a foil to assert that wisdom from God is of more value than any of these stones. In Cant 5:10-16, such language is used as a way to express the loveliness and beauty of "my beloved." In all three usages, the terms voice the extreme case—extreme arrogance, extreme value of wisdom, extreme loveliness. Aaron is to be clothed in the extremes of pride, value, and loveliness. Israel has at its disposal no better language with which to make that point.

Now we may rightly ask, How could this language be used for this community, either by the tradition in the wilderness, where the text places itself, or in the exile, where it is placed by critical scholarship? In either canonical or critical reading, the community is in a situation of little wealth and surplus. If this community of erstwhile slaves (or of subsequently marginated people) has no such wealth, then the cultic extravagance, or rhetoric about alleged cultic extravagance, is an act of hope whereby Israel, in its worship and imagination, takes on a splendor that the world will nowhere else permit it. This community, permitted so little, endows its priest with "glorious adornment" (v. 2) as a vigorous, hopeful protest against its concrete context.

As we have come to expect, we are told little about the breastplate's liturgic function. The only hint of function we have is the mention of Urim and Thummim, which will be the work and trust of Aaron (v. 30). While the meaning of Urim and Thummim is enigmatic, it probably refers to lots (dice) that are used to determine the will of God. In Deut 33:8-9, the Urim and Thummim are entrusted to Levi, so that in our text it is the Aaronide line of the house of Levi that claims and administers the lots.

This priesthood has enormous power, because it is entrusted to make known the will of God, discerned precisely through this priestly mechanism.[168] The breastplate is apparently garb that makes the lots visible and enhances their authority. As the ephod is to bring all of Israel into the presence of God, so the breastplate, filled with all the names, brings the purpose of God fully into the company of Israel.

28:31-35 The Robe. The priest is to be dressed in a way worthy of entering into the awesome presence of the holy God. Verse 35 adds a note that is odd and enigmatic. In a descriptive account that accents the visual, the "sound" (קול *qôl*, "voice") of the robe is emphasized. Presumably the bells are to sound according to the priest's movement, with the sound indicating his coming and going. Such sounds will at least signal that the priest is moving about, doing his work. Perhaps the sound related to coming and going is concerned with access to the holy for the people.

The statement becomes even more enigmatic in the last clause, which takes us completely by surprise: "that he may not die." This suggests that the work of the priest is a dangerous, life-and-death matter. We do not know whether his dysfunction means he will be struck down by God or destroyed by the people. One way or the other, the priests had better get it right with the bells.

168. Pixley, *On Exodus*, 200, speaks of the "hegemonic function" of priestly religion.

28:36-38 The Rosette. This reference is to a blossom or shining object, some kind of golden ornament worn on the priest's forehead (turban). The insignia on it, "Holy to Yahweh," identifies the unambiguous, unqualified loyalty and devotion of the priest. The phrase suggests that "Aaron" is not a priest to the people but is concerned only for the glory of Yahweh.

Every contact within the holiness of Yahweh, however, is freighted with risk and dangers. The risk of "Aaron" is that if the offering is not suitable, the priest, and not the people, is at fault. The purpose of the priest's activity, and therefore of this insignia, is to ensure that the offering "finds favor" (רצון *rāṣôn*), that it is ritually proper and, therefore, acceptable. Otherwise, the priest must be prepared to suffer the consequences.

28:39 The Tunic and Turban. The purpose of the turban is to carry the rosette. It also is to be made of fine material artistically adorned.

28:40-43. This chapter culminates in a general statement about the sons of Aaron that corresponds to vv. 1-5 concerning Aaron. We may note two triads of terms that speak about the authority and function of priesthood. The authority of Aaron and his sons is expressed in three verbs in v. 41: *anoint* (משח *māšaḥ*) *ordain,* (מלא *mālē'*i.e., "fill the hand"), and *consecrate* (קדש *qādaš*). These are roughly synonymous terms that concern investing the priests with holy power and authority. The actual ordination of Aaron and his sons is delayed until Leviticus 8–9; attention should be paid to Lev 8:6-9, which is a quite specific and intentional enactment of the commands of Exodus 28.

The future of Aaron and his sons is also expressed in a triad (v. 43). The priests are to function at "the tent of meeting, the altar, and the holy place." These are three distinct elements of the apparatus that is to ensure the real presence of God. Of the three, the most interesting is the tent. This phrase reflects a tradition different from, and likely older than, that of "tabernacle." It specifies an actual face-to-face meeting to which only priests have access, and in which they participate on behalf of the people. Moreover, in the tent of meeting, according to the older traditions, God does not reside there but comes specifically for the meeting. Thus it accents the freedom of God, who only comes to meet as God chooses. Reference to the risk of death is made again, suggesting that this is an urgent, dreadful activity, important to the community and risky for the priest (v. 43).

REFLECTIONS

1. The polity and liturgical practice centered around Aaron tends to order rather than to dynamism, to stability rather than change, to symmetrical structure rather than to liberating transformation. Thus the office of the priest is to enact, embody, and guarantee orderliness of life with God. This text is ostensibly placed in the wilderness and is taken critically to be located in exile. Both wilderness and exile are situations of extreme disorder, i.e., of chaotic conditions. One might imagine that liturgical communities in such contexts would take great care to enact order that overrides the palpable disorder of life.

Moreover, if life is to be ordered in a way that dramatically triumphs over disorder within the sphere of the cult, then the beauty, loveliness, and elegance of this lavish portrayal intend to assert the good rule of God against the meanness, ugliness, and social experience wherein life is cheap and thin. The patient, almost tedious directions for ephod, breastplate, robe, and rosette are the patient, trustful preparation for a glorious moment of epiphany when life is reconfigured in a splendor not otherwise available.

The beauty and order of the priest, moreover, are fully subsumed by the holiness of God. While Israel may be grateful for holy presence, there is here no hint of intimacy or coziness. Therefore, what Israel must have—access to the holy through the offer of beauty and order—comes only at high risk.

2. The majestic splendor and richness of the religious establishment is rarely simply liturgical and aesthetic, but it characteristically spills over into commodity fetishism, in which the risk and dread of the priestly function is overridden by the power and grandeur of the office.

Conversely, splendid adornment becomes offensive as an end in itself when the community no longer understands itself in wilderness or exile. What is not offensive in "churches of poverty" becomes offensive in "churches of affluence."

To be sure, there is no explicit word of criticism in this text. One may wonder, however, if the text is so completely without irony that one so well appointed could be under threat of death. If there is no irony here, then at least in a canonical arrangement that moves from chaps. 25–31 to chap. 32 (admittedly a different textual tradition), it is clear that "Aaron" is indeed seduced by his own "glorious adornment." Thus the full affirmation and the devastating critique of Aaron live close together. The affirmation, the temptation, and the critique belong intrinsically to the office of priesthood and to any handler of holy things.

3. The priestly genealogy—the sense that holiness is an inherited prerogative—is here handled innocently. While the text unqualifiedly speaks of Aaron's four sons (v. 1), we know in Lev 10:1-3 that two "dropped out of ministry" for their presumptuousness. There is no inherited privilege in being holy.

4. The administration of Urim and Thummin (v. 30) suggests that the priestly office is to probe the mind of God in ways that give guidance to the people. This notation warns against two dangers. On the one hand, there is danger in assuming that there is no more to covenantal responsibility than good common sense or the "reason of this age." The priest is called to a different mode of knowledge to which only the priest has access. This is odd knowledge, indeed!

On the other hand, the device of Urim and Thummin may ensure that such priestly teaching really comes from God, and is not simply a reflection of the passions or interests of the priest. There is no complete, sure safeguard against this latter distortion, but the tradition understands the problem. For that reason, the "will of God" is mediated in ways outside mere priestly articulation.

5. The purpose of priesthood is "meeting" (v. 43). This text believes that, done well and carefully, meeting is possible. Such a way of understanding guards against both worship that is moralistic, didactic, and instructive and worship that is excessively therapeutic and narcissistic. Both didactic and therapeutic tendencies tend to *talk about* the meeting, rather than to *enact* such a meeting with this one who is profoundly holy and yet genuinely present.

6. The letter to the Hebrews finds the imagery of this priesthood poignant for articulating the claims of Jesus Christ (Heb 10:11-25). It is there insisted that Jesus did decisively, "once for all" what the priests of the old order could never fully accomplish. There is, to be sure, an inevitable dimension of supersessionism in this claim. However, the accent in Hebrews is not on displacing the old priestly provisions. Rather, the point is to affirm and celebrate the completeness and adequacy of Jesus in continuity with the old order. Jesus has taken the guilt of the community and made it an acceptable sacrifice (cf. Exod 28:38; Heb 10:22).

7. To some extent, this chapter affirms that "clothes make the priest." In Zech 3:4-5, the high priest Joshua is said to be guilty of violating his priestly office. But his "filthy clothes" are removed, and he is "clothed with festal apparel."

The notion of taking off "filthy clothes" and putting on new clothes and thereby being made new is taken up in powerful, metaphorical ways in Ps 132:9, 16, 18 (cf. 2 Chr 6:41). The imagery may be used positively in celebration of newness, as in Isa 61:10. Or the same imagery may be used negatively concerning judgment, as in Ezek 26:16.

This imagery is also used eschatologically for a vision of the blessed end, when the saints of God are clothed in pure, white linen (see Rev 3:5, 18; 4:4; 7:9; 15:6; 19:14). Note, moreover, how it relates to the transformation wrought in baptism: "You were taught to put away your former way of life, your old self, corrupt and deluded by its lusts, and to be renewed in the spirit of your minds, and to clothe yourselves with the new self, created according to the likeness of God in true righteousness and holiness" (Eph 4:22-24 NRSV).

The process of faith is the process of being "reclothed," as were the priests, as was the man summoned to sanity in Mark 5:1-20, and as are all the faithful. It continues to be a crucial pastoral issue that very many yearn to be "reclothed" in righteousness and salvation, and many yearn to be reinscribed with a new "belonging."

EXODUS 29:1-46, ORDINATION OF PRIESTS

COMMENTARY

Chapter 28 has been concerned with the proper dress and appearance of the priesthood of Aaron. Chapter 29 continues with specifics about ordination, consecration, and authorization. The chapter is a technical manual that appears to consist in directives given for officials who must conduct the specific rituals of ordination. We are given concrete directives on performance but almost no interpretive hint of the significance of the acts prescribed. Matters of significance are perhaps passed on orally, or taken for granted in that small community of privilege and expertise.

The chapter begins with authorization from God to proceed with the ordination (v. 1), and it concludes with a theological crescendo concerned with presence (vv. 43-46). Between is a series of obscure ritual activities that seem to be organized around a series of quite specific offerings. Moses is to "make priests" of the family of Aaron (v. 1). Thus the ultimate authority of Moses is preserved, from whom the priests derive their authority (cf. 7:1-2).

29:1-3. Then follows a series of consecrating acts. The materials needed for the consecration include a young bull and two rams who are "perfect" (תמים *tāmîm*), unleavened bread, cakes with oil, and wafers. The repeated reference to "unleavened," of course, recalls the festival provisions of chaps. 12–13, and anticipates v. 46, concerning the exodus.

29:4-9. The candidates for priesthood are to be washed (purified) and clothed. The inventory of clothing derives from chap. 28, though here the "rosette" of 28:36 is a "diadem" (v. 6; נזר *nēzer*). The candidate is then anointed with oil, i.e., peculiarly and distinctively designated.

29:10-14. The procedure requires the altar and the blood of the bull. The altar has been authorized in 27:1-10 (not to be confused with the one authorized in 30:1-10). The offering that is given from the residue of the bull is termed a "sin offering" (v. 14).

29:15-18. The blood of one of the rams is also used for the altar. The residue of the ram is given as a burnt offering, an "offering by fire" (v. 18), which is said to yield a smell that is offered up to Yahweh (cf. Lev 1:9).

29:19-21. The blood of the second ram is used on the priestly candidates. The person—the very body—of the priest is being ordained. That is, the priesthood is concerned not so much with what a priest *does*, but who he *is*. Accent is ontological rather than functional, a very "high" view of priesthood. The outcome of this act, which presumably has overlooked nothing of the priest, is that the priest "shall be holy." The formula קדש הוא (*qādaš hû*), as Gerhard von Rad has shown, is a liturgical verdict, in which the subject is "reckoned" or declared to be of this status.[169]

Thus the priest is *made* holy by these human, authorized actions.

29:22-28. The second ram is used in two ways. Part of the residue of this ram is mixed with the bread, cake of bread, and wafer (vv. 22-25; cf. v. 2). It is held by the priestly candidate and offered as an "elevated offering." The verb used to describe this offering is נוף (*nwp*), which apparently means there was a rhythmic gesture preliminary to this sacrifice. The other part of the second ram, the breast and thigh, which have been held back from the fire, are now offered as a "peace offering" (vv. 26-28). This offering belongs especially and peculiarly to the priestly candidate.

29:29-30. Provision is made for the sons of Aaron to receive the vestments and insignia as an inheritance from Aaron. Clearly the tradition is concerned to assure genealogical legitimacy and continuity in office.

29:31-37. The meat of the second ram is to be eaten by the priestly candidate. No one else shall eat of it, and none shall be left over. This section of the text is dominated by the threefold use of כפר (*kāpar*, "atonement"), the same term from which "mercy seat" in 25:17-22 derives. The eating of the food and the offering of a sacrifice do the work of atonement.

29:38-42. Finally, provision is made for a daily sacrifice. It is not clear how this provision relates to the preceding material. We are told in v. 35 that seven days are required for the process of ordination. This provision may intend that two lambs are offered for each of the seven days of the ritual of ordination. In any case, this offering, morning and night, is a grain offering and a drink offering (v. 41).

It is clear that this primitive ritual activity (primitive because it seems so elemental and pre-rational, and because we do not understand it) is the process whereby *holiness is created* in the community, holiness that authorizes and qualifies a few, select persons to go to the very core of God's holiness on behalf of the people. Thus the text refers regularly to the "tent of meeting" (vv. 10-11, 30, 32, 42). In the developing theory of presence, the "tent of meeting" performs a very different function from the tabernacle. In the tabernacle, God "dwells" (שכן *šākan*). In the "tent of meeting," God comes for specific engagements. One is struck by the odd

169. Gerhard von Rad, "Faith Reckoned as Righteousness," *The Problem of the Hexateuch and Other Essays* (New York: McGraw-Hill, 1966) 125-30. He regards such categorizing as a priestly verdict that determines the status of the object assessed by priestly expertise.

juxtaposition of such an ambitious religious intention and the daily specifics whereby that intention is actualized. That meeting with the holy God is wrought through rams and bulls and blood and kidney and liver and flour and wafers! The transcendent holy is mediated in and through the stuff of daily life. Moreover, the accent is on the physical practice and not on thoughts or ideas or "knowledge." Holiness is made by proper doing.

The middle section of this chapter appears to be a report on a series of ritual activities (vv. 10-42). However, it may also be that this material is, in fact, organized to give formal, systematic structure to the range of different sacrifices belonging to the priestly office. These include sin offering (vv. 14, 36), burnt (whole) offering (vv. 18, 25, 42), elevation offering (v. 24), peace offering (v. 28), grain offering (v. 41), and drink offering (v. 41).

These same offerings are more systematically presented in Leviticus 1–7.[170] The priestly office is portrayed here as very well developed with technical specificity that we can no longer explicate. It also seems clear that the offerings have a series of intentions that likely cover the gamut of human suffering, joy, need, and gratitude.

170. Older studies of the sacrificial system of the priests from which one can still learn include, H. H. Rowley, *Worship in Ancient Israel: Its Forms and Meanings* (Philadelphia: Fortress, 1967) 111-43; Hans-Joachim Kraus, *Worship in Israel: A Cultic History of the Old Testament* (Richmond: John Knox, 1966); and George Buchanan Gray, *Sacrifice in the Old Testament* (Oxford: Clarendon, 1925). These and all other studies are now displaced, however, by the magisterial work of Milgrom, *Leviticus 1–16*.

29:43-45. The chapter concludes with the first hint of theological intentionality that we have encountered in a long while. At the center of this conclusion is an affirmation of priesthood, which makes all else possible (v. 44). On the basis of this properly established priesthood, the text can declare the full presence of God. This includes three affirmations concerning (1) the availability of God's glory (v. 43); (2) the promise "I will dwell [*šakan*] among the Israelites" (v. 45; cf. 25:8); and (3) a promise, "I will be their God" (v. 45). This latter statement echoes and reiterates the covenant formula of 6:7, but here is stated only the one side of the relation. This is God's resolve to take up a new habitation, fully present in sovereign, life-giving power even without consideration of Israel's readiness or responsiveness.

29:46. The final statement of the chapter is especially remarkable. It not only refers to the exodus, but also reasserts the formula of acknowledgment. Then, remarkably, the old liberation formulas are joined to an affirmation concerning the abiding, dwelling presence of God. By bringing together "brought out" (יצא *yāṣāʾ*) and "know" (ידע *yādaʿ*) with "dwell" (*šakan*), this verse joins together liberation with presence and historical event with ritual stability. It holds together the "recital" and the "pattern," and in a canonical mode joins chaps. 1–15 and 25–31. This juxtaposition is made possible by a rightly performed ordination.

REFLECTIONS

1. These human actions of Moses, at God's command, are about the work of "making holiness," of generating holy reality. Religious communities, synagogues and churches, are always in the process of "making holy"—meals, persons, buildings, times, and places. "Making holy" is a daring, awesome enterprise that imagines ways in which the mystery of God in all its inscrutable power may be available to us.

Two dangers are present, however. On the one hand, there is the easy, ready distortion of taking the process of "making holy" as automatic. Then it becomes a tool for control and manipulation. This is the temptation to be "at ease in Zion," a temptation faced in every religious establishment and to which there is regular, predictable yielding. The other danger is an urbane attitude that believes such primitivism is beneath us and that life can be better ordered around morality and reasonableness. With this attitude, life is emptied of surplus power and significance and reduced to one horizontal plane.

2. The process of "making holy" requires an ongoing and complex action of self-giving. We may be dazzled by or impatient with the rich vocabulary for offerings, thinking it pretentious or overly scrupulous, especially since we do not know enough to decode the vocabulary. We may, however, ponder what it means to have such a rich variety of vocabulary and practice.

Any community has a rich, refined, and carefully nuanced vocabulary for what matters most to it. Thus apple growers in the Northwest of the United States have a legion of words for "apple," making necessary distinctions that outsiders cannot master. Israel, in the same way, is a community whose preoccupation is with "offerings" in all seasons of life. At least in this text, Israel's life is shaped and defined by the richness of "offering business." It is clear that the capacity to "make holy" depends on the fullness of giving. Where there is no rich offering, there will be very little "making holy." In a community that is unable or unwilling to give or to yield, the outcome can only be profanation, whereby neighborhood, environment, and finally self become mere objects, commodities for exploitation.

3. The letter to the Hebrews asserts that the work of Jesus Christ displaces all older patterns of priesthood. In Hebrews 7:11-14, the "order of Aaron" is explicitly mentioned. It is affirmed of Jesus Christ: "Unlike the other high priests, he has no need to offer sacrifices day after day, first for his own sins, and then for those of the people; this he did once for all when he offered himself" (Heb 7:27 NRSV).

While this is a christological claim that dispenses with the old order of Aaron, we shall not understand the argument about the new priesthood of Jesus Christ without attending to the details of the old text. Jesus Christ does not override the categories of priesthood, nor does he dismiss them as old fashioned or superstitious. Rather, these requirements for a genuinely holy priest are honored, enacted, and fulfilled. In our society of enormous isolation, many persons seek a priest who can be with them and for them in the dangerous zones of holiness or in the terrible profanation of life where holiness is lost. This yearning is for more than a counselor or an intercessor. It is a yearning for "atonement." The work of the priest is to reach behind all the issues that are more easily available and back to the core issue of presence, wherein rests the inscrutable gift of our humanness. The priest is the one who can take our offered selves and let them be the material through which God's own holiness is known.

EXODUS 30:1-10, THE INCENSE ALTAR

COMMENTARY

This section concerning the incense altar concludes Yahweh's first, most extended speech to Moses. In 27:1-8, we have already had authorization of an altar, presumably the altar of burnt offerings (cf. 30:28). The altar in this text is different in every way from that one. It is different in its measurements. It is to be overlaid with gold instead of bronze, indicating its greater importance, and it is specifically for the purpose of offering incense to God.

We may observe three items about this particular altar. First, it is carefully placed in relation to our cultic furniture (v. 6), which the text tradition delights in naming and reviewing. Second, the offering of incense is to be made regularly, twice a day, to perpetuity (v. 7). No reason is given for this regularity. The offer of incense is perhaps derivative of royal courts, in which the most exotic spices are to be used to create a most pleasing environment for the sovereign. Again, notice how this aesthetic tradition attends to all of the senses.

Third, in a belated thought, not fully integral to its context, v. 10 provides special priestly opportunity and responsibility, once each year on the Day of Atonement (*Yom Kippur*). On that day, "Aaron" shall do the peculiar work of atonement through blood. This is the most holy and most crucial priestly activity (cf. Leviticus 16).

REFLECTIONS

1. The priestly responsibility of offering fragrant incense morning and night to perpetuity suggests a rigorous, uncompromising discipline, sustained through thick and thin. The priestly tradition understands that "the practice of the presence" is not an *ad hoc* affair and does not take place in fits and starts. It requires regular, sustained, ordered, intentional efforts. Moreover, those efforts are promised no specific pay-outs or results. They are simply what must be done. Such discipline is required of any who would enter the presence of the Holy One.

2. The offer of fragrance involves the expenditure of resources in order to create a pleasing environment for one who is important and warrants special deference. Thus the offer itself is a dramatic enactment of honor and deference, the bestowal of prestige. The incense to make God's place pleasant is not unlike expensive preparation for the coming of a VIP, who must be protected from the sordidness of daily life. A Christian tradition speaks of prayer as a suitable "aroma" to God, indicating how this practice of incense can be taken metaphorically. Such a practice can be taken as appropriate "court action" that pays homage to one who peculiarly warrants such deference.

3. The priest has the capacity and responsibility once a year to perform the dangerous, crucial act of atonement. The writer of Hebrews is familiar with the language of the Exodus text concerning the Aaronides. On the one hand, the priest is said to enter the Holy Place "year after year" (Heb 9:25). On the other hand, "every priest stands day after day" (Heb 10:11 NRSV). What we have affirmed as regular discipline and repeated activity is interpreted in Hebrews as a recognition that none of these priestly acts is ever sufficient or adequate.

In contrast to that need for repetition, so runs the argument, the priestly offering of Jesus—his own blood—is not so inadequate or incomplete that it must be repeated again and again. Instead, this offering is done "once for all," never to be done again (see Heb 7:27; 9:25-28; 10:11-14). The accent on "once for all" is pervasive and is sharply polemical against the Aaronide provision.

The second contrast made to Aaron is that the priest offers blood that is not his own for atonement (cf. Heb 9:25), but from bulls and goats that cannot be effective (cf. Heb 10:4). By contrast, the blood (i.e., life) of Jesus is his own; therefore, it has sure efficacy.

One does not need to probe the intention of the manipulation of blood, nor does one need to engage in militant supersessionism, to appropriate this teaching. The point of the argument is that the offer of Jesus' own life for the sin of the world is sufficient and complete for all time. The letter to the Hebrews provides the ground for sure celebration of a most evangelical kind, a certitude that intends to counter the anxious practice of having to do atonement all over, again and again.

Moreover, if the imagery of adequate atonement is transferred to our "Age of Anxiety," it is enormously reassuring to affirm "once for all" that everything needed, everything hoped for, and everything required has been resolved by this beloved person. Therefore, there need be no anxiety, no restlessness, no tentativeness, no fear, no uncertainty. (Neither was the action of "once a year" in Exodus perceived as a terrible thing to repeat but a wondrous assurance of being able to deal with the problem of sin.)

The claim of Heb 10:21-23 does not need to be aimed at Judaism in a mood of supersessionism. Its critical relevance in our time is in relation to the anxiety of profane secularization that leaves the core of our humanness endlessly unresolved and perpetually at risk. In the face of our obsessive, repetitious, unsatisfying rituals of secularism, this decisive priestly claim has an urgent pertinence.

EXODUS 30:11–31:11, OTHER PRIESTLY MATTERS

This portion of text includes the middle five of Yahweh's seven addresses to Moses, each of which specifies an element in the general Aaronide arrangement for Presence.

Exodus 30:11-16, The Atonement Money

COMMENTARY

Maintaining the structures of presence costs money. This speech gives the "stewardship" angle. This is a rather odd speech in context, containing almost none of the usual references to the cultic apparatus. It provides that all Israelites will be "signed up" (counted and registered in the census) as belonging to the community of the redeemed. However, membership costs. Every adult must pay a set fee, one half shekel, to maintain the machinery of presence. Moreover, the very payment itself is an act of remembering where one belongs, who one is, and what one owes. Each time the money is given, the giver will recall that he or she has been "ransomed" (כפר *kāpar*). This concrete act of payment will recall and make available the whole mystery of faith. This is, indeed, a sacramental use of money.

REFLECTIONS

This provision is stated in careful, rather archaic language. The intent of the instruction, however, is not difficult or obscure. Maintenance of cultic practice costs money. There is ground here for stewardship, which holds together very well the particularity of the "service of the tent of meeting" and the large action of God, which is to be remembered. One may observe that the taxing arrangement of v. 15 is regressive; rich and poor pay the same. Perhaps this regressive arrangement reflects the indifference of this tradition to matters of justice, since the provision for equal payment contrasts sharply with the notice of 16:16-18.

Exodus 30:17-21, Basin for Washing

COMMENTARY

Yahweh's third speech provides for yet another cultic instrument. Its purpose is the ritual cleansing of the priesthood, in order that the priests should enter the zone of holiness clean and pure. The seriousness of the provision is underscored by the double warning, "that they may not die" (vv. 20-21; cf. 28:35, 43). The ritual provision again makes clear the ominous nature of approaching the holy and the high risk in which the priest operates. The text appears to be related to 1 Kgs 7:23-39, in which the "basin" is described as part of the Solomonic establishment.

REFLECTIONS

God cannot be approached carelessly or casually. It may be that a heavy emphasis on "free grace" in much recent theology, rooted in a particular reading of Paul, has suggested that disciplines of purity are not important for communion.

"Washing" concerns being well qualified for the holy. In the cultic traditions of the OT, one must have "clean hands" in order to enter the shrine (Ps 24:4). In Pss 26:6 and 73:13, there is a "washing in innocence." While the phrase may have become metaphorical, it is plausible that such a washing was a specific ritual act (see also Ps 51:2; Isa 1:16). More generally, attention may be given to the significance of baptism (see Acts 22:16; 1 Cor 6:11; Titus 3:5; Heb 10:22; Rev 1:5), and reference might be made to the washing by Jesus in John 13:1-11. Jesus' severe warning "Unless I wash you, you have no share with me" (John 13:8) does not seem remote from our text.

Exodus 30:22-38, Anointing Oil and Incense

COMMENTARY

The fourth (vv. 22-33) and fifth (vv. 34-38) speeches of Yahweh to Moses share a common concern: the preparation and use of precious spices in order to produce perfumes for anointing the holy apparatus. The action of anointing the holy furniture with pleasing smells is an act of ritual adornment bespeaking deference and perhaps purification. The richly endowed, carefully prepared oil is to be used on all the temple furniture and upon the priests. Verses 32-33 and 37-38 suggest how serious is the act of anointing. This particular oil, especially prepared for Yahweh's habitat, cannot be otherwise used, on pain of excommunication.

REFLECTIONS

The practice of holiness mobilizes all of life and attends to all the senses. Thus the practice of holiness "smells good." (Notice the contrast to the "bad odor" in the liberation narrative [7:21; 8:14].) The OT is aware that a "good smell" in worship may cause worship to degenerate into bribery and manipulation. See the prophetic strictures of Isa 1:11-15 and Amos 4:4-5. The relentless critique of the sacrificial system in Heb 10:5-6 explicitly quotes the prophetic strictures. Thus the polemic in Hebrews against "acceptable sacrifice" joins cause with the prophetic strictures, but it intends to make a very different point, one that is christological rather than ethical.

In utilizing such critiques, one must be careful not to fall into a "knee-jerk Protestantism" that condemns worship in principle. Old Testament scholars agree that the prophetic critique of worship is aimed at distortion of ritual practice and not at sacrifice per se.

The reference to myrrh (v. 23) and frankincense (v. 34), moreover, suggests Matt 2:11, concerning the "adoration of the magi." The other two obvious OT practices to which Matthew may refer concern the use of spices by royalty (see Esth 2:12; Ps 45:8) and by lovers (Cant 3:6; 4:6, 17; 5:1, 5). All of these uses of precious spices—in relation to royalty, love, and holiness—concern deference, allegiance, extravagance, and devotion. If the Matthew text can be brought into the sphere of our text, then the wise ones knew they were entering into the zone of the holy in approaching the child. Such imagery concerning the sphere of the holy is not primary in Matthew, but it could not fail to be on the horizon of the Jewish listener to that story.

Exodus 31:1-11, Two Skilled Artisans

COMMENTARY

Yahweh's sixth speech to Moses concerns the pertinent, practical question of how the actual work on the tabernacle will be completed. This text thus parallels 30:11-16 in that it is about the practical implementation of the pattern.

The work has been entrusted to two skilled artisans, Bezalel and Oholiab. Beyond their pedigrees and competence, nothing is known of them. It is remarkable that with the complete domination of the text by Moses (and to a lesser extent by Aaron) the names of the senior craftsmen have not been lost. Three items are worth noting. First, this text forms something of a summary and a conclusion to the longer speech, because it names and reiterates the long list of authorized elements for the tabernacle (vv. 7-11), all of which are the responsibility of these two artisans.

Second, these men are consummately skilled to work in every medium required (vv. 4-5). They are endowed with wisdom, discernment, and knowledge. It is worth noticing that "wisdom" here is quite practical. Consistent with the aesthetic sensibility of this text, wisdom is not excessively cerebral. It takes wisdom to create a place for God's holiness that is visually adequate and pleasing to smell. Third, the workmen are filled with God's Spirit, energized and authorized to use their enormous skill in ways befitting the holy (v. 3).

REFLECTIONS

The text explicitly states what is everywhere assumed in God's address to Moses: Creating a home for holiness is *human work*. That human effort, however, is powered and driven by the wind of God. If Fretheim is correct in relating these texts to creation, then this action entrusted to Bezalel and Oholiab is indeed a new creation fitted for holiness, generated by God's wind, which was the initial agent of creation (Gen 1:2). This text suggests that artistry is a creative act. These artists are, in a proper sense, "inspired" to do this awesome work.

It is important that the triad of "artists-wisdom-Spirit" converge precisely in this text, which we might have expected to be parochial and confined to a narrower range of cultic interests and perceptions. Very recent secularization notwithstanding, the religious community since ancient times has been the central context and habitat for genuinely creative artistry. The work of the Spirit is evident not only in dramatic acts of liberation but in the awesome work of making a new world possible, gathered about God's holiness. With reference to literature, George Steiner has argued that certain kinds of art depend on the reality and presence of the Holy One.[171] In this text, likewise, the connection between genuinely creative art and the power of God's Spirit is decisive for making the earth a suitable place for God's presence. An inadequate doctrine of creation, a failure to value creativity as a gift of God, has caused the church to fail to appreciate or appropriate art as a gift of the Spirit. These artisans are indeed agents of God's powerful Spirit, which makes new life possible.

171. George Steiner, *Real Presences* (Chicago: University of Chicago Press, 1989). More broadly, see Ralph Harper, *On Presence: Variations and Reflections* (Philadelphia: Trinity Press International, 1991).

EXODUS 31:12-18, THE SABBATH

COMMENTARY

This is God's seventh and final speech to Moses from the mountain, and it is quite unlike the preceding six in its concern and in its vocabulary. It has no interest in things liturgical or priestly, nor is it preoccupied with presence. It is, rather, concerned with sabbath as rest (and not as worship), a concern that touches primarily the public, economic sphere of Israel's life.

The speech consists in a series of imperatives followed by motivational clauses introduced by the particle כִּי (*kî*). This speech is roughly chiastic:

A Keep sabbath as a sign (v. 13).
  B Keep sabbath, for violators will be
     executed (v. 14).
  B´ Keep sabbath, for violators will be
     executed(v. 15).
A´ Keep sabbath as a sign (vv. 16-17*a*).
Conclusion: Yahweh rested (v. 17*b*).

31:12-13. The work stoppage on sabbath, the breaking of the vicious cycle of production and consumption, is a sign for all the world to see. What will be known through this freighted gesture is that Yahweh "makes Israel holy" (sanctifies) (cf. 19:6). This is an extraordinary claim; it asserts that Israel is fitted and qualified to enter the realm beyond realms, to participate in the joy, well-being, and power of God's own life. It is noteworthy in this text that entry into God's holiness does not depend on particular cultic scruples of clean and unclean, as we might expect (cf. 30:17-21), but only on a willing, obedient work stoppage.

31:14. The sabbath is "holy," freighted with the power for life. This requirement of holy rest in Israel is so urgent that violators shall "surely die." We have seen this formula מוֹת יוּמַת (*môt yûmāt*) in the legal series of 21:15-17. The phrasing is an ominous, formal, legal death sentence that is reserved in Israel as punishment for the most dangerous and objectionable affronts. The formula of excommunication at the end of v. 14, "cut off from among the people," may be an attempt

to back off from and tone down the severe threat of the death penalty.

We may nevertheless ponder why such a seemingly innocent matter as sabbath carries such a severe sentence. The answer, of course, is that violation of the sabbath is not as innocuous as it seems. This text is still powerfully infused by the exodus narrative. The kingdom of Pharaoh still represents the quintessence of a life lived for productivity (see 5:13-14; 16:19-21). This text evidences anxiety that any violation of sabbath as obedient work stoppage means being seduced by the production values and rewards of Pharaoh, which will predictably end in slavery. Thus "profaning" the sabbath means jeopardizing all that is most precious and definitional about Israel's existence in the world and its loyalty to Yahweh.

31:15. In reverse order, vv. 15-17*a* reiterate the command and warning of vv. 13-14. Verse 15 again evokes the death sentence, *môt yûmāt*, though this time the following formula of excommunication is absent. Abraham Heschel has seen that in Gen 2:1-4*a*, the very first thing God "hallows" (makes holy), is time—not a place (shrine) or a person (priest). The hallowing of time permits Israel in the end to confess "My times [all of them] are in your hand" (Ps 31:15 NRSV).[172]

Violating sabbath is to withhold for self that which rightly belongs to God. Clearly the reason for withholding for self is in order to have joy, well-being, and security on one's own terms and without reference to or reliance upon God. Violation of sabbath as a gesture of self-sufficiency means in the end to overthrow all that is crucial and definitional in Israel's faith (cf. Deut 8:17-20).

31:16-17a. Thus Israel's refusal of such self-sufficiency, shunning such profanation, and resisting the seductiveness of productivity, endlessly reenacts this sign. The sign is "forever."

Both Israel's destiny and Israel's danger are forever. The notion of a perpetual covenant

---

172. See Abraham Heschel, *The Sabbath: Its Meaning for Modern Man* (New York: Farrar, Straus, and Young, 1951).

as the reference point of sabbath is a relation for all time that cannot be disrupted. This affirmation of perpetual covenant is made in a limited number of texts, all of which appear to be dated to the exile. Thus in Gen 9:8-17 God's promise after the flood is that there will be no more jeopardy to the relation. It is remarkable that in the acute disruption and discontinuity of exile Israel's faith affirms the durability and reliability of covenant! (See Isa 54:9-10; 55:3; Jer 31:35-37; 33:20-25; Ezek 16:60-62; 34:25-31; 37:24-28. See also Gen 17:2-21; Lev 26:40-45; Pss 89:3-4, 33-34; 105:8, 10.)

31:17b. The last part of v. 17 contains a remarkable affirmation. On the one hand, as expected, rest is linked to God's own rest on the seventh day of creation (Gen 2:1-4*a*). Rest is not recuperation for the next day's work, but is the goal and climactic event of all creation, the point of it all. This quite explicit reference to the Genesis text supports the hypothesis that Exodus 25–31 is consciously and deliberately related to the seven days of creation, which culminate in rest. It supports the hypothesis both in its sequence of seven speeches like seven days and in the larger substantive claim that the goal of creation is God's palpable glory in the midst of Israel.

On the other hand, this text, perhaps inadvertently, makes an affirmation that is quite unexpected and has no counterpart in the Genesis text: Yahweh "was refreshed." The term translated "refreshed" is נפשׁ (*nepeš*); as a noun it means "life/self" or in older translations, "soul." As a verb, it means to be "lifed, selfed, souled," to be given more of one's *nepeš*. The form in our text is *niph'al*, which could be translated passively as in the NRSV, "was refreshed," though the agent of refreshment is implied and not named; or it could be rendered in the reflexive, "refreshed self." The verb of *nepeš* occurs in only two other places. In 23:12, as here, it is used in relation to sabbath rest, so that an ox, donkey, homeborn slave, or resident alien may be "refreshed." In 2 Sam 16:14, as David flees Absalom, he "refreshed himself in the Jordan."

What is utterly astonishing about v. 17 is that the sabbath is for God to be refreshed, *nepheshed*, given back God's own, diminished self. With either a passive or a reflexive translation, the point is still the same. The inescapable inference is that in six days of creation God worked very hard, and God's own self had been diminished through that exertion. This usage is all the more astonishing in the Priestly tradition, which tends to present God primarily in terms of majestic transcendence. For a moment here, the text lets the reader see God from the other side, the side of frailty and vulnerability.

This point about God and sabbath is quite in tension with the notion that God rests in supreme confidence and assurance about the reliability of creation. Verse 17 thus provides a wondrous juxtaposition concerning God. At the same time, this is the God whose magnificent and serene power made heaven and earth, and yet who is exhausted and needs to recuperate. The sabbath is a sign that Israel is linked to perpetuity with this majestic, vulnerable God. Nobody can be an endless agent of productivity without a break—nobody, not even Yahweh. Israel trusts in and is utterly devoted to this glorious One who overrides Pharaoh's production schedule and who authorizes joyous rest as definitional to the life and destiny of creation.

31:18. God's long speech, which begins in 25:1, now comes to an end. It is finished! The whole pattern has been disclosed. The blueprint is complete. Moses and Israel now know everything that needs to be known about living with the holiness of God.

When God finishes, however, a remarkable outcome is reported. The whole, long speech is not written down for formal transmission. What is written down is only the two tablets (לחת העדת *lūḥōt ha'ēdūt*) which are placed in the ark (cf. 25:16). That is all, and that is everything. In the very moment of utterance, the tradition asserts that the other commands (20:1-17), not the ones now being uttered, are primary. They are the ones given in stone for all time.

This verse creates something of a "canon within the canon," instructing the community in what counts the most. And what counts the most, so that it is formalized and transmitted in writing, is not tabernacle provisions but the commandments.

Moreover, the elevation and priority of the two tablets are made as dramatic and unambiguous as possible by the affirmation that the two tablets are written with "the finger of God" (cf. Deut 9:10). Only twice in the tradition of Exodus is the "finger of God" mobilized. Here the "finger of God" is to bring Israel to a new, covenantal obedience. In 8:19, the "finger of God" dispatches the gnats and defeats the pretense of the empire (cf. Luke 11:20). The two uses are, in fact, intimately related, and together they witness to the unity of intention in the book of Exodus. Both in sending gnats (the story of liberation) and in giving the Torah (the rules for new community) Yahweh acts powerfully and decisively to make new, liberated, covenantal life possible for Israel.

REFLECTIONS

1. In our contemporary situation, sabbath is an urgent check on the *ideology of productivity*, which in turn is rooted in a myth of scarcity used to justify the great surpluses of the empire (cf. 1:11; Gen 47:7-20). The state acts as though there is not enough; therefore, the supreme virtue is in producing and accumulating more.

The ideology of productivity is subtle in its force and variegated in its presence. The most obvious manifestation is the work ethic, whereby one must work harder to achieve more in order to prove one's worth. But, of course, there are other ways to gain "more" besides the "old-fashioned way" of earning it. There is a leisure culture of more games, more expensive shoes, more victories, more entertainment, and more sex. There is a cult of gracious living that specializes in better stereo equipment, better wines, more vacations, a nicer home or better neighborhood, and a better school for the children. And there is a narcissistic cult of more jogged miles and more eating disorders, which is only another mode of a brick quota.

These several self-indulgences are not much removed from the "fool" in Luke 12:16-20 who was in his own ideology of productivity and who could not entertain the thought of sabbath. That story, as with our text, understands that a life that cannot imitate the creator in rest is in the end self-destructive. If the goal of life is, as in chaps. 25–31, the presence of God, then it is clear that a life committed to endless productivity is empty of the promise of God and cut off from the power of holiness. Such a life abandons the exodus narrative and, in the end, violates the very fabric of creation.

2. The main point about sabbath is not worship but the stoppage of work. That fact is noteworthy, especially in this larger text (chaps. 25–31), which is consumed by worship. Such an awareness invites us to rethink the meaning of worship. In this context, worship is God's creation engaged in joyous rest. It may give pause that it is largely the communities at the social margin who maintain restful, playful delight in the act of worship. The reason why worship is such a delight in these contexts is that it is a genuine sabbath, such a contrast to zones dominated by Pharaoh's production schedules. Too much worship has become too heavy, too didactic, too insistent, and too promotional to be a genuine sabbath. As proposed here, worship is a place in which to "enjoy God."

3. Consideration of sabbath provides a context for raising issues about the ultimate purpose of life. In a production-oriented life, we do not reflect much on an ultimate goal or destiny, being too busy with the next quota or assignment. Commitment to production programmatically screens out questions of ultimate goal or destiny, and one is fated to live a penultimate existence. Conversely, a practice of peaceful "at homeness" with God brings us close to an ultimate "at homeness" with God (cf. Heb 3:1–4:11). The fact that this passage on sabbath is placed last in God's speech to Moses suggests that sabbath belongs as the final question of faith and as the final goal of existence. That is, its literary placement bespeaks its eschatological significance.

4. Our text is more than moral instruction about work stoppage. It affirms the very structure and fabric of creation, as willed and practiced by the creator. Rest is not just a Mosaic idea or an outcome of the exodus, as might be suggested in Deut 5:12-15, but belongs to the core and structure of reality. God is not anxious about the world and not worried that it will fall apart. On the seventh day, God is not indispensable, for creation has enough momentum, viability, and coherence that it can, for one day, work on its own. And just as the creator has much confidence in the viability of creation, so also Israel is invited to trust that no human agent is indispensable for creation.

A "market ideology" has given many of us a powerfully atheistic notion of creation. We view all of creation as open to commodity manipulation. All of creation is for sale, for use, or for hoarding. But creation belongs to God and is not reducible to our management, coercion, or purchase. Thus sabbath is an act whereby we may restore and reaccept our proper relation to creator and to creation. Creation is not an object to administer but is a fabric and network of life-giving resources, functioning on its own before us and without us, generous in its sustenance, reliable for us if we will trust and receive (cf. Ps 104:27-28 as a confident conclusion to vv. 1-26). All of this God had to trust in God's own moment of being "refreshed." God trusts creation, and God is restored. We need not do otherwise.

5. Finally, the difficult question posed by this text is whether sabbath is a viable, practical undertaking in our busy, driven world. The hard fact is that sabbath cannot be added on to an ideology of production. There will never be enough time or energy or will or leisure or peaceableness for sabbath, as long as one is in pursuit of one more achievement, one more sale, one more commodity, one more party, or one more advance. The issue of sabbath, while it has practical economic outcomes, is first of all an eminently pastoral, spiritual one. It concerns being weaned away from the deep disorder of distrust, anxiety, and self-sufficiency that haunts all modern people.

M. Tsevat affirms that sabbath is a day to renounce autonomy and to give one's life back to God in gratitude and trust.[173] Freedom to do that requires life in a community intent upon liberation and covenant, a community that is confident that coveting is inappropriate in a world where "your heavenly father knows all you need" (see Luke 12:30).

This teaching on sabbath is oddly juxtaposed to the extensive provisions for tabernacle and priesthood (25:1–31:11). The logic of this juxtaposition is in the awareness that right living (sabbath) and right worship (tabernacle) go together. When one can trust enough in the holy power of Yahweh, one may be eligible for entry into the presence of the glory, utterly at home even in exile. The *practice of sabbath* and the *embrace of the holy* likely do not come in sequence, but are practices common to life with Yahweh.

173. Matitiahu Tsevat, "The Basic Meaning of the Biblical Sabbath," in *The Meaning of Job and Other Biblical Studies: Essays on the Literature and Religion of the Hebrew Bible* (New York: KTAV, 1980) 39-52, esp. 48.

EXODUS 32:1–34:35

SIN AND RESTORATION

OVERVIEW

These three chapters are crucially and peculiarly placed in the book of Exodus. According to scholarly consensus, they belong to the early sources of the book (JE), and so are a continuation of chaps. 19–24. Indeed, in the usual reading informed by critical scholarship, one reads directly from 24:18 to 32:11, skipping over the intervening materials of chaps. 25–31.

With a more recent accent on canonical reading, we must ask about chapters 32–34 in their immediate context, even when a conventional source analysis is accepted. Before chaps. 32–34 come 25–31, with the command for building the tabernacle. After chaps. 32–34 come 35–40, with the implementation of that command. Thus chaps. 32–34 disrupt the expected sequence of command (chaps. 25–31) and performance (chaps. 35–40). The sequence of command-disruption-implementation is likely an important and intentional theological arrangement.

Formally, the disruption of God's command is like the sequence of Genesis 1–2 (creation), 3–8 (sin), and 9:1-17 (new covenant). Exodus 32 is something like a paradigmatic break in the world intended by God for Israel. That formal sequence of creation, sin, and new covenant, however, may be further illuminated if one considers closely the relation between chaps. 25–31 and chap. 32. The most striking commonality is the figure of Aaron, who is authorized as the singular priest (chaps. 28–29), but who perverts Israel's faith in chap. 32. Thus it is possible that chaps. 32–34 present a polemic against the very Aaron so celebrated in chaps. 28–29, in favor of Moses' faith and leadership.

When we turn to chaps. 32–34 itself, we see again that an intentional design has been wrought in the material (helpfully discussed by Moberly).[174] These three chapters are likely made up of quite distinct materials. While chap. 32 concerns the offense of the calf, it has no particular relation to chap. 33. In like manner, the theophanic disclosure of 34:6-7, the resolve to make covenant (v. 10), and the proclamation of covenant law (vv. 11-26), likely reflect an old practice of covenant making that has no connection to broken covenant.

These materials have now been formed, as Moberly shows, into a new configuration around a pattern of sin (chap. 32), dialogue and negotiation (chap. 33), and new covenant (chap. 34). When arranged in this way, the materials are not simply concerned with a moment of crisis in Israel's past, but make a remarkable theological statement that has continuing force and significance. Yahweh has a will, capacity, and yearning for the restoration of broken covenant with Israel. This new beginning, which is enacted in chap. 34, is made possible (or necessary) because of the fierce insistence of Moses. In the assertion of 33:19, in the self-disclosure of 34:6-7a, and in the answer to the petition in 34:10, Israel receives an articulation of God's fierce, unwarranted graciousness, in the face of a profound act of disobedience. This is precisely the theological conclusion that would be most important to the exilic makers of canon. Put another way, the exile is exactly such a context of violation and brokenness that requires a fresh gift of Yahweh's mercy.[175]

In the end, we can appropriate this assertion of Yahweh's unfettered graciousness in two ways. If read critically, i.e., according to source analysis, the relation of Sinai is

174. R. W. L. Moberly, *At the Mountain of God: Story and Theology in Exodus 32–34,* JSOTSup 22 (Sheffield: *JSOT,* 1983).
175. See Walter Brueggemann, "A Shattered Transcendence? Exile and Restoration," in *Biblical Theology: Problems and Perspectives; In Honor of J. Christian Beker,* eds. Steven J. Kraftchick, et al. (Nashville: Abingdon, 1995).

reconstituted on a firmer basis. If read canonically (as the book stands), even Aaron's waywardness does not preclude the miracle of

fidelity and presence. Either way, the final form of the text shows that Israel's future depends on Yahweh's inordinant fidelity.

EXODUS 32:1-35, THE GOLDEN CALF

COMMENTARY

According to conventional source analysis, 32:1 resumes the narrative of 24:14 (or 24:18). Even without such a critical distinction, however, 32:1 follows appropriately as a narrative account after 24:14, for the intervening material (24:15–31:18) takes place on the mountain between God and Moses.

32:1-6. For forty days and nights, Israel is without Moses and without access to God. Indeed, they are so anxious for Moses' return that they seize an initiative of their own to have access to God, without reference to Moses or his demanding scruples (32:1).

The next best source of theological authority (after Moses) is Aaron, thus they appeal to him (v. 1). According to the narrative, Aaron is Moses' brother and aide. As the story develops, however, Aaron becomes Moses' competitor and the progenitor of a priestly line and style that are in principle deeply at odds with Mosaic faith.

In vv. 1-6, Moses is absent, still on the mountain. The only players in the immediate drama are "the people" and Aaron. The people are intensely religious, awaiting an alternative to Moses. They appeal to Aaron: "Make for us gods!" The appeal is a crude and frontal assault on the first and second commandments (20:1-6). In the interest of religious survival, Israel proposes to have gods who are the products of their own invention.

Aaron obliges. He takes an offering of the wealth and jewelry of Israel (cf. 25:1-7; 35:5-9; 36:3-7). The difference of this offering from that of Moses, of course, is in its intent. Moses acts to make the presence of Yahweh possible, according to the promise and command of Yahweh (25:3-8), whereas Aaron acts on his own hook, thus anticipating a rival to Yahweh.

While the people instigate the action, Aaron takes the important initiatives and authorizes the religious adventure. He casts

the image of a calf (on which see Exod 20:4). The god Israel makes for itself is a calf. Nowhere in the OT are we given any clarity about the calf, which in this narrative stands almost as an empty cipher for idolatry. It is plausible that it was no more a departure from Yahwism than was the ark, but was simply one more object upon which the invisible God sat or rode. In 1 Kings 12, in his break with Jerusalem and with the Davidic house, Jeroboam chooses a calf as a symbol of presence, an alternative to the ark. His choice of a calf may be innocent (cf. 1 Kgs 12:27-30). Notice that Aaron's dummy formula (32:4) is precisely paralleled by Jeroboam (1 Kgs 12:28). Our narrative, however, if understood in terms of that religious-political controversy, may be a polemic against the northern rivalry to Jerusalem. It may also be that the calf (i.e., bull) is a powerful symbol of some form of Canaanite fertility religion (cf. Hos 13:2). In that case, the calf symbolizes a way to secure one's own existence, to govern fertility, without recourse to the commands of Yahweh. Either way, the calf invites sharp polemic from the Mosaic purists in Israel.

The people immediately respond to the calf with the affirmation "These are your gods" of the exodus, who "brought you up out of the land of Egypt" (v. 4). Aaron then consolidates this new theological arrangement by building an altar, proclaiming a festival, and receiving offerings (vv. 5-6). That is, Aaron authorizes and constitutes a full alternative liturgical practice. His lame excuse is that Moses, who is clearly still on the mountain with Yahweh (i.e., at risk), is forgotten: "We do not know what has become of him" (v. 1). Short memory!

The elements of this new liturgic practice around these newly cast gods is not incongruent with the intention of the earlier text. In terms of form, Aaron does what Moses has authorized: An altar has been authorized (20:24), and burnt offerings and offerings of well-being are permitted, exactly the ones offered here (20:24). The festival (חג ḥag) has been the aim of the liberation from the beginning, and the celebration in eating and drinking seems to replicate the awesome act at the mountain (24:11).

The failure of Aaron, upon which the narrative does not yet comment, is that this newly authorized worship is distorted at its very core, because the God of the exodus cannot be "produced," by either the whim of the people or the inventiveness of the priest. The true God of the exodus is a lively subject and not a manipulatable object. Thus a deep contrast may perhaps be signaled in the final word of v. 6: They "rose up to revel" (צחק ṣaḥēq). The term *revel* may indicate self-indulgence. This sentence reiterates "eat and drink" from 24:10, but to very different effect. In place of the expression "gaze upon God" in 24:10, we have "rose up to revel." Whereas 24:10 is fully directed to God, 32:6 is an act of self-reference and, we may imagine, self-indulgence.

32:7-14. The narrative moves abruptly from Aaron's initiative to the conversation between God and Moses on the mountain. God speaks first (vv. 7-10). God knows fully what Aaron has done. The speech of Yahweh is in the form of a prophetic lawsuit. First, there is an indictment, indicating the violation of commandment by Israel (vv. 7-8). Yahweh's speech is terse. Yahweh's decisive role in the life of Israel has been disregarded. Israel has accepted an *ersatz* god, completely misconstruing the exodus. They are no longer "my people," but "your people" (v. 7).

Second, Yahweh proposes to burn Israel with wrath, to nullify the covenant and to eradicate Israel (vv. 9-10). The covenant from the outset has been conditional. Yahweh here expresses no restraint or reservation and is not excessively committed to Israel. Moreover, God proposes that for Moses alone there will be a "great nation." God is prepared to scuttle Israel as the promised "great nation," and to reassign and redeploy the great Abrahamic promise of Gen 12:2 to Moses. The lawsuit speech portrays Israel as the deep adversary of Yahweh, who is prepared to terminate Israel and begin again with Moses.

Moses responds at length to Yahweh's speech (vv. 11-13), acting as a daring intercessor on behalf of Israel for the first time. The cause would seem hopeless in light of Yahweh's rage. At great risk to himself, Moses throws himself against the wrath of Yahweh. Moses' speech is in two parts. The first part, in the form of two questions, is a motivation to persuade Yahweh to have a change of heart (vv. 11-12a). Moses identifies Israel as "your people" (v. 11, contra v. 7), appeals to the exodus, and warns that the proposed destruction of Israel will create an impression among the watching Egyptians that the exodus was a bad scheme on Yahweh's part (cf. Num 14:13-16).

Second, on the basis of that appeal to Yahweh's pride and vanity, Moses issues three demanding imperatives to God: Turn (שוב sûb) from your anger, change (נחם niham) your mind, and remember (זכר zākar) your promises (vv. 12b-13). Moses seeks to contextualize the present crisis for God by situating Israel in the midst of the old promises of Genesis. To that end, Moses quotes a classic unconditional promise from Gen 15:5. This is a telling appeal, because it is precisely on the basis of these old memories and promises that the exodus was at first undertaken at all (cf. 2:24; 3:6, 16; 6:8).

The exchange thus features two speeches with two parts each: God in a lawsuit speech: indictment and sentence; Moses in intercession: motivation and petition.

The narrator adds tersely that, on the basis of Moses' appeal, Yahweh has a change of mind (*nḥm*, v. 14). Moses' petition is effective and moves Yahweh away from the harsh resolve of the lawsuit speech. Such freedom on God's part is, of course, a problem for scholastic theology, which wants an immutable God, but such a God stands in deep tension with the biblical presentation of God.[176]

32:15-29. The terrible theological distortion enacted by Aaron (vv. 1-6) has in fact been overcome by the daring intervention of Moses (vv. 7-14). Now Moses must come to see for himself what Yahweh has already seen

---

176. See Terence E. Fretheim, *The Suffering of God: An Old Testament Perspective*, OBT (Philadelphia: Fortress, 1984); and Francis I. Andersen and David Noel Freedman, *Amos: A New Translation with Introduction and Commentary*, AB 24A (New York: Doubleday, 1989) 638-79.

(vv. 15-29). Moses' response to the sorry situation of compromised Israel is twofold.

32:15-20. First, Moses, alone except for Joshua (cf. 24:2, 13), sees and responds all alone. Here the narrative is at pains to describe with precision the two tablets of the covenant, which are in fact the main issue in the narrative. They are not the work of Moses (but see 34:27). The tablets are "the work of God," the writing of God (v. 16). They provide an angle of vision for Moses and a deep contrast to the Aaronide accomplishment. The sounds coming from the camp at the foot of the mountain are no longer the singing of Miriam(cf. 15:20-21) but of those who eat and drink and dance and revel (vv. 18-19; cf. v. 6).

Now Moses' "anger burned hot" (v. 19). Ironically, the phrase is the same as in v. 11. In his innocence, Moses has talked Yahweh out of the rage. But now Moses, upon witnessing the scene, reacts with the same rage as that of Yahweh. In his anger, Moses breaks both religious symbols, the tablets he carries and the calf he despises (vv. 19-20). The breaking of the tablets shows that the commandment-based covenant with Yahweh is abrogated. The breaking of the calf with the powerful, violent verbs *burn, grind,* and *scatter* is to make Israel choke on its own perversion. Moses' action indicates that Israel's relation with Yahweh, so carefully wrought at Sinai, has been quickly and completely nullified.

32:21-24. Moses' second response of Moses involves his confrontation with Aaron, his brother turned competitor and nemesis. Moses speaks to Aaron only briefly (v. 21). He asks a question, but the question is also a heavy accusation. Aaron is permitted the longer speech (vv. 22-24), but speeches of self-justification are characteristically long.

First, Aaron chides his brother, trying to talk him out of his massive anger as Moses has talked Yahweh out of anger. Now a third time, the phrase is used, "anger burns hot" (יחר-אף *yiḥar-'ap*). Aaron suggests Moses' anger is somewhat overwrought and inappropriate. "You know," says Aaron (as do I), "that this people Israel is inclined to evil." Aaron deftly "triangles" with Moses against Israel, seeking Moses as his ally, skillfully exempting himself from the crisis. It is as though Aaron is not at all involved in the trouble.

Aaron continues in v. 23, saying that, given the demand of Israel, Aaron is only marginally involved, and Moses is inappropriately upset with him. Aaron's account of what happened is reliable, until he comes to his own role. In his version he is scarcely involved at all! Aaron's single act, so his report goes, is to collect gold and cast it into the fire; that is all. Aaron's last line (he is permitted to speak no more) is a marvelous act of abdication, "Out came this calf!" (v. 24). The calf itself is the subject of the verb. Nobody did it, certainly not Aaron!

Aaron's shrewd speech seeks to exonerate himself at the expense of the people. His argument, lacking any conviction, is not unlike that of the man and the woman in Gen 3:12-13: Everyone else, but not me. Fretheim asserts, "It is Genesis 3 all over again."[177]

32:25-29. Moses' third response, after the initial reaction with Joshua (vv. 19-20) and after the confrontation with Aaron (vv. 21-24), is a quite public response that seeks to deal with the public damage of the treasonable act. Moses observes the scene. The problem is that the people are "without restraint" (פרע *pārûaʿ*), which is a cause of mockery among the observing nations (cf. v. 12). The same term is used, ironically enough, in 5:4, wherein Pharaoh describes Israel, who has not kept at its work (cf. Prov 29:18). It is clear to Moses that such "running wild" must be stopped. It is incongruous with the character of Israel and the God with whom Israel is allied. The intention of the liberation of the exodus was not to create a people "on the loose."

Moses' strategic response to a people out of control is to summon those who will to stand with Yahweh against the Aaronide travesty (v. 26). Notice that Moses does not summon folk to his side but to Yahweh's cause. That is, Moses preempts Yahweh (as he characteristically does), so that his enemies are the enemies of God (cf. 23:22).

Those who respond to Moses' summons are "the sons of Levi," a priestly order linked to Mosaic authority (cf. 2:1; 6:16-25). There can be little doubt that in a late period, they were rivals to the powerful Zadokite

---

177. Fretheim, *Exodus,* 279. It is instructive that in this great exposition of sin in the OT, Karl Barth, *Church Dogmatics* IV (Edinburgh: T. & T. Clark, 1956) 358-513, sets the text of Exodus 32 alongside Genesis 3 (as well as 1 Samuel 8 and 1 Kings 21).

priesthood, which claims Aaronide root-age.[178] In the earlier period, it may be that the Levites were a "revolutionary cadre" who provided the will and theological legitimacy for the Mosaic revolution.[179] They were the ones with a radical social vision rooted in a radical discernment of Yahweh. If that is who the Levites were, then it is not surprising that they rally here to the summons of Moses to act for the purity and fidelity of Israel against a perverse, compromising tendency. Thus a deep and fundamental theological issue concerning the nature of Yahweh and the faith of Israel is overlaid with a vigorous rivalry between priestly orders.

As is characteristic when Moses is involved, Israel is once again embroiled in a staggering, costly "either/or." Either one is with Yahweh (and Moses), or one is under threat. The Levites here demonstrate their singular devotion to a Mosaic vision of faith by their readiness to execute the distorters—3,000 of them, including their own relatives. The Levites, through this act, are "ordained" and receive a blessing from Moses (cf. 12:33 and 39:43 on Moses as a giver of blessing). This becomes the foundational authorization for this priestly order. Thanks to the unlimited and unhesitating fidelity of the Levites, Israel is purged of the aberration wrought by Aaron and is placed in a position to be reconstituted as a covenant people. The courage of the Levites gives Israel a future.

32:30-35. There is, however, unfinished business for Moses and for Yahweh. Moses' concern is with a "great sin." The phrase occurs in v. 21, and now is the *leitmotif* of vv. 30-31. The "great sin" is unfinished business. Moses first of all indicts the people for this action (v. 30). He is in no way romantic or "therapeutic" about the guilt of Israel nor about the jeopardy in which it has placed itself. Moses will seek to "make atonement" (כפר *kāpar*), a task assigned in the later source to Aaron (cf. 29:36-37). Moses' effort

178. See the hypothetical reconstruction of this rivalry by Cross, *Canaanite Myth and Hebrew Epic,* 195-215. See as well the way in which Hanson, *The Dawn of Apocalyptic,* has taken this struggle as a way to understand the recurring tensions concerning the nature of Judaism.

179. The phrase is used by Gottwald, *The Tribes of Yahweh,* 496, cf. 688. Behind Gottwald lies the explication of Max Weber, *Ancient Judaism* (Glencoe, Ill.: Free Press, 1952) 169-93, concerning the pivotal importance of the Levites for the revolutionary strain in Israelite faith. Hans Walter Wolff, "Hoseas Geistige Heimat," *TLZ* 81 (1956) 83-94, has proposed that Hosea as well as Deuteronomy reflects that radical commitment of the Levitical tradition.

at atonement is not the performance of a priestly act, but a conversation in which he seeks to persuade God away from God's great anger (vv. 31-32). Moses begins his address to God, nonetheless, with a full acknowledgment of Israel's sin (v. 31).

Moses' central appeal is telling, for both the force of its rhetoric and Moses' inability to speak a full sentence (v. 32). It is structured as a double "if": "if . . . if not." However, the structure fails with the first "if." We expect a protasis and an apodosis, "if . . . then." But Moses can think of nothing to say that will balance the possibility of the first "if." He might have said, "If . . . then you will be honored," or "If . . . then we will be obedient," or "If . . . then the nations will see you vindicated." But the sentence is incomplete, and the thought is broken off. Moses cannot utter it. He cannot think of a gain to be made by the sheer forgiveness of Yahweh.

The rhetoric then shifts to a second "if" in which Moses entertains a negative from God. It is on this second "if" that the force of the rhetoric falls. In an almost Job-like challenge to God, Moses wants, if God will not forgive, to be blotted out (מחה *māḥâ*) along with all the other Israelites. Moses stands in complete solidarity with recalcitrant Israel. He does not wish to be exempted from the wrath, as God has proposed in v. 10. Moses does not want to go on with Yahweh in the absence of Israel. Perhaps Moses plays "brinkmanship" with God, rather like threatening to resign from the government if he does not get his way. His speech is at least enormously daring, and perhaps noble as well.

God, however, will not be intimidated, nor will God be blackmailed, even by Moses (vv. 33-34). God will give nothing of what Moses asks. God will neither "forgive their sin" nor "blot out" Moses. God is perfectly capable of making distinctions in judgment, the very distinctions Moses wishes to forestall. God's punishment of Israel is no business of Moses, and he may not interfere with divine judgment. Thus God will "blot out" (*māḥâ*) (v. 33).

However, God has other work for Moses to do. Moses is to go to "the place"—the land of promise. Moses will be led and protected by an angel, and Moses is to get on with God's resolve (cf. 23:20, 23). Then God's speech adds a heavy conclusion: nevertheless, "I will punish" (פקד *pāqad*). Its effect is twofold. First, it reminds us that Yahweh's initial burning wrath (v. 10) is unassuaged. Second, it separates the positive function of Moses from the unfinished negativity of Yahweh.

This awesome confrontation between Yahweh and Moses is skillfully narrated, showing God working massive judgment. Even while the "great sinners" stand under judgment, the Mosaic community (including the Levites) is still the carrier of the promise. Neither the judgment nor the promise is permitted to crowd out each other. God has preserved God's sovereign capacity to adjudicate and to make distinctions. In the end, the calf-makers, the Aaron crowd, get their plague (v. 35). There is a "blotting out." The commandment will not be broken with impunity, and the God of the commandments will not be mocked. The commandments persist, and the Moses community stands ready to obey them.

REFLECTIONS

1. The narrative concerning Aaron introduces us to Israel's primordial (original?) sin. This narrative not only reports an episode, but presents to us a paradigm of Israel's most foundational waywardness. The "great sin" (vv. 21, 30-31) is to substitute an available, produced God for the sovereign one who is not immediately available and who is not made with hands. The first and second commandments require receiving, accepting, and obeying this God. The reality of this God causes Israel to live in endless jeopardy.

Israel, however, cannot tolerate the risk of faith (exemplified by the absence of Moses), so it incessantly seeks to reduce that risk by domesticating God to manageable proportion. The people who seek to reduce faith to palpable certitude are intensely religious, hungry for god(s) (v. 1). Their hunger, however, fails to deal with the reality of this God, and so the very community in partnership with this God becomes a factory for the production of more available, palpable gods.

2. The text stands by itself as a model of sin, punishment, intercession, and forgiveness. Its rich themes present a recurrent drama in the life of faith. We may enter the drama of the text more intensely, however, if we take it in the larger context of the book of Exodus. On the one hand, following critical source analysis, this text (together with 33–34) follows promptly after 19–24. On that reading, Israel's first act after its covenant oath of 24:3, 7 is a deep violation of covenant. Thus we are left, as was Israel, with the following questions: Is this the end? Will covenant be restored? The delicate, mixed ending of the episode in vv. 33-35 shows Israel struggling with this unresolved question.

On the other hand, if we take the final form of the text, chap. 32 comes after chaps. 28–29, which accent the enormous power, prestige, splendor, and wealth of the Aaronide office, perhaps suggesting that Aaron succumbs to the temptations of his office. It is possible to read the conflict as Moses vs. Aaron, Levites vs. Zadokites, or torah priests vs. temple priests. In more simple fashion, it may be enough to see the power of distorted desire among those who benefit too well from holy things, who lose critical self-awareness, and who begin to think they are the producers of the holy. The narrative suggests that this dreadful God "blots out" those who take unto themselves the production of holiness.

3. Insofar as this text is theological, i.e., concerned with God's life and self-presentation, we can see how the easy "both/and" of Aaron and the hard "either/or" of Moses exhibit the profound tension in God's own life. The tension is not simply the work of the narrator, nor is it only a quarrel between Moses and Aaron kicked upstairs. This tension of mercy that forgives and sovereignty that will not be mocked is an endless adjudication for the God of the Bible, who permits no final or systematic resolve. It is a tension we all know in our most intimate and treasured relations. In Exodus the crisis is kept raw, alive, and unresolved. It must be kept so for Moses and for Israel, as it is even for God's own life. This tension is what makes Moses' intercession so dangerous, so urgent, and so future-producing.

EXODUS 33:1-23, MOSES SEEKS ASSURANCE

COMMENTARY

The conclusion of chap. 32 leaves Israel in acute crisis, under assault from Yahweh. Chapter 33 is a narrative concerning "next steps." Those next steps are fragile and tentative; Israel under Moses is in a precarious position. The crisis concerns the plausibility and continuation of Israel's existence as a people. Because Israel is formed from "no people" into a people of the covenant, the abrogation of the covenant implies the termination of Israel. The stakes are very high, because this "people" may become again "no people," exactly what the prophet Hosea envisions (Hos 1:8; cf. 2:23).

That crisis of continued existence, however, is transposed in this chapter into a crisis of God's presence. Only upon the condition of *God's presence* is *Israel's existence* viable. This chapter is the most thorough and sustained struggle with the problem of presence in the entire OT. It is made up of three rhetorical elements. First, vv. 1-6 constitute something of a conclusion to chap. 32, juxtaposing the promise and the danger of Yahweh's presence. Second, vv. 7-11 report on a most elemental and direct mode of confrontation between Yahweh and Moses. Third, vv. 12-23 report on a dramatic encounter between Yahweh and Moses, culminating in a promised theophany (concluded in chap. 34). In all three episodes, one can sense a profound tension concerning Yahweh's way with Israel. Through the episode of the calf, that relationship has lost whatever innocence it may have had. Now Yahweh's will for the relationship is characteristically qualified by the awareness that Israel has betrayed Yahweh. That is an irreversible reality that will endlessly haunt both parties.

33:1-6. The first move beyond the disaster of chap. 32 consists of an oracle of Yahweh to Moses (vv. 1-3) and a narrative response to the oracle that reiterates something of Yahweh's speech (vv. 4-6). The oracle itself is a stunning act of God's graciousness (vv. 1-3). Yahweh might have kept silent, and therefore been absent to Israel. But Yahweh still intends a future for Israel and still expects to be obeyed. The imperative "go" (לך *lēk*), remarkably, is the same verb initially addressed to Abram in Gen 12:1. The speech is dominated, moreover, by the exodus verb for "go up" (עלה *ʿālâ*). The NRSV renders the verb in its first use as "leave." Thus Israel is to "go up" from Sinai as Yahweh "brought up" (*ʿālâ*) Israel from Egypt. Verse 1 in fact gathers together the whole of Israel's faith tradition, including the liberation of Exodus and the promise of Genesis. Moreover, in vv. 2-3*a*, the two great memories of promise and liberation are powered by a reference to the future in the land. As in 23:23, the angel is promised and the enemies are named who are to be overcome. The land to be given is richly described in a reminiscence of the promises of 3:8, 17. Thus in vv. 1-3*a* the oracle of Yahweh asserts that the entire tradition in all its power and authority is still operative. The calf episode has not disrupted Yahweh's intentionality for Israel. Yahweh's resolve has endured past the moment of rage (cf. Isa 54:7-10).[180]

Such a resounding affirmation, however, is poignantly qualified in v. 3*b*. One more time, Yahweh uses the exodus verb: "I will not go up" (v. 3). Yahweh will not be on the way with Israel. The reason is that Israel is

---

180. On this text, see Brueggemann, "A Shattered Transcendence?" and "This Is Like . . . " *Pulpit Digest* (May/June, 1991) 5-8.

"stiff-necked"—stubborn and resistant. Were Yahweh to be directly involved with this people, Yahweh would consume and exterminate them. Yahweh's anger over the calf is enough in check to permit this new declaration of fidelity, but just barely. There will be an exodus; Israel will "go up." But Israel must go alone. Its obduracy has cost the full presence of God.

In providing a mode of presence, the narrative has distinguished between "an angel" and "I." In 23:22-23, "the angel" becomes, as the rhetoric moves on, Yahweh's own person. Here, however, the distinction is maintained. Israel is assured of a great deal, but not of everything. Israel has enough on which to go, but it does not have Yahweh's own personal accompaniment. The angel does not here become "I," because "I" am not going.

The people's response (vv. 4-6) has at its center a reiteration of part of the oracle just uttered (v. 5). Again the threat of Yahweh's presence is affirmed. Also, an act of obedience is voiced in v. 5 that was not in the original oracle of vv. 1-3. Israel must "remove its ornaments" (vv. 5-6), which seems to refer to gold rings like those in 32:2-3, out of which the calf was made. Moreover, the verb translated "stripped themselves" (נצל *nāṣal*) is the same verb used in 3:22 and 12:36 for the seizure of Egyptian valuables. Israel, now possessing wealth and ostentation, is to free itself of such decorations; Israel is to do to itself what it has done to Egypt. Quite clearly, the narrative perceives the ornaments as a seduction and, therefore, a threat.

Three connections may be made concerning the removal of the ornaments. First, there is no doubt a reference here to the materials used for the calf. In this post-calf situation, reconstituted Israel, constituted by God's mercy and in spite of God's rage, is to unburden itself of such provocative possessions. The calf episode lurks for a perfectly possible reenactment. Second, the uses of the verb *nāṣal* suggest that the narrative intends to contrast the empty-handed circumstance of the slaves, who are free to take from their masters (3:22; 12:36), with the full-handed community of Sinai, which now stands under the seduction and danger known by the Egyptians. Third, less directly, this imperative may contain a critique of the priestly portrayal of

Aaron as exotic in garb and appearance (chap. 29). Moses, by contrast, always represents lean, stripped-down obedience.

Because Yahweh speaks, Israel has a post-calf possibility. But it must forego the commodities that seduce and distort. Israel willingly obeys (vv. 4-6), as it did in Gen 35:1-4. In v. 5, this unburdening becomes the precondition of Yahweh's next act: "I will decide what to do to you." This entire paragraph displays a people in severe jeopardy. God has now laid down stringent requirements for the future, and Israel accepts those requirements.

33:7-11. These verses stand in stark contrast to the threat and demand of vv. 1-6. They tell about a most primitive, characteristic, and recurring mode of God's presence. It is noteworthy that these verses do not tell of a particular meeting, but a reliable, regularly operative mode of presence. While the narrative accent of "the tent" is straightforward, we are told very little about it.

The tent is commonly regarded as perhaps the most primitive and elemental cultic device Israel has for God's presence. A device that both makes God available and allows for God's freedom, it is not to be confused with the more sophisticated and developed "tabernacle" (25:1), which seems to derive in part from the tent. We may observe the following features in this paragraph.

The tent is thoroughly and exclusively a Mosaic enterprise. It serves, embodies, and enhances Moses' authority. Most likely, the mention of Joshua in v. 11 (as in 32:17) serves to prepare us for his coming authority after Moses.

The tent is a place to which Yahweh really does come to speak to Moses, face to face. The mode of Yahweh's coming, however, is a visible "pillar of cloud." As is characteristic in the tradition, this text struggles to affirm full presence but also to make sure that God is not impinged upon or presumed upon.

There is a real meeting (v. 11); Moses speaks to God face to face. Indeed, the text suggests an intimate conversation between friends. Thus the text moves between intimate conversation and regal formality (cf. Gen 18:17; Isa 41:8). Through the person of Moses, there is genuine access to Yahweh. Moreover, this access has not been diminished by the calf episode. We are not told what transpires in that access and conversation, but the context permits us to believe that the conversation includes the sovereign affirmation of promise, the sovereign insistence upon command, and the daring intercession of Moses. In the hiddenness of this transaction, full communion between God and Israel is enacted.

The people play a minimal, secondary role in the meeting. They are only observers, not participants. If a person has a petition, it can be taken to the tent (v. 7). Presumably the function of the people is to watch in awe, wonder, and amazement, for in this meeting between the cloud-hidden God and God's friend, their destiny is resolved. There is nothing here of the threatening disruption that the meeting causes at Sinai (19:16-25).

33:12-23. The reference to the tent (vv. 7-11) is almost a pause to relieve the pressure of the narrative. As we have seen, the possibility of Israel's future survival and well-being depends on Yahweh's promise and presence. The reference to the tent might have given assurance on this point. Nonetheless in v. 12, Moses takes up the conversation as though neither the promise of an angel (v. 2) nor the regularity of the tent (vv. 7-11) is operative. This narrative is divided into two parts, an exchange about presence (vv. 12-16) and a final resolution by God to grant a less than complete self-disclosure (vv. 17-23). (The precise breaking point of the material into these two parts is somewhat uncertain, but it does divide in two sections, one dominated by Moses and the other by Yahweh.[181])

33:12-16. We are given two speeches by Moses, with only one brief utterance by Yahweh in v. 14. In Moses' first speech (vv. 12-13), the verb translated "know" (ידע *yāda*) is used three times:[182]

> You have not let me know.
> You said, "I know."
> Show me (הודעני *hôdi'ēnî*),
> that I may know.

Moses wants to know, to have certitude. He can only know if God lets him know, for

only God knows (cf. the rhetoric of Jer 11:18). What Moses wants to know is "whom you will send." Moses wants to know about the future and the mode of God's presence with Israel. The text obviously is unrelated to vv. 1-3, where the one to be sent is an angel. We are dealing here with a distinct voicing of Israel's crisis of presence.

The verb for "see" is used twice as an envelope for the speech: "See" (v. 12) and "consider" (v. 13). The last phrase is a motivational clause. Moses asks that God let him know because this is "your people" (contra 32:7). As in Num 11:11-15, Moses is clear and insistent that Israel belongs to Yahweh, and that Yahweh cannot escape responsibility.

This intense petition does, indeed, evoke a response from Yahweh (v. 14). It is a terse response consisting of only four words, but it contains everything needed. It is an assurance that "my face" will go—i.e., Yahweh's own self. Childs observes that God's promise in v. 14 is given only to Moses, "to you" (singular).[183] Moses' continuing prayer is to include Israel in the assurance. Thus in v. 16, he prays, "I and your people." The promise is for a much more intense and immediate presence than either the angel of v. 2 or the cloud of v. 9. The promise of "rest" is an allusion to the land (cf. vv. 2-3*a*). Thus Yahweh seems to give Moses everything for which he asks.

The mood of Moses' second speech (vv. 15-16) is not obvious. On the one hand, his response seems like a second sharp insistence, as though Moses has not yet gotten satisfaction and must insist one more time. On the other hand, Moses' insistence may be a statement back to Yahweh, receiving the promise and underscoring how indispensably important God's presence is. In either case, Moses affirms that the "face" is crucial. Again, the exodus verb "go up" (*'ālâ*) is used. Moses asserts that the "going up" from Sinai should not be undertaken if Yahweh has no intention of following through into the wilderness.

The reason for Moses' resistance is that without the evidence of continued presence, Israel will appear to be on its own, abandoned. Moses' leadership will be fragile and ineffective. Finally, in v. 16, Moses utters his decisive confessional statement. It is only Yahweh's presence that marks Israel

---

181. See Walter Brueggemann, "The Crisis and Promise of Presence in Israel," *HBT* 1 (1979) 47-86.

182. See James Muilenburg, "The Intercession of the Covenant Mediator (Ex. 33:1*a*, 12-17)," in *Words and Meanings*, eds. Peter R. Ackroyd and Barnabas Lindars (Cambridge: Cambridge University Press, 1968) 159-81.

183. Childs, *The Book of Exodus*, 594-95.

as distinct! Notice that in this last exclamation, the word *face* is used in a different way: "face of the earth." And Moses once more identifies Israel as "your people." The primary point, however, is that Israel's only claim to uniqueness is Yahweh's accompaniment. Moses' verdict may be an insistence, or it may be yet an acknowledgment in gratitude of the assurance of v. 14. I am inclined to think it is an insistence. Moses in this passage always wants more from God, and what he has by way of presence is never enough.

33:17-23. The dialogue continues. Yahweh responds once more to Moses and seems to give over to Moses all that has been asked. In v. 12, Yahweh had assured Moses that he had "found favor." In v. 16, Moses asks for a sign that he has "found favor." Now in v. 17, Yahweh asserts yet again that Moses has "found favor." The point is established! Yahweh is fully committed to Moses and to the future Moses will give to Israel. This assurance is heightened by Yahweh's final utterance in v. 17, once more using the verb *know.* Moses is fully known by Yahweh. Yahweh knows Moses' name! Notice that the use of the verb has been inverted. Moses wants to know, but now he is "known."

Moses, one more time, is relentless (v. 18). He has now received assurance of "face," "rest," and "favor." Now he asks one more request: "Show me [i.e., cause me to see] your glory." The verb *see* is used yet a third time, introducing another mode of God's presence. "Glory" bespeaks God's awesome, shrouded, magisterial presence, something like an overpowering light. It is in this passage as though the request for glory is to draw even closer, more dangerously, more intimately, to the very core of God's own self.

In his request, Moses has reached the limit of what even he may ask in his venturesome courage. Yahweh takes Moses' petition seriously, but will not grant the request. God will not let even Moses crowd into the hidden core of God's own life.

Yahweh's response to Moses' request consists in four powerful affirmations, with a massive negative at the end (vv. 19-23). The four affirmations are assertions of what God will do:

I will make all my goodness pass before you.
I will proclaim before you, my name, "Yahweh."
I will be gracious to whom I will be gracious.
I will show mercy upon whom I will show mercy.

The four statements voice an astonishingly generous, yet guarded, commitment to Moses. The first resolve concerns God's "goodness" (טוב *tôb*), i.e., Yahweh's generous, friendly power for life. The term *goodness* can be used as a synonym for *shalom*, and thus refers to the material blessings of creation. In our context, this promise parallels the concerns of vv. 3 and 14. In response to Moses' request to see glory, this is a manifestation of God's good gifts but not Yahweh's own self.

The second promise concerns God's name and embodies the full disclosure of Yahweh's sovereign character. This phrasing perhaps looks back to 3:14 and 6:2 and anticipates 34:6-7. The third affirmation concerns the completely unfettered capacity of Yahweh to be generous. The term translated "gracious" (חן *ḥēn*) is the same word rendered "favor" in vv. 12, 16, and 17. It generally concerns God's capacity to be unconditionally generous but most specifically refers to Yahweh's resolve to be generous to Moses. The fourth affirmation concerning "mercy" is parallel in structure and content to the third, and it again asserts Yahweh's capacity to act positively as Yahweh chooses. Jack R. Lundbom has shown that the literary structure of these last two promises, as in 3:14, is a rhetorical device used to terminate a conversation abruptly.[184]

To be sure, these four affirmations do not explicitly concern Israel, but they do seem to reassure Moses on the future attentiveness of Yahweh toward Israel in its hazardous journey. Life goes on for Israel only because Yahweh is free, gracious, and merciful.

The negative of v. 20, which comes upon us abruptly, is an exceedingly odd statement. Moses had asked to see the "glory." Yahweh refuses to show the "face." To be sure, both "glory" and "face" concern presence and access to Yahweh. "Glory," however, is less direct, seeming to honor Yahweh's majestic hiddenness. Thus Moses asks to glimpse God

---

184. Jack R. Lundbom, "God's Use of the *idem per idem* to Terminate Debate," *HTR* 71 (1978) 193-201.

in God's transcendent splendor, but Yahweh's refusal is as though Moses has been more disrespectful than he had in fact been. Perhaps Yahweh ups the ante and attributes more to Moses than Moses had dared, only to make the refutation more credible. In this last utterance, God draws a protective cover around the inscrutable mystery of God. The motivational clause of v. 20 suggests that God's refusal to be seen is because such "seeing" is too dangerous. This conclusion in v. 20 is in profound tension with 24:10-11, where the mountain party "gazed upon" God. Clearly the tradition is not concerned to harmonize all these assertions. It is enough to notice that the struggle for and with God's presence is complicated and hard fought. It admits of and requires a diversity of articulations, none of which can alone say all that must be said.

After the negative qualification of v. 20, Yahweh finally goes far in letting Moses stand in the presence (vv. 21-23). This final response

seems not to be concerned for the hiddenness of Yahweh but for the safety of Moses. Yahweh's offer to Moses is indeed gentle and protective. Yahweh finds for Moses a safe place to stand and watch "with me." This statement is filled with specific phrasing about the physical presence of Yahweh: "my glory, my hand, my back, my face." It is as though God plays peek-a-boo with Moses. Moses is permitted to look, just as the face of glory is past, and what Moses is permitted to see is the back side, the rear end of God—but not the face! The only thing he is denied is that for which he has never asked, the "face." It is worth noting that all we have is a promise of a distinctive disclosure to Moses. Nowhere are we ever told that the encounter does take place (cf. 34:5-6). The passing of God's glory seems always to be in prospect.[185]

185. Hans Urs von Balthasar, *The Glory of the Lord I: Seeing the Form* (New York: Crossroad, 1982) 317-31, concludes that "the Biblical experience of God is always proleptic."

REFLECTIONS

1. Life goes on, even after the calf episode! In these verses, the text reasserts the power of the old promise and the validity of the exodus (v. 1). It reiterates the enduring promise of the land. God's whole life with Israel from the beginning continues to operate, the calf notwithstanding. The sin of Aaron has not disrupted the power of God's intentionality, any more than the flood disrupts God's fidelity to Noah (Gen 8:20-22; 9:1-17), any more than the exile interrupts Israel's covenant (Isa 49:14-15; 54:7-10; Jer 31:31-34).

The amazing response of God to the events of chap. 32 is at the heart of biblical faith. The voicing of God's continued faithful resolve is first of all as an imperative: "go." Because God continues in fidelity, Israel, even after the calf, must continue in obedience.

2. The primary condition for a resumed relation with Yahweh in this chapter is the "stripping of ornaments" (vv. 4, 6). Chapters 32–33 are deeply aware of the destructive power of "commodity fetishes," of endless fascination with natural objects that are mistakenly supposed to enhance worth. It may be in our interpretative context that the "ornaments" that seduce are not material but psychological, moral, intellectual, or dialogical. Perhaps so, but we must not move too far from commodities, particularly in a consumer society wherein greed generates brutality and skewed neighbor relations. In these chapters, Israel is indeed "rich in things and poor in soul." The requirement for resumed covenant is divestment and unburdening of the accoutrements of self-sufficiency, which impede and finally preclude a "hearing" relationship. In his encounter with the "rich young ruler" (Mark 10:17-22), Jesus' comments on riches (vv. 2-27) are not far removed from this stern demand of Yahweh for divestment.

3. The primary agenda of this entire chapter revolves around the awareness that *survival* depends on *presence*. *Survival* means exactly the durability of a cultural system that can provide a "home" for individual persons. *Presence* means the holy source of covenantal life in our very midst. The juxtaposition suggests that the survival of a durable cultural system depends on the known, acknowledged power of holiness in its midst. In *Real Presences*, George Steiner persuasively argues that where God is not present, certain kinds of literature and art become impossible.[186] One may extrapolate from Steiner's argument that without God, certain kinds of social relationships are precluded.

The two great modern social experiments of Eastern communism and Western capitalism have struggled in different ways with this juxtaposition. It is now relatively easy to see that in the communism of Eastern Europe (perhaps most visible in Romania, Albania, and the former Soviet Union), where the holy dimension of covenant was denied, social relationships became increasingly brutal and empty. As a consequence, fear became pervasive, human dignity diminished, and creation as a life-giving system was nearly destroyed.

It is not so easy to see, or palatable to notice, that a Western free-market system in a different way evidences the same risks. "Presence" is little more evoked in a consumer economy than in a statist system. In the end, the results are not so different, wherein human dignity fails and life becomes paralyzing and empty. A market society devalues persons who have no productive capacity and relates rapaciously to the environment.

4. The calm, almost flat episode of the tent suggests that in this community of post-calf, stiff-necked people, meeting is nonetheless possible (vv. 7-11). We may imagine that in our secularized society, such a notion is too odd to entertain. But that community, like ours, had little inclination for such a meeting. It was, however, prepared to offer its petitions and to watch in awe and amazement. The meeting is not a big public meeting, when it happens. The meeting depends on the daring of one person who is prepared on behalf of the community to risk God's holiness and to treat the terror of holiness face to face, as "best friend."

5. In v. 16, Moses actualizes a crucial principle of community. He understands that even this Israelite community, in and of itself, possesses no marks of specialness. Moses would refuse to brood about the "marks of the church," and would opt for the radical principle that the church's only claim is its close solidarity to the God who invites camaraderie. The temptation for any community is to imagine that its specialness is its own peculiar property. The point applies first of all to religious communities. Derivatively, it applies as well to national states and every other kind of group that imagines itself to be special.

6. Moses' performance in vv. 12-18 is a model for daring, insistent prayer. He prays with enormous *hutzpah*, and is prepared to crowd God in insistent ways. First, he asks to know *God's ways*. Then he insists on the *face as accompaniment*. Finally, he asks to see the *glory*. Moses refuses to let God determine the limits of asking. This model of Jewish prayer offers much to learn for Christians, whose piety is characteristically too deferential.[187]

We may note two other features of this prayer. It is intensely theological, concerned with the person and presence of God. Moses' mind does not wander onto other agendas, but stays fixed on presence as the crucial issue for his people. Second, Moses knows when to stop, for after vv. 21-23 he goes no further. Moses is a model for prayer, because he takes into full and knowing account the one with whom he must

---

186. Steiner, *Real Presences*, 70, suggests that a refusal to face "presence" leads to "a misreading of man's place in the natural world." While Steiner refers to the objectivism rooted in Descartes and Kant, his insight is not far removed from the struggle for presence in our text, and for a right reading of reality.

187. On the legitimacy and cruciality of such prayer, see Claus Westermann, "The Role of the Lament in the Theology of the Old Testament," *Int* 28 (1974) 20-38; and Moshe Greenberg, *Biblical Prose Prayer as a Window to the Popular Religion of Ancient Israel* (Berkeley: University of California Press, 1983) esp. 11-14. On the efficacy of such prayer, see Harold Fisch, *Poetry with a Purpose: Biblical Poetics and Interpretation* (Bloomington: Indiana University Press, 1990) 108-14.

do business. He acknowledges not only the sovereignty of God but also his own considerable freedom in prayer.

7. The God who responds to Moses is genuinely self-giving. We might not have expected this in the light of chap. 32. This God, however, is fully attentive to the insistent petitions of Moses. God does grant to Moses that God's own face will be present on the journey. God agrees to show goodness to Moses. Most of all, God, in uncompromised freedom, is utterly gracious and utterly merciful. This is not cheap grace; neither is it a blanket offer for any and all. The text suggests, nonetheless, that the God of Moses extends God's self in extreme ways, in order to meet the needs and yearnings of Israel.

8. Only in the final moment is there a limit to presence. The limit on accessibility and intimacy is the limit of God's own inscrutable holiness. This accent is, of course, in tension with God's self-giving. God holds in non-negotiable and unending tension self-giving and the self-reserve that makes self-giving possible. God is endlessly at work in this tension, upon which the vitality of biblical faith depends.

Derivatively, there is in this tension a model for humanness. The keeping or holding of self belongs in tension with the giving of self. To fall out on either side is to destroy the prospect of a serious relation. We are most "God-like" when this tension is kept visible and operative. Too much traditional Christianity has one-sidedly urged self-giving. As a counterpart, secular ideology urges the complete keeping of self. This text suggests that neither posture by itself will bring us to full humanness. We are called to imitate the God who is shown in this text, the God who both holds and gives away.

9. The culmination of this chapter is a vision of God (vv. 22-23). It is, however, a vision that embodies exactly the tension and juxtaposition we have seen all through the chapter. Moses does get to see God—but not God's face. Moses' *"seeing"* is honored—but not fully. Moses anticipates Paul: "For now we see in a mirror, dimly, but then we will see face to face" (1 Cor 13:12 NRSV).

The experience of seeing God might have been given peculiarly to Moses (33:11), but Paul knows such communion is not given to us. Moses' *knowing* is honored—but not fully. Moses here again anticipates Paul: "For we know only in part, and we prophesy only in part; but when the complete comes, the partial will come to an end. . . . Now I know only in part; then I will know fully, even as I have been fully known" (1 Cor 13:9-10, 12 NRSV). The seeing is "dimly"; the knowing is "in part." But "dimly" and "in part" are enough.

EXODUS 34:1-28, RENEWAL OF THE COVENANT

COMMENTARY

This chapter forms the conclusion to the great triad of chaps. 32–34. Together they express a great dramatic moment in Israel's life with Yahweh: chap. 32, broken covenant; chap. 33, intercession and the crisis of presence; chap. 34, renewed, restored covenant.

Chapter 34 provides the dramatic moment whereby Israel, by the graciousness and mercy of Yahweh (cf. 33:19), and by the office of Moses, is restored to be God's covenant partner. The text may be divided into three parts, though such a division fails to deal with the detail and complexity of the several elements: (1) initial theophany and petition preparatory to renewed covenant (vv. 1-10), (2) divine decree concerning covenant stipulations (vv. 11-26), (3) conclusion of the covenant, which preserves the stipulations of covenant for generations to come (vv. 27-28).

34:1-10. The main business of this encounter is to make possible the survival of Israel into the future as the people of Yahweh. The personal interaction of Yahweh and Moses intends to serve the larger purpose of forgiveness, reconciliation, and restoration of the relation with Israel that had been broken by the calf episode.

That drama of restoration has the sternness of command at its center. In vv. 1-3, Yahweh issues to Moses a decree of three items concerning the renegotiation of covenant. The first item is "the two tablets" for the commands of Yahweh (v. 1). Heretofore the tablets had been mentioned in two connections. In 24:12, Yahweh gives Moses the two tablets of command. In 32:15-20, the tablets are destroyed in anger, symbolizing the destruction of this relation based in command and obedience. Now the tablets are reissued. This time Moses must supply the blank tablets upon which Yahweh will write the commands that are at the core of the covenant.

The second item of the initial decree is that entry into the sphere of the holy requires ritual preparation (v. 2). These requirements closely parallel the initial provisions of 19:10-11. This time, however, the instruction applies only to Moses, for only Moses will approach the mountain.

The third item is that Moses alone will conduct this encounter (v. 3). The contrast with the first meeting is clear. This time there are no elders, no people, no priests, not even Aaron. Moses has gained a monopoly in the narrative, perhaps through his daring and singular obedience in chap. 32 or perhaps through his relentless insistence in chap. 33.

Moses then presents himself for the theophany to which he alone has been summoned (vv. 4-7). Moses is obedient. He goes alone, with the tablets. (The ritual preparation is not mentioned.) Primary attention is given, rather, to the descent and speech of Yahweh (vv. 5-7). Yahweh's descent seems to allude to the promise of God's passing presence in 33:22-23, a theophany that has been promised but never, so far as we are told, enacted. This report, however, of a "passing" provides no detail to match the expectations

of 33:22-23. The only parallel between the two texts is the reuse of the verb for "pass before" (עבר ʿābar).

This text, in contrast to 33:22-23, is not interested in any visual encounter, but only in the speech of Yahweh, as indicated by the double use of the verb *proclaim* (קרא qārāʾ). The first use utters the awesome name of God, without any commentary or delineation, as in 33:19. All else is commentary on the unutterable name, now uttered in Moses' ear. (The awesomeness of the name here is reminiscent of 3:14 and perhaps also recalls the warning of 20:7.)

The second use of the verb, in v. 6, introduces one of the most remarkable and important utterances in the OT. It is not unambiguously clear that Yahweh (and not Moses) speaks. I shall accept the more common assumption that Yahweh is the speaker. Thus the speech of vv. 6-7 is Yahweh's self-disclosure, revealing to Moses the fullness of God's character and intentionality. Nowhere before this speech has anyone been privileged to hear directly a disclosure of what is most powerful and definitional for God's own life.

The proclamation begins with a double utterance, "Yahweh, Yahweh," in which the name is even more starkly and poignantly put than in 33:19 or 34:5. This double utterance enunciates and makes powerfully present the majestic, inscrutable sovereignty of Yahweh in the life of Israel. Verses 6-7, then, are an exegesis of the content of that name, which divides into two parts.

On the one hand, Yahweh is wondrously generous and forgiving (vv. 6-7a). This affirmation is profoundly important in this context, for it is exactly and only Yahweh's generosity that will restore Israel to covenant. The declaration employs seven terms to make this assertion. These seven elements provide the core vocabulary of the OT for the affirmation of God's awesome graciousness:

Merciful (רחום raḥûm). Phyllis Trible has effectively made the case that this term is related to the noun *womb* (רחם reḥem), and thus speaks of the kind of positive inclination a mother has toward her child, a "womb-like mother-love."[188]

188. Phyllis Trible, *God and the Rhetoric of Sexuality*, OBT (Philadelphia: Fortress, 1978) chap. 2.

Gracious (חנון *hannûn*). This term refers to completely gratuitous positive inclination, given without cause or warrant, unmerited favor. It is used in 33:12, 16-17 in reference to the "favor" Moses receives from God.

Slow to Anger (ארך אפים *'erek 'apayim*). The phrase literally is "long-nosed." It apparently suggests that whatever "heat of rage" there was in Yahweh's anger has a chance to cool off, as it must be breathed out the long nostril. This phrasing is crucial in the light of 32:10 and 12, where the phrase is literally "heat of my nostrils." Thus the heat of 32:10, 12, which destroys, is here seen to have a cooling mechanism.

Abounding in Steadfast Love (רב-חסד *rab-ḥesed*). Katharine Sakenfeld has shown that *ḥesed* refers to sustained covenantal solidarity.[189] This formula affirms that Yahweh has a great capacity and resolve to remain loyal in covenantal commitment to Israel. In this context, the phrase suggests that Yahweh will "put up with" a great deal because of Yahweh's own powerful resolve to sustain covenant, even when the partner reneges. (In Isa 54:8-10, even exile does not disrupt God's abiding *ḥesed*.)

Faithfulness (אמת *'ĕmet*). This term is frequently used in a pair with *ḥesed* and is a close synonym. It witnesses to Yahweh's complete reliability. The phrase *"ḥesed we'ĕmet"* occurs frequently and is echoed in the christological formula "grace and truth," in John 1:14, 17.

Keeping Steadfast Love (*ḥesed*), for the thousandth generation. This formula reiterates the term *ḥesed* and assures that God's *ḥesed* continues to operate for a long time, and for a host of subjects.

Forgiving (נשא *nāśā'*). The verb literally means "lift," which here means to relieve covenant violators of the burden of their violation. The verb here governs Israel's primary vocabulary for sin, including the three most common words for covenant violation, *iniquity, transgression*, and *sin*.

The use of the seven terms has cumulative impact. It is not possible or necessary to delineate precisely the meaning of each term by itself, for the effect of the whole is to assure Moses (and Israel) that God is deeply

189. Katherine Doob Sakenfeld, *The Meaning of Hesed in the Hebrew Bible* (Missoula, Mont.: Scholars Press, 1978).

committed to sustaining covenant with Israel, even when the other party is careless and unresponsive, as Israel had been in chap. 32. It is crucial and precisely characteristic of this God that the statement of self-disclosure is given in the moment when God is most deeply offended and Israel is most profoundly in jeopardy.

On the other hand, this same God who is so generous and forgiving also responds in sovereign ferocity to affront (v. 7*b*). This time there are only two terms, two negatives as over against seven positives. They are, however, weighty and severe. God will not acquit (נקה *nqh*). This takes the form of an infinitive absolute. God will *really* not pardon! God will not overlook or ignore violations of covenant. Second, God will "visit" (פקד *pāqad*) covenant sanctions upon the community for generations to come. God will not be mocked, and grace is not cheap. Moreover, God has a long and powerful memory for being wronged. The travesty of Aaron in chap. 32 is a serious matter that continues to have decisive impact on the relation Yahweh will have with Israel.

This is an astonishing disclosure of God, which tells Moses (and us) as much about the God of the Bible as any verse can. We may observe four matters about this formulation. First, this is no doubt a highly stylized liturgical formula reflecting Israel's mature and disciplined theological reflection. Fretheim observes that it echoes, in inverted order, the assertion of 20:5. Taking it, as we do, as God's self-disclosure, this formulation is not exhausted in its particular use after the calf episode, but provides an enduring reference point in Israel's life with God. This characterization of God is always and everywhere about God *in relation*. No "attribute" of God is given here concerning God's own character in itself—e.g., omnipotence, omniscience—because Israel characteristically is unconcerned with such categories. God is by character and definition in Israel a God who always stands in relation toward the people.

Second, structurally and at the heart of this formulation is a profound, unacknowledged, and unresolved contradiction. It is explicit in the double use of the term *iniquity* (עון *'āwōn*), which is "lifted" (*nāśā'*) and "visited upon" (*pāqad*). That is, God *forgives* iniquity, and God *punishes* iniquity. The contradiction, however, is not confined to this one double usage but is reflected all through the rhetoric. God does deal with violators of covenant in two very different ways that cannot be logically or in practice harmonized. Moreover, the formula itself gives no hint of how to work out this contradiction.

It is inadmissible to resolve the tension programmatically or systematically. Israel has discerned that there is in the very core existence of Yahweh a profound and durable incongruity: God inclines to be utterly *for the other*, and God characteristically is for *God's own self.*[190] That twofold inclination most marks the God of the Bible, over against more lyrical, more benign, more romantic, and more domesticated gods.

That contradiction makes the God of the Bible interesting, credible, and dangerous. This God is interesting, because one does not know ahead of time who God will be or how God will act. This God is credible, because this contradiction corresponds fully to the way we find our own life with others being enacted. This God is dangerous, because just when almost "deciphered" and made predictable, this God surprises us and keeps us off balance. Serious biblical faith requires a readiness to live precisely with and in the midst of this terrible, double-minded danger, which leaves God's partners always exposed and at risk.

Third, while this contradictory self-disclosure of God has a more general significance, here it pertains to the immediate crisis of Israel. It is in that post-calf situation that Yahweh is generous and severe. Even in that crisis, or especially in that crisis, the narrative provides no hint of adjudication of Yahweh's options. Moses knows only that the conversation requires him to face fully the possibility and risk of Yahweh, for Israel has no other ground for its future.

Fourth, Phyllis Trible, David Noel Freedman, and a host of other scholars have shown that this stylized creed-like formulation forms the basis of much of Israel's subsequent reflection upon the character of God.[191] Thus, for

example, in Num 14:18-19 Moses prays back to Yahweh Yahweh's own self-disclosure, and he holds Yahweh to the terms of that self-disclosure. Yahweh nonetheless inclines to act ferociously toward the offenders (vv. 21-23). Thus, even where God's generosity prevails, Yahweh is unsettled and yearns in continuing ways to act differently.

In other texts, it is clear that the contradiction has been resolved by choosing a side as a theological affirmation. Thus in Ps 145:8-9, the doxology of Israel voices only the generosity of Yahweh, whereas in Nah 1:2-3, the affirmation stresses God's severity (cf. Joel 3:21). In Jonah 4:2, the creed is stated in its positive force, but it is an affirmation that the narrator, in deep irony, has the speaker reject. This remarkable self-disclosure of Yahweh is inordinately supple and open to various theological tilts and uses.

For Moses at the mountain, it is not at all clear how the statement will play for Israel's future. It may be, taken dramatically, that Yahweh also is not yet clear on this future. While the options are stated, the specific implementation for this case at the mountain is yet to be determined. In this determination, Moses in his boldness has a role to play.

On the basis of God's rich self-disclosure, Moses now makes a petition (vv. 8-9) to which Yahweh responds (v. 10). Moses' petition is that Yahweh should choose the first option (generosity) instead of the second (severity), though the latter is fully available to God and perhaps warranted in light of chap. 32. Moses' petition relates to three themes of the preceding narrative. First, the premise of the petition is that Moses has found "favor" with Yahweh. Although Moses prays on a conditional "if," he has already been told that he has favor with Yahweh (33:12, 16-17). Thus Moses has a legitimate and credible place from which to address Yahweh. Second, Moses prays yet again for presence. It is Yahweh's willingness to be engaged with Israel on the way that will make or break Israel's future. Third, Moses acknowledges that Israel is "stiff-necked" (cf. 32:9; 33:5). In so doing, he prepares the way for Yahweh to enact the second half of the self-disclosure: "visiting iniquity."

Only now, with these three notes sounded, does Moses allude to the possibility of newness, just disclosed in vv. 6-7*a*. And even

190. See Walter Brueggemann, "A Shape for Old Testament Theology I: Structure Legitimation," *CBQ* 47 (1985) 28-46; "A Shape for Old Testament Theology II: Embrace of Pain," *CBQ* 47 (1985) 395-415.

191. Trible, *God and the Rhetoric of Sexuality*, chap. 1; David Noel Freedman, "God Compassionate and Gracious," *Western Watch* 6 (1955) 6-24.

here, Moses does not use the exact language of the self-disclosure. He appeals to the offer that Yahweh will "forgive" (lift), but he uses a new, powerful term: *pardon* (סלח *sālaḥ*). (See the same term in a parallel usage in Num 14:19.) In effect, Moses petitions Yahweh to enact generosity, to act in mercy, graciousness, steadfast love, and faithfulness toward this stiff-necked people who deserve only punishment. Moreover, Moses prays against the clear warning of 23:21 that God "will not pardon" (*nāśā*). Moses' appeal to God's generosity is with the full awareness that God's severity is appropriate and warranted.

The petition is intensified at the end of v. 9 with an appeal to the larger tradition of the promise of the land: "inherit us"—i.e., regard us as your special and beloved possession (cf. Jer 12:7-13, in which God abandons God's very own "inheritance"). Everything now hangs in the balance for Israel. Moses has uttered his best, most passionate appeal. In the instant between vv. 9 and 10, Yahweh must decide.

Yahweh's response is like a salvation oracle uttered in response to a petition, as in 14:13-14. It is long and exaggerated, but it is the resolve of Yahweh that opens for Israel a new future. Yahweh has accepted Moses' petition. In this moment of utterance, Yahweh has put aside the calf episode and is prepared to move on afresh from this point. Moses has won from Yahweh precisely the generosity necessary for Israel to have any future.

The promise of Yahweh, as a way to implement a renewed covenant, is to perform "wonders" that have not yet been "created" (ברא *bārā*). Yahweh will do before Israel and for Israel what no people has ever seen. The hyperbolic language is reminiscent of the plague rhetoric of 9:18 and 10:14. The text does not identify what these "wonders" will be. In the larger tradition, they may refer either to miracles in the wilderness or power for the entry into the land. In either case, these occurrences will make clear to Israel, and to the watching nations, that the holy power of Yahweh has been fully and passionately mobilized for the sake of this people.

The last phrase of v. 10 is a reprise, reiterating the promise of the verse. The rhetoric invites Israel to be astonished, and even suggests that Yahweh is rather overwhelmed

with the resolve just announced. As Israel's life was initiated by the wonders of Egypt, so Israel's life now renewed will again be marked by wonders. Thus v. 10 voices a decisive turning point in the larger narrative. The severity of chap. 32 and the unresolved question of presence in chap. 33 have now been fully overcome and wondrously resolved.

This new beginning is rooted in Yahweh's mercy—and in nothing else. It is accomplished, however, through Moses' courage and tenacity.

34:11-26. The act of sovereign generosity promptly becomes a summons to singular obedience. The God who will make covenant (v. 10) is a jealous God (v. 14) who will not tolerate any positive inclination toward any competing God. This list of commands may well be a very old, complete collection existing independently and functioning in some part of the community as a code alternative to the Decalogue.

In the completed form of the Sinai tradition, of course, no question arose that this collection could ever rival the Ten Commandments. Thus in this collection, what we have is another, perhaps well-known collection that is no rival to the Decalogue, but is placed in a secondary position to reiterate some elements of the covenantal command. It may be that this collection aims at the particular temptations evident in the calf episode.

This collection is based on the promise that God is about to displace other peoples to give the land to Israel (v. 11). This motif is already present in 3:8 and 17, in the covenantal conclusion of 23:23-33, and may indeed be the point of the "wonders" in 34:10. In any case, this collection of laws concerns exactly a decision to order the new land differently, in obedience to Yahweh.

If the conquest of the land is seen as a "peasant revolt," it is plausible that this text reflects competing and conflicting notions of land management. Against the more usual, exploitative land practices of the established economy, the community of Moses holds to a radical egalitarian vision. This legal collection is devoted to a defense and authorization of those alternative land practices, which reflect God's intention for covenant.

Two general points are worth considering. First, the claims of Yahweh are deeply linked to socioeconomic practice. Thus faith in Yahweh is not merely a religious exercise but a decision about social values, commitments, and practices. Second, this radical alternative vision of land practice admits of no compromise. The covenant insists on a clear "either/or" concerning the land. Any attempt to work a compromise will eventuate in distortion and finally abandonment of a covenantal possibility. Pixley observes, "To enter into pacts with the rulers of Canaan would be to renounce the whole movement that began in Egypt with the exodus and the victory over Pharaoh."[192] Just as the possibility of covenant concerns social practice, so also does the risk of violating covenant. That is, the "snare" of an alternative is not a supernatural threat (v. 12), but the danger of compromise on equitable social practice.

The covenant with Yahweh precludes alliances with those who do not adhere to Yahwism (vv. 12-16). "Yahweh is jealous"; Yahweh has a socioeconomic intention that admits of no halfway measures. This teaching holds together the danger of alternative religious symbolism (v. 13) and the power of other gods (vv. 15-16), along with cooperation with other peoples in their agricultural practices (vv. 12-15). Other ways of handling the land and ordering social power will have a costly theological outcome.

Verse 17 is perhaps a succinct closure to the long instruction of vv. 12-16. The "casting of idols" is exactly what Aaron had done, and it led Israel away from Yahweh and away from a faith focused on commands.

After this passionate and general urging to avoid entangling alliances with gods or human neighbors (vv. 12-16), the text now proceeds to voice a series of five ritual activities that are to give formal, public expression of allegiance to Yahweh as the true Lord of the land (vv. 17-26). Moberly suggests that these verses give specificity to the general claims of vv. 11-16.[193] To enact and confess Yahweh as Lord of the land is a polemic against Baalism as a religious claim; it is also a polemic against all other systems of political security and economic productivity.

The Festival of Unleavened Bread recalls the exodus (v. 18). The community to be settled in the land is to recall regularly its rootage in the miracle of liberation and especially its hurried departure from bondage.

The offer of the firstborn of livestock—cows, sheep, and donkeys—affirms Yahweh as Lord of the land (vv. 19-20). The provision exempting (through "redemption") the firstborn son from the demand indicates that this is clearly an agricultural requirement and no longer entertains any primitive thought concerning human sacrifice (cf. 13:13). Thus while rooted in the exodus demand of the firstborn (cf. 4:22, 11:5), this provision has moved a long way toward concrete agricultural practice.

The practice of work stoppage on the sabbath is a sacramental assertion that human beings exist neither from nor for productivity, but for well-being in the land (v. 21; cf. 20:8-11).

The festivals of Weeks, First Fruits, and Ingathering are observances of harvest (v. 22). They affirm quite concretely that Yahweh is the giver of crops that sustain the life of Israel.

The offering of First Fruits, like that of the firstborn in vv. 19-20, bespeaks the debt owed to Yahweh, which is acknowledged in ritual performance (v. 26).

These laws all govern ritual practice. But they all have agricultural-economic dimensions and function in a polemical way to fend off alternative economic practices that contain temptations to manipulative self-sufficiency. (On v. 26 as a polemical prohibition, see 23:19*b*.)

The theoretical intention of this set of commands is most evident in vv. 23-24. Israel shall act out its Yahwistic commitments in a public way three times a year. It may be that "three times" came to reflect a stable festival calendar, or perhaps it reflects the decisive times in the rhythms of agricultural life. In a less structured way, it may be that "three times" means "regularly and periodically." In any case, the agricultural community is always under severe temptation to imagine that the land is not subject to the concerns of liberation and covenant, and that other, less costly economic practices might work as well.

Verse 24 adds a curious and powerful notice. It makes two assertions. First, it promises that the zone of land managed

192. Pixley, *On Exodus,* 158.
193. Moberly, *At the Mountain of God,* 98.

covenantally will continue to expand. Such a claim might relate to military success. It might also be a promise that covenantal land and neighbor practices will be economically effective, so that more and more land (and land owners) will want to share in these practices. Second, it affirms that Yahwistically managed land will not be threatened by ("coveted") other economic systems while its owners are in pilgrimage to Yahweh. Those who do not submit their land to the destructive pressures of credit, interest, and profit will not be subject to land seizures that are the inevitable outcome of coveting.

What emerges from this list is a daring social proposal: (a) that the land can indeed be ordered in different, covenantal ways; and (b) that different land ordering must be given explicit symbolic, liturgical expression. Aaron's abortive theological coup was in fact a seductive *commodity fetishism* that is inherently a partner of *economic coveting.* The requirements of vv. 11-26 are designed to guard against such a preoccupation with commodities. The required sacramental acts are to symbolize and mediate a very different system of values and practices that make covenantal life possible and effective.

34:27-28. The conclusion of making covenant and the conclusion of Moses' long stay on the mountain (cf. 24:18, 32:1) concern writing.[194] God instructs Moses to write down "the things" (words) that are the substance of covenant. Moberly has argued well that there is an insoluble tension between vv. 27 and 28.[195] In v. 27, it is apparently the commands of vv. 11-26 that are to be written, but in v. 28, the "ten words" refer to the Decalogue.

What may matter is not the harmonization of these two verses, but that the covenant consists in written commands that persist and endure from generation to generation. In both written forms of covenantal requirement, the materials of vv. 11-26 in v. 27 and the Decalogue in v. 28, what is crucial is the magisterial "either/or" of Yahweh's will. Thus the culmination of covenant shows that Israel's life has now begun again by a God who generously moves beyond the crisis of the calf, but who jealously insists on complete obedience. The writing commanded by Yahweh is so that this massive contrast between Israel and its cultural, agricultural context may be always again available for Israel in time to come.

---

194. See the subtle argument of Carol Kern Stockhausen, *Moses' Veil and the Glory of the New Covenant: The Exegetical Substructure of II Cor. 3:1-4, 6,* Analecta Bibleca 116 (Rome: Pontifical Biblical Institute, 1989) 106-7.

195. Moberly, *At the Mountain of God,* 101-6.

REFLECTIONS

This chapter concerns an astonishing renewal of covenant. It is a renewal made exclusively from God's side in the face of Israel's profound "stiff-necked" character. The interpretive center of the passage may be "beginning again." In Christian proclamation, this theme is often flatly taken simply as a statement of grace. This chapter makes clear that the prospect of beginning again is marked at the outset by risk, uncertainty, and ambivalence, and it is marked at the end by rigorous, uncompromising demand.

1. Verses 6-7 witness to the profoundly personal reality of Yahweh's presence to Israel. That reality is marked by an open-ended, unresolved two-sidedness. This God is at the same time capable of inordinate generosity (mercy, graciousness, steadfast love, faithfulness) and an assaulting severity (visiting iniquities).

For many people, such an unresolved quality in God is deeply distressing. On the one hand, conventional orthodoxy prefers a settled God, with these matters neatly harmonized in a logical fashion. On the other hand, a liberal tendency will easily imagine that God's generosity has "evolved" past and superseded God's severity. Both are forms of reductionism, seeking to domesticate God and deny God's continued capacity for choosing more than one way in the world. Moreover, we are no more honest or better off if we imagine that these tensions have all been overcome in Christian supersessionism, for honest Christian faith must continue to struggle with the oddness of this God.

To seek to resolve in programmatic fashion the intentional uncertainty of vv. 6-7 is to miss out on the main point: Moses and Israel must come to terms with God's surprising, magisterial freedom. The reductionism so convenient to us ends either in a strict retributionism that confines God to a set of moral statements, or in an easy affirmation that makes God endlessly accepting and forgiving. If God should be distorted in either of these more comfortable directions, then we are continuing the work of Aaron and producing a God more to our liking. As Fretheim concludes: "There is no predictability or inevitability about the divine grace. This serves as a reminder that the community of faith ought not live close to the margins of God's patience (cf. Rom 6:1)."[196]

2. The ground of the new covenant is rigorous demand. The covenant requires that Israel undertake complete loyalty to God in a social context where attractive alternatives exist. In that ancient world, the attractive alternative was the established religion of the inhabitants of the land, with all its altars, pillars, and sacred poles—its technology to ensure productivity. In our own Western context, *mutatis mutandis*, the attractive alternatives to covenanted faith are likely to be the techniques of consumerism, which provide "the good life" without rigorous demand or cost and without the covenantal requirement of the neighbor. Then, as now, the jealous God calls for a decision against that easy alternative.

The sketch of the practical "either/or" here given Israel is concerned with two dimensions of public life. On the one hand, the "either/or" is to be practiced liturgically. This is evident from the festal calendar authorized in this set of commands. The text provides a steady sequence of liturgical acts in order to give sustained, visible sacramental embodiment to the "either/or."

On the other hand, these several liturgical gestures are in fact public assertions that the blessings of the land come from Yahweh and belong to Yahweh. In that folk society, the liturgical gestures point to economic realities. In this sequence of religious acts, Israel refuses Canaanite perceptions of the land and insists that ownership, management, and governance of the land are all under the rule of Yahweh.

It is possible, through this bifocal acknowledgment of liturgy and land, that the land (i.e., the economy) might be kept free of the rapacious, competitive practice (vv. 23-24) that destroys the possibility of community. In this text, Moses is doing the difficult interpretive work of transposing the covenant of the wilderness mountain to an agricultural economy.

I suggest that our comparable work is to transpose the covenant of the God of an agrarian economy to the governance of a post-industrial society. That work, like the interpretive work of Moses, will need to be liturgically inventive and economically critical. In a North American context, Wendell Berry has, in a series of novels, imagined that the land could indeed be part of a different social fabric.[197] Thus the deep "either/or" of the covenant is not simply a rigorous religious act, but is a mandate to organize differently the practice of property (land, economics) and the symbols that justify and legitimate those practices (liturgy).

3. The concluding act of writing (done by Moses in vv. 27-28 and by Yahweh in v. 1) gives body, continuity, and visible shape to Israel's new possibility. Writing solidifies the claims of covenant and makes them enduringly available to ongoing generations. It amounts at least to the production of a powerful tradition and perhaps to the production of an authorized canon that shapes communal imagination in normative ways.

In our current theological context, there is a kind of romantic attraction to what is new and spontaneous, which has the effect of scuttling tradition. Some of this scuttling is not done from hostility or resistance as much as from ignorance. Many persons do

196. Fretheim, *Exodus*, 307.
197. See Berry, *The Memory of Old Jack* (New York: Harcourt, Brace, Jovanovich, 1975); *Nathan Coulter* (San Francisco: North Point, 1985); *The Wild Birds: Six Stories of the Port William Membership* (San Francisco: North Point, 1986).

not know that biblical faith (and the communities that practice it) is an ongoing struggle with a body of explicit teaching. Biblical faith is not a series of isolated events or of momentary inclinations, but is a corpus of teaching that has continuing authority. The written corpus requires and permits endless liberated interpretation, so that there is no ethical scholasticism here. This community, receiver of God's radical graciousness, is addressed in a resounding and unending "either/or." This "people of the book" is destined by the decree of this jealous God to struggle with this "either/or," both in terms of its symbolic expressions (liturgy) and in its economic practice (land).

EXODUS 34:29-35, MOSES' SHINING FACE

COMMENTARY

The second meeting at the mountain is now completed. Moses had "gone up" in 34:4, and now "comes down." During that time, the impossible is wrought: A renewed covenant is established with this stiff-necked people. There remains now the difficult work of Moses' reentry into Israel's life after his extraordinary rendezvous at the mountain. After this meeting, Moses is no ordinary person, for he has entered deeply into God's own life. He has seen the back side of God's glory (33:22-23). He comes down with face shining, reflecting the awesome presence. In this difficult passage, two motifs are at work that are not easily reconciled.

On the one hand, Moses is the go-between for Yahweh and Israel, as authorized in 20:18-21. He regularly speaks with God (33:11), and he regularly reports to Israel. The tradition treats the subject as though no further explanation is required. Moreover, even in the older tradition, that function is given a workable institutional form (33:7-11).

On the other hand, this paragraph makes clear that there is an exotic dimension to Moses' mediatorial function. This is no ordinary matter. One cannot lightly or routinely move back and forth between an audience in God's glory and communication in Israel. Thus the text describes a device used by Moses as an acknowledgment of this stunning movement. We are told that his face "shone" (קרן qāran; v. 29) and that a "veil" (מסוה masweh; v. 33) was used to dim the glow.

We are told neither the problem with the shining face nor why the glow has to be toned down. It may be that the veil is a protection

for the Israelites. Or it may be that the glow of God needs protection from common contact, which would cheapen or trivialize it.

Against either possibility, however, the routine is that the veil is removed for purposes of communication with both God and Israel and is worn only between such times of communication. Thus it is exceedingly difficult to determine its purpose or function. It appears that the urgency of communication (word) takes priority over the danger of exposure (light).

The problems intensify when we consider two crucial words in this odd practice. First, shine (qāran) seems clear enough, except that no other uses of the term in the OT have this meaning. The conventional meaning in many places is "horn," which is the basis for Michelangelo's famous presentation of Moses with horns. If the verb translated "shine" derives from that for "horn," this may suggest a shaft of light not unlike a horn, but the usage is in any case most peculiar. (The rendering "shine" is already taken up in the LXX.)

In like manner, the term veil (masweh) is nowhere else used in the OT, although the context would seem to require this meaning. As indicated above, however, we cannot determine its purpose.

We may do better with this enigmatic narrative by focusing on its larger concern in relation to the book of Exodus. Two matters seem important.

First, the glory of God, the pure, dazzling light of presence is the way in which Yahweh is disclosed to Israel. (Note well that this is quite in contrast to an announcement of commands. While the commands depend on speaking and listening, this is a visual contact that has no identifiable or expressed content.) Earlier, it was in triumph over Pharaoh that Yahweh "got glory" (14:4, 17). In the second half of the book of Exodus, the text is concerned with glory as an institutional form of presence, whereby Yahweh can lead, govern, and instruct Israel (24:15-18; 40:34-38). We do not need to labor over the precise meaning of "shine" and "veil" to see that the text is concerned with the power, significance, authority, and danger of God's glory, without which Israel will not be Israel.

Our text stands midway between two other texts concerning God's glory in Israel's life that seem to figure in a Priestly theory of presence. This text looks back to 24:15-18, where Moses enters the cloud and communes with the glory. This paragraph provides a transition from the covenant making of chaps. 19–24 to the theme of cultic presence in chaps. 25–31. Moses goes deeply into the mystery of God with all of its danger, and receives guidance for the ways in which presence can be mediated and made available.

At the same time 34:29-35 looks forward to 40:34-38, the culmination of the text concerning glory as presence. The inscrutable glory of God comes to inhabit the tabernacle, which God authorizes in chaps. 25-31 and Moses instigates in 36–40. Now the glory as presence is no longer at the mountain, but is in the mobile shrine, always with Israel. Thus our text belongs to a self-conscious theory of glory that moves in dramatic narrative stages from mountain to tabernacle via Moses:

24:15-18	34:29-35	40:34-38
glory at the	glory brought	glory in the
mountain	via *Moses*	*tabernacle*

Moses' descent from the mountain is a device for the awesome coming of heavenly glory to dwell in the midst of Israel.

Second, in this text, especially as it is located between 24:15-18 and 40:34-38, Moses is strategically indispensable for God's gift of glory to Israel. As a result, all others, including Aaron and the priests (v. 30), are only passive recipients of what Moses has accomplished. Moses is the one who does not flinch in his insistence before God and who wants to see the glory (33:18). Moses is the one protected by God while the glory passes by (33:22; 34:6-8). Moses, a human agent, is the one who makes possible the glory of God in the midst of Israel.

That glory threatens Israel, and it enlivens Israel. It is not necessary, finally, to decipher completely the problematic verb *shine* and the difficult noun *veil.* We can see enough in this text to know that in the person (body, face) of Moses, a new contact between heaven and earth, between Yahweh and Israel, has come about. Israel is rightly frightened, but Israel is also able to receive its life as God inscrutably gives it.

REFLECTIONS

This is the key text in making "glory" pivotal for God's way in Israel. The term *glory* is elusive, but nonetheless saturates the primal language of the church. Thus the church sings and prays: "Glory be to the Father and to the Son and to the Holy Ghost; as it was in the beginning, is now, and ever shall be, world without end. Amen." And "For thine is the kingdom and the power and the glory, forever and ever. Amen."

Moreover, in the core events of the life of Jesus (birth, resurrection), the church has insisted that the glory of God was visible. The pivotal events in the biblical story, and in the story of Christian faith, concern the awesome entry of heavenly, holy mystery, into human experience. The Bible struggles to find ways to speak about this awesome entry, and one of its preferred, most effective ways is "glory."

1. Imagine a life context in which the glory of God has been completely nullified. The result would be a completely one-dimensional, flattened, profane existence. The outcome of such a profane existence is sure to be brutality, in which any affront against the neighbor is possible and permitted. Such brutality inevitably ends in despair, because there is no "surplus power" to generate any alternative. In handling this text, the interpreter must be aware that many people live at the brink of such a profane existence in which there is no ray of "glory," no power beyond self, and no opening to hopefulness. This text is precisely for such hopelessness.

The news of this text is that in spite of stiff-necked resistance, the glory of God is not necessarily withheld. In Israel's discernment, human life is kept open to the presence, the power, and the possibility of God.

2. The narrative of the transfiguration of Jesus (Matt 17:1-8; Mark 9:2-8; Luke 9:28-36) is marked by the appearance of dazzling glory. As Moses is the one through whom God's glory comes to earth, so now Jesus is the mediatorial figure who brings God's splendid authority into the midst of the disciples. Everything pivots, so the Gospels confess, on this one visited, transformed man!

3. Paul has taken up this narrative of Moses in order to make a statement about the priority, superiority, and cruciality of Jesus in 2 Cor 3:7-18.[198] In making this claim for Jesus, Paul uses our text's themes, but turns the text against Moses. Whereas the veil seems to be a protective device in our text, for Paul it is a blocking mechanism for Jews "whenever Moses is read" (2 Cor 3:15), so that the covenant is inevitably misread. As Richard B. Hays has shown, Paul's strategy is to make a contrast between the glory shown in Moses and a "greater glory" (3:10-11). But that contrast, according to Paul, is already known to Moses, who anticipates the full glory in Christ. Thus Moses becomes "a symbol of unveiling as well as of veiling. Moses prefigures Christian experience, but he is not a Christian. He is both the paradigm for the Christian's direct experience of the spirit and the symbol for the old covenant to which that experience is set in antithesis."[199]

Derivatively, Paul makes a different use of the notion of "veil" and "glory" in 2 Cor 4:3. Here also Paul takes the veil as a block to seeing the glory of the gospel. Only this time the subject is not Jesus but "unbelievers," whose minds are blinded "to keep them from seeing the light of the gospel of the glory of Christ, who is the image of God" (2 Cor 4:4 NRSV). In this text, Paul connects the light of the gospel with the creator's command for light in the world (Gen 1:3). In the end, it is "in the face of Jesus Christ" that one sees the "glory of God." While Paul's interpretive methods may strike us as unduly polemical, the positive point from the text should not be missed. He shares with the Exodus text the claim that the glory of God has become available on earth. To be sure, he locates it not in Moses' face but in the face of Jesus, but his claim moves in the very same categories as the Exodus text.

4. Less directly, the Fourth Gospel dares to speak as well of the glory of Jesus: "We have seen his glory, the glory as of a father's only son, full of grace and truth" (John 1:14 NRSV); "Father, glorify your name. Then a voice came from heaven, 'I have glorified it, and I will glorify it again' " (John 12:28 NRSV).

The words are so familiar to us that we miss their daring claim, a claim as daring as our text makes about the Sinai experience. The text claims to "gaze upon the glory of Jesus!" The Fourth Gospel not only reassigns the glory of God to the person of Jesus, but it also locates the glory of Jesus precisely in the cross (John 12:23). In the shame and shattering of crucifixion, Jesus' sovereign splendor is manifest. Here we are at the core claim of Christian faith, and we do well not to misunderstand. It is not urged that the cross is a step along the way to glory, as an instrumental achievement anticipating the resurrection. Rather, in the crucified one the glory of God is shattered and transposed, so that the vocation of suffering for others is made into the presence of God's power.

---

198. On Paul's use of this text, see Stockhausen, *Moses' Veil and the Glory of the New Covenant;* and Richard B. Hays, *Echoes of Scripture in the Letters of Paul* (New Haven: Yale University Press, 1989) 122-53.

199. Hays, *Echoes of Scripture in the Letters of Paul,* 142, 144.

---

5. This appearance of God's splendor in human affairs is not an easy theme to interpret or proclaim. Moses in any case had it right (33:16): The presence of God makes Israel's life distinctive. Indeed, God's presence makes all creation different.

Without this One of holy, dangerous splendor, life may indeed be reduced to banal control and self-indulgence, to the management of technique, the trivialization of human dignity, and the self-serving devouring of the earth. In our memory and in our own time, the most extreme cases of such disregard of glory include the diabolical drama of Auschwitz, the savagery of Hiroshima, and the heinous abuse of the Soviet gulags, where life is cheap, humanity is diminished, and where winds of life chill, and then cease.

The steadfast witness of the synagogue and the church, of Moses and Jesus, is that Auschwitz, Hiroshima, and the gulags are not the true or decisive narrative of creation. The glory will descend in its unbearable brightness and make all things new. That glory from God is carried in the faces and persons of odd, strange human models—Moses and Jesus. This is not a summons that all should be "carriers," for those carriers are chosen only in God's inscrutable power and freedom. It is, rather, an invitation to Aaron, to the Israelites, and to all who "behold" to notice the glory of God in the faces of those who refuse the golden calf, who stand in the breach to see the glory, and who bring the tablets and let life begin again. God's glory is never far from God's command, which authorizes the revamping of all of life. There is dread in the coming of this glory, but there is also inordinate, practical possibility. For all of his shining, Moses' work is on earth, with this people.

EXODUS 35:1–40:38

ISRAEL'S OBEDIENT WORK

OVERVIEW

These chapters of dutiful obedience match the commands of chaps. 25-31. Like chaps. 25–31, they are judged to be a Priestly characterization of a shrine that will host God's glory. They show Israel (and Moses) fully obedient to Yahweh's command. Read in canonical sequence, they show that after the sin of chap. 32 and the new beginning of chap. 34, Israel must again do its obedient work. This section concludes with the full coming of God's glory (40:34-38). The fullness of creation has now been enacted. The erstwhile slaves now can live anew in the presence of the gracious, awesome One who wills to be with this people. In this final act of God's coming in the midst of Israel, the circumstance of bondage is now completely reversed. Israel can, at the end of Exodus, continue its journey to the land of promise.

EXODUS 35:1–36:7, MATERIALS FOR THE TABERNACLE

COMMENTARY

In the last chapters of the book of Exodus, the text is preoccupied with the problem and possibility of hosting the holy. The plan for providing a viable home for the holy is God's own plan given to Moses on the mountain (chaps. 25–31). The actual construction of the vehicle for presence, however, is human work, to be done on earth, after Moses descends from the mountain (chaps. 35–40). The actual implementation is orderly and intentional. It must begin with the mustering of adequate materials and personnel (the concern of our present unit). The offering for the necessary materials is narrated in three sections: the command (vv. 4-9), the offering itself (vv. 20-29), and the cessation of the offering (36:3-7). The countertheme of personnel is given in two parts, as recruitment (vv. 10-19) and response (35:30–36:2).

35:1-3. In v. 1, Moses assembles the congregation of Israel. The reference, both as a verb (*assemble*) and as a noun (*assembly*), is thoroughly ecclesiological. This is a religious body, without reference to any state official.

The purpose of the assemblage is to perform the commands of chaps. 25–31. Israel, as convened by Moses, exists for obedience (cf. 19:8; 24:3, 7). This Israel is quite contrasted with Israel in chap. 32, a community of radical disobedience.

It is odd and remarkable that the first command after the sin and renewal of chaps. 32–34 concerns sabbath (vv. 2-3). In the corresponding section of chaps. 25–31, sabbath is the final concern (31:12-17). Thus sabbath is the last command (31:12-17) and now the first reiteration (35:2-3). Said another way, sabbath concerns bracket the material of chaps. 32–34. This community is preoccupied with sabbath as the quintessential mark of obedience, for in sabbath, life is willingly handed back to Yahweh in grateful rest (cf. chap. 16).

35:4-9. Moses' first act after coming down from the mountain is to authorize an offering, to gather materials for the tabernacle. The specifics of the offering are precisely those of 25:3-7. The tabernacle is to be made out of the best that Israel can provide. The offering is to be brought by those of "generous heart" (cf. 25:2). The term translated "generous" (נדיב *nĕdîb*) refers to an offering that is spontaneous and unrequired. It is not a much-used term, but regularly refers to generosity for the sake of the temple. The most important parallel to our passage is 1 Chronicles 28–29, where David collects the materials with which his son Solomon will construct the Temple. The people respond generously to David's appeal (29:5-9). His prayer in 29:10-19 acknowledges to Yahweh the people's generous offering and affirms that the offering is not commensurate with Yahweh's own generosity to Israel.

Thus the language as well as the generosity and intensity of leader and people is closely paralleled between Moses and David, tabernacle and Temple. God will be adequately housed only when the people give generously and abundantly. This is Moses' program for the materials.

35:10-19. Moses' second need is to assemble competent personnel to do the required work. Because the tabernacle is to be a work of beauty, the work must be done by skilled and gifted craftspersons. Those required are said to be "wise" (i.e., "skillful"; חכם *ḥākām*). This passage reiterates the inventory of the main features of the tabernacle from the commands of Yahweh: the tabernacle itself (v. 10; cf. 25:9; 26:1-6), the tent (v. 11; cf. 26:7-14), the ark (v. 12; cf. 25:10-16); the mercy seat (v. 12; cf. 25:17-22) the table (v. 13; cf. 25:23-30); the lampstand (v. 14; cf. 25:31-40); the altar of incense (v. 15; cf. 30:1-10); the altar of burnt offerings (v. 16; cf. 27:1-8), the court (v. 17; cf. 27:9-19), and the priestly vestments (v. 19; cf. 28:1-43).

35:20-29. The offering authorized in vv. 4-9 is now received. Two rhetorical features dominate this report of unprecedented generosity. First, it is clear that behind the financial transaction of the offering, which is a considerable matter in and of itself, is a deeply felt religious motivation. Thus the paragraph is saturated with phrases of religious motivation: "heart stirred," i.e., lifted (v. 21); "spirit willing" (v. 21); "willing heart" (v. 22); "hearts moved," i.e., lifted (v. 26); "hearts willing" (v. 29).

The picture presented is a community so convinced of its covenantal affirmations and so taken up in its conviction of the truth of its liberation narrative that it acts completely beyond the usual calculations of prudence and caution.

The second rhetorical feature pervasive in this paragraph is the word *all* (כל *kōl*), suggesting that the offering and its intent are utterly comprehensive. On the one hand, the word is used to describe the participation of all the people (vv. 20-26, 29). The contributors include men and women, leaders and people, and each gives at the point of personal strength, those who have goods and those who have skill. On the other hand, *all* is used for the totality of materials and the totality of the work to be done as well (vv. 22, 24, 29).

The use of the phrases concerning religious motivation and the recurring "all" of comprehensiveness yield a picture of a community alive, bestirred, and energized to act well outside itself and well beyond any conventional practice. This is indeed a once-in-a-lifetime effort for a once-for-all-time theological purpose. The text is enormously restrained, providing no clues as to the cause or driving power of this economic gesture. Aside from the ground of the act in God's own stirring, we may suggest four reference points for such uncalculating generosity.

First is the promise and expectation that the offering will provide a tabernacle in which the very presence of God will dwell. That in itself is sufficient reason for generosity. The Israelites are convinced that their offerings will let the gifts and guarantees of heaven come among them.

Second, as a sequel to chap. 32, Israel has now come face to face with God's incredible graciousness and willingness to begin again with this stiff-necked people. Moreover, this offering poignantly contrasts the disastrous offerings brought to Aaron (32:2-3). In this gesture, Israel has a chance to redress that terrible deed of disobedience.

Third, reading across the book of Exodus and the journey from liberation to presence (cf. 29:43-45), this offering is a response to the wonder of liberation. The people who in their destitute condition had to seize silver and gold from the Egyptians (cf. 3:21-22;

11:2-3; 12:35-36) are now able to give from their abundance. This Israel, unlike the desperate slave community, knows that it is much better to give than to receive.

Fourth, taken critically, the opportunity to construct a home for the holy means that Israel has a chance to put behind it the terrible season of absence called "exile." In the post-exilic period when this text was put into its final form, Israel is indeed beginning again, after "the absence," with the glorious God who has now promised to be present (cf. Ezekiel 40–48). Thus Israel's new beginning is an act of profound generosity by the God who has been so generous in liberation (chaps. 1–15), in covenant making (chaps. 19–24), and in forgiveness (chaps. 32–34). Israel is about the happy work of completing a transaction in which both parties, God and Israel, practice uncommon generosity.

35:30–36:2. As the need for money in 35:4-9 is resolved in 35:20-29, so the requirement of trained personnel in 35:10-19 is now resolved in 35:30–36:2. In 31:1-11, God specifies Bezalel and Oholiab as the key workmen, and they are now authorized. One is struck by the practical, commonsense approach to the construction project. Just as the project requires real financial resources, so also it requires trained and skilled artisans. Moses and Aaron are not builders of tabernacles! This is not work for the religious leaders but requires a very different kind of ministry.

The most striking feature of vv. 30-35 is that Yahweh is the subject of the section, while Bezalel and Oholiab are only objects and recipients of Yahweh's actions: Yahweh has called by name (v. 30); Yahweh has filled (vv. 31, 35); and Yahweh has given heart ("inspired," v. 34).

It is all Yahweh's doing! Yahweh has called, authorized, equipped, and inspired. As a result, the workmen are peculiarly competent for the work. The rhetoric of the chapter, in order to make a proper account, uses an extended series of words to characterize these workmen. Thus in v. 31, four words are used for competence: *spirit, skill, intelligence,* and *knowledge.* In v. 32, a series of materials is enunciated, and in v. 35 a more comprehensive list is given. Moreover, these workmen are equipped to teach others (v. 34), no doubt those who will work under

their supervision. In this entire arrangement of adequate personnel, Moses plays a subordinate role. These are competent laypersons, authorized directly by Yahweh. Their commitment and skill correspond in personnel to the generosity of the money. The program is both well financed and well staffed.

Chapter 36:1-2 provides summary statements on the leadership of Bezalel and Oholiab and a host of other craftspersons. Two points are stressed: They are uncommonly skilled, and they are keenly motivated. Moreover, both their skill and their motivation are the work and gift of Yahweh.

36:3-7. However, concerning the careful preparations, which are both precise and prudent, one unforeseen factor causes Moses' speech to pause momentarily in its march toward obedient construction (36:3-7). Until this point, this portion of the text has developed two themes symmetrically: (1) concerning material offering—command (35:4-9) and response (35:20-29); (2) concerning skilled personnel—command (35:10-19) and response (35:30–36:2). In this fifth element of the unit, however, the text breaks beyond this symmetrical pattern. Beyond command and response, there is now a third, very odd element concerning the offering: The artisans are overwhelmed by too much material! This is generosity run rampant.

The workmen report to Moses an overwhelming supply of goods, and Moses must order a cessation of offerings. Three rhetorical elements express the intensity of the offerings. First, the Israelites bring offerings "morning by morning" (v. 3; see what is perhaps a parody of this in Amos 4:4). Second, twice the adverb עוֹד (ʿôd) is used (vv. 3, 6). It is rendered "still kept" and "anything else," suggesting repeated, reiterated action. Third, twice the term די (dê) is used, rendered "much more than enough" (v. 5) and "more than enough" (v. 7). In v. 7 the term is matched with הותר (hôtēr), so that the Hebrew construction is "enough and some left over" (cf. Mark 6:43; Mark 8:8). The term *dê* regularly means "sufficient, all that is needed," and suggests "overflowing blessing" (cf. Mal 3:10).

We are not told why there was such an overflow of commitment and generosity on the part of Israel. Clearly this is an extraordinary moment in Israel's liturgic life, in which generosity toward God and God's promised presence is unprecedented. The only explicit comment in the text concerning motivation is that the people have "generous hearts and willing spirits." The construction of the tabernacle in chaps. 36–39, at the command of chaps. 25–31, begins, not in calculated obedience, but in unfettered, undisciplined, extravagant devotion. Israel's response is indeed commensurate with the awesome self-giving of Yahweh.

REFLECTIONS

This text portrays a stewardship dream come true, in which the motivation for giving is pure and untroubled and in which the generosity of Israel is staggering. The text may be a model for giving when a community stands, on the one hand, reflecting on God's forgiving generosity, and on the other hand, in anticipation of God's full presence.

1. The assumption of the chapter is that Israel has a "generous heart" and a "willing spirit." The text does not reflect on the psychological aspects of such disposition. Perhaps the best commentary on this generous inclination is voiced in Ps 51:10-17. In this prayer of supplication, the speaker invokes the language of creation, asking God to begin again, to give the Spirit (wind [רוח *rûaḥ*]) that makes one as new as on the first day of creation. The speaker prays that his heart (organ of loyalty [לב *lēb*]) and spirit (capacity for energy [*rûaḥ*]), which had become disaffected from Yahweh, might again be renewed, restored, and engaged for Yahweh. All of this is accomplished through forgiveness. From that restored heart and spirit will come acceptable sacrifice and offerings for rebuilding (vv. 17-19).

In Num 14:24, Caleb has a "different spirit," and in Ezek 36:26-27 Israel in exile will be given "a new heart and a new spirit," suited for obedience. All of these uses concern beginning again out of exile, out of alienation. These texts perhaps illuminate for us the ground of generosity in our chapter. Either directly from the glory of Sinai (Exod 24:15-18; 25:1–31:17; with a source reading), or directly from the mercy of chaps. 33–34 (with a canonical reading), Israel is at a moment of new beginning, as new and fresh as new creation. (Recall that in 34:10, the verb *create* [ברא *bārā*] is used for God's powerful, wondrous new beginning.) In that moment, nothing impedes generosity, nothing qualifies extravagance. The only compelling motivation for generous stewardship is a theological awareness that life is a pure gift and that gratitude is the only fitting posture for life.

2. The text is characteristically realistic in its recognition that the chance of hosting God's holiness requires a concrete strategy that must be financed. Religion that is significant and sustaining costs money, and Moses does not hesitate to commandeer Israel's wealth.

The narrative and prayer of David in 1 Chronicles 28–29 concerning the gathering of materials for the Temple are likely related to our text, and they provide the best exposition. In his prayer, David speaks Israel's most programmatic statement concerning astonishment that he and his people could offer worthy, acceptable offerings. David then acknowledges that the offering is a return of God's own gifts (cf. v. 14). Thus David asserts, "All this abundance . . . comes from your hand and is all your own" (1 Chr 29:16 NRSV).

In response to the prayer, finally, the people offer to Yahweh "a thousand bulls, a thousand rams, and a thousand lambs . . . and sacrifices in abundance for all Israel" (1 Chr 29:21; cf. Mic 6:6-7). No wonder "they ate and drank before the LORD on that day with great joy" (v. 22 NRSV; cf. Exod 19:10-11)!

This remarkable act of stewardship is a dramatic assertion against every notion of self-sufficiency. The psychology and economics of autonomy, of being "self-made," are enormously powerful among us and constitute the fundamental ideology of modern consumerism. That psychology teaches that humans are isolated individuals capable of self-sufficiency. Commensurately, that economics teaches that each is entitled to all that can be acquired. The result of such ideology is a grudging, thin capacity for giving, sharing, or sacrifice.

The strategy of these texts is not to coerce or manipulate or to "nickel and dime" in order to get enough money. Rather, both Moses and David directly counter the fundamental assumptions of autonomy and self-sufficiency. Once it is established that life itself is pure gift, then generosity and gratitude flow easily and readily. These texts (Exod 36:3-7 and 1 Chr 29:6-22) are a powerful alternative to the kind of self-deceiving amnesia reflected in Deut 8:17: "Do not say to yourself, 'My power and the might of my own hand have gotten me this wealth' " (NRSV). A habitat for God's holiness will never be constructed by self-made persons but only by those who are continually moved by the extraordinary gift of new life.

3. A series of NT texts come to mind around this theological theme of evangelical generosity: In his instruction to his disciples, Jesus urges: "You received without payment; give without payment" (Matt 10:8 NRSV). In urging would-be disciples to consider seriously the cost of commitment, Jesus uses an analogy: "For which of you, intending to build a tower, does not first sit down and estimate the cost, to see whether he has enough to complete it?" (Luke 14:28 NRSV). Paul utilizes the metaphor of building for growth in faith: "For we are God's servants, working together; you are God's field, God's building" (1 Cor 3:9 NRSV). In commenting on the work of a steward and warning against autonomy, Paul uses rhetoric reminiscent of 1 Chr 29:14: "What do you have that you did not receive?" (1 Cor 4:7 NRSV) In his great appeal for the "collection" with a reference to exodus manna and a christological reference, Paul appeals for generosity: "So we want you to excel also in this generous undertaking" (2 Cor 8:7 NRSV). Before the writer of Ephesians moves to the imperatives of the Christian life, he ends with a lyrical affirmation of God's inordinate generosity: "Now to him who by the power at work within us is able to accomplish abundantly far more than all we can ask or imagine, to him be glory in the church and in Christ Jesus to all generations, forever and ever. Amen" (Eph 3:20-21 NRSV).

These texts (and many others) suggest that theological foundations lead the community of faith to share its wealth with liberality. Those theological foundations serve to counter the ideology of the world, which moves from fear and ends in selfishness. In the place of fear, faith invites gratitude. In the place of selfishness, faith ends in extravagant generosity.

4. This text knows that the stewardship required for the tabernacle includes "time and talents." "Hosting the Holy" requires many skills, gifts, and competencies that are not "religious." Along with the two master-artisans, Moses seeks out "all who are skillful" (35:10; 36:2). Moreover, the skill is a gift from God (36:2), which may be energized and motivated by God's stirring. Thus, long before the Reformers, this text understands the cruciality of "secular vocation." This is even more important, since it occurs in a Priestly text wherein priests are regarded as the key players in the life of Israel. Here it is clear that the priestly corps fully depends on secular workers who understand their work in terms of the claims of God.

Because the tabernacle is a thing of beauty and artistic sensitivity, one may find in this text a warrant for a community of artists who work to make available "expressions of surplus" that witness to the holy dimension of all of life. That is, the tabernacle is more than something "churchy." It is a sign and vehicle that the community is inhabited by holiness. The religious leaders in this text have profound respect, as well as need, for artisans who are their indispensable allies. The work of this alliance is to make sure that Israel need not live in "real absence," in a profane existence devoid of awe, amazement, and God-given vitality.

EXODUS 36:8–39:43, THE WORK OF CONSTRUCTION

COMMENTARY

With adequate resources (35:4-9, 20-29; 36:3-7) and personnel (35:10-19; 35:30–36:2), the actual work on the tabernacle can now proceed. These texts are closely connected to the commands given earlier (chaps. 25–31). Commentaries rightly handle these texts by referring to the corresponding command. Not much more needs to be said or can be said about these texts. We may make four general observations.

First, the texts closely correlate to the commands of Yahweh. The construction of the tabernacle is a sustained act of obedience. Israel characteristically affirms that as command is issued by the God of glory, so observance is human work done on earth. Obedience is indeed a mode of communion between holy God and responding people.

Second, this is nitty-gritty human work. Not much is made of that fact in this text, but we must keep it in mind. Thus we may imagine the real cutting of lumber, real measuring of frames, real decisions about design and technique, informal conferences and tactical decisions along the way. Tabernacle construction is human work.

Third, in this long sequence of texts, Moses is for the most part absent. To be sure, there are some third-person singular pronouns for which the antecedent is unclear. With the authorization of work in 35:30–36:3, however, it is more probable that Moses stayed out of the actual work. The construction is done by those who have the skill to do it.

Fourth, the actual work of construction moves toward the culminating drama of presence in chap. 40, wherein Moses again becomes decisive. The workers are marked with an awesome religious intentionality: They are making possible the presence.

The text is divided into four sections: the construction of the tabernacle (36:8–38:20), an audit of expenditures (38:21-31), the preparation of priestly attire (39:1-31), and a concluding summary statement (39:32-43).

36:8–38:20. In large measure, the commands of chaps. 25–27 and parts of chap. 30 are implemented: 36:8-38, concerning the tabernacle, refers to 26:1-37; 37:1-5, concerning the ark, refers to 25:10-14; 37:6-9, concerning the mercy seat, refers to 25:17-20; 37:10-16, concerning the table, refers to 25:23-29; 37:17-24, concerning the lampstand, refers to 25:31-39; 37:25-28, concerning the altar of incense, refers to 30:1-5; 37:29, concerning oil and incense, refers to 30:22-25; 38:1-7, concerning the altar of burnt offering, refers to 27:1-8*a;* 38:8, concerning the bronze basin, refers to 30:17-18; and 38:9-20, concerning the court, refers to 27:9-19.

To be sure, there are some small departures from the texts of command, by way of omission, reordering, and in a few cases by addition. (The priority of the tabernacle in chap. 36 before the furnishings in chaps. 37–38 seems logically preferable to the sequence in chaps. 25–27.) On the whole, however, the variations in content and order do not need to concern us. The most important and consistent omissions are comments about the theological function of items. However, these omissions make good sense, because this is a report on construction and not a building manual. Except in details that for our purposes are insignificant, the tabernacle is built according to specifications.

38:21-31. These verses present something like a formal, final, and complete audit of the finances, divided into two parts. First, the three responsible officers are identified (vv. 21-23). It is as though they are the signatories to the final contract. The inclusion of Ithamar surprises us in this context. While we have encountered his name elsewhere (6:23; 28:1), we have had no clue that he is involved in the construction of the tabernacle. His name keeps the project securely related to the priestly houses and their influence.

The second part of this report concerns the expenditure of funds (vv. 24-31). This passage is especially interesting when set in juxtaposition with the texts concerning the offerings in 35:4-9, 20-29 and 36:3-7. While the community may give freely, lavishly, and spontaneously, those responsible for the project must be precise, in order to both cover actual costs and give account of their management.

The formal audit is in three parts, concerning three previous materials used. First, gold is the most precious and most sparingly used metal (v. 24). The second metal reported is silver (vv. 25-28). This must have been the normative material because it receives the most attention in the text. Two matters are noticed. First, the amounts used relate to an actual census tax (on which, see 30:11-16). This procedure for raising money contrasts with the freewill offering mentioned earlier. This text suggests that the project is so ambitious that it requires institutional discipline to raise the money, even beyond uncommon generosity. In any case, the text does not acknowledge any tension between the two modes of finance. The second element related to silver is a detailed accounting of the uses made of it, as though the leadership wants to be clear on where every penny is spent. The third metal, bronze, is used for lesser objects (vv. 29-31).

This audit suggests a report with no questions outstanding and no bills left unpaid. The report evidences care, precision, and comprehensiveness.

39:1-31. The preparation of attire for the Aaronide priesthood is again closely guided by the commands given to Moses and again with some variations: 39:2-7 constructs the ephod, authorized by 28:6-14; 39:8-21 constructs the breastplate, authorized by 28:15-28; 39:22-26 constructs the robe, authorized by 28:31-34; 39:27-29 constructs the tunic, authorized by 28:39; 39:30-31 constructs the rosette, authorized by 28:36-37.

Seven times (39:1, 5, 7, 21, 26, 29, 31) it is asserted, "As the LORD had commanded Moses." This formula is absent in chaps. 36–38 concerning the tabernacle, but it is used with reference to Aaron. Perhaps its repeated usage serves to subordinate the priesthood of Aaron to the tradition of Moses, a recurrent accent of Exodus. Conversely, the formula may also function to give strong legitimacy to the house of Aaron.

39:32-43. This unit reports the completed construction of the tabernacle and all its equipment. The main body of the text provides an inventory of the fixtures (vv. 33-41). Although this list is somewhat more detailed it corresponds to the list in 35:10-19. The two lists together form an envelope for the long text on construction (chaps. 35–39). Moreover, this list of fixtures roughly corresponds to the general outline, of chaps. 25–31 and 36–39. Everything needed is supplied to make the presence possible in Israel.

Primary interest in this passage will be carefully focused on the beginning and end (vv. 32-33*a*, 42-43). The beginning statement, which clearly draws to a close the general statement on construction, contains three interesting features. First, the work is "finished" (כלה *kālâ*). This is not in any way an exceptional word. It is of interest here, however, because the same word is used in a similar formula for the completion of the Temple (see 1 Kgs 6:9, 14, 38; 9:1, 25; 1 Chr 28:20; 2 Chr 8:16). Our text clearly intends the tabernacle to be an anticipation of the Temple.

Second, the introductory formula asserts that all is done "just as the LORD had commanded Moses." This tabernacle is in full compliance and should make presence possible.

Third, the tabernacle is "brought" to Moses. This suggests that Moses has indeed stayed out of the construction. The presentation to him is a formal one, not unlike the legal process of a contractor's handing over a new building to the owner. At this moment, Moses accepts responsibility for the building. Correspondingly, Bazalel, Oholiab, and Ithamar (cf. 38:21-23) disappear from the text. Mosaic activity is screened out of construction (36:9–39:31), just as the workmen have no part in the subsequent Mosaic work of legitimation in 40:1-33.

The conclusion of this passage contains corresponding themes (vv. 42-43). First, though the term *finish* is not used, the formula of completion parallels v. 32: "had done all of the work." Second, the formula "just as the LORD had commanded Moses" is twice repeated. Third, the unit ends with the succinct but freighted statement, "Moses blessed them"—i.e., the Israelites who had done the work. This refers to a powerful gesture of well-being, which Moses is fully authorized to pronounce. This act indicates that he approves the work. Moreover, the act of blessing may mark for Israel a transition to chap. 40 and a commendation to the presence.

We may note one other matter concerning the conclusion. Only two other uses of *bless* in Exodus pertain to Moses. In 12:32, Pharaoh in his anguish petitions Moses, "Bring a blessing on me too!" Moses ignores the petition, and Pharaoh remains unblessed. Here the Israelites do not ask or seek a blessing from Moses, but they nonetheless receive one. The connection to 12:32 once again dramatically contrasts Egypt in the absence of blessing, with Israel, the people where the power for life is given.

The other usage is in 32:29, where Moses acknowledges that the Levites are blessed. They, like the workmen on the Temple, are models of tenacious faithfulness.

REFLECTIONS

While commanded by Yahweh, the work of constructing a house for the holy is human work, and it must be done well. The specificity and concreteness of the work protest against any tendency to make communion with God easy or "spiritual." This God needs *a place* that is reserved precisely for this holiness. The creation of such a place, moreover, requires a combination of passion, generosity, competence, and devotion.

We may identify two other notes about this building project: (1) There is a careful audit and accounting of funds. This fact attests once again to the unembarrassed materiality of the project. (2) The building is "finished," but the conclusion of this chapter is still penultimate. The building is an act of hope and expectation. This can be a people prepared (cf. Luke 1:17) and a place prepared, but all the preparation finally leaves Israel waiting. The place for God's holiness is not finally readied for presence until God readies it.

EXODUS 40:1-33, MOSES FINISHES THE WORK

COMMENTARY

Now Moses reappears in his full power. Since 35:6, the project (and the text) have been turned over to the artisans who construct the holy place. The tabernacle is "finished" (39:32), except that it is not in fact finished until Moses finishes it. The construction of 36:8–39:31 has been the work of the laity. That action must now be matched and done again by Moses, before it is done effectively. These verses are constructed as command (vv. 1-15) and performance (vv. 16-33); thus they repeat in miniature the same pattern of command and performance in chaps. 25–31 and 35–39.

Yahweh speaks to Moses (vv. 1-15), this time to issue the decisive commands concerning the tabernacle. In this speech, Moses is the subject of a long series of imperative verbs that now finally put in place the tabernacle and all its furnishings. This series of verbs serves as a technique for reiterating (yet one more time) all the elements of the tabernacle that have been authorized in chaps. 25–31, summarized in 35:10-19, implemented in 36:8–39:31, and summarized again in 39:32-41. All of these lists vary in detail, but they refer to the same pattern and plan. Moses is instructed to take action on the "first of the first," a new year, at the beginning (v. 2).

Perhaps the most important matter of these commands is the series of pivotal verbs addressed to Moses: *anoint, consecrate,* and *wash.* Moses is to mark with oil (משח *māšaḥ*; vv. 9-11, 13, 15). Through the anointing, Moses is to "make holy" (קדש *qādaš,* vv. 9-11, 13). Moses is to wash Aaron and his sons, and so purify the priesthood. The most intense outcome of the three verbs is that the altar of burnt offering will become "most holy," i.e., "holy of holies" (v. 10). Moses must transpose the visible objects that have been constructed into something they have not been, and could not be, without his authority.

Even the priesthood of Aaron comes to its existence only through Moses and derives its very life from Moses. Indeed, it is startling and telling that in this extended Priestly sequence of chaps. 25–40 (which does not include 32), Aaron, the paradigmatic priest, is only a passive recipient of God's action through Moses. (And in chap. 32, the only text in which Aaron acts, he does less than well!) The priestly office of Aaron is legitimate and important to Israel, but it belongs on a plane of authority quite secondary to, and derived from, the unrivaled, elemental, and personal power of Moses.

Once more, the text reviews the complete inventory of all that is to house the holy. Three matters in the course of this recital of obedience may interest us. First, Moses does act on the "first day." In the constitutive mystery of liturgy, this is something of a primordial event, whereby Israel begins again. So Joseph Blenkinsopp draws a compelling parallel between creation, which is "finished" (Gen 2:1), and tabernacle, which is "finished."[200]

Second, it is striking that of the three crucial verbs we have cited in God's command, only one is present. Nowhere in this text of obedience is the verb *anoint (māšah)* or *consecrate (qādaš)* used. The third verb, *wash,* occurs twice. In its second usage (v. 31), Moses is not, as the Hebrew text has it, even the single subject of the verb, for Aaron and his sons now join in the washing. Thus Moses' action seems to be greatly reduced.

But, third, the most striking rhetorical feature is that Moses "did as Yahweh commanded." After this general statement in v. 16, the formula occurs seven times in a subordinate position (vv. 19, 21, 23, 25, 27, 29, 32). Seven times may bespeak total, complete obedience. It may also reflect the shape of "new creation," which takes place in seven acts. Moses has done all, and everything is "finished."

The verb rendered "finished" has already been used in 39:32, where the workmen have finished. Now, however, Moses finishes with theological authorization (v. 33). The verb for "finish" (*kālâ*) here is the one used in Gen 2:1 to conclude the work of creation. In this cultic action of Moses, however, this is a new "finishing." A new world begins in a new time. The new creation is not yet visible in the world. It is offered to Israel only in worship. What now happens in worship, therefore, is more than the completion of creation begun in Gen 1:1–2:4*a.* It is the initiation of a new creation wherein the power and presence of God are fully present in the earth.

200. Blenkinsopp, "The Structure of P," 275-92.

REFLECTIONS

Moses has initiated, at the behest of God, a mode and means whereby God's very self can now be present in the world. This text does not lend itself to the notion that holy acts can be undertaken or replicated by any among us. In this text, we are permitted a glimpse into the awesome, inscrutable moment of authorization, in which an enduring and reliable religious practice is made possible. Having this text is like being present at the institution of a sacrament. Israel expresses a conviction that, in this irrepeatable moment, a way has been opened whereby the holy God becomes present, palpable, and visible in the earth. God who has bestowed upon us sacraments as "visible means" of "invisible grace."

1. Moses' inimitable act is one of full, comprehensive, and massive obedience. Moses neither initiates nor imagines the tabernacle. It is all given through the magisterial speech of God.

2. The fact that Moses' obedience is voiced seven times, and the fact that this is the "first day," suggests that this is a new act of creation in which the world begins again. In this text, we are "present at creation." (This text in its final form is dated closely to the time of Isa 43:18-19, when another poetic figure in Israel sang lyrically about a "new thing" wrought by God.) This text obviously accepts that what is done in the cultic apparatus is indeed real work that affects everything decisively.

3. In a profane, self-sufficient society like ours, interpretation will usefully dwell on the specificity of religious symbolism that powerfully transforms reality. Against both profanation and universalizing religion, the symbolization completed by Moses is specific. Moses is seen to be the one who "makes holy" at a time and place, and thereby institutes a fresh possibility in a world that has become flat and hopeless. Without denigrating morality, piety, social policy, or doctrine, this text affirms that holy acts by holy persons in holy places give access to the liberating, healing, forgiving power of the holy God.

4. The work is finished! Everything has been done that can be done. This cultic horizon is now kept open eschatologically. Everything is now completed and in readiness, awaiting God's assured coming. But even now, Moses and Israel engage only in an act of hope.

This text has powerful echoes in the Fourth Gospel. In John 19:30, the declaration from the cross, "It is finished" (τετέλεσται *tetelestai*) is a triumphant cry asserting that God's purpose has been fully accomplished. In John 4:34, 5:36, and 17:4, Jesus asserts that he will finish God's work. These fundamental religious figures (Moses and Jesus), who defy our explanation, do indeed accomplish something transformative and irreversibly intended by God.

This daring statement of completion, which still waits for the presence, invites us to reflect on God's continuing work of "finishing" our lives as creatures.

Biblical hope, for both Jews and Christians, is always the celebration of what is finished and the waiting for that yet to be finished. In this text, the accent is on what is finished. Nonetheless, there is waiting, for Moses' splendid, perfectly constituted "holy place" still awaits its awesome Inhabitant. It is always like that with our human ways of hosting the holy—keeping all in readiness, waiting for the One whom we invite to "come be our guest" (cf. Matt 25:1-13).

EXODUS 40:34-38, THE GLORY OF THE LORD

COMMENTARY

The work on the tabernacle was finished (כלה *kālâ*; 39:32). Moses' work of legitimating the tabernacle is also finished (*kālâ*; 40:33). Everything that could be done by human agents is now complete. What remains unfinished is that which only Yahweh can do. Yahweh had promised, "Have them make me a sanctuary, so that I may dwell [שׁכן *šākan*] among them" (25:8 NRSV). Now the sanctuary is complete, and Israel awaits the Dweller for whom the tabernacle is constructed.

This is obviously the literary conclusion of the book of Exodus. It is also the theological conclusion of a priestly theory of presence and the liturgical culmination of the work commanded in chaps. 25–31 and enacted in 36:8–40:33. Indeed, for the book of Exodus, it is for this moment and this event of presence that all of creation has been preparation. Creation is God's work with the goal of God's full and glorious presence. The tabernacle is the vehicle through which the glory of God sojourns with Israel. It is also the means by which the glory of God can be present in sovereign ways in the midst of the whole earth.

This brief text explicates two quite distinctive but related themes: presence (vv. 34-35) and guidance (vv. 36-38). In the first, God is static, settled, and stationary. In the second, God is on the move and under way. Each theme is important to the completed tradition of Israel and to the faith of Israel.

40:34-35. The affirmation of presence is expressed in two devices: cloud and glory. The "cloud" does not refer to an overcast sky, but is a standard device to signify presence and at the same time to keep God hidden, remote, and inaccessible. The cloud "covers"—i.e., surrounds—the tabernacle and "settles" (*šākan*) upon the tent of meeting. The "glory," in contrast, is a bright light that is nearly physical in its power and appearance. It "fills" the tabernacle, so forcefully that even Moses cannot enter the place.

The intent and effect of "cloud" and "glory" are to assert that the cult Moses has authorized does indeed host the real presence of God, which has faithfully, specifically, visibly, and powerfully come. This presence-filled place becomes the center and focus of Israel's life. This company of erstwhile slaves now becomes the caretakers, custodians, and "possessors" of the very place and device where the glory of God has chosen to dwell on earth. God has taken up habitation, not in the world's grand palaces, but among a slave band in the wilderness. In 24:15-18, a closely related text, the cloud and the glory are at the mountain. The process of 25:1–40:33 has transferred the cloud and the glory from the mountain to the tabernacle, thus making the presence mobile.

40:36-38. The process of making the cloud and the glory mobile prepares us for a very different theme. Now the verbs are active: "take up" (עלה *'ālâ*) and "journey" (נסע *nāsa'*). The tabernacle is the locus of cloud and glory, but the cloud would "lift up and go." In this second part of the paragraph, the "glory" is not mentioned, but now the cloud is paired with "the fire." This pairing looks back to 13:20-22; cloud and fire are devices for protection and guidance for sojourning Israel, both day and night. These concealing forms of presence accompany and lead Israel in its dangerous travels. Gerhard von Rad has suggested that "glory" is a vehicle for presence that has displaced the more primitive and material (and, therefore, awkward) presence in the ark.[201] Given that possibility, reference should be made to Num 10:33-36. In that text, the cloud is over Israel, but it is the ark that sits, acts, and rests in order to guide and protect Israel. One can see that, in the collage of ark-cloud-fire-glory, Israel struggles to articulate presence that is powerfully known and confidently trusted but that has not been made directly available for administration.

This passage accomplishes for Israel two important gains. First, it has provided a centering place of reliable, abiding presence. Second, because of the presence, this community cannot stay centered in a place but must be on the move. This is a profound tension both in the character of God and in the destiny of Israel. God yearns to be in an available place for Israel, but this God is always on the move (cf. 2 Sam 7:6-7). Israel wants a safe place, but must be on the way, powered by a promise yet unfulfilled.

This tension is well accomplished in this paragraph, so that vv. 34-35 address the need for a place, and vv. 36-38 address the need for a traveling presence. This shrewd theological tradition speaks about and affirms both.

---

201. Von Rad, *Studies in Deuteronomy,* 37-44. For a more recent and comprehensive review of the problem, see T. N. D. Mettinger, *The Dethronement of Sabbath: Studies in the Shem and Kabod Theologies* (Land: CWK Gleerup, 1982).

Reflections

1. There is an assurance in this text that the very presence of God abides, continually, reliably, enduringly. Moreover, that abiding presence is not just a good idea or a personal experience. Rather, it is a visible, identifiable, liturgic enactment to which the community has recourse and in which the community may have confidence. The visible, institutional place of worship is a place of real presence.

To be sure, the Reformed tradition is uneasy and nervous about such claims, and there have no doubt been overstatements and abuses of the gift of presence, often in the interest of elitism and priestly advantage. Nonetheless, the claim of presence, championed as we might expect by a Priestly tradition, is a powerful insistence that zeal for "reform" does not lead the community to live in the "real absence." God is willing to be present with God's people.

The tabernacle establishment and its claim of presence do indeed curb God's freedom to come and go at will. But it is God's own command that has authorized this liturgic arrangement. Whatever limitation on God's freedom is required by sustained cultic presence, it is a limitation growing out of God's own resolve and commitment. This conviction of centered, cultic presence is crucial to the wilderness community. It is likewise crucial to a community of faith that makes its way in a world of emptied, one-dimensional profanation.

2. The God who stays is the God who goes, travels with, and keeps safe. God's people are not sent out alone in the world, for alone they lack resources for survival. Already in the ancestral stories of Genesis, the recurrent promise is, "I will be with you" (Gen 28:15; 46:4; cf. Exod 33:14). Our text seeks to express in concrete, visible ways the willingness and capacity of Yahweh to travel with this people. This willingness distinguishes the God of the Bible from other kinds of gods bound to a place.

The conviction of God's "traveling mercies" is evident in a variety of texts. Among the more familiar are Pss 23:4*a*; 91:9-13; and 121:5-7. Israel knows that in every dangerous circumstance, its path is transformed because of this accompanying presence.

3. This particular text has managed to join two themes that are not easily related. The ideas of a place of presence and a traveling guidance are in tension. This text uses "glory" for the notion of a placed presence, "fire" for traveling presence, and "cloud" for both. The imaginative quality of the affirmation is not unlike the later, daring affirmation of the Trinity in the early church, a liturgical formulation for holding together what is in profound tension. The connection of *faithful abiding* and *powerful accompaniment* is exactly what we experience in our most treasured, intimate human relations. It is no less so for the God of Israel.

4. The Priestly presentation of these claims of presence may strike us as somewhat crude, primitive, and mechanical. The Bible makes no apology for that, and neither should we. I suggest two reasons for refusing such a critique. First, if such a notion of abiding presence and powerful accompaniment seems awkward, then consider the alternative of a profane world without presence. Indeed, the brutalizing world of technological consumerism is a world of "real absence." In that world, there is no ordering center to which one may refer, but only endless, fleeting reference points. Life with a "real absence" is a world likely to be fraught with anxiety and to end in exhaustion and despair. This is not a special pleading for faith but a recognition that humans are indeed marked by fragility, vulnerability, and mortality. For such persons, the reality of presence matters enormously, even though we have poor ways in which to speak about it. In the end, one may not mumble somewhere between real presence and real absence. One must face that it is a stark either/or. Israel has cast its lot and voiced its text in a conviction of presence. Israel has concluded that "absence" is for fools (cf. Pss 10:4; 14:1; Luke 12:20-21).

Second, this crude, elemental notion of presence is characteristic of the biblical "scandal of particularity." It may be that "God is everywhere." But this God who is everywhere has chosen and designated times and places. Israel's faith does not operate with generalities and generic claims but is always concrete. Thus it is congruent with Israel's way in the world to confess that in this construct of the tabernacle, the omnipresent God has taken up residence, and Israel has guarded crucial access to holiness.

5. These two themes of presence are in the NT transposed into christological affirmations, where Jesus has become the mode and place of real presence.

The theme of *abiding presence* is taken up particularly in the Fourth Gospel. Jesus promises those who keep the word that he will "make a home with them" (14:23). The Fourth Gospel witnesses to Jesus' assured presence in the church. He is the One who "abides."

The theme of *traveling fidelity*, on the other hand, is more fully reflected in the synoptic portrayal of Jesus. He is "on the way" with his disciples, instructing and guiding them (cf. Mark 10:32). Indeed, much of his ministry with his disciples is "conversation on the way." The conclusion of Matthew's Gospel is a summons to put the church on the way: "Go" (Matt 28:19). It is precisely to that company of travelers that Jesus promised, "I am with you always" (Matt. 28:20).

Thus in both modes the presence is reassigned to Jesus. The affirmation that is enacted by Moses and embodied by Jesus is that in staying and in going, the faithful do not live in a world of absence but before a Presence whose glory and splendor transforms everything.

6. The ultimate promise of the gospel, already given as the "gospel beforehand" by Moses, is that God's presence will be fully known on earth. Thus it is promised concerning the new heaven and new earth:

> The tabernacle of God is among mortals.
> He will tabernacle with them as their God;
> they will be his people,
> and God himself will be with them.
> (Rev 21:3, author's translation)

The noun and verb translated "tabernacle" echo the noun משׁכן *miškān* ("tabernacle") and the verb שׁכן (*šākan*, "to sojourn"). What Moses has made possible locally will in the end be true cosmically. The earth shall be filled with the glory of God, and all creation shall be fully inhabited by God's glory. All of that is already present inchoately in our text. It is taken as a promise from Moses that God's healing presence and God's protective accompaniment are intended for all the earth. And when that presence and accompaniment are fully actualized, it is no wonder that heaven and earth break out in wondrous doxology.

In the meantime, until the full coming of presence, the daily pastoral word is much more concrete and immediate. But it is the same word. God intends not only that slaves be rescued but that rescued slaves be transformed in, by, for, and with divine presence.

We are at the finish of Exodus. The workmen finished (39:32). Then Moses finished (40:33). And now God has finished (40:34-38). The seer of Revelation also anticipates a "finish" (Rev 21:3). In our candid self-knowledge, we pray hungrily that God should "finish" for our good. Our prayer for this presence, however, is not a desperate prayer. It is urgent, but it is also confident and bold. Such confidence is grounded in, and informed by, the sacramental enactment by Moses in this text before our very eyes. We dare also say, "It is finished." That lyrical affirmation is part celebration and part anticipation, all grateful, joyous, and confident.

THE BOOK OF LEVITICUS

INTRODUCTION, COMMENTARY, AND REFLECTIONS
BY
WALTER C. KAISER, JR.

THE BOOK OF
LEVITICUS

INTRODUCTION

F ew books of the Bible challenge modern readers like Leviticus. In fact, even the most venturesome individuals, who aspire to read through the whole Bible, usually run out of enthusiasm as they begin to read this third book of the Bible. However, such initial discouragement may be mitigated when we realize that Leviticus discloses the character of God in important ways. One central concern involves the oft-repeated injunction: "Be holy, for I am holy" (11:44-45; 19:2; 20:26). (The Hebrew root for "holy" [קדש *qōdeš*] occurs as a verb, noun, or adjective 150 times in Leviticus.) Moreover, this book calls upon both priests and people constantly to "distinguish between the holy and the profane [common], between the unclean and the clean" (10:10).

THE NAME LEVITICUS

The Greek translators called this third book of the Bible *Leuitikon*, "the Levitical book." Our English title derives from the Greek one, but through the Latin translation. Oddly, the Levites, as such, are mentioned only in 25:32-34, even though all Israelite priests were members of the tribe of Levi.

Leviticus belongs to the section of the Bible that Jewish tradition designated as the *Torah*, "law" or "instruction." This sense of תורה (*tôrâ*)—an extension of that noun in passages such as Deut 1:5; 4:8; 17:18-20; 33:4—applies to everything from Genesis to Deuteronomy. Eventually this same corpus of material came to be known (since 160 CE) by the Greek term *Pentateuch*, the "five-sectioned" work.

As with most works in antiquity, this third book of the Torah is identified by its opening word ויקרא (*wayyiqrā*), "And he [the LORD] called"). The rabbinic name for this book is *tôrat kōhănîm*, a title that can be translated "instruction *for* the priests" (hence, rules and regulations by which priests will conduct their services) or "instruction *of* [or *by*] the priests" (hence, teaching and guidance offered to the people by the priests). This double dimension of the rabbinic title allows us to understand the dual focus of Leviticus: The priesthood is instructed in proper rules for officiating, observing purification, and administering at the sanctuary; but the priests also teach the people what God requires of all Israelites.

THE CONTENT OF LEVITICUS

Except for the brief historical narratives in 10:1-7 and 24:10-16, the book of Leviticus focuses initially on instructions, many of which involve worship of the most holy God as well as the purity of the people. Oversight of such worship is given over to Aaron and his sons, that part of the tribe of Levi designated for the task of officiating at the altar.

The first seven chapters present the laws of sacrifice. Chapters 1–3 articulate the spontaneously motivated sacrifices (burnt, grain, and peace), chaps. 4–5 deal with sacrifices required for expiation of sin (sin and guilt), and chaps. 6–7 rehearse these same five sacrifices, with special emphasis on directions for the priests.

The second main section (chaps. 8–10) concentrates on the priesthood. After their installation (chap. 8), the priests begin to officiate (chap. 9). However, improper officiating could lead to death, as in the case of Aaron's two sons, Nadab and Abihu (chap. 10).

The focus changes to matters of purity in chaps. 11–15. Chapter 11 lists the marks and the names of clean and unclean animals. But impurity of various sorts may also arise from childbirth (chap. 12), from skin diseases and various infections in houses and clothing (chaps. 13–14), and from aspects relating to the sexual life (chap. 15).

Chapter 16 appears central to the life of the worshiping community. One of the best known of all the sections in Leviticus, it is read in the synagogue on Yom Kippur. On this day, according to the ancient prescriptions, the high priest entered the innermost sanctum of the sanctuary with the blood of a goat that had been sacrificed as a sin offering. Afterward, a second goat was released, never to be seen again in the camp.

With chaps. 1–16 as the first major block, chaps. 17–27 constitute the second division, most of which is often termed the Holiness Code. It opens with a prologue (chap. 17) and ends with an epilogue (26:3-46). Chapters 18–20 deal with holiness in the family, especially its sexual activity. Chapters 21–25 return to the ritual life of the community with regulations for the priests, Israelite marriages, mourning rites, and the holy days and feasts. Probably no biblical chapter is quoted or alluded to more in prophetic literature than Leviticus 26. It portrays the alternative prospects for either reward or punishment, depending on Israel's obedience or disobedience.

Most scholars consider chap. 27 to be an appendix. It speaks to the matters of redemption of persons, animals, or lands dedicated to the Lord by vow. Its closing formula (v. 34) is almost a repetition of 26:46.

The content of Leviticus exhibits a plan and a reasonably clear structure. Basically, chaps. 1–16 are addressed to the priests, while chaps. 17–27 focus on priestly instructions for the people. The first division provides directions concerning acts of officiating and purifying directed to the priests, while the second division emphasizes holiness among all Israelites. Despite this basic distinction, chap. 11 fits better in the holiness section (chaps. 17–27), since it provides the first reference to the theme of holiness (11:44-45). Indeed, 11:46-47 ("These are the regulations [tōrâ] concerning animals. . . . You must distinguish between the unclean and the clean") may have originally been part of the holiness law, but it may have been moved forward since it stipulates a basic duty of the priests—namely, to "distinguish between the holy and the profane, between the unclean and the clean" (10:10).[1]

LITERARY FORM OF LEVITICUS

The formula "the LORD said to Moses" (or a similar one) occurs fifty-six times. (In three of these fifty-six formulations, Aaron is named along with Moses [11:1; 14:33; 15:1], and once

---

1. Baruch A. Levine, *The JPS Torah Commentary: Leviticus* (Philadelphia: Jewish Publication Society, 1989) xvi-xvii.

Aaron is addressed alone [10:8].) Seventeen of the twenty-seven chapters begin with the formula "And the LORD said. . . ." Leviticus, more than any other OT book, claims to be a divine word for humanity.

Even though the Greek and Latin origins for the name of this book would tend to limit it as a manual for priests from the tribe of Levi, who indeed are mentioned nearly two hundred times, approximately half of the divine address formulas specifically involve all the people. For example, 1:2 states, "Speak to the Israelites and say to them."

Only in the epilogue to the Holiness Code (26:3-46) does a prose composition appear. Two other narratives make brief appearances: the tragic death of Aaron's sons Nadab and Abihu (10:1-7), and the incarceration and stoning of the blasphemer (24:10-16).

Aside from these brief narratives, Leviticus is a book of rituals and laws. The style we encounter here is very similar to what we would expect in legal documents. Leviticus is filled with specialized terminology, technical vocabulary, and repeated formulaic statements. Even words used frequently in other parts of Scripture are often highly nuanced in their usages in this book.[2]

To summarize: Leviticus is a book that offers rituals and prescriptions for officiating priests and a purified people.

THE PURPOSE OF LEVITICUS

The book is given to Israel so that the people might live holy lives in fellowship with a holy God. But that intent does not tell the whole story, for a greater purpose is also served in furnishing Israel with laws that secure their well-being: They are to be a blessing to the nations. As expressed in the covenant with Abraham (see Gen 12:2-3), these beneficiaries of God's covenant are to be mediators of blessing to the nations at large. Seen in this light, the Levitical laws are intended to train, teach, and prepare the people to be God's instruments of grace to others. Consequently, one of the key purposes for the law of Leviticus is to prepare Israel for its world mission. What Israel communicates most immediately to the nations is the character of God, especially the deity's unapproachable holiness. Israel's disclosure of God's holiness to the nations is visible primarily through the sacrificial system. All can see that any sin, no matter what the status or rank of the individual, is an offense against a holy God.

The importance of God's holiness is also evident in the severity of the penalties attached to some of the laws in Leviticus. Although we mortals are often tempted to play down the seriousness of sin, God's holiness demands intolerance of sin and impurity.

However, God's holiness also involves a positive side: "The LORD, the LORD, the compassionate and gracious God, slow to anger, abounding in love and faithfulness, maintaining love to thousands, and forgiving wickedness, rebellion and sin" (Exod 34:6-7 NIV). What the austere law demands, and what mortals find themselves unable to do, a loving and forgiving Lord provides in the same law that upholds so high a standard. Mercy and remission of sins are available for all who turn to God with a repentant heart.

One of the most frequently repeated terms in Leviticus is *atonement;* it occurs almost fifty times. In connection with the sacrifices, the members of the Israelite community heard the reassuring words repeatedly offered: "The priest will make atonement for [that person's] sin, and [that one] will be forgiven" (e.g., 4:20, 26, 31, 35).

Leviticus 17:11, 14 provides a key statement regarding atonement: "Because the life of a creature [literally life of the flesh] is in the blood." Blood outside the flesh is equivalent to death; however, blood in all creatures makes possible life. Somehow, according to the prevailing belief among ancient Israelites, animal blood could affect mortal sin. Some have suggested that a sacrifice was effective because of an accompanying divine word.

Some Christian readers think the Levitical law was intended to be typical and prophetic of Messiah and his work of redemption. Perhaps some such thought pattern prepared John the

---

2. As Levine (*JPS Torah Commentary* xviii-xix) has shown by citing three such formulas.

Baptist for his sudden declaration when he met Jesus of Nazareth for the first time: "Look, the Lamb of God, who takes away the sin of the world!" (John 1:29b NIV).

One more purpose for Leviticus must be noted: to teach Israel and all subsequent readers how to worship God. True worship can best be expressed by joining the visible forms of the religious life with holiness of the worshiper's life. The external forms are important, but they do not suffice to denote the proper worth and value that a person is attempting to express to God. Although persons must not divorce the sacred from the secular, since God is Lord over all, they must be able to distinguish between what is holy and what is common or profane, between the clean and the unclean. But the holiness of God dictates that any approach to God must acknowledge the yawning gulf between the character of God and the character of all humans. Thus the distinctions between the holy and the ordinary help mortals to realize that God is unapproachably different from humans.

THE MEANING OF SACRIFICE

Whereas the word *sacrifice* in today's common usage means something of value that a person gives up for the sake of some greater value, it did not have that connotation in the ancient world of Israel and its neighbors. For the ancients, *sacrifice* meant a religious rite, something someone offered to some deity or power.

Our English word *sacrifice* comes from a Latin word meaning "to make something sacred, [or] holy." As the object is offered, it passes from the common or mundane world to the sacred realm; it is consecrated. The heart of the sacrificial act, then, is the transference of property from the profane to the sacred realm. The most common Hebrew equivalent for "sacrifice" is קרבן (*qorbān*), meaning "something [that is] brought near [to the altar]." Thus the connection of sacrifice with the altar and meeting place with God is evident in the OT. But what is brought must be a מתנה (*mattānâ*, a "gift"). That probably explains why game and fish were unacceptable as sacrifices, since, as David declared, "I will not sacrifice to the LORD my God burnt offerings that cost me nothing" (2 Sam 24:24 NIV).

In the last century, a huge literature has developed on both the *origin* and the *significance* of sacrifice in the OT and the ancient Near East.[3] Of the two, the question of origin has been the most exasperating, since neither the OT nor the cultures of the ancient Near East provide clear evidence about the subject. Scholars have propounded a number of theories, but no theory has ever commanded anything approaching a consensus. Some have suggested that sacrifices originally belonged either to totemic practices or to ancestor worship.[4] But such speculative theories have now been abandoned.

Generally, researchers in comparative religions have identified four purposes for sacrifice: (1) to provide food for the deity; (2) to assimilate the life force of the sacrificial animal; (3) to effect a union with the deity; and (4) to persuade the deity to give the offerer help as a result of the gift.[5] Some think the first three purposes are not found in Israel and the fourth is in evidence only to a lesser degree than elsewhere in the Near East.

"The feature which distinguishes Israelite and Canaanite rituals from those of other Semitic peoples is that, when an animal is sacrificed, the victim, or at least a part of it, is burnt upon the altar. This rite did not exist in Mesopotamia or in Arabia, but it did exist among the Moabites and the Ammonites, according to allusions in the Bible [1 Kgs 11:8; 1 Kings 18; 2 Kgs 5:17; John 10:18-27; Jer 7:9; 11:12, 13, 17; 32:29]."[6] Clearly, there are strong affinities in the terms and practices for sacrifice between the west Semitic peoples.

Our knowledge of west Semitic peoples comes from three sources: (1) allusions to or condemnations of the ritual practices in Moab, Ammon, and Edom found in the Bible; (2) inscriptions

3. For analysis of the earlier discussion, see D. Davies, "An Interpretation of Sacrifice in Leviticus," *ZAW* 89 (1977) 387-99.
4. One of the standard books is Roland de Vaux's *Ancient Israel: Its Life and Institutions,* trans. John McHugh (New York: McGraw-Hill, 1961); see chap. 12, "The Origin of Israelite Ritual," 433-46. De Vaux's work continues a line of study set forth in J. Pedersen, *Israel, Its Life and Culture* (Copenhagen: V. Pio-P. Branner, 1926) vols. 1 and 2 (Copenhagen: Branner og Korch, 1940) vols. 3 and 4.
5. As set forth by Jacob Milgrom, *Leviticus 1-16,* AB (New York: Doubleday, 1991) 440.
6. De Vaux, *Ancient Israel,* 440, see also 438.

from Phoenicia or its colonies to its cultic practice; and (3) the terms for sacrifice used in the texts from Ras Shamra, i.e., ancient Ugarit. De Vaux provides evidence for the first source in the quotation above. Evidence for the second can be found in the Phoenician and Punic inscriptions. The most important of these are the Carthage price list and the price list of Marseilles, a stone taken from North Africa. These lists fix the amount of money to be paid for each type of sacrifice, including the portion of the sacrifice that is given to the priest and the part that is given to the person making the sacrifice. The four sacrifices mentioned are the *minḥâ*, the *kālîl*, the *sewaʿat*, and the *šelem kalil*. In the *kālîl*, almost everything is burned on the altar except for a small portion given to the priest. In the *sewaʿat*, the breast and the leg are given to the priest and the rest to the person making the sacrifice. At Ras Shamra, archaeologists have discovered texts dating from the fourteenth century BCE with a number of similar terms to those used in Israel's sacrificial vocabulary. They include *dbh*, "sacrifice" (cf. Hebrew זבח *zebaḥ*); *šlmm*, "peace offering" (cf. Hebrew שלמים *šĕlāmîm*); *šrp*, "burnt offering "; and perhaps *ʾtm*, "guilt offering(?)" (cf. Hebrew אשם *ʾāšām*).

Accordingly, whether through close contact with each other or through other means as yet unnoticed, there were some very strong connections with at least the sacrificial terms, and in some cases with some of the practices, in the west Semitic world of the first and second millennia BCE.

But if the origin of sacrifice in Israel and the ancient Near East remains elusive, what may we say about the religious significance of sacrifice? Some anthropologists and historians of religion offer explanations based on cross-cultural comparisons and emphasize the social function of such rituals.[7] These judgments may be based on slim analogies. Also, some Christian readers have moved beyond the evidence by using NT sacrificial concepts to explain the meaning of the OT sacrificial system. Both parties can err by reading into the situation outside materials before the text itself is given a chance to speak.

Some scholars have argued that sacrifice symbolically expresses the interior feelings of the person making the offering. But, as such, it can be an act with many aspects: It is a gift to God, but it is more; it is a means of achieving union with God, but it is more; it is a means of expiating sin, but it is more. Often all three aspects are present, including a response of a conscience motivated by a desire to obey God.

As a *gift*, the act of sacrifice acknowledges that everything a person has comes from God (see 1 Chr 29:14). And just as a contract between men is often sealed by sharing a meal together (cf. Gen 26:28-30; 31:44-54), so also *communion* and *union with God* are often achieved by sharing a sacrificial meal together. Moreover, since the life of the sacrificial animal is symbolized by its blood (Lev 17:11), sacrifice also carries *expiatory* value.

Some scholars have focused on the polemics of the prophets against sacrifices as an indication that they condemned outright the practice of sacrifice (e.g., Isa 1:11-17; Jer 7:21-22; Hos 6:6; Amos 5:21-27; Mic 6:6-8). But such a conclusion misunderstands the prophets. Never did they intend their words to be taken as an unconditional condemnation of the cult and its sacrifices. Instead, theirs was a qualified negation in which they said in effect, "What is the use of *this* [offering sacrifices] without *that* [a proper heart relationship as the basis for offering sacrifices to God]?" Or to put the proverb in another form: "Not this, but that," which is another way of saying, "Not so much this as that." The prophets were opposed to formalism and the mere external practice of religion without corresponding interior affections or repentance of the heart (e.g., 1 Sam 15:22; Isa 29:13).

No less concerned were the wisdom writers who verbalize the same message: "The LORD detests the sacrifice of the wicked,/but the prayer of the upright pleases him" (Prov 15:8 NIV); or "The sacrifice of the wicked is detestable—/how much more so when brought with evil intent" (Prov 21:27 NIV); and "To do what is right and just/is more acceptable to the LORD than sacrifice" (Prov 21:3 NIV).

As a result of such evidence, the older thesis that the pre-exilic prophets repudiated rituals, especially sacrifice, has now been abandoned.[8] It was the abuse, not the practice, of the cult

---

7. For an excellent recent example, see G. Anderson, "Sacrifice and Sacrificial Offerings (OT)," *The Anchor Bible Dictionary*, 5:871-86.

8. For a convenient listing of these scholars dating from 1885 with Julius Wellhausen to P. Volz in 1937, see Milgrom, *Leviticus 1–16*, 482. The thesis of this group of scholars "has been unanimously and convincingly rejected by its successor," argues Milgrom, by scholars such as H. H. Rowley, Y. Kaufmann, R. Rendtorff, and R. de Vaux.

itself that the prophets so thoroughly condemned. For them, ritual activity had no efficacy or value if it was not preceded and motivated by genuine repentance and a proper intention.

However, two texts have continued to haunt biblical scholars since they seem to claim that Israel did not offer sacrifices in the wilderness and was not commanded to do so. The two texts are found in Jeremiah and Amos:

> This is what the LORD Almighty, the God of Israel, says: Go ahead, add your burnt offerings to your other sacrifices and eat the meat yourselves! For when I brought your forefathers out of Egypt and spoke to them, I did not just give them commands about burnt offerings and sacrifices, but I gave them this command: Obey me, and I will be your God and you will be my people. (Jer 7:21-23a NIV)

> Even though you bring me burnt offerings and grain offerings,
> I will not accept them . . . .
> Did you bring me sacrifices and offerings
> forty years in the desert, O house of Israel? (Amos 5:22, 25 NIV)

The NIV has added "just" to Jer 7:22, but this is of little help in rendering the על-דבר (ʿal-děbār, NRSV "concerning"; NIV "about"). The dilemma posed by Jeremiah's text, which appears to disclaim any command or knowledge of a practice of sacrifice in the wilderness, is solved by translating ʿal-děbār as "for the sake of." This meaning for ʿal-děbār is clearly attested in passages such as Gen 20:11, 18; and Ps 79:9. Jeremiah announced that God had not spoken "for the sake of" sacrifices and offerings, i.e., for sacrifices in and of themselves. Jeremiah (chaps. 7–10) provided a strong denunciation of the people's penchant for carrying out external religion without any corresponding interior intentions and desires. Indeed, the very sacrifices named by Jeremiah, the עלה (ʿōlâ) and the זבח (zebaḥ), could apply only to those voluntarily brought by individuals and not to those of the community as a whole.

The solution for the Amos text is different. His question drips with sarcasm and hyperbole. Did Israel indeed bring sacrifices and offerings to the Lord during those forty years in the wilderness? Amos inquired with more than a slight touch of sarcasm. The implication of Amos's pointed barb seems to be that Israel had lifted their sacrifices up to the idols they had made for themselves. Once again the priority of the heart and the intentions is asserted over the mere external performance of the cult.

But this whole discussion raises a further point: What counts for righteous behavior in the OT? Is it the act itself, or does it also involve the disposition and the intent of the sacrificer? Even though many have tried to make the case for the former, attributing most, if not all, of OT cultic and moral practice to the mere carrying out of perfunctory acts, forms, and rituals, the case for intentionality as a major factor in OT cult cannot be avoided. Proverbs 21:27 denounces bringing sacrifices with evil intent (בזמה bězimmâ). Sanctification begins with a declaration that someone intends to sacrifice and then continues with an announcement that the individual intends to follow through with it. One story in Scripture reports how a mother attempted to dedicate stolen money to the Lord by making an oral declaration (see Judg 17:3).

At times, scholars have offered rationalistic explanations for the sacrificial system in the OT. Moses Maimonides (1135–1204 CE) develops such an approach to the sacrificial legislation when he describes it as a concession to human frailty. As this line of thinking goes, the Israelites could not imagine a religion without sacrifice, such as they had witnessed while in Egypt. Thus sacrifices to Yahweh were permitted to wean the Israelites away from making sacrifices to other deities. In this view, sacrifices were a temporary expedient due to the pressure of idolatry. However, Maimonides draws no such conclusion but goes on to affirm that when Messiah returns, the sacrificial rites must again be ready and the Temple must be rebuilt for Messiah's use.[9]

---

9. Nachmanides did not agree with the explanation that sacrifices were merely to protect Israel from falling into idolatry. He argued that Abel and Noah brought sacrifices at a time when idolatry had not yet appeared.

The sacrificial cult came to an end when the Romans burned the Temple in 70 CE and ordered that it not be rebuilt. Another institution, the synagogue, had arisen during the years of the Babylonian captivity. It was a place of prayer and study, but it made no provision for sacrifices.

THE HOLINESS CODE

Leviticus 18–23 and 25–26 were first identified as an independent corpus in 1866 by K. Graf.[10] Graf also proposed Ezekiel as the author of this corpus, for Graf found many linguistic ties with the book of Ezekiel. In 1874, A. Kayser accepted Graf's thesis and noted other linguistic characteristics that he had observed, while adding, most significantly, Leviticus 17.[11] Then in 1877, A. Klostermann gave the corpus, Leviticus 17–26, its name—the Holiness Code—and explored its ties with Ezekiel.[12] However, Julius Wellhausen ensured that this hypothesis would have a permanent berth in the scholarly literature.[13] Wellhausen maintained that Leviticus 17–26 occupied a singularly distinct position within the Priestly (P) document, which he dated to the last years of the exile.

In the late nineteenth and early twentieth centuries the debate about Leviticus 17–26 continued. In 1894 and 1899, L. Paton published several articles in which he sought to identify three primary strata in this code: the original holiness material, a pre-Priestly corpus that was built on the deuteronomistic program for centralization, and a work by a Priestly redactor.[14] In 1912, B. D. Eerdmans attacked the concept of an independent Holiness Code, for in his view no basic structure held the whole corpus together. He complained that other texts in the Pentateuch issued calls for holiness (e.g., Exod 19:6; 22:30 [31]; Lev 11:44-45; Deut 7:6; 14:2, 21; 26:19; 28:9), so holiness could not be limited to this section.[15] Moreover, the alleged distinctive vocabulary of the Holiness Code occurred in other OT texts. S. Küchler supported Eerdmans's position,[16] but scholars, in the main, were not persuaded by Eerdmans's and Küchler's objections.

G. von Rad's *Studies in Deuteronomy* (1947 [German]; 1953 [English ed.]) marked a dramatic change in the direction of research on the Holiness Code.[17] Von Rad emphasized that this material ought to be attributed to the Yahwist, since the deity's role as speaker was emphasized by the repeated formula "I am Yahweh." With this argument, von Rad started a trend that focused on the growth and development of the sections within the Holiness Code.

In 1961, H. G. Reventlow completed a comprehensive study on the code in which he argued that this corpus evolved at the ancient yearly covenant festival, including traditions from Israel's arrival at Mount Sinai.[18] Older materials came from the wilderness period but were supplemented by later elements. The preacher who delivered the sermons found in this code was probably Moses' successor.

R. Kilian returned to the source-critical approach in 1963 as a means for identifying two major redactions in the basic code.[19] And again, in 1964, C. Feucht promoted the independent existence of the Holiness Code, declaring that it was made up of two collections.[20] But in 1966, K. Elliger published his commentary on Leviticus with a denial that the Holiness Code ever had an independent existence.[21] He theorized that the material was grafted onto the Priestly materials in two stages, each with a supplement, thereby leaving us with four identifiable layers

---

10. K. Graf, *Die geschichtlichen Bücher des Alten Testaments: Zwei historische-kritische Untersuchungen* (Leipzig: T. O. Weigel, 1866).

11. A. Kayser, *Das vorexilischen Büch der Urgeschichte Israels und seine Erweiterungen: Ein Beitrag zur Pentateuch-kritik* (Strassburg: C. F. Schmidt's Universitäts-Buchhandlung, 1874).

12. August Klostermann used the term *Holiness Code* for the first time in "Beiträge zur Entstehungsgeschichte des Pentateuchs," *Zeitschrift für Lutherische Theologie für die gesamte Lutherische Theologie und Kirche* 38 (1877) 416. Later he incorporated the term in *Der Pentateuch: Beiträge zu seinem Verständis und seiner Entstehungsgeschichte* (Leipzig: U. Deichert'sche Verlagsbuchhandlung, 1893) 368-69. See also Klostermann's "Ezechiel und das Heiligkeitsgesetz" in the same volume, 419-47.

13. Julius Wellhausen, *Die Composition des Hexateuchs und der historischen Bücher des Alten Testaments* (Berlin: Georg Reimer, 1889) 152-54.

14. For a comprehensive analysis of the positions and bibliography in this discussion of the Holiness Code, see H. T. C. Sun, "An Investigation into the Compositional Integrity of the So-Called Holiness Code (Leviticus 17-26)" (Ph.D. diss., Claremont, 1990).

15. B. D. Eerdmans, *Alttestamentliche Studien 4: Das Buch Leviticus* (Giessen: Töpelmann, 1912).

16. S. Küchler, *Das Heiligkeitsgesetz Lev 17-26: Eine literarkritische Untersuchung* (Königsberg: Kümmel, 1929).

17. G. von Rad, *Studies in Deuteronomy*, trans. D. Stalker (London: SCM, 1953).

18. H. G. Reventlow, *Das Heiligkeitsgesetz: Formgeschichtlich untersucht* (Neukirchen: Neukirchener Verlag, 1961).

19. R. Kilian, *Literarkritische und formgeschichtliche Untersuchung des Heiligkeitsgesetzes* (Bonn: Peter Hanstein, 1963).

20. C. Feucht, *Untersuchungen zum Heiligkeitsgesetz*, Theologische Arbeiten 20 (Berlin: Evangelische Verlagsantstalt, 1964).

21. K. Elliger, *Leviticus*, HAT (Tübingen: Mohr, 1966).

---

in Leviticus 17–26. In 1976, A. Cholewinski concluded that the Holiness Code had not gone through a major Priestly redaction; instead, Leviticus 17–26 was composed by members of a priesthood who belonged to the deuteronomistic circle.[22]

Most recently, H. T. C. Sun has analyzed both the history of the discussion and the compositional history of the Holiness Code.[23] In his view, the Holiness Code had no existence prior to its present location in the text. His conclusion was based on three arguments: (a) The texts in the Holiness Code appear to be of widely varying ages; (b) there is no conclusive evidence that a compositional layer extends throughout the entire corpus; and (c) some texts appear to have been composed as supplements for other materials in the corpus. Therefore, even though blocks of material appear to stand together (e.g., chaps. 18–20, 21–22, 23 and 25), no overall structure unites all of Leviticus 17–26.

Consistent with Sun's work, some scholars express doubts about the Holiness Code as a self-contained, independent document. As a result, some conclude that the holiness corpus was composed in its present position in Leviticus as a continuation of the concerns for ritual purity found in chaps. 11–15.[24]

These chapters, more than any others in the book, emphasize the holiness of God and the fact that Israel is also called to be holy. One command is repeated: "Be holy because I, the LORD your God, am holy" (19:2; 20:7, 26; 21:6, 8), along with a similar declaration: "I am the LORD, who makes them holy" (21:15, 23; 22:9, 16, 32).

The book consistently reminds the reader, "I am the LORD." This refrain, or the expanded one listed below, appears more than thirty times in this latter section (e.g., 18:5; 19:14; 21:12; 22:2; 26:2). Or again: "I am the LORD your God" (e.g., 18:4; 19:3; 20:7; 24:22; 26:1). Finally, this holiness section in Leviticus repeatedly admonishes the reader, "You must obey my laws and be careful to follow my decrees" (e.g., 18:4; 19:3; 20:8; 22:31; 25:18; and throughout chap. 26).

Although these chapters have a distinctive style and content, the absence of any introductory formula in 17:1 would seem to work against the hypothesis that they constitute a volume of laws inserted into Leviticus. Moreover, scholars have been unable to discern an overarching organization, which, if present, would indicate that the chapters had a life of their own outside the book.

Readers may find it difficult to locate chap. 17 in the Holiness Code. It could just as easily be grouped with the preceding chapters with their emphasis on directions for the priests. Yet, though it does not specifically mention the concept of holiness, chap. 17 contains some of the other terminology typical of the holiness section. Chapter 17 may be best regarded as a transitional chapter between the two major sections of the book.

To summarize: Leviticus 17–26 does not appear to be a single, systematic, and consistently ordered document; instead, it is a collection of materials grounded in the affirmation of God's holiness. Chapter 17 functions as a hinge chapter between the first major division, addressed mainly to the priests, and this second major division, which concerns itself with the conduct of the general public.

UNITY, AUTHORSHIP, AND DATE OF LEVITICUS

The colophon at the conclusion of the book places the site for its composition at Sinai at the time when Israel stopped during the first year of the exodus from Egypt: "These are the commands the LORD gave Moses on Mount Sinai for the Israelites" (27:34). This sentiment, of course, stands in contrast with Num 36:13, which has a similar colophon but locates the place for the composition of the materials "on the plains of Moab by the Jordan across from Jericho" (NIV).

Much in Leviticus is consistent with the claim that Israel was still in the wilderness wanderings at the time that most of these laws were promulgated, e.g., the people were dwelling "in

---

22. A. Cholewinski, *Heiligkeitsgesetz und Deuteronomium: Eine vergleichende Studie,* AnBib 66 (Rome: Biblical Institute Press, 1976).
23. See note 14 above.
24. This is the conclusion of John E. Hartley, *Leviticus,* WBC (Dallas: Word, 1992) 259-60.

the camp" (4:12; 9:11; 10:4-5; 14:3; 17:3; 24:10). Their sanctuary is routinely referred to as the "tent of meeting." Outside the camp lies "the desert" (16:21-22). And entrance into the land of Canaan lies in the future (14:34; 18:3; 19:23; 20:22; 25:2).

The aforementioned references, along with the prominent formula "The LORD said to Moses," help explain why both the synagogue and the church held to the essential unity of this book and to a Mosaic authorship until well into medieval times. The internal claims of the book, in their present shape, argue for the beginning of the forty years of wandering as the canonical setting for Leviticus, with Moses, Aaron, and the Israelites of that generation as the ones who are addressed.

This traditional view stood as the scholarly consensus, with very few exceptions, until the rise of the critical method in the sixteenth and seventeenth centuries. Today, most biblical scholars think that Leviticus (and parts of Genesis, Exodus, and Numbers) originated during post-exilic times in conjunction with the Priestly source, often designated as "P." Julius Wellhausen provided one important formulation of that position.[25]

In Wellhausen's view, the earliest days of Israel's worship were simple, spontaneous, and fairly unstructured. Accordingly, whereas it seemed possible to sacrifice wherever one chose in the days of Samuel (see 1 Sam 16:2), King Josiah, during the 621 BCE revival, made a strong case for limiting sacrifice to the Temple in Jerusalem (see 2 Kings 23). As a result, many scholars have argued that Leviticus reflects this notion of worship at a central shrine. Moreover, with the collapse of the institutions of the kingdom and the Davidic monarchy, the priestly guild in Israel had its first real opportunity to assert its point of view—especially after the Babylonian exile.

Another argument often used on behalf of a late dating for P, and therefore of Leviticus, depends on differences between the books of Kings and Chronicles. Since most scholars agree that Chronicles is post-exilic, and since Chronicles has much to say about worship, whereas Kings has very little to offer on the subject, the similarities between P and Chronicles, especially emphasis on ritual matters, suggest that most of the materials in Leviticus derive from the same period as Chronicles—namely, the post-exilic era.

More recently, Yehezkel Kaufmann, among others, has put forth a third and mediating position. Taking aim at the central thesis of Wellhausen, Kaufmann observes that "fixity in times and rites and absence of 'natural spontaneity' characterize the festivals of ancient Babylonia, Egypt, and all known civilizations. Annual purifications are likewise ubiquitous. . . . That these elements are found in P rather than in JE or D is, in itself, no indication of lateness."[26]

Kaufmann argues that P is pre-exilic but not Mosaic. His reasons are: (a) the laws, institutions, and the terminology of P do not fit in with the post-exilic books of Chronicles, Ezra, and Nehemiah; (b) Deuteronomy and Joshua quote Leviticus along with other P passages, suggesting that P comes before, not after, D;[27] and (c) the rules for war and certain other rituals more closely approximate those mentioned in Judges and Samuel than any other period of time. Scholars who follow this mediating position tend to date P to the early seventh century BCE.

For those who have watched the accumulation of the epigraphic materials gathered from the archaeological discoveries of this century, it comes as little surprise that substantial material in Leviticus appears similar to ancient Near Eastern materials from the second millennium BCE.[28]

Still, it is too early to call for a conclusion to this debate between the traditional, critical, and mediating positions on the date and authorship of Leviticus. If we were to emphasize comparisons with ancient Near Eastern texts, some might discern a tendency for dating Leviticus to the pre-exilic period. Scholars who focus primarily on the internal data will tend to side with the critical resolution, i.e., a post-exilic date, to this question. Pentateuchal studies remain in flux, as

25. Julius Wellhausen, *Prolegomena to the History of Israel*, trans. W. Robertson Smith (New York: Meridian, 1957). Originally published in 1878.

26. Yehezkel Kaufmann, *The Religion of Israel*, trans. and abr. M. Greenberg (Chicago: University of Chicago Press, 1960) 178.

27. See, for instance, Milgrom, *Leviticus 1–16*, 9-10. Milgrom follows this discussion with fifteen other arguments for P's antiquity.

28. For example, see E. A. Speiser, "Leviticus and the Critics," in *Yehezkel Kaufmann Jubilee Volume*, ed. M. Haran (Jerusalem: Magnes, 1960) 29-45. Also see William W. Hallo, "Leviticus and Ancient Near Eastern History," in *The Torah: A Modern Commentary*, ed. W. Gunther PLant (New York: Union of American Hebrew Congregations, 1981) 740-48.

the recent studies of Blenkinsopp, Cross, Moberly, and Rendtorff, among others, demonstrate.[29] It is now abundantly clear that there is no sole, higher-critical position; rather, there are a number of quite diverse ways by means of which to understand the origins of the Pentateuch and, hence, Leviticus.

THE THEOLOGY OF LEVITICUS

The keynote to the book of Leviticus is holiness to the Lord, a phrase occurring some 152 times. Leviticus 20:26 exemplifies this concept: "You are to be holy to me because I, the LORD, am holy, and I have set you apart from the nations to be my own."[30]

Leading the way and serving as a model for all other aspects of holiness is the holiness of the deity. In its basic ideology, holiness involves a double separation: distinct *from* and separate *unto/to* someone or something. Thus, God as creator is separate from all creatures. This is the so-called *ontological* gulf that separates beings. God is immortal, omnipotent, omniscient, and totally different from all creatures. But there is another gulf: a *moral* gap between humanity and God because of human sinfulness.

This latter emphasis appears in the second major division of Leviticus (chaps. 17–26). Here individuals are called to act, think, and live holy lives patterned after the norm established by the character of God. The accent is, normally, on the moral rather than the ceremonial and ritual aspects of life.

The first major division of Leviticus treats primarily the sacrificial order and the distinctions between the unclean and the clean. Although the theme of holiness is mentioned directly only once (11:44-45), behind both the sacrificial instructions and the concerns over defilements is the overriding concern for the holiness of God. A holy God graciously provides these rituals to make it possible for mere mortals, who are also sinners, to walk in fellowship with one who is pure. Israel is taught, both in word and in deed, what the holiness of God entails.

The laws of holiness are addressed not to selected individuals but to the entire community of Israel. Instead of attempting to produce a selected group of pure individuals, the laws aim at producing a holy people, a holy nation, who collectively will be a royal priesthood, a rich treasure belonging to God (see Exod 19:5-6). The demonstration of this consecration to God is to be displayed by the whole nation in every walk and area of life: family life, community affairs, farming, commerce, and worship of God. Among the ethical duties entailed in this life of holiness by the total community, the book singles out sexual holiness for special emphasis. Even in this most intimate area, holiness of life demands control and regard for the sanctity of life (and not ascetic abstinence).

Holiness has more dimensions than just the vertical aspect of our relations with the divine and the interior dimension of basic self-integrity. There is also the horizontal relationship with others, which comes to full expression in 19:18*b* (often termed the Golden Rule): "Love your neighbor as yourself." Hillel used this verse to summarize the entire Torah: "What is hateful to you, do not do to your fellow."[31] Likewise, Jesus declared that this commandment is second in importance only to the command to "love the Lord your God with all your heart and with all your soul and with all your mind and with all your strength" (Mark 12:28-31 NIV; quoting Deut 6:4-5).

Many have suggested that the "neighbor" in 19:18*b* is a fellow Israelite, but lest some think that this observation limits the scope of this injunction, 19:34 requires this same love to be shown to the resident alien in their midst. And the love extended to such non-Israelites is to be the same sort of love with which Israelites love each other (v. 34*b*).

---

29. See J. Blenkinsopp, *The Pentateuch: An Introduction to the First Five Books of the Bible*, ABRL (New York: Doubleday, 1992); Frank M. Cross, *Canaanite Myth and Hebrew Epic: Essays in the History of the Religion of Israel* (Cambridge, Mass.: Harvard University Press, 1973); R. Moberly, *The Old Testament of the Old Testament: Patriarchal Narratives and Mosaic Yahwism* (Minneapolis: Fortress, 1992); and R. Rendtorff, *The Problem of the Process of the Transmission of the Pentateuch*, trans. J. Schullion, JSOTSup 89 (Sheffield: JSOT, 1990).

30. See John G. Gammie, *Holiness in Israel*, OBT (Philadelphia: Fortress, 1989).

31. Rabbi Hillel, *Sabb.* 31a.

For those who fail to measure up to the standard of God's holiness, this same Lord has provided a number of reconciling sacrifices. Leviticus describes five major sacrifices. These Israelite sacrifices are unique (even though the institution of sacrifices is common throughout the ancient Near East, many with some of the same names for the sacrifice and often specifying some of the same parts of the animal in the ritual) in their treatment of blood, especially in the expiatory sacrifices.[32]

The word for and notion of "atonement" become important at this point; it occurs forty-five times in this book. The verb כפר (*kipper*, "to atone") used to be understood as cognate with the Arabic root that means "to cover."[33] Thus it was said that the sins in the OT were covered over by the blood of the animals (and in Christian terms, until the final and all-sufficient sacrifice of Christ). However, the meaning "cover" does not adequately convey the meaning of this term in Leviticus. The Hebrew verb is used in causative stem (the *piel*) and as such probably is a denominative verb taken from the noun *kōper*, which means "a ransom." Consequently, the verb carries the meaning "to pay a ransom" or "to ransom, deliver by a substitute."

The related noun *kappōret* is used as the name for the lid on the ark, variously translated as the "mercy seat" or "atonement cover." The same lid is labeled in Greek the ἱλαστήριον (*hilastērion*), a word directly applied to Christ's atoning work in Rom 3:25: "God presented him [Jesus] as a sacrifice of atonement" (NIV).

This concept of delivering and ransoming from sin by means of a substitute is most forcefully expressed in Leviticus 16 and the great Day of Atonement, Yom Kippur. In part it is a ritual of purification for the sanctuary itself and its furniture. It does involve that, to be sure; but three times the text refers explicitly to the atonement made "on behalf of" (literal translation of בעד *ba'ad*; "make atonement *on behalf of* " the high priest and his family [16:11]; "make atonement *on behalf of* " all the congregation of Israel [16:17, 24]), whereas this combination of prepositions is not used with reference to the tabernacle. The uncleanness of the sanctuary and its furniture is due to ("because of," מן *min*, literally "from" [16:16, 19]) the uncleanness and sinfulness of the Israelites.

The one sin offering on the great Day of Atonement is divided into two parts, as the presence of the two goats attests. The first goat is slain and its blood is taken into the holy of holies, behind the veil, where the high priest dares to enter only on this one day every year. The blood of the first goat is placed on the lid of the ark of the covenant, called here the "atonement cover" (16:14-15). After Aaron emerges from the tent of meeting, he is to lay his hands on the head of the second goat, confess all the sins of all Israel, and send the goat away into the desert. In graphic and concrete terms, the rite symbolizes two aspects in the remission of sins: Sins are *forgiven* on the basis of a substitute that gives its life so the people can go free, and sins are *forgotten* and removed, as the psalmist says, "As far as the east is from the west,/so far has he removed our transgressions from us" (Ps 103:12 NIV).

This does not, of course, exhaust all possible meanings of the various sacrifices. In addition to the expiatory sacrifices, mainly in the sin and guilt offerings, the sacrifices bring the believer closer to God through communion, dedication, service, worship, and thanksgiving. However, foundational to all of the offerings is the atonement for sin by blood, i.e., through the life of a victim, which serves as a substitute for the offerer.

Leviticus has as one of its main purposes to teach Israel how to distinguish "between the holy and the common, and between the unclean and the clean" (10:10). No less significant is the theology of cleanness in this book, for the word *unclean* occurs 132 times and the word *clean* appears 74 times!

Just as the sacrificial laws and the theology of atonement are provided to promote ethical holiness as separation from sin, so also the laws on the clean and the unclean are given to promote ritual holiness as a separation from defilements that come as barriers in the worship of

---

32. See R. J. Daly, *The Origins of the Christian Doctrine of Sacrifice* (Philadelphia: Fortress, 1979) 30: "Comparative religion has been unable to find a highly illuminating parallel for the OT blood rites." Also, D. J. McCarthy, "The Symbolism of Blood Sacrifice," *JBL* 95 (1969) 167-76; and Leon Morris, *The Apostolic Preaching of the Cross* (Grand Rapids: Eerdmans, 1956) 110-11, 122-24.

33. See J. Hermann, "*kipper* and *koper*," in *Theological Dictionary of the New Testament*, trans. G. Bromiley (Grand Rapids: Eerdmans, 1965) 3:303-10. Hermann concluded by saying, "It would be useless to deny that the idea of substitution is present to some degree" (310).

God. Thus holiness has both an ethical and a ritual side. Being unclean does not mean the same thing as being dirty, just as being pure means more than being physically clean. "Cleanliness is next to godliness" is not the operating adage for chaps. 11–15. Instead, what is profane (literally what is distant or outside the Temple) and unclean temporarily disqualifies a person from coming into the presence of God. On the other hand, to be holy or clean indicates one who is fit or qualified to enter into the presence of God. It is not always possible to identify what makes something common/profane or unclean. Therefore, from the standpoint of many worshipers, some of the items in the lists of clean/unclean appear to have an arbitrary quality, just as the line drawn around Mount Sinai when Moses ascended it to receive the Ten Commandments was an arbitrary line that neither people nor beasts were to cross on penalty of death. When an individual comes into the presence of a holy God, a line of demarcation must be drawn; otherwise, the worshiper's entrance may trivialize what is absolutely set apart from all of life. And when the profane is blended into the sacred, there is always a loss of the absolute otherness and transcendence of God. Thus some of the boundaries drawn here may seem arbitrary, but drawing the line remains necessary.

When the Almighty confronts Moses at the burning bush (see Exod 3:1-6), the Almighty tells Moses to take off his sandals because the ground he is standing on is holy. It is conceivable to imagine that Moses might well have protested, "But why?" But Moses is informed it is imperative that he do so because the ground on which he is standing is holy ground. Again, Moses might have responded, "But, Lord, what do you mean this is holy ground? Didn't sheep and goats pass over this same spot as recently as this very day? How could such ordinary, common ground be holy?" And the answer is simply this: The presence of God at the burning bush demands that Moses worship God—visibly, concretely, bodily, as well as with his inner spirit. That episode helps us understand both a certain arbitrariness in distinguishing the sacred from the secular and the radical difference between God and everything else in creation.

Mary Douglas has argued that cleanness is a matter of wholeness or normality. Using anthropological categories, she presses the case that animals are clean when they conform wholly to the class to which they belong. Animals that split the hoof and chew the cud are "normal," but those who lack one of these characteristics are "unclean" according to this scheme: They do not wholly conform to their class.[34] However, it remains difficult to define what is normal or clean. All creatures, as they came from the hand of the Creator, were pronounced "good"; therefore, it is difficult to see why only the clean animals, for example, should be regarded as normal. There are many imponderables here that almost all interpreters frankly confess are baffling. But on the central point there can be little room for doubt: A holy God demands that we draw the line between the sacred and the secular, the clean and the unclean, the holy and the common.

THE PRESENT-DAY USE OF LEVITICUS

The question most contemporary readers of this book raise is this: Of what use can the book of Leviticus be for us today? The answer, of course, must not be contrived or involve a manipulation of the text, as some have done by allegorizing and reducing the book to a series of symbols with modern values and meanings. Philo, some of the early church fathers, and Cabalistic interpreters have already traversed this route—with minimal results!

First and foremost, in all attempts of modern persons to worship God, the fact of God's absolute otherness and transcendence must influence all initial thoughts about approaching or entering into the divine presence. However, that sense of divine transcendence must also signal the divine separateness from sin and help create the call for followers of God to be holy. God's mercy is available to those who are penitent, as exemplified in this book.

But if the age and strange features of these rituals cause a stumbling block, let us realize that, although the Aaronic priesthood and blood sacrifices have disappeared, the spiritual truth they

---

34. Mary Douglas, *Purity and Danger*, rev. ed. (London: Routledge & Kegan Paul, 1978) 53.

signal remains constant. Some would say that what Leviticus depicts in a specific ritual points to a later type that would fulfill in the abstract what had earlier been put in a more figurative form.

In addition to ritual prescriptions, Leviticus includes civil laws. Nowhere are modern readers encouraged to attempt to reintroduce the theocracy of Israelite days to our generation. But just as contemporary legal experts read old legal cases to discern the abiding principles, so also readers of Leviticus can use the civil laws contained here in the same way. In so doing, we will find that impartiality in the administration of justice, fairness in the treatment of the poor, provision for unemployed persons, and scrupulous honesty in all business dealings are demanded as the minimal standard for people who are called to be holy as their Lord is holy.

Finally, for those who have difficulty understanding the abstract and theological language of the NT concerning the forgiveness of sins and atonement, the book of Leviticus could serve as an introduction, a primer with big pictures and big print. In it everything is put in the concrete rather than in abstract, philosophical, or theological terms. In the NT, the book of Hebrews capitalizes on this advantage and brilliantly argues its case about salvation and atonement.

In short, Leviticus helps present an overarching view of God, humans, and the physical world. We need only note that the eschatological picture of how history concludes involves a reference to God's holiness. For, on that day, even the bells on the horses and the inscriptions on the pots and pans will have emblazoned on them: "HOLY TO THE LORD" (Zech 14:20 NIV). Leviticus is the book par excellence about this holiness. God remains the quintessence of holiness; and the deity's creatures can hardly offer to be less in their aspirations and in their everyday conduct.

BIBLIOGRAPHY

Bamberger, Bernard J. *The Torah: A Modern Commentary: Leviticus.* New York: Union of American Hebrew Congregations, 1981. A reissue and a slight expansion of a significant work that appeared seventeen years earlier.

Bush, George. *Notes, Critical and Practical on the Book of Leviticus.* New York: Newman and Ivison, 1852 (reprinted, Minneapolis: James & Klock, 1976). A classic evangelical exegetical and theological commentary.

Calvin, John. *Commentary on the Four Last Books of Moses.* Grand Rapids: Eerdmans, reprint of 1852 translation. This is the best representative of pre-critical Reformed thinking and theology.

Gammie, John G. *Holiness in Israel* OBT. Philadelphia: Fortress, 1989. The most thorough treatment of the concept of holiness available in English.

Harris, R. Laird. *The Expositor's Bible Commentary.* 12 vols. Grand Rapids: Zondervan, 1990. 2:500-654. This commentary includes detailed word studies and outlines the implications of Leviticus for biblical theology.

Harrison, Roland K. *Leviticus: An Introduction and Commentary.* Downers Grove, Ill.: InterVarsity, 1980. Insightful for college-level lay Bible study groups and for brief overviews of the text in personal Bible study.

Hartley, John E. *Word Biblical Commentary: Leviticus.* Dallas: Word, 1992. This commentary provides a comprehensive bibliography on each section of Leviticus along with detailed exegetical notes from a conservative point of view. It includes an essay on the history of the exposition of Leviticus.

Keil, C. F., and Franz Delitzsch. *Biblical Commentary on the Old Testament.* Vol. 2, *The Pentateuch.* Translated by J. Martin. Grand Rapids: Eerdmans, 1956. This book, though dated on historical and archaeological matters, still holds interest because of its influence in conservative theological circles.

Kellogg, S. H. *The Book of Leviticus.* The Expositor's Bible. 3rd ed. Minneapolis: Klock & Klock, 1978 (reprint of 1899 edition published by A. C. Armstrong). A classic that is readable and theologically stimulating.

Levine, Baruch A. *The JPS Torah Commentary: Leviticus.* Philadelphia: JPS, 1989. A masterful exegetical commentary that is fully informed by recent linguistic and archaeological advances.

Micklem, Nathaniel. *The Interpreter's Bible.* 12 vols. Nashville: Abingdon-Cokesbury, 1953. 2:1-134. An excellent representative of mid-twentieth century scholarship, written for an ecumenical Christian readership.

Milgrom, Jacob. *The Anchor Bible: Leviticus 1-16.* New York: Doubleday, 1991. The first of a projected two-volume commentary that will probably be the benchmark for all studies on Leviticus in the foreseeable future.

Noordtzij, A. *Bible Student's Commentary: Leviticus.* Translated by Raymond Togtman. Grand Rapids: Zondervan, 1982 (originally published in Dutch by J. H Kok, B. V. Kampen, 1950). An excellent example of continental evangelical thought and exegesis in 1950, one that interacts with historical-critical studies.

Noth, Martin. *Leviticus: A Commentary.* Old Testament Library. Philadelphia: Westminster, 1965. A standard historical-critical commentary.

Wenham, Gordon J. *The New International Commentary on the Old Testament: The Book of Leviticus.* Grand Rapids: Eerdmans, 1979. The most recent evangelical contribution, which examines rhetorical features of the text as a basis for discerning structure and NT theological parallels.

OUTLINE OF LEVITICUS

III. Leviticus 11:1–15:33 The Regulations on Clean and Unclean

    11:1-47 The Clean and the Unclean
    12:1-8 The Uncleanness of Childbirth
    13:1–14:57 The Uncleanness of Skin and Fungus Diseases
    15:1-33 The Uncleanness of Genital Discharges

IV. Leviticus 16:1-34 The Great Day of Atonement

V. Leviticus 17:1–26:46 The Holiness Code

    17:1-16 The Prologue: Holiness in Eating
    18:1-30 Holiness in Sexual Behavior
    19:1-37 Holiness in Social Ethics
    20:1-8, 27 Holiness in Worship
    20:9-26 Holiness in Family Relations
    21:1–22:16 Holiness in the Priesthood
    22:17-33 Holiness in Sacrificial Offerings
    23:1-44 Holiness in Observing the Festivals
    24:1-23 Holiness Contrasted
    25:1-55 Holiness in Land Ownership
    26:1-46 The Alternatives: Blessing or Curse

VI. Leviticus 27:1-34 Epilogue: Entire Dedication to the Lord

LEVITICUS 1:1–7:38

THE LAWS OF SACRIFICE

LEVITICUS 1:1–6:7, LAWS FOR THE FIVE MAJOR OFFERINGS

OVERVIEW

So foreign to our day is the whole institution of sacrifice that even the word itself raises totally different expectations and connotations. We tend to think of a sacrifice as a loss we have suffered or something we have deprived ourselves of for one reason or another. Thus we make sacrifices during Lent or during a national emergency.

But these concepts are not to be equated with the sacrifices mentioned in Leviticus. Instead of regarding a sacrifice in a negative way as something that someone must give up for some greater good, it signifies the joyous dedication of something valuable to one's Lord.

Indeed, the word *sacrifice* comes from a Latin word meaning "to make something holy." As such, sacrificing is fully in accord with the main theme of holiness stressed in Leviticus.

The most common Hebrew equivalent for our English word *sacrifice* is קרבן (*qorbān*), meaning "[that which is] brought near [to the altar or presence of God]."

Nowhere in the Bible is there any indication as to how sacrifices got started. The scholarly literature is replete with various theories, but none can be demonstrated as the correct solution. The most that can be said is that the institution of sacrifice can be attested all over the ancient Near East. Even though many of the same terms and parts of the ritual seem to be shared, Israelite sacrifices exhibit some unique features. One is the part that blood plays in the ritual. We will say more on this later (also see the "Introduction"). From a canonical standpoint, God had accepted sacrifices from the time of Cain and Abel (see Gen 4:1-16). Noah offered burnt offerings as he emerged from the ark (see Gen 8:20). Moreover, Abraham offered sacrifices (see Gen 22:9), as did Jacob (see Gen 46:1) and the congregation of Israel (see Exod 10:25). But, then, so did the Midianite Jethro, Moses' father-in-law, offer (or participate in offering) sacrifices before he joined up with the Israelites exiting from Egypt (see Exod 18:12).

Chapters 1–7 make up the first main section of the book of Leviticus. But there are clearly defined subsections within these seven chapters.

Chapters 1–3 take up three types of offerings that are voluntarily brought to the altar. A separate chapter is given to each: the whole burnt offering; the grain offering; and the peace offering. An introductory formula is provided for these three chapters in 1:1-2a, but there is no closing formula. The only possible candidate for such a closing formula, 3:16b-17 appears to be little more than a restatement of the thought already announced in chap. 3.

Chapter 4, chap. 5 and the first part of chap. 6 form a second subsection. They deal with two more sacrifices that are given for the expiation of sins: the sin offering (4:1–5:13) and the guilt offering (5:14–6:7). There is an introductory formula in 4:1-2a, but as with the previous three chapters, there is no closing formula.

The next subsection (6:8–7:21) in some ways repeats the instructions given for the five offerings, but the emphasis this time is on regulations to Aaron and his sons. This third subsection is further divided in half by the repeated "The LORD said to Moses" (6:8, 19), both of which are further divided by the repeated "These are the regulations . . . " (6:8*b*, 25; 7:1, 11).

The law on the sacrifices closes with a fourth and final section (7:22-36). The first portion is directed to all the congregation of Israel wherein the eating of fat and blood is strictly forbidden (7:22-27). The second portion spells out the share of the offerings to be given to the priests (7:28-36).

A concluding formula in 7:37-38 wraps up the total package of legislation given in chaps. 1–7.

Leviticus 1:1–3:17, The Three Voluntary Offerings

OVERVIEW

Chapters 1–3 outline the three principal types of sacrifices regularly offered by individual Israelites, by their families, kings, and leaders, or often by the entire congregation. Since they could be offered as stand-alone sacrifices, or as part of a variety of other celebrations, they tended to serve multiple functions in the community.

Leviticus 1:1-17, The Whole Burnt Offering

COMMENTARY

The introduction to the whole burnt offering has a somewhat unusual expression. Generally, in the OT, the Lord "speaks" or "says" rather than "calls." In fact, the word *Lord* is inserted in our translations of the first clause (literally "And he called"), even though it occurs in the second clause. The Jerusalem *Targum* renders it, "And the Word of God called." However, it is clear that Leviticus is a sequel to the erection of the tabernacle in Exodus. The unusual Hebrew syntax suggests, as many commentators have observed, that this opening verse of Lev 1:1 begins where Exod 40:34-35 leaves off.

As the cloud of glory fills the recently completed tabernacle and prevents all access to its interior, the Lord calls to Moses, who now stands outside the tabernacle, from the midst of the Shekinah ("the divine presence") glory residing over the ark of the covenant.

The voice of God, which had boomed out from Sinai, now calls out from the tent of meeting. No longer does God speak with a loud thundering voice, as upon Mount Sinai, but presumably in kinder and gentler tones. But the first words from the tent of meeting are words of grace, concerned about maintaining fellowship with God through sacrifice and atonement for sin. Even the name for the tabernacle, the tent of meeting, implies a coming together of two parties by previous appointment. Having taken possession of the tent of meeting (a name that first appears in Exod 27:21), the Lord speaks "from" or "out of " the place where the deity has come to reside (the same place is called God's "dwelling place" in Lev 15:31; 26:11) among Israel, in contrast to the previous speech from the clouds. Thus, by gracious provision, God has condescended to appoint a place to "dwell" among the people in a special way and manifest the divine will to them. *Tabernacle* has become the more standard term for this place, based on the Latin term *tabernaculum,* meaning "tent" or "wooden hut." The word *meeting* derives from the Hebrew verb meaning "gather" or "come together" (See Josh 11:5; Neh 6:2) in the niphal stem. The same Hebrew verb, יעד (*yāʿad*), can also mean to meet with someone with the purpose "to reveal" something when the term is used of the Lord (see Exod 25:22; 30:6; Num 17:4); thus the tabernacle likewise is a tent of revelation. As mediator and people meet before the Lord, the Lord will reveal the holy will from the tent of meeting.

This is only the third time that the Lord "called" to Moses; the first was at the burning bush (see Exod 3:4), and the second was on Mount Sinai (see Exod 19:3). Leviticus is part of the ongoing historical narrative, for the laws about the sacrifices and ceremonies are given to describe what Aaron and his sons will do now that they have been ordained to the office of priest (chaps. 8–9). Accordingly, Leviticus stands at the center not only of the Pentateuch but also of Israel's story of the move to nationhood, with the exodus from Egypt and the entry into the land of promise on either side.

Nevertheless, the laws in Leviticus contain a sort of built-in obsolescence, for they are given to Moses after the pattern of what God had shown him on the mount (see Exod 25:8, 40). These laws, then, are only copies or types: The real or actual ones remain with the living Lord. The laws are designed to mold Israel into being a "holy nation" (Exod 19:6), according to the model of God, whose own self is "holy." What remains unchanging through all the ages is the holiness of God; however, the expressions of that holiness are subject to change. What Moses receives, he is to "speak to the Israelites." Thus he will be a prophet of God and act as the Lord's mediator to the nation (see Deut 18:15-22; Ps 105:15; Hos 12:13) and an intercessor to God when they sin (see Exodus 32–34; Num 12:6-15).

Before proceeding with specific directions about the various sacrifices, 1:2 gives a general case that applies to all offerings. In fact, v. 2 uses the standard legal form that introduces general cases: כִּי (kî, "when," "if"). Individual legal cases are introduced with a separate word: אִם (’im, "if "; see 1:3, 10, 14; 3:1). Even the word קָרְבָּן (qorbān, "offering") is the general term that applies to all offerings. Qorbān is related to the verbal stem "to draw near," "to approach," and it is used for bringing something to God, whether it be a sacrifice or a gift made to the Lord (cf. Num 7:3, 10; Neh 10:35). Therefore, it is something that one "brings near to" God, and as a consequence, the person enjoys God's nearness (see Ps 73:28). The term qorbān occurs in Mark 7:11 in a negative context, because some Pharisees claimed that the gifts they had dedicated to God prevented them from supporting their parents. Any gift, therefore, brought to the altar and dedicated to God is given this general name of offering. Indeed,

the very wood used to burn the sacrifices on the altar is called qorbān in Neh 10:34 because it too is "brought near to" the Lord.

One further general instruction is given before the specific details for each sacrifice are taken up. Only five kinds of living creatures are acceptable for sacrifices—namely, of animals: cattle, i.e., beef or horned domestic animals and sheep and goats from the flock, including the young of each kind eight days of age and older (22:27); and of fowl: turtledoves and pigeons (1:14; 5:7; 12:6, 8; 14:22, 30; 15:14, 29). Wild animals, or hunted game, are not allowed as sacrifices for several reasons: (a) They are not taken from one's possessions; (b) only perfect animals can serve as sacrificial offerings; (c) only tame, gentle, and harmless animals can be sacrifices because of their serviceability to humanity; and (d) only what costs the offerer something can be given, for David declared, "I will not sacrifice to the LORD my God burnt offerings that cost me nothing" (2 Sam 24:24 NIV). The prophet Malachi rhetorically asked his audience in a later day, " 'When you bring injured, crippled, or diseased animals and offer them as sacrifices, should I accept them from your hand?' says the LORD" (Mal 1:13 NIV).

Notice that no "must" or demand is indicated here; the message is addressed to those who, in covenant relation with God and out of a heart filled with gratitude, desire to express that appreciation before God. What gives the offering its greatest value, from the human side of the act, is its voluntariness and its spontaneity.

Before taking up the six parts of the whole burnt offering, the name, antiquity, and function of this offering must be considered. This offering may well have been known as the "whole offering" (Hebrew כָּלִיל kālîl), for that term formed part of the name for this offering in 1 Sam 7:9 ("Then Samuel took a suckling lamb and offered it up as a whole burnt offering [עוֹלָה כָּלִיל ‘ôlâ kālîl] to the LORD" [NIV]). Moreover, the root kll occurs in Ugaritic (a Canaanite alphabetic script whose language is very close to Hebrew) and Punic, meaning "whole."

However, it appears that another name, "that which ascends" (Hebrew עֹלָה ‘ôlâ), replaced the name for "whole" (kālîl), perhaps at a time when the skin of the burnt offering was given to the officiating priest (Lev 7:8). Thus the name "whole" may have seemed inaccurate and misleading. Nevertheless, the term ʿōlâ indicates that, except for the skin, the whole animal is burned. It "goes up" to God or in smoke, and none of it is eaten by priest or worshiper.

The law of the whole burnt offering comes first, even though it is not first in the order of ritual: That spot belongs to the sin offering, and the burnt offering follows in second place. Why, then is it placed first here? Probably because it is the most ancient of the offerings and it is the one in the most constant use. Noah and Abraham brought burnt offerings and peace offerings, but there is no notice of sin or guilt offerings until Leviticus. Moreover, a burnt offering is offered each morning and evening. On every one of the feast days, except the Day of Atonement, where the sin offering is the central act, the burnt offering is the most important sacrifice.

The purpose or function of the burnt offering is a little more complicated than it may seem at first glance. The explicit purpose assigned in 1:4 is "to make atonement for [the individual]"; therefore, it has both propitiatory (to avoid the deserved wrath of God against sin) and expiatory (to appease and cleanse from sin) functions. As Rabbi Ibn Ezra observed, this expression in v. 4 may well be an abbreviation of the full formula in Exod 30:12, to serve as "a ransom for [a] life" (NIV). Accordingly, the favorable acceptance of the burnt offering signals God's willingness to be approached; it also serves as a substitute ransom that averts the deserved wrath of God. Three times Leviticus assigns this expiatory role to the burnt offering but always in connection with the sacrifice of the sin offering (9:7; 14:20; 16:24). Ezekiel also seems to attribute this same expiatory role to the burnt offerings (see Ezek 45:15, 17) but, again, in connection with other offerings.

But other functions are assigned to the burnt offering. Saul appears to connect it with his desperate need to entreat God: " 'I have not sought the LORD's favor.' So I felt compelled to offer the burnt offering" (1 Sam 13:12 NIV). Does this mean that Saul's purpose is to appease God, or is it to render God homage or thanksgiving? Or is he hoping for expiation of his sins? However, in other texts,

such as Lev 22:17-19 and Num 15:3, burnt offerings are joyful acts of fulfilling vows and making freewill offerings to God. In the binding of Isaac to be a burnt offering (see Genesis 22), it is an act of obedience and a dedication of everything back to God in thanksgiving for all that God had first given Abraham. Thanksgiving is not out of place when persons offer this sacrifice after childbirth, healing, and release from bodily pollution (Lev 12:6; 14:13, 19; 15:30). Thus the range of purposes for the burnt offering is quite broad.

Where a combination of sacrifices is observed, the burnt offering frequently appears as the first sacrifice in the ritual. This may seem to favor the suggestion that it is the inviting offering; i.e., it is employed to attract the favor of God. Thus it desires a response from God as much as it pledges the entirety of one's being to God by giving of this totally offered substitute.

The ritual for sacrifices of all types involves six identifiable parts: (1) the presentation of the victim, (2) the laying on of the hand(s), (3) the slaughtering of the victim, (4) the sprinkling of the blood, (5) the sacrificial burning, and (6) the sacrificial meal. Although some differences appear in the various sacrifices, each will exhibit all, or most, of these six parts of the offering ritual.

First comes the presentation of the victim in the whole burnt offering. While the final three parts of the ritual are done by the priest for the offerer, the first three parts are usually reserved for the one drawing near with a gift to God. The offerer must bring the victim.

The place of presentation is prescribed as being "at the entrance to the tent of meeting" (1:3). This restriction to the entrance to the tabernacle takes direct aim at the ever present tendency in Israel toward idolatry. By so specifying, the worship of God is set apart from all worship of false gods. And all forms of self-will in worship are also prohibited. The mode and conditions for the worship of God cannot be other than what God appoints. To think and act otherwise are to offer non-acceptable worship to God.

The acceptance of the sacrifice means that the one making the offering can also find acceptance with God. When God accepts the sacrifice, that is good enough indication that God also accepts the offerer. The zone in which this is to be accomplished is "before the LORD" (literal rendering of 1:3c). By this second reminder, the law specifically limits sacrifice to a particular area by the altar in the sanctuary courtyard to the interior of the tent of meeting.

The concept that sacrifices are pleasing to God is further raised by the oft-repeated phrase "an aroma pleasing to the LORD" (1:9, 13, 17). This phrase is used forty-three times in the OT and only in this expression. The word *pleasing* comes from the same root as the word *rest,* implying that the sacrifice brings peace between God and the worshiper. If the picture is an anthropomorphic one depicting God like a human being smelling the odor from the sacrifices, it is problematic for those who see Leviticus as P material, since P is supposed to minimize anthropomorphisms. To make matters even more complicated for the P thesis, Ezekiel and later literature avoid this expression and the verb for "smelling" that often goes with it. However, instead of being an anthropomorphic figure of speech here, it may be little more than a stock phrase of the language that endures long after the conception of God as literally smelling something.

One other consideration must be made about the nature of this sacrifice. Is the victim offered as an "offering made by fire" (1:9)? It is clear that it is immolated as a holocaust, but the Hebrew term אשה (*'iššeh*) is probably to be connected not with אש (*'ēš*), "fire," but with the Ugaritic root *itt,* "gift." Surprisingly enough, such sacrifices are described in 21:6 as "the bread of their God" (KJV). Therefore, the priests are not to defile themselves, since "they present the offerings made to the LORD by fire [or as gifts of/to the LORD], the food of their God, they are to be holy" (21:6; cf. 3:11, 16; 21:21). If the translation of "offering made by fire" is correct, it cannot be used as it is for the portions that the priests eat (2:3, 10; 7:31, 35) and for the bread of presence (24:7, 9). The addition of the word for "bread" alongside this term of uncertain translation may add some force to translating it "food offering" as NEB and GNB favor.

The second act of the ceremony of the burnt offering is the laying on of the hand(s). At first it appears that nothing more is indicated than declaring that it is the offerer's property, whose right it is to give it back to God. But that would leave this question: Why is this ceremony confined to bloody sacrifices? Certainly nonbloody sacrifices are just as much the property of the offerer, who has the right to give.

The laying on of the hand(s) may originally have been a legal and juridical procedure. When Moses appointed Joshua leader over Israel, he laid his hands on him (see Num 27:18-23; Deut 34:9). The people laid their hands on the Levites (see Num 8:10) and thereby formally substituted the Levites for each firstborn in Israel. Likewise, when they laid hands on the one convicted of blasphemy (see Lev 24:10-16), they transferred the obligation from their heads to the blasphemer. But the fullest symbolic expression of what the imposition of hands means is to be found in the ceremony of the Day of Atonement. There Aaron was ordered to lay his hands on the head of one of the goats of the sin offering (Lev 16:21) and "confess over it all the wickedness and rebellion of the Israelites—all their sins—and put them on the goat's head." Members of the early church laid hands on Paul and Barnabas as they designated them for special service (see Acts 13:2-3).

But even more than the idea of substitution is meant here. This symbolic act, which in later Hebrew would be known as *semikhah* for the verb "to lay," means to lean heavily on the victim, not to lightly rest the hand on it. The force of the verb סמך (*sāmak,* "to rest heavily on [something or someone]") is illustrated in Ps 88:7: "Your wrath lies heavily upon me" (NIV). The offerer is heavily resting on the fact that the victim is procuring from God the needed atonement and acceptance. When the hands are laid on the victim, the one making the offering has to take it by faith that the victim will, in God's merciful provision, symbolically express what the offerer deserves but is now excused by virtue of another who substitutes life for life.

Sometimes the question is raised, Was this part of the ceremony done with one or two hands? Leviticus 16:21 clearly specifies both hands. But that is why others have seen a distinction between that function on the Day of Atonement and what is specified here. However, the Mishnah, tractate *Menahoth* 93a, notes that two hands are everywhere required. The Hebrew consonantal text in 1:4 merely reads ידו (*ydw*), which the MT invariably vocalizes as singular (*yādô*) but which is equally possible to render as a dual form (*yādāw*), for both words are written the same way in the ancient unvocalized text.

The conclusion to this evidence is persuasive: The purpose of the laying on of hands is to transfer the spiritual qualities (in this case one's sin and impurities) from the one doing the ceremony to the one offered as a sacrifice. The idea of substitution, however, is more all-encompassing than the idea of transference of sin, identification of the offerer with the animal, or ownership of the animal. The laying on of hands makes it clear that when the life of the sacrifice is poured out in death, it is just as if the person who brings the offering dies.

The promise that follows is that the sacrifice "will be accepted on [that person's] behalf to make atonement for [that one]" (1:4c). *Atonement* is a key word in Leviticus, for it appears here almost fifty times (along with almost another fifty times in the rest of the OT), usually in association with the priest making atonement by means of a sacrifice. The word does not mean "to cover," even though a verb in a different Hebrew stem (the Qal) using the same consonants appears in Gen 6:14 meaning "to smear with pitch," "to caulk" or in that sense, "to cover." Rather than resorting to this single usage of the verb in Gen 6:14 as the root meaning of this word, Hebrew grammar is better served by deriving this verb from the noun of the same consonants meaning "a ransom" (see Num 35:31; Isa 43:3). Since the verb "to atone" is used only in the intensive stem (the Hebrew piel), it is better to understand it as a denominative verb meaning "to give a ransom" or "to deliver or atone by a substitute." Even the lid to the ark of the covenant, called the "mercy seat" in the KJV, is literally "a place of atonement."

The slaughter of the victim is the third part of the ceremony and the last act performed by the offerer (1:5). But it may well be that the third-person singular form of the verb, "he is to slaughter," is used here in an impersonal sense, "one is to slaughter," a usage seen often in the Hebrew text of Leviticus.[35] This would

explain the apparent contradiction between the thought in Leviticus that the offerer must slaughter the victim and the claim in Ezek 44:10-11 that the Levites are authorized to do so in the eschatological times. Both the LXX and the Samaritan Pentateuch render the verb as plural, thereby allowing for either or both the offerer and the priests to participate. This does not necessarily mean that the Greek and Samaritan versions had a different text before them, for it again is only a matter of vocalizing the same consonantal text.

Our text uses the technical term for ritual slaughter, which involves slitting the throat of the animal. So drastic is the penalty for the offerer's sin that it demands death. The wages of sin is death; but in this case, it means death for the sacrificial victim.

The tendency seemed to be to turn over the duties of slaughtering the animals to the Levites or priests as 1 Chr 23:31 notes. In the days of King Hezekiah, the skinning of the animals was performed by the priests, who being too few in number required the help of the Levites (see 2 Chr 29:34). And whenever the offerers were not ceremonically clean, the Levites had to step in again to kill the sacrifice in the days of Hezekiah (see 2 Chr 30:17). Later, in the days of King Josiah, the Levites slaughtered all the Passover lambs (see 2 Chr 35:6).

The sprinkling of the blood follows. Since only the priests are allowed to ascend the altar (see 1 Sam 2:28), they have to perform the rest of the ritual. The directions to the priest on the use of the blood from the sacrifice vary in each offering. For example, in the sin offering the blood assumes a central role, but here in the burnt offering it is not as dominant. However, the idea of atonement by the blood is not absent even in the burnt offering; therefore, the sprinkling of the blood cannot be omitted, even it if takes a lesser role.

Leviticus 1:5*b* reads, "Then Aaron's sons the priests shall bring the blood and sprinkle it against the altar on all sides at the entrance to the Tent of Meeting." It is difficult to say precisely how the blood was handled since quite a bit of blood was involved and different verbs are used with a range of meaning from "sprinkling" with one's finger or with a bunch of hyssop (14:7) to "dashing," "throwing," or "pouring" (1:5, 11; 3:2, 8, 13; 9:18).

---

35. See George Bush, *Notes, Critical and Practical, on the Book of Leviticus* (New York: Newman & Ivison, 1852; reprint, Minneapolis, James & Klock, 1976) 15, 44, *passim.*

However, in Num 19:18-21 both verbs of "sprinkling" and "throwing" are used as synonyms. The NT understood the concept as one of sprinkling as well (cf. the use of Exod 24:8 in Heb 9:19).

Whether the blood was thrown "against" the altar or poured "on" it is another question. Again, the preposition can have either meaning. Because the fire was no doubt very hot, it was necessary to stand back some distance. Nevertheless, the blood was part of the sacrifice, and so we conclude that part of it was thrown "on" the altar "round about" or "on all sides." To argue that the blood was not part of the offering because it was the life of the animal (17:10-14) and must therefore be returned to God by placing it alongside the altar lest the offerer be considered a murderer is to avoid the symbolism of substitution and the wholeness and completeness of the burnt offering.

The atoning work is completed in the sprinkling of the blood. In this act of presenting and sprinkling the blood on the altar, the life of the innocent victim is presented to God as a ransom and a substitute for the sinner. All of this is done at the altar, the designated place where God promised to meet persons bringing an offering.

The use of the blood is the prerogative of the priest alone. The offerer must leave to the priests the presentation of the blood toward God. The pouring out or sprinkling of the blood, the very life of the victim, constitutes the real virtue of the sacrifice. No doubt, it is deliberately calculated to remind the offerer that each person deserves to have one's own blood shed for sins. Thus, without the shedding of blood, there is no hope of having any sins remitted.

The sacrificial burning is the fifth part of the ritual. First, the animal has to be "skinned" or "flayed" (1:6a). Only the skin (which is to be given to the priests; see 7:8), the crop of a bird, and the animial's viscera are exempted from the whole burnt offering; everything else is burned on the altar: That is the distinctive aspect of the whole burnt offering. To prepare the animal for this total holocaust, it has to be "cut up into its parts" (1:6b). Before the pieces are carefully arranged on the altar (1:8), the priests are to "put fire on the altar" (literally "shall give fire" 1:7). This probably

means to stir up the fire or to stoke it, for the divine command is that the fire is to be kept burning continually (6:12). The carefully arranged wood also is intended to stoke up the fire for the burnt offering about to be offered.

To prevent any pollution of this sacred offering, 1:9 advises that the internal portion of the animal and its legs must be washed with water. Nothing extraneous or corrupt must come into contact with what has been set aside to be presented to God. The viscera of the animal (made unclean by the presence of undigested food) and the legs (possibly contaminated by contact with excreta or with the ground) are to be washed with water.

Now the total offering is to be burned on the altar (1:9b). However, the writer does not use the usual word for consuming something with fire. The verb appears to be derived from the noun for "smoke." Furthermore, since in Hebrew and several of the Semitic languages the word for "incense" appears to be derived from the word for "smoke," it is safe to say that the burned parts of the sacrifice rise in smoke as if they are a perfume or an incense to God.

Thus the holocaust, or the whole burnt offering, with the exception of the skin of the animal or the crop of a bird and the viscera, is entirely dedicated to the Lord and ascends heavenward as a sweet-smelling aroma to the Lord.

Those who are not as wealthy, who cannot offer one of the large domestic horned cattle, can bring a sheep or a goat (1:10-13) from the flock. It too has to be a "male without defect" (1:10). Whereas v. 5 does not specify, v. 11 orders that the animal from the flock be slaughtered on "the north side of the altar," just as the text specifies for the sin offering (4:24, 29, 33; 6:25), the guilt offering (7:2), and offerings performed for ceremonial cleansing (14:13).

As a further concession to the poor people of the land, either a dove or a pigeon can be brought as a whole burnt offering. Thus Mary, the mother of our Lord, brought such an offering (see Luke 2:22-24).

The ritual for sacrificing the dove or pigeon has several unique features. The expression in 1:15, "wring off the head," is probably overtranslated in the NIV, for one need only twist or yank the head to disjoin it from the top of the vertebrae. That would be sufficient to kill the bird; thus the head need not be completely severed. The removal of "the crop with its contents" (1:16) is an uncertain translation. Instead, it has recently been suggested that the word translated "crop" actually was the bird's tail, which directs its flight. If so, we are being given instructions on how to clean a bird. Jacob Milgrom argues that the rare word in v. 16 should be rendered "crissum." The crissum is made up of the loose fatty material that can be removed by cutting through the bird's tail wing: "The anus is removed along with the tail. However, the anus separates from the intestines when it is removed. This leaves a portion of the intestines exposed. By pulling on these, the rest of the intestines can be pulled from the abdomen like a string attached to the gizzard."[36]

36. Milgrom, *Leviticus 1–16*, 171, quoting his student S. Pfann.

Only later in the Second Temple times was the decision made to add the requirement that the gizzard of the bird should be removed as well as its intestines. But the crop contains no excrement, as do the lower intestines; therefore, Scripture does not require this addition. The bird is offered with all of its feathers except for the tail, contrary to some translations.

The "ashes" (literally "fatness"); 1:16c are created mainly from the suet. These ashes are placed on the east side of the altar. There does not appear to be an apparent reason for choosing this side of the altar.

In all three types of victims, whether from the cattle, flock, or two types of birds, everything is given up to God in its entirety (with the exceptions of the skin and viscera). The only missing aspect of the six-part ceremony is the sacrificial meal. Since everything is dedicated wholly to the Lord, there is no provision for sharing a portion with the priests or in a communal meal. The whole is burned on the altar.

REFLECTIONS

The details for the ritual of the whole burnt offering appear so exotic and foreign to our experience that little, if anything, is expected by way of contemporary relevance. However, the reverse is the case. For those who have difficulty understanding and appreciating all the abstract forms used in NT theology to explain Christian concepts of redemption, concepts that often seem to relate more to Greek philosophical thought than to modern concerns, Leviticus offers a real breakthrough. The concepts are not abstract in Leviticus; rather, they are brutally concrete. The pictures are large and terribly real. In Leviticus, abstract thinking and theologizing are reduced to a huge primer.

1. Though sometimes the OT sacrificial system is understood in harsh and legalistic terms, in the NT, Jesus was critical of abuses of the concept of sacrifices.

At their best and in their own context, the sacrifices described in Leviticus are offerings made to God flowing freely from grateful hearts. As the commentary notes, there is no "must" or demand about the sacrifices; sacrifices grow out of a covenant relationship with God.

So, far more than sheep, goats, or birds, the offerings described in Leviticus are signs of our deeper and richer desire to make an offering of ourselves to God. At the conclusion of his masterful *The Denial of Death,* Ernest Becker states, "Who knows what form the forward momentum of life will take in the time ahead or what use it will make of our searching. The most anyone of us can seem to do is to fashion something—an object or ourselves—and drop it into the confusion, make an offering of it, so to speak."[37] At the core of Leviticus is a conviction that human life is most rich, beautiful, and free when, amid the confusion of life, people fashion themselves into offerings to God.

37. Ernest Becker, *The Denial of Death* (New York: Free Press, 1973) 285.

2. The proper mode for worshiping God is not left to human invention; it is by divinely revealed instruction. All self-will in worship is prohibited; the offerer must come on the terms of faith, trusting God and bringing only what God has indicated will be acceptable. The human temptation to add or delete terms or requirements as to the mode and condition for presenting oneself to God is ever present, but this impulse must be firmly resisted.

3. What worshipers offer to God must be the best, most perfect of its kind, and it must cost something. To give to God what costs little or nothing is to invite divine displeasure against the work of our own hands, as the audience of Malachi's day learned (see Malachi 1). Just as King David refused to accept as a gift something that he could in turn offer to God, since he would be giving what cost him nothing (see 2 Sam 24:24), so modern persons should resist the temptation to send to the house of God whatever we could just as well do without or whatever we are trying to get rid of. Almost every community has its share of stories about the person who saved the used tea bags to send to the missionaries, or persons who boxed up all the unsold clothes from the garage sale to send them to homeless people near or far. Is this not a modern variation on the ancient malpractice of offering to God sacrificial animals that were injured, crippled, or diseased (see Mal 1:13)? The widow "put in more than all the others" (Luke 21:3*b* NIV) who were placing their offerings in the Temple treasury as Jesus and his disciples watched, because she gave herself first, and then out of the poverty of what she had to live on, she gave the best she had. That is costly giving, and so it was commanded and taught in bold relief in the whole burnt offering.

4. The whole burnt offering depicts in type what Christ our Savior did on our behalf when he wholly surrendered to the will of the Father. Just as the innocent sacrificial victim submissively yielded its life on behalf of the offerer, "so also through the obedience of the one man [Christ] the many will be made righteous" (Rom 5:19 NIV). Christ "being found in appearance as a man,/ he humbled himself/ and became obedient to death—/ even death on a cross!" (Phil 2:8 NIV).

5. As the burnt offering was "an aroma pleasing to the Lord" (Lev. 1:17), so Christ became exactly the same for all who believe on him. The apostle Paul was making that very point when he urged in Eph 5:1-2, "Be imitators of God, therefore, as dearly loved children and live a life of love, just as Christ loved us and gave himself up for us as a fragrant offering and sacrifice to God" (NIV). The death of Christ, like that of the sacrificial animal, was like perfume that pleased God.

6. The sacrifices are not called the "food" of God (Lev 21:6) because they are in any sense something that the deity needs to be sustained. Psalm 50:8-15 sharply rebukes that idea. After all, argues the psalmist, God owns "the cattle on a thousand hills" (Ps 50:10 NIV); "the world" and "all that is in it" (Ps 50:12 NIV) belong to God. The concept of the food of God must not be understood here in any material sense. Rather, it symbolizes the thanksgiving, loyalty, commitment, and desire for nearness that the sacrifices express. That is the food of God.

7. The whole burnt offering of Leviticus 1 is reflected in the Pauline admonition in Rom 12:1: "Therefore, I urge you, brothers [meaning also 'and sisters'], in view of God's mercy, to offer your bodies as living sacrifices, holy and pleasing to God—this is your spiritual act of worship" (NIV). Nowhere is the call to total commitment of one's life put in a more graphic way. Just as the whole burnt offering was consumed on the altar, in a similar manner Paul exhorted believers to place their whole selves at the disposal of the living God. Such self-giving would be as "living sacrifices" rather than as dead victims. Such an act of consecration is something pleasing to God, even as the aroma of the sacrificial smoke was said to be perfume to the Lord.

Leviticus 2:1-16, The Grain Offering

COMMENTARY

Scripture preserves two types of grain offerings: one that accompanies animal sacrifices, and an independent offering. This offering is regularly prescribed as an accompanying sacrifice with the burnt offering and the peace offering. Its auxiliary function is well attested in the historical books of the OT (e.g., Josh 22:23, 29; Judg 13:19, 23; 1 Sam 1:24; 2:29; 3:14; 10:3; 1 Kgs 8:64; 2 Kgs 16:13, 15). This fact probably accounts for its being introduced second in the order of the sacrifices in Leviticus. The grain offering is also one of the three sacrifices (along with the burnt offering and the peace offering) that produces "an aroma pleasing to the LORD" (1:9, 17; 2:2, 9, 12; 3:5, 16).

The precise connotation for the name of this offering is difficult to determine (since its meaning is never explicitly stated), even though the Hebrew name for it (מנחה *minḥâ*) is well known and exhibits a number of meanings. For example, it can mean a "gift" or a "present," such as Jacob sent to his brother, Esau (see Gen 32:13), or as he later sent to Joseph in Egypt (see Gen 43:11). It can also refer to both an animal and a grain offering, as a sort of generic term for any type of offering, as with Cain's and Abel's offerings (see Gen 4:3, 5). In nonreligious usages, it meant "tribute," the money paid by a vassal king to his overlord (see 2 Sam 8:6; 1 Kgs 4:21). It is likely, then, that the *minḥâ* is a present or gift made to God. The worshiper brings the sacrifice as a gift in recognition of God's supreme authority and in the hope of gaining God's favor and blessing.

The KJV calls this a "meal offering," meaning in the English of that day "food-offering." Other translations come closer to the mark by calling it a "cereal offering," even though it specifies the choicest part of the wheat grain rather than any of the other grains. This criticism, of course, must also be made of the label "grain offering."

This offering is made of semolina, the inner kernels of the wheat grain. Leviticus 2:1 says that the offering is to "be of fine flour" (סלת *sōlet*). In Exod 29:2, *sōlet* is identified as "semolina of wheat." This semolina is identified with grits, for in rabbinic tradition, "A sieve lets through the flour but retains the *sōlet*" (*'Abot* 5:15).

Although it is made to God by fire, the grain offering never implies that a life is being given to God, as is true of the burnt offering. Also, the grain offering does not require the laying on of hands, as the burnt offering does, for there is no idea of transfer or substitution. The dominant idea is that this is a gift to God from the produce of the soil—namely, the inner kernels of the wheat grain.

Not only must the grain offering be a product of the soil, but it must be grown by cultivation. In this way it represents the result of human labor. In addition to human labor in growing it, there is the work of grinding, sifting, and, in some cases, cooking it that further emphasizes the investment of labor. Therefore, just as an aspect of the whole burnt offering emphasizes the consecration of the person to God, so the grain offering represents a similar consecration of the results of one's labors to God.

Three kinds of grain offerings are described here: (1) grain offerings of uncooked grain (Lev 2:1-3); (2) cooked grain offerings and general requirements for this offering (Lev 2:4-13); and (3) grain offerings of firstfruits (Lev 2:14-16). Some have supposed that the various implements used, such as the oven, the baking pan, or the frying pan, represent what different classes of people were likely to have owned. The poorer classes ate parched grain since they usually could not afford an oven or a baking pan. Regardless of the individual means, God is willing to accept all at whatever economic level they come. The size or the status of the gift, as indicated by the mixtures and the method of cooking, is not to keep the worshiper from presenting the grain offering.

Wheat was the most highly prized of all the grains. In offering the inner kernels of wheat, the best of the grains, one is offering the best to God. It also represents what is the most labor-intensive to produce, given the grinding and sifting required to produce this special form of wheat grits.

After the offerer brings the semolina wheat grits to the altar, Aaron's sons take a portion of the offering and add oil to it. Oil is applied in five different ways: pouring (v. 1), mixing (v. 4), spreading (v. 4b), frying (v. 7), and adding (v. 15). The oil is the ubiquitous olive oil of that part of the world. Olive oil also represents the intense labor of the offerer, for the olives had to be crushed—i.e., put into heavy presses with enormous beams used as levers weighted with heavy stones—and ground up. The same olive oil is used to anoint the leaders, priests, and Levites for their offices. Indeed, that oil comes on a gravity feed from the two olive trees into the seven-branched lampstand or menorah in Zech 4:1-3. There it is explained to the two symbolic olive trees, the high priest Joshua and the Davidic governor Zerubbabel, that it is " 'not by might nor by power, but by my Spirit,' says the LORD Almighty" (Zech 4:6 NIV). Thus the grain offering, when kneaded with the olive oil, in whatever form, teaches Israel that in all the work offered as a gift to God, the in-working and enabling agent is the Spirit of God. Elsewhere oil is associated with the Spirit of God (see 1 Sam 10:1; 9-11). But oil is also associated with joy (see Ps 45:7; Prov 27:9; Isa 61:3).

A pinch of incense is also usually added to the grain offering (Lev 2:2, 15-16). It is not a late addition to the grain offering, as some have suggested, for incense burners have been discovered from periods of Israelite occupation much earlier than the time of Jeremiah.[38]

The incense mentioned in 2:2 is actually frankincense. Frankincense is a fragrant gum resin that comes from three different species of *Boswellia* trees, native to southern Arabia and Somaliland on the African coast.

Instead of conjecturing that the frankincense or incense is to cover up the odors of the whole burnt offerings, which are said to be an aroma pleasing to God, it is better to note with the text that the frankincense is a

"memorial"[39] to God (2:2). Even though the rest of the grain offering is to go to the priests, the frankincense is to be given totally to God as a memorial. In that it ascends totally to God, it may symbolize the prayers and praise of God's people. Because Psalms 38 and 70 use a similar form in their title lines as the word translated "memorial" in Lev 2:2, some have speculated that these two psalms were recited as "petitions" with the offering of the grain offering. The same word used in the titles to these two psalms occurs in 1 Chr 16:4, meaning "to make petition" or "to bring to remembrance." The portion that the priests take out of the grain offering, then, is a "memorial," or in "remembrance" of God's supreme dominion over all. It put the priests in mind of the divine promise in the covenant to accept the services the people render to God. As Ps 20:3 enjoins, "May [God] *remember* all your sacrifices/ and accept your burnt offerings" (emphasis added, NIV). This is similar to what an angel told the Roman centurion Cornelius in Acts 10:4: "Your prayers and gifts to the poor have come up as a *memorial gift* before God" (emphasis added, NIV).

The sin offering (Lev 5:11) and the jealousy offerings (Num 5:15) specifically say that no oil or incense is to be mixed with them. These offerings bring iniquity and sin to mind rather than all that Israel holds and enjoys because of the gracious provision of the sovereign covenant-maker. Both the sin and the jealousy offerings are devoid of the elements that make the whole burnt offering and the grain offering an aroma pleasing to the Lord.

The prohibition of yeast (or, as it is called in many versions, "leaven") and honey from the grain offerings is of special interest. Yeast was forbidden at the time of the exodus and

---

38. A point made by Gordon J. Wenham, *The New International Commentary on the Old Testament: Leviticus* (Grand Rapids: Eerdmans, 1979) 68 n. 1, citing as evidence Ruth Amiran, *Ancient Pottery of the Holy Land* (Jerusalem: Massada, 1969) 302- 6.

39. The precise meaning of this Hebrew word, 'azkārātāh, is uncertain. If it is understood as an *Afel* form, it would mean "that which calls to mind," or "a memorial portion," coming from the verb *zākar*, "to remember." Another way to view it would be to take it from the noun *zeker*, meaning "a commemorative object." In that case, the word in Lev 2:2, 9, 16; Leviticus 5:12; Leviticus 6:15 (Heb. 6:8); 24:7; Num 5:26 would mean "a token portion." The Akkadian vocabulary has *zikru,* "an effigy," "a double." This would strengthen the position for the second option; however, we still think the first meaning of "memorial" is preferable. Actually, both concepts say nearly the same thing: The grain offering, in both views, would be a sign that the worshiper has been taught and reminded of the fact that everything is owed to God, but God is pleased to accept a portion of the sacrifice as a "token" of it, while releasing the rest of the offering for consumption by the priests. Thus this offering is a "tribute" or "a gift that fulfills the covenant," while reminding the offerer that God deserves to have everything that we are and have.

the first Passover (see Exod 12:15; 13:3, 7) because Israel was to leave in haste; there was no time to wait around for the yeast to rise (see Exod 12:39). However, we must be careful of claiming that all leaven symbolizes decay and corruption and thus refers to evil in every instance where it appears in Scripture. That is not so: The loaves of the firstfruits were made with yeast (see Lev 23:17, 20), and even honey was introduced into the first-fruits offered in Hezekiah's time (see 2 Chr 31:5). Nevertheless, in the context of the grain offering, it still seems fair to conclude that yeast and honey may be excluded to avoid all suggestions of wickedness, malice, moral decay, and spiritual corruption.

Even though Israel was to be brought to a "land of milk and honey," the widespread use of honey in the pagan cults must have brought this strong aversion to its use in Israelite sacrifices. In the Ugaritic myths of the Canaanite religion, the hero Keret offers honey to the chief Canaanite god, El. Instances could be multiplied from Akkadian cuneiform sources in Mesopotamia and ancient Syria. Accordingly, the offerings made to God must be absolutely free of everything corrupt among God's people.

In 2:13, one other requisite is added to the grain offering: salt. Salt is just the opposite of honey and yeast in that it symbolizes preservation from corruption. It is found in every sacrifice. The best clue to its meaning is in the phrase "the salt of the covenant of your God" (2:13). Often, covenants, in that day and this, were sealed and confirmed by a formal meal in which the parties partook of salt together, thus concluding the pact. Therefore, solemn covenants are described in Scripture as "[covenants] of salt" (see Num 18:19; 2 Chr 13:5). The effect of this concept is to render the expression "the salt of the covenant of your God" as a "covenant made binding by salt." Salt cannot be destroyed by fire or the passing of time. The addition of salt is a deliberate act to remind the offerer that the covenant relationship the act symbolizes is an eternal and binding relationship. God will never forsake the worshiper—and the one bringing the offering has a duty to remember to do all that the covenant teaches.

The grain offering is unique in specifying that a portion goes to Aaron and his sons: "It is a most holy part of the offerings made to the LORD by fire" (2:3b). Only a small part of the grain offering is offered by the priest to the Lord as a "memorial"; the larger portion is given to Aaron and his sons. And most surprisingly of all, that portion is called "a most holy part"! The Hebrew expression used here is the standard way of expressing the superlative degree: "holiness of holinesses," or "most holy." The expression occurs only with the grain, sin, and guilt offerings (2:3; 6:17[cf. Heb 6:10], 25 [cf. Heb 6:18]; 7:6) in distinction to the rest of the sacrifices, which are designated as "sacred" (the peace offering, firstfruits of the harvest, firstfruits of the animals, and all that is devoted, i.e., part of the חרם ḥērem to the Lord [see Num 18:12-19]). These designations of the "sacred" and the "most holy" are always used with the portions to be eaten. That is why the burnt offering is left off the list of "most holy," since no one is to eat any of it.

This distinction, then, between things that are *lighter in holiness* and things that are *most holy* is fairly common among the Jewish communities and in the Egyptian and Hittite cultic texts.[40] "The lighter holy things" may be eaten by persons who are not priests in any place in the encampment, or within Jerusalem, so long as they are ceremonially clean. They include all peace offerings made by particular individuals, the paschal lamb, the tithes, and the firstlings of cattle. But "the most holy things" are to be eaten by no one, or by none except Aaron and his sons, in the sanctuary (6:16-26). Included in this category are all burnt offerings, all sin offerings, and all peace offerings made for the whole community. The grain offering is put into this category of "most holy" as well. A particular sacredness is attached to it because of its use of the inner kernels of the wheat and because of its being set aside for the priests to be eaten in the sanctuary.

This distinction between the sacred and the most holy among the sacrificial instructions supports the argument for a similar distinction within the whole law of God. Many moderns have great difficulty seeing any distinction between the moral law of God and the civil and ceremonial aspects of that same

---

40. See Jacob Milgrom, *Cult and Conscience: The Asham and the Priestly Doctrine of Repentance* (Leiden: Brill, 1976) 41-43.

law. However, by Christian times the rabbis were distinguishing between the light and the heavy aspects of the law, just as Jesus referred to the "weightier matters of the law" (Matt 23:23 NRSV). The separation between the "sacred," or lighter holy things, and the "most holy" things helps us to see that such distinctions were not late fictions concocted by apologists who were hard pressed to find any contemporary relevance for certain legal portions of Scripture.

Three types of cooked grain offerings are mentioned in vv. 4-10. Verse 4 mentions the one baked in an "oven." The oven was partially embedded in the ground in a circular pit, usually four to five feet deep and three feet in diameter, with plastered walls, or it was cylindrical, a three-foot-high unglazed earthen vessel with an opening about fifteen inches wide in diameter at the top that gradually widened toward the bottom, where a hole was placed to remove the ashes conveniently. In both models, the bread was baked by heating the oven to glowing embers in the bottom. Then large oval or round cakes, not thicker than pancakes, were thrown against the sides of the oven. The cake was not turned since it was thin and could, in most cases, be removed in three minutes. If it were not removed in time from the sides of the oven after its moisture had been removed, it would fall into the fire and be wasted. The bread thus produced was usually soft and flexible, and it could be rolled up like paper, a type of falafel. If it stayed in the oven too long, it could become crisp and hard.

Verse 5 speaks of another type of cooking instrument: a "griddle." The griddle was made of either clay [41] or iron (see Ezek 4:3). The latter form is a convex plate of iron (copper often still being in use for some) placed about nine inches from the ground by supporting stones. With a slow fire beneath it, it produces cakes very similar to those stuck to the sides of the oven, but it is a much slower process.

---

41. Milgrom mentions some clay griddles found at Gezer (*Leviticus 1-16,* 185) and described and illustrated in *IDB,* vol. 1 (Nashville: Abingdon, 1962) 1:462, fig. 48.

The last cooking instrument mentioned is a "pan" in v. 7. Apparently, the main difference between the griddle and the pan was that the pan had a lid. Originally, they were shallow earthen vessels resembling our frying pans, then other metal forms appeared.

The prescriptions in this chapter conclude with the third type of grain offering: the grain offering of the firstfruits to the Lord (2:14-16). The firstfruits of all the harvest are to be brought each year to the Lord as the real owner of all the land and what it produced. In this line of thinking, the Israelites have the status of tenants (see Exod 22:29; 23:19; 34:26; Lev 23:9; Deut 26:1-2).

The ears of grain are to be brought to the Lord in the form in which they are to be eaten: roasted first in the fire so as to dry out the moisture, and then ground in a mill, usually between two stones. Whether these grains could be barley as well as wheat is unknown. The term *firstfruits* is applied to barley in 2 Kgs 4:42 but to wheat in Num 28:26. To this day, Arabs roast barley as described here, but not wheat, due to its flat taste.

This offering, like all the cooked grain offerings, is mixed with oil and presented with incense. Once again, the priest takes a handful and burns that portion to the Lord mixed with the oil and all the incense. The remainder, as in the other grain offerings, belongs to the priests, though that is not explicitly stated this time. Since the priests are given no land among the tribal inheritances, they depend on this provision from the Lord and the people for their daily bread.

The crushing or bruising of the "firstfruits" will play a large role in the typology of both the OT and the NT. Christians identify the resurrection of Christ as the "firstfruits of those who have fallen asleep" (1 Cor 15:20 NIV). They see this typology also in the fact that Christ sanctified himself, "that they too may be truly sanctified" (John 17:19 NIV). Thus, to sanctify the first part of the harvest is to sanctify the whole harvest.

REFLECTIONS

The grain offering symbolized the dedication of a person's life, and especially one's labor, to God. This central thesis is illustrated in the following applications to our contemporary lives.

1. If the whole burnt offering required that the entire animal be burned on the altar (except the skin and viscera) to signify the consecration of the whole life to God, why was such a small part of the grain offering placed on the altar since it too indicated a total surrender of the person to God? The answer is readily available: All of the grain offering was presented to God, even if only a small portion was placed in the fire on the altar. Thus the Lord accepted the entire grain offering. The limited portion of the grain offering that was burned was offered as a "memorial," thereby signifying that the offerer served the Lord in all thoughts and labors in life. In the grain offering, Israel and all subsequent generations are reminded that God's claim upon us for full consecration covers everything, even the very food that we eat. Thus, as Paul directed, "So whether you eat or drink or whatever you do, do it all for the glory of God" (1 Cor 10:31 NIV).

2. The idea that the grain offering was a "memorial" (2:2; cf. NRSV) also signifies that one purpose of an offering is to jog memories. We often think of an offering only in the task-oriented sense; that is, we put money in the offering plate to pay for the church expenses, to feed hungry people, to send the youth choir to choir camp, and so on. In other words, we tend to think of offerings as means to get things done. To be sure, getting things done is a worthy reason to make an offering, but Leviticus suggests that one of the most basic reasons we make offerings is not so that something will get done but so that something will be brought to mind.

First, an offering brings to our minds the blessings of God in our lives. At Christmas, we give a necktie to Uncle Joe, not because he really needs another tie, but because the very act of giving a gift brings our loving relationship to the surface. In the same way, we make offerings to God, not because God needs what we offer, but because we need to have our relationship with God continually brought to mind. Making an offering, in this sense, is like participating in the Lord's Supper; we do so "in remembrance" of God's merciful acts.

Second, and more radical, Leviticus suggests that offerings are made to jog God's memory! As noted in the commentary, Ps 20:3 states, "May [God] remember all your sacrifices/ and accept your burnt offerings" (NIV). This is picture language, of course; there is no notion here that God is forgetful, a divine absent-minded professor who needs to be reminded of things. The claim, rather, is that by making an offering, we become present to God. An offering, then, is a form of prayer. It is a way of making active, visible, and concrete what is always tacitly true: our communion with God. In this sense, offerings "bring us to God's mind."

3. The grain offering was one main source of income for the priesthood. The laity were responsible to their ministers to care properly for them. The responsibility to provide for those in ministry still rests with the people of God, even though the ancient grain offerings have ceased to be required or encouraged. (Paul made that point abundantly clear in 1 Cor 9:13-14.) In every dispensation, God has prescribed a demonstrated concern toward those who have devoted themselves to the ministry of "most holy things." To avoid participating in this responsibility, or to do so in a shabby manner that forces economic pressures on those who should be busy about the things of God, is ultimately to demean both the Lord, whom worshipers say they wish to serve, and the service roles God has given. In the long run it reflects on the claims of the laity. How can such miserly pittances be an expression of the lordship of their sovereign

Lord? Those who are called and who faithfully labor in the Word and the holy things of God are to be competently and adequately supported.

4. The tendency to import into our worship of God such negative leavening influences as are found in the wickedness and corruption of our day is all too tempting. But we must maintain constant vigilance to make sure that our worship does not imitate pagan practices or exhibit the leaven of hypocrisy.

5. In accord with the usage of leaven in this text, there are other instances where leaven/yeast symbolizes wickedness in its various forms. For example, Paul warns in 1 Cor 5:7, "Get rid of the old yeast that you may be a new batch without yeast—as you really are. For Christ, our Passover lamb, has been sacrificed" (NIV). Paul goes on to warn in v. 8, "Therefore, let us keep the Festival, not with the old yeast, the yeast of malice and wickedness, but with bread without yeast, the bread of sincerity and truth" (NIV).

6. All promises and covenants with God should be seasoned with "salt," for our word and our practice should be as permanent and binding as the sacrifices where salt indicated the same reality. The apostle Paul must have had the same metaphor in mind when he urged in Col 4:6 that our life-style should always be marked by graciousness; in fact, it ought to be "seasoned with salt." Likewise, Jesus taught in Mark 9:49*b*-50, "Every sacrifice will be salted with salt. Salt is good; but if salt has lost its saltiness, how can you season it? Have salt in yourselves, and be at peace with one another" (NRSV).[42] Rather than exhibiting decay, corruption, hypocrisy, and negativism, the call is for a purifying and preserving effect on all of life by each individual. Salt is the symbol of our friendship with our Lord and a pledge of our faithfulness to the holiness God has called us to display.

7. The distinctions between what is sacred and what is most holy remind us that distinctions within the one law of God were not only possible but required. Such fences around portions of the law appear to make it arbitrary to a certain extent; yet, in other ways they teach us that God is so totally different from us (both in being and in behavior) that it is crass presumption for worshipers to lunge headlong into worship practices that fail to remind us of this distinction. All that God made is good and may be employed for the good of humanity, but how, where, and why these things are used must also be a consideration, especially when we mortals seek to worship the holy God.

8. The One to whom the "firstfruits" pointed was Christ, who was "bruised" (or "crushed") for our iniquities (see Isa 53:5). Christ is the "Firstfruit" par excellence (see 1 Cor 15:20) because his resurrection signaled the possibility of the resurrection of others.

9. Christ is also the "bread of God . . . who comes down from heaven and gives life to the world" (John 6:33 NIV). Regarded in this manner, the grain offering was a type of Christ who is to come, the One symbolized in the Lord's Supper. As the grain was bruised and crushed to make the sacrifice for the ancient Israelite, so the living Bread was bruised and crushed for all who would believe.

---

42. The sentence "every sacrifice will be salted with salt" is omitted from the primary NRSV text but is reported in a textual note as included by some ancient authorities.

Leviticus 3:1-17, The Peace Offering

COMMENTARY

According to a later section in the laws of the sacrifices, 7:11-16, the peace offerings are of three kinds: sacrifices of thanksgiving, of vows, and of freewill offerings.

The name for this offering has puzzled commentators from earliest days. The traditional rendering of the Hebrew שלמים (*šĕlāmîm*) as "peace offerings" (assuming that it derives from שלום *šālôm*, "peace") reflects a rendering borrowed from the Vg's *pacificus* and the LXX εἰρηνικός *eirēnikos* (although the LXX uses no less than three terms to render this one Hebrew term). Both mean "that which relates to peace." Accordingly, the idea is that this sacrifice signifies a peaceful, harmonious relationship between the worshiper and God.

More recent interpreters have favored other renderings as the name for this sacrifice: (a) "the well-being offering" (NRSV) (taken from שלם *šālēm*, "whole," "sound," "harmonious"); (b) "the shared offering" or "the fellowship offering" (NIV) (taken from the fact that it always involves God, the donor, and the donor's friends and family, and the priests); (c) "the gift of greeting offering" (taken from the Ugaritic epic of Keret who offers a "tribute," "gift of greeting" to an attacking commander, called a *šalamūna*); and (d) "the recompense offering" (based on *šillēm*, "repayment," "recompense"). Since all of these are based solely on etymologies, they are no more than mere educated guesses. It is clear, however, that the idea of "peace" (*shalom*) includes the concepts of wholeness, health, and well-being and the cessation of hostilities.

The peace offering, like the whole burnt offering and the grain offering, is represented from a canonical standpoint as being in use prior to the days of its codification in Leviticus. It appears in Gen 31:54, related to the covenant formed between Jacob and Laban. In Exod 18:12, Jethro, Moses' father-in-law, joined Aaron and all the elders in sharing a peace offering. There is even an instance of an improper use of this offering by Israel as part of the golden calf episode (see Exod 32:6).

One of the most detailed illustrations of the ceremony of the peace offering is in 1 Samuel 9. The "invited guests" partake of what has been first blessed (the fat portions, which are then offered up to the Lord on the altar), and the remainder is boiled in pots and served to the guests in rooms nearby. The main function of the peace offering is to express friendship, fellowship, and peace with God. To conclude that its only purpose is to provide meat for the table is to assume a minimalist view of what is happening in this offering.

To say that no thoughts of expiation or of atonement are connected with this offering is going too far. This is true only to a limited degree, for 3:5 carefully requires that the peace offering must be burned "on the altar *on top of the burnt offering that is on the burning wood* " (emphasis added). The connection between the two offerings cannot be stated more clearly: The burnt offering is foundational in sequence and logically prior to the ritual and the significance of the peace offering. Furthermore, all six parts of the ritual mentioned in our discussion of chap. 1 are present in chap. 3, namely, (1) the presentation, (2) the laying on of hands, (3) the slaughter of the victim, (4) the sprinkling of the blood, (5) the sacrificial burning, and (especially here) (6) the sacrificial meal. The first four parts, though the text does not dwell on them in 3:1-2, still carry the symbolic and typical significance they carry in the other blood offerings. There still is the innocent victim. The offerer must still present the victim by faith. The blood of the slain victim must still be shed in the place appointed by God and applied to the altar, thereby indicating the vertical dimension of the sacrifice. The basis of the communion and fellowship shared in the peace offering rests, therefore, on the atonement signified in the animal sacrifice. No single offering can set forth all the facets that needed to be taught to Israel through the whole sacrificial system. All five types of sacrifice were needed before the whole picture of what was involved in the process of restoring and maintaining humans in fellowship with God could be gained.

The plan for chap. 3 is fairly straightforward and falls into three paragraphs, just as chaps. 1–2 do. The three divisions are (1) peace offerings of cattle (3:1-5); (2) peace offerings of sheep (3:6-11); and (3) peace offerings of goats, (3:12-17). Each of the three paragraphs ends with a different remark that the offering is "an aroma pleasing to the LORD" (v. 5), "an offering made to the LORD by fire" (v. 11), or "an offering made by fire (but see our discussion on 1:9), a pleasing aroma" (v. 16). Some would make a separate fourth paragraph for vv. 16c and 17, entitling it the law of suet and blood. But since it is so brief, and since it applies to all of the prescriptions for all the peace offerings, it is better to regard it as a closing colophon to the whole chapter.

The fact that there is a sacrificial meal in connection with this sacrifice has attracted unfair comparisons with similar meals in the ancient Near Eastern world. But the peace offering does not exhibit any mystical union with the deity or any other expression of a sensuous-magical form. These suggestions can be categorically rejected for several reasons: (a) The all-consuming holiness of God sets the peace offering apart from pagan sacrificial meals, where thoughts of a relationship of a blood kinship linkage were present; (b) the initiative for the presence of God rests with God and not with any mystical participation in the divine; and (c) the sacrifice is eaten "before the LORD" (see Deut 27:7), not "with the LORD"—thus humans are not entertaining God at a feast, but God is banqueting mortals. This last point is most important. Here is one of the most instructive contrasts and striking distinctions between all other sacrificial meals in the ancient Near East and Scripture. The host is the deity, not mortals! The meal has to be eaten at God's house, not at a place of the offerer's choosing. Invited guests, along with the donor and the priests, all sit down at the table of the Lord. Although the offerer brings the victim, which also serves as the food for the banquet, the ownership of the victim has already changed hands when it is offered to God, similar to the other blood offerings. From that moment onward, the victim is no longer the property of the offerer, the priest, or the community; it belongs to God! Having

received the victim, God now directs how it is to be used.

First, the Lord directs that a portion of it is to be burned on the altar: only the fat, as we shall see. Then, God instructs that the priests, servants who minister at the altar, must receive the specified pieces after the fat has been burned on the altar (and not before that, as the sons of Eli did so wickedly in 1 Sam 2:12-17). The remaining portion, which is by far the largest part, is given as a feast for the worshiper, family, and friends. Had there been any hint of any mystic participation in the life of the divine, surely the order of the service would have been reversed, and God would have demanded more than the fat; certainly there would have been some eating of the meat together, at the very minimum. But none of that appears here. The regulations used for selecting the animals to be offered are different in several respects from those of the materials specified for the whole burnt offering. The most noticeable change is that doves and pigeons are not permitted in the peace offering. This is not to discriminate against poor people; instead, due to the birds' smallness, they would not provide ample food for a meal.

The second most noticeable feature is that a female is permitted as well as a male animal (3:6; and possibly v. 12, though the text is not completely clear; עז 'ēz sometimes, however, refers only to a female, a nanny goat). This in no way indicates that it is a second-class sacrifice or one of a lesser status. Instead, it provides for greater liberty of choice, especially since the purpose of this sacrifice is to conclude with a sacrificial meal shared by the offerer with family and friends.

To emphasize the point of greater liberty of choice in the animal, a third exception to the rules for materials used in the whole burnt offering can be observed. It is, perhaps, even more striking than the other two exceptions. Even though the general rule for the peace offering is the same as for the burnt offering, i.e., "an animal without defect" (3:1), in the case of the freewill offerings, 22:23 allows even greater freedom by providing that one might offer a cow or sheep that "is deformed or stunted"! This could not be done, however, in connection with any other type of peace offering. The latitude permitted in this one case is explained because the chief aspect of this form of peace offering is to be the offerer's spontaneous expression of love and joy for God. It does not have a particular occasion as the basis for the act; it is completely impulsive, instinctive, and automatically done almost as a spur-of-the-moment deed. This is not to deny what has already been affirmed, i.e., that the ideas of representation, substitution, propitiation and expiation have a place in peace offerings, as indeed they do have in all offerings involving blood, but that is not the chief intent here. Moreover, since the leeway of offering the less expensive birds does not exist in this offering, a concession is made, no doubt, to help the poorer worshipers in acts of participation.

The ritual itself, as has been noted, is identical to the burnt offering through the first four parts: (1) the presentation of the victim, (2) the laying on of hands, (3) the slaughter of the sacrifice, and (4) the sprinkling of the blood against the altar (3:1-2). From that point the ceremony is distinctive, for the burning of the sacrifice and the sacrificial meal (parts five and six of the sacrificial ritual) are markedly different from the burnt offering.

Whereas the whole animal (except the skin and viscera) is burned in the whole burnt offering, in the peace offering only the fat is placed on the altar as an offering to God. The fat referred to here is not the ordinary fat entwined in the musculature of an animal, called שומן (šûmān) in rabbinic Hebrew, but the fat that covers or surrounds the kidneys, the liver, and the entrails (3:3), called חלב (ḥeleb) in Hebrew. This fat protects the vital parts of the body and functions as an energy reserve in maintaining the life of the animal. The kidneys, in the eastern Mediterranean world, were thought to be the seat of the emotions, feelings, and conscience. Often, the kidneys are linked with the heart in representing this idea (see Pss 7:9; 26:2; Jer 17:10; 20:12—"kidneys" translated as "mind" in the NIV).

When a sheep is used, "its fat [אליה 'alyâ], the entire fat tail cut off close to the backbone" (3:9), is an additional requirement. The reference here is to a special breed of sheep still found in the Near East known as the fat- or broad-tailed sheep (Ovis laticaudata). The tail grows several feet and generally weighs about fifteen pounds; however, some have been known to reach fifty and even eighty pounds! Sometimes shepherds used low platforms on wheels to support the tails and to prevent them from dragging on the ground and breaking out in sores.

No symbolism is directly assigned to the fat, as with most of these sacrifices. However, from the culture, times, and Scripture, it is possible to conclude that fatness represents the richest and the best part of the animal. Leviticus 3:16 concludes this chapter with the affirmation that "all the fat is the LORD's"; thus the theology of the action is firmly established. The idea that fat is valuable perplexes many readers in today's Western culture, who are trying to reduce their weight by not eating fat. But our culture does not need to add fat to our diet. Since we get it from so many sources we can afford to be selective and choosy. The ancients never ate this fat alone, but mixed it into many of their dishes with lean meat. They also used it as a substitute for butter and oil. It was especially palatable in boiled rice; the oil from the fat of this sheep's tail made the rice into an outstanding dish. It is interesting to read stories of those who went through severe shortages of food in Eastern Europe during World War II and during the Russian occupation of those lands. What was sought more than anything else was some lard or fat to nourish their vitamin-starved bodies. Only in extreme cases such as these, when fat is absent altogether, do we begin to realize the vital function that fat performs in our bodies.

The other distinctive feature of the peace offering is the sacrificial meal. After the priests burn the specified fat on the altar as the portion that is the Lord's, the breast is given for all the priests and the right shoulder to the priest who officiates (7:30-34). The greatest part by far is left for the offerer and family and friends, i.e., all who are ceremonially clean. If the peace offering is for thanksgiving, all of it has to be eaten on the same day it is offered. If it is a vow or freewill offering, i.e., a voluntary offering, part of it may be eaten on the day it is offered and part of it on the next day; however, if any remains on the third day, that part cannot be eaten but must be burned with fire (7:16-18; 19:5-8).

The meal has three specifications that are to be closely followed. First, it is to be a feast that is an occasion of great joy to the Lord, representing the labors of the donor's hands. Second, the meal is to be eaten by the donor before the Lord at the sanctuary and not at the donor's home. And third, the meal is to include all members of the donor's family and any Levite or priest who might be passing through the neighborhood.

The ancient Near East offered many examples of similar sacrificial meals. Isaiah 65:11 notes that some idolatrous Israelites "spread a table for [the god] Fortune/and [filled] bowls of mixed wine for [the goddess] Destiny" (NIV). When the participants ate and drank in the feasts set for pagan deities, they expressed the same desire that Israel did for friendship, communion, and closeness to their gods. That is the thought behind such biblical sentiments as "You prepare a table before me/ in the presence of my enemies" (Ps 23:5 NIV), the parable of the great banquet (see Luke 14:15-24), the homecoming of the prodigal son for whom the father killed the fatted calf (see Luke 15:23), and the parable of the wedding banquet (see Matt 22:1-14).

At first, the emphasis in the description of the peace offering is on offering up the fat pieces to the Lord. Later on, the spotlight will fall on the meal itself as the grand culmination of this offering. In this later aspect of the sacrifice, the startling factor is that the victim that symbolizes, as it does in all offerings of blood, the satisfaction and substitution for the donor's sin becomes the food on the table for the same offending donor.

Leviticus 3:17 concludes with a stern prohibition on eating blood or fat. "This is a lasting ordinance for the generations to come," warns v. 17, a sentence that occurs seventeen times in Leviticus. The same ban on blood and fat does not appear in Deut 12:15-16, 21-24 because these verses relate to a separate set of ceremonial circumstances. The reason for the ban on blood, however, is that blood in the flesh is life itself, something that only God owns and has control over. In a similar way, the ban on fat is in effect because it surrounds the organs thought to be at the center of a person's being. It also represents the best, and as such it too belongs to God.

REFLECTIONS

We humans can have peace with God but not peace without a price. The peace offering must be understood as it so often appeared in practice: linked with the whole burnt offering. It was placed on top of the fire for the whole burnt offering. Therefore, we are never far away from the redemptive concepts shared in all the sacrifices that involved blood. But this sacrifice sets forth several unique contributions, again in concretely graphic terms.

1. All peace offerings, whether presented as a thanksgiving, supplication, or vow, were to be offered on top of the burnt offering on the altar, thus indicating that the sacrifices of praise, petition, or vow were grounded on the atonement. Many Christian readers understand this to suggest that no matter what service or praise the offerer presents to God, the only way such worship can be made acceptable is on the basis of the atonement of Christ. The only possible way mortals can ever find acceptance and be able to offer to God fitting worship is through the access Christ provided in his obedience and death on a cross.

2. Peace offerings gather up the many meanings of peace: not only the end of warfare and hostility but also mental, physical, and spiritual health. In our culture, there is a gradual reawakening to the fact that illness is more than an isolated, clinically treatable condition. Illness involves the whole self; a brokenness anywhere in our lives affects us everywhere, and the popularity of alternative forms of healing today testifies to people's hunger to treat the spiritual side of illness as well as the clinical. One meaning of the peace offering is that our hopes for wholeness rest finally in God. To be ill becomes, then, not just a concern of physicians and a matter for antibiotics; it becomes a concern of God and a matter for prayer.

3. Whereas in pagan ritual humans gave a feast for God, in the biblical prescription of the peace offering that is reversed: God hosted mortals at the banquet. As soon as the sacrifice was presented to God, it was no longer the property of the offerer or the community. The victim belonged to God. The host of the meal was not the donor but the Lord. That is why the animal had to be eaten at God's house and not at the donor's house or anywhere else in town. All of this strikes at the heart of a popular religious notion: that mortals can make God their friend by doing something or giving something to the deity. That is certainly excluded here. Instead, God does the inviting and provides the occasion for joy. Once the possibility exists for God and humans to enjoy the state of being at one with another (our word *atonement,* the state of being "at one" [with God]), a fellowship is possible that restores the disruption that sin introduced.

4. The prohibition against eating any fat or blood will be explained in the supplemental materials on the law of the peace offering (7:22-27) and in the central declaration (17:11-16). The fat referred to, of course, was limited to the fat specified for the sacrifices; there the law was absolute. To use any portions of the fat specifically set aside for offering to God on the altar in the peace offering, the sin offering, or the guilt offering was to steal what had been appropriated for God. But the prohibition on blood covered all situations since "the life of the flesh is in the blood" (17:11; literal rendering). As such, all life belonged to God. Thus, in these two prohibitions, Israel was reminded of two important facts: (1) God's claim on humans is for their "best," and (2) only life is valuable enough to depict the grounds of atonement with God, as a life was spilled out and the blood yielded up in death on behalf of another.

To treat the "blood of the covenant" as a common or "unholy thing" is offensive, the writer of Hebrews warns (10:26-29 NIV). Such an offense exposes the perpetrators to a much more severe punishment than what came upon those who "rejected the law of Moses" and therefore died without mercy. It is tantamount to "[insulting] the Spirit of grace" (Heb 10:29 NIV). In fact, continues the writer of Hebrews, "It is a dreadful thing to fall into the hands of the living God" (v. 31 NIV). Modern believers must be careful not to undervalue or to despise and regard as something uncouth the sanctity of the blood of the sacrifices, especially the sacrifice of the One to which these offerings pointed.

5. A later regulation concerning the peace offering ordered that none of the peace offering was to remain until the third day presumably to prevent decay. But this provision would one day remind Israel of the Antitype who was to come. Psalm 16:10 affirms that God would not let the "Holy One see decay" (NIV) for he too was raised on the third day from the grave. Is this the source for the Pauline affirmation that Christ "was raised on the third day *according to the Scriptures"* (1 Cor 15:4; emphasis added, NIV)? This certainly is a more convincing source than the text traditionally pointed to in Hos 6:2: "After two days he will revive us;/on the third day he will restore us" (NIV).

Leviticus 4:1–6:7, Two New Atoning Offerings

OVERVIEW

The last two of the five major offerings differ from the first three in several ways. The assumption in the first three offerings seems to be that most were acquainted with the burnt offering, grain offering, and peace offering because of previous experience with them. But in the two offerings that are now to be described, the sin offering and guilt offering, a more detailed description of the meaning and purpose of each is necessary.

Neither offering appears in the narratives of the present canonical order of texts prior to Mosaic times; in fact, Job offers whole burnt offerings where technically, based on what is taught here, he should have offered sin offerings (see Job 1:5; 42:8). But if Job is located, as some believe, in the patriarchal times, the situation agrees with what has been observed elsewhere.

In the view of the older historical-critical school, as best summarized by Julius Wellhausen, these two offerings did not appear until the seventh or, better still, the sixth and fifth centuries BCE, when they presumably took the place of monetary penalties, such as are mentioned in 2 Kgs 12:16. But this line of reasoning appears to reverse what one would normally expect. Usually, the concrete act of the ceremony would later be replaced by the abstract payment of goods or money. And if the allusion to the priests "[feeding] on the *sins* of my people" (Hos 4:8, emphasis added, NIV) is a direct reference to the provision made in the sin offering for the priests to eat a portion of the sacrifice (the Hebrew word for "sins" is the same word used for the "sin offering"), this is a clear eighth-century BCE

reference to the regulation in Lev 6:25-26. The prophets Micah (6:7) and Ezekiel (40:39; 42:13; 43:19; 44:27, 29; 45:17; 46:20) treat the sin offering as if it had been in existence prior to their times as well. One of the most difficult arguments for the classical Wellhausian thesis to handle, in this regard, is the failure of Leviticus to make any provision for the sin of the "king"! Provision is made for the forgiveness of the sin of the "leader," but not a word about the "king." This suggests that the text could reflect a time prior to the first king in Israel, i.e., prior to c. 1000 BCE.

There is a second major difference between the two offerings described in chaps. 4–6 and the ones in chaps. 1–3. The first group of offerings are usually voluntary. But for the sin and guilt offerings, a specific offense makes their presentation necessary (4:1, 13, 22, 27; 5:1, 14; 6:2 [MT 5:21]).

The distinctions between the sin and guilt offerings are sometimes very difficult to draw. Provisions for both of them are very similar (7:7: "the same law applies to both the sin and the guilt offering"), and the Hebrew word אשם (*ʾāšām*) has two distinct connotations, both used in this section: (1) a "guilt offering" (e.g., 5:15-16) and (2) a "penalty" (e.g., 5:5-6). Failure to observe this distinction has led some (e.g., the KJV) to designate 5:1-13 as a section on the guilt offering, even though vv. 11-12 specifically call it a "sin offering."

Leviticus 4:1–5:13, The Sin Offering

COMMENTARY

The law of the sin offering is divided into four sections with an unusual sliding scale of responsibility for each worshiper. The four sections are (1) the sin offering for the high priest (4:3-12); (2) the sin offering for the congregation (4:13-21); (3) the sin offering for the leader (4:22-26); and (4) the sin offering for the individual (4:27-35). Added to these four distinct sections is 5:1-13, where special instructions are given for other circumstances in the use of the sin offering.

4:1-2. A general introduction serves as the opening rubric with the expression, "When [כי *kî*] anyone [נפש *nepeš*] sins." This same

idiom appears again in 5:1, 15. The subsections are likewise clearly demarcated; however, rather than use the conditional word *kî* ("when," "if") they use the word אם (*ʾim*, "if"; 4:3, 13, 27, 32; 5:7, 11; also see 5:14, 17 in the guilt offering). Many of the sections close with the formula of absolution, "The priest will make atonement for him for the sin he has committed, and he will be forgiven" (4:35; 5:13; and in the guilt offering 5:18, 26 [MT 6:7]). The only exception to this use of a separate word *ʾim*, "if," for the subordinate sections is the unusual and rare usage of the word אשר (*ʾăšer*, "if," "whoever") in 4:22 in regard to the ruler or tribal leader. The reason for this departure from the norm is not altogether clear.

The name of this offering presents a problem, just as the name of the other offerings proves difficult. All ancient and modern translations name it the sin offering. However, many modern commentators vehemently protest this rendering as being inaccurate on all grounds: etymological, morphological, and contextual!

The grammatical grounds for this objection are somewhat technical. The noun, it is argued, does not derive from the basic stem (called the qal by Hebrew grammarians), which indeed means "to sin," "to do wrong"; instead, the noun comes from the intensive form of the verb (called the piel by grammarians), which means "to cleanse," "expurgate," or "to decontaminate." Therefore, it is argued, this offering should be called the purification offering, not the sin offering.

Added to this objection is the contextual argument. This offering is also used by women recovering from childbirth or from a hemorrhage (12:6, 8; 15:25-30), by those completing a Nazirite vow (Num 6:13-14), and when a newly constructed altar is dedicated (8:15). Naturally, there can be no question of sinning in these cases.

However, in 4:2, 3, 22, 27 the verb "to sin" appears in the very chapter that uses the debated cognate term as a noun. Therefore, this offering deals with sin and its consequences in many, if not most, situations. But the impression is left that this is the only offering that deals with sin and its consequences; that, of course, is incorrect. The other sacrifices involving blood also speak to this point or rest on the fact that it has been accomplished in an accompanying offering.

The chief argument for changing the traditional name of the sin offering to the purification offering or the offering of purgation is the reason given in 16:16-20 on the Yom Kippur ritual, where this offering plays a central role. The sacrifice, made from the first goat of the two specially chosen on the day for this offering, which for the moment we will leave unnamed here, is to be slain and taken into the holy of holies this one time each year. The high priest is to sprinkle the blood of this sacrifice on the top of the ark of the covenant and in front of it. This is done, comments 16:16, to "make atonement for the Most Holy Place because of the uncleanness and rebellion of the Israelites, whatever their sins have been." It is further contended that blood of this sacrifice (or of any other, for that matter) is never applied to any person; it is put on the "horns [the projections of the four corners] of the altar" (the altar of incense in the holy place in front of the curtain that divided the two main sections of the sanctuary, on the Day of Atonement; or in other cases on the horns of the altar in the open courtyard of the sanctuary), against the sides of the altar, or at the base of the altar (e.g., 8:15). Since nowhere else does the text indicate any other purpose for this offering, it is assumed that the purpose of purging the sanctuary is the correct one.

Admittedly, the conclusion is an extrapolation from one piece of data in 16:16 retrojected over the whole range of sin offerings. Furthermore, 16:16 may be a form of synecdoche, where the part, the most holy place, is said to be infected and stained by the sins of the whole nation. If it is this figure of speech, the conclusion that this purges only the sanctuary is too minimalist in its view of the effects and results of this sacrifice.

A much broader view of the purpose of the sin offering is to regard it as providing a way of atonement for specific sins done by representative leaders, by individuals, or by all the people. Moreover, its purpose also provides for graded levels of responsibility for all sin. If the question about the major difference between the sin offering and the guilt offering remains, the answer is: It is in the nature of the sin. The sin offering covers a number of general sins, while the guilt offering deals with sins involving injury to other persons or those that detract from the worship of God. Thus, in the guilt offering, provision is made for restitution and a fine along with the usual pardon and forgiveness.

The most amazing part of the discussion on the sin offering is the massive confusion on the expression to sin "unintentionally" (4:2; בשגגה *bišĕgāgâ*). It has been all too traditional by commentators of all theological stripes to describe this term as limiting the effectiveness of these offerings to sins committed inadvertently or unknowingly.

The problem with this rendering, however, is that the root שָׁגַג (*šāgag*) means "to err," "go astray," "to wander." Never is the idea of intent part of the meaning. That aspect has been added to the noun form that regularly means "error" or "mistake."

The same expression is translated as sinning "unintentionally" in the guilt offering (5:15-18), yet the sins listed in 6:2-3 are clearly overt acts of rebellion against the law of God: stealing, lying, cheating, extorting, and false swearing. And surely the high priest cannot be excused of any culpability on the grounds of ignorance of the law!

At the center of this storm over the proper meaning of this term, traditionally translated "unintentional," is Num 15:22-31. But once again the contrast is not between sinning in ignorance of the law and sinning deliberately. The issue in Num 15:30 is one of defiance, sinning "with a high hand," as the Hebrew put it. This evokes the ancient sign of the upraised, cocked arm with the clenched fist waved menacingly against heaven and its occupant. Num 15:30-31 deliberately says that this person "blasphemes the LORD" and "[despises] the LORD's word" (NIV). This is the closest parallel in the OT for the NT's unpardonable sin against the Holy Spirit.

As R. Laird Harris correctly contends, "The sense of the verb *šāgag* will be adequately caught if in all the verses concerned here in chaps. 4–5, the phrase 'sins unintentionally' is rendered [instead] by 'goes astray in sin' or 'does wrong' or the like."[43] The same would be true for the passages in Num 15:22-29; they sinned "wrongly" or "in error" rather than "unintentionally." Even in the manslaughter passages (see Num 35:11-22; Josh 20:3-5), it is best to say that it was "by mistake."

The sin offering is unique in distinguishing between the rank and the status of the offenders and in specifying whether the blood is applied to the outer altar or to the altar of incense inside the sanctuary. Each of these may now be considered in turn.

4:3-12. The sin of the "anointed priest" is given first position for consideration. The expression "anointed priest" (4:3; see also 6:22 [MT 6:15]) is somewhat unusual since

Aaron and his sons were anointed. But based on 16:32 and 21:10 (cf. Exod 29:29), it is clear that the title refers to Aaron, or the current presiding high priest, since the two titles are synonymous in these contexts.

This offering begins the same way as the other sacrifices: The worshiper brings the animal to the entrance of the tent of meeting, lays his hand(s) on its head, probably states why the sacrifice has been brought, and then slaughters it by himself or with the help of the priest. From this point the ceremony is unique. Whereas the blood of the burnt and peace offerings is splashed against the side of the altar, in the sin offering the blood is caught in a basin and used in a variety of ways according to the office, status, and responsibility of the person making the offering. Part of the blood is poured out at the base of the altar, but the rest is either sprinkled seven times in front of the curtain that divided the holy of holies from the holy place or put on the four horns of the incense altar. (For the sin offering of a tribal leader or a member of the community, the blood is applied to the four horns of the large altar in the open court of the tabernacle.)

The high priest, then, is to bring a bull calf (פַּר *par*, a "calf"; not to be confused with שׁוֹר *šôr*, an "ox" that served as the victim in the peace offering) without any defect as his sin offering (4:3). The choice of the sacrificial victim is determined by two considerations: the rank or position of the person who sins, and the ability of the person to provide a more costly sacrifice. Thus, the higher a person stands in the theocratic order of governing and ministry, the more costly the offering required. Also, the guilt of any sin is proportional to the rank and position of the offender. One conclusion must be drawn immediately: The guilt of sins committed by those in positions of religious authority is heaviest of all. The reason for this law of graded responsibility is set forth in 4:3—the high priest brings guilt on all the people.

Although individual responsibility is stressed, especially in the latter prophets such as Jeremiah and Ezekiel (e.g., Ezek 18:4: "The soul who sins is the one who will die" [NIV]), an equal emphasis is placed on the collective or corporate effects of sin on a community. Persons in such high positions can bring enormous effects, for good or ill, upon a group, a city, a region, or a whole country.

43. R. Laird Harris, "Leviticus," in *The Expositor's Bible Commentary*, ed. Frank E. Gaebelein, 12 vols. (Grand Rapids: Zondervan, 1990) 2:547-48.

This effect may take place in several ways. In some cases, the people may be tempted to indulge in sins they ordinarily would never think to try until they hear or see the public example of their spiritual leader doing the same or some similar outlandish sin. In other cases, the priest may involve the people in the very act that God condemns, by teaching or permitting it. In still other cases, the mere failure to carry out faithfully the high calling of one's own holy walk with God may leave a vacuum that opens up the nation to moral and spiritual decline. In all cases, however, the priests are to be teachers of the people (see Deut 33:10; Mal 2:6) and lead pure, holy, exemplary lives for others to follow. When the high priest falls into sin, not only is he guilty before God, but so is the whole nation tainted and placed under God's judgment.

The imposition of hands once again is to denote that the victim is the donor's substitute. The blood is sprinkled seven times in front of the curtain, behind which the Shekinah ("the divine presence") glory resides, where the presence of God remains in the camp. Then the blood is applied to four horns, or projections, on the altar of incense, intimating that there is no acceptance of the offender's prayers and intercessions to God (the smoke of the incense is often likened to prayers ascending to God) until that one is absolved by the life of an intervening victim and the blood is applied to the altar.

What remains so strikingly significant about the sin offering of the high priest is that no part of the animal comes near the altar except portions of the blood (already described) and the fat portions said to belong to God (see the earlier discussion of the peace offering). None of the sacrifice is shared with either priest or people. Instead, the bull calf is carried outside the camp, skin and all, to be burned by fire on the ground. Surely, this act, more than many of the other parts of the ritual, must have driven home in the minds of all thoughtful Israelites that the state of the guilt of sin is so great that it forces one to be excluded from one's own people until being reconciled by some substitute. The loneliness and the shame of being left to burn on the outskirts of the camp are enough to depict the shame and the reproach that sin brings into the life of the offender. No altar is used for burning the offering outside the camp; the sacrifice is placed on the wood on the ground where the ash pile is (4:12). This absence of an altar only adds to the reproach already attached to this sacrifice because of the sin it deals with.

4:13-21. The sin offering for the whole congregation follows the same order of ceremony, except in this instance the elders bring the bull calf. Some have been perplexed over whether there is a difference between the "community" (עדה ‘ēdâ; vv. 13, 15) and the "assembly" (קהל qāhāl; vv. 13, 14). Among some Jewish commentators, the word here translated "community" is taken to mean the supreme court of justice in ancient Israel, i.e., the Sanhedrin. However, the word as used in the OT has a much broader meaning; the two terms are often used interchangeably (see Exod 12:6; Num 14:5), as is probably the case here.

The whole community has sinned by breaking some commandment and thus has fallen into error, begins v. 13. However, the fault "is hidden from the assembly," or "the matter is hidden from the eyes of the assembly" (v. 13), i.e., it is not brought out in the open before the worshiping congregation. It is clear, however, that the people have done "what is forbidden in [one or more] of the LORD's commandments" (v. 13). Who actually broke the silence and how it was made known is not disclosed here. It may have come through prophecy, a vision, or the Urim and Thummim. The point is that the congregation now has this sin out in the open (v. 14). The sin offering has to be brought by the elders on behalf of all the people. The elders, acting as representatives for all the people, place their hands on the head of the bull (v. 15). The rest of the ritual follows exactly what is spelled out for the high priest's ritual. This is how the priest "will make atonement for them" (v. 20).

4:22-26. The sin offering for a tribal leader (נשיא nāśî’) is not as serious as that of the high priest or the whole congregation. He is required to bring only a male goat, and the blood is not taken into the tent of meeting but is sprinkled on the altar of burnt offering in the open court of the sanctuary. Thus the victim is of lesser value than that for the high priest and whole congregation, but it is more valuable than that for a private individual.

The civil leader is also held accountable to God and not just to the people (or in our day, the electorate) for the execution of the trust of that office. God holds civil leaders, then, to a higher standard than that of individual persons. This refers to all official acts of the office and all private actions. No distinction is raised in this text between sin resulting from some act in office or in one's private life: both are culpable and carry the same requirement of the more expensive sacrifice. High office gives no immunity to sin or to the need for divine forgiveness.

4:27-35. The sin offering of the common people is taken up last in this descending order of four sin offerings; it can be either a female goat (4:28) or a female lamb (4:32). If the previous three sin offerings teach that no persons are high in position or office as to be above the need for God's cleansing, so here we are taught that no persons are so lowly and poor in their station in life that their sins are not worth the trouble of forgiving or that they should be overlooked. If anything, this section on the common folk bulks larger than the previous sections to make sure that no one is left out of the means of grace simply for lack of enough of this world's goods to make a sacrifice.

The unusual addition is found in v. 31. When the portion of fat is burned on the altar for the ordinary person, as is required in all the sin offerings that involve bloody sacrifices, it is declared to be "an aroma pleasing to the LORD." It may be inferred that this is true of all the sin offerings, just as it is declared in the peace offerings. But the point remains that only with regard to the ordinary person is this portion said to be an aroma pleasing to God. If it is meant to be distinctive in this situation, this word must be intended as special comfort to the lowest class of people: They too share in the same hope, mercy, and grace of God, even though their sacrifices are less costly, glamorous, and flamboyant in comparison to all the others listed in this chapter.

5:1-13. Leviticus 5:1-4 specifies some sins for which a sin offering is necessary. The first instance is the duty and obligation of a witness to come forward regarding something seen or heard that, if left unreported, will offend the interests of truth or justice (5:1). Truth and justice cannot and will not be served when

the populace refuses to become involved. It is a sin to assume the attitude that individuals are responsible only for themselves and their loved ones.

Having contact with anything ceremonially unclean, even if the person is at first unaware of the fact, requires a sin offering (5:2-3). This is not just in the interest of public health; uncleanness also brings temporary disqualification from worship of the living Lord and the accompanying guilt of sin.

A false oath is displeasing to the Lord (5:4). Once again, not being fully aware of the falsity of what is said does not constitute an excuse. A person must atone with a sin offering.

An individual who is unable to offer either a female goat or a female lamb must bring two birds (two doves or two pigeons) as an offering (5:7-10): one as a sin offering and the other as a whole burnt offering (v. 7*c*). The order of these two sacrifices is deliberate: First, peace with God is to be won by means of the sin offering, and then the gift of the whole burnt offering can be accepted.

But the provision of God reaches to the poorest of the poor. If the price of two doves or two pigeons, which were just as plentiful in the cities of that day as they are in ours, is beyond the humble means of the offerer, two quarts of fine flour will be acceptable (5:11-13). The point is that *some* type of offering must be made, even when the prescribed one is unattainable due to economic pressures. However, unlike the offering of oil in the grain offering, the fine flour is to be given without any olive oil or incense added. This is a sin offering; it has to demonstrate the awfulness and loathsomeness of sin.

While the principle remains that without blood there is no atonement, here is another case of an understood *ceteris paribus*, "all other things being equal," in that it permits flour to be used in what is basically a blood offering. However, in this instance there is no equality in the economic levels; therefore, the principle does not apply to each level of society. This one exception tends to prove the rule, but an exception it surely is, mercifully provided by a loving Lord. Nevertheless, a distinction is made with the grain offering so that there is no adorning sin with frankincense and olive oil.

REFLECTIONS

The most prominent feature of the sin offerings is the expiation of guilt by the sacrifice of a substituted victim. But the most astounding provision is the sliding scale of graded responsibility. From these two central truths we can legitimately make a number of observations.

1. The guilt of sin in God's sight is proportional to the rank, office, and responsibilities of the offender. At the head of this sliding scale must come those who are in religious authority. The NT restates this principle in several ways: "From everyone who has been given much, much will be demanded; and from the one who has been entrusted with much, much more will be asked" (Luke 12:48 NIV). That is the reason, no doubt, why the half-brother of our Lord, James, taught "not many of you should presume to be teachers, my brothers, because you know that we who teach will be judged more strictly" (Jas 3:1 NIV).

2. This law of the sin offering also teaches that religion is not just a personal or an individual matter. Responsibility is attached also to the associations of individuals in their collective groups as nations, cities, communities, corporations, societies, and religious affiliations. While there is individual sin, there also is such a thing as the sin of the whole community or congregation. Associations can be held just as responsible for sin of a whole group as they can be held accountable for the sin of a private person. In modern Western democratic societies, it seems taken for granted that religion is a matter of concern only to the individual and to no one else. We assume that there is no way in which we can be implicated in the guilt of the sin of the whole group by virtue of our association with that group, and that we therefore bear no responsibility for relief, confession, or petition for the removal of any judgment that hangs over us. But this text makes all such opinions a delusion. It further urges our involvement in the corporate whole.

3. The sin of noninvolvement in the cause of justice and truth is strikingly set forth as a crime against God and society. This text demands involvement. The recent rash of cases of persons' being beaten and brutalized in our cities while numerous people watch but refuse to come to the aid of the victims, either during the attack or during the court trial, is a blight on the honor and reputation of any city or society and on the cause of truth and justice. But all too frequently, the norm for the actions of modern men and women has fallen far short of God's standards.

4. The law of God that required atonement by the shedding of blood—i.e., by the death of a substitute—is set aside in the exceptional case where the person is unable to bring an offering of either animals or birds. This provision should go a long way in relieving the charges of a harsh legalism in the Levitical law, for it shows that whatever is said often has a suppressed "if" or "unless" with it. This exception seems not to be in operation only when the law is based on the character of God. God cannot change; hence, there is not a chance that the moral law based on the nature and character of God will be modified. But in instances where moral law is illustrated by setting forth ceremonial or civil provisions, each provision of the law is subject to the rule "all other things being equal." Only in this manner can God be said to be immutable and yet graciously responsive to the needs of the people.

Leviticus 5:14–6:7, The Guilt Offering

COMMENTARY

The fifth and final offering in chaps. 1–6 is the guilt offering. As with each of the previous four offerings, there is debate on its precise name.

The KJV renders it as the "trespass offering," but that name fails to communicate that among the central issues in this offering is the problem of lying, or dealing fraudulently, especially in religious matters. The case for its use by the KJV is that "trespass" usually denotes an invasion of the rights of others, of either their property or their service. But the KJV uses the opening terms in 5:15 (תמעל מעל *tim'ōl ma'al;* literally "trespass a trespass"; cf. NIV) as the basis for naming this offering.

The current preference for the name (אשם *'āšām*) of this offering seems to be reparation offering, since its provisions place so much emphasis on redressing the wrong that is committed.[44] The meanings of the verbal form of this offering are twofold: (a) "to incur liability [to someone]" (when it is followed by the preposition *to* or *for* with a personal object), and (b) "to feel guilt" (without a personal object). The meanings of the noun form are also dual: (a) the reparation, i.e., the money paid for redressing a wrong, and (b) the reparation or guilt offering. The case made by Jacob Milgrom is that even though the verb *'āšām* means "is guilty" and its noun *'āšām* means "guilt," these meanings are attested only in noncultic texts. This same verb and noun, as used in cultic texts, argues Milgrom, have one of the four consequential meanings mentioned already. One needs to add to this discussion the findings of Leon Morris in favor of the rendering "guilt" even in these cultic texts.[45]

Actually, the two sides (guilt offering and reparation offering) are not all that far apart. The former stresses the cause, and the latter stresses the need to redress the incurred guilt. Thus, to reduce the amount of exotic-appearing terms, we have decided to stay with guilt offering. However, if it is insisted that

reparation offering is more technically correct since the verb from which this name probably derives is what is known in Hebrew grammar as a stative verb, we will not dissent.

The arrangement of the law of the guilt offering is fairly simple. There are two sections: Lev 5:14-19 deals with the violation of any of "The LORD's holy things" (v. 15), and Lev 6:1-7 (MT 5:20-26) deals with violations of human property rights.

5:14-19. The expression "sins unintentionally" appears in 5:14, 18 in several versions, just as we observed in Lev 4:2, 13, 22, 27 and also in Num 15:25, 27, 28. But the comment made in Leviticus 4 must be made here as well: The Hebrew term does not include the idea of intentionality. An adequate translation in all these cases will be to define this as a sin committed "mistakenly" or "in error." The contrast in Num 15:25-28 is not between sins that are unknown and sins that are known. The traditional teaching that concludes that forgiveness is available for the sins about which we are ignorant while no forgiveness is available for known sins is faulty. It rests on a misinterpretation of Numbers 15. The contrast in Numbers 15, however, is between sins of error and sins of defiance. The expression in Num 15:30, to sin "with a high hand" (literal translation), is explained in context as a defiant and blasphemous attack on God. Therefore, the expression in our text deliberately speaks to those whose sins are committed "in error" or "mistakenly" but not with an attempt to mock God or, as it were, to take on heaven in a frontal attack, thereby blaspheming God.

The guilt offering, as already remarked in the discussion of the sin offering, is very similar to that sacrifice. But some major differences exist. Whereas the sin offering emphasizes the idea of expiation of sin, the guilt offering represents the same atonement with God by stressing the reparation that has to be paid for the wrong committed. Just as the whole burnt offering symbolizes the total consecration of the person and the peace offering symbolizes fellowship with God, so

---

44. See the lengthy discussion by Milgrom, *Leviticus 1–16*, 339-61.
45. Leon Morris, "'āshām," *EvQ*, 30 (1958) 196-210.

the guilt offering (with the sin offering) offers reinstatement of the offerer to full covenantal relationship with God.

Uniquely, the guilt offering is never offered by the congregation; it is used only by individuals. The situations the guilt offering describes are scarcely attributable to the whole congregation.

Another distinctive feature of this offering is the restriction imposed on the animal used. Only one animal is acceptable: "A ram from the flock, one without defect and of the proper value in silver, according to the sanctuary shekel" (5:15). There is no distinction between the rich or the poor, the high or the lowly. The debt incurred, along with the resulting guilt, is such that a valuable offering must be brought. Fortunately, the text does not demand a bull, which would have put it hopelessly out of the reach of many. Nevertheless, it holds the standard high and demands that all meet it.

This offering has one other most unusual feature. The priest has to appraise the male sheep (as appears from Lev 27:8, 12) to make sure that it does not fall below a certain standard. This whole phrase ("proper value") is an old technical term, as the fossilized Hebrew ending of ךָ- (-kā, "by you") attests (and as a result, the ending is not to be translated). It appears in the vows (Lev 27:2) and in Num 18:16. Ephraim Speiser concludes that the appearance of such antique terms in Leviticus argues for an early date of this legislation.[46] The "shekel" must be of full weight and on the standard set by God, not mortals: "the sanctuary shekel" (v. 15). Human standards do not measure up to the high standards of God in this case.

The guilty person is not allowed to gain even a temporary advantage in the use of goods or services thus falsely appropriated, for v. 16 demands that along with the offering of a ram, the offender must add "a fifth of the value to [what has been taken]." This would counter any interim disadvantage suffered by the one wronged. It would also prevent those who would wish to take advantage of another by merely restoring what had been taken without making any reparations for its

loss during the time it was gone and presumably being used free of charge.

No other offering makes it as clear as this one that sin is treated as a debt. Among many ancient peoples—including the Hebrews, Arabs, and later, the Romans—sheep, but particularly rams, were used as a means of payment for debts and tribute. Thus Mesha, king of Moab, annually gave the king of Israel one hundred thousand lambs, and the wool of one hundred thousand rams (see 2 Kgs 3:4) as his tribute money. Isaiah intoned in a later passage, "Send lambs as tribute to the ruler of the land" (16:1 NIV). This fact reinforces the concept that the guilt offering is given because sin places the offender under debt.

The designation "the LORD's holy things" points to all that is the property of the Lord in a special sense. To mistakenly appropriate the parts of the sacrifice that belong to the Lord or to use the tithe or some other things vowed or dedicated to the Lord is to violate this category and to place oneself in need of making a guilt offering. In the singular, this word is translated as "holiness" or "sanctuary." But in the plural form, used in this designation, it appears to refer to all the things specially dedicated by mortals to God.

Leviticus 5:17-19 takes up a second type of trespass for which the guilt offering is provided to give relief. It deals with instances where the conscience troubles the individual, but for some reason, the offender cannot say precisely why. Leviticus 5:17 specifically says the person cannot tell why this guilt occurs. Since the person has done "what is forbidden in [one or more] of the LORD's commands" (v. 17), it hardly appears to be a case of ignorance of the law. Nor is it a matter of subsequent knowledge of the law. Instead, it appears to be a sensitized conscience suddenly convicting the individual so that one begins to sense guilt and to feel responsible for what has been done. As R. Laird Harris comments, "Guilt in the biblical sense is not just a feeling but a condition. There may be known transgressions that bring feelings of guilt, but there is also a condition of guilt before God, caused by sins known or unknown."[47] However, even though vv. 17-18 repeat the disclaimer that the offender "does not know" it is a transgression, the point is made that ignorance of

46. Ephraim A. Speiser, *Oriental and Biblical Studies* (Philadelphia: University of Pennsylvania Press, 1967) 124-28.

47. Harris, "Leviticus," 2:551.

the law was no excuse for not observing it. Ignorance cannot affect the fact of the condition of guilt or of the necessity of making subsequent satisfaction to be restored to one's covenantal relationship with God.

The law of this offering is given in more detail in 7:1-7. Only a ram is accepted. It is brought by the guilty person along with a confession of the fault. Next, the priest slays the animal, but the blood is not applied this time, as it is in the sin offering, to the horns of the altar. Instead, the blood is sprinkled against the altar in the courtyard on all sides. The reason for this difference in the application of the blood is that the guilt offering represents the need for *satisfaction* for the trespass committed; expiation is symbolized more fully in the sin offering.

As it is with the sin offering, where only the fat parts are placed on the altar, so it is with the guilt offering. The fat tail, the fat that covers the inner parts of the ram, the two kidneys with the fat on them, and the covering of the liver are all burned on the altar. Then, similar to the sin offering, the rest is to be eaten only in the holy place by the priests.

6:1-7. The second section of the guilt offering deals with the trespasses against one's fellow human beings. Just as the previous section focuses on trespasses against God and requires full restitution with the added compensation of 20 percent along with a ram as a guilt offering, so also the law requires the same in the five illustrations of sins against one's neighbor.

The first case (6:2) takes up the matter of leaving something on deposit with others only to learn that it has been kept, sold, or used unlawfully as if it had been one's own. Aspects of this law are announced in the civil code of Exod 22:9-11.

The second point treats all cases of fraud (v. 2c). The expression used here appears only once: "the placement in [or of] the hand" (author's trans.; cf. NIV). This seems to refer to stipulations made in partnerships where a bargain is struck and hands are shaken on the deal. Thus this sin seems to include all acts of misrepresentation of goods and services to obtain a better price than what one should get for the goods and services delivered, or a failure to deliver what was agreed upon in the handshake.

The third sin is robbery. It is something taken by force or under the duress and threat of force: otherwise known as extortion. Exodus 22:7, 15 deals with cases where the theft can be proven; but what is one to do when there are no witnesses? That is the problem in Lev 6:2c. The NIV rendering of "or stolen" is a little too tame for the vigor of this expression.

Oppression is fourth on this list of sins. It is a matter of fraudulently taking advantage of an employee, buyer, or seller. When the tax collector Zacchaeus came to the Lord, he had to acknowledge this sin and make it right. He imposed a fourfold restitution to all persons he had wronged (see Luke 19:8).

The fifth and final instance of sinning against one's neighbors is in assuming that "finders, keepers" legitimizes "losers, weepers." However, under biblical law, a person who finds something is obligated to search for its rightful owner, for retaining the found item defrauds and injures the proper owner.

The reference to swearing falsely in v. 5 does not apply to the last named sin, as if it is only a matter of finders vehemently denying that they have found what they now declare to be their own. No, it applies equally to all five cases mentioned in vv. 2-4. The temptation is always present for individuals to lie and swear falsely to gain a financial edge over their neighbors. With the false oath, the appeal is made not only to mortals to believe their false words but to God to act as a witness of the truthfulness of the false words! That makes a bad thing even worse.

But the very act of swearing falsely raises this dilemma: How can the guilt offering provide forgiveness and satisfaction for an oath that Exod 20:7 and Deut 5:11 state is such a misuse of God's holy name that it will not be a matter on which one will be held guiltless? However, when the guilty party comes forward and confesses this sin (as another version of this law has it in Num 5:5-7), it too will be forgiven. Exodus 22:1, 7, 9 makes it clear that when a person is guilty of any of the offenses noted here and is convicted by witnesses in court before the person voluntarily confesses, a double, fourfold, or fivefold restitution is required for the damages done to one's neighbors. On the other hand, the voluntary acknowledgment mollifies the penalty so that only a fifth part, or 20 percent, needs to be added to the offering of the male sheep.

Of course, the five sins specified here are merely examples. If all instances of possible sins were raised at this point, or at any other, Leviticus would be filled with lists of sins. The law of Num 5:5-10 goes beyond the law of Lev 6:1-7 in that it touches on what is to be done if the victim against whom the crimes listed here has, in the meantime, died.

The description of the guilt offering ends in Lev 6:7, much as the repeated sentence in the sin offering: "The priest will make atonement . . . before the LORD, and [that one] will be forgiven for any of these things . . . that made [that one] guilty." Once again, the purpose of the sacrifice is to effect a reinstatement into the favor and blessing of God. The most beautiful word comes at the conclusion of the sin and guilt offerings: *forgiven.* Everything depends, at this point, solely on the words spoken by the priest and grounded in the authority of the One in whose name he pronounced these words of relief.

REFLECTIONS

1. Over and over again, sin is portrayed in Scripture as a debt. That is why we are taught in the Lord's prayer to pray, "Forgive us our debts" or, as another reading has it, our "trespasses." Twice in the parables Jesus depicts the sinner as a debtor to God: the parable of the unmerciful servant, who being forgiven much seizes another who owes a much smaller debt and throws him into prison until he has paid all (see Matt 18:21-35), and the parable about the money lender, who forgives one huge and another minor debt (see Luke 7:41-42). So connected was this thought of debt with our sin that our present English word *ought* is the old preterit form of *owe*, as demonstrated in Tyndale's NT, where he translated Luke 7:41, "There was a certain lender, which *ought* him five hundred pence" (emphasis added). Clearly, all mortals are debtors to God, unable to pay back even a fraction of what we owe. Yet, God is an easy creditor, who personally provides the reparation we are unable to pay.

2. God claims from all persons certain rights of property. Nothing, not even our forgetfulness or inadvertence, will exonerate us from this obligation. The charge made in Malachi's day must be recalled every time this principle is raised: "Will a [person] rob God? Yet you rob me. But you ask, 'How do we rob you?' In tithes and offerings" (Mal 3:8 NIV). Thus taking what rightfully belongs to God, whether it is tithes, offerings, vows, time, talents, or gifts, is tantamount to robbing God. For this reason the apostle Paul teaches in 2 Cor 8:7 that believers are to "excel in this grace of giving" (NIV) just as we abound in the other graces and gifts from the Lord.

3. Humans also have rights, just as God has rights. When these rights are violated, it is a matter for divine justice, even though the act is against mere mortals. Human rights cannot be grounded in certain implied or observed values that are said to be actually or potentially present in one's fellow creatures. Human rights are grounded in the divine declarations of truth and justice and in the fact that men and women are made in the image of God.

4. In a most amazing statement, Isa 53:10 asserts that God made the life of the suffering servant "a guilt offering" (NIV). The very same word is used in Lev 5:14–6:7 for the ritual of the guilt offering. Thus Isaiah declares that the Servant of the Lord, the Messiah, gave up his life in death as a guilt offering on behalf of sinners who were too heavy in debt to help themselves. In this way, the death of Christ became a perfect reparation offering, for just as the ram of the guilt offering was appraised "according to the sanctuary shekel," so Jesus was assessed and given a divine verdict in Matt 3:17: "With him I am well pleased" (NIV).

5. The sin offering represents the passive aspect of the death of Christ in that he met the demands of the law by dying in the place of sinners. But the guilt offering represents the active aspect of the work of Christ in that he carried out the will of God completely by an act of voluntary obedience. This is hardly a moral influence theory of the death of Christ; it is payment of a debt to render satisfaction plus reparation for the wrong committed, thus making reinstatement to the covenant family possible.

LEVITICUS 6:8–7:38, INSTRUCTIONS FOR THE PRIESTS

OVERVIEW

To complete the directions for the offerings, 6:8–7:38 goes over much of the same material as in the first five sacrifices described in 1:1–6:7. At first glance, the repetition seems to the modern reader superfluous. Various modern explanations give one reason or another for this apparent redundancy, but the best clue is found in the text itself. Leviticus 1:2 and 4:2 introduce the materials in their sections under the rubric "Speak/Say to the Israelites." Over against this heading for the contents of 1:1–6:7 is the new rubric in 6:9 (MT 6:2) and 6:25 (MT 6:18): "Give Aaron and his sons this command: 'These are the regulations'" (תורת *tôrat*).[48] In fact, in this second section of 6:7–7:38 the people are addressed in only three paragraphs (7:11, 22, 28).

The difference, then, between the two sections is a difference in emphasis. Leviticus 1:1–6:7 concerns mainly the worshiper, but Lev 6:8–7:38 focuses on the officiating priest(s). This generalization is not without certain crossovers, for some items primarily addressed to the people by their very nature also affected the officiating priest.

Within the sections the order of the sacrifices also differs. In the opening chapters of Leviticus the order is burnt, grain, peace, sin, and guilt offerings. In the last two chapters of this first major section of the book the order is burnt, grain, the high priest's daily grain, sin, guilt, and peace offerings.

Leviticus 6:8–7:38 can be subdivided into the following nine paragraphs: the perpetual burnt offering (6:8-10); the daily grain offering (6:14-18); the priests' daily grain offering (6:19-23); the sin offering (6:24-30); the guilt offering (7:1-10); the peace offering (7:11-21); the prohibition on eating fat or blood (7:22-27); the priests' portion of the peace offering (7:28-36); and summary (7:37-38).

Each of these paragraphs opens with either "The LORD said to Moses" (6:19; 7:22, 28) or "This is the instruction for the . . . offering" (literal translation; 6:14; 7:1, 11, 37). Twice the two rubrics come together in the same opening line (6:8-9, 24-25). A colophon ends the first major section of Leviticus (7:37-38), just as concluding summaries exist elsewhere in the book (11:46-47; 13:59; 14:54-57; 15:32-33).

The colophon in 7:37-38 summarizes the whole legislative section on the sacrifices: "These, then, are the regulations for the burnt offering, the grain offering, the sin offering, the guilt offering, the ordination offering and the fellowship offering, which the LORD gave Moses on Mount Sinai on the day he commanded the Israelites to bring their offerings to the LORD, in the Desert of Sinai." The fact that 1:1 is revealed in the tabernacle, while 7:38 places it at Mount Sinai, has led some to attribute the rubric of 1:1 as a heading just for 1:2– 6:7. Thus the colophon refers, in this view, only to 6:8–7:38. The thought is that Lev 6:8–7:38 was revealed at the same time that Exodus 29 was given, while Moses was on Sinai; Lev 1:1– 6:7, in this view, would have come later. While this solution is possible, it cannot be demonstrated as certain.

---

48. Hebrew *tôrâ* is incorrectly rendered "law" in these contexts. Instead, Torah is now viewed as being derived from the stem *y-r-h*, "to cast," "to shoot," as one would shoot an arrow, for instance. In the hiphil stem of the Hebrew verb, *hôrâ* would mean "to aim, or direct toward something"; therefore, "to point out the way," "to instruct." The conclusion is that "instruction" is the best rendering for the word *torah*.

Leviticus 6:8-13, The Perpetual Burnt Offering

COMMENTARY

Five times in this paragraph the burden of this instruction for the priests is stressed: The fire on the altar in the courtyard of the sanctuary is not to go out (6:9*b*, 12, 13*b*). It is to be kept going day and night.

These verses are informed by the law of the "continual" or "perpetual" offering (תמיד *tāmîd*) in Exod 29:38–46, where we are told that two yearling lambs are to be sacrificed, one each morning and the other each evening (cf. Num 28:3-8; see also 2 Kgs 16:15; Ezek 46:13-15). The whole burnt offering sacrificed each morning and evening forms the foundation for all the other sacrifices. Since no other offering is placed on the altar after the evening sacrifice of the whole burnt offering, the fire has to be tended all night to make sure it does not go out. The whole burnt offering makes atonement each evening for the sins of that day; but come the next morning, it is necessary to atone for the sins of the preceding night. Thus the perpetual whole burnt offering reminds Israel of its need for continual repentance, cleansing, prayer, and thanksgiving to God.

The priest's instructions also include what he is to wear as he removes the ashes from the altar of the burnt offering. To indicate the sacredness of even the ashes, his directions specify that he wear his linen garment, a linen, incidentally, that is made not of the common flax but of the type imported from Egypt. The ashes are deposited beside the altar until the priest once again completely changes his garments, for otherwise the people might be sanctified (see Ezek 44:17, 19) if he were to go outside the sanctuary wearing them; the linen garments are to be used exclusively in the sanctuary. Then the ashes are removed to a clean place outside the camp.

One of the main reasons for maintaining the fire on the altar is to signify that the altar, originally lit by fire from heaven (Lev 9:24), is the divinely approved means for receiving atonement and for expressing uninterrupted worship of Yahweh.

REFLECTIONS

1. One emphasis of this passage is on the ceaseless quality of service to God. The fire on the altar must always be kept burning as a sign that the dedication and consecration the Lord desires from us are not to be occasional but continuous, perpetual, and habitual.

This ceaseless service is to be understood not as exhausting but as hopeful. The worship of God never ends. Even when the night comes and the sanctuary candles are extinguished, somewhere in the world the sun is rising and the morning praises of God are beginning. Even when we are asleep, the God of Israel never slumbers, and God's watchful eye is ever vigilant (see Ps 121:3).

2. With the beginning of each new day there ought to arise a new resolve to dedicate ourselves to God. And before we retire each evening, the ardor of our devotion should be stirred up, not extinguished.

Leviticus 6:14-18 The Daily Grain Offering

COMMENTARY

The grain offering appears in the same sequence here as in the earlier section of Leviticus. This offering, unlike the one described in chap. 2, is not brought by the ordinary Israelite; instead, this daily grain offering is part of the continual or perpetual burnt offering.

First the priest takes a handful of fine flour mixed with oil and together with incense burns it on the altar as a "memorial portion" (see the discussion of this term in 2:2). The remainder of the offering is considered "most holy" (2:3; 6:17). The grain offering, the sin offering, and the guilt offering are said to be "most holy" (6:17, 25; 7:6); that is, only Aaron, his sons, and their descendants can eat any part of these offerings, and then only within the holy place of the tabernacle courtyard.

The expression in 6:18c and 27a, "Whatever touches it [or the flesh] will become holy," is problematic. But in line with the principles of 7:19-20, it would be better if the expression were translated "*Who* ever touches it will become holy," since the Hebrew simply says, "All who touch it." This question must have concerned Israel much, for we find it still being raised in Hag 2:12-13. Apparently, according to Haggai, holiness was not as contagious as uncleanness was. Nevertheless, a warning still had to be issued about touching the most holy sacrifices. What the text means by "become holy" is not certain, even though similar expressions occur elsewhere (see Exod 29:37; 30:29; Deut 22:9). It may

imply that by touching or eating a portion designated "most holy," laypersons expose themselves to the potential wrath of God unless they undergo an act of purification.[49]

Once again, we meet this distinction between the common and the holy (see the discussion on this matter in 2:10). Notice that when the altar is consecrated in Exod 29:37 and its furniture in Exod 30:29, they are said to be "most holy" with the result that everything put on the altar or the tabernacle furniture also is said to be holy.

Having said all of that, the solution may rest in a proper understanding of the Hebrew verb יקדש (*yiqdāš*), which has usually been translated "will become holy" (presumably as a result of contacting sanctified objects or substances). But the problem of a contagious holiness still remained on this basis. While the verb קדש (*qādaš*) may connote a resultant holiness, here it seems to refer to what occurred prior to its contact with the sacred. Therefore, with Baruch A. Levine, it is proposed that a better translation is "must be in a holy state" if it is to touch the altar or any of these dedicated things.[50] Incidentally, such a view also makes the answer of Haggai more understandable.

49. Ellinger, *Leviticus*, 97, as cited by Wenham, *Leviticus*, 121.
50. Levine, *The JPS Torah Commentary*, 37-38.

REFLECTIONS

1. Holiness is not something that acts like a contagious disease. Sin can be caught and is easily transmitted, but holiness does not work that way.

2. The daily offering of fine flour to God signifies Israel's daily consecration and dedication to the Lord.

3. Since God created all things, both the common and the holy must be received as gifts from above and not divorced from each other. But the common must be distinguished from the holy due to the presence of sin in the world, which God originally created "good."

Leviticus 6:19-23, The Priests' Daily Grain Offering

COMMENTARY

This offering is not mentioned in the list of the five major ones; therefore, along with the continual or perpetual burnt offering and the

daily grain offering, we are being given new instructions.

The chief difference between the high

priest's grain offering and the daily grain offering, or even the regular grain offering, is that it must be completely burned on the altar; none of it is to be eaten (v. 23). This same principle is enunciated in the sin offering; if the priest brings the sin offering, the entire animal has to be burned without any of it being eaten (4:3-12). Since the offering is for the high priest, he in no way can at one and the same time be a partaker and a mediator of what he brings out of his own need for atonement and dedication to God.

Verse 20 refers to this as a "regular" (תמיד *tāmîd*) grain offering. Accordingly, it is not limited to the time when the high priest is installed into his office as an initiation offering. The expression in v. 20, "on the day he is anointed," may point to the fact that when Aaron, or any high priest, was anointed, his sons brought this offering from that day onward. How the anointing of the priests in general differed from the anointing of the high priest is not known. But the offerings specified in connection with the anointing of the high priest do not seem to include the daily grain offering. Leviticus 8:26 refers to a basket of bread made without yeast and another made with oil and a wafer, but no mention is made of this grain offering. Since v. 20 specifically directs this instruction to "Aaron and his sons," this solution seems to resolve most of the difficulties. This solution understands the pronominal suffix on the direct object marker in v. 20 in a distributive sense so that it reads, "On the day each [of all the priests] is anointed."[51]

51. As suggested by A. Noordtzij, *Bible Student's Commentary: Leviticus,* trans. Raymond Togtman (Grand Rapids: Zondervan, 1982) 77.

REFLECTIONS

1. The priest's offering must be totally burned since he symbolically bears the sins of the people in his office as a mediator. However, no one figuratively bears his or her own sins, nor can one bear them oneself. That is another reason why the system of sacrifices reveals its weaknesses and its anticipation of a sacrifice that can overcome these imperfections.

2. Hebrews 7:27 uses this loophole to show how Christ's priesthood was superior to that of Aaron's priesthood: "Unlike the other high priests, he does not need to offer sacrifices day after day, first for his own sins, and then for the sins of the people. He sacrificed for their sins once for all when he offered himself" (NIV). Verse 28 goes on to clinch the point: "For the law appoints as high priests men who are weak; but the oath, which came after the law, appointed the Son, who has been made perfect forever" (NIV).

Leviticus 6:24-30, The Sin Offering

COMMENTARY

Leviticus 6:24–7:34 takes up offerings that have already been discussed in 3:1–6:7. These now concern the people at large, whereas the preceding group in 6:8-23 deals mainly with the priests.

The sin offering is included in the category of "most holy" (see the discussion of this term at 6:17). Also, on the improbable translation of "Whatever [or whoever] touches any of the flesh will become holy," a better rendering (as already indicated 6:18) is this: "Everything that touches any of the flesh [now that it has been brought into the courtyard of the tent of meeting] must [itself] be in a holy state." That is why garments that have been accidentally splattered with blood during the ceremony of the sin offering must be washed in the holy place. If washing is impossible, say in the case of a clay pot in which the meat was cooked and thus had penetrated the clay, it has to be destroyed (v. 28). The distinction between the holy and the common is thereby maintained once again.

While the priests can eat the sin offering in the holy place, they cannot eat it if the priest himself brings it (v. 30). It has to be totally burned just as the previous offering specifies, and for the same reason.

REFLECTIONS

1. Only persons consecrated to God could touch any part of this sacrifice once it was devoted to God. That was especially true of the blood of the offering, for should any of it fall on the garment of even a priest who stood nearby, it had to be thoroughly cleansed. The gulf between what was common/ordinary and what was holy was huge, and mortals disregarded it to their own hurt.

2. The NT teaches that Christ was made to be sin for us so that we might be redeemed. It is not without significance, then, that such reverential and holy treatment was given to the dedicated sacrifice and all its parts. Such an example suggests the type of deferential attitude that believers should show to the mysteries of our redemption in Christ.

Leviticus 7:1-10, The Guilt Offering

COMMENTARY

The close connection of the guilt offering with the sin offering is made explicit in v. 7—both are regarded as "most holy" (v. 6c). Once again, their consumption is strictly limited to the Aaronic priesthood (v. 6a).

This offering is to be slaughtered at the same site where the burnt offering is (1:11; 7:2). The rites for the guilt offering are the same as those for the sin offering, except for the way in which the blood is disposed. The blood of the guilt offering is sprinkled around the altar, whereas the blood of the sin offering is put on the horns of the altar (cf. 4:34; 7:2b).

The fatty tissues are to be burned on the altar as a reparation sacrifice, corresponding to the instructions given for the peace offering (3:9-10). The remainder of the offering, then, belongs to the priests; however, its consumption is restricted to male members of the priesthood, who may eat it only in the precincts of the sanctuary.

No mention is made of the laying on of hands as appears in the sin offering (4:4), but since these two offerings are treated as having the same law (7:7), presuming its presence here as well is reasonable.

The officiating priest is also given all the grain offering that had been cooked, whether in an oven or a pan or on a griddle (7:9). The same rule applies to the hide of the guilt offering; it too belongs to the officiating priest.

REFLECTIONS

1. These provisions for the priests enunciate the distinct principle that those who minister at the altar are to share in the sacrificial offerings. This theme will again be announced in 1 Cor 9:13 and 10:18.

2. A corollary of the first reflection is that it is the responsibility of the Lord's people to support those who minister the gospel (see 1 Tim 5:17-18), lest they be distracted from their primary task and be forced to give less of themselves and their time to the primary call of God. Although it was not specifically mentioned previously in connection with this offering, the priest was allowed to keep the animal hide for himself. It must have been valuable, since animal hides were often used as mattresses by night and as carpets to sit on by day.

3. The hide may well have acquired a special significance, through the laying on of hands, in that the guilt of the person was transferred to the animal. When the offerer left behind the skin of the animal, the symbolism may well have been that the offerer left his guilt behind and departed from the sanctuary in a purified state. Thus sins were forgiven through the atoning sacrifice, but they were also forsaken and removed, which was pictured in abandoning the hide to the care of the priest.

Leviticus 7:11-21, The Peace Offering

COMMENTARY

The ritual of the peace offering has already been discussed in chap. 3, but now more specific orders are given to the priests on how this offering is to be observed.

The *peace offering* is actually a collective term for three types of offerings: the eucharistic or thank offering (v. 12), the votive offering (v. 16), and the freewill or voluntary offering (v. 16). The peace offering also is the only one that the laity are allowed to eat.

The eucharistic, or thanksgiving, offering is given on occasions of praise, thanksgiving, or confession. The word תודה (*tôdâ*, "thanksgiving") covers the ideas of thankfulness and confession of sin (see Josh 7:19; Ezra 10:11). As urged in Psalm 107, this sacrifice is to be offered as a token of gratitude for a number of mercies and favors received, such as recovery from sickness, preservation on a journey, deliverance at sea, and rescue from captivity (see Ps 107:22). The writer of Hebrews had this sacrifice in mind when he wrote, "Through Jesus, therefore, let us continually offer to God a sacrifice of praise—the fruit of lips that confess his name" (13:15 NIV; an allusion to Hos 14:2*d*). The same offering is mentioned in Pss 56:12-13; 116:17; Jer 17:26; 33:11; Amos 4:5. Indeed, the liturgical formula used with this offering may appear in Jer 33:11: "Give thanks to the LORD Almighty,/ for the LORD is good;/ his love endures forever" (NIV; cf. Pss 100:4-5; 106:1; 107:1; 118:1; 136:1). The occasion, then, is some moment recalled from the past when God intervened and thus provided an opportunity for the offerer to be grateful and to rejoice in the goodness of the Lord.

The oblations required for this peace offering, along with the usual bull, goat, or sheep, include pancakes mixed with pure oil, but unleavened, inasmuch as part of them is to be offered up to God on the altar with the fatty pieces. Leaven, however, is not prohibited from another part of the offering, i.e., the bread given to the priests, which is not burned on the altar.

All thanksgiving offerings are to be eaten on the same day they are offered, whereas the other peace offerings may be eaten on the second day but never on the third day. For this reason the thanksgiving offering stands first among the class of peace offerings. This rule may also be required to make sure that the thanksgiving offerings are shared with poor people (v. 15). Poor people are invited on the condition that they are ceremonially clean (see 1 Sam 20:24-26; Pss 21:5; cf. Ps 22:25-26). Since the sacrifice belongs to God, who in turn graciously grants it to be shared with the offerer's friends and poorer neighbors, no part of it is to be left around to be diverted to any other use or to putrefy.

The other two types of peace offerings, the votive and the freewill, are often mentioned together in Scripture as they are here in v. 16 (see Lev 22:21; Num 15:3; Deut 12:6,17). The votive offering is made to fulfill a vow made during an emergency of life (see Gen 28:20; Judg 11:30-31; 1 Sam 1:11; 2 Sam 15:8). Israelites are not required to make vows, but if they make them, they must to keep them (see Eccl 5:4-6). The freewill offering comes as a spontaneous impulse of the heart in gratitude to God (see 2 Chr 31:14; 35:8-9; Ps 54:6). The unusual aspect of the freewill offering is that it is not subject to the same stringent rules applied to the other sacrifices. It can be from an animal that is "deformed and stunted" (Lev 22:23b). Here is the single exception to the rule that all animals offered for sacrifice have to be perfect and without blemish. The passage that grants this single exception warns the offerer that this exception will not be accepted even for the companion votive offering, for returning to God anything less than perfect will reflect on the perfection of God's most gracious gifts to the people.

Leviticus 7:20-21 warns that all who participate in eating the sacrificial meal must be ritually clean. Should someone violate this rule, "that person must be cut off from his people" (v. 21). This penalty appears some twenty-five times, usually with regard to a ceremonial violation. It is associated with capital crimes only three times (Exod 31:14; Lev 17:14; 18:29). This phrase appears to be used in various ways, often meaning some kind of excommunication rather than capital punishment. For many sins of even greater magnitude, provision is made for removal of the sin by God's atonement. Furthermore, since 17:10 and 20:3-6 are clear that it is a divine rather than a human punishment, it would be best to understand it as God cutting off the offenders from their kin instead of a premature death.[52]

52. See the discussion by Milgrom, "Karet," in Leviticus 1-16, 457-60. Milgrom lists nineteen cases in the Torah of karet. He concludes that either extirpation (of a person's line of descendants) or premature death is to be seen in these cases of "cutting off."

REFLECTIONS

1. The peace offerings stress that God values more than the mere word of praise and thankfulness. The tangible response of the sacrifice has the effect of backing up the verbal profession of gratitude and appreciation for all that God has done on behalf of the worshiper. Similarly, 1 John 3:18 encourages believers to love, not just in word or speech, but in deed and in truth.

2. The motivating force behind the peace offerings is the desire to express appreciation and gratitude. Accordingly, Christians are still being urged to make their petitions known to God with thanksgiving (see Phil 4:6) and to continue in prayer with thanksgiving (see Col 4:2), giving thanks in everything, always, to God (see Eph 5:20).

Leviticus 7:22-27, The Prohibition on Eating Fat or Blood

COMMENTARY

Whereas the previous material in chaps. 6–7 is directed to the priests, these verses address the people.

The prohibition on eating fat is not an absolute injunction; it applies only to the fat of beasts offered in sacrifice. The rule also applies to clean animals that have died a natural death or have been killed by wild animals. In both additional cases the animal is made unclean because its death may have come due to disease or contact with unclean wildlife; the resulting uncleanness makes it unsuitable for food. The main principle, however, is that the fat belongs to the Lord (3:16).

The prohibition on the use of blood as food, however, is absolutely universal. Whether the blood comes on the occasion of the sacrificial feasts or some other setting makes no difference. The reason is given in 17:11-12: "For the life of a creature is in the blood, and I have given it to you to make atonement for yourselves on the altar; it is the blood that makes atonement for one's life. Therefore I say to the Israelites, 'None of you may eat blood, nor may an alien living among you eat blood' " (cf. Lev 3:17; Deut 12:16; 15:23).

REFLECTIONS

While nothing may seem more remote from the modern believer than these two prohibitions, two most important principles underlie these directions. These principles state how sinful beings can enter into fellowship with a reconciling God.

1. The first principle is that happy communion with God rests on the willing consecration of the best fruit of our lives to God. Just as the peace offering, the sin offering, and the guilt offering required that all the fat be laid on the altar in dedication to God, so we are reminded that we owe God our best.

2. The second principle recognizes the supreme sanctity of the sacrificial blood of the Lamb of God on our behalf. It is a tacit acceptance of the fact that the death of a substitute in our place, as symbolized by the loss of blood from the flesh of the animal sacrifice, is the only grounds for our acceptance into fellowship with God.

Leviticus 7:28-36, The Priests' Portion of the Peace Offering

COMMENTARY

All the people are addressed in these verses, which form a supplement to the peace offering regulations in vv. 11-21. The special emphasis is on the fact that offerers are to bring the peace offering with their own hands (v. 30) so as to prevent anyone's thinking that coercion is involved (cf. 8:27-28).

The priests are entitled to a portion of the peace offering (v. 35). They are assigned two parts: the breast (v. 30) and the right thigh (v. 33).

The right thigh probably indicates the right hindquarter, even though Deut 18:3 and Philo[53] are occasionally incorrectly used to argue that "the thigh of the right [side]" (literal translation) means the right shoulder. What further contributed to the shoulder interpretation was the archaeological excavation of a Lachish Canaanite temple (destroyed about 1220 BCE) that uncovered the right forelegs of a number of species found near an altar, mostly untouched by fire.[54] But the choicest part of the animal was the hindquarter; therefore, this is the preferred interpretation. Moreover, whenever the same Hebrew term is applied to humans in Scripture, the leg, not the arm, is signified.

The breast is said to constitute a "wave offering" (תנופה *těnûpâ*), which seems to mean moving the arms back and forth in a horizontal motion (v. 30). The right thigh is, according to the AV, offered as a "heave offering" (תרומה *těrûmâ*; v. 32), presumably because of its being related to the Hebrew verb "to exalt," "to raise," or "to lift." The NIV does not translate the term this way; instead, it has "as a contribution." The NRSV has "as an offering," and the TNK has "as a gift."

The wave offering, according to the several translators of the English Bible and the works of Jewish commentators, was toward the sanctuary, while the so-called heave offering was a vertical motion toward heaven and thus dedicated to the Lord. However, based on an Egyptian relief from Karnak, Jacob Milgrom argues persuasively that the so-called wave offering should now be understood as

---

53. *Laws* 1.145.53
54. See G. Ernest Wright, *Biblical Archaeology* (Philadelphia: Westminster, 1960) 15.

an elevation offering, a ritual of elevating and lifting the offering in dedication to God.[55]

The so-called heave offering may now be understood as "gift," coming from the verb *rûm*, meaning "to give a gift."[56] This is further collaborated by the fact that in every instance where *tĕrûmâ* is used, it is always "to the LORD," never "before the LORD"— as happens when *tĕnûpâ* appears. Thus the breast is said

to be a "dedication" (*tĕnûpâ*) before the Lord, first, and then it along with the leg is to be a "contribution" or "gift" (*tĕrûmâ*) to the officiating priest. If a difference be sought between these two terms, it is that only certain items underwent a ritual ceremony of "dedication" in the sanctuary itself, while a "contribution" may have represented only the first stage in giving anything to God according to Jacob Milgrom. However, finality on these matters must await the further results of study in lexicography.

55. Milgrom, "The *Tĕnûpâ*," in *Leviticus 1-16*, 461-72.
56. Milgrom, "The *Sôq Hatterûmâ*," in *Leviticus 1-16*, 473-81.

REFLECTIONS

1. In the act of elevating the breast, the priests both dedicate this portion to their Lord and acknowledge their dependence on God as the supplier of their food.

2. Both the dedication and the contribution teach us that it is the will of God that those who give up secular occupations to devote themselves to the ministry of the house of God are to be supported with the offerings of God's people. This would hardly need to be said today, except that some small groups deny this privilege to the clergy and its responsibility to the laity. The apostle Paul came to the same conclusion in 1 Cor 9:13-14; for him the principle had not been set aside, but still held.

Leviticus 7:37-38, Summary

COMMENTARY

These last two verses are written in the style of a colophon, which normally gives the title or designation of the contents, date when it was written, name of the owner, and the scribe who wrote the materials.

The case is sometimes made that the legislation of the section just concluded or certain parts of it were not given "from the tent of meeting" (1:1), but were uniquely given "on Mount Sinai" (7:38). But the case is not beset with dualities or contradictions as may be

at first supposed, for while it is true that the expression "on/in Mount Sinai" (בהר *bĕhar* may mean "in/on/at Mount [Sinai]") usually refers to the peak itself, it may also be true that some of these instructions had indeed been given for the first time while Moses was still on the mount. It may also be true that these instructions were given "in [the area] of Mount Sinai." Thus, already in the wilderness of Sinai, Israel had worshiped God with these same sacrifices.

LEVITICUS 8:1–10:20

THE INAUGURATION OF WORSHIP
AT THE TABERNACLE

OVERVIEW

Even though most tend to think of the book of Leviticus as a book of laws, it is actually the continuation of the story of Israel's history, providing the setting for the laws on worship. Nothing strengthens this judgment more than the section of Leviticus that is before us, chaps. 8–10.

This second section of Leviticus is a narrative account of the consecration of the tabernacle and of Aaron and his sons as the priests of that tent of meeting (chap. 8), of the induction of the Aaronic priesthood into the duties of their offices (chap. 9), and of the awesome judgment that falls on two of Aaron's sons who violated an instruction with regard to carrying out the duties of their offices (chap. 10). Therefore, the style is more descriptive than in the previous seven chapters, and it carries on the story of Israel, which was begun earlier.

One of the most noticeable features of chaps. 8–10 is the remarkable frequency with which the statement "Moses did as the Lord commanded him" (or its equivalent) appears. This statement (or ones similar to it) appears sixteen times in these three chapters alone (8:4, 5, 9, 13, 17, 21, 29, 34, 36; 9:6, 7, 10, 21; 10:7, 13, 15). Fidelity to the Word of God given in the blueprint God laid out on Mount Sinai is stressed repeatedly, especially with the instructions given for the ordination of Aaron and his sons in Exodus 28–29.

In fact, so careful was Moses to follow the directions given to him on the mount that practically every verse in chap. 8 is a quotation or an adaptation of the commands given in Exodus 29–30. We may see this in the following list of parallel passages[57]:

Exodus 29–30	Leviticus 8
29:1-3	8:2
29:4-6	8:6-8
29:7	8:12
30:26-29	8:10-11
29:8-9	8:13
29:10-14	8:14-17
29:15-18	8:18-21
29:19-20	8:22-24
29:22-25	8:25-28
29:26	8:29
29:21	8:30
29:31-32	8:31
29:34	8:32
29:35-37	8:33-35

Moses' strict adherence to the revealed will of God could not be demonstrated more elaborately than by means of this close paralleling of the instructions given in Exodus. All of these sacred instructions were fulfilled in accordance with the aim stated in Exod 29:43-46 and Lev 9:23—i.e., so that "the glory of the Lord [would appear] to all the people" and "dwell among the Israelites."

One other remarkable feature in these texts deserves special mention. After God had given the instructions for the installation of the priests in Exodus 29, the story of Israel's sin at the golden calf (see Exodus 32–34) interrupted the continuation of plans for the design and erection of the tabernacle, its services, and its officiants. One willing participant in the whole fiasco was Aaron, the man marked out to be the future high priest. Even though Moses intervened and saved the people from certain destruction, there was no assurance that Aaron would be named high priest. Indeed, the garments for Aaron had been completed, but he played no part in

---

57. This list appears in Wenham, *Leviticus*, 131 n. 1.

the services of Exodus 40. Would Aaron be named, or would he be by-passed and permanently debarred from the office?

We are surprised by the grace and forgiveness of God when Leviticus 8 makes it clear that Aaron will be named high priest, serving along with his sons. After failing as a leader, he is reinstated. This turn of events makes the lapse of Nadab and Abihu (chap. 10) all the more startling. Was their sin any more grievous than that of their father? We are left pondering this question and the remarkable uniqueness of the holiness of God.

The precise chronology for the events of these chapters cannot be fixed with certainty. What is known is that Moses had set up the tabernacle on the first day of the first month in the second year after the exodus (see Exod 40:2, 17). And according to Leviticus 8–9, the consecration of Aaron and his sons lasted seven days (8:33). The only suggestion that can be made is that the "eighth day" mentioned in Lev 9:1 may be the same as the first day of the first month of the second year after the exodus mentioned in Exod 40:17. But then there is the problem of the twelve days mentioned in Numbers 7, when each of the chieftains of the twelve tribes brought gifts for twelve days after Moses had finished setting up the tent of meeting. The Talmud felt obliged to harmonize the data; therefore, it concluded that the dedication program began on the twenty-third day of the twelfth month. Moses officiated for the last seven days of the month; the eighth day of Lev 9:1 came on the first day of the first month, as noted in Exod 40:2, 17, when Aaron assumed the priestly duties from that point onward. That was the same day that Moses "finished setting up the tabernacle" (Num 7:1 NIV) and discharged his responsibilities to the priests. Then the first of the princes came on that first day of the priestly leadership (see Num 7:12). All of this is possible, but the text gives us no assurance that the harmonization is secure.

LEVITICUS 8:1-36, CONSECRATION OF AARON AND HIS SONS

COMMENTARY

8:1-5. Before the services of worship can begin, the consecration of the tabernacle and the priests who will serve in it is necessary. But such consecration presupposes the call of God on the lives of those who will serve. Thus the installation of Aaron and his sons begins with the command of God, "Take Aaron and his sons . . ." (literal translation; v. 1).

Aaron's family had been selected to be the line through which the priests of Israel would come, even though all the other Levites, to which Aaron and his family also belonged, would carry all the other related duties of the sanctuary. No one might intrude into that perpetual appointment; it was to remain in Aaron's family.

Aaron was indeed succeeded by Eleazar, his oldest living son, after the death of Nadab and Abihu. Eleazar's line was traced for at least seven generations until the death of Eli in the days of Samuel. On Eli's death, the line was removed from Eli's sons, because of their wickedness, to the descendants of Ithamar, Aaron's other son. However, in the time of Solomon the line returned again to Eleazar's descendants and continued until the Babylonian captivity. Joshua, the high priest after the return from the Babylonian exile, was also from this line, but after his time the appointments became irregular and uncertain. In fact, under Roman occupation, no attention was paid to the original instructions for succession in this office, as it often was sold to the highest bidder, whether that bidder was from Aaron's family or not.

From its inception, however, priesthood was not from human beings, but from God. The high priest could act only under divine appointment.

Moses is instructed to gather all the nation together at the door of the tent of meeting (v. 3). Naturally, such a feat, if literally understood, was a logistical impossibility. Moreover, to hold that many people for all seven days of the consecration would stretch the limits of accommodations in the area of the tabernacle. Perhaps it is best to understand this command as an illustration of the figure of speech called synecdoche, where the whole is put for a part—or as it was in this case, all the congregation is put for the elders and principal people of Israel who represented the entire group, as Lev 9:1 seems to confirm.

The consecration ceremonies involve four main parts: the washing (v. 6), the investiture (vv. 7-9), the anointing (vv. 10-13), and the sacrifices (vv. 14-32). Moses acts as the mediator who represents God throughout, since no ordained priest has preceded Aaron in this office. Nowhere is Moses' distinctive role in these ceremonies brought out more clearly than in the sacrifices. Portions that normally would be eaten by the priests are either totally burned on the altar, thereby being given to God, or are given to Moses (see the discussion of the sin offering above).

8:6. This verse records the washing ceremony. The ceremonial washing signifies the inward purification of the spirit. Often the OT requires washings and ablutions, as it does for the one cured of "leprosy" (Lev 14:8-9) or the one who experienced bodily discharges (Leviticus 15). The same word is used for washing away "the filth of the women of Zion" (Isa 4:4 NIV). Washing is a means of restoring persons and things to a state of being made clean (see Num 31:23-24). The symbolism points to cleansing from the defilements of sin that acted as impediments to carrying out the office of the priesthood. Scripture also frequently links the concepts of "clean hands" and a "pure heart" (see Pss 24:4; 73:13; Isa 1:16).

By NT times, washing would be linked with the "washing with water through the word [of God]" (Eph 5:26 NIV), the "washing of rebirth and renewal" (Titus 3:5 NIV), and having "our hearts sprinkled to cleanse us from a guilty conscience and having our bodies washed with pure water" (Heb 10:22 NIV).

Later specifications would determine that this washing was done behind a linen sheet and involved washing the priests' entire bodies. After this, whenever the priests went into the sanctuary, they were required to wash only their hands and feet (see Exod 30:19-21; 40:30-31).

8:7-9. These verses describe the investiture. Eight pieces are assigned to the official uniform of the priests—four are shared with all priests, and four are distinctive to the office of high priest. The garments reflect the office and not the individual. There is no mention of sandals, for the priests probably ministered in their bare feet, just as Moses and Joshua were instructed in their encounter with the living God (see Exod 3:5; Josh 5:15).

The first garment (assuming that the priest is already wearing linen breeches) is a "tunic," or undergarment. It is worn against the naked body, extends to the knees and has short sleeves (cf. Exod 20:26; 28:42). The tunic is held in place by a "sash." Over this is placed a purple "robe," woven into one piece (cf. Exod 28:31-35), reaching to the knees, and adorned with cloth pomegranates made of three different colors of yarn, each pomegranate alternated with a golden bell, all attached to the bottom of this garment. A shoulder garment, an "ephod," forms a type of vest held in place by a waistband. This ephod supports a "breastpiece," a square piece of cloth measuring about ten inches square and made of the same cloth as the ephod. This breastpiece is studded with jewels,[58] symbolizing each of the twelve tribes, and is folded in half so as to form a pouch to hold the "Urim" and "Thummim." The meaning of these two terms remains elusive, though "Lights" and "Perfections," respectively, are the two most frequent suggestions. In form they probably resembled flat stones, similar to the פורים (*pûrîm*), i.e., the dice used for casting lots in the book of Esther. First Samuel 14:41-43 attaches the verb "to cast" or "to throw down" in connection with the use of these two objects. Thus they were probably something like a pair of dice used by the priest to receive a yes, no, or neutral reply to questions put to the Lord by the priest.

On Aaron's head is placed a "turban," a headdress that differs both in name and in design from that worn by the other priests. Attached to it is a gold plate, a sacred diadem,

---

58. See Walter C. Kaiser, Jr., "Exodus," in *The Expositor's Bible Commentary,* 467, for further discussion on Exodus 28–29. On the identity of the jewels, see A. Paul Davis and E. L. Gilmore, *Lapidary Journal* (Dec. 1968) 1124-28, 1130-34.

inscribed with the words "HOLY TO THE LORD" (see Exod 28:36).

8:10-13. Before the priests are anointed to their service, the tabernacle and all that pertains to it must be anointed with oil. The anointing oil is a unique combination of four choice spices, which is not to be duplicated under any circumstances (cf. Exod 25:6; 30:22-33): myrrh, cinnamon, cane, and cassia.

The purpose of the anointing is to set the person or object apart for the service of the Lord. The anointing, not the oil, signals something or someone who has been chosen by the Lord. Only when the priests are on the verge of commencing their work can they and the sanctuary be anointed.

Scripture often connects the act of anointing with the receiving of God's Spirit. This is the case for Saul (see 1 Sam 10:1-10) and for David (see 1 Sam 16:13). The connection is clearly seen in Isa 61:1 where the servant of the Lord announces, "The Spirit of the Sovereign LORD is on me,/ because the LORD has anointed me" (NIV). Jesus applies this verse to himself in Luke 4:18. The apostle Peter declares much later that God "anointed Jesus of Nazareth with the Holy Spirit" (Acts 10:38 NIV), for that indeed is what the name Messiah means, "Anointed [One]."

Ordinary priests have small quantities of anointing oil applied to them with the finger, but the oil is "poured" on Aaron's head. It runs down on his beard and the robe of the ephod (see Ps 133:2).

8:14-32. This passage describes the sacrifices connected with the investiture. Three of the main sacrifices are part of the consecration ceremony: first the sin offering, then the burnt offering, and finally the peace offering.

8:14-17. The sin offering symbolizes the further need for cleansing. The washing of Aaron cannot effectively deal with his need for expiation of the guilt of his sins. Apparently, the ablution can care only for defilements of nature, by bringing renewal and regeneration through the Word of God and the Holy Spirit; but there remains the need for dealing with the removal of objective guilt and the need for forgiveness for the sin that caused the guilt.

The animal of choice for this occasion is the most costly of all: a bull, the same animal

ordered for the sin offering of the anointed priest in chap. 4. Aaron and his sons lay their hands on the victim to clearly indicate that it is their substitute.

The ceremony takes place as described in 4:3-12, except that the blood is not taken into the holy place to be smeared on the horns of the altar of incense; instead, it is put on the altar of burnt offering in the courtyard to sanctify the altar and to prepare it for the next offering Aaron is to make. Moreover, Aaron and his sons have not yet been inducted into their offices, so they cannot enter the holy place yet. Another major difference between this consecration ceremony's sin offering and any other sin offering is that neither Aaron nor his sons are to eat any of this sin offering. The one for whom the sin offering is made must not eat of its flesh; it is to be burned outside the camp after the requisite parts have been offered on the altar (vv. 8:16-17). In this way, "atonement" is also made "for [the altar]" (v. 15). Even the impurities of the altar itself have to be removed.

8:18-21. Now that reconciliation has been effected through the sin offering, the priest offers the burnt offering. This offering signals the complete dedication of the lives of the priests in accordance with the directions of Lev 1:10-13 and Exod 29:15-18.

Once again, the major difference in this offering is that the priests being installed take the part of ordinary worshipers, while Moses performs the priestly aspects of the sacrifice.

8:22-30. The ceremony culminates in a special aspect of the peace offerings described in chap. 3. As in the previous sacrifices, Moses takes the part of the officiating priest. This is especially clear in that the breast of the animal, normally given to the officiating priest, is given to Moses. And the right thigh, normally also assigned to the officiant, is added to the portions burned on the altar, which all belong to God. This strengthens the idea that the ordination of Aaron is carried out jointly by God and Moses.

The sacrificial animal for this peace offering is a "ram" or, to be more specific, "the ram for the ordination" (v. 22). The Hebrew term for "ordination" is מלאים (*millu'îm*), i.e., "fillings." The fuller form of this expression is "to fill the hands." The significance of this phrase comes out immediately in vv. 25-27.

Moses places the fat, the fat tail, and all the fat around the inner parts of the ram along with the right thigh of the ram on three differently made pieces of bread, all of which he puts into the hands of Aaron and his sons as a sign of their priestly office. Thus Aaron and his sons have their hands filled. Apparently, Moses next slides his hands under theirs and waves the contents of what fills the hands of those being dedicated back and forth in dedication to God.

Since the right thigh normally belongs to the priests (7:32), in these rites of dedication they are surrendering a portion that is theirs to God. Thus only when the priests are of service to others can they in any way benefit from it. When it is offered on their own behalf, it is improper for them to benefit from any of the sacrifice.

Later on, in the dedication of the Levites (see Num 8:9-14), the men themselves are waved before the Lord as a wave offering. The conclusion is the same: As the priests give what fills their hands, or even as they dedicate themselves, they just as surely devote themselves to God for service as their gift to God.

An even more remarkable feature about this peace offering is the way the blood is used (v. 23). It is applied to the tip of Aaron's right ear, the thumb of his right hand, and his right big toe instead of being thrown against the altar, as is usual for this offering (3:2, 8, 13). Having previously anointed Aaron with oil, Moses now consecrates him with blood.

This act is surely another instance of the part standing for the whole—in this case, the entirety of his body; he is to be totally consecrated to the service of God in the tabernacle. But the rest of the symbolism is just as clear: Aaron's ear must ever be attentive to the word of the Lord; his hand ever ready to do the work of God; and his feet ever alert to run in the service of the One who called him. Therefore, just as the blood ratifies the covenant at Sinai with all of Israel (see Exod 24:8), and as the same ceremony involving smearing the right ear, thumb, and toe of the cleansed leper signals his being restored to communion with God (Lev 14:14), so also the blood designates Aaron as God's person for the office he is being called to fill (Lev 8:30).

The repetition of the ritual in v. 30 appears at first to be out of place and in conflict with Exod 29:21. However, it is similar to the rite with the leper in Lev 14:10-20, where the remaining oil is poured on the leper's head after the sin offerings have been completed; it is an exact replica of the provisions mentioned here. This is a better solution than suspecting the presence of "later hands" inserting dissonant material into the text.

8:31-32. The ordination ceremony of dedication and consecration is now followed with a meal. This meal also confirms the covenant made between God and the house of Aaron. Given the seriousness of this meal, however, everything that is left over has to be burned and not left until the next day as in certain of the peace offerings. In this regard, the holiness of the act of ordaining is stressed; this act, no doubt, belongs to the category of the things treated as "most holy" (6:25, 29).

8:33-36. These verses treat one more aspect of the ordination services. To avoid any possible contamination or defilement, Aaron and his sons are to remain in the sanctuary precincts for seven days. It would appear from Exod 29:35, 37 that a bull is to be offered on each of the seven days, perhaps accompanied by a burnt offering. The duties for these priests will not begin until the eighth day after the mediators of the old covenant are themselves sanctified.

REFLECTIONS

1. The ordination of Aaron is but one of many biblical examples of God's calling flawed and broken people to places of leadership. We can think of Jacob the trickster, David the adulterer, Paul the persecutor, Peter the one who denied Jesus, and many others. Hebrews 7:28 makes the identical point we have just made: "For the law appoints as high priests men who are weak; but the oath, which came after the law, appointed the Son, who has been made perfect forever" (NIV). The contrast between previous high priests and the Savior as our high priest could not have been any greater. The amazing thing is that God will still use persons with infirmities; God does not demand perfection to permit the services ordained to be rendered.

2. Originally, all Israel was called to be a "kingdom of priests" (Exod 19:6 NIV), but the sin at the golden calf prevented that from happening. However, that original call for all laity to be a royal priesthood never was forgotten. It was repeated for believers after the resurrection of Christ (see Rev 1:6; 5:10). Contemporary believers have been made kings and priests unto God; indeed, they have been given "an altar from which those who minister at the tabernacle [had] no right to eat" (Heb 13:10 NIV).

3. Just as the Urim and Thummim were used to ascertain the will of God, some have pointed to Ps 19:7-8 (Hebrew vv. 8-9) as a modern equivalent for guidance today, where the same two words may be weakly reflected: "The law of the LORD is perfect" (תמימה *tĕmîmâ*; the same root as Thummim); and "The commands of the LORD are radiant,/ giving light (מאירת *mĕʾîrat*; the same root as Urim] to the eyes" (NIV). Perhaps, but the words are related only in their root forms and any assumed connection is not immediately clear.

4. What is most immediately necessary for service to the living God is cleansing. We must be cleansed and washed to be used in the service of God. Today this washing comes by means of the Holy Spirit's using the Word of God (see John 13:10; Eph 5:26; Titus 3:5; Heb 10:22).

LEVITICUS 9:1-24, THE INAUGURATION OF THE TABERNACLE SERVICE

COMMENTARY

After a whole week dedicated to the ordination services, Aaron is now ready to commence his ministry as the fully installed high priest. Significantly enough, his work commences not on the seventh day but on the eighth day—the first day of the week. Surely, this is something more than mere happenstance, for repeatedly the eighth day of the week, i.e., "the first day" or "the day after the Sabbath," will be specified in the list of the feasts given in Leviticus 23 (e.g., 7, 11, 15, 16, 35, 36, 39). To what degree this is symbolic or a type of the change in the day of worship that is to come must await our discussion of the Feast of Firstfruits and the Feast of Tabernacles in connection with chap. 23.

The first day of worship at the tabernacle begins with Moses summoning Aaron and his sons along with the "elders of Israel," acting, no doubt, as the representatives of the people (v. 1). Five times in this chapter Moses issues commands, or Aaron and his sons act on the basis of the commands (vv. 2, 5, 6, 7).

Once again, Aaron is instructed to offer a sin offering and a burnt offering, just as he has been doing for the past seven days. If anything emphasizes the sheer tedium and the repetitious nature of the sacrificial system, by now the point must have impressed itself on Aaron. A more perfect sacrifice and a more perfect officiant are needed. But the repetition on this eighth day is probably necessary, since Aaron must also publicly acknowledge that he too is a sinner in need of God's forgiveness. Even though Aaron has been lifted to the office of high priest, he needs atonement just as much as anyone else. The closer one follows the Lord in obedience and service, the more conscious that person becomes of how short each individual falls from the holy standard of God. So it is with Aaron; hence the need for further sacrifices!

Aaron may have been astonished when Moses ordered him to bring a bull calf (vv. 2-3). This is the only time in the sacrificial instructions where a calf is prescribed for an offering. Was the point of such a command, as many Jewish writers have supposed, to call back to his memory his sin of involvement with the golden calf? (See Exodus 32.) And since we are speculating about that matter, was the requirement of a "ram" for his burnt offering another attempt to help him recall that Abraham had sacrificed a ram, rather than his son Isaac? (See Genesis 22.) These two questions merely introduce intriguing connections and analogies to other parts of the canonical witness.

Meanwhile the people are to prepare themselves for a series of offerings, but only in their proper order: The sin offering is to come first, then the burnt offering, followed by the peace offering with the grain offering.

The purpose for all these offerings is clearly stated twice: "For today the LORD will appear to you" (v. 4c) and "So that the glory of the LORD may appear to you" (v. 6b). That is described in Exod 24:16-17. But in each of these statements, the emphasis falls on the theological concept of "the glory of the LORD."

The glory of the Lord is more than just the visible manifestation of God in fiery displays and effulgences of glory. It signals the very presence of God in the sheer weight of the divine person and the fact that God is immediately present.

Probably the cloudy pillar by day, which became a pillar of fire by night, was the visible manifestation of the fact of God's presence. The same glory that had settled on Mount Sinai when Moses was on the mount, and had led them in the wilderness thus far, is now the glory that will always be present in the tabernacle. Prior to this, it appears, God's glory had already descended on the finished tabernacle (see Exod 40:34), but now that same glory will ratify the ministry about to be undertaken at this place. With the evidence of divine glory, all worship, liturgy, and sacrifices will now be meaningful. Without that glory, worship, no matter how exact, will be worthless.

As the congregation draws near, especially in the persons of the elders who now act as leaders, Aaron begins by slaughtering the calf as his sin offering (v. 8). Then, in ritual details we rarely see in other passages, Aaron's sons assist him by collecting the blood in a basin; it is clear that these sons enter into the ministry with Aaron on the very same day he begins to serve. The blood is brought to Aaron; he, in turn, dips his finger into the blood and puts the blood on the horns of the altar in the courtyard. In that regard, the details once again differ slightly from those given in 4:3-12 (see the comment on 8:15). The rest of the blood is poured out at the base of the altar where the fat, the kidneys, and the covering of the liver are being totally burned as a sin offering to God. The remaining flesh and hide of the calf are to be burned up outside the camp (v. 11). This, then, is the high priest's public admission of his sinfulness and his desire to receive God's expiation for his sins.

As a sign of Aaron's complete self-surrender to God, he next offers a whole burnt offering (vv. 12-14). First his sons hand him the blood (which Aaron sprinkles against the altar on all sides), then they pass him the ram "piece by piece" (although Aaron first washes the unclean portions, such as the inner parts and the legs), and then they hand him the head—all of which are to be totally consumed on the altar to indicate his complete dedication to God.

Now that Aaron and his sons are in a right relationship with the Lord, they can begin to make atonement for the people. Four sacrifices are brought on behalf of the people: a goat as a sin offering to cleanse the altar (vv. 3, 15), a calf and a lamb for a whole burnt offering (vv. 3, 16), a grain offering (vv. 4, 17), and a cow and a ram as a peace offering (vv. 4, 18).

What is new and of importance in the discussion of these sacrifices is the *order* in which they are presented here: always first the sin offering, then the burnt offering with its grain offering, and last, as always, the peace offering. The sin offering provides the grounds for all the other offerings in that it offers both propitiation and expiation from all sin by the shedding of the blood of a substitute. The burnt offering symbolizes the offerer's full surrender to God just as the victim is totally given back to God as a whole burnt offering. Likewise, the grain offering symbolizes the consecration of the fruits of one's labors to God as a total dedication for God's use. Only then is it possible to announce that fellowship in the joy, peace, and life with God is now possible as God and mortals commune around the table of the shared sacrifice of the peace offering. The order of the sacrifices, then, is determined by a law of the spiritual life: Perfect fellowship with God in peace, joy, and life is possible only after one has fully consecrated to God all that one is and produces; but one is unable to consecrate anything to God until one's sin has been forgiven and the wrath of God against all unrighteousness has been satisfied.

This first day of divine services at the tabernacle ends with a double blessing from Aaron. In a motion characteristic of prayer directed toward God, Aaron raises his hands and blesses the people. Whether the words of the famous benediction that now appear in Num 6:24-26 were in use at that time is impossible to say. But the solemnity and joy of granting a blessing on the people are particularly detailed as a part of the priestly office in Deut 10:8. Not only is the tribe of Levi to carry the ark of the covenant and to stand before God to minister, but the Levites are "to pronounce blessings in [God's] name" as well.

To conclude the day, Moses takes Aaron into the tabernacle for the first time. Moses goes with Aaron, in all likelihood, to instruct him on how he is to burn incense on the golden altar, light the lamps, and set the bread of presence in order.

As both men emerge from the tabernacle, they once again bless the waiting congregation. Then the "glory of the LORD appeared

to all the people" (v. 23), and "fire came out from the presence of the LORD and consumed the burnt offering and the fat portions on the altar" (v. 24). This act stamps God's approval on the proceedings of the day and all that led up to it through the past week. No doubt, the sacrifices that Aaron has placed on the large altar are still burning and are not as yet completely consumed. But in an instant they are consumed by a divine fire, perhaps from the holy of holies where now God has taken up permanent residence. Such a fiery display must have made a most memorable impression on the minds of all who saw it: The burning of sacrifices symbolized the acceptance and response of the Lord, who had commanded that the offerings be brought.

Scripture frequently employs fire as the symbol of God's presence and work (see Deut 4:24; Ps 18:8-14; Ezek 1:4). That fiery presence can depict Messiah's coming in judgment (see Mal 3:2; Matt 3:11; Luke 3:16) or it can be the occasion of great joy, thanksgiving, surprise, and relief, as it is here in Lev 9:24. So overwhelmed with joy and adoration are the people that they let out a shout, even though they simultaneously fall face down in awesome respect and fear at the awfulness of God's mighty presence (cf. Judg 6:21; 1 Kgs 18:38; 1 Chr 21:26; 2 Chr 7:1).

Only on three other occasions has God shown approval and acceptance by sending fire in the OT: at the birth of Samson (see Judg 13:15-21), at the dedication of Solomon's Temple (see 2 Chr 7:1), and at Elijah's Mount Carmel contest with the prophets of Baal (see 1 Kgs 18:38). This is certainly a great conclusion to a most significant day in the life of Israel.

REFLECTIONS

Apart from all its pomp and ceremony, the purpose of this worship ritual rings so clear that it remains the key teaching point of the whole chapter: Worship that does not function in the light of the presence of God is worthless, empty, and vain. To miss the glory, i.e., the presence of God, is to miss everything in worship. The glory of God transforms ordinary ritual into divine worship. This leads to several other considerations.

1. Worship at its most profound level is communion with God, the experience of God's intense presence, what Leviticus calls "the glory of the LORD." Sometimes, however, we miss the glory of God in worship because we are looking for something too exalted. We want the sermon to move us to tears, the music to carry us to the heights, the prayers to reveal the secrets of our hearts. Occasionally, such profound experiences do happen in worship, but most of the time God is present to us in smaller, quieter, less-dramatic ways. A prayer phrase here, the face of a child over there, the curious way the hymn we least like nonetheless compels our attention—sometimes these are the vessels God chooses to convey glory.

2. Full consecration of persons and their works must precede fellowship with God. All too many worshipers have aimed at fellowship within the group as the primary purpose of worship without first counting the cost of loving self-surrender to God as a prerequisite for any and all fellowship—whether it be with God or with one another.

3. A cleansed conscience that has received God's atonement must precede a full consecration of the person and service for God. It is possible to give of oneself in numerous acts of self-devotion and sacrifice with an aim of exhibiting the love of God to others, yet such altruism may remain empty and hollow if it does not spring out of a heart motivated with the realization of the expiation and forgiveness that come from the One "who had no sin [but was made] to be sin for us" (2 Cor 5:21 NIV).

4. Aaron's concluding benediction is reminiscent of another high priest's conclusion to his ministry. When Christ had finished his earthly ministry, he too lifted up his hands and blessed his disciples as he ascended into heaven (see Luke 24:50).

LEVITICUS 10:1-20, THE DEATH OF NADAB AND ABIHU

COMMENTARY

10:1-7. While it is still the eighth day of the installation and inaugural ceremonies of the tabernacle services, the events of 10:1 unfold. Suddenly, for what reasons we do not know, the two eldest of Aaron's four sons, Nadab and Abihu, "took their censers, put fire in them and added incense; and they offered unauthorized fire before the Lord" (v. 1). In the midst of the most solemn and impressive set of ceremonies, on what might well have been one of the happiest days for Aaron and his family, all is tragically turned into a moment of deep loss and judgment.

We are unable to ascertain what precisely happened from the texts before us. Many suggestions have been posed. Some attach the blame to the *manner* in which the two sons lighted their firepans. The "unauthorized fire" or "strange fire" (אש זרה *'ēš zārâ*) is understood, in this view, to mean they used hot coals that did not come from the altar in the sanctuary courtyard. It is true, of course, that Moses was careful to warn Aaron on the

Day of Atonement to take "coals from the altar before the Lord" (Lev 16:12), just as he instructed Aaron to do on another occasion of the Korah, Dathan, and Abiram uprising (see Num 16:46).

Others suggest the problem may have been that Nadab and Abihu offered this fire at the wrong *time*. Moses' instructions were very specific with regard to the order of the sacrifices, but nothing here suggests that was the problem plaguing the two men. The event mentioned here no doubt took place toward the evening of that eighth day. Accordingly, the two men may have performed some ceremony that belonged to another part of the day.

Others have suggested that the *place* was incorrect. Perhaps they wanted to offer their incense on the golden altar, thereby usurping Aaron's sole privilege and designated task. Or perhaps they wished to go inside the veil to the holy of holies where only the high priest was allowed to go once a year.

The connection with strong drink and the possibility of *intoxication* cannot be ruled out, given its otherwise unexplained proximity and discussion in this very same context (10:8-11). This may have impeded the ability of the two brothers to think and act responsibly in a situation that called for their highest degree of alertness, caution, and sensitivity.

The more one studies this text, the greater the impression arises that the situation may have involved a combination of some or all of the above suggestions. One thing is certain: The offense is by no means accidental. There is a sudden reversal of everything that has been taught on the day to all of Israel. What is most holy and sacred to the Lord is suddenly trivialized in some unexplained way so as to make what has been set apart for God now common, trite, and secular.

Exodus 30:9 warns that no "strange incense" (KJV using the same adjective זרה *zārâ*, "alien," "strange") is to be offered on the altar before the Lord. Perhaps from this warning it should have been enough of an obvious inference that the same would apply to "strange/alien fire" offered to God.

The phrase at the end of v. 1, "which he did not command them" (literal translation), is the figure of speech known as *meiosis;* that is, a negative expression is stated when the opposite affirmation is emphatically implied (cf. Ps 78:50; Prov 12:3; 17:21). Thus, even though we may not be able to point to the precept that Nadab and Abihu expressly violate, what they do is clearly "contrary to [God's] command" (1 *d*).

What takes place, however, is certain and decisive. Fire comes out from the presence of God and consumes Nadab and Abihu. What has moments before been a sign of divine approval, acceptance, and approbation (as the fire falls on the sacrifice) is swiftly turned into an expression of divine disfavor and wrath. While still serving in their priestly tunics, the men are struck down. But the fire does not consume their tunics, for v. 5 notes that they are still in this priestly garb when they are carried outside the camp by Mishael and Elzaphan, the two sons of Aaron's uncle, Uzziel.

Moses uses this occasion to teach a powerful lesson on the holiness and worship of God (v. 3). Moses refers to something the Lord said at an earlier occasion, but a statement that is not an explicit part of the canonical record we now possess. Some think that the principle cited here may have been alluded to in Exod 19:22: "The priests, who approach the LORD, must consecrate themselves, or the LORD will break out against them" (NIV). Others suppose that the allusion is to Exod 29:43: "I will meet with the Israelites, and the place will be consecrated by my glory" (NIV). But these texts preserve only a certain tenor of the principle raised in Lev 10:3. Maybe that is all Moses means by his statement that the Lord spoke the following words.

The point is that those who by virtue of their office are called to draw near to God constantly place themselves in a perilous, as well as a privileged, position. Whatever they do or fail to do, they must bear in mind that God is absolutely unique above all other creatures. Any act, or failure thereof, that may detract from the deity's absolute holiness, and thus tend to treat God in a light, trite, or unthinking manner, would immediately expose those who draw near to possible danger. If God is not sanctified by those who are supposed to know best, by virtue of their constant opportunity to draw near in acts of serving the people for God, God will be sanctified in the eyes of the people by swift judgment and wrath upon all trivializers of the ministry.

Aaron's two remaining sons, Eleazar and Ithamar, are not allowed to handle the dead bodies of their two fallen older brothers, even though contact with the corpse of a close relative does not, in general, defile members of the priesthood (21:1-2). The reason for this prohibition, then, is not that they are on the threshold of commencing their ministries; instead, it is due to the fact that they are about to eat the "most holy" sacrificial meals of the offerings made that day (10:12-14).

Not only are they to refrain from carrying out the corpses, but Aaron and his sons are told not to "uncover" their heads or tear their garments in grief over what has happened (v. 6). The Hebrew root for "uncover," variously rendered as to "become unkempt" (NIV), "to dishevel" (NRSV), or to "bare" (TNK) their heads, is the word פרע (*pāra*). Its primary meaning is "to make free" or "to uncover"; accordingly, it must connote something like letting one's hair become disarrayed or disheveled while mourning for the dead.[59] Thus none of the usual signs of grief and mourning for the dead are to be seen among them as they minister at the altar. Failure to heed this command could have resulted in death to Aaron and his remaining sons as well as wrath on the whole congregation of Israel. Once again, the significance of corporate solidarity is illustrated in the way that the sins of the leaders could have a negative impact on the people, even though they have not personally done anything to provoke the negative response.

These priests are to continue on even in the midst of this dire emergency in their families because "the LORD's anointing oil [is] on [them]" (v. 7). This anointing signifies that the call to the service of God takes precedence over every other earthly affection. This injunction later on becomes law, as Lev 21:10, 12 demonstrates.

10:8-11. Immediately, the text plunges into a warning to Aaron and his sons about the evils of intoxication while ministering in the house of God. Surely, some link is present, or vv. 8-11 are left dangling with no context or setting. Even if one posits editorial insertions, they are extremely clumsy ones. No wonder, then, that older Jewish commentators thought there was a connection, and Nadab and Abihu had drunk wine to excess. In their view (and ours), this circumstance provides the occasion for the warning found here in vv. 8-11.

Even though the biblical text says that wine is given to humanity to cheer their hearts (see Ps 104:15; cf. Judg 9:13), it also contains some stern warnings against drunkenness. The text condemns drinking to excess and the resulting ugly, degrading, and foolish behavior (see Gen 9:20-27; Prov 23:29-35; 31:4-7; Isa 5:11-12; Amos 2:8).

But vv. 8-11 do not take up all these issues; they merely forbid priests to drink intoxicants while performing sacred tasks.

A question arises whether Israel knew about "strong drink" (שכר *šēkār*) at this time. The term may refer to any kind of intoxicating drink, whether made from corn, apples, honey, dates, or other fruit. Islamic peoples in many parts of the world refer to one of the four prohibited drinks as *Sakar*, meaning an intoxicating beverage. We also know that the ancient Egyptians made liquor from fermented barley.[60] So we can conclude that the technology for making strong or fermented drink was available at this time.

The reason given for this prohibition against wine and intoxicating drinks is that the priests are serving in the sanctuary. Intoxicants would cloud the mind and darken the understanding in such a way that priests would not be able to distinguish "between the holy and the common, between the unclean and the clean." Even though all things were created good by God, not everything is equally holy and equally dedicated to God. Some things have been "removed from the Temple" (the literal meaning of *profane*) and, therefore, are for common use. By maintaining this distinction between the two, the priests would continually remind themselves and their congregants of the wide gulf that yawned between a holy God and a sinning people.

10:12-15. The instructions given previously concerning the use of the grain offerings (6:18) and the peace offerings (7:30-34) are repeated. It would appear that Moses wants to remind Aaron and his sons anew about these matters in light of the events of the day. The emphasis falls on who might eat which portions of these sacrifices and where they must be eaten. But all of this has been stated previously. The oft-repeated category of "most holy" (v. 12) and the identity of the courtyard of the sanctuary as "a holy place" (v. 13) underscore the constant care taken to distinguish between the holy and the common, the clean and the unclean.

10:16-20. A misunderstanding erupts between Moses and Aaron's two sons, Eleazar and Ithamar, over the disposal of the goat of the sin offering. When Moses learns that this goat has been burned up rather than eaten in the holy place by the priests, he becomes angry. Since it is a sin offering, it is

---

59. Milgrom notes the Akkadian root *pertu* actually denotes "the hair of the head" (*Leviticus 1-16*, 608). Thus the Hebrew cognate *pr'* has something to do with the hair of the head. But what it is cannot be defined exactly because of the wide range of meanings for this root—from figurative contexts such as Exod 32:25 where the people were "out of control" (NIV; Hebrew *paru'*) to legal texts such as Lev 13:45; Num 5:18; Num 6:5.

60. This is reported by Herodotus 27.7. A similar claim, though extended throughout the ancient Near East, is made by Diosdorus Siculus in book 1 of Osiris. The Greek and Latin forms of *Sheker* and *Sikera* or *Sicera* may be the origins for English *cider*, a term used for fermented juice from apples. Eventually, the word *sugar* may have had its origins here as well.

"most holy" (v. 17); it should have been eaten in the sanctuary. Furthermore, its blood is not taken into the sanctuary (v. 18), as 4:16-18 requires. How can the guilt of the community be taken away (v. 17) when violations of what God commanded are allowed to take place? Verse 17 lays down an enormously important theological principle when it states that God had given the portion of the sin offering to be eaten in the sanctuary "to bear the iniquity of the congregation" (KJV). "To bear" is from the verb נשׂא (nāśā), "to lift up," "to bear away"). These sins are in some sense transferred to the priests on behalf of the people. It was to this role that the early church appealed in understanding Jesus Christ as the ultimate mediator who would come to bear our sins in his own body (see 1 Pet 2:24), the "Lamb of God, who *takes away* [bears away] the sin of the world" (John 1:29, emphasis added, NIV).

Apparently, Aaron had ordered his sons to burn the whole offering, so he seems to step in and take responsibility for any deviation from the command. But in Aaron's view, he has no other choice than to do what he has done. First, Aaron refers obliquely to the events of the day by saying, "Such things as . . . have happened to me" (v. 19). He deliberately avoids referring to his sons Nadab and Abihu by name.

But then Aaron conscientiously resists eating the sin offering in the holy place with his two youngest sons because he is not absolutely sure whether he and his sons will be permitted to do so on a day when God's wrath is revealed against his family. By saying this, he implies that he shared in the sinfulness of his two oldest sons when they sinned. Accordingly, even though Aaron and his two youngest sons have not personally sinned, their consciences are so awakened to the holiness of God, and to their tendency to sinfulness, that they hesitate to venture into areas where they have no explicit directions.

Moses also is unable to give an immediate answer to this query; therefore, he withdraws his accusations and remains silent. Where God has not spoken, God's servants do best to remain silent. A new principle is set forth, therefore, that would be appealed to on other occasions: Sometimes the circumstances alter what is often perceived at face value to be an unalterable law. Later on, David would have his men eat of the bread of presence when they were hungry and without any provisions, even though the law strictly limited that bread to be eaten only by the priests (see 1 Sam 21:1-9). Hezekiah would also make a temporary change in the rules for the time for eating the Passover due to extenuating circumstances (see 2 Chr 30:18-20).

Some have held that Aaron was uncertain about eating the portions of the sacrifice because he and his sons were in mourning. It is possible to infer from Deut 26:14 that mourners were not allowed to partake of devoted foods. Had this rule also been in effect at this time, perhaps Aaron had extrapolated an application of the same principle to his own situation. However, he and his sons had been warned against any outward sign of mourning, so it is doubtful that this explanation helps.

REFLECTIONS

1. One principle highlighted in this account about Nadab and Abihu's sin is that intentions, no matter how earnest and goodwilled they are, cannot be a substitute for genuine piety of the heart and obedience to the declared will of God.

2. Those who, by virtue of their office and ordination, are privileged constantly to approach God's presence are also exposed to danger when God is not honored through their ministries. That special sense of nearness to God is an opportunity that must not be defrauded in the worship experience, lest times of corporate worship by the group end up being mere will-worship, with God being created in the image of humans. The will and needs of mortals must not be substituted for a high view of God. The primary focus must be on the nature, works, and being of God, which must be central in all true worship.

3. The effect that disciplining Nadab and Abihu had on Aaron and his sons is the same result that the apostle Paul expected discipline would have on the members of the church at Corinth. In 2 Cor 7:11, Paul was pleased that godly sorrow experienced by the members there had led to earnest care, indignation against all sin, an alarm against evil, a genuine concern, and a desire to see that justice was done. In such instances, by the grace of God, that kind of godly sorrow leads to repentance without regrets.

4. If the penalty here seems to be unduly harsh, the response is that ministers, like the Aaronic priests, should be above all reproach (see 1 Tim 3:3, 8). Moreover, as stated in Luke 12:48, "To whom much has been given, much will be required" (NRSV). That is why James invoked the double indemnity rule for those who teach, for they are responsible not only for themselves, but also for those they teach (3:1).

5. The priests were to be good examples of distinguishing between the holy and the common. If they were not models in this most important area, the whole law of God would be made a mockery, and a holy God would quickly have been devalued into an ordinary person who "belonged to this age" (i.e., the literal meaning of *secular*). So significant were these words that the Lord spoke them directly to Aaron rather than going, as usual, through Moses.

LEVITICUS 11:1–15:33

THE REGULATIONS ON CLEAN AND UNCLEAN

OVERVIEW

The third major section in the book of Leviticus deals with the issue of clean and unclean and defilement by dead bodies. Few chapters in the Bible present more difficulties for the application of biblical materials to the modern day for the contemporary reader than Leviticus 11–15. But the religion espoused in this book is not limited to the spheres of the spirit and inner person; rather, faith is carried over into every mundane sphere of life.

Chapters 11–15 consider various types of uncleanness and how persons might be cleansed from their defiling and contaminating effects. The distinctions between the clean and the unclean are set forth under four headings: the clean and unclean foods (chap. 11); the uncleanness of childbirth (chap. 12); the uncleanness of skin and fungus diseases (chaps. 13–14); and the uncleanness of genital discharges (chap. 15).

But how do these chapters fit into the argument and plan of the book of Leviticus as it has come down to us in its present canonical form? Gordon J. Wenham[61] suggests that these five chapters had two vital links in their canonical context: one that looked back to 10:10, and the other that looked forward in anticipation of the ceremonies on the Day of Atonement in chap. 16, especially 16:16. The backward-looking text called for a distinction to be made between the holy and the common, between the clean and the unclean. But no less connected was the text in 16:16 declaring that the ceremonies on the Day of Atonement were necessary "because of the uncleanness . . . of the Israelites." Without the background explanation of chaps. 11–15, much of the significance of chap. 16 would be missed.

The narrative literary form in chaps. 8–10 and chap. 16 frames the intervening section of the laws, for the story of the Torah continues to be an ongoing narration that acts as the framing device for the whole. To argue that the laws provide the grid on which the narrative hangs is to reverse the logic; it is to run counter to the reality of the nation of Israel and its history.

In chaps. 11–15 we move from the sanctuary, which occupies the center of attention in chaps. 1–10, to the sphere of everyday mundane life of an Israelite. Immediately, we are struck by the emphasis on the concept of being clean or unclean. But neither notion originates in the physical realm or even the ethical sphere. In other words, being unclean has nothing to do with being dirty or being in need of a shower. Instead, these terms focus on the cultic and ritual sphere; they deal with being personally qualified and ready to meet God in worship.

Simply put, being clean makes a person fit and suitable for entering into the worship of God. Cleanness is not the same thing as holiness, though clean and holy are intimately linked. In fact, without cleanness, there can be no holiness. Thus, to be holy, one has to first experience the condition of ritual and ceremonial cleanness by means of washing, fasting, and abstaining from certain foods or sexual unions (see Exod 19:10; Num 11:18; Josh 3:5; 1 Sam 16:5).

Holiness, as we will discover in the Holiness Code of Leviticus 17–26, cannot be contrived, manipulated, or induced externally as if it is magical or a substance-like essence that one can put on to wear. On the contrary, holiness circumscribes a person as totally set apart for God's use. It marks a person, a

---

61. Wenham, *Leviticus,* 161.

community, or even an object as belonging entirely to the Lord. These holy persons are subject to God's will and are bound by the specific demands that God makes on each person so dedicated.

Another clue to the meaning of these terms can be found in the close relationship observed between uncleanness and sin. A person is rendered unclean by being involved in the following sins: being in contact with the worship of foreign gods (Jer 2:7, 23; 3:2; 7:30; Hos 6:10); consulting mediums or spiritists (Lev 20:6); using mourning rites borrowed from foreign cults (Lev 19:27-28; Deut 14:1); or engaging in religious prostitution (Lev 19:29). Other sources of uncleanness are related to various sexual phenomena and functions: discharges, menstruation, or copulation (Leviticus 15).

Given the understanding of God as a living person, additional forms of uncleanness involve coming into contact with a corpse (Lev 21:1-4, 11; Num 6:6-7; 19:11-16), a carcass (Lev 11:8, 11, 24-40), a grave (Num 19:16), or any skin or fungus disease (Leviticus 13–14). Each involvement temporarily disqualifies a person from entering into the presence of God for worship.

Although the emphasis on the external qualifications carries the potential danger that Israelite religion might be thought of only in terms of an externalization of faith, it is not meant to be left there. It has as its main thrust the attempt to call the community to a holistic concept of worship—one that involves the body, the soul, and the spirit. This linking of clean hands and a pure heart is evident in Psalms 15 and 24:4.

Leviticus 11:44 plainly states that the people are to be holy because the Lord is holy. Accordingly, the people are not to make themselves unclean by eating unclean things, such as creatures that crawl along the ground. But that text, helpful as it is in supplying the main rationale for the long list of foods included, does not explain why the unclean foods have a defiling effect.

This vacuum, as usually happens when this sort of phenomenon appears, has touched off a search for the principle behind the approval of some animals and foods and the disapproval of others.

The earliest explanation was a moralistic one given by Philo of Alexandria; his conclusion was that the laws were given to teach *self-denial*. To discourage excessive indulgence, certain foods were to be avoided. A thousand years later Maimonides, in partial agreement, made a similar case for *self-control*.

Others argued that the connection was a *mystical* one between the body and the soul. That thesis was perpetuated by an overly literal LXX translation of Lev 11:44 as, "You shall not defile your *souls.*" But the Hebrew original text often used "soul" (נפשׁ *nepeš*) as another way of saying the personal pronoun "you" or, as it appeared with a pronominal suffix here, "yourselves."

Some tried to take refuge in an *allegorical* interpretation of the animals mentioned here. Therefore, it was argued that the behavior and habits of some of the animals exercised certain influences on the character of those who ate them as food. Thus the revengeful character of the camel tended to impart a vindictive propensity in its eater. And the hog's predilections, it was claimed, rendered its eaters gross and sensual. But none of that could be demonstrated, and it usually struck most observers as being extremely fanciful. For instance, what can be said, given this view, of an unclean animal, such as a lion, being used as the symbol of our Lord?

Another approach has been to champion the view that the distinctions are purely *arbitrary*. God is the only One who knows the rationale behind these rules. The most we can say is that they were given to test our obedience.

In more recent times, many readers of Scripture favor another reason for the distinctions between clean and unclean; they argue that the underlying principle was *hygienic*. The divine mind knew of the dangers of tapeworm, trichina in pork, tularemia in rabbits, and infection and spoiling in shellfish, and therefore restricted all potentially dangerous foods for the sake of the health of Israel. That is why, so the argument goes, Jewish people tend to live longer than their fellow citizens, even when they live under sanitary conditions that are worse than those of their compatriots. Now all of this may be very close to some of the truth on this matter, but observing salutary *results* is not necessarily the same as discerning the *intent* for issuing these dietary restrictions.

The most celebrated solution offered to this problem in recent times has come from Mary Douglas.[62] Using the field of social anthropology, she suggests that uncleanness has a *symbolic* significance. When the social background is kept in mind, argues Douglas, certain natural groupings emerged. For those who shepherded sheep and goats, it was natural to regard those animals as clean. The animals in that class appeared to conform to the similar norms desired in humans. The holiness desired in mortals had as its corollary standards of cleanness desired in animals. The division between clean and unclean corresponded to the division between holy Israel and the Gentile world. Thus, for Douglas, the notion of wholeness or normality was the key to determining the distinctions in the animal realm: Those animals, birds, and fish that conform wholly to the class to which they belong are those that are "clean." Any deviation from normality within a particular class (such as insects walking on all fours, thereby creating confusion with other realms) rendered that member unclean. She illustrates this by saying that the dietary code "rejects creatures which are anomalous, whether living between two spheres, or having defining features of members of another sphere, or lacking defining features."[63] Only the clean species have all the criteria of their class. Douglas's view emphasizes the similarities between clean animals and righteous Israelites. However, Douglas's category of "normality" seems to run opposite to the creation account, where all creatures that came from God's hand were called "good." Even some of the animals that conformed to their own class were not called clean. Interesting and detailed as Douglas's proposal is, it does not answer many of these key questions.[64]

What are we left with? If none of these attempted explanations can supply us with the principle behind these rather esoteric laws, how can any contemporary application be made from directions so foreign to our own culture and times?

The answer may be simpler than all those that have been given thus far. It may well be that in addition to any hygienic *results*, which may have been attached as secondary reasons for these distinctive laws, their main purpose was to forever mark Israel off from all the other nations. The purpose, then, was to demonstrate Israel's *separateness*.

Nothing becomes more cumbersome and immediately marks one as set apart as the request for certain unique foods when it comes time to sit down around a table. The difference such dietary restrictions cause would always be present on almost every possible social contact that could be made with any other people in the ordinary course of daily events. Israel would be marked for all time by the oddities of diet and thus would ever be both an unwilling and a willing witness to a unique attachment to God. It was part of Israel's call to be separate and distinct from all the other nations. It was one more mark of that distinctiveness, both in calling and in mission for the nation.

Jacob Milgrom comes to a similar conclusion.[65] He calls attention to the three divine covenants, which he arranges in three concentric circles: the Noachic covenant made with all humankind (see Gen 9:1-11), the outermost circle; the covenant made with Israel (see Gen 17:2; Lev 26:42), the next circle; and the covenant of a lasting priesthood (see Num 25:12-15; Jer 33:17-22), the innermost circle of the three. These three circles, Milgrom advises, were matched by another set of three circles that divided up the animals: (a) all animals are permitted for all humankind, except their blood (see Gen 9:3-5); (b) the edible few are given to Israel (see Leviticus 11); and (c) from this edible group, only the domesticated and perfect specimens could qualify as sacrifices to the Lord (see Lev 22:17-25). Thus there was a congruency between the two concentric circles: all animals—humankind; few animals—Israel;

62. Mary Douglas, *Purity and Danger*, 53. Douglas follows the thesis set forth by the Emile Durkheim school, which contends that the customs and rituals of any society reflect its values. Therefore, the way a society's taxonomy works will afford us an insight into how that society's values work. Douglas applies Durkheim's theory to Leviticus 11, using her own theory of dirt, which is matter out of place. "Order" is fine; "disorder" is dirt. Douglas discovered that the Lele tribe of Africa had a very complex set of dietary regulations. This started her inquiry into Leviticus 11. Incidentally, A. S. Meigs, in the article "A Papuan Perspective on Pollution," *Man* 13 (1978) 304-18, gave a stinging criticism of Douglas's theory of dirt, arguing that many things may be out of place, but only a few pollute.

63. Mary Douglas, *Implicit Meanings: Essays in Anthropology* (Boston: Routledge & Kegan, 1975) 266.

64. For a critique of Mary Douglas's thesis, see Harris, "Leviticus," 2:526-30.

65. Milgrom, "[Excursus] E. The Ethical Foundations of the Dietary System: 3. The Prohibited Animals," in *Leviticus 1-16*, 718-36.

and sacrificial animals—priests. This bond between the choice of Israel and the choice of Israel's food is made explicit in Deuteronomy 14 where the chapter begins (v. 2) and ends (v. 21) in an inclusio that frames the proper foods with the theology that Israel is to be "a holy people." Moreover, this emphasis on separation appears four times in the scope of two and a half verses in Lev 20:24*b*-26. And specifically included in that description of holiness is the call for Israel to be separate from the nations and selective in diet.

The identical approach can be found as early as the *Letter of Aristeas,* written by a first-century BCE Egyptian Jew. It declared:

An additional signification [of the diet laws] is that we are *set apart* from all men. For most of the rest of mankind defile themselves by their promiscuous unions, working great unrighteousness, and whole countries and cities pride themselves on these vices. Not only do they have intercourse with males, but they even defile mothers and daughters. But we have kept apart from these things.[66]

We believe this explanation of separateness is the most meaningful explanation for these laws.

66. *Letter of Aristeas,* 151-52.

LEVITICUS 11:1-47, THE CLEAN AND THE UNCLEAN

COMMENTARY

The Torah contains two lists of clean and unclean animals: Leviticus 11 and Deut 14:3-20. The similarities between these two chapters constitute one of the greatest blocks of shared texts in the Pentateuch.

Naturally, this raises questions about which list came first and why two lists were needed. The prevailing view, following the late-nineteenth-century school of Wellhausen, is to treat Deuteronomy 14 as the more ancient of the two lists.

But is the prevailing view convincing? A better case can be made for giving Leviticus 11 the nod for priority. Several reasons in support of a reversal of the conventional wisdom on this point should be noted: (a) Leviticus 11:2-3 merely specifies quadrupeds, while Deut 14:4-5 proceeds to name ten such clean animals; (b) Lev 11:20-23 limits the edibles in one category to four types of flying insects, but Deut 14:20 opens it up to "any winged creature that is clean you may eat" (NIV); (c) Lev 11:4-6 constantly repeats the reason why certain animals may not be eaten, but Deut 14:7 feels no need to give such reasons (perhaps assuming that such information was already in hand); and (d) Leviticus 11 addresses only the Israelite, but Deut 14:21 must now reckon with the additional presence of the "resident alien," (גר *gēr*), who

dwells in their midst.[67] This alien is one to whom the carcass can be given or sold. There would have been no need for including such a provision when the Israelites were journeying in the wilderness in Leviticus, but as they come into residential life in Deuteronomy, the need is obviously present. We can even see a revision of an older provision found in Lev 11:39-40 that permitted Israelites to eat meat from dead animals that were clean, so long as they washed themselves after eating. But by the time Deut 14:21 was written, it had become an absolutely forbidden act; thus Deuteronomy must reflect a time after Leviticus was given a different type of cultural setting. Regardless of when the final form of Leviticus was fixed, it seems clear that the author of Deuteronomy 14 had a text of Leviticus 11, which he used.

The structure of Leviticus 11 falls into six divisions marked out in the Hebrew text by זה (*zeh,* "this" [masculine]), זאת (*zō't,* "this" [feminine]) and אלה (*'ēlleh,* "these"), in

67. This list is from Noordtzij, *Bible Student's Commentary,* 119-20. More recently, Milgrom concludes his "Excursus B. Deut 14:4-21, An Abridgment of Lev 11" by saying, "The cumulative evidence of this investigation [698-704] points, without exception, in one direction. All the additions, omissions, protuberances, inconcinnities, and inconsistencies that mark off Deut 14:4-21 from Lev 11 can be explained by one premise: D had the entire MT of Lev 11 before him, which he copied, altered, and above all abridged to suit his ideological stance and literary style" (*Leviticus 1-16,* 704).

vv. 2, 9, 13, 24, 29, and 46. The resulting outline is clean and unclean land animals (vv. 1-8); clean and unclean aquatic creatures (vv. 9-12); clean and unclean flying creatures (vv. 13-23); pollution from land animals (vv. 24-28); pollution from swarming creatures (vv. 29-45); and summary (vv. 46-47).

11:1-8. Surprisingly, both Moses and Aaron are addressed together as the chapter begins. Perhaps Aaron is included here (and in 13:1; 14:33; and 15:1) because the priests are particularly charged with "[distinguishing] . . . between the unclean and the clean" and with the task of "[instructing] the Israelites" (10:10-11).

The edible land animals are listed first in vv. 2-3. The hoof of these animals must be split, and they must be ruminants. These include the ox, the sheep, and the goat (see Deut 14:4); later, Deut 14:5 adds seven wild animals to this category.

Four other animals do not meet these criteria: the camel, the coney or rock badger, the hare or rabbit, and the pig. Some split the hoof (e.g., the pig) but do not "chew the cud" while others meet the reverse criteria. The ones chewing the cud, but without split hoofs, are the camel (the single-humped dromedary is intended here), the Syrian coney, and the hare. Of course, "chew the cud" does not mean a ruminant that possesses four stomachs. When Hebrew uses this term, it means the crosswise moving of the jaw while chewing, rather than any elaborate theory of multiple stomachs that allowed regurgitation and rechewing of the cud before it was swallowed and digested.

Were the four animals listed as unclean placed there because of hygienic reasons as potential disease carriers, as William Foxwell Albright proposes,[68] or were they excluded from the list of clean animals because, as Mary Douglas claims, they fail to meet the criteria of their taxonomy? Jacob Milgrom argues that neither of these two explanations fits since, in Albright's theory, these would merely be samples of other animals that would be unfit for the table, and in Douglas's theory, if they are listed because they do not fit the criteria, the list must be complete. However, Milgrom finds that only six animals

fall into the lists of vv. 4-8: The four listed in vv. 4-8 and two others. One of the two not listed is the llama, which is a ruminant, but its hoofs are not split. It is indigenous to South America (along with its relatives, the alpaca and the guanaco). The other is the hippopotamus, which is split-hoofed but is a nonruminant, existing in the marshy areas of the Philistine coast (perhaps discussed in Job 40:15-24). Milgrom concludes that the criteria came first and then the animals were disqualified. But in the case of the pig, he thinks that it was so abominated that the revulsion came first and then the criteria were made deliberately to disqualify it.[69]

Israel's diet, then, is to be limited to three domesticated species: cattle (the ox and the cow), sheep, and goats. These same three animal groups are also allowed in the innermost circle as sacrifices by the priests. Because Israel occupies the second of Milgrom's three concentric circles, seven additional wild animals are allowed. It is not always possible to identify all of the animals in the lists of Leviticus 11 and Deuteronomy 14, since, according to one expert, as many as 60 percent of the Hebrew terms for the creatures in these lists are unknown or are of dubious identification.[70] From the list of seven wild animals in Deut 14:5, the first three may be confidently identified: the roe deer, the gazelle, and the fallow deer. They are not to be used as sacrifices on the altar (although the faunal remains at an archaeological excavation of an altar room from the eleventh to eighth centuries BCE at Tel Dor revealed bone fragments of twenty-eight deer).[71] Both types of deer are also listed among the Ugaritic sacrificial animals at the Canaanite site of Ugarit.

11:9-12. The criteria for distinguishing which water creatures are clean or unclean are limited to whether they have fins and scales. Fish that possess both are free swimming and may be eaten (v. 9); but those without fins or scales may not (vv. 10-12). Those in the latter category are more likely to be scavengers that dwell in the mud bottoms; consequently, they might carry parasites.

68. William Foxwell Albright, *Yahweh and the Gods of Canaan* (Garden City, N.Y.: Doubleday, 1968) 175-81.

69. Milgrom, *Leviticus 1–16*, 728.

70. As cited by Wenham, *Leviticus*, iii.

71. As reported by Milgrom, *Leviticus 1–16*, 723, citing P. Wapnish and B. Hesse.

11:13-23. No principle is set forth in vv. 13-19 for distinguishing the birds that are clean. Although many of the modern equivalents for many of the creatures in this whole chapter are uncertain, based on the current state of our lexicographical knowledge, it is easy to see that the birds listed here are all birds of prey. They feed on carrion, or garbage, and nest and roost in ruins or desert places. Because they eat flesh with blood in it, Mary Douglas points out that they break the covenant law that they, along with mortals, were expected to keep and are therefore unclean.[72]

A distinguishing mark is set forth for all the noxious pests that fly and "walk on all fours" (v. 20). They too are said to be "detestable," just as the fish without fins and scales are (v. 12). The pesky insects included here are flies, mosquitoes, and cockroaches. The term שׁרץ (šereṣ) broadly includes all sorts of vermin: rodents, reptiles, worms, insects, and the like.

Only four locusts or grasshoppers are declared to be clean. Although we cannot give their modern equivalents, the added distinguishing feature that they possess over those that, like them, go on all fours is that they have "jointed legs for hopping" (v. 21). The key illustration of one who lived on locusts was John the Baptist (see Mark 1:6). No one in the OT is known to have eaten locusts.

11:24-47. At this point in the chapter, a change is apparent. Thus far the discussion has been about what is clean or unclean. But other types of questions come to mind as well. What happens if someone accidentally touches something unclean? What is one to do about dead things? And on and on go the questions.

Three sources of uncleanness that help answer some of the remaining questions are now listed: contacting carcasses of unclean land animals (vv. 26-28), contacting carcasses of animals that "move along the ground" (vv. 29-38), and contacting carcasses of clean animals (vv. 39-40). All dead animals are unclean, and they will pollute anyone who comes into contact with them. Unless an animal has been slaughtered in the prescribed manner, it will contaminate all who come

72. Douglas, *Purity and Danger,* 56.

into contact with it. This is true even for an animal that would otherwise be described as clean (v. 39). This pollution is temporary, lasting only until evening of the day it is contacted (vv. 24, 25, 27, 28, 31, 32, 39, 40).

Verse 32 presents a new situation. Any object used in one's everyday existence that comes into contact with the carcass of one of these animals itself becomes unclean. Articles made of wood, cloth, hide, or sackcloth are to be washed, but the easily replaced clay pottery has to be smashed and replaced (v. 33). Likewise, pottery kilns or ovens and cooking pots made of pottery are to be smashed for the same reason.

If, however, food is present in the pot when it is contaminated by a carcass, it would depend on whether the food is dry or wet. If it is dry, it remains clean; but if it is food prepared with water, it is unclean (v. 34). The same logic is used on seed; if the seed is wet and a carcass falls on it, it is defiled (vv. 37-38). The exception comes when running water is present, such as in a spring or a cistern; they are not polluted by such contact (v. 36).

What if a clean animal dies a natural death or is killed by other animals (vv. 39-40)? Contacting such carcasses does make one unclean; whoever eats of it or picks it up has to wash the clothes and remain unclean until evening. Leviticus 17:15 increases the stringency of this rule further by requiring the person to bathe as well. Later rabbinical thinking directed that it was only the flesh that defiled; but the hide, bones, and horns were exempt from this injunction. However, Lev 7:24 exempts only the fat for use from clean animals found dead or torn by wild animals. Even the fat is not to be eaten but used only for other purposes.

This chapter concludes with one rule, apparently returning to the cases mentioned in vv. 20-23 and 29-38 (especially v. 31): "Every creature that moves about on the ground is detestable" (v. 41). Here is the summary of the whole case in this complicated chapter. Israel is to be different because it has been called to be holy (v. 44). This call to holiness is stressed by its repetition in the space of two verses (44-45). It will appear in this direct form of "be holy, because I am holy" three more times in this book (Lev 19:2;

20:7, 26). Indeed, here is the sole purpose for all of the distinctions between the clean and the unclean. God called Israel to be separate and distinct from everything else so that Israel might carry out the mission given in the Abrahamic covenant: "In you all the families of the earth shall be blessed" (Gen 12:3*b* NRSV).

REFLECTIONS

1. The Levitical food laws were the physical expressions of the call for holiness in the totality of Israel's life. The laws were meant to make Israelites sensitive to the need to distinguish between the sacred and the secular in every area of their lives. Holiness could not be practiced merely in the religious realm, with all other areas free and open only to the common. God looked for wholeness, completion, and separateness in every aspect of one's life-style.

The distinction between clean and unclean reminded Israel of its election to be a holy people called for a holy purpose. Similarly, in the NT believers are called to be part of a holy people, a chosen race, a royal priesthood, and a holy nation (see 1 Pet 2:9). Just as Israel was reminded of this fact in the very mundane act of eating, so Christians are to put their minds "on things that are above, not on things that are on earth" (Col 3:2 NRSV). Holiness of life must penetrate the secular, as well as the sacred, realm of existence.

2. The NT teaches that these food laws, as was true of all of the ceremonial law, are no longer binding on Christians. Since observance of these laws marked one as a faithful member of the Jewish nation, the Gentiles did not share in this mark of identification. This is not to say that no abiding principles remained valid for all times and peoples; it merely removed the necessity of rigid observance of all its details.

In Mark 7:19, Jesus "declared all foods clean" (NRSV). By so saying, Jesus abrogated the distinction that had held up to this time between clean and unclean foods. The apostle Peter was surprised to learn this same principle in his contact with the Gentile Cornelius (see Acts 10:11-16). Peter had to be told three times that he was not to call common or unclean what God had cleansed. It finally dawned on Peter that, while it had been previously unlawful for a Jew to associate with or to visit anyone of another nationality, "God [had now] shown [him] that [he] should not call any man impure or unclean" (Acts 10:28 NIV).

The apostle Paul enlarges on the theology of clean and unclean when he affirms, "As one who is in the Lord Jesus, I am fully convinced that no food is unclean in itself. But if anyone regards something as unclean, then for him it is unclean" (Rom 14:14 NIV); and "Food does not bring us near to God; we are no worse if we do not eat, and no better if we do" (1 Cor 8:8 NIV). Paul's grand conclusion is: "So whether you eat or drink or whatever you do, do it all for the glory of God" (1 Cor 10:31 NIV). The call for holiness and promoting the glory of God has not lessened between the OT and the NT; only the means we use to demonstrate it. The call for holiness affects all of life, even though there is no longer a specified list of clean or unclean foods that we must honor.

LEVITICUS 12:1-8, THE UNCLEANNESS OF CHILDBIRTH

COMMENTARY

While chap. 11 deals with uncleanness that is outside humans in the external world, chaps. 12–15 deal more with uncleanness found within the human constitution itself and not in the outside environment. The problem of cleanness for a holy people is not merely one of contact with the external world, but also pollution that comes from within. This double-edged confrontation with the demands of holiness also teaches Israel to be aware of the two sources from which sin might arise: both within and outside the person.

The structure of this brief chapter is as follows: command to Moses (v. 1); uncleanness due to childbirth (vv. 2-5), including birth of a son (vv. 2-4) and birth of a daughter (v. 5); sacrifices after the time of purification (vv. 6-7); and alternative sacrifices for the poor (v. 8).

This brief law prescribes the period of purification after a woman has given birth and the sacrifices she is to offer at the completion of these days.

The law begins by using the resultative form of the Hebrew verb "to sow seed." In the niphal stem of this verb, it usually means "to become pregnant" or "to conceive" (cf. NIV). But in the resultative form (as it appears in Gen 1:11-12, "plants bearing seed" [NIV]), it denotes something like "produces offspring" or, in the stative form of the resultative, "comes to the completion of her pregnancy" and gives birth to a son.

This law continues with the provision that the mother who delivers a son remains unclean for seven days, similar to her condition after her monthly period. This connection with her monthly menses is made in vv. 2 and 5. That law is given in greater detail in 15:19-24.

In the week following the birth of a male, the woman is not only unclean in herself, but anyone or anything that touches her is unclean as well. She is not allowed, either, to touch any hallowed thing or to come into

the sanctuary. Presumably, she is not allowed marital relations with her husband or contact with persons in her household.

On the eighth day the son is circumcised. Even though the mother must not enter the sanctuary or contact any sacred things for another thirty-three days, she can reestablish normal relations with persons in her household. The circumcision of her son cuts her days of purification in half.

Circumcision, of course, had been given as a sign of God's covenant in Gen 17:10-14. The rite of circumcision, as such, was not unknown in the ancient world. According to Jer 9:25-26, it was known among the Egyptians, Edomites, Ammonites, Moabites, and Arabs. In Hellenistic times in Egypt, it was limited to the priests. Everywhere else, outside Israel, it appeared to have functioned as a puberty rite that prepared a man for marriage. Thus Ishmael was circumcised at age thirteen (see Gen 17:25). This may have been the situation in Israel prior to the covenant made with Abraham, for Hebrew philology tends to support that thesis. In Hebrew a "son-in-law," or a "daughter's husband," literally means "one who undergoes circumcision" (חתן *ḥātān*), while "father-in-law," or "wife's father," is literally "circumciser" (*ḥōtēn*). Apparently, then, God took a ceremony already known and reconstituted it as a new symbol of a special relationship with Israel and as a mark of the covenant.

If the newborn is a daughter, both periods of time are doubled; the seven days are stretched to fourteen, and the remaining thirty-three are increased to sixty-six. This doubling of the time has been an occasion for much speculation. We must be careful not to think that a greater sinfulness is attached to a female than to a male. If that is so, why are the sacrifices specified at the end of the period the same for both a male and a female? Furthermore, the fact of childbirth itself involves no sin offering. Rather, contrary to the normal order, a whole burnt offering is made first, and then a sin offering is given on the forty-first or eighty-first day, depending on whether the baby is male or female.

Those who flee to Leviticus 27 to argue that the valuation of males as opposed to females is two to one make the mistake of confusing the value of female *services* at the sanctuary in comparison to male services. But the text gives no support to those who try to establish intrinsic worth of the sexes based on the values established there. This passage does not prove that women are inferior to men.

Nevertheless, the real reason for the doubling of the time for purification escapes modern interpreters. *Jubilees* 3:8-14 and the Mishnah give an etiological explanation for the difference: Adam was created at the end of the first week of creation and entered Eden on the forty-first day, while Eve was created at the end of the second week and was finally admitted to the Garden of Eden on the eighty-first day.

Occasionally, some of the rabbis have attempted a biological explanation: The male embryo is completely formed in forty-one days but the female in eighty-one. Aristotle said the male was formed in forty days but the female in three months; Hippocrates answered with thirty days for the male and forty-two days for the female.

Whatever the reason, a great deal of comparative material could be cited to indicate that the parturient undergoes a longer period for a girl than for a boy.[73] But it must be stressed once again: A longer period of time for purification is not necessarily a sign of lesser social standing or worth. This is jumping categories and assuming that we know the reasons for the differences in time duration—which we do not know!

Certainly, we must not conclude that there is anything unclean or sinful in bearing children. Has not the Creator approved and blessed this function (see Gen 1:28)? The difficulty that this passage, and others like it in Leviticus 15, raises is that acts that are both blessed and approved are also said in this context to bring defilement. The point must be a

symbolic or typological one rather than a condemnation of either the act of sexual union or the children who are born from it. What this text does say—in fact, it emphasizes three times in vv. 4-5 and 7—is that it is the blood of the woman's discharge that makes her unclean. That is vastly different from saying that the sexual union, or the child who was born, makes her unclean. In any case, we must not confuse ritual impurity with sinfulness or moral worth.

Many cultures preserve the same views about the postpartum state. The best explanation to date is the one that equates all bodily discharges, regardless of their cause, with death. The acts of begetting and giving birth present the very moments in time when life and death come together. Since the loss of blood can sometimes lead to death, the threat is always present in childbirth. And any discharge is always a reminder of what could be seen in decaying corpses: Discharges can cause corruption. Hence the connection here with the loss of blood, even though blood, on the other hand, is also the most effective means for reconciling the sinner with God. Therein lies the mystery of this book.

Two offerings are prescribed at the completion of the mother's purification—a burnt offering and a sin offering. It is surprising that a burnt offering is placed first when the usual order prescribed in these offerings is to deal with the sin question first (see the commentary on 9:2-4). The reversal of that pattern here adds further evidence to the point that childbearing in itself is not sinful. The whole burnt offering is one of dedication to God and gratefulness for God's goodness during the delivery and God's protection of the child during the critical days of infancy.

The second offering is a sin offering to "make atonement for her" (vv. 7-8). Is this to bring her back into fellowship with the living God after she has been absent for forty to eighty days? One thing for sure, the external cessation of the flow of blood is somehow connected with her being declared ceremonially clean after the sacrifice of the sin offering. Perhaps the lesson to be learned is not that the act of conception is sinful, but that all who conceive are also at one and the same time sinners; even those born cannot escape the sinful human condition (see Ps 51:5).

---

73. See Milgrom for additional sources and examples (*Leviticus 1-16*, 750). In this century, a physician has attempted to give a medical reason for the postnatal discharge being longer for the delivery of females than males, but nothing there justifies a doubling of the time. See D. I. Macht, "A Scientific Appreciation of Leviticus 12:1-5," *JBL* 52 (1933) 253-60.

Provision is made for those who, like Mary in Luke 2:21-24, are too poor to offer the expensive offering of a year-old lamb. Two doves or two young pigeons can be sub- stituted, one for the burnt offering and one for the sin offering. How graciously God con- tinues to look out for persons who are desti- tute and have very little of this world's goods.

REFLECTIONS

1. The male baby was circumcised on the eighth day; but why that day? We would have guessed that the seventh day would have been chosen, for even though it is the Sabbath, babies will still be circumcised if that is when the eighth day comes. The sug- gestion here is that since circumcision had a spiritual impact by means of the associated idea of a circumcision of the heart (see Deut 10:16; Jer 4:4; Rom 2:29), so eight was a number symbolic of the new creation on the first day of the week. So frequently in the feast days do we see not only the seventh day but also the eighth day being described as a day holy to the Lord. There may be a typological anticipation of the new covenant, with its pointing to the first day of the week when Christ arose from the dead, he who is called the Firstfruits of all who will one day likewise be raised by him from the dead.

2. Love, marriage, and human sexuality are never described in the Bible as dirty, unclean, or sinful. The discussion in this chapter on the discharge of blood does not challenge the testimony of Scripture elsewhere that sexual love is a good gift to be cherished.

3. An estimate of the low status of women in the OT receives a bad rap when pas- sages like this one or Leviticus 27 are used. Proverbs 31, with its poem of the "woman of valor," demonstrates that the ancient Israelite woman wielded power in the home equal to that exercised by her husband. Those who cite the tenth commandment (see Exod 20:17; Deut 5:21) to demonstrate that a wife was merely a husband's "chattel" or possession overlook the fact that the wife is listed first, not as part of the possessions of the husband, but because she is the first-named member of the household. This point is confirmed by the fact that a wife could never be sold, even if she was a captive in war (see Deut 21:14).

LEVITICUS 13:1–14:57, THE UNCLEANNESS OF SKIN AND FUNGUS DISEASES

COMMENTARY

Leviticus 13–14 takes up various patho- logical phenomena referred to by the Hebrew term צרעת (ṣāraʿat), originally understood as a "stroke," from an alleged verbal root that implies someone is "struck [by God]." This etymology, however, remains elusive. The Greek translators rendered the Hebrew term as λέπρα (lepra), meaning "a scaly condi- tion," which in turn was introduced into the Vg. Apparently, during the Middle Ages lepra was identified with the disease we now call leprosy. Formerly, the Greeks referred to this same disease as *elephantiasis Graecorum* or *elephas*.

A nineteenth-century Norwegian physi- cian named Hansen identified the micro- organism (*Mycobacterium leprae*) that causes the real leprosy (1871), so it has been customary to refer to that disease as Hansen's Disease, or Hansenitis. Under most circum- stances, Hansen's disease is not contagious. It develops slowly and exhibits distinctive characteristics. It changes color; It develops growths on the skin; and most uniquely of all, the affected parts experience a loss of sensitivity to pain. In extreme cases, the extremities, the nose, the eyes, and the hair rot and fall away.

Hansen's disease is known in only two principal types. The nodular or lepromatous form is characterized by the appearance of soft, spongy lumps on the skin and a general thickening of the skin tissues. Often these lumps will develop into painless ulcers that secrete pus if they are left unattended. Meanwhile, the mucous membranes of the nose and throat begin to degenerate, affecting, in the disease's advanced stages, other internal organs. The other form of Hansen's disease is the anesthetic or tuberculoid variety. This form is less severe, but its main telltale sign is a degeneration of nerves in the skin. This results in a discoloration of patches of skin that no longer have any sensation. Frequently, ulcers develop on these affected patches. In severe cases the extremities fall off. Often this disease lasts as long as thirty years. The favored medication for Hansen's disease is chaulmoogra oil, a derivative from the seed of an Indian shrub. Today various antibiotics have been used and some unusual results have come from the use of thalidomide.[74]

Clinical leprosy has been around for a long time. Some have supposed its existence in India and China in 4000 BCE. The disease is attested in Mesopotamia in the third millennium BCE, and there is at least one case of it in an Egyptian mummy.

The most difficult question for the exegete is whether the Hebrew term ṣāraʿat is to be equated with Hansen's disease. Interestingly enough, even though everyone will agree that ṣāraʿat is of uncertain etymology, almost all modern commentators are adamant on the point that it cannot mean leprosy. Why there is such intransigence on this one aspect of the argument is baffling unless it is to protect modern sufferers of this malady from the stigma of being under the judgment of God.

Ṣāraʿat surely includes many more ailments than Hansen's disease, but it would appear that Hansen's disease is one of them. In the Greek world lepra was a generic term

for multiple skin diseases, just as the word cancer is used today as a generic term to describe any type of malignant growths. But there are numerous types of cancer, some that respond to treatment and some that do not. Therefore, ṣāraʿat is probably also a general term for a wide class of skin diseases, one of which no doubt includes leprosy.

Most render ṣāraʿat as "scales" or a "scaly [affliction]." Medical personnel who have studied these chapters have come up with a variety of suggestions for the plethora of diseases described under the general term ṣāraʿat. Among the suggestions have been eczema, psoriasis, impetigo, favus, and vitiligo. Yet no one of these identifications has commanded the agreement of the rest of the scholarly community. For example, some complain that such chronic skin diseases as these will not disappear or even change within a one- or two-week period when the priest examines those suffering from these so-called scaly conditions in chap. 13. Therefore, Jacob Milgrom settles simply for "scale disease" as his translation for the Hebrew ṣāraʿat.[75] We are in general agreement with this conclusion, except that Milgrom is too certain, on very slim grounds, that one manifestation of this scale disease was not leprosy.[76] But this conclusion is too confident in an area where all must admit a great deal of puzzlement. Others, such as J. Preuss,[77] are not that confident and do not hesitate to include leprosy in this category.

There are several reasons for equating ṣāraʿat with leprosy, at least in some of the biblical texts. First, except for Lev 13:9-11, only the earliest stages of the disease are described; therefore, some of its distinctive features that come at the end of the disease are not yet present. Second, since it was desirable to get the earliest possible identification of leprosy, other forms of skin disease were noted and acted upon promptly; not everything described here is leprosy. Third, the objection that highly contagious persons like the assumed leprous Naaman and Gehazi would not be left to walk around in society is countered by the fact that modern medical

74. See the following discussions of leprosy and skin diseases in the Bible: S. G. Browne, *Leprosy in the Bible* (London: Christian Medical Fellowship, 1970); E. V. Hulse, "The Nature of Biblical 'Leprosy' and the Use of Alternative Medical Terms in Modern Translations of the Bible," *PEQ* 107 (1975) 87-105.

75. Milgrom, *Leviticus 1–16,* 817.
76. Milgrom, *Leviticus 1–16,* 816.
77. As noted by Milgrom, *Leviticus 1–16,* 816. J. Preuss, *Biblisch-talmüdische Medizin,* trans. F. Rosner (New York: KTAV; reprint, New York: Sanhedrin, 1978). The original edition came from Berlin (S. Karger, 1911).

opinion is not at all sure that leprosy is that contagious.

The conditions exhibited in other parts of Scripture seem to indicate something more serious than a mere case of psoriasis. Aaron's words to Moses are almost incomprehensible if Miriam was not struck with leprosy, for he pleaded, "Do not let her be like a stillborn infant coming from its mother's womb with its flesh half eaten away" (Num 12:12 NIV). Surely these words answer the objection that the use of the Hebrew word *ṣāra'at* (see Num 12:10*b*) is never connected with rotting or mutilation of the body. Psoriasis is bad enough, but it never caused half the flesh to be eaten away. Healing a case of leprosy, complained the king of Israel when a letter arrived asking him to heal the foreign enemy leader Naaman of his "leprosy" (2 Kgs 5:1), was equated with being "God . . . [with the ability to] kill and bring back to life" (2 Kgs 5:7 NIV). No doubt Naaman had exhausted all the regular avenues for help in Syria, and he remained uncured. His attitude indicated that his problem was something more serious than a scaly skin condition.

We conclude that leprosy is mentioned in this chapter, especially where the person is declared to be "unclean," but a vast number of other skin conditions is also represented by the one Hebrew term *ṣāra'at*.

Leviticus 13:1-59 provides a description of various scaly diseases: discoloration (vv. 2-8); swellings (vv. 9-17); ulcers (vv. 18-23); burns (vv. 24-28); ringworm (vv. 29-37); rashes (vv. 38-39); baldness (vv. 40-44); life-styles of certified carriers (vv. 45-46); and scaly disease in clothing (vv. 47-58).

Chapter 14 rehearses cleansing rituals for scaly diseases, particularly cleansing ritual after healing (vv. 2-31) and cleansing ritual for houses (vv. 34-53).

13:1. The descriptions of the diseases that follow in chaps. 13–14 are not to be judged by the state of ancient learning at that time or as the product of folklore and pagan therapeutic practices. Leviticus 13:1 decisively affirms that the Lord reveals these matters to both Moses and Aaron. This material is not to be compared to the Greek temples and the god Asclepius, the deity of healing. The role of Aaron and his sons in these matters is entirely ritualistic; there is no attempt at giving medical treatment or cures. Thus chaps. 13–14 do not present a combination of a religious observance along with a center for medical treatment. The concern, as in this whole section of chaps. 11–15, is to present all persons in such a condition as to make them qualified and fit to enter into the worship of God as holy persons.

13:2-8. The first type of scaly disease is that of discoloration. As soon as an area of skin on the body changes its appearance, appearing to be different from the skin around it, especially if the hair in the area turns white, the person is placed under quarantine for a week (v. 4). Both forms of Hansen's disease start with a pink or white discoloration of the skin; that appears to be what is suspected here. If at the end of that first week the symptoms are inconclusive, the person must be isolated for yet another week before being examined by the priest and declared to be clean. If subsequent to the person's being pronounced clean the infection begins to spread, the person must go to the priest again and be pronounced unclean. This first test applied by the priest, then, turns on two criteria: Has the hair turned white? Is the affected area deeper than the skin? The person who is pronounced clean may have had no more than a rash or an allergic reaction. Once pronounced clean, a person can resume a normal life after washing all the clothing.

13:9-17. The second type of scaly disease involves swelling. In this case, the diagnosis involves sores on the skin that are abnormally white mixed in with some patches of normal color. In this situation, the whitened membranous cavity has also turned the hair white, and there is a lesion exhibiting ulcerating tissue.

This is a "chronic skin disease" (v. 11) and may be a documented case of Hansen's disease. Typically in Hansen's disease, the hairs growing on the affected area break off, split, or become depigmented. Also, in that disease, the shiny white vesicles rupture and discharge a white substance. This is probably the nodular or lepromatous form of leprosy (vv. 9-11).

But if the skin condition covers a person's whole body from head to foot (vv. 12-17)—yet no swellings, sores, lesions, or ulcerations are connected with it—it is probably something like vitiligo (*acquired leucoderma*), a condition where the skin loses its normal color and becomes white. Since it is only a condition where the skin loses its pigmentation, this individual can be pronounced clean. But should sores and lesions break out subsequently, that person's status would be changed from clean to unclean.

The constant emphases of chaps. 13–14 are on being clean and being unclean. In these two chapters alone, variations of "clean" (טהר *ṭāhēr*) appear thirty-six times while forms of "unclean" (טמא *ṭāmē*) occur thirty times. Only four times does the word טמא (*nirpā*), "be healed") occur.[78] Accordingly, we are involved in ritual questions here and not medical ones.

13:18-23. Another condition involves a boil or an ulcer on the person's skin that has healed and then suddenly erupted where the ulcer had been. If there is discoloration of the hair, it is treated as being very serious and once again could have been a clinical form of leprosy. But if the swelling is pale, not deep, and without any white hairs, it is a minor inflammation of old scar tissue. It might be no more than staphylococci or another skin disease known as carbuncle. In this case the priest may pronounce the person clean.

13:24-28. Similar provisions are made for suspicious symptoms following a burn. When a burn produces a pustule, it presents a potentially unclean condition, especially when the hair changes color and the infection penetrates deep into the layer of skin that carries the nerves. The quarantine procedures are the same once again: seven days in isolation with an examination by the priest. If the infection has spread, that one is pronounced unclean; however, if there is no change in the affected area and it has not spread, the priest is to pronounce the person clean (v. 28).

13:29-37. Still another type of skin disease involves an "itch" on the scalp, and also in the beard for men. This condition is serious enough to be called a נגע (*nega*, "a plague"; v. 29 KJV; cf. NIV). In v. 30 it is called a נתק (*neteq*), from the root meaning "to tear off"; in this context it means any tearing off of scabs by scratching. Some have rendered it "scall," meaning any scaly or scabby disease

of the skin, even though the word technically refers to the condition of the hair follicles. It is a situation where the hair follicles are being "torn" from the scalp after "splitting."

The critical telltale sign in this instance is the presence of yellow hair, a condition characteristic of favus. Favus belongs to the ringworm group of afflictions (*tinea tonsurans* or *tinea favosus*). Ringworm is usually found among children and is contracted by a fungus found around animals. Normally, this ringworm invades the scalp, penetrating the skin and forming yellow saucer-like crusts. It is an infectious disease that requires treatment.[79] Others, less convincingly, have suggested that it is a severe case of acne.

Verse 31 is problematic, for as it stands it does not represent the opposite of v. 30, as we would expect. If v. 30 has recessed lesions and yellow hair in the affected area, the reverse of this would be no recessed lesions and no yellow hair in v. 31. However, v. 31 has no recessed lesions and no black hair. C. F. Keil suggests emending the Hebrew text from שחר (*šāḥōr*, "black") to צחר (*ṣāhōr*, "yellow").[80] But such a change would be unnecessary since it fails to understand the progressive stages of moving into the state of being declared clean. Verse 30 records two symptoms, but in v. 31 it has been reduced to only one symptom: the absence of normal black hair, a condition that equals the presence of yellow hair, even though the other symptom has now left the person. Since a final determination cannot be made as yet, the quarantine is continued.

13:38-39. These verses raise another case. Patches of skin, in this example, go completely white. In Hebrew it is termed בהק (*bōhaq*, "brightness"). Here the hair is not discolored, and it is only skin deep. The RSV uses the obsolete English word *tetter* for the set of skin disorders represented here. They would include eczema, impetigo, acne, and perhaps herpes simplex. The person is pronounced clean.

13:40-44. While ordinary baldness is not equated with anything unclean, another type

---

78. Milgrom, *Leviticus 1–16*, 817, quoting the statistical work of Wright and Jones.

79. I am indebted to R. K. Harrison, *Leviticus: An Introduction and Commentary* (Downers Grove, Ill.: InterVarsity, 1980) 144-45, for his clear discussion on this point and on several other key points in this chapter. His discussion of Leviticus 13 is one of the best I have seen.

80. C. F. Keil, *The Pentateuch* (Grand Rapids: Eerdmans, 1950) 2:381.

of baldness evidences reddish-white membranous cavities on the scalp. If the sore begins to ooze, it probably is serious and belongs to the types of skin diseases that make a person unclean. The rest of the procedure is the same as for all the other cases.

13:45-46. When the diagnoses of these skin diseases find that they are defiling, sufferers must rip up their clothes, let their hair become unkempt, and, while covering their lips, cry, "Unclean! Unclean!" to anyone who approaches them. Moreover, they have to live alone outside the camp in isolation from the congregation. All three of these actions—tearing the clothes (cf. Gen 37:34; 2 Sam 1:11), messing up the hair, and covering the lower part of the face (cf. Ezek 24:17, 22; Mic 3:7)—are signs of mourning for the dead. So serious is the state of uncleanness that it is similar to the state of death. Living outside the camp is not equivalent to our modern idea of "getting away from it all," as Gordon Wenham reminds us, but is living in the place most removed from the presence of God, a place to which the sinner and the impure were banished (Lev 10:4-5; Num 5:1-4; 12:14-15; 31:19-24).[81]

13:47-58. The discussion moves from skin diseases to types of mold that affect clothing and other household articles. However, the same word that has been used for the "scaly diseases" (צרעת *ṣāra ʿat*) of the skin is used for abnormal surface conditions that show fungoid or sporoid infections. The operating principle is that disease, like all forms of uncleanness, is transmitted by contact (cf. Lev 11:24-40).

The presence of a greenish or reddish mold in the warp and woof of the fibers of a garment, in an animal skin garment, in a household article, or in the walls of a dwelling was enough to place it under suspicion of the regular seven-day quarantine. The reference to "the warp and woof" (vv. 48-49, 51-53, v. 56-59) seems strange here since it cannot refer to two different types of yarn, in that Israelites were forbidden to mix yarns and material in garments (see Deut 22:11). But the reference to the warp is to the vertical, drawn threads on the loom, and the woof designates the threads woven in by means

of the shuttle, going across horizontally. The mold or mildew, then, is not just a surface matter; it has penetrated into the very fabric itself.

The process for declaring an article clean or unclean is once again invoked. After the examination of the garment or article, each is shut up for a week. If at the end of that time the mold has spread, the article is declared unclean and has to be burned (v. 52). But if the mildew or mold has not spread, the priest orders it to be washed and isolated for another seven days. And if after another week's wait there is no improvement or the damage has spread, it is destroyed.

13:59. The concluding verse of this chapter reiterates the theme of this section: These are the regulations on clean and unclean. Clearly, the law of cleanness does not focus solely on the spiritual aspect of cleanness; rather, it puts both physical well-being and spiritual vitality together and demonstrates that men and women worship God holistically. It is impossible in this view, either to be holy or to worship a holy God without meeting the conditions for holiness by being made clean.

14:1-32. It would be a serious blow to the picture of God's gracious character if chap. 13 were to stand by itself with no hope for restoration and cleansing once someone is found to be unclean. Chapter 14 provides the companion piece to chap. 13. It deals with the ceremonies for the restoration of the healed leper or fellow sufferer of scaly diseases.

The ceremonies for the restoration of these former sufferers are staged in two parts. The first takes place outside the camp. The second takes place inside the camp on the eighth day following the first ceremony. This latter ceremony consists of offering every major type of sacrifice except the peace offering. After being anointed, the newly declared clean worshiper is once more a full member of the covenant of God with all its rights and responsibilities.

14:2-9. First comes the ritual outside the camp. Since the individual is still unclean in the sight of the law, it is impossible, to go to the priest or to the sanctuary inside the camp. Instead, one has to summon the priest to come outside the camp and examine the skin.

If the priest is convinced that the person is cured, two live clean birds are brought to the priest along with some cedar wood, scarlet yarn, and hyssop. Then the priest orders that one bird be killed over a clay pot filled with fresh water taken from a stream or spring that is flowing. The blood of the slain bird is received in this clay pot with fresh water. Next, the other bird, the cedar wood, the scarlet yarn, and the hyssop are all dipped into the clay pot with the blood of the slain bird. The priest then takes the hyssop, perhaps bound with the cedar and the scarlet yarn, and sprinkles blood from the clay pot seven times on the one newly pronounced clean. Then the bird stained with the blood of the slain bird is released and set free to return to its nest. The person for whom the ceremony has been performed washes the clothes, shaves off all the hair, bathes in water, and finally comes home to the camp. But this is just the beginning of the restoration process.

On the seventh day, the individual shaves again and undergoes another ritual bath for cleansing to be fit to enter the tabernacle courts on the eighth day (v. 9).

The exact meaning of the symbolism here is not altogether clear. Even the identity of the hyssop is not secure since there are several varieties: thyme, sage, or the gray-green marjoram plant (*Origanum maru*). The last-named variety appears to be correct, since it is used in Samaritan Passover celebrations.

The slaying of one bird and the releasing of the other are certainly also filled with symbolism. But of what? The two clean birds are characteristic of the holy nation. The bird's blood sprinkled on the individual undergoing this rite identifies that one as once again restored to the fellowship of the congregation. Thus a death makes possible the restoration.

The release of the other bird probably symbolizes the new life that the cured person has been given. Accordingly, it is not by means of death alone but also by the release of life that new life can now be experienced. Many see the same pattern here in the two birds as is evident in the two goats on the Day of Atonement—especially in the release of the scapegoat (16:21-22), i.e., sins forgiven on the basis of a substitute and sins forgotten as the led-away goat is removed, never to return to the camp.

14:10-20. On the eighth day (vv. 10-11), a concept that is becoming familiar to us by now, the once unclean person appears before Yahweh in the tent of meeting with a male lamb for a guilt offering, a male lamb for a sin offering, a ewe lamb for a burnt offering, and about one-third of a bushel (about 6 quarts or 6.5 liters) of fine flour ("three-tenths of an ephah") for a grain offering along with about two-thirds of a pint of oil.

The oil and the lamb for the guilt offering are consecrated to the Lord by lifting them up as an elevation offering. (On the issue of a wave offering, see our comments on 7:28-36.) It is most unusual to hear that the whole lamb is elevated in dedication to God. Then the male lamb is slain as prescribed in the guilt offering.

What follows in vv. 14-20 is most astonishing! As is true in the ordination ceremony of the high priest, where Moses uses the blood of the sacrifice with specially dedicated oil (see comments on 8:22-24), so here the blood of the guilt offering is used with ordinary oil, which the cleansed Israelite brings. The priest anoints the person's right ear, the thumb on the right hand, and the big toe of the right foot, first with the blood of the offering and then with the oil. The significance is the same for the cleansed person as it is for the priest: God sets apart ears to hear God's voice, hands to perform the works of righteousness, and feet to walk in the way of the Lord.

Just as the priest is anointed with holy oil, so also the cleansed person is anointed with oil; however, it is ordinary oil. The officiating priest would pour some of the oil in the palm of his hand, and then with his right forefinger, he would sprinkle some of the oil seven times before the Lord (v. 27). With the remaining oil in his hand, the priest would put the oil on the same places where he had smeared the blood: the offerer's right ear, right thumb, and right big toe (v. 28). What is left of the oil in the palm of his hand the priest applies to the head of the one who is to be cleansed in order "to make atonement" (v. 29) for the person.

14:21-32. The prominence given to the guilt offering can be seen not only in the special use of the blood, as already described, but also in the fact that no diminution is allowed for bringing the lamb as a guilt offering even though all the other offerings can be diminished because of a person's poverty (vv. 21-22). Some may question why the guilt offering should receive such prominence. Two answers are generally given. First, the guilt offering serves as a reparation and satisfaction for the person's long absence from the service of God while he or she was in an unclean state. (But why is this not required after a lengthy illness [cf. Luke 8:43]?) Second, the guilt offering is necessary because the seriousness of this illness may suggest that it is the result of some sin the person committed. (But the thesis that all illness or suffering is the result of sin is too reductionistic and was condemned by Jesus [see John 9:2-3].) Neither answer is completely satisfactory, though if preference is to be given, the first is better than the second. A good response to the first objection, however, might be that it is not the duration of the absence from the sanctuary worship services that is in question, but the nature of the ailment from which deliverance is gained; it is like a dead person's being brought back to life. No doubt more of a renewed consecration of life is being symbolized, for note that this guilt offering deviates slightly from the standard guilt offering in that both the lamb and the two-thirds of a pint of oil are treated as an elevation offering, thereby signifying the person's self-surrender to God.

The sin offering that comes next signifies purification and the purging of uncleanness. Then come the whole burnt offering and the grain offering, both of which indicate the offerer's total dedication to do the will of God and thankfulness and gratitude for being healed.

As with the cleansing of the woman after childbirth (chap. 12), so special concessions are made on the other three offerings (sin, burnt, and grain) for persons who are unable to afford the standard offerings. While the guilt offering standard remains the same, a dove or a young pigeon can be substituted for each of the sin and burnt offerings. Also the grain offering is reduced to one-tenth of an ephah (about two quarts, or approximately two liters) of fine flour along with the two-thirds of a pint of oil.

14:33-53. A final section in chap. 14 deals with some sort of mold, blight, rot, or fungal growth that produced discoloration or recessed lesions in the plaster or mud used to cover the stones forming the walls of buildings.

14:34-42. The symptoms are the same as they are for צרעת (*ṣāra'at*) in humans and those affecting leather and fabrics. The situation has the potential for being something like the plague of God (v. 34; literally "I will afflict an eruptive plague upon a house") and it was treated as contagious and dangerous.

When a homeowner reports this condition to the priest, the priest orders that the building be emptied of its contents before he inspects it. It is a precautionary move, since everything must be declared unclean if the house comes under quarantine. The priest then inspects the place. If he detects greenish or reddish lesions on the plaster-facing of any of the stones, either inside or outside the building, he imposes a quarantine for seven days.

At the end of the seven days, he makes a second inspection. If the affected area has enlarged, the priest orders the removal of the infected stones with their plaster to an unclean place outside the camp reserved for such materials, and new stones and plaster are to be put in their stead.

14:43-47. Now if after all these precautions the plague persists and breaks out once more, the building or house is leveled—all its wood, stones, mud, and plaster are taken outside the camp or city. It is unclean! What is more, all who have entered the building in the meantime, have slept there, or have eaten there during its period of quarantine are to launder their clothes.

14:48-53. Alternatively, if the priest has not noticed any enlargement of the infected area, the dwelling is pronounced clean and the owner can proceed with the ritual of purification. These rites conform to those performed for a person who has recovered from leprosy or a scaly disease (14:1-7).

Two live birds are brought to the priest. One is slain over an earthen vessel containing fresh water. Then the other bird, the cedar wood, the scarlet yarn, and the hyssop are dipped in the vessel containing the fresh water and the blood of the slain bird. The priest then sprinkles the dwelling with the blood and water mixture seven times to purify it with the bird's blood (vv. 51-52). Finally, the live bird is released in the open fields outside town.

The paralleling of this rite of purification with the purification of humans is almost exact. The only difference is that instead of shaving the hair, as humans must do, it is paralleled by scraping the plaster from the building stones. And instead of applying blood and oil to the building, which is done for humans, blood and water are combined to be applied to the dwelling.

14:54-57. These verses summarize the range of chaps. 13–14. Enveloped in these two chapters are the "regulations" (תורת *tôrāt*) given by God (vv. 54, 57). Nothing in these chapters even approaches anything like magic, folklore, or the lore about the gods in pagan literature. It is fair, reasonable, rational, and cautious in its approach to preserving the physical health of the community.

REFLECTIONS

1. Leviticus 14 is unique in being the only section in the Law where hyssop is used in connection with cleansing. The psalmist made a reference to such cleansing with his prayer "Cleanse me with hyssop, and I will be clean;/ wash me, and I will be whiter than snow" (Ps 51:7 NIV). Just as the person once afflicted with leprosy or some other scaly disease would go to the priest after recovering and was pronounced clean when blood and water were applied by a hyssop branch, so the psalmist sought a cleansing touch.

2. God is concerned not only about our souls but also about the welfare of our bodies. We are to remember that same inclusive ministry when it comes to deciding what indeed is the mission of the church. A concerned approach that does not lose perspective on either the spiritual or the physical aspects of human life is in keeping with the expressed will and ways of God.

3. Although leprosy was sometimes imposed as a punishment from God (see Miriam's case in Num 12:10; Gehaz's case in 2 Kgs 5:27), it was by no means the indication par excellence of sin. Biblical authors had better metaphors for sin, such as blindness, stiff-neckedness or obduracy of the will, and hardness of heart. The real tragedy of the severe cases of skin disease, like leprosy, was the person's isolation from fellowship with God and from the people of God. The force of the application to be made in these two chapters, then, is that any and all types of uncleanness separate us from God. The holiness to which this book constantly calls its audience is that of separation *to* God, avoiding what separates us *from* God.

4. The cleansing ritual for the leper, or other sufferers of seriously affected skin diseases, took place outside the camp. Thus, just as the priest had to go outside the camp in pronouncing the person clean, so also Christ went to the cross outside the city walls to atone for human sin (see Heb 13:12).

5. The bird that was killed and the bird that was released alive are graphic illustrations of the double affirmations of Paul that Jesus was put to death for our trespasses but was raised from the dead for our justification (see Rom 4:25). The sprinkling of blood on the leper was a sign that one's life was cleansed through a life vicariously offered up on one's behalf. That offering was accepted in trust by the person needing to be cleansed. But the releasing of the live bird indicated that new life was given, as if one had just come back from the dead.

6. In the two-bird ritual, the blood represented the basis for one's justification, while the anointing oil, in addition to the sprinkled blood, indicated the sustaining presence of God's Holy Spirit. Thus the cleansing of the sufferer argued against a life of selfish pursuit of one's own goals apart from God; the cleansing enabled the one who had been unclean to live in righteousness and holiness with God.

7. The act of smearing the blood on the right ear, right thumb, and right big toe was done to reflect an inclusive claim on a person's total body. It indicated that every area of one's life was affected by the atonement.

LEVITICUS 15:1-33, THE UNCLEANNESS OF GENITAL DISCHARGES

COMMENTARY

Let it be said immediately that coition and the legitimate use of one's sexuality are meant as gifts to creatures from the Creator for their enjoyment. But this chapter does not address the question of the legitimacy of sex or its satisfaction; rather, it deals more narrowly with certain qualifications, or lack thereof, for entering into the presence of God in corporate worship.

Some have thought that chap. 15 would be placed more accurately just prior to chap. 12—thereby grouping the uncleanness that comes from genital discharges with the uncleanness that comes from childbirth. This suggested relocation of the chapter only indicates that the organizing principle for this section has not yet been discovered.

The organizational principle may instead be that the various uncleanness laws were arranged, as Gordon Wenham suggests, according to the length of time that the affected person was unclean.[82] Chapter 11 deals with food laws that can bring permanent uncleanness. Chapter 12 limits the uncleanness of childbirth to a maximum of eighty days. Chapters 13–14 specify that the uncleanness lasts as long as the skin disease persists, but the maximum time for uncleanness with genital discharges (chap. 15) is merely one week.

Whatever the real explanation is, chaps. 11–15 are preparatory to the central event in the book, the Day of Atonement. Leviticus 16:16 makes clear that the basic purpose of these laws of clean and unclean is to teach Israel a sensitivity to uncleanness and sin, in whatever form they manifest themselves. Moreover, the Israelites are to be careful

about defiling the tabernacle by entering it in an unclean condition.

The outline for this chapter is a beautiful example of symmetry and balance. It treats ritual uncleanness in men first (vv. 2-17) and then ceremonial uncleanness in women second (vv. 19-30). In both cases, it takes up forms that are chronic and sporadic; however, the pattern is reversed in the women's section from the way it appears in the men's section, thereby giving a chiasmic pattern (a literary device where A, B appears B, A in the parallel situation). The final touch of artistic balance can be seen in the verse that joins the male/female sections; v. 18 mentions coition of male and female in the act of oneness as originally designed by the Creator in Gen 2:24.

15:1-18. This chapter deals with a number of different discharges from the sexual organs. The word בשׂר (*bāśār*, meaning "flesh," "meat," "body," or even "man") probably is used in this context as a euphemism for the male sex organ, a sense it carries in Gen 17:13 and Ezek 16:26 (literally Ezekiel says, "The Egyptians, your neighbors, [the ones] big of flesh" [גדלי בשׂר *gidlê bāśār*]; cf. Ezek 23:20).

The word for "emission" (זוב *zôb*) is rare with this nuance of meaning, for it appears with this sense of emission only in Leviticus. Its meaning is clarified in v. 3 by another rare word רר (*rār*) from the noun ריר (*rîr*), meaning "slimy juice" or "saliva" (see 1 Sam 21:14 [English 13]; Job 6:6); thus a male discharge runs from his "flesh" periodically.

It is almost impossible to say precisely what this emission is. Some are unhappy with the attachment of these meanings to the sexual organs only, preferring that the text would have used the word זרע (*zera'*, "seed" or "sperm") in this immediate context if that is the meaning. But the disorder does

82. Wenham, *Leviticus*, 216.

not appear to come from any intestinal malfunction or related areas of the body; therefore, all suggestions that the emission comes from hemorrhoids, diverticulitis, or the like are probably incorrect. Instead, it is either a milder form of gonorrhea or a discharge of mucus from inflammation in the urinary tract.

Additional reasons why this cannot be a case of hemorrhoids are: (a) there is no mention of any loss of blood, a factor that would hardly have escaped some comment in a context such as the book of Leviticus; and (b) v. 19 uses "flesh" (*bāśār*) for a woman's vagina—thus the use of "flesh" for a man's penis seems to be required in this context.

The reference to a "stopped" or "blocked" discharge (v. 3) can mean only that the emission has ceased. If it means that the male urethra is blocked, this male is in a lot more trouble than anything these laws consider.

The presence of this discharge, though not as serious as the other forms of uncleanness spoken of in Leviticus 11–14, makes a person unclean (v. 3). Anything that the affected male sits on (a chair in v. 6 or a saddle in v. 9) is just as unclean as the bed he sleeps on (vv. 4-5), and therefore is as unclean as the flowing male himself is unclean. And whoever touches any of the affected things is also unclean, for direct contact transmits uncleanness (v. 7). The unclean person has to be careful to wash his hands, for that is another way to convey the ritual impurity (v. 11). Spittle from an unclean male (v. 8) pollutes just as much as the cooking vessels are affected when he touches them (v. 12).

The solution for this state of ritual uncleanness is not as complicated as in the cases previously discussed. The unclean man has to wait only seven days, wash himself, and on the eighth day bring two doves or two young pigeons, the least expensive of all the sacrifices, to the priest for a sin offering and a burnt offering (vv. 13-15). This solution indicates that these disorders are nowhere near the level of seriousness associated with the scaly skin diseases in chaps. 13–14.

The more intermittent or spasmodic emissions come from the emission of semen (vv. 16-17). This seems to be what Deut 23:10 refers to as a nocturnal emission, an involuntary discharge of semen that indicates no abnormality of the sex organ. While ejaculated semen is judged enough of a pollutant to make a person ceremonially unclean (just as it was likewise regarded by other Semitic peoples, the Egyptians, the Greeks, and the Romans), it does not require any sacrifices for purification. The man has only to wash himself and any affected clothing; he is unclean until evening comes. The purpose, then, seems only to prevent what is a legitimate, but ceremonially unclean, act from encroaching upon what is holy.

At the center of this chapter on discharges from sexual organs is v. 18, which deals with intercourse between a husband and a wife. It is not entirely clear why sexual intercourse should make the partners unclean, since it would seem to be the fulfillment of the divine command given in Gen 1:28. Perhaps these discharges were viewed as defiling because they were thought to contain dead matter. What the text actually provides is the mere declaration that both partners are judged to be ceremonially impure after coition. It is merely a ritual uncleanness in which both are temporarily disqualified until sundown from approaching God's holiness. Both have to bathe after engaging in the sex act. That is why sexual intercourse is not permitted before a person performs religious duties or participates in God's wars (sometimes called "holy wars"). This same idea is found elsewhere in the OT (see Exod 19:15; 1 Sam 21:5-6; 2 Sam 11:11).

15:19-30. This section deals with female discharges. A woman's uncleanness comes from her monthly period (a thought already raised in Lev 12:2, 5), called in the Hebrew her נדה (*niddâ*), a root that is to be compared to the cognate Akkadian term *nadû*, "to cast," "to hurl," or "to throw." Thus the status of a woman during menstruation is that she is unclean (cf. Gen 31:35).

Even though the *niddâ* lasts, as a rule, only four days, her period of uncleanness is for seven days (12:2). She remains isolated during this time. Should a man touch her during this time, much less have sexual relations with her, each is liable to divine punishment (Lev 18:19; 20:18; Ezek 18:6; 22:10). Should her period begin while she is having intercourse with her husband, he too will be unclean for seven days.

At face value it would seem that every female beyond the age of puberty spent one week a month out of contact with the rest of society. But some have argued that a monthly menstrual cycle is a fairly recent phenomenon, due more to the change in modern Western society than a change in female physiology. In earlier times, three things kept the monthly cycle from happening as frequently as it does today: (a) Most persons married shortly after puberty, (b) children were not weaned until they were two or three years old, and (c) most persons desired large families, so the children tended to come one after another.[83]

This law is given not to demean women but, as Bernard J. Bamberger comments, to protect women from the importunities of their husbands at a time when they are physically and emotionally not ready for coitus.[84] Perhaps, more than any other sign, this demonstrates that a husband does not have sovereignty over his wife or her body; that she owes only to God.[85]

More chronic female discharges are discussed in vv. 25-30. If a flow of blood continues beyond the menstrual cycle or there is another abnormal discharge, the time of uncleanness is extended for as long as the condition lasts. That was the situation with the woman mentioned in the Gospels, who had suffered from the aggravation for twelve years (see Matt 9:20-21; Mark 5:25-33; Luke 8:43-48). It is remarkable that Jesus did not rebuke her for making him unclean. In desperation the woman acted contrary to the Levitical laws and moved into society in one last desperate attempt simply to touch the Master, hoping thereby to be healed.

Identifying all the possible sources of the bleeding mentioned in this section on chronic female discharges is impossible. Again it has been suggested that gonorrhea is one of the diseases, but no evidence makes this suggestion secure.

As soon as the woman's complaint clears up, she waits seven days and then offers one bird as a sin offering and another as a burnt offering (note the order of the offerings). Since the problem lasts more than a week, sacrifices are required just as they are for the defiling matters raised in 12:1–15:12.

15:31. The laws on genital discharges conclude with a purpose statement. One of the most unusual forms of the verb for "to separate" is placed in command form (הזיר *hizzîr*) from the root נזר (*nāzar*, "to cause to avoid," "to be separate from"). From this form we also get our word *Nazirite*. The only other place where this verb occurs, naturally, is in the Nazirite law, which also stresses the idea of separation (see Num 6:2, 3, 5-6, 12). The Samaritan Pentateuch and the Syriac Version read in this place הזהיר (*hizhîr*, "to warn") instead of "to separate." But the form seems to be well established in its Numbers 6 setting as a separation "to the LORD" and a separation "from" the things Nazirites pledged not to involve themselves in (Num 6:3 NIV). These laws are to call Israelites away from uncleanness so that when they go to the tabernacle, they will not defile it and as a result die in their uncleanness. They are simultaneously called to be separated unto their God. All of these laws on the clean and unclean are directed at securing a proper degree of reverence for the person and presence of God. Since the tabernacle is the place where God chose to be gloriously manifest, nothing is allowed to come into its precincts that will lower its general esteem and significance. A God who is holy demands a corresponding preparatory cleansing for all who draw near.

15:32-33. There are few, if any, real parallels in the ancient Near East with the provisions given in this closing formula, except in the case of leprosy. The holiness of God could not have been set forth in a more dramatic way. If God is to dwell in the midst of this people, the purity of the community, and especially the purity of God's sanctuary, must be safeguarded.

83. Wenham, *Leviticus,* 223-24.

84. Bernard J. Bamberger, "Leviticus," in *The Torah: A Modern Commentary,* 850.

85. See the extended argument in Walter C. Kaiser, Jr., *Toward Old Testament Ethics* (Grand Rapids: Zondervan, 1983) 198-99.

REFLECTIONS

1. A list of prohibitions in the area of human sexuality should not be misinterpreted to mean that sex is somehow wrong and merely tolerated by God because that is the only way the human race can multiply. Rather, these ritualistic regulations must be balanced against other divine regulations God gave about the sexual side of life.

2. God never intended that a husband should exercise tyrannous power over his wife and her body; therefore, the mandate provided a time of respite for the woman during her menstrual cycle to remind the husband that God, not the mate, was Lord over her life.

3. The change signaled within the NT regarding clean and unclean distinctions is brought out once again in the story of the woman who had a hemorrhage for twelve years but who dared to touch Jesus. She was not the only unclean person Jesus touched. He touched the dead daughter of Jairus (see Mark 5:41) and a leper (see Matt 8:3), and he allowed a sinner to wipe his feet (see Luke 7:36-39). Surely a new age had dawned with the coming of the Messiah. Jesus took the same view toward the laws about bodily uncleanness that he took toward the food laws; he pronounced all things clean. Such teaching led Jesus into direct conflict with the Pharisees (see Mark 7). Jesus emphasized that more was at stake in the matter than an external act; internal preparation and the consent of the heart and mind were also important considerations. This internal feature was already present in the OT, but it tended to be overlooked with all the stress on performance of the act itself.[86]

4. While the main reason for giving these laws on genital discharges was to maintain ritual cleanness, many of the same laws had relevance elsewhere and were not restricted in their application to a single area of life. For example, the law on menstrual uncleanness is found in a ceremonial context in Leviticus 15, but it occurs again in Lev 18:19 among laws that have a broader and much more universal significance. Thus, there may have been accompanying moral principles, or hygienic reasons, that undergirded what appeared to be limited to a ritual observance.

86. See the argument that Old Testament ethics are internal in Kaiser, *Toward Old Testament Ethics*, 7-10.

LEVITICUS 16:1-34

THE GREAT DAY OF ATONEMENT

COMMENTARY

C hapter 16 represents the climactic and pivotal point of the whole book. The event it describes would be known later on in Israel as *Yom Kippur*, a shortened form from the sacred writer's יום הכפרים (*yôm hakkippûrîm*). Here, then, is the single most important day, and most characteristic ritual, in all of the legislation of the Pentateuch. Such a central place did this day hold in the sacred calendar of events that the rabbis referred to it simply as *Yoma;* it was *"the* day."

The reason this day was esteemed so highly was that it depicted the sacrificial expiation for *all* sin, except blasphemy against God (see Num 15:30; there called the "sin with a high hand"), as well as the consequent removal of the guilt and remembrance of sins against individuals. For devout Jews, it remains to this day the climax, indeed the crowning event, of the religious year. One of the best-known melodies to be associated with this day is that of *Kol Nidre.* All over the world on this day, which comes on the Gregorian calendar somewhere at the end of September or the beginning of October, Leviticus 16 is read in celebrating synagogues. Reform Judaism, however, has replaced Leviticus 16 with Leviticus 19 in the morning reading for Yom Kippur, focusing on the ethical rather than the ritual requirements of repentance. Reform Judaism has, however, retained the traditional *haftarah* (the parallel reading from the Prophets in the synagogue service following the lesson from the Torah) of Isa 57:14–58:14, which declares that fasting and rote prayers are valueless unless they are accompanied with inward regeneration and unless they lead to works of service for poor and helpless persons.

Leviticus 16:1-2 begins with a reference to the events of 10:1-2. This has exasperated some who believe that chap. 16 should have been placed right after chap. 10—just for that reason. However, such a relocation would be a major mistake, for the lesson embodied in the death of Nadab and Abihu in chap. 10 would have been wasted. Any approach to God demands extreme care, self-examination, and the ability to meet the qualifications for coming into God's presence. That necessitates the intervening five chapters. Chapters 11–15 dramatize the point that all mortals are exposed to the liability of being disqualified from meeting with God due to contacting uncleanness in foods, decay, death, disease, and sex.

Rarely are we given such a graphic description of what God has done for humanity as we are treated to on the Day of Atonement. Once every year a substitutionary atonement provides for all the sins of all the people. Some have seen the main purpose of the events of this day to be limited to making atonement for the holy of holies (v. 16). But if that were the only purpose for the events of this day, it would miss the clear statements that there is to be a sacrifice "for" (בעד *bĕʿad*) Aaron himself, for Aaron's household (v. 6), and "because of" (מן *min*, "by reason of") the uncleanness [chaps. 11–15] and rebellion of the Israelites" (v. 16; cf. vv. 33-34).

The structure of chap. 16 is not as clear as the structure of other chapters. There are a number of recurring phrases and statements, such as "to make atonement" (vv. 6, 11, 17, 24, 33, 34) and "This/it is to be a lasting ordinance for you" (vv. 29, 31, 34). The chapter is slightly confusing because it uses a typical Hebrew pattern of outlining the ritual first and then it returns to describe it in greater detail. We can discern the following elements: introduction (vv. 1-2); the sacrificial animals and priestly garb (vv. 3-5); an outline of the ceremonies (vv. 6-10); the ritual of the Day of Atonement (vv. 11-28), which includes preparations of the high priest (vv. 11-14), the forgiveness of sin (vv. 15-19), the removal of sin (vv. 20-22), the washing of the participants (vv. 23-28); and the spiritual preparation of the people (vv. 29-34).

16:1-2. We are startled to learn that this day is revealed not to Aaron, the high priest, but to Moses. Clearly, Moses retained his function as spokesperson for God and the receiver of revelation, even after the installation of Aaron as high priest.

The first injunction that Moses gives to Aaron, in light of the death of Aaron's two sons, is (literally) "not to go at any time into the Most Holy Place behind the curtain" (v. 2). This is not to be taken as a total prohibition, but it exhibits a characteristic Oriental negative that seems at first to be all-encompassing, only to have its qualifiers follow immediately (e.g., Deut 1:35, but see vv. 36, 38; Josh 11:22*a*, but see v. 22*b*; 1 Cor 1:14*a*, but see vv. 14*b* and 16). The point is that Aaron alone is to enter the most holy place in the tabernacle only this one day of each year.

16:3-5. Even though Aaron is to conduct the ritual, he too is a sinner, just like the people for whom he is offering the sacrifices. Thus he has to bring a bull as his own sin offering and a ram as a burnt offering (v. 3). The people bring two male goats for their sin offering (note that both goats form one sin offering) and a ram for their burnt offering (v. 5).

As the ceremony begins, Aaron must divest himself of the richly ornamented robes of his office and clothe himself, instead, with the white linen garments of an ordinary priest. Of the eight garments worn by the priests, four are of linen (shirt, shorts, sash, and turban) and are called the white garments (see Exod 39:27-29), while the other four are called the golden garments because of the rich gold embroidered on them (see Exod 28:4-5).

This divestiture is more than pageantry; it is an eloquent symbol of the servant role that the high priest must assume on this day as he takes upon himself the form of an ordinary mortal while retaining in his person all the powers of his high priestly office.

Accordingly, the Day of Atonement is a day of sorrow, repentance, and humiliation over the sins committed. Even the high priest clothes himself in the simple and unspectacular garments of the other priests to demonstrate his humility. Only at the end of the day

is he to resume his dress in the extraordinary robes of his office (vv. 23-24).

16:6, 11-14. After Aaron offers the bull as a sin offering for himself and his sons, he is to take some of the blood of the bull and sprinkle it not outside the curtain leading to the most holy place, as in the sin offering of the priest in 4:3-12, but right inside the most holy place, at or toward the mercy seat. However, to go into this innermost sanctum of the tabernacle, he must prepare a censer full of hot coals from the altar of burnt offering. Taking this censer and two handfuls of fine incense, he enters the most holy place. At that point he drops the incense into the censer to create smoke and conceal the presence of God, who is closely connected with the כפרת (*kappōret*), variously translated as the "mercy seat" or "lid/cover of the ark."

Obviously, *kappōret* is derived from the verb כפר (*kipper*), meaning "to purify" or "to ransom by means of a substitute" (see the discussions of this word at 1:4). On top of the ark (there is no word here for "lid" or "cover" in Hebrew unless one incorrectly understands *kipper* to mean "to cover") were two cherubs facing each other and extending out to the width of the room (see Exod 25:17-22). The LXX renders *kappōret* in the Greek ἱλαστήριον (*hilastērion*, "instrument of propitiation"). Because of what was transacted at this spot every year on the Day of Atonement, it became known as God's seat of mercy from which atonement was granted. The notion that it formed a footstool for God's feet comes from Ps 99:1, which extolls the Lord who reigns and who "sits enthroned upon the cherubim" (NRSV). Whether the Lord is seated or not may be answered by the fact that this is an exalted figure of speech to portray that the Lord was really present in the tent of meeting and was currently reigning on earth.

But there can be no doubt about the propitiatory nature of what takes place in this most holy place, the innermost sanctum of the tabernacle. Aaron then sprinkles the blood of the bull, slain for himself and his family, seven times, either upon or toward the mercy seat. The high priest must enter behind the veil alone without anyone else in the tabernacle. In the mystery of the silence and the loneliness of his work, he ministers on behalf of his soul, and on behalf of all Israel (v. 17).

16:7-10. The second part of the ceremony involves the two goats. They form *one* sin offering for all the sins of all Israelites who truly "afflict your souls" (vv. 29, 31 KJV), i.e., were repentant and sorrowed over their sins. More will be said about this point when we come to discuss those verses.

When the two goats are seen as one sin offering, only one conclusion can be reached with regard to their connection with each other. The one goat makes possible the expiation of the sins laid on it, and thus it is the *means* of expiating and propitiating Israel's sins, while the other goat exhibits the *effects* of that expiation.[87] The role each goat will play is decided by casting lots.

The Mishnaic tractate *Yoma* fills in the details on this part of the ceremony, along with an elaborate description of the other portions. In the simplest outline of events, as the two goats stand before the high priest, he uses the Urim and Thummim to determine which will be the sacrificial goat and which will be sent away, or he puts two lots into a jar: one saying "to the LORD," and the other "to Azazel." If the latter system is used, Aaron places his hand on one goat as he draws one lot and on the other goat as he draws the other lot.

16:15-19. The first goat is to be sacrificed as a sin offering for all the sins of all the people. The blood of this animal is also taken, this one time each year, behind the veil that separated the two rooms in the tabernacle, and is sprinkled seven times on or toward the mercy seat. The means of forgiveness could not have been stated more strongly. The goat becomes the substitute for the people. Nevertheless, it still is an animal and not a person. And what really makes the ceremony effective is not some magical ingredient in the blood or the ritual itself; it is the declaration of forgiveness by the high priest, based on the authority of the God who promises forgiveness.

16:20-22. Next, the second goat is led away from the camp so that it can be lost in the wilderness. Having made atonement for

himself, his family (in his first trip into the holy of holies), and the people of Israel (now in this second trip into the holy of holies), Aaron comes out of the tabernacle once again into the courtyard. He places his hands (the Hebrew ceremony of *Semikhah*, discussed in 1:4) on the head of the live goat as he confesses over it "all the wickedness and rebellion of the Israelites—all their sins—and [puts] them on the goat's head" (v. 21).

The ceremony of the imposition of hands is conclusive on the point that it pictures a transfer of sin to the head of another. Even though what we see is true only in a typical fashion, it nevertheless effectively demonstrates that expiation and propitiation are taking place. Yet so real is this transfer of wickedness, sin, and rebellion on the head of this substitute that the man who takes the goat into the wilderness, as he leads it away, is himself said to become polluted and made unclean because of his contact with the sin-laden goat.

This one sin offering comes in two parts, since the first goat that dies cannot be brought back to life to transact the second part of the ritual. It clearly sets forth the teaching that sins are *forgiven* on the basis of a substitute (the first goat), and sins are *forgotten* and removed from us, as the psalmist said, "as far as the east is from the west,/ so far has he removed our/ transgressions from us" (Ps 103:12 NIV). The first animal pictures the *means* used for atonement—i.e., the shedding of the blood of an innocent substitute— and the second animal pictures the *effect*, the removal of the guilt.

The most difficult question in this chapter concerns the meaning of the statement that the goat is "for/to Azazel" (לעזאזל *la ʿăzāʾzēl*) in vv. 8, 10, and 26. The meaning of this term has proven to be most difficult, and the solutions are legion. Several older rabbinical writers and Targumists took Azazel to be the name of *the place* to which the goat was led. It was supposed that it was a rough and rocky place with a precipice from which the goat was thrown down. That is found, for example, in *Tg. Neb.* in v. 10. The Arabic version favored this solution, for they substitute for *la ʿăzāʾzēl*, "to the Mount Azaz," or to the rough mountain (which roughness Azaz depicts).

---

87. As used here, *expiation* is the act of atoning for an offense while *propitiation* is the act of satisfying the person who has been offended. It is possible for a person to be expiated without being propitiated, especially when one is implacable and demands more than what is rightfully his or hers. Contrariwise, it is possible for a person to be propitiated without being expiated if one is too easily satisfied. The sin offering mentioned here involved both expiation and propitiation.

Others have argued that if this second goat is presented alive "to/for Yahweh" in v. 10, the parallel phrase must be understood as a name as well, "for Azazel." But who is Azazel? It is supposed that he must be a *desert demon* capable of feeding on an animal laden with the sins of the entire nation. This view is generally the one most frequently adopted today. Josephus apparently adopted something close to this view, for he employed the LXX translation of this term as ἀποτροπίασμος (*apotropiasmos*, "the Averter") and said, "The goat is sent away into a remote desert *as an Averter of ills*" (*apotropiasmos*).[88] Some of the early Church Fathers such as Origen, attempted to show that Azazel was the devil. In later Jewish literature, Azazel appears as a demon (*Enoch* 8:1; 9:6). The difficulty with this view is that the very next chapter of Leviticus warns against offering any sacrifices to demons (17:7). Therefore, most who hold this view attempt to show that the goat is in no way an offering to the demon. But the disclaimer is difficult to maintain if the reason for adopting this view is that it is parallel to the expression used "for Yahweh," which does function as a single sin offering!

A simpler view is to see Azazel as a compound word made up of עֵז ('*ēz*, "goat") and אָזַל ('*āzal*, from the verb "to go away" or "to lead away"). Thus, the second goat is the "goat of going/leading away," named in older English the "Scapegoat" (by which they meant in that day what we would mean by Escape-goat). New evidence reveals that Ugaritic (an early Canaanite language that is cognate to Hebrew) did exhibit such compound nouns. *Escape-goat* is a better term than the older Scapegoat, (a word that apparently was coined by William Tyndale, the sixteenth-century English Bible translator) since in today's parlance a scapegoat is one who gets stuck with doing jobs others do not wish to do, and therefore, it would have been more appropriately applied to the first goat. In Num 29:11, this Escape-goat is called "the sin offering for atonement."

16:23-28. Having made atonement for himself, his fellow priests, the sanctuary, and the people, the high priest enters the tabernacle one more time. He removes his white linen attire in which he has performed the

ceremonies up to this point. He then washes himself thoroughly "in a holy place" (v. 24), presumably somewhere in the sanctuary itself. Now that he has completed the work of atonement, it is appropriate for him to take up the beautiful robes and the splendor of his office once more. When he emerges from the tent of meeting in his splendor, he offers burnt offerings for himself and for the people (v. 24), along with the fat of the sin offering (v. 25). He and the people are able to approach the Lord once more with their sacrificial gifts.

16:29-34. Very little, if anything, has been said so far about the people's responsibilities or duties in this whole ceremony. Even though what Aaron has accomplished focuses mainly on the people, they do not play a major part in this event. However, vv. 29, 31, and 34 make it clear that what is being done is to be a permanent rule for the future. It is all the more striking, then, that this Day of Atonement is not mentioned elsewhere in the OT. The three so-called pilgrimage festivals of Passover, Weeks, and Tabernacles, where all the men of Israel journeyed to Jerusalem for these days, are often mentioned but never this day! The day of purification mentioned in Ezek 45:18-20 comes on the first day of the seventh month. Zechariah 3:9 does not refer to this day either. The only explicit references to the Day of Atonement are in Heb 9:7 and the apocryphal work of Sirach 50. If the suggested solution to this unexplainable silence on the Day of Atonement is to say that the Day of Atonement was a late invention of the post-exilic period, as the school of Julius Wellhausen was fond of saying, the question will be this: Where is the ark of the covenant with its mercy seat, a feature so essential to the ceremonies of this day? That piece of furniture was only a memory by the post-exilic period, for it appears nowhere in the later years before the exile, and Jer 3:16 says it will not come to anyone's mind anymore.

The Day of Atonement is to be held "on the tenth day of the seventh month" (v. 29; see also 23:26-32; 25:9). This date is six months after the celebration of Passover. The seventh month was known in post-exilic times as Tishri (September-October). It was autumn by then, and the early rains had begun to fall. Plowing and sowing would not begin until the next month.

But the most important duty for the people is reserved almost to the last in these instructions that otherwise are given mainly for Aaron and his sons. The people are to "deny [themselves]" (vv. 29, 31) or "afflict [their] souls" (KJV). The expression ענה נפש ('nh npš) involves the verbal root from the word ענה ('ānâ) which in the piel form means "to humble oneself." It appears frequently in the instructions for the Day of Atonement (Lev 16:29, 31; 23:27, 32; Num 29:7). The only other places where this expression occurs are in Ps 35:13-14 and in Isa 58:3, 5 (hence the reason for reading this selection from the Prophets on the Day of Atonement in the synagogues). For the psalmist, the humbling of oneself is defined by its association with fasting: "I put on sackcloth/and humbled myself with fasting./ . . . I went about mourning." Likewise in Isaiah 58, it is connected with fasting.

The principle, then, is one of contriteness and godly sorrow for the sins committed during the year. While all sins, including all wickedness and even outright rebellion against God (v. 21) are forgivable, there is no mechanical or purely rote manner in which carte blanche is given to all persons, regardless of their inner disposition. The heart attitude has to accompany the request for forgiveness. This aspect of fasting and humbling oneself can be seen on days of national repentance (see Judg 20:26; 1 Sam 7:6; Esth 4:16). At these times people mourn over their sins (see 1 Sam 31:13; 2 Sam 3:35) and through self-denial call out to God for forgiveness and deliverance.

So significant is this day that it is called a "sabbath of rest" (v. 31). That expression is used of the sabbath itself (see Exod 31:15; 35:2; Lev 23:3) and of the sabbatical year (see Lev 25:4). But here and in Lev 23:32 it is used of the Day of Atonement. On such a day there is to be a complete cessation of all nonessential activities and work. This holiday from all forms of normal activities applies to everyone, including the native-born and the alien living in Israel's midst.

The chapter closes in v. 34 with another reminder that this event is to be an annual affair. It also makes explicit that all that is done has as its main reason to make "atonement . . . for all the sins of the Israelites." One more postscript is added: Moses carried out all that the Lord had told him to do on this day.

REFLECTIONS

1. Here on the holiest of days, the Day of Atonement, Aaron is to exchange his high priestly clothes for the vestments of an ordinary priest. At the moment when his duties are the most urgent, his garments are the most humble, pointing to the fact that leadership in the community of faith is, at its heart, servant leadership.

All acts of ministry—whether they are performed by ordained clergy or laypeople, whether they are preaching a sermon, officiating at a eucharist, handing a bowl of soup to a homeless person, teaching a child in church school, listening to a worried friend, or standing up for the right in a difficult situation—are acts of service done by people who know what it means to suffer, to fail, to struggle, to live as less than perfect people. Deeds of mercy are done, in the words of Henri Nouwen, by "wounded healers."

2. The putting off of the glorious robes of the high priestly office and the donning of the white linen garments of an ordinary priest picture what Christ did when he temporarily set aside the glory he had with the Father to take upon himself the form of a man, even that of a servant, in his incarnation (see Phil 2:5-11). This same humble mind-set, argues the apostle Paul in Phil 2:5, ought to characterize the believing community today.

3. Aaron had to proceed carefully behind the veil or curtain that divided the holy place from the most holy place, but that veil was split from top to bottom when Christ gave the final sacrifice at God's mercy seat (see Matt 27:51; Mark 15:38). This rending of the veil was interpreted by the author of Hebrews as God's announcement of human freedom now to enter into the divine presence, the way being opened by our Lord's death on the cross (see Heb 10:19-22).

4. Although traditional theology has insisted that the only sins that could have been forgiven under the old law of Moses were sins of ignorance and sins of inadvertence, this text boldly decries such a meager view by announcing that "all sin," even "transgressions" can be forgiven. Since the term פשע (*peša'* v. 21) means not only "transgression" but also "revolt" and "rebellion," it is clear that the forgiveness of God encompasses every sin except blasphemy or sinning against the Holy Spirit (see Num 15:27-31; cf. Heb 10:26-31). God will forgive sin and will remember it against us no more (see Ps 103:12; Mic 7:19; 1 John 1:7, 9).

5. Aaron, also a sinner, had to make atonement for himself first before making atonement for the people. But Christ, being pure and sinless, did not need to offer a sacrifice for himself (see Heb 7:26-28). Thus, mortals, even in the office of high priest, are weak; but how fortunate we are to have One, in the person of Jesus of Nazareth, who is not so afflicted!

6. The annual nature of the Day of Atonement with its repetition of the sacrificial ritual is in strong contrast to our Lord's once-for-all sacrifice (see Heb 9:24). By one act of giving his life in death for all mortals, he has permanently secured forgiveness of sin for all who will claim it.

7. Some are willing to accept divine forgiveness, but they say neither they nor God can ever forget what they have done. If ever there was a text in Scripture that released men and women from the act of sin, its consequences, and the objective reality of the guilt that results, this is the text. Sins were forgiven on the basis of a substitute; sins were forgotten and removed from being a consideration in that one and same sin offering.

LEVITICUS 17:1–26:46

THE HOLINESS CODE

OVERVIEW

C hapters 17–26 constitute a distinctive unit, dealing with the theme of holiness. Ever since the days of A. Klostermann in 1877,[89] it has been traditional to refer to these chapters as the Holiness Code. In 1889, Julius Wellhausen attempted to show that within the Priestly document, these chapters form a unique source of their own, with their own distinctive vocabulary and style, yet bearing some points of contact with the Book of the Covenant in Exodus 20–23, and some parts of Deuteronomy and Ezekiel.[90]

There is no question that these chapters exhibit a uniqueness rarely observed in other chapters. Most noticeable are the constant reference to holiness and the constant exhortation to "be holy because I, the LORD your God, am holy" (NIV 19:2; 20:7, 26; 21:6, 8). There is also the repeated declaration that "I am the LORD your God" (18:4, 30; 19:3, 4, 10, 25, 31, 34; 20:7; 23:22, 43; 24:22; 25:17, 55; 26:1). So there is no question that this is a very unified and unique set of materials. To some, this continues to imply a separate origin from the rest of Leviticus.

But many recent scholars believe that the evidence does not justify the conclusion that these chapters constituted a separate volume of laws that had been inserted into the framework of Leviticus. First of all, there is no evidence in the introduction to chap. 17 that there has been a switch in sources. In fact, the introductory formula of 17:1 is

very much like that of previous chapters (cf. 1:1; 4:1; 6:1). Second, a fair amount of material in these chapters has links with what has appeared in chaps. 1–16. For example, 17:10-15 recapitulates matters already taken up in 7:26-27, and 17:15-16 links up with 11:39-40. Third, this section has hardly anything to say about the place of priests in the sacrifices—as if it assumes that that matter has already been described elsewhere and is granted as undergirding the holiness section. And finally, internal clues within these chapters support claims that the author of the first division (chaps. 1–16) uses the same format in the second (chaps. 17–27).

There is one major difference between the two divisions, however. Whereas the first one pictures Moses addressing mainly Aaron the high priest along with his sons, this second division focuses almost entirely on the Israelite people. Almost every chapter opens with a directive to speak to the people themselves; very little is said in chaps. 17–26 directly to the priests, except for the one block of text beginning in chapter 21.

Leviticus 19:2 sounds the theme of the holiness section: "Be holy because I, the LORD your God, am holy." The areas of life in which holiness is required may be seen in the following structural elements: in eating (17:1-16); in sexual behavior (18:1-30); in social ethics (19:1-37); in worship (20:1-8, 27); in family relations (20:9-26); in the priesthood (21:1–22:16); in sacrifical offerings (22:17-33); in observing the festivals (23:1-44); as contrasted (24:1-23); in land ownership (25:1-55); and the alternatives: blessing or curse (26:1-46).

---

89. Klostermann, "Beiträge zur Entstehungsgeschichte des Pentateuchs."

90. Wellhausen, *Die Composition des Hexateuchs und der historischen Bücher des Alten Testaments*, 152ff.

LEVITICUS 17:1-16, THE PROLOGUE: HOLINESS IN EATING

COMMENTARY

Classifying this opening chapter of the Holiness Code is difficult, for it has very strong affinities with several of the teachings in chaps. 1–16. Some have even doubted that this chapter should be attached to the holiness section that follows because (1) it does not mention once the concept of holiness, a theme that is so distinctive of most of the chapters included in 17–26; (b) it contains no moral injunctions so characteristic of this section; and (c) it forms no natural connection with what follows in chaps. 18–26.

But this appraisal may be a bit hasty. There are some phrases that chap. 17 shares in common with the rest of the section. But perhaps the best way to view this chapter is to conclude that it acts as a bridge chapter linking itself especially to chap. 16 and linking the two major divisions of the book, viz. chaps. 1–16 and 18–26. In some ways this chapter could stand alone, much as chap. 16 stands alone. Yet chap. 16 summarizes chaps. 1–15. In a similar way, chap. 17 sets the tone for what is to come in chaps. 18–26.

If it is difficult to locate chap. 17 in its sectional context, it is fairly simple to discern the chapter's internal structure. After an introductory formula, as usual for this book, four paragraphs present four concerns about the eating of meat. Each paragraph is introduced with this formula: "If a man from the house of Israel or from a resident alien sojourning among you . . ." (literal translation). This formula is found in vv. 8, 10, and 13; however, a shortened form of it occurs (without reference to the resident alien) in v. 3. This, then, allows us to identify several elements: introductory formula (vv. 1-2); prohibition of clandestine sacrificial slaughter (vv. 3-7); prohibition of sacrifices outside the tabernacle (vv. 8-9); prohibition of eating blood (vv. 10-12); and rules on eating wild game (vv. 13-16).

17:1-2. Instead of commanding Moses to speak only to Aaron, or to Aaron and his sons, this introductory formula adds for the first time, "And to all the Israelites." This section will concentrate on laypersons and the possible mistakes that they may make if they do not pay attention to these injunctions. The community is to take heed, for "this is what the LORD has commanded" (v. 2). The same phraseology is used in 8:5 and 9:6.

17:3-7. The first paragraph immediately plunges us into a problem of interpretation. Verses 3-4 warn that no one is to slaughter any meat except in front of the tent of meeting. But Deut 12:20-25 allows those who are too far from the tabernacle/temple site in Jerusalem to butcher their own meat where they live without going through the sacrificial formalities—just so long as they eat only what is clean and they thoroughly drain the blood from it.

Even this difference would be no problem, for it appears that the law in Deuteronomy assumes a settled state in the land; therefore, it really spoke to issues that would be effective only after Israel was in the land. Thus the law in Leviticus 17 came first, since it seems to reflect those times when Israel was still in the wilderness. The problem is v. 7, which concludes this first paragraph by saying, "This is to be a lasting ordinance for them and for the generations to come." If "this" refers to the whole paragraph of vv. 3-7, there is a major problem.

Several responses can be made to this problem. First, this law applied to the animals typically used in sacrifices: the ox/cow (i.e., male or female of that bovine species), sheep, or goats. That restricts the law on one side.

Then there is the word for "kill" (שחט *šāhat*). Seven different words for various forms of killing appear in the OT, but this one is used in an overwhelming number of cases for killing animals for sacrifice. Only when it refers to the "slaughter" of a people does it evidence a major deviation from this general rule. So settled were the translators of the NIV on this meaning that they translated the word as "to sacrifice."[91] That this interpretation is secure may be gathered from v. 5 where in a parallel text to this verb, the word זבח (*zābaḥ*), "to sacrifice," appears. Therefore, the law did not command that no meat could be butchered anywhere in the land except in front of the tabernacle. What it restricted was butchering those domestic animals that were used for sacrifices anywhere but at the sanctuary. The law was aimed at preventing the possibility of sacrificing at other altar installations, which always raised the horror of idolatry and pagan worship in the midst of Israel.

This law, we conclude, was given specifically to bring a halt to laity offering sacrificial animals in the open fields (v. 5). There could be no rival to the living God or to the worship Israel was to bring to God. In fact, in v. 7 the verb זנה (*zānâ*, "to commit harlotry," "to go astray," "to prostitute [oneself]") is used. This verb proved to be correct in both a literal and a figurative sense, for as Israel built the competing altars with the one in the courtyard of the tabernacle (and the one later on at the Temple), they began to fall into ritual prostitution at the pagan sites and prohibited altars. The prophets of Israel used no term more frequently for the people's apostasy, in both a literal and a figurative sense, than this word for harlotry.

But what about the fact that this law was to be for all time? Given the interpretation offered here, this would be the rule: It was part and parcel of the centralized worship concept so strong in Deuteronomy. Another possibility, though not strongly favored here, is that the antecedent to the "this" of v. 7*b* is the command given in v. 7*a*—Israel was no longer to offer any sacrifices to the goat idols.

But before we discuss what these "goats" were, notice the penalty for disobedience of this command. The individual would be considered "guilty of bloodshed" and "must be cut off from his people." The offense was as serious as murder! Whether all the cases of "cutting off" involved capital punishment is difficult to say. Occasionally, it may have involved excommunication from the people of God, when the offense was not moral, but ceremonial. But this division of the question

is modern, and a firm basis for such mercy cannot be identified in the text.

Originally, the word translated "goat-gods/demons" (שעירם *śĕʿîrîm*) signified "hairy ones," or "rough, shaggy, or rugged" creatures. Subsequently, it was applied to male goats and then to mythical creatures in half-human and half-goat form.

Lower Egypt had a flourishing worship of goats. It gave rise to the worship of the god Pan in Greek and Roman times, one similar to Christian popular depictions of the devil: a goat form with a tail, horns, and cloven hoofs. So frightening were these depictions of this pagan god that our word for terror comes from the god Pan, i.e., *panic*. It can now be seen why the threat of cutting off is given in v. 7*b*. That had been the warning of Exod 22:19; any Israelite who sacrificed to any other god would be cut off.

The reference here must be to some kind of goat worship, probably not unlike what appeared in Lower Egypt. Joshua 24:14 alluded to the fact that the forefathers of the Israelites had worshiped other gods before Abraham came from Ur of the Chaldees ("worshiped beyond the River") and had also indulged in false worship "in Egypt." A goat worship did flourish in the delta region, which involved, in part, goats copulating with women votaries.

17:8-9. The second regulation prohibits other types of sacrifices people might wish to offer somewhere other than in the tabernacle area. The wisdom of such a restriction can be quickly gathered from reading the subsequent history of the nation of Israel. Disobedience to injunctions, such as these, led to idolatry on practically every high hill in Judah and Israel. It was the snare that finally destroyed both the northern and the southern kingdoms.

This prohibition applies to the resident alien as much as it does to any Israelite. The reason for this rule is the same as for Israel: to discourage the aliens from sacrificing to pagan gods.

Even more serious is offering a whole "burnt offering" to anyone other than the Lord (v. 8). Total dedication, which this offering symbolizes, is owed only to Yahweh. There is no question of eating some of the meat in a sacrificial meal when "burnt offering" is used; thus, not even the excuse that

91. See Victor P. Hamilton's discussion of this Hebrew root in *Theological Wordbook of the Old Testament*, eds. R. Laird Harris, Gleason L. Archer, Jr., and Bruce K. Waltke, 2 vols. (Chicago: Moody, 1980) 915-16.

one needed to butcher some meat for personal use could be used with this offering. It is offered up *totally* on the altar.

17:10-12. The third paragraph deals with the prohibition on eating blood. Again, the resident alien is as much obligated to keep this law as is the Israelite.

This rule had been in force ever since God allowed Noah to eat meat; it was on the condition that he would thoroughly drain the animal's blood before eating it (see Gen 9:4). This is not the only place where this law reappears (see Lev 7:26-27; Deut 12:16, 23; 15:23; 1 Sam 14:32-34).

Why is there so strong a prohibition? Two explanations are given in this text. The first is "For the life of a creature is in the blood." The word translated "life" is נֶפֶשׁ (*nepeš*), which has a wide assortment of meanings, such as "throat," "soul," "appetite," "life," and "person." The word translated "creature" is בָּשָׂר (*bāśār*), which also has a wide range of meanings, including "flesh," "body," "the male reproductive organ," and "creature."

What is v. 11 claiming, then? It is claiming that creatures are living and vital, so long as their blood is in their flesh; but when their blood is separated from the *bāśār*, the creatures are no longer alive! The vitality of the creature is directly linked with its blood. Since there is such a strong link, those who obey and refuse to eat the blood of the animal honor the life of the animal. To honor this injunction is to honor life; to despise this injunction is to despise life.

But a second reason is given for this prohibition on blood in v. 11. The blood has been given not for eating but for making "atonement for yourselves on the altar ; it is the blood that makes atonement for one's life." The understanding of this explanation will literally determine one's whole approach to the book of Leviticus and the sacrificial institution as a whole. It is the most explicit statement on the role and meaning of the blood in the sacrificial system.

Basic to the whole theory of sacrifice in the OT is the concept of substitution. The life of the victim is substituted for the individual human life in such a way that the offender averts the necessity of forfeiting his or her own life, which God could have demanded because of the offense committed. Had not

the life of the substituted victim intervened, exposure to the divine wrath would mean certain death to the offender. But the blood, symbolizing the lifeblood of the victim yielded up in death, comes between the offender and the wrath of God to rescue the offender from the just penalty for the sin.

This would also explain the meaning of the formula "to make atonement for yourselves." The sacrifice literally serves as "a ransom" for the lives of those under the threat of death. Therefore, God graciously chooses to accept the blood of the sacrifices in lieu of the lives of humans, i.e., the blood of humans. It is not that the blood atones for sin by setting the life of the animal free, a view that is held by writers like Roland de Vaux,[92] but the blood delivers or ransoms by means of a substitute; it ransoms by delivering the payment of life itself! Instead of requiring that the offender pay a monetary sum (as was permitted in Exod 21:30 for an owner of a bull who had been known to gore people and who killed a man or a woman), the life of the animal is substituted for the offender's life.

Another case that demonstrates the same point of substitution is the commission of a murder by an unknown perpetrator in the open fields (see Deut 21:1-9). Measurements are to be made to determine which town is the closest to where the corpse lay. The elders of the closest town are to bring a young heifer and lead it down to a stream. There they are to break its neck so that the blood pours back into the earth, apparently since the very ground cries out against this outrageous assault on human life, as it did when the blood of Abel fell on the ground (see Gen 4:10-13)—until Cain was punished for what he had done. The elders then wash their hands with water over the slain heifer and declare, "Our hands did not shed this blood, nor did our eyes see it done" (Deut 21:7 NIV). The heifer's blood is accepted as a substitute for the lives of all who live in the town closest to the corpse, and it is accepted as an "atonement" (Deut 21:8 NIV). Thus, the people are not held guilty for the blood-life of this innocent slain person.

92. Roland de Vaux, "Les sacrifices de porcs en Palestine et dans l'Ancient Orient," BZAW 77 (1958) 250-65; also *idem, Ancient Israel,* 448-49.

The blood, therefore, effects deliverance from the exposure to death by exchanging one life for another. The preposition ‫ב‬ (bĕ) has been understood as an instrumental bet ("the bet of means," i.e., ransomed by means of blood) or the bet of price, which usually occurs in legal texts (i.e., ransomed in the place of [the offender's] life). The parallel between Exod 21:23 ‫נפש תחת נפש‬ (nepeš taḥat nāpeš, "a life in place of a life") is restated as nepeš bĕ-nepeš, "a life in exchange for a life," showing that the one is taken as the price for the other or is exchanged for the other. Each understanding of the preposition is very close to the other in meaning, and makes a strong case for substitution. The instrumental use of bet is usually preferred slightly over the bet of price.[93]

Blood is efficacious because it represents life when it is in the flesh or body of a being. But when the blood is separated from the flesh or the body, that is a sure sign of death. And when that death is directly associated, not with something in the victim, but with something in the one laying hands on it and marking it as being in someway one with that person, one life is being given up so that another life can go free.

17:13-16. The fourth and final paragraph sets forth rules about eating wild game killed in hunting. The previous rules in 17:2-10 deal only with domestic animals such as the bovine class.

93. See Levine, The JPS Torah Commentary, 115-16.

Wild animals can be killed away from the tabernacle, but the blood prohibition still applies. Wild animals are not subject to being considered for sacrifices at the altar; therefore, it does not matter where they are butchered. However, they must be thoroughly drained of all blood because the reasons cited in v. 11 still hold. One reason is repeated in v. 14—"because the life of every creature is its blood" (occuring twice in this verse).

Anything that is found dead, is killed by another animal, or expires naturally is not to be eaten, since its blood would have coagulated in its veins and arteries and the one who ate that meat would be guilty of violating life itself. Only strangers and resident aliens are allowed to eat such meat (see Deut 14:21), but Israelites and proselytes are to refrain from doing so. This rule does not contradict the rule in Leviticus but adds a provision not mentioned in Leviticus. Both texts agree that Israelites should not eat any meat in the category mentioned here.

Should people innocently eat what they did not know had not been properly drained of blood because it fell in one of these above cases of wild game, it is their duty to bathe and to launder their garments in order to be qualified to worship God again. They remain unclean until the evening of the same day (v. 15).

Every clean wild animal killed in the field is to be bled completely, and then its spilled blood is to be covered over with earth (v. 13).

REFLECTIONS

1. The principle of a vicarious substitutionary atonement observed in this passage receives its highest expression in the death of Jesus Christ on the cross at Golgotha. It is possible for those who have offended God, and who are thus worthy of death, to receive atonement and reconciliation with God because of the lifeblood of Christ offered on our behalf as a reconciling means (see Rom 5:9-11). So strong is the proposition that the blood makes atonement that Heb 9:22 lays it down as immutable: "Without the shedding of blood there is no forgiveness" (NIV). Thus, in the NT view, the sacrificial system anticipated and foreshadowed the one and only perfect sacrifice that was to come in the death of Christ. While all agree that his death and resurrection are central to Christian theology in some significant way, the issue of the blood, and what it means, has continued to be one of the most hotly contested issues in modern ecclesiastical history.

2. The prohibition on drinking blood is one of the few ritual obligations passed down to the early church at the Jerusalem Council. Although Gentile believers were not required to observe the ceremonial law, they were enjoined to "abstain from food sacrificed to idols, from blood, from the meat of strangled animals and from sexual immorality" (Acts 15:29 NIV). Two of the four "requirements" came from Leviticus 17—abstaining from eating an animal that had been killed by strangulation, since its blood would not have been properly drained out, and abstaining from eating blood.

Are these two requirements permanent and binding on Christians today? Certainly, no one can make a case for unchastity as being the biblical norm today, so that provision still remains. And Paul also discussed the freedom of the believer to eat meat offered to the idols. Only if eating such meat would wound one's weak conscience or would be misinterpreted by pagans observing Christians doing so would Paul refrain from partaking of meat previously offered to idols (see 1 Corinthians 8; 10:23-33). Paul may have held the same judgment about eating things strangled and eating blood, but this is difficult to say. Certainly, the apostle did not wish to offend any Jewish believers; he would have tended, therefore, to have kept these two principles from Leviticus 17, even where the conditions mentioned in 1 Corinthians 8 and 10 were absent and thus might have permitted him to participate. The question of the continuing force of abstaining from blood and things strangled is more difficult than the other two items in the Jerusalem Council's list of four, since the other two rules involved theological reasons for their prohibition. That is what makes the question of permanence more difficult. It is doubtful that an appeal to eating Christ's body and drinking his blood signals a reversal of the ancient prohibition, for that would be a confusion of the figurative for the literal. While the figure used by our Lord is striking (especially in light of the revealed rule in Leviticus), if it were taken literally, its interpreters would be just as misguided as were those who thought Christ attacked the Temple itself when he claimed he would raise up his temple in three days after it was destroyed!

3. Even though there is nothing wrong in itself with killing an animal in one place rather than another, we are taught a principle of unusual importance: Holiness demands that we abstain from what is in itself wrong and immoral, and that we must keep ourselves from doing lawful and necessary things in ways and in circumstances that may outwardly compromise our otherwise clear testimony as Christians.

4. It is not enough that we as believers abstain from things that are prohibited by God (e.g., in Israel's day it was certain foods), but we must also use what is permitted in such a way that will be well pleasing to God, avoiding even the appearance of evil.

5. All that is connected with God and with the worship of God is to be treated with reverence. Modernity has often lost the sense of the sacredness of everything associated with the divine. The trite, flippant, and irreverent way in which many sacred things are treated today is a public disgrace. Treating irreverently things that are associated with God or with the worship of God can be a mockery of God. Believers must exercise greater caution. If what this text teaches about domestic animals that are connected with the sacrificial order of the altar is true, surely the same principle that denies crossing over the lines of the sacred and the secular applies for all other things connected with the living God.

LEVITICUS 18:1-30, HOLINESS IN SEXUAL BEHAVIOR

COMMENTARY

Chapters 18–20 form a distinct section within the Holiness Code of chaps. 17–26. It begins with a formal introduction in 18:1-5 and concludes with a formal closing in 20:22-26.

Four areas where holiness must be exemplified are set forth in these three chapters, including sexual behavior (18:1-30), social ethics (19:1-37), worship (20:1-8, 27), and family relations (20:9-26). Chapters 18–19 mainly contain moral prohibitions, but chap. 20 has more penal sanctions.

In addition to the prominence given to the theme of the holiness of God as the basis for holiness in the lives of all persons ("Be holy because I, the LORD your God, am holy" [19:2; 20:7, 26; 21:8; and twice previously in 11:44-45]), there is the constant repetition of the formula "I am the LORD your God." Beginning with 18:2, this declaration appears almost fifty times in these three chapters. This affirmation is almost identical to the one that introduces the Ten Commandments in Exod 20:2 and Deut 5:6. It is an assertion of the absolute supremacy and sovereignty of God found in the frequent reminder that "I am the LORD." It also is an obvious allusion to the episodes in Exod 3:15 and 6:2-4 where Yahweh discloses the divine self to Moses and the nation of Israel by this name for the first time.[94]

Chapters 18–20 are unique in the history of morals and ethics, both in grounding their ethical injunctions in the repeated formula of divine self-asserveration and in the way that the institutions of marriage and the family are made the hallmarks and foundations for building morality. None have put it more succinctly than J. H. Hertz. His view is that these chapters set forth

the foundation principles of social morality. The first place among these is given to the institution of marriage . . . the cornerstone of all human society. . . . Any violation of the sacred character of

marriage is deemed a heinous offense, calling down the punishment of Heaven both upon the offender and the society that condones the offence.[95]

Chapter 18 is divided into four sections containing four warnings: against the customs of pagan nations (vv. 1-5); against incestuous and illicit sexual unions (vv. 6-20); against Canaanite sexual deviations (vv. 21-23); and about the consequences of neglecting these rules (vv. 24-30).

Chapter 18 is one of the most systematic and complete collections of laws in the Torah on the subject of incest and forbidden sexual unions. More than any other text, it outlines which unions are permissible and which are forbidden.

The biblical family is organized along patrilineal lines with the father being the head of the family. The nuclear family is founded on six relatives, who are "flesh relations": father, mother, son, daughter, brother, and sister. This definition can be indirectly determined by noting that, according to 21:2-3, any of the priests are permitted to attend the funeral of any one of these six relatives, even though contact with a corpse normally defiles a priest.

Two key principles shape the definition of what is considered incest in this law on sexual behaviors: (1) שאר (šĕ'ēr, "flesh relations") also known as blood relations or as consanguine relations; and (2) לגלות ערוה (legallôt 'erwâ, "to uncover the nakedness") a euphemism for "having sexual relations with [someone]," hence a principle of sexuality. The šĕ'ēr relatives are in a different category from the members of the family related by virtue of marriage. The only exception to the 'erwâ prohibition is the levirate marriage, which according to Deut 25:5-10 allows, if not requires, a man to raise up a male heir with his brother's widow. With the interaction of these two principles of "flesh

---

94. See the altogether unique argument of Moberly, *The Old Testament of the Old Testament,* 21-35.

95. J. H. Hertz, *Leviticus* (London: Oxford University Press, 1932) 172.

relations" and "sexual relations," all sexual unions in chap. 18 are defined as either legitimate or illegitimate.

The prohibitions noted in chap. 18 are in no way meant to be an exhaustive list of all possible combinations of unions. In dealing with the more obvious violations against normative chastity, it sets patterns for inferring principles of interpretation not directly addressed.

18:1-5. The scope of the whole chapter is set out in v. 3. The emphasis on "doing" can best be captured in a literal translation: "According to the *doings* of the land of Egypt, where you used to live, you shall not *do:* and according to the *doings* of the land of Canaan, where I am bringing you, you shall not *do:* neither shall you live by their statutes." Instead, Israel is *to do* God's decrees and statutes, and to keep them in mind while going about the business of living (v. 5). The accent falls on an approved life-style as opposed to forms of living that Israel had seen in Egypt and, apparently, would soon see demonstrated in Canaan.

Israel had been called to be a holy nation, a royal priesthood, or a kingdom of priests (see Exod 19:5-6). Any and all trifling with the customs observed among the pagan nations of Egypt or Canaan would mock the call to holiness that had been issued to the nation. It was common for the royal line in Egypt to intermarry brothers and sisters. Even a pharaoh like Rameses II claimed he was sired by the relations his mother had with the goat-god Ptah. The Canaanites were no more exemplary models of sexual behavior, for the Canaanite Ugaritic texts were lewd in their references to the gods and goddesses and their unrestrained copulation with one another and with animals. The warning was not prudish in the least; it was extremely realistic caution about the surrounding sensate societies of those days.

Men and women will fare much better if they will follow God's laws. This chapter is addressed to those who claim the Lord as their God. In fact, that affirmation literally frames this chapter in vv. 2 and 30. Only those who already have this Lord as their God are commanded to walk in God's ways so that they might live (v. 5). Keeping the law will not lead to eternal life, as some have mistakenly

thought this verse teaches, but it will lead to an abundant life.[96] The phrase "will live by them" means that life will be lived in accordance with God's laws and commandments. The subsequent history of interpretation finds both Christian and Jewish commentators attempting to have this phrase reinterpreted to say, "[A person] shall perform, so that [as a result] he or she may acquire life by keeping them." But this result, as one can see, is contrived both in its understanding of "life" and in its unusual construal of the syntax.

18:6-20. This section deals with all types of incestuous and illicit sexual relations. The section begins in v. 6 with a general statement that underlies all prohibitions on the various kinds of incestuous and wrong sexual relations, insisting that its rules apply to everyone. The Hebrew has איש איש (*ʾîš ʾîš*), meaning literally "man, man," but idiomatically "no one," i.e., "none of you," perhaps implying not only Israelites, but all humans, whether Hebrew or Gentile: "No one is to approach [a euphemism for 'to have sexual intercourse with'; cf. Gen 20:4 or Isa 8:3] any close relative [literally 'to all (any) remainder of his flesh' אל־כל־שאר בשרו *ʾel-kol-šĕʾēr bĕšārô*] to have sexual relations." For the fourth time in the first six verses of this chapter, this principle is sealed, as it were, with a signature that underscores the significance of what has just been said: "I am the LORD." To act differently from this rule's directions would be to make common cause with the customs of the Egyptians and the Canaanites. Such unnatural alliances were sanctioned with some frequency in Egypt between a man and his sister or half-sister. Another form of the same injunction against incest is Paul's rebuke to a man who had committed incest with his mother (see 1 Cor 5:1).

If v. 6 deals with the principle of relatives who are related by virtue of blood relations in the *šĕʾēr*, "flesh," v. 7 announces a similar principle but from the standpoint of affinity by virtue of sexual relations (*ʿerwâ*). Verse 7 forbids sexual relations with one's natural mother. Literally the Hebrew text reads: "The nakedness of your father, that is [ו *wĕ*] the nakedness of your mother, you shall not

96. For a full discussion of this issue, see Walter C. Kaiser, Jr., "Leviticus 18:5 and Paul: 'Do This and You Shall Live (Eternally?)," *JETS* 14 (1971) 19-28; also *idem, Toward an Old Testament Theology* (Grand Rapids: Zondervan, 1978) 110-13.

uncover; she is your mother—you shall not uncover her nakedness." Because the husband and the wife "become one flesh" (Gen 2:24 NIV), to "uncover the nakedness of " (i.e., "to have sexual relations with") one partner is equivalent to exposing the other partner. The husband and the wife are so identified in marriage that they are no longer two. Only sexual relations with the mother is intended in this example even though the father is just as much implicated since he alone should have access to his wife's sexuality. Deuteronomy 27:20 underscores the same thought by saying, "Cursed is the man who sleeps with his father's wife, for he dishonors his father's bed" (NIV). In a similar manner, the nakedness of a brother's wife is exclusively the brother's nakedness (Lev 18:16). The married partners truly are "one flesh."

Incest is forbidden with one's mother (v. 7), stepmother (v. 8; in that a man and his wife are one flesh even if he should die or divorce her), sister (v. 9), granddaughter (v. 10), half-sister on the father's side (v. 11), paternal aunt (v. 12), maternal aunt (v. 13), paternal uncle's wife (v. 14), daughter-in-law (v. 15), brother's wife (v. 16), stepdaughter or granddaughter (v. 17), or wife's sister while the wife is still living (v. 18). These various prohibitions embrace six relationships of consanguinity—i.e., blood relations (vv. 7, 9-13)—and eight cases of affinity (by virtue of sexual relations) in marriage (vv. 8, 14-18).

There is some question about v. 9 with its clause "whether she was born into the household or outside" (literal translation). It may well be that the meaning is one who is one's father's daughter, and thus born into that household, or one who is born outside that household, when the mother is not part of that household. In effect, then, it would distinguish between one who is born from one's father by another woman or one who is born from one's mother by another man.

It is clear, then, that biblical law forbids unions between close blood relatives and, in certain cases, between persons who are connected by marriage. Some relationships that are not present may strike us as being strange, e.g., there is no prohibition of a union between a father and a daughter. However, this is to be inferred from the prohibition

on the union between grandfather and granddaughter (v. 10). There is no warning against a union between an uncle and a niece, but that too is to be inferred because a union between a nephew and an aunt is mentioned in v. 14.

Polygamous marriages within a family, apparently, are discouraged by the prohibition on a man marrying his wife's sister during the lifetime of the wife (v. 18). This not only bars polygamous marriages of two sisters; it also bars marriage to the sister of a divorced wife. A widower, apparently, may marry his late wife's sister.[97]

Adultery is considered in v. 20. It consists of a married or an engaged woman having sexual relations with someone who is not her husband. It was traditionally argued that a married man having intercourse with a single woman was judged to be sinful but such action did not constitute adultery and warrant the accompanying death penalty (vv. 24-30). The law here deals only with the violation of another's marriage, and to do so renders one unclean, a matter regarded as most serious by the Holiness Code (vv. 24-30).

18:21-23. The third section warns against the indulgences of the Canaanites. However, grouped with these aberrations are the issues of profaning the name of God (v. 21b), homosexual acts (v. 22), and bestiality (v. 23).

Why Molech worship (v. 21) should suddenly intrude into this discussion of sexual relations cannot be determined exactly, since we still do not know exactly what this cult involved.

The conventional wisdom on this matter usually declares that Molech was a heathen god to whom infants were sacrificed. His worshipers called him מלך (*Melek*, "king"), but the biblical writers could not abide this offense, so they took the vowels from the word בשת (*bōšet*, "shame") and substituted them into *melek* to get *mōlek*, or as English has it *Molech*.

Human sacrifice was known in the ancient Near East, for the Moabite king Mesha sacrificed his oldest son at a time of national crisis (see 2 Kgs 3:27), but to whom he sacrificed his son we do not know. First Kings 11:7 also

---

97. For further discussion on this important v. 18, see Kaiser, *Toward Old Testament Ethics*, 116, and the arguments of S. E. Dwight, *The Hebrew Wife or the Law of Marriage* (New York: Leavitt, 1836) 105-27.

links Molech with the Ammonites, but elsewhere the Ammonite god is called Milcom. No one has ever found a god named Melek in any extrabiblical source.

It is also true that the Canaanites burned their children (see Deut 12:31) as offerings to the gods, but the sacrifice is never linked directly with Molech; nor does the name of a god appear in a similar passage (see Deut 18:10). Only this passage in Lev 18:21 and Jer 32:35 speaks of children being offered to Molech; but there is not a word about fire in these two contexts. The only passage where Molech and fire are connected is in 2 Kgs 23:10. Some say the children were only made to walk between two fires as a symbol of dedication to Molech, while others tell stories of children being tossed back and forth over a fire until they were burned. Others think that Molech was shaped like a huge potbelly stove in which a roaring fire was placed. Children offered to him were placed on the image's outstretched arms; then they rolled down the arms and fell through the image's mouth into the hot fire.[98]

Traces of this form of infanticide have been found in Carthage, North Africa, a known outpost for the late Phoenician-Canaanite society.[99] Evidence has now come from a Late Bronze Age temple in Amman, Jordan, ancient Rabbath-Ammon, capital of the Ammonites. It is also known that during the reigns of Manasseh and Amon, kings of Judah, Molech worship was practiced just outside Jerusalem at Topheth, in the valley of Hinnom. Manasseh even sacrificed his children to this god! (See 2 Chr 36:6.) So disgusting was the practice that King Josiah, Manasseh's grandson, ordered the Molech installation razed to the ground, and the place was subsequently renamed Gehenna, the awful symbol of hell.[100]

Giving children to Molech is here said to lead to the profanation of the name of God (v. 21 b).[101] The direct opposite of holiness is חל (ḥōl, "profane" or "common"), or what

has been taken away from the Temple. Thus, in one word, "to profane" a holy God and to profane a people is to place two opposite principles in mortal combat with each other. And in this case, the "name" of God stands for God's person, character, teaching, and qualities. To make any of these aspects of God common or cheap is to attack the very person of God.

Homosexual behavior carries strong disapproval (v. 22), perhaps because it too is connected with Canaanite practices or because it is an act considered contrary to human nature. This verse labels it an "abomination," and it is included in the abominations condemned in vv. 26-30. The root from which *abomination* comes means "to hate" or "to abhor." The practice itself, not the person, is despised or hated. The practice is considered by many to be condemned throughout Scripture (see Gen 19:1-38; Lev 20:13; Judg 19:22-23; Rom 1:27; and 1 Cor 6:9). Others would argue that many of these texts imply sexual activity that is exploitive, violent, lustful, or connected with pagan cults and thus cannot be used to condemn homosexual behavior as such. This text, however, does not allow for permissible homosexual activity, but the context may suggest such activity implied Canaanite practice to Israel.

It has been argued that this law on homosexual behavior has been removed in Christian times, since it appears in the ceremonial law. Thus, it is argued, forbidding homosexual acts would be like forbidding unclean foods today. But this challenge forgets that this law is in the Holiness Code with its vigorous moral emphasis; therefore, others would argue that its content is still binding on us today. It is just as normative today as are the laws of blood relations, laws of affinity, laws on incest, laws on adultery, and laws against unjust weights and measures.

Homosexual behavior, until recently, has been regarded as an unnatural, perverted, or degenerate form of sexual relations by most Jewish-Christian morality. Many would argue that this reflects limited Israelite understandings and social context (similar to attitudes on women and slaves) and texts like Lev 18:22 are not to be considered eternally binding. These issues cannot be resolved in the discussion of this text alone. For that reason the

98. For documentation, see the *Talmud, Sanh.* 64b. and Diodorus *History,* 20.14, and *IDB* 4:154a. Also see N. H. Snaith, "The Cult of Molech," VT 16 (1966) 123ff.

99. See Roland de Vaux, *Studies in Old Testament Sacrifice* (Cardiff: University of Wales Press, 1964) 56-90.

100. A. R. W. Green, *The Role of Human Sacrifice in the Ancient Near East* (Missoula: Scholars Press, 1975).

101. For a fuller study of the meaning of "name," see Walter C. Kaiser, Jr., "Name," in the *Zondervan Pictorial Encyclopedia of the Bible,* ed. M. C. Tenney, 5 vols. (Grand Rapids: Zondervan, 1975) 4:360-70.

rigid condemnation and description of homosexual acts found in v. 22 will anger many modern readers who have become more tolerant of homosexual practices than they have of any critiques of it. The subject arouses violent emotions on both sides of the issue, but there can be no doubt about this text's position on the matter. The Holiness Code does not consider homosexual activity between men (women are not considered) acceptable and judges it an abomination.

No less reprehensible is another practice found among the nations of antiquity: bestiality. Sexual congress between humans and animals is unconditionally forbidden (see Exod 22:19; Lev 18:23; 20:15-16; Deut 27:21). To cross over boundaries set by God is to introduce confusion and mixtures that are condemned as being unnatural from the divine point of view. This theme, however, is a frequent one in the myths. Usually, a woman couples with a beast or a god in the guise of a beast. It too stands under the divine indictment of a God who had no female consort and who had no congress with any animals, as did the gods of antiquity.

18:24-30. This chapter on sexual behavior concludes with a set of warnings. To avoid being "vomited out" (vv. 25, 28) of the holy land that God would give to Israel, men and women would do well to observe all the commandments of God. For just as the Canaanites had been expelled from the very same territory prior to the coming of Israel for disobeying the very same moral principles of a holy God, so it would happen to Israel for the same reasons.

REFLECTIONS

1. Sexual purity is only one part of the larger morality that is mandatory for all who would live a godly and righteous life before a holy God. However, sexual holiness may be the first line of practical defense for all who are on the road to living a holy life devoted to God. To give free course to our passions, appetites, and hungers in this area is ultimately to turn loose the controls over every other area of our lives.

2. It is surprising to be asked today if the rules of consanguinity and affinity are still of permanent authority in our contemporary world, for the reasons given are just as valid and foundational now as they were then. The theology of "one flesh" and the relation of blood between members of the same family hold now just as they did then.

3. Important to the well-being of a society is the relation of a man and a woman in the building of a family. While not always able to control and set civil law in modern democratic societies, the church must refuse to compromise where civil law ignores or runs directly counter to the will of God. What contravenes the law of God must be labeled an attack on God's call for mortals to be holy.

On the other hand, a warning must also be issued against the opposite tendency, i.e., to lay heavier burdens on the conscience of the populace than God has first placed there in Scripture. While we resist the tendency to license on the one hand, fairness and truthfulness demand that we proceed with extreme caution when this list of prohibitions in the sexual area is extended by extremely slender grounds of analogy and unfair inference. While trying too hard to avert falling into the ditch on one side of the road, one may fall into the ditch on the other side.

4. When a nation continues to flout the moral standards set by God, that nation can expect the same terrible conclusion to its sovereignty and existence that has come upon every other society in history thus far. This principle was turned into a key warning in Jer 18:7-10. Let the nations beware, because God is not mocked. Whatever a nation sows by way of moral travesty, it will certainly reap—whether there is agreement with the divine morality in the present consensus or not.

LEVITICUS 19:1-37, HOLINESS IN SOCIAL ETHICS

COMMENTARY

Leviticus 19 is one of the grand chapters of the whole book of Leviticus. In American Reform Judaism it is one of the most quoted and most often read chapters, especially since it is assigned as the Torah reading for Yom Kippur afternoon in that tradition.

The masthead for this chapter is v. 2 "Be holy because I, the LORD your God, am holy." To illustrate just how all-embracing this standard is, a list of examples is given in chap. 19 from almost every area of life. So representative and so wide is the range of the laws and commandments found in this chapter that it might be characterized as a brief Torah. Moreover, the refrain that is repeated no less than fifteen times is: "I am the LORD [your God]," which marks the end of almost every one of the sixteen paragraphs (the full formula appears in vv. 3, 4, 10, 25, 31, 34, and 36; the shorter form, "I am the LORD," appears in vv. 12, 14, 16, 18, 28, 30, 32, and 37).

This chapter may appear somewhat arbitrary and heterogeneous in that it appears to mix up moral, civil, and religious injunctions. But we need only note how foundational the Ten Commandments are to these laws to realize that they illustrate deeper ethical principles. The fact that the Ten Commandments are the formative principles can be seen from the following list of parallels:

Ten Commandments	Leviticus 19
1 and 2	v. 4
3	v. 12
4 and 5	v. 3
6	v. 16
7	v. 29
8 and 9	vv. 11, 16
10	v. 18

This is not to imply that Leviticus 19 is a revision of the Decalogue; on the contrary, chap. 19 is a further reinforcement and a practical illustration of it.

The structure of chap. 19 is easily divided into three main sections with a number of subsections, each usually set off by the refrain, "I am the LORD [your God]." The first section (vv. 3-8) deals with two fundamental duties of life: to honor parents (v. 3) and to reverence God (vv. 4-8). The second section (vv. 9-18) explores holiness in neighborliness, specifically regard for the poor (vv. 9-10), regard for the truth (vv. 11-12), regard for the employee and the helpless (vv. 13-14), regard for the rich (vv. 15-16), and regard for one's neighbor (vv. 17-18). The third section (vv. 19-36) examines further holiness in all areas of life, including against certain mixtures (v. 19), regulating slavery and concubinage (vv. 20-22), regulating firstfruits (vv. 23-25), prohibition of eating blood (v. 26*a*), prohibition on divination (v. 26*b*), prohibition on sorcery (v. 26*c*), prohibition on pagan mourning rites (v. 27), prohibition on tattooing for the dead (v. 28), prohibition on sacred prostitution (v. 29), reverence for God's sabbath and sanctuary (v. 30), prohibition on necromancy (v. 31), respect for the elderly (v. 32), respect for the alien (vv. 33-34), and honesty in trading (vv. 35-36).

The constant theme in chaps. 18–26 is holiness.[102] This theme, which has already appeared in 11:44-45, is the motto and central emphasis of the book of Leviticus. The level of ethical performance expected of all persons was that of an imitation of the very character of God: "Be holy because I, the LORD your God, am holy." Holiness is the essential nature of God, as Isa 6:3 announces: "Holy, holy, holy is the LORD of hosts!" (NRSV). In fact, Isaiah is the very same prophet who calls God קְדוֹשׁ יִשְׂרָאֵל (*qĕdôš Yiśrāʾēl*, "the Holy One of Israel" [Isa 1:4]).

Holiness stands as the foundational principle in the long list of precepts set forth in this chapter. Holiness is the object of all of the moral and ceremonial law. But since God sets the norm and defines just what holiness does and does not include, God's holiness acts both as model and as motivating force in

---

102. See Gammie, *Holiness in Israel,* 1-70.

the development and maintenance of a holy character. To make sure that the point is not lost, fifteen times the sixteen subsections end with the reminder that "I am the LORD [your God]."

The concept of holiness has exercised a major influence in recent generations of scholars, if for no other reason because of the book *The Idea of the Holy* by the Protestant theologian Rudolf Otto.[103] Religion, Otto argues, cannot be reduced to ethics, as was the tendency of the reigning liberal theology of that day. Human nature has a religious aspect that responds to the mysterious and the awesome, a reality that can be embraced only in the word *holy* or the experience of the "numinous." But for Otto, holiness is an affective experience, not one anchored to the character of God.

Otto makes no mention, strangely enough, of Leviticus 19, the key chapter in the Bible on holiness. In his zeal to assert a unique character for religion, he ends up making the ethical aspect of holiness a mere "extra." But Leviticus 19 insists that faith and ethics are necessary aspects of the same coin, though they are by no means identical. Faith must demonstrate its authenticity by the way it operates in the ordinary affairs of life. The religious life of faith must have ethical outcomes if it makes a claim to authenticity.

The character of God stands behind the moral duties for humanity. Other ancient religions did not appeal to the person, nature, and actions of their deities as the basis for moral thinking and acting (cf. Psalm 82). Often the pagan deities were more sensual and debased in their actions and character than the mortals who strove to worship them. Not so with Yahweh, who is holiness itself and a model for all.

19:3-8. The first division of the law of holiness sets forth two fundamental duties for the social and religious life: to honor one's parents (v. 3) and to reverence God (vv. 4-8).

Pride of place in the law of holiness goes to honoring one's parents. This precept is first announced in the fifth commandment (see Exod 20:12). But it should not surprise us that honoring one's parents is placed at the head of this list of precepts, especially since

parents function in a very real sense to introduce a child to God during the early years. Notice that the mother is mentioned first, and then the father, reversing the order given in the Ten Commandments. Here, then, is the foundation of all holiness as it is worked out in the sphere of relationships with others.

The second foundational principle is to be found in reverence for God; however, it is not to be taught by direct precept. Instead, three injunctions set forth this reverence for God: Keep the sabbath (v. 3*b*), avoid idolatry (v. 4), and observe the peace offering (vv. 5-8).

But why are these three commands selected from all the possible ones that could have been selected? Perhaps it is because Israel is more liable to fail in these three areas than in any others in the law.

The sabbath law appears frequently: fifteen times in Exodus, twenty-four times in Leviticus, three times in Numbers, three times in Deuteronomy, and sixty-one times in the rest of the books of the OT. The sabbaths could refer to the annual feasts, the sabbatical year, and the weekly sabbath. Yet for all the emphasis in the text, this law seems more like positive law (i.e., a law that depends for its authority on the mere command of God) than like moral law (i.e., a law that depends for its authority on the character and nature of God).

God is Lord of time and, therefore, worthy of a designated portion of time for the worship, service, and honoring of God's name. However, the sabbath is simply positive law in that it specifies the seventh day and grounds its observance in the example of God's action in creation and in the work of delivering Israel from Egypt. But when the law of sabbath worship and rest came into conflict with humanity's love for gain, pleasure, recognition, and haste to become wealthy, a form of idolatry was immediately introduced. Unfortunately, an insatiable greed has generally stamped out the designation of regular times to be set aside in reverence for God (cf. Amos 8:5).

Just as pervasive in the OT are the references to proscribing all forms of idolatry. The second of the Ten Commandments warned Israel against this ever-present danger, but to little avail. Lest the point be lost on modern generations, the nature of idolatry did not

103. Rudolf Otto, *The Idea of the Holy*, trans. J. W. Harvey (New York: Oxford University Press, 1958).

reside simply in erecting a physical icon and in offering worship to that icon; instead, it was to be found in making any goal, person, institution, or allegiance equal to, or above, one's commitment to the living God. In that sense the danger of idolatry is still rampant today.

It is much more difficult to see how failure to observe the peace offerings would have a detrimental influence on reverencing God in one's heart—at least, it does not seem, at first, to be on the same level as the previous two injunctions in this set of three. But the offerer is liable to disobey the provisions of the peace offering (the most frequently offered of all the sacrifices, since it is a shared fellowship meal with many). In an attempt to economize, be thrifty, and be careful to save, Israel would be tempted to retain the food that remained until the third day, even when God had commanded them not to do so (cf. Lev 7:15-18). Disobedience and reverence for God do not go hand in hand. Reverence for God demands that service to God be performed in the prescribed manner. This is the order of holiness—everything else is only self-will.

19:9-18. The second division of this chapter on social ethics and practical holiness embraces five precepts in five paragraphs, all relating to the duties of persons to other persons. Each closes with the characteristic refrain of this law of holiness, "I am the LORD." Five pentads illustrate the law of holiness as it applies to neighborliness.

The first pentad (vv. 9-10) seeks to help poor people by legislating that the three chief products of agriculture—the grain, the product of the vine, and the fruit of the trees—are not to be harvested entirely; some is to be left for poor to glean. Holiness must manifest itself in regard for poor people. As we shall see in 25:23, the Lord is the ultimate owner of everything; thus the land is a gift from the Lord. If the landowners are only stewards of the land and all that it produces, there is no reason to be selfish and stingy. Holiness begins with one's treatment of poor people; but grasping, covetous, and stingy personalities are not holy persons.

The rights of poor people at harvest time appear again in Lev 23:22 and Deut 24:19-22. Disadvantaged members of the society have a right to harvest the edges of the fields;

they are not to depend on voluntary gifts alone.

If the first pentad condemns stinginess, the second relates to outright stealing, lying, and fraud (v. 11). Further, such blatant theft and deception cannot be covered by false swearing in God's name (v. 12) for that is a profanation. Holiness demands the honoring of others' possessions and integrity in dealings with one another. Holy persons refuse to steal (eighth commandment), to lie (ninth commandment), or to fortify their prevarications by a vain use of God's name (third commandment).

The use of fraud to oppress the wage earner or helpless persons is opposed in this third pentad (vv. 13-14). The deuteronomic law takes up the same cause (see Deut 24:15), and the prophets lash out against such blatant injustice (see Isa 3:14; Jer 22:3). The principle is no less important in our own day: No one is to take advantage of another person's vulnerability in order to get work done at lower wages or to call in mortgages for the slightest legal loophole or momentary lapse in the payments. Just as reprehensible is the practice of retaining someone's daily wages when the person is depending on them to purchase food to assuage hunger that very day (see Deut 24:15; Jas 5:1, 4).

The same principle carries over into all acts of vilifying, defaming and treating with contempt persons who are deaf or blind (v. 14). This law prohibits ridiculing these disabilities; but it is just as concerned about someone taking advantage of the vulnerability of those who are so exposed. To care for deaf and blind persons is related here to the fear of God, and their care is related to the character of God: I am the Lord.

To stop the wrong inference that God is only the God of the poor, the helpless, and the disadvantaged persons of society, this pentad (vv. 15-16) stresses regard for rich people, showing that partiality can go both ways! The rights of rich people are not to be violated, nor are they to be slandered any more than those of poor people are to be.

The last pentad in this section on holiness in neighborliness (vv. 17-18) is itself the culmination of this climactic chapter in Leviticus. Verse 18, "Love your neighbor as yourself," has been called the Golden Rule (though we do not know who coined that name). This rule is the summary of this whole section on holiness, which expresses itself in neighborliness. So comprehensive are these simple and familiar words that they embrace all morality and fair dealing with all other mortals. This injunction goes right to the core of the matter and declares that the state of one's heart toward one's neighbor is the determining factor in being as holy toward the neighbor as God is holy. No one is to hate a brother in the heart (v. 17). It would be better to openly rebuke a brother rather than brood over a matter. Wise persons profit from such rebukes, but fools reject them (see Prov 9:8; 15:12; 19:25; 27:5). Offering a rebuke is not just a matter of doing one's civic duty or acting out of self-interest; it is also done out of concern for the whole community—that it too will not ultimately have to share in the guilt as the fruit of some of the actions deserving rebuke come home to rest on the community.

Each of the five paragraphs on neighborliness closes with the motive clause "I am the LORD" (vv. 10, 12, 14, 16, 18). They climax, however, in v. 18. There is also a build-up of words for one's neighbor in these pentads, for vv. 17-18 use four different words to describe that individual: *brother, fellow citizen, people,* and *neighbor.*

19:19-36. The third main section of chap. 19 covers fourteen areas of life, all grouped under the general heading of "keep my decrees" (v. 19).

The first decree warns against mixing cattle, seed, or materials in garments. Thus the crossbreeding of animals, the sowing of two different seeds in the same field in a type of hybridization, and the weaving of two different fabrics into a single article of clothing are deemed to be unnatural associations. But why? The second and third examples are mentioned again in Deut 22:9, 11 with another unnatural association intervening there in v. 10—the prohibition of yoking an ox and a donkey to the same plow. This last example is fairly easy to explain: Too great an expectation would be placed on the weaker donkey in such an arrangement. But what of the other associations and mixtures? What principle lies behind their prohibition?

The reason may have been to maintain the created orders "according to its kind." However, mules were used in Israel from the time of David (see 2 Sam 13:29; Deut 18:9; 1 Kgs 1:33; Deut 18:5), and that would require us to see this as a very early regulation. The perspective of Leviticus often seems motivated by a concern for what seems "natural," and this extends to matters that modern perspectives would consider inconsequential and of little moral significance.

The law of vv. 20-22 deals with the act of sexual intercourse between a master and a slave woman who is promised to another but who has not yet been ransomed or given her freedom. The case is similar to the one mentioned in Exod 21:7-8. If the same act is committed with a free woman, and both are guilty, both are liable to capital punishment (see Deut 22:23-24). Instead of dealing with the issue of slavery or concubinage, the law focuses solely on the issue of inflicting harm on someone else's property. Since the slave woman in question has already been promised to a free man, a guilt offering of a ram must be sacrificed at the tent of meeting. It is a sin. But since sexual intercourse does not take place with a betrothed free woman, the death penalty is not imposed. The "due punishment" spoken of in v. 20 is the Hebrew בקרת (*biqqōret*), probably meaning "indemnity," for the Akkadian verb *baqāru* meant "to make good on a claim," "to indemnify." This is the only time this word occurs in the HB. Some sort of payment must be imposed to be paid to the one who suffers the loss along with the necessary guilt offering.

S. H. Kellogg's comment again is most incisive and thoughtful:

By thus appointing herein a penalty for both the guilty parties such as the public conscience would approve, God taught the Hebrew the fundamental lesson that a slave-girl is not regarded by God as a mere chattel: and that if, because of the hardness of their hearts, concubinage was tolerated for a time, still the slave-girl must not be treated as a thing, but as a person, and indiscriminate license could not be permitted.[104]

104. S. H. Kellogg, *The Book of Leviticus,* 3rd ed. (Minneapolis: Klock & Klock, 1978; reprint of A. C. Armstrong & Son, 1899) 405-6.

Although this command grants some recognition of humanity and rights to slaves, it does not address the institution of slavery itself. Here we can only recognize the moral limitations of Israel even as it struggles to discern and embody God's will in the social order.

The third law (vv. 23-25) restricts eating fruit from a fruit tree during the first three years when the fruit has not yet reached its full form, is tart, and can be considered undeveloped. That fruit is to be regarded as "forbidden" (literally "uncircumcised"). The Hebrew word here is ערל ('ārēl), the same stem as the noun ערלה ('orlâ), usually translated "foreskin." Literally the clause in v. 23 reads "You shall trim its foreskin as foreskin." The trees, then, are seen as having foreskins that have not yet been circumcised and dedicated to the Lord.

What grows on the fruit trees in the fourth year is called "holy, an offering of praise to the LORD" (v. 24; cf. Isa 62:9). The increase of the yield will be as a result of the blessing of God (v. 25).

For the fourth time in this book (3:17; 7:27; 17:10-14), the Israelites are forbidden to eat anything with blood still in it (v. 26a). Given the context here, this law warns about the pagan practice of such eating, where eating things with blood in it was a regular occurrence (cf 1 Sam 14:24; Ezek 33:25).

The next four laws prohibit divination (v. 26b), sorcery (v. 26c), mourning rites of the pagans (v. 27), and bodily lacerations on behalf of the dead (v. 28). The word for "divination" reflects a de-nominative verb based on the noun for "snake," since snakes were used in charms and incantations. Sorcery, on the other hand, was a form of soothsaying, where omens were read from the clouds, since the verb was associated with the Hebrew noun for "cloud." Thus the forms, movements, and positions of the clouds, along with other heavenly bodies, were believed to give information and omens about the future. But God's people have been given a revelation, so they have no need to consult the occult world. In fact, they are warned not to do so (see Deut 18:9-14).

Verse 27 prohibits the shaving of hair off the head or beard as a sign of mourning (see also Deut 14:1; Jer 16:6; Ezek 44:20; Amos 8:10), since these practices were known to exist in the Astarte-Tammuz cult of Syria and Arabia. The mourning is not discouraged—only its identification with the pagan rites carrying idolatrous connotations.

The cutting of one's body on behalf of a dead person (v. 28), presumably to appease the demons from tormenting the corpse when they saw the blood shed, is equally reprehensible. Such practices were attested in Israel (see Jer 16:6; 41:5). But any thought that an offering of human blood would procure the favor of the pagan deity was not part of Israel's faith.

The two Hebrew words usually translated "tattoo marks" appear only here in the OT. But since they occur with the word meaning "to write," the sense seems to be clear even if final certainty eludes us. According to 3 Macc 2:21, though much later in time, an ivy leaf was tattooed on the bodies of the adherents of Dionysus. Once again, another pagan practice is prohibited because of Israel's call to holiness.

Another area of life in the ancient Near East that needed regulation was that of religious prostitution (הזנותה hazenôtāh, v. 29). Canaanite teaching asserted that the fertility of the land, its animals, and its people depended on "consecrated women," more frequently called in Hebrew קדשה (qĕdēšâ, Gen 38:21; Deut 23:18; Hos 4:14), or a cult prostitute, giving their bodies in acts of sacred prostitution. In fact, in this one word qĕdēšâ (prostitute), everything "sacred" (קדוש qādôš) is brought into mortal combat with everything opposed to God—all within the scope of words both coming from the same Hebrew roots!

The context for v. 30 seems strange and intrusive until we realize that this verse appears again verbatim in 26:2. There it is directed against pagan practices. This intent would explain its appearance at this point as well. Rather than going to the pagan installations to practice their sorcery, divination, mutilations, and bloodletting acts, the Israelites should express reverence and fear in the observance of the day of worship to Yahweh at the place where the sanctuary is set up. Few restraints on immorality and unholiness are equal to the frequent remembrance of God in the sanctuary.

Attempts to consult the dead spirits by way of necromancy are prohibited (v. 31). Allegedly, the supposed spirit of the dead person (אֹב 'ōb, translated here "medium" since allegedly the spirit of the dead could later enter a person and become a "medium" through whom control could be exercised over the spirit) was able to give communications to the living (see 1 Sam 28:7-11; Isa 8:19). But such methods of obtaining information are strictly forbidden. Seeking out such spirits leads to uncleanness, which in turn leads to exclusion from worship of the one true living God.

Respect for aged and elderly persons is enjoined in v. 32. Age, according to Prov 16:31 and 20:29, is a "crown of splendor" (NIV). Due to the experience that the years bring, such persons often stand in the same relation to younger persons that parents stand to children. And to show respect for aged persons is simultaneously to walk in the fear of God.

Another member of Israel's society is the resident alien (vv. 33-34). Harassment of aliens is likewise prohibited in this call to holiness, for nothing must be done to an alien that is disallowed to a citizen of Israel (see Exod 22:21; Lev 25:14, 17; Jer 22:3; Ezek 18:7, 16). Noordtzij calculates that the OT warns "no fewer than thirty-six times of Israel's obligation to aliens, widows, and orphans.[105] Most important here, Israel's obligation is to be motivated by the memory that they had been aliens in Egypt. Since God delivered Israel, they are to see this as moral motive for just treatment of aliens.

This list of precepts for the expression of holiness concludes with vv. 35-36 urging honesty in trading. God also is concerned about honest weights and measurements. Holiness does not allow for dishonesty in the marketplace either (see Deut 25:13-16; Prov 11:1; 20:23). But in the days of the prophet Amos, the merchants made "the ephah small/ and the shekel great" (Amos 8:5 NRSV; cf. Mic 6:10-11). Here too the memory of the exodus from Egypt is invoked, though it is unclear why it is specially connected to honest weights and measures.

The chapter closes with one final exhortation: "Keep all my decrees and all my laws and follow them. I am the LORD" (v. 37). The authority of the Lawgiver is evident one more time in this chapter literally peppered with direct reminders of the same fact.

105. Noordtzij, *Bible Student's Commentary*, 207.

REFLECTIONS

1. Holiness cannot be regarded as an optional luxury of a believer's life-style. If Lev 19:2 sets the mark high at "be holy because I, the LORD your God, am holy," the NT sets it just as high: "Be perfect, therefore, as your heavenly Father is perfect" (Matt 5:43 NIV). The standard is not abstract or philosophical but personal and concrete; it represents the very character and nature of the Lord. When Jesus urged Christians to be perfect, he was making the same demands for holiness as those found here in Leviticus 19.

2. In Leviticus, the people of God are called to be holy, not because holiness is an arbitrary religion game that God wants played, but because God is holy. Because God is holy, God's people are to be holy by being like God in the world. We can, therefore, do away with all the cartoon pictures of the sanctimonious holy person wearing a halo and a prudish glare. To be holy is not to be narrow-minded and primly pious; it is, rather, to imitate God. To be holy is to roll up one's sleeves and to join in with whatever God is doing in the world.

That is why, in this great chapter on moral holiness, the emphasis falls on social justice. Produce should be left in the fields for poor people to glean. Neighbors should be dealt with honestly. Wages should be paid promptly. Disputes should be settled with equity and fairness. In Leviticus, if you want to be holy, don't pass out a tract; love your neighbor, show hospitality to the stranger, and be a person of justice.

3. Holiness is so essential to the whole process of believing that the writer of Hebrews could say, "without holiness no one will see the Lord" (12:14*b* NIV). Thus, the *spirit* of all the laws listed in Leviticus 19 remains unchanged, even though the formal expression of some of these same principles will, and often does, change. At every step in life, the call to holiness confronts us: in the field, at home, in business, with friends, with aliens and foreigners, in acts of worship, and in the family.

4. So formative was Leviticus 19 in the life of the early church that some have convincingly argued that the book of James in the NT is a sermon or series of abstracts from sermons based on Lev 19:12-18.[106] Most have seen that Jas 2:8 uses the "royal law" found in Lev 19:18: "Love your neighbor as yourself." But what has been missed is the fact that every verse in that section of Leviticus 19 is commented on except v. 14. An outline of the similarities between the two shows this:

Leviticus 19:	James:
12	5:12
13	5:4
[14]	[0]
15	2:1, 8
16	4:11
17*b*	5:20
18*a*	5:9
18*b*	2:8

106. Luke T. Johnson, "The Use of Leviticus 19 in the Letter of James," *JBL* 101 (1982) 391-401; Walter C. Kaiser, Jr., "Applying the Principles of the Ceremonial Law: Leviticus 19; James," in *The Uses of the Old Testament in the New* (Chicago: Moody, 1985), 221-24; *idem*, "James's View of the Law," *Mishkan* 8/9 (1988) 9-12.

LEVITICUS 20:1-8, 27, HOLINESS IN WORSHIP

COMMENTARY

Chapter 20 acts as a natural sequel to chaps. 18–19 in that it specifies the punishments attached to disobedience of the laws given in the preceding statements on holiness. Chapter 20, then, is mainly a penal code. It can be divided into two sections: the penalty for worshiping Molech and going to mediums and spiritists (vv. 1-8, 27), and penalties for sinning against the family (vv. 9-26). Both sections open with the same formula, "If a man . . . "; include strong exhortations calling for holiness of life (vv. 7-8; 22-26); and end with exhortations to holiness.

There is one major difference between chaps. 18–19 and chap. 20. The laws in the previous two chapters are apodictic[107] in form (meaning they are similar in form to the Ten Commandments, with its formula of "you shall . . ."); the laws in chap. 20, on the other hand, are casuistic in form (meaning they are in the form of case laws that begin with, "If a man . . ." or "When . . ."), and the laws of chap. 20 also state what the penalties will be for persons who break the apodictic laws of chaps. 18–19.

The brief reference to Molech[108] worship in 18:21 (see the discussion there for more detail) is here expanded, both in what will come to those who worship Molech and in what will happen to the community that fails to carry out the sentence prescribed.

107. This distinction between apodictic and casuistic laws was first pointed out by Albrecht Alt, *Essays on Old Testament History and Religion,* trans R. A. Wilson (Oxford: Blackwell, 1966) 81-132.

108. See Levine, "Excursus 7: The Cult of Molech in Biblical Israel," in *JPS Torah Commentary,* 258-60, for a good discussion on this topic. Levine sides with de Vaux, *Studies in Old Testament Sacrifice,* 52-90, against Moshe Weinfeld, "On Burning Babies," *Ugarit-Forschungen* 4 (1972) 133-54. Weinfeld argues that the Molech cult did not actually involve child sacrifice in Israel.

To halt the spread of pagan worship, this law threatens all Israelites and aliens living in Israel who might be tempted to indulge in such practices. The technical expression in v. 4 that describes the legislative body is "people of the land" or "people of the community" (עם הארץ *'am hā'āreṣ*). This body, then, is charged with carrying out the sentence of death by stoning if the law is disobeyed. There is some evidence that the expression "people of the land" may have referred originally to the indigenous inhabitants of Canaan (cf. Gen 23:7; 42:6; Num 13:28). But by now, it is employed as the term for the legislative or authoritative body instead of restricting it to the native population, or to the male landowners, as others have tried to limit it.

Death by stoning is the Hebrew form of execution. It is prescribed for blasphemy (see Lev 24:16), idolatry (see Deut 13:6-10), failure to observe the sabbath (see Num 15:32-36), incorrigible children (see Deut 21:18-21), adulterous wives (see Deut 22:21, 24), and involvement in occultism (Lev 20:27). In each of these cases, the witnesses for the prosecution are ordered to cast the first stones. The fact that they are called witnesses (as described in Deut 17:1-7) suggests that a trial under the control of a judge preceded the execution. Never does the text explain exactly why stoning is appropriate punishment, but the inference seems to be that it is the community's way of rejecting the same sins (see Deut 17:7) and refusing to acquiesce to the same sins in their midst. They do not want the community also to be held guilty by tacitly approving these sins.

As noted above, the first reference to Molech in the Torah occurs in Lev 18:21. The verbs generally used in connection with this cult are "to hand over," "to give," "to devote," and "to [make the children] pass through fire" (Deut 18:10, NRSV). King Ahaz is reported to have "burnt his children in the fire" (2 Chr 28:3 KJV), although a simple textual emendation renders "made his sons pass through fire" (NRSV; עבר *'ābar* instead of בער *bā'ar*, the same verb used in Deut 16:10). Second Kings 23:10 reports that King Josiah puts an end to child sacrifice, which used "the fire to Molech" (NIV).

Is the expression "pass through fire" equivalent to "burn in the fire"? Morton Smith demonstrates that the two are indeed equivalent.[109] The proof is in Num 31:22-23, for in this text, the expression "passed through fire" (NRSV) is used of gold, silver, bronze, iron, tin, and lead, which must be put into the fire to be refined. Thus, to pass one's child through the fire, the child had to be submerged, or put into the fire, in the same way that these metals had to be "passed." Accordingly, despite much scholarly controversy about whether the children really were made to pass through the fire in the OT, the conclusion is that they were the objects of child sacrifice. The prophets Jeremiah and Ezekiel were more than justified in their abhorrence of such outrageous activities among the people of God (see Jer 7:31; 32:35; Ezek 20:26, 31). Moreover, two of the Judahite kings in the seventh century BCE (Manasseh and Amon) sponsored the cult of burning children as sacrifices. Cultures that turn away from God soon begin to manifest the irrationality of such a decision, often in violent and dehumanizing forms. One needs only to witness the declination of human rights in the Third Reich of Germany to illustrate that point!

God's name is profaned (see 19:12) when worship is offered to something or someone other than to God. It also simultaneously renders God's sanctuary defiled and impure (20:3). This will be true if the cult is introduced into, near, or even apart from that sanctuary by one professing allegiance to Yahweh and claiming to be part of the people of God. Moreover, such profanation arouses God's wrath.

God and the sanctuary are defiled whenever God is worshiped in any other place or in any other manner than has been commanded. The word meaning to "profane" God's name (v. 3) is the same word used in 19:29: "Do not prostitute your daughter" (literal translation). Thus, while honor or reverence is due to God alone, God is profaned, desecrated, made abominable, and prostituted whenever that honor or reverence is lavished on ancient or modern idols. God will never share glory with another (see Isa 42:8).

Verses 4-5 deal with the effect of non-involvement on this same problem. Should Israel merely close its eyes to child sacrifice

109. Morton Smith, "A Note on Burning Babies," *JAOS* 95 (1975) 477-79.

by not prosecuting such cases, divine judgment will intervene. The family, clan, tribe, or nation that thinks it can help such a person escape judgment by taking a "hands-off" policy will itself be exposed to divine judgment! The inference, of course, is that the whole nation, or larger group, is indeed the brother's keeper. Negligence, in this case, will lead to drastic results.

Another form of infidelity to Yahweh is treated in vv. 6 and 27. This sin has already been alluded to in 19:31. Consulting mediums and spiritists in the hopes or belief that they possess supernatural powers is another form of stealing glory from God and robbing God of the worship that belongs exclusively to the deity. King Saul exhibited the dreadful outcome of the warning given here (see 1 Chr 10:13-14). It is another form of profaning and prostituting the worship of God.

Thus the sections end with an exhortation. Verse 7 is a repetition of 11:44a. The consecration enjoined here on the people of God is one in which they are to separate themselves from all corrupt and idolatrous practices in the nations around them. To substitute child sacrifice, necromancy, and a number of other outrageous abominations for the rightful worship of Yahweh is not only a profane desecration of the holy name and sanctuary of God, but it is a deadly game as well. It leads to severe judgment from God. God wants personal and corporate holiness, not the abominations of the nations.

REFLECTIONS

1. The Hebrew theology of holiness incorporated the twin notions of separation and purity. When applied to worship, holiness dictated that worship had to be separate from any worship given to any other deity, idol, or supernatural being. To involve oneself with any other form or loyalty would also bring uncleanness and disqualification for approaching the house of God.

2. False worship of competing idolatries and religions also had the effect of prostituting and profaning the reputation, honor, character, and person of Yahweh. There is a sense in which contemporary forms of pluralism that urge an eclectic or syncretistic response to the God of Abraham, Isaac, and Jacob will also come under the same indictment this passage makes for those who worshiped Molech and similar substitutes for the living God.

3. Western Christians may find it hard to believe that what they do, or do not do, has an effect on the whole group, but that is what is taught here. In our democratized and individualized Western society, the philosophy is "live and let live." But God's call for holiness will not let Westerners off the hook so easily. Rampant social and moral evil, left unchecked by any group that ought to act, will be laid at the doorstep of the house of God first and then on the steps of the whole nation. One need only to consult history's final verdict on the Third Reich in Germany for the truthfulness of this judgment.

LEVITICUS 20:9-26, HOLINESS IN FAMILY RELATIONS

COMMENTARY

With the exception of v. 9, vv. 9-21 deal exclusively with sexual sins that have already been discussed in chap. 18. Sins against the family are as much a concern of holiness as are other areas of life.

But why was v. 9 placed among this set

of precepts and sanctions dealing with sexual sins—and at the head of this list? Could it be that this law, which repeats the command of the fifth commandment, was the all-embracing principle on matters of the family? If it were, as we suspect it was, the examples that followed were viewed as an attack on the basic command to honor the various relationships found in families, of which honoring one's father and mother was the most foundational.

Verse 9 is also quoted in Matt 15:4 and Mark 7:10. In the worlds of the OT and the NT, parents symbolize God's surrogate authority on earth. Whereas the fifth commandment calls for honoring these surrogates, the sin here involves cursing parents. "To honor" in Hebrew is literally "to make heavy," "to make glorious"; but "to curse" in Hebrew means literally "to make light of," "to lessen [someone in the eyes of others]." The two form a pair of antonyms: heavy/light, bless/curse. Thus all that has the effect of tearing down the esteem, place of honor, respect, and authority of the most basic unit of the family. Ultimately, it has the effect of destroying the fiber of society itself.

So significant is the offense against one's parents that it calls for the death penalty. But this is not the only offense sharing that sanction. The death penalty is also prescribed as the proper sanction in Israel's theocracy for adultery (v. 10), incest with a mother, stepmother, daughter-in-law, or mother-in-law (vv. 11-12, 14), homosexual behavior and sodomy (v. 13), and bestiality (vv. 15-16). Whether incest with a half-sister or a full sister (v. 17) and relations with a woman in her monthly cycle (v. 18) are placed in the same category depends on the interpretation of the phrase "must be cut off."

Many offenses listed in the "cutting off" contexts are also listed as sins punishable by the death penalty. But "cutting off" is contrasted with judicial execution in 20:2-5, in that the one who escapes stoning must be "cut off." Could this signify something different from capital punishment? Some have argued convincingly for some of these contexts where the expression "cut off" occurs that it means excommunication from the community of God. The situation is far from being clear to those of us who are removed so

many centuries from the vocabulary nuances and practices of that day. Surely in most of the cases, there appears to be a threat of punishment from God in the form of some kind of premature death.

Nevertheless, the death penalty might also merely indicate the seriousness of the crime without calling for its actual implementation in every case. In fact, there is very little evidence that many of these sanctions were ever actually used in ancient Israel. In only one case is no commutation of the sanction ever allowed; that is in first-degree murder. The law strictly warns, "Do not accept a *ransom* for the life of a murderer, who deserves to die. He must surely be put to death (Num 35:31 NIV, emphasis added). The word emphasized is כפר (*kōper*), a "deliverance or a ransom by means of a substitute."

Traditional wisdom, both in the Jewish and in the Christian communities commenting on this verse, interpreted it to mean that in the fourteen to nineteen other cases (the count is variously given) calling for capital punishment in the OT, it was possible to have the sentence of death commuted by some appropriate *kōper* that a judge would determine. Thus the death penalty showed how serious the crime was, and the provision of a substitute, either of money or of some other reparation, allowed the individual's life to be spared in every case, except where that individual had not spared someone else's life by malice and forethought, i.e., in first-degree murder.

Each of the crimes listed in vv. 10-21 already appears in Leviticus and has been discussed in our commentary on chap. 18.

A few unique expressions occur in vv. 10-21 that do not appear in chap. 18. For example, vv. 9, 11-13, 16, and 27 add to the sanction of the death penalty this provision: "Their [his] blood will be on their [his] own head[s]." The meaning is that the offenders are justly punished and have no one else to blame but themselves for the consequences that ensue. Revenge cannot be taken on those who bring such persons to trial; the offenders have to bear full responsibility for their acts.

In vv. 20-21 there is the statement, "They will die childless." The Hebrew word translated here "childless" is literally "unfruitful." It cannot mean that God will send some miracle to prevent procreation of children or introduce barrenness into the womb, for the expression is used of one who already had five sons in Jer 22:30. But since that king's five sons were made eunuchs (see Isa 39:7), they did not receive the inheritance of the Davidic throne, and in that sense, therefore, the king was left "childless and unfruitful." That would seem to be its meaning in this text as well.

Another interesting idiom is found in the Hebrew word for "marries" in vv. 14 and 17. It is from the verb לקח (lāqaḥ, "to take"), an expression found in Hos 1:2. However, in these contexts, the couples lived together without the benefit of a public wedding; thus it was a secondary use of the term in this context, since in the eyes of God it was not a proper marriage.

Another anomaly occurs in v. 14. If a man had sexual relations with a mother and her daughter concurrently, all three "must be burned in the fire, so that no wickedness will be among you." Usually, the incineration was preceded by stoning (see Josh 7:25). We may presume the same here unless other evidence is forthcoming.

But the most unusual word appears in v. 17. The Hebrew word חסד (ḥesed), usually translated "loving kindness," "mercy," "steadfast love," or "grace," has here the meaning of "disgrace." The only other time this word has such an antonymic meaning is in Prov 14:34: "But sin is a *disgrace* to any people" (NIV, emphasis added). Could the word have been chosen to make the point that what should have been a legitimate union, bringing the covenantal love God intended, had

been distorted into mere passion and lust? It would appear that was exactly what the writer intended in this ironic use of the word that otherwise would have meant "grace."

This section calling for holiness in the family closes with another exhortation to holiness (vv. 22-26). Israel is again reminded to avoid the customs of the nations, the very point made in chap. 18. In fact, since the same holiness is required of all, even if they are not part of the promised people of God, that is why the Canaanites, and other offending nations like them, are vomited forth from the countries they once inhabited.

Israel will possess their inheritance, which is called fourteen times in the Pentateuch "a land flowing with milk and honey" (only five more uses of this expression appear in the rest of the OT). So green and fertile will be the hills of the land of Canaan be that the cattle grazing on them will produce an abundance of milk and the bees will manufacture honey (the only form of sweetener used in that day), so that the inhabitants can eat their fill.

Oddly enough, in the midst of these moral precepts and warnings against pagan affections in the religious realm, is a reminder about the laws of cleanness (v. 25). But what appears to be out of place here (and belongs instead to chap. 11) is attached to what has been considered out of place there (when 11:44-45 quotes the holiness injunction that most judge to be more at home in 19:2 and its contexts). The point, however, is that the writer of Leviticus did not wish the two to be separated; cleanness and holiness are twin concepts. One cannot stand without the other.

REFLECTIONS

1. One of the most impressive commentaries on this situation was made by S. H. Kellogg in 1899. Although his day was almost a century away from the contemporary issues we face in our time, Kellogg's words turn out to be almost prophetic:

The maintenance of the family in its integrity and purity is nothing less than essential to the conservation of society and the stability of good government. . . . The Church must come to the full recognition of the principles which underlie this Levitical code; especially of the fact that marriage and the family are not merely civil arrangements, but Divine institutions; so that God has not left it to the caprice of the majority to settle what shall be lawful in these matters. Where God has declared certain alliances and connections to be criminal, we shall permit or condone them at our peril. God rules, whether modern majorities will it or not; and we must adopt the moral standards of the kingdom of God in our legislation, or we shall suffer. God has declared that not merely the material well-being of [a person], but *holiness,* is the moral end of government and of life; and He will find ways to enforce His will in this respect. "The nation that will not serve Him shall perish." All this is not theology, merely, or ethics, but history. All history witnesses that moral corruption and relaxed legislation, especially in matters affecting the relations of the sexes, bring in their train sure retribution, not in Hades, but here on earth. Let us not miss of taking the lesson by imagining that this law was for Israel, but not for other peoples. The contrary is affirmed in this very chapter (vv. 23, 24), where we are reminded that God visited His heavy judgments upon the Canaanitish nations precisely for this very thing, their doing of these things which are in this law of holiness forbidden. Hence "the land spued them out." Our modern democracies, English, American, French, German, or whatever they be, would do well to pause in their progressive repudiation of the law of God in many social questions, and heed this solemn warning. For despite the unbelief of multitudes, the Holy One still governs the world, and it is certain that He will never abdicate His throne of righteousness to submit any of His laws to the sanction of a popular vote.[110]

2. The NT position on the penalties of this section has not always been easy to describe. On the one hand, Christ seems to endorse the death penalty for cursing one's parent (see Matt 15:4; Mark 7:10). Yet, on the other hand, our Lord did not insist on the death penalty for the woman taken in adultery (see John 7:53—8:11). It is true, of course, that the legal case against the woman taken in adultery broke down since the witnesses all fled. Jesus knew the woman was guilty, for when he forgave her, he told her to go and sin no more. But had the witnesses returned, even though she had been divinely forgiven, the consequences and penalty of her sin might still have had to be enforced. Even the apostle Paul concludes his list of similar sins in Rom 1:18-32 with "those who do such things deserve death" (NIV).

What, then, can be the purpose of such punishments as listed in these biblical laws? Deuteronomy 19:19b-20 explains, "You must purge the evil from among you. The rest of the people will hear of this and be afraid, and never again will such an evil thing be done among you" (NIV). Gordon Wenham, in discussing this text, finds five principles here for contemporary application:[111] (1) The offender must receive the legal desert. (2) Purging evil from one's midst cannot refer to the offense itself, which could not be undone, but to the guilt that rested on the land and its inhabitants. (3) Punishment is meant to deter others from committing the offense (see Deut 13:11; 17:13; 21:21). (4) Punishment allows the offender to make atonement and to be reconciled with society. (5) The punishment allows the offender to recompense the injured party rather than try to repay the state.

110. Kellogg, *The Book of Leviticus*, 430-31.
111. Wenham, "Excursus I: 'Principles of Punishment in the Pentateuch,' " in *Leviticus*, 281-86.

LEVITICUS 21:1–22:16, HOLINESS IN THE PRIESTHOOD

COMMENTARY

The holiness law moves from a consideration of what is expected of ordinary laypersons (chaps. 18–20), to the expectations and manifestations of holiness in religious leaders, the priests (21:1–22:16). The standards for the priests are obviously higher than those for the laity.

The rhetorical markers in chaps. 21–22

are clear and regular. Six times the formula "I am the LORD, who makes him [them] holy" appears as a colophon. This formula acts as a divider of the various subjects, and it appears at 21:8, 15, 23; 22:9, 16, and 32. The last paragraph of 22:17-32 is separated from the rest of these two chapters, even though it has the same closing formula, because the opening rubric in 22:17 is addressed to all Israel along with Aaron and his sons. The opening line of address in 21:1 does not include Israel but is made only to "the priests, the sons of Aaron." Therefore, it seems best to block off the last paragraph and deal only with the first five addressed to the priests as a separate division.

The five sections are rules for mourning and marriage of ordinary priests (21:1-8); rules for mourning and marriage of the high priest (21:9-15); physical impediments to the ministry of the office of the priesthood (21:16-24); impediments to eating food reserved for the office of the priesthood (22:1-9); and restrictions on entitlement to eat the portions reserved for the priesthood (22:10-16).

Even though all the nation is called to be holy to the Lord, there appear to be degrees of successively higher holiness, just as there is a threefold division in the sanctuary and a threefold increase in the degree of holiness in the outer court, the holy place, and the holy of holies. In the outworking in the nation of Israel, the three divisions are the people, the priesthood, and the high priest himself. On the forehead of the high priest an inscription is placed that reads, "HOLY TO THE LORD" (Exod 39:30). These two chapters, then, will move the discussion of holiness from the laity in general (covered in the preceding chapters) first to demands laid on the priests and second to those laid on the high priest. The principle observed here will be an abiding one that special privilege and honor place those on whom they are conferred under special obligations to a higher level of holiness of life.

21:1-8. Holiness of life among the regular priesthood may be observed in two additional requirements not imposed on the ordinary laity: rites of mourning for the dead (21:1-6), and rites of marriage (21:7-8).

With regard to the first, ordinary priests are not to defile themselves by coming into contact with a corpse, for dead bodies are judged to be unclean (see Num 5:1-4; 19:11-13). Thus the only funerals that a priest can attend are those of "close [relatives]" (v. 2). The meaning here is the same as is discussed in 18:6. To make sure that there is no confusion, they are listed in vv. 2-3 as one's mother, father, son, daughter, brother, and unmarried sister. The same six relatives are listed in Ezek 44:25, but along with the LXX, the Syriac Peshitta, and the Samaritan reading of the present text in 21:2, "father" is listed before "mother," rather than the reverse order in the present text of 21:2! The only surprising feature here is the absence of the priest's wife from this list. The rabbinic view was that she was tacitly included among the "close relatives." An appeal to Ezek 24:15-18 would not help at this point, since the priestly prophet was forbidden to mourn the death of his wife as the public had expected him to do. But given where the general public's knowledge and practice of God's law were at that time, this is certainly no guide as to what was normative. If the wife were included, it will have to be purely an inference that a wife is always regarded as nearer her husband than one's own father and mother. The validity of the inference must be grounded in the fact that the wife is called "one flesh" with her husband.

A curious note appears in 21:4. Literally, the text reads "He must not make himself unclean, being *a leader* [or chief man] among his people" (emphasis added). The Hebrew word for "leader" or "chief" is the infamous **בעל** (*ba'al*, "Baal"). Nowhere else in the Bible does this word have the meaning of "leader" or "chief" as it must have in this text. The rest of the verse appears to anticipate 21:7, which warns priests not to join themselves in marriage to a woman of doubtful character. Others, however, believe the verse refers to defilement by means of attending a funeral of someone who is related to the priest only through marriage (an in-law) and not through blood. The former interpretation, first proposed by Keil, seems preferable.[112]

Further restrictions are added for funerals that the priest is allowed to attend among his blood relatives. He must not shave his head or the edges of his beard because the custom was observed in pagan mourning rites

112. Keil, *The Pentateuch*, 2:430.

(vv. 5-6; cf. Lev 19:27-28; Deut 14:1). Nothing that could be interpreted as profaning the name of God is allowed, for each priest is to be holy to the Lord. After all, they are the ones who are to officiate at the sacrifices and to present the "food of their God" (v. 6*b*).

Certain women are also excluded from consideration for marriage to a priest (vv. 7-8). Women who are defiled by virtue of prostitution or divorce are barred from marrying a priest. No matter how innocent the divorcee, she cannot marry a priest. The law of holiness jealously guards against even the appearance of impurity. Therefore, holiness demands that there be a visible separation from death as well as a separation from every possible sign of the operation and presence of sin and uncleanness. The word *holy* occurs four times in v. 8. Surely, that is being emphasized.

21:9-15. This passage treats the claims of holiness on the life and character of the high priest. The closing refrains in vv. 8 and 15 give us some objective data for grouping the subject matter in this way. However, v. 9 appears to float between the two sections. Perhaps it is placed after the colophon in v. 8 to make the point that what is said about the life of the family applies to the ordinary priests and to the high priest. Holiness in the priesthood must be evidenced in the life and activities of the priest's family. If a daughter of a priest makes her livelihood by practicing prostitution, her sin is to be punished. But since she has been exposed to greater privilege, and presumably has greater knowledge than most, her punishment is all the heavier. Presumably, she is to be stoned after being tried and proven guilty beyond any shadow of a doubt (see the discussion on 20:14), and then her body is to be burned.

Even tighter standards are required for the high priest. Because he is anointed with oil and ordained to wear the garments of his office, he is forbidden to exhibit the normal expressions of grief (such as letting his hair appear disheveled and tearing his clothes; v. 10), enter a place where there is a dead body (v. 11), or marry anyone except a virgin (v. 13). To do any of these things is to defile and profane his being set apart to God, and it desecrates the sanctuary of God. Although ordinary priests are allowed to attend the funeral

of six blood relatives (v. 2), the high priest must not attend even the funeral of his father and mother (v. 11). In fact, the high priest is not to leave the sanctuary (v. 12). Since no living quarters are provided in the tabernacle or its courts, it is doubtful that the high priest is forced to be a lifetime prisoner, as it were, in the house of God. Rather, the expression must mean that this job is one in which he is on call around the clock; no other commitment must draw him away. Yahweh's claim on him takes precedence over every other natural tie in life.

The anointing oil is literally called a "crown [נזר *nēzer*] of anointing oil" (v. 12*b*). This can be understood in either of two ways: The golden plate, called a "crown" in Exod 29:6, is anointed while it is on his head as the high priest is being installed, or the anointing oil appears as an appositional phrase that explains the crown. The LXX understands it in this latter fashion, since it has no word in the Greek for crown, apart from the reference to the anointing oil.

The high priest must marry one who is a "virgin" (בתולה *bĕtûlâ*), from the verbal root *bātal*, "to separate," "to set apart," "to seclude." As applied to a virgin, it means one who has been separated and secluded from intercourse with men. In this way, there can be no possible defilement of the offspring of the priesthood (v. 15).

21:16-24. The presence of any physical defect on the bodies of the priests is an impediment to their ministering at the sanctuary. The principle is given in v. 17 that "none of [Aaron's] descendants who has a defect may come near to offer the food of his God." In vv. 18-20, a list of various bodily deformities is given to illustrate this law. A proviso, however, is attached immediately in vv. 21-23, allowing those who have been debarred because of such physical maladies to eat of the priestly portions, whether they are of the "holy" things or of the "most holy" portions assigned to the priests. The only requisite is that the priests should be ceremonially clean when they share these portions.

The twelve defects listed here are not all identified with certainty. Being blind and being lame are clear, but "disfigured" and "deformed" are not clear (v. 18). The "disfigured" (חרם *ḥārum*) is likely a "split nose" (cf.

KJV), with the corresponding deformation of the palate causing a distortion in the voice. The reference to "crippled foot or hand" is probably related to the inability to always reset properly broken legs and arms because of the state of the practice of medicine in that day. The word גבן (gibbēn), which occurs only in v. 20, is taken to mean "hunchback" in the Vg and the LXX, but the older Jewish tradition translated it as "misshapen[ed] eyebrows." The word for "dwarfed" is the same one used of the "gaunt" and "thin" cows and grain in Pharaoh's dream (see Gen 41:3-4) or of the incense in Lev 16:12. In that case, it may be consumption, but others think it may be a type of eye problem. The "eye defect" in v. 20 may be "running eye" or "eye discharge." Two more terms in v. 20 appear to point to skin diseases followed by a reference to "damaged testicles," which is probably a case of hernia.

Holiness is not restricted to concerns about the interior being of a person; it is a concern for one's total wholeness and complete separation to God with purity. Mercy and compassion are shown to persons with deformities in that they too can eat with the other priests the portion assigned to them; nevertheless, the standard of wholeness is vividly illustrated by excluding from priestly service persons who evidenced any of these twelve maladies.

22:1-9. The fourth section in these instructions for the priests deals with possible impediments that would keep the priests from eating their portions. Priests in all categories, whether officiating or not, are warned in this paragraph not to partake of the priestly portions assigned to them when they are unclean, whether it is a skin disease (cf. chaps. 13–14), a discharge (cf. chap. 15), or contact with a dead body (cf. 11:39). In all these cases, they are temporarily disqualified from eating the priestly food on pain of being "cut off" (v. 3). Failure to abstain from eating under these conditions is failure to "respect the sacred offerings" (v. 2). The translation "to treat with respect" (NIV), or "to deal carefully with" (NRSV; נזר nzr, "to separate," from which comes our word Nazirite), is to be preferred over to "separate themselves" (KJV) or "to keep away" (RSV). At all costs, the priests are to avoid "[profaning God's] holy name" (v. 2). Thus God's character and

person and the sanctuary itself will be profaned when the holy things attached either to God's name or to the sanctuary are defiled, i.e., when they are offered or eaten by persons who are unclean and who are, therefore, temporarily disqualified from meeting with God or from appearing in the holy presence.

The possibility of being contaminated merely by touching something unclean (vv. 4-8) is reminiscent of the question that the prophet Haggai brings up on this same issue (see Hag 2:10-19). The illustrations of unclean things contacted are some types of skin diseases or leprosy, a corpse, an emission of semen, or some forbidden creature. The individuals will be unclean until they bathe and "the sun [goes] down."

22:10-16. The final set of instructions for the priests responds to two questions: Of all the people attached to a priest's family, such as a guest or a hired worker, who is entitled to partake of the priestly portions (vv. 10-13)? And what if someone who is not entitled to eat of the sacrificial portions assigned to the priests accidentally eats some of them (vv. 14-16)?

The answer to the first question is that even though the "guest" and the "alien" are both non-Israelite in origin, only the resident alien who resides with the priestly family can partake of priestly food. The guest and the "hired worker" are considered to be outside the family, for they are only temporarily attached to the family. A daughter married to someone other than another priest is judged to be outside the family by virtue of her marriage. However, if the daughter's marriage comes to an end through the death of her husband or through divorce, and there are no children in that union, she can return to her father's priestly household and eat of the portions assigned to them. Also, a slave born to the priestly home can eat of the portions of the family, for that person is a permanent member of the family.

In the event that a disqualified person accidentally (בשגגה bišgāgâ) eats some of the priestly portion (vv. 14-16), the offender must provide a full restitution of what is eaten plus a fifth more as a penalty. Accidental deeds are not to be treated as deliberate violations of the law of God; nevertheless, they are desecrations of what God has set apart as holy, hence the restitution and the attached penalty.

REFLECTIONS

1. Although the law was abolished as to its letter, the principles embodied in its spirit are still to be recommended to contemporaries. For example, spiritual privilege and honor carry with them special obligations for holiness of life. Thus it is not enough, in evaluating believers for high positions of service in the body of Christ, to compare them with the best of persons in this world, or even in the church, as graded on the average; a higher level of dedication, holiness, and spiritual achievement must be evidenced if they are to occupy positions with such dignity as teachers or rulers of God's flock. A more stringent obligation to holiness in life-style is laid on these leaders than is laid on the laity.

2. The holy character of the leader must be reflected in the leader's family. Especially leaders in the church should possess a good character (see Acts 6:3; 1 Tim 3; Titus 1:5-11), and their spouses (see 1 Tim 3:11) and their children (see 1 Tim 3:4; Titus 1:6) should also be models for the community to observe and follow.

3. The priests, both in their persons and in their work, were types or models of Christ, who would come as the Lamb without blemish and without spot, holy, undefiled, and separate from sinners (see Eph 5:27; Rev 19:7-8; 21:2). Christ is specially called that Great Priest in Heb 4:14. He is not only the perfect High Priest (see Heb 7:26), but he is also the one who gave himself for the world in his priestly role (see Heb 9:14; 1 Pet 1:19; 2:22).

LEVITICUS 22:17-33, HOLINESS IN SACRIFICIAL OFFERINGS

COMMENTARY

While there is some connection between this section and the preceding five sections in 21:1–22:16 in that all six sections conclude with the closing formula, or colophon, "I am the LORD, who makes you/him/them holy," this sixth section is addressed to all Israel (22:17-18*a*) and the priests, whereas the previous five are addressed exclusively to the priests (21:1). Therefore, treating it separately is best.

The concern in this section is for a jealous maintenance of the holiness of God in the quality of the offerings brought to God's house. The first requirement is that they are to be "without defect" (vv. 19-21; see 1:3, 10; 3:1, 6; 4:3, 23, 28; cf. Mal 1:8, 13). Only for a freewill offering is an exception to this rule allowed: An animal can be brought that is not altogether perfect but is "deformed or stunted" (v. 23). But such an imperfect victim is not acceptable in making a vow

to God. The prophet Malachi alludes to this very exclusion for the vow offerings when he sharply denounces the "cheats" who have an acceptable male in their flocks and who vow to give it to the Lord, "but then [sacrifice] a blemished animal to the LORD" (Mal 1:14 NIV). Can this be the way a great king ought to be treated? asks Malachi.

This unblemished animal has to be a male (see 1:3). It has to come from the cattle, sheep, or goats, not from the wild animals, which belong to no single offerer in particular. There can be no defect in the animals, such as "warts or festering or running sores" (v. 22). The sacrificial animal cannot be a gelding, i.e., castrated in any one of the four ways mentioned in v. 24: bruised, crushed, broken, or cut. Some have taken the clause here in v. 24 to mean that one was not to castrate any animal in the land for any purpose, but our versions are probably correct in taking it to apply only to sacrificial animals.

The second requirement is that this law about not offering blemished animals must be enforced when foreigners make sacrifices to the Lord (v. 25). Offering discount bargains where the holiness of God is involved is to be strictly forbidden; otherwise the offering will not be accepted by the Lord.

The third requirement sets a minimal limit on the age of a sacrificial animal. It has to be no less than eight days old (v. 27), and the mother and its young are not to be slaughtered for sacrifice on the same day (v. 28). One reason why the eighth day is chosen is that an animal is not fit for eating before the eighth day, hence its inappropriateness for sacrifice.

This section closes (vv. 29-30) by repeating the command already given in 7:15 that the meat of the thank offering is to be eaten on the same day in which it is offered.

A concluding admonition is given in vv. 31-33. Israel is urged, once again, to keep God's commands and to obey them. Doing anything less amounts to profaning the name of the Lord. The word חלל (*hillēl* [piel]) means to "demean," "degrade the sacred to the level of the חל (*hōl*), the profane, or secular." Over against the human tendency to degrade God stand God's holiness, lordship, and gracious act of redeeming Israel from Egypt.

REFLECTIONS

1. Offering God the leftovers and scraps of our time, energies, funds, and talents is akin to vowing to give to God our best and then coming with whatever we can spare.

2. The ceremonial law has been repealed in its outward form, since the final and perfect sacrifice of Christ has been offered, yet it abides in its spirit and intention in that we profane the name or sanctuary of God by unholy lives or by lawless worship that fails to acknowledge that God is a great king, priest, and prophet after the orders of David, Aaron-Melchizedek, and Moses, respectively.

LEVITICUS 23:1-44, HOLINESS IN OBSERVING THE FESTIVALS

COMMENTARY

Holiness, thus far, has been related to holy persons, holy things, and holy places. But now in chap. 23 it is extended to holy times. The laws relating to the annual fast, the Feast of Trumpets, and the three annual festivals are brought together into one place and put into their chronological order along with the law of the sabbath.

Just as chaps. 18–19 use the formula "I am the LORD your God" to act as a colophon and a divider between subsections, so also chap. 23 is divided into two main divisions by the appearance of this same formula in vv. 22 and 43, giving the spring festivals in the first division (vv. 1-22) and the autumn festivals in the second division (vv. 23-43).

These two main divisions are divided again by another subset of closing colophons that use another repeated formula: "This is to be a lasting ordinance for the generations to come, wherever you live" (vv. 14, 21, 31, 41). Several other formulas occur, but they do not appear to govern the structure. They include "the appointed feasts of the LORD" or "the LORD's appointed feasts" (vv. 2, 4, 37, 44); "sacred assemblies" or "holy convocations" (vv. 2, 3, 4, 7, 8, 21, 24, 27, 35, 36, 37); and "do no regular work," "do not work on that day," or "do no work at all" (vv. 7, 8, 21, 25, 30, 31, 36).

The resulting outline suggested by these structural guides is this: introduction (vv.

1-2); the sabbath (v. 3); the spring festivals (vv. 4-22), which include Passover and Unleavened Bread (vv. 5-8), Firstfruits (vv. 9-14), and Feast of Weeks (vv. 15-22); the autumn festivals (vv. 23-44), which include the Feast of Trumpets (vv. 23-25), the Day of Atonement (vv. 26-32), and the Feast of Tabernacles (vv. 33-44).

23:1-2. Eleven times in this chapter the phrase "sacred assembly" occurs either in the singular or in the plural. The Hebrew מקראי קדש (*miqrāʾê qōdeš*) is a somewhat ambiguous expression in the Holiness Code, though it also occurs six times in Numbers 28–29 and twice in Exod 12:16 but nowhere else. The verbal root of the first of these two words is קרא (*qārāʾ*), meaning "to summon," "to invite," or "to proclaim." Thus the word for "assembly" might also be translated as "convocation" or "convention." The second word, of course, is the repeated word in Leviticus for "holy." Accordingly, it is an occasion when the community is summoned for common worship and celebration—in holy or sacred assembly.

The other expression used in the introduction is the "appointed feasts of the LORD." The Hebrew word מועד (*môʿēd*) is derived from a verb meaning "to fix" or "to appoint." These are "set" times when the community is to meet to worship and to rejoice in the Lord. This calendar of holy convocations or sacred assemblies is meant primarily for the laity rather than the priests.

The Torah preserves three lists of the festivals and holy days to the Lord: one in the Book of the Covenant, this one in the Holiness Code, and one in Deuteronomy. Each has a distinctive emphasis and often a unique name for each of these celebrations. Exodus 23:12-19, as part of the Book of the Covenant, lists the sabbath and the three pilgrimage festivals (the Festival of Unleavened Bread, the Spring Harvest Festival, and the Festival of Ingathering). Deuteronomy 16:1-17 names Passover, the Festival of Weeks in the late spring, and the Festival of Tabernacles in the autumn. Numbers 28–29 also has a calendrical listing of these feasts including the sabbath, new moon, and all the festivals and holy days, but its emphasis is on the proper offerings that go with each of these occasions. Another brief listing is given in Exod 34:17-26, which is related to the same content given in Exod 23:12-19.

The purpose of the section in Leviticus is set forth in the first verse: It is to give a catalog of "the appointed feasts of the LORD." Only three celebratory events are left out: new moons, the sabbatical year, and the jubilee. But the ones mentioned are listed as sacred times or seasons of worship. These are to be "sacred assemblies." This phrase cannot always refer to the summons of the people to the central sanctuary, for in Exod 34:23 Israel was summoned to the tabernacle only for the feasts of Passover and Weeks and the Day of Atonement. Therefore, this must be a call for local gatherings for worship, such as would take place later at the synagogues.

23:3. The first of this series of appointed times is the sabbath (v. 3). Many have found the inauguration of the list with the sabbath to be most natural, for the whole series of sacred times is based on the sabbatical principle in the number seven. For example, the weekly sabbath comes on the seventh day. There are seven festivals in the year: Passover, Unleavened Bread, Weeks, the day of rest, the Day of Atonement, Tabernacles, and the day after Tabernacles. The duration of each of the great festivals of Unleavened Bread and Tabernacles is seven days. The Feast of Firstfruits, or of Weeks, comes at the end of seven weeks on the fiftieth day. The seventh month is especially holy to the Lord, for it contains three annual times of sacred assembly: the Feast of Trumpets on the first day, the great Day of Atonement on the tenth day, and the Feast of Tabernacles or Ingathering, which lasts for seven days, from the fifteenth day. The sabbatical year comes in the seventh year; but at the end of seven sevens of years, the seventh sabbatical year is the great year of jubilee, the great year of rest, restoration, and release. Thus the number seven has a special place in the order of worship for Israel.

The holiness of the sabbath day is emphasized in the strongest terms possible. It is a שבת שבתון (*šabbat šabbātôn*, a "sabbath of sabbatism," [author's trans.]) or to render this Hebrew superlative form another way, it is "the most restful cessation" (v. 3, author's trans.). The sabbath is to be observed by abstaining from all daily tasks. The fact that the sabbatical year is also called a "sabbath of sabbaths" (25:4, author's trans.) is an indication that the prohibition against work is not to be understood as an absolute, for some minor tasks, such as caring for the animals and the like, must always be carried out. The principle, however, stands. Regular work is to come to a halt in favor of a day of rest for humanity and for the worship of the Lord God.

The Hebrew term *šabbat,* ("sabbath") literally means "to cease," "to stop," "to desist," "to be idle." The Creator gave the day to allow a person to "catch one's breath" (cf. the Hebrew word וינפש *wayyinnāpaš,* Exod 23:12, 31:17). This day is intended to be a time of relief, respite, and up-building of all who have labored for the preceding six days.

At one time it was popular among scholars to say that the Hebrew sabbath was derived from the Babylonian *abattû,* even though the names were not etymologically related. The Babylonian celebration came on the seventh, fourteenth, nineteenth, twenty-first, and twenty-eighth days. In the Babylonian sphere, those days were the concern mainly of the king, soothsayer, and sorcerer since the special dangers created on those days by the activity of demons made it advisable to refrain from doing any official acts. Instead of claiming that they were days of rest, relaxation, and restoration as the OT teaches, the Babylonians viewed their set of times listed above as "evil day(s)" or times when it was unlucky to work.[113]

The sabbath is ever to be valued as the grandest solemnity in the worship of God. Since it is not to be eclipsed or supplanted in the future, it is given pride of place in the list of sacred assemblies.

23:4-8. Verses 4-22 introduce the spring festivals of Passover and Unleavened Bread, and the Feast of Weeks. The most detailed laws on the Passover and Unleavened Bread are given in Exodus 12–13. The Leviticus list offers a simple reminder of these celebrations (vv. 5-8). The reference to the Passover is the briefest of all in v. 5, which asserts that it is to begin "at twilight on the fourteenth day of the first month." The Hebrew expression בין הערבים (*bên hā'arbāyim,* "between the

evenings") has given rise to two explanations: (1) between sunset and dark (Aben-Ezer, Qaraites, Samaritans, Keil, and Delitzsch) or (2) between the decline of the sun (three to five o'clock) and sunset (Josephus, Mishnah, and modern practice in Judaism). With Deut 16:6, the time should be fixed as the time "when the sun goes down," i.e., the same time set for lighting the lamps in the tabernacle (see Exod 30:8) and offering the daily evening sacrifice (see Exod 29:39). The first month in which this celebration took place was called Nisan (March-April), when the barley harvest was ready to begin.

The Passover commemorates Israel's deliverance from Egypt by the mighty hand of God.[114] It also marks the establishment of the nation of Israel. On the day following Passover, the Feast of Unleavened Bread begins. It lasts for seven days and is one of the three pilgrimage celebrations (along with the Feast of Pentecost, i.e., "weeks," and the Feast of Tabernacles) in which all adult males in Israel go to the central sanctuary for its observance (see a fuller description in Num 28:16-25; Deut 16:1-8). While all references to the slaying of the paschal lamb are omitted in this context, vv. 6 and 8 mention the eating of the "bread made without yeast" (the round yellow cakes or "matzos") and the sacrifices made by fire to the Lord. Thus the paschal lamb was probably slain on the fourteenth day of the month, and the blood was applied to the doorposts and lintels, indicating that the death angel could "pass over" the household that was under the redemptive coverage of a substituted life. In the Feast of Unleavened Bread the first and seventh days are declared to be days for sacred assemblies to the Lord in which no work is to be done (vv. 7-8).

23:9-14. On the eighth day following Passover, and the seven days of Unleavened Bread ("on the day after the sabbath"; vv. 11, 15), it is decreed that "a sheaf of the first grain you harvest" (v. 10) is to be brought to the Lord to be consecrated by the priest in a ceremony of waving or (as we have argued earlier) elevating it before the Lord. The reference is to a sheaf of barley, which is the first to ripen in the spring. In this celebration

---

113. See the attempt made by Stephen Langdon to derive the Jewish sabbath from the Assyrian and Babylonian unlucky days (*Babylonian Menologies and the Semitic Calendars* [London: Oxford University Press, 1935]). This work followed the line of argumentation that had been set by Friedrich Delitzsch in *Die grosse Täuschung* 1 (1920) 99f.

114. For a detailed study of the etymology and meaning of the word *Passover,* see J. B. Segal, *The Hebrew Passover* (New York: Oxford University Press, 1963) 95-100. For a detailed commentary on the Passover and the Feast of Unleavened Bread, see Kaiser, "Exodus," 371-84.

of the Feast of Firstfruits, the elevation offering of the sheaf of barley is accompanied by a burnt offering of a year-old lamb (v. 12), a grain offering of approximately four quarts of fine flour mixed with oil (v. 13) and a drink offering of approximately one quart of wine (v. 13). This drink offering is mentioned in Exod 29:38-42, but this is the first time it is mentioned in Leviticus.

Verses 9-14 seem to many commentators to describe a rite similar in purpose to the Feast of Unleavened Bread (v. 14) but with quite a different ceremony. The day for the ceremony is an ambiguously specified "sabbath." This may reflect an originally separate observance in early Israel (or in a particular sanctuary), but in its present context it appears that the intent is to assimilate it into the Feast of Unleavened Bread.

In consecrating the first part of this harvest to the Lord, the whole harvest is thereby dedicated to the Lord. Now the barley can be eaten by all, since Israel receives it as a gift from God. But more is implied than the ethical lesson that God is the bountiful giver of all the harvest. Israel is declared to be God's "firstborn" in Exod 4:22. That is true of God's work in redeeming the nation out of Egypt, and it is to be the NT pattern for all of soteriology, "first for the Jew, then for the Gentile" (Rom 1:16 NIV). The nation, then, just as the harvest, symbolically signifies the consecration of all the nations in that a part of the nations is called to be God's "firstborn."

But even the dedication of the harvest and the dedication of the nation do not exhaust the type. It is specifically declared that following the Passover, on "the day after the sabbath," the first day of the week, the sheaf[115] of firstfruits is to be presented to Yahweh. Some debate has centered on what "sabbath" is meant here in vv. 11 and 15. If it is the regular Saturday sabbath, the sheaf is always waved or elevated before the Lord on Sunday, regardless of the date of Passover. Others, however, argue that the "sabbath" referred to is the Passover, which means that the sheaf is waved on the fifteenth of Nisan. The first

view is to be preferred, since the Feast of Weeks comes exactly fifty days later and is also said to be on the "day after the seventh sabbath" (v. 16).

23:15-22. The Feast of Weeks (so called because it is celebrated after a week of weeks, or seven weeks after Firstfruits) is called the Feast of Harvest in Exod 23:16 and the "firstfruits of the wheat harvest" in Exod 34:22 (NIV; cf. Num 28:26). Since it follows Passover and Unleavened Bread by fifty days, it came to be known as "pentecost," or "fiftieth," from the Greek πεντηκοστή (*pentēkostē*). It is a one-day celebration (see Deut 16:9-12) of rejoicing over the abundant gifts of food that God has given in the harvest.

The Feast of Firstfruits marks the *beginning* of the harvest with the presentation of the first sheaf of barley to the Lord (v. 10), but now the Feast of Pentecost, or Weeks, celebrates the *completion* of the wheat harvest, which generally lasted from the end of April well into the month of June, depending on the location in Israel, the soil, and the slowness of the season. The firstfruits of barley come from the field, but the "offering of new grain [of wheat]" (v. 16) comes as prepared food. Both the firstfruits and the new grain offerings, however, are unlike the grain offering of chap. 2, for both represent the ordinary food of the people.

The new grain offering is accompanied by seven male lambs, one young bull, and two rams. These are to be offered as a burnt offering to the Lord along with the grain and drink offerings. Another male goat is to be offered as a sin offering, and two yearling lambs are to be sacrificed as a peace offering. The two lambs are to be "waved" or, as argued earlier, "elevated" to the Lord in dedication (v. 20).

This festival, as all others in this sabbatical series, is celebrated with a complete cessation of all regular labors, thus picturing the great sabbath that will follow the harvest that comes at the "end of the age" (Matt 13:39 NIV). In the Feast of Pentecost, God is celebrated as the sustainer of Israel and provider of daily food. Israel, in turn, expresses full consecration and fellowship with Yahweh in the offerings lifted up on that day.

In the NT "Firstfruits" came to symbolize for early Jewish Christians that Christ "our Passover" would be raised from the dead and

---

115. The Hebrew term usually translated here as "sheaf" is contradicted by rabbinic exegesis and Jewish tradition (*Menahoth* 66a, 68b). Both the Septuagint and the Mishnah, which devotes a separate tractate called *Hallah* to this matter, speak of dough and cakes made from the grain in regard to both barley and wheat. Numbers 15:20 speaks of the *'ōmer* of firstfruits in the form of cakes as well; thus it is difficult to say for certain which translation is correct.

be the earnest or promise of the resurrection of all others who hoped to be raised from the grave. The presentation of the new grain at the Feast of Pentecost came to symbolize the raising up of "the church of the firstborn" (Heb 12:23 NIV; cf. Jas 1:18) as constituent parts of a unified body on that sacred day (cf. later on the great event of Pentecost where three thousand were added to the church by the work of the Holy Spirit in Acts 2). Yet, this work cannot be the final work of God for the people, for the two loaves of bread are "baked with yeast" (v. 17), indicating the imperfection of the attainment of the loaves that must also await God's final work of redemption. Because the loaves are made with yeast, i.e., leaven, just like the daily bread of the Israelites, they are not placed on the altar (2:11) but are elevated before the Lord in dedication.

The spring festivals conclude (v. 22) with the reminder already noted in 19:9 (cf. Deut 24:19) that the edges of the field are not to be harvested but are to be left for poor people to harvest.

The autumn festivals begin in the busy seventh month and include the Feast of Trumpets and the Feast of Tabernacles with the solemn Day of Atonement between the two (23:23-44).

23:23-25. The Feast of Trumpets inaugurates this most sacred month of all. The first day of this sabbatical month is sanctified in accordance with the principle already observed: The consecration of a portion of anything signifies the consecration of the whole. Thus, if the first day is holy to the Lord, so is the whole month.

In later times, especially from the Seleucids onward, this day would be known as New Year's Day (השנה ראש *rōʾš haššānâ*). Trumpets were blown on several occasions in Israel, though not always the same type of trumpets, but on this occasion people throughout the land joined in as they were able from sunrise to sunset. It was not the same as the traditional noise-making that has come to be associated with New Year's Day in the rest of the world when the fortunes of the coming year are very much in the forefront of most thinking; it was to be a festival of celebration to the Lord and of commemorating it with praise to God.

23:26-32. The Day of Atonement comes on the tenth day of the seventh month. It is the only day divinely announced as a fast in the whole OT, even though tradition added several other days of fasting (see Zech 7:2-5; 8:19). This day has already been described in chap. 16, but here it is placed in its relationship to the other annual events of celebration to the Lord.

The emphasis in this paragraph is on the necessity of denying oneself (vv. 27, 29, 32). The same call to inspect one's interior motivations and sorrow over one's sin is the concluding note in the discussion of this same day in chap. 16 (vv. 29, 31). Here, once again, Israel is being warned that the forgiveness of sin on this day is not an automatic carte blanche type of an affair; it has to be accompanied by real repentance or, as the idiom literally says, by "afflicting oneself." This day also is a day sacred to the Lord in which no work is to be done (vv. 28, 31). On this day, the high priest makes atonement for the sins of the people; thus it is a solemn day rather than a day of festivities.

23:33-44. The final event in this septenary series is the Feast of Tabernacles (vv. 33-44). It begins on the fifteenth day of the seventh month and lasts for seven days (v. 34). It is also known as the Feast of Booths and Feast of Ingathering. The historical occasion that it celebrates is the end of the harvest season. During this festival, Israel again lives in booths made of branches of palms, willows, and other trees, as a reminder of the time the Israelites spent in the wilderness wanderings after the exodus. As the harvest is gathered in, it becomes a time of great joy and thanksgiving to God.

As with the other week-long festivals, the first and the last days are to be observed as sabbaths to the Lord. No work or labor is to be carried out on these days. Once again, however, the eighth day following these days is to be a "sacred assembly" (v. 36a); it is "the closing assembly" (v. 36b). The unique term used only here in this chapter is עצרת (*ʿặṣeret*), meaning "to shut up," "to close," hence the closing day or concluding day of the Feast of Tabernacles. The same term is applied to the concluding day of the Feast of Unleavened Bread in Deut 16:8. Josephus noted that the concluding day of the Feast of

Pentecost was called *asartha*, apparently from the Greek word that attempted to reproduce the Hebrew word for "to close."

This "last" day of the feast or, as the Gospel of John later calls it, "the great day" of the feast (John 7:37 NRSV), is so labeled because of the great solemnity of the assembly.

The Sadducees understood that the branches were to be used for making temporary booths or shelters, but the Pharisees, and most adherents of modern Judaism, tie one branch of palm, three branches of myrtle, and one branch of willow together. These they carry in the right hand, but in the left hand they carry a branch of citron, with its fruit left on it. With these they form a procession to their synagogues on each of the seven days, marching around their reading desks as Joshua did around the walls of Jericho and singing "Hosannah." On the last day of the feast, which the rabbis called "the great Hosannah," they process seven times around the same areas, as their ancestors did around Jericho.

Another ceremony on this occasion is the pouring out of water. One of the priests takes a golden pitcher to the pool of Siloam or Bethesda and, after filling it with water from that place, returns by the gate on the south side of the Temple, which became known from this event as the Water Gate. Silver trumpets sound to announce the priest's arrival. He advances directly to the top of the altar, where two basins stand, one with wine for the ordinary drink offering and the other for the water that he brings. The priest pours the water into the empty basin, then mixes the water and wine together, and pours out both as a libation. Nothing in the Mosaic laws reflects this practice, but authority for it is usually traced to Isa 12:3: "With joy you will draw water/ from the wells of salvation" (NIV). It is to this event that Jesus probably refers in the Gospel of John report: "On the last and greatest day of the Feast, Jesus stood and said in a loud voice, 'If anyone is thirsty, let him come to me and drink. Whoever believes in me, as the Scripture has said, streams of living water will flow from within him' " (7:37-38 NIV).

This feast depicts the completion of the physical and the spiritual harvests. Most beautifully, the joy, rejoicing, and happiness of the reunion of everyone, after all the arduous hours of labor have been completed, lie at the heart of this festival. The typical significance of this feast is discussed in Zechariah 14. There is coming a day when the Lord will be king over the whole earth, the Lord will be one (with no more rivals from pagan idols or competing loyalties from the people), and the divine name will be the only name (vv. 5, 9, 16). Then, all the nations will keep the Feast of Tabernacles, and the words "HOLY TO THE LORD" will be written on everything, even the most ordinary utensils (v. 20). Thus the Feast of Tabernacles signifies the completion of the great world harvest at the end of the age.

REFLECTIONS

1. In Israel, holiness was not confined to people and objects but also extended to times and seasons. Life was not an unbroken highway leading endlessly to more of the same. Here and there along the way there were holy oases of refreshment, celebration, and commemoration—sabbaths, festivals, and special days of awe and praise.

The special times of holiness aimed to disclose what was true of all time, that it belongs to God. The purpose of a sabbath, for example, was not to be the one and only holy day in the week. Instead, the sabbath brought to visibility the holiness of all days. A sabbath or a festival was like a kiss between lovers. It gathered into a special moment what is always true. Just so, a Tuesday was as holy as a sabbath, but it took the "kiss" of the sabbath to make that clear.

2. The case for anticipating a change from the seventh day to the first day of the week as the new sabbath is found in chap. 23 with its frequent references to the "day after the sabbath" (vv. 11, 16), to the "eighth day" (vv. 36, 39), or to the "first day" (vv. 7, 35) as being days of sacred assembly when no work is to be done. But even more impressive are the references to the Firstfruit that was to come on the eighth day and to Pentecost also coming on the eighth day (vv. 11, 16). Often in this series of annual events, both the seventh day and the eighth day are called most holy days equally set aside to God as sacred and devoid of all labor.

3. The typical meaning of the feasts and sacred seasons discussed in Leviticus 23 has already received mention in the commentary, but it is well to collect the comments here in one place. The Passover and the Unleavened Bread pointed forward to Christ, our Passover, who was slain for the sins of the world. Pentecost pointed forward to the spiritual ingathering of the firstfruits of the world harvest that was to come, some fifty days after the presentation of the barley sheaf that symbolized the resurrection from the dead of the One who himself was the firstfruits of all who had died. The Feast of Tabernacles signified the completion of the harvest begun at Pentecost; it marked the new age when the fruits of all labors would be enjoyed, just as the harvest of ingathering at the end of the year signified.

4. The religious life depicted here, as elsewhere in the Bible, is not one of gloom and doom but of joy. Just as Neh 8:10 proclaimed, "The joy of the LORD is your strength" (NIV), so all the set times of sabbatical rest were to be times of joy and celebration. Instead of the sabbath and its associated festivals being days of stern repression with negative rules and prohibitions on work, "There remains, then, a Sabbath-rest for the people of God" (Heb 4:9 NIV). Every temporal celebration was intended to point toward the eternal joy that was to come when the final sabbath rest came to the people of God.

5. It is little wonder, then, that the apostle Paul seized on this crucial point of "firstfruits" in the Feast of Weeks in 1 Cor 15:20 and declared the resurrection of Christ on Easter Day to be "the firstfruits of those who have fallen asleep" (NIV). When Christ rose from the dead on the first day after the sabbath, he became the firstfruits of the harvest of all those who had died in faith and who were awaiting the resurrection of their bodies from the dead. The NT writers frequently employed this figure of "firstfruit(s)" (see Rom 8:23; 11:16; 16:5; Jas 1:18; Rev 14:4).

LEVITICUS 24:1-23, HOLINESS CONTRASTED

COMMENTARY

A number of puzzles confront the interpreter of chap. 24. The greatest enigma is the connection of this chapter with what has preceded it in chap. 23 and with what follows in chap. 25. Another is the principle of organization that mixes the two topics of rules regulating the holy place with the sudden intrusion of the case of the blasphemer. The final puzzle is the lack of clear structural markers in the repeated clauses and phrases that have been present in many of the surrounding chapters.

The problem of the connection with what has preceded chap. 24 in chap. 23 can be eased somewhat by noting that the completed ingathering of the harvest's grain and fruit in the previous chapter is now to have a portion of it used in the sanctuary as olive oil for lighting the seven-branched lampstand (vv. 1-4), and another portion will be used as grain to produce the twelve loaves placed each week on the table of presence (vv. 5-9).

The story of the blasphemer is probably brought to the fore because of the need to know if the law for native-born persons must also be applied to foreigners. The answer is that it does, as v. 22 plainly attests.

The mixture of the story of the blasphemer (vv. 10-23) with instructions for the lampstand and the table of the bread of presence may be that this problem of blasphemy arose right after Moses had given his directions for the festivals that appear in chap. 23, or after Moses had given his instructions for the two rituals in the tabernacle that appear first in this chapter. But it may also have been occasioned by an inquiry that came about this time as to whether these laws also applied to foreigners. It is difficult to suggest any other plausible connections for such an abrupt change of topics.

The only structural clues appear in v. 22, "I am the LORD your God" (a colophon that appears repeatedly in chap. 19); v. 3, "This is to be a lasting ordinance for the generations to come" (cf. 3:17; 10:9; 16:29; 17:7; 23:14, 21, 31, 41); and v. 9, a "regular share" (cf. 6:11 [English 18]; 7:34; 10:15). But these three clues are enough, along with the distinctive change in subject matter, to indicate that there are three main divisions in this chapter: vv. 2-4, 5-9, and 10-23.

24:2-4. These verses repeat the regulations for the lampstand previously given in Exod 27:20-21 with slight changes. In them, directions are given for the light that is to burn in the holy place from evening until morning. The people are to furnish the oil for the seven-branched lampstand in the holy place on the south, or lefthand side, as one faced into the tabernacle.

The oil is to be "clear oil of pressed olives" (v. 2). This oil is extracted from unripened olives beaten and pounded in a mortar rather than crushed in a mill. The pulpy mass is then placed in a basket, and the oil, without mixture of other parts of the olive, drips through the basket, giving a clear, pure oil that burns with little or no smoke.

The oil is given by the people so that, though the holy place is attended by the high priest, the light illuminating it is a gift from all the people. In that sense, here is a service that all the people of Israel render in their devotion to God.

Night after night the seven-branched lampstand is tended so that the light will burn throughout the dark hours. There is to be no intermission.

The significance of the olive oil and the burning of the lamps before the Lord in front of the veil that separated the holy place from the holy of holies can best be found in Zech 4:1-14. There the seven-branched lampstand symbolized Israel as God's congregation, who in turn was to give the light of life to the world. In Zechariah's vision, the oil flowed to the golden lampstand through two golden pipes from two olive trees on either side of the lampstand. The explanation that Zechariah was given about this oil was, " 'Not by might nor by power, but by my Spirit,' says the LORD Almighty" (4:6 NIV). Thus the nation's ability to share this light with the world depended on the supply that came from the Spirit of God and the ministry of the high priest in the holy place. Thus the identification of the lampstand with the people, with the dynamic for sharing their light with the nations of the world as coming from the Holy Spirit, does not appear to be inconsistent with the analogy of other Scripture.

24:5-9. The next illustration of holiness is the ordinance of the preparation and presentation of the bread of the presence. It is placed in two rows of six each on the specially designated table made of pure gold on the north side of the tabernacle, or the right side as one faced into the tabernacle. Thus, just as the lampstand is of "pure gold" (v. 4), so the table is of "pure gold" (v. 6). The themes of purity and holiness are never far from view in this book.

Each sabbath day a new set of twelve loaves is placed before the Lord because the priests eat the previous set at the end of the week. Along with the loaves some "pure incense" (v. 7) is placed, perhaps in golden spoons or cups (cf. Exod 37:16). The incense has first been burned as a "memorial portion . . . to be an offering made to the LORD by fire" (v. 7b).

Because incense is a symbol of prayer (see Ps 141:2), there may also be the intimation that both our physical and our spiritual food are to be received and sanctified by prayer. Surely, it is God who supplies our daily bread; the weekly dedication of the twelve loaves, representing the twelve tribes of Israel, acknowledges the same truth in a most concrete, but graphic, way.

24:10-23. If the preceding two ordinances depict how holiness is observed, the story of the blasphemer certainly shows how holiness is defiled. The chapter, then, must deliberately present a stark contrast of the two attitudes toward holiness.

Israel is commanded in Exod 22:28, "Do not blaspheme God" (NIV). But here, in one of the rare narrative passages in Leviticus, a case is offered where someone actually blasphemed the "Name." No one knew what to do, for the problem seems not to have arisen before. Therefore, the offender was placed in penal incarceration until God would reveal to Moses what should be done to the individual.

To make matters worse, the blasphemer was of mixed parentage. His mother was an Israelite, but his father was an Egyptian. Apparently, the blasphemer's father was a proselyte to the Jewish faith along with the "many other people" (Exod 12:38 NIV) who went up out of Egypt along with Israel when they left. If the guilty person was somewhere between twelve and twenty years old, the conversion of this Egyptian father must have come some years prior to the Exodus, for these events take place within a year or two of Israel's exodus from Egypt.

At any rate, a physical fight broke out between a full-fledged Israelite and the man of mixed parentage. In the heat of the fight, the man of mixed parentage blasphemed "the Name [of the LORD]." The verb used for "blasphemed" is ויקב (*wayyiqqōb*), coming from the root that means "to pierce," "to bore," or "to strike through" or, by extension, "to specify," "to pronounce explicitly," or "to identify," a type of "striking through or wounding" with the tongue. But when this verb is placed with the second verb in this passage, ויקלל (*wayĕqallēl*, "to curse"), the second verb is made into a sort of adverbial phrase: "He pronounced by cursing blasphemously."

The result would be death for the blasphemer. The story of Naboth (see 1 Kgs 21:10-13) demonstrates that the death penalty for blasphemy was not a dead law without any teeth for implementation. In fact, Job's wife urged her husband to "curse God" (Job 2:9 NIV) and thus end his suffering and his life quickly! The ultimate charges that were brought against Jesus and Stephen were charges of blasphemy, for which both were judged worthy of capital punishment (see Matt 26:65-66; Acts 6:11-15).

The genealogy of the blasphemer's Israelite mother is of more than passing interest. She was from the tribe of Dan, the tribe that would eventually move to the far north and set up the calf at the temple of Dan (along with the parallel one at Bethel, for the ten northern tribes that broke away from Judah and Benjamin after the death of Solomon). In their view, the Temple at Jerusalem had become illegitimate.

The blasphemer cursed "the Name," which of course meant the name of God (v. 11). This verse and v. 16 are of special interest to the Jewish people, for on them they have based the well-known belief that it is unlawful to pronounce the name of "Yahweh," substituting, instead, the name *Adōnay*, "Lord," (אדני) which the LXX also represented by κύριος *kurios*. This is why almost all English versions now render "Yahweh" by "LORD" in capital and small capital letters to distinguish it from the regular appearance of *Adōnay*, which is rendered in upper and lower case as "Lord."

Reviling "the Name" (השם *haššēm*), even in the heat of passion, is not something that God will treat as a rather small infraction. "The Name" expresses who God is par excellence. It stands for God's own self, character, nature (see Ps 20:1; Luke 24:47; John 1:12); doctrine (see Ps 22:22; John 17:6, 26); and ethical teachings (see Mic 4:5).[116]

Thus the offender was placed "in custody" (במשמר *bammišmār*, "in the guardhouse") until the Lord would reveal what to do. This is one of four episodes in the Torah where Moses has to make a special inquiry of God about what to do prior to his rendering a legal decision (see Num 9:6-14; Num 15:32-36; 27:1-11). These four passages are discussed at length by Philo and the rabbis, who were troubled because Moses was unable to handle these cases on his own. However, they also clearly show Moses' dependence on God's revelation. He acted under divine orders, and not on his own!

---

116. For a validation of this extended meaning of the "name," see Kaiser, "Name," in *The Zondervan Pictorial Encyclopedia of the Bible*, 4:360-66. Also see Kaiser, *Toward Old Testament Ethics*, 87-88, 132-33.

The divine instruction is that the blasphemer is to be taken outside the camp, where all capital punishments were executed, and there he is to be stoned. First, all who heard him blaspheme are to act as witnesses by placing their hands on the head of the accused man. Hearing, as well as seeing, is a form of witnessing in the biblical law. The entire congregation is to participate in the stoning, for all have been adversely affected by the act of the single individual. Such an affront awakens the anger of God against the whole community—until they deal with it. The imposition of hands symbolizes the transfer of responsibility of guilt from the people to the offender; in this case, the offender turns victim, just as much as it does when their hands are laid on a sacrificial animal (1:4; 16:21).

This incident of blasphemy, then, provides a further occasion for spelling out some other related principles of biblical law in vv. 16-22. In all of the cases discussed here, the penalty is to be the same for the resident alien as for the full-fledged Israel (vv. 16, 22). The six laws in this section are arranged in a careful chiasmus.[117] They appear as follows:

A. Whether an alien or native-born (v. 16)
   B. takes the life of a human being (v. 17)
      C. takes the life of someone's animal (v. 18)
         D. whatever he has done must be done to him (v. 19)
         D´. As he has injured the other, so he is to be injured (v. 20)
      C´. Whoever kills an animal (v. 21 a)
   B´. whoever kills a man (v. 21 b)
A´. the same law for the alien and the native born (v. 22)

These laws are announced in Gen 9:6; in Exod 21:12-14, 18-25, 35-36; and later in Deut 19:21. The repetition of these laws in this context indicates that they apply equally to aliens and to full-fledged Israelites.

The law code of Num 35:9-34 stipulates exceptions to the rule of capital punishment when it is an accidental manslaughter case. Moreover, there is strong reason to suspect

that these laws do not require literal retaliation, as the famous "eye for eye," or as it was known in Roman jurisprudence, the *lex talionis*, seems to advocate. Only in the case of deliberate and premeditated murder does Num 35:31 exclude any type of "ransom" or "substitute" being used as compensation, since men and women are made in the image of God. But this one instance where no exclusion is permitted means, as the rabbis and older commentators opined, that all other cases calling for the death penalty can be compensated by some type of "ransom."

The rabbis correctly argued that v. 18 uses the formula "life for life" (נפש תחת נפש *nepeš taḥat nāpeš*), which means that a live animal can be substituted for the one that has been slain, or its equal. Thus the guilty party can offer either an animal in place of the one killed or its equivalent value. If that is so, the identical formula that appears in the *lex talionis*, i.e., "x" *taḥat* "x" (as in "eye for eye, tooth for tooth"), must mean compensation is likewise possible rather than some form of bodily mutilation or personal retaliation against the offending party. In fact, v. 21 reinforces this interpretation by ordering restitution in the case of an animal.

However, some were dissatisfied with this solution because its main proof centers on animals, not humans. The response to this objection has been to call attention to Deut 22:29, where a man who rapes a virgin is instructed to give a compensation of silver to her father (תחת אשר ענה *taḥat ʾăšer ʾinnāh*, literally "in lieu of having forced her"). Accordingly, just as *taḥat* ("in place of" or "instead of") in that case indicates compensation, so *taḥat* in the law of Lev 24:20 ("eye" *taḥat* "eye") indicates possible compensation rather than personal mutilation and retaliation of the offender. This principle was originally given to the judges in the Covenant Code (see Exod 21:1, 6; 22:8); the principle was not given to the general public as wholesale permission to vindicate oneself of whatever injustice one felt had occurred. The rule of "eye for eye" meant nothing more to the judges in Israel than "make the punishment fit the crime," or in modern parlance, "bumper for bumper," "fender for fender" in automobile

117. Wenham calls this feature "a concentric pattern [named] a palistrophe" (*Leviticus*, 311-12).

accidents; do not try to make a major capital gains out of an accident one has suffered by inventing other subsidiary (and often, imaginary!) ailments that must be compensated for at outrageous prices!

The case of the blasphemer ends, however, with the threatened judgment being carried out by the whole congregation (v. 23). Apparently, the blasphemer did not repent or offer compensation.

REFLECTIONS

1. Both the lampstand and the table of consecrated bread are mentioned in Heb 9:2. No special meaning is given to them in that verse, but Jesus mentions the bread of presence (see Matt 12:1-8 and its parallels in Mark 2:23-28 and Luke 6:1-5). In each instance, Jesus uses the action of the high priest, who shared the bread of presence with David and his hungry men, as an example of the fact that positive rules (such as this one that limits the eating of this bread to the priests alone, and the requirement that no work be done on the sabbath) are meant not to place mortals in bondage but to serve human good. The day is meant to be for the good of humans and not to obligate and enslave humans to the rule.

2. The lampstand functioned as a symbol of the people as a light to the nations, spreading the gospel through the energizing power of the Holy Spirit. Zechariah 4:1-14 completes this symbolism in a very explicit way, as does Rev 1:12-13, 20. Surely, whether it is Israel or the church, the principle is the same: "'Not by might nor by power, but by my Spirit,' says the LORD Almighty" (Zech 4:6 NIV).

3. In this sense, Israel was exactly what Jesus declared all believers to be: "You are the light of the world" (Matt 5:14, 16 NIV). Therefore, all must so let their light shine that all might see it and glorify their Father who is in heaven. In a similar way in Rev 1:12-13, Christ appears (in a vision to John the evangelist) to be walking in the midst of seven lampstands, caring for and watching over their burning. The seven lampstands are expressly said to be the seven churches in Asia (see Rev 1:20).

4. The bread of presence was the consecration to God of the labor and work of the Israelites' hands, just as the grain offering symbolized (chap. 2). However, rather than this being an offering from an individual, as in chap. 2, here it is the collective and organized capacity of the whole people and the total fruits of their labors.

5. In our day when swearing and cursing in the name of the Lord have become so common, the law against the blasphemer comes as startling news. Our culture, be it pagan, Christian, or whatever, needs to be warned that God will not hold anyone guiltless who persists in using the divine name, character, doctrines, or teachings as the basis for selfish expressions of wonderment, oaths, or demands.

LEVITICUS 25:1-55, HOLINESS IN LAND OWNERSHIP

COMMENTARY

In many ways, chap. 25 continues the sabbatical cycle observed in chap. 23. The principle of the weekly sabbath is now extended to a sabbatical rest set for every seven years for the land and for what it produces. And that principle is extended once again to seven seven-year cycles, after which is to be the jubilee year.

The structure of this chapter is marked by the key rhetorical device seen in chap. 19, i.e., "I am the LORD your God" (vv. 17, 38, 55). Not only does each of these formulas signify the close of a section (or as we have previously labeled them, colophons), but also they are joined to a rather extended closing theological exhortation. Thus chap. 25 can be divided into three major sections: a sabbath jubilee for the land (vv. 1-22); the redemption of property in the jubilee (vv. 23-38); and the redemption of a slave in the jubilee (vv. 39-55).

Leviticus 25 is indeed unique among all the chapters of the Torah, for it is the only chapter that deals with the subject of land tenure in ancient Israel. Two other complementary passages on the same subject appear briefly in the Torah: Exod 23:10-11, which specifies that every seventh year (without calling it a sabbatical year) the land is to be left fallow, and Deut 15:1-6, which imposes a moratorium on all debts every seventh year.

The Wellhausian school incorrectly regarded the year of jubilee as a priestly invention exhibiting utopian fantasies that dated from the time of the exile. But to argue that case, one had to disregard the many points of contact between Leviticus 25 and the agricultural regulations of many other ancient peoples. Israel's law, of course, never was limited to the socioeconomic motivations that the other nations demonstrated, for Israel's motivations were also clearly religious, as v. 23 affirms. But there was another hurdle that the Wellhausian thesis had to overcome. If Leviticus 25 came *after* Deut 15:1-6, its legislation would represent a retrogression and an undoing of the benefits that Deut 15:1-6 extended, for Deuteronomy endorsed the year of agricultural release and also added further economic relief to poor persons and extended the principle to the area of debts. It is best, then, from the point of view of theological development to see the Covenant Code's Exod 23:10-11 as coming first, followed by Leviticus 25, and ending in the Torah with Deut 15:1-6, instead of placing Leviticus 25 last as this theory proposed.

A "sabbath of the land" was probably observed during the pre-exilic period, even though we have no direct evidence from the time of the first Temple. But there is ample evidence of such an observance from the period just before the common era. First Maccabees 6:49, 53 reports that the city of Beth-zur had to surrender to the Syrians; the city lacked adequate provisions to endure the siege because the attack came in a sabbatical year. The historian Josephus also reports this incident along with other similar examples.[118] But even if the argument is that there is no evidence that Israel ever observed this law of the sabbatical year and the year of the jubilee during the pre-exilic period, the incident of a sabbatical release of slaves followed by taking them back into slavery, which is rebuked by Jeremiah (34:14), shows that the sabbatical and jubilee laws are known even if disregarded.

25:1-22. The introduction in v. 1 notes that this legislation came to Moses while he was on Mount Sinai. Israel had remained for one year at Sinai and did not move on until the twentieth day of the second month of the second year after their exodus from Egypt (see Num 10:11-12). All that is related here in Leviticus probably took place in the first month of the second year, immediately after the setting up of the tabernacle (see Exod 40:17).

Even though their entry into Canaan will not be for another thirty-eight years, as far as Moses knows at this point it is imminent. Therefore, he instructs them that when they enter the land that the Lord their God is giving to them, the "land itself must observe a sabbath to the LORD" (v. 2). Every seventh year, even the soil is to be given a year of rest, just as God's creatures and the persons made in God's image are given a rest every seven days. This rest is to be a "sabbath of sabbatism" (v. 4), a phrase we have commented on as it appears in 16:31 and 23:3, 32. The superlative form of the expression indicates the intensity of its import and the fact that it is to be a complete cessation of work and a complete rest.

During this seventh year, when the land lies fallow, no landowner is to lay exclusive claim to anything that happens to sprout on its own from the seed that has fallen into the ground from the previous year's harvest; everyone can eat of the land regardless of whose property it grows on. Even the

---

118. *Antiquities of the Jews* 11.8.6; 13.8.1; 14.10.6.

vineyards are to be left "unpruned" (v. 5), a word derived from the same root from which the word *Nazirite* comes. Just as a Nazirite is one who is "separated" unto God and who, therefore, lets his hair grow without shaving it, so the vineyards are consecrated and separated unto the Lord and left untouched by the pruning hook and knife.

The sabbatical year is to be observed by both the "hired worker" (שכיר *śākîr*) and the "temporary resident" (תושב *tôšāb*) "who live among" the Israelites (v. 6). The second term is rather unusual, but it refers to the practice of billeting employees on the land of their employers, especially when these workers are from foreign lands. Some have suggested the meaning of "bound laborer"[119] for this second term, since v. 35 refers to an Israelite "holding" the person as one would "hold" a resident alien.

To demonstrate that God is the ultimate owner of everything, nothing is to be harvested in the seventh year. The natural produce of the land is to feed poor people (see Exod 23:11). The wildlife is to be given a chance to repopulate itself. Moreover, enough food is promised in the sixth year to carry the people through this sabbatical year. And during this sabbatical year, the law is to be read to the people at the Feast of Tabernacles (see Deut 31:10-13).

After seven sabbatical years, totaling an interim of forty-nine years, a ram's horn is to be sounded (v. 9) on the tenth day of the Day of Atonement throughout the land to mark the commencement of the year of jubilee (vv. 9-11) in the fiftieth year. Thus it would appear that two holy years came back to back—the forty-ninth and fiftieth years. However, having two fallow years in a row would not appear to be very practical. This problem has been relieved in the book of *Jubilees* (written about 200 BCE) by making the jubilee year fall on the sabbatical year, i.e., the forty-ninth year. Apparently, one is not to begin counting the forty-nine years in v. 8 *after* a certain date, but the fifty years are to be counted just as the fifty days in 23:15-16 are reckoned from Sunday to Sunday inclusive. This would mean that the sabbatical year on which the counting begins is the first of the fifty years (i.e., the last year of the previous seven years); thus

119. Levine, *The JPS Torah Commentary*, 170-71.

the seventh sabbatical year is the fiftieth year counted.[120]

The septenary system reaches its pinnacle in this fiftieth year. The name of this year is probably taken from the Hebrew word יובל (*yôbēl*), meaning a "ram" in Arabic, because the year is signaled with the blowing of the ram's horn or the שפר (*šôpār*), as it is also called in v. 9.[121]

The jubilee year is to be hallowed or consecrated (v. 10), just as the sabbath day is set apart to the Lord. In this year, "liberty" or "freedom" (דרור *děrôr*) is to be proclaimed throughout the land (v. 10). This, of course, is the source of the famous inscription on the Liberty Bell in Independence Hall in Philadelphia, Pennsylvania.

Very similar to the Hebrew term is the Akkadian concept of *andurāru*, which was an edict of release proclaimed by the Old Babylonian kings and on into the later periods. In the edicts, the kings declared a moratorium on all debts and bondage. In a similar way, Jer 34:15 records a time when King Zedekiah proclaimed a *děrôr*, "a release" of all slaves as the Babylonians drew near to the city of Jerusalem. In Isa 61:1 a *děrôr*, "release," is proclaimed for prisoners. Jesus read from this same text in Isa 61:1-2a in the synagogue and then commented that it was being fulfilled right in front of the people's eyes that very day (see Luke 4:16-21).

The liberty proclaimed is threefold. First, it means liberty for the man who has become dispossessed from his family inheritance of the land and who can now return to it. Second, it means liberty for every Hebrew slave who can become a free person once again. And third, it means liberty or release from the toil of cultivating the land, for the land is to lay fallow all year long and produce only what comes up on its own without any sowing, cultivation, fertilization, or harvesting.

The regulations for the year of jubilee are probably equivalent to those for the "year of freedom" mentioned in Ezek 46:17. Liberty

120. So argues Noordtzij, *Bible Student's Commentary*, 251. Also, in part, Harris, "Leviticus," 2:635. See also S. B. Hoenig, "Sabbatical Years and the Year of Jubilee," *JQR* 59 (1969) 222-36, for similar conclusions but from a different standpoint.

121. Bush, *Notes, Critical and Practical, on the Book of Leviticus*, 253-54, suggests a number of other, but less likely, derivations for jubilee, including Jubal, the inventor of music in Gen 4:21; the Hiphil form of the verb יבל *ybl*, meaning "to recall," "to bring back," or "to restore" as in restoring liberty to the slaves; or the peculiar sound made by the instrument itself.

means that the Hebrew slaves can leave the service of their masters and return to the possessions, lands, and homes that they had to abandon. Even those who have had their ears pierced with an awl (see Exod 21:2, 6) as a sign that they would serve their masters forever are free to leave, for the "ever" in the terms of their agreement is superseded by the year of jubilee. All previous leases on the land are terminated, for the property in this year reverts to the original owners. The sale of the fields is nothing more than the sale of a certain number of harvests until the year of freedom and release comes in the fiftieth year (vv. 13-18, 23-28). Purchases of any farmland are to be on the basis of the number of years remaining until the next jubilee.

Repeatedly, the Israelites are warned "not [to] take advantage of each other" (vv. 14, 17). The reason is simple: "I am the LORD your God" (v. 17); therefore, "fear your God" (v. 17; cf. vv. 36, 43). Once again, a key characteristic of the Holiness Code is this appeal to the fear of God. What follows is an exhortation to obey God's laws and commandments (vv. 18-22). The promise is that if Israel will live as if all transactions take place under the eyes of God, they will find security and a reward for living obedient and God-fearing lives. Those who question, "What will we eat in the seventh year if we do not plant or harvest our crops?" (v. 20) are answered that the Lord will provide so abundantly in the sixth year that it will last into the seventh year. And even while they are planting in the eighth year, they will be eating from the super harvest of year six, given by the Lord. In fact, the old crop from the sixth year will be their supply in the ninth year, since the ground may have become rock hard from not being farmed in the seventh year, and thus the harvest might be slightly off even in the eighth year (vv. 21-22).

25:23-38. The central theology of this section, however, is found in vv. 23-24. The Lord declares that "the land is mine." Thus the land and the crops belong to the Lord. For this reason the land cannot be sold forever. Jezebel failed to comprehend this fact, which Ahab conveniently forgot to tell her. Naboth could not sell, trade, or substitute his land at any price or inducement (see 1 Kings 21), for the ultimate owner of the land forbade such

practices. What is true of Israel, in a larger sense, is true of all lands, for Ps 24:1 teaches that the earth is the Lord's and all that is within the earth.

God gave the land to the people in a rather miraculous way. Therefore, they are viewed as God's tenants, and the land is not to be sold in perpetuity. If it does become necessary for someone to temporarily give up the land, there is always the right of redemption of the land in the interim before the year of jubilee. The owner, or a near relative, can pay off the years of crops remaining until the jubilee, and thus the land will be redeemed. This close relative who redeems the land is known by the famous term גאל gōʾel, the "kinsman-redeemer" (NIV; cf. the famous picture, using the same term, of Boaz in Ruth 3:12–4:6).

The situation is different for persons who live in houses in a walled city (vv. 29-31). Houses in walled cities are more the fruit of the people's labor than the land in the country is; that land is the immediate gift of God. The sale of a house in the city is final if at the end of the first year following the sale the seller does not exercise his option to buy it back. The rules of reversion to the original owner in the year of jubilee do not apply to these situations. Apparently, this provision is made to encourage strangers and proselytes to settle among the people. Even though they cannot purchase land in Canaan, they can purchase and own houses in the walled cities so that they can live and trade among the Israelites. The same permissions do not apply to villages without walls in the country; there the perpetual ownership of the land by the Lord applies, and God gave that land only to Israel. The rules of the year of jubilee apply to the unwalled villages just as they apply to all the farmland in the country.

Leviticus 25:32-34 examines the case of the Levites. The homes in the forty-eight Levitical towns are given to them in perpetuity. They can never be alienated from them. God wants to show favor and watch-care over those who minister in that special service. These same principles continue in many countries to this day with special housing allowances being made for the clergy.

Provision is also made for the one who is "unable to support himself" (vv. 35-38). The Hebrew for this expression is literally "his hand wavers." Relief is to be extended to a native Israelite just as much as to a resident alien or a temporary resident in their midst. But on no account is any "interest" (v. 36) to be charged for such help. Interest in those days could run 30 percent and higher.[122] The word for "interest" in v. 36 is נשֶׁךְ (nešek, "to bite," as a serpent bites). Some have argued that this interest charge for the loan was "bitten off" before the rest of the principal was granted. Thus, on a one-hundred-shekel loan, a debtor might get only seventy shekels since the 30 percent was taken right off the top at the start. But whatever the meaning, no one is to take advantage of another person's calamity to profit from it and to seize the moment to advance oneself over one's neighbors. Such cruel exactions are nipped in the bud, and the Israelites are reminded that the Lord God brought them up out of slavery free of charge (v. 38). After all, "I am the LORD your God" (v. 38). In this context no one is allowed to escape the duty of showing love and a helping hand to others. All this is to be done without any interest charges being made.

25:39-55. A second case of need is that of persons who have indentured themselves to pay off a debt (vv. 39-43). Numerous circumstances could bring people to such desperate straits. Persons reduced to extreme need might have no other choice than to sell themselves to another to pay off that debt. Parents might sell a child for a stipulated sum and for a specified number of years to help finance a shortfall for whatever reasons. Someone found guilty of theft, but unable to make restitution, might be sold among the Jewish people by the judicial process. Such individuals are not to be sold as bondservants in a public manner but are to be treated in a private and honorable way. Neither are they to be "[ruled] over . . . ruthlessly" (v. 43) as Pharaoh's taskmasters treated Israel (the same term appears in Exod 1:13 of the Egyptians' cruelty). Inhumanity to one another is forbidden and is not to be permitted under any circumstance.

Verse 42 states why no Israelite can ever be anyone else's slave: "Because the Israelites

are my servants." Even this thought may sound offensive to us moderns who prefer to think of God as our Father and of ourselves as sons and daughters. But the Israelites thought of God as Lord and themselves as servants of the Lord. Though they were servants in name only, the point was that they were never to sell their bodies to anyone else; only their service and labor could be sold. In the year of jubilee, if not redeemed prior to that time, all Israelites were to go free, regardless of the terms of their servitude.

The Israelites can own male and female slaves (vv. 44-46) from the non-Israelite residents of Canaan or from the neighboring nations. Nevertheless, kidnapping, the method by which much of the modern abuse in slavery is realized, is a capital offense (see Exod 21:16). The law also carefully guards violence and tyranny of the master over these non-Israelite slaves, even granting the slaves immediate release from the indenture if any type of mark, scar, or physical impairment is seen on the body as a result of the master's abusive treatment (see Exod 21:20-21, 26-27).[123]

The final situation dealt with in this chapter is that of Israelites who indenture themselves to aliens (vv. 47-55). The owners of the enslaved Israelites must, however, recognize the right of redemption and the year of release in the jubilee. Every effort must be made to redeem the Israelites out of the hands of non-Israelites and to make the servitude as brief as possible. The price and the monetary equivalent of the release must be calculated as the time remaining until the next year of jubilee, minus the labor already rendered, deducted from the price for which the people sold themselves into bondage. In the meantime, the owners of the Israelites must "not rule over [them] ruthlessly" (v. 53).

The law of chap. 25 ends with a reminder that individual Israelites, as well as Israel as a whole, belong to the Lord as servants. As such, they are God's possessions, for the Lord their God brought them out of the land of Egypt.

122. See the discussion of this complex subject in Kaiser, "The Question of Interest and Usury," in *Toward Old Testament Ethics,* 212-17.

123. See the discussion of these passages in Kaiser, *Toward Old Testament Ethics,* 101-5, and *idem,* "Exodus," 432-34.

REFLECTIONS

Robert North neatly organizes the four lessons that might be learned from Leviticus 25.[124] They include social justice, social worship, personal virtues, and Messianic typology.

1. According to North, the jubilee was intended to prevent the accumulation of all the wealth of the nation in the hands of a few. Under the jubilee law, every Israelite's freedom and legal right to family land were guaranteed. Once in the lifetime of every generation (every fifty years), what might have been lost through debts could be recovered in the jubilee year. Therefore, this law prevented all monopolies that might come from an unfettered capitalism as well as a total communism that placed all property in the hands of the state. Land belonged to God, who in turn placed it on permanent lease in the hands of families. Thus the unity of the economy was found in the family rather than in an artificial organization created by the state or a corporation.

2. The jubilee, as one of the sabbatical years, was an extension of the sabbath day. It was the joining together of the concerns of religion and the concerns for society. Men and women could not be satisfied merely with performing religious duties, for they had to carry out the effects of their religion by helping those who had fallen into debt and had lost their lands. Moreover, this day of jubilee began with the Day of Atonement when worshipers were remorseful and contrite before God. That was the impetus for the threefold repetition of the command to "fear God" in this chapter. Mercy is as much a desideratum as is sacrifice (see Hos 6:6; Matt 9:13; Matthew 12:7).

3. Love and mercy toward one's neighbor lay at the heart of the jubilee legislation. If all Israel were but "aliens and [God's] tenants" (v. 23), the transitory nature of all mortals on this earth and the habitations we occupy must be acknowledged. The same point is made about Christians in Heb 11:10—we are but strangers and pilgrims here as we look forward to another city, whose builder and maker is God. If God cares for sparrows, and promised to provide more than enough in the sixth year to carry Israel through the sabbatical year, can God not also care for us in the same way? No wonder we are urged to cast all our cares on God (see 1 Pet 5:7). Moreover, persons who place their priorities right by seeking first God's kingdom and righteousness will find all the other cares managed by their Lord (see Matt 6:33).

4. In the messianic typology, North points to Jesus' use of the word *release* from Lev 25:10 in Isa 61:1 as he read from the Isaiah scroll in the synagogue (Luke 4:16-21 NIV). The reference to the "year of the LORD's favor" in that same Isaianic passage is probably an allusion to the jubilee year principle. The messianic age will bring release to captives and liberty to all the oppressed. This age began when Christ appeared the first time, but it will be completed when he returns the second time and "[restores] everything" in a new heaven and a new earth (Acts 3:21 NIV; 2 Pet 3:13).

5. John Bright summarizes the theology of this passage as one that:

> seeks to tell us that the land is God's and that we live on this earth as aliens and sojourners, holding all that we have as it were on loan from him (vs 23); that God narrowly superintends every business transaction and expects that we conduct our affairs in the fear of him (vss 17, 36, 43) dealing graciously with the less fortunate brother in the recollection that we have all been recipients of grace (vss 38, 42). And that is normative ethics![125]

124. Robert North, *Sociology of the Biblical Jubilee* (Rome: Pontifical Biblical Institute, 1954) 213-31.

125. John Bright, *The Authority of the Old Testament* (Nashville: Abingdon, 1967) 153. See also the discussion of three other attempts to treat the problem of contemporary application of the jubilee law in Kaiser, *Toward Old Testament Ethics*, 217-21.

LEVITICUS 26:1-46, THE ALTERNATIVES: BLESSING OR CURSE

COMMENTARY

Leviticus 26 and Deuteronomy 28–30 constitute some of the most important and moving chapters in the whole of the Pentateuch. These chapters were quoted or alluded to literally hundreds of times by the four major and twelve minor prophets. But these chapters are also emotionally tender chapters, for the Lord laments the prospect of having to chastise the people as they rebel and become ungrateful.

Chapter 26 is structured very carefully. The key formula, used in several previous chapters of this Holiness Code, now appears once again: "I am the LORD your God" (vv. 1, 2, 13, 44, 45). As in chap. 19, here again we have a double formula at the beginning (vv. 1-2) and at the end (vv. 44-45) of the chapter. Verse 13, then, forms the middle divider between the blessings section and the curses that follow it.

The largest section, by far, is that on the curses (vv. 14-39). The curses divide themselves into six parts, usually with the introductory clause of "If [after all this] you will not listen to me . . ." (vv. 14, 18, 21, 23, 27), and the accompanying threat of "I will punish you for your sins seven times over" (vv. 16, 18, 21, 24, 28). This adding of judgments and increasing the tempo and severity of the visitations from God is also used in Amos 4:6-12. There the prophet Amos concluded after each announced judgment, "'Yet you have not returned to me,' declares the LORD" (vv. 6, 8-11 NIV). Consequently, the northern ten tribes had better be "[prepared] to meet [their] God" (v. 12 NIV). It was as if the prophet and the Lord were counting with each judgment, 1-2-3-4-5, much as a referee would count for a wrestler whose shoulders were pinned to a mat. And then the referee rendered his verdict, only in this case he said, in effect, "Enough! Get ready for the destruction of the country!"

Based on these phrases, the following components can be identified: four foundational commandments (vv. 1-2), six blessings

for obedience (vv. 3-13), six threatened curses for disobedience (vv. 14-39), promise of future restoration (vv. 40-45), and summary (v. 46).

26:1-2. The opening verses summarize the first four commandments of the Decalogue and, therefore, rehearse in a nutshell a person's whole duty to God. Verse 1 prohibits all forms of idolatry because the Lord is God. The Hebrew word for "idols" in this first verse is אלילם (*'ĕlîlîm*), which technically means "nothings," "zeroes." Surely, the term alone is enough to drown the concept of any rivals to the living God with contempt. This summarizes the first two commandments of the Ten Commandments.

The next verse calls for observing God's sabbaths (the fourth of the Ten Commandments) and reverencing God's sanctuary, which covered in principle the ground of the third commandment, which focuses on the name of God. The sabbath included not just the weekly sabbath day, but all the days of holy convocation in the total sabbatical system treated in chaps. 23 and 25. Raising the sabbath and the sabbatical principle at this point is especially appropriate, since the weekly sabbath in particular is a sign of God's covenant with Israel (see Exod 31:12-17). And God's sanctuary is the continuing visible sign of God's presence in the midst of Israel.

26:3-13. There follow, then, the six blessings. Everything depends on Israel's obedience in following the decrees and commands of the Lord (v. 3). The promises mentioned here are of a temporal sort and apply primarily to Israel, but they are sufficiently uniform in nature to describe God's special providence for all individuals who make up all the nations on earth.

The first is the promise of rain (v. 4), introduced with the verb "I will give" (as in vv. 6, 11). The rain will come "in its season," meaning the seasonal former and latter rains. The rains, when they came, were concentrated in the months of October through April. For as the abundance of rain falls only during the rainy season, so the crops are able to grow and to mature during the dry season. The threshing will continue, promises this text, until the time of harvesting the grapes (approximately from early June until September), and the grape harvest will continue until time for planting rolls around again. These conditions are almost Edenic, or at least idyllic enough to fit eschatological times, for Amos promised the same thing in the coming age:

"The days are coming," declares the LORD,
"when the reaper will be overtaken by the
    plowman
and the planter by the one treading grapes."
                              (Amos 9:13 NIV)

The second blessing that obedience will bring is "peace in the land" (v. 6). Nothing will remain to terrorize, frighten, or trouble the thoughts of those who will walk with God in perfect obedience. On the other hand, immorality, reckless living, and unrighteous governing, thinking, and worshiping will invite both civil and foreign disturbance of the peace.

Third, God promises to remove the savage beasts from the land. In the earlier days, lions and bears still inhabited the land of Canaan and continued to be sources of potential danger at times when the supply of food got scarce or when they wandered into the settled areas of habitation (see Exod 23:29; Judg 14:5; 2 Kgs 2:24). But if Israel obeys, God will increase the number of the people, and the rule of the wild beasts will be restricted and contained.

Fourth, Israel will be successful when enemies come against it, for five Israelites will chase a hundred enemy soldiers and a hundred Israelites will take on ten thousand hostile opponents (vv. 7-8). Obedient believers will act as a united force; that is why they can, with the Lord's help, achieve such outstanding feats of victory against such overwhelming odds. Joshua enlarged on this promise by saying, "One of you routs a thousand, because the LORD your God fights for you, just as he promised" (23:10 NIV). Thus it happened that two of David's thirty valiant men experienced this kind of help as one slew 800 men and the other killed 300 men at

one time (see 2 Sam 23:8, 18; 1 Chr 11:11). Gideon's band of 300 men experienced the same kind of deliverance when they routed 135,000 Midianites (see Judg 7:1–8:12).

The fifth promise of God to the obedient people is the increase of their numbers and fruitfulness of their crops and cattle (vv. 9-10). The terminology used here verges on being legal language, for God's promise declares, "I will keep my covenant," or as it is in the Hebrew, "I will cause to rise up [or cause to stand] my covenant." God will have respect for the people, i.e., God will turn toward them with favor. When God's face is toward the people, they prosper (see Num 6:24-27; Ps 67:1-7), but when God turns away from them (see Hos 5:15), they experience misery and shame.

The sixth and final blessing promised (vv. 11-13) is the indwelling presence of God in their midst. God's tabernacle will be set up in the midst of the people, and there God will condescend to take up residence among the people. Both promises of indwelling, whether in the Shekinah glory that resided in the pillar of cloud by day and the pillar of fire by night, which also abode in the tabernacle and went before Israel as they journeyed, are the hallmarks of the presence of God. The immortal deity promises to "walk among" Israel (v. 12) and be their God, and they will be called the people of God.

The combination of these three promises form the oft-repeated (approximately fifty times) tripartite formula of the promise theme found in the OT and the NT: "I will be your God, you shall be my people, and I will dwell in the midst of you." This God set Israel free from bondage in Egypt (v. 13) and enabled Israel to walk without despondency and without the yoke of the heavy burdens of making bricks.

26:14-39. Suddenly, the text changes in v. 14 from the six blessings to the extended discussion of six curses that will be visited on Israel with increasing intensity to punish any disobedience. These threatened punishments are very similar to the ones listed in Deut 28:15-68; 29:18-28. Israel's rejection will not be an abstract abandonment of formal rules and regulations. It will be a turning away from the Lord, for these are the Lord's decrees, laws, commands, and covenant.

They are not Israel's laws or laws of some human.

The first curse will come in the form of "sudden terror." The Hebrew root is בהל (*bhl*, "to be terrified" or "to be confused"). A state of confusion, perplexity, and terror about what is going on is the result of being disoriented from God. Physical ailments will follow in the train of this confusion and fear: "wasting diseases" (such as consumption, dysentery, cholera, typhoid fever, typhus, malaria, tuberculosis, and various types of cancer), and a "fever" that results in the loss of eyesight (v. 16; perhaps something like acute purulent conjunctivitis that spreads rapidly from eye to eye and person to person). Now, instead of five chasing one hundred, Israelites will flee when no one is pursuing them (v. 17).

A second set of curses is set forth in vv. 18-20—all conditioned on the fact that the disobedience continues and that no response has been given to the first set of curses that God sends to turn them back. The judgment of God will be turned up "seven times" higher (v. 18; see also 21, 24, 28). The number seven is a definite number for an indefinite amount of increase in the severity of the judgments. The number seven is also chosen, no doubt, as a reminder of the whole religion in which the number seven and the sabbatical principle function so frequently, e.g., the seventh day, the seventh month, the seventh year. By reason of Israel's continued provocation of God, its troubles will also become more aggravated, not as a retaliatory device on God's part, but as a further stimulus to capture Israel's attention. If Israel had obeyed simply by hearing the word of God, there would have been no need to capture its attention through the events of history. Alas, the text predicts that Israel will often turn tone-deaf to the proclaimed word, and so the same love of God that sent the word of the prophets will now send a message of love in the tragedies of life, hoping that the nation will be forced by desperation to cry out to God for forgiveness and love once again. The whole exercise is solely to capture the hearts of faith so that Israel can live by a faith that expresses itself in obedience once again.

In this second series of curses, it will be as if the sky is sealed up and the rain is unable to break through. What has previously been promised about the rain coming in its season when Israel walks in obedience with God (v. 3) is now withdrawn because of disobedience. The heavens will seem to be turned into iron, and the ground will become as hard as bronze from the sun beating down unmercifully on the dry land. Trying to work the soil will be a fruitless task (v. 20), for it will only be a waste of strength. Neither will the trees yield their fruit. It will all be a hopeless cause. Israel is warned not to attempt to wander away from the Lord in disobedience, for the results predicted here will be awesome and mind-boggling.

The third curse will result in wild animals being let loose in their towns and countryside (vv. 21-22). This is the reverse of the blessing promised in v. 6*b*, where God promises that the beasts will be held in check and be removed far from the populated and farmed areas in deference to Israel's obedience. Ezekiel knew the reality of this threat, for he too warned about the presence of wild animals for a disobedient nation (see Ezek 5:17; 14:15, 21). Once again, the heat is turned up "seven times over" (v. 21). So desperate will conditions become that the beasts will no longer find food in the fields; therefore, the savage brutes will roam into the settled areas preying on livestock, children, and even adults (cf. 2 Kgs 17:25-26).

The fourth curse is the threat of war (vv. 23-26). The fact that all this is coming personally from the Lord is stressed in the text by the reduplication of the personal pronoun "I, [yes] I" (v. 24; cf. vv. 16, 28, 32 in the Hebrew text; NIV and NRSV render some of these repetitions of the pronoun "I" as "I myself").

The previous three curses are intended to lead the people to repent; alas, they have only made the people more adamant and resolute in their sin and disobedience.

This threat of war carries with it the accompanying cousins of plague, captivity, enslavement, and possible famine. The "sword" will fall upon the people "to avenge the breaking of the covenant" (v. 25). There is no way the Israelites can back out of the covenant, for the sword of their enemies will rise up by way of judgment against them. As the people flee from the sword into the walled cities, the crowding together will lead to an outbreak of pestilence that will kill both humans and animals (cf. Amos 4:10). Eventually, the city walls will be breached, the women will probably be violated, and the populace will be forced to go into internment in exile. In the meantime, as the besieged city awaits the inevitable, bread itself will become so scarce that one oven will be more than adequate for ten women to bake in, and the bread will be so little in volume that it will need to be doled out by weight (v. 26; cf. Hos 4:10; Mic 6:14).

If repentance still is not forthcoming, in this future day when Israel abandons the Lord and the covenant, a fifth curse will be imposed on top of the other judgments (vv. 27-33). As Israel's hostility toward the Lord grows, so does the Lord's "anger" or "fury" (v. 28). The famine will lead to the most horrible spectacle of any imaginable, for parents, out of desperation, will eat the flesh of their children (v. 29). Unfortunately, this prophecy was no mere idle threat, for as Deut 28:53-57 also warned, cannibalism did occur in some of Israel's most critical hours, especially during the Babylonian siege of Jerusalem (see 2 Kgs 6:28-29; Jer 19:9; Lam 2:20; 4:10; Ezek 5:10).[126]

Furthermore, the spectacle of the idols erected to Baal and Astoreth will need to be destroyed once and for all. The word used for the "idols," (גלולים *gillûlîm*), is the worst word imaginable in Hebrew. Ezekiel used this word thirty-nine times as he drew a parallel between human excrement and the form of the idol images. It is the most contemptuous term possible in the Hebrew language. So much for the biblical writer's estimate of what the idols were all about!

The cities will be laid waste, it is further warned, along with "your sanctuaries" (v. 31);apparently, the plural reference is to all the pagan installations, as opposed to "my sanctuary" in v. 2! No more will the delightful aromas of the sacrificial offerings be the bases for God's pleasure; they will be things of the past.

So desolate will the land become that even Israel's enemies will be appalled. In the meantime, those who survive all of this will be scattered among the nations, and the diaspora will be on (vv. 31-33). This will be the sixth, and final, curse. While the nation is in exile,

126. See also Josephus *War* 6.15-32 [3-4].

the land will enjoy the sabbatical years that Israel failed to observe (v. 34). Based on the 70 years of Babylonian exile, it appears that the nation went 490 years without observing what Leviticus 25 urges (see Jer 25:11). This would be a period from approximately King Saul's time (c. 1100 BCE) until the fall of Jerusalem in 587 BCE. There is no need, however, to work out any exact number of years, for it appears to be a round number dealing with a rather extended period when Israel forgot God.

Meanwhile, those who are left in the land (vv. 36-37), who once lived in "stubborn pride" (v. 19), will now be reduced to frightened cowards, whose hearts are made so "fearful" (מרך *mōrek*, from the verb meaning "to be soft," "to be tender") that a falling leaf will send them into panic. Moreover, those who go into exile will see their numbers diminish steadily, and they will "waste away" in the land of their captivity (vv. 38-39).

26:40-46. But God will not totally abandon the covenant or forget the obligation to complete what has been promised. This third and final section of the chapter has as its central promise that God will "remember" the covenant with Jacob, Isaac, and Abraham and will "remember the land" as well (v. 42). Actually, there is no Hebrew word to represent the word *with* before each of the patriarchs. Thus the translation should place the emphasis on God's covenant; and Abraham, Isaac, and Jacob may merely be addressed in the vocative here: "I will remember my covenant, O Jacob; my covenant, O Isaac; my covenant, O Abraham."

But in the biblical context, remembering is more than a cognitive activity; remembering is equivalent to doing. Thus the Lord remembers the covenant with the patriarchs when observing the vigor with which the Egyptians pressed the Israelites into making bricks in Egypt (see Exod 6:5-6). When the Lord "remembered" Hannah (see 1 Sam 1:19), it was more than a sudden recollection of what she had been asking for in prayer in the preceding years; instead, she became pregnant as God acted on the request she had been making in prayer for a son. In a similar way, the Lord remembered the "holy covenant" with Abraham and the house of David (Luke 1:72 NIV), and as a result, Jesus was born.

Therefore, God would likewise remember the promise made with Israel about the land, for God's covenants and promises are "irrevocable" (Rom 11:28-29 NIV).

What the people of Israel need to do is to "confess their sins and the sins of their fathers" (v. 40). The principle of the unity of the generations and the corporate solidarity of the nation is repeatedly appealed to in the OT.[127] Although Deut 24:16 makes it clear that children must not be put to death for the sins of the fathers (as does Ezekiel 18), there is another sense in which what the individual does has such an effect on the whole group that its benefits or judgments are shared with the whole group. Thus, when Abraham was blessed, so were his descendants (see Gen 26:2-5); when Achan sinned, all "Israel . . . sinned" (Josh 7:11 NIV). Just as one traitor can have devastating effects on the survival of the whole battalion, so one sinner (or one saint) can affect the whole group. Confession, then, must be more than a request for forgiveness for one's personal sins; it must also be for the group and nation that one is part of. If there is no acknowledgment of the sin that has led to the dispersion of the nation, Hosea represents God as promising not to return to the nation "until they acknowledge their guilt" (Hos 5:15 NRSV). For the nation had committed "treachery" (מעל ma'al), i.e., they had betrayed and attacked what had belonged to God (Lev 26:40; a concept also found in Ezek 17:20; 18:24; 39:23; cf. Lev 5:14-16), and they had provoked an encounter ("made me hostile") between themselves and God (Lev. 26:41).

What is needed is repentance by Israel. More than a physical circumcision, they need a "circumcision of the heart" (a concept found in Deut 10:16; 30:6; Jer 4:4; 9:25-26; Acts 7:51; Rom 2:29). Actually, God's law never emphasizes merely the external practice of religion; it all begins in the heart, or it is not at all real.[128] Human beings might look on

the outward appearnaces, but the Lord looks on the heart (see 1 Sam 16:7). The Israelites need to humble themselves first, as illustrated by the humble and corporate prayer of Daniel (see 9:4-19). They also need to "pay for their sin" (v. 41). And pay they will, for Isa 40:1-2 had to comfort the people in the Babylonian exile who had paid "double for all her sins" (NIV).

"Yet in spite of [all] this" (v. 44), God will never totally abandon or reject the people forever. God can never completely destroy them after all that has been promised and done for them. To deny what has been promised to Israel would require a denial of God's own self. Therefore, a day will come when "all Israel will be saved" (Rom 11:26, 29 NIV). As late as 518 BCE, much later than the return from Babylon in 536 BCE, the prophet Zechariah still held out the same hope that Lev 26:44-45 promised:

I will restore them
  because I have compassion on them. . . .
I will signal for them

  and gather them in.
Surely I will redeem them;

  they will be as numerous as before.
Though I scatter them among the peoples,

  yet in distant lands they will remember me.
They and their children will survive,
  and they will return. . . .
and there will not be room enough for them.
(Zech 10:6-10 NIV)

God is the Lord (v. 45) and will act on the basis of the covenant.

The chapter concludes with a summary (v. 46), reminding all that these are the decrees, laws, and regulations that the Lord established on Mount Sinai with the Israelites through the Lord's servant Moses.

---

127. See the discussion "Corporate Solidarity," in Kaiser, *Toward Old Testament Ethics*, 67-70.
128. On the case for Old Testament ethics as internal, see Kaiser, *Toward Old Testament Ethics*, 7-10.

REFLECTIONS

1. The significance of singling out the sabbath and the sanctuary may be exactly as Andrew Bonar concluded: "All declension and decay may be said to be begun whenever we see these two ordinances despised—the *Sabbath* and the *Sanctuary.* They are the *outward* fence around the *inward love* commanded in ver. 1."[129]

2. The promises and blessings of God do not exempt God's people from obedience. Instead, they were meant to be encouragements to keep on believing and remain obedient to God's expressed will. In the same way, these blessings and promises were not meant to exempt the people of God from praying for what might be realized; rather, they were given to instruct them and us as to what we should pray for, lest we pray in error and thereby miss the intended proofs of God's love.

3. The judgments and curses of God were never visited on mortals in a vindictive way, but ever and always as another proof that God loved and cared so much that if the people refused to hear the word that had been sent, God would speak to them out of the events of life, so that erring believers might all the more quickly be restored to favor.

4. It would be the height of inconsistency to affirm that God would forgive Israel's sin when the people confessed their sin and the sin of their fathers, but then deny the second half of the promise that God would restore Israel to their land once again (vv. 42, 44-45). To affirm one part of the promise is to affirm the other part about the land. In a similar way, Jesus implied that when "the times of the Gentiles are fulfilled" (Luke 21:24 NIV), and Jerusalem is no longer trodden down under the feet of the Gentiles, the city and the land will be restored to Israel again.

5. The call to "remember" the Lord, even as it is given in the invitation in the celebration of the sacrament or ordinance of the eucharist, is an invitation to do more than to go through a cerebral exercise. Instead, it calls for the accompanying deeds that are in conformity with the gracious works of this One who has done so much for us. In a like manner, all calls to remember the Lord in the OT text are invitations to action and life-styles that evidence our gratitude and appreciation for all that has been done for us.

6. There are corporate aspects to sin that our Western individualism quickly casts aside. But the fact remains that believers are their nation's keepers. Therefore, what affects the poor, the disenfranchised, the weak, the despised, the immoral, the hateful, and wrathful persons in our society also affects the whole group sooner or later—both for ill and for good. There is no way in which children of God can claim that these matters are of no concern to them. Rather, they must be occasions for acts of compassion, deeds of mercy, and prayers of forgiveness for the whole group, whether they are part of the believing community or not. Otherwise, where will God find persons to stand in the gap and be among that remnant for whom the majority might still experience divine love and mercy?

7. The promise that God would come and dwell in the tabernacle would receive a new impetus when the living Word would become flesh and would "tabernacle in the midst of us" (John 1:14, author's trans.). But even the incarnate Messiah who walked on earth among mortals for thirty years would pale in comparison with the final epiphany of Christ (see Rev 21:3), who would one day forever come to dwell among the people of God.

129. Andrew A. Bonar, *A Commentary on Leviticus* (London: Banner of Truth Trust, 1966) 473 [originally published in 1846]. Emphases belong to Bonar.

LEVITICUS 27:1-34

EPILOGUE: ENTIRE DEDICATION TO THE LORD

COMMENTARY

Almost everyone has noticed how chap. 27 appears to be somewhat anticlimactic, for the previous chapter, with its alternative prospect of blessings or curses, depending on how people have responded to God's covenant, surely makes an appropriate conclusion to the book. But it is not necessary to suppose that chap. 27 is mislocated or even that it is a later addition to the book.

A fairly straightforward explanation might well be that what has preceded in chaps. 1–26 has all been by way of obligatory duties mandated by Israel's Lord; what follows in chap. 27 is of an optional nature. Indeed, the special vows listed in chap. 27 are not to be required of anyone, for Deut 23:22 expressly teaches, "But if you refrain from making a vow, you will not be guilty" (NIV). Accordingly, the threats and promises of chap. 26 could not apply; that is why this chapter is not placed within the scope and compass of the earlier chapters. In that sense, then, the placement of this material at the end of the book is exactly where it should be.

Nevertheless, the instinct to make vows to God, even though they are not mandated, and even though there is no sin in refraining from doing so, has always been part of the human heart. Three impulses lead persons to offer vows: (a) the desire to procure something from God in exchange for making a vow, (b) the desire to thank God for some special favor God granted, and (c) the urge to spontaneously express love to the Lord.

The biblical text often refers to vows. Jacob offered vows to God while he was at Bethel (see Gen 28:20-22); Jephthah made his foolish vow as he went off to battle (see Judg 11:30-31); Hannah made her vow to God in the sanctuary at Shiloh, if God would grant her a son (see 1 Sam 1:11); and Absalom

offered his vow at Geshur, if the Lord would allow him to return to Jerusalem (see 2 Sam 15:8). Many other vows are made or commented on (see Deut 23:22-24; Pss 22:25; 61:5, 8; 65:1; 66:13-14; 76:11; 116:14; Prov 20:25; Eccl 5:3-4; Isa 19:21; Jonah 1:16; Nah 1:15; Mal 1:14).

Since there will always be occasions for making some kind of vow to God, a series of questions arises in connection with the practice. First, what objects, beings, or possessions can one properly offer to God? Second, what if, after the stress or impulse of the moment has passed, someone who has vowed something suddenly feels that it has been a mistake and wants to be free to recall it? Third, if one can recall a vow, what are the conditions and what are the penalties?

This chapter seeks to settle these types of questions, among other matters. Two of the three sections of this chapter are marked off by clear formulas that function as rhetorical devices for such divisions of the text. The first two sections begin with "if anyone" (איש כי *'îš kî*) in vv. 2 and 14. The subsidiary cases are introduced by "and if" (ואם *we'im*) in vv. 4, 5, 6, 7, 8, 9, 11, and 13 in the first section dealing with persons and animals and in vv. 16, 17, 18, 19, 20, and 22 in the second section dealing with the dedication of houses and lands. No such formulas or rhetorical devices can be observed in the third section; it appears to be more of a potpourri of items collected in one place for the sake of convenience.

The resulting structural components derived from the rhetorical devices already noted are as follows: introduction (v. 1); dedication of persons and animals (vv. 2-13), including vowing persons (vv. 2-8), vowing clean animals (vv. 9-10), vowing unclean animals (vv. 11-13); dedication of houses and lands (vv. 14-24), including vowing houses (vv. 14-15), vowing lands (vv. 16-24); assorted rules on other types of vows (vv. 25-33), including the sanctuary shekel value (v. 25), restrictions on vows (vv. 26-33).

Chapter 27, then, rules that persons may vow to God persons, beasts belonging to them, their dwelling places, or the right to some part of their lands. On the other hand, "the firstborn of an animal" (vv. 26-27), anything "devoted to destruction" (vv. 28-29), and the "tithe" (vv. 30-33) may not be used as special vows to God because they already belong to God and are naturally due to God by way of a previous dedication.

27:2-13. The first law is the law of vowing persons (vv. 2-8). It is the most basic kind of vow. In it persons dedicate themselves or their children to the service of God. Thus a person would be attached to the sanctuary as a servant to carry out duties in connection with its elaborate sets of jobs. In this manner, young Samuel was vowed to the Lord by his mother, and he remained there in the service of the sanctuary (see 1 Samuel 1–2).

Normally, however, the tribe of Levi provided more than enough labor power to carry out the various duties. In this case, the "equivalent value" (v. 2) of the service would be donated to the sanctuary in silver. One key source for understanding this system of equivalents is 2 Kgs 12:4-5, where King Jehoash of Judah needed funds to carry out the repair of the Temple. Jehoash said to the priests, "Collect all the money [silver] that is brought as sacred offerings to the temple of the LORD—the money collected in the census, the money received from personal vows כסף נפשות ערכו *kesep napšôt ʿerkô*, "silver equivalent of persons"] and the money brought voluntarily to the temple" (NIV). The term ערך (*ʿerek*, "equivalent") is the identical term used in Lev 27:2-5. This allows us to see that most did, as a matter of fact, commute their dedicated service into silver, which was then donated to the sanctuary for such needs as those indicated in Jehoash's renovation of the Temple.

The translation of v. 2 has not always been agreed upon by all for the verb יפלא (*yapliʾ*), with the final *aleph*, presumably a variant for the final *heh* in the root פלה (*pālâ*, meaning

"to set apart"). But it also reflected the verb פלא (*pālāʾ*, "to do difficult things, in a wondrous or glorious manner"). Thus the NIV has rendered it "to make a special vow." The noun for "vow" is נדר (*nēder*), which refers to the substance of what is vowed, not the act of vowing itself or its pronouncement.

The following estimation of values for votive offerings was operative:

Age	Male	Female
20 to 60 years	50 shekels	30 shekels
5 to 20 years	20 shekels	10 shekels
Over 60 years	15 shekels	10 shekels
1 month to 5 years	5 shekels	3 shekels

The highest value goes to the male who is in the prime of life and whose ability to carry out the work connected with the sanctuary is at its peak. The lower valuation of females has nothing to do with any perceived notion of worth or alleged negative attitudes toward women. The differentiation in estimates of value is not tied to personal worth, dignity, or esteem; instead, it has to do with the fact that much of the work involves such heavy labor as carrying the weight of heavy beasts offered as sacrifices, which normally men are able to assume more readily than most women. Thus the chart of values represents *labor value*, not personal value. The same factor can be seen in persons over sixty years of age, for their strength also would have subsided; thus their valuation is lowered. But this does not indicate that the society considers older people of less worth than younger people.

These valuations are large, for an average person earned only one shekel per month.[130] Apparently, the values are deliberately set high to restrain persons from easily vowing themselves or their children in the heat and passion of the moment.

It is also possible to vow animals to the Lord for the sanctuary (vv. 9-13). If the vowed animal can be used for a sacrifice, in that it is one of the clean animals, the vow is unalterable and irrevocable. Should persons making the vow change their minds and think that, for some reason, the vow is a mistake or too

---

130. See de Vaux, *Ancient Israel*, 76. De Vaux obtained this figure of one shekel per month from the Code of Hammurabi. Since slaves generally went for thirty to fifty shekels each, it would appear that in the legal limit of six years for Hebrew slaves, an indentured person would pay off approximately twice his value during the seventy-two months at one shekel per month.

generous and attempt to substitute an inferior animal (see Mal 1:8), both animals, the vowed one and the substitute, are considered holy, and both are therefore forfeited to the sanctuary.

Bargaining is not permitted. The decision and the value set by the priest are final (v. 12). If the vowed animal is an unclean animal, the priest then sets a price value on it, presumably for which it will then be sold, and the proceeds will go to the sanctuary.

Persons who wish to redeem an unclean animal that has been vowed can do so by adding another 20 percent value to its price before buying it back. This provision appears to be included to extricate persons from what they later consider to be rash vows.

27:14-24. A house can be vowed to the Lord (vv. 14-15). However, if the one vowing the house wishes to redeem it, the person has to pay a fifth more in price into the treasury of the sanctuary to do so. The houses referred in this case, however, appear to be ones inside the walled cities that can be bought and sold (cf. 25:29-31); houses that are part of the family estate cannot be bought and sold in perpetuity, as chap. 25 advises.

Consecration of land for a vow is much more complicated (vv. 16-24), since in the year of jubilee it reverts to its owner. Two cases are treated here. The first case (vv. 16-21) involves a field that belongs to an Israelite by inheritance, and the second case (vv. 22-24) of a field that has come to someone by a purchase. What is clear is that the land itself is not consecrated but the crops that it may produce until the year the land is due to be returned to its original owners.

In evaluating the land, the priest is to set its value according to the amount of seed it requires to obtain a certain yield (v. 16). The formula used here is the extent of the area required to sow a field with a homer of seed. The term חמר (*hōmer*) usually indicated a dry measure equal to the load a donkey (hence its derivation from חמור *hămôr*) could carry, estimated to be from 3.8 to 6.5 bushels. In Ezek 45:11, a homer equals ten ephahs (approximately 134 to 241 liters or 29 to 53 gallons).[131]

The point is that the value of the field is the value of the amount of seed it took to sow it.

Verse 16*b* is somewhat ambiguous, depending on the reference of the word *seed*. Does it refer to the "harvest [seed]" of the land, or does it refer to the "seed [that was sown]" in the field? Wenham and Roland de Vaux argue in their commentaries for the crop or harvest as the meaning, but most others take it the way we have argued for here—the amount of seed needed to sow a field.[132]

The situation in vv. 20-21 is ambiguous. One view is that the man who vowed a field turned around and sold the same field to another man, which would result in a penalty, such as v. 21 mentions. That shady dealer would lose everything, including the return of the field when the year of jubilee rolled around again. Another view is that the man gave the land to the tabernacle without redeeming it; in that case it was an irrevocable gift. Or it was likewise an irrevocable gift if he sold the land for use until the jubilee; at that time, of course, it must still revert to the sanctuary in the year of jubilee. This later case would make it similar to our modern future bequests. A third view is that the man dedicated the land to the sanctuary, but the priests did not have time to work the land. Therefore, the one making the vow worked the land for them, paying the redemption money while keeping the produce for himself. But if that person decided to lease the field to another person, the field did not revert to the one making the vow in the year of jubilee; it went instead to the sanctuary.

It is impossible to say which of these three views is the correct one, for the passage is so brief. It is clear, however, that the provision is meant to be penal, for the field during the time of the vow belonged to the Lord in a special sense.

A somewhat different case is taken up in vv. 22-24. A person purchases land that does not belong to his paternal inheritance and then dedicates it to the Lord. In the year of jubilee, that land goes back to its original owners according to the law of Lev 25:28. However, the man must pay the full estimated value of the crops that land would produce up to the year of jubilee, for if the

---

131. See de Vaux *Ancient Israel,* 202. Wenham, *Leviticus,* 340, mentioned that in Mesopotamia the standard price for barley was one shekel per homer. This would make the annual valuation of one shekel per a year for a field of one homer to be quite appropriate in this context of Leviticus 27.

132. Wenham, *Leviticus,* 340 and n. 8; de Vaux, *Ancient Israel,* 168.

owner exercised his right of redemption in the interim, the vow would go unfulfilled. To avoid having any liens against the land and to protect the original owner's right to redeem the land at any time, the instruction is that the vow is to be paid up front in full.

27:25-33. The remaining verses deal with three classes of property, which are excluded from being dedicated by vows to the Lord. First, the value of the "sanctuary shekel" is set at "twenty gerahs to the shekel [or twenty grains of silver]" (v. 25). A shekel weighed a half ounce (twelve grams), but there was a lot of variation, depending on local standards. All disputes, however, were to be settled by weighing against the sanctuary shekel, which functioned as a sort of bureau of weights and measure.

The first of the three cases discussed here is the "firstborn of an animal" (vv. 26-27). The firstborn of a clean animal already belongs to the Lord (see Exod 13:2, 15; 34:19); therefore, it cannot be given back to the Lord a second time. If the vow involves an unclean animal—e.g., a donkey—it can be redeemed by paying a fifth more, according to the value usually set on it by the priests. If the one making the vow does not choose to redeem it, however, the animal will be sold according to its value and the money given to the sanctuary.

The second case involves the exclusion of vowing things already "devoted to destruction" (vv. 28-29). The law of חרם (*ḥerem*)[133] seems the strangest of all the laws to Western readers, who have no analogies with which to compare it. But just as there is a positive consecration of persons and things to God, so there is a negative setting apart of some persons and things for destruction. To be sure, this is not something that was done often or precipitously. Only after a long period of chasing men and women with goodness and kindness did God dedicate something for destruction, as in the case where certain cities were marked off (e.g., in the conquest, the city of Jericho), or persons and things in those proscribed places were marked off for final and total annihilation. Historically, this practice of *ḥerem* was associated with wars. This practice of *ḥerem* was also recorded as being in

vogue among Israel's neighbors in ancient times, for King Mesha of Moab (a contemporary of King Ahab; see 2 Kgs 3:4) devoted to his god Chemosh the towns he conquered for destruction. This he recorded, with the use of the equivalent cognate Moabite word to the Hebrew *ḥerem*, in his famous Moabite Stone.

In the biblical context, *ḥerem* is carried out as a punishment. To take some of the souvenirs of war from a site placed under this "ban," or under "devotion to destruction," as Achan took from the Jericho military theater (see Joshua 7), and then try to dedicate them to the Lord as a part of a vow is to take something that already is dedicated and offer it, as it were, a second time. It already belongs to the Lord!

There are also judicial dedications to destruction, when certain of the Lord's commandments are violated (see Exod 22:20; Lev 20:2; Deut 13:13-16).

Verse 28 presents to both ancient and modern interpreters a serious difficulty, for one would not ordinarily speak of personally and voluntarily proscribing one's possessions or a field, much less someone else's things. Normally, such a serious matter was imposed from a divine source or by those in judicial or leadership positions. The rabbis gave two closely related explanations to the same problem: (a) Verse 28 may be speaking of a person who vowed to devote his property, or (b) it may be speaking of one who took an oath on some other matter, but who failed to carry out that oath; consequently, that person's property was forfeited as *ḥerem*. In both cases the oath was a binding obligation; no longer could it be thought of as a voluntary act.

Finally, there is the matter of tithes (vv. 30-33). Two types are discussed: a tenth of all the produce of the field, and a tenth of the flocks and herds. Here, then, is the third and last of the exclusions to what can be vowed to the Lord. Since the tithe is already owed, as it were, to the Lord, it cannot be made the object of a special vow. It is impossible to give away what already belongs to another; that is the case of the tithe. Numbers 18:21 affirms the same principle: A tenth of all that a person earned was to be given to the Levites for the service of the tabernacle.

---

133. For a fuller explanation of all that was involved in this "ban," see Kaiser, *Toward Old Testament Ethics*, 74-75.

The Wellhausian school objected that since Deuteronomy did not mention any other tithe than the produce of the field, the reference to the tithe of the flock was an indication that its inclusion in our present book of Leviticus depended on a late Priestly source from the post-exilic period. But it is possible to urge the exact opposite from the same evidence: that we have here in Leviticus the earliest form of the law on the tithe. Furthermore, Jacob promised a tenth of all that God had given him (see Gen 28:22). Surely that included a tenth of all the increase of his flocks, since he specialized in tending animals at the time. Even earlier than the time of Jacob, Abraham promised to give tithes to Melchizedek (see Gen 14:20).

The book of Leviticus ends with the closing formula of v. 34, referring to all the commands that God had given on Mount Sinai. This colophon refers not only to the opening verse of chap. 25 but also to the total legislation that covered the contents of Leviticus.

REFLECTIONS

1. Do the vows mentioned here, or any others similar to them, have a place in NT ethics and the life of faith? This is an important question, for a great deal of theology hangs on it in many circles. Note, however, that nowhere in the OT are vows represented as anything other than personal, *voluntary* promises made to God. Nowhere in either the OT or the NT do we find the practice of vowing urged, recommended, or mandated. Nevertheless, given the religious impulse of persons to make vows, the writer of Leviticus used the occasion as an opportunity to educate individuals in the legitimate bounds within which vows might be used. Thus Deut 23:22 reminds us that persons are not sinning if they refuse to make a vow. The regulations given in Scripture are meant more as a check against entering into consecrations rashly than as a recommendation for using such devices.

Ecclesiastes 5:5-6 summarizes these points best when it teaches, "It is better not to vow than to make a vow and not fulfill it. Do not let your mouth lead you into sin. And do not protest to the temple messenger, 'My vow was a mistake.' Why should God be angry at what you say and destroy the work of your hands?" (NIV). Thus while vows are nowhere forbidden, there is little, if anything, to say that they are approved. Our Lord's condemnation of the Pharisee's abuse of the vow to justify neglect of one's parents does not imply the propriety of vows in the present era. Nor can we find a permanent example in the apostle Paul's vows (See Acts 18:18; 21:24-26), for they are illustrations of what Paul did without any normative teaching for the church. We conclude, therefore, that nothing urges us to make vows to God, but a great deal is said to warn and caution persons who do make vows and who fail to carry through on them.

2. A most practical question emerges as to the Christian's continued obligation to give a tithe, or one-tenth, of all that is earned. Nothing is mentioned about a specific amount for the tithe in the NT or in the first century of the church. In the fourth century of the church, Jerome, Augustine, and others began to advocate the law of the tenth, or a tithe, for the church. This system passed down through the medieval and Reformed churches. But now that the church in Canada and the United States is not tied to the state, the urgency for some form of steady support has become all the more important.

Two elements must be distinguished in the matter of the tithe: One is moral, and the other is legal. The moral aspect is that believers are urged to set aside to God a fixed proportion of their income. The legal aspect is the precise amount of one-tenth. The moral principle is best stated in 1 Cor 16:2, where Paul urges, "On the first day of every week, each one of you should set aside a sum of money in keeping with [one's] income" (NIV). In that the exact amount is not specified, this principle should not lead to impulsive or capricious giving. Instead, there is to be an orderly, clearly thought-out method of regular giving. But how much? The average minimal giving in the OT was a tenth, but the NT answers with another formula: "See that you also excel in this grace of giving. . . . For you know the grace of our Lord Jesus Christ, that though he was rich, yet for your sakes he became poor, so that you through his poverty might become rich" (2 Cor 8:7, 9 NIV). Our conclusion must be that if a tenth was the minimal amount under the law, how can Christians do any less? Perhaps we should consider not how little but how much we can give, seeing how richly blessed we are in Christ.

3. The book of Leviticus has as its supreme lesson the fact that holiness consists of a full and total consecration of one's whole person to the Lord. It is likewise a call to separate oneself from all that defiles and separates one from being as holy as the Lord God is holy. Leviticus also teaches that the only way to attain this high ideal of holiness, both in its initial inception and in its daily renewal, is through the atoning sacrifice and sole mediation of the High Priest appointed by God. Thus it stands written, "Be holy because I, the LORD your God, am holy" (19:2b).**1.** Holiness is not something that acts like a contagious disease. Sin can be caught and is easily transmitted, but holiness does not work that way.

2. The daily offering of fine flour to God signifies Israel's daily consecration and dedication to the Lord.

3. Since God created all things, both the common and the holy must be received as gifts from above and not divorced from each other. But the common must be distinguished from the holy due to the presence of sin in the world, which God originally created "good."

THE BOOK OF NUMBERS

INTRODUCTION, COMMENTARY, AND REFLECTIONS
BY
THOMAS B. DOZEMAN

THE BOOK OF
NUMBERS

INTRODUCTION

TITLE, STRUCTURE, AND CONTENT

T wo titles are associated with the fourth book of Moses. The title "Numbers" comes from the Vulgate (Vg, *Numeri*) and the Septuagint (LXX, *Arithmoi*). The talmudic name חומש הפקודים (*ḥômeš happĕqûddîm*, "the fifth of the census totals")[1] would also correlate most closely with the title "Numbers." A second title, "In the Wilderness," comes from the Masoretic Text (MT), where pentateuchal books are named either by their opening word or by a significant word in the first sentence. The two titles provide different points of view concerning the central themes and structure of Numbers.

Numbers. The title "Numbers" focuses on the characters in the book. It underscores the census of Israel, which takes place twice over a forty-year period. The first (or exodus) generation is counted in chap. 1 on Year 2, Month 2, Day 1 after the exodus (Num 1:1). A second generation is numbered in chap. 26, most likely in the fortieth year after the exodus. No date is given for this census, but it takes place after the death of Aaron in Num 20:22-29, which is dated as Year 40, Month 5, Day 1 in Num 33:38. Dennis T. Olson has argued that the numbering of Israel is the clue to the structure and thematic development of the book.[2] The two-part division results in the following structure: chapters 1–25, The Old Generation of Rebellion; chapters 26–36, The New Generation of Hope.

Comparison between the two halves of the book reveals thematic development. Numbers 1–25 contains stories of rebellion. The establishment of the wilderness camp in Numbers 1–10 provides background for conflict. The people complain about the lack of meat in Numbers 11. They refuse to risk their lives to conquer Canaan in Numbers 13–14. And they continue to rebel against God and Moses in Numbers 16–17; 20–21; and 25. Rebellion leads to the death of the first generation. Numbers 26:36 focuses on the second generation. It is a story of hope.

---

1. See *m. Yoma* 7:1; *m. Menaḥot* 4:3.
2. Dennis T. Olson, *The Death of the Old and the Birth of the New: The Framework of the Book of Numbers and the Pentateuch*, BJS 71 (Chico, Calif.: Scholars Press, 1985) 83-124.

Rebellion gives way to negotiated solutions (Num 27:1-11; 31:14-15; 32:1-42), and the promise of land once again takes center stage (Numbers 27; 34–36).

In the Wilderness. The title "In the Wilderness" accentuates the setting of the book. The goal of Numbers is for Israel to leave the wilderness and enter the promised land of Canaan. The interrelationship of characters continues to be important to the book when the focus is on the setting. But it is their journey through the wilderness that provides the key to the plot structure. Numbers separates into three parts when the wilderness setting is emphasized: 1:1–10:10, Forming Community Around a Holy God; 10:11–21:35, The Wilderness Journey; 22:1–36:13, Preparing for Canaan on the Plains of Moab.

Numbers 1:1–10:10 contains revelation concerning the camp and the tabernacle. It takes place in the wilderness of Sinai. The purpose of instruction is to ready the people for Yahweh to dwell in the tabernacle at the center of the Israelite camp. The central theme is the holiness of God and its effects on Israel. Israel is counted in Numbers 1. The twelve tribes, priests, and Levites are arranged within the camp in Numbers 2. The Levites become the center of focus in Numbers 3–4. They guard the tabernacle at the center of the camp. Numbers 5–6 contain camp laws, which illustrate ways in which the holiness of God could be defiled. Numbers 7:1–10:10 narrows the subject matter from the social organization of the camp to the dedication of the tabernacle. This section includes sacrifices by each tribe, the observance of Passover, and preparation for the wilderness march.

Numbers 10:11–21:35 tells of the tragic wilderness journey of the first generation. The literature is organized around conflicts in which Israel rebels against God and the leadership of Moses. The people complain about food in Numbers 11–12 and question the ability of Moses to lead them through the wilderness. Israel doubts that God can bring them safely into the promised land in Numbers 13–15. The refusal of the first generation to enter Canaan leads to their death in the wilderness. Numbers 16–17 contains a series of conflict stories in which the priestly leadership of Moses and Aaron is challenged. Numbers 18–19 provide guidelines for approaching God. And Numbers 20–21 chronicles the deaths of Miriam and Aaron to provide the transition from the first to the second generation.

Numbers 22:1–36:13 describes the second generation of Israelites on the plains of Moab. The topics in this section anticipate an imminent possession of Canaan. Numbers 26:1 is a new census of the second generation. Numbers 28–29 provides instruction for worship in the land. Numbers 35 lists cities of asylum in Canaan. And Numbers 27; 32; 34; and 36 contain laws of inheritance. There is also a change of focus. Numbers 10:11–21:35 has an internal focus, exploring how rebellion by Israel threatens the holiness of God. Numbers 22:1–36:13 examines external threats to Israel in the story of Balak and Balaam in chapters 22–24 and the sin at Baal Peor in Numbers 25.

LITERARY FORM AND CONTEXT

Critical Study. Modern interpretation has focused on the literary formation of Numbers and its relation to the other books of the Pentateuch (Genesis, Exodus, Leviticus, and Deuteronomy). George Buchanan Gray outlined the literary formation of Numbers at the turn of the century using the documentary hypothesis.[3] According to this theory, the Pentateuch is composed of four literary sources (JEDP) written independently of each other. The Yahwist (J) was a tenth- or ninth-century BCE history. It was composed either during the united monarchy of David and Solomon (1000–922 BCE) or in the southern kingdom of Judah shortly after the split of the kingdoms (922 BCE). The Elohist (E) was an eighth-century BCE history, written for the northern kingdom of Israel (922–722 BCE). The book of Deuteronomy (D) is a seventh-century BCE document associated with the reform of Josiah in 621 BCE. And the Priestly (P) history was written in the sixth century BCE in the wake of the Babylonian exile (587–539 BCE).[4]

---

3. George Buchanan Gray, *Numbers*, ICC (Edinburgh: T. & T. Clark, 1903) xxix-xxxix.
4. Joseph Blenkinsopp, "Introduction to the Pentateuch," in *The New Interpreter's Bible Commentary*, vol. 1 (Nashville: Abingdon, 2015) 7-9.

Gray concluded that Numbers was composed of J, E, and P. Examples of J include Israel's departure from Sinai (Num 10:29-32), request for meat (Num 11:4-15, 18-24*a*, 31-35), and a portion of the Balaam narrative (Num 22:22-35). The story of the seventy elders (Num 11:16, 17*a*, 24*b*-30), the vindication of Moses (Num 12:1-15), the embassies to Edom and to the Amorites (Num 20:14-21; 21:21-24*a*), and most of the Balaam narrative (Numbers 22:1–24) derive from E. J and E were separate histories that spanned the books of Genesis, Exodus, Numbers, and possibly also Joshua. They were combined in the seventh century BCE. The sign JE represents their combination.[5]

Gray also identified the work of a priestly school (P) in Numbers and concluded that most of the literature in Numbers belongs to this school. The symbol P represents a body of literature that includes both law and narrative. The distinctive literature within P is designated by the symbols Pg, Ps, and Px. Pg is a priestly history of sacred institutions, written after the Babylonian exile. It is composed independently of JE. Examples include the organization of the camp and dedication of the tabernacle in Num 1:1–10:10 and most of the laws dealing with life in the land of Canaan in Numbers 26–36. Gray also concluded that the priestly history (Pg) was expanded with additional stories (Ps) and legal material (Px). Thus the literature of the priestly school was not unified. He judged the war against Midian in Numbers 31 to be a narrative addition (Ps) and the directions concerning unintentional sin in Numbers 15:22-31 to be a legal addition (Px). The present form of Numbers results from the combination of the distinct literary sources (JE plus P).[6]

There are a number of lasting results from Gray's work. We know that Numbers was not written by one author, but contains literature spanning the history of Israel. This literature is preserved in two general histories, with different theological perspectives. There is a pre-priestly stratum of literature (JE), which makes up a small portion of the book. It consists of stories about Israel's wilderness wandering, beginning with their leaving Sinai in Numbers 10:29-36, and it continues through the account of Balaam in Numbers 22–24. Gray used the symbol JE to underscore that this literature was not unified. There is also a priestly stratum of literature (P). Most of Numbers derives from the priestly tradition. Priestly literature opens (Num 1:1–10:10) and closes (Numbers 26–36) the book. Priestly narrative and law are also woven throughout the middle portion of the book (e. g., Num 15:17-21, 22-31; 16:8-11; 17:1-5; 19). Two guidelines for interpretation emerge from the work of Gray. First, priestly theology dominates in the book of Numbers; the commentary will focus on priestly theology. Second, Numbers also contains a history of composition. Thus many stories will yield more than one meaning, since they include priestly and pre-priestly versions.

Two developments in pentateuchal studies influence the present commentary. Both are departures from the documentary hypothesis evident in Gray's commentary. The first is the character and date of pre-priestly literature in Numbers. Gray dated J in the ninth century and E in the eighth century BCE. A consequence of his early dating was the distinction of the J and E histories from Deuteronomy (D), written in the seventh century BCE. Thus, for Gray, there was no D literature in Numbers. Martin Noth sharpened this distinction by arguing that J and E in the Tetrateuch (Genesis, Exodus, Leviticus, and Numbers) were clearly separated from Deuteronomy (D).[7]

More recent research indicates a closer relationship between JE and D. The theme of covenant, for example, with Abraham (Genesis 15) and Israel (Exodus 19:1-34) carries through to Deuteronomy 1–11.[8] The same is true with other themes, such as the promise of land (e.g., Genesis 12; 24; Exodus 13; 30–33; Numbers 14; Deuteronomy 1–11; and Joshua 1).[9] The points of continuity between the Tetrateuch and Deuteronomy have prompted a reevaluation

---

5. Gray, *Numbers*, xxxi-xxxii.

6. Gray, *Numbers*, xxxiii-xxxix.

7. Martin Noth, *Numbers*, trans. James D. Martin, OTL (Philadelphia: Westminster, 1968) 4-11. Noth extended the argument to include later deuteronomistic (Dtr) additions, which tied Deuteronomy to the Deuteronomistic History (Joshua, Judges, Samuel, and Kings).

8. See Lothar Perlitt, *Bundestheologie im Alten Testament*, WMANT 36 (Neukirchen-Vluyn: Neukirchener Verlag, 1969); and Thomas B. Dozeman, *God on the Mountain*, SBLMS 37 (Atlanta: Scholars Press, 1988) 37-86.

9. Susan Boorer, *The Promise of Land as Oath: A Key to the Formation of the Pentateuch*, BZAW 205 (Berlin: de Gruyter, 1992); and Thomas B. Dozeman, *God at War: Power in the Exodus Tradition* (Oxford: Oxford University Press, 1996) 42-100.

of the pre-priestly history.[10] John Van Seters maintains the name "Yahwist" to describe this history, but he redates the material from the early monarchical period to the exile. He also detects influence between J and Deuteronomy. But, according to Van Seters, J was written after Deuteronomy and the Deuteronomistic History (Joshua, Judges, Samuel, and Kings). Thus it represents a later perspective and not an earlier one.[11] Other names for the pre-priestly history include Erhard Blum's designation of it as "D-Compo-sition." This term designates literature in the Tetrateuch, Deuteronomy and the Deuteronomistic History.[12] Thus, for Blum also, there is a literary relationship between the Tetrateuch and Deuteronomy. In previous studies I have employed the term "deuteronomistic" to indicate the same close relationship between the pre-priestly Tetrateuch and Deuteronomy.[13]

The brief overview indicates how terminology is open to debate at the present time. In this commentary, I will simply use the term "pre-priestly" to indicate a history that is earlier than priestly tradition. It is composed in the late monarchical or the exilic period. It contains material from earlier periods in Israel's history as well, and it extends from Genesis through Kings.[14] Thus there is literary interdependence between the pre-priestly history in Numbers and Deuteronomy. Commentary will often include comparison between similar stories in these two books.

The second departure from the documentary hypothesis is the literary character of priestly tradition. Gray interpreted P as a history that was written independently of JE. The relationship between priestly and pre-priestly literature took place only when the distinct histories were combined to form the canonical Pentateuch. Thus the interweaving of the two histories was not important for interpretation. Martin Noth expressed doubts about this conclusion. He noticed more interaction between the two histories in the composition of P, concluding that P played a formative role in determining the literary shape of Numbers. This was true not only for the introduction (Numbers 1–10) and conclusion (Numbers 26–36), but also for the middle section, where Gray identified the JE narrative. Priestly writers provided the basic literary design of this section, according to Noth, by the way in which they had gathered the literature together in Numbers 11–12; 13–15; and 16–19.[15]

More recent scholars have continued to question whether the documentary hypothesis provides the best model for interpreting priestly tradition in Numbers. Wenham noted in passing that the composition of Numbers may be more the result of editors who interrelated older material with commentary.[16] Budd also questioned whether priestly tradition might better be interpreted as "midrashic commentary" on older literature, rather than an independent literary source. He took a middle position in his commentary. Priestly tradition is more than commentary, but not an independent document. P incorporates older material, according to Budd, along with interpretative comments, while also providing its own distinctive structure.[17] I, too, will interpret priestly tradition as a redaction of pre-priestly literature, rather than an independent history. This change in perspective assumes a dialogue between traditions in the formation of Numbers. As a result, interpretation must pay attention to the themes that arise in priestly literature and to the ways in which additions by priestly writers reinterpret and restructure the pre-priestly history.

Literary Form. According to Jacob Milgrom, Numbers contains the greatest variety of literature of any book in the Bible. He lists fourteen distinct genres: narrative (Num 4:1-3), poetry (Num 21:17-18), prophecy (Num 24:3-9), victory song (Num 21:27-30), prayer (Num 12:13), blessing (Num 6:24-26), lampoon (Num 22:22-35), diplomatic letter (Num 21:14-19), civil law (Num 27:1-11), cultic law (Num 15:17-21), oracular decision (Num 15:32-36), census list

10. Blenkinsopp, "Introduction to the Pentateuch," 312-13.

11. John Van Seters, *In Search of History: Historiography in the Ancient World and the Origins of Biblical History* (New Haven: Yale University Press, 1983); and *The Life of Moses: The Yahwist as Historian in Exodus-Numbers* (Louisville: Westminster/John Knox, 1994).

12. Erhard Blum, *Studien zur Komposition des Pentateuch, BZAW* 189 (Berlin: de Gruyter, 1990).

13. Dozeman, *God on the Mountain* and *God at War*.

14. See Dozeman, *God at War*, 42-100, 171-83, for discussion of the pre-priestly history as including Genesis through Kings. For further discussion of terminology, see D. Carr, *Reading the Fractures of Genesis: Historical and Literary Approaches* (Louisville: Westminster John Knox, 1996) 143-293, who uses "Non-P" to designate pre-priestly tradition.

15. Noth, *Numbers*, 4-12.

16. Gordon J. Wenham, *Numbers: An Introduction and Commentary*, Tyndale Old Testament Commentaries (Leicester: Inter-Varsity, 1981) 20-21.

17. Philip J. Budd, *Numbers*, WBC 5 (Waco, Tex.: Word, 1984) xxii.

(Num 26:1-51), temple archive (Num 7:10-88), and itinerary (Num 33:1-49).[18] The literature, moreover, spans the history of Israel. The distinct literature within Numbers can be summarized in four stages of composition: (1) individual poetry, stories, records, and law; (2) the pre-priestly history; (3) the priestly history; and (4) the canonical book of Numbers.

Individual Poetry, Stories, Records, and Law. *Poetry.* Ancient poetry is concentrated in the story of Balaam in Numbers 22–24, but it is also woven throughout Numbers. The poems are very diverse in content. They include songs of war, water, blessing, prophecy, and even a foreign song:

6:24-26, priestly blessing;
10:35-36, Song of the Ark;
21:14-15, an excerpt from the Book of the Wars of Yahweh;
21:17-18, Song of the Well;
21:27-30, ballad over Heshbon;
23:7-10, 18-24; 24:3-9, 15-24, oracles of Balaam.

Stories, Inheritance Records, and Itineraries. Individual stories and other records were also in circulation prior to their incorporation into the pre-priestly and priestly histories. Topics include land inheritance, temple practice, and life experiences from the desert. Numbers also contains travels lists, known as itineraries. These lists are most likely from royal archives, perhaps associated with military campaigns:[19]

20–21,*[20] conquest in the Transjordan;
21:4-9, cult of Nehushtan;
21:10-20, itinerary list;
25:1-5, sin at Baal Peor;
32,* inheritance;
33,* itinerary list.

Law. There is debate surrounding the origin of priestly law. The majority view in the modern era was that priestly law is exilic or post-exilic in origin.[21] This conclusion has been countered by more recent arguments in favor of locating early forms of priestly law in the monarchical period.[22] The debate is difficult to resolve because all priestly law has been edited well into the post-exilic period. Possible examples of pre-exilic priestly law include the following:

5:5-10, restitution
5:11-28, the wife suspected of adultery
6:1-22, Nazirite vow
15:1-31,* law of sacrifice
19, red heifer
28–29,* aspects of the cultic calendar
30,* law of vows
34,* inheritance
35,* levitical cities.

The Pre-priestly History. Pre-priestly literature is concentrated in the middle portion of Numbers. It begins with Israel's departure from Mt. Yahweh in Num 10:29-36 and ends with a summary of the wilderness travel in Numbers 33. The pre-priestly history separates into two

---

18. Jacob Milgrom, *Numbers,* JPS Torah Commentary (Philadelphia: JPS, 1990) xiii.
19. See G. I. Davies, "The Wilderness Itineraries and the Composition of the Pentateuch," *VT* 33 (1983) 1-13.
20. The asterisk (*) indicates that a section of literature contains writing from more than one author.
21. See Julius Wellhausen, *Prolegomena to the History of Ancient Israel,* trans. J. S. Menzies and A. Black (Gloucester: Peter Smith, 1983; first published in 1883).
22. See Y. Kaufmann, *The Religion of Israel,* trans M. Greenberg (Chicago: University of Chicago Press, 1961).

parts. It begins by outlining the complaints of Israel over food, water, and leadership (Numbers 11–12; 16) and the loss of the land by the first generation (Numbers 13–14). Numbers 20–21 provides transition from wilderness wandering to conquest of the Transjordan by the second generation. Numbers 22–24 and 25:1-5 explore threats to Israel by other nations. The story concludes with an account of Israel's inheritance of the Transjordan (Numbers 32) and a summary of the wilderness journey (Numbers 33). Pre-priestly literature includes the following:

10:29-36,* departure from Mt. Yahweh;
11:1-3, murmuring;
11:4-35, complaint about food and the selection of the seventy elders;
12,* conflict between Moses, Miriam, and perhaps Aaron;
13–14,* loss of the land;
16,* conflict between Moses and Dathan and Abiram;
20:14-21, conflict with Edom;
21:1-3, defeat of the king of Arad;
21:4-9, fiery serpents;
21:10-20, leaving the wilderness;
21:21-35, defeat of the Amorite kings Sihon and Og;
22–24,* the threat of Balak and the blessing of Balaam;
25:1-5, sin at Baal Peor;
32, inheritance of the Transjordan;
33,* summary of itinerary stops.

Pre-priestly literature in Numbers is part of a history that includes the promise of land and nationhood to the ancestors in Genesis, as well as liberation from Egypt and the establishment of covenant at the mountain of God in Exodus. The departure of Israel from Mt. Yahweh in Numbers 10:29-36 indicates that the pre-priestly history once followed immediately after the establishment of covenant in Exodus 19–34. The role of the tent of meeting in Exodus 33 and Numbers 11–12 provides further support for this conclusion. In both Exodus 33 and Numbers 11–12, the tent of meeting is located outside the Israelite camp. This is unusual in the Pentateuch, because priestly writers place the tabernacle at the center of the camp in Exodus 35–40, Leviticus, and Numbers 1–10. As a result, Exodus 33 and Numbers 11–12 stand out in their present narrative context. But, in the pre-priestly history, Exodus 33 and Numbers 11–12 would have followed in rapid succession. The return of the tent of meeting in Deut 31:14-23 as the setting for the commissioning of Joshua to replace Moses suggests that the pre-priestly history also incorporated the book of Deuteronomy. The commissioning of Joshua leads into the conquest stories of the book of Joshua. Central themes of the pre-priestly history include the unfulfilled promise of land to the ancestors and the necessity of conquest to acquire it, salvation from Egypt as an event of liberation that provides an initial stage toward conquest, faith as fear of God that is able to withstand tests in the wilderness, the revelation of law, the establishment of covenant, and the idealization of Moses as a prophetic leader and teacher of law.

The Priestly History. Most literature in Numbers belongs to the priestly history. The priestly writers frame the pre-priestly history with law. Camp legislation is introduced in Numbers 1–10, while inheritance law and cultic legislation now conclude the book in Numbers 26–36. The priestly writers also add their interpretation to the conflict stories in Numbers 11–25 and interweave law with the narratives in Numbers 15; 18–19. The story of the loss of land in Numbers 13–14 includes a priestly interpretation, and it concludes with laws concerning life in the land in Numbers 15. A priestly leader, Korah, is added to the conflict with Dathan and Abiram in Numbers 16–17. This conflict, too, is followed by legislation in Numbers 18–19. Numbers 20–21 is less of a transition to the second generation for the priestly writers. They emphasize instead the death of Miriam and Aaron, as well as the sin of Moses. Israel's arrival on the plains of Moab in Numbers 22 signals transition from wilderness wandering to preparation for Canaan in the priestly history, although the death of the first generation is not complete until the second census in chap. 26. Priestly literature includes the following:

1:1–10:10, legislation concerning the camp and the tabernacle;
10:11-28, departure from Sinai;
12,* conflict between Moses, Miriam, and Aaron;
13–14,* loss of the land;
15,* law concerning life in the land;
16–17,* conflict between Moses and Korah;
18–19, law concerning the priesthood and death;
20:1, death of Miriam;
20:2-13, sin of Moses and Aaron;
20:22-29, death of Aaron;
25:6-18, sin at Baal Peor;
26, second census;
27:1-11, inheritance of the daughters of Zelophehad;
27:12-23, death of Moses;
28–29,* offerings and cultic calendar;
30,* law of vows;
31, law of booty;
33,* summary of Israel's itinerary stops;
34,* inheritance;
35,* levitical cities;
36, inheritance of the daughters of Zelophehad.

Priestly literature in Numbers is part of a history that begins with the story of creation in Genesis 1:1. It also includes the promise of land and nationhood to the ancestors in Genesis, the liberation from Egypt, and the establishment of the nation at the mountain of God in Exodus. The central event at Mt. Sinai is the revelation of the tabernacle cult. Its plans are revealed to Moses in Exodus 25–31, when the כבוד יהוה (*kĕbôd YHWH*, "the glory of Yahweh") descends on Mt. Sinai in Exod 24:15-18. Exodus 35–40 describes the construction of the tabernacle. It concludes with a theophany in Exod 40:16-38, when the *kĕbôd YHWH* leaves Mt. Sinai to enter the tabernacle. The book of Leviticus recounts the revelation of the sacrificial cult and the sanctification of the priesthood. These events also conclude with a theophany in Lev 9:23-24, when the *kĕbôd YHWH* appears at the altar in front of the tabernacle. The formation of the camp in Numbers 1–10 completes the revelation at Mt. Sinai in the priestly history. This episode, too, is marked by a theophany in Nums 7:89, when Moses enters the tabernacle to speak with God before the mercy seat.

The conclusion to the priestly history is not clear. There is evidence of editing by priestly writers in Deuteronomy. In particular, they enclose the book of Deuteronomy with the death of Moses. It is announced in Num 27:12-23 and 31:1-2, but not fulfilled until Deut 32:48-32 and 34:1-8. The framing may indicate that their history ends with the death of Moses.

The priestly history addresses the tragedy of the exile (587 BCE), when Israel lost their land to the Babylonians. One of its aims is to explore how Israel can once again be the people of God in the land of Canaan in the post-exilic period (539 BCE). Central themes of the priestly history include creation as the primary context for interpreting salvation, the relationship of creation and covenant, the unfulfilled promise of land, the holiness of God and the demand that it places on Israel to be holy like God, the importance of the sanctuary, the revelation of law, the atoning power of cultic ritual, the need for a sanctified priesthood, the danger of impurity, and the idealization of Moses as a priestly mediator.

The Canonical Book of Numbers. Numbers undergoes a final literary transformation. It is indicated by the way in which the book is presently framed. Numbers 1:1 opens with the statement, "The LORD spoke to Moses in the wilderness of Sinai, in the tent of meeting." The book closes in Num 36:13 with the similar theme: "These are the commandments and the ordinances that the LORD commanded through Moses to the Israelites." The effect of these verses is to separate the literature in Numbers to some degree from the other books in the Pentateuch. The opening and closing verses emphasize the authoritative nature of the literature. The framing also suggests a transformation of genre from history to law. The literature is not so much an episode in a larger history, when it is confined to Numbers. Instead, it resembles more a book of divine law revealed by God to Moses.

METHOD OF STUDY AND PRIESTLY RELIGION

Method of Study. The prominence of priestly ritual law in Numbers has made interpretation difficult. The rituals are not explained; their meaning is assumed. The layout of the camp (Numbers 2); distinctions between priests, Levites, and laity (Numbers 3–4); the dedication of the tabernacle with sacrifices (Numbers 7–9); and laws of inheritance (Numbers 27; 34–36) are outlined in detail without explanation. Gordon Wenham notes that the "sheer bulk of ritual law in the Pentateuch indicates its importance to biblical writers." Yet few of these texts have worked their way into the lectionary cycles of the church. Readings from Numbers in the *Revised Common Lectionary* are limited to three: the priestly blessing in Num 6:22-27, the selection of the seventy elders in Numbers 11, and the healing power of the copper snake in Num 21:4-9. The reason for the absence of Numbers in Christian teaching and preaching, according to Wenham, is that priestly ritual has been judged "dull to read, hard to understand, and apparently quite irrelevant to the church in the twentieth century."[23]

Social anthropologists have opened a window of interpretation into ritual law within the Bible. Anthropologists are trained to interpret living societies. Their research ranges from the most important events in a society to the everyday exchange between members. In most instances, the rules of interaction are known by all and thus usually unexplained. These rules reflect the deepest values of a people, and adhering to them gives rise to ritual behavior. They include important events like birth, marriage, worship practices, and burial of the dead. Yet other rules are mundane, like how and what people eat or acceptable forms of greeting each other on the street.[24] It is usually the outsider or foreigner who becomes aware of such rituals by unintentionally breaking them. All travelers know how easy it is to break the rules of another society.

Priestly laws are the unexplained rituals of ancient Israel. They take up most of the Pentateuch because they reveal their deepest values. Anthropologist Mary Douglas brought insight into the interpretation of priestly law with her study of Leviticus 11.[25] This text outlines the laws for clean and unclean food, known as "kashrut" (כשרות *kašrût*), kosher food law. The chapter consists of a long list of animals, fish, birds, and insects that are edible (clean) and inedible (unclean). Yet the underlying reason why only some split-hoofed animals were edible or why certain fish and birds were clean while others were not elude modern interpreters. Priestly writers gave no explanation, and the study of individual laws provides no insight.

Douglas assumed that the meaning of the text was in the interrelationship of all the laws and not in any one law. She concluded that what made something unclean was that it did not move as other land, air, or water creatures. Unclean animals, therefore, did not clearly conform to their species. The same was true for fish, birds, and insects. They broke the order (or natural law) of creation and thus were not fit for human consumption (at least by godly people). Priestly writers never state this principle. It only emerges when all the laws in Leviticus 11 are read together. The study of food laws in Leviticus 11 provides three important guidelines for interpreting priestly law in Numbers.

(1) Priestly law is concerned with the order of creation. Order, purity, and even holiness are interrelated in priestly law. The source of life is the holiness of God, which fashions order in the

23. Wenham, *Numbers,* 25-29.

24. See, e.g., Thomas W. Overholt, *Cultural Anthropology and the Old Testament,* Guides to Biblical Scholarship, Old Testament (Minneapolis: Augsburg Fortress, 1996); and Robert R. Wilson, *Sociological Approaches to the Old Testament* (Philadelphia: Fortress, 1984).

25. Mary Douglas, *Purity and Danger: An Analysis of the Concepts of Pollution and Taboo* (London: Routledge and Kegan Paul, 1966), 41-57.

world. Life flourishes in a well-ordered creation. Disorder creates a condition that is threatening to holiness and all life in creation. It allows for impurity, which is not simply disorder, but, in its most extreme form, death.[26] Impurity is like a virus to the holiness of God. It can spread through contact, creating chaos and death in its wake. Priestly law is meant to safeguard the holiness of God from contagious impurity by reinforcing the order of creation. Eating habits are part of the system of safeguards for the holiness of God. So are the camp regulations in Numbers.

(2) The meaning of priestly ritual is not in any one law, but in the interrelationship of all the laws. Only by examining all the laws in Leviticus 11:1 was Douglas able to show that the principle of locomotion was the decisive factor for biblical writers in judging animals clean or unclean. The same is true for priestly law in Numbers. Theological insight requires that all the laws be interrelated. As a result, individual stories or laws in Numbers must be interpreted within the larger complex of literature.

(3) Priestly ritual has symbolic meaning. It creates a comprehensive worldview in which God, humans, and the created order are interrelated. Douglas concluded that in Leviticus 11 laws about animals were carried over into the human world. Thus just as animals separated into unclean (inedible), clean (edible), and sacrificial, so also humans separated into Gentile (unclean), Israelite (clean), and priest (sacrificial). Clean people eat clean food, and only priests sacrifice. The laws concerning the layout of the Israelite camp in Numbers will also have symbolic significance about God, about humans, and about creation.

Priestly Religion. Interpretation of Numbers requires an understanding of priestly religion. This is not an easy task for a modern Christian. We envision God as an intimate friend who dwells within us. We sing about "what a friend we have in Jesus." The focus of our piety is not on the vast gulf between God and ourselves, but on our own close, personal, and individual relationship with God. We may fear God, but it is the respect due a powerful companion. Our friendship with God leads to spontaneous prayer. These conversations take place at any time and in any location. They are not restricted to organized worship. They do not require special rituals. There is no need for a priest to mediate our prayer. And prayer certainly is not confined to church buildings. In fact, we envision our own bodies as the temple of God. The temple, sacrificial rituals, and God's relationship to humans are different in priestly religion.

Temple. The center of priestly religion is God dwelling in the Temple. When Solomon completed the Jerusalem Temple, he stated to Yahweh, "I have built you an exalted house, a place for you to dwell in forever." The same is true for the tabernacle in priestly religion. It is where God dwells on earth. Yahweh states to Moses, "Have [Israel] make me a sanctuary, so that I may dwell among them." The plans for the tabernacle in Exodus 25–31 are a pattern of God's heavenly home. Construction of the tabernacle allows God to descend to earth. Thus it connects heaven and earth. It is the *axis mundi*—the central point of creation where heaven and earth link.[27] All communication with God is channeled through cultic rituals in the tabernacle.

Temples are located on symbolic mountains. Solomon's Temple is on Mt. Zion (Psalm 48). Pre-priestly writers associate the tent of meeting in Exodus 33 with Mt. Horeb, which is also the mountain of theophany in Deuteronomy 4–5. Numbers 10:33-34 identifies the desert sanctuary of God as Mt. Yahweh. Priestly writers locate the tabernacle on Mt. Sinai (Exod 24:15-18). Yahweh has many mountain homes. Mountains symbolize the presence of God in the Temple and the role of the Temple in connecting heaven and earth. Different mountains indicate distinct forms of worship. Contemporary church architecture provides a partial analogy. Denominations favor distinct styles for church buildings because of different forms of worship. Churches are built with and without altars, with center aisles or in the round. But nearly all churches have steeples. Steeples convey the same message as mountains: They reach up to heaven and indicate communication between heaven and earth. The difference is that for ancient Israel temples are the only place where God can be approached.[28]

---

26. See Milgrom, *Numbers*, 344-46; and Kathrine Doob Sakenfeld, *Numbers: Journeying with God*, ITC (Grand Rapids: Eerdmans, 1995) 17-20.

27. Gary A. Anderson, "Introduction to Israelite Religion," in *The New Interpreter's Bible*, vol. 1 (Nashville: Abingdon, 1994) 277-79.

28. Dozeman, *God on the Mountain*.

Sacrificial Ritual. Sacrifice and liturgical rituals result from the indwelling of God in the Temple. Worship rituals in the tabernacle, therefore, do not conjure up the presence of God. They are a response to Yahweh, who is already there. The word for worship is "work" or "service" (עבדה *ǎbōdâ*). It states that sacrifice and worship rituals are acts of service to God, who has chosen to dwell with Israel.[29] Two-way communication results from the work of worship. Humans serve God through sacrifice. They also express their hopes and fears and seek blessing from God. In the process, God reveals law and makes promises.[30] Thus the act of worship manifests the presence of God in the sanctuary in a more concrete way through ritual drama.

Sacrificial ritual in priestly religion continues in Christian sacraments. Baptism and eucharist result from prior actions of Jesus. Thus their observance by Christians is a response to God, who has chosen to dwell with us. Observance in worship is an act of service to God, in which Christ is made manifest through two-way communication. In baptism, for example, God forgives sins and defeats death. The congregation makes confession of faith to live a sin-free life and celebrates new life in Christ. Sacraments also provide partial analogy to the central role of the tabernacle in priestly religion. In most cases, they require ordained clergy for their administration. And they are usually performed publically at a sanctuary with established rituals.

God and Humans. Priestly religion does not envision God as an intimate friend of individuals. The starting point for priestly writers in Numbers is the gulf between God and humans. They achieve this by emphasizing the holiness of God. The word "holy" (קדש *qōdeš*) means "to be separate." God is separate from humans in two different ways.

First, holiness distinguishes God from all things common. This is the separation between the sacred and the profane. God is sacred (holy), and humans are profane (common). This contrast makes God dangerous to humans.[31] Priestly writers convey this message by symbolizing the holiness of God as fire. Fire destroys life, but when applied carefully it can also purify. Priestly writers introduce the *kěbôd* YHWH in Exod 24:17 as a devouring fire. Wholeness is another metaphor to contrast the sacred and the profane. Holiness is complete, and the profane world is not. The contrast between the sacred and the profane is prominent in the arrangement of the camp in Numbers 1–4.

Second, holiness also creates a contrast between health (purity) and disease (impurity). The contrast between purity and impurity intensifies the danger of God to humans. God embodies health, purity, and life. Death is the source of disease and all impurity. Thus corpses become a source of impurity for the priestly writers. Evil actions are also disease that pollutes and eventually kills a society. God is repelled by all forms of impurity. The contrast between purity and impurity is a central topic in the laws of defilement in Numbers 5–6.

The goal of priestly religion is to bring a holy God and a profane people together through the tabernacle cult. The arrangement of the camp and selection of Levites provides an ordered way for the sacred and the profane to dwell together. The *kěbôd YHWH* also seeks to purify the tabernacle and the priesthood (Exodus 29; 40; Leviticus 9), allowing God to dwell with Israel. Ritual observance at the tabernacle monitors the health of Israel and transforms them into a holy people. But this transformation is not a story of intimate friendship. It is more an epic drama. Communication with God is not spontaneous and individual. It is ritualized and communal, requiring priestly intercessors. The reason for the heroic or grand scale to the drama is the holiness of God: Israel needs the *kěbôd YHWH* for life, but the source of their life can be a consuming fire.

THEOLOGICAL THEMES

The book of Numbers is a rich resource of theological reflection on community. Israel's formation at Sinai and the journey with God through the wilderness are intended to be a continuing model of how the people of God live out their faith in this world. The central theological

---

29. Anderson, "Introduction to Israelite Religion," 279-80.
30. Wenham, *Numbers,* 29-30.
31. David P. Wright, "Holiness: Old Testament," in *Anchor Bible Dictionary,* 6 vols. (New York: Doubleday, 1992) 3:237-49.

themes in Numbers are embedded in the interplay of the wilderness setting, the journey toward the promised land, and the interaction of characters along the way.

Wilderness Setting. The wilderness is the primary setting for the book of Numbers. Israel is encamped in the wilderness of Sinai (Num 1:1) at the outset of the book, and the wilderness continues to be the setting for their journey toward the promised land of Canaan through Numbers 21. It is replaced by "the plains of Moab" in the Transjordan in Num 22:1.

The wilderness provides more than geographical background in Numbers. Biblical writers also use it to reflect theologically on salvation history. Gerhard von Rad characterized salvation history as a "canonical history."[32] It is a mixture of historical experience and cultic legend, recounting divine acts of salvation that formed the nation of Israel. The central topics of salvation history include the promise of land to the ancestors, the exodus, the wilderness wandering, the revelation at Sinai, and future life in the land of Canaan. The wilderness setting takes on a wide range of theological meanings in Numbers.

Place of Birth. The wilderness can represent Israel's birth as a nation. It is the setting for stories of Israel's youth and innocence, when they were courted by God (see Hos 2:16-17; 9:10). The formation of the camp in Numbers 1–10 is part of these positive stories. The wilderness is the place where Israel is organized, when structures of leadership are defined, when their relationship to God is revealed, and when systems of worship and government are developed.

Place of Testing. The wilderness also symbolizes a time of transition between slavery in Egypt and life in the land. A time of transition is not the same as a time of origin. This is a more complex meaning, in which an age of innocence is replaced by a time of testing. The test is whether Israel is able to live the life of faith outside the promised land. Testing gives rise to the possibility of failure, in which case the wilderness may be a negative time of rebellion, rather than a positive time of innocence and courtship (see Ezek 20:10-17). The failed journey of the first generation in Num 10:11–21:35 contains many negative stories of testing and rebellion.

Homeless Place. The destruction of a city or an entire land is often symbolized by the wilderness. The prophet Isaiah, for example, writes, "The fortified city is solitary, a habitation deserted and forsaken, like the wilderness" (Isa 27:10). Desolation imagery underscores that biblical writers do not view the wilderness as a natural home or an inviting setting.[33] It lies outside the security of civilized structures and is a dangerous place. Stories of complaint about food (Numbers 11) and water (Num 20:2-13) accentuate the danger of traveling through the wilderness. Divine judgment on the "rabble" in Numbers 11 and Moses' loss of the promised land in Num 20:2-13 underscore the need for faithful action in the desert.

A Place Outside of Civilization. The wilderness can take on a more subversive theological meaning as a symbol that criticizes civilization and encourages one to seek God outside its structures.[34] Yahweh is a God of the desert in Israel's oldest poetry, and not a God of the city (Deut 33:2; Judg 5:5; Ps 68:9, 18; Hab 3:3-4).[35] Often biblical heroes like Hagar (Genesis 16–18) and Moses (Exodus 3) must flee oppressive structures of civilization to find some form of salvation or relief in the wilderness. In these stories, Yahweh is presented as a God who is encountered outside of the confines of civilization and the nation-state. Encountering God in the desert puts one in tension with culture at large. Numbers participates in this subversive imagery. That Yahweh chooses to live in a desert tabernacle, rather than the temple of a king, is a criticism of civilization, with its many forms of security that seek to subvert faith in God. Failure to see the threats of society leads to death in the wilderness, while critical insight provides a path toward new life in the land.

---

32. Gerhard von Rad, *Old Testament Theology I*, trans. D. M. G. Stalker (New York: Harper and Bros., 1962) 126, 129. See also Thomas L. Thompson, "Historiography [Israelite]," *ABD* 3:209-10.

33. Shemaryahu Talmon, "The 'Desert Motif' in the Bible and in Qumran Literature," in *Biblical Motifs in Origins and Transformations*, ed. A. Altmann, Philip W. Lown Institute of Advanced Judaic Studies, Brandeis University Studies and Texts 3 (Cambridge, Mass.: Harvard University Press, 1966) 39-44.

34. Herbert N. Schneidau, *Sacred Discontent: The Bible and Western Tradition* (Baton Rouge: Louisiana State University Press, 1976) esp. 104-57.

35. The poems are characterized as the "March in the South" theophany tradition. A common feature of this poetry is that Yahweh dwells in the desert, not in the city. See Dozeman, *God on the Mountain*, 121-26; and Richard J. Clifford, *The Cosmic Mountain in Canaan and the Old Testament*, HSM 4 (Cambridge, Mass.: Harvard University Press, 1972).

New Creation. The wilderness is also the location for God's continuing work in creation. Sabbath re-emerges in the wilderness for the first time after Genesis 1. Signs of providence in water and food bring to the foreground the implications of salvation for all of creation. God is certainly active in creation within the wilderness, but the wilderness is not sacred or holy.[36] The land of Canaan represents a different quality of divine presence in creation, where God will actually dwell in the land. It represents the fulfillment of salvation for Israel and for this world. Second Isaiah underscores the distinction between the wilderness and the promised land, which he symbolizes as a garden in Zion. The wilderness is a road (Isa 40:3) and a place of miracles (Isa 41:18-19) that signals and may even lead to the return of Zion (Isa 53:3). But the wilderness is not Zion. The same is true for the wilderness in Numbers. It is a place of journey and miracles.[37] But the goal of the story is envisioned at the end of the book. One day God will dwell in the land with Israel (Num 35:34).

Promise of Land. The promise of land is central to the plot of Numbers for both pre-priestly and priestly writers. But theological reflection on how Israel achieves their promised home is different in the two histories. The distinct theologies are indicated by divergent travel routes through the wilderness. The two routes can be illustrated as follows.

Pre-priestly Kadesh Sequence of Travel	Priestly Paran Sequence of Travel
	[a] Sinai to Paran (10:12)
[1] from Mt. Yahweh (10:33)	
(Three days journey)	
[2] Kibrothhattaqvah to Hazeroth (11:35)	
	[b] Hazeroth to Paran (12:16)
KADESH/ZIN—Spy Story (13:21, 26)	PARAN
—Spy Story (13:21, 26)	Spy Story (Num 13:3, 26)
—Dathan and Abiram (chap. 16)	—Korah (Num 16–19)
—Edom (20:14-21)	
	—[c] to Kadesh/Zin (20:1)
[3] Kadesh to Mount Hor (20:22)	

The sequence of travel in the pre-priestly history begins with Israel's departure from Mt. Yahweh on a three-day journey (10:33) to Hazeroth (11:35). The wilderness of Zin, or Kadesh, is an important setting in the pre-priestly history, even though it lacks a clear itinerary notice in the present form of Numbers. Israel arrives at Kadesh in the second year of their exodus from Egypt. It is the setting for the loss of the land in Numbers 13–14 (13:21, 26). The challenge to the leadership of Moses by Dathan and Abiram (chap. 16) and an unsuccessful negotiation with the Edomite king to cross his land (20:14-21) also take place at Kadesh. Israel leaves Kadesh when they journey to Mt. Hor (20:22).

Priestly writers change the sequence of travel. Israel departs from Sinai rather than Mt. Yahweh. Their next significant stopping point is the wilderness of Paran. This is stated both at the outset of their journey from Sinai (Num 10:12) and immediately preceding the spy story (Num 12:16). As a result, Paran is firmly established as the location of the spy story, which creates confusion in the present form of Numbers 13–14. The insertion of Paran results in Israel's arriving at Kadesh at the end of their wilderness trek in the fortieth year after they left Egypt (Num 20:1).

The two versions of travel represent different theologies of the promised land. Pre-priestly writers view the promised land from the wilderness location of Kadesh. Priestly writers achieve a different vantage point from Paran.[38] The two perspectives are expressed most clearly in the story of Israel's loss of the promised land in Numbers 13–14.

Kadesh and Holy War. Pre-priestly writers emphasize that Israel must acquire the courage to undertake holy war to leave the wilderness and to enter the promised land. Possession of the

---

36. Max Oelschlaeger, *The Idea of the Wilderness: From Prehistory to the Age of Ecology* (New Haven: Yale University Press, 1991) 41-53, esp. 50-51.
37. Robert L. Cohn, "Liminality in the Wilderness," in *The Shape of Sacred Space: Four Biblical Studies,* AAR Studies in Religion 23 (Missoula, Mont.: Scholars Press, 1981) 7-20.
38. See the detailed study of the different travel routes by Baruch A. Levine, *Numbers 1–20,* AB 4A (New York: Doubleday, 1993) 48-72.

promised land requires a conquest of indigenous peoples no matter how dangerous such a war may appear. Holy war is an act of faith in the promises of God. The failure of the first generation to leave the wilderness in Numbers 13–14 is because they lack the courage of conquest. Joshua sends out spies from Kadesh to reconnoiter the southern border regions of the land. Upon their return, they report the goodness of the land and how fearsome the people appear to be, like the giant Anakim (Num 13:22-24, 26-30), which prompts rebellion (Num 14:2-4). Rebellion in this account is fear of the giants to the point where the people lose faith in God to lead them to conquest. Divine judgment and the subsequent failure of the first generation to leave the wilderness is because the people lack the courage of conquest.

Paran and the Goodness of Creation. Priestly writers change the setting of Numbers 13–14 to Paran, and they introduce a new theology of the promised land. These writers eliminate the central role of conquest as the means for leaving the wilderness. Instead, they emphasize Israel's need to see the goodness of God in creation. In this account, Moses no longer sends out spies, but "explorers" from each tribe to evaluate the entire land of Canaan. Their goal is not espionage on the fortifications at the southern border of Canaan, but assessment of the quality of the whole land that Yahweh has promised. Thus the spies travel to the northernmost border of the land of Canaan (Num 13:21*b*). Rebellion is not the fear of conquest, but the failure of the people to judge the land "good" (Num 13:31-33). The first generation still dies, but the plot no longer pushes ahead to an account of holy war. Priestly writers interpret the wilderness more in relationship to creation than to an exodus and conquest. Entering the promised land, in their version of the story, requires proper perception of its goodness, rather than a conquest of indigenous peoples.

Characters. The development of characters in Numbers evolves around the problem of how to build a theocratic society in the wilderness. The central character is Yahweh, and all other characters are defined in relation to God. The goal is to devise a way in which a holy God can be brought into relationship with humans who do not share this quality, and, hence, are at risk in the presence of God. Characters separate into three general groups: God, who embodies holiness; Israel, who lives in the sphere of holiness; and the nations, who live outside of the sphere of holiness.

God. There is unresolved tension in God that is central to the book of Numbers. It is the tension between holiness and covenant. Divine holiness results in separation from humans and creation. Holiness means that God is unlike creation and even repulsed by the pollution of sin. Covenant describes God's commitment to humans and creation in spite of sin.[39] God enters into a covenant with all of creation at the end of the flood in Gen 9:1-17. God makes a covenant with Abraham in Genesis 17, and God forms a covenant treaty with Israel in Exodus 19–34. Covenant is not easily harmonized with holiness, because it describes the relationship between God and humans, rather than separation. The result is a tension between divine holiness and Yahweh's commitment to creation and relationship with humans. The formation of a theocratic society around the wilderness tabernacle is the attempt to fulfill the divine obligations of covenant while safeguarding holiness.

The tension between holiness and covenant is never really resolved in the book of Numbers. Divine obligation to creation and to Israel fuels the plot of the story. Covenant prompts the exodus (Exod 6:2-8). It is also the driving force in the establishment of the wilderness sanctuary, when God descends from Mt. Sinai into the tabernacle (Exod 40:35-36). Covenantal concern is manifested in divine communication with Moses (Num 1:1), in leading and guiding through the wilderness (Num 9:15-23), in the providential care of food and water (Numbers 11; 20), in healing (Num 21:1-9), in the quality of loving kindness (Num 14:18, 20), and in blessing (Num 6:21-27). The holiness of God emphasizes that divine leading is never casual and that divine grace is anything but cheap. Yahweh's repulsion to sin is underscored by the holy war imagery of the ark of the covenant (Num 10:33-36), by the precise details of the camp and priesthood (Num 1–10:10), and by the destructive power of divine wrath conceived in the wilderness (Num 11:1-3; 25).

---

39. See Dozeman, *God on the Mountain,* 57-65.

The tension between holiness and covenant makes God dynamic and open to change. Obedience reinforces divine obligation (Caleb and Joshua in Numbers 13–14). Resistance to divine leading (Num 11:1-3), lack of faith in divine providence (Numbers 11), rejection of God's new creation (Numbers 13–14), and the worship of other gods (Numbers 25) prompt judgment and separation between God and Israel. Yet, even at these times, zealous action on behalf of God (Numbers 25), healing icons (Num 20:4-9), cultic rituals (Numbers 15), and intercession (Numbers 14) can persuade God to relent from acts of judgment.

Israel. Israel is the direct object of God's saving activity. They are formed out of divine covenantal obligation. Israelites are singled out for divine favor with the promise of land (Numbers 15). They experience special providence (Numbers 11) and divine guidance (Num 9:15-23). They are the ones who gather around the sanctuary and live in close proximity to God (Num 1–10:10). And, because of their special status, they are required to embody the qualities of divine holiness through cultic observances (Num 1–10:10; chaps. 28–29), in their march through the wilderness (Numbers 11–21; 25), and in their future life in the land of Canaan (Numbers 15; 35). Failure to do so results in death (Numbers 13–14; 25).

Numbers also explores forms of leadership for Israel. Leaders provide different ways for Israel to approach God, who dwells at the center of the camp. Divine holiness in the tabernacle is protected through the hierarchy of priests and Levites camped around it. Priestly leaders also provide a safe means for Israel to approach God through worship (Numbers 3–4; 8; 16–18). The seventy elders provide prophetic leadership in governing the people (Numbers 11). Numbers also outlines the role of lay tribal leaders (Numbers 1) and Nazirites (Numbers 6). The role of Moses throughout Numbers also provides theological reflection on both prophetic and priestly leadership. He models prophetic, charismatic leadership (Numbers 11–12); priestly, non-charismatic leadership (Numbers 16–18); and other intercessory roles (Numbers 13–14; 25).

The Nations. The nations are defined more in relationship to divine holiness than to covenant. They are separate from God and live outside of the wilderness camp. Some are associated with Canaan. They may be mythologized as giants, such as Anak, or the descendants of the Nephilim (Num 13:25-33). Others are simply described as ethnic groups, like the Amalekites, the Hittites, the Jebusites, and the Amorites (Num 13:27-29). In general, the nations are opponents of God who must be defeated by Israel in holy war, like Sihon, the Amorite king (Num 21:21-32), and Og of Bashan (Num 21:33-35). Divine concern for the nations is also evident in Numbers. The intercession of Moses in Num 14:13-19 is successful in part because of God's concern for the nations.

Other people and groups blur the line between "Israel" and "the nations." Resident aliens are one example of non-Israelites included in the camp (Num 9:1-14) and in Israel's future life in the land (Numbers 15; 35). "The rabble" in Num 11:4, on the other hand, represent members of the camp who belong outside the sphere of holiness. Balaam is a non-Israelite seer who knows Yahweh (Numbers 22–24), and the Midianites represent an entire ethnic group whose relationship with Israel is ambiguous. Jethro, or Hobab, the father-in-law of Moses, is a Midianite, whose guidance Moses requests (Num 10:29-32). Yet a Midianite woman threatens the purity of the Israelite camp in Numbers 25.

The following study will explore in more detail the theological themes of Numbers in two parts. A commentary section will interpret the meaning of the literature in the context of ancient priestly religion. Important words, the literary structure of chapters, distinct authorship, and divergent theological perspectives will be described. Reflections sections will include summaries of the central theological themes of pre-priestly and priestly writers. The reinterpretation of Numbers in New Testament literature will also be explored where applicable. And more concrete application for contemporary preaching and teaching will also be offered.

BIBLIOGRAPHY

Ashley, Timothy R. *Numbers.* NICOT. Grand Rapids: Eerdmans, 1993. A new translation and careful philological study from an evangelical perspective.

Budd, Phillip J. *Numbers.* WBC 5. Waco, Tex.: Word, 1984. A commentary with extensive review of the history of interpretation. Special attention is given to the history of composition of Numbers.

Gray, George Buchanan. *Numbers.* ICC. Edinburgh: T. & T. Clark, 1903. A classic commentary in the modern period. Full discussion of the history of composition is combined with detailed study of ancient Israelite religion.

Davies, Eryl W. *Numbers.* NCB. Grand Rapids: Eerdmans, 1995. A thorough and recent philological study based on the Revised Standard Version

Levine, Baruch A. *Numbers 1–20.* AB 4A. New York: Doubleday, 1993. A new translation of the text. Commentary is the most up-to-date comparative study of priestly terms in their larger ancient Near Eastern setting.

Milgrom, Jacob. *Numbers.* JPS Torah Commentary. Philadelphia: JPS, 1990. Commentary focuses on the meaning of priestly terms and is based on the New JPS translation. Seventy-seven essays at the end of the commentary summarize a lifetime of research by one of the foremost interpreters of priestly tradition.

Noth, Martin. *Numbers.* OTL. Philadelphia: Westminster, 1968. A classic historical-critical commentary.

Olson, Dennis T. *Numbers.* Interpretation. Louisville: Westminster John Knox, 1996. An insightful commentary comparing the fate of the first and second generation of Israelites to leave Egypt.

Sakenfeld, Katharine Doob. *Journeying with God: A Commentary on the Book of Numbers.* ITC. Grand Rapids: Eerdmans, 1995. A theological summary of Numbers paying particular attention to issues of purity and impurity in priestly religion.

Wenham, Gordon J. *Numbers: An Introduction and Commentary.* Tyndale Old Testament Commentaries. Leicester: Inter-Varsity, 1981. Commentary focuses on the structure of Numbers. Careful attention is given to the contribution of anthropology for interpreting priestly ritual.

OUTLINE OF NUMBERS

I. Numbers 1:1–10:10, Forming Community Around a Holy God at Sinai

    A. 1:1–6:27, Holiness and the Camp
        1:1–2:34, The First Census and the Arrangement of the Camp
        3:1–4:49, The Role of the Levites in the Cult, in the Camp, and on the March
        5:1–6:27, Camp Legislation to Prevent Defilement
    B. 7:1–10:10, Holiness and the Tabernacle
        7:1–8:26, The Dedication of the Tabernacle and the Levites
        9:1–10:10, The Celebration of Passover and Preparation for the Wilderness March

II. Numbers 10:11–21:35, The Wilderness Journey of the First Generation

    A. 10:11-36, Leaving Sinai
    B. 11:1–19:22, Murmuring and Death in the Wilderness
        11:1–12:16, Conflict Over Prophetic Leadership
        13:1–15:41, Conflict Over the Land
        16:1–17:13, Conflict Over Priestly Leadership
        18:1–19:22, Guidelines for Approaching God
    C. 20:1–21:35, Leaving the Wilderness

NUMBERS 1:1–10:10

FORMING COMMUNITY AROUND A HOLY GOD AT SINAI

OVERVIEW

Priestly authors compiled Num 1:1–10:10. The central theme underlying this section is holiness. Detailed instructions about the arrangement of the camp (Numbers 1–2), the different roles of priests and Levites (Numbers 3–4), the measures necessary to prevent contamination of the camp site (Numbers 5–6), and the elaborate process of dedicating the tabernacle (Num 7:1–10:10) are necessary responses to God's holiness.

Two points of tension provide insight into divine holiness: God is the source of all holiness; holiness is not inherent to creation or to humans. By its very nature, therefore, holiness divides. Its sacred character is set apart from our everyday, profane world.[40] As a result, the entrance of Yahweh into the Israelite camp is carefully orchestrated by priestly writers. The process extends for fifty-six chapters from Exodus 19 through Numbers 10. The camp legislation in Num 1:1–10:10 concludes a large section of literature about the revelation of Yahweh at Mt. Sinai in Exodus 19–40 and the formation of the sacrificial cult in Leviticus.

All movement in Exod 19:1–Num 10:10 is about Yahweh's descent from heaven to the tabernacle at the base of the mountain, where Israel is camped. Several attempts are necessary. The original descent of God (Exod 19:16-19) is aborted (Exod 19:20-25). The reason is that there were not enough safeguards to receive the holy presence of God. Yahweh states to Moses that more secure boundaries are necessary. These include stronger fences to keep the people back and a purified priesthood to mediate for Israel. A partial analogy might be nuclear energy. Its power is awesome, but dangerous, requiring complex structures to safeguard its radiation from humans and from our environment.

A second attempt at divine descent succeeds (Exod 24:15-18), when the כבוד יהוה (*kĕbôd YHWH*), "glory of the Lord," settles at the crest of Mt. Sinai to meet alone with Moses. This meeting results in blueprints for the tabernacle cult. The architectural plans of Exodus 25–31 guide the construction of the tabernacle in Exodus 35–40. The tabernacle allows God to descend from Mt. Sinai and enter into the sanctuary. But no one can get into the tabernacle, not even Moses (Exod 40:34-35).

The book of Leviticus opens with Moses outside of the tent of meeting, or tabernacle, as he is addressed by God (Lev 1:1). The divine instructions outline cultic procedures for approaching God, allowing Moses and Aaron to enter the tabernacle in Lev 9:23. Their entrance unleashes a theophany of the *kĕbôd* YHWH in the altar and blessing on the people (Lev 9:24). But even this situation ends in the death of Aaron's two eldest sons, Nadab and Abihu; fire from the altar burns them (Lev 10:1-3). The remainder of Leviticus explores other rituals that will allow the priesthood to approach God safely as representatives of the people.

Numbers 1:1 begins with Moses in the tent of meeting itself, rather than standing outside, as was the case in Lev 1:1. The opening verse indicates progress in the construction of safe procedures to approach God. The subject matter of Num 1:1–10:10 builds upon Leviticus by turning attention from ritual and sacrifice to the more external issues of forming community and creating society around a holy God. The layout of the camp in relation to the tabernacle at its center

40. David P. Wright, "Holiness: Old Testament," *ABD* 237-49.

introduces degrees of holiness, depending on how close a person or place is situated to the tabernacle.[41] There are degrees of holiness among priests, Levites, and people as well as among the tabernacle, the camp, and the wilderness area outside the camp. The

41. J. Milgrom, *Cult and Conscience: The Asham and the Priestly Doctrine of Repentance*, SJLA 18 (Leiden: E. J. Brill, 1970).

closer to God, the holier. Gradations of holiness are a form of sacramental theology. Priestly writers describe how holiness emanating from the tabernacle creates a new social, political, and environmental order for Israel. The arrangement of the camp, the order for marching through the wilderness, and the role of priests and Levites describe the ethics of holiness.

NUMBERS 1:1–6:27, HOLINESS AND THE CAMP

OVERVIEW

These chapters outline the effects of divine holiness on Israel's social organization. The central question is how Israel should organize itself around Yahweh, who dwells in the sanctuary. The answer requires a detailed description of the interrelationships of characters in the wilderness camp. Such mundane matters as the organization of the tribes and their position within the camp take on a sacramental quality because of the nearness of the tabernacle.

Chapters 1–2 sketch the priestly ideal of religious community. Chapter 1 describes the social organization of Israel as twelve tribes with twelve lay leaders representing each tribe. Priestly writers employ a variety of social terminology to explore the nature of the community. The singling out of the Levites at the close brings into focus how the numbering and organization of Israel is being undertaken with an eye on the tabernacle. Chapter 2 describes the arrangement of the camp. Tribes are clustered in groups of three, surrounding the tabernacle from four directions. Throughout this chapter, placement within the camp carries theological significance. Campsites designate different relationships to the tabernacle.

Chapters 3–4 change the focus from the congregation of Israel at large to the Levites. The genealogy of Moses and Aaron is followed by a description of the function of the Levites. They are substitutes for the firstborn. The chapters close with a description of their ancestral houses, their number, their duties, and, finally, their placement in the camp in relationship to the tabernacle.

Chapters 5–6 describe camp legislation aimed at preventing defilement. Selective legislation from community to marriage relationships is presented to illustrate conditions or actions that might threaten holiness in the camp. Examples include leprosy, the relationship of neighbors, and jealousy within marriage. The law of the Nazirite follows, and the section closes with the priestly blessing on the people in the camp.

Numbers 1:1–6:27 is an idealistic picture of community to which the people of God must strive. The ideal character of the literature is reflected in its structure. Divine command (Num 1:1-3) to organize the people and the camp concludes with a priestly blessing (Num 6:21-27). Proper organization allows for the safe access to holiness, unleashing blessing on the camp.

Numbers 1:1–2:34, The First Census and the Arrangement of the Camp

COMMENTARY

Numbers 1–2 recounts the census of the first generation of Israelites and the organization of the campsite. The two chapters are closely interrelated in subject matter and in literary design. Read together, they provide the overall organization of the congregation of Israel and their lay leadership, as compared to Numbers 3–4, where attention will turn to the non-lay leadership in the camp, consisting of priests and Levites.

Numbers 1–2 is organized loosely around divine command and fulfillment. The structure is especially clear in Numbers 1, which opens with a stereotypical introduction, "The LORD spoke to Moses . . . " (see, e.g., 2:1; 3:5, 14, 40, 44; 4:1, 17, 21), indicating that all the following instructions are divine speech to Moses. The chapter concludes in v. 54 with the notice that the divine instructions were fulfilled "as the LORD had commanded Moses" (variations occur in 2:34; 3:51; 4:37, 41, 45, 49; 5:4; 8:4, 22; 9:20-23). Numbers 2:1-2 introduces a second divine command: "The LORD spoke to Moses and Aaron. . . . " Its fulfillment is indicated in 2:32-34: "The Israelites did just as the Lord had commanded Moses."

1:1. The place of divine instruction is the tent of meeting. (See Exodus 25–31 for a detailed description.) The Hebrew noun translated "meeting" (מוֹעֵד *môʿēd*) in the phrase "tent of meeting" (אֹהֶל מוֹעֵד *ʾōhel môʿēd*) comes from the verb יעד (*yāʿad*), whose root meaning is "to appoint," "to meet," or "to gather by appointment." The noun *môʿēd* can take on religious connotations by signifying appointed times and places when God and humans meet.

Appointed times are sacred festivals. The purposes of stars in Gen 1:14, for example, is to mark the liturgical year with its religious festivals. Here the noun *môʿēd* is translated "seasons," thus signifying sacred time as compared to ordinary or profane time. The distinction between sacred and profane time is illustrated in Numbers in the description of

Passover as having to be kept "at its appointed time" (בְּמוֹעֲדוֹ *bĕmôʿădô*, 9:2), or when God states to Moses that the trumpet must be blown "at your appointed festivals" (מוֹעֲדֵיכֶם *môʿădêkem*, 10:10).

The tent of meeting in v. 1 signifies a sacred place. In this instance, the noun *môʿēd* is the location where God and humans meet and where heaven and earth touch (see the section "Priestly Religion" in the Introduction). In biblical tradition, sacred places like sanctuaries are often described using mountain imagery. The divine descent from Mt. Sinai to the sanctuary results in the tent of meeting becoming Israel's sacred place. It is the location where God now dwells and where the ark is lodged.

The indwelling of Yahweh in the tent of meeting is reinforced by the word "tabernacle" (מִשְׁכָּן *miškān*), which is frequently used by priestly authors to describe the wilderness sanctuary (over 40 times in Numbers; see 1:51). The noun "tabernacle" comes from the verb שכן (*šākan*), meaning "to dwell." This verb most likely refers to an impermanent dwelling of the divine. Thus God is able to leave this sanctuary home, if Israel does not maintain proper standards of holiness and justice.[42]

The two terms "tent of meeting" and "tabernacle" are not synonymous. The tent of meeting may represent an ancient tradition in which God was encountered in a tent for the purpose of receiving oracles (see Exod 33:7-11 and the Commentary on Numbers 11:1–12:16). Regardless of their earliest meaning, the tent of meeting and the tabernacle are brought together by priestly authors to designate the one wilderness sanctuary. The account of the divine descent into the sanctuary in Exod 40:34-35 illustrates how

---

42. See Frank M. Cross, *Canaanite Myth and Hebrew Epic: Essays in the History of the Religion of Israel* (Cambridge, Mass.: Harvard University Press, 1963) 298-99; Tryggve N. D. Mettinger, *The Dethronement of Sabaoth: Studies in the Shem and Kadob Theologies*, ConBOT 18 (Lund: CWK Gleerup, 1982) 80-97.

the terms are interchanged by the priestly writers.

The setting and time of the divine instruction in v. 1 intertwine the book of Numbers with other books in the Pentateuch. Reference to the wilderness of Sinai interrelates Num 1:1–10:10 with Exodus 19–40 and the book of Leviticus (see the Overview). The dating of events reinforces this interrelationship. The book of Numbers begins on Month 2, Day 1, Year 2 from the exodus. The following outline illustrates the important dates from the exodus in the priestly history.

I. The Exodus from Egypt (Exod 12:1),
Month 1, Day 14, Year 1, The First Passover

II. Encampment at Sinai (Exod 19:1),
Month 3, Year 1
A. The Tabernacle (Exod 40:2), Month 1, Day 1, Year 2
B. Census (Num 1:1), Month 2, Day 1, Year 2
C. Late Observance of Passover (Num 9:1), Month 2, Day 14, Year 2

III. Departure from Sinai (Num 10:11), Month 2, Day 20, Year 2

The system of dating is a priestly invention aimed at interpreting the liturgical calendar. It is not a historical chronology in any modern sense of the term.[43] Careful attention to dating and chronology provides insight into priestly theology, and not history. The exodus is a watershed event for the priestly authors. It ushers in a new age of salvation that is signified as Year 1. This is similar to the later distinction between B.C. and A.D. in classical Christian chronology, where the birth of Christ becomes the watershed event in time.

The events in the book of Numbers occur in the second year after the exodus. The entire period of Irael's encampment in the wilderness of Sinai, however, bridges the first and second years from Month 3, Year 1 (Exod 19:1), to Month 2, Day 20, Year 2 (Num 10:11). Thus Israel's stay at Sinai encompasses roughly one liturgical year. The significant event marking the transition from the first to the second year is the construction of the tent of meeting/tabernacle. It is completed on New Year's day of Year 2 (Month 1,

Day 1, Year 2). The book of Numbers begins in the following month (Month 2, Day 1, Year 2) with the census of the people. The events in Num 1:1–10:10 last nineteen days.

1:2-3. God commands Moses in v. 2 to take a census of the "whole congregation of Israelites." The phrase combines distinct terms for designating the people. "Israelites" is from the Hebrew בני-יישראל (běnê-yiśrā'ēl), which is translated more literally "sons of Israel." It emphasizes kinship. In his study of social terminology, Norman Gottwald notes that the strictly biological meaning "sons" could become "an extended metaphor for describing clusters of persons according to certain common functions or traits." A contemporary example of this process would be the phrase "sons of liberty" in colonial North American history.[44]

Kinship language is reinforced in v. 2 by the terms "clans" and "ancestral houses" as descriptions of smaller groups within the Israelite community. The Hebrew משפחות (mišpāḥôt) is translated more naturally as "families" rather than "clans." It is avoided in English because the word most certainly refers to more than a nuclear family. It may be used to refer to a whole tribe (Judg 17:7) or more likely to an association of families within a tribe (Josh 7:14). The "ancestral houses" would appear to designate a group that is smaller than a "clan" or "family" (see Josh 7:14). The Hebrew בית-אב (bêt-'āb, "father's house") is a patriarchal term that most likely signifies an extended family, including parents, children—married sons with their wives and unmarried daughters—as well as resident aliens. There is fluidity in the use of these terms throughout the book of Numbers. "Ancestral house," for example, may be equated with a "tribe" already in v. 4, while the meaning of "clan" varies widely in the second census of chap. 26. The terminology reinforces a vision of the wilderness community as being related by genealogy.

The term "congregation" does not signify family ties. The Hebrew noun עדה ('ēdâ), derives from the verb יעד (yā'ad), meaning "to appoint," "to meet," or "to gather by appointment." This same verb was discussed earlier in association with the tent of meeting.

43. See J. Hughes, *Secrets of the Times: Myth and History in Biblical Chronology,* JSOTSup 66 (Sheffield: Sheffield Academic, 1990).

44. N. K. Gottwald, *The Tribes of Yahweh: A Sociology of the Religion of Liberated Israel,* 1250–1050 BCE (Maryknoll, N.Y.: Orbis, 1979) 239-44.

In some instances, "congregation" may designate a smaller group within Israel (27:3). The use of the terms "clans" and "ancestral houses" in v. 2 to describe smaller social units illustrates the preference of priestly writers to designate the entire community as the congregation. The priestly writers use the term "congregation" more than eighty times to designate the people in the wilderness. The congregation is that group of people who gather around the tent of meeting. Thus the act of gathering around the sanctuary as a community becomes the defining characteristic. In this case, proximity to holiness supersedes kinship. The LXX translation of ʿēdâ as "synagogue" underscores the liturgical background of the term "congregation."

Other uses of "congregation" in the book of Numbers elaborate on the term's social significance. In addition to gathering around the sanctuary, the congregation deliberates on the report of spies (14:5, 7) and has the power to reject the promise of land (14:27, 35, 36). The congregation is responsible for the purity of worship (15:24-26) and the people (31:16). The congregation also consults on legal matters (35:12, 24-25).

The purpose of the census is stated in v. 3. It fulfills the divine command from Exod 30:11-16, in which the census is a prerequisite for the people to live in proximity to the sanctuary. God tells Moses that a sanctuary tax is required of each adult male as an atonement for the people and that the money is to be used in service to the tabernacle. The collection of this tax is confirmed in Exod 38:26, where the number of registered males is given as 603,550. There are many parallels between the census of Numbers 1 and the sanctuary census in Exodus. Both number males twenty years of age and older (Exod 30:14; 38:26; Num 1:3); both use the verb "to consider" or "to muster" to describe the registration of the males (the verb פקד *pāqad*, Exod 30:12; Num 1:3; and the noun פקדים *pĕquddîm*, Num 1:21, 22, 24, etc.) Moreover, the number given for the census is the same (Exod 38:26; Num 1:43). The parallels to Exod 30:11-16 underscore the religious dimension of the census in Numbers 1. Numbering and organizing the people are a necessary safeguard for the community to live in the presence of God.

The census is also intended to prepare the community for war and to organize them into a regimented militia. The description of those being numbered in v. 3 includes military terminology. The combination of the verb יצא (*yāṣāʾ* "to go out") and the noun צבא (*ṣābāʾ*, "war," "warfare," "service") indicates military action ("to go to war"), even though the noun *ṣābāʾ* can also describe religious service to the sanctuary (4:1, 23, 30). The priestly writers describe Israel's marching out of Egypt during the night of Passover with the same words (Exod 12:41), and the military meaning of the phrase is also clear in the war against Midian (Num 31:14, 36). War terminology encourages an interpretation of those being registered (*pĕquddîm*; 1:21, 22, 44, etc.) as forming regiments or army units. The military emphasis of the census underscores how God's presence with Israel not only transforms them as a people, but also puts them in conflict with other nations and cultures. As the congregation assembled around God, Israel becomes a militia representing holiness in a profane world. The march through the wilderness becomes a military campaign for God.

1:4-16. Leaders are chosen from each tribe. Verses 4 and 16 frame the actual listing of leaders in vv. 5-15. The tribe of Reuben begins the list of twelve tribes. Reuben also launches tribal lists in the choosing of the spies (chap. 13) and in the second census (chap. 26). The tribe of Judah begins lists that describe the order of the camp (chap. 2), the offerings presented to the tabernacle (chap. 7), the order of marching (chap. 10) through the wilderness, and the inheritance of the land (chap. 34). There may be an idealization of Judah in the distribution of the different tribal lists. Reuben is prominent in the numbering of the people and, more important, in the loss of the land. Judah heads tribal lists in more positive stories, including worshiping at the tabernacle and marching through the wilderness toward the promised land (see Commentary on 2:3-31).

The list of tribal leaders in vv. 5-15 proceeds in a stereotypical form: The tribe is named, followed by the name of the chosen leader and his father's name. The first entry provides illustration: from Reuben, Elizur son of Shedeur. The tribes of Reuben, Simeon,

Judah, Issachar, and Zebulun are listed in this way (vv. 5-9) before the pattern is interrupted in v. 10, where Ephraim and Manasseh are listed as sons of Joseph. The original pattern returns for the remaining five tribes of Benjamin, Dan, Asher, Gad, and Naphtali (vv. 11-15).

The names in vv. 5-15 are, for the most part, confined to chaps. 1–10, where they appear four times (in chaps. 1; 2; 7; and 10). Scholars have sought with limited success to place these leaders in a particular historical setting of ancient Israel. George Buchanan Gray concluded that the list of names was not historical and that its composition was late,[45] while Martin Noth thought that the list was old and that it contained historical information about tribal Israel.[46] The debate is unresolvable. Yet, even if the list is ancient, the place and function of the leaders in a particular historical setting have been lost. Without a precise social context, what stands out is the distinctly theological composition of the names. Divine titles are often incorporated into a person's name to form a sentence. A number of names incorporating elements of names for the divine appear in the list, including Elizur ("El is my rock"), Shedeur ("Shaddai is light"), and Pedahzur ("the Rock has redeemed me"). A notable exception is the absence of the divine name Yahweh in any of the leaders' names.

The listing of tribal leaders (vv. 5-15) is framed in vv. 4 and 16 with a variety of terms that are meant to describe their social functions. The tribal leaders are designated as "the heads of ancestral houses" (v. 4), the "chosen ones from the congregation" (v. 16), the "leaders of ancestral tribes" (v. 16), and the "heads of the divisions of Israel" (v. 16). The language is difficult to sort out. "Leader" (נשׂיא nāśîʾ), "head" (ראשׁ rōʾš), and "division" (אלף ʾelep) may be descriptions of leadership roles from as early as Israel's pre-monarchical period. Yet, their usage and combination with other terms (like "congregation" and "ancestral tribe") point to a later time, suggesting that priestly authors are combining a rich history of social terminology. Theology would appear to take precedence over sociological precision in the portraits of lay leadership.

45. Gray, *Numbers*, 7-8.
46. Noth, *Numbers*, 18-19.

The language in vv. 4 and 16 provides insight into the idealization of lay leadership in priestly tradition. The notion of being "chosen" in v. 16 has political (Ezek 23:22) and cultic (1 Sam 9:13) meaning. The further description of these persons as "heads of the divisions of Israel" points to their responsibility as military leaders. These varied terms are carried over into the different roles the leaders perform in chaps. 1–10. They assist Moses in assembling the people for census (chap. 1), present offerings at the tabernacle (chap. 7), and lead the people in their military march through the wilderness (chaps. 2; 10).

1:17-47. The census of the first generation of Israelites is recorded in these verses. The setting and time of this census are stated in vv. 17-19, a repetition of v. 1. It takes place on Month 1, Day 1 in the wilderness of Sinai. Verses 20-43 list the registration of twenty-year-old males by tribe, beginning with Reuben, the firstborn. Verses 44-47 provide a summary conclusion. The procedure for counting in vv. 20-43 is stereotypical: Tribal identification is followed by the number. The summary of Reuben in vv. 20-21 provides an example of the two-part form: (1) the descendants of Reuben: their lineage in their clans, by their ancestral houses according to the number of names, individually, every male from twenty years old and upward, everyone able to go to war; (2) those enrolled of the tribe of Reuben were 46,500.

The first part of the census repeats many of the sociological terms introduced in v. 2. Males twenty years of age and older are numbered according to tribe, clan, and ancestral house. The additional word "lineage" (תולדות tôlēdôt, also translated as "generations") is added to the opening line. This is the same word used by the priestly authors to organize the book of Genesis ("These are the generations of . . ." [Gen 2:4; 5:1; 6:9; etc.]). Its appearance in the census accentuates the familial character of the wilderness group.

The number of males for each tribe is extremely large. The total of the census in Numbers 1 is 603,550 males over twenty years of age. George Buchanan Gray provides a detailed summary of the problems that arise when one attempts to interpret the census numbers literally as representing the number of people migrating from Egypt to Canaan.

This number of males would require a total population of over 2,000,000 people in the Sinai peninsula.[47] So many people would overwhelm the environment of the Sinai. Moreover, the large total conflicts with other traditions in which the number of fighting males during Israel's tribal period is significantly less (see the reference to 40,000 males in Judg 5:8).

The numbers most likely have symbolic and theological value for the priestly writers. But deciphering what exactly they intended has proven elusive to modern interpreters. Two possibilities arise from the larger storyline of the Pentateuch. First, the enormous size of the wilderness group may signal the fulfillment of the divine blessing of fertility first promised to Abram in Gen 12:1-3. The census of Numbers 1 indicates that the Israelites have indeed become "a great nation." Second, the number of fighting males underscores Israel's potential power as God's "fighting host or militia." This military emphasis is reinforced by a phrase that repeats throughout the census: The males are all "able to go to war."

More precise interpretations of the numbers have also been offered. Philip J. Budd has suggested that the number of males represents theological reflection on the description of the tabernacle in Exodus 25–31. Exodus 38:26 uses the same figure of 603,550 for males over twenty, who were required to pay a half-shekel tax for the tabernacle. This figure may be derived from the cost of bases and hooks in the construction of the tabernacle. Exodus 38:27-28 states that the bases and hooks for the tabernacle required 100 talents (1 talent = 1,000 shekels) and 1,775 shekels of silver. The total shekels were 301,775 shekels. A half-shekel tax for this amount totals 603,550, the number of the census in Exod 38:26 and in Numbers 1.[48] Others suggest that the numbers are an instance of gematria—a process of valuation in which letters from the alphabet have a certain numerical worth. Georg Fohrer has noted that the numerical value of the Hebrew "sons of Israel" is 603, which when multiplied by 1,000 nears the figure in Numbers 1. The figure 603,551 is achieved when

the numerical value of the Hebrew "all the heads" (כל־ראש *kol-rōʾš*) is included.[49] M. Barnouin regards Babylonian astronomy as the key to the numbering system by priestly writers. He argues that the tribal figures correspond to celestial movements that form the Babylonian calendar. In this case, the priestly writers' aim is to place the wilderness community in the widest social and cosmological context possible.[50] As a result, the numbering of the people has universal significance. The different hypotheses are tentative. Each illustrates, however, that the priestly authors are producing a highly stylized and theological history of Israel.

1:48-53. In these verses, the Levites are separated out from the other tribes. The text divides into two parts. Verses 48-50*a* define the special role of the Levites. They are not to be numbered with the other Israelites, because they are assigned special duties in caring for the tabernacle. Three special functions are spelled out in vv. 50*b*-53. The Levites perform service in the tabernacle (vv. 50, 53); they carry the tabernacle and its vessels on Israel's wilderness march (vv. 50, 51); and they must pitch their tents around the sanctuary, thus providing a buffer zone between the sanctuary and the congregation of Israel (v. 53).

The language in vv. 48-53 has given rise to different interpretations concerning the tasks of the Levites. The point of debate concerns the meaning of the concluding phrase in v. 53. The NRSV translation reads, "the Levites shall perform the guard duty of the tabernacle." The Hebrew is more ambiguous: "the Levites shall keep [שמר *šāmar*] the service [משמרת *mišmeret*] of the tabernacle." Interpretation hinges on what the "service of the tabernacle" means.

One reading emphasizes the cultic and religious work required of the Levites. Baruch Levine follows this line of interpretation and concludes that the "service" of the Levites must be defined in the context of their religious duties to God. In performing these duties, they contain the rage (קצף *qeṣep*) of God, mentioned in v. 53. Levitical service stops the divine wrath, which might

---

47. Gray, *Numbers*, 9-15.
48. Budd, *Numbers*, 8-9.

49. Georg Fohrer, *Introduction to the Old Testament*, trans. David E. Green (Nashville: Abingdon, 1968) 184.
50. M. Barnouin, "Les Recensements du Livre des Nombres et l'Astronomie Babylonienne," *VT* 27 (1977) 280-303.

otherwise destroy the camp like a fire burning out of control. Thus they encircle the tabernacle in the camp, they carry the holy artifacts, and they care for both.[51]

Another reading emphasizes the relationship of the Levites to the congregation of Israel, rather than their service to God. This interpretation emphasizes more the role of Levites as protectors of the sanctuary. Jacob Milgrom follows this line of interpretation when he concludes that the phrase "to watch" or "to keep" (*šāmar*) a "service" (*mišmeret*) means "guard duty." The NRSV translation also reflects this interpretation. In this case, the service of the Levites is to keep Israel from coming too near to the divine. Divine rage results from encroachment by humans into the sacred space of God, which would be certain death.[52] The levitical encampment represents a border, and their service is both border guard and customs duty. The reason for guard duty is that all non-Levites are "outsiders" to the sacredness of the tabernacle (v. 51).

1:54. Chapter 1 concludes by underscoring that all divine commands have been completed.

2:1-2. These verses introduce a second divine command, this time directed to Moses and Aaron. The subject changes from the numbering of Israel to their arrangement in the campsite. The motivation behind the careful arrangement of the camp is the tent of meeting, which is situated at the center of the camp. The tribes are to be arranged around the tent of meeting (e.g., on its four sides), and they are to camp at some distance from it. The space between the tent of meeting and the tribes is not stated; Josh 3:4 may provide some help, since it states that the Israelites were required to leave a space of 2,000 cubits (1,000 yards) between themselves and the ark.

2:3-31. The arrangement of the tribes is delineated here. The language is stereotypical: Tribes are listed in groups of three, the names of lay leaders (chap. 1) are repeated, and the total number for every tribe is given. The literary structure of this section is determined by the geography of the campsite.

East of the Tent of Meeting (vv. 3-9)
Judah
Issachar
Zebulun

South of the Tent of Meeting (vv. 10-16)
Reuben
Simeon
Gad

The Tent of Meeting in the Center of the Camp (v. 17)
Levites

West of the Tent of Meeting (vv. 18-24)
Ephraim
Manasseh
Benjamin

North of the Tent of Meeting (vv. 25-31)
Dan
Asher
Naphtali

This outline illustrates how three tribes camp on each side of the tent of meeting, resulting in four groups of three tribes each. Moreover, there is a hierarchy in the relationship of the three tribes on each side. Judah, Reuben, Ephraim, and Dan are singled out as lead tribes. They are described as the "regimental encampment" (דגל מחנה *degel maḥănēh*, vv. 3, 10, 18, 25), in contrast to the others, who are designated simply as "tribes" (מטה *maṭṭeh*, "tribe"). Baruch Levine has demonstrated that the word דגל (*degel*) designates "a unit of the Persian military . . . where soldiers lived with their families."[53] His research underscores how priestly authors have incorporated military terminology from the exilic period and later to describe their ideal vision of Israel's early wilderness camp.

There is an additional distinction made in the placement of each regimental encampment around the sanctuary. Judah has first position (vv. 3-9). Its regiment is located on the east side of the tent of meeting; thus it guards the opening to the tent of meeting. Judah camps in the center of its regiment, with the tribes of Issachar and Zebulun on each side. Second comes Reuben to the

51. Levine, *Numbers 1–20*, 1-20, 141-42.
52. Milgrom, *Numbers*, 9-10, 342-44.
53. Levine, *Numbers 1–20*, 148.

south (vv. 10-16), with the tribes of Simeon and Gad camped on each side. West of the tent of meeting is the regiment of Ephraim (vv. 18-24), accompanied by Manasseh and Benjamin. Finally, to the north lies Dan (vv. 25-31), flanked by Asher and Naphtali. Each ancestral house most likely had its own insignia or banner that marked their campsite (see vv. 1-2).

The arrangement of the regimental encampments on the four sides of the tent of meeting is also meant to provide the order for marching. This is indicated in the closing line of each section (vv. 9, 16, 24, 31). Thus the insignia or banner leads each ancestral house on its processional march through the wilderness.

The outline of vv. 3-31 illustrates how the order of the tribes changes from the census in chap. 1 to the arrangement of the camp in chap. 2. The change of order provides insight into the theological perspective of the priestly writers. The tribe of Reuben is the firstborn of the eponymous ancestors (see Genesis 29–30; 35). Thus it would be expected that Reuben would begin any listing of the tribes, as is the case in the first census in chap. 1, the second census in chap. 26, and the list of spies in chap. 13. But Reuben gives way to the tribe of Judah in the arrangement of the camp (chap. 2), in offerings for the tabernacle (chap. 7), in the order of marching toward the land (chap. 10), and in land distribution (chap. 34). As noted in the Commentary on 1:4-16, comparison suggests that the tribe of Reuben is associated with the numbering

of Israel and with the loss of the land, while the tribe of Judah is associated with marching toward Canaan and acquiring the land. The contrast between the two lists is less a polemic against Reuben than an emphasis on the favored status of Judah, the representative tribe of the southern kingdom. The priestly writers see Israel's future with Judah, and the favored status of this tribe is reflected in their ideal vision of the camp. Judah camps in the central position on the east side of the tent of meeting so as to protect the door of the sanctuary.

Verse 17 underscores that the tent of meeting and the camp of the Levites are at the center of the four regimental encampments and the order of their marching. The camping arrangement of the priests and the Levites around the tent of meeting is described in more detail in chap. 3. Again, a heirarchy emerges in which the Aaronid priests camp to the east of the tabernacle (3:38), the Kohathites to the south (3:35), the Gershonites to the west (3:23), and the Merarites to the north (3:35).

2:32-34. Three summary conclusions end the chapter. First, v. 32 gives the total number of Israelites as 603,550, a repetition from 1:46. Second, v. 33 underscores that the Levites were not included in the total number of Israelites, a repetition of 1:47 (vv. 32-33 do not include the military imagery from 1:46-47). Third, v. 34 notes the successful completion of the divine instructions in vv. 1-2 and closes by anticipating Israel's march through the wilderness.

REFLECTIONS

1. The priestly writers view the entire world from the perspective of the camp, with the tabernacle representing the center point. This is not a common way of writing theology in contemporary culture. But location does influence each of us as we view the larger world. Consider a poster that came out several years ago by Steinberg entitled "A New Yorker's View of the World." The Hudson River is pictured as the outer reaches of the globe, because of the centrality of New York City for those who live in it. The poster illustrates how important even secular locations can become in structuring a vision of the world. The tabernacle plays an even stronger role in the priestly writer's view of the world. It was not simply a familiar or comfortable place to live. It is where Yahweh dwells.

Comparison of the priestly camp to other theological uses of geography, maps, and city plans in the Bible may assist further in understanding this genre of writing. The prophet Isaiah employs geographical descriptions of a new creation or a new Zion to describe the character of salvation (see Isa 65:17-25). The prophet Ezekiel provides a closer parallel to the priestly writers in Numbers 1–2. He, too, describes salvation geographically. It includes a new temple (Ezekiel 40–45), which produces life-giving water (Ezek 47:1-12). The prophet goes on to locate the Temple (Ezek 47:13-23) and the tribes in the land (Ezekiel 48). The book of Revelation provides an inner-biblical interpretation of the wilderness camp of the priestly writers. The camp becomes the new Jerusalem, which descends from heaven filled with divine glory. It is square, with three gates on each side to represent the twelve tribes of Israel (Rev 21:9-15).

Biblical writers employ geography to envision the salvation of God on earth. It is meant to be read symbolically. Yet, geographical imagery does remind us that salvation in the Bible is not an escape from this world to heaven. Rather, it is a transformation of it into the kingdom of God. Priestly writers provide a model for any church to envision its role in community. Write a map of the life of your church. Where is it located in your neighborhood, village, or city? What are its outer reaches? Where has it transformed the social character of its environment?

2. The priestly vision of religious community incorporates two perspectives, identity and mission, which continue to provide a paradigm for Christian community. Identity results from an inward focus on the relationship of Israel to God in the camp. It characterizes the Israelites as a holy people. It is the starting point for community. Mission results from an outward focus on the relationship of Israel to the world. Priestly writers employ military language to describe Israel's mission.

Identity is formed in worship. It is the first act in becoming a Christian community. When the focus of priestly writers is turned inward, toward the indwelling of God in the tabernacle, the Israelite camp is like a worshiping community. The presence of God forms their identity as a holy people. The arrangement of the camp is an outgrowth of the indwelling of God in the tabernacle at its center. Life in the camp, moreover, separates Israel from the profane world. The same is true in contemporary worship. Worship separates; it is where we acquire our identity as the people of God. We die to the world in baptism and feast with Christ in the eucharist. We also acquire a new ethical vision for life through preaching.

The inward focus of the camp is never an end in itself for priestly writers. Identity leads to mission. Thus the congregation encamped around the tabernacle can be transformed into an army that marches out through the wilderness. The military march is an outward focus. It explores Israel's relationship with the larger world. The militaristic language is symbolic and theological. Priestly writers do not glorify war (see the Commentary and Reflections on Numbers 31:1–33:56). War imagery accentuates the conflict between the holiness of God and the profane world, but with an eye on the people of God. Israel is caught up in this conflict. Life with God in the camp puts Israel in opposition to any form of security that would subvert faith in God. Thus their relationship to the world outside the camp is described with images of war. It accentuates the conflict between faith and culture. This tension is no less true for the church today. Worship gives rise to mission, and mission requires the church to continue the same wilderness march. We, too, appropriate war imagery to describe mission. This is not a glorification of war, but a theological statement about the many tensions that exist between the life of faith and our surrounding culture.

The priestly writers provide a continuing paradigm for Christian community. Identity without mission is self-indulgent religion. Mission without identity is not religion at all. Healthy Christian community requires a constant interrelationship of the two.

3. Numbers 1 provides guidelines for reflecting on the theological significance of administration. The chapter illustrates the priestly concern for order. It is important that the people are numbered precisely. Each group requires lay leaders. Levites are separated from other groups to encircle the tabernacle. Even the writing style of the chapter reflects this concern for balance. The divine commands (1:1) are fulfilled (1:54). The choosing of lay leaders (1:5-15) and the counting of the people (1:17-47) repeat the same phrases. All things are done decently and in good order. The aim of priestly writers, however, is not administration for its own sake. The ordering of the camp is a dynamic response to the presence of God in the community. Administration is intended to foster a new community in the wilderness.

Numbers 1 is not meant to be read in isolation. The larger literary context of the priestly history provides insight into the dynamic role of administration. In the creation story of Genesis 1, order subdues chaos, allowing for a rich diversity in creation. Yet, one need not scratch the surface very deeply to realize that the order of creation is a thin membrane, vulnerable to puncture and to the chaotic forces that swirl beneath its skin.[54] Tending to the structure of creation, therefore, has cosmological significance for priestly writers. The return to chaos (the flood) illustrates the consequences of ignoring the details.

The exodus from Egypt inaugurates a new creation for priestly writers. It is Year 1 of a new era, when Israel has passed through the chaotic waters of the Red Sea. Administrating the camp in Numbers 1 is part of this larger drama. Every detail of life in the wilderness matters, because the proper ordering of life and worship secures the presence of God.

Numbers 1 provides a continuing resource for evaluating administration. Power is easily abused for self-interest. Law, ritual, and hierarchy cannot be ends in themselves. Administration is always a dynamic response to the presence of God in community. It requires clear theological grounding. The goal of administration continues to be the creation of community in God's new creation. From the perspective of the priestly writers, serving on the board of trustees, chairing church committees, and participating in newsletters all strengthen the presence of God in community.

4. Numbers 1 contains a vision of community in which organization allows for innovation and difference. Priestly writers never state this explicitly. Instead, the message is embedded in the terminology used to describe Israel. The priestly vision of community in the wilderness holds together myriad social terms that, when interpreted historically, appear contradictory. The most prominent contrast is membership in the group through kinship ("the sons of Israel") and through participation in worship ("the congregation"). These terms form different communities; yet, they exist side by side in Numbers 1. The bringing together of potentially conflicting terms indicates that priestly authors envision something new in the wilderness that defies past social models. Their vision can be summarized in the following manner: Social innovation takes place within the careful ordering of the community, and not in its destruction. And community does not require uniformity. Competing visions of community are allowed to exist together rather than in competition.

5. Numbers are important to the priestly writers. They seem preoccupied with the size of Israel. The commentary indicated that it may signify power and blessing. We, too, focus on numbers as a sign of power and of blessing. Bigger is often judged to be better. The emergence of megachurches is an example. The priestly writers provide two guidelines for reflecting on the size of our churches. The first is in the census. The significant message in numbering Israel is not the size of the group, but that each tribe and every member is accounted for and organized in the camp. The point of counting members is not to stress how large each tribe may be, but to ensure that no one is lost in the wilderness. The second point of emphasis is the large numbers. They are difficult to interpret. They do underscore the size of the group as a fulfillment of divine blessing, but they also emphasize that Israel is prepared to fulfill its mission. This is why the

---

54. See Jon D. Levenson, *Creation and the Persistence of Evil: The Jewish Drama of Divine Omnipotence* (San Francisco: Harper & Row, 1985) 14-50, 66-127.

census is limited to males twenty years of age and older. The message of the priestly writers for our contemporary setting is that size must determine mission, not prestige. Larger churches may have the resources to undertake mission projects that are out of the reach of smaller congregations. Numbering members is one way to gauge mission.

6. The need to appease the wrath of God in the selection of Levites requires comment about priestly religion. God is not an intimate friend in priestly religion. The priestly writers stress, instead, the gulf between God and humans (see Introduction). God is holy and thus separate from humans. The indwelling of God bridges the gulf, but the combination of the sacred and the profane is a volatile mix. The priestly writer's concern for order is aimed at avoiding harmful consequences of living with God. Divine wrath results from any casual approach to God.

Divine wrath is not divine anger. The Israelites are not sinners in the hands of an angry God. They are redeemed humans who now live in the presence of the divine. They have access to power beyond their imagination. Such power is dangerous, because it will always effect change. Thus it must be approached carefully. The starting point of the priestly writers is the power of God to transform and make new. The wrath of God is a necessary by-product of such power. Electricity provides a partial analogy. The flow of generated electricity is constant. When properly wired, it can light and heat our homes. But when an exposed cord is touched with the bare hand, electricity has the power to kill.

The message of the priestly writers translates directly to contemporary Christians. Christians have access to the same power of God through sacraments. Baptism and participating in the eucharist will always effect change in us. Thus casual participation is dangerous, since we are held accountable once we lay claim to the power of God.

Numbers 3:1–4:49, The Role of the Levites in the Cult, in the Camp, and on the March

COMMENTARY

Numbers 3–4 turn from the Israelite congregation in general to focus on the specific role of the Levites in the cult, in the camp, and on the march. In priestly tradition, all cultic personnel—including Moses, Aaron, and Miriam—are descended from their ancestor Levi. Priestly writers outline the genealogy of Levi in Exod 6:16-25 into three clans of Gershon, Kohath, and Merari. This three-part division is reflected in Numbers 3–4, and it repeats in the levitical genealogy of 26:57-62. Figure 1 presents a partial genealogy of Levi.

All priests evolve from the eponymous ancestor Levi, the third son of Jacob's first wife, Leah (Gen 29:31-35). The folklore surrounding Levi and the Levites is that they are violent in service to Yahweh. Levi and Simeon destroy the family of Shechem to avenge the defilement of their sister, Dinah (Gen 34:25-31). This action is cursed in the last words of Jacob (Genesis 49). The

patriarch characterizes it as uncontrolled and denies the Levites land in Canaan because of their violence (Gen 49:5-7). The Levites also slaughter 3,000 of their own family and friends to purge Israel from the sin of worshiping the golden calf (Exod 32:25-29). This action is praised in the song of Moses (Deuteronomy 33). Deuteronomy 33:8-11 attributes their priestly status (as the ones who consult the Thummin and the Urim) to their loyalty to Yahweh, even at the cost of family and children. Read together, these traditions account for the special status of the Levites as priests (Deuteronomy 33) who are without land in Canaan (Genesis 49). The special role is rooted in violence, motivated by allegiance to God. The violence is both praised (Deut 33:8-11) and cursed (Gen 49:25-29).

The priestly writers provide their own interpretation of the Levites in Numbers 3–4. Many historical problems surround the priestly presentation of the Levites. The genealogy of Levi in Num 26:57-62 indicates that the division of three clans in Numbers 3–4 is not original. Numbers 26:58 divides the house of Levi into five clans: Libnites, Hebronites, Mahlites, Mushites, and Korahites. This structure most likely reflects an earlier genealogy of Levi. Numbers 26:57 replaces the five-clan structure with the three-clan structure of Exod 6:16-25 and Numbers 3–4, thus bringing the older genealogy into conformity with other priestly genealogies of Levi. Such modification suggests that the priesthood underwent change during the exilic period. Conflict between priestly families during the exile is evident in Ezek 44:11-13. The genealogy of Levi as three clans in Numbers 3–4 may represent the structure of the priesthood during the post-exilic period.

The division between Aaronide priests and Levites in the book of Numbers may also be an innovation by priestly writers during the period of the exile.[55] There does not appear to be a distinction between priests and Levites in the book of Deuteronomy, written toward the end of the monarchical period. In Deuteronomy, the term "levitical priests" (הכהנים הלוים *hakkōhănîm halwiyyim*) is a general reference for all priests (Deut 17:9, 18; 24:8; see also Deut 18:1; 21:5).[56] Yet, Numbers 3:1–4 assumes a clear distinction between Aaronide priests and all other Levites, even though they share the same family tree.

The difference between Aaronide priests and Levites in priestly tradition is indicated by their rites of ordination. Priests are consecrated to achieve their status of holiness. Levites undergo purification to assume their role in guarding the tabernacle. Levites achieve a position of holiness between that of Aaronide priests and the congregation of Israel in general. The consecration of the Aaronide priesthood was a central topic in the book of Leviticus, where the sacrificial system was described. The purification of the Levites becomes the focus in Numbers. Their role in the setting of the tabernacle and the camp is described in Numbers 1; 3–4; 8.

The literary structure of Numbers 3–4 follows the pattern of divine command and fulfillment. The stereotypical introduction, "The LORD spoke to Moses . . ." occurs seven times. Yahweh commands the Levites to be separated from the congregation of Israel (1:5), to be substitutes for all Israelite firstborn (3:11), and to be counted from one month of age and older (3:14). The command to be substitutes for all Israelite firstborn repeats in 3:44. Then God commands that the Kohathites from thirty to fifty years of age be counted and assigned duties for transporting the most holy objects of the tent of meeting (4:1) and that they not look at the holy objects in the tabernacle (4:17). The Gershonites and the Merarites from thirty to fifty years of age must also be counted and assigned duties for moving the remainder of the tent of meeting (4:21). The number of commands (seven) may be intentional, since it signifies completeness in priestly tradition. An additional command to number all Israelite firstborn appears in 3:40, where the verb "to say" (אמר *'āmar*) replaces the verb "to speak" (דבר *dābar*), bringing the total number of introductory commands to eight.

The introductions divide loosely between a first census, in which the Levites are numbered to determine their role as substitutes for all Israelite firstborn, and a second census, in which each levitical ancestral house is assigned duties. Statements indicating fulfillment of the divine commands reinforce this two-part structure. Moses fulfills the requirements of the first census in 3:42, and he collects the redemption money in 3:51 "as the LORD had commanded." The fulfillment of the second census is recorded in 4:34-49.

3:1-10. The Levites are separated from the congregation. Verses 1-4 provide a genealogy of the Aaronide priesthood, and vv. 5-10 describe the Levites' relationship to the Aaronide priests.

3:1-4. Two introductory formulas are combined in these verses, both of which link chaps. 3–4 with a larger genealogical structure that runs throughout the Pentateuch. The two phrases are the *Toledot* (from תולדות *Tōlēdôt*, "Generations") formula ("This is the lineage of Moses and Aaron") in v. 1 and a naming formula ("These are the names of the sons of Aaron") in v. 2.

---

55. For a brief overview of the problems surrounding the history of the Levites, see Levine, *Numbers 1–20*, 171-78, 279-90; and M. D. Rehm, "Levites and Priests," *ABD* 4:297-310.

56. For a listing of references to Levites in Deuteronomy, see Rehm, "Levites and Priests," *ABD* 4:303-5.

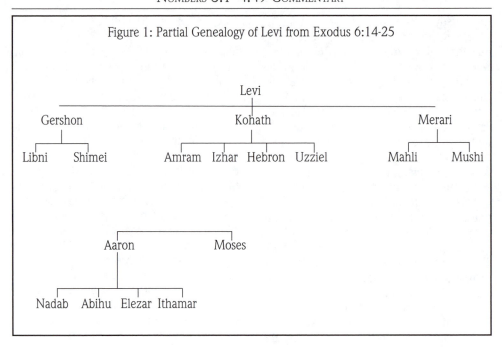

Figure 1: Partial Genealogy of Levi from Exodus 6:14-25

Most instances of the *Toledot* occur in Genesis. Yet the appearance of the phrase in Num 3:1 indicates that the priestly writers use the formula to emphasize the important role of Moses and Aaron in history. Its overall structure can be summarized in the following manner.

Several features of the *Toledot* provide insight into the priestly history. The story of creation in Genesis 1 is outside the structure of the *Toledot*. The special position of Genesis 1, outside of all genealogical development, allows for the story of creation to be both the beginning and the end of the priestly account of salvation history. The circular design to the priestly history encourages a reading of the *Toledot* structure both forward (from Genesis 2 to Numbers 3) and backward (from Numbers 3 to Genesis 2). The circular design of the *Toledot* structure reinforces the emphasis of priestly writers both to establish Israel's identity and to describe their mission as the people of God.

When the *Toledot* is read forward (from Genesis 2 to Numbers 3), it is a story of identity. The priestly history provides a genealogical account of salvation history as a process of divine election from the earliest humans to the wilderness generation. The first *Toledot*

describes "the generations of the heavens and the earth" (Gen 2:4*a*). The scope of the *Toledot* narrows from all the families of the earth (Adam, Noah) to the Israelite ancestors (Abraham, Isaac, and Jacob) and, finally, to the genealogy of the Israelite priesthood in Num 3:1. This process of separation identifies Israel as the people of God.

When the *Toledot* is read backward, it provides a blueprint for mission. It is an outline of how the people of God must transform this world into the ideal of Genesis 1. Israel's mission in the priestly history is not simply to transform Israel (Jacob, Isaac, Abraham) or even all humans (Noah, Adam), but the very heavens and the earth themselves.

The circular design of the priestly history underscores how the genealogy of Moses and Aaron is the apex of salvation history. It is the turning point, where history moves back toward its ideal origin. Social and cosmological transformation must begin with the Aaronide priesthood and the Levites. They encircle the tabernacle and provide the starting point for guiding divine holiness into the world.

A naming formula in Num 3:2, "These are the names of the sons of Aaron . . . ," has been added to the *Toledot*. This formula is

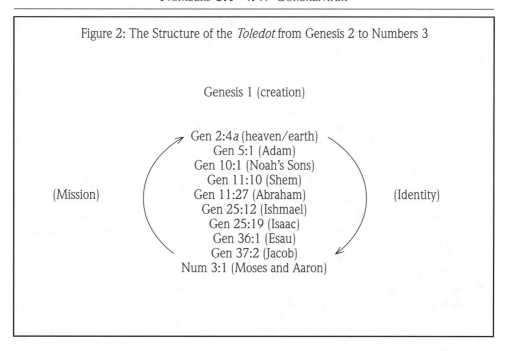

Figure 2: The Structure of the *Toledot* from Genesis 2 to Numbers 3

Genesis 1 (creation)

(Mission)

Gen 2:4*a* (heaven/earth)
Gen 5:1 (Adam)
Gen 10:1 (Noah's Sons)
Gen 11:10 (Shem)
Gen 11:27 (Abraham)
Gen 25:12 (Ishmael)
Gen 25:19 (Isaac)
Gen 36:1 (Esau)
Gen 37:2 (Jacob)
Num 3:1 (Moses and Aaron)

(Identity)

used more randomly throughout the Pentateuch to identify descendants of Ishmael (Gen 25:13), Esau (Gen 36:10, 40), Jacob (Gen 46:8; Exod 1:1), Levi (Exod 6:16), lay leaders (Num 1:5), spies (Num 13:16), the daughters of Zelophehad (Num 27:1), and tribal leaders in the land (Num 34:17, 19). The formula in Num 3:2 introduces Aaron's four sons, Nadab, Abihu, Eleazar, and Ithamar.

Numbers 3:3-4 recounts the death of Aaron's elder two sons, Nadab and Abihu. The reason for their death is that "they offered illicit [or strange] fire before Yahweh" (author's trans.). This is a reference to Leviticus 10:1, when Nadab and Abihu were killed by God immediately after the theophany of the כבוד יהוה (*kĕbôd YHWH*, "glory of God") in the altar of the tabernacle. Scholars debate just what is meant by the phrase "strange fire" (אש זרה *'ēš zārâ*). The larger context of Leviticus 10:1 suggests that Nadab and Abihu sought to hoard holiness, rather than to use their special position as Aaronide priests as a means for channeling holiness to the entire congregation. Thus Moses warns Aaron immediately after the death of Nadab and Abihu that divine holiness is meant for "all the people" (Lev 10:3). The role of the priests and, more specifically, the Levites is certainly

meant to provide boundaries between the sacred and the profane. Such boundaries, however, are not for the purpose of hoarding holiness for a few, but for holiness to influence as many as possible.

3:5-10. This section describes the relationship of the Levites to the Aaronide priesthood and to the congregation. The Levites are positioned between the priesthood and the congregation for the purpose of serving both groups in front of the tabernacle (vv. 6-7). George Buchanan Gray describes the Levites as a caste of servants for the priests.[57] This paragraph is filled with technical language that is not immediately apparent in translation. The command in v. 5 for Moses "to set them [the Levites] before Aaron the priest" indicates subordination, which is reaffirmed in v. 9 with the divine command to Moses: "you give the Levites to Aaron and his descendants." The verb "to give" (נתתה *nātattâ*) in this context is a technical term for dedication that signifies subordination.

The tasks of the Levites are twofold. They are "to perform duties" (שמרו את-משמרת *šāmĕrû 'et-mišmeret*) for the priests and congregation in front of the tent of meeting and

57. Gray, *Numbers*, 21.

"to do the service" (עבדת‎-את לעבד‎ la'ăbōd 'et-'ăbōdat) of the tabernacle. Jacob Milgrom has argued that the phrase "to perform duties" indicates guard duty.[58] Thus one of the tasks of the Levites is to guard the outer court of the tabernacle from encroachers. The second task is the hard labor of maintaining and transporting the tabernacle, which is described later in the chapter. The language used to indicate hard labor has overtones of slavery that will influence the special role of the Levites as substitutes for the firstborn. They are claimed by God as slaves for the divine. The threat of death to encroachers in v. 10 underscores the sacredness of the tabernacle and its danger to outsiders.

3:11-51. The purpose of the first census is to number all Levites one month of age and older. The reason for determining this number is that the Levites are to function as substitutes for all Israelite firstborn, who otherwise would be claimed by God. The theme of substitution frames this section. The divine claim on the Levites as substitutes for the firstborn is stated in vv. 11-13. The command to number the Levites by their ancestral houses occupies the central section in vv. 14-39. And the issue of substitution for the firstborn returns in vv. 40-51.

3:11-13. These verses separate into three parts. Verse 11 begins the unit with the introduction, "Then the LORD spoke to Moses." Verse 12 states the divine claim on the Levites as acceptable substitutes for the firstborn. Although it is not stated in v. 12, the claim is on firstborn males. This is made clear in v. 40, where God requires Moses to count all firstborn males in the camp to determine how many persons are required for substitution. Verse 13 provides a historical reason for the divine claim on the firstborn by anchoring it in the exodus.

The text states that all firstborn are claimed by God and, thus, are considered holy in Israelite religion. Legal texts such as Exod 22:29-30 and 34:19-20 confirm the sacred status of the firstborn. Exodus 22:29 bluntly states that "the firstborn of your sons you shall give to me." The divine claim on the firstborn may have risen from the creative power of God as the giver of life. Perhaps there was a relationship with the Festival of First Fruits,

also known as Weeks. This was a one-day festival in the spring, occurring fifty days after the Festival of Unleavened Bread, *Massot* (Exod 23:14-17). The few passages that mention the firstborn are not clear on this point, however. Another reason for the divine claim may have been that the firstborn assumed responsibility for burial and even worship of deceased parents. Remnants of such ancestral worship are evident in texts like Deut 26:1-14 (see esp. v. 14). Just how the holy status of the firstborn influenced early cultic practice is also unclear. Whether there was a special ritual, redemption, or even sacrifice of the firstborn is difficult to determine. Stories like the attempted sacrifice of Isaac in Genesis 22 appear to be polemics against child sacrifice. But it is not clear whether Genesis 22 is a late story polemicizing against an earlier Israelite practice or against non-Israelite cultic practice. In any case, Exod 34:20 speaks of redemption for the firstborn son rather than sacrifice.

Verse 13 roots the holy status of the Israelite firstborn in the exodus. The divine claim on the firstborn is historicized through the climactic final plague. The death of all firstborn Egyptian children and livestock at midnight (Exod 11:4-8; 12:29-32) is judgment on the Egyptians and their gods (Exod 12:12). God spares the Israelite firstborn in the priestly history through the substitution of a one-year-old male lamb. This becomes the Feast of Passover (Exod 12:1-13; see also the non-priestly account in Exod 12:21-27). In this ritual, the blood of the lamb on the doorpost was a sign for God not to kill the Israelite firstborn at midnight.

The divine claim on the Israelite firstborn is a direct result of their being spared on Passover. Exodus 13:11-16 states that the sparing of the Israelite firstborn during the midnight plague in Egypt results in their becoming a special divine possession. Thus all firstborn were to be given over to God through sacrifice or redeemed in some way through substitution. The special status of the firstborn would begin once Israel entered the land of Canaan (Exod 13:15).

Numbers 3:13 follows the same line of interpretation as does Exod 13:11-16. It, too, states that the sacred status of the firstborn is a direct result of their being spared during

---

58. Milgrom, *Numbers,* 16.

the first Passover. Priestly writers, however, make three changes in Numbers. First, they describe the firstborn explicitly as having a holy status ("I consecrated for my own all the firstborn in Israel"). Second, they require redemption of the firstborn already in the wilderness, rather than commencing the requirement with Israel's future life in the land. As a result, the holy status of the firstborn is a present reality for priestly writers. Third, the priestly writers also provide a one-time means of substitution through the levitical priestly caste, who are dedicated to God.

3:14-39. The role of the Levites as substitutes for the firstborn requires that they be counted. Verses 14-20 provide an introduction to the section with the divine command to number the Levites. All levitical males from one month of age and older are to be numbered according to their ancestral houses. The reason for beginning at one month is unclear. The census of the congregation in chap. 1 began at the age of twenty, which appeared to correspond with the age of military service. The Levites, by contrast, are being numbered for the purpose of redemption of the firstborn and not for military service. Thus it appears that all levitical males of any age could function as a substitute. In his commentary on Numbers, W. Gunther Plaut notes that in Jewish tradition "a child must live a month before being considered fully viable" and that a child who dies earlier than one month of age is considered a stillborn.[59] Whether a similar tradition is at work already in the priestly writing cannot be determined, but remains a possibility.

The census of the Levites is introduced in v. 14 with the expected divine command, "Then the LORD spoke to Moses." The fulfillment of the divine command follows immediately in v. 16, even though the census continues to v. 51. Verse 16 reads, "So Moses enrolled them according to the word of the LORD [עַל־פִּי יהוה *'al-pî YHWH*], as he was commanded." The phrase "as he was commanded" is the expected language for indicating fulfillment of a divine command (see 1:54; 2:34). The additional phrase "according to the word of the LORD" is new, and it appears to create an unnecessary repetition.

The purpose of this repetition may be to call attention to the levitical census and to underscore that their census is distinct from the general census of the people. Jacob Milgrom has gone so far as to argue that the phrase should be translated "oracle," thus signifying that the census of the Levites was actually taken by God rather than by Moses.[60] In this case, the role of Moses in the process is to record the divine count, rather than to undertake it himself. Milgrom's interpretation may account for the place of the fulfillment of the divine command already in the introduction, since the remainder of the section would consist of the recording of the divine count and not the count itself.

The census is separated into the three levitical ancestral houses of Gershon (vv. 21-26), Kohath (vv. 27-32), and Merari (vv. 33-37). Each paragraph follows the same structure: (1) a list of the clans of each ancestral house; (2) the number of males one month of age and older; (3) their placement in the camp; (4) the head of the ancestral house; and (5) a list of their responsibilities with regard to caring for the tabernacle (see Fig. 3, "The Levitical Ancestral Houses"; see also Commentary on 4:1-33).

Verses 38-39 turn attention from the levitical ancestral houses to the Aaronide priesthood, not for the purpose of numbering them, but to finish out the arrangement of the camp. The encampment of Moses and the Aaronide priesthood on the east side of the tabernacle is noted in v. 38, along with a description of the Aaronide priests' tasks within the tabernacle (as opposed to the other levitical houses, who labored outside). The total number of levitical males one month of age and older is given in v. 39 as 22,000.

3:40-51. The purpose of the census to substitute Levites for Israelite firstborn is restated. Verses 40-43 provide the number of firstborn Israelite males one month of age and older as 22,273. This census conflicts with the census of twenty-year-old males in chap. 1, where the total given was 603,550 (1:46). Harmonizing the two counts would require that each Israelite family have at least 14 children. The focus of the priestly writers, however, does not appear to be the census total from chap. 1, but the 22,000 Levites

59. W. Gunther Plaut, *Numbers, The Torah: A Modern Commentary* 4 (New York: Union of American Hebrew Congregations, 1979) 26.

60. Milgrom, *Numbers,* 19.

Figure 3: The Levitical Ancestral Houses

	Gershon	Kohath	Merari
1. Clans	Libnites	Amramites	Mahlites
	Shimeites	Izharites	Mushites
		Hebronites	
		Uzzielites	
2. Numbers	7,500	8,600	6,200
3. Placement in the Camp	West	South	North
4. Head of Ancestral House	Eliasaph son of Lael	Elizaphan son of Uzziel	Zuriel son of Abihail
5. Task	Tabernacle	Utensils	Frames

who were numbered in 3:14-39. Comparison indicates 273 more firstborn Israelites than Levites. The excess of 273 firstborn is important, because it creates a situation in which the priestly writers can provide a paradigm for redemption beyond the number of Levites. Each firstborn Israelite beyond the number of Levites must be redeemed at the price of five shekels, payable to the Aaronide priesthood. Substitution is also extended to cattle in v. 41. Levitical cattle substitute for firstborn cattle of the people of Israel. There is conflict between this law and 18:17, which states that all firstborn cattle must be sacrificed to Yahweh, rather than being redeemed. Moses fulfills the divine command in vv. 49-51.

4:1-49. Numbers 4:1 describes a second census. Its purpose is to define and distribute the workload of the Levites. The age of those counted changes from one month of age and higher to males between the ages of thirty and fifty (vv. 3, 23, 30). Divine command (vv. 1, 17, 21) indicates a hierarchy among the Kohathites (vv. 1-20), the Gershonites (vv. 21-28), and the Merarites (vv. 29-33). Moses undertakes the count in vv. 34-49.

All the Levites are placed under the direction of the Aaronide priests, but even here there is a difference in hierarchy. The Kohathites are supervised by Eleazar (v. 16), while the Gershonites and the Merarites are under the oversight of Ithamar (vv. 28, 33). The distinction in supervision arises from the separate jobs assigned to the ancestral

houses. The Kohathites transport the most holy objects, while the Gershonites and the Merarites transport the remainder of the tabernacle and its court.

The tasks of the Kohathites are outlined in vv. 5-15. Once the Aaronide priests have packed the most holy objects, they must carry them on the march. These objects include the ark in the holy of holies (vv. 5-6), the table of showbread (vv. 7-8), the lampstand (vv. 9-10), the golden altar (v. 11), and all the utensils in the sanctuary (v. 12) as well as the altar of burnt offering in the courtyard (vv. 13-14).

Degrees of holiness are indicated by the position of the objects in the tabernacle and its courtyard. The most holy location is the holy of holies. The intensity of holiness lessens as one moves further from this location. Categories of holiness are maintained by the colors of the wrappings and by the process of packaging the objects for the march through the wilderness.

The most holy status of the ark is signified by the use of a veil in its storage for travel (v. 6). During periods of encampment, this veil separates the ark in the holy of holies from other objects in the tabernacle. There are two other wrappings for the ark in addition to the veil. Fine leather (perhaps from dolphin skin) surrounds the veil, which is itself covered with a blue cloth.

The table of showbread, the lampstand, the golden altar, and the utensils from the sanctuary are wrapped in blue cloth and then placed in fine leather. The altar of burnt offering in the courtyard is wrapped in purple and then placed in a fine leather covering.

Thus the packaging changes from the holy of holies (ark) to the sanctuary of the tabernacle (table of showbread, lampstand, golden altar, and utensils) to the courtyard (altar). This distinction is carried through to the colors. Note that on the march the ark would be the only blue object. All other objects have fine leather as their outer wrapping, although they are distinguished beneath by blue and purple cloth. The transportation of the holy objects is by far the most dangerous task of the Levites, and it elevates the status of the Kohathites. But even with their elevated position, they are warned never to touch the objects directly (v. 15). Only Aaronide priests are properly safeguarded for this task (vv. 17-20).

The task of the Gershonites is outlined in vv. 21-28. They are to carry the curtains of the tabernacle, its top, and all hangings from the court. The task of the Merarites is described in vv. 29-33. They are to carry the frames, bars, and pillars of the tabernacle and its court.

Moses fulfills the divine command in vv. 34-49. The section separates into four repetitive paragraphs: vv. 34-37, vv. 38-41, vv. 42-45, and vv. 46-49. In the first three sections, Moses and Aaron are described as counting the Kohathites (vv. 34-37), the Gershonites (vv. 38-41), and the Merarites (vv. 42-45) between the ages of thirty and fifty before their totals are given (Kohathites, 2,700; Gershonites, 2,630; Merarites, 3,200). A summary statement indicates the successful completion of the census. The final paragraph in vv. 46-49 follows the same structure in providing the total number of Levites, which is 8,580.

REFLECTIONS

1. The idealization of hierarchy in the priestly writer's vision of the camp requires careful theological reflection by modern interpreters, especially since priestly writing is often judged in the modern context as advocating elitism. Hierarchy in priestly theology is not for the purpose of limiting power to the few, but to distribute holiness to as many as possible. Thus, in teaching and preaching Numbers 3–4, it is important to remember that the focus of priestly writers is on the whole camp and not on individual members. This is true even when the topic narrows to the Levites or the Aaronide priesthood.

The starting point of priestly writers is the separation between God and humans (see Introduction). The incompatibility of holiness to our everyday world requires that a select few acquire a special status to serve the sacred for the many. Selection is not for privilege, but for service. Language of slavery is used to describe the role of the Levites (Num 3:5-10). The task of the Levites to carry the sacred objects of the tabernacle illustrates how holiness is not meant to be hoarded, but shared. These actions enable God to live in the camp and to move through the wilderness with Israel.

The Pauline vision of the body in 1 Corinthians 12 provides a New Testament analogy to the priestly vision of the camp. Paul, too, underscores that there are varieties of gifts in the church. But his focus, like that of the priestly writers, is on the whole body and not on the individual parts. All gifts, according to Paul, derive from the power of God (1 Cor 12:6). Gifts are evaluated, moreover, by whether they contribute to the common good (1 Cor 12:7) and not by the social position of a person with a particular gift. A camp of only Levites or Aaronide priests would be like a human body with only eyes and no ears (see 1 Cor 12:14-26). The diversity of the entire community is always stronger than any one person or group for both the priestly writers and Paul.

The priestly vision of the camp and the Pauline vision of the body challenge contemporary individualism in two ways. First, they remind us that the indwelling of God is not for individual persons to have a private relationship with God or to acquire prestige over others. It is intended to strengthen the community. The death of Nadab and Abihu (Num 3:2) indicates the rejection of such spiritual elitism by the priestly writers. Second, the distribution of leadership roles is always in service to the larger group. The Levites substitute for the firstborn, thus providing life to the community. The apostle Paul makes the same point when he concludes that honor and rank do not go together in the body of the church (1 Cor 12:24-25). Rank is always for the purpose of service to the weaker members. Weaker members hold the position of honor in the community.

2. The distinction among priests, Levites, and lay Israelites allows for theological reflection on different types of calling and ordination in the contemporary church. Degrees of holiness in the geography of the camp determine distinct ordinations. Three degrees of holiness emerge from the architecture of the tabernacle and its court. There is the holy of holies, where the ark is housed and God dwells (Num 4:5-6); the sanctuary of the tabernacle, where the holy objects, consisting of the table of showbread, the lampstand, the golden altar, and the utensils are housed (Num 4:7-12); and the outer court, where the altar of burnt offering is located (Num 4:13-14). The degrees of holiness give rise to the separation of priests and laity as well as to distinctions within the priesthood itself. Aaronide priests labor within the sanctuary. They are protected from death in viewing the sacred objects. Kohathite Levites rank higher than Gershonite and Merarite clans, because they carry the most sacred objects. The link between priests and laity is forged when all Levites substitute for the firstborn, thus providing a way for all Israelites to live in the camp.

We still evaluate ordination in much the same way within the contemporary church. We often think of preaching as separating ordained clergy from laity. This may be true in some churches, but it is the administration of the sacraments that provides the clearest line between clergy and laity. Baptism and the eucharist are the most holy rituals of the church. They are priestly functions of ministry that take place in the front or altar area of the church. The ordination required to discharge the sacraments is usually the most restricted of all offices in the church. But there are also many other ministries and offices in the church that broaden the role of leadership. Bishops, elders, deacons, and commissioned teachers are just a few examples of offices that emerge from the indwelling of Christ in the church. Gradations of holiness continue in the church for the same reason as in Numbers 3–4: God calls people to different tasks in order to disburse holiness through the community.

3. The divine claim on Israelite firstborn and their redemption by the Levites introduces language of service, salvation, and identity that lives on in Christian tradition. Numbers 3:11-13 states that God made the Israelite firstborn holy by not killing them during the night of Passover, when the Egyptian firstborn were destroyed. Firstborn, therefore, are a divine possession: "They are mine," says Yahweh. The divine claim of possession means that they should be given over to God, whether through sacrifice or through some other symbolic action. Levites redeem the firstborn by releasing them from their legal obligation through substitution. The Hebrew word "to redeem" (פדה pādâ) means "to buy back," implying that something is lost to the original owner. The thought behind Numbers 3 is that God, the Savior of Israel in Egypt, is compensated by the Levites. They are given over to God, they take on a special service in the camp, and they even lose their rights to the land. The identity of the Levites is formed in this act of substitution.

Redemption through substitution becomes a model for interpreting the ministry of Jesus and the life of all Christians. Jesus substitutes divine form for human and in this action acquires identity, according to the apostle Paul (Phil 2:6-11). The pattern continues in his own life, when Paul writes of himself, "It is no longer I who live, but it is Christ who lives in me. And the life I now live in the flesh I live by faith in the son of God, who lived in me and gave himself for me" (Gal 2:20 NRSV). In both of these instances, substitution leads to service and identity.

4. Numbers 3–4 illustrates the concern of the priestly writers to transform the entire environment of Israel. The smallest details take on importance. Holiness permeates objects like the ark, the table, the lampstand, the altar, and the utensils. It is even reflected in the different colors associated with the tabernacle: violet, purple, and crimson. We continue this practice in Christian tradition. The Christian year is made up of sacred seasons or times, like Advent, Epiphany, Lent, Easter, and Pentecost, which contrast to regular or ordinary time. Our seasons of worship are also distinguished by colors. For example, Advent and Lent are purple, Easter is white, and Pentecost is red. Ordinary time is green. Colors reflect different degrees of holiness just as in priestly tradition. Every church also has sacred objects. Some are objects common to all churches, like communion utensils or baptismal basins. Others are unique to local churches. Windows, paintings, artwork, or a special cross may each enrich our religious life. Paying attention to sacred objects in our church and the changing colors of the Christian year makes us conscious of the many concrete ways God changes the details of our lives.

5. The contemporary church is rediscovering how important the earth is for human health. The priestly history provides an important resource for reflecting on environmental theology. The *Toledot* formula in Num 3:1 indicates that Israel's life in the camp is part of a larger history that extends back to the origins of creation itself. Humans are defined as part of the earth. Salvation apart from the "heavens and the earth" would make no sense to the priestly writers (see the *Toledot* in Gen 2:4*a*). The quest of Israel within salvation history, according to priestly writers, is to rediscover the lost world of Genesis 1.

Numbers 5:1–6:27, Camp Legislation to Prevent Defilement

COMMENTARY

The legislation in Numbers 5–6 builds on the arrangement of the camp and the census in chaps. 1–4. The sections are tied together around the common problem of how Israel is to live in the presence of divine holiness. In chaps. 1–4, the holiness of God in the tabernacle gave rise to the social organization of Israel, the arrangement of the camp around the tent of meeting, and the role of the Levites. Chapters 5–6 present legislation to protect the holiness of the camp from impurity.

Biblical impurity and its relation to holiness requires definition. The holiness of God creates two different contrasts: sacred versus profane and pure versus impure.[61] The contrast of sacred versus profane is the contrast between the holy and the common. It has

dominated Numbers 1–4. Holiness separates by its very nature. God is holy; humans are not. They are common or profane. Thus care must be taken in bringing the two together. Humans must conform to divine holiness, symbolized as completeness. The quest for holiness requires taking on the order of holiness. The priestly writer's concern for order in the camp (chaps. 1–4) represents the desire to conform to holiness.

The dangers of physical and social impurity to the camp are central in chaps. 5–6. God's holiness remains the central theme. But the contrast is not between the sacred and the profane. It is between health and disease. The quest for completeness is replaced with medical images. Holiness is health. It must be protected from infection, contamination, pollution, and impurity. Contact with

61. Milgrom, *Numbers,* 334-46.

a corpse or the acquiring of a skin disease defiles. The medical language also describes the ethical life of Israel. Evil actions are contagious disease that pollutes and eventually kills the social body like cancer in a human body. The most basic contrast between holiness and impurity is life and death. The holiness of God is life. All forms of impurity, whether physical disease or immoral behavior, are death. The two are incompatible.

The laws of impurity in chaps. 5–6 are arranged in relationship to the tabernacle. They move from the outside of the camp (5:1-4) to the inside of the camp (5:5–6:21). The laws that focus on life within the camp (5:5–6:21) move in closer orbits toward the tabernacle at the center. Numbers 5:5-10 represents the broadest circle in the camp. It explores social relationships that defile. Numbers 5:11-31 narrows the circle. It turns attention to defilement within marriage relationships. Numbers 6:1-21 represents the smallest circle. It addresses the special human-divine relationship resulting from the Nazirite vow. This vow is the only way a non-priestly Israelite could attain a holy status. The section closes in 6:22-27 with the priestly blessing on the congregation. It is God's response to the purity of the camp. Comparison to Lev 9:22 indicates that the priestly blessing emanates from the door of the tabernacle, thus completing the movement toward the center of the camp.

Divine command and fulfillment reinforce the overall design of chaps. 5–6. The list of impurities in 5:1-4 requiring a person to be placed outside the camp is introduced by divine command in v. 1 ("The LORD spoke to Moses") and concludes with the notice of fulfillment in v. 4 ("The Israelites did so . . . as the LORD had spoken to Moses"). The different laws concerning relationships in the camp are introduced with divine command ("The LORD spoke to Moses," 5:5, 11; 6:1). They lack the formula of completion, however. The reason may be that they constitute ongoing legislation for the camp, rather than specific requirements to be implemented at the time of command. The priestly blessing on the congregation and the camp in 6:22-27 replaces the formula of completion.

5:1-4. This section is structured into four parts. It begins with the divine command in

v. 1. The content of the command is stated in vv. 2-3a. Three forms of impurity threatening the purity of the camp are listed: (1) a skin disease described in Hebrew as צרעת (ṣāraʿat); (2) abnormal bodily discharges from the genitals; and (3) contact with a corpse. Any male or female with these conditions threatens the purity of the camp and must be expelled. Verse 3b states that the purpose of the legislation is not to protect people from disease, but to protect God's holiness from these threatening conditions. Verse 4 closes the unit by underscoring the completion of the command by the congregation.

The laws in vv. 1-4 stress that the life-giving power of holiness must be protected. But what exactly is being protected, and where is the conflict? Mary Douglas has argued that laws of impurity are symbolic of larger cosmological realities.[62] From her perspective, the point of conflict in Num 5:1-4 is not the specific diseases, but what they symbolize. The holiness of God at the center of the camp gives life that is whole and complete. The order of the camp is an outgrowth of divine holiness; as such, it reflects this abundant life. The camp symbolizes a whole new age of salvation. Following the interpretation of Douglas, we might conclude that the diseases and other impurities listed in v. 2 represent the disruption of the unblemished order of holiness symbolized by the camp. In other words, they represent different forms of "dirt" that must be removed to protect the order (or cleanliness) of the camp.

Jacob Milgrom takes the work of Douglas a step further. He concludes that each of the three forms of impurity listed in v. 2 represents the power of death in somewhat different ways.[63] Thus, according to Milgrom, the conflict addressed in vv. 1-4 is not simply order versus disorder, but the life-giving power of holiness versus death. The contamination to camp members by contact with a corpse clearly illustrates the conflict between holiness and death.

Defilement from skin disease addresses the same conflict. Although this condition is translated "leprosy" (צרעת ṣāraʿat), the term most likely encompasses a variety of skin disorders described in more detail in Leviticus

62. Douglas, *Purity and Danger.*
63. Milgrom, *Numbers,* 344-46.

13–14. Once again, it is not the health consequences of the disease that force a person from the camp, but its association with death, which is incompatible with holiness. The story of Miriam in Numbers 12:1 provides illustration. When she acquires *ṣāraʿat* as punishment for opposing Moses, Aaron exclaims that her condition makes her like one of the dead (12:12).

The contrast between holiness and death is also the rationale for the impurity of discharge. The Hebrew word for "discharge" (זוב *zôb*) simply means "one flowing." Comparison to Leviticus 15, however, makes it clear that the context concerns abnormal discharge from the genitals of either males or females. Abnormal flowing of blood and semen, the sources of life, also symbolizes death.

In summary, vv. 1-4 outline two forms of power and their spheres of influence: life-giving holiness and death. Holiness emanates from God and is located in the tabernacle. Its sphere of power is the camp. The incompatibility of holiness and death demands that all signs of the latter be banished from the camp.

5:5–6:21. The perspective shifts in Num 5:5–6:21 from signs of death that must be banished from the camp to relationships within the camp that are incompatible with holiness. The topic changes from ritual impurity to moral offenses. The goal of the laws also appears to change. Their aim is no longer to remove threatening persons (or conditions) from the sphere of the holy, but to keep offenders within the camp. Thus restoration for violations of camp holiness is an important aspect of the legislation in this section.

5:5-10. These verses deal with the breakdown of community relationships. The first part of v. 5 underscores the broadly based social dimension of this law. It is addressed to all men and women in the camp. The violation described in v. 6 with the Hebrew phrase כי יעשו מכל-חטאת האדם (*kî yaʿăśû mikkol-ḥaṭṭōʾt hāʾādām*) occurs only in this verse. It could be translated as "wrongs committed against another human" or as "wrongs committed by any human." The difference is whether the last word in the phrase, "the human" (האדם *hāʾādām*) is interpreted as a subjective genitive ("wrongs committed by any human") or as an objective genitive ("wrongs committed against another

human"). Similar language occurs in Lev 6:1-7 (Lev 5:20-26 MT), where the former interpretation is intended. But the phrase in v. 6 is not exactly the same. The details of restitution in vv. 6-10 suggest that the sin being addressed is one of defrauding a neighbor, which favors the translation "wrongs committed against another human."

The issue in these verses is not secular crime, however, but the violation of the sacred. The closing phrase of v. 6 makes this clear. It states that cheating and stealing "break faith with Yahweh." The Hebrew word "to break faith" (מעל *māʿal*) in conjunction with the preposition "with/against" (ב *bĕ*) is precise in indicating some form of sacrilege. God tends to be the offended party when this syntactical construction is used. Thus, for example, Moses is told by Yahweh in Deut 32:51 that he must die on Mt. Nebo and not enter the promised land, because Moses "broke faith [*māʿal*] with [*bĕ*] God" when he angrily struck the rock, instead of sanctifying God in the people's midst (see Numbers 20). The reason for the sacred dimension to community relationships in Num 5:5-10 is that the camp is the sphere of holiness. Holiness permeates all action.

The sacred character of the law is reinforced at the close of v. 6 when the offender is described as "incurring guilt." The Hebrew word for "guilt" (אשם *ʾāšām*) is a central term in the priestly description of Israel's cultic system. Guilt is a legal condition. It describes a situation resulting from illegal action. The removal of the condition of guilt requires ritual purification and restitution. The word is used no fewer than four times in vv. 6-8. A verbal form of the Hebrew word *ʾāšām* is used in vv. 6 and 8, while a noun form occurs in vv. 7 and 8. The noun has at least two meanings in priestly writing. It can designate a particular kind of sacrifice that is meant to alleviate guilt (as it does in 6:12); more specifically, it can indicate the actual content that is required for restitution. Verse 7 illustrates this latter meaning when it states that the one who has stolen must make full repayment "for what he has stolen" (the Hebrew translates literally, "his" *ʾāšām*).[64]

The Hebrew verb meaning "to be guilty" is stative. Such verbs do not describe action,

64. Milgrom, *Numbers,* 35.

but the state or condition of something resulting from action (e.g., you cannot "cold" someone, but you can "be cold"). The stative aspect of the Hebrew verb is rendered in English as "is guilty" or, as in the case of the NRSV translation of v. 6, "incurs guilt." What the NRSV translation suggests is that defrauding in the camp becomes sacrilege that gives rise to a condition of guilt, which is incompatible with holiness.[65] The imagery is medical. Such a person infects the camp with pollution, and a contaminated camp is incompatible with a holy God. The infected person must be cured. The offender must make confession, pay back the principal amount of what he or she stole, and add 20 percent (v. 7). These actions alleviate the condition of guilt created by the theft. Health is achieved. The offender is allowed to remain in the camp and continue living within the sphere of God's holiness.

A slightly different interpretation of vv. 6-7 has been offered by Jacob Milgrom, who argues that the Hebrew verb "to be guilty" can take on a psychological dimension when used without an object (as is the case in v. 6). In such instances, Milgrom suggests, the more accurate translation is "feel guilt."[66] Verses 6-7 state, according to Milgrom, that the offender must first feel guilt (become aware of his or her sin). Only then is confession meaningful and the reparation of guilt efficacious.

Verse 8 clarifies that restitution of theft remains a requirement even after the death of the injured party. The reason given for this requirement is that ultimately God is the offended party. Verse 8 closes by adding that God allocates the guilt offering to the priests. Verses 9-10 comment on the legislation of v. 8 by clarifying which priests receive the donation. The donation belongs to the priest who collects it.

5:11-31. These verses narrow the focus from relationships between all persons in the camp (vv. 5-10) to marriage. The danger of defilement is no longer defrauding in general, but adultery. The law is stated at the beginning (vv. 12-14) and the end (vv. 29-30) of the legislation.[67] It is aimed at a wife, who is suspected of "going astray." The verb "to

65. Levine, *Numbers 1–20*, 188-89.
66. Milgrom, *Cult and Conscience*, 3-12.
67. See M. Fishbane, "Accusations of Adultery: A Study of Law and Scribal Practice in Numbers 5:11-31," *HUCA* 45 (1974) 35-36.

go astray" (שטה *śāṭâ*) in vv. 12 and 29 can mean wickedness in general (Prov 4:15), but v. 13 makes it clear that sexual infidelity is intended. If the charge is true, such a wife is described as being unfaithful to her husband (v. 12) and thus defiled (v. 29).

The phrase in v. 12 indicating unfaithfulness (מעל *māʿal*) to (ב *bě*) a husband is unique, since (as noted in the Commentary on 5:6) this expression tends to be used to indicate sacrilege, with God as the object. The repetition is certainly meant to relate the two laws. The unique usage in v. 12 may also be intended to indicate that adultery is a violation against God and, hence, a threat to the holiness of the camp. Such a broad interpretation of v. 12 is supported by v. 29, where the act of "going astray" is explicitly said to result in defilement (טמא *ṭāmēʾ*), thereby associating adultery with sacrilege. Genesis 20:6 provides an additional instance of adultery as sacrilege. Abimelech's potential sleeping with Sarah is described as sin against God. The religious dimension of the law is indicated by its frequent use throughout this section (vv. 12, 13, 14 [twice], 19, 20, 27, 28, 29).

Verses 15-31 outline a judicial ritual for determining the guilt or innocence of a suspected adulteress. The rationale for the ritual is that adultery is sacrilege. A woman guilty of such an action threatens the camp with contamination, not because she is ritually unclean from sexual intercourse, but because she is ethically unclean from violating her marriage relationship. The aim of the detailed ritual, therefore, is not to assuage a husband's jealousy (an infraction of civil law), but to avoid defilement of the camp (an infraction of sacred law). The magical character of the ordeal (vv. 15-28) for determining the guilt or innocence of the woman underscores the sacred dimension in which the law is meant to function.

Verse 15 states the condition for the ritual ordeal. A husband who suspects his wife of sexual infidelity must bring her to the priest along with a special offering, described as a "grain offering of jealousy" and a "grain offering of remembrance."

Verses 16-18 outline cultic instructions for the ritual ordeal. The priest places the woman before God (v. 16). He takes "holy water" and mixes it with dust from the floor of the tabernacle in an earthen vessel (v. 17). He also loosens the woman's hair and puts the special offering of jealousy and remembrance in her hands (v. 18).

Verses 19-26 prescribe an oath and accompanying sacrifices. The priest recites an oath while holding the mixture of water and dust in his own hands. The oath functions as a curse if the woman is guilty. Her "womb will discharge" and her "uterus will drop." The woman accepts the oath on herself by stating, "Amen, Amen" (vv. 19-22). The priest then writes down the words of the oath, washes the parchment in the mixture of water and dust, and makes the woman drink the potion while he sacrifices the grain offering of jealousy and remembrance (vv. 23-26).

Verses 27-28 indicate that the woman's reaction to the potion will determine her guilt or innocence. If she is guilty, the curse of the oath will take effect. If innocent, she will be immune to the curse and continue to conceive children.

The ritual contains technical language that is no longer clear to modern readers. The various descriptions of the offering in v. 15 ("offering of jealousy," "offering of remembrance," and "bringing iniquity to remembrance") lack precise parallels. Reference to "holy water" (מים קדשים *mayim qĕdōšim*) in v. 17 is not explained and occurs nowhere else in the Old Testament. Perhaps the combination of water and dust symbolizes life and death. The symbolic significance of loosening the woman's hair in v. 18 may indicate mourning (Lev 10:6), a state of defilement as in leprosy (Lev 13:45), or shame.

Even more problematic is "the water of bitterness that brings a curse" (v. 19). The description of this potion is important for interpreting the entire ordeal, since it is the centerpiece of the ritual. Yet no clear consensus has emerged concerning the meaning of the word המרים (*hammārîm*). It is translated as "bitterness" in the NRSV and "bitter" in the NIV, from the root consonants מרר (*mrr*), "to be bitter." Other Hebrew roots have been suggested, which result in very different interpretations, including "water of rebellion" from the root מרי *(mry*, "to rebel")[68]

and "water of instruction or revelation," from the root ירה (*yrh*, "to teach").[69]

The effect of the potion on the woman raises further questions. If the woman is innocent, she will be immune to the negative effects of the potion and will "be able to conceive children" (v. 29). If she is guilty, the potion will make her womb discharge and her uterus drop (vv. 21, 27). Interpreters are divided on the matter of whether the woman is pregnant. If pregnant and guilty of adultery, the phrase would mean that the potion induces an abortion. Innocence would result in a full-term delivery. If the woman is not pregnant and guilty, the phrase would indicate that the potion renders her physically unable to have children.

The process of the ritual has also prompted conflicting interpretations. Some scholars question whether the text is describing one ritual or a combination of distinct rituals and offerings. Martin Noth separated the text into a meal offering and a drink offering. He also identified three different forms of divine judgment. Holy water held secret power of judgment. The oath, in the form of a curse, could also trigger divine judgment. And the writing of words in a book was yet a third form of judgment.[70] More recent interpreters tend to view the text as describing one complex ritual.[71] But even here there is debate about whether the ritual should be characterized as an ordeal.

Such a magical ritual ordeal is unusual in the OT. There are other rituals from the ancient Near East in which guilt or innocence of a person is determined by a water ordeal. In the Code of Hammurabi, for example, a person accused of sorcery must go through a river ordeal to determine guilt or innocence,[72] as must a wife accused of adultery by a third party.[73] The closest parallel in the OT is Exod 32:20, where a similar ordeal may be implied when Moses makes the Israelites drink water mixed with powder from the destroyed golden calf. Perhaps the drinking of this mixture determined who would be killed by the Levites (Exod 32:25-29).

68. *BDB*, 598a; and G. R. Driver, "Two Problems in the Old Testament Examined in the Light of Assyriology," *Syria* 33 (1956) 73-77.

69. H. B. Brichto, "The Case of the SOTA and a Reconsideration of Biblical 'Law,'" *HUCA* 46 (1975) 66-67.

70. Noth, *Numbers*, 48-49.

71. Milgrom, *Numbers*, 350-54.

72. James H. Charlesworth, ed. *Ancient Near Eastern Texts* (New York: Doubleday, 1985) 2:166.

73. Charlesworth, ed. *Ancient Near Eastern Texts*, par. 130-31, 171.

Tikva Frymer-Kensky questions whether Num 5:11-31 should be categorized as a trial by ordeal. She notes that the trial by ordeal includes two important features: The god's decision is manifested immediately, and the result of the ordeal is not the penalty for offense, requiring that the society execute judgment. Numbers 5:11-31 departs from both of these features. The divine decision is not immediately known at the end of the ritual, and the execution of judgment is reserved for God alone.[74] The second point is made explicit in v. 31, which states that the "woman shall bear her iniquity." The Hebrew of "to bear iniquity" (נשא את-עונה *nāśā’ ’et-‘ăwōnāh*) means that any punishment must come from God and not from the husband or the larger society, thus protecting the woman, to a certain degree, from her husband's jealousy.

The drinking of a magical potion certainly provides a strong parallel to the trial by ordeal. The differences highlighted by Frymer-Kensky, however, are significant. At the very least, they accentuate the theological aim of the priestly writers to address the danger of defilement to the camp, which in the end must be determined by God alone, and not by the people.

6:1-21. These verses describe the Nazirite. The name "Nazirite" comes from the Hebrew verb נזר (*nāzar*), meaning "to separate." Verse 3 states that a Nazirite is potentially any woman or man from the congregation who makes a vow to be separate or dedicated to God for a period of time. The act of vowing is described with the Hebrew פלא (*pālā’*). When used in conjunction with the word "vow" (נדר *neder*), it means simply "to fulfill a vow." The verb may indicate the need for an explicit statement by the person making the vow. Martin Noth thought that the verb also expressed an extraordinary pledge to God, since the verb can also mean something marvelous.[75] The consequence of such a vow was certainly special ordination. It resulted in lay Israelites' achieving a holy status. This special relationship between God and humans is the last to be explored in Numbers 5–6.

The holy status of Nazirites means that such persons are divine property during the period of their vow. They are separated out for God. The holy state of Nazirites may exceed that of regular priests. Nazirites occasion a third type of relationship that, if broken, would defile the camp. The purpose of priestly writers in these verses is to address potential problems of defilement that might arise in conjunction with the Nazirite vow. The particular details of the vow and the circumstances under which someone becomes a permanent Nazirite (e.g., Samson or Samuel) are not mentioned. Instead, vv. 1-8 provide enough conditions for addressing two potential situations of defilement. The first concerns accidental contamination from a corpse (vv. 9-12). Exposure to a dead family member, for example, contaminates a Nazirite, rendering such a person unable to fulfill the vow. The second (vv. 13-20) is guidelines for ending the vow and thus leaving the holy state of a Nazirite. The unit closes with a summary in v. 21.

Verses 1-8 describe the requirements for temporary Nazirite vows. Three restrictions characterize Nazirites during the period of their vow.

First, Nazirites cannot consume wine or any grape products, including raisins (vv. 3-4). The rationale for this prohibition is not given. George Buchanan Gray has suggested that abstinence from grape products represents a rejection of the settled agricultural life represented by Canaanite culture.[76] The story of the drunkenness of Noah (Gen 9:18-29) reflects a similar suspicion of Canaanite civilization. A rejection of agrarian culture in the Nazirite vow may be intended to symbolize intensified dependence on God.

Second, Nazirites cannot cut their hair during the period of the vow (v. 5). The story of the Nazirite Samson (Judges 13–16) illustrates how hair symbolizes strength. Refraining from cutting the hair during the period of the vow and offering it in sacrifice during the closing ritual (Num 6:18) most likely symbolizes the Nazirites' total dedication to God during their vow.

Third, the Nazirite cannot touch a corpse (v. 6), because the Nazirite is holy during the period of the vow. Holiness and death are

74. T. Frymer-Kensky, "The Strange Case of the Suspected Sotah (Numbers V 11-31)," *VT* 34 (1984) 24.

75. Noth, *Numbers,* 55.

76. Gray, *Numbers,* 61-63.

incompatible. Nazirites would lose their state of holiness through contact with a corpse. The Nazirite vow takes precedence over all other relationships, including family. The Nazirite, therefore, is forbidden even to attend the funeral of a parent or sibling (vv. 7-8).

Once the requirements of the Nazirite vow are spelled out in vv. 1-8, the remainder of the text explores the dangers of defilement to those who undertake the vow. Verses 9-12 focus on cleansing from accidental defilement. Verses 13-20 outline proper procedures for ending the vow.

The cultic instructions in vv. 9-12 address the problem of corpse contamination to a Nazirite. Exposure to a corpse defiles a Nazirite, making him or her unable to fulfill the vow. The obligation of the vow remains in place, requiring the Nazirite to repeat the period of consecration. Verses 9-12 are aimed at decontaminating both the sanctuary and the Nazirite, so that the person could begin the vow anew and thus fulfill the obligation to God. The text states that a contaminated Nazirite must undergo a seven-day period of purification, at the end of which his or her hair must be shaved (v. 9). On the eighth day, two turtle doves or pigeons are presented to the priest for sacrifice at the door of the tent of meeting (vv. 10-11). The first sacrifice is a sin offering, which purges the sanctuary from pollution. The second is a burnt offering, which may invoke divine presence. After rededication, the Nazirite presents a guilt offering of a one-year-old male lamb for expiation for the broken vow. Then the vow begins anew (v. 12).

A second situation in which Nazirites are vulnerable to defilement is the ending of their vow. Verses 13-20 outline the proper ritual for avoiding contamination when leaving the holy state of the Nazirite. The location of the rite is the door of the tent of meeting (v. 13). A complex series of sacrifices is required, including a burnt offering, a sin offering, an offering of well-being, and grain and drink offerings (vv. 14-15). The question arises as to why such a complex ritual is required and, more precisely, why a sin offering is necessary at the close of the period of the vow. Jacob Milgrom, who cites the medieval commentator Ramban (1194–1270 CE), is most likely correct that "self-removal from the sacred to the

profane realm requires sacrificial expiation."[77] During the sacrifice, the consecrated hair of the Nazirite was shaved and destroyed in the fire to ensure that it not become the cause of some future defilement (v. 18). The priestly portion of the sacrifice is described in vv. 19-20; the unit ends by stating that after the ritual, the Nazirite can again drink wine.

6:22-27. A priestly blessing on the congregation closes the section on camp defilement in Numbers 5–6. The blessing in vv. 24-26 has been woven into its present framework (vv. 22-23, 27).

The act of blessing is deeply rooted in Israelite culture. It bears a wide range of meaning. On the one hand, Jacob's stealing of Esau's blessing and the latter's inability to acquire another from his father, Isaac (Gen 27:30-38), provides a glimpse into the near magical power of blessing. In that story, to bless is to bestow power for fertility and well-being, which, once spoken, takes on a life of its own. On the other hand, the expression of divine blessing appears to be no more than a stereotypical exchange for "Hello." The book of Ruth provides an example of how the invocation of divine blessing was part of the everyday language of greeting, for example, when the harvesters welcome Boaz with the words, "The LORD bless you" (Ruth 2:4).

The cultic use of divine blessing, as in vv. 24-26, functions someplace between the two examples noted above. The cultic use of the priestly blessing was widespread by the late monarchical period. Similar cultic language is richly attested in other liturgical literature. Psalm 129:8, for example, concludes with a priestly blessing on the worshipers, "The blessing of the LORD be upon you. We bless you in the name of the LORD" (see also Pss 128:5; 133:3; 134:3). The Hebrew inscription "the LORD bless you and keep you and be with you" was found on a jar at Kuntillet 'Ajrud in the upper Sinai, dating from the eighth-century BCE. This inscription indicates the use of a blessing very similar to Num 5:24-26 already in the middle of the monarchical period. The discovery of the priestly blessing in a burial cave in the area of Jerusalem known as the Valley of Hinnom (contemporary Keteph Hinnom) is even more striking. The blessing is written on two silver amulets that date from the late seventh century BCE.

77. Milgrom, *Numbers*, 48.

An amulet is an object believed to give magical powers of protection against evil to the one who wears it. The discovery of such an amulet in a grave raises further questions of whether the priestly blessing was meant to function in association with the dead. Baruch Levine suggests that the priestly blessing may have protected the dead on their way to Sheol.[78]

The priestly blessing has a simple structure, consisting of three lines, each of which contains two verbs: bless-keep (protect), shine-grace, lift-peace. The name "Yahweh" appears once in each line, in association with the first of the paired verbs.

Yahweh bless you and keep you;
Yahweh make his face to shine upon
  you and be gracious to you;
Yahweh lift up his countenance upon you—
  and give you peace

Two readings are possible from this structure. The six verbs could be interpreted to describe distinct actions of God. They can also be interpreted in pairs. The first verb in each line summarizes an activity of God upon the worshiper, and the second describes the results of God's actions. The use of the name "Yahweh" as the subject for only the first verb in each sentence favors the interpretation in which the verbs are paired.[79] The result is a threefold blessing. The first emphasizes concrete gifts—blessing and security (guarding). The second stresses the hope that God will be well disposed toward the person (to lighten or shine upon the worshiper) and thus temper judgment with mercy (to be gracious). The third asserts that God will pay attention (lift his face), thus providing fullness of life (peace). David Noel Freedman notes a variety of subtle stylistic devices in the Hebrew that aid in carrying out the meaning of the priestly blessing. These include a progression in the numbers of words (3, 5, 7) and consonants (15, 20, 25) in each line. The progression is framed by an opening ("The LORD bless you") and a closing ("and give you peace") cola of the same length (7 syllables in Hebrew).[80] Numbers 6:22-23, 27 frames the priestly blessing within the context of Numbers 5–6.

These verses take the form of divine instruction for the Aaronide priesthood. Numbers 6:22-23 indicate that the blessing is meant to function as a concluding benediction (vv. 22-23) to the instruction for camp purity in chaps. 5–6. Numbers 6:27 clarifies that it is God (rather than the priests) who blesses Israel.

The literary setting has puzzled scholars,[81] prompting some even to suggest that the text has been displaced from Lev 9:22, where Aaron is also described as blessing the people from the door of the tent of meeting.[82] But the function of the blessing as a concluding benediction on the camp and the congregation does correspond to other cultic uses of the priestly blessing in the Psalms (e.g., Psalm 129:1), suggesting that its present context is less arbitrary than many have suspected.

The overall design of Numbers 5–6 provides additional guidelines for interpreting the priestly blessing in its present context. The placement of the priestly benediction at the door of the tent of meeting follows naturally upon the inward movement of the laws of defilement. These laws began with contamination requiring expulsion from the camp (5:1-4), followed by three types of relationships within the camp with the power to defile. These relationships moved in an ever-closer orbit to the tabernacle at the center of the camp—from defrauding in general (5:5-10), to adultery (5:11-31), and through to the Nazirite vow (6:1-21). The location for expiatory rituals has tended to follow the same movement. The laws of defrauding and adultery require that the offender be presented "to the priest" (5:9, 15), while the defiled Nazirite must go "to the door of the tent of meeting" (6:10, 13). The door of the tent of meeting is also the location for the priestly blessing on the congregation (see Lev 9:22).

The priestly blessing has at least two functions in its present literary context. It provides yet another safeguard against defilement by blanketing the camp with the power of divine blessing. It also concludes Numbers 5–6 with a description of the ideal camp. The ideal is where God pays particular attention to persons, where blessing and security drive out the power of death, and where the achievement of wholeness and peace is possible.

78. Levine, *Numbers 1–20*, 236-44, esp. 242-43.
79. P. D. Miller, Jr., "The Blessing of God," *Int.* 29 (1975) 240-51.
80. D. N. Freedman, "The Aaronic Benedictions," in *No Famine in the Land*, ed. J. W. Flanagan (Missoula, Mont.: Scholars Press, 1975) 411-42.
81. See, e.g., Milgrom, *Numbers*, 51.
82. Gray, *Numbers*, 71.

REFLECTIONS

1. The priestly writers encourage us to reflect theologically on the role of the church in health care. Medical care in modern society is increasingly separated from the life of faith. Doctors operate and prescribe medicine to combat disease. Ministers support the emotional needs of the family and the patient. We acknowledge the importance of both for human health, but the vocations are clearly separated between the physical and the spiritual. The priestly writers would have a difficult time understanding our clear separation of roles. Religion and health are more closely interwoven in their worldview. Their starting point in Numbers 5–6 is God as the source of both physical and moral health. Thus religious laws of defilement embrace both bodily and social diseases. Both are signs of death equally opposed by God.

What would it mean to translate the priestly worldview into our life? Their teaching on social defilement is not all that different from our own. We understand the power of social disease in the contemporary church. We employ the power of God to combat violence, greed, racism, the breakdown of the family, and many other illnesses that plague our society. And we expect God to bring about social change. Our expectations for God are less concrete when we shift from social to physical disease. The priestly teaching on physical defilement and the role of God in healing is more of a challenge. Yet their view of holiness requires that the church be actively involved in health care.

Employing the power of God to combat physical disease does not put the church in opposition to any other form of medical care. Cancer treatment requires operations and chemotherapy. But priestly writers would say that the church also has its own medicine to combat illness. And the New Testament witness to Jesus supports them. Jesus was a healer. It is one of the few things that both his followers and his opponents could agree about (Mark 4:20-27). This power is passed on to his followers. The sacraments of the church are a repository of Jesus' healing power. The water of baptism makes us new. The blood and body of Jesus flow in our veins through communion. These sacraments are resources for health to be dispensed freely by the church. Many churches have additional rituals of healing, some involving oil. The priestly writers infuse all dimensions of life with holiness. They encourage us to combat social and physical disease with the same expectation of change. Racism and cancer are both signs of death equally opposed by God.

2. The priestly laws of defilement are aimed at creating a healthy community. The details of their laws do not apply to the modern world. Skin diseases, semen, menstrual discharges, and contact with the dead are not the significant points to communicate when teaching Numbers 5–6. Two principles are important for healthy community. First, laws of defilement are universal to the human condition. They are not aimed at certain classes of people or races. All persons are liable for defilement. Second, the laws of defilement are inclusive in their intent. They are aimed at keeping people in the camp within the sphere of holiness, and not driving them away. Disease is identified so that it can be cured. It is not used to exclude anyone. This is especially evident with the laws of defilement within the camp (Num 5:5–6:21). They are aimed at restoration, not expulsion. It is also true with the laws requiring a person to leave the camp (Num 5:1-4). The larger body of priestly law includes rituals for reentry into the camp for those who have suffered skin disease (Leviticus 13–14), those who have had bodily discharges (Leviticus 15), and those who have been contaminated from contact with a corpse (Numbers 19). A healthy community has God at its center, cares equally for each member, and is socially inclusive.

3. The ritual ordeal of the suspected adulteress (Num 5:11-31) confronts the contemporary reader with a host of obstacles for interpretation. Much of the language of the text is no longer clear even to experts. The role of magic in the trial by ordeal is foreign to contemporary religious practice, and the unequal treatment of a husband and a wife regarding fidelity in marriage is viewed as unjust in contemporary society. Thus Numbers 5–6 forces the reader to think clearly about principles of interpretation. The central task is to determine how Scripture that is historically specific can function authoritatively for a contemporary reader, to whom the text may not only be unclear in its details, but even immoral in its prescribed practice as well.

The starting point for teaching this text is the association of adultery with sacrilege in Num 5:12. As noted in the commentary, the phrase "to break faith with" indicates that God is the offended party. Thus, even though the husband brings the woman to the priest in a "spirit of jealousy" (Num 5:13-15), the ordeal focuses on God and the woman, not the husband. Jealousy on the part of a wife is not mentioned. The limited focus on the husband's jealousy reflects the patriarchal society of ancient Israel. The priestly writers most likely shared the belief that sexual activity of a woman is an offense against the man, whether it be the woman's father or her husband (Deut 22:13-29).

Tikva Frymer-Kensky may be correct that the shift in focus from husband to God as judge is meant to protect the woman from her husband's jealousy in a patriarchal society. The principle underlying the ritual is that the accused is innocent until proven otherwise by God, in spite of jealousy. The aim of the ritual is to maintain the marriage relationship in a society where men are in sole control. Our ideal of marriage departs from the priestly writers. We seek an even distribution of power between the husband and the wife. But the aim of the priestly writers—to maintain a marriage even at the moment of jealousy—remains an important principle. But their limited application to men is too narrow for us. A contemporary interpretation would expand the principle to include a "spirit of jealousy" in both the husband and the wife. The destructive power of jealousy can infect both men and women in our society in ways that priestly writers could never have imagined.

4. Drinking "the water of bitterness" presents another obstacle in the interpretation of the trial by ordeal. The ability of the priest to make a potion that releases supernatural powers borders on magic, and "magic" is a bad word in the Judeo-Christian tradition. The God of the exodus cannot be manipulated through incantations or through sorcery (Deut 18:9-14). The power of Jesus cannot be induced through divination or bought with money (Acts 8:9-25). These confessions appear to conflict with the drinking of a magical potion. Why the aura of magic in warding off defilement? What is it about holiness and defilement that forced priestly theologians to incorporate rituals that did not easily fit into their own central beliefs?

Interpretation must focus on the power of God in the ritual. The point of emphasis is not on the ability of the priest to manipulate God with the use of a potion. It is, rather, on the tangible way in which holiness infiltrates the body of the woman. The setting of the ritual as self-curse focuses only on negative consequences. The requirement that a wife invoke God to destroy her uterus because of a husband's jealousy is so offensive that we are inclined to stop the process of interpretation. The underlying rationale, however, is worthy of reflection: The ingestion of holy water has health consequences (v. 16). It is the attempt of the priestly writers to communicate the physical effects of holiness that has pushed them to the limit of their theological discourse. Christians continue to share in their uneasy quest. We, too, confess that holiness is physical and that it infiltrates our bodies through tangible sacraments of water, wine, and bread.

5. The Nazirite vow provides a model for temporary leadership that is grounded in community. The Nazirite vow is a special calling of laypersons for a designated period of time. The content of the Nazirite vow does not appear to be the central point, and the priestly writers provide no reason for undertaking the Nazirite vow. What is emphasized is that laypersons take on a special calling for a limited period of time. It is done in public, and not in private. It is official, requiring rituals of commencement and conclusion, and it has communal and life-style consequences. The Nazirite is required to separate from everyday routine. Separation is not retreat from the world; Nazirites are not hermits. They remain part of the congregation, but their holy status brings them in a closer orbit of the tabernacle at the center of the camp. The Nazirite vow is a suggestive model for laypersons in the contemporary church to commit themselves to a special ministry for a limited period of time.

6. The priestly blessing (Num 6:22-24) is the most familiar passage in Numbers 5:1–6. The central message of the blessing is stated in the closing Hebrew word, שלום (šālôm), translated "peace." In English, "peace" connotes the absence of war. It can also describe a state of tranquility. These meanings are also in the Hebrew. But the peace of God in the priestly blessing embraces even more aspects of life, inluding good health, security, inner harmony, wellness, material prosperity, and a long life. The broad and rich meaning of "peace" in the priestly blessing reinforces the role of holiness in the life of Israel to bring about both social and physical health.

It was noted in the Commentary that the priestly blessing provides an ideal vision of the camp and that it functions as a conclusion to the laws of defilement in Numbers 5–6. The ideal of the priestly blessing continues in contemporary Jewish and Christian worship. It is included in most lectionary cycles as a topic for preaching. The blessing of God also continues to be the last word in many of our Sunday liturgies as a closing benediction.

The central task in preaching this text is to explore what blessing means. Is the bestowal of a blessing sacramental, or is it no more than a socially polite activity? What is it that we recieve at the close of a worship service? Is real divine power transmitted in blessing, or is the preacher simply telling us that the worship service is nearly over? The latter point creates a problem for interpreting the priestly benediction. Notice how the introduction to the priestly blessing (Num 6:22-23) stresses that only priests can bless. It is not a casual activity. The conclusion (Num 6:27) indicates how close the text is to the world of magic. The author must clarify that the priest does not possess the power to bless independently of God. The need for such clarification underscores that divine blessing has independent power that can be let loose in the congregation.

NUMBERS 7:1–10:10, HOLINESS AND THE TABERNACLE

OVERVIEW

The scope of the literature narrows in 7:1–10:10 from the effects of holiness on the camp to the tabernacle at its center. The subject matter also changes from the social organization of Israel to cultic rituals associated with the care and dedication of the sanctuary. Numbers 7–8 details the dedication of the tabernacle and the Levites. Numbers 9:1–10:10 describes the celebration of Passover and an account of theophany in the tabernacle, which prepares Israel for the wilderness march.

Numbers 7–8 progresses from rituals of dedication outside of the tabernacle (7:2-88) to divine instruction inside (7:89–8:26). In the first scene, leaders from each tribe present gifts at the altar in front of the tabernacle. The second scene takes place inside the tabernacle. It includes instruction for the lighting of the menorah and the duties of the Levites. The two parts are linked by the account of Moses entering the sanctuary to receive revelation from God (7:89).

Numbers 9:1–10:10 addresses cultic matters that prepare Israel for its wilderness march. The section opens with Passover instruction in 9:1-14. The instructions include special provisions to postpone the feast for those unable to celebrate it at the appointed time. Numbers 9:15-23 is an account of theophany in the tabernacle. The section also includes a description of how the cloud will lead Israel on its wilderness journey. Numbers 10:1-10 concludes the section by describing the trumpets associated with the tabernacle and their use. They organize Israel for marching in the wilderness and for waging holy war in the land of Canaan.

The tabernacle is the center of focus throughout Numbers 7:1–10:10. Its significance is described in two ways: by its location in the camp and by its function in Israel's wilderness journey. The placement of the tabernacle at the center of the camp symbolizes its important role in Israel's cultic and communal life. The theophany to Moses indicates that the tabernacle is the location where God dwells. Rituals associated with the tabernacle explore its significance in Israel's history of salvation. The Passover provides a point of continuity with the past by underscoring how the God in the tabernacle is the Savior of the exodus. The cloud probes the significance of the sanctuary in Israel's present life as a guide in the wilderness. The trumpets also probe the present significance of the tabernacle when they are used to organize Israel for journeying in the wilderness. They also point to the future in their role of calling Israel to holy war in the promised land.

Numbers 7:1–8:26, The Dedication of the Tabernacle and the Levites

COMMENTARY

Numbers 7–8 explore the role of the tabernacle. The dedication of offerings by the twelve tribes in chap. 7 highlights the tabernacle's central role among the tribes. The chapter describes the presentation of sacrificial gifts at the altar by each tribe. The interior of the tabernacle becomes the setting for the dedication of the Levites in chap. 8.

7:1. This verse provides transition from the campsite in chaps. 1–6 to the dedication of the tabernacle in 7:1–10:10. The tabernacle is dedicated twice while Israel is encamped at Mt. Sinai (Exodus 19–Numbers 10), after its initial construction (Exodus 40) and again after the organization of the camp (Numbers 7). The chronology of Exodus 19–Numbers 10 suggests that the two dedications take place at the same time. The initial dedication takes place on Month 1, Day 1 of Year 2 after the exodus (Exod 40:1, 16). It is the day that Moses "set up the tabernacle." The second dedication appears to be on the same day. Numbers 7:1 reads: "On the day when Moses had finished setting up the tabernacle. . . ."

If the two dedications are interpreted as having taken place on the same day, then chronological time is suspended during the formation of the priesthood and cult in Leviticus and the organization of the congregation and camp in Numbers 1:1–6. It resumes in Num 7:1 (Month 1, Day 1, Year 2), when events once again follow a clear sequence of action, with twelve days of dedication offerings (Num 7:2-88); the dedication of Levites on the thirteenth day (Num 8:5-26); Passover on the fourteenth day (Num 9:1); a special observance of Passover one month later on Month 2, Day 14, Year 2 (Num 9:11); and the departure from Mt. Sinai on Month 2, Day 20, Year 2 (Num 10:11). The framing of events in Leviticus and Numbers 1–6 with the dedication of the tabernacle may be intended to accentuate its central role in the formation of the priesthood and the camp.

The disregard of chronology from Exodus 40 through Numbers 7 has bothered both ancient and modern interpreters. The rabbis note violations of sacrifice that occur in Num 7:1-88 because of the chronological problems, including the offering by a private individual that overrides the requirements of sabbath.[83] Jacob Milgrom has offered a modern resolution to the problem by translating the phrase "on the day" (ביום *běyôm*) in Num 7:1 indefinitely as "when," so that it need not designate the same day as Exod 40:2, 16.[84]

7:2-88. Sacrifice is important throughout Numbers 7. The priestly theology of sacrifice occurs primarily in the book of Leviticus, where it becomes clear that sacrifice can mean many things in ancient Israelite religion, including a means of expiation as well as a process of gaining union with God.[85] A basic meaning of sacrifice, however, is gift, and it is this meaning of sacrifice that stands out in these verses.

Dedication offerings are central to this section. Events take place in the courtyard of the tabernacle. The offerings are spontaneous gifts from the laity, not prompted by divine command. Initial gifts concern transportation of the tabernacle (vv. 2-9). The leaders of the tribes (see Commentary on 1:1–2:34) present a general offering of six wagons and twelve oxen for transporting it. Their gifts are distributed to the Gershonite and the Merarite Levites, since they are responsible for transporting the tabernacle. Two wagons and four oxen are given to the Gershonites to carry the curtains and coverings of the tabernacle (see 4:21-28), while four wagons and eight oxen are presented to the Merarites to carry the frames and other supporting material (see 4:29-33).

Verses 10-88 are an extensive account of gifts presented by each tribal leader over a twelve-day period. The order of gift-giving follows the sequence of tribes, in which Judah is first, rather than Reuben (see Commentary on 1:1–2:34). Each tribe brings identical gifts:

Grain Offering (מנחה *minḥâ*)
1 silver plate (130 shekels in weight = approx. 65 ozs.)
1 silver basin (70 shekels in weight = approx. 35 ozs.)
(both containing choice flour and oil)

Incense (קטרת *qĕṭōret*)
1 gold dish (10 shekels in weight = approx 5 ozs.)

Burnt Offering (עלה *'ōlâ*)
1 bull
1 ram
1 male lamb (one year old)

Sin Offering (חטאת *ḥaṭṭā't*)
1 male goat

Well-Being Offering (שלמים *šĕlāmîm*)
2 oxen
5 rams
5 male goats
5 male lambs (one year old)

The gifts presented by each tribal leader include all the central sacrifices in priestly tradition except the guilt offering (אשם *'āšām*).

The grain offering is prescribed in Leviticus 2, and its ritual is outlined in Lev 6:14-18. Grain offerings include choice floor, with oil, frankincense, and salt of the covenant, but never leaven. A portion is offered to God as smoke on the altar, while the remainder becomes the property of the priesthood.

Incense is associated with a number of sacrifices. An altar of incense stands inside the tabernacle (Exod 30:1-10).

The burnt offering (lit., "offering of ascent") could be from the herd, the flock, or even fowl. It is described in Leviticus 1 as an offering of atonement, but such a description is never repeated in priestly literature. Levine argues that the purpose of this offering was to attract God's attention by giving a gift that is totally consumed on the altar.[86] The ritual is described in Lev 6:8-13, where it is clear that the burnt offering was a continuous offering to God.

The sin offering alleviated the guilt of specific wrongful acts by cleansing or purging a person. For this reason, Milgrom has argued that the sacrifice is better translated as the purification offering.[87] It is described in Leviticus 4, and its ritual is outlined in Lev 6:24-29.

The offering of well-being, or peace offering, emphasizes fellowship and allegiance between the worshiper and God. Humans

83. *Sifre Num.* 51.

84. Milgrom, *Numbers,* 362-64.

85. See G. A. Anderson, "Sacrifice and Sacrificial Offerings," *ABD* 5:870-86, esp. 871-73.

86. B. Levine, *In the Presence of the Lord* (Leiden: E. J. Brill, 1974) 20-27, esp. 22-27.

87. J. Milgrom, *Studies in Cultic Theology and Terminology,* ed. J. Neusner, Studies in Judaism in Late Antiquity 36 (Leiden: E. J. Brill, 1983) 67-69.

consume the sacrifice in an atmosphere of joy and celebration. It is described in Leviticus 3, and its rituals are outlined in Lev 7:11-36 in association with thanksgiving, votive, and freewill offerings.

The presentation of the gifts by each tribe is described with the hiphil form of the Hebrew verb קרב (*qārab*), translated "to present" or "to bring near." The verb does not clarify whether the gifts are actually sacrificed or given as resources for future sacrifice. The order of the sacrifices suggests that actual sacrifice is not taking place. Within the cult, the sin offering was usually first, since it purified the sanctuary and the worshiper for worship itself. It would then be followed by a burnt offering, in which God's readiness to respond would be tested, giving way to the sacrifice of well-being. In contrast to this expected order of sacrifices, the sin offering comes after the burnt offering in the listing of gifts by the tribal leaders. The importance of the proper ordering of the offerings is still reflected in many Christian liturgies in which the confession of sin and divine pardon leads into the proclamation of a divine word and the eucharistic banquet.

The order of sacrifices suggests that the gifts are presented to the priesthood as resources for the cult. Levine has strengthened this interpretation. He notes that the tabular format of the records in 7:2-88 conforms to the manner in which temples kept track of their holdings.[88] These verses may be an example of bookkeeping from the archives of the Temple. The content of the gifts, however, is likely intended to convey the theological point that each tribe donates equally to the maintenance of the tabernacle, regardless of the tribe's size. The section also stresses that donations are spontaneous gifts to the Temple.

7:89. The opening phrase in this verse presents a problem. The Hebrew translates, "When Moses went into the tent of meeting to speak with him. . . ." The puzzle is the pronoun "him" (אתו *'ittô*). There is no mention of the divine name to provide an antecedent for the pronoun. As a consequence, scholars have argued that the verse is a late redactional insertion.[89] Note how the NRSV

has resolved this problem by changing the pronoun "him" to the proper name "the Lord." Regardless of the transmission history of this verse, it is clear that this verse signals transition from the sacrificial gifts outside of the tabernacle (vv. 2-88) to the divine instruction to Moses inside the shrine (chap. 8). The iconography within the tabernacle and the actions of Moses communicate the priestly writer's theology of divine cultic presence. Three aspects of v. 89 require commentary: the function of the verse within Numbers 7–8; the significance of the iconography in the description of the ark; and the role of this verse in the progression of events at Mt. Sinai (Exodus 19–Numbers 10).

First, 7:89 is pivotal for interpreting the overall structure of Numbers 7–8. Once this verse is in place, the divine speeches to Moses (8:1, 8, 23) concerning the menorah and the Levites acquire a more specific location within the tabernacle/tent of meeting. Change of location signals a new topic: from the tribal gifts (7:2-88) to rituals within the tabernacle and the divine claim on Levites as substitutes for Israelite firstborn (chap. 8). This claim separates Levites from the congregation, allowing them to approach the tabernacle as guardians of the shrine.

Second, the description of how God spoke with Moses in v. 89 is rich in priestly iconography. The priestly writers use visual imagery to communicate the presence of God. The fire of the כבוד יהוה (*kĕbôd YHWH*) is a central symbol for the presence of God throughout the revelation at Mt. Sinai (Exod 24:15-18; 40:34-35; Lev 9:23-24). But there are no representations or statues of God in the priestly tabernacle. Explicit statues of Yahweh would constitute idolatry for the priestly writers. Thus there is only a divine voice in the tabernacle.

The voice of God is located between the two cherubim that frame the mercy seat, which forms the top of the ark of the congregation. "Cover" is a more accurate translation than "mercy seat" for the Hebrew כפרת (*kappōret*). The translation "mercy seat" may derive from the rite of atonement that takes place at the ark (Leviticus 16). The name for the ark as "ark of the congregation" is distinctive to the priestly writers, who also identify the people of Israel as the "congregation"

---

88. Levine, *Numbers 1–20*, 264.
89. Gray, *Numbers,* 77.

(4:5; Exod 25:22; 26:33, 34). The Hebrew העדת (*hā'ēdut*) signifies that Israel is a people in covenant with God. Thus the NRSV translates the Hebrew phrase ארן העדת (*'ărōn hā'ēdut*) as "ark of the covenant," instead of "ark of the congregation" (NIV, "ark of the Testimony").

The iconography in the tabernacle is not an invention of the priestly writers. These objects were important in Israel's worship throughout the monarchical period. The priestly writers have reinterpreted the cherubim and the ark from the Jerusalem Temple of the monarchical period in order to describe how God was present with Israel even during the exile. The wilderness tabernacle represents this new period in Israel's worship life. It represents change within tradition. In the Jerusalem Temple, God was described as being enthroned upon two cherubim (Ps 99:1-5), massive winged statues ten cubits in height (one cubit = 18-22 inches), each with a single wing span of five cubits (1 Kgs 6:23-28; 8:7). Their wings stretched the width of the inner chamber of the Temple, touching in the middle to form a throne for God. The ark was placed in front of the wings of the cherubim as a footstool for God (Ps 99:1-5). Such iconography gave religious expression to Israel's belief that God dwelled or was enthroned in the Temple and ruled the land of Israel through the Davidic king.

The wilderness shrine is a theological response to the fall of the nation, the destruction of the Temple, and the loss of the monarchy in 587 BCE. The cherubim remain in the tabernacle, but they have been diminished in size and function. They are reduced from 10 cubits in height to figurines that sit on the cover of the ark, which has the dimensions of 2½ x 1½ cubits. No mention is made of divine enthronement, and the ark assumes a more central place of significance. It may yet be a footstool, if the Hebrew word for its covering (כפרת *kappōret*) is related to the Egyptian word meaning "sole of foot."[90] But its significance derives from the fact that it contains God's revelatory words from Mt. Sinai ("testimony"), and not that it provides a footrest for the enthroned God. The reinterpretation of the ark influences the function of

the cherubim, who now appear as guardian angels of divine law in the wilderness, rather than as supports for divine enthronement in the land.[91]

Third, v. 89 plays an important role in the progression of events at Mt. Sinai (Exodus 19–Numbers 10). Speech between God and Moses in the innermost part of the tabernacle concludes a process of revelation that began with the theophany of Yahweh on Mt. Sinai in Exodus 19. The original description of the ark, with its cover and two cherubim, appears in Exod 25:10-22. There Moses receives the blueprints for the tabernacle on the summit of Mt. Sinai. God also promises to meet with Moses in the tabernacle at the base of the mountain and to speak with him from above the cover of the ark. Numbers 7:89 fulfills that divine promise. It also emphasizes that the tabernacle is a location of divine speech for priestly writers, preserved as law. The emphasis on the cultic presence of God as speech is also evident in Exod 33:7-11, where Moses is described as entering the tent of meeting outside the camp to receive divine oracles. Priestly writers have combined this tradition of the tent of meeting with their description of the tabernacle, now at the center of the Israelite camp.

8:1-26. Moses is instructed in two matters regarding cultic personnel while inside the tabernacle. The first concerns Aaron and the menorah (vv. 1-4), and the second shifts to the role of the Levites (vv. 5-26). The format of divine command and fulfillment returns, providing structure for the two sections. Each separates into three parts: (1) divine instruction (vv. 1-2 and 5-19), (2) the execution of the instruction (vv. 3 and 20-22), and (3) further clarification of the topic (vv. 4 and 23-26).

8:1-4. The setting up of the lampstand, or menorah (מנורה *měnôrâ*), by Aaron is part of the dedication of the tabernacle. His action brings to conclusion a series of references to the menorah. The first command focused on its construction (Exod 25:31-40), which was fulfilled in Exod 37:17-24. A second divine command (Exod 30:8; Lev 24:1-4) indicated that lay Israelites were responsible to

---

90. M. Gürg, "Eine neue Deutung für kapporet," *ZAW* 89 (1977) 115-18.

91. For brief discussion, see T. N. D. Mettinger, *The Dethronement of Sabaoth: Studies in the Shem and Kabod Theologies,* ConBOT 18 (Lund: CWK Gleerup, 1982) 87-88.

supply oil for the lamp and that Aaron and his sons were required to tend to its regular evening burning. Numbers 8:1-4 fulfills this command.

The divine instruction in vv. 1-2 is not so much about Aaron's responsibility to burn the menorah as it is on how the lights should be burned, especially their direction toward the altar. The details accentuate the divine presence in the tabernacle. The fifth vision of the prophet in Zechariah 4:1 may provide insight into the function of the menorah, for he equates the seven lights with the eyes of God.

The menorah has additional symbolism. It is described with botanical imagery in Exod 25:31-40. Its shaft is called a stem (קנה *qāneh*), and its receptacles for lamps are branches (קנים *qānîm*). In her study of the menorah, Carol Meyers concludes that it is a stylized tree of life, symbolizing fertility in nature and the life-giving power of God. Such symbolism is common throughout the ancient Near East. Yet the construction of the tabernacle menorah points in particular to influence of Egyptian craft techniques.[92] When focus is limited to the OT, the image of the menorah as a stylized tree invites comparison to the tree of life in the garden of Eden (Gen 3:22-24). It relates the divine presence in the tabernacle to creation and holds out hope that Yahweh is able to restore fertility even in the wilderness.

8:5-26. This section focuses on the purification and dedication of the Levites. The Levites have been separated out for special attention throughout chaps. 1–8. They were separated from the other clans during the census (1:48-53). Chapters 3–4 detailed their separate census, service to the tabernacle, and special role as substitutes for Israelite firstborn. These verses now describe the process of dedication and status of the Levites in the camp. Divine command (vv. 5-19) and fulfillment (vv. 20-22) structure the section. A supplement specifying the age span for levitical service in the tabernacle ends the section (vv. 23-26). Commentary will focus on three topics: the purification and dedication of the Levites (vv. 5-14); the role of the Levites in ransoming the Israelite firstborn (vv. 15-18);

and the ability of the Levites to atone for Israel (v. 19).

Verses 5-14 describe the dedication of the Levites for service and the ritual they must undergo in order to be purified. The process moves from purification (vv. 6-7) to sacrificial rites in the larger setting of the congregation (vv. 9-14).

Levites are not Aaronide priests. The distinction is significant. Aaronide priests must be consecrated (קדש *qādaš*) before assuming their office (Exodus 29; Leviticus 8). Consecration makes priests holy, allowing them to handle sacred objects in the tabernacle and to officiate at the altar. Levites are not consecrated. They are purified (טהר *ṭāhēr*) and presented to God as a divine possession. Purification separates Levites from the congregation, but purification does not result in Levites' achieving the holy status of priests. Levites do not handle sacred objects, they do not officiate at the altar, and they do not actually enter the tabernacle for their service. They guard it, and they carry it.

Verses 5-7 describe the purification of Levites through three actions. They are sprinkled with water of purification; they shave their entire bodies; and they wash their clothes. The practice of shaving for purification was mentioned in relation to the Nazirite vow in 6:9 and is prescribed in the purification of lepers in Lev 14:8. The washing of clothes also occurs in the purification of lepers (Lev 14:8), and was part of Israel's ritual of consecration in preparing for the initial theophany on Mt. Sinai (Exod 19:10).

The sprinkling of water is more difficult to interpret. The Hebrew translates literally "water of sin" or "sin offering" (מי חטאת *mê ḥaṭṭā't*). The term occurs nowhere else in the OT, hindering translation and interpretation. The absence of water in the sin offering makes the literal translation unlikely. Gray has suggested that the phrase "water of cleansing" (מי נדה *mê niddâ*), which is made from the ashes of the red cow (19:9), may also be the water in the levitical purification.[93] The aim of the ritual process is similar, to purify the Levites. The goal of purification has influenced the NRSV translation "water of purification" and the NIV's "water of cleansing." Completion of the three-step purification of

92. Carol Meyers, "Lampstand," *ABD* 4:141-43; and her more extended study, *The Tabernacle Menorah*, AASOR Dissertation Series 2 (Missoula, Mont.: Scholars Press, 1976).

93. Gray, *Numbers*, 79.

the Levites leads to public rituals of sacrifice before the tabernacle.

Verses 9-13 describe the sacrifice of two bulls on the altar before the tent of meeting. The ritual begins with the entire congregation of Israel (perhaps represented by its elders) laying hands on the Levites (v. 10). The Levites in turn lay their hands on the bulls (v. 12), thereby linking the congregation, the Levites, and the sacrificial bulls in the ritual. These actions are punctuated with two elevation offerings by Aaron (vv. 11, 13).

The elevation offering is most likely a dedication to God. Its use in this ritual signifies that the Levites are being given to God as an offering. The elevation offering itself is a two-part ritual surrounding the sacrifice of the bulls. The Levites are given over to God for service by the congregation of Israel in the first elevation offering (v. 11). It emphasizes the separation between the Levites and the congregation of Israel that takes place in the laying on of hands. The sacrifice of the two bulls, on whom the Levites have laid hands, completes their transfer as a sacrifice from the congregation to God (v. 12). One bull is a sin offering and the other a burnt offering. The Levites are atoned by the bulls, allowing the Levites, in turn, to atone for Israel (v. 19). The second wave offering associates the Levites with the Aaronide priests as a result of their dedication to God (v. 13). They now "stand before Aaron and his sons."

The process by which Levites substitute for the Israelite firstborn is clarified in vv. 14-18. First, as a result of the ritual, Levites become a divine possession (v. 14). God states to Moses in v. 16: "They are unreservedly given to me from among the Israelites." Second, as a divine possession, Levites substitute for Israelite firstborn (vv. 16-18). The divine claim on the firstborn is rooted in the exodus, when God spared the Israelite firstborn, while killing all Egyptian firstborn (see the story in Exod 11:5-8; 12:29-30; and the priestly interpretation in Exod 12:12-13; see also the Commentary on Num 3:11-13). Third, once the Levites have substituted for the Israelite firsborn, God gives them to the Aaronide priesthood for service. God states in v. 19: "I have given the Levites as a gift to Aaron and his sons from among the Israelites."

Verse 19 states further that the Levites atone for Israel. This is not the same as their role of substitution for the Israelite firstborn. Nor is levitical atonement the blood-rite priests perform to purge the sanctuary of impurities that would otherwise drive God from the tabernacle (see, e.g., the ritual of the Day of Atonement in Leviticus 16). In fact, the Levites do not actually perform atonement themselves. Only priests can undertake this action. Instead, atonement is performed with the Levites through their position in the camp. Their role of atonement presupposes the dangerous presence of God in the sanctuary. They protect the Israelites who live in close proximity to God.[94]

The atonement performed by Levites is more along the lines of a ransom payment to God for protection. Exodus 30:11-16 provides an analogous understanding of atonement with regard to money. In this text, a temple tax on each Israelite is described as a ransom (atonement) payment for their lives, which protects them from any plague that might break out from the temple. The ransom is not an attempt to change divine motive, as if God required an extortion from humans in exchange for their lives. Nor is the ransom intended to be an indicator of human motive. The problem is not motive at all. Rather, the need for ransom arises when a holy God and the profane world are brought together. They are incompatible. Purification allows Levites to approach closer to the sanctuary than ordinary Israelites and even to carry it when journeying through the wilderness. Their guard duty provides a buffer zone between God in the tabernacle and the Israelite camp.

Verses 20-22 narrate the fulfillment of the divine commands concerning the Levites. Verses 23-26 are an addendum to the chapter, stating the age requirements for levitical service—from twenty-five years of age to fifty.

94. See Milgrom, *Numbers*, 369-71.

REFLECTIONS

1. The tribal offerings in Num 7:2-88 provide a model for church giving. God does not compel gifts from the tribes. The tribes spontaneously give gifts to God. There is no immediate benefit for the tribes as a reward for their giving. And all gifts are of equal value; no gift is better than another. Gift-giving by the tribes, moreover, is one of their last actions at Mt. Sinai. It signals their readiness to journey with God through the wilderness.

G. Van der Leeuw states that giving is essentially three things: It is personal, because the gift is part of oneself; it creates communion, because the personal nature of the gift creates a bond between the giver and the recipient; and it is reciprocal, because gifts prompt gifts. Van der Leeuw continues that the exchange of gifts creates a bond between God and the people of God: "The principal feature [of giving] is not that some-one or other should receive something, but that the stream of life should continue to flow."[95]

The priestly writer's vision of gift giving fits Van der Leeuw's definition. Yahweh rescued Israel in the exodus. Israel receives providential care in the wilderness, and their camp is flooded with the life-giving power of holiness. These actions alone, however, do not conform to Van der Leeuw's definition of gift giving, because they have not yet generated an equal response in Israel. The saving power of God becomes a transforming gift for Israel when they participate in the same power of giving. It is the dynamic interaction of gift giving between God and Israel that transforms the camp and readies Israel for their journey. The apostle Paul also understood the power of giving. The death of Christ is God's gift to him. In return, Paul gives his life back to God. Gift prompts gift, and in the process new life is created (Gal 2:19-20).

We live in a materialistic culture that threatens the priestly vision of giving from many directions. Too many church budgets are raised through guilt, coercion, or the promise of rewards. We tend to emphasize the gift over the spontaneous act of giving. Pledge cards have levels of giving. Large donors acquire disproportionate privilege in the community. These are signs of weakness in the church. Nowhere is wealth a category for evaluating persons in the priestly camp. And our tendency to emphasize the gift actually hinders God's holiness from becoming a gift to us. This is not the principle of the priestly writers. We give in order to give, not to receive. In the process, the stream of life—holiness itself—becomes stronger. This is not a message for pledge Sunday. It is a message for every Sunday.

2. Contemporary worship revolves around preaching. The priestly writers remind us in Numbers 7–8 that worship rests on liturgical drama and sacrifice. The work of worship has its own rhythm of transformation, indicated by the order of sacrifices. Baruch Levine summarizes the liturgy of sacrifices in three steps: The sin offering purified, making the sanctuary ready for worship. The burnt offering followed as an invocation to God, signaling God's readiness to respond to worshipers. The offering of well-being culminated the process; it was a sacred meal shared by priest and worshipers in the presence of God.[96]

Sacrifice is also foundational for Christian worship, even though the slaughter of cattle is replaced by the blood of Jesus. The ordering of sacrifices structures our own worship. We approach God every Sunday with confession of sin, seeking divine pardon to purify us for worship. We offer prayers of invocation, the Word of God is proclaimed, and we share a sacred meal.

---

95. G. Van der Leeuw, *Religion in Essence and Manifestation,* trans. J. E. Turner (Princeton: Princeton University Press, 1986) 350-60.
96. Levine, *Numbers 1–20,* 263-64.

Preaching is essential to Christian worship. It provides vision, motivation, and inspiration for living. But preaching is not a sacrament, and it loses its power to transform when it is detached from the larger sacramental drama of worship. Preaching clarifies the power of God in our lives, but it is our participation in sacraments that brings us into communion with God. Worship is one of our gifts to God that strengthens holiness in our community.

3. The priestly writers understood the important role of symbols and icons in the worship of God. The Protestant church rests on the power of the Word. Jesus is the incarnate Word. Scripture is the written Word. And preaching is the spoken Word. But the emphasis on the Word often leads to the neglect of visual symbols for worship or even to rejection of religious icons as forms of idolatry. This is unfortunate, because God communicates through visual symbols. Numbers 7–8 is filled with sacred objects. The sacrificial altar, the cherubim, the ark, and the menorah all play a role in worship. These objects are not idols. They communicate the power and presence of God visually rather than through words. The interrelationship of iconography and divine speech in the revelation to Moses (Num 7:89) indicates the commitment of priestly writers to both words and sacramental icons in their theology of divine presence within the sanctuary.

The priestly writers provide us with a model to identify our own religious icons and to develop new ones. Many of the sacred objects in our local churches are universal symbols. They may be baptismal fonts and communion utensils. Each church will also have its own sacred objects. These may be windows, tapestries, paintings, statues, and furnishings. It is important to identify and use these objects for worship and teaching. They define community.

Priestly writers also provide a model for creating new religious symbols. We saw in the commentary that the cherubim and the ark represent new designs of traditional objects that reflect the changing circumstances of Israel. The contemporary church faces the same challenge that faced the priestly writers: Traditional symbols require constant reinterpretation as our culture changes. Television, computers, and other forms of communication require new designs for our traditional sacred objects. It is the priestly writers who provide biblical guidelines to meet this challenge.

4. There is no analogy for Levites in the contemporary church, which makes their role in the priestly camp difficult to understand. We have clergy in the church, whether priest or minister, and we have laity. But a Levite is neither. They represent a third category between priests and laity. Their dedication ceremony in Num 8:5-22 indicates that they are living sacrifices in the camp. Levites substitute for the divine claim on firstborn, serve the priesthood, and allow the camp to function by atoning for all Israelites.

Every church has Levites, whether we acknowledge it in the organizational structure of our church. Every church has members who substitute for others by taking on extra responsibility. They serve on committees beyond their appointed time. They teach Sunday school or vacation Bible school for an extra term. They clean the church on Saturday, paint a room, or set up coffee on Sunday. They are the first ones called in an emergency. Such persons relieve someone else of responsibility every time they take on an extra task. They ransom other members from God's claim on their time. They are living sacrifices of great value.

The apostle Paul understood the important role of Levites when he wrote in Rom 12:1: "Present your bodies as a living sacrifice, holy and acceptable to God, which is your spiritual worship" (NRSV). God claims all Christians as a living sacrifice. There are always members in our churches who fulfill this claim for others.

Name your Levites. Honor them publicly in special ceremonies. The priestly writers provide a model with their dedication ceremony in Num 8:5-22. Lay hands on them to signify their role as substitutes who ransom other members. Indicate in some concrete way the value of their service. The modern equivalent of two bulls for the public dedication of Levites would challenge the annual budget of many churches today.

Numbers 9:1–10:10, The Celebration of Passover and Preparation for the Wilderness March

COMMENTARY

Numbers 9:1–10:10 is transitional between the organization of the camp and the tabernacle cult and Israel's march through the wilderness. As a result, the literature can be interpreted in two different ways: as a conclusion to the revelation of law and the cult at Mt. Sinai (Exodus 19–Numbers 10) and as an overview of the priestly interpretation of the wilderness journey (Numbers 11). Each vantage provides a somewhat different interpretation. As a concluding section, the repetition of theophany functions as the final snapshot of how Yahweh is present in the tabernacle. The final word of priestly writers is that God is available both day and night, but is not to be taken for granted. As an introduction to the following material in Numbers, the commentary on the cloud and the trumpets provides guidelines of how Israel must follow God in the wilderness. Three sections of commentary follow: 9:1-14, the celebration of Passover; 9:15-23, the role of the cloud on the wilderness march; 10:1-10, the function of the trumpets.

9:1-14. Passover concludes the organization of the camp and prepares Israel for the wilderness march. The literary setting of the Passover instruction is important for its interpretation in priestly tradition. It is introduced during the exodus (Exodus 12), and it concludes the revelation at Mt. Sinai (Num 9:1-14). Passover originally saved the firstborn sons of Israel from death in Egypt (Exodus 12), and Passover defines Israel as the congregation of God after the revelation, construction, and dedication of the tabernacle at Sinai. Thus Passover is Israel's constitutional feast. Participation in it solidifies the congregation as the people of God, whether native Israelite or resident alien. It prepares them to journey with God in the wilderness.

These verses do not contain the ritual for the observance of Passover; its statutes are mentioned only briefly in vv. 3, 11-12. The text presupposes the instruction from Exod 12:1-20, where Passover (Exod 12:1-14) is combined with unleavened bread (Exod 12:15-20). Passover is celebrated in households (Exod 12:3-4). The Passover lamb was a one-year-old male, selected on the tenth day of the month and slaughtered at twilight on the fourteenth day (Exod 12:6). Its blood was placed on the doorframe (Exod 12:7). The meat with the intestines was roasted over a fire and eaten with unleavened bread and bitter herbs. Any remaining meat was to be burned the next morning (Exod 12:8-10).

Verses 1-14 separate into three parts: the observance of Passover (vv. 1-5); the problem of observance posed by those who are unclean (vv. 6-8); and the solution to the problem by the creation of a second observance one month later (vv. 9-14).

Verses 1-5 recount both the divine command to observe Passover and its fulfillment. It takes place on the fourteenth day of the first month, most likely in the spring, probably the month Nisan, which corresponds roughly to April. This date is one month earlier than the beginning of the book (1:1), where God addresses Moses on the first day of the second month. The point of emphasis, however, is on the observance of a second Passover one month later. The emphasis on the second month places 9:1-14 within the chronology of Numbers 1–10 (see the Commentary on 7:1).

Verses 6-8 confirm the focus on a second observance of Passover one month later. The text presents a situation in which some Israelites were unable to observe Passover because of having been contaminated by contact with a corpse. They complain to Moses and Aaron about their dilemma, prompting Moses to seek a solution from God.

Verses 9-14 give the divine solution. A second Passover is sanctioned one month later. The solution is narrated in 2 Chronicles 30 in relation to Hezekiah's reformation. The divine decree to Moses, however, goes well beyond the problem of corpse contamination. God states three additional stipulations: Those who are on a trip and thus unable to observe Passover may also participate in the feast during the second month; resident aliens who choose to meet the requirements may also participate in Passover; and lack of participation by any Israelite will result in his or her being cut off from the congregation. Each of these declarations provides insight into the meaning of Passover for the priestly writers.

First, the problem posed by travel suggests the centralization of Israel's cult, which occurred in the seventh century BCE under the influence of the deuteronomic movement. Cult centralization with regard to Passover is narrated in the story of Josiah's reform (2 Kings 23, which required that all Israelites journey to Jerusalem to celebrate Passover as a national feast. This same practice is evident in Deut 16:5-7 and may also lie behind Num 9:1-14. The celebration of Passover as a family feast in Exod 12:1-20, however, raises questions about the exact details of Passover observance by the priestly writers.

Second, the stipulation regarding the resident alien is a signal that the wilderness setting of the priestly history is not to be taken literally. Resident aliens presuppose Israel's life in the land of Canaan. There could be no resident aliens in the wilderness, since all Israel would fall under this category. The emphasis on the resident alien signifies that membership in the congregation is open to outsiders. The priestly writer's vision of the camp is not limited to the twelve tribes of Israel. The inclusive character of the congregation is also reflected in the priestly writer's description of Passover at the exodus (Exod 12:43-49).

Third, Passover is the only feast in which all Israelites are required to participate (v. 13). Participation in Passover defines membership in the congregation. Conversely, avoidance of this constitutional feast results in being "cut off" from the group—most likely excommunication, but possibly even death. The unique status of Passover clarifies the importance of its celebration at the close of Israel's time at Sinai, where the community has been defined and organized for the first time.

9:15-23. This section describes the cloud associated with the tabernacle. The cloud symbolizes the presence of God. It is a common symbol throughout the ancient Near East to indicate the presence of the divine. The Akkadian word *melammu* designates a halo or bright disk that would surround a god or any other person or object that shared in divine power. The root of the imagery is most likely associated with the sun, especially viewed through mist or at the time of an eclipse, when there is a diffuse radiance around it. The encircling radiance, rather than the sun itself, is the *melammu* that in ancient Israelite religion becomes the cloud.

Psalm 97:1-2 provides illustration. This psalm celebrates the presence of God in the Temple with the imagery of enthronement:

The LORD is king! Let the earth rejoice;
let the many coastlands be glad!
Clouds and thick darkness are all around him;
righteousness and justice are
the foundation of his throne.
(Ps 97:1-2 NRSV)

God is not literally seen in this psalm—Yahweh dwells in thick darkness. Yet the psalmist is confident of the divine presence because the radiance of God appears in the form of the cloud. The cloud both symbolizes divine presence in the cult and also hides God from the direct view of worshipers. Sometimes this dual function of the cloud—to reveal and to hide God—is represented by a cultic mask. The long tradition in Christian art of portraits of Jesus and the saints with halos surrounding their heads is a continuation of the symbolism of the *melammu*, or cloud.[97]

Priestly writers interrelate two aspects of divine presence: God's presence in the tabernacle (vv. 15-16) and the cloud as a guide in

97. For examples of iconography and a detailed examination of the cloud imagery in its ancient Near Eastern context see G. E. Mendenhall, "The Mask of Yahweh," in *The Tenth Generation: The Origins of the Biblical Tradition* (Baltimore: The Johns Hopkins University Press, 1973) 32-66.

Israel's wilderness march (vv. 17-22). Verse 23 provides a concluding summary by clarifying the divine authority behind the cloud.

Verses 15-16 state that when Moses set up the tabernacle, a cloud covered it continually, day and night. During the night, the cloud appeared as fire. The larger literary setting of this description is important for interpretation, since the cloud provides the framework for the priestly legislation at Mt. Sinai in Exodus 19–Numbers 10.

A "thick cloud" was first mentioned in the pre-priestly account of theophany in Exod 19:16. It was accompanied by thunder, lightning, and a blast of a trumpet to indicate the presence of God on the mountain. The image of the cloud is developed further by the priestly writers in their account of theophany on Mt. Sinai (Exod 24:15-18) and when God enters the tabernacle (Exod 40:34-38).

The priestly writers refine the imagery of the "thick cloud" (Exod 19:16) on Mt. Sinai in three ways in their description of theophany on the mountain (Exod 24:15-18). First, they state that the "glory of the LORD [כבוד יהוה *kĕbôd YHWH*]" resides within the cloud. When Moses ascends Sinai to receive plans for the tabernacle the cloud surrounds the *kĕbôd YHWH* (Exod 24:16). Second, the *kĕbôd YHWH* is a divine fire. The appearance of the glory of Yahweh was like a consuming fire on the top of Mount Sinai (Exod 24:17). And third, the cloud and the *kĕbôd YHWH* are not the same thing. The cloud first covers Mount Sinai (Exod 24:15), before the *kĕbôd YHWH* settles on it (Exod 24:16).

The cloud and the *kĕbôd YHWH* reappear in the tabernacle upon its completion (Exod 40:34-38). This theophany allows the priestly writers to transfer the presence of God from Sinai to the tabernacle. The *kĕbôd YHWH* now fills the tabernacle (Exod 40:35). The cloud and the *kĕbôd YHWH* remain separate. The cloud once again covers the *kĕbôd YHWH* (Exod 40:34). Yet the cloud also takes on a new role at the conclusion of this theophany. The "cloud of Yahweh" is able to lead Israel in the wilderness journey, appearing as fire at night (Exod 40:36-38).

The priestly writers return to the topic of the cloud in v. 15. They date this theophany to the same day as its first appearance on the

tabernacle (Exod 40:34-38). Verse 15 begins, "On the day [וביום *ûbĕyôm*] the tabernacle was set up, the cloud covered the tabernacle" (see Exod 40:2, 16). The similar dating suggests that priestly writers are providing further commentary on the presence of God in the tabernacle at the close of Israel's stay at Mt. Sinai. Comparison with Exod 40:34-38 suggests three points of emphasis in Num 9:15-16. First, the priestly writers state explicitly that the cloud continually covered the tabernacle (v. 16). God is always available to Israel in their wilderness march. Second, there is no mention of the *kĕbôd YHWH* in Num 9:15-16, as there was in Exod 40:34-35. They have been separated throughout the previous theophanies. The absence of the *kĕbôd YHWH* may be cautionary warning at the end of Israel's time at Mt. Sinai that Yahweh is elusiveness in the wilderness. The presence of the cloud over the tabernacle does not guarantee the glory of Yahweh within the sanctuary. Third, the role of the cloud as a wilderness guide is greatly expanded from Exod 40:34-38. The brief concluding description (Exod 40:36-38) becomes the central topic (Num 9:17-22).

Verses 17-22 provide a detailed summary of how the cloud guides Israel in the wilderness march. Verses 17-18 make clear that when the cloud arose from the sanctuary, Israel marched, and when it descended, they camped. Verses 19-22 reinforce the message through a variation in Israel's routine of travel and rest. Rest periods might include one night (v. 21), days, a month, or even longer periods of time (v. 22).

In following the cloud, Israel is "keeping the charge of the LORD" (vv. 19, 22). This expression may connote guard duty, as it does when used to describe the Levites (1:53). So precise a meaning in reference to the entire congregation of Israel seems unlikely. Here it appears that the charge of the congregation is the more general requirement that they follow the cloud in its rhythm of leading them through the wilderness. The imagery of travel with periods of unequal rest may refer to the priestly cultic calendar (see Numbers 28–29), where distinct feasts require different periods of rest. Observing these festivals throughout the liturgical year is how Israel "keeps the charge of the LORD" as they journey through the wilderness.

10:1-10. God commands Moses to make two silver trumpets (חצוצרת *ḥăṣōṣĕrōt*). Josephus describes trumpets as narrow tubes, roughly eighteen inches in length, with a bell-shaped end.[98] Such instruments are common in Egyptian iconography. Reference to these particular trumpets is most common in priestly texts. They contrast to the שׁוֹפר (*šōpăr*, Exod 19:16, 19; 20:18) and the יבל *(yōbēl*; Exod 19:13), also mentioned during theophany at Mt. Sinai. Both of these terms refer to a smaller instrument in the shape of a ram's horn. The silver trumpets are mentioned only one other time in Numbers, during Israel's holy war against Midian (31:6). They occur frequently in Chronicles (1 Chr 13:8; 15:24, 28; 16:6, 42; 2 Chr 5:12; 13:12; 15:14; 20:28; 29:27).

Verses 1-2 describe the construction and purpose of the trumpets. They are made of hammered silver and are used both to summon the congregation and to prepare the camp for travel.

Verses 3-7 are a series of different signals for which the trumpets were used during Israel's wilderness march. When both trumpets are blown, the Israelites are to gather at the door of the tent of meeting (v. 3); one trumpet blast calls only the leaders (v. 4); one long blast signals that the east side of the camp is to set out (v. 5); a second long blast starts the south side of the camp (v. 6).

Verse 8 assigns responsibility for the blowing of trumpets to the Aaronide priests. According to 2 Chr 5:12, the total Aaronide priests who blow the trumpet are numbered at 120.

Verses 9-10 turn from the wilderness setting to the land, describing two more functions of the trumpets once Israel is in Canaan: They will summon the people to holy war (v. 9), and they will call Israel to the observance of feast days (v. 10). The books of Chronicles illustrate the role of the trumpets in holy war. They are associated most frequently with the ark (1 Chr 13:8; 15:24, 28; 16:6, 42) and are blown during battles (2 Chr 13:12; 20:28). The trumpets summon the people for assembly during the dedication of the Jerusalem wall (Neh 12:35, 41) and when the foundation of the post-exilic Temple is completed (Ezra 3:10).

Verse 10 concludes with a divine promise: Blowing the trumpets will prompt God to remember Israel, punctuated by the statement, "I am Yahweh [אני יהוה *ănî YHWH*], your God." The final phrase is a revelation of the divine name, Yahweh, known as the self-introduction of God.[99] It is part of Israel's cultic life at least as early as the eighth century BCE. The prophet Hosea used it to express Yahweh's exclusive claim on Israel (Hos 12:10; 13:4, and the exilic prophets Ezekiel (e.g., Ezek 37:6) and Second Isaiah (e.g., Isa 42:8) used it frequently. When the phrase "your God" is added to the self-introduction, the relationship between Yahweh and Israel is emphasized.

The priestly writers use the self-introduction of Yahweh throughout the events of the exodus and revelation at Mt. Sinai. The commission to Moses (Exod 6:2, 7); the plagues (e.g., Exod 7:17; 10:2); and salvation at the sea (Exod 14:4, 18) are actions that reveal the name Yahweh. The establishment of the tabernacle cult (Exod 29:46), with its laws (e.g., Lev 19:11, 13, 16; 18:2, 5; 25:17, 38), also reveal the name Yahweh. Israel acquires power to communicate with God through the gift of the divine name, Yahweh. In the book of Numbers, the divine claim on the Israelite firstborn (3:13) was a revelation of the name Yahweh. Numbers 10:10 now closes the entire revelation at Mt. Sinai with a similar theophany of the name.

98. Josephus *Antiquities of the Jews* 3.291. See the discussion of musical instruments by Ivor H. Jones, "Musical Instruments," *ABD* 4:934-39, esp. 936.

99. Walter Zimmerli, *I Am Yahweh*, ed. Walter Brueggemann, trans. D. W. Stott (Altanta: John Knox, 1982).

REFLECTIONS

1. Passover continues to be a constitutional feast for Christians. The Lord's supper is rooted in a Passover meal between Jesus and his disciples (Matthew 26; Mark 14; Luke 22). Jesus is the paschal lamb (John 1:29; 1 Cor 5:7). Even his bones are not broken in crucifixion, fulfilling priestly law (John 19:36; cf. Num 9:12). Participation in the Lord's supper defines the community. It is life-giving and dangerous, requiring preparation and self-examination. And it is inclusive (1 Cor 11:17-34). The Lord's supper is also expanded beyond the Passover rite of the priestly writers to include the death and resurrection of Jesus. The observance of Passover on Maundy Thursday of holy week demonstrates both its central role in Christian tradition and its reinterpretation. Churches gather to observe the seder meal (Passover) on Thursday evening. But it is followed by the three-day passion of Jesus, Good Friday through Easter Sunday, rather than the seven days of unleavened bread.

2. The imagery of the cloud over the tabernacle emphasizes the presence of God with Israel. It is not a symbol of God in heaven, separated from this world. The cloud over the tabernacle empowers Israel to "keep the charge of Yahweh" concretely in their march through the wilderness. The tradition of the cloud reappears in the transfiguration of Jesus (Matt 17:1-8; Mark 9:2-8; Luke 9:28-36). Too often this tradition is interpreted apart from its background in priestly tradition. Jesus' journey up the mountain is misinterpreted to indicate his separation from this world. The message of the transfiguration is just the reverse. It attests to the descent of God into our world in the person of Jesus, like the cloud over the tabernacle.

The tradition of the cloud in Luke-Acts provides illustration. The transfiguration of Jesus (Luke 9:28-37) employs the imagery of the cloud to highlight the presence of God, not separation. Jesus is on the mountaintop praying (Luke 9:29; see Exod 24:15-18). Moses and Elijah join him (Luke 9:30). Divine glory appears to the disciples (Luke 9:32; see Exod 24:17; 40:34-35) and is covered by the cloud (Luke 9:35; see Exod 24:15, 18; 40:34-38). The visual imagery of theophany culminates in a divine voice (Luke 9:35; see Exod 24:16; Num 7:89). The cloud returns during the ascension of Jesus (Acts 1:6-11) to cover him while he rises to heaven (Acts 1:9). The disciples are drawn away from this world by the event. They stand "gazing up toward heaven" (Acts 1:10). Two angels bring them back to earth with the question, "Men of Galilee, why do you stand looking up toward heaven?" (Acts 1:11). Once they turn their focus to Jerusalem rather than to heaven, they too are transfigured with the fire of the Holy Spirit (Acts 2:1-3). The message of the ascension is the same as that of the transfiguration. Both accentuate the immanence of God in this world, not the separation. The message of the cloud in biblical literature is that God is not encountered gazing into heaven. Following the cloud anchors us firmly in this world.

3. Priestly writers envision the life of faith as a wilderness journey in which God is the guide (Num 9:15-23). Success on this journey is moving in rhythm with God. Two features are noteworthy in preaching and teaching this material. First, the journey is long. The impression of the literary style in Num 9:15-23, with its complex syntax and many repetitions, is that Israel is about to embark on a long journey. The journey will include repeated stops of days, weeks, and even longer periods. Second, the journey has no clear ending. The emphasis is more on the rhythm of the cloud than on its destination. Israel keeps the charge of Yahweh by staying in harmony with the cloud's movement. The absence of a clear ending suggests that the life of faith rests more on the process of journey through the wilderness than on its conclusion. Yet, the final instruction on the trumpets forces a qualification of this conclusion. Journey for its own sake cannot be the final word of salvation in the priestly history. There is the divine promise of land, and it is introduced in conjunction with the trumpets. They bridge the wilderness march (Num 10:1-7) and life in the land (Num 10:9-10). The different signals of the trumpets even provide directions for finding the gift of the land in the wilderness. Moving and resting with God, following the signals of the trumpets for assemblies, marching, engaging in holy war, and observing feast days bring the promise of land near at hand.

4. Trumpets are important throughout the revelation at Mt. Sinai. They signal the presence of God and direct the people of God. The ram horns are blown during the theophany on the mountain (Exod 19:13, 16; 20:18). The priestly description of the silver trumpets adds further details for how God directs the people of God through the sound of the horn.

Trumpets continue the same role in the New Testament. They signal the end of history in Matt 24:30-31. This apocalyptic vision of the end also embraces the imagery of the cloud and the *kĕbôd YHWH*. Jesus is the Son of Man, who descends from heaven in glory on a cloud. Accompanying angels take over the priestly role of blowing the trumpets to assemble the elect from around the world. The apostle Paul takes up the imagery of the trumpet to signal the raising of the dead at the end of history (1 Cor 15:52). The book of Revelation provides the most extended account of trumpets at the end of history. Six angels blow trumpets in Revelation 8, prompting disruptions of nature and judgment on the wicked. A seventh angel sounds a trumpet in Rev 11:14-19 to announce the coming of the kingdom of God.

5. The legislation concerning the camp and the tabernacle concludes with a revelation of the divine name, Yahweh (Num 10:10). The phrase "I am Yahweh" is described as a self-introduction in the Commentary. Revelation of the divine name is a gift from God. God grants power to those who possess the name. Jacob's wrestling with God at the Jabbok River (Gen 32:22-32) illustrates the power of knowing names. Jacob wrestles all night with an unnamed divine being. Jacob overpowers his opponent and requests a name. He is never told the name, but in the process Jacob reveals his own name. As a consequence the opponent overpowers Jacob and renames him "Israel." Jacob concludes that next morning that his opponent was God, but the name "Yahweh" was never revealed to him. He names the location of his struggle simply "Peniel" ("The Face of God"). God reveals the special name, "Yahweh," to Moses at the outset of the exodus (Exod 3:13-15). The plagues reveal the power of the name "Yahweh" throughout the events of the exodus. The legislation at Mt. Sinai also reveals the name. Possession of the name "Yahweh" empowers Israel. They become God's people."

New Testament writers also employ the self-introduction to reveal the name "Jesus." The power of name is revealed to the disciples when Jesus approaches them walking on water (Mark 6:50). The disciples fear, thinking Jesus is a ghost. Jesus responds, "I am do not fear." The statement "I am" is a self-introduction like "I am Yahweh." When the high priest later asks Jesus whether he is the Messiah (Mark 14:62), Jesus responds, "I am." The use of "I am" as a divine name is developed most extensively in the Gospel of John.[100] Jesus is the "I am" (John 7:24, 28, 58; 13:19). Revelation of the name "Jesus" empowers believers to make requests to God (John 14:13; 17:23). Christian prayer arises from the power of the name. It is God's gift to us. When we punctuate our prayer "in the name of Jesus," we claim the power of God. We are empowered, like Israel at Sinai, to be the people of God. Jesus promises that whatever we ask in his name, God will do (John 15:16). Prayer offered in the name of Jesus and answered by God brings glory to God (John 14:13). Priestly writers would say that it strengthens holiness in our community and in our churches.

---

100. See Raymond E. Brown, *The Gospel According to John (I–XII)*, ed. D. N. Freedman (New York: Doubleday, 1966) 533-38.

NUMBERS 10:11–21:35

THE WILDERNESS JOURNEY OF THE FIRST GENERATION

OVERVIEW

The holiness of God was the central theme of Num 1:1–10:10. The construction of the tabernacle (Exodus 25–40), the implementation of the sacrificial system, and the consecration of priests (Leviticus), as well as the organization of the camp and dedication of Levites (Numbers 1–10) allowed for the *kĕbôd YHWH* to descend from the summit of Sinai and dwell in the midst of Israel. Throughout this section, the people have remained in their encampment at the base of the mountain.

Israel departs from Mt. Sinai in Num 10:11–21:35. This section depicts the journey of the first generation of Israelites as a tragic story leading to death. The section is dominated by conflicts among God, Israel, and Moses that arise on the wilderness journey. Such conflicts were not possible as long as Israel was encamped at Mt. Sinai. Three of these conflicts are prominent: Challenges concerning leadership appear in chaps. 11–12 and 16–17. They frame a more central

conflict (chaps. 13–14) over how Israel is to acquire the promised land of Canaan. Signs of hope are interspersed in legislation that points ahead to Israel's life in the land (chaps. 15; 18–19).

Conflicts over leadership center on Moses, whose authority is challenged twice. The charismatic and prophetic leadership of Moses is central to Numbers 11–12. Chapters 16–17 focus on his non-charismatic, priestly leadership. Resolution of conflicts through divine judgment serves to define more clearly these distinct leadership roles within the wilderness community. Chapters 13–14 describe the failure of the first generation of Israelites to secure the promised land of Canaan. Their failure, however, provides guidelines for success by a future generation (chaps. 15; 18–19). Chapters 20–21 provide transition from the failed journey of the first generation of Israelites to the second generation, who successfully undertake holy war.

NUMBERS 10:11-36, LEAVING SINAI

COMMENTARY

There are two accounts of Israel's departure from Mt. Sinai. Numbers 10:11-28 is the priestly account. It incorporates language, characters, and tribal organizations from 1:1–10:10. The priestly writers recount Israel's march from Sinai to Paran as a carefully orchestrated military maneuver with the tabernacle and the ark at the center of their march. They focus on the congregation of Israel as a whole and locate every tribe in

the processional march, with God at the center. The repetition of language from Numbers 1–10 gives their version of departure a retrospective focus, as though the priestly writers wished to conclude the organization of the camp by showing how the Israelites moved through the wilderness.

Numbers 10:29-36 is the first occurrence of the pre-priestly history. It describes Israel's departure from Mt. Yahweh, with the ark of the covenant leading them three days in advance. The pre-priestly account has incorporated an even older hymn (10:35-36) about the role of the ark in holy war. No mention is made of the Israelites on the march. The focus, instead, is on the guidance of God. Divine leadership gives this account a forward focus, anticipating the conflicts over leadership that will take center stage in the following chapters.

10:11-12. The priestly account of leaving Sinai is tied to the closing celebrations surrounding the tabernacle in 9:1–10:10. The date of departure is on Month 2, Day 20 of the second year after the exodus, allowing for the completion of the second Passover prescribed in 9:1-14. The cloud guides Israel, as was described in 9:15-23.

Verse 12 indicates Israel's travel route through the wilderness. The priestly writers state that the people set out by stages from the wilderness of Sinai and that the cloud settled next in the wilderness of Paran. The priestly writers repeat this information in 12:16: "The people set out from Hazeroth, and camped in the wilderness of Paran." The wilderness of Paran thereby frames the pre-priestly version of Israel's departure from Mt. Yahweh (v. 33) and the events at Kibrothhattaveh and Hazeroth in chaps. 11–12 (these locations are stated in 11:35.) The priestly writers also change the setting of the spy story (chaps. 13–14; see 13:3, 26) and the rebellion of Korah (chaps. 16–19) from Kadesh to Paran. Israel leaves the wilderness of Paran in 20:1, when they arrive at Kadesh/Zin.

The priestly writers indicate important events by the rest stops in the wilderness journey. The summary of travel indicates that Paran is the most important setting for the priestly writers in the wilderness travel of the first generation (10:11–21:35). Although the priestly writers provide some commentary to the events in chaps. 11–12, they point ahead to the loss of the promised land (chaps. 13–15) and the rebellion of Korah against the Aaronide priesthood (chaps. 16–19) in the wilderness of Paran.

The exact location of the wilderness of Paran is unclear. It is described as a desert site between Midian and Egypt in 1 Kgs 11:18. This corresponds with similar references to Paran in Abram's war with the five kings

(Gen 14:6) and to Ishmael and Hagar's home (Gen 21:21). The priestly writers' insertion of Paran in the spy story (Numbers 13–14) indicates some association with Kadesh, suggesting a larger area in the northern Sinai peninsula, rather than a specific station in the wilderness.

The wilderness of Paran also has theological significance. In ancient poetry, Paran is Yahweh's desert mountain. God is described as "the Holy One from Mount Paran" (Hab 3:3). In another poem (Deut 33:2), Yahweh wages holy war from Mt. Paran to rescue Israel. The priestly writers may be influenced by this tradition of theophany in emphasizing the wilderness of Paran. It was noted in the Introduction that the travel route has theological meaning for both the pre-priestly and the priestly writers. But the priestly writers have also reinterpreted the theological significance of Paran from the ancient poetry. It is neither a mountain home of God nor a setting for salvation. Instead, Paran has become the wilderness region where the first generation rebelled against God. As a result, God does not rescue Israel from Mt. Paran, but instead wages holy war against them in the wilderness of Paran.

10:13-28. This section describes the organization of Israel on the march. The image of the congregation as a regimented militia ties this account of its departure to the census in chap. 1 and to the organization of the camp in chap. 2. Numbers 10:14 contains the military phrase "the standard of the camp" (דגל מחנה *degel maḥănē*) from Numbers 2:3, 10, 18, 25 to describe the four tribes that lead each regiment (Judah, Reuben, Ephraim, and Dan). The phrase "whole company" (צבא *ṣābāʾ*), designating those under the lead tribes, also repeats military language from Numbers 2. Thus the wilderness march bears overtones of holy war for the priestly writers.

Israel's organization on the march includes a description of the four standards, the leaders of each tribe (see Commentary on 1:1–2:34), and the transportation of the tabernacle with its holy objects by the three levitical families (see Commentary on 3:1–4:49). The priestly vision of Israel on the march in the wilderness can be illustrated in the following manner:

Standard 1 (Front)
Judah (Nahshon ben Amminadab)
Issachar (Nethanel ben Zuar)
Zebulun (Eliab ben Helon)
The Tabernacle
Gershonites
Merarites

Standard 2
Reuben (Elizur ben Shedeur)
Simeon (Shelumiel ben Zurishaddai)
Gad (Elisaph ben Deuel)
The Holy Objects
Kohathites

Standard 3
Ephraim (Elishama ben Ammihud)
Manasseh (Gamaliel ben Pedahzur)
Benjamin (Abidan ben Gideoni)

Standard 4 (Rear Guard)
Dan (Ahiezer ben Ammishaddai)
Asher (Pagiel ben Ochran)
Naphtali (Ahira ben Enan)

10:29-32. Verses 29-36 constitute a second account of Israel's departure, this time from Mt. Yahweh rather than from Mt. Sinai. Verses 29-32 report an exchange between Moses and his father-in-law, Hobab the son of Reuel. Moses requests his guidance and promises him a share in the goodness that Yahweh promises Israel. Hobab refuses and states his intention to return to Midian (v. 30). Moses repeats the request (vv. 31-32), adding that Hobab knows the terrain and can serve as the eyes for Israel in their wilderness journey. Moses again promises him a share in God's goodness, but receives no response from Hobab. The guiding role of the ark immediately following this exchange (vv. 33-36) suggests that God replaces Hobab in leading Israel on their wilderness journey.

There are several pentateuchal traditions about Moses' father-in-law. He is introduced as Reuel, the Midianite priest (Exod 2:15-22). His name changes to Jethro, the Midianite priest in the revelation to Moses on the mountain of God (Exod 3:1; 4:18) and in his visit to Moses after the exodus (Exod 18:1). Thus the name "Hobab, the son of Reuel, the Midianite" (Num 10:29-32) is unexpected and constitutes a third name. This name also

occurs in Judg 4:11 to describe the father-in-law of Moses, where Hobab is a Kenite rather than a Midianite.

All pentateuchal stories about the father-in-law of Moses belong to the pre-priestly history. Thus the retention of three different names has puzzled interpreters. One suspects a rich tradition of folklore on how Israelites and Midianites are related. Midianites play a prominent and positive role in Israel's earliest accounts of their origins. They appear three times in the pre-priestly history: (1) prior to the exodus, when Moses receives his initial command to free Israel (Exod 2:15-22; 3:1–4:20); (2) before the revelation at Sinai (Exodus 18); and (3) at the conclusion of the revelation at Sinai (Num 10:29-32). The Midianites provided safe haven for Moses (Exodus 2–3). Moses marries the Midianite Zipporah, and they have two sons, Gershom and Eliezar. Zipporah rescues Moses from an attack by God (Exod 4:24-26).

Stories about Moses' father-in-law frame the account of revelation at the sacred mountain. Jethro provides guidance in matters of worship and government (Exodus 18) prior to covenant ceremony between God and Israel (Exodus 19–24; 32–34). And the refusal of Hobab to lead Moses (Num 10:29-32) at the end appears less an abandonment than a transfer of leadership from himself to God, symbolized by the ark. These stories would have followed in rapid succession in the pre-priestly history without the extended description by the priestly writers of the tabernacle cult (Exodus 25–31; 35–40; Leviticus; Numbers 1–10). The Midianites receive a negative interpretation by the priestly writers. They plot with Balak to destroy Israel in the story of Balaam (Numbers 22–24), and Israel wages holy war against them (Numbers 25).

10:33-36. The departure of Israel (vv. 33-34) is followed by a poem about the ark (vv. 35-36). The poem is highlighted in the Hebrew Text (MT) by a pair of "inverted nuns" (*nun* is the letter *n* in the Hebrew alphabet). Such bracketing is rare in the Hebrew Bible; it may be a way by which scribes indicated the insertion of older poems into their present literary context.[101]

---

101. Levine, *Numbers 1–20*, 318-19, for examples of this same scribal practice in Greek texts.

Israel's travel route through the wilderness is described in vv. 33-34. Israel departs from Mt. Yahweh on a three-day journey, with the ark leading them an additional three days. The cloud also hovers over Israel during the day (v. 33). The "three-day" journey most likely has religious and, perhaps, liturgical significance, since the exodus from Egypt was also a three-day journey (Exod 5:3; 15:22). No destination is provided (Num 10:12). The aim of the ark, "to seek out" (תור *tûr*) a resting place may be an addition by the priestly writers. They use this verb repeatedly to describe the activity of the spies in chaps. 13–15.

The pre-priestly interpretation of the ark is central in this story. It leads Israel in their wilderness march, in contrast to the priestly version, where the ark travels in the middle of the tribal procession (3:27-32; 11:11-28). The poem (vv. 35-36) indicates the role of the ark in war. It represents God's power as a holy warrior who scatters enemies before returning to Israel. The poem is a couplet and may have served as a battle cry. The first line describes Yahweh's ability to attack the enemy. The NRSV translation "Arise" (NIV, "Rise up") does not convey the military imagery of the Hebrew קומה (*qûmâ*). It signifies advancing for the purpose of attacking. Psalm 68:1 employs the same language to describe the power of God in holy war. The second line envisions the successful return of Yahweh from battle along with the Israelite army. The verb "return" (שוב *šûb*) indicates that Yahweh rests on the ark. It is the divine throne, which symbolizes God's presence with Israel.

The ark is one of the most significant cult objects in Israel's history. The poem in vv. 35-36 may be an ancient liturgy, indicating the ark's original role in holy war. Such an interpretation corresponds with the stories in 1 Samuel 4–7, where the ark also represents the presence of God in war. The monarchy reinterpreted the ark by incorporating it into the iconography of the Temple as the footstool of the enthroned God (Ps 99:1-5). Previous commentary on Num 7:89 took note of how priestly writers renamed the ark as "the ark of the congregation" and how they gave it a more central place in the tabernacle as the location where God would speak with Moses and as the source of divine mercy.

The pre-priestly writers provide yet another interpretation of the ark in v. 33 by naming it "the ark of the covenant [ארון ברית *ʾărôn běrît*]" This name is common in Deuteronomy (e.g., Deut 10:8, 31:9, 25) and in the Deuteronomistic History (e.g., Josh 3:3; 4:7; Judg 20:27; 1 Sam 4:3; 1 Kgs 3:15; 6:19; 8:1). The emphasis is on the Ten Commandments, which are contained within the ark on two stone tablets. The ark is holy because it contains the stipulations between God and Israel. The use of the term "ark of the covenant" in the pre-priestly history suggests that its authors share the theological perspective contained in Deuteronomy and in the Deuteronomistic History. God is present with the people of God through divine words codified as law. The law of God leads Israel in the wilderness march to the promised land.

REFLECTIONS

1. Israel's departure from Sinai envisions the life of faith as a journey with God. The imagery of journeying with God remains central to the Christian life. The life of Jesus is portrayed in the Gospels as a journey through the wilderness to Jerusalem. The disciples encounter Jesus as they journey on the road from Emmaus to Jerusalem (Luke 24). Numbers 10:11-36 contains specific insights for exploring the contemporary significance of this theme.

First, the larger literary context clarifies that journeying is not the first action for Israel in following God. The first action is worship. Numbers 1–10 is foundational for Israel's journey. The cultic icons of the tabernacle, the cloud, and the ark lead Israel. Without worship, the life of faith has no fuel or direction.

Second, Israel's journey with God is in the wilderness. It is not in the land. The theological significance of the wilderness (see Introduction) is important for interpretation.

Yahweh is a desert God. Journeying with Yahweh takes one away from the security of home, land, and country. It destablizes Israel and transforms them. The same is true for the contemporary church. Baptism makes us citizens of Christ's church. Residency in the church creates new allegiances. The old passes away. We are propelled on a journey with God that may lead us away from the security of home and country.

Third, the positive role of Hobab, Moses' father-in-law, indicates the inclusive nature of community in the wilderness journey. Leadership may arise from unexpected persons, like Hobab the Midianite. Twice Moses offers Hobab a share in the goodness of God. The second offer is left open-ended. It is not Moses and Israel who decide to include Hobab in the wilderness camp, but the Midianite himself.

Fourth, God is three days ahead of Israel. The ark advances to protect Israel from enemies and to search for a resting place. It was noted in the commentary that this image has theological significance in the pre-priestly history. It continues in the New Testament. Jesus leads the church from the other side of Easter. The passion of Jesus from Good Friday through Easter also places him three days ahead of us. According to the writer of Hebrews, this makes Jesus a pioneer who lives on the frontier of a new salvation (Heb 2:10). He destroys death and seeks out a resting place for the church. Following Jesus, according to the writer of Hebrews, is like journeying with God through the wilderness (Hebrews 3–4).

2. The prominence of war imagery to depict the life of faith is an obstacle for teaching and preaching. Israel is a militia (Num 10:11-28), and the leading of God is glorified as victory over an enemy (Num 10:29-36). This imagery continues to be prominent in the church. The passion of Jesus is envisioned as a war against death, and Christians are soldiers of Christ. Teaching about holy war requires careful reflection on both its violent imagery and its social implications. Holy war is a theological metaphor to describe the conflict between God and death. The violent imagery indicates the power of death. Its grip on the world is strong; it is able to wage war against God and influence human society. God battles death in its many forms.

There are always social implications to holy war. Specific actions vary widely in the Bible. In Num 10:11-36, Israel must join in God's battle against death. Israel is Yahweh's militia. The demands are concrete and influence their way of life. But holy war does not describe political and military actions in support of the nation and its land. The Israelites have no land in Num 10:11-36. They are Yahweh's militia in the wilderness. They wage holy war by maintaining God's holiness, which may put them in conflict with others. The wars against the king of Arad (Num 21:1-3), King Sihon (Num 21:21-32), and the Midianites (Numbers 31) are instances of holy war.

The life and passion of Jesus are another model for waging holy war. Conflict is also central to the story of Jesus. He wages holy war by suffering for others, and in his suffering he defeats the power of death. In the case of Jesus, holy war theology becomes the basis for pacifism. Some Christian communities continue to wage holy war against death by turning the other cheek in social situations of violence. The two examples indicate broad social implications of holy war in the Bible from activism to pacifism. What they have in common is that conflicts of holy war are not determined by national policy. They are made clear through revelation in the church.

3. The symbolism of the ark is important for preaching, teaching, and worship. The commentary for Numbers 7:89 and 10:29-36 has outlined its significance throughout Israel's history of worship. It continues to inform Christian worship in two different ways. First, the holy war imagery of the ark is incorporated into the cross of Jesus. The cross symbolizes God's defeat of death. Its central place in our worship indicates the victory of God and the cost to God in winning this war. Thus there is victory in this symbol, but always at the price of suffering. The cross also becomes the standard or banner for the Christian church in our faith journey, in much the same way as the ark led Israel. The message is not one of triumphalism, but of challenge. The ark led Israel on a risky wilderness journey, filled with testing. The same is true when the cross becomes the emblem of the church. Jesus tells his disciples to pick up their cross and follow him. Second, the ark also indicated the central place of God's law in leading Israel. The title "ark of the covenant" pointed to the Ten Commandments contained in the chest. This symbolism of the ark continues in the central role of Scripture within Christian tradition. It is revelation that provides a road map for the Christian journey through the wilderness.

4. Biblical writers embrace both history and mythology to describe the power of God in the life of Israel. They describe historical periods and specific locations and infuse them with theological meaning. Thus their stories combine historical realism with supernatural actions of God. The use of Paran by the priestly writers is an example. It is both a location in the wilderness and the home of God. The same is true for many other locations in Israel's journey through the wilderness. There is a reason for this method of writing. Biblical writers always look for God in history, but they refuse to reduce the power of God to the events of history. This method of writing theology has become unfamiliar in the modern period of the church. We separate history and mythology, and often we force a choice between the two. The fundamentalist and modernist debate provides illustration. One perspective stresses solely the historical reliability of the wilderness stories. The other reduces historical tradition to ideas. Both interpretations are dissatisfactory because they are at odds with biblical literature. Preaching the wilderness stories requires the same easy movement between myth and history evidenced by the biblical writers.

NUMBERS 11:1–19:22, MURMURING AND DEATH IN THE WILDERNESS

OVERVIEW

These chapters outline the tragic wilderness journey of the first generation. The literature is organized around three conflicts, in which Israel rebels against God and the leadership of Moses.

Chapters 11–12 explore the prophetic leadership of Moses through a series of complaints. Numbers 11:1-3 introduces the section with a general story of complaint by the rabble in the camp, who are destroyed by fire. Israel murmurs about the lack of food in 11:4-35, prompting Moses to complain about his leadership role. Transfer of his prophetic spirit to the seventy elders becomes the central topic. Numbers 12 emphasizes the unique status of Moses as a prophetic leader when Miriam and Aaron challenge his privileged role to speak with God.

Chapters 13–15 tell how the first generation of Israelites lost the gift of the land.

Chapters 13–14 recount the spying out of the land, the fear of Israel to wage holy war, and their inability to see the goodness of the land. Chapter 15 concludes the episode with legislation about sacrifices that Israel must perform when they eventually enter the land.

Chapters 16–17 explore priestly leadership in the wilderness camp. Chapter 16 tells of a rebellion against Moses by Dathan and Abiram, two leaders from the tribe of Reuben. Their story is combined with another rebellion by the Levite Korah, who challenges the priestly leadership of Moses and Aaron. Chapter 17 is the story of Aaron's budding staff, which confirms his leadership role as priest.

Chapters 18–19 are laws providing guidelines for approaching God in the tabernacle. Chapter 18 outlines the requirements for tithing, and chap. 19 contains the ritual for purification from corpse contamination. Guidelines for purification from the dead conclude the episode on a note of hope. Contamination from death can be purged from the community with the ashes of the red heifer. Murmuring and death in the wilderness are not God's last word for Israel.

Two themes are developed in 11:1–19:22. The first is death in the wilderness. Complaints by the first generation about Mosaic leadership and their rejection of the promised land create a tragic story. The people's rebellion results in their aimless wandering and eventual death. The second theme is the leadership of Moses. Rebellion is often against his leadership.

The Murmuring Stories. Numbers 11:1–19:22 is organized around episodes of complaint, known as the murmuring stories.[102] Threatening situations in the wilderness cause Israel to protest their present condition. Their complaint is accompanied by a longing to return to slavery in Egypt. The murmuring stories begin at the exodus when the Israelites complain to Moses at the Red Sea during the attack by Pharaoh. They prefer their life of slavery in Egypt over the risky journey with God through the wilderness (Exod 14:11-12). Two rounds of murmuring stories follow their initial complaint at the Red Sea. The first sequence occurs in the march from Egypt to Sinai (Exodus 15–17). The second takes place during Israel's journey from Sinai to the plains of Moab (Num 11–19:22). The two sequences are separated by the revelation at Mt. Sinai (Exodus 19–Numbers 10). The formation of covenant and the creation of the tabernacle cult change God's response to the murmuring stories from assistance to judgment.

The Israelites raise three complaints in their initial journey from Egypt to Sinai (Exodus 15–17). The first concerns bitter or diseased water (Exod 15:22-26).[103] The second is about the lack of food in the wilderness (Exodus 16), and the third complaint is over the absence of water (Exod 17:1-7). The

initial murmuring stories address the major environmental problems that arise in following God through the wilderness. Each problem is an appropriate concern about divine providence, prompting assistance from God. In the first story, Yahweh provides a way for Moses to purify the water. The crisis of food is solved by the miracle of manna, and in response to the third complaint, Moses draws water out of a rock. Israel's complaints do not indicate their lack of faith in God's leading. Instead, they occur during a period of courtship between God and Israel. God tests Israel in the incident of bitter water (Exod 15:22-26), and Israel tests God in their request for water from the rock (Exod 17:1-7). Complaint does not lead to divine judgment, but to rescue. The first sequence of murmuring stories corresponds to the prophet Hosea's interpretation of the wilderness as a period of innocence, when God courted Israel (Hos 2:14-15).

Numbers 11:1–19:22 repeats the murmuring stories about food (11:4-35) and water (20:2-13). The problem of health also returns in 21:4-9. Other murmuring stories include a general complaint about the wilderness (11:1-3), a protest about the threatening inhabitants in the land of Canaan (chap. 14), and further criticism of the leadership of Moses and Aaron (chaps. 16–17). Murmuring after the events of Sinai changes God's response from assistance to judgment. The murmuring stories in 11:1–19:22 illustrate the loss of faith of the first generation and their eventual death in the wilderness.

The murmuring stories also provide a loose structure to the death of the first generation. Two stories of complaint frame the second wilderness period. The complaint of the rabble occurs as Israel leaves Sinai (11:1-3). There is also a complaint about food as the people leave the wilderness (21:4-9). Both stories are general complaints about the conditions of life in the wilderness. Each prompts immediate divine judgment. The first murmuring brings divine fire on the camp, while the second brings forth deadly fiery serpents. The immediacy of divine judgment indicates how the mood has changed from the period of courtship in Exodus 15–17. Murmuring is no longer appropriate testing of God's providence after the revelation of law, construction

102. George W. Coats, *Rebellion in the Wilderness: The Murmuring Motif in the Wilderness Traditions of the Old Testament* (Nashville: Abingdon, 1968).

103. Norbert Lohfink, " 'I am Yahweh, your Physician' (Exodus 15:26): God, Society and Human Health in a Postexilic Revision of the Pentateuch (Exod. 15:2b, 26)," in *Theology of the Pentateuch: Themes of the Priestly Narrative and Deuteronomy,* trans. Linda M. Maloney (Minneapolis: Fortress, 1994) 35-95.

of the cult, and establishment of covenant at Mt. Sinai. It is rebellion against God and the leadership of Moses.

The Leadership of Moses. Divine judgment on the first generation allows for development in the leadership role of Moses as an intercessor. His prayer often stops divine judgment. The enhanced role of Moses as intercessor alerts the reader to issues of leadership that run throughout the murmuring stories

in 11:1–19:22. The complaint about meat (chaps. 11–12) explores Moses' prophetic leadership. He models intercession by averting divine anger when Israel rejects the promised land and God wishes to destroy them immediately (chaps. 13–15). The priestly leadership of Moses and Aaron is central to the rebellion by Korah (chaps. 16–17). Thus models of leadership emerge from the conflicts between the first generation and Moses.

Numbers 11:1–12:16, Conflict Over Prophetic Leadership

COMMENTARY

Numbers 11–12 is a collection of stories compiled to explore the prophetic leadership of Moses. Prophetic leadership is charismatic. The word *charisma* means "gift" in Greek. Moses is a gifted person. His power arises from his personality, and not from an inherited office of leadership. He is set apart from others, filled with the divine Spirit. He speaks with God face to face; he speaks for God to the community; and he intercedes on behalf of the people.

Chapters 11–12 describe the nature of Moses' charismatic leadership from different perspectives. Numbers 11:1-3 functions as an introduction, defining the mood and interaction of characters. Numbers 11:4-35 juxtaposes two different complaints—one by the people about the lack of meat and another by Moses about the burden of leadership. The complaint of Moses dominates the story. It provides the occasion to explore how his charismatic spirit can be transferred to others. The conflict between Miriam, Aaron, and Moses in Numbers 12 emphasizes the unique quality of Moses' prophetic spirit. Taken together, these stories explore the nature of charismatic leadership in the wilderness community.

11:1-3. This is an odd story, striking both in its context and in its content. It is a negative story about complaint, for which the reader is unprepared, especially after the account of Israel's leaving Sinai in 10:11-36. Its unexpected appearance at the outset of Israel's journey signals a change of mood in

the book of Numbers from the formation of community at Sinai (chaps. 1–10) to conflict in the wilderness journey (chaps. 11–19). Conflict will provide opportunity for biblical writers to define more clearly the character of community and the leadership role of Moses.

Verses 1-3 lack specific details. They begin abruptly with an unexpected complaint by the people. Just as abruptly, God sends down fire to destroy rebels in the camp. The story moves quickly to a resolution and a concluding etiology. The location of this event is named Taberah (תבערה *tab'ērâ*; from בערה [*bĕ'ērâ*, "burning"]), because God uses fire to punish the people. The sequence includes the five basic elements in the murmuring stories: (1) complaint by the people; (2) divine punishment; (3) the cry of the people; (4) intercession by Moses; and (5) the end of divine judgment. This structure is somewhat different from the initial murmuring stories in Exodus 15–17, where complaint was not followed by divine punishment.

The language of vv. 1-3 introduces themes that the biblical writers will be addressing in chaps. 11–19. The Hebrew word translated "to complain" (אנן *'ānan*) in v. 1 appears only twice in the Hebrew Bible. The other occurrence is in Lam 3:39, where the negative character of complaint in Num 11:1-3 is reinforced. The author of Lam 3:37-39 states: "Who can command and have it done,/ if the LORD has not ordained it?/ Is it not from the mouth of the Most High/ that good and bad come?/ Why should any who draw breath complain/ about the punishment of their sins?" (NRSV). The writer of Lamentations leaves no room for the type of complaint signified by the Hebrew word *'ānan*. Numbers 11:1-3 shows how such complaint can actually prompt divine punishment.

Verse 2 states that divine fire destroyed all persons at the "outlying parts of the camp." Placement within the camp indicates moral action. The commentary on chaps. 1–10 provides illustration. God dwells at the center of the camp. The holiness of God radiates from the tabernacle and enhances life throughout the camp. The area outside the camp is of a different quality. Thus someone suffering from skin disease must be put outside the camp to avoid contaminating the community within the campsite (chap. 5). It is doubtful that priestly writers composed 11:1-3, but the pre-priestly authors are working with a similar understanding of holiness and community. Complaint does not characterize the people of God. Those who complain are not transformed members of the community. Their action places them at the edge of the camp. Divine fire at the edge of the camp defines the boundaries of community. Such borderline persons are pruned from the camp by fire. Yet Moses has the ability to intercede on behalf of those who are God's people. Thus conflict defines community and the leadership role of Moses. Both themes will continue throughout Numbers 11–19.

11:4-35. This is a distinct murmuring story. It is separated from vv. 1-3 by a new complaint, this time about the lack of meat in the wilderness. The story also occurs at a different location. The concluding etiology in v. 34 locates the story at Kibroth-hattaaveh ("graves of craving") as compared to Taberah ("burning") in v. 3. Verses 4-35 are also separated from chap. 12 by the itinerary notice in v. 35. The people journey from Kibroth-hattaaveh to Hazeroth for the next complaint story.

The juxtaposition of the themes of the people's desire for meat (vv. 4-9, 13, 18-23, 31-34) and Moses' complaint about the burden of leadership (vv. 10-12, 14-17, 24-30) raises questions concerning the authorship of these verses.[104] It is possible that the

leadership theme was added to a complaint story about meat. The problem of leadership is embedded in that story and cannot be read independently of it, while the complaint about meat can be read as an independent story. Yet, it is not possible to distinguish the authors of the different themes. A careful study of the motifs favors a unified reading of the story. I read the entire account in vv. 4-35 as a pre-priestly complaint story, in which the subordinate theme of leadership is the central problem. Thus complaint about meat provides the setting for exploring how the charismatic spirit of Moses is distributed to others, first to the seventy elders and then to Eldad and Medad.

11:4-15. The opening section provides the setting and circumstances for the story. The complaint about meat is introduced in vv. 4-9. Verse 4 is important. It states that certain members of the camp, described as the "rabble" (אספסף *'ăsapsup*) had a strong "craving" (תאוה *ta'ăwâ*). Because the term translated "rabble" occurs only once in the OT, it is difficult to know exactly what the biblical writers meant by using it. The rabble does not represent all the people, since the writers explicitly state that the activity of this group eventually affects all the Israelites.

The distinction in groups raises the question of identity. That the rabble is a sub-group of persons who have been gathered into the camp is basic to the Hebrew word, which includes the verbal form "to gather" (אסף *'āsap*). This may be a reference to the "mixed crowd" that left Egypt with Israel (Exod 12:38), but the language is not the same. It is more likely that the term indicates a fringe group that is defined by its action. The latter interpretation provides insight into the Hebrew word (האספסף *hā'sapsup*), whose ending (סוף *sôp*) could mean "end," thus designating those gathered at the outer circumference of the camp: Their act of craving defines them as fringe members of the camp.

The craving for meat sets the story in motion. It affects all Israelites who join in the complaint, and it continues to the end of the story, where the Hebrew word "craving" (*ta'ăwâ*) becomes part of the place name, Kibroth-hattaavah. The craving for meat is a rejection of manna, the wilderness food first given to Israel in Exodus 16. This is indicated

104. Noth, *Numbers,* 83-85.

by an extended description in vv. 7-9 of the different ways that manna was served and eaten in the wilderness. The reference to manna indicates that the rabble has rejected divine providence in the wilderness through their desire for meat.

The story takes an unexpected turn from the complaint about the lack of meat to the problem of leadership. Verse 10 describes the circumstances in the camp. The people are crying at the openings of their tents. God is angry over their complaint for meat, and Moses also hears the crying of Israel and judges the situation to be very evil. The five elements of the murmuring story outlined in vv. 1-3 indicate intercession by Moses as the next action. Instead of seeking a remedy through intercession, however, Moses complains about the burden of leadership (vv. 11-15).

The exchange between Moses and God provides commentary on two previous stories. The first is Exodus 18, where Jethro advised Moses on the organization of the camp and recommended more leaders to govern the people. This story provided a prelude to the revelation of law at Sinai. The second story is Exodus 33, where Moses negotiated with God to continue leading Israel after the incident of the golden calf (Exodus 32). God desired to destroy Israel as punishment for the idolatry of the calf (Exod 32:9-10). Moses interceded for Israel and persuaded God not to destroy them (Exod 32:11-14). Exodus 33 contains a second intercession by Moses, in which he persuades God to accompany Israel in the wilderness. He states to Yahweh:

"See, you have said to me, 'Bring up this people'; but you have not let me know whom you will send with me. Yet you have said, 'I know you by name, and you have also found favor in my sight.' Now if I have found favor in your sight, show me our ways, so that I may know you and find favor in your sight." . . . He [Yahweh] said, "My presence will go with you, and I will give you rest." (Exod 33:12-14 NRSV)

Exodus 33 provides the background for interpreting the problems of leadership in Num 11:10-15. The description of the Israelites crying at the openings of their tents (v. 10) repeats the setting of Exod 33:7-11, where the Israelites are sitting at the entrances of their tents. The points of contact between Exodus 33 and the leadership story in Num 11:10-15 continue in Moses' speech. In his opening complaint, Moses poses the question, "Why have I not found favor in your sight?" This question presupposes Exod 33:12-23, where the phrase was at the center of the successful attempt to persuade God to lead Israel through the wilderness. Moses' complaint about leadership (vv. 12-15) is rooted in a theological problem about divine guidance and presence that was first addressed in Exodus 33.

The problem of leadership in vv. 12-15 is the conflicting expectations of Moses by God and the Israelites. Food is the central metaphor for addressing the problem. Moses' complaint juxtaposes God's (v. 12b) and the Israelite's (v. 13) views of appropriate food for the wilderness journey, each indicating different leadership models. Moses first states God's expectations for leadership. He raises a rhetorical question, meant as a complaint: "Did I conceive all this people? Did I give birth to them?" The implied answer to his question is that Moses did not give birth to Israel but that God has, which provides the force for the quotation about food in v. 12b: "Then why are you telling me, 'Carry them in your bosom as a nurse carries a suckling child?' " The imagery is feminine, involving conception and breast feeding. The expectation of God is that Moses will nurture Israel to maturity in the wilderness, eventually bringing them to the promised land. Manna in the wilderness symbolizes this stage in the Israelites' religious development. The view of the Israelites is contrasted to God's in v. 13. They do not want to mature through the wilderness journey. They want meat now. Moses quotes their demand in his complaint to God, "Give us meat to eat!" The impossibility of providing the two diets at the same time illustrates the burden of leadership. Two views of leadership collide in these quotations. God advocates breast feeding as a natural outgrowth of conception and birth over against the people, who want meat, and Moses is caught in the middle.

Moses concludes his complaint by appealing to the divine favor bestowed upon him in Exodus 33. As far as Moses is concerned, divine favor in the present contradictory situation is death, which he requests. Death is better than the burden of leadership (v. 15). Two other prophets request death from God. Jonah wishes for death when a worm destroys a bush that has been giving him shade (Jonah 4:8). The prophet Elijah also requests death while fleeing from Jezebel in the wilderness (1 Kgs 19:4). His story provides a closer parallel to Moses, since Elijah is also a charismatic leader who believes that he is alone in following God.

11:16-23. God responds to both the problems of leadership and the Israelites' demand for meat in this section. The complaint by Moses about leadership is countered with instruction in vv. 16-17 on how to select seventy elders who will share in his spirit. The inner-biblical connections between Num 11:16-17 and Exodus 33 are again present. As was the case in Exodus 33, the tent of meeting is situated outside the camp, where it signifies a more prophetic encounter with God. Both Exodus 33 and Numbers 11 contrast the priestly writers' view that the tent of meeting is at the center of the camp and is equated with the priestly cult of the tabernacle.

The placement of the tent of meeting outside the camp signals that the complaint over leadership is meant to address problems of charismatic or prophetic leadership, rather than priestly leadership. This focus becomes even clearer from the details of the divine instruction. The seventy elders are scribes who, when stationed in front of the tent of meeting outside the camp, will received a portion of the spirit (רוח *rûaḥ*) of Moses, which will enable them to govern the people. The spirit of Moses refers to the spirit of prophecy (see Amos 9:7). The spirit is also central in the charismatic leadership of judges (Judg 3:10; 11:29). The word "scribe" (שמר *šōṭēr*) describes those who write documents, although their role in Numbers 11 is broader and includes administration. Reference to seventy may be symbolic. This number occurs frequently in the Old Testament. For example, there are seventy sons of Jacob (Exod 1:5); seventy elders accompany Moses upon the mountain (Exod 24:9-11); seventy princes are killed by Jehu (2 Kgs 10:6). The number seventy also is institutionalized in the

Sanhedrin, the judicial body in Palestine during the Roman period.

God responds to the request for meat in vv. 18-23. The people are to consecrate themselves, an action they have not undertaken since the initial revelation of God on Mt. Sinai (Exod 19:10). God repeats the complaint of the people in v. 18, quoting their earlier words now as an indictment: "You have wailed in the hearing of the LORD, saying, 'If only we had meat to eat! Surely it was better for us in Egypt.' " Yahweh concludes that they will eat meat for no less than an entire month, until it comes out of their noses and becomes repulsive to them (vv. 19-20*a*). The reason for the negative tone is that the people's request for meat is really their rejection of the nurturing presence and providence of God in their midst (v. 20*b*).

The section ends with an aside in vv. 21-23, in which Moses reminds God of the 600,000 Israelites and the great quantities of cattle and fish needed to feed them. This number is a repetition of Exod 12:37, where this same number of people were described as having left Egypt. God responds to Moses with a rhetorical question: "Is the LORD's power limited?" The implied answer, no, moves the story to its completion in vv. 24-35.

11:24-35. The divine instructions are accomplished in this section. The selection of seventy elders is narrated in vv. 24-30. They are placed around the tent located outside the camp (v. 24). God descends in a cloud, takes some of the spirit of Moses, and places it on the seventy, causing them to prophesy momentarily (v. 25). The language in v. 25 is precise. It indicates that the seventy elders became ecstatic prophets when they received the spirit of Moses. The form of the verb "to prophesy" is hithpael, a form used to describe Saul when he was possessed by God and fell into a prophetic frenzy (1 Sam 10:10-11). But, just as the text is precise about the mantic behavior of the seventy elders, it is also equally explicit in stating that their behavior ceases.

The message of the story is paradoxical. The pre-priestly writers emphasize the importance of charismatic and prophetic leadership in the wilderness community. They state that elders from the people are able to participate in the power of the spirit of Moses, and thus they become charismatic leaders of the people. On the other hand, the pre-priestly writers do not want charismatic leadership to be uncontrolled. Thus the prophetic frenzy that overtakes the seventy elders and authenticates them is momentary and is not repeated. The story suggests that the pre-priestly writers idealize the power of prophecy, while they also wish for its traditional role to cease. Perhaps this is why the seventy elders were described earlier as "scribes"—that is, inspired writers and interpreters of tradition, rather than classical prophets who spoke new words from God.

A similar development is evident in Deut 17:15-22. A prophet like Moses, who speaks oracles from Yahweh, is idealized (Deut 17:15-19). The Israelites are encouraged to look for another prophet like Moses. They will know that such a prophet has arisen when his spoken oracles are fulfilled (Deut 17:20-22). This criterion for judging the truth claims of a prophet, however, eliminates the power of prophetic oracles. The word of a prophet must be obeyed when it is spoken, not when it is fulfilled. The message of Deuteronomy 17 contains the same paradoxical message as Numbers 11. The prophetic spirit of Moses is idealized, while the traditional role of prophets is eliminated.

But charismatic power by definition cannot be completely controlled. The story of Eldad and Medad (vv. 26-30) emphasizes this point. It is a minority report to the previous story of the seventy elders. Verse 26 states that Eldad and Medad "were registered." Critics debate whether this means that they were numbered among the seventy elders, or simply were members of the community. In any case, the text clearly states that they were not at the tent of meeting outside the camp but within the camp. The Spirit of God spilled out upon them, causing the two to go into ecstatic frenzy like the seventy elders. Eldad and Medad represent the unpredictable side of charismatic leadership and hence a challenge to the orderly control of the spirit of Moses in vv. 24-25.

Joshua assumes a central role in the story of Eldad and Medad. He embodies the prophetic spirit of Moses more than does any other character in the Pentateuch. Joshua is introduced as the Israelites' gifted leader in holy war (Exod 17:8-13). He accompanies Moses onto Mt. Sinai to receive the tablets of the law (Exod 24:12-15; 32:17-19). His role in Num 11:26-30 links to Exodus 33, which states that Joshua remained in the tent of meeting alone when Moses left it. Joshua is a charismatic leader with a special role in the tent of meeting. He is concerned about the unpredictable presence of God's Spirit outside the tent of meeting in the camp. Wishing to control the spirit, he urges Moses to make Eldad and Medad stop prophesying: "My lord Moses, stop them!" (v. 28). This demand evokes a response from Moses: "Are you jealous for my sake? Would that all the LORD's people were prophets, and that the LORD would put his spirit on them!" Thus Moses rejects the desire of Joshua to control the transmission of his spirit to the seventy elders. He states that he does not hoard his own charismatic power; indeed, he wishes that all the people were prophets.

The exchange between Joshua and Moses ends in v. 30 with Moses gathering the seventy elders back into the camp. The use of the verb "to gather" (ʾāsap) repeats language from the opening section of the story (vv. 4-11). The incorporation of the seventy elders into the camp will be a contrast to those who leave the camp for meat in the following section.

The episode concludes by returning to the request of the Israelites for meat (vv. 31-35). Yahweh sends a wind from the sea that brings quails. The word "spirit" (rûaḥ), now meaning "wind" (v. 31), interrelates the selection of the seventy elders and the theme of meat. The story is miraculous and fantastic. Quails drop from heaven all around the camp (but not in it) until they are piled up two cubits deep (approx. 36-44 inches). The people who run out of the camp to catch these birds collect quail for two days, until the least that any one person possesses is ten homers of quail (approx. 89 bushels). But the feast no sooner begins than God kills the people with the meat still between their teeth. Thus all persons who chose to leave the camp for meat also choose death in the wilderness. The result is another pruning of the wilderness community. The miracle of quail answers the divine rhetorical question from v. 23,

"Is the LORD's power limited?" Indeed, nothing is too difficult for God, but in this case the miracle comes with a price. Hence, the name of the place is "Graves of Craving" (Kibroth-hattaavah).

12:1-16. Chapter 12 is part of the prepriestly history. The placement of the tent of meeting outside the camp ties chaps. 11 and 12 together. The broader literary connection to Exodus 33:1 continues, with the appearance of the pillar of cloud (v. 5; Exod 33:10). The literary relationships indicate that the pre-priestly history progressed from covenant renewal (Exodus 32–34) to the conflicts over prophetic leadership (Numbers 11–12). There are also signs of additional priestly authorship: the characters of Miriam and Aaron, the seven-day period of purification from leprosy for Miriam (vv. 14-15; prescribed in Leviticus 13–14), and the reference to Paran in the closing itinerary notice (v. 16).

The charismatic leadership of Moses remains the central theme in the controversy between Miriam, Aaron, and Moses in this chapter, in which Miriam and Aaron claim the same prophetic authority as Moses. The central point of tension throughout the chapter is the need to maintain a hierarchy of authority among characters. Thus chap. 12 moves in the opposite direction of chap. 11, where the central problem was how the charismatic spirit of Moses could be passed on to the seventy elders, and even influence all members of the camp (11:29). The challenge from Miriam and Aaron sets in motion a story of divine revelation and punishment with a four-part structure.

12:1-3. These verses do not follow smoothly from chap. 11. Moses has no sooner told Joshua of his wish that all the people were prophets (11:29) than Miriam and Aaron challenge his own exclusive role of speaking for God. These opening verses present two problems for interpretation: determining why these particular characters are involved in the story and discerning the content of the challenge from Miriam and Aaron.

Why are the priest Aaron and his sister, Miriam, the ones who challenge Moses' special status as a charismatic leader? One would expect such a challenge from a more charismatic figure like Joshua or even the seventy elders, who now possess the spirit

of Moses. Some scholars argue that Aaron is a late addition to the story and that Miriam alone originally challenged Moses.[105] Implied in this interpretation is the view that in early Israelite culture women played a more central and charismatic role, which was played down in later tradition.[106] The strength of this argument is that women assume charismatic leadership roles in the OT. In Exod 15:20, Miriam is presented as a charismatic prophet like Deborah (Judges 5) when she sings her victory song after the defeat of the Egyptian army at the sea. From this perspective, the anomaly of having a priest claim the charismatic spirit of Moses is resolved by interpreting the story at an earlier level of tradition. The challenge in Numbers 12 is between the two charismatic leaders of the exodus, Moses and Miriam.

The weakness of that interpretation is that it is difficult to edit out the character of Aaron. Often the verbal tenses presuppose two opponents against Moses, while the structure of the story, with its levels of intercession, implies all three characters. Even if one reconstructs a fairly coherent story with only Moses and Miriam, it still does not address Aaron's role in the present form of the story. Thus the problem of how many characters are involved is not easily resolved. It becomes even more problematic if we assume that Numbers 12 was written, or at least edited, by priestly authors, since this story is critical of Aaron, who ordinarily functions as their hero.

The reason for the central role of Miriam and Aaron in challenging Moses' charismatic authority may be their role in the exodus. They are the only other characters called prophets. Aaron is described as the prophet of Moses in Exod 7:1, while Miriam is called a prophet in Exod 15:20. In fact, outside of Miriam and Aaron, the only other character described as a prophet in the entire Pentateuch is Abraham (Gen 20:7), whose intercession for Abimelech provides background for interpreting Moses' mediation for Miriam

105. Martin Noth, *A History of Pentateuchal Traditions,* trans. Bernhard W. Anderson (Chico, Calif.: Scholars Press, 1981) 180-81.

106. For the role of Miriam in tradition, see P. Trible, "Subversive Justice: Tracing the Miriamic Traditions," in *Justice and the Holy: Essays in Honor of Walter Harrelson,* ed. D. A. Knight and P. J. Paris (Atlanta: Scholars Press, 1989) 102; and R. J. Burns, *Has the Lord Indeed Spoken Only Through Moses? A Study of the Biblical Portrait of Miriam,* SBLDS 84 (Atlanta: Scholars Press, 1987) 119-20.

in Num 12:11-15. The familial relationship of Miriam, Aaron, and Moses in priestly tradition may be another reason for their having this central role (Num 28:59). The family setting implied in the central characters of Numbers 12:1 also provides some context for the dispute over marriage that initiates the conflict.

Aaron and Miriam present two distinct complaints to Moses in vv. 1-2 that are not easily related. In v. 1, they complain about Moses' intermarriage to a Cushite woman. The topic changes in v. 2, when they question Moses' status as the only person to speak for God. The second challenge concerning Moses' special role as spokesperson for God conforms to the larger topic of charismatic authority. But the complaint concerning his wife appears to be isolated from the larger themes of the chapter.

Intermarriage between Israelites and foreigners was forbidden in the post-exilic period. The emergence of this law may have provided the background of this story for both the pre-priestly and the priestly writers. Deuteronomy 7:3 states that Israel is to make no covenants with the people of the land, including intermarriage. Numbers 25 illustrates the corrupting influence of intermarriage with the Moabites (the pre-priestly version) and the Midianites (the priestly account). Ezra 9–10 recounts the policy in the post-exilic period whereby all foreign wives were sent away to their homes of origin. The complaint of Miriam and Aaron thus represents the policy on intermarriage in that Moses' marriage to a Cushite woman conflicts with this teaching.

Reference to Moses' marriage to a Cushite appears only in Num 12:1. The more developed tradition is that he married the Midianite woman Zipporah (Exodus 2–4, 18). The land of Cush refers to ancient Nubia (the kingdom south of Egypt), which is modern-day Ethiopia. Sporadic references to Cush in the OT suggest that it symbolized the outermost southern boundaries of the world for ancient Israel (Gen 2:13; Esth 1:1; 8:9). In this role it takes on exotic associations as a place of wealth (Job 28:19; Isa 45:14) and as a land populated by near mythic warriors, like Nimrod (Genesis 10).

The marriage of Moses to a Cushite woman stands in uneasy tension with authoritative teaching on intermarriage. It challenges the prescribed boundaries of the camp, and it is this quality that interrelates the two complaints of Miriam and Aaron in vv. 1-2. Their challenge concerning the special status of Moses as the authorative voice for God (v. 2) cannot be separated from their complaint concerning his marriage to the Cushite (v. 1). The two reinforce each other. By arguing that God also speaks through them, Miriam and Aaron are adding authority to their criticism of Moses' intermarriage. Their claim, furthermore, is supported by law. They represent the power of tradition; Moses has violated tradition.

Yet God supports Moses over against traditional law. Verse 3 sets the stage for refuting the challenge to Moses' authority, stressing his special quality as a devout person: "Moses was very humble, more so than anyone else on the face of the earth." The description of Moses as being humble (עָנָו ʿānāw) is not a psychological assessment. It describes his status before God. The "humble" are those who seek God (Pss 22:27; 69:33), hear God (Ps 34:3), rejoice in God (Ps 63:33), and do justice and righteousness (Isa 11:4). As a consequence, God hears the humble (Ps 10:17), saves them (Pss 76:10; 149:4), instructs them (Ps 25:9), and does not forget them (Pss 9:13; 10:12, 17). His humble nature makes Moses' status before God qualitatively different from that of any other person, including the other heroes of the exodus—Aaron and Miriam. His authority is not in any office, but in his personal qualities. Thus his actions are models of faithfulness to be repeated, not criticized.

Moses' marriage to a Cushite stands in uneasy tension with emerging teaching on intermarriage. It is an instance of innerbiblical interpretation, in which a story qualifies a broader teaching. The violation of marriage law is justified by Moses' personal quality of humility, and not by his having a special office of leadership. In this respect, Numbers 12 continues to explore the charismatic authority of Moses. The breaking of expected boundaries through marriage provides a point of contact with the unexpected spilling over of Moses' spirit onto Eldad and

Medad in the previous story. Both stories challenge the structures of tradition. Each illustrates how charismatic power breaks boundaries. Joshua complained about this quality of uncontrolled ecstatic prophecy within the wilderness community by Eldad and Medad. Aaron and Miriam, the siblings of Moses, now complain about this quality in Moses' marriage, because it blurs the boundaries of the wilderness community.

12:4-10. This section describes God's response to the challenge of Aaron and Miriam. God suddenly calls Moses, Miriam, and Aaron to the tent of meeting outside the camp (v. 4). The presence of God is indicated by the pillar of cloud at the entrance of the tent (v. 5).

A divine oracle is given to Miriam and Aaron (vv. 6-8). The divine speech makes explicit the message implied in the narrator's comment in v. 3—namely, that Moses is incomparable, more humble than any person on earth. His charismatic authority is beyond that of the prophetic office. To prophets, Miriam and Aaron are told, God reveals messages through dreams and riddles (v. 6). To Moses, God speaks "mouth to mouth" (פה אל-פה *peh 'el-peh*). The phrase "mouth to mouth" occurs only in Num 12:8. The NIV and the NRSV use the translation "face to face" to indicate the relationship between this oracle and Exodus 33:1, where the special status of Moses is established: "Yahweh used to speak to Moses face to face, as one speaks to a friend" (Exod 33:11). In 12:7, Moses is described as Yahweh's servant, entrusted with God's house. Thus Moses is trustworthy. He has even been allowed to see the form of God. The description of Moses links to the earlier account of his descent from Mt. Sinai with a shining face as a result of his nearness to God on the mountain (Exod 34:29-35).

The point of the divine oracle is that such direct communication with God is beyond that of prophets and places Moses in a special category. His charismatic authority transcends traditional categories. Consequently, prophets like Aaron and Miriam should fear Moses and certainly not challenge his special

charismatic authority (v. 8) or his actions, including his intermarriage with the Cushite woman. Because Miriam and Aaron have not feared Moses, God strikes Miriam with severe leprosy so that her skin is white as snow (cf. Exod 4:6; 2 Kgs 5:27).

12:11-15. Miriam's leprosy provides the opportunity for Moses to demonstrate his special status as a charismatic leader. Aaron addresses Moses deferentially as "my lord" in acknowledging his and Miriam's sin. He requests intercession by Moses for Miriam, whose situation threatens to become like that of a stillborn baby (v. 12). Moses intercedes, requesting that God heal Miriam. Healing was God's first promise to Israel in the wilderness (Exod 15:26), and now Moses calls forth that power (Num 12:13).

The response of God to Moses' intercession is puzzling. Yahweh states, "If her father had but spit in her face, would she not bear her shame for seven days?" (v. 14). Spitting in the face may be a sign of contempt (Deut 25:9), an insult (Isa 50:6), or a source of impurity (Lev 15:8). The phrase may also be playing with sounds in the larger story. Rhetorically the verbal phrase "had but spit" (ירק ירק *yārōq yāraq*) repeats the sound (the literary device called paranomasia) of the opening challenge of Miriam and Aaron in v. 2: "Only [הרק *hăraq*] through Moses does the LORD speak?" The intention of such a sound play is reinforced by the similar rhetorical device in the exchange between Aaron and Moses in the previous verses, where Aaron pleads to Moses for help through negative requests ("Do not let [אל-נא *'al-nā*]" in vv. 11-12), are translated into a positive petition to God by Moses in v. 13, "O God, please [אל נא *'ēl nā'*]."

12:16. The special status of Moses is illustrated by his successful intercession. Miriam is healed, but not without first being banished from the camp for seven days (see the instructions for leprosy in Leviticus 13). At the end of seven days, she is brought back into the camp, and Israel departs from Hazeroth to Paran (v. 16), the setting for the spy story in priestly tradition.

REFLECTIONS

Numbers 11–12 is a rich resource for theological reflection on the nature of community, the importance of prophetic leadership, and the uneasy relationship between tradition and social change.

1. The introductory story in Num 11:1-3 is a strong reminder that our identity as the people of God is determined by what we do, not by what we say or by our social location. We often prefer to identify ourselves on the basis of other criteria. But God recognizes us by our actions. When members of the wilderness community judge their journey as misfortune, God prunes them from the camp by fire. The rabble who complain about meat reinforce the same conclusion. They are not named individually. Anyone who craves meat more than the nourishment of God belongs to this group. The act of leaving the camp for meat determines identity. The stories illustrate how fluid our identity is as the people of God; it can change over time. Pruning takes place on the basis of life-style. A central goal in preaching and teaching these stories is to determine what we crave in the contemporary church that puts us in conflict with God's leading. The object of our craving changes. The meat desired by the rabble may be money, employment, or social prestige. The message of the story remains the same, however: God recognizes us by what we do. If we leave the camp in pursuit of the thing we crave, then we forfeit our identity as God's people. We die with the meat still in our teeth.

The conflict over food also contains a message about providence and the Christian life. The Christian life is goal oriented. It is like a wilderness journey. We make goals in life. We seek to discern the will of God in our planning; yet we often want God to conform to our timetable. The fast pace of modern life intensifies this desire. When we force God to accommodate to our life-style, we may turn providence into a commodity that serves our self-interest. The complaint over meat explores this temptation. Israel is at the outset of their wilderness journey, living on manna provided daily by God. Yet they desire meat. Spiritual growth in God's time is in conflict with the rabble, who desire divine grace on their own terms. Their desire for providence on their own terms creates ambiguity in determining who makes up the people of God in the camp.

Numbers 11 contains an important message for the contemporary church. Spiritual growth is not fast food. God often works on a different clock from that of our short-sighted, fast-paced culture. The rabble could not conform to God's timetable and were purged from the community. Those who remained in the camp and ate manna continued to journey with God. Sometimes God tests us by making us slow down.

2. A biblical understanding of charismatic leadership is crucial for the contemporary church. Contemporary culture is fixated on individual personalities. Celebrities attract our attention on television and in newsprint. They determine many trends in our society through advertising. Our tendency to worship fame has infiltrated the church, where we all too often are attracted by the superficial personality of individual preachers. But celebrity status in contemporary society and in the church is not the same as charismatic leadership. At the outset of the commentary, it was noted that prophetic leadership is charismatic and that the word *charisma* in Greek means "gift." Charismatic power is the quality of an individual's personality. It describes a gifted person whose personal strength makes him or her stand out from others. But charismatic persons are not necessarily famous. Max Weber adds a sociological dimension to charismatic leadership, concluding that such leaders are often agents of change during times of social crisis.[107] Numbers 11:1–12 provides a rich resource for evaluating the strengths and weaknesses of this form of leadership.

---

107. Max Weber, *Essays in Sociology,* ed. and trans. H. H. Gerth and C. Wright Mills (Oxford: Oxford University Press, 1946).

Too often charisma is used for self-promotion in our individualistic society. One reason for this is that charisma highlights individuals, hence the danger to confuse it with fame. Yet charismatic leadership is never about self-promotion. It is aimed at building community. The role of Moses in Numbers 11–12 provides illustration: He rejects self-promotion. He complains to God that his leading the people alone is inadequate. Thus it is Moses the charismatic leader who forces God to devise a way to pass on Moses' spirit to the seventy elders. His goal is not fame, but the distribution of his spirit to all members of the community, even when it threatens other leaders, like Joshua. Numbers 12:3 states the ideal: The most charismatic leader is the most humble person on earth. Humility is selflessness before God and others. Such persons do not hoard power jealously; they give it away. In preaching and teaching this story, it is important to clarify that Moses is not a celebrity. He is a charismatic leader.

The ability to intercede for others through prayer is a form of charismatic leadership. Intercession is certainly not limited to prophets. Priests intercede for the community through sacraments, a role that also has the power to influence God. But intercession through prayer in Numbers 11–12 is associated with Moses' prophetic leadership. The introductory story of murmuring in Num 11:1-3 accentuates Moses' power to stop divine judgment through prayer. The story of the quail in Num 11:4-35 develops Moses' role to intercede. His prayer provides a model for lamenting. He has expectations that arise from his past relationship with God. Thus he is able to complain to God about the burden of leadership. God hears his lament and responds to it. The conflict between Moses, Miriam, and Aaron in Numbers 12 demonstrates Moses' power to prompt divine healing through prayer. Intercession in each of these instances is more prophetic than priestly. In each case, God's actions are influenced through persuasion rather than by set rituals, and Moses changes divine action by interceding as a prophet.[108] Prophetic intercession is an important part of corporate worship. But it is not limited to public occasions. The discipline of private prayer is a form of charismatic leadership. Not all persons have this gift; yet all communities need such leaders.

Preaching is a form of charismatic leadership. But it is the role of the seventy elders in Numbers 11 that provides the model for Christian preaching, not Moses. The seventy elders receive a portion of Moses' spirit; thus they are charismatic leaders—but not of the quality of Moses. The seventy elders do not receive revelations, as was the case with classical prophets and Moses. When the spirit of Moses enters them, they prophesy only momentarily. Their charismatic leadership, then, is like that of a scribe. In Numbers 11, this means that they have responsibility to govern the community. The seventy elders govern by interpreting and applying the revelation received by Moses to Israel's life in the camp. In doing so, they model preaching in Christian tradition. Preaching is not classical prophecy. Preachers do not speak with God face to face, nor do they receive new oracles from God. Preaching is inspired interpretation. The truth claims of any sermon must be authenticated by Scripture. Thus ministers of the Word are a continuation of the office of the seventy elders. This analogy also provides insight into the goal of preaching. The role of the seventy elders was to apply the law of Moses to Israel's life; thereby they governed the people. The same is true in Christian preaching. The proclamation of the Word in worship is heard when it is applied to the life of the community.

3. The Spirit of God cannot be controlled by human structures. It is a force for change that blows where it will. Thus there is always a subversive quality to communities that are attuned to charismatic leadership. Numbers 11–12 conveys this message in the story of Eldad and Medad. They illustrate how the charisma of God can appear in members who were not supposed to have such power. Their prophesying illustrates that the boundaries of even minimal forms of hierarchy can be broken immediately by

---

108. P. D. Miller, Jr., *They Cried to the Lord: The Form and Theology of Biblical Prayer* (Minneapolis: Fortress, 1994) 262-80.

the uncontrollable Spirit of God. The role of Moses in this episode illustrates how an ideal charismatic leader will promote and recognize such power in unexpected places, rather than view it as a challenge to his own authority, as did Joshua. The subversive character of charisma continues into the next story, where Miriam and Aaron challenge Moses because of his Cushite wife. Their complaint illustrates the way in which the charisma of God can break external boundaries as well as internal ones. The marriage of Moses to the Cushite is no less subversive to the structure of the community than was the unexpected prophesying of Eldad and Medad. When Numbers 11–12 are read together, they illustrate how charisma breaks established boundaries both within and outside of communities. Charismatic leadership forces communities to be self-critical, because the power of God can appear in unexpected forms, places, and persons.

Numbers 13:1–15:41, Conflict Over the Land

COMMENTARY

Chapters 13–15 are pivotal in the book of Numbers. They tell the story of why the first generation of Israelites to leave Egypt lost the gift of the promised land (chaps. 13–14). The story concludes with legislation concerning sacrifices that Israel must observe when the next generation eventually enters the land (chap. 15). The episode introduces a distinctive method of composition, in which one account of a story is supplemented with an additional interpretation.[109] This method of composition allowed the biblical writers to present more than one interpretation in telling a single story. It occurs in the most important stories in the Pentateuch, including the flood story (Genesis 6–9), the exodus account (Exodus 1–15), and the revelation of God and forging of the covenant at Mt. Sinai and Mt. Horeb (Exodus 19–34; Deuteronomy 4–5). Given the importance of the loss of the promised land, it is not surprising that multiple interpretations of this story have been preserved in the Pentateuch. Deuteronomy 1:19-46 contains one such interpretation, while two additional versions are woven into Numbers 13–15. These interpretations present different perspectives on the nature of salvation, conceived as the divine gift of land, and, more particularly, how the people of God are to live in this world in order to realize the promise of salvation. A brief synopsis

of Deut 1:19-45 provides a point of departure for commentary on Numbers 13–15.

The loss of the land by the first generation of Israelites is an important story in Deuteronomy. In Deut 1:19-46, Moses recounts the tragedy to the second generation who are preparing for conquest, thus setting the stage for the whole book. The story separates into four parts: First, preparation for conquest (Deut 1:19-23) takes place at Kadesh-barnea, where the people request spies to scout out proper routes for invasion. Second, the act of spying out the land (Deut 1:24-25) is associated with the Wadi Eschol. The reconnaissance of the spies is for the purpose of war; yet they also bring back fruit, which provides the basis for a good report of the land itself. Third, the main section of the story consists of reactions to the spies' report by the people, by Moses, and by God (Deut 1:26-40). The people are unwilling to invade the land because they fear its inhabitants. The indigenous people are greater than they, the cities are fortified, and the giant race of the Anakim are present (Deut 1:26-28). Moses calls the people to faithfulness and holy war by reminding them of the power of God, which they witnessed in Egypt and in the wilderness (Deut 1:29-33). With the exception of Caleb and Joshua, God denies the first generation life in the land, promising instead to give it to their children (whom they feared would become booty if they invaded the land; Deut 1:34-40). Moses also is not allowed to enter the land because of the rebellion of the people. In his place, Joshua is appointed to lead

---

109. This method of writing by supplementation is also called "redaction" and "conflation" in biblical studies, depending on one's overall view of the formation of the OT. See J. Trebolle, "Conflate Readings in the OT," *ABD* 1:1125-28; Blenkinsopp, "Introduction to the Pentateuch," *NIBC* 1:1-16.

the second generation in their invasion, while the first generation is directed to travel back into the wilderness. Fourth, the story ends with an account of a frantic and failed conquest because of the absence of God (Deut 1:41-46).

Deuteronomy 1:19-46 is not an independent story. Several important questions arise that cannot be answered simply by reading these verses. How did the people know about the fierce population, the fortified cities, and the Anakim? The spies' report does not contain this information. How did God know that Caleb had a different spirit from the other spies and that, as a consequence, he should receive land immediately? There is no mention of Caleb in the entire story. Then, too, when did Israel ever say that their children would be booty if they invaded the land? The literary genre of Deut 1:19-46 is a speech by Moses in which past events are recounted. The logical gaps in his speech suggest that it be read in conjunction with a pre-priestly version of Numbers 13–15. Thus Deut 1:19-46 provides a starting point for interpreting Numbers 13–15.

Two very different interpretations of why Israel lost the promised land are woven into the four-part story in Numbers. A pre-priestly version of the story shares many features with Deut 1:19-46, and it has been supplemented with a priestly interpretation of events. A brief summary of both points of view provides an overview for more detailed commentary of Numbers 13–15.

The pre-priestly version of Numbers 13–14 includes 13:17b-20, 22-24, part of 26, 27-30; 14:1b, 3-4, part of 5, 8-10a, 11-25, 39-45. This version locates Israel at Kadesh (13:26) and describes the spies' mission as reconnaissance for a conquest of the southern part of the land (13:17b-20). The spies go as far north as Hebron, take grapes from the Wadi Eschol, and bring back a report concerning the richness of the land and the fierceness of its people (13:22-24, 26-30). The Israelites murmur in response to the spies' report (14:1b, 3-4). The central portion of this story is dominated by God's desire to destroy Israel and the intercession of Moses to save them (most of 14:11-25), before it closes with an account of a failed attempt at conquest (14:39-45). The pre-priestly account of

Numbers 13–14 contains many similarities to Deut 1:19-46 and, in most cases, fills in the gaps that exist in the latter version.

The priestly interpretation of Numbers 13–15 includes 13:1-3, 17a, 21, 25, part of 26, 32-33; 14:1a, 2, 5, part of 6, 17, 10b, 26-38; 15:1-41. This version changes the location of Israel's encampment to Paran (see the travel notice in 12:16 as well as references in 13:3, 26). The mission of the spies is reinterpreted from reconnaissance for invasion to an assessment of the land itself (13:17a). As a consequence, the spies go all the way to the northern boundary of Canaan in order to explore the entire land (13:21, 25). Failure is not a result of their fear to invade, but the negative assessment of the land as terrain that eats its inhabitants (13:31-33). The bad report of the land angers God (14:26-38). The priestly writers also extend the story beyond the failed conquest of the pre-priestly version with the revelation of new law that points ahead to Israel's future life in the land (chap. 15).

13:1-20. This section describes Israel's preparation for conquest. It divides into a divine command to Moses (vv. 1-3), a list of tribal leaders (vv. 4-16), and Moses' instructions to the spies (vv. 17-20). The pre-priestly version of the spy story does not begin with a divine command. Instead, it commences with Moses' instructions that the spies proceed into the Negeb hills for reconnaissance (vv. 17b-20). An evaluation of the land is important to their mission. Moses instructs them to evaluate the land and its environment (vv. 18a, 20). Is the soil rich or poor? Are there trees? In addition they must gather fruit. The central portion of the instruction, however, focuses on the inhabitants and their fortifications (vv. 18b-19). Are the people strong or weak, many or few? Are their cities fortified? The focus is on gathering information for conquest. The notification that instruction took place in "the season of the first ripe grapes" (v. 20) may be pre-priestly or a later addition by priestly writers. It establishes the time of year in which grapes could be gathered in the Wadi Eschol.

The priestly writers change the dynamics of the story by adding the divine command in vv. 1-3 and by reinterpreting the mission of the spies in v. 17a. Verses 1-3 turn the spy story into a structure of divine command and fulfillment that predominates throughout chaps. 1–10. It even includes the introduction, "And the LORD spoke to Moses" (see 1:1; 2:1; 3:5, 14, 40, 44; 4:1). The priestly writers also change the mission of the leaders with the command in v. 17a, which the NRSV translates as, "Moses sent them to spy out the land of Canaan" (NIV, "Moses sent them to explore Canaan"). The Hebrew word translated "to spy out" is תור (tûr). The precise translation of the Hebrew is important for interpretation, especially since the NRSV translation is misleading. The primary meaning of the word is not the act of spying for the purpose of conquest. It is used in wisdom literature to describe how one searches for wisdom (Eccl 1:13; 2:3; 7:25) and how the righteous give advice to friends (Prov 12:26). Persons who embody this action during the reign of Solomon are described as "traders" (1 Kgs 10:15/ 2 Chr 9:14). In fact, only once is this verb used to describe the activity of spying with an aim toward invasion (Judg 1:23), and there the object of the activity is clearly a city. Neither people nor cities are ever the object of the verb in Numbers 13–15. Instead, the mission of the leaders is always directed to the land itself (13:16, 21, 25, 32 [twice]; 14:6-7, 36, 38), or more specifically the "land of Canaan" (13:1, 17)—a designation for the promised land that is characteristic of priestly authors (e.g., Gen 11:31; 12:5; 13:12; 16:33; 17:8).[110]

The meaning of the Hebrew word tûr is central to the priestly interpretation of Numbers 13–15. Of its twenty-three occurrences in the OT, twelve are in priestly additions to Numbers 13–15. Two additional occurrences also appear to be priestly commentary on the leading of the cloud in the wilderness march (at the end of Num 10:33-34 and in the account of the spy story in Deut 1:33, where the imagery of God's leading with the cloud also appears to be a priestly insertion).

Some commentators translate the verb in Numbers 13–15 as "to scout out" and underscore that such activity need not be of a military nature,[111] but the translation "to explore" may be even closer to the intended meaning

(so NIV). Sean McEvenue concludes that the priestly writer's interpretation of the mission of the leaders is that "they are to know with their own eyes the good thing which Yahweh is about to give them, and they are to evaluate it, giving a favorable evaluation of it to the people."[112] The priestly writers' focus in the story is on the land, not the inhabitants. Theirs is not a story of conquest, but a theological assessment of the gift of salvation, conceived of as land.

Verses 4-16 provide a list of leaders from each tribe who are sent into the land. Most names on the list are unique to this passage. Whether this list was always part of the story or a later addition is difficult to confirm. Priestly writers are certainly fond of providing lists of tribal leaders (e.g., chaps. 1; 2; 7; 10; 26; 34). The list in these verses begins with the tribe of Reuben, as do the two census accounts by the priestly writers in Numbers 1 and 26. But the names are different from those of the first census. One argument for including the list of leaders in the pre-priestly version of the story is that Caleb and Hoshea (= Joshua) are central characters in the story, and both are included in the list. Moreover, it is doubtful that the pre-priestly story actually begins with v. 17b, since the syntax presupposes a specific list of characters like the list of leaders in vv. 4-16. In its present context, however, the list is framed by priestly material (vv. 1-3, 17a), where emphasis falls on the mission of the leaders "to explore" the land.

13:21-33. The mission of the spies and their report is described in this section. Verses 21 and 22 each begin with the same word, "they went up" (ויעלו wayya'ălû). The repetition indicates two interpretations of the same event.

13:21. This verse constitutes the priestly description of the journey of the explorers. The command couples the verb "to go up" with the verb "to explore" (תור tûr) in order to describe the purpose of their mission as a theological evaluation of the land. In view of this, the priestly writers indicate that the parameters of their mission included the entire land of Canaan, extending from the wilderness of Zin in the south to Rehob, near Lebo-hamath, a city located in the extreme north of the land (1 Kgs 8:65).

---

110. Sean E. McEvenue, *The Narrative Style of the Priestly Writer*, AnBib 50 (Rome: Pontifical Biblical Institute, 1971) 118-20.
111. See, e.g., Milgrom, *Numbers*, 100.

112. McEvenue, *The Narrative Style of the Priestly Writer*, 121.

13:22-24. This section is the pre-priestly account of the mission. It is limited to the southern boundary of the land, from the Negeb north to the city of Hebron, which is south of Jerusalem and adjacent to the Dead Sea. Here the mission is one of reconnaissance along the southern border for the purpose of conquest. Two points are stressed in the pre-priestly account of the mission. The first concerns the richness of the land in the Wadi Eschol (12:23-24), where the spies cut down a cluster of grapes so heavy that two men are required to carry it on a pole. This story closes in v. 24 by giving a name to this region: The valley is named "grape-cluster" (אשכול *'eškôl*) because of this event.

The second point of emphasis concerns the inhabitants (v. 22). The spies encounter Ahiman, Sheshai, and Talmai—a race of giants descended from Anak. This clan of giants acquires a near mythological status in stories about the conquest. They are mentioned in the account of the spy story in Deut 1:19-46 and in the story of Caleb's conquest of Hebron in Josh 14:12, 15; 15:13-19. Joshua is also described as killing indigenous Anakim in the hill country, leaving the remnants of this race of giants to live in Gaza, Gath, and Ashdod (Josh 11:21-22). They eventually give birth to Goliath, the giant killed by David (1 Samuel 17). The Anakim giants are mythologized even further in Deuteronomy 2, when they are also identified with the Rephaim, another superhuman race of giants (1 Chr 20:4-8) of whom Og of Bashan is one of the last descendants (Deut 2:11, 20). He required a sixteen-foot iron bed (Deut 3:11).

13:25-33. The report of the spies is recounted in this section. Again there are two versions. The pre-priestly spy story includes part of v. 26 ("And they came to Moses . . . at Kadesh, brought back word to them . . . and showed them the fruit of the land") and all of vv. 27-31. The spies declare the land rich in resources, stating that "it flows with milk and honey" (v. 27). But their report is dominated by an evaluation of the inhabitants and their fortifications. The people are strong, the cities are fortified, and the giant Anakim dwell there (v. 28). In addition to superhuman foes, they also report more a traditional list of opposing nations: Amalekites in the Negeb; Hittites, Jebusites, and Amorites in

the hills; and Canaanites flanking the land by the sea and the Jordan River (v. 29). Variations of this list of enemy nations occur both in the Pentateuch (e.g., Gen 15:21; Exod 3:5, 8, 17; 32:3; Deut 1:7; 7:1; 20:17) and in the book of Joshua (Josh 3:10; 5:1; 11:1), always in stories about the promise of land and the conquest. In the pre-priestly story, Caleb is singled out from the other spies (v. 30). He acts on behalf of Moses by quieting the people, and he encourages them to undertake the conquest. But the group of spies counter his report with a negative one: The people will not be able to conquer the land because the inhabitants are stronger than they (v. 31). The loss of the land in the pre-priestly story arises from the fear of conquest.

The priestly writers' report of the spies includes part of v, 26 (reference to Aaron, the congregation, and the wilderness of Paran) and vv. 32-33. It also contains an assessment of the land and the population. But both are different. The report of the land takes place at Paran (v. 26), and it contradicts the pre-priestly version. The spies do not report that the land is good or that it "flows with milk and honey." Instead, they give a bad report of the land. The Hebrew phrase "bad report of the land" (דבת הארץ *dibbat hā'āreṣ*) is limited to the priestly version of the story (v. 32; 14:36, 37), and it includes a sense of defamation or slander. They state that the land eats its inhabitants (v. 32).

The report of the population in the land does not contradict the other version, although it does reinterpret it. The inhabitants are, indeed, great in size (v. 32). Descendants of Anak (v. 33), these giants are also identified with the Nephilim. The Nephilim are only mentioned twice in the OT, here and at the outset of the flood story (Gen 6:4). Both instances fit in well with priestly views concerning the need for proper boundaries in the world and how the violation of such boundaries creates defilement. Genesis 6:1-3 describes how divine beings took human wives. God, fearing their offspring, limited the human lifespan to 120 years. This story, with its focus on the mortality of humans, may very well be a pre-priestly introduction to the flood. Genesis 6:4 goes beyond Gen 6:1-3 by providing additional commentary, identifying the divine-human offspring as Nephilim ("fallen ones"). This interpretation fits in well with priestly theology in the Pentateuch.

Nephilim are not just heroic human giants. They are freaks of nature, because they blur the boundary between divine and human, originally established in creation. Nephilim are not intended for this earth, and their presence triggers the flood. The identification of the Nephilim in the land of Canaan (v. 33) accentuates its unnaturalness by recalling the monstrous conditions of the pre-flood world. Only the freakish Nephilim could live in a land that ate its inhabitants. Certainly nothing good could come from such land. The loss of the land in the priestly interpretation arises from slandering Canaan, rather than reporting on its goodness.

14:1-38. This section recounts various reactions to the spies' report by the people (vv. 1-4), by Moses and Aaron (v. 5), by Joshua and Caleb (vv. 6-10*a*), and by God. Moses assumes the role of intercessor (vv. 10*b*-38).

14:1-4. The reaction of the people is the same in both the pre-priestly and the priestly stories. They murmur, wishing they had died in Egypt or in the wilderness. They complain about divine leading, which, in their view, has brought them to the point of being slaughtered, and they fear that their children will become booty in a foolhardy invasion doomed to fail.

14:5. The response of Moses and Aaron to the report of the spies and to the murmuring of the people is stated in this verse: "[They] fell on their faces before all the assembly of the congregation of the Israelites." This posture usually signifies reverence. It could be an act of homage to a person, as when the brothers of Joseph fall on their faces before him (Gen 44:14; 50:18). More commonly, however, it is an act of reverence to God during a theophany. Thus the Israelites fall on their faces during the first revelation of God at the altar (Lev 9:24; see also Josh 5:14). But it can also signify anger, as in the case of Cain, when his offering was not accepted by God (Gen 4:5). Moses and Aaron are described as falling on their faces five times in Numbers. Two times they fall on their faces before the congregation (14:5; 16:4), two times before God (16:22, 45), and once the two actions are combined (20:6). When this ritual action

takes place before the congregation, it signifies anger as a response to murmuring. During theophany, it is an act of homage that leads to intercession on behalf of the people. The response of Moses and Aaron in this verse, therefore, should be interpreted as anger against the people. Although the phrase is wide-ranging in biblical literature, this ritual act before the congregation appears to be commentary by the priestly writers.

14:6-10a. Joshua and Caleb respond to the people in this section. It is for the most part pre-priestly material, although there is some priestly commentary. The pre-priestly version includes the reference to "Joshua ben Nun and Caleb ben Jephunneh" (v. 6), the verb "to say" (אמר *'āmar*, v. 7), and all of vv. 8-9. They reaffirm God's power to fulfill the promise of land (v. 8), and they call the people to holy war with the command that they "not fear" (v. 9). The priestly writers reinterpret the mission of Joshua and Caleb as exploration (תור *tûr*) of the land (vv. 6-7). They insert the ritual act of tearing their clothes as a sign of mourning (v. 6), and they include a positive assessment of the land as a minority report that counters the previous negative report of the land. Thus Joshua and Caleb state in v. 7: "The land that we went through [as explorers] is an exceedingly good land." The priestly writers also portray the congregation's attempt to stone Joshua and Caleb (v. 10a).

14:10b-38. The glory of Yahweh (כבוד יהוה *kĕbôd YHWH*) appears at the entrance of the tent of meeting in v. 10b. God's reaction to the spies' report and the murmuring of the people appears in vv. 11-38. This section can be separated into pre-priestly (vv. 11-25) and priestly (vv. 10*b*, 26-38) interpretations (although there is some priestly editing throughout vv. 11-25). The two sections are demarcated by repetition of divine questions to Moses, each of which employs different terminology. The pre-priestly version begins in v. 11: "How long [עד-אנה *'ad-'ānâ*] will this people [עם *'ām*] . . . ?" as compared to the priestly interpretation in v. 27: "How long [עד-מתי *'ad-mātay*] shall this wicked congregation [עדה *'ēdâ*]. . . ?" Each version moves to a point where God makes an oath, "as I live [חי-אני *ḥay-'ānî*]" (vv. 21, 28), that the murmuring generation of Israelites will not inherit the land. But the specific interpretations of the pre-priestly and the priestly writers are very different.

14:11-25. God complains that the people have rejected divine leading and do not believe in divine power, even though they have seen signs of it both in Egypt and in the wilderness (vv. 11, 21-22). As a result, the promised land is denied to all adults in the group except Caleb, who has a different spirit from the rest (vv. 23-24). The Israelites are then commanded to journey south along the Red Sea road (v. 25).

The central portion of the pre-priestly account (vv. 12-20) explores Moses' intercessory role, which, as noted, was first introduced in 11:1-3 and expanded upon in chaps. 11–12 (esp. 11:11-15). Some scholars argue that the intercessory role of Moses is a late addition to chaps. 13–15. Their reasons are that the section could be removed from 14:11, 21-25 without influencing the outcome of the story—more important, that Moses is not presented as interceding for Israel in Deut 1:19-46, which presupposes the pre-priestly account of the spy story in Numbers 13–14.[113]

The following commentary includes the intercession of Moses as part of the original account. This feature is not easily removed from the story. His actions are central for the delay of the promise of land to the next generation. Also, the role of Moses as intercessor is an important feature throughout the wilderness stories in Numbers 11–21. It reaches back to earlier wilderness stories (Exod 15:22-26) as well as to Moses' actions at Sinai (Exodus 32–34), making its removal from Numbers 14 even more difficult. Finally, gaps in Deut 1:19-45 have already illustrated how selectively this story has been constructed from Numbers 13–14. The absence of Moses' intercession for Israel in Deut 1:19-45 may be because it serves no purpose in an address to the second generation, who must now prepare for holy war. Instead, what matters (and what is stressed in Deut 1:19-45) is the need for the second generation to be courageous and not fear their impending invasion, as did the first generation.

The need for intercession in the pre-priestly story arises when God decides to destroy Israel and to form a new nation (v. 12). Moses intercedes for the people with a two-part argument about God's character. The first argument concerns holy war. He reminds God that killing off Israel at this point would lead the indigenous nations of the land to conclude that Yahweh is unreliable, incapable of fulfilling the promise of land.

The second argument turns on Yahweh's ability to change and thus forgive. This argument is presented as Moses selectively quotes the revelation of God's attributes from Exod 34:6-7. The literary context of Exod 34:6-7 aids in its interpretation. This revelation follows the intercession by Moses in Exodus 33 for the continuing presence of God with Israel. Despite Israel's sin in the golden calf episode (Exodus 32), Yahweh announces the decision to continue to lead Israel by revealing aspects of the divine character to Moses: (1) mercy and grace; (2) slow to anger; (3) rich in loving kindness and willing to dispense it to thousands; (4) bearer of iniquity; (5) yet not willing to cancel all guilt (6) so that punishment for iniquity might be extended to offspring to the fourth generation.

Exodus 34:6-7 is a liturgical confession about divine forgiveness in a culture that stressed collective responsibility and guilt. In this cultural setting, deferment of punishment was interpreted as the forgiving character of God. On the basis of these attributes, Moses asks God to forgive Israel (Exod 34:8-9). In Exodus 32–34, God's ability to defer punishment to a later generation allows Israel's story to continue after the incident of the golden calf. But such action gives rise to the proverb "The parents have eaten sour grapes, and the children's teeth are set on edge" (Ezek 18:2).

The intercession of Moses in Num 14:12-19 is an inner-biblical interpretation of Exod 34:6-7. In Num 14:17, Moses recalls God's earlier revelation and recites it in v. 18. Although the motifs of mercy, grace, and the dispensing of loving kindness are absent, the quotation by Moses does not appear to change the overall meaning of Exod 34:6-7. The people are still viewed collectively over several generations. The call for forgiveness in v. 19, therefore, is a request for deferment of punishment, like Exod 34:6-7.

---

113. See Gray, *Numbers,* 155-59; McEvenue, *The Narrative Style of the Priestly Writer,* 94n. 4, 97-99; and N. Lohfink, "Darstellungskunst und Theologie in Dtn 1,6-3,29," *Bib* 41 (1960) 117-18.

The divine response to Moses in vv. 20-24 goes beyond his request; in doing so, it reinterprets Exod 34:6-7. God agrees to forgive in v. 20 as Moses requested. As a result, the entire nation is not destroyed instantly. In fact, no one is killed immediately in the pre-priestly story. But delayed execution does not lead to the gift of the land. Instead, the people are instructed to travel back into the wilderness on the Red Sea road (v. 25). The collective understanding of the people means that all members of the exodus generation—even Moses—must forfeit the land (with the exception of Caleb). This view is expressed in Deut 1:19-46, where Moses states that he cannot enter the land because of the people's murmuring.

What is new is that God redefines deferment of punishment by limiting its execution to the generation responsible for the sin. They may not die instantly as God had wished, but they will die in the wilderness without ever having reached the promised land. Thus God rejects deferment of punishment to later generations and, with it, the notion of accumulated guilt. The result of this new limitation on the traditional understanding of forgiveness is that the promise of salvation becomes intergenerational. This gives rise to a reversal of the traditional understanding. Divine forgiveness in the pre-priestly story means that the promise of land to Israel is deferred to a later generation, and not the punishment due their faithless ancestors.

14:26-38. Priestly writers provide their own interpretation of God's response in this section. They also reframe the dialogue between God and Moses in vv. 11-25 by describing more precisely how God was present in the tabernacle and how God leads Israel in the wilderness. In v. 10*b*, the priestly writers state that "the glory of Yahweh appeared on the tent of meeting," and they return to the topic of Yahweh's "glory" two more times (vv. 21-22). These insertions bring the appearance of God into conformity with the central role that the glory of Yahweh assumes in priestly descriptions of theophany (Exod 24:12-18; 40:34-38; Lev 9:23). In v. 14, the priestly writers also emphasize how God leads Israel day and night with the pillar of cloud and the pillar of fire, respectively, which is how they described the wilderness

march in 9:15-23. But their theological evaluation of the loss of the land is contained in 14:26-38.

The priestly version of God's response to the murmuring of the people begins with their typical introduction, "And the LORD spoke to Moses and Aaron" (v. 26). The priestly writers move even further from the traditional way of viewing the people collectively over several generations. In fact, it is not clear whether the priestly writers view even a single generation collectively. Instead, they focus on detailed retribution for distinct groups, measured out in proportion to the offense. Thus God punishes the people according to what they have actually said (v. 28). Those who murmured will die in the wilderness rather than live in the land with God (v. 30). These persons include those who were numbered in the census (chap. 1) as being over twenty years of age (v. 29); Joshua and Caleb are the only exceptions. The children will inherit the land instead of their parents (v. 31). Furthermore, the length of the punishment is determined by the offense. The forty days of exploring the land will be translated into forty years of wilderness wandering (vv. 34-35). The leaders, who actually defamed the land with their evil report, die instantly before God (vv. 36-37). Because the priestly writers appear to stress individual responsibility, it is not surprising that a second story is necessary to explain why Moses was not allowed to enter the land (see 20:1-13).

14:39–15:41. The episode concludes with an account of Israel's failed attempt at conquest (14:39-45), which is supplemented by the priestly writers with divine law about Israel's future life in the land (chap. 15).

14:39-45. The pre-priestly story ends with an account of profane war. Moses tells the people of the divine decision to defer the gift of land, which prompts confession of sin and the decision to invade (v. 40). Moses condemns this decision as yet another transgression against God. It can only lead to the slaughter of the people, because God will not fight for them (vv. 41-43). The closing scene of the story has the people ascending into the hills for battle, while the ark of Yahweh remains in the camp (v. 44). The inevitable consequence is narrated in v. 45: The people are pummeled all the way to the city of Hormah, a location south of Hebron.

15:1-41. The priestly writers provide a more positive ending to the loss of the land in chaps. 13–14 by ending the story with legislation (chap. 15), which emphasizes Israel's future life in the land and, hence, God's commitment to fulfill the promise of salvation. Thus the law in this chapter is meant to provide commentary on the actions in chaps. 13–14. The chapter separates into three parts. An initial division between vv. 1-16 and 17-31 is indicated by the repetition of vv. 1-2 in vv. 17-18. This repetition includes the stereotypical introduction, "The LORD spoke to Moses, saying: Speak to the Israelites and say to them" (vv. 1-2*a*, 17-18*a*), and a reference to life in the land, which gives the law a future orientation, "When you come into the land . . ." (vv. 2*b*, 18*b*). A third section, vv. 32-41, contains legislation intended for the wilderness setting.

15:1-16. This section contains detailed prescriptions of what ingredients should accompany different sacrifices. Verses 3-16 state that every offering by fire, whether a whole burnt offering or a sacrifice in which only part of the animal is burnt, must be accompanied by both a grain offering and a drink offering. Similar requirements with slightly different measurements also appear in Leviticus 2 and Ezek 46:5-7, 11, 14. The following guidelines are given in vv. 4-10 (a hin is approx. 3.6 liters and an ephah is approx. 22 liters):

Animal	Grain Offering (and oil)	Drink Offering (wine)
Lamb	$\frac{1}{10}$ ephah + ($\frac{1}{4}$ hin)	$\frac{1}{4}$ hin
Ram	$\frac{2}{10}$ ephah + ($\frac{1}{3}$ hin)	$\frac{1}{3}$ hin
Bull	$\frac{3}{10}$ ephah + ($\frac{1}{5}$ hin)	$\frac{1}{5}$ hin

A refrain throughout these verses is that the sacrifices are a "pleasing odor for the LORD" (vv. 3, 7, 10, 13, 14). The conception of God as being attracted to sacrifice by its aroma is rooted in the mythology of the ancient Near East. In the *Epic of Gilgamesh,* for example, Utnapishtim, the survivor of the flood, describes his sacrifice to the gods after the flood:

The gods smelled the savor,
The gods smelled the sweet savor,
The gods crowded like flies about the sacrificer.[114]

The OT parallel to Utnapishtim occurs when Noah sacrifices to God after the flood with the result that "the LORD smelled the pleasing odor" (Gen 8:21). Priestly writers use this phrase both in Leviticus 1–3 and in Numbers 15 to indicate that an offering is accepted by God and, hence, will effect power from God. Verses 11-16 underscore that the basis of the requirements for sacrifice are rooted in the gift of the land. Verse 13 states that all native Israelites (אזרח *'ezrāḥ,* sing.) are required to perform the sacrifices listed in vv. 4-10. A native Israelite is one who owns land.

Priestly writers also extend the law to the resident alien (גר *gēr,* also the "stranger" or "sojourner"), if they choose to participate. The priestly writers incorporate resident aliens into civil law and cultic practice in a number of different ways. For example, the resident alien must avoid leaven during the observance of unleavened bread (Exod 12:19), must not work on the Day of Atonement (Lev 16:29-31), must refrain from eating blood (Lev 17:10-12), must abide by Israelite sexual practices (Lev 18:26), must not sacrifice to Molech (Lev 20:2), and must undergo purification if defiled by a corpse (Num 19:10). They must have access to cities of refuge (Num 35:15). Furthermore, resident aliens may observe cultic rites like Passover if they undergo circumcision (Exod 12:48-49; Num 9:14) and other sacrificial rituals (Lev 17:8; 22:18-20; Num 15:26). The laws concerning the resident alien provide a social and theological window into Israel's self-identity, because the Israelites viewed themselves as resident aliens in a land that God owned (Lev 25:23).

Two points stand out in these verses. First, the promise of land is not negated by the disobedience of the congregation, nor is it even in question. The detailed legislation on sacrifice underscores that Israel will, indeed, live in the land. Second, specific details of the sacrifices emphasize the productivity of the land. When Israel lives in the promised land, there will be cattle, grain, oil, and wine

114. *The Epic of Gilgamesh,* ll. 159-61 in *ANET,* 95.

for repeated sacrifices to God. This picture of fertility counters the bad report of the leaders (13:32-33). A land that eats its inhabitants does not produce the abundance of meat, meal, oil, and wine listed in vv. 1-16.

15:17-31. This second section of legislation is also directed to Israel's future life in the land. Verses 17-21 anchor the legislation firmly in the future context of the land when God states that a donation from the first batch of dough is required whenever anyone eats "bread of the land" (vv. 19-20). The Hebrew word translated "dough" (עריסה *'ărîsâ*) is not clear. The translation "dough" is from the Septuagint, but it may also refer to barley food, or even more likely a baking vessel. Similar legislation is repeated in Ezek 44:30 and Neh 10:38. The point of the legislation in Num 15:17-21 is that the donation is required from generation to generation. This law sets the stage for the priestly writers to return to the topic of corporate and individual responsibility that is central to Numbers 13–14.

Verses 22-31 explore three types of transgression in order to illustrate the limitations of forgiveness and the different ways in which forgiveness operates: unintentional corporate sin (vv. 22-26); unintentional individual sin (vv. 27-29); and intentional sin (vv. 30-31). Verses 22-26 explore unintentional corporate sin. If an act of transgression is committed without the people's knowing it, corporate forgiveness of both native Israelites and resident aliens is possible. Forgiveness, in this case, requires that the priest sacrifice a bull for a burnt offering and a male goat for a sin offering. This ritual atones for the entire congregation. (It is also outlined in Lev 4:13-21.)

Verses 27-29 describe how unintentional individual transgression can be forgiven. The sacrifice of a female goat by the priest atones for either a native Israelite or a resident alien. (This ritual is also described in Lev 4:27-31.)

Verses 30-31 are the point of emphasis in the section. They describe high-handed transgression. The Hebrew phrase "high-handed" (ביד רמה *běyād rāmâ*) also was used to characterize Israel as it left Egypt (Exod 14:8), where it is translated "boldly." In the legal context of Num 15:30-31, "high-handed" transgressions are best interpreted as intentional or premeditated sin. There is no forgiveness for premeditated transgression. Such

persons must bear their guilt, which means that they are "cut off" (כרת *kārat*) from the people. The exact meaning of this phrase in priestly tradition is not clear. It may have a collective sense, meaning a family line is discontinued. This meaning would qualify the more individual focus of 14:26-38. But it may also be more individual in its meaning, in which case it would signify a loss of status, excommunication, death, or even a judgment by God after death. The bad report of the land by the leaders of Israel (who die instantly) and the murmuring of the people (who are condemned to die in the wilderness) are instances of premeditated transgression that fall under the final category.

15:32-41. The third section of law in this chapter switches from the setting of the land to the wilderness. Verses 32-36 describe the case of a person collecting sticks on the sabbath who is taken into custody and brought to Moses for judgment. The infraction is without precedent, requiring special revelation for a resolution. Other instances where an ambiguous situation demanded new law in the form of an oracle from God include the blasphemer (Lev 24:10-23), the second Passover (9:6-13), and the rights of the daughters of Zelophehad (27:1-11; 36:1-12). In none of these situations is there clear precedent in priestly law—even though the non-priestly Book of the Covenant does prescribe legislation against blasphemy (Exod 22:28[27]).

But the incident in vv. 32-36 is perplexing, because the priestly writers do indeed address sabbath law in a number of different places. The priestly theologians prescribe sabbath law in the Decalogue (Exod 20:10-11), where work is forbidden because of the structure of creation (Gen 2:1-3). They return to the topic during the revelation of the tabernacle (Exod 31:12-17; 35:1-3), reiterating the prohibition against work and including an additional prohibition against home fires on the sabbath. Again their argument is based on an analogy with creation. Thus, when Israel is at a loss of what to do with the person gathering sticks on the sabbath, the reader is also at a loss, because there is, in fact, clear precedent for action from other texts. The rabbis saw the problem and suggested that the new thing requiring an oracle from God is not sabbath law, but the nature of the punishment.

More modern commentators speculate that the ambiguity of the situation involves gathering wood and whether that is work.[115]

The wilderness setting for the story offers yet another perspective for interpretation. From this point of view, vv. 32-36 address the question of whether sabbath observance is tied only to the land or is in effect in all places. The emphasis on the wilderness as the setting for the legislation (v. 32) suggests that the point of clarity in the divine oracle is that sabbath law is always in effect, whether Israel is in its land or not. The basis for the universal requirement of sabbath law in priestly tradition arises from the structure of creation (Gen 2:1-3). It is simply part of the intended fabric of this world. Thus, in the priestly history, sabbath reemerges immediately in the wilderness in conjunction with the providential gift of manna (Exod 16:22-31). And because sabbath observance is universal in scope, picking

115. See, e.g., Milgrom, *Numbers*, 126, 408-10.

up sticks on this day—even in the wilderness outside of the land—is a capital offense against God, requiring the death penalty.

The priestly writers close the unit in vv. 37-41 by calling Israel to remember God's legislation through the act of sewing blue tassels to the corners of their garments (see the parallel in Deut 22:12). Blue tassels are intended to be an aid to faithful living in that such symbols will remind the Israelites of Yahweh's promise of land; the priestly writers state the principle in v. 39. Looking at the blue cords will prevent the Israelites from exploring (13:1, 17, 21, 25, 32 [twice]; 14:6, 7, 36, 38) according to their own hearts' desire, which led to adultery (14:33) and loss of the land. Thus tassels are a sign of hope about a future life in the land. Finally, the authority for the divine commands is rooted in Yahweh's power as demonstrated in the event of the exodus (v. 41).

REFLECTIONS

1. The central role of creation in the priestly writers' account of the Israelites' loss of the land is timely for the contemporary church. The Israelites fail to see the value of the land. Even worse, their leaders give a bad report that defames it. They conclude that the land of Canaan eats its inhabitants and that only unnatural Nephilim are able to live in its environment.

The priestly writers' version of Israel's pivotal sin in the wilderness reads like a parable of the contemporary church. God's good gift of creation is nearly absent in our worship life. We focus on our personal relationship with Jesus and our social responsibility to other humans. Both are essential to the Christian life. But each rests on a more foundational divine gift: the earth itself. We have failed to identify ourselves as creatures of God within the ecosystem of the earth, and our blindness has given rise to "bad reports" of the land, which defame the earth.

A central goal in preaching and teaching this story is to explore ways in which we have defamed the earth by being blind to its goodness. Environmental pollution, overdevelopment, and irresponsible use of resources are ways in which we slander the earth through blindness. We no longer need to mythologize the results of such pollution as did the priestly writers. We have abundant evidence of Nephilim created by our toxic environment. And the result of our blindness is the same as that of the wilderness generation of Israelites: We lose God's gift of the land.

Preaching on the environment must move beyond a message of doom and judgment. The priestly writers are not pessimists. The power of God's promise means that pollution is not the last word on the land. Atonement for moral blindness is possible. The priestly writers also point ahead to a future vision of a rich and productive earth. When God's promise is fulfilled, Israel will recognize their produce as a gift from God and return it through sacrifice. Priestly writers not only envision a bright future based on God's promise, but they also provide guidelines for Israel's present life in the wilderness. The future vision of the land begins by organizing the wilderness journey within the rhythm and cycles of creation. Sabbath rest is the first act in living in harmony with creation.

Sabbath law is about worship. The first step in addressing our abuse of the earth is to celebrate its gift in worship; otherwise, we remain blind. We are only beginning to awaken to the central role of creation in Jesus' proclamation of the kingdom of God. Identifying the earth as God's gift of salvation and ourselves as creatures within it brings God's kingdom into view. We must return to the insight of the ancient Israelites that they were resident aliens on God's land. We continue to sojourn on God's property, and our worship must include recognition of this gift. Leadership in environmental ethics will then flow from our worship life.

2. There is a growing conflict in the church between social justice and environmental theology. The argument is that the church has limited resources and cannot undertake two distinct missions. The message of Numbers 13–15 is that the two cannot be separated. The pre-priestly writers interpret the loss of the land as a failure of holy war. Holy war often symbolizes struggles for social justice in the Bible. The exodus is Yahweh's holy war against the oppressive empire of Egypt. It is an event of liberation for Israel. The message of the pre-priestly writers is that the Israelites fear to risk their lives for social justice, and as a consequence they lose the gift of salvation. The priestly writers emphasize the important role of seeing the goodness of the land in order to possess it. They stress a theology of creation. Both interpretations are interwoven in Numbers 13–15; neither is given precedence. The message arising from the composition of Numbers 13–15 is that social justice and environmental justice are inseparable.

3. The message in the loss of the land is salvation, not judgment, when interpretation focuses on God. Three insights into the character of God are important for preaching. First, God is able to change. This is the central message of the story. The Israelites' rejection of the land should have stopped the story of salvation. They broke the conditions of their covenant by refusing to follow God, sealing their fate. God continues the story by changing the conditions of their relationship. Yahweh's forgiveness of Israel indicates a transformation by God, not by Israel. There is no such thing as fate in the Bible. The future is open, because God is in a personal relationship with the Israelites. The result is that Yahweh is steadfast, constant, and enduring, according to biblical writers. Second, God's grace is most clear during times of judgment. It is the crisis of the loss of land that brings forth new insight into Yahweh's mercy. Third, the mercy of God goes beyond our expectations. Moses presented his best argument to God, requesting that God defer punishment at the present time, so that the Israelites might endure the wilderness march. God shatters Moses' meager request by eliminating deferred punishment altogether and replacing it with the promise of land as the point of continuity between the generations. The result is that the transforming power of salvation (not guilt) passes from generation to generation.

4. Moses models intercession in Numbers 13–14. He approaches Yahweh on the basis of tradition. He quotes the best liturgy at his disposal (Exod 34:6-7). He presents additional arguments to dissuade God from judgment, including past promises by Yahweh to the Israelites and the perception of God by other nations. Moses is idealized, moreover, both as a prophet (Num 14:11-25) and as a priest (Num 14:26-38) as he mediates for the people. The power to intercede is not limited to any one office. Central to Moses' intercession is the knowledge that Yahweh is able to change judgment into forgiveness. But what is most striking in this story is that even Moses, the greatest intercessor, underestimates Yahweh's ability to transform disaster into hope. The message that arises from this story is that there is no limit to the power of intercession. Moses demonstrates that it is not possible to undervalue the persuasive power of intercession with God. Yahweh is full of surprises. Jesus models the same boldness in his intercession with God, and he encourages his disciples to do the same (see John 14–17).

5. The message of the loss of the land is judgment when interpretation focuses on the Israelites. A sermon on the Israelites is a meditation on the destructive power of fear. Fear blinds the first generation to God's leading. Fear turns salvation into a fool-hardy enterprise that will ensure the death of children. Fear changes the good gift of the land into a place of death. Fear transforms other humans into monsters (Anakim) and freaks of nature (Nephilim). And an immature response to fear leads to a suicidal war. Fear in each case is a form of death. God has the power to defeat it, but not inde-pendent of the Israelites. Thus the first generation dies in the wilderness because they refuse to let go of their fear and give it to God.

The task of preaching is to discern the destructive power of fear in contemporary life. What keeps your congregation from following God's leading? Is it fear of losing money or the risk of changing a life-style? Do members of your church mask their fear by belittling or slandering the salvation of God? Have any concluded that the land is not worth the risk and, therefore, is a foolhardy endeavor? Do members in your church turn other humans into monsters and thus feed racism? Is God's gift of creation respected or abused? The destructive power of fear can push the promised land further into our future, as it did for the Israelites in the wilderness.

Numbers 16:1–17:13, Conflict Over Priestly Leadership

COMMENTARY

Numbers 16–17 explores priestly leader-ship in the wilderness community through a series of challenges to the authority of Moses and Aaron. This section provides a counter-part to Numbers 11–12, where charismatic, prophetic leadership was examined. Priestly leadership is not charismatic. It does not arise spontaneously through the power of person-ality, as was the case in Numbers 11–12. Rather, it emerges in response to holiness. The formal structures of the priestly office are meant to protect people from the danger of divine holiness, while also providing a safe means to worship God. The Aaronide priests are noncharismatic leaders. They are born into their leadership role, not called like the seventy elders. They lack the visible signs of charismatic authority evident in the seventy elders, whose ecstatic behavior confirmed their divine call. Numbers 16–17 examine the proper exercise of priestly power.

Numbers 16:1-2 lists the many characters who come into conflict with Moses. They include a Levite from the family of Kohath named Korah, two Reubenites named Dathan and Abiram, perhaps a third character named On, also a Reubenite, and 250 unnamed lead-ers of Israel. Scholars have long noted that the cast of characters in 16:1-2 do not appear to be original. On plays no role in the story, and reference to him may actually be the result of textual corruption. Even with the absence of On, Reubenites and Levites do not form a natural coalition, which has raised the ques-tion of whether the characters come from dif-ferent authors. This suspicion is strengthened by the tradition in Deut 11:6, where Dathan and Abiram appear independently of Korah. Their complaints also appear to be separated in Numbers 16–17.

Deuteronomy 11:6 provides a window into the pre-priestly version of the story. It states that Dathan and Abiram, both Reu-benites, were swallowed up by the earth in the wilderness, along with their entire households. All the Israelites witnessed this event. The narrative account to which Deut 11:6 refers is contained in Num 16:25-34, suggesting that much of this material was present before priestly writers reworked the story. Dathan and Abiram also play a central role in Num 16:12-15, which provides the conflict leading to their destruction in 16:25-34. In this section, they complain about Moses' leadership using language similar to other murmuring stories. Moses has made himself prince, they charge, even though he has led Israel from fertile Egypt to die in the wilderness. The exact contours of the Dathan and Abiram story are difficult to determine, because these men play such a subordinate role in the present form of the story, in which they are referred to only five times (16:1, 12, 24, 27 [twice]).

The priestly writers have thoroughly reworked the story of Dathan and Abiram, adding a new conflict between Korah, Moses, and Aaron over priestly leadership. In fact, they have supplemented and edited the material to such an extent that the present form of the story is, for all practical purposes, their interpretation. Korah now dominates the conflict. He is referred to eleven times (16:1, 5, 6, 8, 16, 19, 24, 27, 32; 17:5, 14) as a Levite who is supported by a congregation of 250 leaders. Together Korah and his supporters challenge the special priestly status of Moses and Aaron. The issue in the priestly version of the story is no longer Moses' ability to lead in the wilderness, but holiness and, more precisely, who has the power and privilege to approach God at the altar.

The priestly editing of the Dathan and Abiram story results in a new drama with three parts: an opening conflict with Korah (Dathan and Abiram) over priestly leadership (16:1-17); theophany and judgment at the tent of meeting to resolve the conflict (16:18-35); and a cultic etiology concerning hammered plates on the altar as a memorial of the conflict (16:36-40[17:1-5]). The priestly writers also extend the story with an additional episode. Numbers 16:41–17:13[17:6-28] is a conflict between all the Israelites and Moses and Aaron. It arises from the deaths of Korah, Dathan, and Abiram, and it follows the same three-part structure of that story: opening conflict, theophany as judgment, and etiological conclusion. The opening conflict is a complaint by the congregation of Israel over the deaths of Korah, Dathan, and Abiram (16:41). The glory of Yahweh (כבוד יהוה *kĕbôd YHWH*) appears at the tent of meeting to judge the Israelites (16:42-50). The episode concludes with an etiology concerning

Aaron's budding staff as a memorial of the conflict and as a sign of priestly authority (chap. 17).

The priestly interpretation of chaps. 16–17 will provide the framework for more detailed commentary. Their reading yields a story line of two episodes: 16:1-40, the challenge to priestly leadership by other leaders; 16:41–17:13, the challenge to priestly leadership by the people.

16:1-40. The challenge to Moses and Aaron by other leaders is the central conflict in chaps. 16–17. It establishes the main themes surrounding non-charismatic leadership, and it sets the stage for the second episode in 16:41–17:12.

16:1-17. The setting and themes for the conflict over non-charismatic leadership are established in this section. The introduction of the challengers in vv. 1-2 is stylized. Three groups are each identified in three ways. A linear genealogy of three generations is given for Korah (Izhar-Kohath-Levi) and for Dathan and Abiram (Eliab-Peleth [= Pellu]-Reuben), while the 250 leaders are described as (1) leaders of the congregation who were (2) chosen from the assembly and (3) are well-known men. The genealogy of Dathan and Abiram presents the most problems for interpretation. The ancestry list assumes that On, the son of Peleth, appears as the result of textual corruption, perhaps repetition of the closing letters of the preceding word. He certainly plays no role in the story, nor does he occur in any other references to this event (27:1-4, Korah; Deut 11:6, Dathan and Abiram; Ps 106:16-18, Dathan and Abiram). The reference to Pellu in place of Peleth is based on the second census of Israel in 26:5-11 (see also Exod 6:14), where Dathan and Abiram are listed in the genealogy of Reuben and are identified with Korah and the 250 leaders. No mention of On appears in this text. The family line of Korah is repeated in the levitical genealogies of Exod 6:16-24 and 1 Chr 6:16-30.

The complaint of the challengers in v. 3 concerns priestly leadership. They oppose the social structure in which priests alone are able to approach God. They counter with an egalitarian vision of the camp, stating that all the congregation is holy, because God dwells in its midst. Indeed, their claim is supported throughout the priestly literature as an ideal for Israel. Repeatedly in priestly tradition, Yahweh promises to dwell in Israel's midst (Exod 29:45), and the people are called to be holy. The opening divine speech at Mt. Sinai envisioned Israel as a "priestly kingdom and a holy nation" (Exod 19:6); this ideal returns throughout the priestly corpus, appearing as recently as the closing verses of the previous story, where Israel is once again called to be holy (15:40). The thrust of the challengers' complaint is that this future ideal is, in fact, a present reality, rendering the structural hierarchy of the priesthood both unnecessary and oppressive.

The egalitarian ideal of holiness leads to the accusation that Moses and Aaron "have gone too far!" (רב-לכם *rab-lākem*) in "exalting themselves above [על *ʿal*] the assembly of the LORD." The form of the verb translated "to exalt yourselves" (תתנשאו *titnaśśě'û*) is used to describe non-charismatic forms of hierarchy and power. Such power is good when it describes Yahweh as the LORD who is exalted over all (1 Chr 29:11), including Israelite kings who reign as God's representatives (2 Chr 32:23) and even the kingdom of Israel (Num 23:24; 24:7). But such power is evil when it is grasped for selfish reasons. Such persons are foolish (Prov 30:31-32), as illustrated by Adonijah, who rashly grasped for the power of kingship (1 Kgs 1:5). The challengers use the term negatively against Moses and Aaron. The expression "to exalt oneself above" signifies oppression. The only other occurrence of this phrase is in Ezek 29:15, where the prophet condemns past Egyptian oppression by describing how the future nation will be lowly, so much so that Egypt "will never again exalt itself above nations."

Moses responds to the challengers in vv. 4-17. His initial response (v. 4) is anger against the congregation: He falls on his face. As was the case in the spy story (14:5), this action signals dissatisfaction and anger. It differs from the same action performed before God, where it signifies reverence (v. 22; 17:10). After the ritual act of falling on his face before the congregation, Moses addresses the challengers in three parts. Two addresses to Korah and his group (vv. 5-7, 16-17) frame a separate confrontation with Dathan and Abiram (vv. 12-15). Thus one detects editing,

in which the priestly interpretation of events in vv. 5-7 and vv. 16-17 has come to dominate the pre-priestly story about Dathan and Abiram.

The confrontation with Dathan and Abiram in vv. 12-15 takes place at their tents. Moses sends for them, but they respond, "We will not go up [לא-נעלה *lōʾ naʿăleh*]!" This expression frames the confrontation in vv. 12 and 14, and it contains a broader complaint against Moses, since it is also used to describe Yahweh's choice of Moses to lead the Israelites into the land of Canaan. Yahweh's commissioning of Moses in Exod 3:8 includes rescue from Egypt ("I have come down to deliver them [Israel] from the Egyptians") and leadership into the promised land ("and to bring them up [ולהעלתו *ûlěhaʿălōtô*] out of that land to a good and broad land, a land flowing with milk and honey").[116] By refusing to appear before Moses, Dathan and Abiram are also rejecting his leadership.

Their complaint to Moses is filled with irony. They state, "Is it too little that you have brought us up [עלה *ʿālâ*] out of a land flowing with milk and honey to kill us in the wilderness?" (v. 13). They employ language of salvation from Egypt, but reverse its meaning. Dathan and Abiram use the word "to go up" (*ʿālâ*) in order to describe their exodus from Egypt, rather than the more traditional word for leaving Egypt, "to go out" (יצא *yāṣāʾ*), as in the phrase, "Yahweh brought Israel out of Egypt" (Exod 13:3, 9, 14, 16).[117] They also use metaphorical language of Canaan ("a land flowing with milk and honey") to describe the land of Egypt. As a result, Moses is accused of leading the people from an Egyptian paradise to die in the wilderness. This accusation echoes the other murmuring stories, where hardships in the wilderness prompt complaint. (See the commentary on the murmuring stories in the Overview to Num 11:1–19:22.)

The complaint of Dathan and Abiram also exceeds the other murmuring stories, because it is not limited to a failure of leadership by Moses. Their complaint includes the

116. J. N. M. Wijngaards, "הוציא and העלה: A Twofold Approach to the Exodus," *VT* 15 (1965) 91-102.

117. H. D. Preuss, "יצא," in *TDOT*, ed. G. J. Botterweck and H. Ringgren (Grand Rapids: Eerdmans, 1990) 6:225-50; Thomas B. Dozeman, *God at War: Power in the Exodus Tradition* (Oxford: Oxford University Press, 1996) 51-53.

accusation that Moses has abused his power. They accuse Moses of having proclaimed himself leader and, in the process, "lording it over" (v. 13, שׂרר *śārar*). The same accusation was lodged earlier against Moses in Exod 2:14, where, in the midst of a dispute between two Hebrews, one asks him sarcastically, "Who made you a ruler [שׂר *śar*] and judge over us?" The verb indicates that the conflict concerns non-charismatic, civil leadership, especially how it is evaluated and justified. This focus ties the pre-priestly Dathan and Abiram story with the priestly writers' story of Korah. The difference between the two is that the former focuses on civil leadership, as opposed to the sacral interests of the priestly writers.

Moses' response in v. 15 provides the model for non-charismatic, civil leadership. His actions come into clearer light when they are compared to the earlier story in Exod 2:11-15, where he was accused of the same abuse. In that account, Moses executed justice on his own. Seeing an Egyptian abuse an Israelite, Moses killed the Egyptian (Exod 2:12). Confronted by an Israelite about the source of his authority, Moses fled Egypt (Exod 2:13-15). He repeats neither of these actions in Num 16:12-15. Confronted by the same charge from Dathan and Abiram, Moses neither executes judgment on his own nor flees. Instead, he turns the matter over to God and provides evidence that he has not abused his leadership power (v. 15): He has not taken a single donkey from any of his accusers, nor has he harmed them in any way. Moses also requests that God vindicate him by not accepting his accusers' sacrifice. Thus the matter is adjudicated in a larger context than Moses' sphere of power.

Priestly writers frame the conflict over civil leadership (vv. 12-15) with the conflict between Moses, Aaron, and Korah over priestly leadership (vv. 5-11, 16-17). The technique of repeating material before (vv. 5-11) and after (vv. 16-17) another episode (vv. 12-15) is called resumptive repetition. The introductory and concluding sections become the points of emphasis as the result of this type of editing.[118] The effect of the repetition is that Korah's confrontation now dominates the narrative. With these additions, the issue

is no longer the ability of Moses to lead Israel into Canaan, but who is allowed to approach God in the sanctuary. The social background for such an inter-priestly conflict about access to the cult is most likely the post-exilic period. H. Gese has suggested that the priestly version of Numbers 16 is intended to clarify the subordinate role of Korahite cultic singers to Aaronide priests in the rituals of the post-exilic Temple.[119]

Although Moses' role changes from civil to priestly leadership, his response to Korah is similar to the incident with Dathan and Abiram. Moses does not adjudicate the conflict himself, but turns the matter over to God (vv. 5-7a), before stating his own criticism of Korah and his company (vv. 7b-11). A ritual is devised (vv. 5-7a) to determine who will achieve holy status and thus be able to draw near to God. The ritual involves censers (מחתות *maḥtôt*), flat bronze pans used to draw ashes from the fire at the altar. In this ritual, however, the censers are used with קטרת *(qĕṭōret)*, "incense," according to the NIV and NRSV translations. The participants are to draw fire from the altar with their censers and place incense on them before God. But the meaning of *qĕṭōret* is difficult to determine. It may refer to either an incense offering or a sacrificial burning.[120] In any case, Moses states that through this action Yahweh will reveal who within the tribe of Levi is allowed to represent the people in God's presence.

The ritual with "censers" and "incense" provides many parallels to Lev 10:1-3, where Aaron's two sons, Nadab and Abihu, also take censers, put fire on them, burn incense before God, and die. The Nadab and Abihu story also defines the leadership role of priests by criticizing a potential abuse of their power. Moses' statement to Aaron in Lev 10:3 provides the point of the criticism in the form of an oracle from Yahweh:

Through those who are near me
I will show myself holy,
and before all the people
I will be glorified. (Lev 10:3 NRSV)

---

118. C. Kuhl, "Wiederaufnahme. Ein Literar Prinzip?" *ZAW* 64 (1952) 1-10.

119. H. Gese, "Zur Geschichte der Kältsänger am zweiten Tempel," in *Abraham unser Vater: Juden und Christen im Gespräch über die Bibel* (Leiden: Brill, 1963) 232-33. See also the work of D. L. Peterson, *Late Israelite Prophecy: Studies in Deutero-Prophetic Literature and in Chronicles*, SBLMS 23 (Missoula, Mont.: Scholars Press, 1977).

120. See M. Haran, "The Uses of Incense in the Ancient Israelite Ritual," *VT* 10 (1960) 116-28, esp. 116-17.

The oracle indicates that priestly offerings at the altar are not for private access to God or for personal benefit or prestige, but for the sake of all the people. From this statement it appears that Nadab and Abihu were killed by God for having performed a private ritual for their own benefit. The literary parallels may signal a continuation of the same theme in the challenge by Korah.

In contrast to Lev 10:1-3, the point of the ritual in Num 16:5-7 is not to criticize the power of priests, but to defend it. Thus the conflict with Korah moves in the opposite direction from the story of Nadab and Abihu. The defense of priestly power is made clear in the speech of Moses (vv. 7b-11): It is not Moses and Aaron who have "gone too far" (רב-לכם *rab-lākem*), but Korah and his company of Levites (v. 7b). The evidence is their dissatisfaction in serving the tabernacle as Levites and their desire for the power of Aaronide priests. Moses states that by questioning the leadership of the priesthood, they are actually rebelling against God. The outcome of the ritual test at the close of the scene (v. 35), where fire destroys those of Korah's company who had burned incense, is already foreshadowed in the speech of Moses.

16:18-35. This section describes the divine execution of judgment on Dathan, Abiram, Korah, and the 250 leaders. Its literary structure is organized by the technique of resumptive repetition, as was also evident in vv. 4-17. The execution of judgment against Dathan and Abiram in the pre-priestly story (vv. 24-34) is framed by priestly material in vv. 18-23 and 35. Interpretation will begin with the judgment against Dathan and Abiram in vv. 24-34, then turn to the reinterpretation of this event by the priestly writers with their new introduction (vv. 18-23) and conclusion (v. 35).

The beginning of the pre-priestly story of Dathan and Abiram is not clear. It most likely included divine instruction to Moses similar to that of vv. 23-24, if not those precise words. The refusal of Dathan and Abiram to meet with Moses prompts Moses to go to their tents, along with the elders of Israel (v. 25). The setting of the story, therefore, is not at the tent of meeting, but at the tents of Dathan and Abiram (v. 28).

God's judgment (vv. 31-34) is preceded by a two-part speech by Moses to Israel (vv. 26-30). First, Moses warns the people to separate themselves from the tents of Dathan and Abiram in order to avoid the judgment that is about to fall on these men and their entire households (vv. 26-27). Second, Moses outlines the test by which Israel will be able to evaluate the complaint by Dathan and Abiram that Moses has abused his power of leadership (vv. 28-30). If nothing happens to Dathan and Abiram and they die natural deaths, then the people will know that Moses was not sent by God (v. 29). But if the ground swallows the households of Dathan and Abiram, sending them down to Sheol alive, then Israel will know that in challenging Mosaic leadership they have rejected God (v. 30). The judgment is executed swiftly in vv. 31-34. The ground swallows the households of Dathan and Abiram, and they descend alive and screaming into Sheol for all Israel to witness.

The priestly writers edit the confrontation with Dathan and Abiram by adding Korah to the story (vv. 24, 27, 32) and by describing Israel as a congregation (v. 24). Perhaps they also insert the emphasis on Israel's coming to a knowledge of God (v. 28), since this is a common motif in the priestly interpretation of the exodus (e.g., Exod 6:7) and in priestly law (e.g., Exod 29:45). Most important, however, the priestly writers frame the story of Dathan and Abiram with a new introduction (vv. 18-23) and conclusion (v. 35). The introduction superimposes the command and fulfillment structure characteristic of priestly literature onto Numbers 16. The instruction of Moses that Korah and his company perform the ritual with censers (vv. 6-7, 17) is carried out in v. 18, before the tent of meeting. Verse 35 brings this ritual to a close by describing how the participants are destroyed by fire.

The centerpiece of the priestly story is the theophany in vv. 18-21 and the intercession by Moses and Aaron in v. 22. The performance of the ritual act with censers (v. 18) prompts the appearance of the glory of Yahweh before the entire congregation of Israel (v. 19) for the purpose of judgment. God commands Moses and Aaron to separate themselves from the congregation, so that all the people can be destroyed with fire (vv. 20-21). The threat of destruction to all Israel is a new element in the story, allowing the priestly writers to idealize Moses and Aaron in the role of priestly intercessors on behalf of the people (v. 22). Their intercession begins with the ritual act of falling on their faces, this time as an act of reverence intended to divert the divine wrath that is about to consume Israel. Moses and Aaron ask God why all the congregation should perish as a consequence of the sin of one person.

The intercession of Moses and Aaron builds on the revelation of individual responsibility, which the priestly writers introduced in the story concerning the loss of the land (14:26-38). There, also, the glory of Yahweh appeared for the purpose of judging the people (14:10). What is different, however, is the view that God supports priestly intercession. As priests, Moses and Aaron appeal to the universal power of God as Creator, rather than to the more particular power of God as Israel's Savior and covenant partner. In his previous roles of intercession (chaps. 11–12; 14), Moses functioned as a prophet who enjoyed special favor in the eyes of God (11:11). His charisma gave him the power to intercede through prayer, and successful intercession grew out of his persuasive rhetorical arguments (14:13-17), reminding God of past covenantal commitments to Israel (14:18) as a basis for forgiveness (14:19).

The priestly intercession of Moses and Aaron in v. 22 lacks rhetorical persuasion and makes no reference to Israel's unique salvation history. Instead, it presents the facts of creation. God is addressed with the more general name *El* ("God"), rather than with the covenantal name, *Yahweh* ("LORD"), in order to emphasize that God is the creative source of all life. The implication of the epitaph "God of the spirits of all flesh" is that such a deity cannot be the source of indiscriminate death. This argument requires no request that God forgive—only that punishment be limited to the guilty. The call for the Israelites to separate themselves from the rebellious group (v. 24) indicates the successful intercession by Moses and Aaron to save the nation of Israel. The deaths of Dathan and Abiram (vv. 24-34), rather than of the entire nation, become one stage of a more selective punishment aimed only at the guilty. The destruction by fire of the 250 participants in

the ritual at the close of the scene completes the punishment of the guilty in the priestly interpretation of the story (v. 35).

16:36-40. The story ends with a cultic etiology concerning the origin of hammered plates on the altar. These plates are made from the censers of the 250 participants in Korah's company who challenged the special status of the Aaronide priesthood and were killed by God. The censers are hammered into plates for the altar because they become holy in the ritual—the cause of death for the participants. By handling holy censers, the 250 participants commit sin worthy of capital punishment. As a consequence, Eleazar, the priest and son of Aaron, now handles the censers and fashions them into a new cultic object that symbolizes priestly authority, with a warning about encroachment: Any person outside of the clan of Aaron who approaches the altar will suffer the same consequences as did Korah and his company. The hammered plates on the altar serve as God's answer to the challenge of v. 3 that Moses and Aaron "have gone too far! All the congregation are holy, every one of them, and the LORD is among them." All the congregation of the wilderness community are not equally holy, and the separation of a special priesthood to approach God is not in itself oppressive.

16:41–17:13. The priestly writers add an entire story to the conflict over priestly leadership in these verses (= 17:6-28 MT) that focuses on all of the people, rather than select leaders. This section repeats the three-part structure of the preceding conflict: complaint, theophany and judgment, and concluding cultic etiology.

16:41. The challenge to priestly leadership by the people occurs on the day following the death of Korah and his company. It begins when the congregation murmurs against Moses and Aaron, accusing them of murdering the "people of Yahweh" (עם יהוה *'am YHWH*). The phrase "people of Yahweh" is not one of the priestly writers' regular designations for Israel. They prefer the word "congregation" (עדה *'ēdâ*), which is, indeed, how Israel is described by the narrator in the opening of this verse. The phrase "people of Yahweh" may indicate a special covenantal relationship between God and Israel in which governance is less hierarchical than the careful stratifications of holiness being advocated by the priestly writers. Note that Moses used this very term in 11:29 in presenting to Joshua the charismatic ideal that "all people of Yahweh [*'am YHWH*] were prophets and that Yahweh would put his spirit on them." The repetition of the phrase in the people's complaint indicates that the priestly writers intend to address the relationship of charismatic and non-charismatic forms of leadership in this story by using Moses' own words from a past story as a challenge to his role as a priest.

16:42-50. Theophany and intercession by Moses and Aaron once again constitute the centerpiece of the story. The description of theophany in vv. 42-45 even repeats the details from vv. 19-21. It, too, begins by establishing a setting at the tent of meeting, where the congregation (rather than Korah) assembles against Moses, prompting the appearance of the glory of Yahweh (v. 19; see v. 42). Yahweh commands Moses and Aaron to separate themselves from their challengers, so their opponents can be consumed instantly with fire (vv. 20-21; see vv. 44-45).

Moses and Aaron again intercede for the people (vv. 46-50). They fall on their faces (v. 45), and Moses directs Aaron to perform a ritual of atonement for the people against divine wrath that has taken the form of a plague. The plague indicates the anger of God that brings death. Exodus 12:13 provides an analogy to this story, where an independent "destroyer" also executed divine judgment on the Egyptians by killing all unprotected firstborn. The ritual of atonement is an antidote that stops the plague.

Moses' instructions underscore the holy status of Aaron, for he is commanded to perform the very ritual that led to the deaths of Korah and his company (v. 46). Aaron takes his censer, puts fire from the altar on it along with incense, and uses the holy fire to appease the avenging wrath, now moving through the camp. The intercessory role of Aaron is emphasized when he leaves the confines of the altar and stands in the midst of the people in order to atone for them (v. 47). Atonement in this context is a rite of expiation that makes appeasement for the people and, in the process, wards off the divine wrath. Such a

ritual of atonement, with a censer rather than blood, is unique to this passage.[121]

Aaron's intercession stops the divine wrath, but not before 14,700 Israelites are killed (vv. 48-49). His actions challenge the opening complaint of the people: "You have killed the people of Yahweh" (v. 41). When the crisis is over, he returns to Moses at the entrance of the tent of meeting (v. 50).

17:1-13. This section contains a cultic etiology about the budding staff of Aaron, which rests in front of the ark of the covenant in the tent of meeting. The story begins with a divine command to Moses (vv. 1-5) that he collect a staff from the leader of each tribe. Many of the social terms used to describe Israel from Numbers 1–4 recur here, such as Israelites, ancestral house, leader; but the focus is on the Hebrew word for "staff" (מטה *maṭṭeh*), which can mean both "staff" and "tribe." Moses is to write the name of each tribal leader on his staff. Aaron represents the Levites. He is to place the staffs before the ark of the covenant, described with the priestly term עדות (*'ēdût*, "testimony"). The one whose staff buds is God's chosen priestly leader. This sign of divine election is intended to stop any further murmuring by the people.

Moses executes the divine command (vv. 6-7) and returns the next day for the results. Aaron's staff is the only one that has budded. It is filled with ripe almonds, visible to all the Israelites (vv. 8-9). Aaron's budding staff is to be placed before the ark. Its symbolic meaning is stated in v. 10: The budding staff of Aaron is a warning to rebels to cease complaining about the role of the priesthood lest they die. Although Aaron's staff functions as a warning to rebellious Israelites in the present construction of the story, the meaning of Aaron's budding staff is actually positive. The choice of almonds may signify watchfulness, as in Jer 1:11. The whiteness of the budding almond may symbolize purity and holiness, as it does in Isa 1:18.[122] In more general terms, the budding staff symbolizes the ability of the Aaronide priesthood to approach God and live.[123] Thus the two cultic etiologies

121. Haran, "The Uses of Incense in the Ancient Israelite Ritual," 122.
122. Wenham, *Numbers*, 139-40.
123. For comparisons to the budding staff of Aaron in other ancient folklore, see Gray, *Numbers*, 216-17.

in chaps. 16–17 complement each other in confirming the necessity of priestly intercessors. The hammered plates on the altar are a warning against encroachment by non-priests, while the budding staff is a sign of the divine choice of the Aaronide priesthood to represent the people before God.

The story ends in vv. 12-13 on a more negative note about the danger of encroachment. Israel expresses its fear to approach God with the question, "Are we all to perish?"

REFLECTIONS

1. The office of priest is often misinterpreted and ignored in the contemporary church. The most prominent current image is the phrase "the priesthood of all believers" (1 Pet 2:5, 9). It has come to mean that all Christians are priests, thereby making a special office of priesthood irrelevant. The roots of this interpretation reflect important conflicts over hierarchy and the abuse of clerical power during the Reformation period. But the lasting effects of these controversies can be harmful to Christian community. Our contemporary interpretation of "the priesthood of all believers" resembles the position of Korah, when he stated that "all the congregation are holy, every one of them." Both judge the special office of priest unnecessary and oppressive. Numbers 16–17 is a strong criticism of Korah, and it presents two challenges to many contemporary churches.

First, when we disperse the office of priest to the entire congregation, clergy fail to claim the full resources of God available through ordination. Ordination to Word (prophetic office) and sacraments (priestly office) continue in most denominations, but the emphasis is on preaching the Word, not administering sacraments. Yet every ordained clergy is both a prophet and a priest. Clergy who preach the Word and interpret Scripture empower churches to live Spirit-filled lives. But God offers additional power to transform humans through baptism and the eucharist, requiring priestly mediation. The ideal of the priestly writers is the claim of Korah that Israel become a kingdom of priests (Exod 19:6). The message of Numbers 16–17 is that the ideal is not yet a present reality. Priestly mediators represent an important step in reaching this goal. They stand between the dead and the living and transmit God's holiness and health to the community (Num 16:48).

Second, congregations fail to realize the dangerous power of Christian sacraments when the office of priest is ignored or casually dispersed to all members. The death of Korah and his followers (Num 16:31-35) indicates that the holiness of God is strong medicine, never to be taken for granted. The same message undergirds 1 Peter. The call for Christians to become a "priesthood of all believers" is embedded in a baptismal sermon (1 Pet 1:3–4:11), the force of which presupposes the essential role of the priestly office in creating Christian community. The audience of 1 Peter consists of new Christians. Baptism has transformed them, creating tension between their former life and their new identity in Christ (1 Pet 1:13-16). They are now exiles in this world on a journey with God (1 Pet 1:17-21; 2:11-12), but they have not yet reached their goal. These new Christians are vulnerable, like newborn infants. The water of baptism is spiritual milk that will make them grow (1 Pet 2:1-3).

The message of 1 Peter is similar to that of Numbers 16–17. The call to be a royal priesthood is the goal for these new Christians (1 Pet 2:4-10) as it is for the priestly writers (Exod 19:6). But the goal has not yet been attained. The Christians in 1 Peter are aliens and exiles like the Israelites in the wilderness, where the life of faith is also a journey between Egypt and the promised land. The mediation of sacraments is the spiritual source for waging war against evil and achieving the goal of salvation (1 Pet 2:11-12). First Peter does not eliminate the office of priest. On the contrary, it presents an argument for the central role of this office in the life of Christians.

2. Numbers 16 provides a model of intercession based on priestly ritual, rather than prophetic words. Aaron stands between the dead and the living to stop the plague from sweeping through the camp. He does not halt the plague through persuasive prayer, but by burning incense and thereby atoning for the people (Num 16:46-48). The healing role of priestly intercession is a distinctive form of ministry. It extends the power of sacraments into the community through rituals. The power of the priest to intercede by action is a reminder that effective ministry is not necessarily saying the right words. Aaron models a ministry of presence. His ritual action calls forth the healing power of God. Sharing the eucharist with homebound members of your church, performing rituals of healing with oil, or simply sitting at the bedside of a sick person is similar to the priestly intercession of Aaron. These are ritual forms of intercession, bringing the power of the sacraments into the lives of Christians. The goal of priestly intercession is to maintain the health of the community by providing safe access to the healing power of holiness.

3. Clergy misconduct through the abuse of power is no less dangerous to Christian community today than it was to the wilderness community of Israel. The complaint of Dathan and Abiram that Moses "lords it over them" (Num 16:13) and Korah's accusation that Moses and Aaron "exalt themselves" (Num 16:3) reflect a long tradition of exploitation by civil and ecclesiastical leaders. The prophets repeatedly condemn the self-interest of princes, kings, and priests. Amos condemned both Jeroboam, the king, and his priest, Amaziah, for turning justice into poison (Amos 7:1). He is followed by Hosea (chaps. 4–5) and Jeremiah (chaps. 7; 26). Prophetic judgment warns us that power is a dangerous gift, easily exploited. Numbers 16–17 are a manual on conflict resolution for people in positions of power. The response of Moses to the challenges of Korah, Dathan, and Abiram provides two criteria for evaluating authentic leadership during times of conflict.

First, leaders do not themselves adjudicate conflicts over their own leadership. In neither the challenge to his civil leadership by Dathan and Abiram, nor that to his priestly leadership by Korah does Moses adjudicate the matter himself. In both instances, he places the challenge to his authority in a larger context than his own sphere of power, so that the outcome is open to public evaluation. In the case of Dathan and Abiram, God was called upon to evaluate the truth of their accusation through a public display of judgment. Due process is followed. The same is true with the challenge to the priestly leadership of Moses by Korah. In both instances, all Israel sees the outcome of the tests. Resolution is always public, not a private agreement among a few.

Second, leadership is authentic when power is used for the good of the whole community, rather than for a select few. Priests and Levites hold office for the sake of the community. They protect people from the danger of holiness, while also mediating its life-giving power to them through rituals. Priests and Levites bear the responsibility for encroachment themselves through substitution. Their office increases their responsibilities, not their privileges.

Numbers 18:1–19:22, Guidelines for Approaching God

COMMENTARY

The priestly writers present detailed guidelines for approaching God in Numbers 18–19. These chapters constitute the third episode to the conflicts surrounding priestly leadership.

The first episode contained complaints by Korah, Dathan, and Abiram about the leadership of Moses and Aaron (16:1-40). The people challenged priestly leadership in the second episode (16:41–17:13). It closed with the people expressing their fear to approach God, "Are we all to perish?" The guidelines for approaching God in chaps. 18–19 are the response to the Israelites' fear of perishing in the presence of Yahweh.

18:1-7. This section provides a response to the fear of Israel expressed in 17:12-13. The section consists of a divine speech directed to Aaron, rather than to Moses (v. 1)—unusual in priestly literature, where nearly all divine speech is directed to Moses. Aaron is addressed directly by God only three other times. Two of them also occur in chap. 18 (vv. 8 and 20), while the one other time appears in Lev 10:8. There Aaron is commanded to maintain purity in a situation of lethal divine wrath (Lev 10:1-2). Thus the direct address to Aaron appears in situations of danger, while also accentuating the authority of the priesthood.

The danger of divine wrath is addressed in 17:5. God tells Aaron that if the priests perform their duties at the sanctuary and at the altar, divine wrath will not strike Israel. Thus the priesthood is a divine gift aimed at protecting Israel from the danger of divine holiness (v. 7). The nature of the gift is spelled out in more detail, as the responsibilities of the priests and the Levites are described. Israel is protected from divine wrath at one level by the Aaronide priests, who perform the duties of the sanctuary and the altar (vv. 1, 3*b*, 5*a*). Any encroachment on the sanctuary becomes their responsibility. Israel is further protected by the Levites, who serve the Aaronide priests. Their subordinate role is indicated (v. 2) through a play on words. The verb stating that the Levites "will be joined" (לוה *lāwâ*) to the Aaronite priests derives from the same root in Hebrew as does the noun "Levi" (לוי *lēwî*). The Levites serve the priests by performing service for the tent of meeting (vv. 2-4), but they are restricted from handling holy utensils or from serving at the altar.

18:8-20. This section is framed by two divine speeches to Aaron (vv. 8, 20). The first speech consists of vv. 8-19. In this section, God outlines the compensation that priests will receive for performing their sacred duties. Such compensation is called emolument, and it consists of either a portion of a sacrifice or a redemption payment. The second speech

actually includes vv. 20-24, although vv. 21-24 have been separated from v. 20 in the Commentary because the focus changes from the Aaronide priesthood to the Levites. Verse 20 appears to be a later addition to a section of priestly law (vv. 8-19, 21-24) in which the compensation for priests (vv. 8-19) and Levites (vv. 21-24) was outlined. In v. 20, God informs Aaron that priests forfeit land ownership as a consequence of their office, because God is their special possession among the people of Israel.

Two kinds of priestly emoluments are described in vv. 8-19. The first is compensation that comes "from the most holy" (מקדש הקדשים *miqqōdeš haqqŏdāšîm*) offerings. These are described in vv. 8-10 as three sacrifices: grain, sin, and guilt offerings (see the Commentary on 7:1-89 for a description of these sacrifices). The sacrifices are described as being reserved for priests "from the fire" (מן־האש *min-hā'ēš*). This phrase most likely refers to offering by fire (see also 15:2). The burnt offering is not mentioned because it is a holocaust, meaning that no portion remains for the priests to eat. Compensation from most holy sacrifices is limited to priests who are ritually clean—that is, they have not been contaminated by skin disease, bodily discharge, or contact with the dead. Furthermore, such compensation can only be eaten within the sacred precinct of the tent of meeting.

The second compensation is from "holy" (הקדשים *haqqŏdāšîm*) offerings and contributions. Unlike the most holy offerings, compensation from holy offerings can be eaten outside of the precinct of the tent of meeting by anyone in a priest's family who is ritually clean. Contributions within this lesser category are described in vv. 11-19. They include all dedicated offerings (v. 11); the first fruits of grain, wine, and oil (vv. 12-13); any devoted thing (v. 14); and the firstborn of clean animals (vv. 15-18). Verse 19, a concluding summary, states that the compensation of priests is a "covenant of salt," which probably connotes permanence. The phrase is used in v. 19 in conjunction with other language that indicates permanence (the compensation is a "perpetual due"). The two other uses of the phrase (Lev 2:13; 2 Chr 13:15) also support such an interpretation. In Lev 2:13, the salting of sacrifices appears to be a binding requirement, while in 2 Chr 13:15 the divine covenant with David is also described as a "covenant of salt," meaning that it is eternal. The phrase may also indicate obligations, since salt was regularly included in sacrifices (Lev 2:13).

The reference to "devoted things" in v. 14 requires comment. It is a translation of the Hebrew word חרם (ḥērem), which means "to separate" or "to set aside." Thus it is one of the words used to designate holiness. Yet the semantics of ḥērem are often negative. It can designate property that is taken away from individual owners and seized by the temple (Lev 27:16-25, esp. v. 21). People, too, can become ḥērem because of worshiping other gods (Exod 22:20) or as booty from holy war (Joshua 1–7). Verse 14 states that priests are allowed to possess devoted property as part of their compensation.

God owns the firstborn, and vv. 15-18 state that the firstborn belong to the priesthood as part of their payment. God's claim on firstborn humans has been addressed twice before in Numbers (3:11-13; 8:14-19; the Levites substitute for them). The divine claim on the firstborn returns in 18:15-18 in the context of compensation for priests. Firstborn of humans and of unclean animals one month of age must be redeemed at the cost of five shekels, which is paid to the priests (vv. 15-16). Clean animals, such as cows, sheep, and goats cannot be redeemed. They are holy, and God does not relinquish claim on them. Their blood must be dashed against the altar, and the fat must be burned, while their flesh becomes compensation for the priests (vv. 17-18).

18:21-24. The divine command to Aaron in v. 20 that priests cannot possess land continues into vv. 21-24, even though the topic changes to levitical compensation. Thus vv. 20-24 constitute a single unit of literature in the present form of the text. Levites are to receive a tithe (or one-tenth of Israel's produce) in return for their service of maintaining the tent of meeting and performing guard duty. The point of emphasis in this section is the role of guarding, which the Levites fulfill in protecting the tent of meeting from encroachment. This role means that the Israelites will not be able to approach the sanctuary. If any layperson does so, the Levites

bear the responsibility for the violation of the sacred space. Thus the responsibility of the Levites as guards becomes another way of alleviating Israel's fear, stated in 17:12-13, that God's presence in their midst is lethal. God's instructions to Aaron indicate that in the future only Levites would perish for any offense of encroachment.

The Levites receive a general tithe from all Israelites for the dangerous task of guarding the sanctuary (v. 21). This compensation substitutes for ownership of land in Canaan (v. 24). In these verses, the priestly writers provide few details on the nature of the tithe. What is clear is that the tithe is not a voluntary donation. It is more like a tax required of all Israelites. Such taxes, which are not unique to Israel, appear to have been a general policy of governments in the ancient Near East. Thus, for example, when Samuel lists the oppressive actions that a king will impose on Israel, he includes a royal tithe levied against all Israelites (1 Sam 8:15, 17).

Royal taxes, moreover, are closely associated with a temple tithe in the ancient Near East because of the intertwining of king and cult. The same close interrelationship also appears to have arisen during Israel's monarchical period. The book of Genesis contains etiologic stories in which the patriarchs legitimate tithing as a royal temple tax to the cultic sites of the kings. Abram tithes to Melchizedek, the king-priest of Salem (= Jerusalem) in Gen 14:20, while Jacob does the same at Bethel in Gen 28:22 (see also Amos 4:4).

The royal tithe becomes more exclusively a temple tax for the priestly writers, who envision a theocracy rather than a monarchy. References to the tithe in Deuteronomy provide some background for this transition. Tithing is addressed in the call for cult centralization in Deut 12:6, 11, 17, where it is required of all Israelites living in the land. The tithe must be brought to the cultic center by each Israelite family unit, who are then required to have a feast at the temple. The act of tithing, therefore, would appear to require a yearly religious pilgrimage to the central sanctuary (although there were exceptions). Individuals could redeem their tithe of produce if the trip from the village to the central cult site was too far.

The emphasis on cult centralization throughout Deuteronomy 12 suggests that this tithing practice was an innovation. The normal practice of tithing during the monarchical period must have occurred in local settings. Thus cult centralization presented new hardships for local levitical priests, whose incomes from tithing would have been cut off. The inclusion of the local Levite, along with all household slaves, in the family feast at the central sanctuary reinforces this conclusion. The more detailed law of the tithe in Deut 14:22-29 provides a solution to the financial problem imposed on local levitical priests through the centralization of the tithe. It prescribes two different tithes. The yearly tithe, described in vv. 22-27, consists of produce (grain, wine, oil) and firstlings of flocks that are given at the central sanctuary, thus conforming to the requirement of cult centralization in Deuteronomy 12. Deuteronomy 14:28-29 states that every third year the tithe is given locally for the Levite, for orphans, and for widows; Deut 26:12 calls this the Year of the Tithe. (Deuteronomy makes no clear distinction between Aaronide priests and Levites.)

The priestly law of the tithe in Num 19:21-24 addresses more specifically the emerging hierarchy of priests that arises from cult centralization, with the distinction between Aaronide and levitical priests. Tithes are clearly compensation to Levites (18:21-24). Thus one of the implications of serving the tent of meeting is that the Levites become responsible for collecting the temple tax. Nehemiah 10:38-39 provides a window into this responsibility when it describes the Levites as traveling from village to village to collect tithes for the post-exilic Temple. This scenario suggests that the priestly writers eliminate the yearly requirement of a pilgrimage by each Israelite family. In the process, they fashion a new office for local levitical priests: tax collection. Perhaps local collection of the tithe was one way in which Levites guarded against the encroachment outlined in Num 18:21-24. In any case, Lev 27:30-33 indicates that tithes consisted of produce and animals. Produce could be redeemed at a 20 percent surcharge, while animals could not be redeemed. The tithe was stored in the central temple (2 Chr 31:5, 6, 12; Neh 12:44; Mal 3:10).

18:25-32. Another implication of the distinction between Aaronide and levitical priests is that Levites themselves must tithe. Their tithe is described in Num 18:25-32. The requirement that Levites tithe is introduced in a divine speech to Moses, not Aaron (v. 25). The divine command is clear: The Levites also must give one-tenth of their wages to the temple. The best portion of the general tithe they receive from Israel must be given to the priest (v. 29). The penalty for withholding the tithe is death (v. 32). The remaining nine-tenths of Israel's tithe consists of levitical wages, which are no longer tied to the sanctuary in any way. This is the meaning of v. 30, where the remaining tithe is reckoned as "produce of the threshing floor, and as produce of the wine press."

19:1-22. Numbers 19 changes the focus from Aaronide priests and Levites (Numbers 18) to ordinary Israelites. The topic of the chapter is corpse contamination and the threat of defilement that it poses to the sanctuary.

Baruch Levine has argued that "the hidden agenda of Numbers 19 is the cult of the dead."[124] It is the belief that the dead lived on as ghosts. Dead ancestors were memorialized in the ancient Near East through burial rituals and continual care through offerings of food and drink. Observance ensured protection from evil.[125] Israelites observed the cult of the dead at least with regard to kings. The burial of Asa in 2 Chr 16:13-14 may refer to such a practice. The prophet Ezekiel lists the burial of kings within the Temple as one of the practices in the monarchical period that defiled the sanctuary, forcing God to abandon it (Ezek 43:6-9).[126] Prohibitions against sacrificing to the dead are stated in the law of first fruits (Deut 26:13-15), again suggesting an ongoing practice. Scholars speculate whether the responsibility of caring for the dead originally fell on the firstborn, giving them sacred status (see the Commentary on 3:11-13).[127]

---

124. Levine, *Numbers 1–20*, 472.
125. Jerold S. Cooper, "The Fate of Mankind: Death and Afterlife in Ancient Mesopotamia," in *Death and Afterlife: Perspectives of World Religions*, ed. Hiroshi Obayashi, Contributions to the Study of Religion 13 (New York: Greenwood, 1992) 19-33, esp. 27-30.
126. One of the innovations of the Josianic reform at the close of the monarchical period was the elimination of ancestral worship, at least as the official practice of the state (2 Kgs 23:15-16).
127. Milgrom, *Numbers*, 432.

In the cult of the dead, the ancestral ghosts remained part of the community, and authority within society remained focused on the past.[128]

The priestly writers oppose worshiping the dead or giving them any authority in the community of the living. Death becomes the most extreme form of defilement for priestly writers. Far from providing power to the living, it pollutes those whom it touches and drives God away. Thus the priestly writers forbid priests to officiate at funerals, removing the mediatorial power of the priesthood from burial ceremonies (Lev 21:1-15). They also remove all burial rituals from the sanctuary. Those contaminated from contact with the dead are expelled from the camp (Num 5:1-4). Rejection of the cult of the dead indicates the priestly writers' future orientation in understanding the power of salvation. They deny past actions of ancestors as determining the fate of Israelites. Authority rests in Yahweh's promise about the future gift of the land. Worship of the ancestors could only lead to death.[129]

Numbers 19 outlines procedures for Israelites to be purified from corpse contamination and thus reenter the camp. Contamination occurs through touching or simply from being in the proximity of the dead. Any person contaminated by death becomes a threat to God's life-giving holiness in the sanctuary. This is the only time that this topic is addressed in the OT. Its placement at this particular juncture in Numbers answers the Israelites' question from 17:12-13: How are they to live in the sphere of divine holiness and not perish? Thus, contrary to many interpreters,[130] chap. 19 is an integral part of the conflicts over priestly leadership in chaps. 16–19. Thomas Mann has gone so far as to argue that holiness and death are the central themes throughout these chapters for the priestly writers and that these themes extend through 20:2-13, where Moses and

Aaron are also condemned to death because of their violation of holiness.[131]

The central ingredient in the ritual in this chapter is the "water of cleansing" (מי נדה‎ mê niddâ). Water bears cleansing properties throughout priestly law. It is used, for example, to cleanse lepers (Leviticus 14). But the water of cleansing is a special potion, derived mainly from the ashes of a red heifer, that has the power to purify those who have been contaminated through contact with the dead. The water of cleansing also appears in 31:23, where it is used as a detergent to purify warriors after holy war.

The four references to the water of cleansing in chap. 19 (vv. 9, 13, 20-21) span three sections. Verses 1-10a describe how the potion is made from the ashes of a red heifer, as well as other ingredients. Verses 10b-13 and 14-22 describe conditions for using the potion: vv. 10b-13 state that the water must be used for both Israelites and resident aliens; vv. 14-22 outline the different conditions that make someone impure.

Scholars debate whether Numbers 19 consists of two sections (vv. 1-13, 14-22) or three (vv. 1-10a, 10b-13, and 14-22).[132] They also question whether the chapter constitutes an original unit of law or is the final result of an ongoing process of supplementation. Verses 10b-13 may, indeed, be a later addition to vv. 1-10a and 14-22, since these verses clarify that contamination from the dead affects both Israelites and resident aliens. The commentary will follow the three-part structure of vv. 1-10a, vv. 10b-13, and vv. 14-22. But even here questions arise concerning the headings to the different sections. Verses 1-10a and vv. 14-22 are introduced with clear headings: "This is the [statute of the] law." Verses 10b-13 begin with the words "a perpetual statute," perhaps a summary conclusion to vv. 1-10a, in which case the middle section consists of vv. 11-13.

19:1-10a. This section consists of legislation aimed at Israelites, not at their priests (v. 2). It describes a ritual of riddance or exorcism, which decontaminates persons from defilement through contact with the dead.

128. George E. Mendenhall, "From Witchcraft to Justice: Death and Afterlife in the Old Testament," in Obayashi, *Death and Afterlife*, 71-72.

129. See 28. Mendenhall, "From Witchcraft to Justice: Death and Afterlife in the Old Testament," 67-81, for discussion of the historical character of ancient Israelite religion and how this perspective conflicted with worship of the ancestors.

130. See, e.g., Noth, *Numbers*, 139.

131. T. W. Mann, "Holiness and Death in the Redaction of Numbers 16:1–20:13," in *Love and Death in the Ancient Near East: Essays in Honor of Marvin H. Pope*, ed. J. H. Marks and R. M. Good (Guilford: Four Quarters, 1987) 181-90.

132. For a summary of positions see Budd, *Numbers*, 209-10.

Verses 1-2 describes the animal to be used, vv. 3-6 the details of the ritual, and vv. 7-10*a* its effects on all the participants. Israel is to present a cow for sacrifice. The Hebrew is unclear, but it would appear that the priestly writers intend that the cow be full grown, and not a calf. Four conditions are stated concerning the cow. It must be red, perhaps to symbolize blood. It must be physically perfect (NIV, "without defect or blemish"; NRSV, "without defect, in which there is no blemish"). The Hebrew word used in this instance, תמימה (*tĕmîmâ*), means "complete" or "whole." The cow must be without blemish, and it must never have been yoked. Gray is probably correct to conclude that the prohibition against a yoke precludes that the animal has been used for profane work, such as plowing.[133] The two cows used by the Philistines to return the ark to Israel (1 Sam 6:7) also meet this requirement, suggesting that they were being presented to Israel for sacrifice.

The ritual is described in vv. 3-6. It required priestly supervision by Eleazar: the cow must be slaughtered in his presence and then burned in fire. The blood of the cow must be sprinkled seven times in the direction of the entrance of the tent of meeting. All of these actions resemble a sacrifice (e.g., Lev 4:6; 14:7; see also the ritual of atonement in Leviticus 16). But the ritual of the red cow takes place outside the camp, away from the altar. Thus it is not technically a sacrifice, even though it is specifically described as a purification (sacrifice) in v. 9. The unique function of the ashes of the red cow to eliminate impurity from corpse contamination partially explains this irregularity, since persons so defiled were banished from the camp (5:1-4). It also provides background for another exceptional feature of the ritual: The blood is burned in the fire along with the skin, flesh, and dung of the cow (v. 5). Blood in the ashes of the red cow is the ritual detergent that purifies,[134] along with three additional ingredients: cedar wood, hyssop, and crimson (v. 6). These ingredients are also used in the purification of the leper (Leviticus 14), but the precise reasons for their combination are not clear. Cedar is aromatic, as is hyssop, which is associated with a ritual of purification in Ps 51:7:

"Purge me with hyssop, and I shall be clean." Crimson, or red, may have symbolic significance in association with blood.

Verses 7-10*a* describe the effects of the ritual on all the participants. The water of cleansing (מי נדה *mê niddâ*) purifies. The Hebrew word translated "cleansing" (נדה *niddâ*) probably comes from a verb meaning "to cast off" (נדה *nādâ*).[135] Gray states that this word tends to describe ritual impurity, such as menstrual blood (Lev 12:2; Ezek 18:6).[136] In the reference to menstruation, Levine notes the ambiguity of whether the casting off describes the flow of blood or the social isolation of women during menstruation.[137] In v. 9, the act of casting off with water removes impurity, hence the translation "water of cleansing." A ritual of washing with water to purify Levites was described in 8:7 as the "water of purification" (מי חטאת *mê ḥaṭṭā't*). This term returns in 19:9, where the water of cleansing is described as a purification offering (חטאת *ḥaṭṭā't*) for ordinary Israelites. The water of cleansing provides a way for Israelites to reenter the camp safely after expulsion on account of corpse contamination (5:1-4), and thus to continue to live in the sphere of divine holiness.

Paradoxically, all three individuals involved in performing the ritual become impure and thus must undergo separate acts of purification, involving the washing of clothes (see also 8:7; Exod 19:10) and bathing before reentering the camp. The priest who supervises the ritual and the layperson who burns the red cow must wash their clothes and bathe before entering the camp at evening. The ritually clean person who gathers the ashes of the red cow is required to wash his clothes before reentering the camp at evening.

19:10b-13. The central point in this section is that both Israelites and resident aliens (see Commentary on 9:1-14 and 15:1-16) are susceptible to defilement from the dead. Purification lasts seven days and requires washing with the water of cleansing on the third and seventh days. Failure to perform the purification ritual results in being cut off from the

133. Gray, *Numbers*, 249.
134. Milgrom, *Numbers*, 159, 438-43.

135. Levine, *Numbers 1–20*, 463.
136. Gray, *Numbers*, 252.
137. Levine, *Numbers 1–20*, 463-64.

congregation, meaning excommunication or perhaps even execution.

19:14-22. This section provides more detailed commentary concerning the circumstances under which someone becomes defiled from contact with the dead (vv. 14-16) and the ritual processes for using the water of cleansing (vv. 17-22). If someone dies inside a tent, all persons and all open vessels in that tent will be contaminated for seven days (v. 14). Here contamination is thought to permeate an entire space irrespective of actual contact with the dead. Defilement from a corpse in an open field, however, requires contact. This form of contamination also lingers for seven days (v. 15). Contamination in the open field is defined more precisely as contact with a human who has been killed or someone who has died of natural causes or even contact with human bones. Thus, according to priestly writers, the impurity of the dead is permanent.[138]

The procedures for purification are outlined in vv. 17-22. Ashes from the red cow must be mixed with running water. The Hebrew in v. 17 differs slightly from the NRSV's "running water" and the NIV's "fresh water." The ashes of the red cow are described as "dust" in Hebrew, while running water is literally "living water" (מים חיים *mayim ḥayyîm*). Living water is water that is not stagnant, but spring fed. A ritually clean person is required to dip hyssop into the potion and sprinkle it on contaminated persons and objects on the third and seventh days (v. 18). As was the case for those preparing the ingredients, the person performing the ritual is also rendered unclean until evening, requiring the washing of clothes and a bath. Verses 21-22 add two further clarifications about ritual impurity: The water of cleansing contaminates through touch, making a person unclean until evening, and contamination from the dead can be spread by touching something that an unclean person has touched. Verse 20 underscores the necessity of purification for any person contaminated by the dead, since they pose a threat to the sanctuary. Failure to follow proper procedures leads to being cut off from the assembly.

---

138. Levine, *Numbers 1–20,* 467.

REFLECTIONS

1. The ritual of cleansing with the ashes of the red heifer is the most detailed treatment of death in the Old Testament. Upon first reading, the priestly theology of death appears to be far removed from the New Testament, where resurrection from the dead is central. The priestly writers do not share a belief in resurrection, but their theology of death informs New Testament teaching in a number of ways.

First, death is defined over against holiness by priestly writers and in New Testament literature. Death is a power that is incompatible with the holiness of God, and thus it defiles. Those infected with corpse contamination are expelled from the camp (Num 5:1-4). In the same way, life in Christ and death are incompatible for Christians (Rom 5:12-21; 7–8).

Second, the power of death is combated through sacraments of atonement. Those contaminated from contact with the dead must be purified with the water of cleansing from the red heifer in order to reenter the camp. Christians, too, are purged from the power of death through sacraments. Baptism defeats death (1 Pet 3:19-21), while the eucharist is a messianic feast in the kingdom of God.

Third, the mediation between holiness and death is a priestly form of leadership. A priest is required to oversee the making of the ashes from the red heifer. In Christian tradition, Jesus becomes the ashes of the red heifer in his role as high priest (Heb 9:11-14). The administration of Jesus' cleansing power through sacraments remains a priestly function of ministry. Power in this situation is rooted not in personality, but in formal structures of healing that emerge from the holiness of Jesus. The defeat of death is central to the priestly writers and to the Christian faith. The points of continuity indicate how influential the priestly theology of death is to the formation of Christian theology and liturgy.

2. There is a future orientation in the priestly writers' view of community that is foundational to Christian teaching. It emerges from their emphasis on individual responsibilty and divine forgiveness, first articulated in Numbers 13–15. The identity of Israel rests on Yahweh's promise of the land, according to the priestly writers, and not on the past actions of the ancestors. This future orientation is carried over into the teaching on death. Dead ancestors are not allowed to influence the living. Death itself is banished from the camp. The identity of the community is formed, instead, by marching ahead to the promised land.

The church extends the future orientation of the priestly writers in its teaching on death. Death is not only banished from the camp, but it is also defeated in the resurrection of Jesus and in the promise of his future return. But the foundation for this teaching rests in priestly tradition. The future orientation of the priestly writers is the building block of Christian sacraments. Baptism creates an eschatological community, in which the past loses authority for Christians because death has been defeated. Christians continue to reflect on past tradition, but only to understand the present and the future, not to worship the past of the ancestors. Christians feast with the saints in the eucharist, but this is not a cult of the dead in which the past holds authority over the present. It is an eschatological banquet in which the present and the future merge in Christ.

3. The laws regarding priestly and levitical tithes provide guidelines for reflecting on the special position of clergy within the church. Two aspects of the priestly office stand out in Numbers 18.

First, priests are paid by the congregation through tithing. Tithing, moreover, is not a gift; it is an obligation of the laity. It is one way in which the congregation of Israel is able to appoach God. Supporting priests and Levites financially allows them to fulfill their office and thus protect Israel from the danger of holiness. The command to support clergy continues into the New Testament. Paul refers to the obligation of Christians to tithe (1 Cor 9:13-14). The author of 1 Timothy is even more direct in demanding pay for preachers and teachers (1 Tim 5:17-18).

Second, priests forfeit land ownership because of their special calling. They are set apart in this respect from other members of the congregation. Numbers 18:20 states that the priests' special status with Yahweh replaces their right to inherit land. Celibacy among Roman Catholic priests provides a partial analogy to the special status of priests in Numbers 18. They give up marriage and family in exchange for their special status with God. Finding an analogy for Protestant clergy is more difficult. Yet the question is important for any clergyperson. What are clergy called to forfeit because of their special status with God?

NUMBERS 20:1–21:35, LEAVING THE WILDERNESS

COMMENTARY

Numbers 20–21 is a loose collection of stories clustered around three general locations: Kadesh, Mt. Hor, and the Transjordan. Kadesh is the location for Miriam's death (20:1), the failure of leadership by Moses and Aaron (20:2-13), and a conflict with the Edomites concerning passage through their land (20:14-21). Mount Hor is the location for Aaron's death (20:22-29), the defeat of the Canaanite king of Arad at Hormah (21:1-3), and the attack by fiery serpents as Israel journeys around Edom on the Red Sea road (21:4-9). A series of Transjordanian locations concludes the section, providing the setting for Israel's defeat of the Amorite kings Sihon and Og (21:10-35).

This synopsis illustrates how chaps. 20–21 provide a transition in the book of Numbers from wandering and death in the wilderness to successful holy war in the Transjordan. The transitional character of this section creates ambiguity about its central themes. It can be read both as a story about the death of the first generation in the wilderness and as a story about the successful inauguration of holy war by the second generation. Its different points of focus have spawned debate among interpreters concerning the place of chaps. 20–21 in the larger structure of the book. This debate may be unresolvable, since the ambiguity has been built into the literature itself by the pre-priestly and priestly authors.

The pre-priestly stories include the following sequence: The conflict with Edom (20:14-21) follows the spy story (chaps. 13–14) and the rebellion of Dathan and Abiram (chap. 16). These stories take place at Kadesh. The defeat of the Canaanite king of Arad (21:1-3) and the attack by fiery serpents (21:4-9) occur in the vicinity of Mt. Hor. And the defeat of the Amorite kings, Sihon and Og (21:10-35), takes place in the Transjordan.

The pre-priestly writers emphasize positive themes in chaps. 20–21, focusing on the second generation's leaving the wilderness and beginning their initial conquest of Transjordan. This conclusion is based on comparison to Deut 1:46–3:17. The death of the first generation is never stated in chaps. 20–21, nor anywhere else in the pre-priestly version of Numbers, but it appears in Deuteronomy. There are differences between Numbers 20–21 and Deut 1:46–3:17, especially with regard to geography. Deuteronomy 2:3-13 notes that Israel went through Edom and Moab, while Num 20:14-21 makes no mention of Moab and enlarges the confrontation with Edom before concluding that Israel did not go through this land. Yet the accounts are similar enough to suggest some form of

relationship between the two, at least concerning the first and second generations.

Reference to the Wadi Zered in Deuteronomy and in Numbers provides an anchor point for discerning the transition from the first to the second generations. In Deuteronomy, the first generation of Israelites dies during the wilderness journey between Kadesh-barnea and the Wadi Zered. Deuteronomy 1:46–2:2 locates the wilderness wandering of the first generation in the region of Mt. Seir. Deuteronomy 2:7 states that the duration of this wandering is forty years. Deuteronomy 2:13-15 adds that travel from Kadesh-barnea to the Wadi Zered took thirty-eight years and that, during this time, the entire first generation of Israelites died. Their deaths provide transition in Deut 2:16-17 to holy war against Sihon and Og by the second generation of Israelites.

The Wadi Zered is also embedded in Num 20:10-20, where it signifies transition from the wilderness to the border of the Amorite kingdom at Arnon (vv. 12-13). This point of transition marks the beginning of holy war in the book of Numbers, just as it does in Deuteronomy. The parallel to Deuteronomy suggests that the second generation is the focal point at this juncture in Numbers. But the exact point of transition between generations is not clear. According to Numbers 20–21, the first generation may have died off already at Kadesh. The story of holy war at Mt. Hor against the King of Arad (21:1-3) may point to action by the second generation, in which case it provides a contrast to the defeat of the first generation at the same location immediately after the loss of the land (14:39-45). Such an interpretation would correspond to the perspective of Deuteronomy, where the first generation never engages in a successful holy war after the spy story. Even without locating the precise point of transition from the first to the second generation in Numbers 20–21, it is clear that the pre-priestly version of events is oriented toward the future conquest of the Transjordan by the second generation.

The priestly writers add three stories. They include Miriam's death at Kadesh, along with an itinerary notice indicating Israel's arrival there (20:1). The failure of leadership by Moses and Aaron is also included at Kadesh

(20:2-13). The priestly writers locate the death of Aaron at Mt. Hor (20:22-29).

The priestly writers focus on the theme of death in the wilderness for the first generation by highlighting both the failure of the leadership and the deaths of the heroes of the exodus—Miriam, Aaron, and Moses. Thus their reading of chaps. 20–21 is not oriented toward a future conquest. In fact, the second generation of Israelites does not become a clear focus of the priestly writers until the second census in chap. 26 (see 26:63-65). For them, the deaths of the first generation are not complete until chap. 25, when Phinehas the priest slaughters all those who worshiped the baal of Peor (chap. 25).

This overview illustrates that interpretation must deal with two points of view in Numbers 20–21. The pre-priestly writers turn their focus toward the land, emphasizing that the second generation of Israelites will leave the wilderness and begin the conquest of the Transjordan. The priestly writers focus on the wilderness in order to explore the theme of the deaths of the leaders of the exodus.

20:1. The section begins with a travel notice that Israel has entered the wilderness of Zin and is encamped at Kadesh. Two terms are used to describe the people: "Israelites" and "the whole congregation." The combination of these terms occurs only in this itinerary notice and in the itinerary notice in v. 22. Some scholars suggest that reference to Kadesh was already present in the pre-priestly story—not as an itinerary notice but to remind the reader that Israel is still encamped there. "The whole congregation" (כל-העדה *kol-hā'ēdâ*) is one of the central phrases used by the priestly writers. This phrase, along with reference to the wilderness of Zin (see 13:21; 27:14; 33:36; 34:3-4, all P) suggest that the itinerary notice is the work of the priestly writers. The date for Israel's arrival at Kadesh in the priestly itinerary lacks reference to year and day. It simply states the "first month." Comparison to 33:38-39, however, indicates that it is the fortieth year of wilderness wandering. The itinerary notice is significant to the priestly history. It places Israel at Kadesh only at the end of the wilderness journey, as compared to the pre-priestly version, in which Israel arrives at Kadesh in the

second year of the wilderness journey (chaps. 13–14).

In spite of their different chronologies, both histories portray Kadesh as the setting for negative stories. In the pre-priestly history, Kadesh was the general location for a series of negative accounts about the first generation of Israelites to leave Egypt. The events take place over an extended period of time and include the loss of the land (chaps. 13–14), the defeat at Hormah (14:39-45), and the challenge to Moses' leadership by Dathan and Abiram (chap. 16). The priestly writers also view events at Kadesh negatively, but their focus is narrowed to a shorter period of time and to the leadership of the first generation of Israelites to leave Egypt. Paran is the place where Israel loses the land. Kadesh, on the other hand, is the place where Miriam dies and is buried (Num 20:1). It is also the place where Moses and Aaron disobey God and lose the gift of the land (20:2-13).

Miriam's death is noted almost in passing. No reason for her death is given, nor is any mention made of mourning rites (cf. the deaths of Aaron in 20:29 and Moses in Deut 34:8). Yet her death is significant because of her role in the exodus, both as the savior of Moses (Exod 2:1-10) and as the one who sang a victory song of salvation at the Red Sea (Exod 15:20-21). Along with Moses and Aaron, she is one of the three leaders of the exodus. Whether her death in the wilderness at Kadesh is meant to be a result of her earlier challenge to Moses' leadership (chap. 12) is unclear; no direct connection is drawn. But her death at Kadesh foreshadows the deaths of Moses and Aaron, the other two heroes of the exodus.

20:2-13. The priestly writers follow Miriam's death notice with a story about the disobedience of Moses and Aaron, which results in their not being able to enter the promised land of Canaan. This story is a continuation of the idealization of Moses as a leader, which has been a central theme throughout chap. 11–21. In this case, however, Moses models the failure of leadership. This section is an outgrowth of the priestly emphasis on individual responsibility, introduced in the story of the loss of the land (14:26-35). Individual responsibility before God means that Moses and Aaron could no longer be denied entrance into the promised land simply because of the collective sin of the people, as was the case in Deuteronomy. Thus the central purpose of this story is clear: The priestly writers recount the sin of Moses and Aaron that denies them entrance into the promised land. In the process, they illustrate failure of leadership in the wilderness community. Yet the interpretation of the sin of Moses has puzzled interpreters. Scholars debate whether his sin lies in striking the rock, in his character, in his speech to the people, or perhaps in some feature no longer recorded in the text.[139]

Verses 2-13 recount a four-part murmuring story about lack of water. It begins with a complaint against Moses and Aaron by the congregation (vv. 2-6) includes motifs found also in other murmuring stories. The people question why Moses has brought them up from Egypt to die of thirst in the desert. The second scene (vv. 7-8) consists of a theophany of the glory of Yahweh at the entrance of the tent of meeting, where Moses and Aaron receive instruction about procuring water. They must (1) take the rod from its position before Yahweh; (2) assemble the people; and (3) speak to the rock in order to bring forth from it water for the Israelites and their cattle. Commentators debate whether the rod in this story belongs to Moses or to Aaron. The location of the rod before Yahweh in the tent of meeting suggests that it is the budding rod of Aaron, since this is where Moses was commanded to place it (17:10).

In the third scene (vv. 8-11), Moses only partially executes the divine order. He takes the rod from before Yahweh and assembles the people. Instead of speaking to the rock, however, he addresses the people and strikes the rock twice with the rod. Thus one aspect of Moses' sin is his failure to follow the divine command, especially the last requirement of speaking to the rock. The final scene (vv. 12-13) consists of a divine speech in which the sin of Moses is described as not having trusted in Yahweh and not sanctifying God before Israel. The word "to sanctify" in Hebrew (הקדיש *hiqdîš*, hiphil from קדש *qādaš*) is a pun on the place name "Kadesh." The two words include the same consonants in Hebrew (ק *q*; ד *d*; ש *š*). The episode concludes with an etiology on the

"waters of Meribah" (מי מריבה *mê mĕrîbâ*). The place name "Meribah" includes the root consonants from the verb "to quarrel" (ריב *rîb*). The etiology combines the quarrelling of Israel with the sanctifying presence of Yahweh: "These are the waters of Meribah, where the people of Israel quarreled [*rîb*] with Yahweh, and by which he showed his holiness [*qādaš*, niphal]."

The etiology indicates that vv. 2-13 are meant to be read as a positive story of divine provision in the wilderness. It is the only murmuring story in the entire book of Numbers that does not prompt divine anger and judgment against Israel. By contrast, the general complaint in 11:1-3; the desire for meat in 11:4-35 (esp. v. 10); the complaint of Miriam and Aaron in 12:9; the spy story in 14:11-12, 26-35; and the Korah, Dathan, and Abiram rebellion in 16:21, 45 all result in divine anger and judgment on the people.

The positive orientation of the need for water in 20:2-13 is reinforced by its many parallels to Exod 17:1-7, where Israel also complains about lack of water without prompting divine punishment. Furthermore, both stories use the verb "to quarrel" (*rîb*) in the complaint of the people, giving both accounts legal overtones (20:3; Exod 17:2). The Hebrew verb translated "to quarrel" (*rîb*) frequently means "to conduct a legal case," while the noun often refers to a lawsuit.[140] The legal dimension of both stories is reflected in their similar etiology of Meribah (20:13; Exod 17:7). The positive character of Israel's legal complaint in these verses is very important for interpreting the sin of Moses. It suggests that Israel's desire for water has been voiced in the proper way and that God intends to respond appropriately by supplying water to them.

Moses' sin includes both his actions and his words to Israel. His sin of action is clear from the synopsis of the story. He does not follow divine instructions in responding to the people's dispute. Striking the rock conveys divine anger in response to Israel's legal claim, when, in fact, there is none. In this action, Moses demonstrates his own lack of faith in the very structures he should uphold. Thus God accuses him of not trusting and, hence, of not being able to mediate divine

---

139. Milgrom, *Numbers*, 448-56.

140. *BDB*, 936; and *KB*, 888b-89a.

holiness in the midst of the people. Moses fails as a leader by not following the appropriate means of communication and accountability between God and Israel.

This sin is compounded by Moses' angry address to Israel before he strikes the rock with this rod: "You rebels!" (המרים *hammōrîm*). The sinful nature of Moses' words comes into full view when they are interpreted against the backdrop of the rebellion of Korah in chaps. 16–17. Israel's complaint in 20:3 first established a connection between these two stories: "Would that we had died [גוענו *gāwa'nû*] when our kindred died [בגוע *bigwa'*] before the LORD!" The word translated "to die" (גוע *gāwa'*) repeats the exclamation of the people at the conclusion of the Korah rebellion (17:12-13): "Are we all to perish [*gāwa'*] [in approaching God]?" The repetition suggests that their legal complaint in 20:2-13 for water may be one way in which Israel is able to approach God without perishing. Yet Moses does not discern the appropriateness of their action. He misinterprets their legal complaint as rebellion against God. In doing so, he fails as a leader by not discerning proper ways for Israel to approach God in the wilderness.

Moses' failure of leadership and his self-indictment are conveyed ironically through Aaron's rod, which he was required to remove from the tent of meeting. It provides yet another connection to the rebellion of Korah. In fact, the budding of Aaron's rod prompted Israel's exclamation of fear in 17:12-13. They were afraid because this rod became a sign to rebels not to complain against God. The structure of 20:2-13, suggests, however, that Israel's legal complaint about water is not an instance of rebellion through murmuring. Indeed, the peculiar divine command to Moses that he take the rod with him when he draws water from the rock, but not wield it against the rock, reinforces the positive context of the people's legal complaint. Thus, when Moses uses the rod to strike the rock, he is doing more than simply disobeying divine instructions. He is also judging the situation as an act of rebellion by the people against God. This action is consistent with his message that the people are rebels. Instead, he becomes the rebel through his misuse of the rod, which prompts his own death sentence, rather than Israel's.

20:14-21. The final story associated with Kadesh concerns Israel's request to pass through the land of Edom. Moses sends messengers from Kadesh to the king of Edom. The account takes the form of diplomatic correspondence, which includes naming the recipient, a messenger formula, identification of the sender and his rank, the present predicament and motive for the message, and finally the request itself.[141]

In v. 14, the recipient of the message is identified as "the King of Edom." This is followed by a messenger formula, "Thus says your brother Israel," including the name of the sender, "Israel," and his rank, "brother." The latter refers to the ancestral story of the brothers Jacob and Esau (Gen 25:19–33:20). Israel's approach of Edom is reminiscent of Jacob's approach to Esau in Genesis 32–33.

Verses 16-17, a description of Israel's present situation, includes a synopsis of the exodus. The ancestors of the Israelites went down to Egypt and lived there many years. But they were oppressed by the Egyptians, prompting their cry to God for help. The Lord heard their cry and sent an angel, who brought them out of Egypt. This summary of the exodus is similar to accounts in Deut 26:5-9 and Judg 11:16-18, though not in all details. The reference to the angel, or more precisely in Hebrew, "divine messenger" (מלאך *mal'āk*) is unique to this version of the exodus. The same word is used to describe the human messengers whom Moses sends to the king of Edom. The most prominent characteristic of the divine messenger is leading Israel in holy war. The divine messenger was present at the confrontation with Egypt at the Red Sea (Exod 14:19), and God promises that the divine messenger will lead Israel in conquest of the land (Exod 23:20-33; 33:2). Thus holy war overtones are present in the message to the King of Edom, but not when the exodus is recounted from the setting of the promised land in Deut 26:5-9 and Judg 11:16-18.

Moses requests permission for the Israelites to pass through the land of Edom on the King's Highway (v. 17), a trade route running north and south from southern Arabia

141. Wenham, *Numbers,* 152.

to Syria. He promises that they will stay on this route, harming no field and drinking no water. The central motif in this request is that the people be allowed to "cross over" (עבר ʿābar) the land, a word that occurs three times in this single verse. The literal meaning of the request "to cross over" is "to travel"—Israel wishes to pass through the land. But the word also bears overtones of conquest. The final refrain in the Song of the Sea (Exod 15:16), for example, describes Israel's conquest as "crossing over" the nations, which in this hymn includes Edom. The language suggests that the central theme of the book of Numbers is changing from wilderness wandering to conquest, even though no holy war against Edom occurs.

Verses 18-21 recount the exchange between Israel and Edom. Both nations are represented by individuals, recalling the ancestral stories of Jacob and Esau, in which the nations of Israel and Edom are represented by persons. Edom refuses Israel's request for passage in v. 18 and even threatens war. Israel responds in v. 19 by repeating the request and offering to pay for water. The story ends in vv. 20-21 with the king of Edom refusing to allow the Israelites to cross over and even meeting them with an army, thus forcing "Israel to turn away from him."

The closing line, "So Israel turned away from Edom," is suggestive. On one level it is a geographical statement. Israel looked for another route to the promised land around Edom. But one wanders if it also reflects Israel's experience during the exile. The title "King of Edom" is certainly anachronistic for the setting of the story, since Edom was an independent state only from the eighth to the sixth centuries BCE, the end of Israel's monarchical period.[142] The treachery of the Edomites in the immediate aftermath of Jerusalem's destruction is specifically mentioned in Israel's anguished lament of the exile (Ps 137:7), and it is also the topic of the exilic prophet Obadiah. Read from the perspective of the exile, the pre-priestly story of Num 20:14-21 functions as an etiology that describes how Israel's brother nation, the Edomites, refused to assist in a time of need, thus causing Israel to turn away from them.

---

142. J. R. Bartlett, "The Rise and Fall of the Kingdom of Edom," *PEQ* 104 (1972) 26-37.

20:22-29. An itinerary notice in v. 22 indicates that Israel leaves Kadesh and arrives at Mt. Hor. Two events are addressed in these verses: the death of Aaron and the passing on of the office of high priest. The story is closely linked with the preceding stories in this chapter. Mount Hor stands in the proximity of Edom, the location of vv. 14-21, and Aaron's death is a result of his earlier disobedience at Kadesh (vv. 2-13). The account of Aaron's death follows the pattern of divine command to Moses (vv. 23-26) and its fulfillment (vv. 27-28). It concludes with mourning rituals (v. 29).

The death of Aaron is a significant event in the book of Numbers and, indeed, in the entire Pentateuch. His death, along with the deaths of Miriam and Moses, will mark the end of the generation of Israelites who were liberated from Egypt. One indication of Aaron's significance is that his death is remembered in two different traditions within the Pentateuch. Deuteronomy 10:6 locates his death at Moserah; Num 20:2-13 places it at Mt. Hor. The complete itinerary list of the wilderness march in Numbers 33 makes it clear that these locations were not regarded as the same. In 33:31-37, Moserah is seven stops removed from Mt. Hor. Both traditions contain a notice of Eleazar's succeeding Aaron as high priest.

The details surrounding the death of Aaron further attest to his importance in tradition. Like Moses (Deut 34:1-8), he dies on a mountaintop and is gathered to his ancestors, prompting mourning for thirty days. The usual period of mourning was seven days (Gen 50:10; Job 2:13). Thus the month-long period of mourning indicates the prominence of Aaron. Moses is the only other person whose death prompted a thirty-day period of mourning (Deut 34:1-8). Numbers 33:38-39 dates Aaron's death to Year 40, Month 5, Day 1 after the exodus from Egypt, making him 123 years old. According to the priestly writers, he undertook the exodus at 83 years of age (Exod 7:7). The phrase "was gathered to his people" is applied to many of the male heroes in the Pentateuch: e.g., Abraham (Gen 25:8); Ishmael (Gen 25:17); Isaac (Gen 35:29); Jacob (Gen 49:33); and Moses (Num 27:13; 31:2; Deut 32:50). It provides a glimpse into Israel's view of Sheol as a place where one is united with ancestors. Whether this was Israel's only view of the afterlife or whether Sheol was limited to men is unclear.

Aaron's death also provides occasion for the priestly writers to model succession of leadership in the office of high priest. The office is inherited; thus it is a non-charismatic form of leadership. There is no transfer of a prophetic spirit or laying on of hands. Instead, Eleazar is invested with the signs of the office. Aaron is stripped of his priestly vestments, and they are placed on Eleazar. The Israelites know that Aaron has died, because they see the priestly vestments on Eleazar. The vestments of the high priest are described in Lev 8:7-9. They include a tunic with sash and robe, the decorated band of the ephod, a breastpiece containing the Urim and Thummin, and a turban with a golden ornament and a holy crown. The procedure for transferring these sacred garments from one high priest to another is described in Exod 29:29-30. The ritual of investiture includes anointing and ordination over a seven-day period within the tent of meeting. These details are not specifically recounted in Num 20:22-29.

21:1-3. These verses tell a story of divine deliverance and a successful holy war against the Canaanite king of Arad in the Negeb at Hormah. The episode is clearly out of place in its present literary context, for it is inserted between the death of Aaron at Mt. Hor (20:22) and Israel's departure from Mt. Hor to travel south around Edom (21:4). Thus it momentarily transports Israel to a military campaign in the north, while the itinerary has them traveling south on the Red Sea road. A tradition of victory against Arad in the Negeb is preserved in Judg 1:16, but Num 21:1-3 does not appear to be the same story. Furthermore, the geographical references suggest that no such kingdom of Arad existed during the Late Bronze Age. Interpretation will focus on the literary purpose of 21:1-3 at this juncture in the book of Numbers.

Numbers 21:1-3 is structured as a story of divine deliverance in a threatening situation. The king of Arad attacks Israel and takes captives (v. 1). Israel asks God for help, vowing to place all the cities of Arad under the חרם (ḥērem) ban (v. 2). Under the ḥērem ban, all property would be given over to God through destruction, rather than becoming booty for the warriors. God hears the Israelites' request and gives the Canaanites to them in battle (v. 3a). As Israel had vowed, they turn all the cities over to God by destroying them. Hence the etiological name "Hormah," from the Hebrew word חרם (ḥērem). Milgrom has suggested that the story is meant to underscore the sin of Moses by presenting his failed attempt at holy war in Canaan after being denied entry into the land.[143] But Moses is conspicuously absent from this story. Furthermore, this is a positive story about Israel, and not about specific leaders.

The setting of the story at Hormah provides a connection to Israel's failed attempt at holy war at the close of the spy story in 14:39-45, which also took place at Hormah. The meaning of the story most likely lies in this repetition. Both stories focus on Israel, rather than on specific leaders, and both are paradigmatic for holy war. The first story provides a negative example of holy war, illustrating what not to do. Divine direction is rejected, war is waged out of desperation, and Israel is defeated. In 21:1-3, holy war is waged as a response to oppression, divine direction is sought before the battle, ḥērem vows are made to ensure that war is not motivated by self-interest, and Israel is successful. Levine's suggestion that the repetition marks a transition from the first to the second generation may also be correct, although there are no clear statements to this effect in the story.[144] What is clear is that the insertion of holy war at Hormah is one more instance of the transition from wilderness wandering to conquest of the promised land in Numbers 20–21.

21:4-9. The final murmuring story occurs when Israel leaves Mt. Hor and journeys south around Edom on the Red Sea road (v. 4). The story moves briskly without providing many details; in this respect, it resembles the first murmuring story after Israel's departure from Sinai (11:1-3). In both instances, general complaint leads immediately to divine punishment, prompting confession by the people and the request for intercession by Moses, whose prayer persuades God to eliminate the punishment. These parallels in structure underscore that the stories of Israel's

143. Milgrom, *Numbers,* 458. For fuller discussion of *ḥērem,* see P. Stern, *The Biblical Herem: A Window on Israel's Religious Experience,* BJS 211 (Atlanta: Scholars Press, 1991); N. Lohfink, "haram," *TDOT* 5:180-99.
144. Levine, *Numbers 1–20,* 60.

wilderness journey from Sinai to the plains of Moab are framed by instances of murmuring and successful intercession by Moses.

Israel's final complaint is directed against both Moses and God (vv. 4-5). It includes the idealization of Egypt, characteristic of most of the murmuring stories. The specific complaint by Israel about the wilderness is presented as incoherent ranting. They have neither bread nor water, yet they do not like the miserable food in their possession!

God responds in v. 6 by sending poisonous serpents to bite and kill many of the people. The translation "poisonous" serpents is from the Hebrew word שרפים (śĕrāpîm), which comes from the verb meaning "to burn" (שרף śārap). These snakes are not simply a natural disaster. They are divine agents of punishment and potential healing. The seraph is mentioned in Isa 14:29 and 30:6-7 as a flying serpent. The seraphim are also active in the call of the prophet Isaiah (Isaiah 6). They are part of the iconography of the Temple, stationed above Yahweh's throne. They are winged creatures, associated with the fire of divine holiness. Their fire is life-threatening; yet, they also are able to purify the prophet. Bronze serpents have been found throughout the ancient Near East, providing ample parallels for interpreting vv. 4-9.[145] Yet the association of the seraphim with Yahweh's throne most likely derives from Egyptian religion, where the raised and swollen head of the cobra is often depicted on the pharaoh's headdress as a protective goddess, Wadjyt. Her function was to spit fiery venom onto the enemies of the king.[146] Thus in Egypt the cobra's function was twofold: to protect and to destroy.

Verses 4-9 illustrate the twofold character of the seraph serpents as well. God sends them to punish Israel for murmuring, but the point of the story is to explore the healing property of the snake. As a consequence, once the people have confessed their sin and requested intercession by Moses (v. 7), God instructs Moses to make a seraph and to place it on a pole or banner as an antidote to the snake bites (v. 8). The story ends with an

account of Moses making a bronze replica of the seraph, called נחש נחשת (nĕḥaš nĕḥōšet, "the serpent of bronze"). This serpent has the power to heal anyone who looks at it. The cultic roots of story in vv. 4-9 may derive from religious practice in the Jerusalem Temple. It contained a bronze serpent named Nehushtan, which was destroyed by King Hezekiah (2 Kgs 18:4).

21:10-20. This section consists of travel notices (vv. 10-13, 16a, 18b-20) and two songs (vv. 14-15, 17-18a). It separates into two parts: vv. 10-18a recount the final stages of Israel's wilderness march to the Arnon River; vv. 18b-20 note Israel's exit from the wilderness and then briefly summarize the journey from Mattanah to Mt. Pisgah.

The travel notices give specific stopping sites with detailed geographical locations, extending from Oboth in the wilderness (v. 10) to a valley in the fields of Moab near Mt. Pisgah (v. 20). The specific locations include Oboth, Iye-abarim, the Wadi Zered, the Arnon River, Beer, Mattanah, Nahaliel, Bamoth, and Pisgah. The location of Oboth (v. 10) is unknown, but it must be south of the Dead Sea. The next stopping point, Iye-abarim (v. 11), is also unknown and may simply be a reference to "the ruins on the other side." The Wadi Zered (v. 12), however, is likely the modern Wadi el-Hesa, which flows into the southern portion of the Dead Sea from the east. The Arnon River (v. 13) is also a firmly fixed point. It flows from the east into the Dead Sea at its midpoint. These two sites indicate that the writers of these verses envision Israel as moving north into the Transjordan on the east side of the Dead Sea. Yet Beer (v. 16), as well as Mattanah, Nahaliel, Bamoth, and Pisgah (vv. 19-20), are all unknown.

The journey of the Israelites into the Transjordan is also recounted in Deuteronomy 2 and in Numbers 33, with different routes and other locations. In Deuteronomy 2, Israel journeys from Kadesh (Deut 2:19, 46) through Edom and Moab (Deut 2:1-13) to the Wadi Zered (Deut 2:13-15), before crossing into Moab at Ar (Deut 2:18). Then they cross the Arnon to battle Sihon (Deut 2:24) from their camp in the wilderness at Kedemoth (Deut 2:26). Comparison with Num 21:10-20 reveals several differences: Israel journeys through Edom rather than around it; nearly

145. See K. R. Joines, "The Bronze Serpent in the Israelite Cult, *JBL* 87 (1968) 245-56.
146. Stephen Quirke, *Ancient Egyptian Religion* (London: British Museum, 1992) 31-32.

all of the sites mentioned in Num 21:10-20 are absent from Deuteronomy, with the exception of the Wadi Zered and the Arnon River; and the reference to Kedemoth in Deuteronomy is absent from Num 21:10-20.

The itinerary in Numbers 33 records Israel's journey to Oboth, Iye-abarim, Dibon-gad, Almon-diblathaim, the mountains of Abarim before Nebo, and, finally, the plains of Moab by the Jordan, opposite Jericho (33:41-48). This list includes neither the Wadi Zered nor the Arnon River, while it locates Iye-abarim in the land of Moab, placing it significantly further north than envisioned by the writers of 21:10-20, where Iye-abarim is south of the Wadi Zered.

The differences between Num 21:10-20, Numbers 33, and Deuteronomy 2, along with the lack of historical detail, suggest that geography is being employed for theological purposes in all of the travel lists. The geographical descriptions that accompany the different sites in Num 21:10-20 provide a window into the theological aims of the authors. The most important description is that of the wilderness. It is mentioned three times in the short section (vv. 10, 13, 18b). The first two references (vv. 10, 13) place Israel in the wilderness. Iye-abarim is in the wilderness at the border of Moab (v. 10). The Arnon River (v. 13) is also described as being in the wilderness, this time at the border of the Amorites. The third reference marks the Israelites' departure from the wilderness as they journey to Mattanah (v. 18b). The three references to the wilderness indicate that one purpose of Num 21:10-20 is to mark the transition from Israel's wilderness wandering to its conquest of fertile land.

This transition is underscored by the inclusion of two songs. The first is about holy war at the River Arnon (vv. 14-15). The second is about the gift of water at Beer (vv. 17-18). Holy war and flowing, spring-fed water mark an end to the wilderness wanderings.

The first song (vv. 14-15) is a fragment of poetry from an anthology of war poems, entitled The Book of the Wars of Yahweh. It is the only example of poetry from this collection. The fragmentary character of the poem is indicated by the first line, "Waheb in Suphah" (את-והב בסופה *'et-wāhēb bĕsûpâ*). The initial word, את (*'et*), is a direct object marker. It has no

translation value by itself. Instead, it indicates that the following phrase is meant to be the direct object of a verb; yet, no verb (or subject) is present. The NRSV and the NIV interpret the Hebrew as a place name, Waheb in Suphah. This reading emphasizes geography through a series of place names: Waheb in Suphah, the Arnon, Ar, and the border of Moab. With this reading, the poetic insertion reinforces the place names of the itinerary in vv. 10-20.

But the title the Book of the Wars of Yahweh also signals that the poem is about holy war. Christensen has proposed a reconstruction of the song that emphasizes the holy war theme of the fragment by reading the direct object marker as a verb, "he came" (אתה *'ātâ*), and the place name, Weheb, as the divine name YHW (without the final H). Also, rather than regarding the Hebrew סופה (*Sûpâ*) as a place name, he interprets the word to mean "whirlwind," as it does in all other instances of its use in the OT. This reading turns the opening phrase into a complete sentence, "Yahweh came in a whirlwind."[147] The use of natural imagery like the whirlwind to describe the approach of Yahweh to aid Israel in holy war is characteristic of ancient poetry (e.g., Judg 5:4; Ps 68:6). As a holy war poem, the song foreshadows the subsequent war with the Amorite kings Sihon and Og in vv. 21-35. In fact, the story of war against Sihon and Og likely occurred at this place in Numbers in the pre-priestly history, making it presently out of sequence.

A second song in vv. 17-18a concerns water. The location for the song is Beer ("well"). Scholars have classified the poem as a work song.[148] Yet, its function in the present text is celebrative. Verse 16 indicates that the water at Beer is a divine gift to the people. The song in vv. 17-18 is Israel's response to God's providence. The people sing, "Spring up, O well!—Sing to it!" The Song of the Well provides yet another point of transition in the book of Numbers from wilderness wandering to fertile land, where water wells simply spring up from the ground. Indeed, Israel officially leaves the wilderness at this point in its journey (v. 18b), moving quickly to the valley in Moab and looking back upon

147. D. L. Christensen, "Num 21:14-15 and the Book of the Wars of Yahweh," *CBQ* 36 (1974) 359-60.

148. Eissfeldt, *The Old Testament: An Introduction*, trans. P. Ackroyd (New York: Harper & Row, 1965) 88.

the wasteland of the wilderness from the top of Pisgah (v. 20).

21:21-35. The defeat of the Amorite kings Sihon and Og is reported three times in the OT. The story in these verses is presented as the original narrative of the victory. Moses recounts the event to the second generation of Israelites in Deut 2:26–3:7, and Jephthah, the judge, tells it to the Ammonite king who claims the territory as his own (Judg 11:19-26). Each of these stories, independent of the others, includes a request by Israel to pass through the kingdom of Sihon, his refusal and attack, Israel's victory at Jahaz, and the conquest of the Amorite kingdom from the Arnon to the Jabbok rivers. But there are differences as well. Numbers 21:27-30 includes a poem that is absent from the other accounts. Numbers 21:33-34 and Deut 3:1-7 extend the story to include the defeat of Og of Bashan. These differences have occassioned debate over the precise interrelationship between the three stories, which has bearing on the composition of the Tetrateuch (Genesis–Numbers), Deuteronomy, and the Deuteronomistic History (Joshua, Judges, Samuel, and Kings).[149] For the purposes of this commentary, it is important to note that there are no indications that Num 21:21-35 is part of the priestly history. All debate concerns the literary character of the pre-priestly history. Thus the conquest of the Transjordan will be interpreted as part of the pre-priestly history.

The request to pass through the kingdom of Sihon (vv. 21-22) is very similar to the story about Edom (20:14-21). Messengers are sent to the king, requesting permission to pass through the land. Promises are made: Travel will be restricted to the King's Highway, and Israel will drink no water, eat no food, or tred on any field or vineyard. There are also differences between the two stories. In 20:14-21, Moses sent messengers to Edom; they recounted the exodus and underscored the kinship ties between the two peoples. In 21:21-22, Israel sends the messengers to

Sihon, the exodus is not recounted, and no kinship ties are claimed.

The war is narrated in vv. 23-32. Verse 23 describes Sihon's attack, which takes place in the wilderness at Jahaz. The exact location of this city is unknown, although Jeremiah also mentions it (Jer 48:21, where it is referred to as Jahzah), and it appears in the Mesha Inscription as a location next to Dibon.[150] The war itself provides a transition from the wilderness to the Transjordan. The wilderness setting for the attack by Sihon signals that the battle is out of place in the book of Numbers, since Israel already left the wilderness on the way to Pisgah (20:18b-20). The battle fits better with the preceding events in 20:10-20, where Israel traveled to the Arnon (20:10-13) and celebrated their holy war victory (20:14-15).

Verses 24-25 and 31-32 outline the extent of Israel's conquest. The central location is Heshbon, the city of King Sihon (v. 25). The Israelites also take all the towns and villages of the Amorites, from the Arnon to the Jabbok as far as the Ammonite border (vv. 24-25). Verses 31-32 confirm the successful conquest and include the capture of Jazer, most likely a location further north (see 32:1). This northern location provides transition to the defeat of Og of Bashan in vv. 33-35.

The accounts of conquest in vv. 24-25 and 31-32 frame a poem about Heshbon (vv. 26-30). Scholars have sought to interpret the Song of Heshbon as an Israelite taunt of Sihon.[151] But v. 26 makes is clear that it is an Amorite ballad, celebrating Sihon's defeat of the Moabites.[152] The song reaffirms this conclusion. Verses 27-29 recount the defeat of the Moabites. Heshbon is identified as King Sihon's (v. 27b), as a result of his conquering the Moabites up to the Arnon. The act of conquest is pictured as fire and flames (v. 28). The Moabites are addressed directly in v. 29 with a lament that their god, Chemosh, has given their sons and daughters over as captives. As a result, the final line of v. 29 states that the Moabites are captives "to an Amorite king, Sihon." But this line is most likely a later addition, since it breaks the poetic structure of parallel lines in vv. 27b-29.

149. See J. Van Seters, "The Conquest of Sihon's Kingdom: A Literary Examination," *JBL* 91 (1972) 182-97; and "Once Again—the Conquest of Sihon's Kingdom," *JBL* 99 (1980) 117-19; J. R. Bartlett, "The Conquest of Sihon's Kingdom: A Literary Re-examination," *JBL* 97 (1978) 347-51. Van Seters argues that Num 21:21-35 is the latest of the three texts, meaning that the pre-priestly history would be later than Deuteronomy and the Deuteronomistic History. Bartlett, on the other hand, argues that Deuteronomy is a later development of the story in Numbers.

150. *ANET*, 320.
151. Noth, *Numbers*, 163-66; Gray, *Numbers*, 300.
152. See Milgrom, *Numbers*, 462-63. 152

Interpretation of the poem becomes much more difficult in v. 30. The opening line is unclear. The NRSV translation, "So their posterity perished from Heshbon to Dibon," follows the LXX, which has changed ניר (*nîr*, "yoke"?) to נין (*nîn*, "offspring"). Hanson has suggested restoring v. 30 so that it reads, "The dominion of Moab has perished."[153] The closing line in v. 30 is also difficult. The NRSV has changed the relative pronoun (אשר *'ăšer*) to the noun "fire" (אש *'ēš*) to translate, "and we laid waste until fire spread to Medaba."

The purpose of the Ballad of Heshbon is difficult to determine. By attributing the song to Israelites, scholars have sought to interpret it as a taunt against the Amorites. But the context resists this interpretation. Perhaps the ballad addresses Israel's relationship with the Moabites, since the defeat of the Moabites by Sihon is the central point of the poem. Jeremiah 48:45-46, where portions of the Ballad of Heshbon reappear as judgment oracles against Moab, provides some support for this interpretation. The message of the Ballad of Heshbon at this juncture in Numbers is that the Moabites have no claim on Israelite property in the Transjordan, since they had been defeated already by Sihon.

The conquest of the Amorites in the Transjordan ends in vv. 33-35 with an account of the defeat of Og, king of Bashan. Yahweh commands Moses to attack Og, and his defeat takes place at Edrei. The subsequent defeat of Og is repeated in Deut 3:1-7. Deuteronomy 3:11 provides further lore on Og of Bashan as one of the last of the Rephaim. His bed measures nine cubits long (approx. 16 feet) and is preserved at the Ammonite city Rabbah.

153. P. D. Hanson, "The Song of Heshbon and David's Nir," *HTR* 61 (1968) 297-320, esp. 304.

REFLECTIONS

1. The power of leadership is dangerous. It can breed arrogance, making people intolerant of conflict and blind to due process. The fall of Moses is a paradigm of such abuse. He is impatient. Moses first demonstrated impatience when he killed the Egyptian taskmaster (Exod 2:11-15), forcing him to flee for his life. In Num 20:2-13, Moses' impatience cost him entry into the promised land. Anger forces him to exploit his power by not following the legal channels of accountability between God and Israel. In the process, he places himself above the law and plays God. The tragedy of the story resides in his blindness and confused motivation. He accuses the Israelites of being rebels in their legal complaint against God, when all the time he is the rebel himself. The continuing message of this tragedy is clear: No one is above the law, not even Moses the law-giver.

2. The paradoxical role of the snakes in the story of the bronze serpent invites theological reflection on their twofold role: Their bite kills; yet, the bronze serpent heals. What makes the snakes kill or heal? The Commentary indicated that the Israelites' complaint in this story is more an impatient tirade than a response to any life-threatening crisis. The people are sick of eating manna, and they desire something more interesting. God's response is to send fiery snakes to torment them. They are divine agents of death in response to Israel's trivial complaints about life in the wilderness. But the bronze snake has the power to heal. It is the medical antidote to the bite of the seraphim. Healing, however, does not just happen independently of the Israelites. The people are required to gaze at the snake in order to access its healing power.

Two themes for preaching emerge from the paradoxical role of the snakes. First, actions by Israel determine whether the seraphim are agents of death or life. Trivial and self-indulgent complaints lead to death. Faith in the power of the bronze serpent heals. This is also the message of Jesus to Nicodemus, when he refers to the story of the bronze snake: "And just as Moses lifted up the serpent in the wilderness, so must the Son of Man be lifted up, that whoever believes in him may have eternal life" (John 3:14-15). Belief in the Son of Man is a requirement for eternal life.

Second, even in their most trivial moment of pointless haranguing, God devises medicine to heal Israel. The message is that Israel cannot become so terminally ill that Yahweh is unable to heal them. Yahweh made this promise in the first wilderness story (Exod 15:22-26). The last story (Num 21:4-9) illustrates its truth. The same message returns in the discourse of Jesus to Nicodemus. The love of God has no boundaries, "for God so loved the world that he gave his only son" (John 3:16).

3. The bronze snake raises questions concerning the role of the church in health care. Does the snake really heal? The relationship between God, the church, and health care is an uneasy topic for contemporary Christians. It can be avoided by reading the story of the bronze serpent metaphorically, as an illustration about trusting in God and avoiding self-indulgent trivia. A more literal interpretation of the healing power of the bronze snake and its application to Jesus (John 3:14-15) requires reflection on Christian sacraments. The healing power of God begins in baptism, when Christians are re-created. It is when God opens the medicine chest, infuses humans with divine serum, and defeats death. Communion contains divine vitamins that give strength. The church claims the promises of God to heal in these two sacraments. They are not metaphors about social formation; they are divine medicine. The healing power of God flows from one's having been re-created in baptism. The teaching of Jesus to Nicodemus reinforces the point when Jesus offers Nicodemus eternal life, telling him that he must be born anew. The reference is not to his funeral, but to his baptism. It is the moment of his new birth.

4. The two battles of Israel at Hormah (Num 14:39-45; 21:1-3) provide some guidelines for reflecting on just war. Warfare that is a response to oppression and includes no aspect of self-gain is possible for the people of God, according to the writers of Num 21:1-3. Here Israel responds to a threat, seeks divine guidance, and bans all personal profit from war. In contrast, war initiated by the people of God and undertaken out of fear for personal gain is condemned in Num 14:39-45. It is war that leads to death in the wilderness. (See the Reflections on 31:1–33:56 for further discussion of the *ḥērem* ban as sacrifice to God.)

NUMBERS 22:1–36:13

PREPARING FOR CANAAN ON THE PLAINS OF MOAB

OVERVIEW

Numbers 22:1–36:13 is the third and final section of the book of Numbers. The central theme of preparation for Canaan builds upon the two previous sections. The holiness of God was the central theme in 1:1–10:10. Holiness provided the backdrop for the priestly writers to explore the organization of the camp around the tabernacle. The wilderness journey of the first generation was the central theme of 10:11–21:35. In this section, both pre-priestly and priestly writers explored the life of faith as a journey with God through the threatening wilderness. Lack of faith expressed in the form of murmuring led to death, while faithfulness required that Israel follow God regardless of the threat. The first generation failed and died, leaving the divine promise of land to the second generation.

The third and final section in Numbers, 22:1–36:13, is signaled by a change of setting from the wilderness to the plains of Moab. This change of setting indicates a transition in theme from the wilderness wandering of the first generation to final preparations for Canaan by the second generation. The setting looks ahead to Jericho across the Jordan River and away from the desert that lies behind. The topics in 22:1–36:13 reinforce the anticipation of imminent possession of the land of Canaan. They include a new census of the people (chap. 26), instructions regarding the cultic calendar of Israel once the people enter the land (chaps. 28–29), cities of asylum in Canaan (chap. 35), and detailed laws concerning inheritance (chaps. 27; 32; 34; 36).

There are two accounts of Israel's final preparation for entering Canaan. The pre-priestly history moves briskly in four stages: the blessing of Balaam, when Israel is threatened by Balak's desire to have them cursed (chaps. 22–24); the sin at Baal Peor (25:1-5); the inheritance of land in the Transjordan (chap. 32); and a summary of Israel's wilderness travels (chap. 33).

The priestly history greatly enlarges Moses' instructions to Israel in 22:1–36:13. Yet it follows in general the outline of the pre-priestly history. The threats to Israel on the plains of Moab are expanded with the addition of the Midianites. The priestly writers include the Midianites with Balak, king of Moab, as those who wish that Israel be cursed (22:4, 7). They also include the Midianites in Israel's sin at Baal Peor (25:6-18), and they add an account of holy war against the Midianites (chap. 31). Thus the Midianites become the central threat to Israel on the plains of Moab.

The priestly writers also expand the second part of the pre-priestly history concerning laws of inheritance. They begin this section with a second census (chap. 26), which signals a new beginning for the second generation of Israelites. Then, inheritance laws for daughters frame an extended section of law governing Israel's possession of the land. The inheritance of the daughters of Zelophehad appears in 27:1-11 and chap. 36. Within this framework, the priestly writers address a range of issues surrounding the inheritance of the land, including the announcement of the death of Moses and guidelines for succession of leadership (27:12-23), a cultic calendar and legislation regarding vows (chaps. 28–30), and holy war (chap. 31). Most noteworthy, they extend the rights of inheritance to include all of the promised land of Canaan (chaps. 34–36). The pre-priestly history is limited in scope to the inheritance of the Transjordan area (chap. 32).

The priestly expansion of 22:1–36:13 was undertaken with an eye on Deuteronomy, since the divine announcement to Moses of his impending death in 27:12-14 is not fulfilled until the closing chapters of Deuteronomy (Deut 32:48-52; 34:1-7). Thus the pattern of divine announcement and fulfillment, so characteristic of priestly writers, is employed at the close of the book of Numbers to incorporate the entire book of Deuteronomy into the final section of their history under the theme of "Instructions for Inheritance."

The preceding summary indicates that most of the literature in Numbers 22:1–36:13 is part of the priestly history, even though the pre-priestly literature provides the general structure for the section. Commentary will proceed in two parts. Chapters 22–25 will explore threats to Israel on the plains of Moab by other nations. Chapters 26–36 conclude the book by looking ahead to Israel's future life in the land.

NUMBERS 22:1–25:18, THREATS TO ISRAEL ON THE PLAINS OF MOAB

OVERVIEW

Points of tension change throughout the book of Numbers. Numbers 1:1–10:10 focused on the internal life of Israel within the camp. The danger of holiness within the tabernacle gave rise to the layout of the camp as a means to protect Israel as they lived in proximity to God. The transition from the stationary camp at Sinai to the wilderness march in 10:11–21:25 continued to focus on Israel's relationship with God. Central themes in this section included lack of faith in the divine promise of land, conflicts over leadership, and various forms of defilement. All of these threats were self-imposed, internal conflicts over land and leadership, and they led to the death of the first generation.

In 22:1–25:18, the point of tension changes from internal to external threats to the wilderness community. This change in focus is signaled by a new setting, the plains of Moab, and by a new cast of characters, the second generation. Two somewhat different external threats are explored. The first is the danger of being cursed by another nation. The story of Balak and Balaam in chaps. 22–24 probes the protective role of God outside the boundaries of the Israelite community. Israel plays no active role in this story. The second external threat is the danger of seduction of worshiping the gods of another nation. In contrast to the threat from Balak and Balaam, Israel is a central character in 25:1-5, where their sin at Baal Peor illustrates how other nations can defile Israel through intermarriage and syncretistic worship, and thus bring death into the camp. The priestly writers intensify this external danger by inserting a series of stories about the Midianites (22:4, 7; 25:6-18).

Numbers 22:1–24:25, The Blessing of Balaam

COMMENTARY

Numbers 22–24 opens with Israel encamped on the plains of Moab beside the Jordan River, across from Jericho. The change in setting marks a transition from the first generation in the wilderness to the second generation. Israel has grown into a great nation, fulfilling the divine blessing of fertility to the ancestors (Gen 12:1-4). The second generation is so numerous, in fact, that it threatens Balak, the king of Moab, in much the same way that the previous generation had threatened Pharaoh in Egypt (Exodus 1–2).

Numbers 22–24 tell how Balak sought to weaken Israel's ability to reproduce by hiring a Mesopotamian diviner named Balaam to curse them.

The Central Theme of Numbers 22–24. The central problem in these chapters is the external threat that Balak poses to Israel through his request to have Balaam curse them. Israel is unaware of this threat. Thus the people play no active role in the story. Yahweh, however, is an active character. Through a series of revelations to Balaam, God protects Israel from the threat of a curse by commanding only blessings from the seer. The whole story ends with Israel remaining unaware of either the threat or God's salvation.

Divine revelation to a non-Israelite diviner is unusual in the Old Testament, and it creates tension for the storytellers. One message of the story is comforting: God's protective care for the people of God is universal in scope, influencing actions well beyond Israel's immediate horizon. Another message of the story is more problematic: The revelation of Yahweh, and even acts of salvation, are not limited to the Israelites or their cultic practices. Balaam, the Mesopotamian, is a Yahwistic diviner, even though he is neither an Israelite nor part of the wilderness community; nor does he participate in the cult of the tabernacle. This tension provides insight into the history of tradition that surrounds Balaam in general and the composition of Numbers 22–24 in particular.

The Legend of Balaam Outside of the Old Testament. The discovery in 1967 at Tell Deir 'Alla of a text about a diviner named Balaam son of Beor has provided unexpected information concerning the legendary significance of Balaam as a diviner who lived in the Transjordan. Tell Deir 'Alla is located near the Jabbok and Jordan rivers. The text was written on lime-plaster, which appears to have covered either a pillar or a wall of an eighth-century BCE temple. One hundred and nineteen fragments of the lime-plaster were recovered, but only twelve pieces fit together.[154] These twelve pieces tell of the night vision of a seer, Balaam son of Beor, who sees a coming disaster, causing him to fast and to weep. Balaam describes his vision of a divine counsel, in which the goddess Shagar (most likely a fertility goddess) and the Shaddai-gods decide to cause a drought on earth. The drought is accompanied by reversals in nature and in society. Balaam warns that darkness will eclipse light, weak birds will overpower stronger ones, the wise will be laughed at by their pupils, and the poor will take the place of the rich.[155] The Deir 'Alla text provides two starting points for interpreting Numbers 22–24. First, the role of Balaam in Numbers 22–24 arises from Israel's larger cultural context, where the character had achieved legendary significance as a diviner by the eighth century BCE. Second, Balaam appears to be a positive character in the Deir 'Alla text, rather than a negative or sinister diviner.

The Poems in Numbers 22–24. These chapters were composed around four poems, or oracles, of Balaam. Israel is the subject of the first three oracles, while the final poem predicts disaster on nations that surround Israel. In the oracles directed to Israel, Balaam addresses the central themes of the Pentateuch. These themes are the divine promises to the ancestors that they would be fertile (e.g., Gen 12:1-4) and that they would possess a land (e.g., Gen 17:1-8). In the first poem (23:7-10), Balaam affirms that the fertility of Israel is a result of God's blessing and that, for this reason, he cannot curse them. In the second (23:18-24), Balaam underscores the reliability of God's promises to Israel against any attempt at divination. And in the third (24:3-9), Balaam predicts that Israel will possess land, become a kingdom, and be successful in warfare. The fourth poem (24:15-24) changes in focus from Israel to other nations. It is a series of smaller oracles about imminent tragedy awaiting a number of nations, including Moab, Edom, Amalek, the Kenites, and Asshur.

The age of the poems is debated. W. F. Albright argued that the poems originated very early in Israel's history, perhaps as early as the thirteenth century BCE, because of similarities in grammar, language, and writing

---

154. See Klaas A. D. Smelik, *Writings from Ancient Israel: A Handbook of Historical and Religious Documents*, trans. G. I. Davies (Louisville: Westminster/John Knox, 1991) 79-92.

155. For translation and exegesis of the Deir 'Alla text, see Jo Ann Hackett, *The Balaam Text from Deir 'Alla*, HSM 31 (Chico, Calif.: Scholars Press, 1984). For interpretation of the role of Balaam in the Deir 'Alla text as a diviner and seer, see Michael S. Moore, *The Balaam Traditions: Their Character and Development*, SBLDS 113 (Atlanta: Scholars Press, 1990) 66-96.

style to other northwest Semitic texts of this period.[156] Others, like George Buchanan Gray and Sigmund Mowinckel, argued that the nationalistic perspective of the poems and their optimistic outlook suggested, instead, the early monarchical period.[157] There is further debate concerning the literary context of the poems. If composed in the thirteenth century BCE, they were meant to be read independently from their present narrative context. Gray writes that "the poems were obviously written to fit into a story of Balaam: see 23:7ff., 18, 20; 24:3, 15; though it is only in the first two that a close structural connection with a story of Balaam is found."[158] Jacob Milgrom extended this argument to suggest that all the poems were composed for the sake of the narrative.[159] If the poems are early and independent, then they constitute the oldest level of tradition in Numbers about a non-Israelite diviner name Balaam. But they may also simply reflect a more archaic writing style that was fashioned for literary effect in Numbers 22–24. Regardless of their date of composition, it is clear that throughout the oracles Balaam is presented in a positive light as a diviner who speaks only what Yahweh reveals to him.

The Narrative in Numbers 22–24. The narrative portions of these chapters contain a history of commentary, which has made the flow of the story uneven (especially in chap. 22). Clarifications within the text about central characters and locations are one indication of additions to the narrative. For example, later writers felt it necessary to identify Balak as the king of Moab (22:4*b*), even though this information was already assumed at the outset of the story (22:2). There is also a more precise identification of Balak's advisers as "elders of Moab" (זקני מואב *ziqnê-mô'āb*, 22:7), in addition to their role as "princes of Moab" (שרי-מואב *śārê-mô'ab*, 22:8, 15, 21). The additional notice that Balaam's home at Pethor on the Euphrates was "in the land of Amaw" (22:5) may also be later commentary.[160]

Later writers also added new motifs and episodes to the story, of which two stand out. The first is the inclusion of the "elders of Midian" (זקני מדין *ziqnê midyān*, 22:4, 7) as co-conspirators with Balak against Israel. The priestly writers are most likely responsible for the addition of this motif to the story, since it provides the basis for their story of holy war against Midian in chap. 31. The second addition is the story of Balaam's journey to Balak (22:22-35). This episode disrupts the larger narrative in a number of ways. It creates a literary tension between the divine command that Balaam go to Balak (22:20) and the divine anger against Balaam for disobeying God by journeying to Balak (22:22). This episode also introduces a negative interpretation of Balaam in what would otherwise be a positive story of a non-Israelite seer. The authors of 22:22-35 may have been priestly writers, but such an identification is by no means clear.

The literary overview of the narrative in Numbers 22–24 indicates a history of composition. The earliest version is a positive story of a non-Israelite seer, Balaam, who serves Yahweh and is unable to curse Israel as Balak requests. Both the poems and the narrative (excluding 22:22-35) idealize Balaam as a seer. He is frequently presented as using the divine name "Yahweh" ("LORD") in Numbers 22–24, which reinforces the positive portrait of him. In the opening narrative (22:1-21), Balaam refers to Yahweh four times (22:8, 13, 18, 19); in one instance, he even confesses that Yahweh is his God (22:18). In the sequence of oracles (22:36–24:25), Balaam continues to use the name "Yahweh," both in the narrative (23:5, 12, 23; 24:13) and in the poetry (23:8, 21; 24:6). Scholars debate whether the positive story of Balaam existed independently or whether it was composed by pre-priestly writers to fit in at this point in their history.[161] A clear resolution to this debate is not possible from a literary study of these chapters.

The addition of 22:22-35 introduces a new interpretation of Balaam as an anti-hero. In this episode, he is presented as a disobedient seer who is more blind to divine leading than is his donkey. The authors of this episode are difficult to identify. They may have

156. W. F. Albright, "The Oracles of Balaam," *JBL* 63 (1944) 207-33. See the review of Albright's work by D. A. Robertson, *The Linguistic Evidence in Dating Early Hebrew Poetry,* SBLDS 3 (Missoula, Mont.: Scholars Press, 1972) 145.

157. Gray, *Numbers,* 313-14; Sigmund Mowinckel, "Die Ursprung der Bil'amsage," *ZAW* 7 (1930) 233-71, esp. 268-69.

158. Gray, *Numbers,* 313.

159. Milgrom, *Numbers,* 467-68.

160. See Gray, *Numbers,* 307-22.

161. See Noth, *Numbers,* 166-94.

been priestly writers, since it is clear that the priestly writers interpret Balaam negatively, associating him with the Midianites in Numbers 31. Thus it is possible that the positive portrayal of Balaam reflects the pre-priestly version of Numbers 22–24 and that the negative reinterpretation of this story is by the priestly writers. In this case, the latter would have included the insertion of the Midianites as co-conspirators with Balak (22:4, 7), along with a negative episode about Balaam's disobedience and blindness (22:22-35). The death of both the Midianites and Balaam in the priestly account of holy war in chap. 31 lends support to this hypothesis.

But the language of Num 22:22-35 does not show clear signs of priestly authorship. In fact, the frequent use of the "messenger of Yahweh" (מלאך יהוה *mal'ak YHWH*, 22:22-27, 31-32, 34-35) is a strong argument against priestly authorship, since this designation of God is not part of their theological vocabulary. In this case, the history of composition does not follow the pattern of pre-priestly and priestly authorship. Thus the literary study of the poetry and the narrative points to several possible histories of composition that may account for the present form of the story of Balaam in Numbers 22–24.

What remains clear is that the story of a non-Israelite Yahwistic seer has prompted a complex history of commentary. The reason for the ongoing commentary is the theological problem that is posed when a non-Israelite seer claims to be a Yahwist, even though he functions outside of Israel's cultic institutions. One suspects that the history of commentary is a compilation of different answers to this theological problem.

The Divine Names. Scholars have used the two divine names, *Elohim* ("God") and *Yahweh* ("LORD") to gain insight into the compositional history of Numbers 22–24.[162] Noth, for example, concluded that two versions of the narrative, Yahwistic (J) and Elohistic (E), are discernible in these chapters. The Elohistic version, according to Noth, includes most parts of 22:2-21 and 22:41–23:27, while the Yahwistic encompasses most of 22:22-40 and 23:28–24:19.[163] The distribution of the divine names in these chapters is, indeed,

striking. But an overview indicates that their use is for literary and theological reasons, and not the result of a history of composition.

The many names used for God in Numbers 22–24 can be summarized as follows: The personal name of God, *Yahweh* ("LORD") appears seventeen times, nine times in speeches by Balaam (22:8, 13, 18-19; 23:3, 8, 12, 26; 24:6, 13), twice by Balak (23:17; 24:11), and five times by the narrator of the story (22:28, 31; 23:5, 16; 24:1). *Elohim* ("God") occurs nine times, once by Balaam (22:38), once by Balak (23:27), and seven times by the narrator of the story (22:9, 10, 12, 20, 22; 23:4; 24:2). The combination *Yahweh-Elohim* ("LORD God") is used twice in speeches by Balaam (22:18; 23:21). Other names for God also appear in speeches by Balaam: *El* ("God"), seven times (23:19, 22, 23; 24:8, 16, 23); *Elyon* ("Most High"), once (24:16); and *Shaddai* ("Almighty"), twice (24:4, 16). The ten references to the "messenger of Yahweh" are confined to the episode of Balaam and his donkey (22:22-25).

The range of divine names employed in Numbers 22–24 indicates that the biblical writers are exploring the different ways in which the God of Israel is known to other people. Thus the variety of divine names serves literary and theological purposes. For example, in the opening scene (22:1-21), Balaam only refers to God as *Yahweh* ("LORD"; 22:8, 13, 18-19), while the narrator of the story uses only the name *Elohim* ("God"; 22:9-10, 12, 20). This technique presents a contrast between the narrator, who speaks in more general language about the God of Israel in relationship to the non-Israelite seer Balaam, and Balaam, who claims knowledge of Yahweh. Such a carefully constructed contrast is not the result of combining two narrative accounts. A stronger hypothesis asserts that the variety of divine names is the work of a single author. Indeed, the result of this technique is a portrayal of Balaam as someone who knows the God of Israel and most of the important names for God. How he chooses to use such knowledge is one of the central tensions of the story. The reticence on the part of the narrator to name Balaam's God as Yahweh simply highlights this tension.

162. Gray, *Numbers*, 309-14.
163. Noth, *Numbers*, 171-75.

22:1-21. This section tells of the fear of Balak, king of Moab. He hears of Israel's defeat of the Amorite kings, Og and Sihon, and he seeks to weaken them by hiring a diviner named Balaam to curse the people. Verses 1-20 provide the setting for the entire story of Balaam (v. 1), outline the nature of the Israelite threat to Balak (vv. 2-4), and describe two missions of Balak to Balaam to hire him to curse Israel (the first mission appears in vv. 5-14, the second in vv. 15-20).

22:1. The setting of the story takes the form of an itinerary notice, but it lacks the location of Israel's departure. It simply states that they journeyed and camped "in the plains of Moab," located more precisely as "across the Jordan from Jericho." The broken form of the itinerary emphasizes the new setting, rather than the point of departure.

The change of setting to the plains of Moab indicates that Israel has left the wilderness. Leaving the wilderness does not fulfill the divine promise of land in the Pentateuch, however, because the plains of Moab are not Canaan. Instead, it signals the fulfillment of the promise of fertility; the second generation has become a great nation once again. The central focus on fertility is underscored by the fear of the Moabites (vv. 2-4); the number of the Israelites terrifies them.

The location "in the plains of Moab across the Jordan from Jericho" is a favorite expression of the priestly writers. It is the location for the second census of Israel (26:3, 63); the waging of holy war against Midian (31:12); the appointing of levitical cities (35:1); the final legislation of Moses in the book of Numbers (36:13); and for the death of Moses (Deut 34:1, 8). The priestly writers' use of this location throughout chaps. 22–36 provides strong evidence for attributing the travel notice in 22:1 to them.[164]

But this itinerary notice may be part of the pre-priestly history along with a similar reference in 33:50—the conclusion to the full list of wilderness travel stops. Verse 1 introduces "the plains of Moab" as the location for two external threats to Israel: the first by Balak (chaps. 22–24) and the second the incident at Baal Peor (25:1-5). The plains of Moab in 33:50 is the setting for the divine command that Israel cross the Jordan and conquer the

Canaanites. Crossing the Jordan for conquest is not a theme in the priestly history.[165] Read together, 22:1 and 33:50 frame the final section of Numbers in the pre-priestly history and point the reader ahead to additional instruction by Moses in Deuteronomy, also in the "land of Moab" (Deut 29:1).

22:2-4. This section describes the nature of the Israelite threat to Balak and the Moabite nation. Verse 3 states that Moab fears Israel. Two words are used to describe their fear, and both are important for interpretation. The first word, "dread" (גור *gûr*) characterizes persons who are confronted by power, either divine (Deut 9:19) or human (1 Sam 18:15), and who are unsure of how such power will be used. The second word, "to be overcome with fear" (קוץ *qûs*) bears connotations of abhorrence. Again, the context of the word indicates a confrontation of power amid the threat of war. The word is used to describe the fear that Ahaz, the Judahite king, had for Damascus and the northern kingdom of Israel during war (Isa 7:16). A more important parallel for Num 22:3 is Exod 1:12, where the fear of the Egyptians over the unchecked population growth of the Israelites is described with the same word.

The reason for the Moabite fear is twofold. Israel's power to wage war is evident from its defeat of the Amorites (v. 1). The more explicit reason, however, is the size of Israel (v. 3). Balak's speech to the Midianites in v. 4 underscores this fact. He fears the impact that so many Israelites will have on the environment of his country: "The horde will now lick up [resources] as an ox licks up the grass of the field." The fertility of Israel fulfills one of two divine promises to the ancestors: population (Gen 12:1-4) and land (Gen 17:1-8). At the outset of chap. 22, the second generation has once again become numerous, just as the first generation had become in Egypt (Exodus 1:1).

The parallel between Numbers 22 and Exodus 1 is important for interpretation. It signals that the change in setting from the wilderness to the "plains of Moab" is more than a transition from the first to the second generation in the pre-priestly history. It also marks for a second time the fulfillment of the divine promise of fertility that was made to the ancestors. The connection to the

---

164. Gray, *Numbers,* 306-7.

165. Gray, *Numbers,* 449-52.

first generation in Egypt goes beyond mere numbers of persons to include a threatening dimension. Israelite fertility in the second generation creates the same dread in the Moabites that it did in the Egyptians (Exod 1:12). The parallels to Egypt will continue with Balak's message to Balaam (vv. 5-6).

The renaming of Balak in v. 4 as the son of Zippor, and the description of him as "king of Moab at that time," provide transition from the opening description of Moabite fear to their plan of action. The meaning of "Zippor" is not clear, although the name appears in a feminine form, "Zipporah" (the wife of Moses).

The closing temporal phrase in v. 4, "at that time" (ההוא בעת *bāʿēt hahî*), to indicate when Balak was king of Moab gives the story a didactic quality. It is a favorite device for narrating historical stories in Deuteronomy (Deut 1:9, 16, 18; 2:34; 3:4, 8, 12, 18, 21, 23; 4:14; 5:5; 9:20 10:1), where past events are recalled for the purpose of teaching. The phrase has a similar didactic function in Num 22:4. As a result, the story is less an unfolding drama than a lesson from the past: how God foiled Balak's plan to hire Balaam to curse Israel.

22:5-14. This section describes the first mission to Balaam, who is introduced in v. 5 by lineage and location. He is the son of Beor. His home is Pethor ("on the river"). "The river" almost always means the Euphrates, accounting for the NRSV translation. Pethor may be Pitru, a location in Syria, south of Carchemish. The additional identification "in the land of Amaw" is unclear; the Hebrew translates "in the land of his people."

Balak's request to Balaam (vv. 5-6) takes the form of a speech to his messengers. His words recount many themes from the exodus. The expression "a people has come out of Egypt" consists of a form of the Hebrew verb "to go forth" or "to go out" (יצא *yāṣā*), with the prepositional phrase "from Egypt" (ממצרים *mimmiṣrayim*). It is used in Exodus to describe the mission of Moses (Exod 3:10-12) and the exodus itself (e.g., Exod 13:3, 8-9; 14:11). As noted, the primary fear of Balak concerns the fertility of Israel. This fear, too, is expressed in language from the exodus. Balak's description of the number of Israelites encamped on his land as "having spread over the face of the earth" recalls the plague of locusts (Exod 10:5). His statement that the number of Israelites implies that "they are stronger than [he]" echoes Pharaoh's fear at the outset of the exodus (Exod 1:9).

The fertility of Israel is a direct result of God's blessing; God states this to Balaam explicitly in v. 12. Balak requests that Balaam curse the Israelites, because cursing, the opposite of blessing, disrupts fertility. The cursed earth in Gen 3:17-19, for example, is transformed from a fertile garden into ground that brings forth thorns and thistles. Thus the objective power of cursing and blessing is central to the story. Balak hopes that having Israel cursed will weaken it, allowing him to drive the Israelites from his land. "Driving out" (גרש *gāraš*) Israel from the land is language of conquest. It occurs in a Moabite inscription (The Moabite Stone or Mesha Stele), in which the king Mesha boasts of conquest over Israel.[166] It also appears elsewhere in the OT, for example, when God promised that the divine messenger would "drive out" the inhabitants of Canaan (Exod 23:20-33).

Balaam possesses the power to curse and to bless. Balak affirms this power in v. 6 with language reminiscent of the divine promise to Abraham (Gen 12:3). Whomever Balaam blesses is blessed, and whomever he curses is cursed. Attributing such power to Balaam indicates that such power is not unique to Israel, but may also be possessed by a non-Israelite. The primeval hero of the flood, Noah, also possessed the power to bless and to curse. He cursed Canaan (Gen 9:25) and blessed Shem (Gen 9:26). The description of Balaam also conveys the objective quality of blessing and cursing, in which the words set into motion powers that cannot be reversed. Isaac's blessing of Jacob by mistake (Gen 27:27-29), and his inability to reverse it upon learning of his error, is similar.

Balaam's power to bless and to curse is described in v. 7 as "divination" (קסם *qesem*). Divination is the science of predicting the future through interpretation of natural phenomena. It took many forms in the ancient Near East, including the casting of lots (1 Sam 14:42-43) and the reading of animal entrails. It was most certainly common in ancient Israel, but it came to be

166. *ANET*, 320-21.

condemned as a practice that conflicted with Yahwistic faith. The clearest statement on this point is Deut 18:9-14, but such teaching is also found in other places; 2 Kings 17:7-23, supports the teaching of Deuteronomy by listing divination as one of the reasons for the destruction of the northern kingdom. Ezekiel, too, condemns the practice (Ezek 13:9). Thus the reference to divination in association with Balaam raises the question of whether the term is meant to be a negative commentary on the seer. It appears not to be. "Diviner" is not a title Balaam claims for himself, and his subsequent actions do not conform to such practice. In fact, the characterization of Balaam as a diviner is made indirectly through the description of the payment of Balak's messengers as "the fees for divination."

Verses 8-14 describe Balaam's intercession with God to discern whether or not to curse Israel. Throughout the passage, Balaam is presented in a positive light. In v. 8 he explicitly states that he is unable to make a decision without instruction from Yahweh. As a result, the episode is structured around Balaam's seeking instruction from God during the night (vv. 8-11) and returning with an answer at dawn (v. 13). Balaam refuses Balak's request to curse Israel.

Several features of vv. 8-14 are important for interpretation. Perhaps the most noteworthy is that Balaam refers to God with the personal name "Yahweh" ("LORD," v. 8). "Yahweh" is the name for God given to Moses in Exodus 3 with the specific instruction that he share this name with Israel. Thus it is not a general epithet for God; rather, it requires knowledge of Israel's unique history of salvation. Balaam's use of the name "Yahweh," then, is astonishing, because he has no knowledge of Israel. Note that in the nighttime exchange between Balaam and God, Balaam has no firsthand knowledge of Israel. Describing the request of Balak (v. 11), Balaam refers generically to "a people" that has come out of Egypt and now covers the land of Moab. His description is merely a repetition of the message conveyed to him (see vv. 5-6). The biblical writers present Balaam as a diviner who has come to possess the special divine name "Yahweh" through independent revelation.

The portrait of God is also noteworthy. God is presented as having a special relationship with a non-Israelite formed outside of the structure of Israel's history of salvation. Nowhere in God's reply to Balaam is Israel referred to by name, nor are they called God's people (v. 12). Instead, God tells Balaam that he cannot curse "the people" because they are blessed. In this brief exchange, the biblical writers succeed in presenting a glimpse into God's relationship with a diviner. The Israelites are peripheral to the scene. In fact, they are unaware of the threat posed by Balak and the intercession of Balaam (v. 13).

22:15-21. This section describes the second mission to Balaam. The language intensifies. Balak sends many more distinguished officials (v. 15). Their message to Balaam is prefaced with the messenger formula, "Thus says Balak son of Zippor. . . . " The message itself is filled with pleas, exclamations, and even demands (vv. 16-17). Nothing should hinder Balaam from traveling to Moab. Balak assures Balaam through his messengers that no price is too high, if only he will come and curse this people. Balaam's response is equally strong (v. 18). No amount of money could make him act contrary to the command of Yahweh, his God. The portrait of Balaam is even more positive as a result of this second mission. Once again, Balaam inquires of God during the night for an answer to Balak's request (vv. 19-20). This time God instructs Balaam to return with the officials of Balak, but to speak only the words that God commands him.

22:22-35. The account of Balaam's journey to Balak is a separate story. Originally the two previous missions of Balak's officials (vv. 1-21) probably continued uninterrupted into v. 36, where Balaam arrives at Moab and informs Balak that he can only speak what God tells him (the command from v. 20).

Several literary features indicate that vv. 22-35 were inserted into the Balaam cycle of stories. Yahweh's anger at Balaam's decision to travel to Moab (v. 22) directly contradicts the divine command that he undertake the trip (v. 20). The portrayal of Balaam changes significantly from a diviner who carefully discerns the direction of God's leading to a blind and impatient seer whose donkey has more sense and clairvoyance than he. The appearance of the messenger of Yahweh is confined to this section; and the internal structure of vv. 22-35, with their three-part repetition of action, also suggests a self-contained story. All of these factors lead to the conclusion that these verses were a later addition to the Balaam cycle of stories, intended to introduce a negative interpretation of the non-Israelite diviner.

Numbers 22:22-35 is folklore—a burlesque, even slapstick story about a clairvoyant animal who speaks a word of common sense to a blind seer. The story divines between a confrontation with the messenger of Yahweh (vv. 22-27) and the interpretation of the message (vv. 28-35).

22:22-27. Verse 22 sets the stage for the story, describing how the messenger of Yahweh blocks the road and functions as Balaam's adversary on his journey to Moab. The word "adversary" (שטן *śāṭān*) is also used to describe God's opponent in Job 1. Here God or the messenger of Yahweh opposes Balaam. There is no clear distinction between the messenger of Yahweh and God in this particular folk tale. Other references to Yahweh's messenger indicate that this manifestation of God is able to wage holy war for Israel (Exod 23:20-33) and to lead Israel through the wilderness (Exod 14:19). Numbers 22:22-35 bears overtones of war, since the messenger states that he seeks to kill Balaam (v. 33).

There are three encounters with the messenger of Yahweh, all seen by the donkey (vv. 23, 25, 27), but not by Balaam or his servants (who disappear from the story after v. 22). The encounters are increasingly intense. First, the messenger of Yahweh forces the donkey from the road (v. 23). Then he forces the donkey against the wall (vv. 24-25). Finally, he blocks the donkey's path altogether, causing it to lie down (vv. 26-27). In each of these instances, the donkey saves Balaam's life, but the diviner is blind to his rescue and responds with increasingly violent acts against the donkey.

22:28-35. The donkey and the messenger of Yahweh address Balaam. The donkey interprets events for Balaam in vv. 28-30, followed by a more detailed interpretation from the messenger of Yahweh in vv. 31-35. Speaking animals are a common feature of folk literature, but they are unusual in biblical stories.

The only other talking animal in the OT is the serpent in the garden of Eden (Genesis 2). In both instances, a talking animal appears not to be unusual to the human character. Balaam does not show surprise that his donkey is able to engage him in conversation; instead, he responds immediately as if they conversed regularly.

The donkey's interpretation of events (vv. 28-30) is based on common sense. It questions why Balaam has beaten it three times. The question casts Balaam in the role of the fool. He has misinterpreted the donkey's actions as ruthless, rather than salvific. If he had a sword, Balaam swears, he would kill the donkey. Yet the nearest sword is in the hand of the messenger of Yahweh, and it is aimed at Balaam! The donkey does not share its clairvoyance with Balaam. Rather, it reflects on experience, reminding Balaam of past service. The donkey questions whether its behavior has ever been ruthless. Balaam responds that no, it has not. The implication of their conversation is that Balaam has no business attributing sinister motive to his donkey, even though he does not understand the animal's unexpected behavior. His accumulated experience with the donkey should suffice to warrant his trust.

Yahweh's messenger provides the second interpretation of the events in vv. 31-35. Finally, Balaam's eyes are opened to the presence of his swordbearing divine adversary, prompting an act of worship. The messenger of Yahweh repeats the donkey's question— why the beatings? The new information supplied by God in vv. 32-33 builds on the commonsense conclusion offered by the donkey. The animal was not acting ruthlessly. On the contrary, it saved Balaam from a divine attack, for God would surely have killed him and left the animal alive. Had the animal acted in response to Balaam's sinister assumption, the diviner would now be dead. His eyes now opened, Balaam confesses his sin, while also claiming ignorance. He then offers to return to his home. The episode ends in v. 35 with the messenger repeating the divine instruction from v. 20 that Balaam continue on in his journey, but speak only what God instructs him to say.

22:36–24:13. Balaam's oracles concerning Israel comprise the heart of the Balaam cycle. The section evolves around three episodes. Numbers 22:36-40 provides both a conclusion to the opening story about Balak's envoys to Balaam (22:1-21) and an introduction to Balaam's three oracles about Israel (22:41–24:13). The three oracles separate into episodes consisting of 22:41–23:12; 23:13-26; and 23:27–24:13. Similar in form, each begins with Balak taking Balaam to a specific location to curse Israel. In each scene, Balaam sacrifices on seven altars, prompting a word from God that leads to a poetic oracle. Balaam's oracles are blessings rather than curses. This unexpected reversal leads in each case to an exchange between Balaam and Balak, in which Balak appears dumbfounded that the diviner has blessed Israel rather than cursed it. Balaam responds that he can only say what God commands him to say. The portrait of Balaam throughout this section is positive. Further commentary will demonstrate that development of character occurs within the repetitive structure of the oracles.

22:36-40. The geographical locations are important to the story. Balak travels to the border of Moab to meet Balaam, who enters the country from the north. The setting is Ir-moab, a site on the Arnon River. Ir-moab should, perhaps, be translated "City of Moab." The location does not correspond to any known contemporary site, but it does relate to a city mentioned in 21:15, 28 called Ar of Moab, the setting for the Moabites' destruction in the Book of the Wars of Yahweh (21:15) and in the Ballad of Heshbon (21:28). These inner-biblical references lend a somber tone to the account of Balaam's arrival in Moab, foreshadowing the downfall of the Moabites.

Ir-moab serves as the setting for an exchange between Balak and Balaam (vv. 37-38). Balak questions why Balaam has been delayed: Did Balaam not think that he, Balak, had the power to honor him? Balaam dismisses this question by introducing divine direction, as opposed to reward from Balak. Balaam states that he is only able to speak the words that God puts in his mouth, a repetition of the divine instruction in vv. 20, 35. Thus this encounter of Balaam and Balak can be read as a continuation either of vv. 1-21 or of vv. 22-35. In either case, Balaam is presented

as a positive character. The scene closes with Balak taking Balaam to Kiriath-huzoth ("City of Streets") for sacrifices.

22:41–23:12. The events surrounding the first oracle progress in three stages. The setting and procedures for divination are described in 22:41–23:6. Balaam's oracle follows in 23:7-10. The concluding exchange between Balaam and Balak is described in 23:11-12. This three-part structure continues throughout the sequence of oracles, along with repetition in actions and dialogue between Balaam and Balak. Variations within the stereotypical actions convey development in the plot.

Numbers 22:41 states both the time (dawn) and the location (Bamoth-baal) of the first oracle. It also describes what Balaam saw from this location, but the Hebrew is ambiguous. The text states literally that Balaam saw "the extremity or outer edge of the people" (קצה העם *qěṣēh hāʿām*). But it does not indicate which outer edge of the people the writer intends. If it is the furthermost edge, then Balaam is viewing the entire people of Israel encamped below Bamoth-baal. If it is the closest edge, then he is viewing only a small section of the people. The NRSV adopts the latter reading: "from there he [Balaam] saw part of the people of Israel."[167] The NEB follows the former reading so that Balaam saw "the full extent of the Israelite host."[168] The two readings provide distinctive plot structures to the story. In each, however, the name "Israel" is an unwarranted addition, since it is absent from the text. The Commentary on 22:1-21 indicated that the absence of a proper name for Israel was important to the perspective of the narrative.

Divination is central to the Balaam oracles, and sight is central to divination. Milgrom writes that in a story about divination "the object must be within sight for a curse to be effective." He quotes Democritus to illustrate the power of the evil eye:

From the eyes issue images which are neither without sensation nor without volition, and are filled with the wickedness and malice of those from whom they proceed: imprinting themselves

167. See Gray, *Numbers*, 342.
168. See Eryl W. Davies, *Numbers*, NCB (Grand Rapids: Eerdmans, 1995) 253-54.

firmly upon the person to be enchanted, they become part of him, and disturb and injure both his body and mind.[169]

The importance of sight for cursing can be interpreted in two ways in the story of Balaam. The NRSV translation of 22:41 yields a three-part plot that increases in scope. Balaam sees only the outer edge of the people for the first oracle (at Bamoth-baal, 22:41–23:12). He sees a greater portion of the people for the second oracle (on Pisgah, 23:13-26). Finally, Balaam views all of Israel for the third oracle (on Peor, 23:27–24:13).

The NEB interpretation (Balaam saw all of Israel from Bamoth-baal) creates a satirical story of reversal, rather than a story that increases in scope and drama. This reading suggests that the first episode (22:41–23:12) is the most threatening, because Balaam is able to fix his eye on the entire people. Balak's inability to induce a curse on Israel, even when Balaam has them firmly fixed in his eye, gives rise to satire: Balak then tries to conjure up a curse by limiting Balaam's view of Israel. In 22:13, Balak takes Balaam to Pisgah, where he can see only part of the people, in the hope that a more limited viewing might induce a curse from Balaam. When this attempt fails (23:13-26), Balak takes Balaam to Peor, where the seer "overlooks the wasteland" (23:27-28). The people are not mentioned in the introduction to the third oracle, nor does Balak refer to the need for Balaam to view Israel. One way to interpret the absence of these motifs is that Balaam has turned away from Israel altogether. Numbers 20:10-20 indicates that Israel has left the desert. Balak provides commentary on this unorthodox action when he states that perhaps he may induce enough divine favor to prompt Balaam into cursing the people (23:27). But this action backfires (24:1-2): Balaam departs from Balak, discontinues his process of divination, and looks upon all of Israel, tribe by tribe, for a final oracle of blessing.

The divination procedure is described in 23:1-6. Balaam requires the construction of no less than seven altars—a sacred number of completeness—each to be used for sacrificing a bull and a ram. These are extravagant

sacrifices, the most valued sacrifices in the book of Leviticus (chap. 4). According to Num 23:2, the sacrifices are performed by both Balak and Balaam. But the inclusion of Balaam may be a latter addition, since the verbs describing the act of sacrificing are third-person singular, referring to Balak alone. The larger context also supports this reading. In 22:36-40, only Balak sacrificed, and in 23:3, when Balaam instructs Balak to remain beside his sacrifice, he uses the second-person singular pronoun, "your sacrifice." The sacrifices are part of a ritual of divination, perhaps intended to prompt God's appearance. The encounter between Balaam and God is separated from Balak and his sacrifices, for Balaam is described as going to a bare height. His aim in 23:3 is to meet Yahweh ("the LORD"; the narrator describes the encounter between Balaam and God by using both the general divine name "God" [v. 4] and the personal name "Yahweh" [v. 5].

The oracle in 23:7-10 constitutes the divine word to Balaam. The Hebrew word for "oracle" is משל (māšāl, v. 7). This word is unusual in the present context, because it is not used to describe the sayings of OT prophets. Yet all of Balaam's speeches are described with this word. Māšāl has a range of meanings, including "parable" or "allegory" (Ezek 17:2), "proverb" (Prov 1:1), and "taunt" (Isa 14:4). It appears that the biblical writers have introduced an element of ambiguity regarding the genre of Balaam's speeches. Read in isolation from their narrative context, Balaam's speeches resemble prophetic oracles. But when the narrative context is emphasized, the oracles provide commentary on surrounding events, in which case they are more like parables or wisdom sayings about Israel's journey with God. The final oracle against the nations (24:15-24) bears characteristics of a taunt.

Balaam's initial oracle consists of three stanzas: 23:7-8 presents the central theme of the poem—namely, the inability of Balaam to curse if it is not God's will; 23:9 describes the distinctive character of Israel; and 23:10 makes allusion to the fertility of Israel. It is composed in synonymous parallelism, a poetic device in which two lines provide variation on a similar theme, of which 23:7 provides an illustration:

169. Milgrom, *Numbers*, 193-94. The quotation is from Plutarch *Symposium* 5.7.6.

"*Balak* has brought me *from Aram*,
> the king of Moab from the eastern mountains:
'Come, *curse* Jacob for me;
> Come, *denounce* Israel!' "

The first pair and the last pair of lines are parallel and synonymous, because they state essentially the same thing. Lines one and two state that Balak commissioned Balaam. The repetition between the lines adds information. Balak is the king of Moab, and Balaam came from Aram by the eastern mountains. Lines three and four state that the content of the commission is a curse. Repetition clarifies the nature of cursing as denouncing and the object of the curse as Jacob/Israel. Synonymous parallelism continues throughout: v. 8 contains two lines that are synonymous, while vv. 9-10 contain four lines consisting of two pairs of synonymous parallelism, like v. 7.

The speech of Balaam takes on different meaning, depending on whether it is read in isolation as a prophetic oracle or in its present narrative context as commentary on the story. When the poem is read in isolation, Balaam's speech resembles prophetic discourse, and the message takes precedence over the messenger. The central theme of the oracle as prophetic discourse is Balaam's inability to curse if it is contrary to God's will. The limited focus on the northern kingdom (e.g., Jacob/Israel) may indicate the original setting of the Balaam oracles prior to their incorporation within the pre-priestly history.

Balaam's speech can also be read as commentary on the larger story. That the biblical writers intend for such a reading is clear from the careful way in which the oracle has been interwoven into its narrative context. The reference to Aram (22:7) harks back to 22:5, where Balaam's homeland was identified as Pethor, a location most likely near the Euphrates. The recounting of Balak's commission that Balaam curse Israel, then, ties the oracle into the opening episode in 22:1-21. Balaam's view of Israel "from the top of the crags" links the oracle to the narrative introduction (22:41). Finally, Balaam's reference to the number of Israelites reinforces the population motif, which prompted Balak to act in the first place (22:5).

The oracle in 23:7-10 loses its prophetic quality when read as commentary on the larger narrative context. What stands out, instead, is the autobiographical nature of Balaam's speech. "I" statements by Balaam come into focus throughout the sequence of the three stanzas. The first two stanzas begin with "I" statements by Balaam that recount past events in the narrative—his commissioning by Balak to curse Israel (v. 7) and his present location "at the top of the crags" (v. 9a). Statements about Israel's present condition conclude each of these stanzas—he cannot curse a people whom God has not cursed (v. 8), and Israel is distinct from the nations (v. 9b). The third stanza reverses this structure. It begins with a statement about Israel's present condition (their great number [v. 10a]), and concludes with yet another self-reference by Balaam. This time Balaam's "I" statement is a wish that he might be like Israel (v. 10b).

Read in the larger context of the narrative, the first episode emphasizes Balaam's coming to knowledge of the nation of Israel, not his inability to curse when doing so is against the divine will. In this regard, it is noteworthy that Israel is named by Balaam, since he did not know the name of the people in his earlier exchange with God (22:11-12). The first oracle indicates development in Balaam. God has revealed to Balaam the name of this people and their special status with regard to God (v. 8) and the nations (v. 9). As a consequence, Balaam wishes to join Israel rather than curse them (v. 10).

Numbers 23:11-12 concludes the first oracle with an exchange between Balak and Balaam that provides insight into these two characters. Balak is angry with Balaam for having blessed Israel rather than cursing them, even though Balaam has not actually blessed Israel in the first oracle. The language of Balak indicates his expectation that Balaam would functioned as a sorcerer. A sorcerer is someone who attempts to alter the future; thus Balak wishes to alter the Israelites' destiny by having Balaam curse them. Balaam responds by repeating a motif that has already occurred in 22:38 and 23:3: He can only speak what God tells him. This response indicates that Balaam sees himself as a diviner, and not as a sorcerer.[170] Diviners predict the future, but they do not seek to alter it. The

170. See Moore, *The Balaam Traditions*, 113-18; and Milgrom, *Numbers*, 469-71.

two perceptions of Balaam's role signal a tension that runs throughout the narrative: Is Balaam's power positive or negative? Balak wishes to use the power of Balaam negatively. But Balaam appears in a positive light as a diviner who conveys the divine will, but does not seek to manipulate it through sorcerery.

23:13-26. The setting for the second oracle is established in vv. 13-17. Balak takes Balaam to a new location at the top of Mt. Pisgah in the field of Zophim. Pisgah appears as one of Israel's traveling stops in 21:20. The location of the field of Zophim, however, is uncertain. The name may be a pun on the meaning of the word "watchers" (צפים *ṣōpîm*). The new setting of the second oracle means that Balaam can only see a part of Israel. As in the first oracle, seven altars are built, and a bull and a ram are sacrificed on each. Balaam departs from Balak to receive a word of divination from God and then returns to him with a message. Note that in this case, however, Balak asks Balaam, "What has Yahweh said?" The question indicates a new understanding in Balak that Yahweh (the LORD) is the deity who empowers Balaam.

Verses 18-24 contain the second oracle of Balaam. It, too, is structured in eleven parallel lines (vv. 18, 19*a*, 19*b*, 20, 21*a*, 22, 23*a*, 23*b*, 24*a*, 24*b*), and it separates into three stanzas. Verses 18-19 contrast Balak and God; vv. 20-22 describe God's power in the history of Israel; and vv. 23-24 turn the focus from God to Israel in order to describe the power of Israel and the futility of seeking enchantments against it. When the oracle is read within the larger narrative context, the direct address to Balak (v. 18) stands out. In contrast to the autobiographical nature of the first oracle, the second oracle is intended to teach Balak about God and Israel.

Verses 18-19 are composed of three parallel lines:

"Rise, Balak, and hear;
  listen to me, O son of Zippor:
God is not a human being, that he should lie,
  or a mortal, that he should change his mind.
Has he promised, and will he not do it?
  Has he spoken, and will he not fulfill it?"

The oracle is addressed to Balak, described in the second line as "son of Zippor." The point

of the oracle is to teach Balak something about God and Israel. The teaching will take place by contrasting Balak and God. Verse 19*a* provides two contrasts: Unlike Balak, God is neither a man (איש *'îš*) nor the "son of a human" (בן-אדם *ben-'ādām*). As a result, God neither "lies" (כזב *kāzab*) nor "changes his mind" (נחם *niḥam*).

The contrast between the divine and the human is used in biblical literature to emphasize that God is not bound to human expectations or desires. The meaning of such contrasts must be determined by the specific context of the text under study. For example, a similar contrast occurs in Hos 11:9, where the incomparability of God to humans is stated in order to emphasize that God is not bound to predictable results of legal justice and thus can change. The contrast between God and humans is meant to emphasize transformation in God's character. Unlike humans, God can forgive, even though the situation requires judgment.

The context of the Balaam oracle is just the opposite of Hosea, since the threatening situation is that Balak wishes to change the future through sorcery. Balaam's response is that such human manipulation is useless in relationship to God. Thus the emphasis in this literary setting is the reliability and constancy of divine promises and blessings, rather than God's ability to change. The background for Balaam's proclamation about divine nature over against human nature might be the words of the psalmist, "Everyone is a liar" (Ps 116:11)—meaning all humans. Balaam's point to Balak would be that God is not "everyone." "Lying" (כזב *kāzab*) in v. 19 refers to more than telling a falsehood. It has to do with failing to fulfill an oracle or a promise (see Hab 2:3). Balaam's revelation to Balak is that God does not fail to fulfill promises.

God does not "change his mind." Again it is important to emphasize the context of the Balaam oracle. The point of this oracle is that God cannot be manipulated through sorcery. No act of magical divination can influence God. When God promises salvation, God is reliable and will not change, even under the threat of outside sorcery (v. 19*b*). There are other stories in which the ability of God to "change his mind" is a central theme, especially where the power of intercession through prayer is at issue. Examples include the intercession of Moses for Israel during the sin of the golden calf (Exod 32:9-14), and the spy story (Numbers 14). The ability of God to change is also an important theme in Jonah 3 and Joel 2. In these texts, the biblical writers encourage intercessory prayer as a way of influencing divine action.

The second stanza (vv. 20-22) consists of four paired lines. The poetic structure of this stanza is less clear than the synonymous parallelism of the opening stanza, although there is repetition between the lines, as is evident in vv. 20-21.

> See, I received a command to bless;
>> he has blessed, and I cannot revoke it.
> He has not beheld misfortune in Jacob;
>> nor has he seen trouble in Israel.
> The LORD their God is with them,
>> acclaimed as a king among them.

But in many cases, as in v. 22, the second line adds new material with little or no repetition:

> God, who brings them out of Egypt,
>> is like the horns of a wild ox for them.

Verses 20-22 describe the power of God in more detail by recounting Israel's history of salvation as an outgrowth of divine blessing. Verse 20 affirms God's intention to bless Israel, and vv. 21-22 state that God is the king of Israel and has rescued Israel through the exodus. Again this information is intended for Balak; he is being called to understand Israel's unique history of salvation.

The third stanza (vv. 23-24) changes from past events of salvation history to the present; note the transitional word "now" in v. 23b. Each verse consists of four paired lines, beginning with a direct address to Balak about his desire for sorcerery:

> Surely there is no enchantment against Jacob,
>> no divination against Israel;

The oracle ends by comparing Israel to a lion:

> Look, a people rising up like a lioness,
>> and rousing itself like a lion!

Comparison of Israel to a lion is unusual (but see Gen 49:9; Deut 33:20; Mic 5:8). In ancient Near Eastern iconography, kings are often pictured as lions on the hunt. The symbolism most likely is meant to underscore the power of the state to protect against the wild forces of nature. Such symbolism ties in well with Balak's concern about the Israelite threat. Balaam's message, then, is that Balak and the Moabite state cannot protect themselves against Israel (v. 24b):

> It [Israel the lion] does not lie down until it has
>> eaten the prey
> and drunk the blood of the slain.

When the imagery of Israel as a lion is viewed within the larger context of ancient Near Eastern iconography, a degree of irony emerges in the story. In the opening scene of the story, Balak expressed his fear of Israel with the imagery of domestic cattle: "This horde will now lick up all that is around us, as an ox licks up the grass of the field" (22:4). The concluding point of Balaam's second oracle is that Balak has underestimated the threat of Israel. They are a lion and not an ox. They will lick up not only the grass of the fields of Moab, but also its people.

The conclusion to the second oracle (vv. 25-26) follows the pattern of the first oracle by presenting an exchange between Balaam and Balak. Balak is angry and prefers that Balaam say nothing at all. Balaam's response is to reaffirm his position: He can only say what God tells him to speak.

23:27–24:13. The third oracle of Balaam follows the general pattern of the previous two. The episode consists of an introduction (23:27–24:2), the presentation of an oracle (24:3-9), and a conclusion (24:10-13). The three sections also include details from the other two. In the introduction, Balak takes Balaam to a new location, Peor, where seven altars are constructed and a bull and a ram are sacrificed on each. The episode concludes with an exchange between Balak and Balaam, in which Balak again expresses anger over the content of the oracle.

The third episode departs from the other two in significant ways. The introduction in 23:27–24:2 contains a series of new motifs. The episode begins with speech by Balak, as before, but his reference to God marks a development in the story. He opines that "perhaps it will please God" that Balaam curse Israel from this new location (23:27). Peor is expected, since each oracle has taken place at a different place. But the notice that Peor overlooked the wasteland departs from the previous episodes, where Balaam's view of Israel was always described. Israel is not mentioned at the outset of the third oracle. Thus the text is ambiguous about what Balaam sees on Peor. Is he looking at Israel or toward the desert from whence they emerged?

Numbers 24:1-2 provides three further points of contrast to the previous episodes. First, Balaam's perception of events is stated: He saw that "it pleased the Lord to bless Israel." Balaam's insight contradicts Balak's opening statement (23:27) that "perhaps it will please God" to curse Israel. Second, Balaam departs from the procedure of seeking omens. The change of practice must be inferred, since the word for seeking omens was not actually used in the earlier episodes. Yet the statement that Balaam did not look for omens "as at other times" clarifies that the writers wish to contrast this episode with the previous ones. Third, Balaam is filled with the "spirit of God" as he gazes over the entire population of Israel, tribe by tribe. The reference to the Spirit is certainly a positive feature, drawing Balaam into the orbit of charismatic leadership, which was explored in chaps. 11–12 in relationship to the seventy elders (see 11:17, 25).

The introduction of the "spirit of God" (24:2) suggests that Balaam achieves a new level of clairvoyance in the third oracle (24:3-9). The content of the oracle supports this interpretation, with its repetition of the technical word for "oracle" (נאם *nĕʾum*) in 24:3-4. This word frequently appears in the oracles of Israelite prophets. Hosea 2:13 provides an example:

I will punish her for the festival days of the Baals,
    when she offered incense to them
and decked herself with her ring and jewelry,
    and went after her lovers,
and forgot me, says the Lord. (NRSV)

This example illustrates that the word "oracle" tends to end prophetic discourses, rather than begin them (as in the saying of Balaam), and that oracles are attributed to God rather than to a human speaker. In spite of these departures in form, it appears that the biblical writers intend to present a positive portrayal of Balaam, whose three oracles about Israel progress in insight and clairvoyance until the third closely resembles the form of Israelite prophecy. The first oracle (23:7-10) was autobiographical, describing Balaam's coming to knowledge of Israel. The second (23:18-24) was directed at Balak; it taught Balak about God and Israel. The third (24:3-9) is prophetic discourse about Israel's fate. It is not intended to be instruction for either Balaam or Balak, but is addressed to Israel (in the opening [v. 3] and closing [v. 9] verses). These are the first occurrences in which Balaam addresses Israel directly in any of his oracles.

The third oracle is structured primarily in parallel lines, separating loosely into three stanzas. The poetic structure of the third oracle departs from the strict parallelism of the previous two. Parallel lines still dominate, occurring nine times (vv. 3, 5, 6a, 6b, 7a, 7b, 8a, 9a, 9b). Unlike the previous oracles, tricolons also appear in vv. 4 and 8b. Verses 3-4 provide an introduction, vv. 5-7 describe the Israelite camp with fertility imagery, and vv. 8-9 describe the power of Israel as an extension of God's power.

Balaam introduces himself as a diviner in 24:3-4. The opening lines are not clear. The NRSV reads:

"The oracle of Balaam son of Beor,
    the oracle of the man whose eye is clear."

The translation suggests clairvoyance, even though the meaning of the Hebrew is uncertain. It assumes that the Hebrew word שתם (*šātam*) means "to be open." But a somewhat similar word, שתם (*sătam*), means "to be closed" in Lam 3:8. Thus the question arises whether Balaam's eye is open or closed. In either case, the intent of the verse is to state that his inner eye is receptive to the revelation of God. Verse 4 reinforces this interpretation:

the oracle of one who hears the words of God [El],
who sees the vision of the Almighty [Shaddai],
who falls down, but with eyes uncovered.

Falling down may refer to an ecstatic trance for the purpose of achieving clairvoyance. Balaam identifies the God of his revelation with two names. The first is a general name for God, "El," and the second is a more specific name for God, "Shaddai." The exact meaning of "Shaddai" is uncertain. It may derive from the word "mountain" or "steppe." This name for God appears in other poetry (Gen 49:25), and it is used by the priestly writers as a name for God during Israel's ancestral period (Gen 17:1; Exod 6:3). Most occurrences of "Shaddai" in the OT appear in the book of Job. It is noteworthy that the Dier 'Allah text (the non-Israelite account of Balaam) also employs "Shaddai" to describe a group of deities.

Numbers 24:5-7 describes the Israelite camp using fertility imagery. Four agricultural metaphors in 24:6 point to Israel's possession of land, as compared to the emphasis on population in the opening episodes of the story. The comparisons between camp and land are in the second person in reference to Israel— "your tents" and "your encampments." The camp is fertile like palm groves, a garden beside the river, the aloe tree, and cedars. The imagery is of a rich and fertile land.

Verse 7 appears to continue the imagery of a fertile land, although it does not follow clearly from vv. 5-6. There is a shift in v. 7 to the third person to describe Israel—"his buckets," "his seed," "his king," and "his kingdom." The water flowing from Israel's buckets in v. 7a signifies prosperity, while the reference to the seed of Israel may refer to posterity or allude to deep roots as a sign of health. Verse 7b concludes the stanza with explicit statements about the future kingdom of Israel. The strength of their king is compared to Agag, the Amalekite king who was defeated by Saul (1 Sam 15:8). The reference to Agag, with its allusions to Saul, points to the possibility that the Balaam oracles may have functioned independently in the northern kingdom. The LXX reinterprets this line in a more eschatological vein by changing Agag to Gog, the legendary enemy of Israel described in Ezekiel 38:1–39.

Numbers 24:8-9 concludes the oracle, introducing the exodus in order to describe Israel's power. Verse 8 repeats 23:22, where God was also described as Israel's Savior through the exodus. The verse extends the imagery of holy war even further: Israel has the power to devour nations, break their bones, and strike with arrows. Verse 9 concludes by returning to the metaphor of a lion, which also ended the previous oracle (23:24). The former reference indicated Israel's ability to attack without relenting. The present metaphor shifts to the power of a lion at rest, secure in its rule. The concluding couplet (v. 9b) returns to the theme of blessing and cursing. Those who bless Israel are themselves blessed, and those who curse Israel are cursed. This two-sided outcome to anyone who interacts with Israel relates the Balaam oracles to the original divine promise to Abram (Gen 12:3).

Numbers 24:10-13 recounts the exchange between Balak and Balaam. Balak is even more angry with Balaam. He claps his hands, restates his original intention that Balaam curse Israel, and reminds Balaam of the reward that he had promised. But Balak also adds new insight to the situation by recognizing that it was Yahweh who hindered Balaam from cursing Israel and receiving reward. Balaam's response in 24:12-13 is stereotypical. He repeats his inability to say anything contrary to Yahweh's direction, regardless of reward.

24:14-25. The final section of the Balaam story contains an oracle against Moab (vv. 15-17) and Edom (vv. 18-19), as well as an additional series of oracles against the nations that will surround Israel (vv. 20-24). The transition to this oracle takes place quickly in v. 14. Balaam tells Balak that he is leaving Moab to return to his own people, but before leaving, he offers Balak advice. The verb יעץ (yā 'aṣ) can take on the meaning "to advise," as in the counsel that Jethro gives Moses in Exod 18:19, or it can mean "to plan," as in the recounting of the Balak story in Mic 6:5. The reference to the future indicates that Balaam's advice to Balak is prophetic. Thus the following oracle is divine revelation about Moab's future in relation to Israel.

The oracle against Moab (vv. 15-17) includes an introduction (vv. 15-16) and a prediction of their fate (v. 17). The introduction repeats language from the third oracle about Israel (24:3-9):

"The oracle of Balaam son of Beor,
the oracle of the man whose eye is clear
[v. 15 = Num 24:4]
the oracle of one who hears the words of God [El],
and knows the knowledge of the Most High [Elyon],
who sees the vision of the Almighty [Shaddai],
who falls down, but with his eyes uncovered."
(v. 16 = Num 24:5)

The first couplet in v. 15 names Balaam and states his clairvoyance with the couplet from v. 3. Verse 16 departs from v. 4, however, with the addition of the line "and knows the knowledge of the Most High [*Elyon*]." The introduction includes a series of important names for God, including El, Elyon, and Shaddai. The divine name *Elyon,* a non-Israelite title for God, first occurs in Gen 14:18-20, 22, where Melchizedech, the high priest of Salem, blesses Abram in the name of Elyon. It is also employed in the Song of Moses, where the "Most High" is described as the creator God, who "apportioned the nations" and "divided humankind" (Deut 32:8).

Verse 17 predicts the fate of Moab. The future orientation of the saying is indicated by its opening couplet. The vision of Moab is "not now," nor is it "near." The content of the eschatological vision contains royal imagery for Jacob/Israel. The reference to a star coming from Jacob is unusual in OT literature; yet, such imagery tends to have royal connotations, as in Isa 14:12, where the king of Babylonian is called "Day Star." The reference to a scepter is more explicitly a reference to royalty, for the scepter is the insignia of kings (Amos 1:5, 8). Balaam's prediction is that a royal figure will rise out of Israel to destroy Moab. This may be a reference to David, who defeats the Moabites (2 Sam 8:2, 13-14). But it need not be anchored in any particular historical period. The oracle may be intended as eschatological discourse, in which case the poem reflects messianic speculation in Second Temple Judaism and even later. Evidence of the messianic interpretation in Second Temple Judaism is reflected in later rabbinic (*Targum Onkelos*) and Christian

(Rev 22:16) tradition. The leader of the Jewish revolt against Rome in the second century CE, Bar-Kochba ("son of the star") illustrates the continuing influence of the messianic reading of Balaam's oracle.

The closing line of v. 17 is not clear. It states that the future royal figure will crush Moab as well as the Sethites. Seth was the third son of Adam and Eve (Gen 4:26; 5:1-8). The inclusion of the Sethites suggests that the author is predicting the defeat of all humanity descended from Seth, which would include the Israelites. Such speculation about the end time is possible, but the rationale for including Israel in this judgment is not immediately apparent. In view of this problem, scholars have also sought a more regional meaning to the Sethites, since it is in parallel with Moab. Egyptian execration texts from the second millennium BCE provide one solution, since they mention a nomadic tribe named Shutu that lived in Canaan.[171]

Verses 18-19 predict the fate of Edom. Both the poetry and the change of subject present problems for interpretation. The identification of Edom with Seir in the first couplet is expected (see Judg 5:4), but the placement of the word "his enemy" (איביו *ʾōyĕbāyaw*) in the second line of v. 18 disrupts the rhythm of the poetry and does not make sense. The Hebrew translates literally, "Edom will be a possession, Seir will be a possession of his enemies." Some interpreters judge "his enemies" to be a gloss, while others suggest that it be transferred to v. 19a to read: "Jacob will rule over his enemies."

The change in subject in vv. 18-19 is also surprising, since Edom has not been part of the Balaam cycle of stories. It may indicate that vv. 18-19 are an addition to an oracle that originally ended with the prediction of Moab's destruction. Yet the language of the poetry ties in to the larger context of Numbers. Israel was not allowed to attack the Edomites in 20:14-21, even though they failed to show Israel hospitality during their journey toward Canaan. The future destruction of Edom could be read as a response to this earlier incident. This interpretation also raises problems, however, since the reference to Ir in v. 19b ties back to Moab rather than to

171. W. F. Albright, "The Oracles of Balaam," *JBL* 63 (1944) 220n. 89.

Edom. It is the city mentioned in the Ballad of Heshbon (21:27-30) and the location where Balak first met Balaam (22:36).

Verses 20-24 are not related to vv. 16-19. It begins with a new introduction, which broadens the scope of Balaam's final oracle to include judgments on Amalek (v. 20), the Kenites (vv. 21-22), and an unnamed nation (vv. 23-24). Unlike vv. 15-19, Israel is not mentioned in these final three oracles. Verses 20-24 may consist of three separate oracles, since the judgment against each nation has a separate introduction. The first two are introduced by the words "Then he [Balaam] looked on . . . and uttered his oracle," while the last oracle only includes the words "he uttered his oracle." Thus vv. 20-24 are best characterized as prophetic oracles against foreign nations, a genre developed extensively in the classical prophets (e.g., Isaiah 13:1–23; Jeremiah 46:1–51).

The future destruction of the Amalekites is predicted in vv. 20-21. The reason for their inclusion at this juncture in the story is not clear. They are remembered as a nomadic tribe that opposed Israel early in its history, but presented no great threat during the monarchical period (Judges 6–7; 2 Sam 12:2-26). The description of them as "first among the nations" is open to several interpretations. It may be historical, but the OT provides very little evidence to evaluate such an interpretation. Another possibility arises from the literary structure of the poetic unit, in which "first among the nations" is an antonym of "end" in the second line.[172] A third interpretation arises from the larger story of the Pentateuch, where the Amalekites are the first nation to attack Israel during its wilderness journey (Exod 17:8-16).

The oracle against the Kenites in vv. 21-22 may arise from an association between Amalekits and Kenites in Israel's national experience (1 Sam 15:6). But Israel's memory of the Kenites is not that they are enemies. According to Judg 4:11, Moses' father-in-law was a Kenite, while in 1 Sam 15:4-9 Saul spares the Kenites in his conquest of the Amalekits because they "showed kindness to all the people of Israel when they came up out of Egypt."

The judgment against the Kenites may have to do more with their occupation as metalworkers, since the name "Kenite" means "smithy." The manipulation of metals is a form of alchemy that took on magical characteristics in the ancient world. It allowed nations to forge new materials for war, for work, and for construction that made a civilized, urban life possible. Verse 22 identifies the Kenites as descendants of Cain, who is the eponymous ancestor of all "smiths" and, indeed, of all forms of civilization, including city building, commerce, and art (Gen 4:17-24). The negative evaluation of Cain in the Pentateuch is partially a judgment against civilization in general. The judgment of the biblical writers is that, in spite of all of its splendor, civilization is built on blood and violence. It began with the murder of Abel by Cain, and it increased to the point where Lamech, a descendent of Cain, kills a youth for merely striking him and boasts about it to his wives (Gen 4:23-24). Thus the judgment against the Kenites may be rooted in a broadly based critique of their manipulation of metal as a central component in the development of civilization and its empires. Balaam states that the destiny of Kain is to burn and to be taken captive by Asshur. In the OT, Asshur nearly always means the Assyrian Empire (Gen 10:22; Isa 10:5), which points to the eighth century BCE as one possible date for the composition of the poem.

The poem ends in Num vv. 23-24 with an additional oracle whose introduction lacks a specific nation as the object of the speech. The poem is nearly impossible to interpret in its present form. It begins as a woe oracle, "Alas!" The NRSV translation ("who shall live when God does this?") follows the MT text, where מִשֻּׂמוֹ (*miśśumô*) is derived from the verb "to determine" (שׂוּם *śûm*). The problem with that translation is that "this" is ambiguous. If "this" is taken to be a person, then it may refer to Asshur from the preceding verse (v. 22). The oracle then traces the downfall of Asshur and an unknown nation named Eber. In the LXX, Eber is taken to be a reference to the Hebrews. Others have conjectured a possible reference to a nomadic tribe or to a descendent of Midian (Gen 25:4). Still other problems of interpretation remain. The downfall of Asshur and

172. See Milgrom, *Numbers*, 209.

Eber is brought about by ships from Kittim. Kittim was a city on Crete (Isa 23:1), but it can also designate Greeks (1 Macc 1:1) and the Romans (Dan 11:30). Such late historical references raise the possibility that subsequent world events affecting the history of Second Temple Judaism have prompted the additions in vv. 20-24. The story of Balaam ends in v. 25 with the diviner returning home.

REFLECTIONS

1. Every church has persons who see the power of God at work outside the community of faith. Their focus of ministry is often beyond the walls of the church. They identify the Spirit of God at work in unexpected places. They form coalitions with non-church groups. They build bridges with other faith communities. Such persons often make other members of their own church uncomfortable, because they are willing to push the boundaries for discerning the Spirit of God in the world. These persons are diviners. They are like Balaam.

Balaam models a third office of leadership in the book of Numbers: the seer. Prophetic and priestly leaders originate from within the worship life of Israel. Their forms of leadership and their responsibilities are distinct; the Commentary on Numbers 11–12 and 16–17 outlines these differences. Yet their sources of authority are similar. Revelation at the tent of meeting is central in the selection of Aaronide priests and the seventy elders. Both require divine confirmation to the entire community, through established forms of revelation. They represent tradition. Prophets channel the Spirit of God within the Israelite camp, and priests mediate the "glory of the LORD" through the tabernacle cult. Their focus of leadership remains within the community of faith.

The seer is a distinct form of religious leadership. Balaam's commission is never provided; he is simply introduced as a diviner. His religious authority is not confirmed through the tent of meeting, like that of prophets and priests. He is an outsider who knows God. The positive role of Balaam models the leadership of the seer. He is an outsider who divines the Spirit of God in Israel. The message of the story is that the reader also discern the Spirit of God in Balaam.

Two insights into the leadership role of the seer emerge from the story. First, a seer does not fear the unknown, as Balak does, whose first reaction to a new people is to destroy them. Instead, a seer seeks insight from God in order to evaluate the unfamiliar. The Israelites are unknown to Balaam; yet, he does not act out of fear. He divines in order to gain insight, not to destroy. Second, a seer builds bridges between people. Balak sought to destroy what was foreign to him. Balaam was able to discern the Spirit of God at work in a new situation, gain insight into others who are different, and make new alliances. He identified with Israel, and his oracles model this process. Balaam acquired self-understanding as he learned more about Israel. In the end, he blesses the people, rather than cursing them.

Every church needs seers in addition to priests and prophets. It is a form of mission. Christians also need to recognize seers in other faith communities. Our contemporary setting requires two additional comments on the seer that are implicit in the story of Balaam, but not articulated. First, the leadership role of a seer is not for the purpose of conversion. Balaam is not an Israelite, nor is the point of his story that he becomes an Israelite. Instead, he is idealized as one who is able to see God's Spirit at work in another community. At the conclusion of the story, he returns to his own home. Second, the clairvoyance of the seer is a gift from God. It does not occur outside of revelation or religious tradition. Balaam is grounded in his own relationship with God. The power of a seer is the ability to identify God's Spirit in others while embracing one's own faith tradition. Recognizing this special gift of leadership strengthens the church, both within its community of faith and in its larger role in the world.

2. Evaluating the authenticity of a seer is a problem. The role of a seer is meant to push us beyond what is familiar and orthodox. Thus, by its very nature, the leadership of the seer often takes away our ability to evaluate. How do we live with seers? How do we know when their divination is the voice of God, encouraging us to move into new and unfamiliar frontiers of faith, or whether it is destructive? The story of Balaam, his donkey, and the messenger of Yahweh answers these questions. Balaam is once again the model, but this time through satire. He represents limited vision in this story, and his donkey takes on the leadership role of the seer.

The central theme of the episode is common sense in community, arising through shared experience. The donkey provides the teaching. Balaam fell prey to the fear of Balak by attributing sinister intentions to the animal when he was unable to understand its motives in veering off the road. The leadership role of the seer is modeled in this action. The seer is often required to lead us off the straight and narrow path to avoid dangers from God that most of us never see. The message of the story is that we evaluate what we cannot see by judging the morality of the seer. The donkey reminds Balaam of past service. Their shared experience warrants trust, even when one of the party is blind to the situation. The messenger of Yahweh confirms the commonsense insight of the donkey. Veering from the path saved Balaam from an attack by God. Recognizing the leadership role of seers is urgent, but evaluating it is even more important. The message of the foolish Balaam and his donkey is that without trust the leadership of a seer will always appear sinister.

3. The role of the church in interfaith dialogue raises many uncertain questions about religious pluralism in contemporary society. Balaam provides a model for evaluating religious persons outside of Judeo-Christian tradition. There is a long tradition in Jewish and Christian theology that knowledge of God is not limited to special revelation, but also includes a more general revelation. Special revelation includes unique events of salvation history and the acts of worship that grow out of those events. The Day of Atonement, for Jews, and Easter, for Christians, are festivals of special revelation. General revelation is the confession that God is also known more broadly through creation. Psalm 19:1 gives voice to general revelation when the psalmist declares, "The heavens are telling the glory of God;/ and the firmament proclaims God's handiwork" (NRSV). General revelation is potentially universal in scope, since any person living in this world has the potential of seeing the power of God in creation.

The story of Balaam fits neither category of special or general revelation. Balaam does not have some vague sense of divinity that emerges from the creation itself. He knows Yahweh through divination; yet, he did not acquire this knowledge from Israel. In fact, he has no knowledge of Israel or of their past history with God. Thus he has not acquired his knowledge of God through Israel's special revelation. But Balaam's knowledge of God is not simply the result of a general revelation, arising through the speech of creation. He is a diviner who performs specific cultic acts at night to prompt revelation. His acts of divination represent another religion, in which, surprisingly, not only El, Elyon, or Shaddai, but also even Yahweh is worshiped. One result of this surprising turn of events is that the story of Balaam confronts readers of the Bible with the revelation that God maintains active and personal relationships with human beings through other religious structures. The challenge for the church is to fashion an understanding of God that is firmly grounded in Christ, while not limiting God's power of salvation to Christian sacraments.

4. The Israelites are not active in the story of Balaam. Their absence allows biblical writers to explore the power of God's providence through blessing. The commentary on the priestly benediction (Num 6:22-27) outlined a variety of meanings that are conveyed in the act of blessing in ancient Israel. Three additional aspects of blessing provide the basis for theological reflection on Numbers 22–24.

First, blessing is evident through population and fertility. God blesses humanity in Gen 1:26-28 to be fertile. God blesses Abram in Gen 12:1-3 with the promise that his family will be fertile and develop into a great nation. This meaning is also evident in Numbers 22, where it is emphasized that Israel is once again a great population. The divine blessing is evident in the growth of Israel's second generation. This theme presents a special challenge to the contemporary church. We continue to confess that every human life and the ability to have children are gifts from God. But a large population is no longer a sign of blessing. It is even becoming a curse on the earth as we continue to strain natural resources to accommodate an ever-increasing number of people. Overpopulation and a limited view of the earth's resources were not topics of reflection for biblical writers.

Second, blessing means well-being, health, and peace. Numbers 22–24 explores the protective power of divine blessing. Israel assumes a passive and defenseless role throughout the drama. The interaction between God, Balaam, and Balak illustrates how God's blessing encircles Israel, protecting them in ways they do not even know. The message of the story is that God's blessing is reliable. The second oracle of Balaam provides commentary (Num 23:18-24). God's promises reach their goal. They cannot be revoked.

Third, blessing is dynamic. It is an active force that pulsates with life and, in doing so, confronts people with the power of God. The opening verses of Numbers 22 underscore the dynamic quality of blessing by emphasizing how Israel threatened Balak and the Moabites. The second generation of Israelites creates the same dread in the Moabites as in the Egyptians who were confronted by the first generation (Exodus 1). Thus Balak's desire to curse them is a response to the active power of blessing that emanates through Israel. Balaam, too, underscores the dynamic quality of blessing in his third oracle when he describes the interactive nature of blessing. Blessing will flow out to those who bless Israel, and it will bring a curse on those who curse Israel. Balaam and Balak represent the two ways in which the divine blessing on Israel can influence other nations. Both are confronted by the power of divine blessing, and each comes to a knowledge of Yahweh. Their separate reactions, however, determine whether divine blessing on Israel leads to their own blessing or to a curse. Balaam recognizes the power of divine blessing on Israel and claims it for himself. Balak, on the other hand, is threatened by Israel and seeks an antidote to their blessing through a curse. In the process, he becomes cursed. The central message in preaching about the dynamic quality of blessing is not the fate of Balaam and Balak, however. It is the reliability of God's blessing for the Israelites. God is active in dynamic ways, even when they are unaware.

5. Balaam is reinterpreted as a negative character in other Old Testament passages, in rabbinical tradition, and in the New Testament. In Numbers 31, Balaam, along with the Midianite kings, is killed by Israel for having induced them to sin at Baal Peor. In Deut 23:1-6, Balaam is accused of seeking to curse Israel. New Testament writers continue the negative interpretation of Balaam. In Rev 2:14, the story of Balaam and Balak is actually reversed, so that it is Balaam who is teaching Balak how he might make Israel stumble, while in Jude 11 and 2 Pet 2:15 Balaam is presented as divining for financial gain. The negative portrayal of Balaam is also in rabbinical literature. Three non-Israelites are singled out as advising Pharaoh on how to treat Israelites in Egypt. Job and Jethro are righteous Gentiles, but Balaam is characterized as being a wicked and blasphemous diviner.[173] He is accused of using his power of divination for greedy purposes.[174]

---

173. *B. Sota* 11a; *B. Sanh.* 106a; *Exod. Rab.* 1:9.

174. *M. Abot* 5:18. See Judith R. Baskin, *Pharaoh's Counsellors: Job, Jethro, and Balaam in Rabbinic and Patristic Tradition*, ed. J. Neusner et al., BJS 47 (Chico, Calif.: Scholars Press, 1983). For additional studies on the Balaam traditions see Moore, *The Balaam Traditions*, and John T. Greene, *Balaam and His Interpreters: A Hermeneutical History of the Balaam Traditions*, ed. Shaye J. D. Cohen et al., BJS 244 (Atlanta: Scholars Press, 1992).

The negative interpretations of Balaam tend to emphasize his greed. This theme grows out of a more fundamental judgment about Balaam as being an idolater and a magician. Idolatry is the belief that there is a power distinct from God that does not transcend the systems of this world. Magic is the desire to utilize this power for personal gain; thus it represents greed in humans."

The history of interpretation illustrates the fluidity of Scripture over time. A positive character in Numbers 22–24 is used negatively in other texts. The teaching on idolatry as greed in the New Testament and in rabbinical literature contains a strong message for our materialistic culture. It warns against reducing God to systems of social power to be used for personal gain. But the negative interpretations of Balaam must not silence his positive portrayal. Reclaiming his positive role in Numbers 22–24 is urgent in our ever-increasingly pluralistic world. The contemporary church requires the leadership of seers who are able to discern the Spirit of God in inter-religious dialogue and to guide us in new forms of social ethics.

Numbers 25:1-19, The Sin of Israel at Baal Peor

COMMENTARY

Numbers 22–25 describes two external threats to Israel. The first (chaps. 22–24) is Balak's desire to conjure up a curse on Israel. The Balaam cycle of stories illustrates God's protective power even at those times when Israel is unaware of it. The second external threat to Israel (chap. 25) involves its active participation in worshiping other gods and in mixed marriages. As a result, the worship of the golden calf at Mt. Sinai (Exodus 32) is repeated on the plains of Moab, with the same consequences for the Israelites.

Numbers 25 contains two stories about how Israel's complicity in external threats to their purity can lead to death. The pre-priestly story (vv. 1-5) treats the threat of worshiping the gods of surrounding nations. The Moabites are the central characters. Israel is described as "the people" (העם *hāʿām*). The daughters of Moab entice the Israelites to worship their gods. The foreign god worshiped by Israel is a local deity named Baal of Peor. Yahweh responds in anger, commanding Moses to punish the leaders of the tribes by impaling them. Judges assist Moses in carrying out the divine decree. Parallels to the story of the golden calf (Exodus 32) include the worship of a foreign god with sacrifice (v. 2; Exod 32:6), divine rage (v. 4; Exod 32:10), and slaughter of the offenders (v. 5; Exod 32:28).

The priestly writers add a second story in vv. 6-18. In this account, an Israelite man publicly brings a Midianite woman into his family. Israel is described with the priestly term "the congregation of the children of Israel" (עדת בני–ישראל *ʿădat bĕnê-yiśrā'ēl*). Sexual imagery indicates the central theme as intermarriage between an Israelite and a Midianite. In response, Phinehas, the priest, spears the couple through their stomachs as they lie in their tent. Divine anger in the form of a plague ceases with this action. Additional parallels to the golden calf appear, including plague as divine punishment (v. 9; Exod 32:35); slaughter of the guilty, resulting in atonement (vv. 8-10; Exod 32:28-30); and the establishment of a special office (Levites to serve Yahweh [Exod 32:28-29] and Phinehas to the perpetual priesthood [Num 25:12-13]).

The differences between the two stories in Numbers 25 are clear: The pre-priestly story warns against worshiping Moabite gods. Moses and the tribal judges assume responsibility for purity of worship. The priestly story moves beyond worship to intermarriage with Midianites, and the priesthood assumes responsibility for Israel's purity. More detailed commentary will bring to light further differences. In spite of their differences, however, both stories share underlying similarities that provide an important starting point for commentary: (1) Other nations present an external threat to Israel; (2) the external threat requires Israel's active participation; (3) resisting the threat implies clear boundaries between Israel and other nations; and (4) both stories qualify the universal focus on revelation of the Balaam cycle of stories.

25:1-5. The account of Israel's idolatry consists of three parts. The event and its location are described in vv. 1-3*a,* the divine response appears in vv. 3*b*-4, and the action of Moses (v. 5) concludes the episode.

The setting of the story is Shittim (v. 1). It is not one of the itinerary notices, but simply states that Israel "was staying" or "dwelt" at Shittim. Similar notices occur in 20:1 and 21:25, 31. Israel dwells at Kadesh (20:1), in the city of the Amorites (21:25), and in the land of the Amorites (21:35). Shittim has no clear modern counterpart. The word translates as the thorny tree "acacias." Shittim wood is used in the construction of the ark and the tabernacle (e.g., Exod 25:5, 10, 13; 26:32, 37). Shittim reappears in the itinerary travel list of Numbers 33 as Abel-Shittim (33:49), and it is associated with the crossing of the Jordan (Josh 2:1; 3:1; 4:18). The literary function of the new setting is that it separates the events in Numbers 25 from the Balaam cycle of stories in Numbers 22–24, which took place while Israel was encamped on the plains of Moab (see 22:1).

Events move quickly in vv. 1-3*a*. The NRSV translation emphasizes a sexual relationship between Israelite men and Moabite women. The Hebrew, however, is ambiguous. The central verb of the sentence is חלל (*ḥālal*), meaning "to pollute," and it is combined with the verb זנה (*zānâ*), meaning "to fornicate" or "to engage in illicit extramarital relations." Thus sexual nuances are undoubtedly part of the story. Leviticus 21:9 uses the latter verb to describe sexual practice, but the language may be intended to describe the worship of other gods, since the verb "to fornicate" can also be used metaphorically to described false worship (e.g., Jer 2:20). The book of Hosea illustrates how both meanings may be combined (Hos 2:7; 4:13-14), and this may also be the case in v. 1b.

The larger context of vv. 1-3*a* indicates that the pre-priestly writers are concerned primarily with the worship of other gods. Israel's act of fornication entails sacrificing to the Moabite deities, eating the food of the sacrifices, and, finally, worshiping Moabite gods. The result (v. 3) is that Israel becomes attached

to Baal of Peor. The Hebrew word describing Israel's attachment is translated "yoked" (צמד *ṣāmad*) in the NRSV and "joined" in the NIV. The idea is not oppression or servitude, but bonding, hence the imagery of fornication to describe Israel's action in relationship to Yahweh. The particular deity is odd, given that Chemosh was the Moabite god. Baal is the Canaanite storm god of fertility who appears in a variety of local manifestations in the OT; in addition to Baal Peor (vv. 1-5), other manifestations include Baal-hermon (Judg 3:3) and Baal-hazor (2 Sam 13:23).

The divine response in vv. 3*b*-4 is anger. Other occurrences of such anger include the golden calf incident (Exod 32:10-11), the divine responses to Israel's murmuring (Num 11:1-3; 11:10, 33), the challenge of Aaron and Miriam (Num 12:9), and Balaam (Num 22:22). Many of these instances are accompanied by a plague, which has prompted commentators to assume a similar situation in Numbers 25. But no mention is made of a plague in the pre-priestly story (vv. 1-5). It is first introduced in the priestly addition (vv. 6-18).

Although God's anger is directed to Israel in general, the chiefs of the people are singled out for judgment in v. 4. The term "chiefs" (ראשים *rā'šîm*) has appeared two other times in Numbers. In 10:4, they are described as heads of the tribes who represent the people at special meetings announced by a single trumpet blast. The chiefs reappear as spies in 13:3. The use of the term in 25:4 suggests that divine judgment is not limited to the guilty but falls indiscriminately on all leaders. They are to be hanged in the sun. Reference to the sun suggests a public execution. The manner of death is most likely impalement. Similar language describes the death of Saul's seven sons (2 Sam 21:6, 9), who were impaled by Gibeonites. Wenham has suggested that the act of impalement in the sun indicates that the corpses were not buried.[175] Such impalement without burial signifies divine curse (Deut 21:22-23) and is actually forbidden in the promised land of Canaan because of its power to defile the land. The text is not clear about the burial of the corpses, but it is clear that the impalement is not meant primarily as a warning to

---

175. Wenham, *Numbers,* 186-87.

Israel. Rather, it functions to appease God by expiating Israel from apostasy.

Moses executes the divine command in v. 5. But instead of impaling the leaders in general, he commands judges to kill only the guilty individuals. Thus there is no correspondence between the divine command of v. 4 and Moses' actions in v. 5. The reference to judges relates this text with Exodus 18, where, upon the advice of Jethro, Moses elected judges to command companies of ten, fifty, one hundred, and one thousand. The relationship between these judges and the chiefs mentioned in v. 4 is not clear. In addition, there is no indication that impalement is used to kill the offenders.

The lack of correspondence has puzzled commentators. Some have suggested that 25:1-5 consists of two different stories, now only partially woven together. But this is unlikely. What is striking about the story is that even though God demands indiscriminate death to appease divine anger, Moses follows the principle of punishing only the guilty. In so doing, Moses is following and extending God's own instructions from the story of the spies, where punishment was reserved for the guilty generation, while grace was extended indiscriminately to the next generation (14:11-25). The action of Moses in v. 5 is an extension of the spy story, in that he is distinguishing between the innocent and the guilty within the same generation. The lack of comment on the striking difference between the divine command and the action of Moses suggests that his method is the proper extension of law and grace from the story of the spies.

25:6-19. The priestly writers add their own interpretation of Israel's sin at Baal Peor. It is a story of intermarriage between an Israelite man and a Midianite woman, who are executed by Phinehas the priest. The story is structured in four parts that modulate between a description of events and divine speeches evaluating the events. Verses 6-9 provide the central narrative, with divine discourse in vv. 10-13 affirming the action of Phinehas. Verses 14-15 return to the story line by providing the names of the executed couple, while vv. 16-18 conclude the episode with a divine judgment on the Midianites.

The priestly version of the sin at Baal Peor is narrated in vv. 6-9. The wording of v. 6 indicates that the priestly writers intend for their story to be read in conjunction with the previous story, even though the connection is at best loose. For the priestly writers, the crisis with Moabites evolves into a crisis with Midianites. The setting for the story is cultic. The congregation is weeping at the door of the tent of meeting. The offense is that an Israelite man brings a Midianite woman into the Israelite camp for the purpose of marriage. The action is described as taking place in the sight of Moses and the congregation, suggesting a public act of intermarriage. The couple is described in v. 8 as being in the tent. The Hebrew word translated "tent" is קבה (*qubbâ*); it occurs only in this story. Scholars debate what the priestly writers intend by using this word. The setting of the story suggests that it may refer to a chamber of the tent of meeting, since Moses and the congregation were weeping at the door of the tent of meeting. Another possible interpretation is that it is a marriage canopy. In either case, it is clear that the imagery of the priestly story is meant to be explicitly sexual. The couple is having intercourse either in the tent of meeting or in a separate marriage tent.

Phinehas is introduced in this story for the first time in the book of Numbers. He is mentioned one previous time in the Pentateuch, in the priestly genealogy of Exod 6:16-25, where he is identified as a grandson of Aaron through the line of Eleazar. His name is Egyptian and means "dark-skinned one." In the genealogy of 1 Chronicles 9, Phinehas is described as chief over all the levitical gatekeepers (see 1 Chr 9:17-20). Phinehas functions as guard of the camp in this story. He is singled out as acting to protect the camp from the pollution of an intermarriage between an Israelite man and a Midianite woman. Phinehas will return in the same role against Midianites in chap. 31, when he leads Israel in a holy war. Thus, in the priestly version of the sin at Baal Peor, Phinehas saves Israel from divine wrath in his role as guard.

Verses 7-9 describe how Phinehas takes a spear, enters the tent where the couple is lying, and stabs either the woman or both of them through the stomach. At this point in the story, a plague is mentioned for the first time. The reader is told that the execution stops the plague, but not before 24,000 Israelites are killed. The action of Phinehas in killing the couple, and its effects in appeasing divine wrath in the form of a plague, parallels the story of Aaron in 16:41-50[17:6-15]. In both stories, priestly acts of ritual intercession provide antidotes to disease that stems from divine wrath.

The central theme in the divine speech of vv. 10-13 is jealousy. God demands an exclusive relationship with Israel. The word "jealousy" (קנא qānā˒) conveys qualities of vigilance, intolerance, and absolute devotion. God states in v. 11 that Phinehas has absorbed God's jealousy ("he was jealous with my jealousy in their midst"). Phinehas's act has a fanatical quality to it, which is idealized in later tradition by Zealots (4 Macc 18:12). In absorbing God's jealousy and acting it out precisely on those who are guilty, Phinehas has saved Israel from God's more indiscriminate punishment of a general plague on all Israelites. Here the action of Phinehas parallels that of Moses from the preceding story (v. 5), in that each hero focuses divine anger on the guilty, rather than on all the people.

The divine speech in vv. 10-13 affirms the action of Phinehas, interprets its significance theologically, and bestows special status upon him and his clan. Phinehas is given a covenant of peace from God. The language may indicate wholeness and health as the Hebrew word "peace" (שלום šālôm) often does (see 6:22-27; Isa 54:10). But, as Milgrom has suggested, it may have a more precise meaning in this case—namely, that Phinehas is protected from revenge by Zimri's clan.[176] In this case, the text would be stating that those who protect the sanctuary from encroachment do not incur blood guilt. Indeed, such action saves Israel. God makes a second covenant concerning the status of Phinehas's clan: They will be priests forever. The enduring quality of the promise is similar to the covenant

176. Milgrom, *Numbers,* 216.

made with King David (Ps 89:29-37). Both are unconditional and permanent.

Verses 14-15 return to the narrative by naming the couple. The Israelite male was Zimri, whose father was Salu, a chief in the tribe of Simeon. The Midianite woman was Cozbi, whose father was Zur, a tribal head. Including the names of the couple gives the incident concreteness. Perhaps their status indicates that the prohibition against intermarriage could not be circumvented by those with power. More certainly, it is clear that the mention of the Midianites serves a larger purpose for priestly writers—eliminating their influence on Israelite religion. The concluding speech by God (vv. 16-18) provides a bridge to chap. 31, where Israel will declare holy war on Midian.

God commands Moses (vv. 16-18) to show hostility (צרור ṣārôr) against Midian, because Midian showed hostility (צררים ṣōrĕrîm) against it. Midian's hostility toward Israel takes the form of trickery or deceit, according to the priestly writers. The Hebrew word used to describe their deceit is נכל (nēkel). It occurs in only two other passages in the OT: It characterizes the action of Joseph's brothers in deciding to kill him (Gen 37:18), and Pharaoh is described as acting in a deceitful manner when he oppressed Israel in Egypt (Ps 105:25). These passages suggest that trickery leads to either death or oppression. For the priestly writers, intermarriage between an Israelite and a Midianite is also trickery, leading to the same outcome. God calls the Israelites to holy war against the Midianites.

Verse 19 is an incomplete sentence. It includes only the phrase "after the plague." The NRSV and the NIV have merged the verse with the second census in Numbers 26. This may be the original intention of the priestly writers. The temporal clause may also have been intended to connect chaps. 25 and 31, "After the plague the LORD spoke to Moses, saying," (31:1). The strength of this interpretation is that Numbers 31 fulfills the divine command to wage holy war against Midian (25:17-18).

REFLECTIONS

1. The Christian life has an irresolvable tension within it. The incarnation of Jesus and his proclamation of the kingdom of God root salvation in this world. Christians are called to embrace life here and now, and all people. The gospel is inclusive. Jesus provides the model by accepting outsiders, like the Samaritan woman (John 4). The pattern continues in Acts as disciples venture out to the ends of the earth. At the same time, discipleship requires radical and even fanatical denial. Everything must be renounced by disciples, according to Jesus (Luke 14:25-33). He even states, "Whoever comes to me and does not hate father and mother, wife and children, brothers and sisters, yes, and even life itself, cannot be my disciple" (Luke 14:26 NRSV). The truth of the gospel cannot be understood by focusing on one pole of the tension or in seeking a resolution between embracing the world and denying it altogether. The tension generates a vision of the Christian life, encapsulated in the saying, "Christians must be in the world, but not of it."

The threats to Israel on the plains of Moab (Numbers 22–25) create the same tension. Balaam, the Mesopotamian seer, breaks all boundaries in demonstrating the universal power of Yahweh in the world (Numbers 22–24). The pre-priestly writers barely make this point before they qualify it with a message of radical exclusion in following Yahweh (Num 25:1-5). The Mesopotamian seer may be a Yahwist, but Israel had better maintain clear boundaries with their more immediate Moabite neighbors. The two stories stand side by side. Neither negates the other, nor is a resolution between them offered. The priestly writers intensify the tension by making it personal. They move from the social domain of the pre-priestly writers to the family and marriage (Num 25:6-19). Their conclusion is that following Yahweh may require renouncing family. Preaching Numbers 22–25 is no different from preaching the Gospels. No single story carries the entire message. The central message in Numbers 22–25 emerges from the tension between the stories. It is that Israel must be in the world (Numbers 22–24), but not of it (Numbers 25).

2. The jealousy of God is an important topic for theological reflection. It is a central theme throughout Numbers 25, both in the story of the Moabites (Num 25:1-5) and in intermarriage between an Israelite and a Midianite (Num 25:6-19). Jealousy is about divine passion. It stresses that Yahweh is not indifferent to Israel or to their relationships in this world. It conveys strong imagery of intolerance for any allegiance outside of the relationship to God. Commentators tend to water down the violent and suspicious characteristics that accompany a description of God as being jealous. But the content of the stories in Numbers 25 suggest just the opposite. God is fanatical in demanding exclusive allegiance—so fanatical, in fact, that punishment is enacted indiscriminately. The jealousy of God is an important message to preach. God is not casual about our commitments. God is jealous about how we worship (Num 25:1-5) and how we live (Num 25:6-18).

Seduction in Numbers 25 aids in interpreting jealousy. It describes the process by which Israel is pulled away from Yahweh, prompting God's jealous reaction. The threats to Israel are external. The pollution represented by Moabites and Midianites, therefore, requires Israel's active participation in order for it to enter the camp. The sexual imagery throughout Numbers 25 indicates the Israelites' active role in seeking partners other than Yahweh, prompting the jealous response.

There is every reason to believe that priestly writers were literal in their message against intermarriage. Laws against intermarriage during the Second Temple period are stated in Ezra 9–10 (see Commentary on 11:1–12:16). One need not continue to read the story literally, however, to preach and to teach its central message. Entering into a relationship with God is filled with passion, and God demands exclusive devotion, requiring that we create boundaries in our lives. In the contemporary church, these boundaries are ethical. The constant factor in reinterpreting this story in the modern world is divine jealousy. God continues to be an enraged spouse whenever we are seduced by other allegiances.

3. There is yet another example of leadership in Numbers 25, which also provides insight into God. Both Moses and Phinehas act on principles that arise from the story of the spies in Numbers 13–15. The principle is that God limits punishment to the guilty. The striking feature of Moses' leadership is that he applies this principle even when it goes against the command of God. God is enraged in Num 25:1-5 and wishes to destroy indiscriminately. Moses departs from the direct command of Yahweh and kills only the guilty. The action of Moses is not determined by the passion of the moment, nor does he resort to direct intercession with God as he has tended to do in the past. Instead, his action is based on God's own instructions from the spy story that punishment be reserved for the guilty.

The lack of intercession to justify Moses' action has prompted scholars to judge the story incomplete. But his action requires no intercession, since the divine principle of punishing only the guilty has already been established. Moses even advances the teaching from the spy story, since he now distinguishes between the guilty and the innocent of the same generation. Phinehas models the same principle in a priestly leadership role. By executing the guilty and halting the plague on all the people, he also qualifies indiscriminate divine wrath so that the innocent are not punished.

The role of Scripture emerges as central in preaching this story. Moses models leadership based on principles of past revelation, not on the passion of the moment. A central message of the story is that God is also bound by the principles of Scripture. Moses does not execute the divine command to kill all of the Israelites. Yet, there is no indication that he is disobeying God. Mosaic leadership in Num 25:1-5 provides a model of searching Scripture to resolve conflict. The rabbis give image to the central role of Scripture by envisioning God as also studying Torah.[177]

177. *m.'Abod. Zar* 3.b.

NUMBERS 26:1–36:13, INSTRUCTIONS FOR INHERITANCE

OVERVIEW

Priestly literature frames the book of Numbers. Chapters 1–10 describe the first generation at Mt. Sinai, fashioning the wilderness camp around the tabernacle. They perish because of rebellion against God. Chapters 26–36 are also priestly tradition, with the exception of chaps. 32–33, which focuses on the second generation preparing for life in the land. The central theme, inheritance, provides a new beginning to the Israelites' quest for the promised land, signaled through repetition in the structure of Numbers. The census of the second generation (chap. 26) repeats the first (chap. 1). There is also a change of leadership. Eleazar replaces Aaron as high priest (26:1), and Joshua succeeds Moses to lead Israel into the promised land (27:12-23). The theme of inheritance loosely organizes chaps. 27–36. Inheritance law of daughters frames the section (27:1-11; 36:1-13), while possession of the Transjordan (chap. 32) and Canaan (chap. 34), along with the distribution of levitical cities (chap. 35) are woven throughout the section.

The census (chap. 26) signals transition from the first to the second generation. The tribes and the Levites are recounted on the plains of Moab.

In chap. 27, the central theme of land inheritance is established with the request by the daughters of Zelophehad to take possession of their father's property, since they lack male siblings. The chapter also includes the announcement of Moses' death and Joshua's succession of him to lead Israel into the land of Canaan.

Divine command to Moses in chaps. 28–30 outlines the sacrificial responsibilities for each day, week, month, and year. The commands include priestly duties for cultic sacrifices, the Israelite cultic calendar for worship festivals, and the obligations of vows by laypersons—especially women.

Holy war is the central theme of chaps. 31–33, and chap. 31 returns to the threat of Midian introduced in the Balaam cycle of stories (chaps. 22–24) and in the priestly version of Israel's sin at Baal Peor (chap. 25). God declares holy war against Midian in chap. 31, providing the occasion to describe the laws pertaining to booty. Chapter 32 outlines the inheritance of the Transjordan as the outcome of war. Chapter 33 reviews the wilderness journey to prepare the Israelites for continued war in Canaan.

The land of Canaan takes center stage in the final section (chaps. 34–36). Chapter 34 describes its boundaries; chap. 35 outlines the Levites' role in the land and their cities of refuge; and chap. 36 closes the book by returning to the topic of inheritance by daughters. The request of the daughters of Zelophehad is modified to ensure that land stays within the possession of the original tribe, regardless of marriage.

Numbers 26:1-65, The Census of the Second Generation

COMMENTARY

Numbers 26 recounts the census of the second generation of Israelites. The chapter consists of divine command to Moses and to Eleazar, the son of Aaron. As in the first census, the Levites are separated out, resulting in the following outline: vv. 1-4, the setting for the census; vv. 5-56, the numbering of the tribes; vv. 57-62, the numbering of the Levites; vv. 63-65, conclusion.

26:1-4. The reference to the plague in 25:19 ties the introduction of the census in Numbers 26 to the story of the sin at Baal Peor. Only after the plague does God command Moses and Eleazar to undertake a new census of the second generation. This sequence suggests that for priestly writers the first generation does not die off completely until the Baal Peor episode. This interpretation of the transition from the first to second generation departs from the pre-priestly history, where the second generation appeared already to be active in the conquest of Og and Sihon in the Transjordan (see Commentary on 20:1–21:35).

These verses loosely parallel the divine command for a census in 1:1-4. In each case, the census is presented as a divine command; the command focuses on males, twenty years of age and older, who are able to go to war. There are also differences, which indicate how the story line in the book of Numbers has progressed. The second command is directed to Moses and Eleazar, as compared to Moses and Aaron. The transition in priestly leadership parallels the change in generations signaled by the new census. The setting also indicates progression from the wilderness of Sinai in chap. 1 to the plains of Moab in chap. 26.

The text of vv. 1-4 presents some difficulties, suggesting that parts of the introduction may have been lost in transmission. First, the wording of the divine command for a census in v. 2 is an abbreviated form of 1:2. The former lacks the division of the Israelites into clans and ancestral houses. Second, and more problematic, is an apparent gap in logic between v. 3 and v. 4. Verse 3 ends with the word "saying," which indicates that v. 4 is a direct quotation of Moses and Eleazar. Yet v. 4 is clearly missing the first part of the quotation. The NRSV translation has supplied the words, "Take a census of the people" in v. 4a (NIV, "Take a census of the men"), even though these words are absent in the

MT. A third and final problem in v. 4 concerns the ending of the verse. Some scholars have argued that the reference to "Israelites, who came out of the land of Egypt" is the second object of the statement, "The LORD commanded." In this case, the second census fulfills a divine command both to Moses and to the first generation of Israelites (i.e., those who came out of Egypt). The NRSV translation interprets v. 4*b* as supplying the heading for the next section concerning the numbering of the second generation. This would appear to be the stronger reading. Yet it, too, creates a problem, since the second generation of Israelites are not those who came out of Egypt.

26:5-56. A literary relationship exists between the list of tribes in Numbers 26 and that in Genesis 46. The difference is that the list in Genesis 46 is about individuals, while Numbers 26 is about clans. The census in Numbers 26 follows a two-part pattern in which each tribe is identified by clan, followed by the total number of able-bodied fighting men over the age of twenty years. Commentary and departures in format are interspersed throughout this pattern with regard to the tribes of Reuben, Judah, Manasseh, and Asher. Careful attention to the commentary and to the departures in format will provide insight into the aims of the priestly writers concerning the second census and its introductory function for the remainder of the book of Numbers (see Fig. 4, "The Structure and Number of the Clans").

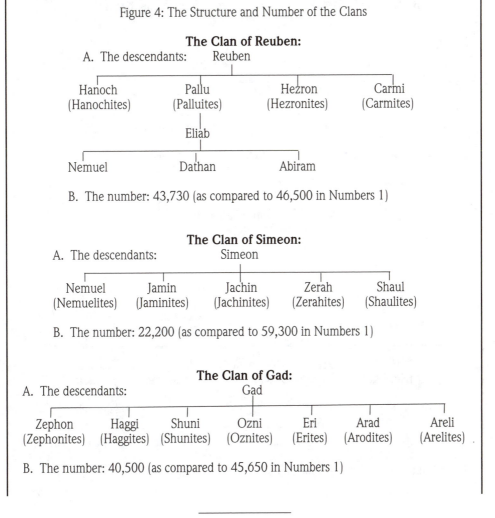

Figure 4: The Structure and Number of the Clans

The Clan of Reuben:

A. The descendants: Reuben

Hanoch (Hanochites) — Pallu (Palluites) — Hezron (Hezronites) — Carmi (Carmites)

Eliab

Nemuel — Dathan — Abiram

B. The number: 43,730 (as compared to 46,500 in Numbers 1)

The Clan of Simeon:

A. The descendants: Simeon

Nemuel (Nemuelites) — Jamin (Jaminites) — Jachin (Jachinites) — Zerah (Zerahites) — Shaul (Shaulites)

B. The number: 22,200 (as compared to 59,300 in Numbers 1)

The Clan of Gad:

A. The descendants: Gad

Zephon (Zephonites) — Haggi (Haggites) — Shuni (Shunites) — Ozni (Oznites) — Eri (Erites) — Arad (Arodites) — Areli (Arelites)

B. The number: 40,500 (as compared to 45,650 in Numbers 1)

The Clan of Judah:

A. The descendants:

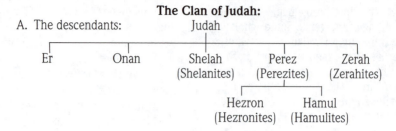

Judah
- Er
- Onan
- Shelah (Shelanites)
- Perez (Perezites)
  - Hezron (Hezronites)
  - Hamul (Hamulites)
- Zerah (Zerahites)

B. The number: 76,500 (as compared to 74,600 in Numbers 1)

The Clan of Issachar:

A. The descendants:

Issachar
- Tola (Tolaites)
- Puvah (Punites)
- Jashub (Jashubites)
- Shimron (Shimronites)

B. The number: 64,300 (as compared to 54,400 in Numbers 1)

The Clan of Zebulun:

A. The descendants:

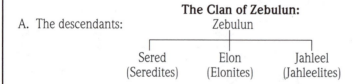

Zebulun
- Sered (Seredites)
- Elon (Elonites)
- Jahleel (Jahleelites)

B. The number: 60,500 (as compared to 57,400 in Numbers 1)

The Clan of Joseph:

A. Manasseh (vv. 29-34)

1. The descendants:

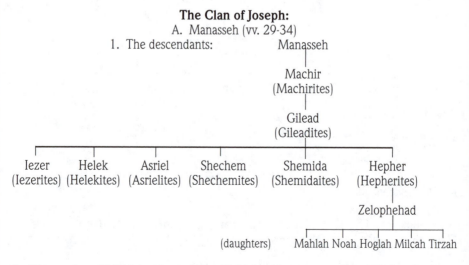

Manasseh
- Machir (Machirites)
  - Gilead (Gileadites)
    - Iezer (Iezerites)
    - Helek (Helekites)
    - Asriel (Asrielites)
    - Shechem (Shechemites)
    - Shemida (Shemidaites)
    - Hepher (Hepherites)
      - Zelophehad
        - (daughters) Mahlah Noah Hoglah Milcah Tirzah

2. The number: 52,700 (as compared to 32,200 in Numbers 1)

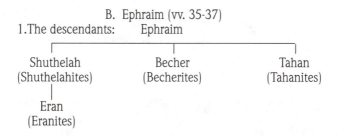

B. Ephraim (vv. 35-37)

1.The descendants: Ephraim
- Shuthelah (Shuthelahites)
  - Eran (Eranites)
- Becher (Becherites)
- Tahan (Tahanites)

2. The number: 32,500 (as compared to 40,500 in Numbers 1)

The Clan of Benjamin

A. The descendants: Benjamin

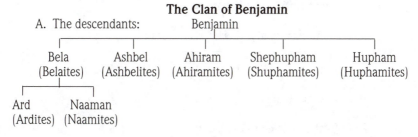

- Bela (Belaites)
  - Ard (Ardites)
  - Naaman (Naamites)
- Ashbel (Ashbelites)
- Ahiram (Ahiramites)
- Shephupham (Shuphamites)
- Hupham (Huphamites)

B. The number: 45,600 (as compared to 35,400 in Numbers 1)

The Clan of Dan:

A. The descendants: Dan
- Shuham (Shuhamites)

B. The number: 64,400 (as compared to 62,700 in Numbers 1)

The Clan of Asher:

A. The descendants: Asher

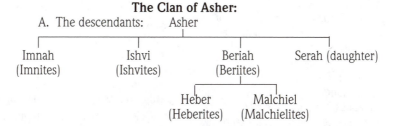

- Imnah (Imnites)
- Ishvi (Ishvites)
- Beriah (Beriites)
  - Heber (Heberites)
  - Malchiel (Malchielites)
- Serah (daughter)

B. The number: 53,400 (as compared to 41,500 in Numbers 1)

The Clan of Naphtali:

A. The descendants: Naphtali

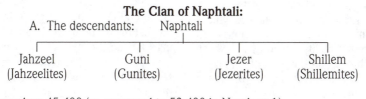

- Jahzeel (Jahzeelites)
- Guni (Gunites)
- Jezer (Jezerites)
- Shillem (Shillemites)

B. The number: 45,400 (as compared to 53,400 in Numbers 1)

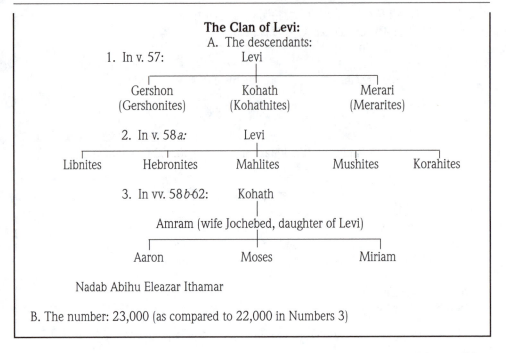

The Clan of Levi:
A. The descendants:

1. In v. 57: Levi

Gershon (Gershonites)   Kohath (Kohathites)   Merari (Merarites)

2. In v. 58a: Levi

Libnites   Hebronites   Mahlites   Mushites   Korahites

3. In vv. 58b-62: Kohath

Amram (wife Jochebed, daughter of Levi)

Aaron   Moses   Miriam

Nadab Abihu Eleazar Ithamar

B. The number: 23,000 (as compared to 22,000 in Numbers 3)

26:5-18. The clans of Reuben in vv. 5-7 have been expanded three generations to include Dathan and Abiram from the conflict with Moses over leadership in chap. 16. In vv. 8-11, the priestly writers associate the rebellion of Dathan and Abiram with the levitical leader Korah. Yet in the census all three leaders appear to have died together by being swallowed up by the earth, as compared to chap. 16, where Korah and his company die separately by fire.

The point of focus is not the manner of the deaths of these characters. Rather, it would appear to lie with the closing line that punishment of the guilty persons does not extend throughout their clan. The continuation of Korah's descendants in v. 11 makes this point explicit. In biblical tradition, the clan of Korah is remembered as temple singers. Psalms like 42, 44–49, 84–85, and 87 are attributed to this clan of Levites. In 1 Chr 9:19, the clan of Korah is described as temple guards. The emphasis on the continuation of the Korah clan beyond the sin of their eponymous ancestor conforms to the priestly emphasis on individual responsibility for sin that has been developed throughout the book of Numbers.

26:19-27. The numbering of Judah departs from the expected format in two ways. First, it records the deaths of two sons, Er and Onan, who "died in the land of Canaan." Second, the clan structure of Judah is extended with an additional generation through the line of Perez. Both of these departures provide commentary on inheritance laws in the land of Canaan through reference to the story of Judah and Tamar in Genesis 38.

The reference to the deaths of Er and Onan harks back to the opening of Genesis 38. Er was the husband of Tamar, killed by Yahweh because of unspecified wicked behavior before having produced any heirs. Onan also is killed by God for not performing the levirate law with Tamar, the widow of Er. The levirate law required that, in instances where a husband died without leaving offspring, the dead man's brother must produce children with his sister-in-law in order to carry on the clan of the lost brother. The levirate law, therefore, has to do with inheritance rights (see Deut 25:5-10; Ruth 4:1-12). In Genesis 38, Onan let his sperm fall to the ground rather than impregnate Tamar, knowing that the offspring would not be his (meaning that these offspring would not enhance his inheritance). Reference to his death in Num 26:19 may be intended to underscore that such behavior continues to be worthy of death in the land of Canaan.

The second departure in the account of the census of Judah is the additional information that his line continued through Perez to include Hezron and Hamul. The significance of naming Hezron and Hamul requires interpretation of the three remaining sons of Judah: Shelah, Perez, and Zerah. All three play a role in Genesis 38. Shelah was the last of Judah's three sons, whom he kept from performing the levirate law with Tamar after the death of Onan. Perez and Zerah are not part of Judah's original offspring in Genesis 38. Instead, they are introduced at the close of the story as twins born to Tamar by Judah, who unwittingly fulfilled the levirate law by impregnating Tamar, whom he thought to be a prostitute. Through a reversal in birth, Perez becomes the firstborn of these twins. The grandchildren of Judah through the line of Perez balance the two lost sons of Judah, and, in so doing, may be intended to affirm the continuing relevance of the levirate inheritance law for the second generation of Israelites, who are about to reenter the land of Canaan.

26:28-43. The clan structure of Joseph departs significantly in form from the other sections of this chapter. The splitting of Manasseh and Ephraim under Joseph is unique among the tribes; it goes back to Genesis 48, where Manasseh and Ephraim are introduced as sons of Joseph. The central event in Genesis 48 is that Jacob blesses the younger Ephraim over the firstborn, Manasseh. The blessing of Ephraim is reflected in the first census in Numbers 1, where Ephraim (1:32-33) is listed before Manasseh (1:34-35). The reversal of the order of Manasseh and Ephraim in chap. 26 is thus noteworthy, given the story of blessing in Genesis 48 and the more prominent place of Ephraim in Numbers 1.

The reversal of order between Manasseh and Ephraim here places Manasseh in the special seventh position within the census. The number seven plays a significant role in the priestly history from the outset, from God's resting on the seventh day (Gen 2:1-3), through the importance of seven in the construction of the tabernacle (Exod 24:12-18), and on into the laws of Jubilee (Leviticus 25:1). In each of these instances, the number seven marks a transition in the priestly history and the incorporation of something new. The

same is true with Manasseh, the seventh clan in the census of the second generation.

The clan structure of Manasseh is also unique in Numbers 26 because of the linear depth of the genealogy. It is structured into seven generations: (1) Joseph, (2) Manasseh, (3) Machir, (4) Gilead, (5) the six offspring of Gilead, (6) Zelophehad, and (7) the daughters of Zelophehad. The intention of the priestly writers emerges at this point. Manasseh is the seventh tribe, and the daughters of Zelophehad are the seventh generation of Manasseh. One begins to suspect that the daughters of Zelophehad will represent a new transition in the priestly history. Indeed, they become central characters in the concluding structure of Numbers, since they frame the remainder of the material in the book (27:1-11; 36:1-13). The new thing that the daughters of Zelophehad represent is the right of daughters to inherit apart from levirate law.

Comparison to other accounts of the genealogy of Manasseh underscores that vv. 25-32 have been constructed for social, literary, and theological purposes, instead of for purely historical reasons. Other descriptions of the genealogy of Manasseh appear in Josh 17:1-3, where Gilead is a son of Manasseh, rather than a grandson (as in Num 26:29). In Num 32:39, Gilead is not a descendant of either Manasseh or Machir, but a city that is conquered by Manasseh and thus given over to the tribe by Moses. Still other genealogies occur in 1 Chr 2:21-23 and 7:14-19.

The comparison illustrates how cities and territories are personified and related in ancient Israelite tradition through genealogy. The daughters of Zelophehad may also have originally represented smaller regions within the territory of Manasseh. Tirzah, the name of one of the five daughters of Zelophehad, appears as a Canaanite city-state on one of the Samaria ostraca.[178] The incorporation of geographical relationships into clan systems, as well as the variety of genealogies, underscores the social and theological function of this genre of literature in the Bible over against a strictly historical purpose. Whatever the origin of the daughters of Zelophehad may have been, in priestly tradition they have

178. Milgrom, *Numbers*, 224-25; Timothy R. Ashley, *Numbers*, NICOT (Grand Rapids: Eerdmans, 1993) 535-37; and J. Sasson, "A Genealogical 'Convention' in Biblical Chronography," *ZAW* 90 (1978) 171-85.

come to represent a transition in inheritance law with regard to daughters. The central point of the genealogy is that daughters who are unable to carry on their clan lines through the levirate law are able to inherit independently. The details of this change in practice will be explained in 27:1-11 and 36:1-13.

26:44-50. The genealogy of Asher is the last to depart from the standard format of the census. The new feature in this genealogy is the listing of Serah as the daughter of Asher. She is the only recorded daughter of an eponymous ancestor; her place in the genealogy of Asher is also noted in Gen 46:17 and 1 Chr 7:30. The purpose for her status in the genealogy is not immediately apparent. One suspects that she is meant to be interpreted in relation to the daughters of Zelophehad, since they are the only women mentioned in the census of non-levitical tribes. If this is the case, her preservation in the clan structure of Asher may illustrate the rights of daughters to inherit independent of the levirate law.[179]

26:51-56. The total number of the second census is given in v. 51 as 601,730, which is slightly smaller than the first census total of 603,550. It is difficult to discern any pattern or overall message in the numbers for each tribe or in the different totals between the first and second census. The tribes that decreased in number include Reuben (-2,770), Simeon (-37,100), Gad (-5,150), Ephraim (-8,000), and Naphtali (-8,000). The tribes that increased in number include Judah (+1,900), Issachar (+9,900), Zebulun (+3,100), Manasseh (+20,500), Benjamin (+10,200), Dan (+1,700), and Asher (+11,900).

Verses 52-56 make it clear that the purpose of the census is to determine the proportion of inheritance for each tribe. These verses most likely reflect a history of interpretation, since two contradictory methods for determining inheritance are proposed side by side. In vv. 52-54, God instructs Moses that inheritance of land will be determined by the size of each tribe. This conclusion fits well with the overall intent of the chapter to determine

the size of each tribe. But the divine instruction moves in a completely different direction in v. 55, where God states that inheritance will be determined by lot. The practice of casting lots to determine divine will is common in biblical literature. The choice of Saul as Israel's leader in 1 Samuel 10 provides some insight into the religious character of casting lots. In that story, Samuel casts lots at the cultic site at Mizpah. The lot eventually falls to Saul, thus indicating to Samuel God's choice of leader.

The revision of the method of inheritance in Num 26:52-56 from the size of each tribe (vv. 52-54) to the casting of lots (v. 55) brings this chapter into conformity with the account of inheritance in the book of Joshua (14:2; 15:1; 16:1; 17:1), even as it creates internal contradiction within Numbers 26. Verse 56 would appear to be still later commentary that seeks to relate the two methods of inheritance. It states that inheritance will be both by lot and by size.

26:57-62. The clan structure of Levi separates into three parts. Verse 57 presents the traditional division of the levitical clans into the three houses of Gershon, Kohath, and Merari; v. 58*a* departs from the traditional division by listing five houses of Libnites, Hebronites, Mahlites, Mushites, and Horahites; and vv. 58*b*-62 provide commentary on the opening genealogy in v. 57.

The first genealogy of the levitical clans (v. 57) begins with the introduction: "This is the enrollment of the Levites by their clans." Following this introduction is the three-part division of the Levites into the houses of Gershonites, Kohathites, and Merarites. This structure is the most prominent tradition of the Levites in the OT. It is first stated in the family genealogy of Gen 46:11. It reappears in the levitical genealogy of Exod 6:16-25 and is reflected in the first census of the Levites in Numbers 3; it also occurs in 1 Chr 5:27–6:34. Within this structure, the three levitical houses split further in the following manner: Gershon (Libnites and Shimeites); Kohath (Amramites, Izharites, Hebronites, and Uzzielites); and Merari (Mahlites and Mushites).

Verse 58*a* begins with a separate introduction: "These are the clans of Levi." This introduction suggests that this verse is not a continuation of v. 57. The content confirms this

---

179. Milgrom (*Numbers,* 226) cites the work of Moses ben Nahman (Ramban), a medieval Jewish commentator (1194–1270) whose reference to the Targum on Serah has "the name of the daughter of the wife of Asher." This reference does not exist in any extant Targum texts. It suggests, however, an interpretation that would relate Serah and the daughters of Zelophehad.

conclusion, since v. 58*a* presents a distinctive genealogy of Levi, consisting of five sons or clans: Libnites, Hebronites, Mahlites, Mushites, and Korahites. These clans have been subordinated under the three-clan structure of the genealogy in v. 57. Scholars speculate that v. 58*a* may represent an older tradition concerning the clan structure of the Levites that was eventually replaced by the more prominent three-part division.[180]

The explanation and additional genealogy in vv. 58*b*-62 are a continuation of the opening genealogy in v. 57. The concern here is with the clan of Kohath, which is not mentioned in the second genealogy of v. 58*a*. When v. 57 and vv. 58*b*-62 are read together, they parallel closely the levitical genealogy in Exod 6:16-25. Both texts trace the family line of Aaron and Moses back to Levi through the ancestors of Amram and Kohath. Both texts also identify the mother of Aaron and Moses, and hence the wife of Amram, as Jochebed. Comparison of these genealogies also brings to light differences, which may indicate the intention of the priestly writers in Numbers 26:1.

Verses 57 and 58*b*-62 weave together information from four previous stories or genealogies. Verse 59 states that Jochebed, the wife of Amram, is the daughter of Levi. This is a reinterpretation of Exod 6:20, where Jochebed is the sister of Kohath rather than of Levi. The identification of Miriam as a sister of Aaron and Moses refers to Exod 15:21,

where Miriam was identified as Aaron's sister when she took on the prophetic role of singing a victory hymn after Israel's salvation at the sea. These identifications certainly provide for a more precise interpretation of the birth of Moses in Exod 2:1-10, since the unnamed mother in this episode can be identified with Jochebed and the sister with Miriam. But one suspects that the intentions of the priestly writers go beyond a desire to provide inner-biblical interpretation on the birth of Moses. The changing status of Miriam in the priestly genealogy may be tied to social developments within the post-exilic priesthood. The nature of these developments, however, is not immediately clear from the text. Her prophetic role of singing in Exod 15:21 may relate to the priestly reinterpretation of prophecy during the post-exilic period, when the levitical temple choir of Korahites takes over the role of prophets (see the prophetic role of the Korahite Levites' singing during holy war in 2 Chronicles 20). Finally, the statement that Nadab and Abihu, Aaron's eldest sons, were killed by God for offering "illicit fire" ties back to Lev 10:1-2 and Num 3:4.

26:63-65. The conclusion to the census refers to the spy story of Numbers 13–14, where God condemned the first generation to death in the wilderness. These verses stress that all of the first generation, who were counted in the wilderness of Sinai, are dead, with the exception of Joshua and Caleb. The point of the conclusion is not so much the death of the first generation as it is the new beginning for the second generation.

180. K. Mühlenbrink, "Die levitischen Überlieferung des Alten Testaments," *ZAW* 12 (1934) 184-231.

REFLECTIONS

1. All churches have a genealogy. The history of every congregation includes important persons, families, and clergy who have shaped the character of community. Genealogies are not simply recorded history. They live on in churches. The persons listed in a genealogy represent the continuing values of a congregation. Leadership is often determined through conformity to the ideals memorialized in the genealogy. Genealogies represent the continuing social power of past tradition. One of the first responsibilities for any minister upon arrival at a new church is to uncover its genealogy. To ignore this central task almost guarantees failure.

The ancient Near East is a far more tradition-based society than is modern Western culture. As a result, at the time of the priestly writers, genealogies exerted even more power over community. This insight provides a window into the radical character of the priestly genealogy in Numbers 26. It is certainly rooted in tradition, with the historic division of the tribes. But its central feature throughout is the inclusion of new heroes into the Israelites' founding genealogy. The daughters of Zelophehad, Serah, and Miriam are memorialized as founding members of the community. The Commentary has illustrated that the incorporation of new characters into the genealogy indicates change in social practice during the post-exilic period with regard to inheritance and leadership.

The genealogy of the second generation provides a model for social change. The starting point for engaging the priestly writers' use of genealogy is to raise the question, Who is in our genealogy and who is left out? Does our idealized past adequately empower our present community? Genealogy is a mirror of our ideals. Thus the way we shape our founding genealogy is one way of introducing change while embracing the power of tradition. The priestly writers provide illustration. They reaffirm the value of levirate law in the genealogy of Judah. At the same time, they introduce inheritance of daughters independent of levirate law in the genealogy of Manasseh. Tradition and change stand side by side. The point of the priestly writers is that the second generation is not simply an extension of the first. They represent both continuity and change in following the leading of Yahweh into the promised land.

2. The genealogy of the second generation probes the character of God and what is required in following God. Numbers 26 provides commentary on the divine promises of nationhood and land first given to Abram (Genesis 12). The central message of the priestly writers is that God is reliable in fulfilling promises and that their fulfillment requires human participation.

One of the central themes of the Pentateuch is the divine promise to the ancestors that they would become a great nation (Gen 12:1-4). The literary structure of the book of Numbers, with its division into a census of the first (chap. 1) and the second (chap. 26) generations, develops this theme in three ways. First, the death of the first generation in the wilderness indicates that disobedience can disqualify an entire generation from God's promise of nationhood. The message is that divine promise requires our participation for its fulfillment. Second, the birth of a new generation in the wilderness emphasizes that hope lies with God, who is faithful to promises. Olson illustrates this point: "Numbers presents a radical and decisive distinction between the old rebellious generation of death and the new generation of hope. . . . The focus is not on a gradual spiritual improvement on the part of the people. Rather, the focus is on the activity of God, who, though intolerant of rebellion, remains faithful to his promise."[181] God's commitment to the promise of salvation lays the basis for individual responsibility in the book of Numbers. Promise of salvation, not human guilt, becomes intergenerational. As a result, the second generation is given the opportunity to participate anew with God in realizing salvation. Third, the census of the second generation illustrates the subtle ways in which God is reliable to promises. The number of Israelites in Numbers 26 illustrates that the divine promise of nationhood was in effect even when Israel was disobedient in the wilderness.

A second theme running throughout the Pentateuch is the promise of land to the ancestors (Gen 12:7). The census of the second generation also develops this theme. The story line of the book of Numbers progresses from the wilderness of Sinai in Numbers 1 to the plains of Moab in Numbers 26, where the city of Jericho in the land of Canaan is already in view. The purpose of taking a census changes along with the new setting. The census of the first generation was for the purpose of war. Preparation for war continues in the census of the second generation, but it is the theme of inheritance that takes center stage. Unlike the first generation, the second is on the threshold of taking possession of the promised land. The second generation not only embodies the fulfillment of the divine promise of nationhood through their numbers, but they are also in a position to receive the divine promise of land.

181. Olson, *The Death of the Old and the Birth of the New,* 180.

The interaction of the two divine promises, nationhood and land, provides a spring-board for teaching and preaching. The contrast between the first and the second generations provides models of failure and success. God is faithful to promises. Some promises, like the promise of nationhood to Israel in the wilderness, are being fulfilled in the present time. The first generation failed to recognize the power of God in their midst and died in the wilderness. The second census is a recognition of God's faithfulness to promise. The Israelites are once again a great nation. Recognition provides the basis for journeying ahead and realizing the future promise of land just over the horizon.

Numbers 27:1-23, Inheritance, Death, and Succession

COMMENTARY

Three events are interwoven in Numbers 27. The chapter begins with a legal claim by the daughters of Zelophehad (vv. 1-11) concerning their right to inherit land in the absence of male offspring. The topic changes from inheritance to death in vv. 12-14. Moses is told by God that he is about to die because of his rebellion in the wilderness of Zin. The divine announcement occasions a transition to the account of Joshua's succession of Moses (vv. 15-23).

27:1-11. This section presents a legal case about inheritance. The daughters of Zelophehad claim the right of inheritance, requiring a special revelation from God. These verses contain the initial ruling, while chap. 36 will return to the topic in order to clarify restrictions on the inheritance of daughters.

The setting for the legal case is stated in v. 2: It takes place at the door of the tent of meeting before Moses, Eleazar the priest, the leaders, and the entire congregation. The genealogy of the daughters of Zelophehad is outlined in v. 1, a repetition of the clan structure of Manasseh from 26:28-35. The problem of inheritance, which the daughters present, is not covered in any of the existing law codes in Torah. This is one of only four stories in which an ambiguous legal situation requires special revelation for its solution; the others are the case of the blasphemer (Lev 24:10-23); the second Passover (Num 9:6-14); and sabbath law (Num 15:32-36).

The daughters present their legal problem in vv. 3-4. Their father has died in the wilderness, leaving no sons to inherit. In view of this situation, they request the right to inherit. The circumstances of the death of Zelophehad are spelled out in detail: He

"died for his own sins." By stating that their father "died for his own sins," his daughters appeal to the principle of individual responsibility for guilt. This statement is contrasted with an alternative possibility—namely, that he might have been a participant in Korah's rebellion. The implication of the contrast is that participation in a sin like the rebellion of Korah could result in loss of land or inheritance rights,[182] even though 26:11 indicates that such sin does not lead to the death of an entire family. Thus it appears that Zelophehad is being described as having died for the general sin of unfaithfulness, which characterized the entire first generation, and not for any particular offense. As a result, no circumstances exist to justify the loss of inheritance to his family. On the basis of this situation, his daughters claim the right to inherit in order to perpetuate the clan name of their father.

Their request is without precedent, and Moses refers the matter to God (vv. 5-11). God concurs with the legal claim of the daughters and provides judgment on the case in v. 7. Moses is to transfer the inheritance of Zelophehad to his daughters, so that they are able to take possession of the land. Three theological foundations undergird the divine ruling. The first is that God owns the land. This principle is stated most clearly in the context of the Jubilee law of Leviticus 25, where God declares divine ownership: "For the land is mine" (Lev 25:23). Second, divine ownership means that the status of Israel is that of a tenant of the land; again see Lev 25:23: "With me you are but aliens and tenants." No

---

182. J. Weingreen, "The Case of the Daughters of Zelophehad," *VT* 16 (1966) 518-21.

humans have an inherent right to any portion of the land, because all receive land as a divine gift. Third, the social implication of this divine gift is that each Israelite's right to a portion of land is inalienable. No parcel of land can be permanently sold or taken away from its clan of origin. Once again, see Lev 25:24: "You will provide for the redemption of the land." Joshua 17:3-6 narrates the fulfillment of the divine ruling in Num 27:5-7: The daughters of Zelophehad each receive a portion of the promised land.

Verses 8-11 extend the claim of the daughters of Zelophehad into four general case laws. The first codifies their situation: (1) If a man dies without sons, then the inheritance is passed on to his daughters (v. 8). The next three case laws go beyond the story of vv. 1-7. These laws emphasize that inheritance in Israel was patrilineal, meaning that inheritance is passed to males through the father's side. Thus, (2) if a man died without sons or daughters, then his inheritance would pass on to his brother or brothers (v. 9); (3) if there were no brothers, then the father's brothers would inherit (v. 10); and (4) if there were no uncles, then the nearest kinsmen of his clan would inherit (v. 11 a). The divine ruling is judged to be "a statute and ordinance" (לחקת משפט lĕḥuqqat mišpāṭ). This designation of divine law occurs only one other time (35:29), as a conclusion to the laws concerning the cities of refuge.

27:12-14. The impending death of Moses is announced by God in this section. God commands Moses to ascend the Abarim mountain range, located on the northern end of the Dead Sea. From there he will be able to see the promised land before he dies. The reason for his sentence is his sin at Meribathkadesh (20:2-13). In this story, the priestly writers advocate the principle of individual responsibility for guilt. Moses cannot enter the promised land of Canaan because of his failure of leadership in not following the legal structures of communication and authority concerning Israel's complaint about water. Instead of following God's instructions, Moses condemns Israel as rebels. The point of the story is that in accusing the Israelites of being rebels, Moses himself becomes guilty of the charge. Thus Moses does not enter Canaan as a result of his own actions, as compared to Deut 1:37; 3:23-29, where he must share vicariously in the collective guilt of the first generation.

The announcement concerning the death of Moses in vv. 12-14 is repeated in Deut 32:48-52 before it is finally fulfilled in Deut 34:1-8. This structure of divine announcement and fulfillment is yet another illustration of how the book of Numbers is meant to be read within the larger context of the Pentateuch. The present structure of the Pentateuch encourages a reading of Numbers 27–Deuteronomy 34 as representing the final series of addresses by Moses to Israel. The remainder of Numbers focuses primarily on inheritance law, while in Deuteronomy Moses recounts the exodus and wilderness periods (Deuteronomy 1–11) to the second generation, as well as the private revelation of God that he received at Mt. Horeb (Deuteronomy 12–26). It is only when the education of the second generation is completed that Moses finally ascends Mt. Nebo in the Abarim range to view the promised land before dying (Deut 34:1-8), thus fulfilling the original divine commandment (Num 27:12-14).

No specific dates are given for the divine announcement to Moses in vv. 12-14. In fact, no specific dates for speeches or narrative events appear again in the book of Numbers. As a result, the timeframe between the announcement (vv. 12-14; Deut 32:48-52) and his death (Deut 34:1-8) is not immediately clear. The introduction to Deuteronomy, however, dates the speeches of Moses in this book to Year 40, Month 11, Day 1 after the exodus. This date was most likely supplied by the priestly writers. The death of Moses in Deut 34:1-8 also shows signs of priestly influence, including the statement that Israel mourned Moses for thirty days after his death (v. 8). Note that the death of Aaron was mourned for the same period of time (Num 20:29).

The manner in which the priestly writers have framed the book of Deuteronomy with dates suggests that Moses' address in Deuteronomy took place on one day and that at the close of the speeches, "on that very day" (Deut 32:48), God commanded Moses to ascend the mountain. In that case, the speeches of Moses and the thirty days of mourning for his death complete the forti-eth year of Israel's journey from Egypt. The absence of dates in Numbers 27–36 raises the question of whether the priestly writ-ers intended for the entire section of Num 27:12–Deut 34:8 to take place on one day. The only story in Numbers 27–36 that pres-ents a problem is the war with Midian in chap. 31. Although that war is not dated, the action of this story and the seven-day require-ment for purification (31:24) require a some-what looser timeframe than the single day in which Moses ostensibly promulgated the book of Deuteronomy.

The dating by priestly writers bears theological significance, underscoring how important the fortieth year is in the priestly history. It is a time of both death and new hope. It is the year when the second genera-tion of Israelites are numbered (Numbers 26) in preparation for the gift of the land. Yet it is also the year in which the leaders of the exodus die: Miriam, Aaron, and Moses. The deaths of the leaders of the exodus began with Miriam (20:1). Her demise at Kadesh in the wilderness of Zin is dated to Month 1 with no year given. Comparison of her death with the deaths of Aaron and Moses indicates, however, that the complete date is most likely Year 40, Month 1. The death of Aaron at Mt. Hor is recounted immediately thereafter in 20:22-29. No date is given in this story, but in 33:38-39 Aaron's death is dated as Year 40, Month 5, Day 1; and 20:29 indicates that his death is followed by thirty days of mourning. Finally, the announcement and death of Moses on Year 40, Month 11, Day 1, along with the thirty days of mourning after his death, complete the forty-year death cycle of the leaders of the exodus. The over-view of dates shows that Miriam and Aaron died in the first half of Year 40 in the priestly history, while the death of Moses concludes the second half of the year. Death and life are thus intermingled in Year 40, leading to the final topic of succession of leadership.

27:15-23. The transfer of the Mosaic spirit to Joshua provides occasion for the priestly writers to explore how charismatic non-priestly power is transferred. This story pro-vides a counterpart to the succession of Aaron by Eleazar in 20:22-29, where the transfer of non-charismatic priestly power was modeled.

The succession of Eleazar was signaled by the transfer of vestments representing the office of high priest. Once the people saw Aaron's vestments on Eleazar, the succession of priestly leadership was complete. The trans-fer of Moses' charismatic spirit is not tied to vestments of an office. Furthermore, succes-sion of Moses' charismatic spirit is initiated by his own request in vv. 15-17.

In v. 16, Moses addresses Yahweh as the "God of the spirits of all flesh." This is the same language of intercession that the priestly writers used in 16:20-22, when Moses and Aaron interceded for Israel during the rebel-lion of Korah. In Numbers 16, reference to the divine Spirit in creation was used to underscore that the creator God could not be the source of indiscriminate death. In chap. 27, the language is employed to argue that Israel will always need a non-priestly leader.

Two images in vv. 15-17 demonstrate that the request of Moses for a leader is about civil or lay leadership. First, the image of a leader who "goes out" (יצא *yāṣā*) and "comes in" (בוא *bô*) before the people has military over-tones. David is described in 1 Sam 18:13 as "going out" and "coming in" while leading his army. The language can also refer more generally to Israel's salvation history. The exodus is an experience of "going out." Yah-weh is described as the God "who brought Israel out from Egypt" (Exod 20:1). The gift of the land is historicized in salvation history as Israel's "coming in" or "entering" the land (Exod 12:25; 13:3). Yahweh is described as the God "who will bring Israel into the land of Canaan" (Exod 13:5). Second, the image of a shepherd is also royal rather than priestly. Kings are described as shepherds of the sheep (1 Kgs 22:17; Ezek 34:6).

The divine response appears in vv. 18-21. Joshua is chosen to succeed Moses in his charismatic role as Israel's military leader. He fulfills the charismatic ideal of leadership in that he already possesses the spirit. The refer-ence to the spirit of Joshua most likely ties this story to Numbers 11, where a portion of the spirit of Moses was placed on the seventy elders. Joshua is not specifically mentioned as being one of the seventy elders, but he is identified in 11:28 as "the assistant of Moses and one of his chosen men." Joshua certainly fulfills the requirements for a lay, charismatic, military leader. He is an Ephraimite (13:8) who plays a role in waging holy war already in Exod 17:9. He accompanies Moses up the mountain in Exod 24:13 and returns with Moses in Exod 32:17 to discover the golden calf. Joshua is associated with the early tradition of the tent of meeting in Exod 33:11, where it functions more as an oracular tent than as a cultic shrine. He is a hero of the spy story (14:6, 30, 38) and eventually the hero of the conquest (the book of Joshua). The succession of Joshua is also noted in Deut 34:9.

The priestly point of view of charismatic lay leaders is evident in the divine instructions for the transfer ritual. As was the case in the selection of the seventy elders, only a portion of the "authority" of Moses will actually be transferred to Joshua. In v. 20 the word "authority" (הוד *hôd*) replaces the language of "spirit" from 11:17, but the point is most likely the same: After Moses, non-charismatic leaders will not have his status, which was a position of authority even above that of priests. Instead, charismatic lay leaders will possess only part of his spirit or authority. Joshua, therefore, will be subordinate to the high priest, Eleazar. Joshua's ritual of ordination makes this point clear. The transfer of charismatic power is accomplished through the laying on of hands, but confirmation of the authority of Joshua must take place through Eleazar, who will discern the character of the charisma through the Urim.

The Urim and Thummim are most likely divining stones used by priests to inquire judgments from God. They are mentioned in Deut 33:8 as belonging to the Levites in general. In this text, the Levites' possession of the Urim and Thummim arises from their zealous devotion to God above family. As a consequence, the Levites acquire three functions: They transmit divine law to Israel, they burn incense, and they sacrifice on the altar. The function of conveying divine judgments through teaching may be associated with the Urim and Thummim.

Priestly writers limit the use of the Urim and Thummim to the high priest. In Exod 28:30, the Urim and Thummim are part of the special garments of the high priest, which include an underrobe made of wool and an ephod, or outer garment, of gold, wool, and linen placed over the underrobe. Over the ephod garment is a breastplate, also made of gold, wool, and linen containing two onyx stones with the names of the twelve tribes of Israel and an additional set of twelve stones. The high priest represented the people before God when wearing the breastplate. The Urim and Thummim could also be attached to the breastplate in a pouch. The high priest would wear the Urim and Thummim in the inner sanctuary when seeking a divine judgment on behalf of the people. The details of the inquiry are not provided. If the Urim and Thummim were stones, however, then the ritual may have resembled the casting of lots, in which questions were posed to God requiring a yes or no answer. The brief statement by Saul in 1 Sam 14:41 provides a glimpse into how the Urim and Thummim functioned as a casting of lots. In this story, Saul requests Urim to designate guilt in himself and Jonathan and Thummim to designate guilt in the people of Israel. The Urim and Thummim are also mentioned in Ezra 2:63 and Neh 7:65 without explanation or comment.

The choice of Joshua to succeed Moses may also provide an illustration of how the Urim and Thummim functioned in ancient Israel in relationship to the high priest. For Joshua's selection to be official, Eleazar, the high priest, "inquired for him [Joshua] by the judgment of the Urim before the Yahweh" (v. 21). The important point in v. 21 is that charismatic leaders must be authenticated by the priest. Their authority was not transferred independently of the high priest.

Verses 22-23 mark the fulfillment of the divine command. Moses takes Joshua to Eleazar and commissions Joshua before the priest and all the congregation of Israel.

REFLECTIONS

1. The priestly writers characterize human life on earth as renting space, not owning land. Their insight provides the starting point for theological reflection on the role of humans in creation and its implications for social ethics.

The central word used to designate family inheritance of land in Num 27:6-11 is נחלה (naḥălâ). In his study of this term, J. Herrmann concluded that it tends to focus on a portion of a tribal possession rather than the land of Canaan as a whole. Thus the term for "inheritance" has a concrete dimension. The land designated as "inheritance" is allotted to someone. The apportionment is by divine ordination, with the result that it is a lasting possession of the family.[183] Thus the laws of inheritance in Num 27:6-11 emphasize the inalienable right of family possession of property.

The story of Naboth's vineyard in 1 Kings 21 illustrates the inalienable right of family inheritance. In this story, Naboth refuses to sell his property to the king because it is his ancestral inheritance. When Ahab offers to pay Naboth full price for the land, Naboth responds, "God forbid that I should give you my ancestral inheritance." The story of Naboth's vineyard brings to light the theological background of inheritance law in ancient Israel. The land is a divine gift to Israel. Possession of a particular allotment of land by an ancestral family transforms the status of that clan into land-tenants of God, who is the owner of the property. Being a tenant of God actually guarantees one rights in God's land as an heir of the gift. Ahab the king, in the story of Naboth's vineyard, understood the theological foundations of land possession. When Naboth refused to sell his land, Ahab's immediate response was to honor the claim. His downfall was in forcing possession of the land for himself.

The present form of the Pentateuch is structured around the theological affirmation that the land of Canaan belongs to God, not to the Israelites. The ancestral stories in Genesis and the salvation of Israel from Egypt are built around the divine promise of land. The laws of inheritance in Num 27:6-11 are part of the same theme. The second generation of Israelites represents the fulfillment of the first promise of God to the ancestors that Israel would one day be a great nation (Gen 12:1-4). They are on the threshold of fulfilling the second promise of God, in becoming tenants of God in the land of Canaan. The promise of land, however, is not fulfilled in the Pentateuch as is the promise of descendants. It remains a goal for Israel to be realized in the near future.

Throughout the Old and New Testaments the imagery of being a tenant on God's land is both an image of salvation and the basis for ethical accountability of the people of God. The image of Israel as a tenant of God in Canaan is a central metaphor for salvation in prophetic literature. The prophet Micah describes the land of Israel as "the portion of the people" (Mic 2:4). Jeremiah describes Canaan as Israel's inheritance from God (Jer 3:19). Judgment in the book of Amos is pictured as the Israelites' losing status as God's tenants in the land because of their unethical behavior (Amos 2:6-16; 7). The parable of the vineyard by the prophet Isaiah (Isa 5:1-7) also presupposes the theological basis of inheritance law, when the prophet declares that Israel will lose the vineyard because they are unworthy tenants.

The same theology of inheritance is taken up in the New Testament. The proclamation of the kingdom of God by Jesus is a continuation of the promise of land to the ancestors (Mark 1:15). God, the Creator, owns the earth and is reestablishing divine rule. Humans are called to recognize God's ownership and become renters in God's land. The apostle Paul often refers to inheritance law to describe salvation in Christ (Rom 8:17; Gal 4:7).[184] The ethical responsibility of inheritance is explored in the parable of the wicked tenants in the vineyard (Matt 21:33-46; Mark 12:1-12; Luke 20:9-19), which represents a Christian reinterpretation of Isa 5:1-7. Christian identity is formed in the understanding that we live as guests and renters in God's creation.

The divine promise of land throughout the Pentateuch, the prophetic call for ethical behavior in God's land, and the central place of the kingdom of God in the ministry of Jesus (Mark 1:15) all remind us that salvation is not simply about people. These related

---

183. J. Herrmann, " נחלה" *TDNT,* ed. G. Kittel (Grand Rapids: Eerdmans, 1965) 3:769-76. See also Christopher J. H. Wright, *God's People in God's Land: Family, Land, and Property in the Old Testament* (Grand Rapids: Eerdmans, 1990) 3-23.
184. Paul L. Hammer, "Inheritance (NT)," *ABD* 3:415-17.

themes affirm that God's salvation is rooted in creation itself. The challenge for the contemporary church is to reaffirm the central role of the earth as part of God's kingdom. Salvation is not restricted to people and population (the promise of fertility and nationhood); it also requires the proper environment for humans (the promise of land). All humans rent space on earth as tenants of God. The church is called to be a model tenant, strengthening the earth, not weakening it. An understanding of salvation that highlights individuals or social systems at the expense of creation misses the central message of inheritance, which runs throughout Scripture.

2. The request of the daughters of Zelophehad for the right to inherit presupposes a situation in which daughters have no legal rights of inheritance. In ancient Israel, sons inherited property in a patrilineal system, while daughters received a dowry to take into marriage (Judg 1:13-15). Given this situation, the request of the daughters of Zelophehad to inherit is certainly meant to provide a model of change within tradition. The structure of the text, with its emphasis on obtaining a special revelation from God, makes this point clear. But the exact nature of the change in inheritance law is unclear.

Two interpretations of the request of the daughters of Zelophehad are possible. First, if the request for inheritance by daughters is meant to be a rejection of the levirate law, then the change in tradition is significant. It would mean that daughters have a right to inherit independent of any male. George Buchanan Gray interpreted the request of the daughters of Zelophehad as such a rejection, because no mention of levirate law is made to resolve the problem of the lack of males to inherit.[185] He further reasoned that a rejection of levirate law would also conform to priestly legislation against incest (Lev 18:16; 20:21). Second, if the request for inheritance by daughters is an extension of levirate law, then less change in traditional practice is intended. The marriage restrictions in Numbers 36 concerning daughters who inherit favors this second reading. It suggests that daughters who held land would turn it over to their husbands after marriage, thus maintaining the patrilineal system of inheritance.

The request of the daughters of Zelophehad for the right to inherit has caught the attention of modern readers because of the issues of gender rights implied in their legal request. A careful reading of Num 27:1-11; 36 certainly emphasizes that change is indeed built into biblical tradition. As such, it provides a basis for evaluating change in gender roles in our own culture. But these texts also underscore how the social background of biblical literature is often far removed from contemporary life and unable to provide concrete models for contemporary social concerns. The power of the text for teaching and preaching is not in its specific teaching on inheritance of daughters, but in its modeling of social change. Priestly writers affirm change in inheritance law as special revelation from God.

3. The book of Numbers has modeled many forms of leadership. Charismatic leadership was outlined in Numbers 11–12. Non-charismatic, priestly leadership came into focus in Numbers 16–19. All leadership in the book of Numbers is derived from Moses; yet, no subsequent leader equals his status. God said as much to Miriam and Aaron in Num 12:6-8. The passing on of only a portion of Moses' spirit to Joshua in Num 27:20 underscores the same point, and Moses himself states the same in Deut 18:15. As the leader of the exodus and the one to receive the special revelation of God from the mountain, Moses is a hero of unparalleled stature. It is this unique quality of Moses that prompts New Testament writers to make comparisons to Jesus—not in the sense that Jesus is Moses, but that, like Moses, Jesus is an incomparable hero who represents something new from God (John 1:17; Rom 5:14).

185. Gray, *Numbers*, 398.

Numbers 28:1–30:16, Priestly Offerings, the Cultic Calendar, and Lay Vows

COMMENTARY

The priestly duties for cultic sacrifices are outlined in chaps. 28–29, while chap. 30 adds material on lay vowing, especially by women. Chapters 28–29 are clearly unified. The chapters are structured as divine command (28:1) and fulfillment by Moses (29:40[30:1]), a common feature of the priestly writers throughout Numbers. The content of these chapters also encourages that they be read as a single unit, since together they describe Israel's worship through one annual cycle.

Numbers 30 is less clear in its relationship to chaps. 28–29; yet, it appears that the priestly writers intend to interrelate chaps. 28–30. No new divine command to Moses at the outset of chap. 30 separates the instruction on vows from the legislation regarding priestly sacrifices in chaps. 28–29. Instead, the instruction concerning vows follows immediately after 29:40[30:1 MT], where it states that Moses conveyed to Israel all of the divine commands. The reference to votive, freewill, burnt, grain, drink, and well-being offerings in 29:39 may have provided the transition from priestly sacrifices in chaps. 28–29 to the topic of lay vows in chap. 30, since vowing often included sacrifices at the cult site. Thus it appears that legislation regarding vows in general, but especially vows by women (chap. 30), has been loosely attached to the information on priestly sacrifices in chaps. 28–29. The result is that chaps. 28–30 present a contrast between lay (chap. 30) and priestly (chaps. 28–29) responsibilities for sacrifices. The emphasis on priestly responsibilities also contrasts with chap. 15, where other lay responsibilities for cultic sacrifice were outlined.

The commentary on Numbers 28–30 will follow the pattern of the priestly writers, in which instructions for priestly sacrifice are arranged by frequency. These sacrifices are followed by the legislation on vowing.

28:1-2. These verses provide a general introduction to chaps. 28–29. Verse 1 indicates that chaps. 28–29 are divine instruction

to Moses. The introduction is vague, making it difficult to integrate this section into the larger design of the book. Two problems stand out. First, no specific location is given for the divine instruction to Moses. The present context of Numbers 28 would suggest that the divine commands follow the commissioning of Joshua by Eleazar at the door of the tent of meeting (27:12-23). Yet, the relationship between these two chapters is not clearly defined. Second, the intended audience indicates that the commands are directed to the Israelites in general, even though the content of the instruction deals primarily with priestly responsibilities for sacrifices. Perhaps the leadership role of Eleazar in the preceding commissioning of Joshua has prompted the priestly writers to outline at this point the comprehensive cultic responsibilities of priests for conducting sacrifices on behalf of Israel. Also, there has been a tendency in priestly tradition to place priestly requirements within the context of all Israel, which may explain why the commands are directed to all Israelites rather than to the priests alone. The focus on all Israel for communicating priestly responsibilities holds the priesthood accountable in their office of mediation. Their power is not intended to be held privately. The deaths of Nadab and Abihu for offering private sacrifices provide a strong warning against separating priestly mediation from the entire Israelite congregation (Lev 10:1-2).

Verse 2 indicates that the focus of chaps. 28–29 is sacred time or, more precisely, "appointed time" (מועד *mô'ēd*). God tells Moses that each offering by fire must be made "at its appointed time." The appointed time refers to sacred seasons that structure Israel's cultic life. Proper observance of sacred time through sacrifice will create a "pleasing odor" to God. (See the Commentary on 1:1–2:34 for further discussion of "appointed time," where the Hebrew word is used in the phrase "tent of meeting" to indicate a sacred place as opposed to its temporal meaning here. See the Commentary on 13:1–15:41 for interpretation of the phrase "pleasing odor.")

The emphasis on God's claim over time is new to the book of Numbers. References to "appointed times" have occurred in relationship to Passover (9:2) and to trumpets (10:10). For the most part, however, the focus of chaps. 1–10 was place, including the legislation concerning the holiness of the camp (chaps. 1–6) and the tabernacle (chaps. 7–10). The central role of setting in the wilderness and the quest for land also gave the travel stories in chaps. 11–25 a geographical focus.

But the divine claim on time is deeply rooted in the priestly history, appearing already in Genesis 1. In this account of creation, the planets and the stars, as well as the sun and the moon, function to direct Israel's worship life. All heavenly bodies exist to indicate sacred or "appointed times" (Gen 1:14-19). The priestly writers state in Gen 1:14 that the stars are "for signs and for seasons and for days and years." The NRSV translation "for seasons" is the same Hebrew word translated as "appointed time" in Num 28:2. Numbers 28–29 provides detailed commentary on Gen 1:14 by outlining the priestly responsibilities for sacrificing on days, months, and seasons of the year. The temporal rhythms of sacrifice outlined in these chapters are meant to put Israel in harmony with God's ideal vision for creation.

28:3-8. The first sacrifice prescribed is "the regular burnt offering" (v. 6). This is the daily offering by the priests, also known as the *Tamid* (תמיד *tāmîd*), from the Hebrew word translated "regular." The regular burnt offering consists of:

Animal	Grain Offering (and oil)	Drink Offering
lamb	$\frac{1}{10}$ ephah ($\frac{1}{4}$ hin)	$\frac{1}{4}$ hin

The daily offering was performed twice each day, once in the morning and again at twilight. Thus two lambs with the accompanying grain and drink offerings were required. Each lamb was to be one year of age and without blemish. This requirement of age and quality continues throughout all festival sacrifices of lambs. The accompanying grain

offering (מנחה *minḥâ*) consisted of choice flour and beaten oil. The drink offering was most likely wine, although v. 7 describes it simply as "strong drink." The proportions of the daily offering are the same as those given in chap. 15 (see the Commentary on 15:1-16 for an explanation of the quantities ephah and hin). The priestly writers anchor the requirement of a daily offering in the revelation at Sinai, described in Exod 29:38-42.

The practice of a daily offering is already evident in the monarchical period. A morning burnt offering and an evening cereal offering are described in 2 Kgs 16:15. The prophet Ezekiel describes only a morning offering, indicating the practice of *Tamid* during the exilic period (Ezek 46:13-15). The practice of a daily offering was so important to Israel that its cessation during the time of Antiochus IV (167 BCE) was interpreted as marking the end of an epoch in Jewish history (see Dan 8:11; 11:31; 12:11). The Christian practice of morning and evening vespers is an outgrowth of the divine requirement for daily offering in priestly tradition.

28:9-10. Sabbath required special sacrifice by the priests. The day was already set apart from others by the priestly writers in their account of creation, when God rested on this day (Gen 2:1-3). The amount of the offering on sabbath was equal to the daily offering, and it was accumulative, meaning that it was offered in addition to the daily offering. Thus sabbath required a double offering. The burnt offering includes:

Animal	Grain Offering (and oil)	Drink Offering
2 lambs	$\frac{1}{10}$ ephah/lamb	$\frac{1}{4}$ hin/lamb

These verses do not explicitly state the amount of oil and wine used in this offering, but only that the grain offering was to be accompanied by oil and the drink offering. The proportions listed above follow the quantities of the daily burnt offering. The only other mention of a requirement for sabbath sacrifice appears in the book of Ezekiel, where the prophet states that the prince (or king) must offer six lambs, one ram, one ephah of grain with the ram, and as much grain with the lambs as he wishes.

28:11-15. The monthly offering by priests was to take place on the first day of the month. Once again, these verses do not explicitly state the amount of oil to be used, but only that the grain offering was to be accompanied by oil. The burnt offering includes:

Animal	Grain Offering (and oil)	Drink Offering (wine)
2 bulls	$3/_{10}$ ephah/bull	$1/_2$ hin/bull
1 ram	$2/_{10}$ ephah	$1/_3$ hin
7 lambs	$1/_{10}$ ephah/lamb	$1/_4$ hin/lamb

+

1 goat as a sin offering

The quantity of the sacrifice on New Moon indicates its importance in the priestly calendar. It equals the number of offerings for Passover and First Fruits. Other references to New Moon in the OT suggest that lunar observance was an old custom in Israel. An observance of New Moon is mentioned in the story of Jonathan and David (1 Sam 20:5, a family meal) and again in the story of the prophet Elisha (2 Kgs 4:23), where it appears that the Israelites visited holy persons on this day. The festival is also mentioned in Amos 8:5 and Hos 2:11. A form of lunar observance occurs in Protestant churches that celebrate the eucharist on the first Sunday of each month.

28:16–29:38. The yearly sacrifices focus on months 1 and 7, with the Festival of Weeks, or First Fruits, occurring between these months. (Its observance, according to Lev 23:15-16, was fifty days after an initial presentation of a sheaf of grain to the priest.) The underlying structure of the yearly festivals of the priestly cultic calendar follows in general an old pattern of worship in Israel, in which the cultic year was organized around three agricultural festivals: a seven-day Feast of Unleavened Bread in spring, followed by First Fruits when they were ready, and concluded by the Feast of Ingathering in autumn. This tri-partite cultic calendar is preserved in Exod 23:14-17 (see also Exod 34:22-23).[186]

But the priestly calendar also indicates change in worship. The Feast of Unleavened

Bread in the spring (Month 1) in Exod 23:15 had become attached to Passover by the time of the priestly writers, while the Feast of Ingathering in autumn (Month 7) in Exod 23:16 was renamed the Feast of Booths, or Succoth (see Lev 23:33-36). The feast days of Blowing the Horn on the first day, as well as Atonement, had also been added to Month 7. The addition of two feasts in Month 7 suggests that for the priestly writers the fall was the high point of worship in the liturgical year.

The purpose of Num 28:16–29:37 is to catalogue the required sacrifices by priests during the yearly festivals. The yearly rituals repeat the cultic calendar outlined in Leviticus 23. This repetition may be intended to contrast lay and priestly responsibilities, as the following outline illustrates:

Comparison of Leviticus 23 and Numbers 28–29 demonstrates that the two cultic calendars complement each other with different emphases. Both are focused on Israel's future life in the land of Canaan. Yet Leviticus 23 outlines the role of lay Israelites during the yearly festivals, while Numbers 28–29 focus on the role of priests. Note, for example, that Leviticus 23 makes no mention of daily or monthly sacrifices, since these activities are performed by priests at the central cultic location independently of lay Israelites. Sabbath is mentioned in both texts, but the emphasis is different in each: Leviticus 23 describes the duties of lay Israelites, while Numbers 28 outlines the priestly responsibilities for sacrifices.

The yearly festivals in Leviticus 23 are also aimed at lay Israelites, as compared to Numbers 28–29, where, once again, the focus is on priestly sacrifices. The festivals in Month 1 provide illustration: In Leviticus 23, Passover is specified as taking place at twilight, thus locating the time of family observance. Unleavened Bread requires two convocations for all Israelites. The ritual associated with First Fruits, or Weeks, is described in detail, and the time of the festival is determined precisely by its focus on lay Israelite participation. In chaps. 28–29, the emphasis is sacrifice by the priests. The same contrast holds true for the festivals in Month 7: The Blowing of the Horn, Atonement, and the Feast of Booths describe the role of lay Israelites in Leviticus 23, as compared to the focus on priestly sacrifices in Numbers 28–29.

186. See "Agricultural and Civil Calendar," *NIB* 1:275.

Figure 5: Cultic Calendars in Leviticus 23 and Numbers 28–29

Leviticus 23
1. Daily Sacrifice (Not Included)

2. Sabbath (Lev 23:3)
   Emphasis: No Work by Israelites
3. Monthly Sacrifice (Not Included)

4. Yearly Festivals (Lev 23:5-43)
   A. Month 1
      (1) Day 14
      Passover (23:5)
      Emphasis: Time (Twilight)
      (2) Days 15-21
         Unleavened Bread (23:6-8)
         Empahsis: Days 15 and 21
         Convocation by Israel
   B. First Fruits (23:9-22)
      Emphasis: Role of Lay Israelites
      (1) First Fruits to Priest
      (2) Sacrifice by Israelites
      (3) Determining Date
   C. Month 7
   (1) Day 1
      Blowing the Horn (23:23-25)
      Emphasis: Convocation by Israel
         No Work
   (2) Day 10
      Day of Atonement (23:26-32)
      Emphasis: Convocation by Israel
         No Work
   (3) Days 15-21
      Feast of Booths (23:33-43)
      Emphasis: Role of Lay Israelites
         (a) Construction of Booths
         (b) Interpretation

Numbers 28–29
1. Daily Sacrifice (Num 28:2-6)
   Emphasis: Sacrifices by Priests
2. Sabbath (28:9-10)
   Emphasis: Sacrifices by Priests
3. Monthly Sacrifice (Num 28:11-15)
   Emphasis: Sacrifices by Priests

4. Yearly Festivals (Num 28:16–29:39)
   A. Month 1
      (1) Day 14
      Passover (28:16)

      (2) Days 15-21
         Unleavened Bread (28:17-24)
         Emphasis: Daily Offerings
         by Priests
   B. First Fruits (28:26-31)
      Emphasis: Sacrifices by Priests

   C. Month 7
      (1) Day 1
         Blowing the Horn (29:1-6)
         Emphasis: Sacrifices by Priests

      (2) Day 10
         Not Named (29:7-11)
         Emphasis: Sacrifice by Priests

      (3) Days 15-21
         Not Named (29:12-38)
         Emphasis: Sacrifice by Priests

Scholars debate the literary relationship between Leviticus 23 and Numbers 28–29. The latter appears to presuppose Leviticus 23:1 at several points.[187] The outline illustrates that neither the Day of Atonement on Month 7, Day 10, nor the Feast of Booths on Month 7, Days 15-21, is specifically named in Numbers 28–29, suggesting a dependent relationship to Leviticus 23. Some scholars interpret the formality of the language and the precise details of Numbers 28–29 as signs of late composition.[188] In general, scholars have assumed that

Numbers 28–29 is a later composition than Leviticus 23. But the complementary nature of the two texts, with their different points of emphasis, may provide sufficient reason for their distinct locations in the priestly history. Even the consensus concerning the later composition of Numbers 28–29 has been challenged recently by Israel Knohl, who argues that the present form of Leviticus 23 represents the latest view of the priestly writers.[189]

The important point for this commentary is the more general conclusion that Numbers

187. Gray, *Numbers*, 402-7; Budd, *Numbers*, 312-15.
188. Noth, *Numbers*, 219-20. Cf., however, L. R. Fisher, "A New Ritual Calendar from Ugarit," HTR 63 (1970) 485-501; and see the criticism of Ashley, *Numbers*, 561.

189. I. Knohl, "The Priestly Torah Versus the Holiness School: Sabbath and the Festivals," *HUCA* 58 (1987) 65-117; and *The Sanctuary of Silence: The Priestly Torah and the Holiness School* (Minneapolis: Fortress, 1995).

28–29 and Leviticus 23 are part of the priestly history, rather than the pre-priestly history. The cultic calendar in Deuteronomy 16 most likely reflects more closely the point of view of the writers of the pre-priestly history. Still, other cultic calendars that contrast both the deuteronomic and the priestly interpretation of festivals include the older calendars contained in Exod 23:14-17; 34:18-26, mentioned above, and most notably Ezek 45:18-25, where a distinctive list of priestly sacrifices is proposed.

28:16. The Passover offering is observed on Month 1, Day 14. No further description is given of Passover, because there are no sacrifices by priests at the central cult on this day. Passover in priestly tradition is a family observance. The priestly interpretation of Passover appears in Exod 12:1-13, 43-49, which states that the Passover offering required one male lamb, one year of age and without blemish. It was to be slaughtered at twilight (see also Lev 23:5) and eaten during the night by families. Numbers 9:1-14 contains legislation granting observance on Month 2, Day 14 for those unable to participate in Passover at its designated time.

28:17-25. The Feast of Unleavened Bread was observed on Month 1, Days 15-21. A convocation of all Israelites was required on the first and last days of the feast. In addition, priestly sacrifice was required on all seven days. The sacrifices are the same as for New Moon, although no drink offering is specifically mentioned. Like the New Moon and sabbath sacrifices, these offerings are in addition to other prescribed sacrifices, like the daily offerings. The burnt offering includes:

Animal	Grain Offering (and oil)
2 bulls	$3/10$ ephah/bull
1 ram	$2/10$ ephah
7 lambs	$1/10$ ephah/lamb
+	
1 goat as a sin offering	

28:26-31. The Feast of Weeks is an agricultural festival that is not fixed in the priestly calendar. Calculations for determining its date are not even given here; more precise directions for its observance are provided in Lev 23:9-22. It was determined by counting fifty days, seven sabbaths from the day on which the sheaf of first fruit was presented to the priests. In Exod 23:16, this feast is called the "festival of harvest," because it celebrated the harvest of barley. Its name in priestly tradition underscores the timing of its celebration: seven weeks after Unleavened Bread. The Feast of Weeks required a convocation of all Israelites and the cessation of all work. (This festival corresponds with Pentecost in the Christian calendar.) The amount of the burnt offering required by priests follows the expected formula of major feasts:

Animal	Grain Offering (and oil)
2 bulls	$3/10$ ephah/bull
1 ram	$2/10$ ephah
7 lambs	$1/10$ ephah/lamb
+	
1 goat as a sin offering	

29:1-6. A horn was blown on Month 7, Day 1. The blowing of a similar horn was used to direct Israel on its march (10:5-6), and later the blowing of a horn will be used for waging war against Midian (31:6). Here the blowing of the horn distinguishes the seventh month from other months, in much the same way that sabbath is distinguished from other days. Thus the New Moon on Month 7 is separated out as a special day of convocation without work. The priestly sacrifices on this day are in addition to the already prescribed New Moon offerings. The amount of burnt offerings required by the priest are:

Animal	Grain Offering (and oil)
2 bulls	$3/10$ ephah/bull
1 ram	$2/10$ ephah
7 lambs	$1/10$ ephah/lamb
+	
1 goat as a sin offering	

29:7-11. The Day of Atonement is observed on Month 7, Day 10. Its name does not appear in these verses, but is derived from Lev 23:27; the complex ritual is outlined in Leviticus 16. The purpose of the Day of Atonement is to purge the sanctuary of the defilement accumulated through human use. The contamination from human sin is transferred to a goat, which is then sent out into the wilderness (Lev 16:20-22). Here it is stipulated that this day is a time of self-denial, which most likely is the practice of fasting. In addition, Israelites were to perform no work and to hold a convocation. The central point of these verses is to outline the requirements for priestly offerings. They include:

Animal	Grain Offering (and oil)
1 bull	$\frac{3}{10}$ ephah
1 ram	$\frac{2}{10}$ ephah
7 lambs	$\frac{1}{10}$ ephah/lamb
+	
1 goat as a sin offering	

29:12-38. The Feast of Booths was celebrated on Month 7, Days 15-21, with an extra day of sacrifice on Day 22. The extra eighth day may be a later addition to the festival. The name of the festival is absent in these verses. Other designations for the fall festival include the Feast of Ingathering (Exod 23:16); during the monarchical period, it is simply referred to as "the Feast" (1 Kgs 8:22), suggesting its predominant role in the liturgical year. The name Feast of Booths derives from Lev 23:34, where it is described with the Hebrew word סכות (*sukkôt*), meaning "booths" or "tabernacles." This word refers to the temporary dwellings of farmers during harvest. These were interpreted by the priestly writers as reminders of Israel's wilderness travels (Lev 23:43). During the festival, all Israel was required to refrain from work and to hold a convocation.

Verses 12-38 are primarily concerned with outlining the extensive sacrifices required by priests during the eight days of the festival. Unique to this festival is the descending number of bull sacrifices from thirteen on Day 15 to seven on Day 21. This pattern accentuates the importance of the number seven. On the seventh day of the festival in the seventh month and on the twenty-first day of the month (3 x 7) seven bulls are sacrificed. The number seven is central throughout the calendar. There are seven feasts, and seven days of observance for Unleavened Bread and Booths. In addition, the seventh day of the week and the seventh month are holy times. Thus the sacrifice of seven bulls on the seventh day of the seventh month is most certainly a significant moment in the liturgical year for the priestly writers. The daily sacrifices on Days 15-21 include:

Animal	Grain Offering (and oil)
1-7 bulls	$\frac{3}{10}$ ephah/bull
2 rams	$\frac{2}{10}$ ephah/ram
7 lambs	$\frac{1}{10}$ ephah/lamb
+	
1 goat as a sin offering	

On Day 22, a day of transition from the Feast of Booths to ordinary time, the sacrifices include:

Animal	Grain Offering (and oil)
1 bull	$\frac{3}{10}$ ephah
1 ram	$\frac{2}{10}$ ephah
7 lambs	$\frac{1}{10}$ ephah/lamb
+	
1 goat as a sin offering	

The total number of sacrifices for the Feast of Booths require no less than 71 bulls, 15 rams, 105 lambs, and 8 goats. These sacrifices are in addition to the daily offerings.

29:39-40. The conclusion to the cultic calendar stresses that the preceding list of sacrifices is intended to be public offerings. Private offerings, like those described in chap. 15, are in addition to the public cycle of sacrifice. The section closes by indicating that Moses fulfilled the divine instructions by relaying the information concerning public offerings to Israel.

30:1-16. This chapter contains instruction by Moses concerning vowing. Vows were most likely accompanied by private offerings, since they include dedication to God at a sanctuary. Hannah, for example, makes a vow at the central cult site of Shiloh. The content of her vow is that if God gives her a male child, she will dedicate that child to God as a Nazirite (1 Sam 1:11). Her son, Samuel, is the dedication of this vow. When Hannah fulfills her vow and brings Samuel to Eli at the temple of Shiloh, however, she also brings a private sacrifice consisting of one "three-year old bull, an ephah of flour, and a skin of wine" (1 Sam 1:24). It may be this link between vowing and lay sacrifice that accounts for the linkage of Numbers 30 with chaps. 28–29.

The story of Hannah illustrates that vows are promises in which a person invokes God's name. These vows are binding in much the same way as covenants. In this chapter, two types of vows are addressed. They are distinguished in translation by the words "vow" (נדר *neder*) and "pledge" (אסר *ʾissār*), which occur in tandem in nearly every verse of the chapter. Although both words require the fulfillment of promises made to God, each designates a different action. The word "vow" indicates a situation in which a person promises to do something for God in exchange for divine help. Jacob illustrates such a vow (Gen 28:20-22) when he promises to construct a sanctuary for God at Bethel, if God protects him on his journey. A "pledge" is a promise that involves an action of self-denial. The Nazirites illustrate this type of vow, since their pledge involved giving up wine. The distinction between "vow" and "pledge" does not continue outside of Numbers 30; the Hebrew word *neder* is used to describe both types of promises. Thus, for example, the abstinence by Nazirites in Numbers 6 is described as a "vow" rather than a "pledge."

This chapter focuses primarily on vows by women. It is the second chapter in the section of chaps. 27–36 to focus on the role of women in ancient Israelite society. Chapter 27 outlined the rights of daughters to inherit, and chap. 30 sketches out situations in which women can make and fulfill vows. Both chapters illustrate that ancient Israelite society was patriarchal, since the intended audience in both appears to be men. Inheritance of daughters takes place only in exceptional situations where there is no male heir. The underlying concern in this chapter is the financial obligations that accompany vows. The legislation regarding vowing by women is primarily concerned to outline the conditions under which either fathers or husbands are able to annul them.

Gordon Wenham has illustrated that the laws on vowing divide into two groups, consisting of vv. 2-8 and vv. 9-15.[190] Each half, in turn, separates into three categories. The first category concerns unbreakable vows. Verse 2 states that any vow made by a man is binding. The complement to this is v. 9, which states that any vow by a widow or divorced woman is also unbreakable.

The second category concerns vows by women that can be annulled by men without penalty. Verses 3-5 state that a father can annul a vow by his daughter, if he immediately expresses disapproval. Such an action by the father will prompt divine forgiveness of the daughter. The complement to this is vv. 10-12, which states that a husband can nullify the vow of his wife, if he expresses disapproval immediately at the time of hearing.

The third category addresses situations in which a husband desires to nullify the vow of his wife after a period of time. Verses 6-8 address the situation in which a husband wishes to annul a vow that was made by his wife and approved by her father prior to their marriage. The law states that husbands may annul the previous vows of their brides without penalty. The complement to this law is vv. 13-15, which state that if a husband does not act immediately to nullify a vow of his wife, then he must bear the guilt for any future action on his part to annul the vow.

190. Wenham, *Numbers*, 206.

REFLECTIONS

1. Our contemporary world is obsessed with time. It is an obstacle to be overcome in reaching goals faster. Manufacturing technology is aimed at a never-ending quest to accomplish more in less time. Computers and the World Wide Web accelerate our communication in order to save time. Family life includes more and more activity in the same twenty-four-hour period. Food is now even evaluated by time—fast food is a growth industry in Western culture. Progress in each of these different areas of modern life is measured by overcoming the limits of time. The priestly writers view time differently in Numbers 28–29. They provide an excellent resource for reflecting theologically on the significance of time in contemporary life and especially sacred time in our worship life.

Time is holy for the priestly writers. The importance of time is not its speed in reaching a goal, but its rhythm in relationship with objects in creation. Thus time highlights interrelationships in creation. Genesis 1 lays the foundation for this insight. Creation is an evolution of opposites, from dark to light, from water to air, from sea to dry land, and from profane time to sacred time. Time, according to the priestly writers, is part of the pattern of contrasts that imposes order on chaos. But priestly writers value time even beyond its role in containing chaos. It holds the key to holiness. The ideal rhythm of time is woven into the pattern of creation, including day and night (Gen 1:3-5), sabbath (Gen 2:1-3), and months and years (Gen 1:14-19). These rhythms are not obstacles to be overcome by humans. On the contrary, human life is enriched when it corresponds to the temporal patterns of creation. Conforming to the rhythm of creation is the only way to achieve holiness.

Sabbath is central to the priestly vision of sacred time. Genesis 1 once again is the source of their teaching. God sanctifies sabbath (Gen 2:3) by resting on this day. Sanctification of sabbath imposes yet another temporal order on creation—sacred and profane time—providing a paradigm for the worship week of humans. This message is clear from the story of manna (Exodus 16), the Decalogue (Exodus 20), the instructions for the tabernacle (Exodus 31 and 35), and the case of the man picking up sticks on the sabbath (Numbers 15). Humans rest on sabbath because God rested on sabbath (Gen 2:1-3). This moment in creation is sanctified.

Only sabbath time is holy, according to the priestly writers. No other part of creation is given holy status in Genesis 1. The earth is not holy. The stars, sun, and moon are not holy. Animals, birds, and humans are not holy. All of these parts of creation are good, but none is sacred. God cannot be identified with objects or creatures in creation. Only time is holy in Genesis 1. God sanctifies the sabbath, because it marks the moment of completion. On sabbath, the finished creation interacts as an organism, alive and in balance. This is what allows for divine rest. The organism is not holy, but the moment of sabbath rest is holy. Any additional work would disrupt the balance of the whole. Thus when humans rest on sabbath, it takes on eschatological significance for the priestly writers. It is a window into this original sacred moment, when the organism of creation conformed to God's intentions.

Priestly writers lay the foundation for their view of sacred time in Genesis 1, but God's claim on time continues into the book of Numbers. The presence of God in the tabernacle influences not only the way Israel is organized in the camp, but also how their days, weeks, months, and years are structured. Thus time itself divides between sacred and profane. Transitional moments in the day (at dawn and twilight), in the week (on sabbath), in the month (on the first day), and in the year (at major festivals) are infused with holiness, creating a contrast with ordinary time. Work is replaced by worship, and sacrificial rites are performed. Participation in the cultic rhythms of Numbers 28–29 is eschatological. It transports Israel to the sacred moment when creation was balanced and God rested.

The change in the observance of sabbath from Saturday to Sunday in early Christian worship accentuates the eschatological nature of sabbath rest established by priestly writers. The resurrection of Jesus prompted Christians to move sabbath from Saturday to Sunday in order to memorialize the resurrection on a weekly basis. Sabbath as Sunday becomes the first day of the new creation in the kingdom of God, ushered in through the passion of Jesus. The message in Christian worship is the same as that of the priestly writers: Time is never an obstacle to be overcome. Just the opposite; we participate in holiness by conforming to the rhythm of God's time in creation.

2. The priestly cultic calendar also provides an occasion to reflect more generally on sacred time in the Christian liturgical year. Christians share the confession of the priestly writers that God claims time, creating a contrast between sacred and profane time. Christians also profess that sacred time provides a rhythm suggestive of God's vision for time. Furthermore, the Christian calendar has evolved from the priestly calendar in Numbers 28–29 in much the same way as the priestly calendar evolved from the older cultic calendar in Exod 23:14-17. Comparison between the priestly and the Christian calendars underscores how the fall festivals in the priestly calendar—those that occur in Month 7—do not continue in Christian tradition. Advent and Christmas are not a continuation of the priestly fall festivals. Instead, they represent a late innovation in Christian tradition that departs from Jewish tradition.

The center of the Christian year is Holy Week in the spring. Holy Week in Christian tradition builds off of the spring festival of Passover in Month 1, Day 14. Passover is embedded in a week-long festival for Christians that now includes the three-day passion of Jesus from Good Friday to Easter Sunday morning, where much of the priestly rituals from the Day of Atonement are relocated. Pentecost is the Christian reinterpretation of the Feast of Weeks in the priestly calendar. Thus the Festival of First Fruits for Christians becomes the gift of the Holy Spirit to the apostles. In this way, the church becomes the first fruits of the kingdom of God. The comparisons underscore how Christians, like the priestly writers, profess that time is holy and that the life of faith must be organized according to the rhythm of God's time.

3. Numbers 28–29 model the power of public intercession through sacrifice. This is true for all the public offerings by the priests, but such power is reflected especially in the *Tamid,* the daily regular burnt offerings, because it occurs independently of a convocation by Israel. The *Tamid* is a form of priestly intercession that takes place every morning and every evening. It is aimed at maintaining the health and well-being of the community as a whole and the entire creation as well. What is noteworthy for contemporary teaching and preaching is that the *Tamid* takes place without the personal involvement of those whom it is intended to benefit. The ritual itself creates an environment of health.

The ever-growing emphasis on individualized and personal religion in modern culture has tended to minimize the power of public intercession like the *Tamid.* As a result, the power of God in contemporary culture is often limited in scope to individual persons, while the action of God to save tends to be conditioned on personal, human involvement. The focus on lay Israelite involvement, emphasized in Leviticus 23, indicates that priestly writers certainly support individual participation in worship. The message of priestly writers in Numbers 28–29, however, is that daily ritual sacrifice by priests also influences God and that such influence is independent of direct lay participation. The *Tamid* is rooted in the belief that the Temple (for Christians, the church) has the power to influence the outcome of world events through ritual intercession. Such intercession actually aids in keeping the world in balance. The message of the priestly writers is that we are more powerful collectively than we are individually. The writer of Matthew states the same insight somewhat differently with the proclamation that the church holds the keys to the kingdom of God (Matt 16:13-20).

4. The patriarchal structure of Numbers 30, in which women play a subordinate role to men, renders the passage socially irrelevant to modern culture, for which the goal is for men and women to have equal status under the law. But the social structure of Numbers 30 should not obscure its essential point: the power of making vows with God. The challenge of Numbers 30 for modern readers is not a literal reading of ancient Israelite social structure, but a literal reading of the power of making vows. Too often, modern interpreters reverse this order and look to ancient texts for irrelevant social models, while ignoring the underlying religious dimension of the text.

Vows imply the active presence of God in the life of people. Vows were often made at times of crisis. Hannah's request for a son (1 Samuel 1) and Israel's request for divine help in war (Num 21:2) illustrate typical situations in which vows were made. The legal background of Numbers 30 underscores how seriously both Israel and God evaluated promises. Vows were not interpreted metaphorically in ancient Israel as expressions of wishful thinking on the part of Israelites. They were legally binding for both

God and humans. Thus vows imply that God is a concrete and active force in human affairs. Ancient Israel expected God to be faithful to the contract. They also held themselves accountable. Thus once spoken a vow took on a life of its own. The NRSV translation in Num 30:2, "he shall not break his word," literally means "to desecrate." Failure to fulfill a vow threatened to profane the sanctuary, influencing the health of the entire community.

Vowing implies an awareness of God in the outcome of concrete human events. This, and not the social structure of the text, is the central message and challenge for contemporary preaching and teaching on Numbers 30. Vows hold God and the person making the vow accountable. They also are public contracts, whose fulfillment strengthens the community of faith. We make vows constantly in the church. There are vows for positions of leadership (ordination vows), marriage, baptism, tithing, and so forth. Numbers 30 reminds us that both God and we have legal obligations when we make vows. The chapter also invites reflection on more individual vows for specific occasions or periods of time. These are less common in the life of the church, but are no less important to the health of a community.

Numbers 31:1–33:56, Holy War

COMMENTARY

Numbers 31–33 are bound together by the theme of war. The section opens with the divine command that Israel destroy the Midianites for their seduction of the people at Baal Peor. Chapter 32 outlines the rules for participation in holy war by the tribes of Reuben, Gad, and Manasseh; these are the tribes who chose to settle in the Transjordan. Chapter 33 recounts Israel's entire wilderness journey as a military march, concluding with the warning that Israel must drive out all of the indigenous people of Canaan if they expect God to lead them in the land.

Both the pre-priestly and the priestly histories emphasize the theme of holy war. The pre-priestly history includes the rules for participation in holy war (chap. 32), along with the review of the wilderness march and the call for holy war (chap. 33). The priestly writers preface the pre-priestly history with the account of holy war against Midian (chap. 31), while adding additional commentary throughout the section.

31:1-54. This chapter tells of holy war against the Midianites. Scholars debate whether this war is historical or fictional.[191] The complete destruction of all Midianite

males without one Israelite fatality suggests that the story is a literary construction by the priestly writers, intended to provide the framework for their interpretation of holy war legislation. The role of the central characters throughout the story is important for discerning the teaching of the priestly writers on war. Joshua does not lead this holy war. Moses and the priests oversee the war. Eleazar the high priest determines what constitutes acceptable booty from holy war, while Phinehas, the son of Eleazar, actually leads the troops.

Holy war against Midian provides the literary setting for the priestly writers to return to the topic of external threats to Israel—the central theme of chaps. 22–25. The story of Balaam (chaps. 22–24) explored the external threat presented by Balak of Moab in seeking to curse Israel, while the sin of Israel at Baal Peor (25:1-5) illustrated the danger of intermingling with surrounding people. The priestly writers weave Midianites into both of these stories. Midianites assist in hiring Balaam to curse Israel (22:4, 7), and they intermarry with Israelites at Baal Peor (25:6-18). Holy war against Midian concludes the topic of external threats to Israel. It represents the most extreme measures for maintaining purity. The divine command that Israel "harass" the Midianites because of the

191. For arguments favoring its historicity, see Milgrom, *Numbers,* 490-91; and Wenham, *Numbers,* 209. For arguments in support of the fictive character of the chapter, see Gray, *Numbers,* 417-20; and Davies, *Numbers,* 320.

incident at Baal Peor (25:16-18) foreshadows the holy war in chap. 31.

Booty is the central concern underlying the rules and procedures for holy war in Numbers 31. Other topics also addressed include the selection and participation of warriors from the tribes, leadership, the role of priests in sanctioning holy war, purification of warriors from contact with the dead, and the price of ransom to the temple. Central topics concerning the booty acquired during holy war include foreign objects and persons that can be taken into the Israelite camp without polluting the community; the division of booty among warriors and other Israelites; and the amount of booty given to priests and Levites. The quantity of booty acquired in the holy war against Midian exceeds 800,000 animals and 16,750 shekels of gold. The unrealistic quantity indicates that plunder from war is the central concern of the priestly writers.

Even more specific is the priestly writers' concern for the role of women as booty. No fewer than 32,000 virgins are taken as booty. This chapter is the fourth time in Numbers 22–36 that the priestly writers turn their attention to women. Chapter 25 addressed the threat of Midianite women to the purity of the Israelite camp; chap. 27 outlined the inheritance rights of Israelite daughters in the absence of a male heir; and chap. 30 described the legal rights of Israelite daughters and wives to make vows. Now, chap. 31 returns to the topic of Midianite women entering the Israelite camp, this time as the spoils of holy war.

Chapters 25 and 31 are meant to be read together. Numbers 25 introduces the threat of intermarriage between Midianites and Israelites, and chap. 31 outlines conditions by which foreign women can become part of the Israelite community. In 25:6-18, intermarriage with Midianites was unacceptable to the priestly writers, since it threatened the purity of the Israelite camp. Holy war, however, eliminates the threat of cultural intermingling, since it envisions the extermination of entire cultures and religions. Under such conditions, chap. 31 suggests that Israelite males are able to assimilate foreign virgins into their families.

Deuteronomy 20 and 21:10-14 provide the background for the priestly legislation regarding booty from holy war. Two features, in particular, provide a starting point for interpreting women as booty. The first is the general law regarding spoils of war in Deuteronomy 20: (1) From cities within the promised land, no booty is allowed; everything must be destroyed (Deut 20:16-18); (2) from all peoples outside the promised land, holy war requires only that all adult males be killed. Acceptable plunder in these instances includes women, children, livestock, and everything else (Deut 20:10-15). The priestly story of holy war against Midian falls under the second category regarding holy war booty, and it even appears to follow the guidelines of Deuteronomy 20. The booty taken by Phinehas and the Israelite warriors in Num 31:9 includes women, children, cattle, flocks, and all other goods.

Deuteronomy 21:10-14 also provides background for interpreting Numbers 31, which states that Israelite males are allowed to marry any woman acquired as booty in holy war. Read in conjunction with the general laws of holy war in Deuteronomy 20, this law implies that Israelites could wed non-virgin foreign women. The larger context of Deuteronomy 21 indicates that such marriages influence inheritance laws. Marriage law is not directly addressed in Numbers 31; yet it, too, would be affected by the story of the war with Midian. The priestly story of holy war against Midian departs from the guidelines of Deut 21:10-14. Moses voices the concern of the priestly writers in Num 31:14-18. His anger over taking male children and non-virgin women as booty indicates priestly opposition to the breadth of the laws in Deuteronomy 20 and 21:10-14. The new law voiced by Moses narrows the scope of acceptable booty to female virgins.

31:1-18. Holy war against Midian is undertaken at divine command (vv. 1-2). God instructs Moses to take vengeance on the Midianites—a response to 25:6-18, where Midianites are blamed by the priestly writers for Israel's sin at Baal Peor. The divine instruction also indicates that this is one of the last commands Moses will receive. After this incident, he will die. The instruction of Moses to Israel is recorded in vv. 3-4, where he states that war with Midian is an execution of divine vengeance. In addition, he indicates the number and distribution of warriors. Israel's army is to include 1,000 male warriors from each of the twelve tribes; thus all tribes participate in holy war equally.

Verses 5-12 are a brief account of the battle, anchoring the institution of holy war in the cult. The troops are led by the priest Phinehas, who already assumed the position of holy warrior when he killed the Midianite woman Cozbi and the Israelite man Zimri for the sin of intermarriage (25:6-18). Now, he leads the Israelite army in executing God's vengeance on the entire nation of Midian for this sin. Not only is Israel led by a priest, but also it takes "vessels of the sanctuary" into battle. The text is not clear about the exact nature of these objects. Scholars suggest three possibilities: holy war clothing for the priest (Deut 22:5), the ark (Num 10:35; 14:44; 1 Sam 4:4), or the trumpets (cited in Num 31:6).[192] The phrase "vessels of the sanctuary" is used earlier in Numbers (3:31; 4:15; 18:3) to indicate furniture, thus favoring a reference to the ark or trumpets over the priestly clothing.

A description of the actual battle against Midian is absent. Instead, vv. 7-12 list the results of the war. Those killed in the battle are listed in vv. 7-8. The Midianite dead include all the males (v. 7), the five kings of Midian (Evi, Rekem, Zur, Hur, and Reba; v. 8/ Josh 13:21), and Balaam son of Beor (v. 8). The booty is listed in v. 9. It includes all Midianite women and children, all cattle and flocks, and all goods. With towns and settlements burned, the army returns to Moses, Eleazar, and Israel on the plains of Moab. (Other wars with Midian in biblical literature include Gideon's war with them in Judges 6–9 and the obscure reference to the Day of Midian in Ps 83:10; Isa 9:3.)

The response of Moses in vv. 13-18 indicates that the priestly writers' focus is on the booty. As noted earlier, the booty taken from the Midianites follows the instructions for holy war in Deuteronomy 20 and 21:10-14. Yet Moses is angry. The cause of his anger is the Midianite women taken as booty (vv. 15-16). He accuses them of seduction in the incident at Baal Peor. The priestly writers also reinterpret the Balaam stories more negatively by accusing the diviner, rather

than the Moabite king Balak, of threatening Israel. Balaam's sin is not having cursed Israel through divination, as King Balak desired in the story of Numbers 22–24, however. Rather, it is the seduction of Israel by Midianite women. The priestly writers are much less generous about granting Balaam an authentic relationship with God outside of the Israelite cult than were the pre-priestly writers. Balaam the diviner, who knows God independently of the cultic rituals of the tabernacle, represents for the priestly writers a type of religious pimp, while the Midianite women are his prostitutes. They must all be killed according to new and more rigorous rules for booty.

Verses 17-18 state the priestly law of booty in both a negative and a positive form. The negative statement is that all male children and non-virgin women must be killed. The positive form of the law is that virgins are acceptable booty. Israelites may keep them "alive for themselves." The meaning of this phrase is not clear. Comparison to Deut 21:10-14 and Judges 21 suggests that it refers to marriage. Deuteronomy 21:10-14 indicates that Israelite men are allowed to marry any women taken as plunder in holy war, without stipulating that the women must be virgins. Judges 21 provides a closer parallel to Num 31:18. In this story, an army of 12,000 soldiers (1,000 soldiers from each tribe, as Moses required in Num 31:4-6) defeats Jabesh-gilead in a holy war. They spare only the virgins, who are then given to the Benjaminites as wives.

31:19-24. The procedures for purifying humans and objects after holy war is outlined in this section. Purification is necessary, because death defiles all participants in war; and contact with the dead threatens the holiness of the camp. Numbers 5:1-4 stated the initial rule that any person defiled by contact with a corpse must be expelled from the camp. Numbers 19 outlined the general procedures for purification from contamination by corpses. Central to the process of purification was the "water of cleansing" made from the ashes of the red heifer. The priestly writers intend that these verses be read in relation to chap. 19, which not only refers to the rituals associated with the water of cleansing, but also describes the legislation with the

192. See Davies, *Numbers,* 323; Gray, *Numbers,* 420.

same language: Both are "the statute of the law that the LORD has commanded" (19:2; 31:21).

These verses also add new information to chap. 19 by applying the purification ritual to war. Soldiers must go through the seven-day ritual outside the camp, with cleansing taking place on the third and seventh days. Verse 19 makes it clear that such purification applies both to Israelite warriors and to their human booty. Finally, 31:21-24 provides the guidelines for purifying objects taken as booty. Eleazar, rather than Moses, outlines these procedures. Metals must pass through fire and be purified with the water of cleansing. Objects that cannot withstand fire are purified only with the water of cleansing. At the end of the process, all clothes must be washed before an Israelite warrior can reenter the camp.

The teaching of the priestly writers is that war pollutes. This is a significant departure from other stories in which participation in war makes soldiers holy. David and his soldiers, for example, are in a holy state in 1 Sam 21:4-5 and thus are able to eat holy bread. In 2 Samuel 11, Uriah the Hittite refuses to have sex with his wife, Bathsheba, because he has been consecrated for war. These stories suggest that participation in war is a sacred act, making its participants holy. For the priestly writers, participation in war requires the most rigorous form of purification. Killing in war does not sanctify its participants but defiles them even when the war has been commanded by God, raising the question of whether there is such a thing as "holy war" in priestly teaching.

31:25-47. The inventory and distribution of booty are outlined in this section. Verses 25-30 provide the formula for distribution. The booty is divided equally among warriors and all other Israelites. The principle of equal distribution of the spoils among warrior and citizen is illustrated in David's defeat of the Amalekites in 1 Samuel 30. Each group is then taxed by the temple at a different rate. Warriors pay 1/500th of their booty to the priesthood, while civilians pay 1/50th of their booty to the Levites. (See Numbers 7; 18; and 28 for other discussion of taxation for the temple and priesthood.)

Verses 31-47 apply the formula of distribution to the Midianite booty. The total booty

from the war with Midian is exceptionally large:

	Total	Warriors/ Citizens	Priests	Levites
Sheep	675,000	337,500	675	6,750
Oxen	72,000	36,000	72	720
Donkeys	61,000	30,500	61	610
Virgins	32,000	16,000	32	320

31:48-54. The chapter closes with the officers' taking a census of the warriors and reporting to Moses that not a single soldier has died in the battle with Midian. They bring a gift of gold and jewelry, weighing 16,750 shekels, to Moses and Eleazar, which, they state, is intended to make atonement for themselves to God. Atonement does not indicate an offering of thanksgiving. Rather, it is a form of ransom to God in order to avoid divine wrath, perhaps associated with the census. Second Samuel 24 tells of a plague that occurred as a result of David's census. Exodus 30:12 states that whenever a census is taken, it must be accompanied by a ransom in order to avoid a plague. Given the priestly teaching on war as an act of defilement, it may be that ransom is required from soldiers because of their participation in war, even though it was sanctioned by God.

32:1-42. The themes of holy war and inheritance are interwoven in this chapter. The opening (vv. 1-5) and closing (vv. 33-42) sections of the chapter focus on the inheritance of the Transjordan by the tribes of Reuben, Gad, and Manasseh. The dialogue between Moses and the tribes of Reuben and Gad in the central section of the chapter (vv. 6-32) concerns participation in holy war as a condition for inheritance. These two themes were likely always related in the chapter. Yet a history of composition lies behind Numbers 32:1, suggesting that the emphasis has changed from inheritance in the pre-priestly history to holy war in the priestly history.[193]

The stories of inheritance in vv. 1-5 and 33-42 are part of the pre-priestly history. They outline the territory and the cities that Israel took over after conquering King Sihon of the Amorites and King Og of Bashan. The request for land and the account of

---

193. The history of composition in Numbers 32 is especially complicated. For an overview of past interpretations, see Budd, *Numbers*, 337-42.

settlement provide continuity with the story of the Transjordanian conquest in chap. 21, where the central theme was holy war. The focus of the pre-priestly narrative in chap. 32 is less on holy war than on the city-building activities of the Transjordanian tribes after the conquest. In the pre-priestly history, chap. 32 is about inheriting land east of the Jordan. The accounts of inheritance are not unified, since the opening section (vv. 1-5) focuses only on the Reubenites and the Gadites, while the closing section (vv. 33-42) suddenly adds Manasseh. The list of cities in chap. 32 contrasts to others found in Deut 3:8-17 and Josh 13:8-13. Some form of the stipulation that participation in holy war is a condition for inheritance (vv. 6-32) is also most likely present in the pre-priestly history, since Deuteronomy and Joshua stress that the conquest of Canaan was a unified invasion by all Israel.

The influence of the priestly writers is also evident throughout Numbers 32. Eleazar the priest plays a prominent role in negotiating with the tribes of Reuben and Gad. Israel is described as the congregation (Exod 32:2), a favorite term of the priestly writers. Details from the priestly account of the loss of the land by the first generation (Numbers 13–14) appear in the speech of Moses (vv. 6-15), and the instruction of Moses to Eleazar about holy war and inheritance (vv. 28-32) conforms to the priestly account of the commissioning of Joshua in 27:12-23. Additions by the priestly writers change the emphasis in chap. 32 from inheritance to holy war, continuing the theme from chap. 31. The war with Midian in chap. 31 outlined the requirements for participation, purification, offerings, and booty in holy war. Chapter 32 returns to the topic of participation in holy war as a prerequisite for inheritance.

The interweaving of holy war and inheritance provides transition in the book of Numbers. When the theme of holy war is emphasized, the chapter provides a contrast to the failure of the first generation (chaps. 13–14) to undertake such a war. The second generation successfully carries out holy war in chap. 21, where Israel wages war against Sihon and Og, and again in chap. 31, where Israel wages war against Midian. Chapter 32 extends the commentary on holy war by outlining the requirements of participation. The theme of inheritance looks toward the conclusion of the story, indicating that the second generation has left the wilderness, already achieved part of its inheritance, and is about to complete the story of salvation by realizing the divine promise of land though conquest.

32:1-5. The order in which the tribes are listed in the opening verse has caught the attention of commentators, because it changes after v. 1. Gad takes precedence over Reuben in vv. 2, 6, 25, 29, 31, and 33. Gad is also the tribe identified most strongly with the Transjordan. The census of David in 2 Sam 24:5, for example, mentions only Gad; the Mesha stone also mentions only Gad.[194]

The tribes of Reuben and Gad are described as owning a great number of cattle, and the land east of the Jordan is rich for grazing. The area of the Transjordan that was of interest to the Reubenites and the Gadites is the land of Jazer and Gilead (v. 2). Jazer was mentioned as a location in the account of the conquest of Sihon (21:32). Gilead may refer to all of the area east of the Jordan, but here it designates a smaller section in the southern region, between the Arnon and Yarmuk rivers (vv. 3, 34-37). The nine towns listed in v. 3 cluster in the southern region of Gilead. These cities are also mentioned in vv. 34-38, where they are distributed between Gad and Reuben. The only variation from the southern location for Gilead appears in v. 39, where Gilead may designate a region further north.

Reuben and Gad make their request to Moses, Eleazar, and the entire congregation of Israel (vv. 3-5). They note that the land of Jazer and Gilead is good for grazing and ask that it be given to them, that Moses "not make [them] cross the Jordan." The Hebrew verb "to cross" (עבר 'ābar) is more than a description of travel, especially when used in conjunction with the Jordan. In such instances, it signifies conquest. The verb is used repeatedly in Joshua 3–5, where Israel's crossing of the Jordan for conquest is described. Thus the request of Reuben and Gad is ambiguous. It may mean that they wish the Transjordan for their inheritance, but it may also mean that they wish to avoid participating in the conquest of the promised land west of the Jordan.[195]

---

194. See "Mesha Stele," *ABD* 4:708-9.
195. Milgrom (*Numbers,* 268) underscores the central role of עבר (*'ābar*) by noting that it is used seven times: Num 32:5, 7, 21, 27, 29, 30, 32.

32:6-27. Moses interprets the request of the Reubenites and the Gadites as a desire to inherit land without participating fully in holy war. This leads to two rounds of negotiations (vv. 6-19 and 20-27). The first round (vv. 6-19) includes a warning by Moses that holy war requires the participation of all Israelites (vv. 6-15). In response, the tribes of Gad and Reuben propose a solution (vv. 16-19). In the second round of negotiations, Moses formalizes the proposed solution into law (vv. 20-24), to which the Reubenites and the Gadites agree (vv. 25-27).

Moses' initial response in vv. 6-15 is anger. He recounts the story of the spies, when the first generation lost the land because they feared holy war. This analogy is made in vv. 6-9 along with two accusations. First, the Reubenites and the Gadites are accused of discouraging the entire group from waging holy war (v. 7). This was the sin of their fathers at Kadesh-barnea (vv. 8-9). Second, they are accused of instigating disunity within the entire group (v. 6). Here is one of the central points of the chapter: Moses asks, "Shall your brothers go to war while you sit here?"

The need for all Israel to participate in holy war is stressed by the way the sin at Kadesh-barnea is recounted in vv. 10-15. Twice the anger of the Lord is cited (vv. 10, 13) as a response to the lack of faith of the first generation. Verses 10-12 state how divine anger resulted in the loss of the land for the first generation of Israelites, with the exception of Caleb and Joshua. Verse 13 describes how divine anger led to forty years of wandering in the wilderness. The point of recounting the original loss of the land is stated in vv. 14-15, where the speech of Moses switches from the past to the present tense. The demand placed on the second generation is that they assume collective responsibility for participation in holy war, at least within the same generation. By not participating in holy war with the other tribes, Reuben and Gad endanger the gift of the land for their entire generation. They threaten to "destroy all this people" (v. 15).

The response by the tribes of Reuben and Gad in vv. 16-19 forges a solution to the requirement that all Israelites participate in holy war. A two-part procedure is outlined in vv. 16-18. First, the tribes of Reuben and Gad will fortify cities for their families and build corrals for their flock (composed of stone walls). Second, a fighting force will join the other tribes in holy war. The language in v. 17 suggests that they even offer to be the shock troops, who will lead Israel in battle. The warriors from the tribes of Reuben and Gad, moreover, will not return to the Transjordan until all fighting is completed. The concluding statement in v. 19, that neither Reuben nor Gad will inherit land as a result of their participation, indicates that their solution to the Moses' accusation is meant to provide a paradigm for participation in holy war by settled tribes, whose involvement is out of obligation to the group, rather than for their own self-interest.

The proposed solution is reformulated by Moses as law (vv. 20-24), to which the Reubenites and the Gadites formally agree (vv. 25-27). Moses formulates the proposal as an oath. Repeatedly in vv. 20-24 he states that the agreement for participation in war is being made "before the LORD." The consequences of the oath are stated in both a positive and a negative form. If the Reubenites and the Gadites fulfill their obligations for holy war, then they will be free of their oath agreement and thus able to inherit land in the Transjordan; the legal background for the fulfillment of such oaths is stated in Deut 24:5. If they renege on their oath, their "sin will find them out." Sin is an active force in this statement. (See the story of Cain and Abel in Gen 4:7, where the same view of sin is expressed.) The phrase implies a curse in an oath situation. But no specific punishments are outlined. Moses ends the statement by implying the positive form of the law. He sends the Reubenites and the Gadites off to build their cities. These tribes agree (vv. 25-27) and promise to join in the holy war on the west side of the Jordan.

32:28-32. The public ratification of the negotiations in vv. 6-27 is stated in this section through repetition of the oaths from vv. 20-24. Those present include Eleazar the priest, Joshua son of Nun, and the heads of the tribes. The leadership structure is reminiscent of 27:15-23, where Joshua was also commissioned before Eleazar. The ratification of holy war legislation before Eleazar anchors holy war firmly in the orbit of the cult. If the tribes are faithful in their participation, they will be allowed to possess the land of Gilead. The negative form in v. 30 is unclear. Lack of fulfillment will result in Reuben and Gad inheriting land west of the Jordan with the other tribes. The confusion is that the consequences of not participating in holy war appear to be positive. Perhaps what is meant is that they will forfeit possession of the Transjordan. The same ambiguity is evident in the earlier negative form of the oath (v. 23). The tribes of Gad and Reuben, however, agree to the oath in vv. 31-32.

32:33-42. The theme of participation in holy war gives way to inheritance in the final section of the chapter. In v. 33, Moses charges the tribes east of the Jordan with securing the towns taken from Sihon and Og. Surprisingly, the tribe of Manasseh is mentioned for the first time in this chapter, along with the tribes of Reuben and Gad. Although Manasseh is absent from the negotiations in this chapter, the presence of this tribe at the conclusion of the chapter conforms to other accounts of land distribution east of the Jordan in Deut 3:13; 4:43; 29:8 and in Josh 12:6; 13:29-31. Verses 34-38 repeat the list of nine towns mentioned at the outset of the chapter, along with five others, which are now distributed between the tribes of Gad (Dibon, Ataroth, Aroer, Atroth-shophan, Jazer, Jogbehah, Beth-nimrah and Beth-haran) and Reuben (Heshbon, Elealeh, Kiriathaim, Nebo, Baal-meon and Sibmah).

Numbers 32 concludes with an independent account of conquest by the tribe of Manasseh (vv. 39-42). Machir conquers the Amorites in Gilead, here a more northern region than the previous references to Gilead at the opening of the chapter. Jair, another ancestor in the tribe of Manasseh, is described as renaming Amorite villages after himself. Independent action by one tribe contradicts the emphasis on holy war as requiring participation by all Israelites. The picture of singular tribes waging war independently conforms to the account of Judges 1.

33:1-56. This chapter provides a transition in the book of Numbers. It looks back to review Yahweh's leading in the wilderness by listing Israel's stopping points in the wilderness march (vv. 1-49), and it looks ahead to the conquest of the promised land with a warning that Israel continue to engage in holy war after crossing the Jordan (vv. 50-56). In the pre-priestly history, this chapter ends the book of Numbers. The review of the wilderness march and the concluding call for holy war probably led to the book of Deuteronomy, where Moses once again reviews the wilderness period and calls the second generation to holy war. In the priestly history, by contrast, Numbers 33 provides a transition to the final section on inheritance in Numbers 34–36.

The list of stopping points in vv. 1-49 has received a great deal of attention. Scholars debate whether the list of forty-two locations is ancient (and the source of the stopping points that run throughout Exodus and Numbers) or a late literary construction. There is clear evidence of priestly additions to the list. The priestly writers add commentary to bring the wilderness march into conformity with their history. They weave their interpretation of the exodus into vv. 1-4 by providing a date, a description of Israel leaving Egypt with a "high hand," and an interpretation of the exodus as a judgment on the Egyptian gods. All of these motifs are part of the priestly account of the exodus (see Exod 7:5; 14:8). The priestly writers also include Pi-harhiroth (v. 7) as the location of the confrontation at the sea in Exod 14:1-4. Finally, priestly writers also include the notice of Aaron's death at the close of the itinerary list; this information derives from the account of Aaron's death in 20:22-29.

Evidence of priestly additions, however, does not solve the problem of the origin or purpose of the list, nor does it clarify the relationship of Numbers 33 to the list of stopping points running throughout Exodus and Numbers. A comparison illustrates the similarities and differences between these accounts of Israel's wilderness travel:

Comparison of the stopping points in Exodus–Numbers and in Numbers 33 indicates that the latter contains many more locations than appear in the travel accounts of Exodus–Numbers. Further comparison throughout Scripture reveals that sixteen of the places mentioned in Numbers 33 occur nowhere else. The obscurity of the locations may indicate that the document, or at least parts of it, is old and that it provides the source for the more abbreviated version in

Figure 6: Israel's Wilderness Travel in Exodus–Numbers and in Numbers 33

Numbers 33	Exodus–Numbers Itinerary Stops and Other Locations	
	Similarities	*Differences*
Ramses	Ramses (Exod 12:37)	
Succoth	Succoth (12:37)	
Etham	Etham (13:20)	
Pi-harhiroth	Pi-harhiroth (14:2)	
		Red Sea-Shur (15:22)
Marah	Marah (15:23)	
Elim	Elim (15:27)	
Red Sea		
Wilderness of Sin	Wilderness of Sin (16:1)	
Dophkah		
Alush		
Rephidim	Rephidim (17:1)	
Wilderness of Sinai	Wilderness of Sinai (19:1)	
		Sinai-Paran (Num 10:12)
		Three days from Mt. Yahweh (10:33)
Kibroth-hattaavah	Kibroth-hattaavah (11:35)	
Hazeroth	Hazeroth (11:35)	
		Hazeroth—Paran (12:16)
Rithmah		
Rimmon-perez		
Libnah		
Rissah		
Kehelathah		
Mt. Shepher		
Haradah		
Makheloth		
Tahath		
Terah		
Mithkah		
Hashmonah		
Moseroth		
Bene-jaakan		
Hor-haggidgad		
Jotbathah		
Abronah		
Ezion-geber		
Wilderness of Zin (Kadesh)	Wilderness of Zin (Kadesh) (13:26; 20:1)	
Kadesh—Mt. Hor	Kadesh—Mt. Hor (20:22)	
Zalmonah		
Punon		
Oboth	Oboth (21:10)	
Iye-abarim	Iye-abarim (21:11)	
		Zered—Mattanah— Nahaliel—Bamoth —Pisgah (region of Moab) (21:12-20)
Dibon-gad		
Almon-diblathaim		
Mountains of Abarim (Nebo)		
Plains of Moab	Plains of Moab (22:1)	

Exodus–Numbers. But such a conclusion is difficult to confirm.[196]

The purpose for preserving Numbers 33 is no more clear than its age. It may indicate pilgrimage sites, as Noth suggested.[197] More promising, however, is the conclusion by Davis.[198] Comparing Numbers 33 with other ancient Near Eastern texts of a similar nature, Davis concluded that it shares characteristics of records associated with military campaigns. The style in which military campaigns were recorded in the ancient Near East progressed in the same manner as do the travel notices: They set out at A and encamped at B; they set out from B and encamped at C. This genre indicates that, regardless of whether Numbers 33 is an ancient source or a late literary creation, in its present journey as a military march. This is certainly how the list functions in the chapter. The successful completion of Israel's military march, indicated by the summary in 33:1-49, provides the background for the command and warning in 33:50-56 that Israel continue its holy war across the Jordan.

The emphasis on holy war is reinforced by commentary in Numbers 33. Narrative commentary is interspersed especially at the beginning and end of the list of stopping points. Commentary at the beginning of the list includes the exodus (vv. 1-4), the location of Etham at the edge of the wilderness (v. 6*b*), the confrontation at the sea (vv. 7*b*-8*a*), and the lushness of the oasis at Elim (v. 9*b*). Commentary at the end of the list identifies the Wilderness of Zin as Kadesh (v. 36*b*) and includes Israel's approach to Edom (v. 37*b*), the death of Aaron (vv. 38-40), the detection of Israel's approach by the Canaanite king of Arad (v. 40), and Israel's entry into the land of Moab (v. 44*b*). The distribution of commentary indicates that it is not so much the wilderness journey that concerns the biblical writers, but a reading of salvation history as a holy war within the structure of an exodus and a conquest. There is no commentary on the wilderness journey from the Red Sea to Kadesh (vv. 10-36). The structure of salvation

196. See Noth, *Numbers,* 242-46; Cross, *Canaanite Myth and Hebrew Epic,* 309-21; G. I. Davies, "The Wilderness Itineraries: A Comparative Study," *TynBul* 25 (1974) 46-81; and *The Way of the Wilderness: A Geographical Study of the Wilderness Itineraries in the Old Testament,* SOTSMS 5 (Cambridge: Cambridge University Press, 1979); and Milgrom, *Numbers,* 497-99.
197. Noth, *Numbers,* 242-44.
198. Davies, "The Wilderness Itineraries," 46-81.

history in this chapter as an exodus and conquest certainly conforms to its literary setting, where the recounting of Israel's history (vv. 1-49) is intended to provide background for the command by God in vv. 50-56 that Israel complete the holy war by conquering Canaan.

Numbers 33 is composed of different kinds of locations. Most of the list consists of precise locations of cities (e.g., Rameses) or of oases (e.g., Elim). But there are also three more general designations of wilderness areas (Wilderness of Sin, Wilderness of Sinai, Wilderness of Zin), as well as the more general reference to the Plains of Moab. (These are indicated in the list above by the use of italics.)

33:1-11. Verse 1 establishes the military nature of the entire chapter. Israel is envisioned as an army or military host under the command of Moses and Aaron (see the Commentary on 1:3). Verse 2 is unusual in describing Moses as writing down the stopping points in Israel's journey. The last occasion on which Moses was described as writing down information was Exod 24:4, where he was described as writing down divine commandments at Mt. Sinai. Thus Moses authors both law and history in the book of Numbers.

The events of the exodus are described in vv. 3-8 and of Israel's journey into the wilderness in vv. 9-11. The description of the exodus separates into the death of the Egyptian firstborn (vv. 3-4) and the confrontation at the sea (vv. 5-8). The recounting of these events tends to follow the priestly interpretation: The exodus is dated to Month 1, Day 15 (v. 3), the day after the Passover. Israel's departure from Egypt repeats the priestly description of the event in Exod 14:8, in which Israel does not sneak away during the night (see Exod 12:29-39), but marches boldly out of Egypt. The additional comment in v. 4 that the exodus took place in full sight of all the Egyptians, who are still burying their firstborn dead, has no parallel in the story of the exodus. But the interpretation of the death of the firstborn as a judgment against the Egyptian gods repeats the priestly account of events in Exod 7:5.

The confrontation at the sea (vv. 5-8) also follows in general the priestly interpretation from Exod 14:1-4. In the pre-priestly story of the exodus, Israel is said to journey from Rameses to Succoth (Exod 12:37) and from Succoth to Etham, located at the "edge of the wilderness" (Exod 13:20). In the pre-priestly version of the exodus, the confrontation at the Red Sea takes place in the vicinity of Etham, which may indicate a location in the wilderness, rather than in Egypt. The priestly writers change the location in Exod 14:1-4 by having Israel turn around and travel back into Egypt to Pi-hahiroth, a site they place between Migdol and the sea, in front of Baal-zephon. The confrontation at the sea in vv. 5-8 shows the same reinterpretation of location as does Exod 14:1-4. Israel travels from Rameses through Succoth to Etham, before turning back to Pi-hahiroth. The comparison of accounts indicates that the pre-priestly writers favor a wilderness location for the confrontation at the Red Sea, while priestly writers place the confrontation in Egypt.

The account of Israel's entry into the wilderness (vv. 9-11) departs from both the pre-priestly and the priestly versions of the exodus. In the pre-priestly version, Israel crossed the Red Sea (Exod 13:18; 15:22) in its journey from Etham (Exod 13:20) to the Wilderness of Shur (Exod 15:22), the location for the story of bitter water at Marah. The oasis of Elim then follows (Exod 15:27). The priestly account follows this sequence but interjects Pi-hahiroth between Etham and the Wilderness of Shur as the location for the confrontation at the sea. The sequence of locations in v. 9 no longer associates the Red Sea with the crossing of water. It is instead a wilderness campsite that Israel reaches only after several days of travel from Elim. The different accounts can be illustrated in the following manner:

Pre-priestly Exodus	Priestly Exodus	Numbers 33
Rameses	Rameses	Rameses
Succoth	Succoth	Succoth
Etham	Etham	Etham
(Edge of Wilderness)	(Edge of Wilderness)	(Edge of Wilderness)
Red Sea (Sea of Confrontation)		
Pi-hahiroth	Pi-hahiroth	
Wilderness	Wilderness	Wilderness
Shur/Marah	Shur/Marah	Eham/Marah

(Three Days Journey)	(Three Days Journey)	(Three Days Journey)
Elim	Elim	Elim
		Red Sea (Wilderness Location)

Etham is interpreted in this chapter both as a particular place and as a more general wilderness region, which replaces the Wilderness of Shur. More significantly, however, the lists indicate two interpretations of the Red Sea—both as the sea of confrontation with the Egyptians and as a wilderness location. These two interpretations run throughout OT literature. In the Song of the Sea in Exodus 15, the Red Sea is the sea of confrontation, where Pharaoh and his army are destroyed (Exod 15:4). This interpretation is reflected in the book of Joshua, where the Red Sea is dried up by God (Josh 2:10), is crossed over by Israel (Josh 4:23), and is the location of Pharaoh's destruction (Josh 24:6). This interpretation is also implied in Exod 13:18 and 15:22, where references to the Red Sea frame the confrontation at the sea. But Exod 13:18 also indicates that the Red Sea can be envisioned as a road through the wilderness. Numbers 21:4 reflects this interpretation, as do Deut 1:40; 2:1. The Red Sea is the setting for God's central act of salvation. Its two interpretations provide commentary on the meaning of divine salvation. It is a single event in time, when Yahweh destroyed the Egyptians, but salvation at the Red Sea also implies journeying with God through the wilderness. The designation of the Red Sea as a place of destruction and a wilderness road carries both of these meanings.

33:12-37. The march of Israel from the Wilderness of Sin (v. 12) to the Wilderness of Zin (v. 37) contains twenty-four stopping points. Fourteen of the stopping points occur only in this chapter, six correspond to travel notices in Exodus–Numbers, and four correspond to an account of Israel's travels in Deut 10:6-9. The locations that occur only in this chapter include Dophkah and Alush (vv. 12b-14a), as well as the twelve locations between Rithmah and Hashmonah (vv. 18b-30a).

The five locations that occur in Exodus–Numbers are as follows: The Wilderness of Sin is the location for the story of manna (Exodus 16). The four stopping points after Alush in vv. 14*b*-18*a* follow loosely the account of Israel's travel in Exodus 17–Numbers 12. Rephidim is the location of the war with the Amalekites (Exodus 17); the Wilderness of Sinai is the location for the revelation of law (Exodus 19–Num 10:10), and Kibroth-hat-taavah is the location of Israel's murmuring for meat and of the selection of the seventy elders (11:4-35). Hazeroth is the location of the confrontation between Aaron, Miriam, and Moses (11:35; 12:16).

Four locations in vv. 20*b*-34*a* correspond loosely to a travel sequence in Deut 10:6-9, which describes Israel's journey after receiving the second copy of the tablets of law. In this account, Israel journeys in the following sequence: Meeroth-bene-jaaken, Moserah, Gudgodah-Jotbathah. Moserah is described in Deut 10:6 as the place of Aaron's death (Mt. Hor in Num 20:22-29; 33:38), while Jotbathah is the location where the Levites were first set apart from the other tribes to guard the ark, in place of receiving an inheritance of land.

This section concludes by tracing Israel's travels from Abronah to Ezion-geber and finally to the Wilderness of Zin, identified as Kadesh. Ezion-geber is most likely located at the head of the Gulf of Akaba (1 Kgs 9:26; 22:48), making the travel distance to Kadesh exceptionally long.

33:38-49. More extended commentary returns in the account of Israel's travels from Kadesh to the Plains of Moab. The purpose of the commentary is to accentuate the theme of holy war. The death of Aaron at Mt. Hor begins the section. His death notice in vv. 38-39 includes information that is lacking in 20:22-29. The date is given as Year 40, Month 5, Day 1 from the exodus, and his age is 123 years. This corresponds to Exod 7:7, where priestly writers date his age as 83 years at the time of the exodus. The death of Aaron

indicates a transition in chap. 33 from wilderness travel to holy war.

Aaron's death is followed immediately by commentary (v. 40) concerning the Canaanite king of Arad. Accentuating the theme of holy war, the writer refers to the story in 21:1-3, where Arad attacked Israel and took captives. Israel's response was to enter into a vow of holy war with God, which was successful. Reference to this event sets the stage for the instruction in vv. 50-56 about Israel's need to wage holy war in Canaan. The additional place sites in vv. 41-49 reinforce the theme of holy war by referring to locations in Israel's war against King Sihon, the Amorite. Oboth (v. 43) is mentioned in 21:10; Iye-Abarim (v. 34) in 21:11; and Dibon-gad (v. 35) in 21:30. The section concludes by noting Israel's present location on the Plains of Moab.

33:50-56. Holy war in Canaan is the central theme of this section. It is signaled by the reference to Israel's crossing over the Jordan (v. 51), which was also central to the negotiations between Moses and the tribes of Reuben and Gad (chap. 32). The holy war material corresponds to similar instruction in the pre-priestly history during the giving of law at Sinai (Exod 23:20-23), in Deuteronomy as teaching by Moses (Deut 7:1-6), and in the Deuteronomistic History as teaching by Joshua (Josh 23:1-13). Israel is to expel the land's inhabitants (v. 52), destroy their idols (v. 52), and take possession of their land (v. 53). The final warning in v. 55, that the inhabitants of Canaan will become a "snare" to Israel if they fail to execute holy war, also repeats language from the same group of texts (Exod 23:33; Deut 7:16; Josh 23:13). The influence of the priestly writers is also evident. The reference to "figured stones" in v. 52 elsewhere occurs only in Lev 26:1, while the allotment of the land in v. 54 repeats the instructions from 26:52-56.

REFLECTIONS

The teaching on war is central in Numbers 31–33, but it also permeates the entire book. The book of Numbers is violent. The opening verses characterize the numbering of Israel at Mt. Sinai as a registration for the draft, focusing on males who are eligible for war (Num 1:3). The march through the wilderness is a military expedition, with each tribe representing a division (Num 11:13-28) led by the ark (Num 10:34-36). The loss of the land is a military failure (Numbers 13–14), culminating in the slaughter of Israelites (Num 14:39-45). The faithfulness of the second generation is charted by military victories over the king of Arad (Num 21:1-3), over Og, and over Sihon (Num 21:10-35). The prominence of war in Numbers requires careful theological reflection. How do we interpret these stories? Is war being glorified in the book of Numbers? Are the Israelite wars models for contemporary ethics of war, so that conquest stories in the Bible call for continuing conquest today? Or is war metaphorical commentary on the life of faith and the need for worshiping communities to maintain purity as the people of God? Whether metaphorical or literal, is violent imagery necessary at all? The following reflections will summarize the teaching on war in the book of Numbers and explore its significance for contemporary Christian teaching.

1. The first important insight is that no unified teaching on war is presented in the book of Numbers. Rather, war is a topic of debate among the different writers of Numbers. Even a brief summary indicates conflict over the significance of killing other human beings in battle.

The battle against the king of Arad (Num 21:1-3) teaches that killing in war is an act of sacrifice to God, requiring the extermination of the entire population. Extermination is described as חרם *ḥērem*, meaning that the enemy is devoted to God as an offering in exchange for divine assistance in battle. Susan Niditch notes the "terrifying completeness" in the *ḥērem* ban as sacrifice. The ethics of such violence, however, are paradoxically rooted in respect for the value of human life. "The ban validates the enemy as human and valuable and does not turn him into a monster worthy of destruction." As a result, the death of each enemy "is a mirror of the self, that which God desires for himself."[199] Sacrificing the enemy to God is an attempt to address the guilt in killing fellow human beings in war. Participation in war, according to this teaching, may be holy, but it is certainly not something to be glorified.

The pre-priestly writers envision war as divine judgment against nations that worship false gods (see the list of nations in Num 13:25-29 and their false worship in Exod 23:20-33). The symbolism of the ark as marching before Israel in the wilderness toward the promised land, scattering enemies before it, and returning to protect the camp (Num 10:34-36) locates God within war (see also Deut 20:1, which encourages Israel not to fear in war because "the LORD your God is with you"). The first generation's fear of invading the indigenous nations of Canaan (Numbers 13–14) is a rejection of God and indicates lack of faith in the divine promise of salvation. The second generation, in contrast, illustrates faith in defeating Og and Sihon in the Transjordan (Num 21:10-35). War in the pre-priestly history is rightful conquest of opponents deserving of death as divine judgment on idolatry. They are defined impersonally as the "other." The indigenous populations of Canaan become the giant Anakim. Such mythologizing dehumanizes them, making their slaughter a just act of divine judgment. The killing of Sihon and Og provides illustration; Og is even identified later as one of the Anakim (Deut 3:11).

The priestly writers interpret war as a necessary evil. War maintains purity in a polluted world. Military imagery characterizes the people of God as a community (Num 1:3) in their journey throughout the wilderness (Num 11:13-28). War itself is sanctioned by God (Num 25:16-18; 31:1). Priests participate in war and even take cultic objects into battle (Num 31:6). But there is no clear indication that Yahweh is actually present in battle, making it holy. To the contrary, participation in war defiles all participants. Killing in war is dissociated from God. Warriors and all objects of war require the most severe processes of purification before reentry into the camp is allowed. War, according to the priestly writers, exacts an enormous price. Killing separates participants from God, even when the cause is deemed just (i.e., sanctioned by God).

199. Susan Niditch, *War in the Hebrew Bible: A Study in the Ethics of Violence* (Oxford: Oxford University Press, 1993) 50. Niditch summarizes a range of teachings on war that provide an excellent resource for a more broadly based study of war in the OT.

The brief summary indicates that war is a debated topic among the writers of Numbers. No single view is presented as the authoritative teaching. The three positions summarized do not exhaust the teaching; war songs (Num 21:14-14, 26-30), the refusal to go to war against Edom (Num 20:14-21), war oracles against the nations by Balaam (Num 24:15-24), and the passive role of Israel during the threat from Balak (Numbers 22–24) add still other voices to the debate on war. Other Old Testament books expand the discussion of how the people of God respond to acts of violence (see, for example, the holy war of Joshua, the pacifism of Isaiah, and the cultic interpretation of war in Chronicles). Too often the pre-priestly teaching of war as justified conquest is allowed to dominate Old Testament teaching on war. Any use of Numbers as a resource for contemporary reflection on war must begin with the understanding that it provides a resource for contemporary debate on war, rather than a single authoritative teaching.

2. Interpretation of war stories in Numbers is complicated by their metaphorical use to address theological themes of faithfulness to God and of the need for Israelites to be separate from the nations. Thus holy war takes on broad theological significance in Numbers. It provides the underlying structure of salvation history as a liberation from Egypt and conquest of the promised land. The wilderness journey in Numbers 33 reflects this theology. It symbolizes Israel's march as one of unconditional faith in the power of God to lead. Compromise with surrounding nations signifies lack of faith that can lead only to doom, causing God to turn against Israel and to use the nations as a "snare" to take the land away from Israel.

More explicit stories of war may also be theological in their intent. The execution of the *ḥērem* ban against the king of Arad at Hormah (Num 21:1-3) may be a theological story about faithfulness to God in a time of crisis, as compared to the faithlessness of the first generation in their earlier battle at Hormah (Num 14:39-45). There is no evidence that the *ḥērem* ban as sacrifice to God was ever practiced. The priestly writers also use war imagery to write theology. The Midianites represent an external threat of pollution. They are a borderline people in the priestly history, with close ties to Israel through Moses. In this position, they are dangerous characters who have the power to seduce Israel, requiring their extermination. The description of the war as the extermination of all Midianites without the loss of one single Israelite indicates that holy war is used metaphorically to address problems of cultural intermingling, hence the focus on booty and especially virgins as potential wives.

War as a metaphor for theology does not eliminate its violent imagery as a model for living a faithful life. Conflict permeates the themes of faithfulness and purity throughout the book of Numbers. Holy war imagery encourages contemporary teachers and preachers to accentuate that the life of faith includes struggle, requiring discipline to fulfill its mission. In the end, however, the metaphorical use of war in Numbers brings one full circle to concrete problems of war and violence—including the role of the church in times of war.

3. Roland Bainton summarizes three historic Christian positions toward war: pacifism, the crusade, and the just war.[200] In the book *War: A Primer for Christians,* Joseph Allen briefly summarizes each position.[201] Pacifism is rooted in the principles that God forbids killing (Exod 20:13), warns against relying on force against enemies (Hos 7:11), and ideally envisions the world at peace (Isa 2:4). These principles are most clearly stated in Jesus' command not to resist evil (Matt 5:39).[202] The crusade includes these features: Justifiable war is a religious conflict between good and evil (Judges 4–5), the goals in war are absolute and unlimited (Deut 7:1-2), and the means of war are unrestrained (Josh 6:21; 8:24).[203] Just-war theory emerged in the fourth and fifth

200. Roland H. Bainton, *Christian Attitudes Toward War and Peace: A Historical Survey and Critical Re-evaluation* (Nashville: Abingdon, 1960) 14.
201. Joseph L. Allen, *War: A Primer for Christians* (Nashville: Abingdon, 1991).
202. Allen, *War: A Primer for Christians*, 16-30.
203. Allen, *War: A Primer for Christians*, 7-15.

centuries CE, when Christian theologians like Ambrose and Augustine began to evaluate the Roman Empire's use of power. Augustine, for example, argued that the state had a moral obligation to protect people, avenge injuries, and restore justice and peace in society. Two principles informed his theology: War should not be waged for selfish reasons, and it should be directed toward helping other people.[204]

The book of Numbers does not separate into the three categories of Christian teaching on war. The crusade model is the clearest of the three, occurring in the conquest stories. There is no clear teaching on pacifism. The inactive role of Israel during the threat by Balak may touch on the topic, since evil is not resisted. But inactivity by Israel is not the central point. The avoidance of war with Edom might also support features of pacifism (Num 20:14-21). Individual principles stated in pacifism and in the crusade model do occur in Numbers. Peace, not war, is the ideal for creation (Num 6:22-27). Killing defiles (Numbers 31). Reliance on one's own power in war is condemned, as is warring for self-interest (Num 14:39-45). And God must declare all war through the cult.

The need for God to declare war leads to the conclusion that there is no teaching on just war in Numbers. Israel is a theocracy in the wilderness throughout the book. All war in Numbers is waged through the sanctuary. No state has the power to declare war in Numbers. Those that do are destroyed (Balak, the king of Arad, Sihon, and Og). The central role of just-war theory in contemporary Christian teaching underscores how theological reflection on war is an ongoing responsibility for the people of God throughout history. The church now evaluates the actions of nation-states in Western history. Such a practice was not envisioned by the writers of Numbers. The absence of just-war theory in Numbers, however, is also a caution for contemporary Christians. We often concede too much power to the state, and thus fail to take full moral authority for the role of the church at times of war. The book of Numbers does not present a single teaching on war, but all of its different writers agree that evaluation of and participation in war are responsibilities of the sanctuary, not of the state.

204. Allen, *War: A Primer for Christians*, 31-52.

Numbers 34:1–36:13, Life in the Land

COMMENTARY

The priestly writers are the authors of the closing section of the book of Numbers. They are also responsible for the overall design of Numbers 26–36. The commentary on chap. 26 indicated that the priestly writers used the second census to show that the divine promise of descendants was fulfilled at this point in Israel's salvation history. The divine promise of descendants (Gen 12:2) is one of two promises of salvation to the ancestors that runs throughout the Pentateuch.

The second promise of salvation to the ancestors is that of land (Gen 12:7). The priestly writers set their focus squarely on this second theme in Numbers 34–36. Chapter 34 outlines the boundaries of the promised land of Canaan and lists the leaders from each tribe who will assist in land distribution. Chapter 35 provides a list of the levitical cities in the land and the laws regarding cities of refuge. Chapter 36 returns one final time to inheritance by the daughters of Zelophehad.

The subject matter of Numbers 34–36 provides two initial insights that aid in interpretation. First, the concluding section of Numbers is about Israel's future life in the land. Second, chaps. 34–36 follow a division between the people of Israel and the Levites that was also important to the priestly writers in the opening section of Numbers 1–10, where Israel's life in the camp was described. Thus the social structure surrounding the holiness of God in the camp is extended to the land.

34:1-15. The spies travel from the Wilderness of Zin in the south to Rehob, near Lebo-hamath in the north, in the priestly version of their mission (13:21). The geographical locations from the spy story return in these verses, where the priestly writers fill in the boundaries of the promised land of Canaan. Two details are noteworthy. The first is that the priestly vision of Canaan in vv. 1-12 is of a large geographical area. The second is that in spite of their expansionist view of the land, the Transjordan is not specifically included in vv. 13-15.

The priestly vision of the promised land in vv. 1-12 does not correspond to its boundaries in any known time in Israel's political history. It is an ideal vision of the land as a divine gift. The description of its borders progresses in a circle that moves in a clockwise direction from south (vv. 1-5), to west (v. 6), to north (vv. 7-9), and to east (vv. 10-12). The circle begins and ends with the Dead Sea. The list of locations includes:

(1) The southern boundary (Num 34:1-5)
    Wilderness of Zin
      along Edom
    Dead Sea
    Akrabbim
    Zin
    Kadesh-barnea
      (outer limit south)
    Hazar-addar
    Azmon Wadi Egypt
    The (Great) Sea
(2) The western boundary (Num 34:6)
    The Great Sea
(3) The northern boundary (Num 34:7-9)
    The Great Sea
    Mount Hor
    Lebo-hamath
    Zedad (outer limit north)
    Ziphron
    Hazar-enan
(4) The eastern boundary (Num 34:10-12)
    Hazar-enan
    Shepham
    Riblah on the East Side of Ain
    Sea of Chinnereth
    Jordan
    Dead Sea

Many of the locations cited in vv. 1-12 are difficult to place. Nevertheless, the listing of exact boundaries for Canaan underscores that, for priestly writers, the promise of land must be interpreted concretely. The fulfillment of promises is not to be sought in another world. God's quest for renewal is aimed at this world.

There appear to be two descriptions of the southern boundary of the land in vv. 1-5, a general description ("the wilderness of Zin along the side of Edom," v. 3*a*) and a more detailed account of specific locations (vv. 3*b*-5). Kadesh-barnea marks the southernmost boundary for the priestly writers. The Great Sea, or Mediterranean, links the southern, western, and northern borders, although the particular location where the northern border meets the Mediterranean is unknown. The furthermost boundary on the north is Zedad. This location is in the vicinity of Lebo-hamath, thus providing a link with the priestly interpretation of the spy story, which mentions "Rehob, near Lebo-hamath" as the northernmost destination of the spies (13:21). But Rehob is not mentioned in chap. 34. The location of Hazar-enan, which provides the corner point for the northern and eastern borders, is also unknown. The eastern border, however, is clearly marked by the Jordan River.

Two related descriptions of the boundaries of Canaan occur in Josh 15:1-12 and Ezek 47:15-20. The description in Joshua begins with the southern boundary, but progresses counterclockwise: south, east, north, west. The eastern boundary is the Dead Sea, while the northern boundary is the northern point of the Dead Sea and includes many more locations than does Numbers 34. Ezekiel 47:15-20 begins with the northern boundary rather than the southern, as in Joshua 15 and in Numbers 34. Like Numbers 34, it also progresses clockwise: north, east, south, west and follows closely the boundaries of Numbers 34.

Surprisingly, the boundaries of the promised land appear to exclude the Transjordan. The eastern boundary of the land mentioned in vv. 10-12 indicates as much, since it runs along the Jordan River. The concluding commentary by Moses in vv. 13-15 reinforces this point. The promised land includes only what is apportioned to the nine tribes west of the Jordan. The land east of the Jordan, taken by the tribes of Reuben, Gad, and half of Manasseh, is regarded by Moses as their inheritance, but he does not include it in the boundaries of Canaan. Cities of refuge, however, are designated for the Transjordan in chap. 35. Perhaps the limitation of the promised land to territory west of the Jordan accounts for Reuben's loss of firstborn status to the tribe of Judah in the priestly list of the tribes in vv. 16-29.

34:16-29. Ten tribal leaders are named to assist Eleazar and Joshua in distributing the land. The number is ten, rather than twelve, because the tribes of Reuben and Gad chose to inherit in the Transjordan. The names of the tribal leaders are new with the exception of Caleb, who, along with Joshua (see Numbers 13–14), is allowed to inherit land.

The order of the tribes follows the direction of the boundaries from vv. 1-15, moving from south to north. The tribes who will settle in the south include Judah, Simeon, Benjamin, and Dan. The Joseph tribes, Manasseh and Ephraim, will settle in the central portion of Canaan. The northern tribes include Zebulun, Issachar, Asher, and Naphtali. The result of listing the tribes from south to north is that Judah heads the list. This, too, may be by design, since the tribe of Judah has headed the list of tribes in situations that point toward the inheritance of the land, including the order of the camp (chap. 2), the presentation of offerings (chap. 7), the order of marching (chap. 10), and now inheritance (chap. 34). These lists contrast other situations in which Reuben heads the lists: the first census (chap. 1), the spy story (chap. 13), and the second census (chap. 26).

35:1-34. The Levites are separated from the other tribes in the promised land, just as they were in the wilderness camp. The divine command to Moses in vv. 1 and 9 indicates the two general topics of the chapter. In vv. 1-8, God states that, unlike other tribes, the Levites will receive no land, because they are a divine possession. Instead, they receive special cities located throughout the land. The levitical cities now complement the tithe that the Levites receive, which was described (18:21-24) as a substitute for inheriting land.

Verses 9-34 return to the topic of the special role of Levites as a divine possession and their ability to protect Israel from the danger of divine wrath. The protective role of the Levites in the camp is now extended to the entire land. God states to Moses that a small number of levitical cities will take on the power of protection that characterized the Levites in the camp. These cities will be havens of refuge for persons who are guilty of certain kinds of homicide. Much of chap. 35 outlines the conditions under which individuals might seek asylum in a city of refuge.

35:1-8. The priestly description of sacrifices for the priests and Levites (18:21-25) contained the divine commandment that the Levites not inherit land. The priestly writers provide further details of this divine command by stating that the Levites will own cities rather than land. This section is introduced as divine instruction to Moses (v. 1) and includes information about the boundaries of a levitical city along with its pastureland (vv. 2-5) as well as the number of such cities and the process by which they will be selected from each tribe's territory (vv. 6-8).

The inheritance of cities instead of land by Levites carries forward a theological design that the priestly writers first developed in their description of the wilderness camp. Four times the Levites were singled out in chaps. 1–10 to indicate their special status as a divine possession and to outline how that status influenced their role in the camp. They were counted separately from the other tribes in 1:48-53, where their role of maintaining a buffer zone between God and Israel was noted. Numbers 2:17 provided a visual illustration of this role by noting how the Levites camped around the tabernacle, creating a protective space between God and the people. Chapters 3–4 described in detail the work of the Levites in caring for the tabernacle and their special status as substitutes for Israel's firstborn. Finally, chap. 8 added further background on the Levites' ability to atone for Israel's firstborn as substitutes. Atonement was understood as a ransom for protection of the firstborn. Such ransom was possible because the Levites were a divine possession. Here, the priestly writers describe how the special status of Levites as a divine possession affects their life in the land.

How the Levites actually lived in the land of Canaan is no clearer from biblical literature than is the history of their development (see the Commentary on 3:1–4:49). The prophet Ezekiel contradicts 35:1-8 by stating that the Levites do inherit land (Ezek 48:3-22). Deuteronomy 18:1-8 provides some agreement with Num 35:1-8 in stating that the Levites do not inherit land. Yet, there is no mention of levitical cities in Deut 18:1-8. In fact, Deut 18:6 suggests that the Levites are scattered throughout all of Israel's cities, and not in specially designated cities. Given the contradictory information in Scripture and the clear signs of theological design by the priestly writers regarding the role of the Levites, scholars debate whether there is any historical value to Num 35:1-8. The debate over the history of levitical cities is complicated, however, by Judges 21, which may contain older tradition concerning such cities. There are clear signs that priestly editing in Judges 21 seeks to make the chapter function as the fulfillment of Num 35:1-8. Chapter 35 may also contain older information on levitical cities from Israel's monarchical period.[205]

Several literary questions arise in vv. 1-8. In an attempt to harmonize the priestly material on levitical cities with Deuteronomy, some commentators have questioned whether the command that Levites "live in" cities (v. 2) indicates possession or some form of leasing. But Lev 25:32-34 makes it clear that the priestly writers intend for Levites to own their cities. The designated pastureland of the cities in vv. 4-5 presents a more puzzling problem. Verse 4 states that pastureland shall extend for 1,000 cubits, while v. 5 expands the dimension to 2,000 cubits. Verses 6-8 change the focus from the dimensions of levitical cities to their number and location. Levitical cities will number forty-eight in all, while six will have special status as "cities of refuge." Selection of levitical cities is to be determined by size, with larger tribes contributing more.

35:9-15. The more narrow topic of levitical cities of refuge is indicated with a new introduction in v. 9. Verse 11 states that cities of refuge function as places of asylum. There

205. See W. F. Albright, "The List of Levitical Cities," in L. Ginzberg, *Jubilee Volume* (New York: American Academy for Jewish Research, 1945) 49-73.

are indications that early in Israel's history the altars of sanctuaries, rather than selected cities, functioned as locations of asylum. Two examples appear in the opening chapters of 1 Kings, where Adonijah competes with Solomon for succession to the throne of David. Upon hearing of the selection of Solomon, both Adonijah (1 Kgs 1:49-53) and Joab, David's general who supported Adonijah for the throne (1 Kgs 2:28-35), flee to the sanctuary and "grasp the horns of the altar" for protection from Solomon. The priestly designation of levitical cities of refuge thus indicates a rejection of the sanctuary altar as the place for asylum. Indeed, contact with the altar kills humans, according to the priestly writers (4:15). The rejection of the altar as the place of refuge is evident in Deuteronomy (Deut 4:41-43) and in the Deuteronomistic History (Joshua 21); thus it is not an innovation by the priestly writers. Scholars debate when the transfer of asylum from altar to designated cities occurred. It may have been early in the monarchical period. Perhaps the prophet Hosea refers to Gilead and Shechem as places of refuge (Hos 6:7-10). Another possible time would be during the reign of Josiah in the late seventh century BCE, when he centralized the cult in Jerusalem.

The specific crime for which the cities of refuge are intended to provide asylum is homicide. Verse 12 indicates that asylum is granted from the avenger (גאל *gō'ēl*). The avenger, or next of kin, performed many duties. Boaz functions as the *gō'ēl* in fulfilling the levirate vow with Ruth (Ruth 3:13). The *gō'ēl* may be called upon to redeem family property or a relative from slavery (Leviticus 25:1). In these cases, the word *gō'ēl* is often translated "redeemer." The shedding of blood is a debt that pollutes the land. In this situation, the *gō'ēl* is responsible for "redeeming" the debt of blood that occurs with homicide. The traditional role of the avenger of blood indicates that justice surrounding murder was a matter of the clan or family. The priestly law in v. 12 does not eliminate the avenger's role. On the contrary, it affirms the role of the avenger and anchors it even more broadly in the theology of the land (vv. 33-34). But the priestly writers do transfer the execution of justice surrounding homicide from the family to the state. The city of refuge functions as an asylum until the guilt or innocence of the one who killed could be determined by a trial before the congregation.

Verses 13-15 indicate the number and location of the cities of refuge and the range of persons having access to their protection. The six cities are distributed evenly on both sides of the Jordan, with three in Canaan and three in the Transjordan. They are not named in this chapter, but they are listed in Deut 4:41-43 and Joshua 21 as Bezer, Ramoth, and Golan in the Transjordan (Deut 4:41-43), and Shechem (Josh 21:21), Golan (Josh 21:27), and Kedesh (Josh 21:32) in Canaan. Cities of asylum functioned for all Israelites, as well as for resident aliens in the land (see the Commentary on 15:1-16).

35:16-28. The priestly writers introduced the distinction between intentional and unintentional sins with regard to sacrifices in chap. 15. Unintentional sins (15:22-29) could be forgiven, while intentional or "high-handed" sins (15:30-31) could not. The priestly writers extend the distinction based on intention to homicide in this section. Verses 16-21 provide criteria for determining intention and the procedure to be followed in executing punishment, while vv. 22-28 outline the procedures that must be followed if someone kills another unintentionally.

Verses 16-21 describe instances of intentional homicide. Guilt can be determined in two ways. First, the object used to kill indicates motive. An iron object (v. 16), a stone (v. 17), or a piece of wood (v. 18) is considered a weapon. The use of such instruments indicates motive to kill. Thus anyone who kills another person with one of these objects is guilty of intentional homicide. Second, motive must be examined independently of weapons. Thus, if someone kills another simply with the fist and it is determined that it was done out of hatred or enmity, then that person is guilty of murder (vv. 20-21). The procedure to be followed in cases of murder is stated in v. 19: The guilty person must be executed by the avenger of blood.

Verses 22-28 describe instances of unintentional homicide. Accidental death through pushing or while working with stone (v. 22) requires a trial by the congregation. Even when the congregation determines that blood was shed unintentionally, there is no such thing as innocence. Absence of motive does not absolve someone from blood guilt. The procedure for unintentional homicide involves the cities of refuge, which function in two ways. First, they shelter persons guilty of shedding blood. Thus they become a type of prison, keeping those who have slain other humans from moving freely about the land. Second, they are places of refuge. Thus the slayer is rescued from the avenger of blood. But, if at any time the slayer leaves the city of refuge, he or she may be killed by the avenger of blood without penalty. The guilt of shedding blood unintentionally can be atoned for only by the high priest, upon whose death all persons guilty of unintentional homicide are atoned for. At that time, they are allowed to leave the city of refuge and return home.

35:29-34. The chapter concludes by stating that the rules surrounding homicide are confirmed civil law. The same designation of law is used with regard to the inheritance rights of the daughters of Zelophehad (27:11).

Three additions to the laws of homicide (vv. 30-32) and a theological grounding for all the laws in the chapter (vv. 33-35) are given. The first addition concerns witnesses. Verse 30 states that no one can be convicted of murder on the basis of only one witness; there must be two or more witnesses. The second concerns convicted murderers. Verse 31 states that no ransom is possible for convicted murderers under any circumstance; they must be executed. The third addition concerns those guilty of unintentional homicide. Verse 32 states that no person guilty of manslaughter is able to ransom an early release from a city of refuge before the death of the high priest. For priestly writers, money cannot atone for the shedding of human blood.

The rationale for the strict laws regarding homicide is provided in vv. 33-34: Blood pollutes the land. The story of Cain's murder of Abel illustrates vividly the polluting power of human blood on the land (Gen 4:10). God knows of Cain's act of murder because the ground screams when Abel's blood soaks into it. Thus murder is a violent act of cosmic proportions that cannot be reduced to mere finances. No monetary expiation is possible for any form of homicide. The debt of blood once shed requires the blood of the perpetrator. Finally, the laws of homicide are placed in the largest context possible: Murder is not simply an act of cosmic consequences, it also influences God, who has chosen to dwell in the land. Human blood that has been shed in the land and not accounted for through proper expiation can drive even God away.

36:1-13. The final chapter of the book of Numbers returns to a problem surrounding the inheritance of the daughters of Zelophehad, first addressed in 27:1-11. As a result, chaps. 27–36 are framed by the theme of the inheritance of daughters in the land. Inheritance in general has also been a central theme throughout the final section of the book. The theme of holy war in chaps. 31–33 emphasized Israel's claim on the land of Canaan, with the concluding paragraph (33:50-56) focusing clearly on the conquest of the land. Chap. 34 outlined the boundaries of land to be inherited, while chap. 35 underscored the danger of defiling the land through the shedding of blood. Chapter 36 returns to the topic of inheritance in order to emphasize the inalienable right of each tribe to dwell in the land.

36:1-4. The original claim of the daughters of Zelophehad in 27:1-11 was that their father had died without sons, thus threatening the family's right to inherit land. On the basis of this situation, they claimed the right to inherit in order to preserve the basic principle that possession of land was inalienable. Their claim is supported by God and extended by Moses (27:8-11) into case law. In the Commentary on 27:8-11, three principles were noted as undergirding the law that extends inheritance rights to daughters: (1) God owns the land; (2) divine ownership means that the land is a divine gift to Israel, whose status in the land is that of a tenant; and (3) each person's right to land is inalienable. As noted earlier, these principles are stated most clearly in the Jubilee law of Leviticus 25.

The daughters of Zelophehad are from the tribe of Manasseh. The leaders of that tribe now address Moses (vv. 1-4) to bring to light a problem in the case law of 27:8-11. The problem concerns intertribal marriage, particularly with daughters like those of Zelophehad, who have inherited land. Under the present law, their possession of land would be transferred to their husbands, in which case the tribe of Manasseh would lose part of its inheritance. In other words, by solving a problem of inheritance at the level of the family, Moses has created a new problem of inheritance at the level of the tribe. Reference to the law of Jubilee in v. 4 is used to confirm that the principle of inalienable rights is being contradicted. The tribal leaders state that at the time of Jubilee the land will permanently transfer to the husband's tribe. This reference to the Jubilee has puzzled commentators, because it applies to debts and not to inheritance (see Leviticus 25). Furthermore, one would expect that a strict application of the Jubilee law would return the land to the tribe of Manasseh. In any case, in Numbers 36 it is used to underscore that the land will leave the possession of the tribe of Manasseh, thus violating their right to inalienable possession.

36:5-12. Moses agrees and adds an addendum to his previous ruling from 27:8-11. The ruling is that daughters who inherit land must marry within their own tribe. Thus the principle of the inalienable right of possession of land by tribes is maintained: "No inheritance shall be transferred from one tribe to another." The section concludes by naming again the daughters of Zelophehad and by stating that they have fulfilled the new law; each has married within the clan of Manasseh.

36:13. The book of Numbers ends with a subscription, stating that the book contains divine commandments delivered to Moses on the plains of Moab. The subscription certainly provides a conclusion to the legislation on homicide in chap. 35 and on inheritance in chap. 36. But upon further analysis, it appears that the subscription is also intended to provide a conclusion to the book of Numbers. A similar subscription occurs at the end of Leviticus, in which Lev 27:34 states that it contains divine commandments presented by Moses at Mt. Sinai. Numbers uses the same conclusion, but changes the location to "the plains of Moab by the Jordan at Jericho." The book of Numbers ends with the promised land of Canaan in clear view of all the Israelites.

REFLECTIONS

1. The central message of Jesus is the good news of a new creation. The Gospel of Mark provides illustration: Jesus begins his ministry with the proclamation that the kingdom of God is near (Mark 1:15). Too often we interpret Jesus' mission as being directed solely at humans. Nothing could be further from the truth. The good news of salvation for humans, according to Jesus, arises in recognizing God's claim on creation and entering into the domain of God's rule. The kingdom of God does not exist solely in the human heart, nor is it limited to human relationships. It embraces the earth and all life within it. The substitution of kinship language for the kingdom of God in contemporary liturgy is well intended in its attempt to avoid overly sexist imagery, but it is an anthropocentric misreading of the gospel. The promise of salvation is much larger than God's relationship with us.

Jesus' proclamation of the kingdom of God is rooted in the message of the priestly writers at the close of the book of Numbers, where the focus rests on God's promise of the land. The priestly writers trace Israel's journey with God through the wilderness and follow its growth from one generation to the next. The promise of descendants explores the importance of Israel's relationship with God. But the goal of salvation in the book of Numbers is the promise of land. The story does not end with the census of the second generation in chapter 26. The promise of descendants alone does not complete the story of salvation history. The second generation still requires land.

The promise of land in the priestly history gives concreteness to salvation history. Numbers 34 even provides specific boundaries. Yet the overall structure of the priestly history suggests that the promise of land reaches out to include all creation. God's commitment to creation in priestly tradition is evident in Genesis 1, when all aspects of the world are judged to be good. The importance of creation for human salvation is made clear by priestly writers in their conclusion to the flood story, where God makes a covenant (Gen 9:1-17) never again to abandon the world through a flood because of the sin of humans. God's commitment to the creation provides the broader context and mission for interpreting Israel's journey with God. Jesus' proclamation of the kingdom of God is an extension of the priestly writers' vision of salvation.

2. The priestly writers' laws of homicide arise from their vision of a new creation. Life has sanctity, and blood defiles the earth. Life in God's land is intended to transform human relationships. All shedding of blood pollutes the land. No amount of money can atone for such bloodshed. Murder is far more than an act against society. It is a violation against creation, inducing a debt to the land. Even accidental death defiles the land. Not a single life is expendable in God's land, according to the priestly writers. Every death must be accounted for in the land economy of the priestly writers. We all understand debt in our contemporary capitalistic society. Our news media spend hours reporting on national debt, interest paid on inter-fund borrowing, trade deficits, and the like. Few of us are free from family or personal debt on property. Imagine our present debt to the earth in the priestly writers' economy of value. There are so many deaths daily in our cities that news organizations cannot report on all of them. With every violent death, we take another loan from the kingdom of God, according to the priestly writers, reducing our equity in God's salvation.

3. The Commentary indicated that asylum in ancient Israel was originally associated with the sanctuary altar. The basic premise of asylum, according to Jacob Milgrom, is "that those who touch the altar absorb its sanctity and are removed from and immune to the jurisdiction of the profane world."[206] The priestly writers remove asylum from the altar to designated cities, and they focus more particularly on sanctuary from blood

---

206. Milgrom, *Numbers*, 504.

vengeance. But the basic principle remains the same: Asylum suspended the normal practice of justice, allowing for evaluation by the congregation. Cities of refuge are difficult to translate into modern society, requiring theological reflection on the role of the church as a place of asylum in modern culture. Certainly redemption takes place in the church. but the social implications of redemption concerning asylum from national law are less clear. The sanctuary movement in North America, for example, provided asylum for migrants from the U.S. Immigration and Naturalization Service, prompting debate among church people whether the action was ethical. Regardless of one's position on this particular issue, the possibility of asylum is a reminder that the church can never be subsumed under the law of any nation-state.

4. The priestly description of levitical cities and of the entire land of Canaan is a vision between utopia and historical reality. Menahan Haran notes how the measurement of each city as an exact square of 2,000 cubits, the Jubilee legislation of release, and even the distinction between Aaronide priests and Levites conforms to an idealized theological program. But realism is mixed throughout. Levitical cities are dispersed away from the temple and even outside of the boundaries of Canaan, not what one might expect from a purely fictional story.[207] The result is that neither utopian fiction nor historical reality is allowed to outweigh the other. They are intertwined in the priestly writers' vision of the land, giving rise to two conclusions at the close of the book of Numbers. First, utopian imagery denotes that the story of Numbers is incomplete. Life in the land with God represents a new quality of life. It is an ideal to be reached at the end of the wilderness journey. Second, the realism of the priestly writers indicates that the ideal vision is obtainable in this world. Biblical writers offer the content of the book of Numbers as a manual for achieving life in the promised land.

207. Menahem Haran, *Temples and Temple Service in Ancient Israel: An Inquiry into the Biblical Cult Phenomena and the Historical Setting of the Priestly School* (Winona Lake: Eisenbrauns, 1985) 122-29.

THE BOOK OF DEUTERONOMY

INTRODUCTION, COMMENTARY, AND REFLECTIONS
BY
RONALD E. CLEMENTS

THE BOOK OF
DEUTERONOMY

INTRODUCTION

THE BOOK AND ITS LITERARY SETTING

The Contents of the Book. Deuteronomy is the fifth book of the Hebrew Bible and is ascribed to Moses, making it the concluding book, or scroll, of the Pentateuch. Its title, which derives from the Greek (Septuagint, or LXX) text of Deut 17:18, indicates that it is a "second law." The title is wholly appropriate, since it describes the law given by Moses in the plains of Moab immediately prior to the crossing of the river Jordan and Israel's entry into the land promised to its ancestors, Abraham, Isaac, and Jacob. It is, therefore, a "second law," or more precisely a second giving of the law that had first been given as the terms of the covenant concluded through the mediation of Moses on Mt. Sinai between the Lord as God and the people of Israel, immediately after their deliverance from slavery in Egypt.

Although it contains two main collections of legal, or quasi-legal, material, the book of Deuteronomy is much more than a book of law. The first of these collections is set out in Deut 5:6-21, where the Ten Commandments are repeated from their first disclosure in Exod 20:2-17. The second collection is to be found in chapters 12–26 and contains an extensive collection of laws and legislative prescriptions (concerning, for example, how law is to be administered). The relationship between the Ten Commandments and the laws of chapter 26 has remained a very important issue for the understanding of the book and its background.

In addition to these collections of commandments and laws there is a narrative beginning in chapters 1–3 that summarizes the story of Israel's life in the wilderness from the first revelation on Mt. Sinai (which Deuteronomy consistently refers to as Mt. Horeb) to the time when the people were ready to launch their assault upon the promised land under Joshua. The narrative conclusion (chap. 34) tells of the death of Moses in the plains of Moab, before the crossing of the Jordan. In addition to this narrative framework there is a significant series of exhortations and warnings in chapters 6–11 and similar admonitory speeches, presented as blessings and curses, in chapters 27–28. Further hortatory addresses and poems in chapters 29–33 complete the framework of the law code. Scholars, therefore, have found it useful to distinguish between the "law code" of chapters 12–26 and the "framework" of chapters 1–11 and 27–34.

Sermon-like speeches and laws may at first appear as unlikely companions in a single literary work, but throughout there is a high level of consistency and homogeneity of style in Deuteronomy that makes it in general the most easily recognized of the entire OT. This closeness of stylistic presentation does not point to one single author, but to a particular group of writers, preachers, and reformers who shared a consistency of purpose that has created a work of coherence, clarity, and intense passion. The writers very evidently set out to compose a comprehensive guidebook for Israel to live as the people of the LORD God.

The Form and Forms of the Book. When we inquire as to the overall form and character of the book, the overall title of "law" proves to be inadequate. Deuteronomy describes its own chief contents as being composed of "law" (תורה *tôrâ*, "instruction," "directive," "guidance") and further defines this as being made up of "decrees, statutes, and ordinances" (Deut 4:44). Certainly there are laws, such as would appear in a statute book for the handling of criminal cases, which are present in the book, but there is much else besides. Moreover, many of the so-called laws are in the nature of religious regulations; some are ethical directives concerning good behavior in the home and in society in general, and some are institutional directives for setting up governmental organizations. Besides all these there are regulations controlling family law and custom. If we seek a comprehensive term to describe what is to be found in the book, then "polity" is almost certainly the most helpful term.

From a formal perspective, there is a surprising shift between the high prominence given to Moses in the framework, particularly in chapters 1–11, and in the lack of reference to Moses in the law code of chapters 12–26, apart from being referred to by inference in the regulation concerning prophecy in Deut 18:18. This accords with the very marked rhetorical style of the exhortations of the framework and the more crisp style of the law code. Obviously the authors of the finished book have drawn material from different sources over an extended period of time. Although they have imposed a general level of stylistic and theological consistency on the work, this variety in the different types of material and its varied origins still shows through.

If the subject matter of the book can best be described as declaring a national "polity" for Israel,[1] extending from constitutional permission for a monarchy (Deut 17:14-20) to rules of personal hygiene in a military encampment (Deut 23:12-14), then its form can best be described as "preached law."[2] It is law only in a modified sense, however, since it is addressed to an entire nation, even demanding that its most important requirements be taught to children (Deut 6:7) and making use of a high degree of exhortation and rhetorical persuasion. Even specific laws that call for precise and careful definition are sometimes supplemented by exhortations to observe them for religious reasons (e.g., in showing generosity to former slaves, Deut 15:12-18).

The formal legal parts of the book can be usefully compared with earlier formulations of laws covering similar cases, most particularly in the law code of Exod 20:22–23:19, which has come to be described as "the book of the covenant" (cf. Exod 24:7). This older law code can clearly be seen to have been available to the authors of the laws of Deuteronomy, who can be shown to have based many of their own rulings on it.[3]

The form of the Ten Commandments has a distinctiveness all its own and requires to be considered separately for its importance in regard to the origins both of these commandments and of the book of Deuteronomy.

The law code proper of chapters 12–26 necessarily invites comparison with the form and structure of comparable law codes of the ancient Near East. The similarities and the contrasts are both worthy of close attention and can be considered in connection with the introduction to that code.

The speeches of warning and exhortation ascribed to Moses are distinctive in their style and represent the most marked and characteristically "deuteronomic" feature of the book. Whoever

---

1. S. Dean McBride, "Polity of the Covenant People: The Book of Deuteronomy," *Int* 41 (1987) 229-44.
2. G. von Rad, *Studies in Deuteronomy*, trans. D. Stalker, SBT 9 (London: SCM, 1953) 11-24.
3. Cf. E. Otto, *Theologische Ethik des Alten Testaments* (Stuttgart: W. Kohlhammer, 1994) 18-31.

the authors were, it is evident that they were accomplished speakers and preachers. A further aspect of the form of the book as a whole relates to the possibility that ancient Near Eastern treaty forms, themselves originally secular in character, may have been employed by its authors to shape the work.[4] While not in itself implausible, at most the extent of this influence would appear to be limited to the introduction of the blessing and curse formulas of chapters 27–29 and will be considered in that connection. Beyond this, support for the assumption of the influence of ancient Near Eastern treaty forms is chiefly in the awareness that the book of Deuteronomy displays many affinities in its forms and vocabulary with the bureaucratic language and conventions of a state administrative circle.

Deuteronomy in the Old Testament. Deuteronomy now appears as the fifth and final book of the five books of Moses that make up the Pentateuch (Genesis–Deuteronomy). In Jewish tradition, all of them are ascribed to the authorship of Moses, and they form the first, and most foundational, part of the canon of the Hebrew Bible. Taken as a whole, they provide the basis for the heirs of Abraham, who are also viewed as persons bound in covenant to the LORD God through the revelation given through Moses on Mt. Sinai (Horeb), to govern their lives as the people of God.

However, so extensive a work as the Pentateuch was certainly not written at one period of history and by one writer alone. It has been brought together from a variety of source documents and traditions in order to present the fullest and most basic constitution of Israel. Within this great anthology, which shows many features of being a "collection of collections," Deuteronomy is neither the earliest nor the latest to have been composed, even though it now forms the last of the five books. Rather, it stands very much as a midpoint, and even a balance point, for the Pentateuch as a whole.

Because Deuteronomy has such a distinctive style and lays down such precise and specific requirements over a number of major issues relating to worship, it has proved helpful in enabling scholars to identify (within certain limits) what is "pre-deuteronomic" from what is "post-deuteronomic." It is not surprising, therefore, that in the course of critical biblical scholarship, which has sought to trace, as far as possible, the main lines of the literary growth of the Pentateuch, the attention to Deuteronomy has been very pronounced. It represents a kind of center, both for the literary composition of the Pentateuch and for the development of Israel's religious life.

Seen in such a light, the book of Deuteronomy, or at least some major part of it, can be said to have once formed an independent work that was later joined to other writings, before finally being given its present position. Whereas we might have expected that these other writings would have been the other books of the Pentateuch, the majority opinion among present-day scholars is that this was certainly not the case. It was instead first joined with the six historical books of Joshua–2 Kings, which in the Hebrew canon make up the Former Prophets (Joshua, Judges, 1–2 Samuel, 1–2 Kings). As a consequence, it has become a widespread scholarly practice to refer to these six books as "the deuteronomic (or deuteronomistic) history" because they explicitly presuppose a tradition of divinely given law by which events and persons are judged. This law, which is sometimes explicitly referred to as a law book, is clearly a body of the laws contained in Deuteronomy. There is also a consensus to accept that the first three chapters of Deuteronomy were composed in order to provide an introduction to this large work, comprising both law book and historical narrative. At most, some parts of Deuteronomy 1–3 may have provided a much more brief introduction to the original deuteronomic law book before it was combined with the history.

During the post-exilic period, the deuteronomic writings were supplemented by a large body of additional material, consisting partly of narrative and partly of additional rulings of a priestly and ritual character. This additional material has usually been described as belonging to a priestly (or P) documentary source, although much of it may actually have been incorporated piecemeal into a combined work. Essentially the Pentateuch can be seen to have been composed of the

---

4. See J. G. McConville, *Law and Theology in Deuteronomy,* JSOTSup 33 (Sheffield: JSOT, 1984). A more cautious and critical position is presented by Dennis J. McCarthy, *Treaty and Covenant,* AnBib 21A (Rome: Pontifical Biblical Institute, 1978) 157-205.

combined deuteronomic and priestly material, together with such earlier (pre-deuteronomic) traditions as had been preserved in conjunction with Deuteronomy.

At this stage, the book of Deuteronomy was separated from the history of the Former Prophets, of which it had at one time been a part, to constitute a separate work that is our present Pentateuch. This contains all the essential traditions and rulings governing the existence and life of Israel as the people of the LORD God, given before Israel entered the promised land. Within this immensely formative document, Deuteronomy can readily be seen to have a most important place. In terms of religious ideas and practice, it marks the first great comprehensive stage in the collecting, harmonizing, and unifying of regulations governing Israelite belief and practice. It represents, therefore, a primary stage in the formation of the Hebrew canon, or "rule," of faith, even though the term as such is not used. Nevertheless, all the main features of defining, controlling, and focusing faith and practice, which later the provision of a scriptural canon sought to supply, are evident in Deuteronomy. It can justifiably be regarded, therefore, as providing a center for the Pentateuch and for the Hebrew Bible as a whole.

In addition to the links between Deuteronomy and the historical books of the Former Prophets, it is also important to note that there are significant contacts between Deuteronomy and the prophecies of Jeremiah. At one time these were explained in terms of an influence, either from the prophet Jeremiah upon the authors of the law book, or vice versa. If the deuteronomic law book, with its distinctive preaching style, were part of a contemporary tradition that the prophet Jeremiah was familiar with, then it could be argued that Jeremiah sometimes made use of this high-flown rhetorical style.

However, all such explanations must now be set aside in favor of a more literary, but potentially more complex, explanation for such noteworthy contacts between a prophet and the authors of a law book. Certainly the evidence that these contacts provide is important for determining the date of Deuteronomy, but their origin can be explained in a rather different fashion from supposing that a direct influence of a prophet upon lawmakers took place. The use of the so-called deuteronomic style in the book of Jeremiah, which is in reality more a matter of a distinctive vocabulary and a distinctive set of theological ideas than a matter of style in the technical sense, is not uniformly present throughout the book. It appears particularly in the narrative sections and in a series of homilies on specific themes and topics. The reason for the presence of these homilies and for the use of this narrative style is to be found in the fact that the extant book of Jeremiah has come down to us in a deuteronomic dress. It has, in fact, been edited in circles that stood close to the authors of Deuteronomy.

Taken overall, therefore, we can identify a situation in which, besides the book of Deuteronomy, the scribes who produced the final form of the history of Joshua–2 Kings and the extant written version of the prophecies of Jeremiah were all deeply influenced by the belief in a Mosaic law given by Moses in the plains of Moab. The law book of Deuteronomy can then be seen to provide an excellent viewpoint for understanding one of the most formative periods in the development of Israel's faith and of the formation of a central part of the biblical literature.

THE CHARACTER OF DEUTERONOMY

Having drawn attention to what has been described as the style of the deuteronomic authors, it is now possible to consider what precisely this style consisted of.[5] In a broad sense, the features that mark a particular author, or group of authors, have to do with the way in which ideas are presented so that the literary purpose is achieved. We can infer the purpose of the authors of Deuteronomy with considerable confidence. It was first and foremost to define a pattern of conduct, especially religious conduct, which was regarded as conforming to the terms of the covenant the LORD God had made with Israel. Such conduct required especially single-minded and exclusive allegiance to worship the LORD God alone. No other God was to be set alongside this one deity, nor was any form of image or physical representation of any god, even of the

---

5. See the comprehensive survey in M. Weinfeld, *Deuteronomy and the Deuteronomic School* (Oxford: Oxford University Press, 1972) 320-65.

Lord, to be tolerated. In accordance with this purpose, sacrificial worship was to be restricted to one location only, which the Lord God would signify. Sanctuaries, cult objects, and religious practices pertaining to other gods and goddesses were all banned and condemned to be actively destroyed. A particular program of festivals was further defined as appropriate to the worship of the Lord God.

Alongside this very stringent code of religious practice was placed a related, and interwoven, code of moral and social behavior, which was partly defined in terms of dealing with criminal behavior through an established, although rather mixed, legal administration. Much further than this, however, were many rules governing family life, military commitments, and commercial dealings that were all intended to bear the stamp of the covenant made between the Lord and Israel.

If defining what God's covenant implied was the primary purpose of the book of Deuteronomy, in parallel with it went the goal of persuading the readers of the book of the rightness and necessity of this. To this end a highly developed rhetorical style of speech is employed, marked by long parentheses, many repetitions, and a strong probing into questions of motive and attitude that search the hearts of the reader. The psychology of faith is richly explored, more so than anywhere else in the entire Bible, with constant appeals to remember, not to forget, to avoid self-satisfied complacency, and to bear constantly in mind the deceitfulness of the human heart. The overall evaluation that the deuteronomic authors place upon the goodwill and good intentions of their readers is not high! They are assumed to be prone to disloyalty, as the deuteronomic authors insist their ancestors had been.

In line with this rich and often intensely passionate appeal to religious loyalty and steadfastness is a deep feeling that Israel is one single people throughout all its generations. The chosen setting in which the laws and exhortations of the book are given is that of Israel, standing poised in the plains of Moab and waiting to cross the river Jordan to take possession of the land. Yet, the author is fully aware that this was a generation that lay in the very distant past, so that the fiction of such a time and place is only thinly maintained. The reality that Israel has long been in the land and that its experience there has often been painful and distressing is frequently evident in the book. Yet, the author uses extensively the phrase "all Israel" and views the passing of the generations as a fact that changes nothing concerning the way in which Israel stands face to face before God. The "here and now" of the authors is both the situation recognized for the readers and that which is selected for the setting of the speeches and laws given through Moses. Moreover, even this collapsing of the interval of time between the generation that first awaited entry into the land and that of the readers is stretched further to embrace the generation that stood at the foot of Mt. Horeb to whom Moses first brought the tablets of law. Israel is one people, and this oneness stretches laterally across all twelve of its member tribes and vertically through its generations.

It is in the rhetorical flourishes and insights into human psychology that the distinctiveness of the deuteronomic vocabulary shows itself most markedly. This is what we should expect, since the defining of behavior requisite to the careful formulation of laws was necessarily governed by the subject matter dealt with. However, alongside the distinctive vocabulary of this preaching style there is also a very evident theological vocabulary relating to the way in which Israel is regarded as being bound to the Lord God and, therefore, must repudiate the forms of illicit religion through which the people have been tempted. These religious traditions, which are ascribed to the former occupants of the land, are regarded as particularly alluring and contrary to the attitude of mind that is appropriate to true worship. So we find that the concept of covenant, the dangers of idolatry, the persistence of the worship of the Baals and Asherah, and the importance of gratitude as an essential component of serving God all stand prominently in view within the deuteronomic horizon.

Whether we consider the topic from a theological, a historical, a political, or a sociological perspective, the subject of the land that had been promised to the ancestors of Israel— Abraham, Isaac, and Jacob—is of paramount significance.[6] The primary gift of God to Israel

---

6. L. Perlitt, "Motive und Schichten der Landtheologie im Deuteronomium," *Deuteronomium-Studien* (Tübingen: J. C. B. Mohr, 1994) 97-108.

under the terms of the covenant is this land. Consequently, the most serious consequence of disobeying the terms of the covenant is threatened as the loss of this land and the possibility of being expelled from it.

However, besides these broad theological and literary features that characterize Deuteronomy, there are other features that are of great interest to the careful reader. Not least among these is the contribution that Deuteronomy makes to the knowledge and evaluation of the development of a system of law in ancient Israel. The fact that it is possible to compare closely the text of the deuteronomic laws with those made earlier in the Book of the Covenant makes it possible to see how new questions had arisen in legal administration and how this had been progressively improved and elaborated. Conversely, several features of the deuteronomic law code reveal that this administration had displayed shortcomings and serious limitations. Furthermore, the fact that, in some cases, later versions of rulings dealing with essentially the same problem are also preserved in the latest parts of the Pentateuch enable us to construct a valuable chronology of legal and ethical development.

THE DATE OF DEUTERONOMY

A question that has loomed prominently in the modern study of the book of Deuteronomy concerns the question of the date at which it was written. In 2 Kings 22–23, the biblical historian recounts how a "book of the law," which was subsequently identified as "the law of the covenant between God and Israel" (2 Kgs 22:11–23:3), was found in the Temple during renovations in the reign of King Josiah (639–609 BCE). This led to an extensive cultic reform in which a complete destruction of the ancient sanctuary of Bethel took place and many of the old Canaanite rural shrines were destroyed in order to centralize sacrificial worship exclusively in Jerusalem. Since the work of the great nineteenth-century biblical scholar W. M. L. de Wette, this law book has been identified with some part, if not the whole, of the book of Deuteronomy. For a time, there was something of a scholarly consensus that the law book thus rediscovered was probably only the law code of Deuteronomy 12–26. Such conclusions must now certainly be substantially modified.

In the present reconsideration of the issues, the value of this piece of historical criticism has been heavily undermined by the recognition that the account of how the law book was discovered is clearly an attempt by the biblical historian to introduce to the reader the law book of Deuteronomy. The story is itself, therefore, a part of the deuteronomic character of the presentation of history in 1–2 Kings and by itself neither confirms nor denies that the book of Deuteronomy was composed somewhere close to that time.[7]

The report of the discovery of the law book in Josiah's time, then, is relevant to an understanding of the date of origin of the book of Deuteronomy, but does not settle the issue. In reality it never could have done, since it leaves unclear how much older the law book was at the time when it was rediscovered. Nor does it explain what part or form of the book of Deuteronomy was given a new life at this time.

Some parts of Deuteronomy cannot have been written as early as King Josiah's reign, since they make allusion to the disasters that befell Jerusalem in the sixth century BCE (e.g., Deut 29:21-28). Other parts could be, and have frequently been held to be, considerably older. Much depends, then, on which part of Deuteronomy is being discussed when the question of time of composition is under consideration. Too much has been built on the assumption that the law code of chapters 12–26 was significantly older in its complete form than the framework of chapters 1–11 and 27–34. The position adopted in the present commentary is that the original law code on which the present code was based almost certainly did originate in Josiah's reign, but that this has been extensively revised and added to in the wake of the disasters that overtook Judah in the sixth century BCE.

---

7. See E. Würthwein, "Die Josianische Reform und das Deuteronomium" *ZTK* 73 (1976) 395-423.

Overall the question of the date at which the book was composed must be regarded as dependent in part on a careful analysis of the various component sections and layers that are evident within the book. Neither the law code of chapters 12–26, nor the book as a whole was composed at a stroke and at one time.

Of great significance is the question of how much of the book was composed after the disastrous events that overtook the kingdom of Judah at the hands of the Babylonian forces at the beginning of the sixth century. Some reflections of these events are evident in the book, although they have frequently been held to be present only in the concluding parts of the framework. The view adopted here is that these events are far more strongly reflected than this and have deeply influenced several major features of Deuteronomy. Most prominent are the demand for cult centralization, the greatly weakened role ascribed to the king, the desacralizing of several aspects of the cultus, and most probably the overall awareness that, in the future, the true Israelite who is loyal to the covenant will be dependent on a written law for guidance. If this is the case, then a great deal of the spiritual character and strategy that have contributed to making the book of Deuteronomy what it is are a consequence of what happened to Judah at the beginning of the sixth century BCE.

However, this does not properly settle the issue of the date of Deuteronomy as a written document. Those scholars are undoubtedly correct who have recognized that some form of connection exists between the book and the steps taken by King Josiah in the late seventh century to reform worship around Jerusalem. The relationship is more oblique, however, than has often been assumed, and in signficant measure the book of Deuteronomy in its final form must be regarded as a long-term product of the reforms initiated by Josiah, rather than simply the prompting cause of those reforms.

After the breakup of the united Israelite kingdom at Solomon's death, the divided kingdoms of Israel and Judah pursued separate paths and eventually the northern kingdom fell prey to Assyrian intervention by the end of the eighth century. Judah survived, though at the cost of painful and humiliating submission to Assyrian demands that only slackened when, by the middle of the seventh century, the Mesopotamian influence weakened. Josiah's measures were essentially an attempt to rebuild a united kingdom of Israel, with its capital in Jerusalem and under a Davidic king, along the lines that tradition credited to David and Solomon.

Josiah was only partially successful in achieving his goal, and his death in battle in 609 BCE set a limit to further restoration of the ideal kingdom of "all Israel." In these reforms, clearly the role of the Davidic monarchy had of necessity been significantly curtailed, since it was the excessive impositions of the monarchy under Solomon that had brought about the earlier breakup (1 Kgs 12:4). However, the relief from Assyrian control in Judah proved to be only short-lived, and Babylonian power swiftly replaced it, thereby putting an end to the belief that God had spared and preserved Jerusalem during the preceding centuries for the sake of Jerusalem and the Davidic kingship.

The disastrous events that brought a fearful siege and eventual surrender of Jerusalem to the Babylonians in 598 and again in 587 BCE ended with the destruction of the Temple in Jerusalem and the removal of the last of the Davidic kings from his Jerusalem throne. All of these events form part of the background to the composition of the book of Deuteronomy and are, in varied ways, reflected in its pronouncements and exhortations. What was left of the old kingdom of Israel, which Josiah had sought to restore and revive, now found itself in ruins. The people were once again in a situation closely akin to that chosen by the author of Deuteronomy for the setting of the book. They stood at the borders of the land, sorely stricken by military defeats that seemed to defy explanation and in danger of losing altogether their sense of nationhood, of commitment to the LORD as God, and of any direction as to how to prepare for a difficult future. More than at any other period in its history the threat of a return to the "old gods" of the land presented Israel with a temptation and appeal that were almost irresistible.

The book of Deuteronomy, together with its supporting historical and prophetic writings, is a magnificent response to this situation of political and religious crisis. It is a serious review of Israel's past and a challenge to renew commitment and loyalty to God and to look for the time when a new Israel would take shape and the land would once again belong to those who had kept faith with the God who gave it.

THE AUTHORS OF THE BOOK

The Authors and Their Interests. To some extent the answers that we have sought to provide to the date of the book go some way toward also answering the question concerning who the authors were. If they were persons who were active over a period of more than a century, then clearly they represented not simply a small interest group that emerged at one moment of crisis, but a movement that retained momentum for a significant length of time. We can best seek to track down more fully who they were from the particular interests they reveal in the book they have left.

Among such interests we can certainly place the high premium they set on the commitment to an exclusive worship of the LORD God alone. No image was to be tolerated of any kind, and no other God was to be set alongside this one deity. That this falls short of an absolute monotheism in which the very existence of any other God is altogether denied may be admitted, but nevertheless the portrayal that is made of such deities is so negative and derisive in its tone as to present them as powerless nonentities that deserve little more than contempt. Certainly the deuteronomic doctrine of God contributed greatly to the emergence of a more fully explicit monotheism in subsequent biblical writings.[8]

It is unlikely that this movement, which aimed at worshiping "the LORD alone," originated among these deuteronomic authors. It certainly found support among several of the eighth-century prophets, and it seems likely that this prophetic influence was an important factor. But so, too, were the political crises that had beset Israel during the eighth century, when the incursions from Mesopotamia effectively broke up the temporary stability that had left the Levant to sort out its own affairs, looking chiefly to Egypt as the major external power to be reckoned with.

The very concept of a law book, the markedly literate social world the book presumes, and the polished rhetorical style, which shares many features in common with the Israelite tradition of wisdom,[9] point us also to recognize that the authors of Deuteronomy had close links with the royal administration, where education flourished. Certainly this must have been the Jerusalem court, even though the general tenor of the deuteronomic attitude to kingship is certainly not that of an ardent pro-Davidic court circle. Many of its most marked features represent a strong expression of antipathy to the high-flown and exaggerated court style of the royal psalms, with their mythological coloring for the place of the king in the world of lesser mortals.

Strongly supportive of the conclusion that the deuteronomic authors themselves stood close to the circles of power that hovered around the king is the fact that the authors of this law book display every confidence in their ability to control the administration of the nation. King Josiah had assumed the throne in Jerusalem as a mere boy, placed there by those described as "the people of the land" (2 Kgs 21:23-24). In particular the control of legal affairs, the expectation of enforcing new legal rulings, combined with the assumption of a right to speak for "all Israel," points to a circle of patrician and skilled administrators.

A further feature of the deuteronomic legislation is to be found in its interest in the cultus and in the levitical priesthood. This has led several scholars to look to a circle of levitical priests, or ex-priests, as the authors of Deuteronomy, perhaps drawn from among those who had been forced from their duties and service in sanctuaries during the eighth-century incursions of Assyria. Yet, overall the intellectual outlook and concern of the book are not priestly. It is, on the contrary, very distinctively non-mystical and unsympathetic to the ideas of priestly cultic power, redolent of a holiness that could kill, which echoes in several of the priestly (P) sections of the Pentateuch.[10] It seems certain that the authors of Deuteronomy were not traditional

---

8. Cf. N. Lohfink, "Gott im Buch Deuteronomium," *Studien zum Deuteronomium und zur deuteronomistischen Literatur* II, SBA 12 (Stuttgart: Katholisches Bibelwerk, 1991) 25-53.

9. Weinfeld, *Deuteronomy and the Deuteronomic School*, 244-81.

10. Weinfeld, *Deuteronomy and the Deuteronomic School*, 282-97.

priests, even though they recognized the value and authority of the services that Israel's priests performed.

Taken together, all of these considerations point to the recognition that the authors of Deuteronomy are unlikely to have belonged to any one professional class. If this were the case, then they have contrived to show a considerable knowledge, not only of governmental administration, but also of ideas that were current among both the prophetic and the priestly circles current in Judah during the seventh and sixth centuries BCE. This is by no means impossible. Nevertheless, if we think in terms of a deuteronomic movement, encouraged and inspired by the strong nationalistic and Yahwistic faith that arose in the wake of the humiliations and sufferings inflicted by Assyria, then we shall certainly be close to the truth. Since, in any case, we know and understand the aims and thinking of the deuteronomic authors from the literature that they have given to us, it is perhaps of only limited value to endeavor to define more precisely who they were. For the most part they remain anonymous, although it is tempting to speculate from the names of men linked with King Josiah, and later the prophet Jeremiah, who may have been among their number.

Deuteronomy and the Northern Kingdom. One of the features of the book of Deuteronomy that has repeatedly attracted the attention of biblical scholars is the extent to which it shows familiarity with, and even a strong empathy with, traditions that appear to have originated within the old northern, or Ephraimite, kingdom of Israel. This region had broken from any allegiance to the Davidic monarchy when Rehoboam became king, and it was effectively dismembered as a political entity at the end of the eighth century BCE by Assyrian intrusion and territorial realignments, including mass deportations of sections of the population.

Scholars as distinct as A. C. Welch,[11] Albrecht Alt,[12] and G. von Rad[13] have drawn attention to different features of the book that show a stong link to territorial, political, and religious aspects of the dismembered northern kingdom. But they have not agreed as to what these northern interests are. More recently, the commentary by E. Nielsen[14] has added further support for such a conclusion. Josiah clearly had political ambitions to regain as much of this lost territory as it was possible to achieve and to restore it to a reborn kingdom of a united Israel. That he was only partially successful in doing so does not weaken the insight that this had been a prime goal he sought to achieve.

The insights gained from this can all too readily be overpressed. In particular, we must conclude that many aspects of the book are to be traced to the devastating effect that Babylonian interventions in Judah at the beginning of the sixth century had upon the veneration for the Davidic dynasty of kings and the Jerusalem Temple. Josiah's reform had encouraged hope that a new era of prosperity for Israel was about to dawn. Now the discrediting of an overconfident and complacent faith in both the Temple and the kingship demanded a major reappraisal of them. It is this reappraisal, and not the resurgence of old northern Israelite traditions, that is most prominent in the deuteronomic legislation.

Nevertheless, set in a guarded perspective, it seems evident that the deuteronomic ambition to present a legislative program that was designed for, and acceptable to, "all Israel" was genuine enough. It could not hope to achieve this by simply retaining the excessive Judahite claims that had first broken the kingdoms apart in the tenth century. It would appear, then, that the deuteronomic movement did not ultimately prevail to establish the final form of the Mosaic Torah. More cult-oriented traditions, almost certainly originating in a central circle of the Jerusalem priestly aristocracy, acquired new impetus and dominance in the post-exilic period. Fundamental, therefore, as the deuteronomic movement was in establishing the central lines of the post-exilic Jewish faith, the final definition of this called for a noticeably different tradition from that of Deuteronomy to be added to it, and in substantial measure to overlay it.

Moses in the Book of Deuteronomy. It is a feature of the book that cannot easily be overlooked that it is prominently presented as the product and teaching of Moses. In chapters 1–11

---

11. A. C. Welch, *The Code of Deuteronomy: A New Theory of Its Origin* (London: Nisbet, 1924).

12. A. Alt, "Die Heimat des Deuteronomiums," *Kleine Schriften zur Geschichte des Volkes Israel II* (Munich: C. H. Beck, 1953) 250-75.

13. G. von Rad, *Deuteronomy,* OTL (Philadelphia: Westminster, 1966).

14. E. Nielsen, *Deuteronomium,* HAT I/6 (Tübingen: J. C. B. Mohr, 1995).

and again in 31–34, this great leader of Israel's formative beginnings dominates the scene. Not only is much of the book presented under the form of a speech of Moses, but also his figure is set in the forefront of faith. To a remarkable extent he is presented as a man who stands over against the great majority of his people. He is a leader, and they need to be led. His faith contrasts with their mean-spiritedness. He is a person of prayer, but they are faithless and full of complaints. He is for going on, when they are for going back. It is not simply that Moses stands between the people and God, as a chosen mediator would inevitably do, but that he is of a different temper and insight from all of them. In heeding the words of Moses, the people of Israel are assured that they will be drawing inspiration from the most worthy of sources.

Certainly the earlier traditions of Israel's origins had given a significant role to Moses as the one who had led the people out of slavery in Egypt, but none of this material had placed so high a valuation upon his person. He is a figure of faith in a way that shows a remarkable new sensitivity concerning what is needed in such a person. He appears as the most worthy of national leaders.

There is no easy, simple explanation of why the deuteronomic authors display so great an interest in Moses. In part it can be seen as a consequence of the feeling of leaderless malaise that the deuteronomic authors diagnosed as part of their nation's ills. They needed a new Moses! Yet this is not sufficient to explain such a prominent new interest in this historic figure. Certainly it cannot be traced to the belief that the authors of the book held any specific professional attachment to Moses, either as a prophet or a priest, for they do not place any significant emphasis on either task, even though Moses is more prophet than priest. Rather, it must lie chiefly in the feeling of disillusionment with the institution of kingship, and in particular with the kings who were of the dynasty of David. They had promised much and had, in the person of Josiah, given cause for hope that the LORD God would once again hold all nations in derision before the power vested in the chosen scion of the house of David (see Ps 2:4-11). This had proved to be a tragically misguided faith, as even those who had placed great confidence in the ambitions of Josiah and his less honorable successors found out so tragically (see 2 Kgs 23:29-30).

We must also recognize that there is present in all the deuteronomic literature a refreshing, if sometimes startling, consciousness that all human institutions are no more than human. Claims to divinity or to possess unlimited access to divine power, when vested in any human being become a serious threat to fundamental features of human society. So the deuteronomic authors put more trust in law than in lawmakers, and more in God than in human beings.

They also shared a remarkably insightful and commendable awareness of the way in which human beings are easily led. The markedly dismissive portrait they present of the contemporaries of Moses, with very few exceptions, reveals much of this social awareness that all human leaders seem readily capable of commanding a following, even when leading their people astray. Accordingly, by presenting the true ideal of human leadership in a figure of the past, who is forthrightly declared to have been more cognizant of the divine ways than any other (Deut 34:10-12), the deuteronomists establish a firm role model through whom all other expressions of human leadership are to be judged. In painting such a picture of the great leader of the nation, they reinforce their claims that the Mosaic law deserves the most urgent and undeviating attention.

DEUTERONOMY IN JEWISH AND CHRISTIAN TRADITION

Deuteronomy in the Hebrew Bible and in Jewish Tradition. To a quite remarkable degree the book of Deuteronomy establishes a standard for the interpretation of the entire Hebrew Bible. This is not surprising, since it is in Deuteronomy that we first hear defined the content of the Mosaic teaching as *torah*. Subsequently, such a title has been employed to characterize the entire contents of the Pentateuch and to establish its essential purpose. Its English translation as "law," by means of its ancient Greek and Latin counterparts, has meant that from a Jewish perspective the entire biblical tradition is understood to consist of law. That it could equally well have been translated as "instruction" or "guidance" is undoubtedly true, although had this been the case the note of authority that has so characterized its reception in Judaism (and Christianity) would certainly have been much reduced.

Moreover, as has already been noted, the fact that the deuteronomic law expresses a development of an earlier code of laws and was itself subsequently used as the basis for yet further elaboration and clarification has meant that it provides a pattern for all subsequent Jewish biblical interpretation. The eventual formulation and publication of a code of Mishnah stands very much in a straight line with the idea that Deuteronomy itself represents a "second giving" of the law of God's covenant. If we are at all to understand the Jewish perspective on the interpretation of the biblical tradition, then we shall undoubtedly need to pay full attention to the fact that Deuteronomy presents its contents as *torah*, and what it implies by doing so.

Deuteronomy in New Testament Perspective. From a New Testament viewpoint, the book of Deuteronomy was clearly a work of immense importance as a central formative work that had shaped contemporary Jewish practice. Allusions to and citations from the book in the New Testament writings are to be found more frequently than is the case with any other Old Testament book. Moreover, it cannot be overlooked that the teaching of Jesus concerning the first, and most important, of all the commandments takes the form of a quotation from Deut 6:4-5 (see Luke 10:25-28). In a similar fashion, the story of the temptation of Jesus in the wilderness uses citations from Deuteronomy as the primary means for countering the suggestions made by Satan (Matt 4:1-11).

However, it is not simply in these specific key moments that the teaching of Deuteronomy has exercised a major influence on the New Testament tradition. More pervasively, it can be recognized that the inward psychologizing and spiritualizing of religious commitment, which is so marked a feature of the deuteronomic teaching, pervades the early Christian tradition. It is the inwardness of faith, the emphasis on attitude beside action, and the focus on love, obedience, and gratitude that have made the deuteronomic teaching so fundamental to New Testament faith.

Moreover, one of the significant aspects of the deuteronomic interpretation of a divine *torah* lies in the way it brings together religious, ethical, and social concerns under a single umbrella. It may be held to have desacralized religion, removing much of the mystical and quasi-magical notions of cultic power. As such it promotes a rather "secularized" interpretation of religious commitment. In another direction, however, it can be held to have spiritualized a wide range of everyday activities, spiritualizing their significance. It can be seen to have moraled and personalized ideas of religious loyalty to a remarkable degree. Not only is the individual called upon to respond to God in obedience, but also such obedience is made the subject of deep heart searching and self-examination. Without the teaching of Deuteronomy, it is hard to see how the religious and ethical arguments that characterize the conflicts between Jesus and his Jewish contemporaries could have arisen. From the perspective of grasping the nature of the New Testament and its reflection of Christian controversies with the contemporary Jewish tradition, a close study of the teaching of Deuteronomy becomes essential.

Deuteronomy in Historical and Ethical Perspective. What has been noted in regard to the place of Deuteronomy in Old and New Testament tradition has viewed it in a predominantly positive and constructive light. On any reckoning its influence in shaping the main lines of biblical tradition has been very strong. Yet, once it is viewed in a wider historical and ethical perspective, a number of serious questions arise that can only be answered negatively.[15] Most prominent in this regard is the uncompromising vehemence with which Deuteronomy demands the wholesale extermination of all ethnic and religious communities that had occupied the land prior to the Israelite conquest. Moreover the very assumption that Israel could be the beneficiary of a divinely given entitlement to conquer, repress, and exterminate an entire population in order to gain possession of their land undermines the many richer ethical and spiritual insights the book contains.[16] It reflects deeply upon not only the concept of Israel as a people of God, but also on the understanding of God that it exemplifies.

---

15. See F. E. Deist, "The Dangers of Deuteronomy: A Page from the Reception History of the Book," in *Studies in Deuteronomy in Honour of C. J. Labuschagne*, ed. F. Garcia Martinez et al. (Leiden: E. J. Brill, 1994) 13-30.

16. Cf. Susan Niditch, *War in the Hebrew Bible* (New York: Oxford University Press, 1994).

From a historical perspective, therefore, the influence of Deuteronomy has been far from uniform and not at all consistently helpful. That there are inherent dangers and defects in its teaching must be frankly reckoned with. Certainly we can moderate this ethical criticism of the book with the help of two important provisos, neither of which adequately resolves the problems raised.

The first of these provisos concerns the fact that the book is an uneven composition; it has many strands. The stratum of legislative demand that calls for the extermination of all the previous occupants of the land and the death penalty for any Israelite who tolerates or encourages the perpetuation of their religion stands alongside much more tolerant and humane considerations for the weak and the oppressed. Even informing on one's neighbor is encouraged if religious loyalty is at stake (Deut 13:6-11). To this extent, the punishment demanded for those who presume to practice the religions of Baal and Asherah and the other traditions of the land's previous occupants stands in contrast with a more considered awareness of the need to show consideration and compassion to the oppressed and to distinguish between distinct categories of foreign aliens (Deut 23:3-8). How and why the frenetic and cruel demand for a rigid exclusivism in promoting the worship of the Lord alone was to be applied in the light of the parallel concern for love and compassion is never adequately made clear from the book's contents. Presumably it was an attitude the authors felt to be necessary when the very survival of their religious tradition was under threat.

The second proviso concerns the fact that, in calling for the extermination of the previous inhabitants of the land, the book was undoubtedly propagating a historical anachronism. These peoples had long since ceased to retain any clear and separate ethnic identity, having undoubtedly largely been absorbed into the Israelite kingdom that flourished under David and Solomon. Yet this does not properly resolve the difficulty, since almost certainly the deuteronomic authors did have in mind a real contemporary community and its leaders, whom they regarded as enemies and who were believed to pose a danger to the program that they themselves were seeking to propagate. Thus we are left with the difficulty that, in seeking to promote a richly ethical and responsible interpretation of Israel's religious faith, the authors of Deuteronomy were prepared to recommend the most uncompromising and repressive measures. Sadly, the long history of humankind's subsequent religious conflicts has shown how many have been willing to follow that lead and have failed to set it under a necessary critical scrutiny.

A further critical perspective on the teaching of Deuteronomy is also a necessary part of the introduction to the book. From within the biblical tradition, one of its most innovative features has been its emphasis on the ideas of Israel's divine election, of its privileged covenant status in relationship to God, and of the many claims to advantage and power that this covenant relationship confers. In itself such teaching can be seen as an important step in seeking to theologize and rationalize the inherited ideas that flourished in the ancient world of competing national powers with national deities, each seeking advantage over others. In many respects the history of international conflict that characterized the ancient Near East during the half millennium from the days of David to the end of the Davidic monarchy witnessed the absurdity of such notions. The impetus toward monotheism and to a concept of one world rendered the belief in many competing gods totally obsolete.

So Deuteronomy stands apart from the confused and confusing picture of a world in which many gods fought for the allegiance of human beings. It moves strongly in the direction of a true monotheism. Yet in order to accommodate its national, as well as its more universal, concepts appropriate to belief in a deity who wielded supreme authority over the universe, it makes use of ideas that have themselves become fraught with danger. In spite of the high place given to the notion of a covenant between the supreme deity and human beings in Deuteronomy and the biblical tradition that drew from it, it remains a limiting and imperfect concept for the expression of religious ideas. All too readily conferred privileges, rather than the call to a spiritual obedience, have assumed the most prominent place, sometimes with disastrous consequences.

BIBLIOGRAPHY

Commentaries:

Craigie, P. C. *The Book of Deuteronomy.* NICOT. Grand Rapids: Eerdmans, 1976. Although rather strongly conservative in its literary and historical perspectives, this remains a useful and clearly written exposition.

Driver, S. R. *Deuteronomy.* 3rd ed. ICC. Edinburgh: T. & T. Clark, 1902. Very dated now in its critical assessments, but a classical work by an outstanding scholar; it is still indispensable for its comments on the Hebrew text and vocabulary of the book.

Mayes, A. D. H. *Deuteronomy.* NCB. London: Marshall, Morgan & Scott, 1979. An exposition from a modern critical perspective that gives an excellent account of the theological and literary developments in which Deuteronomy arose.

Miller, P. D. *Deuteronomy.* Interpretation. Louisville: Westminster John Knox, 1990. Written in nontechnical language and aimed at the preacher and general reader; places high emphasis on the ethical and religious issues raised by Deuteronomy.

von Rad, G. *Deuteronomy.* OTL. Philadelphia: Westminster, 1966. A strikingly fresh theological understanding of Deuteronomy that has remained central to subsequent research; although brief in compass, it is valuable for its insights into central issues of biblical theology.

Thompson, J. A. *Deuteronomy.* Tyndale Old Testament Commentaries. London: IVF, 1974. Conservative in outlook and rather too dependent on analogies between Deuteronomy and ancient Near Eastern treaty documents, this is nevertheless a clear and positive exposition.

Weinfeld, M. *Deuteronomy 1–11.* AB 5. New York: Doubleday, 1991. Although so far incomplete, this commentary is indispensable for the serious student because of its summaries and accounts of early and medieval Jewish interpretation. When used in conjunction with Weinfeld's study of the religious and ethical background to the book, it provides a well-balanced account of the central place of Deuteronomy in the growth of the OT and the development of ancient Israelite religion.

Special Studies:

Braulik, G. *The Theology of Deuteronomy. Collected Essays of Georg Braulik OSB.* Bibal Collected Essays 2. Translated by Ulrika Lindblad. N. Richland Hills, Tex.: Bibal, 1994. Along with N. Lohfink, the author has played a central role in research into the legal structure and ethical background of Deuteronomy.

Christensen, D. L., ed. *A Song of Power and the Power of Song: Essays on the Book of Deuteronomy.* Sources for Biblical and Theological Study 3. Winona Lake: Eisenbrauns, 1993. An excellent resource for the serious student; it brings together a wide range of the most significant critical essays reflecting contemporary research into the background and interpretation of Deuteronomy.

Haran, M. *Temples and Temple Service in Ancient Israel.* Oxford: Oxford University Press, 1978. An essential resource for understanding the priestly and ritual background reflected in the legislative prescriptions of Deuteronomy.

Harrelson, W. *The Ten Commandments and Human Rights.* OBT. Philadelphia: Fortress, 1980.

N. Lohfink, ed. *Das Deuteronomium: Entstehung, Gestalt und Botschaft.* BETL 68. Leuven: J. P. Peeters, 1985.

———. *Studien zum Deuteronomium und zur deuteronomistischen Literatur I.* SBA 8. Stuttgart: Katholisches Bibelwerk, 1990.

———. *Studien zum Deuteronomium und zur deuteronomistischen Literatur II.* SBA 12. Stuttgart: Katholisches Bibelwerk, 1991.

———. *Studien zum Deuteronomium und zur deuteronomistischen Literatur III.* SBA 20. Stuttgart: Katholisches Bibelwerk, 1995.

———. *Theology of the Pentateuch: Themes of the Priestly Narrative and Deuteronomy.* Translated by L. M. Maloney. Minneapolis: Augsburg Fortress, 1994. A sample of the work of an author who has become an outstanding world authority on the book of Deuteronomy.

Olson, D. T. *Deuteronomy and the Death of Moses.* OBT. Minneapolis: Augsburg Fortress, 1994.

von Rad, G. *Studies in Deuteronomy.* Translated by D. Stalker. SBT 9. London: SCM, 1953.

Weinfeld, M. *Deuteronomy and the Deuteronomic School.* Oxford: Oxford University Press, 1972.

OUTLINE OF DEUTERONOMY

DEUTERONOMY 1:1–3:29

INTRODUCTION TO ISRAEL'S STORY

OVERVIEW

L ike many introductions to a major piece of literature, the introduction to the book of Deuteronomy hides much behind its simplicity and brevity. It presents a central guide to the significance and authority of the words that follow and establishes for them a unique place within the social and religious history of Israel, as well as within the literary structure of the Hebrew Bible.

In order to appreciate its character, it is essential to bear in mind certain central critical observations regarding chapters 1–3 and their significance for the book of Deuteronomy and for the writings that follow it. In a major, pathfinding work on the history of the books of Joshua, Judges, 1–2 Samuel, and 1–2 Kings, Martin Noth argued that Deuteronomy 1–3 must be regarded as the introduction, not simply to the law book of Deuteronomy, but to the entire narrative history that follows in these six books.[17] Following the order of the Hebrew canon, these books belong together as "the Former Prophets" (the book of Ruth appears separately among the five scrolls). So the book of Deuteronomy provides the beginning for the history of Israel under the monarchy that follows it, a history that Noth believed could be appropriately described as "the Deuteronomistic History." Seen as a whole, since it comprises a work of substantial length, the Deuteronomistic History offers a record of God's polity for Israel in the law book and an account of how the nation had subsequently fared under this code of laws. Israel did well when it displayed obedience, but experienced disaster when the people turned back from it.

Against such a background, we can see that Deuteronomy 1–3 contains a short historical résumé describing the adventures of

Israel from the time of God's revelation at Mt. Horeb to the eve of the people's crossing of the river Jordan and their entry into the land promised to their ancestors. In order to provide such a historical setting for the giving of the law that forms the heart of the book, the writers employed information drawn from narrative sources that are still preserved in parts of Genesis–Numbers. So it partially summarizes a story that has already been told.

The law of Deuteronomy is presented as a speech of Moses given on the eve of this crossing and the subsequent conquest, recapitulating with elaborations and variations the law already given through Moses at Mt. Horeb. So the book's title as "a second law" is quite fitting. The introductory narrative's historical continuation is to be found in the account of Moses' death (chaps. 31 and 34) and the preparations for crossing the river Jordan under Joshua (Joshua 1–11).

Noth's case for recognizing this larger literary setting and purpose for the introduction to Deuteronomy has been widely accepted and must be upheld as valid, with two major cautionary provisos. The first of these is that many scholars have rightly sought to give recognition to the intricate, and rather piecemeal, composition of Deuteronomy 1–3. A basic text appears to have been progressively enlarged and expanded in several stages. A second significant point has been argued by S. Mittmann[18] in claiming that a part of this ground text was aimed at providing an introduction to the Decalogue of Deut 5:6-21. On any reckoning, this "Commandment Code" must be regarded as the central "law"

---

17. M. Noth, *The Deuteronomistic History,* JSOTSup 15 (Sheffield: JSOT, 1981). The original German text was published in 1943.

18. S. Mittmann, *Deuteronomium 1,1-6,3 literarkriotisch und traditionsgeschichtlich untersucht,* BZAW 139 (Berlin: de Gruyter, 1975). A review of the problems is presented in L. Perlitt, "Deuteronomium 1-3 im Streit der exegetischen Methoden," *Das Deuteronomium. Entstehung, Gestalt und Botschaft,* ed. N. Lohfink, BETL 68 (Leuven: Peeters, 1985) 149-63; L. Perliit, *Deuteronomum-Studien* (Tübingen: J. C. B. Mohr, 1994) 32-49.

of Deuteronomy and as a key to understanding the aims and assumptions of the deuteronomic movement. The more detailed code of Deuteronomy 12–26 can then be seen as an elaboration and outworking of this central, and relatively brief, list of commandments.

In this light, the introduction of Deuteronomy 1–3 serves a twofold goal: It prepares for the declaration of the basic commandments by Moses, unwaveringly placing him as the central figure in affirming the divine origin and authority of Israel's law, and it shows that Israel's history had a beginning *before* it entered the land promised to its ancestors. Law and narrative history, therefore, are the central means used by the deuteronomists to present their message explaining what it meant for Israel to be the people of the LORD God.

We should not be surprised, then, that there is some unevenness of form and content in chaps. 1–3, which is to be explained by recognizing that more than one editorial hand has been at work. Yet, the precise analysis and ordering of this compositional process remain uncertain, and little is to be gained by pressing the various scholarly conjectures to the point of assurance.[19] More significant is the recognition that the many rough edges in the literary flow of these introductory chapters are themselves a result of the need to bind the book of Deuteronomy closely to the

four books that precede it (i.e., Genesis–Numbers). It is not difficult to recognize that the authors of Deuteronomy have drawn upon narratives, still preserved in these preceding books, that tell of the revelation of the LORD God to the patriarchs and to Moses. So Deuteronomy has a special place in the Hebrew Bible and represents a uniquely important literary bond. It forms the final section of the five books of the Pentateuch—the books of Moses—but also joins directly and closely to the story that follows in those books that the Hebrew Bible describes as the Former Prophets. The introductory chapters thus fulfill a key role in establishing this literary bond.[20]

Since the wide acceptance of Noth's study has led to a strong emphasis on the connections between Deuteronomy and the Former Prophets, it is salutary to bear in mind the importance of the fact that its present canonical form and shape also tie it inseparably to Genesis–Numbers. It forms the final book of Moses, declaring repeatedly and unequivocally that Israel's origins began with Moses and not with the kingship that occupies so large a place in the story that follows. The nation had its start before the land was entered and conquered, and not after this had been achieved. It began with a covenant made on Mt. Horeb and with a law embodied in this, not with laws made and administered by kings and a royal court.

19. A valuable survey of positions is to be found in N. Lohfink, "Dtn 1,6–3,29," in *Studien zum Deuteronomium und zur deuteronomistischen Literatur I*, SBA 8 (Stuttgart: Katholisches Biblewerk, 1990) 15-44.

20. A review of the issues is to be found in N. Lohfink, "Deuteronomum und Pentateuch. Zum Stand der Forschung," in *Studien zum Deuteronomum und zur deuteronomistischen Literatur III*, SBA 20 (Stuttgart: Katholisches Bibelwerk, 1995) 13-38.

DEUTERONOMY 1:1-5, EDITORIAL PREFACE

COMMENTARY

Bearing these preliminary remarks in mind, we can note the points that the introduction to the book establishes in 1:1-5: (1) The words that follow are the work, and carry the unique authority, of Moses, the great founding father of Israel (note especially the threefold references to Moses in vv. 1, 3, 5). (2) They were given to Israel in the wilderness, before the crossing of the river Jordan and the entry into the land (v. 3). The author's perspective as one living within this

land is made clear in v. 5 with the reference to "beyond the Jordan." (3) By defeating King Sihon of the Amorites and King Og of Bashan, Israel has a claim to certain territories east of the Jordan; this point has been drawn from Num 21:21-35 and is taken up again later. What history proved about Israel's claims to the land is a feature that was clearly of great importance to the author. Past events carried a strong contemporary relevance. (4) What Moses sets out in this second act of lawgiving is not a new or different law from that which had already been given, but rather represents an exposition and reaffirmation of that law. The Hebrew verb באר (*bē'ēr*, piel) used in v. 5 for "to expound" is unusual (cf. 27:8; Hab 2:2) and suggests both amplification and emphasis as well as "making plain," all of which are features that well characterize the book of Deuteronomy.

Taken as an introduction both to the book of Deuteronomy and to the larger history that follows it, some significant features are brought out in these verses. Israel's law is neither a "law of the land" nor a "law of the king" (one may compare King Hammurabi's famous law code). Israel's law is truly a divine law and stands above both land and kingship. Moreover, this law is addressed to the entire nation—"all Israel" (v. 1). Even children are to be taught the law and are expected to respond to it in a manner appropriate to their age (6:20).

The victories over Sihon and Og (v. 4) in the region to the east of Jordan take on something of an exemplary role. They show that, when obedient to the law, Israel can win great victories. Throughout the deuteronomic literature the questions of military organization and effectiveness appear prominently as major issues. So stories of defeat and victory achieved in the past constantly assume exemplary status.

REFLECTIONS

The most striking and fundamental feature of the introduction to Deuteronomy is its emphasis on Moses and the revelation of God given at Mt. Horeb. This man and this event provide the point of origin of the religion and faith of Israel, through which God had disclosed the special divine calling and destiny of Israel. Israel's very existence was bound up irrevocably to faith. This faith gave assurance of the reality of God and of the divine engagement with the world and its peoples. It was also, and inevitably, a fragile and vulnerable faith, since the demands of God's revelation and the divine covenant could be refused. Deuteronomy is very, almost excessively, conscious of this vulnerability. Faith is a question of human responsiveness, and such responsiveness may not be forthcoming. Deuteronomy has much to say about the shadowy side of Israel's beginnings, the acts of failure, the timid refusals to rise to the challenge that God's calling had made possible, and the denial of the great vision of the promise that Moses had made possible from the beginning.

It is wholly in line with this biblical consciousness of the vulnerability of faith that the early rabbinic commentators were struck by the contrast between the eleven-day journey from Mt. Horeb to Kadesh-barnea and the thirty-eight-year interval before Israel finally set out to cross the Wadi Zered (2:14). Time had passed, and a generation had died out, all because the majority of Israelites lacked the courage and faith to act according to God's promise. So there had been, from the very beginning, a faithless generation.

The entire deuteronomic literature is imbued with this sensitivity to the psychology of faith. It records a noble story of the past and sets out an insightful constitution for the moral life of the nation. Yet, above both these informational literary tasks it makes an urgent appeal for faith and courage. This document was evidently intended to be read in public worship, and seems constantly aware that its readers and hearers were facing a challenge similar to that which confronted the first generation traveling with Moses to the borders of the promised land. That entire generation had failed, with the result that it—along with Moses—died before entering the land. Only their children, rearmed spiritually under the leadership of Joshua, had ventured to believe that God's promise would be fulfilled and that they would enjoy the fruits of freedom the exodus had given to their forebears.

It is on account of this intense faith consciousness that the book of Deuteronomy has retained its appeal and been able to continue to speak to succeeding generations. The generation lost in the wilderness was a perpetual reminder that the summons to faith is inescapable and essential for every subsequent generation.

DEUTERONOMY 1:6-45, FAITH AFFIRMED, TESTED, AND JUDGED

COMMENTARY

The story of Israel's beginnings up to the eve of entry into the land is now sketched out more fully by means of certain incidents, selected because they bring to the surface key constitutional and theological motifs.

1:6-8. The first of these key motifs is that of the promise of the land given to Israel's first ancestors (Gen 12:7; 15:18).[21] This theme is the *leitmotif* that now binds the entire Genesis story to that of the exodus and the revelation at Mt. Horeb. It gives coherence to the wide variety of local and tribal traditions that constitute the story of the patriarchal period of Israel's existence (Genesis 12–50). In its developed literary form, it appears as one of the ways in which local and individual narrative memories, which naturally focused on specific regions and clans, were woven together into a larger whole. Tribal tradition became national tradition, since each tribe had its own particular story to tell to make its own contribution to the larger picture.

This summary history was consequently able to bring together a wide compass of ancestral traditions belonging to each of Israel's member clans and tribes. It set them under one overarching heading: God's promise of the land. This, then, provides a central theological motif, because the land is presented as belonging to Israel as the outworking of a divine purpose and the product of divine action. So the theology of God as Land-giver functions as a unifying principle, bringing diverse stories and memories about settlement of the land into one connected story.

The phrase "the LORD our God" (v. 6) is typically deuteronomic, occurring no less than twenty-three times in the book. Even more common is the expression "the LORD your/our God," which is to be found no less than 276 times. The title "Amorite" is widely attested in Mesopotamian documents from the second and third centuries BCE to

designate "west land" or "westerner." In biblical usage, it is found alongside the related title "Canaanite" to describe the pre-Israelite inhabitants of the territory Israel had settled. Predominantly Amorite peoples occupied the hill country, whereas the Canaanites were settled mainly along the coastal areas (see Josh 13:3-4). The extent of the land Israel was destined to occupy is regarded from a perspective of its maximum coverage; yet even this appears to be heavily idealized (see 11:24; Josh 1:4). That the land itself was the subject of an older covenant made between the LORD God and Abraham is described in Gen 15:18-21, but significantly the covenant there lacks any element of a binding set of obligations that dominate the deuteronomic presentation of the covenant at Horeb.

1:9-18. The deuteronomist has clearly drawn his information regarding the institution of an order of lay judges from the literary sources now preserved in Exodus 18 and Numbers 11. Noticeably, the complaint by Moses concerning the heavy burden imposed by having to adjudicate the disputes that arose between members of the community, which in Numbers 11 is directed toward God, is here directed toward the people. The deuteronomic author has evidently felt a need to heighten the image and role of Moses. The placing of this action at this point highlights the importance to Israel of a fair and acceptable system of juridical authority vested in reputable leaders chosen from among the tribes (v. 13). Throughout the legal section of the book (chaps. 12–26), the question of the administration of law receives considerable attention and reflects a variety of institutional responsibilities, embracing priests, elders, and appointed judges.[22]

Comparison with other peoples of the ancient Near East reveals the prominent role of kingship in establishing and promoting

---

21. W. Brueggemann, *The Land: Place as Gift, Promise and Challenge in Biblical Faith,* OBT (Philadelphia: Fortress, 1977).

22. J. C. Gertz, *Die Gerichtsorgainisation Israels im deuteromistischen Gesetz,* FRLANT 165 (Göttingen: Vandenhoeck & Ruprecht, 1994).

systems of law administration.[23] This was evidently true to a significant extent for ancient Israel, as various narrative reports show. It was, inevitably, open to abuse so that a highly critiqued aspect of the institution of monarchy was that it failed to institute and maintain a responsible judicial system over which the king personally presided, at least in a nominal fashion (see Jer 22:15-17). It is apparent that the deuteronomic concern to place the issue of law and legal administration at the head of its requirements, as is achieved by setting this summary report here, reflects the prominence given to the matter. Fundamental to the entire deuteronomic outlook is a concern with public justice, and underlying this ambition is a scarcely disguised awareness of the complexity of the many issues raised and the vulnerability of existing systems to abuse and corruption. The high profile accorded to Moses as the supreme lawgiver has in part been shaped by the consciousness that Israel's kings had often fallen short in this regard.

Verse 15 occasions some difficulty concerning the manner of choice of the judges. Since v. 13 has shown that the power to choose the appropriate individuals was to rest with the people, it is surprising to find here that those chosen are simply approved by Moses and are already designated as "leaders of your tribes." This might point to a mere twelve such judges, whereas Numbers 11:1 specifies seventy elders. Furthermore, although the title "commanders" (שָׂרִים śārîm) could be construed widely to describe various types of officials, the division of the people into thousands, hundreds, fifties, and tens suggests patterns of military organization and obligation. Probably the inclusion of the verse was intended to allow this wider jurisdiction of the judges for military activity. It provides one of a larger number of indications that, at the time of the composition of this introduction, Israel was aware that it was itself deeply threatened militarily. Arrangements for local community defense were necessary and involved the raising of a civil militia.

1:19-33. Once again this historical survey by the deuteronomic author makes direct use of older written sources that are now preserved in Numbers 13–14. The literary

dependence on the part of Deuteronomy is evident, but there are some significant variations. These would appear to have been introduced in order to highlight the central theme that failure to occupy the land immediately was a result of misguided fear on the part of the people and faithlessness toward God.

Mayes points out that the deuteronomist not only summarizes the story contained in his source, but also presupposes that the reader is familiar with it.[24] The reiteration of the divine promise of the land and its accompanying injunction to show no fear or alarm at the danger and immensity of the task are characteristic deuteronomic themes (vv. 21, 29). The gift of the land is both a promise and a divine command to act. The proposal to send out spies to evaluate and report on the nature of the territory to be conquered is presented as originating from the people themselves: "All of you came to me and said. . . ." There is a collective responsibility for the mission and a shared culpability for the consequences of it.

1:34-45. The earliest version of the story clearly possessed much local flavor and focused in detail on the contrast between the attitude of Caleb, with his consequent position of privilege, shared with Joshua (Num 14:6, 24, 30, 38), and that of the people more generally. This motif is retained, but serves now to contrast Caleb's faithfulness with the lack of it from the wider community. He is said to have displayed "complete fidelity to the LORD." The popular response to the spies' report, advocating caution and promoting fear, is presented as a fundamental reason for disobeying the divine command to proceed immediately to prepare for entry into the land. The reprehensible and unbelieving attitude of the community as a whole, with the exceptions of Joshua and Caleb, is made the subject of particular emphasis (v. 27). The people even go so far as to accuse God of perpetrating a vindictive deceit upon them by leading them on to disaster. Throughout the reader is directly drawn into the story by being shown contrasting attitudes in which his or her own loyalties and sympathies would be bound to agree with those of the narrator. Those who choose the path of

23. K. W. Whitelam, *The Just King: Monarchical Judicial Authority in Ancient Israel* (Sheffield: JSOT, 1979).

24. A. D. H. Mayes, *Deuteronomy,* NCB (London: Marshall, Morgan & Scott, 1979) 127.

disobedience through fear pay a heavy price for their timidity!

Taken as a carefully selected incident, the report of which is drawn from older sources relating to the conquest and settlement of the land, the narrative seeks to demonstrate that success in the occupation and enjoyment of the land was entirely a matter of obedience to God's clearly given commands and to an unwavering trust in the reliability of the divine promises. These had been given first to the patriarchal ancestors of Israel and subsequently reaffirmed through Moses. Such a call for undeviating faith in God, no matter how daunting the danger or massive the task, is wholly in line with the later narrative of Joshua 1–9. This is itself undoubtedly a late narrative compilation on the part of the deuteronomic school. It recounts how the occupation of the land was finally achieved in a swift coordinated campaign in which obedience or disobedience toward the divine law was the deciding factor. In both Deuteronomy and the book of Joshua the historical recollections and reconstructions of the past are made to elucidate from them lessons of faith. These lessons relate consistently to questions of faith in the promises of God and the neccessity for obedience to a clearly known divine law.

The report of the popular dismay at God's anger over the people's response and their subsequent regret for their lack of faith (vv. 41-45) is employed as a means of further reinforcing the central message. It is a message that holds together both the deuteronomic understanding of warfare and the conviction that Israel's occupation of the land and its obedience to God's law are inseparably linked. The LORD's presence must remain in the midst of the people if they are to secure victory (v. 42). Without this presence, no victory can be won and defeat becomes inevitable. It is in line with this that the eventual conquest of Jericho is presented, not as a battle but as a

ritual procession led by priests (Josh 6:1-21). Faith and obedience to the law, not military expertise and force of arms, are the needful elements of security and assurance for the retention of God's gifts. For Deuteronomy, the most central of those gifts was the gift of the land.

In Num 14:43, 45 the enemy is identified as "the Amalekites and Canaanites" so that their designation here as "Amorites" (v. 44) is a mark of the general leveling shown by the deuteronomic author in using this term for the pre-Israelite occupants of all the land. The concluding affirmation in v. 45 that God refused to listen to the remorse expressed by the people for their lack of faith reveals the strength of the deuteronomic doctrine of divine retribution. Some offenses against God's commands are such that human entreaties, no matter how passionately felt and expressed, cannot bring about a withdrawal of the divine anger.

The theme that prayerful entreaty and intercession may sometimes prove to be unavailing is an important feature of the deuteronomic understanding of Israel's history. This appears to have become even more marked in those parts of the deuteronomic literature that derive from the latest period of the composition of the book. The theme is explored extensively in the lengthy account of Moses' intercession in Deuteronomy 9. Although a clear chronology is unobtainable for the various stages of theological development of the deuteronomic movement, such evidence as we have points to a deepening sense of foreboding and a consciousness of the depth of the divine anger. If this is true, it would also serve to relate to, and perhaps in part explain, the level of frenetic intensity, combined with merciless severity, with which the demand for enforcing obedience to the law is presented in certain parts of the books of Deuteronomy and Joshua.

REFLECTIONS

Two issues immediately call for attention in surveying this summary report of Israel's generation-long sojourn in the wilderness after the revelation on Mt. Horeb. The occupation of the land is understood as an unquestioned consequence of God's purpose and gracious will toward Israel. No thought is given to the needs, feelings, or survival of the existing occupants of that land. They appear only as shadowy, half-identifiable people whose misfortune it was to have been in the way of a more favored people. The deuteronomic literature is uncompromising on the issue. Such a partisan attitude accords badly with either modern Jewish or Christian awareness of the universal sovereignty and grace of God. This view may be mitigated to some extent by recognizing its historical inadequacy as a way to understand and interpret the many extensive, and usually violent, population movements that shaped several millennia of human settlement in the ancient Near East. Such movements and extensive migrations occurred, invariably with triumphant consequences for the victors and no pity or redress for the vanquished.

The rise of Israel as a nation toward the end of the second millennium BCE was one particular instance of a complex pattern of similar actions that took place over the region. The deuteronomic literature is the biblical record of one such instance among many similar major social and political movements, and that record survives with a distinctive theological interpretation stamped upon it.

Of special importance to us is the fact that it is the deuteronomic movement and its literary achievements that established the best-known paradigm for such developments by creating a canonical biblical interpretation for Israel's version. In spite of intense historical research and the use of comparative data to show how it comes about that nations and a national consciousness emerge, the full details of how Israel stepped onto the historical stage of national history can be traced only imperfectly. The early history of many of its constituent tribes and of the regions where they settled is far from clear. What we are left with is a single coordinated theological interpretation of a series of past events that saw within them unfolding images of divine grace, beneficence, and a summons to courage and a high moral vision.

Alongside these images were set also some negative metaphors of divine anger, retribution, and discriminatory punishment and rejection. It then becomes no easy task to isolate the more positive imagery, ideas, and symbols from the less helpful negative concepts and themes.

One way in which this can be attempted is by recognizing that the deuteronomic construct of how Israel came to birth as a nation was itself the product of men and women facing a major crisis.[25] The book itself suggests at many places that it was composed at a time when the continuance of Israel's existence as a state, with a land and kingship of its own, was all but at an end. The deuteronomic literature is essentially a twilight literature, written in the shadow of catastrophe when much of Israel's territory had already been lost, when defeat had faced the nation many times, and when the great expectations associated with the days of David and Solomon were a richly colored memory.

In a very powerful way the authors felt that their own contemporaries, the hearers and readers of the book, were facing the same threats and dangers that had faced their forebears who had first entered the land. A new generation of Anakim (giants) had come upon the scene and had threatened to take and keep possession of the land. Nor can the authors of the book hide their conviction that many of their contemporaries were displaying the same fear and defeatist thinking that had kept the generation that had first sent spies to reconnoiter the land imprisoned in the wilderness. The call to faith and obedience was urgent; the belief that, however great the opposition, the LORD God was greater still fired their imagination. The fervor of their appeal is unmistakable. It is in large measure this sense of urgency and its accompanying call to firmer loyalty to God that have made the book of Deuteronomy a rich source of spiritual resources for both Jews and Christians. That this call to loyalty should have fallen short of recognizing that the Canaanites, too, were human beings and also children of God should not hide from us the fact that there is a better, as well as an insidiously dangerous, aspect to the deuteronomic theology.

---

25. See W. Brueggemann, *The Land,* 46: "It is as though Israel's traditionists had intuitively known that this is the hour of destiny; as though Israel knows that hard, disciplined reflection is never more needed than at this moment, when the new situation of land requires a new Israel with a new faith."

DEUTERONOMY 1:46–3:29, THE FIRST CAMPAIGNS—PEACEFUL AND MILITARY

COMMENTARY

1:46–2:8a. The author continues his story by reporting a journey that has already been recounted in Num 20:14 concerning the Israelites' passage through the territory of Edom. By the time the author wrote, Edom and Esau had evidently come to be effectively identified as one. This had taken place as a result of the westward spread of Edom into Seir, a territory that had been occupied by the descendants of Esau. The awareness of a blood relationship between Jacob and Esau (Gen 27:1-45) accounts for the insistence on a peaceful passage through the territory of Esau's descendants. Their land had been assigned to them by the LORD God (v. 5), and any provisions acquired from them by the Israelites had to be paid for (v. 6). The mention of this need to buy provisions gave rise to the slightly jarring note that God provided for Israel all necessary sustenance during the forty-year wilderness period (v. 7). This was believed not to exclude the purchase of goods, although no indication is made of whence the purchase money would come.

Altogether the narrative down to 3:11 recounts five encounters with nations settled east of Jordan that follow a closely similar pattern.[26] In three of them, Edom, Moab, and Ammon, peaceful negotiations avoid any conflict. However, in the last two, involving Sihon and Og, hostilities arise that enable and entitle Israel to take possession of their respective territories. Undoubtedly this motif of using historical traditions to maintain a claim on territory was an important feature of deuteronomic writing. From a purely historical perspective, most of the land east of the Jordan appears to have been lost to Israel subsequent to the death of Solomon. Nevertheless, we must take it as highly probable that changing allegiances and feuding among local clans led to many fluctuations of political and religious

affiliation. We cannot, therefore, assume that there was a fixed and settled border in Transjordan, or across much of the land occupied at some stage by the Israelites. Certainly also the Mesopotamian incursions into the region from the ninth century BCE on led to further shifts and realignments. The deuteronomic author here was clearly endeavoring to maintain a political horizon that retained a contemporary relevance for his time. A relatively conciliatory attitude toward the Edomites is commanded in 23:7-8.

2:8b-23. The next ethnic community settled east of the Jordan whose territory had to be crossed was that of Moab. How Israel did so in order to reach its own promised land is recounted in vv. 8b-18. This is followed by a brief warning concerning the necessity for avoiding conflict with the people of Ammon (v. 9); further elaboration of this particular caution is then given in v. 37. Apparently the route envisaged by the author for Israel's journey did not require incursion into Ammonite territory, which lay still farther to the east.

The injunction not to harass Moab follows the pattern of the preceding report of avoiding conflict with Edom. It has no precise counterpart in the earlier source used by the author, but was introduced to complete the picture of the long journey from Kadesh to the land. The tolerant and peace-seeking attitude toward both Moab and Ammon contrasts sharply with the more hostile and uncompromising sentiment expressed in the law of 23:3-6. Obviously, allegiances changed at different periods during the time covered by the composition of the deuteronomic literature. We must assume that changing political events had led to quite fundamental changes of attitude on the part of the Israelites. We may particularly bear in mind that the story of the Ammonite involvement in the protection of the murderers of the Judahite governor Gedaliah after the disaster of 587 BCE (Jer 41:15) provides evidence of friction. For almost two centuries, in fact, it appears

---

26. For these nations, see J. R. Bartlett, "The Moabites and Edomites," in *Peoples of Old Testament Times*, ed. D. J. Wiseman (Oxford: Oxford University Press, 1973) 229-58; M. Noth, *Aufsätze zur biblischen Landes und Altertumskunde I*, ed. H. W. Wolff (Neukirchen-Vluyn: Neukirchener Verlag, 1971) 391-433.

that the military pressures imposed on the region from Mesopotamia inevitably led to fluctuating, and often treacherous, shifts of allegiance.

The brief note in v. 14 concerning the period of thirty-eight years spent in the wilderness accords with the author's affirmation that the entire generation that had spurned God's promise and been fearful of attempting to enter the land had to die out. This was to be their punishment for their lack of courage and disobedience. The interval of thirty-eight years shows that the author has deducted two years to account for the time in reaching Mt. Horeb and the period spent there and at Kadesh. The punishment is here restricted (cf. 1:35) to those who were of age for military service ("warriors," NRSV). It is in accord with this conviction that no military action could be undertaken before these adults had passed from the scene, since the LORD was no longer in Israel's midst (1:42).

The point that the generation who died in the wilderness was experiencing God's punishment for their fearfulness is hardly consistent with the emphasis that has been put on God's special provision for the people during these years (2:7); but in reality two separate theological points are being made. On one side, God's faithfulness and care are exemplified, while on the other the divine punishment of disobedience is also revealed.

The explanatory notes in vv. 10-12 and 20-23 concerning the identities and character of the pre-Israelite inhabitants of the land are of special interest and display an antiquarian flavor.[27] Already the report of the spies had brought information concerning the height of the inhabitants. Now various names are ascribed to them: Emim, Anakim, Rephaim, Zamzummim, and Avvim. The name "Rephaim" is not an ethnic term, and appears in Ps 88:10 and Isa 14:9 as a title for the spirits of the dead. It seems to convey the meaning "healer" or "restorer." What is apparently the same name is found in Ugaritic as an honorific title for the god Baal. Emim are mentioned in Gen 14:5, Anakim in Num 13:33 and Judg 1:20; and Avvim in Josh 13:3. These latter are undoubtedly understood to

have been the original occupants of southwest Palestine, but it is in any event probable that frequent population shifts took place in the region. Both the difficult climate and the vulnerable political situation vis-à-vis Egypt brought frequent changes. From the perspective of tracing historically some of the major ethnic movements of the region, the mention of the displacement of the Avvim by the Caphtorim from Caphtor (Crete) indicates their likely links with the Philistines, whose origin from Caphtor is elsewhere referred to (Jer 47:4; Amos 9:7).

2:24–3:11. The fact that the disobedient and fainthearted generation that had refused to undertake an immediate march to occupy the land had died out is now fully recognized by the author. A worthier and more faith-engendered enterprise could now begin. Forceful dispossession of the previous inhabitants of the land would now have to commence, and two instances from Israel's historical tradition are adduced to bear this out.

From the author's point of view, these stories serve a double purpose, on the one hand establishing the claim that the land promised to Israel included territory to the east of Jordan. Throughout the report the writer's own location west of the Jordan is presupposed. On the other hand, these accounts of victories gained east of the Jordan provided exemplary instances of how success in conquering the land was to be achieved. Victory would be a gift of God so that great emphasis is placed on the elements of panic and confusion the enemy were to experience, reducing their defense to the point of being ineffective.[28] King Sihon of Heshbon and King Og of Bashan are the example cases that show that victory comes from the LORD and brings with it the right to take possession of conquered territory.[29]

The narrative at this point draws upon material from Num 20:17, 19 and 21:21-23, which has been adapted to bring out the deuteronomist's particular religious interests. It especially concerns the art of warfare, beginning with a characteristic emphasis on the psychological factors—the generating of fear

27. See L. Perlitt, "Riesen im Alten Testament. Ein literarisches Motiv im Wirkungsfeld des Deuteronomismus," in *Deuteronomium-Studien* (Tübingen: J. C. B. Mohr, 1994) 205-46.

28. See M. C. Lind, *Yahweh Is a Warrior: The Theology of Warfare in Ancient Israel* (Scottdale, Pa.: Herald, 1980) 147-48, "Reliance upon Yahweh's Miracle."

29. For the historical background, see J. R. Bartlett, "Sihon and Og, Kings of the Amorites," *VT* 20 (1970) 257-77.

and foreboding in the hearts of the enemy (v. 25) and the demand for unflinching courage and faith on the part of Israel's warriors. It is noteworthy that the possibility of avoiding conflict altogether is raised in vv. 27-29, with the offer of a peaceful passage through Sihon's territory. We may compare the instructions for the conduct of war set out in 20:1-20. The discrepancies and unevenness further bear out that the deuteronomic law book was produced from varied materials over a period of time and is far from being homogeneous and unified.

The refusal to accept Israel's offer of peace then provides a reason for the beginning of conflict, which in turn entitles Israel to take possession of Sihon's territory, which is now considered to have become forfeit.[30] The point is of interest since it further reflects the deuteronomic sensitivity to questions of human responsibility and the unresolved tensions that lie hidden in the phrase "God had hardened his spirit" (v. 30).

The narrative brings to light the fact that Heshbon was Sihon's chief city so that the region over which he ruled was not extensive. Kingship did not necessarily imply leadership either of a large territory or of a large national community. He appears more to have been an urban chieftain than the ruler of a nation. His control was mainly a regional one, and the point is important for understanding the rise of monarchy as an institution in which territorial, rather than kinship, factors played a large role.

The narrative concerning the defeat and dispossession of the two kings from Transjordan enables us for the first time to perceive details of the distinctive and prominent deuteronomic theology of warfare.[31] It has become customary to describe this deuteronomic doctrine as that of "holy war," although serious caveats and objections need to be considered in regard to such a title. Most especially it must be regarded as extremely doubtful that the deuteronomic authors were simply reflecting a far older and widely practiced set of conventions regarding the conduct of war. Certainly both contemporary experience and past customs and

conventions are to be traced in the deuteronomic presentation, but ultimately its distinctive, and effectively unique, character must be recognized. So, too, is it necessary to draw attention to several highly stylized and theoretical features that are introduced into it.

It is important to the deuteronomic interpretation of warfare that it is chiefly considered from the point of view of the conquest and retention of the land. So it was seen as a religious duty, and those who participated in it were consecrated to their task. In turn this consecration imposed restraints and set limits on what could be gained from the victorious outcome of such battles. It is certainly not the case that such a deuteronomic understanding of a form of consecration to warfare was intended only in the case of defensive battles. On the contrary, almost all that is presented on the subject is subordinated to the claim that the gift of the land that Israel occupied was a direct gift from God.[32] It had been promised to Israel's ancestors and so belonged to Israel as a consequence of its election by the LORD God. It is this promise and the related claim to a special election that rendered the commitment to take the land in warfare a religious task.

The most striking aspect of the deuteronomic doctrine of warfare is the claim that the primary qualifications demanded of Israel were faith and courage. The victory would come as a gift of God, a situation exemplified in the story of the conquest of Jericho. Little real fighting would be necessary, and the elements of religious ritual were every bit as important as the task of actual fighting. Through and through the conduct of war is viewed as a supernatural activity in which Israel's warriors would face little risk to themselves, if only they exemplified the right kind of courage and obedience.

Considering the period at which this deuteronomic doctrine of warfare emerged, we can feel certain that it represents a heavily theologized and theoretical response to Israel's deep consciousness of military weakness. In the two centuries from the middle of the eighth century BCE to the middle of the sixth, Israel and Judah had suffered fearsome defeats in the face of the imperial spread of Mesopotamian power. Neither Israel's own

30. Niditch, *War in the Hebrew Bible*, 127-28.
31. Von Rad, *Studies in Deuteronomy*, 45-59, and *Holy War in Ancient Israel*, trans. Marva J. Dawn (Grand Rapids: Eerdmans, 1991) 115-27; M. C. Lind, *Yahweh Is a Warrior*, 146-68.

32. Brueggemann, *The Land*, 45-53.

military strength nor that which could be called upon by the formation of alliances with Egypt and other neighboring powers proved adequate to face such a threat. The deuteronomic doctrine, therefore, must be viewed as an attempt to piece together a new understanding of warfare and a new explanation for the seeming failures of national policy. It has undoubtedly drawn upon beliefs, customs, and a military awareness that made its novelties and strong claims for acts of divine intervention a further cause for total obedience to the LORD as God. As a practical formula for military reorganization and renewal, it appears strained and unconvincing. Yet as a basis for appeal for a new sense of national reawakening and a renewal of national pride, it merits close attention for its spiritual intensity.

The emphasis on the sovereignty of the divine power to give victory is well brought out in v. 33 with its insistence that "the LORD gave him over to us." Even so, the unevenness of the deuteronomic ideology reappears once it is recognized that the actions of the people in these battles do not properly conform to those laid down later in the regulations of 20:10-18.

3:12-17. Bashan was an area in Transjordan, to the north of Gilead, highly regarded for its rich, fertile land, which is the meaning its very name conveys (Amos 4:1; Mic 7:14). No older pre-deuteronomic account has been preserved of the defeat of King Og, although Josh 12:4 reports the ruler's name and tells of his control over this rich territory. Verse 2, which appears as a parenthetical addition, reiterates the primary injunction to show no fear in the face of a powerful enemy.

The story of Israel's journeyings and experiences under the leadership of Moses is now brought to a conclusion with a summary account of the allocation of land east of the Jordan to the tribes of Reuben, Gad, and Manasseh. The region on the east of the river Jordan that is here claimed for Israel was very extensive, stretching from Mt. Hermon in the north to the boundary of Moab at the river Arnon in the south. The central region of Gilead was divided by the Jabbok. All told, the deuteronomic historical narratives appear to show a special anxiety to reaffirm Israel's claim to this desirable region, noted for its

agricultural lushness and contrasting with the more rugged hill country to the west of Jordan and the semi-desert region to the south. Not least was this Transjordanian territory felt to be of great significance for the security of the Jordan valley and the protection of its trade routes.

The vulnerability of the region to incursions from the east, from which aggressive marauding tribespeople came repeatedly, accounts for much of its violent history. During the period of Israel's monarchy, it appears that this area of the Transjordan was subjected to a whole series of conflicts, bringing constant realignments of allegiance. Little clear historical recollection has been preserved of Reuben's checkered and unfortunate history. At a very early period in the emergence of Israel as a nation it appears to have suffered as a consequence of its exposed position. That the tribal territory of Manasseh straddled the Jordan was important to its survival within Israel. Those tribes who had settled in the attractive lands to the east of Jordan were too exposed to a variety of threats to be able to maintain themselves with any confidence. It is also noteworthy that the settlement of Israelite tribes to the east of the Jordan posed something of a problem for the deuteronomist's concern with the centralizing of worship in Jerusalem; as a result, the issue receives separate attention in Josh 22:1-34. Overall it seems clear that the deuteronomist was aware of the weak position of the tribes settled east of the Jordan, but that his convictions concerning the oneness of Israel, understood in a very wide compass, has encouraged attention to their territory.

Joshua 12:4 records that King Og of Bashan belonged among the Rephaim (cf. Deut 3:13). The writer here clearly regarded this as evidence of Og's great stature and strength, leading to the intriguing antiquarian notice in v. 11 regarding his iron bed. The REB follows a scholarly suggestion that this can best be understood as a reference to a "sarcophagus of basalt." That it should have been thirteen feet long and six feet wide (NRSV, "nine cubits by four") would then not be so surprising. It would, in fact, be factually quite feasible and would indicate little regarding the king's actual physical stature.

Much of the information set out here regarding the tribal settlements of Israel has been drawn from Num 32:9. Nevertheless it has been added to, and tailored into, a carefully structured unity. A measure of difficulty appears in that v. 12 reports that the half tribe of Manasseh was allocated the territory of Bashan and the northern half of Gilead. This has then been amplified in v. 15 to record that Gilead was ascribed to Machir, who was one son of Manasseh, whereas Bashan was given to another son, Jair. A judge named Jair is mentioned in Judg 10:3-5 as having originated from Gilead and is said to have judged Israel for twenty-two years. This would be in accord with 1 Chr 2:21-22, which makes Jair the great-grandson of Manasseh's son Machir. It may be that the author here was seeking to systematize such evidence as he had, but it is also necessary to bear in mind that the same name could frequently recur across several generations.

The overall purpose of this narrative unit is clear: It is concerned to trace the story of Israel's beginnings from the time of the revelation of God on Mt. Horeb to the eve of the people's entry into the land. Some supplementation of the original narrative appears to have taken place with a view to adding interesting additional detail and clarifying information mentioned only briefly in the basic account.

3:18-29. Essentially the original account of the first campaign to occupy the land, which dealt with the region of Transjordan, appears to have been drawn by the author from material preserved in the book of Numbers. Nevertheless, it has been carefully systematized and filled out. The historical details have been set in the background in order to illuminate more fully certain basic theological themes that the deuteronomists regarded as matters of great importance.

Prominent among these themes is the uniqueness of the leadership afforded by Moses, who now dominates the scene.[33] It is a remarkable feature of chaps. 1–11 that the name and achievements of Moses are given immense emphasis that contrasts with the absence of his name from chaps. 12–26.

In this first campaign, where his presence is evident, Moses' personal conduct contrasts

with the lamentably poor response shown by the Israelites more generally to the privileges and opportunities that had been granted to them. Where he shows obedience and faith, the people display distrust and fear. So Moses himself is exonerated from all blame, and it is the people who must carry the guilt of this. We may note nevertheless that, according to v. 26, Moses was forced to suffer on the people's account; so he had to share the privations and punishment of the people whose leader he had become. It is more a shared punishment than a vicarious punishment, but it is not difficult to see that it could later be understood in this fashion (see 32:51; Num 20:12).

The leadership of Moses is clearly intended to be exemplary, and his success is only vitiated because the people as a whole fail to heed his commands, or do so only reluctantly. So the people enjoy success in their military campaigns while the leadership of Moses remains available to them. They are able without difficulty to conquer the territories of Sihon and Og and to deal effectively with Edom and Moab. When we seek to find some explanation for this exceptional emphasis on one man, which the deuteronomic authors have obviously taken some pains to stress beyond what their sources declared, two points emerge. The first of these is provided by the portrayal of the confused, defeatist, and timid spirit displayed by the majority in Israel. This was evidently an attitude of mind that the writer clearly believed reflected the mood of his own readers. They were tempted to relapse into the same mood of defeatist despair, lacking worthy leadership. Yet they themselves could no longer enjoy the direct leadership of Moses, who had himself not entered the land.

So this gave rise to the second of the points regarding this unusual emphasis. If the people could no longer enjoy the leadership of Moses, they could bask in the benefit of the great gift Moses had brought to them. This was the gift of the law of the LORD, and this is the message the book of Deuteronomy was concerned to present. It was, indeed, the great legacy Moses had given to Israel.

It might have been assumed that the leadership of Moses was simply handed on to his successor in the person of Joshua (vv.

33. See G. W. Coats, *Moses: Heroic Man, Man of God,* JSOTSup 57 (Sheffield: JSOT, 1988).

21, 28). Yet, there is a subtle delicacy and distinctiveness in the manner in which the deuteronomists present the succession of Joshua. He is not another Moses, since there could never be such a figure, but Joshua is most emphatically the successor to the great leader. So his role is significantly different, and his task is to ensure that the commands and instructions of Moses are faithfully carried out. He is the administrator of a new order, and this new order is that of living in accordance with the law that Moses had revealed to the people. In a sense, Joshua is the first deuteronomist, since he is the leader of the generation that was called upon to shape its life and actions in accordance with what had been laid down by the founding father of the nation. To this extent, the very uniqueness of Moses makes the succession

of Joshua indispensable. The lawgiver must give way to the first administrator of the law. This issue is so important that it is dealt with further in chaps. 31 and 34.

The concluding geographical note leaves Israel poised at the border of the promised land and being brought face to face with a new temptation. Halted in the valley opposite Beth-peor, the Israelites face the dangerous possibility of accepting and worshiping the gods of the land they are about to occupy. The reference to the location must intend the same place referred to as Baal-peor, which is clearly presumed in 4:3 to be the case. In Josh 13:20, the location is connected with Mt. Pisgah (cf. Hos 9:10). As often occurred, the name of the deity and his sanctuary has served to provide a name for the entire town.

REFLECTIONS

The entire deuteronomic theology of war is composed of the various exhortations, regulations, and narratives that deal with the military aspects of Israel's national life. Precisely because this theology of war enters so strongly and extensively into the larger biblical narrative tradition, it has given rise to some of the sharpest and most keenly felt objections to the morality of the biblical revelation. A number of considerations need to be borne in mind that may offer some reasoned understanding of this feature of Deuteronomy.

A number of political and religious concerns, closely bound up with the deuteronomic authors' contemporary anxieties, may be discerned. From a political and legal standpoint, it mattered greatly to affirm that the whole land promised to Abraham's descendants had been occupied and settled by Israel. The previous inhabitants had simply been wiped out. Not only was this a gross exaggeration, but it fits badly with the deuteronomic writers' insistence, given in the narrative history that follows, that Israel was persistently and deeply led into disloyalty to God by the temptation to emulate the religion of those who survived in the land. The theory of a wholesale extermination of the previous inhabitants of the land was intended to give assurance that Israel's forebears had at first enjoyed a good and unrestricted start to life in the land. Furthermore, it was necessary to reassert the claim that the entire land had at one time belonged to Israel by right of conquest.

However, even the felt need to provide a clean sheet for the record of Israel's origins in the land, with its highly selective and stylized character, cannot account for the insensitivity and cruelty with which the demand for a religiously motivated genocide is expressed. This fact alone forces us to recognize that the deuteronomic authors were keenly aware of Israel's weakness when faced with the contemporary threat from the military might of Babylon. Behind that more than a century of humiliating subjugation to the Assyrians had effectively led to the loss of a large part of the territory occupied by the northern tribes and had left a legacy of almost abject helplessness on the part of those who remained. Faced with forces that had developed effective techniques of siege breaking and whose cohorts were manned by well-trained and unpitying soldiers, Israel's weakness was all too evident. So we can understand, even if we cannot justify, that Deuteronomy responded to such a threat by a new harshness and severity of its own and by reasserting with a passionate zeal the conviction that the LORD God was greater than all the powers ranged against them. So this book idealized the past in order to compensate for the inadequacies of the present. Most striking of all, the deuteronomic authors sought to rearm faith as a means for combating the sense of helplessness they so readily associate with their readers. All was not lost, and a new commitment of faith could bring a new age in which even the great achievements of Joshua would no longer appear strange and out of place.

Yet, we dare not overlook the impassioned commitment to military force and expectations that the deuteronomists express. Even allowing its presence in other parts of the biblical literature, there exists within it a great consciousness of the cruelty and barbarity of war and of the irreplaceable gift of peace and security. At best, all that the modern reader can hope to salvage from the shadowed and dangerous encouragement the deuteronomists give to warfare as a means of achieving the divine will are some elements of its psychological and spiritual relevance. The appeal to courage and faith, and even to an unremitting resistance to evil, has provided a rich imagery for a portrayal of human life as a "spiritual warfare." We may compare especially John Bunyan's extensive use of both the language and the ideas drawn from the deuteronomists in his work *The Holy War Made by Shaddai upon Diabolus for the Regaining of the Metropolis of the World* (1682).

DEUTERONOMY 4:1–11:32

THE COMMANDMENTS OF GOD

DEUTERONOMY 4:1-43, THE GREAT SUMMONS TO OBEDIENCE

OVERVIEW

The deuteronomic literature is through and through colored by its use of speeches, prayers, and occasional historical reflections that have a strong impact on the reader. In the case of speeches, which are made by the leading figures within the narrative, the distance between the original hearers of the speech and the readers of the book is swallowed up. The message takes on a degree of timelessness. Such speeches and prayers are characterized by some of the most searching theological reflections to be found anywhere in the OT. This amply confirms the widely recognized feature that the deuteronomic movement was heavily innovative in its theological grasp and intentions.

The speech that is here ascribed to Moses has been introduced into the narrative of the lawbook at a relatively late stage.[34] Almost certainly it can be recognized as one of the very latest units to have been composed and incorporated into the book. This is borne out by the reference in v. 3 linking the speech to Israel's encampment at Baal-peor, waiting to cross the Jordan and to enter the land. This event, with all its tensions and temptations, is seen as a decisive moment for Israel's past,

calling for special caution and heart searching. Yet the speech is wholly deuteronomic in its character and clearly recognizes that many of the former citizens of Israel had, by this time, been dispersed into exile among the nations (vv. 27-31). This fact adds to the awareness that acute temptations and difficulties were facing many Israelites in a perilous and uncertain future. In a quite special way, therefore, it addresses these people (v. 29), recognizing their yearning at a distance for the land and conscious that it was, for the present at least, lost to them (cf. Jer 29:12-13). It urges them not to abandon their loyalty to the LORD God, reassuring them that they, in turn, will not be abandoned by God.

The difficult situation of such people, separated from the Temple and its ministry, is reflected in v. 9, which introduces an injunction to make the commandments the subject of teaching within the home, particularly emphasizing the necessity of instructing children in them. This consciousness that the law was not simply a matter for elders and recognized officials, but a textbook to be used for instruction in the home, becomes a highly distinctive characteristic of Deuteronomy. It is a book for a whole community and for everyone who cares about the LORD God, not simply a charter for leaders and officials.

---

34. N. Lohfink, "Verkündigung des Hauptgebots in der jüngsten Schicht des Deuteronomiums (Dt 4,1-40)," in *Studien zum Deuteronomium und deuteronomistischen Literatur I*, SBA 8 (Stuttgart: Katholisches Bibelwerk, 1995) 167-92.

Deuteronomy 4:1-20, A Warning Against Idolatry

COMMENTARY

In its content, this great hortatory speech falls into two parts (vv. 1-20 and 21-40) that nevertheless remain closely interlinked. The first part declares unequivocally that on Mt. Horeb the LORD made a covenant with Israel that had as its central feature a series of ten commandments, written on two stone tablets (v. 13). This is the first point at which the deuteronomic author has explicitly described the events that took place on Mt. Horeb as constituting a covenant agreement. It becomes one of the key themes, encapsulated in the key term "covenant" (ברית *bĕrît*), by which the bilateral commitments between the LORD as God and Israel as a people are described.[35] Its usage is spread rather unevenly throughout the book of Deuteronomy and the literature influenced by it, strongly pointing to the conclusion that it was not an original part of the deuteronomic theological vocabulary, but was introduced into it at a particular stage. A major consequence of its use was to indicate both a conditional element in Israel's special relationship to the LORD God and a heightened sense of the exclusiveness of the moral and spiritual demands imposed on Israel. This provides the basis for the second part of the speech in v. 21.

A transition to this second section is provided by vv. 15-20, which focus attention on the demands of the second commandment, with its complete rejection of the use of any image or idol in the worship of God. It is a complete rebuttal of the validity of any such image, uncompromising and far-reaching in its firmness. Only in the prophetic passage in Isa 44:9-20 do we find any comparable treatment of the theological objections to idolatry. The speech here clearly recognizes that idolatry had remained a persistent and powerful temptation to Israel, by its very vigor clearly

indicating that this was a temptation Israel had not often resisted.

The origins and primary reasons for the rejection of the use of images for God in Israel remain obscure and have been heavily discussed.[36] The very associations of images with alien forms of religion in which the LORD had either no place at all or only a very subordinate one within a larger pantheon would clearly have strengthened the call to reject their use. It is likely also that iconographic imagery was closely linked to aspects of cultus involving fertility rituals, which the more carefully guarded features of the Israelite religious inheritance strongly opposed. Idols, therefore, had many unwelcome associations. To what extent an unapproved tradition in the use of idols, involving images among which even the LORD God could be represented, was present in ancient Israel has never become wholly clear from archaeological research. It seems likely that such representations existed, but that they may have been subjected to much official opposition and condemnation.

Certainly in the deuteronomic movement the prohibition of the use of images was one of the most keenly felt, and strongly argued, features pertaining to the Israelite tradition. It is also a feature in which the passionate condemnations of the deuteronomists have left the strongest imprint on the biblical literature. Accordingly, a special interest attaches to the explanations and theological justification for this rejection, set out here. Valuable as it is, it nonetheless falls short of providing a wholly convincing rationale for so major a feature of religion.

As to the speech itself we may confidently regard its balanced literary structure as indicative that it has been constructed as a unity. Throughout it displays the strong rhetorical style that is so characteristic of the deuteronomists. This, in itself, provides evidence that behind the book of Deuteronomy stands a

35. For the deuteronomic background of covenant terminology, see L. Perlitt, *Bundestheologie im Alten Testament,* WMANT 36 (Neukirchen-Vluyn: Neukirchener Verlag, 1969); D. J. McCarthy, *Old Testament Covenant: A Survey of Current Opinions* (Oxford: Blackwell, 1972); D. R. Hillers, *Covenant: The History of a Biblical Idea* (Baltimore: Johns Hopkins University Press, 1969); E. W. Nicholson, *God and His People: Covenant and Theology in the Old Testament* (Oxford: Oxford University Press, 1986).

36. W. Zimmerli, "Das Zweite Gebot," *Gottes Offenbarung. Gesammelte Aufsätze,* Theologische Bücherei 19 (Munich: Kaiser Verlag, 1963) 234-48.

well-established and effective preaching style that must have become part of an intense preaching and didactic activity within the community.

4:1-8. The opening part of the address declares that what Moses presented to the people consisted of "statutes and ordinances." These key terms used in legal administration are further defined in v. 8 as constituting תורה (*tôrâ*).[37] This term, which has familiarly entered into the English-language biblical tradition, more widely denotes "instruction" or "direction." Clearly it includes laws, but much else besides. It was an appropriate term by which to describe cultic instruction, but it could also be used to describe moral direction. It cannot have been a distinctive neologism on the part of the deuteronomists, but their use of it, particularly to describe the varied contents of Moses' teaching, undoubtedly raised its importance for the development of Israel's religious life. Taken as a description of the material set out in the book of Deuteronomy, it can helpfully be described as "polity,"[38] since what is set out covers a great deal of direction for the constitutional structure of Israel as a national community.

The importance of this comprehensive designation of the divine revelation as Torah cannot easily be overestimated. No other requirement, whether passed as a royal edict, imposed as a local priestly convention, or revealed through a prophet could displace it or override it. It offered a categorical rule of life. At the same time, this comprehensiveness, expressed through its being linked with other, more diverse titles of a predominantly legal character, asserted that it carried an all-sufficient authority. It was a rule of life, controlling public behavior as well as religious practice and political affairs. Taken as a whole it offered a guidebook for education and contained a wisdom that established life goals and guidelines for all human living. To some extent, its all-encompassing role as a direction for human life is modified and limited by its being presented as the conditions

of a covenant between Israel and God, but it nevertheless remains both a human document and a national one.[39]

Here, as repeatedly in the book, we encounter a strong emphasis on the various psychological aspects relating to religious loyalty and spiritual sincerity. So there are repeated exhortations concerning the commandments to "watch . . . do not forget . . . nor let them slip from your mind." This is combined with a strong emphasis on the inner psychological dimension of obedience. The people must not "become complacent" or "act corruptly" (i.e., be guilty of self-delusion, v. 25).

4:9-14. In these verses, the author presupposes that the reader is fully familiar with the events that took place on Mt. Horeb and are recorded in Exodus 19–20. He expects the reader to know this story well and to have reflected upon it, taking full cognizance of the impressive awesomeness of the events that occurred.

Through skillful literary artistry, the author brings into unity three distinct generations of Israelites: "You once stood before the LORD your God at Horeb." However, the adults of the first generation had died in the wilderness, and a new generation now stood poised to enter the land. Yet this community, too, is the author's backward projection into the past, since he is wholly mindful of the readers and hearers whom he now addresses. All three generations are nevertheless one people who constitute "all Israel," united through their generations. From within this unity, Moses still speaks to the present generation.

The nature of the "fire" (vv. 11-12) on Mt. Horeb has provided few useful clues to the original location of the mountain or its geological character. It is only since early Christian times that its identification with Jebel Musa, the highest mountain of the Sinai peninsula, has been firmly claimed. Other possibilities for a location closer to the oasis of Kadesh, and even more distant ones, have been canvassed in an effort to defend the interpretation of the "fire" on the mountain as a manifestation of volcanic activity. Yet this latter claim would carry the entire episode

37. See B. Lindars, "Torah in Deuteronomy," in *Words and Meanings: Essays Presented to David Winton Thomas,* ed. P. R. Ackroyd and B. Lindars (Cambridge: Cambridge University Presss, 1968) 117-36; G. Braulik, "Die Ausdrücke für 'Gesetz' im Buch Deuteronomium," *Studien zur Theologie des Deuteronomiums,* Stuttgarter Biblische Aufsatzbände 2 (Stuttgart: Katholisches Bibelwerk, 1988) 11-38.
38. S. Dean McBride, "Polity of the Covenant People: The Book of Deuteronomy," *Int* 41 (1987) 229-44.

39. G. Braulik, "Deuteronomy and Human Rights," in *The Theology of Deuteronomy: Collected Essays of Georg Braulik, O.S.B.,* trans. Ulrika Lindblad, Bibal Collected Essays 2 (N. Richland Hills, Tex.: Bibal, 1994) 131-50.

much too far to the east to be a convincing alternative. The theophany tradition that was so central to the Israelite recollection of the significance of the mountain has undoubtedly woven together various images.[40] Some of these appear to be natural phenomena such as storms and volcanic activity, but features of a sanctuary, with its altar fire burning, have been woven into the tradition as well. So, by itself, the fire imagery, which was in any case a widely established feature of a divine presence, enables us to determine little at all about the original location of the holy mountain.

4:15-20. The strong polemic against idolatry in these verses proceeds to deal with the central theme of the speech as a whole. The temptation posed by the sanctuary at Baal-peor has rendered it necessary. It concerns the vital necessity of maintaining the second commandment, prohibiting any Israelite from using an image as a focus for worship. From within the context of the Ten Commandments, this second commandment (5:8-10) presumes that such an image would be some form of the representation of the LORD God, since to worship any other deity alongside the LORD was already precluded. In reality, however, it seems probable that the subjects covered by the first two commandments could readily become intertwined.

The reference in v. 17 to the likeness of any human or animal form greatly extends the prohibition to cover creatures that could be understood as consorts, or servants, of the LORD God. In general, in the ancient Near East deities were conceived of as being grouped into pantheons in which a number of deities were placed in a certain order and were themselves pictured as being surrounded by a number of lesser deities and heavenly servants, some with human form and some with part-human or animal form. The world of the gods was portrayed as comparable to the earthly world, but populated by a mixture of beings.

Alongside the representations of human-like and animal-like beings existed many stylized symbols that were also thought to possess divine power, or at least to make such

power accessible. Prominent among these were portrayals of the sun and the moon and other heavenly bodies (v. 19). So an "image" could take many forms, and even the biblical narrative tradition contained recollections of the use of symbolic artifacts, used in the Jerusalem Temple as symbols of special potency (1 Kgs 6:23-36). The prophet Ezekiel's descriptions of bizarre imagery in the very heart of the Jerusalem Temple reveal how complex such symbolism could become (Ezek 8:5, 10). More important, the repeated condemnations of it in prophecy make plain that the use of such symbolism, what each symbol was thought to mean or convey, and whether it was acceptable within the Israelite tradition of worship were all highly contested issues. It would certainly appear that the deuteronomic authors, and the exilic age more generally, marked a period when a much more stringent interpretation of the second commandment became strenuously advocated.

The polemic set out here, that Israel heard a voice but saw no form of deity when the LORD God was revealed as being present at Mt. Horeb (v. 15), does little to clarify the reasons why such a prohibition arose in Israel and why it was felt to carry such immense importance. From a practical perspective, however, it is not difficult to see why, with the deuteronomists and the period of the exilic age, the issue had become a major one. If Israel were to retain any clear uniformity and identity within its religious tradition, then the use of unrestrained and uncontrolled iconography of any form of deity whatsoever existed as a major threat. Images could mean almost anything and could readily be associated with more than one deity, with such bewildering lack of positive control or integrity that their use could not be tolerated at all. Indeed, it seems highly probable that it was the recognition that this was already the situation for many Israelites that made the intensity of the deuteronomic polemic so necessary. Without the rejection of the plethora of images and symbols that had become commonplace, the deuteronomists saw that Israel's religious tradition would simply disintegrate. (See Reflections at 4:21-43.)

---

40. The development of such a tradition from a variety of traditional features is proposed by Jörg Jeremias, *Theophanie, Die Geschichte einer alttestamentlichen Gattung,* WMANT 10 (Neukirchen-Vluyn: Neukirchener Verlag, 1965).

Deuteronomy 4:21-43, A Warning Against Complacency

COMMENTARY

4:21-31. The second part of Moses' speech begins in these verses and provides a passage that both develops the theme of the divine fire and combines it with a further warning concerning the threat posed by idolatry. It strengthens the notion of God's consistent and implacable hostility to any form of disobedience against the commandments. The LORD is a devouring fire and a deity whose will cannot be flouted or thwarted. Proof of this fact is found in the tradition that even Moses could fall victim to the divine anger, not on his own account but on account of the faithlessness of the disobedient generation who had perished in the wilderness. They represented a perpetual example, whose misfortune and punishment existed as a warning for all the later generations of Israelites.

Verse 26 adopts the legal formula of summoning heaven and earth as witnesses, since God has no peer among human beings to act as witnesses to the veracity of the divine revelation. Since the summoning of witnesses was a prominent feature of the form of ancient Near Eastern vassal treaties, it could well be that it is on the analogy of such a political-legal formulation that this deuteronomic usage has been based. Yet even this is not a necessary conclusion, since the role of witnesses in lawsuits was familiar enough to the deuteronomists; more important, it was very familiar to every Israelite, so that the employment of such a mode of address would have been readily understood.

The threat voiced in v. 27 that God's punishment for disobedience would take the form of the people's being dispersed among the nations points strongly in the direction of a late origin for this speech, almost certainly after the disasters of 598 and 587 BCE had taken place. As a specific threat, however, it is in line with the deuteronomic concern with the land.

Disobedience to God's covenant and its commandments would result in failure to enjoy life in the promised land. Moses himself is made the prime example of this, although in his case it was not as a consequence of his personal disobedience, but that of his contemporaries. He was debarred from enjoying entry in the land, with all its fruits, on account of the disobedience and unbelief of others. Now the message is spelled out very clearly that failure to respond fully to God's basic demands by showing unswerving loyalty and rejecting any form of idolatry would result in punishment and expulsion from the land. This was clearly the fate that had already befallen some in Israel, whose loss was already known to the readers of Deuteronomy (v. 27).

In this context, it is important to recognize that the concept of "exile among the nations" is already, in this deuteronomic address, beginning to take on a more comprehensive and rounded form as a doctrine of a scattering that could become a long-term condition. Dispersal among the nations was assuming the status of becoming the major threat to the entire nation.

The large-scale deportations to Babylon in 598 and 587 BCE, which already followed even larger mass deportations perpetrated by the Assyrians after the fall of Samaria in 722 BCE, had generated a picture of all Israel effectively returning to the "wilderness." There is, however, an important message of hope set out in vv. 29-31, with its assurance that, even there, God would not abandon them (cf. 1 Kgs 8:45).

4:32-43. The final section of this address in vv. 32-40 returns to the theme of the covenant between God and Israel. It is couched in the heavily rhetorical form that characterizes much of the deuteronomic writing, effectively demonstrating that much of the material in the introduction to the law code was spoken before it came to be written down. The use of rhetorical questions ("For ask now about former ages," v. 32), the emphasis on all the manifestations of God's presence and power ("by trials, by signs, by wonders," v. 34), and the identification of the contemporary hearers of the deuteronomic address with the first generation that had witnessed God's action

("Before your very eyes") all bear the marks of skilled preachers and persuaders.

The reference in v. 37 to the claim that God "loved your ancestors" reveals the interesting manner in which the deuteronomic authors treat the earlier patriarchal period. So far as its historical details are concerned, these writers offer little by way of specific references to either the persons or the events recounted in the book of Genesis. It is not, however, a period that had little meaning for Israel, since it is presented as one in which a continued and purposeful providence was manifested.

The concluding section raises more strikingly than anywhere else in the deuteronomic literature the question of the full extent of the conditional element in Israel's covenant relationship with God. All the rhetoric and warnings are based on the dangers Israel faced and the possibility that disobedience would bring a terrible outburst of the divine wrath and a permanent scattering among the nations. Yet the reflection on this possibility in vv. 37-40 shrinks from this ultimate conclusion without giving a final verdict. All the passion and rhetoric the deuteronomists can call to their aid is directed toward warding off such a terrible threat.

Could the covenant ultimately be broken off permanently and forever on God's side because of the people's disobedience? No answer is given, and in any case it was wholly in line with the deuteronomic theology that it would be events themselves, not theological theorizing, that decided the issue. So far as the present was concerned, all was not yet lost. The land could be held, the exiles could return to their former homeland, and a new nation could arise from the ashes of the old.

A brief note is inserted in vv. 41-43 concerning the establishing of cities of refuge east of the river Jordan. This prepares the way for the next major section, which introduces the primary commandments of the covenant between God and Israel. It has been placed here to complete the details of the arrangements made by Israel for life under the law and in order to maintain the claim to territory east of the Jordan. The establishing of cities of refuge to which a person accused of murder could flee to avoid peremptory vengeance is dealt with in 19:1-10, where the manner of their functioning is more fully explained; but it is not made clear that three of the cities of refuge were to be located east of the Jordan, nor is the precise identification of these sites clarified.

It was obviously important to maintain the jurisdiction of Israelite law across its entire territory, in much the same manner that it was important to provide suitable opportunity for Israelite worship throughout its entire land. For that reason, as a kind of preparation for the further declaration of the divine law (which is made in v. 44), the narrator has recognized that, in upholding Israel's claim to possess territory across the Jordan, the necessary facilities for the proper administration of this claim had to be provided. So this list has been introduced at this point. The names of the cities concerned are in agreement with those mentioned in Josh 20:8, which almost certainly provides the source of the author's information.

To the uninitiated reader, the inclusion of the list makes an awkward interruption of the text, but the reasoning that underlies it is a carefully considered one. The sign and "proof" of Israel's claim to territory was that the divine law was upheld and authoritative there. In similar fashion, Mesopotamian rulers set up tablets of law in order to demonstrate the system of justice that applied as "the law of the land." For Israel's law to be applicable required that the authority for its administration was fully in place. Accordingly, the narrator explains that this had been done as soon as Israel had opportunity to act.

REFLECTIONS

The theological perceptiveness and depth of this great speech ascribed to Moses undoubtedly represent a classical exposition of the deuteronomists' skill and artistry. Their tools are the tools of rhetoric, and their aim is to persuade the reader that faith in God and the scrupulous avoidance of all idolatry are wholly desirable and beneficial goals in life. So they set about imparting to their readers a renewed sense of who they really are and what dangers are currently facing them. Yet this is achieved by identifying the present readership with a generation that had long since passed away. They can even appeal to present readers to believe that they actually witnessed some of the events they can only have known as stories and names from a distant past.

Even more startling, they are shown to be waiting to cross over the Jordan and to begin life as a nation—an event that even their most distantly and carefully remembered forebears would not have experienced directly. Yet, in some sense, through the power of the spoken and written word, the past lives again for them, since they can find in it the key to their own situation. The richness of the land encourages them to believe the word of God and take possession of the land; yet, the sanctuary of Baal-peor and the temptations of idolatry raise a sinister threat to the enjoyment of the land.

The weapon by which the folly of idolatry is countered is an appeal to historical events and to the absurdity of idolatry. Since God's glory and power had been revealed on Mt. Horeb, then an image made of stone or wood could convey nothing of the true majesty of God. It was more appropriate and meaningful to recall the unimaginable glory of fire and smoke filling the heavens than to suppose that a man-made artifact could conjure up divine power.

For the modern reader, the question of idolatry appears to pose no threat at all, if it is viewed simply in terms of using visual aids to conjure up images and memories of God and the divine power. Even Paul in the Epistle to the Colossians interprets idolatry in terms closer to the tenth, rather than the second, commandment when he describes its error as that of covetousness (Col 3:5). For the biblical tradition, the intensity of opposition to idolatry appears to lie in its pretentiousness of claiming that God can be manipulated and used to serve some desirable human goal. It turns God into an object and makes human beings the subject who can conjure up divine power to suit themselves. Over against this the biblical presentation, mediated through storytelling and metaphor, presents God as the subject who always finds us and calls us out of a darkness that we cannot penetrate. The very domain of God is that of impenetrable fire that we cannot enter and explore. The most terrible blasphemy is to believe that God can be kept "in one's pocket." To suppose that we can describe God or present a portrait of divinity is to lose the biblical sense that only the verbal images of fire and light convey insight of the truth about God. When we think that we can see something more than this, we begin to deceive ourselves.

For the modern world, the effective opposite to a religious interpretation of life would appear to be a secular one. An image of one god is no more and no less meaningful than an image of any other. Some may simply appear more beautiful and elegant than others. There is, nonetheless, a salutary warning in the biblical shrinking away from idolatry that demands serious consideration. Religious faith has immense power, and when such faith is misdirected or misrepresented, then quite fearful consequences can ensue. So often the effective opposite of real faith in a real God appears to be a distorted and defective search for images of a false deity. Bogus religions are with us still in abundance, flourishing in the very tolerance the deuteronomic authors would have rejected. By losing awareness of the dimension of transcendence and mystery that must clothe any language we employ to describe the Creator and Sovereign of the universe, the very universe itself becomes trivialized and the majesty of life is brought into contempt.

DEUTERONOMY 4:44–5:5, INTRODUCTION TO THE COVENANT LAW

COMMENTARY

The narrative introduction in 4:44-49 prepares for the disclosure of the divine law that is to be the hallmark of the covenant relationship between God and Israel. The law proper is then prepared for by a speech of Moses couched in the first person in 5:1-5. This speech adds the personal authority of Moses to the law and explains the time and circumstances of its revelation to the people. The law itself, in the form of the Ten Commandments, then follows in 5:6-21. These commandments are formulated as the direct speech of God, adding a yet higher level of authority to them as the unmistakable demand placed upon Israel as the people of the LORD God.

The addresses from Moses that follow the disclosure of these commandments in 5:22–11:32 serve as a means of emphasizing their importance, warning of the dangers and temptations of neglecting or disregarding them, and adding further exhortations to observe them. The law code that follows in 12:1–26:19 then serves as a fuller elaboration and explication of these basic Ten Commandments. So the book of Deuteronomy itself is presented as an ellipse with its focus on two collections of law. The first of these is brief, sharply declaratory in form, and repeats, with minor variations, the list of commandments the reader of the books of Genesis–Numbers will already be familiar with from Exod 20:2-17. Moses himself refers to such an earlier disclosure in 5:4-5.

However, this sense of an elliptical structure with two separate law collections is more apparent than real, and it is evident that the deuteronomic authors did not intend to imply that there were two separate "covenant" law codes; nor did they in any way recognize or assume this to be the case. God's covenant law was one law. The fundamental and primary declaration of that was the Decalogue of Deut 5:6-21. The law code of chaps. 12–26, even though it is formulated very differently, is viewed as an explication and commentary of the essential commandments of 5:6-21. It is regrettable that, in attempting to unravel the literary sequence by which the component elements of Deuteronomy were composed and brought together, many scholars assumed that the "original" law of Deuteronomy was that of chaps. 12–26 and that the introduction of the Ten Commandments into chap. 5 was a secondary development from a literary point of view. This was claimed even when it was recognized that the Ten Commandments were written earlier than the laws of chaps. 12–26 and were initially formed as an independent collection.

However, it remains clear from the Mosaic exhortations of 5:22–11:32 that the Ten Commandments stand at the head of all that the deuteronomic authors understood by the concept of God's covenant law. The more detailed collections of regulations and case law collected into the code of chaps. 12–26 appear as an elaboration of this primary law, and actually bear significant indications that they owe much of their own structure and order to the desire to maintain this. (The connection between the Ten Commandments and the order of the law code of chaps. 12–26 is dealt with more fully in the Commentary on 12:1-28.)

4:44-49. In the light of these considerations, the transitional introduction to the Ten Commandments, which begins in v. 44, serves to bind the whole series together. It is, then, not simply the preamble to the Ten Commandments, but to the whole collection of 4:44–26:32. While it would be overly hasty to assume that this large literary unit ever existed in precisely its present form and textual content, nevertheless it is reasonable to infer that it provides us with the best guide to what the "original" shape of Deuteronomy was. Even when we accept that many expansions have been introduced into this, it offers a reasonable guide to the core issues that shaped the deuteronomic movement.

The opening declaration in vv. 44-45 offers us the fullest description of how the deuteronomic authors themselves understood their literary work. It is especially noteworthy in view of the fact that much of the deuteronomic literature consists of narrative, as we have already encountered, and, in chaps. 6–11, of hortatory speeches. Yet here the heart of the deuteronomic writing is described as "instruction" (תורה *tôrâ*), which consists of "decrees" (עדת *ʿēdōt*), "statutes" (משפטים *mišpāṭîm*), and "ordinances" (חקים *ḥuqqîm*). These are all predominantly legal terms, although it is difficult to defend the claim that they had previously pertained only to very precisely defined areas of legal and administrative affairs. In any case, we must ultimately be guided by the actual content of the deuteronomic writing, which contains many laws, but also much in the way of religious directives for worship, besides some fundamental constitutional matters covering kingship, military service, and even family customs relating to marriage settlements. Overall the material is comprehensive in scope and was obviously intended to be so.

Furthermore, since the Ten Commandments form a primary formulation of demands that are not in the strictest sense laws at all, we sense that they were aimed at achieving a maximal level of coverage. All life is to be brought under the umbrella of God's authority and to conform to a call for righteous living. God's covenant touches every area of life and reaches into every home and every corner of daily activity. So it was appropriate that the opening declaration concerning God's law should make it abundantly clear that no other law stood above that which God has given. So there is a transcendent, otherworldly dimension to God's law, even though it is wholly directed toward very practical, this-worldly affairs. It sanctifies everyday life by showing that every activity engages human life with responsibilities and demands that fall under the designation of "holy." This is what it means for Israel to be a holy people.

Verses 46-49 then simply recapitulate the outline story of the situation in which Israel found itself when Moses declared to them, for a second time, the demands of the covenant law first given on Mt. Horeb. At first appearance, such a summary may appear repetitive, as also does the strong affirmation that it was a law mediated through the person of Moses. Both the situation and the name of the great leader, however, were vital for the entire deuteronomic claim that this was a binding law for all Israel. The miscellany and variety of traditions that had at one time characterized the different tribal and regional communities of Israel were now emphatically combined into one.

Indeed, the claim to unity—one God, one land, one people, one law—was a vital and indispensable feature of what the authors of Deuteronomy were striving for. The opposite threat was not simply disunity, although this was obvious, but the realization that disunity would inevitably lead to diversity, disintegration, and death—the death of Israel among the nations once its belief in its own nationhood had been eroded to the point of emptiness. Memories of Israel's past were not a luxury to be savored in quiet contemplation but a reality to be seized and held on to as the very lifeblood through which Israel could survive as a people. So the deuteronomic rhetoric is not a piece of cosmetic artistry, but a determined effort to hold on to the very core of what it meant to be Israel.

5:1-5. The declaration concerning the covenant made on Mt. Horeb makes plain that the commandments that constitute the heart of God's law belong inseparably to that covenant. So it is especially affirmed that this was not simply a reassertion of an ancient covenant made with Israel's ancestors (v. 2), but that it is central to the birthplace of the nation on Mt. Horeb. The covenant, therefore, was binding upon the entire nation and was inseparable from its religious commitment to the Lord as God. There could be no effective retention of a faith commitment to the LORD as God that did not, in the very nature of that commitment, include as a central feature the recognition of the Ten Commandments and the necessity of their observance. So faith and morality belonged together, as did deliverance (from Egyptian slavery) and law (embodied in the commandments). Freedom without law would be no freedom at all.

REFLECTIONS

The situation the deuteronomists saw themselves addressing highlights the special relevance of their work. They were calling upon their readers to think back to first principles in order to deal adequately with a new and threatening era, one in which disaster had succeeded disaster and the surviving remnant of Israel was facing the dissolution of the very institutions that had held it together. Because of the threat to the Davidic monarchy and the prospect that even the Temple and its priesthood would not be forever available to give shape and structure to life, Israel was facing a new, and more perilous, Jordan crossing in which dispersion among the nations was a serious threat. Only by reclaiming the central truths concerning the LORD as God, the covenant of Horeb, and the fundamental commandments that it presented could the nation's life be held together.

The political and historical consequences of this had become terrifyingly evident by the time the deuteronomic movement took hold. That movement had striven to recover the unity and "soul" of the nation by looking back to its beginnings. Unity was now to be sought, not in the institutions of kings and priests, but in the fundamentals of law, justice, and family life. So what is now unfolded in this remarkable presentation of the law of the covenant given to Israel by Moses on Mt. Horeb is a carefully considered judgment concerning everything that was deemed essential for Israel to be, and to remain, Israel.

The picture given of Moses "standing between the LORD and you" (5:5) once again bridges the gap of the generations. By this powerful rhetorical device, the figure of Moses once again confronts a new generation with his disclosure of the voice of God. Such an assertion does not correspond to any one specific incident recorded in the earlier narratives in which Moses acted as mediator between the people and God. In the earlier reports, the leader had ascended the mountain, and only seventy elders had been permitted to accompany him as representatives of the people (Exodus 24:1). However, it is the overall portrayal of Moses as the indispensable mediator who could interpret the will of God that forms the essential basis of the claim that Moses stood between them and God. So it is not simply in the narrow historical sense that Moses acted as go-between for every man, woman, and child within Israel. In a wider, theological and figurative sense, Moses was the mediator without whom the nation could not have come to birth and without whose words it could not survive. Once again the ordinary mass of human beings who constituted the community of Israel are portrayed in a less than flattering manner. They are "afraid because of the fire" (5:5); yet Moses dare not be afraid, since his negotiating between the LORD and the people is vital for their existence.

The role of Moses as mediator between God and human beings may suggest to Christian readers a similar role of Jesus. For instance, the Gospel of Matthew, with the five major discourses of Jesus, may reflect the Evangelist's view of Jesus as a new Moses offering a new Torah that fulfills the old.

DEUTERONOMY 5:6-21, THE TEN COMMANDMENTS: THE COVENANT RULE

OVERVIEW

In a quite fundamental way, the Ten Commandments dominate the book of Deuter- onomy, as they have tended to dominate popular perceptions of the entire Hebrew

Bible.[41] They represent law in a very basic sense, even though they are not laws in a technical and formal manner. Moreover, their very dominance has generally been found to lie in the fact that they represent a form of "higher law" that stands behind and above all human systems of law.

However, from a strictly literary perspective they constitute simply one series, or collection, of laws presented as having been given at Mt. Horeb (Mt. Sinai in the Exod 20:2-17 account). Since a large part of the Pentateuch from Exod 19:1 to Deut 34:12 consists of a wide variety of collections of laws and regulations, one might have expected that the Ten Commandments would simply be submerged within this larger framework. Yet, this is not so. By their presentation in the foremost experience of revelation on the mountain (Exodus 20) and their repetition on the eve of the entry into the land (Deuteronomy 5), they are placed in positions of pre-eminence. These commandments possess an importance above and beyond that of other laws contained within the narrative. It is a recognition of this importance in Jewish and Christian tradition that has set them apart as deserving special attention and as being representative not simply of laws, but of principles, and even human rights, that still matter greatly to human society.

Certainly, from both a historical and a literary point of view, this series of Ten Commandments has raised many searching and complex questions.[42] The very fact of their being set out twice calls attention to them. All the more does this occasion surprise from a narrative structural perspective, in that their first expression in Exodus 20 fits awkwardly in a larger narrative setting in which the tablets upon which they were inscribed were destroyed. The second set of tablets (Exod 34:10-26) then contains a rather different series of laws, which are no longer ten in number.

However, it is the relationship between the list of commandments in Exod 20:2-17 and those in Deut 5:6-21 that calls for the closest examination. Essentially the commandments are the same, although the wording of some of them is rather different, and, in particular, the sabbath commandment in Exod 20:8-11 is noticeably longer and more elaborate. This commandment also shows a connection with, and a dependence on, the creation narrative of Gen 1:1–2:4a, which is of post-exilic date and is ascribed to the priestly (P) source. In seeking to defend the historical and literary priority of the Exodus 20 version of the commandments, therefore, scholars have found themselves compelled to accept that a number of later additions and elaborations have been made to it. In fact, to make such a defense at all has consistently called for recognition of an older, more basic form of the Ten Commandments, sometimes described as a Primary Decalogue.[43] All such concern to unravel the complex literary history of the Ten Commandments, and to defend a very early literary origin for them, probably in a rather different form, raises a host of questions that require separate consideration. Certainly, even from a purely literary perspective, the conclusion seems assured that the list of the commandments was inserted in the narrative of Exodus 20 at a late stage. The case for claiming that this version was the more original, therefore, must be regarded as very dubious.

We must proceed on the basic premise that the formulation of the Ten Commandments in Deut 5:6-21 remains their earliest literary presentation. Because of their importance, a further listing of them was brought forward to introduce them into Exodus 20 at a relatively late stage in the final formation of the Pentateuch. Certainly, these Ten Commandments are thoroughly in keeping with the aims, the tenor, and the literary techniques of the deuteronomists. Moreover, they represent for the deuteronomists the expression

---

41. The literature on the Ten Commandments is now very extensive. Among recent studies the following are particularly accessible and significant: E. Nielsen, *The Ten Commandments in New Perspective,* trans. D. J. Bourke, SBT second series 7 (London: SCM, 1968); J. J. Stamm and M. E. Andrew, *The Ten Commandments in Recent Research,* SBT second series 2 (London: SCM, 1967); Anthony Phillips, *Ancient Israel's Criminal Law: A New Approach to the Decalogue* (Oxford: Blackwell, 1970); Walter Harrelson, *The Ten Commandments and Human Rights,* OBT (Philadelphia: Fortress, 1980).

42. For the special importance of the Deuteronomy 5 version of the Decalogue, see N. Lohfink, "The Decalogue in Deuteronomy 5," in *Theology of the Pentateuch: Themes of the Priestly Narrative and Deuteronomy,* trans. Linda M. Maloney (Edinburgh: T. & T. Clark, 1994) 248-64.

43. Lohfink ("The Decalogue in Deuteronomy 5," 248), while setting aside the case for a more primitive list of ten prohibitions, suggests that the present series may have arisen as an expansion of the sabbath commandment, thereby effectively reversing the usual order of literary growth. Since it is certain that the formulation of the Ten Commandments has made use of earlier material, it would appear of limited value to speculate of what form such a list may have taken and what it may, or may not, have included.

of the most basic demands imposed on Israel by God's covenant made on Mt. Horeb. They represent Torah in a manner that no other brief summary account can possibly rival. The remainder of the Torah is, in effect, simply an elaboration and enlargement of these basic commands.

All of these considerations do not of themselves tell us about the actual date of origin of the Ten Commandments, nor do they imply that they are not fundamentally the work of Moses. Yet they are the work of Moses in essentially the same sense and with the same literary and historical provisos that pertain to the book of Deuteronomy as a whole. We can then more directly address the question of the literary origin of this vitally significant ethical masterpiece.

The Date of Origin of the Ten Commandments. To a number of scholars, it has appeared that the literary formulation of the Ten Commandments can be of no earlier date than the remainder of Deuteronomy and should almost certainly be ascribed to a relatively late period in the history of Israel under the monarchy. It may even be later still. To others it has appeared a highly probable, if not virtually certain, conclusion that these commandments represent the most clearly attested legacy of the work of Moses. If they are not to be credited to so great a figure, then who else could lay claim to a work of such eminent ethical value and significance?

Yet, when focused in sharper detail, two such contrasting conclusions are merely reflections of larger questions that can be answered with more clarity and confidence. They show that the original question is really rather inadequately formulated and that we are called upon to answer broader issues in order to recognize this.

On one side, we can define the question simply in terms of asking at what stage the verbal written list of Ten Commandments, as we now possess them in Deut 5:6-21, was made. The answer to this would seem to be that it was made either contemporaneously with, or perhaps somewhat earlier than, the remainder of Deut 4:44–26:19. It certainly appears likely that such a list of Ten Commandments was composed earlier as an independent document, and some such list may have existed from a very early period of

Israel's history. To make such a deduction, however, is inevitably a speculative proceeding, and it has usually carried with it the belief that the original form was briefer and probably consisted simply of ten prohibitions, all with a similar formal structure.

There seems little point in rigorously pursuing such historical speculations, however, since they effectively form a subject area of their own and lead to no certain results. It is sufficient to note that we have no firm support outside the present text for claiming a very early date for the written Ten Commandments.

On the other side exists the more directly ethical, and not purely literary, question concerning the stage at which the demands now contained in these individual commandments became binding upon Israel. This is to ask at what period these basic commandments, and the conduct they seek to regulate, became formative features of Israel's faith, fundamental to its recognition of the LORD as the God who had made a covenant with Israel as a people.

The answer to this would certainly carry us much further back and bring us closer to the person and work of Moses. What the formulation of these Ten Commandments has endeavored to achieve is a focusing and clarifying of the most basic demands that belong to the worship of the LORD as God. They are not, therefore, a novel creation of the deuteronomists, introducing fresh moral ideas and demands. Rather, they are a bold and effective attempt to focus emphatically on certain fundamental features of faith in the LORD as God that had a long history.

When we ask about an era in which human beings first recognized the folly of wanton killing, unchecked theft, or carefree adultery, we look in vain for clear dates, for certain fundamental ethical demands belong inescapably to all human society. The ancient Near East amply attests the deep concern on the part of human communities to control, suppress, and punish violent and socially disruptive behavior. For millennia, in fact, it belonged to the protective role of the kin group to deal with such matters. The problems and issues the commandments deal with can then be seen to be of varying periods in their origin, many of them as old as human civilization. It is in their concern to deal with these problems in a fundamental and practical way that the commandments display their great originality. So we must face the fact that it is essentially the deuteronomists who have formulated this literary list of Ten Commandments in this unique fashion.

The Ten Commandments as Fundamental Teaching. The creative innovation brought by the Ten Commandments lies in bringing together a basic series of ten primary demands, in formulating them in a readily memorable fashion, and in highlighting their significance as basic to all human life, when it is to be lived "before God." Their originality lies not in their "discovery" of new ethical demands, but in their stress on the importance of these basic demands for human living.[44] They combine this emphasis with a simple listing technique devised for teaching purposes by using the number ten. So their importance lies not in the novelty of discovering new areas of life that needed to be controlled and regulated, since these belong to the human situation as such, but to a special emphasis that is focused on them.

Second, it is clearly of the utmost importance to the Ten Commandments as a comprehensive list that they combine duties to God and duties to fellow human beings. In a significant measure, it is this combination, making the recognition of a transcendent God the foundation for a respectful and truly moral concern for other human beings, that marks their distinctiveness. In effect, they recognize that the question of what duties exist toward other persons is also a question concerning who these other persons are. It recognizes that the answer lies in the fact that they, too, are children of God, deserving of the regard that derives from the createdness of all things and all people. So morality and moral obligation have a divine origin and meaning.

It has often been customary to draw attention to the negative aspects of the formulation of the commandments in that eight of the ten are set out as prohibitions: "You shall not. . . ." However, this is less significant than may at first glance appear. There is no real basis for the attempts that have sometimes been advocated for recasting all ten as original prohibitions. This is simply to rewrite the commandments—a hazardous proceeding! In any event, the subject areas covered were clearly of far greater importance than the tidiness of maintaining a consistent form. Furthermore, once the manner in which the extended law code of Deuteronomy 12–26 is recognized as being structured as an amplification of the Ten Commandments, then such a criticism becomes even more markedly misplaced. It depends on the conduct being dealt with whether a prohibition or an injunction is the most appropriate form for the commandment.

Form of the Commandments. The question of the form of the commandments has been much discussed, and only certain main features can be examined in detail. It is, as a foremost consideration, of great significance that they are presented as direct speech of God. It is otherwise almost always only prophets who adopt so bold a formula for their utterances. Yet, in the case of the commandments, this direct-speech formula accords fully with the religious dimension that pervades them all and gives to them their unique authority. Even to reduce them to the level of the speech of Moses would deprive them of some element of their remarkable authority. They belong unequivocally to the spiritual understanding and meaning of life. To recognize that these commandments are the voice of God is a paramount consideration.

The distinctive commandment form of address (usually called "apodeictic" from the pioneering study by A. Alt)[45] in which active prohibition, or demand, is expressed adds rhetorical vigor to this sense of authority and separates them from more familiar legal formulations—i.e., case laws (Alt, casuistic laws). That it represents a direct adaptation and shift from a form of clan (or family) instruction in which the familial head controlled the conduct of the kin group appears an unnecessary conclusion. Nonetheless, the point is important in showing that the direct apodeictic form was not a uniquely legal device, nor was it exclusive to a narrow pattern of teaching and authority. We must reaffirm that, essentially, form follows content, rather than dictates it.

44. E. Otto, *Theologische Ethik des Alten Testaments* (Stuttgart: W. Kohlhammer, 1994) 215-19, describes the Ten Commandments as presenting the sum of the divinely authorized and ordained ethic of the Hebrew Bible.

45. A. Alt, "The Origins of Israelite Law," in *Essays on Old Testament History and Religion*, trans. R. A. Wilson (Oxford: Blackwell, 1966) 79-132.

In similar fashion, the much explored attempt to bring fresh illumination to the form of the commandments by comparing them with ancient Near Eastern treaty formulations must be set aside as having little bearing on the understanding of the Decalogue. This is not to deny that such treaties may, more broadly, have exercised some literary influence on the deuteronomists. The commandments, in the form they now possess, make eminent sense in and for themselves as a major feature of the deuteronomic measures to ensure Israel's survival. Two centuries of painful history have served to shape and direct those measures.

A further issue relates to the number ten and to its function within the overall purpose of the list. Basically this may be held as a useful didactic device, almost certainly drawn from reference to the ten fingers of a person's hands. That such commandments were incised on tablets of stone and retained inside the sacred ark as a covenant document (31:9-13, 24-26) can at most be seen as a secondary concern to heighten their significance for Israel's faith, rather than as a feature that dictated their formulation. Their relative brevity can owe nothing to such lapidary preservation, since other Near Eastern law codes, inscribed on stone tablets, could be of considerable length and discursiveness.

We may conclude, in consequence, that studies of the distinctive form of the Ten Commandments, illuminating and extensive as they have been, should not lead us to attempt to regard the form as uniquely meaningful. Certainly it should not encourage us to attempt to redraft any of the commandments in an attempt to re-create a more original Primary Decalogue. Such attempts are too speculative to offer a serious basis for research. Since the issues covered by the commandments were of primary importance to society, it is evident that other attempts to deal with them would have been made.

Contents of the Ten Commandments. It is surprising, in view of the relative brevity of a list of a mere ten commandments, that uncertainty has existed on precisely how the division into ten separate commandments should be counted. Furthermore, in view of their exceptional significance, it is surprising that certain of them remain a little obscure as to their precise meaning and intent, notably in relation to the misuse of the divine name and the range of conduct covered by the prohibition against unlawful killing (murder, v. 17).

It has also been a matter of considerable concern that, precisely on account of their formulation as commandments, they lack any specific indication of what punishment is to be meted out to offenders. Since they are tied closely to the sense of a covenant relationship that exists between the LORD God and Israel, it could be assumed that exclusion from the covenant community would be the inevitable and appropriate punishment. Yet this is not spelled out, and the seriousness of the offenses dealt with must be held not to be of equal importance. In the case of the tenth commandment, which warns against covetousness, it is difficult to envisage any effective form of punishment. The attempt to elevate all ten of the commandments to cover capital crimes involving the death penalty must be set aside as highly implausible. We are left, then, with a list of commandments that deal with fundamental religious and social issues, some of which overlap with offenses for which specific legal action is called for.

The opening declaration of v. 6 unswervingly ties the commandments to the LORD God, who has delivered Israel out of the slavery of Egypt. Certainly the awareness of a commitment to God as a primary assumption permeates all the commandments. It is Israel's faith that must shape its conduct. From a historical perspective, this has frequently been seen as a limitation of the commandments, since they appear as eliciting a special demand from Israelites and Jews, and in a strictly formal sense are not necessarily applicable to all humankind. Yet, in historical retrospect and with minor adjustments (notably in connection with the sabbath), the commandments have readily been recognized as a universal human document. Their concern is for the welfare of human beings as such and for the harmony and good order of all human society. This does not claim for them a level of absolute authority, since too many issues are either left unclear or left out, for this to be possible. Nevertheless, they have been expounded and understood within both Judaism and Christianity as an essentially universal ethical document of immense value.

Deuteronomy 5:6-7, The First Commandment

COMMENTARY

The demand "You shall have no other gods before me" (the marginal note in the NRSV, suggesting "besides" instead of "before," is relevant) must be intended to preclude the acceptance of other gods alongside, and in addition to, the LORD. However, it could also imply "in preference to," which was undoubtedly important to the deuteronomic emphasis on the uniqueness and sovereignty of the LORD as God. It falls short of a strict monotheism, since it does not deny the existence of other deities. Since also it is addressed to Israelites ("you"), it leaves untouched the legitimacy of the worship of other gods by other peoples (cf. 4:28). Obviously this was an unclear area of polemic, and the commandment was directly aimed at achieving a pragmatic rejection of acceptance of other deities alongside the LORD in Israel, rather than attempting a more theoretical monotheism. In other features of the deuteronomic apologetic there is a more positive assertiveness in denying that other deities have any power to obstruct, or frustrate, the sovereign will of the LORD as God. (See Reflections at 5:21.)

Deuteronomy 5:8-10, The Second Commandment

COMMENTARY

The prohibition on the use of images returns to a subject that has already been dealt with polemically in the speech ascribed to Moses in 4:15-20. The assumption certainly appears to be that such images would be images of the LORD God, although elsewhere the rejection of all symbolic imagery as representative of divine powers is maintained. Iconographic symbolism of various kinds was effectively the norm in ancient Near Eastern religions so that the absolute rejection of them for the worship of the LORD in Israel is striking. All the more is this the case when we recognize that certain forms of iconography, especially the cherubim (cf. 1 Kgs 6:23-30), existed within the Jerusalem Temple itself. Clearly the dividing line between symbols was not easily drawn, and this becomes even more marked when we consider the use of various forms of geometric symbolism within worship. (See Reflections at 5:21.)

Deuteronomy 5:11, The Third Commandment

COMMENTARY

The reference to "the third and fourth generation of those who reject me" points to a deep sense of the solidarity of the extended family living within a single household. Four generations within one household was the maximum that was likely to be encountered.

The precise aim of the third commandment is more obscure in the precise range of activities that it sought to prohibit than might at first appear. The Hebrew specifically prohibits the invoking of God's name to what is "empty," "void," "false" (שׁוא *šāwʾ*). It could be construed as referring to false and deceitful oaths, or even a false image or idol. Most probably, however, it refers to the use of the divine name to back up a wide range of harmful or false utterances. These would have included magical utterances as well as deceitful oaths. Modern English versions have endeavored to show the wide range of harmful activities covered by offering a slight paraphrase of the Hebrew; e.g., GNB, "for evil purposes." While the Bible generally shows a deep concern with the threat of perjury in legal affairs, it is also conscious that the line between magic and religion was often difficult to define.

It should also be noted that the reference to "the name of the LORD your God" refers to God in the third person, although the commandments as a whole are the direct speech of God (hence, "my name" might have been expected). This feature, however, simply reflects that instructional material from teaching in the cultus, as well as in legal matters, has been secondarily incorporated into the commandment form. It is, in any case, not at all surprising that in a prohibition of this nature, it was advantageous to identify precisely the divine name that was not to be subjected to misuse. The name expressed the very reality and being of God, so that to misuse it or to trivialize its use was a serious affront to the very foundations on which the commandment form rested. (See Reflections at 5:21.)

Deuteronomy 5:12-15, The Fourth Commandment

COMMENTARY

In v. 12, the fourth commandment is the first of the two that abandon the prohibition form. It has been suggested, therefore, that it may have existed earlier in a form such as "You shall do no work on the sabbath day." Yet this would represent a far more fundamental change than might at first appear, since to keep the day "holy" (קדש *qādaš*) involved positive obligations of prayer and worship, rather than simple abstention from work. The parallel clause in Exod 20:8 reads "Remember [זכר *zākar*] the sabbath day to keep it holy," which occasions some surprise in view of the considerable emphasis the deuteronomic exhortations and admonitions place on "remembering" as a religious obligation.

The sabbath combines two features, making it likely that its observance was itself a combination of two elements of religious tradition. The first of these was the importance of reckoning time within a sacred calendar, so that the division of time into weeks, months, and years was seen as part of the sacred order of life (see Gen 1:14). The sabbath, therefore, was an especially "holy" day because it marked a basic temporal division of life and its holiness served to regulate the entire week. At the same time, the importance of rest and relaxation, especially in periods when work was a particularly heavy burden (cf. Exod 23:12; 34:21) served an important purpose for human well-being. So the necessity of granting rest to all creatures, even slaves and domestic animals, was important. Time and space both formed elements within the structure of life that had to be observed by confessing their holiness. Human beings did not create the order of time, but experienced it as something given and, therefore, to be accepted and consecrated.

It seems likely that the sabbath title was itself originally closely linked to the lunar cycle of the calendar, probably as the day of the full moon ("new moons and sabbaths"). Since this was linked to a seven-day periodic cycle, the use of the term has been extended to cover every seventh day, rather than only one within the lunar cycle.

The enlargement of the sabbath commandment in vv. 13-15 is noteworthy and indicative of the kind of expansion that has suggested that at least in this case the original wording was shorter. If this is true, it would serve to confirm a perspective corroborated elsewhere in the OT that this particular commandment was especially vulnerable to indifference and neglect. We may note that trading on the sabbath appears commonplace in the time of the prophet Amos (Amos 8:5) and that even the rigor of Nehemiah could not achieve the willing observance of sabbath, but that he had to be content with rendering it impossible for traders to enter Jerusalem on the sabbath (Neh 13:15-22). The aim of the expansion here is clearly to apply persuasion in order to encourage its effective observance, especially in granting sabbath rest as a concession to slaves (vv. 14-15). That it was ever customary to enforce it by imposing capital punishment (cf. Num 15:32-36) appears very unlikely. Once again, we can note the great importance the deuteronomists attached to rhetoric and the art of persuasion. (See Reflections at 5:21.)

Deuteronomy 5:16, The Fifth Commandment

COMMENTARY

The commandment to honor father and mother, like the preceding one, is couched in a positive form. Older legislation (cf Exod 21:15, 17) shows that the striking or cursing of a parent was treated with the utmost seriousness so that, if this commandment were to be recast into the negative prohibition form, it would greatly narrow the activities it sought to preclude. As it stands, the positive formulation was clearly of great significance in seeking to secure respect for parents in terms of obedience and seeking the overall welfare of the family unit over which the parents presided. Such a demand also possessed strong economic overtones, since the problems of old age and failing health could undoubtedly impose severe economic strains.

That this commandment, like the preceding one, has also been given a supplemental promissory extension ("that your days may be long") is a further instance of the recognition made by the commandments that it was impossible to legislate for a right attitude. The hope instead is to encourage that attitude through persuasion. Such an assurance concerning the attainment of a secure old age shows that the problems of aging were especially in view in the framing of the commandment.

The high profile given to the question of old age, and the strains and temptations that this could bring within a family unit, is marked out by its inclusion in the list of ten primary obligations. Expectations and calculations show that average life expectancy cannot have been very high in ancient Israel— certainly not in comparison with modern developed societies.[46] Yet a high infant mortality rate was a major feature of life for all ancient societies, and those who reached adulthood could clearly hope to reach a full span of years (see Psalm 90). That many such adults passed the point where they could usefully work may have provided a serious temptation for poverty-stricken households to exclude them from active participation in the household routine or even to expel them altogether. (See Reflections at 5:21.)

46. The problems in calculating life expectancy in ancient Israel are dealt with in H. W. Wolff, *Anthropology of the Old Testament*, trans. Margaret Kohl (London: SCM, 1973) 119-20.

Deuteronomy 5:17, The Sixth Commandment

COMMENTARY

The prohibition "You shall not kill [murder]" was clearly not intended to preclude necessary killing in time of war or capital punishment. Still less can it have had in mind questions relating to the slaughter of animals, although this was not a matter of complete indifference (cf. Gen 9:5-6). The Hebrew verb translated "murder" (רצח *rāṣaḥ*) is not the simple expression for any sort of killing, but relates to various forms of violent illegitimate acts of slaughter. Since there were clear laws dealing with homicide and the difficulties that could arise in regard to distinguishing it from accidental killing (cf. 17:8; Exod 21:12-14), it is evident that the translation "murder" must be rather inadequate in connection with this particular commandment. It was evidently designed to exclude various forms of wanton killing, but would appear particularly to envisage actions in which the normal legislative processes would be unlikely, or even powerless, to act.

This prohibition would relate directly to vengeance killing, for which a person accused of a serious crime was peremptorily punished without resort to investigation and a fair trial. It is evident that a custom of clan-based "blood revenge" was widely current in biblical times and proved difficult to eradicate. It is also noteworthy that the unjustified killing of a thief is made the subject of special legislative provision (see Exod 22:2-3). Clearly there were ways of indulging in wanton killing that slipped through the laws against homicide, and it is all such actions that are prohibited by this commandment. (See Reflections at 5:21.)

Deuteronomy 5:18, The Seventh Commandment

COMMENTARY

The prohibition against adultery raises once again the concern of the commandments to protect the family as a unit and to ensure the right of the paternal head of the household to the paternity of his children. This leaves open the question of whether the charge of adultery was limited to women, so that sexual promiscuity of adult males was tolerated (see the story of Judah's visit to a supposed prostitute in Genesis 38:1). Obviously the commandment, by itself, is not entirely clear on this point, making the supplementary laws dealing with such sexual matters in chaps. 22–23 of great importance. It is noteworthy that such sayings as Prov 30:20 recognize the difficulties of proving a woman's adulterous conduct and the danger posed by an unreasonably suspicious husband is dealt with in 22:13-21. Similarly, it is a feature of the biblical tradition that it retains the archaic provision for trial by testing in respect of a wife accused of infidelity (Num 5:11-31). (See Reflections at 5:21.)

Deuteronomy 5:19, The Eighth Commandment

COMMENTARY

The prohibition against theft occasions surprise on account of its inclusion in a series of commandments that, for the most part, relate to matters either beyond the regular competence of the law to deal with or to such matters that stood on the border between clear-cut offenses that the law could handle and those that were unclear or could easily be flouted. Obviously simple theft by itself could not have been considered a capital crime, and there is no reason for limiting the commandment to the kidnapping of persons, which would have been a capital offense (cf. Exod 21:16).

Undoubtedly the growth of prosperity in ancient Israel and the building of large and opulent households in a society in which many persons were gravely impoverished created major inequalities between the wealthy and the near destitute. The protection of property, therefore, became a matter of increasing prominence for the law to deal with, especially when matters of proof of ownership were difficult to establish. Clearly theft was often an occasion for unresolvable disputes and dissensions, which the intervention of third parties could not always be relied upon to settle (cf. Exod 22:9). Accordingly we find that such matters as the use of false weights (25:13-15) and the removal of territorial boundary markers (19:14) were forms of cheating and theft that ancient courts often found difficult to deal with for lack of satisfactory evidence. (See Reflections at 5:21.)

Deuteronomy 5:20, The Ninth Commandment

COMMENTARY

The offense of bearing false witness against another person primarily concerns perjury in a legal proceeding (Exod 23:1). The ease with which false acusations might be brought against an innocent person is well illustrated by the story of Naboth's vineyard (2 Kgs 21:16, esp. vv. 8-10). That such cases could include the leveling of capital charges against an enemy was clearly a major problem for ancient society. In many psalms, the complaint of the psalmist is that he or she is suffering as a result of malicious accusations and that only God can truly bring a verdict of innocence.

Not only could malevolent accusations of a very serious kind lead to the punishment, and even death, of the accused person, but it is also clear that a related problem existed in regard to the laws of evidence. Since major accusations required a minimum of two witnesses if they were to be upheld, it was clearly a great temptation for a plaintiff to secure the support of a person to act as a second witness and, in so doing, commit perjury (cf. the provision of 19:15-21). The person may have acted with some misguided feeling of trust, but would thereby undermine completely the protective procedures of the law.

Certainly the inclusion of this particular commandment further strengthens the broad recognition that the entire series of commandments was specially designed to support and back up the resources of the law, rather than to exist as an independent series of laws as such. They do not circumvent the normal juridical processes, and they were clearly not intended to do so. They were, however, fully conscious that the law was a fragile and limited instrument for the good order of society and that, for its effectiveness, it required a positive and law-respecting attitude on the part of the entire community. (See Reflections at 5:21.)

Deuteronomy 5:21, The Tenth Commandment

COMMENTARY

The injunction "Neither shall you covet" would appear to overlap with the eighth commandment, prohibiting theft, since the "vigorous desiring" that is denoted by coveting would undoubtedly include the nurturing of desires and the plotting of schemes whereby the property of a neighbor might become one's own. The weakness of the case for seeing a particularly strong and active intention behind the verb and the concern to recognize a more serious offense than mere desiring has led Anthony Phillips to suggest that this commandment entailed plotting to deprive an elder of his status.[47] Yet the argument for such an interpretation rests largely on a concern to defend the overall claim for the commandments that they relate to serious forms of criminal behavior. Once such an assumption is left aside, there is no difficulty in taking the command at its plain surface meaning. It is a prohibition against the harboring of a dangerous and selfish attitude of mind in which a wide variety of potential criminal actions could be nurtured. As such it is indicative of the deep attention given in the series of commandments as a whole to those broad issues of morality that extended beyond the law, but that the legal system was designed to serve.

There is much in Deuteronomy to indicate that it was addressed to a community for whom the implementation of the demands of the law was often weak and uncertain. The community, therefore, needed to ensure that it was not "lawless" in the larger sense that there was no regard for basic human rights and for protection from violence. The

47. Anthony Phillips, *Ancient Israel's Criminal Law: A New Approach to the Decalogue* (Oxford: Blackwell, 1970) 149-52.

extension of the list to include property belonging to a neighbor that might arouse covetous desires is quite possibly an expansion of what was originally a much briefer formulation. It is, nevertheless, surprising that it should include a wife among the property of another, even though the commandments already include a prohibition against adultery.

This commandment fulfills a valuable role in contributing to a wider understanding of the purpose of the series of Ten Commandments, which were to be learned as a part of basic education, rather than set out in a court of law. It shows that they cannot have been laws in the formal juridical sense. However much coveting could be recognized as a dangerous and undesirable attitude of mind, it was scarcely the kind of offense that could be made subject to legal action or redress. Moreover, the claim that has sometimes

been raised that the commandment ethic represents a rather negative ideal by failing to recognize the inwardness of true morality clearly cannot be sustained in this particular case. It is of special interest for the fuller understanding of the social development of ancient Israel that those commandments that deal with property appear to recognize most fully the weaknesses endemic to the legal processes available to the community. Ownership of goods and property, the protection of honest trading practices, and the restraint of exploitative commercial deals were all well recognized as immensely important benefits for the health and good order of the community. They were, at the same time, notoriously difficult areas to guard from abuse by the limited and haphazard legal processes available to ancient Israel.

REFLECTIONS

The Ten Commandments must be recognized as one of the great contributions the Hebrew Scriptures have made to humankind, certainly to the development of Western civilization. The Ten Commandments came into existence as a teaching aid, concerned with the moral education of a whole community. It is appropriate, therefore, that they be recognized as deliberately limiting their compass to a mere ten fundamental issues. The remarkable feature is that, in doing so, they nevertheless maintain an extraordinary comprehensiveness. The range of conduct they cover is extensive, and their breadth becomes all the more evident once the needless criticism that they are merely negative is set aside. If later generations developed a form of casuistry, seeking to keep the letter of the law but to deny its spirit and intention, then this was certainly never within the purview of those who compiled such a list.

Those who preserved the commandments were only too conscious that the law and its processes were vulnerable to abuse and could be treated as rather blunt instruments for attaining effective redress for wrongs suffered. Already by the time of Deuteronomy it was evident that many Israelites would be compelled to live under the jurisdiction of foreign powers, with all the limitations that this imposed and the unlikelihood of obtaining justice from well-established juridical systems. For much of their history, in fact, Jews have had to become self-regulating so far as many areas of conduct are concerned. Recognition of this necessity for all human beings is, to a significant degree, present in the Ten Commandments. "Morality is too important simply to be left to the law and its officers." Such at least would appear to be a major assumption undergirding the concern of the Ten Commandments.

It is regrettable that a misinformed apologetic has led to a misguided tendency to contrast the supposed externalism and supposed negativity of the Ten Commandments with the more emphatically inward and positive love orientation of the New Testament tradition. Clearly the Ten Commandments were not concerned to cover every possible area of social and ethical concern. Nor could they have done so. Their primary aim was to restrain abuses and to prevent the deficiencies of the authorized legislative system from destroying community life. This aim the commandments have clearly served very effectively to maintain.

It is a paramount feature of the Ten Commandments that they combine religious duties with those toward the family and the community more generally. In a secular, modern social context, it is not difficult to see that this appeal to an ultimate transcendent authority can cause problems. The commandments do not formally purport to be for all humankind but for Israel, and they might seem to lose a certain degree of their claim upon us when they are regarded simply as a series of demands imposed by an ancient God upon an ancient people. Yet to think in such terms is to misread the commandments.

The great value and historical importance of the Ten Commandments lie in their focus on certain fundamental issues that belong to the human condition. They recognize that the right ordering and protection of humans from abuse and exploitation are of the utmost importance to human survival and human happiness. Still today it becomes necessary to appeal to such fictive concepts as "natural law" and "natural justice" in order to protect the awareness that there is a measure of ultimate concern that belongs to the welfare of human beings. So even though the mode of appeal employed by the commandments seems to require modification and adaptation, the centrality of the issues with which they deal is unaffected. Whether we express such a feeling of ultimate demand in terms of "God says . . ." or "human dignity requires . . ." the issues remain quite fundamentally the same. Seen in the context of ancient Israel's life, the Ten Commandments can still be reflected upon profitably and seriously as one of the great ethical documents of humankind. They have proved to be a primary contribution made by the biblical tradition to the shaping of civilization.

DEUTERONOMY 5:22–11:32, MOSAIC EXHORTATIONS

Deuteronomy 5:22-33, The Request for a Mediator and the Authority of the Commandments

COMMENTARY

This section rounds off the preceding declaration of the Ten Commandments by reporting the manner of their reception by Israel. It then paves the way for the long series of exhortations and admonitions that form the main content of chaps. 6–9. There is a certain measure of ambivalence in the fact that vv. 22-27 reaffirm the fearful and awesome nature of the LORD as God. The fear-inspiring majesty that had been revealed on Mt. Horeb is now experienced afresh, once the commandments have been repeated. It is as though the commandments themselves are in some measure a manifestation of the presence of God. As the people hear once again the demands that are presented, by that

very experience, they encounter God afresh. All the traditional elements that constitute a theophany are again manifested here—fire, cloud, impenetrable darkness, and an awesome sound (thunder).

Taken as a whole, these features marvelously combine the sense of a genuine revelation with the inevitable hiddenness of God. The people have heard the divine voice again as the commandments have been repeated to them. They cannot doubt that God is present with them still through the divine law and that, even though they are now poised on the banks of the Jordan ready to enter the land, all the majesty and awe of the presence manifested on Mt. Horeb will accompany them. Where the law is read and heard, there God is truly present. God reveals both the majesty and the otherness that belong to the very essence of deity, and yet remains essentially hidden. God cannot be seen, touched, or defined, yet through the commandments given on Mt. Horeb the majesty of a divine otherness is felt and known.

A note of ambivalence colors the account of Israel's response to the giving of the commandments in vv. 22-27. The people are terrified at what they have felt and heard, so they turn again to Moses, asking that he act as mediator for them. Alongside this is the contrasting motif that it had been a unique and remarkable privilege for them to see God and still remain alive (vv. 24, 26). The two themes run in parallel and are not easily reconciled. It is in consequence of this that many interpreters have seen here the work of an editor who has expanded upon the original narrative in the same vein that runs through chap. 4. However the text has been brought to its present shape, there is a necessary complementarity about the two themes. God is the holy One who inspires fear and dread, manifesting a reality that cannot be grasped. Yet such fear and dread are themselves uplifting and irresistibly fascinating. Israel had enjoyed a unique privilege in encountering God. The enduring legacy of that encounter was that the Israelites could live life at a new level through their reception of, and obedience to, the divine commandments.

The importance of the role of Moses as mediator continues to dominate chaps. 6–9. There are, however, certain related themes needing to be dealt with. Since the commandments are presented as having been inscribed on two stone tablets (v. 22), written by the very hand of God and received by Moses, their divine origin could not be stated more forcibly. They are of God, and it becomes fundamental to their role and effectiveness that this divine origin should be permanently recognized.

On account of this divine origin, they required no list of specific punishments for disobedience, since it is fundamental to the deuteronomic perspective that Israel's very relationship to God would be placed in jeopardy were Israel to disobey these commandments. Only in the list of blessings and curses set out in the epilogue to the book as a whole in chaps. 27–30 is there an attempt to focus on the question of what would happen to Israel were it to fail to live up to its high calling. Through and through Israel's relationship to God is seen as conditional. Yet, only when the terms of blessing and cursing are spelled out in detail do the full consequences and risks of this conditional status become explicit.

Throughout the structure of the book, therefore, there is a certain momentum that gathers strength, in which the possibility of disaster becomes ever more openly recognized. But this does not extinguish the element of hope. Rather, it serves to reinforce it. Hope is not a predestined future from which Israel cannot escape. Rather, it is an opportunity to be seized and striven for in much the same manner as the nation's forebears had seized their opportunity when they crossed the Jordan and set foot on the new territory. When faced with the vital question of how this rich and hopeful future could be grasped, the deuteronomists give one clear and unequivocal answer—by paying heed to the commandments God had given and following their guidance faithfully.

The reception of the Ten Commandments by the people is then further reflected upon in vv. 28-33. Their ultimate purpose is well expressed in v. 33. It is to promote a way of life that would be prosperous and beneficial to the social and political well-being of Israel: "and that you may live long in the land." The theme of the temptations of life in the land, combined with the potential threat of being expelled from it, now begins to hover like the shadow of a bird of prey over the remainder of the book. It is a theme that is more broadly enlarged upon in the great work of history that follows the law book from the deuteronomic authors. The theme generates a somber mood, and at times it gives rise to a frenetic intensity of aggressive demand and intolerance, which characterizes the entire theological outlook of the deuteronomists.

So Moses, and the first generation of the nation who enjoyed the prospect of entry into the land, were looking to a future that the readers of the book knew only too well still eluded them. They could empathize with that earlier band of nation seekers, since they shared their expectations, and yet were equally fearful of its consequences. If there were an advantage that the original readers of Deuteronomy enjoyed—but was not appreciated by their national ancestors about whom the book was written—it was a realization attained through hindsight of the importance of the commandments God had given. If only that earlier generation had heeded God's law, then the people would not now be faced with the prospect of beginning again.

So there is an unmistakable sense of tension that permeates Deuteronomy and that now unfolds with remarkable intensity in a series of exhortations and warnings, ascribed to Moses, that set out clearly the choices facing Israel. There is, woven into them, a certain wistfulness in which the authors of the book read back some of their own emotional stresses and anxieties: "If only they had such a mind as this" (v. 29); "You must be careful to do . . ." (v. 32). Repeatedly the warning note is sounded in Deuteronomy. There is a consciousness that Israel is wavering in its loyalty and is as uncertain of the outcome of its own painful choices as that first generation had been. Quite clearly the "if only" is meant with utmost seriousness. All kinds of unknown threats and dangers lay awaiting the people, just as that earlier generation had experienced them when they first set foot on the bed of the river Jordan. The only guidance they possessed by which to negotiate the perils they faced was in the commandments by which they could be assured of divine protection and support.

REFLECTIONS

It is appropriate that the giving of the Ten Commandments should be followed by a formal sequel that summarizes their central importance for the life and future of Israel. This short episode binds together two very distinct and differing interpretations of the divine transcendence. On one side is a physical awesomeness that is unbearably terrifying and potentially destructive—storm clouds, fire, unbearable light. But the disclosure of the commandments calls forth a life-enhancing moral seriousness. God is the author of life and the source of love. The divine law is itself a body of truths concerning the high dignity of human beings and the immense seriousness of the moral responsibility they bear. Only those who pay no heed to the ethical dimension of the divine nature and who pay no regard to this moral priority have need to fear God. So, for all their seeming brevity and simple directness, the Ten Commandments are awesome in their significance. They hold the key to human welfare and the possibility of building a truly God-willed order of life on earth.

The deuteronomic modes of address continually fluctuate between the singular and the plural. Sometimes it appears that the authors of the work are addressing one solitary person, as though the future of God's law and the future life of the nation hung wholly upon the response of that one person. At other times, the plural form of address is employed, creating a more profound sense of the social nature of the community and of the collective responsibility shared among all its members.

A key toward understanding the relationship between these two dimensions of human identity—the individual and the collective—is found in the deuteronomic portrait of Moses. More than any other person, he is presented as distinctive and unique. When others are afraid, he is fearless. When others are in despair, he is fired with courage. When others would turn back, he is for going on. He stands alone, and yet he is never alone. On him rests the survival of the nation, and without him they cannot go forward. In the conclusion to Deuteronomy's narrative, Moses himself dies in the wilderness, being debarred from the future that he has made possible for others. Yet even this failure to enjoy the fruits of his own vision is not on his own account. He must forfeit his future, so that the nation might have theirs! With such perceptive awareness of the complex intertwining of collective and individual elements of human responses, the deuteronomic literature sees a profoundly spiritual and theological dimension in the concept of community.

A whole plethora of phrases ("Be careful. Do not forget. If only . . .") indicate how firmly and confidently the deuteronomists point to the simplicity of the way to the future. If Israel willed, it could readily and immediately enjoy the fruits of the land, with the prospect of unclouded days ahead. Yet the very repetitions and passionate pleading indicate that the deuteronomists were all too conscious that it had not been that simple and could not be so. The Israelites so easily could have achieved everything that was promised, yet they singularly failed to do so. The deuteronomic authors do not disguise this feeling from their readers, who were already looking back on a ruined nation. So even within this insistence on the simplicity of God's directive, with a mere ten brief commandments being all that was necessary to unlock the gate to an almost paradisaical future, there is a consciousness of the faulty humans with whom God had to work. Deep within the human psyche lie forces and leanings that are not so easily governed, so that even Moses had to be denied the future that he strove so unselfishly to bring to others.

Deuteronomy 6:1-25, The Call to Diligent Observance

COMMENTARY

The giving of the Ten Commandments provides a fitting climax to the entire story of God's action with, and toward, Israel, which has occupied the books of Genesis through Numbers. It has three central themes: the promise to the ancestors of the nation that Israel would enter and occupy a land "flowing with milk and honey"; the exodus from Egypt, which rescued the people from slavery; and the giving of the law, now enshrined in the Ten Commandments.

A summary of these events now provides the basis for a renewed appeal to make ready for the crossing of the Jordan to take possession of the land (v. 1). The immediate threat posed by the present inhabitants of the land and the task of defeating them is taken as a relatively minor difficulty. More serious and prolonged is the threat posed by the temptation to forget the law that Moses had just reaffirmed. So before all other dangers are faced, there must be a carefully nurtured preparation—spiritual, psychological, and practical—to ensure that this law would never be forgotten. It must remain imprinted on the mind of every single Israelite, both young and old. Chapter 6, then, was carefully constructed, and its component themes are easily identified.

6:1-3. The opening section focuses afresh on the centrality of the law as the climactic gift of God. Israel's story, from the days of the patriarchs to the eve of the conquest,

has now reached its climax, and the time has come to set in motion the plans and forces to bring Israel to its triumphant achievement. Israel can now contemplate the prospect of life in the land, where the people will enjoy an untroubled and undiminished future.

6:4-9. These verses set out the requisite attitude of mind needed to maintain the centrality of the commandments' authority. They must be taught to children from their earliest days, worn as a sign on the body, and fixed permanently upon the doorways of every house (vv. 8-9). The response to be aroused by explaining the meaning of this sign is later set out in vv. 20-25 (cf. Exod 12:24-27; 13:11-16). In between, there is a parenthesis (vv. 10-19) that breaks up the straightforward formula of the sign, followed by its explanation. This parenthesis contains a series of admonitions reinforcing the demand of the first commandment. The LORD alone is to be feared as God, and all temptation to act otherwise must be rigidly and firmly rejected. This parenthesis appears to have been inserted later into the original unit and serves to add yet more emphasis to a feature that was already heavily stressed.

Many of the most basic of the deuteronomic characteristic features come to the surface in this chapter, so that it has quite appropriately become one of the most often repeated, and readily memorable, parts of the book. Of prominent interest is the command to love God (v. 5), which, from this point onward, becomes a central aspect of the entire biblical tradition, shaping much of the Jewish and Christian spirituality that has been built upon it. For Deuteronomy, this demand for a loving attitude toward God is closely related to the concept of moral obedience. It reflects an attitude of giving priority to the demands of God. Commentators have regarded it as being closely linked to the teaching of the prophet Hosea (esp. Hos 11:1), in which God's exceptional love for Israel is stressed. There is to be a strong reciprocal bond of affection and commitment between Israel and the LORD as God.

Attempts to explore the similarities and parallels between the deuteronomic teaching and the form and characteristics of international treaties have noted that a demand for love is to be found in both of them.[48] If the deuteronomic authors were familiar with this treaty form, then it could be argued that they have consciously adapted this important demand for a loving attitude on the part of an Israelite worshiper toward God on the analogy of the treaty between a vassal partner and an overlord.

Yet such an argument appears strained and implausible in view of the importance of the issue and the widespread feature in Deuteronomy of pointing out the necessity for the nurturing of a right attitude toward God. Since love is vitally important in family life, and since there is widespread use throughout the biblical tradition of employing kinship metaphors to describe divine-human relationships, the employment of the love concept by the deuteronomists can hardly occasion surprise. It is simply one further example of the introduction of human metaphors and analogies to describe the fundamental features of the spiritual life.

A further important aspect of the deuteronomic teaching is evident in the injunction to teach "these words" (הדברים האלה *haddĕbārîm hā'ēlleh*), which must refer to the Ten Commandments, to children. The inference is clear that those who are addressed are regarded as lay citizens of Israel who will carry out such instruction in their homes. Such a practice reflects an important similarity between the teaching of Deuteronomy and the biblical wisdom tradition (see, e.g., 4:9; Prov 2:1).

The confessional affirmation of the Shema (v. 4) is very terse, so that ascertaining the precise meaning is fraught with uncertainties. "The LORD is our God, the LORD alone" (cf. NIV; REB). The Hebrew affirmation falls short of expressing a clear-cut denial of the existence of other deities, but is adamant that there is only one LORD God who is to be worshiped by Israel. This, then, amounts to a denial that the LORD can have more than one manifestation (i.e., a denial that the deity could be known in different forms, or manifestations, in different sanctuaries), and it is a firm rejection of the notion that there could be any consort or retinue of lesser gods surrounding the LORD.[49] This latter feature was clearly virtually the norm in traditional forms of Canaanite religion, where one deity was supreme but other gods and goddesses served as helpers and servants. There would also appear to be substantial evidence that unofficial practice in Israel frequently countenanced the acceptance of other gods alongside the LORD. That this was the case, even though not officially approved, lends weight to the conviction that it was a concern to repudiate such practice that has motivated the form of the confessional recital of faith here.

It is possible to construe either literally or metaphorically the instructions in vv. 8-9 to bind this confessional affirmation "as a sign on your hand" and to fix them to the doorposts of the house. If taken metaphorically, the implication would be that the commandments are to be remembered at all times. The force of the construction can then be understood as "when you are at home and when you are away."

The injunction has consistently been understood literally within Jewish tradition, giving rise to the use of phylacteries, small leather containers to hold the texts of Exod 13:1-10, 11-16; and Deut 6:4-9; 11:13-21 inscribed on scrolls (cf. Matt 23:5). It seems

48. W. L. Moran, "The Ancient Near Eastern Background of the Love of God in Deuteronomy," *CBQ* 25 (1963) 77-87. For a review of the issue, see D. J. McCarthy, "Notes on the Love of God in Deuteronomy and the Father-Son Relationship Between Yahweh and Israel," in *Institution and Narrative: Collected Essays*, AnBib 108 (Rome: Pontifical Biblical Institute, 1985) 301-4.

49. G. Braulik, "Das Deuteronomium und die Geburt des Monotheismus," *Studien zur Theologie des Deuteronomiums*, SBA 2 (Stuttgart: Katholisches Bibelwerk, 1988) 257-300.

probable that a literal understanding was intended from the outset, making the use of such important confessional texts affirming religious loyalty and identity a counterpart to the widespread use of semi-magical amulets and religious jewelry among non-Israelite peoples. Such amulets were thought to provide divine healing power (cf. Ezek 13:18) and would certainly have been familiar objects to the deuteronomic authors. It would have been a positive form of religious apologetic, therefore, to provide continued reminders of the commandments and of the need for total loyalty to the LORD as God—a requirement that could easily be infringed by resorting to popular semi-magical practices.

6:10-19. This parenthetical section reiterates commands that have already been given and marks a further aspect of the extent to which the deuteronomic writers were conscious of human weakness. Security, prosperity, and the general feeling that God's promises had been fulfilled could readily lead to a sense of complacency (v. 11; cf. 8:11-20). In such a circumstance a belief could arise that the requirements of the divine law were no longer important and could safely be set aside. So there could emerge an attitude of indifference to the divine law and a feeling that God's gifts, having once been received, would not subsequently be taken away. Once given, they would forever be the spiritual possession of Israel. Against all such complacency, the authors of these exhortations offer a sharp rebuke.

It is likely that we should recognize that behind such forms of spiritual psychologizing the deuteronomic authors were seeking not simply to forestall future eventualities, but were also very mindful of attitudes and events that had already overtaken Israel. We are entitled to assume, therefore, that in this rather pessimistic exploration of the psychology of apostasy these authors were assessing the mood and attitude of some of their readers. Clearly they had encountered such a spirit and were here concerned to oppose it by uncovering its element of self-delusion. It belonged to their belief, and the entire strategy of their work, to set the Mosaic *torah* in the forefront of the life of Israel, out of a conviction that this had never really been the case in the past. So the disasters that had already

overtaken the nation were, to the knowledge of these authors, entirely explainable. The right attitude toward the law of God on the part of Israel had been seriously lacking from the earliest times since the nation had taken possession of the land.

The central understanding of what constituted the sum of Israel's religious duties is then set out clearly in v. 13: Israel must fear the LORD, serve God unswervingly, and invoke no other divine name in affirming its oaths. The contrast between this and the simple formula of Israel's visible commitment to God set out in Exod 23:17 is quite noteworthy. Formal outward duties toward the LORD are certainly required (and are specified in 16:1-17), but alongside this, and undergirding them, lies a prior commitment of attitude that would affect every part of the year and every aspect of life. It is this concern to match outward observance with inward attitude and reflection that forms so large a feature of what is new and striking in Deuteronomy. The entire understanding of religious commitment has taken on a more inward, and more recognizably spiritual, stance. It is on this account that the book has acquired a central place in the formation of a reasoned theological explication of what constitutes the service of God.

Once again the element of conditionality in Israel's relationship with the LORD is given renewed emphasis. The author does not shun from declaring what failure to adhere to God's demands will entail: "he would destroy you from the face of the earth" (v. 15).

The warning against putting the LORD God "to the test" (נסה *nāsâ*, v. 16) can most readily be understood in the present context as a reference to the temptation to see whether God would, indeed, punish Israel if it failed to adhere to the law—i.e., the test would be a bold flouting of God's law to see if punishment would ensue. This fits closely the general theme of the unit, and it would be out of place to see here a reference to seeking a "sign" from God as indicative that a prophetic word was to be fulfilled (as in Isa 7:10, 14).

6:20-25. The unit that brings the section to a conclusion is important for the manner in which it formulates a short credo-like summary of Israel's history as an answer to the question put by children concerning the "sign" of God's law, which was binding upon

Israel. The use of short historical summaries of the past as a demonstrative affirmation of the love of God toward Israel and the reason why this people were bound to respond to this love by obedience is a major feature of the deuteronomic rhetoric. It comes to its fullest expression in the more elaborate summary set out in 26:5*b*-10*a* and can more fully be examined there. Its importance lies in the manner in which it reflects the consistent deuteronomic assertion that God's law is a further manifestation of the divine grace that belongs with, and is related to, God's deliverance of the people from Egypt. Deliverance and response are both seen to be expressions of the same divine love without which Israel could not exist. So the law itself is viewed as an instrument of grace.

REFLECTIONS

The most striking and memorable feature of this entire hortatory address concerning the importance of God's commandments and the steps Israel must take to ensure that it never forgets them lies in its command to love God. All the familiar vocabulary of worship concerning the necessity to fear God, to revere God's name, and to offer service and gifts at a sanctuary at the appropriate times of the year is fully present in Deuteronomy. Yet now there comes a fresh, and less obviously expected, demand that seeks to provide motivation and reason for all the rest: Israel is to *love* God. Clearly elements of tension and near contradiction can readily arise, since it is a far from straightforward undertaking to show love toward a power that may hurl one swiftly to destruction and may take away everything that one possesses. Yet, with this intrusion of the concept of love into the framework of the deuteronomic understanding of faith and spirituality a breakthrough of immense importance has been made. In fact, the strong emphasis placed on all the gifts and benefits God has showered upon Israel represents a move in the direction of recognizing the *loveliness* of God. God becomes the supreme expression of love, motivating, inspiring, and making possible a deeper understanding of the nature of love in the lives of human beings.

Were it not for the placing of such a demand in a position of great prominence here, it could be claimed that the assertions concerning the requirement to love God and to confess the divine love in the Old Testament are often muted. Sometimes assertions of God's love are severely modified by the limits placed on them. The LORD God has many enemies, and the focus placed on the concept of divine wrath frequently reduces worship to a cringing submissiveness. Features of a more violent portrayal of the divine being then come to the fore. Yet it must be recognized that the understanding that love lies at the heart of worship is a leaven that must ultimately affect the entire understanding of faith. There is, therefore, a direct path from the command in Deuteronomy to love God to the New Testament assertion in 1 John 4:8: "Whoever does not love does not know God, for God is love."

A second aspect of the deuteronomic teaching emerges very forcibly in Deuteronomy 6. This concerns the heavy psychologizing of faith and all its concerns. Commitment to God cannot simply be presented as the performance of certain outward duties that will be publicly observed and recognized. Rather, all knowledge of God becomes a matter of heart searching and looking inward. The authors seem to display an almost Freudian awareness that self-delusion is always a possibility in religion. So there may arise a sense of complacency that calculates in a mean-spirited fashion that sufficient regard for God and the divine demands has been made and that no outward signs of divine wrath are likely to overwhelm the formally correct worshiper.

For Deuteronomy, however, such can never be the obedience that God seeks, which must ultimately flow out from a sense of love toward God. Again there is a note of duality and ambivalence in the overall perspectives set out in Deuteronomy. At times the most violent and cruel responses are demanded by way of punishment upon those who refuse the message of God's love. Yet alongside these harsh demands, tempering them and ultimately outlasting them, is an awareness that true faith and a true spirit of obedience can only be attained from within the human spirit. So the key words for understanding the kind of obedience that is sought after lie in the injunctions: "Observe diligently"; "Remember . . ."; "Love!"

The short unit (6:20-25) that brings this hortatory address to a close is also of great significance for the overall grasp of the message of the Pentateuch in its full compass. This concerns the combining of a message of deliverance and liberation with a call for obedience and a high regard for God's command. The Pentateuch is a story of freedom and promise. But it is also a call to obedience and righteousness. There can be no liberation without law and no freedom without justice.

All too easily there can arise within religious reflection an imbalance precisely because one feature is emphasized to the detriment of another. So the threat of legalism and the pursuit of righteousness as a path to salvation can become stultifying and self-destructive. But Deuteronomy is in no sense a legalistic book, affirming only the awesome demands of the law with threats and warnings lest it be disobeyed. Such elements are certainly present, but they are combined with an assertion of divine love and grace, which calls for a similar attitude of love by way of response. It recognizes that, for the divine love and grace to become real and effective in human society, it must be reciprocated in human actions. So the path is left open for the recognition that to love God is loving to obey the divine commandments.

Deuteronomy 7:1-26, When You Live in the Land

COMMENTARY

The look ahead to a future life in the land that Israel was shortly to occupy affirmed that it was to be lived in the light of the commandments of God (6:1-2). Careful safeguards were to be implemented to ensure that Israel forgot neither these commandments nor their inescapable link to the promise of God through which the land had been occupied. Forgetfulness and complacency were clearly inner spiritual temptations to which the nation could all too easily fall prey (6:10-13). Yet a more visible and persistent hazard needed also to be considered in the form of the presence of sanctuaries to alien deities, like that at Baalpeor, and especially the deeply rooted traditional religious practices of the people already occupying the land.

7:1-6. Three fundamental rules are laid down with uncompromising sternness to obviate the dangers to Israel posed by these alluring temptations. First the former occupants of the land themselves were to be exterminated: "You must utterly destroy them" (v. 2). No treaties or covenants that might qualify this demand were to be entertained (v. 3).

It is the most uncompromising demand for genocide, based on religious principles, that could possibly be expressed. In historical and theological perspective, we are bound to seek some degree of qualification, and hermeneutical distance, to place between the modern world and such a horrifying demand.[50] Nevertheless, it is appalling in the fearfulness of what it demands and contrasts strangely with the preceding affirmation concerning the loving aspects of God and of obedience. Deuteronomy presents us with several strange anomalies and paradoxes!

As a second step, no intermarriage was to be tolerated between the young people of Israel and those of the groups already inhabiting the land who are, somewhat inconsistently, assumed to have survived the calls for their removal. In this demand we can recognize a deep-seated and long-established feature of societies in which kinship played a prominent role. This was the practice of

---

50. The subject of the deuteronomic repudiation of any acceptance of peace with the inhabitants of the land is covered by G. Schmitt, *Du sollst keinen Frieden Schliessen mit den Bewohnen des Landes*, BWANT V:11 (Stuttgart: W. Kohlhammer, 1970) 13-24, 131-44.

endogamy (marriage within the larger kin group; cf. Gen 24:1-9), although such marriage was necessarily restricted within kinship affinities to preclude the most immediate family kin.

In view of the concern to preclude intermarriage of Israelites with former inhabitants of the land, it is surprising to find that the important ruling presented in the law code of Deuteronomy (21:10-14) takes it for granted that an Israelite man might take as a wife a woman taken as a prisoner of war. In this case, it would undoubtedly have involved the crossing of a wide ethnic gap. Almost certainly such a ruling stands closer to actual practice in Israel, whereas the hortatory injunction of v. 4 represents a stylized concern to remove every temptation from Israel whereby God's law might be neglected.

The third instruction, designed to remove the danger of Israel's becoming enmeshed in practices and beliefs of the former religion of the land, demands that all the physical symbols of that religion be destroyed (v. 5). The justification for this action is that Israel is a people holy to the LORD God (v. 6).

The use of the term "holy" (קדוש *qādôš*) in such a context is itself full of distinctive meaning. It represents one of the most basic and lastingly significant aspects of the deuteronomic teaching.[51] In origin, the concept of holiness related directly to the sphere of cultic activity and connoted a quality of separateness and of being imbued with a special divine power. So holiness is not only a quality of persons and things, but also a power possessed by them. It was applicable primarily to holy places and objects, but it naturally extended, in a quasi-physical fashion, to cover those persons whose activities required that they work in close proximity to, and relationship with, such objects (cf. the experience of Moses in Exod 3:5).

In itself, therefore, the direct application to persons was not the remarkable feature of the deuteronomic teaching on holiness, but rather the extension of it to cover an entire nation. Israel as a whole was regarded as a holy nation. The formulation of v. 6, therefore, combines cultic and legal vocabulary in

a way that has had lasting consequences for Jewish and Christian thinking.

A further important part of the deuteronomic understanding of the term "holy" lies in the assertion that the covenant relationship between Israel and the LORD God was itself the consequence of a unique act of divine choice. So the vocabulary of divine election is introduced as a vital part of Israel's thinking about the nature and meaning of its unique relationship to the LORD as God. Once again we find an extended application of a basic traditional concept, a feature that repeatedly characterizes the deuteronomic movement. Old ideas are given new clothes, and this process is consistently in the direction of adding the colors of ritual and worship to fundamental political and ethical terminology. It is not surprising, then, that scholars have found it difficult to determine whether Deuteronomy can best be understood as the work of priests or that of lawyers. So many features of both areas of social life are brought together and skillfully combined. On one hand, religion is partially secularized, but on the other hand, secular life is sacralized in a new way. This then is part of what it means for Israel to be a holy nation.

The very existence of Israel as a nation-state, together with the life within it that is to be regulated and shaped by the observance of the Ten Commandments, is recognized as the goal of a prior act of God's choice.[52] Close study of the background to this deuteronomic teaching brings to light a clear and discernible shift of thought. The concept of divine choice in early Israel was directly related to two institutions: God's choice of Mt. Zion as the location for the divine abode (cf. Psalm 78) and God's choice of the Davidic dynasty to provide a line of kings under whom Israel might live and be governed (cf. Psalms 89; 132).

Now the foreground of the divine purpose is taken up with Israel itself as a nation. The whole people is chosen; the whole nation is holy! So an important shift takes place, almost certainly anticipating, if not directly reflecting, the already accomplished fact that both the

51. J. G. Gammie, *Holiness in Israel,* OBT (Minneapolis: Fortress, 1989) 106-16; M. Weinfeld, *Deuteronomy and the Deuteronomic School* (Oxford: Oxford University Press, 1972) 225-32.

52. A valuable study of the whole concept of election in relation to Israel is to be found in H. Wildberger, *Jahwes Eigentumsvolk,* ATANT 37 (Zurich: Zwingli Verlag, 1959). See also Paul D. Hanson, *The People Called: The Growth of Community in the Bible* (San Fransisco: Harper & Row, 1987) 167-76.

Davidic kingship and the Temple that stood on Mt. Zion might be lost to Israel. Would Israel's chosen status be forfeited because of such disasters? Clearly the deuteronomic authors give a clear and resounding no to such a possibility. Israel itself as a people is the object of God's choice. King and Temple might serve them and symbolize the reality of this election, but they do not themselves embody it or empower it.

7:7-11. This section forms a short parenthesis, almost certainly brought into the text at a late stage, that digresses more fully on the question of the mystery of divine election. Taken at a merely surface level, the belief that Israel had been selected to exist in a unique relationship to God could relapse into a doctrine of self-justification and self-congratulation. It is a risk endemic to all concepts of being especially chosen and favored. It could, in fact, become an article of faith that would encourage the very complacency 6:10-13 had warned Israel to resist. Accordingly, this parenthesis both warns against this, arguing that it would be a complete misreading of the situation, and reasserts the inscrutable and unqualified nature of divine love (v. 8).

The author then proceeds to reaffirm, if any such reaffirmation were still needed, that Israel has been chosen by God and must therefore maintain its obligations toward the divine covenant that was the consequence of this choice (v. 9). Very clearly, all the references in this section to the divine law presuppose them to be the commandments given at Mt. Horeb—i.e., the Ten Commandments.

This unit is particularly important on two counts. First, it brings into sharp focus an awareness of the existence and potential destiny of other nations. The command that the nations that had previously occupied Israel's land should be exterminated was recognized as inadequate, although we here encounter a distinction between those nations who were rival claimants to the land and more distant nations, with whom Israel must deal. Already the journey through the wilderness had highlighted the possibility of such a distinction.

A second issue, also of considerable importance, now emerges into the light of day and concerns the question of the permanence of the covenant relationship between the LORD God and Israel. Could this covenant be annulled? Could Israel forfeit its unique and privileged position before God? The assertion in v. 10, which declares that God "repays in their own person those who reject him," would appear to indicate that this conditional uncertainty was indeed the case. Yet, it is noteworthy that the warning is couched in the singular form, indicating that it envisaged that it would be individuals who might turn away from their privileged status, without the entire nation's falling away and being destroyed as a result. The question of the conditional element within the deuteronomic covenant theology was to become one fraught with serious consequences for later generations of Jews, and also to become one that intruded itself into Christian apologetic toward Jews (cf. Romans 9–11); it raises too large a set of questions to be considered here. Clearly the deuteronomic authors did not believe that such a falling away had happened, and they clearly hope to forestall its ever happening.

7:12-16. This section resumes the assurance that obedience to the law will bring great success and prosperity to Israel so that the nation as a whole will have no need to remain in fear of its former inhabitants. Essentially it centers upon an affirmation of divine blessing (vv. 13-16) that closely follows the traditional formulas of blessing proclaimed in the rituals of Israel's worship. What is promised covers the full range of traditional benefits to be desired: fertility in flocks and herds and in the soil, healthy children, and protection from illness and disease. All those people who stood in the way of Israel's possession of the land would be quickly removed. We can well summarize all these benefits as comprising "life," a concept that lies at the heart of the deuteronomic understanding of the meaning of salvation.

What is especially significant for an understanding of the deuteronomic theology is that this "life" is set within the context of the covenant and is made conditional upon obedience to the commands that stand at the center of this covenant. Effectively it asserts that without obedience to the commandments there can be no blessing. The consequences of this for the overall understanding of worship, as seen by the deuteronomists, is far reaching. Ritual and prayer, with all their many forms and requirements, are not effective, save within this larger context of covenant life. The commandments hold the key to the path of blessing—a feature that is taken up afresh in the latter part of the book.

7:17-26. The problem of the nations who were already settled in the land then occupies the final section of the chapter. From the point of view of the deuteronomists, seeing the threat posed by these nations at a considerable distance in time from the direct encounter with them when Israel settled in the land, their existence provided opportunity for fundamental theological reflection. The same fundamental outlook on the question of the threat and the perils of warfare with these people is then set out. God will give victory as a reward for loyalty. The reassuring promise of v. 22 that the nations of the land could only be destroyed piecemeal and over time stands in obvious tension with the admonition that Israel is to make a quick end of them (v. 2). It is possible that it has been introduced out of a positive historical knowledge that there had not, in reality, been any wholesale slaughter of the previous inhabitants of the land.[53] More plausibly, however, the reassurance has been introduced into the text at a late stage in order to offer some clear explanation as to why the presence of these people and their religious establishments would remain a serious temptation for later generations of Israel. Overall, there is considerable incongruity in

the reasoning that the previous inhabitants would have to remain for some time until the number of Israelites was sufficient to prevent the land's being overrun by wild animals.

The final warning against the temptation of seizing possession of the images of gods or any other cult objects that had belonged to the former inhabitants serves as a further reinforcement of the deuteronomic polemic against religious images. It is basically this sin of which Achan and his household are accused in Josh 7:20-21, when they are charged with having taken "a beautiful mantle from Shinar" from among the spoils of the city of Ai, an offense for which they pay the ultimate price. The infringement is against the rules of holy war, which are assumed to be a necessary part of Torah, and the offense is given vaguely cultic overtones. The terminology used in Deuteronomy to describe the unacceptibility of such religious objects is that they are "an abhorrent thing" (v. 26). The concept of "abhorrence"/"abomination" (תועבה *tôʿēbâ*) is important for the deuteronomists (cf. 18:10; 22:5) and is used to justify the rejection of a number of objects and practices as hostile to the essential meaning of God's law.[54] Elsewhere it is widely used by the sages in the book of Proverbs to describe unacceptability within the moral sphere, although older usage links it closely to cultic objects and actions. Objects used within one religious tradition are regarded as abhorrent to the god of another.

53. G. Schmitt, *Du sollst keinen Frieden schliessen mit den Bewohnen des Landes,* 134, cites the observation of P. Kleinert, published in 1870, that in historical reality there had been no such wholesale slaughter of the previous inhabitants so that the deuteronomic demand represents an idealized and fictionalized perspective on the past.

54. See Weinfeld, *Deuteronomy and the Deuteronomic School,* 226, 265-70.

REFLECTIONS

Taken as a whole, Deuteronomy 7 reflects theologically on the problem posed by the previous inhabitants of the land. It is noteworthy that, in the basic form of the promise of the land given to the patriarchs of Israel, the question of the existence of these peoples is not properly taken into consideration. Yet it was clear to the ancient writers that rich, arable farmland, which is the warm and glowing picture given of the land of Israel, would not be left unoccupied. A "return to the wild" is a condition of curse that is sometimes used in prophetic threats of future defeat and destruction, both for Israel and for other nations.

Accordingly, the realization that the land Israel occupied had had previous inhabitants becomes an increasingly prominent feature of the deuteronomic picture of the course of Israel's early history—a conquest of the land—and of its subsequent problems—a mixture of non-Israelite religious traditions with many sanctuaries and cult objects. The theological response made to this realization is twofold in nature. First, there is a dramatic theology of warfare, with the belief that victory in war is entirely a gift of God, and the deuteronomic authors have already provided the reader with outline summaries of how such campaigns involve supernatural, divine intervention, sending the enemy into a panic and depriving them of the power to resist.

The second feature of the deuteronomic concern with the existence and religious activities of the previous inhabitants—the Canaanites—is one of religious apologetic. It is primarily the relics of the religion of these peoples that are claimed to have brought disunity and idolatry to Israel in the past. The continued existence of such relics and practices is a threat in the present as well. So the portrayal of the danger posed by the previous occupants is viewed as a present religious one, since the integrity and purity of Israel's faith are held to have been established at the beginning, but progressively lost thereafter.

It is reasonable to conclude that the deuteronomic authors were fully aware that among their readers were many who still held fast to the wide variety of amulets, cult objects, and general religious bric-a-brac with which daily life was surrounded. Almost certainly many of these readers did not regard the retention of these pious artifacts as hostile to God or a flagrant infringement of the commandments. For many readers, these were no more than ancient features of community life and household religion with which they were understandably reluctant to part. The vigor with which the fear is expressed that Israel will continue to venerate the "old gods" of the land and will perpetuate practices that originated before Israel occupied it reveals something of the situation in which the deuteronomic authors found their readers.

By far the most adequate explanation for this fear, and for the ruthless punishments demanded for breaking the rule of maintaining an exclusive purity in the worship of the LORD God, is that it emerged after the Jerusalem Temple had been destroyed in 587 BCE. This single event had dealt a massive blow to the prestige and credibility of the traditional worship of the LORD God. With the destruction of Jerusalem went the destruction of much that had been popularly believed about the power of God to protect the people of Judah. In such a time of crisis, it is fully understandable that there was a widespread popular return to the simple, long-established forms of religion associated with households, local communities, and local shrines that had a strong domestic flavor and enjoyed a seemingly ineradicable following. The deuteronomic polemic represents a major fighting back for the maintenance of an "official" expression of Israel's faith. The fuller outworking of this is then to be seen in the greatly reinterpreted expression of cultic life that the deuteronomic lawmakers set out in Deuteronomy 12–13.

It was important for the deuteronomic polemic—if it was to achieve its goal of retraining, unifying, harmonizing, and strengthening faith in and commitment to the LORD as God—that veneration of the "old gods" be eradicated. Since their antiquity could not be denied, it was important that their orthodoxy and acceptability to the LORD be challenged. A major feature of the deuteronomic theology is that it identifies those features of Israel's religious tradition that it repudiates as belonging to the former inhabitants of the land.

As a feature of religious apologetic, this aggressive repudiation and rejection of popular and quasi-magical forms of religion is recognizable as a survival technique that has left a powerful legacy within both Judaism and Christianity. Exclusivism in religion, combined with a sharp intolerance of any alien religious tradition, can readily become regressive and destructive. Strong and forceful moves to promote a fuller and firmer hold on the positive aspects of faith seem almost invariably destined to align themselves with harsh, and often cruel, reactions against all that threatens them. In order to establish what is new and positive, the hostility to what is old and familiar becomes aggressive and destructive.

Within the biblical tradition this awareness of bold affirmation and repressive defensiveness becomes very pronounced in Deuteronomy and the writings it has influenced, pointing strongly to the situation of crisis out of which it emerged. Since situations of crisis can be reconstructed only in part, we can only partially understand the justification of radical exclusivism. However, this fact in itself does little to soften the dangerous and destructive tendencies of such exclusivism. That it represents a violent and iconoclastic repudiation of well-established religious traditions in order to retain faith in Israel's God in the wake of unexpected catastrophe can readily be recognized. Nevertheless, in seeking to embrace for faith in the LORD God of Israel a painful experience of disaster, it has left a dangerous legacy of intolerance that has in turn set in motion further tragedies.

Deuteronomy 8:1-20, Take Care to Remember God's Commandment

COMMENTARY

The warnings concerning the threat that will be posed by the presence, and more particularly the religious artifacts and practices, of the former occupants of the land is now followed by a sermon addressed directly to the heart of every Israelite. Its message is passionate and consistent: "Take care to remember that the LORD God who gave you the land, also gave you the commandments to observe."

8:1-10. The address opens with its fundamental theme: "This entire commandment that I command you today you must diligently observe" (v. 1). What follows is essentially a sermon on this text, amplifying its importance and pointing out the likely personal temptations that will be encountered and that might lead to failure to fulfill such a demand. The conclusion is sharp and decisive: "If you do forget . . . you shall surely perish" (v. 19).[55] The sermon raises yet again the question of the extent to which the deuteronomic theology of covenant contains a radical conditional element that could contemplate the annihilation of Israel as a nation. Here the warning seems clear enough that the possibility exists that Israel, as a nation, could perish from the land. At the same time, this was evidently what the deuteronomists believed was now inevitable. Theirs is a kind of "last appeal,"

contemplating the possibility of disaster, but hoping to avert it.

By appealing to "this entire commandment," the author was clearly referring to the Ten Commandments, rather than to any wider range of laws. There are sufficient signs of variation in the chapter to suggest that an earlier unit (vv. 7-11a) has subsequently been amplified in close conformity with the message of 4:1-40. Yet overall the signs of a resultant unity are strong, with evidence of a chiastic structure.

The danger of forgetting the LORD God focuses on two issues that are closely interrelated and that envisage different contents for what has been forgotten. The first is that Israel may forget the providential care of God during the years in the wilderness (vv. 2-5), a period of trial and testing in which a parental discipline had been imposed on the people. This represents an interesting and important development of the theme concerning what the wilderness period of Israel's existence signified. For the prophets Hosea and Jeremiah, it had been a honeymoon time in Israel's life (Jer 2:2-8; Hos 2:14; 9:10). Ezekiel, however, placed a more radically negative interpretation on this phase of Israel's history (Ezek 20:10-26). He regarded it as having been as fully a time of religious unfaithfulness as was all of Israel's subsequent history. For this prophet, no part of Israel's past had been untainted by a deep inner obsession with idolatry, thereby sharply implying that the roots

---

55. The necessity of remembering as a primary religious duty is a fundamental aspect of the deuteronomic theology. See B. S. Childs, *Memory and Tradition in Israel*, SBT 37 (London: SCM, 1962) 45-56.

of such idolatry lay in Israel's inner consciousness, and not in historical circumstances.

The deuteronomic position marks a kind of neutral middle ground. The wilderness period was neither wholly good nor wholly bad, but an occasion when the challenges and temptations of disobedience had first been fully felt. The outcome of Israel's wilderness period had then proved to be that Israel had been taught a lesson and had been humbled by it. The meaning must clearly be that Israel had experienced sufficient adversity at that time and had learned the inner deceitfulness of the human heart, so that such punishment as had been inflicted amounted to a severe lesson. So it was a time of trial during which the seriousness of Israel's intent to maintain loyalty to God's covenant had been tested and the consequences of disobedience had begun to be felt. Throughout there is the assumption that the experience of deprivation had forced upon Israel the necessity of depending on God's provision—even right up to the point when severe hunger and thirst threatened personal disaster.

This interesting spiritual interpretation of the harshness and vulnerability of life in the semi-desert of the Sinai region has given rise to some of the most theologically perceptive and memorable features of the entire book. The manna that was to be found on some of the scrub vegetation of the region, and is the product of insect secretion that is edible and possesses a sweet taste, is interpreted as a supernaturally provided food from God. Its meaning, however, is found not simply in its nutritional value for desert travelers, but in its role as a sign of God's providential care. More than this, it becomes a sign that the acknowledgment of such direct dependence upon God is its ultimate purpose. So we are brought to a justly famous and meaningful pronouncement: "One does not live by bread alone, but by every word that comes from the mouth of the LORD" (v. 3).

A third feature of the experience of Israel's wilderness generation is then added and places further emphasis on the overall interpretation that it was a time of testing and of demonstration of divine providence: "The clothes on your back did not wear out and your feet did not swell these forty years" (v. 4). The comment is repeated in 29:5 and

is made into a meaningful symbol of divine providence in Nehemiah's great prayer reviewing Israel's history (Neh 9:21).

The saying reflects the richly varied manner in which the deuteronomists combine practical and spiritual features in using inherited historical traditions to generate a doctrine of divine providence. In this case, the central point made is that God's care is sufficient for all human need. To ask for more than this becomes a mark of human arrogance and greed, with a consequent loss of the essential perception that the most fundamental of all human needs are spiritual. Accordingly, the Word of God is the most precious gift, and it alone makes possible life within the divine order.

8:11-20. By contrast, the abundant provisions of life within the boundaries of the promised land rendered possible a life of richness and prosperity (vv. 7-10). Wheat, barley, vines, figs, pomegranates, olives, and honey all amount to an abundance and variety of diet that contrast dramatically with the sparse rations of the wilderness years. It is precisely this richness and abundance that is seen as a temptation to forget God and the divine commandments (vv. 11-14). It then becomes a striking reflection of the way in which the physical terrain and climate in the biblical lands have been shaped into a series of spiritual lessons about the human condition and the inter-relationship between bodily and spiritual needs. The one becomes the guidebook to the other.

For such a small region, Palestine reveals a great variety of ecological features. These vary from the semi-desert of the south and east to the sub-tropical vegetation in the upper Jordan valley. In consequence, the mixed possibilities of agriculture, the major variations of climate, and the harshness of the more mountainous and desert regions all create problems and uncertainties for the maintenance of a settled population. For many areas, drought and consequent famine remain regular threats, whereas violent storms manifest the violence, as well as the beneficence, of the rainfall. The author here brilliantly interprets these uncertainties and variations as a combination of privileges, tests, and temptations to which each inhabitant is called upon to make an appropriate spiritual response.

This response is unerringly seen as a need to remember the LORD God. Abundance and prosperity are signs of God's grace and beneficence, but such welcome beneficence can quickly turn to manifestations of divine anger when the God-ordained pattern of life is flouted (vv. 15-16).

The concluding section in vv. 19-20 presents a solemn adjuration that to forget that the LORD is God and to tolerate and pursue the worship of other gods would plunge Israel into the pit of destruction: "I solemnly warn you today that you shall surely perish" (v. 19). The covenant itself makes known the conditions of security, prosperity, and survival in the land. So the possibility of ultimate failure to heed the simple lessons of the wilderness years could lead to an even more drastic failure to remain secure and prosperous in the land that God had given. If Israel could not take note of the message inherent in the basic traditions about its own past, it would have to learn more fearful and destructive lessons within its own history in the present. It was not as if there was not ample evidence in all that Israel knew of its own past to take the solemn warning to heart: "Like the nations that the LORD is destroying before you, so shall you perish" (v. 20). Evidently, this was not yet a catastrophe that had actually come to pass. Yet it was an imminent possibility that the deuteronomic author recognized and strove with great rhetorical artistry to impress upon the reader.

REFLECTIONS

Coming immediately after the alarming and ruthless injunctions of chapter 7, with their insistence that Israel spare no effort to root out every one of the previous occupants of the land and the relics of their detested religions, the artistry and spiritual perceptiveness of chapter 8 provide a splendid and welcome relief. It is unquestionably one of the most memorable and instructive passages in the entire book. It is small wonder, then, that this chapter has provided the basis on which the meaning and message of the temptations of Jesus in the wilderness are constructed (Matt 4:1-11). Human life can have no higher wealth and no more necessary sustenance than that provided by the Word of God. Whereas most people spend their lives seeking to secure themselves from famine by ensuring a plentiful food supply and from cold and destitution by surrounding themselves with fine and warm clothing, they fail to see that the most basic of all essentials for life is to be found in the Word of God. Real poverty is poverty of the spirit, and even those who feel secure because they have no fear of hunger and destitution may fail to see this. Indeed, the opposite result may obtain and the very plentiful supplies of food and clothing may lead to a complacency that encourages the thought that "God is no longer necessary for my life."

So the deuteronomic authors draw out from a vague and historically little-known phase of Israel's earlier existence some remarkable lessons. In the forefront is the perceptive observation that it is in the memory of years of famine and want that the value of an abundance of food and clothing is most fully appreciated. The privilege of possession becomes the richer and the more genuinely appreciated when it can be accepted in the shadow of want. So far as precise details are concerned, it seems evident that a good deal of historical and literary license has been taken with the facts and conditions of Israel's life in the wilderness. Neither the unexpected discovery and sweetness of manna nor the food offered by exhausted quail or other wild creatures found in the wilderness could possibly supply food for an entire nation for thirty-eight years. Yet it is sufficient for the authors to realize that there are unexpected manifestations of God's providential care that even the hard pressed and the near destitute may find. So this unexpected provision and the conviction that even worn-out clothes could last a little longer to protect a nation on the march provide the basis for important spiritual lessons.

However much we may be inclined to dismiss the poetic exaggeration and special pleading of the author, we can only marvel at his insight into truths that have continued to have a profound influence on the spiritual tradition of both Jews and Christians. There may be more to be learned in times of trial and deprivation than can possibly be learned in times of wealth and plenty. Moreover, spiritual truths may become more apparent and more readily accepted in such times as well. Consistently, the Bible and the spiritual tradition built upon it have viewed with suspicion and criticism the dangers of wealth and plenty. It is not that these desirable attainments are wrong in themselves, but that they become an occasion for neglect of a more profound spiritual truth: Without an inward peace and an awareness of God, the most lavish of possessions can appear tawdry. So the New Testament parable can present the hearing and responding to the gospel message as a discovery comparable to the finding of a treasure of incalculable price that makes the surrender of all other treasures an easy option (Matt 13:45-46).

A further feature characterizes the remarkable artistry and insight of this chapter in its ability to deduce searching lessons from the basic facts of geology, climate, and ecology. The wilderness, with all its hazards, provides the basis for important tests of character and personal resilience (8:15). By contrast, the richer agricultural land of Israel offers the opportunity for rich farming and the building of fine homes. In such a land trade can bring yet greater wealth (8:12-13). Here, however, more subtle temptations may arise in that complacency and a sense of self-achievement may displace the due recognition that there is nothing that was not ultimately a gift of God. Even the power to achieve anything is itself God's gift (8:17-18). Success and prosperity, too, therefore, are tests of character, in their own way more subtle and more dangerous than the wilderness. Whereas the wilderness poses an open and readily recognized challenge, the settled land offers instead a hidden allure that may, in the end, prove more effectively destructive of the knowledge of God and of the divine covenant. So the message is clear: "Remember the LORD your God, for it is he who gives you power to get wealth" (8:18 NRSV).

Deuteronomy 9:1-7, Be Prepared and Be Humble

COMMENTARY

This brief sermon urging Israel yet again to prepare themselves for the crossing of the Jordan and the entry into the land serves as a transition piece. It summarizes and reinforces the call to courage, loyalty, and obedience as the three prerequisites for entry into the land. At the same time it introduces a further admonitory note. The entire corpus of traditions concerning Israel's status as a people in covenant with the LORD God could have a damaging and misleading effect. The promise of the ancestors, the making of the covenant on Mt. Horeb, and the giving of the law could all have the consequence of encouraging Israel to believe that it was a very remarkable and special people. Had not the LORD God chosen them from among all peoples to be a chosen and privileged nation, pre-eminent above all others on this account?

The preparation for crossing the Jordan and occupying the land could reinforce this conviction still further. God was about to drive out and destroy peoples who were already settled there—and these people included the Anakim, a race of powerful giants! Surely such a people must be very special indeed to merit so many privileges and to have received so many advantages from God.

This short sermon faces the issue squarely and knocks away completely any such complacent belief. The nations who were about to be expelled and destroyed from the land were deeply tainted with the spirit and deeds of wickedness (vv. 4-5). It was not, therefore, because of Israel's righteousness that such privileges and opportunities were being accorded to them. Rather, it was as a necessary punishment visited on the erstwhile occupants of the land, whose evil deeds called for judgment. The terms employed to describe the conduct that is respectively described as either bad or good, wicked or righteous, has a directly legal background. Yet their reference here appears extended to cover a wide range of activities, of which the major offense is to be found in their false religious beliefs and practices. So legal terminology is employed to condemn what are fundamentally false religious pursuits. From the author's perspective, these pursuits could then be seen readily to flout the requirements of the Ten Commandments.

The message concerning God's gracious election of Israel has a double-edged significance. It represents a marvelous privilege and opportunity, but it is also not without its element of warning and danger. If the previous occupants of the land had been dispossessed and destroyed because of their wickedness, should not Israel be fully warned of the possibility of the same fate awaiting them should they, in turn, prove to be disobedient?

Two contrasting comments then add further force to this note of warning. First, God had given this privileged opportunity to Israel because of the promise given on oath to the national ancestors: Abraham, Isaac, and Jacob (v. 5). Second, and more ominous, Israel must look into its own heart to see what sentiments resided there. The historical traditions the nation had so jealously preserved would reveal a darker side to the nation's conduct in the past and the dangerous inner propensities of spirit that had all too often been displayed. They were a stubborn people and had been rebellious against God since the day they had come out of Egypt (vv. 6-7).

REFLECTIONS

Short as it is, this further exhortation to courage and boldness in facing the challenge of taking possession of the land, even from the grip of such feared opponents as the Anakim, touches a very salutary note. God's election does not mean groundless and unmerited favoritism. Were that the case, God would have been shown to flout the very righteousness the covenant declared and upheld. That God must be fair and just, and therefore no supporter of undeserved favoritism, is strongly argued by Peter in Acts 10:34-35. God does not, and cannot, have favorites, since it is the divine purpose to uphold justice and righteousness. Even to entertain the idea that this could be the case is an affront to the very character of divinity.

A deeper aspect of this deuteronomic teaching is its probing of human thought and attitudes. It searches the inner recesses of the human heart. Pride was one of the medieval church's seven deadly sins. It becomes even more deadly when it takes the form of spiritual pride, which may occur even though it is established on the most worthy spiritual premises of God's gifts and assurances. Hidden feelings of stubborn rebelliousness may remain cloaked behind an outward display of good behavior. Yet, however well masked they are, the sentiment of pride will eventually show up. So the deuteronomic author here probes into the inner motives and attitudes of every person, demanding an introspective soul-searching that is remarkable in a document that has sometimes mistakenly been held to be legalistic in its tendencies. God's acts of election call for an inner response, summoning feelings of gratitude and love and resisting any temptation to human self-congratulation: "Let the one who boasts, boast in the LORD" (1 Cor 1:31 NRSV).

Deuteronomy 9:8–10:11, The Great Intercessor

COMMENTARY

The warning to Israel that, as a nation, it was a people prone to rebelliousness against God (9:7) is now backed up by a long sermon demonstrating more fully this very point. Israel should not, on its past record, trust in itself. It could only trust in Moses and the power of intercessory prayer.[56] The text for this sermon is provided by the historical report, now preserved in Exod 32:1-35, that told how the Israelites, even while Moses was on Mt. Horeb in conversation with God, had manufactured an image of a golden calf. So the very historical tradition Israel had retained demonstrated that from the very beginning of Israel's spiritual journey, which began at Mt. Horeb, deep sin had been committed against the second commandment. Even while the covenant was in the process of being made, Israel was in the process of flouting one of its most solemn requirements.

Before even the writing on the tablets, written by the finger of God, had been seen by human eyes, and before they had been handed over to the people, these people were enmeshed in idolatry. The message is taken as decisively clear that, when left to their own devices, the people invariably go deeply astray. At the time when they were waiting at the foot of the mountain, the effrontery of such an act is taken to have been so serious that it would have brought an end to Israel's hopes of fulfilling God's promise to them. Had it not been for the intercession of Moses, they would have perished there and then. He had placed his own person between God and the people and had been willing to die with them, rather than see everything that had been promised come to nothing.

The narrative is complex from a literary point of view. It has been given its present literary location because it serves to illustrate and reinforce the warning of 9:7: "You have been rebellious against the LORD from the day

you came out of the land of Egypt" (NRSV). Yet from a narrative viewpoint it appears out of historical sequence, particularly when set beside similar historical narratives in Deuteronomy 1–3. It deals with an event that had occurred at Mt. Horeb at the time when negotiations for the covenant were still being completed and before Israel had ventured farther into the wilderness.

The story is told here by Moses in the first person, and it interprets this act of spiritual betrayal from his point of view. In contrast, the report of the event in Exodus 32 saw the action from the people's, and Aaron's, perspective.

The narrative in its final form is certainly not from one single literary mold. The report of the final outcome of the events that occurred and of the reprieve that was granted to Israel is given in 10:10-11. This is linked directly to a great prayer of intercession ascribed to Moses in 9:25-29. The intervening instructions concerning the need for the making of a sacred ark (10:1-5) and for the placing of this in the custody of the Levites (10:6-9) have been introduced at this particular point to show where the law of God was to be found and from whom it could be heard. To some degree it implies, without explicitly declaring, that the ark and the law of God replaced any need in Israel for the kind of symbolic image of deity that had been sought after in the manufacture of the golden calf.

The account of the actual intercession of Moses appears to be given twice. It is first reported in 9:18-19, where no actual prayer is recounted, and then again in 9:25-29, where the vital text of the prayer is given. It certainly appears, therefore, that a shorter report of Moses' action has undergone a measure of subsequent expansion. The central core of the original report, which focuses on the issues of the necessity for complete obedience to God's commandments and the efficacious power of prayer, can be seen to be based directly on the account given in Exodus 32. In its enlarged form, with the subsequent expansions, the major emphasis is placed on

---

56. The fullest recent study by E. Aurelius, *Der Fürbitte Israels. Eine Studie zum Mosebild im Alten Testament,* ConBOT 27 (Lund: Almqvist & Wiksell International, 1988) 8-56, is most valuable. See also S. E. Balentine, *Prayer in the Hebrew Bible,* OBT (Minneapolis: Fortress, 1993) 19, 21; H. Graf Reventlow, *Gebet im Alten Testament* (Stuttgart: W. Kohlhammer, 1986) 229-35.

the rebellious tendency Israel had persistently displayed, which is viewed with an almost fatalistic and despairing inevitability. Left to itself, Israel is almost beyond the hope of redemption. Without a spiritual giant of the stature of Moses, Israel would have perished at the very beginning of its existence as the chosen people of the LORD God. The warning from this presentation is clear: When no comparable figure to that of Moses exists, then Israel must take even greater care to remain obedient to God's commandments. The mediatorial role of Moses carries over to affirm the mediation provided by God's law.

We can note some of the most prominent features that make this account of Moses' intercessory prayer a central basis for the expression of the deuteronomic theology. It reveals how human beings are related to God through prayer and the vital role that spiritual leadership plays in building this relationship. The covenant between God and Israel is presented as synonymous with the Ten Commandments, which were inscribed on the two tablets. These are then described as "the tablets of the covenant" (9:9, 11, 15; cf. 4:13). The dramatic action of Moses in smashing the tablets (9:17) is both a mark of the leader's anger, which itself reflects the anger of God, and also a deliberate sign-action. It aimed at demonstrating in visible fashion the fact that the people had broken the covenant on their side so that it would now be regarded as no longer valid and in force. Only the prayer of Moses alters the situation to rescue the covenant from this act of annulment. In making such a gesture of breaking the tablets it seems highly probable that Moses is enacting a dramatic gesture comparable to that employed in negotiating and revoking major international treaties.

The formal expression of the people's disobedience is given outward and visible form in the manufacture of an image of a calf, cast from gold. Similar images of bull calves, made either from clay or wood overlaid with metal, have been found at a number of sites in the Holy Land. The bull-calf form, symbolizing strength and fertility, was a popular image so that the portrayal of such an image at this vital moment in Israel's history was undoubtedly intended as a typical example of the way in which Israel had flouted the demands of the

second commandment throughout a long history. The bull-calf images set up by Jeroboam I at Bethel and Dan (1 Kgs 12:28-29) were probably especially in the author's mind, in which case a degree of political feeling has intruded into the account, since such images were proof of the indifference to the demand for one single sanctuary at the place the LORD would choose.

We are clearly left with the question of what precisely the rationale was for such images and how it came about that they were so widely popular for so long throughout Israel's history. Undoubtedly such an image expressed both male power and fertility, making it a suitable symbol of the life-giving power of God. Since the Jerusalem Temple possessed images of cherubim (winged lion-like creatures; cf. Ezek 10:14), it may be asked why the cherubim images were acceptable, while the bull-calf images were not. No clear answer can be given to show precisely how the image was believed to relate to, and embody the power of, that which it symbolized.

Undoubtedly the bull-calf image was thought to be more than a pedestal for the invisible deity. Yet the manner of identity between the deity and its image is never clearly or directly stated. To some extent the two were never wholly identified, although the sense of the power of deity in a suitable image that represented divine presence (the Hebrew uses the word פנים [pānîm] for "face, presence") was all-important. Not only does the deuteronomic theology reject the sexual associations of the bull-calf image, but it also strongly opposes the sense of immediacy in the identity between deity and image that was fundamental to the religious symbolism of the entire ancient Near East. It has been noted, and is relevant to the deuteronomic theology, that in the ancient Near Eastern texts from Ugarit the god El is frequently described as having the form of a bull. Yet so is the deity Baal, indicating that there was no restriction of the most popular power and fertility symbolism to one single deity. That bull imagery had been popularly linked with the LORD God of Israel, therefore, is wholly understandable.

Many sections of the population of ancient Israel had simply adopted the imagery of a bull calf as a suitable symbol for deity, basing the practice on the older tradition that had existed in the land. This almost certainly went back to the time of the very beginning of the domestication of cattle for agricultural use and for food. Many of the most widely used forms of such an image would appear to have been retained in the homes of individual families, so that their presence at the major shrines was not the only manifestation of their presence. Even centralized control over the practice at Israel's sanctuaries would not eradicate the popularity of such symbols. The deuteronomists now seek to repudiate all further use of such iconography from the homes and rural shrines of Israel. It had become, in their skillful reworking of the ancient tradition, a tangible expression of all that was most tempting, and yet seemingly most ineradicable, in the inherited legacy of the religious life in the land. This deuteronomic narrative polemic then appears as the expression of a major effort to remove these popular religious bull-calf images and their associated customs from the homes and thought world of Israel.

So the account of the great intercessory prayer of Moses serves a dual pupose. On the one hand, it reveals the deceitfulness of sin by showing how seemingly natural and inevitable it was that Israel should fall into idolatry if it failed to give the most strenuous heed to the Ten Commandments. On the other hand, it also exalted the memory and image of the person of Moses. Without him Israel would have perished at its very beginning. He was the spiritual giant who towered above all others, since not even the patriarchs had carried the destiny of the nation on their shoulders in quite the fashion that Moses had done. Israel had been spared, not for its own sake, but for the sake of God's honor and for the sake of the self-denying intervention of Moses.

Before the final outcome of Moses' great work of intercession is reported in 10:10-11, two short narrative reports are inserted in the story. The first of these (10:1-5) tells of the making of an ark, and the second (10:6-9) of the resumption of the journey and the setting apart of the Levites to carry and keep custody of the ark. The reason for their inclusion here, which introduces a rather disconnected flow to the story of Moses' prayer and its successful outcome, must lie in their relevance to the custody and proclamation of the law. Since these commandments were vital to Israel's obedience, it was essential to know where the law was kept and who its custodians were. The answers to these questions were that the tablets containing the commandments had been entrusted to the Levites, who were commissioned by God to retain custody of the ark and to convey God's blessing to the people. In this way, the ark and the Levites between them maintained much of the unique ministry of Moses on behalf of the people. In turn, this perspective tells something of considerable importance about the authors of Deuteronomy and about their major theological reassessment of one of the leading features of Israel's worship.

The early history of the ark in ancient Israel is shrouded in obscurity. It is introduced to us as a mobile sanctuary in Num 10:34-35, where the accompanying invocation and prayers indicate that it had a close link to the concept of the LORD God as Israel's Leader in battle. The fact that it could be addressed directly as though it were God reveals how closely the divine presence was believed to be linked to it. This fact has given rise to the belief that, in spite of its name and box-like form, it was regarded as the throne of the invisible deity seated upon it. However, doubts remain as to its original significance and role since its name clearly implies that it was a container of some description. Its connection with warfare and the belief in God's leadership and power in battle appear as the most certain of its associations.

Not until the time of King David was the ark brought to Jerusalem and established permanently in a tent there (2 Sam 6:12-19). From this time onward, at least, it was evidently regarded as the most important of Israel's sacred artifacts and as a feature that made the shrine of Jerusalem more important than others, even before the Temple was built there. So the presence of the ark in Jerusalem played an important part in making the city the political capital of all Israel and in relating the traditions of it to one of the oldest features of Israel's religious inheritance.

For the deuteronomists, this older interpretation of the ark called for considerable modification, and it is this deuteronomic reinterpretation that is now set out in 10:1-5. It has been widely recognized as among the latest literary units to have been introduced into the book. It is also quite likely that an older account of the making of the ark once stood after Exod 33:6, where it would have followed the account of the making of the golden calf. With the literary reshaping of the Pentateuch in its later stages, this account was regarded as no longer relevant and so was lost, being replaced by the deuteronomic revised viewpoint.

It is a striking feature of the deuteronomic theology that the direct identification of the ark with the presence of God is effectively set aside and its role as a container contrastingly emphasized. It is regarded as the focal shrine memorializing and expressing the covenant between Israel and the LORD as God. So it could even be described as "the ark of the covenant," although this cannot have been its earliest designation, and its original relationship to any covenant ideology appears doubtful. Later Jewish tradition was of the belief that several of the most important relics of Israel's national history had been kept in it (cf. Heb 9:4).

It is, however, not difficult to see that when the Judean state collapsed in 587 BCE and the Temple of Jerusalem was destroyed, the significance of the ark effectively perished with it. It is possible that the ark had not even survived that long and had been removed earlier, but this appears unlikely. In any case, as a symbol of the divine power to bring victory in battle, the ark now became totally discredited. For its deuteronomic reinterpretation, however, its significance now lay not in what it was in itself, but solely in what it contained: the sacred book of Torah. Since that law of God's covenant had not perished, then the loss of the ark no longer mattered greatly. An allusion to its loss and to the unimportance of this for Jerusalem's future is to be found in Jer 3:15-16, and this note must undoubtedly be credited to a deuteronomic editor of Jeremiah's prophecies.

The short narrative in 10:6-9 carries us back to the period of Israel's wilderness journeyings. Its inclusion here must be a consequence of the desire to show both that the ark had accompanied the Israelites in the wilderness and that it was in the custody, and under the protection of, the Levites. The brief note in 10:9 explaining that the Levites had

no permanent inheritance of land, but were maintained by the gifts of the people for their role of ministry before the LORD, introduces us to them and to their significance for the deuteronomists, showing that they, too, were agents of the covenant relationship.

The role of the Levites, as set out in the book of Deuteronomy, has aroused considerable discussion and deserves close attention, since it undoubtedly served to magnify their importance to Israel's life.[57] It presents a seemingly ambivalent attitude toward them. As in the brief note here, the Levites are recognized as guardians, and by implication interpreters, of the law of the covenant. So they are revered as faithful teachers who were authorized as the law's interpreters and also as those who could be expected to promote allegiance to it with the utmost zeal. At the same time, there are several passages in the book, especially in the law code section (chaps. 12–26), which align them so directly with the poor as to suggest that they were a relatively impoverished group whose claim on the people for support was in need of strong encouragement. G. von Rad in particular has seen the close association of the Levites with the authors of Deuteronomy to be one of identity.[58] The powerful rhetorical preaching style that colors chaps. 6–9 could then reflect the work of teaching Levites, who were the strongest and most respected of those whose loyalty to the LORD God was above question. That such loyalty to God was their prime duty (cf. the story of the ruthlessness in displaying loyalty to the LORD in Exod 32:25-29) could then serve to explain, if not to justify, those parts of the book that advocate complete ruthlessness in demanding adherence to the LORD.

Attractive as some aspects of this attempt to identify the Levites as Deuteronomy's authors is, it appears, by itself, to be too incomplete an understanding of the latter. Other aspects of the work point strongly to other interests and traditions. More significant for an understanding of the deuteronomic interpretation of the distinctive position of the Levites is the question of their priestly status. While

57. M. Haran, *Temples and Temple Service in Ancient Israel* (Oxford: Oxford University Press, 1978) 58-83; Aelred Cody, *A History of Old Testament Priesthood,* AnBib 35 (Rome: Pontifical Biblical Institute, 1969) 125-45; A. H. J. Gunneweg, *Leviten und Priester,* FRLANT 89 (Göttingen, 1965); J. A. Emerton, "Priests and Levites in Deuteronomy," *VT* 12 (1962) 128-38.
58. Von Rad, *Studies in Deuteronomy,* 60-69.

Deuteronomy assumes that all priests are Levites, it clearly recognizes that many Levites are teachers, rather than priests, and are not formally carrying out priestly duties. In seeking to relate the situation of the law book to Josiah's reform, this was understood by von Rad to point to those Levites who had been displaced as a result of the Assyrian incursions into northern Israel during the eighth century BCE.

However, the deuteronomic awareness that the Levites were in special need of consideration for support from Israel's tithes and charitable gifts, and that they were not all fulfilling priestly duties, can be far better explained as a consequence of what had happened in 587 BCE, when the Temple was destroyed. The Levites had been effectively left without an altar to serve. As custodians of Israel's sacral traditions they were, nevertheless, able to fulfill a primary role as teachers and guides for prayer. It is in such a capacity that the deuteronomic legislation seeks to retain for them a primary function as guardians of Israel's faith.

REFLECTIONS

The story of Moses' great act of intercession, and the role of intercessory prayer generally in the biblical portrait of religious life, marks a high point of deuteronomic theology. We have consistently noted the turning to an inner spiritual dimension of faith that characterizes so much of this book. It is wholly consonant with this that the history of Joshua–2 Kings, which carries so many of the trademarks of deuteronomic thinking, should also present many of the great turning points of the national history being negotiated through sermons or prayers.

Whereas the inherited patterns of religion in the ancient Near East had consistently been physical, external, and visual in form, that of Deuteronomy is contrastingly inward, rational, and reflective. In general the human endeavor to make the divine world accessible through ritual and the veneration of artifacts is regarded by the deuteronomists at best with suspicion and at worst with deep hostility. Without an inner probing and searching of the heart, there could be no true access to the world of divine power and a divine presence. Almost all other forms of religious activity are viewed as largely adjuncts to prayer. Only by acts of remembering, heart searching, and loving can the human mind seize the key to the heavenly realities. Even the most august and respected of Israel's shrines could be no more than a place where the divine name could be found, through which prayer could be offered. In fact, even prayer offered from a distant land toward this place would be heard and honored (1 Kgs 8:44).

Yet prayer could easily lapse into the most isolated and individualistic expression of religious faith. Instead of promoting a sense of community and shared faith within a larger congregation, it could become isolationist and solipsistic, with each individual Israelite praying on a spiritual island of his or her own making. Yet, according to the deuteronomic perspective, prayer was never to be isolationist, and so intercessory prayer was one of its most basic and fundamental expressions. Individuals were bound up with one another in the community of faith, enabling the strong to carry the weak and the stumbling and fainthearted to be carried along by those of courage and insight. In all Israel's history there was no one whose courage and insight could match those of the figure of Moses.

The interjection of the two narratives in 10:1-9 regarding the ark and the Levites brings us face to face with an important aspect of the deuteronomic thinking. We have already noted the striking manner in which the forms of address used in the sermonic exhortations to the reader introduce a note of contemporaneity in regard to events of the past. The generations of Israel who stood at the foot of Mt. Horeb or who waited anxiously to set foot across the river Jordan to enter the promised land or who now constituted the surviving readership to whom Deuteronomy was addressed, all made up one Israel. A timeless unity bound the generations of the nation together to make them one so that decisions and choices of the past remained real options for the present. Israel was facing the same challenges and possibilities that its earlier generations had faced.

This is an important rhetorical device employed in Deuteronomy to create a sense of urgency and immediacy. The past lived on in that it had left open future choices and decisions that each Israelite man and woman still faced. It is, however, more than a skillfull literary technique, since the authors clearly believed that God's choice of Israel and the covenant that had been made with the people were lasting covenants. The consequences remained real and valid for the generations who had passed since the Jordan was first crossed.

For this ongoing reality of the covenant to be accepted and realized within Israel there needed to be a continued ministry of teaching, prayer, and responsiveness to keep alive the blessing that the covenant had brought. Israel would remain on its land, its fields and flocks would prosper and be fertile, and the power that had defeated all Israel's enemies so victoriously at the beginning would still give victory in later years (cf. the role of the ark and the Levites in achieving the model victory at Jericho, Josh 6:12-21). So the ministry of the Levites, the making and care of the sacred ark, the reading and hearing of the law, and all the rites and customs that gave vitality and visible expression to religion had to be maintained. Israel would then continue to be a blessed people.

This awareness that salvation could be a *present* condition, and not merely an event that had happened in the past, was a vital aspect of the deuteronomic theology. For all the careful historical focus on events of the past, and not least the lessons of the failures and rebelliousness of the past, the present mattered greatly to the deuteronomic authors.

Deuteronomy 10:12–11:7, The Law Carries Both Curse and Blessing

COMMENTARY

The sermons that have advocated and reinforced the covenant commandments by a process of exhortation and reflection on past events are now brought to a climax by further admonitions. These recapitulate points that have already been made, but lend a further note of urgency to the consciousness of the covenant and its law. The demands of the covenant are both simple and yet inexhaustible. They can easily be remembered, and yet the nature of the human mind and the inevitable temptations of alien religious traditions make constant vigilance a necessity. One thing that is constantly needed is to fear God, to pursue the path marked out by the divine laws and to hold to them by maintaining an unbroken attitude of love toward God. "Only to fear the LORD your God" (v. 12) remained a perpetual admonition and command. Yet this one thing posed a demand that knew no limit, since it was a demand that could only be responded to with the whole of one's being—heart, soul, and mind.

10:12-22. Once again the unique privilege and opportunity that have been conferred on Israel as a consequence of the mysterious act of God's choice of them are reasserted (v. 15). Israel could neither evade nor deny the opportunity that lay ahead. Nevertheless, it was not an opportunity to be faced lightly. It was no easy thing to be the recipient of God's choice and call. The LORD was to be celebrated as God of gods, Lord of lords, and One who could not be swayed or bribed by human plans or devious practices. Accordingly, vv. 18-19 digress to assert that Israel's conduct must show the same pattern of right dealing as that displayed by the divine nature. It is noteworthy that the interpretation of what such right acting entailed for the orphan, the widow, and the stranger (or resident alien) was to provide each with food and clothing. The point is subsequently taken up more fully in the law code of chaps. 12–26.

The appeal to the historical tradition regarding Israel's origins as slaves in the land of Egypt (vv. 19, 22) is used by the deuteronomists on several occasions to sustain a basic ethical injunction of care and empathy toward the weaker and more destitute members of society. In this way, the very "national" tradition of Israel was one in which a sensitivity to those who were deprived and abused held a prominent place. For the deuteronomists, the very understanding of righteousness included a strong bias toward the weak and the poor.

The point is a significant one and serves to explain the distinctive nature of the commandments and the remarkable deuteronomic concern to combine a strong demand for an inward disposition of love with a sharply defined formal system of legislation. Clearly love and law were in no way regarded as concepts that stood in contrast. It is precisely this combination of law and an ethic of love that makes it impossible to interpret the Ten Commandments as representing a system of law in an exclusively juridical sense. They were to be the guideposts of a social order built on an ethic of unity and of a responsive concern to a knowledge of divine love.

The theological nature of the deuteronomic ethic is reinforced by a return once again to the insistence that reverence for the LORD as God, and unswerving loyalty to the divine commandments, demanded an exclusive use of the name of the LORD alone when sacred oaths and vows were needed (v. 20). This single-minded emphasis reveals the theological underpinning of the deuteronomic ethic. Without a prior exclusive reverence for the LORD as God, the fundamental grounds for accepting the demands of righteous action would be undermined.

11:1-7. These verses provide further insight into the deuteronomic theology of worship and the manner in which this is combined with a strong moral demand. Israel was called upon to obey the commandments of God—a point that has already been established as the controlling theme of chaps.

5–11. Yet it should never appear difficult or unwelcome to Israel to yield this obedience, since the people had themselves witnessed the saving power of the LORD as God. Once again the sense of contemporaneity and the rhetorical bridge that bound together Israel's many generations create a sense of unity and reassert the claim of God on every generation of Israel. The truths of the past became the springboard of action for the present.

At a first reading, the insistence that the readers of the book "must acknowledge his greatness" (v. 2) would appear to be unremarkable. Yet it glosses over the point already made earlier regarding the period of thirty-eight years spent wandering aimlessly in the wilderness until the generation that had shown complete distrust of God's Word had died out. Those whom the author so emphatically insists have most reason to trust and acknowledge the power of God from the evidence of what their own eyes had witnessed are assumed to be most at risk to disobey the commandments of God.

The point made in v. 2 that "it was not your children" becomes all the more remarkable when it is recognized that the text of Deuteronomy was quite evidently and consciously being addressed to a much later generation still. The great power of God had been demonstrated to the full to those Hebrew slaves who had experienced the marvelous deliverance from Egypt and who had witnessed the overthrow of the pursuing Egyptian army (v. 4). That generation had been given firsthand knowledge of who the LORD God was and of the divine majesty. Yet all this had taken place with the most immense consequences for the present, which the author brings out with a kind of double entendre in the key phrase "to this day" (עד היום הזה *'ad hayyôm hazzeh,* v. 4). It is both the day when Moses addressed Israel as the people faced the prospect of entering the land and it is the day of the reader who stands trembling with anxiety and concern as to whether there can be any future at all for the remnant of Israel. The former glory now appeared to be sadly tarnished. Israel's spiritual armor had rusted, and its moral courage in believing the Word of God had been gradually ebbing away. The reawakening call of Deuteronomy is that "this day" is still "God's today." Salvation is viewed as a reality that has consequences for all succeeding generations of Israelites. Past events prove the possibility of present salvation.

At this point, the narrative takes up a more unexpected point. Not only had there existed an external threat from the Egyptian forces that had pursued Israel, but there was also a more insidious threat from within in the figures of Dathan and Abiram, who had rebelled against the authority of Moses. A point of special interest regarding the method of the deuteronomic writer appears in that it is evident that the source of the information presented here is the report of the rebellion given in Numbers 16. There, where the present priestly text is now preserved, "all the men of Korah," along with Dathan and Abiram, are the rebels who suffer dire punishment for their folly. The deuteronomic author, however, must have followed an earlier version of the pentateuchal source (JE?) that mentioned only Dathan and Abiram and not Korah.

The reference to this internal threat comes unexpectedly at this particular point. Nevertheless, it fits in well with the broader deuteronomic perspective that Israel not only faced external enemies, spearheaded by powerful foreign peoples with massive armies, but also internal ones, led by rebels from within the nation. More threatening and dangerous still in the eyes of the deuteronomists was the threat that every man, woman, and child within the nation would forget the greatness of God's achievements in the past. The lessons of the past needed to be learned all over again, and the courage of the few, which had given birth to the nation and had dared to believe the Word of God, had to be learned all over again.

REFLECTIONS

Few subjects can appear more confusing and difficult for the untutored mind than the uses of history. What is it that history teaches? For some it may appear to have no lessons or meaning at all, while for others it may, as in Marxist dogma, operate as if on rails, to "prove" that one consequence necessarily follows another and that society is moving in unstoppable necessity toward a classless utopia. To some people, one period of history appears much like any other, illustrating the same features and uncovering the same mix of human vision and human weakness. To others all episodes of human history are utterly unique and unrepeatable and, therefore, incapable of teaching anything at all that might be relevant to another period.

In fact, history sometimes teaches us easily discernible truths, and sometimes history teaches us nothing at all. Certainly much seems so startlingly to repeat itself that one generation finds itself having to fight again the battles and learn again the lessons that earlier generations had fought and learned. As the biblical Ecclesiastes could repeat as a proverbial maxim, "There is nothing new under the sun" (Eccl 1:9). Yet there is an element of uniqueness about the past that makes the course of history unforeseeable and the study of it so fascinating. To a noticeable extent, each generation of the human race has had to work out its own salvation.

The brief period that Israel's ancestors spent marching from the oasis of Kadesh to the banks of the river Jordan, after they had wasted a fruitless lifetime of a generation meandering aimlessly in a wasteland, provided the deuteronomic authors with object lessons for their own generation. These lessons learned about the past and already recorded in Israel's national history were also lessons for the present, when read and interpreted discerningly. And such is what the deuteronomists have done in using these stories. They are, in effect, sermons, and the "texts" for these sermons are provided by extracted records from episodes reported in earlier material, for the most part still preserved for us in the Pentateuch.

The method of the deuteronomic authors is relatively easy to follow, and the rhetorical skill with which the reader is invited to heed the message of the past is unmistakable and highly praiseworthy. When we examine closely the theological undergirding that has shaped the way the stories are retold and the lessons that are deduced from them, we see that these writers have resorted to simple paradigms with a rather simplistic presentation, suggesting that the same features are repeated from one generation to the next. Nowhere is this deuteronomistic style of making history fit into a formula more evident than in the framework to the book of Judges.

It would be a mistake, however, to regard the deuteronomic interpretation of history as a fixed and stylized sequence of repetitions, in which only the names of persons and locations change but the essential outcome appears predetermined. Hidden within these anecdotal paradigms is a very powerful and existential view of the past. While the past is seen to conform to certain patterns, what these patterns bring to the fore is the sense of challenge and uniqueness that belongs to each situation, a sense that a time has come that is full of opportunity and danger, and that it will not come again. By such a theological reflection the past events of Israel's beginning period become the text for showing the reader the challenge of the present. The sense that repeatedly faces the reader is one of wistful reflection: "If only they had. . . ." Some people behaved well in the past, but some behaved badly and foolishly. So the opportunity passed them by, and a time of spiritual richness was lost. Yet no serious reader can fail to see how he or she is still being faced with the same challenge: "Today, if you will hear his voice. . . ." So the message of the past becomes a call to action in the present. The very fact that there existed an open gateway in the past reveals that there are still gates that may be opened in the present.

Deuteronomy 11:8-32, Be Diligent to Keep the Commandments

COMMENTARY

A final sermon brings the introduction to the deuteronomic law code to a close and summarizes the message of what has been declared in the previous addresses of chaps. 5–11. The message remains unequivocal: The Ten Commandments are vitally important and must never be forgotten. So the opening words, "Keep then this entire commandment" (v. 8), are effectively complemented by the concluding injunction: "You must diligently observe all the statutes and ordinances that I am setting before you today" (v. 32). In the center of this section (vv. 18-21), we are presented with a further summary recapitulation of the various injunctions as to how Israel may learn to keep these important commandments. Here we find repeated directives that have already been made earlier. Israel must learn to keep the words of the commandments consistently in mind—to bind them as a sign to the hand, to teach them to children, and to think upon them wherever and whenever it is practically possible. All of

this further insistence upon the central position of the commandments is necessary for one overriding reason: Continued settlement in the land and retention of its ownership are conditional upon doing so.

A number of features in the section carry us deeply into the theological world of the deuteronomists. Taken in their entirety, the series of commandments can be summed up by the singular term "the commandment" (המצוה *hammiṣwâ*, v. 8; cf. 5:31). Virtually every blessing of life that made it sustainable are presented as being dependent upon obedience to these basic demands.

What is striking in contrast to the appeal to history as a motivating reason for such observance in 10:12–11:7 is that here an appeal is made to the beauty, the fertility, and the general desirability of Israel's land, shortly to be won and occupied, that provides such a motive. Since scholars have frequently contrasted the biblical appeals to history and historical recollection with an appeal to the natural world and the natural order of things, the section here deserves the closest attention. In a poetic and somewhat exaggerated fashion, the very geology and climate of the biblical landscape is made into an assertion concerning the directness of God's concern with it: "The eyes of the LORD your God are always on it, from the beginning of the year to the end of the year" (v. 12).

Such attention to the fertility and desirability of the biblical territory is highly meaningful when read in the context of the religious tradition of the ancient Near East. It is wholly typical of the deuteronomistic theology to contrast the Israelites' land favorably with the seemingly hostile territory of Egypt (v. 10). Yet more immediately relevant for an appreciation of the significance of the deuteronomic theology is its consciousness of the popular appeal of Canaanite religion on account of its claim to uphold the vitality and seasonal efficacy of the natural order of life. Baal and his consort Anat were presented as givers of "life," so that it can be misleading to focus exclusively on their appeal as givers of "fertility" in abstraction from this. The fertility of fields and flocks, the productivity of the soil, and the seasonal regularity of the rainfall were all regarded as aspects of life. Such life could then be regarded as the gift of the Cannanite deities, whose rituals were designed to promote its preservation and continuance.

Baal was lord of storms and thunder, master of the rainfall, and on this account he was revered as the giver of life. Anat, his heavenly consort, was both his defender and his helper and the bearer of new life. By controlling the seasonal order, these deities brought life to the soil and security to the people whose very existence depended on its productivity and on the health of flocks and herds. Because drought and consequent famine were ever-present threats, neither god nor goddess could easily be ignored.

Keeping in mind an awareness of this intense Canaanite preoccupation with rainfall and the fertility of the soil, one can see the special significance of the description of Israel's land as one "flowing with milk and honey" (v. 9). Whereas the land of the Israelites was irrigated by the seasonal rainfall, Egypt was dependent upon irrigation "by foot" (v. 10), an allusion to the need for human effort to power the mechanical systems in use in ancient Egypt. The fact that the human-designed systems of irrigation made the Nile and its surrounding land into "the granary of Egypt" and that Israel's ancestor Jacob had fled to Egypt in order to find food in a time of famine is tactfully passed over. The author has made use of an understandable degree of poetic license to express his own overpowering delight in the land of Israel and the horror with which he contemplates the possibility of its loss.

Awareness of the variations of climate and the marginal levels of rainfall in the semi-desert regions of Israel's land are here employed to promote a sense of the immediacy of its dependence upon God. The coming of the rains in the spring and fall of the year becomes a vital mark of a beneficent providence and so makes the question, "Who is it who gives the rain?" a primary one for religion (v. 14). In a very real sense, it was the same awareness and the raising of the same question that were a prominent feature of Canaanite religion and that made Baal, lord of storms and thunder, so forceful a factor in the Canaanite mythology and pantheon. What is then particularly striking in this homily is the interposing of obedience to the Ten Commandments as a vital requirement for the life-sustaining climate of the region to be maintained. Not Baal, but the LORD God of Israel is the giver of life. The LORD God alone is the life-ensuring One without whose cooperation and power the fertility of the land would wither away. So this important combining of ethical demand with natural promise results in a powerful moralizing and spiritualizing of the interpretation of nature.

We can well appreciate the note of urgency in the warning: "Take care, or you will be seduced into turning away, serving other gods and worshiping them" (v. 16). Precisely because the gods and goddesses of Canaan were venerated as "deities of the land," who were its sustainers and protectors, it was an inevitable temptation for those who lived on it, and who were dependent upon its produce, to feel under obligation to them. All the more must this have been the case when the LORD God of Israel was regarded as merely the God of Mt. Horeb who had intervened to rescue the nation's ancestors in Egypt. The sense of geographical and temporal distance made the appeal of "the gods of the land" appear more immediate and relevant to the people of Israel once they had settled in it.

The concluding section of this sermonic address in vv. 26-31, which brings to a close the whole series of homilies advocating careful observance of the commandments beginning in chap. 6, proclaims both the promise of blessing and the threat of curse. This theme then returns far more extensively in chaps. 27–29.

The simple contrasting of the consequences of blessing and curse in vv. 26-30 serves to set the commandments once more in the very forefront of all life and activity. Whether the one or the other is to be the experience of Israel will be wholly determined by whether Israel, taken as a single entity, displays obedience to the commandments. This highlights the pre-eminence attached to religious commitment, combined with a concern for morality, which is embodied in the commandments. Both here and even more fully in the larger exposition of the hope of blessing and the threat of curse in chaps. 27–29, there are important elements of the harmonization and integration of a wide variety of human experiences into a consolidated pattern. For many people, concepts of blessing and, even more particularly, of curse were treated in a quasi-magical fashion. They were believed to possess a vitality of their own. Persons, families, and places could all be thought of as being the subjects of curse or of blessing. Certain individuals were regarded as being capable of uttering words of either blessing or curse that could not thereafter be canceled. Some persons could be thought of as having been "born under a curse," while others were thought of as "children of blessing." It was no insignificant matter for the deuteronomic authors, therefore, to seek to discern a coherence and wholeness in the entire arena of life by insisting that both blessing and curse lay in the hands of the One God, who had spoken to Israel through the commandments.

Behind concepts of blessing and curse there lay a deep consciousness throughout the entire ancient Near East of the power of the spoken word. Words uttered in the name of a deity, whether threatening or reassuring, were words fraught with power. It is the consciousness of this fact that makes inclusion of the misuse of the name of the LORD an important prohibition among the commandments (5:11). To link the powerful name of God with words spoken in deliberately contrived malice, or in order to secure undeserved protection, was to abuse the divine name.

Since words declaring curse or blessing from any god were words of special significance, especially was this so when such words were spoken with appeal to the name of Israel's God. All too easily the fear of such words plunged innocent people into a sea of fear and anxiety that would become destructive. Conversely, the misguided belief that words promising security and prosperity would be unstoppable in their effect could breed a dangerous complacency. A considerable importance, therefore, attaches to what Deuteronomy has to teach on this subject. It presents a feature that permeates the book as a whole and marks the whole deuteronomic outlook in insisting that all faith and spiritual understanding are subject to God's ethical demands.

Religion must inevitably be related to the language and concepts of power and authority. But both power and authority may be abused when they become separated from the wider ethical needs and demands of the human community. Since blessing and curse may be seen as the outworking of human power and authority, then it matters greatly that there should be a tight integration of spiritual, ethical, and political authority. It is just such integration that Deuteronomy seeks to promote and to bring about.

How successful the writers of Deuteronomy were in achieving this in practice we do not adequately know. But we can see in its prescriptive assertions concerning the subordination of all spiritual and political agencies to the ultimate authority of one God that it recognized the central significance of the issue: It declared an unequivocal no to the belief that religious power, even when designed to bring about blessing, could be bestowed without regard for the most fundamental notions of right and wrong. God offers "blessing, if you obey the commandments of the LORD your God . . . and the curse, if you do not" (vv. 27-28).

REFLECTIONS

The careful reader may at first be taken aback by the repetitiveness and seeming overstatement of the deuteronomic emphasis on the commandments of God. So exaggerated is the concern that its repetitiveness sounds rather obsessive. Everywhere, every day, and without exception, the commandments are to be remembered and reflected upon. Moreover, the author of the homilies urging obedience to these commandments probes into the human psyche to uncover the temptations and self-justifying reasonings that might lead any Israelite, once settled safely in the land, to neglect to obey them. The passage of time and the comfort and complacency induced by success are seen to present inevitable temptations. Why should the biblical writers be so insistent, and why should they be so negative in their assessment of how future generations of Israelites would behave? Could it not be assumed that, having once seen and known what was good and right, obedience to God's commandments would commend itself so obviously to everyone as to elicit a natural and unforced obedience? Clearly the deuteronomists did not think so.

The reasons for such negative assessments immediately reveal themselves. First, behind the deuteronomic homilies lies a deep and long experience of human life and attitudes that have given rise to these warnings. The writers were well aware of what had happened in the later years of Israel's life under a monarchy. All Israel's systems of law, of government, of education, and of religious practice and instruction had been severely tested and found wanting since the time when Israel's ancestors had crossed the Jordan and settled in the land. Those very institutions that had claimed so much for themselves—the kingship, the priesthood, the civil judges, and the wealthy heads of families—had all claimed more than they had delivered in promising the success of a healthy, moral, and prosperous nation.

It is for this reason that so much of the Hebrew Bible that deals with the period from the conquest of the land to the collapse of the first Jewish state is a literature of protest. The stories point to weaknesses, betrayals, and failures, and only seldom to a few outstanding leaders and reformers who summoned the nation back to higher goals and worthier ideals than they had achieved. The prophets, with their decisive invective and threats, are more characteristic of the voices from this past than are the words of epic storytellers and poets of triumphant success. By the time of the deuteronomists, Israel felt itself to be lingering under judgment and in need of a new beginning and a return to more fundamental values than it currently embraced. It looked for the recapturing of such values and ideals in the figure and teaching of Moses.

The warnings and admonitions set out here by the deuteronomists were not speculative probings in the darkness, but were themselves the result of serious reflection and deep, heart-searching questions concerning the mysterious nature of evil and the possibilities of self-deception that every human being must feel. There is a mystery of iniquity that means that it is one thing to promulgate good laws and another to ensure that they are obeyed. It is relatively easy to teach high ideals, but another story altogether when it comes to winning acceptance for them. Kings may celebrate righteousness and justice as the very foundations on which their thrones rest, but that celebration does not prevent them from following in the footsteps of Ahab. Loyalty to one LORD God could quickly become confused and undermined by fear of magical powers and age-old respect for local traditions and conventions. The deuteronomic portrait of the actions of Jeroboam I, whatever its precise historical basis, is profoundly insightful (1 Kings 12). The capacity for pandering to human weakness and naïveté may cloud the vision of better things for any community. Nations may be born in moments of splendid insight and glorious endeavor, only to perish in a wasteland of disillusionment and self-deception. The modern social historian and shrewd observer of behavior will find similar enough pictures of the human scene in our time.

In the shaping of these deuteronomic sermons, the repetition of the emphatic conditional warning is meant with the most intense seriousness: "Take heed . . . do not forget . . . days will come when you will indeed be tempted to forget the LORD God and to set aside the divine commandments." So there is a powerful and meaningful catalog of explanations and admonitions, uttered in a highly charged rhetorical style to which every generation of Israelites was urged to pay attention. Even when all the outward signs of obedience would appear to be intact and secure, there could nevertheless arise a deceptive inner aversion to them. Those who felt most assured of their rectitude had reason to be most watchful lest they be the ones to lead Israel astray.

It is important that the spiritual depth of the deuteronomic concern to teach love for God, and to go so far as to demand that it be given with a whole heart and mind and effort, should have its counterpart in a recognition of the inwardness and deceptiveness of evil. Even circumcision itself—the physical proof of submission to the covenant of God—must be matched with a circumcision of the heart (Deut 10:16). Consciousness of the covenant and all that it stood for had to motivate the inner springs of thought and action. This was true because it is in the heart also that forgetfulness, complacency, and indifference to the love of God arise. Evil can no longer be regarded simply as the fault of society, of other people, or even of one's own past mistakes. It has to be traced deep down into the inner workings of the human heart. Wherever the deuteronomists had been nurtured in their understanding of the nature of evil, it was clearly no simple doctrine of ritual error or social oppression. It demanded a degree of personal self-examination. It is this aspect of the deuteronomic teaching that has made it such a powerful instrument in the shaping of both Jewish and Christian piety. To suppose that the Hebrew Bible thinks of sin only in formal and external categories is to fail to heed the very warnings that Deuteronomy declares so loudly.

The second feature of these homilies is their intense moralizing of faith, which they express through repeated calls to obey the commandments. To the modern reader, it may appear self-evident that true religion is about love, honesty, truthfulness, and integrity in all aspects of conduct. Without such virtues faith and worship lose their meaning and become lifeless formalities. Yet such convictions were not normal, or widespread, in the ancient world. Even in the modern world they are less commonplace than might be supposed. Religion that promises power, but evades the insistent demands of right speaking and right dealing, possesses an ever-current appeal.

All such belief is an illusion, and the deuteronomic authors of these memorable homilies assert the point with all the passion and vigor that their rhetoric could express. Without the commandments, all faith would become empty and all devotion would be robbed of its real connection with God. The love of God can never be an excuse for evading the demands of the commandments. On the contrary, it is just such love that opened the range of possibilities for human living that the commandments disclosed.

DEUTERONOMY 12:1–26:19

THE DEUTERONOMIC LAW CODE

OVERVIEW

That a new beginning is to be found at 12:1 is evident from the clear introductory formula: "These are the statutes and ordinances. . . ." It marks the commencement of a law corpus that extends as far as 26:15. The issues dealt with by these laws can be outlined as follows: 12:1–14:21, laws dealing with unity and purity of worship; 14:22–16:17, regulations concerning the sacred divisions of time; 16:18–18:22, order within the community and the officials of the state; 19:1–21:9, matters of life and death; 22:1-30, boundaries of life and society; 23:1–25:19, matters of general conduct; and 26:1-15, first fruits and tithes.

It will be seen from this summary that a wide range of religious, personal, and social matters are dealt with. In contrast, a number of concerns that one might have anticipated to be present in a law code that aimed at being fully comprehensive are not covered. Many issues relating to property, marriage, and health do not appear, whereas some of the issues that are covered appear to be relatively peripheral. Nevertheless, a comparison of the material in the deuteronomic law code with the forms and content of other ancient Near Eastern legal collections has proved highly instructive.

The Date of the Code of Deuteronomy 12–26. With the rise of a historical-critical approach to the study of the book of Deuteronomy in the nineteenth and early twentieth centuries it became a widely accepted opinion among scholars, to the point of becoming almost a consensus conclusion, that the law code of chaps. 12–26 represented the oldest part of the book of Deuteronomy. It was widely regarded as the "original" Deuteronomy. The introduction of chaps. 5–11 and the epilogue of chaps. 27–32 were then regarded as later expansions of this original text. The historical "preamble" of chaps. 1–3 could

then be taken as a still later addition, with 4:1-40 being brought in as one of the very latest expansions to the book. Such a comprehensive set of conclusions regarding the literary growth of the book, however, cannot now be sustained quite in this form, even though no firm consensus has been able to replace it.

Many of the observations that gave rise to this reconstruction of a straightforward process of aggregation of the material remain valid, even though the conclusions based on them must now be viewed with circumspection. Undoubtedly there is material of varying dates set both in the introductory chaps. of 5–11 and in the laws of chaps. 12–26. Reconstructing a precise literary chronology of this development, however, is fraught with uncertainty. Moreover, the belief that much of the material in Deuteronomy, including some of the most influential theological developments to be found in chaps. 12–26, is to be dated after the debacle of 587 BCE had occurred must now be seriously considered. Whereas the earlier critical views of the growth of Deuteronomy fully allowed for the presence of post–587 material in the framework of the book, it must now be regarded as certain that this observation applies to the code as well.

This is the case not only in respect of the prominent issue of the law of centralization of the cultus (12:1-28), but also in regard to the constitutional regulation for the monarchy (17:14-20). We cannot then simply draw the conclusion that the laws of chaps. 12–26 were in their present form before the introduction and epilogue were added to them.

The Diversity of Laws in Deuteronomy 12–26. The reader of the law code of chaps. 12–26 will be struck by the sharp contrasts that are evidenced within it. The extreme severity of the punishments prescribed for those who fail to maintain the purity of worship demanded in 12:1–14:21

contrasts starkly with the emphasis on love and charity that emerges in other sections of the legislation (e.g., 15:7-11). Moreover, the relatively humane and practical attitude toward non-Israelites, whether resident aliens or members of a foreign nation (e.g., 23:3-6), contrasts with the barbarism that demands the extermination of the previous inhabitants of the land (12:30-32; 13:12-60). Overall, too, the intermingling of rules concerning the conduct of worship and the observance of prescribed festivals mixes awkwardly with detailed instructions for the administration of law in a precise juridical sense.

When examined more closely still, it is striking that the formal administration of law does not lie securely in the hands of one single set of officials. Instead there is a threefold division between the authority of established officials appointed to administer law, elders of the community, and levitical priests, since a number of legal responsibilities are assigned to them as a court of last resort. Clearly at varying stages each of these groups could become involved in examining and adjudicating both civil disputes and criminal offenses.[59]

We must also consider the question of the precise literary and social character of the law code of chaps. 12–26. In what sense is it a law code, and for whom, precisely, was it written? It has already been noted that its overall character can be described as one of prescribing a "polity" for a nation-state.[60] It is clearly not simply a handbook for legal officials, since it is addressed to responsible adult members of the Israelite community more widely. It deals with several matters that would broadly have come under the purview of the levitical priests concerning the timing of the major religious festivals and the activities to be undertaken at them. Included also, however, are matters relating to family law, including marriage obligations and questions involving inheritance. Domestic arrangements too, therefore, fall within its scope. It is wide ranging, if not properly comprehensive, and shows every sign of having been built up

from more than one source over an extended period of time.

A further feature of the code is that it includes some rulings of a highly theoretical character that still carry the appearance of being unworkable. This concerns such matters as the laws of debt release (15:1-11). There is good reason to question whether the brutal laws aimed at the extermination of apostate members of the community could ever seriously have been implemented on a wide scale under the safeguards laid down for capital crimes, such as murder and rape. They appear more to be intended as a deterrent than as a workable set of laws. Their threatened penalties are more in line with the intense passion and rhetoric of the sermons in the introduction than with the cautionary safeguards of the laws dealing with crimes of violence.

The Deuteronomic Law Code and the Book of the Covenant of Exod 20:22–23:19. In many of its judicial rulings, the deuteronomic law code shows connections and affinities with the similar collection of laws in Exod 20:22–23:19, which has come to be known as "the Book of the Covenant."[61] This was clearly the earliest Israelite law collection that was given a formal statutory position in Israel's legal administration. It shows many points of contact with similar law collections of the ancient Near East, making it evident that a long history of keeping written records of legal decisions existed and was familiar to the ancient Israelites. That this code of laws could have been composed and used in the period when Israel was still a tribal society, as argued by M. Noth,[62] is doubtful. Rather it must itself have arisen under a period of monarchic rule, probably in northern Israelite territory, among a governmental circle familiar with Near Eastern practice.

For an understanding of the deuteronomic laws it is important to recognize that the evidence points uniformly to the conclusion that the deuteronomic material is later than that of the Book of the Covenant and that, in part, the deuteronomic laws were designed to

59. See J. C. Gertz, *Die Gerichtsorganisation Israels im deuteronomistischen Gesetz,* FRLANT 165 (Göttingen: Vandenhoeck & Ruprecht, 1994).

60. L. Perlitt, "Der Staatsgedanke im Deuteronomium," in *Language and Theology in the Bible: Essays in Honour of James Barr,* ed. S. E. Balentine and J. Barton (Oxford: Oxford University Press, 1994) 182-98.

61. E. Otto, "Vom Bundesbuch zum Deuteronomium. Die deuteronomische Redaktion in Dtn 12-26," in *Biblische Theologie und gesellschaftliche Wandel.Festschrift für N. Lohfink, S.J.,* ed. G. Braulik, W. Gross, and S. McEvenue (Freiburg: Herder Verlag, 1993) 260-78.

62. M. Noth, "The Laws in the Pentateuch: Their Assumptions and Meaning," in *The Laws of the Pentateuch and Other Essays,* trans. D. R. Ap-Thomas (Edinburgh: Oliver & Boyd, 1966) 1-107.

expand, clarify, and, where necessary, modify the rulings of the Book of the Covenant. It is certain, therefore, that the deuteronomic lawmakers were able to draw upon the older law collection.[63]

The Deuteronomic Law Code and the Ten Commandments. Significant for present understanding of the nature of the code of chaps. 12–26 are the indications that the ordering of its legal material, with minor modifications and adaptations, is structured on the basis of the Ten Commandments. This has been argued by Braulik[64] and is set out in the work of Olson,[65] who lists the links with the commandments as follows:

1. First Commandment—Deut 12:1–13:18, No Other gods to Be Worshiped.
2. Second Commandment—14:1-21, God's Name to Be Honored.
3. Third Commandment—14:22–16:17, The Sabbath to Be Remembered.
4. Fourth Commandment—16:18–18:22, Parents and Civil Authority to Be Respected.
5. Fifth Commandment—19:1–22:8, Issues of Life and Death.
6. Sixth Commandment—22:9–23:18, Prohibition of Adultery.
7. Seventh Commandment—23:19–24:7, Prohibition of Theft.
8. Eighth Commandment—24:8–25:4, Prohibition of False Testimony.
9. Ninth Commandment—25:5-12, Prohibition of Coveting a Neighbor's Wife.
10. Tenth Commandment—25:13–26:15, Prohibition of Inordinate Desiring.

The possibility of such a recognition simply confirms what we can in any case readily deduce from the theological emphases of the book of Deuteronomy: that the deuteronomic "law, Torah" par excellence is embodied in the Ten Commandments. The broader spectrum of laws and religious regulations set out in the law code, and that in many cases correlate directly with legislative material in ancient Near Eastern law codes, are to be interpreted as an amplification of these commandments.

Of great significance for understanding the structure of Deuteronomy 12–26 is the fact that the particular issues that fall under a particular commandment heading are not always transparently clear. Moreover, there are certainly some rulings that fall outside any such watertight listing, either because they have been inserted secondarily or because they form "link" passages, assisting in forming a bridge between separate groups of rulings. It would then appear to be the case that the major legal "source" for the deuteronomic legislation has been provided by the older Book of the Covenant, but this required substantial revision and amplification in order to render it a more suitable guidebook for the post–587 restoration of Israel. In such a light, the ordering of chaps. 12–26 to conform to the pattern of the Ten Commandments can only have represented a stage of final redaction.

The Deuteronomic Law Code and Ancient Near Eastern Laws. There are close affinities between the form of many of the legislative pronouncements contained in Deuteronomy 12–26 and that of ancient Near Eastern law codes. Predominantly these are a type of "case law" (or casuistic law, to use A. Alt's terminology)[66] in which a particular offense is described as a hypothetical event, and the appropriate action to be taken by way of imposing punishment is laid down. It would certainly appear that the source for the determining of such considered judgments lies in records of actual cases dealt with. In any case, the connection with the legal tradition of the ancient Near East was already initiated in the Book of the Covenant and so is simply carried further in the deuteronomic revisions of this.

Interspersed with properly legal pronouncements in Deuteronomy is a wide variety of religious instructions concerned with requirements for worship as well as exhortations and provisions for matters of state concerning the institution of kingship and the role of prophets. It comes as a surprise that Moses' name is absent from the laws,

---

63. See E. Otto, *Theologische Ethik des Alten Testaments,* 175-208; and "Aspects of Legal Reforms and Reformulations in Ancient Cuneiform and Israelite Law," in *Theory and Method in Biblical and Cuneiform Law,* ed. B. M. Levinson, JSOTSup 181 (Sheffield: Sheffield Academic, 1994) 160-96.

64. G. Braulik, "The Sequence of Laws in Deuteronomy 12:1–26 and in the Decalogue," in *A Song of Power and the Power of Song: Essays on the Book of Deuteronomy,* ed. D. L. Christensen, Sources for Biblical and Theological Study 3 (Winona Lake: Eisenbrauns, 1993) 313-35; and "Zur Abfolge der Gesetze in Deuteronomium 16,18–21,23. Weitere Beobachtungen," *Biblica* 69 (1988) 63-91.

65. Dennis T. Olson, *Deuteronomy and the Death of Moses,* OBT (Minneapolis: Fortress, 1994).

66. Alt, "The Origins of Israelite Law," 88-103.

although the framework implies that he is the spokesman of them. This is then reinforced in the law dealing with false prophecy in 18:15-22, which presumes the direct speech of Moses as being himself a true prophet. In other respects, the laws are anonymous, although they are throughout expressed with an absolute level of authority commensurate with their origin as divinely given and ordained.[67]

It is predominantly the presence of provisions of a cultic nature that betrays unmistakably their origin in a situation after the catastrophe of 587 BCE, which effectively put an end to the old Israelite state and with it an established temple cultus. All the indications are that what we are presented with in the law code of Deuteronomy 12–26 is a programmatic legislative document designed for the administration of a restored state of Israel after the debacle that had brought an end to the old kingdom. Its basis, however, lies in an earlier document of a predominantly juridical nature, showing close affinities with Mesopotamian legal practice and originating in the first half of the seventh century BCE. That this original "proto-Deuteronomy" was already in existence to enable it to form the basis for Josiah's reform in the latter half of that century would appear highly probable. However, it underwent considerable expansion during the latter half of the sixth century to form the present code of chaps. 12–26. Certainly the religious and nationalistic circle behind Josiah's reform also stand behind the book of Deuteronomy.

In this law code, as in the case of the book as a whole, a central core of material that bears a direct relationship to the long-standing tradition of written law in the ancient Near East has been adapted and expanded by its incorporation into a distinctively Israelite framework and structure. What was initially a system of legal administrative rulings compiled at a time of fundamental national and legal reform has been developed into a program for the renewal of Israel after a period of national disaster.

67. Lohfink, "Das Deuteronomium; Jahwegesetz oder Mosegesetz? Die Subjektzuordnung bei Wortern für 'Gesetz' in Dtn und in der dtr Literatur," 157-66.

DEUTERONOMY 12:1–14:21, LAWS DEALING WITH THE UNITY AND PURITY OF WORSHIP

Deuteronomy 12:1-28, The Law of the Central Sanctuary

COMMENTARY

The most prominent and widely discussed feature of chaps. 12–26 is to be found in its prescription for one single sanctuary where alone an altar was to be set up and where officially approved sacrifices and burnt offerings were to be made to the LORD God of Israel. In conjunction with this there is to be a corresponding freeing of the usual festive slaughter of domestic animals from cultic restraints so that their killing and eating are made into a purely secular, or profane, act (12:20-28). We have no reason to doubt that at least by the end of the seventh century BCE the identity of this central sanctuary was taken to be Jerusalem, since the reforming activities of Josiah's reign openly presuppose this.[68] Behind this, however, from the time of Solomon's building of a Temple in Jerusalem, the centralization formula is openly associated with that city in the narratives of 1 Kings (1 Kgs 11:32, 36; 14:21; 2 Kgs 21:7; 23:7).

In a formal sense it is evident that the claim to a centralized cultus is carried back by the deuteronomic legislation to the time of Moses

68. See R. E. Clements, "Deuteronomy and the Jerusalem Cult Tradition," VT 15 (1965) 300-312. The extensive discussion concerning the law of cult centralization is fully reviewed in E. Reuter, Kultzentralisation. Entstehung und Theologie von Dtn 12, BBB 87 (Frankfürt: Herder Verlag, 1993).

through the prescription for the building of an ark and the setting of it in a tent of meeting. Wherever these cult objects are carried is then taken as fulfilling the requirements of a centralized cult until the time when the ark is carried into Jerusalem (2 Sam 5:6-10) and a tent was set up for it there. From that point, Jerusalem became the designated shrine, and a Temple was built there in Solomon's reign. In historical, rather than theological, perspective, it was evidently the building of the celebrated Temple in Jerusalem that provided the effective moment of cult centralization in Israel. Even this action established a pre-eminent national sanctuary, rather than an exclusive one. Not until Josiah's time were active steps taken to restore the central role of the Jerusalem sanctuary to the position of unrivaled pre-eminence it had lost. Since the Jerusalem Temple enjoyed a close association with the Davidic royal dynasty, whose power and privileges it was intended to convey, it represented a political, as much as a religious, institution. In celebrating the deity who was believed to dwell there, it necessarily also celebrated the royal house whom God was believed to have chosen to rule over Israel.

12:1-4. Verse 1 provides a fresh description of the contents of the law code of chaps. 12–26, describing it as being made up of "statutes and ordinances." This compares closely with 4:45, but lacks the designation "decrees" (NRSV), which is set alongside the other two there. The term "ordinances" (משפטים *mišpāṭîm*) must certainly identify the juridical rulings that constitute the oldest part of the law code. "Statutes" (חקים *ḥuqqîm*) would then aptly fit as a description of the regulations contained in chaps. 12–26 concerning what is specifically due to the LORD God. Horst has defined them as the "charter rights of YHWH," comparing them to a form of "Privilege Law" in which tenants of a medieval lord were given protection and rights of land use, in return for which they were required to render certain dues back to the lord.[69]

69. F. Horst, "Das Privilegrecht Jahwes," originally published in 1930 and reprinted in *Gottes Recht. Studien zum Recht im Alten Testament,* Th B12 (Munich: Kaiser Verlag, 1961) 150-54. On the two terms, see N. Lohfink, "Die huqqim umispatim und ihre Neubegrenzung durch Dtn 12,1," *Studien zum Deuteronomium und zur deuteronomistischen,* 229-56.

Overall the broad scope of the issues dealt with in the law code indicates that in its present form it was intended to serve as a comprehensive policy document for the religious, social, and moral life of Israel in its entirety. It addresses the reader as "you," allowing a very open transition from the narrative setting of Moses addressing the gathered community of Israel in the plains of Moab to a timeless inclusiveness in which all Israelites of all generations are included. The contents of the code, however, leave it in no doubt that Israel is assumed to constitute a nation like other nations, to possess a territory of its own, and to have the authority to administer all its civil and religious affairs, including those of the highest levels of government. From a literary and historical perspective, it is evident that this represents something of an ideal situation, since several aspects of Deuteronomy show it to be a program for reform and restoration that was shaped after the collapse of the surviving kingdom of Judah in 587 BCE. What level of freedom was allowed under the Judean puppet administration during the period of Babylonian control is unclear, as also is the extent to which the deuteronomic authors were justified in their expectations of exercising political control.

Many of the same observations apply in respect of the authority of the assumed speaker of the laws, which remains that of the person of Moses. He addresses the reader directly and refers consistently to the LORD God in third-person speech forms, but nevertheless assumes an absolute and unquestioned right to obedience on all matters—religious, civil, and personal.

After the introduction in v. 1, the preparation for establishing right and appropriate worship in the land is spelled out. Verses 2-4 affirm the bold demand that characterizes one of the more uncompromisingly assertive aspects of the deuteronomic legislation. Israel is to identify and destroy all the sanctuaries, altars, religious artifacts, and symbols that had previously existed in the land. There was to be a new beginning, achieved by the rooting out of every vestige of the previous religious life that existed within it. Since there was to be no continuance of veneration for the former gods and goddesses worshiped in the land, all that pertained to them was to be sytematically destroyed. The location and character of these older sanctuaries are described in such a way as to make their identity easily recognized and so as to explain their dangerous nature.

The description of these worship sites as being "on the mountain heights" (v. 2) shows that they were predominantly of a rural character. They could apparently be found "under every leafy tree," because such vegetation revealed the life-giving fertilizing power of the deities who were believed to make available and to release their divine life-sustaining energy there. On hills and mountain heights they could be regarded as being situated near the divine realm above the clouds.

At such sanctuaries were to be found a few simple, but nevertheless essential, religious symbols: an altar where offerings could be slaughtered and burned, alongside a sacred pole and a stone pillar. These appear to denote respectively the male and female aspects of the life-producing and sustaining power of God. It seems probable that many of these sacred columnar symbols bore explicit sexual symbolism (cf. Ezek 16:17).

Side by side with these larger fixed symbols would have been images, usually set up in small sheltered structures, to which prayers could be addressed. The relative simplicity of such furnishings and their location in open-air sites outside the major cities appear to have been characteristic of them.

The rural character of these pre-Israelite sanctuaries described in the deuteronomic law is significant. Certainly before the Israelite occupation of the land all the major cities had at one time been centers of celebrated and important sanctuaries. This fact becomes evident from the stories of Israel's ancestors preserved in Genesis. Many of the city names were acquired on the basis of the sanctuaries that lay within their boundaries.

The rural character of this pattern of religion, of which the deuteronomic authors disapprove so strongly, is noteworthy since the portrait of Israelite life the deuteronomic legislation presupposes is quite markedly urban in character. This accords also with the fact that the general tradition of legal development in the ancient Near East also displays a major role for the great cities that served as centers of administration and culture. It is

not difficult to discern, therefore, that, hidden within the opposition between the Israelite Yahwistic tradition of religion promoted by Deuteronomy and that which is rejected as belonging to the former inhabitants, lie broader social and cultural differences. Deuteronomy represents a strongly centralized pattern of administration, operated through city life, whereas the amorphous, varied, but persistently popular forms of rural unofficial religion appeared to hinder and be a threat to this.

These wider considerations concerning the context in which the deuteronomic law of centralization appears indicate that it represents a strong concern to uphold and protect a form of official Israelite religion over against a more mixed and varied conglomerate of traditions and customs that possessed a more domestic and unofficial character. At the same time, this observation needs to be modified by the recognition that the strong concern of the deuteronomists that the fundamental principles of the knowledge and worship of the LORD God of Israel should be taught to children in every home and should become an inseparable feature of everyday life brought about a new form of domesticated religion. In the deuteronomic legislation, in spite of the importance attached to the centralization of the cultus, this cultus itself impinges less forcibly and directly upon the life of the people as a whole. There is a marked element of de-sacralizing and de-mythologizing the older forms and customs of Israelite religion, especially when we compare the deuteronomic theological ideas with many features still retained in the Jerusalemite psalmody.

12:5-12. The second of the features contained in this distinctive deuteronomic formula for the chosen sanctuary is that it was to be the location where the LORD God's name would be placed.[70] Much discussion has focused on this definition of the chosen sanctuary, which has clearly been designed to avoid the implication that God's actual presence could be found in the Temple. We have noted that this appears as a consequence of what had happened with the

---

70. Von Rad, *Studies in Deuteronomy*; T. N. D. Mettinger, *The Dethronement of Sabaoth: Studies in the Shem and Kabod Theologies*, ConBOT 18 (Lund: C. W. K. Gleerup, 1982) esp. 59-62.

Temple's destruction in 587 BCE. God dwells in heaven, not on earth, but can make the divine power available to Israel through the placing of God's name. In some sense the divine name then appears as a kind of surrogate or mediating power through which God remains accessible without actually being present. An emphatic deuteronomic emphasis on God's dwelling in heaven is placed in the mouth of Solomon for the prayer at the dedication of the Temple in 1 Kgs 8:27-30. In the later priestly theology that dominates the final form of the pentateuchal accounts of the Mosaic tabernacle, the presence of God is designated as a manifestation of the divine "glory" (Exod 40:34-38).

Since the deuteronomic authors do not themselves define precisely what role the name fulfills, it is unhelpful to seek to establish a doctrine of the name as a manifestation of divine eminence that is then to be contrasted with the aspect of transcendence implicit in the idea that God dwells in heaven. The term "name" (שֵׁם šēm) is essentially no more than the deuteronomic explanation for the significance of the Temple as a place for prayer and as the designated location to which tithes and burnt offerings were to be brought. The distinctive form of "name theology" appears fundamentally to have originated as a reformulation and reinterpretation of the older formula for the setting up of an altar to the LORD in the Book of the Covenant (Exod 20:24).

In this way the directness of the identity between the earthly and the heavenly divine dwelling places is relaxed, without altogether losing the sense of the uniqueness of the earthly sanctuary and the reality of the divine power manifested there. The result was undoubtedly a strong reinforcement of the sense of otherness and transcendence belonging to the LORD as God, without forfeiting the belief in the importance of a special sanctuary with all its traditional symbolism. Clearly this deuteronomic development was conscious of the damaging effect on Israel's theology that had been brought about by the threat to, and eventual destruction of, the Jerusalem Temple at the hands of foreign armies.

The primary function for the sanctuary chosen by the LORD as God (vv. 6-7) is that it should be the location to which all Israel's offerings are brought. The list of these is comprehensive and was clearly intended to be all-inclusive in order to preclude the presentation of unorthodox offerings elsewhere. The emphasis on eating together and rejoicing in the presence of God is characteristic of the deuteronomic interpretation of worship as a celebratory occasion. That certain of the offerings would be made in acts of contrition and self-abasement is not discounted, but the more festive tone is presented as the more typical.

Verses 8-12 reiterate the basic demand set out in the preceding section, but offer a further explanation for the evident fact that Israel had not always restricted holy offerings to the one designated sanctuary chosen by the LORD God. Clearly Israelites could not have been expected to do so until they had entered and occupied the land as a nation. Only then would they enjoy the "rest" (i.e., the permanent security and peace) that God had promised to them.

12:13-19. These verses appear to be the oldest section of the pronouncements dealing with the rules for cult centralization. It reasserts the vital importance of the ruling contained in the Book of the Covenant that Israel's burnt offerings were to be presented only at the altar specifically designated for that purpose by the LORD God. More significant is its freeing of most forms of slaughter of domestic animals for food, placing them on a level with animals caught and killed in the hunt (v. 15). This action must undoubtedly be a departure from previous practice in which all forms of the slaughter of domestic animals had been bound by the tightly knit rules of the cultus. It would appear that this concession had been rendered necessary by the requirement that burnt offerings and tithes should be presented only at the designated central sanctuary.

It was necessary, in amplifying this concession for the slaughter of domestic animals for food, to make plain that it did not represent an abrogation of the tithe offering (vv. 17-19). This was still required, since its origins indicate that it was a deeply embedded feature of the concept of a natural cycle of life. As the new life of the crops appeared each season, so it was necessary that the appropriate portion should be set apart for God as a gift for the deity, the giver of life. It served also as a means of support for the levitical priesthood, and this requirement is especially reaffirmed (v. 19). What is a new and startling innovation in the deuteronomic reformulation of the demand for the tithe is the concession spelled out in 14:24-27, decreeing that, if the distance to the central sanctuary should prove too far away to carry the tithe offering there, then it was to be sold and fresh produce bought so that it would remain possible to hold a festive meal in the presence of God.

The designation of the appointed sanctuary leaves no doubt that one single sanctuary was intended (vv. 14, 18), and the context in which this demand is set shows that it was closely connected with, if not originally intended to uphold, the concern to preclude an uncontrolled, haphazard range of cultic activities. Older non-Israelite forms of ritual activity, linked almost certainly with other deities besides the LORD God of Israel, would continue if there were not a tightly monitored central priestly oversight. It is this that the deuteronomic authors were concerned to establish.

The injunction to be careful to show special favor to the Levites (vv. 18-19) was evidently inserted at this point because they had at one time resided close to the sanctuaries where they would assist in the presentation of the festal offerings. They would then naturally expect to be invited to share in the meal in return for this help. The freeing of some animal slaughter from the strict religious requirements pertaining to offerings created a situation in which the needs of the Levites could easily be overlooked. Their mention here introduces one of several instances where Deuteronomy points to the activities of Levites that were not exclusively priestly in character. Although the Levites were to serve as priests, the service of the sanctuary was evidently not their only duty within Israel.

Overall the purpose of the demand for cult centralization would appear to be clearly evident. It was to maintain a pure cultus. Nor can we doubt that the sanctuary where this demand was implemented was Jerusalem. But was it always intended to be so? The recognition that many aspects of the deuteronomic legislation show a northern Israelite background has suggested that possibly some major sanctuary in the north was originally the chosen location. Yet it would seem extremely unlikely that this should have been the case,

not least because Josiah's reforming activities specially targeted the chief rival sanctuary to Jerusalem for destruction and desecration (2 Kgs 23:15-20). If some other location than Jerusalem were the intended location, then no adequate evidence now remains to defend such a claim. On the contrary, not only was Jerusalem assumed to be the chosen location, but also there is a wealth of evidence to support the belief that the claims to the unique pre-eminence of Jerusalem-Zion as the sanctuary uniquely chosen and blessed by the LORD God had a very long history in Israel. It had only been subjected to question when the two kingdoms were divided (1 Kgs 12:25-33).

How far King Josiah's reign witnessed an effective centralizing of worship in Jerusalem remains historically unclear. That some major attempt was made to refurbish and reinvigorate the unique claims of the Jerusalem Temple in his day appears certain. Yet it was in the wake of the Temple's destruction in 587 BCE that the demand for centralization in Jerusalem acquired a fresh importance. This event also gave renewed impetus to such a demand, precisely because it had put a serious question mark against this sanctuary. The very trust that had been placed in it and the high-flown celebration of its power to secure Israel's defense against all enemies had proved misdirected. Moreover, its links with the monarchy and with Davidic dynastic rights to kingly status over Israel had also proved ill founded. After 587 BCE there were many reasons why the Temple site in Jerusalem should be abandoned along with the ruined building. The deuteronomic demand for the retention of the practice of bringing tithes to Jerusalem and prohibiting ritual slaughter at any other sanctuary secured a place for Jerusalem in Israel's future.

Certainly the interpretation of Jerusalem's role as a sanctuary was much changed and its function within the religious life of the community was much revised with it. Nevertheless the deuteronomic law of cult centralization effectively defended Jerusalem's unique place within Israel's cultic history, exalting it as the sole legitimate place to which tithes and sacrificial offerings could be brought.

12:20-28. Taken together the twofold concessions toward a secularizing and demythologizing of two fundamental cultic activities—the presentation of the tithes and the slaughter of domestic animals for food—represent a major shift in cultic legislation introduced by Deuteronomy. The concessions have, in the first instance, been rendered necessary for the reason that the law code itself describes: "If the place where the LORD your God will choose to put his name is too far from you" (v. 21; cf. 14:24). That there were other important considerations after the Temple had been destroyed cannot be doubted. It also appears likely that for whoever had formulated the deuteronomic legislation, the older cultic notions of holiness held little attraction. For all their attention to matters of ritual and cultic life, their intellectual world had closer affinities with that of lay administrators than with that of a class of priests. So there is throughout many aspects of their work a remarkable atmosphere of demythologization and de-sacralization of life. It cannot then have been too difficult a step for them to take to value most cultic actions as expressions of gratitude and affection for God, rather than of obligatory encroachment into the mysterious sphere of a mystic life force that permeated the natural world.[71]

71. See M. Weinfeld, *Deuteronomy and the Deuteronomic School* (Oxford: Oxford University Press, 1972) 191-224.

There was, however, an inevitable danger in granting permission for a regular pattern of non-cultic slaughter of animals. The very roots of all such ritual actions that involved the taking of life and the shedding of blood, even that of domestic animals, was that blood was regarded as sacred. No blood could be shed in total innocence, since it required interference with the very life force of the natural order of the world. Was it not likely, then, that if such slaughter was not undertaken with the blessing of the LORD God of Israel it would be performed in the name of some other deity? Such would appear to be the fear behind the special provisions and distinctions laid down in vv. 20-28. A careful distinction was to be made between the profane slaughter of animals that was now permitted and the sacred donations and burnt offerings that were to be brought to the central sanctuary (vv. 26-27). The latter were sacred and required a cloak of ritual protection. The former were not and needed no such cultic situation or assistance. The one proviso remained that, since the blood was sacred, it was to be poured out on the ground (v. 24). It was not to be consumed.

REFLECTIONS

The law of the central sanctuary in Deuteronomy 12 marks the most obvious and readily recognizable platform of the deuteronomic legislation in the entire book. The claim for cultic centralization at one single sanctuary highlights a major attempt to regularize and control forms of ritual activity and cultic expression at the foremost of Israel's shrines. The theme of centralization, used as a means of establishing uniformity and of eliminating deviations and a plurality of religious expressions, represents a combination of ideological and pragmatic considerations.

As a testimony to the inner spiritual development of Israel's faith, the forthright demand for the centralization of all cultic activity at one single sanctuary represents something of an extreme development. Coming as it undoubtedly did at the very close of a period when the Temple of Jerusalem had dominated the religious life of Judah, it represented a triumph for the unique claims of this historical sanctuary. It might have been expected, therefore, that the deuteronomic theology of the sanctuary and its cultus would have been characterized by the themes of Mt. Zion, its unique claims to divine pre-eminence, and its assurance of a unique measure of divine protection. In fact, we should certainly have expected it to express in full measure the Zion theology that is still preserved for us in the celebratory psalms of Zion (especially Psalms 46, 48, 84). Yet it does not do this, and these particular Zion themes are wholly absent from the deuteronomic formulations of faith. At most the notion that one particular sanctuary had been especially "chosen" by the LORD God of Israel retains the outer shell of such a Zion theology.

Even more startling, the very concept of a divine "presence" at the sanctuary and the assurance that this one sanctuary could offer a blessing found at no other place have been abandoned. They have been replaced by a theology of the divine "name," linking the sanctuary to a relationship with the LORD God in which prayer and moral obedience held pride of place. Even though the chosen sanctuary represents something external to the worshiper, it nevertheless demands a relationship with God in which an inner spiritual seeking and remembering are as important as the outward location. It could then be boldly asserted that the significance of the chosen sanctuary is as valid for those who remained at a distance from it as for those who daily lived their lives in its shadow. Even the concept of dwelling in the house of God took on a broader spiritual meaning.

It is here, more profoundly than in any other of its assertions, that the remarkable tensions and paradoxes of the deuteronomic theology and spirituality appear. Because it was to stand alone as the sole valid place to which offerings could be brought and where the name of God would be established on earth, the central sanctuary is exalted in importance in Deuteronomy above anything that had previously pertained to Israelite worship. At the same time, the role played by this one solitary house of prayer and ritual service was balanced against the opening out and domestication of religious activity, so that every home, and even every child's nursery, would be a place where the name of God would be remembered and the commandments taught. As the cultus became more tightly controlled and monitored, much of its purpose and usefulness was replaced by a far simpler work of teaching, nurturing, and honoring the name and demands of God in everyday life. In a real sense the doors of the inner sanctuary of the Temple, which the high priest alone was permitted to enter, were opened and the presence of God, which was revered and honored there, was made available across the length and breadth of Israel.

Such a religious development became all the more important because the next generation of Israelites, instead of crossing the River Jordan to enter the land as Joshua and the first generation after Moses had done, found themselves crossing in the other direction into exile. It was understandable that they could be dismissed and even ridiculed by some as those who "had gone far from the LORD" (Ezekiel 11). It was the deuteronomic theology that assured them that they had not gone beyond the range of the divine care and love. They could, indeed, "sing the songs of Zion in a foreign land" (Psalm 137). God would maintain their cause.

Deuteronomy 12:29–13:18, The Perpetual Temptation: Apostasy

COMMENTARY

The admonitory address in 12:29–13:18 represents the reverse side of the concern for purity of religious practice and integrity that motivates the law of the central sanctuary. It reinforces this with a style loosely based on typical case-law legislation: "If prophets arise . . . if anyone . . . if you hear. . . ."

12:29-32. This introductory unit to the regulations dealing with persons who seek to lead Israel into apostasy explains why such fierce regulations were necessary. The barbarism of the practices that were associated with the gods worshiped by the previous inhabitants included horrifying forms of child sacrifice.

This repugnant practice, the precise details of which remain obscure, even though they are clearly credible, constitutes an important aspect of the deuteronomic polemic against the older religious life of the land.[72] It was clearly based on firm knowledge and recognizable traditions. At several points the deuteronomic polemic concerning certain of Judah's rulers mentions that the kings were guilty of such practices (Ahaz, 2 Kgs 16:3; 17:31; Manasseh, 2 Kgs 21:6). That the practice was more widespread is attested by the prophet Jeremiah (Jer 7:31), in whose time the high place of Tophet, in the valley of Ben-Hinnom in Jerusalem, is identified as the location where such actions were carried out. In several OT passages such actions are linked with Moloch (or Molk). Later Judaism, as testified by the translation of this word in the Greek and Latin versions, took this to be the name of a deity to whom such child offerings were dedicated. More probably it designates the type of offering intended, or even its purpose in fulfillment of a vow.

The prophet Ezekiel (Ezek 20:25-26; cf. Ezek 16:20) refers to the currency in Israel of an evil law (= religious custom) that was assumed to require the sacrifice of a firstborn child. This would appear to be a reference to the "giving" to God of the firstborn child in Exod 22:28-29 (cf. Exod 13:1-2). That the firstborn of animals were sacrificed to God is certain (Exod 13:11-15; 34:19-20) However, it is clear that in historical times such actions concerning the sacrifice of human infants were discounted by the claim that the firstborn could be redeemed. Overall the evidence concerning any widespread prevalence of the sacrifice of human infants, either to some non-Israelite deity or even in the name of the LORD was not widespread. Yet certainly such actions did take place (see 1 Kgs 16:34; 2 Kgs 3:27), although the instances that provide circumstantial detail show it to have been a relatively rare occurrence. That child sacrifice was practiced seems certain nevertheless, and the deuteronomic author here has undoubtedly made use of this knowledge to justify the severity of the actions called for in eliminating all traces of the worship of the former inhabitants of the land.

13:1-5. It is evident that the activities of prophets could not easily be regulated. Their voices could be raised in support of novelties and innovations in religion as powerfully as in support of a return to fundamental loyalties. The mechanism of appeal employed by prophets was that displayed in their own preaching and rhetorical skills. There could therefore be false prophets as well as true ones. Such truth and falseness lay not only in whether they were able to foresee the outcome of events, but also in their claims to disclose a valid understanding of God's will for human society. So prophets might appear who would turn the minds of people back to the veneration of discarded gods and goddesses or to the practices, now cloaked in the name of the LORD God of Israel, that had marked the worship of these ancient deities.

With its interest in establishing firm lines of control over the entire range of Israel's religious life, it is no surprise that Deuteronomy is alone among Israel's law books in including restrictions and regulations that sought to distinguish the work of true prophets from false. The confrontation between the prophets Jeremiah and Hananiah recounted in Jeremiah 28 shows how two contrasting messages, each purporting to derive from the LORD God of Israel, could cause confusion. The legislation in Deut 13:1-5, however, is concerned more directly with the activities of prophets who urged the worship of other deities besides the LORD. That this should have happened is wholly intelligible, but becomes especially so if we recognize that this ruling has arisen in the wake of the destruction of the Jerusalem Temple by the Babylonian armies. Such an action would inevitably have been popularly interpreted as a sign of the powerlessness of Israel's God to protect even the Temple upon which the divine name was set.

In the wake of such an event there must have been many prophetic voices loudly declaring that such a disaster had happened because the "old gods" of the land had been offended at having been abandoned. The very zeal for the exclusive worship of the LORD would have been turned into an argument for its own mistakenness. In the deuteronomic ruling, such false prophets are condemned and repudiated. Their falseness is seen to lie in their attempts to seduce Israelites away

72. See R. de Vaux, *Ancient Israel: Its Life and Institutions*, trans. John McHugh (London: Darton, Longman & Todd, 1961) 441-46.

from an exclusive worship of the LORD as God. Whatever their apparent credibility as prophets and dream interpreters, if they incited Israelites to acknowledge any other god than the LORD God of Israel they were automatically to be identified as false and punished accordingly. This was to take the form of public execution by stoning (v. 5).

In the description of the false prophets, it is striking that they are regarded as being closely allied to interpreters of dreams (v. 1), which would appear to be a rather limited form of semi-religious activity. It is otherwise only in popular wisdom tales that dream interpretation receives wide attention in the biblical tradition, despite its similarity to prophecy in its claim to be able to foresee future events. It is primarily the mantic wisdom portrait of the figure of Daniel that otherwise links prophecy and dream interpretation closely together. In making such an association between dreams and prophetic speech, the deuteronomic authors would certainly appear to establish a significant gap between their own work as lawmakers and prophetic oracle giving. This evidence would certainly indicate that the links between these zealous reforming writings and the actual prophets was a rather tenuous one. Such a description jars considerably with the recognition that Moses was a prophet (cf. 18:15; 34:10).

Although the deuteronomists appear to have favored such vigorous and forthright prophets as Jeremiah, their own estimate of prophecy, at least in chap. 13, appears seriously compromised. While favoring those who proclaimed an uncompromising loyalty to the LORD as God, they recognized the dangers of unregulated prophecy and saw its role within the life of the nation as a relatively marginal one.

The formula used to justify the execution of false prophets ("So you shall purge the evil from your midst," v. 5) represents a particular purpose for imposing punishment that is several times used by the deuteronomic authors. It is evidently a purely religious categorization of evil and retains many of the features of the taboo-like concept of "guilt" (עָוֹן 'āwōn), which viewed it as a form of infection that could bring harmful consequences upon an entire community. By punishing the false

prophets so severely, the Israelite community was thought to be protecting itself.

13:6-11. There can be no question but that the deuteronomic authors felt the threat of apostasy to be very real and urgent, regarding it as the major challenge to the survival of Israel as a people and a massive threat to Israel's hope of retaining occupancy of the land promised to their ancestors. Much of the sense of a crisis situation and of the feeling that few people could be wholly trusted to carry out the deuteronomic demands is revealed in this further elaboration of the insistence that any person who was found to be guilty of encouraging the worship of other gods than the LORD God of Israel was to be put to death. There is a threefold pattern in what is demanded in this unit. Most striking of all is the recognition that such disloyalty to the LORD God could arise within members of one's own household. The most immediate kin—brother, sister, son, daughter, or even a person's own spouse—could be responsible for abandoning faith in the LORD and turning to other gods. So an Israelite who wished to be loyal to the nation's ancestral faith was commanded to inform upon his or her most immediate relatives, eyeing them with suspicion and reporting on even their most private conversations. Also, and in stark contrast to the more consistent deuteronomic demands for love and compassion to those who are the weaker members of society, there was to be no pity or compassion shown. Religious loyalty was to be set above every other form of kinship and community bond, and all natural feelings were to be set aside.

Another feature is also of importance. This is to be found in v. 11 and relates to the intention that the brutal punishment meted out to an offender was intended to serve as a warning to others. The victims of such a cruel repression of apostasy were to be used as examples to ensure that others were suitably impressed to take heed of the warning.

It is a point of significant legal interest to note that no provisions are laid out in line with those required for similar cases in 17:6 that a minimum of two witnesses were required for the charge to be upheld. Since informing on members from within one's closest kin group would usually require the disclosure of private information, it is evident that such supporting testimony would usually have been difficult to obtain. It must also be regarded as certain that the overall intention of this harsh legislation was to deter, and it can hardly have anticipated that a large number of cases would ensue. Nor, in fact, are we made aware in respect of the deuteronomic law code generally what degree of effective authority the lawmakers possessed to implement their policies. There are clearly several indications that suggest that this was not high and that the exilic revision of the original deuteronomic law code was an attempt to establish guidelines and policies for a future that remained politically very uncertain. It is worthy of note that, at a later time, even so influential a figure as Nehemiah was unable to take direct action against those who flagrantly broke the sabbath rules. He had to be content simply with making their trading activities unworkable (Neh 13:15-22).

13:12-18. The last of the three cases concerning apostasy from commitment to the LORD as Israel's God envisages a situation in which entire towns are guilty of such defection. A significantly new point arises in that, in addition to the total destruction of all the inhabitants of the town, their livestock and all their possessions are to be destroyed along with them. They are regarded as having been infected with the non-Israelite religious practices, and among the spoil taken from them would certainly have been some objects of an expressly religious nature. The degree of hostility that is expressed is startling, as is the belief that a quasi-physical threat would arise from the retention of any of these objects.

The case that most immediately relates to the injunction of v. 17, "Do not let anything devoted to destruction stick to your hand," is that reported of Achan at the time of the Israelite conquest. His appropriation of a "mantle from Shinar" and a large quantity of silver and gold were held responsible for Israel's failure to capture Ai at the first attempt (Josh 7:1-26). It is only in a very extended sense that the original requirement of the so-called holy war devotion of all captured persons and objects to the "ban" (חרם *ḥērem*) can be said to cover the character and purpose of what is described here. The purpose is wholly religious in intent, regarding any object that has been associated with an alien religious tradition as dangerously unacceptable. It is fit only to be destroyed, whatever its value.

In several respects this further demand for the elimination of all objects, persons, and practices associated with the mixed religious traditions that existed in the land before the Israelites established in it their unique worship of the LORD God is surprising. It would appear, superficially at least, to be of a highly theoretical nature. Especially is this the case when the demand for the elimination of religious rivals is viewed in the actual historical context the deuteronomic authors were facing in Judah in the mid-sixth century BCE. It must, nevertheless, reveal to us something of that situation. Evidently the representatives of the pure Israelite faith that the deuteronomists strove for were not that powerful and evidently could not count on widespread support within the land. Whole towns were regarded as likely to defect from their ancestral faith. Throughout Deuteronomy we are made constantly aware that, in demanding so stringent an interpretation of what loyalty to God demanded, its authors were not only introducing a new rigidity and intolerance of defectors, but also desperately trying to secure a faith that they believed to be in danger of being lost.

In view of the appalling consequences that such cruelly harsh judgment of religious apostasy has had in the history of the interpretation of Deuteronomy,[73] it is open to question whether the authors of Deuteronomy were in any position to carry it into effect. This must certainly remain a matter of uncertainty, even though this fact does little to lessen its bitter message. Many aspects of the deuteronomic legal requirements appear to display a markedly theoretical character, setting a program for the future that it was hoped to enforce, rather than recording one that had actually shaped the life of a community. To this extent, the severity of what is demanded must certainly reflect the deep anxieties of the deuteronomic authors to impose their will upon an unwilling community.

73. See F. E. Deist, "The Dangers of Deuteronomy: A Page from the Reception History of the Book," in *Studies in Deuteronomy in Honour of C. J. Labuschagne on the Occasion of His 65th Birthday,* ed. F. Garcia Martinez et al. (Leiden: E. J. Brill, 1994) 13-30.

REFLECTIONS

The modern reader, influenced by two and a half thousand years of religious history, will perhaps experience anxiety and shock at the uncompromising intolerance and harshness with which these cruel demands are set out. One is shocked not only by the bland resort to capital punishment for purely religious offenses, but also by the lack of protection against their being abused and misapplied and the insistence that there be no feelings of compassion and pity for those so treated. The urgent necessity for religious tolerance in modern secular societies, coupled with the historical knowledge of trials and executions carried out upon many hapless victims, requires that these laws be viewed in their more limited historical context, rather than as a broad spiritual demand. Yet even in such a limited setting the reasons why they arose in ancient Israel, by whom they were invented, and how far they were actually carried into effect all remain obscure.

It is certainly important to recognize inherent dangers of such legislation. We need to read it critically, in the light of later Jewish and Christian moral ideals. It can in no way be elevated to provide a pattern for modern religious goals, and modern attempts to appeal to it, even in a modified fashion, are fraught with the gravest dangers.

The first requirement, therefore, is certainly that we should set these harsh regulations in their historical context and recognize the significance of their considerable limitations. It is almost impossible to know whether they were ever carried into effect in more than a few instances. Clearly, even the story of Achan's punishment is intended to support the legislation, rather than provide a certain historical reflection of its implementation. By the time the laws were incorporated into the deuteronomic law code, it was certainly the case that only very limited power and authority remained in the hands of the religious authorities. These laws, in their character, represent something of a middle stage between the age-old holiness restriction, exemplified in the book of Numbers, that believed God would intervene directly to punish infringements of the laws of holiness, and the rather more political assumptions of the state legislative authorities, who believed that it was their duty to protect the community from religious apostasy. After the collapse of the Judean state in 587 BCE (the most plausible period when these laws were composed), it is far from clear that the continuing political authority in Judah possessed either the will or the authority to implement such rules as are advocated by the deuteronomists.

When we ask, then, who was responsible for having composed and advocated such a harsh policy of religious uniformity and repression, it would appear that it arose among a group of reforming zealots who sought to restore Israel's national pride and religious integrity in the face of the threat of its imminent dissolution. They undoubtedly found inspiration and traditional examples for their policy in the circles of Yahwistic Levites; they may well have included some Levites among their numbers. The reforming zeal of certain prophets also gave them traditional encouragement.

These historical observations, however, do little to soften the stern rigor that is demanded as a way of countering the undoubtedly real threat of religious apostasy and national defection from faith in the LORD as Israel's God. At most we can understand such measures by reflecting that the crisis situation both in politics and in religion that the deuteronomists must certainly have faced has spawned a reaction of extreme severity. The terrible consequences of witch-hunts and religious persecutions in the much later experience of seventeenth-century Europe and North America highlight the dangers of this deuteronomic teaching.

A twofold anxiety reverberates through Deuteronomy 13. On one side lies the question of how the disasters Israel had experienced could have been avoided. On the other side is the question concerning how a repetition of such disasters in the future might be prevented. Israel's prevalent resort to idolatry and the popularity of a mixture of religious customs and activities that involved recognition of minor deities besides the LORD God appeared primarily to blame. It is the determination to eradicate such practices at whatever cost to individual lives and freedom that is expressed in this chapter.

There have been attempts to rescue some spiritual meaning and integrity for these deuteronomic demands by a form of spiritualizing interpretation. The threats and dangers the legislation seeks to counter are viewed, not as physical enemies and opponents, but as hidden spiritual enemies who are to be defeated solely by faith and continued allegiance to the one LORD God.

Nevertheless, the stratum of religious intolerance in the deuteronomic legislation is abundantly evident. The modern reader is forced to remember the terrible history of religious intolerance and the social disasters to which it has given rise, and to remember as well the critique from later New Testament and rabbinical perspectives upon what is demanded in Deuteronomy 13.

Deuteronomy 14:1-21, Maintaining the Holiness of God's Name

COMMENTARY

The fundamental requirement that Israel should worship the LORD God alone and that it should devote all offerings and tithes to this one deity at the place set apart as the sole legitimate place of worship demanded further amplification. A more detailed set of rules was needed to explain and demonstrate those varied aspects of life and activity where the holy regard for the LORD as God could be imperiled. Accordingly the distinctions between "holy" and "profane" needed to be fully defined. Entering the world where such distinctions prevailed meant entering a complex domain of categories, ideas, and demarcations that do not readily translate into comparable categories of modern life.

Verse 1 affirms, rather unexpectedly, the conviction, clearly both ancient and deeply felt, that the Israelites comprised a nation who were all "children of the LORD your God." Clearly in the deuteronomic context this affirmation was to be interpreted metaphorically, thereby asserting the close and unbreakable relationship that bound Israel to God.[74] A more carefully worded deuteronomic pronouncement of what was implicit

in Israel's special relationship to God is then given in terms of Israel's having been chosen by God; thus it had become God's uniquely treasured possession. All of this meant that Israel was holy to the LORD God (v. 2).

Thus it is possible to see this entire section as an elaboration of the second commandment, defining what it meant for Israel to uphold the correct use of the divine name.[75] Since the name of God was required to be set apart as holy, the proper observance of all that was implicit in holiness formed an indispensable guideline for daily life. The consequence of this demand was that a wide range of everyday concerns, especially those involving food, had to be carefully monitored and the rules of holiness maintained. It was as if the whole of Israel's life were set under a great umbrella of the sacred and this protecting shelter kept in proper repair because God's name was attached to it.

We must then proceed to ask what this notion of holiness entailed. Of all the major religious concepts of antiquity, the concept of holiness has proved to be one of the most difficult to reinterpret into a modern setting.[76] It is evident that, even by the time of the NT writings, the varied meanings attached to

---

74. The importance of Deuteronomy 14 as a reflection of the deuteronomic worldview is well set out by A. D. H. Mayes, "Deuteronomy 14 and the Deuteronomic World View," in Martinez, *Studies in Deuteronomy in Honour of C. J. Labuschagne on the Occasion of His 65th Birthday,* 165-82.

75. Olson, *Deuteronomy and the Death of Moses,* 70-73.
76. See J. G. Gammie, *Holiness in Israel,* OBT (Minneapolis: Fortress, 1989) 102-24.

holiness were sufficiently mixed and indistinct to make it a problematic term for use in a Christian context. Similarly with Judaism, the partial overlap with notions of purity and cleanliness, as well as of acceptability to God, called for a complex and prolonged series of reinterpretations.

This complexity is due, in part at least, to the fact that in ancient times the idea of holiness was given a physical, or quasi-physical, connotation. Holiness was a quality attached to places, persons, or things. At the same time, this quasi-physical property of holiness was fundamentally linked to ideas of separation and distinctness. Consequently it involved the careful marking of boundaries. The holiness associated with God demanded, by this very affinity, a careful separation from all that was unclean and that could threaten this holiness. Holiness and uncleanness, if allowed to come together, were a dangerous mixture. Just as idolatry and the worship of gods other than the LORD God of Israel broke into and threatened the purity of worship, so also uncleanness threatened the boundaries of Israel's holiness.

It is in the light of this that Deut 14:1-21 reaffirms the understanding that Israel was a people holy to the LORD God, and then proceeds to show how this called for a careful screening of actions and creatures that might bring uncleanness, thereby threatening Israel's holiness. This could occur either in a purely individual fashion or more broadly in regard to the nation as a whole. So there could be no self-laceration or symbolic disfiguring for the dead (v. 1), nor could the people eat anything that was abhorrent to God and so constituted an abomination (תועבה *tôʿēbâ*). We see here that an original body of relatively basic and concise legislation has been expanded by the inclusion of more extensive details relating to which animals were to be regarded as clean and which as unclean (vv. 4-20). The listing of the clean and unclean creatures relates closely to the comparable list in Leviticus 11. An original catalog of ten clean animals (Deut 14:4b-5), followed by a list of ten unclean birds, has later been amplified by the inclusion of a further list of birds taken from Lev 11:18, which brings the total to twenty.

For the modern reader, this defining of the distinction between clean and unclean animals has led to substantial problems of understanding. The context clearly shows that these dietary rules originally belonged within the larger context of a distinction between what was holy and what was profane. To eat anything that was classed as "unclean," which described the fundamental category to which the creature belonged and not its temporary condition, is here regarded as an infringement of the demand that Israel should be a holy people. All the people's activities were required to conform to the rules governing the distinctions between holiness and uncleanness.

While Israel remained a national community, it is evident that a broad social consensus established an easily enforced pattern of activities that reduced the risk of casual or unintentional breaking of the rules concerning holiness. However, once the Jewish communities found themselves increasingly living a scattered existence, intermixed with non-Jewish communities, these dietary rules became more difficult to enforce and, therefore, subject to closer attention and care. Once this situation had occurred, such rules themselves became important badges of religious commitment and identity, as they have remained for certain sections of the Jewish community to the present day.

It is evident that these dietary rules functioned as rules of hygiene, and it is largely in such terms that they have subsequently been understood in Jewish tradition. For example, the consumption of carrion-eating birds, such as the vulture, carried an evident health risk. It seems unlikely, however, that such hygienic considerations formed more than one possible feature for the rationale of such a list.[77] In seeking to establish a safe and secure order of life, ancient societies established a complex system of symbols in which an order of creation was perceived. It was a matter of primary importance to uphold this social symbol system that rejected "disorderly," or "mixed," forms of life. Boundaries of cleanness and wholeness had to be recognized and maintained. So, for example, the eating of fish that lacked both fins and scales was prohibited.

---

77. Most influential in recent study has been the work of anthropologist Mary Douglas, *Purity and Danger: An Analysis of Concepts of Pollution and Taboo* (London: Routledge and Kegan Paul, 1966) 53.

What is surprising in the biblical account of creation in Genesis 1 is that it fails to incorporate any mention of the existence of such unclean forms of animal life, which only become apparent to the reader in the account of the great flood (cf. Gen 7:2). The fact that all creation could be defined as "good" (e.g., Gen 1:4, 10) can only be understood in a relative sense that does not include the clean/unclean distinction. Even the story of the great flood only partially resolves the question of the non-edibility of unclean creatures.

By the time the list in Deut 14:1-21 was compiled, Israel had become well aware of the differing dietary habits pertaining to neighboring communities, so that their association with the worship of idols and alien deities would have added an intensified feeling of rejection to those creatures defined as unclean. Already such a distinction may have influenced Deuteronomy, even though it cannot have been an association with non-Israelite religion that gave rise to the compilation in the first instance.

Undoubtedly the boundary that was feared most of all, and that consequently needed to be observed with the greatest possible care, was that relating to life and death. So Israel had to keep itself well clear of participating in forms of self-mutilation for the dead, no matter how symbolic and restrained such behavioral patterns were (v. 1). It was also essential for Israel to avoid eating the carcass of a clean animal that had died of apparent natural causes (v. 21). It is against such a background also that we must understand the prohibition against boiling a kid in its mother's milk (v. 21). Life and death could not be mixed in such a fashion. The action thus referred to is prohibited elsewhere in earlier legal formulations (Exod 23:19; 34:26). These older prohibitions strongly point to such a practice as having once formed part of a ritual action, possibly itself intended to assist in ensuring safe childbirth or some related concern.

The fact that matters relating to death form the beginning and end of the series (vv. 1, 21) seems clearly to point to a deliberate pattern of inclusio to show that death marked a kind of ultimate boundary. In Israel in particular the ultimate nature of death is strongly recognized, thereby precluding forms of ritual and mythology that laid claim to a consistent crossing and recrossing of the boundary between life and death.

REFLECTIONS

There is a certain historical irony in the fact that the biblical dietary laws became so pronounced a feature of Jewish life. Clearly this had already taken place by the close of the formation of the Hebrew Bible, even though it is in the New Testament and the Mishnah that the wider consequences of this become apparent. Even the prohibition against boiling a kid in its mother's milk, the original significance of which has remained relatively obscure, has become a major identifying feature of Jewish food hygiene through the ages. At the same time, these rules, which were aimed at achieving a measure of careful conformity to the perceived order of the natural world, have in the passage of time become archaic and have instead functioned largely as distinguishing features of traditional faith and religious commitment.

At a very early stage of the parting of the ways between Judaism and Christianity, the Jewish dietary laws concerning clean and unclean food became a primary cause for the separation of the two communities (see Mark 7:17-23; Acts 10:9-16). At the same time, it is firmly recognizable that the Jewish rules relating food to the concept of a divine Torah contributed strongly to maintaining a close relationship between the concept of holiness and everyday patterns of life. From being a concept concerning the mysterious power, and inherent dangers, of the divine order of life, holiness came to be largely related to practical hygiene and healthy living.

A further consideration involves another primary issue of contemporary concern. That human beings should exercise control, or dominion, over the animal and natural world (Gen 1:28) can be easily, and dangerously, misinterpreted to imply complete human freedom to exploit natural resources and the natural environment without restraint. The destructive consequences of doing so, leading at times to the extinction of valued forms of animal and plant life and the devastation of large areas of the earth, reducing once fruitful areas to wastelands, have all been visible effects of such uncontrolled exploitation.

It is important that the modern reader recognize that the biblical concept of holiness included a wide recognition of the divine createdness and orderliness of all things, viewing all creation as part of a grand design that had to be respected and upheld. While it would be too much to claim that the concept of holiness as set out in Deut 14:1-21 consciously presented a clear-cut awareness of an ecological balance in the natural world, it is undoubtedly significant in its recognition that the human species belongs within a larger whole.

The biblical perspective is clearly one of concern to accept the wholeness of the natural world, to recognize and learn its innate orderliness and patterns, and to act so as to maintain and respect the various features of this order, so far as it touched upon human life. The very biblical notion of creation is itself a declaration of belief in one world. Human beings are seen to be part of this natural order of life, which even extends to inanimate objects. Although it is not difficult for the modern reader to note that the biblical distinctions between clean and unclean creatures include much that is primitive and unscientific, the fact that such distinctions were made points to fundamentally important principles. There exists a pattern and inter-relatedness between all creatures, in which even unclean creatures have a positive place and role to play. Life is believed to involve a complex intermeshing of different forms and expressions that all contribute distinctive features to make up the whole.

A further feature of the listing of animals in Deut 14:1-21 relates to teaching about the fixed and unalterable boundary between life and death. The passages of birth and death are of the most extreme significance and demand the greatest care. Accordingly, the passage into life itself, which takes place at birth for human beings and for flocks and herds, was surrounded with special prayers and rites. This mysterious cycle of life is also seen in the pattern of the seasons and of vegetational growth. But most of all it was seen in the passage from life into death, even the death of an animal. Such an event brought into play processes of decay and dissolution, which are mysterious and frightening. For human beings this is especially true, since death marks a departure and the crossing of a frontier that can never thereafter be recrossed.

Death marks the end of an individual existence and the transition to a new, and less welcome, form of being that could not be fully understood. It was impossible for persons of antiquity to confront death as a "natural" event, for all the circumstances that related to it pointed to its unnaturalness and, therefore, its dangerous character. The reflective disquisition on the fact of death in Ecclesiastes 8 reflects the immense problems in coming to terms with death as a part of the natural order and, therefore, as part of a divine design. It is not surprising, then, to find that Canaanite religion conceived of death in wholly unnatural and hostile terms as personified in the figure of Mot, the archenemy of Baal, the giver of life.

It is evident that, when confronted with the reality of death in the presence of a corpse or in the solemn duty of taking leave of a dead person at a funeral, a wide range of customs and rituals existed, some of which blatantly challenged the belief in the sovereignty of the LORD as God. It is also evident that such customs and rituals could pose serious problems for the loyal Israelite, since death was itself understood to be a form of uncleanness, the effects of which had to be countered.

Even in the modern world it is recognizable that, when faced with the presence of death, it becomes all too easy to relapse into an anxious evasiveness and pretense, rather than to accept that God is the one and only deliverer who enables us to contemplate the existence of another world beyond the boundary of death. So the biblical prohibitions warning against engaging in customs and rituals that evade the reality of death as itself a feature of the God-given order still carry a relevant message concerning the sacredness of life and the fact that God alone, as Lord of life, is also Lord of death.

DEUTERONOMY 14:22–16:17, REGULATIONS CONCERNING THE SACRED DIVISIONS OF TIME

Deuteronomy 14:22–15:23, The Worship of God in the Sacred Order of Time

COMMENTARY

14:22-29. The section that now follows concerns the temporal order in that the passage of time, like the dimension of terrestrial space, was viewed as part of the sacred order of things; 14:22 marks the transition to those dues required to be given to God in return for the privilege of divine protection. Both in the annual seasons and in the larger context of the progression through the years, time was regarded as the gift of God and as a carefully designed and ordered dimension of the natural world. The fact that the heavenly bodies could be interpreted as visible signs of the passage of time (Genesis 1) enables us to see that the Israelites saw the world as a created whole, so that space and time were interlocking arenas subject to certain sacred rules. In just the same way that it was necessary in the terrestrial and animal realms to observe the fixed distinctions between locations and species, so also it was essential to maintain and acknowledge the sacred nature of the temporal realm.

To "observe the sabbath day to keep it holy" (5:12), therefore, was not simply a convenient way of enjoying a break within a busy routine. It was, rather, the acknowledgment of the immense mystery and inescapability of the passage of time. It was, in its link to the story of creation (cf. Gen 2:2-3), a recognition of the createdness of time and of the distinction between the "now" of present human experience and the "then" and "hereafter" that can only be thought about, but never actually experienced. So the marking and observance of the sabbath by prayer and rest from work formed the simplest and most basic of the distinctions that shaped and ordered the temporal realm.

The first of the rules concerning time is set out in 14:22-29 and concerns the offering of the tithe of the produce of the fields. All the harvest—grain, wine, and oil—was to be divided and marked off in this fashion, as were also the firstlings of flocks and herds. At first glance, the rules appear more in the nature of a tax rather than an act of recognition of the movement of time. Yet it was precisely the life-giving effect of the progress of the seasons that made the yielding of the tithe and the offering of firstlings actions that acknowledged the divine power present in the progress of time.

The tithe undoubtedly had very ancient origins, serving both as a gift and, more important, as an act of consecration. It maintained the orderliness and integrity of the cycle of life. And it expressed the return to God of some part of what the worshiper had received from God, since, just as some of the crop had to be retained for seed, so also some further part had to be handed back for the use of the divine giver. So the tithe came to fulfill many significant purposes. It reminded the worshiper that, in harvesting the crops or counting the offspring of flocks and herds, there had occurred an act of receiving, and not simply of producing. The worshiper had participated in a life-sustaining cycle in which he or she had co-operated, but over which only God had ultimate control.

It was also of great importance to the deuteronomic authors that the tithe fulfilled a second role in providing a supply of food for the support of the levitical priesthood and the poor of the community. They, too, held a place within the larger community, and it was essential that they, too, be provided for and that their basic needs be met.

At a third level, one of the key ways by which the deuteronomists understood the power and value of worship was that of remembering. The Israelite citizen was repeatedly urged to remember that all the major benefits of life—land, freedom, fertility, and a welcoming climate—were gifts from God. By such acts of remembering it was intended to engender a feeling of gratitude and an awareness of dependence that renewed the desire to remain loyal to God and to display a proper obedience to the divine commandments. So the calculation and yielding up of tithes was a formal temporal requirement that gave outward expression to the inward act of remembering.

Against such a background of allied purposes being served by the offering of tithes, we can understand the unusually bold pronouncement of the deuteronomistic legislation that permitted the sale of the actual tithe offering and the use of the money gained in this fashion to buy other goods at the location of the central sanctuary. The offering could be eaten there "in the presence of the Lord your God" (vv. 23-24). This is clearly a concession to the recognition that the demand for the restriction of formal offerings to one single centralized sanctuary could result in some worshipers' residing at too great a distance from this sanctuary for it to be practical to carry the offerings there. It represents one of the relatively few major elements in the deuteronomic legislation outside the actual formulation of the law of the sanctuary that seeks to compensate and allow for its consequences. It has been noted by several scholars that a large element of unreality pertains to such a law at a time when the social and political unity of Judah and Israel were progressively being broken apart.

The unique significance of such a concession is that it amounts to a desacralizing of the actual tithe itself, which is thereby no longer regarded as holy in itself. Offerings attain this holiness only through their relationship to the loyalty and religious intention of the worshiper, who uses such a gift to acknowledge the sovereignty of God over the cycle of the natural world.

The ruling that the tithe of every third year was to be wholly given for the benefit of the Levites marks a further element of the deuteronomic legislation that recognized that the Levites were in special need of support— a feature already remarked upon in connection with the social and political affinities of the deuteronomists. It is, at the same time, startling in its assumption that such a system of triennial additional support for the Levites, who are assumed in any case to benefit from the usual tithe offering, would be sufficient to enhance their situation within the community.

15:1-11. A further feature in the deuteronomic concern for the sacred observance of the order of time is presented with the legislation demanding the acceptance of a year for the remission of debts at the end of a forty-nine-year cycle. The Hebrew word for "remission" (שמטה *šĕmiṭṭâ*) means literally "letting fall"; it occurs in Exod 23:11 in relation to the cultivation of land. In that context, it undoubtedly meant "to leave uncultivated" and referred to the practice of allowing land to remain fallow every seventh year. Thereby the natural life cycle of the land, as God's gift, could be honored and its vitality renewed. Through such a practice we can recognize the importance of the acceptance of a cyclical pattern operating in the temporal order. Just as the seasons of the year evidence a pattern of use, decay, and renewal, so also a similar pattern can be observed through a sequence of years.

Here the law has been transferred across to the larger realm of commerce and property transactions, and is primarily applied to the making of loans for commercial purposes. By the time this deuteronomic legislation was formulated Israel had moved deeply into a capital-acquiring, land-owning economy in which wealth and poverty were prominent features. It is taken for granted that debts would be incurred for the purchase of land and other property and that there would be further, risk-laden business ventures. For the successful, these could lead to the amassing of considerable wealth and the acquisition of influence and power. For the less fortunate, such ventures could lead to ruin and destitution. So the more egalitarian patterns of life that had operated reasonably well in the social structure of extended families and clans, where property was largely held in trust throughout a large group, were eroding and being replaced by more individualistic patterns of economic life. Some people were doing considerably less well than others, and the legislation proposed by the deuteronomists was evidently designed to alleviate the consequences and effects of this and to make possible a recurring pattern of renewals and restarts, based on the analogy of agricultural routines.

It is assumed that debts will have been incurred for commercial ventures. Where these ventures have prospered it is then further taken for granted that the debt will have been repaid; if not, the debtor is not to be saddled with the burden of it beyond the set period of six years.

This legislation concerning the year of "release" has proved something of a puzzle for commentators. How could such a law have been upheld without the imposition of a form of negative interest, in which the value of the capital sum would have steadily depreciated over a period of six years? The "mean thinking" outlined in v. 9 appears to be a perfectly sensible response to the situation and to have implied that a fixed cycle of seven years was envisioned. This would have meant a cycle in which all loans were made and incurred within an already established timetable. Undoubtedly the proximity of the time of remission would have brought an effective standstill to a wide range of financial and property loans. The legislation, therefore, appears to be unduly theoretical, so much so as to render it unworkable except as a form of social charity.

The most positive estimate of it would appear to be a recognition that without some form of larger social restraint the unchecked operation of commercial pressures and risks brought business activity to the level of uncontrollability, leaving the successful virtual monopolistic rulers and locking the less fortunate into debt and poverty from which they could not escape. The proposed legislation set out here can then be viewed as an attempt to break into this situation by limiting the extent to which the commercial and financial pressures of the economy could be allowed to shape and control society more generally.

From a purely literary perspective, the original brief formulation of the legislation appears to have been expanded in the manner in which it defines the neighbor, referred to in v. 2 as a "member of the community" (אח 'āḥ; lit., " brother").[78] Similarly the warning against mean thinking in vv. 7-11 appears to be a later addition to the original ruling. It recognizes quite openly the difficulty that would arise in persuading free citizens, who would themselves have faced quite regularly major financial risks in farming, to maintain in spite of these risks an exceedingly generous spirit. Such observations serve only to strengthen the awareness that this was an area of legislation that sought to build on a long-standing history of cyclical renewal in agriculture and that assumed a strong sense of obligation concerning the wider moral and social problems of wealth and poverty.

Behind all such laws we can discern the shifting social and economic patterns of Israelite life in which some measure of accommodation to the commercial practices of the ancient Near East was sought. It perceives the need for sophisticated commercial development, but at the same time tempers this with traditions and rules that reflect older patterns of a kinship-based society concerned with protecting the weaker and less fortunate members of society. The deuteronomic legislation, which is incorporated into a deep awareness of the divine ordering of the temporal realm, reflects much of the "in-between" character of Israelite life at the close of the monarchic period. Much adaptation in the forms of economic activity and social urbanized community life had brought great changes. Yet these could bring, and probably to some degree already had brought, disruptive and disturbing transformations in society. The consequences had been far from ethically helpful, or even commercially successful, so that this deuteronomic ruling proposes

78. Perlitt, "Ein einzig Volk von Brüdern. Zur deuteronomischen Herkunft der biblischen Bezeichnung Bruder," 50-73.

important ameliorating restrictions to restrain commercial activity.

In spite of its idealistic character, this particular deuteronomic law gives voice to some of the most passionately expressed pleas on behalf of the poor that are to be found in the Bible. The tersely worded command, "Open your hand to the poor" (v. 11), spells out a great depth of feeling concerning social justice that permeates the legislation of Deuteronomy. It marks an attempt, as does the book of Deuteronomy more largely, to marry conscience to legislative action. It frankly recognizes that laws, especially those regulating commercial activity, cannot function effectively unless there is a willingness to implement them with a genuine compassion and integrity of respect for the entire community. Even the fact that there is any legislation at all reveals the recognition that mere appeals to goodwill are an insufficient basis for any society to implement justice and compassion in its activities. Law requires love, but love also demands law!

15:12-18. The third of the commitments enjoined in this section dealing with the temporal realm concerns the acquisition, retention, and release of slaves. In line with the general tenor of the entire section, the emphasis is on generosity and the showing of compassion toward a fellow Israelite. In this case, the slave, whether a man or a woman, is understood to be a member of the community, a "brother." Clearly this is how the term 'āḥ is intended to be understood in this passage, indicating an ethnic affiliation rather than membership in a particular social class. It is closely equivalent to the concept of an "Israelite," a term the deuteronomists do not employ, even though the legislation implies such a concept.

The use of the term עברי ('ibrî) is to be explained from the fact that it has been taken and adapted, like the deuteronomic law itself, from the older law concerning slavery in Exod 21:2-6. In this case, the term 'ibrî certainly carried the connotation of social status, indicating the legal situation of a person who had fallen into slavery. The law in Deuteronomy was intended to provide an amendment to the older law and to modify its effect and purpose in a number of ways. Male and female slaves are placed on an equal footing

(v. 17b), and provision is to be made to enable a released slave to maintain a viable position in the community (vv. 13-15).

Most striking of all, however, the law requiring the release of slaves after six years of service sets the whole question of such release within the larger context of the remission of debts. This release is assumed to take place within the fixed seven-year cycle requiring the remission of debts, rather than to represent the usual period of service into which a person would be sold to work as a slave. The law presupposes throughout that the situation of slavery has been occasioned through debt. In dire circumstances, a person might sell either himself or members of his or her family (see Amos 2:6) into slavery as a means of paying off a debt. But there were other ways in which people might be enslaved in ancient Israel, as in the ancient Near East generally. Some prisoners of war were kept as slaves, some slaves were victims of kidnapping (see the law of Exodus 21:1), and some persons may have been sold into slavery. The restriction of the present law to deal only with Hebrew slaves—i.e., those who were ethnically from the community—does not take into account those other slaves who were of alien origin and whose servitude was assumed in most cases to be permanent. The implication, therefore, is that this ruling was concerned primarily with ameliorating the consequences of debt slavery.

The fact that the legislation in Exodus deals only with the case of male slaves, whereas that in Deuteronomy is extended to cover females as well, reveals something of the changing social status of women by the time the deuteronomic legislation was written. Since the slave was clearly expected to be accorded certain minimal rights, in regard to both length of servitude and protection against abuse (Exodus 22, which deals with cases of physical injury resulting in a slave's death), their social position was evidently only a little lower than that of the hired laborer, whose employment is referred to in v. 18.

Verse 15 is an appeal to the tradition of the experience of Israel's ancestors as slaves in Egypt (cf. 5:15; 16:12; 24:18, 22), according to which the Egyptians furnished the departing Israelites with gifts before sending them away (Exod 3:21-22; 11:2; 12:35-36). Quite certainly the legislative requirement of providing adequate means for a released slave to function as an independent citizen has served to shape this unexpected feature of the narrative tradition.

The law dealing with the release of slaves reveals much of the same ambivalence and complexity that are found more broadly in this section covering temporal matters affecting social and commercial activity. On one side we find a deep compassion and studied realism concerning the humiliation and deprivation of status and protection to which fellow Israelites were subjected when sold into slavery. Over against this is a well-intended appeal to a spirit of generosity and goodwill designed to alleviate the worst consequences of slavery. The tightening up of the law in order to prevent exploitation and cruelty is evident, although the difficulty in doing much in this direction is everywhere evident. The appeal to the goodwill of the slave-owning citizen is then made in order to improve the lot of the slave.

A striking and alarming instance of the operation of this appeal for generosity and compassion concerning the release of slaves is provided by the report in Jer 34:8-22. When Jerusalem was under siege by the army of Babylon, those citizens who owned slaves released them. The reasoning behind this action was almost certainly largely selfish and cynical: It relieved the owners of the responsibility of providing food for these unfortunates. When the siege was temporarily lifted, the former slaveowners repossessed them, assuming, prematurely as it turned out, that the threat of defeat and starvation had passed. The prophet Jeremiah's unrestrained condemnation of such a cruel and cynical act is ample evidence that he shared wholly the spirit of compassion and concern that underlies these deuteronomic regulations.

15:19-23. The law concerning the dedication of the firstborn males in the herds and flocks belonging to Israelites upholds an ancient ritual tradition. The birth of these animals was the manifestation of new life, and so they were to be returned to God, as the giver of life, in the form of a sacrifice. Together with the offering of firstfruits in the harvest as a means of promoting and upholding the cyclical order of the natural world, such offerings acknowledged the sovereignty of God over the temporal realm. New life implied the regenerative power of God in the world and, accordingly, had to be acknowledged with gratitude and honor. Behind the practice we can discern deep convictions regarding the belief that all life is a consequence of divine energy and power, which must be channeled and protected to ensure its continuance.

Throughout the many regulations for the ordering, upholding, and proper understanding of worship and the temporal order that are to be found in Deuteronomy, we can sense a deep spirit of respect for its given nature. Time is a gift of God, as much a feature of the shaping and structuring order of things as is space itself. It possesses measurements and symbols that can be noted and acknowledged. At the same time, it imposes limits on human activities. Just as human work potential was not to be exploited to the point of exhaustion, but was to be restrained by the renewing and life-restoring gift of the sabbath, so also the land was not to be exploited to the point of denuding it of its productiveness. Similarly, all commercial and social life was to be placed within boundaries that gave place for the renewing and regenerating life of God. Even capital acquisition, debt, and slavery were not conditions that could be allowed to run in perpetuity. They belong within the human scheme of things and require limits and boundaries, giving room for the renewing miracle of God's grace and power.

REFLECTIONS

The section that began in 14:22 and extends as far as 15:23 represents an amplification of the law of the sabbath, a law that reflects a consciousness of the divine order of time. Time is as much a gift of God as is the territorial domain of space. In the modern world, astrophysics has reawakened our own awareness that there exists a space-time continuum, so that all that exists does so within a framework of created time. We should not feel surprise, then, that in much the same way that we feel a compunction to devote some space to God by the establishing of a sanctuary, or holy place, that expresses to others and reminds us of the divine relatedness of space, so also time calls for the same degree of sacred setting apart.

The most elementary and foundational setting apart of time is that which occurs with the sabbath, a brief interval of one day in a sequence of seven, marking this divine givenness of time. It is important, therefore, that the biblical record traces the origin of the sabbath back to creation itself, thereby fitting it into a foundational level of the world's existence. It is also significant that the worshiper is called upon both to observe (i.e., "keep and acknowledge") the sabbath day and to remember to sanctify it through prayer and thanksgiving. It is a time set apart for celebration and rejoicing; it is altogether regrettable that, in the course of an overzealous interpretation in both Judaism and Christianity, the sabbath should at times become a day fraught with anxiety and boredom. Its primary function is to establish a pattern of renewal, enabling the exhaustion and stress of a work-laden week to be relieved by a revitalizing opportunity and freedom for renewal. Even the slave was to enjoy the freedom the sabbath provided, since no other human being was empowered to demand the wholeness of a person's time, which belonged to God the Creator.

The legislation within the present section, however, is not focused on the sabbath directly, but with other intervals and consequences in the passage of time. These focused on three particular issues. The first of these is the passage of the seasons in the agricultural year and the process of birth, maturity, and rebirth within the flocks and herds. The passing of the old into decay and inaction, followed by subsequent renewal with new growth and new births is evident. Time formed a part of the enabling stream of life, since it made visible and effective the experience of decay and renewal. It was vitally important, therefore, that this cycle of the seasons should be sanctified by marking its progress with appropriate offerings to God.

The second of the patterns of decay and renewal that is dealt with concerns commercial transactions in which debts were incurred. Some debt escape provision was called for lest a state of permanent indebtedness, with a consequent permanent crippling of a person's ability to participate in normal business life and activity, should be brought about. The legislation has consistently appeared strange and unworkable, even though the charitable and compassionate reasons for its introduction are laudable enough and clearly possess much ethical value. It marked an attempt to prevent a situation in which citizens could be permanently tied down with a burden of unrepayable debt. The deuteronomic legislation strived to avoid this situation with rulings that established an outer limit to the time scale of debt and sought, by doing so, to avert the consequences that would place an impossible burden on an individual household.

The pattern of such legislation, like the title "a year of release" (lit., "letting fall," "leaving alone"), has evidently been carried over from an agricultural setting with its institution of a fallow year. So economic and commercial activities were not to be allowed to determine and destroy an individual's life in such a way that ignored the God-ordained pattern of decay and renewal.

However unworkable such a legislative rule appears to be in purely commercial terms, it nevertheless reflects certain profound truths concerning the nature of human life and of the world order. The book of Deuteronomy clearly reveals a picture in which Israel's social and economic transformation, which characterizes the nation's development during the period of the monarchy, had brought major social inequalities and injustices. The prophets, particularly Amos, Micah, and Isaiah, cried out forcefully against the effect of these changes. Yet their only response appears to have been to appeal for the growth of a national conscience over the issue. The deuteronomic legislation, however, seeks to achieve more than this, by making law follow the dictates of the prophetic conscience. It seems unlikely that such laws proved practically workable or could easily have been put into effect. The issues they deal with, however, have remained powerful and significant, not least during the nineteenth and twentieth centuries. The consequences of uncontrolled capitalistic activity have repeatedly incurred world-shattering consequences to the detriment of other aspects of human social development.

The law attempts to translate into legislative regulation the biblical concern to subordinate commercial activity to a larger range of moral and social factors that shape human life and social development. Just as the sabbath provided a breathing space within the working week, so also the year of release was designed to provide a kind of commercial breathing space within the temporal realm.

The third of the issues dealt with relates to slavery, and in particular to the practice of debt slavery, in which a person sold oneself or members of one's family into slavery in order to pay off debts that had otherwise become unrepayable. The analogy with the sabbath, and with the regulation for the year of release, becomes evident. Even the misfortune of being sold into slavery was not to become a life sentence for an individual. For that to occur, human dignity and human freedom would be so deeply undermined that it would contradict the belief that all human beings had been fashioned in the image of God. So a limit was set, based on the cycle of six plus one. Thus an Israelite's slavery would be brought to an end with the arrival of the year of release and the possibility of a new beginning.

It is in this regard that a particular level of human interest is introduced into the legislation, since it openly recognized that, after six years of slavery, the unfortunate citizen in such a situation would not have remained in the same condition he or she had been in before misfortune struck. Life is never as simple as that! In order to be a truly free citizen it would be necessary to have capital to buy property and to begin again. Moreover it was quite likely that, if the slave was a young person, he or she would have reached puberty and probably would have contracted a marriage while enslaved. All these eventualities had to be taken into account. So the deuteronomic legislation is frank and realistic, even when it falls back upon rather idealistic appeals. Freedom would not be freedom if the capital to work and farm as a free citizen were lacking. Marriage commitments had to be balanced against the rights and expectations of the former lord and owner of the slaves, whose outlay also needed to be protected.

The rulings that are ultimately set out resort to a fundamental deuteronomic appeal to the slaveowner to be generous and compassionate in dealing with a former slave. A slaveowner had to remember that Israel's own ancestry could be traced back to men and women who had themselves been slaves in Egypt. It was essential, therefore, to treat slaves with understanding and compassion, realizing that it was only by the grace of the LORD God that one's own family was no longer in such a position.

How effective such appeals were to careful land- and slaveowners, on whose goodwill there were evidently many demands, remains wholly unknown. But the fact that such appeals are present and mark an important feature of the deuteronomic laws is itself significant. Laws cannot embrace every possible eventuality or deal with every aspect of a situation. They can be abused, misinterpreted, or applied so callously and unthinkingly as to undermine the very justice they were intended to maintain. So it was vital that the hearer or reader of the law should regard every fellow citizen as a human being, feeling the same pains and loyalties as well as facing the same dangers and challenges. It was essential to remember, when surveying one's misfortunes and mistakes, that these were risks that might subsequently befall oneself. So it was necessary that law should be administered and tempered by love, a demand that shapes the memorable saying of Lev 19:15: "You shall love your neighbor as yourself."

Deuteronomy 16:1-17, The Festival Calendar

COMMENTARY

For the community of ancient Israel, the passage of time was characterized most dramatically by the routines and processes of agriculture. There was a time for sowing and a time for harvesting, a time for plowing and readying the soil for the coming season of growth and a time for reaping, threshing, and storing the crops. Each of these seasons of the agricultural year was accompanied by an appropriate religious festival, and this festival was inevitably closely bound up with memories and recollections of the divine power and beneficence that had made agricultural growth possible.

In the life of the Canaanite peoples from whom Israel had taken over the land, these festivals were also present and were inevitably closely patterned on the seasonal activities that marked the winning of crops from the soil. Such had certainly been the case for several thousands of years, probably with little variation in the rituals of seasonal activity. The major festivals were interpreted, and in a measure sanctified, by the telling of myths and stories of the work and exploits of the gods who watched over the activities of the human beings who strove to gain from the soil the food to sustain life. With a kind of impertinent boldness, such mythology could even view the gods as enjoying their leisure, while their human slaves worked for the life-sustaining food, some of which they also would enjoy. So farming and religion went hand in hand.

It is in taking full account of this intimate bond between religion, mythology, and the agricultural year, as it was experienced by the previous inhabitants of the land, that we can see the reasoning behind the deuteronomistic fervor to promote a fresh understanding of seasonal time. The sanctuaries, holy places, rituals, and stories of the gods and goddesses of the land, which the deuteronomists sought strenuously to remove from the memorials and sacred sites of the land, were deeply ingrained in daily life. There was an understandable reluctance on the part of ordinary people, bordering closely on a kind of incomprehension, to abandon beliefs and practices upon which the very productivity of the land seemed to depend. So the most vital and inescapable requirement for the provision of an interpretation of time that fully honored the LORD as God was one in which the festivals of the agricultural year were celebrated wholly in honor of this one divine name.

The festival calendar[79] presented in 16:1-17 marks the final section of the collection of laws dealing with the sanctification of time. It provides us with one of the most forthright indications of the manner in which the aims of the deuteronomists have led to revisions of earlier customs. Older formulations of Israel's list of annual religious celebrations are to be found in Exod 23:14-19 and 34:18-26. We must assume that these formulations, already in written form, were available to the deuteronomistic authors.

By comparing the different calendars of events and their carefully prescribed wording, we can trace a number of changes that have been introduced over time. Even though we cannot always know when these changes were actually introduced, they nevertheless reveal the directional trend of religious development in Israel. These festivals undoubtedly marked a high point in the year and established the most evident public face of religious life. All families everywhere were bound to participate, since the life of the entire community depended on the success of the farming year. Moreover, such festivals provided the most powerful activities that generated a form of social bonding. They were joyous celebratory occasions, so that to have absented oneself or one's family from them would have been to turn one's back on the community as a whole. To do so would have been unthinkable, so that even the slaves and resident aliens, to whom much of what was done may have appeared strange, were required to participate.

---

79. See "Agricultural and Civil Calendar," in *The New Interpreter's Bible*, vol. 1 (Nashville: Abingdon, 1994) 275.

In large measure, the aims of the deuteronomists can be seen quite clearly to have been to consolidate, to unify, and to "Israelitize" the festivals, which already had a long history behind them. They were to be performed in honor of the LORD God alone, to be divested of any of the sexual connotations and implications that the idea of new life invariably suggested to an ancient society, and to recall the slavery and humble, landless origins from which Israel had sprung.

16:1-8. From a literary perspective, the most remarkable new feature of the regulations set out in 16:1-17, when compared with the earlier formulations of the book of Exodus, is to be found in the close conjunction of the celebration of Passover with that of Unleavened Bread in the springtime of the year. Although there may have been some older connection between the two simply because they both took place in the same season, the Passover was essentially a festival for sheep farmers, whereas that of Unleavened Bread was related to a cereal harvest from the sown land. In such distinctions lay deep differences of economy, life-style, and necessarily of religious concern. So it is certainly the deuteronomistic sacred calendar that has formally striven to connect the two together and to provide for each a single coherent relationship to Israel's tradition of the exodus.

The Passover celebration took on a close association with the tradition of Israel's deliverance from slavery in Egypt. By doing so, it elevated the sense of salvation and protection afforded by the sacrificial and blood-smearing rituals of the passover event into a memorializing of that event, which marked the nation's birth. It represents a striking example of the manner in which a far older religious celebration, linked originally to a change of pasturage in the spring and to a warding off of dangerous powers, could become thoroughly "Israelitized." The combination of act and word could be transformed by adding new words to outdated forms. More than any other single seasonal religious event, Passover expressed and proclaimed the manner and circumstances of Israel's beginnings and the unique indebtedness to the LORD as God.

The title "Passover" is applied both to the sacrificial lamb, which provided the central ritual material for the celebration, and to the

act of celebration itself. The oldest narrative account of its introduction into Israel is given in Exod 12:29-39 (usually ascribed to the pre-deuteronomic source J). However, this narrative record was enlarged in the post-exilic age, with evident post-deuteronomic features. It seems certain that in the process of this literary development much of the tradition available to the deuteronomistic authors has been discarded.

The term "Passover" (פֶּסַח *pesaḥ*, from פָּסַח *pāsaḥ*, "to hop," "to leap") refers to the divine grace in "passing over" Israel when "the angel of the LORD" threatened the firstborn of Egypt with death (Exod 11:5). Yet this is a very strained and implausible explanation for the origin of the name, and it remains a strong possibility that we should regard the actual verb here as a homonym meaning "to protect," since protection was clearly the primary purpose of the ritual.

The celebration was to take place during the first month of the year, Abib (March-April; cf. Exod 13:4; 23:15). The later post-exilic festival calendar established this date more precisely as the fourteenth or fifteenth day of Abib.

It is reported in 2 Kgs 23:21-22 that the Passover had not been celebrated by Israel from the time of the judges until the reign of King Josiah (cf. Josh 5:10-12). However, it is improbable that it was an entirely fresh restoration in Josiah's reign of a custom from so far back. Passover must have remained a significant celebration among some elements of the community throughout the monarchic era, possibly among the more marginal, sheep-farming segment. All the indications are that it was the purpose of the deuteronomistic legislation to regularize, standardize, and reinterpret religious celebrations that had previously been observed in a more haphazard fashion. It would then certainly appear that this was true of the spring celebration, which the deuteronomists now sought to establish as a unified festival of Passover-Mazzot, effectively combining the two celebrations into a single event.

The original Festival of Mazzot (Unleavened Bread) is related to the agricultural year, designed to establish an interval between the using up of the leavened meal from one year and the introduction of new leaven from the new year's first crop. In the narrowest sense, it was not a religious celebration performed at a sanctuary, but a domestic provision related to the grain harvest and the food supply. It even possessed certain hygienic considerations.

Yet the original farming connotations are left aside in the acquisition of a new significance in terms of eating the bread of affliction as an act of remembering the season of affliction Israel's ancestors had experienced in Egypt. Old festival celebrations were filled with new content, and, in the process, ritual actions that can be traced to an agricultural context were invested with new meaning that related them overtly to Israel's historical commitment to the LORD as God.

16:9-17. The other two festivals specified in the deuteronomistic legislation, the Feast of Weeks (vv. 9-12) and the Feast of Booths (vv. 13-17), complete the religious observances of the year. They, too, possess an obviously agricultural character. The celebration of Weeks was to take place seven weeks after the first cutting of the early harvest. The post-exilic, amplified regulations for the celebration of this festival, set out in Lev 13:15-16, require that it be held on the fiftieth day after the sabbath following the offering of the first sheaf. This gave to it the title "Pentecost" (πεντηκοστή *pentēkostē*, "fiftieth"). It marked the complete harvesting of the grain crop and required that an appropriate offering, related to the size of the yield, be made.

Unlike the events of Passover and Mazzot, which recalled painful episodes from the nation's past, the Feast of Weeks was through and through a joyful celebration. It provided opportunity for thanksgiving for the food supply for the coming year. Such a reassuring provision contrasted with the scarcity of food that had pertained in Egypt (v. 12). Firm insistence is made that the entire household, including slaves, should join in the celebration, along with the disadvantaged, non-landowning members of the community, which included resident aliens, orphans, and widows.

The third of the annual festival celebrations is defined as the Festival of Booths, which, like Mazzot, lasted seven days (v. 13). This festival was celebrated when the last of the produce of the agricultural year—the vintage and olive harvests—was acknowledged

with gratitude. Since this celebration took place in the late summer, its outdoor nature was characterized by the making of simple shelters from branches and scrub foliage, forming the booths, or tabernacles, in which the celebrants protected themselves from the cool night air. In turn, these rough shelters were later reinterpreted as imitations of the temporary shelters made by the Israelites when they fled from Egypt and set out into the wilderness.

It is in this fashion that the deuteronomistic interpretation, or more strictly reinterpretation, of Israel's agricultural festivals has drawn all of them into a relatively coherent and consistent pattern of worship. They mark the passage of the seasons, originally being locally related to the harvest, but later fixed at specific days within particular months. Their original agricultural character was not abandoned, but was overlaid with a distinctive theological set of images and ideas.

It would be easy to overstate the primary agricultural significance of these celebrations. They were primarily signposts and markers of the passage of time throughout the year. This could be recognized to possess a pattern of rise and fall, of new birth, followed by decay and death until the new season heralded a resurgence of new life. Naturally the harvesting of the crops provided the materials with which this process of decay and revitalization could be recognized and expressed. Yet they were far more than simple token gifts of gratitude for an adequate food supply. They enabled the entire community to become part of this seasonal rise and fall of the passage of time. Men and women grew accustomed to the passing of the weeks and months in which their own life cycle was mirrored in a simpler, more basic form. God was "the living God," and in worshiping this life-bestowing power people are looked to be renewed with new life.

It is clear that, in giving new meaning to these festivals and in emphasizing their significance as memorials of events from the national past, the deuteronomists were concerned to break with aspects that were no longer regarded as helpful. At the same time, it is evident from the demand for compulsory participation in these celebrations that they were also seen to be vitally important moments of social bonding and renewal. Being present on such occasions was the most obvious and deeply felt way an individual family knew that they were part of the community of the LORD God.

For the deuteronomists it is wholly in line with the concern to coordinate and regularize the celebration of these festivities that they were required to be performed at the one central sanctuary (vv. 6, 11, 15). Obviously this imposed considerable difficulties and restrictions on their actual performance, since it is unthinkable that whole communities would vacate their towns and homesteads to journey to Jerusalem for seven days or more. Such a restriction became increasingly difficult because of the ever-enlarging dispersion of the Judean population into scattered and loosely connected settlements. The breakup of the former nation and the progressive migration into more distant lands turned the original population of a single nation into a miscellany of aliens resident in many lands. Except in the context of a pilgrimage, the celebration at a central sanctuary became progressively more difficult. Nevertheless, the importance of the deuteronomistic legislation cannot be overstated, and the religious foundations of the dispersion were laid firmly on the memorializing and celebration of a national past, with a strong forward look to its re-creation at a future time. It is among these foundations that the sacred festival calendar of ancient Israel held a place of exceptional significance. The deuteronomistic legislation provided a pattern of ritual that was readily adaptable and required only basic domestic materials for performance.

It seems certain that the primary aim of the deuteronomists had been to create a closer uniformity of practice and to promote a healthy sense of national unity in honor of the one LORD God. In historical reality, it appears most probable that it was less the creation of a new unity than the prevention of further disunity of religious practice that was its greatest achievement. It is noteworthy that, in the fifth century BCE, the Jewish community established at Yeb (Elephantine) in Egypt celebrated the Passover, even though it is evident that much of their practice and religious outlook were highly heterodox from the standards set by the deuteronomists. Nevertheless, the sacred festival calendar marked the passage of time through the year in very much the same way that the observance of the sabbath marked the passage of days into weeks. Time itself was sanctified and made holy by being filled with religious content and meaning.

REFLECTIONS

Religion implies a strong measure of continuity, so it is not surprising to find in Deuteronomy a series of regulations promoting the observance of three major religious festivals throughout the year. Nor should we be surprised that these festivals bear all the indications of close connections with the practice of agriculture. Quite certainly these celebrations had belonged inseparably to the skills and techniques of raising crops from the land and husbanding flocks and herds with only limited subsistence and rainfall. They were, in many of their details, ancient by the time of Moses. Their origins must go back to the very earliest stages of organized agriculture in the ancient Near East.

The deuteronomistic festival calendar is not, however, simply a calendar of the agricultural year. Rather, it has been transformed by associating each of the main seasonal celebrations with events from Israel's national past. The renewing of the farming year has been transformed into a celebration of human freedom—Passover freedom from the slavery of Egypt, the wickedness of human oppression and obstinacy in Pharaoh's refusal to let Israel go free, and the entitlement to own land, to plant crops, and to own flocks. Passover had been turned into a festival of human freedom, not only in the narrowly political sense, but also in its recognition that to live meant to be free to enjoy the fruits of life in food, well-being, and pride of possession. So Israel's gifts of the land are seen first and foremost as the fruits of the larger gift of historic acts of deliverance.

The rituals were recast in the form of mini-dramas that reenacted significant moments from the past so that entire families could feel themselves caught up once again in the great turning points by which the nation of Israel had been given birth.

The modern reader is inevitably surprised at the way these ancient festival celebrations combine the physical with totally spiritual connotations. There is no sharp dichotomy between the benefits and the blessings of the material world and the inner meaning and "message" the worshiper is bidden to draw from the celebration. Most striking to our modern perspective is the total absence of any sense of distinction between wealth and poverty in the manner in which the celebration takes place. The entire community is not simply invited to take part, but is duty bound to do so. Even those who stood most at the margins of society were required to participate. These celebrations relate to the community in its entirety and wholeness, so that all can be seen to benefit from the food that sustains them. The festival celebrations exemplify a belief in the essential unity and oneness of the community before God.

By the time the written deuteronomistic legislation regarding the calendar of sacred festivals was composed, Israel was on the verge of national collapse. In fact, by this period much of the nation had already succumbed to the destructive impact of Mesopotamian imperialism upon the region. One of the remarkable features of this reworking and revitalizing of an ancient festival calendar, therefore, lies in the way it provided a simple pattern of ritual and celebration that could take place even far away from the central sanctuary for which it had originally been designed. Even Israelites living in the lands of their dispersion could continue sanctifying and "nationalizing" the passage of the seasons, even in environments in which the original agricultural connections became less and less evident.

The world of commerce was also incorporated into a seasonal calendar of time that had wholly different origins and significance from the historical events it commemorated. Acts of national thanksgiving survived as reminders that Israel had once been a nation and could become so again. Recollections of events that freed them from slavery continued to provide for Jews a self-image of people who were free, responsible, and law-abiding in their commitment to the larger social environment. This was true because such concepts were woven into the very meaning of time and history.

Few features of the biblical worldview contrast more directly with a modern secular worldview than in the understanding of time. For the secularist, time represents no more than an undifferentiated stream of possibility in which no one aspect is qualitatively distinguished from any other. Modern cosmology, by the unimaginable eons of time over which it has traced the processes of creation, has served to remove the sense of the creativity of time from the realms of everyday living. Similarly, time has been given a predominantly oppressive and negative quality—it is always "running out," like the sand from an hourglass.

In contrast, the biblical perception of time calls attention to its rhythmic, cyclical patterns. It is regrettable that, in a desire to magnify the historical sequential nature of time as a process, beginning at creation and proceeding to an as yet unknown end point, an earlier generation of biblical scholarship sought to denigrate the significance of the rhythmic, cyclical aspects of the Hebraic portrayal of time. Beginning with the visible symbols of the heavenly bodies and their observable and predictable movements, the biblical portrayal of time regarded it as a rhythmic, cyclical order. The cycle of seven days in which the regular occurrence of the sabbath presented both a period of rest and renewal and a recapturing of the potential of the primal sabbath of creation (Gen 2:2-3) provided the model of a larger pattern.

Days, weeks, and years were brought together in a pattern in which work and leisure, followed by times of release and recommencement, formed part of a divine plan. For the ancient Israelites who participated in and formulated this sacred calendar, time did not conform to the pattern of an undifferentiated stream. It had its moments of rise and fall, death and rebirth. In regarding time as "holy" and in accepting its given place in the divine scheme of things, the Israelites accepted a balance that conformed to the natural rhythm of life.

It is helpful to reflect on whether the modern secular perception of time has destroyed this balance and, by denying its natural rhythms, generated a far more stressful, uncontrolled, and uncontrollable environment. Because time is no longer perceived as holy, and not, therefore, subject to religious imagery and obligations, it has instead become a bewildering maze that can only be negotiated with patience and care. Rest and leisure no longer possess a "natural" and given place within the scheme of things, with the strange consequence that for some it is difficult to find room for it at all, while others look for ways to fill its boredom.

So we moderns have had to learn techniques of "time management" as a means of dealing with the unregulated and unmanageable pressures of a pattern of time that has no formal order. The abandonment of any attempt to understand time in relation to the natural rhythms and patterns of life and the seasonal order has meant that life in the modern world has become a markedly stress-inducing and destabilizing affair.

It is also important to reflect that the abandonment of religious connotations and associations for many of the major turning points of the seasonal calendar has resulted in a greatly weakened sense of its social connotation. Whereas the ancient festival days recalled the essential, if largely ideal, belief in the unity and united origins of the community, the modern secular marking of time retains few indications of such an ideal unity. As a consequence, a sense of otherness and alienation emphasizes the distinctions and differences within community life, rather than a calling back to a primary feeling of a common heritage.

DEUTERONOMY 16:18–18:22, PUBLIC AUTHORITY AND LEADERSHIP

OVERVIEW

The section 16:18–18:22 moves into a new area of legislation and concerns questions of public authority and leadership.[80] In the broad context of the Ten Commandments it appears as an elaboration of the commandment concerning the honoring of parents, since this marked the primary and most basic form of acknowledgment of a concept of social order. Parenthood, with all the responsibilities and commitments of the family as the primary kin group, established the groundwork for a wider spectrum of authority and leadership that provided a structural backbone for society as a whole. So the natural authority that arose within the family is taken as indicative of a necessary and given order that enables economic, moral, and household discipline to be managed and controlled.

Ultimately these forms of public authority can be seen to cover four specific areas of activity. In turn, these conferred authority upon and required submission to four professional, or semi-professional, social classes: the judiciary, which depended primarily on a body of publicly appointed judges; the levitical priesthood, which emerged from a particular family lineage; the monarchy, which traced its origin

---

80. J. C. Gertz, *Die Gerichtsorganisation Israels im deuteronomistischen Gesetz*, FRLANT 165 (Göttingen: Vandenhoeck & Ruprecht, 1994) 28-97; U. Rütersworden, *Von der politischen Gemeinschaft zur Gemeinde. Studien zum Dt 16,18–18,22*, BBB 65 (Frankfurt: Herder Verlag, 1987); N. Lohfink, "Distribution of the Functions of Power: The Laws Concerning Public Offices in Deuteronomy 16:18–18:22," in *A Song of Power and the Power of Song: Essays on the Book of Deuteronomy*, ed. D. L. Christensen, Sources for Biblical and Theological Study 3 (Winona Lake: Eisenbrauns, 1993) 336-52; E. Otto, "Von der Gerichtsordnung zum Verfassungsentwurf. Deuteronomische Gestaltung und Deuteronomistische Interpretation im Žmtergesetz. Dtn 16,18–18,22," *Wer ist wie du, HERR, unter den Göttern? Studien zur Theologie und Religionsgeschichte Israels für Otto Kaiser zum 70. Geburtstag*, ed. Ingo Kottsieper et al. (Göttingen: Vandenhoeck & Ruprecht, 1994) 142-55.

to an act of divine choice and appointment, but that in practice was dependent upon a unique family dynasty; the charismatic prophets, who represented a divinely selected and appointed class of leadership.

All of these groups of public leaders are viewed as necessary for the proper maintenance of social order, although how their relative levels of authority were to be balanced against one another is not spelled out. Each is necessary and to some extent exists within a kind of social oligarchy. It is not made clear how an operating balance between the various competing interests was to be achieved. There is an underlying assumption that each of these classes of leader administers the higher authority of God and that some kind of divine ordering and balance would manifest itself.

We should not be surprised, then, that no predetermined method of resolving conflicts of authority within Israelite society is laid down. The significance of what is set out in the deuteronomic legislation lies in its acceptance of a specific place for each of four main forms of authority, allowing each to serve as a check and balance over the other three areas. In this way, there would be no monopoly of public authority that could lead to abuses of power. In this regard, the most striking feature, when viewed against the larger context of the ancient Near East, is the limited authority accorded to the kingship as a public institution. Its existence appears to be conceded, rather than warmly demanded, and it is set under a positive code of restraints.

It is also noteworthy that even the basic form of authority in which parents exercised control over their children is placed under certain limits. This indicates a clear recognition that no one form of authority, however basic, was allowed to exercise a dominant position over the others.

From the perspective of the time of origin of the legislation set out here, a measure of openness has to be accepted. The provision for the institution of monarchy clearly points to the expectation of the continuance of this institution, but even this appears as one of the latest insertions into the section as a whole. It is provided for in such a manner as to suggest that its continuance was uncertain and that

the institution of a monarchy was not essential to Israel's existence as a nation.

The time scale within which this legislative section concerning public leadership and authority was composed cannot be determined with any certainty, and such a question need not be thought of as an issue of great significance. The provisions set out in this section endorse a situation concerning the institutional life of ancient Israel, which emerged over a very long period. They point to a fundamental trend in the organizational structure and life of the society, rather than to a sudden reformation. Certainly we should regard them as being related to the major changes in Israel's political existence that occurred during the reign of King Josiah (639–609 BCE). Yet many of these changes likely were consequential upon the changes introduced during this king's reign, rather than serving as the immediate cause of them. If we may single out one feature that is wholly remarkable, it is that the monarchy is provided for; instead of being the foundational basis on which all other features of the state are based, however, it is itself presented as simply one part of a higher divine order for society.

Broader policy shifts can be discerned within the area of the major reduction in the power of the monarchy. The kingship is given little overt instruction as to its function, either militarily or judicially. The primary concern is that this institution should endorse and uphold the Mosaic (deuteronomic) constitution, and not act outside its scope. Also evident is a broad recognition that society functions primarily as a collection of townships with little power ascribed to the heads of larger family groups of clans and tribes. The elders of towns are presented as more directly active as a resource of authority, rather than family or clan chiefs, although presumably these elders came from powerful families. Nevertheless, it is the strong focus on cities and towns as the seats of local administration that betrays the strong development of urbanized communities.

Another feature of this deuteronomic concern with public leadership and authority is that it points to a situation in which the more formal structure of a nation-state is no longer regarded as the sole ultimate authority. Claims to the righteousness and justice that uphold the royal throne are no longer made. Instead legal disputes are handled under a variety of lesser powers, including those of the levitical priesthood and the elders of local townships. It would certainly appear to be the case that the final form of the picture set out in these regulations envisages a community in which a strong and effectively administered central government could no longer be relied upon. This would point to the conclusion that the final draft of this legislation was made after the debacles of 598 and 587 BCE, when the central Jerusalem administration collapsed. Although the framework of a national monarchic state is retained, the historical figure of Moses and the concept of a written Torah provide the constitutional foundations upon which the whole polity is established.

Few factors impinge more heavily upon the harmony and well-being of society than its forms and structures of public authority. This is especially true in those areas that control legal powers, social and family policy, and commercial protection and promotion. Ultimately the justification for all such exercise of public leadership is traced back to the supreme authority of God, from whom all forms of human authority are derived. This is most emphatically expressed in the Pauline assertion that "the powers which exist are ordained of God," but it underlies all the Hebraic biblical presentation of the nature of a divine social order. It also becomes evident in a far wider spectrum of political and social order of the ancient Near East.

So far as claims to a religious basis for political order are concerned, two patterns appear prominent: the monarchy and a priestly theocracy. The monarchy, in which the royal power is itself presented as absolute, is derived directly from God, making it a theocracy. Ironically, it is typically portrayed in the biblical reports of the pharaonic administration of Egypt with its unlimited powers carried to the lengths of absurdity.

A second form of divine rule through human agency may also lay claim to unlimited power when a priestly theocracy is allowed to dominate. In practice it appears that both in Egypt and in Babylon an administration established on a balance between kingly and priestly rule prevailed. Yet even in these forms of state development the necessity for careful protection of both royal and priestly power remained essential, and the need for constant vigilance was paramount.

From the biblical perspective it would appear that a considerable level of residual authority remained with the heads of major family and tribal groups. Furthermore, repeated challenges to kingly authority by individual prophets is a marked feature of the historical tradition. Clearly such prophets could not have been unsupported and unconnected with popular feeling and the local interests of the community, whose interests they voiced. Overall, therefore, the biblical tradition is strongly critical of kingship as an institution and relatively unsympathetic toward the claims to public authority of the most celebrated priestly families. Thus a special interest attaches to the deuteronomic presentation of the forms and duties vested in these different expressions of public leadership and authority.

Deuteronomy 16:18–17:13, Judicial Authority

COMMENTARY

The major series of deuteronomic regulations authorizing the setting up of such public leaders is set out in 16:18–17:13. It concerns the setting up of an order of juridical officials to oversee the administration of law. Who exactly was to be given the duty of selecting and installing such legal officials is not made explicit, but it would appear to be the community itself. Traditionally such selection would have rested in the hands of the royal administration, and it cannot be ruled out that this was originally intended here. The royal court claimed complete authority over the administration of justice, making this a major feature of the beneficent claims of kingship for the community. Failure to uphold such a juridical system is made a primary prophetic accusation against King Jehoiakim

(Jer 22:13-17). If those who were appointed under the deuteronomic legislation were to be given office through the centralized royal administration, then it is also to be borne in mind that this opened the way to conflicts of loyalty between such officials and the heads of local townships and clans.

The very existence of the deuteronomic law code, with its many important contacts with legal procedures and formulations, which are well evidenced from the wider world of the ancient Near East, indicates the high level of skill and sophistication that was required. Such persons were not simply judges in the modern sense, but were held responsible for careful record-keeping of cases dealt with and for obtaining familiarity with the rulings and principles of legislation that had developed over a long period in the ancient Near East. Clearly such a legal official would be held responsible for controlling the conduct of cases and for ensuring the fairness of the proceedings. There is an abundance of testimony from the speech forms used by prophets, as well as from reports of cases, that a well-established protocol for the hearing of cases was observed.

16:18-20. The remarkably forthright declaration of the principles of impartiality and evenhandedness in the administration of cases set out in vv. 19-20 undoubtedly reflects long experience of actual situations. The custom of presenting gifts as a token of friendship and esteem readily developed into the corruption of giving bribes to secure a favorable verdict. Probably just as difficult to eradicate was the practice of honoring powerful and wealthy families in such a manner that their influence could easily be secured to subvert justice. In a society where kinship loyalties had traditionally provided a powerful bonding factor in upholding social harmony and cohesion, it could often prove difficult to override such loyalties in the interest of justice. The very concepts of loyalty and integrity (to one's family) could actually serve to undermine, rather than foster, a true spirit of justice.

That the task of a judge in ancient Israel could be a difficult one to fulfill honorably, and was persistently susceptible to abuse, becomes evident from the repeated sharp strictures of both prophets and the authors of

proverbial instruction concerning the administration of justice. By reading between the lines of what is demanded, it is not difficult to recognize the prevalence of familiar forms of distortion and abuse. Clearly major problems arose for the administration of justice over the difficulty in assessing the truthfulness of witnesses and the rudimentary nature of the laws of evidence. In consequence, a high premium was placed on the insight, experience, and resolute determination of legal officials to ensure fair trials. These requirements for the selection of suitable officials for the task, as set out in 16:20, point us to recognize that the administration of justice formed a high priority for the general harmony and well-being of ancient Israelite society.

Issues concerning the administration of justice are further dealt with in 17:8-13, which provides for a way of dealing with cases of a serious nature in which the local judicial process, presided over by a judge, was unable to come to a satisfactory verdict, providing the basis for what we might describe as a system of appeals. The intervening regulations that are set out in 16:21–17:7 deal with fundamental questions of religious disloyalty and apostasy. Three specific cases are considered: (1) setting up a sacred pole as an Asherah or a stone pillar as a related non-Israelite cult symbol; (2) presenting a defective animal as a sacred offering to God; and (3) open blasphemy.

16:21-22. Clearly the practice of establishing simple, and basically primitive, shrines to a local deity had a long history in the land occupied by Israel. Such simple sanctuaries were local features that could often claim to have existed from times of great antiquity and were not, therefore, to be ignored or set aside. The sharp deuteronomic polemic against them indicates that they enjoyed a good deal of popular support. For the authors of Deuteronomy, these shrines are now viewed as a serious threat to the purity and integrity of the worship of the LORD as God. It seems highly probable that in many instances the local communities that venerated such symbols regarded them as acceptable adjuncts to the worship of the LORD as Israel's God. They could also readily provide explanations for why the one great God of Israel should have appeared in many forms.

Throughout the Deuteronomic History we find a consistent zeal and fervor to maintain a rigid religious purity, with every indication that forms of religious practice that had at one time appeared acceptable, and even normal, within Israel were now outlawed and classed as objectionable and dangerous. Moreover, the deuteronomists, who were themselves clearly not priests, had no restraint in expecting to use the full force of the law to implement their stringent demands.

It is not at all clear why these prohibitions against long-established, and now rejected, cultic features should have been introduced into a series of instructions for the administration of justice. We may consider that they were felt to be necessary at this point because the simple resolution of difficult legal cases by the Levites at a local sanctuary, as laid down in the older Book of the Covenant, were in need of revision when only one central sanctuary was permitted. Resort to any traditional, but non-Yahwistic, sanctuary as a place where difficult legal matters could be settled, therefore, was firmly outlawed. It had become necessary to preclude that the concern to deal with local juristic problems should have led to any recognition of small sanctuaries that were repudiated on religious grounds. In other words, it was not to be permitted that non-Yahwistic sanctuaries should be tolerated simply because they were needed for settling legal disputes.

17:1. The use of blemished animals as sacrificial offerings is prohibited by the ruling laid down in this verse, which defines such an offering as an "abomination" (תועבה *tôʿēbâ*) to God. This was undoubtedly a significant term in the vocabulary of evil and wrongdoing for the deuteronomists, since it expressed a strong note of divine repugnance, without entering further into discussion of how it conflicted with the divine order of life. Neither this nor the preceding prohibition gives any ruling on the punishment to be imposed on offenders, should they be guilty of contravening the deuteronomic ruling.

17:2-7. This is not the case, however, with the third of the condemnatory prohibitions, which concerns a blatant infringement of the first commandment. It brings us face to face once again with the extremely harsh treatment demanded by the deuteronomic

legislators for any citizens who defected from a total commitment to the worship and devotion to the LORD as God. This was brought out earlier in the rulings of chap. 13 concerning incitement by prophets to turn away from exclusive loyalty to the LORD. The situation envisaged in the present law concerns acts of outright apostasy. It would seem most probable that it has been introduced at this point as a further elaboration of the prohibition against the retention of non-Israelite cult symbols that was raised in 16:21–17:1. The penalty for blatant acts of apostasy is unequivocal and final: Any person found guilty of such an offense was to be put to death.

It is clear that such cases represented extremely dangerous instances where the legal system could be abused and where unscrupulous persons could concoct a charge of apostasy in order to avenge themselves upon people against whom they held a grudge. Thus the rules governing witnesses and their evidence are reaffirmed in 17:6-7 to ensure that those who made such accusations were directly implicated in their consequences. The presence of this ruling may reflect on the fact that such cases called for the most careful judicial handling. More probable, however, it seems that the whole stratum of harsh anti-apostasy legislation in Deuteronomy, imposing capital punishment for such offenses and calling for the extermination of non-Israelite residents in the land, marks a consistent, coherent, but relatively late, stratum in the growth of the deuteronomic corpus. After the political disasters that witnessed the collapse of the Judean state in 587 BCE, a harsh and bitter attempt was made to effect a religious "cleansing" of the land from those elements of the population who had abandoned their exclusive loyalty to the LORD as God, or who had never observed such a commitment.

17:8-13. The ruling set out concerning legal cases that could not be resolved through the usual judicial processes maintains the ancient custom of settling such disputes by resorting to the services of a priest at a sanctuary. In most cases, this would have called for the use of the sacred lot, rather than depending on any kind of special priestly legal expertise. It is of interest that the type of dispute envisaged as needing such priestly resolution is primarily one that involved physical violence (v. 8). The various kinds of bloodshed mentioned refer to distinctions between intentional and accidental assaults leading to the death of the victim. A similar understanding must apply to the phrase "one kind of assault and another." In such cases, the intention of the assailant was of critical importance, but was obviously frequently difficult to determine. Similarly, even accidental injury could be brought about through culpable negligence on the part of a person's ill-judged actions. The issues relating to "one kind of legal right and another" must refer to claims over property in which proof of ownership could often be difficult to establish.

The recognition of the difficulties inherent in such cases, where the expertise and experience of a judge could be most heavily tested, reflects two prominent features of ancient Israelite law. The first concerns the relatively undeveloped laws of evidence, for which a verdict depended on assessing the accused person's intention at the time of the offense. The second concerns the reluctance in such cases in which insufficient and inconclusive evidence was available to allow the case to be dropped altogether. Belief that a divine decision could be obtained in spite

of the difficulties of the case by resorting to the help of a levitical priest at a sanctuary enabled the determination of disputes lacking adequate proof by a different route altogether. The results may often have been arbitrary, but were simply imposed on the persons concerned.

The conclusion set out in vv. 12-13 specifying the death penalty for anyone who refused to accept the verdict of the priest in such instances can be taken to indicate that the arbitrary nature of the verdicts arrived at in such cases could often give rise to further bitterness and recrimination. Quite evidently, even the inclusion of provisions to involve the priestly authorities in settling difficult legal cases was only a partial, and apparently contested, means of assistance. Overall the picture we obtain from the regulations providing for a wide-ranging legal system in ancient Israel reflects the importance of a system of criminal justice in maintaining peaceful and non-violent relationships in society. At the same time, the provisions that are made highlight the difficulties that all such systems experience and the need for protecting the innocent as well as punishing the guilty.

REFLECTIONS

The provision of publicly appointed judges, combined with a strong insistence on the necessity for their impartiality and integrity in the performance of their duties, reflects the high importance the development of law encounters in any society. We find ample evidence of such developments throughout the ancient Near East, and they are well represented in the legal sections of the Old Testament. The belief in a foundation of law that undergirds and protects all human societies was one of the major products of the rise of civilization in the ancient Near East. The achievements of (even partial) justice have provided a legacy from which all of Western civilization has benefited.

From as far back as clear historical evidence can take us it was initially the members of a person's own clan or tribe who sought to protect individuals and to impose punishment on wrongdoers. Family heads and tribal chiefs used their wisdom and experience to sort out disputes and to settle quarrels. When members of other clans and tribes were involved, a system of blood revenge operated as far as could be attained. Quite often such a primitive system of justice based on avenging wrongdoing must have been cruel and have caught up many innocent persons in its actions. To establish a system of redress and punishment based on individual responsibility and guilt, therefore, stood in the forefront of building a fairer and more peaceful society. Yet to achieve this called for considerable care and experience of human behavior. Questions of responsibility and guilt consistently called for ways of determining the relative degrees of guilt when two persons were caught up in a violent quarrel. Fairness demanded insight into matters of intentions and self-control. So inevitably forms of law that set out the principles and guidelines by which men and women should be judged became carefully worded and carefully balanced statements. Time and again the verdicts that were to be reached depended on the good sense, integrity, and fair-mindedness of the persons who judged the case. Perhaps more precisely it was the people themselves, including both the victim and the accused, who were to "judge" the case, and it was the responsibility of the judge to show how this was to be done and to ensure, so far as was possible, that it was done.

Yet even with the best of intentions all forms of public authority could be abused and manipulated to serve more selfish and partisan ends. Even kings could abuse their authority, as is amply shown by the biblical portrait of the Egyptian pharaoh in the story of how Israel suffered oppression in Egypt. So in any township or city, judges were fallible human beings who could behave in unsatisfactory ways.

It is in the light of this that much of the biblical tradition, even when it boldly upholds a public judicial system and supports the necessity for its operation in a civilized society, is constantly aware of its vulnerability and limitations. Whether we look at biblical stories of how royal figures such as Ahab could distort justice to support their selfish aims (1 Kings 21), how prophets complained of major abuses perpetrated by high public figures (Jeremiah 22), or even how psalmists and sages warned of corruption and injustice in judicial affairs, we are brought face to face with an awareness of the problems that the cry for justice entailed.

It is important in the light of this to note how persistently the biblical tradition of justice focuses not simply on the insistent demand "justice and only justice shall you pursue," but that it recognizes the many hindrances to this. All judicial systems are subject to limitations and weaknesses and can rise no higher than the honesty and conscientiousness of the persons who administer them. It is a major feature of the Ten Commandments that they frankly recognize these difficulties and endeavor to counter them. The prohibition against wrong use of the divine name, the sharp repudiation of giving false evidence ("bearing false witness," KJV), and not least the prohibition against coveting a neighbor's property indicate that possessing good laws is not sufficient in itself to create a just and worthy society. Personal honor and integrity also have a role to play, as does a willingness to seek out and deal with public wrongs. Laws can be no more "lawful" than the willingness and determination of those who administer them.

We sense once again the importance that Deuteronomy, and the biblical tradition more generally, attaches to the claim that justice and righteousness are fundamental features of the divine order of life. They are not simply human constructions for the convenience of men and women living in society, but are gifts of God by which a truly holy and righteous world order can be achieved. In many respects, we can see how basic, and sometimes inadequate, the laws set out in the Bible appear to be when compared with the more sophisticated legal formulations with which we work in the modern world. Nevertheless, the insights, principles, and especially the sense of the divine basis for law that the Bible presents remain valid for our acceptance and recognition. We, too, are called upon to pursue justice and righteousness with impartiality and fervor, since the lives, freedom, and well-being of all human beings depend on this. If we are sometimes tempted to feel superior to persons in antiquity, we may nonetheless profit from the clarity and directness with which they set out the goals of righteous living.

Deuteronomy 17:14–18:22, Kings, Priests, and Prophets

COMMENTARY

17:14-20. Central to the understanding of public authority in ancient Israel was acceptance of the king as supreme earthly ruler. So we are now given instructions for the setting up of a monarchy as the first of three primary institutions for the administration and life of the community. The other two are those of priests and prophets. Already the regulations concerning the appointment of law officials have presupposed acceptance of an order of levitical priests. Now we are presented with an explicit instruction concerning the place, character, and function of the king in ancient Israel. It is unique within the Pentateuch as a formulation declaring the constitutional position of the king and the basic duties that are entrusted to him. We can, however, note that the hymnic celebrations of the Davidic king in a significant number of psalms forthrightly express an absolute claim for the divine choice and support for the kingly office. What is surprising about the deuteronomic ruling is that it regards the monarchy as a permitted concession, rather than a necessary foundation of national existence. We may contrast the very different perspective given in Lam 4:20, where the kingship is regarded as indispensable.

So the regulations governing the kingship that are set out in these verses are distinctive for the quite modest claims made for the king and for the restrictions placed on the role and prestige of the public office. It cuts the monarchy down to size, clearly showing it to be a human institution, subject to normal human temptations. Undoubtedly this guarded attitude must reflect the uncertainty with which the deuteronomists viewed it.[81] It is also a noteworthy feature that the particular limitations imposed on the king in vv. 16-17 are aimed at preventing another ruler of the character of Solomon, whose excesses had effectively caused the breakup of the old united kingdom that David had built. There

can be no doubt at all that the reason for this cutting down to human dimensions of the office of king was a consequence of Israel's experience and an awareness of the dangers of the oppressiveness kings could bring. The prophet Samuel's warning concerning kings and their excessive claims and demands (1 Sam 8:11-18) was a message the deuteronomists had taken to heart.

In order to appreciate the special character of what the deuteronomists declare concerning Israel's kings, we must see it against the background of the ancient Near Eastern world.[82] Fundamental to this context was the claim that kings were appointed by God, chosen and supported by an act of divine will, enabling kings to exercise a form of "divine" rule on earth. Human kings were presented as acting on behalf of, and in the place of, God. So kingship purported to be a form of theocracy in which the human agent, whether claimed as "son of God" or simply as the "anointed of God," exercised a divine rule. So whatever kings did was claimed to be by divine authority and to possess an absolute, unquestionable right. Human societies simply "received" their kings as emissaries of God, rather than choosing and appointing them. It is on account of such excessive claims that kingship could consistently appear as a powerful, but inherently oppressive, form of government.

Yet kingship was not all bad, and it is impossible to consider the rise and success of the progress of civilization in the ancient world without it. Kings were powerful, relatively efficient, and militarily successful. They claimed to administer justice, to deter brigands and robbers, and to put down all forms of wrongdoing. They presented themselves as the friends of widows and the weak. In order to fulfill all these duties, they produced great codes of law, amassed powerful armies, promoted trade, built great temples and palaces, and founded schools and colleges of scribes.

---

81. F. Crüsemann, *Der Widerstand gegen das Königtum. Die antikönigliche Texte des Alten Testaments und der kampf um den frühe israelitischen Staat,* WMANT 49 (Neukirchen-Vluyn: Neukirchener Verlag, 1978); G. E. Gerbrandt, *Kingship According to the Deuteronomistic History,* SBLDS 87 (Atlanta: Scholars Press, 1986) esp. 89-115.

82. This background is excellently described in H. Frankfort, *Kingship and the Gods: A Study of Ancient Near Eastern Religion as the Integration of Society and Nature* (Chicago: University of Chicago Press, 1948).

So they achieved much, but frequently did so at a terrible human cost.

Looking at kingship in such a light, we can understand the carefully moderated acceptance of kingship that the deuteronomists advocate. Kingship, even that of the revered house and dynasty of David, was an institution that had a tarnished history.

Nevertheless, the assertion that the ruler was to be "a king whom the LORD your God will choose" (v. 15) maintains the long-standing tradition that kings were not humanly appointed but were the subject of divine election. Such had certainly been declared with regard to the dynasty of David (Pss 89:3-4; 132:11-12), and the restriction of succession to members of this dynasty must certainly have been intended by the deuteronomists.

The rule of the king, further, expressly spells out that the king was to be "one of your own community" (מקרב אחיך *miqqereb 'aheyka*; lit., "one from among your brothers"). This has a twofold significance, consciously emphasizing the human status of the king and eliminating the mythological language of the king's origins from a divine birth, making him "Son of God," as in Egypt. Also, it ensured that the king was a native Israelite, thereby precluding that a foreigner could usurp the throne of Israel. In all of this the deuteronomic legislation very plainly sets limits to the titles, religious claims, and supernatural status of the king, such as had surrounded the varied portraits of kingship current in antiquity. The king is very clearly a human figure with a particular task to perform within the life of Israel as a nation.

Historically we can place the origins of this deuteronomic view of kingship in the situation of Josiah's reign. This was a period in which a major attempt was made, in the disastrous aftermath of a century of Assyrian interference, to reestablish a single united people of Israel under a native ruler of the house of David. The price that such a ruler had to pay was that he should not repeat the excesses of Solomon.[83] So the roots of this deuteronomic reformed view of a limited monarchy are to be traced back to the political situation of Josiah's reign. However,

more than this would appear to underlie the surprising degree of uncertainty concerning whether there needed to be a continuing Davidic monarchy in Israel at all. Certainly for Josiah's reform the supporting role of the king was vital to the whole success of the program. We must conclude, therefore, that this level of doubt expressed in vv. 14-20 regarding the future of the institution has entered in the wake of the disastrous blow to the Jerusalem monarchy in 587 BCE. After that, its future was far from clearly evident, and the noncommittal historical note in 2 Kgs 25:27-30 corroborates this to be the later deuteronomic viewpoint.

The requirement that the king should have prepared a copy of the written law of Moses (vv. 18-19), which is a reference to the deuteronomists' own law code, and that he should read from it "all the days of his life" accords with the report of David's instructions to Solomon (1 Kgs 2:1-4). It has all the marks of being a rather idealistic demand that affirmed the priority of Moses and the Mosaic law over the institution of kingship. It would support the overall deuteronomic demand that the historical figure of Moses and the Mosaic written law should provide the basis for limiting the absolute freedom of the king to control religious, military, and legal affairs.

18:1-14. The next major institution to be subjected to the legislative purview of the deuteronomists is that of the priesthood. Here the deuteronomic instructions make provision for all Levites to serve as priests, whether they were already resident in the city of the central shrine or whether they had earlier been resident in other towns, but now wished to continue their ministry at the central sanctuary (vv. 6-7). The ruling explicitly specifies that they are then to enjoy equal privileges and rewards for their services as those of other priests working in the city. (That this privilege was not conceded is reported in 2 Kgs 23:9.)

The origin of the Levites as a class of religious ministrants is shrouded in historical uncertainty and cannot be brought into a wholly clear light. It is claimed both here and elsewhere in the Bible that they at one time constituted a separate tribe, but became scattered as a consequence of a major upheaval that befell them (cf. Genesis 34). Yet this

---

83. This historical background to the changed perception of kingship in Josiah's time is described in R. Albertz, *A History of Israelite Religion in the Old Testament Period,* trans. J. Bowden (London: SCM, 1994) 1:198-206.

claim is not easily substantiated, and such a portrayal of the origins of what was essentially a varied range of religious devotees bears traces of a highly stylized and theoretical account of persons who had no specific territorial holding of their own. Their primary characteristic was an unswerving and uncompromising loyalty to the LORD as sole deity and a concomitant expertise in the knowledge of divine service that qualified them to be priests.

Certainly at an earlier time in Israel not all priests were Levites (even David's sons could become priests; 2 Sam 8:18), but this simply reflects that early Israel lacked any narrowly defined summary of the duties exclusive to priests. It was undoubtedly held from an early period of Israel's development that it was advantageous for a priest to be a Levite (cf. Judg 17:12-13). It would appear, therefore, that the deuteronomic legislation moves strongly in the direction of imposing some uniformity by permitting all Levites to serve as priests. However, such a situation was more than a little theoretical if by the time this legislation was set out the Jerusalem Temple had been destroyed and the levitical communities scattered.

That they did not all do so becomes clear from subsequent definitions of priestly duties and restrictions contained in the book of Ezekiel and the later priestly (P) parts of the Pentateuch. In fact, in the post-exilic age, the Levites became a class of second-rank sanctuary ministers. Their duties especially concerned the more verbal aspects of public worship with the offering of public prayer, the singing of psalms, and the delivery of sermon-like exhortations.

The deuteronomic concern to set out a program for the worship of Israel at only one central sanctuary involved a number of competing, and often conflicting, claims relating to the history of the priesthood. The events of the sixth century BCE had undoubtedly brought not only disruption to the activities of the Jerusalem priesthood, but also serious divisions within it. These conflicts were not easily resolved, and when the time came for the rebuilding and refurbishing of the destroyed Temple fresh compromises became necessary. In fact, the entire period is shrouded in obscurity so far as the history of the priesthood is concerned.[84] The deuteronomic ruling concerning the role of the Levites and their potential status as priests marks an important step in defining their position within the nation. From the evidence of the existence of levitical cities, it would appear that not all Levites were involved with the service of a sanctuary. Thus the deuteronomic ruling points to a firm encouragement for the Levites to become more fully involved in Israel's cultic affairs.

Two particular points concerning the levitical priesthood are well reflected in the deuteronomic legislation. The first is its recognition that the Levites were wholly dependent upon the gifts and tithe offerings of the people. Since they possessed no substantial tribal territory of their own, the Levites' adherence to the traditional allegiance to the LORD as God was their title-deed to a role in Israel's life.

If the overall perspective adopted by this commentary—that Deuteronomy 12–26 reflects a concern to legislate for religious renewal in the wake of the disasters of 587 BCE—is valid, then this degree of concern for the welfare of the Levites is particularly fitting. Without a fully functioning Temple and temple cultus to administer, the position of the levitical priesthood had become precarious. So it was especially significant that the deuteronomists were deeply committed to securing the survival of the levitical priesthood.

It is certainly also a matter of significance for the development of Israel's priesthood that the deuteronomic instructions and provisions brought a variety of priestly duties and activities under a single, uniform set of regulations. In the wider concern to eradicate deviations of practice and to expunge the risk of continuing resort to non-Yahwistic deities and rituals, the priestly function itself has here become more closely defined.

Since priestly duties involved the service of the altar, the careful and ritually acceptable slaughter and presentation of sacrifices were among the more obvious of priestly functions. Yet, alongside these duties were many others involving instruction in prayer, the obtaining of oracles, and the handling of a range of

84. Haran, *Temples and Temple Service in Ancient Israel*; Cody, *A History of Old Testament Priesthood*.

issues covering matters of hygiene and ritual purity. Although many areas relating to the latter either do not appear at all or do so only marginally in the deuteronomic law book, it can be concluded that the deuteronomic provisions for the priesthood generated a strong unifying impulse. This was not an accidental offshoot of the reformers' work, but rather represented a positive tendency designed to uphold an integrated and unified tradition. So far as the deuteronomists were concerned, all worship was a matter of wider concern to society and to the possibility of maintaining an Israelite state. Therefore, it needed to be carefully regulated and supervised. The deuteronomic tendency to treat matters of religious allegiance and worship as matters involving the state and its legislative powers is a striking aspect of its assumptions and interests. It is wholly in line with this deuteronomic tendency that precise instructions are given concerning which parts of the sacrificial offering and what proportion of the first fruits were to be given to the Levites as their due (vv. 3-4).

The inclusion of a series of prohibitions concerning cultic and quasi-cultic activities set out in vv. 9-14 can be seen as a practical consequence of the endorsement given to the approved levitical priesthood. With a faithful and loyal order of priestly servants, Israel would have no need to resort to the mixed range of rituals and divinatory practices that are outlawed here. It would appear that many of them had been popular and widely used responses to a variety of social needs, especially those concerned with health and hygiene.

The reference to making a son or daughter "pass through fire" (v. 10) marks a particularly repugnant form of religious commitment attested in the OT (cf. 2 Kgs 21:6). It relates to human sacrifice, as condemned in 12:31. The remaining categories of cultic activity that are outlawed in vv. 10-14 relate to forms of oracle giving, divination, and the manipulation of magic powers through the uttering of spells or counterspells. In this we encounter a particularly influential aspect of the deuteronomic theology, which strove to eliminate any form of acceptance of or deference to arbitrary spiritual powers, whether they were believed to be beneficial or harmful. All

spiritual powers and controls, whether public or private, are made subject to the overriding sense of the unique, personal, and gracious nature of the LORD as God. Belief in the sovereignty of one divine controlling power and its superiority to all human powers and to all forms of spiritual power to which human beings might claim access was of paramount importance. No compulsive manipulation of divine forces, secret invocation of divine names and titles, or even appeal to the spirits of departed ancestors was to be permitted in Israel. All worship is personalized and subjected to recognized categories of reasoned personal communication. Personal prayer, not magical formulas, is the basis for humans' communication with God and with the divine world. Public worship was to be saturated with awareness that symbols, words, and ritual actions could only be adjuncts to support this personal communion of human beings with God. Neither ritual nor the spoken word could be depersonalized so as to provide a mechanistic interpretation of spiritual realities.

18:15-22. So far we have been introduced to the roles of three classes of public institutional authority: royal, juridical, and priestly. In the course of time, each was liable to acquire a degree of rigidity and permanence in the wielding of power. For both kings and priests authority was based on an inherited status, conferred upon them as a birthright. In consequence, the public power structures based on these roles easily became inflexible. They tended to become detached from actual personal needs, and so became unresponsive to the changing religious and social circumstances of the community. To counter this inflexibility, prophets offered a measure of corrective challenge and the possibility of innovation.

We are now introduced to a fourth, and more controversial, class of public leaders. These were the prophets who would arise from time to time to bring a new word from God that could affect both the national and the private lives of persons in Israel.

Taken in its broad compass, the picture of ancient Israelite religion given to us by the biblical writings is of a spiritual and religious life in which prophets figured very prominently. This accords with the realities of the situation as they were actually experienced. Prophets consistently and regularly appeared as charismatically endowed, and often richly eloquent, speakers and preachers. Their authority was claimed to be, and was usually accepted as, direct, God-given, and unconfined to any one family, locality, or tribal group. To outsiders and opponents, prophets appeared to be self-appointed speakers, but to their followers they were God-appointed revealers of truth that came through no other avenue of spiritual knowledge.

Prophets gave expression to a fundamentally different kind of authority from that of priests and kings precisely because it appeared as a spontaneous breaking-in of knowledge and truth from God alone. The speech forms used by such prophets conformed to this claim to a divine origin, in which they presented themselves as the very mouth of God to speak to Israel. It is this spontaneous, uncontrolled—and uncontrollable—feature of prophetic activity that made it both a powerful instrument for change and renewal and a danger to all attempts at religious conformity and orthodoxy. In the light of their concern to create and impose a uniform Mosaic Torah, it is understandable that the deuteronomists should have viewed prophets and their activities with some misgivings. Already we have encountered the sharp ruling and ferocious penalties that endeavored to deal with any prophet who presumed to speak a message in the name of a deity other than that of the LORD God of Israel (13:1-5). Yet prophecy could not be altogether denied, and it appears that the rigorous contention, which the deuteronomists so eagerly endorsed, that Israel should worship the LORD alone as God was itself a product of prophetic tradition. Besides which, prophets must often have received a strong popular following in ancient Israel, making any attempt to limit or nullify their activities quite impossible. So the deuteronomic legislative ruling concerning prophets bears a twofold requirement: Prophets should be "from among your own people" (i.e., native Israelites), and they should be "like Moses."

Although it has been argued that there may have existed in Israel a specific order of official prophets who would fulfill an inter-tribal role for the whole community and would thereby have a national significance "like Moses," no firm evidence for this is available. Rather, the formulation must be not the reconstruction of an ancient office within the nation, but a major attempt by the deuteronomists to see prophecy in perspective. The importance of prophecy could not be denied, but its haphazard and random appearance meant that it had to be treated with great care. It is for this reason that this legislation allows prophecy a place in the religious and public life of Israel, but hedges it about with restrictions. Prophets must be "like Moses," by which it is intended to affirm that their teaching must accord with the words and spirit of Moses as Israel's unique leader.

The second test for the acknowledgment of a true prophet is that the prophet's messages should be proved true by the actual outcome of events (v. 22). This must be judged a reasonable, but in practice rather unhelpful, test to apply. Since prophecies often took the form of warnings and threats in times of crisis, it may have been of little assistance to find that such warnings were true when it was too late to heed their message. Similarly the reverse situation would be equally valid. Yet in truth the ruling, for all its theoretical nature, provides an important guide to the way in which prophecy was understood by the deuteronomists.

Already there existed a substantial body of written tradition of the words and messages of earlier prophets that are now preserved for us. These messages, emanating from as early as the eighth century BCE from such figures as Amos and Isaiah, had foretold the terrible disasters Israel had subsequently suffered. So this deuteronomic ruling serves as a form of endorsement and approval for these figures, recognizing that they had formed a genuine succession in the spirit of Moses. In substantial measure, their words had already shown themselves to be true prophecies by the time that deuteronomic legislation was composed, and it is the need to draw attention to this that has occasioned its composition. We may compare the rough and ready guide to the differences between true and false prophecy that is set out in Jer 28:8-9, where the influence of the deuteronomists is certainly evident.

In large measure it agreed well with the overall sense of crisis they felt and with their urgent appeals for obedience to the law Moses had given for the deuteronomic authors to point to the way in which prophecies of doom had already proved true to events. The distinctive word of prophecy could not be ignored as a valid and authoritative word from God. Yet this did not open the door for every prophet to be heard and listened to with confidence. Many prophets came with deceitful messages of false hope, just as Hananiah had endeavored to beguile the hearers of Jeremiah (Jer 28:1-4; 29:8-9). Not every prophetic message was from God, and only that which was in agreement with the terms and spirit of Moses and the law was to be accepted.

Overall the presence of prophets within the national life of Israel, both in a larger historical perspective and in the contemporary scene, provided the deuteronomists with an unsettling and complex agency of religious leadership. It claimed an immediate and unquestioned authority and could thereby easily endanger the zeal for conformity and unswerving loyalty the deuteronomists demanded. Yet it had held a rich and influential place in Israel's history and was, in any case, widely respected. The prophets' place could not be denied and had contributed much to the deuteronomic sense that Israel's present crisis had been foretold by divine warnings. So the formula that is put forward is that all true prophets must be "like Moses," thereby drawing a line around the range of their teaching and at the same time indicating that Moses was a more than ordinary prophet.

REFLECTIONS

The fourfold listing of public leadership authorized by the deuteronomic legislators represents a uniquely balanced assessment of the power structures of human societies in general. A striking mixture of leadership based on inherited status and popular acclamation jostles alongside religious and social factors in shaping public life. Kings are brought down from their high thrones, but prophets, too, who could sometimes appear as kingmakers, are commissioned for their work within strict limits. Law officers are heralded as the custodians of justice and fairness, but their task is seen to be almost impossible to fulfill without the added input of priestly agents who could pronounce a verdict from God.

In an avowedly religious writing like the book of Deuteronomy, we might have expected to find evidence of claims for a priestly hierarchy, such as existed in many ancient societies and have occasionally reappeared in Christian history. Throughout the ancient Near East also we find that all writing of a political nature has emerged from within powerful monarchies in which the role of the king is presented as supreme and beyond all question. Such portrayals of the kingly office as absolute and as the only divinely approved form of human government find some limited expression in the Old Testament (see Psalm 2). Yet much of the biblical literature offers a more truthful and circumscribed portrait of kings, revealing their weaknesses and corruptibility. The deuteronomic ruling, therefore, places their power within necessary restraints and openly insists that they are themselves simply servants of a higher power and a more perfect justice.

Perhaps most of all we might have expected to find in the deuteronomic rulings an endorsement of prophecy as the sure and certain word from God to guide the people of Israel along a difficult and uncharted course. Yet here, too, we find major limitations, even if their expression is so brief and simplistic as to be difficult to apply to individual cases. Prophets, like kings, were to be administrators and leaders in a social order that had been laid down by Moses and ultimately looked to God as its author and founder.

So we find in Deuteronomy a sensitive balance in which judges, kings, priests, and prophets are each accorded an appropriate, if rather loosely defined, range of authority. Very markedly the royal power is sharply curtailed and set under a higher power based on the tradition of Moses. Priestly authority and the right of priests to claim the economic support of the community are firmly endorsed, but are placed within boundaries that exclude a range of mantic activities that are now viewed as dangerous and subversive. All priestly claims to be able to negotiate with the spirits of departed ancestors or to pierce the hidden mysteries of the future are eliminated. Israelite priests could not be shamans wielding magical power, nor could prophets and soothsayers ply their trade, preying on popular griefs and fears.

No indication is given as to how the judges and law officers were to be appointed, and this may well have been left open for local communities to decide. To what extent the royal administration exercised influence on this matter is left unclear.

The picture generated by this deuteronomic legislation concerning public authority left significant areas of overlap between the separate lines of interest and control. Township elders appear still to have exercised considerable power in local affairs, but no sharp line defining each respective sphere of influence is drawn. Nor is it evident how disputes were to be settled when conflicts of interest arose. However, the legislation provides an interesting recognition that a variety of insights and interests was appropriate to the good ordering of a society. In particular, legal disputes were not left under the exclusive control of any one professional group or section of the community. Some degree of interactive checks and restraints is envisaged that conceived of Israelite society as functioning as an organic unit. For the health of the whole, each part was required to be vitally active and consciously alert.

Undergirding the whole picture of society that is presupposed by these rules governing public authority is an affirmed divine foundation. Israel is conceived of as existing by an act of divine election, and so its social order is to be shaped by a polity given by Moses in the name of God. The concept of divine revelation colors and illuminates everything; yet, it is not a traditional theocracy in which kings or priests assume the role of deity. In place of an autocratic, and easily corruptible, imperial bureaucracy there is an awareness of a need for flexibility and the embracing of change. In spite of its form and reputation as a law book, Deuteronomy is strongly committed to granting the freedom of responsible officers to deal with a wide range of basic matters on an ad hoc basis. Unlike the later developments of Jewish life in which a vast number of rules and instructions were formulated to cover everyday activities, Deuteronomy leaves much to the good sense and integrity of responsible citizens.

Particular importance attaches to the deuteronomic concern to allow that a variety of channels of public jurisdiction were to be recognized and given the freedom to act in concert, and even to react upon each other. Nor is any undue emphasis placed here on the strictly religious, over against the more openly secular, structures of the community.

It is not by mere chance that the deuteronomic movement as a whole has been viewed as providing a kind of center or balance point for the entire development of the Old Testament. It quite evidently marked a point of transition, consciously aware that, with the decline and eventual collapse of the kingdoms of Israel and Judah between the eighth and sixth centuries BCE, an experiment had come to an end. Israel had entered the world of nations, had striven to express a divine ideal within this national reality, and had fallen apart in the face of unstoppable pressures from Mesopotamian imperialism. From within this declining national ethos the deuteronomists sought to retrieve many of the fundamental values and achievements it had brought to birth. A commitment to law, justice, brotherly love, and national solidarity had established ideals that were worth preserving for the future.

Such ideals, however, remain weak and powerless unless they are incorporated into the operating structures of social and political life. It is never sufficient to have just laws. It is essential that such laws be administered justly. Similarly, the righteous authority of judges and rulers to put down wrongdoing and punish the lawless can only work when these officers of the state act justly. More subtly still, both priests and prophets can uphold a vision and awareness of the spiritual dimension of life. Yet these persons, too, can distort their offices to pander to the fears and sufferings of a community by preying on those fears. Even religion can be abused and traded for spurious claims to know what cannot be known and to deal in unholy fire!

DEUTERONOMY 19:1–21:23, MATTERS OF LIFE AND DEATH

OVERVIEW

The series of laws that now follow deals with issues of life and death. They can helpfully be regarded as having been brought together to provide an elaboration and explication of the sixth commandment ("You shall not murder," 5:17). This commandment applied to more than simply the overt criminal acts that can be covered by the modern criminal category of murder. Even the ancient laws covering this crime encountered difficulties with the necessity for distinguishing between a deliberate act of killing, the causing of death by accident, and the varying degrees of culpability that could emerge between the two extremes. At the very least, the commandment against unjustified killing raised a host of questions concerning the intention of the offender, the possibility of provocation, and the extent to which social conventions of revenge may have played a role.

When we add to these variable factors the indirect responsibility for a person's premature death, a vast number of further issues arise. Injury might lead to dangerous infections, resulting in prolonged suffering and

death, and carelessness and indifference can lead to an innocent person's suffering a fatal accident. Who, then, was to blame? Homicide was seldom a simple matter, and further complexities arose when the circumstances of death were suspicious, but no obvious culprit could be found. The stories in 2 Samuel present excellent examples of the problem of apportioning blame for homicide, as in the case of David's responsibility for Uriah's death (2 Sam 12:9) and Joab's responsibility for the killing of Abner (2 Sam 3:26-30).

Overall the problem of distinguishing between intentional and accidental killing occasioned difficulties for the lawmakers of antiquity, as it still does today. When we add to these problems the accountability for accidental death or for the death of a slave, we can see that the direct commandment "You shall not murder" opened up a range of further issues. Issues of life and death stretched into areas that, at first reckoning, appeared to be only peripherally related to the question of murder.

Deuteronomy 19:1-21, Issues of Life and Death: Murder

COMMENTARY

The three issues that come first under the purview of this section of the deuteronomic legislation deal with the provision of three cities of refuge west of the river Jordan (vv. 1-13), the removal of a neighbor's boundary marker (v. 14), and the question of what kind of evidence was admissible to substantiate

a criminal charge, especially if it carried the death penalty (vv. 15-21).

19:14. It certainly appears out of place that the shifting of a boundary marker should have been included among rules dealing with offenses that carried the possibility of capital punishment. It may be that such a criminal act had come to be regarded as so serious a problem that it had to be deterred by the most serious punishment. It cannot, in any case, altogether be ruled out that such actions had given rise to violent quarrels in which deaths had occurred.

We must also keep in mind that the problem attendant upon the illegal shifting of boundary markers may have been introduced at this point precisely because it illustrated the major problems attendant upon the laws of evidence admissible in legal cases. Without any form of mapping procedure it is likely that it was virtually impossible to attain proof that a marker had been moved. The particular problem would then have been brought into the series of cases concerning issues of life and death, since it highlighted the importance of securing admissible evidence. Beyond this we can note that the primacy of land as the most basic form of wealth made any attempt to deprive a citizen of it a serious matter. To be cheated out of land eroded the very ability of a farmer to maintain himself and his family.

19:1-13. The regulations set out concerning the provision of three cities of refuge west of the river Jordan was an important matter for the administration of law. Their existence greatly affected the possibility of giving a fair trial to an accused person. Any person who was suspected of or accused of involvement in the death of another could flee to a designated city in order to secure a fair trial. By presenting oneself at such a location, the accused person was to be protected from any of the victim's family members who were seeking immediate vengeance. In Num 35:6, 11, these cities are described as "cities of refuge," although that precise title is not employed here. The setting apart of three similarly functioning cities east of the Jordan is dealt with in Deut 4:41-43 as well, drawing special attention to the importance attached to such provision in Israel's legal administration. It would certainly appear that the passage in 4:41-43 is of later origin than the law of 19:1-13. It elaborates on the clause of 19:8-10 that allows for the designation of additional cities "in the event of Israel's territory being enlarged." In the final shaping of the book of Deuteronomy, adequate account had to be taken, not only of the ideal borders

of the territory of Israel, but also of the fact that many loyal citizens had by this time been scattered outside the traditional territory of Israel.

We can take it for granted that the designation of specific cities as places of refuge was a feature of considerable antiquity in Israel and was not simply a deuteronomic measure aimed at compensating the loss of protection afforded by the many sanctuaries extant in the earliest period. Such cities were of vital significance if a credible and uniform system of law were to operate within the nation. This is not to suppose that, prior to their introduction, Israel was essentially a lawless society, but rather that the power to administer justice and to punish criminal acts was almost exclusively the prerogative of the heads of the large extended families. Their impartiality could not be relied upon, and, in any event, when dealing with offenses perpetrated by those outside of their immediate kin group a straightforward practice of vengeance taking was the norm. True justice meant fairness for all, and this involved preventing the taking of innocent life in cases where the guilty could not be reached or identified and ensuring that any accused person was given an opportunity to present whatever defense he or she could offer. The process of law was deeply committed to protecting the innocent by ensuring that punishment was never arbitrary or untried.

So the purpose of designating cities of refuge was not to provide a means whereby offenders could protect themselves from the due course of justice, but to provide places where a proper examination of the charges could be made and a verdict arrived at by a more impartial court than would be presented by the victim's family or local townspeople. For the system to work effectively, it was necessary that experienced and trained officials be available in the cities to which the criminal had fled in order for proper legal procedures to be followed. The situation once again draws special attention to the point that, when we consider the difficulties encountered in biblical times for the administration of justice, and when we listen to the persistent cries preserved in the literature of the period of those who felt denied this, it is clear that it was primarily in matters of procedure that the greatest difficulties arose. It was usually possible to discern what distinguished right from wrongful actions, but problems arose with the need for a procedure to ensure that the innocent were not punished with the guilty, or even instead of them.

Where serious crimes were concerned, especially those in which the death of a person was involved, the custom of exacting punitive revenge by a near relative of the victim existed as a long-standing and publicly acknowledged tradition. It represented a rough and ready means of protecting against crime and was chiefly operated from within a social setting in which kin groups and kinship obligations were paramount.

The term used here to identify the pursuer of the accused as "the avenger of blood" (גאל הדם gō'ēl haddām) indicates a person who was expected to be acting "in hot anger" (יחם לבבו yēḥam lēbābô, v. 6). It strongly suggests that such a pursuer would be a near relative of the victim who would be seeking revenge. However, it is possible that the townspeople of the victim may have acted to appoint such an avenging deputy. In any case, it is the elders of the victim's city (v. 12) who are charged with seeking out and punishing the accused. The Hebrew is sufficiently open to allow that such elders may have been those from the designated city to which the fugitive had fled. In this case, it is possible that they would have been regarded as especially experienced in handling such matters and fully conversant with the law. In any case, it was an issue of importance for the avenging person to obtain some degree of public recognition of the elder's intentions and purpose lest he should later be accused of the fugitive's death. Behind these procedures and the provision of designated cities for the sorting out of serious legal offenses it appears that a primary concern was to enable the community more broadly to implement a proper distinction between accidental and intentional killing. Such a need involved careful examination of witnesses and the assurance that punitive action was not taken simply on the word of a single witness. Overall, we can see why more than one community could become caught up in such procedures and why it was necessary to allow time for the investigation of the charges to be conducted fully.

19:15-21. The need to distinguish manslaughter from murder raised serious problems concerning the admissibility of evidence and the broader background of the relationship between the accused person and the victim. The formula in v. 11 makes plain that a primary factor in determining guilt was whether a previous history of enmity between the two persons was known. It is in this regard that the laws of evidence set out in this section are significant. The important issues dealt with concern the requirement that at least two witnesses be available to substantiate the guilt of the accused person. This must often have proved a major obstacle to the prosecution of a satisfactory case. Many murders would have taken place where no reliable witnesses could be found. The danger posed by a malicious witness, which is dealt with in v. 16, would then sometimes have referred not simply to a totally false accusation (as in the instance of the charges against Naboth, 2 Kings) but to a person who could be persuaded to come forward with corroborative evidence that had no real basis of truth. The harsh punishment of bearing false witness testifies to the serious problem for justice posed by the danger of perjury. In general, in the biblical period the laws of evidence were relatively undeveloped and unsophisticated. This fact alone must undoubtedly have been a strong factor in keeping alive the older tradition of justice by revenge when the legal system was unable to deal with a case satisfactorily.

Another significant way the instructions set out here reflect the development of the ancient Israelite legal system concerns the variety of legal, or quasi-legal, authorities who could become involved in the handling of a particular case. The rules governing proceedings in the cities of refuge for a person accused of homicide refer to the authority of city elders (v. 12). In the rules of procedure against a witness accused of perjury, reference is made to both priests and judges. It would have been unusual, but not impossible, for all three classes of judicial authority—elders, priests, and judges—would all have been involved at the same time. It seems likely, therefore, that a substantial measure of openness was left so that, in changing social circumstances, any of the three sources of legal expertise could become involved in a particular case. In general it seems that an appeal to the priests to settle a dispute was not so much a question of their independent legal knowledge, but rather of their access to the sacred lot, which could be called upon to reach a verdict when other means failed.

The sternness of the rule of making the punishment equal to that which might have been inflicted on the accused person—"life for life, eye for eye, tooth for tooth," the *lex talionis* (v. 21)—is a reflection on the problem posed by perjury. It is not a deliberate relapse into expressly physical forms of punishment involving maiming, which the

biblical law codes largely shun, but a deep realization that harsh dissuasive measures were needed to deal with offenses that could undermine the entire legal system. The same general observation may well account for the unexpected inclusion of a warning against the removal of a neighbor's landmark (v. 14). Where the legal system showed itself to be vulnerable, it inevitably countered by calling for very severe punishments. Carried to an extreme, this approach to the problems of law appears in the gross demands for capital punishment for those who repudiated the Mosaic legal system altogether by blatant apostasy.

REFLECTIONS

The three laws set out in Deuteronomy 19 are centered especially on cases of homicide and the varying circumstances by which a person could be held responsible for another's death. The foremost distinction lay between determining whether it had been done intentionally or accidentally. The guideline concerning proof of earlier enmity between the parties concerned could only serve as a very rough and provisional guide. Obviously even two friends could fall out, and one might become violent in a dangerous, and perhaps uncharacteristic, fit of rage. Similarly in the course of daily work, it might be possible to misuse a tool or weapon so recklessly as to endanger another person's life.

In such circumstances, it was wholly understandable that the immediate relatives and dependents of the victim should seek revenge for what had happened. This is a state of affairs that can be traced far back into the kinship structures of tribal groups. Wanton violence and killing were not tolerated within any normal community of human beings. Yet conflicts and quarrels between families and tribes might often go unpunished when there was no effective means of imposing punishment across family and tribal boundaries. The growth of systems of law that operated on a territorial, and ultimately a nationwide, level was of the utmost importance. It became compellingly necessary once large townships and cities embraced a wide mixture of tribal and ethnic groups. Therefore, it became the goal of a satisfactory legal system to deal with all human beings on an equal footing—a feature that is partially affirmed in the deuteronomic concept of membership in the community (lit., of "brothers"). Although this fell short of treating all human beings as standing on an equal footing, it nevertheless marked a major step forward and cut directly across the family and clan boundaries that must still have molded the feelings controlling moral attitudes within the nation.

So acts involving bodily violence, sometimes resulting in death, needed the greatest care to determine whether they should be treated as criminal acts. The law needed to protect innocent persons as well as to punish the guilty. Such cases largely turned on assessment of intention, and so raised the question as to how such intentions could be discovered, and when discovered, how they could be proved. The problems were clearly many, and the modern reader is well aware that they remain fundamental aspects of our own legal system.

For Christian readers, the presumption in the Sermon on the Mount of personal responsibility for nurturing good attitudes (Matt 5:21-26) intensifies the debate about the issue. Moreover, the dangers of too easily and hastily giving way to feelings of anger are strongly emphasized. When pressed even further, the modern reader is made aware of the fact that issues of provocation may also be summoned in defense of a person who commits a violent crime (Matt 5:38-42). Once we begin to judge our actions, and the actions of others, we are forced to recognize that the motives and restraints that determine them are many and complex.

Each of us has limits beyond which, if we are pushed, we may experience an emotional explosion. So even when we are compelled to judge others for the sake of public well-being and justice, we know that we are never wholly and completely innocent of the desires for revenge and for hurting those who have hurt and wounded us. It is in such a context that the very personal admonition of Jesus is to be heard and reflected on. It is not too subtle and illusory to suggest that sometimes the very strength and fervor of our anxiety to see punishment brought upon wrongdoers lies not in an altruistic desire to protect others around us, but in a half-conscious guilty fear that we, too, given the right circumstances, can become dangerous and violent persons. All too easily we can overlook the fact that the stark simplicity and terse formulations of the Old Testament laws hide from us the deep and considered judgments that undergird them.

It is important to give room to the sophisticated concern of the biblical teachers of proverbial wisdom that whether we are peaceable or violent persons may lie far back, before we ever commit either peaceful or angry actions. The person who consorts with violent persons is likely to become as violent as those companions (Prov 1:10-19). Similarly, by yielding to impulses of ill temper or outbursts of violence, a person will smooth the path to more ill-tempered and violent outbursts at a later time. Every day of our lives we are becoming new persons as a consequence of the emotions we yield to or learn to contain. Ultimately when we ask ourselves what kind of person we have become, we may look back on actions of which we are ashamed. We may not have realized at the time what our actions would lead to, and we shall probably have dismissed them as "uncharacteristic." Nevertheless, what was uncharacteristic yesterday can quickly develop into what is all too characteristic today.

Deuteronomy 20:1-20, Issues of Life and Death: Warfare

COMMENTARY

We are now presented with two sections concerned with Israel's conduct in time of war. Already we have noted the strong and forthright manner in which the deuteronomic legislation deals with issues involving the aims and conduct of war, and the subject has left an indelible stamp on the entire deuteronomic theology and ethic. Here we are brought face to face with two speeches, the first of which was to be delivered by a priest to the assembled soldiers before a battle (vv. 2-4). This is followed by another that was to be delivered by undefined officials at a similar time (vv. 5-8). Only after these formal speeches had been made were the mustered military forces to be returned to the charge of their commanders (v. 9).

The first speech, which was to be given by a priest, sets out the religious nature of the

battle that was to come and gives assurance that it would be God who would accompany the forces to fight against Israel's enemy and give the victory. The address by the officials allows a modest number of exemptions from military service on what could be regarded as compassionate grounds. These include the building of a new house, the planting of a new vineyard, or engagement to be married.

However, when we look at the implications more closely we see that the reasons for exemption have less to do with compassion for persons with overriding personal commitments than with larger issues concerning morale in battle. The central issue is that of courage and wholehearted commitment in battle. Those who were preoccupied with personal concerns and undue anxieties about their personal survival could be the cause of undermining the morale of the entire army (v. 8). Throughout there appears a realization that morale was a subtle and complex factor in battle and that even a few defaulters could sap the determination of the army.

A central issue that permeates both speeches is the claim that warfare was a religious duty in which victory could only come directly from God. For such victories to be obtained the primary requirements were not military technology but unbroken moral courage and unwavering faith in the power of God to give success. This is exactly the formula that is singled out as bringing success in defeating kings Sihon and Og (2:24–3:13) and that is claimed to have brought about the overthrow of Jericho at the outset of the campaign to claim possession of the land (Josh 6:1-27).

The entire ideology relating to warfare in Deuteronomy has been labeled that of "holy war," and it has been held to represent an ancient Israelite concept of obligation for military action that the deuteronomists resuscitated from an earlier period. Certainly a number of ancient ideas and customs relating to warfare have been called upon by the deuteronomists to create their particular presentation regarding Israel's military potential. Overall the book of Deuteronomy is a startlingly and dangerously militaristic work, reflecting the situation its authors saw to be facing Israel. Nevertheless, it appears doubtful in the extreme that what the deuteronomists propose as a way for Israel to achieve great success in its military campaigns represents a viable and ancient practice that was being revived at the close of the monarchic period. Such an assumption would not explain the highly theological and theoretical tone of what is demanded and the extraordinary claim that warfare could largely be left in the hands of the priests.

The ideology of warfare that is set out in Deuteronomy must be held as largely a creation of the deuteronomists themselves, although undoubtedly drawing upon various elements of custom and tradition.[85] These elements served the deuteronomists' purpose in

stressing the religious over against the strictly military and technological features of ancient warfare. Overall the view of warfare in Deuteronomy must be regarded as a response to the calamities and disasters that had befallen the twilight years of the kingdom of Judah in the late seventh and early sixth centuries BCE. It represents the deuteronomists' answer to the catastrophe of 587 BCE and to the military prowess of Assyria and Babylon. It evidences much the same tone and manner as the prophet Isaiah in repudiating the boastful claims of the Assyrian Rabshakeh when calling upon the citizens of Judah to surrender.

It is highly dubious whether the deuteronomic program for battle can be regarded as significantly more than a theoretical set of rules for the conduct of war; therefore, it is one that was never properly put to the test. It is more concerned with theology and the belief in the divine control of history than with what happened on the battlefield. As with many features of the law code of Deuteronomy 12–26, a core of established rules and customs has been incorporated into a larger framework of religious ideology aimed at renewing and reestablishing the central role of faith in the LORD God as the key to Israel's future. It is true that it reflects experience of war, but this would appear largely to have been the tragic battles Israel and Judah fought in defense of their land once the grip of Mesopotamian rule on the Levant had tightened. In recognizing Israel's weakness and helplessness in the face of Mesopotamian military strength, Deuteronomy looks to a renewed faith in God as a basis for defense.

Once this background is taken fully into account and full cognizance is taken of the religious, rather than the military, features of what is demanded, we can better understand the distinctive character of Deuteronomy's perspective on warfare. It looks for divinely wrought miracles, rather than effective campaign strategies. It portrays as the exemplary guide to success in warfare the qualities shown in the defeat of Goliath by the boy David, in whom the virtues of faith and courage were the primary qualifications for victory (1 Sam 17:45-47). It is in line with this religious and theological interpretation of warfare that the deuteronomists saw warfare primarily as a means for the taking

---

85. This point is particularly well presented in A. Rofé, "The Laws of Warfare in the Book of Deuteronomy: Their Origins, Intent and Positivity," *JSOT* 32 (1985) 23-44. See also Von Rad, *Studies in Deuteronomy,* 45-59, and *Holy War in Ancient Israel,* 115-27; Millard C. Lind, *The Theology of Warfare in Ancient Israel* (Scottdale, Pa.: Herald, 1980) 146-68.

and retaining of possession of the land. The demand for the annihilation of the previous inhabitants is wholly in line with this aim (vv. 17-18). For the deuteronomists, war was a God-ordained means of land acquisition and religious purification.[86]

An unfortunate consequence of the assumption that the deuteronomic theology of warfare represents a viewpoint that was typical and widely adopted in ancient Israel is that its demands have frequently been regarded as characteristic of ancient Israel as a whole. This is not the case, as its religious purpose and highly theoretical nature bear out. There is much in the literature that points to Israel's warfare as having been more restrained and less theologically charged than either the book of Deuteronomy or the historical writings it has influenced would suggest.

Certainly the late reflections on the reasons for Israel's defeat at the hands of the Babylonian ruler Nebuchadnezzar (Jer 27:5-7) would point to the eventual abandonment of the exaggerated hopes of God-ordained victory that the deuteronomic doctrine led some to expect. At most we must conclude that the biblical writings contain a variety of viewpoints concerning warfare and its demands. Accordingly the emphatic deuteronomic doctrine on the subject must be set in a larger context that shows it to have been an unusually one-sided portrayal of the aims, methods, and possibilities warfare proffered to ancient Israel. It is certainly not the only viewpoint regarding war the Bible contains.

Some awareness that different situations called for different responses and that the harsh demand for the extermination of all the previous occupants of the land on religious grounds was an extreme position is shown by the qualification set out in vv. 10-14.

86. Niditch, *War in the Hebrew Bible*, 28-55.

In this case, it is urged that, before a town was besieged, terms of surrender should be offered to its inhabitants, with forced slave labor being the price such surrender incurred (v. 11). After the capture of a town that had been besieged and defeated, only the men were to be put to death, with the women, children, and property falling to the victors as spoil (v. 13). However, the addition of vv. 15-18 limits these concessions to towns outside the land of Israel proper. The concession is important for two reasons. The first lies in its recognition that Israel's aims and practices in the conduct of war were unusual and abnormal for warfare in the ancient world. More significant, it also recognizes that the reasons for this harsh and unyielding demand were wholly religious in nature, once again revealing how the deuteronomic concern with the first commandment has ultimately colored its entire legislative program.

When examined from a historical-critical perspective, both in regard to other literary developments within the deuteronomic movement and in the light of a knowledge of the practice of warfare in antiquity, the distinctively deuteronomic character of what is demanded in the conduct of war can be clearly and readily seen. It represents far more than the revival of an ancient practice of the so-called holy war, even though some elements of ancient custom have been incorporated into it. Nor is it at all likely that it represents a serious attempt during the reign of King Josiah to restore some military credibility after the disastrous consequences of more than a century of Assyrian control. In sum, it marks a particular stratum of deuteronomic thought that viewed warfare in precisely the same manner as it viewed the administration of criminal law, as a means whereby the purity of Israel's religion, as expressed in the deuteronomic law code, could be enforced.

REFLECTIONS

The aims and methods of warfare as set out in this deuteronomic passage are among the most disturbing and dangerous of all the teaching that is to be found within the book. The realization that this ideology of warfare has an exclusive religious basis and motivation, and that it has frequently been said to constitute a doctrine of "holy war," has heightened, rather than softened, the intense moral objections to it. It is nothing less than a demand for a policy of religious and ethnic genocide. Clearly its total contradiction to the Christian demand for the love of one's enemy (Matt 5:43-45) stands out starkly. The deuteronomic viewpoint has created a popular image of the militaristic aggressiveness of Old Testament literature generally, by the very drama and abnormality of the story of how Jericho was captured as the first of the campaigns within the land, when the deuteronomic formula was held to have been adopted.

Various lines of Christian and Jewish apologetic have repeatedly been adopted with a view to rescuing the demands for such genocidal belligerence from its obvious, and directly literal, consequences. The first is essentially a hermeneutical ploy and endeavors to isolate the demand for faith, courage, and unconditional loyalty to the LORD God from its genocidal expression. So it is argued that the demand for the slaughter of those who practice idolatry and who repudiate their loyalty to the LORD God may be set aside, to be replaced by a more tolerant and reasoned policy of persuading such persons to see the error of their ways. Loyalty to God is applauded and endorsed, but the method demanded for dealing with God's enemies is repudiated. Whatever merit lies in such a stance, it cannot be said to deal effectively with the heart of the problem without facing more directly the dangerous nature of any such demand for violence against religious opponents. Too much of Jewish and Christian history has been stained with blood by those who did not realize that the deuteronomic demands should not be taken literally. In this regard, the firm repudiation of such a doctrine of genocide in the New Testament needs to be given its full weight.

Possibly a more fruitful path has been pursued by those who, like John Bunyan in *The Holy War*, have sought to regard the concept of a biblically justified holy warfare typologically as an allegory of the conflict between good and evil for control of the human soul. It is not a doctrine of how Israelites should deal with Canaanites, but a doctrine outlining the demands, difficulties, and dangers of the spiritual warfare that every serious believer in a righteous God must face. Not only does Bunyan allegorize the broad concept of warfare into a spiritual struggle, but also, in his marginal notes, he connects individual acts of heroism and violence to particular virtues or temptations. It must undoubtedly be recognized that an imaginative, spiritually uplifting, and purposeful set of guidelines for the pursuit of the spiritual life can be wrung from even the most unlikely sources. Provided the imaginative reader is fully aware of the literary technique that is being adopted, and of the inherent dangers of the literal interpretation of the material, then quite positive and constructive ideas and guidelines can be adduced.

Yet neither of these two hermeneutical approaches has engaged seriously enough with the moral dangers and threats posed by the literal interpretation of the text. They have arisen primarily out of a deep consciousness that the literal demands of the text are totally unacceptable and have usually failed to face this issue seriously enough. Clearly the intention of the original authors of the text, insofar as we can understand it, was that their demands should be taken seriously. Moreover the very seriousness of their intent was a vital reason for the harsh and uncompromising measures they proposed to adopt. We are compelled, therefore, to face up to this serious demand for genocide as a product of a community that undoubtedly believed that it should have been attempted, even if history suggests that it was not actually undertaken.

It is the more historical perspective, relating both to the circumstances and to the background of the deuteronomists and of what we can discover historically concerning the manner in which Israel took possession of the land and waged warfare in defense of it, that has drawn most attention from modern critics. Undoubtedly the previous Canaanite inhabitants of the land Israel occupied were not exterminated. There is a deep illogicality inherent in the deuteronomic doctrine that they had been. Had this been the case, the fervor to remove all relics of the religion of these people and all knowledge of their customs would not have been needed.

Yet whatever amelioration of anxiety and conscience such modern historical knowledge may give to the critical reader of the text, it nevertheless fails to deal adequately with the moral and historical problems it raises for us. The very existence of the deuter-onomic doctrine of religious warfare and its methods demands that we acknowledge that it clearly came into existence as a serious ideology of a segment within ancient Israel. That this community felt itself to be threatened and its survival to be in doubt if such measures were not adopted may also be granted. That the historical Canaanites and their immediate ethnic descendants were no longer easily to be found may be granted. Nevertheless, there clearly were in existence people whom the deuteronomic authors identified as Canaanites and whom they feared so greatly, and detested so fer-vently, that the deuteronomists called for their total extermination. Who exactly these people were and why such a sharp and fearful conflict with them had arisen remains totally obscure. Yet certainly it appears that such a community existed and that, under the guise of fighting an ancient ideological battle concerning the uniqueness of Israel's God, the deuteronomists pieced together a harsh religious doctrine concerning the purpose, methods, and possibilities of warfare (the fruits of which they expected to be miraculous).

The Commentary has sought to interpret the manner and content of the deutero-nomic legislation against the background of the twilight days of Judah's history. The movement certainly continued its activity after the final collapse of Judah and the destruction of its Temple in 587 BCE. Yet it appears not to have survived this catastro-phe for very long, so that new movements carried the future spiritual and intellectual movements of the new Judaism in very different directions. Most prominent among these new directions were a more tolerant spirit, the hope of an ultimate spread of the knowledge of the LORD God to all nations and peoples, and a willingness to live, work, and learn alongside non-Jewish neighbors. So a broader intellectual outlook accompanied a more tolerant spirit, and the excesses of the deuteronomic calls for genocide were left aside. The attempts that have arisen from time to time to reactivate the deuteronomic demand for a renewed religious warfare in the face of some new spiritual crisis have only served to reinforce the moral objections to it. In interpreting it, therefore, it is valuable that its literal meaning should be frankly recognized, its dire consequences properly appraised, and its moral limitations reasserted.

Deuteronomy 21:1-23, Issues of Life and Death: Murder, Capital Offenses, and Inheritance

COMMENTARY

A total of six separate rulings are pre-sented in chap. 21, dealing broadly with mat-ters relating to the boundary between life and death. Included among them are questions of inheritance, and hence of the protection and preservation of the family name and house-hold. It is possible to see in the structure of the units a chiastic pattern (ABCC'B'A'), a literary device used to connect the rulings. Overall the concern is to counter the disruptive con-sequences of death in the life of a family and of the community more generally. There is evident a desire to discern a coherent bound-ary between life and death and a drawing

together of anxieties and beliefs relating to religion with those that relate more directly to basic legal and ethical concerns.

21:1-9. The first of the rulings deals with the matter of the discovery of a dead body in the open countryside. Two factors imme-diately become evident: the likelihood that a murder has been committed, with the perpe-trator of the crime remaining unknown, and a religious conviction that any unburied corpse would defile the land and thereby destroy its holy, life-upholding character.

The response to this situation is twofold. First, the elders of the town nearest to the place where the body was discovered must take responsibility for its safe burial in a location where the land has not been used for farming. They are to take the body to a wadi where there is running water to perform a ritual that will remove the defilement associated with a corpse. The land will then be protected against the defiling effect of the presence of death upon it. The ritual involves breaking the neck of a heifer that has never been worked. Then the elders are required to wash their hands over the carcass of the dead heifer. At the same time, a formal declaration of their innocence of the crime and a prayer that the guilt it has incurred may be forgiven are made.

The reasoning behind these carefully specified actions is not openly expressed. Clearly, from a practical viewpoint, it was an acknowledgment that the crime was taken seriously, but that nothing further could be done to identify the circumstances of the death or to apprehend the person, or persons, responsible for it. However, behind this avowal of innocence we discern that the killing of the unworked heifer at a place not used for agriculture indicates that the action was intended to remove the consequences of the probable crime from the sphere where it might bring harm. The ritual reenacted the original killing by substituting the heifer for the victim and carrying its attendant blood guilt away from the life-supporting productive land of the nearby township. The land's holiness was preserved and its legal system affirmed, even though no actual proceedings were undertaken.

21:10-13. The second of the regulations presented concerns the treatment of a woman taken as a captive in war and subsequently married by her captor, or purchaser.[87] She was to be allowed a full month's mourning for the loss of her former home and parents, after which she could become the wife of an Israelite citizen. The ruling demands that she then be fully integrated into the community and family, being given the full status of an Israelite woman. This newly acquired status guaranteed her a full measure of freedom commensurate with other Israelite women.

She was to be regarded as a full member of the household and not demeaned as a slave-wife. The implication is clearly that life in Israel was characterized by a particular status as a mother and wife and that this status was to be granted to all the wives of the household, irrespective of their origin. They were assumed to be responsible for bearing children who would then bring new life into the community, so it was vital that they, too, should acquire a normal position in the household commensurate with their age. The ruling is concerned with the life and growth of the household within society more generally, and the aim is to protect this new life by noting the boundaries that were to be upheld and those that were not. The circumstances of a woman's origin were not to form a permanent barrier once her marriage had taken place.

21:14. The ruling that follows is essentially a rider to the primary declaration.[88] It asserts that the status acquired by becoming a wife and potential mother in Israel was unalterable and could not thereafter be withdrawn. Such a woman could not be returned to the level of a slave after her marriage to an Israelite citizen, since this circumstance had brought to her full recognition as an Israelite woman.

21:15-17. A further ruling is in the same vein, but covers a wider range of possible cases than that of the children of a woman who had been elevated from slave status of a prisoner of war to become a wife and potential mother. The firstborn son of an Israelite household enjoyed a unique status as the primary heir of the family and was accordingly entitled to a significantly increased share in the family inheritance. More than this, it was the privilege and duty of the firstborn son to become the head of the family estate. In the course of time, when the father had to surrender his control over family affairs through physical weakness or death, then the eldest son would assume his mantle.

The ruling set out here simply asserts that, in a household in which there is more than one wife, the status of the firstborn son was unalterable. It is a matter of particular interest that the reason why a father might attempt to remove this status is assumed to

87. C. J. H. Wright, *God's People in God's Land: Family, Land, and Property in the Old Testament* (Ann Arbor: Books on Demand, 1990) 213-16.

88. Wright, *God's People in God's Land*, 193.

lie, not in the ill favor of the son or his lack of business ability, but in the unloved status of the mother. Not only might a paternal head of a household seek to take revenge on an unloved wife by depriving her son of the inheritance to which he was entitled, but also the potential influence of a more favored, or more probably a younger, wife was not to be allowed to disrupt the established structure of the household or the status of its individual members. Clearly such a ruling had in its favor the need to preserve the customary rights and good order of a household as well as the necessity for eliminating the possibility of continuous intrigue and squabbling within a polygamous family.

It is noteworthy that David's reported action in supporting the claim of Solomon to succeed to the throne of Israel (1 Kgs 1:15-31) appears to contravene this ruling. In general, such a firm imposition of the rights of inheritance within a family was concerned to maintain a secure social order. It carries special interest in regard to the royal household of Judah and Israel, where an extensive practice of polygamy prevailed and where the process by which an heir apparent was chosen is not fully known. Obviously primogeniture was important, but it seems unlikely to have been an exclusive factor. Unfortunately, insufficient information is provided to clarify the procedure, although the practice of naming the mother of the royal successor indicates the special status she acquired through her son's position. This is wholly in line with the present ruling, which closely connects the mother's position with that of the inheritance of the family estate. The need to preserve and promote the economic strength and integrity of the household was a primary feature, with far-reaching consequences for the health and stability of society more generally.

21:18-21. The ruling that follows allows for the death penalty to be inflicted on a rebellious and wanton son.[89] It continues on the same general principle as the preceding regulation. Maintaining the vitality and good order of the household was fundamental to the interests of the larger community. It marked one of the boundaries of life, since once the economic strength of a household had been undermined, the viability of that household

more broadly was placed in jeopardy. All its members could be threatened, even though the trouble had arisen on account of a single one of them.

It is in the light of the importance of the household in general as the primary economic unit of society that the relatively severe and uncompromising discipline enjoined here is to be understood. As well as permitting, in certain circumstances, the complete removal of a troublesome son, it also takes full account of the fact that this was a practice that could easily be abused. In such cases, this action would frustrate the intention of the ruling that precedes it. The possibility that a troublesome son might even be put to death by his parents is in line with the generally stern approach advocated by Israel's sages and educators in endorsing the need for strong parental discipline.

In the case envisaged, the procedure for examining the culprit and enforcing the harsh penalty is noteworthy. All that the parents were permitted to do was to report the matter to the elders of the town, who would then initiate their own investigation. Only after they had been satisfied that the accusation was justified could the death penalty be inflicted. The cruel method of execution by stoning was preferred in cases where a wide measure of shared responsibility for the verdict and its consequences was to be upheld. Those who had made and approved the charges had to carry the risk of blood guilt for their actions. When this was a whole township, then the whole community was to be involved.

D. Olson points out that in the Mishnah, where this particular ruling is evaluated, so many qualifications were introduced to determine the nature of the rebellious son's guilt that it is unlikely that the punishment was ever carried out.[90] Clearly we can discern beneath the surface of the ruling a deep consciousness that polygamous households could often be torn apart by fierce feuds. The broader context of the ruling given is that relating to the cycle of life, death, and new birth, which inevitably shaped and characterized the life of an extended family. There is accordingly a strong concern to protect the strength and hope inherent in every new life within a household. This was especially

89. Wright, *God's People in God's Land*, 77-78, 230-31.

90. Olson, *Deuteronomy and the Death of Moses*, 98.

important where that new life was the formal heir to the family's estate. All too easily the jealousies and feuds of one generation could be carried forward into the next with disastrous consequences. Family survival and stability were important, but all too easily the tensions that arose within it could destroy the very entity that should have been protected.

21:22-23. The last of the rulings contained in the chapter deals with the necessity for the removal of the corpse of an executed criminal on the day of the execution. There was obviously a temptation for the community to display the victim's body for exemplary purposes. The motive for the requirement set out in the present rule is firmly spelled out: The decaying corpse in the open countryside would defile the land (v. 23). Death is treated as a living force with its own power to replicate itself and to endanger the lives of others. It is no surprise to find that in Canaanite mythology a deity named Mot ("Death") appears in various legendary guises as a kind of anti-God.

All the more would the defiling effect of a corpse left in the open be felt to constitute a danger when the dead person had been executed as a criminal. Execution by hanging from a tree marked out the victim as a person under God's curse. It is this observation that is taken up and commented upon by Paul in Gal 3:3 in reference to the atoning work of the death of Jesus by crucifixion, itself taken as a form of hanging from a tree.

REFLECTIONS

The series of rulings set out in this chapter deals with the mysterious cycle of life and death and with the need for noting the boundary between the two. In general, it might have been supposed that a clear-cut dividing line existed between life and death that everyone would recognize. However, the problem of noting and observing the boundary was brought about because all kinds of circumstances can arise in which actions in life fail to take account of the seriousness of this dividing line and, in consequence, fail to allow its ultimacy to be recognized. We can see this most clearly in respect to the concern to protect the progeny within a family from the effects of actions that were not of their own making. In particular, the right of the firstborn was to remain inalienable. The mother who had been born a slave and had borne children to the man who had taken and married her could not afterward be returned to the status of a slave. New life was a God-ordained reality that was not to be interfered with or manipulated to accommodate the whims and preferences of a capricious head of a household.

The underlying assumptions that govern these rulings represent a mixture of traditional religious concern about death, viewing it in a quasi-physical fashion as a power of supernatural dimensions that had to be feared and that could have ongoing consequences, as the spread of disease from a rotting corpse so obviously exemplified. Woven into this mixture of concerns, sometimes rather taboo-ridden in nature, lie a wider concern for justice, a righteous order of family life, and the promotion of health and well-being in society. So religious and legal considerations become intertwined. Boundaries have to be noted and their reality upheld. Life must be separated from death so that just as death itself marked a final shutdown on a human life, so also did birth bring about the opening of a new scene, with new potential and new opportunities.

Throughout the chapter there is the deep conviction that all life is sacred and a gift from God. Hence the taking of innocent life, even when its cause cannot be explained, must be atoned for. Those associated with the taking of a life must be absolved from guilt, both to declare their innocence and to explain their inability to bring the culprit to justice. Only so could the natural cycle of justice be fulfilled. When the established law required the taking of the culprit's life in punishment for a capital crime, even then the seriousness of such an act needed to be publicly recognized so that the corpse of the executed person had to be removed on the same day as the execution for proper burial. All taking of life represented acts of intrusion into the sphere of the sacred, whether this was justified in the punishment of a criminal or unexplained in the finding of a corpse in the country.

It is the awareness of the sacredness of life that marks out marriage as a step in life's journey with immense, potentially immeasurable, consequences. Even when the marriage was to a woman who had been taken as a captive and turned into a slave, that marriage could never be reduced simply to a master/slave relationship. Marriage, with its expectation of bringing new life into being, could not thereafter be regarded as a matter of no consequence.

By a similar reasoning, the firstborn son of such a marriage would retain unalterably the rights and privileges that came to him from that union. Even the contention that a son was unworthy of his position and privilege within a household and that his status brought shame and the risk of disaster to a household had to be treated with the greatest circumspection. If the accusation was proved to the satisfaction of the town elders, then he was potentially subject to the death penalty. If it was not proved, then he retained his position within the family.

All these rulings represent the outworking of a belief in the sanctity of life, its unique quality as a divine gift, and the necessity of guarding and upholding its power within the family and the community at large. Legal matters relating to life and death were never merely legal matters, since they marked the encounter of humankind with the most demanding and uncrossable of all barriers—that which separated the living from the dead. To take life, whether by a criminal act or in judicial punishment, was to enter into the religious domain. To give birth to new life as a wife and mother was similarly to participate in a process in which God was also involved.

All of this has much to instruct the modern reader regarding the strong feelings, scruples, and sensitivities that colored life in the biblical world. Life had an incommensurate value that could not be matched by mere monetary compensation, any more than a newly discovered corpse could be quietly buried as though nothing untoward had happened. All life had to be accounted for, to the community at large so far as this was possible, but to God always, since the Author and Giver of life could be reckoned to watch over every creature.

Few aspects of the impact of a secular worldview on modern life highlight more directly our different attitude from the people of antiquity than in this question of the sanctity of life. Abortion, invitro fertilization, and euthanasia pose deep moral concerns and uncertainties. Yet the issues do not end here, since it is possible, even while adopting a guarded and responsible attitude to these issues, to lose sight of lesser questions.

Life for every individual is a unique, unrepeatable experiment and adventure. It happens to each of us only once. Consequently its opportunities, possibilities, and dangers have to be faced anew by each person individually. With each new birth there is a new divine act of creation. So the boundaries between life and death, as this ancient legislative compilation reminds us, are not simply the moments of birth and death. These we can mark by essential religious services, reminding ourselves and the community that something remarkable and unique has taken place. Yet the boundary between life and death is more widely felt than is to be comprehended in these dramatic experiences. There are many moments when the resurgence of life over death may be established by our choices and actions. Conversely some experiences can so diminish life and its quality that we may sense that death itself has made inroads upon us.

A further reflection is important in view of the fact that it has sometimes been argued that the fundamental commandment "Thou shalt not kill" ("do no murder") is too negative to provide an adequate guideline for normal conduct. This was capriciously and cynically put by the Victorian poet A. H. Clough in his satirical poem "A Decalogue for Today":

Thou shalt not kill, but need not strive
officiously to keep alive.

Such a viewpoint is contrary to the message and purpose of the commandment, as the present chapter of legislation fully bears out. Acknowledging the boundary between life and death, and acting accordingly, is a vital requirement for living. To act negligently so that another's life is lost or so that serious injury results (cf. Deut 22:8) is as much a failure to heed the commandment as is a willful act of murder. It is the sanctity of life itself that needs to be protected and upheld.

The question of the boundary between life and death was of great concern in ancient Israel, since it formed a significant border between morality, religious feeling, and social responsibility. So questions of primal anxieties as to what lies beyond the grave mingled with the practical affairs of inheritance and family structure, as well as determining whether someone could be held responsible when a death occurred accidentally or indirectly. In our secular world, we have sought, by using a host of euphemisms and verbal screens, to hide from ourselves the natural fear of death. In trying to remove the demons of fear, we have often only driven them underground. It is a great merit of the deuteronomic legislation that, however much it may appear to simplify the mysteries of life and death, it frankly recognizes that they cannot be ignored.

DEUTERONOMY 22:1-30, MAINTAINING THE DIVINE ORDER OF LIFE

COMMENTARY

The group of laws that now commence relate to a wide range of issues governing both social responsibility and personal conduct. They have, as a common connecting principle, a concern to maintain the proper boundaries of life and to uphold the realm that we should describe as "the natural order." In some of them, the anxiety to respect what are considered to be the boundaries of a given created scheme of things is very prominent, whereas in others it is less clearly apparent. Braulik sees this unit as marking a transition from the topic of "preserving life" to that of "sexuality."[91] These laws are concerned with marriage, the raising of a family, and the protection of the household, and they represent a pattern of order that could only be satisfactorily maintained provided that its structural boundaries were protected and upheld.

Certainly the upholding of the sexual order represents a central concern, since the gender distinction between male and female is perceived to be one of the foremost of the structural boundaries of the created world.

However, within the central concern to clarify and define the boundaries of sexual conduct and to protect against sexual abuses, there are several other foundational lines that are perceived as lending support and stability to society. Regulations protecting these boundaries act like fences to keep everything in its place and to prevent the falling apart of society as a result of a breach in the invisible boundaries that contain it.

22:1-4. As well as protecting the integrity of the family, the first of the regulations (vv. 1-3) can be interpreted as an elaboration of the commandment concerning the avoidance of coveting a neighbor's wife or property. The matter of finding oxen or sheep straying across the known limits of a neighbor's

91. G. Braulik, "The Sequence of Laws in Deuteronomy 12:1-26 and in the Decalogue," 322, 332.

property, or more simply of discovering a stray animal, the ownership of which was not known, on one's own land imposed an obligation. This obligation consisted simply of returning the stray beast to its rightful owner. The need to respect a neighbor as a fellow citizen of Israel who enjoyed the same right to respect and protection as one sought for oneself extended also to property. This necessity even extended as far as the obligation to return any object belonging to a neighbor that might be found by chance. As the legislation is set out, it appears as a fuller elaboration of the earlier law contained in Exod 23:4-5.

The ruling that lost property must be returned to its rightful owner may at first appear as a transparently obvious duty. However, it was clearly a matter of considerable importance in regard to the question of respecting established boundaries. The head of a family could expect to be master of the property that belonged to his household. There were, however, necessary limits to this right, so that what is decreed here sets out certain limits as a matter of principle. When a neighbor's animal strayed onto another person's property, then it was the duty of that person to return it. Location did not determine ownership, even when the rightful owner of lost property was not immediately known.

A further extension of this principle is then affirmed in v. 4 by its imposition of an obligation to come to the help of a neighbor's beast, even when the misfortune that had befallen it occurred on public land. The obligation to assist an injured animal extended across the boundaries defined by ownership.

22:5. A more subtle and psychologically more complicated ruling is put forward here by the introduction of a number of regulations governing the protection of sexual boundaries. These rules prohibit the practice of transvestism as a forbidden crossing of one of the foremost distinctions established at creation (Gen 1:27). The boundary defined by gender was regarded as all-pervasive. It is possible that some forms of transvestism were practiced in cultic ceremonies of which the deuteronomists disapproved, so that they are here outlawed as idolatrous and non-Israelite. However, the overall context of the ruling shows that it

was concerned to uphold what were perceived to be given boundaries of the natural order, rather than being a further ruling to outlaw acts of apostasy from the LORD God.

We can reasonably assume that some persons in ancient Israel experienced problems and difficulties in establishing their gender orientation, as has been the case in human society generally. However, the ruling set out here must certainly be interpreted as based on the fundamental awareness that formal gender distinctions marked one of the formative structural boundaries of life. Such boundaries were not to be blurred or willfully crossed. To do so would amount to a negation of the divine order.

It is significant that the prohibition against transvestism is not sanctioned by any specific punitive measure to be taken against those who contravene its demands. It is not difficult to recognize that any such punitive action would have been difficult to enforce, but it is also clear that the social sanction of shame and repudiation by the community at large would have carried a considerable force. The formula that expresses this awareness of social stigma and repudiation is that certain actions are described as "abhorrent to the LORD your God." The use of such a formula draws attention to the fact that, quite apart from setting out a legal code for action against civil and criminal misdemeanors, the book of Deuteronomy contains much that reflects the less overtly enforced ethos of the community. It was taken as natural that such an ethos should have been regarded as an expression of the mind and will of God.

22:6-7. The prohibition contained in v. 6 regarding the rather limited protection that was to be afforded to wild birds displays a concern to maintain the boundary between life and death by a refusal to take the mother with the fledgling birds and eggs. Since the mother provided the womb from which life came, then, when the eggs and fledglings were taken, presumably for food, life and death were not to be mixed together. In this fashion the respect for life and the need to avoid entanglement with death were maintained by not permitting death to overrule life completely.

22:8. The regulation demanding that an adequate protective parapet be built on the roof of a house to reduce the risk of accidents follows a similar concern to protect life. The rooftop of a house, whether it was built of mudbrick or stone, was a part of the living space of an ancient Israelite's home. It could be expected that it would be in use throughout much of the year. Failure to ensure that it incorporated reasonable protection against injury and death through accidental falls was adjudged to incur blood guilt. That such a term is used at all for injury caused in this fashion is noteworthy since it is otherwise almost exclusively applied to cases of homicide or the willful inflicting of serious bodily injury.

It would appear from these rulings that the ancient Israelite legislators were uncomfortable with the notion of an accident for which no responsibility could be apportioned. Accordingly even the earlier legislation regarding an unpremeditated act that resulted in a person's death is described as having been brought about by "an act of God" (Exod 21:13). We have already noted a deep concern in the legislation in 21:1-9, dealing with the discovery of a corpse in open country, to ensure that no blood guilt was incurred simply because the real culprit was not known and could not be apprehended. The local community was required to demonstrate that it was innocent of the crime.

It is noteworthy that the Jewish sage referred to as Qohelet, writing in the third century BCE (Eccl 9:11-12) seems to have been the first to have left a written recognition of the concept of pure chance that could bring about personal accident or misfortune for which no one, not even God, was directly to be blamed.

22:9-11. Three rulings set out in these verses quite directly reflect the importance of maintaining the given boundaries of the natural order and of avoiding any willful crossing of them. A vineyard was not to be planted with the seed of another crop, since this would mix the two and contravene a given order of life. The very force of life would be confused if the established boundaries of its many varied manifestations were not respected. It is rather surprising that the mixing of crops that is contemplated was to have occurred in a vineyard. A parallel ruling in Lev 19:19 specifies that it was not to be

undertaken in a field. This would appear to have provided a broader, and more plausible, context, since it is the principle of mixing different crops in a single field that is prohibited. However, the deuteronomic formulation appears to have been content simply to specify a typical and reasonably likely case of infringement, whereas the ruling in Levicitus is more tersely formulated and is focused on the general principle. It is in line with this that the deuteronomic ruling specifies a penalty, in that both crops would become forfeit to the local sanctuary, whereas in Leviticus this is not specified.

The prohibition against plowing with both an ox and a donkey (v. 10) was not the result of a compassionate concern to avoid using together two beasts of unequal strength. It is possible that the verb translated "plow" (חרשׁ *ḥāraš*) should be taken to imply "mate together," thereby occasioning the miscegenation of species. However, none of the standard English versions follow such a suggestion, which appears instead to have arisen out of a desire to find a rational explanation for a procedure that otherwise might have appeared insignificant. It would comply with the larger context, which is concerned with avoiding any mixture of species. However, it is possible to understand the verb in its literal sense and to interpret it as a prohibition against bringing animals together in any fashion that might lead to miscegenation.

A similar concern to maintain the observed order of things, and of avoiding any unwarranted mixture, appears further in the regulation of v. 11, which prohibits the making of garments of a combination of wool and linen; this ruling is also repeated in Lev 19:19. The Hebrew uses a noun "mixed stuff" (שׁעטנז *ša'aṭnēz*), which is clearly a loan word, to describe the mixed cloth. It may indicate that such clothing was intended to have special, semi-magical power, either for the cure of illnesses or for the warding off of evil spirits. It has then simply been brought into line with a general concern to avoid crossing the given boundaries of life, save in certain specified exceptional cases.

22:12. The ruling concerned with the making of tassels on the four corners of a cloak is related to a practice of unknown origin. In Num 15:38-39, it is explained in terms of symbols to remind members of the community of Israel that they possessed obligations to uphold the divine commandments. The very general nature of this obligation strongly suggests that the original purpose of such tassels was either unknown or had come to be regarded as inappropriate, so that it required to be replaced by a more general reason.

22:13-30. The remaining six rulings in the section are all concerned with marriage and sexual relationships. This undoubtedly provided one of the most central and important areas of the given boundaries of life, which called for especially careful handling. At a basic level it represented a particularly difficult feature of life to grasp conceptually, just as it also marked an area of potentially disruptive, and even destructive, social force if its boundaries were not respected.

Gender differences were quite evidently perceived to be fundamental to life, reaching across from the human sphere to embrace also the animal world and even the sphere of vegetation. Male and female principles were widely perceived to pervade all creation, and it is a striking exception that the OT does not carry this through into the divine sphere, which the rest of the ancient Near East so clearly did. The boundaries of gender and sexuality, therefore, had to be respected, as we have already seen in regard to human dress codes.

More than this was entailed, however, since at times these boundaries had to be crossed in order to permit sexual relationships to lead to the establishment of wholly new households (cf. Gen 2:24). Moreover the making of such relationships and marriages required the crossing of the boundaries of the most close-knit family kinship structures, since incestuous sexual connections were precluded and a wide degree of openness in permitting marriages to take place outside the immediate kin group was permitted. Already the ruling of 21:10-14, which allowed marriage to a woman who had been taken as a prisoner of war illustrates this fact. Some boundaries might have been, and even had been, crossed in normal sexual activities, but these trespasses in turn established new boundaries that could not thereafter be broken.

Accordingly sexual relationships called for very careful handling, and a considerable number of subordinate protective rulings were required in order to set appropriate limits. These guaranteed protection and stability so that proper order could be upheld within the sphere of sexual activity. Throughout the regulations there is a pervasive awareness that a sexual relationship implied the crossing of a boundary that could not thereafter be uncrossed. Accordingly the loss of a woman's virginity and the setting up of a sexual partnership in marriage could never thereafter be ignored either by the individuals concerned or by the kin groups to which each of them belonged. Nor was this solely a matter that concerned the procreation of children, since major financial implications were also tied up with marriage.

The first of the cases that the deuteronomic legislation deals with (vv. 13-19) concerns precisely the recognition that marriage and the commencement of a sexual relationship brought into being a wholly new situation that had not before existed. Such a relationship could not thereafter be denied or revoked simply by an accusation on the part of the husband that the wife was not a virgin at the time of the marriage. The parents of the woman are then given the responsibility of providing to the town elders evidence of the woman's virginity at the time of the marriage. If this evidence is taken to be sufficient and satisfactory, then a heavy fine, amounting to one hundred shekels of silver (v. 19), was to be imposed on the husband and paid over to the wife's father. Such a sum must have represented a very substantial amount of capital. Thereafter the husband is refused any right to divorce the woman, who, together with her family who had been responsible for her, was regarded as having been subjected to a considerable level of social shame as a result of the false accusation regarding her virginity.

Very little indication is given to indicate why the husband might have been tempted to behave in such a fashion. He is said simply to have accused his bride of wanton or capricious conduct. However, it is more evident from the response that the woman's parents make in repudiation of such accusations that a primary concern lay in the charge that the bride was not a virgin at the time of her marriage. There is an imputation that the woman's family may have known this and acted deceitfully in marrying her off, when her value as a bride would have been reduced. The paternity of her children would then be put in doubt. There is also the very real possibility that the husband might have been acting out of unreasoned jealousy. Having taken a bride in good faith, he could not simply afterward revoke his responsibilities.

The "proofs of virginity" the parents are to bring to the elders are usually taken to be the bloodstains resulting from the first sexual union. However, it has very plausibly been argued that the reference is to proofs of menstruation, showing that the woman was not pregnant at the time of her marriage.

Verses 20-21 deal with the situation when no proofs of the woman's virginity could be produced. In this event, the accusations are assumed to be justified, and the woman was to be returned to the entrance of her father's house. She was then to be publicly executed by stoning. The location is significant, since it is throughout assumed that she was in the custody of her father until the time of her marriage. He is then held to have been responsible for ensuring that she remained a virgin until the time of her marriage. Throughout the male domination of women is heavily marked, since the woman passes from the custody of her father to that of her husband.

The whole situation is noteworthy and was clearly aimed at ensuring the man's right to certain knowledge of the paternity of his children. The harsh punishment for the woman's failure to fit in with these demands is striking, especially as there is a strong measure of responsibility leveled at her father. The severity of the assumed offense is measured by its being categorized as an act of "outrage" (נבלה *nĕbālâ*; cf. the purging formula used in 5:18). In view of the penalty to be inflicted, the KJV's translation "folly" appears remarkably weak. In the prophetic literature, Hos 2:2 and Jer 3:8 point to a situation in which the woman's punishment for such action is only that she should be divorced. In the light of this, the deuteronomic legislation demands a stricter enforcement of the moral code regarding charges of sexual misconduct.

Verses 22-29 deal with cases of rape and adultery. The fundamental ruling is set out directly in v. 22. If a man is found having sexual intercourse with the wife of another man, then both are to be put to death. The method of execution is not specified, but the formula for purging evil from Israel is expressed, which most plausibly indicates death by stoning. The primary concern must certainly be to protect the husband's rights to the paternity of his children. At the same time, the close interconnection between a social kinship structure and the complex boundaries posed by human sexuality points to a fervent anxiety to protect the formal lines of these distinctions.

A number of subordinate considerations are then introduced that have a direct bearing on the broader concern to preclude irregular sexual relationships. The first of these appears in vv. 23-27 and relates to a situation in which the woman is a virgin and is engaged to be married, but the formal marriage has not yet taken place. If, in this circumstance, the woman is found in an illicit sexual union, then both she and the man concerned are held to be equally guilty and are to suffer the same penalty as if the woman were already married. The ruling is important in establishing the contractual importance of the engagement arrangement, since this is taken as tantamount to marriage itself. The formal financial arrangements that were a part of the marriage contract are assumed to have been completed so that the husband-to-be has already acquired certain basic rights over his future bride.

The severity of the punishment, which is one of a number of instances in which capital punishment is laid down for a sexual offense, was obviously designed to have a strong deterrent effect. This is further borne out by the employment of the purging formula, indicating the strong concern to influence the conduct of Israel as a whole. It may well indicate that, in spite of the concern to ensure that young women remained under the supervision and custody of responsible males, there was a deep awareness that such offenses as are dealt with were often difficult to prove and disturbing in their social effect.

However, the situation raises a further important consideration, since it was necessary to allow that the woman may have been seized, overpowered, and raped against her will. Thus a qualification is introduced calling for the fullest and most severe punishment to be inflicted on the woman only in cases where the offense took place within the township boundaries. Outside of these it is assumed that the woman would have been unable to cry out and summon help to protect her. The hypothetical situation in which she is portrayed as doing so is then described extensively in vv. 25-27. The conclusion is drawn that, in such a case, only the man is deserving of death, while the woman is presumed to be innocent of any intention to violate the terms of her engagement.

At first reflection the case appears to express a perfectly reasonable and straightforward situation. Its ruling, however, is of considerable interest and importance for the insights it provides into the social implications of human sexuality. Attention has been drawn to the range of boundaries that controlled the structure of human society, in which those concerning sexual relationships were of paramount importance. In the case of the rape of an unmarried woman, a major social boundary had been transgressed. This is shown by the situation envisaged in the ruling in vv. 28-29, concerning the case of a young unmarried woman who is seized and raped by a man who may or may not be married. The culprit is then obliged to compensate the unmarried woman's father with fifty shekels of silver. He is also required to marry the woman with no subsequent entitlement to divorce her. Clearly, by his having established a sexual relationship with her it is assumed that a boundary had been crossed. The consequences of this had then to be fully accepted both by the man and by the victim, together with her family.

The ruling highlights the special significance of the case covered by vv. 25-27 in which the woman is presumed to be innocent of having committed an offense since it took place in open country. Although declared to be innocent, no indication is given as to what her future status would be, although she was engaged to be married at the time she was taken by another man. The discerning critic will note throughout that the rulings display a rather hypothetical nature since, although the concessionary caveat of v. 24 applies when no help to prevent an offense was available, the case defined in v. 28 requires that the offending couple be caught in the act.

From a legal perspective it becomes apparent in these regulations, as in many of the provisions contained in the deuteronomic law code, that a particularly weak feature of the legislative processes of ancient Israel concerned rules governing the admissibility of evidence. The sense of fairness and the general desire on the part of the elders who are made responsible for administering the laws to maintain order with compassion were obviously of paramount importance. It would appear that the rulings arrived at were intended to provide guidelines and to be related to particular cases as the situation demanded.

A concluding ruling in v. 30 prohibiting the marriage of a son to his father's wife serves as a connecting link between the rules of sexual conduct that have preceded it and those that follow. Together they cover fundamental issues regarding the structural boundaries of the community. It may be presumed here that the designated father's wife was a stepmother of the son and that the father was presumed to be dead by the time of the marriage. The background concerns that are envisaged, therefore, are those relating to questions of inheritance. The biblical laws provide evidence of a widespread and long-held assumption that a son could inherit his father's wives and concubines (Gen 35:22; 49:4; 2 Sam 3:7; 16:22; 1 Kgs 2:22). These latter figure as part of the household capital.

REFLECTIONS

Two considerations will appear uppermost to the modern reader of these deuteronomic laws. The first is to note the firm and unmodified patriarchal structure of ancient Israelite society. This male-oriented world assumed throughout that, from birth to death, the place of every female member of the community was determined by her relationship to men. Initially this relationship was to her father, who remained her effective guardian and owner until the time of her marriage to an agreed suitor. This patriarchal dominance is startlingly shown by the fact that the young woman's father was required to be compensated if she was seized and raped in open country before formal arrangements for her betrothal and marriage had been negotiated (22:29). The culprit was then compelled to marry his victim with no right for a subsequent divorce. The young woman's wishes were not even considered. To the modern reader, such heavy restrictions placed on the ability of a woman to initiate and control her position in society must appear deeply disturbing and demeaning.

The second consideration that must strike the modern reader very forcefully is the pervasive awareness that sexual relationships could not be regarded, and treated in law, simply as a private matter between two consenting adults. A much wider social context was recognized as being affected by all such relationships. Behind all of the rules governing sexual behavior we are made deeply aware that human sexuality was never simply an individual matter, since it concerned the families from which the individuals came and the children they were likely to produce and for whom they had to accept responsibility. Sexual relationships could not be treated simply as the concern only of the two central parties.

So far as the male domination of social and sexual relationships is concerned within this patriarchal structure, some degree of protection of women's rights and participation in family and social life was afforded. She was protected against malicious accusations and slanders regarding her virginity on the part of a husband who became jealous or who wished for some reason to be rid of a wife he had taken (22:13-19). If the charge could reasonably be disproved to the satisfaction of impartial judges, then no divorce was possible. On the other hand, if no such proof were forthcoming, the woman could be put to death as an adulteress (v. 27) on the basis of her husband's accusations against her.

A woman was also afforded some protection in the case of rape when it could be assumed that she had been overpowered and had been unable to cry out for help. A further limiting consideration to the male domination of women's position in society is the ruling in 22:30 that a woman who had been widowed could not thereafter be passed on like other family property to the son and heir.

Behind all of these rules governing sexual behavior, we are made deeply conscious that sexual relationships introduced a distinctive boundary in society that gave rise to many complications. That this boundary was set up to protect male interests, both personal and economic, is markedly evident and must appear deeply disturbing in a modern setting. Perhaps also it should be noted that the entire legal structure of the community appears to have been heavily affected by questions of property, inheritance, and the protection of capital within a family context generally. Sexuality and sexual desire are little reflected upon as issues in themselves. Rather, on account of the importance of the preservation and extension of a family, sexuality is safeguarded within this larger setting.

Throughout these rulings is an assumption that it was the male members of society who had the power to initiate relationships between the sexes, even though the woman who was guilty of adultery or who was the unwilling but unprotected victim of certain forms of rape paid a terrible price for her vulnerability. This background highlights the important changes introduced in Israel by the new and liberating teachings of Jesus about equality before God.

DEUTERONOMY 23:1–25:19, MATTERS OF GENERAL CONDUCT

Deuteronomy 23:1-18, The Boundaries of the Community

COMMENTARY

The legislation we have been considering until now has presumed that a clear distinction can be drawn between the Israelite proper, the resident alien who had settled within Israel, and the foreigner whose place within the Israelite community was purely temporary. The weak and exposed position of such a person then needed to be protected by certain conventions of hospitality and did not assume any permanent adoption within the community of Israel (cf. 14:21). Such persons may have been caravan traders and emissaries from foreign lands. Obviously individuals and their families could move from one status to another, but only within certain well-established limits and conventions.

The deuteronomic literature makes membership in the Israelite community a matter of paramount importance and effectively addresses its own demands and standards to men and women who were assumed to belong within this community of privilege. In fact, by its historical recollections and direct modes of address, Deuteronomy functions as literature that actively promotes a sense of belonging within this community.

Yet who did belong within this people, and where were its boundaries to be drawn? In the traditional portrayal of its own national origins, Israel was made up of a group of twelve tribes that comprised large extended families. Accordingly a sense of kinship and family structure belonged indispensably to a person's sense of identity. Birth and family origin were evidently of paramount importance. Each person also existed, however, within a series of networks that centered first on the immediate family circle of parents, children, and their close relatives. Around this circle were larger circles to be drawn of a wider extended family who might all exercise varying degrees of influence and authority over

an individual. Such families could draw other members into their embrace through marriage, the acquisition of slaves, and negotiations in which persons from other regions were adopted into the extended family on a client basis. As a result, only as a kind of notional outer limit did the idea of being an Israelite figure significantly. For the most part the more immediate circle defined the necessary pattern of relationships that governed social and religious life.

It is strongly arguable that the book of Deuteronomy contributed a great deal to strengthen and reinforce the awareness that a marked boundary separated those who were within Israel from those who stood outside the privileges of the covenant community.[92] The deuteronomic legislation both idealizes the boundaries of Israel by its concepts of membership (lit., "brotherhood") and at the same time seeks in practical terms to regularize and define the status of those who belonged within the community. To a very meaningful degree such membership carried far-reaching consequences, since the person who betrayed his or her primary allegiance to the LORD as God could pay a terrible price for doing so (cf. 13:12-18).

Much of the explanation for this heavy deuteronomic attention to the boundaries of the community must lie within the particular historical and social context in which the law book was composed. A strong sense that the people of Israel were threatened with breakup and dissolution and that the ready-made givenness of clan and tribal affiliations no longer played a decisive role pervades Deuteronomy. We cannot evade the conclusion that it was precisely the fact of this social breakup and disorientation that provided the

---

92. Braulik, "Deuteronomy and Human Rights," 131-50.

major background concern the deuteronomists were anxious to address.

23:1-8. What we find as a set of rules defining the limits of the Israelite community is a list of exclusions. The first two categories arise directly out of concern with the sexual boundaries that were dealt with in the preceding section. By appearing here, they serve as a useful transition element in the overall structure of the laws. The other exclusions arose from historical, ethnic, and less obviously defined considerations. A major point of concern relating to these factors must have been connected with the particular social and historical context in which Deuteronomy was composed. It is probable that these rules of exclusion had a very early origin, possibly from as far back as the pre-monarchic period. They may have emerged at a major border city, such as Gilgal in the Jordan valley, where trade and communication routes met. Joshua 2:9-11 and 9:9-10 reflect situations in which the acceptance of outsiders into the Israelite cultic community required to be dealt with. It seems unlikely, however, that before the deuteronomic legislation sought to regularize the situation there was any uniform Israelite policy on such matters. Individual clan and tribal groups pursued their own preferences according to local circumstances. It would then have been a consequence of the disruption arising from Assyrian interventions in the late eighth century BCE that a more considered policy was called for.

Obviously the question of membership in the Israelite community, with its consequent privileges, was a point of importance for individual families and even whole clusters of families at every stage throughout the nation's history. The necessity for regularizing and standardizing conventions of community allegiance in the age of Josiah, with the desire to reestablish a united Israel, made this a major social issue. It became all the more urgent after the disaster of 587 BCE, when large-scale movements of population took place and normal administrative practices collapsed altogether.

So it appears as an issue of unique importance in the context of the deuteronomic concern to integrate a code of practice applicable to all members of the community. All who claimed that they were full members of the Israelite covenant community and loyal worshipers of the LORD God had to establish their claims for acceptance by the recognized authority. As a result, what had no doubt earlier been varied and uncoordinated conventions needed to be fixed within a single set of rules. Whereas the separate individual rulings were almost certainly of considerable antiquity and here given a somewhat rationalized explanation, we are here presented with a set of rules to establish the cultic and social boundaries applicable to all Israelites. For the deuteronomic authors, the question of who was within and who was outside the recognized boundaries of the covenant people was of the utmost importance. It could ultimately prove to be a matter of life or death if the strict terms of the demands of religious loyalty were implemented.

After the collapse of the old Judahite state, membership in the cultic community, even without a continuing sacrificial cultus in the Temple, became a vital and irreplaceable badge of acceptance within society. The final composition of this list of community membership would therefore appear to have taken place sometime during the middle of the sixth century BCE.

The ruling in v. 1, which excludes any male whose sexual organs had been severely damaged or removed, represents an ancient sensitivity to the belief that sexual potency was a mark of divine blessing and wholeness. In consequence, any serious impairment of sexual health, which was a humiliation frequently inflicted on males defeated in battle, represented a separation from the life-giving power of the living God.

Similarly, the ruling in v. 2, which excludes the progeny of illicit sexual unions from the cultic community, must refer to those children who were born to women whose relationships conflicted with the regulations previously laid down for married status. The permanent exclusion of the Ammonites and the Moabites from entry into Israel, even to the tenth generation (vv. 3-6), reflects the long-standing antipathy and conflict between Israel and these peoples. The term "tenth generation" should probably not be taken literally, but simply implies no limit to the exclusion.

It seems highly probable that both Ammon and Moab had callously exploited Israel's weakness after the Babylonian campaign of 588–587 BCE, thereby adding further support to a date for the list at this time (for Ammonite involvement in Israel's misfortunes, see Jer 41:15). By plundering Israelite villages and harrying refugees from the Babylonian forces, these people had added further wounds to a long history of bitter suspicion and conflict.

The adducing of historical motives in v. 4 in the form of a tradition relating back to the beginning period of Israel's journeyings in the wilderness contains some unexpected features. Deuteronomy 2:29 relates that the Moabites gave food and drink to Israel at this time, although nothing is said in respect of the Ammonites on this matter. In order to provide a suitable reason, however, the deuteronomic author makes reference to the anti-Israelite stance of Balaam, the Moabite prophet (Numbers 22–24).

The prophetic oracles against Moab preserved in the prophetic literature of the OT (Isa 15:1–16:14; Amos 2:1-3) show how intense was the bitterness felt toward the Moabites. It is the awareness of the strength of this hostility that forms a significant feature of the context of the story of Ruth.

It comes as something of a surprise that a relatively open and more relaxed attitude is adopted toward both the Edomites and the Egyptians. In spite of the vigorously unsympathetic, even hostile portrayal of the Egyptian pharaoh in the story of the exodus, it is evident that close political and commercial relationships existed between Israel and Egypt. For two centuries both Israel and Judah had relied, rather unwisely, on promises of Egyptian military support against the Assyrians and the Babylonians.

In the case of the Edomites, it is noteworthy that 2:1-8 identifies Edom with Esau, the brother of Jacob/Israel. This identification had its origins in the Edomite occupation of the region of Seir, a territory where Esau's descendants established their settlements. Overall it is apparent that membership in the cultic community of Israel had, by the time these rulings were formally promulgated as law, taken on a range of major social, economic, and political consequences.

23:9-14. The rulings set out in these verses concern the hygienic conditions that were to prevail in the Israelite military camp. Two features come prominently to the fore. The first is that warfare was perceived to be an activity when extra precautions were necessary because of its hazardous nature. It was also regarded as a partially sacred activity that has drawn to it rather misleadingly the idea of "holy war." Warfare entailed the shedding of blood so that warriors were required to be protected from any blood guilt that might be incurred by acts of killing. It was also important that a military camp should be so arranged that the divine presence would be secured, since it was this presence that ensured victory according to the deuteronomic theology of warfare.

In a practical perspective, it is also to be borne in mind that, with large numbers of men living in hastily prepared and ill-protected conditions, disease became a serious threat and proper handling of food was easily neglected. The basic, if seemingly mundane, requirements for personal hygiene set out in vv. 12-13 made practical good sense. It is a consistently developed feature of Deuteronomy that warfare and military service were mandatory obligations for all able-bodied male members of the community. What is envisaged in the deuteronomic literature is a citizen army, rather than a professional fighting elite.

23:15-16. The law regarding the right of slaves to receive protection and the right to permanent domicile in the community occasions some degree of surprise. The Babylonian law code of Hammurabi required that fugitive slaves be returned to their former masters. The ruling here reflects a more humanitarian concern that recurs in the deuteronomic legislation, especially in regard to the protection of slaves. It found explicit justification in the traditional memory of the period of slavery suffered by Israel's ancestors in Egypt. God alone was the ultimate judge of all human conduct, so the commercial and social interests that it was the business of the state legislation to protect had to be subordinated to this belief in an ultimate divine order of right.

The choice granted to a slave to take up residence in any of Israel's cities exhibits a considerable degree of personal freedom.

The formula that is used ("in any place they choose in any one of your towns") links this freedom of choice with the freedom of God in establishing the location of the nation's central sanctuary (cf. 12:5). It also recognizes frankly that full social freedom was not simply a matter of status but also one of opportunity to express and fulfill a normal pattern of life. A comparable concern is reflected in the admonition to ensure that a freed slave had sufficient capital to set up a viable homestead (cf. 15:12-18).

This protection and right of domicile for a runaway slave can be considered a development of the earlier law of Exod 22:21 prohibiting the oppression or exploitation of an alien.[93] In a similar fashion, this adduces as a motive the experience of Israel's ancestors in Egypt: "you were aliens in the land of Egypt." Certainly there are close similarities, but it is improbable that Israel simply equated the status of a slave with that of a resident alien, although clearly a runaway slave would seek recognition as an alien in a foreign region. Both categories of persons represented disadvantaged, and consequently vulnerable, members of the community, so that the attitude of the deuteronomists appears as the outcome of a conscious broadening of concern for classes of weak and oppressed persons.

23:17-18. In these verses, the practice of cultic prostitution appears as an acknowledged fact in ancient Israel during the period of the monarchy and to have required the employment of both male and female practitioners. The deuteronomic literature displays a sharp hostility to the practice; this hostility must certainly have represented a long-held antipathy to the practice in the official

Israelite cultus (cf. Gen 38:21-2; 1 Kgs 14:24; 15:12). In its origin in the ancient Near East, the custom appears widely attested and to have been related to rituals in which sexual union was performed as a type of sympathetic magic designed at reactivating the natural forces of life. The prohibition of such activity to the daughters and sons of Israel points firmly in the direction of recognizing that those employed in such services were usually of foreign, non-Israelite origin. The ruling here is surprising in that, while prohibiting such ritual service to Israelites, the law nevertheless frankly recognizes the freedom of such activities to continue. A further discouragement of such activity is maintained by prohibiting that any fee paid for such practice should be contributed to the temple treasury. It would appear that this had at one time been an established custom.

The name given to a male prostitute in v. 18 is "dog" (כלב *keleb*), which appears to have strong pejorative tones. Less plausibly, it could be understood in the sense of "faithful follower." The use of such a name needs to be considered in conjunction with the general hostility to all forms of cult prostitution. The deuteronomic attitude is clearly hostility and repudiation, but not to the point where it possessed the assurance and authority to bar the practice altogether. Although the deuteronomic authors usually assume with great confidence that they have, or can expect to have, the authority to implement their legislative proposals, this is one of a number of instances in the book where their ability to do so faced some inevitable limitations. In this regard, there are significant similarities between the authors of Deuteronomy and the sages of Proverbs in condemning and repudiating popular forms of prostitution, while at the same time acknowledging its prevalence.

93. C. van Houten, *The Alien in Israelite Law,* JSOTSup 107 (Sheffield: Sheffield Academic, 1991) 45, 87-88.

REFLECTIONS

The laws set out in Deut 23:1-18 deal with defining the boundaries of the community, ethnically, socially and, to a lesser extent, morally. The legislation about community membership was a matter of primary concern and was to be exemplified by participation in the formal worship of the sanctuary at the major festivals. Membership established privileges and brought assurances concerning welfare and opportunities for prosperity within the national life. Ideally the covenant instituted on Mt. Horeb and expressed through the Ten Commandments determined the nature of this covenant community. However, human communities are living entities that necessarily create their own boundaries. The orderliness and well-being of the entire group could be threatened from within by disruptive sexual behavior, so rules were set forth to regulate behavior and to contain consequences within proper limits. At the edges also, a community's general stability and vitality could be threatened by the intrusion of unwelcome outsiders.

At the same time, the need to show vigor and firmness in maintaining the internal purity and integrity of the community had to be tempered with the need to display compassion and openness. So Israel had to accept the right of entry of aliens and foreigners on a regulated basis and especially to show a humanitarian protection and right of residence to fugitive slaves, since to have denied this would have made a mockery of Israel's own central tradition concerning its origin in an act of divine deliverance from slavery in Egypt.[94]

All such concerns are real and pressing issues in the modern world. The enthusiasm to maintain high standards and firm boundaries all too readily becomes harsh and unrealistic. Yet openness and laxity can equally easily tear away the very heart of the commitment to a sense of high calling established through God's election and covenant promises.

What we are faced with in these laws are ancient perceptions showing where boundaries were to be drawn. Attention is fixed on the manner in which historical and kinship obligations had to be modified in the light of the need to maintain the health and compassionate outreach of a caring society.

94. Braulik, "Deuteronomy and Human Rights," 145.

Deuteronomy 23:19–25:4, Justice and Compassion in the Community

COMMENTARY

The makeup of a community is a complex reality, bearing all the characteristics of growth, like a living body, rather than of a fixed structure, like a building. This sensitivity to the vitality of a community in terms of growth and decay is well reflected in the earliest narratives of the Hebrew patriarchs shown in the book of Genesis. It places a marked emphasis on the extended family and on ties of kinship as providing a set of values and associations that require to be acknowledged in all aspects of life. The consciousness of clan and tribal affiliation continues to be reflected strongly in the stories relating to the earliest phase of Israel's settlement in the land and in the accounts of the origins of the Israelite monarchy. For Deuteronomy, the concept of Israel's divine election and of a covenant bond between the nation and the LORD God embraced these kinship ties, vesting them with a powerful religious significance and creating the idea that the entire nation was a people of one kin. So they could be portrayed pictorially as one large family, which the Hebrew expressed in its patriarchal fashion as "a nation of brothers."

Quite clearly various factors contributed to the breakdown of this feeling of social solidarity, which appears to have been strongest in the earliest period of Israel's life. It may well be that it was never more than a projected ideal that was only partially felt by the various member clans and tribes. For the most part, it becomes consistently evident that in the earliest times a sense of identity and belonging was generated most firmly through the immediate affiliation of the extended family and clan, rather than of the nation in its broad extent. We can see that, over time, other factors, especially those of regional associations and status within a city or community, became important.

In this process of development from tribal groups to cities inevitable changes occurred in patterns of religious loyalty. Greater prosperity emerged, but the increased acquisition and influence of wealth created new social boundaries, which gave rise to fresh problems. Accordingly it became the business of the law to monitor and control these.

Far too little is known regarding the development of the Israelite economy, although it would appear from the legislation in the book of Deuteronomy that ownership of land, the protection of rights of inheritance, and general expectations of prosperity and well-being were all matters that were accorded high priority in the attention of Israel's lawmakers. The position of families within the community could not be viewed in isolation from matters of property and wealth. These contributed to defining the status of a family. It is evident from the deuteronomic laws that silver had become a means of exchange and a highly prized form of capital. Mercantile enterprise was common, and contacts with other nations for purposes of trade were generally experienced. For all the consciousness of military threats and political uncertainties that surround the final form of the book, the broad outlook of the book of Deuteronomy can be described as one of general economic stability. Israel, as it is portrayed within the laws, is a community of opportunity and of social and commercial sophistication.

It is against this background that the laws set out in 23:19-25 are to be interpreted. To an extent, they reflect a guarded acceptance of the principle that it was the duty of the law to protect capital, to promote commercial enterprise, and to secure respect and encouragement for personal industry and effort. Over against this, however, there appears a deep consciousness that, if left unregulated, economic enterprise and protectiveness could undermine the very basis of the community with its kinship values and commitments. A nation of landowners and mercantilists could not easily also be a nation of brothers and sisters.

The laws set out in 23:19–25:4 are predominantly aimed at achieving a balance between accepting the necessity for commercial enterprise and the protection of family capital, while at the same time setting limits to both. They may broadly be seen as an elaboration of the aims and intentions that undergird the commandment "You shall not steal" (5:19). They establish guidelines to show what constituted misappropriation of

another's property and what was required to uphold the traditional compassion of the extended family to protect the weaker and more vulnerable members of the community.

23:19-23. The law here protects against the prevalent practice of usury, in which excessive rates of interest were charged on loans of capital and on goods purchased. As a result, the borrower, assumed to be already in economic constraints, was mercilessly exploited. The response exhibited by this legislation is to prohibit the taking of any interest at all from a fellow Israelite, but to allow it, with no specified restrictions, from foreigners. The custom of such selective business dealings was probably not wholly an innovation at this point of time, since it is probable that local, kinship-based trading practices of this kind were quite common. What is new is the extension of this pattern to cover an entire national, covenant-based community. The status as a citizen of Israel could, from this time, carry quite major economic consequences.

The law concerning the fulfillment of vows must similarly reflect the uncertainties of the economic order. Vows to present goods and produce to the sanctuary at the end of the harvest or of some commercial enterprise could readily prove to be inconvenient, or even hopelessly optimistic, in their calculation. Behind all such actions often lay the unexpressed belief that such vows might serve as a form of inducement to God so that the enterprise would be blessed. Any delay in paying what had been vowed is here prohibited out of the theological conviction that words spoken to God, even in secret, were binding promises in which the integrity and good faith of the giver were at stake. Undoubtedly we find throughout biblical history evidence of the belief that vows were a sign of the trustworthiness and good faith of the true worshiper. Gifts to God were an evident proof of the reality of faith in the divine governance of the world (cf. Eccl 5:4-6).

23:24-25. The reality of the economic order, tempered by the necessity to display compassion and charity to a needy neighbor, are reflected in these two laws. The background assumption to them is undoubtedly that of a long-standing custom that allowed a local person or a traveler to pluck grapes from a neighbor's vineyard when passing through.

A similar convention existed with regard to the standing grain in a neighbor's field at harvesttime. To allow a modest plucking of the crop was a mark of hospitality and goodwill, but was quite evidently never intended to provide an impoverished neighbor with a continued means of charitable support. So a charitable concession could easily be abused when it was exploited by deliberate scroungers. Both laws then provide illuminating expressions of the deuteronomic spirit and of the general social context in which its legislative program was developed. Old customs, nurtured in a world of neighborly trust and the conventions appropriate to a close-knit community with strong kinship ties, were overtaken by a harsher economic environment in which those customs were susceptible to exploitation.

Where vines were grown and fields planted with crops for commercial purposes rather than home use, new protective measures were called for. Even neighbors could become greedy and exploitative in using old customs to get something for themselves at another's expense. This ruling, therefore, is aimed at protecting the rights of the landowner while at the same time seeking to preserve what was valuable of the neighborly attitudes of ancient customs.

From the perspective of legislative development, these laws also serve to highlight the inevitable reflections and ramifications consequent upon the broad sweep of the commandment prohibiting stealing. It sought to determine what constituted theft in specific circumstances and endeavored to show that this was not incompatible with ancient customs of a charitable nature. We may presume that these rulings still left open a rather indeterminate area of judgment for local elders to define when a reasonable right had been abused.

24:1-4. The law that prohibits the remarriage to her former husband of a woman who had subsequently been divorced by him and married to another is of special interest.[95]

95. The issue is discussed in G. Wenham, "The Restoration of Marriage Reconsidered," *JJS* 30 (1979) 36-40; R. Westbrook, "The Prohibition of Marriage in Deuteronomy 24:1-4," *Studies in Bible*, ed S. Japhet, Scripta Hierosolumitana 31 (Jerusalem: Magnes, 1986) 385-405; E. Otto, "Das Verbot der Wiederherstellung einer geschiedenen Ehe. Deuteronomum 24,1-4 im Kontext des israelitischen und jüdäischen Eherechts" *UF* 24 (1992) 301-9.

There are no close parallels to it in other ancient Near Eastern law codes, and the reasoning that underlies it is not wholly clear. It appears also to be awkwardly placed, since it might have been expected to appear alongside the other laws concerning sexual behavior in 22:13-30. It can best be regarded as a transition piece that concerns property rights and inheritance as well as sexual behavior.

The ruling itself is clear enough and is further reflected in the prophetic report of Hosea 1–3 and the saying recorded in Jer 3:1-2. It reveals an underlying awareness that such action could only promote social confusion and would make nonsense of the proper boundaries of sexual conduct. The circumstances that are said to have brought about the divorce in the first instance ("because he finds something objectionable about her," v. 1) are vague and ill-defined. Similarly, the situation envisaged is one in which the woman is then divorced again by her second husband on the grounds that "he dislikes her." The second husband is then assumed to be still living at the time when the proposed remarriage to the first husband occurs. Overall the background conviction expressed by the law recognizes the seriousness of marriage, permits rather arbitrary grounds for divorce, but takes full account of the fact that divorce introduces considerable complications in the preservation of acceptable social boundaries. While some degree of arbitrariness in permitting divorce in the first place is allowed, any relapse into a fickle marital exchange is prohibited. The concern is to exclude the possibility altogether of remarriage to a former spouse after a divorce. Such action would represent a serious breach of respect for acknowledged social structures.

24:5. The law grants the unusual concession that a newly married man was to be freed from military or other public service for one year after his marriage. The underlying assumption appears to be that marriage is a solemn undertaking that establishes a new household unit within society. Therefore, it both carries obligations and fulfills certain promises in regard to the upholding and extension of the extended family unit. It is assumed that children would result from the marriage and thereby secure the future of the new household unit, preserving the name of the husband should he fall victim in his military service. Such concern for the protection of a new family unit was important for society, and by granting this concession to a newly married man his adulthood and manhood would be confirmed. Widows with children, especially sons, were more favorably placed than widows without offspring, as the book of Ruth illustrates (cf. Ruth 1:11-13).

The law serves as a noteworthy attempt to define the boundary between private right, closely linked to the values of the extended family, and public duty. To yield complete priority to one consideration over the other would ultimately have jeopardized the future health and well-being of society as a whole. It also has relevance in displaying an awareness that, even in times of military emergency, it was not appropriate that one generation should be sacrificed in the expectation that a future generation would thereby benefit from what they had forgone. Each generation is seen as a whole in and for itself, with its own expectation of establishing families and households in which an individual adult male would ensure that his name was preserved.

24:6. This law is a sharp reminder of the level of poverty that could be experienced in ancient Israel. The two millstones with which grain would be ground into flour are regarded as forming a basic minimum of household utensils. Without them, a family would be reduced to begging and would lose all ability to remain self-supporting. It is prohibited, therefore, that such vital domestic utensils be taken as a pledge against a loan of provisions or money of any kind. Such a ruling reflects on the way in which the protection of property and the authority of the law to enforce commercial, or loan, transactions was subjected to specific limits. When the enforcement of such transactions would reduce a fellow Israelite to the point of complete destitution, then to do so was prohibited. Similar limits to the enforcement of business transactions are set out in vv. 10-13.

24:7. The law that prohibits kidnapping follows the differently worded, but essentially equivalent, law of Exod 21:16. The subject of kidnapping is also covered in the law code of Hammurabi, which deals with the kidnapping of an infant son of a free citizen. This would certainly suggest that the crime, intended for

the acquisition of slaves, was a serious one in antiquity. In a tribally structured community, members of an alien tribe could readily have been regarded as reasonable targets for such hostile acts, with marauding bands capturing and enslaving their unfortunate victims, many of whom would have been children. It appears as a prevalent and deeply disruptive aspect of ancient banditry, which the centrally based authority of the urban communities strove hard to control and eliminate.

The directive that such a prohibition applied only to "another Israelite" is a surprising, and rather disturbing, weakening of the basic principle of the law. It is occasionally a feature of the deuteronomic legislation that it is made to apply only to Israelites, allowing a lower standard of conduct to operate toward outsiders (cf. 14:21; 15:3; 23:20). This reflects the strong background of election and covenant ideology that permeates the legislation, extending privileges and status to all Israelites, but at the same time heightening in a negative fashion a sense of exclusion for those outside the privileged circle.

24:8-9. Concern for neighborly conduct toward a fellow Israelite also motivates the law regarding the prevention of the spread of infectious skin diseases. A considerable debate has taken place regarding the precise medical identification of the skin disease, or diseases, covered by the Hebrew word צרעת (ṣāraʿat).[96] No satisfactory evidence has arisen to indicate that the disease was leprosy, which became a scourge in medieval times, but was not known in the ancient Near East. The complex rulings set out in Leviticus indicate a recognition that some skin afflictions were more contagious, and therefore more dangerous, than others; but precise identification was difficult. All the indications are that various types of skin afflictions were covered by the term ṣāraʿat and that it was left to the experience and traditional knowledge of the levitical priest to pronounce the level of risk posed by the condition. The purpose of the law here was clearly to protect the community at large from heedless and uncaring persons who might have been tempted to ignore whatever warnings had been given regarding

---

96. The varied range of diseases and manifestations (since the term is also used of buildings) covered by the Hebrew term is examined in the light of modern medical and scientific understanding in David P. Wright and R. N. Jones, "Leprosy," *ABD* 4:277-82.

their condition. By remaining in active social circulation, they risked infecting other people. The law, in effect, sought to give a measure of authority and control to the priests over such matters. Nevertheless, it leaves open the question of what further active steps could be taken to restrict the movements of a person who was unwilling to comply with the priestly restraints.

The adducing of the example of Moses' sister Miriam (Num 12:14-15) is an instructive instance of the awareness that the law lacked any specific penalty and that difficulties could arise in seeking to enforce restrictions on an uncooperative member of the community. The biblical tradition recounts that Miriam had been afflicted with a severe skin disease as punishment for her critical attitude toward Moses. The author clearly intends to warn that a similar misfortune could befall any Israelite who flouted the restrictions demanded by the law of v. 8. Throughout there is a fundamental assumption that affliction with disease, and any consequent recovery from it, were matters that lay entirely in the hands of God to control. Hidden within this also lies the belief that disease could be a punishment for sin, an assumption that is challenged in the book of Job.

24:10-13. The rulings set out in these verses return to deal with issues arising from the economic order. Once again they concern the treatment of a neighbor who has fallen upon hard times and who has been compelled to seek a loan of goods or silver. Even the most necessary items of personal clothing could be offered and taken in pledge against a loan. When proceeding to take possession of the pledge, the creditor was not permitted to enter the house of the debtor. Nor, if the pledge took the form of the debtor's only cloak, could this last piece of property be withheld overnight. Throughout there is a deep consciousness of the disruptive consequence that the legally backed enforcement of commercial transactions could have on the social life and stability of a community. The caring and neighborly concern that would almost certainly have been strongly felt within communities in which the values of the extended family were still strongly maintained could easily be broken and undermined in the

harsher context of the economic life of large urban communities.

The deuteronomic law is at pains to protect and uphold the personal rights of possession of property and aims to protect—and where necessary enforce—the honoring of commercial and monetary dealings. Yet there were limits, and these limits established new restrictions that were to be respected. Fundamental among these was the boundary established between Israelites and non-Israelites, which had come to acquire a paramount significance in the deuteronomic horizon. There was also a boundary set by an individual's household, which became an expression of his or her individual citizenship and a sanctuary of privacy. Thus it could not be invaded arbitrarily, even in the legitimate act of taking possession of something given in pledge to secure a loan.

If the item pledged was the cloak that was vital to the well-being and personal identity of a citizen, then, under the same principle, this was to be returned at nightfall. The duty of the law to protect commercial dealings was thereby set within certain limits that could not be crossed. At all stages of Israelite/Jewish history in the biblical period, it appears that debt slavery represented a real, and potentially deeply disturbing, threat. In upholding the economic order, wider issues of a humanitarian kind could be set aside. Children could be sold off in order to pay debts (Amos 2:6), and starvation and ruination faced an impoverished family.

24:14-15. Problems of poverty and the economic order also surface in the law regarding the prompt payment of wages. The ruling presupposes that labor was normally paid for on a daily basis and that those who were available for work on these terms were wholly dependent upon what they earned. It is significant that, as in the case of the previous laws dealing with the limits imposed on the enforcement of monetary dealings, these are addressed to those who are assumed to be members of the free landowning section of the community. The appeal is essentially one that sought to maintain a sensitive and fair attitude toward the poorer members of society, as well as to those who could suddenly find themselves thrown into unexpected poverty. The motive for such a charitable disposition is held to lie with God, who is the protector of the poor, so that the ungenerous person, even when legally in the right, might nevertheless incur guilt from God (v. 15).

24:16-18. The same line of argument to support a compassionate and caring interpretation of justice reverberates through the three laws that follow. Of great importance is the ruling in v. 16, which precludes the infliction of the death penalty on the children of the actual culprit. The rule is cited in 2 Kgs 14:6 in connection with Amaziah's execution of his father's murderers, but the sparing of their children.

The law is concerned with the administration of human justice, rather than with the effect of divine punishment on a family or community, and so, in this respect at least, it stands apart from the warning given in the Decalogue (5:9). We may also note the cruel punishment inflicted upon Achan's entire household in Josh 7:24 and the severe punishment urged for those who transgress the first commandment (Deut 13:15).

The principle behind the law was clearly felt to be important and reflects directly on the way in which the development of a centralized system of law, administered through law officers and elders, was able to check and restrain the custom of vengeful mutilations and killings that characterized the strong vengeance orientation of family solidarity in early Israel. Repeatedly we find that the deuteronomic legislators were concerned to secure fairness and parity of treatment across the whole community. How effective such a legal code was in the manner of its operation is impossible to determine and clearly depended much on the good sense of those who administered it.

The awareness of an "all Israel" consciousness that strongly pervades the book of Deuteronomy, setting a sharp distinction between those who were within the community and those who were outside it, is reflected in the law of v. 17. The resident alien and the orphan belonged within the basic community, yet lacked the full support that would ordinarily have been afforded by a surrounding kinship circle. As a result, they became more than usually vulnerable to exploitation and abuse. They enjoyed only a dependent,

client status in society,[97] so they had to rely on the protection and representative mediation of others if they were to secure legal or financial redress in contentious matters. They were, therefore, especially vulnerable and virtually powerless if they were unable to obtain the support of a patron. The admonition here, which once again falls back on the historical recollection of Israel's ancestral origins in the slavery of Egypt, warns categorically against any exploitation of this weakness. We can once again perceive the real degree of sensitivity the deuteronomic legislators display toward recognizing that a system of law could be no more just and fair than the level of integrity and goodwill shown by those who administered it. Even laws carved on tablets of stone were powerless if those who were responsible for applying those laws were indifferent to the claims of society's weakest members. An added touch of authority is thus imposed on the administration by the concluding comment: "therefore I command you to do this" (v. 18).

24:19-22. These admonitions concerning the requirement to leave a forgotten sheaf of grain or the gleanings of the olive trees and vines for the poorer members of society to harvest must certainly reflect an ancient custom. It was a way of providing some assistance for the poor that enabled them to share both in the workload of harvest and in its rejoicing and fruits. Obviously such charitable provision made available a necessary means of subsistence for the landless and provided an important means of social bonding and collective sharing. The community was ultimately seen as a single entity that could prosper as a whole, but in which even the least fortunate were to participate.

25:1-3. The legislation concerning the manner and circumstances in which a punishment of flogging was to be administered provides a valuable insight into the way Deuteronomy envisaged the application of its legal rulings. A dispute between two persons, evidently over a serious matter in view of the potential punishment, was to be brought before judges who would decide on the guilt or innocence of the accused person.

---

97. The deuteronomic legislation on the subject of the resident alien, and its social background, is well covered in van Houten, *The Alien in Israelite Law,* 68-108.

If the guilty verdict were upheld, then the punishment of flogging was to be carried out in the presence of the judge. He was also to ensure that the punishment was administered exactly as had been determined and that it was neither lessened nor exceeded. A maximum number of lashes, forty, is then prescribed in v. 3 on the grounds that to exceed this number would lead to the neighbor's being "degraded in your sight." It was the custom in later Jewish practice for this to be limited to thirty-nine in order to avoid any accidental overstepping of the number (cf. 2 Cor 11:24).

25:4. The ruling in this verse gives a measure of protection for animals by affirming that an ox was not to be muzzled while treading out the grain. The ruling has consistently been understood literally in rabbinic interpretations, which must certainly be regarded as correct. In 1 Cor 9:9, Paul understands the ruling allegorically as indicating that workers deserve their reward. Clearly the issue had become a matter of discussion in learned Jewish circles, and the fact that it displays a concern for the welfare of animals is significant. Creation was looked upon as a coherent reality, the order of which needed to be respected in all its parts.

REFLECTIONS

The series of laws that commenced in 23:19 ranges over a number of issues that appear, at first glance, to have little in common. Yet this seeming randomness in the subject matter is more apparent than real, since the prevailing concern is to mark out exceptions in the rigorous application of certain laws. In consequence, there is a relatively broad basis of attention to situations in which human welfare and dignity, or even that of animals, are protected against overly zealous administration of justice.

The upholding of the right of a citizen to pick grapes or pluck grain from a neighbor's vineyard or field maintains a customary freedom, while aiming to prevent deliberate theft or exploitation of another's property. Similarly the refusal to allow a neighbor to enter the house of another in order to take possession of property that had been offered in pledge guaranteed the neighbor's independence and right of privacy in his or her own home.

This series of rulings reveals a sensitive and practical attitude toward the administration of law and justice. To press one facet or ruling of the law to the detriment of other matters of moral and social concern would have been to make a mockery of the law. There is displayed here a genuine recognition that laws protecting property and possessions could easily enforce the rights of the property owner at the expense of the dignity and social standing of another. Property could become a cause of division and dissension in an unwelcome and unforeseen way. As a broad principle, it appears that it was felt to be the business of the legal system to uphold the binding nature of legal transactions, to enforce payment of debts, and to defend the enterprise of landowners in farming and developing their land commercially without interference and exploitation by envious neighbors. Yet all such developments could trespass heavily on ancient customs aimed at providing some protection and support for the poorer members of society. The law, if pressed too zealously, could lead to sharper social and economic divisions, with the poor becoming poorer and the rich getting richer. To prevent the breakup of a community and the consequent loss of human dignity if the poor became utterly destitute, some restraining guidelines were necessary, thus the guidelines illustrated by these laws. Ultimately even working animals represented an important resource that deserved to be respected and protected.

These laws make us aware that it is the business of the law to protect the community as a whole, and not just the more successful members of it. The earlier structure of Israelite society had leaned heavily upon the commitment of the extended family to protect its weaker members and to provide the conditions for sharing property and its benefits widely throughout the group. But fundamental shifts in Israel's economy, a series of moves toward more sophisticated and diverse forms of urban living, and increased openness to the larger world of the ancient Near East had all made heavy inroads into these older structures with their strong sense of kinship values. Progress was welcome, but it often came at a price that the smaller rural communities of Israel could ill afford. Wealth and the promotion of trade threatened to undermine many of the older values and supportive customs. Accordingly a major interest in the legislation set out here indicates a concern to retain what could be preserved of these older values and customs by setting limits to the rights of the landowning section of the community.

The attitude that it displayed regarding personal property is of particular interest, since there is a bold recognition of its importance to individual persons. Considerations of health, of human dignity, and of the need for a person to retain a minimum of resources to be self-supporting all came under the purview of the lawmakers. As a result, such unlikely sounding possessions as a millstone, a cloak, or other items of personal property that might be used as a token pledge to secure a loan are all made the subject of specific rulings. There emerges a sensitivity to the recognition that what a person is as a member of the community cannot properly be separated from that person's basic possessions. Food, warmth, work, and the right to privacy in one's own house are all viewed as central features of an individual's dignity. Therefore, it becomes the duty of the law to consider property in its relationship to a person's overall position in society. What was a minor item for the wealthy could represent a priceless treasure to the poor.

Deuteronomy 25:5-19, Protecting the Family

COMMENTARY

The laws that now bring the present section to a close appear to have only a slight connection with those that have preceded them. Yet this lack of connection is more apparent than real, since the overall concern of the laws set out in vv. 5-12 is with the need to protect the family. More precisely, they are concerned to protect the economic interests of the family by safeguarding its capital and its importance as an inheritance. We have already noted in Deuteronomy that the family unit is focused in a relatively narrow way on an individual household and its property rather than the much larger extended kin group. We have seen how this could be threatened by irresponsible sexual behavior on the part of the head of the family and, more directly, by misconduct on the part of the women of the household, whether wives or daughters, for whom the family head was responsible.

Yet the household was not simply a kin group built around a sense of belonging. A prime concern of the law prohibiting adultery

was a need to ensure the family head of his right to the paternity of the children his wives were expected to bear him. He was entitled to be assured, in accordance with the commandment prohibiting adultery (5:18), that his children were truly his. They would become part of the economic unit of the household and would eventually become its heirs. So the viability and success of the household as a primary unit of society depended on the extent to which there were legitimate heirs to its wealth and a willingness on their part to concern themselves with its welfare. The security of a household and its property were very much a matter entrusted to its male head and the eldest son, who could expect to take his father's place in due course. It then became a matter of honor that this heir apparent should pay proper respect to his parents, once they passed an effective working age. The law permitted harsh measures to be taken against a wastrel son, while at the same time it strove to ensure that the inheritance rights of each son were fully protected in accordance with birth order. The boundary lines of such matters were of the utmost significance. Where it might well have seemed practical to allow the head of the household to act as he saw fit in planning for future eventualities, the law fully recognized the dangers of doing so. In a polygamous household, bitter tensions could arise to bring the family to the point of destruction. Accordingly there was a deep interest on the part of society more generally to concern itself with the rights and expectations of wives and their children.

25:5-10. The law regarding levirate marriage (the title is taken from the Latin *levir*, "husband's brother") gives formal approval to measures aimed at coping with a situation in which a woman was widowed without having a son to assume the male role within the household.[98] The custom appears to rest on a well-established practice that most probably operated on an ad hoc basis. It seems unlikely that it was either a common practice or that it was legally enforceable. Had it been the normal convention in the circumstance of early widowhood, it is hard to understand why in the OT the misfortunes and near destitution of widows and orphans appear to be a persistent, and acutely felt, social problem.

The requirement that a widow could not be married outside the family was evidently intended to ensure that the property of the deceased husband remained within his family's control. It also marks a situation in which the patriarchal structure of Israelite society was itself closely guarded, since, had women been entitled to inherit ancestral property in accordance with the prescription given in Num 27:8, the problem would not have arisen. As it is, the concern of the law is to provide the possibility of the birth of a male heir to the deceased, who would eventually take responsibility for the family estate. Accordingly, the explanation for the marriage to the deceased husband's brother set out in vv. 5-6 is that it should lead to the birth of a male heir who would then be counted as the original husband's firstborn for the purposes of inheritance.

The narrative episode of Gen 38:12-30 goes further even than this in recognizing all the offspring of such a relationship

as constituting the family of the deceased brother. However, the point is not of major importance, since the intention of the arrangement was achieved once a firstborn son to the deceased had been born. The overall concern is with the economic preservation of the original household, rather than with the regulation of sexual relationships or the provision of a home for an unfortunate widow. The contrary law contained in the holiness code (Lev 18:16; 20:21), which forbids the contracting of such levirate marriages, is probably later in origin but must also reflect the fact that such a practice had never been widely adopted.

It is the shadow of this unease concerning the practice that has given rise to the further regulations in vv. 7-10, which provide for the possibility of the husband's brother opting out of any such commitment. The reasons why this might be desirable followed two main paths. A primary factor would certainly be that the husband's brother might himself be in a position to acquire his brother's property, adding it to property of his own. This could readily have arisen when the brother was in line to take over a family estate that would have gone to his deceased brother. By marrying his widowed sister-in-law, he would be reducing his own household's prospects. It could also have been the case that the value of his own property might be diminished and his status in the community lessened if a major entitlement remained in the name of his dead brother.

The law frankly recognizes the possibility of such a refusal to implement the requirement of marriage to a widow. Accordingly, the right to make such a refusal is upheld, but it is countered to some extent by imposing a ceremony of public shaming and humiliation. This took the form of a ritualized action of removing the sandal from the non-compliant brother's foot and spitting in his face. Clearly the offense, such as it is, is regarded as failure to uphold the integrity of a family and its estate. The sandal was the token of "walking over" a piece of land as a sign of ownership. Its removal signified that the owner of the sandal had not shown proper regard for his (extended) family's property.

The demand that such a ceremonial act of shaming be carried out is interesting, since shame was clearly a matter that exercised

98. R. Westbrook, *Family and Property in Biblical Law*, JSOTSup 113 (Sheffield: Sheffield Academic, 1991) 69-89.

a powerful influence on patterns of social behavior. It was, however, primarily a social matter and is clearly one that the deuteronomic lawmakers do not otherwise consider a major means of enforcing right conduct.

Overall the problem that the custom of levirate marriage sought to deal with was one occasioned by the growth of wealthy property-owning households. It can then be seen in the context, and against the background, of the older strong sense of kinship ties and the heavily protective desire to keep property and wealth within the immediate extended family. Formal codes of social legislation like that of Deuteronomy came strongly to the fore as society became more urbanized and more affluent. It is understandable, therefore, that the book of Deuteronomy should have felt it a prime duty to give the full backing of the law to commercial loans and transactions and to the right of owning and developing private property. At the same time, it clearly remained fully sensitive to the moral value latent in kinship ties. Therefore, it could resort to the language of family membership (brotherhood and sisterhood) as a means of evoking a strong sense of mutual responsibility. In the case of the legislation for levirate marriage, which was obviously not a common practice, it tries to retain something of the older commitment to the extended family in a more commercially minded age.

25:11-12. The law that follows provides the only example among the OT laws in which physical mutilation is prescribed as a legal punishment, apart from the broad reference to the practice in the *lex talionis* (cf. 19:21). The quarrel outlined in v. 11 is described as one between "brothers" (אחים *'āḥîm*); it may have been intended in a narrow literal sense (as in the NRSV) or be understood to cover any male member of the community. The context could favor the narrower and more literal interpretation, since the concern was evidently not simply with immodest or unseemly behavior, but with an action that could result in preventing a male member of a household from producing offspring. The harshness of the punishment prescribed would then become more readily intelligible in a situation that would not simply have been humiliating to a man, but would have had major consequences for him.

25:13-16. The concluding law covers the problem of a trader working with different kinds of weights, all carrying the same nominal value. The general problem of maintaining a fair system of standard weights and measures was quite evidently a persistent problem for ancient society once the practice of barter as well as of direct sales with monetary values was in widespread use. By using a heavier weight for buying than for selling, it was easy to cheat the unwary. It must certainly have been one of the most widespread forms of cheating simply because it was difficult for the purchaser to detect or for the authorities to stamp out (cf. Ps 12:2; Prov 20:23; Amos 8:5). Even standard weights employed in antiquity suffered considerable variation through wear and tear, besides which there may also have existed regional variations, since new weights were balanced from older, worn ones. One of the most desirable benefits of official royal oversight of trading practices was a concern to enforce standard weights. Nevertheless, even with these efforts, it seems probable that the honesty of the officials was little superior to the dishonesty of the traders. Against such a background, the deep disgust at such cheating is expressed by the idea of such practices as constituting an "abomination" (תועבה *tô'ēbâ*).

25:17-19. The remarks concerning Amalek and the necessity for maintaining a continued hostility and watchfulness toward this people bring an unexpected note to the conclusion. The verses would appear to have been added at a late stage in order to round off the series of regulations and laws, probably at a time when Amalekite brigands became a renewed threat to the Israelite community. The historical reference to Amalekite treachery is to Exod 17:8-17, although the accusation made here goes beyond the details recorded there. In any event, this historical memory can scarcely have provided a sufficient basis for the unrelenting animosity and distrust that are expressed. Israel's experience had clearly shown the Amalekites to be unsatisfactory people with whom to have any dealings whatsoever and persons with whom it was impossible to make real peace, in spite of attempts to do so.

REFLECTIONS

The laws contained in 25:5-19 appear to be a miscellany, but, as with the preceding group, a number of underlying basic concerns draw them together. The major interest lies in preserving the family household as an integrated unit and in upholding its viability. The death of any prominent male member of a household posed a potential threat to its economic strength since there had then to take place either a handing over of the deceased person's estate to his male heirs or a fundamental realignment of expectation within the surviving male family members. Without any males to administer a household's capital stock, its future was placed in jeopardy or collapsed altogether (as envisaged by Qoheleth in Eccl 4:7-8; 5:13-17). Obviously it was impractical to apportion the estate in equal shares to all, even to only the male children, since this would have broken up its consolidated value. We may assume that its capital value was often not great, with many persons being dependent upon it. To have divided an estate into equal shares, however attractive this may have appeared in simple fairness, would have destroyed its viability, since this was largely in terms of arable land.

In the light of this need, the eldest son, ordinarily the firstborn (and assumed to have reached adulthood by the time such a major responsibility fell to him) had the lion's share. Yet this privilege also carried immense responsibility since it meant that all the other members of the family, especially the women, were almost entirely dependent upon him. In a polygamous household in which there may be many sons, it is obvious that rivalries within the family could become bitter and sometimes violent. Much was at stake, then, and the structure of the household unit, with its roots in the extended family, was closely tied to the economic viability of the whole community. Strong households made for strong townships, provided a reasonable harmony, and common interest was established between them. In the case of the premature death of the head of a household, the problems became greatly exacerbated, especially if the inheriting son were still a minor. Personal interests had to be subordinated to the need to hold together the value of the household's capital assets and to the concern to keep this under efficient male control.

From the perspective of hindsight, and with a less narrowly structured pattern of social groupings in which male domination can no longer be conceded, the limitations of the Israelite situation become apparent. We can at best seek to understand it and to understand the motives and concerns that gave rise to it. We should also recognize that such legislation as is presented here was itself a reflection of social attitudes and assumptions that had grown up over many centuries, and even millennia.

Of special interest to us is the recognition of the importance of building strong and positive relationships within a household. Throughout the book of Proverbs, the sages who were its authors offer strong warnings against disruptive behavior within a household. Quarrelsome speech, nagging complaints, undisciplined children, as well as violent and uncontrolled anger are all made the targets of their admonitions. At first it may appear a rather trivial concern with matters that are a part of ordinary human experience. However, the sages clearly regarded such matters important, because any conduct that could bring dissension and conflict within a household might eventually bring the entire household to ruin. The strong biblical emphasis on the family as the foundational unit of society is important and relevant to the modern world. It represents a major line of defense against dehumanization and economic weakness, since the household unit is crucial for coping with varied human demands. At the same time, it is important, in seeking to defend and protect family life, to recognize those factors that can make it vulnerable or that can lead to its becoming an oppressive, rather than a liberating and supportive, institution. One aspect of the legislation in Deuteronomy is the manner in which it seeks to achieve a shift of focus from a social context in which dependence on the family was all-important to one in which a wider range of conventions and attitudes retained its strengths, while at the same time seeking to curtail its weaknesses.

Clearly the strongest and most successful families in ancient Israel had the resources with which to protect themselves from the economic misfortunes of life. There were, however, weaker members of the community who lacked an effective basis of family support, such as resident aliens and freed slaves, or who had been unfortunate enough to fall victim to misfortune, such as those widowed early in life and no longer within range of their families. The story of Ruth skillfully captures a scenario in which two women, Ruth and her mother-in-law, Naomi, find themselves in such a situation.

One of the measures adopted by the deuteronomic legislators with a view to retaining the benefits of the family values of Israelite society, as it had existed in its earliest phase, is to classify every member of the community as a "brother" or "sister." To learn to think of other members of society as part of one great national family was clearly aimed at enhancing respect for them and protecting their interests. Yet more than a purely verbal basis of support is needed if family life is to be protected in Israel and if the weaker members of the community are to be kept from starvation and destitution. So there are important legislative steps to be taken, aimed in part at guaranteeing that families behave responsibly by ensuring consistency and fairness in matters of inheritance and by seeking to assist them to retain their economic viability. A cornerstone in this policy is undoubtedly that of seeking to ensure that deaths, particularly that of the patriarchal head of a successful family, did not become a destructive event for the family's future.

DEUTERONOMY 26:1-19, LITURGY AND THANKFULNESS

COMMENTARY

The significance and attractiveness of the two liturgical confessions that bring to a close the main legal section of Deuteronomy can scarcely be overrated. Each provides an illuminating glimpse into the minds of the deuteronomists and reveals why this law book has been so influential in the development of both Jewish and Christian thought.

It should be noted that Deuteronomy 26 provides a carefully structured inclusio to balance the opening of the more directly worded instructions for the establishment of a central place of worship in chap. 12. There the primary importance of the sanctuary is declared, with its controlling position in shaping the life of the community in all its aspects. It is described with relative simplicity as a place at which prayers could be made and to which offerings could be brought. It was to be a sanctuary where God would become accessible to the people by the presence there of the divine name. In chap. 26 we have a concluding resumption of the theme

concerning the central place worship was to have in the life of every member of the Israelite nation. Whereas chap. 12 provides the means and institutional structure for the religious dimension of Israel's life, chap. 26 fills this structure with content and ideas. And whereas chap. 12 determines the outward pattern and location of worship, chap. 26 determines the shape of the liturgical prayers, confessions, and theological meaning of worship.

Most of all this content is set out as an expression of the thankfulness with which Israel was to celebrate before God the immensity of the gift that the divine choosing, calling, and preservation of the nation had made possible. From a literary and historical perspective, it should be noted that, contrary to the widely canvassed view of Gerhard von Rad[99] that this confessional recital of God's

99. G. von Rad, "The Form-critical Problem of the Hexateuch," in *The Problem of the Hexateuch and Other Essays,* trans. E. W. T. Dicken (Edinburgh: Oliver & Boyd, 1965) 3.

gracious dealings with Israel had an early origin, its relatively late deuteronomic composition must be fully recognized.[100] It marks a late, and revisionist, view of the meaning of worship for Israel, rather than a very early one. It is pervasively and characteristically an expression of the deuteronomic understanding of worship and of the embedding of all social relationships and moral seriousness in this.

To be an Israelite was to be a beneficiary of a long history of God's gracious providence and care, which had made slaves into free and prosperous citizens. This is the message that echoes through the confessional recital of the past in 25:5-10*a*. This summary account has been constructed and worded on the basis of the outline history of Israel's origins, now contained in Genesis–Numbers. Clearly only a part of the present tradition was available to the deuteronomists, although the main structural outlines had been established in the form with which we are familiar.

26:1-4. The introductory rubric explains the circumstances in which this confessional recital was to be made. A token gift of the firstfruits of the harvest was to be placed in a basket and handed to the priest at the central sanctuary (v. 2). The priest was then to place this basket of gifts before the altar as a gesture acknowledging that the produce belonged to God. It represents a part of what God had given to the worshiper. The occasion for this action was evidently intended to be the Festival of Ingathering, which took place in the late summer (14:22-29). The whole procedure, which is carefully specified, is an open acknowledgment that the land itself is a gift from God. It has acquired this religious significance because it was the land that had been promised on oath by God to the nation's ancestors (v. 3).

The handing over of the basket of fruit and produce is only one part of the prescribed act of worship. Probably rituals that were not all that dissimilar had been performed in honor of the local Baals by non-Israelites. As important as the presentation of the gift was

the confessional declaration showing how the land had been given to Israel's ancestors when they were landless and impoverished.

26:5-10a. These verses contain what can best be described as Israel's confession of faith. It was a kind of creed, declaring the story of God's actions that had shaped the nation's faith. It anchored Israel's possession of the land to its knowledge of God and tied both to events from the nation's past. In this fashion, Israel's faith was inseparably linked to the territory on which the produce had been grown and elicited from the story of the past a message concerning the nature and purpose of God. It was this message that gave assurance, faith, and hope for the future.

Such a confession defines the Being of God in an oblique manner by affirming and recalling those actions through which God had become known and accessible to Israel. It transforms a simple act of giving into an assertion of the gracious and generous nature of God and avers yet again the dependence of the worshiper on God for the sustenance that makes life possible. It renounces, by implication, any claim upon God other than that of God's own gracious and outgoing nature. Israel had been brought into existence by divine grace and continued to be saved by grace alone. In this simple thanksgiving ceremony, the declaration of that grace was reaffirmed as Israel's continually renewed confession of faith.

The detailed elements of the historical summary that constitutes this creed are brief and are drawn from the outline part of the story that binds together the narrative of the present books of Genesis to Joshua. The "wandering Aramaean" (the phrase ארמי אבד [’ărammî ’ōbēd] conveys the sense of "vulnerable" or "destitute," since a landless person was without security of food and protection) was Jacob, who had sought refuge from famine in the land of Egypt. It was while he was in Egypt that his descendants had grown to such numbers that they were reckoned to constitute a "nation." For the deuteronomic authors of this creedal confession, the sheer growth in number of the Israelites is regarded as the primary factor that had elevated them to nationhood.

This affirmation draws attention to the unexpected omission in the recited account

100. See L. Rost, "Das kleine geschichtliche credo," *Das kleine Credo und andere Studien zum Alten Testament* (Heidelberg: Quelle & Meyer, 1965) 11-25; N. Lohfink, "Zum 'kleinen geschichtlichen Credo' Dtn 26,5-9," and "Dt,6-9: Ein Beispiel altisraelitischer Geschichtstheologie," in *Studien zum Deuteronomium und zur deuteronomistischen Literatur I*, SBA 8 (Stuttgart: Katholisches Bibelwerk, 1990) 263-304.

of Israel's beginnings of any mention of the covenant made on Mt. Horeb (Sinai). In the exodus story, it is especially the revelation of God on the sacred mountain and the making of the covenant between the LORD God and Israel that elevated Israel to the status of nation (Exod 19:5-6). Yet here this status is seen as having already been conferred by the growth in number of Jacob's descendants. Surprisingly the report of the making of the covenant on Mt. Horeb is passed over in silence.

For von Rad and Noth, this failure to make reference to the Horeb event was seen as a significant guide to the manner in which Israel's tradition concerning its past had been built up, with the tradition of the revelation on Mt. Horeb being grafted in at a relatively late stage.[101] It is questionable, however, whether this omission is particularly significant and whether it represents a valid conclusion that can be drawn. In any case, once the fact that this creedal recital of the story of Israel's origins is seen to be a deuteronomic composition, then the basis for drawing such conclusions is largely removed.

The reason for the absence of any reference to the events of God's revelation on Mt. Horeb must lie in the theological motives that led to the formulation of this historical summary as a concentration on God's reaching out to Israel. The Horeb revelation, with its code of commandments, together with the entire deuteronomic legislation, which gave sharper definition to the demands of the covenant, belonged to the sphere of Israel's response. In this regard, the entire law code of Deuteronomy 12–26 is viewed as a spelling out of the content and purpose of the revelation made on Horeb. The covenant at Horeb and the covenant made in the plains of Moab (29:1) are not two different covenants, but two occasions for affirming what is viewed essentially as one covenant relationship, brought about by God's election of Israel. Seen in such a light, the purpose of recalling how God had stretched out a mighty hand to bring Israel out of Egypt "with a terrifying display of power and with signs and wonders" (v. 8) was aimed at showing that all Israel possessed had been given to it. Israel's duty to obey these laws was a necessary way of responding to all the privileges to which its continued existence on the land bore testimony. God was Israel's inescapable benefactor to whom it both had been and forever would be totally indebted. Without God, Israel was nothing.

We cannot leave aside consideration of the centrality of the importance of land for the larger perspective of the theology of the deuteronomists. Throughout the years in which the deuteronomic movement came into being and through which it had flourished and gained maturity, the threat of the loss of the land had grown in scale to be a major threat. For much of the nation, it had already become a reality by the time this confessional recital was composed. The roots of this aspect of deuteronomic theology are traceable to the shock and alarm that had arisen when the first Assyrian depredations of Israel's territory had occurred during the latter half of the eight century BCE. By the beginning of the sixth century, when the deuteronomic movement reached maturity, very little of the original territory that had constituted the Davidic-Solomonic empire remained under the control of Jerusalem. In reciting the tradition of how the land had originally been given to Israel, each surviving member of this once great nation was recalling what had been his or her ancestral inheritance.

This fact lends added force to the emphasis on the manner in which Israel had been brought out of Egypt, "with signs and wonders." This distinctive deuteronomic formulation (cf. 4:34; 6:22; 7:19; 11:2-3; 29:2; 34:11)[102] reflects directly the central theme of the plague narrative (Exodus 6–12) and of the providential wonders by which Israel had been sustained in the wilderness. Such actions on God's part served to provide evidence that the LORD was indeed God and that the exercise of divine power was the reason for Israel's escape from Egypt, survival in the wilderness, and conquest of the land. It had not been in Israel's power to achieve these victories, since they were gifts conferred by the power of God.

101. A critical survey of the problem arising from this is presented in E. W. Nicholson, *Exodus and Sinai in History and Tradition* (Oxford: Blackwell, 1973) 1-32.

102. For the significance of this formula in the deuteronomic presentation of the exodus from Egypt, see B. S. Childs, "Deuteronomic Formulae of the Exodus Traditions, *Hebräische Wortforschung. Festschrift zum 80. Geburtstag von Walter Baumgartner,* SVTP 16 (Leiden: E. J. Brill, 1967) 30-39.

Such a theological message clearly had taken on a special relevance at a time when Israel was contemplating the greatness of the past and was staring a more ruinous present in the face. By recalling the gracious divine purpose that had brought Israel into being in the first place, a firm basis for hope for the future was established.

26:10b-15. The second of the confessional recitals by which Israel was to affirm the giving of firstfruits of the land to God and the tithe of the produce for the upkeep of the Levites and the care of the destitute is more functional. The requirement that Israel should tithe the increase of all its produce annually was established in 14:22, whereas here the tithe is reckoned only at the end of a three-year period. The annual levy is then counted as the firstfruits. No specific reference is made to the requirement that this offering be presented at the central sanctuary, as laid down in 14:23 and 15:20, although this should probably be taken for granted.

Throughout the chapter the emphasis is firmly placed in demonstrating that the giving of this triennial tithe for the upkeep of the sanctuary servants and the destitute (for the three categories of the needy: resident aliens, orphans, and widows; cf. 1:16; 14:29) was to be fulfilled "in accordance with your entire commandment that you commanded me" (v. 13) and was not a voluntary act of charity. To this extent the confessional recital represents a stringent declaration of the importance of the tithe as a visible expression of Israel's observance of the law. This conforms also with the requirement that a full declaration be made that the commandments had been kept in their entirety. The offerings had not been spoiled by having been eaten, or set apart, while the worshiper was in an unclean (cultically unacceptable) condition.

In this fashion the offering of the triennial tithe became an act of wider significance than simply providing support for the ministers of Israel's worship and giving charitable assistance to the poor. It was a public expression of the religious good standing and the law-abiding faithfulness of the worshiper. To have been negligent in this offering would have had serious consequences for membership within the community as a whole. The effect was clearly twofold: It both reinforced the importance of the tithe as a sign of the willingness to keep the commandments in their full range, and it ensured that the tithe was not reduced to a mere optional extra that could be treated with indifference.

There is a measure of dignity and open-ended expectation in the prayer with which this second confessional recollection of the past is made: "Look down from your holy habitation, from heaven . . . and bless your people Israel" (v. 15). The past could be remembered with gratitude; the present could be viewed only with anxiety and alarm; the future could now be striven for and secured by renewing obedience to God's commandments.

26:16-19. The concluding section affirms that the covenant between God and Israel, the laws for which have been set out in the preceding chapters and give to this covenant a human dimension, has been agreed upon, sealed, and ratified.[103] Both parties to the covenant are fully aware of the terms and consequences relating to it and have willingly agreed to abide by them. Israel is therefore already bound to the commandments and has been so since its entry into the land.

From a literary perspective, this section completes the framework to the laws that began in 12:1, and it links directly to the exhortation by Moses (11:1-32) for Israel to keep the commandments. The preparatory period in the wilderness has come to an end, and now the promises and expectations for the future need to be fulfilled. There is, therefore, a note of dramatic finality about the time reference: "this very day." The time of preparation is over. The period of fulfillment has begun when obedience must prevail.

From a formal perspective, there can be little reason to doubt that the pattern of covenant making portrayed here, together with much of the terminology employed, has been drawn and adapted from international treaty making between nations and cities. To such treaties, God, or the respective deities named by the signatory parties, could be invoked to act as witness and guardian. The fundamental difference here is that the LORD God is one party to the covenant and Israel is the other. There is no invoking of third parties to act

---

103. See N. Lohfink, "Dt 26,17-19 und die Bundesformel," *Studien zum Deuteronomium und zur deuteronomistischen Literatur I,* SBA 8 (Stuttgart: Katholisches Bibelwerk, 1990) 211-61.

as witnesses or patron overseers, because the LORD God acts throughout as initiator, guardian, and witness to it.

At the same time, there is a solemn and serious intent behind the securing of agreement from all the people of Israel. This is further reinforced in the following section (27:1-10) by affirming that Moses was accompanied by the elders of Israel (27:1) and the Levites (27:9), who act as the people's representatives. All Israel has been drawn into the covenant with the LORD as God since its entry into the land.

We should not overlook the point that the strongly worded formula insisting that "this very day" saw the covenant bond between Israel and God inaugurated is repeated in each and every day in which Israel continues to exist. A renewed immediacy of the commandments is brought into being every time they are read and remembered. By them Israel must live, and no letup in their importance is contemplated. So the repetition of the today formula in vv. 17-18 carries forward to each

new day Israel's obligation, which forms its response to God's covenant making.

It is significant that not only has Israel been bound to God by the covenant and has thereby become committed to keeping the commandments, but also God is bound by what is promised from the divine side. Israel will be set high above all nations (v. 19). The formula that follows is ambiguous whether the reference to "fame, praise, and honor" refers to Israel (NRSV and NIV) or to God (NEB and REB).

Clearly the text displays a certain level of reticence in suggesting that Israel has a claim on God by which the LORD is bound to bless them and to keep them secure in their land. The divine initiative and sovereignty are carefully protected. Nevertheless, the covenant implies that the bond between Israel and God carries obligations for God as well as for Israel. It is God who has taken the initiative to deliver, uphold, and render holy the people of Israel.

REFLECTIONS

Few passages in the book of Deuteronomy have attracted quite so much attention as the short confessional recital of Deut 16:5-10a. The reason for this lies in its history-centered emphasis. It portrays God as "the God who acts" by constructing a brief review of particular past events relating to Israel's origins, which paints a picture of the love, purpose, and power of God. Without defining the attributes of God in the conventional language of classical theology, it nevertheless infers and implies many of those attributes. So the worshiper can sense that he or she knows God because of events that bear directly on the worshiper's own experience and perceptions of the world.

Moreover, because these events are related directly to the situation of the worshiper, making reference to the land on which the crops offered to God had been grown, a bridge is built between the past and the present and between God and human beings. The realization that it was my ancestor who was landless and destitute and that it was my forebears who were slaves and my predecessors who first entered and took possession of this land made faith personal and real.

Seen in this light, the importance of well-planned worship and a well-structured liturgy becomes obvious. Such worship forms a continuous bridge between the generations and between the unseen world of God and the known earthly realm of home and work. Worship becomes a process of bonding in much the same way that an infant becomes bonded to its mother—through care and contact. Far from such worship's being an optional extra, it fulfills a vital role in life. It establishes an indispensable sense of identity, relating the individual to the larger community in which life has to be lived and generating a sense of orientation and hope to the environment and its future. All this in a mere half dozen verses!

To contrast this emphasis on the action of God in directing events with other, especially Canaanite, religious traditions—suggesting that whereas they represented gods of nature, Israel worshiped a God of history—has undoubtedly been a serious misinterpretation of the situation. Undoubtedly it was a widespread feature of much ancient Near Eastern religion, as indeed of religions generally, to claim that a god, known by whatever name, had the power to initiate and control events. It is hard to see how it could have been otherwise if the deity concerned were not regarded as impossibly remote and inaccessible. It belongs to the most basic notion of divinity that gods possess power over events, persons, and processes in this world. At most the contrast suggested has relevance in relation to a degree of emphasis on historical processes or the natural order. In a very real way, most of the world's great religious traditions have focused attention on the power of God, or the gods, to intervene directly in human activities and affairs, either at a national or a personal level. We can understand that a deity who did nothing at all for human beings would attract few worshipers, since it is the consciousness of divine power that lies at the heart of faith.

It is scarcely adequate as an interpretation of the specific setting in Deuteronomy 26 to contrast the idea of a God of history with a God of nature, since the chapter is directly related to the offering of the fruits of the soil. The very fact that the Israelite worshiper was commanded to recite this short summary of Israel's early history as an accompaniment to the presentation of a harvest thank offering relates the gifts of nature very directly to the land and to the historical events through which Israel had come to possess it. It is very much a scholarly abstraction to separate too sharply God's power in nature from God's power in history, since these are simply modern abstractions by which we grasp our experience of the world in its totality.

Absolute contrasts between history and nature and between the God of history and the gods of nature, therefore, are mistaken. We can discern a remarkable wholeness and balance in the Israelite confession of faith. God is related personally and directly to each Israelite's actual situation. Faith is tied indissolubly to the demands, tasks, and necessities of daily life. The world of faith and the world of food, clothing, and territory are one world.

A similar significance attaches to the omission in this confession of any reference to the giving of the law on Mt. Sinai. In view of all that has been noted concerning the importance of the concept of covenant law to Deuteronomy and the fact that this chapter is clearly intended to serve as a kind of summarizing conclusion to the specific legal parts of the book of Deuteronomy, it becomes unthinkable to suppose that the author quite intentionally bypassed any reference to the giving of the law. Only by taking the confession out of its present context altogether could this assumption be made. To some degree, it is probably this fact that has led the author to give added emphasis to the law in the shorter second confession (26:12-15). This was to be recited in accompaniment to the offering of the triennial tithe, where the bringing of the tithe is a public act of avowing that the worshiper intends to keep the commandments in their entirety.

Overall the recital of God's providential care, which has given Israel the land, and the acknowledgment that there are laws that belong to the covenant by which Israel must respond to God belong together. Law and grace are two parallel manifestations of God's commitment to Israel. Obedience to God is not a way of gaining God's favor, but a proper way of responding to it. It is because all of life's most precious assets can be seen as having derived from God that an obedient path of rightly using these assets is a proper human response.

In the theology of Deuteronomy, special importance attaches to this linking together of law and grace in that the book is deeply committed to emphasizing both concepts. It is because God is gracious that God gives the law. To emphasize one aspect to the detriment of the other or to take objection to Deuteronomy because it places the Ten Commandments so high in the divine scheme of things would be to distort the balance the book expresses. All the more does this become evident when we take full account of the way in which the central law code of the book (chaps. 12–26) is given a historical framework and an epilogue that looks to the future of Israel.

The very structure of the law code in chapter 12 begins with instructions for the building of a sanctuary and the setting up of an altar where God's presence would continue to be made available to Israel. This sanctuary would be the location of the divine name, making God accessible to the people, but at the same time providing a center of focus for the people and the place to which prayers could be offered. The same law code then concludes here with a resumption of the instruction to bring to God a thank offering. Law is set within a context of prayer and worship, which themselves form part of the armory of grace that has been given to Israel.

DEUTERONOMY 27:1–30:20

EPILOGUE

OVERVIEW

The section that begins in 27:1 and extends to 30:20 has all the appearance of being a rather randomly shaped miscellany, providing an epilogue to the giving of the law through Moses, which has now been completed in all its essentials. In this epilogue, the four chapters are broadly held together by the themes of blessing and curse, with a marked predominance of the latter. It appears that life under the law has more things that may go amiss and bring pain than it possesses of positive blessings. This appearance of one-sidedness may be partly due to the usefulness of curses as a didactic tool, exercising an admonitory role. It may also be due in part to a consciousness that historically Israel had failed to live up to its obligations to keep God's commandments. To this extent, the book of Deuteronomy carries something of a "last chance" appeal to restore the commandments to their rightful place in the daily agenda of Israel's existence.

Even granted such ameliorating comments regarding the heavy weight of curses that now unfold, it must be clearly stated that, in spite of the formulaic language, the major part of the curse section that colors the epilogue is not a true series of curses at all. In essence, a curse is the invoking of harm and evil upon a specified enemy, or wrongdoer, whether known or unknown. Curses are a form of negative prayer, aimed at inflicting hurt. We find here, however, that a substantial section of the material formulated under the heading of curse is not really a curse at all. It is, rather, a stylized confessional reflection on the historical experience of Israel. It contains much that is a shrill cry of pain for all that Israel has suffered and brings this cry to God in confession, since the commandments have been grievously neglected. It even goes so far as to pinpoint specific events and sufferings that can quite readily be related to known historical events.

DEUTERONOMY 27:1-10, THE LAW IS BOTH BLESSING AND CURSE

COMMENTARY

As an opening presentation of this epilogue to the deuteronomic law code, renewed instructions are given for the setting up of a monument to the commandments at a suitable location west of the river Jordan. This monument is to be located on Mt. Ebal, in fulfillment of the instruction first given in 11:29-30.

Such monuments were not unusual in antiquity; the law tablet of King Hammurabi is undoubtedly the most famous. Special interest attaches here to the precise detail that it

was to be constructed from a heap of large stones covered with plaster (vv. 2, 4) so that the words could more readily be inscribed upon it. Clearly the author was familiar with such a technique of rendering a stone surface more amenable to an ancient script.

The directive in v. 2, which insists upon the stone's being set up "on the day that you cross over the Jordan into the land that the LORD your God is giving you," certainly points to a location close to the western bank of the Jordan, which would appear to exclude the more distant location of Mt. Ebal. This was close to Shechem, a city that repeatedly appears as a central location of Israel's earliest covenant traditions. Verse 4 understands the law table set up on Mt. Ebal to be a second set of memorial symbols, in addition to the stones set up immediately after the Israelites' crossing of the Jordan. There would appear to be some confusion, then, with the stone monuments set up at Gilgal, on the west bank of the Jordan, which were directly associated with Israel's entry into the land (Josh 4:1-9). Either the time reference is to be understood very loosely as indicating no more than "the time when . . ." or more likely the report here represents a drawing together of the tradition concerning the ancient stone circle of Gilgal with the inscribing of the Ten Commandments on stone tablets (Deut 5:22) and the knowledge of a monumental pillar set up on the sacred Mt. Ebal.

The example of such law monuments as the law code of Hammurabi would indicate that they could serve not only as memorials to great rulers and their achievements, but also as important territorial boundary markers, signifying the rule of justice that prevailed in the land. They laid claim to the land as a region in which the rule of law was upheld and, when set out in the name of and bearing the image of the ruler of the land, they affirmed the justice of that ruler. In the case presented here, the fact of such a monument declared that justice in the land was inseparably linked to the name of the LORD God.

From the perspective of the history and development of law, it is noteworthy that this tradition reflects, even in a rather incomplete fashion, the long-established convention that related law to territory. The monument indicated that the law of God given through Moses represented the law of the land, modifying and extending the connection between law and established political authority.

Mount Ebal (v. 4) was traditionally associated with the curse, whereas Mt. Gerizim was the sacred mountain of the Samaritan community. It is then a matter of some importance that the text of the Samaritan Pentateuch records the name of Mt. Gerizim here. It may be that the Hebrew (MT) text is the original one and that this was subsequently altered in the Samaritan tradition to accord

directly with Samaritan territorial claims. It is equally possible, however, that the Samaritan recording of the name "Gerizim" here is the older tradition and that the change was introduced after the break between Samaritans and Jews had occurred.

The building of an altar constructed from natural, uncut stones on which sacrifices of burnt offerings were to be made is prescribed in vv. 5-7. The instruction represents something of an enigma, since the deuteronomic law of cult centralization explicitly precluded the making and use of any such altar for formal cultic worship outside "the place which the LORD your God will choose." This was clearly a reference to Jerusalem, so that an altar on Mt. Ebal (or Gerizim) would have contradicted such a limitation. It certainly appears strange that the author here appears to be indifferent to the demand for the centralized control of the cultus at one place. Either he was well aware that an altar had once been in use on Mt. Ebal, or it may simply be the case that an altar on Mt. Ebal may have been regarded as permissible, and even necessary, until such time as the ark had been brought into Jerusalem. The historical narratives recounting Israel's actions immediately after the conquest are fully aware that an authorized cultus had been in use from the earliest crossing of the Jordan.

The story of the setting up of this monument to the law of the covenant reflects the intensity of the author's concern to relate the keeping of the commandments to the formal conduct of worship. The horizons of the deuteronomic author are firmly bounded by the political history of the Israelite people as a nation, together with all the institutional features of a national life. These included acceptance of a single, unified government that could administer law and a sanctuary through which the cultus could be regulated. At the same time, this law is presented as the product of a divine revelation that was made prior to the formation of the nation in all the range of its territorial and social expression. Accordingly, the law is seen to have existed before Israel's organized national life, since the formation of the nation was seen to be the consequence of the covenant between the LORD God and Israel. So, in the eyes of the deuteronomic authors of the book of the law, the entire territory west of the Jordan that Israel occupied was "the land of the law." It was wholly appropriate, therefore, that from the very outset of Israel's entry into the land, the claim of the law upon it should be affirmed and memorialized.

REFLECTIONS

Long before formal history ever came to be written, human beings marked their achievements and sent signals into the future by the raising of monuments. Some of these monuments, in the form of sacred stone pillars and circles of great stones arranged in a meaningful pattern, still exist. They stand as mute witnesses to human triumphs and values that can be recaptured only very inadequately. They speak of a sense of the divine power and purpose for humankind that could be visualized and expressed in no other way than through the setting up of a symbol that could not be ignored.

Ancient Israel was familiar with such stone circles and pillar monuments that had become familiar landmarks by the beginning of the biblical period and were already ancient by that time. The pillar that stood on Mt. Ebal was evidently among the most familiar of such historic landmarks, while the great circle of stones that stood beside the river Jordan at Gilgal was another. But what was it that these great monuments witnessed to? Even to think of them in terms of merely human achievements and triumphs of early engineering skill would be to distort and falsify the message they expressed. In truth, they were human achievements, setting forth as they did signs of the immense physical effort and engineering skills that made their erection possible. Yet the intention behind their creation lay elsewhere, since it was to point to the world behind and beyond that which can be seen. They sought to embody a transcendent meaning in a very earthly symbol.

For the deuteronomic authors, mindful of the long traditions that had made the prominent heights of Mt. Ebal and Mt. Gerizim into major national monuments, the question was what they signified. It seems likely that a great variety of popular interpretations existed, linked to the separate tribes and clans who visited these sites. This consciousness of mixed tribal and partisan traditions is still later reflected in the manner in which the later Jewish and Samaritan communities saw in these two distinct mountain heights an expression of their own jealously guarded traditions.

For the deuteronomic authors, however, the twin realities of these mountains testified to the twin realities for which Israel had come into existence. These were the law of Moses, which constituted Israel's national charter, and the blessing and curses that such a law activated into real life.

The introductory speeches ascribed to Moses have emphasized well enough the either/or nature of the challenges and decisions facing Israel. The very setting of the deuteronomic law book on the eve of Israel's entry into the land highlights this sense of a choice facing Israel and its future. There was a path leading to blessing and success and a path leading to failure and despair. The author of the epilogue to the book now seeks with considerable artistry and skill to focus attention on this existential dimension of the future. Just as every person must choose between two paths (cf. Psalm 1), so also now an entire nation found itself at a similar point in its history. The monument on the mountain of Ebal served as a kind of signpost from the past, continually pointing to that fork in the road where the momentous decision for or against God's covenant had to be made.

The concept of the law as a gift of divine grace, which makes possible a life lived in an aura of blessing, points to an understanding of human existence that recognizes that life has a potency. Whereas we have grown accustomed to thinking of infancy and childhood as an age of innocence from which we slowly fall away as experience and failures make us conscious of what we might have become, but failed to be, the biblical perspective is rather different. Infancy and childhood are ages of potency, and all our life is a stage of becoming.

Just as the deuteronomic author could look back on the beginning period of Israel's history as a time of challenge and choices, so also each human life is a continual process of meeting such challenges and making choices. It belongs to our human condition to "become what we are," which is a child of God, created in the divine image and destined to seek and find fellowship with the Creator. In order to achieve this, however, it is necessary to follow that pattern and way of life that accords with the divine image and purpose. So there is a need for God's law to serve as a map by which to trace a route through the complex paths of life.

It is in this context that the Old Testament perspective concerning the centrality of Torah, which means "guidance" or "instruction" as fully as it means "law," must be understood. Law becomes a directive for living, but it is a directive that speaks of curse as well as blessing. The contrast between the two serves as a warning that Torah is not simply about knowing what is right, but choosing the right path. To know what is right is the gift and grace of the law. Yet knowing is not the same as choosing and doing. Failure to respond in a positive fashion means that the very law that was designed to bring blessing becomes a monument of misery and despair by reminding us of all that we failed to achieve.

The tensions between law and grace, with which the apostle Paul wrestles so vehemently in Romans and Galatians, are not tensions that first emerged in the New Testament period. Already they have begun to come to the surface in a quite sharp and pointed fashion in the book of Deuteronomy. It is one of the advantages of turning back to Deuteronomy in the light of Paul's inner conflicts and turmoil to see why law is both a means of grace and a threat of curse.

For those setting out on the path of entry into the land promised to Israel's ancestors, the law appeared at first as the indispensable key to success and achievement. Yet for those, like the deuteronomic authors, looking back over what had happened since the death of Moses there was a consciousness of failure and disaster. The law had been the guidebook Israel had failed to follow. Accordingly the epilogue to the code of laws (chaps. 27–30) brings a consciousness of this fact very forcefully to the reader. The book of Deuteronomy is an optimistic document, setting out a story full of promise and hoped-for achievement. Yet hidden away in many of its warning speeches and poetry is a very gloomy and despairing note. It is a warning concerning the curse of the law and the pain of regret felt by authors surveying the prospect of a world that might have been. Only by coming to terms with this note of gloom and near despair does a fresh message of hope and renewal come to the surface.

DEUTERONOMY 27:11-26, BEHAVIOR NOT PERMITTED IN ISRAEL

COMMENTARY

The general assertion that disobedience to the law of God could place an individual Israelite under the curse now leads to a highly distinctive formal series of curses in which particular forms of conduct are outlawed. The careful formal structure and the particular deeds that are forbidden strongly suggest that the series was at one time an independent formulation. It would then have been introduced at this point because it provides an excellent illustration of the way in which disobedience to the law could result in a person's being placed under a curse.[104] It is also noteworthy for the manner in which it shows how the set forms of public worship could be used to reinforce and influence moral conduct, especially over conduct that might appear marginal and difficult to control by any other means.

Among modern scholars, Albrecht Alt,[105] in his pioneering study of the form of the Ten Commandments, drew special attention to this series of twelve curses since they illustrated how an appeal to divine authority and an implicit threat of direct punishment from God could be used to shape fundamental matters of social behavior. In arguing that the Ten Commandments were originally composed for instruction and declaration within a form of worship, a feature that had earlier been proposed by Mowinckel, Alt drew attention to this dodecalogue of curses. Although there is some overlap with the contents of the commandments, it is not specifically the particular actions condemned that provide the point of comparison. A feature that is explicit in some of these curses is that they concern wrongful actions that would have been carried out in secret. Alt went further than to accept that this was true of those deeds where their private and secret nature was explicitly mentioned and proposed that it was actually true of all. There are substantive reasons for thinking that this was the case and that the actions outlawed in these curses, with the exception of the first and last, which are almost certainly additional to an original ten, were all deeds that would have been carried out privately and away from public knowledge. Such an understanding has a significant bearing on the interpretation of certain of them, which might otherwise be understood more broadly.

The reason why these particular actions are singled out and made the subject of publicly recited curses, to which the individual members of Israel are required to respond with a cry of "Amen," is that they dealt with matters that could not reasonably have been dealt with by the processes of law. This was not because the actions were not "illegal" in the sense that they were contrary to the commands and spirit of the law. Rather, it was precisely because these actions were carried out privately that it was highly improbable that any formal public action could have been taken against them.

It is noteworthy that no specific penalty is attached to these curses, since "living under a curse" must have been regarded as a dangerous and potentially serious condition. That it necessarily carried with it the implication that such persons would have been outlawed from the community, or even regarded as being under sentence of death, can by no means be taken for granted. It would have been left open as to what effect the curse would bring.

The form of the curse was not the only way in which the rituals and formal proceedings of the cultus were employed to influence individual conduct in a direct and publicly recognized fashion. We find that admission to the Temple could also carry with it strong admonitions regarding the forms of conduct that God hated and would render a person unfit to appear in the divine presence in the sanctuary (cf. Psalms 15; 27). There are good reasons, therefore, for accepting that, in a slightly modified form, this dodecalogue of curses once existed as a separate composition and that, like the short listing of the Ten Commandments, it was intended as a means of reminding worshipers of the moral demands of God's holiness. God could be expected to take action against the person who knowingly flouted the divine order of life.

There is little reason to suppose that this list of curses for public recital was very much earlier in its origin than the time of the deuteronomic authors of the law book. It has then been incorporated into the epilogue to the law code as a formal example of the way in which the law made it essential to distinguish between following the path of blessing and following the way of the curse.

Almost certainly the present list of twelve curses has been enlarged from a more original list in which only ten such curses were included.[106] The first, which concerns the general prohibition against worshiping alien

104. For the relationship between these curses and the law, see E. Bellefontaine, "The Curses of Deuteronomy 27: Their Relationship to the Prohibitive," in *A Song of Power and the Power of Song: Essays on the Book of Deuteronomy,* ed. D. L. Christensen, SBT 3 (Winona Lake, Ind.: Eisenbrauns, 1993) 256-68.

105. Alt, "The Origins of Israelite Law," 114-22.

106. H. Gese, "Der Dekalog als Ganzheit betrachtet," *Vom Sinai zum Zion. Alttestamentliche Beiträge zur biblischen Theologie* (Munich: Chr. Kaiser, 1974) 71-72.

gods, and the last, which is little more than a repeated summary of all the preceding prohibitions, have then been added in order to bring the number up to twelve. The reason for this proceeding can only be that it was felt appropriate to make the number of curses equivalent to the number of the tribes of Israel, whose representatives are held to have been present for the public recital of the curses.

27:11-14. The introduction to the list in vv. 11-13 describes the twelve tribes of Israel as gathered together and divided into two groups of six. One group is then placed on Mt. Gerizim for the blessing, and the second group is located on Mt. Ebal for the curses. In this way, the author has made the declaration of the list of twelve curses fit directly into a narrative context relating to the Israelites' entry into the land, the designation of the two historic mountains as centers of blessing and curse, and the presence of all twelve tribes in the land after their crossing of the Jordan.

The tribal names have been taken from the list of the sons of Jacob, set out in the narrative of Genesis 29–30. The first group appears to be the more favored tribes, which is appropriate to their proximity to the mount of blessing. These comprise the sons born to Jacob's wives, Leah and Rachel. The second group is made up of the descendants of Jacob's concubines, together with Reuben and Zebulon. The first group was the tribes who had settled in the central and southern territories, which corresponds with their favored associations of blessing. The latter group had settled the less favored territory of Galilee and the Transjordan.

Overall it appears that this assembling of representatives of the tribes, if not the whole nation of tribes, in such a massive convocation is a literary device of the deuteronomic author. It suits the broad theological affirmation that all Israel equally came under the law and so all were equally subject to the contingencies of blessing and curse. It was also a point at issue that the list of twelve activities subjected to the formula of curse were prohibited to all Israel.

27:15. There are strong reasons for concluding that the first and last of the twelve curses have been added to an original list of ten. The first of them relates to the setting up

of an image "in secret," presenting a particular variation of the more familiar prohibition against the use of any image at all in worship. It could have been the case that, since the series of curses relates to actions and activities that were unlikely to be dealt with by the normal processes of public prosecution and punishment, a scribe felt it appropriate that this offense, which was taken by the deuteronomic authors with the utmost seriousness, also deserved to be included.

By establishing the nature of the first offense as one committed in secret, we can recognize that the formal use of ritual curses against potential offenders was intended to operate as an adjunct to the law. Actions that the law was unlikely to deal with are nonetheless reprehensible, and those who commit them deserve to be outlawed from the community.

The curses, therefore, serve as a form of public condemnation, inviting ostracism from the community and asking God to punish the offender, but without offering any clear indication of how this would come about. To a considerable extent, the instruction that those assembled are required to respond to the levitical declaration of the curse with a loud "Amen" shows that it was a matter of individual conscience and sense of guilt that made the curse effective. At the same time, the recital of such curses gave a powerful declaration of the will of the community, affirming that those who committed certain actions were banished. There is, then, a degree of affinity with the use of the formula that declared certain objects or actions "abhorrent to the LORD," thereby showing that they were wholly contrary to the divine will. They caused offense and a sense of outrage.

27:16. The curse upon those guilty of dishonoring their parents relates directly to the offense covered by the laws of Exod 21:17 and Lev 20:9. It is obviously closely connected with the commandment of the Decalogue that enjoins the honoring of parents (5:16). The fact that essentially all of these rulings deal with substantially the same moral issue of showing respect for parents, making provision for them, and acting so as to maintain the strength and integrity of the household is significant. Clearly an outright act of cursing parents, or rejecting them when they became infirm, was a particularly detestable offense. At the same time, the different verbal formulations used indicate that whether a positive or negative construction was used was a relatively minor issue.

27:17. The prohibition against the removal of a neighbor's boundary marker concerns an issue that has already been dealt with, potentially very severely, in the legislative ruling of 19:14. Its reappearance here further demonstrates the sensitivity to the problem that was felt and further illustrates the point that it was one for which effective action through processes of law was difficult to obtain. Both this and the preceding curse relate to forms of conduct that would have been undertaken furtively and in private, where it would be difficult to produce satisfactory proof to enable action to be taken.

27:18-19. Much the same background of furtive, unprovable misconduct is illustrated by the deliberate misleading of a blind person, which is cursed in v. 18. It is closely paralleled by the admonition of Lev 19:14, which deals with abuse of both blind and deaf persons. It is linked here to a general injunction not to deprive handicapped or disadvantaged members of the community from access to the public processes of justice (v. 19), which belongs alongside the widely expressed deuteronomic concern to grant to such persons the same privileges that other members of the community enjoyed (14:29; 16:14).

27:20-23. The curses set out here deal with sexual relationships. The curse upon sexual contact between a man and his stepmother (v. 20) must be compared with the law of 22:30, which precludes a marriage between two such persons. This raises the issue of whether the conduct that is made the subject of the curse envisages a marriage or simply a casual sexual encounter. In view of the preceding curses, which relate to misconduct of a secretive and furtive nature, it would appear that it is the latter situation that is envisaged. Since a marriage with a stepmother, who is probably assumed to be widowed, was already precluded, the intention here may have been to prohibit the sexual abuse of a woman who is likely a member of the same household as the man upon whom the curse is laid. By taking advantage of a woman who was a dependent member of the

household, the culprit could probably escape public detection.

A similar background of private, secretive activity would then be covered by the curse upon anyone who had had sexual contact with an animal (v. 21). An earlier legal prohibition against such acts is found in the laws of the Book of the Covenant in Exod 22:19. It seems highly likely that such bizarre sexual acts once formed part of rituals aimed at securing special power through the life force present in the animal. It would have displayed some of the same reasoning that made the visual portrayal of various forms of mixed human and animal creatures a prominent feature of the religious symbolism of ancient Egyptian religion. A more complete and wide-ranging list of forbidden sexual relationships is set out in Lev 20:13-21.

It seems highly probable that this list of curses against forbidden sexual behaviors was not intended to be a redrafting of marginal cases relating to family law. Israelite custom had at one time clearly not precluded marriage to a halfsister (Gen 20:12; 2 Sam 13:13), although a later prohibition is found in Lev 18:9; 20:17. Rather, the curses were aimed at prohibiting sexual abuse, especially of vulnerable female members of a household who would be unlikely to have effective means of redress against a senior male. Unmarried sisters, halfsisters, and widowed in-laws were all likely to have been part of a household and, therefore, susceptible to sexual abuse. It is certainly a prominent feature that the list of curses regarding such actions focuses directly on the issue of sexual relationships.

27:24. The extent of the harm inflicted on another person covered by this curse is not precisely defined. The RSV's "strikes" has been strengthened in the NRSV to "strikes down" (נכה *nākâ*). Clearly a violent blow leading to death or serious injury is primarily in mind, although it is not explicitly spelled out whether there was any intent to kill. That such an act is said to be carried out in secret points to a carefully planned attempt to inflict harm upon another.

27:25. Bribery was a persistent problem throughout the ancient world, and it appears only to have increased in its effectiveness with the introduction of more complex and sophisticated legal systems. The particular offense of receiving payment to shed innocent blood would have covered payments made for "contract killing," but more probably it refers to the committing of perjury in a capital lawsuit that could lead to the death penalty's being imposed upon an innocent person, thereby amounting to murder.

27:26. The concluding curse effectively summarizes all the preceding ones and serves to reinforce the level of authority that attaches to them. It adds nothing new and appears to have been introduced primarily with a view to increasing the number of such curses to twelve, thereby matching the number of tribes said to have been present to affirm them.

Overall this series of curses, in which the entire community bound itself to refrain from actions that might otherwise go unpunished, was clearly intended to augment the efficacy of the law, rather than to add to its demands in any specifically detailed fashion. Some of the conduct that is outlawed would have been undetected because of its secretive nature, but other actions may have lacked

effective witnesses to make a reliable prosecution possible.

The formulation as a series of curses is essentially artificial and achieves little more than the simple declaration that certain types of conduct were "abhorrent to" God. A curse in the fullest sense was believed to possess a measure of dynamic efficacy, invoking divine action to harm a specified person or group. Here the curse form has been converted essentially into a didactic device to draw popular attention to conduct the community as a whole would not tolerate. The popular response whereby each member present acknowledged the wrongfulness of such prohibited actions is expressed by the utterance of the single word *Amen.* This in itself was used as a way of personalizing and directing the message of the curse to each person present. What we find here appears to have been a further didactic means introduced by the deuteronomists to fill some of the gaps brought on by a laxity in moral order and family discipline. The deuteronomists recognized quite openly that there were several important areas of conduct that could not appropriately be handled by the established legal arrangements.

REFLECTIONS

It is a significant and thought-provoking point of awareness that the Old Testament has frequently been characterized by Christians as a book of law. The book of Deuteronomy, possibly rather more directly than any other Old Testament writing, appears to exemplify this commitment to law. Yet we have already had much opportunity to note that the deuteronomic authors were primarily interested in presenting law as both a gift of the grace of God, which had brought Israel into existence in the first place, and a way through which Israel could enjoy a life of blessing. It would be a mistake, then, to interpret the book of Deuteronomy as a whole as presenting law as a kind of negative contrast to the concept of divine love and an ethic of grace.

So in a very profound sense, the book of Deuteronomy, like the Old Testament as a whole, is a book about law. Yet law itself has more than one sense, which becomes very complex when put in a theological context. In the first, and most obvious, manner, law refers to those statutes that represent pronouncements of a legal system through which human conduct in society is to be governed. It stretches across many areas of conduct in families and in business as well as between neighbors. It regulates all sorts of morally reprehensible behavior, from violence and wanton killing to cheating and taking advantage of disadvantaged and helpless members of the community.

For any citizen of the modern world, the administration and trust in a system of law are vital if a community is to live at peace with itself and if the full potential of human opportunities is to be realized. At the same time, we are all too conscious that law can be a very blunt and imperfect instrument by which human conduct and affairs are to be regulated. Laws have to be administered fairly, and, in much of modern life, it becomes impossible to devise a law to cover every situation that might arise. We have become all too conscious of these problems in connection with such painful issues as sexual abuse within a family and with problems of corruption among those who are called upon to uphold the law. Quite obviously the knowledge that "there is a law against it!" does not mean that particular forms of undesirable conduct never take place. It only means that the law cannot do everything.

It is against such a backdrop that we can see the considerable relevance of the series of curses in Deuteronomy 27. It would appear as a strange and objectionable proceeding were we to conduct such a public ritual of cursing in a modern setting. Yet we are forced to do many things that are surprisingly similar. We are called upon to educate people concerning undesirable forms of conduct; we are impelled to teach respect for the law and for the needs and rights of other human beings. Education for right conduct is as important as the legal system that is called upon to enforce it.

We can certainly go further than this, since it is also a prevalent modern concern that legal systems are often very clumsy and inadequate social institutions for handling many personal matters. To mislead a blind person on the road so that he or she stumbles into a wall or a ditch will appear to most people a very cruel form of a practical joke. Yet it would make little sense to formulate a law against such behavior, for the root of the problem lies in a lack of compassion and an inability of some persons to empathize with the needs and difficulties of others. Only by educating for compassion and for respect for each individual can we address some behaviors. Such concerns require instruction, example, and teaching, rather than laws.

In a more deeply philosophical vein, this list of public curses highlights the awareness that all systems of law must ultimately reckon with a fundamental understanding of human nature. The dignity of all human beings, and, therefore, their right to command respect and compassion, is in the final resort a question for theology and not simply a matter of what is educationally useful. The understanding that human beings are fashioned in "the image of God" (Gen 1:26) is a basic biblical assertion that seeks to encapsulate this sense of human dignity and human potential. It is in educating to declare the religious nature and destiny of humankind that both the importance and the limitations of human laws can best be understood.

DEUTERONOMY 28:1-68, GOD'S ORDER: BLESSING AND CURSE

COMMENTARY

The surprisingly long series of blessings and curses found in Deuteronomy 28 provokes discussion and comment on account of its somber and threatening tone. Curses outnumber blessings by a considerable margin and give the impression that the overall effect of the deuteronomic legislation was predominantly negative. There were more things that could go wrong than could go right! There is undoubtedly some justification for this impression, and a detailed examination of several of the features of the list of curses will show how and why it has arisen.

It is important, therefore, that we remember that this section forms part of the epilogue to the law code; and to a significant extent it reflects an awareness of how Israel has fared under the law. There is, in consequence, a sense of failure and non-achievement since Israel has not kept the law. This sensitivity to failure and to the belief that in retrospect the law of Moses had proved to be Israel's undoing can, however, only be regarded as a superficial and limited sense of what this long section of blessing and curses has to teach.

From a formal perspective two issues have dominated discussion of the chapter and have a very direct bearing on its interpretation. The first of these concerns the presence of comparable lists of threats and curses in ancient Near Eastern vassal treaties. Considerable discussion has taken place over the extent to which the overall shape of Deuteronomy, as well as several of its basic constituent parts, have been influenced by, and even directly adapted from, these vassal treaties. Certainly in the later Assyrian treaty documents, for example, the enumeration of a long and deliberately intimidating list of curses that will befall the vassal should the demands of the treaty not be complied with is very marked. These certainly bear comparison with the curses that appear in Deuteronomy 28:1, although there is no reason for supposing that specific wording was adapted to one from the other. From a literary perspective, therefore, it is undoubtedly conceivable that the authors of Deuteronomy were familiar with the employment of a series of threatening curses of warning and admonition to encourage the vassal to stick to the terms of the treaty.

However, to concede this point draws attention to a rather formal literary aspect of Deuteronomy, and it seems highly probable that the addition of the blessings and curses in this chapter was made at a relatively late stage in the composition of the book. They do not fit the nature and content of the laws that have occupied the central part of the book since these laws prescribe their own punishments and penalties where necessary and do not need additional reinforcement by a further series of punitive threats. It is primarily the setting of the law code within the larger context of a review of Israel's history and its experience as a nation that has occasioned the inclusion of these curses.

This perception is more fully confirmed when we look at the particular content of the curse lists. For the most part they cannot truly be regarded as curses in the formal sense at all but are more in the nature of a historical reflection on the history of Israel and its present situation. Even the actual verbal formulation as curses is abandoned throughout most of them so that we are presented with a broad declaration that failure to keep the terms of the covenant law will result in punishment. This is then followed by a detailed look at specific circumstances relevant to Israel in this light.

It becomes clear from close examination that the present chapter is not from a single hand. An initial section in vv. 1-46 represents the foundational basis of the whole. Even this primary unit bears all the hallmarks of having been built up around a relatively concise core text that has then undergone expansion. The concluding verses are then introduced as an editorial transition piece preparing for the historical perspective that follows. The intention throughout appears to be essentially didactic and reflective, rather than offering a real attempt to provide additional warnings to Israel concerning the dangers of any failure to keep the law. Although there are some overlaps with the kind of admonition contained in the secular vassal-treaty form, the situation in Deuteronomy is essentially of a different nature. Overall there is a broad desire to teach the seriousness of the law, closely comparable with the general message that is to be found in the prologue to the law book in the speeches of Moses in chapters 6–9.

A second section has subsequently been joined on in vv. 47-57 that gives a further and noticeably even more threatening tone to the curses. It spells out with added detail the horrors of life under the curse, although it refrains altogether from using the formal structure of cursing or the relevant vocabulary. Rather it points to events that have clearly already befallen Israel and seeks to understand these in the light of the situation threatened by the curse for those who disobey the law. In such a setting the notion of curse is little more than a very open and broad way of coming to terms with the mysterious nature of evil and the specific misfortunes that have overtaken Israel.

A further section has then been added even later in vv. 58-68, offering yet more detailed instances of the almost unbearable pain of life under God's curse. It quite directly relates this to the post–587 BCE circumstances when many former citizens of Judah had been forced to become refugees, fleeing into exile and slavery. A sense of inevitable retribution for disobedience to God's covenant law is provided by the fact that these very refugees sought asylum back in Egypt, willingly selling themselves as slaves and so reversing completely the story of how Israel's ancestors had been rescued by the hand of God from there. Because the present generation of Israel had failed to remember that its ancestors had been slaves in Egypt, they were compelled by the irony of divine justice to find out what that really meant!

We are certainly faced here with a progressive series of literary additions. The second of these (vv. 47-57) bears unmistakable indications that it was composed shortly after the siege and destruction of Jerusalem in 588–87 BCE. Its message illustrating the agony and suffering of the people of Judah shows significant connections of theme and purpose with the book of Lamentations.

Similarly the third section (vv. 58-68) bears all the marks of having been written later still, when the pain and wretchedness of those refugees who had fled from Judah could be readily envisaged. There is no doubt a deliberate element of poetic license in this in which the author has imaginatively reconstructed the plight of destitute people selling themselves into slavery rather than facing death by starvation. Nevertheless, the verses have been designed to fit the present context very skillfully, alerting the reader to interpret the text, not in a documentary and historical fashion as a testimony of the last days of Moses, but as a contemporary warning of the plight into which fellow-Israelites had fallen in recent days. Once again the author collapses the long historical distance between the men and women who followed Moses through the wilderness and were awaiting the moment to enter the land and those who were experiencing the present time of distress. Israel is one Israel, both laterally through the twelve tribes and also vertically through its many generations.

Both of these later sections can be seen to be rhetorically molded literary compositions aimed at offering contemporary relevance for the reader concerning the reality of the curses that have been listed. By drawing on memories and events from the reader's recent past, they serve to intensify the message that disobedience to God's law would bring the most terrifying consequences. For the author these events served to confirm the urgency of the warnings. Only the first of the sections retains the formal blessing-curse structure, and even

this exhibits substantial modifications from the true curse form.

From a historical and theological viewpoint this series of three rhetorical "curses" is a forward-looking epilogue that abandons the narrative perspective of the situation in the plains of Moab and establishes the setting for the second giving of the law. Already the admonitory addresses in chapters 6–9 have made clear that Israel faced a decisive either/or challenge. To obey the law that Moses had given would bring success and lasting security and peace; to flout its demands would conversely lead to appalling suffering and catastrophe. The epilogue now draws on recent memory to confirm this very point.

It is arguable that a first intimation of this more somber note of warning for Israel is to be found in the first address concerning blessing and curse in vv. 1-46. Here for the first time is a marked indication that curse will, in the end, prove to be a more powerful feature of Israel's history than blessing. As soon as we move on to examine the addresses of vv. 47-57 and 58-68, we are made yet more conscious of the predominance of curse. Moreover, it becomes incontrovertibly clear that we are no longer contemplating possible events of an uncertain future but instead are looking back on certain events of a grievously painful past. Not only is there a wealth of circumstantial detail that carries us beyond the generalizations of hard choices, but we are also given terrifying pictures of recent events. This is especially the case in the last discourse. No longer is the question: "Will curse rather than blessing be the fate of Israel?" Instead, there is a deeper theological anxiety that asks whether God can have any future purpose for Israel at all, if it must lead to such terrible personal suffering. Has not the law itself become a curse, and has it not acted as a millstone around Israel's neck to plunge it into a whirlpool of disaster?

28:1-46. The primary address in 28:1-44 begins in vv. 1-14 with a restatement of the meaning and possibility of blessing that would accrue to those who obeyed the commandments. The theme throughout is transparently clear and thoroughly deuteronomic in its character: "If you will obey the LORD your God by diligently observing all his commandments" (vv. 1, 13b-15). The commandments hold the key to understanding life, prosperity, and security. All aspects of human need are claimed to be covered by the comprehensive sweep of God's law since they relate to family life, agriculture (v. 4), and military success (v. 7). The message is twofold in its thrust: The righteousness of the law is the key to human happiness; therefore, the opposite truth must also be entertained, that where such success and prosperity are lacking there must have been a neglect of obedience to the commandments.

The somber note of this necessary deduction is then spelled out explicitly by the curse formulations of vv. 16-44. The concluding summary in vv. 45-46 then serves as a transition piece reiterating a conclusion that has become obvious: Disobedience will bring terrible consequences. The verses prepare the reader for the harsher message to come in the sections that follow.

So far as the basic unit of vv. 1-44 is concerned, we are clearly still very much in the theological thought world of the deuteronomists. Retribution for good to those who obey and for ill to those who disobey is the key feature. We hear the confident deuteronomic doctrine that God is wholly just and fair in all dealings with the people of Israel. The covenant has made the terms clear so that there can be no impugning of the idea of the divine justice. Israel can remain assured that it receives from God only what it deserves.

The date of composition of this section is best indicated by the reference in v. 36 to the removal of the king of Judah to a foreign land. This is most probably a reference to the imprisonment and removal into exile of King Jehoiachin in 598 BCE (cf. 2 Kings 20), rather than to the events of 587 BCE when King Zedekiah was removed from his royal throne in Jerusalem altogether and taken to Babylon and to his death there. Had these latter disastrous and final consequences for the Davidic kingship already taken place, it seems unlikely that the lesser misfortune that befell Jehoiachin would alone have been referred to. If this is the case, then the original unit must have been composed during the period of political upheaval consequent upon Judah's first disastrous encounter with the might of Babylon in 598 BCE and the even worse disasters of 587 BCE.

The language employed in this lengthy disquisition on the possibilities of either blessing or curse, especially that used in the much shorter blessing section, is strongly reminiscent of the celebratory language of worship. Conversely, the language of the curse section gives explicit expression to the kinds of misfortune that could readily have been invoked at almost any time upon Israel's enemies. All that has changed is that these curses envisage Israel itself becoming the LORD's enemy. To a significant extent it is arguable that the whole section represents a particular adaptation of the kind of prophetic threat/curse that a cultic prophet would have been expected to deliver against the enemies of Israel.

Such "national" curses were simply developments of the more personal style of curse in which an individual invoked evil upon another in the name of a particular deity. The belief that words had power in themselves, especially when reinforced by the power of a god, meant that they were believed to be capable of bringing harm upon those who were named as the targets of the curse.

There is in this deuteronomic setting a considerable shift from this primitive stage of word-magic since the belief in the power of words to bring harm is wholly subsumed under the larger notion that it is the law of God alone that has the power to bring blessing or to inflict harm. There can then be no other, unforeseen power that would occasion harm; still less could the belief be upheld that random curses brought with them power to inflict injury and hurt.

In spite of the overweight of curses over blessings in vv. 1-44, there is nonetheless a profoundly rational and systematizing theology undergirding it. It shares much in common with the view of the authors of proverbial wisdom, who entertained a strong confidence in the justice that pervaded all things and in the effective outworking of a pattern of retribution in daily life.

The transitional unit in vv. 45-46 introduces into the message of blessing and curse a more deeply disturbing warning regarding the power of God's commandments. When things go wrong because Israel has disobeyed the law, there will be no avenue of escape from the terrible and inevitable retribution that will come. Justice will be done, and it will be seen to have been done when Israel remembers the commandments of God and surveys its own history in their light. The commandments themselves will be the "sign and portent" of disaster for future generations. The wording is very significant since it carries a deliberate echo of the triumphant assurance with which Deuteronomy had recorded the story of how the LORD God had brought up Israel from Egypt "with signs and wonders."

Respecting the epilogue to the law code, the message of 28:1-46 is of a different theological character from the admonitions of chapters 6–9. The latter are prospective in viewpoint and educative in intention. The former, however, is retrospective of Israel's actual history and serves as a theodicy, justifying God's ways with Israel. What has happened is what could have been expected to happen in view of Israel's behavior since it entered the land.

The predominance of curses over blessings in chapter 28 can then find its explanation in the conviction that this is in fact how Israel's history has proved to be. Disaster had come, and what was needed at this juncture was an explanation for it. Where many had simply drawn the conclusion that the LORD God of Israel was impotent when faced with the conflicting power of the gods of surrounding nations, the deuteronomic author endeavors to reassert the truth of the LORD's sovereignty. Israel had been called by God to fulfill the demands of the law. Now it must be content to be judged by it.

In the light of this distinctive use of a series of curses to present a theodicy of the final collapse of the first Israelite kingdom, we can discern some significant undercurrents in the theological message that is set forth. Most striking is the insistence on the sovereign power of the LORD God. The theological stance is very close to that of the prophecies ascribed to Isaiah in Isaiah 37:22-29. It is the LORD God of Israel who controls the power processes of historical events and not the supposedly superior gods of Mesopotamia.

So we find in vv. 20-37 no fewer than ten assertions that what has happened has been determined by the LORD God:

v. 20, "The LORD will send upon you . . .
v. 21, "The LORD will make the pestilence cling to you . . .

v. 22, "The LORD will afflict you . . .
v. 24, "The LORD will change . . .
v. 25, "The LORD will cause you . . .
v. 27, "The LORD will afflict you . . .
v. 28, "The LORD will afflict you . . .
v. 35, "The LORD will strike you . . .
v. 36, "The LORD will bring you . . .
v. 37, " . . . among all the peoples where the LORD will lead you.""

Behind these assertions lies a firm intention to reaffirm one of the central tenets of a true monotheism: The LORD God of Israel is a sovereign deity over all other claims to godhood. Though the existence of other gods is not denied (cf. v. 36), their powerlessness before the LORD God of Israel is heavily emphasized and their uselessness shown in that they are not real gods at all but merely objects of wood and stone.

A striking feature of this basic series of blessings and curses lies in the incompleteness of the picture it offers concerning what the future will hold for Israel under the curse. Verse 20 envisages the possibility that Israel may be destroyed, and this threat of complete annihilation is repeated further in vv. 21-24. The transitional summary in v. 45 reaffirms the warning yet again. Some slight concession appears to be introduced in v. 36, giving a glimpse of Judah's king and his people being taken into exile, where they will be forced to serve alien gods. No more substantial expression of hope for the future than this is provided.

28:47-57. When we turn to the addition in vv. 47-57, there is a significant shift both in formal structure and theological viewpoint. The literary form of the curse is abandoned altogether and instead graphic illustrative detail is given of Israel's sufferings at the hands of an unnamed enemy. The agent of God's punishment is specified as "a nation from far away" (v. 49). No fuller identification is made, but Babylon must certainly be intended. The most striking feature is the detailed description of a prolonged and horrifying siege that will bring unendurable famine and will lead to gruesome acts of cannibalism (vv. 53-57), even involving parents and their children. These are undoubtedly no longer generalized sketches of human suffering but rather are specific recollections of horrors that took place in Jerusalem during the Babylonian siege of Jerusalem between the years of 588–587 BCE. There is, therefore, a close similarity of date and theological intention between this rhetorical address and the book of Lamentations.

Overall the purpose of the address appears to have been to provide a full confession on Israel's part, insisting that it has been guilty of disobedience to God's laws. The element of theodicy is strongly present in the implied insistence that it is not the powerlessness of Israel's God that has brought about the nation's misfortunes but rather the terrible indifference shown to the divine commandments given through Moses.

28:58-68. The final addition in vv. 58-68 is important, not for any fuller theological development of the theodicy, but for the clear and extensive message concerning Israel's exile. Of great interest is the last great shift in deuteronomic theology and the embracing of the notion of a painful and lasting flight from the land of Israel and a prolonged period of exile. Still no hint at all is made of an eventual end to this exile and to a return to the land once conquered by Israel under Joshua. For a nation for which the land had occupied so prominent and central a position, the awareness of expulsion from it takes on a singularly threatening character. One of the closest parallels to the passage is in Jer 25:10-14, with its realization that a long and painful time of exile is the fate that awaits Israel.

A particular feature of this passage lies in the attention given to those who would flee to Egypt (vv. 60, 68) and offer themselves for sale as slaves (v. 68). Egypt appears to be the preferred destination of the Judean survivors who fled there after the murder of Gedaliah (cf. Jer 43:1–44:30), and the return there is seen as a tragic reversal of the original deliverance. The exodus had given birth to Israel as a nation, and the return to seek refuge in that land takes on the character of a loss of nationhood. Noteworthy, too, is the complete absence of any further reference to the group of exiles from Judah who had been taken to Babylon in 598 BCE, together with the Davidic ruler Jehoiachin. At this point the expectation that the renewal of Israel as a nation would come about when those who had been taken to Babylon returned to their native land has not been defined clearly enough to show how the rebirth of Israel would come about.

Obviously, the fate of those who had either been taken as exiles to Babylon or who had fled to neighboring lands such as Egypt had come to preoccupy the deuteronomic authors. Yet even up to this point hope for the continuance of some form of government and stability in the land had not been altogether abandoned, and expectations of the exiles' eventual return has no firm place in Israel's hope.

By the time the prophecies of Isaiah 40–55 and the major prophetic collections of Jeremiah and Ezekiel had been given a literary shape, all hope for Israel's future had become focused on a return from Babylon of those who had been forcibly taken there. This was clearly the situation that emerged by the beginning of the sixth century BCE. In the meantime all confidence in the surviving administration in the ruined land of Judah had been abandoned, and with this one of the central planks of the deuteronomic theology had perished.

REFLECTIONS

There is a surprising appropriateness in the manner in which the deuteronomic law code is followed by an epilogue that declares the role of the law in human experience. Why should a person be obedient to the law, and what are the benefits to be obtained by doing so? The first part of Deuteronomy 28 responds to these unfocused questions in the most straightforward and predictable way: Those who obey the law will be blessed and will achieve happiness and prosperity (Deut 28:2-14); conversely, those who disobey the law will be cursed and will suffer misfortune and ruin (vv. 16-44). Such is the deuteronomic doctrine of retribution that governs both the law book and the written story of Israel's history shaped by its doctrines. God is a God of justice, and divine retribution is inevitable.

However, it is not only the deuteronomic writings and much of the biblical literature but also the experience of life that encourage such a belief. Were it not so, we should have neither need nor respect for law and good behavior since it is a fundamental conviction that they point us to recognize the order and moral structure of our world and of the place of human beings within it.

Yet if a doctrine of retribution is true, it is certainly not the whole truth about life and cannot therefore be made into a universal truth that is always valid. Evildoers often do not get their deserts, and correspondingly very good people may suffer horrendous misfortunes. The book of Job is the richest biblical exploration of the doctrine of retribution. So theologians conclude that the shadow of the cross stretches not only across the whole of the biblical literature but in a very real sense across the whole of life. The problem of unmerited pain and undeserved misfortune becomes a major part of the human story.

The fact that the simplest enumeration of blessings and curses in an either/or choice begins the epilogue of Deut 28:1-44 (the blessings of vv. 3-6 contrast directly with the curses of vv. 16-19 and may well have been adapted from a simple formula used in worship) draws attention to the shifts and differences of thought that emerge in the additions that have subsequently been joined to it.

Verses 47-57 were undoubtedly added in the wake of the setbacks and disasters that befell Judah once the kingdom came under Babylonian control and King Jehoiakim was foolhardy enough to rebel. The nightmare consequences of the sieges of Jerusalem in 599–598 BCE and again in 588–587 are then brought more directly into the picture. Although the simple doctrine of retribution is still held on to, it is already evident from the horrifying instance of cannibalism that the doctrine had worn extremely thin! A simple doctrine that men and women only suffer what they deserve surely did not account for this. At the least it forcibly raised the point that those who were responsible for bringing about a situation (the king and the royal administration) were not the only ones to suffer its consequences. Many innocent persons were brought down in the judgment.

It seems clear that these additions, which are in a formal sense merely illustrations of what it means to live under God's curse, actually do far more than this. They raise the question whether a simple teaching that evil and misfortune are a consequence of disobedience to God's law is really enough to explain the facts of the real world! Clearly the author has drawn upon known instances of barbarism, and the miseries that befell the inhabitants of a city under siege cannot properly be fitted into any such doctrine. The mystery of evil goes deeper than this, and it is pointless to give inadequate answers to such major questions.

Very much the same problem, arising out of the same circumstances, appears in the laments brought together in the book of Lamentations. The author is confessing guilt and unburdening his grief and shock but is also trying to focus a question that remains blurred and only half defined. Can such appalling actions as are attested in Deut 28:33-57 (cf. Lam 2:20), in which every vestige of normal human feeling and compassion is overthrown, really have been intended by God as a punishment?

At a single stroke the very framing of such a question forces us to recognize that "theology after the holocaust" can never be the same as it was before. New depths of human misery have been plumbed; new horrors have been inscribed on the walls of human history; new nightmares have been experienced that can never afterward be erased from human consciousness. The unknown author of Deut 28:47-57 has not given us an answer but has set a question before us that would have been very much easier to ignore.

The second of the additions made to the simplistic assertions of the blessing-curse formulation is also profoundly interesting. This is given in vv. 58-68 and represents a straightforward updating of Israel's story in the wake of what happened to a large section of the population of Judah after the events of 587 BCE. Thousands were compelled to flee from their homes, to confront a burned and ravaged countryside, and to come to terms with the unwelcome truth that homes, households, and freedom had all been lost.

With bitter irony the picture given in these verses is of a tragic reversal of the triumphalist story of Israel's beginnings portrayed in Deuteronomy 1–3. The plight of slavery in Egypt, the sound of the taskmaster's lash, and the humiliation of being sold as a slave in the marketplace—all these miseries had been part of the traditional story of everything that God had rescued Israel from. Now Israel was once again to experience these cruel sufferings. The wheel of fate seemed to have turned full circle!

However, the message the author of these verses draws from this ironic contrast between Israel's beginnings and endings is not a fatalistic doctrine of despair. As Jesus was later to appeal to the citizens of Jerusalem in the name of God, "If you, even you, had only recognized on this day the things that make for peace! But now they are hidden from your eyes" (Luke 19:42), so there is here a poignant awareness that God's possibilities are never exhausted. God had given Israel a lifeline of hope through the revelation of the commandments, but Israel had refused to grasp it. For those readers who were still indifferent to the claim of these commandments, the message had now become very plain. The pain of the past, however, did not eliminate the reality of hope for the future.

DEUTERONOMY 29:1–30:20, THE GREAT FAREWELL ADDRESS OF MOSES

COMMENTARY

The art of rhetoric and speech making was highly prized and highly developed by both the ancient Greeks and Romans. Moving the minds of fellow human beings by artistry with words—appealing, informing, cajoling, and persuading—has been among the most influential of human artistic achievements. Because it is an art that has been exploited by demagogues and abused in the pursuit of dangerous and selfish ends, it is one that many responsible and educated people view with suspicion. It is an art that can easily be misused and that can unleash feelings and ambitions that eventually lead to great suffering and destruction.

Yet, rightly used and directed, a skillfully prepared and delivered speech can take on a life-transforming importance. Few persons, in fact, can claim that they have never been so deeply moved by a powerful speech or sermon that they have changed the direction of

their lives. Certainly the speech that is presented in Deut 29:1–30:20 as the farewell address of Moses to the people of Israel is a brilliant example of the rhetorician's art. It appears as the third of the great addresses of Moses that make up the book of Deuteronomy.[107] Studied from the perspective of its rhetorical techniques and stylistic devices it stands out as among the most brilliant dramatic compositions that the Old Testament contains.

Clearly an addition to the original law book of Deut 4:44–16:19, the speech is also of considerable historical and theological significance in that it is addressed specifically and openly to a community of Israel who found themselves at a wholly new juncture in

107. An excellent critique and exposition of the speech, with an analysis of its rhetorical techniques, is presented in Timothy A Lenchak, "Choose Life!" A Rhetorical-Critical Investigation of Deuteronomy 28, 69-30, 20, AnBib 129 (Rome: Pontifical Biblical Institute, 1993).

their national history. They had by this time been driven out from the land promised to their ancestors, Abraham, Isaac, and Jacob. This land, which represented God's central material gift to Israel and by which they had been embodied a nation, had by this time been lost. Through its possession they had been able, however imperfectly, to express their nationhood and to fulfill the promise of freedom that had been assured by their deliverance from Egypt. From it all that sustains life could be obtained in such abundance that they had become the envy of less fortunate neighbors. Thereby the promises implicit in the covenant God had made on Mt. Horeb had found a measure of fulfillment. Yet by the time this address was composed the land had been ravaged and its productivity ruined. Even more disturbing, it no longer remained under the political control of those whose religious loyalty meant that it could safely be entrusted to their care. For the deuteronomic authors Israel had been driven into exile— a picture that is graphically and effectively drawn in 28:58-68.

This new situation exhibited with considerable realism the human vulnerability of Israel. In the eyes of the deuteronomists it was also a fearful confirmation of the importance of obedience to the law of Moses. Yet, even beyond these two glaring physical facts, it was a fundamental theological problem. Without possession of the land how could there be an Israel at all? A restored nation could only come into being by a new journey through the wilderness and a new act of taking possession of the land. In a remarkable way, therefore, the situation that the deuteronomic authors used to reaffirm the central importance of the law of Moses—Israel waiting in the plains of Moab and poised to cross the Jordan into the promised land—had to be repeated. Israel was once again exiled in the wilderness; as a nation it was once again wrestling to break free from bondage to alien nations; it had once again to recross the Jordan and repossess the land.

In the form of a farewell speech by Moses to the assembled people of Israel, this splendid address is delivered to an Israel that had been driven into exile. It was a people landless, demoralized, and confused—a people seeking to find a path of hope in a situation

that seemed hopeless. So a wide array of rhetorical skills is used as a means of appeal to reawaken and rearm Israel morally and spiritually. The very faith in the power of the LORD God that seemed to have been discredited and largely disowned by the people is now summoned back into being. The address is therefore a supreme appeal to faith, courage, and hope. If ever the art of rhetoric was needed, it was needed now!

Seen against such a background the speech emerges as a strong appeal to faith, urging Israel to accept its past failures, to recognize its hopeless position without faith in God, and to return to a renewed loyalty to the covenant and its commandments. A new beginning was possible, and a new day would dawn when the failures of the past and the wretchedness of the present would be set behind Israel. A new life would open up for the people once they had resettled in their ancient homeland.

The speech of 29:1–30:20 must be regarded as a unity, although it divides into separate sections. Throughout it displays a coherence and consistency of theme, style, and purpose. It undoubtedly belongs to the latest among the strata of material that has been incorporated into the book and displays several important theological and literary links with the viewpoint of Jer 24:1-24; 25:1-10; 30:18-22; 31:1-34. Its central message is the insistence on the possibility of repentance and the return of Israel to nationhood as part of a great purpose that God would bring about. The situation of those addressed is clearly described in 30:1. Israel's disobedience after the first settlement in the land and its being scattered among the nations in punishment for turning to other gods is presupposed as having taken place. Now a new choice faced the people: They could either abandon God and the covenant altogether, as the fainthearted among them had already begun to do, or they could return in sincerity and truth to keep God's covenant and to remain unwaveringly loyal to the LORD as God.

The appeal of the address is clear and decisive, and the situation in which the original hearers/readers were placed is allowed to show through very clearly. The address has a threefold purpose: It makes clear that, by the grace of the LORD God, Israel's renewal is a genuine possibility; it thrusts aside the objections that could be raised against trusting in this possibility; and it uncovers and refutes the unspoken thoughts of despair and disillusionment the people secretly nursed. The whole message is set out with great psychological insight and outstanding rhetorical skill.

(1) The opening declaration of 29:1 sets the scene by establishing the genuineness of Israel's opportunity to repent and in pointing to the new situation this would bring about. Israel is once again poised on the edge of the land, exactly as its ancestors were when they stood across the Jordan in the plains of Moab. Just as Moses' address to their ancestors had amounted to a new covenant "in addition to the covenant made with them at Horeb" (v. 1), so also this "new covenant" was a fresh possibility once again. In effect, what is envisaged is not so much a totally new covenant, but rather a renewed covenant.

This is the first point at which the deuteronomic legislation has been explicitly presented as being a new covenant in addition to that made on Horeb. This does not contain a new additional set of commandments but is rather a restatement of the Horeb covenant. Its secondary and supplementary character had become necessary because Israel had failed to observe its terms and to grasp the importance of its commandments. Verse 4 declares categorically that throughout its generations Israel had consistently not grasped the greatness of God's power. The immediate reference in its historical guise is to the tradition of Israel's rebellion in the wilderness, now understood symbolically as a repeated obstinacy and willful disobedience that lay hidden in the hearts of the people. It is the "blindness and deafness" of which the prophet Isaiah had accused them (Isa 6:10), and it is the "stiff-necked obstinacy" that the prophet Jeremiah had found among his contemporaries.

The accusation serves to highlight the truth that the thirty-eight years spent wandering in the wilderness were symbolic of the whole failed history of Israel in the land from the time of the conquest under Joshua to the removal of Zedekiah from the throne in 587 BCE. From the author's point of view the accusation was still true that "but to this day the

LORD has not given you a mind to understand, or eyes to see, or ears to hear" (v. 4). The phrase "but to this day" establishes again the sense of contemporaneity between Moses addressing Israel in the plains of Moab and the author addressing Israel as it now found itself scattered among the nations. Accordingly, the idea of a second covenant made on the plains of Moab established the grounds for confidence that Israel could reenter and repossess the land as Joshua had done. By seeing its situation in this light Israel could experience a renewing of its commitment to the covenant at Horeb as Moses had urged the people to do centuries before. There are significant connections of historical context and theological ideas with the promise of the new covenant of Jer 31:31-34.

The essential content of the message is then made incontrovertibly plain in the words of 30:1-5, which leaves no uncertainty as to what Israel, scattered and demoralized as it was, must now do: "Return to the LORD your God" (v. 2); "The LORD will restore your fortunes and have compassion on you" (v. 3). This will then lead to God's further initiative in renewal: "gathering you again from all the peoples" (v. 3); "The LORD will bring you into the land that your ancestors possessed, and you will possess it" (v. 5).

The possibilities that faced Israel as it reflected on the renewal of the Horeb covenant made on the far side of the river Jordan is thereby clearly stated. Yet the message made a demand on the present generation, the same demand that had been made on every Israelite since the original Horeb covenant had been established: They must choose between following the way of God or abandoning it. They could either remain totally loyal to the covenant, obeying its commandments (vv. 15-20), or they could turn away; but in doing so they would also abandon the promise of hope altogether. In this case they would be throwing away the only lifeline that was within their grasp.

With magnificent evangelical passion the author makes a final appeal: "Choose life so that you and your descendants may live" (v. 19). One thing alone remained for Israel to do; the remainder lay in the power of God. Nevertheless, this one act was the essential key that would enable them to pass through the doorway of hope. Choose life!

(2) The second of the aims of this address is to thrust aside the objections that the survivors of Israel nursed in their hearts, that made such a message of hope appear impossible. Foremost among these was the belief that God's actions and power were not sufficient for such a restoration. The influence the LORD God of Israel possessed over the course of human affairs was not enough to ensure Israel's eventual success. So ran the unexpressed objections to returning at this point of history to a deep and exclusive commitment to the LORD as God. Had not the entire course of events in the years of Judah's final demise given proof of God's powerlessness before the gods of the nations?

The response to this objection is to look back once again to the story of Israel's beginnings when the nation journeyed through the wilderness. There God had shown extraordinary providential care for Israel (vv. 5-6), and there great victories had been won over King Sihon of Heshbon and King Og of Bashan (v. 7; cf. Deut 2:26–3:17). The territory on the far side of the Jordan occupied by Reuben, Gad, and part of Manasseh had been swiftly claimed. When faith and loyalty had been strong and Moses' leadership still a reality, then Israel had been assured of success.

The second of the objections that were aroused concerned the uncertainty and confusion surrounding the requirement that Israel should obey the commands of the covenant. How could the people know that they had fulfilled what was required? Here the author of the address presents a very central feature of God's covenant with Israel. It did not involve mysterious, unknown, or unfulfillable demands on the part of God. The commandments were clear, plain, and fully knowable by every citizen in Israel, both young and old: "The secret things belong to the LORD our God, but the revealed things belong to us and to our children forever, to observe all the words of this law" (v. 29).

It could not be denied that there was a mysterious side to God's Being that humans did not, and could not, know. What mattered was that the truths that concerned humankind had been fully disclosed in the covenant. Essentially the same truth is reaffirmed in

30:11-14 in words that leave no doubt as to the central position the deuteronomists saw the law of God to hold. These words are vitally and centrally related to the biblical concept of divine revelation and of a moral order of life that is indissolubly linked to it.

A third objection that must have been openly spoken and not merely privately reflected on is found in vv. 22-26. The key element is the ruined state of the land, forcefully described in v. 23: "all its soil burned out by sulfur and salt, nothing planted, nothing sprouting, unable to support any vegetation, like the destruction of Sodom and Gomorrah, Admah and Zeboiim." The picture must have been unforgettably etched on the minds of many of the hearers and readers of this remarkable sermon.

However, in a masterful twist of rhetorical artistry, the words of this objection are not placed on the lips of the hearers and readers. Instead, they are put into the mouths of the children of future generations of Israelites and of foreigners who will comment on such devastation—and they will know precisely the reason why such devastation had come! It is "because they abandoned the covenant of the LORD, the God of their ancestors" (v. 25). Children as yet unborn and foreigners who survey the scene from outside will know the truth that the Israelites want to hide from themselves. It is not the powerlessness of the LORD God that is responsible for the ruin of the land but the disobedience and faithlessness of the people of Israel. They blame God, but they should look into their own hearts where they will see that they can only blame themselves. Such is the writer's rhetorical skill that even a seemingly unanswerable objection does have an answer when men and women "have a mind to understand" (v. 4).

(3) The third aim of this long address is to uncover and remove the fears and disillusionment that had reduced the author's readers to near despair. Why did the situation and the future outlook appear so different to the author from the way it appeared to the readers? To answer this question the author probes deeply into the psychology of faith. Faith is a perspective on life and the world that requires a proper understanding. Just as the first generation of Israelites in the wilderness had failed miserably to understand the

call and challenge of God (v. 4), so also, the author implies, many of his contemporaries still do not understand. The human mind is deceptively liable to seek easy answers to complex questions. As a consequence, there are those who are ready to turn aside from trusting God at the first sign that the situation has become difficult: "It may be that there is among you a man or woman, or a family or tribe, whose heart is already turning away from the LORD our God" (v. 18). The deuteronomic account of their ancestors wandering in the wilderness provided many examples of such a cowardly lack of faith (Deut 8:1-10).

Alongside such mean-spirited faithlessness there was also the temptation to indulge in a selfish complacency. People were saying to themselves: "We are safe even though we go our own stubborn ways" (v. 19). By self-indulgently contemplating their own remarkable good fortune in at least surviving, they were willing to abandon altogether any concern with larger issues of faith and national destiny in order to look after themselves, thus paying no attention to the larger fate of the nation.

All such want of faith the author describes as "a root sprouting poisonous and bitter growth" (v. 18). Clearly these were thoughts that the author was hearing daily, or, if they were not openly spoken, they certainly represented widely felt but unspoken reflections of despondency and despair. By drawing them out into the open and putting them in plain speech, such thoughts could be shown up for the self-centered, unworthy, and faithless realities that they were. Those who were too timid to speak such words would thereby be shamed into admitting to themselves that they had entertained them.

Another objection also came to the author's attention and must certainly have cut deeply into the message of hope. Its essential thought line ran: Even granting that all that is said about the covenant, its law, and its promise for the future, does not the covenant itself, backed up by the entire past history of Israel, show that the same disasters would overtake the nation again? If disobedience to the law carried such terrible consequences, and if the nature of Israel in the future remained what it had been in the past, would not the same consequences inevitably befall Israel yet again? One way or another the nation was doomed!

This serious objection is countered by the words of 30:6: "God will circumcise your heart and the heart of your descendants so that you will love the LORD your God with all your heart and with all your soul, in order that you may live." God would transform the inner mind and spirit of Israel by "circumcising" the hearts of the people in order to implant the will to obey the commandments. The theology is virtually identical to that expressed in Jer 31:33-34 and Ezek 36:25-27. By a spiritual transformation the power of God would create a new spirit of obedience within every Israelite. God would give the power and the willingness to obey.

To some extent a certain level of ambivalence and inconsistency in the author's presentation is discernible here. After such a strong emphasis on the need to obey the commandments and on the terrible consequences of failure to do so, it is remarkable that God's love and compassion are so great that in the future God will give Israel the power to obey. The sharpness of earlier warnings is to this extent compromised. However, in spite of this inconsistency, it is very significant that this same issue was to recur more than once in both Jewish and Christian attempts to combine the concepts of law and grace. That law should be an instrument of grace and that grace should bring us to fulfill God's law have remained important emphases in Christian exegesis through such different figures as Paul, Augustine, and Martin Luther.

With this threefold armory of rhetoric—stating a clear and decisive message, showing its conformity to all that its readers truly believed, and exposing the shamefulness and emptiness of those who were inclined to reject it—the author concludes with a renewed challenge: "Choose life so that you and your descendants may live!" (30:19).

The address clearly belongs to the middle of the sixth century BCE, closely contemporaneous with the book of Lamentations and displaying many connections with the edited collection of Jeremiah's prophecies, which bears a deuteronomic stamp.

Taken in the context of its origin, the deuteronomic movement had striven desperately to avert the disasters that had befallen the surviving kingdom of Judah at the hands of the Babylonians. In its aftermath they found a land that was economically ruined, politically divided, and spiritually demoralized.

In this splendid speech ascribed to Moses, this late deuteronomic author makes a decisive appeal for a renewal of faith and loyalty. Rightly discerning that spiritual confusion was the foremost issue to be dealt with, in this address he introduces into the deuteronomic theology a new dimension of hope. No longer could the future be hoped for in terms of averting catastrophe. It needed to be seen in terms of renewal and recovery after the worst had taken place.

REFLECTIONS

In many ways this outstanding example of the ancient preacher's art needs little by way of further reflection. It contains so many timeless truths, and its allusions and references to events are reasonably self-explanatory within the overall perspective of the deuteronomic movement. Nevertheless, it has a powerful contemporary relevance in its strong emphasis on issues of personal faith. In a modern secular world where religion appears so frequently as a matter of choice, embraced and held on to by relatively few persons in a society that has largely grown indifferent to religion, its central importance for human development is easily overlooked. The author of this address recognizes that faith and loyalty to God are central antidotes to despair. Hope in God becomes a larger, surer, and more comprehensive basis of hope than is to be found anywhere else.

Despair of the future is a kind of social disease. Whether that social sickness is a consequence of the turmoil and ruination caused by warfare, as this ancient author witnessed, or whether it is caused by deprivation, unemployment, and social alienation, the effects are very similar. Hopelessness generates despondency. It deenergizes and dehumanizes persons so that they no longer reach to grasp the possibilities that life brings. It generates impulses of self-pity and self-condemnation. It begins to regard death as a welcome release instead of the closure of the period of opportunity.

So the appeal to faith and hope is not merely a religious appeal to generate support for religious enterprise but an appeal to enter into a full humanity. It is an appeal to seek out the deep wellsprings of human ambition and to expect the future to be open and desirable. It is an appeal to discover afresh what it truly means to be a human being.

Seen in this light the appeal to faith set out here gains greatly from the recognition that it originates in the worst of times. It is a call to hope that emerged out of a situation of deep gloom and emptiness. Not simply a challenge to embrace particular articles of faith or partisan leanings, it is, rather, an appeal to heart searching and self-examination, a remarkably personal and direct challenge that highlights the way in which, in the final analysis, faith is a necessity for every human being.

As a rhetorical composition made with great skill and based on a tradition of preaching eloquence, it makes an appropriate "last sermon" from the person and genius of Moses. It bears close comparison with the roughly contemporary and similarly directed speech ascribed to Joshua in Josh 24:1-28. In view of popular familiarity with the latter speech, it is surprising that this address of Moses has not been more fully explored. It brings out many of the same points made in the address of Joshua; it counters similar popular objections and expresses the same fundamental challenge to make firm decisions of faith. It is, then, a fitting testimony to the figure of Moses as a giant of faith, leaving a clear call to face the future with courage and with hope.

DEUTERONOMY 31:1–34:12

APPENDIX

OVERVIEW

Although the figure of Moses and the acclamation of his leadership as the unique mediator between God and Israel dominate the book of Deuteronomy, nevertheless, the book prepares Israel for life without the presence of this unique leader. Because the written law is the legacy and testament of Moses to Israel, Deuteronomy gives details of the preparations for the leader's inevitable death. It contains instructions that are designed to show how the contents of this book of law are to be preserved, protected, and administered.

What we now encounter in the final chapters of the book is an appendix that provides details concerning where the law book was to be kept, who were to be its trusted custodians, and what arrangements were to be made to ensure that Israel remained familiar with its contents. In addition to these essential preparations, there is a practical note on the fact and circumstances of Moses' death, together with two beautiful hymnic poems, the Song of Moses and the Blessing of Moses, that provide a kind of summary of what Moses means to all the future generations of Israel. In spite of their ascription to Moses,

these cannot have been composed directly by him since they refer to events that happened long after his death. Nevertheless, they brilliantly convey the sense of a person whose gift to humankind was the gift of faith and for whom the greatest blessing that can be afforded is the discovery of this faith.

In addition to the arrangements for the preservation and custody of the law book, instructions are given for the installation of Moses' successor, Joshua, and an address entrusting him with his high task.

From a literary perspective this appendix to the law book displays considerable unevenness. Both of the major poems have clearly been added to the text at a late stage, but even allowing for this the flow of events is ragged. The basic themes concerning arrangements for the law book, the succession of Joshua, and the fact of Moses' death before the crossing of the Jordan are referred to at more than one point and intersect each other. It can only be concluded that these materials were added as a supplement to the law book and that this literary process of revision resulted in repetitions.

DEUTERONOMY 31:1-29, PREPARATIONS FOR LIFE UNDER THE LAW OF MOSES

COMMENTARY

The primary text (31:1-13) covers two basic issues: First, Moses acknowledges to Israel that he is old and will soon die (v. 1). Accordingly, he commissions Joshua as his successor (vv. 1-8).[108] Second, he writes down

the law hitherto spoken to Israel (v. 9). This is placed in the custody of the levitical priests (vv. 9-13) with instructions for it to be read every seventh year (v. 10). The two essential

---

108. Coats, "Legendary Motifs in the Moses Death Reports," 181-91; N. Lohfink, "Die deuteronomistische Darstellung des übergangs der Führung Israels von Moses auf Josue. Ein Beitrag zur alttestamentlichen

Theologie des Amtes," *Studien zum Deuteronomium und zur deuteronomistischen Literatur I,* SBA 8 (Stuttgart: Katholisches Bibelwerk, 1990) 83-97; G. W. Coats, *The Moses Tradition,* JSOTSup 161 (Sheffield: Sheffield Academic, 1993) 76-81; and *Moses: Heroic Man, Man of God,* 145-54.

concerns are then outlined. The injunction to Israel in 31:13 reads like a suitable final admonition for the book.

However, 31:14–32:44 resumes and repeats both issues concerning the law book and the leadership succession and also a third theme and theological viewpoint relating to the disobedience of Israel. This is then used as a basis for introducing the Song of Moses. The theme of this song is the sovereign greatness of Israel's God, the national disobedience, and Israel's eventual vindication by God. The introduction is in 31:16-22, and the matter of Joshua's succession to leadership is taken up afresh in 31:23, followed by arrangements for the law's preservation. The precise literary and compositional sequence that has led to this unevenness is not wholly clear, although it would certainly appear that the insertion of the Song of Moses at a late stage has disrupted a smooth narrative sequence.

A number of broad literary observations must also be made. It is evident that in its original form the law book of Deuteronomy must have been composed as an independent and self-contained work. At a significant second stage of development, it was adapted to provide the opening section of the history that now stretches across six books from Joshua to 2 Kings. Within this larger literary setting the Mosaic handing over of the leadership of the nation to Joshua became an important issue. Joshua became a link figure who brought together the story of the giving of the law with the story of how the land was conquered.

As a third phase of literary growth, Deuteronomy was once more separated from the historical work and reformulated as the final book of the Pentateuch. It then rounded off the story of Moses' achievements; more important, it made the Pentateuch a kind of constitutional charter for the nation of Israel, given through Moses and completed before Israel entered the land. It thereby applied to everyone included in the covenant, not merely to those living within the land. This point held considerable significance for later generations of Jewish readers.

From a historical and theological perspective the material contained in Deuteronomy 29–34 reflects a number of major issues regarding the nature of religious leadership and of the importance of sacred Scripture as a witness to, and product of, God's revelation to Israel. Moses was the supreme revealer and spokesman of God throughout his lifetime. Yet his inevitable death would remove from Israel this source of guidance and judgment (31:1).

With Moses no longer present in their midst, how would Israel face the future? Who, or what, would replace this divine guidance? Clearly no single person, not even one as obedient and courageous as Joshua, could do so. The primary response to this need is found in the provision of the book of the law that is placed in the custody of the levitical priests. From this time on Israel would be "the people of the book."

One of the implications of this action is that the levitical priests would now take responsibility for teaching and administering the law. However, as we have already seen, the urgent need to teach the commandments of God is made a responsibility of every household (cf. Deut 6:7). All Israel was to be caught up in learning, obeying, and teaching God's commandments. Life after Moses would necessarily, therefore, be of a significantly different order from what it had been while Moses was still alive.

In many respects the more surprising feature of the arrangements made for Israel after the death of Moses is that Joshua is entrusted with national leadership. It might have appeared that the provision of the law book would have made this unnecessary. We can, then, best understand the role of Joshua and the according to him of a leadership role as preparation for the ultimate introduction of a monarchy. The deuteronomic historian then shows how a leadership succession emerged from Moses to Joshua, from Joshua to the judges, and then ultimately to the kingship that finally results in the dynasty of David. This picture accords with the law of the king in Deut 17:14-20, which permits such an institution but views its primary responsibility as one of knowing and administering the Mosaic law.

The provision for the reading of the law every seventh year at the Festival of Booths (31:10) is significant. The interval between readings would appear to be unusually long if such an act were intended as an effective instrument of education. At most it would symbolically demonstrate that the law was a fundamental feature of Israel's faith and worship. Nevertheless, it would seem very probable that the reading of sections of the law in a service of worship, and in particular at the Feast of Booths (Tabernacles) held in the fall of the year, was a feature of the Israelite cultus. Certainly in later Jewish worship the giving of the law on Mt. Sinai (Horeb) came to be the foremost focus for thanksgiving at the fall celebration. Just as worship was an occasion to recall the providential care of God in the past, so also the reading of the law was a way of ensuring that Israel remained mindful of its proper response in the present.

The second of the major provisions in installing Joshua as leader concerned the transition from life in the wilderness (preparation) to life in the land (fulfillment). From a literary perspective we have already noted that this established a narrative continuity between the period of revelation at Horeb and in the plains of Moab and the period of active response in Joshua and all that followed.

A more restrained and hidden motif, however, would also appear to be found in the background to such an action. This concerned the eventual introduction of the monarchy, which the law book permits but does not absolutely require (Deut 17:14-20). There is abundant evidence from the way 1 and 2 Samuel and 1 and 2 Kings deal with the monarchy that the deuteronomic authors viewed the institution very critically. Yet they certainly did not preclude it, provided that it acted within the confines set by the divine commandments in the law book (Deuteronomy 17: cf. also 1 Kings 2). So Joshua's installation is shown to be a necessity in order to provide Israel with military leadership, a task that is eventually seen as the primary one fulfilled by a king.

The report of the manner of Joshua's installation in 31:7-8, 23 employs a well-established formula, strongly suggesting that it was drawn from a cultic, or possibly a civil, ceremony for such appointments. Certainly behind the rather heavy emphasis placed by the deuteronomic authors on warfare and on Israel's military commitments lies an awareness of the nation's vulnerability to Mesopotamian power during the eighth and seventh centuries. Consistently the unspoken question arises as to how Israel can compensate for this weakness, and the answer given is that God must fight on their behalf. Only with such divine support can Israel match and overpower the strength of its enemies. So Joshua is bidden to be a man of courage and faith, ensuring that both he and all his soldiers are wholly devoted to the LORD God.

The section dealing with the tent of meeting in 31:14-15, 23 shows close parallels to Exod 33:7-11, presenting the tent as a simple sanctuary that the later priestly pentateuchal author has elaborated into the tabernacle. This is a temple in all but name and clearly prefigures the building of the Temple that Israelite tradition recognized as the work of Solomon.

The deuteronomic author here does not go so far as the later priestly writer in elaborating the details of the sanctuary but nevertheless uses the tradition concerning such a tent of meeting to show how the cultus instituted by Moses had been performed before the Temple was built. The emphasis in v. 3 on the assurance that the presence of the LORD will go with Israel has not been fully harmonized with the deuteronomic doctrine that the name of God will make God's presence available. The concern for God's presence with the people was especially relevant in connection with the installation of Joshua as leader since he would have to lead them into battle.

The issue of Moses' succession is further resumed in 34:9 and Josh 1:1-9, where the installation formula is repeated. This repetition has become necessary, as well as that concerning the manner and time of Moses' death, in order to allow for the inclusion of the two major poems, the Song of Moses and the Blessing of Moses, which round off Moses' literary legacy to Israel. The era of Moses is complete before the age of conquest and life in the land can begin. This accords with the literary division between the Pentateuch and the narrative history of the former prophets (Joshua–2 Kings) that follows. The division may appear to be primarily a literary feature, but it had considerable significance for contemporary readers, many of whom, like Moses, now found themselves excluded from the land, either by exile to Babylon and elsewhere or by being forced to flee to other lands for refuge. For such people the land promised to the nation's patriarchal ancestors had once again become a hope for the future rather than a present reality.

The placement of the book of the law in the custody of the levitical priests (31:9, 25-26) placed a responsibility on them to become both its guardians and its administrators. It would certainly appear likely that prominent Levites were among the leading figures of the deuteronomic movement. It would also seem likely that, with such a trust given into their hands, the levitical priests also now assumed a new role as interpreters of the law.

The ruling that the book, or scroll, of the law should be kept beside the ark accords with its functional role, which is how the deuteronomic law book interpreted its significance. God's relationship to Israel was mediated through the covenant rather than through the symbolism of "presence" in a temple and its furnishings. As a visible token that God was "with" Israel the ark had served in the pre-Temple period as a reminder of the LORD's leadership in battle (cf. Num 10:45-46). By interpreting the central sanctuary as the location of the divine name, the ark had almost become irrelevant save as a container for the scroll of the covenant law. The belief that Israel had neglected such a central role

for the law draws forth yet another reminder that the nation could again in the future fail to fulfill the possibilities implicit in its elect covenant status. Future generations "will surely act corruptly, turning aside from the way that I have commanded you" (v. 29).

Such an adverse warning of future apostasy on the part of Israel serves to provide a suitable scene-setting introduction to the Song of Moses (32:1-43). The requirement that the Israel of the future must learn to become "the people of the book" allows the possibility that yet again the people may choose to disobey the covenant commandments. What then? The response to such a question is given in vv. 16-22: Because God will then no longer be able to speak to the people through the law, which they have rejected; instead, they will have to learn through the punishments and disasters that will befall them. This advance warning of Israel's future apostasy then serves to prepare the reader for the message of the Song of Moses. In it, the strongest warnings are given against faithlessness and religious disloyalty. At the same time, and with consummate skill, the poem declares the message of hope that, in spite of future disloyalty, God will ultimately ensure that the people of Israel are vindicated and that they will triumph over their enemies.

REFLECTIONS

Life after Moses would never be the same again! That Moses was about to die becomes an important feature of the book of Deuteronomy. Once Moses was dead and had become a figure of past history, buried in the wilderness before Israel had even crossed the Jordan, a new order would prevail. In a very real sense, it is not only the book of Deuteronomy but also the entire Old Testament that owes its existence to the death of Moses. It was the need for guiding, shaping, and advancing an order of life without Moses that made the writing of the book of the law essential. Had Moses lived forever, then every generation of Israel would have been able to enjoy the benefits of his inspiration and leadership in the same way as had those who had followed him in the wilderness.

The impression left by the biblical accounts of Israel's time spent in the wilderness is that the entire story of the nation would have been very different had Moses been immortal. Later generations would not have been so easily led astray or so willing to abandon their faith and high destiny, had Moses been able to rebuke and chide them as he had done to the faithless generation in the wilderness.

Yet such was not possible, for even the most outstanding of human leaders must die, and the task they have worked at must be carried on by others. So it becomes important that there be a successor to Moses, chosen while Moses was still alive so that he could be introduced to and accepted by the people during Moses' lifetime. Almost certainly this is what took place in later years with Israel's kingship, since the time of transition to a new ruler was fraught with unrest and dangers. A crown prince had to be appointed while the existing ruler was still living in order to secure a smooth transition in the threat of rival claimants.

Yet the situation was different with Moses! A successor, even a man of the stature and skill of Joshua, could not be another Moses. Something irreplaceable would have disappeared from the nation's life. Accordingly it was necessary that special and unique provisions be made so that the teaching and spiritual leadership Moses had given should be preserved in a new way for future generations. This could come about through the writing down of the book of the law, which Moses had personally given in the name of God. Through the preservation and reading of this book of law, Moses would live on. His guidance would be permanently enshrined in a book, which would eventually grow to comprise the five books of Moses, the Pentateuch (Genesis–Deuteronomy). Through them the unique gift of Moses would contribute to each new generation of Israelites. Moses would, in a sense, be contemporary with them all.

Seen in such a light, all biblical religion is built on Torah, "instruction." It is founded on a collection of writings that make possible defiance of death and its destructiveness. It requires scribes, interpreters, and custodians, because it is a faith that requires both literacy and literature. It demands scholars and scholarship, since otherwise the truth once committed to these ancient scrolls would be lost. Both Jews and Christians then become "people of the book" and are able to share in the benefits of the revelation given to Moses.

At many, and probably all, periods of their respective histories, both Jews and Christians have encountered problems from those who have believed that this book-orientation of their religion is irksome and tiresome. Should not religion be free and completely open to wherever the Spirit may lead? Such has been the reasoning of those who have felt constrained by the need for biblical instruction. Yet such freedom has all too often become a byway to disaster, akin to exploring a land without a map.

This is not to decry the need for openness and fresh spiritual leadership, but to recognize the importance of a firm basis of truth enshrined in the belief in God's past revelation to Moses and the prophets and, above all, in Jesus of Nazareth. There is certainly also a danger that the very scrolls and books that make up the Bible have been turned into an unreasoned fetish—symbols of divine action that no longer speak or contain any message by which we can chart life's journey.

In a remarkable manner, the picture set out in Deuteronomy 31 dealing with the arrangements that would become necessary once Moses had died expresses a constantly repeated pattern of faith and understanding. The work of Moses would be enshrined in a book, but there was still a need for continued leadership by new generations of persons like Joshua. The combination of God's order for Israel's future was that the given truth of the law should inspire fresh leadership as represented by Joshua. The book of the law alone would not be sufficient, yet neither would leadership without the law prevail. It would quickly go astray, just as the book of Judges portrays Israel doing once Joshua had passed from the scene.

The balance between the two kinds of authority—the authority of the book and the authority of the charismatic leader—must be firmly kept, even though it cannot be rigidly defined. At times, biblical religion has become "bookish" and textbound, knowing the words of the law but denying its spirit (cf. 2 Cor 3:6). At other times, new prophets of "the Spirit" have arisen, claiming the power and appearance of spiritual leadership, but all too readily going astray by departing from the foundation laid within the biblical text. In a very real way, all subsequent Jewish and Christian experience, both in its high points and in its failures, has been a coming to terms with the fact that Moses is dead.

DEUTERONOMY 31:30–32:52, THE SONG OF MOSES

COMMENTARY

The poem of 32:1-43, which forms the Song of Moses, has already been introduced in 31:16-22, so that 31:30 links back to 31:22. The narrative continuation in 32:44-52 then resumes the report of the arrangements for Moses' death and tells of how the great leader was refused permission by God to enter the land, but was instead allowed to ascend Mt. Nebo in order to see it.

The song must certainly have been composed as an independent unit and, as its literary setting shows, has been incorporated into the book at a late stage. In vocabulary and style, it is a composition of a very different type from the legal and hortatory addresses of Deuteronomy, being highly poetic in its imagery. Nevertheless its inclusion rests on its suitability as a further warning to Israel against continued disobedience and apostasy. Its concluding message of hope that Israel, in spite of its unfaithfulness, will ultimately be vindicated by God conveys an important additional perspective to the deuteronomic viewpoint. The impact of the repeated warnings and curses could have left an expectation of the future that was ultimately negative and threatening. Instead, the song brings an assurance of Israel's ultimate triumph among the nations.

Literary Form. The basic imagery and form of the song are that of the presentation of a lawsuit, modeled closely on features that would have characterized the presentation of a case in a court of law. Both the chosen vocabulary and the speech forms adhere to this purported setting in bringing an indictment against Israel. This is then abandoned at 32:28 when the narrator, who assumes divine authority, turns to accuse the nations of misunderstanding. Finally, in 32:39-42 a verdict is declared against these unnamed nations who have been guilty of foolishness and wanton violence. A concluding summons to the gods of the nations to praise the LORD in 32:43 then reaffirms the divine plan to cleanse the land.

The fact that it is initially the nation of Israel that is indicted invites comparison with the use of a similar lawsuit form by certain prophets (e.g., Isaiah 1). In turn, this prophetic usage invites comparison with the form of international vassal treaties, which set out in a formal legal manner the requirements imposed on a vassal by his sovereign overlord. It displays a distinctively set form. However, all the indications are that the song here is a distinctive artistic composition that has simply used the basic lawsuit form, with which most readers would have been familiar, for rhetorical purposes. It presumes that God is both judge and plaintiff, and it accuses both Israel and foreign nations. The use of the lawsuit form provides the basis for an effectively reasoned challenge against Israel, but then turns to make it a reason for hope by its assurance of vindication over the nations. Overall there are some similarities with the didactic style of the wisdom literature as well as with the use of legal language by Israel's prophets in justifying threats against Israel.

Time of Origin. So far as the time of composition of the song is concerned, it is evident from the references to Israel's misfortunes and defeats in battle (vv. 22-33) that a long and painful history has confirmed the seriousness of the warnings against apostasy that have already been given. Israel has proved itself disobedient, and defeats and sufferings have already come (vv. 23-24). But precise details of how Israel has been defeated, or by whom, are lacking, and the impression is created that it is a situation that has existed for some time.

A primary purpose of the song is to provide assurance that punishment will eventually come to Israel's enemies, who have tormented and ravaged the land. The time for this punishment is held to be not far off. It seems likely that the poem was originally composed independently, almost certainly in the post-exilic age, and very possibly at a time when Deuteronomy had come to form the final part of the Pentateuch. If this is the case, then the ascription to Moses (31:22) can only be understood as a literary device that has used the figure of the great leader to stress the authority and relevance of the message the song contains. Its appropriateness lies in its message of Israel's vindication.

Formal Structure. The highly poetic form of the song means that it poses many problems for the translator as a consequence of textual uncertainties. It makes full use of the prophetic device in which God speaks directly in the first person, declaring what the present situation is and what is about to happen. At other points, it adopts a distinctly wisdom didactic manner. All told, this mixing of formal rhetorical speech forms with an incomplete adoption of a trial scene points to an author well versed in literary poetic skills.

Content. The song divides into separate units, with a major turning point between v. 27 and v. 28, where the speaker turns to rebuke Israel's enemies. They are accused of failing to understand what has really happened when they have inflicted torment and misfortune upon Israel. God then declares that the time for action against these enemies will soon come, which will lead to Israel's vindication. A concluding appeal to the gods of the defeated nations to praise the LORD is made in v. 43, rounding off the note of assurance that, in spite of present appearances, God will vindicate the people.

32:1-9. God is Israel's Creator and Sustainer. Yet the people are accused of having forgotten this fact and have dealt treacherously against their divine benefactor. They have abused the divine care. All the more is this a punishable offense because Israel was the most favored of all nations from the time of its creation (vv. 8-9). The title used for God in v. 8, "Most High" (עליון 'elyôn), refers to the LORD God, but was an ancient title that could be used to celebrate any divine power who sat at the head of a pantheon of gods. It has been chosen here to give poetic expression to the mythical idea of many deities, of which the LORD was head, with Israel being uniquely the LORD's people and the lesser deities acting as guardians of other nations. The NRSV follows the text of a Qumran fragment and of the Septuagint. It reflects a belief that there were many gods for other nations, with

the LORD being only the chief among them. Later scribal objections to this use of a polytheistic idea, even for poetic purposes, has occasioned the variant readings of v. 8 (see the NRSV's marginal note).

32:10-18. The affirmation of the LORD's unique providential care of Israel moves on to the theme of the years spent wandering through the wilderness and the miraculous manner in which the survival of Israel was ensured. The author views the entire wilderness experience as one demonstrating the total sufficiency of God's care for the people. The traditional stories of how the people were fed with manna and quail from the skies and water from the rock have been made the subject of poetic hyperbole in v. 13. They are then linked in v. 14 to the richness of Israel's land. The rare name "Jeshurun" for Israel (v. 15; cf. 33:5, 26; Isa 44:2) makes an apparent verbal play on the concept of uprightness. Yet Israel has turned its back on God through complacency, taking for granted the richness and sufficiency of the land and provoking God to anger by turning to worship false gods and demons (vv. 16-17).

32:19-27. Having seen how the people have responded to the care lavished upon them, God determines that they must be punished in order to bring them to their senses. The form this punishment will take is then determined as attacks by unnamed enemies, who are described as "no people" and "a foolish nation" (v. 21). We can only assume that a succession of foreign invaders is intended here (Assyria, Babylon, Persia) and that the titles are deliberately derogatory. That it is the work of God is explicitly shown by being spoken throughout by the poet in the first person, assuming the role of both creator and judge. In a subtle change of theme, God pauses to reflect that the punishment of Israel may be misunderstood as a mark of divine weakness, thereby demanding that further action be taken to dispel such a mistaken view (v. 27).

32:28-32. The theme that Israel's enemies are "a foolish people" is further explored in vv. 28-31 by showing that the exaggerated and arrogant nature of their claims cannot possibly be true (v. 30). Imagery of God as Israel's "Rock" (צור ṣûr) and the poetic assurances that God will give stunning victories to those who put their trust in divine aid are all turned around. Because this has not happened, then it can only be that God has been angry with Israel, not because the divine power is inadequate to meet such demands.

32:33-38. These verses then turn sharply against the enemies for their cruel and wanton behavior. At this point the poem indulges in a degree of moral inconsistency. God has had to use these cruel enemies to punish Israel, but will now turn to exact vengeance on them for their own false religion (v. 37). The gods who guide these nations, like guardian angels, will appear to be greater than the LORD! Then it will be Israel's turn to be the object of divine compassion (v. 36). Great play is now made of the emptiness and powerlessness of the gods of the nations, who can do nothing to protect them from the vengeance of the LORD God. At this point, the claims of "the gods of the nations," which were alluded to in v. 8, are shown to be worthless, demonstrating that in reality these are no gods at all.

32:39-43. The final unit of the Song of Moses (vv. 39-42) makes a forthright declaration that the LORD has complete power over all peoples so that when the time comes for vengeance upon Israel's enemies, this power will prove to be unstoppable. An unexplained feature arises in the description of the enemy as "the long-haired enemy." The reference may be not to a particular physical characteristic, but to the fact that warriors wore their hair long as a mark of consecration or as a sign of leadership. The final summons to praise in v. 43 is startling in calling upon the heavens to praise God's people and in summoning all the lesser gods to worship the LORD.

32:44-52. This short unit summarizes the challenging and admonitory element contained in the Song of Moses (vv. 44-47). It warns that the threat of apostasy on the part of Israel is real ("no trifling matter") and that failure to take the warning to heart could jeopardize Israel's continued settlement of the land. From the writer's viewpoint, these were eventualities that had already become real and serious threats. The narrative of vv. 48-52 then picks up the announcement from 31:21 that Moses had brought the people to the very border of the promised land.

The story of how Moses ascended Mt. Nebo to view the promised land, now being fully aware that he would not be allowed to enter it, contains a number of instructive features. Most prominent is the warning that Moses was not to be allowed to enter the land because he had broken faith with God. In 3:26, the author firmly stated that Moses was innocent of doubting God and that it was the people who had sinned. However, the priestly writer of Num 20:1-13 has developed the notion that Moses, too, had been led to question whether God could bring water from the rock. Therefore, he had been led to sin against God. The accusation that Moses had failed to maintain the divine holiness among the Israelites appears to have called for a deliberate play upon the name of Meribath-kadesh (cf. Num 20:13, 24; 27:14). This form of the name for the oasis of Kadesh appears as a priestly coining, probably because it was the location where conflict and contention (מריבה *měrîbâ*) had arisen. Historically the name almost certainly owes its origin to the fact that disputes were brought there for judgment. In this unexpected charge against Moses, it is taken to imply that he had been contentious over the matter of holiness.

The author here has undoubtedly been influenced by the priestly tradition, using the brief note here to record Moses' offense, which serves to reinforce the connection between sinning against the LORD and taking possession of the land. The close literary link with the priestly (P) tradition of the Pentateuch indicates the late stage at which the note has been brought in here, almost certainly when the book of Deuteronomy had been combined with Genesis–Numbers to form the closing chapter of the story of Israel's beginnings.

From the reader's perspective, Moses' exclusion from the land had undoubtedly become a major issue in view of the seeming hopelessness of the situation for those who had been exiled from their homeland. The recollection of the tradition that Moses himself had been denied entry into the land gave a dimension of hope and encouragement for its repossession.

❖   ❖   ❖   ❖

EXCURSUS: MONOTHEISM AND THE SONG OF MOSES

The theme that permeates the theological message of the Song of Moses (Deut 32:1-43) is that of monotheism. God is one, and there is no other who is comparable in power or purpose. In a strictly formal sense, the poem does not declare a monotheistic faith, for it repeatedly refers to the existence of other deities besides the LORD God of Israel. They first appear in 32:8 as the guardians of the non-Israelite nations, with each one being allocated a particular nation and territory to watch over. They reemerge in 32:16 as "strange gods" and in the following verse as "deities they had never known" and "new ones recently arrived." In the context of the deuteronomic religious polemic, such a dismissive charge fits rather awkwardly, since the primary accusation concerning the deities Israel was repeatedly tempted to worship is that they were the gods of the former occupants of the land. The primary point is that all such gods are weak and powerless beside the God of Israel, and they must submit to the will and purpose of the LORD. All of this is already conveyed in the opening section, where an early form of a creation myth is alluded to in which the Most High God (the LORD) is the primary creator figure, using the lesser gods as servants.

The gods worshiped by other peoples are referred to again in 32:37 and in the final summons to praise in 32:43. Such references appear to conflict with the declaration of a more absolute monotheistic faith in 32:39, which denies any power at all to other gods. We may regard the tension that arises between faith in one absolute deity and the belief that other gods have a relative degree of authority apportioned them by the Most High God as partly poetic hyperbole and partly a desire to show how weak other gods really are. It can be argued that if other nations believe their gods exist, then in some sense they do exist for them. The poet does not finally resolve the issue, but uses the idea of non-Israelite gods in order to emphasize to the fullest possible extent the absolute power of the LORD (cf. Ps 96:4-5).

It may at first glance appear to be a somewhat unexpected development that the Song of Moses, the great architect of Israel's faith, should be equivocal over the question of monotheism and whether other gods besides the LORD have real existence. Yet such an inference is more apparent than real, because the direction of this poem is to show the sovereign power of the LORD in all the history of Israel. When things went well for Israel, it was because God was showing mercy to the people. When things went badly, it was because it was necessary that they be punished.

Yet these other nations rashly assumed that their gods were greater and more powerful than the LORD God of Israel (32:27). Such was certainly not the case, but merely a foolish misunderstanding, for, in fact, no god is greater than the LORD God of Israel. Because this is true, then ultimately the power of this God will prevail on earth, bringing judgment over Israel's enemies and providing vindication for Israel.

A subordinate theme of the poem is the relationship between many gods and many nations. The conventional mythical perspective in which each nation has its own deity is assumed in 32:8, so that the various competing claims among them for precedence are assumed to have a measure of validity.[109] Yet this can only on the surface seem to be the case, but cannot be so in reality. Once it is admitted that one God is superior to all other gods, then these others cannot be gods at all. They must be mere idols, since the very essence of divinity is the concept of creative power. Once that creative power

---

109. The importance of such a belief for the rise of nation-states in the ancient Near East is shown by Daniel I. Block, The Gods of the Nations: Studies in Near Eastern National Theology (Winona Lake, Ind.: Eisenbrauns, 1988).

is made subordinate and relative to a superior power, then these so-called deities are reduced to mere appearances. So, by a rather historical form of polemic, the poet insists that there can only be one true God.

The debate over one God or many, which reverberates through the Old Testament, can be reduced to a rather arid and abstract debate about theories and speculations. More relevant is the question of a single all-powerful and all-encompassing divine will that controls the universe. That there should be lesser powers (sons of gods, demons, idols, no gods) then becomes irrelevant. It is the issue of the sovereignty of the LORD God of Israel that is so majestically argued for in this song.

❖　　❖　　❖　　❖

REFLECTIONS

There is a consistent undercurrent of practicality about the faith expressed in this poem. Although it employs the formal language concerning God and the divine power as Creator, it focuses all such faith on more immediately knowable and practical issues. These concern the way in which Israel saw itself and its situation. That the latter was a time of frustration, tension, and suffering is readily apparent. In highly poetic language, Israel's present time of crisis is echoed in 32:24-25. Bitter pestilence and "the teeth of beasts" have been sent against the people. There is no respect of person, either on the grounds of age or gender (32:25). The hidden question in such experiences is, Why has God allowed this to happen? The poem's answer is to argue that it had become necessary for a time, but that the time would soon pass. Rather than abandon faith in God's control over events, the author believes that it is possible to explain them in terms of the complex character of God. The divine will for the loyalty and uprightness of Israel had to be combined with the belief that Israel's enemies were God's enemies, too, and must eventually be punished. So the issue of monotheism, which can easily slip back into becoming sterile and theoretical, must be rescued from this by focusing on the way in which it helps to explain the mixed and complex nature of the way we experience life. It is far better that we retain a sense of the oneness and wholeness of human history and human experience, than that we seek to explain away its varied faces by supposing that rivalries and conflicts between a multitude of gods are their cause.

DEUTERONOMY 33:1-29, THE BLESSING OF MOSES

COMMENTARY

Another poem is brought in as the final utterance of Moses, through which he is able to survey and to "bless" all the future generations of Israelites. It bears close comparison with the similar blessing of Jacob in Gen 49:1-28 and, less directly, with the list of the Israelite tribes in Num 1:5-15. Behind both this poetic prayer and the one ascribed to Jacob we are confronted with the intense belief that so great a figure could both foresee the destiny of each tribe and pronounce blessing upon each.

The poem is essentially split into two parts with a hymnic praise of God in vv. 2-5 and 26-29. This then serves as a framework for the blessing formula for each tribe, which captures for each a divine message concerning their individual destiny. Moses thereby gives to each tribe his own gift of divine understanding and power, and at the same time the diverse gifts and characteristics of each tribe are recognized and affirmed to be gifts of God.

33:2-5, 26-29. Almost certainly we must conclude that the two elements of the poem were originally separate, the framework being taken from a psalm celebrating the kingship and triumphant power of the LORD God. It shares many features and a common vocabulary with the "enthronement psalms," which celebrate the power of God over creation and over all Israel's potential enemies. It must certainly be of early pre-exilic origin, but it is unlikely to have been written earlier than the building of the Jerusalem Temple.

A particularly memorable feature of the poem is the description of a divine theophany in vv. 2-3, in which God is seen as coming in triumph to Israel from Mt. Sinai and the southern hill country to appear before Israel in their land. Similar theophanic descriptions appear in Ps 68:7-10, 17-23 and Hab 3:3-15.[110] The divine passage from the southern mountains conveys many of the features of a powerful electrical storm in which dark clouds and brilliant flashes of lightning display both the power and the wrath of God. Such storm-theophany imagery appears in Ps 29:3-9, and there are many indications that the Canaanite Baal tradition drew heavily upon the conception of Baal as a god of storms and thunder who rode upon the clouds (cf. 33:26). It is noteworthy, however, that the LORD comes from Sinai, pointing to an amalgamation of the historical tradition concerning God's unique act of self-disclosure on Mt. Sinai (Exodus 19–24) with the more stereotypical imagery of a divine theophany in a thunderstorm. The reference to Mt. Sinai is unique in the book of Deuteronomy; elsewhere the mountain of revelation is consistently referred to as Mt. Horeb (see the Commentary on 1:2). The linking of the divine appearance with the giving of the law is possibly an editorial attempt to combine traditional cultic language with the central importance attached to the law.

In a similar fashion, the note that "there arose a king in Jeshurun" (v. 5) could refer either to Moses as king or, more probably, to the celebration of the LORD as divine King over Israel. While Israel lived under a human monarchy, the conception prevailed that the earthly ruler was the servant and representative of God, who was the heavenly King. So human kingship mirrored the divine. Nevertheless, the idea of divine kingship was flexible, which subsequently gave rise to ideas of a theocracy in which no earthly king was needed.

The second part of the framework (vv. 26-29) proclaims many of the established features of the psalms that express the theme of God's kingship (esp. Psalms 95–100). These verses focus especially on God's triumph over all other deities and the destruction of Israel's enemies (vv. 27, 29), so that Israel can live in peace. These enemies, who are essentially regarded as constituting a potential, rather than an immediate and known threat to Israel's security, are not identified. The psalm itself is an affirmation of divine triumph and victory that was designed to promote and achieve such peace and safety.

The use of this hymnic declaration of the LORD's victories at this point has considerable theological significance for its reflection of a subtle change of context in its future hope. There can be no doubt that in its original cultic context it was a stereo typical formula aimed at declaring that any potential aggressor against Israel would be swiftly dealt with (cf. Ps 2:10-11). However, here the overall context at the close of the book of Deuteronomy reflects a situation in which Israel's vulnerable position among the nations of the world was prominently in mind. How will Israel ultimately fare in the world of nations, and how will the God of Israel prove victorious in a world that venerates many strange gods? No longer is the situation abstract and undefined. Through Israel's experience, it proves to be vitally significant. As a consequence, the dimension of hope was pressed further into the future in the expectation of a more distant, but ultimately more glorious, triumph over the nations in which Israel would be vindicated in their land. This hope is clearly set out in the shaping of the canonical books of prophecy, but is less clearly evident in the pentateuchal collection. Here the psalm has effectively been read as prophecy.

110. J. Jeremias, *Theophanie, Die Geschichte einer alttestamentlichen Gattung,* WMANT 10 (Neukirchen-Vluyn: Neukirchener Verlag, 1965).

33:6-25. The central part of the blessing of Moses consists of sayings directed to the traditional twelve tribes, each of which was descended from Jacob, the nation's ancestor. The listing of the twelve tribes is variously arrived at between the tribal genealogies of Num 1:5-15 and 26:5-62 and the "blessing" compositions. Here the name of Simeon is missing, but is compensated for by the fact that Joseph is divided into two, with Ephraim and Manasseh each constituting a complete tribe. The precise history of each of these tribes is impossible to trace, and it is questionable whether such a list of short, and sometimes cryptic, sayings such as are preserved in the blessing-poems provide sufficient information to reconstruct the earliest stages of the tribal history.[111] Even the significance of the well-preserved tradition concerning the existence and inter-relationship of the twelve tribes before the formation of the Israelite state under Saul and David remains shrouded in uncertainty.

Two major historical questions make it difficult to arrive at a date for the composition of this list of sayings. The first question relates to the sense of tribal awareness that prevailed in Israel. Quite certainly during the period of the monarchy, the territorial upheavals, especially those brought on by Mesopotamian interference in the region, led to a disintegration of the older sense of tribal unity that had held Israel together. Increasingly, the effective solidarity of the twelve-tribe group, based on a feeling of kin-based "belonging," waned. It was the purpose of such "blessing" sayings, then, to promote and preserve such feelings.

Second, it is not clear whether these sayings were originally independent or were an expression of the concern to keep alive the memory of an original "family" of twelve tribes who shared a common ancestor. The fact that the names of these twelve were not uniformly preserved argues against this, but evidently the number twelve remained significant. All we can conclude is that these tribal sayings seek to encapsulate the destiny of each of the member tribes and that it was important for the author of the blessing of Moses to keep alive the consciousness of this. It is plausible that the inclusion of the blessing

111. H.-J. Zobel, *Stammesspruch und Geschichte*, BZAW 95 (Berlin: Alfred Töpelmann, 1965).

in Deuteronomy 33, on the eve of the move into the promised land, was made at the time when the book of Deuteronomy became the final chapter of the written Torah, the five books of Moses.

33:6, Reuben. The first saying is addressed appropriately to Reuben, the first-born of Jacob. It recognizes the fact that, within the biblical period, Reuben had become a very small tribe, so much so that its actual history is no longer reported in the extant tradition. It remained little more than a name and a memory.

33:7, Judah. This saying takes full account of the separateness of this tribe and its problem with unnamed adversaries. Who these might have been, and why this tribe had become separate from the remainder of Israel ("his people") is not explained. It may be that the saying originated in the period of the divided monarchy. Judah's enemies are likely to have been Edom and Moab, the other national groups settled in the south and to the east of the Jordan valley. When compared with the Judah saying in the blessing of Jacob (Gen 49:10), it is significant that the rise of Israel's kingship from within Judah is now passed over.

33:8-11, Levi. The saying addressed to Levi is the longest of those preserved in the blessing. It appears to be composite in origin, having been expanded by the addition of vv. 9b-10. Verse 11, then, would have been the original conclusion to the Judah saying. The original Levi saying allocates to them a role in dispensing priestly oracular judgment through the Urim and Thummim (cf. 1 Sam 14:18-19). The Massah and Meribah incident is recounted in Exod 17:1-7, where the link with Levi can only be through the testing of Moses. The unflinching and cruel loyalty of Levi refers to the incident in Exod 32:25-29, but must also, more generally, have been related to their historic commitment to total loyalty to the LORD God of Israel, to whose service they were dedicated. Their role as teachers of the law fits closely with the task envisaged for them by the deuteronomists and became increasingly their responsibility in the early post-exilic age.

33:12, Benjamin. This saying alludes to Benjamin's favored status as the youngest, and especially loved, son of Jacob (Gen

44:20); it probably also contains a hidden political message. Many features of the Israelite tradition, as reflected in Deuteronomy, reveal a deep suspicion of the Judahite claims to superiority among the tribes, to which the tribe of Benjamin fell victim. The conflict over the beginnings of the kingship between Saul (a Benjaminite) and David (a Judahite) were evidently a long-felt source of tension.

33:13-17, Ephraim and Manasseh. The Joseph saying is particularly long and is full of nature imagery regarding the fertility of the land occupied by the tribes of Ephraim and Manasseh. It rejoices in the fertility of the soil and its productivity ("choice fruits of the sun"; "rich yield of the months"; v. 14) and presupposes that the Joseph tribes are the most favored of Israel. The explicit mention of both Ephraim and Manasseh in v. 17 must have originated with the author's desire to ensure that all twelve tribal names received a mention in the blessing. The fact that the saying is so forthright in favoring the Joseph tribes, coupled with the omission of any mention of Judah's kingly status, would fit the broad deuteronomic reflection of an "all Israel" perspective. It is a further reflection of the broad Ephraimite (northern) traditions preserved in the book.

33:18-19, Zebulun and Issachar. These two northern tribes had settled on the hinterland of the Phoenician seaports of Tyre and Sidon and were evidently able to benefit from the maritime trade that developed in the first millennium BCE. Hence, they could be said to "suck the affluence of the seas." The OT preserves relatively sparse information concerning them.

33:20-21, Gad. The strongest of the tribes settled to the east of the Jordan, Gad is reputed for its belligerent and aggressive character (cf. Gen 49:19). This tribe appears to have absorbed much of the territory of its neighbor, Reuben, and was undoubtedly settled in the rich cultivated region in the upper Jordan valley. No obvious explanation appears as to why Gad was especially praised for having "executed the justice of the LORD."

33:22, Dan. The metaphor of Dan as "a lion's whelp that leaps forth from Bashan" is probably best explained as referring to the fact that this tribe had settled in the forested region of the upper Jordan, where, in antiquity, wildlife abounded. The region, with its ready access to the trading routes to Syria and Mesopotamia, made it an important security frontier for Israel, but also left the tribe vulnerable. Accordingly, its toughness was both needed and celebrated as its great virtue.

33:23, Naphtali. This tribe was settled to the north and west of the Sea of Galilee and is another of the twelve tribes about which little historical information is preserved in the biblical tradition. The rich territory that was their traditional land holding has drawn for them a very favored picture in this blessing, but little concrete detail can be gleaned from it.

33:24-25, Asher. The desirable settlement area of this tribe is reflected in the high level of blessing ascribed to it, but once again the reference to their military prowess ("Your bars are iron and bronze," v. 25) indicates the threats that were constantly endangering their ability to hold on to this might. The concluding saying, "and as your days, so is your strength," gives assurance that this tribe will prove strong enough to withstand these attacks.

REFLECTIONS

The blessing of Moses is appropriately set as the final hymnic assurance to bring both the book of Deuteronomy and the entire collection of the Mosaic Torah to a close. It has been a law addressed to Israel, full of warnings, threats, and exhortations to heed the Word of God and to be obedient to the law that has been given to Israel through the covenant. Now Moses is to bid final farewell to the nation he has led and nurtured for a full generation. Like a youth leaving home to go to a distant city to learn or work, Israel is being released to face an uncertain future. The message of the blessing is one of the most prayerful desires for the nation's success and well-being. Moses has bequeathed to the tribes all that he has to give them. The tribes, in return, have revealed the responsive, as well as dangerous, aspects of who they are. Now all that remains is to commit them all to God.

The author undoubtedly felt a great significance attached to the sense of wholeness and inclusiveness of Israel at this point. Certainly by the time Deuteronomy came to be written the fortunes of several of the tribes had long been clouded and almost totally lost. More relevant than the breakup and dispersion of the tribal groupings that had characterized the earliest form of Israel was the exiled and fugitive status that had befallen much of the nation. This fate is well reflected in the formulas of curse that characterize chapters 28–30.

But curse cannot be the ultimate fate of Israel as a nation, and the grounds for believing this are set out here in the context of the hymnic celebration of God's power. So this final formulaic blessing with which Moses parts from the tribes and their representatives is a final pointer to trust in the power of God as the only source and assurance of ultimate success. It is, in the most literal sense, a poem that bids, "Fare well!"

DEUTERONOMY 34:1-12, THE DEATH OF MOSES

COMMENTARY

The final chapter of Deuteronomy has undoubtedly been given its present shape by the editor who made it the final chapter of the Pentateuch. It reports the death of the great leader Moses, with further emphasis that he did not set foot in the land (v. 4) and with a renewed declaration that Joshua was fully empowered as the successor to Moses (v. 9). The final word is a eulogy in praise of Moses as the unequaled leader of the nation. His physical strength was unimpaired (v. 7), but more pertinent, he was able to wield a miraculous divine power against Pharaoh and all his servants, more than any other leader or prophet in Israel (vv. 10-12).

This ascription of Moses' unique miracle-working power is significant as a reflection of the conception of charismatic leadership with which he was believed to have been endowed, and as a mark of a distinct shift of emphasis from that which prevails more extensively in the book of Deuteronomy. Until now, the emphasis has been on Moses' ability to prevail with God in prayer (9:25-29), his unflinching courage and commitment at a time when the majority of the nation had been discouraged and cowardly in the face of the report of the

spies (1:26-45), and his mediation with God on Israel's behalf in bringing the tablets of the law by which they can live as a nation. The transition to a more priestly, power-conscious sense of virtue is quite striking.

In the final form of the biblical books of law, the emphasis on righteousness and justice, rather than priestly power and authority, is uppermost. It is noteworthy that in v. 10 Moses is described as a prophet, in whom the prophetic skills were more fully developed than in any other. This accords with the law relating to true and false prophets in 18:18, where Moses is introduced as a superior prophet. Overall if one title more than any other is sought to describe the role Moses has played in Israel, it is "prophet." In the end, however, Moses' very uniqueness makes it impossible to describe his role as that of prophet, priest, military commander, or king. At different times, he fulfills tasks appropriate to each one of these roles. Yet he surpasses them all and thereby ties Israel to a person and a past history from which it can never afterward be separated. He is the one "whom the LORD knew face to face."

ABBREVIATIONS

BCE	before the Common Era
ca.	circa
CE	Common Era
cent.	century
cf.	compare
chap(s).	chapter(s)
d.	died
Dtr	Deuteronomistic historian
esp.	especially
fem.	feminine
HB	Hebrew Bible
l(l).	line(s)
lit.	literally
LXX	Septuagint
masc.	masculine
MS(S)	manuscript(s)
MT	Masoretic Text
n(n).	note(s)
neut.	neuter
NT	New Testament
OG	Old Greek
OL	Old Latin
OT	Old Testament
par(r).	parallel(s)
pl(s).	plate(s)
SP	Samaritan Pentateuch
v(v).	verse(s)
Vg	Vulgate
\\	between Scripture references indicates parallelism

Names of Pseudepigraphical and Early Patristic Books

Apoc. Abr.	*Apocalypse of Abraham*
2–3 Apoc. Bar.	Syriac, Greek *Apocalypse of Baruch*
Apoc. Mos.	*Apocalypse of Moses*

Ascen. Isa.	*Ascension of Isaiah*
As. Mos.	*Assumption of Moses*
Barn.	*Barnabas*
Bib. Ant.	Pseudo-Philo, *Biblical Antiquities*
1–2 Clem.	*1–2 Clement*
Did.	*Didache*
1–2–3 Enoch	Ethiopic, Slavonic, Hebrew *Enoch*
Ep. Arist.	*Epistle of Aristeas*
Gos. Pet.	*Gospel of Peter*
Herm. Sim.	Hermas, *Similitude(s)*
Ign. Eph.	Ignatius, *Letter to the Ephesians*
Ign. Magn.	Ignatius, *Letter to the Magnesians*
Ign. Phld.	Ignatius, *Letter to the Philadelphians*
Ign. Pol.	Ignatius, *Letter to Polycarp*
Ign. Rom.	Ignatius, *Letter to the Romans*
Ign. Smyrn.	Ignatius, *Letter to the Smyrnaeans*
Ign. Trall.	Ignatius, *Letter to the Trallians*
Jub.	*Jubilees*
POxy	B. P. Grenfell and A. S. Hunt (eds.), *Oxyrhynchus Papyri*
Pss. Sol.	*Psalms of Solomon*
Sib. Or.	*Sibylline Oracles*
T. Benj.	*Testament of Benjamin*
T. Dan	*Testament of Dan*
T. Iss.	*Testament of Issachar*
T. Job	*Testament of Job*
T. Jud.	*Testament of Judah*
T. Levi	*Testament of Levi*
T. Naph.	*Testament of Naphtali*
T. Reub.	*Testament of Reuben*
T. Sim.	*Testament of Simeon*

Names of Dead Sea Scrolls and Related Texts

CD	Cairo (Genizah text of the) Damascus Document
DSS	Dead Sea Scrolls
8HevXII gr	Greek scroll of the Minor Prophets from Naḥal Ḥever
Q	Qumran
1Q, 2Q, etc.	numbered caves of Qumran, yielding written material; followed by abbreviation of biblical or apocryphal book
1Q28b	Rule of the Blessings (Appendix b to 1QS)
1QH	Thanksgiving Hymns (Qumran Cave 1)
1QM	War Scroll (Qumran Cave 1)
1QpHab	Pesher on Habakkuk (Qumran Cave 1)
1QpPs	Pesher on Psalms (Qumran Cave 1)
1QS	Rule of the Community (Qumran Cave 1)
1QSa	Rule of the Congregation (Appendix a to 1QS)
1QSb	Rule of the Blessings (Appendix b to 1QS)
4Q175	Testimonia text (Qumran Cave 4)
4Q246	Apocryphon of Daniel (Qumran Cave 4)
4Q298	Words of the Sage to the Sons of Dawn (Qumran Cave 4)
4Q385b	fragmentary remains of Pseudo-Jeremiah that implies that Jeremiah went into Babylonian exile. Also known as ApocJer^C or 4Q385 16. (Qumran Cave 4)

4Q389a	several scroll fragments now thought to contain portions of three pseudepigraphical works including Pseudo-Jeremiah. Also known as 4QApocJer[e]. (Qumran Cave 4)
4Q390	contains a schematized history of Israel's sin and divine punishment. Also known as psMos[e]. (Qumran Cave 4)
4Q394–399	Halakhic Letter (Qumran Cave 4)
4Q416	Instruction[b] (Qumran Cave 4)
4Q521	Messianic Apocalypse (Qumran Cave 4)
4Q550	Proto-Esther [a-f] (Qumran Cave 4)
4QFlor	Florilegium (or Eschatological Midrashim) (Qumran Cave 4)
4QMMT	Halakhic Letter (Qumran Cave 4)
4QpaleoDeutr	copy of Deuteronomy in paleo-Hebrew script (Qumran Cave 4)
4QpaleoExod	copy of Exodus in paleo-Hebrew script (Qumran Cave 4)
4QpNah	Pesher on Nahum (Qumran Cave 4)
4QpPs	Psalm Pesher A (Qumran Cave 4)
4QPrNab	Prayer of Nabonidus (Qumran Cave 4)
4QPs37	Psalm Scroll (Qumran Cave 4)
4QpsDan	Pseudo-Daniel (Qumran Cave 4)
4QSam	First copy of Samuel (Qumran Cave 4)
4QTestim	Testimonia text (Qumran Cave 4)
4QTob	Copy of Tobit (Qumran Cave 4)
11QMelch	Melchizedek text (Qumran Cave 11)
11QPs[a]	Psalms Scroll (Qumran Cave 11)
11QT	Temple Scroll (Qumran Cave 11)
11QtgJob	Targum of Job (Qumran Cave 11)

Targumic Material

Tg. Esth. I, II	First or Second Targum of Esther
Tg. Neb.	Targum of the Prophets
Tg. Neof.	Targum Neofiti

Orders and Tractates in Mishnaic and Related Literature

To distinguish the same-named tractates in the Mishnah, Tosefta, Babylonian Talmud, and Jerusalem Talmud, *m., t., b.,* or *y.* precedes the title of the tractate.

'Abot	'Abot
'Arak.	'Arakin
B. Bat.	Baba Batra
B. Meṣ.	Baba Meṣiʿa
B. Qam.	Baba Qamma
Ber.	Berakot
Dem.	Demai
Giṭ.	Giṭṭin
Ḥag.	Ḥagigah
Hor.	Horayot
Ḥul.	Ḥullin
Ket.	Ketubbot
Maʿaś.	Maʿaśerot
Meg.	Megilla
Menaḥ.	Menaḥot

Mid.	Middot
Moʿed Qaṭ.	Moʿed Qaṭan
Nazir	Nazir
Ned.	Nedarim
p. Šeqal.	pesachim Šeqalim
Pesaḥ.	Pesaḥim
Qidd.	Quddušin
Šabb.	Šabbat
Sanh.	Sanhedrin
Soṭah	Soṭah
Sukk.	Sukkah
Taʿan.	Taʿanit
Tamid	Tamid
Yad.	Yadayim
Yoma	Yoma (=Kippurim)

Other Rabbinic Works

'Abot R. Nat.	'Abot de Rabbi Nathan
Pesiq. R.	Pesiqta Rabbati
Rab.	Rabbah (following abbreviation of biblical book—e.g., Gen. Rab. = Genesis Rabbah)
Sipra	Sipra

Greek Manuscripts and Ancient Versions

Papyrus Manuscripts

$\mathfrak{P}^1$	third-century Greek papyrus manuscript of the Gospels
$\mathfrak{P}^{29}$	third- or fourth-century Greek papyrus manuscript
$\mathfrak{P}^{33}$	sixth-century Greek papyrus manuscript of Acts
$\mathfrak{P}^{37}$	third- or fourth-century Greek papyrus manuscript of the Gospels
$\mathfrak{P}^{38}$	fourth-century Greek papyrus manuscript of Acts
$\mathfrak{P}^{45}$	third-century Greek papyrus manuscript of the Gospels
$\mathfrak{P}^{46}$	third-century Greek papyrus manuscript of the letters
$\mathfrak{P}^{47}$	third-century Greek papyrus manuscript of Revelation
$\mathfrak{P}^{48}$	third-century Greek papyrus manuscript of Acts
$\mathfrak{P}^{52}$	second-century Greek papyrus manuscript of John 18:31-33, 37-38
$\mathfrak{P}^{58}$	sixth-century Greek papyrus manuscript of Acts
$\mathfrak{P}^{64}$	third-century Greek papyrus fragment of Matthew
$\mathfrak{P}^{66}$	second- or third-century Greek papyrus manuscript of John (incomplete)
$\mathfrak{P}^{67}$	third-century Greek papyrus fragment of Matthew
$\mathfrak{P}^{69}$	third-century Greek papyrus manuscript of the Gospel of Luke
$\mathfrak{P}^{75}$	third-century Greek papyrus manuscript of the Gospels

Lettered Uncials

א	Codex Sinaiticus, fourth-century manuscript of LXX, NT, Epistle of Barnabas, and Shepherd of Hermas
A	Codex Alexandrinus, fifth-century manuscript of LXX, NT, 1 and 2 Clement, and Psalms of Solomon
B	Codex Vaticanus, fourth-century manuscript of LXX and parts of the NT

C	Codex Ephraemi, fifth-century manuscript of parts of LXX and NT
D	Codex Bezae, fifth-century bilingual (Greek and Latin) manuscript of the Gospels and Acts
G	ninth-century manuscript of the Gospels
K	ninth-century manuscript of the Gospels
L	eighth-century manuscript of the Gospels
W	Washington Codex, fifth-century manuscript of the Gospels
X	Codex Monacensis, ninth- or tenth-century manuscript of the Gospels
Z	sixth-century manuscript of Matthew
Θ	Koridethi Codex, ninth-century manuscript of the Gospels
Ψ	Athous Laurae Codex, eighth- or ninth-century manuscript of the Gospels (incomplete), Acts, the Catholic and Pauline Epistles, and Hebrews

Numbered Uncials

058	fourth-century fragment of Matthew 18
074	sixth-century fragment of Matthew
078	sixth-century fragment of Matthew, Luke, and John
0170	fifth- or sixth-century manuscript of Matthew
0181	fourth- or fifth-century partial manuscript of Luke 9:59–10:14

Numbered Minuscules

33	tenth-century manuscript of the Gospels
75	eleventh-century manuscript of the Gospels
565	ninth-century manuscript of the Gospels
700	eleventh-century manuscript of the Gospels
892	ninth-century manuscript of the Gospels

Names of Nag Hammadi Tractates

Ap. John	Apocryphon of John (also called the Secret Book of John)
Apoc. Adam	Apocalypse of Adam (also called the Revelation of Adam)
Ep. Pet.	Letter of Peter to Philip
Exeg. Soul	Exegesis on the Soul
Gos. Phil.	Gospel of Philip
Gos. Truth	Gospel of Truth

Ancient Versions

bo	the Bohairic (Memphitic) Coptic version
bo^{mss}	some manuscripts in the Bohairic tradition
d	the Latin text of Codex Bezae
e	Codex Palatinus, fifth-century Latin manuscript of the Gospels
$f\!f^{2}$	Old Latin manuscript, fifth-century translation of the Gospels
Ir^{lat}	the Latin translation of Irenaeus
latt	the whole Latin tradition (including the Vulgate)
mae	Middle Egyptian
sa	the Sahidic (Thebaic) Coptic version
sy	the Syriac version
sy^{s}	the Sinaitic Syriac version

<u>Other Abbreviations</u>

700*	the original reading of manuscript 700
ℵ*	the original reading of Codex Sinaiticus
ℵ¹	the first corrector of Codex Sinaiticus
ℵ²	the second corrector of Codex Sinaiticus
𝔐	the Majority text (the mass of later manuscripts)
C²	the corrected text of Codex Ephraemi
D*	the original reading of Codex Bezae
D²	the second corrector (c. fifth century) of Codex Bezae
f^1	Family 1: minuscule manuscripts belonging to the Lake Group (1, 118, 131, 209, 1582)
f^{13}	Family 13: minuscule manuscripts belonging to the Ferrar Group (13, 69, 124, 174, 230, 346, 543, 788, 826, 828, 983, 1689, 1709)
pc	a few other manuscripts

Commonly Used Periodicals, Reference Works, and Serials

AAR	American Academy of Religion
AASOR	Annual of the American Schools of Oriental Research
AB	Anchor Bible
ABD	*Anchor Bible Dictionary*
ABR	*Australian Biblical Review*
ABRL	Anchor Bible Reference Library
ACNT	Augsburg Commentaries on the New Testament
AcOr	*Acta Orientalia*
AfO	*Archiv für Orientforschung*
AfOB	Archiv für Orientforschung: Beiheft
AGJU	Arbeiten zur Geschichte des antiken Judentums und des Urchristentums
AJP	*American Journal of Philology*
AJSL	*American Journal of Semitic Languages and Literature*
AJT	*American Journal of Theology*
AnBib	Analecta Biblica
ANEP	J. B. Pritchard (ed.), *The Ancient Near East in Pictures Relating to the Old Testament*
ANET	J. B. Pritchard (ed.), *Ancient Near Eastern Texts Relating to the Old Testament*
ANF	*Ante-Nicene Fathers*
ANRW	*Aufstieg und Niedergang der römischen Welt*
ANTC	Abingdon New Testament Commentaries
ANTJ	Arbeiten zum Neuen Testament und Judentum
APOT	R. H. Charles (ed.), *The Apocrypha and Pseudepigrapha of the Old Testament*
ASNU	Acta Seminarii Neotestamentici Upsaliensis
ATANT	Abhandlungen zur Theologie des Alten und Neuen Testaments
ATD	Das Alte Testament Deutsch
ATDan	Acta Theologica Danica
Aug	*Augustinianum*
AusBR	*Australian Biblical Review*
BA	*Biblical Archaeologist*

BAGD	W. Bauer, W. F. Arndt, F. W. Gingrich, and F. W. Danker, *Greek-English Lexicon of the New Testament and Other Early Christian Literature*, 2nd ed. (Bauer-Arndt-Gingrich-Danker)
BAR	*Biblical Archaeology Review*
BASOR	*Bulletin of the American Schools of Oriental Research*
BBB	Bonner biblische Beiträge
BBET	Beiträge zur biblischen Exegese und Theologie
BBR	*Bulletin for Biblical Research*
BDAG	W. Bauer, W. F. Arndt, F. W. Gingrich, and F. W. Danker, *Greek-English Lexicon of the New Testament and Other Early Christian Literature*, 3rd ed. (Bauer-Danker-Arndt-Gingrich)
BDB	F. Brown, S. R. Driver, and C. A. Briggs, *A Hebrew and English Lexicon of the Old Testament*
BDF	F. Blass, A. Debrunner, and R. W. Funk, *A Greek Grammar of the New Testament and Other Early Christian Literature*
BEATAJ	Beiträge zur Erforschung des Alten Testaments und des antiken Judentum
BETL	Bibliotheca Ephemeridum Theologicarum Lovaniensium
BEvT	Beiträge zur evangelischen Theologie
BHS	*Biblia Hebraica Stuttgartensia*
BHT	Beiträge zur historischen Theologie
Bib	*Biblica*
BibInt	*Biblical Interpretation*
BibOr	Biblica et Orientalia
BJRL	*Bulletin of the John Rylands University Library of Manchester*
BJS	Brown Judaic Studies
BK	*Bibel und Kirche*
BKAT	Biblischer Kommentar, Altes Testament
BLS	Bible and Literature Series
BN	*Biblische Notizen*
BNTC	Black's New Testament Commentaries
BR	*Biblical Research*
BSac	*Bibliotheca Sacra*
BSOAS	*Bulletin of the School of Oriental and African Studies*
BT	*The Bible Translator*
BTB	*Biblical Theology Bulletin*
BVC	*Bible et vie chrétienne*
BWA(N)T	Beiträge zur Wissenschaft vom Alten (und Neuen) Testament
BZ	*Biblische Zeitschrift*
BZAW	Beihefte zur Zeitschrift für die alttestamentliche Wissenschaft
BZNW	Beihefte zur Zeitschrift für die neutestamentliche Wissenschaft
CAD	*The Assyrian Dictionary of the Oriental Institute of the University of Chicago*
CB	*Cultura Bíblica*
CBC	Cambridge Bible Commentary
CBOTS	Coniectanea Biblica: Old Testament Series
CBQ	*Catholic Biblical Quarterly*
CBQMS	Catholic Biblical Quarterly Monograph Series
ConBNT	Coniectanea Neotestamentica or Coniectanea Biblica: New Testament Series
ConBOT	Coniectanea Biblica: Old Testament Series
CP	*Classical Philology*
CRAI	Comptes rendus de l'Académie des inscriptions et belles-lettres

CRINT	Compendia Rerum Iudaicarum ad Novum Testamentum
CTM	*Concordia Theological Monthly*
DJD	Discoveries in the Judaean Desert
EB	Echter Bibel
EI	*Encyclopaedia of Islam*
EKKNT	Evangelisch-katholischer Kommentar zum Neuen Testament
Enc	*Encounter*
EncJud	C. Roth and G. Wigoder (eds.), *Encyclopedia Judaica*
EPRO	Etudes préliminaires aux religions orientales dans l'empire romain
ErIsr	*Eretz-Israel*
EstBib	*Estudios bíblicos*
ETL	*Ephemerides Theologicae Lovanienses*
ETS	Erfurter theologische Studien
EvQ	*Evangelical Quarterly*
EvT	*Evangelische Theologie*
ExAud	*Ex Auditu*
ExpTim	*Expository Times*
FAT	Forschungen zum Alten Testament
FB	Forschung zur Bibel
FBBS	Facet Books, Biblical Series
FFNT	Foundations and Facets: New Testament
FOTL	Forms of the Old Testament Literature
FRLANT	Forschungen zur Religion und Literatur des Alten und Neuen Testaments
FTS	Frankfurter Theologische Studien
GBS.OTS	Guides to Biblical Scholarship. Old Testament Series
GCS	Die griechischen christlichen Schriftsteller der ersten [drei] Jahrhunderte
GKC	Emil Kautzsch (ed.), *Gesenius' Hebrew Grammar*, trans. A. E. Cowley, 2nd ed.
GNS	*Good News Studies*
GTA	Göttinger theologischer Arbeiten
HALAT	*Hebräisches und aramäisches Lexikon zum Alten Testament*
HAR	*Hebrew Annual Review*
HAT	Handbuch zum Alten Testament
HBC	*Harper's Bible Commentary*
HBT	*Horizons in Biblical Theology*
HDB	*Hastings' Dictionary of the Bible*
HDR	Harvard Dissertations in Religion
HeyJ	Heythrop Journal
HNT	Handbuch zum Neuen Testament
HNTC	Harper's New Testament Commentaries
HR	*History of Religions*
HSM	Harvard Semitic Monographs
HSS	Harvard Semitic Studies
HTKNT	Herders Theologischer Kommentar zum Neuen Testament
HTR	*Harvard Theological Review*
HTS	Harvard Theological Studies
HUCA	*Hebrew Union College Annual*
IB	*Interpreter's Bible*
IBC	Interpretation: A Bible Commentary for Teaching and Preaching
IBS	*Irish Biblical Studies*
ICC	International Critical Commentary

IDB	*The Interpreter's Dictionary of the Bible*
IDBSup	supplementary volume to *The Interpreter's Dictionary of the Bible*
IEJ	*Israel Exploration Journal*
Int	*Interpretation*
IRT	Issues in Religion and Theology
ITC	International Theological Commentary
JAAR	*Journal of the American Academy of Religion*
JAL	Jewish Apocryphal Literature Series
JANESCU	*Journal of the Ancient Near Eastern Society of Columbia University*
JAOS	*Journal of the American Oriental Society*
JBL	*Journal of Biblical Literature*
JETS	*Journal of the Evangelical Theological Society*
JJS	*Journal of Jewish Studies*
JNES	*Journal of Near Eastern Studies*
JNSL	*Journal of Northwest Semitic Languages*
JPS	Jewish Publication Society
JQR	*Jewish Quarterly Review*
JR	*Journal of Religion*
JRH	*Journal of Religious History*
JSJ	*Journal for the Study of Judaism in the Persian, Hellenistic, and Roman Periods*
JSNT	*Journal for the Study of the New Testament*
JSNTSup	Journal for the Study of the New Testament Supplement Series
JSOT	*Journal for the Study of the Old Testament*
JSOTSup	Journal for the Study of the Old Testament Supplement Series
JSP	*Journal for the Study of the Pseudepigrapha*
JSS	*Journal of Semitic Studies*
JTC	*Journal for Theology and the Church*
JTS	*Journal of Theological Studies*
KAT	Kommentar zum Alten Testament
KB	L. Koehler and W. Baumgartner, *Lexicon in Veteris Testamenti libros*
KEK	Kritisch-exegetischer Kommentar über das Neue Testament (Meyer-Kommentar)
KPG	Knox Preaching Guides
LCL	Loeb Classical Library
LTQ	Lexington Theological Quarterly
MNTC	*Moffatt New Testament Commentary*
NCBC	New Century Bible Commentary
NHS	*Nag Hammadi Studies*
NIB	*The New Interpreter's Bible*
NIBC	*The New Interpreter's Bible Commentary*
NICNT	New International Commentary on the New Testament
NICOT	New International Commentary on the Old Testament
NIGTC	The New International Greek Testament Commentary
NJBC	*The New Jerome Biblical Commentary*
NovT	*Novum Testamentum*
NovTSup	Supplements to Novum Testamentum
NPNF	*Nicene and Post-Nicene Fathers*
NTC	New Testament in Context
NTG	New Testament Guides
NTS	*New Testament Studies*
NTT	*Norsk Teologisk Tidsskrift*

OBC	*The Oxford Bible Commentary*
OBO	Orbis Biblicus et Orientalis
OBT	Overtures to Biblical Theology
OIP	Oriental Institute Publications
Or	*Orientalia* (NS)
OTG	Old Testament Guides
OTL	Old Testament Library
OTM	Old Testament Message
OTP	*Old Testament Pseudepigrapha*
OTS	*Oudtestamentische Studiën*
PAAJR	*Proceedings of the American Academy of Jewish Research*
PEFQS	Palestine Exploration Fund Quarterly Statement
PEQ	*Palestine Exploration Quarterly*
PGM	K. Preisendanz (ed.), *Papyri Graecae Magicae*
PTMS	Pittsburgh Theological Monograph Series
QD	Quaestiones Disputatae
RANE	Records of the Ancient Near East
RB	*Revue biblique*
ResQ	*Restoration Quarterly*
RevExp	*Review and Expositor*
RevQ	*Revue de Qumran*
RSRel	*Recherches de science religieuse*
RTL	*Revue théologique de Louvain*
SAA	State Archives of Assyria
SB	H. L. Strack and P. Billerbeck, *Kommentar zum Neuen Testament aus Talmud und Midrasch,* 6 vols. 1922–61
SBAB	Stuttgarter biblische Aufsatzbände
SBB	Stuttgarter biblische Beiträge
SBL	Society of Biblical Literature
SBLDS	SBL Dissertation Series
SBLMS	SBL Monograph Series
SBLRBS	SBL Resources for Biblical Study
SBLSCS	SBL Septuagint and Cognate Studies
SBLSP	SBL Seminar Papers
SBLSS	SBL *Semeia* Studies
SBLSymS	SBL Symposium Series
SBLWAW	SBL Writings from the Ancient World
SBM	Stuttgarter biblische Monographien
SBS	Stuttgarter Bibelstudien
SBT	Studies in Biblical Theology
SEÅ	*Svensk exegetisk årsbok*
SJLA	Studies in Judaism in Late Antiquity
SJOT	*Scandinavian Journal of the Old Testament*
SJT	*Scottish Journal of Theology*
SKK	Stuttgarter kleiner Kommentar
SNTSMS	Society for New Testament Studies Monograph Series
SOTSMS	Society for Old Testament Studies Monograph Series
SP	Sacra Pagina
SR	*Studies in Religion/Sciences religieuses*
SSN	Studia Semitica Neerlandica
ST	*Studia Theologica*
SUNT	Studien zur Umwelt des Neuen Testaments
SVT	Supplements to Vetus Testamentum

SVTP	Studia in Veteris Testamenti Pseudepigraphica
SWBA	Social World of Biblical Antiquity
TB	Theologische Bücherei: Neudrucke und Berichte aus dem 20. Jahrhundert
TD	*Theology Digest*
TDNT	*Theological Dictionary of the New Testament*
TDOT	*Theological Dictionary of the Old Testament*
TextS	Texts and Studies
THKNT	Theologischer Handkommentar zum Neuen Testament
TLZ	*Theologische Literaturzeitung*
TOTC	Tyndale Old Testament Commentaries
TQ	*Theologische Quartalschrift*
TSK	*Theologische Studien und Kritiken*
TSSI	*Textbook of Syrian Semitic Inscriptions*
TToday	*Theology Today*
TynBul	*Tyndale Bulletin*
TZ	*Theologische Zeitschrift*
UBS	United Bible Societies
UBSGNT	*United Bible Societies Greek New Testament*
UF	*Ugarit-Forschungen*
USQR	*Union Seminary Quarterly Review*
UUÅ	Uppsala Universitetsårsskrift
VC	*Vigiliae Christianae*
VT	*Vetus Testamentum*
VTSup	Supplements to Vetus Testamentum
WA	M. Luther, *Kritische Gesamtausgabe* (= "Weimar" edition)
WBC	Word Biblical Commentary
WBT	Word Biblical Themes
WMANT	Wissenschaftliche Monographien zum Alten und Neuen Testament
WTJ	*Westminster Theological Journal*
WUNT	Wissenschaftliche Untersuchungen zum Neuen Testament
ZAH	*Zeitschrift für Althebräistik*
ZAW	*Zeitschrift für die alttestamentliche Wissenschaft*
ZNW	*Zeitschrift für die neutestamentliche Wissenschaft und die Kunde der älteren Kirche*
ZTK	*Zeitschrift für Theologie und Kirche*